ROBERT NORTH S.J.

ELENCHUS OF BIBLICA

1990

EDITRICE PONTIFICIO ISTITUTO BIBLICO
ROMA 1993

ROBERT NORTH S.J.

ELENCHUS OF BIBLICA

1990

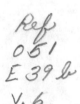
EDITRICE PONTIFICIO ISTITUTO BIBLICO
ROMA 1993

© 1993 – E.P.I.B. – Roma

ISBN 88-7653-599-3

EDITRICE PONTIFICIO ISTITUTO BIBLICO
Piazza della Pilotta, 35 - 00187 Roma

Regrets

Into this year's Index on p. 1023 are inserted all the items with author *Alonso*, unfortunately omitted from the 1989 Index. Also there on p. 1090 under the name *Laberge* L. it is indicated that the numerous book-reviews due to this name in the 1988 Index were erroneously inserted under Labarge M.

Another curious error has crept into this year's Index. Between *Browne* and *Bryce* in some cases is omitted the *first* item-number; or, if it was the *only* one, also the surname may have been omitted: despite our strenuous efforts.

Our Index gives no **titles** except in the rare cases where no **person** responsible could be found indicated.

Deploranda: In Indice hujus anni p. 1023 supplentur sub cognomine **Alonso** *plures articuli anni praecedentis; item p. 1090 recensiones* **Laberge** *pro 1988; et hoc ipso anno deesse possunt aliquot numeri (rarius cognomina) inter* **Browne** *et* **Bryce**.

Tituli *non dantur in Indice per se.*

Taking liberties

The first duty of a bibliography is to be *relentlessly accurate* in reproducing titles exactly as they are given in the original source. Our p. 6 calls attention to our apparent toleration of some deviations from this norm.

We avoid Roman numerals (periodical-volume, Bible-chapter); and also italics (for cited titles or foreign words), which we reserve for authors not of books; or for sites (in the Index). The ten digits after books indicate (without naming) ISBN; and following this, a few digits preceded by hyphen indicate paperback, second volume, or otherwise as in context. Eight digits indicate the ISSN of periodicals. The AA order-number for dissertations is in a form like 90-55678. For ExpTim we usually indicate the editor's 1st/2d top choice.

Our brief citation of 'arresting' items from reviews by no means indicates agreement; the criticism itself may be *sub judice*.

Excusantur rarae variationes in citando.

Acronym-policy

The list of sigla (periodical abbreviations) of this *Elenchus* was once adopted as normative by many biblical reviews, but has now usually been abandoned in favor of the IATG/TRE list; or a special listing (Biblica; CBQ). This was in part because ever since 1967 efforts were made to use longer abbreviations that would give the reader at least a *hint* of the true title, instead of mere acronyms (initial letters only). We have tried to follow this policy but with some shortening. Thus for ÉPROER we have long found ÉPR sufficient; so now we are trying FRL, BW, BSO (for FRLANT, BWANT, BSOAS). Note especially now Bt (for Bibliotheca/que/k, even BiblETL), since Bt is not likely to be mistaken for Bibl(ical); similarly Bbg, Bn for Bibliography, Bulletin. We hope that Mg for Monograph and Pg for Philolog-y/ical (also RPg and RBgPg) will compensate by their unmistakableness for any oddness they may have. It is disconcerting if abbreviations are changed too often; but a certain keeping pace with progress cannot be avoided.

Sigla hujus Elenchi talia eliguntur (vel gradatim mutantur) quae quadamtenus, etsi quam brevissime, integrum titulum adumbrent.

New section-headings

As indicated by bold-face italics in the Table of Contents p. 5, our overweight Comparative Religion section has been subdivided. 'What is religion?' is now put in a class by itself; though naturally not always easy to distinguish from 'Centers and schools' (M3.2) or 'Experts' (M3.3).

Also inevitably somewhat arbitrary is the further division into 'Comparison of religions' either without (M3.4) or with Christianity (M3.5). For 'Sects', again a hazy term, is reserved M3.6. – 'Mythology' is M3.8.

Greek religion too has now been divided into its polytheistic (M5.1), philosophical (M5.2), and Hellenistic-mystery aspects (M5.3).

Similar divisions of Greek/Hellenistic history, and especially New Testament era Roman history, will be more prominent in next year's Table of Contents.

Subdividitur nunc 'Quid est religio?' a 'centris/peritis historiae religionis' et 'comparatione sine/cum christianismo', deinde 'sectis', 'mythologia', sicut ex **Indice systematico** *(M3) apparet; item M5 pro religione graeca (Q5 et Q8s clarius anno venturo).*

4

Index systematicus – Contents

5

AA	Ann Arbor
Amst	Amsterdam
B	Berlin
Ba/BA	Basel/Buenos Aires
Barc	Barcelona
Bo/Bru	Bologna/Brussel
CasM	Casale Monferrato
CinB	Cinisello Balsamo
C	Cambridge, England
CM	Cambridge, Mass.
Ch	Chicago
Da: Wiss	Darmstadt, WissBuchg
DG	Downers Grove IL
Dü	Düsseldorf
E	Edinburgh
ENJ	EnglewoodCliffs NJ
F	Firenze
FrB/FrS	Freiburg-Br/Schw
Fra	Frankfurt/M
GCNY	Garden City NY
Gö	Göttingen
GR	Grand Rapids MI
Gü	Gütersloh
Ha	Hamburg
Heid	Heidelberg
Hmw	Harmondsworth
J	Jerusalem
K	København
L	London
LA	Los Angeles
Lp	Leipzig
Lv(N)	Leuven (L-Neuve)
M/Mi	Madrid/Milano
Mkn/Mp	Maryknoll/Minneapolis
Mü	München
N	Napoli
ND	NotreDame IN
Neuk	Neukirchen/Verlag
NHv	New Haven
Nv	Nashville
NY	New York
Ox	Oxford
P/Pd	Paris/Paderborn
Ph	Philadelphia
R/Rg	Roma/Regensburg
S/Sdr	Salamanca/Santander
SF	San Francisco
Sto	Stockholm
Stu	Stuttgart
T/TA	Torino/Tel Aviv
Tü	Tübingen
U/W	Uppsala/Wien
WL	Winona Lake IN
Wmr	Warminster
Wsb	Wiesbaden
Wsh	Washington
Wsz	Warszawa
Wu/Wü	Wuppertal/Würzburg

Nota Bene – in citing titles from this Elenchus

1. We strive to give the original form of titles as accurately and identically as possible. But every bibliography has certain 'conventions' or adaptations in the interest of its own internal clarity and consistency; thus for example a title is never given in ALL CAPITALS even when it is so in the original. Our major warning is this: we use the **semicolon [;]** to set off the **subtitle**, where the original uses a colon, dot, or separate line. Also, like many bibliography and library catalogues, we do **not** capitalize every word in English-language titles.

For **quotation-marks**, we are following always British usage:

Normally ' ';

Quotes-within-quotes " "

even where the original may have „ " or «».

2. The **price** is rounded off, in the interest of brevity, clarity, and coping with inflation. Thus $12.95 will appear as $13 even where the cited source has $12.95. Less often: £20 for 19.90; DM 50 for 49,80.

3. In principle each volume contains only books and articles published **within that year** or earlier; thus this volume 6 contains the writings dated 1990. However, to be as up-to-date as possible, we include: *a)* periodicals officially dated 1990 even though published late; *b)* periodical-volumes including **partly** 1990, but also the part published in 1991 (= 1990s); *c)* **Source** for 1989 books, usually by volume-number (without year-number) of a later periodical [thus TDig 39,182; but BL 92,35 since it has no volume-numbers]; so also for **dissertations**.

4. We have progressively been moving **away from the front** those materials which are less directly biblical. Thus a book given in A-section for its first appearance (so that its number can be used for → renvoi), if repeated in later volumes (with book-reviews), will be in the section where it fits best. — 'Summary reports of meetings' (not needed for renvoi) are now shunted from A2.2 to Y7.2. 'Revelation', formerly B3.2, is now H1.7. Hermeneutic materials not strictly biblical have been moved from B2 to J9 (linguistic analysis).

5. The Table of Contents (systematic index, p. 4-5) prints in **boldface** those categories which have been relocated, or new categories; thus changes made in the history of religion sections in general, and in particular the history of Greek religion, as explained above on p. 3. Other changes, on Islam and NT era history, also noted there, will be focused in next year's Index.

Citando hinc

Adhibemus:
Intra titulum ;
ante subtitulum
[***non** sicut originale*]

Semper
'[" "]'
non ,' *vel* «».

Pretium numero
rotundo: $20 *pro*
$19.95, *etiam*
contra *fontem*
ibidem citatum.

Annus voluminis
late interpretandus;
sub 1989
etiam 1989-90, vel
1989 tarde
editum, vel
(numerus voluminis
sine anno) pro
fonte *libri 1989.*

Datur tendentia
movendi titulos
non biblicos ab
initio versus
finem libri;
sic compilationes
in voluminibus
post primam
mentionem.

Index systematicus
(et synopticus)
monstrat
innovationes;
e.g. nunc
B4.4-6 de influxu
biblico in
litteraturam.

Acronyms: **Periodica** - Series (small).
8 fig. = ISSN; *10 fig.* = ISBN; *6/7* = DissA.

❹: *arabice,* in Arabic.
AAR [Aids]: American Academy of Religion (➤ JAAR, not PAAR) [Aids for the Study of Religion; Chico CA].
AAS: Acta Apostolicae Sedis; Vaticano. 0001-5199.
AASOR: Annual of the American Schools of Oriental Research; CM.
Abh: Abhandlungen Gö Lp Mü etc.; ➤ DOG / DPV.
AbhChrJüDial: Abhandlungen zum christlich-jüdischen Dialog; Mü, Kaiser.
AbrNahr: Abr-Nahrain; Lv, Peeters.
AcAANorv: Acta ad archaeologiam et artium historiam; R, Inst. Norv.
AcArchLov: Acta archaeologica Lovaniensia; Lv.
AcBg: Académie royale de Belgique; Bru.
Acme; Mi, Fac. Lett. Filos. 0001-494X.
AcNum: Acta Numismatica; Barc. 0211-8386.
Act: Actes/Acta (Congrès, Colloque).
ActAntH: Acta Antiqua; Budapest.
Acta PIB: Acta Pontificii Instituti Biblici; Roma.
ActArchH/K: Acta Archaeologica; Hungarica, Budapest. 0001-5210 / København. 0065-101X.
ActClasSAfr: Acta Classica; Cape Town.
ActIran: Acta Iranica; Téhéran/Leiden.
ActOrH/K: Acta Orientalia: Budapest. 0044-5975 / K (Soc. Or. Danica, Norveigica). 0001-6438.
ActPraeh: Acta Praehistorica/Archaeol.; B.
ActSum: Acta Sumerologica; Hiroshima, Univ. Linguistics. 0387-8082.
ActuBbg: Actualidad Bibliográfica; Barc. 0211-4143.
ADAJ: Annual of the Department of Antiquities, Jordan; 'Amman.
ADPF: Association pour la diffusion de la pensée française; Paris ➤ RCiv.
Aeg: Aegyptus; Milano. 0001-9046.
ÄgAbh: Ägyptologische Abhandlungen; Wb.
ÄgAT: Ägypten und Altes Testament; Wiesbaden. 0720-9061.
AegHelv: Aegyptiaca Helvetica: Basel Univ. Äg. Sem. (Univ. Genève).
ÄgLev: Ägypten und Levante; Wien. 1015-5014 [1,1990].

ÄthF: Äthiopische Forschungen; Stu.
AevA: Aevum Antiquum; Mi, Univ. Cattolica/ViPe. [1 (1988)]. 88-348-1701-5.
Aevum; Milano [anche Univ. Catt.].
AfER: African Ecclesial Review; Eldoret, Kenya.
AfJB: African Journal of Biblical, Studies; Ibadan. [1,1 (1986)].
AfO: Archiv für Orientforschung; Graz.
AfTJ: Africa Theological Journal; Arusha, Tanzania. 0856-0048.
AGJU: Arbeiten zur Geschichte Antik. Judentums und des Urchristentums; Leiden.
AIBL: Académie des Inscriptions et Belles-Lettres; P ➤ CRAI. – AIEMA ➤ BMosA.
AION [-Clas]: Annali (dell')Istituto Universitario Orientale [Classico] ➤ ArchStorAnt di Napoli.
AIPHOS: Annuaire de l'Institut de Philologie et d'Histoire Orientales et Slaves; Bru.
AJA: American Journal of Archaeology; Princeton NJ. 0002-9114.
AJS: Association for Jewish Studies Review; CM 0364-0094 [6 (1981); Newsletter (10, 1985) 0278-4033].
Akkadica; Bruxelles/Brussel.
al.: et alii, and other(s).
ALGHJ: Arbeiten zur Literatur und Geschichte des hellenistischen Judentums; Leiden.
Al-Kibt, The Copts, die Kopten; Ha.
Altertum (Das); B. 0002-6646.
AltOrF: Altorientalische Forschungen; B. 0232-8461.
AmBapQ: American Baptist Quarterly; Valley Forge PA. 0015-8992.
AmBenR: American Benedictine Review; Richardton ND. 0002-7650.
Ambrosius, bollettino liturgico; Milano. 0392-5757.
America; NY. 0002-7049.
AmHR: American Historical Rev.; NY.
AmJAncH: American Journal of Ancient History; CM.
AmJPg: American Journal of Philology; Baltimore. 0002-9475.
AmJTPh: American Journal of Theology and Philosophy; W. Lafayette IN.
AmMessianJ: The American Messianic Jew; Ph.

AmNumM: American Numismatic Society Museum Notes; NY.

AmPhTr: Transactions of the American Philosophical Society; Ph.

AmstCah: Amsterdamse cahiers voor exegese/bijbelse theologie; Kampen.

AmstMed ➤ Mededelingen.

AmStPapyr: American Studies in Papyrology; NHv.

AnAASyr: Annales Archéologiques Arabes Syriennes; Damas.

Anadolu; Ankara, Univ.

AnArStorAnt: Annali di Archeologia e Storia Antica.

Anatolica; Istanbul. 0066-1554.

AnatSt: Anatolian Studies; London.

AnAug: Analecta Augustiniana; R.

ANaut: Archaeonautica; P. 0154-1854.

AnBib: Analecta Biblica. Investigationes scientificae in res biblicas; R. 0066-135X.

AnBoll: Analecta Bollandiana; Bruxelles. 0003-2468.

AnBritAth: Annual of the British School at Athens; London.

AnCalas: Analecta Calasanctiana; Salamanca. 0569-9789.

AnCÉtRel: Annales du Centre d'Études des Religions; Bru.

AncHB: Ancient History Bulletin; Calgary/Chicago. 0835-3638.

AnChile: Anales de la Facultad de Teología; Santiago, Univ. Católica.

AnchorB: Anchor Bible; Garden City NY.

AncHRes: Ancient History ['Ancient Society' till 1987]; Resources for Teachers; Sydney. 0310-5814.

AnCist: Analecta Cisterciensia; Roma. 0003-2476.

AnClas: Annales Universitatis, sectio classica; Budapest.

AnClémOchr: Annuaire de l'Académie de théologie 'Ochrida'; Sofya.

AnCracov: Analecta Cracoviensia (Polish Theol. Soc.); Kraków. 0209-0864.

AncSoc: Ancient Society. Katholieke Universiteit; Leuven. 0066-1619.

AncW: Ancient World; Ch. 0160-9645.

AndrUnS: Andrews University Seminary Studies; Berrien Springs, Mich. 0003-2980.

AnÉCS: Annales Économies Sociétés Civilisations; P. 0395-2649.

AnEgBbg: Annual Egyptological Bibliography; Leiden.

AnÉPH: Annuaire ➤ ÉPHÉ.

AnÉth: Annales d'Éthiopie; Addis-Ababa.

AnFac: Let: Annali della facoltà di lettere, Univ. (Bari/Cagliari/Perugia).

— Ling/T: Annal(es) Facultat(is); linguarum, theologiae.

AnFg: Anuario de Filología; Barc.

Ang: Angelicum; Roma. 0003-3081.

AnglTR: Anglican Theological Review; Evanston IL. 0003-3286.

AnGreg: Analecta (Pont. Univ.) Gregoriana; Roma. 0066-1376.

AnHArt: Annales d'histoire de l'art et d'archéologie: Bru.

AnHConc: Annuarium Historiae Conciliorum; Paderborn.

ANilM: Archéologie du Nil Moyen; Lille. 0299-8130.

AnItNum: Annali (dell')Istituto Italiano di Numismatica; Roma.

AnJapB: Annual of the Japanese Biblical Institute; Tokyo ◑ ➤ Sei-Ron.

AnLetN: Annali della Facoltà di lettere e filosofia dell'Univ.; Napoli.

AnLovBOr: Analecta Lovaniensia Biblica et Orientalia; Lv.

AnnTh: Annales Theologici; Roma.

AnOr: Analecta Orientalia: Roma.

AnOrdBas: Analecta Ordinis S. Basilii Magni; Roma.

AnPg: L'Année Philologique; P. ➤ 1098.

AnPisa: Annali della Scuola Normale Superiore; Pisa.

AnPraem: Analecta Praemonstratensia; Averbode.

AnRIM: Annual Review of the Royal Inscriptions of Mesopotamia Project; Toronto. 0822-2525.

AnRSocSR: Annual Review of the Social Sciences of Religion; The Hague. 0066-2062.

ANRW: Aufstieg und Niedergang der römischen Welt ➤ 828.

AnSacTar: Analecta Sacra Tarraconensia; Barcelona.

AnSemClas: Annali del Seminario di Studi del Mondo Classico; N, Univ.

AnStoEseg: Annali di Storia dell'Esegesi; Bologna.

AntAb: Antike und Abendland; Berlin. 0003-5696.

AntAfr: Antiquités africaines; Paris. 0066-4871.

AntClas: L'Antiquité Classique; Bru.

AntClCr: Antichità classica e cristiana; Brescia.

Anthropos; 1. Fribourg/Suisse. 0003-5572. / [2. Famiglia; Roma].

Anthropotes; Roma, Città Nuova.

AntiqJ: Antiquaries Journal; London. 0003-5815.

Antiquity; Gloucester. 0003-5982.

Ant/ka: ⊖ Anthropologiká: Thessaloniki.

AntKu: Antike Kunst; Basel. 0003-5688.

Anton: Antonianum; Roma. 0003-6064.

AntRArch: Antiqua, Rivista d'Archeologia e d'Architettura; Roma.

AnTVal: Anales de Teología, Universidad de Valencia.

AntWelt: Antike Welt; Feldmeilen.

Anvil, Anglican Ev. theol.; Bramcote, Nottingham. 0003-6226.

AnzAltW: Anzeiger für die Altertumswissenschaft; Innsbruck. 0003-6293.

AnzW: Anzeiger der österreichischen Akademie; Wien. 0378-8652.

AOAT: Alter Orient und Altes Testament: Kevelaer/Neukirchen.

AOtt: Univ. München, Arbeiten zu Text und Sprache im AT; St. Ottilien.

Apollonia: Afro-Hellenic studies; Johannesburg, Rand Afrikaans Univ.

Aram: Oxford.

Arasaradi, journal of theological reflection: Tamilnadu, Madurai (3/2, 1990).

ArBegG: Archiv für Begriffsgeschichte (Mainz, Akad.); Bonn.

ArbGTL: Arbeiten zur Geschichte und Theologie des Luthertums, NF; B.

ArbKiG: Arbeiten zur Kirchengeschichte; B.

ArbNTJud: Arbeiten zum NT und zum Judentum: Frankfurt/M. 0170-8856.

ArbNtTextf: Arbeiten zur Neutestamentlichen Textforschung; B/NY.

ArbT: Arbeiten zur Theologie (Calwer); Stu.

ArCalc: Archeologia e calcolatori; F, Univ. Siena [1 (1990) 88-7814-072-4].

ARCE → J [News] AmEg.

Archaeología; Wrocław. 0066-605X.

Archaeology; Boston. 0003-8113.

Archaeometry; L. 0003-813X.

ArchAnz: Archäologischer Anzeiger; Berlin. 0003-8105.

ArchAth: ⊖ Archaiología; Athēna.

ArchBbg: Archäologische Bibliographie zu JbDAI; Berlin.

ArchClasR: Archeologia Classica; Roma. 0391-8165.

Archeo, attualità del passato; Milano.

Archéologia; (ex-Paris) Dijon, Faton. 0570-6270 → Dossiers.

ArchEph: ⊖ Archaiologikē Ephēmeris; Athēnai.

ArchInf: Archäologische Informationen; Bonn.

ArchMIran: Archäologische Mitteilungen aus Iran, N.F.; Berlin.

ArchNews: Archaeological News; Tallahassee FL. 0194-3413.

ArchRCamb: Archaeological Reviews from Cambridge (Eng.). 0261-4332.

ArchRep: Archaeological Reports; Wmr, British Sch. Athens. 0570-6084.

ArchStorAnt: [= a *third* AION] Archeologia e Storia Antica; Napoli, Univ. Ist. Or./Cl. 0393-070X.

Arctos, Acta Philologica Fennica; Helsinki. 0570-734X.

ArEspArq: Archivo Español de Arqueología; Madrid. 0066-6742.

ARET/S: Archivi Reali di Ebla, Testi/Studi; Roma, Univ.

Arethusa; Buffalo NY. 0004-0975.

ArFrancHist: Archivum Franciscanum Historicum; Grottaferrata.

ArGlottIt: Archivio Glottologico Italiano; Firenze. 0004-0207.

ArHPont: Archivum Historiae Pontificiae; Roma.

ArKulturg: Archiv für Kulturgeschichte; Köln. 0003-9233.

ArLtgW: Archiv für Liturgiewissenschaft; Regensburg. 0066-6386.

ArOr: Archiv Orientální; Praha. 0044-8699.

ArPapF: Archiv für Papyrusforschung; Leipzig. 0066-6459.

ArRefG: Archiv für Reformationsgeschichte; Gütersloh.

ArSSocRel: Archives de Sciences Sociales des Religions; Paris.

ArTGran: Archivo Teológico Granadino; Granada. 0210-1629.

ArztC: Arzt und Christ; Salzburg.

ASAE: Annales du Service des Antiquités de l'Égypte; Le Caire.

AsbTJ: Asbury Theological Journal; Wilmore, KY.

AshlandTJ: ... Theological J. (Ohio).

AsiaJT: Asia Journal of Theology; Tokyo.

ASOR: American Schools of Oriental Research; CM (**diss.:** Dissertation Series).

Asprenas... Scienze Teologiche; Napoli.

At[AcBol/Tor/Tosc]: Atti [dell'Accademia... di Bologna / di Torino / Toscana].

ATANT: Abhandlungen zur Theologie des Alten & Neuen Testaments; Zürich.

ATD: Das Alte Testament Deutsch. Neues Göttinger Bibelwerk; Gö.

AteDial: Ateismo e Dialogo; Vaticano.

AtenRom: Atene e Roma; Firenze. 0004-6493.

Athenaeum: Letteratura e Storia dell'antichità; Pavia.

Atiqot, English edition; J, Dept. Ant.

AtKap: Ateneum Kapłańskie; Włocławek. 0208-9041.

ATLA: American Theological Library Association; Menuchen, NJ.

Atualização, Revista de Divulgação Teológica; Belo Horizonte, MG.

AuCAfr: Au cœur de l'Afrique; Burundi.

AugL: Augustinus-Lexikon ➤ 829.

AugLv: Augustiniana; Leuven.

AugM: Augustinus; Madrid.

AugR: Augustinianum; Roma.

AugSt: Augustinian Studies; Villanova PA.

AulaO: Aula Orientalis; Barc.

AusgF: Ausgrabungen und Funde; B.

AustinSB: Austin (TX) Sem. Bulletin.

AustralasCR: Australasian Catholic Record; Sydney. 0727-3215.

AustralBR: Australian Biblical Review; Melbourne.

AVA: ➤ Bei AVgA.

BA: Biblical Archaeologist; CM. 0006-0895.

Babel (translation); Budapest, Akad.

BaBernSt: Basler und Berner Studien zur hist./systematischen Theologie; Bern.

Babesch: Bulletin Antieke Beschaving; Haag. 0165-9367.

BaghMit: Baghdader Mitteilungen DAI; Berlin.

BAH: Bibliothèque Archéologique et Historique (IFA-Beyrouth).

BAngIsr: Bulletin of the Anglo-Israel Archaeological Soc.; L. 0266-2442.

BangTF: Bangalore Theological Forum.

BaptQ: Baptist [Historical Soc.] Quarterly; Oxford. 0005-576X.

BArchAlg: Bulletin d'Archéologie Algérienne; Alger.

BarIlAn: Bar-Ilan Annual; Ramat-Gan. 0067-4109.

BAR: British Archaeology Reports; Ox.

BAR-W: Biblical Archaeology Review; Washington. 0098-9444.

BArte: Bollettino d'Arte; Roma.

BAsEsp[Or/Eg]: Boletín de la Asociación Española de Orientalistas / de Egiptología (2, 1990); Madrid.

BASOR: Bulletin of the American Schools of Oriental Research; Atlanta. 0003-097X.

BASP: Bulletin, American Society of Papyrologists; NY. 0003-1186.

BAusPrax: Biblische Auslegung für die Praxis; Stuttgart.

Bazmaveb (Pazmavep; Armenian); Venezia.

BBArchäom: Berliner Beiträge zur Archäometrie; Berlin. 0344-5098.

BBB: ➤ BiBasB & BoBB.

BbbOr: Bibbia e Oriente; Bornato BS.

BBelgRom: Bulletin de l'Institut Historique Belge; R. 0073-8530.

Bbg: Bibliographia/-ly.

BBudé: Bulletin de l'Association G. Budé; Paris.

BBVO: Berliner Beiträge zum Vorderen Orient: B, Reimer.

BCanadB: Bulletin of the Canadian Society of Biblical Studies; Ottawa.

BCanMedit: Bulletin of the Canad. Mediterranean Institute ➤ **BMes.**

BCentPrei: Bollettino del Centro Camuno di Studi Preistorici; Brescia. 0057-2168.

BCentProt: Bulletin du Centre Protestant d'Études; Genève.

BCH: Bulletin de Correspondance Hellénique; Paris. 0007-4217.

BCILL: Bibliothèque des Cahiers de l'Institut de Linguistique; Lv/P.

BCNH-T: Bibliothèque Copte de Nag Hammadi -Textes; Québec.

BEcuT: Bulletin of ecumenical theology; Enugu, Nigeria [2,1 (1989)].

BeerSheva: ❶ Annual: Bible/ANE; J.

BÉF: Bibliothèque des Écoles françaises d'Athènes et de Rome; R. → MÉF.

BEgS: Bulletin of the Egyptological Seminar; NY.

BeitATJ: Beiträge zur Erforschung des Alten Testaments und des Antiken Judentums; Bern. 0722-0790.

BeitAVgArch: Beiträge zur allgemeinen und vergleichenden Archäologie; Mü, Beck.

BeitBExT: Beiträge zur biblischen Exegese und Theologie [ipsi: BET]; Frankfurt/M.

BeitEvT: Beiträge zur evangelischen Theologie; München.

BeitGbEx: Beiträge zur Geschichte der biblischen Exegese; Tübingen.

BeitHistT: Beiträge zur Historischen Theologie; Tübingen.

BeitNam: Beiträge zur Namenforschung N. F.; Heid. 0005-8114.

BeitÖkT: Beiträge zur ökumenischen Theologie; München, Schöningh. 0067-5172.

BeitRelT: Beiträge zur Religionstheologie; Wien-Mödling.

BeitSudan: Beiträge zur Sudanforschung; Wien, Univ.

Belleten (Türk Tarih Kurumu); Ankara.

Benedictina; Roma.

Berytus (Amer. Univ. Beirut); K.

BethM: ❶ Beth Mikra; Jerusalem. 0005-979X.

BÉtOr: Bulletin d'Études Orientales; Damas, IFAO.

BFaCLyon: Bulletin des Facultés Catholiques; Lyon. 0180-5282.

Bib → Biblica; Roma. 0006-0887.

BibAfr: La Bible en Afrique [francophone]; Lomé, Togo.

BiBasB: Biblische Basis Bücher; Kevelaer/ Stuttgart.

BiBeit: Biblische Beiträge, Schweizerisches Kath. Bibelwerk; Fribourg.

BibFe: Biblia y Fe; M. 0210-5209.

BibIll: Biblical Illustrator; Nv.

BibKonf: Biblische Konfrontationen; Stu.

Bible Bhashyam: Kottayam. 0970-2288.

Biblica: commentarii Pontificii Instituti Biblici; Roma. 0006-0887.

Biblos 1. Coimbra; 2. Wien.

BibNot: Biblische Notizen; Bamberg. 0178-2967.

BibOrPont: Biblica et Orientalia, Pontificio Istituto Biblico; Roma.

BibTB: Biblical Theology Bulletin; St. Bonaventure NY. 0146-1079.

BibTSt: Biblisch-Theologische Studien; Neukirchen-Vluyn. 0930-4800.

BibUnt: Biblische Untersuchungen; Regensburg.

BIFAO: Bulletin de l'Institut Français d'Archéologie Orientale; Le Caire. 0255-0962.

Bijd: Bijdragen, Filosofie en Theologie; Nijmegen. 0006-2278.

BijH: Bijbels Handboek; Kampen = World of the Bible; GR → 830.

BiKi: Bibel und Kirche; Stuttgart. 0006-0623.

BInfWsz: Bulletin d'Information de l'Académie de Théologie Catholique; Warszawa. 0137-7000.

BInstArch: Bulletin of the Institute of Archaeology; London. 0076-0722.

BIP[Br]: Books in Print, U.S., annual; NY, Bowker [British, L, Whitaker].

BiRes: Biblical Research; Chicago. 0067-6535.

Biserica ... Ortodoxă; Bucureşti.

BIstFGrec: Bollettino dell'Istituto di Filologia Greca, Univ. Padova; R.

Bits and bytes review; Whitefish MT. 0891-2955.

BJG: Bulletin of Judaeo-Greek Studies; Cambridge Univ.

BJRyL: Bulletin of the John Rylands Library; Manchester. 0301-102X.

BKAT: Biblischer Kommentar AT; Neuk.

BL: Book List, The Society for Old Testament Study. 0309-0892.

BLCéramEg: Bulletin de liaison ... céramique égyptienne; Le Caire, IFAO. 0255-0903.

BLitEc [Chr]: Bulletin de Littérature Ecclésiastique [Chronique]. Toulouse. 0007-4322 [0495-9396].

BLtg: Bibel und Liturgie; Wien-Klosterneuburg. 0006-064X.

BMB: Bulletin du Musée de Beyrouth.

BMeijiG: Bulletin of the Christian Research Institute Meiji Gakuin Univ.; Tokyo (23, 1990).

BMes: Bulletin, the Society for Mesopotamian Studies; Toronto.

BMosA [ipsi **AIEMA**]: Bulletin, étude mosaïque antique; P. 0761-8808.

BO: Bibliotheca Orientalis; Leiden. 0006-1913.

BoBB: Bonner Biblische Beiträge; Königstein.

Bobolanum, teologia; Wsz. 0867-3330. (1, 1990).

BogSmot: Bogoslovska Smotra; Zagreb. 0352-3101.

BogVest: Bogoslovni Vestnik; Ljubljana.

BonnJb: Bonner Jahrbücher.

Boreas [1. Uppsala, series]; 2. Münster, Archäologie. 0344-810X.

BProtF: Bulletin de la Société de l'Histoire du Protestantisme Français; P.

BR: Bible Review; Wsh. 8755-6316.

BRefB: Bulletin, Reformation Biblical Studies: Fort Wayne.

BritJREd: British Journal of Religious Education; London,

BRöG: Bericht der Römisch-Germanischen Kommission DAI; Mainz. 0341-9312 (71, 1990).

BrownJudSt/StRel: Brown Judaic Studies / Studies in Religion; Atlanta.

BS: Bibliotheca Sacra; Dallas, TX. 0006-1921.

BSAA: Boletín, Seminario Estudios Arte y Arqueología; Valladolid.

BSAC: Bulletin de la Société d'Archéologie Copte; Le Caire.

BSeptCog: Bulletin of the International Organization for Septuagint and Cognate Studies; ND.

BSignR: Bulletin Signalétique, religions; Paris. 0180-9296.

BSLP: Bulletin de la Société de Linguistique; Paris.

BSNAm: Biblical Scholarship in North America; Atlanta, SBL.

BSNEJap ➔ Oriento.

BSO: Bulletin of the School of Oriental and African Studies; London. 0041-977X.

BSoc[Fr]Ég: Bulletin de la Société [Française] d'Égyptologie; Genève [Paris].

BSoGgIt: Bollettino della Società Geografica Italiana; R. 0037-8755.

BSpade: Bible and Spade; Ballston NY.

BStLat: Bollettino di Studi Latini; N.

BSumAg: Bulletin on Sumerian Agriculture; Cambridge. 0267-0658.

Bt: Bibliotheca/-que.

BTAfr: Bulletin de Théologie Africaine; Kinshasa.

BTAM: Bulletin de Théologie Ancienne et Médiévale; Louvain. ➔ RTAM.

BtEscB/EstB: Biblioteca Escuela Bíblica; M / de Estudios Bíblicos, Salamanca.

BtETL: Bibliotheca, ETL; Leuven.

BThemT: Bibliothek Themen der Theologie; Stuttgart.

BtHumRef: Bibliotheca Humanistica et Reformatorica; Nieuwkoop, de Graaf.

BtHumRen: Bibliothèque d'Humanisme et Renaissance; Genève/Paris.

BtMesop: Bibliotheca Mesopotamica; Malibu CA.

BToday: The Bible Today; Collegeville MN. 0006-0836.

BTrans: The Bible Translator [Technical/ Practical]; Stu. 0260-0943.

BtScRel: Biblioteca di Scienze religiose; Roma, Salesiana.

BTSt: Biblisch-theologische Studien (ex-Biblische Studien); Neukirchen.

BtStor: Biblioteca di storia e storiografia dei tempi biblici; Brescia.

BTT: Bible de tous les temps; P.

BtTPaid: Biblioteca Teologica; Brescia, Paideia.

BTZ: Berliner Theologische Zeitschrift; Berlin. 0724-6137.

BuBbgB: Bulletin de Bibliographie Biblique; Lausanne (1, 1990).

BUBS: Bulletin of the United Bible Societies; Stu.

BudCSt: Buddhist-Christian Studies; Honolulu, Univ. 0882-0945.

Burgense; Burgos. 0521-8195.

BurHist: Buried History; Melbourne. 0007-6260.

BVieChr: Bible et Vie Chrétienne; P.

BViewp: Biblical Viewpoint; Greenville SC, Jones Univ. 0006-0925.

BW: Beiträge zur Wissenschaft vom Alten und Neuen Testament; Stuttgart.

BySlav: Byzantinoslavica; Praha. 0007-7712.

ByZ: Byzantinische Zeitschrift; München. 0007-7704.

Ⓖ Byzantina; Thessaloniki.

Byzantion; Bruxelles.

ByzFor: Byzantinische Forschungen; Amsterdam.

BZ: Biblische Zeitschrift; Paderborn. 0006-2014.

BZA[N]W: Beihefte zur ➤ ZAW [ZNW].

CAD: [Chicago] Assyrian Dictionary; Glückstadt. ➤ 9439.

CADIR: Centre pour l'Analyse du Discours Religieux; Lyon ➤ SémBib.

CAH: Cambridge Ancient History²; Cambridge Univ. ➤ 831.

CahArchéol: Cahiers Archéologiques; Paris.

CahCMéd: Cahiers de Civilisation Médiévale; Poitiers.

CahDAFI: Cahiers de la Délégation Archéologique Française en Iran; Paris. 0765-104X.

CahÉv: Cahiers Évangile; Paris. 0222-8741.

CahHist: Cahiers d'Histoire; Lyon.

CahIntSymb: Cahiers Internationaux de Symbolique; Mons, Belgique.

CahLV: Cahiers voor Levensverdieping; Averbode.

CahRechScRel: Cahiers de Recherche en Sciences de la Religion; Québec.

CahSpIgn: Cahiers de spiritualité ignatienne; Québec.

CahTrB: Cahiers de traduction biblique; Pierrefitte France. 0755-1371.

CahTun: Les Cahiers (de la Faculté des Lettres) de Tunisie; Tunis.

CalvaryB: Calvary Baptist Theological Journal; Lansdale PA. 8756-0429.

CalvinT: Calvin Theological Journal; Grand Rapids MI. 0008-1795.

CalwTMon: Calwer Theologische Monographien (A: Biblisch); Stuttgart.

CamCW: Cambridge Commentary on Writings of the Jewish and Christian World.

CanadCR: Canadian Catholic Review; Saskatoon.

Carmel: Tilburg.

Carmelus: Roma. 0008-6673.

Carthage Conservation Bulletin; Tunis.

Carthaginensia; Murcia, Inst. Teol. 0213-4381.

CathCris: Catholicism in crisis; ND.

CathHR: Catholic Historical Review; Wsh. 0008-8080.

Catholica (Moehler-Institut, Paderborn); Münster.

Catholicisme: Paris ➤ 833.

Catholic Studies, Tokyo ➤ Katorikku.

CathTR: Catholic Theological Review; Clayton/Hong Kong.

CathTSocAmPr: ➤ PrCTSAm [AnCTS].

CATSS: Computer assisted tools for Septuagint studies: Atlanta ➤ SBL.

CBQ: Catholic Biblical Quarterly; Washington, DC. 0008-7912.

CC: La Civiltà Cattolica; R. 0009-8167.

CCGraec/Lat/Med: Corpus Christianorum, series graeca / latina / continuatio mediaev.; Turnhout.

CdÉ: Chronique d'Égypte; Bruxelles.

CEB: Commentaire évangelique de la Bible; Vaux/Seine ➤ Édifac.

Center Journal; Notre Dame.

CERDAC: (Atti) Centro di Ricerca e Documentazione Classica; Milano

CERDIC: Centre d'échanges et de recherches sur la diffusion et l'inculturation du christianisme.

CETÉDOC: Centre de Traitement Électronique des Documents; Lv.

CGL: Coptic Gnostic Library ➤ NHS.

CGMG: Christlicher Glaube in moderner Gesellschaft; FrB.

ChCu: Church and Culture; Vatican.

CHermProt: Centre d'Herméneutique Protestante.

ChH: Church History; Indiatlantic FL.

CHH: Center for Hermeneutical Studies in Hellenistic & Modern Culture; Berkeley.

Chiea [ChAfC]: Nairobi, Catholic Higher Institute of Eastern Africa.

CHIran: Cambridge History of Iran ➤ 834.

Chiron: Geschichte, Epigraphie; München.

CHistEI: Ⓗ Cathedra, History of Eretz-Israel; Jerusalem.

CHist-J: Jerusalem Cathedra.

CHJud: Cambridge History of Judaism ➤ 835.

Chm: Churchman 1. (Anglican); London: 0009-661X / 2. (Humanistic); St. Petersburg FL: 0009-6628.

ChrCent: Christian Century; Chicago. Christus; 1. Paris; 2. México.

ChrJRel: Christian Jewish Relations; L.

ChrNIsr: Christian News from Israel; J.

ChrOost: Het Christelijk Oosten; Nijmegen.

ChrSchR: Christian Scholar's Review; Houston TX.

ChrT: Christianity Today; Carol Stream IL. 0009-5761.

ChSt: Chicago Studies; Mundelein IL. Church: NY, Nat. Pastoral Life.

ChWoman: The Church Woman; NY. 0009-6598.

CistSt: Cistercian Studies; ed. Getsemani KY; pub. Chimay, Belgium. Citeaux; Achel, Belgium. 0009-7497.

Cithara: Judaeo-Christian Tradition; St. Bonaventure (NY) Univ.

CiTom: Ciencia Tomista; S. 0210-0398.

CiuD: Ciudad de Dios; M. 0009-7756.

CivClCr: Civiltà classica e cristiana; Genova. 0392-8632.

CiVit: Città di Vita; Firenze. [0]009-7632.

Claret: Claretianum; Roma.

ClasA: [formerly California Studies in] Classical Antiquity; Berkeley.

ClasB: Classical Bulletin; Ch. 0009-8137 (ᴱAsbury Coll., Wilmore KY).

ClasJ: Classical Journal; Greenville SC. 0009-8353.

ClasMed: Classica et Mediaevalia; København. 0106-5815.

ClasOutl: The Classical Outlook; Ch [ed. Miami Univ. OH]. 0009-8361.

ClasPg: Classical Philology; Chicago. 0009-8361.

ClasQ: Classical Quarterly NS; Oxford. 0009-8388.

ClasR: Classical Review NS; Oxford. 0009-840X.

ClasWo: Classical World; Pittsburgh. 0009-8148.

CLehre: Die Christenlehre; Berlin. Clio, studi storici; N.

CMatArch: Contributi e materiali di archeologia orientale; Roma, Univ.

CNRS: Conseil National de Recherche Scientifique; Paris.

CogF: Cogitatio Fidei; Paris.

ColcCist: Collectanea Cisterciensia; Forges, Belgique.

ColcFranc: Collectanea Franciscana; Roma. 0010-0749.

ColcT: Collectanea Theologica; Warszawa. 0137-6985.

ColcTFu: Collectanea theol. Universitatis Fujen = *Shenhsileh Lunchi*; Taipei.

CollatVL: Collationes, Vlaams... Theologie en Pastoraal; Gent. Colloquium; Auckland, Sydney.

ColStFen: Collezione di Studi Fenici; Roma, Univ.

ComLtg: Communautés et Liturgies; Ottignies (Belgique). Commentary; NY. 0010-2601.

CommBras: Communio Brasiliensis: Rio de Janeiro.

CommND: Communio USA; Notre Dame. 0094-2065.

CommRevue: Communio [various languages, not related to **ComSev**]: revue catholique internationale; Paris.

CommStrum: Communio, strumento internazionale per un lavoro teologico; Milano. Communio deutsch ➤ **IkaZ.**

ComOT: Commentaar op het Oude Testament. Kampen.

CompHum: Computers and the Humanities; Osprey FL. 0010-4817.

CompNT: Compendium rerum Iudaicarum ad NT; Assen. Compostellanum; Santiago de Compostela.

ComRatisbNT: Comentario de Ratisbona; Barc.

ComSev: Communio; Sevilla. 0010-3705.

ComSpirAT/NT: Commenti spirituali dell'Antico / Nuovo Testamento; Roma.

ComTeolNT: Commentario Teologico del NT; Brescia.

ComViat: Communio Viatorum; Praha. 0010-7133. Suspended after 33/2, 1990.

ConBib: Coniectanea Biblica OT/NT; Malmö.

Conc: Concilium, variis linguis; Paris etc. [deutsch = ➤ IZT].

ConcordJ: Concordia Journal; St. Louis. 0145-7233.

ConcordTQ: Concordia Theological Quarterly; Fort Wayne.

ConsJud: Conservative Judaism; NY. 0010-6542.

Contacts/Orthodoxe, de théologie et spiritualité; P. 0045-8325.

ContrIstStorAnt: Contributi dell'Istituto di Storia Antica; Milano, Univ. Sacro Cuore.

Coptologia [also for Egyptology]: Thunder Bay ONT, Lakehead Univ.

CouStR: Council for the Study of Religion Bulletin; Macon GA, Mercer Univ.

CovQ: Covenant Quarterly; Chicago.

CRAI: Comptes rendus de l'Académie des Inscriptions et Belles-Lettres; P.

Cretan Studies; Amst.

CRIPEL ➤ SocUÉg.

CriswT: Criswell Theological Review; Dallas.

Criterio; Buenos Aires. 0011-1473,

CritRR: Critical Review of Books in Religion: Atlanta (1, 1988 ➤ 4,947*).

CrkvaSv: Crkva u Svijetu; Split.

CrNSt: Cristianesimo nella Storia; Bologna. 0393-3598.

CroatC: Croatica Christiana; Zagreb.

CrossC: Cross Currents; West Nyack NJ. 0011-1953.

Crux: Vancouver. 0011-2186.

CSacSN: Corpus Sacrae Scripturae Neerlandicae Medii Aevi; Leiden.

CSCO: Corpus Scriptorum Christianorum Orientalium; Lv. 0070-0401.

CuadJer: Cuadernos Bíblicos, Institución S. Jerónimo; Valencia.

CuadFgClás: Cuadernos de Filología Clásica; M, Univ.

CuadTeol: Cuadernos de Teología; Buenos Aires.

CuadTrad: Cuadernos de Traducción y Interpretación; Barc.

CuBíb: Cultura Bíblica; M: AFEBE. 0211-2493.

CuesT: Cuestiones Teológicas; Medellín.

CuH: Culture and History; K.

CurrTMiss: Currents in Theology and Mission; St. Louis. 0098-2113.

CyrMeth: Cyrillomethodianum; Thessaloniki.

D: director (in Indice etiam *auctor*) Dissertationis.

DAFI: Délégation Archéologique Française en Iran (Mém); Paris.

DAI: Deutsches Archäologisches Institut (Baghdad etc.) ➤ Mi(tt).

DanTTs: Dansk Teologisk Tidsskrift; København.

DanVMed/Skr: Dansk. Videnskabornes Selskap, Hist./Fil. Meddelelser / Skriften; K.

DBS [= SDB].

DeltChr: Deltion tes christianikēs archaiologikēs hetaireias: Athēna.

DeltVM: Ⓖ Deltío vivlikôn meletôn, Bulletin Études Bibliques; Athēnai.

DHGE: Dictionnaire d'Histoire et de Géographie Ecclésiastiques; P ➤ 836.

Diakonia; Mainz/Wien. 0341-9592; Stu.

DialArch: Dialoghi di Archeologia; Mi.

DiálEcum: Diálogo Ecuménico; Salamanca. 0210-2870.

Dialog; Minneapolis. 0012-2033.

DialTP: Diálogo teológico; El Paso TX.

DictSpir: Dictionnaire de Spiritualité; P. ➤ 837.

Didascalia; Rosario ARG.

Didaskalia; Lisboa.

DielB: Dielheimer Blätter zum Alten Testament [ipsi DBAT]; Heid.

Dionysius: Halifax. 0705-1085.

Direction; Fresno CA.

DiscEg: Discussions in Egyptology; Oxford. 0268-3083.

Disciple, the (Disciples of Christ); St. Louis. 0092-8372.

DissA: Dissertation Abstracts International; AA/L. -A [= US]: 0419-4209 [C = Europe. 0307-6075].

DissHRel: Dissertationes ad historiam religionum (supp. Numen); Leiden.

Divinitas, Pont. Acad. Theol. Rom. (Lateranensis); Vaticano. 0012-4222.

DivThom: Divus Thomas; Piacenza. 0012-4257.

DizTF: Dizionario di Teologia Fondamentale ➤ 837.

DJD: Discoveries in the Judaean Desert; Oxford.

DLZ: Deutsche Literaturzeitung; Berlin. 0012-043X.

DMA: Dictionary of the Middle Ages; NY ➤ 838.

DocCath: Documentation Catholique; Paris.

DoctCom: Doctor Communis; Vaticano.

DoctLife: Doctrine and Life; Dublin.

DOG: Deutsche Orient-Gesellschaft: B.
Dor ⇸ JBQ.
DosB: Les dossiers de la Bible; P.
DossHA: Histoire et archéologie, les dossiers; Dijon.
DowR: Downside Review; Bath. 0012-5806.
DPA: Dizionario patristico e di antichità cristiane; Casale Monferrato ⇸ 838*.
DrevVost: ❸ Drevnij Vostok; Moskva.
DrewG: The Drew [Theological School] Gateway; Madison NJ.
DumbO: Dumbarton Oaks Papers; CM. 0070-7546.
DutchMgA: Dutch Monographs in Ancient History and Archaeology; Amst.
E: editor, Herausgeber, a cura di.
EAfJE: East African Journal of Evangelical Theology; Machakos, Kenya.
EAsJT: East Asia Journal of Theology [combining NE & SE AJT]; Tokyo. 0217-3859.
EAPast: East Asian Pastoral Review; Manila. 0040-0564.
ÉcAnn: Écoutez et Annoncez, mensuel; Lomé, Togo [6 (1984)].
ÉchMClas: Échos du Monde Classique/Classical Views; Calgary. 0012-9356.
ÉchSM: Les Échos de Saint-Maurice; Valais, Abbaye.
EcOr: Ecclesia Orans, periodica de scientiis liturgicis; R, Anselmiano [1,1 (1984)].
ÉcoutBib: Écouter la Bible; Paris.
EcuR: Ecumenical Review; Geneva. 0013-0790.
EDIFAC: Éditions de la Faculté libre de Théologie Évangélique; Vaux/Seine.
EfMex: Efemerides Mexicana; Tlalpan.
Egb: Ergänzungsband.
ÉglRur après 488 (1987) ⇸ Sève.
ÉglT: Église et Théologie; Ottawa.
EgVO: Egitto e Vicino Oriente; Pisa.
ÉHRel: Études d'histoire des religions.
Eikasmós, Quaderni di Filologia Classica; Bo, Univ. (1, 1990).
Einzb: Einzelband.
EkK [Vor]: Evangelischer-katholischer Kommentar zum NT; Z/Köln; Neukirchen-Vluyn ['Vorarbeiten'].
EkkT: ❸ Ekklēsía kaì Theología; L.

Elenchos, ... pensiero antico; Napoli.
Ellin? ; ❸ Thessaloniki.
Emerita: (lingüística clásica); M.
Emmanuel: St. Meinrads IN/NY. 0013-6719.
Enc. Biblica ⇸ EnṣMiqr.
EncHebr: ❿ Encyclopaedia Hebraica; J/TA.
Enchoria, Demotistik/Koptologie; Wsb.
EncIran: Encyclopaedia Iranica; L.
EncIslam: Encyclopédie de l'Islam. Nouvelle édition; Leiden/P ⇸ 890.
EncKat: Encyklopedia Katolicka; Lublin ⇸ 891.
Encounter (theol.); Indianapolis.
EncRel: (1) ᴱEliade M., The encyclopedia of religion; NY ⇸ 841; (2) Enciclopedia delle Religioni; Firenze.
EncTF: Enciclopedia di Teologia Fondamentale; Genova ⇸ 843.
EnṣMiqr: ❿ Enṣiqlopediya miqrā'ît, Encyclopaedia Biblica; Jerusalem.
Entschluss: Wien. 0017-4602.
EnzMär: Enzyklopädie des Märchens; B ⇸ 3, 860.
EOL: Ex Oriente Lux ⇸ 1.Jb/2. Phoenix.
Eos, ... philologia; Wsz. 0012-7825.
EpAnat: Epigraphica anatolica; Bonn.
ÉPHÉ[H/R]: École Pratique des Hautes-Études, Annuaire [Hist.-Pg. / Sc. Rel.]; Paris.
EpHetVyz: ❸ Ephēmeris tēs Hetaireías Vyzantinōn Spoudōn; Athēnai.
EphLtg: Ephemerides Liturgicae; R.
EphMar: Ephemerides Mariologicae; Madrid.
ÉPR: Études préliminaires aux religions orientales dans l'Empire romain; Leiden.
Eranos[/Jb]: Acta Philologica Suecana; Uppsala / Jahrbuch; Fra.
ErbAuf: Erbe und Auftrag; Beuron.
Eretz-Israel (partly ❿); J. 0071-108X.
ErfTSt/Schr: Erfurter Theologische Studien/ Schriften.
ErtFor: Ertrag der Forschung; Darmstadt, Wiss. 0174-0695.
EscrVedat: Escritos del Vedat; Valencia. 0210-3133.
EsprVie: Esprit et Vie: 1. [< Ami du Clergé]; Langres; 2. Chambray.
EstAgust: Estudio Agustiniano; Valladolid. 0425-340X.
EstBíb: Estudios Bíblicos; Madrid. 0014-1437.

EstDeusto: Estudios de (Universidad) Deusto; Madrid. 0423-4847.
EstE: Estudios Eclesiásticos; Madrid. 0210-1610.
EstFranc: Estudios Franciscanos; Barcelona.
EstJos: Estudios Josefinos; Valladolid.
EstLul: Estudios Lulianos; Mallorca.
EstMar: Estudios Marianos; Madrid.
EstMonInstJer: Estudios y Monografias, Institución S. Jerónimo (bíblica); Valencia.
EstTrin: Estudios Trinitarios; Salamanca.
EstudosB: Estudos Bíblicos; Petrópolis.
ÉtBN: Études Bibliques, Nouvelle Série; Paris. 0760-3541.
ÉtClas: Les études classiques; Namur. 0014-200X.
ÉtFranc: Études Franciscaines; Blois.
ETL: Ephemerides Theologicae Lovanienses; Leuven. 0013-9513. ➤ **Bt.**
ÉtPapyr: Études [Société Égyptienne] de Papyrologie; Le Caire.
ÉtPgHist: Études de Philologie et d'Histoire; Genève, Droz.
ÉTRel: Études Théologiques et Religieuses; Montpellier. 0014-2239.
ÉtTrav: Études et Travaux; Varsovie.
Études; Paris. 0014-1941.
Euhemer (❷ hist. rel.); Wsz. 0014-2298
EuntDoc: Euntes Docete; Roma.
EurHS: Europäische Hochschulschriften / Publ. Universitaires Européennes; Bern.
Evangel; Edinburgh. 0265-4547.
EvErz: Der evangelische Erzieher; Frankfurt/M. 0014-3413.
EvJ: Evangelical Journal; Myerstown.
EvKL: Evangelisches Kirchenlexikon; ➤ 844.
EvKom: Evangelische Kommentare; Stuttgart. 0300-4236.
EvQ[RT]: Evangelical Quarterly [Review of Theology]; Exeter.
EvT: Evangelische Theologie, NS; München. 0014-3502.
EWest: East and West | 1. L / 2. R.
EWSp: Encyclopedia of World Spirituality; NY/L.
ExAud: Ex auditu; Princeton. 0883-0053.
ExcSIsr: Excavations and Surveys in Israel < Ḥadašot; J. 0334-1607.
Expedition; Ph. 0014-4738.
Explor [sic]; Evanston. 0362-0876.

ExpTim: The Expository Times; Edinburgh. 0014-5246.
ExWNTT ➤ 868.
F&R: Faith and Reason; Front Royal VA. 0098-5449.
FascBib: Fascículos bíblicos; Madrid.
Faventia: classica; Barc. 0210-7570.
fg./fil.: filologia/co, filosofia/co.
FgNt: Filologia neotestamentaria; Córdoba, Univ.
FidH: Fides et Historia; Longview TX.
FilT: Filosofia e teologia; Napoli.
FoiTemps: La Foi et le Temps. NS; Tournai.
FoiVie: Foi et Vie; Paris. 0015-5357.
FolOr: Folia Orientalia, Polska Akademia Nauk; Kraków. 0015-5675.
Fondamenti; Brescia, Paideia.
ForBib: Forschung zur Bibel; Wü/Stu.
ForBMusB: Forschungen und Berichte, Staatliche Museen zu Berlin.
ForGLProt: Forschungen zur Geschichte und Lehre des Protestantismus; Mü.
ForJüdChrDial: Forschungen zum jüdisch-christlichen Dialog; Neuk.
ForKiDG: Forschungen zur Kirchen- und Dogmengeschichte; Gö.
Fornvännen; Lund. 0015-7813.
ForSystÖ: Forschungen zur Systematischen & Ökumenischen Theologie; Gö.
ForTLing: Forum Theologiae Linguisticae; Bonn.
Forum [= Foundations & Facets]; Bonner MT. 0883-4970.
ForumKT: Forum Katholische Theologie; Münster. 0178-1626.
FOTLit: Forms of OT Literature; GR, Eerdmans.
FraJudBei: Frankfurter Judaistische Beiträge; Fra.
FranBog: Franciscanum, ciencias del espíritu; Bogotá. 0120-1468.
FrancSt: Franciscan Studies; St. Bonaventure, NY. 0080-5459.
FranzSt: Franziskanische Studien; Pd.
FraTSt: Frankfurter Theologische Studien; Fra, S. Georgen.
FreibRu: Freiburger Rundbrief. ... christlich-jüdische Begegnung; FrB.
FreibTSt: Freiburger Theologische Studien; Freiburg/Br.
FreibZ: Freiburger Zeitschrift für Philosophie und Theologie; Fribourg.

FRL: Forschungen zur Religion und Literatur des Alten und NTs; Gö.

FutUo: Il futuro dell'uomo; Firenze, Assoc. Teilhard. 0390-217X.

Ⓖ *Graece*; title/text in Greek.

GCS: Die Griechischen Christlichen Schriftsteller der ersten Jahrhunderte; B.

GdT: Giornale di Teologia; Brescia.

GeistL: Geist und Leben; Wü. 0016-5921.

Genava (archéologie, hist. art); Genève. 0072-0585.

GenLing: General Linguistics; University Park PA. 0016-6553.

Georgica: Jena/Tbilissi. 0232-4490.

GerefTTs: Gereformeerd Theologisch Tijdschrift; Kampen. 0016-8610.

Gerión, revista de Historia Antigua; Madrid, Univ. 0213-0181.

GGA: Göttingische Gelehrte Anzeigen; Göttingen. 0017-1549.

GItFg: Giornale italiano di filologia; Napoli. 0017-0461.

GLA/NT: Grande Lessico dell'A/NT (< TWA/NT); Brescia ⇥ 845.

GLÉCS: (Comptes rendus) Groupe Linguistique d'Études Chamito-Sémitiques; Paris.

GLern: Glaube und Lernen; Zeitschrift für theologische Urteilsbildung; Göttingen, VR [2 (1987)].

GLeven: Geest en leven [continuing OnsGLev] 65 (1988); Eindhoven.

Glotta: griech.-lat.; Gö. 0017-1298.

Gnomon; München. 0017-1417.

GöMiszÄg: Göttinger Miszellen ... zur ägyptologischen Diskussion; Göttingen. 0344-385X.

GöOrFor: Göttinger Orientforschungen; Würzburg.

GöTArb: Göttinger Theologische Arbeiten; Göttingen.

GraceTJ: Grace Theological Journal; Winona Lake IN. 0198-666X.

GraecChrPrim: Graecitas Christianorum Primaeva; Nijmegen, van den Vegt.

Grail, ecumenical quarterly; Waterloo.

GreeceR: Greece and Rome; Oxford.

Greg[LA/Inf.]: Gregorianum; R, Pontificia Universitas Gregoriana [Liber Annualis / Informationes PUG].

GrOrTR: Greek Orthodox Theological Review; Brookline. 0017-3894.

GrRByz: Greek, Roman and Byzantine Studies; CM. 0017-3916.

GrSinal: Grande Sinai; Petrópolis.

Gymn: Gymnasium; Heid. 0342-5231.

Ⓗ *(Neo-)hebraice*; (modern) Hebrew.

HaBeiA: Hamburger Beiträge zur Archäologie. 0341-3152.

Ḥadašôt arkeologiyôt Ⓗ [News]; J.

HalleB: Hallesche Beiträge zur Orientwissenschaft; Halle. 0233-2205.

Hamdard Islamicus [research]; Pakistan. 0250-7196.

Handes Amsorya [armen.]; Wien.

HarvSemMon/Mus: Harvard Semitic Monographs / Museum Series; CM.

HarvStClasPg: Harvard Studies in Classical Philology; CM.

HarvTR: The Harvard Theological Review; CM. 0017-8160.

HbAltW: Handbuch der Altertumswissenschaft; München.

HbAT/NT: Handbuch zum Alten/Neuen Testament; Tübingen.

HbDG: Handbuch der Dogmengeschichte; Freiburg/B.

HbDTG: Handbuch der Dogmen- und Theologiegeschichte; Göttingen.

HbFT: Handbuch der Fundamentaltheologie; FrB ⇥ 846.

HbOr: Handbuch der Orientalistik; Leiden.

HbRelG: Handbuch der Religionsgeschichte; Göttingen.

HbRwG: Handbuch Religionswissenschaftlicher Grundbegriffe; Stuttgart ⇥ 5,897.

HDienst: Heiliger Dienst; Salzburg. 0017-9620.

HebAnR: Hebrew Annual Review; Columbus, Ohio State Univ.

HebSt: Hebrew Studies; Madison WI. 0146-4094.

Hekima; Nairobi.

Helikon (Tradizione e Cultura Classica, Univ. Messina); Roma.

Helinium; Stockholm.

Hellenika; Bochum. 0018-0084; ⇥ *Elliniká*.

Helmantica; Salamanca, Univ.

Henceforth; Lenox MA.

Henoch (ebraismo): Torino (Univ.).

Hephaistos, Theorie / Praxis Arch.; Ha.

HerdKor: Herder-Korrespondenz; Freiburg/Br. 0018-0645.

HerdTKom, NT: Herders Theologischer Kommentar zum NT; FrB.

Heresis; Carcassonne. 0758-3737.

Hermathena; Dublin. 0018-0750.

Hermes; Wiesbaden. 0018-0777.

HermUnT: Hermeneutische Untersuchungen zur Theologie; Tü. 0440-7180.

HervTS: Hervormde Teologiese Studies; Pretoria.

Hesperia (American School, Athens); Princeton. 0018-098X.

Hethitica. Travaux édités; Lv.

HeythJ: Heythrop Journal; London. 0018-1196.

HistJ: Historical Journal; Cambridge.

HistJb: Historisches Jahrbuch; Mü.

Historia; 1. Baden-Baden: 0018-2311; 2. Santiago/Chile, Univ. Católica.

HistRel: History of Religions; Chicago. 0018-2710.

HLand[S]: Das Heilige Land (Deutscher Verein) Köln [(Schw. Verein); Luzern].

Hokhma; Lausanne. 0379-7465.

HolyL: Holy Land: J, OFM. 0333-4851 ➤ **TerraS.**

Homoousios; Buenos Aires.

HomP: Homiletic and Pastoral Review; New York. 0018-4268.

HomRel: Homo religiosus (histoire des religions); Louvain-la-Neuve.

HorBibT: Horizons in Biblical Theology; Pittsburgh. 0195-9085.

Horizons (College Theology Society); Villanova PA. 0360-9669.

Hsientai Hsüehyüan (= Universitas); Taipei.

HSprF: Historische Sprachforschung. 0044-3646.

HUC | A: Hebrew Union College [+ Jewish Institute of Religion] Annual; Cincinnati.

Humanitas; 1. Brescia; 2. Tucuman.

HumT: Humanística e Teologia; Porto.

HWomenRel: History of women religious, news and notes; St. Paul MN.

Hypom: Hypomnemata; Göttingen, VR.

HZ: Historische Zeitschrift; München. 0018-2613.

IBMiss: International Bulletin of Missionary Research; Mp.

ICC: International Critical Commentary; Edinburgh.

IClasSt: Illinois Classical Studies; Urbana. 0363-1923.

IFA[O]: Institut Français d'Archéologie (Orientale, Le Caire / Beyrouth).

IglV: Iglesia Viva; Valencia/Madrid.

IkaZ: Internationale Kath. Zeitschrift [= Communio]; Rodenkirchen. 0341-8693.

IkiZ: Internationale kirchliche Zeitschrift; Bern. 0020-9252.

Immanuel (ecumenical); J. 0302-8127.

Index Jewish Studies ➤ **RAMBI.**

IndIranJ: Indo-Iranian Journal; (Canberra-) Leiden. 0019-7246.

IndJT: Indian Journal of Theology; Serampore.

IndMissR: Indian Missiological Review; Shillong.

IndogF: Indogermanische Forschungen; Berlin. 0019-7262.

IndTSt: Indian Theological Studies; Bangalore, St. Peter's.

InfPUG ➤ Greg.

InnsBeiKultW/SpraW/TS: Innsbrucker Beiträge zur Kulturwissenschaft / Sprachwissenschaft / Theologische Studien.

Interp: Interpretation; Richmond VA. 0020-9643.

IntJNaut: International Journal of Nautical Archaeology L/NY. 0305-7445.

IntJPhR: International Journal for the Philosophy of Religion; Haag.

IntJSport: International Journal of the history of sport; London.

IntRMiss: International Review of Mission; London. 0020-8582.

Iran; London. 0578-6967.

IrAnt: Iranica Antiqua; Leiden.

Iraq; London. 0021-0889.

IrBSt: Irish Biblical Studies; Belfast. 0268-6112.

Irén: Irénikon; Chevetogne. 0021-0978.

IrTQ: Irish Theological Quarterly; Maynooth. 0021-1400.

ISBEnc: International Standard Bible Encyclopedia[3]; GR, Ferdmans ➤ 847.

Islam, Der: Berlin. 0021-1818.

Islamochristiana; Roma, Pontificio Istituto di Studi Arabi. 0392-7288.

IsrEJ: Israel Exploration Journal; Jerusalem. 0021-2059.

IsrJBot/Zool: Israel Journal of Botany 0021-213X / Zoology 0021-2210: J.

IsrLawR: Israel Law Review; Jerusalem. 0021-2237.

IsrMusJ: Israel Museum Journal; Jerusalem.

IsrNumJ[SocB]: Israel Numismatic Journal, J [Society Bulletin: TA].

IsrOrSt: Israel Oriental Studies; Tel Aviv. Istina; Paris. 0021-2423.

IVRA (Jura); Napoli.

IZBG ➜ 378: Internationale Zeitschriftenschau für Bibelwissenschaft und Grenzgebiete; Pd. 0074-9745.

IZT: Internationale Zeitschrift für Theologie [= Concilium deutsch].

JAAR: Journal, American Academy of Religion; Atlanta. 0002-7189.

JACiv: Journal of Ancient Civilizations: Chang-chun, Jilin (4, 1989).

J[News]AmEg: Journal [Newsletter] of the American Research Center in Egypt [ARCE]; Winona Lake IN.

JAmScAff: Journal of the American Scientific Affiliation (evang.); Ipswich MA. 0003-0988.

JANES: Journal of the Ancient Near Eastern Society; NY, Jewish Theol. Sem. 0010-2016.

JanLing[Pract]: Janua Linguarum [Series Practica]; Haag / Paris.

JAOS: Journal of the American Oriental Society; NHv. 0003-0279.

JapJRelSt: Japanese Journal of Religious Studies; Nagoya.

JapRel: Japanese Religions; Tokyo.

JArchSc: Journal of Archaeological Science; London/New York.

JAs: Journal Asiatique; P. 0021-762X.

JAsAf: Journal of Asian and African Studies; Toronto / Leiden.

Jb: Jahrbuch [Heid, Mainz...]; Jaarbericht.

JbAC: Jahrbuch für Antike und Christentum; Münster i. W.

JbBerlMus: Jahrbücher der Berliner Museen; Berlin.

JbBTh: Jahrbuch für biblische Theologie; Neukirchen.

JbEOL: Jaarbericht van het Vooraziatisch-Egyptisch Genootschap Ex Oriente Lux; Leiden.

JbEvHL: Jahrbuch des Deutschen Evangelischen Instituts für Altertumswissenschaft des Heiligen Landes; Firth.

JBL: Journal of Biblical Literature; Atlanta. 0021-9231.

JBlackT: Journal of Black Theology; Atteridgeville SAf.

JbLtgH: Jahrbuch für Liturgik und Hymnologie; Kassel.

JbNumG: Jahrbuch für Numismatik und Geldgeschichte; Regensburg.

JbÖsByz: Jahrbuch der Österreichischen Byzantinistik; W. 0378-8660.

JBQ: Jewish Bible Quarterly (< Dor le Dor); J. 0792-3910.

JChrB: Journal of the Christian Brethren Research Fellowship; Wellington NZ [122,1990].

JChrEd: Journal of Christian Education; Sydney. 0021-9657.

JCS: Journal of Cuneiform Studies; CM. 0022-0256.

JDharma: Journal of Dharma; Bangalore.

JdU: Judentum und Umwelt; Frankfurt/M.

JEA: Journal of Egyptian Archaeology; London. 0307-5133.

JEcuSt: Journal of Ecumenical Studies; Ph, Temple Univ. 0022-0558.

Jeevadhara; Alleppey, Kerala.

JEH: Journal of Ecclesiastical History; Cambridge. 0022-0469.

JEmpT: Journal of empirical theology; Kampen.

JeronMg: Institución S. Jerónimo (bíblica), estudios y monografías; Valencia.

JESHO: Journal of Economic and Social History of the Orient; Leiden.

JEvTS: Journal of the Evangelical Theological Society; Wheaton IL.

JewishH: Jewish History; Leiden. 0334-701X.

JFemR: Journal of Feminist Studies in Religion; Chico CA. 8755-4178.

JField: Journal of Field Archaeology; Boston, Univ. 0093-4690.

JGlass: Journal of Glass Studies; Corning, NY. 0075-4250.

JHistId: Journal of the History of Ideas; Ph, Temple Univ. 0022-5037.

JHMR: Judaica, Hermeneutics, Mysticism, and Religion; Albany, SUNY.

JhÖsA: Jahreshefte des Österreichischen Archäologischen Institutes; Wien. 0078-3579.

JHS: Journal of Hellenic Studies; London. 0075-4269.

JIndEur: Journal of Indo-European Studies; Hattiesburg, Miss.

JIntdenom: Journal, Interdenominational Theological Center; Atlanta.

JIntdis: Journal of the Society for Interdisciplinary History; CM, MIT.

JJC: Jésus et Jésus-Christ; Paris.

JJS: Journal of Jewish Studies; Oxford. 0022-2097.

JJurPap: Journal of Juristic Papyrology; Warszawa.

JLawA: Jewish Law Annual (Oxford).

JMeditArch: Journal of Mediterranean Archeol.; Sheffield. 0952-7648.

JMedRenSt: Journal of Medieval and Renaissance Studies; Durham NC.

JMoscPatr: [Engl.] Journal of the Moscow Patriarchate; Moscow.

JNES: Journal of Near Eastern Studies; Chicago, Univ. 0022-2968.

JNWS: Journal of Northwest Semitic Languages; Leiden.

JPersp: Jerusalem perspective.

JPrehRel: Journal of Prehistoric Religion; Göteborg. 0283-8486.

JPseud: Journal for the Study of the Pseudepigrapha; Sheffield. 0951-8207.

JPsy&C/Jud/T: Journal of Psychology and Christianity; Farmington Hills MI. 0733-4273 / ... and Judaism; New York / ... and Theology; Rosemead CA.

JQR: Jewish Quarterly Review (Ph, Dropsie Univ.); WL. 0021-6682.

JRArch: Journal of Roman Archaeology; AA.

JRAS: Journal of the Royal Asiatic Society; London.

JRefJud: Journal of Reform Judaism; NY. 0149-712X.

JRel: Journal of Religion; Chicago. 0022-4189.

JRelAf: Journal of Religion in Africa; Leiden. 0022-4200.

JRelEth: Journal of Religion and Ethics; ND (ᴱRutgers). 0384-9694.

JRelHealth: The Journal of Religion and Health; New York.

JRelHist: Journal of Religious History; Sydney, Univ. 0022-4227.

JRelPsyR: Journal of Religion and Psychical Research; Bloomfield CT.

JRelSt: Journal of Religious Studies; Cleveland.

JRelTht: Journal of Religious Thought; Washington DC.

JRit: Journal of ritual studies; Pittsburgh/Waterloo ON.

JRMilit: Journal of Roman Military Equipment Studies; Newcastle. 0961-3684 (1,1990).

JRPot: Journal of Roman Pottery Studies: Oxford.

JRS: Journal of Roman Studies; London. 0075-4358.

JSArm: Journal of the Society for Armenian Studies; LA.

JSav: Journal des Savants: Paris.

JScStR: Journal for the Scientific Study of Religion; NHv. 0021-8294.

JSemant: Journal of Semantics; Oxford. 0167-5133 (7,1990).

JSemit: Journal for Semitics / Tydskrif vir Semitistiek; Pretoria, Unisa.

JSHZ: Jüdische Schriften aus hellenistischer und römischer Zeit; Gütersloh.

JSS: Journal of Semitic Studies; Manchester. 0022-4480.

JSStEg: Journal of the Society for the Study of Egyptian Antiquities [ipsi SSEA]; Toronto. 0383-9753.

JStJTht: Jerusalem Studies in Jewish Thought; J (2,1982).

JStJud: Journal for the Study of Judaism in the Persian, Hellenistic, & Roman Periods; Leiden. 0047-2212.

JStNT/OT: Journal for the Study of the NT/OT; Sheffield, Univ. 0142-064X / 0309-0892. → JPseud.

JStRel: Journal for the study of religion [formerly Religion in Southern Africa]; Pietermaritzburg, Natal.

JTS: Journal of Theological Studies; Oxford/London. 0022-5185.

JTSAfr: Journal of Theology for Southern Africa; Rondebosch.

Judaica; Zürich. 0022-572X.

Judaism; NY. 0022-5762.

JudTSt: Judaistische Texte und Studien; Hildesheim.

JWarb: Journal of the Warburg and Courtauld Institutes; London.

JwHist: Jewish History; Haifa.

JWomen&R: Journal of Women and Religion; Berkeley.
JyskR ➤ RJysk.
Kadmos; Berlin. 0022-7498.
Kairos (Religionswiss.); Salzburg. 0022-7757.
Karawane (Die); Ludwigsburg.
Karthago (archéologie africaine); P.
KAT: Kommentar zum AT: Gütersloh.
KatBlät: Katechetische Blätter; Mü.
KatKenk: Katorikku Kenkyu < Shingaku; Tokyo, Sophia. 0387-3005.
KBW: Katholisches Bibelwerk; Stu [bzw. Österreich, Schweiz].
KeK: Kritisch-exegetischer Kommentar über das NT; Göttingen.
KerDo: Kerygma und Dogma; Göttingen. 0023-0707.
KerkT: Kerk en Theologie; Wageningen. 0165-2346.
Kernos, religion grecque; Liège.
Kerux, a journal of biblical-theological preaching; Escondido CA. 0888-8513 (5,1990).
Kerygma (on Indian missions); Ottawa. 0023-0693.
KGaku: ❹ Kirisutokyo Gaku (Christian Studies); Tokyo, 0387-6810.
KingsTR: King's College Theological Review; London.
KirSef: ❺ Kiryat Sefer, Bibliographical Quarterly; Jerusalem, Nat.-Univ. Libr. 0023-1851. ➤ Rambi.
KIsr: Kirche und Israel, theologische Zeitschrift; Neukirchen. 0179-7239.
KkKS: Konfessionskundliche und Kontroverstheologische Studien; Paderborn.
KkMat: Konfessionskundliches Institut, Materialdienst; Bensheim.
KleinÄgTexte: Kleine ägyptische Texte; Wb.
Kler: ❻ Klēronomia; Thessaloniki.
Klio; Berlin. 0075-6334.
KLK: Katholisches Leben und Kirchenreform im Zeitalter der Glaubensspaltung; Münster.
KölnFG: Kölner Jahrbuch für Vor- und Frühgeschichte; B. 0075-6512.
KomBeiANT: Kommentare und Beiträge zum Alten und N.T.; Düsseldorf.
Kratylos (Sprachwissenschaft); Wsb.

KřestR [TPřil]: Křest'anská revue [Theologická Příloha]; Praha.
KTB/KUB: Keilschrifttexte/urkunden aus Boghazköi; B, Mann/Akademie.
Ktema; Strasbourg, CEDEX.
KuGAW: Kulturgeschichte der Antiken Welt; Mainz.
KvinnerA: Kvinner i arkeologi i Norge; Bergen, Historisk Museum.
KZg: Kirchliche Zeitgeschichte; Gö.
LA: Liber Annuus; J. 0081-8933. ➤ SBF.
Labeo, diritto romano; N. 0023-6462.
Landas: Journal of Loyola School of Theology; Manila,
Language; Baltimore. 0097-8507.
LAPO: Littératures Anciennes du Proche-Orient; Paris, Cerf. 0459-5831.
Lateranum; R, Pont. Univ. Lateranense.
Latomus (Ét. latines); Bru. 0023-8856.
Laur: Laurentianum; R. 0023-902X.
LavalTP: Laval Théologique et Philosophique; Québec.
Laverna, Wirtschafts- und Sozialgeschichte; St. Katharinen. 0938-5835 (1,1990).
LDiv: Lectio Divina; Paris, Cerf.
LebSeels: Lebendige Seelsorge; Wü/FrB.
LebZeug: Lebendiges Zeugnis; Paderborn. 0023-9941.
Lěšonénu (Hebrew Language); J.
LetPastB: Lettura pastorale della Bibbia; Bologna, Dehoniane.
Levant (archeology); London.
LexÄg: Lexikon der Ägyptologie; Wsb ➤ 848.
LexMA: Lexikon des Mittelalters; Mü/Z ➤ 849.
LexTQ: Lexington [KY] Theological Quarterly. 0024-1628.
LGB: Lexikon des Gesamten Buchwesens²; Stu ➤ 933.
LIAO: Lettre d'Information Archéologie Orientale; Valbonne, CNRS. 0750-6279.
LIMC: Lexicon iconographicum mythologiae classicae; Z. ➤ 934.
LimnOc: Limnology & Oceanography; AA.
LinceiR/Scavi/BClas: Accademia Nazionale dei Lincei. Rendiconti / Notizie degli Scavi / Bollettino Classico. 0391-8270: Roma.

LingBib: Linguistica Biblica; Bonn. 0342-0884.

Lire la Bible; P, Cerf. 0588-2257.

Listening: Romeoville IL.

LitLComp: Literary and Linguistic Computing; Ox. 0268-1145.

LFrühJ: Literatur und Religion des Frühjudentums; Wü/Gü.

LitTOx: Literature and theology; Ox.

LivLight: The Living Light (US Cath. Conf.); Huntington. 0024-5275.

LivWord: Living Word; Alwaye, Kerala.

LoB: Leggere oggi la Bibbia; Brescia, Queriniana.

LogosPh: Logos, philosophic issues in Christian perspective; Santa Clara.

Logotherapie; Bremen.

LOrA: Langues orientales anciennes; Lv. 0987-7738.

LPastB: Lettura pastorale della Bibbia: Bo.

LStClas: London studies in classical philology [8, Corolla Londiniensis 1]; Amst.

LtgJb: Liturgisches Jahrbuch; Munster/Wf.

Lucentum; prehistoria, arqueologia e historia antigua; Alicante, Univ.

LumenK: Lumen; København.

LumenVr: Lumen; Vitoria.

LumièreV: Lumière et Vie; Lyon. 0024-7359.

Luther [Jb]; Ha. 0340-6210 [Gö].

LuthMon: Lutherische Monatshefte; Hamburg. 0024-7618.

LuthTJ: Lutheran Theological Journal; North Adelaide, S. Australia.

LuthTKi: Lutherische Theologie und Kirche; Oberursel. 0170-3846.

LuxB: Lux Biblica; R, Ist. B. Evangelico (1,1990).

LVitae: Lumen Vitae; Bru. 0024-7324.

LvSt: Louvain Studies.

Ⓜ magyar: *hungarice*, en hongrois.

ᴹ: *mentio, de eo*; author commented upon.

Maarav; WL. 0149-5712.

MadMitt [B/F]: DAI Madrider Mitteilungen [Beiträge/Forschungen]; Mainz.

MAGA: Mitteilungen zur Alten Geschichte und Archäologie; B.

Maia (letterature classiche); Messina. 0025-0538.

MaimS: Maimonidean Studies; NY, Yeshiva Univ./KTAV (1,1990).

MaisD: Maison-Dieu; P. 0025-0937.

MgANE: Monographs on the Ancient Near East; 1. Leiden; 2. Malibu.

Manresa (espiritualidad ignaciana); Azpeitia-Guipúzcoa.

Manuscripta; St. Louis.

Mara: tijdschrift voor feminisme en theologie.

MarbTSt: Marburger Theologische Studien; Marburg.

MARI: Mari, Annales de Recherches Interdisciplinaires; Paris.

Marianum; Roma.

MariolSt: Mariologische Studien; Essen.

MarŠipri; Boston, Baghdad ASOR.

MarSt: Marian Studies; Washington.

Masca: Museum Applied Science Center for Archaeology Journal; Ph.

MasSt: (SBL) Masoretic Studies; Atlanta.

MastJ: Master's Seminary Journal; Sun Valley, CA (1,1990).

MatDClas: Materiali e discussioni per l'analisi dei testi classici; Pisa. 0392-6338.

MatKonfInst: Materialdienst des konfessionskundlichen Instituts; Bensheim.

MatPomWykBlb: Materiały pomocnicze do wykładów z biblistyki; Lublin.

Mayéutica; Marcilla (Navarra).

MDOG: Mitteilungen der Deutschen Orientgesellschaft; B. 0342-118X.

Meander: Wsz Akad. 0025-6285.

Med: Mededelingen [Amst,]; Meddelander.

MedHum: Mediaevalia et Humanistica (Denton, N. Texas U.); Totowa.

MeditArch: Mediterranean Archaeology; Sydney. 1030-8482.

MeditHistR: Mediterranean historical review Tel Aviv Univ.; L. 0951-8967.

MeditQ: Mediterranean Quarterly; Durham NC.

MedvSt: Mediaeval Studies; Toronto. 0076-5872.

MÉF [= **MélÉcFrR**]: Mélanges de l'École Française de Rome/Ath (Antiquité). 0223-5102.

MélSR: Mélanges de Science Religieuse; Lille.

Mém: Mémoires → AIBL ... AcSc, T...

MenQR: Mennonite Quarterly Review; Goshen, Ind.

Mensaje; Chile.

Meroit: Meroitic Newsletter / Bulletin d'informations méroitiques: Paris, CNRS.

MESA: Middle East Studies Association (Bulletin); Tucson, Univ. AZ.
MesCiv: Mesopotamian Civilization; WL.
MesopK: Mesopotamia: Copenhagen Studies in Assyriology; København.
MesopT: Mesopotamia (Archeologia, Epigrafia, Storia ... Torino); (pub. F).
Mesorot [Language-tradition researches]; Jerusalem.
MESt: Middle Eastern Studies; L.
MetB: Metropolitan Museum Bulletin; New York. 0026-1521.
MethT: Method and theory in the study of religion; Toronto.
Mêtis, Anthropologie grecque; P.
Mg: Monograph (-ie, -fia); → CBQ, SBL, SNTS.
MGraz: Mitteilungen der archäologischen Gesellschaft; Graz.
MgStB: Monographien und Studienbücher; Wu/Giessen.
MHT: Materialien zu einem hethitischen Thesaurus; Heidelberg.
MiDAI-A/K/M/R: Mitteilungen des Deutschen Archäologischen Instituts: Athen / Kairo / Madrid / Rom 0342-1287.
MidAmJT: Mid-America Journal of Theology: Orange City, Iowa.
Mid-Stream, Disciples of Christ; Indianapolis. – Midstream (Jewish); NY. 0026-332X.
Mikael; Paraná, Arg. (Seminario).
MilltSt: Milltown Studies (philosophy, theology); Dublin. 0332-1428.
Minerva: 1. filología clásica; Valladolid; 2. (incorporating Archaeology Today); L (1,1990).
Minos (Filología Egea); Salamanca. 0544-3733.
MiscCom: Miscelánea Comillas, estudios históricos; M. 0210-9522.
MiscFranc: Miscellanea Francescana; Roma (OFM Conv.).
Mishkan, a theological forum on Jewish evangelism; Jerusalem.
MissHisp: Missionalia hispanica; Madrid, CSIC Inst. E. Flores.
Missiology; Scottdale PA.
Mitt: Mitteilungen [Gö Septuaginta; Berliner Museen ...]; → MiDAI.
Mnemosyne, Bibliotheca Classica Batava [+ Supplements]; Leiden.

ModChm: Modern Churchman; Leominster, Herf.
ModJud: Modern Judaism; Baltimore.
ModT: Modern Theology; Oxford.
MonSt: Monastic Studies; Montreal. 0026-9190.
MondeB: Le Monde de la Bible: 1. P. 0154-9049. – 2. Genève.
Monde Copte, Le: 0399-905X.
Month; London. 0027-0172.
Moralia; Madrid.
MsME: Manuscripts of the Middle East; Leiden. 0920-0401.
MüÄgSt: Münchener Ägyptologische Studien; München/Berlin.
MüBei[T]PapR: Münchener Beiträge zur [Theologie] Papyruskunde und antiken Rechtsgeschichte; Mü.
MünstHand: Münsterische Beiträge zur Antiken Handelsgeschichte; St. Katharinen. 0722-4532.
MüStSprW: Münchener Studien zur Sprachwissenschaft; Mü. → AOtt.
MüTZ: Münchener Theologische Zeitschrift; St. Ottilien. 0580-1400.
Mus: Le Muséon; LvN. 0771-6494.
MusHelv: Museum Helveticum; Basel.
MUSJ: Mélanges de l'Université Saint-Joseph (rediviva); Beyrouth [51 (1990): 2-7214-5000-X].
MusTusc: Museum Tusculanum; København. 0107-8062.
MuzTA: ⊕ Muzeon Ha-Areṣ NS; TA.
NABU: Nouvelles assyriologiques brèves et utilitaires; 0989-5671.
NachGö: Nachrichten der Akademie der Wissenschaften; Göttingen.
NarAzAfr: ⊖ Narody: Peoples of Asia and Africa; Moskva.
NatGeog: National Geographic; Washington. 0027-9358.
NatGrac: Naturaleza y Gracia; S.
NBL: Neues Bibel-Lexikon 1988 → 850.
NBlackfr: New Blackfriars; London. 0028-4289.
NCent: The New Century Bible Commentary (reedited); Edinburgh / GR.
NChrIsr: Nouvelles Chrétiennes d'Israël; Jérusalem.
NDizTB: Nuovo Dizionario Teol.B → 851.
NduitseGT: Nederduits-Gereformeerde Teologiese Tydskrif; Kaapstad. 0028-2006.

NedTTs: Nederlands Theologisch Tijdschrift; Wageningen. 0028-212X.
Neotestamentica; Pretoria; NTWerk.
Nestor, Classical Antiquity, Indiana Univ.; Bloomington. 0028-2812.
NESTR: Near East School of Theology Review; Beirut.
News: Newsletter: Anat[olian Studies; NHv]; Targ[umic and Cognate Studies; Toronto]; ASOR [Baltimore]; Ug[aritic Studies; Calgary]; ↠ JAmEg.
NewTR: New theology review: Ch. 0896-4297.
NHC: Nag Hammadi Codices, Egypt UAR Facsimile edition; Leiden.
NHL/S: Nag Hammadi Library in English / Studies; Leiden.
NHLW: Neues Handbuch der Literaturwissenschaft: Wsb, Athenaion.
Nicolaus (teol. ecumenico-patristica); Bari.
NICOT: New International Commentary OT; Grand Rapids, Eerdmans.
NigJT: The Nigerian Journal of Theology; Owerri.
NIGT: New International Greek Testament Commentary; Exeter/GR.
NJBC: New Jerome Biblical Commentary ↠ 2036.
NOrb: NT & Orbis Antiquus; FrS/Gö.
NorJ: Nordisk Judaistik.
NorTTs: Norsk Teologisk Tidsskrift; Oslo. 0029-2176.
NoTr: Notes on Translation; Dallas (4,1990).
NOxR: New Oxford Review; Berkeley.
NRT: Nouvelle Revue Théologique; Tournai. 0029-4845.
NS [NF]: Nova series, nouvelle série.
NSys: Neue Zeitschrift für systematische Theologie und Religionsphilosophie; Berlin. 0028-3517.
NT: Novum Testamentum; Leiden. 0048-1009.
NTAbh: Neutestamentliche Abhandlungen. [N.F.]; Münster.
NTAbs: New Testament Abstracts; CM. 0028-6877.
NTDt: Das Neue Testament deutsch; Gö.
NTS: New Testament Studies; L (Studiorum NT Societas).
NTTools: Leiden. 0077-8842.

NubChr: Nubia Christiana; Wsz.
Nubica; Köln (1,1990).
NumC: Numismatic Chronicle; London. 0078-2696.
Numisma; Madrid. 0029-0015.
NumZ: Numismatische Zeitschrift; Wien. 0250-7838.
Numen (History of Religions); Leiden.
NuovaUm: Nuova Umanità; Roma.
NVFr/Z: Nova et Vetera; 1. Fribourg S. / 2. Zamora.
NZMissW: Neue Zeitschrift für Missionswissenschaft; Beckenried, Schweiz. 0028-3495.
ObnŽiv: Obnovljeni Život; Zagreb.
OBO: Orbis Biblicus et Orientalis: FrS/Gö.
OEIL: Office d'édition et d'impression du livre; Paris.
ÖkRu: Ökumenische Rundschau; Stuttgart. 0029-8654.
ÖkTbKom, NT: Ökumenischer Taschenbuchkommentar; Gütersloh / Würzburg.
ÖsterrBibSt: Österreichische Biblische Studien; Klosterneuburg.
Offa, ... Frühgeschichte; Neumünster. 0078-3714.
Ohio ↠ JRelSt: Cleveland.
OIAc/P/C: Oriental Institute Acquisitions / Publications / Communications; Ch.
OikBud: Oikumene, historia; Budapest.
Olivo (El), diálogo jud.-cr.: Madrid.
OLZ: Orientalistische Literaturzeitung; Berlin. 0030-5383.
OMRO: Oudheidkundige Mededelingen, Rijksmuseum Oudheden; Leiden.
OneInC: One in Christ (Catholic Ecumenical); Turvey, Bedfordshire.
OnsGErf: Ons Geestelijk Erf; Antwerpen. ↠ GLeven.
OpAth/Rom: Opuscula Atheniensia / Romana; Swedish Inst.
OPTAT: Occasional Papers in Translation and Textlinguistics: Dallas.
Opus, storia economica (Siena); R.
Or: ↠ Orientalia; Roma.
OraLab: Ora et Labora; Roriz, Portugal.
OrAnt[Coll]: Oriens Antiquus [Collectio]; Roma.
OrBibLov: Orientalia et Biblica Lovaniensia; Lv.
OrChr: Oriens Christianus; Wsb.

OrChrPer[An]: Orientalia Christiana Periodica [Analecta]; R, Pontificium Inst. Orientalium Stud. 0030-5375.
OrGand: Oríentalia Gandensia; Gent.
Orientalia (Ancient Near East); Rome, Pontifical Biblical Institute. 0030-5367.
Orientierung; Zürich. 0030-5502.
Orient-Japan: Orient, Near Eastern Studies Annual; Tokyo. 0743-3851; cf. ❹ Oriento. 0030-5219.
Origins; Washington Catholic Conference. 0093-609X.
OrJog: Orientasi, Annual ... Philosophy and Theology; Jogjakarta.
OrLovPer[An]: Orientalia Lovaniensia Periodica [Analecta]; Lv. 0085-4522.
OrMod: Oriente Moderno; Napoli. 0030-5472.
OrOcc: Oriente-Occidente. Buenos Aires, Univ. Salvador.
OrPast: Orientamenti Pastorali; Roma.
Orpheus: 1. Catania; 2. -Thracia; Sofya (1,1990).
OrSuec: Orientalia Suecana; Uppsala.
OrtBuc: Ortodoxia; Bucureşti.
OrthF: Orthodoxes Forum; München.
OrTrad: Oral Tradition; Columbia. MO.
OrVars: Orientalia Varsoviensia; Wsz. 0860-5785.
OstkSt: Ostkirchliche Studien; Würzburg. 0030-6487.
OTAbs: Old Testament Abstracts; Washington. 0364-8591.
OTEssays: Old Testament essays; Pretoria. 1010-9919.
OTS: Oudtestamentische Studiën; Leiden. 0169-9555.
OTWerkSuidA: Die Ou Testamentiese Werkgemeenskap Suid-Afrika; Pretoria.
OvBTh: Overtures to Biblical Theology; Philadelphia.
Overview; Ch St. Thomas More Asn.
OxJArch: Oxford Journal of Archaeology; Ox. 0262-5253.
❺: *polonice,* in Polish.
p./pa./pl.: page(s)/paperback/plate(s).
PAAR: Proceedings of the American Academy for Jewish Research; Ph.
Pacifica: Australian theological studies; Melbourne Brunswick East.

PacTR: Pacific theological review: SanAnselmo, SF Theol.Sem.
Palaeohistoria; Haarlem.
PalCl: Palestra del Clero; Rovigo.
PaléOr: Paléorient; Paris.
PalSb: ❺ Palestinski Sbornik; Leningrad.
PapBritSR: Papers of the British School at Rome; London.
PAPS: Proceedings of the American Philosophical Society; Ph.
PapTAbh: Papyrologische Texte und Abhandlungen; Bonn, Habelt.
PapyrolColon: Papyrologica Coloniensia; Opladen. 0078-9410.
Parabola; New York.
Paradigms; Louisville KY.
ParOr: Parole de l'Orient; Kaslik.
ParPass: Parola del Passato; Napoli. 0031-2355.
ParSpV: Parola, Spirito e Vita; Bologna.
ParVi: Parole di Vita; T-Leumann.
PasT: Pastoraltheologie; Göttingen.
PastScPast: Pastoral / Sciences pastorales; psych.sociol.théol.; Ottawa.
Patr&M: Patristica et Mediaevalia; BA.
PatrMedRen: Proceedings of the Patristic, Mediaeval and Renaissance Conference; Villanova PA.
PatrStudT: Patristische Studien und Texte; B. 0553-4003.
PBSB: Petite bibliothèque des sciences bibliques; Paris, Desclée.
PenséeC: La Pensée Catholique; P.
PEQ: Palestine Exploration Quarterly; London. 0031-0328.
PerAz: Peredneaziatskij Sbornik; Moskva.
Persica: Leiden.
PerspRelSt: Perspectives in Religious Studies (Baptist); Danville VA.
PerspT: Perspectiva Teológica; Belo Horizonte.
Pg/Ph: philolog-/philosoph-.
PgOrTb: Philologia Orientalis; Tbilisi.
Phase; Barcelona.
PhilipSa: Philippiniana Sacra; Manila.
Philologus; B. 0031-7985.
Phoenix; Toronto. 0031-8299.
PhoenixEOL; Leiden. 0031-8329.
Phronema: Greek Orthodox; Sydney.
Phronesis; Assen. 0031-8868.
Pneuma, Pentecostal; Pasadena.
PoinT: Le Point Théologique; P.

Polin: Polish-Jewish Studies; Oxford.

PontAcc, R/Mem: Atti della Pontificia Accademia Romana di Archeologia, Rendiconti/Memorie; Vaticano.

PrPeo [< CleR]: Priests and People; L.

PracArch: Prace Archeologiczne; Kraków, Univ. 0083-4300.

PraehZ: Praehistorische Zeitschrift; Berlin. 0079-4848.

PrakT: Praktische theologie; Zwolle.

PraktArch: ⑥ Praktika, Archeology Society Athens.

PrCambPg: Proceedings of the Cambridge Philological Soc. 0068-6735.

PrCTSAm: Proceedings Catholic Theological Society of America; Villanova.

PredikOT/NT: De Prediking van het OT / van het NT; Nijkerk.

Premislia Christiana; Przemyśl (2, 1988s).

Presbyteri; Trento.

Presbyterion; St. Louis.

PresPast: Presenza Pastorale; Roma.

PrêtreP: Prêtre et Pasteur; Montréal. 0385-8307.

Priest (The); Washington.

PrincSemB: Princeton Seminary Bulletin; Princeton NJ.

PrIrB: Proceedings of the Irish Biblical Association; Dublin.

Prism; St. Paul MN.

ProbHistChr: Problèmes de l'Histoire du Christianisme; Bruxelles, Univ.

ProcClas: Proceedings of the Classical Association; London.

ProcCom: Proclamation Commentaries; Ph.

ProcGLM: Proceedings of the Eastern Great Lakes and Midwest Bible Societies; Buffalo.

ProcIsrAc: Proceedings of the Israel Academy of Sciences & Humanities; Jerusalem.

Prooftexts; Baltimore.

PrOrChr: Proche-Orient Chrétien; Jérusalem. 0032-9622.

Prot: Protestantesimo; R. 0033-1767.

Proyección (mundo actual); Granada.

ProySal: Proyecto Centro Salesiano de Estudios; Buenos Aires.

PrPg/PrehS: Proceedings of the Philological/Prehistoric Society; Cambridge.

PrSemArab: Proceedings of the Seminar for Arabian Studies; London.

Prudentia (Hellenistic, Roman); Auckland.

PrzOr[Tom/Pow]: Przegląd Orientalistyczny, Wsz: [Tomisticzny; Wsz / Powszechny, Kraków].

PT: Philosophy/Theology: Milwaukee, Marquette Univ.

PubTNEsp: Publicaciones de la Facultad Teológica del Norte de España; Burgos.

PUF: Presses Universitaires de France; P.

Qadm: Qadmoniot ❶ Quarterly of Dept. of Antiquities; Jerusalem.

Qardom, ❶ mensuel pour la connaissance du pays; Jerusalem, Ariel.

QDisp: Quaestiones Disputatae; FrB.

Qedem: Monographs of the Institute of Archaeology: Jerusalem.

QLtg: Questions Liturgiques; Lv.

QRMin: Quarterly Review [for] Ministry; Nv. 0270-9287.

QuadCatan / Chieti: Quaderni, Catania / Chieti; Univ.

QuadSemant: Quaderni di Semantica; Bologna.

QuadSemit: Quaderni di Semitistica; Firenze.

QuadUrb: Quaderni Urbinati di Cultura Classica; Urbino. 0033-4987.

Quaerendo (Low Countries: Manuscripts and Printed Books); Amst.

QuatreF: Les quatre fleuves: Paris.

QüestVidaCr: Qüestions de Vida Cristiana; Montserrat.

QumC: The Qumran Chronicle; Kraków (1,1990).

❶: russice, in Russian.

R: recensio, book-review(er).

RAC: Reallexikon für Antike und Christentum; Stuttgart → 853.

Radiocarbon; NHv, Yale. 0033-8222.

RAfrT: Revue Africaine de Théologie; Kinshasa/Limete.

RAg: Revista Agustiniana Calahorra.

RAMBI: Rešimat Ma'amarim bemadda'ê ha-Yahedût, Index of articles on Jewish Studies; J. 0073-5817.

RaMIsr: Rassegna mensile di Israel; Roma. 0033-9792.

RArchéol: Revue Archéologique; Paris. 0035-0737.

RArchéom: Revue d'Archéométrie; Rennes.

RArtLv: Revue des Archéologues et Historiens d'Art; Lv. 0080-2530.

RasArch: Rassegna di archeologia; F (9,1990).
RasEtiop: Rassegna di Studi Etiopici; R/N.
RAss: Revue d'Assyriologie et d'Archéologie Orientale; Paris.
RasT: Rassegna di Teologia; Roma [ᴱNapoli]. 0034-9644.
RazF: Razón y Fe; M. 0034-0235.
RB: Revue Biblique; J/P. 0035-0907.
RBén: Revue Bénédictine; Maredsous. 0035-0893.
RBgNum: Revue Belge de Numismatique et Sigillographie; Bruxelles.
RBgPg: Revue Belge de Philologie et d'Histoire; Bru. 0035-0818.
RBBras: Revista Bíblica Brasileira; Fortaleza.
RBíbArg: Revista Bíblica; Buenos Aires. 0034-7078.
RBkRel: The Review of Books and Religion; Durham NC, Duke Univ.
RCatalT: Revista Catalana de Teología; Barcelona, St. Pacià.
RCiv: Éditions Recherche sur les Civilisations [Mém(oires) 0291-1655]; P ➤ ADPF.
RClerIt: Rivista del Clero Italiano; Milano. 0042-7586.
RCuClaMed: Rivista di Cultura Classica e Medioevale; R. 0080-3251.
RÉAnc: Revue des Études Anciennes; Bordeaux. 0035-2004.
RÉArmén: Revue des Études Arméniennes. 0080-2549.
RÉAug: Revue des Études Augustiniennes; Paris. 0035-2012.
REB: 1. Revista Eclesiástica Brasileira; Petrópolis. 2. ➤ RNEB.
RÉByz: Revue des Études Byzantines; Paris.
RECAM: Regional Epigraphic Catalogues of Asia Minor [AnSt].
RechAug: Recherches Augustiniennes; Paris. 0035-2021.
RechSR: Recherches de Science Religieuse; Paris. 0034-1258.
RecTrPO: Recueil de travaux, Proche-Orient ancien; Montréal.
RefEgy: Református Egyház; Budapest. 0324-475X.
ReferSR: Reference Services Review; Dearborn MI, Univ.
RefF: Reformiertes Forum; Zürich.

RefGStT: Reformationsgeschichtliche Studien und Texten: Münster.
RefJ: The Reformed Journal; Grand Rapids. 0486-252X.
Reformatio; Zürich. 0034-3021.
RefR: Reformed Review; New Brunswick NJ / Holland MI. 0034-3072.
RefTR: Reformed Theological Review; Hawthorn, Australia. 0034-3072.
RefW: Reformed World; Geneva. 0034-3056.
RÉG: Revue des Études Grecques; Paris. 0035-2039.
RÉgp: Revue d'Égyptologie; Paris.
RÉJ: Revue des Études Juives; Paris. 0035-2055.
RÉLat: Revue des Études Latines; P.
RelCult: Religión y Cultura; M.
RelEdn: Religious Education (biblical; Jewish-sponsored); NHv.
Religion [... and Religions]; Lancaster. 0048-721X.
RelIntL: Religion and Intellectual Life; New Rochelle NY, College. 0741-0549.
RelPBei: Religionspädagogische Beiträge; Kaarst.
RelSoc: Religion and Society; B/Haag.
RelSt: Religious Studies; Cambridge. 0034-4125.
RelStR: Religious Studies Review; Waterloo, Ont. 0319-485X.
RelStT: Religious Studies and Theology; Edmonton. 0829-2922.
RelTAbs: Religious and Theological Abstracts; Myerstown, Pa.
RelTrad: Religious Traditions; Brisbane. 0156-1650.
RencAssInt: Rencontre Assyriologique Internationale, Compte-Rendu.
RencChrJ: Rencontre Chrétiens et Juifs; Paris. 0233-5579.
Renovatio: 1. Zeitschrift für das interdisziplinäre Gespräch; Köln: 2. (teologia); Genova.
RepCyp: Report of the Department of Antiquities of Cyprus; Nicosia.
RépertAA: Répertoire d'art et d'archéologie; Paris. 0080-0953.
REPPAL: Revue d'Études Phéniciennes-Puniques et des Antiquités Libyques; Tunis.

REspir: Revista de Espiritualidad; San Sebastián.

ResPLit: Res Publica Litterarum; Kansas.

RestQ: Restoration Quarterly; Abilene TX.

Résurrection, bimestriel catholique d'actualité et de formation.

RET: Revista Española de Teología; Madrid.

RÉtGC: Revue des Études Géorgiennes et Caucasiennes; Paris. 0373-1537 [< Bedi Kartlisa].

RevCuBíb: Revista de Cultura Bíblica; São Paulo.

RevSR: Revue des Sciences Religieuses; Strasbourg. 0035-2217.

RExp: Review and Expositor; Louisville. 0034-6373.

RFgIC: Rivista di Filologia e di Istruzione Classica; Torino. 0035-6220.

RgStTh: Regensburger Studien zur Theologie; Fra/Bern, Lang.

RgVV: Religionsgeschichtliche Versuche und Vorarbeiten; B/NY, de Gruyter.

RHDroit: Revue historique de Droit français et étranger; Paris.

RHE: Revue d'Histoire Ecclésiastique; Louvain. 0035-2381.

RheinMus: Rheinisches Museum für Philologie, Frankfurt. 0035-449X.

Rhetorik [Jb]; Stu / Bad Cannstatt.

RHist: Revue Historique; Paris.

RHPR: Revue d'Histoire et de l'Philosophie Religieuses; Strasbourg. 0035-2403.

RHR: Revue de l'Histoire des Religions; Paris. 0035-1423.

RHS ➤ RUntHö; RU ➤ ZRUnt.

RHText: Revue d'Histoire des Textes; Paris. 0373-6075.

Ribla: Revista de interpretación bíblica latinoamericana; San José CR.

RIC: Répertoire bibliographique des institutions chrétiennes; Strasbourg ➤ 1063.

RICathP: Revue de l'Institut Catholique de Paris. 0294-4308

RicStoB: Ricerche storico bibliche; Bologna. 0394-980X.

RicStorSocRel: Ricerche di Storia Sociale e Religiosa; Roma.

RIDA: Revue Internationale des Droits de l'Antiquité; Bruxelles.

RIMA ➤ AnRIM.

RINASA: Rivista dell'Istituto Nazionale di Archeologia e Storia dell'Arte; Roma.

RitFg: Rivista italiana di Filologia Classica.

RItNum: Rivista Italiana di Numismatica e scienze affini; Milano.

RivArCr: Rivista di Archeologia Cristiana; Città del Vaticano. 0035-6042.

RivArV: Rivista di Archeologia, Univ. Venezia; Roma.

RivAscM: Rivista di Ascetica e Mistica; Roma.

RivB: Rivista Biblica Italiana; Bologna, Dehoniane. 0393-4853.

RivLtg: Rivista di Liturgia; T-Leumann.

RivPastLtg: Rivista di Pastorale Liturgica; Brescia. 0035-6395.

RivScR: Rivista di Scienze Religiose; Molfetta.

RivStoLR: Rivista di Storia e Letteratura Religiosa; F. 0035-6573.

RivStorA: Rivista Storica dell'Antichità; Bologna. 0300-340X.

RivVSp: Rivista di Vita Spirituale; Roma. 0035-6638.

RJysk: Religionsvidenskapeligt Tidsskrift (Jysk/Jutland); Aarhus. 0108-1993.

RLA: Reallexikon der Assyriologie & vorderasiatischen Archäologie; B ➤ 853*.

RLatAmT: Revista Latinoamericana de Teología; El Salvador.

RNEB: revision of New English Bible ➤ 1975.

RNouv: La Revue Nouvelle; Bruxelles. 0035-3809.

RNum: Revue Numismatique; Paris.

RoczOr: Rocznik Orientalistyczny; Warszawa. 0080-3545.

RoczTK: Roczniki Teologiczno-Kanoniczne; Lublin. 0035-7723.

RömQ: Römische Quartalschrift für Christliche Altertumskunde...; Freiburg/Br. 0035-7812.

RomOrth: Romanian Orthodox Church News, French Version [sic]; Bucureşti.

RPg: Revue de Philologie, de Littérature et d'Histoire anciennes; Paris, Klincksieck. 0035-1652.

RQum: Revue de Qumrân; P. 0035-1725.
RRéf: Revue Réformée; Saint-Germain-en-Laye.
RRel: Review for Religious; St. Louis. 0034-639X.
RRelRes: Review of Religious Research; New York. 0034-673X.
RRns: The Review of Religions; Wsh. 0743-5622.
RSO: Rivista degli Studi Orientali; Roma. 0392-4869.
RSPT: Revue des Sciences Philosophiques et Théologiques; [Le Saulchoir] Paris. 0035-2209.
RStFen: Rivista di Studi Fenici: R.
RSzem: Református Szemle; Budapest.
RTAM: Recherches de Théologie Ancienne et Médiévale; Louvain. 0034-1266. → BTAM.
RTBat: Revista Teológica (Sem. Batista); Rio de Janeiro.
RThom: Revue Thomiste; Toulouse/Bru. 0035-4295.
RTLim: Revista Teológica; Lima.
RTLv: Revue théologique de Louvain. 0080-2654.
RTPhil: Revue de Théologie et de Philosophie; Épalinges. 0035-1784.
RuBi: Ruch Biblijny i Liturgiczny; Kraków. 0209-0872.
RUntHö: Religionsunterricht an höheren Schulen; Dü. (RU → ZPrax).
RVidEsp: Revista vida espiritual; Bogotà.
RZaïrTP: Revue Zaïroise de Théologie Protestante.
SAA[B]: State Archives of Assyria [Bulletin]; Helsinki.
SacEr: Sacris Erudiri; Steenbrugge.
Saeculum; FrB/Mü. 0080-5319.
Sales: Salesianum; Roma. 0036-3502.
Salm: Salmanticensis; S. 0036-3537.
SalT: Sal Terrae; Sdr. 0211-4569.
Sandalion (Sassari); R, Herder.
SAOC: Studies in Ancient Oriental Civilization: Ch, Univ. 0081-7554. → OI.
Sap: Sapienza; Napoli. 0036-4711.
SapCro: La Sapienza della Croce; R.
sb.: subscription; price for members.
SbBrno: Sborník praci filozoficke fakulty; Brno, Univ.

SBF/Anal/Pub [min]: Studii Biblici Franciscani: 0081-8933 / Analecta / Publicationes series maior 0081-8971 [minor]; Jerusalem. → LA.
SBL [AramSt / Mg / Diss / GRR / MasSt / NAm / SemP / TexTr]: Society of Biblical Literature: Aramaic Studies / Monograph Series / Dissertation Series / Graeco-Roman Religion / Masoretic Studies / Biblical Scholarship in North America / Seminar Papers 0145-2711 / Texts and Translations. → JBL; CATSS; CritRR.
SBS [KBW]: Stuttgarter Bibelstudien; Stuttgart, Katholisches Bibelwerk.
ScandJOT: Scandinavian Journal of the Old Testament; Aarhus.
ScEsp: Science et Esprit; Montréal. 0316-5345.
SCHN: Studia ad Corpus Hellenisticum NT; Leiden.
Schönberger Hefte; Fra.
Scholars Choice; Richmond VA.
SChr: Sources Chrétiennes; P. 0750-1978.
SCompass: Social Compass, revue internationale de sociologie de la religion: Lv.
ScotBEv: The Scottish Bulletin of Evangelical Theology; E. 0265-4539.
ScotJT: Scottish Journal of Theology; Edinburgh. 0036-9306.
ScotR: Scottish Journal of Religious Studies; Stirling. 0143-8301.
ScrCiv: Scrittura [scrivere] e Civiltà; T.
ScrClasIsr: Scripta Classica Israelica; J.
ScriptB: Scripture Bulletin; London. 0036-9780.
Scriptorium; Bruxelles. 0036-9772.
ScripTPamp: Scripta theologica; Pamplona, Univ. Navarra. 0036-9764.
Scriptura; Stellenbosch. 0254-1807.
ScriptVict: Scriptorium Victoriense; Vitoria, España.
ScuolC: La Scuola Cattolica; Venegono Inferiore, Varese. 0036-9810.
SDB [= DBS]: Supplément au Dictionnaire de la Bible; Paris → 854.
SDH: Studia et documenta historiae et iuris; Roma, Pont. Univ. Lateran.
SecC: The Second Century; Malibu CA. 0276-7899.
Sefarad; Madrid. 0037-0894.
SEG: Supplementum epigraphicum graecum; Withoorn.
Segmenten; Amsterdam, Vrije Univ.

SeiRon: Seisho-gaku ronshū; Tokyo, Japanese Biblical Institute.

SelT: Selecciones de Teología; Barc.

SémBib: Sémiotique et Bible; Lyon ➜ CADIR. 0154-6902.

Semeia (Biblical Criticism) [Supplements]; Atlanta. 0095-571X.

Seminarios; Salamanca.

Seminarium; Roma.

Seminary Review; Cincinnati.

Semiotica; Amsterdam. 0037-1998.

Semitica; Paris. 0085-6037.

Semitics; Pretoria. 0256-6044.

Sens; juifs et chrétiens; Paris.

SeptCogSt: ➜ B[ulletin].

Servitium; CasM (ᴱBergamo).

SEST: South-Eastern [Baptist] Seminary Studies; Wake Forest NC.

Sevārtham; Ranchi.

Sève = Église aujourd'hui; P. 0223-5854.

SGErm: ℗ Soobščeniya gosudarstvennovo Ermitaža, Reports of the State Hermitage Museum; Leningrad. 0432-1501.

ShinKen: ℗ Shinyaku Kenkyū, Studia Textus Novi Testamenti; Osaka.

ShnatM: ℗ Shnaton la-Mikra (Annual, Biblical and ANE Studies); TA.

SicArch: Sicilia archaeologica; Trapani.

SicGym: Siculorum Gymnasium; Catania.

Sidra, a journal for the study of Rabbinic literature; Ramat-Gan.

SIMA: Studies in Mediterranean Archaeology; Göteborg.

SixtC: The Sixteenth Century Journal; St. Louis (Kirksville). 0361-0160.

SkK: Stuttgarter kleiner Kommentar.

SkrifK: Skrif en Kerk; Pretoria, Univ.

SMEA: Studi Micenei ed Egeo-Anatolici (Incunabula Graeca); Roma.

ŠMišpat: Šnaton ha-Mišpaṭ ha-Ivri, Annual of Jewish Law.

SMSR: Studi e Materiali di Storia delle religioni; Roma.

SNTS (Mg.): Studiorum Novi Testamenti Societas (Monograph Series); Cambridge.

SNTU-A/B: Studien zum NT und seiner Umwelt; Linz [Periodica / Series].

SocAnRel: Sociological analysis (sociology of religion); Chicago.

SocUÉg: Sociétés Urbaines en Égypte et au Soudan; Lille.

SocWB: The Social World of Biblical Antiquity; Sheffield.

Soundings; Nashville. 0585-5462.

SovArch: ℗ Sovyetskaja Archeologija; Moskva. 0038-5034.

Speculum (Medieval Studies); CM. 0038-7134.

SPg: Studia Philologica. 0585-5462.

SpirC, SpirNC: La Spiritualità cristiana / non-cristiana; R ➜ 5,907.

Spiritus; Paris. 0038-7665.

SpirLife: Spiritual Life; Washington. 0038-7630.

Sprache; Wien. 0038-8467.

SR: Studies in Religion / Sciences Religieuses; Waterloo, Ont. 0008-4298.

ST: (Vaticano) Studi e Testi.

ST: Studia Theologica; K. 0039-338X.

StAägK: Studien zur altägyptischen Kultur; Hamburg. 0340-2215.

StAChron: Studies in Ancient Chronology; London. 0952-4975.

Stadion, Geschichte des Sports; Sankt Augustin. 0178-4029.

StAns: Studia Anselmiana; Roma.

StANT: Studien zum Alten und Neuen Testament; München.

StAntCr: Studi di Antichità Cristiana; Città del Vaticano.

Star: St. Thomas Academy for Research; Bangalore.

StArchWsz: Studia archeologiczne; Warszawa, Univ.

Stauròs, Bollettino trimestrale sulla teologia della Croce: Pescara.

StBEC: Studies in the Bible and Early Christianity; Lewiston NY.

StBEx: Studies in Bible and Exegesis; Ramat-Gan.

StBib: Dehon/Paid/Leiden: Studi Biblici; Bo, Dehoniane / Brescia, Paideia / Studia Biblica; Leiden.

StBoğT: Studien zu den Boğazköy-Texten; Wiesbaden.

STBuc: Studii Teologice; Bucureşti.

StCatt: Studi cattolici; Mi. 0039-2901.

StCEth: Studies in Christian Ethics; Edinburgh. 0953-9468.

StChrAnt: Studies in Christian Antiquity; Wsh.

StChrJud: Studies in Christianity and Judaism; Waterloo ON.

StClasBuc: Studii Clasice; Bucureşti.

StClasOr: Studi Classici e Orientali; R.

StCompRel: Studies in Comparative Religion; Bedfont. 0039-3622.

StDelitzsch: Studia Delitzschiana (ᴱMünster); Stuttgart. 0585-5071.

StEbl: Studi Eblaiti; Roma, Univ.

StEcum: Studi Ecumenici; Verona. 0393-3687.

StEgPun: Studi di Egittologia e di Antichità Puniche (Univ. Bo.); Pisa.

StEpL: Studi Epigrafici e Linguistici sul Vicino Oriente antico; Verona.

STEv: Studi di Teologia dell'Istituto Biblico Evangelico; Padova.

StFormSp: Studies in Formative Spirituality; Pittsburgh, Duquesne.

StGnes: Studia Gnesnensia; Gniezno.

StHJewishP: Studies in the History of the Jewish People; Haifa.

StHPhRel: Studies in the History and Philosophy of Religion; CM.

StHRel [= Numen Suppl.] Studies in the History of Religions; Leiden.

StIran: Studia Iranica; Leiden. 0772-7852.

StIsVArh: Studii şi cercetări de Istorie Veche şi arheologie; Bucureşti. 0039-4009.

StItFgC: Studi Italiani di Filologia Classica; Firenze. 0039-2987.

StiZt: Stimmen der Zeit; FrB. 0039-1492.

StJudLA: Studies in Judaism in Late Antiquity; Leiden. 0169-961X.

StLeg: Studium Legionense; León.

StLtg: Studia Liturgica; Nieuwendam.

StLuke: St. Luke's Journal of Theology; Sewanee TN.

StMiss: Studia Missionalia, Annual; Rome, Gregorian Univ.

StMor: Studia Moralia; R, Alphonsianum. 0081-6736.

StNT: Studien zum Neuen Testament; Gütersloh; STNT ➤ Shin-Ken.

StNW: Studies of the NT and its World; E.

StOr: Studia Orientalia; Helsinki, Societas Orientalis Fennica. 0039-3282.

StOrL: Studi Orientali e Linguistici; Bo, Univ. Ist. Glottologia (1,1983).

StOrRel: Studies in Oriental Religions; Wiesbaden.

StOvet: Studium Ovetense; Oviedo.

StPatav: Studia Patavina; Padova. 0039-3304.

StPatrist: Studia Patristica; Berlin.

StPhilonAn: Studia Philonica Annual; Atlanta.

StPostB: Studia Post-Biblica; Leiden.

StPrace: Studia i Prace = Études, Wsz. Streven: 1. cultureel; Antwerpen. 0039-2324; 2. S.J., Amst.

StRicOrCr: Studi e Ricerche dell'Oriente Cristiano; Roma.

StRom: Studi Romani; Roma. Stromata (< Ciencia y Fe); San Miguel, Argentina. 0049-2353.

StRz: Studia Religioznawcze (Filozofii i Socjologii); Wsz, Univ.

StSemLgLing: Studies in Semitic Language and Linguistics; Leiden.

StSp (Dehoniane) ➤ 854*.

StSpG (Borla) ➤ 855.

StTNeunz: Studien zur Theologie und Geistesgeschichte des Neunzehnten Jh.; Gö.

StudiaBT: Studia Biblica et Theologica; Pasadena CA. 0094-2022.

Studies; Dublin. 0039-3495.

StudiesBT: Studies in Biblical Theology; L.

Studium; 1. Madrid; 2. R –0039-4130.

StVTPseud: Studia in Veteris Testamenti Pseudepigrapha; Leiden.

STWsz: Studia theologica Varsaviensia; Warszawa.

SubsBPont: Subsidia Biblica; R, Pontifical Biblical Institute.

SudanTB: Sudan Texts Bulletin; Ulster, Univ. 0143-6554.

Sumer (Archaeology-History in the Arab World); Baghdad, Dir. Ant.

SUNT: Studien zur Umwelt des NTs; Gö.

SUNY: State University of New York; Albany etc.

Supp.: Supplement ➤ NT, JStOT, SEG.

Supplément, Le: autrefois 'de VSp'; P.

SvEx: Svensk Exegetisk Årsbok; U.

SVlad: St. Vladimir's Theological Quarterly; Tuckahoe NY. 0036-3227.

SvTKv: Svensk Teologisk Kvartalskrift; Lund.

SWJT: Southwestern Journal of Theology; Fort Worth. 0038-4828.

Symbolae (graec-lat.); Oslo. 0039-7679.

Symbolon: 1. Ba/Stu; 2. Köln.
Synaxe; annuale, Catania.
Syria (Art Oriental, Archéologie); Paris, IFA Beyrouth.
SyrMesSt: Syro-Mesopotamian Studies (Monograph Journals); Malibu CA.
Szb: Sitzungsberichte [Univ.], phil.-hist. Klasse (Bayr./Mü. 0342-5991).
Szolgalat ⓜ ['Dienst']; Eisenstadt, Ös.
❶: *lingua turca*, Turkish; – ᵀtranslator.
Tablet; London. 0039-8837.
TAik: Teologinen Aikakauskirja / Teologisk Tidskrift; Helsinki.
TaiwJT: Taiwan [Presbyterian Sem.] Journal of Theology; Taipei.
TAJ: Tel Aviv [Univ.] Journal of the Institute of Archaeology. 0334-4355.
TAn: Theology Annual; Hongkong.
ṬanṭurYb: Ecumenical Institute for Theological Research Yearbook; J.
TArb: Theologische Arbeiten; Stu/B.
Tarbiẓ ❶ (Jewish Studies); Jerusalem, Hebr. Univ. 0334-3650.
TArbNZ: Texte und Arbeiten zum neutestamentlichen Zeitalter; Tü.
TArg: Teología; Buenos Aires.
Target, translation studies; Amst (1, 1989).
TAth: Ⓖ Theología; Athēnai.
TAVO: Tübinger Atlas zum Vorderen Orient [Beih(efte)]; Wiesbaden.
TBei: Theologische Beiträge; Wu.
TBer: Theologische Berichte; Z/Köln.
TBR: Theological Book Review; Guildford, Surrey.
TBraga: Theologica; Braga.
TBud: Teologia; Budapest, Ac. Cath.
TBüch: Theologische Bücherei. (Neudrukke und Berichte 20. Jdt.); München.
TCN: Theological College of Northern Nigeria Bulletin; Bukuru.
TContext: Theology in Context, English ed. [7 (1990) ➤ TKontext 11]. 0176-1439.
TDeusto: Teología-Deusto; Bilbao/M.
TDienst: Theologie und Dienst; Wuppertal.
TDig: Theology Digest; St. Louis. 0040-5728.
TDNT: Theological Dictionary of the NT [< TWNT]; Grand Rapids ➤ 5,811.
TDocStA: Testi e documenti per lo studio dell'Antichità; Milano, Cisalpino.

TDOT: Theological Dictionary of the Old Testament [< TWAT] GR ➤ 856.
TEdn: Theological Education; Vandalia, Ohio.
TEdr: Theological Educator; New Orleans.
TEFS: Theological Education [Materials for Africa, Asia, Caribbean] Fund, Study Guide; London.
Téléma (réflexion et créativité chrétiennes en Afrique); Kinshasa-Gombe.
Teocomunicação.
Teresianum; Roma.
TerraS / TerreS: Terra Santa: 0040-3784. / La Terre Sainte; J (Custodia OFM). ➤ HolyL.
TEspir: Teología Espiritual; Valencia.
TEuph: Transeuphratène [Syrie perse]; P.
TEV: Today's English Version (Good News for Modern Man); L, Collins.
TEvca: Theologia Evangelica; Pretoria, Univ. S. Africa.
TExH: Theologische Existenz heute; Mü.
Text; The Hague. 0165-4888.
TextEstCisn: Textos y Estudios 'Cardenal Cisneros'; Madrid, Cons.Sup.Inv.
TextPatLtg: Textus patristici et liturgici; Regensburg, Pustet.
Textus, Annual of the Hebrew Univ. Bible Project; J. 0082-3767.
TFor: Theologische Forschung; Ha.
TGegw: Theologie der Gegenwart in Auswahl; Münster, Regensberg-V.
TGL: Theologie und Glaube; Pd.
THandkNT: Theologischer Handkommentar zum NT; B.
THAT: Theologisches Handwörterbuch zum AT; München. ➤ 1,908.
Themelios; L. 0307-8388.
Theokratia, Jahrbuch des Institutum Delitzschianum; Leiden/Köln.
Ho Theológos; Fac. Teol. Palermo.
30D: Thirty days in the Church and in the world [< Trenta giorni]; SF.
THist: Théologie Historique; P. 0563-4253.
This World; NY.
Thomist, The; Wsh. 0040-6325.
Thought; NY, Fordham. 0040-6457.
TierraN: Tierra Nueva.
Tikkun; Oakland CA.
TimLitS: Times Literary Supplement; L.
TItSett: Teologia; Brescia (Fac. teol. Italia settentrionale).

T-Iusi: Teología, Instituto Universitario Seminario Interdioc.; Caracas.

TJb: Theologisches Jahrbuch; Leipzig.

TKontext: Theologie im Kontext; Aachen. 0724-1682. ➤ TContext[o].

TLond: Theology; London. 0040-571X.

TLZ: Theologische Literaturzeitung; Berlin. 0040-5671.

TolkNT: Tolkning [commentarius] av Nya Testamentet; Stockholm.

TorJT: Toronto Journal of Theology.

TPast: Theologie en pastoraat; Zwolle.

TPhil: Theologie und Philosophie; Freiburg/Br. 0040-5655.

TPQ: Theologisch-praktische Quartalschrift; Linz, Ös. 0040-5663.

TPract: Theologia Practica; München/Hamburg. 0720-9525.

TR: Theologische Revue; Münster. 0040-568X.

TradErn: Tradition und Erneuerung (religiös-liberales Judentum); Bern.

Traditio; Bronx NY, Fordham Univ.

Tradition, orthodox Jewish; NY.

TRE: Theologische Realenzyklopädie; Berlin ➤ 857.

TRef: Theologia Reformata; Woerden.

TRevNE: ➤ NESTR.

TRicScR: Testi e ricerche di scienze religiose; Brescia.

TrierTZ: Trierer Theologische Zeitschrift; Trier. 0041-2945.

TrinJ: Trinity Journal; Deerfield IL. 0360-3032.

TrinSemR: Trinity Seminary Review; Columbus.

TrinT: Trinity theological journal, Singapore.

TrinUn [St/Mg] Rel: Trinity University Studies [Monographs] in Religion, San Antonio TX.

Tripod; Hong Kong.

TRu: Theologische Rundschau; Tübingen. 0040-5698.

TS: Theological Studies; Baltimore. 0040-5639.

TsGesch: Tijdschrift voor Geschiedenis; Groningen.

TsLtg: Tijdschrift voor Liturgie; Lv.

TStAJud: Texte und Studien zum Antiken Judentum; Tübingen. 0721-8753.

TsTKi: Tidsskrift for Teologi og Kirke; Oslo. 0040-7194.

TsTNijm: Tijdschrift voor Theologie; Nijmegen (redactie). 0168-9959.

TStR: Texts and Studies in Religion; Lewiston NY.

TSzem: Theologiai Szemle; Budapest. 0133-7599.

TTod: Theology Today; Princeton. 0040-5736.

TU: Texte und Untersuchungen, Geschichte der altchristlichen Literatur; Berlin.

Tü [ÄgBei] ThS: Tübinger [Ägyptologische Beiträge; Bonn, Habelt] Theologische Studien; Mainz, Grünewald.

[Tü]TQ: [Tübinger] Theologische Quartalschrift; Mü. 0342-1430.

TürkArk: Türk Arkeoloji dergisi; Ankara.

TUmAT: Texte aus der Umwelt des ATs; Gütersloh ➤ 858.

TVers: Theologische Versuche; B. 0437-3014.

TViat: Theologia Viatorum; SAfr.

TVida: Teología y Vida; Santiago, Chile. 0049-3449.

TWAT: Theologisches Wörterbuch zum Alten Testament; Stu ➤ 859.

TWiss: Theologische Wissenschaft, Sammelwerk für Studium und Beruf; Stu.

TWNT: Theologisches Wörterbuch zum NT; Stuttgart (➤ GLNT; TDNT).

TXav: Theologica Xaveriana; Bogotá.

TxK: Texte und Kontexte (Exegese); Stu.

Tyche, Beiträge zur alten Geschichte, Papyrologie und Epigraphik; Wien.

Tychique (Chemin Neuf); Lyon.

TyndB: Tyndale Bulletin; Cambridge.

TZBas: Theologische Zeitschrift; Basel. 0040-5741.

UF: Ugarit-Forschungen; Kevelaer/Neukirchen. 0342-2356.

Universitas; 1. Stuttgart. 0041-9079; 2. Bogotá. 0041-9060.

UnivT: Universale Teologica; Brescia.

UnSa: Una Sancta: 1. Augsburg-Meitingen; 2. Brooklyn.

UnSemQ: Union Seminary Quarterly Review; New York.

UPA: University Press of America; Wsh/Lanham MD.

Update [religious trends]; Aarhus.

URM: Ultimate Reality and Meaning; Toronto.

VAeg: Varia Aegyptiaca; San Antonio. 0887-4026.
VBGed: Verklaring van een Bijbelgedeelte; Kampen.
VChrét: Vie Chrétienne; P. 0767-3221.
VComRel: La vie des communautés religieuses; Montréal.
VDI: ⑬ Vestnik Drevnej Istorii; Moskva. 0321-0391.
Veleia, (pre-) historia, filología clásicas; Vitoria-Gasteiz, Univ. P. Vasco.
Verbum; 1. SVD; R; - 2. Nancy.
Veritas; Porto Alegre, Univ. Católica.
VerkF: Verkündigung und Forschung; München. 0342-2410.
VerVid: Verdad y Vida; M. 0042-3718.
VestB: Vestigia Biblica; Hamburg.
VetChr: Vetera Christianorum; Bari.
Vidyajyoti (Theological Reflection); Ranchi (Delhi, Inst. Rel.St.).
VieCons: La Vie Consacrée; P/Bru.
VigChr: Vigiliae Christianae; Leiden. 0042-6032.
ViMon: Vita Monastica; Arezzo.
ViPe: Vita e Pensiero: Mi, S. Cuore.
VlsLang: Visible Language; Cleveland.
VisRel: Visible Religion, annual for iconography; Leiden. 0169-5606.
VitaCons: Vita Consacrata; Milano.
VizVrem: ⑬ Vizantijskij Vremennik; Moskva. 0136-7358.
VO: Vicino Oriente; Roma.
Vocation; Paris.
VoxEvca: Vox Evangelica; London. 0263-6786.
VoxEvi: Vox Evangelii; Buenos Aires.
VoxRef: Vox Reformata; Geelong, Australia.
VoxTh: Vox Theologica; Assen.
VSp: La Vie Spirituelle; Paris. 0042-4935; ➜ Supp. 0083-5859.
VT: Vetus Testamentum; Leiden. 0042-4935.
WDienst: Wort und Dienst; Bielefeld. 0342-3085.
WegFor: Wege der Forschung; Da, Wiss.
WeltOr: Welt des Orients; Göttingen. 0043-2547.
WesleyTJ: Wesleyan Theological Journal; Marion IN. 0092-4245.
WestTJ: Westminster Theological Journal; Philadelphia. 0043-4388.
WEvent: Word + Event; Stuttgart.

WienerSt: Wiener Studien; Wien.
Wiss: Wissenschaftliche Buchhandlung; Da.
WissPrax: Wissenschaft und Praxis in Kirche und Gesellschaft; Göttingen.
WissWeish: Wissenschaft und Weisheit; Mü-Gladbach. 0043-678X.
WM: Wissenschaftliche Monographien zum Alten/Neuen Testament; Neukirchen.
WoAnt: Wort und Antwort; Mainz.
Word and Spirit; Still River MA.
WorldArch: World Archaeology; Henley.
World Spirituality ➜ EWSp.
Worship; St. John's Abbey, Collegeville, Minn. 0043-9414.
WrocST: Wrocławskie Studia Teologiczne / Colloquium Salutis; Wrocław. 0239-7714.
WUNT: Wissenschaftliche Untersuchungen zum NT: Tübingen.
WVDOG: Wissenschaftliche Veröffentlichungen der Deutschen Orient-Gesellschaft; Berlin.
WWorld: Word and World; St. Paul.
WZ: Wissenschaftliche Zeitschrift [... Univ.].
WZKM: Wiener Zeitschrift für die Kunde des Morgenlandes; Wien. 0084-0076.
Xilotl, revista nicaraguense de teología.
YaleClas: Yale Classical Studies; NHv.
Yuval: Studies of the Jewish Music Research Centre [incl. Psalms]; Jerusalem.
ZäSpr: Zeitschrift für Ägyptische Sprache und Altertumskunde; Berlin. 0044-216X.
ZAHeb: Zeitschrift für Althebraistik; Stuttgart. 0932-4461.
ZAss: Zeitschrift für Assyriologie & Vorderasiatische Archäologie; Berlin. 0048-5299.
ZAW: Zeitschrift für die Alttestamentliche Wissenschaft; Berlin. 0044-2526.
ZDialekT: Zeitschrift für dialektische Theologie; Kampen.
ZDMG: Zeitschrift der Deutschen Morgenländischen Gesellschaft; Wiesbaden.
ZDPV: Zeitschrift des Deutschen Palästina-Vereins; Stu. 0012-1169.
ZeichZt: Die Zeichen der Zeit, Evangelische Monatschrift; Berlin.

Zeitwende (Die neue Furche); Gü.
ZeKUL: Zeszyty Naukowe Katolickiego
Uniw. Lubelskiego; Lublin. 0044-4405.
Zephyrus; Salamanca. 0514-7336.
ZEthnol: Zeitschrift für Ethnologie;
Braunschweig. 0044-2666.
ZEvEthik: Zeitschrift für Evangelische
Ethik; Gütersloh. 0044-2674.
ZfArch: Zeitschrift für Archäologie:
Berlin. 0044-233X.
ZGPred: Zeitschrift für Gottesdienst
und Predigt; Gütersloh.
Zion: ⊕; Jerusalem. 0044-4758.
ZIT: Zeitschriften Inhaltsdienst Theo-
logie; Tübingen. 0340-8361.
ZKG: Zeitschrift für Kirchengeschich-
te; Stuttgart. 0044-2985.
ZkT: Zeitschrift für katholische Theo-
logie; Innsbruck. 0044-2895.
ZMissRW: Zeitschrift für Missions-
wissenschaft und Religionswissen-
schaft; Münster. 0044-3123.

ZNW: Zeitschrift für die Neutestamentliche Wissenschaft und die
Kunde des Alten Christentums; Ber-
lin. 0044-2615.
ZPapEp: Zeitschrift für Papyrolo-
gie und Epigraphik; Bonn. 0084-
5388.
ZPraxRU: Zeitschrift für die Praxis
des Religionsunterrichts; Stu.
ZRGg: Zeitschrift für Reli-
gions- und Geistesgeschichte; Köln.
0044-3441.
ZSavR: Zeitschrift der Savigny-
Stiftung (Romanistische) Rechtsge-
schichte: Weimar. 0323-4096.
ZSprW: Zeitschrift für Sprachwissen-
schaft; Gö. 0721-9067.
ZTK: Zeitschrift für Theologie und
Kirche; Tübingen. 0513-9147.
ZvgSpr ➤ HSprF.
Zwingliana; Zürich.
Zygon; Winter Park FL. 0591-2385.

I. Bibliographica

A1   *Opera collecta* .1 **Festschriften,** memorials.

1 *a*) Collected essays (signed reports with tit. pp. — titles and pages): CBQ 52
(1990) 182-193 . 370-8 . 579-586 . 772-5. – *b*) *Epp* E. J. (*al.*), Collected
essays: JBL 109 (1990) 169-178 . 361-371 . 547-558 . 737-749. – *c*) ᴱ*Ernst*
Juliette, Mélanges et recueils: AnPg 60 (pour 1989) p. 871-6. – *d*) ETL 66
(1990) 9*-17* ('opera quae analysi subiecta sunt') & 137*s (VT opera
collectiva); – *e*) **LuJb** mingles all kinds of compilations in its first section
with number-prefixes 0-, but has at the end an index, of which one
Stichwort is 'Festschrift' [12 items vol. 57, p. 369]. – *f*) The appreciated
'Recueils et mélanges' in **RB** was replaced in 1990 by the greatly-amplified
'Ouvrages reçus' of J.-M. *Rousée*, ➤ 991. – *g*) **RHE** 86 (1991) 77* under
'Histoire universelle' has a long string of Festschriften (many about
theology; none about 'universal history'), though others are distributed
according to the particular topic.

2 *a*) ᴱ**Leistner** Otto, Internationale Bibliographie der Festschriften von den
Anfängen bis 1979², [I-II, 812 p.; 967 p.] III. Sachregister und Nachträge.
Osnabrück 1989, Biblio. 449 p. – *b*) **Zeller** Otto & Wolfram, Inter-
nationale Jahresbibliographie der Festschriften, 8 für 1987; 9 für 1989.
Osnabrück 1989, Dietrich. 495 [+?] 717 + 596 p.; 584 + 903 + 421 p.
[AnPg 60 p. 871].

3 ALKIM U. Bahadır, 1915-1981: Hatıra Sayısı (in memoriam), ᴱ**Dinçol** Ali M.,
al. AnAraşt = JbKlAsF 10 (1986). Istanbul c. 1990. 553 p.; bibliog. 3-13.
$20. 30 art., 14 infra.

4 AMIRAN Ruth: Eretz-Israel 21, ᴱ**Eitan** A., *al.* J 1990, Israel Exploration Soc. 110* p. + ❸ 258, portrait; ill. $60. 14 art. + 26❸, infra [BL 92,11, A. R. *Millard*; RB 99,292, tit. pp.; OLZ 87,261, G. *Pfeifer*].

4* ANGELI Wilhelm: Fs. 65. Gb., ᴱ**Kremser** Manfred: Mitteilungen der Anthropologischen Gesellschaft in Wien 118s (1988s). 412 p.; ill.; portr.; Bibliog. 5-7 (*Ruttkay* Elisabeth). 3-85028-182-2. 29 art.; 2 infra.

5 (Otmar) von ARETIN Karl; CHRISMAN Miriam U. (➤ 37*); SCHÄFER Gerhard; 1988 Festschriften on modern Europe [LuJb 57 (1990) p. 322].

6 ARNOLD Walter: Proclaiming Christ in Christ's way; studies in integral evangelism, 60th b., ᴱ**Samuel** Vinay. Ox 1989, Regnum. 228 p.; ill. 1-870345-07-X. 16 art. [ZIT 90,78].

7 ARTZI Pinḥas; Bar-Ilan Studies in Assyriology, ᴱ**Klein** Jacob, *Skaist* Aaron. Ramat-Gan 1990. 295 p., 16 pl. 965-226-100-9 [BL 92,117, W. G. *Lambert*]. 12 art., infra.

8 ASCHKENASY Yehuda: Tora met hart en ziel, 65ᵉ verjaardag: Kath. Theol. Univ. Amst. & B. Folkertsma Stichting voor Talmudica. Hilversum 1989, Gooi & S. 379 p. [ETL 64,16*].

8* ASSFALG Julius: Lingua restituta orientalis, Festgabe, ᴱ**Schulz** Regine, *Görg* Manfred: ÄgAT 20. Wsb 1990, Harrassowitz. xxv-419 p.; portr.; Bibliog. xiii-xxv. 3-447-03113-1. 47 art.; 23 infra.

9 BALIL ILLANA Alberto, mem. † 23.VIII.1989: BSAA 56 (1990). 599 p.; bibliog. p. 7-24.

10 BALTHASAR Hans Urs von: Gestalt und Werk, ᴱ**Lehmann** K., *Kasper* W. Pa 1989, Bonifatius. 359 p. DM 48. 3-921204-03-8. – ᴿTsTNijm 30 (1990) 414 (H. E. *Mertens*).

11 BANDLE Oskar; Fs., ᴱ**Naumann** Hans P., *al.*: Beiträge zur nordischen Philologie 15. Basel 1986, Helbing & L. viii-316 p. 28 art. – ᴿRBgPg 68 (1990) 788 (C. *Peeters*).

12 BAPAT P. V.: Amala Prajñā, Aspects of Buddhist Studies. Delhi 1989, Sri Satguru. xxx-574 p.; bibliog. p. xxv-xxx. rs. 600. 60 art. – ᴿIndIranJ 33 (1990) 285s (tit. pp.).

BAUD-BOVY Samuel, Mem., Symposion, Griechische Musik 1986 ➤ 718*.

13 BAVEL Tarsicius J. van; Collectanea Augustiniana, ᴰ**Bruning** B., *al.* = Augustiniana 40 (Lv 1990) + 41 (1991), 428 p. + p. 429-1074; portr.; biobibliog. xv-xxxviii (J. Van *Houtem*). [NRT 113,237, V. *Roisel*; TsTNijm 31,431, A. *Lascaris*].

14 BECK Hans-Georg: Fest und Alltag in Byzanz, ᴰ**Prinzing** G., *Simon* D., Mü 1990, Beck. 227 p.; 3 fig. [Klio 73, 685-7, C. *Ludwig*].

15 BECK Heinrich: Actualitas omnium actuum, ᴱ**Schadel** E. 1989 ➤ 5,22: ᴿTVida 31 (1990) 76-79 (Anneliese *Meis*).

16 BECKERATH Jürgen von: 70. Gb.: Hildesheimer ÄgBeit 30, ᴱ**Eggebrecht** Arne, *Schmitz* Bettine. Hildesheim 1990, Gerstenberg. xxvii-264 p.; 19 pl.; Bibliog. xi-xxvii (*Martin* Karl). 3-8067-8116-8; 22 art., 17 infra. [OLZ 86, 264, K. A. *Kitchen*, tit. pp., comments].

17 BERG Karl: Uni trinoque Domino, Festgabe Erzbischof ~, 80. Gb., ᴱ**Paarhammer** Hans, *Schmölz* Franz-Martin. Thaur 1989, Österr. Kulturverlag. 496 p. Sch. 520 [TR 86,249].

18 BERGER Ernst: Kanon, ᴱ**Schmidt** Margot: AntKunstBeih 15. Basel 1988. viii-380 p. + x-104 pl. [Nikephoros 2 (1989) 225]. – ᴿRÉG 103 (1990) 286s (F. *Chamoux*).

19 BERLINGER Rudolph: Agora = Perspektiven zur Philosophie, Jb. (Amst 1988, Rodopi). lix-442 p. [AnPg 60 p. 872, 'dépouillé'].

20 BIEMER Günter, Das Geheimnis spüren — zum Glauben anstiften, Gb. EBissinger Albert, *Tzschaetzsch* Werner. FrB 1989, Herder. 290 p.; p. 277-290 Bibliog. DM 58 [TR 86,533; tit. pp.; ZkT 113,130, M. *Heizer*].

21 BISCHOFF Bernhard: Scire litteras; Forschungen zum mittelalterlichen Geistesleben, EKraemer Sigrid, *Bernhard* Michael: AbhBayrAkad 99. Mü 1988, Beck. 438 p. [AnPg 60, p. 872: part. dépouillé].

21* BJØRNDALEN Anders Jørgen, 23.III.1928-14.I.1989, mem. = TsTKi 60,4 (1989). p. 245-318; portr.; biobibliog. 247-254 (M. *Sæbø*), 313-8 (A. *Aschim*).

22 BLACKWELDER Boyce W. (1913-1976) mem.: Listening to the Word of God, ECallen B. L. Anderson IN 1990, Warner. xiv-172 p. 0-87162-516-4 [NTAbs 34,378]. 8 art., mostly NT.

23 BLANC Haim 1926-1984: Studia linguistica et orientalia ~ memoriae dedita, EWexler Paul, *al.*: Mediterranean Language and Culture Mg 6. Wsb 1989, Harrassowitz. viii-314 p.; portr.; biobibliog. p. 1-9 (S. *Somekh*). 27 art.; 3 infra.

23* BLOK D. P.: Festbundel 65ste Verjaardag, EBerns J. B., *al.* Hilversum 1990, Verloren. 397 p. 35 art. [BeiNam 26,431, D. *Stellmacher*].

24 BOERS Hendrikus W.: Test and Logos; the humanistic interpretation of the New Testament, EJennings Theodore W.: Homage Series. Atlanta 1990, Scholars. xvi-306 p.; bibliog. with summaries, 295-306. 1-55540-508-8. 17 art., infra [TR 87,427, tit. pp.].

25 BOGAERT Raymond & LOOY Hermann Van, Opes atticae, miscellanea philologica et historica, EGeerard M., *al.* = Sacris Erudiri 31. Steenbrugge/Haag 1989s, St.-Pietersabdij/Nijhoff. 483 p.; 34 pl.; biobibliog. ix-xx / xxi-xxix. Fb. 2200. 0071-7667. 39 art.; plures infra.

26 BOHREN Rudolf: Lobet Gott; Beiträge zur theologischen Ästhetik, 70. Gb., ESeim Jürgen, *Steiger* Lothar. Mü 1990, Kaiser. 205 p.; Bibliog. (*Brates* Ulrich), 195ss. 3-459-01841-0. [ZIT 90,582, tit. pp.] 19 art.; 5 infra.

FBOSCH David, dialogue 1990 → 579.

27 BOSL Karl: Gesellschaftsgeschichte, 80. Gb., ESeibt Ferdinand. Oldenbourg 1988, Collegium Carolinum. I. 506 p.; 11 pl.; II. 498 p., foldout map. DM 138. – RSpeculum 65 (1990) 800s (some tit. pp.).

28 BOUNNI Adnan: Resurrecting the past; a joint tribute to ~, 62d b., EMatthiae Paolo, *al.*: Uitgaven 67. Leiden 1990, Nederlands Historisch-Archaeologisch Instituut te Istanbul. xxxvi-407 p.; portr.; 140 pl.; biobibliog. xxxi-xxxvi. 90-6258-067-X. 27 art.; infra.

29 BOURCIER Élisabeth: Ténèbres et lumière, essais en hommage (par) *Carrive* Lucien, *al.*: Ét. Anglaises 9. P 1988, Didier. 142 p. – RRHR 207 (1990) 110-2 (B. *Cottret*).

30 CAMBITOGLOU Alexander: *Eumousia*; ceramic and iconographic studies, EDescoeudres Jean-Paul: MeditArch Supp 1. Sydney 1990, Univ. xxii-256 p.; 52 pl.; bibliog. xix-xxii. 0-909797-17-X. 38 art.; 3 infra.

31 CARNEY James: Sages, saints, and storytellers; Celtic studies, EÓ Corráin Donnchadh, *al.*: Mg 2. Maynooth 1989, Sagart. xvi-472 p.; color. front. £28 [RHE 85,394*]. – RSpeculum 65 (1990) 709 (tit. pp.).

32 [CARPANETO] Cassiano da Langasco: Studi in onore di Padre ~. Genova 1989, Prov. Cappuccini. 148 p.; ill. [RHE 85,394*].

33 CHABRET FRAGA Antonio: Homenatge ['Sagunto']-1988; present. *Aranegui Gascó* Carmen. Valencia 1989, Generalitat. 252 p.; portr. 84-7579-751-2. 8 art. sobre Sagunto, → d760.

34 (I) CHAMPOLLION Jean-François; L'Égypte, Bonaparte et Champollion, exposition bicentenaire, Hôtel de Balène. Figeac 1990, Assoc. Bic. Champollion. 78 p.; ill. 2-906398-01-2. 5 art., infra; + catalogue.

35 (II) Hommage de l'Europe à CHAMPOLLION: Mémoires d'Égypte, présent. **Ladurie** Emmanuel L. Strasbourg 1990, La Nuée Bleue. 253 p.; (color.) ill. 2-7165-0258-7. 15 art., infra. – RUniversitas 45 (1990) 915 (H. *Vogt*).

36 CHAPLAIS Pierre: England and her neighbours, 1066-1453, E**Jones** M., *Vale* M. L 1989, Hambledon. xxiv-326 p.; 6 fig. [RHE 85, p. 240*].

36* CHASTEL André: Il se rendit en Italie. R/P 1987, Elefante/Flammarion. 698 p.; ill. [RHE 86,76*].

37 CHICAGO-LAMBETH 1886-8: Quadrilateral at One Hundred; essays on the centenary of the Chicago-Lambeth Quadrilateral 1886/88 - 1986/88, E**Wright** J. Robert. Cincinnati 1988, Forward. ix-229 p. £17.50. 0-264-671-78-3. – RCathHR 76 (1990) 97 (H. J. *Ryan*); ScotBEv 7 (1989) 45-47 (D. F. *Wright*).

37* CHRISMAN Miriam Usher, The process of change in early modern Europe, E**Bebb** Philipp N., *Marshall* Sherrin. Athens OH 1988, Ohio Univ. vii-218 p. [LuJb 57, p. 322, indicating 4 items there cited].

38 CLARK J. Desmond: 70th b., E**Philipson** David N., *Harris* J.W.K. = African Archaeological Review 5 (1987). 207 p. £25 (private persons £15). – RBInstArch 26 (1989) 231 (A. *Hooper*).

38* COLPE Carsten: Loyalitätskonflikte in der Religionsgeschichte, 60. Gb., E**Elsas** Christoph, *Kippenberg* Hans, *al.* Wü 1990, Königsberg & N. ix-386 p. 28 art. [CritRR 4,502 tit. pp.], 6 infra.

39 CORBO Virgilio C.: Christian archaeology in the Holy Land; new discoveries; essays in honour of ~, O.F.M., E**Bottini** G.C., *Di Segni* L., *Alliata* E.: SBF maior 36. J 1990, Franciscan. xix-596 p.; ill.; phot.; bibliog. xv-xix (Bottini); map p. 590; index of places (*Alliata*) p. 591-6, with grid-reference of each. 31 art., infra [RB 98,615, J. *Murphy-O'Connor*].

39* CORISH Patrick J.: Religion, conflict and coexistence in Ireland, E**Comerford** Richard V. Dublin 1990, Gill & M. 360 p.; bibliog. p. 278-292. £35 [TR 87,342]

40 CUTTINO George P.: Documenting the past; essays in medieval history, E**Hamilton** J.S., *Bradley* Patricia J. Wolfeboro NH 1989, Boydell & B. x-239 p. $53 [RHE 85, p. 239*]. – RSpeculum 65 (1990) 1089s (tit. pp.).

41 DANKER Frederick W.: CurrTMiss 17,4.6 (1990) 258-297. 418-461.

41* a) DILIGENZA Luigi: Studi in onore di Mgr. ~, E**Ianniello.** Aversa 1989, Fabozzi. xvi-386 p. [RHE 86,77*].

— b) DIOP cheikh Anta: Sciences et civilisations africaines. Fort-de-France 1989, Revue Martiniquaise des Sciences/Lit 6. 153 p. 0990-7866 [OIAc Oc90].

— c) DOSTÁLOVÁ Råžena: Byzantinoslavica 50,1 (1989).

42 DÖLLINGER J.J. Ignaz von: Geschichtlichkeit und Glaube; zum 100. Todestag, E**Denzler** Georg, *Grasmück* Ernst L. Mü 1990, Wewel. 498 p.; Bibliog. p. 486-495. DM 68 [TR 87,431, tit. pp.].

42* DOORNINK-HOOGENRAND J.C.: Geschiedenis in Zutphen; over geschiedschrijving, geschiedbeoefening en historisch besef, E**Looper** B., *Riemens* J.C. Zutphen 1988, Walburg. 143 p. *f* 32 [RHE 86,357*].

43 DOVER Kenneth: 'Owls to Athena', essays on classical subjects presented to Sir ~, E**Craik** E.M. Ox 1990, Clarendon. xv-413 p., portr.; bibliog. p. 401-9. 0-19-814478-4. 42 art.

44 DOWEY Edward A.[J]: Probing the Reformed tradition; historical studies in honor of ∼, [E]McKee Elsie A., *Armstrong* Brian G. Louisville 1990, Westminster/Knox. 461 p. bibliog. p. 459-461 (*Burrows* Mark S.). 0-664-21916-0 [TDig 37,380; TR 86,525 & ZIT 90,507, tit. pp.; RHPR 71,391, M. *Arnold*]. – 22 art.; 10 infra. – [R]TTod 47 (1990s) 354 (M.P. *Engel*).

45 DULLES Avery: Faithful witness; foundations of theology for today's Church, 70th b., [E]O'Donovan Leo J., *Sanks* T. Howard. NY 1989, Crossroad. xiii-235 p. $23. 0-8245-0896-3 [NTAbs 34,192; NewTR 4/1,94, Mary E. *Hines*; RelStR 17,147, J. *Buckley*].

46 *a*) EICHENSEER Caelestis: Latine sapere, agere, loqui, [E]Sigridis Albert. Saarbrücken 1989, Soc. Latina. 220 p.; portr. [AnPg 60, p.872; dépouillé].

— *b*) ELANSKAJA Alla I.: JCopt 1 (1990) [portr.; bibliog. p.1-12 (P. *Nagel*); brief word end of p.x]. 155 p.; 7 pl. 1016-5558. 10 art.; infra.

46* ERBEN Johannes: Deutsche Sprachgeschichte; Grundlagen, Methoden, Perspektiven, 65. Gb., [E]Besch Werner. Fra 1990, Lang. 485 p. [Bei-Nam 26.433-447, Stefanie *Stricker*].

EWIG Eugen, Colloquium zum 75. Gb. 1988/90 → 732*.

47 FINNISH EXEGETICAL SOCIETY 50th Anniv.: The Law in the Bible and in its environment, [E]Veijola T. Helsinki/Gö 1990, Finnish Exeg. Soc. / Vandenhoeck & R. 186 p. DM 58. 951-9217-06-1 / 3-525-54000-0 [BL 91,25, B.S. *Jackson*].

47* FLANDERS Henry Jackson[J]: With steadfast purpose; essays on Acts, [E]Keathley N.H. Waco 1990, Baylor Univ. xi-345 p.; portr.; 27-p. biog. (W.L. *Pitts*). $20. 15 art. [NTAbs 35,247: authors, topics; no pp. or titles].

48 FOREVILLE Raymonde: Mediaevalia Christiana XIe-XIIIe siècles, [E]Viola Coloman E. Tourn 1989, Univ. xxxiv-382 p.; bibliog. ix-xxix. F 290 [TR 86,525 no tit pp.].

49 FÓTI László 1944-1985: Studia in honorem, [E]Pölöskei Ferenc: Studia Aegyptiaca 12, Budapest 1989, Univ. Chaire d'Égyptologie. 435 p.; ill.; portr. 963-462-542-8. 17 art.; infra.

50 FOX Helmut: Ökumenisch leben, 60. Gb., [E]Mercker H., *Wibbing* S. Landau/Pfalz 1990, Ev.-Kath. Sem. [ZAW 103,165 → 2436].

51 FOX Marvin: From ancient Israel to modern Judaism; Israel in quest of understanding [first of 4 volumes to contain 56 essays], [E]Neusner Jacob, *al.*: BrownJudSt 159. Atlanta 1989, Scholars. xxiv-292 p. $48; sb. $32. 1-55540-335-2 [BL 91,21, S.C. *Reif*]. – Vol. 2-4. BrownJudSt 173-5; 315 p.; 254 p.; 235 p. [all 4 $300; sb. $200: RelStR 16,356].

52 FULLER Reginald H.: Christ and his communities, [E]Hultgren Arland J., *Hall* Barbara: AnglTR Supp. 11. Evanston IL/Cincinnati 1990, Forward Movement. xxviii-153 p.; $8. portr.; biobibliog. xi-xxiv (*Kahl* R.M., *Burke* G.P.). 12 art., infra [NTAbs 34,283].

53 GABBA Emilio: Studi di storia e storiografia antica, Pavia 1988. 179 p. 10 art.; 5 infra.

53* GAMBER Klaus, Gedenkschrift: Simandron, der Wachklopfer, [E]Nyssen Wilhelm. Köln 1989, Lüthe. 347 p. [ZkT 113,357, H.B. *Meyer*].

54 GAMPL Inge; 60. Gb., [E]Melichar Erwin, *Potz* Richard, = Österreichisches Archiv für Kirchenrecht 39,1s (1990). viii-275 p. 17 art., 3 infra.

55 GARD Donald: Anxiety, guilt and freedom; religious studies perspectives, [E]Hubbard Benjamin J., *Starr* Bradley E. Lanham MD 1990, UPA. ix-278 p. $40.25; pa. $18.50. 0-9191-7683-4; -4-2. 14 art. [TDig 38,250].

56 GEIJER Agnes: Opera textilia variorum temporum, 90th b., ᴱEstham Inger, *Nockert* Margareta: Museum Studies 8. Sto 1988, Hist. Museum. 168 p.; phot. 91-7192-742-5. 19 art.; 2 infra.

57 GEMELLARO G., Solidarietà, nuovo nome della pace; studi sull'Enciclica 'Sollicitudo rei socialis' di GIOVANNI PAOLO II, offerti a Don ~, ᴱToso M.: Problemi d'oggi. T-Leumann 1988, Elle Di Ci. 230 p. – ᴿClaretianum 29 (1989) 400s (S. M. *González Silva*).

58 GHISELLI Alfredo: Mnemosynum, 70° compleanno. Bo 1989, Pàtron. xxi-561 p. Lit. 80.000 [Maia 43,237, Elisa *Mignogna*]. – ᴿSileno 16 (1990) 361-3 (C. *Nicolosi*).

GHUL Mahmud mem. 1923-1983: symposium 1984 → 801.

59 GIBB Hellmuth Otto F.: Festschrift. Fra 1989, Luther-Konf. Hessen-Nassau. 467 + 30 p.; Bibliog. 4-16 [TR 86,521], DM 36.

60 GIOVANNI DELLA CROCE, IV centenario della morte: Teresianum 40,2 (1989) 289-433; 41,2 (1990) 323-587.

60* GIUNTA Francesco: Mediterraneo medievale: Biblioteca di Storia e Cultura Meridionale 2. Soveria Mannelli CZ 1989, Rubbettino. xxix-1287 p. (3 vol.) [RHE 86,82*].

61 GRAF ZU DOHNA Lothar: Reformatio et reformationes, 65. Gb., ᴱMehl Andreas, *Schneider* Christian: Wissenschaft und Technik 47. Da 1989, Technische Hochschule. 482 p.; ill. 3-88607-069-7 [ZIT 90,441] 18 art.; 4 infra.

61* GRANE Leif: Teologi og tradition, ᵀGrosbal Thorkild, *al.* Århus 1988, Arus. 197 p. [LuJb 56, p. 164].

62 GRILLI Alberto: Scritti in onore di ~, ᴱScarpat Giuseppe = Paideia 45. Brescia 1990. 477 p.; portr. [BStLat 21,130, V. *Viparelli* (+ 212s, tit. pp.)] 24 art., 3 infra.

63 GROËR Hans Hermann Kard.: Servitium pietatis, 70. Gb., ᴱCoreth Anna, *Fux* Ildefons. Maria Roggendorf 1989, Sal Terrae. 431 p. 290 p. [RHE 86,77*].

64 GRZYBEK Stanisław: ❷ Studium Scripturae anima theologiae, ᴱChmiel Jerzy, *Matras* Tadeusz. Kraków 1990, Polskie Towarzystwo Teologiczne. 376 p.; portr.; bibliog. p. 7-19 (Matras). 83-85017-53-4. 32 art. (2 deutsch, 1 franç.; 29 ❷ with summaries).

65 GSCHWANTLER: ᴱReichert Hermann, *Zimmermann* Günter. W 1990 [announced in HistRel 29,189].

65* GY Pierre-Marie O.P.: Rituels, ᴱClerck P. de, *Palazzo* E. P 1990, Cerf. iv-490 p.; 36 fig. F 335 [RB 98,456 & TR 87,439, tit. pp.; RHE 86,141* 'Guy'; EsprVie 101,203, F. *Rouillard*; JTS 42,823, K. *Stevenson*; MaisD 187,137, B. *Fischer*; NRT 113,276, A. *Toubeau*].

66 HABERMAS Jürgen: 60. Gb., Habermas und die Theologie; Beiträge zur theologischen Rezeption; Diskussion und Kritik der Theorie kommunikativen Handelns, ᴱArens Edmund. Dü 1989, Patmos. 270 p. DM 40 pa. – ᴿTLZ 115 (1990) 222-4 (W. *Pfüller*).

66* HACKETT Stuart C.: The logic of rational theism, exploratory essays, ᴱCraig William L., *McLeod* Mark S.: Problems in contemporary philosophy 24. Lewiston NY 1990, Mellen. 250 p. $60. 0-88946-369-7 [TDig 38,277] 12 art.

67 HAHN István mem., 28.III.1913-26.VII.1984: Studia classica: AcAntH 32,1s (1989). 211 p.; portr.; p. 207-9 evocatio (J. *Harmatta*).

67* HALKES Catharina J. M.: Zij waait waarhen zij wil; opstellen over de Geest, ᴱBons-Storm R., *al.* Baarn 1986 Ten Have. 159 p.; ill. [RHE 84, p. 373*].

68 HALLIDAY Michael: Language topics. Ph 1988, Benjamins. 1160 p. (2 vol.) 75 art. – ᴿRBgPg 68 (1990) 709-724 (L. K. *Engels*: team-work conspicuous; astonishingly coherent).

69 HAMMERSCHMIDT Ernst: Collectanea Aethiopica, 60. Gb.: = Äthiopische Forschungen 26. Stu 1988, Steiner. 233 p. – ᴿAcOrK 51 (1990) 257-261 (K.-G. *Prasse*).

69* HANDY Robert T.: Altered landscapes; Christianity in America 1935-1985, ᴱLotz David W., *al.* GR 1989, Eerdmans. xi-387 p. $28; pa. $18 [CritRR 4, 327, E. T. *Linenthal*].

70 HANHART Robert: Studien zur Septuaginta, 65. Gb., ᴱFraenkel Detlef, *al.*: Mitteilungen des Septuaginta-Unternehmens 20 / AbhGö p/h 3/1990. Gö 1990, Vandenhoeck & R. 368 p.; portr. DM 160. 3-525-82477-7 [ZAW 103,459, tit. pp.; BL 91,45, A. G. *Auld*].

70* HARI Robert mém.: BSocÉg 13 (Genève 1989). 184 p.; portr.; bibliog. p. 5-7. 23 art., 11 infra [BO 48,447, C. *Cannuyer*].

71 (I) HARRELSON Walter J.: Perspectives on the Hebrew Bible, ᴱCrenshaw James L. [Macon GA 1988, Mercer Univ. 116 p.; 5-7 brief biobibliog. 0-86554-330-5] seems identical with PerspRelSt 15,4 (1988) with anomalous pagination [➤ 4,1876; the other articles also are cited in our volume 4].

72 (II) HARRELSON Walter: Justice and the Holy, ᴱKnight Douglas A., *Paris* Peter J.: Homage Series. Atlanta 1989, Scholars. xxxix-369 p.; bio-bibliog. xix-xxxvi; phot. $45; sb./pa. $30. 20 art. [JBL 109,747, tit. pp.].

73 HECKSCHER Williams S.: The verbal and the visual. NY 1990, Italica. – p. 225-247, *Vickers* Michael, Wandering stones; Venice, Constantinople, and Athens [Antiquity 64,694].

74 HEIDEGGER Martin: Kunst und Technik, Gedächtnisschrift zum 100. Gb., ᴱBiemel Walter, *Herrmann* Friedrich-Wilhelm von. Fra 1989, Klostermann. 459 p. – ᴿTPhil 65 (1990) 451-3 (G. *Haeffner*, auch über Gedenkschrift Japan und Heidegger 1989, ᴱ*Buchner* Harmut).

75 HELD Moshe, † 6.VI.1984 [I. Linguistic studies 1988 ➤ 5,81]; II. Semitic studies: Journal of the Ancient Near Eastern Society 19 (1989). NY 1989, Jewish Theological Seminary. viii-181 p.; bibliog. p. vii-viii [VT 41,377, R. H. *O'Connell*].

76 HENKYS Jürgen: '... Das tiefe Wort erneun', 60. Gb., ᴱSchultze Harald, *al.* B-Brandenburg 1989. Ev.-K. Sprachenkonvikt. 467 p., bibliog. p. 449ss [TLZ 115,573; iii. 'Bibel, Lehre und Tradition'; ZIT 90,798, tit. pp.] 35 art., 5 infra.

77 HIMMELMANN Nikolaus: Beiträge zur Ikonographie und Hermeneutik, ᴱCain Hans-Ulrich, *al.*: BonnJbb Beih 47. Mainz 1989, von Zabern, x-539 p.; 86 pl. [AnPg 60 p. 871 & dépouillé].

78 HINTZE Fritz: Studia in honorem, ᴱApelt Dietlind, *al.*: Meroitica 12. B 1990, Akademie. 390 p.; portr.; V pl.; p. 385-390, Bibliog. (*Hintze* Ursula †). 3-05-000976-4. 28 art.; 13 infra.

79 HOENIGSWALD Henry: Fs 70th b., ᴱCardona George. Mü c. 1990, Narr. [OIAc S90 ➤ 9593].

80 *a*) HÖRNER Hadwig, [H]Ermēneumata, 60 Gb., ᴱEisenberger Herbert: BiblKlasAltW NF 79. Heid 1990 Winter. 345 p., VI pl., portr. 3-533-04155-7; pa. -4-9. 17 art., 6 infra [Salesianum 53,798: *Mühlenberg* E. su Mt 20,1-16; *Grillmeier* A. su LEONZIO B.; *Sallmann* K. sulla musica in AGOSTINO: settore intero su G. NISSA].

— *b*) HOLTER Åge: Det levende ordet, sytti årsdag, ᴱAsheim Ivar, *al.* Oslo 1989, Univ. 196 p. – ᴿTsTKi 61 (1990) 153 (O. J. *Jensen*).

80* HORNUNG Maria: Mundart und Name in Sprachkontakt, 70. Gb.:
Beiträge zur Sprachinselforschung 8.   W 1990, VWGÖ (Verband der
wissenschaftlichen Gesellschaften Österreichs). 406 p. 23 art. [BeiNam
26,358, Maria G. *Arcamone*].

81 HUBBELING Hubertus G. (1925-1986) mem.:   Belief in God and intellectual
honesty, EValdhuis Ruurd, *al.*: Philosophia religionis 26.   Assen 1990,
Van Gorcum.   vii-205 p.; bibliog. p. 185-192. *f* 49,50 [TR 87,259: 11 art.,
tit. pp.].

81* HÜRTEN Heinz: Festgabe, Vom Sinn der Geschichte, 60. Gb., EDickerhof
H.   Bern 1988, Lang.   681 p. – RZSav-Kanon. 107 (1990) 384s (R.
Morsey) [RHE 85,394*; TR 85,252, tit. pp.].

82 HUNT Joseph I.:   The Psalms and other studies on the Old Testament,
70th b., EKnight Jack C., *Sinclair* Lawrence A.   Nashotah WI/Cincinnati
1990, Seminary/Forward. xii-203 p. $10.   22 art., infra [BibTB 21,80, J.
Burns].

83 HURLEY Denis: Shaping English liturgy; studies in honor of [Durban S.
Africa] Archbishop ∼, EFinn Peter C., *Schellman* James M.   Wsh 1990,
Pastoral.   493 p. $35 pa.   0-912405-72-4 [TDig 38,87].

84 HYDE John Kenneth, 1930-1986, mem.:   Towns and Townspeople in
medieval and renaissance Europe: BJRylL 90,3 (1990) 3-212; portr.; biog.
3-11 (B. *Pullan*). 14 art.; → g872.

85 HYLDAHL Niels: 60. Gb. = DanTTs 53,4 (1990).

86 HYMAN Arthur: Of scholars, savants, and their texts; studies in philosophy and religious thought.   NY 1989, Lang.   263 p. [JAAR 58,327].

86* IGLESIAS Juan: Estudios en homenaje, ERoset Jaime (*Álvarez Barrés* Ale-
gría). M 1988, Univ. Complutense.   I. xxiv-563 p.; portr.; biobibliog. xvii-
xxiv; II. viii + p. 565-1106; III. viii + p. 1107-1688. 84-600-5403-9. 111 art.

87 IMMOOS Thomas,   Das Gold im Wachs, 70. Gb., EGössmann Elisabeth,
Zobel Günter.   Mü 1988, Iudicium. 555 p. – RNZMissW 45 (1989) 143-5
(F. *Kollbrunner*).

88 INEICHEN Gustav: Variatio linguarum; Beiträge zu Sprachvergleich und
Sprachentwicklung, 60. Gb., EKlenk Ursula, *al.* Stu 1989, Steiner
xvii-332 p.   RSalesianum 52 (1990) 936s (R. *Gottlieb*: titoli senza pp.).

89 JASHEMSKI Wilhelmina F.:   Studia Pompeiana (I) et classica (II), ECurtis
Robert I.   New Rochelle 1988s, Caratzas.   xxi-330 p.; xxi-271 p.; ill.;
portr.; bibliog. (I) xix-xxi.   16 + 15 art.; 10 infra.   0-89241-423-5; -4-3
(set -5-1).

90 JELOČNIK Aleksandr: Studia numismatica labacensia, 70 b., EKos Peter,
Demo Željko: Situla 26. Ljubljana 1988, Narodni Muzej.   330 p.; ill.;
portr.; bibliog. p. 327-330.   86-80651-13-3. 24 art.; 3 infra.

91 JERPHAGNON Lucien: Du banal au merveilleux, mélanges offerts à ∼,
EBonnamour Jacqueline: Cahiers de Fontenay 55-57.   S. Cloud 1989,
E.N.S..   374 p.; portr.; bibliog. p. 11-14. F 100.   0395-8418 [ÉTRel
65,660]. 19 art., 3 infra.

92 JOLY Henri, † 1989: *a*) RTPhil 122 (1990): l'hommage p. 297-302 [→ m504]
et la bibliographie p. 431s semblent encadrer les onze articles, tous sur le
Néant en Grèce ancienne [→ a920]; – *b*) Recherches sur la philosophie et
les langues 2.   Grenoble 1990, Groupe Ph.Langage.   470 p. [RTPhil
123,452, S. *Imhoof*].

93 JUNG Hans-Gernot: Vernünftiger Gottesdienst; Kirche nach der Barmer
theologischen Erklärung, 60. Gb., EScholz Frithard, *Dickel* Horst.   Gö
1990, Vandenhoeck & R.   374 p.; ill.; Bibliog. p. 363ss [ZIT 90,660, tit.
pp.; TLZ 116,261, G. *Heintze*]. 20 art.; 3 infra.

94 KERFERD George: The criterion of truth, essays, with (text, tr., notes)
   PTOLEMY, On the kriterion and hegemonikon, EHuby Pamela, *Gordon*
   Neal. Liverpool 1989, Univ.   xiv-301 p. [AnPg 60, p. 873].
95 KERKHOFS Jan: Kerkelijk leven in Vlaanderen anno 2000; emeritaat;
   EBuickens J., *Cooreman* P.: Nikè-Didachè. Lv 1989, Acco.   443 p. [ETL
   66,10*].
96 KHOURY Adel T.:   'Ihr alle aber seid Brüder', 60. Gb., EHagemann
   Ludwig, *Pulsfort* Ernst: Wü Forsch. Miss/Rel. Wiss. 2/14.   Wü/
   Altenberge 1990, Echter/Telos.   640 p.; Bibliog. 629-637. DM 75 pa. [TR
   86,161; TPhil 65,631; ZkT 113,318s, K. *Piskaty*].
97 KLOPSCH Paul, EKindermann Udo, *al.*: Arb. Germanistik 492. Göppingen
   1988, Kümmerle. vi-633 p. DM 128 pa. – RSpeculum 65 (1990) 511s (tit.
   pp.).
97* KNOCH Otto B.:   Die Freude an Gott — unsere Kraft, 65. Gb., EDe-
   genhard Joachim, *al.*   Stu 1990, KBW.   viii-499 p. DM 76.
98 KNOWLTON Edgar C.J: East meets West, EHadlich Roger L., *Ellsworth*
   J. D.   Honolulu 1988, Univ. Hawaii.   xii-336 p. [AnPg 60, p. 873 &
   dépouillé].
99 Das KÖLNER PRIESTERSEMINAR im 19. und 20. Jahrhundert, Feier des
   250jährigen Bestehens, ETrippen N.: Studien zu Kölner KG 23.   Siegburg
   1988, F. Schmitt.   xiii-366 p.; 16 pl. [ETL 64,16*].
100 KÖRBER-GROHNE Udelgard: Der prähistorische Mensch und seine
   Umwelt, 65. Gb., EKüster Hansjörg: Berichte zur Vor- und Frühgeschichte in Baden-Württemberg 31.   Stu 1988, Theiss.   430 p.; 140 fig.
   DM 125.   3-8062-0799-2. – RHelinium 29 (1989) 152-4 (L. J. *Kooistra*);
   Offa 46 (1989) 404s (H. *Kroll*: 33 Art., botanisch, meist Baden-
   Württemberg).
100* KÖTTING Bernhard: 80. Gb.: JbAC 33.   Münster 1990, Aschendorff.
   277 p.; portr.; ill. 3-402-08535-6; pa. -4-8.
101 KOSTELECKY Alfred: Pax et Justitia, 90. Gb., EKaluza Hans W., *al.*   B
   1990, Duncker & H.   xxviii-651 p. DM 248.   3-428-06879-3 [TPQ 138/3].
102 KRISTELLER Paul Oskar: [I.] Florilegium columbianum.   NY 1987,
   Italica.   x-206 p. [AnPg 58,814]. – II. Supplementum Festivum, EHankins
   J. 1987 → 4,89.
103 KRÖTKE Wolf: Wahrzeichen, ESchröder Richard, *al.*   B 1988, Ev.
   K.-Union [< IZBG 36, p. 112 → 4040].
104 KUEN Heinrich: Studien zur romanischen Wortgeschichte, 90. Gb.,
   EErnst Gerhard, *Stefenelli* Arnulf.   Stu 1989, Steiner.   195 p. – RSalesianum 52 (1990) 931s (R. *Gottlieb*, titles sans pp.).
105 KUHN Helmut: 'Anodos', EHofmann Rupert.   Weinheim 1989, Acta
   Humaniora.   viii-380 p. – RForumKT 5 (1989) 302 (B. *Haneke*).
106 KUITERT H. M.:   Geloof dat te denken geeft, EGäbler K. U., *al.*   Baarn
   1989, Ten Have.   336 p. [ETL 66,12*; NedTTs 45,166 (A. van den *Beld*);
   TsTNijm 31,104, T. *Veerkamp*].
107 KUPPER J.-R.:   De la Babylonie à la Syrie, en passant par Mari, 70e
   anniv., ETunca Önhan.   Liège 1990, Univ.   xi-273 p.; ill. 20 art., infra
   [BO 48,553, M. *Stol*].
107* KUTTNER Stephan,   The two laws; studies in medieval legal history,
   EMayali L., *Tibbetts* A. J.: StudCanonLaw 1.   Wsh 1990, Catholic Univ.
   xii-248 p.; 3 fig. $40 [RHE 86,104*].
108 LANGEMEYER Georg B.:   Universität und Toleranz; der Anspruch des
   christlichen Glaubens, 60. Gb., EKlimek N.   Essen 1989, Ludgerus.   263 p.
   [RHE 86,77*].

108* LANOWSKI Jerzy: Eos 78/1 (1990). 248 p.; portr.; biobibliog. p. 11-24-39. 24 art., 2 infra.

109 LAUFFER Siegfried mém.: Khostia, résultats des explorations, I. Études diverses dédiées à ∼, ᴱFossey John M.: McGill Mg Arch 5. Amst 1986, Gieben. xvii-139 p. 90-70265-70-2. – ᴿAntClas 59 (1990) 570s (R. Laffineur). – II. Boiotika 1986/9 ➤ 746.

109* LAURENTIN René: Kecharitōménē, présent. Ouvrard Pierre (Univ. Angers). P 1990, Desclée. 735 p.; portr.; biobibliog. p. 29-36. 2-7189-0430-5. 16 art. (Écr. S.) + 21 (ét. mariales) + 18; plusieurs infra.

110 LEACH B. Foss, Saying so doesn't make it so, ᴱSutton Douglas G.: New Zealand Archaeological Mg 17. Otago 1989, NZ Arch. Asn. vi-304 p.; ill. 0-9597915-0-7. 16 art. – ᴿAntiquity 64 (1990) 575 (not clear whether 'anthropoloty' is a new science or a misprint).

111 LÉVÊQUE Pierre: Mélanges [I, 1988 ➤ 5,118] IIs, Anthropologie et société; IV. Religion, ᴱMactoux Marie-M., Geny Evelyne: Ann. Besançon 377.404.413. P 1989-90, BLettres. xxix-440 p.; ill. 2-251-60377-8; -404-9; -413-3. 29 + 32 + 30 art.; 16 infra [TR 87,433, tit. pp.].

112 LEVI Primo, mém.: RaMIsr 56,2s (1989) 191-345; phot. 13 art. (su lui), ᴱDella Torre Stefano.

113 LEWIS Hywel D.: Religion, reason and the self, ᴱSutherland Stuart R., Roberts T.A. Cardiff 1989, Univ. xiv-173 p. £20 [TR 86,527]. – ᴿNBlackf 71 (1990) 466 (M. Wynn: includes Swinburne R., meaning of the Bible; Sutherland S., concept of religion).

114 LICHTHEIM Miriam: Studies in Egyptology, ᴱIsraelit-Groll Sarah. J 1990, Magnes. I. xii-506 p.; pl. 1-9 (p. 507-516); II. p. 517-1128. 965-223-733-7. 20 + 30 art.; 19 infra [ZAW 103,171].

115 LIPTZIN Sol: 90th b.: JBQ 19,4 (1990s) 223-277; portr.

116 LLEDÓ Emilio: Historia, lenguaje, sociedad; homenaje a ∼, ᴱCruz M., al.: Crítica/Filosofia. Barc 1989, Crítica. 480 p. [CommSev 23 (1990) 151].

117 LÖFGREN Oscar: On both sides of al-Mandab; Ethiopian, South-Arabic and Islamic studies, 90th b., ᴱEhrensvärd Ulla, Toll Christopher: Transactions 2. İstanbul 1989, Swedish Inst. [viii-] 168 p.; phot.; bibliog. p. 155-168 (Nordesjö Hans). 91-22-01289-3. 15 art.; 3 infra. – ᴿZDMG 140 (1990) 381s (E. Wagner: tit. pp.).

117* LØKKEGAARD Frede: Living waters; Scandinavian Orientalistic studies, 75th B., ᴱKeck Egon, al. K 1990, Museum Tusculanum. ix-419 p.; portr. 87-7289-083-5. 33 art.; 13 infra.

118 LØNNING Per: Tjeneste — tro og tanke, 60-år, ᴱAmundsen Arne B., al. Oslo 1988, Nye Atheneum. 208 p. Nk 198. – ᴿNorTTs 90 (1989) 52s (T. Wyller: comments; no tit. pp.).

119 LOHMEYER Ernst [1890-1946]: Freiheit in der Gebundenheit; zur Erinnerung an den Theologen ∼, 100. Gb., ᴱOtto Wolfgang. Gö 1990, Vandenhoeck & R. 191 p.; Bibliog. p. 4s.181-191 (Lührmann D.). DM 28 pa. 3-525-53588-0 [CritRR 4,505, tit. pp.; NTAbs 35,96; TLZ 117,18, W. Wiefel]. 2 items on Lohmeyer; 3 infra ➤ m43.

LOOY Hermann Van, Opes atticae 1989s ➤ 25.

120 LORTZ Joseph (1887-1975), Beiträge zur Reformationsgeschichte und Ökumene, zum Gedenken an ∼, ᴱDecot R., Vinke R.: Mainz Inst. Eur. Gesch., Rel. G 30. Stu 1989, Steiner. viii-396 p. DM 120 [TS 51,188].

121 LURKER Manfred: Mnemosyne, 60. Gb., ᴱBies Werner, Jung Hermann: Bibliographie zur Symbolik, Ikonographie und Mythologie Egb 2. Baden-Baden 1988, Koerner. 245 p.; ill. [AnPg 60, p. 874 & dépouillé].

121* MCCORMICK Richard A.: Moral theology; challenges for the future,
     ᴱCurran Charles E. NY 1990, Paulist. viii-400 p. $18. 0-8091-3168-4
     [TR 87,436, tit. pp.; RelStR 17,341, Dolores L. *Christie*].
122 MALHERBE Abraham J.: Greeks, Romans, and Christians, 60th b.,
     ᴱBalch David L., *al.* Mp 1990, Fortress. xv-404 p.; bibliog. 367-371
     (*Peterson* Stephen L.). 0-8006-2445-7. 22 art., infra [CritRR 4,497 &
     RB 99,295, tit. pp.; NTAbs 35,232].
122* MARTYN J. Louis: The conversation continues; studies in Paul and
     John, 65th b., ᴱFortna Robert T., *Gaventa* Beverly R. Nv 1990,
     Abingdon. 400 p. $27. 0-687-09634-0. 16 art. [TR 87,426 & RB 99,298,
     tit. pp.].
     MATSON Frederick R. 1986/8 ➤ 812.
123 *a*) MENDEZ ORTIZ Rafael, in memoriam: Arte y poblamiento en el SE
     peninsular durante los ultimos siglos de civilización romana, ᴱGonzález
     Blanco Antonino: Antigüedad y cristianismo 5. Murcia 1988, Univ.
     679 p.; portr.; ill. 0214-2165. 32 art.
— *b*) MIKAT Paul: Staat, Kirche, Wissenschaft in einer pluralistischen
     Gesellschaft, 65. Gb., ᴱSchwab D., *al.* B 1989, Duncker & H. 899 p.
     [RHE 86,77*].
123* *a*) MEYER Paul W., Faith and history, ᴱCarroll John T., *al.* Atlanta
     1990, Scholars. viii-377 p. $50; sb. $35. 1-55540-383-2. 22 art. [CritRR
     4,500, tit. pp.], all infra.
— *b*) MOLETTE Charles: L'histoire des croyants, mémoire vivante des hommes
     [1. Travaux de ~]; 2. Hommage a mgr. ~, ᴱWaché B. Abbeville 1989,
     Paillart. [339 p.] p. 345-950 [RHE 86,77*].
124 MORAN William L.: Lingering over words; studies in Ancient Near
     Eastern literature, ᴱAbusch Tzvi, *al.* HarvSemSt 37. Atlanta 1990,
     Scholars. viii-524 p.; portr.; biobibliog. ix-xviii. $35; pa. $22. 1-55540-
     502-9. 31 art., infra [RB 48,449, tit. pp.].
125 MORENO CASAMITJANA Antonio y VILLEGAS MATHIEU Beltrán,
     biblistas: Anunciare tu verdad: AnChile 39 (1988). Santiago 1990,
     Pontificia Universidad Católica. 329 p. 0069-3596. 12 art., infra.
125* MORESHET Menahem: Studies in the Hebrew language and the
     Talmudic literature, ᴱKaddari M. Ramat-Gan 1989, Bar-Ilan Univ. –
     ᴿBSO 53 (1990) 585 (L. *Glinert*).
126 MOSS Rosalind mem.: A dedicated life, ᴱJames Thomas G. H., *Malek* J.
     Ox 1990, Griffith Institute, Ashmolean Museum. lx-110 p.; 10 pl.; map.
     0-900416-56-4. Only brief tributes [OLZ 87,239, U. *Luft*].
127 MÜLLER Ernst Wilhelm: Die Vielfalt der Kultur; ethnologische Aspekte
     von Verwandtschaft, Kunst und Weltauffassung, 65. Gb., ᴱKohl Karl-
     Heinz, *al.* B 1990, Reimer. c. 680 p.; Bibliog. p. 671 ... 3-496- 00388-X.
     44 art.; ➤ G5.5, *Lang* B.
127* MÜLLER-WIENER Wolfgang: IstMitt 39 (1989); portr. 595 p.; 56 pl.
128 NARR Karl J.: Urgeschichte als Kulturanthropologie; 70. Gb. = Sae-
     culum 41,3s (1990) 179-349.
129 NEWMAN *a*) centenary essays: Faith & Reason 15,4. Front Royal
     1989, Christendom. 170 p. [TR 86,526, no tit. pp.]; dedicated to
     memory of SCHODER R. – *b*) Newman today, ᴱJaki S. 1989 ➤ 532; –
     c) Newman J. H. 1801-1890: ᴱMerrigan Terrence = LvSt 15,2s (1990)
     100-110.
130 NICHOLAS Barry: New perspectives on the Roman law of property, 70th
     b., ᴱBirks Peter. Ox 1989, Clarendon. vii-233 p.; portr. £25. 17 art. –
     ᴿClasR 40 (1990) 331-3 (J. *Crook*).

131 NIEMEYER Gerhart: The good man in society; active contemplation, EGuegen J.A., al. Lanham MD 1989, UPA. xxiv-326 p. $27.50; pa. $15.75 [JTS 41,824].

132 NIPKOW Karl Ernst: Bildung – Glaube – Aufklärung; zur Wiedergewinnung des Bildungsbegriffs in Pädagogik und Theologie, 60. Gb., EPreul Reiner, al.: Münster Comenius-Inst. Gü 1989, Mohn. 354 p., ill. 21 art. [ZIT 89,567], 3 infra.

133 NYÍRS Tamás: Köszöntő/Fs. 70. Gb., EGelejiné Neubauer Irén, al. Budapest 1990. 526 p.; phot.; biobibliog. p. 517-525. 963-400-237-4. 76 art.; 5 infra.

133* OBERMAN Heiko A.: AUGUSTINE, the harvest, and theology, EHagen K. Leiden 1990, Brill. vii-375 p.; portr. [NRT 114,909, R. Escol].

134 ÖZGÜÇ Tahsin: Armagan, Anatolia and the Near East, EEmre K., Hrouda B., Mellink M., Özgüç N. Ankara 1989, Türk Tarih Kurumu. xviii-525 p.; 141 pl. [OIAc S90].

135 ORBE Antonio: Compostellanum 35,1s + 36,1s (1990s). 359 p.; ...

136 O'RIORDAN Sean: History and conscience, EGallagher Raphael, McConnery Brendan. Dublin 1989, Gill & M. viii-319 p. £9 [JTS 41,346]: moral theology.

137 PACK Frank: Johannine studies, EPriest J.E. Malibu CA 1989, Pepperdine Univ. xxiv-309 p.; bibliog. (E.N. Whatley). $20. 0-932612-20-2. 15 art. [NTAbs 34,110: topics, no tit. pp.].

138 PERROT Jean: Contribution à l'histoire de l'Iran, EVallat François. P 1990, RCiv. xxi-320 p.; portr.; ill.; biobibliog. vii-xxi. 2-86538-209-1. 28 art., infra.

139 PETERS George W.: Bilanz und Plan; Mission an der Schwelle zum Dritten Jahrtausend, 80. Gb., EKasdorf Hans, Müller Klaus W., Ev. Mission C-2. Bad Liebenzell 1988. 504 p. – RNZMissW 45 (1989) 306s (F. Kollbrunner); ZMissRW 74 (1990) 84s (H. Waldenfels).

140 PINBORG Jan mem.: Linguistic theory, EBursill-Hall G.L., al.: Studies in the History of the Language Sciences 47. Amst/Ph 1990, Benjamins. – RLatomus 49 (1990) 198-200 (Colette Jeudy, gives pages as 133-146 in title, and in text speaks of [? this] third volume).

141 PLEZIA Marian: Munera philologica et historica. Wrocław 1988, Polska Akad. Nauk. 239 p.; portr. [AnPg 60, p. 874].

142 PÖGGELER Otto, Philosophie und Poesie, 60. Gb., EGethmann-Siefert Annemarie: Spekulation und Erfahrung 2/7. Stu 1988, Frommann-Holzboog. xiii-452 p.; 374 p. – RTPhil 65 (1990) 134-6 (J. Splett: Grab Jesu; Maria bei HEGEL; Christlichkeit des frühen HEIDEGGER...).

143 POZZI Giovanni: Forme e vicende, EBesomi O., al.: Medioevo e Umanesimo 72. Padova 1988, Antenore. xxxviii-626 p.; ill. [RHE 85,395*].

144 RAABE Paul: Respublica Guelpherbytana, Wolfenbütteler Beiträge zur Reinaissance- und Barockforschung, EBuck August, Bircher Martin: Chloe 6. Amst 1987, Rodopi. 709 p.; portr. [LuJb 57 (1990) p. 321, 5 items cited].

145 RAMM Bernard L.: EGrenz Stanley J. = PerspRelSt 17,4 (1990) 101 p.; bibliog. 87-101 (Murdina MacDonald) [Not designated as a Festschrift, but all the articles are about him; and the fascicle abnormally has a separate page-numbering].

145* REINECKE John E. mem.: Pidgin and Creole languages, EGilbert Glenn C. Honolulu 1987, Univ. Hawaii. x-497 p. $35. – RBSO 53 (1990) 197-9 (J. Wansbrough, also on HOLM J., THOMASON S., creole).

146 REINELT Heinz: Die alttestamentliche Botschaft als Wegweisung, 65.
Gb., ᴱZmijewski Josef. Stu 1990, KBW. 453 p.; phot.; Biobibliog.
405-442. DM 39. 3-460-32901-7 [TR 86 (1990) 337 & ZAW 102 (1990)
437s: tit. pp.]. 22 art., infra.

147 RENDTORFF Rolf: Die Hebräische Bibel und ihre zweifache Nachgeschichte, 65. Gb., ᴱBlum Erhard, al. Neuk 1990, Neuk.-V. xiii-736 p.,
portr. DM 98 [KIsr 5,93 adv.; ZIT 90,871, tit. pp.; Protestantesimo 46,73,
J. A. Soggin]. 3-7887-1353-4. 54 art., infra.

148 REYNOLDS Joyce: Images of authority, 70th b., ᴱMackenzie Mary M.,
Roueché Charlotte: Supp. 16. C 1989, Pg. Soc. 228 p. £15 pa. – ᴿArctos
24 (1990) 183 (J. Aronen); ClasR 40 (1990) 445s (S. D. Goldhill).

149 RICHÉ Pierre: Haut Moyen-Âge; culture, éducation et société, ᴱSot
Michel. La Garenne-Colombes 1990, Publidix. 630 p.; portr.; bibliog.
p. 15-22 (Vulliez Charles). 2-7338-0089-0. 41 art.; 5 infra.

150 RIEF Josef: Freiheit in Gemeinschaft und Fortschrift, 65. Gb., ᴱSchäfer
Philipp. Passau 1989, Passavia/Univ. 135 p.; ill.; Bibliog. 121s. 3-
922016-88-X. 6 art.; 1 infra [< ZIT 90,440]. – ᴿForumKT 6 (1990) 319s
(L. Scheffczyk); TPQ 138 (1990) 394 (A. Riedl).

151 RILEY Derrick: Into the sun; essays in air photography in archaeology in
honour of ~, ᴱKennedy David. Sheffield 1989, Univ. Dept. Archaeol.
x-211 p.; 82 fig. £20. 0-906090-36-9. – ᴿAntiquity 64 (1990) 418s (R.
Nikitsch).

152 ROBINSON James M.: I. Gospel origins and Christian beginnings; II.
Gnosticism and the early Christian world; (both) ᴱGoehring James E., al.:
Forum Fascicles. Sonoma CA 1990, Polebridge. I. xxix-214 p.; portr.;
bibliog. xiii-xxvii (Kathleen E. Corley); II. xxiv-200 p.; biog. xxi-xxiv (S.
Patterson); general bibliog. I, 179-197; II. 162, 184. $30 (each?) pa.
0-944344-151; -6-X. 12 + 11 art.; infra.

152* a) ROSEMAN Yehuda † 1987, mem.; Facing the future; essays on contemporary Jewish life, ᴱBayme Steven. NY 1989, KTAV/American Jewish
Committee. xxvi-234 p. $13 [CritRR 4,391, Deborah D. Moore].

— b) ROSENMEYER Thomas G.: Cabinet of the Muses; essays on classical and
comparative literature, 70th b., ᴱGriffith Mark, Mastronarde Donald: SBL
Homage. Atlanta 1990, Scholars. xiv-402 p. $40. 26 art. [RelStR 17. 358,
D. E. Oakman].

153 ROUX Georges: Architecture et poésie dans le monde grec, ᴱÉtienne
Roland, al.; Coll. nᵒ 19. Lyon/P 1989, Maison de l'Orient/de Boccard.
303 p.; ill. [CRAI (1969) 526s, Pouilloux; AnPg 60, p. 675 & dépouillé].

154 SACCHI Paolo: Biblische und judaistische Studien, ᴱVivian Angelo: Judentum und Umwelt 29. Fra 1990, Lang. xxvi-709 p.; 3 pl.; bibliog. xv-xxvi.
3-631-43180-5. 35 art., 32 infra. – ᴿLA 40 (1990) 513-5 (A. Mello).

155 ST. AMANT C. Penrose: [8 articles about him, including bibliog.]:
PerspRelSt [17,1 (1990) or supplement to 16,4 (1989), 95 p. < ZIT 90,165].
SALESIANA, obra, en Colombia, centenario 1990 → 3721.
ᶠSÁNCHEZ VAQUERO José 1990 → 684*.

156 SCHÄFER Gerhard Fs. ᴱBrecht Martin: Verein für Württembergsche
Kirchengeschichte, BL88. S 1988, Scheufele. 507 p. [LuJb 57 (1990)
p. 322, with indication of 10 items there cited].

156* SCHAUF Heribert: Geist und Kirche; Studien zur Theologie im Umfeld
der beiden Vatikanischen Konzilien, ᴱHammans H., al. Pd 1990,
Schöningh. x-585 p.; portr. DM 78 [491-523, Berning V., Konservatismus
und Fortschritt ... H. SCHELL; 299-322, Bäumer R., M. J. SCHEEBEN in
den kirchenpolitischen Auseinandersetzungen um das I. Vat.].

157 SCHLÜTER Johannes: Mit Kopf, Herz und Hand. Pd 1988, Bonifatius. 252 p. DM 38 [TPQ 138,180].

158 SCHMID Karl: Person und Gemeinschaft im Mittelalter, 65. Gb., ᴱAlthoff Gerd, al. Sigmaringen 1988, Thorbecke. xviii-651 p.; portr.; 29 fig.; map. DM 116. – ᴿSpeculum 65 (1990) 509.

158* SCHMITZ Josef: Erfahrung des Absoluten — absolute Erfahrung; Beiträge zum christlichen Offenbarungsverständnis, 65. Gb., ᴱHilberath Bernd J. Dü 1990, Patmos. 239 p. DM 40. 10 art.; 5 infra [TR 87,82; TsTNijm 31,437, A. *Brants*].

159 SCHNUTTGEN Hildegard: Women in history, literature and the arts [30 years service], ᴱBaird-Lange Lorrayne Y., *Copeland* Thomas A. Youngstown 1989, State Univ. 420 p. $20 [JAAR 58,160].

160 *a*) SCHOW Niels I. [1754-1830]: Miscellanea papyrologica, in occasione del bicentenario dell'[a sua, 1788] edizione della Charta Borgiana, ᴱCapasso Mario, al.; pref. *Pintaudi* R.: Papyrologica Florentina 19. F 1990, Gonnelli. xi-334 p., portr.; p. 335-569, LI pl. 50 art.; 4 infra.

— *b*) SCHÜTZINGER Heinrich, 65. Gb. = BibNot 47 (1989) 114 p.

160* SCHULER Einar von: Gedenkschrift 28.X.1930-15.II.1990, ᴱMarazzi Massimiliano, *Wilhelm* Gernot: Orientalia 59,2 (1990) 101-332; pl. VIII-XVII.

161 SCHWAIGER Georg: Papsttum und Kirchenreform; historische Beiträge, 65. Gb., ᴱWeitlauff Manfred, *Hausberger* Karl. St. Ottilien 1990, EOS. xx-812 p.; ill.; Bibliog. 787-811. DM 98 [RHE 86,192, H. *Wolf*; TR 86,163, tit. pp.] 1 infra. – ᴿMüTZ 41 (1990) 298s (G. L. *Müller*); TüTQ 170 (1990) 311s (R. *Reinhardt*).

162 SCOTT Nathan A.ᴶ: Morphologies of faith; essays in religion and culture in honor of ∼, ᴱGerhart M., *Yu* A. Atlanta 1990, Scholars. 396 p. $40; pa. $25 [JAAR 58,745; RelStR 17,344; TS 52,195].

162* ŠEBESTA Giuseppe: Scritti e nota bio-bibliografica per il 70° compleanno. Trento 1989, Biblioteca comunale. 492 p. [Salesianum 53,763; 28 autori; *Ferrari* M., su MENDEL].

163 SEE Klaus von: Idee, Gestalt, Geschichte; Studien zur europäischen Kulturtradition, ᴱ[Wolfgang-]Weber Gerd. Odense 1988, Univ. 722 p.; portr. Dk 500 [BeiNam 26,98s, II. *Schottmann*]. ᴿSpeculum 65 (1990) 1093s (tit. pp.).

164 SEGERT Stanislav: *Sopher mahir*; Northwest Semitic studies presented to ∼, 70th b., ᴱCook Edward M.: Maarav 5s (1990) [also:] WL 1990, Eisenbrauns. 384 p.; portr.; bibliog. 345-384. 0-931464-56-0 [BL 91,12, J. *Barr*]. 20 art.; infra.

165 SELLNOW Werner: Eigentum; Beiträge zu seiner Entwicklung in politischen Gesellschaften [...Ägypten; Rom], 70. Gb., ᴱKöhn Jens, *Rode* Burkhard. Weimar 1987, Böhlau. 324 p. – ᴿZSavR 106 (1989) 709-713 (T. *Meyer-Maly*).

166 SHEFFIELD UNIV. 40 years biblical studies: The Bible in three dimensions, ᴱClines David J. A., al.: JStOT supp 87. Sheffield 1990, JStOT [Ithaca NY, Cornell $50]. 408 p. £35. 1-85075-227-3. 20 art.; infra (*Rogerson* J., *Bruce* F., on Sheffield 19-23 / 25-27) [TDig 37,346; ETRel 66,431, D. *Lys*; TLZ 117,649, K.-M. *Beyse*; VT 41,489, H. *Williamson*]. – ᴿZAW 102 (1990) 440 (tit. pp.) [OTAbs 14, 99s: titles sans pp.; N.B. all the left-hand pages of this issue have erroneously at the top 13 (1990)].

167 SÖLLE Dorothee: Gotteslehrerinnen, 60. Gb., ᴱSchottroff L., *Thiele* J. Stu 1989, Kreuz. 254 p. DM 29,80. 3-7831-0992-2. – ᴿTsTNijm 30 (1990) 423s (C. *Claassen*).

SPIRA Andreas: Studien zu GREGOR von Nyssa 1990 ➔ 695.

168* STACKMANN Karl: Ja muz ich sunder riuwe sin. Gö 1990, Vandenhoeck & R. vi-274 p. 15 art. [BeiNam 26,259, A. *Masser*].
169 STÉFANINI Jean mém.: Grammaire et histoire de la grammaire, ᴱBlanche-
Benveniste Claire, *al.* Aix 1988, Univ. Provence. 694 p.; portr. [AnPg 60,
p. 875].
170 STEINBACH Ernst: Der Wirklichkeitsanpruch von Theologie und Religion;
die sozialistische Herausforderung ∼ 70. Gb., ᴱHenke Dieter, *al.* Tü 1976,
Mohr. xxiv-238 p., portr. 3-16-138542-X. 16 art.
170* STEITZ Heinrich; ᴱBöcher Otto: Ebenburg-Hefte 21 = Blätter für
Pfälzische KG 54 (Osterbach 1987) 123-294; Bibliog. 131-9 (*Wulfert* H.)
[LuJb 56, p. 163]. – p. 141-151, *Benrath* Gustav A., Reformatoren vor den
Reformatoren; p. 153-190, *Weber* W., M. LUTHER im Spiegel der Kunst
des 19. und 20. Jhts.
171 STÖGER A.: Weihbischof ∼, Exeget zwischen Bibelkommission und
Offenbarungskonstitution, ᴱStaudinger F., *Wurz* H. St. Pölten 1989
[SNTU A-15,101; TPQ 139,113, C. P. *März*]. 10 art. ⇢ vol. 7, 1991.
171* STOODT Dieter: Unterwegs für die Volkskirche, 60. Gb., ᴱFederlin
W. L., *Weber* E. Fra 1987, Lang. 707 p. [ETL 66, p. 11*].
172 STRATOS Andreas N.: Byzantion; I. Histoire, art, archéologie; II.
Théologie et philologie, ᴱStratos Nia A. Athens 1986s, auct. cx-306 p.;
X pl. – 443 p., ill. [AnPg 60, p. 875]. – ᴿSpeculum 64 (1989) 509s (*Arbagi*).
173 STRUGNELL John: Of scribes and scrolls; studies on the Hebrew Bible,
intertestamental Judaism, ᴱAttridge Harold W., *al.* Lanham MD 1990,
UPA. 298 p. $52.25; pa. $33 [TS 52,191; NTAbs 35,234]. 0-9191-7902-7;
pa. -3-5. 25 art.; infra [BL 92,7, A. J. *Brooks*].
174 SUDBRACK Josef: Gottes Nähe, religiöse Erfahrung in Mystik und
Offenbarung, 65. Gb., ᴱImhof Paul. Wü 1990, Echter [TR 86,346; ZIT
90,369: both with tit. pp.; PrzPow 273,568, S. *Obirek*; TPhil 66,303, G.
Switek]. – ᴿArTGran 53 (1990) 347s (A. *Segovia*); GeistL 63 (1990) 79s
(Maria *Ottl*).
174* SZABÓ Árpád: AcAntH 31,3s (1985-8).
175 SZNYCZER Maurice: Hommages à ∼, Semitica 38s. P 1990, Maisonneuve. 189 + 203 p.; ill.; bibliog. (*Fauveaud-Brassaud* Catherine):
(2,)187-199. 25 + 24 art.; 22 infra. 2-7200-1076-6; -7-4.
175* TALLEY Thomas J.: Time and community; studies in liturgical history
and theology, ᴱAlexander J. Neil. Wsh 1990, Pastoral. xi-338 p. $35
[JTS 42,821, G. *Woolfenden*: L. HOFFMAN on Jewish background to
three-week Roman Lent; R. TAFT 'trenchant detective work' on Hagia
Sophia and Palestine churches].
176 TESTINI Pasquale † 1989: Miscellanea in memoria di = RivArchCr 66
(1990). 324 p.; fot.; bibliog. p. 13-24 (V. *Saxer*).
176* THOME A., Der menschenfreundliche Gott, ᴱFeilzer H., *Heinz* A.,
Lentzen-Deis W. Trier 1990, Paulinus [ZAW 103,161 ⇢ 3832].
177 TORRES FONTES Juan, Homenaje. Murcia 1987, Univ. 1804 p. (2 vol.).
– ᴿCuadernos de Historia de España 70 (BA 1988) 281-8 (P. de *Forteza*)
[< RHE 86,78*].
178 TORRES RODRÍGUEZ Casimiro [colaborador]: Compostellanum 35,3s
(1990) 367-375 (M. J. *Precedo Lafuente*) [-...].
179 TOYNBEE Joselyn mem.: Image and mystery in the Roman world [1986],
ᴱHuskinson J., *al.*, Gloucester 1988, Sutton. 88 p.; portr. 0-9514135-0-3. 3
art., infra.
180 TROMP Nico: 'Gelukkig de mens'; Opstellen over Psalmen, exegese en
semiotiek, ᴱBeentjes Panc, *al.* Kampen c. 1990, Kok. 267 p.; portr.;
Eng. summaries p. 255-261; bibliog. p. 244-253 (*Adriaanse* Jan, *al.*; the

actual date of the volume is skilfully suppressed throughout, but most of the bibliography stops with 1990; on p. 247 there is a single) [(? anticipation of) 1991]. 90-242-3068-3. 18 art., infra.

180* TYLOCH Witold: Euhemer 31,4 (Wsz 1988): his influence on philology, Qumranica, Ugaritica, Hebraica, Judaica, African, Christian, and religious studies [NTA 34,144].

181 UKRAINE: *Marusyn* Myroslav, abp. [*al.*] ❻ The introduction of Christianity in Kievan Rus': AnOrdBas 13 (Sacri Millennii 988-1988) 3-14 [-404; 405-538, Bibliographia, *Patrilo* I.].

181* UTRECHT Studentengezalschap Excelsior: Uit de sjoek geklapt; christelijke belangstelling voor joodse traditie, 23e lustrum, EBerg M. van den, *al.* Hilversum 1986, Gooi & S. f 37,50. – RNedTTs 43 (1989) 62s (J. S. *Vos*).

182 VALLS Ignacio: Homenaje a ∼. Valencia 1990, Fac. Teol.

182* VEREECKE Louis: = Studia Moralia 28,1s (1990). 9 art. [ZIT 91,244] 245 p. + p. 330-602; biobiblio. 7-23 (S. *Majorano*) 523-550, *Tremblay* R., L' 'Exode', une idée maîtresse de la pensée théologique du Cardinal Joseph RATZINGER?

183 VERMES Geza: A tribute to ∼, Essays on Jewish and Christian literature and history, EDavies Philip R., *White* Richard T.: JStOT supp 100. Sheffield 1990, Academic. 406 p.; portr.; bibliog. p. 383-8. 1-85075-253-2. 21 art., infra [ETL 62,145, J. *Lust*; ÉTRel 66,592, J. *Léonard*; JStJud 22,127, F. *García Martínez*; JTS 42,643, W. *Horbury*; NTAbs 35,326].

VILLEGAS Beltrán 1990 ➔ 125, MORENO A.

184 VITESTAM Gösta, 70th b. 1991: OrSuec 38s (1989s) [largely from the 2d Scandinavian Symposium for Semitic Studies organized by him, Kivik, Sweden, 16-18 Aug. 1990]; xvi-210 p.; portr.; xii-xvi, Tabula gratulatoria; biobibliog. 203-8 (T. *Kronholm*).

VITTINGHOFF Friedrich, Kolloquium 1989 ➔ 770.

185 WALTHER Hans: 70 Gb., Onomastica Slavogermanica XIX, EEichler Ernst: AbhLp p/h 73/2. 257 p.; ill.; 245-51, Bibliog. seit OSG 7 (1972) 197s (*Lutz* Jacob). 3-05-001003-7. 24 art.

185* WARD W. R.: Protestant evangelicalism; England, Ireland, Germany and America c. 1750-c. 1950, ERobbins Keith: StEcclHist Subsidia 7. Ox 1990, Blackwell. xii-369 p. £35 [TR 87,171].

186 WATANABE Kin-Ichi: Collected papers dedicated to ∼: Studies in the Mediterranean World, Past and Present, 11. Tokyo 1988, Hitotsubashi Univ. iv-311 p.; bibliog. 293-304 [ByZ 82,350] ➔ g880.

WATERBOLK H. T. 1988 ➔ 827.

187 WEGMAN Herman. Omnes circumstantes; contributions toward a history of the role of the people in the liturgy, ECaspers Charles, *Schneiders* Marc. Kampen 1990, Kok. viii-320 p. f 50 [TR 86,439; tit. pp.] 17 art.; p. 51-77 *Rouwhorst* Gerard, Actes de Thomas.

188 WEILER Anton G.: Die fonteyn der ewiger wijsheit; 25-jaar hoogleraar, EBange Petty, *Kort* P. de: Middeleeuwse Studies 5. Nijmegen 1989, Katholieke Universiteit. 258 p. f 35 [RHE 85,395*; TR 87,523].

188* WESEMANN Paul: Iustus iudex, 75. Gb., ELüdicke Klaus ...: Münsterischer Kommentar zum Codex Iuris Canonici Beih 5. Essen 1990, Ludgerus. xxiv-728 p. [TR 87,173, plures tit. pp.; 185-196, *Beyer* Jean, Die christliche Ehe ist Sakrament].

189 WILLEBRANDS Johannes card.: Promoting unity; themes in Lutheran-Catholic dialogue, 80th b., EAnderson H. George, *Crumley* James R.J. Minneapolis 1989, Augsburg. xii-112 p. $12 pa. 0-8066-2453-1.

190 WINSNES A. H.: Spor etter mennesket, mem. 100th b. [† d. 1972],
   EBliksrud Liv, Aarnes Asbjørn. Oslo 1989, Aschehoug. 333 p. Nk 228. –
   RNorTTs 91 (1990) 173-5 (Karstein M. Hansen).
191 Woś Jan Władysław: Studi offerti, 50° compleanno; EBianchi G. F
   1989, Mandragora. 238 p. – RAevum 64 (1990) 621s (A. F. Dziuba);
   StPatav 37 (1990) 719 (L. Sartori; p. 712-4 A. Dziuba su un libro del
   Woś).
192 YARSHATER Ehsan: Iranica varia, papers in honor of prof. ~; present.
   Amin D., al.: Acta Iranica 3/30. Leiden 1990, Brill. xxxii-291 p.; XVI
   pl. + portr.; biobibliog. ix-xxxii (M. Boyce, G. Windfuhr). 90-
   6831-226-X. 32 art.; 6 infra [OLZ 86,308, W. Sundermann, tit. pp.
   comment].
192* ZÜRICH 2000-Jahr-Jubiläum: Stadt und Fest; zu Geschichte und Gegenwart europäischer Festkultur, EHugger P., al.: Univ. phil. Fakultät.
   Stu 1987 [Nikephoros 2 (1989) 222].

A1.2 Miscellanea unius auctoris.

193 Aland Kurt, Supplementa zu den Neutestamentlichen [1979: noch 9] und
   den Kirchengeschichtlichen Entwürfen [1960: auch 9], 75. Gb., EKöster
   Beate, al. B 1990, de Gruyter. vii-516 p.; Bibliog. p. 487-514. DM 198
   [TLZ 116,415, W. Wiefel]. 3-11-012142-5. 19 art., 6 infra. – RETL 66
   (1990) 455 (F. Neirynck).
194 Alberigo Giuseppe [➤ 7964], La Chiesa nella storia: BiblCuRel 51.
   Brescia 1988, Paideia. 335 p. 88-394-0411-2. – RJEH 41 (1990) 146s (A.
   Black).
195 Alexander Edward, The Jewish idea and its enemies. New Brunswick NJ
   1988, Transaction. 264 p. $25. – RJRel 70 (1990) 490s (D. Singer).
196 Alföldy Géza, Die Krise des römischen Reiches [2 inedita + 20]. Wsb
   1989, Steiner. 541 p. – RRÉLat 67 (1989) 358 (A. Chastagnol).
196* Alston William P., Divine nature and human language; essays [1979-88]
   in philosophical theology. Ithaca NY 1989, Cornell Univ. xi-279 p.
   $38.50; pa. $13.50 [HeythJ 32,554, B. Hebblethwaite).
197 Armstrong Arthur H., Hellenic and Christian studies: Collected Studies
   324. Aldershot 1990, Variorum. xii-317 p. [original numberings kept].
   0-86078-273-5. 15 art.; 4 infra.
198 Baldwin Barry, Roman and Byzantine papers [third collected studies]:
   London StClasPg 21. Amst 1989, Gieben. 691 p. – RSalesianum 52
   (1990) 927 (R. Della Casa: titoli senza pp.).
199 Betz Hans-Dieter, Hellenismus und Christentum: Gesammelte Aufsätze
   I. Tü 1990, Mohr. viii-303 p. 3-16-145574-6. 16 art. [CritRR 4,498,
   tit. pp.; TLZ 116,424, F. Horn].
200 Betz Otto, Jesus der Herr der Kirche; [20 1958-86] Aufsätze zur biblischen Theologie II. Qumran-Paulus-Gnosis: WUNT 52. Tü 1990, Mohr.
   viii-514 p. DM 188 [RB 98,295, tit. pp.; Carthaginensia 7,260, R. Sanz
   V.; Salesianum 53,577, R. Vicent; TLZ 116,154, W. Wiefel; TPQ 139,320,
   A. Fuchs; ZkT 113,302, R. Oberforcher]. 3-16-145505-3. 3 inedita,
   infra; + 2.
201 Bieler Ludwig, Ireland and the culture of early medieval Europe,
   ESharpe Richard: Collected Studies 263. L 1987, Variorum. xii-322 p.
   £32. 0-86078-213-5. 22 art. – RJEH 41 (1990) 81s (D. N. Dumville); JTS
   41 (1990) 268-271 (C. E. Stancliffe: not unified like Sharpe's 1986 edition
   of Bieler articles on St. Patrick).

201* **Blandino** Giovanni,   Problemi di teologia; una ricerca di sintesi[2]. R 1989, Univ. Lateranense / Coletti. 262 p. Lit. 24.000. – RDivThom 93 (1990) 158s (L. *Elders*: hypothèses hasardeuses).

202 **Bolognesi** Giancarlo,   Studi glottologici filologici orientali. Brescia 1990, Paideia. xliii-431 p.; fot.; bibliog. xxxi-xliii. Lit. 80.000.   88-394-0459-7. 15 art., → 9623.

202* **Bourassa** François,   Redenzione e sacrificio.   Vaticano 1989, Libreria. 214 p. Lit. 36.000. – REsprVie 100 (1990) 208 (P. *Jay*: articles d'une revue, français [T]; centon de phrases tirées de discours pontificaux; pour l'Année Sainte, semble-t-il).

203 **Browning** Robert,   History, language and literacy in the Byzantine world [art. 1978-89]: CS 299.   Northampton 1989, Variorum.

204 **Bruce** Frederick F.,   A mind for what matters; collected essays.   GR 1990, Eerdmans.   x-325 p. $20.   0-8028-0446-2.

205 **Brümmer** Vincent,   Over een persoonlijke God gesproken; studies in de wijsgerige theologie.   Kampen 1988, Kok Agora.   182 p. *f* 27.75. – RKerkT 40 (1989) 254-6 (A. van de *Beek*).

206 **Brunt** P. A.,   Roman imperial themes [2 inedita; 16 reprints with addenda].   Ox 1990, Clarendon.   551 p. [JRS 81,199, G. P. *Burton*]. 0-19-814476-8.   5 infra.

207 **Burckhardt** Titus [1908-1984],   Mirror of the intellect; [25] essays on traditional science and sacred art, TE*Stoddart* William.   Albany 1987, SUNY.   270 p. $44.50; pa. $15. – RCritRR 2 (1989) 470-2 (J. W. *Morris*: comparative religion).

208 **Caporale** V.,   Teologia e antropologia, saggi.   N 1990, D'Auria.   230 p. Lit. 25.000. – RRasT 31 (1990) 620 (A. *Barruffo*).

209 **Casaroli** A. card.,   Nella Chiesa per il mondo; Omelie e discorsi [per il 50° sacerdotale]; pref. *Guitton* Jean. Mi 1987, Rusconi.   502 p. Lit. 28.000. – RDivThom 92 (1989) 187-9 (G. *Perini*).

210 **Cavarnos** Constantine,   New library [his reviews of 52 books 1948-88] I. Belmont MA 1989, Institute for Byzantine.   176 p. $11; pa. $8.   0-914744-81-X; -2-8 [TDig 37,352].

211   **Chadwick** Owen,   The spirit of the Oxford Movement; tractarian essays [15, 1954-87].   C 1990, Univ.   ix-324 p. $49.50 [TS 52,155, F. M. *Jelly*].

212 **Clark** Grahame,   Economic prehistory; papers in archaeology.   C 1989, Univ.   xviii-638 p.; ill. $50.   0-521-34481-6. – RAntiqJ 69 (1989) 339s (I. *Longworth*: clear concise English selected from 40 years).

213 **Clines** David J. A.,   What does Eve do to help? and other readerly questions on the OT: JStOT supp 94.   Sheffield 1990, Academic.   178 p. £18.50.   1-85075-248-6 [BL 91,69, J. F. A. *Sawyer*: six powerful and witty essays mostly from SBL meetings; CBQ 53,517, Alice L. *Laffey*]. – RExp-Tim 101,2 3d-top choice (1989s) 355 (C. S. *Rodd*: hilariously funny; more serious on Nehemiah); TLond 93 (1990) 479s (Grace I. *Emmerson*: good).

214 **Colpe** Carsten,   Das Siegel der Propheten; historische Beziehungen zwischen Judentum, Judenchristentum, Heidentum und frühem Islam: ArbNZ 3.   B 1990, Inst. Kirche & J.   271 p. DM 24.80.   3-923095-83-X. 9 art. [NTAbs 34,405].

215 **Constable** Giles,   Monks, hermits and Crusaders in medieval Europe: Collected Studies 273.   L 1988, Variorum.   346 p. £34.   0-86078-221-2 [Speculum 64,778].   11 art., his third collection. – RJEH 40 (1989) 411s (H. E. J. *Cowdrey*).

216 **Cooper** Eli L.,   Insights to Scripture.   Lanham MD 1986, UPA.   xvi-180 p. [KirSef 62 (1988s) p. 25].

216* **Cox** Harvey, Göttliche Spiele; meine Erfahrungen mit den Religionen, [T]*Kohlhaas* Radbert. FrB 1989, Herder. 235 p. DM 36. 3-451-21541-1. – [R]ZkT 112 (1990) 345s (K. H. *Neufeld*: does this really help any?); ZRGg 42 (1990) 378 (K. *Ebert*).

217 **Crouzel** Henri, Les fins dernières selon ORIGÈNE: CS 320. Aldershot, Hamps 1990, Variorum. x-341 p.; portr. 0-86078-369-2. 14 art. (pagination orig.); 5 infra.

218 **Crowe** Frederick E., Appropriating the LONERGAN idea [9 essays on Lonergan, 13 others on applications], [E]*Vertin* Michael. Wsh 1989, Catholic University of America. xiv-410 p. $50. 0-8132-0668-5 [TDig 37,257].

219 **Curran** Charles, Tensions in moral theology (10 revised articles). ND c. 1989, Univ. 214 p. $20. – [R]America 160 (1989) 455-7 (Lisa S. *Cahill*).

219* **Delcor** Mathias, Environnement et tradition de l'AT: AOAT 228. Kevelaer/Neuk 1990, Butzon & B./Neuk.-V. xiv-458 p. DM 93 [TR 87,250]. 3-7666-9675-0/ Neuk 3-7887-2339-9. 25 art.; 8 infra.

220 **Demougeot** Émilienne, L'empire romain et les barbares d'Occident (IVe-VIIe siècles); scripta varia [1956-88]: Réimpressions 4. P 1988, Sorbonne. 420 p.; 3 maps. [AnPg 60, p. 877].

221 **Dillon** John, The golden chain; studies in the development of Platonism and Christianity: CS 333. Aldershot, Hamps 1990, Variorum. viii-322 p., 28 art. (original pagination).

222 **Dondaine** A., Les hérésies et l'Inquisition, XIIe-XIIIe s., documents et études, [E]*Dossat* Y.: Collected Studies 314. Aldershot 1990, Variorum. x-340 p. £42 [RHE 85, p. 269*].

223 **Dover** Kenneth J., The Greeks and their legacy; collected papers [I. 1987 → 4,181] II: Prose literature, history, society, transmission, influence. Ox 1988, Blackwell. ix-334 p. £37.50. – [R]AmJPg 111 (1990) 112-5 (C. W. *Wooten*); ClasR 39 (1989) 370-2 (H. *Lloyd-Jones*).

224 **Dray** W. H., On history and philosophers of history. Leiden 1989, Brill. 256 p. *f* 135 [RHE 85, p. 184*].

225 **Duft** Johannes, Die Abtei St. Gallen; Beiträge zur Erforschung ihrer Manuskripte; Ausgewählte Aufsätze in überbearbeiteter Fassung, I.; 75. Gb., [E]**Ochsenbein** Peter, *Ziegler* Ernst. Sigmaringen 1990, Thorbecke. xiv-274 p. 20 fig. + 24 color. DM 72 [RHE 86,181, A. *d'Haenens*].

226 **Dunn** James D. G., Jesus, Paul, and the Law; [9 reprinted] studies in Mark and Galatians. L/Louisville 1990, SPCK/Westminster-Knox. x-277 p. $20 pa. 0-281-04436-8 / 0-664-25095-5 [TDig 37,357; NTAbs 34,376]. – [R]ExpTim 102 (1990s) 246s (A. *Chester*); Tablet 244 (1990) 986 (D. L. *Edwards*); TLond 93 (1990) 482s (J. A. *Ziesler*).

227 **Dunn** James D. G., The living word [... 6 essays on biblical authority]. Ph 1987, Fortress. iv-196 p. – [R]RelStR 15 (1989) 153 (R. H. *Fuller*).

228 **Egan** Joseph M., The fullness of time; essays in biblical chronology. Elmira NY 1990, Sator. [viii-] 388 p. $17.

228* **Esposito** Mario † 1961, [E]*Lapidge* Michael, Irish books and learning in mediaeval Europe, CS. Aldershot 1990, Gower. xii-320 p. [RHE 86,132, F. *Grannell*].

Fessard Gaston, HEGEL, le christianisme et l'histoire [inedita] 1990 → k873.

229 **Fleckenstein** Josef, Ordnungen und formende Kräfte des Mittelalters; Ausgewählte Beiträge. Gö 1989, Vandenhoeck & R. x-601 p. DM 124. – [R]TLZ 115 (1990) 204-6 (G. *Haendler*).

230 **Flint** V. I. J., Ideas in the medieval west; texts and their contexts [14 art. 1964-88]: CS 268. L 1989, Variorum. 344 p. – [R]StMon 32 (1990) 233-7 (M. Odile *Garrigues*).

231 **Foss** Clive, History and archaeology of Byzantine Asia Minor [12 reprints]: Collected Studies 315. Aldershot 1990, Gower. x-324 p. 0-86078-263-8 [OIAc Oc90].

232 **Fouyas** Methodios, Theological and historical studies; a collection of minor works 9-11. L 1986-8, Thyateira House. 352 p.; 479 p.; 284 p. – RRTLv 21 (1990) 106s (A. de *Halleux*).

233 **Furley** David, Cosmic problems; essays on Greek and Roman philosophy of nature. C 1989, Univ. xiv-258 p.

234 **Garuti** Adriano, Il Papa patriarca d'Occidente? Studio storico dottrinale [articoli di Antonianum 1985-90]: Antoniana 2. Bo 1990, Ed. Francescane. 280 p. Lit. 30.000. – RAntonianum 65 (1990) 404-6 (U. *Betti*).

235 **Gatti** Guglielmo, Topografia ed edilizia di Roma antica [art. 1934-79]: Studi e materiali del Museo della Civiltà Romana 13. R 1989, Bretschneider. 406 p.; ill.

236 **Gilkey** [Langdon] on TILLICH. NY 1990, Crossroad. xvi-215 $25 [TS 52,370, R. *Modras*].

237 **Gleason** Philip, Keeping the faith; American Catholicism past and present. ND 1987, Univ. 285 p. $25. – RJAAR 58 (1990) 281-3 (P. W. *Carey*: he holds that continuity with past has become problematic since Vatican II).

238 **Goffart** Walter, Rome's fall and after [12 art. 1963-89 + 1 ineditum]. Ronceverte WV 1989, Hambledon. viii-371 p. $45. 1-85285-001-9. – RCathHR 76 (1990) 820-2 (K. F. *Morrison*); JEH 41 (1990) 700s (R. *Collins*).

240 **GOGARTEN** Friedrich (100. Gb.), EGöckeritz Hermann G., Gehören und Verantworten, ausgewählte Aufsätze. Tü 1988, Mohr. 352 p. DM 89. 3-16-145389-1. – RActuBbg 26 (1989) 55 (J. *Boada*).

241 **Green** Peter, Classical bearings [16 art.]; interpreting ancient history and culture. L 1989, Thames & H. 328 p. £18. – RClasR 40 (1990) 528 (P. *Walcot*).

241* **Gruen** Erich S., Studies in Greek culture and Roman policy [1985 Semple Lectures]. Cincinnati ClasSt NS 7. Leiden 1990, Brill. x- 209 p. 90-04-09051-7.

242 **Gy** Pierre-M., La liturgie dans l'histoire [20 reprints depuis 1950]: Liturgie. P 1990, S. Paul-Cerf. 332 p. F 349 [NRT 113,276, A. *Toubeau*].

242* **Hall** B., Humanists and Protestants 1500-1900. E 1990, Clark. x-380 p. £20. 0-567-09531-3 [BL 91,17; TLZ 116,439, H. R. *Guggisberg*; TS 52,557, J. C. *Olin*].

243 **Halleux** André de, Patrologie et œcuménisme; recueil d'études: BlETL 93. Lv 1990, Univ./Peeters. xvi-892 p. Fb 3180. 90-6186-404-6 / P 90-6831-263-4 [Irénikon 64,427, B. *Lanne*; JEH 42,629s, L. R. *Wickham*; NRT 113,771, V. *Roisel*; RTLv 22,239, G. *Thils*; TR 87,48, B. *Studer*].

243* **Hamp** Vinzenz, Weisheit und Gottesfurcht; Aufsätze zur alltestamentlichen Einleitung, Exegese und Theologie, ESchmuttermayr Georg. St. Ottilien 1990, EOS. 396 p. DM 48 [TR 86,425]. 3-88096-698-2. 22 art. 1949-74.

244 **Hastings** Adrian, The theology of a protestant Catholic ['a Roman Catholic ... against the deeper rigidities within the whole central Christian tradition']. L/Ph 1990, SCM/Trinity. x-213 p. £10.50. 0-334-02441-2 [RelStR 17,148, J. J. *Buckley*; TsTNijm 31,334, W. *Boelens*]. – RExpTim 102 (1990s) 215 (J. *Kent*); Tablet 244 (1990) 1411s (R. *McBrien*).

244* **Heckel** Martin, Gesammelte Schriften; Staat, Kirche, Recht, Geschichte; ESchlaich Klaus: Ius ecclesiasticum 38. Tü 1989, Mohr. xx-612 p.; xx + p. 613-1267 [LuJb 57 (1990) p. 323, indicating 8 items].

245 **Heymel** M., Zur Verherrlichung Israels; Vorträge und Predigten. Fra 1990, Lang. 3-631-42793-X [BL 91,158].

246 **Hidal** Sven, Israel och Hellas; studier kring Gamla testamentet och dess verkningshistoria [6 reprints, 4 inedita]: Religio 27. Lund 1988, Teologiska Institutionen. 130 p. Sk 50. 0280-3723 [BL 91,126, G.W. *Anderson*: fresh]. – ᴿTsTKi 61 (1990) 294 (Terje *Stordalen*).

247 **Hirsch** Samson R., Studies on Isaiah and essays on the Psalms: Hirsch heritage 4. NY 1986, Feldheim. xxi-604 p. [KirSef (1-3: 42, n° 4285); 62 (1988s) p. 28].

247* **Hödl** Ludwig: Welt-Wissen und Gottes-Glaube in Geschichte und Gegenwart, 65. Gb. ['Ausgewählte Aufsätze, gesammelte Forschungen'], ᴱ*Gerwing* M. St. Ottilien 1990, EOS. 315 p. DM 68 [RHE 86,311*].

248 **Hommel** Hildebrecht, Symbola; kleine Schriften zur Literatur und Kulturgeschichte der Antike [I. 1976: AnPg 47, p. 820]; II: Collectanea 5. Hildesheim 1988, Olms. 504 p. [AnPg 60, p. 878].

249 **Hooker** Morna D., From Adam to Christ; essays on Paul. C 1990, Univ. viii-198 p. $49.50. 0-521-34317-8 [NTAbs 35,113; RB 98,453, tit. pp.; NBlackf 72,539, J.D.G. *Dunn*].

250 **Horst** P.W. van der [ᴱ*Mussies* G., 21] Studies on the Hellenistic background of the New Testament: TheolReeks 10. Utrecht 1990. 242 p. – ᴿFgNt 3 (1990) 170s (J. *Mateos*).

251 **Hughes** Kathleen †, Church and society in Ireland A.D. 400-1200 (19 art.), ᴱ*Dumville* David: Collected Studies 258. L 1987, Variorum. 380 p.; front.; 8 maps. £32. – ᴿJTS 41 (1990) 266-8 (C.E. *Stancliffe*).

252 **Hunger** H., Epidosis, gesammelte Schriften zur byzantinischen Geistes- und Kulturgeschichte, ᴱ*Horändner* W., *al.* Mü 1989, Maris. 512 p.; 21 fig. DM 78 [RHE 86,311*].

252* **Jacques** Émile, Jansénisme, Antijansénisme; acteurs, auteurs et témoins [17 reprints]. Bru 1988, Perfectiora [RHE 86,481, R. *Aubert*].

253 **Jenkins** David E., [< Living with questions 1969 + 6 new items] Still living with questions. L/Ph 1990, SCM/Trinity. 226 p. £11. 0-334-02439-0. – ᴿExpTim 102 (1990s) 186s (G.T. *Eddy*).

254 **Kaplan** Mordecai M. [d. 1983 aet. 102]: Dynamic Judaism; the essential writings of ~, ᴱ*Goldsmith* Emanuel S., *Scult* Mel. NY 1985, Schocken / Reconstructionist. 263 p. $13 pa. – ᴿRelStT 8,1s (1988) 85 (E. *Segal*).

255 **Kasper** Walter, a) Theology and Church [Theologie und Kirche 1987 ➤ 3,340, but omitting the 5 'foundational' essays of the 15], ᵀ*Kohl* Margaret. NY/L 1989. Crossroad/SCM. xiv-231 p. $23. – /0-334-02358-0. – ᴿExpTim 101 (1989s) 217 (R. *Butterworth*); TS 51 (1990) 527-9 (L. *Örsy*); TTod 47 (1990s) 359 (J. *Gros*). – b) La théologie et l'église [➤ 7908], ᵀ*Hoffmann* J.: CogF 158. P 1990, Cerf. 454 p. F 188. – ᴿÉtudes 373 (1990) 570s (R. *Marlé*). – c) Transcending all understanding; the meaning of Christian faith today [lectures on various occasions], ᵀ*Ramsey* Boniface. SF 1989, Ignatius. 124 p. $8. 0-89870-856-9 [TDig 37,271]. – ᴿNewTR 3,3 (1990) 112-4 (Z. *Hayes*, also on his 'Theology and Church').

255* **Kaufmann** Franz-Xaver, Religion und Modernität; sozialwissenschaftliche Perspektiven. Tü 1989, Mohr. 286 p. DM 58 [HerdKor 44,351].

256 **Kermode** Frank, An appetite for poetry [collected essays... canon, history of biblical interpretation]. CM 1989, Harvard. 242 p. $22.50 [RelStR 17,163, J. *Sykes*].

257 **Kilpatrick** George D. † 1989, The principles and practice of New Testament textual criticism; collected essays, ᴱ*Elliott* J.K.: BtETL 96. Lv 1989, Univ./Peeters. xxxviii-489 p. Fb 3000. 90-6186-413-5 / 90-

683-292-8. 69 art., 6 infra [RB 99,296, tit. pp.; Neotestamentica 25,429, J. H. *Petzer*; NRT 113,753, X. *Jacques*; TLZ 117,32, B. M. *Metzger*].

258 **Knox** Bernard M. W., Essays ancient and modern. Baltimore 1989, Johns Hopkins Univ. xxxv-312 p. – [R]NY Review of Books 36,16 (1989) 45s (*Griffin*) [AnPg 60, p. 878].

259 **Küng** Hans, Reforming the Church today; keeping hope alive [15 art. since 1970], [T]*Heinegg* Peter, *al.* NY 1990, Crossroad. vi-198 p. $19. 0-8245-1045-3 [TDig 38,171; TS 52,365, F. M. *Jelly*: some 'apparently' inedita].

260 **Küng** Hans, *a*) Une théologie pour le troisième millénaire; pour un nouveau départ œcuménique [3 inédits + 7]. P 1989, Cerf. 381 p. F 130. – [R]NRT 112 (1990) 749 (L. *Renwart*). – *b*) Kentering in de theologie; naar een oecumenische theologie van de postmoderne tijd [6 hermeneutic reprints + 4 inedita]. Hilversum 1989, Gooi & S. 288 p. ƒ 49,50. 90-304-0466-3. – [R]CollatVL 20 (1990) 339 (W. Van *Soom*: 3 inedita); TsT-Nijm 30 (1990) 98 (H. J. van *Hout*).

261 **Lane** Dermot A., Christ at the center; selected issues in Christology. Dublin 1990, Veritas. 165 p. £8 [NRT 113,896, L. *Renwart*].

262 **Lasserre** François, Nouveaux chapitres de littérature grecque (1947-1986) [65e anniv.]: Lausanne, PubFacLet 31. Genève 1989, Droz. xii-277 p. [RBgPg 69,183, tit. pp.; RPg 63,290]. – [R]AntClas 59 (1990) 351s (Monique *Mund-Dophchie*).

263 **Liebeschütz** J. H. G. W., From Diocletian to the Arab Conquest; change in the Late Roman empire [20 art. 1959-88]: CS 310. Aldershot 1990, Variorum. xiv-336 p.; portr. [Gnomon 63,617, R. *Klein*]. – [R]OrChrPer 56 (1998) 521s (V. *Poggi*).

264 **Liebman** Charles S., Deceptive images; toward a redefinition of American Judaism [2 inedita + 5]. New Brunswick 1988, Transaction. x-114 p. $28 [RelStR 17,48, W. *Silverman*].

265 **Lohfink** Norbert, Studien zum Deuteronomium und zur deuteronomistischen Literatur I [13 art. 1950-77]: SBAufs 8. Stu 1990, KBW. 392 p. DM 39. 3-460-06081-6 [RB 98,294; tit. pp, BL 91,83, A. D. H. *Mayes*: judges too modestly the enduring worth of his contributions, thus regrettably omitting his 1964 [F]*Rahner* article]. – [R]OTAbs 13 (1990) 309 (R. E. *Murphy*); ZAW 102 (1990) 449s (H.-C. *Schmitt*).

266 **Lubac** Henri de, Théologie dans l'histoire I. La lumière du Christ [8 art.], préf. *Sales* Michel; II. Questions disputées et résistances au racisme. P 1990, D-Brouwer. 224 p., F 130 / 425 p. [RTPhil 123,120, J. *Borel*]. – [R]ZkT 112 (1990) 353s (K. H. *Neufeld*).

267 **Luis Iglesias** A., Reina y madre; grandes temas marianos. M 1988, PS. 493 p.; 504 p. – [R]Salmanticensis 36 (1989) 244s (E. *Llamas*).

268 **Mackay** Donald [scientist, † 1987], [E]*Tinker* Melvin, The open mind and other essays. Leicester 1988, Inter-Varsity. 247 p. $11. 0-85110-640-4. – [R]ExpTim 101 (1989s) 36 (A. *Ford*).

268* **Maggioni** Bruno, Uomo e società nella Bibbia: Già e non ancora 147. Mi 1987, Jaca. 221 p. [Salesianum 53,771, C. *Bissoli*].

269 **Marshall** I. Howard, Jesus the Saviour; studies in NT theology. L 1990, SPCK. 329 p. £10 pa. 0-281-04432-5. – [R]Evangel 8,4 (1990) 24 (H. C. *Bigg*); ExpTim 102 (1990s) 88 (O. E. *Evans*); TLond 93 (1990) 483s (D. de *Lacey*).

270 **Mateos** Juan, La utopía de Jesús [6 art.: Bautismo; criterio de verdad etc.]: En torno al NT 8. Córdoba 1990, Almendro. 173 p. 84-86077-82-6 [NTAbs 35,258]. – [R]Iter 1 (Caracas 1990) 140 (J.-P. *Wyssenbach*).

271 **Meier** John, The mission of Christ and his Church; studies in Christology and Ecclesiology: Good News studies 30. Wilmington c. 1990, Glazier. $18 [JBL 109/2, adv.; Interpretation 45,430, D. R. *Bauer*]. 0-89453-795-4. 16 art.; ➤ 8986.

272 **Mélèze-Modrzejewski** Joseph, Droit impérial et traditions locales dans l'Égypte romaine: Coll. Studies 321. Aldershot 1990, Gower. 336 p. 0-85078-270-0 [OIAc Oc90].

Mesters C., Defenseless flower 1089 ➤ 1215.

272* **Mitchell** Basil, How to play theological ping-pong and other essays on faith and reason, E*Abraham* William J., *Prevost* Robert W. L 1990, Hodder & S. 218 p. £9 [TR 87,346].

273 **Möhler** J. A., Nachgelassene Schriften, Kopien von *Lösch* Stephan, E*Reinhardt* R.; I. E*Rieger* B., Vorlesungen, Entwürfe, Fragmente: KkKSt 52. Pd 1989, Bonifatius. 201 p. DM 92 [RHE 85,394*].

274 **Moltmann-Wendel** Elisabeth, Wenn Gott und Körper sich begegnen; feministische Perspektiven zur Leiblichkeit: Siebenstern 496. Gü 1989, Mohr. 158 p. DM 24,80. 3-579-00496-4. – RTsTNijm 30 (1990) 424 (C. *Claassen*).

275 **Mooney** Christopher F., Boundaries dimly perceived; law, religion, education and the common good. ND 1990, Univ. 200 p. $26 [JAAR 58,327].

275* **Moortgat** Anton, Kleine Schriften zur vorderasiatischen Altertumskunde (1927-1974), E*Moortgat-Correns* Ursula. Damaskus 1990, Amani [Bonn, Habelt in Komm.] 551 + 156 p. [28 art. + 38 R + obit., Fs.: OIAc F91,16].

276 **Morales** *Marín* José, Religión, hombre, historia; estudios NEWMANianos. Pamplona 1989, EUNSA. 302 p. – RScripTPamp 22 (1990) 983-6 (L. F. *Mateo-Seco*).

276* **Napiórkowski** Stanisław C., ☻ Matka Mojego Pana [mother of my Lord] (problemy-poszukiwania-perspektywy). Opole 1988, Ś. Krzyża. 358 p. [RTLv 22,118, Z. *Kijas*].

277 **Neusner** Jacob, Ideas of history, ethics, ontology, and religion in formative Judaism: RelStJud 4. Lanham MD 1988, UPA. xix-189 p. $19.75. 0-8191-7142-5 [NTAbs 34,412: 8 essays].

278 **Neusner** Jacob, Lectures on Judaism in the Academy and in the Humanities [15 art.] / in the history of religions [17 art.]: S. Florida Judaism 1s. Atlanta 1990, Scholars. xi-270 p.; xi-377 p. $60; $73. 1-55540-413-8; 80-4 [NTAbs 35,129].

279 **Noordmans** O., Ontmoetingen — De actualiteit der Historie II: Verzamelde werken 4 [6,1986 ➤ 5,332*]. Kampen 1988, Kok. 517 p. ƒ90. 90-242-2607-4 [TsTNijm 30,225].

280 **Oort** J. van, AUGUSTINUS, facetten van leven en werk [reprints]. Kampen 1989, Kok. 111 p. ƒ22,50. 90-242-4815-9. – RTsTNijm 30 (1990) 204 (M. *Lamberigts*).

280* **Pavan** card. Pietro, Scritti, E*Biffi* F., 1. L'anelito dell'uomo alla libertà; 2. Ascese e attese del lavoro umano. R 1989, Città Nuova. xxiii-444 p.; xvii-412 p. Lit. 50.000 ciasc. [NRT 113,271, L. *Volpe*].

281 **Pearson** Birger A., Gnosticism, Judaism, and Egyptian Christianity: StAntiquity&Chr. Mp 1990, Fortress. xix-228 p. $30. 0-8006-3104-8 [NTAbs 35,130]. 10 art. 1972-86 updated; 3 inedita; 2 infra. – RExpTim 102 (1990s) 248 (C. *Tuckett*).

282 **Penna** Romano, Letture evangeliche; saggi esegetici sui quattro vangeli: Studi e Ricerche Bibliche. R 1989, Borla. 238 p. Lit. 25.000. 88-263-0742-3 [NTAbs 34,386: from Lateran classes].

283 **PERLER** Othmar, Sapientia et caritas; gesammelte Aufsätze zum 90. Gb., ᴱ**Damme** Dirk van, *Wermelinger* Otto: Paradosis 29. FrS 1990, Univ. xiv-630 p. 3-7278-0684-2. 31 art.; 3 infra [RB 98,455, tit. pp.; JTS 42,435, W. *Frend*].

284 **Pikaza** Xabier, Dios como espíritu y persona; razón humana y misterio trinitario: Koinonia 24. S 1989, Secr. Trinitario. 471 p. 84-85376-79-X. – ᴿActuBbg 27 (1990) 90 (J. *Vives*).

284* **Post** Stephen G., A theory of *agape*; on the meaning of Christian love. Lewisburg PA 1990, Bucknell. 126 p. $35; pa. $8.75 [CritRR 4,458, K. B. *Lyon*].

285 **Poulat** Émile, Poussières de raison [articles 1978-87]. P 1988, Cerf. 180 p. F 94. – ᴿCathHR 75 (1989) 525s (F. *Busi*, also on Liberté laïcité).

285* **Poupard** Paul, L'église au défi des cultures [12 conférences]. P 1989, Desclée. 172 p. F 125. – ᴿSpiritus 31 (1990) 456s (M. *Oger*).

286 **Pulgram** Ernst, Practicing linguist; essays on [I. Language; and II.] Languages (1930-1985). Heid 1988, Winter. 345 p. – ᴿSalesianum 52 (1990) 228s (R. *Gottlieb*).

287 **Robert** Louis, Opera minora selecta; épigraphie et antiquités grecques. Amst 1989s, Hakkert [not = ➤ 5,344]. Vol. 6 (Nᵒ 131-157) 1989: xi-719 p.; XIII pl.; vol. 7 (Nᵒ 158-181) 1990: xi-794 p.; VII pl. 90-256-0976-7; -7-5.

288 **Rodríguez Adrados** Francisco, Nuevos estudios de lingüística general y de teoría literaria. Barc 1988, Ariel. 332 p. ᴿKratylos 34 (1989) 163s (*Zgusta*).

289 **Roloff** Jürgen, Exegetische Verantwortung in der Kirche; Aufsätze, ᴱ*Karrer* Martin. Gö 1990, Vandenhoeck & R. 399 p. 3-525-58155-6. 15 art.; 3 infra [TLZ 117,257, E. *Schweizer*].

290 **Rosenthal** Franz, Muslim intellectual and social history: CS 309. Aldershot 1990, Variorum. x-326 p. 0-86078-257-3. XVI art.; 2 infra.

291 **Rostagno** Sergio, Teologia e società; saggi sull'impegno etico: Sola Scriptura 13. T 1989, Claudiana. 168 p. Lit. 22.000 [TLZ 116,378, J. E. *Vercruysse*]. – ᴿCC 141 (1990,4) 521s (F. *Cultrera*); Protestantesimo 45 (1990) 228 (S. *Merlo*); Salesianum 52 (1990) 443 (P. *Carlotti*: Valdese).

292 **Ruckstuhl** Eugen, Jesus im Horizont der Evangelien: Aufsatzband 3. Stu 1988, KBW. – ᴿStPatav 37 (1990) 397s (A. *Moda*).

293 **Runia** David T., Exegesis and philosophy; studies on PHILO of Alexandria. CS 332. Aldershot 1990, Variorum. x-308 p. 0-86078- 287-5. 12 reprints + 1 ineditum infra ➤ k2.1.

293* **Sacchi** Paolo, L'apocalittica giudaica e la sua storia: BiblCuRel 55. Brescia 1990, Paidcia. 375 p. Lit. 47.000 [JStJud 22,150, F. *García M.*: ZAW 103,456; J. A. *Soggin*].

294 **Sales** Michel, Le corps de l'église, études sur l'Église une, sainte, catholique et apostolique: Communio. P 1989, Fayard. 261 p. [TPhil 65,320].

295 **Sanders** E. P., Jewish law from Jesus to the Mishnah; five studies [inedita]. L/Ph 1990, SCM/Trinity. xii-404 p. 0-334-02455-2; pa. -102-2.

296 **Scharlemann** Robert P., Inscriptions and reflections; essays in philosophical theology. Charlottesville 1989, Univ. Virginia. 254 p. $35 [Interp 45,216, G. *Green*]. – ᴿTTod 47 (1990s) 196.198 (D. S. *Blix*).

297 **Scholem** Gershom, De la création du monde jusqu'à Varsovie [8 art., la plupart < Judaica 4, Fra 1984], ᵀ*Hayoun* M.-R.: Patrimoines, Judaïsme. P 1990, Cerf. 261 p. F 230. 2-204-04085-1 [BL 91,145, N. de *Lange*].

298 **Schottroff** L., Befreiungserfahrungen; [20 reprint] Studien zur Sozialgeschichte des Neuen Testaments: TBü 82. Mü 1990, Kaiser. 381 p.

DM 98. 3-459-01823-2. 20 art. [NTAbs 35,97; TsTNijm 31,428, J. *Negenman*]. – ᴿSNTU A-15 (1990) 212 (A. *Fuchs*).

299 **Schürmann** Heinz, Studien zur neutestamentlichen Ethik, ᴱ*Söding* Thomas: SBAufs 7. Stu 1990, KBW. 382 p. DM 30. 13 art. [RB 98,296, tit. pp.]. 3-460-06071-9. – ᴿStPatav 37 (1990) 401-3 (G. *Segalla*).

300 **Segalla** Giuseppe, Introduzione all'etica del NT [articoli 1977-87, *al.*]: Biblioteca Biblica 2. Brescia 1989, Queriniana. Lit. 30.000. – ᴿAnnTh 4 (1990) 443-7 (B. *Estrada*); RasT 31 (1990) 410 (V. *Fusco*); StPatav 37 (1990) 602-625 (G. *Leonardi*).

301 **Serra** A., E c'era la madre di Gesù... (Gv. 2,1); saggi di esegesi biblico-mariana (1978-1988). Mi/R 1989, 'CENS'/Marianum. vii-665 p. Lit. 50.000 [NTAbs 34,402]. – ᴿAsprenas 37 (1990) 512s (A. *Rolla*).

302 **Siri** Giuseppe, † 1989, Opere (24 volumi), ᴱ*Lanzi* Nicola 1983- . – ᴿDivThom 92 (1989) 233-8 (G. *Perini* 1-6).

303 **Smit** M.C., † 1981, De eerste en tweede geschiedenis; nagelaten schriften, ᴿ*Klapwijk* J.: Verantwoording 1. Amst 1987, Buiten & S. 239 p. ƒ 34,50. 90-6064-528-6. – ᴿNedTTs 44 (1990) 360 (H.M. *Vroom*: philosophy of religion).

304 **Splett** Jörg, Leben als Mit-Sein; vom trinitarisch Menschlichen. Fra 1990, Knecht. 128 p. – ᴿMüTZ 41 (1990) 299-301 (G.L. *Müller*).

305 **Stemberger** Günter, Studien zum rabbinischen Judentum: Biblischer Aufsatzband 10. Stu 1990, KBW. 416 p. 3-460-06101-4. 12 art.; meist < Kairos.

306 **Stenger** W., Strukturale Beobachtungen zum NT [8 Art + 5 mit *Schnider* F.]: NT Tools 12. Leiden 1990, Brill. vii-320 p. ƒ 135. 90-04-09113-0 [NTAbs 34,380].

307 **Täubler** Eugen [1879-1953], Ausgewählte Schriften zur Alten Geschichte [22], ᴱ*Alföldy* Géza: Heid. Althist. Beit. 3. Stu 1987, Steiner. 343 p. – ᴿGGA 242 (1990) 237-245 (W. *Nippel*: Bibel, Ägypten...); Henoch 12 (1990) 331s (B. *Chiesa*).

307* **Talley** J., Worship; reforming tradition [revised reprints]. Wsh 1990, Pastoral. ix-155 p. $12 pa. 0-912405-70-8 [MaisD 187,141, J.J. *Fradet*; TDig 38,190].

308 **Talmon** Shemaryahu, Gesellschaft und Literatur in der hebräischen Bibel: GesAufs 1. Neuk 1988, Neuk.-V. 233 p. 3-7887-0749-13. – ᴿUF 22 (1990) 514s (O. *Loretz*).

309 **Thils** Gustave, Primauté et infaillibilité du pontife romain à Vatican I [= 1969 abrégé + 1972 abrégé] et d'autres études d'ecclésiologie [9 reprints + 4 inédits]: BiblETL 89. Lv 1989, Peeters/Univ. xii-422 p. – ᴿRHE 85 (1990) 491 (R. *Aubert*); ScEsp 42 (1990) 361a (A. *Naud*); TS 51 (1990) 757-9 (J.T. *Ford*: what Vatican I really said, in view of what it intended to reject); ZkT 112 (1990) 355 (K.H. *Neufeld*).

310 **Tibiletti** Carlo, Raccolta di studi [37, dal 1949; su TERTULLIANO, CLEMENTE A., AGOSTINO...], ᴱ*Blanco* M.G., *al.*: Univ. Macerata lett/fil 48. R 1989, Viella. xx-702 p. – ᴿSalesianum 52 (1990) 783s (S. *Felici*).

311 **Timm** Hermann, Diesseits des Himmels; von Welt- und Menschenbildung, Facetten der Religionskultur [12 reprints]. Gü 1988, Mohn. 194 p. DM 58 pa. – ᴿTLZ 115 (1990) 97s (P. *Heidrich*: Fortsetzung seiner ungewöhnlichen Bücher).

311* **Touati** C., Prophètes, talmudistes, philosophes [20 reprints 1954-85]: Patrimoines Judaïsme. P 1990, Cerf. 315 p. F 198 [NRT 113,914, X. *Jacques*].

312 **Trudinger** P., Not in the mainstream; biblical essays 'in the eddies' [21 art., several NT]. Kingston ON 1988, Frye. vii-121 p. 0-919741-05-3 [NTAbs 34,104].

313 **Ullendorff** Edward, From the Bible to Enrico CERULLI; a miscellany of Ethiopian and Semitic papers: ÄthF 32. Stu 1990, Steiner. 235 p. DM 70. 3-515-05593-2 [BL 91,24, M. *Knibb*].

314 **VANHETLOO** Warren: retirement [18 of his own articles]: Calvary Baptist Theological Journal 6 (Lansdale PA 1990). 174 p.; phot.; bibliog. 171-4.

315 **Veijola** Timo, David: Gesammelte Studien zu den Davidüberlieferungen des Alten Testaments: Publ. 52. Helsinki/Gö 1990, Finnish Exeg. Soc. / Vandenhoeck & R. 184 p. DM 58. 051-921707-X / 3-525-53591-0 [BL 91,24, R. *Clements*; ZAW 103,312, tit. pp.].

315* **Vergote** Ant., Explorations de l'espace théologique; [35] études de théologie et de philosophie de la religion: BiblETL 90. Lv 1990, Univ/ Peeters. xvi-709 p. Fb 2000 [NRT 113,254, L. *Volpe*; TsTNijm 31,447, P. *Vermeersch*; ZkT 113,314, K. H. *Neufeld*].

316 **Vernant** Jean-Pierre, Myth and society in ancient Greece [9 art. 1953-88], TLloyd Janet. NY 1988, Zone. 279 p. $27; pa. $15. 0-942299-16-7; -7-5. – RRelStR 16 (1990) 339s (R. A. *Swanson*).

317 **Vernant** Jean-Pierre, *Vidal-Naquet* Pierre, Myth and tragedy in ancient Greece [➤ 4,b807], TLloyd Janet. NY 1988, Zone. 527 p. $33; pa. $19. 0-942299-18-3; -9-1.

317* **Vilanova** Evangelista, La fe cristiana entre la sospecha y la inocencia [artículos (< catalán)]: Nuevos desafíos. Estella 1990, VDivino. 276 p. – RLumenVr 39 (1990) 452 (F. *Ortiz de Urtaran*).

318 **Wagner** Falk, Was ist Theologie? Studien zu ihrem Begriff und Thema in der Neuzeit [reprints]. Gü 1989, Mohn. 504 p. DM 148. 3-579-00180-9. – RTsTKi 61 (1990) 300s (J.-O. *Henriksen*: not merely a reordering of 15 years' articles); TsTNijm 30 (1990) 212 (A. *Brante*).

319 **Weiser** Alfons, Studien zu Christsein und Kirche: Biblischer Aufsatzband 9. Stu 1990, KBW. 373 p. 3-460-06091-3. 19 art.

320 **Westlake** H. D., Studies on THUCYDIDES and Greek history (19 reprints + 1 ineditum]. Bristol 1989, Classical. vii-310 p. £10. RClasR 40 (1990) 359-361 (S. *Hornblower*).

321 **Wirszubski** Chaim, ❿ Between the lines; Kabbalah, Christian Kabbalah and Sabbatianism [collected articles], TIdel Moshe. J 1990, Magnes. 13 + 222 p. – RTarbiz 60 (1990s) 131-8; Eng. V (Y. *Liebes*).

321* **Wojtyła** Karol, I fondamenti dell'ordine etico [11 art. 1955-70]. Bo 1989, CSEO. 174 p. Lit. 35.000. – RCC 141 (1990,2) 95-97 (F. *Cultrera*).

322 **Wolff** H. W., Iss dein Brot mit Freuden; Alttestamentliche Ermutigungen [< Predigten 'Wie ein Fackel' 1980]: FrB 1990, Herder. 126 p. DM 10. – RZAW 102 (1990) 464s (H.-C. *Schmitt*).

A1.3 *Plurium compilationes* **biblicae.**

322* **Aulard** S., *al.*, Parole de Dieu et exégèse [25e anniv. Dei Verbum]: CahÉv 74. P 1990, Cerf. 67 p. F 25. 0222-9714 [NTAbs 35,229].

323 E**Auneau** Joseph, (*Monloubou* L.), [présent. *Paul* André], Les Psaumes et les autres Écrits: Petite Bibliothèque des Sciences Bibliques, AT 5. Tournai/P 1990, Desclée/Proost France. 476 p. 2-7189-0458. 8 art.; infra.

324 E**Bach** Alice, The pleasure of her text; feminist readings of biblical and historical texts [< UnSemQ]. Ph 1990, Trinity. xii-148 p. [RelStR 17,348, W. L. *Humphreys*].

325 ᴱ**Bianchi** Enzo, *a*) 'Dinanzi a te la benedizione e la maledizione'; – *b*) 'Il ritorno': ParSpV 21s. Bo 1990, Dehoniane. 286 p.; 16 art. / 286 p.; 16 art. Lit. 16.000 each; both 20.500, outside Italy 26.000.

325* ᴱ**Bilde** Per, *al.*, Religion and religious practice in the Seleucid Kingdom: Studies in Hellenistic Civilization 1. Aarhus 1990, Univ. 269 p.; bibliog. 237-253. Dk 211 / $36. 87-7288-322-7. 11 art., infra.

326 ᴱ**Bloom** Harold, The Gospels [9 reprints; *Frei* H., *Frye* N., *Schüssler Fiorenza* E,; *Girard* R. ...]: Modern critical interpretations. NY 1988, Chelsea. vii-187 p. $24.50. 0-87754-911-7 [TDig 36,370].

326* ᴱ**Cameron** Ron, [p. 1-6; 35-69 on Baptist] The apocryphal Jesus and Christian origins: Semeia 49. Atlanta 1990, Scholars. v-176 p. 6 other art., infra.

327 **Camponovo** C. & 8 autres, Peuple parmi les peuples; dossier pour l'animation biblique: Essais Bibliques 18. Genève 1990, Labor et Fides. 240 p. 2-8309-0622-5 [BL 91,105, B. P. *Robinson*: Swiss identity-quest].

328 ᴱ**Carson** D. A., Teach us to pray; prayer in the Bible and the world. GR/Exeter 1990, Baker/Paternoster. 362 p. $15. 0-8010-2537-0 / 0-85364-495-0 [NTAbs 35,117].

328* ᴱ**Cohen** Shaye D., *Greenstein* Edwards L., The state of Jewish studies. Detroit 1990, Wayne State Univ. (for Jewish Theol. Sem.) 277 p. 0-8143-2195-X [OIAc JJ90].

329 **Desreumaux** A., *Schmidt* F., Moïse géographe 1988 → 5,e823 (ind. !): ᴿAnÉCS 45 (1990) 462-4 (B. *Lepetit*); JJS 41 (1990) 122-4 (P. S. *Alexander*); LavalTP 46 (1990) 251s (P.-H. *Poirier*).

329* ᴱ**Detweiler** Robert, *Dory* William G., The daemonic imagination; biblical text and secular story. Atlanta 1990, Scholars. 232 p. $16 [JAAR 58,745].

330 **Ebach** J., *al.*, Die Bibel gehört nicht uns: Einwürfe 6. Mü 1990, Kaiser. 207 p. DM 32. 3-459-01867-4. 5 art. [BL 92,104, A. G. *Auld*: common theme 'our understanding of the Bible requires to be liberated from our expectations of it'; WEINRICH M., SCHELLONG D.; *al.* infra].

330* ᴱ**Eid** V., Prophetie und Widerstand: Theologie zur Zeit 5. Dü 1989, Patmos. 294 p. DM 32,80. 3-491-77706-2 [ZAW 102,456: *Kegler* J., Prophetischer Widerstand, 90-141]. – ᴿTsTNijm 30 (1990) 110 (R. *Weverbergh*).

331 ᴱ**Emerton** J. A., Studies in the Pentateuch [< VT]: VT supp 41. Leiden 1990, Brill. vii-253 p. *f*120. 90-04-091-95-5 [BL 91,13; RB 98,293, tit. pp.].

332 ᴱ**Engberg-Pedersen** T., *Lemche* N. P., Tradition og Nybrud; Jødedommen i hellenistisk tid [... Seleucids, Daniel, Judith, Sirach ...]: Forum for bibelsk eksegese 2. K 1990, Mus. Tusc. 240 p. Dk 150. 87-7289-091-6 [BL 91,136, K. *Jeppesen*, no tit. pp.].

333 ᴱ**Firmage** Edwin B., *al.*, Religion and law; biblical-Judaic and Islamic perspectives. WL 1990, Eisenbruns. xii-402 p. $37.50 [AndrUnS 28,190; VT 41,491: H. *Williamson* '1985/90'].

334 ᴱ**Flesher** Paul V. M., Society and literature in analysis: New perspectives on ancient Judaism 5. Lanham MD 1990, UPA. xiv-189 p. $29.75. 0-8191-7614-1 [JStJud 22,273s, W. J. van *Bekkum*: H. van *Broekhoeven* applies Mary DOUGLAS group-grid to Sir & Sap; NTAbs 35,264]. 8 art., 3 infra.

335 ᴱ**Flothkötter** H., *Nacke* B., Das Judentum — eine Wurzel des Christlichen; neue Perspektiven des Miteinanders. Wü 1900, Echter. 224 p. DM 29. 3-429-01318-6 [NTAbs 35,256].

335* EFrohnhofen Herbert, Christlicher Antijudaismus und jüdischer Anti-paganismus, ihre Motive und Hintergründe in den ersten drei Jahr-hunderten: HaTheolSt 3. Ha 1990, Steinmann & S. viii-206 p. DM 62. 3-927043-13-3 [Bijdragen 51,466].

336 EGammie J. G. †, Perdue L. G., The sage in Israel and the Ancient Near East. WL 1990, Eisenbrauns. xiv-545 p. $42.50. 0-931464-46-3. 36 inedita, infra [ZAW 103,456 & RB 99,293, tit. pp.]. – RLA 40 (1990) 503-6 (A. Niccacci).

337 EGarmus L., Sociologia das comunidades paulinas: EstudosB 25. Pe-trópolis 1990, Vozes. 64 p. 4 art. [NTAbs 35,111].

338 EGoldscheider C., Neusner J., Social foundations of Judaism [15 art.]. ENJ 1990, Prentice-Hall. xvi-288 p. $13. 0-13-818683-9 [NTAbs 35,125].

EGordon C., Rendsburg G., Eblaitica 2, 1990 → e319.

340 EHansson G., Bible reading in Sweden; studies related to the translation of the New Testament 1981: AcU psych./soc. rel 2. Sto 1990, Almqvist & W. 171 p. 91-554-25410 [BL 91,57; G. W. Anderson: immensely valuable and thorough survey, so apparently it proves '36 percent of Sweden's population read the Bible'].

EHeinrichs W., Studies in Neo-Aramaic → 9401.

EHolbrook, Issues in Hebrews 1989 → 6698.

343 Jones Bruce W., [Hallo William J.] al., The Bible in the light of cuneiform literature; Scripture; Scripture in Context 3: Ancient and Near Eastern Texts and Studies 8. Lewiston NY 1990, Mellen. 490 p. $90. 0-88946-219-4.

344 EJüngel Eberhard, Die Heilsbedeutung des Kreuzes für Glaube und Hoffnung der Christen: ZTK Beih 8. Tü 1990, Mohr. 93 p. 0513-9147. Ebeling G., p. 3-29; Becker Jürgen, p. 30-49; Härle Winfried, p. 50-69; Jörns Klaus, p. 70-93.

345 EKämpchen Martin, Liebe auch den Gott deines Nächsten; Lebens-erfahrungen beim Dialog der Religionen: Tb 162. FrB 1989, Herder. 208 p. DM 16. – RZkT 112 (1990) 348 (I. Jorissen: das höchstaktuelle Thema verdient sorgfältigere Behandlung).

347 EKark Ruth, The land that became Israel; studies in historical geography [preliminary to 1989 J conference]. NHv/J 1990, Yale Univ./Magnes. 332 p.; 30 fig. $27.50 [JAAR 58,159]. 965-223-719-1.

348 EKasher A., al., ⊕ Man and law in Eretz-Israel in antiquity. J 1986, Yad Ben Zvi. xxiv-243 p. 16 art., infra. – RJStJud 21 (1990) 263-5 (M. Mach: tit. pp. and summaries, but with no indication of whether it was a meeting).

349 EKatz David S., Israel Jonathan I., [FPOPKIN Richard H. p. ix] Sceptics, millenarians and Jews: Studies in Intellectual History 17. Leiden 1990, Brill. x-293 p. 90-04-09160-2. 14 art.

350 EKertelge Karl, Metaphorik und Mythos im NT: QDisp 126. FrS 1990, Herder. 298 p. DM 69 [TR 87,164 & RB 98,451, tit. pp.; TsTNijm 31,428, S. Noorda]. 3-451-02126-9.

350* EKertelge Karl, Saggi esegetici su La Legge nel NT [Das Gesetz im NT: QDisp 108, 1985/6 → 2,382], TLaurenzi Maria C.: Parola di Dio II. CinB 1990, Paoline. 244 p. Lit. 20.000. 88-215-1950-3.

351 EKrawutscke Peter W., Translation and interpreter training and foreign language pedagogy. Binghamton 1989. SUNY. 178 p. [JAAR 58,740].

351* EKugel J. A., [on David], Poetry and prophecy; the beginnings of a literary tradition [10 art.]: Myth and Poetics. Ithaca NY 1990, Cornell Univ. ix-251 p. $32.50; pa. $12. 0-8014-2310-4; -9568-7 [NTAbs 35,266].

352 ᴱLaboa Juan M., El postconcilio en España. M 1988, Encuentro. 475 p. – ᴿMiscCom 47 (1989) 338-340 (M.J.B).
353 *Lamarche* Paul, *al.* La Bibbia alle origini della Chiesa [= BTT 1, p. 19-125 seules], ᵀ: StBPaid 92. Brescia 1990, Paideia. 170 p. 88-394-0441-4.
354 ᴱLaperrousaz Ernest-Marie, La protohistoire d'Israël; de l'exode à la monarchie. P 1990, Cerf. 343 p. F 170. 2-204-04128-9 [cover gives also ISSN 0768-2980 but there is no series-title]. 7 art.; infra.
354* ᴱLentzen-Deis Fritzleo, *Mora Paz* C., *a)* Jesús en la reflexión exegética y comunitaria; – *b)* Avances metodológicas de la exégesis para la praxis de hoy: Evangelio y cultura 1s. Bogotá 1990, Paulinas [AcPIB 9/7, 550].
355 ᴱLindars Barnabas, Law and religion; essays on the place of the law in Israel and early Christianity [13 essays of the Manchester Erhardt seminar: on OT, Jesus, Paul]. 1988, J. Clarke. 209 p. £25. 0-227-69707-3 [ExpTim 102,127].
355* ᴱLink F., Paradigmata; literarische Typologie des Alten Testaments, I. Von den Anfängen bis zum 19. Jh.; II. 20. Jh.: Schriften zur Literaturwissenschaft 5. B 1989, Duncker & H. 953 p. [ZAW 102,444, tit. pp.].
356 ᴱMack B.L., *Robbins* V.K., Patterns of persecution in the Gospels: FF. Sonoma CA 1989, Polebridge. x-230 p. $20 pa. 0-944-344-08-0 [NTAbs 34,112].
357 ᴱMcKnight Scot, Introducing New Testament interpretation: Guides to NT exegesis 1. GR 1989, Baker. 197 p. $12 pa. 0-8010-0260-8. 7 authors. – ᴿSWJT 33,2 (1990s) 57s (L.L. *Cranford*).
358 ᴱMindlin M., *al.*, Figurative language in the Ancient Near East [... *Jacobsen* T., *Lambert* W., *Talmon* S.]. L 1987, Univ. Sch. Or. Afr. xiii-155 p. ➤ 4,a888; £10. – ᴿBSO 52 (1989) 122s (C.H. *Gordon*).
359 ᴱNeusner J., *a)* Ancient Judaism, debates and disputes II [largely book-reviews]: S. Florida studies in the history of Judaism 5. Atlanta 1990, Scholars. xiii-230 p. $55. 1-55540-479-0 [NTAbs 35,128]. – *b)* with *Frerichs* E.S., Approaches to ancient Judaism 6., Studies in the ethnography and literature of Judaism [... *Drower* E.; comments on STEINSALTZ, URBACH, MOORE]: BrownJudSt 192. Atlanta 1989, Scholars. xiv-204 p. $55. 1-55540-411-1 [NTAbs 34,274; RelStR 17,178, M.S. *Jaffee*].
360 ᴱNí Chatháin Próinséas, *Richter* Michael, Irland und die Christenheit, Bibelstudien und Mission [i. Der Bibeltext im frühen Mittelalter (*McNamara* M.), 7-55; ii. Bibeltext und Exegese, 59-199; iii. Literarische Grundlagen, Rechtstexte, 203-307; iv. Mission, 311-412; v. Die Iren und die Westslaven, 415-470]: Tü Eur-Zentrum. Stu 1987, Klett-Cotta. xii-523 p. [Salesianum 53,411].
361 ᴱOrmiston Gayle L., *Schrift* Alan D., The hermeneutic tradition, from Ast to Ricoeur: Intersections. Albany 1990, SUNY. xii-380 p. 0-7914-0136-7 [12 reprints; II. awaited, From Nietzsche to Nancy].
362 ᴱPastore C. [AT-NT], La inculturación del evangelio: EstT 3. Caracas 1988, ITER. 166 p. bs 120. 980-300-220-1 [NTAbs 35,259].
363 ᴱPerdue Leo G., *Gammie* John G., Paraenesis, act and form: Semeia 50. Atlanta 1990, Scholars. vi-71 p. 11 art.; infra.
365 ᴱPhillips Gary A., (p. 7-49) Poststructural criticism and the Bible; text/history/discourse: Semeia 51 (1990) vi-240 p. – 8 other art., infra.
366 ᴱPopkin Richard H., Millenarianism and Messianism in English literature and thought, 1650-1800 [8 essays on NEWTON, *al.*]: ➤ 4,5759;

Clark Library Professorship 10. Leiden 1988, Brill. 210 p. $34. 90-04-08513-0. – ᴿÉTRel 65 (1990) 284s (H. *Rost*).

367 ᴱ**Radday** Y. T., *Brenner* A., On humour and the comic in the Hebrew Bible [essays, some new, from various authors]: JStOT supp 92 / BLit 23. Sheffield 1990, Almond. 328 p. $30. 1-85075-241-9; pa. -701-1 [BL 91,91, R. B. *Salters*; ETL 67,416, J. *Lust*; ÉTRel 66,589, J. *Lys*]. 14 art., infra.

368 ᴱ**Ratigan** Virginia K., *Swidler* Arlene A., A new Phoebe; perspectives on Roman Catholic women and the permanent diaconate. KC 1990, Sheed & W. vi-111 p. $8 pa. 1-55612-357-4 [TDig 38,179].

Ratzinger J., *al.*, Mission et formation du prêtre: Chemins de crêtes 3, 1990 ➤ 672*b*.

370 ᴱ**Robertson** M. J., *Lane* W., The Gospels today; a guide to some recent developments: The NT Student 6. x-178 p. Ph 1990, Sowers/Skilton [Acta PIB 9,457; NTAbs 35,107]. 11 art., infra.

370* ᴱ**Sánchez Caro** José M., *al.*, Introducción al estudio de la Biblia [en 10 vol.; 2. Biblia y Palabra de Dios, **Artola** A., 1989 ➤ 5,1447] 1. La Biblia en su entorno. Valencia/Estella 1990, Inst. S. Jerónimo/VDivino. 589 p. 84-7151-691-8. 7 art.; infra.

371 ᴱ**Schwartz** R. M., The book and the text; the Bible and literary theory [12 art.]. Ox 1990, Blackwell. xi-313 p.; 3 fig. $50; pa. $19. 0631-16861-3; -2-1 [NTAbs 34,380].

372 ᴱ**Shanks** Hershel, *Cole* Dan P., Archaeology and the Bible; the best of BAR. Wsh 1990, Biblical Archaeology Society. I. Early Israel, xi-325 p.; II. Archaeology in the world of Herod, Jesus and Paul; ix-293 p. [except for (vol. 2) p. 23-53, the color illustrations of the original are reproduced in black and white. The six sections of each volume (2-7 art. each) are followed by 'After Words']. 0-961-30895-8; -6-6 (both -3-1).

373 ᴱ**Silva** V. da, Categorias de Marginalidade na Biblia: EstudB 21. Petrópolis 1989, Vozes. 79 p. [NTAbs 34,124: WOLFF G. on cross, ZANINI O. on Paul].

375 ᴱ**Smith** Dennis E., How Gospels begin: Semeia 52. Atlanta 1990, Scholars. viii-192 p. 6 art., infra.

376 ᴱ**Stemberger** Günter, Die Juden; ein historisches Lesebuch: B-Reihe 410. Mü 1990, Beck. 348 p.; ill. 3-406-34002-4. 58 reprints.

377 ᴱ**Stone** M. E., *Satran* D., Emerging Judaism; studies on the fourth and third centuries B.C.E. Mp 1989, Fortress. xlv-178 p. $15 pa. 0-8006-2090-9 [NTAbs 34,139].

378 ᴱ**Sylva** Dennis H., Reimaging the death of the Lukan Jesus: BoBB 73. Fra 1990, Hain/Athanäum. vii-231 p DM 98. 3-445-09128-5 [NTAbs 34,388]. – ᴿSNTU A-15 (1990) 168 (A. *Fuchs*); TR 86 (1990) 162 (tit. pp.).

379 ᴱ**Tollers** Vincent L., *Maier* John, Mappings of the biblical terrain; the Bible as text [issue 33/2 of the Bucknell Review, mostly from Modern Language Asn meetings]. Lewisburg PA 1990, Bucknell Univ. 372 p.; 5 fig. $21. 0-8387-5172-5 [NTAbs 35,98].

380 ᴱ**Trotta** G., Gerusalemme: Collana ACLI. Brescia 1900, Morcelliana. 208 p. [AnStoEseg 8,714, M. *Pesce*].

381 ᴱ**Warner** Martin, The Bible as rhetoric; studies in biblical persuasion and credibility. L 1990, Routledge. 224 p. £25; pa. £9. 0-415-06317-8; -4409-X.

381* ᴱ**Weder** H., Die Sprache der Bilder; Gleichnis und Metapher in Literatur und Theologie: Zeitzeichen 4 / Siebenstern 558. Gü 1989,

Mohn. 129 p. DM 14,80. 3-579-00558-8 [NTAbs 35,108: *Bovon* F., Kingdom; *Harnisch* W. Mk 12 ...].

382 EWeiss J.G., Papers of the Institute of Jewish Studies, London, I [Jerusalem 1964, Hebrew Univ.: *Urbach* E. on slavery; *Werblowsky* R. on *bittaḥôn, Loewe* R. on hermeneutic, *Stern* S. on Al-Hariz]ᵀ: Brown Classics in Judaica. Lanham MD 1989, UPA. xxi-210 p. $26.75. 0-8191-2276-6 [NTAbs 34,279 'witness to state of Jewish learning nearly 30 years ago' (*Neusner* preface)].

A1.4   *Plurium compilationes* **theologicae.**

383 EAkoun André, Le monothéisme; mythes et traditions [E*Caquot* André, Orient sémite, p. 12-193; E*Simon* Marcel, Christianisme primitif, p. 195-251]. P 1990, Brepols. 476 p.; ill. 2-503-82376-9.

384 EArens Edmund, HABERMAS und die Theologie; Beiträge zur theologischen Rezeption; Diskussion und Kritik der Theorie kommunikativen Handelns. Dü 1989, Patmos. 270 p. – RTPhil 65 (1990) 290-2 (T. M. *Schmidt*).

385 EArvind Sharma, Women in world religions, intr. *Young* Katherine K. Albany 1987, SUNY. xii-302 p. – RJRel 69 (1989) 140-2 (Nancy A. *Falk* compares with EKING Ursula, Women in the world's religions 1987).

385* EBan Joseph D., Christological foundation for contemporary theological education. Macon GA 1988, Mercer Univ. 272 p. $30. → 5,432; 0-86554-313-5 [RelStR 17,51, A. *Dunnavant*]. RInterpretation 44 (1990) 216.218 (D. P. *Henry*).

386 EBarr Marleen S., *Feldstein* Richard. Discontented discourses; feminism / textual intervention / psychoanalysis. Urbana 1989, Univ. Illinois. viii-250 p. $30; pa. $12.50. – RRelStR 16 (1990) 327 (Kathryn A. *Rabuzzi*).

387 *Bartóla* A., *al.* [→ 1750] Miscellanea bibliothecae apostolicae Vaticanae III: ST 333, Vaticano 1989, Biblioteca. 370 p.; ill. 88-210-0619-0. 7 other art.

388 EBaum Gregory, *Coleman* John, Sport [... (p. 6) as an alternative to religion]. E 1989, Clark. xiii-133 p. [RelStR 17,236, J. L. *Price*].

389 EBeard M., *North* J., Pagan priests; religion and power in the ancient world. L 1990, Duckworth. xii-226 p.; 31 fig. £24. 0-7156-2206-4. 9 art., 4 infra [BL 91,104, R. J. *Coggins* on KUHRT Amélie, Nabonidus and the Babylonian priesthood].

390 EBennett Gareth, To the Church of England [8 on LUTHER and after, 8 more contemporary]. L 1988, Churchman. 256 p. £6. 1-85093-110-0. – RExpTim 101 (1989s) 55s [R. *Lunt*: severe only on that unhappy 'unjust, snide, acid' preface, not identified further, but see → 4,8864].

391 Bertini F., *al.*, Medioevo al femminile. Bari 1989, Laterza. xxvi-195 p. Lit. 28.000. 8 art.; *Cardini* F., EGERIA e Dhuoda. – RRenovatio 24 (1989) 652s (A. *Ceresa-Gastaldo*).

392 EBirch Charles, *al.*, Liberating life; contemporary American approaches to ecological theology. Mkn 1990, Orbis. ix-293 p. $17 pa. [NewTR 4/3, 103, Elizabeth *Dreyer*].

392* EBolle Kees W., Secrecy in religion: Numen supp. 49. Leiden 1987, Brill. xvi-164 p. $42 [TR 87,248]; largely pre-1972; 2 reprints; theme vague.

393 EBraaten Carl E., Our naming of God; problems and prospects of God-talk today. Minneapolis 1989, Fortress. 163 p. $13. – RTS 51

(1990) 565s (T. W. *Tilley*: more past than future); TTod 47 (1990s) 357 (R. H. *King*: from Ch Lutheran).

394 ᴱ**Brennan** Teresa, Between feminism and psychoanalysis. L 1989, Routledge. viii-271 p. $55; pa. $16. – ᴿRelStR 16 (1990) 326 (Kathryn A. *Rabuzzi*).

394* ᴱ**Bresch** Carsten, *al.*, Kann man Gott aus der Natur erkennen? Evolution als Offenbarung: QDisp 125. FrB 1990, Herder. 175 p. DM 36 [TR 87,217, G. L. *Müller*; p. 346 tit. pp.]. 10 art., 3 infra.

395 ᴱ**Brovelli** Franco, Liturgia, temi e autori; saggi di studio sul movimento liturgico: EphLtg subs. 53. R 1990, ed. Liturgiche. 278 p. Lit. 30.000. 6 art. [TR 87,352].

395* ᴱ**Bryant** M. Darrol, *Flinn* Frank, Interreligious dialogue; voices from a new frontier [24 items]. NY 1989, Paragon. xx-234 p. $25. – ᴿTS 51 (1990) 374 (C. *Hallisey*).

396 ᴱ**Cassese** M., Religioni per la pace. R 1987, ASAL. 340 p. Lit. 25.000. – ᴿProtestantesimo 45 (1990) 159s (F. *Ferrario*).

397 ᴱ**Chaunu** Pierre [& 5 art.], The Reformation. Gloucester/NY 1989, A. Sutton/St. Martin's. 296 p. $30/$50. 0-86299-635-X [RelStR 17,168, R. *Kolb*]. – ᴿExpTim 102 (1990s) 58 (P. N. *Brooks*).

398 ᴱ**Cobb** John B.ᴶ, *Ives* Christopher, The emptying God; a Buddhist-Jewish-Christian conversation: Faith Meets Faith. Mkn 1990, Orbis. xx-212 p. $30; pa. $15.

399 ᴱ**Collet** Giancarlo, Theologien der Dritten Welt; ᴇᴀᴛᴡᴏᴛ als Herausforderung westlicher Theologie und Kirche: NZMissW Supp. 37. Immensee 1990. 359 p. Fs 48. – ᴿMüTZ 41 (1990) 389-394 (P. *Schmidt-Leukel*); NRT 112 (1990) 772 (J. *Masson*).

400 ᴱ**Colombo** Giuseppe, L'evidenza e la fede: Quaestio. Mi 1988, Glossa. 470 p. Lit. 48.000. 88-7105-000-2. – ᴿActuBbg 26 (1989) 206 (M. *Cuyás*).

401 **Communio**, Revue catholique internationale 15 (P 1990): **1.** Résurrection de la chair; – **2.** La modernité – et après; – **3s.** L'Europe; – **5.** L'Église dans la ville; – **6.** Former des prêtres; les vingt-cinq ans du Concile. c. 130 p. F 44 chaque.

402 **Concilium** [now Ph/L., Trinity/SCM] (1990) Eng.; **1.** On the threshold of the Third Millennium, ᴱ*Hillyer* P., – **2.** The ethics of world religions and human rights, ᴱ*Küng* H., *Moltmann* J., – **3.** Asking and thanking, ᴱ*Duquoc* C., *Florestan* C.; – **4.** Collegiality put to the test, ᴱ*Provost* J., *Walf* K.; – **5.** Coping with failure, ᴱ*Greinacher* N., *Mette* N.; – **6.** 1492-1992, The voice of the victims, ᴱ*Boff* L., *Elizondo* V. c. 190 p. $13 each. – Italiano 26 (1990). Brescia, Queriniana. Lit. 12.000 each. Français etc.; deutsch = IZT 26.

402* ᴱ**D'Costa** Gavin, Christian uniqueness reconsidered; the myth of a pluralistic theology of religions. Mkn 1990, Orbis. xxii-218 p. $35; pa. $17 [RelStR 17,340, P. C. *Hodgson*].

403 **Dichiarazione** 'Mysterium Filii Dei' (21 febbraio 1972) [documenti authentici ed altri a proposito]: Congregazione per la Fede, DocStudi 1. Vaticano 1989, Editrice. 63 p. [NRT 113,303, A. *Harvengt*].

403* **Dinzelbacher** Peter, *Bauer* Dieter R., Heiligenverehrung in Geschichte und Gegenwart. Ostfildern 1990, Schwabenverlag. 375 p. 3-7996- 0679-2. 18 art.; → 8278, *Kellermann* D.

404 ᴱ**Doré** Joseph, [p. 8-16. 171-216] Sur l'identité chrétienne: Relais-études. P 1990, Desclée. 222 p.; F 125 [Études 374,138, R. *Marlé*].

404* ᴱ**Dudley** Martin, *Rowell* Geoffrey, Confession and absolution. L 1990, SPCK. xii-212 p. $10. – ᴿTLond 93 (1990) 497s (C. J. A. *Hickling*).

405 ᴱ**Dupré** Louis, *Saliers* Don E., Christian spirituality; post-Reformation and modern; EWSp 18. NY 1989, Crossroad. xxvi-566 p. $49.50. – ᴿCathHR 76 (1990) 858-861 (L. *Bouyer*).

406 ᴱ**Fabella** Virginia, *Park Sun Ai Lee,* We dare to dream; doing theology as Asian women: Hong Kong Asian Women's Resource Centre / Manila EATWOT Women's Commission. Mkn 1900, Orbis. x-156 p. $13 [TDig 37,390].

407 ᴱ**Fitzer** Joseph, Romance and the rock; nineteenth century Catholics on faith and reason [14 texts: *Chateaubriand... LeRoy*]: Texts in Modern Theology. Minneapolis 1989, Fortress. ix-386 p. $20. – ᴿTS 51 (1990) 755-7 (P. *Misner*: excellent choice; comments identify too strongly with an approach admitted to be passé).

408 ᴱ**Ford** David F., The modern theologians; an introduction to Christian theology in the twentieth century ➤ 5,1461 [I. individuals, mostly continental; II. types, Britain-US]. Ox 1989, Blackwell. 342 p.; 330 p. £35 each, pa. £11. 0-631-15371-3; 2-1; pa. -6807-9; -8-7. – ᴱExpTim 101,3 top choice (1989s) 65-67 (C. S. *Rodd*).

409 ᴱ**Gannon** Thomas M., World Catholicism in transition. NY 1988, Macmillan. xiv-402 p. $35. – ᴿRelStR 16 (1990) 79 (G. *Gilmore*: first-class sociological reflection).

410 ᴱ**Gelineau** Joseph, Dans vos assemblées; manuel de pastorale liturgique²ʳᵉᵛ [¹1971]. P 1989, Desclée. 688 p. (2. vol.) F 350. – ᴿEsprVie 100 (1990) 359s (P. *Rouillard*).

410* ᴱ**Gelpi** Donald L., Beyond individualism; toward a retrieval of moral discourse in America. ND 1989, Univ. 230 p. $21 [JRel 71,452, M. L. *Cook*].

411 *a)* ᴱ**Gerhards** Albert, Die grössere Hoffnung der Christen; eschatologische Vorstellungen im Wandel: QDisp 127. FrB 1990, Herder. 184 p. [TPhil 65,631].

— *b)* ᴱ**Gesché** A., Création et salut: Publ. 47. Bru 1989, Fac. univ. S.-Louis. 166 p. Fb 550 [NRT 113,616, G. N.].

411* ᴱ**Gilmont** Jean-François, La Réforme et le livre; l'Europe de l'imprimé (1517-v. 1570) [16 auteurs, chacun avec sommaire en anglais]: Histoire. P 1990, Cerf. 533 p. F 120. 2-204-04130-0 [NRT 113,783, B. *Joassart*].

412 ᴱ**Goldingay** John, Signs, worders and healing; When Christians disagree. Leicester 1989, Inter-Varsity. 192 p. £5.50. 0-85110-796-6. – ᴿExpTim 101 (1989s) 54 (J. *Wilkinson*: 3 medics, 3 pastors).

413 ᴱ**Griffin** D., Sacred interconnections. Albany 1990, SUNY. 227 p. [TS 51,572].

414 ᴱ**Griffiths** Paul J., Christianity through non-Christian eyes: Faith Meets Faith. Mkn 1990, Orbis. 286 p. $30; pa. $15. 0-88344-661-8; -2-6. – ᴿExpTim 102 (1990s) 254 (M. *Forward*).

415 ᴱ**Halder** Alois, *al.*, Religionsphilosophie heute; Chancen und Bedeutung in Philosophie und Theologie: Experiment RelPh 3. Dü 1988, Patmos. 395 p. DM 56 pa. – ᴿTLZ 115 (1990) 369-371 (H. *Moritz*).

415* ᴱ**Ranson** Patric, Saint AUGUSTIN; Les dossiers H. P c.1989, L'âge d'homme. 492 p. 39 art.; p. 479-487 *Morello* A.-A., Sous le soleil de Satan, roman augustinien, roman de la grâce. – ᴿRÉAug 35 (1989) 365-8 (G. *Madec*, tit. pp., 'pour assurer un minimum d'objectivité'; 'le choix de Flasch K., Delumeau J. n'est pas innocent').

416 ᴱ**Harvey** Anthony, Theology in the city — a theological response [or rather several] to Faith in the City 1985. L 1989, SPCK. 132 p. £7. – ᴿMonth 250 (1989) 390s (R. *Darwen*).

416* EHauerwas Stanley, *Jones* L. Gregory, Why narrative? Readings in narrative theology. GR 1990, Eerdmans. 367 p. $30 [RelStR 17,147, R. P. *Scharlemann*].

417 *a*) EHeinonen Reijo, *al.*, Religionsunterricht und Dialog zwischen Judentum und Christentum. Åbo 1988, Akademi. 207 p. – RNorTTs 90 (1989) 124-6 (Sigurd *Hjelde*).

— *b*) EHogg J., Die Ausbreitung kartäusischen Lebens und Geistes im Mittelalter, I: AnalCart 63. Salzburg/Lewiston NY 1990, Inst. Anglistik/Mellen. 250 p.; 9 fig. [RHE 86, p. 237*].

417* *a*) EHorgan Thaddeus D., Walking together; Roman Catholics and ecumenism twenty-five years after Vatican II. GR 1990, Eerdmans. xii-148 p. $13 [TR 87,171].

— *b*) EHorosz William, *Clements* Tad, Religion and human purpose. Dordrecht 1987, Nijhoff. 307 p. $64.50. – RCritRR 2 (1989) 474-6 (J. H. *Whittaker*).

418 EHorton Michael, The agony of deceit; what some TV preachers are really teaching. Ch 1989, Moody. 266 p. $13. – RBS 147 (1990) 503s (F. D. *Lindsay*: Reformed Covenant discrediting of gaudy superficiality of much contemporary televangelism).

419 EHsia Po-Chia, The German people and the Reformation. Ithaca 1988, Cornell Univ. 303 p. $33. – RSixtC 21 (1990) 293s (B. *Nischan*).

420 Hunt Richard A., *al.*, Clergy assessment and career development [35 essays on testing candidates for ordained ministry]. Nv 1990, Abington. 224 p. $20 [RelStR 17,135, S. S. *Ivy*].

421 EHutchison William R., Between the times. C 1989, Univ. 332 p. $39.50. – RTTod 47 (1990s) 190.192s (E. B. *Holifield*).

421* EIdel Moshe, *McGinn* Bernard, Mystical union and monotheistic faith, an ecumenical dialogue. NY 1989, Macmillan. iv-252 p. $30 [CritRR 4,258 260, G. H. *Tavard*].

422 EJacobs J., Is Pinksteren voorbij? Het tweede Vaticaans oecumenisch concilie tussen geschiedenis en actualiteit. Hilversum 1989, Gooi & S. 111 p. ƒ19,50. 90-304-0508-2. – RTsTNijm 30 (1990) 97 (F. van *Leeuwen*).

422* EKer Ian, *Hill* Alan G., NEWMAN after a hundred years. Ox 1990, Clarendon. xvi-470 p. $85. 22 authors [TS 52,563, G. *Magill*].

423 EKienzler K., Der neue Fundamentalismus; Rettung oder Gefahr für Gesellschaft und Religion?: Bayer. Kath. Akad. 136. Dü 1990, Patmos. 124 p. DM 26,80. 3-491-77794-1. – RTsTNijm 30 (1990) 428s (P. A. van *Gennip*).

424 EKing Edward B., *Schaefer* Jacqueline T., Saint AUGUSTINE and his influence in the Middle Ages 3. Sewanee TE 1988, Univ. South. 124 p. – RSpeculum 65 (1990) 795s (tit. pp.).

425 EKirkpatrick Dow, Faith born in the struggle for life; a rereading of Protestant faith in Latin America today [25 art.]. GR/Exeter 1988, Eerdmans/Paternoster. xv-328 p. £11.75. 0-8028-0355-5. – RExpTim 101 (1989s) 350 (A. *Kee*).

426 EKunstenaar Marion T., Der eigene Freiraum; Frauen in Synagoge und Kirche [ned.], TMünden Ursula. Offenbach 1989, Burckhardt. 160 p. DM 18. 5 Art. [2 Jüd.; 3 Kath.]. – RKIsr 5 (1990) 81s (Julie *Kirchberg*).

426* ELimouris Gennadios, Icons, windows on eternity; theology and spirituality in color [essays by 29 authors]. Geneva 1990, WCC. x-228 p.; 16 pl. – RTS 51 (1990) 745-7 (J. L. *Empereur*).

427 ᴱLittell Franklin H., A half century of religious dialogue 1939-1989; making the circles larger: TorStT 46. Lewiston NY 1989, Mellen. 355 p. $70 [TR 87,347]. 0-88946-926-1.

427* ᴱLuneau René, *Ladrière* Paul, Le rêve de Compostelle; vers la restauration d'une Europe chrétienne? P 1989, Centurion. 366 p. – ᴿScEsp 42 (1990) 375-380 (J. *Grand'maison*: résolument contre le néo-triomphalisme de RATZINGER, ETCHEGARAY, JEAN-PAUL II... 'une théologie romaine inacceptable'; mais laissant plusieurs points sous silence).

428 ᴱMackey James P., An introduction to Celtic Christianity. E 1989, Clark. 440 p. £20. – ᴿIrBSt 12 (1990) 195-8 (R. B. *Knox*).

428* ᴱMainwaring Scott, *Wilde* Alexander, The progressive Church in Latin America: Helen Kellogg Institute project (8 art.). ND 1989, Univ. xii-340 p. $33. – ᴿMissiology 18 (1990) 478s (sr. T. M. *O'Reilly*).

429 ᴱMangum John M., The new faith-science debate; probing cosmology, technology, and theology. Mp/Geneva 1989, Augsburg-Fortress/WCC. cx-165 p. – ᴿRelStR 16 (1990) 529 (D. W. *Musser*).

430 ᴱMarshall Paul A., *al.*, Stained glass; worldviews and social science [Amst (Reformed) Free Univ.; Toronto Institute for Christian Studies]. Lanham MD 1989, UPA. 187 p. $12.50. – ᴿTorJT 6 (1990) 119-121 (M. J. *Schuck*).

431 ᴱMarx Jacques, Religion et tabou sexuel: ProbHistR. Bru 1990, Univ. 159 p. 2-8004-1018-3. 12 art.

431* ᴱMarz Bernd, Alles für Gott? Priester sein zwischen Anspruch und Wirklichkeit. Dü 1990, Patmos. 208 p. DM 29,80 [TR 87,438].

432 ᴱMennekes Friedhelm, Zwischen Kunst und Kirche; Beiträge zum Thema Das Christusbild im Menschenbild [cf. infra ➤ d514, *Grinten*; auch ➤ 1,b996]. Stu 1985, KBW. 276 p. DM 9,80. 3-460-32361-2. – ᴿBijdragen 51 (1990) 100s (J. *Besemer*).

432* *a)* ᴱMoore Robert J., Carl JUNG and Christian spirituality [12 reprints]. NY 1988, Paulist. xii-252 p. $13 [RelStR 17,334, H. *Coward*]. – *b)* ᴱwith *Meckel* Daniel J., Jung and Christianity in dialogue; faith, feminism, and hermeneutics: Jung and spirituality. NY 1990, Paulist. ix-265 p. $13 pa. 0-8091-3187-0 [TDig 38,273]. 12 art.

433 Neufeld K. H., ᵀᴱ*Ullrich* Lothar, Probleme und Perspektiven dogmatischer Theologie. Lp 1986, St. Benno. 558 p. – ᴿTrierTZ 98 (1989) 236s (A. *Dahm*).

434 ᴱNeuhaus Richard J., The believable futures of American Protestantism: Encounter 7. GR 1988, Eerdmans. ix-154 p. $9 pa. – ᴿCalvinT 25 (1990) 107s (J. D. *Bratt*).

435 ᴱNeumann Peter H. A., 'Religionsloses Christentum': WegFor 204. Da 1990, Wiss. – ᴿNorTTs 91 (1990) 185s (T. *Wyller*).

436 ᴱNichol Todd, *Kolden* Marc, Called and ordained; Lutheran perspectives on the office of the ministry. Minneapolis 1990, Augsburg Fortress. xii-226 p. $15 pa. – ᴿCurrTMiss 17 (1990) 466s (T. *Peters*: fracas quelled or increased?).

437 ᴱNiemann F. J., Jesus der Offenbarer I-II Texte zur T.; Fundamentaltheologie 5,1s. Graz 1990, Steyer. 151 p.; 216 p. je DM 29,80. – ᴿMüTZ 41 (1990) 400 (A. *Kreiner*).

438 ᴱOelmüller W., Theodizee — Gott vor Gericht? Mü 1990, Fink. 120 p. DM 28. – ᴿOrientierung 54 (1990) 243-5 (C.-F. *Geyer*).

439 ᴱOhlig K., Christologie I-II: Texte zur Theologie, Dogmatik 4,1s. Graz 1989, Styria. 227 p., 239 p. je DM 29,80. – ᴿMüTZ 41 (1990) 302s (A. *Kreiner*).

440 ᴱOkure Teresa, *Thiel* Paul van, *al.*, Inculturation of Christianity in Africa [32 art., mostly < AfER]: Spearhead 112-4. Eldoret 1990, Gaba. 259 p. [TContext 8/2, 134, H. *Janssen*].

441 ᴱPacker J. L., *Fromer* P., The best in theology [1. -] 2. Carol Stream IL c. 1989, ChrTod. 0-91746-318-8. – ᴿJStOT 48 (1990) 126s (R. S. *Hess*: on OT, 4 review articles).

441* ᴱPelikan Jaroslav, The world treasury of modern religious thought. Boston 1990, Little Brown. 635 p. £19. – ᴿPrPeo 4 (1990) 423-5 (E. *Hulmes*).

442 ᴱPeter Rodolphe †, *Roussel* Bernard, Le livre et la Réforme ⇒ 4,k112 [= Revue française d'histoire du livre, fasc. 50]. Bordeaux 1987, Bibliophiles de Guyenne. 278 p. – ᴿBibHumRen 51 (1989) 508-510 (Irena *Backus*).

443 ᴱPeters Ted, Cosmos as creation; theology and science in consonance [Berkeley IGM science center lectures]. Nv 1989, Abingdon. 288 p. – ᴿTS 51 (1990) 568s (F. R. *Haig* praises especially I. BARBOUR).

444 ᴱPlaskow Judith, *Christ* Carol P., Weaving the visions; new patterns in feminist spirituality. SF 1989, Harper. viii-359 p. $30; pa. $13. – ᴿJRel 70 (1990) 276s (Joann W. *Conn*).

445 ᴱReese Thomas J., Episcopal conferences; historical, canonical, and theological studies. Wsh 1989, Georgetown Univ. xii-296 p. $20. – ᴿHomPast 90,7 (1989s) 71s (K. *Baker*: all ten articles oppose the Roman position); NewTR 3,4 (1990) 110s (J. M. *Huels*).

446 **Riccardi** Andrea, *al.*, Stranieri nostri fratelli, verso una solidarietà multirazziale. Brescia 1989, Morcelliana. 175 p. Lit. 16.000. – ᴿSapienza 43 (1990) 467s (B. *Belletti*).

447 ᴱRobbins Thomas, *Anthony* Dick, In gods we trust; new patterns of religious pluralism in America²ʳᵉᵛ. New Brunswick NJ 1990, Transaction. xiv-544 p. $23 pa. 0-88738-800-9 [TDig 38,167: expanded (to) 22 essays].

448 ᴱRobinson-Hammerstein Helga. The transmission of ideas in the Lutheran Reformation. Dublin 1989, Irish Academic. 192 p. [RelStR 17,169, J. L. *Farthing*].

449 ᴱRothschild Fritz A., Jewish perspectives on Christianity [*Baeck* L., *Buber* M., *Rosenzweig* F., *Herberg* W., *Heschel* A., each with a Christian reaction]. NY 1990, Crossroad. x-363 p. $29.50. 0-8245-0937-4 [TDig 38,168].

450 ᴱRuether R., *Keller* R., Women and religion in America 3, 1900-1968. SF 1990, Harper & R. 409 p. $16 [JAAR 58,161].

451 ᴱRuf Henry, Religion, ontotheology and deconstruction. NY 1989, Paragon. xiii-238 p. $25; pa. $13 [CritRR 4,463s, R. S. *Gall*].

452 ᴱSauter Gerhard, Rechtfertigung als Grundbegriff evangelischer Theologie; Textsammlung: TBü 78. Mü 1989, Kaiser. 322 p. DM 38 pa. 3-459-01741-4 [TLZ 115,138] – ᴿTsTNijm 30 (1990) 215 (G. P. *Hartvelt*].

453 ᴱSchaffenorth G., *Thraede* K., 'Freunde in Christus werden ...' Die Beziehung von Mann und Frau als Frage in Theologie und Kirche. B 1977, Stein. 146 p. [TrierTZ 98,227].

454 ᴱSchaumberger Christine, *Maassen* Monika, Handbuch feministischer Theologie. Münster 1986, Morgana. 415 p. DM 29,80 [EvKomm 23, 348].

455 **Schaumberger** Christine, *Schottroff* Luise, Schuld und Macht; Studien zu einer feministischen Befreiungstheologie, mit Bibelstellenregister. Mü

1988, Kaiser. 296 p. DM 49. – ᴿEvKomm 22,10 (1989) 52 (Hildburg *Wegener*).

456 ᴱ**Schroeder** W. Widick, *Gamwell* Franklin I., Economic life; process interpretations and critical responses: Studies in Religion and Society. Ch 1988, Center ScStRel. 269 p. $27; pa. $16. – ᴿJRel 70 (1990) 472s (G. *Dorrien*).

456* ᴱ**Smith** Joseph, *Handelman* Susan A., Psychoanalysis and religion [12 art.]: Psychiatry and the Humanities 11. Baltimore 1990, Johns Hopkins Univ. xxi-252 p. $36 [CritRR 4,417, R. L. *Underwood*].

457 Solidaridad, nuevo nombre de la paz; comentario interdisciplinar a la encíclica 'Sollicitudo rei socialis'. Bilbao 1989, Mensajero. 213 p. – ᴿRET 50 (1990) 93s (L. *González-Carvajal Santabárbara*).

458 ᴱ**Strain** Charles R., Prophetic visions and economic realities; Protestants, Jews, and Catholics confront the bishops' letter on the economy. GR 1989, Eerdmans. 257 p. $14 pa. – ᴿCalvinT 25 (1990) 310-313 (S. V. *Monsma*: a document and a book that can help all faiths in their striving for economic justice).

459 ᴱ**Swatos** William H.ᴶ, Time, place, and circumstance; [eleven] neo-Weberian studies in comparative religious history [... Judges in Israel, charismatic authority]: Contributions to the study of religion 24. Westport CT 1990, Greenwood. xii-229 p. $40. 0-313-26892-4 [TDig 38,90].

460 ᴱ**Tennekes** J., *Vroom* H. M., Contextualiteit en christelijk geloof: Amst VU Bezinningscentrum 19. Kampen 1989, Kok. 176 p. ƒ34,50. 90-242-538-96. – ᴿTsTNijm 30 (1990) 424 (G. J. W. van *Rossum*).

461 ᴱ**Thistlethwaite** Susan B., *Engel* Mary P., Lift every voice; constructing Christian [liberation] theologies from the underside. SF 1990, Harper & R. v-329 p. $16. 0-06-067992-1 [NTAbs 35,136].

462 ᴱ**Tillman** William M.ᴶ, Understanding Christian ethics; an interpretive approach [13 art.]. Nv 1988, Broadman. 286 p. – ᴿSWJT 33,2 (1990s) 51 (B. *Dominy*: BELLINGER W. H. OT, LEA Thomas O. NT: models of conciseness).

462* ᴱ**Vesey** Godfrey, The philosophy in Christianity [14 invited papers]. C 1990, Univ. xvi-244 p. £11. 0-521-37578-9. – ᴿExpTim 102 (1990s) 154 (D. P. *Pailin*).

463 ᴱ**Vorgrimler** H., Gotteslehre I-II: Texte zur Theologie, Dogmatik 2,1s. Graz 1989, Styria. 135 p.; 215 p. je DM 29,80. – ᴿMüTZ 41 (1990) 302s (A. *Kreiner*).

464 ᴱ**Walker** Andrew, Different gospels; Christian orthodoxy and modern theologies: C. S. Lewis centre. L 1989, Hodder & S. 253 p. £8. 0-340-42631-4. – ᴿExpTim 101 (1989s) 56s (B. G. *Powley*); Tablet 243 (1989) 1060 (J. *Todd*: Christianity must use contemporary language, but along with it come assumptions).

465 ᴱ**Weinrich** Michael, Theologiekritik in der Neuzeit; theologische Texte aus den 18. bis 20. Jh.: Reader Theologie. Gü 1988, Mohn. 191 p. DM 34. 3-579-00294-5. – ᴿActuBbg 26 (1989) 61 (J. *Boada*).

465* **Wimbush** Vincent L., Ascetic behavior in Greco-Roman antiquity; a sourcebook: Studies in Antiquity and Christianity. Mp 1990, Fortress. xxviii-514 p. $42. 0-8006-3105-6.

466 **Zimoń** H., ⊕ Z badań... Researches on religion and popular religiosity [ᶠLublin Univ. chair of History/Ethnology of Religions 1958-88]. Wsz 1988, Verbinum [Antonianum 65,390, C. *Teklak*].

467 ᴱZinser Hartmut, Religionswissenschaft; eine Einführung. B 1988, Reimer. 300 p. DM 29,50. 3-4960-0935-7. – ᴿNedTTs 44 (1990) 334s (J. G. *Platvoet*); RHR 207 (1990) 413-6 (A. *Caquot*).

A1.5 *Plurium compilationes* **philologicae** *vel* **archaeologicae.**

467* a) Las abreviaturas en la enseñanza medieval y la transmisión del saber. Barc 1990, Univ. [AcPIB 9/7, 551].
— b) ᴱAllen Jeffner, *Young* Iris M., The thinking muse; feminism and modern French philosophy [by 10 American feminists]. Bloomington 1989, Indiana Univ. 215 p. $32.50; pa. $12 [CritRR 4,484-6, Ladelle *McWhorter*].
468 ᴱAngeli Bernardini Paola, Lo sport in Grecia: Storia e società. Bari 1988, Laterza. xxxvii-262 p.; 27 pl. 10 art. – ᴿRFgIC 118 (1990) 303-6 (M. *Vetta*).
468* Asali K. J., Jerusalem in history. Buckhurst Hill 1989, Scorpion. 295 p. [RB 98,632: 300-63 B.C. by *Franken* H. J., *Mendenhall* G.; Roman-Byzantine by *Wilkinson* J.].
469 ᴱBaldi Philip, Linguistic change and reconstruction methodology [Workshop Stanford July 1987]: Trends in Linguistics 45. B 1990, Mouton-G. xii-752 p. 0-89925-546-9. – *Hodge* Carleton T., The role of Egyptian within Afroasiatic.
470 ᴱBapty Ian, *Yates* Tim, Archaeology after structuralism; post-structuralism and the practice of archaeology. L 1990, Routledge. xii-314 p. 9-415- 04500-2. 10 art., 2 infra.
470* Becker-Colonna Andreina, *al.*, Akhenaton; la caduta degli dèi [Testi]. R 1990, Cirua. 176 p.; ill.
471 ᴱBender Thomas, The university and the city, from medieval origins to the present. NY 1988, Oxford-UP. x-316 p. £30. 0-19-505273-0. – ᴿJEH 41 (1990) 100s (A. R. *Cobban*).
472 ᴱBenedetti Gaetano, *Rauchfleisch* Udo, Welt der Symbole, Interdisziplinäre Aspekte des Symbolverständnisses. Gö 1988, VR. 253 p. DM 29. – ᴿTZBas 45 (1990) 381s (W. *Neidhart*).
473 ᴱBinder G., *Effe* B., Krieg und Friede im Altertum. Trier 1989, Wiss.-V. 245 p. – ᴿGymnasium 97 (1990) 277s (L. *Voit*).
474 ᴱBinder Gerhard, Saeculum Augustum [I. 1987 ⇸ 3,483] II. Religion und Literatur: WegFor 512, 1988 ⇸ 4,436; ᴿRPg 63 (1989) 346-8 (A. *Vassileiou*).
475 Buonocore M., [cf. ⇸ 4,g823] Miscellanea Bibliothecae Apostolicae Vaticanae I-III: ST 329.331.333. Vaticano 1987, Bibliotheca. 260 p.; 2 fig.; 22 pl. / 329 p.; 17 fig.; 10 pl. / 370 p.; 55 pl. [RHE 85, p. 286*].
475* ᴱBuonocore M., Miscellanea Bibliothecae Apostolicae Vaticanae IV: ST 338. Vaticano 1990. 399 p.; ill. 88-210-0626-3. 14 art.; p. 365-383, *Sheehan* William, Hebrew incunabula (Nᵒ 1-12, Biblia); p. 89-129, *Izbicki* T., Ecclesiological mss.
476 ᴱCameron A., History as text; the writing of ancient history. L 1989, Duckworth. 208 p. [ByZ 83,144].
478 ᴱCavallo Guglielmo, Le Biblioteche nel mondo antico e medievale 1988 (²1989) ⇸ 5,538b; 88-420-3256-5; 8 art., 5 infra. – ᴿViPe 72 (1989) 72-74 (Alessandra *Tarabochia Canavero*).
479 ᴱClarke G., *al.*, Reading the past in late antiquity. Rushcutters Bay 1990, Pergamon/Australian Natl. Univ. xv-370 p., map [RHE 85,184*]. 0-08-034407-0.

480 ᴱCohen Ralph, The future of literary theory. NY 1990, Routledge. xx-445 p. $20 [RelStR 17,246, R. *Detweiler*].

481 ᴱDentzer Jean-Marie, *Orthmann* Winfried, Archéologie et histoire de la Syrie [I...] II. La Syrie de l'époque achéménide à l'avènement de l'Islam: SchrVorderasArch 1. Saarbrücken 1989, S-DV. 579 p.; 216 fig.; 9 maps. 3-925036-34-2. 30 art., infra. – ᴿAntClas 59 (1990) 594-6 (C. *Delvoye*).

482 ᴱDijk Teun Van, Discourse and literature; new approaches to the analysis of literary genres [12 art.]: Critical Theory 3. Amst 1985, Benjamins. vi-245 p. – ᴿRBgPg 68 (1990) 761-3 (J. *Walravens*).

483 ᴱDonadoni Sergio, L'uomo egiziano: Storia e società. R 1990, Laterza. xi-348 p. Lit. 35.000. 88-420-3662-5. 9 art.; plures infra.

484 ᴱEaton-Krauss Marianne, *Graefe* Erhart, Studien zur ägyptischen Kunstgeschichte: HildÄgBeit 29. Hildesheim 1990, Gerstenberg. x-113 p.; ill.

485 ᴱFisiak Jacek, Historical linguistics and philology: Trends in Linguistics 46. B 1990, Mouton-G. xi-401 p.

485* *a*) ᴱFronzaroli Pelio, Miscellanea eblaitica 2/3 = Quaderni di Semitistica 16/17. F 1989s, Univ. vi-203 p.; 7 art.; infra [vol. 3 è un solo studio di *Conti* G. ⇢ e316a].

— *b*) ᴱGitin S., *Dever* W., Recent excavations in Israel; studies in Iron Age archaeology 1989 ⇢ 5,543 [BL 92,32, K. W. *Whitelam*; ZAW 103,455, tit. pp.: p. 23-58 Ekron-Miqne].

— *c*) ᴱGarnier Bernard, *al.*, Introduction à la métrologie historique. P 1989, Economica. – ᴿRHist 292 (1989) 423s (Lucie *Fossier*).

486 ᴱHaas Jonathan, The anthropology of [pre-state] war. C 1990, Univ. xiv-242 p. $30. 0-521- 38042-1 [Antiquity 65,133].

486* ᴱHackett John, Warfare in the ancient world. L 1989, Sidgwick & J. 256 p.; ill. 0-283-99591-2. 11 art., 4 infra.

487 ᴱHalperin David M., *al.*, Before sexuality; the construction [... via politics, medicine, customs] of the erotic experience in the ancient Greek world. Princeton 1990, Univ. xx-526 p.; ill. $59.50. 0-691-03538-5 [Antiquity 64,941].

488 ᴱHarmatta J., From Alexander the Great to Kül Tegin; studies in Bactrian, Pahlavi, Sanskrit...: Coll. Sources Pre-Islamic Central Asia 4. Budapest 1990, Akad. 215 p.; ill. 963-05-5539-5. 3 art. infra.

488* ᴱHerzog Reinhart, Restauration und Erneuerung; die lateinische Literatur von 284 bis 374 n.Chr.: HbAltW 8/5. Mü 1989, Beck. xxix-559 p. [RHE 86, p. 388-393, W. *Evenepoel*].

489 ᴱIrmscher Johannes, Einführung in die klassischen Altertumswissenschaften. B 1986, VEB. 356 p. – ᴿSileno 15 (1989) 297-300 (E. V. *Maltese*).

489* James P. J., *al.*, Studies in ancient chronology 1, Bronze to Iron Age chronology in the Old World; time for a reassessment? L 1990, Univ. Inst. Archaeology. 143 p.; 4 maps. £8. – ᴿBAnglsr 10 (1990s) 96-99 (R. M. *Porter*).

490 ᴱKaltenbrunner Gerd-Klaus, Im Anfang war das Spiel; Schöpfertum und Glück zwischen Arbeit und Freizeit: Initiative 71. FrB 1987, Herder. DM 12,80. – ᴿTPQ 137 (1989) 109s (C. *Schacherreiter*).

491 ᴱKelso William M., *Most* Rachel, Earth patterns; essays in landscape archaeology. Charlottesville 1990, Univ. Virginia. ix-319 p.

492 ᴱKemp Peter, *Thill* Georges, Le triomphe des biotechnologies; la domestication de l'animal humain. Namur 1988, Presses Univ. – ᴿRNouv 46,4 (1990) 93 (D. *Vinck*).

493 ᴱLamberg-Karlovsky C.C., Archaeological thought in America. NY 1989, Cambridge-UP. 357 p.; 35 fig. – ᴿAJA 94 (1990) 679s (P.N. *Kardulias*).

494 ᴱLaurens Anne-France, Entre hommes et dieux; le convive, le héros, le prophète: AnnLitt Besançon 391. P 1989, BLettres. 199 p.; 18 fig. – ᴿAntClas 59 (1990) 433s (Vinciane *Pirenne-Delforges*).

495 ᴱMojsisch Burkhard, Sprachphilosophie in Antike und Mittelalter: Bochumer Studien zur Philosophie 3. Amst 1986, Grüner. vii-448 p. $38. – ᴿJAOS 110 (1990) 356-360 (R.M. *Frank*: mostly on Aristotelian-Arabic confrontation: ENDRESS G., KUHN W.).

496 *a*) Les mystères de l'archéologie; les sciences à la recherche du passé. Lyon 1990, Presses Univ. / Caisse Monum. Hist. 387 p. [RArchéom 14,109].

— *b*) ᴱScarcia Amoretti Biancamaria, Sguardi sulla cultura sciita nel Deccan / Glances on Shi'ite Deccan culture: RSO 64.1s (1990) 236 p. 8 art.; Eng. summaries p. 235s.

497 ᴱNewmeyer Frederick J., Linguistics; the Cambridge survey; I. Linguistic theory; [II.] III. Language, psychological and biological aspects; [IV.]. C 1983, Univ. x-500 p.; ix-350 p. – ᴿBSLP 84,2 (1989) 148-151 (P. *Swiggers*: tit. pp.).

498 ᴱ[Schmitt] **Pantel** Pauline, Storia delle donne in occidente I. L'antichità, ᴱ*Duby* Georges, *Perrot* Michelle, ᵀ*Cataldi Villari* Fausta, *al.* [II-V (*al.*)]. Bari 1990, Laterza. xvii-598 p. Lit. 45.000. 88-420-3659-5. 11 art., 4 infra.

499 **Piazzoni** A.M., *Vian* P., Manoscritti Vaticani latini 14666-15203, catalogo sommario: ST 332. Vaticano 1989, Biblioteca. xxviii-305 p. [RHE 85,189*].

500 ᴱRast Walter E., (*Zeiger* Marion) Preliminary reports of ASOR-sponsored excavations 1983-7: BASOR supp. 26. Baltimore 1990, Johns Hopkins Univ. 177 p.; ill. 0003-097X. 5 art., infra.

500* ᴱSchindler S., *Zimprich* H., Ökologie der Perinatalzeit [... vorgeburtliches Seelenleben]. Stu 1989, Hippokrates. 211 p. DM 98 [TR 87,415, K. *Thomas*: hardly adds to GRABER, HAU, RASKOVSKY, VERNY; no theological advertence].

501 ᴱSimpson W.K., Religion and philosophy in ancient Egypt: Yale Egyptological Studies 3. NHv/Wmr 1989, Yale Univ./Aris & P. xii-159 p. £21. 0-912532-18-1 / 0-85668-520-8 [BL 91,130, N. *Wyatt*].

502 ᴱThompson H.O., Archaeology in Jordan: AmUnivSt 9/55. NY 1989, Lang. xvii-283 p. Fs 89. – ᴿZAW 102 (1990) 461 (tit. pp.).

503 ᴱTreuil René, *al.*, Les civilisations égéennes du Néolithique et de l'Âge du Bronze: Nouvelle Clio 1-ter. P 1989, PUF. 633 p.; 64 fig.; 8 maps. F 198. 2-13-042280-2. – ᴿAntClas 59 (1990) 498-473 (C. *Delvoye*).

504 ᴱTuana Nancy, Feminism and science [14 essays from Hypatia, a Journal of Feminist Philosophy]. Bloomington 1989, Indiana Univ. xi-249 p. [RelStR 17,137, Kathryn A. *Rabuzzi*: Helen LONGINO's 'Can there be a feminist science?' spells it out with terms like 'pion' and 'muon'].

505 ᴱWinquist Charles E., The archaeology of the imagination: JAAR Thematic Studies 48/2 (no date; citations only to 1979). 118 p. 8 art. [*Altizer* T., *Crossan* J., *Funk* R. ...].

A2 **Acta** *congressuum* .1 **biblica** [*Notitiae, reports* ➔ Y7.2].

506 *Ablondi* Alberto present. [Di *Sante* Carmine, *al.*, 10 discorsi, Roma] Ebrei ed ebraismo nel Nuovo Testamento: Assoc. Ebr.-Cr. R 1989s,

Dehoniane. I. 73 p.; II. 125 p.; III. (1990) 141 p. Lit. 16.000; 13.000; 12.000. 88-396-0270-4; -265-8; -304-2. 5 + 5 + 5 art.; 9 infra. – ᴿAsprenas 37 (1990) 496-9 (V. *Scippa*).

506* ᴱ**Amersfoort** J. van, *Oort* J. van, Juden und Christen in der Antike [Patristische Arbeitsgemeinschaft, Utrecht 2.-5. Jan. 1989. Kampen 1990, Kok. 150 p. 90-242-4926-0. 8 art.; infra.

507 ᴱ**Assaf** David, The Bible and its world; proceedings of the Tenth World Congress of Jewish studies, J August 16-24, 1989; division A. J 1990, World Union of Jewish Studies. 284 p. + ◐ 134 [+ 6 other volumes]. 0333-9068 [OIAc S90].

508 — ᴱ**Assaf**, Proceedings of the Tenth World Congress of Jewish Studies, Aug. 16-24, 1989; B. History of the Jewish People; 1. ◐; 2. J 1990, World Union. 612 p.; 590 p. 0333-9068 [OIAc Oc90].

509 — **Cohen** Susie, Index of the Proceedings of the World Congress of Jewish Studies, First (1947) to Eighth (1981). J 1985, World Union of Jewish Studies. [xiv-] 120 p. 0333-9068.

510 ᴱ**Babcock** William S., Paul and the legacies of Paul [Southern Methodist/Dallas University conference 1987]. Dallas 1990, SMU. xxviii-426 p. $32.50; pa. $17. 0-87074-305-8; -6-6 [CritRR 4,496, tit. pp.].

511 ᴱ**Backus** Iréna, *Higman* F., Théorie et pratique de l'exégèse; Actes du IIIᵉ colloque international sur l'histoire de l'exégèse biblique au XVIᵉ s. (Genève, 31 août - 2 septembre 1988). Genève 1990, Droz. 449 p. [ÉTRel 66,606s, H. *Bost*; RHE 85,370*].

512 ᴱ**Bar-Asher** Moshe, ◐ *Meḥqarim* ... Studies in Jewish language; Bible translations and spoken languages: Actes du IIᵉ Congrès international du Misgav Yerushalayim, Institut de recherche sur le judaïsme sépharade et oriental. J 1986. 62 p. + ◐ 161 p. – ᴿRÉJ 149 (1990) 194-6 (C. *Aslanoff*).

513 Bible et Informatique; méthodes, outils, résultats; Actes du Second Congrès international, Jérusalem 9-13 juin 1988: Debora 5. P/Genève 1989, Champion-Slatkine. 655 p. 37 art. – ᴿRTLv 21 (1990) 360 (P.-M. *Bogaert*).

514 BIBLIA, associazione laica di cultura biblica; convegni [1986-9 ➤ 5,563]: *a*) *Fiores d'Arcais* Francesco, moderatore, Giacobbe, o l'avventura del figlio minore: Bocca di Magra, 9-12.II.1989; 192 p.; 9 art.; infra. – *b*) *Stefani* Piero, moderatore, Un libro, molte letture; leggere la Bibbia oggi: Napoli 28-30.IV.1989; 110 p. – *c*) La violenza nella Bibbia: Mantova 31.III - 1.IV.1990; 128 p.; 6 art.; infra. Settimello Fi 1990, Biblia.

514* ᴱ**Blaisdell** Charles R., Conservative, moderate, liberal; the biblical authority debate [Christian Theol. Sem. Sept. 27-28, 1989]. St. Louis 1990, 'CBP'. xix-136 p. $15 pa. [JBL 110,565].

515 ᴱ**Blau** J., Academy of the Hebrew Language, 100th anniversary: two panel sessions of Tenth World Congress (J 1989) = Lešonenu 54,2-4 (1989s) xvii + p. 97-325.

516 ᴱ**Botha** J. E., Reading Revelation [Unisa seminar 1987]. Pretoria 1988, van Schaik. 160 p. r 19.75. – ᴿNeotestamentica 24 (1990) 157s (J. G. van der *Watt*).

517 ᴱ**Bourgeois** H., *Gibert* P., *Jourjon* M. [enseignement interdisciplinaire Fac. cath. Lyon, 1985s], La cause des Écritures; l'autorité des Écritures en Christianisme. Lyon 1989, Fac. cath. 128 p. – ᴿEspVie 100 (1990) 537s (L. *Walter*); RHPR 70 (1990) 484 (A. *Benoît*).

518 ᴱ**Brekelmans** Christian, *Lust* Johan, Pentateuchal and Deuteronomistic Studies: IOSOT Congress 13, Aug. 27 - Sept. 1, 1989: BiblETL 94. Lv

1990, Univ./Peeters. 307 p. 90-6186-423-2 / Peeters 90-6831-306-1 [NRT 113,905, J.-L. *Ska*; TsTNijm 31,426, A. van *Wieringen*]. 22 art.; infra.

518* ᴱ**Brinner** William M., *Ricks* Stephen D., Studies in Islamic and Judaic traditions [four Denver Univ. meetings 1981 (➤ 3,523; 5,b127) - 1984]: BrownJudSt 110.178. Atlanta 1986/9, Scholars. xiii-273 p.; xi-247 p. $29; pa. $25; $54. 1-55540-047-7, -8-5; -373-5 [TDig 38,190].

519 ᴱ**Brooke** George J., *Lindars* Barnabas †, Septuagint, scrolls and cognate writings, international symposium Manchester 1990: SeptCog 33. Atlanta 1990, Scholars. viii-657 p. $45; pa./sb. $30. 17 art., infra.

519* ᴱ**Brooks** R., *Collins* J.J., Hebrew Bible or Old Testament? Studying the Bible in Judaism and Christianity [ND conference 1989]: Christianity and Judaism in antiquity 5. ND 1990, Univ. xiv-242 p. 0-268-01090-0 [BL 92,103, A.G. *Auld*; but Josephine M. FORD develops *her* themes; NTAbs 35,123].

520 [ᴱ**Cazelles** Henri,] Unité et diversité dans l'Église; texte officiel de la Commission Biblique Pontificale [réunion annuelle] et travaux personnels des membres: Teologia & Filosofia 15. Vatican 1989, Editrice. 348 p. Lit. 40.000. 88-209-1643-6 [BL 91,121, B.P. *Robinson*]. – ᴿNRT 112 (1990) 894 (X. *Jacques*).

521 ᴱ**Collins** Raymond F., The Thessalonian correspondence: Colloquium Biblicum Lovaniense XXXVIII, Aug. 16-18, 1988: BiblETL 98. Lv 1990, Univ./Peeters. xv-546 p. Fb 3000. 90-6186-329-5 / 90-6831-262-6. 37 art.; infra [NRT 113,764-6, X. *Jacques*, titres sans pp.].

521* Colloquium on transportation in biblical research in the 19th-20th centuries, Jerusalem 10-13 Sept. 1984. Strasbourg 1984, European Science Foundation. 39 p. [abstracts: KirSef 62 (1988s) p. 25].

522 ᴱ**Dahan** Gilbert, *Nahon* Gérard, La culture juive en France du Nord au moyen âge, de Rashi aux Tosafistes, le Talmud de France; colloque internat. (Paris-Troyes, 3-5 déc. 1990], 'Argument' [program and summaries]: RÉJ 149 (1990) 459-530.

522* ᴱ**Dan** J., The age of the Zohar: Proceedings of 3d International Conference on the History of Jewish Mysticism [1st 1986; 2d 1987 ➤ 5,578]: Jerusalem Studies in Jewish Thought 8 (1989) [JStJud 21,327]; 250-298, *Gruenwald* J., From Talmudic to Zoharic homiletics (p. 277-284 on Nm 6).

523 ᴱ**Donnelly** Doris, Mary, woman of Nazareth; biblical and theological perspectives [ND symposium 1988]. NY 1990, Paulist. iii-188 p. $10 pa. [Horizons 18,337s, F.M. *Jelly*].

524 ᴱ**Dungan** David L., The interrelations of the Gospels; a symposium led by M.-É. *Boismard*, Jerusalem 1984: BiblETL 95. Lv 1990, Univ./ Peeters. xxxi-672 p. Fb 3000. 90-6186-396-1 / P 90-6831-261-8. 22 art., some with response [RB 98,451, tit. pp.; TPQ 139,121, A. *Fuchs*]. – ᴿExpTim 102 (1990s) 213 (Meg *Davies*).

525 ᴱ**Duperray** Ève, Marie-Madeleine dans la mystique, les arts et les lettres; Actes du colloque international, Avignon 20-22 juillet 1988. P 1989, Beauchesne. 360 p. F 180. – ᴿHumT 2 (1990) 260s (H.M.S. *Pereira*); VSp 143 (1989) 838s (G. *Barnaud*).

526 ᴱ**Firmage** Edwin B., al., Religion and law; biblical-Judaic and Islamic perspectives [conference Univ. Utah & Brigham Young, 5-8.III.1985]. WL 1990, Eisenbrauns. xii-401 p.; 18 fig. $37.50. 0-931464-39-0. 21 art.; 17 infra. – ᴿOTAbs 13 (1990) 303s (L. *Greenspoon*: titles sans pp.).

526* *a)* FORNI Enrico M., mem., Antropologia biblica e pensiero moderno; Atti del Convegno Internazionale Modena 15-17 sett. 1988: AnStoEseg 7,1 (1990) 368 p. [29-43, Forni su Spinoza; 21-27, *Melandri* E. su Forni].

— b) ᴱ**Fürst** G., Gottes Wort in der Sprache der Zeit; 10 Jahre Einheitsübersetzung [Tagung 1989]: Hohenheimer Protokolle 35. Stu 1990, Diözese Rottenburg. 124 p. DM 25 pa. 3-926297-24-7 [NTAbs 35,231; authors sans tit. pp.].

527 ᴱ**García Martínez** Florentino, The texts of Qumran and the history of the community; proceedings of the Groningen Congress on the Dead Sea Scrolls (20-23 August 1989), I. Biblical texts: II. Non-biblical texts; III. The history of the community: RQum 14, 54-56 (1989s) 183-323. 331-495. 503-676.

528 ᴱ**Ghiberti** G., La Bibbia, libro sacro, e la sua interpretazione; simposio per il XL dell'ABI (Milano 2-4 giugno 1988): RicStoB 2/2. Bo 1990, Dehoniane. 138 p. Lit. 15.000 [NTAbs 35,256]. 11 art.

529 ᴱ**Ghiberti** G., La missione nel mondo antico e nella Bibbia; XXX settimana biblica nazionale (Roma 12-16 sett. 1988): RicStoBib 2/1. Bo 1990, Dehoniane. 211 p. Lit. 35.000 [NTAbs 35,256]. 11 art.

530 ᴱ**Gilbert** Maurice, La sagesse de l'AT² [Leuven 1978/9] 1990 → 3551 [p. 397-425, authors' additional notes and bibliography update; OTAbs 14,101, tit. pp.].

530* Giudaismo e cristianesimo: FIST 9. T 1990, Federazione Interreligiosa per gli Studi Teologici [AcPIB 9/7, 550].

531 **Goldenberg** David M., present., Translation of Scripture; proceedings of a conference at the Annenberg Research Institute May 15-16, 1989; JQR supp. 1990. WL 1990, Eisenbrauns. $22.50. 13 art. [JQR 81,150, titles, no pp.].

531* ᴱ**Guelich** Robert A., Prophetic and/or apocalyptic eschatology: North Park Sem. Symposium, Chicago Oct. 12-14, 1990: Ex Auditu 6 (1990). 145 p. 12 art.; infra.

532 ᴱ**Heller Willensky** S. O., *Idel* M., The concept of God in Jewish theology [plus another Haifa conference on 13th century Jewish thought]: Studies in Jewish Thought. J 1989, Magnes. p. 7-27, *Gruenwald* I., Changing concepts of God in Jewish thought [< JStJud 21,338].

533 ᴱ**Henten** J. W. van, *al.*, Die Entstehung der Jüdischen Martyrologie → 5,a99 [Workshop Leiden 6-8.IX.1984]: StPostB 38. Leiden 1989, Brill. vii-271 p. *f* 118. 90-04-08978-0. [TLZ 116,655, S. *Schreiner*; Tit. pp. in TR 86 (1990) 522; ZAW 102 (1990) 442; plures infra].

534 ᴱ**Hoftijzer** J., *Kooij* G. van der, The Balaam text from Deir 'Alla re-evaluated; proceedings of the international symposium, Leiden 21-24 August 1989. Leiden c. 1990, Brill. xi-324 p. 90-04-09317-6.

535 ᴱ**Holbrook** Frank B., Symposium on Daniel [2 & 8]: Dan/Rev 2. Wsh 1986, Adventist Biblical. xii-557 p. $10 pa. – ᴿAndrUnS 27 (1989) 243-5 (R. M. *Davidson*, also on vol. 1, ᴱ**Shea** W. H. 1982; and 3).

536 ᴱ**Jackson** B. S., Jewish Law Association Studies 4. The Boston conference volume. Atlanta 1990, Scholars. 190 p. $30. 1-55540-433-2 [NTAbs 34,409].

537 ᴱ**Jackson** Bernard S., Jewish Law Association 1986 conference, Ramat Rahel: Jewish Law Annual 8 (1989). first part. NY 1989, Harwood [HebSt 31,268 tit. sans pp.].

538 ᴱ**Jagersma** H., Job, studies over en rondom een bijbelboek [Bru Prot. Studieweek april 1989]. Kampen 1990, Kok. 112 p. Fb 338. – ᴿCollatVL 20 (1990) 442 (P. *Schmidt*).

538* ᴱ**Kaestli** Jean-Daniel, *Poffet* Jean-Michel, *Zumstein* Jean, La communauté johannique et son histoire; la trajectoire de l'évangile de Jean aux deux premiers siècles (cours 1987s Fribourg, Genève, Lausanne, Neuchâtel): Monde de la Bible. Genève 1990, Labor et Fides. 389 p. 2-8309-0596-2. 17 art., infra.

539 ᴱ**Kannengiesser** Charles, ORIGEN of Alexandria and his world [colloquy ND Apr. 11-13, 1986, 18th centennial of Origen's birth]: ChrJudAnt 1. ND 1988, Univ. viii-373 p. $25. – ᴿCathHR 76 (1990) 98s (G. H. *Ettlinger*, 'instead of merely listing titles').

539* ᴱ**Kapera** Zdzisław J., The first international colloquium on the Dead Sea Scrolls (Mogilany near Cracow, May 31-June 2, 1987): [0015-5675] FolOr 25 (1989). p. 1-155. zł 1200. 19 art.; infra.

540 ᴱ**Kasher** Aryeh, *al.*, Greece and Rome in Eretz Israel, 'collected essays', but rather Conference Yad Ben-Zvi, Haifa and Tel Aviv Universities, March 1985. J 1990, Yad Ben-Zvi/Israel Exploration Soc. [v-] 172 p. 965-217-074-7. 15 art.; infra.

540* ᴱ**Kottek** Samuel S., Third international symposium on medicine in Bible and Talmud, Jerusalem, December 7-9, 1987: Koroth 9, special issue (1988). 280 p. 30 art.; 9 infra.

541 ᴱ**Kuyt** A., *Uchelen* N. A. van, History and form, Dutch studies in the Mishnah [Amst Palache Inst. Feb. 1988]: Publ. Palache 4. Amst 1988. vii-107 p. – ᴿJSS 35 (1990) 319-321 (A. P. *Hayman*).

541* *Lafontaine* René, présent., L'écriture âme de la théologie; Actes du colloque Bru 17-19 sept. 1989: IET 9. Bru 1990, Institut d'Études Théologiques. 222 p. Fb 635 [Études 374,137, R. *Marlé*; RHPR 71,477, A. *Birmelé*]. – ᴿEsprVie 100 (1990) 679-681 (É. *Cothenet*).

542 **Léthel** François-M., présent., L'Évangile de Jésus; rencontre spirituelle et théologique, Centre Notre-Dame de Vie: Spiritualité 6. Venasque 1990, Carmel. 304 p 2-900424-11-9. 13 art., 8 infra; p 9-22, *Lustiger* card. Jean-Marie, Le Christ prophétie et sacrement. – ᴿEsprVie 100 (1990) 675 (É. *Cothenet*).

542* ᴱ**Liberti** Vittorio, I laici nel popolo di Dio; esegesi biblica: Studio Biblico Teologico Aquilano 10. R 1990, Dehoniane. xv-148 p. 88-396-0320-4 [RB 98,457, tit. pp.] 13 art., infra.

543 ᴱ**Lightstone** Jack N., Society, the sacred and Scripture in ancient Judaism — a sociology of knowledge [Canadian Torah/Nomos group]. Waterloo 1988, W. Laurier Univ. 126 p, $17.50. 0-88920-975-8. – ᴿExpTim 100 (1988s) 436 (C. *Middleburgh*: it is a 'compilation' of papers given at the meetings).

543* ᴱ**Long** B. O., Rethinking the place of biblical studies in the academy [1989 conference]. Brunswick NJ 1990, Bowdoin College. iii-28 p. [papers by *Fontaine* C., *Phillips* G., *Poland* L.].

544 ᴱ**Lull** David J., Society of Biblical Literature 1990 seminar papers, 126th meeting Nov. 17-20, New Orleans: SemP 29. Atlanta 1990, Scholars. ix-644 p. 1-55540-548-7. 39 art.; infra.

545 ᴱ**Maier** Gerhard, Der Kanon der Bibel [Arbeitskreis für evangelikale Theologie, 6. Kongress, Tübingen 27.-30. Aug. 1989]. Ba/Wu 1990, Brunnen/Brockhaus. 200 p. DM 29. 3-7655-9354-0 / 3-417-29354-5 [BL 91,116, J. *Barton*]. 8 art., infra.

545* ᴱ**Marchadour** Alain, [p. 173-183] Origine et postérité de l'évangile de Jean; XIIIe congrès de l'ACFEB, Toulouse 1989: LDiv 143. P 1990, Cerf. 339 p. F 207. 16 art.; infra [TR 87,339 & RB 99,297, tit. pp.].

546 [*Matras* Tadeusz, Bericht], Materiały z sympozjum biblistów polskich w Łodzi (13-14.IX) 1988: RuBi 42,1 (1989) (1-) 65-67 [61s, 63s, homilies, *Ziółek* W., *Langkammer* H.].

546* ᴱMuraoka Takamitsu, Melbourne symposium on Septuagint lexico-graphy: SBL SeptCog 28. Atlanta 1990, Scholars. xvi-136 p. $20; sb./pa. $15. 1-55540-486-3; -7-1. 4 art. [BL 91,48; sans tit. pp.].

547 ᴱNiditch Susan, Text and tradition; the Hebrew Bible and folklore; Proceedings... Amherst College Apr. 28-May 1, 1988: Semeia Studies. Atlanta 1990, Scholars. $30; sb./pa. $20. 1-55540-440-5; -3-3 [ZAW 103,310 & RB 99,294, tit. pp.; BL 91,88, R. P. *Carroll*: titles sans pp.; excellent].

548 ᴱOrmsby Eric L., Moses MAIMONIDES and his time [...M. and St. THOMAS as biblical commentators; Wsh Catholic Univ. conference Oct. 1985]: Studies in philosophy and the history of philosophy 19. Wsh 1989, Catholic University of America. vii-180 p. $20. 0-8132-0649-9 [TDig 37,277].

548* ᴱOsborn Eric, *McIntosh* Lawrence, The Bible and European literature; history and hermeneutics [Melbourne Queen's College United Theol. Fac. 15-18 May 1987. Melbourne 1987, Academia. vii-252 p. $30. 21 art. − ᴿCritRR 3 (1990) 462s (E. J. *Epp*).

549 ᴱPetersen William L., Gospel traditions in the 2nd century; origins, recensions, text, and transmission [Proceedings, Notre Dame April 13-17, 1988]: Christianity and Judaism in Antiquity 3. ND 1990, Univ. xi-174 p.; map. $22 [RHE 85,209*]. 0-268-01022-6. 8 art.; infra. − ᴿVigChr 44 (1990) 408-411 (G. *Quispel*).

550 **Propp** William H., *al.*, The Hebrew Bible and its interpreters [4th San Diego Conversation in Biblical Studies. May 18-19, 1986]: UCalSD Biblical and Judaic Studies 1. WL 1990, Eisenbrauns. 225 p. 0-931464-52-8. 6 art. + 3 by the editors, infra [BL 92,22, A. G. *Auld*; OTAbs 14,103, R. E. *Murphy*].

551 ᴱRevell E. J., VIII international congress of the International Orga-nization for Masoretic Studies, Chicago 1988: SBL Masoretic Studies 6. Atlanta 1990, Scholars. viii-138 p. $18; sb./pa. $12. 1-55540-387-5. 12 art.; 3 infra. − ᴿZAW 102 (1990) 444s (tit. pp.).

551* ᴱ**Richard** Earl, New views on Luke and Acts [< CBA seminar, ᴰ*O'Toole* R., from 1976 on]. Collegeville MN 1990, Ltg/Glazier. 196 p. 0-8146-5704-4. 11 art.; infra.

552 ᴱ**Ries** J., *al.*, Le epistole paoline nei manichei, i donatisti e il primo Agostino [1988]: StPatr 5. R 1989, Ist. Augustinianum. 168 p. − ᴿAsprenas 37 (1990) 375s (L. *Fatica*); ScripTPamp 22 (1990) 601-6 ('Albero' *Viciano*).

552* ᴱ**Roth** Wolfgang, Interpretation as scriptural matrix; a panel on FISHBANE's thesis [Ch April 15, 1989]: BiRes 35 (1990) 36(-57, *al.* ➔ 1280).

553 ᴱ**Schmied-Kowarzik** Wolfdietrich, Der Philosoph Franz ROSENZWEIG (1886-1929), Internationaler Kongress, Kassel 1986; I. Die Herausfor-derung jüdischen Lernens; II. Das neue Denken und seine Dimensionen. Fr 1988, Alber. 1060 p. DM 198. 3-495-47655-5. − ᴿActuBbg 26 (1989) 187-9 (J. *Boada*).

554 [YADIN mem. conference NY 1985], ᴱ**Schiffman** L. H., Archaeology and history in the Dead Sea Scrolls: Kevorkian; JPseud supp 8; JSOT/ASOR Mg 2. Sheffield 1990, JStOT. 296 p. £30. 1-85075-221-4. − ᴿJJS 41 (1990) 259s (G. *Vermes*); JStJud 21 (1990) 285-291 (F. *Garcia Martinez*: tit. pp.; lengthy analyses).

554* ᴱ**Schwartz** Regina, The book and the text; the Bible and literary theory [conference]. Ox 1990, Blackwell. xi-313 p. £35; pa. £10 [JTS 42,471, D. *Jasper*, high quality].

555 ᴱShaked Saul,   Irano-Judaica; studies relating to Jewish contacts with Persian culture throughout the ages.   J 1982-90, Ben-Zvi Inst.   I. 1982, 222 p. + ❻ 134 p.; II. ᴱwith *Netzer* Amnon, Jerusalem conference 1987: 1990; ix-254 p.   965-235-001-X; -032-X.   15 art., 8 infra.

556 *a*) SOTS bulletin for 1990: 65th winter meeting, L 3-5.I.1990: *Johnstone* W., presidential address *îš lᵉpî oklô* [Ex 13-37 vs. Dt 16,1-8 on Passover]; – *Brett* M. G., Motives and intentions in Gn 1; – *Healey* J. F., The God of Abraham, Ishmael and Nebaioth — an alternative covenant?; – *Smith* Carol, 'The woman who brings death' or 'the man who causes chaos'?; – *Whybray* R. N., Eces 3,2-8; – *Jackson* B. S., Practical wisdom and literary artifice in the Covenant-Code. – 66th Summer Meeting, Aberdeen 16-19.VII.1990: *Davies* G. I., Hosea and his religious background; – *Elwolde* J. F., God and sexuality; – *Chester* A., Messianism, eschatology and political context; – *Nicol* G., The death of Joab and the accession of Solomon; – *Trible* P., Miriamic fragments; – *Perlitt* L., Heroes or giants?; – *Porter* J. R., Reign of Saul; – *McKeating* H., Ezekiel, a prophet like Moses?

— *b*) ᴱSteinmetz David C.,   The Bible in the sixteenth century [Duke 2d colloquy, Sept. 23-25, 1982]: MgMedRen 14.   Durham NC 1990, Duke Univ.   vi-263 p. $32.50.   0-8223-1012-0 [RB 99,299, tit. pp.; TDig 38,348].   11 art., infra.

556* ᴱStine Philip C.,   Bible translation and the spread of the Church the last 200 years [Princeton Oct. 29-31, 1988]: Studies in Christian Mission 2.   Leiden 1990, Brill.   xii-154 p.   90-04-09331-1.   9 art.; 3 infra.

557 ᴱStockwell Eugene L.,   WCC World Conference on Mission and Evangelism, San Antonio 1989: IntRMiss 78,311s (1989) 259-453; 409-415, *Schwantes* Milton, Notes on the Bible studies.

557* ᴱThéobald C. ['groupe de Sèvres'],   Le canon des Écritures; études historiques, exégétiques et systématiques [*Aletti* J.-N., *al.*]: LDiv 140.   P 1990, Cerf.   573 p.   2-204-03137-2.   10 art., infra.

558 ᴱTheraios P., *al.*,   L'Ancien Testament dans l'Église [VII Sém. Chambésy]: ÉtT 8.   Genève 1988, Centre Orthodoxe.   254 p. – ᴿSalesianum 5? (1990) 164s (M. *Cimosa*).

559 Tollet D., dir.,   Politique et religion dans le judaïsme ancien et médiéval [Sorbonne P-IV, Centre d'Études Juives, 8-9.XII.1987, avec exposition, L'art juif au Moyen Âge]: Relais 7.   P 1989, Desclée.   368 p.; 6 pl. F 235.   2-7189-0412-2. – ᴿÉTRel 65 (1990) 534s (Jeanne-Marie *Léonard*); NRT 112 (1990) 916s (X. *Jacques*).

559* Turchia, crocevia di culture e religioni [colloquio Iskenderun... sett. 1989]: Turchia, la Chiesa e la sua storia 1, Soc. Eteria e Cappuccini di Parma.   R 1990, Pont. Ateneo Antonianum.   175 p. [Salesianum 53,764s: *Nobile* M., religione ittita; *Padovese* L., primo cristianesimo; *Cocchini* F., Paolo; anche Concilio di Efeso; *Mafa* M. G., Apocrifo di Pietro; *Migliarini* M., Tecla; *Siniscalco* P., Il pellegrinaggio; *Kapitanovic* V., Crociati].

560 ᴱVeijola Timo,   The Law in the Bible and its environment [Finnish Exeg. Soc. 50th Anniversary Lectures 1988s]: Publ. 51.   Helsinki/Gö 1990, F. Exeg. Soc./Vandenhoeck & R.   vi-186 p. 9 art., infra.   3-525-54000-0 [RB 98,144s, F. *Langlamet*: tit. pp. comment].

560* ᴱVervenne M.,   Exodus, verhaal en leidmotief [Lv 18-19.VIII.1989].   Lv 1989, Acco.   175 p. ƒ25,75.   90-334-2180-1.   7 art.; infra [TsTNijm 31,95, tit. pp.]. – ᴿCollatVL 20 (1990) 456 (P. *Schmidt*).

561 ᴱWarner Martin,   The Bible as rhetoric; [eleven invited] studies in biblical persuasion and credibility: Warwick Studies.   NY 1990, Routledge.   x-

236 p. $55; pa. $16.   0-415-03617-8; -4409-X [TDig 38,48]. – RTLond 93 (1990) 478s (M. *Wheeler*).
561* EWillems G. F.,   Élie le Prophète; Bible, tradition, iconographie: colloque Bru Inst. Iudaicum, 10-11 nov. 1985. Lv 1988, Peeters. 272 p. Fb 1280. 90-6831-147-6. 8 art. + 6 sur la *metánoia* [NTAbs 34,140].
562 EWise Michael O., *Golb* Norman, Qumran and Apocalyptic; the 'end of days' in ancient Judaism and in the Dead Sea Scrolls: symposium Chicago Univ. 18 Nov. 1988: JNES 49,2 (1990) 101-194. 8 art., infra.
563 EWoude A. S. van der,   In quest of the past; studies on Israelite religion, literature and prophetism; papers read at the joint British-Dutch OT conference, Elspeet 1988: OTS 26. Leiden 1990, Brill. 123 p. ƒ80. 90-04-09192-0 [BL 91,25, R. N. *Whybray*]. 8 art., infra.
564 WYCLIF [John, 1320-1384] e la tradizione degli studi biblici in Inghilterra: convegno centenario 1984, Univ. Genova. Genova 1987, Melangolo. 155 p. 6 art. – RSTEv 1 (1989) 93 (P. *Bolognesi*).
564* EWyk W. C. van. Studies in the Succession narrative: OTSSA 27th (1984), 29th (1986), Pretoria 1986, OT Soc. 379 p. 0-86979-653-4.

A2.3   **Acta congressuum theologica** [reports ➤ Y7.4].

565 EAbraham K. C.,   Third World theologies; commonalities and divergences, 2d Ecumenical Assembly Dcc. 1986, Oaxtepec, Mex. Mkn 1990, Orbis. xix-216 p. $15 pa. 0-88344-681-2 [TContext 8/2, 129, G. *Evers*; TDig 38,192].
566 EAguer Héctor,   El origen del universo; simposio San Miguel 1.IX.1990 = Stromata 46,3s (1990) 235-273.
567 EAlcalá Ángel,   The Spanish Inquisition and the inquisitorial mind [symposium 1983 ? Boulder]: Atlantic Studies on Society in Change 49. Highland Lakes NJ / NY 1987, Atlantic Research / Columbia Univ. 680 p. $65. – RCathHR 75 (1989) 497s (W. J. *Callahan*).
567* All-Asia conference on evangelization: Indian Missiological Review 11 (Shillong 1989) 203-328 [< TContext 7/2,32].
568 Almås Kirsten, *al.*, Presterollen — en kvalitativ undersøkelse om det å være prest i Den norske kirke. Trondheim 1989, Tapir. 327 p. – RNorTTs 91 (1990) 180-3 (T. S. *Dokka*).
569 La América española en la época de las Luces; tradición – innovación – representaciones [Coloq. Hispano-Francés, Univ. Burdeos 18-20.IX.1986]. M 1988, Cultura Hispánica. 423 p. – RScripTPamp 22 (1990) 611-6 (J. C. *Martín de la Hoz*).
570 EAmos Thomas L. †, *Green* Eugene A., *Kienzle* Beverly M., De ore Domini; preacher and word in the Middle Ages [Western Michigan Univ. meeting 1987]: Studies in Medieval Culture 27. Kalamazoo 1989, Western Michigan Univ. xiv-269 p. – RRHE 85 (1990) 825-7 (P. H. *Daly*, tit. pp.; note aussi le colloque Assise 1990, LvN 1992).
571 EAntes Peter, *Pahnke* Donate, Die Religion von Oberschichten; Religion-Profession-Intellektualismus: Jahrestagung Rel. G. 19. Marburg 1989, Diagonal. 316 p. DM 32. – RTLZ 115 (1990) 731-3 (H.-J. *Diesner*).
572 EApczynski John,   Theology and the University [14 of the papers of the College Theological Society 1987 meeting]: CTS Annual 33. Lanham MD 1990, UPA. xiv-275 p. $38.50; pa. $19.25. 0-8191-7472-6; -3-4 [TDig 38,45].
572* Ars celebrandi; sympozjum wykładowców liturgiki — Katowice 1988 [Bericht, *Rojewski* A.]: RuBi 42 (1989) 161-238 [-240].

573 [*Augustijn* C., *al.*] Geestelijke vernieuwing en sociale verandering; de vroege Reformatie in de Nederlanden: Doopgezinde Bijdragen NR 12s (1986s). Amst 1987, Doopgezinde Kring. 316 p.; 25 fig. 90-701654-87-6.

573* EBeck H., *Quiles* J., Entwicklung zur Menschlichkeit durch Begegnung westlicher und östlicher Kultur; Akten des IV. Interkontinentalen Kolloquiums zur philosophischen In-sistenz-anthropologie, 1.-6. September 1986 an der Universität Bamberg: Triadik und Ontodynamik 1. Fra 1988, Lang. 391 p. – RTPhil 65 (1990) 136-8 (J. *Splett*: R. PANIKKAR; M. DHAVAMONY; M. DELIA über WOJTYŁA...).

574 EBeckley Harlan R., *Sweeney* Charles M., James M. GUSTAFSON's theocentric ethics; interpretations and assessments [symposium 1985]. Macon GA 1988, Mercer Univ. 255 p. $35 [CritRR 4,261s, T.F. *Sedgwick*].

574* EBeierwaltes Werner, Begriff und Metapher; Sprachform des Denkens bei ERIUGENA; Vorträge des VII. Internationalen Eriugena-Colloquiums, W-Reimers-Stiftung, Bad Homburg 26.-29. Juli 1989: Abh Heid p/h 1990/3. Heid 1990, Winter. 233 p. 3-533-04259-6; pa. -8-8. 13 art.

575 EBeinert Wolfgang, Braucht Liebe (noch) die Ehe? [zwei Tagungen 1988, kath. Fak. Regensburg]. Rg 1988, Pustet. 149 p. DM 22,80. – RTPQ 137 (1989) 422 (B. *Lies*).

575* EBertalot Renzo, *Franceschetti* Franco, Riscoperta della festa; Corso S.A.E. [Segretariato Attività Ecumeniche] gruppo romano: Le Spighe R 1990, Borla. 139 p. Lit. 15 000. 88 263-0832-2. 10 art.; 5 infra.

576 EBlanchi Enzo, *Manicardi* Luciano, La carità nella Chiesa: Azione Cattolica Bari 29 sett.-1 ott. 1989. Magnano VC 1990, Qiqajon. 51 p.

577 EBiemer Günter, *Fries* Heinrich, Christliche Heiligkeit als Lehre und Praxis nach J.H. NEWMAN /Newman's teaching on Christian holiness [12. internat. Newman-Kongress, FrB Sept. 1987]. Int. Newman-Studien 12. Sigmaringen 1988, Regio-GL. 316 p.; 277 p. je DM 60. 22 art. [TLZ 115,131]. – RGeistL 63 (1990) 392 (R. *Siebenrock*); MüTZ 41 (1990) 111-4 (A. *Loichinger*); ZkT 112 (1990) 227 (S. *Renoldner*).

578 EBogensberger Hugo, *Zauner* Wilhelm, Versuch, über Gott zu reden [Symposium Linz, März 1986]: Forum St. Stephan 4. St. Pölten 1987, NÖ Pressehaus. 116 p.; maps. – RTPQ 137 (1989) 87s (A. *Habichler*: 'können wir die Aussagen der Offenbarung heute mit weniger einseitigen Akzenten verstehen?').

579 FBOSCH David, Mission in creative tension, a dialogue with ~ [S. Africa Missiological Sec. secr.] 60th b., EKritzinger J.N.J., *Saayman* W.A. Pretoria 1990, Missiol. Soc. 269 p. 19 art. [TContext 9/1, 24s.136, H. *Janssen*].

580 EBrakelmann Günter, *Rosowski* Martin, Antisemitismus; von religiöser Judenfeindschaft zur Rassenideologie [Referate...]. Gö 1989, Vandenhoeck & R. 204 p. DM 21,80. – RKIsr 5 (1990) 186s (Julie *Kirchberg*).

581 EBrink Jean R., *al.*, The politics of gender in early modern Europe [i. 'The witch as focus for misogyny': Tempe AZ 1989]: SixtC Essays 12. Kirksville MO 1989, SixtC. 168 p. $30. 0-940474-12-3 [TDig 37,380].

582 EBryder Peter, Manichaean studies; proceedings of the First International Conference on Manichaeism [Lund Univ. 1987]: StAfrAsRel 1. Lund 1988, Plus Ultra. x-294 p. $30. 91-86668-24-2 [NTAbs 35,123: authors, topics]. – RScripTPamp 22 (1990) 973-5 (A. *Viciano*).

583 EBuehler Pierre, Humain à l'image de Dieu; la théologie et les sciences humaines face au problème de l'anthropologie [cours 1985s]: Lieux

théologiques 15, 1989 ➤ 5,447: ᴿFoiTemps 20 (1990) 280s (G. *Harpigny*); NRT 112 (1990) 611s (J.-P. *Prévost*).

584 ᴱ**Burnham** Frederic B., Postmodern theology; Christian faith in a pluralist world [NY Trinity Episcopal Church conference on G. LINDBECK 1984]. SF 1989, Harper & R. vii-117 p. $18 pa. – ᴿNewTR 3,3 (1990) 114s (S. *Bevans*); TTod 47 (1990s) 220.222 (D. R. *Griffin*).

584* ᴱ**Burrell** David B., *McGinn* Bernard, God and creation; an ecumenical symposium. ND 1990, Univ. xii-328 p. $30.

585 ᴱ**Bustros** Salim, *al.*, Pour une théologie contemporaine du Moyen-Orient, Harissa 15-18 oct. 1987. Beyrouth 1988, S. Paul. 322 p. $23. – ᴿÉTRel 65 (1990) 152 (J.-P. *Gabus*: inégal); BLitEc 91 (1990) 232 (S. *Légasse*); IndTSt 26 (1989) 181s (L. *Ray*).

586 ᴱ**Cameron** Nigel M. D., The power and weakness of God; impassibility and orthodoxy; papers presented at the Third Edinburgh Conference in Christian Dogmatics, 1989. E 1990, Rutherford. vi-140 p. £7.90. 0-946068-43-7. 6 art., infra.

586* ᴱ**Caplan** Lionel, Studies in fundamentalism [London Univ. Or-Afr anthropology seminar (6 items) + 3 added]. Albany 1988, SUNY. 216 p. $49.50; pa. $17. 0-88706-519-8. – ᴿRExp 87 (1990) 652 (B. J. *Leonard*).

587 ᴱ**Caquot** A., *Canivet* P., Ritualisme et vie intérieure / Religion et culture: Société Ernest Renan, Histoire des Religions, colloques 1985 et 1987: PoinT 52. P 1989, Beauchesne. 200 p. F 90 [RTLv 22,102, A. *Haquin*].

587* ᴱ**Charlesworth** James H., Jews and Christians; exploring the past, present, and future [Philadelphia May 1987]. NY 1990, Crossroad. 258 p.; ill. 0-8245-1012-7. 9 art. [*Martini* C. M. (sent) ital. 27-33; Eng. 19-26]; 2 infra. – ᴿTTod 47 (1990) 481 (W. H. *Becker*).

588 *a*) Chiesa e missione: StUrbaniana 37. R 1990, Urbaniana. 645 p. Lit. 60.000. 22 art. [TR 87,169, tit. pp.]. P. 69-95, *Testa* Emmanuele, Popolo-nazioni e universalismo nell'Antico Testamento.

— *b*) ᴱ**Christenson** L., Welcome, Holy Spirit; a study of charismatic renewal in the Church [1982s studies commissioned by 1981 Finland Lutheran meeting]. Minneapolis 1987, Augsburg. 418 p. $17. – ᴿCriswT 4 (1989s) 422-6 (J. *Pretlove*: raises some questions for Baptists).

— *c*) Christian lay spirituality and basic ecclesial communities: 16th theological workshop, Changhua July 26-29 (1990) ◉ = ColcFuJen 86 (1990) 461-580. Grouped by (four) religious congregations, plus one on ecology.

589 **Ciolini** Gino, *al.*, Cristo nel pensiero contemporaneo: Firenze, Convegni di S. Spirito 4. Palermo 1988, Augustinus. 122 p. Lit. 13.000. – ᴿETL 66 (1990) 441 (A. de *Halleux*: 'huitièmes entretiens humanistes florentins'; titre s'applique à l'introd. seule); Salesianum 52 (1990) 176s (C. *Cantone*).

590 ᴱ**Cirillo** Luigi, Codex Manichaicus Coloniensis; Atti del 2° Simposio internazionale (Cosenza 27-28 maggio 1988): Studi e ricerche 5. Cosenza 1990, Marra. 115 p. Lit. 20.000. 6 art., 3 infra. – ᴿEWest 40 (1990) 363-5 (G. *Gnoli*).

591 ᴱ**Cohen** Norman J., The fundamentalist phenomenon; a view from within; a response from without [15 papers, NY Nov. 1988]: Starkoff Studies in Ethics. GR 1990, Eerdmans. xiii-266 p. $15. 0-8028-0447-0 [TDig 37,363].

591* ᴱ**Collet** Giancarlo, Theologien der dritten Welt; EATWOT als Herausforderung westlicher Theologie und Kirche: NZMissW Supp. 37. Immensee 1990, NZMissW. 359 p. Fs 48 [TR 87,256: *Kohlbrunner* F. Africa, 51-100; *Frei* Fritz, Asia, 101-131; Collet, Latin America, 133-141; *al.*].

592 ᴱ**Corliss** Roger, *Knitter* Paul F., Buddhist emptiness and Christian Trinity; essays and explorations [Hawaii conference 1984]. NY 1990, Paulist. iv-109 p. $9 [TS 52,381, J. A. *Bracken*, also on ᴱCoʙʙ and Aʙᴇ M.].

593 ᴱ**Corsini** Eugenio, *Costa* E., [I.; ᴱ**Barbaro** Filippi, II], L'autunno del diavolo; 'Diabolos, dialogos, daimon', convegno di Torino 17-21 ott. 1988. Mi 1990, Bompiani. I. 679 p.; II. 565 p. Lit. 60.000 ciasc. 88-452-1554-7; -5-5. 42 + 32 art.; 10 infra.

593* Les courants chrétiens de l'Aufklärung en Europe, Congrès de Varsovie, 25 juin-1 juillet 1978, II: Miscellanea Historiae Ecclesiasticae 6, Bibliothèque de la RHE 68. Bru 1987, Nauwelaerts. [vi]-383 p.; *Stella* P. sur 'les traductions de la Bible dans le cadre des courants culturels de l'époque' [sans titre ni pages, RHE 86,205].

594 ᴱ**Coward** Harold, Hindu-Christian dialogue; perspectives and encounters [Calgary Univ. research project]: Faith meets faith. Mkn 1990, Orbis. xix-281 p. $30, pa. $15. 0-88344-634-0; -3-2 [TDig 38,65].

595 ᴱ**Creel** Austin B., *Narayanan* Vasudha, Monastic life in the Christian and Hindu traditions; a comparative study [Univ. Florida Feb. 16-19, 1985]: Studies in comparative religion 3. Lewiston NY 1990, Mellen. xiii-593 p. $100. 0-88946-502-9. 19 art. [TDig 37,375].

596 ᴱ**Daly** Robert J., In all things; religious faith and American culture [Boston Jesuit conference, April 1989]. KC 1990, Sheed & W. ix-221 p. $15 [NewTR 4/3, J. *Nilson*].

597 ᴱ**David** M., Western colonialism in Asia and Christianity: EATWOT Working Commission on Church History [1. Asia and Christianity 1985] 2. Bombay 1988, Himalaya. 179 p. rs 90. – ᴿEcuR 42 (1990) 178s (S. *Sunquist*).

598 ᴱ**Davis** Stephen T., Death and afterlife [California conference 1987]. L 1989, Macmillan. xi-211 p. £35. – ᴿTLond 93 (1990) 398s (R. *Swinburne*).

599 ᴱ**Denis** H., Le mariage, un sacrement pour les croyants [groupe de travail, fac. théol. Lyon]: Recherches Morales. P 1990, Cerf. 275 p. F 140. – ᴿNRT 112 (1990) 441s (A. *Toubeau*).

600 Dios y el hombre al encuentro; Actas de la 2ª Semana de Teología, Madrid, 25 al 27 de septiembre de 1989: RET 50,2s (1990) 147-340. 6 art.; 293-317, *García Murga* José R., El Dios bíblico; 267-292, *Pikaza* Xabier, Religión y Teodicea; Dios y el futuro del hombre sobre el mundo.

601 ᴱ**Distante** Giovanni, La legittimità del culto delle icone 1987/8 ↦ 4,552: ᴿRThom 90 (1990) 132-4 (D. *Cerbelaud*).

602 [Dominicos de Andalucía], V Centenario del descubrimiento de América; Actas del I Congreso Internacional, Sevilla 21-25 de abril de 1987. M 1988, Deimos. 1011 p. 40 art. – ᴿCrNSt 11 (1990) 402-6 (H.-J. *Prien*, deutsch).

603 ᴱ**Dou** A., Experiencia religiosa [XV Reunión 'J. de Acosta', Granada 6-10.IX.1988]. M 1988, Univ. Comillas. 340 p. – ᴿMiscCom 48 (1990) 290-2 (Jean de Dieu *Mandangui*).

 ᴱ**Drobner** Hubertus R., *Klock* Christoph, Studien zu Gʀᴇɢoʀ von Nyssa, St. Andreas 1990 ↦ 695, Sᴘɪʀᴀ.

604 ᴱ**Duchrow** Ulrich, *Liedke* Gerhard, Shalom; biblical perspectives on creation, justice and peace [deutsch 1987 ↦ 3,6821; 4,8262]. Geneva 1989, WCC. 198 p. – ᴿNorTTs 91 (1990) 177s (K. *Nordstokke*).

 ᴱ**Duperray** Ève, Marie Madeleine dans la mystique, les arts et les lettres; Actes du colloque international Avignon 20-22.VII.1988: 1989 ↦ 525.

605 **Durand** Jean-Paul, présent., État contemporain et liberté religieuse; quel interlocuteur pour l'Église catholique [colloque P, Inst. Catholique 8-10 déc. 1989]: SuppVSp 175 (1990) 1-192 [p. 5-27, *Poulat* Émile, Le grand absent de Dignitatis humanae (Vat. II): l'État].

606 Ebraismo e antiebraismo, immagine e pregiudizio [F 1986s]. F 1989, Giuntina. xi-295 p. Lit. 30.000. – ᴿRaMIsr 56 (1989) 349-355 (M. *Chamla*).

606* *a*) Ecumenismo e catechesi: Atti SAE (La Mendola, Trento) 26.VII-3.VIII.1986. N 1987, Dehoniane. 454 p. Lit. 22.000. – ᴿProtestantesimo 45 (1990) 74s (E. *Genre*: CORSANI B., Bibbia e catechesi). – *b*) Eucaristía y Trinidad [symposium oct. 1989]: Semanas Est. Trin. 24. S 1990, Secr. Trinitario. 270 p. [NRT 113,585, R. *Escol*].

607 ᴱ**Elders** Léon, La doctrine de la révélation divine de saint Thomas d'AQUIN; Actes du symposium Rolduc 4-5.XI.1989; StTomistici 37. Vaticano 1990, Libreria. 278 p. Lit. 30.000. 12 art., infra [TR 87,342, tit. pp.; Divinitas 35,293, D. *Vibrac*; NRT 113,269, R. *Escol*].

608 L'Éthique à venir; une question de sagesse? une question d'expertise? Actes du colloque 29-31 oct. 1986, Univ. Québec à Rimouski. Rimouski 1987, Groupe Éthos. 492 p. – ᴿScEspr 40 (1988) 393-5 (Denise *Couture*).

609 ᴱ**Ettore** Franco, La teologia biblica, natura e prospettive, in dialogo con Giuseppe *Segalla* (p. 15-42. 203-210): Saggi 27. R 1989, A.V.E. 229 p. Lit. 28.000. 6 art. – ᴿRivScR 4 (1990) 278-280 (A. *Pitta*).

610 ᴱ**Fabian** A.C., Origins [Darwin College lectures]. C 1988, Univ. 168 p. £13. 0-521-35189-8. – ᴿExpTim 101 (1989s) 223.

611 ᴱ**Fares** Diego J., Jornadas-Coloquio, 'Libertad cristiana y preocupación social', Buenos Aires, Univ. del Salvador, 29 mar.-19 abr. 1989: Stromata 45,1s (1989). 171 p.

612 ᴱ**Feenstra** Ronald J., *Plantinga* Corneliusᴶ, Trinity, incarnation, and atonement; philosophical and theological essays [Marquette Univ., Milwaukee April 14-16, 1988]: Library of Religious Philosphy 1. ND 1990, Univ. xii-256 p. $30. 0-268-01870-7 [TDig 37,388; RelStR 17,141, P.C. *Phan*].

612* ᴱ**Felici** Sergio, La mariologia nella catechesi dei Patri (età prenicena), Convegno Altioris Latinitatis, Roma 18-19 marzo 1988: BiblScRel 88. R 1989, LAS. 260 p.; 7 fig. Lit. 30.000. 88-213-0189-3.

613 ᴱ**Ferretti** Giovanni, La ragione e i simboli della salvezza oggi; Atti del Quarto Colloquio su Filosofia e Religione, Macerata 12-14 maggio 1988: Univ. Macerata 53. Genova 1990, Marietti. 195 p. 88-211-8588-5 [15-32, *Ricœur* P., Miti della salvezza; 67-83, *Bodei* R., La salvezza laica; 93-108, *Tilliette* X., ... filosofia romantica; 125-141, *Pagano* S., HEGEL] ➤ 7710*.

613* ᴱ**Fischer** Hermann, Paul TILLICH, Studien zu einer Theologie der Moderne [100. Gb. Ringvorlesung Univ. Hamburg 20.VIII.1986]. Fra 1989, Athenäum. 366 p. DM 58 [TR 87,296, W. *Schüssler*, vieles über die 12 Art.].

614 ᴱ**Franck** Eskil, Din uppståndelse bekänner vi [We confess your resurrection], föredrag och samtalsinledningar från konferens i Båstad 1 maj 1987. Sto 1988, Verbum. – ᴿSvEx 55 (1990) 176-8 (C. *Cavallin*).

615 ᴱ**Fürst** Gebhard, Glaube als Lebensform; der Beitrag Johann Baptist HIRSCHERS [1788-1865] zur Neugestaltung christlich-kirchlicher Lebenspraxis und lebensbezogener Theologie [Tagung Diözese Rottenburg-Stuttgart]. Mainz 1989, Grünewald. 163 p. DM 48. – ᴿTLZ 115 (1990) 877-9 (S. *Mette*).

616 *a*) Génesis – do sonho à esperança da terra prometida; – *b*) Apocalipse – novos céus e nova terra: IX/X Semana Bíblica Nacional. Lisboa 1987/8, Difusora Bíblica. 197 p.; 214 p. – ᴿHumT 10 (1989) 266 (H. *Alves*).

616* ᴱ**George** Timothy, John CALVIN and the Church; a prism of reform [4 Davidson College colloquia 1982-8]. Louisville 1990, W-Knox. 276 p. $15 [TTod 42,249, B. W. *Farley*].

ᴱ**Gerardi** Renzo, La creazione [settimana teologica Oristano 1988] 1990 → 7647.

617 ᴱ**Gervers** Michael, *Bikhazi* Ramzi J., Conversion [to Islam] and continuity; indigenous Christian communities in Islamic lands, eighth to eighteenth centuries [Univ. Toronto conference, 23-25 Oct. 1986]: Papers in mediaeval studies 9. Toronto 1990, Pontifical Inst. Med. Stud. 559 p.; 6 maps. $49.50 pa. 0-88844-809-0 [TDig 37,355: the great majority of the world's Christians fell under Muslim rule in its first century].

617* ᴱ**Giannantonio** P., Alfonso M. de LIGUORI e la società civile del suo tempo; Atti del Convegno internazionale per il bicentenario della morte 1787, Napoli etc. 15-19 maggio 1988: Archivum Romanicum 243. F 1990, Olschki. iv-366 p.; p. 367-379. Lit. 128.000 [RHE 86,362*].

618 ᴱ**Gignoux** Philippe, La commémoration; colloque du centenaire [1986] de la Section des Sciences Religieuses de l'École Pratique des Hautes Études: ÉPHÉR Bibl. 91. Lv 1988, Peeters. 405 p. [OIAc F91,10, titles sans p.]. 90-6831-123-9. 31 art.; 18 infra.

619 ᴱ**Gössmann** Elisabeth, *Bader* Dietmar, Warum keine Ordination der Frau? Unterschiedliche Einstellungen in den christlichen Kirchen [Tagung Erzdiözese Freiburg]. Mü 1987, Schnell & S. 120 p. DM 18. – ᴿTLZ 115 (1990) 392s (K.-M. *Siegert*).

620 ᴱ**Gordan** Paulus, Säkulare Welt und Reich Gottes: Salzburger Hochschulwochen 1987. Graz 1988, Styria. 252 p. Sch. 220. – ᴿTPQ 138 (1990) 278 (F. *Reisinger*).

621 ᴱ**Gort** J., *al.*, Dialogue and syncretism, an interdisciplinary approach: Currents of Encounter. Amst/GR 1989, Rodopi/Eerdmans. 230 p. *f*95; pa. *f*36. – ᴿNRT 112 (1990) 631 (J. *Masson*).

621* ᴱ**Grootaers** J., *Soetens* C., Sources locales de Vatican II: Symposium Lv / LvN [23-25 oct. 1989]: Instrumenta Theologica 8. Lv 1990, Fac. Godgeleerdheid. 98 p. [RTLv 22,415, G. *Thils*].

622 ᴱ**Gründer** Karlfried, *Rengstorf* Karl-H., Religionskritik und Religiosität in der deutschen Aufklärung: Wolfenbütteler Stud. Aufklärung 11. Heid 1989, Schneider. 214 p. DM 54 [TR 86,255, tit. pp.] 43-54, *Gawlick* G., REIMARUS; 101-111, *Rengstorf*, LESSING.

623 ᴱ**Hamann** Louis J., *Buck* Harry M., Religious traditions and the limits of tolerance [Gettysburg and Wilson colleges colloquy 1987]. Chambersburg PA 1988, Anima. 155 p. $13. – ᴿRelStR 15 (1989) 54 (F. X. *Clooney*).

623* ᴱ**Harran** Marilyn J., LUTHER and learning; the Wittenberg University [Springfield OH 1983] Luther symposium. Cranbury NJ 1985, Susquehanna Univ. 144 p. $19.50. – ᴿCritRR 3 (1990) 284s (B. A. *Gerrish*).

624 ᴱ**Heering** J. P., *al.*, De kerk verbouwen; [Een huis om in te wonen, G.] DINGEMANS' ecclesiologie critisch bekeken [Studiedag 1988]: Leidse lezingen. Nijkerk 1989, Callenbach. 151 p. *f*29,50. 90-266-0186-7. – ᴿTsT-Nijm 30 (1990) 215s (F. *Haarsma*).

625 ᴱ**Heinonen** Reijo E., *al.*, Religionsunterricht und Dialog zwischen Judentum und Christentum [Grankulla, Finland, 9-13 Aug. 1987, Luth. europ. Komm. für Kirche und Judentum]. Åbo 1988, Akademi. 207 p. –

RSvTKv 65 (1989) 128 (B. *Johnson*); TLZ 114 (1989) 626s (G. *Kehn-scherper*).

625* EHeinz H., *al.*, Versöhnung in der jüdischen und christlichen Liturgie [Augsburg Juli 1989]: QDisp 124. FrB 1990, Herder. 232 p. DM 48 [NRT 113,276, L.-J. *Renard*; TsTNijm 31,17, H. *Wegman*].

626 EHelleman Wendy E., Christianity and the Classics; the acceptance of a heritage [Toronto conference June 1984]: Christian Studies Today. Lanham MD 1989, UPA. 219 p. $29.50; pa. $14.50. 0-8191-7577-3; -8-1 [TDig 37,353].

626* Herausgefordert durch die Armen, Dokumente 1976-86 EATWOT [Ecumenical Association of Third-World Theologians]: Theologie der Dritten Welt 13. FrB 1990, Herder. 229 p. DM 38. – RMüTZ 41 (1990) 389-394 (P. *Schmidt-Leukel*).

627 EHillerbrand Hans, Radical tendencies in the Reformation: Studies 9. Kirksville MO 1988, Sixteenth Century. 140 p. $30. – RCritRR 3 (1990) 386-8 (M. L. *Wagner*: 'Kirksville... USA-GDR IREX sponsored').

628 EHorst Ulrich, Wahrheit und Geschichtlichkeit; Ringen um einen lebendigen Glauben [Salzburg Dez. 1988]: Kath. Akad. Bayern 131. Dü 1988, Patmos. 133 p. DM 22,80. – RTGL 80 (1990) 212 (W. *Beinert*).

628* EHoutepen Anton, De verscheidenheid verzoend? Actuele thema's uit het gesprek Rome-Reformatie toegleicht aan de hand van de thesen van H. FRIES en K. RAHNER (1983). Leiden/Utrecht 1989, Interuniversitaire Instituut voor Missiologie en Oecumenica. 251 p. *f* 29,50 [TR 87,348].

629 EHudson Anne, *Wilks* Michael, From Ockham to Wyclif ➜ 5,472 [Oxford April 1985]. Ox 1987, Blackwell. xv-486 p. £35. – RHeythJ 31 (1990) 341 (N. P. *Tanner*).

629* EHyland John, Mary in the Church [Marist Brothers centenary 1984]. Athlone 1989, Veritas. 178 p. – RMilltSt 26 (1990) 103s (Éilis *Ní Thiarnaigh*).

630 EIdel Moshe, *McGinn* Bernard, Mystical union and monotheistic faith; an ecumenical dialogue. NY 1989, Macmillan. xi-252 p. [RelStR 17,149, J. T. *Pawlikowski*].

631 EIserloh Erwin, Johannes ECK (1486-1543) im Streit der Jahrhunderte; internationales Symposion [Ingolstadt/Eichstätt 13-16. Nov. 1986]: RefGStT 127. Münster 1988, Aschendorff. iv-275 p. DM 84. – RRHE 85 (1990) 468 (J.-F. *Gilmont*).

632 EJaki Stanley L., NEWMAN today; NY Wethersfield Inst. conference, Oct. 14-15, 1988. SF 1989, Ignatius. 232 p. $15. 0-89870-242-9 [TR 87,168, tit. pp.]. – RPrPeo 4 (1990) 240-3 (P. *Hodgson*).

633 EJasper David, *Wright* T. R., The critical spirit and the will to believe; essays in nineteenth-century literature and religion [3d National conference, Durham 1986]. L/NY 1989, Macmillan/St. Martins. xii-239 p. £35. 0-333-45791-9. 14 art. – RExpTim 101 (1989s) 379 (M. J. *Townsend*); TLond 93 (1990) 313 (Frances *Knight*).

633* Jori Alberto, *al.*, La responsabilità ecologica [rencontre d'universités catholiques]: Qualità della vita 10. R 1990, Studium. 204 p. Lit. 19.000 [NRT 113,935, L. *Volpe*].
EJüngel E., Heilsbedeutung des Kreuzes 1990 ➜ 7780*.

634 EKippenberg H. G., Genres in visual representations; proceedings of conference 1986 Reimers-Stiftung. Bad Homburg = VisRel 7 (1990). xix-307 p. 90-04-09094-0. 17 art.; 4 infra.

635 EKlein Goldewijk B., *al.*, Bevrijdingstheologie in West-Europa, Teksten van het symposium nov. 1987 Nijmegen: Kerk en theologie in context

2. Kampen 1988, Kok. 178 p. ƒ29,80. 90-242-3195-7. – RTsTNijm 30 (1990) 318 (M. van *Tente*).

636 EKoehler T. A., Proceedings of the [35th ➤ 3,653*; 36th ➤ 2,452] 37th ... Mariological Society Tampa May 28-29, 1986: Marian Studies 37 (1986). 279 p. – RTLZ 115 (1990) 618 (H. *Beintker*).

637 EKrätzel H., *al.*, Verantwortung der Kirche für Europa; interdisziplinare Gespräche zwischen Orthodoxen und Katholiken [Kolympari, Kreta 20.-25.IX.1988]. Wien 1989. – RAtKap 114 (1990) 164-6 (J. *Bagrowicz*).

637* EKüng H., *Tracy* D., Paradigm change in theology [1983]. NY 1989, Crossroad. 250 p. $34.50. 0-8245-0925-0. – RExpTim 101 (1989s) 315s (D. *Fergusson*); Horizons 17 (1990) 347s (J. *McCarthy*); Month 250 (1989) 438s (P. *Endean*); Tablet 244 (1990) 858 (A. *Dulles*: underemphasizes needed aspects); TTod 47 (1990s) 74.76s (P. *Sponheim*).

638 EKulka Otto D., *Mendes-Flohr* Paul R., Judaism and Christianity under the impact of National Socialism [symposium Jerusalem, June 1982]. J 1987, Hist. Soc. / Shazar Centre. 558 p. – RCathHR 75 (1989) 310-2 (E. C. *Helmreich*); *Soggin* J. A. ➤ 4,b393.

638* ELambrecht J., *Kenis* L., Leven over dood heen; verslagboek van een interdisciplinair Leuvens colloquium. Amerfort 1990, Acco. 334 p. Fb 720 [NRT 113,451, A. *Toubeau*].

639 La Novalesa; ricerche, fonti documentarie, restauri, Abbazia della Novares; XV centenario della nascita di S. Benedetto, Atti del Convegno-Dibattito, 10-12 luglio 1981. Torino 1988, Archivio di Stato / Comunità Benedettina SS. Pietro e Andrea. 595 p.; 109 p.; ill. [RHE 85,341*].

639* El laicado en la Iglesia: XXI Seminario Español de Derecho, 1989.

640 ELapointe Guy, Crise de prophétisme hier et aujourd'hui; l'itinéraire d'un peuple dans l'œuvre de Jacques GRAND'MAISON; Actes du colloque 5-7 oct. 1988: Héritage et projet 43. Montréal 1990, Fides. 353 p. [NRT 113,633, L. *Volpe*].

641 ELemopoulos George, Your will be done; [Greek etc.] Orthodoxy in mission [Kavalla, April 16-24, 1988]. Geneva 1989, WCC. 267 p. $13.50. – RCalvinT 25 (1990) 284-7 (J. R. *Payton*).

641* ELeonardi C., *Menestò* E., La tradizione dei tropi liturgici; Atti del convegno, Parigi 15-19 ott. 1985 - Perugia 2-5 sett. 1987: Centro Perugia 3. Spoleto 1990, Centro Medioevo. xvi-479 p.; ill. [RHE 86,58*].

642 Lévêque Pierre, présente [p. 7-9; 129-131], Les rites de passage dans l'Antiquité (rencontre Univ. Rome / Besançon / ÉcFr ...): MÉF 102,1 (1990) 7-137. 8 art.; 3 infra.

642* a) La libertà religiosa fattore di pacificazione ; Atti del Seminario interdisciplinare, Antonianum Roma (23-25 nov. 1989) = Antonianum 65,3s (1990) 417-660.

— b) Libri, idee e sentimenti religiosi nel Cinquecento italiano; Atti del convegno promosso dall'Istituto di Studi Rinascimentali (Ferrara, 3-5 aprile 1986). Modena 1987, Punini. 212 p. – RCrNSt 11 (1990) 628s (S. *Giombi*).

643 ELivingstone Elizabeth A., 9th international conference on patristic studies, Oxford 1983: Studia Patristica 18. Kalamazoo 1985-90, Cistercian. I. 1985 (➤ 1,609); II. 1989, Critica, classica, ascetica, liturgica; x-402 p.; 50 art. – III. 1989, x-594 p., 42 art. – IV. 1990. vii-390 p., 48 art. [I. 0-87907-350-0]; II-IV (Lv Peeters) 90-6831-233-2 [-2-4 vol. III; -01-0 vol. IV].

643* Livingstone Elizabeth A., Studia patristica (Oxford 1987): TU 1990 ➤ 5,696: JTS 42,313 (L. *Wickham*).

644 **Llamas** Enrique, present., Doctrina y piedad mariana en España en torno al III Concilio de Toledo (a. 589) [43° Seminario de Estudios Marianos, Toledo]: EstMar 55 (1990). 408 p.

644* ᴱ**Llamas** Enrique, present. La Encíclica 'Redemptoris mater'; la madre del Redentor en la vida de la Iglesia [Semana Nacional de Estudios Marianos, Zaragoza 6-12.VI.1988] = EstMar 54 (1989). 308 p.

645 ᴱ**Loades** David, *Walsh* Katherine, Faith and identity; Christian political experience; Anglo-Polish colloquium Hist. Eccl. Comparée, 9-13 Sept. 1986: Studies in Church History subsidia 6. Ox 1990, Blackwell [for Eccl. Hist. Soc.]. xiii-173 p. [TDig 38,159]. 13 art.

646 **Lønning** Inge, present. [p. 9-18] Lᴜᴛʜᴇʀs Theologie als Weltverantwortung; Absichten und Wirkungen / Responsibility for the world; Luther's intentions and their effects; Referate und Berichte des 7. Internationalen Kongresses für Lutherforschung, Oslo, 14.-20. August 1988: LuJb 57 (1990) 5-286. 12 Art. (5 infra ➤ k570) + 16 Berichte (254-6, *Baeder* Siegfried, Luther als Ausleger der hl. Schr.).

646* ᴱ**Lopez** Donald S.ᴶ, *Rockefeller* Steven C., The Christ and the Bodhisattva [week symposium 1984, Middlebury College]. Albany 1987, ꜱᴜɴʏ. viii-274 p. $44.50; pa. $15. – ᴿJRel 70 (1990) 496s (D. W. *Chappell*).

647 ᴱ**Lucal** John, *Laubier* Patrick de, Travail, culture, religions [2ᵉ colloque Genève 1986]. FrS 1988, Univ. 197 p. – ᴿScEsp 42 (1990) 224-7 (J.-G. *Vaillancourt*).

647* LUTHER, town and gown: colloquium Gettysburg ᴘᴀ Oct. 25, 1989 = Lutheran Theol. Sem. Bulletin 70,1 (1990) 1-57 [TR 87,78].

648 ᴱ**Luyten** N. A., *Scheffczyk* Leo, Veränderungen im Menschenbild; Divergenzen der modernen Anthropologie [Tagung Görres-G.]. Fr 1987, Alber. 308 p. – ᴿForumKT 5 (1989) 319s (A. *Ziegenaus*).

649 ᴱ**MacDonald** Michael H., *Tadie* Andrew A., G. K. Cʜᴇꜱᴛᴇʀᴛᴏɴ and C. S. Lᴇᴡɪꜱ, The riddle of joy [conference 1987, Seattle & Seattle-Pacific Universities]. GR 1989, Eerdmans. xvi-304 p. 17 art. [Salesianum 53,572, G. *Abbà*]. – ᴿTLond 93 (1990) 241s (G. *Irvine*).

650 ᴱ**McDonnell** James, *Trampiets* Frances, Communicating faith in a technological age [London Communications Centre seminar in Dayton 1988]. Middlegreen, Slough 1989, St. Paul (Dayton Univ.) 175 p. $19. 0-85439-314-5 [TDig 37,354]. – ᴿExpTim 102 (1990s) 158s (W. D. *Horton*).

650* ᴱ**McEvenue** Sean E., *Meyer* Ben F., Lᴏɴᴇʀɢᴀɴ's hermeneutics; its development and application [Concordia conference 1986]. Wsh 1989, Catholic University of America. vi-313 p. $45. 0-8132-0670-7 [OTAbs 14,102, R. E. *Murphy*].

651 ᴱ**Marinelli** Francesco, *Baronio* Luciano, Carità e politica; la dimensione politica della carità e la solidarietà nella politica [convegno Univ. Lateranense / Caritas italiana]: Fede e Annuncio 29. Bo 1990, Dehoniane. 462 p. Lit. 42.000. 88-10-20321-6. P. 185-205, Aspetto biblico, *Vanni* Ugo.

652 ᴱ**Marshall** I. Howard, Christian experience in theology and life [FEET (Fellowship of European Evangelical Theologians) 1984 conference]: Scottish Bulletin of Ev. Theol. Special Study 2. Leicester 1988, Paternoster. vii-198 p. £8. 0-946068-32-1. – ᴿExpTim 101 (1989s) 93 (D. *Tripp*: Max Tᴜʀɴᴇʀ on NT spiritual gifts).

653 ᴱ**Marshall** Paul A., *Vandervennen* Robert E., Social science in Christian perspective [1978 Toronto conference]. Lanham ᴍᴅ 1988, UPA. 358 p. – ᴿTorJT 6 (1990) 326-330 (L. *Cormie*: delayed by death of B. Zʏʟꜱᴛʀᴀ).

653* ᴱMensen Bernhard, Fünfhundert Jahre Lateinamerika [St. Augustin/ Bonn 1988s]: Völker und Kulturen 12. Nettetal 1989, Steyler. 152 p. DM 28. 6 art. [TR 87,283, N. M. *Borengässer*: detaillierte Analysen].

654 ᴱMorino M., Verbo de Dios y palabras humanas; en el XVI centenario de la conversion cristiana de San AGUSTÍN [actos académicos, 15 ponencias]. Pamplona 1988, Eunsa. 327 p. – ᴿRelCu 35 (1989) 481 (P. *Langa*).

655 ᴱMeyer-Bisch Patrice, *Durand* Jean-Paul, Les devoirs de l'homme; de la réciprocité dans les droits d'homme, vᵉ colloque, Fribourg/S., 1987: SuppVS 168 (1989). 174 p. 7 art.

656 ᴱMiguel José M. de, El hombre, imagen de Dios; XXIII Simposio de Teología Trinitaria, Salamanca, 17-19 octubre 1988: EstTrin 23 (1989) 129s (sumario); 3-127, 4 art., 2 infra.

657 Miscellanea historiae ecclesiasticae, VI. Congrès de Varsovie (25 juin-1 juillet 1978), II. Les courants chrétiens de l'Aufklärung en Europe de la fin du XVIIᵉ siècle jusque vers 1830: BiblRHE 68. Lv 1987, RHE. 383 p. Fb 1400. – ᴿRTLv 21 (1990) 357s (G. *Thils*).

658 ᴱMoltmann Jürgen, Religion der Freiheit; Protestantismus in der Moderne [Tagung März 1989]. Mü 1990, Kaiser. 106 p. DM 12,80. – ᴿHerdKor 44 (1990) 346 (U. *Ruh*).

659 ᴱMorales José, Religión, hombre, historia; estudios Newmanianos. Pamplona 1989, Eunsa. 302 p. pt. 2850 [RTLv 21,404].

659* MORCELLI Stefano A. 1737-1821: Atti del Colloquio Milano-Chiari 2-3 ott. 1987. Brescia 1990, Morcelliana. 241 p. Lit. 35.000. 88-372-1371-9.

660 ᴱMugambi J. N. K., *Magesa* Laurenti, The Church in African Christianity, innovative essays in ecclesiology [ecum. meeting Mar. 1990, Sagana]: African Challenge 1. Nairobi 1990, Initiative [TContext 8/2, 133, H. *Janssen*].

661 ᴱNeuhaus Richard J., American apostasy; the triumph of 'other' gospels [NY Rockford conference Jan. 1987]: Encounter 10. GR 1989, Eerdmans. 137 p. $9 pa. [P. *Berger*, A. *Dulles*, al.]. ᴿCriswT 4 (1989s) 201-3 (B. *Stancil*).

662 ᴱNeusner Jacob, al., Religion, science, and magic, in concert and in conflict [Brown Univ. conference 1987]. NY 1989, Oxford-UP. xii-294 p.; 5 fig. $30. 0-19-505603-5 [NTAbs 34,137].

663 ᴱObelkevich Jim, al., Disciplines of faith; studies in religion, politics and patriarchy [35 art. from July 1983 Religion and Society Workshop]: History workshop series. L 1987, Routledge-KP. 581 p. $11. – ᴿCritRR 2 (1989) 478-480 (J. *Geller*).

664 ᴱOlivieri Marco M., Theologie heute? [colloquio Castelli, R 3-6.I.1988]. R 1988, CEDAM. 720 p. Lit. 80.000. – ᴿTrierTZ 99 (1990) 159s (R. *Weier*).

664* Örsy Ladislas [83-98, The development of the concept of protos in the ancient church], al., The 'Protos' and his jurisdiction; VIII Congress of the Society for the Law of the Oriental Churches, Santiago de Compostela, Sept. 20-27, 1987: Kanon 9 (Wien 1989). c. 420 p. [< ZIT 89,751].

665 ᴱOzment Steven, Religion and culture in the Renaissance and Reformation [from a meeting intended to be on 'Cities and their cultures...']: Essays 11. Kirksville MO 1988, SixtC. 136 p. [CritRR 4,335, Paula S. *Fichtner*].

666 Paolo VI e i problemi ecclesiologici al Concilio; colloquio internazionale di studio, Brescia 19-21 sett. 1986: Publ. 6/7. Brescia/R 1989, Ist. Pao-

lo VI / Studium. xviii-719 p. Lit. 90.000. – ᴿNRT 112 (1990) 429s (L.-J. *Renard*).

666* Papers and reports of the Disciples of Christ – Roman Catholic international commission for dialogue, 1988-9: Mid-Stream 29,3 (1990) 199-336; 199-207, 247-256 *Tillard* J.M.-R., Ministry and apostolic tradition.

667 ᴱ**Pastore** Corrado (p. 11-33), La inculturación del evangelio [IV Seminario ITER, Caracas marzo/mayo 1987]. Caracas 1988. 166 p. 6 al. art. – ᴿREB 50 (1990) 1020 (J. *Clasen*).

667* ᴱ**Penzo** Giorgio, SCHOPENHAUER e il Sacro [seminario Trento 26-28.IV.1984]: IstScRel. Bo 1987, Dehoniane. 156 p. 10 art. [Salesianum 53,787, C. *Cantone*; titoli; osservazioni sull'ambito di 'sacro' incluso R. GIRARD (= ? 'violenza fondatrice')].

668 ᴱ**Péronnet** Michel, Naissance et affirmation de l'idée de tolérance, XVIᵉ-XVIIIᵉ siècles; Actes du 5ᵉ Colloque J. Boisset: Centre Hist. des Réformes et du Protestantisme. Montpellier 1989, Univ. III. 416 p. 2-905397-35-7. – ᴿÉTRel 65 (1990) 383s (H. *Bost*).

669 ᴱ**Petit** Jean-Claude, *Breton* Jean-Claude, Jésus-Christ universel? Interprétations anciennes et appropriations contemporaines de la figure de Jésus; Actes du Congrès de la Société canadienne de théologie, Montréal 27-29 oct. 1989: Héritage et Projet 44. Montréal 1990, Fides. 273 p. 2-7621-1519-1. 14 art.; 7 infra [NRT 113,897, L. *Renwart*; TR 87,347, tit. pp.].

669* ᴱ**Peura** Simo, *Raunio* Antti, LUTHER und Theosis; Vergöttlichung als Thema der abendländischen Theologie... Fachtagung Helsinki 30.III-2.IV.1989: Agricola-Schr. A-25. Helsinki/Erlangen 1990, Agricola/Luther. xv-200 p. DM 65. 951-9047-24-7. 10 art. [163-186, Peura, Die Teilhabe an Christus bei Luther; 27-48, *Slenczka* Reinhard, Die Gemeinschaft mit Gott als Grund und Gegenstand der Theologie; Vergöttlichung als ontologisches Problem; 187-214, *Huovinen* Eero, Opus operatum; ist Luthers Verständnis von der Effektivität des Sakraments richtig verstanden? [< TR 87,167]. – ᴿLuthTKi 14 (1990) 173-7 (G. *Martens*).

670 PFLUG: ᴱ**Neuss** Elmar, *Pollet* J.V., Pflugiana, Studien über Julius Pflug 1499-1564; ein internationales Symposium: RefGStT 129. Münster 1990, Aschendorff. x-233 p. DM 78 [TPQ 139,435, G.B. *Winkler*; TR 87,255]. 9 art.; 2 infra ➤ 741.

670* *a*) ᴱ**Pottmeyer** H.J., Kirche im Kontext der modernen Gesellschaft; zur Strukturfrage der römisch-katholischen Kirche [Tagung Erzd. Freiburg 1988] Mü/Z 1989, Schell & S. 124 p. – ᴿNRT 112 (1990) 612s (A. *Toubeau*); ZkT 112 (1990) 230s (J. *Morel*).

— *b*) [*Poulat* Émile p. 11-34; *Beckford* James A. p. 45-64], Actes de la 20ème Conférence Internationale de Sociologie des Religions (21-25 août 1989, Helsinki): Social Compass 37,1 (Louvain 1990) c. 190 p. [< ZIT 91,113].

671 ᴱ**Quispel** G., Gnosis, de derde component van de Europese cultuurtraditie [Amst 1986]. Utrecht 1988, 'HES'. 280 p. 90-6194-446-5 [NTAbs 34,275].

671* La ragione e i simboli della salvezza oggi, Atti del IV Colloquio su Filosofia e Religione, Macerata 12-14 maggio 1988. Genova 1990, Marietti; p. 39-66 *Alonso Schökel* L.

672 *a*) **Ratzinger** Joseph card., *al.*, The Catholic priest as moral teacher and guide [Symposium Ph (Overbrook) 1990]. SF 1990, Ignatius. 176 p. $13. 0-89870-312-3. – *b*) [Ratzinger p. 1-26, ᴱ*Chantraine* G.], *al.*, Mission et

formation du prêtre: Chemins de Crêtes NS 3. Namur 1990, Culture et Vérité. v-103 p. 2-87299-099-9 [EsprVie 101,140, C. *Bouchaud*]. 3 art., infra.

672* ᴱ**Rauch** Albert, *Imhof* Paul, Das Priestertum in der einen Kirche; Diakonat, Presbyterat und Episkopat [Ök. Symposion, Regensburg 1985]. Aschaffenburg 1988, Kaffke. 255 p. DM 34 pa. – ᴿÖkRu 39 (1990) 364-6 (C. *Oeyen*).

673 **Rémond** René, présent., Nouveaux enjeux de la laïcité; Actes des colloques 'Laïcité et débats d'aujourd'hui' (La Croix) et 'Pluralité des religions et État laïque' (Centres Sèvres/Pompidou)... P 1989, Centurion. 273 p. F 130. – ᴿEsprVie 100 (1990) 522-5 (L. de *Naurois*).

673* ᴱ**Remy** G., Tradition et renouvellement en théologie; Actes du Colloque Metz (avec Trèves) 21-22 oct. 1988]. Metz 1990, Univ. 147 p. [NRT 113,620].

674 La riforma gregoriana e l'Europa; congresso internazionale Salerno, 20-25 maggio 1989, I. Relazioni: Studi Gregoriani 13. R 1989, LAS. xi-433 p. Lit. 50.000 [TR 87,429].

674* ᴱ**Rippin** Andrew, Approaches to the history of the interpretation of the Qur'ān [Conference Univ. Calgary 1985; 14 art.]. Ox 1988. xi-334 p. £37.50. – ᴿJSS 35 (1990) 333-5 (N. *Calder*).

675 ᴱ**Ritsema** Rudolf, Gleichklang oder Gleichzeitigkeit – Concordance or coincidence [Ascona 17.-25. Aug. 1988]: Eranos-Jb 57 (1988). 336 p. 9 art.; 1 infra ➤ 4859.

676 ᴱ**Rodante** S., La Sindone; indagini scientifiche; Atti del IV Congresso nazionale di studi sulla Sindone, Siracusa 17-18 ott. 1987. T 1988, Paoline. 442 p. Lit. 40.000. 88-215-1603-2 [NTAbs 33,389].

677 **Rollin** Francis, présent., Environnement, création, éthique; échos du Congrès de l'ATEM (Association des théologiens pour l'étude de la morale), Strasbourg 5-8 sept. 1988 = SuppVSp 169 (1989) 202 p. 13 art., 3 infra.

679 ᴱ**Rowdon** H. H., Into all the world; papers on world mission today; understanding it, practising it, teaching it [1987 London conference] = Christian Brethren Review 40 (Exeter 1989). 128 p.; £4.50. 0263-466X [NTAbs 34,127].

680 ᴱ**Rudolph** Kurt, *Rinschede* Gisbert, Beiträge zur Religion/Umwelt-Forschung; Tagung... Eichstätt 5.-8.V.1988: Geog. Rel. 6s. B 1989, Reimer. 262 p.; 205 p. DM 48 [TR 86,345, tit. pp.].

681 ᴱ**Ruggieri** Giuseppe [*Alberigo* G. present.], Église et histoire de l'Église en Afrique; Actes du Colloque de Bologne, 22-25 octobre 1988: Religions-SP 18. P 1988, Beauchesne. xxv-390 p. F 294 [TR 87,345, tit. pp.; TS 52,173, J. C. *McKenna*].

681* ᴱ**Rusecki** Marian, ᴾ *Z zagadnień...* Dei problemi sulla visione cristiana del mondo. Lublin 1989, KUL. 228 p. [Antonianum 65,392, C. *Teklak*].

682 ᴱ**Russell** Robert J., *Stoeger* William R., *Coyne* George V., Physics, philosophy and theology [Vatican observatory conference 1988] 1988 ➤ 5,2095: ᴿTS 51 (1990) 151-3 (J. F. *Haught*).

683 ᴱ**Ryan** C., The religious roles of the papacy; ideals and realities, 1150-1300 [Toronto 13-16.V.1985]: Papers in Mediaeval Studies 8. Toronto 1989, Pont. Inst. Mediaeval Studies. xii-476 p.; 8 pl. C$55. 15 art. – ᴿCathHR 76 (1990) 345-7 (J. C. *Moore*); RHE 85 (1990) 742-7 (S. *Hanssens*).

684 *a*) La salvezza oggi 1988/9 ➤ 5,735: ᴿCC 141 (1990,3) 307-9 (A. *Wolanin*); – *b*) Le salut aujourd'hui [éd. française de La salvezza oggi 1989 ➤ 5,735], ᴱ*Tomko* J.: vᵉ Congrès de Missiologie, Urbanianum, R

5-8.X.1988]. R 1990, Urbaniana Univ. 176 p. Lit. 30.000. – ᴿSalesianum 52 (1990) 771-3 (U. *Casalegno*); StPatav 37 (1990) 408s (G. *Segalla*).

684* ꜰSÁNCHEZ VAQUERO José [65. cumpl.]: 1 Hispano-Polaco, 'Tolerancia y intoleranza religiosas en dos paises confesionalmente católicos' (Salamanca 10-13 oct. 1989) = Diálogo Ecuménico 25,82s (1990) 197-589; color. fot.; 201-9 biobibliog.

685 ᴱSantantoni A., [*Bonifazi* A., S. Scr.., *al.*] Rinati dall'acqua; un viaggio attraverso il battesimo: Liturgia-Strumenti 1. Assisi 1989, Cittadella. 196 p. Lit. 18.000. – ᴿAsprenas 37 (1990) 525s (A. *Petti*).

685* ᴱScharlemann Robert P., Theology at the end of the century; a dialogue on the postmodern with Thomas J. J. ALTIZER, Mark C. TAYLOR, Charles E. WINQUIST: Studies in Religion and Culture. Charlottesville 1990, Univ. Virginia. 160 p. $28.50. 0-8139-1246-6 [TDig 38,292].

686 ᴱScheffczyk Leo, Rationalität, ihre Entwicklung und ihre Grenzen [Kolloquia 1986s Görresg.]: Grenzfragen 16. FrB 1989, Alber. 500 p. DM 68. 3-495-47659-9. – ᴿActuBbg 27 (1990) 79s (J. *Boada*).

686* *a)* **Schillebeeckx** Edward, present. Congresso teologico internazionale, [Lovanio] 1990, Alle soglie del terzo millennio = Concilium 26,1 (1990) [→ 402 Eng.] 131 p. 6 art.

— *b)* ᴱSchindler David L., Catholicism and secularization in America; essays on nature, grace, and culture [Communio conference]. Huntington IN 1990, Our Sunday Visitor. 236 p. $8. 0-87973-450-7 [TDig 38,256]. 13 art.; *Kasper* W., *Dupré* L., *Novak* M., *Bouyer* L., *Rousseau* Mary..., *al.*

687 ᴱSchlemmer Karl, Gottesdienst, Weg zur Einheit; Impulse für die Ökumene [Symposion Passau 20.-21.X.1988]: QDisp 122. FrB 1989, Herder. 142 p. DM 32. – ᴿTGL 80 (1990) 228 (M. *Kunzler*).

688 ᴱSchmithals Walter, Existenz und Sein; Karl BARTH und die Marburger Theologie [3.-6.I.1988]. Tü 1989, Mohr. 75 p. DM 29. – ᴿNorTTs 91 (1990) 250s (S. A. *Christoffersen*).

688* *a)* ᴱSchnaubelt Joseph C., *Van Fleteren* Frederick, Collectanea Augustiniana; Augustine, 'Second Founder of the Faith' [16th Centenary of his conversion, symposia 1986-7, Villanova Univ.]: Villanova Augustinian Historical Institute. NY 1990, P. Lang. xvi-517 p. 0-8204-1184-1. 30 art.; 9 infra.

— *b)* ᴱSchnaubelt Joseph C., *al.*, Anselm Studies [I. 1983] II (5th Int. St. Anselm Conference, Villanova Univ. 16-21.IX.1985). White Plains NY 1988, Kraus. xiv-634 p. $55. – ᴿCritRR 3 (1990) 323-6 (J. R. *Berrigan*).

689 ᴱSchneider T., Mann und Frau — Grundproblem theologischer Anthropologie [Tagung St. Pölten 1988]: QDisp 121. FrB 1989, Herder. 222 p. DM 38. – ᴿNRT 112 (1990) 442s (A. *Toubeau*).

689* ᴱSchnucker Robert V., Calviniana; ideas and influence of Jean CALVIN [... one of a series of symposia]: Essays 10. Kirksville MO 1988, SixtC. 388 p. $30 [CritRR 4,340, M. *Klauber*].

690 [Schrotenboer Paul, final coordinator] Christ's rule — a light for every corner; papers of the RES conferences [mission, theology, youth]. Harare, Zimbabwe May 24-28, 1988. GR 1988, Reformed Ecumenical Council. 252 p. $7 pa. – ᴿCalvinT 25 (1990) 91-93 (R. R. *Recker*).

690* Giovanni SCOTO nel suo tempo; L'organizzazione del sapere in età carolingia, Atti del XXIV convegno storico internazionale, Todi 11-14 ott. 1987. Spoleto 1989, Centro Medioevo. xii-609-ix p.; 9 fig. [RHE 86,125*].

691 ᴱSeligman Adam B., Order and transcendence; the role of Utopias and the dynamics of civilizations [Hebrew University seminar 1985-7]: In-

ternational studies in sociology and social anthropology 50. Leiden 1989, Brill. vii-158 p. 90-04-08975-6. p. 13-30-43, *Seligman*, 'Christian Utopias and Christian salvation'; 'The Eucharistic Sacrifice and the changing utopian moment'.

692 ᴱ**Sheils** W. J., *Wood* Diana, Voluntary religion [groups outside official churches; 1985-6 meetings, Ecclesiatical History Society]: Studies in Church History 23. Ox 1986, Blackwell. xvi-521 p. £29.50. – ᴿJTS 40 (1989) 268-270 (Brenda M. *Bolton*).

692* ᴱ**Sheils** William J., Women in the Church, papers read at the 1989 summer meeting and the 1990 winter meeting of the Ecclesiastical History Society: Studies in Church History 27. Ox 1990, Blackwell. xxii-515 p.; ill. £27.50 [TR 87,163, tit. pp.].

693 ᴱ**Siegele-Wenschkewitz** Leonore [ihr Beitrag 'Feministische Theologie ohne Antijudaismus', Ev. Akademie Arnoldshain], Verdrängte Vergangenheit, die uns bedrängt; feministische Theologie in der Verantwortung für die Geschichte: Tb 29. Mü 1988, Kaiser. 280 p. DM 24,80. – ᴿKIsr 5 (1990) 80s (Julie *Kirchberg*).

693* **Simon** René présent., Mal et compassion; Actes du congrès de sept. 1989 de l'ATEM, Asn des théologiens pour l'étude de la morale: SuppVSp 172 (1990) 1-159.

694 Solidaridad nuevo nombre de la paz; comentario interdisciplinar a la encíclica 'Sollicitudo rei socialis': TDeusto 19. Bilbao 1989, Univ/ Mensajero. 213 p. – ᴿNRT 112 (1990) 443s (C. *Mertens*).

694* **Spindler** Marc présent., Des missions aux Églises; naissance et passation des pouvoirs, XVIIᵉ-XXᵉ s.: Actes Bâle 27-31 août 1989: CERDIC 10. Lyon 1990. 303 p. F 130. – ᴿRHE 85 (1990) 845-9 (M. *Cheza*, sur ce que l'on appelait jadis 'l'indigénisation'; aussi sur les sessions CERDIC 'inculturation' 1983/4/6/7/7/8).

695 ꜰ**Spira** Andreas: Studien zu Gregor von Nyssa und der christlichen Spätantike [7. Kolloquium G. Nyssa, St. Andrews 1990], ᴱ**Drobner** Hubertus R., *Klock* Christoph: VigChr supp. 12. Leiden 1990, Brill. xii-418 p. *f* 180. 90-04-09222-6 [OrChr 75,264, W. *Gessel*; RHE 85,96*; ScripTPamp 23,1018, J. *Alviar*; TR 87,428, tit. pp.]. 21 art.; 4 infra. – ᴿVigChr 44 (1990) 312 (tit. pp.).

696 [*Świerzawski* Wacław, wprowadzenie], Dwadzieścia pięć lat odnowy liturgicznej: RuBi 42,1s (1990) 5-8 [-91, *al.*].

697 Teologia e scienze nel mondo contemporaneo [Simposio Angelicum 1989]: Studia Univ. S. Thomae R 31. Mi 1989, Massimo. 278 p. Lit. 30.000. – ᴿAsprenas 37 (1990) 518 (A. *Russo*).

698 ᴱ**Ternes** Charles M., Actes du colloque international Éliade-Dumézil, Luxembourg avril 1988 (avec Centre d'histoire des religions, Louvain). Luxembourg 1988, Courrier de l'Éducation nationale, numéro spécial. 144 p. [RTLv 22,271, J. *Étienne*].

699 ᴱ**Tomm** Winnie, The effects of feminist approaches on research methodologies [Calgary 22-24.I.1987]. Waterloo ᴏɴ 1989, W. Laurier Univ. x-259 p. – ᴿSR 19 (1990) 390s (Monique *Dumais*).

700 La tradizione, forme e modi: XVIII incontro di studiosi dell'antichità cristiana, Roma 7-9 maggio 1989: AugR Stud 31. R 1990, Institutum Patristicum. 466 p. 30 art.; 12 infra [TR 87,526, tit. pp.].

702 ᴱ**Triacca** A. M., *Pistoia* A., Liturgie et anthropologie: S. Serge 36, 27-30.VI.1989: EphLtg Subs 55. R 1990, Ltg. 301 p. Lit. 48.000 [TR 86,351, tit. pp.].

703 ᴱValentini D., La teologia; aspetti innovatori e loro incidenza sulla ecclesiologia e sulla mariologia [congresso Roma 3-7.I.1988]. R 1989, LAS(alesiano). 374 p. – ᴿCarthaginensia 6 (1990) 227s (F. *Martínez Fresneda*); Laurentianum 31 (1990) 622 (E. *Covi*).

705 ᴱWeinzieri Erika, Christen und Juden in Offenbarung und kirchlichen Erklärungen vom Urchristentum bis zur Gegenwart [Symposion...]: Grundfragen 34. Salzburg 1988, Geyer. 189 p. – ᴿTPQ 137 (1989) 306 (R. *Zinnhobler*).

706 ᴱWhite Ronald C., *Fischer* Eugene J., [Catholic-Reformed] Partners in peace and education. GR 1988, Eerdmans. 143 p. $10.25. 0-8028-0346-6. – ᴿÉTRel 65 (1990) 292s (J.-M. *Prieur*).

707 ᴱWillaime Jean-Paul, Vers de nouveaux œcuménismes; les paradoxes contemporains de l'œcuménisme; recherches d'unité et quêtes d'identité [Centre de sociologie du Protestantisme, colloque Strasbourg 1987]: Sciences humaines et religions. P 1989, Cerf. 250 p. F 132 [TR 86,171, tit. pp.]. – ᴿÉTRel 65 (1990) 650s (J.-M. *Prieur*); FoiVie 89,2 (1990) 96-99 (G. *Vahanian*); NRT 112 (1990) 929 (A. *Harvengt*); RHPR 70 (1990) 404s (*ipse*).

709 ᴱWister Robert J., Priests, identity and ministry [Catholic Educational Asn study group; Scripture, *Senior* Donald; patristics, *Cunningham* Agnes...]. Collegeville MN 1990, Glazier. 160 p. $10 pa. 0-89453-784-9 [TDig 38,81].

710 ᴱZerfass Rolf, Erzählter Glaube — erzählende Kirche → 4,a930 [Tagung Goslar 1986]: QDisp 116. FrB 1988, Herder. 203 p. DM 39. – ᴿNRT 112 (1990) 259s (L. *Renwart*).

711 ᴱZoccali V., L'eucaristia, progetto di Dio per il mondo [settimana Gambarie d'Aspromonte 22-27.VIII.1987]. Reggio Calabria 1988, Ist. Sup. Sc. Rel. 202 p. – ᴿAsprenas 37 (1990) 251 (S. *Cipriani*).

712 ᴱZucal Silvano, La Weltanschauung cristiana di Romano GUARDINI [Trento 1985/6]: IstScRel 13. Bo 1988, Dehoniane. 495 p. Lit. 35.000. – ᴿTGL 80 (1990) 357 (A. *Schilson*).

713 ᴱZulehner Paul M., Pluralismus in Gesellschaft und Kirche — Ängste, Hoffnungen, Chancen [kath. Tagung Freiburg Erzdiözese Mai 1987]. Mü 1988, Schnell & S. 104 p. DM 19 pa. – ᴿTPQ 137 (1989) 421 (J. *Singer*).

A2.5   *Acta* philologica *et* historica [reports → Y7.6].

714 Actes de la première rencontre internationale de dialectique grecque, CNRS, Nancy/Pont-à-Mousson, 1-3 juillet 1986: Verbum 10. Nancy 1988, Presses Univ. 291 p. F 200. – ᴿKratylos 34 (1989) 72-79 (E. *Risch* †).

715 ᴱAffeldt W., (*Vorwerk* U.), Frauen in Spätantike und Frühmittelalter; Lebensbedingungen, Lebensnormen, Lebensformen: Beiträge zu einer internationalen Tagung, Freie Univ. Berlin, 18.-21. Februar 1987. Sigmaringen 1990, Thorbecke. 347 p.; 8 pl. DM 68 [RHE 85,471*].

715* L'Afrique dans l'Occident romain (Iᵉʳ s. av. J.-C. - IVᵉ s. ap. J.-C.), Actes du colloque (Tunis), Éc. Fr., Rome 3-5 déc. 1987: CollÉcFR 134. P 1990, de Boccard. viii-624 p.; ill. [RHE 86,81*].

716 ᴱArcher Léonie J., Slavery and other forms of unfree labour [→ 4,434]: History Workshop. L 1988, Routledge. xii-307 p. 0-415-00203-6; pa. -4-4. – ᴿJRS 80 (1990) 194 (Jane *Gardner*: severe).

716* ᴱBahner Werner, *al.*, Proceedings of the Fourteenth International Congress of Linguists, Berlin/DDR August 10-15, 1987. B 1990, Akademie. xi-938 p.; p. 939-1835; p. 1836-2818. 3-05-000655-2; -6-0; -7-9 [all -4-4]. ➤ 469.

717 ᴱBakirtzis Charalambos, Byzantine Thrace, image and character: First International Symposium for Thracian Studies, Komotini May 28-31, 1987: ByzF 14 (1989); fasc. 1, ix-710 p., 38 art. (half ☉); fasc. 2, 280 pl.

718 ᴱBarbera André, Music theory and its sources; antiquity and the Middle Ages: conference ND Apr.30 - May 2, 1987. ND 1990, Univ. xiv-319 p. $50. – ᴿManuscripta 34 (1990) 245.

718* BAUD-BOVY Samuel, Mém.: Griechische Musik und Europa; Antike, Byzanz, Volksmusik der Neuzeit, Symposium 9.-11. Mai 1986, Würzburg, ᴱBrandl Rudolf M., Konstantinou Evangelos: Orbis Musicarum 3. Aachen 1986, Herodot. 120 p. [AnPg 60, p. 871; 'dépouillé'].

719 ᶠBENNETT Emmett L.ᴶ [symposium Madison wɪ 1988], Problems in decipherment, ᴱDuhoux Y., al.; BCILL 49. LvN 1989, Peeters. 216 p.; 54 fig. Fb 650. 90-6831-177-8. – ᴿAntClas 59 (1990) 454-7 (M. Leroy).

720 ᴱBolognesi G., Pisani V., Linguistica e filologia; Atti del VII convegno internaz. di linguisti [Milano 12-14.IX.1984], 1987 ➤ 4,671: ᴿHenoch 12 (1990) 101s (B. Chiesa).

721 ᴱBoss G., Seel G., PROCLUS et son influence; Actes du Colloque de Neuchâtel juin 1985. Z 1987, Grand Midi. xiii-308 p. 2-88093-107-X. 14 art.

722 ᴱBuck August, Klaniczay Tibor, Das Ende der Renaissance; europäische Kultur um 1600: Vorträge, Wolfenbütteler Rena.For. 6. Wsb 1987, Harrassowitz. 239 p. [LuJb 56, p. 164].

723 ᴱCampanile Enrico, Alle origini di Roma; Atti del Colloquio tenuto a Pisa il 18 e 19 settembre 1987: Testi Linguistici 12. Pisa 1988, Giardini. 100 p. – ᴿSalesianum 52 (1990) 475s (R. Bracchi).

724 ᴱCanfora Luciano, Liverani Mario, Zaccagnini Carlo, I trattati nel mondo antico; forma, ideologia, funzione; Istituto Gramsci, seminario di antichistica, Roma 14-15 marzo 1986: Saggi di Storia Antica 2. R 1990, Bretschneider. 256 p. 88-7062-687-3. 9 art.; infra.

724* ᴱCastrén Paavo, Ancient and popular healing; symposium on ancient medicine, Athens 4-6 Oct. 1986. Helsinki 1989, Athens Finnish Institute. 125 p. [AnPg 60, p. 653: dépouillé].

725 Chomarat ., al., ÉRASME; Actes du colloque international (Tours 1986): TrHumRen 239. Genève 1990, Droz. viii-452 p. [RHE 85,450*].

726 Cirene e i Libyi [R/Urbino 1981]: Quad. Archeologia della Libia 12. R 1987, Bretschneider. 432 p., 554 fig.; 11 pl. Lit. 700.000. – ᴿArctos 24 (1990) 184 (Heikki Solin).

727 ᴱClarke G. W., (Eade J. C.), Rediscovering Hellenism; the Hellenic heritage and the English imagination [Australia meeting 1985]. C 1989, Univ. xiv-364 p. 10 art. – ᴿRelStR 16 (1990) 340 (W. M. Calder).

ᴱCohen David, Les langues chamitosémitiques 1988 ➤ 9813*.

727* a) ᴱContamine G., Traduction et traducteurs au Moyen Âge, Actes du colloque internat. CNRS, Institut de recherche et d'histoire des textes, 26-28 mai 1986: Documents, études et répertoires. P 1989, CNRS. xxiii-381 p. F 370 [RHE 86,384*].

— b) ᴱHamesse Jacqueline, Fattori Marta, Rencontres de cultures dans la philosophie médiévale; traductions et traducteurs de l'Antiquité tardive au XIVᵉ siècle; Acts du Colloque international de Cassino 15-17 juin 1990: Textes, Congrès 11-1. LvN 1990, Univ. Inst. Médiév. viii-402 p.; ill. 17 art., 3 infra.

728 ^E**Danien** Elin C.,   The world of Philip and Alexander; a symposium on Greek life and times: Public Forum 1.   Ph 1990, Univ. Museum. ix-114 p.   0-934718-94-6 [OIAc F91,5: *Graham* A., *Romano* D. & I., *McClellan* G., *al.*, titles sans pp.].

728* Deutscher Altphilologenverband, Tagung Bonn 1988, 3. Teil = Gymnasium 97,2 (1990) 97-130, 3 Art. über 5 Gelehrte.

729 ^E**Diehle** A.,   L'Église et l'Empire au IVe siècle: Entretiens sur l'Antiquité Classique 34.   Genève 1989, Hardt.   viii-365 p.   Fs 68. – ^RClasR 40 (1990) 392s (N. *McLynn*).

730 ^E**Dionisotti** A. C., *al.*,   The uses of Greek and Latin, historical essays [colloquium June 1986]: Surveys and Texts 16.   L 1988, Univ. Warburg Inst.   vi-248 p.   £10.   0-85481-071-4.   14 art.; MOMIGLIANO on Jewish and Christian Sibylline oracles; P. J. *Schmidt* on TIMPANARO's LACHMANN. – ^RClasR 39 (1989) 374-6 (H. *Lloyd-Jones*); JRS 80 (1990) 265 (P. *Hainsworth*).

731 ^F**DISANDRO** Carlos A..,   Semanas de estudios romanos [6 (1978) - 11 (1984)] 3s. Valparaiso 1986, Univ. Católica.   317 p. – ^REmerita 58 (1990) 365s (M. *Conde*).

731* ^E**Ebert** Joachim,   *Zimmermann* Hans-Dieter,   Innere und äussere Integration der Altertumswissenschaften: Konferenz zur 200. Wiederkehr der Gründung des Seminarium Philologicum Halense 1987: Wiss. Beit. Halle 1989/36.   271 p. [AnPg 60, p. 870, dépouillé].

732 ^E**Eder** Walter,   Staat und Staatlichkeit in der frühen römischen Republik [Kolloquium Berlin, Juli 1988].   Stu 1990, Steiner.   627 p. – ^RRÉLat 68 (1990) 220s (D. *Briquel*).

732* EWIG Eugen, Colloquium zum 75. Gb., 28.V.1988; Beiträge zur Geschichte des Regnum Francorum, ^E**Schieffer** H.: Francia supp. 22. Sigmaringen 1990, Thorbecke.   172 p. DM 68 [RHE 85,397*].

733 ^E**Fiaccadori** Gianfranco,   Autori classici in lingue del Vicino e Medio Oriente; Atti del III, IV, e V Seminario 'Recupero di testi classici' [Brescia 21.XI.1984; R 22-27.III.1985; Padova-Venezia 15s.IV.1986].   R 1990, Ist. Poligrafico.   216 p.   88-240-0059-2. 18 art.; 1 infra.

733* ^E**Fisiak** Jacek,   Historical linguistics and philology [Poznań April 20-23, 1988]: Trends in Linguistics, StMg 46.   B 1990, Mouton de Gruyter. xi-401 p.   3-11-012204-9.

734 ^E**French** D. H., *Lightfoot* C. S.,   The eastern frontier of the Roman Empire; Proceedings of a Colloquium held at Ankara in September 1988: British Institute of Archaeology at Ankara Mg 11 / BAR-Int 553.   Ox 1989.   xxxiv-615 p. (2 vol.) 0-86054-700-0.

734* FRINGS Theodor (1886-1968): Sprache in der sozialen und kulturellen Entwicklung; Beiträge eines Kolloquiums zu ehren ~, ^E**Grosse** Rudolf: Abh Sächs. Akad. Lp/ph/h 73/1.   B 1990, Akademie.   447 p.; ill.   3-01-000864-4.   46 art.; 2 infra.

735 ^E**Garzya** Antonio,   Metodologia della ricerca sulla tarda antichità; Atti del primo convegno dell'Associazione di Studi Tardoantichi, Napoli 16-18.X.1987.   N 1989, D'Auria.   604 p.   88-7092-043-7.   41 art.; → g991.

736 ^E**Gebauer** G.,   Körper- und Einbildungskraft; Inszenierung des Helden im Sport: Historische Anthropologie 2.   B 1988 [Nikephoros 2 (1989) 222].

737 **Gimbutas** Marija present. [p. 193-6], Second International Conference on the Transformation of European and Anatolian culture 4500-2500 B.C. [Dublin Sept. 15-22, 1989]: JIndEur 18,3s (1989) 193-383; 19,1s & 3s (1990) 1-224. 225-448.

738 ᴱGallacher Patrick J., *Damico* Helen, Hermeneutics and medieval culture [Albuquerque 1989, Medieval Acad.]. Albany 1989, SUNY. xv-287 p. $49.50; pa. $17 [RHE 85, p. 284*].

739 ᴱGargiulo T., Documentare il manoscritto, problematica di un censimento; Atti del Seminario di Roma, 6-7 aprile 1987. R 1987, Centrale Catalogo Biblioteche [RHE 85,347*].

740 ᴱGrant John N., Editing Greek and Latin texts; papers given at the XXIIIrd Annual Conference on Editorial Problems, Univ. Toronto, 6-7. Nov. 1987. NY 1989, AMS. xii-197 p. $29.50 [RHE 85,347*]. – ᴿGreeceR 37 (1990) 254 (P. *Walcot*: REEVE, GOOLD, TARRANT fine).

741 ᴱGualdo G., Cancelleria e cultura nel Medio Evo; comunicazioni presentate nelle giornate di studio della commissione, Stoccarda, 29-30 agosto 1985, XVI Congresso Internaz. di Scienze Storiche. Vaticano 1990, Archivio Segreto. viii-341 p. [RHE 85, p. 357*].

742 ᴱHaiman John, Iconicity in syntax: symposium Stanford 24-26.VI.1983: Typological Studies in Language 6. Amst/Ph 1985, Benjamins. vi-403 p. – ᴿArGlotIt 74 (1988) 102-8 (P. *Cuzzolin*).

742* Holloway B. Ross, present., Rome's Alpine frontier; Proceedings of the conference held at the Center for Old World Archaeology and Art, Brown Univ., Providence RI, Sept. 27, 1986, in RArtLv 21 (1988) 1-50. 5 art. → g465.

743 ᴱHoward-Johnston J.D., Byzantium and the West, c. 850-c. 1200; Proceedings of the XVIII Spring Symposium of Byzantine studies, Oxford 30.III-1.IV.1984: ByzF 13 (1988). 332 p., XLI pl.

744 ᴱIrmscher Johannes, Historiker-Kongress, Stuttgart 1985, Journée Byzantine. ByzF 15 (1990) 327-416. 10 art.; 331-3, archéologie, *Condurachi* E.; 335-344, Altertumswissenschaft, *Dostálová* Rŏžena.

744* ᴱJouan François, *Deforge* Bernard, Peuples et pays mythiques; Actes du Vᵉ Colloque du Centre de recherches Mythologiques de l'Université de Paris X, Chantilly 18-20 sept. 1986: Vérité des Mythes. P 1988, BLettres. 269 p. [Salesianum 53,761, R. *Della Casa*: titoli senza pp.; H. *Limet*, Dilmun; M. *Alexandre*, Gen 2,8-15].

745 Krafft Peter, TSCHIEDEL –, Concentus hexachordus; Beiträge zum 10. Symposium klas. Philologie in Eichstätt (24.-25. Februar 1984): [Univ. cath.] Eich. Beiträge 13. Rg 1986, Pustet. 196 p. – ᴿRPg 63 (1989) 397s (Édith *Weber*).

745* ᴱLandsberg Marge E., The genesis of language; a difference in judgment of evidence [Symposium Vancouver 20-23 Aug. 1983]: Studies in anthropological linguistics 3. B 1988, Mouton de Gruyter. xv-278 p. – ᴿSalesianum 52 (1990) 487s (R. *Bracchi*).

746 LAUFFER Siegfried zu ehren [→ 109]: Boiotika: Vorträge vom 5. Internationalen Böotien-Kolloquium, Univ. Mü 13.-17. Juni 1986, ᴱBeister Hartmut, *al.*; ArbAltGesch. 2. Mü 1989, Maris. 380 p.; ill. [AnPg 60, p. 874: dépouillé].

747 ᴱLaurens Annie-France, Entre hommes et Dieu; le convive, le héros, le prophète [enquête Montpellier]: CentreHistAnc 86. Besançon 1989, Univ. Annales Litt. 201 p. [RHR 208,327-331, P. *Schmitt-Pantel*].

748 Lévêque P., prés., Rites de passage: *a*) Passage et efficacité sociale; – *b*) *Musti* Domenico, La teoria delle età e i passaggi di status in Solone; – *c*) *Cantarella* Eva, 'Neaniskoi', classi di età e passaggi di 'status' nel diritto ateniese; – *d*) *Mactoux* Marie-Madeleine, Esclaves et rites de passage; – *e*) *Torelli* Mario, Riti di passaggio maschili di Roma arcaica: MÉF 102,1 (1990) 7-9 / 11-35 / 37-51 / 53-81 / 93-106.

749 ᴱLobato A., Homo loquens; uomo e linguaggio; pensieri, cervelli e macchine [symposia Soc. Int. T. Aquino, R. 1986, 1987]: Philosophica 2. Bo 1989, Dehoniane. 286 p. [CommSev 23,153].

750 ᴱLonis Raoul, L'Étranger dans le monde grec [colloquium Nancy 1987]. Nancy 1988, Presses Univ. 191 p. F 180. 2-86480-362-3 [139-158, *Baslez* M.-F., Les communautés d'Orientaux dans la cité grecque; 169-191, *Orrieux* C., La parenté entre Juifs et Spartiates; 1 Mcb 12:20-23 non authentique]. – ᴿBO 47 (1990) 258.

751 ᴱLorenzini Amleto, La comunicazione nella storia; un itinerario nello sviluppo dei rapporti sociali; preistoria, Mesopotamia, Egitto, Africa nera, India, Americhe; pref. *Orfei* Ruggero: Società italiana telecomunicazioni. Pomezia 1989, Sarin. 326 p.; ill. 7 art.; p. 29-61 preistoria, *Tosi* Maurizio; 63-153, Vicino Oriente Antico, *Pettinato* Giovanni; 155-185, Egitto faraonico, *Roccati* Alessandro.

752 ᴱMalkin Irad, *Hohlfelder* Robert L., Mediterranean cities; historical perspectives [mostly Palestine ports; Haifa conference 1986]. L 1988, F. Cass. 200 p.; ill. £18. – ᴿGreeceR 37 (1990) 258 (P. *Walcot*).

752* [Mandilaras B. G. org.] Proceedings of the XVIII Internat. Congress of Papyrology, Athens 25-31 May 1986. Athens 1988, Greek papyrological soc. 491 p., 16 pl.; 523 p., 19 pl. [ArPapF 37,65-68, detailliert (? G. *Poethke*)].

753 ᴱManuli Paola, *Vegetti* Mario, Le opere psicologiche di GALENO; Atti del terzo colloquio galenico int. Pavia 10-12 sett. 1986: StPensieroAnt 13. N 1988, Bibliopolis. 333 p. Lit. 40.000. 88-7088-179-2. – ᴿAntClas 59 (1990) 339s (A. *Touwaide*).

754 *Markey* T. L., *Greppin* John A. C., present., When worlds collide; the Indo-Europeans and the Pre-Indo-Europeans: Rockefeller Foundation Bellagio/Como 8-13 Feb. 1988: Linguistica Extranea Studia 19. AA 1990, Karoma. 401 p.; map. 0-89-720-090-X. 21 art.; 7 infra.

755 ᴱMassaut Jean-Pierre, Colloque érasmien de Liège, commémoration du 450ᵉ anniversaire de la mort d'Érasme: Fac. Liège ph/lett 247. P 1987, BLettres. x-313 p. [LuJb 57, p. 321; 8 items cited].

755* ᴱMastino A., L'Africa romana; Atti del VI convegno, Sassari 16-18 dic. 1988: Univ. Dip. Storia 14. Sassari 1989, Gallizzi. 416 p.; p. 417-838; ill. Lit. 100.000 [RHE 86,81*].

756 ᴱMommsen Wolfgang J., Leopold von RANKE und die moderne Geschichtswissenschaft [Symposium, 100. Todesjahr]. Stu 1988, Klett-Cotta. 270 p. – ᴿHistTheor 28 (1989) 78-94 (T. H. *Von Laue*).

757 Motte André, présent., Oracles et mantique en Grèce ancienne [Actes du Colloque ...]: Kernos 3 (1990) 366 p. 28 art.

758 ᴱMurray Oswyn, *Price* Simon, The Greek city from Homer to Alexander [Oxford seminar 1986/7]. Ox 1990, Clarendon. xv-372 p.; 19 fig.; IV pl. 0-19-814888-7. 14 art., 2 infra [GreeceR 38,102, P. J. *Rhodes*].

758* ᴱMurray Oswyn, Sympotica; a symposium on the Symposium. Ox 1990, Clarendon. 345 p.; 14 fig.; 24 pl. £50. 0-19-814861-5 [Antiquity 64,941].

759 ᴱMusti Domenico, Le origini dei Greci; Dori e mondo egeo [colloquio Roma 11-13 apr. 1983]. R 1986, Laterza. xxv-443 p. Lit. 55.000. – ᴿMeditHistR 5 (1990) 85-87 (D. *Asheri*: leaves the questions unsolved).

760 ᴱNicolet Claude, Du pouvoir dans l'antiquité; mots et réalités [conférences 1983s]: ÉPHE 4/3, Gréco-Romain 16 / Cah Glotz 1. Genève 1990, Droz. 238 p. 15 art.; 5 infra.

761 ᴱOroz Reta José, Actas del I Simposio del latín cristiano [Madrid, 10-13 nov. 1987] = Helmantica 40 (1989). 523 p. 44 art.

762 ᴱPailler J.-M., Actualité de l'Antiquité, Actes du colloque Pallas / Univ. Toulouse. P 1989, CNRS. 270 p. - ᴿAnÉCS 45 (1990) 961-3 (Y. Thébert).

762* [Baurain Claude, al., présent.] Phoinikeia Grammata, function and diffusion of writing in the Ancient Mediterranean, IXᵉ colloque: Documents de travail, tables rondes. Liège 1989, Univ. 160 p. 14 art.; 12 infra [p. 150-164, Hadas-Lebel M., L'hébreu, écriture et culture; n'est que des facsimiles avec observations écrites à main].

763 ☺ Praktiká... Acta, 1st. International Nicopolis symposium, 23-29 Sept. 1984. Preveza 1987, Chrysos. 595 p. - ᴿEllinika 40 (1989) 486-495 (D. K. Samsaris).

764 ᴱRaaflaub K. A., Toher M., Between Republic and Empire; interpretations of Augustus and his principate [for 50th anniversary pf R. SYME's 1989 Roman Revolution, largely 1987 Brown Univ. conference]. Berkeley 1990, Univ. California. xxi-495 p. $75. 0-520-06676-6 [NTAbs 35,131].

765 ᴱRijksbaron A., al., In the footsteps of Raphael KÜHNER [150th anniv. of Ausführliche Grammatik der griechischen Sprache 1986], Proceedings II. Amst 1988, Gieben. - ᴿSalesianum 52 (1990) 230 (R. Della Casa).

766 Friedrich RÜCKERT Dichter und Sprachgelehrter in Erlangen, 9. Colloquium Regionalforschung. Neustadt/Aisch 1990, Degener [ZAW 103,167] → 3692.

767 St. Louis Univ. 17th Conference on Manuscript Studies, 12-13 Oct. 1990: Manuscripta 34 (1990) 201-215.

768 ᴱSchmitz Bettina, Steffgen Ute, Waren sie nur schön? Frauen im Spiegel der Jahrtausende [Vortragsreihe Hildesheim 1985]. Kulturgeschichte der Antiken Welt 42. Mainz 1989, von Zabern. 329 p.; 161 fig. 3-8053-1073-0. 7 art.; infra.

768* ᴱSolin Heikki, Kajava Mika, Roman Eastern policy and other studies in Roman History; proceedings of a colloquium at Tvarminne 2-3 October 1987: Comm. Hum. Litt. 91. Helsinki 1990, Soc. Scientiarum Fennica. 174 p. [BeiNam 26,365, D. Eibach; Tyche 6,243, G, Dobesch].

769 ᴱVerdin H., al., Purposes of history; studies in Greek historiography from the 4th to the 2nd centuries B.C.; proceedings of the international colloquium Leuven 24-26 May 1988: StHellenistica 30. Lv 1990, Peeters. xxx-385 p. [OIAc S90].

770 VITTINGHOFF Friedrich; Religion und Gesellschaft in der römischen Kaiserzeit, Kolloquium zu Ehren von ~, ᴱEck W. [p. 15-51]: Kölner Hist. Abh. 35. Köln 1989, Böhlau. vii-293 p. DM 54 [RHE 85, p. 236*; TR 86,524, tit. pp.].

771 ᴱVoelke André-Jean, Le scepticisme antique; perspectives historiques et systématiques; Actes du Colloque international Univ. Lausanne, 1-3 juin 1988: RTPhil Cah 15. Genève 1990. 215 p. 14 art. [RTPhil 123,107, S. Imhoof].

772 ᴱWeijers Olga, Terminologie de la vie intellectuelle au Moyen Âge: colloque Leiden/Haag 20-21 sept. 1985. Turnhout 1988, Brepols. 114 p. [RHE 84, p. 329*].

773 ᴱWeijers Olga, Vocabulaire du livre et de l'écriture au moyen âge; actes de la Table Ronde, P 24-26 sept. 1987: Civicima 2. Turnhout 1989, Brepols. 252 p.; 13 facsim. Fb 1500 [RHE 86,203, R. Gryson, tit. pp.; observations].

773* ᴱWeiler Ingomar, (*Grassl* Herbert), Soziale Randgruppen und Aussenseiter im Altertum: Symposion Graz 21.-23. Sept. 1987. Graz 1988, Leykam. 168 p.; ill. [AnPg 59, p. 812].

774 ᴱWinkes Rolf, The age of Augustus: Interdisciplinary conference, Brown Univ. Apr. 30 - May 2, 1982: Archaeologia Transatlantica 5. LvN 1985, Art & Archaeology. 208 p. 13 art.

775 ᴱZinko Christian, Akten der 13. Österreichischen Linguistentag, Graz, 25.-27. Oktober 1985 [+ Salzburg 1983]: VgSprW Arbeiten 1. Graz 1988, Leykam. 338 p. DM 58,60. – ᴿKratylos 34 (1989) 163-5 (R. *Schmitt*).

A2.7   *Acta* orientalistica.

776 ᴱArbel Benjamin, *al.*, Latins and Greeks in the Eastern Mediterranean after 1204 [22d Byzantine-Crusade spring symposium, Nottingham 26-29 March 1988]. Totowa ɴᴊ 1989, Cass [= MeditHistR 4,1 (1989)]. viii-245 p. £18. – ᴿJRAS (1990) 389s (P. W. *Edbury*).

776* ᴱCreed Austin B., *Natavarian* Vasudha, Monastic life in the Christian and Hindu traditions; a comparative study [1985 meeting]: StCompRel 3. Lewiston ɴʏ 1990, Mellen. xiii-593 p. $100 [RelStR 17,334, F. X. *Clooney*].

777 ᴱDiem Werner, *Falaturi* Abdoljavad, XXIV. Deutscher Orientalistentag 26.-30. Sept. 1988, Köln; Ausgewählte Vorträge [60 aus 180 ungefähr]: ZDMG Supp 8. Stu 1900, Steiner. ix-611 p.; XXIII pl. DM 178. 3-515-05356-5. 61 art.; 7 infra [BL 91,126, J. F. *Healey*: WEDEL on Pentateuch] (XXIII. ᴱ*Schuler* E. von, 1985/9, ➤ 5,823*).

777* [ᴇᴛᴛɪɴɢʜᴀᴜsᴇɴ Richard mem. ᴰ*Bier* Carol M., ᴱSoucek Priscilla P., Content and context of visual arts in the Islamic world, Colloquium NYU 2-4 April 1980. Univ. Park 1988, Penn State Univ. xx-277 p. £42.50. – ᴿBSO 53 (1990) 342s (Barbara *Brend*).

ᴱGarcin Jean-Claude, L'habitat traditionnel dans les pays musulmans, rencontre Aix-en-Provence 6-8 juin 1984/8 ➤ d146.

778 ᴱHornung E., Zum Bild Ägyptens im Mittelalter und in der Renaissance [Symposion Basel 7.VI.1986]: OBO 95. FrS/Gö 1990, Univ./VR. 241 p.; 11 pl. Fs 64. 3-7278-0669-9 / VR 3-525-53725-5 [BL 91,127, K. A. *Kitchen*: entertaining].

779 ᴱJungraithmayr Herrmann, *Müller* Walter W., Proceedings of the fourth international Hamito-Semitic congress, Marburg, 20-22 Sept. 1983. Amst 1987, Benjamins. xiv-609 p. *f* 200. 90-272-3538-4. – ᴿBO 47 (1990) 289-292 (H. J. *Stroomer*).

779* ᴱLavenant René, V Symposium syriacum 1988, Katholieke Universiteit Leuven 29-31 août 1988: OrChrAn 236. R 1990, Pont. Inst. Studiorum Orientalium. 745 p. 42 art., 9 infra.

780 ᴱNagel Peter, Carl-Sᴄʜᴍɪᴅᴛ-Kolloquium an der Martin-Luther Universität [27.-29. April 1988: geb. 1868, † 1938]: WissBeit 1990/23. Halle 1990, Univ. 301 p.; 8 fig. 3-86010-251-6. 25 art.; als Koptologe, Nagel p. 9-24; als Kirchenhistoriker, *Winkelmann* Friedhelm, 25-35; als Patristiker, *Treu* Kurt, 37-41; als Papyrologe, *Poethke* Günter, 43-47. 11 *al.*, infra.

780* ᴱRippin Andrew, Approaches to the history of the interpretation of the Qur'ān [colloquium Calgary April 1985]. Ox 1988, Clarendon. xii-334 p. 0-19-826546-8. 13 art. – ᴿBO 47 (1990) 248 [titles without pp.]; BSO 52 (1989) 340-4 (J. *Burton*); JRAS (1990) 385s (G. R. *Hawting*).

781 ᴱRooney J., St. Thomas and Taxila [Sirkap visit 47 A.D.]; a symposium on Saint Thomas. Pakistan Christian History, 1. Rawalpindi 1988, Christian Study Centre. 41 p.; 3 fig.; 4 maps [NTAbs 35,270].

781* Scholz P. [Bericht S. 433-449], Sechste Internationale Konferenz für nubische Studien in Uppsala, 11.-16. August 1986 = Nubica I-II (Köln 1990, J. Dinter) 433-668. 17 art.; 4 infra.

782 ᴱZimmermann Albert, Cremer-Ruegenberg Ingrid, Orientalische Kultur und europäisches Mittelalter [24. Kölner Mediävistentagung 1984]: Miscellanea Mediaevalia 17 ➤ 5,826: B 1985, de Gruyter. ix-440 p. DM 212. 26 art. – ᴿFranzSt 71 (1989) 106 (A. Pattin).

A2.9   Acta archaeologica [reports ➤ Y7.8].

783 Abou Zayd Shafiq, present. [p. xi-xii] First International Conference, The Nabataeans, Oxford 26-29 Sept. 1989: Aram 2,1s (1990). xii-447 p.; Mém. STARCKY Jean 1909-1988, bibliog. 1-5 (Z. al-Muheisen, Dominique Tarrier]. 29 art., infra.

783* ᴱAerts Erik, Klengel Horst, The town as regional economic centre in the Ancient Near East: Proc. 10th Economic History Congress Section B-16, Leuven Aug. 1990: Studies in Social and Economic History 20. Lv 1990, Univ. 115 p. 90-6186-392-9 [OIAc Oc90].

784 Archaeological Institute of America, 91st general meeting, Boston 27-30.XII.1989: AJA 94 (1990) 297-344: 300-word summaries of 186 papers with author index; only 9 noted infra.

786 ᴱAveni Anthony F., World archaeoastronomy [2d Oxford conference, Merida MEX, Jan. 1986]. C 1989, Univ. 512 p.; 199 fig. £75. 0-521-34180-9. – ᴿAntiquity 64 (1990) 697s (I. J. Thorpe: Assyria... also China, Wisconsin, Peru).

787 ᴱBar-Yosef O., Vandermeersch B., Investigations in Southern Levantine prehistory: BAR-Int 497. Ox 1989. viii-350 p. 0-86054-637-3 [OIAc Oc90].

788 ᴱBell Martin, Limbrey Susan, Archaeological aspects of woodland ecology [Environmental Archaeology symposium, Bristol Sept. 1981]: BAR-Int 146. 333 p. £14. – ᴿBInstArch 26 (1989) 236s (W. H. Bonner).

789 Bérard Claude, présente, Images et société en Grèce ancienne; l'iconographie comme méthode d'analyse; Actes du colloque international, Lausanne 8-11 févr. 1984: Cah. Archéol. Romande 36. Lausanne 1987. 248 p. – ᴿRArtLv 21 (1988) 179-181 (F. de Callatay).

790 ᴱBerman Lawrence M., The art of Amenhotep III, art historical analysis; papers presented at the international symposium, Cleveland 20-21 Nov. 1987. Cleveland 1990, Museum of Art / Indiana Univ. xii-92 p.; 27 pl. 0-940717-01-8. 8 art.; infra.

790* ᴱBest Jan G.P., Vries Nanny M.W. de, Thracians and Mycenaeans, Proceedings of the Fourth International Congress of Thracology, Rotterdam, 24-26 Sept. 1984: Frankfort Found. 11. Leiden 1989, Brill. 306 p. 90-04-08864-4. 23 art., 3 infra.

791 ᴱBintliff John, Extracting meaning from the past [meeting Bradford 1987]. Ox 1988, Oxbow. 98 p.; 7 fig. £7 pa. 0-946897-15-8. – ᴿAntiquity 64 (1990) 195s (N. Merriman).

791* [ᴱBuchner Edmond], Akten des XIII. Internationalen Kongresses für Klassische Archäologie, Berlin 1988, DAI. Mainz 1990, von Zabern. xvii-701 p.; 143 fig.; 91 pl. 3-8053-1099-4. 273 art., plures infra.

792 ᴱCalder William M.ᴵᴵᴵ, *Cobet* Justus, Heinrich SCHLIEMANN nach hundert Jahren [Symposion Bad-Homburg, 5-9.XII.1989]. Fra 1990, V. Klostermann. 460 p.; ill. 3-465-02266-1. 21 art., 7 infra.

793 ᴱCarancini G., Miscellanea protostorica. R 1990, Bretschneider. v-410 p. – ᴿRÉLat 68 (1990) 247 (R. *Adam*).

793* ᴱChristenson Andrew L., Tracing archaeology's past; the historiography of archaeology [1987 Scholars' Conference]. Carbondale 1990, Southern Illinois Univ. xi-252 p. $30. 0-8093-1523-8. 17 art. – ᴿAJA 94 (1990) 485 (T. C. *Patterson*).

794 Clutton-Brock J., The walking larder; problems of domestication, pastoralism and predation [Southampton 1986 World Archaeological Congress]. L 1989, Unwin Hyman. 368 p.; ill. £40. 0-04-445013-3. – ᴿHelinium 30 (1990) 154s (A. T. *Clason*).

794* Coulson William D. E., *al.*, Archaic Greek architectural terracottas (International Conference) = Hesperia 59,1 (1990) 11s (-324).

795 Criscuolo Lucia, *Geraci* Giovanni, Egitto e storia antica dall'Ellenismo all'età araba; bilancio di un confronto: Atti del colloquio internazionale, Bologna 31 agosto - 2 settembre 1987. Bo 1989, Clueb. ix-716 p. 46 art.

796 ᴱCurtis John, Bronze-working centres of western Asia c. 1000-539 B.C. [3-day British Museum colloquium, July 1986]. L 1988, Kegan Paul. 342 p.; 183 fig. £30. 0-7103-0274-6. – ᴿAntiquity 64 (1990) 172s (W. T. *Chase*: J. *Tubb* on Palestine, A. *Leahy* Egypt, I. *Winter* N. Syria; Curtis, Assyria ...).

797 ᴱDepeyrot Georges, *al.*, Rythmes de la production monétaire, de l'Antiquité à nos jours [colloque Paris, 10-12 janvier 1986]: NumLov 7. LvN 1987 [1990], Séminaire de Numismatique M. Hoc. xvi-775 p.; XIII pl.; maps. Fb 6950 [RBgNum 137,213-6, H. *Frère*; RNum 33,281, M. *Amandry*].

798 ᴱDriel-Murray C. van, The sources of evidence; proceedings of the fifth Roman military equipment conference (Nijmegen 1987): BAR-Int 476. Ox 1989. viii-377 p.

799 ᴱEaton-Krauss Marianne, *Graefe* Erhart, Studien zur ägyptischen Kunstgeschichte [Münster 1987]: Hild.ÄgBeit 29. Hildesheim 1990, Gerstenberg. x-112 p.; 26 pl. 3-8087-8117-6. 5 art.; 3 infra.

800 FINLEY Moses I. mém.: La cité antique? Paris, Collège de France 22-24.IX.1988: Opus 6-8 (1987-9). 17 art. [Announced with Opus 5 (1986)].

801 GHUL Mahmoud: Arabian Studies in honor of ~; Symposium at Yarmouk University, Dec. 8-11, 1984: Inst. Archaeology series, 2. Wsb 1984, Harrassowitz. 177 p. + ❹ 160 p. 3-447-02796-7 [OIAc JJ90]. – ᴿLA 40 (1990) 483s (P. *Kaswalder*).

801* ᴱHaas Volkert, Hurriter und Hurritisch; Konstanzer Altorientalische Symposien 2, Xenia 21. Konstanz 1988, Univ. 318 p. 3-87940-324-4. 10 art.; infra.

802 ᴱHarris David R., *Hillman* Gordon C., Foraging and farming; the evolution of plant exploration [Southampton World Archaeological Congress 1986]. L 1989, Unwin Hyman. xxxiii-733 p.; ill. £50; pa. £20. – ᴿBInstArch 26 (1989) 268-270 (J. *Chapman*).

803 ᴱHastorf Christine A., *Popper* Virginia S., Current paleoethnobotany; analytical methods and cultural interpretations of archaeological plant remains [1985 symposium, Society for American Archaeology; where?]: Prehistoric Archaeology and Ecology. Ch 1989, Univ. xii-236 p.; 61 fig. $25; pa. $10. – ᴿAJA 94 (1990) 345 (Jane *Fitt*).

804   ᴱHenrickson Elizabeth F., *Thuesen* Ingolf, Upon this foundation; the 'Ubaid reconsidered; symposium Elsinore May 30 - June 1, 1988: Niebuhr Inst. 10 [0902-5499]. K 1989, Mus.Tusc. 478 p. 87-7289-070-3 [OIAc S90].

805   ᴱHershkovitz I., People and culture in change; proceedings of the Second Symposium on Upper Paleolithic, Mesolithic and Neolithic populations of Europe and the Mediterranean basin: BAR-Int 508. Ox 1989. 2 vol., 563 p. £35. 0-86054-649-7. – ᴿAntiquity 64 (1990) 687s (M. *Zvelebil*, J. *Lewthwaite*: disappoints).

806   ᴱHerz Norman, *Waelkens* Marc, Classical marble; geochemistry, technology, trade: Proceedings Lucca 9-13.V.1988, NATO ASI Applied Sciences 153. Dordrecht 1988, Kluwer. xvi-428 p.; ill. 90-247-3793-1. 49 art.; 5 infra [See also d69 infra].

807   ᴱHesberg Henner von, *Zanker* Paul, Römische Gräberstrassen; Selbstdarstellung – Status – Standard; Kolloquium München 28.-30. Okt. 1985. Bayr. Akad. Abh. NF 95. Mü 1987, Beck. 312 p.; 93 fig.; 58 pl.; 5 plans. – ᴿGnomon 62 (1990) 734-9 (C. *Compostella*).

808   Hours Francis, hommage [bibliog. 13-16]: Préhistoire du Levant II. Processus des changements culturels: Colloque CNRS 30 mai - 4 juin 1988, org. *Aurenche* O., al. = Paléorient 14/2 (1988), 345 p.; 34 art. et 15,1 (1989) 290 p., 21 art.

808* ᴱIngold Tim, What is an animal [and what (from when) is a human]? Southampton 1986 One World Archaeology 1. L 1988, Unwin Hyman. xviii-189 p.; 15 fig. £28. 0-04-945012-5 [Antiquity 65,147, A.J. *Legge*].

809   ᴱKelley A. L., Papers of the pottery workshop, 3d internat. congress of Egyptology, Toronto, Sept. 1982. Toronto 1983, Royal Ontario Museum. 43 p.

809* ᴱKrzyzaniak Lech, *Kobusiewicz* Michał, Late prehistory of the Nile Basin and the Sahara; Proceedings of the International Symposium, Polish Acad., Poznań 11.-15.IX.1984: Studies in African archaeology 2. Poznań 1989, Arch. Museum. 547 p.

810   ᴱManzanilla L., Studies in the neolithic and urban revolutions: CHILDE colloquium, Mexico 1986: BAR-Int 349. Ox 1987. 381 p.; 33 fig. [AcArchH 43,430, E. *Bánffy*].

811   Massa-Pairault Françoise-Hélène, présente, Crise et transformation des sociétés archaïques de l'Italie antique au Vᵉ siècle av. J.-C.; Actes de la Table Ronde, École Française de Rome / Unité de Recherches Étrusco-Italiques CNRS, Rome 19-21 nov. 1987: Coll. ÉcFrR 137. R 1990, École Française. [vi-] 426 p. 2-7283-8308-8. 20 art., 3 infra.

811* ᴱMastroroberto Marisa, Archeologia e botanica; Atti del Convegno di studi sul contributo dell Botanica alla conoscenza e alla conservazione delle aree archeologiche vesuviane, Pompei 7-9 aprile 1989: Soprintendenza Mg 2. R 1990, Bretschneider. 117 p. [Salesianum 53,762].

812   ᶠMatson Frederick R., A pot for all reasons; ceramic ecology revisited [1986 American Anthropological Asn symposium in honor of ∼], ᴱKolb Charles C., *Lackey* Louanna M. Ph 1988, Temple Univ. xxv-261 p.; 54 fig. 10 art. – ᴿAJA 94 (1990) 488s (Karen D. *Vitelli*: 'special publication of Cerámica de cultura maya et al.').

812* ᴱMiller Daniel, al., Domination and resistance: One World Archaeology 3. L 1989, Unwin Hyman. xx-332 p. 0-04-445023-2. P. 229-239, *Larsen* Mogens T., Orientalism and Near Eastern archaeology.

813   ᴱMilles Annie, al., The beginnings of agriculture [Cardiff 18-21 Sept. 1987]; Symposia Environmental Archaeology 8: BAR-Int 496. Ox 1989. xii-267 p. 0-86054-636-5. 12 art.; 3 infra.

813* ᴱMiroschedji P. de, L'urbanisation de la Palestine à l'âge du Bronze ancien; bilan et perspectives des recherches actuelles; Actes du Colloque d'Emmaüs, 20-24 oct. 1986: BAR-Int 527. Ox 1989. £28.

814 *a*) ᴱMoe Dagfinn, *Hicks* S., Impact of prehistoric and medieval man on the vegetation; man at the forest limit: meeting Ravello Dec. 9-10, 1989: PACT 31. Strasbourg 1990, Conseil de l'Europe. 116 p. 0257-8727. 14 art.

— *b*) ᴱMook W.G., *Waterbolk* H.T., Proceedings of the Second International Symposium ¹⁴C and Archaeology, Groningen 1987: PACT 29. Strasbourg 1990, Conseil de l'Europe. 459 p. 0257-8727. 33 art. 3 (Levant) infra.

814* ᴱMorphy Howard, Animals into art [Southampton 1986]: One World Archaeology 7. L 1989, Unwin Hyman. xiv-465 p.; 25 colour. pl. £50. – ᴿBInstArch 26 (1989) 285s (J.M. *Hoadley*).

815 ᴱNelson Ben A., Decoding prehistoric ceramics [partly Vancouver ʙᴄ symposium 1979]. Carbondale 1985, S. Illinois Univ. xv-441 p.; 82 fig. $35. 0-8093-1189-5. – ᴿJField 17 (1990) 93-98 (C.C. *Kolb*, also on *Rice* P.M. 1987).

815* ᴱNelson Sarah M., *Kehoe* Alice B., Powers of observation; alternative views in archaeology [section Nov. 1987 Chicago meeting of American Anthropological Asn]: Archaeological papers 2. Tempe 1990, Amer. Anthrop. vii-119 p. 0-913167-42-6 [OIAc Ja91].

816 O'Connell Kevin G., *al.*, 'A hundred years of excavation at Tell el-Hesi'; a symposium sponsored by the Palestine Exploration Fund and the joint expedition to Tell el-Hesi, 19 June 1990: PEQ 122,2 (1990) 83-86 (-132).

816* ᴱOtte Marcel, L'homme de Neandertal, Actes du colloque international de Liège (4-7 dec. 1986), 1. La chronologie (*Schwarcz* H.P.); 2. L'environnement (*Laville* Henri) [3.-8., *al.*]; ÉtRechArch 28s [30-35]. Liège 1988, Univ. 143 p., Fb 950; 222 p., Fb 1100; ill. – ᴿHelinium 30 (1990) 126-9 [208-13] (S. *De Laet*).

817 ᴱPasquinucci Marinella, *Menchelli* Simonetta, La cartografia archeologica, problemi e prospettive: Atti del Convegno internazionale, Pisa, 21-22 marzo 1988. Pisa 1989, Amm. Provinciale. 308 p. 15 art.; 3 infra.

817* Picazo Marina, *Sanmartí* Enric, Ceràmiques gregues i helenistiques a la península ibérica, Taula Rodana Empúries 18-20 març 1983: Mg Emporitanes 8. Barc 1985, Inst. Prehist. 168 p. 84-85060-45-8 [BO 48,272-7, Luisa *Ramos Sainz*].

818 ᴱPinsky Valerie, *Wylie* Alison [organizers of respective symposia], Critical traditions in contemporary archaeology; essays in the philosophy, history, and socio-politics of archaeology. C 1990, Univ. 160 p. $54.40. 0-521-32109-3. – ᴿAntiquity 64 (1990) 965s (U. *Veit*, Eng.).

818* Puglisi Salvatore M., mem.: L'interpretazione funzionale dei dati in paletnologia, giornate di studio, giugno 1988: Origini 14,1 (1988s). R [1991], Univ. 88-7597-131-5/. 358 p. + 359-780. 38 art.; 4 infra.

819 ᴱRoodenberg J., Aceramic neolithic in S.E. Turkey, Round Table June 2-4, 1986, Istanbul. Leiden 1988, Ned. Inst. Nab. Oosten. vii-232 p. *f* 102,50. – ᴿBInstArch 26 (1989) 232s (J. *Mellaart*).

820 ᴱRoueché C., *Erim* K.T., Aphrodisias papers; recent work on architecture and sculpture [London King's College 1987]: JRS supp. 1. AA 1990, Univ. Michigan. 160 p. $30.

821 ᴱRupp David W., Western Cyprus, connections; an archaeological symposium, Brock University, St. Catherines ᴏɴᴛ March 21-22, 1986:

SIMA 77. Göteborg 1987, Åström. 240 p. – ᴿPEQ 122 (1990) 147-9 (Carolyn *Elliott*).

822 ᴱ**Sancisi-Weerdenburg** Heleen, Achaemenid history: *a*) with *Kuhrt* Amélie [III. 1985/8 → 4,713] IV. Centre and Periphery; Groningen 1986; – *b*) with *Drijvers* J.W., V. The roots of the European tradition, Groningen 1987. Leiden 1990. Nederlands Instituut voor het Nabije Oosten. xv-274 p.; xii-170 p.; ill. 90-6258-404-7; -5-5. 17 art. + 11 art.; 5 + 2 infra.

822* ᴱ**Sancisi-Weerdenburg** Heleen, *al.*, Continuity and change; proceedings of the [8th and] last Achaemenid history workshop, April 6-8, 1990, Ann Arbor. Leiden [BO 47/1 back cover ad, with complete data on the preceding volumes; 4 & 5 in 1990; 6 & 7 for 1991].

823 ᴱ**Schneider** Laurie, Phrygian art and archaeology [AIA colloquium 1987]: Source, [journal of] notes in the history of art 7,3s special (1988). NY 1988, Ars Brevis. 71 p. $25. 0737-4453 [BO 48,266, M. van *Loon*].

823* ᴱ**Seeden** Helga, Processes of neolithization: International Congress of Anthropological and Ethnological Sciences, Zagreb 24-31.VIII.1988: Berytus 36 (1988). 193 p. [Cf. → 5,832, ᴱ*Aurenche* O., Néolithisations 1986/9].

824 Transition periods in Iranian history, Actes du Symposium FrB 22-24 mai 1985: StIran Cah 5. Lv 1987, Peeters. 264 p. Fb 2000. – ᴿBO 47 (1990) 432s (tit. pp.).

825 ᴱ**Tzalas** Harry, Tropis 1, First international symposium on ship construction in antiquity [Piraeus 1985], proceedings. Athens 1989, Hellenic Institute/Nautical Tradition. 297 p.; 146 fig. – ᴿIntJNaut 19 (1990) 345s (F. *Hocker*: 1987 and 1989 acta awaited shortly).

826 **Vadas** F., present., International prehistoric conference, Szekszárd 9.-19.V.1985. Szekszárd 1986, B. B. Adám Muzeum. 387 p.; ill. – ᴿBonnJbb 189 (1989) 547-550 (J. *Petrasch*).

826* ᴱ**Voorrijs** A., *Ottaway* B. S., New tools from mathematical archaeology, 5th Int. Symposium Kraków/Mogilany May 24-29, 1989. Kraków 1990, Polish Academy. vi-126 p. – ᴿHelinium 30 (1990) 291s (F. *Verhaeghe*: information packed into modest presentation).

827 ᶠ**WATERBOLK** H. T.: Archaeology and landscape; symposium 19-20 Oct. 1987, ᴱ**Biersma** M., *al.* Groningen 1988, Univ. 206 p.; ill. ƒ 29,50. 90-367-0104-X. – ᴿHelinium 30 (1990) 146-8 (S. De *Laet*).

827* ᴱ**Watkins** Sarah C., *Brown* Carol E., Conservation of ancient Egyptian materials [conference Bristol Dec. 15-16, 1988]. L 1988, UK Institute for Conservation. 1-871656-02-8 [OIAc JuJ89].

A3 *Opera consultationis* **Reference works** 1. *plurium* **separately** *infra*.

828 **ANRW**: Aufstieg und Niedergang der römischen Welt, II. Principat, ᴱ**Haase** Wolfgang: [→ 5,878] **18**, 3-4, Religion; Heidentum; die religiösen Verhältnisse in den Provinzen, Forts. 1990, xii + p. 1659-2211; xii + p. 2213-2797. – **33**, 1.2, Sprache und Literatur: Allgemeines 2 Jht; Einzelne Autoren der traianischen und frühhadrianischen Zeit, 1990: xxv-847 p; xii + p. 849-1647 (alles über TACITUS). B, de Gruyter. 3-11-010382-6; -2630-3; -0375-3; -89-3. – ᴿAntClas 59 (1990) 424s . 525s (M.-T. *Raepsaet-Charlier*, 36,1; 10,1); AnzAltW 43 (1990) 35-39 (G. *Radke*, 16,3); ÉtClas 58 (1990) 290 . 414 (A. *Wankenne*, 36,3; 10,1); Gnomon 62 (1990) 462-4 (W. *Kissel*, 32,5); Gymnasium 97 (1990) 370-4 (F. *Bömer*; 11,1; 18,2; 33,1; 36,3: tit. pp.); Irénikon 63 (1990) 299-301 (A. L.); NTAbs 35,262 (18,3s); Numen 37 (1990) 96-109 (A. *Wasserstein*, 16,3; 8,1; 19,1s;

21,1s); RelStR 16 (1990) 272 (O.R. *Mueller*, 20,1s); ZSavR 106 (1989) 725-7 (D. *Nörr*, 20,1; 36,1).

829 **AugL:** Augustinus-Lexikon, ᴱ**Mayer** Cornelius [I, 1-3, 1986-8 ➤ 2,637*... 5,879], I, Fasc. 4, Asinus-Bellum. Ba 1990, Schwabe. col. 481-640. DM 39. 3-7965-0874-X. – ᴿAntClas 59 (1990) 407s (H. *Savon*, 3); Bijdragen 51 (1990) 206s (M. *Schneiders*, 1-3); IrTQ 56 (1990) 69-71 (G. *Watson*, 3); JEH 40 (1989) 451 (H. *Chadwick*, 3); Stromata 46 (1990) 209s . 425-7 (F.J. *Weismann*, 1-4).

— [apparently unrelated to AugL] **Hensellek** Werner, **Schilling** Peter, Specimina eines Lexicon Augustinianum (SLA), erstellt auf Grund sämtlicher Editionen des CSEL; 1987 ➤ k255.

830 **BijH:** [ᴱ**Woude** A. van der], World of the OT 2, 1989 ➤ 5,880: ᴿBL (1990) 29 (J.R. *Bartlett*); BTrans 41 (1990) 355s (D.J. *Wiseman* contrasts with Bɪᴍsoɴ's identical title); HebSt 31 (1990) 264s (A. *Luc*); Vidyajyoti 53 (1989) 634s (P.M. *Meagher* compares with Roɢᴇʀsoɴ J. 1988).

831 **CAH:** Cambridge Ancient History 4, Persia, Greece and the Western Mediterranean c. 525 to 479 B.C., ᴱ**Boardman** John, *al.* C 1988, Univ. ➤ 4,785; 5,881: 0-521-32804-2; -30580-2. – ᴿAntClas 59 (1990) 475s (M.-T. *Raepsaet-Charlier*); RArchéol (1990) 423-6 (P. *Briant*).

832 **CAH** 8: ᴱ**Astin** A.E., Rome and the Mediterranean to 133 B.C. C 1989, Univ. xiii-625 p. 0-521-23448-4.

833 Catholicisme, ᴱ**Mathon** G., *al.* [XII, 54,1988 ➤ 5,882]: ᴿBLitEc 91 (1990) 145 (S. *Légasse*, 52-54); Gregorianum 71 (1990) 610s (J. *Galot*, 54); NRT 112 (1990) 785 (L.-J. *Renard*, 55-57); RHE 85 (1990) 208s (R. *Aubert*, 55).

834 **CHIran** 2. ᴱ**Gershevitch** I. 1985 ➤ 1,885... 5,883: ᴿArOr 58 (1990) 181-3 (M. *Shaki*); BSO 52 (1989) 151s (D.O. *Morgan*, 6).

835 **CHJud:** The Cambridge history of Judaism, ᴱ**Davies** W.D., Finkelstein Louis, 2. The Hellenistic age 1989 ➤ 5,884; 18 art., infra [JAAR 58,326 '1990']. – ᴿExpTim 102 (1990s) 55 (R. *Coggins*, 2: seriously flawed, outdated at birth); RechSR 78 (1990) 471s (A. *Paul*, 2).

836 **DHGE:** Dictionnaire d'Histoire et de Géographie Ecclésiastiques, ᴱ**Aubert** R. [XXIII,135, 1989 ➤ 5,885]: XXIII,136, Henneberg-Henryków, col. 1025-1280; Vol. XXIII (137, col. 1281-1518: 2-7063-0173-2). – XXIV,138, Herlet-Herzog 1-256. P 1990, Letouzey & A. F 66. 2-7063-0181-3 – ᴿNRT 112 (1990) 782s (N. *Plumat*, 133-6); RHE 85 (1990) 524s (H. *Silvestre*, 135).

837 **DictSpir:** Dictionnaire de Spiritualité, ᴱ**Rayez** A., *al.* [XIV, 92-94, 1989 ➤ 5,886]: XIV, 95 & XV, 96-98. P 1990, Beauchesne. – ᴿBLitEc 91 (1990) 146 (S. *Légasse*, 89s); DivThom 92 (1989) 198-214 (G. *Perini*, 89-94); Manresa 62 (1990) 91 (M. *Alcalá*); NRT 112 (1990) 783s (L.-J. *Renard*, 95-98); OrChrPer 56 (1990) 214-6 (V. *Poggi*, 92-94); REspir 49 (1990) 635-7 (J. *Damián Gaitán*, 89-94]; RET 50 (1990) 191-4 (M. *Gesteira Garza*, 92-94); RHE 85 (1990) 522s (R. *Aubert*, 92-98); RHPR 70 (1990) 340s (M. *Chevallier*, 92-94).

837* **DizTF:** Dizionario di Teologia Fondamentale, ᴱ**Latourelle** R., *Fisichella* R.: Pont. Univ. Gregoriana. Assisi 1990, Cittadella. p. 395-403, *Gilbert* Maurice, Esegesi integrale.

838 **DMA:** Dictionary of the Middle Ages, ᴱ**Strayer** Joseph R. [11, - textiles 1988 ➤ 4,792] 12, Thaddeus legend - Zwart 'Noċ'. NY 1989, Scribner's. xv-751 p. 0-684-18278-5.

838* **DPA:** Dizionario patristico e di antichità cristiane, ᴱ**Di Berardino** Angelo, 1-3, 1983-8 ➤ 4,793: ᴿStromata 45 (1989) 467 (F.J. *Weismann*).

839 — Dictionnaire encyclopédique du christianisme ancien [1983-8 ⇥ 65,731 ... 5,888], ᵀᴱVial François. P 1990, Cerf. xxxi-1279 p.; xxiv + p. 1281-2641. 2-204-03017-1; -4182-3 [ÉTRel 66,444, J.-D. *Dubois*; RTLv 21,401]. – ᴿMondeB 66 (1990) 63 (P. *Maraval*).

840 **EncIslam:** Encyclopedia of Islam², ᴱ**Bosworth** C. E., *al.* [VI, 107-110, 1989 ⇥ 5,889] VI, 113s, Mar'ashis-Mawlid, p. 896-1044; VII, 115s, Mifrash-Mirwaḥa, p. 1-128; 90-04-09369-9. Leiden 1990, Brill. – ᴿOLZ 85 (1990) 517-521 (M. *Greskowiak*, vol. 1-5).

841 **EncRel:** Encyclopedia of Religion, ᴱ**Eliade** M., 1987 ⇥ 2,585... 5,892: ᴿCritRR 2 (1989) 1-22 (H. H. *Penner*); 23-40 (W. S. *Green* on Judaism); 41-56 (J. O. *Duke* on Christianity); 57-76 (Jane D. *McAuliffe*, Islam); 77-104 (D. *Brooks*, Hinduism); 105-116 (M. D. *Eckel*, Buddhism).

842 — ᴱ**Eliade** Mircea, Religion, history and culture: 5 [+ others dubiously coming] paperback abridgments from Encyclopedia of Religion (1988) ⇥ 2,585]. Basingstoke 1989, Collier-Macmillan. 0-02-897211-2; -212-0; -402-6; -403-4; -404-2. £10 each. – ᴿExpTim 101 (1989s) 309s (P. *Bishop*: curious selections; and the publisher has ceased).

843 **EncTF:** ᴱ**Ruggieri** Giuseppe, Enciclopedia di Teologia Fondamentale I, 1987 ⇥ 4,797: ᴿActuBbg 26 (1989) 23-25 (J. *Boada*); Protestantesimo 45 (1990) 229s (F. *Ferrario*); RTLv 21 (1990) 234s (E. *Brito*).

844 **EvKL:** Evangelisches Kirchenlexikon, ᴱ**Fahlbusch** E., II, 1987 ⇥ 5,894: ᴿCarthaginensia 6 (1990) 226 (F. *Martínez Fresneda*, 2); ÖkRu 39 (1990) 510-2 (H. *Vorster*); SixtC 21 (1990) 728s (R. *Jütte*, 1s: Eerdmans translation under way); TLZ 115 (1990) 665-7 (E. *Winkler*); TPQ 138 (1990) 73 . 272 (R. *Zinnhobler*, 5s); TRu 55 (1990) 372-7 (L. *Perlitt*, 1: 'Benin und Bhutan, aber nicht Bethlehem'); ZkT 112 (1990) 361 (L. *Lies*, 2/6).

ExWNT: ᴱ**Balz** Horst, *Schneider* Gerhard, ⇥ 868, Exegetical dictionary of the New Testament I. Aaron-Enoch, 1990: the single items in their German form, with author, were noted in ⇥ vol. 60-64.

845 **GLNT:** Grande Lessico del Nuovo Testamento [< TWNT, ᴱ*Kittel* G.], ᵀᴱ**Montagnini** Felice, *al.* [XIV, 1984 ⇥ 65,739]. XV. Brescia 1988, Paideia. – ᴿProtestantesimo 45 (1990) 61-63 (B. *Corsani*).

846 **HbFT:** Handbuch der Fundamentaltheologie 1-4, ᴱ**Kern** Walter, *al.*, 1985-8 ⇥ 1,898... 5,896: ᴿCommSev 22 (1989) 96-99 (M. de *Burgos*, 1-4); HerdKor 43 (1989) 190 (U. *Ruh*, 4); TPQ 138 (1990) 275-7 (F. *Reisinger*, 1-4).

847 **ISBEnc:** International Standard Bible Encyclopaedia, ᴱ**Bromiley** G. 4 (1988) ⇥ 5,898: ᴿVidyajyoti 54 (1990) 541s (P. M. *Meagher*, 4).

848 **LexÄg:** Lexikon der Ägyptologie [⇥ 5,899], Indices Lfg. 52, p. 241-351; Wsb 1990, Harrassowitz. 3-447-03057-7.

849 **LexMA:** Lexikon des Mittelalters, ᴱ**Mariacher** B. [IV, 10, 1989 ⇥ 5,901], V, 1s. Mü 1990, Artemis. – ᴿAnBoll 108 (1990) 222s (J. van der *Straeten*, 4); AnHConc 21 (1989) 212 . 433 (G. *Kreuzer*, 4/5-10); AnPraem 66 (1990) 89s (L. *Horstkötter*, 4/5-10); ColcFran 60 (1990) 753s (O. *Schmucki*); JTS 41 (1990) 731s (H. *Chadwick*, 4/8ss); Numen 37 (1990) 277-9 (P. S. van *Koningsveld*, 1-4 on Judaism); OrChrPer 56 (1990) 217s (V. *Poggi*); RBén 100 (1990) 594 (P. *Verbraken*, 4/8-10); RHE 85 (1990) 783-5 (J. *Pycke*, all 1988/9); TR 86 (1990) 466s (R. *Köttle*, 1-4); TRu 55 (1990) 188-199 (M. A. *Schmidt*, 2s); ZkT 112 (1990) 231s (H. B. *Meyer*, 4/8-10).

850 **NBL:** Neues Bibel-Lexikon, ᴱ**Görg** Manfred, *Lang* Bernhard (Lfg. 1s, 1988s ⇥ 4,804; 5,902), Band I. Z 1990, Benziger. xvi-965 col.; 12 fig. 3-545-23074-0. – ᴿNubica 1s (1990) 361s (P. *Scholz*); ZAW 102 (1990) 453 (H.-C. *Schmitt*); ZkT 112 (1990) 91s (J. M. *Oesch*, Lfg. 1).

851 **NDizTB:** Nuovo dizionario di teologia biblica, ERossano P., al. 1988
→ 4,806; 5,903: RQVidCr 147 (1989) 130 (P. *Busquets*); RuBi 43 (1990)
170 (J. *Chmiel*); STEv 1 (1989) 209 (P. *Bolognesi*).

852 — Nuevo diccionario de teología bíblica, TE*Requeña* Eloy, *Ortiz* Alfonso.
M 1990, Paulinas. 2025 p. 84-285-1357-0.

853 **RAC:** Reallexikon für Antike und Christentum, EDassmann Ernst [XV,
115, 1989 → 5,904]: XV, 116, [Hippokrates] Hippolytus - Hispania. Stu
1990, Hiersemann. col. 481-640. 3-7772-9010-6. – RNRT 112 (1990) 132s.
784 s (N. *Plumat*, 105-112; 113-5); RPg 63 (1989) 384-7 (J. *André*, 13s).

853* **RLA:** Reallexikon der Assyriologie, EEdzard Dietz O., al. [VII, 1-4
(1987-9) → 5,905]; VII, 5s-7s -Medizin (Ende des Bandes). B/NY 1990, de
Gruyter. p. 321-631. 3-11-010441-5; -2-3.

854 **SDB:** Supplément, Dictionnaire de la Bible, EBriend J., al., XI [62,1988
→ 4,809; 5,906], 63-64A, Salut-Samuel. P 1990, Letouzey & A. col.
737-1056. F 350.

854* **StSp:** Storia della Spiritualità, EBarbaglio G. Bo 1988 [→ 5,908],
Dehoniane: RRasT 30 (1989) 393s (L. *Borriello*, 1; 3C; 8).

855 **StSpG:** Storia della Spiritualità, EGrossi V. Roma 1989 [→ 5,909],
Borla: RCarthaginensia 6 (1990) 205 (J. F. *Cuenca*, 1).

856 **TDOT:** Theological dictionary of the Old Testament, EBotterweck G. J.,
Ringgren H.; TGreen David E. VI, yôbēl-yātar. GR 1990, Eerdmans.
xxi-491 p. Most of the separate articles with their authors are given for
TWAT III,5-9 (1980-2) → 859. – RCriswT 2 (1988) 426-8 (G. L. *Klein*).

857 **TRE:** Theologische Realenzyklopädie, EMüller G., al. [18,1989 → 5,911]
19, Kirchenrechtsquellen-Kreuz. 1990; 818 p. DM 396. – 20. Kreuz-
züge-Leo XIII. 1990; 793 p. 3-11-012355-X; -655-9. – Register zu Band
1-17. B 1990, de Gruyter. 229 p. DM 118. 3-11-010479-2. – RBib-
HumRen 51 (1989) 253-5. 730s (I. *Hazlett*, 16s); ÉTRel 65 (1990) 301s (B.
Reymond, 17); JEH 41 (1990) 74-76. 324-6. 512-4 (O. *Chadwick*, 13-17);
NRT 112 (1990) 133s (L.-J. *Renard*, 17s); ÖkRu 39 (1990) 256 (H. *Krüger*,
18); Protestantesimo 45 (1990) 70. 323s (J. A. *Soggin*, 18s); TPQ 138
(1990) 281 (G. *Bachl*, 17); TR 86 (1990) 279-284 (R. *Bäumer*, 17s); TRu 55
(1990) 380-3 (E. *Grässer*, 14-17); TZBas 46 (1990) 383s (W. *Rordorf*,
16-18); ZkT 112 (1990) 362 (L. *Lies*, 18).

858 **TUmAT:** Texte aus der Umwelt des Alten Testaments [2/5, 1989 → 5,912],
3, Lfg. 1, **Römer** W. H. P., *Soden* W. v., Weisheitstexte. Gü 1990, Mohn.
188 p. DM 138; sb. 118. 3-579-00072-1 [BL 91,129, W. G. *Lambert*]. –
RZkT 112 (1990) 92s (F. *Mohr*, 2/3).

859 **TWAT:** Theologisches Wörterbuch zum Alten Testament, EFabry H.;
Ringgren H. [VI. 8-11, 1989 → 5,913] VII. Lfg. 1-2, qôṣ-rā'âh, col. 1-256;
Lfg. 3-5, rā'âh-rāṣāh, col. 257-640. Stu 1990, Kohlhammer. DM 84; ...
3-17-010733-X; -1553-7. [BL 91,14, R. N. *Whybray*: irritatingly illogical
arrangement]. – RTLZ 115 (1990) 191-3 (J. *Heller*, 6).

A3.3   *Opera consultationis* **biblica** *non excerpta infra* – **not subindexed.**

860 EAchtemeier Paul J., Harper's Bible dictionary 1985 → 1,913... 5,915;
also Bangalore 1990, Theol. Publ. Nº 85: RJAOS 110 (1990) 586-9 (D.
Marcus: 40 errors plus 20 typos, but an outstanding work); Vidyajyoti 54
(1990) 540 (P. M. *Meagher*).

861 **Bellinger** Gerhard [cf. → 890], al., Dictionnaire illustré de la Bible [1985],
TE*Cannuyer* Christian. P 1990, Bordas. 600 p. F 399. – RÉtudes 373
(1990) 282 (Nicole *Gueunier*: traduction parfois 'cahotique').

862 **Beneker** Wilhelm, Das will ich wissen; Bibellexikon zum AT. Wü 1987, Echter. 172 p.; 104 color. pl. DM 16,80. – RTPQ 137 (1989) 80 (Roswitha *Unfried*).

863 **Bocian** Martin, Lexikon der biblischen Personen, mit ihrem Fortleben in Judentum, Christentum, Islam, Dichtung, Musik und Kunst 1989 → 5,922; DM 38: RBLtg 63 (1990) 60s (C. *Dohmen*); EvKomm 23 (1990) 438s (E. *Stammler*); JBQ 19 (1990s) 40s (S. *Liptzin* regrets that data from Yiddish and modern Hebrew literature are not included); Salesianum 52 (1990) 893 (R. *Sabin*); TLZ 115 (1990) 673 (R. M.).

864 E**Bogaert** P.-M., *al.*, Dictionnaire encyclopédique de la Bible 1987 → 3,888 ... 5,923: RRBibArg 52 (1990) 128 (A. J. *Levoratti*: presented as updated second edition of VAN DEN BORN, but 87% of the items are enrirely new).

865 E**Coggins** R. J., *Houlden* J. L., A dictionary of biblical interpretation [146 contributors]. L/Ph 1990, SCM/Trinity. xvi-751 p. £35. 0-334-00294-X / [BL 91,11, G. I. *Davies*: TORREY the only item on a 20th-century scholar; currently fashionable movements are mostly treated by enthusiastic practitioners]. – RExpTim 101 (1989s) 375s (R. *Lunt*); ScotBEv 8 (1990) 142-4 (I. H. *Marshall*); TLond 93 (1990) 475-7 (Λ. E. *Harvey*); TsTNjim 30 (1990) 305 (L. *Grollenberg*).

866 E**Douglas** J. D., *Tenney* M. C., NIV compact dictionary of the Bible [< NIntDB], E*White* C. GR 1989, Zondervan. xxix-672 p. 0-310-33180-3 [NTAbs 34,98].

867 E**Elwell** Walter A., *a)* Baker Encyclopedia of the Bible 1988 → 5,933: RCriswT 4 (1989s) 196s (P. A. *Bernhardt*: the 178 evangelical contributors sometimes ignore more recent views); RelStR 16 (1990) 63 (W. L. *Humphreys*); Themelios 16 (1990s) 29 (K. A. *Eckleberger*); *b)* = (?) **Elwell** Walter A., Marshall Pickering Encyclopedia of the Bible 1990. 1079 p. + 2210 p. £29.50 each. 0-551-01970-0; -2052-0. – RExpTim 102 (1990s) 180 (C. S. *Rodd*).

868 **ExWNT** [→ 60,880 ... 1,894], Eng. Exegetical Dictionary of the New Testament, E**Balz** H., *Schneider* G., 1., T*Howard* V. P., (Aaron-asaleutos), *Thompson* J. W. (Asaph-Enôch). GR/E 1990, Eerdmans/Clark. xxiv-463 p. £30. 0-8028-2409-9 / 0-567-09540-1 [NRT 113,425s, X. *Jacques*].

869 **Fouilloux** Danielle, *al.*, Dictionnaire culturel de la Bible. P 1990, Cerf/ Nathan. 304 p. F 100. 2-204-04028-2 / 2-09-08810-7 [BL 91,14, B. P. *Robinson*: good (and worth translating) for looking up allusions puzzling to students of the arts]. – RÉtudes 373 (1990) 281s (Nicole *Gueunier*).

870 **Fritz** Volkmar, Kleines Lexikon der Biblischen Archäologie: Bibel-Kirche-Gemeinde 26, 1987 → 5,935: RSNTU-A 14 (1989) 290s (B. *Baldauf*).

871 E**Gentz** William H., The dictionary of Bible and Religion 1986 → 2,618; 3,906: RCriswT 2 (1988) 440s (D. S. *Dockery*).

872 **Goosen** Louis, Van Abraham tot Zachariah; thema's uit het Oude Testament in religie, bildende kunst, literatuur, muziek en theater. Nijmegen 1990, SUN. ill. *f* 39,50. 90-6168-329-7 [PhoenixEOL 37/1, 67s, M. L. *Folmer*].

873 E**Hennig** Kurt [*Paul* S., *Viviano* B., *Stern* E.], Jerusalemer Bibellexikon. Stu-Neuhäusen 1990, Hänssler. xv-987 p.; ill. 3-7751-1271-5.

874 E**Longton** Joseph, *Poswick* Ferdinand, La Bible de A à Z: Maredsous. Turnhout 1989, Brepols. Par ordre alphabétique: I. Animaux, plantes, xxv-135 p. – II. Objets, arts, xxv-107 p. – III. Personnages, xxv-294 p. – IV. Mœurs, xxv-201 p. – V. Livres bibliques, xxv-212 p. – VI. Histoire du

texte biblique, xxv-135 p. 2-503-50023-4; -4-2; -5-0; -6-9; -7-7; -8-5 [ÉTRel 66,443s, C.-B. *Amphoux*: utiliser avec prudence].

875 **Lurker** Manfred, Dizionario delle immagini e dei simboli biblici [²1987 ➤ 3,926 (➤ 4,856)], ᵀ*Limiroli* M. R., ᴱ*Ravasi* G. CinB 1990, Paoline. xiv-257 p.

876 **Lurker** Manfred, ❷ Słownik obrazów i symboli biblijnich [Wörterbuch biblischer Bilder² 1987], ᵀ*Romaniuk* Kazimierz. Poznań 1989, Pallottinum. – ᴿAtKap 114 (1990) 503-5 (J. *Warzecha*).

877 **McLeish** Kenneth & Valerie, Longman's guide to biblical quotations. Harlow, Essex 1986, Longman. vi-415 p. [KirSef 62 (1988s) p. 38].

878 **Manser** Martin H., Vom Reichtum der Bibel; Bibelzitate [The Lion concise book of Bible quotations 1982],ᵀ. Mödling 1988, St. Gabriel. 576 p. Sch. 220. – ᴿZkT 112 (1990) 222s (M. *Hasitschka*).

879 ᴱ**Mills** Watson E., (Baptist Professors of Religion), Mercer dictionary of the Bible. Macon GA 1990, Mercer Univ. $55; pa. $27.50. 0-86554-299-6; 373-9 [TDig 37,374].

880 **Müller** P.-G., Lessico della scienza biblica [1985 ➤ 1,960], ᵀ*Gatti* Enzo: LoB 3.11. Brescia 1990, Queriniana. 221 p. Lit. 30.000 [NRT 113,904, J.-L. *Ska*]. 88-399-1691-1.

881 ᵀᴱ**Myers** Allen C., The Eerdmans Bible dictionary [Dutch 1950, ²1975 but further revised] 1987 ➤ 4,862: 5,958: ᴿEvQ 62 (1990) 181-3 (J. *Barclay*).

882 **Sáenz-Badillos** Ángel, *Targarona Borras* Judit, Diccionario de autores judíos (Sefarad, siglos X-XV): Estudios de cultura hebrea 10. Córdoba 1988, Almendro. xii-227 p.; ill. 84-86077-69-9.

882* ᴱ**Richards** L. O., The Revell Bible Dictionary. Old Tappan NJ 1990, Revell. xii-1156 p.; ill.; 96 maps. 0-8007-1594-2 [NTAbs 35,235].

883 ᴱ**Schlatter** T., Calwer Bibellexikon⁶ [¹c. 1960]. Stu 1989, Calwer. x-734 p.; 48 pl., 14 maps. DM 48; pa. 29,80. 3-7668-3031-7; -28-7 [NTAbs 38,234: fuller captions and new color photos for text retained as NTAbs 6 p. 135].

884 **Schulz** Carl, Die biblischen Sprichwörter der deutschen Sprache [1860], ᴱ*Mieder* Wolfgang. Bern 1987, Lang. lviii-202 p. [KirSef 62 (1988s), p. 500].

885 ᴱ**Walker** William O., Harper's Bible pronunciation guide 1988 ➤ 5,971: ᴿParadigms 6,2 (1990s) 50s (S. L. *Cox*).

886 ᴱ**Williams** D., New concise Bible dictionary [< ᴱ*Douglas* J., ²*al.*], Leicester/Wheaton 1989, Inter-Varsity/Tyndale. xii-595 p.; 32 pl. £9. 0-85110-641-2 / 0-8423-4697-X [NTAbs 34,381].

A3.5   *Opera consultationis* **theologica** *non excerpta infra.*

887 ᴱ**Aparicio** [➤ 5,965:] *Rodríguez* Ángel, *Canals Casas* Joan, Diccionario teológico de la vida consagrada. M 1989, Claretianas. xxvii-1987 p. – ᴿCarthaginensia 6 (1990) 376s (F. *Martínez Fresneda*); Manresa 61 (1989) 411s (I. *Iglesias*).

888 **Bachmann** E. Theodore & Mercia B., Lutheran churches in the world; a handbook² [¹1979 in 'Lutheran World']. Minneapolis 1989, Augsburg. 631 p. $33. 0-8066-2371-3 [TDig 37,343].

889 ᴱ**Bäumer** R., *Scheffczyk* L., Marienlexikon 1988 ➤ 4,819; 5,917*: ᴿNRT 112 (1990) 455s (L.-J. *Renard*: takes over the Lexikon der Marienkunde which stopped publication in 1967 after one volume); TGL 80 (1990) 357-9 (W. *Beinert*).

890 **Bellinger** G.J. [cf. ➤ 863], Enciclopedia delle Religioni [1986 ➤ 5,919], T. Mi 1989, Garzanti. 862 p. Lit. 44.000. – RAsprenas 37 (1990) 127s (G. *Ragozzino*).

891 **Bouyer** L., Dictionnaire théologique² [¹1963]. P 1990, Desclée. 351 p. [NRT 113, 295, L. *Renwart*].

892 **Bowden** John, Who's Who in theology. L 1990, SCM. viii-152 p. 0-334-02464-1.

893 ᴱ**Cancik** H., *Gladigow* B., *Laubscher* M., Handbuch religionswissenschaftlicher Grundbegriffe [I. 1988 ➤ 5,897]; II. Apokalyptik-Geschichte. Stu 1990, Kohlhammer. 500 p. DM 98. 3-17-010531-0 [BL 91,10]. – RRHR 207 (1990) 432-4 (A. *Caquot*, 1); TsTNijm 30 (1990) 112 (E. *Cornélis*, 1).

894 ᴱ**Canobbio** G., Piccolo lessico di teologia. Brescia 1989, Morcelliana. 364 p. Lit. 28.000. – RAsprenas 37 (1990) 517 (Diana *Pacelli*: a chi destinato?).

895 ᴱ**Compagnoni** F., *al.*, Nuovo dizionario di teologia morale. CinB 1990, Paoline. 1554 p. Lit. 78.000. – RRasT 31 (1990) 524s (B. *Marra*).

896 ᴱ**Crim** K., The perennial dictionary of world religions [= pa. for 1981 Abingdon Dictionary of Living Religions]. SF 1989, Harper & R. xviii-830 p. $20 pa. 0-06-061613-X [NTAbs 34,235].

897 ᴱ**Cully** Iris V. & Kendig B., Harper's encyclopedia of religious education. SF 1990, Harper & R. xxiii-717 p. $35. 0-06-061656-3 [NTAbs 34,375].

898 ᴱ**Davies** J.G., A new dictionary of liturgy and worship [¹1972]. L 1989, SCM. xvi-544 p.; ill. 0-334-02209-6.

899 **de Fiores** S., *Goffi* T., Dicionario de Espiritualidade, T*Leal Ferreira* Isabel F. São Paulo 1989, Paulinas. 1208 p. – RREB 50 (1990) 747s (E.F. *Alves*).

ᴱ**Di Berardino** Angelo, Dictionnaire encyclopédique du christianisme ancien [DPA 1983-8] ➤ 839.

901 **Drehsen** Volker, Wörterbuch des Christentums 1988 ➤ 4,831; 5,929: RTPQ 138 (1990) 74 (R. *Zinnhobler*).

902 ᴱ**Eicher** Peter, Neue Summe Theologie, [< ᴱ*Lauret* B., *Refoulé* F., Initiation à la pratique 1982s ➤ 64,335 ...: 1. Der lebendige Gott; 2. Die neue Schöpfung;] – 3. Der Dienst der Gemeinde. T*Suchla* Peter. FrB 1989, Herder. 528 p. DM 65. 3-451-20694-3. – RActuBbg 27 (1990) 68 (J. *Boada*); TLZ 115 (1990) 626-631 (R. *Slenczka*: thorough adaptation retaining only half the articles of Initiation/pratique 1982).

903 — ᴱ**Eicher** Peter, Dictionnaire de théologie, TE*Lauret* Bernard [T*Jossua* P. ➤ 4,834; 5,931]: RRTLv 21 (1990) 359s (J. *Ponthot*).

904 — ᴱ**Eicher** Peter, Diccionario de conceptos teológicos, 1. Amor-Liturgia ➤ 5,932; II. Magisterio-Verdad; TE*Moll* Xavier. Barc 1989s, Herder. 659 p.; 642 p. – RActuBbg 27 (1990) 86s (J. *Boada*, 1); BibFe 16 (1990) 154 (A. *Salas*); Carthaginensia 6 (1990) 231s.375 (F. *Martinez Fresneda*: 'renovación de los CFT, Madrid 1979'); CiTom 117 (1990) 385s (L. *Lago*); CommSev 23 (1990) 436s (M. *Sánchez*); EstTrin 23 (1989) 341s / 24 (1990) 510s (J.M. de *Miguel*, 1/2); LumenVr 39 (1990) 81.536 (F. *Ortiz de Urtaran*); RTLim 24 (1990) 298s (N. *Strotmann*; dimensión bíblica, U. *Berges*).

905 ᴱ**Engelhard** P., Dizionario di citazioni cristiane. T 1988, Gribaudi. 188 p. Lit. 12.000. – RDivThom 92 (1989) 195-7 (G. *Perini*).

906 **Enns** Paul, The Moody handbook of theology. Ch 1989, Moody. 688 p. 0-8024-3428-2. – RScotBEv 8 (1990) 149 (H. *Taylor*: 'biblical theology' section not what the Bible is about).

907 ᴱ**Ferguson** Everett, *al.*,   Encyclopedia of early Christianity: Ref. Humanities 846.   NY 1990, Garland. xx-983 p. $95 [TR 87,252]. 0-8240-5745-7. – ᴿCathHR 76 (1990) 819s (R. B. *Eno*).

908 ᴱ**Groot** Aart de,   Biografisch Lexicon voor de geschiednis van het Nederlandse Protestantisme [I. c. 1980], 2-3.   Kampen 1983/8, Kok. 488 p., 428 p. *f* 89 + 125. – ᴿTLZ [106 (1981) 578s] 115 (1990) 253s (S. de *Boer*, Eng.).

909 **Kennedy** Richard,   The international dictionary of religion.   NY 1984, Crossroad. 256 p.; ill. ['profusely']. – ᴿRelStT 8,3 (1988) 46-48 (P. W. R. *Bowlby* does not recommend).

910 ᴱ**Khoury** Adel T.,   Lexikon religiöser Grundbegriffe 1987 → 3,920 ... 5,943: ᴿTLZ 115 (1990) 489-491 (T. *Holtz*).

911 **Koch** Traugott, *al.*,   Fe cristiana y sociedad moderna [CGMG 1980s → 62,852] 28.   M 1989, SM.   191 p.   84-348-2806-5. – ᴿActuBbg 27 (1990) 69.146 (J. *Boada*, 28; 11).

912 ᴱ**Komonchak** J. A., *al.*,   The new dictionary of theology 1987; also Dublin, Gill & M. → 3,923 ... 5,946; £50; 0-7171-1552-6: ᴿPrPeo 4 (1990) 456s (M. Cecily *Boulding*); ScotBEv 7 (1989) 117-9 (D. F. *Wright*: why capitalize Jewish and Catholic but not christian?); Themelios 16 (1990s) 29s (G. *Bray*).

913 ᴱ**La Brosse** Olivier de, *Rouillard* P.,   Dictionnaire des mots de la foi chrétienne² 1989 → 5,947: ᴿCarthaginensia 6 (1990) 223 (F. *Martínez Fresneda*).

914 **Lang** Jovian P.,   Dictionary of the liturgy.   NY 1989, Catholic.   687 p. $11. – ᴿHomPast 90,6 (1989s) 76s (R. M. *Nardone*: includes how to pronounce 'Mary').

915 ᴱ**Lippy** Charles H., *Williams* Peter W.,   Encyclopedia of the American religious experience; studies of traditions and movements.   NY 1988, Scribner's . 1872 p. (3 vol.) $225. – ᴿCritRR 3 (1990) 299-302 (M. G. *Toulouse*); JRel 69 (1989) 417s (P. *Gleason*).

915* **LTK**³-Project ᴱ**Kasper** Walter: HerdKorr 44 (1990) 583-8.

916 **Masson** Hervé,   Manual de herejías [Dictionnaire], ᵀ.   M 1989, Rialp. 400 p. – ᴿCarthaginensia 6 (1990) 393s (V. *Sánchez*: French title better).

917 **Miethe** Terry L.,   The compact dictionary of doctrinal words.   Mp 1988, Bethany.   224 p. $7. – ᴿBS 147 (1990) 237 (R. P. *Lightner*: omits common terms like posttribulational, limited atonement, common grace, rapture).

918 ᴱ**Nyssen** W., *al.*,   Handbuch der Ostkirchenkunde.   Dü 1989, Patmos. xx-273 p. DM 38,80. – ᴿTsTNijm 30 (1990) 216s (A. J. van der *Aalst*: 'ISBN 3-491-777477-2').

919 [**Pacomio** L., *Ghiberti* G.], ᵀᴱ*Ortiz* Alfonso,   Diccionario teológico inter-disciplinar I-IV [→ 63,806]; Verdad e Imagen 66-69, 1982; 598 p.; 603 p.; 1018 p. – ᴿFranBog 30 (1988) 91-94 [directores].

920 ᴱ**Pelliccia** G., [→ 5,964:] *Rocca* G.,   Dizionario degli Istituti di Perfezione 8, Saba-Spirituali, 1988; ᴿCathHR 76 (1990) 319s (R. L. *Burns*); JEH 40 (1989) 615s (O. *Chadwick*); RHR 207 (1990) 109s (A. *Guillaumont*).

921 ᴱ**Poupard** Paul,   Diccionario de las religiones 1987 → 4,865*a*; 5,960*b*: ᴿHumT 10 (1989) 257s (J. *Monteiro*).

922 ᴱ**Reid** Daniel G., *al.*,   Dictionary of Christianity in America.   DG 1990, Inter-Varsity. $40.   0-8308-1776-X [TDig 37,49]. – ᴿAndrUnS 28 (1990) 184-6 (G. R. *Knight*: better than 'IV' 1988 New dictionary of theology); NewTR 3,2 (1990) 92s (R. J. *Schreiter*: good).

923 ᴱ**Rotter** Hans, *Virt* Günter,   Neues Lexikon der christlichen Moral. Innsbruck 1990, Tyrolia.

923* ᴱRuh Ulrich, *al.*, Handwörterbuch religiöser Gegenwartsfragen.² FrB 1989, Herder. 520 p. DM 29,80 [¹58!]. 3-451-21612-4. – ᴿLuthTKi 14 (1990) 44s (H. *Brandt*).
924 **Sartore** Domenico, *Triacca* A.M., Nuevo diccionario de liturgía, ᵀᴱ*Canals* Joan M., 1987 ⇝ 4,868: ᴿTeresianum 40 (1989) 242 (M.D. *Sánchez*).
925 ᴱ**Schütz** Christian, Praktisches Lexikon der Spiritualität 1988 ⇝ 5,967; 3-451-21063-0: ᴿManresa 61 (1989) 186s (P. *Cebollada*); TPhil 65 (1990) 317s (G. *Switek*); ZkT 112 (1990) 477s (H. *Rotter*).
926 ᴱ**Stein** Gordon, The encyclopedia of unbelief. Buffalo 1985, Prometheus. xvi-819 p. [2 vol.] 0-87975-307-2. – ᴿScotBEv 7 (1989) 119 (D.F. *Wright*: promotes rather than describes).
927 *Widmann* Peter, Tegin Pʀᴇɴᴛᴇʀs teologiske encyklopædi: DanTTs 52 (1989) 190-204 [< ᴢɪᴛ 89,702].

A3.6   *Opera consultationis* **philologica** *et* **generalia**.

928 ᴱ**Aurox** Sylvain, Les notions philosophiques; dictionnaire: Encyclopédie Philosophique Universelle 2. P 1990, PUF. I. 1515 p. II. -2297. 2-13-041-440-0.
929 ᴱ**Brunner** Hellmut, *al.* (Meyers Lexikonredaktion), Lexikon Alte Kulturen, I. A-Fir. Mannheim 1990, Meyer. 704 p. 3-411-07302-2 [OIAc S90].
930 ᴱ**Goulet** Richard, Dictionnaire des philosophes antiques I, Abam(m)on à Axiothéa. P 1989, CNRS. 841 p. F 425. 2-222-04042-6. – ᴿJRAS (1990) 376s (S.P. *Brock*); VigChr 44 (1990) 304-8 (D.T. *Runia*: magnificent).
931 ᴱ**Howatson** M.C., The Oxford companion to classical literature [replacing same title of *Harvey* P.]. Ox 1989, Univ. 615 p.; 6 maps. A$55. 0-19-866121-5. – ᴿAncHRes 20 (1990) 190s (R. *Pitcher*).
932 ᴱ**Kennedy** George A., The Cambridge history of literary criticism 1989 ⇝ 5,942: ᴿRÉLat 68 (1990) 202-4 (H. *Zehnacker*).
933 **LGB:** Lexikon des gesamten Buchwesens² [¹1937], ᴱ**Corsten** Severin, *al.* [II. 145-152, 1989 ⇝ 5,928*]; Lfg. 18. Bergisch Gladbach 1990, Lubbe.
934 **LIMC:** Lexicon iconographicum mythologiae classicae, ᴱ**Kahil** Lilly, IV, 1988 ⇝ 4,852; 5,951: ᴿAJA 94 (1990) 504s (Brunilde S. *Ridgway*); AntClas 59 (1990) 557-9 (C. *Delvoye*); Archaiognosia 4 (1985s) 199-213 (M.A. *Tiverios* ☺); RÉG 103 (1990) 287-9 (F. *Chamoux*).
934* **LIMC:** V. Herakles-Kenchrias. Z 1990, Artemis. I. Texte, xxix-1047 p.; II. Planches, 709 p. (652 pl.) [RÉG 104,597, F. *Chamoux*].
935 **Lübker** Federico, Il lessico classico; lessico ragionato dell'antichità classica⁶ [1882], ᵀ**Murero** Carlo A. [1898], ᴱ**Mariotti** Scevola. Bo 1989, Zanichelli. viii-1345 p. – ᴿSalesianum 52 (1990) 779s (R. *Della Casa*).
936 ᴱ**Ritter** Joachim †, *Gründer* Karlfried, Historisches Wörterbuch der Philosophie 7, P-Q. Basel 1989, Schwabe. [xvii-] 1842 col. DM 298. – ᴿJbAC 33 (1990) 244-6 (K. *Bormann*).
937 **Schmitt** Hatto H., *Vogt* Ernst, Kleines Wörterbuch des Hellenismus. Wsb 1988, Harrassowitz. xiii-745 p.; 6 fig.; 30 pl.; 2 maps. DM 78. 3-447-02036-9. – ᴿGnomon 62 (1990) 128-131 (F.W. *Walbank*); Gymnasium 97 (1990) 377s (Ilona *Opelt*); ZAW 102 (1990) 307 (O. *Kaiser*).
938 **Veh** Otto, Lexikon der römischen Kaiser, von Augustus bis Iustinianus I, 27 v.Chr. bis 565 n.Chr.³ʳᵉᵛ. Mü 1990, jetzt ill. [Tyche 6,251, G. *Dobesch*].

939 Verzeichnis der im deutschen Sprachbereich erschienenen Drücke des
XVI. Jahrhunderts: Band 12, Lut-Mann: Mü Bayerische Staatsbibliothek / Wolfenbüttel Bibliothek. Stu 1988, Hiersemann. 692 p. – ᴿLuJb
57 (1990) 295s (H. *Junghans*: 4336 printed items on Luther; p. 296-315
on 19 other Luther-related bibliographies).
940 ᴱ**Walther** Karl K., Lexikon der Buchkunst und Bibliophilie 1987 ➤ 5,972
[auch Lp. 1987, VEB; 386 + 396 p.]: ᴿDLZ 111 (1990) 1-5 (Anneliese
Schmitt).

A3.8 *Opera consultationis* **archaeologica** *et* **geographica.**

941 ᴱ**Assfalg** Julius, Kleines Wörterbuch des christlichen Orients. Wsb 1975,
Harrassowitz. xxxiii-460 p.; 25 fig.; 16 pl.; 6 foldouts. – ᴿBSACopte 29
(1990) 156s (A. *Sidarus*).
942 **Bojnurdi** Kazem M., The great encyclopedia of Islam ['Persian version';
an 'Arabic version' is awaited]. Tehran 1989. I. Ab-Ali Davud, xxiv-
714 p.; ill.; maps. – ᴿJRAS (1990) 383s [C. *Melville*'s comparisons with
EncIslam² ('corrected' by putting the old errors in new guise; this one is
more 'Islamic' but not reactionary propaganda) hint that 'Persian version'
does not exclude its being in English).
943 **CAD:** Chicago Assyrian Dictionary, ᴱ**Reiner** Erica [13 'Q' 1982 ➤ 63,784]
17: 'S' part 1. Ch/Glückstadt 1989, Univ. Oriental Inst. / Augustin.
XXVIII-492 p. 0-918986-55-9 [BO 48,314].
944 ᴱ**Embree** Ainslee T., Encyclopedia of Asian history [Iran and farther
east]. NY/L 1988, Scribner's / CollierMacmillan. xiii-528 p.; 538 p.;
516 p.; 478 p. $325. – ᴿJRAS (1990) 382s (D. O. *Morgan*, editor: useful for
his work).
945 **Henze** Dietmar, Enzyklopädie der Entdecker [II. 1985 ➤ 2,9838*], 3/13,
Low-McMinn. Graz 1989, Akademisch. 127 p. DM 98. – ᴿDLZ 111
(1990) 123s (K.-R. *Biermann*).
947 ᴱ**Kirschbaum** Engelberg [Bd. 1-4], *Braunfels* Wolfgang [Bd. 5-8], Lexikon
der christlichen Ikonographie. FrB 1990 = 1968-76, Herder. 8 vol.
DM 358. – ᴿZkT 112 (1990) 495s (R. *Pacik*).
948 ᴱ**Mostyn** Trevor, *Hourani* Albert, The Cambridge Encyclopedia of the
Middle East and North Africa. C 1988, Univ. 504 p.; ill. £30. – ᴿJRAS
(1989) 314s (Isabel *Miller*).
949 Reallexikon zur deutschen Kunstgeschichte, Lfg. 98-100, Fisch-Flache.
Mü 1988/90/91. col. 129-512 [NRT 113,933, Y. *Torly*].
950 [*Stadler* Wolf] ᴱ**Wiench** Peter, Lexikon der Kunst [Mal-Oel 1987s
➤ 5,973]; 9-12. FrB 1989/90, Herder. je DM 178. – ᴿTrierTZ 98 (1989)
232 (E. *Sauser*); ZkT 112 (1990) 491 (H. B. *Meyer*).
951 **Yarshater** Ehsan, Encyclopaedia Iranica [2, 1985 ➤ 3,949; 4,874], 4, fasc.
8, Cappadocia-Carpets. L 1990, Routledge-KP. p. 785-896. 0-7100-9131-
1 [OIAc S90]. – ᴿBSO 53 (1990) 522-4 (J. B. *Russell*, 2); JAOS 110 (1990)
777s (A. S. *Shahrazi*, 2); JRAS (1989) 148s (C. *Melville*, 2); StIran 19
(1990) 125-8 (J. *Calmard*, 2).

A4 **Bibliographiae** .1 **biblicae.**

AnPg 'Testamenta' [= NT] ➤ 1098.
952 **Asurmendi** Jesús, *al.*, Des livres au service de la Bible; guide bibliographique: CahÉv 69. P 1989, Cerf. 99 p. F 30. 0222-9714.
953 *Auneau* Joseph, Bulletin biblique: MaisD 182 (1990) 139-152.

954 *Best* Ernest, Recent continental NT literature [9 books]: ExpTim 101 (1989s) 235-9.

954* Bibliotec [computer program]; Good News New Testament and concordance. Swindon 1988, Bible Soc. 80 p.; 3 discs; £45. – ᴿBTrans 41 (1990) 147 (H. P. *Scanlin*).

955 **BL:** Society for Old Testament Study, Book List, ᴱ*Auld* A. Graeme, [Edinburgh/Leeds/Birmingham] 1991. 170 p. 0-905495-10-1. The valuable criticisms, dense even when brief, and on the whole supportive, are now frequently enlarged to a full page.

956 *a*) *Breder* Wilhelm [+ 9 Andere] Bibliographische Dokumentation; Lexikalisches und grammatisches Material; – *b*) *Loersch* Sigrid, Dokumentation über neu entdeckte Texte: ZAHeb 3 (1990) 98-125; Register 128-132 / 126s.

957 — *Görg* Manfred, Zur 'bibliographischen Dokumentation' in der 'Zeitschrift für Althebraistik': BibNot 52 (1990) 11s.

957* **Brisman** Shimeon, A history and guide to Judaic encyclopedias and lexicons: Jewish Research Literature 2. Cincinnati 1987, HUCA. xxvi-502 p. 0-87820-909-3.

958 **BTAM:** Tables du tome 14 (19 1990) [new computerized norms]: BTAM 14 (5,1990) 800-871 (E. M.).

958* *Chavannes* B.-P., Les livres [sur le judaïsme]: FoiVie 89,1 (1990) 93-106.

959 *Clarke* E. G., Targum bibliography: NewsTarg 14/1 (1987) 2-11; 14/2, 4-8; 15/1 (1988) 2-8; 15/2, 2-7; 16/1 (1989) 2-10; 16/2 (1990) 2-9.

960 Computer Programs: NIVᴾᶜ version 1.00 / Scripture fonts version 1.1. GR 1990, Zondervan. $300 / $100 [OTAbs 14,236s, Mary Ann *Stachow*]. ➤ 967.

962 *Delcor* Mathias, *Husser* Jean-M., Chronique d'Ancien Testament: BLitEc 91 (1990) 133-144.

963 *Dion* P. E., The Jews during the Persian period; a bibliography [over 400 items plus topical index]: NewsTarg supp 5. Toronto 1990, Univ. NE Studies. 29 p. $5. 0704-5905 [BL 91,45 '59005'].

964 *a*) *Dirksen* P. B., De Peshitta van het O.T. in de recente literatuur; – *b*) *Horst* Pieter W. van der, Nieuwe literatuur over het jodendom [Zuidema W. ⁵1988; Harl M. ...]: NedTTs 43 (1989) 265-277 / 229-236.

964* **Di Segni** Riccardo, Catalogue of the manuscripts of the library of the Collegio Rabbinico Italiano, Rome, Italy: Alei Sefer supp. Ramat-Gan 1990, Bar Ilan Univ. [iv-] 204 p. 0334-4754.

965 Dissertation Abstracts-A 49,1-6 (1988), 7-12 (1989), reprinted in StudiaBT 17 (1989) 84-115. 199-230 [N.B. 'Other Fuller dissertations', only 230s (*Watts* K. Analogy and category); p. 83 and 198 state that notice of dissertations *not* in Diss-A will also be published here, but so far there is no indication of such].

966 Dissertationen und Habilitationsschriften [44 deutsch, 6 franç., je 2 Eng. ital español] 1986s: BZ 34 (1990) 155-9.

967 *Faiman* David, Mac[intosh Zondervan Electronic software package] Bible version 2.0: JBQ 19 (1990s) 42-46: highly praised, with examples [and a gematria appendix: Ps 42 King James version has 'shake' 42 words from the beginning and 'spear' 42 words from the end; since 'he' was 42 years old in 1610, he may have been one of the panel responsible for the book's outstanding English; but letters p. 210 point out that it is Ps 46, not 42; and the 42 should be 46 both from beginning and from end; Shakespeare was 46 in 1611].

968 **Fitzmyer** Joseph A., An introductory bibliography for the study of Scripture[3] [[1]1961 with *Glanzman* G., [2]1980]: SubsBPont 3. R 1990, Pontificio Istituto Biblico.   xv-217 p. Lit. 18,500 [NRT 113, 749, X. *Jacques*]. 88-7653-592-6.

969 *Giesen* Heinz, Botschaft und Geschichte; Hilfen zum Umgang mit der Heiligen Schrift [BAUER-ALAND, PRITCHARD Bibelatlas, KNOCH Synopse ...]: TGegw 33 (1990) 297-303.

970 *Gotenburg* Erwin, Bibelwissenschaft [Theologische Bibliographie]: TR 86 (1990) 73-75 [-88]. 161-3 [-176]. 249-251 [-264]. 337-340 [-352]. 425-8 [-440]. 521-3 [-534].

971 **Grossfeld** B., A bibliography of Targum literature [I. 1972 ⮞ 54,924; II. 1977 ⮞ 60,952; 61,1206]; III. [items 1823-2846].   NY 1990, Sepher-Hermon. xx-91 p. $39.50. 0-87203-132-2 [BL 91,46, G. *Vermes*].

972 **Hughes** John J., Bits, bytes and biblical studies 1987 ⮞ 3,965... 5,1639: [R]CritRR 2 (1989) 136-8 (J. L. *Boyce*).

973 *a) Hughes* John J., Beyond word processing; – *b) Scrimgeour* Andrew, The computer as a tool for research and communication in religious studies: CritRR 3 (1990) 1-43 / 45-59.

974 **Hupper** W. G., Index to English periodical literature on the Old Testament and Ancient Near Eastern studies, I, 1987 ⮞ 3,966; II, 1988 ⮞ 4,890: [R]BL (1990) 17: A. G. *Auld* compares to PURVIS' less-complicated Jerusalem volume, but with no clue to how this vol. 2 relates to vol. 1.

975 [E]**Hupper** William G., An index to English periodical literature on the OT and ANE studies, III/IV: ATLA 21. Metuchen NJ 1990, Scarecrow. xxxvii-783 p. $79.50. / xlvii-544 p. 0-8108-2319-5; -93-4.

976 [E]*Ibach* Robert D., Periodical reviews [signed lengthy summaries of select items]: Bibliotheca Sacra 147 (1990) 194-8 . 231-3 . 480-4 . 480-4.

Index international des dissertations doctorales en théologie et en droit canonique présentées en 1989: RTLv 21 (1990) ⮞ 1034: ÉcrS 539-548, N⁰ 31-173.

978 **IZBG:** Internationale Zeitschriftenschau für Bibelwissenschaft und Grenzgebiete, [E]**Lang** Bernhard, *Minner* Elisabeth, 36 (1988-90). Dü 1990, Patmos. 507 p. Items from 33 contributors, mostly with signed summary, English or German, about half each. Remarkably interesting and accurate; only a rival would notice such trifles as Tiago (Portuguese for James) under Titus n⁰ 1651; and the Greek capital sigma generally given as E (1748). – [E]TAth 61 (1990) 887-9 (P. *Simotas*, Ⓖ).

979 *Kaestli* Jean-Daniel, présent: Bulletin de bibliographie biblique 1 [AT 1989-90 + une recension] (Lausanne 1990). 52 p.

980 *Kealy* Seán P., Gospel studies since 1970: IrTQ 56 (1990) 161-9.

981 **Lazcano González** Rafael, Fray Luis de LEÓN, bibliografía. M 1990, Rev. Augustiniana. 278 p. – [R]RHE 85 (1990) 503 (J.-F. *Gilmont*: poète, exégète ... carences graves, format non indiqué).

982 *Meagher* Patrick M., More and more of Pauline studies [18 books, most infra]: Vidyajyoti 54 (1990) 353-368.

983 *Lichtenberger* H., Dokumentation über Neuveröffentlichungen aus den Qumranfunden: ZAHeb 3 (1990) 232-4 [-5, *Loersch* Sigrid, ... über neu entdeckte epigraphische Texte].

984 *Paul* André, Bulletin du judaïsme ancien [JOSÈPHE, PHILON, mystique juive ...]: RechSR 78 (1990) 449-479.

985 *Piñero* Antonio, New Testament philology bulletin [bibliography with brief description of most items, and Scriptural index only at end]: FgNt 3

(1990) 85-98.175-189 [101-5, 'Libros recibidos' also contains a 5-line presentation of each].

986 *Raab* Hamutal, ❸ Indexes to articles, words, subjects 36 (1971s) - 50 (1985s): Lešonenu 54,1 (1989s). 90 p.

987 **Rábanos Espinosa** R., *Muñoz León* D., Bibliografía joánica; evangelio, cartas y apocalipsis 1960-1986: Bibliotheca Hispana Biblica 14. M 1990, Cons. Sup. Inv. 752 p. 84-00-07033-X [NTAbs 35,106]. – ᴿStLeg 31 (1990) 285s (C. de *Villapadierna*).

988 **Rakover** Nahum, The multi-language bibliography of Jewish Law. J 1990, Library of Jewish Law.

989 RENDTORFF Rolf, Bibliographie 1949-90 (*Miltenberger* J.): DielB Beitr 11. Heid 1990. vii-52 p. [ZAW 103,307].

990 *Rodd* Cyril S., [Twenty] Recent NT commentaries: ExpTim 101 (1989s) 184-190.

990* *Rosso Ubigli* Liliana, Gli apocrifi (o pseudepigrafi) dell'Antico Testamento; bibliografia 1979-1989: Henoch 12,3 (1990) 259-321; Eng. 321, continuation of CHARLESWORTH 1981, though less comprehensively.

991 *Rousée* J.-M., Ouvrages reçus, RB 97 (1990) 146-158 . 302-320 . 621-640, has here become a veritable Bulletin, subdivided by areas (OT, NT, Judaism, archeology ...), with critical reports of some 400 words; and strewn among them a relatively few Festschriften or similar compilations: mostly without titles/pages especially in the earlier fascicles (but given for e.g. ᶠWESTERMANN p. 628, ᶠHARRELSON 625, ᶠBENNETT 622; also for HUCA 60 p. 626; BRIEND, Protohistoire 628).

992 *Scholer* David M., Bibliographia Gnostica, supplementum XIX: NT 32 (1990) 349-373.

993 ᴱ**Schwantes** M., Bibliografia bíblica latino-americana I. 1988 [BL 91,23, J. M. *Dines*] II. Petrópolis 1990, Vozes. 312 p. (1500 títulos) [REB 50,1023].

994 *Stover* M., Bible study in the computer age: ChrTod 34,11 (1990) 55-59 [< NTAbs 35,13].

994* *Szier* Barbara, Polska bibliografia biblijna za rok 1987/8: RoczTK 36,1 (1989) 73-84.

995 *Vattioni* Francesco, Saggio di bibliografia semitica 1988-9: AION 49,4 (1989) 397-455.

996 *Vouga* François, Bulletin du NT [i. Marc; ii. Paul; iii. paroles et paraboles de Jésus]: ÉTRel 63 (1988) 79-98.

997 *a)* **Weisbard** Phyllis H., *Schonberg* David, Jewish law; bibliography of sources and scholarship in English. Littleton CO 1989, Rothman. xviii-558 p. $57.50 [RelStR 17,174, M. S. *Jaffee*].

— *b)* *Wenham* David, Survey of NT articles 1988 and 1989: Themelios 15 (1989s) 91; 93-101 (not at end of fascicle) Index to volumes 1-15.

997* Zeitschriftenschau: ZAW 102 (1990) 121-141.263-293.421-437 [Bücherschau 141-167 . 293-319 . 437-466]. – ZNW 81 (1990) 149-151 . 284-286.

A4.2 *Bibliographiae* **theologicae.**

998 *Arató* Pál, Bibliographia historiae pontificiae: ArHistPont 27 (1989) 465-740.

999 *Bériou* Nicole, Bulletin d'histoire des doctrines médiévales; pastorale et spiritualité: RSPT 74 (1990) 466-476.

1000 *Bertuletti* Angelo, *al.*, Schede bibliografiche [Problemi metodologici 1989]: TItSett 15 (1990) 341-411, SScr. 353-360.

1001 BÉRUBÉ Camille, Bibliographie 1933-1990: ColcFranc 60 (1990) 709-731 (O. *Schmucki*).

1001* Bibliografia Lul·lística: EstLul 28 (1988) 85-89 (93-114 ressenyes). 243-248 (-282); 29 (1989) 79-81 (-95). 181-6 (-211).

1002 EBierzychudek Eduardo, Bibliografía teológica comentada del área iberoamericana 13 (1985). BA 1988, ISEDET (ev.). 604 p. – RCiTom 117 (1990) 190 (J. L. *Espinel*).

1003 *Borgman* Erik, Promoties in de theologie [dissertations, with summary more concise than TLZ, but including details of author's birth and employment]: TsTNijm 30 (1990) 82-85 . 187-191 . 302-4.

1004 E*Boudens* R., *al.*, Elenchus bibliographicus 1989: ETL 66,2s (1990) 648* p., 11463 items; has no major section on either archeology or philology, but ample coverage, not coextensive with ours, for History of Religions (in general and especially Islam, Hinduism, Buddhism).

1004* *Buchrucker* Armin-Ernst, Frauen und Göttinnen — zur feministischen Theologie [Bücherschau]: LuthTKi 14 (1990) 19-24.

1005 Bulletin bibliographique de la liturgie [récensions signées], QLtg 70 (1989) 178-206 . 265-286; 71 (1990) 50-80 . 138-152 . 297.

1005* CARAMELLA Santino, guida bibliografica: Ho Theológos 6 (1988) 3-359 (fasc. intero, F. *Armetta*).

1006 **CritRR:** Critical review of books in religion 1989 / 1990; EGaventa Beverly R., Atlanta 1989s, Scholars. vi-496 p. / 487 p. $20 [NTAbs 35,231]. 0894-8860.

1006* *Dagorski* Bazyli, Przegląd csasopism / Patristica in periodicis 1989: VoxPa 17 (1989) 1019-1052.

1007 **Dante** Francesco, Storia della 'Civiltà Cattolica' (1850-1891), il laboratorio del Papa: Il pensiero politico e sociale dei cattolici italiani 14. R 1990, Studium. 287 p. Lit. 28.000 [TR 87,261].

1007* *Davie* Martin, A survey of Church History articles [from the years] 1986-9: Themelios 15 (1989s) 63-66.

1008 **Dawsey** James, A scholar's guide to academic journals in religion: ATLA 23, 1988 ➤ 5,1037: 0-8108-2135-4. – RIExp 87 (1990) 534 (Melody *Mazuk*); Tablet 243 (1989) 735 (M. *Walsh*: hard to see what it is for, though it is entertaining and calls Tablet 'the oldest and most respected periodical of the English-speaking world').

1009 *De Klerk* Peter, Calvin bibliography 1990: CalvinT 25 (1990) 225-248.

1010 *Desvoyes* R., *al.*, Origine et étapes de l'Ami du Clergé [Esprit et Vie, centenaire]: EsprVie 100 (1990) 562-7 (-575, 577-592).

1011 *Díaz* G., *al.*, Settimo Congresso Internazionale di Storia dell'Ordine Agostiniano [Roma 25-29.X.1985]; relazioni bibliografiche: AnAug 52 (R 1989) 356-362 (-398).

1012 *a)* Recent [completed] dissertations in religion [not *yet* using the 'new' section-titles given on p. 132, which still have no 'Bible' or 'Old Testament' except under Ancient Near East (but four sections of 'Judaism') and no 'New Testament' except under 'Christian Origins']; many infra; – *b)* Dissertations in progress: RelStR 16 (1990) 186-191 / 285-291.

1013 DOMMERSHAUSEN Werner, Bio- und Bibliographie [70. Gb.]: TrierTZ 98 (1989) 75-78 (R. *Bohlen*).

1014 *Doré* Joseph, Les collections de théologie en France: RICathP 33 (1990) 161-187.

1015 *Durand* G.-M. de,   Bulletin de patrologie: RSPT 74 (1990) 623-648.

1016 ^E**Evers** Georg,   Annotated bibliography / Summaries of selected articles / Book surveys / Reports about theological Conferences / Indices: Theology in Context [7,2 (1990)] 8/1, 15-112 / 113-128 / 129-141 / 143-155 = TKontext 11,2 & 12,1, roughly the same pages in German.

1017 *Fares* D. J., *Astigueta* D.,   Fichero de revistas latinoamericanas: Stromata 46 (1990) 449-494; Sagrada Escr. 461-3; elenco de revistas p. 445-7.

1018 GARDEIL Ambroise, ❷ Sus escritos y método del trabajo: STWsz 28,1 (1990) 56-95 (T. *Pikus*); español 95s.

1019 *a*) ^E*Gliściński* Jan, [*Obrycki* Kazimierz],   Biuletyn patrystyczny; – *b*) ^E*Piwowarski* Władysław,   Biuletyn socjologii religii; – *c*) ^E*Kowalek* Władysław,   Biuletyn misjologiczno-religioznawczy: ColcT 59,1 (1989) 129-135; 2,129-138 [4,145-152] / 2,113-128; 3,105-113 / 4,131-144.

1020 *Gorsuch* Richard L., *al.*,   The Church and the computer: RExp 87/2 (1990) 185-193 (-299).

1021 *Granado* Carmelo,   Boletín de literatura antigua cristiana [... SChr]:   EstE 65 (1990) 339-350.

1022 GUARDINI Romano: Polska bibliografia: STWsz 28.1 (1990) 280-290 (Iwona *Borla*).

1023 *Gy* Pierre-Marie,   Bulletin de liturgie; documents liturgiques médiévaux: RSPT 74 (1990) 111-9.

1024 Habilitationen / Dissertationen im akademischen Jahr 1989/90:   TR 86 (1990) 509s / 510-519.

1025 *Häussling* Angelus A., *al.*,   Gottesdienst der Kirche...:   ArLtgW 31 (1989) 152-222 [-479].

1026 *Häussling* Angelus A., *al.*,   Literaturbericht: ArLtgW 32 (1990) 55-106 (-295 *al.*; 394-426, *Kirchberg* Julie, *Minz* Karl-Heinz, Liturgie und Judentum).

1027 **Hanawalt** Emily A.,   An annotated bibliography of Byzantine sources in English translation.   Brookline MA 1988, Hellenic College.   37 p. $2.50. – ^RRelStR 16 (1990) 349 (P. *Viscuso*).

1028 *Hausberger* Karl,   Thèses d'habilitation allemandes, histoire de l'Église: RHE 85 (1990) 470-2.

1029 *Haverals* M.,   Bibliographies: RHE 85 (1990) 1*-182* . 183*-145*, 347*-614*.

1030 *Heath* Peter,   Bibliographical survey IV, Between reform and Reformation; the English Church in the fourteenth and fifteenth centuries: JEH 41 (1990) 647-678.

1031 HEIMING Odilo K. 1898-1988, Gestalt und Bibliographie eines grossen Liturgiewissenschaftlers: ArLtgW 31 (1989) 119-151 (E. v. *Severus*, Paula L. *Hey*).

1032 **Heiser** W. Charles,   Theology Digest book survey 37 (1990) 42-96 . 147-195 . 247-296 . 341-392.

1033 *Hendrix* G.,   À propos de manuscrits médiévaux: RTAM 57 (1990) 263-277.

1034 Index international des dissertations doctorales en théologie et en droit canonique presentées en 1989: RTLv 21 (1990) 521-589 (539-548, AT-NT; 523-539, finder par institution). – N.B. p. 142, Mémoires de license (20): **Bailly** J. J., La mention de Sara en Hébreux 11,11, ^D*Bogaert* P.; **Szmatula** Dominique, Les commentaires patristiques sur Isaïe d'ORIGÈNE à JÉRÔME; état de la question, ^D*Gryson* R.

1035 *Irmscher* J.,   100 Jahre des Corpus der 'Griechischen christlichen Schriftsteller': CrNSt 11 (1990) 357-362 [< ZIT 91,37: 'der Corpus'].

1035* Istina, Tables I-XXXV, années 1954-1990: Istina 35,4 (1990) 353-448; à part F 65.

1036 *Ivy* Steven S., Pastoral assessment; issues and directions [5 books 1976-87]: RelStR 16 (1990) 212-8.

1037 *Jossua* Jean-Pierre, Bulletin de théologie littéraire: RSPT 74 (1990) 293-311; p. 297, GROSJEAN Jean, La reine de Saba; Samson 1989.

1038 JPsy&T 16 (1988) 49-123, cumulative index vol. 1-15.

1039 **Korros** Alexandra S., *Sarna* Jonathan D., American synagogue history; a bibliography and state-of-the field survey. NY 1988, Wiener. ix-247 p. $30 [RelStR 17,197, S. *Heilman*, E. *Holifield*].

1040 *Kraft* Robert A., Offline; computer assisted research for religious studies – 32: CouStR 20 (1991) 50-52.

1041 KUC Leszek K. † 4.VI.1986: bibliografia: STWsz 27,2 (1989) 233-246 (J. *Jędrys*).

1041* a) *Lachmann* Rainer, Zum Stand der Diskussion über die Methoden im Religionsunterricht; ein Literaturbericht; – b) *Rickers* Folkert, Religionspädagogische Bibliographie 1988 für den deutschen Sprachraum: JbReligionspädagogik 6 (Neuk 1990) 111-132 / 265 ... [< ZIT 91,118].

1042 LECLERCQ Jean, Bibliographie III: StMon 30 (1988) 417-440 (A. M. *Altermatt*).

1043 LLULL Ramón: Bibliografia 1984-5 / [después sin fecha]: EstLul 26 (1986) 99-106 / 269-272; 27 (1987) 109-113 . 253-5.

1044 LØGSTRUP K. E.: **Hansen** Karstein M., ~ 's forfatterskap 1930-1987; en bibliografi: Acta Jutlandica teol. 15. Århus 1987, Aarhus Univ. – ᴿNorTTs 91 (1990) 62 (S. H. *Birkeflet*).

1045 *Lumpe* Adolf, Bibliographie: AnHConc 20 (1988) 498-500; 21 (1989) 231-240 . 469-480.

1046 **Magnuson** Norris A., *Travis* William G., American evangelicalism. 1990, Locust Hill. 495 p. $45 [JAAR 58,740].

1047 *Matabosch* Antoni, Justícia, pau i integritat de la creació (JPIC); publicacions entorn del programa del consell ecumènic de les esglésies (1983-1990): RCatalT 15 (1990) 203-211: 34 items with analysis.

1048 *Meijer* Alberic de, Bibliographie historique de l'Ordre de Saint-Augustin 1985-1989: AugLv 39,3 (1989) 189-392.

1049 *Merino* Marcelo, Indices vol. xiii-xxii (1981-1990): ScripTPamp 22,4 (1990), 360 p.

1050 Milano, Università Cattolica del Sacro Cuore; catalogo delle pubblicazioni periodiche possedute dalla biblioteca, I-II. Mi 1977-, Vita e Pensiero. Supp. Periodica, 1985; III. Aggiornamento, 1991s. 88-343-1504-9; -8-7.

1051 *Montagnes* Bernard, Chronique d'histoire religieuse: RThom 90 (1990) 652-667.

1052 MÜLLER Norbert, Bibliographie 65. Gb.: TLZ 115 (1990) 474-7 (Roija *Weidhas*).

1053 OLEJNIK Stanisław: Spis publikacji: STWsz 28,2 (1990) 151-7 (J. *Pryszmont*).

1054 ᴱO'**Malley** John W., Catholicism in early modern history, a guide to research: Reformation Guides to Research 2. St Louis 1988, Center Reformation Research. vi-342 p. – ᴿCathHR 76 (1990) 127s (Elisabeth G. *Gleason*).

1055 Pelas revistas: REB 50 (1990) 265-272 . 506-512 . 760-8 . 1029-35 [siglas 27 (1967) 248].

1056 Periodical literature [by periods]: CathHR 75 (1989) 192-201 . 367-377 . 544-555 . 765-778; 76 (1990) 178-189 . 442-456 . 648-661 . 918-826.

1057 *Peterson* Stephen L., The more things change, the more things change; theological libraries in the 1990s: TEdn 26,2 (1989s) 137-151.

1058 *Pié y Ninot* Salvador, Boletín bibliográfico de teología fundamental: RCatalT 15 (1990) 213-223.

1059 *Pöhlmann* Horst G., Zeitschriftenschau: NSys 31 (1989) 109-124 . 327-335; 32 (1990) 85-92 . 343-355.

1060 *Poirier* Paul, Ancienne littérature chrétienne et histoire de l'église [21 livres]: LavalTP 46 (1990) 246-268.

1061 Revista Española de Teología, índice de los 50 años: RET 50,4 (1990) 479-534, Table of Contents of the issues in chronological order; 534-588, entire titles classed by subject; 588-598, alphabetical author-index without titles.

1062 Revista de Revistas; RET 50 (1990) 119-139 . 356-369.

1063 **RIC,** Répertoire bibliographique des institutions chrétiennes 35s, ᴱ**Zimmermann** M., *al.* Strasbourg 1989s, CERDIC. – ᴿNRT 112 (1990) 785s (L. *Volpe*).

1064 *Riedl* Gerda, 'Neues Zeitalter' versus 'Neuer Bund'; Aspekte christlicher Standortsbestimmung, eine kommentierte Bibliographie: ForumKT 6 (1990) 131-9.

1065 *Ruello* Francis, Bulletin d'histoire des idées médiévales: RechSR 78 (1990) 131-158.

1066 **Schadel** Erwin, Bibliotheca Trinitariorum 2/2. Mü 1988, Saur. xxxvii-594 p. DM 148. – ᴿColcFranc 60 (1990) 349s (O. *Schmucki*); ZRGg 42 (1990) 184s (W. *Kern*).

1067 *Segovia* Augusto, Boletín de historia de la teología 1500-1800: ArTGran 52 (1989) 207-241.

1068 *Seim* Jürgen, *al.*, 50. Jahrgänge 'Evangelische Theologie' [1934 ...] Der Neuanfang 1946: EvT 50 (1990) 488-495 [-524, ... Schuld].

1069 Significant ecumenical journals, table of contents (titles sans pp.; addresses at end) [and books.] Bibliographia œcumenica: EcuR 42 (1990) 79-83 . 182-6 . 371-6 [84s . 187-191 . 377-380 (366-370)].

1070 TETTAMANZI Dionigi [nuovo vescovo di Ancona-Osimo, bibliografia]: ScuolC 117 (1989) 543-662.

1071 *a) Théobald* Christoph, Bulletin de théologie dogmatique; question de Dieu et Trinité; – *b) Dumortier* F.-X., Théologie pratique; – *c) Bourgeois* Henri, Théologie sacramentaire: RechSR 78 (1990) 97-130 . 241-268 / 293-303 / 591-624.

1072 Theologische Examensarbeiten [Diplom-, Dissertation, meist Lizentiat]: ZMissRW 74 (1990) 73-82.

1073 *Thomas* N. E., *al.*, Selected annotated bibliography on missiology, Q. The Americas; R. Asia; S. Europe; T. Oceania: Missiology 18 (1990) 107-110 . 237-240 . 377-380 . 500-3; (annotated) Books Received 111-124 . 241-255 . 381-390 . 504-513.

1074 TORRANCE Thomas F., bibliography 1941-89: ScotJT 43 (1990) 225-262 (I. R. *Torrance*, his son, continuing and correcting B. *Gray* in ᶠTorrance 1976).

1075 *a) Tretter* H., Bibliographie; – *b) Röhling* Horst, Zeitschriftenschau: OstkSt 38 (1989) 82-104 . 233-280 . 348-371; Index 372-382 / 73-81 . 218-232.

1076 *Trevijano Etcheverría* Ramón, Bibliografía patrística hispano-luso-americana 6: Salmanticensis 37 (1990) 75-119.

1077 *Vidal* Marciano, Diez años de teología moral... Revistas 1980-1989: Moralia 12,2s (M 1990) 127-377 [11,4 (1989) 331-370: en 1988].

1078 VÖLKER Walther, 1. Juli 1896 - 2. Oktober 1988 Bibliographie ab 1920: TLZ 115 (1990) 778-782 (Ingo *Jungbluth*).

1079 VRIES Joseph de [3.I.1898-26.XII.1989]: Bibliographie: TPhil 65 (1990) 579-588 (H. *Scheit*, Hanna *Lauterbach*).

1080 WAGNER Siegfried, Bibliographie 60. Gb.: TLZ 115 (1990) 921-6 (D. *Mathias*).

1081 *Wainwright* Geoffrey, Recent continental theology, historical and systematic [23 books]: ExpTim 101 (1989s) 148-153.

1082 *Walls* A. F., Bibliography on mission studies: IntRMiss 78 (1989) 107-128 . 237-256 . 467-494; 79 (1990) 111-134 . 239-260 . 395-417 . 517-539.

1083 *Werblowsky* R. J. Z., Book survey: Numen 37 (1990) 110-131.

1084 **Youssif** Pierre, A classified bibliography on the East Syrian liturgy. R 1990, Yogam (Pont. Inst. Or.) xxxii-155 p. Lit. 20.000. – ᴿMuséon 103 (1990) 377 (A. de *Halleux*).

1085 ZARAGOZA Y PASCUAL Ernesto [n. 1944], Bibliografía monástica: StMon 31 (1989) 407-423 (A. *Linage Conde*; further confrères' bibliographies in 32, 1990).

A4.3   *Bibliographiae* **philologicae** *et* **generales.**

1086 **Abercrombie** John R., Computer programs for literary analysis. Ph 1984, Univ. Pennsylvania. 203 p. – ᴿVeleia 6 (1989) 312s (M. A. *Gutiérrez Galindo*).

1087 *Balconi* Carla, *al., a*) Testi recentemente pubblicati [... Gn 1,1-5 in samaritano]; – *b*) Bibliografia metodica... Egittologia, papirologia: Aegyptus 70 (1990) 259-297 [297 in basso] / 309-370; indice 371-6.

1088 *Bell* R. M., *Cwuwenberghe* E. H. G. Van, The medieval and early modern data bank (MEMDB): Tijdschrift voor Geschiedenis 103 (Groningen 1990) 260-278 [< RHE 85,347*].

1088* **Berkowitz** Luci, *Squitier* Karl A., [Thesaurus linguae graecae, computerized data base of all Greek literature from Homer to Middle Ages: 3100 authors, 9400 titles, 65,000,000 words] Canon of Greek authors and works³. NY 1990, Oxford-UP. lx-471 p. $40. 0-19-506037-7 [TDig 38,191].

1089 Bibliographische Beilage 1-4: Gnomon 62 (1990) *1-152* [81-94, 1990 zu erwartende Neuerscheinungen].

1090 **Bratkowsky** Joan G., Yiddish linguistics; a multilingual bibliography. NY 1988, Garland. xiv-407 p. – ᴿJQR 80 (1989s) 148-155 (D. L. *Gold* adds 24 pre-1959 items and queries some classifications).

1091 **Busa** Roberto, Fondamenti di informatica linguistica 1987 ➤ 5,1093: ᴿHenoch 12 (1990) 102-4 (P. G. *Borbone*).

1092 **Chastagnol** A., *al.*, L'Année épigraphique [pour] 1985. P 1988, PUF. – ᴿLatomus 49 (1990) 729-733 (R. *Chevallier*); – [pour] 1986: ᴿRÉLat 67 (1989) 392s (P. *Grimal*).

1093 Classical and medieval philology, classical archaeology and ancient history in Sweden in the years 1988-9 [Univ. Uppsala, Stockholm, Göteborg, Lund]: Eranos 88 (1990) 167-189.

1094 ᴱ*Cockshaw* P., *Silvestre* H., Bulletin Codicologique: Scriptorium-Bru 42 (1988) 1*-138* . 139*-277*; 43 (1989) 1*-211* . 213*-319*.

1095 *Cupaiuolo* Giovanni, Notiziario bibliografico (1988/9) / (1989-90) [in alphabetical order of Latin authors, then 'disciplines']: BStLat 19 (1989)

311-385 / 20 (1990) 290-330. 503-536 [NB p. 238-310 / 184-289. 439-502: imponente Rivista delle riviste].

1096 *Damon* C. E., *McNamee* K., Index 1-25 (1963-1989): BASP 26,1s (1989) 1-44; 45-87, list of ostraca, papyri, and inscriptions discussed.

1097 ᴱ*Davis* Ann S., Guide to reprints; an international bibliography of scholarly reprints. Kent 1989. xiv-1976 p.

1098 ᴱ**Ernst** Juliette, *al.*, L'Année philologique 58 (1987). P 1990, BLettres. xxxvii-1088 p.; 15312 items. 0184-6949. We continue to be baffled by the plural subtitle 'Testamenta' p. 370-391, containing only New Testament items; but we have found especially usable the sections on Mélanges, Sport, and Médecine.

1099 *Giacomini* Paola, Le banche dati dell'epigrafia; esperienze e prospettive: ArchCalc 1 (1990) 295-304.

1100 ᴱ**Gualdo** Germano, Sussidi per la consultazione dell'Archivio Vaticano; lo schedario Garampi...²ʳᵉᵛ: Colc 17. Vaticano 1989, Archivio. xxvii-449 p. Lit. 60.000. – ᴿColcFran 60 (1990) 757s (V. *Criscuolo*).

1101 ᴱ*Hohlweg* A., *Papademetriu* H., Bibliographische Notizen und Mitteilungen: ByZ 81 (1988) 97-245. 344-585; 82 (1989) 323-530; 83 (1990) 142-410.

1102 **Lith** S. M. E. van: Aegyptus, index of articles vol. 1-50, 1920-1970: StAmstelEpPap 2. Amst 1974, Hakkert. v-183 p.

1103 **Luey** Beth, Handbook for academic authors 1987 ⮕ 5,1102: ᴿRelStR 16 (1990) 132 (J. L. *Price*).

1104 *Misuri* Patrizia, Bibliografia sullo Scetticismo antico (1979-1988): Elenchos 11 (1990) 257-334.

1105 *Packer* Margaret M., Research in classical studies for university degrees in Great Britain and Ireland: BInstClas 37 (1990) 177-207, in progress; 208-213 completed.

1106 **Pellegrin** Élisabeth, Bibliothèques retrouvées 1988 ⮕ 5,1104: ᴿRPg 63 (1989) 391s (J.-P. *Rothschild*).

1107 *Pirenne-Delforge* Vinciane, *Loucas* Ioannis, Revue des Revues [Actes de Colloques]: Kernos 3 (1990) 401-6 [303-8].

1108 Rassegna delle Riviste / Novità in Libreria: Informazione Filosofica 1 (1990) 64-70 / 71-80 [2, 71-76 / 77-84; 3, 66-71 / 72-80].

1108* Rassegna bibliografica: Ivra [38 (1987)] 39 (1988) 297-483.

1109 *Staritsyn* A. N., ⊕ Index of literature on the ancient world published in the USSR in 1986: VDI 192 (1990) 215-227; 735 items.

1110 Text 10 (1989) 167-183; indices 1-10 (1981-9).

1111 *Tucker* C. W., Greek and Latin literature in translation, 1990 survey: ClasB 65,2 (1990) 153-169 [< NTAbs 34,368].

1112 *Vavřínek* Vladimir, *Tůma* Oldrich, Bibliographie: Byzantino-Slavica 50 (1989) 95-163. 238-308; – 51 (1990) 75-176. 256-323.

1113 Veranstaltungen, Veranstaltungsvorschau: ZSem 12 (1990) 133-164. 247-261. 408-418.

1114 *a) Wächter* Otto, Bibliothekrestaurierung heute; – *b) Mayerhöfer* Josef, Das Buch wahrt sich; die Zukunft von Buch und Bibliotheken zwischen Informationsgesellschaft und Lesegesellschaft: Biblos 38 (W 1989) 12-16 / 1-11 [34-47. 101-112. 180- 5. 264-8, Bibliographie; auch 39 (1990) 50-56. 116-127 (174-181). 230-3. 290-6].

A4.4   *Bibliographiae* **orientalisticae.**

1115 **Behn** W. H., Index islamicus 1665-1905; a bibliography of articles on Islamic subjects in periodicals and other collective publications. Millersville PA 1989, Adiyok. xxx-870 p. $125. – ᴿJSS 35 (1990) 378s (C. E. *Bosworth*: 635 periodicals imposingly excerpted, despite some few inconsistencies).

1115* Coptic bibliography 8, 1990 [ᴱ*Orlandi* Tito], Roma 1990, Centro Italiano Microfiches. 4 fasc.: 1. Numerical list, 92 groups of some 3 p. each; – 2. Introduction, subject list (10 groups: Gnosticism, Bibbia, etc.), numbered separately, from 10 to 76 each. – 3. Index, 67 p. – 4. Supplement, 20 p.

1116 *Deller* Karlheinz, Bibliography of Neo-Assyrian – 1988 and updates: SAAB 2 (1988) 129-135.

1117 *Guzman* Diane, *Gow* Mary, Reviews of Egyptological literature, Sept. 1986-Sept. 1987/Sept. 1987-Sept. 1989: BEgSem 8 (1986s) 131-147; 9 (1987s!) 83-105.

1118 **OIAc: Jones** Charles E., Oriental Institute Research Archives. Ch 1990, Univ. Oriental Inst. [The first three issues for 1991 appear in a larger format, followed by Aug.-Oct. inaugurating an entirely new periodical, No. 1 of 202 p.].

1118* **Khosho** Francis K., Twin rivers bibliography; Assyrian, Chaldian and Syrians past and present. Springfield IL 1987, auct. 0-9619310-1-9 [OIAc JJ90].

1119 KLÍMA Josef, 80 Gb., Bibliographie 1930-1988: AltOrF 17 (1990) 191-219 (B. *Hruška*, J. *Prosecký*).

1120 *Magee* Diana, The Egyptological bibliography of Percy E. NEWBERRY (1896-1949): JEA 76 (1990) 149-155.

1121 *Mazza* F., *al.*, Bibliografia 18 (1989): RStFen 18 (1990) 235-263 (-266 index auctorum).

1122 *Nemat Nejat* Karen R., A bibliography for cuneiform mathematical texts: ➤ 75, Mem. HELD M., JANES 19 (1989) 119-133.

1123 Philologia orientalis; a description of books illustrating the study and printing of Oriental languages in Europe (by R. *Smitskamp*), 2. (17th cent.). Leiden 1983, Brill. 220 p.

1124 *Scholz* Piotr O., (*Wacker* Erhard), Materialien zu einer für die Nubienforschung relevanten Bibliographie 1: Nubica 1s (1990) 313-351.

1125 Serta historica antiqua 16: **Amelotti** Mario, L'Egitto augusteo tra novità e continuità; una lettura della più recente bibliografia. Ist. Storia Antica. Genova 1989, Univ. 88-7689-051-3.

1126 *Thissen* Heinz-Josef, Demotistischer Literaturbericht XVII: Enchoria 17 (1990) 133-152.

  Yousif Pierre, A classified bibliography on the East Syrian liturgy 1990 ➤ 1084.

A4.5 *Bibliographiae* **archaeologicae.**

1129 Archäologische Dissertationen: ArchAnz (1990) 143-8.

1130 BAGATTI Bellarmino †, Bibliografia: LA 40 (1990) 397-442 (G. C. *Bottini*).

1131 **Barouch** Giovanna, Publications on archaeological excavations and surveys in Israel 1979-1984: ʿAtiqot-Eng. 18 supp. J 1989, Antiquities Dept. 95 p.

1132 Bibliographie zur Ur- und Frühgeschichte 1989: AusgF 35 (1990) 273-308.

1133 *a) Buccellati* Giorgio, Cybernetica mesopotamica [... computer]; – *b) Sailhamer* John H., A database approach to the analysis of Hebrew narrative: ➤ 164, ᶠSEGERT S., *Sopher* 1990, 23-32 / 319-335.

1134 BUCHHOLZ Hans-Günter, Bibliographie: MDOG 122 (1990) 219-233 (H. P. *Gumtz*); phot. p. 3 (70. Gb.).

1135 Bulletin of the Canadian Society for Mesopotamian Studies, Index nᵒ 1-20: BCanadMesop 20 (1990) 29-35.

1136 *Decker* Wolfgang, *a*) Bibliographie zum Sport im Alten Ägypten für die Jahre 1986 bis 1989 (V); – *b*) mit *Hermann* Werner, Jahresbibliographie zum Sport im Altertum 1989: Nikephoros 2 (1989) 185-215 / 217-238.

1137 *Delvoye* Charles, Chronique archéologique: Byzantion 60 (1990) 493-531.

1138 *Djindjian* François, Nouvelles tendences méthodologiques dans le traitement de l'information en archéologie: ArchCalc 1 (1990) 9-13; Eng. 13.

1139 *Fagan* Brian, BAR, British Archaeological Reports; 750 volumes, 200 still in print; a browse through the catalog: JField 17 (1990) 229-234.

1140 *Finney* Paul C., Early Christian art and archaeology II. (A.D. 200-500); a selected bibliography 1945-1985: SecC 6 (1987s) 203 ... [< ZIT 90,114].

1141 *Guermandi* Maria Pia, ALADINO; verso un sistema computerizzato per lo studio e l'analisi dei dati archeologici: ArchCalc 1 (1990) 263-293; Eng. 294.

1142 **Hermann** Werner, *Neudecker* Richard, Archäologische Bibliographie 1990: DAI. B 1991, de Gruyter. viii-563 p. 0141-8308.

1143 *Heymann* Florence, *Dollfus* Geneviève, Bibliographie annuelle générale: Paléorient 14,2 (1988) 321-345; 15,2 (1989) 161-187; 16,2 (1990).

1144 **Jacquet-Gordon** Hélène, Bulletin de Liaison du Groupe international d'étude de la céramique égyptienne 14 (1990). 45 p.

1145 Kern Institute Annual Bibliography of Indian Archaeology 23 for 1970-72. Leiden 1984, Reidel. 241 p. – ᴿOLZ 85 (1990) 80s (H. *Plaeschke*).

1146 *Laere* R. Van, Tables des tomes 113 (1967) à 135 (1989): RBgNum 136 (1990) 1-345.

1147 *Lieber* Erik, Index to JAmEg (ARCE, Journal of the American Research Center in Egypt) vol. I-XXVI (1962-1989): JAmEg 27 (1990) 199-217.

1148 *Moscati* Paola, Bibliografia 1989: Archeologia e calcolatori 1 (1990) 327-331.

1149 Numismatic literature 1235 (1990): semiannual bibliography of articles on coins by region, ancient then modern.

1150 *Peyn* Ortrun, List of accessions to the library [1988-9]: AntiqJ 70 (1990) 167-237.

1151 **Prodhomme** J., La préparation des publications archéologiques; réflexions, méthodes et conseils pratiques: Documents d'Archéologie Française 8, 1987 ⇒ 4,1044: ᴿHelinium 30 (1990) 123s (P. *Verhaeghe*, Eng.).

1152 *Verga* Flaminia, Rassegna archeologica: StRom 38 (1990) 422-430.

1153 *Vseviov* L. M., ⑥ Soviet works on archaeology; 1988 bibliographical index: SovArch (1990,4) 271-288; 454 items.

II. Introductio

B1 *Introductio* .1 *tota vel VT* – **Whole Bible or OT.**

1154 **Arenhoevel** Diego, Introduzione all'AT; il libro sconosciuto [Das fremde Buch 1985], ᵀ. Assisi 1989, Cittadella. 145 p. – ᴿSalesianum 52 (1990) 429 (M. *Cimosa*: piccolo, prezioso).

Artola A., *Sánchez* C. J., Biblia y Palabra de Dios: Introducción al Estudio de la Biblia 2, 1982 ²1990 ⇒ 1502 [1. ⇒ 370*].

1155 **Baldermann** Ingo, Einführung in die Bibel³ʳᵉᵛ: Uni-Tb 1486, 1988
➤ 4,1051; 5,1130: ᴿProtestantesimo 45 (1990) 217s (G. *Conte*).
1156 **Barucq** A., *al.*, Écrits d'Orient ancien et sources bibliques 1986 ➤ 2,602*;
4,1131: ᴿSTBuc 40,2 (1988) 126 (A. *Marinescu*).
1157 **Barucq** A., *al.*, Scritti dell'Antico Vicino Oriente e fonti bibliche, ᵀ*Nono*
Paola: PiccEncB 2, 1988 ➤ 4,1052; 5,1132: R 1988, Borla. 295 p. Lit.
30.000. – ᴿBenedictina 36 (1989) 574-6 (L. *De Lorenzi*).
1158 ᴱ**Bigger** Stephen, Creating the OT 1989 ➤ 5,1133: ᴿTLond 93 (1990)
314s (I. W. *Provan*).
1159 **Campbell** Antony F., The study companion to OT literature; an approach to the writings of pre-exilic Israel and exilic Israel [... level of
literary structures (and contemporary theology)]. Wilmington 1989,
Glazier. viii-504 p. $20. 0-8953-586-2 [TS 52, 387, J. C. *Endres*].
1160 ᴱ**Cimosa** Mario, *Mosetto* Francesco, Parola e vita; una introduzione
alla Bibbia. T-Leumann 1988, Elle Di Ci. 398 p. Lit. 14.000. 88-01-
14785-6. 28 art: *Bonora* A., *Cipriani* S., *Ravasi* G.; al. infra.
ᴱ**Clements** R. E., The world of ancient Israel 1989 ➤ g607.
1161 **Coggins** R., Introducing. the Old Testament: Oxford Bible Series. Ox
1990, UP. xi-165 p. £25; pa. £9. 0-1921-3154-7; -255-5 [BL 91,69, P. R.
Davies: gets the point]. – ᴿExpTim 101,10 2d-top choice (1989s) 290-2
(C. S. *Rodd*: superb); TLond 93 (1990) 315 (R. F. *Carroll*: informative and
judicious); TZBas 46 (1990) 569 (M. *Keller*).
1162 **Craigie** Peter C., The OT, its background, growth, and content 1986
➤ 2,797... 5,1135: ᴿMastJ 1 (1990) 78s (T. *Finley*).
1163 **Drane** J., Introducing the OT 1987 ➤ 4,1065; 5,1136: ᴿAnglTR 71
(1989) 310-2 (M. H. *Floyd*).
1164 **Ewert** D., A general introduction to the Bible [= ²From ancient tablets
to modern translations; ¹c. 1982]. GR 1990, Zondervan. 284 p. $13. 0-
310-45371-2 [NTAbs 35,93].
1165 **Gillieron** B., La Bible n'est pas tombée du ciel; l'étonnante histoire de sa
naissance. Aubonne 1988, Moulin. 115 p. – ᴿProtestantesimo 45 (1990)
138 (B. *Subilia*: autore pastore svizzero).
1165* **Goldbrunner** Josef, Corso biblico; riflessioni sulla storia della salvezza,
I. L'Antico Testamento; II. Nuovo Testamento; ᵀ*Paiusco* Luisella, *Riboldi*
Enea. Brescia 1990, Queriniana. 110 p.; 116 p. 88-399-3091-4; -2-2.
González Echegaray J., *al.*, La Biblia en su entorno: Introducción al estudio
de la Biblia [1. ➤ 1502] 2, 1990 ➤ 370*.
1166 **González-Núñez** Ángel, La Biblia; los autores, los libros , el mensaje.
M 1989, Paulinas. 323 p. 84-285-1278-7. – ᴿActuBbg 27 (1990) 194 (X.
Alegre S.); BibFe 16 (1990) 304s (M. *Sáenz de Santa María*: no científico,
no divulgación; gigantesco esfuerzo de síntesis); EstAg 25 (1990) 452 (C.
Mielgo).
1167 **Gottwald** Norman, The Hebrew Bible, a socio-literary introduction 1985
➤ 1,1183... 5,1143: ᴿCritRR 3 (1990) 129s (G. T. *Sheppard*).
1168 **Gottwald** Norman K., Introdução socioliterária à Bíblia hebráica [1985
➤ 1,1183], ᵀ*Álvarez* Anacleto: Bíblia e sociologia. São Paulo 1988,
Paulinas. 651 p. 85-05-00774-3. – ᴿPerspT 22 (1990) 241s (J. *Vitório*).
1169 **Hallo** William W., *al.*, The Bible in the light of cuneiform literature:
Scripture in Context 3: ANE TextsSt 8. Lewiston NY 1990, Mellen.
xii-486 p. 0-88946-219-4 [OIAc S90].
1170 **Harrington** Wilfrid J., ❾ Klucz do Biblii, praef. *Vaux* R. de [1965 ²1984
➤ 65,1007], ᵀ*Marzęcki* Józef. Wsz 1984, Pax. 608 p. [KirSef 62 (1988s)
p. 27].

1171 **Humphreys** W. Lee, Crisis and story; an introduction to the Old Testament² [¹1980]. Mountain View CA 1990, Mayfield. xvii-377 p.; ill. 0-87484-934-9.

Josipovici Gabriel, The book of God; a response to the Bible 1988 → 1643.

1172 **Laffey** Alice L., An introduction to the OT; a feminist perspective 1988 → 4,1075; 5,1150: ᴿAnglTR 71 (1989) 207s (Katharine D. *Sakenfeld*: qualified praise); CritRR 2 (1989) 170-3 (Naomi *Steinberg*); HebSt 31 (1990) 192-4 (Eleanor *Amico*: a valuable resource); Interpretation 44 (1990) 81 (J. L. *Sullivan*: favorable; sharpens our skills as interpreters).

1173 **Laffey** Alice L., Wives, harlots and concubines; the Old Testament in feminist perspective. L 1990, SPCK. xii-243 p. £10. 0-281-04492-9 [BL 91, 114, G. I. *Emmerson*: a sad book].

1174 **Lambiasi** Francesco, Breve introducción a la Sagrada Escritura [1985], ᵀ1988 → 5,1076: ᴿTVida 31 (1990) 356s (M. A. *Ferrando*).

1175 **Lang** Bernhard, Die Bibel, eine kritische Einführung: Uni-Tb 1594. Pd 1990, Schöningh. 255 p. [TR 87,73].

1176 **Mertens** Heinrich A., Manual de la Biblia; aspectos literarios, históricos, arqueológicos, histórico-religiosos, culturales y geográficos del Antiguo y Nuevo Testamento [Hebraische Bibelkunde], ᵀ*Gancho* Claudio. Barc 1989, Herder. 872 p. – ᴿActuBbg 27 (1990) 199s (X. *Alegre* S.); CommSev 23 (1990) 277 (M. de *Burgos*); EstTrin 24 (1990) 508s (J. L. *Aurrecoechea*); Manresa 62 (1990) 465s (J. I. *Macua* P.); NatGrac 37 (1990) 317s (F. F. *Ramos*); RelCu 36 (1990) 687 (M. A. *Martín Juárez*).

1177 ᴱ**Mulder** Martin J., *Sysling* H. Mikra 1988 → 4,317; 5,1157: ᴿAndr-UnS 28 (1990) 175-7 (J. E. *Miller*); Antonianum 65 (1990) 105s (M. *Nobile*); BO 47 (1990) 188s (J. W. *Wevers*); BZ 34 (1990) 130-2 (C. *Thoma*; unter 'NT-Rezensionen'); HebSt 31 (1990) 218-222 (B. *Halpern*); Interpretation 44 (1990) 415s (C. *Bernas*); JSS 35 (1990) 317s (S. *Brock*); JTS 41 (1990) 575-8 (N. *de Lange*); StPhilonAn 2 (1990) 223-6 (D. T. *Runia*); WestTJ 52 (1990) 151-3 (M. *Silva*).

1178 **Ohler** Annemarie, Grundwissen AT Werkbuch 2s 1987s → 2,810... 5,1159: ᴿBLtg 63 (1990) 121s (L. *Schwienhorst-Schönberger*).

1178* **Ohler** Annemarie, Studying the OT, from tradition to canon [1972s], ᵀ*Cairns* D. 1985 → 1,1198... 5,1160: ᴿDialog 28 (1989) 159 (M. *Throntveit*: somewhat simplistic and outdated).

1179 **Rendtorff** Rolf, Introduction à l'Ancien Testament 1989 → 5,1162: ᴿLavalTP 46 (1990) 406s (J.-J. *Lavoie*); Masses Ouvrières 432 (1990) 80s (F. *Dumortier*).

1180 **Rendtorff** Rolf, Introduzione all'Antico Testamento; storia, vita sociale e letteratura d'Israele in epoca biblica [1983, ³1988 → 64,1025], ᵀ*Garrone* Daniele: Piccola biblioteca teologica 22. T 1990, Claudiana. 412 p. Lit. 42.000 [Asprenas 38,390, V. *Scippa*].

1181 **Rogerson** John W., *Davies* Philip R., The OT world 1989 → 5,1163: ᴿEvQ 62 (1990) 355 (K. T. *Aitken*); ExpTim 101 (1989s) 48 (C. S. *Rodd*: 'OT as studied today'); Vidyajyoti 54 (1990) 542s (P. M. *Meagher*).

1181* **Rogerson** John [OT], *Avis* John [NT], *Rowland* C. [Inter-T], The study and use of the Bible. GR/Basingstoke 1988, Eerdmans/Marshall Pickering. [xii-] 415 p. 0-8028-0196-X / 0-551-01519-5.

1182 **Schmidt** Werner H., *al.*, Altes Testament: Grundkurs Theologie 1 (aus 10), Urban-Tb 421, 1989 → 5,1165: ᴿTLZ 115 (1990) 20 (L. *Wächter*); TPQ 138 (1990) 185s (F. *Hubmann*).

1183 **Smend** Rudolf, Die Entstehung des Alten Testaments⁴ [= ¹1980]: TWiss 1. Stu 1989, Kohlhammer. 242 p. DM 32.

1184 **Soggin** J. Alberto, Introduction to the OT³ [1987 → 3,1169]ᵀ 1989
→ 5,1170: ᴿCurrTMiss 17 (1990) 77 (R.W. *Klein*); OTAbs 13 (1990)
204s (L. *Boadt*).

1185 **Stachowiak** Lech, Wstęp do Starego Testamentu: Wstęp do Pisma Ś.
2. Poznań 1990, Pallottinum. 496 p.

1186 **Walton** John H., Ancient Israelite literature in its cultural context; a
survey of parallels between biblical and ancient Near Eastern texts. GR
1989, Zondervan. 249 p. $20. – ᴿBA 53 (1990) 176 (V.H. *Matthews*).

1186* ᴱWoude A.S. van der, Inleiding tot de studie van het Oude Testament
1986 → 3,1173 [!4,1198]: 90-242-27763: ᴿNedTTs 43 (1989) 54 (M.D.
Koster).

B1.2 'Invitations' to Bible or OT.

1187 **Aurelio** J., Skipping stones; the OT in a new light. NY 1990, Crossroad. 143 p. $10 [TS 51,571].

1188 **Barbiere** Flavio (ingegnere elettronico), La Bibbia senza segreti. Mi
1988, Rusconi. 468 p. Lit. 35.000. – ᴿHumBr 44 (1989) 601s (M. *Orsatti*).

1189 *Batista* I., The Bible and Christian theological education: JIntden 15,1
(Atlanta 1987s) 102-117 [< NTAbs 35,3].

1190 **Beauchamp** Paul, Parler d'Écritures saintes 1987 → 3,1177... 5,1180:
ᴿTéléma 15,2 (1989) 73s (R. *De Haes*).

1191 **Beauchamp** Paul, Hablar de las escrituras santas; perfil del lector actual
de la Biblia → 5,1181: ᵀ*Arias* Isidro, 1989; 84-254-1661-2: ᴿActuBbg 27
(1990) 55 (R. de *Sivatte*); CiTom 117 (1990) 379s (M. *Itza*); LumenVr 39
(1990) 339-341 (U. *Gil Ortega*: rico de enseñanzas, no de fácil lectura);
PerspT 22 (1990) 275-7 (J.K.).

1192 **Beauchamp** Paul, Leggere la Sacra Scrittura oggi (Con quale spirito
accostarsi alla Bibbia) [Parler d'Écr. 1987 → 3,1177], ᵀ*Frattini* Luigi.
Sorgenti di Vita 19. Mi 1990, Massimo. 126 p. 88-7030-724-7. – ᴿPalCl
69 (1990) 606 (G. *Lavarda*).

1193 **Beck** Eleonore, La mia Bibbia. R 1988, Città Nuova. 280 p.; ill.
(*König* P.). – ᴿStMon 32 (1990) 253s (O. *Divi*).

1194 **Brown** Raymond E., Responses to 101 questions on the Bible. NY 1990,
Paulist. v-147 p. $6 pa [JBL 109,753]. 0-8091-0443-1; pa. -3188-9.

1195 **Chouraqui** André, Il pensiero ebraico: LoB 3,10, 1989 → 5,1184: ᴿSt-
Patav 37 (1990) 193s (G. *Segalla*).

1196 *Collins* R.F., On reading the Scriptures: Emmanuel 96,2 (1990) 70-
73.98-101 [< NTAbs 34,286].

1197 **Czajkowski** M., Biblia dziś odczytana. Wsz 1988. 179 p. – ᴿRuBi 43
(1990) 179s (J. *Warzecha*).

1198 **Ebach** J., *al.*, Die Bibel gehört nicht uns: Einwürfe 6. Mü 1990, Kaiser.
3-459-01867-4 [BL 91,158].

1199 *Echegaray* Hugo, Comentario bíblico; tiempo y fidelidad: Paginas
14,96 (Lima 1989) 6-13.

1200 *Gallup* [... poll] Georgeᴶ, *Castelli* Jim, Americans and the Bible [... how
education affects views of Bible authority or involvement in Bible groups]:
BR 6,3 (1990) 37s.

1201 **Geisler** Norman, *Brooks* Ron, When skeptics ask [good questions but
do not listen to the answers]. Wheaton ɪʟ 1990, Victor. 348 p. $18. – ᴿBS
147 (1990) 485 (F.R. *Howe*).

1202 **Gibert** P., L'Ancien Testament: Parcours. P 1989, Centurion. 124 p. –
ᴿEsprVie 100 (1990) 539 (L. *Walter*).

1203 **Greeley** Andrew M., *Neusner* Jacob, The Bible and us; a priest and a rabbi read Scripture together. NY 1990, Warner. xv-228 p. $25. 0-446-51522-1 [TDig 37,366].

1204 **Hanegraaff** J., Met de Torah is het begonnen [I. 1988 ➤ 5,1193 N.B. -ff]; II. De voortgang van het Woord in Tenach en Septuagint. Nijkerk 1989, Callenbach. 354 p. *f*47.50. 90-266-0175-1. – ᴿKerkT 41 (1990) 67 (P. A. *Elderenbosch*); TsTNijm 30 (1990) 86 (J. *Holman*: queries).

1205 **Hanson** R. P. C. & A. T., The Bible without illusions 1989 ➤ 5,1194: ᴿTLond 93 (1990) 477s (S. W. *Need*).

1206 **Jérôme,** moine de Sept-Fons, Jalons pour l'Ancien Testament³ [¹1951], ᴱ*Olive* Patrick, abbé: Ad Solem. Genève 1990, Martingay. 96 p. – ᴿEsprVie 100 (1990) 382s É. *Ricaud*: approche très religieux de 1948).

1207 *Josipovici* Gabriel [➤ 1643], The Bible in focus [7th JStOT lecture]: JStOT 48 (1990) 101-122.

1208 **Kopp** Johanna, Das Alte Testament — ein Buch für heute; Zugänge zu den Büchern der Geschichte Israels 1989 ➤ 5,1203: ᴿTPQ 138 (1990) 398s (Roswitha *Unfried*).

1209 **Larue** G., The supernatural, the occult, and the Bible. Buffalo 1990, Prometheus. 303 p. $22 [TS 52,191].

1210 **Llamas** Román, La Biblia de Francisco PALAU, II. Temas bíblicos 1988 ➤ 5,8180*: ᴿEstE 65 (1990) 232s (R. M. *Sanz de Diego*).

1211 **Manacorda** Mario A., Lettura laica della Bibbia. R 1989, Riuniti. 184 p. Lit. 14.000. – ᴿCC 141 (1990,2) 196s (G. L. *Prato*).

1212 **Marchadour** Alain, Grandi temi biblici [1987 ➤ 4,227], ᵀ*Scaglioni* Vittoria, ᶠ*Moroni* Giancarlo. Brescia 1990, Queriniana. 80 p. Lit. 10.000. 88-399-3066-3.

1213 *Martin Juárez* M. A., Leer la Biblia; reflexiones metodológicas sobre el AT: RelCult 34 (1988) 309-334.

1214 **Mattam** Zacharias, Opening the Bible; meeting Christ in the Scriptures. Bangalore 1988, KJC. xii-336 p. rs 50. – ᴿVidyajyoti 54 (1990) 314 (R. J. *Raja*).

1215 **Mesters** Carlos, Defenseless flower; a new reading of the Bible [1970s conferences], ᵀ*McDonagh* F. L/Mkn 1989, Catholic Institute for International Relations/Orbis. viii-175 p. £14. 1-85287-055-9 / US 0-88344-596-4 [BL 91,86, R. J. *Coggins*]. – ᴿTS 51 (1990) 557 (M. L. *Cook*).

1216 ᴱ*Metzger* B. M., *al.*, Faszinierende Welt der Bibel [Great events 1987 ➤ 3,353], ᵀ*Meyer* I. FrB 1988, Herder. 200 p. DM 50. – ᴿSNTU-A 14 (1989) 289s (A. *Fuchs*).

1217 **Noakes** Susan, Timely reading; between exegesis and interpretation [GADAMER H., DERRIDA J.]. 1988 ➤ 4,1131: ᴿSpeculum 65 (1990) 1030-2 (G. *Mazzotta*).

1218 **Oden** Robert A., The Bible without theology 1987 ➤ 3,269... 5,1209: ᴿCritRR 2 (1989) 142-5 (H. C. *White*).

1219 **Peters** F. E., Judaism, Christianity, and Islam; the classical texts and their interpretation; 1. From covenant to community; 2. The Word and the Law and the People of God; 3. The works of the Spirit. Princeton 1990, Univ. xxv-408 p.; xxv-395 p.; xxv-408 p. $15 each pa.; $75 bound in one volume. – ᴿManuscripta 34 (1990) 246 (companion to his Children of Abraham).

1220 *a) Pousset* Édouard, La Bible comme univers; – *b) Vallin* Pierre, La Bible, objet culturel ou livre chrétien: ➤ 379, Canon 1990, 512-521 / 541-558.

1221 **Pigeaud** Olivier, Petit guide biblique. P 1989, Bergers & Mages. 91 p. F 40. 2-85304-070-8. – RÉTRel 65 (1990) 631s (G. *Balestier-Stengel*).

1222 **Power** J., History of salvation; introducing the Old Testament[2] [= [1]Set my exiles free 1967 + new intr.]. Dublin/NY 1989, Gill & M/Alba. 201 p. £6.   0-7171-1719-7 / US 0-8189-0566-2 [BL 91,91, R.J. *Coggins*: no advertence to the many new developments].

1222* *Premnath* D. N., The Old Testament in its cultural background and its implications for theological education: Asia JT 2 (1988) 98-105 [12-97 *al.*, ecumenical cooperation in India especially in theological education].

E**Radday** Yehuda T., *Brenner* Athalya, On humour and the comic in the Hebrew Bible 1990 ⇒ 367.

1224 **Ravasi** Gianfranco, L'Antico Testamento e le culture del tempo; testi scelti: Studi e Ricerche Bibliche. R 1990, Borla. 622 p. 88-263-0819-5.

1124* **Renckens** H. E. J., De bijbel mee maken; omgangsvormen en proefteksten. Kampen 1988, Kok. 234 p. *f* 39. 90-242-3395-X. – RNedTTs 43 (1989) 333 (P. B. *Dirksen*).

1225 **Roos** Klaus, Habt ihr keine Ohren, um zu hören? Reiz-Texte zur Bibel für Predigt und Gruppenarbeit. Mainz 1990, Grünewald. 128 p. DM 19,80. – RTGL 80 (1990) 341 (R. *Dillmann*: Hauptziel 'die LeserInnen zur Auseinandersetzung mit der hl. Schrift zu reizen' p. 15).

1226 **Schilling** Alfred, 'Verstehst du auch, was du liest?' Vom rechten Umgang mit der Bibel: Tb 1585. FrB 1988, Herder. 157 p. DM 12,90. – ETR 86 1990) 190s (O. B. *Knoch*).

1227 **Smith** Morton, *Hoffman* R. J., What the Bible really says 1989 ⇒ 5,418: RBR 6,5 (1990) 12s (Paula M. *McNutt*).

1228 **Strapazzon** Valentin, 30 questions sur la Bible: C'est-à-dire, 1989 ⇒ 5,1219: REsprVie 100 (1990) 235s (L. *Monloubou*).

1229 **Stuhlmueller** C., New paths through the OT 1989 ⇒ 5,1220: RVidyajyoti 54 (1990) 494s (P. M. *Meagher*).

1230 **Weinreb** Freidrich [sic], Roots of the Bible, an ancient view for a new outlook [Dutch], TKeus N. Brauntaon 1986, Merlin. 585 p. [KirSef 62 (1988s) p. 36; no indication that roots is to be taken botanically].

1231 **Woodrow** Martin [OT], *Sanders* E. P. [NT], People from the Bible. L 1987, P. Lowe. 180 p.; color. ill. (Heseltine J., *al.*) [KirSef 62 (1988s) p. 493].

B1.3   *Paedagogia biblica* – **Bible-teaching techniques.**

1232 *Asurmendi* Jesús, Enseigner l'Ancien Testament: RICathP 33 (1990) 127-135.

1233 **Bobrowski** Jürgen, Biblische Symbole im Spiel erfahren; Grundlagen und Praxis des Bibliodramas: ev. Diss. DCornehl. Hamburg 1989s. – TR 86 (1990) 515.

1233* **Brereton** Virginia L., Training God's army; the American Bible school, 1880-1940. Bloomington 1990, Indiana Univ. xix-212 p. $27.50. 0-253-31266-3 [TDig 38,253].

1234 **Camponovo** O., *al.*, Peuple parmi les peuples; dossier pour l'animation biblique; TPerillard Marianne. Essais Bibliques 18. Genève 1990, Labor et Fides. 240 p. 2-8309-0622-5.

1235 **Höffken** Peter, Elemente kommunikativer Didaktik in frühjüdischer und rabbinischer Literatur [pädag. Hab.-Diss. Bonn 1984]: Rel.-Pädagogik 1, 1986 ⇒ 2,855: RTR 86 (1990) 408-410 (D. *Dormeyer*).

1236 **Kaynor** Keith, The Bible visual resource book for do-it-yourself Bible scholars. Schaumburg IL 1989, Regular Baptist Press. 332 p.; maps, graphs, charts. $13 pa. – ᴿBS 147 (1990) 496 (F. D. *Lindsey*).

1237 ᴱ*Lavarda* Girolamo, Catechisti e operatori pastorali devono conoscere la Bibbia; contenuti essenziali di un'indispensabile iniziazione: PalCl 68 (1989) 1155-1160.

1238 *LaVerdiere* E., Sowing the seed: Church 6,4 (1990) 43-46 [47, *Martini* C. M. on lectio divina: < NTAbs 35,140].

1239 *Mesters* Carlos, The Bible and the new evangelization: VerbumSVD 31 (1990) 361-388.

1240 **Pastore** Corrado [ᴱ*Stéfani* Luciano, *al.*], *a*) Un pueblo, un libro; introducción a la Biblia; – *b*) La Biblia en la catequesis: Escuela de Catequistas 1s. Caracas c. 1990, Salesiana. 48 p.; ill. / 32 p. 980- 6007- 46-8 (both).

1241 *Reinmuth* Titus [Neh 5,1-13 ...] Alttestamentliche Exegese in der Berliner Wirklichkeit [unter Rubrik: 'Visitation']: BTZ 7 (1990) 119-135.

1242 **Sari Scamatra** F., La Bible [de Jérusalem] en questions; 3024 questions [pour joueurs autour d'un tableau, 504 cartes avec la réponse au verso ...]. Tournai 1990, Marquain. Fb 3000 [NRT 113, 466, G. M.].

1243 **Schinzer** Reinhard, Spielräume in der Bibel; Anregungen für den Umgang mit der Bibel in Gruppen. Gö 1989, Vandenhoeck & R. 180 p. 3-525-61298-2. P. 9-12, 'Ärger mit Onesimus' [Phlm] + 11 *al.*

1244 *Schwarz* J. E., Twenty popular adult Bible study programs: WWorld 10,1 (St. Paul 1990) 60-69 [< NTAbs 34,150].

1245 *a*) *Stachel* Günter, Bibelunterricht als Erlernen der Sprache des Glaubens; – *b*) *Raske* Michael, Feministische Theologie, ein prophetischer Ausbruch; – *c*) *Voss-Goldstein* Christel, *al.*, Frauen machen Geschichte; geschichtliche Hintergründe der Frauenfrage und deren prophetische Deutung: KatBlätt 115 (Mü 1990) 52-57 / 84-86 / 94-100 (-124) [< ZIT 90,200].

1246 *Uwalaka* Mary Angela, Biblical apostolate in African universities: Biblical Pastoral Bulletin 10 (Nairobi 1990) 44-51 [< TContext 8/1,19].

1247 **Weber** Hans-Ruedi, Esperimenti di studio biblico; nuovi metodi e tecniche [... per gruppi], ᵀ*Comba* F.: Piccola Bibl. Teol. 20. T 1989, Claudiana. 240 p. Lit. 24.000. 88-7016-098-X. – ᴿActuBbg 27 (1990) 205s (X. *Alegre* S.); BbbOr 32 (1990) 251s [F. *Sardini*]; StPatav 37 (1990) 199s (G. *Segalla*: zelo missionario ed ecumenico).

B2.1 Hermeneutica.

1248 **Arasola** K., The end of historicism; Millerite hermeneutic of time prophecies in the OT [diss. Uppsala 1989]. U 1990, Univ. x-226 p. [NRT 113, 906, J.-L. *Ska*].

1249 *Armstrong* Arthur H., *a*) Philosophy, theology and interpretation; the interpretation of interpreters [< Eriugena 1979/80, 7-14]; – *b*) Pagan and Christian traditionalism in the first three centuries A.D. [< StPatr 15, 1975/84, 414-431]: → 197, Hellenic and Christian Studies 1990, X (p. 7-14) / IX (p. 414-431).

1250 *a*) *Berger* Klaus, Hermeneutik und Ästhetik; – *b*) *Martin* Gerhard M., Bild – Licht – Körperbild; zu einer 'Kritik der Bilder' anhand einiger Logien des Thomas-Evangelium: → 28, ᶠBOHREN R., 1990, 47-51 / 69-76.

1251 **Betti** Emilio, L'ermeneutica come metodica generale delle scienze dello spirito [²1972], ᴱ*Mura* Gaspare. R 1987, Città Nuova. 213 p. – ᴿZSavR 106 (1989) 713-9 (M. J. *Schermaier*).

1252 **Biser** Eugen, Die Bibel als Medium; zur medienkritischen Schlüsselposition der Theologie: Szb Heid p/h 1990,1. Heid 1990, Winter. 37 p.; ill. 3-533-04257-X.

1253 *Burkill* M., The principles of Bible interpretation: Churchman 103 (L 1989) 40-52 [< NTAbs 34,4].

1254 ᴱ**Carson** D. A., *Woodbridge* J. D., Hermeneutics, authority, and canon 1986 ➤ 2,240; 3,1248: ᴿCriswT 4 (1989s) 413-5 (D. L. *Akin*).

1255 **Chevalier** Jacques M., Semiotics, romanticism and the Scriptures: Approaches to Semitics 88. B/NY 1990, Mouton de Gruyter. vii-364 p. 3-11-012224-4 / 0-89925-819-8.

1256 *Childs* Brevard S., Critical reflections on James BARR's understanding of the literal and the allegorical: JStOT 46 (1990) 3-9.

1257 **Cochran** Shelley E., Liturgical hermeneutics; the lectionary as an agent of biblical interpretation: diss. Drew, ᴰ*Doughty* D. Madison NJ 1990. 270 p. 90-32120. – DissA 51 (1990s) 2051-A; RelStR 17,191.

ᴱ**Coggins** R. J., *Houlden* J. L., A dictionary of Bible interpretation 1990 ➤ 865.

1257* ᴱ**Connolly** John M., *Keutner* Thomas, Hermeneutics versus science [GADAMER and 3 other Germans' essays]. ND 1988, Univ. viii-176 p. – ᴿJRel 70 (1990) 287-9 (J. J. *Jackson*).

1258 **Contides** Theodosios, Ⓖ Biblical interpretation; notes on the interpretative method of Farados [*Pharantos* Megas, Ⓖ Orthodox teaching on God, Athena 1985]: DeltioVM 19,1 (1990) 60-69; 19/2, p. 78, comment of Farados.

1259 **Cowley** Roger W., Ethiopian biblical interpretation 1988 ➤ 4,1186: ᴿExpTim 101 (1989s) 49s (J. D. *Ray*); JRAS (1990) 378-382 (*Getatchew Haile*); JSS 35 (1990) 181-3 (E. *Ullendorff*).

1260 **Croatto** J. Severino, Biblical hermeneutics 1987 ➤ 3,1252 ... 5,1256: ᴿTorJT 6 (1990) 350-3 (J. D. *Evers*).

1261 **Croatto** J. S., Die Bibel gehöhrt den Armen [Hermenéutica bíblica 1984 = Biblical Hermeneutics 1987], ᵀ*Schroeder* C.: ÖkExH 5. Mü 1989, Kaiser. 100 p. DM 19,80 [NTAbs 34,98].

1262 *Crouzel* Henri, Le rôle de l'exégèse spirituelle dans la prise de conscience du contenu de la tradition et dans le développement du dogme: ➤ 700, Tradizione Aug 1989/90, 341-9.

1263 *a*) *Davies* P. R., Do Old Testament studies need a dictionary? [the metalanguage of scholarship]: – *b*) *Thiselton* Anthony C., On models and methods; a conversation with Robert MORGAN [Biblical Interpretation 1988]; – *c*) *Brett* Mark G., Four or five things to do with texts; a taxonomy of interpretative interests; – *d*) *Fowl* Stephen E., The ethics of interpretation, or What's left over after the elimination of meaning?: ➤ 166, ᶠSheffield 1990, 321-335 / 337-356 / 357-377 / 379-398.

1264 **Denison** James C., Prolegomena to theological hermeneutics; a critical evaluation of the proposals of J. V. Langmead CASSERLEY regarding the nature of biblical and theological language: diss. SW Baptist Theol. Sem. 1989. 257 p. 90-14712. – DissA 51 (1990s) 193-A.

1264* *Dumermuth* C. F., Number symbolism; a biblical key: AsiaJT 4,1 (1990) 108-119 [< ZIT 91,203].

1265 *Fee* G. D., Issues in evangelical hermeneutics; hermeneutics and the nature of Scripture: Crux 26,2 (1990) 21-26; 26/3, 35-42 [< NTAbs 35,6].

1266 **Fishbane** Michael, The garments of Torah; essays in biblical hermeneutics [5 inedita; 5 1975-88]: 1989 ➤ 5,259: ᴿHebSt 31 (1990) 135-141 (S. *Lasine*).

1267 **Fishbane** Michael, Biblical interpretation in ancient Israel 1985 ⇒ 1, 1308...5,1260: ᴿNedTTs 44 (1990) 60s (A. van der *Kooij*); TTod 47 (1990) 433-5 (J. A. *Sanders*).

1268 *Franklin* R. L., Certainty and interpretation [our faith is 'certain' if we see it as a pathway to deeper understanding rather than a fortress to be defended]: Pacifica 3 (1990) 139-156.

1269 **Goldingay** J., Approaches to Old Testament interpretation² [= ¹1981 + postscript]. Leicester 1990, Apollos. 207 p. £10. 0-85111-415-6 [BL 91, 111].

1270 **Graham** William A., Beyond the written word 1987 ⇒ 4,1200; 5,1263: ᴿHistRel 30 (1990s) (Marilyn R. *Waldman*); Vidyajyoti 54 (1990) 44 (G. *Gispert-Sauch*).

1271 **Groves** Joseph W., Actualization and interpretation in the Old Testament: SBL diss. 86, 1987 ⇒ 3,1263... 5,1265: ᴿÉTRel 65 (1990) 621 (D. *Lys*).

1272 *Güttgemanns* Erhardt, Gēmatriyyā' und Lᵉchēshbōn: LingBib 64 (1990) 23-51; Eng. 51s.

1273 *Güttgemanns* Erhardt, Was ist ein 'Text'? [*Ijsseling* Samuel, Rhetorik und Philosophie 1988]: LingB 63 (1989) 106-142.

1274 **Gusdorf** G., Storia dell'ermeneutica, ᵀ*Guidobaldi* M. P. Bari 1989, Laterza. 516 p. – ᴿEuntDoc 43 (1990) 539s (P. *Miccoli*).

1275 **Hall** D. R., The seven pilleries of wisdom [common bad norms: a modern idea is better than an ancient one; probable can be taken as certain; NT world-view modernized; argument from silence; everything is product of environment; one author always uses same style; NT authors were specialists]. Macon GA 1990, Mercer Univ. viii-137 p. $19. 0-86554-3669-0.

1276 *Haręzga* Stanisław, En pneumati jako zasada interpretacji pisma św. we wschodniej tradycji kościoła: RuBi 43 (1990) 111-121: 'In the spirit' as basis of the interpretation of Scripture in the eastern tradition of the Church.

1277 a) *Hennaux* Jean-Marie, Sens tropologique de l'Écriture et problèmes d'aujourd'hui; – b) *Théobald* Christoph, L'Écriture, âme de la théologie, ou le christianisme comme religion de l'interprétation: ⇒ 541*, L'Écriture âme 1989/90, 145-161 / 109-132.

1278 *Hobbs* E., Hermeneutical cartography; a modest proposal [to cope with diversity in hermeneutics; authors must recognize this and show cognizance of which kind they are using; then 'a new typology' is needed to locate the various approaches in relation to each other]: CHS 59 (1990) 5-11; responses 17-31 [NTAbs 34,287].

1279 *Hooker* Morna D., Interpreting the Bible; methods old and new [excitement and allure of the new (post-modernist) literary critical approaches (would) run riot without the 'traditional' historico-critical methods]: EpworthR 17,1 (1990) 69-77 [< NTAbs 34,287].

1280 a) *Hoppe* Leslie J., Biblical interpretation in ancient Israel [FISHBANE M., 1985]; an introduction; – b) *Haak* Robert D., At the borders of the text; – c) *Viviano* Pauline A., Methodology, chronology, scribes and inspiration: ⇒ 552*, BiRes 35 (1990) 37-43 / 44-50 / 51-57.

1281 *Hultgren* A. J., Exploring the boundaries of biblical interpretation [natural, what we do not know; imposed, by church or academic bodies; disputed, i.e. feminist/liberationist challenges]: Dialog 28,4 (St. Paul 1989) 257-262 [< NTAbs 34,146].

1282 *Janse van Rensburg* N. A., 'n Samevatting en kritiese evaluasie van B. S.
CHILDS se kanoniese benadering: SkrifKerk 9,1 (Pretoria 1988) 22-32
[< NTAbs 34,146].

1283 ᴱJohnson Bo, *Kieffer* René, Text och tolkning; Uppsatser om bibel-
tolkningens problem: Religio 20. Lund 1985, Teologiska Institutionen.
196 p. – ᴿSvEx 55 (1990) 93-95 (P. *Block*).

1284 **Johnson** Elliott E., Expository hermeneutics; an introduction. GR
1990, Zondervan. 330 p. $20. 0-310-31460-4. – ᴿBS 147 (1990) 234s
(R. B. *Zuck*: how does one know if his interpretation of a Bible text rather
than a conflicting interpretation is correct?).

1285 *Karasszon* István, Ⓜ The science of hermeneutics today: TSzem 33
(1990) 32-34.

1286 *Kraft* Heinrich, Hermeneutisches; zur allegorischen Auslegungsweise:
TZBas 46 (1990) 333-8.

1287 **Kugel** James L., *Greer* Rowan A., Early biblical interpretation 1986
→ 2,905 ... 5,1272: ᴿCriswT 4 (1989s) 183s (D. S. *Dockery*); SecC 7
(1989s) 184s (J. J. *Collins*).

1288 **Larkin** William J., Culture and biblical hermeneutics; interpreting and
applying the authoritative word in a relativistic age 1988 → 4,1216;
5,1273: ᴿBS 147 (1990) 495 (E. E. *Johnson*); CalvinT 25 (1990) 105s (S.
Greidanus); Evangel 8,1 (1990) 23s (G. W. *Grogan*); ExpTim 101 (1989s)
249 (A. C. *Thiselton*).

1289 *Lategan* B., Introducing a research project on contextual hermeneutics:
Scriptura 23 (Stellenbosch 1990) 1-5 [< NTAbs 35,8].

1290 **Laurant** Jean-Pierre, Symbolisme de l'Écriture... Pitra/Méliton 1988
→ 4,1217; 5,1274: ᴿRÉAug 36 (1990) 210s (A. *Le Boulluec*).

1291 *Lee* D., Taking ourselves more seriously [... in interpreting Scripture,
more attention needs to be given to the present cultural context of the
interpreter]: Anvil 6,2 (1989) 149-159 [< NTAbs 34,5].

1292 *Lerner* Berel D., Faith, fiction and the Jewish Scriptures: Judaism 39
(1990) 215-220.

1293 *a) Lodahl* Michael E., Jews and Christians in a conflict of interpretations; on questioning the 'Judeo-Christian tradition'; – *b) Olthuis*
James H., A cold and comfortless hermeneutic or a warm and trembling
hermeneutic; a conversation with John D. CAPUTO; – *c) Lundin* Roger,
The cult and culture of interpretation: ChrSchR 19 (1990) 332-344 /
345-362 / 363-387 [< ZIT 90,588].

1294 **McEvenue** Sean E., *Meyer* Ben F., LONERGAN's hermeneutics; its
development and application. Wsh 1989, Catholic University. vi-313 p.
$45 [CBQ 53,172].

1295 **McKim** Donald K., A guide to contemporary hermeneutics 1986
→ 2,258 ... 5,1277*: ᴿGraceTJ 10 (1989) 79s (D. S. *Dockery*).

1296 **Macky** Peter W., The centrality of metaphors in biblical thought; a
method for interpreting the Bible: StBeC 19. Lewiston 1990, Mellen.
320 p. $70. 0-88946-619-X.

1297 *Mahlmann* Theodor, Kritischer Rationalismus [POPPER Karl...]: → 857,
TRE 20 (1990) 97-121 [65-96, al. Kritik (Bibelkritik, Hermeneutik),
kritische Theorie].

1298 **Maier** Gerhard, Biblische Hermeneutik. Wu 1990, Brockhaus. 404 p.
DM 50 pa. [TR 86,521].

1299 *a) Makarushka* Irena, NIETZSCHE's critique of modernity; the emergence
of hermeneutical consciousness; – *b) Fischer* David H., Self in text, text
in self: ⟶ 365, Semeia 51 (1990) 193-214 / 137-154.

1300 *Marrion* M., Biblical hermeneutics in the Regula Benedicti: StMon 30 (1988) 17-40.

1301 *Meyer* Ben F., A tricky business, ascribing new meaning to old texts [AUGUSTINE, LONERGAN succeeded; HEGEL, Northrop FRYE failed]: Gregorianum 71 (1990) 743-760; franç. 761.

1302 **Molina Palma** M. A., La interpretación de la Escritura en el Espíritu ᴰ1987 → 3,1277 ... 5,1279: ᴿEstE 65 (1990) 76s (A. M. *Artola*).

1303 **Morfino** Mauro M., Leggere la Bibbia con la vita; la lettura esistenziale della Parola, un aspetto comune all'ermeneutica rabbinica e patristica. Magnano ᴠᴄ 1990, Qiqajon. 192 p.

1304 **Morgan** R., (*Barton* J.) Biblical interpretation 1988 → 4,1231; 5,1280: ᴿCritRR 3 (1990) 82-84 (J. J. *Collins*); Interpretation 44 (1990) 204-206 (D. L. *Bartlett*: careful, provocative); JRel 70 (1990) 447s (J. D. *Levenson*); TEdn 26,1 (1989s) 114 (D. J. *Harrington*: best available today); TR 86 (1990) 362s (O. B. *Knoch*).

1306 **Mura** Gaspare, Ermeneutica e verità; storia e problemi della filosofia dell'interpretazione. R 1990, Città Nuova. 516 p. – ᴿEuntDoc 43 (1990) 560-2 (P. *Miccoli*).

1307 **O'Connell** Colin, A study of Heinrich OTT's theological development; his hermeneutical and ontological programme: diss. McMaster, ᴰ*Robertson* J. Hamilton 1989. – RTLv 22, p. 586.

1308 *Piattelli* Alberto, L'interpretazione di fede della Bibbia da un punto di vista ebraico: → 514*b*, Un libro 1989/90, 31-33.

1309 **Piret** P., L'Écriture et l'Esprit 1987 → 3,1283 ... 5, aussi 1283: ᴿTelema 16,1 (1990) 73s (R. *Capoen*).

1310 **Pleitner** Henning, Das Ende der liberalen Hermeneutik am Beispiel Albert SCHWEITZERs: diss. Heidelberg 1990s, ᴰ*Berger*. – RTLv 22, p. 686.

1311 **Prickett** Stephen, Words and the Word; language, poetics and biblical interpretation 1986 → 2,918 ... 5,1284: ᴿÉTRel 65 (1990) 621s (J. *Pons*, D. *Lys*).

1312 **Resweber** Jean-Paul, Qu'est-ce qu'interpréter? Essai sur les fondements de l'herméneutique 1988 → 4,1287: F 119; 2-204-02929-7: ᴿScEsp 42 (1990) 223s (J.-C. *Petit*).

1313 *Riley* W., On the location of meaning in a sacred text: ProcIrB 13 (1990) 7-23 [< NTAbs 35,8].

1314 **Roitman** Betty, Feu noir sur feu blanc; essai sur l'herméneutique juive 1986 → 2,921, 'Rojtman': P 1986, Verdier. – ᴿRÉJ 149 (1990) 152-6 (R. *Goetschel*).

1315 *Scharlemann* Robert P., The measure of meaning in reading texts: Dialog 28 (1989) 247-250 [< OTAbs 13,128, p. 121].

1316 **Schleiermacher** Friedrich, Herméneutique, ᵀ*Simon* Marianna; préf. *Starobinski* Jean, 1987 → 3,1287: ᴿRTLv 21 (1990) 235-7 (E. *Brito*).

1317 **Scott** Edwin E., The nature and use of Scripture in the writings of Clark H. PINNOCK and James BARR: diss. Baptist Theol. Sem., ᴰ*Young* J. T. New Orleans 1989. 210 p. 90-20108. – DissA 51 (1990s) 2427-A.

1318 *Seynaeve* Jaak, NEWMAN's biblical hermeneutics: → 129*c*, LvSt 15 (1990) 282-300.

1319 *Stucki* Pierre-André, La compréhension en herméneutique; un héritage de BULTMANN: LavalTP 46 (1990) 31-42.

1320 ᴱ**Tardieu** Michel, Les règles de l'interprétation 1987 → 3,569 ... 5,1295: ᴿBZ 34 (1990) 289s (Jutta *Hausmann*); ÉTRel 65 (1990) 447s (C.-B. *Amphoux*); JAAR 58 (1990) 314-8 (E. V. *McKnight*).

1321 *Theissen* Gerd, L'herméneutique biblique et la recherche de la vérité religieuse: RTPhil 122 (1990) 485-503; Eng. 578.

1322 **Untergassmair** F. G., *Kappes* M., Zum Thema, Wie wörtlich 1987 ➤ 3,1234 ... 5,1298: ᴿSNTU-A 14 (1989) 219 (A. *Fuchs*).

1323 **Wallace** M. I., The second naiveté; BARTH, RICŒUR, and the New Yale theology [FREI H., HOLMER P., LINDBECK G.]: Studies in American Biblical Hermeneutics 6. Macon GA 1990, Mercer Univ. xv-130 p. $25; pa. $17. 0-86554-357-7 [NTAbs 35,237].

1324 *Watson* D., The spiritual interpretation of the Bible: Friends' Quarterly 25 (Ashford, Kent UK 1989) 248-262 [< NTAbs 34,10].

1325 **Whitman** Jon, Allegory 1987 ➤ 4,1260; 5,1300: ᴿSalesianum 52 (1990) 911 (P. T. *Stella*).

1326 *Williams* Rowan, *a*) The literal sense of Scripture: ModT 7 (1990s) 121-134: – *b*) Der Literalsinn der Heiligen Schrift: EvT 50 (1990) 55-71.

1326* *Willis* John T., Prophetic hermeneutics: RestQ 32 (1990) 193-208 [< ᴢɪᴛ 91,14].

1327 **Wind** H. C., *a*) Historie og forståelse; filosofisk hermeneutik³ [¹1976]. 121 p.; – *b*) Religion og kommunikation; teologisk hermeneutik. Aarhus 1987, Univ. 170 p. – ᴿTsTKi 60 (1989) 111-123 (J.-O. *Henriksen*: against Postmodernism).

1328 **Wolde** Ellen van, Van tekst via tekst naar betekenis: TsTNijm 30 (1990) 333-361; Eng. 361.

1329 **Wyckoff** John W., The relationship of the Holy Spirit to biblical hermeneutics: diss. Baylor. 1990. 275 p. 91-02025. – DissA 51 (1990s) 2786-A.

B2.2 **Structuralismus biblicus** (generalior ➤ J9.4).

1330 **Diaz Castrillón** Clara M., Leer el texto ... manual estructural 1988 ➤ 5,1304; ᴿTeresianum 41 (1990) 690s (A. *Vaz*).

1331 **Greenwood** David, Structuralism and the biblical text: Religion & Reason 32, 1985 ➤ 1,1358 ... 5,1306: ᴿBZ 34 (1990) 121s (N. *Lohfink*).

1332 **Milne** Pamela J., Vladimir PROPP and the study of structure in Hebrew biblical narrative: BLit 13, 1988 ➤ 3,1309 ... 5,1307: ᴿCBQ 52 (1990) 321-3 (B. O. *Long*); CritRR 3 (1990) 166s (P. L. *Day*).

1333 *Milne* P. J., The patriarchal stamp of Scripture; the implications of structuralist analyses for feminist hermeneutics: JFemStRel 5 (1989) 17-34 [< ETL 66, p. 166*].

1334 **Patte** D., The religious dimensions of biblical texts; GREIMAS's structural semiotics and biblical exegesis: SBL Semeia Studies. Atlanta 1990, Scholars. xi-293 p. $32; pa. $21. 1-55540-385-9; -6-7 [BL 91,119, R.P. *Carroll*: distinguishes thymic and veredictory semiotic systems, but rewarding].

1335 **Patte** D., Structural exegesis for New Testament critics: GuidesBS. Mp 1990, Fortress. x-134 p. $8 pa. 0-8006-2396-7 [NTAbs 34,239: 'not simply a revision of 1976 What is structural exegesis³']. – ᴿFoiVie 89,5 (1990) 100s (G. *Vahanian*).

ᴱ*Phillips* Gary A., Poststructural criticism and the Bible: Semeia 51 (1990) ➤ 365.

B2.4 *Analysis* **narrationis** *biblicae* (generalior ➤ J9.6).

Alonso Schökel Luis, Arte narrativa en Josué-Jueces-Samuel-Reyes 1990 ➤ 2861.

1336 **Alter** Robert, L'arte della narrativa biblica [1981 → 62,1456], ᵀ*Gatti* Enzo: Biblioteca Biblica 4. Brescia 1990, Queriniana. 229 p. 88-399-2004-8.

1337 **Bar-Efrat** Shimon, Narrative art in the Bible: JStOT supp 70, 1989 → 5,1312: ᴿCritRR 3 (1990) 106-8 (Gail M. *Eifrig*); JTS 41 (1990) 136 (Meg *Davies*: examples mostly Gn-Sam, but no Joseph-Ruth).

1338 ᴱ**Bühler** P., *Habermacher* F., La narration 1988 → 4,a911; 5,385: ᴿCritRR 3 (1990) 64s (E. J. *Epp*); RSPT 74 (1990) 299 (J.-P. *Jossua*: excellent, mais HABERMAS manque).

1339 *Comstock* G. L., Truth or meaning; RICŒUR versus FREI on biblical narrative: HervTS 45 (1989) 741-760 [< NTAbs 35,4].

1340 **Culbertson** Diana, The poetics of revelation; recognition and the narrative tradition: StAmBHerm 4. Macon GA 1989, Mercer Univ. xii-189 p. $25; pa. $17. 0-86554-319-0; -51-8 [NTAbs 34,107]. 'Poetics' is taken to mean '(power to) make (a change, *šûb/metánoia*) in the reader'.

1341 **Ellingsen** M., The integrity of biblical narrative; story in theology and proclamation. Mp 1990, Fortress. 128 p. 0-8006-2407-6 [NTAbs 35,92].

Eskhult Mats, Studies in verbal aspect and narrative technique in biblical Hebrew prose: AcU StudSemU 12, 1990 → 9158.

1343 **Eslinger** Lyle, Into the hands of the living God: JStOT supp 84, 1989 → 5,1316: ᴿBiblica 71 (1990) 561-4 (Adele *Berlin*: 'narrative ontology', attributing inconcinnities to the varying perspectives of characters, implied author, real author, rather than to editorial accretions).

1344 **Funk** R. W., The poetics of biblical narrative 1988 → 4,1273; 5,1318: ᴿForum 5,3 (1989) 61-68 (H. *Boers*) & 69-78 (J. *Camery-Hoggatt*) & 79-86 (G. A. *Phillips*) [summaries in NTAbs 35,6s]; Interpretation 44 (1990) 102.104 (J. A. *Darr*); TorJT 6 (1990) 111-4 (J. D. *Evers*).

1345 *Greenstein* Edward L., Deconstruction and biblical narrative: Prooftexts 9 (1989) 43-71.

ᴱ**Hauerwas** S., *Jones* L., Why narrative? 1990 → 416*.

1346 *Kelber* Werner H., In the beginning were the words; the apotheosis and narrative displacement of the logos: JAAR 58 (1990) 69-98.

1347 **Kort** Wesley A., Story, text, and scripture 1988 → 4,1276; 5,1322: ᴿJAAR 58 (1990) 125-7 (E. W. *Amend*); RelSt 25 (1989) 405s (J. L. *Houlden*).

1348 ᴱ**McConnell** Frank, The Bible and the narrative tradition 1987 → 2,385 ... 4,1278: ᴿHeythJ 31 (1990) 212s (J. *Barton*).

1349 **Powell** Mark A., What is narrative criticism?: Guides to Biblical Scholarship, NT. Mp 1990, Fortress. xi-125 p. $8 [TS 52,401]. 0-8006-0473-3.

1350 **Savran** George W., Telling and retelling 1988 → 4,1282; 5,1330: ᴿCBQ 52 (1990) 728s (R. C. *Culley*: some but not all changes are significant); CritRR 3 (1990) 177-9 (D. *Jobling*); HebSt 31 (1990) 237-9 (A. *Cooper*); Prooftexts 9 (1989) 264-7 (Alice *Bach*).

1351 *Simon* Uriel, Minor characters in biblical narrative: JStOT 46 (1990) 11-19.

1352 **Ska** Jean Louis, 'Our fathers have told us'; introduction to the analysis of Hebrew narratives: SubsBPont 13. R 1990, Pontificio Istituto Biblico. viii-129 p. Lit. 17.000. 88-7653-593-4 [BL 91,95, W. G. E. *Watson*: useful reference manual; heavily annotated glossary].

1353 *a) Smith* Dennis E., Narrative beginning in ancient literature and theory; – *b) Parsons* Mikeal C., Reading a beginning / beginning a reading; tracing literary theory on narrative openings; – *c) Malbon*

Elizabeth S., *Tannehill* Robert C., reponses: ➤ 375, Semeia 52 (1990) 1-9 / 11-31 [33-41 bibliog.] / 175-184 . 185-192.

1354 **Stegner** W. Richard, Narrative theology in early Jewish Christianity 1989 ➤ 5,1331; 0-8042-0265-6: ᴿSWJT 23 (1990s) 68 (E. E. *Ellis*).

1355 *Stroup* George, Theology of narrative or narrative theology? A response to 'Why narrative?': TTod [32 (1975) 133-173] 47 (1990s) 424-432.

1356 **Vanhoozer** Kevin J., Biblical narrative in the philosophy of Paul RICŒUR; a study in hermeneutics and theology [diss. C, ᴰ*Lash* N.]. C 1990, Univ. xiii-308 p. $49.50. 0-521-34425-5 [NTAbs 35,98]. – ᴿExpTim 102 (1990s) 152 (R. *Morgan*: against chilling echo of BARTH and J. D. SMART 'Two centuries of biblical and historical criticism have in large part silenced the Scriptures, even in the Church').

B2.6   *Critica reactionis lectoris* – **Reader-response criticism.**

1357 **McKnight** Edgar V., The Bible and the reader 1985 ➤ 1,1658 ... 5,1340*: ᴿCritRR 3 (1990) 73-75 (G. A. *Phillips*).

1358 **McKnight** Edgar V., Postmodern use of the Bible... reader-oriented 1988 ➤ 5,1340: ᴿCBQ 52 (1990) 758s (A. K. M. *Adam*); CritRR 3 (1990) 75-78 (R. M. *Fowler*); ÉTRel 65 (1990) 441s (D. *Lys*); JAAR 58 (1990) 719s (Lynn *Poland*); RExp 87 (1990) 338-340 (J. D. W. *Watts*: the most complete so far, though omitting GADAMER and RICŒUR); TS 51 (1990) 174 (Marie-Eloise *Rosenblatt*).

1359 **Moore** S. D., Literary criticism and the Gospels; the theoretical challenge [narrative criticism, reader-response, poststructuralism]. NHv 1989, Yale. xxii-226 p. $25. 0-300-04525-5 [NTAbs 34,249].

1360 *Porter* S. E., Why hasn't reader-response criticism caught on in New Testament studies? LitTOx 4,3 (1990) 278-292 [< NTAbs 35,141].

1361 *Scott* Bernard B., The birth of the reader [Mt opening provides orientation to the work ...]: ➤ 375, Semeia 52 (1990) 83-102.

B3   *Interpretatio ecclesiastica*   .1   **Bible and Church.**

1362 **Abraham** William J., The logic of evangelism. GR 1989, Eerdmans. ix-245 p. $13. 0-8028-0433-9 [TDig 37,247].

1363 **Auza Bernadita** C., The noninfallibile magisterium and theological dissent: diss. Angelicum, ᴰ*Henchey* J. Roma 1990. 608 p. – RTLv 22, p. 617.

1364 **Averill** Lloyd J., Religious right, religious wrong; a critique of the fundamentalist phenomenon. NY 1989, Pilgrim. 196 p. $10. – ᴿJRel 70 (1990) 640-2 (R. S. *Appleby*); TTod 47 (1990s) 107 (D. G. *Hart*).

1365 **Barton** John, People of the book? The authority of the Bible in Christianity 1988 ➤ 4,1294: ᴿJTS 41 (1990) 212-4 (W. D. *Stacey*); RelStR 16 (1990) 145 (W. L. *Humphreys*); ScotJT 43 (1990) 267-9 (Frances M. *Young*).

1365* **Blanco** Michael H., The hermeneutics of 'The Fundamentals' [fundamentalist periodical 1910-15]: diss. Pennsylvania State 1990, ᴰ*Harvey* F. 287 p. 90-32249. – DissA 51 (1990s) 2057-A.

1366 [Signed by C. & L. *Boff* amid 100 others] A missão eclesial do teólogo; subsídios de leitura e elementos para um diálogo em torno à 'Instrução sobre a vocação eclesial do teólogo': REB 50 (1990) 771-807.

1367 **Boone** Kathleen C., The Bible tells them so ^D1989 ➤ 5,1351: ^RInterpretation 44 (1990) 330s (R. *Hutchinson*); JRel 70 (1990) 463-5 (R. S. *Appleby*); RExp 87 (1990) 343s (D. S. *Dockery*).

1368 *Brugues* Jean-Louis, L'exercice du Magistère romain ordinaire [< Oss-Rom franç. 20.III.1990]; EsprVie 100 (1990) 268-270.

1369 **Burke** Cormac, Autoridad y libertad en la Iglesia [1988], ^T: Patmos 192, 1988 ➤ 4,1303; 5,1358: ^RAnnTh 4 (1990) 221-3 (A. *Cirillo*); RET 50 (1990) 351s (M. *Gesteira*: pero autoridad no excluye corrección fraterna).

1370 *Burtchaell* James, Too bad to be true [the new loyalty oath is slippery and vague... speaks with the authority of the scribes, not that of Jesus, ... so 'could not have come from Rome']: Tablet 243 (1989) 388..390.

1371 ^E**Caplan** Lionel, Studies in religious fundamentalism 1988 ➤ 4,537; 5,1359: ^RRelSt 25 (1989) 250-2 (B. P. *Wilson*).

1372 ^FCHADWICK Henry, Christian authority, ^E**Evans** G. R. 1988 ➤ 4,23: ^RJTS 41 (1990) 781-3 (S. *Sykes*).

1373 *a*) *Citrini* Tullio, A proposito dell'indole pastorale del magistero; – *b*) *Angelini* Giuseppe, Indole pastorale e oggetto morale del magistero: TItSett 15 (1990) 130-149; Eng. 149 / 150-171; Eng. 171.

1374 *Colombo* Giuseppe, Per la lettura dei testi del magistero (in margine alla 'Istruzione sulla vocazione ecclesiale del teologo'): TItSett 15 (1990) 293-304.

1375 *a*) *Dinter* Paul E., Rome, America and orthodoxy; *b*) *Toolan* David S, Catholic Theological Society's response to Rome: America 163 (1990) 79-83 / 76-78.

1376 *Dulles* Avery, *a*) The teaching mission of the Church and academic freedom; – *b*) The Church and the universal catechism: America 162 (1990) 397-402 / 201-3.218s (189-200); 206-212, *al.*).

1377 *a*) *Dulles* Avery, The question of dissent [there is much that is timely in the 24.V.1990 Instruction]; – *b*) *Örsy* Ladislas, The limits of magisterium [it oversteps]: Tablet 244 (1990) 1066-8.

1378 *Duquoc* Christian, The Curia sews it up [Instructio 27.VI.1990: 'there is no longer the slightest risk that the possibilities laid open by Vatican II will have any practical expression'; a hymn of praise to centralism]: Tablet 244 (1990) 1097s.

1379 **Echols** James K., Charles Michael JACOBS, the Scriptures, and the Word of God; one man's struggle against biblical fundamentalism among American Lutherans: diss. Yale. NHv 1989. 252 p. 90-15242. – DissA 51 (1990s) 892s-A.

1380 **Ellingsen** Mark, The evangelical movement; growth, impact, controversy, dialog 1988 ➤ 5,1367; $25: ^RAnglTR 71 (1989) 452s (L. P. *Fairfield*); TTod 47 (1990s) 186s (C. M. *Gay*).

1381 **Evans** Rod L., *Berent* Irwin M., Fundamentalism; hazards and heartbreaks ➤ 5,1369. Peru IL ; 0-8126-9081-8: ^RJPsy&T 17 (1989) 81 (W. F. *Hunter*); RExp 87 (1930) 652 (B. *Leonard* puts Berent first).

1382 *Fahlbusch* Erwin, Römischer Fundamentalismus; eine kritische Betrachtung der Konfrontation von Lehramt und Theologie: KkKMat 41 (Bensheim 1990) 87-91 [< ZIT 90,790].

1383 *Farmer* Ron, The 'transmission of tradition' and the 'academic freedom – ecclesiastical control' debate; three models: PerspRelSt 17 (1990) 129-139.

1384 *Fischer* Hermann, Rezeption in ihrer Bedeutung für Leben und Lehre der Kirche; Vorläufige Erwägungen zu einem undeutlichen Begriff [nur seit 10-20 Jahren]: ZTK 87 (1990) 100-123.

1385 *a) Forte* Bruno,   La lettura di fede della Bibbia nel mondo cattolico; – *b*) *Garrone* Daniele,   L'interpretazione di fede della Bibbia da un punto di vista protestante: ➤ 514*b*, Un libro 1989/90, 37-63 / 67-77.

1386 *Fuchs* Josef,   The absolute in morality and the Christian conscience [... in relation to 'what is so absolute and universally valid in morality that ... the Church's magisterium can declare it binding for all peoples and times']: Gregorianum 71 (1990) 697-711; deutsch 711.

1387 *Gamberoni* Johann,   'Exegetae et pastores' [zu NÜBOLD Elmar, Entstehung und Bewertung der neuen Perikopenordnung des Römischen Ritus für die Messfeier, ᴰ1986 Pd ᴰ*Renning* H.]: TGL 80 (1990) 316-326.

1388 *Giovanni Paolo II*, Costituzione Apostolica 'Ex corde Ecclesiae' sulle Università Cattoliche: Seminarium 42,4 (1990) 605-632; 657-729, 7 commentarii (633-655 sommari ital. Eng. franç. portug. deutsch); 603s *Laghi* Card. Pio, present.

1389 *González Montes* Adolfo,   Tradición, Escritura, Magisterio y desarrollo doctrinal de la fe (Congreso Luterano-Católico, Estrasburgo 1988): Diál-Ecum 25 (1989) 75-105.

1389* *a) González-Montes* Adolfo,   Apostolicité de la foi et de la doctrine; tradition, écriture, Magistère et développement doctrinal de la foi; – *b*) *Gesteira-Garza* Manuel,   Autorité et obéissance dans l'Église; – *c) Pie i Ninot* Salvador,   L'apostolicité de l'église et le ministère de l'évêque: PosLuth 38 (1990) 322-339 / 363-390 / 340-362.

1390 *Greinacher* Norbert,   Demokratisierung der Kirche: TüTQ 170 (1990) 253-266.

1391 *Grossi* Vittorino,   La coscienza storica tra Bibbia e Tradizione (L'Istruzione sullo studio dei Padri della Chiesa nella formazione sacerdotale) [10.XI.1989]: Lateranum 56 (1990) 653-678.

1392 *Haag* Herbert,   Streit um die Bibel unter fünf Päpsten [... 'die Atmosphäre der Angst, des Misstrauens, der Willkur und der Unfreiheit, in die PIUS X die katholische Bibelwissenschaft gestürzt hatte ... eine Periode tiefster Erniedrigung wie wohl nie in der Geschichte der Kirche' ... LAGRANGE als Bahnbrecher]: TüTQ 170 (1990) 241-253.

1393 **Hartog** JohnᴵᴵI,   Enduring to the end; Jehovah's Witnesses and Bible doctrine. Schaumberg IL 1987, Regular Baptist. 168 p. $6 pa. – ᴿGrace-TJ 10 (1989) 256s (W. E. *Glenny*: serves as good summary of the orthodoxy from which they differ).

1394 *a) Hasitschka* Martin,   Fundamentalistische und kirchliche Bibelauslegung; – *b) Palaver* Wolfgang,   Amerikanischer Fundamentalismus; zur Problematik der Vermischung von Religion und Politik: ➤ 1416, Eindeutige Antworten?², 1988, 125-132 / 41-62.

1394* *Hünermann* Peter,   Das Lehramt und die endliche Gestalt der Glaubenswahrheit; Überlegungen zur römischen Instruktion über die kirchliche Berufung von Theologen: HerdKor 44 (1990) 373-7.

1395 *Jean-Paul II,* Constitution Apostolique 'Les universités catholiques' [15 août 1990]: EsprVie 100 (1990) 548-560.

1396 **Jodock** Darrell,   The Church's Bible; its contemporary authority 1989 ➤ 5,1380*; 0-8006-2326-0: ᴿThomist 54 (1990) 730-5 (M. I. *Raposa*); TS 51 (1990) 781 (W. S. *Kurz*).

1397 ᴱ**Johnston** Robert K.,   The use of the Bible in theology; evangelical options 1985 ➤ 2,960...5,1381: ᴿCriswT 2 (1988) 448-450 (C.L. *Bomberg*).

1398 [ᴱ*Kasper* Walter], Commission Théologique Internationale,   L'interprétation des dogmes [oct. 1989]: EsprVie 100 (1990) 211-219. 225-231 [225-7, dogme et Écriture Sainte].

1399 **Kaufman** Philip S., Why you can disagree... and remain a faithful Catholic 1989 ➤ 5,1384: ᴿHorizons 17 (1989) 155s (J. P. *Hanigan*); RelStR 16 (1990) 245s (J. T. *Ford*: encourages further disagreeing).

1400 *Kent* John, The decade of evangelism 4.... and conservative Christianity: ExpTim 102 (1990s) 227-230.

1401 *Knox* R. Buick, The Bible in Irish Presbyterianism II: IrBSt 12 (1990) 26-40.

1402 *Koffeman* L. J., Het spreken der Kerk; mogelijkheden en grenzen in een geseculariseerde samenleving: KerkT 41 (1990) 117-130.

1403 *La Potterie* Ignace de, Il Cristo-Verità secondo la Scrittura e la Tradizione: commenti all'Istruzione sulla vocazione ecclesiale del teologo 2: OssRom (19.IX.1990) 1 . 6.

1404 **Lawrence** Bruce B., Defenders of God; the fundamentalist revolt against the modern age. SF 1989, Harper & R. 306 p. $25. – ᴿTTod 47 (1990s) 183s (D. G. *Dawe*).

1405 **Lee** Philip J., Against the Protestant Gnostics 1987 ➤ 3,1342; 4,1336: ᴿAnglTR 72 (1990) 334-9 (J. *Woolverton*); CalvinT 25 (1990) 82-84 (A. J. *Griffioen*); Dialog 27 (1988) 152s (Sharon Z. *Ross*).

Leprieur François, Quand Rome condamne 1989 ➤ m122.

1406 *Mahoney* Jack, Forgotten truths of Vatican II... must we keep silent?: Tablet 243 (1989) 8s. Masthead p. 2 top wrongly gives volume number as 242.

1407 **Marsden** George M., Overcoming fundamentalism... Fuller 1987 ➤ 3, 1348... 5,1389: ᴿCathHR 75 (1989) 333s (R. D. *Shields*); JAAR 58 (1990) 131-3 (J. H. *Gill*: Fuller as history of how 'evangelicals' came to differ from 'fundamentalists').

1408 *Martínez Sierra* Alejandro, Magisterio y teología: MiscCom 48 (1990) 3-19.

1409 **Mattai** Giuseppe, Magistero e teologia; alle radici di un dissenso 1989 ➤ 5,1390: ᴿCollatVL 20 (1990) 340 (E. Vanden *Berghe*); EstAg 25 (1990) 458s (J. V. *González Olea*); ETL 66 (1990) 438s (A. de *Halleux*).

1410 *a) Mattai* Giuseppe, Magistero e teologia; alle radici di un dissenso; – *b) Cipriani* Settimio,... un difficile ma ineludibile rapporto: Asprenas 37 (1990) 27-40 [117s, ᴿ*Pifano* P. del libro omonimo] / 41-58.

1411 *Mieth* Dietmar, Der überflüssige Treueid oder: Das Credo genügt: TuTQ 170 (1990) 140-2.

1412 *Moingt* Joseph, Religions, traditions et fondamentalismes: Études 373 (1990) 215-226.

1413 *Moser* Theresa, *al.*, Preliminary report of the [US] C(atholic) T(heological) S(ociety) committee on [the newly-promulgated] profession of faith / oath of fidelity: Horizons 17 (1990) 103-127.

1414 *a) Murray* Robert, The teaching Church and the thinking Church; – *b) Mahoney* Jack, 'The ecclesial vocation of the theologian'; some theological reflections: Month 251 (1990) 310-319 / 303-309.

1415 **Naud** André, Le magistère incertain 1987 ➤ 5,1397: ᴿTS 51 (1990) 181s (L. *Örsy*: highly praised in Europe).

1416 ᴱ**Niewiadomski** Józef, Eindeutige Antworten? Fundamentalistische Versuchung in Religion und Gesellschaft² [¹1988 ➤ 4,397], aktualisierte Auflage: Theologische Trends 1. Thaur 1988, Österr. Kulturverlag. 211 p. 3-85395-134-1. 8 art.; 5 infra. – ᴿDiakonia 21 (1990) 141s (Regina *Brandl*).

1417 *Noll* M.A., Bible scholarship and the evangelicals: Religion and Intellectual Life 6,3s (New Rochelle 1989) 110-124 [96-109, *Osiek* C. feminist, reprint; < NTAbs 34,6].

1418 *O'Brien* David J., The Church and Catholic higher education: Horizons 17 (1990) 7-29.

1419 **Örsy** Ladislas, The Church, learning and teaching; magisterium, assent, dissent, academic freedom 1987 ➤ 4,1346; 5,1400: ᴿNRT 112 (1990) 114s (L. *Volpe*); RExp 87 [not 88 as top] (1990) 531 (E.G. *Hinson*); Vidyajyoti 53 (1984) 101 (G.V. *Lobo*).

1420 *Örsy* Ladislas, Magisterium and theologians [Cong. Faith 24.V.1990]: America 163 (1990) 30-32.

1421 *Örsy* Ladislas, An oath too far [imposed 6.I.1990]: Tablet 244 (1990) 442-4 [726, 'Priests and people'].

1422 **O'Meara** Thomas F., Fundamentalism; a Catholic perspective. NY 1990, Paulist. 103 p. $6 [TR 87,258].

1423 **Osmer** Richard R., A teachable spirit; recovering the teaching office in the Church. Louisville 1990, W-Knox. xi-298 p. $15 [TS 52, 566, Agnes *Cunningham*: a new paradigm for Protestantism].

1424 *Palácio* Carlos, Teologia, magistério e 'recepção' do Vaticano II: Persp-Teol 22 (1990) 151-169.

1425 *Pastore* Corrado, *Mesters* Carlos, La Biblia y la nueva evangelización: Palabra de Vida 23, Dossier Secorve [Dei Verbum 25 años; Evangelización de América, 500 años] (Caracas 1990, Secretariado de Religiosos) 3-6 (73-79 sobre Apoc 21,1-5; Is 43,16-21; 65,17-26; Lc 4,16-30) / 19-44 [7-18 . 45-63, documentos; 63-72 Valle Edenio].

1426 *Peter* Carl J., Theses on Christian memory, hope and assent; the current theological debate about dissent: CommND 16 (1989) 233-243.

1426* *Pissarek-Hudelist* Herlinde, Ein Katechismus für die Weltkirche? Bemerkungen und Rückfragen zu einem römischen Entwurf: HerdKor 44 (1990) 237-242 [dazu *Ratzinger* J. 341-3].

1427 *Primetshofer* Bruno, Die Bestellung Akademischer an katholisch-theologischen Fakultäten Österreichs: ➤ 54, ᶠGAMPL I., ÖsAK 39,1s (1990) 153-161.

   Ratzinger Joseph (*Neuhaus* R.) Biblical interpretation in crisis / Schriftauslegung im Widerstreit 1989 ➤ m203.

1428 [*Ratzinger* Joseph], Congrégation pour la Doctrine de la Foi: Instruction sur la vocation ecclésiale du théologien 24.V.1990: EsprVie 100 (1990) 401-410; *jaune* 202s, résumé du secrétariat de l'épiscopat français.

1429 **Reese** T.J., The universal catechism [project circulated 1989] reader; reflections and responses. SF 1990, Harper & R. vii-237 p. $20 [NRT 113, 457, L. *Volpe*].

1430 *a*) *Rikhof* Herwi, Vatican II and the collegiality of bishops; a reading of Lumen Gentium 22 and 23; – *b*) *Grootaers* Jan, The collegiality of the synod of bishops; an unresolved problem; – *c*) *Valentini* Donato, An overview of theologians' positions: ➤ 402, Concilium (Ph/L 1990, 4) 3-17 / 18-30 / 31-42 [-139 *al.*].

1431 *Rivinius* Karl J., Fundamentalismus; eine Herausforderung für Kirche und Mission [LEFEBVRE; Opus Dei]: TGL 80 (1990) 495-511.

1432 *Roach* Richard R., The magisterium and the academy; honest teaching of Catholic theology requires open acknowledgment of the Magisterium: HomP 90,8 (1990) 51-59.

1432* *Robinson* Bernard, Whither Catholic biblical studies?: PrPeo 4 (1990) 278-81 [251-277 reprints of *Lattey* C. 1945, *al.*].

1433 **Robinson** Robert B., Roman Catholic exegesis since Divino Afflante ...: SBL diss. 111, 1988 ➤ 4,1349; 5,1409: ᴿCritRR 3 (1990) 84-87 (S. E. *McEvenue*: fascinating; 'goes from LAGRANGE to LOHFINK. But what precisely is it about? What did its author intend?'); JAAR 58 (1990) 723s (J. V. *Apczynski*).

1434 ᴱ**Seckler** Max, Die schiefen Wände des Lehrhauses; Katholizität als Herausforderung 1988 ➤ 5,353: ᴿTPhil 65 (1990) 297s (K. *Schatz*).

1435 *Shelley* John C., The gift of ambiguity ['fundamentalism is essentially the denial or escape from ambiguity']: PerspRelSt 17 (1990) 5-11.

1436 **Silva** Moisés, Has the Church misread the Bible? The history of interpretation in the light of current issues 1987 ➤ 3,1365 ... 5,1413: ᴿBL (1990) 115 (J. *Barton*: learned and intelligent).

1437 *Simons* Eberhard, Toleranz und Wahrheit; die Provokation des Fundamentalismus: UnSa 45 (1990) 4-13.

1438 *Simpfendörfer* Gerhard, Fromm in der säkularen Kultur; Bibel und Schöpfung im Fundamentalismus: EvKomm 22,11 (1989) 40-44.

1439 *Singer* Johannes, Fundamentalismus und katholische Weite: TPQ 138 (1990) 203-213.

1439* a) *Sordet* Jean-Michel, L'emploi [fondamentaliste] de l'Écriture; – b) *Widmer* Gabriel-P., Intégrisme et fondamentalisme [réplique *Lengronne* Fabrice]; – c) *Blocher* Henri, Le fondamentalisme, non évangélique: Hokhma 41 (1989) 53-71 / 42 (1989) 36-51 [57-64] / 52-56.

1440 **Teeple** H. M., I started to be a minister; from fundamentalism to a religion of ethics [... how biblical scholars work]. Evanston 1990, Religion & E. xii-265 p. $20. 0-914384-03-1 [NTAbs 34,380].

1441 **Thils** Gustave, La profession de foi et le serment de fidélité: RTLv Cah 23. P 1989, Procure. 60 p. Fb 200. – ᴿEsprVie 100 (1990) 76 (H. *Wattiaux*).

1442 **Thils** Gustave [p. 11-74], *Schneider* Theodor [p. 75-123], Glaubensbekenntnis und Treueid; Klarstellungen zu den 'neuen' römischen Formeln für kirchliche Amtsträger. Mainz 1990, Grünewald. 143 p. DM 19,80 [TR 87,82].

1443 **Torrey** R. A., The fundamentals; the famous sourcebook of foundational biblical truths [the twelve volumes c. 1900 which made 'fundamentalism' a household word; reduced to one volume of 64 articles]. GR 1990, Kregel. 714 p. $17 pa. – ᴿCalvinT 25 (1990) 324s (J. *Bolt*: today of mostly antiquarian value).

1444 *Valadier* Paul, Turning the clock back (the universal catechism draft buries the spirit of Vatican II documents; sees faith as a body of knowledge to be acquired rather than a way of life to be experienced; and emphasizes the supernatural at the expense of the human]: Tablet 244 (1990) 784s.

1445 *Vallin* Pierre, Théologies de la tradition [... séduction du fondamentalisme]: Études 372 (1990) 231-241.

1446 **Visser 't Hooft** Willem A. †, Lehrer und Lehramt der Kirche 1986 ➤ 3,8028: ᴿZkT 112 (1990) 368-370 (L. *Lies*).

1447 *Vogel* Traugott, Evangelium – Schrift – Kirche; eine Problemanzeige zum reformatorischen Schriftprinzip: TLZ 115 (1990) 653-666.

1448 *Weakland* Rembert, Church in the market-place [Bible and natural law guided U.S. bishops' social documents]: Tablet 244 (150th anniversary issue, May 19, 1990) 606-8.

1449 *Wenz* Günther, Kerygma und Dogma; Erwägungen zum Verhältnis von

Schrift, Bekenntnis und Lehramt in der Perspektive lutherischer Theologie: KerDo 36 (1990) 2-36; Eng. 36.

B3.2 *Homiletica* – **The Bible in preaching.**

1449* *Achtemeier* Elizabeth, Preaching from the OT. Louisville 1989, W-Knox. 200 p. $14. 0-664-24080-1. – ᴿMid-Stream 29 (1990) 338s (D. E. *Stevenson*).

1450 **Bailey** R., Jesus the preacher. Nv 1990, Broadman. 128 p. $11. 0-8054-6007-1 [NTAbs 35,99].

1451 *Bataillon* Louis-Jacques, Les images dans les sermons du XIIIᵉ siècle: FreibZ 37 (1990) 327-395.

Beaudean J., Paul's theology of preaching ᴰ1988 → 5,5813.

1452 **Best** Ernest, From text to sermon² 1988 → 4,1362; 5,1421: ᴿScotBEv 8 (1990) 129s (M. A. W. *Allen*).

1453 *Brovelli* Franco, L'omelia; elementi di riflessione dal dibattito recente: ScuolC 117 (1989) 287-329.

1454 **Brueggemann** Walter, Finally comes the poet; daring speech for proclamation [Beecher Lectures]. Mp 1989, Fortress. 142 p. $9. 0-8006-2394-0. – ᴿRExp 87 (1990) 516s (R. *Bailey*); TTod 47 (1990s) 226 (D. E. *Gowan*).

1455 *Brueggemann* Walter, The preacher, the text, and the people: TTod 47 (1990s) 237-247.

1456 **Burghardt** Walter J., Lovely in eyes not his; homilies for an imaging of Christ. NY 1988, Paulist. 218 p. $7 pa. – ᴿLvSt 15 (1990) 416s (P. J. *Judge*: his 5th); TorJT 6 (1990) 377s (T. *Harding*).

1457 **Burr** Amanda, New life for the old, old story; a guide for developing story sermons. 1989, Thornsbury-BB. 150 p. $25. 0-945253-06-0 [Interpretation 44,332].

1458 *Cipriani* Settimio, Il carisma di pensare Dio e l'uomo a voce alta: Presbyteri 24 (1990) 581-593.

1458* *Dennison* James T.ᴶ, Building the biblical-theological sermon, I. Perspective; II. Text and context: Kerux, a journal of biblical-theological preaching 4,3 (1989) 30-43; 5,1 (1990) 32-46.

1459 *Edwards* O. C.ᴶ, Preaching in the late Middle Ages [three 1989 books]: AnglTR 72 (1990) 447-454.

1460 **Engemann** Wilfried, Kritik der Homiletik aus semiotischer Sicht; ein Beitrag zur Grundlegung der Predigtlehre: Hab.-Diss. ᴰ*Kehnscherper*. Greifswald 1989s. – TR 86 (1990) 509.

1461 *Engemann* Wilfried, Wider den redundanten Exzess; semiotisches Plädoyer für eine ergänzungsbedürftige Predigt: TLZ 115 (1990) 786-800.

1462 ᴱ**Farmer** David A., *Hunter* Edwina, And blessed is she; sermons by women [US, 22]. SF 1990, Harper & R. viii-247 p. $19. 0-06-062335-7 [TDig 37,342].

1463 **Forde** Gerhard O., Theology is for proclamation. Mp 1990, Augsburg Fortress. viii-199 p. $11. – ᴿCurrTMiss 17 (1990) 463s.466 (J. C. *Rochelle*).

1464 *Francis* Mark R., Liturgical preaching and pastoral care: NewTR 3,2 (1990) 65-77.

1465 *Goldingay* J., Preaching on the stories in Scripture: Anvil 7,2 (1990) 105-114 [< NTAbs 35,7].

1466 **Gradwohl** R., Bibelauslegungen aus jüdischen Quellen, 4. Die [19] alttestamentlichen Predigttexte des 6. Jahrgangs. Stu 1989, Calwer. 336 p. DM 34. 3-7668-3016-3 [< NTAbs 34,268].

1467 **Green** Michael F., Illustrations for biblical preaching[2] [[1]1985] 1989 ➤ 5,1431; $20: [R]CriswT 4 (1989s) 213s (C. *Ward*).

1468 **Greidanus** Sidney, The modern preacher and the ancient text 1988 ➤ 5,1432: [R]CalvinT 25 (1990) 98-102 (H. D. *Schurings*: a jewel on homiletics and hermeneutics); ExpTim 101 (1989s) 220 (J. M. *James*).

1469 *Hennig* Gerhard, Die Bibel, das Evangelium und die Predigt; Erinnerungen an eine reformatorische Entdeckung für Prediger und Predigerinnen: TBei 21,1 (Wu 1990) 24-31 [< ZIT 90,174].

1469* **Jabusch** Willard F., The spoken Christ; reading and preaching the transforming word. NY 1990, Crossroad. xii-131 p. $14. 0-8245-1015-1 [TDig 38.272].

1470 *a) Jörns* K.-P., Exegese und Homiletik: – *b) Thadden* R. von, Das Feuer der Reformation — ausgebrannt? Gedanken über die Zukunft des Protestantismus: Pastoraltheologie 79,1 (Gö 1990) 10-25 / 2-9 [< ZIT 90,201].

1471 *Josuttis* Manfred, Predigt – Rede – Mythos; Einsichten und Aufgaben heutiger Homiletik: VerkF 35,2 (1990) 59-84.

1472 *a) Kidner* Derek, Preaching from the Old Testament; – *b) Selman* Martin, Preaching OT law: Evangel 8,4 (1990) 10-14 / 15-20.

1473 **Kwon Sook,** The influence of a high view of preaching on the homiletical principles and practice of D. M. *Lloyd-Jones*: diss. [D]*Kromminga* C.: Calvin Theol. Sem. ii-103 p. + bibliog. – CalvinT 25 (GR 1990) 333s.

1474 *Lahidalga Aguirre* J. M. [de p. 52], Fray Luis de GRANADA; la predicación como arte y carisma: LumenVr 39 (1990) 147-168.

1475 **Leggett** Donald A., Loving God and disturbing men; preaching from the prophets. GR 1990, Baker. vii-208 p. $13. 0-8010-5660-8 [BL 91,115, R. A. *Mason*).

1476 *Leimgruber* Stephan, Karl BARTHs Predigtverständnis im Vergleich zur neueren Homiletik: FreibZ 37 (1990) 174-193.

1477 **Long** T. G., Preaching and the literary forms of the Bible 1988 ➤ 5,1435: [R]BL (1990) 107 (R. *Davidson*); CurrTMiss 17 (1990) 148s (D. W. *Kuck*); QRMin 10 (1990) 105-7 (D. M. *Greenhaw*).

1478 **Long** Thomas G., The witness of preaching. Louisville 1989, Westminster/Knox. 216 p. $14 pa. – [R]CalvinT 25 (1990) 290-2 (W. M. *VanDyk*).

1479 *Long* Thomas G., The use of Scripture in contemporary preaching: Interpretation 44 (1990) 341-352.

1480 *Longère* Jean, La prédication médiévale: MaisD 177 ('Mystagogies' 1989) 49-66.

1481 **Lowry** Eugene L., How to preach a parable; designs for narrative sermons. Nv 1989, Abingdon. 173 p. $13. 0-687-17924-6. – [R]RExp 87 (1990) 512s (C. *Bugg*).

1482 *MacArthur* John F.[J], The mandate of biblical inerrancy; expository preaching: MastJ 1,1 (1990) 3-15.

1483 **Martin** Hervé, Le métier de prédicateur à la fin du Moyen Âge (1350-1520) [diss. Paris IV, 1986]. P 1988, Cerf. 720 p. F 292. – [R]RBgPg 68 (1990) 479-483 (H. *Platelle*); RHPR 70 (1990) 366-8 (J.-M. *Mehl*).

1484 **Miller** Calvin, Spirit, word, and story; a philosophy of preaching. Dallas 1989, Word. 246 p. $16. 0-8499-0691-1. – [R]RExp 87 [not 88 as top] (1990) 517s (R. *Bailey*).

1485 *Oberholzer* J. P., Ou-Testamentiese perspektiewe op die definisie van die prediking: HervTS 46 (1990) 647-655 [< OTAbs 14, p. 207].

1486 *Oftestad* Bernt T., Lehre, die das Herz bewegt; das Predigtparadigma bei Martin CHEMNITZ: ArRefG 80 (1989) 125-153; Eng. 153.

1487 *Osten-Sacken* Peter von der, Jesu Weinen über sein Volk; Predigt über Lukas 19,41-44: ➤ 147, ᶠRENDTORFF R., Hebr. Bibel 1990, 555-9 [567-573, *Steiger* Lothar, über Joh 19,38-42 (Der Tobiasdienst); 561-5, *Rau* Gerhard, über Gen 1; 575-9, *Sundermeier* Theo, über Gen 12,1-9].

1488 *a) Reymond* Bernard, La prédication et le culte protestants entre les anciens et les nouveaux médias [p. 537 'la viva vox Evangelii devenait pour les Réformateurs... non solum scripta sed etiam imprimata' (sic)]; – *b) Cochand* Nicolas, L'évangélisation est-elle encore possible? (à propos du télévangéliste américain Bob SCHULLER): ÉTRel 65 (1990) 535-560 / 561-8.

1489 ᴱ**Saperstein** Marc, Jewish preaching 1200-1800; an anthology: YaleJud 26. NHv 1989, Yale Univ. 470 p. $45. – ᴿCalvinT 25 (1990) 307-310 (V. *Vander Zee*: can trigger Christian preachers' creativity).

1490 **Shuger** Deborah K., Sacred rhetoric; the Christian grand style in the Renaissance [Tridentine... Protestant]. Princeton 1988, Univ. 289 p. $32.50. – ᴿJAAR 58 (1990) 144-6 (Retha M. *Warnicke*).

1491 **Smith** Christine M., Weaving the sermon; preaching in a feminist perspective. Louisville 1989, W/Knox. 164 p. $16 pa. – ᴿInterpretation 44 (1990) 328-330 (J. *Benedict*).

1492 **Smith** Frances L., Gender and the framing of exegetical authority in sermon performances: diss. Georgetown. Wsh 1990. 261 p. – 91-08658. – DissA 51 (1990s) 3728-A.

1493 *Staniek* Edward, ❷ The secrets of good preaching according to St. AUGUSTINE: RuBi 42 (1989) 302-8.

1494 *Stordalen* Terje, Det eksegetiske objekt [Eng. p. 272 'Text as exegetical object'] og teologiens enhet: TsTKi 61 (1990) [131-144, *Hegstad* H., *al.*] 255-272.

1495 **Theissen** G., Die offene Tür; biblische Variationen zu [25] Predigttexten. Mü 1990, Kaiser. 188 p. DM 29,80. 3-459-01858-5 [NTAbs 35,260].

1496 **Vogels** Walter, Reading and preaching the Bible; a new semiotic approach 1985 ➤ 3,1294... 4,1397: ᴿVidyajyoti 53 (1989) 517s (R. J. *Raja*).

1497 **Williamson** C. M., *Allen* R. J., Interpreting... anti-Judaism 1989 ➤ 4, 1499; 5,1446*: ᴿTTod 47 (1990s) 225s (R. L. *Brawley*).

1498 **Wilson-Kastner** Patricia, Imagery for preaching. Mp 1989, Fortress. 108 p. 0-8006-1150-0. – ᴿRExp 87 (1990) 518s (R. *Bailey*).

1499 **Wolff** Hans W., Old Testament and Christian preaching 1986 [a collection of sermons] ➤ 2,1007; 3,1404: ᴿDialog 28 (1989) 72s (M. A. *Throntveit*).

1500 **Zerfass** Rolf, (*Roos* Klaus), Spruchpredigt: Grundkurs Predigt 1. Dü 1987, Patmos. 192 p. DM 29,80; sb. 26. 3-491-72166-9. – ᴿBijdragen 51 (1990) 97s (J. *Besemer*).

ʙ3.3 Inerrantia, inspiratio [Revelatio ➤ H1.7].

1501 **Archer** Gleason L., Encyclopedia of Bible difficulties [defending inerrancy... alleged discrepancies] 1982 ➤ 63,777; 64,769: ᴿMastJ 1,1 (1990) 75-78 (J. E. *Rosscup*).

1502 **Artola** Antonio M., *Sánchez Caro* José M., Biblia y Palabra de Dios: Introducción al estudio de la Biblia [I. ➤ 370* supra] 2, 1989 ➤ 5,1447: ᴿActuBbg 27 (1990) 191 (X. *Alegre* S.); Angelicum 67 (1990) 579s (J.

Salguero); EfMex 8 (1990) 395-7 (C. *Junco Garza*); EstAg 25 (1990) 451 (C. *Mielgo*); Salmanticensis 37 (1990) 359-361 (G. *Pérez*).

1503 *Bourgeois* H., *Gibert* P. [inner testimony], *Jourjon* M. [Fathers], La cause des Écritures; l'autorité des Écritures en christianisme. Lyon 1989, PROFAC. 128 p. F 55 pa. 2-84317-038-1 [NTAbs 34,234]. – ᴿMasses Ouvrières 432 (1990) 83s (A. *Fournier-Bidoz*); RTLv 21 (1990) 94s (C. *Focant*).

Burkhardt Helmut, Die Inspiration heiliger Schriften bei PHILO von Alexandrien ᴰ1988 → 9987.

1505 *Cole* Alan, Ⓜ What shall we do with the Bible? The authority and relevance of the Bible in the modern world [< Australia Béguin lecture 1989], ᵀ*Mayer* Judit: TSzem 33 (1990) 141-7.

1506 **Conn** Harvie M., Inerrancy and hermeneutic; a tradition, a challenge, a debate. GR 1988, Baker. 276 p. 0-8010-2533-8. – ᴿExpTim 101 (1989s) 249 (A. C. *Thiselton*).

1506* *Dawson* David, Against the divine ventriloquist; COLERIDGE and DE MAN on symbol, allegory and Scripture: LitTOx 4 (1990) 293-310 [< ZIT 91,11].

1507 *a) Dietrich* Bernard C., Oracles and divine inspiration; – *b) Couloubaritsis* Lambros, L'art divinatoire et la question de la vérité; – *c) Vernière* Yvonne, La théorie de l'inspiration prophétique dans les Dialogues pythiques de PLUTARQUE: → 757, Oracles = Kernos 3 (1990) 157-174 / 115-122 / 359-366.

1508 **Fackre** Gabriel, Authority; Scripture in the Church for the world: The Christian story, a pastoral systematics 2. GR 1987, Eerdmans. xii 366 p. $15. – ᴿScotJT 43 (1990) 117-9 (A. P. F. *Sell*).

1509 **Gabel** Helmut, Inspirationsverständnis im Wandel; die Neuorientierung der katholischen Inspirationslehre im Umfeld des Zweiten Vatikanischen Konzils: kath. Diss. Mainz 1990, ᴰ*Schneider* T. 540 p. – RTLv 22, p. 617.

1510 *Geisler* Norman L., Is inerrancy incompatible with the free will defence?: EvQ [55 (1983) 177] 62 (1990) 175-8.

1511 **Goldingay** John, Theological diversity and the authority of the OT [< 1983 Nottingham diss.] 1987 → 3,1415... 5,1454: ᴿCBQ 52 (1990) 318-320 (D. C. *Benjamin*: a work of the kind of biblical theology which continental scholars eschew); RTLv 21 (1990) 491s (J. *Vermeylen*); Themelios 15 (1989s) 66-68 (D. G. *Deboys*).

1512 *Gunn* David M., Reading right; reliable and omniscient narrator, omniscient God, and foolproof composition in the Hebrew Bible: → 166, ꟳSheffield 1990, 53-64.

1513 *Hanson* Paul D., Biblical authority reconsidered: HorBT 11,2 (1989) 57-79.

1514 *a) Jakubiec* Czesław, Ⓓ De inspiratione Sacrae Scripturae secundum constitutionem Dei Verbum; reflexiones et animadversiones; – *b) Jelonek* Tomasz, Veritas S. Scripturae secundum Dei Verbum: → 64, ꟳGRZYBEK S. 1990, 115-125 / 140-9.

1515 *Jelen* Ted G., *al.*, Biblical literalism and inerrancy; a methodological investigation: Sociological Analysis... of Religion 51 (Wsh 1990) 307-314 [< ZIT 90,869].

1516 *Jenson* R. W., Can a text defend itself? an essay de inspiratione scripturae: Dialog 28,4 (St. Paul 1989) 251-256 [< NTAbs 34,147].

1517 **Jodock** Darrell, The Church's Bible, its contemporary authority. Mp 1989, Fortress. xi-173 p. $13. 0-8006-2326-6 [TDig 37,368]; ᴿRExp 87 [not 88 as top] (1990) 495s (B. J. *Leonard*).

1518 ᴱ**Kantzer** Kenneth S.,   Applying the Scriptures [ICBI (inerrancy) summit
   3] 1978/87 ➤ 3,548:   ᴿSTEv 1 (1989) 85s (P. *Bolognesi*).

1519 *a) Minear* Paul S.,   Inclusive language and biblical authority; – *b) Price*
   C. P.,   Revelation as our knowledge of God: ➤ 123*, ᶠMEYER P.,   Faith
   1990, 335-351 / 313-334.

1520 **Pinnock** Clark H.,   The Scripture principle 1985 ➤ 1,1461 … 5, also
   1461:   ᴿChrSchR 19,1 (GR 1989) 66-72 (D. *Brown*; 73-78, Pinnock
   response) [< NTAbs 34,148].

1521 — **Roenfeldt** Raymond C. W.,   Clark H. PINNOCK's shift in his doctrine
   of biblical authority and reliability; an analysis and critique: diss.
   Andrews, ᴰ*Dederen* R.   Berrien Springs MI 1990. – RTLv 22, p. 604.

1522 ᴱ**Radmacher** Earl, *Preus* Robert,   Hermeneutics, inerrancy, and the
   Bible [International Council on Biblical Inerrancy, Summit II, Chicago
   Nov. 10-13, 1982] 1984 ➤ 65,431; $21:   ᴿMastJ 1/1 (1990) 93-96 (J. E.
   Rosscup).

1523 *Reck* Reinhold,   2 Tim 3,16 in der altkirchlichen Literatur; eine wir-
   kungsgeschichtliche Untersuchung zum Locus classicus der Inspirationslehre: WissWeis 53 (1990) 81-105.

1524 *Ring* R. E.,   Does the Bible contain doctrines about itself? [neither the
   word Bible nor its concept is in it]:   Dialog 28 (St. Paul 1990) 119-122
   [< NTAbs 34,289].

1525 *Russell* J. M.,   PITTENGER on biblical authority; a processive approach:
   Encounter 51,4 (1990) 359-376 [< NTAbs 35,142].

1526 *a) Schüssler Fiorenza* Elisabeth,   The crisis of scriptural authority; interpretation and reception; – *b) Jodock* Darrell,   The reciprocity between
   Scripture and theology; the role of Scripture in contemporary theological
   reflection: Interpretation 44 (1990) 353-368 / 369-382.

1527 **Trembath** Kern R.,   Evangelical theories of biblical inspiration 1987
   ➤ 3,1430 … 5,1467:   ᴿJTS 41 (1990) 322-4 (J. *Barr*: lack of contact with
   biblical exegesis — and the Bible has even less about inspiration than
   MACQUARRIE's Theology).

1528 *Vogt* Hermann J.,   Die Lehre des ORIGENES von der Inspiration der
   Heiligen Schrift; ein Vergleich zwischen der Grundlagenschrift und der
   Antwort auf Kelsos: TüTQ 170 (1990) 97-103.

1529 *Wiefel* Wolfgang,   Die Autorität der Schrift und die Autorität des
   Evangeliums: TLZ 115 (1990) 641-654.

           B3.4   **Traditio.**

1530 *Beeck* Franz Jozef van,   Tradition and interpretation: Bijdragen 51
   (1990) 257-271.

1531 **Bunnenberg** Johannes,   Lebendige Treue zum Ursprung; das Traditions-
   verständnis Yves CONGARs: Walberberger St. Theol. 14, ᴰ1989 ➤ 5,1474:
   ᴿActuBbg 27 (1990) 65s (J. *Boada*); NatGrac 37 (1990) 123 (A. *Villalmonte*); NRT 112 (1990) 749s (J. *Famerée*); TLZ 115 (1990) 697-9 (R.
   Slenczka); TS 51 (1990) 545-7 (W. *Henn*); TsTNijm 30 (1990) 211s (P. van
   Leeuwen). ZkT 112 (1990) 321-4 (K. H. *Neufeld*).

1532 *a) Chauvet* Louis-Marie,   La notion de tradition; – *b) Selles* Jean-Marie,
   La notion de tradition dans le judaïsme rabbinique; une textualité de
   l'oralité: MaisD 178 ('La Tradition' 1989) 7-46 / 47-79.

1533 *Gaboriau* Florent,   Sur le concept de tradition: RThom 90 (1990)
   373-408.

1534 *a) Grech* Prosper, Le tradizioni neotestamentarie e la 'traditio catholica'; – *b) Mazzanti* A. M., La tradizione 'segreta' in CLEMENTE di Alessandria: ➤ 700, Tradizione 1989/90, 31-37 / 205-211.

1535 ᶠHANSON Richard P. C., Scripture, tradition and reason, ᴱ**Bauckham** R. *al.* 1988 ➤ 4,60: ᴿJEH 40 (1989) 262s (S. G. *Hall*); ScotJT 43 (1990) 403-6 (T. A. *Hart*).

1536 *Kasper* Walter, Das Verhältnis von Schrift und Tradition; eine pneumatologische Perspektive: TüTQ 170 (1990) 161-190.

1537 *Mihălţan* I. (en roumain), Tradition, Écriture, Église: OrtBuc 40,4 (1988) 59-73.

1538 *Minnerath* R., La Tradition chrétienne de Paul à Origène: AnHConc 20 (Pd 1988) 182-215 [< NTAbs 35,2].

1539 **Noll** Mark A., Between faith and criticism; evangelicals, scholarship, and the Bible in America 1986 ➤ 3,1353; 4,1453: ᴿCriswT 4 (1989s) 203s (D. S. *Dockery*).

1540 *Oberforcher* Robert, Überlieferung und Erstarrung; bibeltheologische Gedanken zur Ambivalenz von Traditionen: TGegw 33 (1990) 134-146.

1541 *Race* Alan, Quarrying tradition: TLond 93 (1990) 380-7.

1541* *Ruh* Ulrich, Das Gottesvolk als Subjekt der Überlieferung; Dogmatikertagung über Tradition und Erneuerung [23.-28. Sept. 1990, Vierzehnheiligen]: HerdKor 44 (1990) 536-9.

1542 *Schott* Rudiger, Die Macht des Überlieferungswissens in schriftlosen Gesellschaften: ➤ 128, ᶠNARR K., Saeculum 41 (1990) 273-316.

1543 *Sesboüé* Bernard, Tradition et traditions [CONGAR Y. M. J., La Tradition et les traditions 1960-3]: NRT 112 (1990) 570-585.

1544 *Trevijano Etcheverría* Ramón, Tradición y teología en los orígenes cristianos: RET 50 (1990) 5-28.

1545 *Wiedenhofer* Siegfried, Grundprobleme des theologischen Traditionsbegriffs: ZkT 112 (1990) 18-29.

B3.5 Canon.

1546 *Aschim* Anders, Det gamle testamente som kanon [*Childs* B. ... theologiens enhet]: TsTKi 61 (1990) 109-118.

1547 **Beckwith** Roger, OT canon of NT church 1985 ➤ 1,1472 ... 5,1470: ᴿBO 47 (1990) 189-192 (H. *Sysling*).

1548 **Blanchard** Yves-M., IRÉNÉE de Lyon — témoin du développement du canon neo-testamentaire: diss. Inst. Cath. ᴰ*Perrot* C. P 1990. 396 p.; 119 p. – RICathP 34 (1990) 193-6. – RTLv 22, p. 596.

1549 *a) Brettler* Mark, Canon; how the books of the Hebrew Bible were chosen; – *b) Greenspoon* Leonard J., Mission to Alexandria; truth and legend about the creation of the Septuagint: BR 5,4 (1989) 12s / 34-37.40s.

1550 **Bruce** F. F., The canon of Scripture 1988 ➤ 5,1472: ᴿEvQ 62 (1990) 180s (R. *Beckwith*); JTS 41 (1990) 207s (also R. *Beckwith*).

1551 *Carlston* C. E., The canon — problems and benefits: Bulletin of Christian Research Institute Meiji Gakuin Univ. Tokyo 23 (1990) 1-22 [< NTAbs 35,138].

1552 **Dunn** James D. G., The living word [Griffiths Lectures + others on canon] 1987 ➤ 4,184: ᴿJTS 41 (1990) 214s (I. H. *Jones*).

1553 *Freedman* David N., The formation of the canon of the OT; the selection and identification of the Torah as the supreme authority of the postexilic community: ➤ 526, Religion & Law 1985/90, 315-331.

1554 *Geoltrain* P., Lettre à Sarah; sur la diversité des corpus [... various collections constituting the OT corpus]: FoiVie 90,5 (1990) 3-9 [83-92, *Monsarrat* V., Jewish history: < NTAbs 35,217].

1555 *Goodman* Martin, Sacred Scripture and 'defiling the hands': JTS 41 (1990) 99-107.

1556 *Hall* Stuart G., Canon and controversies; some recent researches in early Christianity [METZGER B. 1987, ROBERTS-SKEAT 1987 and six others]: JEH 40 (1989) 253-261.

1557 **Hernando** James D., IRENAEUS and the Apostolic Fathers; an inquiry into the development of the New Testament canon: diss. Drew, ᴰ*Pain* J. Madison NJ 1990. 376 p. 90-32121. – DissA 51 (1990s) 2053-A; RelStR 17,194.

1558 *Howard* G., Canon; choosing the books of the New Testament: BR 5,5 (1989) 16s [< NTAbs 34,2].

1559 ᴱ**Kaestli** J.-D., *Wermelinger* O., Le canon de l'AT 1984 → 1,477 ... 3,1453: ᴿVT 40 (1990) 243s (W. *Horbury*).

1560 *Kalin* Everett R., Re-examining New Testament canon history; I. The canon of ORIGEN: → 41, ᶠDANKER F., CurrTMiss 17 (1990) 274-282.

1561 **McDonald** Lee M., The formation of the Christian biblical canon 1988 → 4,1446; 5,1480: ᴿHorBT 12,1 (1990) 102s (F. A. *Spina*); Interpretation 44 (1990) 300s (J. S. *Siker*); PerspRelSt 17 (1990) 267-9 (M. D. *Greene*, also on BRUCE F., BARTON J.).

1562 *Macholz* Christian, Die Entstehung des hebräischen Bibelkanons nach 4 Esra 14: → 147, ᶠRENDTORFF R., Hebr. Bibel 1990, 379-391.

1563 *a*) *Maier* Gerhard, Der Abschluss des jüdischen Kanons und das Lehrhaus von Jabne; – *b*) *Stadelmann* Helge, Die Reform Esras und der Kanon; – *c*) *Betz* Otto, Das Problem des 'Kanons' in den Texten von Qumran; – *d*) *Neudorfer* Heinz-Werner, Das Diasporajudentum und der Kanon: → 545, Kanon 1989/90, 1-24 / 52-69 / 70-82 / 83-101.

1563* **Maier** Gerhard, Der Kanon der Bibel: MgStudBücher 354. Giessen 1990, Brunnen. vi-199 p.

1564 **Metzger** B., Canon of NT, 1987 → 3,1456 ... 5,1482: ᴿAmHR 95 (1990) 127 (H. C. *Kee*); BR 5,2 (1989) 6 (G. *Howard*); BTrans 41 (1990) 145s (P. *Ellingworth*); CathHR 75 (1989) 470s (J. P. *Kelly*); HeythJ 31 (1990) 333 (G. *Stanton*); IrTQ 56 (1990) 75s (D. *Brown*); WestTJ 52 (1990) 152-5 (R. B. *Gaffin*: valuable despite reserves on theology).

1564* **Morgan** Donn F., Between text and community; the 'Writings' un canonical interpretation. Mp 1990, Fortress. x-164 p. 0-8006-2406-8.

1565 *Oakes* Edward T., The usurped town; the canon of Scripture in postmodern aesthetics: CommND 17 (1990) 261-280 [< OTAbs 13,10].

1566 *Patterson* L. G., IRENAEUS and the Valentinians; the emergence of a Christian scripture: → 643, StPatr 18,3 (1983/8) 189-220.

1567 ᴱ**Reventlow** Henning, *Sparn* Walter, *Woodbridge* John, Historische Kritik und biblischer Kanon in der deutschen Aufklärung [Wolfenbütteler Symposion Dez. 1985]: W-Forsch 4, 1988 → 5,602: ᴿTLZ 115 (1990) 210-2 (W. *Sommer*).

1568 *Salmon* M., The function of canon and the quest for inclusive language: Prism 5,2 (1990) 50-56 [< NTAbs 35,148].

1569 **Sanders** James A., From sacred story to sacred text; canon as paradigm 1987 → 3,1466 ... 5,1492: ᴿCriswT 4 (1989s) 191s (D. S. *Dockery*).

1570 **Stuhlhofer** Franz, Der Gebrauch der Bibel von Jesus bis Euseb; eine statistische Untersuchung zur Kanonsgeschichte; Vorw. *Riesner* R. 1988

➤ 4,1461; 5,1494:   ᴿRÉAug 35 (1989) 180s (A. *LeBoulluec*); TLZ 115 (1990) 671 (T. *Holtz*).

1570* *a) Swarat* Uwe, Das Werden des neutestamentlichen Kanons; – *b) Riesner* Rainer, Ansätze zur Kanonbildung innerhalb des Neuen Testaments; – *c) Schnabel* Eckhard, Die Entwürfe B. S. CHILDS und H. GESE bezüglich des Kanons; – *d) Stuhlhofer* Franz, Die altkirche Kanonsgeschichte im Spiegel evangelischer Literatur: ➤ 545, ᴱ*Maier* G., Kanon 1989/90, 25-51 / 153-164 / 102-152 / 165-197.

1571 *a) Théobald* Christoph, Le canon des Écritures; l'enjeu d'un 'conflit des facultés'; – *b) Trublet* Jacques, Constitution et clôture du canon hébraïque: ➤ 557*, Canon 1990, 13-73 / 177-236.

1572 *a) Vallin* Pierre, La formation de la Bible chrétienne; – *b) Haulotte* Edgar, Formation du corpus du NT; recherche d'un 'module' génératif intertextuel; – *c) Marty* François, Le canon des Écritures; mémoire pour un avenir; – *d) Sesboüé* Bernard, Essai de théologie systématique sur le canon des Écritures: ➤ 557*, Canon 1990, 189-236 / 255-439 / 495-512 / 523-539.

1573 **Vasholz** Robert I., The Old Testament canon in the Old Testament Church [sic]; the internal rationale for Old Testament canonicity: ANE TSt 7. Lewiston NY 1990, Mellen. [viii-] 105 p. $50.   0-88946-084-1.

1574 *Veltri* Giuseppe, Zur traditionsgeschichtlichen Entwicklung des Bewusstseins von einem Kanon; die Yavneh-Frage: JStJud 21 (1990) 210-226.

1575 **Ziegenaus** Anton, Kanon; von der Väterzeit bis zur Gegenwart: HbDG 1/3a/2. FrB 1990, Herder. 252 p. 3-451-00747-9. – ᴿZkT 112 (1990) 341s (K. H. *Neufeld*).

1576 *Ziegenaus* Anton, Die ungleiche Bibel; das Problem der deuterokanonischen Schriften: ForumKT 6 (1990) 85-102.

B4   *Interpretatio humanistica* – .1 **The Bible and man.**

1577 *Alonso Schökel* Luis, Meditazione per la terza età: VConsacr 26 (1990) 830-6.

1578 **Augustin** M., Der schöne Mensch im AT und im hellenistischen Judentum 1983 ➤ 64,1537 ... 3,1471:   ᴿNedTTs 44 (1990) 249s (K. A. D. *Smelik*).

1579 *Bosman* H., Tweede naïwitet [second naiveté] en Derde Wêreld; teologiese nadenke oor die Ou Testament: TEv 23 (Pretoria 1990) 45-56 [< OTAbs 14,83].

1580 *Chang* Anna, ⊖ Transcendence and joy [in the Bible and in Christian tradition]: ColcFuJen 83 (1990) 103-117.

1581 *Genest* Hartmut, Gottesglaube und Arbeitsethos: ➤ 76, ᶠHENKYS J. 1989, 318-325.

1582 **Harris** J. Gordon, Biblical perspectives on aging 1987 ➤ 3,1472; 5,1504: ᴿCritRR 2 (1989) 134-6 (L. R. *Bailey*: do mythological texts indicate social attitudes?).

1583 *Homerski* Józef, ⊕ The labor of man [człowiek] in the Old Testament: ➤ 64, ᶠGRZYBEK S. 1990, 103-114; Eng. 114.

1584 *Hsu* Aloysius, ⊖ Psychological growth seen from the Scripture: ColcFuJen 85 (1990) 395-409 [< TContext 8/2, p. 35].

1585 *Ibarmia* Francisco, Teología del dolor en la Biblia: REspir 49 (1990) 197-228.

1585* *Maraval* Pierre,   Modèles bibliques de l'hospitalité chez les Pères:
→ 182*, ᶠVEREECKE L.,   StMor 28 (1990) 27-41.

1586 **Minois** George,   Storia della vecchiaia dall'antichità al Rinascimento.
Bari 1988, Laterza.   357 p. – ᴿSalesianum 52 (1990) 156s (C. *Semeraro*: il
mito del vecchio saggio spesso non corrisponde alla realtà).

1586* **Navone** J.,   Teologia del fallimento² 1988 → 4,9272:   ᴿREspir 49 (1990)
160s (J. *García Rojo*).

1587 **Reboul** Hélène,   Vieillir dans la Bible.   P 1990, Chalet.   112 p. F 52. –
ᴿEsprVie 100 (1990) 675 (É. *Cothenet*).

1588 **Tacke** H. † 1988, Mit den Müden zur rechten Zeit zu reden; Beiträge zu
einer bibelorienterten Seelsorge.   Neuk 1989, Neuk-V.   272 p. DM 34.
3-7887-1302-X. – ᴿTsTNijm 30 (1990) 322 (G. *Heitink*).

1589 *Zani* Lorenzo,   L'accoglienza nella Bibbia: Presbyteri 24 (1990) 59-
66 . 137-146 . 213-223 . 299-308 . 384-388 . 458-466 . 619-624 . 698-704 .
776-782.

B4.2   *Femina, familia;*   **Woman in the Bible** [→ H8.8s].

1590 **Archer** Léonie J.,   Her price is beyond rubies; the Jewish woman in
Græco-Roman Palestine [< London diss. 1983 + death-ritual]: JStOT
supp 60.   Sheffield 1990, Academic.   335 p. £27.50.   1-85075-079-3 [BL
91,33, G. I. *Emmerson*]. – ᴿOTAbs 13 (1990) 301s (A. A. *Di Lella*).

1591 **Aschkenasy** Nehama,   Eve's journey; feminine images in Hebraic literary
tradition,   1986 → 4,1479; £25.45:   ᴿJJS 41 (1990) 139s (G. *Abramson*);
Judaism 39 (1990) 113-118 (Zvia *Ginor*, also on FUCHS E. 1987).

1592 ᴱ**Bach** Alice,   The pleasure of her text; feminist readings of biblical and
historical texts.   Ph 1990, Trinity.   xii-148 p.   0-334-02479-X.

1593 ᴱ**Bal** Mieke,   Anti-covenant 1989 → 5,625:   ᴿÉTRel 65 (1990) 440s
(Françoise *Smyth*: démasque 'l'absurde mais jusqu'ici efficace prétension
des sciences bibliques à une objectivité ...'); TTod 47 (1990s) 112 (D. T.
Olson).

1594 **Bal** Mieke,   Lethal love 1987 → 3,1482; 5,1513:   ᴿOTAbs 13 (1990) 302
(W. J. *Urbrock*).

1594* *Bartolomei* Maria Cristina,   Il soggetto e la parola dell'altro; a proposito della interpretazione femminista della Bibbia: → 526*a, AnSto-
Eseg 7,1 (1990) 323-334.

1595 **Berkovits** Eliezer,   Jewish women in time and Torah.   Hoboken 1990,
KTAV.   143 p. $15.   0-88125-311-1 [TDig 38,48].

1596 *Bronner* Leila L.,   The changing face of woman from Bible to Talmud:
Shofar 7,2 (W. Lafayette IN 1989) 34-47 [< OTAbs 13,219].

1597 **Brooten** Bernadette J.,   Women leaders in the ancient synagogue 1982
→ 64,1503 ... 4,1485:   ᴿSecC 7 (1989s) 59s (A. J. *Saldarini*).

1598 **Brown** Cheryl Anne,   Women in rewritten Bible; Studies in [Ps.-PHILO]
'Liber antiquitatum biblicarum' and JOSEPHUS' 'Antiquities of the Jews':
diss. Graduate Theological Union.   Berkeley 1989. 222 p. 90-29090. –
DissA 51 (1990s) 2052-A.

1599 **Bührig** Marga,   Donne invisibili e Dio patriarcale, ᵀ*Leibbrand* Mirella.   T 1989, Claudiana.   115 p. – ᴿLaurentianum 31 (1990) 615s (F.
Raurell).

1599* *a) Camp* Claudia V.,   The female sage in ancient Israel and in the
biblical Wisdom literature; – *b) Fontaine* Carol R.,   The sage in family
and tribe; – *c) Harris* Rivkah,   The female 'sage' in Mesopotamian

literature (with an appendix on Egypt): → 336, Sage 1990, 185-203 / 155-164 / 3-17.

1600 **Cantor** Aviva (*Hamelsdorf* Ora), The Jewish woman 1980-1985. Fresh Meadows 1987, Biblio. ix-139 p. – RJQR 81 (1990s) 151 (Rachel R. *Adler*: 11-area bibliography).

1601 *Carr* B., Synergy toward life; a paradigm for liberative Christian work with the Bible [... feminist rewriting and mutual transformation of Scripture]: QRMin 10,4 (1990) 40-58.

1602 *Chmiel* Jerzy, ⊘ New aspects of the biblical view of marriage and family in the 'Familiaris Consortio': RuBi 42 (1989) 284-290.

1603 EDay Peggy L., Gender and difference in ancient Israel 1989 → 5,391: ROTAbs 13 (1990) 199s (M. S. *Smith*).

1604 **Dumais** Monique, Les femmes dans la Bible, 1985 → 1,1517 [español 1987 → 5,8800]: RÉglT 30 (1989) 127s (Micheline *Lagué*).

1605 *Eller* Cynthia, Relativizing the patriarchy; the sacred history of the feminist spirituality movement: HistRel 30 (1990s) 279-295.

1606 **Engelken** Karen, Frauen im alten Israel; eine begriffsgeschichtliche und sozialgeschichtliche Studie der Frau im AT [< Inaug. Diss.]: BW 130. Stu 1990, Kohlhammer. ix-256 p. DM 79 pa. 3-1701-1034-9 [BL 91,109, C. S. *Rodd*]. – ROTAbs 13 (1990) 303 (C. T. *Begg*).

1606* *Fatum* Lone, En kvindehistorie om tro og køn: DanTTs 53 (1990) 278-299 [< ZIT 91,5].

1607 *French* Valerie, What is central for the study of women in antiquity?: Helios 17 (Lubbock TX 1990) 213-220.

1608 *Goeden* Roland, Die Bibel über 'Mann und Frau' 2: NT: Religion Heute (1990,1) 45-53 [< ZIT 90,359].

Goldenberg Naomi R., Returning words to flesh; feminism, psychoanalysis, and the resurrection of the body 1990 → 8955.

1610 *Gruber* Mayer I., Breast-feeding practices in biblical Israel and in Old Babylonian Mesopotamia: → 75, Mem. HELD M., JANES 19 (1989) 61-83.

1611 *Huckett* J.A., Can a sexist model liberate us? Ancient Near East 'fertility' goddesses: JFemStRel 5 (1989) 65-76 [< ETL 66,118*].

1612 **Jeansonne** Sharon P., The women of Genesis; from Sarah to Potiphar's wife. Mp 1990, Fortress. 152 p. 0-8006-2419-X. – RExpTim 102 (1990s) 86 (C. S. *Rodd*, also on ARCHER L.).

1613 EKeay Kathy, Men, women and God [1985 conference, 17 art.] 1987 → 4,1503; 0-551-01501-2: RScotBEv 7 (1989) 58s (Shirley A. *Fraser*).

1614 **Lacocque** A., The feminine unconventional; four subversive figures in Israel's tradition [Susanna, Judith, Esther, Ruth]: OvBT. Minneapolis 1990, Fortress. xvi-144 p. $9. 0-8006-1559-X [BL 91,114, G.I. *Emmerson*: not tendentious].

1615 ELesko Barbara S., Women's earliest records; from Ancient Egypt and Western Asia; Proceedings of the Conference on Women in the Ancient Near East, Brown Univ., Providence Nov. 5-7, 1987: Brown JudSt 166, 1989 → 5,851: RBA 53 (1990) 119s (Patricia C. *Wood*).

1616 [Navè] **Levinson** Pnina, Was wurde aus Saras Töchtern? Frauen im Judentum: Siebenstern 495. Gü 1989, Mohn. 192 p.; 8 fig. DM 19,80. – RKIsr 5 (1990) 82 (Julie *Kirchberg*).

1617 ELiberti V., La famiglia nella Bibbia 1987/9 → 5,587*: RAsprenas 37 (1990) 372s (A. *Rolla*).

1618 *Magnus* Shulamit, 'Out of the ghetto'; integrating the study of Jewish women into the study of 'the Jews': Judaism 39 (1990) 28-36 [383s, self-defense of D. *Biale*; 508 rejoinder].

1619 **Maillot** Alphonse, Éve, ma mère; étude sur la femme dans l'AT 1989 → 5,1538:   ᴿEsprVie 100 (1990) 236 (L. *Monloubou*); RHPR 70 (1990) 257s (P. de *Robert*).

1620 *Maillot* Alphon[s]e, La femme dans l'Ancien Testament: FoiVie 89,2 (1990) 27-45.

1621 **Mayer** Günter, Die jüdische Frau in der hellenistisch-römischen Antike 1987 → 3,1508; 4,1509:   ᴿNedTTs 43 (1989) 339s (P. W. van der *Horst*); UF 22 (1990) 510 (O. *Loretz*: notes without comment p. 103-127, Frauennamen).

1622 **Meyers** Carol, Discovering Eve; ancient Israelite women in context. Ox 1988, Univ. → 4,1510; xiv-238 p. £19.50. 0-19-504934-9. – ᴿBA 53 (1990) 43-45 (D. *Edelman*); BL (1990) 109 (B. P. *Robinson*); BR 6,4 (1990) 10s (R. S. *Kraemer*); CBQ 52 (1990) 530-2 (Gale A. *Yee*: Eve is 'Everywoman' who lived in ancient Israel; 'biblical women' were mostly exceptional; fine but needs a further stage: why is the Bible so misogynist?); CritRR 3 (1990) 162-6 (Naomi *Steinberg*); CurrTMiss 17 (1990) 144 (R. W. *Klein*); JAAR 58 (1990) 511-3 (Mieke *Bal*); JAOS 110 (1990) 158 (D. J. *Gilner*: based more on preconceptions than on biblical and other available data); JRel 70 (1990) 84s (Phyllis A. *Bird*); TEdn 26,1 (1989s) 121-3 (D. A. *Knight*); TLond 93 (1990) 66s (Grace I. *Emmerson*); ZAW 102 (1990) 156 (H.-C. *Schmitt*).

1624 *Neu* Rainer, Patrilokalität und Patrilinearität in Israel; zur ethnosoziologischen Kritik der These von Matriarchat: BZ 34 (1990) 222-233.

1625 **Plaskow** Judith, Standing again at Sinai; Judaism from a feminist perspective. SF 1990, Harper & R. xix-282 p. $22. – ᴿTS 51 (1990) 732s (Barbara A. *Cullom*).

1626 *Plaskow* Judith, Sind die Juden schuld am Patriarchat? Gegen christlich-feministische Mythenbildung: Junge Kirche 51 (Bremen 1990) 434-6 [< ZIT 90,596].

1627 *Pushparanjan* A., The Bible and the family; the Word of God challenges the Indian family: Vidyajyoti 54 (1990) 327-336.

1628 **Ruud** Inger Marie, Women and Judaism; a select annotated bibliography. NY 1988, Garland. xxiv-232 p. – ᴿJQR 81 (1990s) 151s (Rachel H. *Adler*; unreliable, baffling).

1629 *Schroer* Silvia, Weise Frauen und Ratgeberinnen in Israel — literarische und historische Vorbilder der personifikierten Chokmah: [< Hab. Vortrag FrS 1989]: BibNot 51 (1990) 41-60.

1630 ᴱ**Skinner** Marilyn, Rescuing Creusa 1987 → 3,772*; 5,1543: ᴿLatomus 49 (1990) 504-6 (Simone *Deléani*); RÉG 103 (1990) 273-5 (O. *Rodari*); WienerSt 103 (1990) 245-9 (Edith *Specht*).

1631 *Thornton* Larry R., A biblical approach to establishing marital intimacy [7 interesting crises noted by W. MᶜRᴀᴇ: 4 months; 3, 5, 6, 7, 11, 27 years]: CalvaryB 6 (1990) 52-70.

1632 **Wegner** Judith R., Chattel or person... Mishnah 1988 → 4,b177: ᴿBA 53 (1990) 117s (M. B. *Peskowitz*); CritRR 3 (1990) 361-4 (R. S. *Kraemer*); JRel 70 (1990) 252s (Carol *Meyers*).

1633 **Weiler** Gerda, Das Matriarchat im alten Israel. Stu 1989, Kohlhammer. 368 p. DM 29. – BL (1990) 116 (J. W. *Rogerson*: scholarship not in the class of 'Fiorenza or Myers'; writes Otto Kehl for 'Otmar Keel'); KIsr 5 (1990) 82 (Julie *Kirchberg*).

1634 **Winter** Urs, Frau und Göttin...: OBO 53, 1983 ➤ 64,1534... 3,1520;
²1987: ᴿZDPV 106 (1990) 185-8 (Helga *Weippert*).

B4.4 *Exegesis litteraria* – **The Bible itself as literature.**

1635 *Alonso Schökel* Luis, Dimensión literaria de la Biblia: ➤ 370*, Introducción I (1990) 369-383.

1636 ᴱ**Alter** Robert, *Kermode* Frank, The literary guide to the Bible [1987],
pa. L 1989, Collins. 678 p. £10. 0-00-686170-9. – ᴿBL (1990) 64 (D.
Clines); CBQ 52 (1990) 505-7 (W. R. *Herzog*: title pretentious and
misleading; rather Literary and some other readings of biblical texts);
CritRR 2 (1989) 127-9 (Alice L. *Laffey*: 'a' guide, not 'the'); Annals of
Scholarship 6/4 ('Religion and the humanities' 1990: W. *Reed*, R. A.
Rosengarten, M. L. *Soards*, < JAAR 58,243 adv.).

1637 **Bloom** Harold, Ruin the sacred truths; poetry and belief from the
Bible to the present 1989 ➤ 5,1549: ᴿJAAR 58 (1990) 479-482 (E. B.
Kabisch).

1638 *Bodrato* Aldo, Bibbia e letteratura; Pentecoste e/o Babele?: HumBr 45
(1990) 450-477.

Campbell Antony F., The study companion to OT [... literary structures]
1990 ➤ 1159.

1639 **Della Terza** Dante, Tradizione ed esegesi; semantica dell'innovazione
da AGOSTINO a De Sanctis. Padova 1987, Liviana. 225 p. Lit. 24.000.
– ᴿViPe 73 (1990) 152-4 (Silvia *Bulletta*).

1640 **Gabel** John H., *Wheeler* Charles B., The Bible as literature; an
introduction² 1989 ¹1986 ➤ 2,1106... 5,1551: ᴿBR 5,4 (1989) 4 . 44
(M. *Brettler*, also on ALTER-KERMODE); EvQ 62 (1990) 284s (A. G.
Newell).

1641 *Gianto* Agustinus, Kitab Suci... Bible and literature: Rohani 37 (1990)
445-450 [AcPIB 9/7, 548].

1642 *Herrero Cecilia* Juan, ¿Puede existir una ciencia en la Literatura?
Problemas epistemológicos de la crítica literaria: Carthaginensia 6 (1990)
169-181.

1643 **Josipovici** Gabriel, The Book of God; a response to the Bible 1988
➤ 4,1073; 5,1553: ᴿBR 6,6 (1990) 10 (J. S. *Ackerman*); CritRR 3 (1990)
71-73 (Pamela J. *Milne*); HebSt 31 (1990) 178-182 (J. G. *Williams*: by an
author of fiction); Interpretation 44 (1990) 318 (A. *Milavec*).

1643* **King** Thomas M., Enchantments; religion and the power of the word.
KC 1989, Sheed & W. xiv-232 p. 1-55612-269-1.

1644 **Lawton** David, Faith, text and history; the Bible in English: Studies in
Religion and Culture. Charlottesville 1990, Univ. Virginia. x-203 p.
0-8139-1325-X.

1645 **Longman** Tremperᴵᴵᴵ, Literary approaches to biblical interpretation
1987 ➤ 4,1529: ᴿMastJ 1 (1990) 89-91 (D. C. *Deuel*: refreshing); ScotBEv
8 (1990) 66s (I. H. *Marshall*).

1646 *Powell* M. A., The Bible and modern literary criticism: Summary of
Proceedings of the American Theological Library Association 43
(Evanston 1989) 78-94 [< NTAbs 34,289].

1647 *Prince* G., The Bible as literature; dealing with presumptions: CounSR
19,2 (Macon 1990) 33.35.37 [< NTAbs 34,289].

Rousseau F., La poétique fondamentale du texte biblique 1989 ➤ 3243.

1649 **Ryken** Leland, Words of delight; a literary introduction to the Bible

1987 ➤ 3,1202: ᴿRelStT 8,1s (1988) 100-2 (K. I. *Parker*: continues his 1984 How to read the Bible as literature).

1650 **Ryken** Leland, *a*) Words of Delight / *b*) Words of Life; a literary introduction to the Bible / NT ➤ 4,4109 [both together are the revision of 1974 Literature of the Bible]. GR 1987, Baker. 382 p.; $16 / 182 p.; $12. – ᴿGraceTJ 10 (1989) 80-83 (B. L. *Woodard*).

1650* *Ryken* Leland, The Bible as literature, 1. 'Words of delight'; – 2. 'And it came to pass'; the Bible as God's storybook; – 3. 'I have used similitudes'; the poetry of the Bible; – 4. 'With many such parables'; the imagination as a means of grace: Bibliotheca Sacra 147 (1990) 3-15 / 131-142 / 259-269 / 387-398.

1651 ᴱ**Schwartz** Regina M., The Book and the text; the Bible and literary theory [passages from ALTER R., BAL M., *al.*]. Ox 1990, Blackwell. xi-313 p. 0-631-16861-3; pa. -2-1.

1652 *Seidl* Theodor, ❷ Metoda literaturoznawcza... Literary OT exegesis: AtKap 115 (1990) 172-186.

1652* *Wilder* A. N., The literary critic and the Bible; George STEINER on The literary guide to the Bible: Religion and Intellectual Life 6,3s (New Rochelle 1989) 17-24 [25-30, *Brooks* C.; 9-16, Steiner's review reprinted].

1653 *Wilder* A. N., Holy Writ and Lit Crit: ChrCent 107 (1990) 790s [< NTAbs 35,12].

1654 **Wright** T. R., Theology and literature: Signposts in theology 1988 ➤ 4,1532: ᴿBL (1990) 117 (J. *Barton*).

B4.5 **Influxus biblicus in litteraturam profanam,** *generalia.*

1655 **Alter** Robert, The invention of Hebrew prose [1790-1932]; modern fiction and the language of realism 1988 ➤ 4,1521: ᴿCritRR 2 (1989) 120-3 (Pamela J. *Milne*).

1656 *Bañeza Román* Celso, Las oraciones [bíblico-]narrativas de la literatura medieval española y sus orígenes: EstE 65 (1990) 317-330.

1657 **Bukowski** Kazimierz, ❷ Biblia a literatura polska. Poznań 1988, Pallottinum. 392 p. – ᴿAtKap 114 (1990) 154s (T. *Lenczewski*).

1658 ᴱ**Corn** A., Incarnation; contemporary writers on the New Testament [essays by 23 novelists and poets on the respective NT books]. NY 1990, Viking. xiv-361 p. $20. 0-670-82504-2 [NTAbs 35, p. 230].

1659 **Damrosch** Leopold ᴶ, God's plot and man's stories; studies in the fictional imagination from MILTON to FIELDING. Ch 1985, Univ. 363 p. $25. – ᴿCritRR 3 (1990) 61s (G. *Taylor*).

1660 **Gallagher** Susan V., *Lundin* Roger, Literature through the eyes of faith. SF 1989, Harper & R. xxvii-193 p. $10 pa. – ᴿBS 147 (1990) 376 (J. A. *Witmer*).

1661 **Hall** Thomas N., Apocryphal lore and the life of Christ in Old English literature: diss. Illinois, ᴰ*Wright* C. Urbana 1990. 269 p. 91-14255. – DissA 51 (1990s) 4115-A.

1661* **Henderson** Heather, The Victorian self; autobiography and biblical narrative. Ithaca NY 1989, Cornell Univ. x-205 p. $30 [JRel 71,637, M. *Woodfield*).

1662 **Jasper** David, The study of literature and religion, an introduction. Mp/L 1989, Fortress/Macmillan. xii-158 p. $13. 0-8006-2325-8/ [TDig 37,368]. – ᴿTLond 93 (1990) 501s (S. *Prickett*).

1662* **Kerby-Fulton** Kathryn, Reformist apocalypticism and Piers Plowman [< diss. York]: Studies in Medieval Literature 7. C 1990, Univ. xii-256 p. $49.50. 0-521-34298-8 [TDig 38,274]. – Piers Ploughman author is Wm LANGLAND [᭼Goodrich J. F., Penguin 1959: CBQ 53,580].

1663 *Kort* Wesley A., 'Religion and literature' in postmodernist contexts: JAAR 50 (1990) 575-588.

1664 ᴱKüng H., *Jens* W., Dichtung und Religion 1988 [1985 ➙ 3,1550; 4,1539; Jens put first]: ᴿTLZ 115 (1990) 531s (K. *Stiebert*).

1665 ᴱKüng Hans, *Jens* Walter, Literature and religion, ᵀ*Heinigg* Peter. NY 1990, Paragon. x-308 p. $23 [TS 52, 385, E. *Ingebretsen*].

1666 **Küng** H., *Jens* W., Maestri di umanità, ᵀ*Moretto* G. Mi c. 1990, Rizzoli. 240 p. Lit. 28.000. 88-17-84005-X. – ᴿRivStoLR 26 (1990) 328-344 (Clara *Leri*: 'La croce e il moderno').

1667 **Lüdde** Maria-Elisabeth, Die Rezeption, Interpretation und Transformation biblischer Motive und Mythen in gegenwärtiger DDR-Literatur: Diss. ᴰ*Hildebrandt*. Greifswald 1989s. – TR 86 (1990) 515.

1668 *Pezzini* Domenico, La poesia della Passione nella tradizione letteraria inglese, dal 'Sogno della Croce' a R. S. THOMAS: RivStoLR 26 (1990) 460-507.

1669 **Remley** Paul G., The biblical sources of the Junius poems [11, p. 1-212: Anglo-Saxon] 'Genesis', 'Exodus', and 'Daniel'; diss. Columbia. NY 1990. 520 p. 91-02453. – DissA 51 (1990s) 3757-A.

1670 ᴱ**Rosenberg** D., Congregation; Jewish writers read the Hebrew Bible 1987 ➙ 4,1543; pa. 1989, $15. 0-15-146350-6.

1671 **Speirs** Nancy J., Hermeneutic sensibility and the Old English 'Exodus': diss. Toronto 1990, ᴰ*Frank* R. – DissA 51 (1990s) 3407-A.

1671* *Yaniv* Shlomo, La Biblia en la balada literaria hebrea: Helmantica 38 (1987) 381-405.

B4.6 *Singuli auctores* — **Bible-influence on individual authors.**

1672 ARNOLD: **Gaffney** Kathleen M., Matthew Arnold, priest of culture; a study of Arnold's religious criticism [Saint Paul and Protestantism 1870; Literature and dogma (a case for the Bible) 1873; God and the Bible 1875]: diss. Baptist Theol. Sem. ᴰ*Howe* C. New Orleans 1990. 226 p. 90-27865. – DissA 51 (1990s) 1659-A.

1673 BÉCQUER: *García Viñó* Manuel, Sobre un posible substrato bíblico en la leyenda de Bécquer 'El Gnomo': RelCu 36 (1990) 667-672.

1674 BUNYAN: *Ward* Graham, To be a reader; John Bunyan's struggle with the language of Scripture in Grace abounding to the chief of sinners: LitTOx 4,1 (1990) 29-49 [< ZIT 90,237].

1674* — *Dawson* David, Allegorical intertextuality in Bunyan and WIN-STANLEY: JRel 70 (1990) 189-212.

1675 CARLYLE: **ApRoberts** Ruth, The ancient dialect; Thomas Carlyle and comparative religion. Berkeley 1988, Univ. California. vii-126 p. 0-520-06116-0. – ᴿLingBib 62 (1989) 128 (W. *Schenk*).

1676 CHAUCER: **Besserman** Lawrence, Chaucer and the Bible; a critical review of research, indices, and bibliography: Ref. Hum. 839. NY 1988, Garland. xx-432 p. $62. – ᴿSpeculum 65 (1990) 939-941 (J. M. *Dean*).

1677 **de Weever** Jacqueline, Chaucer name dictionary; a guide to astrological, biblical, historical, literary, and mythological names: RefHum 709. NY 1988, Garland. 451 p. $50. – ᴿSpeculum 65 (1990) 968s (Linne R. *Mooney*).

1678 COLERIDGE: *Bilik* Dorothy, JOSEPHUS [on Cain], Mosollamus, and [Coleridge S.] The Ancient Mariner: StPg 86 (1989) 87-95.

1679 DONNE: **Stevens** Timothy S., Things that belong to the way; John Donne's sermons on the penitential psalms: diss. Northwestern, ᴰ*Cirillo* A. Evanston IL 1990. 289 p. – 91-14641. – DissA 51 (1990s) 4134s-A.

1680 DOSTOYEVSKY: **Arnold** Eberhard, *al.*, The Gospel in Dostoyevsky. Rifton NY 1988, Plough. 260 p.; ill. (Eichenberg F.) $9.50. – ᴿCurrTMiss 17 (1990) 306s (J. C. *Rochelle*).

1681 EMERSON: **Waters** Laura O., Hymns of the pearl; Gnostic impulses in Emerson and MELVILLE: diss. SUNY. Binghampton 1990. 383 p. 90-28131. – DissA 51 (1990s) 1616-A.

1682 KÉPES: *Ferenc* Mrs. David, Ⓜ The image of God and biblical motifs in the lyric poetry of Géza Képes: TSzem 33 (1990) 42-47.

1683 MILTON: *Kee* James M., Typology and tradition; refiguring the Bible in Milton's Paradise lost: ➤ 365, Semeia 51 (1990) 155-175.

1684 **Lee** Terrence O., (Re)Imagining Satan in 'Paradise Lost'; (re)valuing the dark side, transgression, and the 'woman's image': diss. Syracuse NY 1990. 248 p. 91-09605. – DissA 51 (1990s) 3754-A.

1684* *a)* *Lewalski* Barbara K., Milton, the Bible and human experience; – *b)* *Nicastro* Onofrio, La grande ribellione e il grande codice; usi radicali della Bibbia nella rivoluzione inglese (1640-1660); – *c)* *Pacchi* Arrigo, HOBBES e la filologia biblica al servizio dello Stato: ➤ 526*a*, AnStoEseg 7,1 (1990) 187-204 / 225-256 / 277-292.

1685 **Martini** Catherine G., Dark with excessive bright; 'Paradise Lost' and the decline of allegory: diss. California. Santa Cruz 1989. 461 p. 90-21410. – DissA 51 (1990s) 865-A.

1686 MUIR: *Slater* R. G. †XI.89, The toy horse [Johannine Christ: last poem in MUIR E. 1949, The Labyrinth]: TLond 93 (1990) 27-30.

1687 NIETZSCHE: **Richards** W. Wiley, The Bible and Christian traditions; keys to understanding the allegorical subplot of Nietzsche's Zarathustra: AmerUnivSt 7/75. NY 1990, Lang. 411 p. $70. 0-8204-1312-7 [RelStR 17,344, J. J. *Buckley*].

1688 O'CONNOR: **Barnes** Linda A., Faith and narrative; Flannery O'Connor and the New Testament: diss. Vanderbilt, ᴰ*Kreyling* M. Nv 1989. 167 p. 90-17606. – DissA 51 (1990s) 504-A.

1689 SHAKESPEARE: **Thompson** Stephen P., Shakespeare and the Elizabethan St. Paul: diss. Iowa 1990, ᴰ*Steele* O. 255 p. 91-03271. – DissA 51 (1990s) 3087-A.

1690 *Rand* Herbert, Biblical influences on Shakespeare's Hamlet [Ps 8,5s; Qoh 12,5; 12,14...; over 1000 allusions to the Bible have been counted in Shakespeare]: JBQ 19 (1990s) 29-33.

1691 SHELLEY: **Shelley** Bryan K., The interpreting angel; Shelley and Scriptura: diss. Oxford 1986. 363 p. BRD-88667. – DissA 51 (1990s) 171-A.

1692 SPENSER...: **Augustine** John H., 'Sole fountain of truth'; Elizabethan poetics and the Reformed theology of Scripture: diss. Minnesota, ᴰ*Clayton* T. Minneapolis 1989. 191 p. 90-19046. – DissA 51 (1990s) 532-A.

1693 WERFEL: **Jaeger** Klaus, Franz Werfel; the Gnostic-religious viewpoint of the [Christianizing] Jewish writer in his critical assessment of his time [in German]: diss. Pennsylvania State 1989, ᴰ*Preisner* R. 296 p. 90-18230. – DissA 60 (1990s) 515-A.

B4.7 *Interpretatio* **athea, materialistica, psychiatrica.**

1694 **Drewermann** Eugen, Tiefenpsychologie und Exegese 1⁶, 1988 ➤ 4,1584; 5,1609; 2. Wunder, Gleichnis, Apokalypse ⁵1989 ➤ 4843.

1694* *Drewermann* Eugen, Schule für das Leben — Leben für die Schule?: Religion Heute 4 (Hannover 1990) 212-9 [< ZIT 91,122].

1695 — *Boada* Josep, Método histórico-crítico, psicología profunda y revelación; una aproximación a E. DREWERMANN: ActuBbg 27 (1990) 5-32.

1696 — *Funke* Dieter [interview], Psychotherapie und Glaube... DREWERMANN: TGegw 33 (1990) 291-6.

1697 — *Gnilka* Joachim, Psicologia del profondo ed esegesi [DREWERMANN E.; Mt 5,1-20], ᵀ*Bonora* A.: RivB 38 (1990) 3-12; Eng. 11.

1698 — ᴱ**Görres** Albert, *Kasper* Walter, Tiefenpsychologische Deutung des Glaubens... DREWERMANN: QDisp 113, 1988 ➤ 4,305; 5,1613: ᴿBogVest 49 (1989) 106-112 (V. *Dermota*, in Slovene); TLZ 115 (1990) 224-6 (H.-M. *Barth*).

1699 — *Kaspar* Peter P., Der Fall DREWERMANN; ein notwendiger Konflikt in Theologie und Kirche: KatBlätt 115 (1990) 339-345 [< ZIT 90,427].

1700 — *Kassel* Maria, *a*) Die Überwindung der menschlichen Angst — das einzige wesentliche Thema der Religion? Zu DREWERMANNS Pathologisierung der Religion durch patriarchale Projektion; – *b*) Bibel und Tiefenpsychologie; eine Sichtung des Streits um E. Drewermann: Diakonia 21 (Mainz 1990) 107-110 / RHöhS 33,1 (1990) 48- [< ZIT 90,273.282].

1701 — *a*) **Lohfink** G., *Pesch* R., Tiefenpsychologie und keine Exegese... Drewermann 1987 ➤ 3,1571... 5,1616: ᴿBijdragen 51 (1990) 202s (J. van *Ruiten*). *b*) **Drewermann** E., 'An ihren Früchten...', G. LOHFINK, R. PESCH, 1988 ➤ 4,1585; 5,1609: ᴿTLZ 115 (1990) 293s (H.-M. *Barth*: 'Ob dieses Buch geschrieben werden musste? Vielleicht doch... Aufschrei'),

1702 — *Lüdemann* Gerd, Träume — die vergessene Sprache Gottes? Zur tiefenpsychologischen Exegese Eugen DREWERMANNS: KkKMaterialdienst 41 (1990) 67-72 [< ZIT 90,721].

1703 — *Martin* Gerhard M., Eugen DREWERMANNS 'Strukturen des Bösen' als Ausgangspunkt eines umstrittenen theologischen Denkweges: TLZ 115 (1990) 321-332.

1704 — *Stolle* Volker, Tiefenpsychologische Schriftauslegung [DREWERMANN E., Markusev.² 1988]: LuthTKi 13 (1989) 16-28.

1705 **Fleischmann** Paul R., The healing spirit. L 1990, SPCK. xii-288 p. £9. 0-281-04451-1. – ᴿExpTim 102 (1990s) 155s (G. T. *Eddy*: wisc, readable).

1706 **Gay** Peter, A godless Jew, FREUD 1987 ➤ 4,1587; 5,1617: ᴿCritRR 2 (1989) 416-8 (L. *Bregman*).

1706* **Küng** Hans, Freud and the problem of God² [Yale 41st Terry Lectures 1979 + 1986 award discourse], ᵀ*Quinn* Edward. NHv 1990, Yale. xiv-168 p. $23.50; pa. $9. 0-300-04711-8; -23-1 [TDig 38,276].

1707 *Reines* Alvin J., FREUD's concepts of reality and God; a text study: HUCA 61 (1990) 219-270.

1708 **Gibert** Pierre, Le récit biblique de rêve; essai de confrontation analytique: Biblique 3. Lyon 1990, Profac. 124 p. [RTLv 22,533, P.-M. *Bogaert*: littéraire mais éclairée par l'analyse freudienne].

1709 *Natoli* Salvatore, Un non credente di fronte alla Bibbia: ➤ 514*b*, Un libro 1989/90, 13-27.
1710 **Pfeifer** Samuel, Die Schwachen tragen; moderne Psychiatrie und biblische Seelsorge. Ba 1988, Brunnen. 216 p. DM 24. 3-7655-2408-5. – ᴿLuthTKi 14 (1990) 37 (Gudrun *Schätzel*).

B5   **Methodus exegetica.**

1711 **Armstrong** Chloe, Oral interpretation of biblical literature. Mp 1968, Burgess. 88 p. 0-8087-0109-6 [not in Elenchus 1968-70].
1712 *Barthélemy* Dominique [pour son doctorat d'honneur], La critique canonique [SANDERS J., CHILDS B.]: RICathP 36 (1990) 191-220.
1713 **Barton** John, Reading the OT; method ... 1984 ➤ 65,1413 ... 3,1581: ᴿTEdn 26,1 (1989s) 116s (J. *Blenkinsopp*).
1715 **Beach** Eleanor F., Image and word; iconology in the interpretation of Hebrew Scripture, with examples from Sumeria: diss. Claremont 1989, ᴰ*Knierim* R. – RelStR 17,193.
1716 **Beattie** D. R. G., First steps in biblical criticism: Studies in Judaism, 1988 ➤ 4,1608; 5,1623; 0-8191-7053-4. – ᴿBL (1991) 64 (W. *Houston*); CritRR 3 (1990) 108s (D. H. *Little*).
1717 *a*) *Blank* Josef, Die systematischen Implikationen der historisch-kritischen Methode; – *b*) *Maier* Gerhard, Grundlinien eines biblischen Schriftverständnisses; – *c*) *Oberforcher* Robert, Fundamentalistische Schriftauslegung als Feindbild der historisch-kritischen Bibelwissenschaft; – *d*) *Fuchs* Othmar, Umgang mit der Bibel als Lernschule der Pluralität; – *e*) *Wenz* Gunther, Kanonbildung und Schriftverständnis in evangelischer Perspektive: UnSa 44,3 ('Schriftauslegung; Ökumenische Chancen und Konflikte' 1989) 186-192 / 193-9 / 200-7 / 208-214 / 215-221.
1718 *Bonora* Antonio, L'esegesi biblica tra 'storia' e 'teologia': TItSett 15 (1990) 191-7.
1719 *Botha* P. J., Resepsieteorie; konkurrent of [or] komplement van die teksimmanente eksegese?: SkrifKerk 10,2 (1989) 113-127 [< NTAbs 34,285].
1720 **Corsani** Bruno, Esegesi; come interpretare un testo biblico 1985 ➤ 2, 1140*: ᴿProtestantesimo 45 (1990) 71s (A. *Adamo*).
1721 *Dohmen* Christoph, Muss der Exeget Theologe sein? oder, Vom rechten Umgang mit der heiligen Schrift: TrierTZ 99 (1990) 1-14.
1722 *Forestell* J. T., A view of the landscape [presidential address, 1989]: RelStT 8,1s (1988) 9-23.
1723 **Fowler** Alastair, Kinds of literature; an introduction to the theory of genres and modes. Ox 1987, Clarendon. viii-357 p. 0-19-812857-6.
1724 ᴱ**Friedman** R. E., *Williamson* H. G. M., The future of biblical studies; the Hebrew Scriptures 1987 ➤ 3,541; 5,1632: ᴿRelStT 8,1s (1988) 103s (P. G. *Mosca*).
1725 **Guillemette** Pierre, *Brisebois* Mireille, Introduction aux méthodes historico-critiques 1987 ➤ 3,1596 ... 5,1635: ᴿCritRR 2 (1989) 133s (J. I. *Hunt*); RTLv 21 (1990) 226s (C. *Focant*); TR 86 (1990) 191s (O. B. *Knoch*).
1726 **Guillemette** Pierre, *Brisebois* Mireille, Introduzione ai metodi storico-critici [1987 ➤ 3,1596], ᵀ*Valentino* C.: Studi e Ricerche Bibliche. R 1990, Borla. 452 p. 88-263-0727-X.
1727 *Hughes* John J., [➤ 972] Computers and the Bible: BAR-W 16,6 (1990) 62-68.

1728 **Johnson-Laird** Philip N., The computer and the mind; an introduction to cognitive science. CM 1988, Harvard Univ. 444 p. $29.50. – ᴿLanguage 65 (1989) 800-811 (S. R. *Anderson*).

1729 *Kugel* James L., The Bible in the university: ➤ 550, Hebrew Bible SD 1986/90, 143-165.

1729* *Landy* Francis, Humour as a tool for biblical exegesis [< JQR 28 (1980) 13-19]: ➤ 367, ᴱ*Radday*, Humour 1990, 99-115.

1730 **Linnemann** E., Historical criticism of the Bible; methodology or ideology? [Wissenschaft oder Meinung? Anfragen und Alternativen 1986], ᵀ*Yarbrough* R.W. GR 1990, Baker. 169 p. $10 pa. 0-8010-5662-4 [NTAbs 35,95: she contends that no truth or usefulness can come from historical-critical method, and renounces her earlier work on it].

1731 **Meynet** Roland, *a)* L'analyse rhétorique; une nouvelle méthode pour comprendre la Bible 1989 ➤ 5,1642: ᴿArTGran 53 (1990) 310s (A. S. *Muñoz*); Études 372 (1989) 713 (J.-N. *Aletti*); FgNt 3 (1990) 167s (J. *Mateos*); QVidCr 154 (1990) 125s (R. *Ribera-Marine*). – *b)* Initiation à la rhétorique biblique 1982 ➤ 63,1254s; 64,3934 ...: ᴿLVitae 44 (1989) 238s (P. *Mourlon Beernaert*).

1732 **Murrmann-Kahl** Michael, 'Religionsgeschichte' und 'Formgeschichte' in ihrer Genese im Kontext der Theologie und Geschichtswissenschaft des 19. und 20. Jahrhunderts: ev. Diss. ᴰ*Wagner* F. München 1990. – 557 p. – RTLv 22, p. 604.

1733 *Nielsen* Kirsten, Intertextuality and biblical scholarship [EAGLETON T., Literary theory 1983, 'political criticism']: ScandJOT (1990,2) 89-95.

1734 *Ozorowski* Edward, ⓟ Bibel – Väter – Theologie; methodologische Überlegungen: STWsz 28,1 (1990) 28-40; deutsch 40.

1735 *Panier* Louis, Lecture sémiotique et projet théologique; incidences et interrogations: RechSR 78 (1990) 199-220; Eng. 163.

1736 **Patrick** Dale, *Scult* Allen, Rhetoric and biblical interpretation [... applied to Job & Gn 1-3]: JStOT supp. 82. Sheffield 1990, Academic. 171 p. £22.50. 1-85075-222-2 [ExpTim 102,222].

1737 **Peck** John, *Coyle* Martin, Literary terms and criticism: How to study literature. Basingstoke 1990, Macmillan. x-177 p. 0-333-36271-3.

1738 *Prinsloo* W.S., Die historics-kritiese metode(s) in perspektief: Skrif-Kerk 9,2 (Pretoria 1988) 196-209 [< NTAbs 34,148].

1739 *a)* *Sevrin* J.M., L'exégèse critique comme discipline théologique; – *b)* *Gesché* Adolphe, Du dogme, comme exégèse: RTLv 21 (1990) 146-162 / 163-198; Eng. 279: two discourses to honor Prof. Joseph PONTHOT at his retirement, 6.X.1989 (p. 133-5, C. *Focant*; & 145).

1740 *Stachowiak* Lech, Stary Testament w świetle ostatnich badań krytycznych (AT in luce recentium investigationum): ➤ 546, RuBi 42 (1989) 1-10.

1741 **Stipp** Hermann-Josef, Textkritik – Literarkritik – Textentwicklung; Überlegungen zur exegetischen Aspektsystematik [... Jos 4,10; 1 K 8,65; Jer 29,14; Joh 7,53-8,11; – 2S 16,10s; 1S 26,14; – Ezech 5,2.12; Sach 11,17]: ETL 66 (1990) 143-159.

1742 ᴱ**Uffenheimer** B., *Reventlow* H., Creative biblical exegesis 1985/9 ➤ 4, 505; 5,1650: ᴿÉTRel 65 (1900) 265s (D. *Lys*).

1742* *Villegas Mathieu* Beltrán, El método de las ciencias bíblicas: TVida 30 (1989) 207-211.

1743 *a)* *Vorster* W.S., The in/compatibility of methods and strategies in reading or interpreting the OT; – *b)* *Nel* P.J., A critical perspective on OT exegetical methodology: OTEssays 2,3 (1989) 53-63 / 64-74.

1744 **Willmes** Bernd, Bibelauslegung — genau genommen; syntaktische, semantische und praktische Dimensionen und Kategorien für die sprachliche Analyse hebräischer und griechischer Texte auf Wort- und Satzebene: BibNot Beih 5. Mü 1990, Inst. B. Exegese. 100 p. DM 8 [TR 87,337].

1745 *Willmes* Bernd, 'Extreme Exegese'; Überlegungen zur Reihenfolge exegetischer Methoden: BibNot 53 (1990) 68-99.

1746 **Wink** Walter, Transforming Bible study² [¹1981 → 62,1181]. Nv 1990, Abingdon. 176 p. $11 [CBQ 52,783].

1747 *Zatelli* Ida, La chiamata dell'uomo da parte di Dio nella Bibbia al vaglio della 'discourse analysis': RivB 38 (1990) 13-25; Eng. 26.

III. Critica Textus, Versiones

D1 **Textual Criticism.**

1748 *Amphoux* C.-B. / *Jourjon* M., Le Centre Jean Duplacy pour l'étude des manuscrits de la Bible: BICLyon 89,113 (1989) 47-51 / 51s [< NTAbs 35,12].

1749 ᴱ**Barthélemy** Dominique, Critique textuelle I-II, 1982/6 → 63,1720... 5,1656: ᴿBZ 34 (1990) 113-6 (J. *Schreiner*).

1750 *Bartola* Alberto, ALESSANDRO VII e Athanasius KIRCHER S.J.; ricerche ed appunti sulla loro corrispondenza erudita e sulla storia di alcuni codici chigiani; → 475, ST 333 (1989) 7-107.

1751 *Bartoletti* Guglielmo, La scrittura romana nelle 'Tabellae defixionum' (saec. I a.C.-IV d.C.), note paleografiche: ScrCiv 14 (1990) 7-42 + 5 charts; 12 pl.

1752 *Bass* George F., A bronze-age writing diptych from the sea off Lycia: Kadmos 29 (1990) only p. 169; 1 fig. p. 168.

1753 *a) Bataillon* L. J., Exemplar, pecia, quaternus; – *b) Irigoin* J., Terminologie du livre et de l'écriture dans le monde byzantin: → 773, Vocabulaire 1987/9, 206-219 / 11-19 [< RHE 85, p. 197*].

1754 **Bat-Yehouda** Monique Z., Les papiers filigranés médiévaux; essai de méthodologie descriptive, I-II: Bibliologia 7s. Turnhout 1989, Brepols. 270 p.; ill. – ᴿAnnBoll 108 (1990) 226s (U. *Zanetti*).

1755 ᴱ**Becker** P. J., *Brandis* T., Glanz alter Buchkunst; mittelalterliche Handschriften der Staatsbibliothek Preussischer Kulturbesitz [Ausstellung 125 codices IX.-XVI. Jahrhundert, B - Brunschwig]. Wsb 1988, Reichert. 272 p.; 125 pl. DM 58. – ᴿRHE 85 (1990) 472 (M. *Haverals*).

1757 ᴱ**Blanchard** Alain, Les débuts du codex [colloquium Paris 3-4.VII.1985] 1989 → 5,778: ᴿJTS 41 (1990) 634-7 (J. N. *Birdsall*).

1758 **Brown** Michelle P., A guide to western historical scripts from antiquity to 1600. L/Toronto 1990, British Library/Univ. 144 p.; 55 fig. £18 [RHE 85,192*]. – ᴿManuscripta 34 (1990) 156.

1759 **Büll** Reinhard, Vom Wachs; Wachs als Beschreib- und Siegelstoff; Wachsschreibtafeln und ihre Verwendung. Fra 1968, Hoechst.

1760 ᴱ**Büsser** F., Early printed Bibles in microfiche [eventually 300, in 30 languages, 1450-1600]. Leiden 1989-, IDC Microform [SixtC 21 (1990) 234 adv.].

1761 *a) Canfora* Luciano, Le biblioteche ellenistiche; – *b) Fedeli* Paolo, Biblioteche private e pubbliche a Roma e nel mondo romano: → 89, Biblioteche² 1989, 5-28 / 29-64.

1762 *Cataldi Palau* Annaclara,   Une collection de manuscrits grecs du XVI
       siècle [... CHRYSOSTOME Hom. Mt./Cor]: Scriptorium 43 (Bru 1989) 35-75.
1763 *Cavallo* Guglielmo,   Libri, scritture, scribi, a Ercolano 1983 ➤ 1,1675*...
       5,1661:   ᴿCdÉ 65 (1990) 172-4 (J. *Lenaerts*).
1764 ᴱ**Cavallo** Guglielmo,   Le strade del testo 1987 ➤ 5,533*a*:   ᴿEmerita 58
       (1990) 146s (J. A. *Ochoa*); Maia 42 (1990) 184-6 (C. *Bevegni*).
1765 **Cavallo** G., *Maehler* H., Greek bookhands 1987 ➤ 5,1662:   ᴿAntClas 59
       (1990) 466s (J. A. *Straus*); Eos 77 (1989) 364-7 (Alina *Brzóstowska*); RÉG
       103 (1990) 353s (A. *Blanchard*).
1766 *Chasson* Timothy,   New uses for an old text in some early Tuscan
       Bibles: Manuscripta 33 (1989) 15-28.
1767 *Crown* Alan D.,   The morphology of paper in Samaritan manuscripts; a
       diachronic profile: BJRyL 71,1 (1989) 71-93; 19 fig.
1768 *Delange* E., *al.*,   Apparition de l'encre métallogallique en Égypte à partir
       de la collection de papyrus du Louvre: RÉgp 41 (1990) 213-7.
1769 ᴱ**Detienne** Marcel,   Les savoirs de l'écriture en Grèce ancienne 1988
       ➤ 5,538 ['de l'écrire']: ᴿAntClas 59 (1990) 457s (A. *Martin*).
1770 ᴱ**Detienne** M.,   Sapere e scrittura in Grecia [parte del raduno di Lilla
       1988, Les savoirs de l'écriture]. R 1989, Laterza. xxi-266 p. – ᴿElenchos
       11 (1990) 357s (G. *Giannantoni*).
1771 **Diethart** Johannes M., *Worp* Klaas A.,   Notarsunterschriften im By-
       zantinischen Ägypten: Mitt. Rainer NS 16. W 1986, Hollinek.   104 p.;
       fasc. of 59 pl. – ᴿCdÉ 65 (1990) 176 (J. *Bingen*).
1771* *a*) *Dotan* A.,   Masoretic rubrics of indicated origin in Codex Leningrad
       (B 19a); – *b*) *Fernández Tejero* E.,   Benedicti ARIAE MONTANI, De
       Mazzoreth ratione atque usu: ➤ 551, ᴱ*Revell*, 8. Kongress 1988/90, 37-44
       / 65-79.
1772 **Dukan** Michèle,   Réglure des manuscrits 1988 ➤ 5,1663:   ᴿSefarad 50
       (1990) 485s (N. *Fernández Tejero*).
1773 ᴱ**Dummer** Jürgen, Texte und Textkritik 1987 ➤ 3,489, DM 150:   ᴿTR 86
       (1990) 452s (G. D. *Kilpatrick*).
1774 *Edwards* Mark U.ᴶ,   Statistics on sixteenth century printing: ➤ 37*,
       ᶠCHRISMAN M., Process of change 1988, 149-163.
1775 Fälschungen im Mittelalter 1986/8 ➤ 4,1662*; 5,1665:   ᴿRTAM 57
       (1990) 287-290 (H. *Silvestre*).
1776 **Fikhman** I. F., ◉ Vvedenie v dokumentalnuyu papirologiyu. Moskva
       1987, Nauka. – ᴿArPapF 36 (1990) 81s [G. *Poethke*]; Enchoria 17 (1990)
       133s (auch G. *Poethke*); VDI 193 (1990) 201-4 (A. I. *Pavlovskaya* ◉).
1777 *Fitzgerald* W., 'Ocelli nominum'; names and shelf marks of famous/
       familiar manuscripts III: MdvSt 50 (1988) 333-348 [< RHE 85,193*].
1778 **Gallo** Italo,   Greek and Latin papyrology 1986 ➤ 2,1167: 4,1664; 5,1668;
       ᴿEos 77 (1989) 376-8 (Krystyna *Bartol*); JEA 76 (1990) 252 (R. S.
       Bagnall: devastating).
1779 ᴱ**Gamillscheg** E., *Harlfinger* D., Repertorium der griechischen Kopisten,
       800-1600, II. Handschriften aus Bibliotheken Frankreichs und Nachträge
       zu den Bibliotheken Grossbritanniens, A. Verzeichnis der Kopisten; B.
       (*Hunger* H.) Paläographische Charakteristika; C. Tafeln: Komm. By-
       zantinistik 3. W 1989, Österr. Akad.   227 p.; 202 p.; 308 p. [RHE 85,
       p. 193*].
1780 *Gasnault* P.,   Les supports et les instruments de l'écriture à l'époque
       médiévale: ➤ 773, Vocabulaire 1987/9, 20-33 [< RHE 85, p. 193*].
1781 *Gasparri* F.,   Lexicographie historique des écritures: ➤ 773, Vocabulaire
       1987/9, 100-110 [< RHE 85,194*].

1782 *a*) *Genest* J.-F., Le mobilier des bibliothèques d'après les inventaires médiévaux; – *b*) *Vezin* J., Le vocabulaire latin de la reliure au moyen âge; – *c*) *Laffitte* M.-P., Le vocabulaire médiéval de la reliure d'après les anciens inventaires; – *d*) *Bourgain* P., La naissance officielle de l'œuvre; l'expression métaphorique de la mise au jour: ➤ 773, Vocabulaire 1987/9, 136-154 / 56-60 / 61-78 / 195-205.

1783 ᴱ**Glénisson** Jean, Le livre au moyen âge 1988 ➤ 4,1666; 5,1669: ᴿRÉJ 149 (1990) 219s (J.-P. *Rothschild*).

1784 ᴱ**Goehring** James E., *al.*, The [Claremont] Crosby-Schoyen codex: CSCOr 521, subs. 85. Lv 1990, Peeters. lxiii-305 p. 0070-0844.

1785 **Grafton** Anthony, Forgers and critics; creativity and duplicity in Western scholarship: Juliet Gardiner books. L 1990, Collins & B. x-157 p. 1-85585-086-9.

1786 *Harrauer* Hermann, Neues aus der Wiener Papyrussammlung: Biblos 38 (1989) 89-93.

1787 **Harris** William V., Ancient literacy. CM 1989, Harvard Univ. xv-383 p.; 6 pl. $42. – ᴿCdÉ 65 (1990) 174s (A. *Wouters*: sans Nᴵᴇᴅᴅᴜ G. 1985).

1788 **Hoffmann** Hartmut, Buchkunst und Königtum im ottonischen und früh-salischen Reich; Mon. Germ. Hist. Schriften 30. Stu 1986, Hiersemann. xx-566 p. + vol. of 310 pl. DM 196 + 166. 3-7772-8640-9. – ᴿJEH 40 (1989) 409-411 (T. *Reuter*); Scriptorium 42 (1988) 266-9 (F. *Heintzer*).

1789 *Hugeux* Vincent, Les manuscrits bibliques roumains [de la Bibliothèque Universitaire de Bucarest avant l'incendie de 1989]: MondeB 64 (1990) 68 seule.

1790 **Hunger** Herbert, Schreiben und Lesen in Byzanz; die byzantinische Buchkultur 1989 ➤ 5,1673; 174 p.; DM 38; 3-406-44491-5: ᴿAevum 64 (1990) 321-3 (C. M. *Mazzucchi*); BySlav 51 (1990) 222s (Růžena *Dostálová*); JbÖstByz 40 (1990) 423-6 (K. *Treu*); Speculum 65 (1990) 702-4 (B. *Baldwin*); WienerSt 103 (1990) 282s (K. *Smolak*).

1791 ᴱ**Jemolo** Viviana, *Moralli* Mirella, Guida a una descrizione uniforme dei manoscritti e al loro censimento. R 1990, Ist. Catalogo Unico Bi-blioteche. 200 p.

1792 **Kaczynski** Bernice M., Greek in the Carolingian age; the St. Gall manuscripts: Speculum Anniv. Mg. 13. CM 1988, Medieval Academy. x-164 p.; $15; pa $8 [Manuscripta 35/1, 70].

1793 *Kvalheim* O. M., *al.*, A data-analytical examination of the Claremont profile method for classifying and evaluating manuscript evidence: Symbolae 63 (Oslo 1988) 132-...

1794 *Letis* Theodore P., The Protestant dogmaticians and the Late Princeton School on the status of the sacred apographa [faithful copies of the autograph Scriptures]: ScotBEv 8 (1990) 16-42.

1795 **Lemaire** Jacques, Introduction à la codicologie 1989 ➤ 5,1675: ᴿRBén 100 (1990) 550 (P.-M. *Bogaert*: une lacune comblée); RTAM 57 (1990) 277-9 (H. *Silvestre*).

1796 *McCormick* Michael, Writing materials, western European: ➤ 827*, DMA 12 (1989) 699-703.

1797 ᴱ**Maloy** Robert, *al.*, The Bible; 100 [text-history] landmarks from the E. P. Prothro collection. Dallas 1990, Bridwell Library, Southern Methodist Univ. No pagination; a few pl.; 6 p. index.

1798 ᴱ**Mandilaras** Vasileios G. [➤ 4,492 'Basil'], Proc. XVIII Congress of Papyrology 1986/8: ᴿRÉG 103 (1990) 307s (P. *Gauderlier*); WienerSt 103 (1990) 243-5 (J. M. *Diethart*).

1799 **Mazal** O., Lehrbuch der Handschriftenkunde 1986 ➤ 4,1672*a*: ᴿByZ 81 (1988) 299s (J. *Irigoin*).

1800 **Mazal** Otto, Zur Praxis des Handschriftenbearbeiters: ElemBuBi 11. Wsb 1987, Reichert. vi-196 p. DM 60. – ᴿScriptorium 43 (1989) 330-4 (Hedwig *Röckelein*).

1801 **Meltzer** Tova, Carl S. KNOPF and the I.A.C. tablet collection: OccP 11. Claremont CA 1987, Institute for Antiquity and Christianity. 36 p.

1803 *Mullins* Phil, Sacred text in an electronic age: BibTB 20 (1990) 99-106.

1804 *O'Dwyer* B. W., Celtic-Irish monasticism and early insular illuminated manuscripts: JRelHist 15 (1988s) 425-435.

1805 **Offenberg** A. K., (*Moed-Van Walraven* C.), Hebrew incunabula in public collections; a first international census: BibHumRef 47. Nieuwkoop 1990, De Graaf. lxxiv-214 p. 90-6004-404-5.

1806 *Palmer* N. F., Kapitel und Buch; zu den Gliederungsprinzipien mittelalterlicher Bücher: Frühmittelalterliche Studien 23 (1989) 43-88; 4 pl. [< RHE 85,192*].

1807 **Pavoncello** Nello, Le tipografie ebraiche minori a Venezia. R 1990, Veneziana. 78 p.; 7 fig.

1808 [*David* & *Van Groningen* B. A.], ⁵**Pestman** P. W., The new papyrological primer [¹1940, Eng. ²1946]. Leiden 1990, Brill. xxii-315 p. 90-04-09348-6.

1808* ᴱ**Piazzoni** Ambrogio M., *Vian* Paolo, Manoscritti Vaticani Latini 14666-15203, catalogo sommario: ST 332. Vaticano 1989, Biblioteca. xxviii-305 p. 88-210-0618-2.

1809 *Ricci Massabò* I, *Chiaberto* S., Un problema di metodo; l'esame dei cinquantadue esempi di scrittura nei suffragi per [l'abate] BOSONE: ➤ 639, La Novalesa 1981/8, 63-76; 3 maps.

1810 *Richard* Francis, Achille de HARLAY de Sancy et ses collections de manuscrits hébreux [Oratoire de Paris 1611-]: RÉJ 149 (1990) 417-442 + 13 fig.

1811 **Richards** Mary P., Texts and their traditions in the medieval library of Rochester cathedral priory: AmPhTr 78/3. Ph 1988. xii-129 p. – ᴿRHE 85 (1990) 395-400 (G. *Fransen*).

1812 **Robinson** James M., The Pachomian monastic library at the Chester Beatty library and the Bibliothèque Bodmer: OccP 19. Claremont CA 1990, Institute for Antiquity and Christianity. 27 p.

1813 *Ruysschaert* José, Les manuscrits hébraïques vaticans; corrections et additions à la liste de 1968 [*Alloy* N., Jerusalem]: ST 333 ➤ 475, ᶠ*Buonocore* M., Miscellanea III 1989, 357-360.

1814 *Saenger* Paul, The separation of words and the order of words; the genesis of medieval reading: ScrCiv 14 (1990) 49-74; 2 pl.

1815 **Schreiner** P., Codices Vat. gr. 867-932, 1988 ➤ 5,1684: ᴿJbÖsByz 40 (1990) 480-7 (H. *Hunger*).

1816 **Seider** Richard, Paläographie der griechischen Papyri 3/1, Urkundenschrift 1. Stu 1990, Hiersemann. xii-422 p. 3-7772-8943-4.

1817 [*Shanks* H.] Bible for a king; J. Paul Getty II reunites abducted Bible manuscripts: BR 5,5 (1989) 42-44; the cover photo of David, attributed to Gérard *David* [1460-1523; detail from his 'Genealogy of the Virgin'] is really from Egbert's Psalter [= / or] 10th century Udine Duomo: BR 6,1 (1990) 6 does not say which.

1818 *Skeat* T. C., Roll versus codex — a new approach? [example of a roll that rolled itself up after 1500 years confirms his ᶠMONTEVECCHI O. (1978) 373]: ZPapEp 84 (1990) 297s.

1819 **Spatharakis** Ioannis, The left-handed evangelist; a contribution to Palaeologan iconography. L 1988, Pindar. 110 p.; 132 fig. 0-907132-49-9. – ᴿJbÖsByz 40 (1990) 493-5 (H. *Hunger*).

1820 *Starr* Raymond J., The [scarcely existent] used-book trade in the Roman world: Phoenix 44 (Toronto 1990) 148-157.

1821 *Stipp* Hermann-J., Das Verhältnis von Textkritik und Literarkritik in neueren alttestamentlichen Veröffentlichungen [BARTHÉLEMY D., TOV E. ... BARTH-STECK, SCHWIENHORST L.]: BZ 34 (1990) 16-37.

1822 **Thorp** Nigel, The glory of the page; mediaeval and Renaissance illuminated manuscripts, Glasgow Univ. Library. L 1987, H. Miller. 228 p.; 42 color facsimiles + others. $48. – ᴿSpeculum 65 (1990) 767s (K. *Gould*).

1823 *Trebolle Barrera* Julio, El texto [y versiones] de la Biblia [en España, *Sánchez Caro* J. M.]: → 370*, Introd. I, 1990, 433-552 [-574].

1824 **Turner** Eric G., ²ʳᵉᵛ*Parsons* P. J., Greek manuscripts of the ancient world 1987 → 4,1680; 5,1687: ᴿKlio 72 (1990) 614-6 (K. *Treu*, auch über CAVALLO-MAEHLER); Mnemosyne 43 (1990) 187-9 (S. R. *Slings*).

1825 ᴱ**Vian** Paolo, La 'raccolta prima' degli autografi FERRAJOLI; introduzione, inventario e indice: ST 336. Vaticano 1990, Biblioteca. xxv-273 p. 88-210-0622-0.

1826 **Wendland** Henning. Die Buchillustration, von den Frühdrucken bis zur Gegenwart. Stu-Aarau 1987, AT-Verlag. 208 p.; 153 (color.) fig. Fs 94. – ᴿDLZ 111 (1990) 621-3 (K. *Kratzsch*).

1827 **Wilson** Nigel G., Scholars of Byzantium [→ 64,1709]. L/Baltimore 1983, Duckworth/Johns Hopkins Univ. ix-283 p. – ᴿJAOS 110 (1990) 167s (S. P. *Cowe*).

D2.1   *Biblia hebraica,* **Hebrew text.**

1828 *Brettler* Marc, Old Testament manuscripts from Qumran to Leningrad: BR 6,4 (1990) 40-42; ill.

1829 *Busi* O., I manoscritti ebraici della Scrittura copiati a Roma tra Due e Trecento: → 154, ᶠSACCHI P. 1990, 535-543.

1830 **Cassuto** Philippe, Qere-Ketib et listes massorétiques dans le manuscrit B 19a: JudUmw 26. Fra 1989, Lang. 289 p. Fs 29. 3-631-42168-0 [BL 91,44, P. *Wernberg-Møller*].

1831 *Chiesa* Bruno, Appunti di storia della critica del testo dell'Antico Testamento ebraico: Henoch 12 (1990) 3-14; Eng. 14.

1832 *Craig* Kenneth E.ᴶ, The corrections of the scribes [Mekilta Ex 15,7; Sipre Num 10,35 and 16 others]: PerspRelSt 17 (1990) 155-165.

1832* *Deist* F.E., Is die Massoretiese teks die Ou Testament?: SkrifK 10 (1989) 9-20 [< OTAbs 14,3].

1833 **Jakerson** Semen M., Ⓖ Hebrew incunabula... Moscow, Leningrad 1988 → 3,969; 4,a224: ᴿFolOr 27 (1990) 270s (E. *Lipiński*).

1834 **Khan** G., Karaite Bible manuscripts from the Cairo Genizah: Genizah series 9. C 1990, Univ. xv-186 p.; 17 pl. £55. 0-521-39227-6 [BL 91,47, J. F. A. *Sawyer*].

1835 **McCarter** P. K., Textual criticism; recovering the text of the Hebrew Bible 1986 → 2,1192... 4,1686: ᴿJJS 41 (1990) 263s (J. *Hughes*).

1836 *Rabe* Norbert, Zur synchron definierten alttestamentlichen Textkritik: BibNot 52 (1990) 64-97.

1837 **Róth** E., *Prijs* L., Hebräische Handschriften: Verzeichnis der orientalischen Handschriften in Deutschland 6 [I 1982] 2. Wiesbaden 1990, Steiner. xxii-206 p. DM 118 [NRT 113,913, X. *Jacques*: vol. 3 prévu].

1839 **Sed-Rajna** Gabrielle, The Hebrew Bible in medieval illuminated manuscripts. NY 1987, Rizzoli. 176 p.; 120 pl. + 60 color. $85.

1840 — *Wieck* Roger S., Visual glories; the Hebrew Bible in medieval manuscripts: BR 5,2 (1989) 29-32 [alludes to alleged prohibition of images, but most of the illustrations do not show the human head replaced by animal, as is the suggested solution].

1841 **Wonneberger** Reinhard, Understanding BHS; a manual for the users of Biblia Hebraica Stuttgartensia[2] corrected and recomposed [[1]1984 ➤ 65,1484]: SubsBPont 8. R 1990, Pont. Ist. Biblico. xii-104 p. 88-7653-5780.

1842 **Würthwein** Ernst, Text des AT[5] 1988 ➤ 4,1697; 5,1711: [R]RÉJ 149 (1990) 188s (A. *Caquot*); SvEx 55 (1990) 115s (L. *Eriksson*).

D2.2   Targum.

1843 **Díez Macho** A., Targum palaestinense in Pentateuchum I. Genesis 1988 ➤ 4,1700: [R]OLZ 85 (1990) 680-2 (G. *Stemberger*).

1844 **Grossfeld** B., *a*) A bibliography of Targum literature 3 [1024 more items]. NY 1990, Sepher-Hermon. XX-91 p. $39.50. 0-87203-133-2 [NTAbs 35,265]. – *b*) Targum Onqelos Gn-Dt 1988 ➤ 4,1703; 5,1719: [R]CritRR 2 (1989) 371s (S. *Kaufmann*).

1845 **Harrington** Daniel J., *Saldarini* A., Targum Jonathan 1987s ➤ 3,1686; 4,1703*: [R]CritRR 3 (1990) 343-8 (E. M. *Cook*, also on Is-Jer-Ezck, some 20 corrections for each); TorJT 6 (1990) 371-5 (E. G. *Clarke*, severe).

1846 **Klein** Michael, Geniza manuscripts of Palestinian Targum to the Pentateuch 1986 ➤ 2,1298 ... 5,1723: [R]BO 74 (1990) 199-203 (B. *Grossfeld*); JStJud 21 (1990) 121-3 (F. *García Martínez*); Lešonenu 53 (1988s) 141-4 (Joshua *Blau*, ◑; Eng. XI).

1847 *a*) Le *Déaut* Roger, The Targumim; – *b*) *Purvis* James D., The Samaritans: ➤ 835, CHJud 2 (1989) 563-590 / 591-613.

1848 **Levine** Etan, The Aramaic version of the Bible; contents and context: BZAW 174, 1988 ➤ 4,1706; 5,1725: [R]BL (1990) 45 (R. P. *Gordon*); CBQ 52 (1990) 525s (M. *Aberbach*); CritRR 3 (1990) 351s (B. *Chilton*); JTS 41 (1990) 147-9 (M. *Casey*).

1849 **Nutt** John W., Fragments of a Samaritan Targum. Hildesheim 1980 = 1874, Olms. vii-172 p. + ◑ 84 p. 3-487-06927-X.

1850 *Samely* Alexander, What Scripture does *not* say; interpretation through contrast in Targum Pseudo-Jonathan: ➤ 146, [F]REINELT H., At. Botschaft 1990, 251-283.

1851 *Shinan* Avigdor, Dating Targum Pseudo-Jonathan; some more comments; JJS [40 (1989) 7-30, *Hayward* R.] 41 (1990) 57-61.

1852 *Somekh* Alberto, Il Targum Onqelos, traduzione o tradizione? ➤ 700, Tradizione 1989/90, 135-150.

D3.1   *Textus graecus* – Greek NT.

1853 *Aland* Barbara, Neutestamentliche Textforschung und Textgeschichte; Erwägungen zu einem notwendigen Thema: NTS 36 (1990) 337-358.

1854 *Aland* B., Die Münsteraner Arbeit am Text des Neuen Testaments und ihr Beitrag für die frühe Überlieferung des II. Jhts.; eine methodologische Betrachtung: ➤ 549, Gospel traditions 1988/90, 55-70.

1855 **Aland** K. & B., Der Text des NTs²*rev* [¹1982 ➤ 63,1795]. Stu 1989, Bibelges. 374 p.; Eng.² (ᵀ*Rhodes* E.) GR/Leiden 1989, Eerdmans/Brill. xviii-366 p. – ᴿNT 32 (1990) 374-9 (J. K. *Elliott*).

1856 **Aland** K. & B., Text of the NT 1987 ➤ 3,1667... 5,1730: ᴿInterpretation 44 (1990) 71-75 (E. J. *Epp*: indispensable but flawed); SvEx 55 (1990) 133s (R. *Kieffer*).

1857 *Aland* Kurt, Der neutestamentliche Text in der vorkonstantinischen Epoche: ➤ 135, ᶠORBE A., Compostellanum 34 (1989) 9-35.

1858 *Aland* Kurt, Die Grundurkunde des Glaubens; ein Bericht über 40 Jahre Arbeit an ihrem Text [< Kunst-Stiftung 1985 ➤ 2,1214*]: ➤ 193, Supplementa 1990, 1-61.

1859 *Aland* Kurt, Il testo della Chiesa [TrinJ ➤ 5,1733], ᵀ: Lux Biblica 1,2 (Roma 1990) 3-28 [< NTAbs 35,12].

1860 *a) Birdsall* J. N., The Western text in the IInd century; – *b) Koester* H., The text of the Synoptic Gospels in the IInd cent.; – *c) Wisse* F., The nature and purpose of redactional changes in early Christian texts; the canonical Gospels; – *d) Delobel* J., Extra-canonical sayings of Jesus; Marcion and some 'non-received' logia; ➤ 549, Gospel traditions 1988/90, 3-17 / 19-37 / 39-53 / 105-116.

1861 *Busto Sáiz* José Ramón, El texto luciánico en el marco del pluralismo textual; estado de la cuestión y perspectivas: EstE 65 (1990) 3-18.

1862 **Comfort** Philip W., Early manuscripts and modern translations of the NT. Wheaton IL 1990, Tyndale. xx-235 p.; 14 pl. $20 [RelStR 17, 362, B. D. *Ehrman*: errors].

1863 **Daniels** Jon B., The Egerton gospel [Greek papyrus]; its place in early Christianity: diss. ᴰ*Robinson* J. M. Claremont 1989. – RelStR 17,194.

1864 **Dunn** Mark R., An examination of the textual character of Codex Ephraemi Syri Rescriptus (C, 04) in the four gospels: diss. SW Baptist Theol. Sem. 1990. 240 p. 90-33446. – DissA 51 (1990s) 2409s-A.

1865 **Elliott** J. K., A bibliography of [the 5442] Greek NT manuscripts: SNTS Mg 62, 1989 ➤ 5,1738: ᴿClasR 40 (1990) 151s (J. N. *Birdsall*); ExpTim 101 (1989s) 29s (J. *Muddiman*); JTS 41 (1990) 209-212 (also J. N. *Birdsall*).

1866 *Epp* Eldon J., The significance of the papyri for determining the nature of the NT text in the 2d century; a dynamic view of textual transmission: ➤ 549, Gospel traditions 1989, 71-103.

1867 *Head* Peter M., Observations on early papyri of the Synoptic Gospels, especially on the 'scribal habits': Biblica 71 (1990) 240-7.

1868 *Kilpatrick* G. D., *a)* The transmission of the NT and its reliability [< Victoria Institute 1957 = BTrans 9 (1958) 127-136]; – *b)* The Greek NT text of today and the Textus Receptus [< Mem. *MacGregor* H. 1965, 189-208]: ➤ 257, Principles 1990, 3-14 / 33-52.

1869 *a) Letis* T. P., The ecclesiastical text redivivus?; – *b) Johnston* P. J., The textual character of the Textus Receptus (received text) where it differs from the majority text in the Gospels of Matthew and Mark: BRefB 1,2 (Fort Wayne 1990) 1-4 / 4-9 [< NTAbs 35,143].

1870 **Merk** A., ᴱ*Barbaglio* G., Nuovo Testamento greco e italiano. Bo 1990, Dehoniane. 47*-858 p. 88-10-80672-2.

1871 *O'Callaghan* José, Papyri manuscripts of the Gospels: ➤ 370, Gospels Today 1990, 13-26.

1872 **Parker** David C., Codex Bezae, an early Christian manuscript and its text: diss. Leiden 1990, ᴰ*Jonge* M. de. – TsTNijm 31,91; RTLv 22, p. 594.

ᴱ**Petersen** William L., Gospel traditions in the second century 1988/9 ➤ 549.

1873 **Petzer** Ja(-Kobus) H.,   Die teks van die Nuwe Testament, 'n Inleiding in die basiese aspekte van die teorie en praktyk van die tekskritiek van die NT: HervTSt supp 2.   Pretoria 1990, NduitsHervKerk.   xviii-353 p.   0-620-14761-X [NTAbs 34,379].

1874 *Petzer* J. H.,   a) Author's style and the textual criticism of the New Testament: Neotestamentica 24,2 ('The language of the New Testament' 1990) 185-197 [391-7, residence-addresses of members of NT Society of South Africa]; – b) A survey of the developments in the textual criticism of the Greek New Testament since UBS³: Neotestamentica 24,1 (1990) 71-92.

1875 *Strothmann* Werner,   Die Handschriften der Evangelien in der Versio [= Textform, nicht Übersetzung] Heraclensis: ➤ 8*, ᶠASSFALG J. 1990, 367-375.

1876 *Taylor* Bernard A.,   Evaluating minority variants within families of Greek manuscripts: BSeptCog 23 (1990) 31-38.

1877 **Westcott** B. F., *Hort* F. J. A.,   Introduction to the New Testament in the original Greek.   Peabody MA 1988 = 1882, Hendrickson. xxxiii-324 + 188 p.   0-913573-94-1. – ᴿRThom 90 (1990) 141s (L. *Devillers*).

D3.2   *Versiones graecae* –   **VT, Septuaginta etc.**

1877* a) *Barr* Robert,   'Guessing' in the Septuagint; – b) *Soisalon-Soininen* I.,   Zurück zur Hebräismenfrage; – c) *Tov* E.,   Renderings of combinations of the infinitive absolute and finite verbs in the LXX — their nature and distribution; – d) *Fernández Marcos* Natalio,   Some reflections on the Antiochian text of the Septuagint; – e) *Smend* R.,   Der geistige Vater des Septuaginta-Unternehmens [R. SMEND senior]: ➤ 70, ᶠHANHART R., 1990, 19-34 / 35-51 / 64-73 / 219-229 / 332-344.

1878 *Bogaert* Pierre-Maurice,   La Septante, passage obligé entre l'exégèse biblique et les autres disciplines de la théologie: RICathP 29 (1989) 63-78.

1879 **Cousin** R.,   La Bible grecque; la Septante: CahÉv supp   P 1990, Cerf. 115 p. F 45.   0222-9706 [NTAbs 35,263].

1880 *Dufresne* Suzy,   À propos de la Bible de la reine Christine [10ᵉ s., Vat. Reg. gr. 1]: Bulletin Antiquaires de France (1988) 176-180; pl. VI.

1881 *Fernández Marcos* N.,   Simmaco [mm siempre] y sus predecesores judíos: ➤ 154, ᶠSACCHI P. 1990, 193-202.

1882 *Greenspoon* L. J.,   Mission to Alexandria; truth and legend about the creation of the Septuagint, the first Bible translation: BR 5,4 (1989) 34-37.40-41.

1882* a) *Hanhart* Robert,   The translation of the Septuagint in light of earlier tradition and subsequent influences; – b) *Collins* Nina L.,   281 B.C.E., the year of the translation of the Pentetuech into Greek under Ptolemy II; – c) *Brock* Sebastian P.,   To revise or not to revise; attitudes to Jewish biblical translation; – d) *Hanson* Anthony †,   The treatment of the LXX on the theme of seeing God; – e) *Ulrich* Eugene C.,   The Septuagint manuscripts from Qumran; a reappraisal of their value; – f) *Grabbe* Lester L.,   The translation techniques of the Greek minor versions; translations or revisions?: ➤ 519, Septuagint, Scrolls 1990/2, 339-379 / 403-503 / 301-338 / 557-568 / 505-556.

1883 **Harl** M., *al.*,   La Bible grecque des Septante 1988 ➤ 4,1732; 5,1756: ᴿLavalTP 46 (1990) 246s (P.-H. *Poirier*, aussi sur Lév.); RHPR 70 (1990) 251s (M.-A. *Chevallier*).

1884 *Harl* Marguerite,   La place de la Septante dans les études bibliques [conférence 24.I.1989, Soc. Hist. Protestantisme Français]:   ÉTRel 65 (1990) 161-9.

1885 *Kaczynski* Bernice M.,   Greek in the Carolingian age; the St. Gall manuscripts [alphabets, grammars, glossaries, Bibles, and liturgies]: Speculum Anniv. Mg. 13.   CM 1988, Medieval Academy of America. x-164 p.; 7 facsimiles. $15; $9 pa. – ᴿSpeculum 65 (1990) 708-711 (D. *Ganz*).

1886 *Müller* M.,   Translatio et interpretatio; om den antikke bibeloversættelses væsen: DanTTs 53 (1990) 260-277 [< NTAbs 35,219].

1887 **Olofsson** Staffan,   The LXX version; a guide to the translation technique of the Septuagint: ConBib OT 30.   Sto c. 1990, Almqvist & W.   viii-105 p.   Sk 122.   91-2201-392-X [BL 91,48, B. *Lindars* without date: the preliminary appraisal he had to make for his ᴰGod is my rock ➤ 9279].

1888 *Orlinsky* Harry M.,   The Septuagint and its Hebrew text: ➤ 835, CHJud 2 (1989) 534-562.

1889 *Paul* G.,   Un centenaire à rappeler; l'édition sixtine des Septante: ➤ 511, Théorie/pratique 1988/90, 413-428.

1890 **Rehkopf** Friedrich,   Septuaginta-Vokabular 1989 ➤ 5,1758:   ᴿTLZ 115 (1990) 670s (T. *Holtz*).

1891 **Sailhamer** John H.,   The translational technique of the Greek Septuagint for the Hebrew verbs and participles in Psalms 3-41: Studies in biblical Greek.   NY 1990, Lang.   325 p. DM 64 [TR 87,250].

1892 *a) Schwartz* Joseph,   Traductions en Égypte gréco-romaine; – *b) Paul* André,   Traductions grecques de la Bible avant la Septante?: ➤ 111, ᶠLÉVÊQUE P., 2 (1989) 379-385 / 4 (1990) 315-328.

1893 *Steyn* G. J.,   *a)* Die ou Griekse vertaling (Septuagint), I. 'n Kort oorsig oor die moontlike ontstaansgeskiedenis: TEv 22,2 (Pretoria 1989) 9-18 [< NTAbs 34,91]; – *b)* Die ou Griekse vertaling (Septuagint) II. 'n Kort oorsig oor die ontwikkelingsgeskiedenis en bestaande teksteorieën: TEv 22,3 (1989) 2-13 [< NTAbs 34,225]; – *c)* Die stand van LXX-navorsing in Suid-Afrika (1978-1989) en die belang hiervan vir die Nuwe-Testamentiese wetenskap: TEv 23,2 (Pretoria 1990) 7-14 [< OTAbs 14,13].

   Tov E.,   The Greek Minor Prophets scroll from Nahal Ḥever [≅ Barthélemy's *kaige*] 1990 ➤ 4033.

1894 **Tov** Emanuel,   A computerized data base for Septuagint studies; parallel aligned text: CATSS 2, 1986 ➤ 4,1742; 5,1760:   ᴿJQR 81 (1990s) 166-8 (A. *Groves*); NedTTs 43 (1989) 143s (E. *Talstra*).

1894* *Waard* Jan de,   Old Greek translation techniques and the modern translator: BTrans 41 (1990) 311-9.

D4   **Versiones orientales.**

1895 *Baarda* Tjitze,   Diaphōnía - symphōnía; factors in the harmonization of the Gospels, especially in the Diatessaron of TATIAN: ➤ 549, Gospel 1989, 133-156.

1896 *Cook* J.,   Recent developments in Peshitta research: JNWS 15 (1989) 39-54.

1897 ᴱ**Dirksen** P. B., *Mulder* M. J., The Peshiṭta 1985/8 ➤ 4,480; 5,1762: ᴿJSS 35 (1990) 518s (R.F. *Gordon*); JTS 41 (1990) 640-2 (R.P.R. *Murray*).

1898 **Dirksen** P. B.,   Annotated bibliography of Peshiṭta OT 1989 ➤ 5,987: ᴿBS 147 (1990) 496s (R. A. *Taylor*); JStJud 21 (1990) 104-8 (S. P. *Brock*).

1899 *Dirksen* P. B.,   [Samuel] LEE's editions of the Syriac Old Testament and the Psalms, 1822-1826: ➤ 563, OTS 26 (1988/90) 63-71.

1899* a) *Dirksen* Peter B.,   The Leiden Peshitta edition; – b) *Perrier* Pierre, Structures orales de la Pešīttā; leurs variantes chez les Pères syriaques: ► 799*, Symposium 5 1988/90, 31-38 / 39-52.

1900 **Strothmann** Werner,   Wörterverzeichnis der apokryphen-deuterokano- nischen Schriften des Alten Testaments in der Peshiṭta: GöOrF 1/37, 1988 ► 4,752; DM 86:   ᴿJSS 35 (1990) 160s (S. *Brock*); ZDMG 140 (1990) 158 (R. *Degen*).

1901 **Bouvarel-Boud'hors** Anne,   Bibl. Nat. Catalogue des fragments coptes I. bibliques, P 1987 ► 4,1753; 5,1764;   ᴿEnchoria 17 (1990) 167s (K. *Schüssler*).

1902 *Emmel* Stephen,   Coptic biblical texts in the Beinecke library: JCopt 1 (1990) 13-28 (Yale: Jg 9,7-19; Jos 7,1-3; Ps 77s; Prov 20s; Dan 8s; Joel 2,19s).

1903 a) *Brashear* William, *Satzinger* Helmut,   Ein akrostischer griechischer Hymnus mit koptischer Übersetzung (Wagner-Museum K 1003); – b) *Browne* Gerald M.,   A Coptic Vorlage for an Old Nubian text: ► 46b, ꟳELANSKAJA Alla I. = JCopt 1 (1990) 37-58; pl. 5-6 / 137-9.

1904 *O'Callaghan* José,   Un codice copto con tre vangeli: CC 141 (1990,4) 483-5.

1905 **Schmitz** F.-J., *Mink* G.,   Liste der koptischen Handschriften des NTs, 2/I, sahid. Ev I., 1989 ► [1,1242 ...] 5,1768:   ᴿEnchoria 17 (1990) 175s (K. *Schüssler*); KerkT 41 (1990) 255s (R. van den *Broek*); NRT 112 (1990) 591s (X. *Jacques*); NT 32 (1990) 96 (J. K. *Elliott*); OLZ 82 (1991) 21-25 (H.-M. *Schenke*); OrChrPer 56 (1990) 212-4 (*Khalil Samir*).

1906 **Zuurmond** R.,   Novum Testamentum aethiopice; The Synoptic Gospels, general introduction — Edition of the Gospel of Mark: ÄthFor 27.   Stu 1989, Steiner.   xv-288 p.; 406 p. [FgNt 4/7, 91]; ᴿOrChrPer 56 (1990) 502 (G. *Raineri*).

1907 **Minassian** Martiros,   a) Synopse des Évangiles en arménien classique. Genève 1986, Fond. Ghoukassiantz.   172 p. – b) Die Textvarianten im Tetraevangeliar cod. 608 der Mechitaristen-Bibkliothek zu Wien: Na- tionalbibliothek 229.   W 1989, Mechitaristen.   80 p.

1908 **Nersessian** Vrej,   Armenian illustrated Gospel-Books.   L 1987, British Library.   x-100 p. £15. – ᴿBSO 52 (1989) 154s (D. M. *Lang*).

1909 **Renoux** Charles,   Le lectionnaire de Jérusalem en Arménie, Le Casoc', I. Introduction et liste des manuscrits: PatrOr 44/4, nº 200.   Turnhout 1989, Brepols.   p. 416-551. – ᴿBLitEc 91 (1990) 239 (A.-G. *Martimort*).

1910 **Schmidt** Karl H.,   Zur Wiedergabe aktiver griechischer Partizipialkon- struktionen in den altarmenischen und altgeorgischen Bibelübersetzungen: ► 8*, ꟳASSFALG J. 1990, 299-302.

1911 *Mgaloblishvili* Tamila,   Juden und Christen in Georgien in den ersten christlichen Jahrhunderten: ► 506*, Juden/Christen 1989/90, 94-100.

1911* *Songulashvili* Malkhaz V.,   The translation of the Bible into [modern] Georgian: BTrans 41 (1990) 131-4.

1912 Al-Kitābu 'l-Muqaddas.   Beirut 1989, Dar al-Mashriq.   2031 p. + 893 p.; maps.

1913 *Pollock* James W.,   Two Christian Arabic manuscripts [one a psalter

916 A.D., followed by nine Canticles (Magnificat etc.) called Surahs]: JAOS 110 (1990) 330s.

1914 *Gryson* Roger, La version gotique des évangiles; essai de réévaluation: RTLv 21 (1990) 3-31; Eng. 144.

D5 Versiones latinae.

1915 **Bischoff** Bernhard, Latin palaeography; antiquity and the Middle Ages [c. 1981, ²1986], ᵀ⁽ʳᵉᵛ·⁾ *Ó Cróinin* Dáibhi, *Ganz* David. C 1990, Univ. xii-291 p.; 23 pl. £35 [RHE 85,556].
1916 *Bogaert* P.-M., *Gryson* R., Centre de recherches sur la Bible latine; rapport d'activité 1989: RTLv 21 (1990) 137-140.
1917 **Boyle** Leonard E., Medieval Latin palaeography, a bibliographical introduction 1984 → 3,1734: ᴿFaventia 10 (1988) 187s (J. *Alturo i Perucho*).
1918 *Brown* M.P., A new fragment of a ix-th-cent. English Bible [...? *in* English]: → 5,1877, Anglo-Saxon England 18 (1989) 33-43 [< RHE 85, p. 193*].
1919 **Fischer** Bonifatius, Lateinische Bibelhandschriften: LatBGesch 11s, 1985s → 1,173; 2,156.1272: ᴿRCatalT 13 (1988) 243s (M. *Gros i Pujol*).
   Fischer B., Die lateinischen Evangelien bis zum 10. Jahrhundert; 3. Varianten zu Lukas 1990 → 5362.
1920 *García de la Fuente* Olegario, El latín bíblico y el latín cristiano: coincidencias y discrepancias: → 761, Helmantica 49 (1987/9) 45-67.
1921 **García-Moreno** Antonio, La Neovulgata; precedentes y actualidad 1986 → 2,1274... 4,1769: ᴿStLeg 31 (1990) 286 (C. de *Villapadierna*).
1922 *González Luis* Francisco, Los cambios de género gramatical en las antiguas versiones latinas de la Biblia; → 761, Helmantica 40 (1987/9) 303-310.
1923 *Gould* Karen, The recovery of a fifteenth-century Flemish Book of Hours [Austin HRC 2]: Scriptorium 43 (Bru 1989) 76-100; pl. 9-12.
1924 **Grimme** Ernst G., Das Evangeliar von Gross Sankt Martin; ein Kölner Bilderzyklus des hohen Mittelalters [jetzt Brüssel]. FrB 1989, Herder. 111 p.; 16 fig. + 32 color. DM 78. – ᴿZkT 112 (1990) 489s (H.B. *Meyer*).
1925 ᴱ**Gryson** R., *Bogaert* P., Recherches sur l'histoire de la Bible latine 1986/7 → 3,544: ᴿRÉAug 35 (1989) 181s (J. *Doignon*).
1926 **Guderian** Gregory A., The palaeography of later Roman cursive: diss. Toronto 1990, ᴰ*Boyle* L. – DissA 51 (1990s) 3491s-A.
1927 *Haendler* Gert, Neue Editionen lateinischer Texte 1988/9 [Vetus Latina Beuron; SChr; CC]: TLZ 115 (1990) 313-7.
1928 *a) Herren* M.W., Evidence for a 'vulgar Greek' from early medieval Latin texts and manuscripts; – *b) Berschin* W., Greek elements in medieval Latin manuscripts: → 4,h971*, Nectar 1988, 57-84 / 85-104; 16 pl.
1929 **Kötzsche** Dietrich, Das Evangeliar Heinrichs des Löwen. Fra 1989, Insel. 145 p.; 16 pl.: ᴿGGA 242 (1990) 34-79 (J. *Fried*: 'Das goldglänzende Buch').
1930 ᵀᴱ**Labriola** Albert C., *Smeltz* John W., The Bible of the poor = Biblia pauperum; a facsimile and edition of the British Library blockbook C.9 d.2. Pittsburgh 1990, Duquesne Univ. ix-190 p. $38; pa. $20. 0-8207-0229-3; -30-7 [TDig 38,48].

1931 **Light** Laura, The Bible in the twelfth century; an exhibition of [39] manuscripts at the Houghton Library. CM 1988, Harvard. 114 p.; 25 pl. – ᴿSpeculum 65 (1990) 456-8 (P. *Verdier*, with no mention of what language).

1932 **NcNamara** Martin, Studies on texts of early Irish Latin gospels, A.D. 600-1200: Instrumenta patristica 20. Steenbrugge/Dordrecht 1990, St. Pietersabdij/Kluwer. xv-248 p. Fb 2200 [RHE 85, p. 210*].

1933 *Nolden* Reiner, Über die Reste einer nordwestfranzösischen Bibel aus der Karolingerzeit in der Stadtbibliothek Trier: Scriptorium 43 (1989) 239-247 [< RHE 85,355*].

1934 *Parker* D.C., A copy of the Codex Mediolanensis [a copy of Jn 13,1-18,36 is in the middle of Quere 39]: JTS 41 (1990) 537-541.

1935 *Popović* Vladislav, Sur l'origine de l'Évangéliaire latin de la British Library, Harley 1775: CRAI (1990) 709-735; 10 fig.

1936 *Strohm* Stefan, Die Bibel mit dem Brustbild des Herzogs Christoph von Württemberg: → 156, ᶠSCHAFER G., BLWKG 88 (1988) 124-177.

1937 **Supino Martini** Paola, Roma e l'area grafica romanesca (secoli X-XII): ScrCiv Bibl. 1. Alessandria 1987, Orso. 432 p. 80 pl. – ᴿScriptorium 43 (1989) 156-8 (R. *Étaix*).

D5.5 *Citationes apud Patres* – **the Patristic Bible.**

1938 Biblia patristica 4. Eusèbe ... 1987 → 4,1787: ᴿRHE 85 (1990) 209 (R. *Aubert*).

1939 *Deun* Peter Van, Un mémoire anonyme sur saint Barnabé [apôtre] (BHG 226e), édition et traduction: AnBoll 108 (1990) 323-335.

1940 *Dolbeau* François, Une liste latine de disciples et d'apôtres traduite sur la recension grecque de Pseudo-Dorothée: AnBoll 108 (1990) 51-70.

1941 **Jefford** Clayton N., The sayings of Jesus in the Teaching of the Twelve Apostles: VigChr supp 11. Leiden 1989, Brill. xvi-185 p. 90-04-09127-0.

1942 *Troncarelli* Pietro, Un codice con note autografe di GIOACCHINO da Fiore (Vat. Barb. Lat. 627): Scriptorium 43 (Bru 1989) 3-34, pl. 1-8.

D6 **Versiones modernae .1** *romanicae,* **romance.**

1943 ᴱ**Casalis** G., *Roussel* B., OLIVÉTAN traducteur 1985/7 → 3,527; 5,1801: ᴿRHPR 70 (1990) 380s (M. *Lienhard*).

1944 Bible chrétienne, Les quatre évangélistes. Sigier/Desclée. – ᴿPensceC 244 (1990) 80-83 (Y. *Daoudal*).

1945 **Chédozeau** Bernard, La Bible et la liturgie en français; l'Église tridentine et les traductions bibliques et liturgiques (1600-1789): Histoire. P 1990, Cerf. 296 p. 2-204-04163-7 [NRT 113,272, N. *Plumat*].

1946 *Engammare* M., La Bible en français à la Dispute de Lausanne; recherche sur l'autorité et l'utilisation d'une Bible en français dans la première moitié du XVIe s.: Zeitschrift für schweizerische Kirchenge-schichte 83 (1989) 205-232 [< RHE 85,370*].

1947 *Monter* William, French Bibles and the Spanish Inquisition, 1552: BibHumRen 51 (1989) 147-152.

Quereuil Michel, La Bible française du XIIIe siècle ... Genèse 1988 → 2086.

1948 ᴱ**Guillén Torralba** J., ᵀCASIODORO DE REINA, La Biblia del Oso, Basilea 1569 Is, Libros históricos [III. Proféticos y sapienciales, ᴱ**Flor Serrano** G.; IV. NT, ᴱ**González Ruiz** J. M.]. M 1987, Alfagua-

ra. 554 + 962 p. [1148 p., 698 p.]. – ᴿRelCult 34 (1988) 417 (M. A. *Martín Juárez*).
1949 **Hauptmann** Oliver † ᴱ*Littlefield* Mark G., Escorial Bible [vol. I: E-4; vol. II:] I. J. 4.2: Spanish Series 34. Madison NJ 1987, Univ. Hispanic Sem. lxxii-646 p.; 6 facsimiles. – ᴿSpeculum 65 (1990) 686-8 (J. F. *Burke*).
1950 Traducciones de la Biblia en español [46, incluido 17 sólo NT: 18 antes de NÁCAR-COLUNGA 1944; dos 'en preparación']: RBibArg 52,37 (1990) 55-59.
1951 *Amigo Espada* Lorenzo, Una aproximación al Pentateuco de Constantinopla (1547) [ladino, comparada con la primera traducción judía en castellano]: EstB 48 (1990) 81-111; Eng. 81.

1952 **Storniolo** Ivo, *al.*, Bíblia sagrada [... pastoral]. São Paulo 1990, Paulinas. 1632 p. [REB 50,501].

1953 Parole del Signore, La Bibbia, traduzione interconfessionale in lingua corrente con fotografie a colori e note. T-Leumann/R 1988, LDC/Alleanza Biblica. 1472 p. – ᴿPalCl 68 (1989) 1199s (A. *Pedrini*).
1954 *Ravasi* Gianfranco, QUASIMODO [Salvatore, 1901-1968; 1946; 1958 con testo greco a fronte] traduttore del Quarto Vangelo: ViPe 72 (1989) 683-691.
1955 **Placerean** Checo, *Beline* Antoni, La Bibie [Gn-Dt] (Friulano). Udine 1988, Ribis. 351 p., (color.) ill.

D6.2   *Versiones anglicae* – **English Bible translations.**

1956 *Banz* Clint, The Anglo-Saxon translations of the Bible: CalvaryB (1990) 44-52.
1956* **Beck** William F. † 1965, God's Word to the nations, NT² [¹1963]. 1989, Biblion. xxiii-672 p. 0-9620063-2-7. – ᴿExpTim 101 (1989s) 190s (F. F. *Bruce*: Lutheran; dignified, refreshing).
1957 The Christian community Bible... for Philippines and Third World. Manila 1988, Claretian *al.* 1147 + 513 p. rs 150. 971-501-283-3. – ᴿVidyajyoti 54 (1990) 153s (P. M. *Meagher*: worth the price).
1958 **Comfort** Philip W., Early manuscripts and modern translations of the New Testament. Wheaton IL 1990, Tyndale. xx-295 p.; 13 pl. $20. 0-8423-0766-4 [NTAbs 35,91].
1959 **Daniell** David, Tyndale's NT 1534: 1989 ➤ 5,1812: ᴿCalvinT 25 (1990) 313-6 (H. *Boonstra*); JTS 41 (1990) 753-9 (P. N. *Brooks*); Times Literary Supplement (L 17.XI.1989) 1273-6 (G. *Hill*) [< NTAbs 34,153: severe].
1960 *Foster* John, ULFILAS, apostle of the Goths [but on the wrong side at Nicea], who gave North Europe its first book, 341: ExpTim 102 (1990s) 173s. ➤ infra 1987.
1961 *Hargreaves* Cecil, Bibles in modern English; are their critics right?: ExpTim 102 (1990s) 68-71.
1962 **Hill** Gary, The discovery Bible, NT [fosters closer attention to the Greek]. Ch 1987, Moody. xxix-591 p.; maps. $18. – ᴿMastJ 1 (1990) 85-87 (R. L. *Thomas*: must be used with caution because of the brevity of the explanations).
1963 King James: *a) James* K. (? author) The majority text and King James 'minority' variations; a look at manuscript witnesses; – *b) Johnston* P. J., Codex Vaticanus (B) plus P₇₅ -- the 'best' text of the NT?; – *c) Pietersma* A., New Greek fragments of biblical manuscripts in the Chester Beatty

Library: Bulletin of the Institute for Reformation Biblical Studies 1,1 (Fort Wayne 1989) 10s / 2-4 / 37-61 [< NTAbs 34,292].
1964 — **Robertson** E., Makers of the English Bible. C 1990, Lutterworth. 222 p. £8 pa. 0-7188-2774-9 [NTAbs 35,235].
1965 **Lathrop** G., *Schmidt* G. R., Lectionary for the Christian People 1986-8. 3 vol. – ᴿDialog 28 (1989) 263-9 (K. P. *Donfried*: eliminates all masculine pronouns for God but retains Lady Wisdom) [NTAbs 34,153].
1966 **Ludlow** William L., The story of Bible translations. NY 1990, Vantage. vii-167 p. $15 [CBQ 53,359].
1967 **NAB,** Revised New Testament. Northport NY/GR 1988 [= 1986 → 4,1811]: ᴿCBQ 52 (1990) 166-8 (M. *Cahill*: this 1986 revision must be regarded as a new translation, though sometimes retaining stilted Gospel quality).
1967* **NIV:** *Boogaart* Thomas A., The New International version; what price harmony?: RRef 43 (1989) 189-203 [< ZIT 91,14].
1968 **NJB:** ᴱ**Wansbrough** Henry, The New Jerusalem Bible [1985 → 1,1827... 3,1775] pocket edition. L 1990, Darton-LT. 1472 p. £7 [leather £19]. 0-232-51890-4. – ᴿHeythJ 31 (1990) 205-9 (L. *Swain*); Month 251 (1990) 446s (R. C. *Fuller*: 'if you say so').
1969 **NRSV:** New Revised Standard version, ᴱ**Metzger** Bruce M. + 30 others. Oxford 1990, Univ. xxi-996 + 298 + 284 p. £12 [£10 without Apocrypha]. 0-19-528330-9 [-9-5]. – ᴿBR 6,3 (1990) 9s (H. *Minkoff*, also on REB and Tyndale); ExpTim 102,3 top choice (1990s) 65-68 (C. S. *Rodd*).
1970 *a*) *Dentan* Robert C., The story of the NRSV; – *b*) *Harrelson* Walter, Inclusive language in the NRSV; – *c*) *Trible* Phyllis, The pilgrim Bible on a feminist journey: PrincSemB 11 (1990) 211-223 / 224-231 / 232-9 [< ZIT 91,145].
1971 *a*) *Fontaine* Carole R., The NRSV and the REB, a feminist critique; – *b*) *Grether* Herbert G., Translators and the gender gap; – *c*) *Throckmorton* Burton H., NRSV-BIB, a NT critique; – *d*) *Bratcher* Robert H., Translating for the reader: TTod 47 (1990s) 273-280 / 299-305/ 281-289 / 290-298.
1972 *a*) *Stek* J. H., The new Revised Standard Version [1980]; a preliminary assessment; – *b*) *Brownson* J. V., Pastor, which Bible?: – *c*) *Metzger* B. M., Handing down the Bible through the ages; the role of scribe and translator: RefR 42,3 (Holland MI 1990) 171-188 / 204-215 / 161-170 [< NTAbs 34,294].
1973 *Wink* W., The new RSV; the best translation, halfway there: ChrCent 107 (1990) 829-833 [< NTAbs 35,16].
1974 **Rashkow** Ilona N., Upon the dark places; anti-Semitism and sexism in English Renaissance biblical translations: Bible and Literature 28. Sheffield 1990, Academic. 180 p. 1-85075-251-6.
1975 **REB** [(ᴱ*McHardy* W. B.) = NEB² → 5,1820]: Revised English Bible with Apocrypha [revision of 1970 New English Bible]. Ox/C 1989, Univ. £10. 0-19-101220-3 / 0-521-50724-3. – ᴿAndrUnS 28 (1990) 137-146 (*Sakae Kubo*: improved, though less spicy); Bijdragen 51 (1990) 195-201 (P. C. *Beentjes*); BL (1990) 60 (K. J. *Cathcart*: 'xvii-236 p.'); EpworthR 17,2 (1990) 68-71 (M. *Hooker*); ExpTim 101 (1989s) 12-16 (C. S. *Rodd*); Friends Quarterly 26 (1990) 109-114 (J. *James*) [< NTAbs 35,46]; HeythJ 31 (1990) 209-211 (H. *Wansbrough* indicates no relation to the 'New English Bible'); PrPeo 4 (1990) 32s (B. *Robinson*).
1976 — **Coleman** Roger, New light and truth; the making of the Revised English Bible. Ox/C 1989, Univ. 90 p. £8, pa. £3. 0-521-38497-4;

-171-1. – ᴿExpTim 102 (1990s) 159; TLond 93 (1990) 46s (L. *Houlden*: like NEB itself, much more a work of the churches than of the academic community ... Anglican and even English role relatively small, 'a strong breeze blows from north of Tweed'... no mention of the fact that far more copies of the Authorized Version are still sold than of any other ... which somebody should analyze).

1977 — *Rogerson* J.W. [OT], *Stanton* Graham N. [NT],   The revised English Bible; new wine in old wineskins?: TLond 93 (1990) 38-41-46.

1978 The New Translation: the letters of the NT. Wheaton IL 1990, Tyndale. v-259 p. £13 [0-8423-0073-7 [NTAbs 35,114].

1979 *Sibley* L., The word made fresh [10 new or revised translations]: ChrTod 34,11 (1990) 53-55 [< NTAbs 35,16].

1980 **Tulloch** Graham, A history of the Scots Bible, with selected texts. Aberdeen 1989, Univ. xii-184 p. 0-08-03722-X; pa. -1-1.

D6.3 *Versiones germanicae* – **Deutsche Bibelübersetzungen.**

1981 Die Bibel nach der Übersetzung Martin LUTHERs mit Apokryphen und Wortkonkordanz. Stu 1990, Deutsche Bibelges. 906 + (Apok.) 176 + NT 306 p. 3-438-01583-8.

1982 — **Gelhaus** Hermann, Der Streit um Luthers Bibelverdeutschung im 16. und 17. Jahrhundert, mit der Identifizierung Friedrich TRAUBs: Germanistische Linguistik 69. Tü 1989, Niemeyer. xiv-317 p. DM 116. – ᴿDLZ 111 (1990) 651-3 (J. *Schüdt*).

1983 Einheitsübersetzung [1979 ⇥ 62,2067a; 63,1889]: Das Neue Testament: Stu Taschenbücher 1. Stu 1990, KBW. 352 p. DM 7,80. 3-460-11101-5.

1984 — **Haacker** K., Brauchen wir eine neue deutsche Bibel? Memorandum zur Tagung 'Gottes Wort in der Sprache der Zeit — 10 Jahre Einheitsübersetzung': TBeit 20 (1989) 269s [NTAbs 34,154 does not indicate site or date of Tagung, or find in Haacker's title any hint either that no new translation was needed, or that another is still needed; instead 'how to work toward an officially recognized translation'].

1985 **Murphy** G. Ronald, The Saxon savior; the Germanic transformation of the Gospel in the ninth-century Heliand. NY 1990, Oxford-UP. xiv-129 p. 0-19-506042-3.

1986 *Reiser* Marius, Das Neue Testament im Spiegel moderner Übersetzungen: TüTQ 170 (1990) 52-64.

1987 *Schäferdiek* Knut, Die Überlieferung des Namens Ulfila; zum linguistischen Umgang mit der Überlieferungsgeschichte: BeiNam 25 (1990) 267-276. ⇥ supra 1960.

1988 ᵀStier Fridolin †, Das Neue Testament, ᴱ*Beck* Eleonore, *al.* Mü/Dü1989, Kösel/Patmos. 580 p. 3-466-20315-5; pa. -4-7 / Dü 3-491-77779-8; pa. -8-7 [NTAbs 34,239: no notes; 12 p. postscript explains aim]. – ᴿErbAuf 66 (1990) 314 (B. *Schwank*: nicht für Gottesdienst); TGL 80 (1990) 512s (J. *Ernst*, auch über Münchener NT Studienübersetzung 1989); TPhil 65 (1990) 593-6 (N. *Lohfink*).

D6.4 **Versiones nordicae** *et variae.*

1989 *a*) *Capelleveen* J.J. van, Prof. dr. Nic. J. TROMP en de Groot Nieuws Bijbel; – *b*) *Beentjes* P., *Wever* Tamis, Het 'kwellende' détail van de vertaler; een interview met Nico Tromp over de Willibrordvertaling:

→ F180*, TROMP N., Gelukkig c. 1990, 215-228 / 229-244 [only these two articles have no English summary].

1990 [**Kamp** W. van der, 1954 NT; *Noordman* H., *al.*, OT 1964-83], Concordantie op de Bijbel in de nieuwe vertaling van het Nederlands Bijbelgenootschap. Kampen 1988, Kok. 1536 p. f79,50. 90-242-2900-6. – RNedTTs 44 (1990) 255 (P. W. van der *Horst*).

1991 **Bondevik** Jarle, Nynorske Bibelomsetjingar; ein bibliografi: Skrift 1. Oslo 1989, Bibelselskapet. – RTsTKi 61 (1990) 226s (R. *Astås*).

1992 **Kirby** Ian J., Bible translation in Old Norse [D1973 London]: Univ. Lausanne, lettres 27. Genève 1986, Droz. – RSpeculum 64 (1989) 985s (E. S. *Firchow*); TsTKi 61 (1990) 226 (R. *Astås*: 'D1873').

1993 *Kruse-Blinkenberg* Lars, Edvard BRANDES som oversætter av Den jødiske Bibel: → 117*, FLØKKEGAARD F. 1990, 181-205.

1994 E**Hansson** Gunnar, Bible reading in Sweden; studies related to the translation of the NT 1981: AcU ps/soc. rel. 2. U 1990, Almqvist & W. 171 p. Sk 125. 91-554-2541-0. 9 art.

1995 *a*) *Harsányi* András, ⑩ KÁROLI Gaspar, his service and the theology of the Vizsolyi Bible on the basis of the glosses; – *b*) *Borsa* Gedeon, ⑩ The Hungarian Bible and printing in the 16th-17th century: TSzem 33 (1990) 150-9 / 160-162.

1996 *a*) *Barbu-Bucur* Sebastian, (roum.) Le chant liturgique dans la Sainte Écriture et la Sainte Écriture dans les hymnes de l'Église Orthodoxe [tricentenaire de la Bible de Bucureşti (1688)]; – *b*) *Dură* Nicolae, (roum.) La Bible de Bucarest (1688); le tricentenaire de la première édition intégrale de la Bible en roumain: STBuc 40 (1988) 5,86-102 / 6,9-29.

1997 *Mitchell* William, James THOMSON and Bible translation in the Andean languages [Quechua, Aymara (in Peru) in the wake of Jesuits GONÇALEZ HOLGUIÉN D. 1607s and BERTONIO L. 1612]: BTrans 41 (1990) 341-5.

D7 *Problemata vertentis* – **Bible translation techniques.**

1997* *a*) *Cameron* Peter S., Functional equivalence and the *mot juste*; – *b*) *Sterk* Jan P., Translating for impact?; – *c*) *O'Thomas* Kenneth J., Making a methodology for exegetical checking of audio Scriptures; – *d*) *Omanson* Roger L., Exegesis; finding out what a text means / What do those parentheses mean?: BTrans 41 (1990) 101-9 / 109-121 / 301-311 / 401-9 (with *Stine* Philip C.) . 205-214.

1998 *Castelli* E. A., Les belles infidèles / fidelity or feminism? The meaning of feminist biblical translation: JFemStRel 6,2 (1990) 25-39 [responses by *Dewey* J., 63-69; *Hutaff* P., 69-74; *Schaberg* J. 74-85: < NTAbs 35,145].

1999 *Clarkson* J.S., Inclusive language and the Church: Prism 5,2 (1990) 37-49 [< NTAbs 35,145].

2000 *a*) *Crim* K. R., Translating the Bible; an unending task; – *b*) *Harrelson* W., Recent discoveries and Bible translation; – *c*) *Metzger* B. M., The processes and struggles involved in making a new translation of the Bible; – *d*) *Van Eck* A. O., The NRSV — why now?: – *e*) *Bennett* A. D., The NRSV, a teaching guide; – *f*) *Boys* M. C., Educational tasks new and old for an ancient yet timely text; – *g*) *Griggs* D. L., The Bible; from neglected book to primary text: RelEdn 85,2 (NHv 1990) 201-210 / 186-200 / 174-184 / 163-172 / 255-278 [222-8, *Walaskay* P.: smoother than Luke himself] / 229-239 / 240-254 [< NTAbs 35,14s: NHv not Ch].

2001 *Durnbaugh* Hedda, 'Steig in das Boot' Der Ruf zum über-Setzen: → 76, FHENKYS J. 1989, 11-24.

2002 *Fick* Ulrich, Ⓜ Why must we cooperate in Bible translation?; ᵀ*Karasszon* István: TSzem 33 (1990) 147-9.
2003 ᴱ**Gibaud** Henri, Les problèmes d'expression dans la traduction biblique; traduction, interprétation, lectures [anniv. Tyndale/Vulgate 7-8 nov. 1986, Angers] 1988 ➤ 4,486; 5,1847: ᴿCBQ 52 (1990) 374-6 (K. R. *Crim*); RevSR 63 (1989) 147 (R. *Kuntzmann*).
2004 **Greenstein** E. L., Essays on biblical method and translation [mostly reprints]: BrownJudSt 92, 1989 ➤ 5,269: ᴿBL (1990) 15 (D. *Clines*).
2004* **Hertzsch** Klaus-Peter, *al.*, Übersetzen und verstehen (Beiträge zur Bibel). B 1987, Ev. B.-Ges. 96 p. 3-7461-0028-3 [BTrans 41,139].
2005 *a) Hess* H. H., Fidelity equivalence [not immune to differing beliefs and assumptions]; – *b) Wallace* D., Textual criticism; is it relevant to the Bible translator?: Notes on Translation 3,3 (Dallas 1989) 1-30 / 4,1 (1990) 1-18 [< NTAbs 35,147s].
2006 *Kytzler* Bernhard, Fidus interpres; the theory and practice of translation in classical antiquity: Antichthon 23 (Sydney 1989) 42-50.
2007 **Martin** R. P., Accuracy of translation and the NIV [insecure]; the primary criterion in evaluating Bible versions. E 1989, Banner of Truth. vi-89 p. $7. 0-85151-546-0 [NTAbs 34,378].
2008 *Mavrofides* S., Ⓖ Two exaggerations in the conceptional translation: DeltioVM 19,1 (1990) 5-12.
2009 *Minkoff* Harvey, Coarse language in the Bible? It's culture shocking: BR 5,2 (1989) 22-27. 44.
2010 **Mounin** Georges, Les problèmes théoriques de la traduction; préf. *Aury* D.: Tel 5. P 1990 = 1963, Gallimard. xii-297 p. 2-07-029464-1.
2011 *a) Müller* Mogens, Translatio et interpretatio; – *b) Nielsen* Eduard, Mødet ved brønden: DanTTs 53 (1990) 260-277 / 243-259 [< ᴢɪᴛ 91,5].
2012 *Omanson* Roger L., Dynamic-equivalence translations reconsidered: TS [50 (1989), *Walsh* J. P. M.] 51 (1990) 497-505 (-8, Walsh rejoinder).
2013 *Orlinsky* Harry M., A Jewish scholar looks at the RSV and its new edition; RelEdn 85 (Ch 1990) 211-221 [< ᴢɪᴛ 90,646].
2014 ᶠPALMER Edwin H., ᴱ**Barker** Kenneth L., The making of a contemporary translation: NIV, 1987 ➤ 3,125; 4,1812: ᴿScotBEv 7 (1989) 55s (P. *Ellingworth*).
2015 *Rashkow* Ilona N., Hebrew Bible translation and the fear of Judaization: SixtC 21 (1990) 217-233.
2015* *a) Sanneh* Lamin, Gospel and culture; ramifying effects of Scriptural translation; – *b) Luzbetak* Louis J., Contextual translation; the role of cultural anthropology; – *c) Whiteman* Darrell L., Bible translation and social and cultural development: ➤ 556*, Bible Translation 1988/90, 1-23 / 108-119 / 120-144.
2016 *a) Sermoneta* Giuseppe, Dall'ebraico in latino e dal latino in ebraico; traduzione scolastica e metodica della traduzione; – *b) Hugonnard-Roche* Henri, Les traductions du grec au syriaque et du syriaque à l'arabe (à propos de l'Organon d'ARISTOTE); – *c) Cavallo* Guglielmo, La circolazione dei testi greci nell'Europa dell'Alto Medioevo: ➤ 727*b, Traductions 1989/90, 149-165 / 131-147 / 47-64.
2017 **Shaw** R. D., Transculturation; the cultural factor in translation and other communication tasks. Pasadena 1988, Carey. xii-300 p. $11. 0-87808-216-6 [NTAbs 34,103]. – ᴿBTrans 41 (1990) 140-2 (P. C. *Stine*).
ᴱ**Stine** P. C., Bible translation and the spread of the Church the last 200 years: Studies in Christian Mission 2, 1990 ➤ 556*.

2018 ᴱStine Philip C., Issues in Bible translation 1988 → 4,502: ᴿJTS 41 (1990) 215-7 (P. *Ellingworth*); Language 66 (1990) 429s (B. M. *Sietsema*).

2019 *Thomas* Robert L., Bible translations; the link between exegesis and expository preaching: MastJ 1,1 (1990) 53-73; 3 fig.

2020 **Waard** Jan de, *Nida* Eugene A., From one language to another; functional equivalence... 1986 → 4,1877; 5,1863: ᴿÉTRel 65 (1990) 622s (D. *Lys*).

2021 *Zyl* A. H. van, Die weergave van Adonaj in 'n Bybelvertaling: SkrifK 7 (1986) 93-98 [< OTAbs 14,16].

D8 *Concordantiae, lexica specialia* – **Specialized dictionaries, synopses.**

2022 *Flis* Jan, ❷ How is a biblical concordance made?; → 546, RuBi 42 (1989) 54-61.

2023 **Grela** Kazimierz, Konkordancja Nowego Testamentu, I. A-Ó; II. P-Z. Kraków 1987, P. Tow. Teologiczne. 499 p.; 548 p. zł 3200. – ᴿRuBi 42 (1989) 80 (J. *Chmiel*).

2024 **Goodrick** E. W., *Kohlenberger* J. R.ᴵᴵᴵ, The NIV exhaustive concordance. GR 1990, Zondervan. 0-310-43690-7 [BL 91,158].

2025 Grosse Konkordanz zur Lutherbibel²ʳᵉᵛ [¹1979]. Stu 1989, Calwer. xvii-1708 p. 3-7668-3029-5.

2026 **Joy** C. R., Harper's topical concordance of the Bible²ʳᵉᵛ [¹1940]. SF 1990 = 1962 = pa. 1976, Harper. ix-628 p. $16. 0-06-064229-7 [NTAbs 35,94].

2027 **Odelain** O., *Séguineau* R., Concordance thématique NT 1989 → 4,1883; 5,1871: ᴿÉTRel 65 (1990) 124s (G. *Balestier-Stengel*); NRT 112 (1990) 587s (X. *Jacques*).

2028 **Rinaldi** G., Biblia Gentium... citazioni 1989 → 5,1872: ᴿHenoch 12 (1990) 247s (J. A. *Soggin*); JStJud 21 (1990) 272-5 (A. *Hilhorst*: an excellent idea; some suggestions for carrying it further); RasT 31 (1990) 95 (E. *Cattaneo*); RivStoLR 26 (1990) 584-7 (G. *Cortassa*).

2029 **Schmoller** Alfred, Handkonkordanz zum Griechischen Neuen Testament [Nᴇsᴛʟᴇ́-Aʟᴀɴᴅ²⁶] 1989 → 5,1873: ᴿÉTRel 65 (1990) 456s (E. *Cuvillier*: réserves, ne remplace pas Mᴏᴜʟᴛᴏɴ); NRT 112 (1990) 588s (X. *Jacques*; le Tamieion d'Otto Schmoller 1869, souvent réédité; ⁷ʳᵉᵛ1938 par son fils Alfred; maintenant 4000 modifications].

2030 **Strothmann** Werner, Konkordanz zur syrischen Bibel; der Pentateuch 1986 → 3,1832b; 4,1887: ᴿZDMG 139 (1989) 428-430 (R. *Degen*).

IV. → K1

V. Exegesis generalis VT vel cum NT

D9 **Commentaries on the whole Bible or OT.**

2031 ᴱBergant Dianne, *Karris* Robert L., The Collegeville Bible Commentary [< pamphlets 1960, new series 1983-6] 1989 → 5,1876; also Dublin, Columba; £40: ᴿCBQ 52 (1990) 528-530 (M. D. *Guinan* compares with Mᴀʏs/Harpers); PrPeo 4 (1990) 202s (R. *Duckworth*); Tablet 244 (1990) 316 (Bernard *Robinson* compares to JBC and NJBC); Vidyajyoti 54 (1990) 102 (P. M. *Meagher*).

2032 ᴱElwell W. A., Evangelical commentary on the Bible. GR 1989, Baker. xi-1229 p. $40. 0-8010-3202-4 [NTAbs 34,99: NT authors sans pp.].

2033 **Federici** Tommaso, Per conoscere Lui e la potenza della Resurrezione di Lui ... ciclo A-C 1987s ➤ 3,216 ... 5,1879: ᴿCC 141 (1990,4) 314 (M. *Parisi,* C) & 623 (G. *De Gennaro,* A²); RuBi 42 (1989) 78s (A. *Durak*); Teresianum 40 (1989) 600s (M. *Diego Sánchez*).

2034 ᴱ**Gaebelein** Frank E., The Expositor's Bible commentary, with NIV; vol. 2 (tenth to appear) *Sailhamer* J.H., Genesis; *Kaiser* Walter C.ᴶ, Exodus; *Harris* R. Laird, Leviticus; *Allen* Ronald B., Numbers. GR 1990, Zondervan. xvi-1008 p. $32. 0-310-36440-X [TDig 37,360].

2035 ᴱ**Mays** James L., Harper's Bible Commentary 1988 ➤ 4,1895; 5,1883: ᴿBS 147 (1990) 116 (S.S. *Ozier*); HomP 90,7 (1989s) 77s (W.G. *Heidt*: a bargain; some queries); Interpretation 44 (1990) 291s (C.B. *Cousar* singles out P. MEYER's Romans); JRel 70 (1990) 81s (J.S. *Hanson*).

2036 **NJBC:** New Jerome Biblical Commentary, ᴱ**Brown** Raymond E., *al.* 1989 ➤ 5,384: ᴿCritRR 3 (1990) 78-82 (K.R. *Crim* compares with Harpers); ExpTim 101,8 top choice (1989s) 225-7 (C.S. *Rodd*); HomP 90,11s (1989s) 84-86 (W.G. *Most:* some good, some not); IrBSt 12 (1990) 153-6 (J.C. *McCullough*); MilltSt 26 (1990) 101-3 (W. *Harrington*); National Catholic Reporter [KC Sept. 1 (1990)] 24 (J.L. *Mays:* much new, all better) [< NTAbs 35,1]; PrPeo 4 (1990) 33-35 (B. *Robinson*); Tablet 243 (1989) 1406s (H. *Wansbrough*); Vidyajyoti 54 (1990) 265s (P.M. *Meagher*).

2037 — Scripture in Church 20,79 (Dublin 1990) 354-360 (B. *McConvery*) [NTAbs 34,283].

2038 **Owens** John J., Analytical key to the [Hebrew verse-by-verse of the] OT, I. Genesis-Joshua 1990; xi-1020 p. ... 4. Isaiah-Malachi. GR 1989, Baker. 941 p. 0-8010-6713-8. – ᴿRExp 87 [not 88 as at top] (1990) 489s (A. *Bean*).

2039 ᴱ**Senior** Donald, The Catholic study Bible. NY 1990, Oxford-UP. xiii-2273 p.; 14 maps. $30. 0-19-928391-0 [NTAbs 34,374]. – ᴿOTAbs 13 (1990) 203 (T.P. *McCreesh*); Tablet 244 (1990) 1233s (H. *Wansbrough* notes some NRSV superiorities amid quandaries).

2040 **Stuart** D., A guide to selecting and using Bible commentaries. Dallas 1990, Word. vi-131 p. $7. 0-8499-3228-9 [NTAbs 35,98].

2041 ᴱ**Vanetti** P., La Bibbia dei Gesuiti di CC⁴ [¹1974]. CasM 1990, Piemme. xxiv-1992 p.; xxiv-716 p.; ill. Lit. 120.000. 88-384-1470-X [NTAbs 35,98].

VI. Libri historici VT

E1 **Pentateuchus, Torah** .1 *Textus, commentarii.*

2042 **Breuer** Marc, Wissen und Wahrheit; ein Kommentar zur Tora, ᵀ*Hausmann* Erich. Zürich 1988, Morascha. vi-348 p.

2043 The five books of Moses, with a newly revised contemporary English translation: Sabbat prayer book. NY 1986, Ateres. 478 + 165 p.; 18 fig. [KirSef 62 (1988s) p. 17].

2044 **Goulet** Richard, La philosophie de Moïse ... commentaire préphilonien 1987 ➤ 3,1849 ... 5,1892: ᴿRB 97 (1990) 296s (M.-J. *Pierre*); RechSR 78 (1990) 461s (A. *Paul,* aussi sur R. RADICE, *al.*).

2045* ᴱ**Reale** Giovanni, (*Radice* R., *al.*), FILONE, Commentario allegorico della Bibbia, 5 vol. 1981-8 ➤ 5,1893 (4,a984, *Kraus Reggiani* C.): ᴿHumBr 44 (1989) 591-4 (B. *Belletti*); StPhilonAn 2 (1990) 177-182 (J. *Dillon*).

2046 ᵀᴱ**Silbermann** A. M., (*Rosenbaum* M.), RAŠI, Solomon ben Isaac, Chumash with Targum Onkelos, Haphtaroth, J 1985, Feldheim. 282 + 29 p.; 277 + 38 p.; 212 + 31 p.; 213 + 21 p.; 241 + 26 p. 0-87306-019-9.

2047 ᵀᴱ**Strickman** H. Norman, *Silver* Arthur M., Abraham IBN EZRA's Commentary on the Pentateuch. NY 1988-, Menorah. 456 p. 0-932232-07-8.

E1 *Pentateuchus* .2 **Introductio; Fontes JEDP.**

2048 **Berge** Kåre, Die Zeit des Jahwisten; ein Beitrag zur Datierung jahwistischer Vätertexte [diss. Norway 1985]; BZAW 186. B 1990, de Gruyter. xi-329 p. DM 148. 3-11-011892-0 [BL 91,65]; ᴿExpTim 102 (1990s) 181 (R. *Coggins*: united monarchy seen to be still likeliest); TüTQ 170 (1990) 225s (W. *Gross*).

2049 **Coote** Robert B., *Ord* David R., The Bible's first history [... Yahwist] 1989 ➤ 5,1906 [not 'first historian']: ᴿBA 53 (1990) 171s (C. *Hauer*); CritRR 3 (1990) 114-6 (A. J. *Hauser*); TorJT 6 (1990) 367-9 (J. *Neeb*); TS 51 (1990) 509s (J. C. *Endres*).

2050 **Friedman** R. E., Who wrote the Bible? 1987 ➤ 3,1857 ... 5,1894: ᴿRuBi 43 (1990) 172s (S. *Mędala*).

2051 **Friedman** Richard E., Wer schrieb die Bibel? So entstand das AT [1987 ➤ 3,1857], ᵀ*Pitschmann* Hartmut. W 1989, Zsolnay. 336 p. DM 38. – ᴿOrientierung 54 (1990) 22-24 (C. *Locher*).

2052 *Goldstein* Bernard R., *Cooper* Alan, The festivals of Israel and Judah and the literary history of the Pentateuch: JAOS 110 (1990) 19-31.

2052* *Loza* José, Pentateuque: ➤ m408, ᴱ*Vesco* J.-L., I.'AT ... École Biblique 1990, 79-117.

2053 **Paran** Meir, Forms of the Priestly style in the Pentateuch; patterns, linguistic usages, syntactic structures; introd. *Haran* Menahem. J 1989, Magnes (Perry Foundation). xvi-400 p. 965-223-692-6 [OIAc Oc90].

2054 ᴱ**Pury** A. de, Le Pentateuque en question 1986/9 ➤ 5,601: ᴿCommScv 23 (1990) 431s (M. de *Burgos*); EstAg 25 (1990) 452s (C. *Mielgo*); ExpTim 101 (1989s) 362-6 (R T *Coggins*, also on *Vermeylen* Isaïe and 6 other recent Continental books); Gregorianum 71 (1990) 779-782 (G. L. *Prato*); JTS 41 (1990) 555-7 (R. J. *Coggins*); RB 97 (1990) 581-594 (J. *Loza*); TüTQ 170 (1990) 69-71 (W. *Gross*).

2055 **Rosenberg** David, The book of J translated from the Hebrew; interpreted by *Bloom* Harold. L 1990, Weidenfeld/Faber & F. [x-] 286 p. 0-571-16111-1.

E1.3 *Pentateuchus,* **themata.**

Blum Erhard, Studien zur Komposition des Pentateuch: BZAW 189, 1990 ➤ 2527.

2057 *De Carolis* Francesco, SPINOZA e la questione del Penteteuco in Francesco LEONI OFMConv (1702-1775): MiscFranc 90 (1990) 459-505 [TR 87,255: 'MF'].

2058 *Dyk* P. J. van, Current trends in Pentateuch criticism: OTEssays 3 (1990) 191-202.

2058* *Fanuli* Antonio, *a*) I libri di Mosè; – *b*) La storia deuteronomistica: ➤ 1160, *Cimosa* M., Parola e vita 1988, 49-86.

2059 *Gorman* Frank H.ᴶ, The ideology of ritual space, time and status in the priestly theology [largely passages of Lev Num; diss. Emory, ᴰ*Hayes* J.]:

JStOT supp 91. Sheffield 1990, JStOT. 259 p. £35. 1-85075-231-1. –
ᴿExpTim 102 (1990s) 150s (R. P. *Carroll*: uses anthropology well, but
omits relation to actual Second Temple world).
2060 *a*) *Greenberg* Moshe, Three conceptions of the Torah in Hebrew
Scriptures; – *b*) *Kraus* Hans-Joachim, Tora und 'Volksnomos'; – *c*)
Marquardt Friedrich-W., Zur Reintegration der Tora in eine evangelische
Theologie: ➤ 147, ꜰRENDTORFF R., Hebr. Bibel 1990, 365-378 / 641-655 /
657-676.
2061 **Guinan** Michael D., The Pentateuch: Message of Biblical Spirituality 1.
Collegeville MN 1990, Liturgical. 138 p. 0-8146-5567-X.
2062 **Halpern** Baruch, The first historians 1988 ➤ 4,d139; 5,1910: ᴿAmHR
95 (1990) 1500s (Shaye *Cohen*); BibTB 20 (1990) 39s (R. *Gnuse*); CBQ 52
(1990) 713s (P. M. *Arnold*: a wonderful writer); Interpretation 44 (1990)
293-5 (J. C. *VanderKam*); JRel 70 (1990) 83s (M. *Brettler*); RExp 87 (1990)
126s (T. G. *Smothers*).
2063 **Jacobson** Bernhard S., *Bina bamikra*, Gedanken zur Tora ❺ ᵀ*Möller*
Avraham. J 1987, Zionistische Weltorganisation, Thora Erziehungs- und
Kulturabteilung für die Diaspora. 506 p. [KirSef (46, Nº 2921) 62 (1988s)
p. 28].
2064 **Krapf** Thomas, Die Priesterschrift und die vorexilische Zeit; Yehezkel
KAUFMANNs vernachlässigter Beitrag zur Geschichte der biblischen
Religion: Diss. ᴰ*Welten*. Berlin 1990s. – RTLv 22, p. 588.
2065 *Licht* Jacob, The Hebrew Bible contains the oldest surviving history:
BR 5,6 (1989) 22-25 . 38.
2066 **Locke** Gutman G., The spice of Torah – Gematria; intr. *Schochet* J. I.
NY 1985, Judaica. xxvii-318 p. [KirSef 62 (1988s), p. 31].
2067 **McEvenue** Sean, Interpreting the Pentateuch: OT Studies 4. Collegeville MN 1990, Liturgical. 194 p. $20 pa. 0-8146-5654-4 [OTAbs 14, 107,
R. E. *Murphy*].
2068 **Mann** Thomas W., The book of the Torah; narrative integrity... 1988
➤ 4,1928: ᴿAnglTR 71 (1989) 436s (S. F. *Noll*); CritRR 3 (1990) 160-2
(D. T. *Olson*); JRel 70 (1990) 450 (R. L. *Cohn*).
2069 **Peli** Pinchas H., La Tora aujourd'hui; la Bible vous parle, ᵀ*Gugenheim*
J. J. P 1988, D-Brouwer. – ᴿSidic 23,1 (1990) 23s (E. *Meir*).
2070 **Rendtorff** Rolf, The problem of the process of transmission in the
Pentateuch, ᵀ*Scullion* J. J.: JStOT supp. 89. Sheffield 1990, Academic.
214 p. 1-85075-229-X.
2070* *Shinan* A., ❺ The numerical introduction in the Aramaic targums on
the Pentateuch: JerStHLit 12 (1990) 85-102 [< NTAbs 35,220].
2071 *Wedel* Gerhard, Samaritanische Uminterpretation der anthropomor-
phismen im Pentateuch: ➤ 777, Or.-Tag. 1988/90, 46-54.
2072 *Wyatt* Nicolas, There and back again; the significance of movement in
the Priestly work [many texts cited]: ScandJOT (1990,1) 62-80.

E1.4   **Genesis;** *textus, commentarii.*

2073 **Adar** Zvi, The book of Genesis, an introduction to the biblical world
❺, ᵀ*Cohen* P. J 1990, Magnes. 165 p. $12. 965-223-7272 [BL 91,62,
B. P. *Robinson*: no 'research' beyond occasional mention of von RAD].
2074 **Arenhovel** Diego, Genesi... 1987 ➤ 3,1881: ᴿSalesianum 52 (1990) 169
(M. *Cimosa*).
2075 ᴱ**Belkin** Samuel, The Midrash of PHILO, vol. 1, Genesis II-XVII, translated into Hebrew from the Armenian and Greek, with commentary based

on parallels from rabbinic literature. NY 1989, Yeshiva Univ. 32 + ❺
298 p. [CBQ 52,587: title given somewhat differently from ➤ 5,9932].
2076 **Bianchi** Enzo, Genesi, commento esegetico-spirituale, I. cap. 1-11. Magnano VC 1990, Qiqajon. 221 p.
2077 *a) Blum* Alexis, Le commentaire sur le Pentateuque de Joseph BEKHOR SHOR; – *b) Touitou* Elazar, Le contexte historique de l'exégèse juive en France sur la partie halakhique du Pentateuque: ➤ 521, RÉJ 149 (1990) 477s / 529s.
2077* **Briscoe** D. Stuart, Genesis: The Communicator's commentary 1. Waco 1987, Word. 413 p. 0-8499-0406-4.
2078 ᴱ**Carrozzi** L., Sant'AGOSTINO, La Genesi difesa contro i Manichei / La Genesi alla lettera: La Genesi 1s. R 1988s, Città Nuova. cxi-270 p.; ill. / 899 p. Lit. 43.000 / 100.000. – ᴿCC 141 (1990,1) 302s. 94s (G. *Cremascoli*).
2079 *Cohen* Chaim, Jewish medieval commentary on the book of Genesis and modern biblical philology, Part I, Gen. 1-18: JQR 81 (1990s) 1-11.
2080 **Díez Macho** Alejandro, Genesis: Targ. pal. 1, 1988 ➤ 4,1700; 5,1919: ᴿHenoch 12 (1990) 112-4 (C. *del Valle*); JStJud 21 (1990) 92-94 (F. *García Martínez*); Muséon 103 (1990) 177-180 (J.-C. *Haelewyck*); RB 97 (1990) 594-9 (P. *Grelot*).
2080* ᴱ**Di Giovanni** Alberto, *al.*, Sant'AGOSTINO, La Genesi I. La Genesi difesa contro i Manichei; libro incompiuto sulla Genesi: R 1988, Città Nuova. cxi-270 p.; ill. Lit. 43.000. – ᴿCC 141 (1990,1) 302s (G. *Cremascoli*).
2081 **Edwards** Burton V., The two commentaries on Genesis attributed to REMIGIUS of Auxerre; with a critical edition of STEGMÜLLER 7195; diss. Pennsylvania, ᴰ*Peters* E. Ph 1990. 452 p. 90-26547. – DissA 51 (1990s) 1729-A.
2082 **Gowan** Donald E., From Eden to Babel; a commentary on the book of Genesis 1-11: Internat. Theol. Comm. 1988 ➤ 4,1939; 5,1920: ᴿBL (1990) 55 (J. *Gibson*: praise); ÉTRel 65 (1990) 611s (D. *Lys*).
2082* **Hamilton** Victor P., The book of Genesis I ch. 1-17: NICOT. GR 1990, Eerdmans. xviii-522 p. $28 [TR 87,249]. 0-8028-2308-4.
2083 *Heymann* Yaacob, Georg GRODDECK (1866-1934) on Genesis [psychoanalytic sanatorium, nicknamed by his students satanarium]: Koroth 9 (1987/8) 84-85.
2083* ᵀᴱ**Hill** Robert C., John CHRYSOSTOM, Homilies on Genesis, 18-45: Fathers 82. Wsh 1990, Catholic Univ. ix-483 p. $35. 0-8132-0082-2 [TDig 38,159].
2084 **Neri** U., Genesi: Biblia 1, 1986 ➤ 2,1386... 4,1948: ᴿHenoch 12 (1990) 114-7 (P. *Sacchi*: esula dal campo di storia e filologia).
2085 *Pavlovskis* Zoja, The pastoral world of HILARIUS' In Genesin [CSEL 23; not of Poitiers; perhaps of Arles]: ClasJ 85 (1989s) 121-132.
2086 **Quereuil** Michel, La Bible française du XIIIᵉ siècle; édition critique de la Genèse: PRomanes 183. Genève 1988, Droz. 421 p. – ᴿRTPhil 122 (1990) 438s (M. *Engammare*).
2087 **Sacks** Robert D., A commentary on the Book of Genesis: AncNETSt 6. Lewiston NY 1990, Mellen. [viii-] 430 p. 0-88946-090-6.
2088 **Sarna** Nahum M., Genesis: JPS Torah comm. 1989 ➤ 5,1932: ᴿCritRR 3 (1990) 174-6 (D. E. *Gowan*).
2089 **Scharbert** Josef, Genesis 12-50: NEchter 16, 1986 ➤ 3,2190; 5,2258: ᴿCBQ 52 (1990) 134s (J. G. *Gammie*).
2090 *Teske* Roland J., A decisive admonition for St. AUGUSTINE? [recorded at outset of De Genesi adversus Manichaeos: he has failed to recognize

that the learned understand also language which the uneducated can understand]: AugSt 19 (1988) 85-92.

2091 ᴱVannini Marco, Meister ECKHART, Commento alla Genesi: 'Ascolta, Israele' 6. Genova 1989, Marietti. xxxiv-178 p. 88-211-8455-7.

2092 *Vilar Hueso* Vicente, Notas marginales de San Juan de RIBERA al Génesis 1-18: → 182, ᶠVALLS I. 1990, 45-73.

2093 **Weitzmann** Kurt, *Kessler* Herbert L., The Cotton Genesis [LXX] 1986 → 2,1395 ... 5,1935: ᴿByZ 82 (1989) 319-321 (Susan P. *Madigan*, Eng.).

2094 **Wenham** Gordon J., Genesis 1-15: Word Comm 1, 1987 → 3,1903 ... 5,1936: ᴿAndrUnS 28 (1990) 100-3 (W. H. *Shea*: well done); CBQ 52 (1990) 143-5 (J. I. *Hunt*: earnest); CritRR 2 (1989) 176-8 (R. S. *Hendel* cautions); EstB 48 (1990) 275s (M. *García Cordero*); TLZ 115 (1990) 580-2 (H.-J. *Zobel*).

2095 **Westermann** Claus, Genesis, abridged, ᵀ*Green* D. E., 1987 → 3,1906; 5,1938: ᴿIrBSt 12 (1990) 48-50 (J. *McKeown*); Pacifica 3 (1990) 239s (C. *Murray*).

2096 **Wit** Hans de, He visto la humillación de mi pueblo; relectura de Génesis desde América Latina. Santiago [Chile] 1988, Amerindia. 289 p. – ᴿIter 1 (Caracas 1990) 130-3 (C. *Pastore*).

2097 **Zlotowitz** Meir, The family Chumash Bereishis, Genesis... concise commentary with haftarahs: Art Scroll Tanach. Brooklyn 1989, Mesorah. [xi] 349 p. 0-89906-012-9; pa. -3-7.

E1.5 *Genesis,* themata.

2098 **Brisman** Leslie, The voice of Jacob; on the composition of Genesis. Bloomington 1990, Indiana Univ. 122 p. $22.50 [JAAR 58,325].

2099 **Erffa** Hans M. von, Ikonologie der Genesis; die christlichen Bildthemen aus dem Alten Testament und ihre Quellen, I. Mü 1989, Dt. Kunst-V. 542 p.

2100 *Friedman* Mira, On the sources of the Vienna Genesis [art-work]: CahArch 37 (1989) 5-17; 10 fig.

Jeansonne Sharon P., The women of Genesis 1990 → 1612.

2101 *Jenkins* R. G., Quotations from Genesis and Exodus in the writings of PHILOXENUS of Mabbug: → 643, StPatr 18,4 (1983/90) 245-81.

2102 **Lacarrière** Jacques, Le livre des genèses. P 1990, Lebaud. 264 p.; (color.) ill. 2-86594-059-4 [OIAc F91,14].

2103 *Martin* John H., Can religions change? A hierarchy of values in Genesis: Pacifica 3 (1990) 1-24 [< ZIT 90,311].

2104 **Prewitt** Terry J., The elusive covenant; a structural-semiotic reading of Genesis: Advances in Semiotics. Bloomington 1990, Indiana Univ. x-146 p. $20. 0-253-34599-5 [OTAbs 14,219, M. K. *Deeley*].

2105 **Rendsburg** Gary A., The redaction of Genesis 1986 → 2,1412 ... 5,1947: ᴿOLZ 85 (1990) 678-680 (E.-J. *Waschke*).

2106 *Savasta* Carmelo, Una ipotesi sulla struttura letteraria di Gen 1-11: RivB 38 (1990) 225-9.

2107 **Thompson** Thomas L., The origin tradition of ancient Israel 1987 → 3,1917 ... 5,1950: ᴿJSS 35 (1990) 138-140 (G. *Garbini*: substantially right; keen intelligence, sensitiveness for biblical narrative).

2108 **Tilby** Angela, Let there be light; praying with Genesis. L 1989, Darton-LT. xii-130 p. £5 pa. – ᴿTLond 93 (1990) 424 (T. *Tastard*).

2109 **Turner** L. A., Announcements of plot in Genesis [diss. Sheffield 1988, ᴰ*Clines* D.: BRDX-91844: DissA 51 (1990s) 3784-A]: JStOT supp 96.

Sheffield 1990.   210 p.   £22.40.   1-85075-260-5 [BL 91, 97, J. A. *Emerton*: dubious discounting of source-criticism and author's intention].

E1.6   **Creatio,** *Genesis 1s.*

2110 *Artus* Walter W.,   Ramón LLULL's concept of creation: EstLul 26 (1986) 23-68.

2111 *Beintker* Michael,   Das Schöpfercredo in LUTHERs Kleinem Katechismus; theologische Erwägungen zum Ansatz seiner Auslegung [Gastvortrag Marburg 26.IV.1988]: NSys 31 (1989) 1-17; Eng. 17.

2112 *Capponi* Filippo,   Note ambrosiane (II) [Hexameron dies V, sermo VII]: LinceiBClas 8 (1987) 79-92.

2113 **Cerbelaud** Dominique,   Les enjeux théologiques de l'interprétation 'trinitaire' de Gn 1:1-2 des origines à Saint Augustin: diss. Strasbourg 1987. – BZ 34,158.

2114 *Cerbelaud* Dominique,   La création ex nihilo en question: RThom 90 (1990) 357-372.

2114* **Cimosa** Mario,   Génesis 1-11; a humanidade na sua origem, [T]*García Soares F.* João A.: PeqComB. São Paulo 1987, Paulinas.   133 p.   85-05-00718-2. – [R]PerspT 21 (1989) 137s (B. *Guzmán*).

2115 **Cupitt** Don,   Creation out of nothing. L/Ph 1990, SCM/Trinity.   213 p. £9.   0-334-02463-3. – [R]ExpTim 102 (1990s) 251 (G. *Slater*: not so much post-dogmatic non-supernatural religion as linguistic analysis).

2115* *Deist* Ferdinand,   Genesis 1-11; oppression and liberation: JTSAf 73 (1990) 3-11 [< ZIT 91,80].

2116 [E]**Ebbesen** S., *Mortensen* L. B.,   Andreas SUNESEN, Hexaemeron 1983/8 → 5,1959:   [R]TLZ 115 (1990) 513 (R. *Söderlund*).

2117 *Elata-Alster* G., *Salmon* R.,   Midrashic interpretation and the discourse of paradox; the 'two creation stories', Genesis 1-2:4a and 2:4b-3:24. AmstCah 10 (1989) 129-143 [< ZAW 103, 126].

2118 *a) Ernst* Stephen,   Der Schöpfer und seine Schöpfung; – *b) Splett* Jörg,   Der Mensch   als Mann und Frau erschaffen; – *c) Waschbüsch* Rita,   Vertrauen, Versohnung, Gemeinschaft; – *d) Bsteh* Andreas,   Begegnung im Raum der einen Schöpfungsgeschichte;   LebZeug 44,3 ('Geschaffen für die Begegnung und die Kultur' 1989) 165-176 / 177-184 / 185-190 / 191-203.

2119 **Ferrucci** Franco,   Die Schöpfung; das Leben Gottes, von ihm selbst erzählt. Mü 1988, Hanser.   406 p. DM 39,80. – [R]EvKomm 22,4 (1989) 51s (H.-V. *Findeisen*).

2120 *French* William C.,   Subject-centered and creation-centered paradigms in recent Catholic thought [... TEILHARD]: JRel 70 (1990) 48-72.

2121 *Gignoux* Philippe,   Hexaéméron et millénarisme; quelques motifs de comparaison entre Mazdéisme et Judaïsme: → 555, Irano-Judaica 2 (1987/ 90) 72-84.

2122 *Illanes* J. L.,   El trabajo en las homilias sobre el Hexamerón de S. BASILIO de Cesarea: → 603, Stud./Nyss. 1990, 299-310.

2123 *Lim* Richard,   The politics of interpretation in BASIL of Caesarea's Hexaemeron: VigChr 44 (1990) 351-370.

2124 **Manaranche** A.,   En séparant le sable et l'eau ... La création: Lumière Vérité.   P 1990, Sarment/Fayard.   298 p.   F 65 [NRT 113, 302, A. *Toubeau*].

2125 *a) Murray* Robert,   The relationship of creatures within the Cosmic Covenant;   *b) McDade* John,   Creation and salvation; green faith and

Christian themes; – *c*) *Echlin* Edward P., Christian wholeism within creation under God: Month 251 (1990) 425-432 / 433-441 / 450-7.

2126 ᴱ**Naldini** Mario, BASILIO di Cesarea, sulla Genesi (Omelie sull'Esamerone): Fond. Valla. Mi 1990, Mondadori. lv-422 p. Lit. 45.000. – ᴿCivClasCr 11 (1990) 325 (Adriana *Della Casa*); Letture 45 (1990) 761s (G. *Ravasi*).

2127 *Napel* Erik ten, The textual tradition of Emmanuel BAR SHAHHARE's Hexaemeron in the light of the monastic school-tradition: ✦ 643, StPatr 18,4 (1983/90) 289-295.

2128 **Nothomb** Paul, Les tuniques aveugles, une lecture inouïe de la Bible des Origines. P 1990, La Différence. 237 p. F 120. – ᴿFoiVie 89,6 (1990) 109s (G. *Vahanian*: récit de la création occulté non moins par le judaïsme que par le christianisme avec la hellénisation).

2129 *Pépin* Jean, Le maniement des prépositions dans la théorie AUGUSTI-NIENNE de la création: RÉAug 35 (1989) 251-274.

2130 *Rosenbloom* Noah H., A post-enlightenment exposition of creationism: Judaism 38 (1989) 460-477.

2131 ᵀ**Rosenthal** Frans, ṬABARI 1. General introduction from the creation to the flood 1989 ✦ 5,1974: ᴿBSO 53 (1990) 402s (A. *Rippin*).

2132 **Savasta** Carmelo, Forme e strutture in Gen. 1-11, 1988 ✦ 5,1975: ᴿZAW 102 (1990) 161 (J. A. *Soggin*).

2133 *Schenk* Wolfgang, Giacomo CASANOVA als Ausleger der Schöpfungsgeschichte der Genesis [Praha 1788]: ComViat 33 (1990) 85-115.

2134 **Schwarz** H., Die biblische Urgeschichte [... Predigte]: Tb 1608, 1989 ✦ 5,1976: ᴿBL (1990) 113 (C. S. *Rodd*.

2135 *Sellew* Philip, Five days of creation? The origin of an unusual exegesis (Ps.-CYPRIAN, De centesima 26): ZNW 81 (1990) 277-283.

3136 ᴱ**Tasini** G. P., In principio; interpretazioni ebraiche del racconto della creazione, I. Il Midrash. R 1988, Città Nuova. 146 p. Lit. 18.000. – ᴿRaMIsr 55 (1989) 167s (Lea *Sestieri*).

2137 *Touitou* Elazar, Rashi's commentary on Genesis 1-6 in the context of Judeo-Christian controversy [... obviously polemical]: HUCA 61 (1990) 159-183.

2138 *Trinkaus* Charles, LUTHER's hexameral anthropology: in (his) ᴱThe scope of Renaissance humanism. AA 1983, Univ. Michigan [ᴿWolfenbütteler Renaissance Mitteilungen 11 (1987) 89-92 (K. *Ley*) ✦ LuJb 57 (1990) p. 322 with indication of 5 other articles cited there].

Walker-Jones A. W., Alternative cosmogonies in the Psalms ᴰ1990 ✦ 3311.

2139 **Alexandre** Monique, Le commencement du livre Genèse I-V; la version grecque de la Septante et sa réception: Christianisme Antique 3 ✦ 4,1976; 5,1952: F 372. 2-7010-1151-5. – ᴿBL (1990) 43 [N. de *Lange*: more detailed than HARL].

2140 *a*) ᴱ*Jeremias* Jörg, Schöpfung in Poesie und Prosa des ATs; Gen 1-3 im Vergleich mit anderen Schöpfungstexten des ATs = JbBT 5 (1990) 11-36; – *b*) *Janowski* Bernd, Tempel und Schöpfung; Schöpfungstheologische Aspekte der priesterlichen Heiligtumskonzeption, p. 37-69; – *c*) *Maier* Johann, Tora und Schöpfung, p. 139-150.

2141 **Tsumura** David T., The earth and the waters in Genesis 1 and 2; a linguistic investigation: JStOT Sup 83, 1989 ✦ 5,1978: ᴿBL (1990) 94 (J. C. L. *Gibson*: shows that both have same cosmology, but leaves us panting for another book on where he stands on the Chaoskampf); ÉTRel 65 (1990) 432s (D. *Lys*); TLZ 115 (1990) 888-890 (E.-J. *Waschke*).

2142 *a) Costacurta* Bruna, Benedizione e creazione in Gen 1,1-2,4a; – *b)* *Bonora* A., 'Maledetta la terra'; il dilagare della maledizione (Gen. 1-11); *c) Stefani* Piero, 'In te saranno benedette tutte le genti!' (Gen 12): ⟶ 325, ParSpV 21 (1990) 23-34 / 9-22 / 35-46.

2143 *Davila* James R., New Qumran readings for Genesis One: ⟶ 173, ᶠSTRUGNELL J., Of scribes 1990, 3-11.

2144 *Anderson* Gary, The interpretation of Genesis 1:1 in the Targums: CBQ 52 (1990) 21-29.

2145 **Dobin** Joel C., [Gen 1,16] The astrological secrets of the Hebrew sages; to rule both day and night. Rochester VT 1983, Inner Traditions. 255 p. [KirSef 62 (1988s) p. 266].

Gen. 1,26: imago Dei:

2146 **Aguilar Schreiber** Milton, L'uomo immagine di Dio; principi ed elementi di sintesi teológica 1987 ⟶ 4,2013: ᴿDoctCom 42 (1989) 63-67 (B. *Mondin*); PerspT 21 (1990) 413s (J. B. *Libânio*).

2147 **Boer** Harry R., An ember still glowing; humankind in the image of God. GR c.1990, Eerdmans. 208 pa. $15 [TTod 47,311 adv.]. 0-8028-0434-0.

ᴱ**Bühler** Pierre, Humain à l'image de Dieu 1989 ⟶ 7160.

2149 *Christen* Eduard, ⓟ Der Mensch als Abbild Gottes und dessen theologische Relevanz: StWsz 27,1 (1989) 5-13; deutsch 14.

2150 *García López* Félix, El hombre imagen de Dios en el AT: EstTrin 22 (1988) 365-382.

2151 *Gerl* Hanna-Barbara, 'Geschaffen nach Gottes Bild und Gleichnis': LebZeug 44 (1989) 47-56.

2152 *Golub* Ivan, Man – image of God (Genesis 1:26); a new approach to an old problem: ⟶ 4,469, ᴱ**Augustin** M., ... 'Wünschet Jerusalem Frieden', IOSOT 1986 (Supplement), 1988, 223-233.

2153 **Hall** Douglas J., Imaging God 1986 ⟶ 2,1456 ... 5,1982. ᴿNedTTs 43 (1989) 72s (H. *Berkhof*).

Hughes Philip E., The true image; the origin and destiny of man in Christ 1989 ⟶ 1174.

2155 **Jónsson** Gunnlaugur A., The image of God; Genesis 1:26-28 in a century of OT research, ᵀ*Svendsen* L.: ConBib OT 26, 1988 ⟶ 4,2017; 5,1985: ᴿInterpretation 44 (1990) 198 (R. P. *Knierim*); NedTTs 44 (1990) 338s (P. B. *Dirksen*); SvEx 55 (1990) 95-98 (S. *Hidal*); TLZ 115 (1990) 418-420 (E.-J. *Waschke*); TR 86 (1990) 14s (O. *Loretz*).

2156 **Leavy** Stanley A., In the image of God; a psychoanalyst's view 1988 ⟶ 5,1987: ᴿRelStT 8,3 (1988) 48s (R. W. *Brockway*: polemical and subjective).

2157 *Martins Terra* J. E., Criados à imagem de Dios; homem e mulher: Atualização (1990) 665-684.

2158 **Merriel** D. Juvenal, To the image of the Trinity; a study in the development of AQUINAS' teaching. Toronto 1990, Pont. Inst. Mediaeval Studies. x-266 p. $29.50. – ᴿTS 51 (1990) 524-6 (D. B. *Burrell*).

2159 *Miller* Calvin, Genesis 1:26: RExp 87 (1990) 599-603.

2160 *Navone* John, The image and glory of God: HomP 91,1 (1990) 64-67.

2161 *Pearson* Birger A., Biblical exegesis in Gnostic literature [Gn 1,26; 2,7; Apocryphon of John (< ᴱ*Stone* M., Armenian 1976) 70-80]: ⟶ 281, Gnosticism 1990, 29-38.

2162 *Włodarczyk* Stanisław, ❷ Człowiek... image of God according to John
CHRYSOSTOM: RuBi 43 (1990) 121-7.

2163 *Aviezer* Nathan, [Gen 1,27-29] Man, the pinnacle of creation: ➤ 115,
ᶠLIPTZIN S., JBQ 19 (1990s) 239-243.

2164 *Salmona* Bruno, L'uomo vicario di Dio nella Creazione (GREGORIO di
Nissa e Giovanni CRISOSTOMO): Renovatio 24 (1989) 589-598.

2165 *a*) *Gradl* Felix, Alttestamentlicher Schöpfungsglaube und seine Konsequenz für die Beziehung zwischen Mensch und Natur; – *b*) *Langemeyer*
Bernhard, Die frohe Botschaft und die Schöpfung: FranzSt 71 (1989)
42-57 / 69-77.

2166 *Graf* Friedrich W., Von der creatio ex nihilo zur 'Bewahrung der
Schöpfung'; dogmatische Erwägungen zur Frage nach einer möglichen
ethischen Relevanz der Schöpfungslehre: ZTK 87 (1990) 206-223.

2167 *a*) *Capulong* Noriel C., Creation and human responsibility, Genesis
1,1-28 [Col. 1,15-20]; – *b*) *Chuang* Su-Jen, The new mission of Asian
Christians, Gn 2,1-17; – *c*) *Russel* Rosemary, Seedtime and harvest, Gn
9,8-17: CTC Bulletin 9,1 (Thailand 1990) 25-31 [32-36] / 40s / 37-39.

2168 *Grünwaldt* Klaus, Wozu wir essen; Überlegungen zu Genesis 1,29-30a:
BibNot 49 (1989) 25-38.

E1.7   *Genesis 1s:*   **Bible and myth** [➤ M3.8].

2168* **Allan** James P., Genesis in Egypt; the philosophy of ancient Egyptian
creation accounts: YaleEgSt 2. NHv 1988, Yale Univ. x-114 p.; 4 pl.
[BO 48,97s, W. *Barta*].

2169 **Anderson** Bernhard W., Creation versus chaos; the interpretation of
mythical symbolism in the Bible 1989 = 1987 ➤ 3,1973... 5,1994: ᴿRel-
StR 16 (1990) 66 (G. W. *Coats*).

2170 **Bilolo** Mubabinge [➤ M6.5], Créateur... memphite/amarn. 1988 ➤ 5,
1995: ᴿSpiritus 31 (1990) 453s (H. *Maurier*).

2171 **Bottéro** J., *Kramer* S. N., Lorque les dieux faisaient l'homme 1989
➤ 5,1996: ᴿEstFranc 91 (1990) 594-6 (M. *Taradach*).

2172 — *Pomponio* Francesco, L'umorismo di Enki-Ea; alcune considerazioni
su una *Summa* mitologica di recente edizione [BOTTÉRO J., KRAMER S.
1989]: RSO 64 (1990) 235-246.

2174 *Coll Compte* Javier, Cosmogonías orientales [... tres serpientes]: BAs-
EspOr 26 (1990) 206-8.

2175 ᵀᴱ**Dalley** Stephanie, Myths from Mesopotamia; creation, the flood, Gilgamesh and others, 1989 ➤ 5,1997: ᴿGreeceR 37 (1990) 254 (P. *Walcot*).

2175* **Day** John. God's conflict with the dragon and the sea 1985 ➤ 1,2051...
4,2031: ᴿBO 47 (1990) 193s (W. *Herrmann*).

2176 ᴱ**Derousseaux** Louis, La création dans l'Orient Ancien: ACFÉB 1985/7
➤ 3,521... 5,1998: ᴿCommSev 23 (1990) 100s (M. de *Burgos*); JRel
70 (1990) 246s (D. A. *Knight*); LavalTP 46 (1990) 107-111 (Elizabeth
Shannon *Farrell*).

2177 **Gibert** Pierre, Bible, mythes et récits de commencement 1986 ➤ 2,1468*
... 5,2000: ᴿGregorianum 71 (1990) 777-9 (E. *Farahian*).

Grinten Franz Joseph van der, *Mennekes* Friedhelm, Mythos und Bibel;
Auseinandersetzung mit einem Thema der Gegenwartskunst 1985 ➤ d514.

2178 **Hutter** Manfred, Altorientalische Vorstellungen von der Unterwelt...
'Nergal und Ereškigal': OBO 63, 1985 ➤ 1,2058.a687... 5,2005: ᴿNed-
TTs 44 (1990) 57s (K. A. D. *Smelik*).

2179 **Kirkpatrick** Patricia G., The OT and folklore study: JStOT supp. 62, 1988 ➤ 4,2039; 5,2006: ᴿBZ 34 (1990) 293s (H. *Seebass*); CBQ 52 (1990) 321s (B. O. *Long*); CritRR 3 (1990) 144s (Kathleen A. *Farmer*); Interpretation 44 (1990) 86.88 (W. *Soll*).

2180 *Kramer* Samuel N., A new Dumuzi myth: RAss 84 (1990) 143-9; 2 phot.; 2 facsim.

2181 *Michalowski* Piotr, Presence at the creation: ➤ 124, ᶠMORAN W., Lingering 1990, 381-396.

2182 *Moye* Richard H., In the beginning; myth and history in Genesis and Exodus: JBL 109 (1990) 577-598.

2183 **Niditch** Susan [➤ 3416] Text and tradition; the Hebrew Bible and folklore [selections with introductions]: SBL Semeia 20. Atlanta 1990, Scholars. ix-261 p. 1-55540-440-5.

2184 **Otzen** B., *al.*, Myter i Det gamle Testamente [= 1973 (Eng. 1980 ➤ 60,2633) + *Jensen* H. on structuralistic analysis, including R. GIRARD's critique]. Frederiksberg 1990, Anis. 243 p. Dk 198. 87-7457-092-7 [BL 91,119, K. *Nielsen*].

2184* ᴱ**Plas** D. van der, *al.*, De schepping van de wereld; mythische voorstellingen in het Oude Nabije Oosten: EOL supp. 1. Muiderburg 1990. xi-182 p.; 10 pl. *f* 34.50. 90-6283-791-3 [BO 48,310].

2185 *Rawi* F. N. H. al-, *George* A. R., Tablets from the Sippar library, II. Tablet II of the Babylonian creation epic [facsimile, transcription, translation, notes]; Iraq 52 (1990) 149-157.

2186 *Reventlow* H., Mythos im AT, in ᴱ**Binder** G., *Effe* B., Mythos (Trier 1990) 33-55 [< ZAW 103,305].

2187 **Salas** Antonio, La Biblia; ¿historia – mito – leyenda?: Nuevos Horizontes 1. M 1990, Biblia y Fe. 128 p.

2188 **Seux** M.-J., *al.*, La création et le déluge d'après les textes du Proche-Orient ancien: CahEv 64 supp. P 1988, Cerf. 99 p. F 45. 0222-9706.

2189 *Vanstiphout* H. L. J., Over de Mesopotamische letterkunde [G. SMITH, Chaldean Genesis 1876...]: RBgPg 68 (1990) 5-53.

E1.8 Genesis 1s: The Bible, the Church, and Science.

2190 **Achtner** Wolfgang, Physik, Mystik und Christentum; eine Darstellung und Diskussion der natürlichen Theologie bei T. F. TORRANCE: Diss. ᴰR-*itschl*. Heidelberg 1989s. – TR (1990) 516.

2190* *Alessandri* Michelangelo, Evoluzionismo e religione: Divinitas 34 (1990) 264-271.

2191 **Ambrose** E. J., The mirror of creation: Theology and science at the frontiers of knowledge 11. E 1990, Scottish Academic. xii-236 p. [TR 87,346]. £12.50. 0-7073-0575-6. – ᴿExpTim 102 (1990s) 154s (R. *Stannard*).

2192 *Arcidiacono* Salvatore, Evoluzionismo 1990: CiVit 45 (1990) 617-628.

2193 **Aviezer** Nathan, In the beginning... Biblical creation and science. Hoboken 1990, KTAV. xii-138 p. $16. 0-88125-328-6 [BL 91,7, L. L. *Grabbe*: biblically naive and uninformed].

2194 **Banner** Michael C., The justification of science and the rationality of religious belief: PhMg. Ox 1990, Clarendon. x-196 p. £25 [TR 87,170].

2195 **Barbour** Ian G., Religion in an age of science (Aberdeen Gifford Lectures 1989-91), I. SF 1990, Harper & R. xv-297 p. $30; pa. $17. 0-06-060383-6 (TDig 37,343). – ᴿAsbTJ 45,2 (1990) 90s (K. J. *Collins*);

ExpTim 102 (1990s) 220 (J. *Polkinghorne*); TTod 47 (1990s) 474.476 (C. B. *Kaiser*).

2196 **Baud** P., *Neirynck* J., Première épître aux techniciens: Réflexion sur les sciences. Lausanne 1990, Presses Polytechniques. 327 p. [NRT 113, 114, A. *Toubeau*].

2197 *Baumann* Ulrike, *Treml* Alfred K., *a*) Schöpfung oder Evolution? ethische Konsequenzen eines Paradigmawechsels; – *b*) *Dauber* Heinrich, Was heisst 'sich ökologisch bilden'?: 132, [F]NIPKOW K., Bildung 1989, 141-155 / 156-170.

2198 *Beek* A. van de, Plantensystematiek en theologie — analogieën en verschillen: KerkT 41 (1990) 26-40.

2199 **Berry** R. J., God and evolution; creation, evolution and the Bible [= [2]Adam and the ape] 1988 → 4,2061; 5,2020: [R]ScotBEv 8 (1990) 68s (J. C. *Sharp*).

2200 **Binns** Emily, The world as creation; creation in Christ in an evolutionary world view: ZchSt. Wilmington 1990, Glazier. 104 p. $5 [CBQ 52,776].

2201 **Bird** Wendell R., The Origin of Species revisited. NY 1989, Philosophical. xvi-551 p.; xix-563 p. $65. – [R]BS 147 (1990) 109s (F. R. *Howe*: high praise).

2202 *Boyd* Robert [sir; physicist; a poem:] Creation: ExpTim 101 (1989s) 41s.

[E]**Bresch** Carsten, Kann man Gott aus der Natur erkennen? Evolution als Offenbarung: QDisp 125, 1990 → 394*.

2203 **Bucaille** Maurice, The Bible, the Qur'an and Science [French [14]1989,] Eng. P [6]1989, Seghers; also in German and in 8 Islamic languages.

2204 *Buckley* Michael J., Religion and science; Paul DAVIES [1983] and JOHN PAUL II [preface to [E]*Russell* R. 1987/8]: TS 51 (1990) 310-324.

2205 **Chalmel** P., L'Évolution, mythe et réalités; la question évolutionniste au regard de la science et de la philosophie aujourd'hui; préf. *Daujat* J. P 1989, Téqui. 156 p. F 89. – [R]DivThom 93 (1990) 219-223 (G. *Perini*).

2206 **Clayton** Philip, Explanation from physics to theology; an essay in rationality and religion 1989 → 5,2034: [R]TTod 47 (1990s) 70. 72-74 (P. L. *Quinn*).

2207 *Corbett* Thomas, Science and religion: IrTQ 56 (1990) 102-113.

2207* *Corradino* Saverio, Athanasius KIRCHER; 'damnatio memoriae' e revisione in atto: Archivum Historicum Societatis Jesu 59 (1990) 3-26.

2208 *Corsi* Pietro, Science and religion 1988 → 5,2035*: [R]JEH 40 (1989) 609-611 (J. C. *Livingston*).

2209 *a*) *Daecke* Sigurd M., Gott der Vernunft, Gott der Natur und persönlicher Gott; natürliche Theologie im Gespräch zwischen Naturphilosophie und Worttheologie; – *d*) *Weissmahr* Béla, Evolution als Offenbarung: → 394*, [E]*Bresch* Carsten. Gott aus Natur? 1990, (9-20) 135-154 (-174) / 87-101.

2210 *Daoudal* Yves, En finir avec l'évolutionnisme [*Denton* M., *Chalmel* P., *Plus* R. & *Kovács* F.; *Thürkauf* M.]. PenséeC 245 (1990) 79-86.

2211 *Davis* Edward B., Newton's rejection of the 'Newtonian world view'; the role of divine will in NEWTON's natural philosophy: Fides et Historia 22,2 (Longview TX 1990) 6-60 [< ZIT 90,694].

2212 **Davis** Percival, *Kenyon* Dean H., Of pandas and people; the central question of biological origins. Dallas 1989, Haughton. 166 p. $18; pa. $14. – [R]BS 147 (1990) 493s (F. R. *Howe*: laudably uses charts and color photos for creation instead of evolution).

2213 *Delzant* Antoine, Un problème résurgent, la science et la foi: → 404, EDoré J., Identité 1990, 51-79.

2214 *Ditfurth* Helmar von, [Gespräch] Gott in der Evolution?: EvKomm 22,3 (1989) 9-13.

2215 **Dress** Willem B., Beyond the Big Bang; quantum cosmologies and God: diss. Amst → 5,2039; Groningen 1989, auct. vii-236 p. – RNedTTs 44 (1990) 351-3 (L. J. van den *Brom*).

2216 **Duboucher** Georges, La science et la foi; thèmes et exigences d'un dialogue: PoinT 51. P 1988, Beauchesne. 130 p. F 63. – REsprVie 100 (1990) 206 (P. *Jay*: important; difficile pour ceux qui n'ont pas une formation scientifique).

2217 *Dupay* Bernard, La révision du procès de GALILÉE [*Pagano* S., *Redondi* P., *Longchamp* J.]: Istina 35 (1990) 191-5.

2218 EDurant John, DARWINISM and divinity 1985 → 2,426...5,2040: RIr-TQ 56 (1990) 151s (A. P. F. *Sell*).

2219 **Elder** Gregory P., Chronic vigour; evolution, biblical criticism, and English theology [Anglicans adapted readily to DARWIN]: diss. California, DLuft D. San Diego 1990. 265 p. 90-33346. – DissA 51 (1990s) 2417-A.

2220 **Finocchiaro** Maurice A., The Galileo affair [→ 5,2041]; documentary history. Berkeley 1989, Univ. California. xvi-382 p. – RAngelicum 67 (1990) 604s (A. *Wilder*: documents rather than history); CathHR 76 (1990) 597-9 (W. A. *Wallace*).

2221 *Fischer* Johannes, Ungeklärte Fragen im Dialog zwischen Glaube und Naturwissenchaft: FreibZ 37 (1990) 441-464.

2222 HAWKING S.: *a*) **Peacock** Roy E., A brief history of eternity; a considered response to S. HAWKING's 'A brief history of time'. 1989, Monarch. 160 p. £7. – RTLond 93 (1990) 407 (J. *Polkinghorne*: too thermodynamic). – *b*) *Arranz Rodrigo* M., Agujeros negros y creacionismo; los escarceos teológicos de un cosmólogo [HAWKING S. 1988; Historia del tiempo, TOrtuño Miguel: Barc 1989, Crítica]: RelCult 35 (1989) 525-554.

2223 **Hawkins** David & Eileen, The word of science — the religious and social thought of C[harles] A. COULSON. L 1989, Epworth. xii-127 p. £6. 0-7162-0462-2. – RExpTim 102 (1990s) 29 (J. *Polkinghorne*).

2223* *Helm* Paul, The contribution of Donald MACKAY [religion/science]: Evangel 7,4 (1989) 11-13.

2224 *Herrero* José M., Narración bíblica y teoría evolucionista sobre el origen del hombre: EscrVedat 20 (1990) 125-148.

2225 **Houtman** C., *al.*, Schepping en evolutie — Het creationisme een alternatief?; Bezinningscentrum 9, 1986 → 2,1513*: RKerkT 41 (1990) 80-82 (L. J. van den *Brom*).

2226 **Houziaux** Alain, La vérité, Dieu et le monde [dialogue science-religion]. Lausanne 1988, Âge d'Homme. – RRHPR 70 (1990) 125-130 (F. de *Lange*).

2227 *a*) *Hrdy* Sarah B., Raising DARWIN's consciousness; females and evolutionary theory; – *b*) *McDaniel* J., Six characteristics of a postpatriarchal Christianity; – *c*) *James* George A., The status of the anomaly in the feminist God-talk of Rosemary RUETHER: Zygon 25,2 (1990) 129-138 / 187-218 / 167-186 [< ZIT 90,730].

2228 EHübner Jürgen, Der Dialog zwischen Theologie und Naturwissenschaft, ein bibliographischer Bericht: ForBEv 41, 1987 → 3,1036...5,2058: RTsTKi 60 (1989) 150-2 (J.-O. *Henriksen*).

2229 *Hübner* Jürgen, KOPERNIKUS, Nikolaus (1473-1543): ⇥ 857, TRE 19 (1990) 591-5.
2230 *Hughes* Gerard J., Science, creation, and providence [POLKINGHORNE J.]: Month 251 (1990) 38-41.
2231 **Jaki** Stanley L., God and the Cosmologists. L 1989 (Regnery Gateway 1990). 288 p.; $11. 0-89526-749-7. – ᴿDowR 108 (1990) 215-8 (D. *O'Keefe*); ExpTim 102 (1990s) 59s (R. *Boyd*); Tablet 244 (1990) 633s (P. *Hodgson*); TLond 93 (1990) 407s (J. *Polkinghorne*).
2232 *Jaki* Stanley L., La Cristologia e l'origine della scienza moderna: AnnTh 4 (1990) 333-347.
2233 *Jongeneel* J. A. B., De ethische zendingstheologie van François E. DAUBANTON (1853-1920); revelatie versus evolutie; kerstening versus beschavingswerk en maatschappelijk werk: NedTTs 44 (1990) 288-307; Eng. 332.
2234 *Knecht* Herbert H., Vérité mathématique et vérité théologique: Hokhma 45 (1990) 47-61.
2235 **Kuhn** Wolfgang, Pietre d'inciampo per il DARWINISMO. Isola del Gran Sasso 1990, DLC. 141 p. [Divinitas 35, 199, D. *Vibrac*].
2236 **Liderbach** Daniel, The numinous universe. NY 1989, Paulist. x-159 p. $10. 0-8091-3060-2. – ᴿCalvinT 25 (1990) 287-290 (C. *Menninga*: good intention, inadequate physics).
2237 **Livingstone** David N., DARWIN's forgotten defenders 1987 ⇥ 3,2047 ... 5,2070: ᴿCritRR 2 (1989) 316-9 (J. C. *Livingston*); Evangel 7,3 (1989) 22s (N. M. *Cameron*).
2238 **Lo Chiatto** Franco, *Marconi* Sergio, Galilée entre le pouvoir et le savoir, ᵀ*Matarasso-Gervais* Simone. P 1988, Alinéa. 296 p. – ᴿIstina 35 (1990) 191-5 (B. *Dupuy*); RSPT 74 (1990) 265s (J. *Courcier*: contre POUPARD).
2239 *Lonchamp* Jean-Pierre, Vers un nouveau concordisme? Vues d'un scientifique de [Dieu dans la création 1989] J. MOLTMANN: Études 372 (1990) 99-109.
2240 ᴱ**Mangum** John M., The new faith-science debate; probing cosmology, technology, and theology 1987/9 ⇥ 5,702; also Mp 1989, Augsburg; 0-8006-2390-8: ᴿExpTim 102 (1990s) 29 (J. *Polkinghorne*); RHPR 70 (1990) 491s (G. *Vahanian*: ever more the problem is not the sciences but the nature of salvation, the Church, and 'la condition verbale de l'homme').
2241 **Minois** Georges, L'église et la science; histoire d'un malentendu, de saint Augustin à Galilée. P 1990, Fayard. 484 p. F 150 [TR 86, 428].
2242 *Molari* Carlo, Razionalità scientifica e razionalità teologica; [a)] metodologie a confronto; – b) *Forte* Bruno, ... quattro tesi provvisorie: RasT 31 (1990) 27-50 / 65-67.
2243 **Moreland** J. P., Christianity and the nature of science, a philosophical investigation 1989 ⇥ 5,2077*; $15 pa.: ᴿBS 147 (1990) 490s (F. R. *Howe*); CalvinT 25 (1990) 132-5 (D. *Ratzsch*); CriswT 4 (1989s) 443s (K. *Spencer*: rather technical, 'non-black non-ravens'); WestTJ 52 (1990) 173-5 (V. S. *Poythress*).
2244 **Nebelsick** H. P., Circles of God; theology and science from the Greeks to COPERNICUS 1985 ⇥ 2,1533 ... 5,2079: ᴿScotBEv 7 (1989) 121s (N. *Cameron*).
2245 *Nowosad* Elżbieta, ✋ From the history of the faith-science relation in the 17th century [I. de *la Peyrère*]: ColcT 59,4 (1989) 89-99; Eng. 99s.
2246 *Patterson* Bob E., Modern science and contemporary biblical interpretation; [Bernard L.] RAMM's contribution: ⇥ 145, PerspRelSt 17,4 (1990) 55-67.

2247 **Paul** Iain,   Knowledge of God; CALVIN, EINSTEIN and POLANYI 1987
➤ 4,2117:   RTLond 93 (1990) 54-56 (C. *Schwöbel*).

2248 **Paul** Iain,   Science and theology in Einstein's perspective 1986 ➤ 3,2058;
4,2118; 0-7073-0449-0:   RScotBEv 7 (1989) 67s (J.C. *Sharp*).

2249 *Podestà* Gustavo,   La teología de la creación y el problema de los
orígenes: ➤ 566, El origen, Stromata 46 (1990) 259-273.

2250 **Polkinghorne** John,   Science and creation 1988 ➤ 5,2085:   RRelSt 25
(1989) 537s (K. *Ward*); Tablet 243 (1989) 321 (P. *Hodgson*); Themelios 16
(1990s) 33 (M. *Tinker*).

2251 **Polkinghorne** John,   Science and Providence; God's interaction with the
world 1989 ➤ 5,2086:   REcuR 42 (1990) 76s (D. *Gosling*); TLond 93
(1990) 56s (C. *Wiltsher*).

2252 **Poythress** Vern S.,   Science and hermeneutics; foundations of contemporary interpretation 6, 1988 ➤ 4,2128; 5,2088:   RExpTim 101 (1989s)
210 (R. *Morgan*; also on 1. SILVA M.: 3. LONGMAN T.); RExp 87 (1990)
352 (D.S. *Dockery*: also on Understanding Dispensationalists).

2253 *Putnam* John J., *al.*, Where did we come from; the people of the earth:
NatGeog 177 (1990) (434) 438-477 (-499).

2254 *a) Reding* José,   Des chances pour l'Évangile dans un monde qui
s'autonomise; – *b) Morren* Lucien,   Réflexions d'un scientifique sur la
pastorale actuelle: LVitae 45 (1990) 7-19 / 20-32.

2255 **Redondi** Pietro,   Galileo heretic, TRosenthal Raymond 1987 ➤ 5,2091:
RCathHR 75 (1989) 516-8 (W.A. *Wallace*); JEH 40 (1989) 433s (R.
Porter); SixtC 20 (1989) 309s (F.J. *Baumgartner*).

2256 **Redondi** Pietro,   Galilei, ketter; de politieke machtsstrijd rond het proces
tegen Galileo Galilei, 1623 [1983 ➤ 64,2144], TBoer Wietse de.   Amst
1989, Agon.   395 p. – RCollatVL 20 (1990) 114 (K. *Vanhoutte*).

2257 **Roberts** Jon H.,   Darwinism and the divine in America; Protestant
intellectuals and organic evolution, 1859-1900: 1988 ➤ 4,2133; 5,2093:
RJAAR 58 (1990) 521-4 (J.C. *Dawson*); JRel 70 (1990) 103s (J.C.
Waldmeir).

2258 **Rolston** Holmes III,   Science and religion 1987 ➤ 3,2067 ... 5,2094:
RCriRR 2 (1989) 425-7 (J.J. *Compton*).

2259 **Santmire** H. Paul,   The travail of nature 1985 ➤ 4,2136: RJRel 69 (1989)
574s (P.W. *Bakken*).

2260 **Scandaletti** Paolo,   Galileo privato.   Mi 1989, Camunia.   278 p. Lit.
28.000. – RCC 141 (1990,4) 96s (G. *Mucci*).

2261 *Schilling* S. Paul,   Chance and order in science and theology: TTod 47
(1990s) 365-376.

2262 *Seckler* Max,   Der christliche Glaube und die Wissenschaft; Überlegungen zu den Dimensionen eines keineswegs sinnlosen Konfliktes:
TüTQ 170 (1990) 1-9.

2263 **Seely** Paul H.,   Inerrant wisdom; science and inerrancy in biblical
perspective.   Portland OR 1989, Evangelical Reform.   [ix-] 216 p. $12 pa.
[CBQ 52,592].

2264 *Sladek* Paulus,   Johann G. MENDEL, rehabilitiert: AnAug 51 (R 1988)
115-9.

2264* **Spanner** Douglas,   Biblical creation and the theory of evolution 1987
➤ 3,2073 ... 5,2098:   REvangel 7,3 (1989) 22 (D. *Watts*).

2265 **Stanesby** Derek,   Science, reason and religion 1988 ➤ 5,2100:   RRelStT
8,3 (1988) 49-51 (A.P.F. *Sell*).

2266 **Stannard** Russell [physicist],   Grounds for reasonable belief.   L 1989,
Scottish Academic.   361 p. £12.50.   0-7073-0581-0. – RExpTim 101
(1989s) 219s (J. *Polkinghorne*).

2267 *Starnes* Colin, AUGUSTINIAN biblical exegesis and the origins of modern science: → 688*a, Collectanea 1986/90, 345-355.
2268 **Stewart** Ian, Does God play dice? 1989 → 5,2057b (index!): ᴿTLond 93 (1990) 331s (P. C. W. *Davies*).
2269 **Tambiah** Stanley J., Magic, science, religion, and the scope of rationality. C 1990, Univ. xi-187 p. £10. 0-521-37631-9. – ᴿExpTim 102 (1990s) 155 (R. *Gill*: challenging).
2270 **Templeton** John M., *Herrmann* Robert L., The God who would be known; revelations of the divine in contemporary science. SF 1989, Harper & R. 214 p. $20. – ᴿBS 147 (1990) 481s (F. R. *Howe*: fascinating, but leaves massive theological problems).
2271 **Trowitzsch** Michael, Technokratie und Geist der Zeit; Beiträge zu einer theologischen Kritik. Tü 1988, Mohr. viii-230 p. DM 39. 3-16-345399-6 [ZTK 87/4 cover adv.].
2272 *a*) *Trowitzsch* Michael, Technokratie als Thema der Theologie; – *b*) *Honecker* Martin, Folgen der Technik: ZTK 87 (1990) 456-470 / 471-486.
2273 **Turner** David H., Life before Genesis; a conclusion, an understanding of the significance of Australian aboriginal culture[2]: Toronto studies in religion. NY 1987, Lang. vii-181 p.; ill. [KirSef 62 (1988s) p. 495].
2274 **Van Til** Howard J., *al.*, Science held hostage; what's wrong with creation science AND evolution 1988 → 5,2108 ['Till']: ᴿCriswT 4 (1989) 435-7 (K. *Spencer*).
2274* *Weighman* Colin, Christian theology in dialogue with science: Churchman 23 (1990) 27-36 [< ZIT 91,76].
2275 **Wright** Richard T., Biology through the eyes of faith. SF 1989, Harper & R. 298 p. $10 pa. – ᴿBS 147 (1990) 492s (F. E. *Howe*: bends Scripture); GraceTJ 10 (1989) 254-6 (D. B. *DeYoung*).
2275* **Zoffoli** Enrico, *a*) Galileo, fede nella ragione e ragioni della fede. Bo 1990, Studio Domenicano. 185 p. Lit. 18.000 [Asprenas 38, 278, P. *Orlando*]; – *b*) Galileo, fede nella ragione, ragioni della fede: SacDoc 35,3s (1990) 255-443 [< ZIT 91,89].

E1.9 *Peccatum originale,* **The Sin of Eden,** *Genesis 2-3.*

2276 *Amit* Yairah, Biblical utopianism; a mapmaker's guide to Eden: UnSemQ 44 (1990) 11-17 [< OTAbs 14,50].
2277 *Anderlini* Gianpaolo, L'uomo, la terra (e Dio) nell'Antico Testamento: BbbOr 32 (1990) 162-179.
2278 *Antelli* Mauro, Stato di natura e peccato originale in ROUSSEAU ed HEGEL: Acme 43 (1990) 5-15.
2279 **Ayán Calvo** J.J., Antropología de S. JUSTINO... Gen 1-3, 1988 → 4, 2158: ᴿSalmanticensis 37 (1990) 243-5 (R. *Trevijano*).
2280 *a*) *Bacq* Philippe, Le péché originel; – *b*) *Tavard* Georges, Satan dans la catéchèse: LVitae 45 (1990) 377-393 / 395-404.
2281 *Bammel* C.P., Adam in ORIGEN: → 5,38*, ᶠCHADWICK H., Making of orthodoxy 1989, 82-93.
2282 *Bastiaensen* Antoon, La *perdrix* animal méchant figure du diable; AUGUSTIN héritier d'une tradition exégétique: → 13, ᶠBAVEL T. van, AugLv 40 (1990) 193-217.
2283 *Bitton* Michèle, Lilith ou la première Ève; un mythe juif tardif: ArScSocRel 35,70s (1990) 113- [? 176: < ZIT 90,862].
2284 *Blandino* Giovanni, The problem of suffering; the original sin: Teresianum 40 (1989) 149-173.

2285 *a*) *Branden* Albert Van den,   La création de l'homme et de la femme
d'après le document Jahviste;   – *b*) *Provera* Mario, Il tema e culto del
serpente nella tradizione biblica e profana;   BbbOr 32 (1990) 193-204 /
209-214.

2286 *Bridgman* Laird P., *Carter* John D.,   Original sin — Oedipal or Pre-
oedipal?: JPsy&T 17 (1989) 3-8. 13s; 9-12, *Vitz* Paul C., *Gartner* J. reply.

2287 **Bur** J.,   Le péché originel 1988 ➤ 4,2161; 5,2128: ᴿEstE 65 (1990) 115s
(J. *Alonso Díaz*).

2288 **Carus** Paul,   The history of the devil and the idea of evil, from the
earliest times to the present day.   La Salle ɪʟ 1974 = 1990, Open Court.
[xx-] 496 p. 0-87548-307-0.

2289 *Chapelle* Albert,   Méditations sur nos 'premiers parents': NRT 112
(1990) 702-717.

2290 *Christe* Yves,   À propos de la création de l'homme du sarcophage de
Crozant (Creuse) et des peintures de Saint-Eutrope des Salles-Lavauguyon
(Haute-Vienne): CahArch 38 (1990) 7-16; 9 fig.

Clines D. J. A.,   What does Eve do to help? 1990 ➤ 213.

2291 *Coetzee* J. C.,   Satan en sy magte in die Nuwe Testament — besonderlik
tenoor die Heilige Gees: SkrifKerk 8,1 (Pretoria 1987) 20-37 [< NTAbs
34,204].

2292 *Cole* Basil,   A note on [JOHN PAUL II] Mulieris dignitatem and the
question of Eve: Angelicum 67 (1990) 121-8.

2293 *a*) *Colombo* Giuseppe,   Tesi sul peccato originale; – *b*) *Biffi* Inos,   La
solidarietà predestinata di tutti gli uomini in Cristo e la loro solidarietà in
Adamo: TItSett 15 (1990) 265-276 / 277-282; Eng. 276.

2294 *Coyle* Kathleen,   A theological reflection on Genesis 3;   *a*) EAPast 27,1
(1990) 40-58 [< TContext 8,73]; – *b*) Month 251 (1990) 287-294.

2295 **Day** Peggy L.,   An adversary in heaven ... *śāṭān* 1988 ➤ 4,2167: ᴿIsrEJ
40 (1990) 319s (A. *Hurovitz*); JBL 109 (1990) 508-510 (M. S. *Moore*); OLZ
85 (1990) 559s (H. *Seidel*).

2296 **Deppe** Rupert M.,   Die Erbsünde in der philosophischen Theologie
Frederick R. TENNANTS; zur Ortung eines naturwissenschaftlich-evo-
lutiv-psychologischen Ansatzes: Theologie im Übergang 11.   Fra 1990,
Lang. vii-384 p. – ᴿForumKT 6 (1990) 152-4 (M. *Hauke*).

2297 **Dohmen** Christoph,   Schöpfung und Tod; die Entfaltung theologischer
und anthropologischer Konzeptionen in Gen 2/3 [kath. H-Diss. Bonn
1988] 1988 ➤ 4,2169; 5,2135; DM 39: SBB 17: ᴿArTGran 53 (1990)
343s (R. *Franco*); CritRR 3 (1990) 116-8 (R. R. *Hendel*); TLZ 115 (1990)
99 (L. *Wächter*); ZkT 112 (1990) 99 (G. *Fischer*).

2298 *Douglas* Mary,   The devil vanishes: Tablet 244 (1990) 513s: against
Western theologians' bypassing of hell and demons, this anthropologist
says 'the teaching on evil will come from Africa, and that is what Afri-
canisation will mean'.

2299 **Drewermann** Eugen, [➤ supra 1694-1704] Strukturen des Bösen; die
jahwistische Urgeschichte in exegetischer / psychoanalystischer / philo-
sophischer Sicht⁶ Tb. ➤ 5,2136: Pd 1988, Schöningh. xciii-413 p.; 680 p.;
lxxxvi-656 p. DM 68. – ᴿZkT 112 (1990) 87-89 (R. *Oberforcher*: käuf-
erfreundlich, heuristisch, innovatorisch).

2300 *Duffy* Stephen J.,   Tiniebla de corazones; una revisión del pecado
original [< TS 49 (1988) 597-621], ᵀᴱ*Forcades* Teresa: SelT 29 (1990)
183-195.

2301 *Franz* Albert,   Die philosophische Idee des Bösen; zur Satanologie
SCHELLINGS und DANTES: TrierTZ 99 (1990) 81-94.

2302 **Franzoni** Giovanni,   Der Teufel mein Bruder; der Abschied von der ewigen Verdammnis, [T]*Grün* Marie-Luise. Mü 1990, Kösel. 166 p. – [R]NatGrac 37 (1990) 448 (A. *Villalmonte*); TGegw 33 (1990) 372s (E. *Grumert*).

2303 *Gardner* Anne, Genesis 2:4b-3; a mythological paradigm of sexual equality or of the religious history of pre-exilic Israel?: ScotJT 43 (1990) 1-18.

2303* **Garrett** Susan R.,   The demise of the devil; magic and the demonic in Luke's Writings 1989 ➤ 5,5036*:   [R]ExpTim 102 (1990s) 22 (N. G. *Richardson*); TS 51 (1990) 557 (A. C. *Mitchell*); TTod 47 (1990s) 310,312 (Antoinette C. *Wire*).

2304 **Giordano** Donato, [his frescoes in] La cripta del Peccato originale a Matera; iconografia e teologia: Quad. Picciano 8. Matera 1989, BMG. 110 p. – [R]Benedictina 37 (1990) 543s (B. *Ferretti*).

2305 **González Núñez** Ángel,   Adán y Eva; el hombre y su porvenir. M 1990, Paulinas. 140 p. – [R]Iter 1 (Caracas 1990) 138 (J.-P. *Wyssenbach*: sumamente competente).

2306 *a) Granado Bellido* Carmelo, Teología del pecado original en PACIANO de Barcelona; – *b) Valero* Juan B., Pecar en Adán según AMBROSIASTER: EstE 65 (1990) 129-146 / 147-191.

2307 *Günzler* Beate, 'Über das Marionettentheater'; [Heinrich von] KLEISTS säkularisiertes Verständnis von Schöpfung, Sünde und Eschaton: NSys 32 (1990) 1-24; Eng. 25.

2307* **Heaney-Hunter** Jo Ann,   The links between sexuality and original sin in the writings of John CHRYSOSTOM and AUGUSTINE: diss. Fordham, [D]*Ettlinger* G. NY 1988. – RTLv 22, p. 597.

2308 **Heinberg** Richard,   Memories and visions of paradise; exploring the universal myth of a lost golden age. Wellingborough, Northamptonshire 1990, Aquarian. xxxi-282 p., 13 pl. 0-85030-955-7.

2309 *a) Hess* R. S., Splitting the Adam; the usage of *'adam* in Genesis I-V; – *b) Wallace* H. N., The toledot of Adam ➤ 331, [E]*Emerton* J., VTS 41 (1990) 1-15 / 17-34.

2310 *Hess* Richard S., Genesis 1-2 in its literary context: TyndB 41 (1990) 143-153.

2311 *Hinschberger* Régine, Une lecture synchronique de Gn 2-3: RevSR 63 (1989) 1-16.

2312 **Holter** Knut, The serpent in Eden as a symbol of Israel's political enemies; a Yahwistic criticism of the Solomonic foreign policy?: ScandJOT (1990,1) 106-112 [OTAbs 13,154 'The servant in Eden'].

2313 *Isenmann* Véronique, Je vous salue, Ève, mère de tous les maux; les deux récits de la création: Gn 1/1-2/4 et Gn 2/4-25; le récit de la chute: Gn 3: ÉTRel 65 (1990) 587-592.

2314 **Jobling** David, The sense of biblical narrative II 1986 ➤ 3,176 ... 5,2146: [R]RelStT 8,3 (1988) 51s (L. *Eslinger*).

2315 *Kennedy* James M., Peasants in revolt; political allegory in Genesis 2-3: JStOT 47 (1990) 3-14: the narrator portrays the first couple as peasant-rebels who must submit to centralized authority.

2316 **Kowalski** Aleksander, Perfezione e giustizia di Adamo nel Liber Graduum [siriaco]: OrChrAnal 232, 1989 ➤ 5,2148: [R]JTS 41 (1990) 815 (S. *Brock*).

2317 **Krondorfer** Bjoern, Play, experimental drama, and the interpretation of biblical narratives; a study of the Open Theatre's production of the Serpent, a ceremony: diss. Temple, [D]*Laeuchli* S. Ph 1990. 91-00302. – DissA 51 (1990) 4153-A; RelStR 17,191.

2318 *Kuhlmann* Helga, Freispruch für Eva?! Eva und der Sündenfall in der feministischen Theologie — Ein Vergleich der Positionen Elga SORGEs und Luise SCHOTTROFFs: BTZ 7 (1990) 36-50.

2319 **Levenson** Jon, Creation and the persistence of evil 1988 → 5,2150*: RCritRR 3 (1990) 150-3 (B. W. *Anderson*).

2320 **Levison** John R., Portraits of Adam in early Judaism from Sirach to 2 Baruch 1988 → 4,2192: RBijdragen 51 (1990) 324 (P. C. *Beentjes*); CBQ 52 (1990) 756 (L. J. *Hoppe*: shows how intertestamental literature ought to be read); ExpTim 101 (1989s) 29 (M. A. *Knibb*); JBL 109 (1990) 133s (L. W. *Hurtado*); JStJud 21 (1990) 126-130 (F. *García Martínez*); Themelios 16 (1990s) 25 (R. *Beckwith*).

2321 *Long* Valentine, Satan: HomP 90,3 (1989s) 53-57 [... Bible sanctions capital punishment].

2322 **Lülsdorf** Raimund, Creatio specialissima hominis; die Wirkweise Gottes beim Ursprung des einzelnen Menschen [Diss. Augsburg, DZiegenaus A.]: Theologie im Übergang 10. Fra 1989, Lang. 378 p. – RForumKT 6 (1990) 239-241 (E. *Fastenrath*).

2323 *Mahn-Lot* Marianne, [Gn 2, Eces 6 > Apc] Îles des bienheureux et paradis terrestre: RHist 281 (1989) 47-50.

2324 **Manaranche** A., Adam, où es-tu? Le péché originel: Lumière Vérité. P 1990, Sarment/Fayard. 221 p. F 59 [NRT 113, 584s, L. *Renwart*].

2325 **Murlière** Frédéric, a) Et leurs yeux s'ouvrirent. Sainte-Foy QUE 1988, Sigier. x-395 p. – RFoiTemps 19 (1989) 399s (G. *Harpigny*). – b) Et ils virent qu'ils étaient nus... Sigier/Charles. 300 p. F 98. – RSpiritus 31 (1990) 454 (P. *Moreau*).

2326 **Martelet** G., Libera risposta ad uno scandalo 1987 → 4,2195; 5,2151: RAsprenas 37 (1990) 238-240 (P. *Pifano*).

2327 a) *Miscall* Peter D., Jacques DERRIDA in the Garden of Eden; – b) *Brown* Schuyler, Biblical imagery and the experience of evil: UnSemQ 44,1 (NY 1990) 1-10 / 151-6 [< ZIT 90,607s].

2328 *Otto* Randall E., The solidarity of mankind in Jonathan EDWARDS' doctrine of original sin. EvQ 62 (1990) 205-221

2329 **Pagels** Elaine, Adam, Eve, and the serpent 1988 → 4,2203; 5,2160: RAnglTR 72 (1990) 221-3 (D. E. *Groh*: 'do we want to continue a doctrine of damaged human liberty so congruent to a particular age?'); CBQ 52 (1990) 168s (Pheme *Perkins*: really on human freedom; fair to AUGUSTINE but less suitably qualified than P. *Brown*); CritRR 3 (1990) 315-7 (Karen L. *King*); Interpretation 44 (1990) 105s (Rebecca H. *Weaver*: delightful, extravagant); JRel 70 (1990) 80s (J. A. *Trumbower*); NorTTs 90 (1989) 243-5 (Øyvind *Norderval*: inspiring); UnSemQ 44,1s (1990) 19-30 (R. A. *Norris*: 'The little engine that could?') [< NTAbs 35,65: 'out to pillory AUGUSTINE'].

2330 **Pagels** Elaine, Adam, Eve et le serpent, TChatenay M. 1988 → 5,2161; 2-08-211186-5: RÉTRel 65 (1990) 300s (J. *Ansaldi*: 5 des 6 chapitres caricaturaux); NRT 112 (1990) 607s (X. *Jacques*).

2331 — *Lamberigts* M., AUGUSTINE, JULIAN of Aeclanum and E. Pagels' Adam, Eve and the Serpent: AugLv 39 (1989) 393-435.

2332 *Pagels* Elaine, a) Adam and Eve and the serpent in Genesis 1-3; – b) Pursuing the spiritual Eve; imagery and hermeneutics in the Hypothesis of the Archons and the Gospel of Philip: → 5,481a, EKing Karen L., Images of the feminine in Gnosticism 1985/8, 412-423 / 187-206 (-210).

2333 **Phillips** John A., Eva; von der Göttin zur Dämonin: Symbole 1987 → 4,2204 (Eng. 5,2165): RStMon 31 (1989) 209 (A. *Izquierdo*).

2334 **Phipps** William E., Genesis and gender; biblical myths of sexuality and their cultural impact. NY 1989, Praeger. xvi-125 p. $33. – ᴿRelStR 16 (1990) 235 (Judith L. *Poxon*).

2335 **Poorthuis** Marcel, Sexisme als zondeval; rabbijnse interpretaties van het paradijsverhaal belicht vanuit de verhouding tussen man en vrouw [iii. de strategie van de slang; iv. de afwezigheid van Adam; v. de verlangen van de vrouw; vi. de zelfgenoogzamheid van de man; vii. de strategie van Eva]: TsTNijm 30 (1990) 234-257; Eng. 258.

2336 **Pottier** Bernard, Le péché originel selon HEGEL; commentaire et synthèse critique; préf. *Chapelle* Albert. Namur 1990, Culture et Vérité. 308 p. Fb 1484. 2-87299-002-X. – ᴿRTLv 21 (1990) 481-3 (E. *Brito*).

2337 *Propp* William H., Eden sketches: ➤ 500, Hebrew Bible SD 1986/90, 189-203 [...Suffering Serpent as benefactor of humanity].

2337* *Ramlot* Léon, La haute stature d'Ève sur toile de fond orientale: ➤ 109*, ᶠLAURENTIN René, 1990, 279-290.

2338 ᴱ**Robbins** Gregory A., Genesis 1-3... intrigue in the garden: Studies in Women and Religion 27, 1988 ➤ 5,2171; 0-88946-549-5: ᴿCBQ 52 (1990) 726s (J. C. *Kesterson*).

2339 *a*) *Rosso Ubigli* Liliana, Demòni ed esorcismi nel giudaismo antico; – *b*) *Sacchi* Pablo, Il diavolo nelle tradizioni giudaiche del Secondo Tempio: ➤ 693, Diavolo 1 (1988/90) 129-141 / 107-128.

2340 *Rottzoll* Dirk U., [Gn 3] '... ihr werdet sein wie Gott, indem ihr "Gut und Böse" kennt' [sexuelle Deutung]: ZAW 102 (1990) 385-391.

2341 **Russell** J. B., Il diavolo nel mondo antico [1977 ➤ 65,1911, ᵀ*Cezzi* F.; i tre libri successivi già tradotti 1986-7-8]. R 1989, Laterza. 217 p. Lit. 12.000. – ᴿBbbOr 32 (1990) 247s (E. *Jucci*).

2341* **Russell** J. B., The prince of darkness 1988 ➤ 4, 2211; ᴿJRel 70 (1990) 458s (C. D. *Nugent*: superb synthesis).

2342 *Scarre* Geoffrey, Demons, demonologists and DESCARTES: HeythJ 31 (1990) 3-22.

2343 *Scheffczyk* Leo, Die Erbsündenlehre des Tridentinums im Gegenwartsaspekt: ForumKT 6 (1990) 1-21.

2344 *Schottroff* Luise, The seduction of Eve and Adam's sin; social historical feminist interpretation of Paul's understanding of sin and freedom: ➤ 24, ᶠBOERS H., Text 1990, 165-174.

2345 **Schüngel-Straumann** Helen, Die Frau am Anfang; Eva und die Folgen. FrB 1989, Herder. 192 p. DM 26,80. – ᴿEstFranc 91 (1990) 585-592 (F. *Raurell*); EvKomm 23 (1990) 349s (Reinhild *Traitler*); Laurentianum 31 (1990) 606-614 (anche F. *Raurell*).

2346 *Schurb* Ken, Sixteenth-century Lutheran-Calvinist conflict on the Protevangelium: ConcordTQ 54,1 (Fort Wayne 1990) 25-... [< ᴢɪᴛ 90,803].

2347 *a*) *Stiglmair* Arnold, Der Befreiergott und seine Engel und Dämonen; – *b*) *Kampling* Rainer, Dämonismus und Exorzismus in der Jesus überlieferung; – *c*) *Gubler* Marie-Louise, Fürchtet euch nicht! Die Botschaft der Engel im NT: Diakonia 21 (1990) 294-300 / 306-314 / 301-6 [323-9, *Müller* Gerhard L.).

2348 **Streeter** Jarvis, Human nature and human sinfulness; Ernest BECKER's anthropology and the contemporary western Erbsünde debate: diss. Southern Methodist, ᴰ*Ogden* S. Dallas 1990. – RelStR 17,192.

2349 **Stürner** Wolfgang, Peccatum und potestas; der Sündenfall und die Entstehung der herrscherlichen Gewalt im mittelalterlichen Staatsdenken: BeitGQMA 11. Sigmaringen 1987, Thorbecke. 276 p. – ᴿArKulturG 71 (1989) 507s (H.-W. *Goetz*).

2350 **Tavard** Georges, Satan: L'horizon du croyant 1988 ➤ 5,2181: ᴿMélSR 47 (1990) 118 (M. *Huftier*); SR 19 (1990) 252s (J.-J. *Lavoie*).

2350* **Tejirian** Edward J., Sexuality and the devil; symbols of love, power, and fear in male psychology. L 1990, Routledge. 254 p. $30 [JAAR 58,536].

2351 **Testa** Emanuele, La legge del progresso organico e l'évoluzione; il problema del monogenismo e il peccato originale 1987 ➤ 3,2075; 5,2182: ᴿÉglT 20 (1989) 488s (W. *Vogels*; informative though ignoring VAN- NESTE); Salmanticensis 37 (1990) 135s (J. L. *Ruiz de la Peña*).

2352 **Toorn** Karel van der, Sin and sanction in Israel and Mesopotamia 1985 ➤ 1,2242 ... 5,2184: ᴿHebSt 31 (1990) 240-6 (P. *Machinist*); JCS 48 (1990) 105-117 (M. J. *Geller*); NedTTs 43 (1989) 332s (M. *Dijkstra*).

2353 **Vanier** Jean, ℗ Mężczyzną i kobietą stworzył ich do życia w prawdziwej miłości: Man and woman he created for life in true love. Kraków 1987, Apostolstwo Modlitwy. 232 p. – ᴿColcT 59,2 (1989) 174s (E. *Kowalski*).

2354 *a) Vannier* Marie-Anne, Saint AUGUSTIN et la création; – *b) Lamberigts* Mathijs, JULIAN d'Éclane et Augustin d'Hippone; deux conceptions d'Adam; – *c) Børresen* Kari E., In defence of Augustine; how *femina* is *homo*?: ➤ 13, ᶠBAVEL T. van, AugLv 40 (1990) 349-371 / 373-410 / 411-428.

2355 ᴱ**Villiers** P. de, Like a roaring lion... demonic powers 1986/7 ➤ 4,508: ᴿCalvinT 25 (1990) 84-86 (R. *Recker*: to read alongside J. WIMBER).

2356 **Wallace** Howard N., The Eden narrative [ᴰ1982 Harvard] 1985 ➤ 1,2243; 2,1603: ᴿOLZ 85 (1990) 428s (E.-J. *Waschke*).

2356* *Wenham* Gordon, Original sin in Genesis 1-11: Churchman 104 (1990) 309-328 [< ZIT 91,74].

2357 **Wolde** Ellen J. van, A semiotic analysis of Genesis 2-3 [diss. Nijmegen, ᴰ*Nelis* J., < *Greimas* A., PEIRCE C.]: StSemNeerlandica 25. Assen 1989, Van Gorcum. 244 p. ƒ42,50. 90-232-2433-7 [OTAbs 14, 220, W. T. *Miller*]. – ᴿCBQ 52 (1990) 732 (W. A. *Vogels*); CritRR 3 (1990) 181-4 (D. *Jobling*); TsTNijm 30 (1990) 86s (J. *Delorme*); ZAW 102 (1990) 318 (H.-C. *Schmitt*).

2358 *Wolde* Ellen van, A reader-oriented exegesis illustrated by a study of the serpent in Genesis 2-3: ➤ 518, IOSOT 13, 1989/90, 11-21.

2359 *Görg* Manfred, Noch einmal zu '*ēd* (Gen 2,6): BibNot 50 (1989) 9s.

2360 *Valantasis* Richard, [Gen 2,7] [The formation of] Adam's body; un- covering esoteric traditions in the Apocryphon of John and ORIGEN's Dialogue with Heraclides: SecC 7 (1989s) 150-162.

2361 *Koch* Klaus, Der Güter Gefährlichstes, die Sprache, dem Menschen gegeben ... Überlegungen zu Gen 2,7: BibNot 48 (1989) 50-60.

2362 *Waldman* Nahum M., [Gen 2,9] What was the actual effect of the tree of knowledge?: JBQ 19 (1990s) 105-113.

2363 *a) Rod-Salomonsen* Børge, KNGDW; Erwägungen zu Gen 2,18; – *b) Rasmussen* Stig, Adam og Eva — associationer, etymologier og litterær semantik: ➤ 117*, ᶠLØKKEGAARD F. 1990, 321-5 / 289-303.

2364 *Eilberg-Schwartz* H., [Gen 2,19] What happens when God invents language [Gen. Rabbah; language and torah existed before the world]: Moment 14,5 (Wsh 1989) 36-41 [< NTAbs 34,85].

2365 *Tosato* Angelo, On Genesis 2:24 [claimed rightly by some to be a gloss, since the sense is complete with verse 23]: CBQ 52 (1990) 389-409.

2365* *Taylor* Barbara B., Surviving Eden — Genesis 3:1-21: RefR 44,1 (1990) 15-18 [< ZIT 91,86].
2366 *Görg* Manfred, Geschichte der Sünde — Sünde der Geschichte; Gen 3,1-7 im Licht tendenzkritischer Beobachtungen: MüTZ 41 (1990) 315-325.
2367 *Bergmann* J., A figura de Maria em Gênesis 3.15: Teocomunicação 18 (1988) 411-424 [< Stromata 45,498].

E2.1 Cain et Abel; *gigantes, longaevi; Genesis 4s.*

2368 *Gutmann* Joseph, Cain's burial of Abel; a legendary motif in Christian and Islamic art [< ᶠ*Orlinsky* H., ErIsr 16 (1982)]: ➤ 5,272, Sacred images 1989, 92-98.
2369 *Pearson* Birger A., Cain and the Cainites [ineditum < Dallas 1983 SBL]: ➤ 281, Gnosticism 1990, 95-107.
2370 *West* Gerald, Reading 'the text' and reading 'behind the text'; the 'Cain and Abel' story in a context of [S. Africa] liberation: ➤ 166, ᶠSheffield 1990, 301-320.
2371 *Jacobson* Howard, [Gn 4,16] The land of Nod ['Naim in the land of the sleepers', Onom. Sac. 182,9]: JTS 41 (1990) 91s.
2372 **Fraade** Stephen D., [Gn 4,26] Enosh and his generation 1985 ➤ 65, 1944... 4,2236: ᴿJAAR 58 (1990) 124 (J. *Neusner*: impressive erudition though limited to a single verse).
2373 *Maller* Allen S., The difficult verse in Genesis 4:26: JBQ 18 (1989s) 257-9.263.
2374 **Hookerman** Jacob, Ⓗ Some Genesis passages [4,1; 6,3; 22,6...]: BethM 36,124 (1990s) 20-28.
2375 *Renaud* B., Les généalogies de l'histoire sacerdotale: RB 97 (1990) 5-30; Eng. 5s.
2376 *Young* Dwight W., The influence of Babylonian algebra on longevity among the antediluvians: ZAW 102 (1990) 322-335.

E2.2 Diluvium, **The Flood;** Gilgameš (Atraḥasis); **Genesis 6...**

2377 **Bailey** Lloyd R., Noah, the person and the story in history and tradition: Studies on Personalities of the OT 1989 ➤ 5,2216; 0-87249-571-X; pa. -637-6: ᴿBA 53 (1990) 120 (J. P. *Lewis*); RelStR 16 (1990) 282 (W. L. *Humphreys*); VT 40 (1990) 381s (J. A. *Emerton*).
2378 *Diakonoff* I. M., *Jankowska* N. B., An Elamite Gilgameš text from Argištihenele, Urartu (Armavir-blur, 8th century B.C.): ZAss 80 (1990) 102-120; 2 pl.; 121-3, facsimiles.
2379 *a*) *Dundes* Alan, The flood as male myth of creation; – *b*) *Roheim* G., The flood myth as vesical dream; – *c*) *Utley* F., The devil in the ark; – *d*) *Kolig* E., Noah's Ark revisited; on the myth-land connection in traditional Australian Aboriginal thought [*al.* Cameroon, Philippines, India, S/Central America]: ᴱ**Dundes**, The flood myth 1988 ➤ 4,2246; 5,2218: 167-182 / 151-165 / 337-356 / 241-248 [183-239.249-319: < CBQ 185-7, P. *Arnold* ('Dundee' p. 186)]: ᴿJScStR 29 (1990) 126 (J. F. *Baggett*).
2380 *Edzard* Dietz O., Gilgameš und Huwawa A. I. Teil: ZAss 80 (1990) 165-190; 191-203. facsimiles.
2381 *a*) *Frazer* J. G., The great flood; – *b*) *Woolley* L., Stories of the creation and the flood; – *c*) *Smith* G. A. (1872), The Chaldean account of the deluge; – *d*) *Hammerly-Dupuy* D., Some observations on the As-

syro-Babylonian and Sumerian flood stories; – c) *Frymer-Kensky* T., The Atrahasis epic and its significance for our understanding of Genesis 1-9; – f) *Kelsen* H., The principle of retribution in the flood and catastrophic myths: ➤ 2379 supra, ᴱ**Dundes** A.,Flood Myth 1988, 113-123 / 89-99 / 29-48 / 49-59 / 61-73 / 135-149.

2382 *George* A. R., The day the earth divided; a geological aetiology in the Babylonian Gilgameš epic: ZAss 80 (1990) 214-220.

2382* a) *Habel* Norman C., The two flood stories in Genesis; – b) *Follansbee* E., The story of the flood in the light of comparative Semitic mythology; – c) *Ginzberg* L., Noah and the Flood in Jewish legend; – d) *Moore* J., Charles LYELL and the Noachian deluge; – e) *Allen* D., Science and the universality of the flood; – f) *Rappaport* R., Geology and orthodoxy; the case of Noah's flood in eighteenth-century thought; – g) *Gould* S., Creationism; genesis vs. geology: ➤ 2379 supra, ᴱ**Dundes** A., Flood Myth 1988, 13-28 / 75-87 / 319-335 / 405-425 / 357-382 / 421-427.

2383 *Keller* Christoph, Freiheitsbelehrung; eine moraltheologische Predigt über die Sintflutgeschichte: ➤ 150, ꟻRIEF J., Freiheit 1989, 7-12.

2384 *Lardet* P., Peuples et langues de CALVIN à BODIN; Moïse historien: ➤ 511, Théorie/pratique 1988/90, 77-111.

2385 a) *Lord* Albert B., Gilgamesh and other epics; – b) *Jacobsen* Thorkild, The Gilgamesh epic; tragic and romantic vision; – c) *Harris* Rivkah, Images of women in the Gilgamesh epic: ➤ 124, ꟻMORAN W., Lingering 1990, 371-380 / 231-249 / 219-230.

2386 **Mielke** Thomas R. P., Gilgamesh, König von Uruk; Roman [a novel]. H-Reinbek 1990, Rowohlt. 635 p.; map. 3-499-12689-3 [OIAc S90].

2387 *Müller* Hans-Peter, a) Gilgamesch-Epos und Altes Testament [➤ ꟻKOCH K., Ernten, was man sät ? 1991] 75-99; – b) Parallelen zu Gen 2f. und Ez[ech] 28 aus dem Gilgamesch-Epos: ZAHeb 3 (1990) 167-178.

2387* *Salvini* Mirjo, Die hurritischen Überlieferungen des Gilgameš-Epos und der Kešši-Erzählung: ➤ 801*, Hurriter 1988, 157-172.

2388 **Stachowiak** Lech, ✪ Potop biblijny — The flood; literary formation, contents of the narrative, theology: Jak rozumieć Pismo święte? Lublin 1988. 186 p. – ᴿRuBi 43 (1990) 172 (J. *Augustynowicz*).

2389 *Stachowiak* Lech, ✪ Die theologischen Grundgedanken der jahwistischen und priesterlichen Fluterzählung (Gen 6,5 - 9,17): ➤ ꟻGRZYBEK S. 1990, 291-301; deutsch 301.

2390 *Tonder* C. A. P. van, Die strukturele opbou van die Atra-ḫasis-epos in die tweede kolom van die eerste tablet: JSem 2,1 (1990) 100-111.

2391 *Veenhof* Klaas R., De interpretatie van de Atrachasis-mythe, een Babylonische oorgeschiedenis: NedTTs 44 (1990) 177-197; Eng. 245 [< OTAbs 14,15].

_____

2392 *Sattler* Steve, [Gn 6,5; 18,20; Jg 19,21] The destruction of the wicked: JBQ 19 (1990s) 22-24.

2393 [Backchine] *Dumont* Simonne, Le mythe chamitique [malediction des noirs] dans les sources rabbiniques du Proche-Orient du début de l'ère chrétienne au XIIIᵉ siècle: RaMIsr 55 (1989) 43-71.

2393* *Ernst* Alexander, 'Wer Menschenblut vergiesst...' Zur Übersetzung von bᵉādām in Gen 9,6: ZAW 102 (1989) 252s; Eng. 253.

2394 *Horowitz* W., The isles of the nations; Genesis X and Babylonian geography: ➤ 331, VTS 41 (1990) 35-43.

2395 *Toorn* K. van der [before], *Horst* P.W. van den [after: Gn 10,8-12]
Nimrod before and after the Bible: HarvTR 83 (1990) 1-29.
2396 *Kornfeld* Walter, [Gn 10,25; 1 Chr 1] Die Listen arabischer Stämme im
Lichte des altarabischen Namensmateriales: → 64, ᶠGRZYBEK S. 1990,
150-6, deutsch.
2397 *Carey* J., The ancestry of Fénius Farsaid [co-builder at Babel according
to an Irish inheritance from Pseudo-PHILO Ant 4-6]: Celtica 21 (Dublin
1990) 104-112 [< NTAbs 35,213].
2398 *Durand* J.M., Fourmis blanches et fourmis noires [... dispersion des
races comme à Babel]: → 138, ᶠPERROT J., Iran 1990, 101-8; 6 phot.
2399 **García Santos** A. Ángel, La Torre de Babel (Gn 11,1-9); estudio
comparativo del texto masorético y el Targum Onqelos [< diss.]. Valencia 1990, Fac. Teol. Ferrer. 89 p.
2400 *García Santos* Angel, *a*) El Targum Onqelos de Gn 11,1-9; análisis de la
traducción: EscrVedat 20 (1990) 167-226; – *b*) Análisis de la forma de
Génesis 11,1-9: CommSev 23 (1990) 169-208.
2401 **Marty** F., La bénédiction de Babel; vérité et communication: La nuit
surveillée. P 1990, Cerf. 272 p. F 139 [NRT 113, 124, J.-P. *Prévost*: le
titre paradoxal semble signifier 'Est-il tellement sûr qu'une langue unique
aurait mieux honoré la vérité?'].
2402 *Noël* Damien, La tour de Babel: Masses Ouvrières [311 (1974) 58-67]
432 (1990) 69-78 [79-191, *Pizivin* D., *al.*].
2403 **Uehlinger** Christoph, Weltreich und 'eine Rede'; eine neue Deutung der
sogenannten Turmbauerzählung (Gen 11,1-9): OBO 101, 1990 → 5,2238;
Fs 155: 3-7278-0697-4 / VR 3-525-53733-6. – ᴿUF 22 (1990) 515s (O.
Loretz).

E2.3 **Patriarchae, Abraham;** *Genesis 12s.*

2404 **Abela** Anthony, [Gn 11-25] The themes of the Abraham narrative;
thematic coherence within the Abraham literary unity of Genesis
11,27 - 25,18 [diss. Rome, Pont. Biblical Institute → 5,2243]. Malta 1989,
Studia. x-141 p. – ᴿBL (1990) 64 (D. *Clines*).
2405 *Bray* G., The promises made to Abraham and the destiny of Israel:
ScotBEv 7,2 (E 1989) 69-87 [< NTAbs 34,347].
2406 *Conrad* Edgar W., Isaiah and the Abraham connection [Abraham is
mentioned only 26 times outside the Pentateuch, 18 quite casually. The
article is by an Australian, but with no perceptible relevance to its group
subtitled 'Australian contextual theology']: AsiaJT 2 (1988) 382-393.
2407 *Deurloo* K.A., Narrative geography in the Abraham cycle: → 563, OTS
26 (1988/90) 48-62.
Hansen G., Abraham in Galatians → 6486.
2408 **Harrisville** Roy A., In the footsteps of Abraham; the figure of Abraham
in the epistles of St. Paul: diss. Union Theol. Sem. Richmond 1990.
384 p. 91-13421. – DissA 51 (1990s) 4162-A.
Köckert Mathias, Vätergott und Väterverheissungen ... ALT: FRL 142, 1988
→ 7012*.
2408* *Lord* A.B., Patterns of Lives of the Patriarchs from Abraham to
Samson and Samuel [comment, *Gunn* D.M.]: → 547, Text/Tradition
1988/90, 7-18 [19-24].
2409 **Poteet** Margaret E., [Gn 11-50] Literary unity in the patriarchal
narratives: diss. Oklahoma 1990, ᴰ*Granger* B. 278 p. 90-33284. – DissA
51 (1990s) 2008-A.

2410 *Quinn* Philip L., Agamemnon and Abraham; the tragic dilemma of KIERKEGAARD's Knight of Faith: LitTOx 4 (1990) 181-193 [< ZIT 90,599].

2411 *Roloff* Jürgen, Abraham im NT [1980; 1982; ?ineditum]: ➤ 289, Verantwortung 1990, 231-254.

2412 **Wieser** F., Die Abraham-Vorstellungen im NT, ^D1987 ➤ 4,2283*: ^RCritRR 2 (1989) 257-9 (G. W. *Buchanan*).

Wilson Marvin R., Our father Abraham; Jewish roots of the Christian faith 1989 ➤ 4389.

2413 *Pons* Jacques, Confrontation et dialogue en Genèse 12-36: ÉTRel 65 (1990) 15-26.

2414 ^E**Becking** B., *Smelik* K.A.D., Een patriarchale leugen; het verhaal in Genesis 12 verschillend belicht 1989 ➤ 5,2265: 90-259-4378-0: ^RTsT-Nijm 30 (1990) 199s (P. *Kevers*).

2415 *Biddle* Mark E., [Gn 12,10-20; 20,1-18; 26,1-11] The 'endangered ancestress' and blessing for the nations: JBL 109 (1990) 509-611.

2416 **Niditch** Susan, Underdogs and tricksters... biblical folklore 1987 [... Gn 12,20] 1987 ➤ 3,2189 ... 5,2266: ^RBR 6,4 (1990) 11.43 (J.R. *Levison*); HebSt 31 (1990) 222-4 (R.S. *Hendel*).

E2.4 Melchisedech, Sodoma; *Genesis 14.*

2417 *Baltzer* Klaus, Jerusalem in den Erzväter-Geschichten der Genesis? Traditionsgeschichtliche Erwägungen zu Gen 14 und 22: ➤ 147, ^FRENDTORFF R., Hebr. Bibel 1990, 3-12.

2417* *a) Delcor* Mathias, La naissance merveilleuse de Melchisédeq d'après l'Hénoch slave; – *b) Paul* André, Intertestament et interprétation biblique; plaidoyer pour une théologie de l'Écriture: ➤ 109*, ^FLAURENTIN R. 1990, 217-229 / 127-137.

2418 *Emerton* J.A., *a)* The site of Salem, the city of Melchisedek (Genesis XIV 16); *b)* Some problems in Genesis XIV: ➤ 331, VTS 41 (1990) 45-71 / 73-102.

2419 **Loader** J.A., [➤ 2437] A tale of two cities; Sodom and Gomorrah in the Old Testament, early Jewish and early Christian traditions: ContrBExTh 1. Kampen 1990, Kok. 150 p. 90-242-5333-0.

2420 *Ménard* Jacques E., Le traité de Melchisédek de Nag Hammadi: RevSR 64 (1990) 235-243.

2421 *Pearson* Birger A., The figure of Melchizedek in Gnostic literature [ineditum < Lv 1988]: ➤ 281, Gnosticism 1990, 108-124.

2422 *Salibi* Kamal, The 'Jerusalem' question [= Salem Ps 76,3 and/or Gn 14,18?]: NESTR 11,1 (1990) 3-18.

E2.5 The Covenant (alliance, Bund); *Foedus, Genesis 15...*

2423 *Brzegowy* Tadeusz, [Gn 15...] ^❾ Théophanies dans les sanctuaires d'Israël: AtKap 112 (1989) 39-53.

2424 **Ha** John, Genesis 15, a theological [Diss. Rome 1986]: compendium of Pentateuchal history: BZAW 181, 1989 ➤ 5,2272: ^RBL (1990) 77 (I.W. *Provan*); ÉTRel 65 (1990) 433 (T. *Römer*); RHPR 70 (1990) 255 (P. de *Robert*); RivB 38 (1990) 515-8 (J.-L. *Ska*, franç.).

2425 **Kreuzer** Siegfried, [Gn 15,13-16 ... Dt 26] Die Frühgeschichte Israels [Ev. Hab.-Diss. Wien 1987]: BZAW 178, 1989 ➤ 5,2274: ^RBL (1990) 81 (A.

Mayes); CBQ 52 (1990) 720-2 (T. B. *Dozeman*); LuthTKi 14 (1990) 88-90 (H. *Brandt*); RivB 38 (1990) 522-5 (G. L. *Prato*).

2426 **Mölle** H., Genesis 15; eine Erzählung von den Anfängen Israels: ForBi 62, 1988 ⇢ 4,2309; DM 56. 3-429-01258-9 [BL 91,87, R. E. *Clements*: some details arbitrary].

2427 *a) Moberly* R. W. L., Abraham's righteousness, Gen XV 6; – *b) Alexander* T. D., The Hagar traditions in Gen XVI and XXI: ⇢ 331, VTS 41 (1990) 103-130 / 131-148.

2428 *Begg* Christopher, [Gen 15,9] Doves and treaty-making; another possible reference [TUmAT 1983, 1/2, 176, Esarhaddon 1,637]: BibNot 48 (1989) 8-11.

ᴱ**Canfora** Luciano, I trattati nel mondo antico 1990 ⇢ 724.

2429 *a) Mendenhall* George E., The suzerainty treaty structure; thirty years later; – *b) Weiss* Bernard G., Covenant and law in Islam; – *c) Hillers* Delbert R., Rite; ceremonies of law and treaty in the Ancient Near East: ⇢ 526, Religion & Law 1985/90, 85-100 / 49-83 / 351-364.

2430 *Talmon* Shemaryahu, '400 Jahre' oder 'vier Generationen' (Gen 15,13-15); geschichtliche Zeitangaben oder literarische Motive?: ⇢ 147, ᶠREND-TORFF R., Hebr. Bibel 1990, 13-25.

2431 **Deurloo** K. A., Hagar en Ismael (Genesis 16 en 21): AmstCah 10 (1989) 9-15 [< ZAW 103,125].

Knauf Ernst A., Ismael 1985 ⇢ b327.

2432 *Dyk* P. J. van, [Gn 16] The function of the so-called etiological elements in narratives: ZAW 102 (1990) 19-33.

2433 **Firestone** Reuven, Journeys in holy lands; the evolution of the Abraham-Ishmael legends in Islamic exegesis. NYU 1990. xxi-265 p. $17 [RelStR 17, 271, J. *Renard*].

2434 **Teubal** Savina J., Hagar the Egyptian; the lost tradition of the matriarchs. SF 1990, Harper & R. xliv-226 p. 0-06-250873-3 [OIAc S90].

2435 **Külling** Samuel R., Zur Datierung der 'Genesis-P-Stücke', namentlich des Kapitels Genesis XVII². Riehen, Schweiz 1985, Immanuel. xxvi-332 p. [KirSef (40, Nᵒ 2307) 62 (1988s) p. 31].

2436 *a) Schmid* H., Ökumene im Genesisbuch [... 17,6]; – *b) Borchert* R., Erziehung im AT: ⇢ 50, ᶠFOX H., Ökumenisch leben 1990, 217-227 / 21-43.

2437 *Loader* J. A., [Gen 18s ⇢ 2419] The sin of Sodom in Talmud and Midrash: OTEssays 3 (1990) 231-245.

2438 *Turner* Laurence A., Lot as Jekyll and Hyde; a reading of Genesis 18-19: ⇢ 166, ᶠSheffield 1990, 85-101.

2439 **Miller** William T., [Gn 18; 22] Mysterious encounters at Mamre and Jabbok: BrownJudSt 50, 1984 ⇢ 65,2002; 2,1668: ᴿJAOS 110 (1990) 125s (A. *Kamesar*).

2440 *Hyman* Ronald T., [Gen 18,14; Nm 11,12] God, Abraham, Moses; a comparison of key questions: ⇢ 115, ᶠLIPTZIN S., JBQ 19 (1990s) 250-9.

2441 *Blenkinsopp* Joseph, The judge of all the earth; theodicy in the midrash on Genesis 18:22-23: JJS 41 (1990) 1-12.

E2.6 **The ʿAqedâ;** *Isaac, Genesis 22 ...*

2442 *Abramson* Glenda, The reinterpretation of the Akedah in modern Hebrew poetry: JJS 41 (1990) 101-114.

2443 *Barth* Lewis M., Introducing the Akedah; a comparison of two midrashic presentations: ⇢ 183, ᶠVERMES G., Essays 1990, 125-138.

2444 *Bergen* Robert D., The role of Genesis 22:1-19 in the Abraham cycle; a computer-assisted textual interpretation: CriswT 4 (1989s) 313-326.

2444* *Exum* J. Cheryl, *Whedbee* J. William, Isaac, Samson, and Saul; reflections on the comic and tragic visions [< Semeía 32 (1984)] → 367, *Radday*, Humour 1990, 117-159.

2445 **Green** Arthur, Devotion and commandment; the faith of Abraham in the Hasidic imagination [Efroymson lectures 1986). Cincinnati 1989, HUC. 99 p. – ᴿHebSt 31 (1990) 171 (F. *Rosenthal*: challenging).

2446 *Hayward* C. T. R., The sacrifice of Isaac and Jewish polemic against Christianity: CBQ 52 (1990) 292-306.

2447 *Reiser* Werner, Isaak darf nicht geopfert werden; Predigt zu 1. Mose 22, 1-14: TZBas 46 (1990) 578-583.

2448 *Rojtman* Betty, Le récit comme interprétation (à partir de Gen. 22 et du Midrach Rabba): TPhil 122 (1990) 157-169; Eng. 295.

2449 **Tschuggnall** Peter, Und Gott stellte Abraham auf die Probe; das Abraham-Opfer als Glaubensparadox: Diss. Innsbruck 1989s, ᴰ*Kern* W. – ZkT 112 (1990) 508; RTLv 22, p. 618; TR 86,510.

2450 *Yerkes* Moshe J., The meaning of Abraham's test; a reexamination of the Akedah: JBQ 19 (1990s) 3-10.

2451 *a*) *Zucker* David J., Conflicting conclusions; the hatred of Isaac and Ishmael; – *b*) *Kaplan* Kalman J., Isaac and Oedipus; a re-examination of the father-son relationship: Judaism 39 (1990) 37-46 / 73-81.

2452 *Alonso Schökel* Luis, [< Dov'è tuo fratello] *a*) Lo sgambettatore, nascita e lenticchie; – *b*) L'astuzia come ideale dell'uomo antico; benedizione testamentaria e pecore screziate: → 514a, Giacobbe 1989/90, 111-124 / 127-147.

2453 *Grandjean* Michel, Pierre DAMIEN lecteur d'AUGUSTIN; à propos de l'interprétation du mariage de Jacob: RÉAug 36 (1990) 147-154.

2454 *Rofé* Alexander, [Gen 24] An inquiry into the betrothal of Rebecca: → 147, ᶠRENDTORFF R., Hebr. Bibel 1990, 27-39.

2455 *Kendrick* W. Gerald, [Gn 21,9; 24,62s; 26,8; 29,17] Selected translation problems in Genesis: BTrans 41 (1990) 425-431.

2456 *Weisblit* Shlomoh, Ⓗ [Gn 21,33] Abraham planted an *ešel* in Beer-Sheba and called [it] *El 'Olam*: BethM 36,124 (1990s) 11-19.

E2.7 **Jacob** and Esau; ladder-dream; *Jacob, somnium, Genesis 25 ...*

2457 *Soggin* J. Alberto, *a*) Da Abramo a Giacobbe; – *b*) Sogni e visioni; la scala di Giacobbe: → 514a, Giacobbe 1989/90, 39-48 / 79-88.

2457* *Görg* M., *šwḥ* (Shuach) [Gn 25,2] — Wege der Namensüberlieferung: BibNot [22 (1983) 25, *Knauf* E.] 47 (1989) 7-9.

2458 *Wilke* Hans-Hermann, Abraham starb alt und lebenssatt (1. Mose 25,8): (ZPrax) RU 20 (1990) 42-44 [< ZIT 90,430].

2459 *Cohen* Jeffrey, [Gen 25,19] These are the generations of Isaac: → 115, ᶠLIPTZIN S., JBQ 19 (1990s) 260-4.

2460 **Hendel** Ronald S., The epic of the patriarch ... Jacob 1987 → 5,2308 [not 'of the Pentateuch' nor 'of the patriarchs']: ᴿBO 47 (1990) 194s (G. W. *Coats*); JAOS 110 (1990) 345 (V. H. *Matthews*); Orientalia 59 (1990) 90s (W. G. E. *Watson*).

2461 *Jeansonne* Sharon Pace, Gen 25: 23 — the use of poetry in the Rebekah narrative: → 82, ᶠHUNT J., Psalms 1990, 145-152.

2462 *Kreuter* Jens A., Warum liebte Isaak Esau? Überlegungen zu *b*ᵉ*pīw* in
Gen 25,28: BibNot 48 (1989) 17s.
2463 *Smith* S.H., [Gn 25,36...] 'Heel' and 'thigh'; the concept of sexuality in
the Jacob-Esau narrative: VT (1990) 464-473.
2464 *Gottfriedsen* Christine, Beobachtungen zum alttestamentlichen
Segensverständnis [Gn 27... WESTERMANN C.]: BZ 34 (1990) 1-15.
2465 a) *Vermeylen* Jacques, Le vol de la bénédiction paternelle; une lecture de
Gen 27; – b) *Kevers* Paul, [Gn 34] Les 'fils de Jacob' à Sichem: ➤ 518,
IOSOT 13, 1989/90, 23-40 / 41-46.
2466 *Siebert* Lothar, Die Jakob-Esau-Erzählung; Arbeitshilfe zu Gen 24-27:
CLehre 43 (B 1990) U-81-91.97-106 [< ZIT 90,634].
2467 **Kuntzmann** Raymond, Le symbolisme des jumeaux 1983 ➤ 64,2325...
2,1690: ᴿAulaO 8 (1990) 149s (G. del *Olmo Lete*).
2468 *Hermisson* Hans-Jürgen, Jakob und Zion, Schöpfung und Heil: ZeichZt
44 (1990) 262-8 [< ZIT 91,25].
2469 *Dresner* Samuel, [Gen 28] Rachel and Leah; sibling tragedy or the
triumph of piety and compassion?: BR 6,2 (1990) 22-27.40-42; ill.
2470 **Dicou** B., [Gn 27s] Jakob en Esau, Israël en Edom; Israël tegenover de
volken in de verhalen van Jacob en Esau in Genesis en in de grote profetieën over Edom: Diss. ᴰ*Deurloo* K., VU. Amst 1990. 310 p. Voorburg
1990, Publiform. 299 p. ƒ39,50. 90-6495-225-6. – TsTNijm 30 (1990) 302;
RTLv 22, p. 587.
2471 *Rosenblatt* Marie-Eloise, [Gen 28,10-22] 'Surely the Lord is in this place';
blessing in the world: Way 30 (1990) 3-15.
2472 *Wyatt* Nicolas, [Gn 28,10-22] Where did Jacob dream his dream?:
ScandJOT (1990,2) 44-57.
2473 *Abrams* Judith Z., [Gn 29] Rachel, a woman who would be a mother:
JBQ 18 (1989s) 213-221.
2474 **Weisman** Zeev, ✪ From Jacob to Israel [ʿAl Yaʿaqob wᵉ-šillubô...]. J
1986, Magnes. 149 p.; 23 fig. 965-223-646-2 [KirSef 62 (1988s) p. 20].
2475 **Sherwood** Stephen K., 'Had God not been on my side'; an examination
of the narrative technique of the story of Jacob and Laban, Genesis
29,1-32: EurUnivSt 23/400. Fra 1990, Lang. xix-433 p. – ᴿLA 40 (1990)
502s (A. *Niccacci*).
2476 *Jonge* Martinus de, [Gen 30,14-18] Rachel's virtuous behavior in the
Testament of Issachar: ➤ 122, ᶠMALHERBE A., Greeks 1990, 340-352.
2477 a) *Zatelli* Ida, Lea e Rachele, dall'esegesi scritturale all'interpretazione
simbolica; – b) *Fiores d'Arcais* Francesco, 'Le storie di Giacobbe' di
Thomas MANN: ➤ 514a, Giacobbe 1989/90, 51-75 / 9-35.

E2.8   **Jacob's wrestling; the Angels;** *lucta, Angelus/mal'ak Gn 31...*

2478 a) *Neufeld* Ernst, [Gen 31] Two views on Jacob; Jacob the wrestler; – b)
Bulka Reuven P., The selling of the birthright; making sense of a
perplexing episode: JBQ 19 (1990s) 92-99.104 / 100-104.
2479 *Gilat* Lipa, ✪ [Gn 31,40] Jacob's blessing on Esau: BethM 36,124
(1990s) 84-90.
2480 *Weimar* Peter, Beobachtungen zur Analyse von Gen 32,23-33: BibNot
49 (1989) 53-81; 50 (1989) 58-94.
2481 a) *De Benedetti* Paolo, La lotta con l'angelo (Genesi 32,25-33); – b)
Sierra Sergio J., Giacobbe nel Midrash; – c) *Rizzi* Armido, La strana
etica di Giacobbe ci intriga: ➤ 514a, Giacobbe 1989/90, 91-108 / 151-174 /
177-192.

2482 *Holmgren* Fredrick C., Holding your own against God! Genesis 32:22-32 (in the context of Gen 31-33]: Interpretation 44 (1990) 5-17.

2483 *Cazelles* Henri, Fondements bibliques de la théologie des anges: RThom 90 (1990) 181-193.

2484 **Giudici** Maria Pia, Gli angeli; note esegetiche e spirituali [franç. 1985 → 2,1697]. R 1984, Città Nuova. 150 p. Lit. 7000. – ᴿPalCl 69 (1990) 92s (A. *Pedrini*].

2485 **Greene** John T., The role of the messenger and message in the Ancient Near East [diss. Boston Univ. 1980]: BrownJudSt 169, 1989 → 5,3317: ᴿJAOS 110 (1990) 752s (S. A. *Meier*).

2486 **Mach** Michael, ❶ Studies in Jewish angelology in the Hellenistic-Roman period: diss. TA 1986. 436 p.; 28 fig. – KirSef 62 (1988s) p. 62.

2487 **Meier** Samuel A., The messenger in the ancient Semitic world [*mal'ak/ mar sipri*] 5,1230*; 1-55590-289-5: ᴿBL (1990) 124 (J. *Sawyer*); CBQ 52 (1990) 724 (R. D. *Nelson*, brief; his function not so much verbatim delivery but being 'a resource-person for clarification of the message'); JBL 109 (1990) 306-8 (J. T. *Greene*); JSS 35 (1980) 501 (L. L. *Grabbe*).

2488 **Santangelo** Maria N., Le Berceau des anges. Lv 1988, Peeters. 220 p. Fb 1200. 90-6381-19-9 [sic in] ᴿAntClas 59 (1990) 453 (J. *Wankenne*: bristling with errors, asserts that the angels exist and are attested in Gn Dan Ezek Tob & NT; but then continues with a 'linguistic' investigation of the 'profane', Phoenician, and 'magic' alphabets).

2489 *Ströter Bender* Jutta, Engel, ihre Stimme, ihr Duft, ihr Gewand und ihr Tanz; Symbole. Stu 1988, Kreuz. 230 p. ᴿStromata 45 (1989) 235s.

2490 *Suurmond* J.-J., Engelen en demonen; exegetisch-theologische en pastorale notities: GerefTTs 90 (1990) 221-235.

2491 **Sheres** Ita, [Gn 34] Dinah's rebellion; a biblical parable for our time. NY 1990, Crossroad. vii-148 p. $18 [TS 52, 388, Kathleen M. *O'Connor*].

2492 *Wyatt* N., [Gn 34] The story of Dinah and Shechem: UF 22 (1990) 433-458.

2493 *Geller* Stephen A., The sack of Shechem; the use of typology in biblical covenant religion: Prooftexts 18 (1990) 1-15.

2494 *Hayward* C. T. T., [Gen 35,1] Jacob's second visit to Bethel in Targum Pseudo-Jonathan: → 183, ᶠVERMES G. 1990, 175-192.

2495 **Cowan** Margaret P., Genesis 38; the story of Judah and Tamar and its role in the ancestral narratives of Genesis: diss. Vanderbilt, ᴰ*Harrelson* W. Nv 1990. – RelStR 17,193.

2496 *Friedman* M. A., [Gn 38] Tamar, a symbol of life; the 'killer wife' superstition in the Bible and Jewish traditions: AJS 15,1 (CM 1990) 23-61 [< NTAbs 35,216].

2497 *Tawa* Habib, Histoire de Thamar et peuple de Thamoud; les récits bibliques et coraniques à la rencontre de l'histoire: RevSR 64 (1990) 271-281.

E2.9   **Joseph;** Jacob's blessings; *Genesis 37; 39-50.*

2498 **Croisier** Faika, L'histoire de Joseph d'après un manuscrit oriental [arabe 16ᵉ siècle, d'un IBN ISÂ Aḥmad, chrétien converti à l'Islam]: Arabiyya 10. Genève 1989, Labor et Fides. 251 p. 2-8309-0135-5. – ᴿÉTRel 65 (1990) 442 (Françoise *Smyth*); RTPhil 122 (1990) 286s (T. *Römer*).

2499 **Dietrich** W., Die Josephserzählung als Novelle und Geschichtsschreibung; zugleich ein Beitrag zur Pentateuchfrage: BTStud 14, 1989 → 5, 2331: ᴿTLZ 115 (1990) 497s (L. *Schmidt*).

2500 *Gauthier-Walter* Marie-Dominique, Joseph, figure idéale du Roi?: Cah-Arch 38 (1990) 25-36; 8 fig.
2501 **Humphreys** W. Lee, Joseph and his family 1988 ➤ 4,2375; 5,2332: ^RCritRR 2 (1989) 168-170 (J. R. *King*).
2502 **Kebekus** Norbert, Die Joseferzählung; Literarkritische und redaktions-geschichtliche Untersuchungen zu Genesis 37-50 [Diss. Münster, ^D*Weimar*]: Internationale Hochschulschriften. NY 1990, Waxmann. 357 p. DM 59 [TR 87,249].
2503 **Koptak** Paul E., Judah in the biblical story of Joseph; rhetoric and biography in the light of Kenneth BURKE's theory of identification: diss. Northwestern. Evanston 1990. 303 p. 90-31943. – DissA 51 (1990s) 2048-A.
2504 **Kugel** J. L., In Potiphar's house; the interpretive life of biblical texts [5 on Joseph; also Ps 137...]. SF 1990, Harper-Collins. v-266 p. $35. 0-06-064907-0 [NTAbs 35,266].
2505 **Longacre** Robert E., Joseph, 1989 ➤ 5,2334: ^RCritRR 3 (1990) 155-7 (W. L. *Humphreys*); HebSt 31 (1990) 200-4 (D. *Pardee*: morpho-semantic part good); WestTJ 52 (1990) 365-8 (R. B. *Dillard*: indispensable approach).
2506 **Premare** A.-L. de, Joseph et Muhammad; le chapitre 12 du Coran (étude textuelle). Aix-en-Provence 1989, Univ. 194 p. – ^RRThom 90 (1990) 678s (J. *Jomier*).
Rodrigues Pereira A. S., Two Syriac verse homilies on Joseph 1989s ➤ 9430.
2507 **Schmidt** Ludwig, Literarische Studien zur Josephsgeschichte: BZAW 167, 1986 ➤ 2,1715 ... 4,2383: ^RRB 97 (1990) 608-610 (J. *Loza*).
2508 **Schmitt** Hans-Christoph, Die nichtpriesterliche Josephsgeschichte... BZAW 154, 1980 ➤ 61,3248 ... 65,2036: ^RRB 97 (1990) 606-8 (J. *Loza*).
2509 *Schuller* Eileen, 4Q372 1, a text about Joseph: ➤ 527, RQum 14,55 (1989s) 349-376.
2510 **Seebass** Horst, Geschichtliche Zeit und theonome Tradition in der Joseph-Erzählung 1978 ➤ 60,2970 ...: RB 97 (1990) 605s (J. *Loza*: retard parce que 'j'avais l'intention d'en parler critiquement, mais le moment ne semble pas encore venu, même si je n'ai pas à dire ici pour quelles raisons').
2511 *Vickrey* John F., [Old English] Exodus and the robe of Joseph: StPg 86 (1989) 1-17.
2512 **Westermann** C., Die Joseph-Erzählungen; elf Bibelarbeiten zu Genesis 37-50 [revised from part of 1966 Calwer Predigthilfen]: Tb 1. Stu 1990, Calwer. 106 p. DM 16,80. 3-7608-3058-9 [BL 91,101, R. N. *Whybray*: for those who know some Hebrew].
2513 **Knauf** E. A., [Gn 37,28] Midian 1988 ➤ 4,2376; 5,2338: ^RBL (1990) 39 (J. R. *Bartlett*); EfMex 8 (1990) 286-8 (R. *Duarte Castillo*); ZAW 102 (1990) 152 (H. C. *Schmitt*); ZRGg 42 (1990) 182s (G. *Lüling*).
2514 *Jeffers* A., [Gen 37...] Divination by dreams in Ugaritic literature and in the OT: IrBSt 12 (1990) 167-183.
2515 *Görg* Manfred, [Gn 37,36] Die Amtstitel des Potifar: BibNot 53 (1990) 14-20.
2516 *Kugel* James, [Gen 39,7...] The case against Joseph: ➤ 124, ^FMORAN W., Lingering 1990, 271-287 [...he changed his mind in the heat of passion, because he then had a vision of Jacob (R. *Huna*, Gen. Rabba)].
2517 *Marcus* David, 'Lifting up the head'; on the trail of a word play in Genesis 40: Prooftexts 10 (1990) 17-27.

2518 **Wills** L. M., [Gn 37-50, Est, Dan] The Jew in the court of the foreign king: HarvDissRel 26. Minneapolis 1990, Fortress. xiii-204 p. $15. 0-943872-95-2 [BL 91,102, F. W. *Coxon*].

2519 *Lichtenstein* Murray H., Idiom, rhetoric and the text of Genesis 41:16: ➤ 75, Mem. HELD M., JANES 19 (1989) 85-100.

2519* **Scharbert** Josef, [Gn 45,3] Ich bin Josef 1988 ➤ 4,2381; 5,1989: ᴿTPQ 137 (1989) 110s (L. *Ruppert*: ➤ Elenchus vol. 5 Index p. 1051: vom Text p. 190 leider ausgefallen).

2520 *Langlamet* François, Arithmétique des scribes et texte consonantique; Gen 46,1-7 et 1 Sam 17,1-54: RB 97 (1990) 379-409; Eng. 379: 409-413, note complémentaire, *Nodet* Étienne.

2521 **Somekh** Alberto, Il commiato di Yaʿaqob (Gen. 49,2-27); un'ipotesi di interpretazione in chiave 'mediterranea': Mi Univ Fac ʟ/f 139, Glottologia 2. F 1990, Nuova Italia. xix-145 p. 88-221-0895-7.

2522 *Ahuviah* Avraham, Gen 49,6: BethM 35 (1989s) 227-236; also Nm 30,2-17; 1 Sam 9,25; 10,16; 15,23; 20 [OTAbs 14,127].

2523 *Heck* Joel D., A history of interpretation of Genesis 49 and Deuteronomy 33: BS 147 (1990) 16-31.

2524 **Syrén** R., The blessings in the Targums [Gn 49, Dt 33] 1986 ➤ 2,1722 ... 5,2141: ᴿCritRR 2 (1989) 381-3 (B. *Chilton*); SvEx 55 (1990) 121-3 (B. *Isaksson*).

2525 *Reardon* Patrick H., [Gn 50,23s; Jos 24,32] Of Joseph, especially his bones: ➤ 82, ꟳHUNT J., Psalms 1990, 153-7.

2526 *Vanhetloo* Warren, Four hundred silent years [Jacob to Moses, 1900 to 1500; also Malachi to the Baptist]: CalvaryB 6 (1990) 14-32.

E3.1   **Exodus event and theme;** *textus, commentarii.*

2527 **Blum** Erhard, [Ex 1-14] Studien zur Komposition des Pentateuch: BZAW 189. B 1990, de Gruyter. x-493 p. DM 148. 3-1101-2027-5 [BL 91,67, A. G. *Auld*: substantial continuation of his Komposition der Vätergeschichte].

2528 ꟳ**Borret** M., ORIGÈNE, Homélics sur l'Exode; SChr 321, 1985 ➤ 2,1725 ... 5,2346: ᴿHelmantica 41 (1990) 396s (Rosa M. *Herrera*).

2529 *Cazelles* Henri, Peut-on circonscrire un événement Exode? ➤ 354, Protohistoire 1990, 29-65 [BL 91,37s, A. D. H. *Mayes*: 'a sometimes rather speculative and uncertain attempt to trace the history of the tradition of a flight from Egypt'].

2530 **Cazelles** H., Autour de l'Exode 1987 ➤ 3,201 ... 5,2347: ᴿSvEx 55 (1990) 98s (T. N. D. *Mettinger*).

2531 ᵀᴱ**Drazin** Israel, Targum Onkelos to Exodus [based on A. *Sperber* and A. *Berliner* editions]: Center for Judaic Studies. Denver/Brooklyn 1990, Univ./Ktav. xiii-383 p. 0-88125-342-1.

2532 **Durham** John I., Exodus: Word Comm. 3, 1987 ➤ 3,2284 ... 5,2351: ᴿEstB 48 (1990) 151s (J. P. *Tosaus*); IrTQ 56 (1990) 73-75 (A. D. H. *Mayes*); Themelios 15 (1989s) 68s (D. *Jackson*); VT 40 (1990) 126s (J. A. *Emerton*).

2533 **Fritz** Maureena, The Exodus experience, a journey in prayer. Winona MN 1989, St. Mary's. 151 p. $12. – ᴿTorJT 6 (1990) 156s (Jackie *Kuikman*).

2534 *García López* Félix, El Dios del Éxodo y la realidad social: EstTrin 21 (1987) 259-281.

2535 *Genuyt* François, La sortie d'Égypte: SémBib 54 (1989) 18-35; 55,1-18; 56,1-17.
2536 **Girón Blanc** Luis-Fernando, Midrás Éxodo Rabbah I, 1989 ↠ 5,2353: ᴿEstB 48 (1990) 143s (M. *Pérez Fernández*).
2537 *Gottwald* Norman K., El 'Éxodo' como evento y proceso; un estudio de la base bíblica de la teología de la liberación: TXav 39 (1989) 385-396.
2538 **Horst** P. W. van der, Joods-hellenistische poëzie ... Ezech. trag. 1987 ↠ 4,2413: ᴿNedTTs 44 (1990) 71s (A. S. van der *Woude*).
2539 **Houtman** C., Exodus [I 1986 ↠ 3,2288] II, 7:14-19:25: CommOudT 1989 ↠ 5,2356: ᴿCBQ 52 (1990) 714-6 (W. A. *Vogels*: philological minutiae so abundant that he neglects theological and existential aspects; he attributes to the reader 'feelings' like joy in war and pleasure in the misery of the dispossessed); GerefTTs 90 (1990) 246s (A. van der *Wal*, 1); NedTTs 44 (1990) 157s (M. D. *Koster*, 1).
2539* **Isabelle de la Source** sr., Le cycle de Moïse (Ex-Lv-Nm-Dt): Lire la Bible avec les Pères 2. P/Montréal 1990, Médiaspaul/Paulines. 253 p. F 85 [NRT 113,466, A. *Harvengt*].
2540 **Johnstone** W., Exodus: OTGuides. Sheffield 1990, Academic. 120 p. £5. 1-85075-239-7. – ᴱExpTim 101 (1989s) 310s (C. S. *Rodd*).
2541 ᵀᴱ**Le Boulluec** A., *Sandevoir* P., L'Exode; traduction du texte grec de la Septante; intr. notes: Bible d'Alexandrie 2. P 1989, Cerf. 394 p. F 185. 2-204-03066-X. – ᴿBL (1990) 44 (N. de *Lange*); ÉTRel 65 (1990) C.-B. *Amphoux*, aussi sur 3. Lévitique); JStJud 21 (1990) 123-6 (A. *Hilhorst*); NRT 112 (1990) 586s (X. *Jacques*); RTLv 21 (1990) 70-74 (P.-M. *Bogaert*).
2542 **Loewenstamm** Samuel E., ✡ *Mesorat yeşi'at Miṣrayim* ... The tradition of the Exodus in its development. J 1987, Magnes. 168 + 10 p.; 24 fig. 965-223-453-2 [KirSef (41, Nᵒ 1884) 62 (1988s) p. 20].
2543 *Lott* sr. Anastasia, Exodus as a soteriological problem; journey – struggle – hope – covenant fulfilment [Bura irrigation resettlement scheme]: AfER 32,1 (1990) 29-41.
2544 *Navone* John, Itinerari biblici, espressione della ricerca di Dio [Esodo; Mosè in Mt; Gesù in Gv e Lc-Atti ...]: CC 141 (1990,3) 238-247.
2545 **Rebula** Aloiz, Jutri čez Jordan [roman, novel]. Celie 1988, Mohorjeva družba. 319 p. – ᴿBogVest 49 (1989) 99-101 (F. *Rozman*).
2546 *Redford* Donald, An Egyptological perspective on the Exodus narrative: ᴱ**Rainey** Anson F., Egypt, Israel, Sinai; archaeological and historical relationships in the biblical period [Tel Aviv symposium 1982 ↠ 3,834]: Biblical Ramesses is not to be identified with Piramesse; Exodus topographical data relate to Saite and Persian periods, not New Kingdom; no reason to link the Exodus specifically to 19th dynasty. Brief response by *Bietak*.
2547 *Sabar* Yona, On the nature of the oral translation of the Book of Exodus in the Neo-Aramaic dialect of the Jews of Zakho: ↠ 164, ᶠSEGERT S., *Sopher* 1990, 311-7.
2548 **Sanderson** Judith E., An Exodus scroll from Qumran 1986 ↠ 3,1737 ... 5,2361: ᴿBZ 34 (1990) 300s (J. *Maier*); JNES 49 (1990) 195s (M.O. *Wise*).
2549 **Sarna** Nahum M., Understanding [↠ 5,2363 'Exploring'] Exodus; the heritage of biblical Israel 1986 ↠ 2,1738; ... 4,2428: ᴿJAOS 110 (1990) 127s (J. *Van Seters*: homiletical; geographical data unreliable).
2550 **Schmid** Rudolf, Esodo, Levitico, Numeri; Dio cammina con il suo popolo [Mit Gott auf dem Weg 1977] ᵀ1987 ↠ 3,2307: ᴿSalesianum 52 (1990) 173 (M. *Cimosa*).

2550* **Schmidt** Werner H.,   Exodus [I-II. 1977/83 ► 3,2308; III. 1988 ► 4, 2429] IV: BK AT.   Neuk 1988. – ᴿTLZ 115 (1990) 735 (J. *Conrad*).

2551 **Sierra** Sergio J.,   RASHI, Commento all'Esodo: Ascolta Israele 5, 1988 ► 5,2367:   ᴿMaia 42 (1990) 88s (A. *Ceresa-Gastaldo*).

2552 **Spreafico** Ambrogio,   Esodo, memoria e promessa; interpretazioni profetiche 1985 ► 1,2397 ... 4,2433:   ᴿRBibArg 52 (1990) 189-191 (J. S. *Croatto*).

2553 **Stiebing** William H.ᴶ, Out of the desert? Archaeology and the Exodus/Conquest narratives 1989 ► 5,2369:   ᴿBA 53 (1990) 118s (G. L. *Mattingly*); JBL 109 (1990) 701-3 (R. G. *Boling*: 15th century date unlikely; 13th only partially; famine may have caused peasant revolt along with 'occasional bands of brigands' and 'a small contingent of escaped slaves from Egypt' p. 187); JScStR 29 (1990) 269s (P. C. *Hammond*).

2554 *Vermeylen* Jacques,   Libération socio-politique et libération plénière (la 'théologie de la libération' et le thème biblique de l'Exode): StMiss 39 (1990) 49-78.

2554* *a) Vervenne* M.   Het boek Exodus, lijnen en standpunten in het onderzoek naar een gegroeid geschrift / Zij stelden vertrouwen in Jahwe en in Mozes zijn dienaar; kanttekeningen bij het zeeverhaal (Ex. 13,17 - 14,31); – *b) Schrijver* G. De,   Exodus en bevrijding in de bevrijdingstheologie: ► 560*, Exodus 1989, 9-49 . 101-120 / 151-167.

2555 **Wevers** J. W.,   Notes on the Greek text of Exodus: SBL SeptCog 30. Atlanta 1990, Scholars. xxvii-678 p. $42; sb./pa. $28. 1-55540-453-7; -4-5 [BL 91,53, W. *Johnstone*].

2556 *a) Wevers* J. W.   Pre-Origen recensional activity in the Greek Exodus; – *b) Ulrich* E.,   A Greek paraphrase of Exodus on papyrus from Qumran Cave 4; – *c) Fraenkel* D.,   Die Quellen der asterisierten Zusätze im zweiten Tabernakelbericht Exod 35-40: ► 70, ᶠHANHART R. 1990, 121-139 / 297s / 140-186.

E3.2   Moyses – Pharaoh, Goshen – *Exodus 1*

2557 **Alonso Schökel** Luis,   *Gutiérrez* Guillermo,   *a)* La misión de Moisés; meditaciones bíblicas: Servidores y Testigos 42, 1989 ► 5,2372:   ᴿActuBbg 27 (1990) 53s (R. de *Sivatte*); BibFe 16 (1990) 146 (M. *Sáenz Galache*). – *b)* Moses, his mission, ᵀ*Livingstone* Dinah.   Slough 1990, St. Paul.   143 p. [AcPIB 9/7,546].   0-85439-345-5.

2558 **Aurelius** Erik,   Der Fürbitter Israels 1988 ► 4,2441; 5,2374:   ᴿBiblica 71 (1990) 116-122 (H. *Cazelles*); CBQ 52 (1990) 106-8 (T. B. *Dozeman*); RB 97 (1990) 85-102 (N. *Lohfink*, Dissens über Dt 9-10); TsTKi 61 (1990) 219s (Terje *Stordalen*).

2559 **Berge** Kåre,   Kallelsen av Moses til profet; momenter til literaturhistorisk plassering av Exodus 3f. [*Schmid* H. H.]: ► 21*, Mem. BJØRNDALEN A., TsTKi 60,4 (1989) 271-280; Eng. 280.

2560 **Chandler** Tertius,   When were Moses and Abraham? Diss. Clayton Univ. 1988. 74 p. – OIAc JJ90.

2561 **Coats** George W.,   Moses, heroic man 1988 ► 4,2448; 5,2378:   ᴿBR 5,2 (1989) 6s (J. S. *Ackerman*).

2562 **Deist** F. E.   *a)* Laat my volk trek; 'n Verhaal van bevryding, Eksodus 1-14.   Cape Town 1988, Tafelberg. – OTEssays 2,3 (1989) 113s (JHP); – *b)* Heads I win, tails you lose; Yahweh and the editor of the exodus story; an historico-aesthetic interpretation of Exodus 1-12: OTEssays 2,3 (1989) 36-52.

2563 *Derrett* J. D. M., A Moses-Buddha parallel and its meaning: ArOr 58 (1990) 310-7.
2564 *Dodson* Aidan, The Canopic chest of Ramesses II [British Museum fragment]: RÉgp 41 (1990) 31-37; 3 fig.; pl. 2.
2565 *Edwards* M. J., Atticizing Moses? NUMENIUS, the Fathers and the Jews: VigChr 44 (1990) 64-75.
2566 *Feucht* Erika, Kinder fremder Völker in Ägypten: StAltÄgK 17 (1990) 177-204.
2567 **Fleg** Edmond, Mosé secondo i Saggi: 'Ascolta Israele', ᵀ*Masarati* Rodi, *al.* R 1989 = 1981 , Dehoniane. 207 p. 88-396-01031.
2568 **Foulke-Ffeinberg** F. X., Moses and his masters. Edinburg TX 1990, CUI. xi-160 p. $19; $10 [CBQ 52,589].
2569 *Fubini* Giorgio, Il Mosè legislatore e il popolo ribelle; la religione mosaica nell'ultima opera di FREUD: RaMIsr 55 (1989) 85-102.
2570 **Getz** Gene A., Mozes; Leven bij het Woord. Haag 1985, Voorhoeve. 122 p. *f*17.50 [KerkT 40,341].
2571 *Gutmann* Joseph, The testing of Moses; a comparative study in Christian, Muslim and Jewish art [< Bulletin of Asia Institute NS 2 (1988)]: ➤ 5,272, Sacred images 1989, XIV, 107-117.
2572 *Helck* Wolfgang, Drei ramessidische Daten [Thronbesteigungsdatum Ramses' II. und Sethos' I. (nur Tag des Monats)]: StAltÄgK 17 (1990) 205-214.
2573 **Kushelevsky** Rella, Moses versus the Angel of Death; development of a thematic unity: diss. Bar-Ilan. Ramat-Gan 1990. – RTLv 22, p. 588.
2574 *Lehmann* [Oskar/Asher, KirSef 62,499], The young Moses, prince of Egypt [Das Leiden des], ᵀ*Hirschler* Gertrude. NY 1987, Judaica. ix-234 p.; ill. (Forst S.).
2574* *a*) *Lust* J., De geboorte van Mozes en Exodus 1-6; Mozes en de profeten; – *b*) *Jagersma* H., Oorsprong en betekenis van Mozes; – *c*) *Outryve* O.-E. van, Het verhaal van de 'plagen' in Egypte: ➤ 560*, Exodus 1989, 63-75. 151-167 / 51-60 / 77-98.
2575 *a*) *McBride* S. Dean, Transcendent authority; the role of Moses in OT traditions; – *b*) *Hay* David M., Moses through NT spectacles; – *c*) *Herzog* Frederick, Moses in contemporary theology; – *d*) *Flynn* Elisabeth L., Moses in the visual arts; – *e*) *McCann* J. Clinton, Exodus 32:1-14, Expository; – *f*) *Baird* William, 1 Corinthians 10:1-13, expository: Interpretation 44 (1990) 229-239 / 240-252 / 253-264 / 265-276 / 277-281 / 286-290.
2575* *Meghnagi* David, The dancer balancing on the tip of one toe; FREUD and the man Moses: ➤ 526*a, AnStoEseg 7,1 (1990) 311-321.
2576 *Milgrom* Jacob, ❺ Magic, monotheism, and Moses' *ṭaʾwiyôt*; BethM 36,124 (1990s) 42-55.
2577 *Opeloye* Muhib O., Confluence and conflict in the Qur'anic and biblical accounts of the life of Prophet Musa: Islamochristiana 16 (1990) 25-41.
2578 **Rice** Emanuel, FREUD and Moses; the long journey home. Albany 1990, SUNY. 260 p. [JAAR 58,741].
2579 *Rorem* Paul, Moses as the paradigm for the liturgical spirituality of Pseudo-DIONYSIUS: ➤ 643, StPatr 18,2 (1983/9) 275-9.
2580 **Schmidt** Werner H., Exodus, Sinai und Mose; Erwägungen zu Ex 1-19 und 24²ʳᵉᵛ [erweiterte Bibliographie]: ErtFor 191. Da 1990, Wiss. viii-176 p. – 3-534-08779-8.
2581 **Schutz** Albert L., Exodus: the Cabalistic Bible; i. The enslavement of Israel and the coming of Moses; ii. God's call. Goleta CA 1985s, Quantal. 35 p.; 54 p. [KirSef 62 (1988s) p. 40].

Seitz C. R., Mose als Prophet 1990 ➤ 3887.
2582 **Sourouzian** H., Les monuments du roi Merenptah: DAI-K Sonderschrift 22. Mainz 1989, von Zabern. ix-237 p.; 36 fig.; 42 pl. 3-8053-1053-6 [BL 91,32, K. A. *Kitchen*: splendid, except in her attributing some Merenptah monuments (with REDFORD) to Ramesses II].
2583 *Strugnell* J., Moses-pseudepigrapha at Qumran; 4Q375, 4Q376, and similar works: ➤ 554, ArchHistDSS 1985/90, 221-256.
2584 *Tronina* Antoni, ❷ Epigraphic attestations of Israel's origins [... Meneptah]: RuBi 42 (1989) 21-27.
2585 **Weimar** Peter, Berufung des Mose [Ex 2,23-5,5]: OBO 32, 1980 ➤ 61,3355 ... 64,2407: ᴿTsTKi 61 (1990) 67s (M. *Sæbø*).
2586 *Winston* David, Two types of Mosaic prophecy according to PHILO: JPseud 4 (1989) 49-67 [< TR 87,64].

2587 **Davies** Gordon, Israel in Egypt, Exod. 1-2: diss. Pont. Gregorian Univ., ᴰ*Conroy* C. Rome 1990. – RTLv 22, p. 587.
2588 *Dijkstra* M., [Ex 1,11] Pithom en Raämses: NedTTs 43 (1989) 89-105; 4 fig.; Eng. 141: Reṭābe and Qantîr.
2589 **Görg** Manfred, Edom und Pitom: BibNot 51 (1990) 9s.
2590 *Weber* Beat, '...jede Tochter aber sollt ihr am Leben lassen!': Beobachtungen zu Ex 1,15-2,10 und seinem Kontext aus literaturwissenschaftlicher Perspektive: BibNot 55 (1990) 47-76.
2591 *Siebert-Hommes* J. C., Mozes – 'vreemdeling' in Midian: AmstCah 10 (1989) 16-20 [< ZAW 103,125].
2592 *Knights* C. H., [Ex 2,20; bSoṭah 11] Jethro merited that his descendants should sit in the chamber of hewn stone [i.e. Sanhedrin, before 30 C.E.]: JJS 41 (1990) 247-253.

E3.3 Nomen divinum, Tetragrammaton; *Exodus 3,14 ...*

2593 *Akao* J. O., Yahweh and Mal'ak in the early traditions of Israel, a study of the underlying traditions of Yahweh/Angel theophany in Exodus 3: IrBSt 12 (1990) 72-85.
2594 *Breton* Stanislas, Quelques réflexions sur la nomination paradoxale de Dieu: RSPT 74 (1990) 591-604.
2595 Celui qui est, ᴱ**Libera** Alain de 1986 ➤ 2,1778 ... 4,2474: ᴿLavalTP 46 (1990) 269s (J.-C. *Petit*).
2596 *Burrell* David, [Ex 3,14 ...] Naming the names of God; Muslims, Jews, Christians: TTod 47 (1990s) 22-29 [-51, symposium; 52-59, summation, *Pederson* Kusumita P.].
2597 *Debès* Joseph, Les mésaventures philosophiques de l'hémistiche biblique Ex 3,14: Masses Ouvrières 430 (1990) 41-47.
2598 *Ellingworth* Paul, The Lord; the final judge of functional equivalence: BTrans 41 (1990) 345-350.
2599 **Fischer** Georg, Jahwe unser Gott; Sprache, Aufbau und Erzähltechnik in der Berufung des Mose (Ex 3-4) [Diss. R 1988, Pont. Ist. Biblico]: OBO 91, 1989 ➤ 5,2390: ᴿErbAuf 66 (1990) 237s (S. *Petzolt*); ETL 66 (1990) 178s (J. *Lust*: not extreme but not superficial); ExpTim 102 (1990s) 123s (R. *Coggins*: important); OTAbs 13 (1990) 306 (C. T. *Begg*); TLZ 115 (1990) 885-7 (C. *Levin*); TüTQ 170 (1990) 71s (W. *Gross*).
2600 *Herrmann* K., Die Gottesnamen KWZW und MSPS [für YHWH] in der Hekhalot-Literatur: FraJudBei 16 (1988) 75-87 [< JStJud 21,112].

2601 *Janowitz* Naomi,   Theories of divine names in ORIGEN and Pseudo-DIONYSIUS: HistRel 30 (1990s) 359-372.
2602 *Kim Ee-Kon*,   🅚 Yahweh the God [of ?] Moses: Sinhak Sasang 68? (Seoul 1989?) 4-29 [TContext 8,70 gives as continuation of 67 (1989) but with page-numbering continued in 69 (1990)].
2603 *Klamer* Aleksy † 1969,   *a*) Les noms hébraïques 'Jahveh' et 'Elohim'; – *b*) The name Jahveh in the light of most recent discussions: FolOr 27 (1990) 5-9 / 11s.
2604 **Kohata** Fujiko,   Jahwist und P in Ex 3-14 [Diss. ᴰ*Schmitt* H.]: BZAW 166, 1986 ➤ 2,1776... 5,2391:   ᴿCBQ 52 (1990) 717-9 (J. E. *Wimmer*: strong case for her thesis).
2605 *Kruse* Heinz,   Der wunderbare Name; zu Herkunft und Sinngehalt des Jahwe-Namens: ZkT 112 (1990) 385-405.
2606 *a*) **Malaguti** M., Tu, ermeneutica di un nome di Dio.   Imola 1988, Martedí. – *b*) *Morandi* Emmanuele,   Ermeneutica e Tomismo: DoctCom 43 (1990) 103-125.
2607 **Mettinger** T. N. D., In search of God ... names 1988 ➤ 4,2477; 5,2392: ᴿExpTim 102 (1990s) 117 (G. *Lloyd Jones*); Interpretation 44 (1990) 415 (Phyllis A. *Bird*); JBL 109 (1990) 313-6 (M. S. *Smith*); TR 86 (1990) 192s (H. *Seebass*); NedTTs 44 (1990) 254s (P. B. *Dirksen*).
2608 **Mettinger** Tryggve N. D.,   Namnet och närvaron; Gudsnamn och Gudsbild i Böckernas Bok.   Örebro 1987, Libris.   222 p.; ill. Sk 260 – ᴿNorTTs 90 (1989) 230-2 (A. S. *Kapelrud*: interesting); TsTKi 61 (1990) 221s (A. *Aschim*).
2609 *a*) *Mettinger* Tryggve N. D.,   The elusive essence; ʏʜᴡʜ, El and Baal and the distinctiveness of Israelite faith; – *b*) *Schmidt* Werner H., 'Jahwe und...'; Anmerkungen zur sog. Monotheismus-Debatte; – *c*) *Stohr* Martin, Keine Korruption des Monotheismus durch Christozentrismus... J. L. HROMÁDKA: ➤ 147, ᶠRENDTORFF R., Hebr. Bibel 1990, 393-417 / 435-447 / 677-688.
2610 *O'Callaghan* José,   Problemática sobre los 'nomina sacra': ➤ 467*, Las abreviaturas en la enseñanza medieval y la transmisión del saber [Univ. Barcelona 1990) 21-36.
2611 *Paściak* Józef, 🅟 Yahwé – nom du Dieu d'Israël: ➤ 64, ᶠGRZYBEK S. 1990, 225-235; franç. 236.
2612 *Scheifler* J. R., ¿Que significa el nombre de Yahvé?:   Christus 628 (Méx. 1989) 58-64 [< Stromata 45,500].
2613 *Stubbens* Neil A.,   Naming God; Moses MAIMONIDES and Thomas AQUINAS: Thomist 54 (1990) 229-267 (nothing on Scripture).
2614 *Delcor* Mathias, *a*) La signification de l'E delphique et Exode 3,14-15 [< ᶠ*Cazelles* H., De la Torah 1981, 361-8]; – *b*) L'interdiction de briser les os de la victime pascale d'après la tradition juive [< L'animal 1985, 71-81]; – *c*) Une allusion à ʿAnath, déesse guerrière en Ex 32,18? [< ᶠ*Yadin* Y., JJS 33 (1982) 145-160]: ➤ 219*, Environnement 1990, 82-89 / 71-81 / 160-175.

———————

2615 *Dulaey* Martine,   Le bâton transformé en serpent; l'exégèse augustinienne d'Ex 4,2-4 et Ex 7,8-12: ➤ 13, ᶠBAVEL T. van, AugLv 41 (1990s) 723-737.
2616 *Blum* Ruth & Erhard,   Zippora und ihr *ḥoten dammîm*: ➤ 147, ᶠRENDTORFF R., Hebr. Bibel 1990, 41-54.

2617 *a) Derby* Josiah, [Ex 4,24-26] Why did God want to kill Moses?; – *b)*
Faiman David, [Ex 12] How many Hebrews left Egypt? [as in Ex; editorial
note remonstrates]: JBQ 18 (1989s) 222-9 / 230-3.
2618 *Diebner* B. J., De besnijdenis van Mozes in het boek Exodus; en geval
dat om verklaring vraagt: AmstCah 10 (1989) 21-36 [< ZAW 103,125].
2619 *Vycichl* Werner, Une erreur de traduction plus que deux fois millénaire
[*par'ō*, 'big house' never with article as 'the king, the shah' nor proper
name; yet (!) can be translated correctly 'the king' or proper name Ar'o
with *p-* prefixed as article]: → 70*, Mém. HARI R., BSocÉg 13 (1989)
183-4.
2620 *Biggar* Nigel, [Ex 6,2-8 ...] Between the Promise and the Promised Land:
ExpTim 102 (1990s) 18s.
2621 *Rendsburg* Gary A., [Ex 6,16-23; 1 Chr 2 ...; Nm 27] The internal consistency and historical reliability of the biblical genealogies: VT 40 (1990)
185-206.
2622 *Kegler* Jürgen, [Ex 7 ...] Zur Komposition und Theologie der Plagenerzählungen: → 147, FRENDTORFF R., Hebr. Bibel 1990, 55-74.
2623 *Krašovec* Jože, Unifying themes in Ex 7,8 - 11,10: → 518, IOSOT 13,
1989/90, 47-66.
2624 **Schmidt** L., Beobachtungen zu den Plagenerzählungen in Exodus
VII 14 - XI 10: StBibl 4. Leiden 1990, Brill. 119 p. ƒ 48. 90-04-09187-4
[BL 91,94, W. *Johnstone*].
2625 *Zevit Ziony*, Three ways to look at the Ten Plagues. BR 6,3 (1990)
16-23 . 42; color. ill.
2626 *Rendsburg* Gary A., [Ex 10,5 *ra'* pun on 'bad' / god Ra] Targum Onqelos
to Exod 10:5; 10:15; Numb 22:5; 22:11: Henoch [10 (1988) 1-15] 12
(1990) 15-17; ital. 17.

E3.4 *Pascha, sanguis, sacrificium:* **Passover, blood, sacrifice,** *Ex 11*...

2627 *Drobner* Hubertus R., Die Deutung der alttestamentlichen Pascha (Ex
xii) bei GREGOR von Nyssa im Lichte der Auslegungstradition der
griechischen Kirche: → 695, Stud/Nyss. 19 /90, 273-296.
2627* *Grelot* Pierre, Un poème acrostique araméen sur Exode 12: → 175,
FSZNYCER M., Semitica 38 (1989s) 159-165.
2628 *Nobile* Marco, [Ex 12; Nb 9,1-5; Jos 5,10-12; 2 R 21-23] Les quatre
Pâques dans le cadre de la rédaction finale de Gen - 2 Rois: → 518,
IOSOT 13, 1989/90, 191-6.
2629 *Vervenne* Marc, The 'P' tradition in the Pentateuch; document and/or
redaction? The 'Sea Narrative' (Ex 13,17 - 14,31) as a test case: → 518,
IOSOT 13, 1989/90, 67-90.
2630 *Sheriffs* Deryck, Moving on with God; key motifs in Exodus 13-20:
Themelios 15 (1989s) 49-60.
2631 **Ska** J. L., Le passage de la mer... Ex 14,1-31: AnBib 109, 1986 → 2,
1803*... 5,2407: RBZ 34 (1990) 126s (J. *Scharbert*); RivB 38 (1990) 521s
(Cecilia *Carniti*).
2632 *Monloubou* Louis, Exode 14-15; la sortie d'Égypte comme acte
liturgique [SKA J.-L., Le passage de la Mer 1986]: EsprVie 100 (1990)
257-261.
2633 *Couroyer* L. B., L'Exode et la bataille de Qadesh [...la réalité de la
traversée de la Mer (Ex 14,1-31) a été — et continue d'être — mise en
doute; peut-être en rapport avec les bas-reliefs de la Qadesh homonyme]:
RB 97 (1990) 321-358; 4 fig.; Eng. 321s.

2634 **Lamberty-Zielinski** Hedwig, Das 'Schilfmeer'; Herkunft, Bedeutung und Funktion eines alttestamentlichen Exodusbegriffs: kath. Diss. ᴰ*Fabry*. Bonn 1989s. – TR 86 (1990) 513.

2635 *Görg* Manfred, [Ex 14,2...] Pi-Hahirot – 'Mündung der Wasserläufen': BibNot 50 (1989) 7s.

2636 *a) Caquot* André, [Ex 15] Cantique de la mer et miracle de la mer; – *b) Valbelle* Dominique, Le paysage historique de l'Exode; – *c) Yoyotte* Jean, La campagne palestinienne du pharaon Merneptah; données anciennes et récentes: ⇸ 354, Protohistoire 1990, 67-85 / 87-107; 4 fig. / 109-119.

2637 **Burns** Rita J., Has the Lord... Miriam 1987 ⇸ 3,2367... 5,2414: ᴿJQR 81 (1990s) 221-6 (Yair *Zakovitch*).

2638 *Trible* Phyllis, Bringing Miriam out of the shadows: BR 5,1 (1989) 14-25.34; color. ill. [5/3, p.4-8 letters].

2639 *Wolters* Al, Not rescue but destruction; rereading Exodus 15:8 [four rare words for the waters 'piling up']: CBQ 52 (1990) 223-240.

2640 *Boyarin* Daniel, Inner biblical ambiguity, intertextuality and the dialect of midrash; the waters of Marah: Prooftexts 10 (1990) 29-48.

2641 *Shim Yong-Súb,* ◎ On the narrative on 'manna' Exodus 16: Samok 129 (Seoul 1989) 150-165 [< TContext 7/2, 56].

2642 **Maiberger** Paul, [Ex 16,15] Das Manna ᴰ1983 ⇸ 64,2457; 1,2471: ᴿJNES 49 (1990) 362s (D. *Pardee*).

2643 **Zenger** Erich, [Ex 17-34] Israel am Sinai; Analysen und Interpretationen zu Exodus 17-34 [Vorträge] 1982 ⇸ 63,2459... 65,2130: ᴿCBQ 52 (1990) 147s (R.B. *Coote*).

2644 **Schmitt** Hans-Christoph, Die Geschichte vom Sieg über die Amalekiter Ex 17,8-16 als theologische Lehrerzählung: ZAW 102 (1990) 335-344.

2645 *Balentine* Samuel E., Prayer in the wilderness traditions; in pursuit of divine justice: HebAnR 9 (1985) 53-74 [< OTAbs 13,219].

2646 *Lerner* Berel D., [Ex 17,11] Could Moses' hands make war?: JBQ 19 (1990s) 114-9.

2647 **Schart** Aaron, Mose und Israel im Konflikt; eine redaktionsgeschichtliche Studie zu den Wüstenerzählungen: OBO 98. FrS/Gö 1990, Univ./VR. 290 p. Fs 69. 3-7278-0672-9 / VR 3-525-53729-8 [BL 91,94, G.I. *Davies*].

2648 **Propp** William H., Water in the wilderness ᴰ1987 ⇸ 5,2417: ᴿBL (1990) 112 (J.R. *Porter*); BO 47 (1990) 454-6 (J. *Day*: unsatisfactory).

2649 **de Rocha Couto** António José, A aliança do Sinai como núcleo lógico-teológico central do Antigo Testamento: diss. R, Pont. Univ. Urbaniana, ᴰ*Testa* E. Valadares 1990. liii-307 p.

2650 **Dozeman** Thomas B., God on the mountain... Ex 19-24: SBL Mg 37, 1989 ⇸ 5,2420: ᴿTLZ 115 (1990) 884s (V. *Hirth*).

2651 **Tronina** Antoni, ⊕ Bóg przybywa ze Synaju [la théophanie dans la lyrique religieuse de l'ancien Israël; Hab.-Diss.]. Lublin 1989, KUL. 180 p. – ᴿFolOr 27 (1990) 271s (E. *Lipiński*).

2651* *Ska* J.L., [Ex 19,6] Popolo sacerdotale e popolo dell'alleanza nell'ANT: ⇸ 542*, I laici 1988/90, 19-38.

E3.5 **Decalogus,** *Ex 20 = Dt 5; Ex 21ss;* **Ancient Near East Law.**

2652 **Ahn Keumyoung,** The Sinaitic covenant and law in the theology of dispensationalism: diss. Andrews, ᴰ*La Rondelle* H. Berrien Springs MI, 1989. – AndrUnS 28 (1990) 147s.

2653 *a) Baanders* B., De tien woorden volgens RASJI; – *b) Reedijk* W. M., De joodse exegese van de Bijbel in de Middeleeuwen: Ter Herkenning 17,3 (1989) 154-168 / 145-153 [< GerefTTs 90,124].

2654 **Brooks** R., The spirit of the Ten Commandments; shattering the myth of rabbinic legalism. SF 1990, Harper & R. xiv-199 p. $22. 0-06-061132-4 [NTAbs 35,123].

2655 *Freedman* David N., The nine commandments; the secret progress of Israel's sins [due to re-touching by final editor, the nine books from Genesis through Kings each successively reveal violation of the first nine commandments: BR 5,6 (1989) 28-37.42 [6,2 (1990) 8s, H. *Shanks* suggests Nabot 1 Kgs 21 as violating tenth (coveting) commandment].

2656 **Harrelson** Walter, Os Dez Mandamentos e os direitos humanos [1980 → 61,3403], T*Mesquitella* Carlos S.: Temas Bíblicos. São Paulo 1987, Paulinas. 258 p. 85-05-00656-9. – RPerspT 22 (1990) 242-5 (J. *Vitório*).

2657 *Lettinga* J. P., Sprachliche Erwägungen zum Text der Zehn Gebote: Fundamentum (Schweiz 1990,1) 37-54... [< OTAbs 13, p. 122].

2658 **McBride** Alfred O., The Ten Commandments, sounds of love from Sinai. Cincinnati 1990, St. Anthony. 158 p. $7 pa. 0-86716-109-4 [TDig 38,72].

2658* **Mesters** Carlos, Befreit – gebunden; die 10 Gebote, das Bundesbuch, T*Brandt* Hermann: Erlanger TB 94. Erlangen 1989, Ev.-Luth. Mission. 117 p. DM 14,80 [TR 87,371, L. *Schwienhorst-Schönberger*].

2659 *Otto* Eckart, Alte und neue Perspektive in der Dekalogforschung: EvErz 42 (Fru 1990) 125-132 [*Schmidt* Heinz, *Maser* Hans G., didaktisch 133-149-162: < ZIT 90,424].

2660 *Rubello* Alfredo M., Sul decalogo 'cristianizzato' e l'autore della Collatio legum mosaicarum et romanarum: RaMIsr 55 (1989) 133-5.

2661 ESegal Ben-Zion, The Ten Commandments in history and tradition, ELevi Gershon: Perry Foundation. J 1990, Magnes. xv-453 p. 965-223-724-8.

2662 *a) Veijola* Timo, Der Dekalog bei LUTHER und in der heutigen Wissenschaft; – *b) Barr* James, Biblical law and the question of natural theology; → 560, Law 1988/90, 63-90 / 1 22.

2663 *Wolfson* E., Mystical rationalization of the commandments in [Moše B. ŠEM ṬOB] *Sefer ha-Rimmon*: HUCA 49 (1988) 217-251 [< ZAW 102,276].

2664 *a) Milgrom* Jo, Some consequences of the image prohibition in Jewish art; – *b) Weinfeld* Moshe, The decalogue; its significance, uniqueness, and place in Israel's tradition: → 526, Religion & Law 1985/90, 263-299 (301-6 response, *Hallet* S.) / 3-47.

2664* *a) Nichols* Aidan, Israels Bilder; alttestamentliche Prolegomena zu einer Christologie des Bildes: IZK 18 (1989) 533-549 [< HerdKorr 44,47]. – *b) Patrich* Joseph, Prohibition of a graven image among the Nabataeans; the evidence and its significance: → 783, Aram 2 (1990) 185-196.

2665 **Prigent** Pierre, [Ex 20,4] Le Judaïsme et l'image [... how there was in early Judaism an alternative trend more tolerant of images; but its art remained exclusively religious-symbolic]: TStAJud 24. Tü 1990, Mohr. xviii-381 p. DM 178. 3-16-14599-1 [BL 91,143, N. R. M. *de Lange*].

2666 **Patrich** Joseph, The formation of Nabatean art; prohibition of a graven image among the Nabateans. J 1990, Magnes. 231 p. 90-04-09256-0 [BL 91,160].

2667 **Schroer** Silvia, In Israel gab es Bilder... : OBO 74, 1987 → 3,2404... 5,2448: RVT 40 (1990) 373s (Judith M. *Hadley*).

Weltman Sheldon J., The biblical polemic against the foreign divine images D1990 → b15*.

2668 **Heschel** Abraham J. [Ex 20,8], Sabbat, seine Bedeutung für den heutigen Menschen [Eng. 1951], ᵀ*Olmesdahl* Ruth: Information Judentum 10. Neuk 1990, Neuk.-V. [vi-] 79 p. 3-7987-1326-7.

2669 *Köckert* Matthias, Das Gebot des siebten Tages: ↠ 76, ᶠHENKYS J. 1989, 170-186.

2670 *Placanica* Antonio, Cum de latrina lapsum Salomona ruina (Walther, initia 3580 E 4852) [Jew fallen into a sewer on sabbath refuses to be pulled out]: Maia 42 (1990) 275-286.

2671 **Robinson** Gnana, The origins and development of the Old Testament Sabbath [diss. Hamburg 1975, ᴰ*Koch* K.]: BeiBTEx 21, 1988 ↠ 4,2538: ᴿBL (1990) 112 (R. J. *Coggins*).

2672 **Spier** Erich, Der Sabbat: Das Judentum 1, 1989 ↠ 5,2449: ᴿJJS 41 (1990) 278s (L. *Jacobs*); Judaica 46 (1990) 242s (F. von *Hammerstein*).

2673 *Kvanvig* Helge S., [Ex 20,14] 'Du skal ikke drive hor ...'; hermeneutiske refleksjoner over det sjette bud [HANSEN... in VOGT 1967; NILSEN... 1966; seksualitet]: NorTTs 90 (1989) 65-86.

2674 *Lohfink* Norbert, Gibt es eine deuteronomistische Bearbeitung im Bundesbuch?: ↠ 518, IOSOT 13, 1989/90, 91-113.

2675 **Schwienhorst-Schönberger** Ludger, Das Bundesbuch (Ex 20,22 - 23,33): Studien zu seiner Entstehung und Theologie [ᴰ1988 ↠ 5,2458]: BZAW 198, B 1990, de Gruyter. xiii-468 p. 3-11-012-404-1.

2676 **Otto** E., Rechtsgeschichte... Ešnunna / Bundesbuch 1989 ↠ 5,2456: ᴿBO 47 (1990) 684-6 (M. *Stol*).

2677 **Otto** Eckart, Wandel der Rechtsbegründungen... Ex XX 22-XXIII 13: StB 3, 1988 ↠ 4,2543; 5,2457: ᴿCBQ 52 (1990) 534-6 (D. *Patrick* compares with NIEHR, both among the best of German scholarship); JBL 109 (1990) 510-2 (T. B. *Dozeman*).

2678 **Schenker** Adrian, [cf. Versöhnung und Sühne 1981 ↠ 62,7615] Versöhnung und Widerstand; bibeltheologische Untersuchung zum Strafen Gottes und der Menschen, besonders im Lichte von Exodus 21-22: SBS 139. Stu 1990, KBW. 110 p. DM 29,80 pa. [JBL 110,708, J. M. *Hamilton*; ZAW 103,169, H.-C. *Schmitt*].

2679 *Cohen* Matty, Le 'ger' biblique et son statut socio-religieux: RHR 207 (1990) 131-158; Eng. 131 ↠ 2758s.

2680 *a*) *Bresciani* Edda, Lo straniero; – *b*) *Loprieno* Antonio, Lo schiavo: ↠ 483, L'uomo egiziano 1990, 235-268 / 197-233.

2681 **Fleishman** Joseph, Studies pertaining to the legal status of the child in Israel and in the ancient Near East: diss. Bar-Ilan. – RTLv 22, p. 588 sans date.

2682 *Ararat* Nissan, [Ex 21ss] 'These are the *mišpāṭîm*' – order of the dispositions [*m'rkt... 'rkym simuyim*]: BethM 36,124 (1990s) 65-73.

2683 **Houtman** C., Het altaar als asielplaats; beschouwingen over en naar aanleiding van Exodus 21:12-14: Kamper Cah 70. Kampen 1990, Kok. 90-242-3250-3 [BL 91,158].

2684 *Carmichael* Calum, [Ex 21,22-25...] Biblical laws of talion: HebAnR 9 (1985) 107-126 [< OTAbs 13,221].

2685 **Draï** Raphaël, Oeil pour oeil; le mythe de la loi du talion: Liens sacrés. P 1986, Clims. 187 p. [KirSef 62 (1988s) p. 26].

2686 *Isser* Stanley, Two traditions; the law of Exodus 21:22-23 revisited: CBQ 52 (1991) 30-45.

2687 *Avalos* Hector, Exodus 22:9 and Akkadian legal formulae: JBL 109 (1990) 116s.

2688 *Cooper* Alan, The plain sense of Exodus 23: 5: HUCA 59 (1988) 1-22 [< OTAbs 13, p. 160].

2689 **Dorff** Elliot N., *Rosett* Arthur, A living tree; the roots and growth of Jewish law 1988 ➤ 5,2468; 0-88706-459-0; pa. -6-4. – ᴿJudaism 38 (1989) 241-4 (M. S. *Konvitz*).

2690 **Gibert** Pierre, Bible et conception de la Loi: ➤ 557*, L'Écriture âme 1989/90, 133-143.

Gordis Robert, The dynamics of Judaism; a study in Jewish law 1990 ➤ a200.

2691 *a) Greenberg* Moshe, Biblical attitudes toward power; ideal and reality in law and prophets (response *Welch* John W.); – *b) Falk* Ze'ev W., Spirituality and Jewish law; – *c) Milgrom* Jacob, Ethics and ritual; the foundations of the biblical dietary laws (response *Wright* David P.]; – *d) Paul* Shalom M., Biblical analogies to Middle Assyrian laws [Dt 25,11s; Is 47,1-4; Ezek 23,24s; Lv 24,10-23]: ➤ 526, Religion & Law 1985/90, 101-112 (113-125) / 127-138 / 159-191 [193-8] / 333-350.

2692 *a) Jackson* Bernard S., Jewish law or Jewish laws?; – *b) Yuter* A., Is Halakhah really law?: ➤ 537, Jewish Law 1986/9 ...

2693 **Malul** Meir, The comparative method in Ancient Near Eastern and biblical legal studies: AOAT 227. Neuk/Kevelaer 1990, Neuk.- V./ Butzon & B. xii-197 p. 3-7887-1354-2 / Kev 3-7666-9709-9.

2694 **Niehr** Herbert, Rechtsprechung in Israel ...: SBS 130, 1987 ➤ 3,2430; 5,2473: ᴿBiblica 71 (1990) 93-95 (A. *Schenker*); BZ 34 (1990) 308-310 (W. *Thiel*); HcbSt 31 (1990) 225s (B. *Lang*).

2695 *Piattelli* Daniela, Diritti umani in Israele ieri e [piuttosto] oggi: StMiss 39 (1990) 243-252.

2696 **Rakover** Nahum, The multi-language bibliography of Jewish law [Oṣar ha-Mišpaṭ I, 1975], II. J 1990, Jewish Legal Heritage Society. [III. Current Legal Problems; and IV. MAIMONIDES: Proceedings of First/Second International Seminar, ᴱ*Rakover*, awaited].

2697 *Renna* Thomas, The Jewish Law according to William of St. Thierry: StMon 31 (1989) 49-68.

2698 *Stern* Marc D., [*al.*] Kosher food and the law: Judaism 39 (1990) 389-401 [-493].

ᴱ**Veijola** Timo, The Law in the Bible and in its environment 1990 ➤ 560.

2699 **Westbrook** Raymond, Studies in biblical and cuneiform law 1988 ➤ 4,2568; 5,2478: ᴿBL (1990) 117 (B. S. *Jackson*); BLitEc 91 (1990) 231s (M. *Delcor*); Orientalia 59 (1990) 85-90 (M. *Mulul.* stimulating); TR 86 (1990) 284-7 (E. *Otto*).

2700 *Cardascia* Guillaume, L'indulgence pour la première faute dans les droits du Proche-Orient ancien: ➤ 86*, ꟳIGLESIAS J., 2 (1988) 651-674.

2701 *Fales* Frederick M., Babylonian slave-documents in the state archives of Assyria: SAAB 2 (1988) 41-57.

2702 *Farber* W., Ḫanum kauft Gadagada; eine altassyrische Selbstverkaufs- Urkunde: AulaO 8 (1990) 197-202 + 6 fig.

2703 *Fleishman* Joseph, The authority of the paterfamilias according to CH[ammurabi] 117: ➤ 7, ꟳARTZI P. 1990, 249-253.

2704 *Limet* H., Actes juridiques paléo-babyloniens: ➤ 107, ꟳKUPPER J.-R. 1990, 35-57.

2705 **Maine** Henry S.,   Ancient Law (1882-8). Tucson 1986, Univ. Arizona. lxxxi-400 p. $13 pa. – ᴿArOr 58 (1990) 94 (F. V.).

2706 *Matthews* Victor H.,   Entrance ways and threshing floors; legally significant sites in the Ancient Near East: Fides et Historia 19 (GR 1987) 25-40 [< OTAbs 13, p. 258].

2707 *Pangas* J. C.,   Notas sobre el aborto en la antigua Mesopotamia: AulaO 8 (1990) 213-8.

2708 *Sauren* H.,   Trois tablettes d'une collection belge et le code d'Ur: OrLovPer 20 (1989) 5-19.

2709 *a*) *Sauren* Herbert,   Aufbau und Anordnung der babylonischen Kodizes; – *b*) *Ries* Gerhard, Altbabylonische Beweisurteile: ZSavR 106 (1989) 1-55 / 56-80.

2710 ᵀᴱ**Seux** M.-J.,   Lois de l'Ancien Orient: CahÉv 56 supp.   P 1988, Cerf. 99 p. F 35. 0222-9706.

2711 **Sick** Ulrich,   Die Tötung eines Menschen und ihre Ahndung... Diss. Stu 1984. x-313 p.; vi-203 p.: ᴿBO 47 (1990) 401s (A. *Skaist*).

2712 *a*) *Théodoridès* Aristide,   La formation du droit dans l'Égypte pharaonique; – *b*) *Zaccagnini* Carlo,   La formazione del diritto in Mesopotamia; – *c*) *Archi* Alfonso, ... nell'Anatolia ittita; – *d*) *Yaron* R., The evolution of biblical law: → 5,824, Formazione del diritto 1988.

2712* *Westbrook* Raymond,   Adultery in ancient Near Eastern law: RB 97 (1990) 524-580; franç. 542.

2713 *Willems* Harco,   Crime, cult and capital punishment (Moʿalla inscription 8): JEA 76 (1990) 27-55.

2714 **Yaron** Reuven,   The laws of Eshnunna²ʳᵉᵛ 1988 → 5,2429: ᴿVT 40 (1990) 361-9 (E. *Otto*).

E3.6   **Cultus,** *Exodus 24-40*.

2714* *Aejmelaeus* Anneli, [Ex 25-31.35-40] Septuagintal translation techniques — a solution to the problem of the tabernacle account: → 519, Septuagint, Scrolls 1990, 381-402.

2715 *Koch* Klaus,   Alttestamentliche und altorientalische Rituale: → 147, ꟳRENDTORFF R., Hebr. Bibel 1990, 75-85.

2716 **Utzschneider** Helmut,   Das Heiligtum und das Gesetz... Ex 25-40; Lev 8-9: OBO 77, 1988 → 4,2604; 5,2499: ᴿCBQ 52 (1990) 545s (J. F. *Craghan*: competently provocative); ExpTim 101 (1989s) 26 (R. *Coggins*); HebSt 31 (1990) 246-9 (N. *Lohfink*: powerful); TLZ 115 (1990) 187-9 (H. *Reventlow*).

2717 *a*) *McCrory* Jeff H.ᴶ, 'Up, up, up, and up'; Exodus 24:9-18 as the narrative context for the tabernacle instructions of Exodus 25-31; – *b*) *Van Seters* John,   Law and the wilderness rebellion tradition, Ex 32: → 544, SBL seminars 1990, 570-582 / 583-591.

2718 **Cohen** Lysbeth,   The Tabernacle, then and now. Sydney 1983, Great Synagogue. 52 p.; ill. (Hodge J.) [KirSef 62 (1988)s) p. 25].

2719 **Koester** Craig R.,   The dwelling of God [diss. Union NY, ᴰ*Brown* R. E.]: CBQ Mg 22, 1989 → 5,2500: ᴿArTGran 53 (1990) 354s (A. *Segovia*); BL (1990) 104 (D. G. *Deboys*: focuses NT); JTS 41 (1990) 590-2 (R. J. *McKelvey*); Laurentianum 31 (1990) 605s (F. *Raurell*).

2720 *Revel-Neher* Elisabeth,   Le signe de la rencontre; l'arche d'alliance dans l'art (ᴰ1981), 1984 → 1,2552... 4,2602: ᴿEpeteris-Byz 47 (1987-9) 471-4 (D. I. *Palla*, Ⓖ).

2721 **Zwickel** Wolfgang,   Räucherkult und Räuchergeräte; exegetische und archäologische Studien zum Räucheropfer im AT [ev. Diss Kiel 1988, [D]*Metzger* ➤ 5,2496]: OBO 97.   FrS/Gö 1990, Univ./VR.   [xii-]353 p. Fs 89. 3-7278-0671-0 / VR 3-525-53727-1 [BL 91,122, J. F. *Healey*].

2722 [E]**Auneau** Joseph,   Le sacerdoce dans la Bible: CahÉv 70.   P 1990, Cerf. 67 p. F 25.   0222-9714.

2723 *Berges* Ulrich,   El sacerdocio en el Antiguo Testamento: RTLim 24 (1990) 189-207.

2724 *Crocker* P.,   Corrupt priests — a common phenomenon: BurHist 26 (1990) 36-43 [< OTAbs 13, p. 222].

2725 *Houtman* C.,   [Ex 28,33s) On the pomegranates and the golden bells of the high priest's mantle: VT 40 (1990) 223-9.

2726 *Fass* David E.,   [Ex 32] The molten calf; judgment, motive and meaning: Judaism 39 (1990) 171-183.

2727 **Hahn** Joachim,   Das 'Goldene Kalb'[2rev]: EurHS 23/154.   Fra 1987, Lang.   298 p. Fs 71.   3-8204-8657-7. – [R]BO 47 (1990) 751-3 (J. *Vermeylen*).

2728 *Holbert* John C.,   A new literary reading of Exodus 32, the story of the Golden Calf: QRMin 10 (1990) 46-68.

2729 *Janzen* J. Gerald,   The character of the calf and its cult in Exodus 32: CBQ 52 (1990) 597-607.

2730 *Mandelbaum* Irving J.,   Tannaitic exegesis of the Golden Calf episode: ➤ 183, [F]VERMES G. 1990, 207-223.

2731 *Riggans* Walter,   Gods, tents, and authority; a study of Exodus 32 and 1 Kings 12:   ➤ 115, [F]LIPTZIN S., JBQ 19 (1990s) 230-8.

2732 *Gunneweg* A. H. J. †,   Das Gesetz und die Propheten; eine Auslegung von Ex 33,7-11; Num. 11,4-12,8; Dtn 31,14f.; 34,10:   ZAW 102 (1990) 169-180.

2733 *Osborn* Noel D.,   [Ex 33,7] Tent or tabernacle? Translating two traditions: BTrans 41 (1990) 214-221.

2734 *Dohmen* Christoph,   'Eifersüchtiger ist sein Name' (Ex 34,14); Ursprung und Bedeutung der alttestamentlichen Rede von Gottes Eifersucht: TZBas 46 (1990) 289-304.

2735 *Houtman* C.,   [Ex 34,29-35] Het verheerlijkte gezicht van Mozes: NedTTs 43 (1990) 1-10; Eng. 52.

E3.7   **Leviticus.**

2736 *Angerstorfer* Andreas,   Überlegungen zu Sprache und Sitz im Leben des Toratargums 4QTgLev [4Q 156], sein Verhältnis zu Targum Onkelos: BibNot 55 (1990) 18-35.

2737 [TE]**Barkley** Gary W.,   ORIGEN, Homilies on Leviticus, 1-16: Fathers 83 [72 was Origen on Gn-Ex].   Wsh 1990, Catholic Univ.   xviii-294 p. $32 [TDig 38,159]. 0-8132-0083-0.

2738 **Freedman** D. N.,   *Mathews* K. A.,   The paleo-Hebrew Leviticus scroll 1985 ➤ 1,2873... 5,2512:   [R]JNES 49 (1990) 196s (D. *Pardee*).

2739 **Harlé** Paul, *Pralon* Didier, Le Lévitique LXX: BAlex 3, 1988 ➤ 4,2613; 5,2513:   [R]ÉglT 20 (1989) 471-4 (L. *Laberge*); StMon 31 (1989) 459 (R. *Ribera-Mariné*).

2740 **Noth** Martin,   Levitico, traduzione e commento [1962 [4]1978], [T]*Dal Bianco* Antonio, [E]*Federici* Tommaso: AT 6.   Brescia 1989, Paideia.   266 p. 88-394-0421-X.

2741 **Péter-Contesse** René, *Ellington* John,   A translator's handbook on Leviticus: Helps for Translators.   NY 1990, United Bible Societies.   ix-458 p. $10.   0-8267-0102-7 [BL 91,160].

2742 **Anderson** Gary A., [Lv 1s] Sacrifices 1987 ➔ 3,2476 ... 5,2520: ᴿJSS 35 (1990) 134s (A. H. W. *Curtis*).

2743 *Knohl* Israel, ❽ [Lv 4,14] The law of sin-offering of the 'Holiness School':   Tarbiz 60 (1990s) 1-9; Eng. I.

2744 *Schenker* Adrian,   Der Unterschied zwischen Sündopfer *chaṭṭat* und Schuldopfer *ascham* im Licht von Lv 5,17-19 und 5,1-6: ➔ 518, IOSOT 13, 1989/90, 115-123.

2745 *Delcor* Mathias,   Le tarif dit de Marseille (CIS I,165); aspects du système sacrificiel punique: ➔ 175, ᶠSZNYCER M., Semitica 38 (1990) 87-94; pl. XVI.

2745* *Auneau* Joseph,   Le bain de purification des prêtres; Lv 8,6 et parallèles: ➔ 109*, ᶠLAURENTIN R. 1990, 103-111.

2746 *Firmage* E.,   The biblical dietary laws and the concept of holiness: ➔ 331, VTSup 41 (1990) 209-215.

2746* *Wright* David P., [Lev 11-16; Num 19] Two types of impurity in the priestly writings of the Bible: ➔ 540*, Koroth 9 sp. (3d symposium 1987/8) 180-193.

2747 **Wang Tai-Il,** Leviticus 11-15, a form-critical study: diss. ᴰ*Knierim* P. Claremont 1990. – RelStR 17,193.

2748 *Wyatt* Nicolas [Lev 11; Deut 14: dietary laws] Symbols of exile: SvEx 55 (1990) 39-59.

2749 *Kehnscherper* Günther,   The 'churching of women'; Leviticus 12 and Luke 2:21-24; the law of purity and the benediction of mothers, ᵀ*Krehayn* J.: ➔ 643, StPatr 18,2 (1983/9) 380-4.

2750 *Crocker* P. T.,   Archaeology, mildew, and Leviticus 14:   BurHist 26 (1990) 3-11 [< OTAbs 13, p. 265].

2751 *Falk* Ze'ev, [Lev 16 ... 19] ❽ The portion Qedoshim; ethics and esthetics: BethMikra 34 (1989) 138-143 [< OTAbs 14,53].

2752 **Scullion** James P., [Lev 16] A traditio-historical study of the Day of Atonement: diss. Catholic Univ., ᴰ*Gignac* F.,   Wsh 1990. – RTLv 22, p. 595.

2753 *a) Janowski* Bernd,   Azazel – biblisches Gegenstück zum ägyptischen Seth? Zur Religionsgeschichte von Lev 16,18-21f [*Görg* M. 1986 ...]; – *b) Malamat* Avraham (Lev 19,18) 'You shall love your neighbor as yourself'; a case of misinterpretation? ['be useful' rather than 'love']; – *c) Crüsemann* Frank,   Die Exodus als Heiligung; zur rechtsgeschichtlichen Bedeutung des Heiligkeitsgesetzes; – *d) Sæbø* Magne,   Bemerkungen zur Textgeschichte von Leviticus; welchen Wert haben die Varianten aus der Kairoer Geniza?: ➔ 147, ᶠRENDTORFF R., Hebr. Bibel 1990, 97-110 / 111-5 / 117-129 / 131-9.

2754 **Sun** Henry T. C.,   An investigation into the compositional integrity of the so-called Holiness Code (Leviticus 17-26): diss. ᴰ*Knierim* R. Claremont 1989. – RelStR 17,193.

2755 **Schwartz** Baruch J., Lv 17-19. ᴰ1987 – OIAc JuJ89.

2756 *Milgrom* Jacob, [Lev 17,11] The modus operandi of the *ḥaṭṭa't* [sacrifice]; a rejoinder: JBL [107 (1988) 609, *Zohar* N.] 109 (1990) 111-3.

2757 *Malamat* Abraham, [Lv 19,18] 'Love your neighbor as yourself'; what it really means [< FRENDTORFF ➤ 2753*b*]: BAR-W 16,4 (1990) 50.

2758 *Schwienhorst-Schönberger* Ludger. [Lev 19,34 ➤ 2679] '...denn Fremde seid Ihr gewesen im Lande Ägypten'; zur sozialen und rechtlichen Stellung von Fremden und Ausländern im alten Israel: BLtg 63 (1990) 108-117.

2759 *a) Hein-Jahnke* Ewald, *Greiner* Gerhard, Gleiches Recht soll euch gelten für Fremde wie für den Einheimischen (Lev 24,22); Versuch einer Ortsbestimmung; – *b) Palmieri* Vito, Ausländer und Asylsuchende aus biblischer Sicht; Texte zum Nachdenken und Handeln: ZPraxRU 20 (1990) 78s / 80-86 [< ZIT 90,647].

2760 *Weinfeld* Moshe, [Lv 25] Sabbatical Year and Jubilee in the Pentateuchal laws and their Ancient Near Eastern background: ➤ 560, Law 1988/90, 39-62.

2760* **Jeyaraj** Jesudason B., *a)* [Lv 25,23; Ex 9,29...] Land ownership in the Pentateuch; a thematic study of Genesis 12 to Deuteronomy 34: diss. Sheffield 1989. 288 p. – Arasaradi 3/2 (Tamilnadu 1990) 37-43. – *b)* Ownership, tenancy and care of land in Leviticus 25-27: Arasaradi 4/2, 18-31.

2761 *Jordan* Gregory D., Usury, slavery and land-tenure; the Nuzi *tidennūtu* transaction: ZAss 80 (1990) 76-92.

2762 **Wright** Christopher J.H., God's people in God's land; family, land, and property in the OT. GR/Exeter 1990, Eerdmans/Paternoster. xx-284 p. $17.

2763 *Krašovec* Jože, [in Slovene] Blessing/Curse and restoration in Lev 26 and Deut 28 and 30,1-10: BogVest 49 (Ljubljana 1989) 3-23; Eng. 20.

2764 **Herman** Menahem, [Lev 27,30...] Tithe as gift; the institution in the Pentateuch and in light of MAUSS's prestation theory: diss. Northwestern, ᴰ*Roth* W. Evanston 1990, 194 p. 90-31917. – DissA 51 (1990s) 2047s-A.

E3.8 *Numeri;* **Numbers, Balaam.**

2764* *a) Culley* Robert C., Five tales of punishment in the Book of Numbers; – *b)* response, *Ben Amos* Dan: ➤ 547, ᴱ*Niditch* S., Folklore 1990, 25-34 / 35-45.

2765 **Doron** Pinchas, Interpretation of difficult passages in RASHI, 3. Numbers. NY 1990, Sepher-Hermon. xviii-328 p. 0-87203-134-9.

2766 **Harrison** R.K., Numbers: Wycliffe exeg. comm. Ch 1990, Moody. xvi-452 p. $26. 0-8024-9261-4 [TDig 38.163].

2767 **Jastram** Nathan R., The book of Numbers from Qumran, Cave IV (4QNumᵇ): diss. Harvard. CM 1990. 263 p. 90-35610. – DissA 51 (1990s) 2418-A.

2768 **Milgrom** Jacob, Numbers: JPS Torah comm. Ph 1990, Jewish Publ. lxi-520 p. $47.50. 0-8276-0329-0 [TDig 37,173].

2769 **Neusner** J., Sifré to Numbers 1986 ➤ 2,1905; 5,2537: ᴿAbrNahr 28 (1990) 137-9 (L.F. *Girón*).

2770 **Pérez Fernández** Miguel, Midrás Sifré Números; versión crítica, introducción y notas: Biblioteca Midrásica, 1989 ➤ 5,2538: ᴿJStJud 21 (1990) 266-8 (J. *Neusner*: a first-rate piece of work, beginning to end; translation accurate wherever checked; Spanish is becoming necessary for studies in Judaism).

2770* **Philip** James, Numbers: Communicator's Commentary 4. Waco 1986, Word. 364 p. 0-8499-0409-9.

2771 *Quast* U., Der rezensionelle Charakter einiger Wortvarianten im Buche
   Numeri: ➤ 70, ᶠHANHART R., 1990, 230-252.
2771* *a) White* Marsha, The Elohistic depiction of Aaron; a study in the
   Levite-Zadokite controversy; – *b) Davies* G. I., The Wilderness itineraries
   and recent archaeological research: ➤ 331, VTSup 41 (1990) 149-159 /
   161-175.

2772 **Destro** A., [Nm 5,1-11] The law of jealousy; anthropology of Sotah:
   BrownJudSt 18. Atlanta 1989, Scholars. xii-189 p. $45. 1-55540-379-4
   [NTAbs 34,268].
2773 *Parente* F., [Num 6,2-21] Die Ursprünge des Naziräats: ➤ 154, ᶠSACCHI
   P. 1990, 65-83.
2774 *Manicardi* Luciano, La benedizione sacerdotale, Nm 6,22-27: ➤ 325*a*,
   ParSpV 21 (1990) 61-82.
2775 *Milgrom* Jacob, [Nm 7] The chieftains' gifts: HebAnR 9 (1985) 221-5.
2776 **Jobsen** Aarnoud, Krisis en hoop; een exegetisch-theologisch onderzoek
   naar de achtergronden en tendenzen van de rebelliecyclus in Numeri
   11:1-20:13 [diss. Bru ᴰ*Jagersma* H.], 1987 ➤ 5,2545; 90-6651-085-4. –
   ᴿNedTTs 43 (1989) 340s (C. *Houtman*); ZAW 102 (1990) 305 (H.-C.
   Schmitt).
2777 *Dion* Paul-Eugène, La *rwḥ* dans l'heptateuque; la protestation pour la
   liberté du prophétisme en Nb 11,26-29: ScEsp 42 (1990) 167-191.
2778 **Diebner** Bernd J., '... for he had married a Cushite woman' (Numbers
   12:1) [cf. DielB 25,5 (1988) 35-95]: ➤ 781, Uppsala Konferenz 1986/
   Nubica Is (1990) 499-504.
2779 *Dawes* Stephen B., Numbers 12.3; what was special about Moses?
   [*'anaw* = 'humble']: BTrans 41 (1990) 336-340.
2780 *Beltrán Torreira* Federico-Marco, [Num 16] Algunas reflexiones en torno
   a las figuras de Coré, Datán y Abirón en las fuentes hispano-visigodas:
   ➤ 761, Helmantica 40 (1987/9) 183-194.
2781 *Murphy* Frederick J., [Nm 16] Korah's rebellion in Pseudo PHILO 16:
   ➤ 173, ᶠSTRUGNELL J., Of scribes 1990, 111-120.
2782 *Maccoby* H., NEUSNER [A religion of pots and pans 1988; Nm 19,1-10]
   and the red cow: JStJud 21 (1990) 60-75.

2783 *Greene* John T., [Nm 22-24] Balaam as figure and type in ancient Semitic
   literature to the first century B.C.E., with a survey of selected post-Philo
   applications of the Balaam figure and type: ➤ 544, SBL seminars 1990,
   82-147.
2784 **Hackett** Jo Ann, The Balaam text from Deir 'Alla 1984 ➤ 65,2375 ...
   4,2668: ᴿAulaO 8 (1990) 147s (G. del *Olmo Lete*).
2785 *Delcor* Mathias, *a)* Bala'am Pātōrāh, 'interprète de songes' au pays
   d'Ammon, d'après Num 22,5; les témoignages épigraphiques parallèles
   [< Semitica 32 (1982) 89-91]; – *b)* Le texte de Deir'Alla et les oracles
   bibliques de Bala'am [< Vienna Congress VTSup 1982, 52-73]: ➤ 219*,
   Environnement 1990, 68-70 / 46-67.
2786 *Dijkstra* M., Is Bileam ook onder de Profeten?: GerefTTs 90 (1990)
   159-185 [< OTAbs 14,29].
   ᴱ**Hoftijzer** J., *Kooij* G. van der, The Balaam text from Deir 'Alla 1989/90.
   ➤ 534.

2787 *Langbein* Martina, Die Bileamerzählung in der Grundschule; Anregungen für ein Fest im Religionsunterricht: EvErz 42,1 (1990) 54-68; ill. [< ZIT 90,275].

2788 *Lemaire* André, [Nm 22s; Gn 36,32] Bala'am/ Bela' fils de Be'ôr: ZAW 102 (1990) 180-187.

2789 *Magonet* Jonathan, Bileams sprechender Esel: KIsr 5 (1990) 45-53.

2790 **Moore** M. S., The Balaam traditions: SBL diss 113. Atlanta 1990, Scholars. $24; sb./pa. $16. 1-55540-327-1; -8-X [BL 91,87, J. R. *Porter*: his intriguing hypotheses could perhaps be related to J, E, D].

2791 *Moore* Michael S., Another look at Balaam: RB 97 (1990) 359-378: franç. 359.

2792 *Müller* Hans-Peter, Die Funktion divinatorischen Redens und die Tierbezeichnungen der Inschrift von Tell Deir'Alla [... Bileam]: → 534, Balaam 1989 185-205.

2793 *Wolters* Al, The Balaamites of Deir 'Alla as Aramean deportees: HUCA 59 (1988) 101-113 [< ZAW 102,275].

2794 **Montes-Peral** Luis Angel, [Nm 23,19; Philo] Akataleptos theos; der unfassbare Gott [kath. Diss. München 1979]: ArbGJ 16,1987 → 3,a279: ᴿStPhilonAn 2 (1990) 201-4 (D. *Zeller*).

2795 *a)* *Zobel* Hans-Jürgen, Bileam-Lieder und Bileam-Erzählung; – *b)* *Knierim* Rolf P., The Book of Numbers; – *c)* *Haran* Menahem, Book-size and the thematic cycles in the Pentateuch: → 147, ᶠRENDTORFF R., Hebr. Bibel 1990, 141 154 / 155-163 / 165-176.

2796 *Levin* Saul, An unattested 'scribal correction' in Numbers 26,59?: Biblica 71 (1990) 26-33.

2797 *Cimosa* Mario, [Num 35,19] Translating *go'ēl ha-dam*, 'the avenger of blood': BTrans 41 (1990) 319-326 [the 'blood' *may* mean 'consanguinity' as in LXX].

E3.9 Liber Deuteronomii.

2798 **Braulich** Georg, Studien zur Theologie des Dts 1988 → 4,188; 5,2568: ᴿTR 86 (1990) 193-5 (T. *Veijola*).

2799 **Buchholz** Joachim, Die Ältesten Israels im Dt: GöTheolArb 36, 1988 → 4,2681; 5,2570: ᴿBZ 34 (1990) 288s (H. *Niehr*); JBL 109 (1990) 121s (L. J. *Hoppe*); NorTTs 90 (1989) 238-240 (H. M. *Barstad*).

2800 **Calvin** Jean, Sermons on Deuteronomy, ᵀ*Golding* Arthur: 16th century facsimile editions. E 1987, Banner of Truth. 1247 p. [KirSef 62 (1988s) p. 497].

2801 **Clements** R. E., Deuteronomy: OTGuides 1989 → 5,2572: ᴿExpTim 101 (1989s) 247 (C. S. *Rodd*: serves to replace his 1968 'God's Chosen People').

2802 **Cortés** E., *Martínez* T., Sifre Dt. Comentario tannaítico al libro del Deuteronomio, Pisqa 1-160. Barc 1989, Herder/FacT. Catalunya. 346 p. 84-600-7183-9. – ᴿEstFranc 91 (1990) 358-360 (J. *Ferrer*); NatGrac 37 (1990) 314s (F. F. *Ramos*); PerspT 22 (1990) 398-400 (L. *Stadelmann*).

2803 **Duncan** Julie Ann, A critical edition of Deuteronomy manuscripts from Qumran, Cave IV: 4QDtᵇ⁻ᵉ⁻ʰ⁻ʲ⁻ᵏ⁻ˡ: diss. Harvard, ᴰ*Cross* F. CM 1989. 182 p. 90-13284. – DissA 51 (1990s) 834-A.

2804 **García López** Félix, Le Deutéronome, une loi prêchée: CahÉv 63. P 1988, Cerf. 67 p. F 24. 0222-9714.

2805 **Labuschagne** C. J., Deuteronomium I-AB (through ch. 11): PredikOT 1987 → 5,2577: ᴿCBQ 52 (1990) 522s (C. T. *Begg*: verse-by-verse good, but his complex number theory out of place in a commentary, especially one claimed 'for preaching'); KerkT 41 (1990) 161-3 (B. *Becking*).

2806 *Levinson* Bernard M.,   Calum M. CARMICHAEL's approach to the laws of Deuteronomy: HarvTR 83 (1990) 227-259.

2807 *Liao* Timothy, ☉ Holy War in Dt: ColcFuJen 83 (1990) 15-39.

2808 *Lohfink* Norbert,   a) Das Deuteronomische Gesetz in der Endgestalt — Entwurf einer Gesellschaft ohne marginale Gruppen: BibNot 51 (1990) 25-40; – b) Das Deuteronomium; Jahwegesetz oder Mosegesetz? Die Subjektzuordnung bei Wörtern für 'Gesetz' im Dtn und in der dtr Literatur: TPhil 65 (1990) 387-391.

2809 **McConville** J.G.,   Law and theology in Dt: JStOT supp 33, 1984 ➤ 65,2294... 5,2579s: ᴿBZ 34 (1990) 122-4 (N. *Lohfink*).

2810 **Miller** P.D.,   Deuteronomy: Interpretation comm. Atlanta 1990, Knox. x-253 p. $22. 0-8042-3105-2 [BL 91,58, A. *Mayes*].

2811 **Neusner** J.,   Sifre to Dt, 1987 ➤ 4,2692: ᴿJQR 81 (1990s) 170-4 (R. *Hammer*, 1).

2812 **Perlitt** Lothar,   Deuteronomium: BK AT 5. Neuk 1990, Neuk.-V. I. (bis Dt 1,18) 80 p. 3-7887-1370-4.

2813 **Perlitt** Lothar,   Riesen im Alten Testament; ein literarisches Motiv im Wirkungsfeld des Deuteronomiums: NachGö p/h 1990, 1. Gö 1990, Vandenhoeck & R. 52 p.

2814 *Perlitt* Lothar,   'Evangelium' und Gesetz im Deuterononium: ➤ 560, Law 1988/90, 23-38.

2815 *Ravasi* Gianfranco,   Benedizione e maledizione nell'alleanza, Dt 27-30: ➤ 325a, ParSpV 21 (1990) 47-59.

2816 **Regt** L.J. de,   A parametric model for syntactic studies of a textual corpus, demonstrated on the Hebrew of Dt 1-30: StSemNeer 24, 1988 ➤ 4,2696; 5,2582; 90-232-2381-0: ᴿBO 17 (1990) 39-52 (C. van der *Merwe*).

2817 **Römer** Thomas,   Israels Väter; Untersuchungen zur Väterthematik im Dt und in der deuteronomistischen Tradition: OBO 99. FrS/Gö 1990, Univ./VR. xvi-639 p. Fs 145. 3-7278-0673-7 / VR 3-525-53730-1 [BL 91,93, A. *Mayes*].

2818 a) *Schäfer-Lichtenberger* Christa,   Göttliche und menschliche Autorität im Deuteronomium; – b) *Lubsczyk* Hans,   Die Bundesurkunde; Ursprung und Wirkungsgeschichte des Deuteronomiums; – c) *Cortese* E.,   Theories concerning dtr; a possible rapprochement: ➤ 518, IOSOT 13, 1989/90, 125-142 / 161-177 / 179-190.

2819 *Stulman* Louis,   Encroachment in Deuteronomy; an analysis of the social world of the D-code: JBL 109 (1990) 613-632.

2820 **Weitenberg** J.J.S., *Leeuw Van Weenen* A. De,   Lemmatized index of the Armenian version of Deuteronomy: SBL SeptCog 32. Atlanta 1990, Scholars. xii-96 p. $20; sb./pa. $15. 1-55540-486-3; -7-1 [BL 91,51: S.P. *Brock*: rather technical companion to Cox edition; no Greek or English equivalents].

2821 *White* Sidnie Ann,   The All Souls [NY Unitarian church which paid for 4QDtⁿ] Deuteronomy and the Decalogue: JBL 109 (1990) 193-206.

2822 **Zobel** Konstantin,   Prophetie und Deuteronomium; die Rezeption prophetischer Theologumena: Diss. ᴰ*Wallis*. Halle-Wittenberg 1989s. – TR 86 (1990) 515.

2823 *Perlitt* Lothar,   a) Dtn 1,12 LXX: ➤ 70, ᶠHANHART R. 1990, 299-311; –

b) Hoc libro maxime fides docetur; Dt 1,19-46 bei M. LUTHER und Johann GERHARD: NSys 32 (1990) 105-112; Eng. 112.

2824 *Millard* Alan R., [Dt 3,11] King Og's iron bed; fact or fancy?: BR 6,2 (1990) 16-21 . 44; ill.

2825 *Lohfink* Norbert, Zum 'Numeruswechsel' in Dtn 3,21f: BibNot 49 (1989) 39-52.

2826 **Knapp** Dietrich, Deuteronomium 4...: GöTArb 35, 1987 ➤ 3,2564... 5,2586: ᴿBiblica 71 (1990) 95-98 (C. T. *Begg*).

2827 *Lichtenberger* Hermann, Dass du nicht vergisst (Devarim-Dtn 4,9); von der Lebenskraft der Tora: TBeit 21,4 (Wu 1990) 196-204 [< NTAbs 35,79].

2828 *Heller* J., [Dt 6,4] Sjemaᶜ als fundament van 'monotheisme'?: AmstCah 10 (1989) 37-44 [< ZAW 103,125].

2829 *a) Moberly* R.W.L., [Dt 6,4] 'Yahweh is one'; the translation of the Shema; – *b) Reimer* D.J., Concerning return to Egypt; Dt XVII 16 and XXVIII 68 reconsidered; – *c) Daniels* D.R., The creed of Dt XXVI revisited: ➤ 331, VTSup 41 (1990) 209-215 / 217-229 / 231-242.

2830 *Giles* Terry, What did the Fathers know? A discussion of Deuteronomy 8:3,16: ProcGLM 10 (1990) 39-51.

2831 *O'Connell* Robert H., Deuteronomy VIII 1-20; asymmetrical concentricity and the rhetoric of Providence: VT 40 (1990) 437-452.

2832 **Langer** G., [Dt 12] Von Gott erwählt — Jerusalem: ÖstBSt 8, ᴰ1988 ➤ 5,2590: ᴿBL (1990) 84 (A. *Mayes*); TüTQ 170 (1990) 72s (W. *Gross*).

2833 *Lohfink* Norbert, Zum rabbinischen Verständnis von Dtn 12,1: ➤ 146, ᶠREINERT H., Dic atl. Botschaft 1990, 157-162.

2834 *Reuter* Eleonore, 'Nimm nichts davon weg und füge nichts hinzu!' Dtn 13,1, seine alttestamentlichen Parallelen und seine altorientalischen Vorbilder: BibNot 47 (1989) 107-114.

2835 **Hamilton** Jeffries M., Social justice and Deuteronomy; the case of Dt 15: diss. ᴰ*Miller* P., Princeton Theol. Sem. 1989. 273 p. 90-30368. – DissA 51 (1990s) 3107-A; RelStR 17,193.

2836 *Plantin* Henry, Deuteronomium [16,13-15] och lövhyddofestens psalmer [50; 81; 94; 82] i bSukka 55a: SvEx 55 (1990) 7-37; Eng. 37s.

2837 *Otto* Eckart, Die keilschriftlichen Parallelen der Vindikationsformel in Dtn 20,10: ZAW 102 (1990) 94s.

2838 **Locher** Clemens, Dic Ehre einer Frau in Israel... Dt 22,13-21: OBO 70, ᴰ1986 ➤ 2,1938... 5,2596: ᴿHebSt 31 (1990) 197-200 (M.J. *Gruber* recommends highly); ZSavR 106 (1989) 601-4 (H. *Kaufhold*).

2839 *Derby* Josiah, [Dt 25,5-10 'yibbum'] The problem of the Levirate marriage: JBQ 19 (1990s) 13-17.

2840 **Harada** Toyoki, The 'historical creed' of the Covenant's people; the theology of Deuteronomy 26,1-19: diss. Pont. Univ. Urbaniana, ᴰ*Federici* T. Roma 1990. lix-84 p. (extr.).

2841 *Lipiński* E., [Dt 26,5-9] 'Mon père était un araméen errant'; l'histoire, carrefour des sciences bibliques et orientales: OrLovPer 20 (1989) 23-47.

2842 *Weissblueth* Shlomo, [Dt 28,47 joy (absent)] ❸ Toward the essence of a day that does not come to pass: BethM 34 (1989s) 44-48 [< OTAbs 14,54].

2843 *Lohfink* Norbert, Dtn 26,6-19; ein Beispiel altisraelitischer Geschichtstheologie [Erstveröffentlichung, Un exemple de théologie de l'histoire... Archivio di Filosofia 39 (1971) 189-199; deutsch in ᴱ*Thomas* F.,

Geschichte, Zeugnis (1976) 100-7]: ➤ 265, Studien zum Dt, 1990, 291-303.

2844 *Laberge* Léo, Le texte de Deutéronome 31 (Dt 31,1; 32,44-47): ➤ 518, IOSOT 13, 1989/90, 161-177.

2845 **Basser** Herbert W., Midrashic interpretations of the Song of Moses [< ᴰ1983 Toronto] 1984 ➤ 65,2326b: ᴿCritRR 2 (1989) 365-7 (J. *Neusner*: complete success).

2846 **Cheng Joong-Ho,** The Song of Moses [Dt 32,1-43] and the Hosea-Pekah conflict: diss. Emory, ᴰ*Hayes* J. Atlanta 1990. x-356 p. 90-27898. – DissA 51 (1990s) 1658-A; RelStR 17,193; OIAc Ja91; RTLv 22,587.

2847 *Irsigler* Hubert, Das Proömium im Moselied Dtn 32; Struktur, Sprechakte und Redeintentionen von V. 1-3: ➤ 8*, ᴱAssfalg J., 1990, 161-174.

2848 *Wiebe* John M., [Dt 32] The form, setting and meaning of the Song of Moses: StudiaBT 17 (Pasadena 1989) 119-163.

2849 **Axelsson** I. E., [Dt 33,2] The Lord rose up from Seir 1987 ➤ 3,2592... 5,2601:   ᴿBL (1990) 66 (J. R. *Bartlett*); SvEx 55 (1990) 100-4 (M. *Ottosson*).

E4.1   *Deuteronomista; Origo Israelis in Canaan;*   **Liber Josue.**

2850 *Bimson* John J., The origins of Israel in Canaan; an examination of recent theories: Themelios 15 (1989s) 5-15 [24, *Deboys* D. review of cognate Hayes J.].

2851 **Coote** R. B., *Whitelam* K. W., Emergence of early Israel 1987 ➤ 3,2595 ... 5,2612:   ᴿJSS 35 (1990) 131-3 (G. *Garbini*: historically improbable); JTS 41 (1990) 129-131 (G. I. *Davies*); RuBi 43 (1990) 173-5 (Maria *Kantor*).

2852 **Coote** Robert B., Early Israel; a new horizon. Mp 1990, Fortress. ix-197 p. 0-8006-2450-5 [BL 91,157].

2853 **Finkelstein** Israel, The archaeology of the Israelite settlement 1988 ➤ 4, 2733; 5,2613:   ᴿJBL 109 (1990) 322-4 (T. L. *Thompson*).

2854 *Finkelstein* Israel, The emergence of early Israel; anthropology, environment and archaeology [Lemche N. 1985; Coote R.-Whitelam K. 1987]: JAOS 110 (1990) 677-686.

2855 *Fritz* Volkmar, Die Landnahme der israelitischen Stämme in Kanaan [Eroberung, Albright; Infiltration, Alt; Revolution, Mendenhall]: ZDPV 106 (1990) 63-77 (-85) 'Übergang nomadisierender [Rand-] Gruppen zur Sesshaftigkeit'.

2855* *Greenspoon* Leonard, The Qumran fragments of Joshua; which puzzle are they part of and where do they fit?: ➤ 519, Septuagint, Scrolls 1990, 159-194.

2856 **Halpern** B., The emergence of Israel in Canaan: SBL Mg 29, 1983 ➤ 65,2337... 4,2738:   ᴿAulaO 8 (1990) 277s (G. del *Olmo Lete*).

2857 **Hoggatt** William L., The emergence of premonarchical Israel (1250-1050 B.C.E.); a sociological understanding of the origin and dynamics of that society: diss. Baylor, 1990. 380 p. 91-02019. – DissA 51 (1990s) 2775s-A.

2858 **Kessler** Rainer, Staat und Gesellschaft im vorexilischen Juda: Diss. Bethel, ᴰ*Crüsemann* F. Bielefeld 1990. – RTLv 22, p. 588.

2859 **Lemche** N. P., Early Israel 1985 ➤ 2,1955... 5,2615:   ᴿRivB 38 (1990) 519-521 (A. *Bonora*); VT 40 (1990) 299s (H. G. M. *Williamson*).

2860 *Lüdy* José H., La historia y los orígenes de Israel: Stromata 46 (1990) 275-291.

2861 *Alonso Schökel* Luis, Arte narrativa en Josué-Jueces-Samuel-Reyes: EstB 48 (1990) 145-169; Eng. 145.

2862 **Arx** Urs von, Studien zur Geschichte des alttestamentlichen Zwölfer-symbolismus, I. Fragen im Horizont der Amphiktyoniehypothese von Martin NOTH [Diss. Bern, Teil]: EurHS 23/397. Bern 1990, Lang. 583 p. DM 120 [TR 87,338]. 3-261-04250-8.

2863 *Coats* George W., The Ark of the Covenant in Joshua; a probe into the history of a tradition: HebAnR 9 (1985) 137-157 [203-220, *McKenzie* S. L., redaction of Kings; < OTAbs 13,270ss].

2864 *Coogan* Michael D., Archaeology and biblical studies; the book of Joshua: ➤ 550, Hebrew Bible SD 1986/90, 19-32.

2865 **Davis** Dale R., No falling words; expositions of the book of Joshua 1988 ➤ 4,2746: RGraceTJ 10 (1989) 83s (A. B. *Luter*: successful midway between aridly scholarly and overly popular).

2866 *Feldman* Louis H., JOSEPHUS's portrait of Joshua: HarvTR 82 (1989) 351-376.

2867 **Hawk** L. Daniel, Every promise fulfilled; a study of plot in the book of Joshua: diss. Emory, DGunn D. Atlanta 1990. 341 p. 91-06723. – DissA 51 (1990s) 3439-A; RTLv 22, p. 588.

2868 **Koorevaar** Hendrik J., De opbouw van het boek Jozua [prot. diss. DJa-gersma H. Bru 1990. Heverlee 1990, Centrum voor bijbelse vorming. 304 p.; Eng. p. 279-293. Fb 940 pa. 90-71813-06-1]. > JStOT supp. – TsTNijm 30,302; RTLv 22, p. 588. – ROTAbs 13 (1990) 310 (C. T. *Begg*).

2869 **O'Brien** Mark, The Deuteronomistic history hypothesis, a reassessment [diss. Melbourne DCampbell A.]: OBO 92, 1989 ➤ 5,2608: RBiblica 71 (1990) 564-7 (R. D. *Nelson*: but Martin NOTH explains so much so well); ETL 66 (1990) 179s (J. *Lust*: 'a CAMPBELL school, between CROSS and SMEND'); RivB 38 (1990) 525-9 (A. *Bonora*); TüTQ 170 (1990) 147s (W. *Gross*).

2870 *Van Seters* John, Joshua's campaign of Canaan and Near Eastern his-toriography: ScandJOT (1990,2) 1-12.

2871 **Floss** Johannes P., Kunden oder Kundschafter?... Jos 2: AOtt 16.26, 1982/6 ➤ 63,2687... 5,2634: RTLZ 115 (1990) 804-6 (H.-J. *Zobel*).

2871* *a*) *Zakovitch* Yair, Humor and theology or the successful failure of Israelite intelligence; a literary-folkloric approach to Joshua 2 [response *Cross* Frank M.]; – *b*) *Wilson* Robert R., Sociological aspects of ancient Israelite ethics [comments, *Middleton* John]. ➤ 547, ENiditch Susan, Folklore 1990, 75-98 [99-104] / 193-205 [207-213].

2872 *Crocker* P. T., [Jos 6] Joshua and the walls of Jericho: BurHist 26 (1990) 100-4 [< OTAbs 14,150].

2873 *Thompson* Yaakov, [Jos 7,25] The punishment of Achan: JBQ 19 (1990s) 25-28.

2874 *a*) *Briend* Jacques, [Jos 9] Israël et les Gabaonites; – *b*) *Lemaire* André, Aux origines d'Israël; la montagne d'Ephraïm et le territoire de Manassé (XIIIe-XIe siècle av. J.-C.) [+ La montagne de Juda]; – *c*) *Kempinski* Aharon, L'installation des clans et des tribus dans le bassin de Beersheba: ➤ 354, Protohistoire 1990, 121-182 / 183-292; map [293-8] / 299-334; 10 fig.

2875 *Barr* James, [Jos 10,3] Mythical monarch unmasked? Mysterious doings of Debir king of Eglon: JStOT 48 (1990) 55-68.

2876 *David* Robert, Jos 10,28-39, témoin d'une conquête de la Palestine par le Sud?: ScEsp 42 (1990) 209-222.

2877 **Cortese** Enzo, Joshua 13-31; ein priesterschriftlicher Abschnitt im deuteronomistischen Geschichtswerk: OBO 94. FrS/Gö 1990, Univ./VR. 122 p. Fs 34. 3-7278-0661-3 / 3-525-53724-7. – ᴿExpTim 102 (1990s) 181 (R. *Coggins*: Argentine author; technical proof that these geographic texts are not Deuteronomistic).

2878 *Pienaar* D. N., Die stad aan die rivier (Jos 13: 16): NduitsGT 30 (1989) 376-382 [< OTAbs 13, p. 162].

2879 *Kallai* Zecharia, The land of the Perizzites and the Rephaim (Joshua 17,14-18): ➤ 518, IOSOT 13, 1989/90, 197-205.

2880 **Koopmans** Willam T., Joshua 24 as poetic narrative [diss. ᴰ*Moor* J. de. Kampen 1990. – TsTNijm 31,89; RTLv 22, p. 588]: JStOT supp. 93. Sheffield 1990, JStOT. xv-522 p. $52.50. 1-85075-247-8. – ᴿExpTim 102 (1990s) 116 (A. G. *Auld*); ZAW 102 (1990) 448 (H.-C. *Schmitt*).

E4.2 *Liber Judicum:* **Richter, Judges.**

2881 *Avner* Tamar, Septuagint illustrations of the Book of Judges in manuscripts of the court school of Saint Louis [< diss.]: ➤ 743, ByzF 13 (1988) 297-317; pl. XXV-XLI.

2882 *Bacher* Shlomo, ✪ Judges/Ruth: BethM 34 (1989) 149-154 [< OTAbs 14,56].

2883 **Becker** Uwe, Richterzeit und Königtum; redaktionsgeschichtliche Studien zum Richterbuch [ev. Diss. Bonn 1989, ᴰ*Gunneweg* A. ➤ 5,2646]: BZAW 192. B 1990, de Gruyter. ix-326 p. DM 126 [ZAW 103,293, H.-C. *Schmitt*].

2884 *Chalcraft* David J., Deviance and legitimate action in the book of Judges: ➤ 166, ᶠSheffield 1990, 177-201.

2885 *Cimosa* M., I giudici, uomini dello Spirito; Debora... Gedeone... Sansone: ➤ 542*, Laici 1988/90, 39-64.

2886 *Exum* J. Cheryl, The centre cannot hold; thematic and textual instabilities in Judges: CBQ 52 (1990) 410-432.

2887 **Hamlin** E. John, At risk in the Promised Land; a commentary on the book of Judges: IntTC. GR/E 1990, Eerdmans/Handsel. xii-182 p. $13 [TR 87,337].

2888 **Klein** Lilian R., The triumph of irony in the Book of Judges: JStOT supp 68, 1988 ➤ 4,2763 ... 5,2651: ᴿBiblica 71 (1990) 567-9 (A. *Wénin*); CBQ 52 (1990) 323s (L. J. *Hoppe*: for an approach to the method, Pᴏʟᴢɪɴ and Wᴇʙʙ preferable); CritRR 3 (1990) 145-7 (Mieke *Bal*); ÉTRel 65 (1990) 612s (Françoise *Smyth*: remarques fines, neuves, utiles); Interpretation 44 (1990) 303s (C. *Mabee*); Themelios 16 (1990s) 23s (D. F. *Pennant*); TLZ 115 (1990) 582s (W. *Herrmann*).

2889 *Trebolle Barrera* J., Textual variants in 4QJudgᵃ and the textual and editorial history of the book of Judges: ➤ 527, RQum 14,54 (1989s) 229-245.

2890 *Washburn* David L., The chronology of Judges; another look: BS 147 (1990) 414-425.

2891 **Webb** Barry G., The book of the Judges, an integrated reading: JStOT supp 46, 1987 ➤ 3,2638 ... 5,2657: ᴿCritRR 3 (1990) 184-7 (J. C. *Exum*); NedTTs 44 (1990) 158s (K. A. D. *Smelik*).

2892 *a*) *Brenner* Athalya, A triangle and a rhombus in narrative structure; a proposed integrative reading of Judges IV and V: VT 40 (1990) 129-138; – *b*) *Fewell* Donna N., *Gunn* David M., Controlling perspectives; women, men, and the authority of violence in Judges 4 & 5: JAAR 58 (1990) 389-411.

2893 *Na'aman* Nadav, Literary and topographical notes on the battle of Kishon (Judges IV-V): VT 40 (1990) 423-436.

2894 **Bal** Mieke, Murder and difference ... Sisera's death 1988 ➤ 4,2772; 5,2663: ᴿCritRR 3 (1990) 103-5 (F. E. *Greenspahn*); HebSt 31 (1990) 96-101 (M. *Brettler*: also on 'Death & dissymmetry'; some serious objections).

2895 *Cohen-Kiener* Andrea, [Jg 4s] Three women [Deborah, Jael, Sisera's mother]: JBQ 19 (1990s) 204s . 203.

2896 **Soden** John M., Prose and poetry compared; Judges 4 and 5 in their Ancient Near Eastern context: diss. Dallas Theol. Sem. 1989. 332 p. 90-20894. – DissA 51 (1990s) 891-A.

2897 **Bechmann** Ulrike, Das Deboralied zwischen Geschichte und Fiktion; eine exegetische Untersuchung zu Richter 5: TheolDiss [Bamberg 1988, ᴰ*Görg* M.] 33: St. Ottilien 1989, EOS. ix-287 p. DM 29.80. – ᴿZAW 102 (1990) 296 (H.-C. *Schmitt*).

2898 **McDaniel** Thomas F., Deborah never sang; a philological study on the song of Deborah (Judges ch. V). J 1983, Makor. 402 p. [KirSef 62 (1988s), p. 31].

2899 *Tronina* Antoni, [Jg 5] ✪ Reconstruction textuelle du Cantique de Débora: ➤ 64, ᶠGʀᴢʏʙᴇᴋ S. 1990, 329-339.

2900 *a*) *Schulte* Hannelis, Richter 5; das Debora-Lied; Versuch einer Deutung; – *b*) *Donner* Herbert, [Ri 6 ...] Ophra in Manasse; der Heimatsort des Richters Gideon und des Königs Abimelech; – *c*) *Hübner* Ulrich, [Ri 11] Hermeneutische Möglichkeiten; zur frühen Rezeptionsgeschichte der Jefta-Tradition: ➤ 147, ᶠRᴇɴᴅᴛᴏʀғғ R., Hebr. Bibel 1990, 177-191 / 193-205; map 206 / 489-501.

2901 **Gibert** Pierre, [Jg 6] Vérité historique et esprit historien; l'historien biblique de Gédéon face à Hᴇ́ʀᴏᴅᴏᴛᴇ; préf. *Caquot* André: Initiations. P 1990, Cerf. 272 p. F 175. 2-204-04029-0. – ᴿEsprVie 100 (1990) 685s (L. *Monloubou*); RTLv 21 (1990) 490s (P.-M. *Bogaert*),

2902 *Waldman* Nahum M., [Jg 6,34] The imagery of clothing, covering, and overpowering [... Akkadian]: ➤ 75, Mem. Hᴇʟᴅ M., JANES 19 (1989) 161-170.

2903 *Costacurta* Bruna, [Giudici 7,21; 19,3; 2 Sam 16,12.26; Geremia 18,22; 1,5: polisemia]: Implicazioni semantiche in alcuni casi di *qere-ketib*: Biblica 71 (1990) 226-239.

2904 *Długosz* Antoni, [Jg 9,8-15; 2 K 14,9] ✪ Kerygmatic meaning of the Old Testament fables: ➤ 64, ᶠGʀᴢʏʙᴇᴋ S. 1990, 50-62; Eng. 63.

2905 *Tångberg* Arvid, Bibel og fabel; bemerkninger til Jotamfabelen Dom 9: ➤ 21*, Mem. Bᴊøʀɴᴅᴀʟᴇɴ A., TsTKi 60,4 (1989) 281-292; Eng. 292.

2906 **Trible** Phyllis, Verhalen van verschrikking; een literair-feministische lezing van bijbelse verhalen [1984 ➤ 65,1331*], ᵀ. Kampen 1986, Kok. 140 p. ƒ24,50. 90-242-0832-7. – ᴿNedTTs 44 (1990) 64s (Fokkelien van *Dijk-Hemmes*).

2907 *Becking* Bob, Iphigeneia in Gilead, over het verstaan van Richteren 11, 29-40: KerkT 41 (1990) 192-205.
2908 **Kaswalder** Pietro A., La disputa diplomatica di Iefte (Gdc 11,12-28); la ricerca archeologica in Giordania e il problema della conquista: SBF Anal 29. J 1990, Franciscan. xvii-364 p. $25.
2909 **Marcus** David, Jephthah and his vow 1986 → 2,1993... 4,2782: RHeb-St 31 (1990) 208-210 (R. G. *Boling*: not death, only celibacy).
2910 *Ellington* John, Translating shibboleth and sibboleth (Judges 12.6): BTrans 41 (1990) 446: 1. 'a word which the people of Ephraim were unable to pronounce correctly'; 2, 'pronounced the wrong way'.
2911 *Na'aman* Nadav, [Jg 12,13 / 6] Pirathon and Ophra [Far'ata 10k S Sabasṭiya rather Ophra]: BibNot 50 (1989) 11-16.
2911* [Jg 13-17] *a) Alter* Robert, Samson without folklore; – *b) Bynum* David E., Samson as a biblical phēr oreskōos; – *c) Lord* Albert B., Patterns of lives of the patriarchs from Abraham to Samson and Samuel [*Gunn* D., response]: → 547, ENiditch Susan, Folklore 1990, 47-56 / 57-73 / 7-18 [19-24].
2912 **Bal** Mieke, [Jg] Death and dissymmetry 1988 → 5,2682: RParadigms 6,2 (1990s) 40s (W. *Bergen*).
2913 *Niditch* Susan, [Jg 13-17] Samson as culture hero, trickster, and bandit; the empowerment of the weak: CBQ 52 (1990) 608-624.
2914 *Trau* H., al., [Jg 16,19...] Symbolic significance of hair in the biblical narrative and in the law [... LEACH E. 1958; HALLPIKE C. 1969]: → 540*, Koroth 9 sp. (3d symposium 1987/8) 173-9.
2915 *Amit* Yairah, Hidden polemic in the conquest of Dan; Judges XVII-XVIII: VT 40 (1990) 4-20 [not vol. 60 as p. 4 top].
2915* *Block* Daniel J., Echo narrative technique in Hebrew literature; a study in Judges 19: WestTJ 52 (1990) 325-341.

E4.3   **Liber Ruth,** *'V Rotuli',* the Five Scrolls.

2916 *Beattie* D. R. G., The Yemenite tradition of Targum Ruth: JJS 41 (1990) 49-56.
2917 **Brenner** Athalya, ✪ Ruth and Naomi; literary, stylistic and linguistic studies in the Book of Ruth [→ 5,2700; title differently]. TA 1988, Kib. Meuchad. 168 p. – RHebSt 31 (1990) 110-2 (M. *Garziel*).
2918 **Cohen** A., 2revRosenberg A.J., The five megilloth; Hebrew text and English translation with an introduction and commentary, I. Song Ruth Lam; II. Eces Est. L 1984, Soncino. 208 p.; 189 p. [KirSef 62 (1988s) p. 485].
2919 *Feeley-Harnik* Gillian, Naomi and Ruth; building up the house of David [*Greenstein* Edward L., response]: → 547, ENiditch S., Folklore 1990, 163-184 [185-191].
2920 **Fewell** Diana N., *Gunn* D. M., Compromising redemption; relating characters in the Book of Ruth: Literary Currents in Biblical Interpretation. Louisville 1990, Westminster/Knox. 141 p. $12. 0-664-25135-8 [BL 91,72, R. P. *Carroll*: good]. – RSWJT 33,3 (1990s) 46s (D. G. *Kent* disagrees but recommends).
2921 *Goldenberg* Gideon, *Zaken* Mordekhay, The Book of Ruth in Neo-Aramaic → 9401, EHeinrichs W., Studies in Neo-Aramaic 1990, 151-7 (simple transcription of tape from Zakho).
2922 **Grant** Reg, The validity of pregeneric plot structure in Ruth as a key for interpretation: diss. Dallas Theol. Sem. 1988. 257 p. 90-08217. – DissA 51 (1990s) 529-A.

2923 **Hubbard** Robert L.[J], The book of Ruth: NICOT 1988 → 4,2793*; 5,2695: [R]BL (1990) 57 (G. L. *Emmerson*: fine); CBQ 52 (1990) 514-6 (Barbara *Green*: interesting but scarcely convincing); CriswT 4 (1989s) 177-9 (D. L. *Block*); HebSt 31 (1990) 176-8 (Eileen *Schuller*).

2924 *Hyman* Frieda C., Ruth – a pure dove of Israel: Judaism 38 (1989) 53-62.

2925 **Kraft** A., *Tov* E., Ruth: Computer-LXX 1, 1986 → 2,2003 ... 4,2795: [R]ÉTRel 65 (1990) 446 (C.-B. *Amphoux*).

2926 *Liptzin* Sol, Reflections; [Der junge David, Viennese poet Richard] BEER-HOFFMAN's image of Ruth: JBQ 19,4 (1990s) 226-9.

2927 **Martel** Gérard de, Commentaria in Ruth e codicibus Genovefensi 45 et Clagenfurtensi 13: CCMed 81. Turnhout 1990, Brepols. 460 p. Fb 5550. 2-503-03811-5; pa. -2-3. – [R]NRT 112 (1990) 921s (V. *Roisel*).

2928 **Martel** Gérard de, Répertoire des textes latins relatifs au livre de Ruth (VIIe-XVe s.): Instrumenta Patristica 18. Steenbrugge/Dordrecht 1990, Sint-Pietersabdij / Kluwer. 273 p. – [R]RBén 100 (1990) 568 (P. *Verbraken*); RHE 85 (1990) 482 (J. *O'Kane*).

2929 **Neusner** Jacob, Ruth Rabbah [→ a219], an analytical translation: BrownJudSt 183. Atlanta 1989, Scholars. xii-209 p. $50. 1-88840-397-2 [NTAbs 34,274].

2930 *Prévost* J.-P., Les rouleaux (Ruth – Le Cantique des Cantiques – Qohéleth – Les Lamentations – Esther): → 323, Psaumes/Écrits 1990, 145-195.

2931 **Sasson** Jack M., Ruth[2] [= [1]1979, minimally corrected] 1989 → 5,2698: [R]CBQ [56 (1981) 113-6] 20 (1990) 727s (M. D. *Guinan*); ÉTRel 65 (1990) 617 (D. *Lys*).

2932 a) *Standaert* Benoît, Petit commentaire du livre de Ruth à la lumière de la tradition juive; – b) *Giannarelli* Elena, Ruth chez les Pères de l'Église; – c) *Kohn* Moshé, Bonté vaut mieux que charité: Sidic 23,2 (1990) 3-13 / 14-17 / 18s.

2933 **Thorsen** Audun I., Fortolkning til Ruts bok 1987 → 3,2662; Nk 59: [R]NorTTs 90 (1989) 242 (K. *Sauge*).

2934 **Zakovitch** Yair, Ⓗ Ruth, introduction and commentary: Mikra le-Yiśra'el, a Bible commentary for Israel. TA/J 1990, Am Oved / Magnes. v-124 p. $17. 965-13-0646-7.

2935 **Zenger** Erich, Das Buch Ruth; Z BK AT 8, 1986 → 3,2664; 4,2804: [R]BZ 34 (1990) 302s (J. *Scharbert*); ETL 66 (1990) 396s (J. *Lust*); TZBas 46 (1990) 283-5 (Ina *Willi-Plein*).

2936 **Zlotowitz** Meir, Ruth, commentaire rabbinique, intr. *Scherman* Nosson; [T]*Halpern* Maguy: La Bible commentée. P 1987, Colbo. 165 p. [KirSef 62 (1988s) p. 485].

2937 *Oikawa* Hirokazu, [Ruth 1s] notion of 'and' in the Coptic translation of the book of Ruth [Ch. 1s, 130 times in Hebrew or Coptic or Greek]: → 114, [F]LICHTHEIM M. 1990, (II) 730-750.

2938 *Gow* Murray D., Ruth quoque — a coquette? (Ruth 4:5 REB): TyndB 41 (1990) 302-311.

E4.4 **1-2 Samuel.**

2939 **Anderson** A. A., 2 Samuel: Word Comm. 11, 1989 → 5,2704: [R]BS 147 (1990) 118s (E. H. *Merrill*: a model commentary, despite diminishing historicity); CriswT (1989s) 387s (R.D. *Bergen*); VT 40 (1990) 380s (J.A. *Emerton*).

2940 **Baldwin** Joyce, 1-2 Samuel: Tyndale OT 1988 ➤ 4,2806; 5,2706: RIrBSt 12 (1990) 149s (Gilian *Keys*).

2941 **Brueggemann** W., First and Second Samuel: Interpretation comm. Louisville 1990, Knox. x-362 p. $25. 0-8042-3108-7 [BL 91,54s, H.G.M. *Williamson*: fresh and challenging, not as 'all to often'].

2941* **Brueggemann** Walter, [spinoff of his 1-2 Sam] Power, providence, and personality; biblical insights into life and ministry. Louisville 1990, W-Knox. 117 p. $9. 0-664-25138-2 [TDig 38,152].

2942 *Dumbrell* W.J., The content and significance of the books of Samuel; their place and purpose within the Former Prophets: JEvTS 33 (1990) 49-62 [< ZAW 103,434].

2943 **Fernández Marcos** Natalio, *Busto Saiz* José R., 1-2 Samuel: Texto Antioqueno de la Biblia Griega 1: TEstCist 1989 ➤ 5,2711: RETL 66 (1990) 180s (J. *Lust*); MiscCom 48 (1990) 289s (*Busto Saiz*); Muséon 103 (1990) 372s (P.M. *Bogaert*).

2944 **Garsiel** Moshe, The first book of Samuel, a literary study of comparative structures, analogies and parallels. J 1990. Ruben Mass. 169 p. [OIAc JJ90].

2945 **Gordon** Robert P., I & II Samuel [Paternoster 1986 ➤ 2,2016... 4,2810], also GR 1988, Zondervan. 365 p. $18. – RCriswT 4 (1989s) 176s (R.D. *Bergen*).

2946 **McCarter** P.K., II Samuel: AnchorB 9, 1984 ➤ 65,2408... 5,2713: RJNES 49 (1990) 363-5 (D. *Pardee*: lots of queries).

2947 **Martini** Carlo M., Samuele, profeta religioso e civile [es. spir. Peru 1990]: Centro Ambrosiano. CasM 1990, Piemme. 160 p. Lit. 22.000 [Asprenas 38,242, A. *Rolla*].

2948 **Morano Rodríguez** Ciriaca, Glosas... VLat 1-2 Sam: TEstCisn 48, 1989 ➤ 5,2716: RETL 66 (1990) 397s (P.-M. *Bogaert*); JTS 41 (1990) 578 (J.K. *Elliott*).

2949 *Moreno Hernández* Antonio, *a*) Dobletes de nombres propios en la Vetus Latina de 1 y 2 Samuel: ➤ 761, Helmantica 40 (1987/9) 365-371; – *b*) Nuevos textos de Vetus Latina (1 Reyes 22), edición y estudio: Emerita 58 (1990) 275-287.

2950 **Ogilvie** Lloyd J., series editor of Communicator's commentary [not Word Commentary, though published by Word Books Publ. Co], given as editor of the separate books in ÉTRel 65,662; 1-2 Samuel is by **Chafin** Kenneth. Irving TX 1990, Word. 404 p. 0-8499-0413-7.

2951 **Polzin** Robert, Samuel and the Deuteronomist II. I Samuel, 1989 ➤ 5, 2719: RCritRR 3 (1990) 172-4 (P.D. *Miscall*); Interpretation 44 (1990) 416 (D. *Jobling* calls this a 'Commentary on 1 Sam.' and seems to make it a volume 2 to his 1980 Moses and the Deuteronomist); TS 51 (1990) 127 (F.L. *Moriarty*).

2952 *a*) *Rofé* Alexander, The nomistic correction in biblical manuscripts and its occurrence in 4QSam[a]; – *b*) *Lübbe* John, Certain implications of the scribal process of 4QSam[c] ➤ 527, RQum 14,54 (1989s) 247-254 / 255-265.

2953 **Trebolle Barrera** Julio, Centena in libros Samuelis et Regum... Variantes textuales...: TEstCisn 47, 1989 ➤ 5,2723: RETL 66 (1990) 181s (J. *Lust*).

2954 **Vogüé** Adalbert de, GRÉGOIRE, Comm. sur 1 Rois [1 Sam 1-2,28]...: SChr 351, 1989; 2-204-03155-0: RGregorianum 71 (1990) 603 (G. *Pelland*); JTS 41 (1990) 720-2 (Margaret *Gibson*); NRT 112 (1990) 268 (A.

Harvengt); ScEsp 42 (1990) 360s (L. *Sabourin*); Studium 85 (R 1989) 727s (Vera *Paronetto*); VigChr 44 (1990) 299-301 (G. J. M. *Bartelink*).

2955 **Zijl** [= Zyl] A. H. van, 1 Samuel: PredikOT, 1988; ➤ 4,2823; 5,2725: RCBQ 52 (1990) 337s (C. T. Begg, 1: good but without actualization and with too many typos); NedTTs 44 (1990) 251-3 (P. B. *Dirksen*, 1); TsT-Nijm 30 (1990) 404 (P. *Kevers*).

2956 *Kotze* Robert J., The circumstantial sentence; a catch-them-all term? A study in sentence relationships in 1 Samuel 1-12: JNWS 15 (1989) 109-126.

2957 **Robert** Philippe de, La formation de 1 Samuel 1 à 7 [prot. diss. Strasbourg 1980 ➤ 62,2895]. Lille 1984, Atelier des Thèses [KirSef 62 (1988s) p. 33].

2958 *Tsevat* Mattitiahu, Abzählungen in 1 Samuel 1-4: ➤ 147, FRENDTORFF R., Hebr. Bibel 1990, 207-214.

2959 **Mommer** Peter, Samuel, Geschichte und Tradition: ev. Diss. DThiel. Marburg 1989s. – TR 86 (1990) 517.

2960 *Brueggemann* Walter, 1 Samuel 1; a ['lively, daring'] sense of a beginning: ZAW 102 (1990) 33-48.

2960* *Zyl* A. H. van, [1 Sam 1,1] Die herkoms en betekenis van die naam Elkana: SkrifK 7 (Pretoria 1986) 219-223 [< OTAbs 14,40].

2961 *Westbrook* Raymond, 1 Samuel 1:8 ['ten sons' in Ashurbanipal]: JBL 109 (1990) 114s.

2962 *Henrix* Hans H., [1 Sam 2] Hannas Gebet – Inszenierung einer Seele: UnSa 45 (1990) 134-141.

2963 *Wallace* Ronald S., Eli and his sons; 1 Samuel 2:11-36 / The word of the Lord was scarce, 1 Sam 3:1-4 / The beginning of a friendship, 1 Sam 3:1-21 / The Ark on the field, 1 Sam 1:4-11: Evangel 7 (1989) fasc. 1, 2-5 . 2,2-4 . 3,2-5 . 4,2-4.

2964 *Cook* Johann, Hannah and/or Elkanah on their way home (1 Samuel 2:11)? A witness to the complexity of the tradition history of the Samuel texts: OTEssays 3 (1990) 247-262.

2965 *Rooy* H. F. van, Prophetic utterances in narrative texts, with reference to 1 Samuel 2:27-36: OTEssays 3 (1990) 203-218.

2966 *Wallace* R. S., a) Old Testament aftermath; an exposition of 1 Samuel 4,12-22: – b) The Ark among the Philistines; 1 Samuel 5 [not 15 as here]: 1-12; Psalm 78:59-66: Evangel 8,3 (1990) 4-6 / 8,4 (1990) 3-6.

2967 *Winter* Yosef, [1 Sam 5; 3s; 12] ❶ The impact of the division into sections on the meaning of the Bible: BethM 35 (1989s) 245-256 [< OTAbs 14,177].

2967* a) *Lust* Johan, [1 Sam 5,6] Edra and the Philistine plague; – b) *Gordon* R. P., The problem of haplography in 1 and 2 Samuel; – c) *Polak* Frank H., Statistics and textual filiation; the case of 4QSam^a/LXX (with a note on the text of the Pentateuch); ➤ 519, Septuagint, Scrolls 1990, 569-597 / 131-158 / 215-276.

E4.5 *1 Sam 7 ... Initia potestatis regiae.* **Origins of kingship.**

2968 **Brettler** M. Z., God is king [diss. Brandeis ➤ 3,3100]: JStOT 76, 1989 ➤ 5,2733: RExpTim 101 (1989s) 247s (J. *Eaton*); VT 40 (1990) 501s (J. A. *Emerton*).

2969 **Eaton** John H., Kingship and the Psalms² ➤ 4,2832*; 5,2735: RJAOS 110 (1990) 159 (J. J. M. *Roberts*).

2970 a) *Edelman* Diana, The Deuteronomist's story of King Saul; narrative
art or editorial product?: – b) *Peterca* Vladimir, Der Bruch zwischen
Samuel und Saul und seine theologischen Hintergründe (1 Sam 15,24-31):
→ 518, IOSOT 13, 1989/90, 207-220 / 221-5.
2971 *Freund* Richard A., From kings to archons; Jewish political ethics and
kingship passages in the LXX: ScandJOT 4,2 (1990) 58-72.
2972 *Howard* David M.ᴶ, The case for kingship in Deuteronomy and the
Former Prophets [*Gerbrandt* E. 1986]: WestTJ 52 (1990) 101-115.
2973 *Jacobs* Irving, Kingship and holiness in the third benediction of the
Amidah and in the Yoẓer: JJS 41 (1990) 62-74.
2974 **Martin** James K., Cultic obligations of kingship during Israel's united
monarchy and possible Ancient Near Eastern prototypes: diss. SW Baptist
theol. sem., ᴰ*Keim* G. Fort Wayne 1990. vii-302 p. 90-14718. – DissA 51
(1990s) 260-A; OIAc Oc90.
2975 **Ntreh** Benjamin A., Transmission of political authority in ancient Israel;
a tradition historical study of the demise and succession of kings in the
Deuteronomistic history and in the Chronicler's history: diss. Lutheran
School of Theology. Ch 1990. 227 p. 90-12904. – DissA 50 (1989s)
3990-A.
2976 *Pattison* George, Violence, kingship and cultus [GIRARD's otherwise
illuminating use of the Bible neglects this aspect]: ExpTim 102 (1990s)
135-140.
2977 **Rosenberg** Joel, King and kin; political allegory in the Hebrew Bible
[diss. 1978 Santa Cruz] 1986 → 3,2692 ... 5,2740: ᴿHebSt 31 (1990) 233-7
(E. *Bellefontaine*); Prooftexts 9 (1989) 257-263 (D. *Damrosch*).
2978 *Schmidt* Ludwig, Königtum AT [*Lanczkowski* Günter, Religionsge-
schichtlich]: → 857, TRE 19 (1990) 327-333 [323-7].
2979 **Springborg** Patricia, Royal persons; patriarchal monarchy and the
feminine principle. L 1990, Unwin Hyman. xv-326 p. 0-04-445376-0
[OIAc Ja91].
2980 **Weiss** Esther, ❺ Israelite monarchy and the tribal factor; conflict and
compromise from Saul to Jeroboam I. J 1987. 417 p.; 28 fig. [KirSef 62
(1988s) p. 20].

2981 **Wénin** André, Samuel et l'instauration de la monarchie (1 S 1-12)...
[diss. PIB, Rome] 1988 → 4,2839; 5,2743: ᴿBL (1990) 96 (R. R. *Gordon*);
CBQ 52 (1990) 734s (P. D. *Miscall*: typical thesis; detail seldom matched
by insight).
2982 *Kőszeghy* Miklós, ❿ 'Give us a king to judge over us'; prehistory of
Israelite kingship, 1 Sam 8,6: TSzem 33 (1990) 166-171.
2983 *Scheffler* Eben, The game Samuel played [... contributing to Saul's
suicide]; a psychological interpretation of the relationship between Samuel
and Saul: OTEssays 3 (1990) 263-273.
2984 *Ben Nahum* Yonathan, [1 Sam 10,10-12; 19,24] What ailed the son of
Kish? [diabetes; < BethM, ᵀ*Luzann* Lolla]: → 115, ᶠLIPTZIN S., JBQ 19
(1990s) 244-9.
2985 **Berges** U., Die Verwerfung Sauls; eine thematische Untersuchung:
ForBi 61. Wü 1989, Echter. xviii-332 p. DM 48. 3-429-01224-4 [BL
90,67, B. *Lindars*].
2986 *Berges* Ulrich, El rechazo de Saul; historia e historiografía en el antiguo
Israel: RTLim 23 (1989) 235-247.

2987 *Catastini* A., [1 Sam 13,16] Un'integrazione nel pergamenaceo greco laurenziano PL III/957: ➤ 154, FSACCHI P. 1990, 105-7.

E4.6 *1 Sam 16 ... 2 Sam: Accessio Davidis.* **David's Rise.**

2988 **Dietrich** W., David, Saul und die Propheten: BW 122, 1987 ➤ 3,2709 ... 5,2750: RÉTRel 65 (1990) 267s (J. *Rennes*).

2989 *Feinglass* Abraham, Abraham COWLEY [17th century Davideis] and the David story: ➤ 115, FLIPTZIN S., JBQ 19 (1990s) 265-273.

2990 **Flanagan** James W., David's... hologram: SocWB 7, 1988 ➤ 4,2855; 5,2752: RBiblica 71 (1990) 411-5 (N. P. *Lemche*: an advance but ill-digestibly intricate); CBQ 52 (1990) 711-3 (T. R. *Hobbs*: fresh and stimulating, though the hologram is not all it is claimed to be); Interpretation 44 (1990) 303 (J. M. *Bracke*); JAOS 110 (1990) 573s (B. *Halpern*: 'Braudelian in scope'); JBL 109 (1990) 329-331 (F. S. *Frick*); VT 40 (1990) 127 (H. G. M. *Williamson*).

2991 *Fokkelman* Jan P., Saul and David, crossed fates: BR 5,3 (1989) 20-32.

2992 **Kaynor** Keith, When God chooses; the life of David. Schaumburg IL 1989, Regular Baptist Press. 332 p. $13. – RBS 147 (1990) 498 (F. D. *Lindsey*), corrected in 148, p. 128.

2993 **Keller** Weldon P., David, the time of Saul's tyranny. Waco 1985, Word. 223 p. [KirSef 62 (1988s) p. 39].

Kugel J. A., David: Poetry and prophecy 1990 ➤ 351*.

2994 **Martini** Carlo Maria, *a*) David sinner and believer [retreat Chad 1988; Piemme 1989, TNeame Alan]. Middlegreen, Slough 1990, St. Paul. xiv-173 p. – 0-85439-322-6. – *b*) David, pecador y creyente [Chad 1988 Eng.], TOrtiz García Alfonso: Servidores y Testigos 44. Sd 1989, SalTerrae. 207 p. 84-293-0853-9. – RActuBbg 27 (1990) 99 (A. M. *Tortras*). – *c*) Du, den ich suche; Wege von David zu Jesus [Tschad Ordensleute-Exerzitien]. FrB 1990, Herder. 207 p. DM 29,80. – RZkT 112 (1990) 485 (B. *Niederbacher*).

2995 *Merrill* Eugene H., The 'accession year' and Davidic chronology: ➤ 75, Mem. HELD M., JANES 19 (1989) 101-112.

2996 **Todd** Judith A., Can their voices be heard? Narratives about women in I Samuel 16 - I Kings 2: diss. Graduate Theological Union, DChaney M. Berkeley 1990. 389 p. 91-00369. – DissA 51 (1990s) 2542s-A; RelStR 17,193.

Veijola Timo, David; Gesammelte Studien zu den Davidüberlieferungen des ATs 1990 ➤ 315.

2997 **Kaiser** Otto, David und Jonathan; Tradition, Redaktion und Geschichte in 1 Sam 16-20; ein Versuch: ETL 66 (1990) 281-296.

2998 *Trebolle* Julio, The story of David and Goliath (1 Sam 17-18), textual variants and literary composition: BSeptCog 23 (1990) 16-30.

2999 **Barthélemy** D., *al.*, Story of David and Goliath: OBO 73, 1986 ➤ 2, 2060 ... 5,2759: RRivB 38 (1990) 235-240 (P. G. *Borbone*: TOV e LUST pubblicati anche altrove).

3000 *Kellermann* Diether, [1 Sam 17,1-58] Die Geschichte von David und Goliath im Lichte der Endokrinologie: ZAW 102 (1990) 344-357; Eng. 357.

3001 *Luciani* Ferdinando, La struttura sintattica di due passi del primo libro di Samuele (18,10-11; 19,9-10): Aevum 64 (1990) 5-16.

3002 *Gordon* Robert P., Word-play and verse-order in I Samuel XXIV 5-8: VT 40 (1990) 139-144.

3002* *Garsiel* Moshe, Wit, words, and a woman: 1 Samuel 25: → 367, Humour 1990, 161-8.

3003 *Strauss* Hans, Über die Grenzen? Exegetische Betrachtungen zu 1 Sam 28,3-25 auf dem Hintergrund bestimmter Strömungen im Rahmen des sogenannten 'New Age': BibNot 50 (1989) 17-25.

3004 *Littlewood* A. R., [1 Sam 28] Michael PSELLOS and [one of his (6) texts on] the witch of Endor: JbÖstByz 40 (1990) 225-231 (228-231, Greek text).

3005 **Vernette** Jean, Peut-on communiquer avec l'au-delà? : C'est-à-dire. P 1990, Centurion. – ᴿEsprVie 100 (1990) 492s (P. *Jay*).

3006 *Spero* Shubert, [2 Sam 1,17-27] An elegy of David; to teach the sons of Judah the bow: JBQ 25 (1990) 155-163.

3007 **Kleven** T., Hebrew style and narrative sequence in II Samuel 1-7: diss. McMaster, ᴰ*Combs* A. Hamilton ON 1990. – RelStR 17, 193.

3008 **Fokkelman** J.P., Throne and city (II Sam. 2-8 & 21-24): Narrative art and poetry in the books of Samuel; a full interpretation based on stylistic and structural analyses [I. 1981 → 63,2962a; 2. 1986 → 2,2042] 3: StSemNeer 27. Assen 1990, van Gorcum. vi-441 p. ƒ85. 90-232-2546-5 [BL 91,158].

3009 *Na'aman* Nadav, [2 Sam 2,9] The kingdom of Ishbaal: BibNot 54 (1990) 33-37.

3010 **Floss** J.P., David und Jerusalem; Ziele und Folgen des Stadteroberungsberichtes 2 Sam 5,6-9 literarwissenschaftlich betrachtet: AOtt 30, 1987 → 3,2738: ᴿZAW 102 (1990) 443 (H.-C. *Schmitt*).

3011 *Brzegowy* Tadeusz, *a)* [2 Sm 6; 24; 1 R 8] ❷ Les théophanies historiques dans le sanctuaire de Jérusalem; – *b)* ❷ Jérusalem, la capitale de l'Oint du Seigneur: ColcT 59,2 (1989) 21-34; franç. 34 / 59,4 (1989) 15-43; franç. 44.

3012 **Ollenburger** Ben C., Zion, the city of the great king...: JStOT supp 41, 1987 → 3,2718... 5,2756: ᴿJTS 41 (1990) 554s (G. W. *Anderson*); NedTTs 43 (1989) 242s (P. B. *Dirksen*).

3013 *Shea* William H., [2 Sam 6:3-8, Uzzah] Further light on the biblical connection of the Beth Shemesh ostracon: AndrUnS 28 (1990) 115-125.

3014 *Murray* D.F., *mqwm* and the future of Israel in 2 Samuel VII 10: VT 40 (1990) 298-320.

3015 *Ackerman* James S., Knowing good and evil; a literary analysis of the court history in 2 Samuel 9-20 and 1 Kings 1-2: JBL 109 (1990) 41-60.

3016 **Fokkelman** Jan P., [2 Sam 9-20] Narrative art... Samuel I, 1981 → 63,2962a... 5,2778: ᴿRelStT 8,1s (1988) 78-80 (L. *Eslinger*).

3017 **Gregory** Mark W., Keret/Succession ᴰ1989. – OIAc JuJ89.

3018 *Wesselius* J.W., Joab's death and the central theme of the succession narrative (2 Samuel IX - 1 Kings II): VT 40 (1990) 336-351.

3019 **Bailey** Randall C., David in love and war; the pursuit of power in 2 Samuel 10-12 [< diss.]: JStOT supp. 75. Sheffield 1990, Academic. 214 p. £26.50. 1-85075-209-5 [BL 91,63, I. W. *Provan*]. – ᴿExpTim 101 (1989s) 376 (C. S. *Rodd*).

3020 *Hentschel* Georg, Der Auftritt des Natan (2 Sam 12,1-15a): → 146, ᶠREINELT H., At. Botschaft 1990, 117-133.

3021 **Jones** Gwilym H., [2 Sam 7; 12; 1 Kgs 1] The Nathan narratives: JStOT supp 80. Sheffield 1990, Academic. 196 p. £25. 1-85075-225-7. –ᴿETL 66 (1990) 398s (J. *Lust*); ExpTim 101 (1989s) 376s (C. S. *Rodd*).

3022 *Smith* Jenny,   The discourse structure of the rape of Tamar (2 Samuel 13:1-22):   VoxEvca 20 (1990) 21-42.

3023 *Hansen* Tracy, [2 Sam 13:1] My name is Tamar: PrPeo 4 (1990) 315-8.

3024 *Mulzer* Martin, [2 Sam 18,19f...] Zur Etymologie von Ahimaaz: BibNot 49 (1989) 17-24.

3025 *Lasine* Stuart,   [2 Sam 19,25-31] Judicial narratives and the ethics of reading; the reader as judge of the dispute between Mephibosheth and Ziba: HebSt 30 (1989) 40-69 [< OTAbs 13, p. 50].

3026 *Anderson* Roger W.[J],   'And he grasp away our eye' ['spy']; a note on II Sam 20,6:   ZAW 102 (1990) 392-396.

3026* *Ben-Yašar* M., [2 Sam 21] Rizpah: BethM 36,124 (1990s) 56-64.

3027 *Rofé* Alexander,   4QSam[a] in the light of historico-literary criticism; the case of 2 Sam 24 and 1 Chr 21:   → 154, [F]SACCHI P. 1990, 109-119.

3028 *Wyatt* Nicolas,   [2 Sam 24,13] David's census and the tripartite theory [DUMÉZIL G.]:   VT 40 (1990) 352-360.

3029 *Lohfink* Norbert,   Welches Orakel gab den Davididen Dauer? Ein Textproblem in 2 Kön 8,19 und das Funktionieren der dynastischen Orakel im deuteronomistischen Geschichtswerk: → 124, [F]MORAN W., Lingering 1990, 349-370.

E4.7   *Libri Regum;* **Solomon, Temple:** *1 Kings ...*

3029* *a) Brueggemann* W.A., The social significance of Solomon as a patron of wisdom; – *b) Whybray* R.N.,   The sage in the Israelite royal court; – *c) Lemaire* A.,   The sage in school and temple; – *d) Leeuwen* R.C. Van, The sage in the prophetic literature; – *e) McCarter* P.K.,   The sage in the dcutcronomistic history; – *f) Blenkinsopp* J.,   The sage, the scribe, and scribalism in the Chronicler's work: → 336, Sage 1990, 117-132 / 133-9 / 165-181 / 295-306 / 289-293 / 307-315.

3030 **Duval** Danièle,   Salomon, sage ou habile dans le texte massorétique et dans la Septante (1 R 2,12-11,43 et 3 Regnorum 2,12-11,43): cath. diss. Strasbourg 1990, [D]*Renaud* B. – RTLv 22, p. 587.

3031 **Faulstich** E.W.,   History, harmony and the Hebrew Kings.   Spencer IA 1988, Chronology Books.   ix-304 p. – [R]JBL 109 (1990) 327-9 (L.K. *Handy*: flaws; compared with HAYES-HOOKER).

3032 **Frisch** Amos A., ❺ The narrative of Solomon's reign in the Book of Kings: diss. Bar-Ilan Univ.   Ramat-Gan 1986.   420 p. – KirSef 62 (1988s) p. 21.

3033 **Long** Burke O.,   1 Kings 1984 → 65,2465 ... 3,2758:   [R]Vidyajyoti 53 (1989) 395s (P. *Meagher*).

3034 *Migliario* Elvira,   Salomone e Vespasiano (Ant. Jud. VIII.2.5): → 53, [F]GABBA E. 1988, 93-100.

3035 **Rice** Gene,   Nations under God; a commentary on the book of 1 Kings: Int. TComm.   GR/E 1990, Eerdmans/Handsel.   xv-198 p.   0-8028-0492-6 / 1-871828-06-6.

3036 **Sträuli** Robert,   Salomo; die Königsquelle.   Z 1989, ABZ.   436 p.   3-85516-007-4 [OIAc F91,20].

3037 *Talshir* Zipora, ❺ The image [i.e. a judgment on the reliability] of the Septuagint edition of the Book of Kings: Tarbiz 59 (1989s) 249-302; Eng. I.

3038 *Wightman* G.J.,   The myth of Solomon: BASOR 277s (1990) 5-22.

3039 *Younger* K. Lawson[J],   The figurative aspect and the contextual method in the evaluation of the Solomonic Empire (1 Kings 1-11): ➤ 166, FSheffield 1990, 157-175.

———————

3039* *Gourévitch* Danielle, [1 Kgs 1,1-4] On the medical tradition of Shunāmitism [... GALEN; COHAUSEN J. 1742]: ➤ 540*, Koroth 9 sp. (1988) 49-61.

3040 *McKenna* Andrew, [1 Kgs 3,16-28] Biblical structuralism; testing the victimary hypothesis; Helios 17,1 ('René GIRARD and western literature' 1990) 71-87.

3041 *Naveh* Joseph, [1 Kgs 4 ...] Nameless people [Alt's theory that 'son of X' implies hereditary office is contradicted by ostraca and Ugarit lists where both 'son of X' and (other) names are nicknames]: IsrEJ 40 (1990) 108-123; 3 fig.

3042 *Kuan* Jeffrey K., [1 Kgs] Third Kingdoms 5.1 and Israelite-Tyrian relations during the reign of Solomon: JStOT 46 (1990) 31-46.

Templum, 1 Reg 6s:

3043 **Endres** John, Temple, monarchy and word of God: MessageBSp 2, 1988 ➤ 4,2919: RBibTB 20 (1990) 128 (R. *Gnuse*); CBQ 52 (1990) 112s (Marilyn M. *Schaub*); CritRR 2 (1989) 160-2 (Pauline A. *Viviano*).

3043* *Gutmann* J., Masorah figurata in the Mikdashyah; the Messianic Solomonic Temple in a 14th-century Spanish Hebrew Bible manuscript: ➤ 551, ERevell S., 8. Kongress 1988/90.

3044 *Knohl* Israel, ☉ Participation of the people in the Temple worship — Second Temple sectarian conflict and the biblical tradition: Tarbiz 60 (1990s) 139-146; Eng. I.

3045 *Ruderman* Abraham, Reconstructing Herod's Temple in Jerusalem [< *Ritmeyer* K. & L., BAR-W 15,6 (1989) 23-42, not BA as indicated]: ➤ 115, LIPTZIN S., JBQ 19 (1990s) 274-7.

3046 *Jacobson* David M., The plan of Herod's Temple: BAngIsr 10 (1990s) 36-66; 1 fig.

3047 **Jacq** Christian, Maître Hiram et le roi Salomon. P 1989, Rocher. 396 p. F 130. – REsprVie 100 (1990) 264-7-*jaune* (C. *Jean-Nesmy*, avec 11 autres romans de religion).

3048 *Eibschitz* E., ☉ Galleries for the water-drawing festival and other buildings in the women's section [of the Temple] (The forms of the buildings; their use and names): Sinai 103/2 (1988) 1-9 [< JStJud 21,338].

3049 *Zwickel* Wolfgang, [1 Kön 7,21] Die Keramikplatte aus Tell Qasīle, gleichzeitig ein Beitrag zur Deutung von Jachim und Boas: ZDPV 106 (1990) 57-62; 1 fig.

3050 *Gupta* R.C., [1 Kgs 7,23] The 'molten sea' and the value of pi [mathematical for circle]: JBQ 19 (1990s) 127-135; 3 fig.

3051 *Sporty* Lawrence D., The location of the Holy House of Herod's temple; evidence from the pre-destruction period: BA 53 (1990) 194-204.

3052 *Łach* Józef, ☉ De oratione Salomonis post Templi dedicationem (1 Reg 8,22-53): ➤ 64, FGRZYBEK S. 1990, 175-9; lat. 180.

3053 **Talstra** Ebele, Het Gebet van Salomo; synchronie en diachronie in de kompositie van I. Kon. 8.14-61, D1987 ➤ 4,2926; 90-6256-571-9: RGregorianum 71 (1990) 213 (C. *Conroy*); NedTTs 44 (1990) 250s (B. *Becking*); TsTNijm 30 (1990) 87 (E. van *Wolde*).

3054 *Bartlett* J.R., 'Ezion-geber, which is near Elath on the shore of the Red [p. 1; 'Read' (*sic*) p. v] Sea' (1 Kings IX 26): ⇒ 563, OTS 26 (1988/90) 1-16.

3055 **Beyer** Rolf, [1 Kön 10,1-13] Die Königin von Saba, Engel und Dämon; der Mythos einer Frau 1987 ⇒ 4,2927; 5,2814: 3-7857-0449-6. – ᴿZDMG 140 (1990) 196 (M. *Krause*).

3056 ᴱ**Daum** Werner, Die Königin von Saba 1988 ⇒ 5,2815: ᴿJRAS (1990) 131-6 (E. *Ullendorff*: illustrations good, text mostly not).

3057 *Scholz* Piotr, Königin von Saba und kein Ende [JANKOWSKI A. 1987; BEYER Rolf 1987; DAUM W. 1988, *al.*]: Nubica 1s (1990) 395-8.

3058 **Hayes** John H., *Hooker* Paul K., A new chronology for the kings... 1988 ⇒ 4,2931; 5,2824: ᴿCBQ 52 (1990) 510-2 (H. O. *Thompson*: chiefly interesting but frustratingly undocumented are the '15 Assumptions' previous chronographers have made while diverging from some biblical data); JAOS 110 (1990) 767-770 (J. W. *Walton*; p. 769, table of dates also of THIELE, BRIGHT, TADMOR); JTS 41 (1990) 134-6 (A. R. *Millard*).

3058* *Talshir* Zipora, Is the alternate tradition of the division of the Kingdom (3 Kgdms 12:24a-z) non-deuteronomistic?: ⇒ 519, Septuagint, Scrolls 1990, 599-621.

3059 *Moore* Mark, [1 Kgs 12,29) Jeroboam's calves; idols or imitations [i.e. representations (of God)]: BTrans 41 (1990) 421-4.

3060 **Toews** Wesley I., Monarchy and religious institution in Israel under Jeroboam I: diss. ᴰ*Sakenfeld* K. Princeton Theol. Sem. 1990. 253 p. 90-30376. – DissA 51 (1990s) 2055-A; RelStR 17,193.

3061 *a*) *Ibáñez Arana* Andrés, El 'hombre de Dios' y el Profeta de Betel (1 Re 12); – *b*) *Hernando* Eusebio, La profecía yahvista como alternativa de la mántica pagana: ScripV 36 (1989) 5-76 / 77-106.

3062 *Brzegowy* Tadeusz, [1 R 12,25-32] ❷ L'origine du sanctuaire de Dan: ⇒ 64, ᶠGRZYBEK S. 1990, 21-32; franç. 32.

E4.8 *1 Regum 17 33: Elias*, **Elijah**.

3063 *Brodie* Thomas L., Luke-Acts as an imitation and emulation of the Elijah-Elisha narrative: ⇒ 369, New views 1990, 78-85. 172-4.

3064 *Hyman* Frieda C., Elijah, accuser and defender: Judaism 39 (1990) 282-295.

3065 **Speyr** Adrienne von, Elijah, ᵀ*McNeil* Brian. SF 1990, Ignatius. 123 p. $8. 0-89870-270-4 [TDig 38,88].

3066 *Miscall* Peter D., [1 K 14,18] Elijah, Ahab and Jehu; a prophecy fulfilled: Prooftexts 9 (1989) 73-83.

3067 *a*) *Smelik* K.A.D., The literary function of 1 Kings 17,8-24; – *b*) *Eynikel* Erik, Prophecy and fulfillment in the deuteronomistic history (1 Kgs 13; 2 Kgs 23,16-18): ⇒ 518, IOSOT 13, 1989/90, 239-243 / 227-237.

3068 **Hauser** Alan J., *Gregory* Russell, [two interpretations of 1 Kgs 17-19] From Carmel to Horeb; Elijah in Crisis: JStOT supp 85 / BLit 19. Sheffield 1990, Almond. 184 p. $25. 1-85075-128-5 [BL 91,77, A. H. W. *Curtis*].

3069 *Loewenthal* E., La storia del fiume Sambaţion [= Gozan 1 Re 17,6 secondo Nahmanide su Dt 32,26]; alcune note sulla tradizione ebraica antica e medievale: ⇒ 154, ᶠSACCHI P. 1990, 651-663.

3070 *Smelik* K.A.D., De weduwe uit Sarefat; de literaire functie van 1 Koningen 17:8-24: AmstCah 10 (1989) 45-56 [< ZAW 103,125].

3071 **Moriarty** Robert K., [1 K 17s] The treatment of the Lord's prophet; a matter of life and death (3 Kingdoms 17:17-24 as hermeneutic key to 17s): diss. Marquette, Milwaukee 1990. 217 p. 91-01419. – DissA 51 (1990s) 2776-A.

3072 *Thiel* Winfried, Zur Komposition von 1 Könige 18; Versuch einer kontextuellen Auslegung: → 147, FRENDTORFF R., Hebr. Bibel 1990, 215-223.

3073 *Stern* Philip D., The *ḥerem* in 1 Kgs 20,42 as an exegetical problem: Biblica 71 (1990) 43-47.

3074 **Yafé** Felipe C., The case of Naboth's vineyard (1 Kings 21); an historical, sociological and literary study: diss. Jewish Theol. Sem., DGreenstein E. NY 1990. viii-325 p. 90-17169. – DissA 51 (1990s) 897-A; OIAc Oc90.

3075 *Phipps* William E., [1 Kgs 22 Huldah] A woman was the first to declare Scripture holy: BR 6,2 (1990) 14s. 44.

3076 *Ibáñez Arana* Andrés, Miqueas Ben Yimlá y los cuatrocientos profetas (1 Re 22): ScripV 36 (1989) 225-277.

E4.9   **2 Reg 1**... *Elisaeus*... Ezechias, Josias.

3077 **Cogan** Mordechai, *Tadmor* Hayim, II Kings: AnchorB 11, 1988 → 4, 2952; 5,2842: RAngelicum 67 (1990) 423-5 (J. *García Trapiello*); Biblica 71 (1990) 98-100 (H. *Engel*: Standardwerk); BL (1990) 54 (I. W. *Provan*); Gregorianum 71 (1989) 585-7 (G. L. *Prato*); HebSt 31 (1990) 125-130 (J. *Van Seters*: some serious shortcomings); JQR 81 (1990s) 155-8 (M. *Brettler*: a magnificent volume, though typesetting is faulty and bibliography stops 1982).

3078 **Hobbs** T. R., 2 Kings: Word Comm. 13, 1985 → 2,2116... 4,2952*: RVT 40 (1990) 242s (J. A. *Emerton*).

3079 *Lemaire* André, Joas, roi d'Israël et la première rédaction du cycle d'Élisée: → 518, IOSOT 13, 1989/90, 245-254.

3080 **Maeijer** F. J. M., Elisha as a second Elijah 1 K 16,29 - II K 11,20. Apeldoorn 1989 [Biblica 71,145].

3081 **Moore** Rick D., God saves; lessons from the Elisha stories: JStOT supp 95. Sheffield 1990. 169 p. £27.50. 1-85075-259-1 [BL 91,117, R. P. *Carroll*].

3082 **Reinhold** Gotthard G. G., Die Beziehungen Altisraels zu den aramäischen Staaten in der israelitisch-jüdischen Königszeit [ev. Diss. 1988 → 5,2843]: EurHS 23/368. Fra 1989, Lang. 552 p.; 18 pl. Fs 35. 3-631-42010-2 [BL 91,41, L. *Grabbe*].

3083 **Stipp** Hermann-Josef, Elischa – Propheten – Gottesmänner 1 Kön 20-22, 2 Kön 2-7 [kath. Diss. Tü 1985]: AOtt 24, 1987 → 3,2808; 5,2845: RBZ 34 (1990) 304-6 (W. *Thiel*); OLZ 85 (1990) 317-321 (H.-J. *Stoebe*: die Mühe lohnt sich).

3084 *Ziolkowski* Eric J., [2 Kgs 2,23] The bad boys of Bethel; origin and development of a sacrilegious type: HistRel 30 (1990s) 331-358.

3084* *Burns* John B., Why did the besieging army withdraw? (II Reg 3,27): ZAW 102 (1990) 187-194.

3085 *Müller* Walter W., Eselfleisch und Taubendreck; zur Hungersnotspeise in Samaria nach 2 Kön 6,25: BibNot 46 (1989) 17-23.

3086 *Oeming* Manfred, [2 Kg 6,28; Jer 19,9...] 'Ich habe einen Greis gegessen'; Kannibalismus und Autophagie der Kriegsnotschilderung in der Kila-muwa-Inschrift, Zeile 5-8, in Alten Orient und in Alten Testament: Bib-Not 47 (1989) 90-106.

3087 **Barré** Lloyd M.,   The rhetoric of political persuasion ... 2 Kgs 9-11: CBQ Mg 20, 1988 ➤ 4,2959; 5,2850: ᴿBiblica 71 (1990) 260-2 (A. *Rofé* would assign the genre differently); JBL 109 (1990) 331-3 (J. *Walsh*); JTS 41 (1990) 558s (R. *Williamson*).

3087* *Ehrlich* sr. Emilia, [2 K 5; Lk 4,27] ❷ Naaman in the Old and New Testament: ➤ 64, ᶠGʀᴢʏʙᴇᴋ S. 1990, 64-79; Eng. 79.

3088 **Minokami** Yoshikazu,   Die Revolution des Jehu [Diss. Göttingen]: Gö-TArb 28, 1989 ➤ 5,2851; 3-525-87391-3: ᴿBL (1990) 40 (A.G. *Auld*: clear but overlooks Tʀᴇʙᴏʟʟᴇ); ÉTRel 65 (1990) 435s (T. *Römer*); ExpTim 102 (1990s) 25 (R. *Coggins*); TLZ 115 (1990) 100 (S. *Timm*).

3089 *Garcia-Treto* Francisco O.,   The fall of the house; a carnivalesque reading of 2 Kings 9 and 10: JStOT 46 (1990) 47-65.

3090 *Levin* Christoph, [2 Reg 12,1-4] Die Instandsetzung des Tempels unter Joasch ben Ahasja: VT 40 (1990) 51-88.

3091 *Loretz* O., *Mayer* W.,   Pūlu – Tiglatpileser III. und Menahem von Israel nach assyrischen Quellen und 2 Kön 15,19-20: UF 22 (1990) 221-231.

3092 *Ben-Zvi* Ehud,   Tracing prophetic literature in the Book of Kings; the case of II Kings 15,37: ZAW 102 (1990) 100-5.

  Chong Joong Ho,   The song of Moses and the Hoshea-Pekah conflict [2 Kgs 15,30; 17,13], ᴰ1990 ➤ 2846.

3093 **Becking** B.,   Die ondergang van Samaria ... 2 Kon 17, ᴰ1985 ➤ 3,2819; 4,2968: ᴿHenoch 12 (1990) 236s (J.A. *Soggin*).

3094 *Na'aman* Nadav, [2 Kgs 17,3-6] The historical background to the conquest of Samaria (720 ʙ.ᴄ.): Biblica 71 (1990) 206-225; franç. 225.

3095 **Camp** Ludger,   Hiskija und Hiskijabild, Analyse und Interpretation von 2 Kön 18-20 ᴰ1990 ➤ 5,2866: ᴿZAW 102 (1990) 441 (E. *Zenger*).

3097 *Hardmeier* Christof,   *a*) [2 K 18-20] Umrisse eines vordeuteronomi-stischen Annalenwerks der Zidkijazeit; zu den Möglichkeiten computer-gestützter Textanalyse: VT 40 (1990) 165-184. – *b*) Prophetie im Streit ... Jes Jer 2 Reg 18-20: BZAW 187, 1990 ➤ 3916.

3098 **Provan** Iain W.,   Hezekiah and ... composition of the drt history: BZAW 172, 1988 ➤ 4,2979; 5,2867: ᴿHebSt 31 (1990) 229-233 (B. *Halpern*); Interpretation 44 (1990) 304.306 (J.C. *McCann*); JAOS 110 (1990) 770s (W.B. *Barrick*); JBL 109 (1990) 122-4 (E.T. *Mullen*); OLZ 85 (1990) 555-9 (W. *Dietrich*); RivB 38 (1990) 95-97 (P. *Bovati*).

3098* *Ruprecht* Eberhard,   Die ursprüngliche Komposition der Hiskia–Jesaja–Erzählungen und ihre Umstrukturierung durch den Verfasser des deuteronomistischen Geschichtswerkes: ZTK 87 (1990) 33-66.

3099 *Jong* S. de,   Het verhaal van Hizkia en Sanherib, 2 Koningen 18:17-19:37; Jesaja 36-37 als narratieve reflectie op de ballingschap: AmstCah 10 (1989) 57-71.

3100 *Millard* A.R., [2 Kgs 18] Please speak Aramaic [against *Garbini* G., History and ideology 1988 claim that Judah's leaders learned Aramaic only in the Exile]: BurHist 25 (1989) 67-73 [< OTAbs 13, p. 37].

3101 *Ben Zvi* Ehud, [2 Kgs 18,19-35] Who wrote the speech of Rabshakeh and when?: JBL 109 (1990) 79-92.

3102 *Anbar* M., [2 Rois 18,34] *kai poû* ... 'et où sont les dieux du pays de Samarie?': BibNot 51 (1990) 7s.

3103 **Gonçalves** Francolino J. [2 Rois 18,17] L'expédition de Sennacherib ... ÉtBN 7, 1986 ⇒ 2,2131 ... 4,2971: ᴿSalmanticensis 37 (1990) 361-3 (F. *García López*).

3104 *Gonçalves* Francolino J., Senaquerib en Palestina y la tradición bíblica: EfMex 8 (1990) 57-69.

3106 *Zawadzki* Stefan, Oriental and Greek tradition about the death of Sennacherib: SAAB 4,1 (1990) 69-72.

3107 *Levin* Schneir, [2 Kgs 23,21] Hezekiah's second passover: JBQ 19 (1990s) 195-8.

3108 *a*) *Conroy* Charles, Reflections on the exegetical task; apropos of recent studies on 2 Kings 22-23; – *b*) *Paul* Maarten J., King Josiah's renewal of the Covenant (2 Kings 22-23); – *c*) *Coggins* R. J., 2 Kings 23,29; a problem of method in translation: ⇒ 518, IOSOT 13, 1989/90, 255-268 / 269-276 / 277-281.

3109 *Lohfink* Norbert, 2 Kön 23,3 und Dtn 6,17: Biblica [zu 70 (1989) 10 n. 19] 71 (1990) 34-42.

3110 *Delcor* Mathias, *a*) Réflexions sur la Pâque du temps de Josias d'après 2 Rois 23,21-23 [< Henoch 4 (1982) 205-219]; – *b*) Les cultes étrangers en Israël au moment de la réforme de Josias d'après 2 R 23; étude de religions sémitiques comparées [< ᶠ*Cazelles* H., AOAT 212 (1981) 91-123]: ⇒ 219*, Environnement 1900, 90-104 / 105-137.

3111 *Smelik* K. A. D., The riddle of [Lachish III] Tobiah's document; difficulties in the interpretation of Lachish [letter] III,19-21: PEQ 122 (1990) 133-138.

3112 *Malamat* Abraham, [final years of] The Kingdom of Judah between Egypt and Babylon; a small state within a Great Power confrontation [Mowinckel Lecture]: ST 44 (1990) 65-77.

3113 *Becking* Bob, Jehojachin's amnesty, salvation for Israel? Notes on 2 Kings 25,27-30: ⇒ 518, IOSOT 13, 1989/90, 283-292.

E5.1   *Chronicorum libri* –   **The books of Chronicles.**

3114 **Becker** Joachim, I. Chronik: NEchter 1986 ⇒ 3,2840 ... 5,2878: ᴿNed-TTs 44 (1990) 253 (P. B. *Dirksen*).

3115 **Crossley** Sanford L., [Chr ...] The Levite as a royal servant during the Israelite monarchy: diss. SW Baptist Theol. Sem. 1989. 218 p. 90-14711. – DissA 51 (1990s) 191-A; OIAc Oc90.

3116 **De Vries** Simon J., 1 & 2 Chronicles: FOTLit 11, 1989 ⇒ 5,2880: ᴿHebSt 31 (1990) 130-3 (K. G. *Hoglund*).

3117 *Díez Merino* L., La onomástica hebreo-aramea como fuente de exégesis bíblica en el Targum de Crónicas: ⇒ 154, ᶠSᴀᴄᴄʜɪ P. 1990, 203-244.

3118 **Dillard** Raymond B., 2 Chronicles: Word comm. 15, 1987 ⇒ 3,2485 ... 5,2881: ᴿCBQ 52 (1990) 318 (Alice L. *Laffey*: valuable especially for less-obvious theological observations of a Christian scholar).

3119 **Duke** Rodney S., The persuasive appeal of the Chronicler; a rhetorical analysis: JStOT supp 88, BLit 25. Sheffield 1990, Almond. 192 p. £22.50 [TR 87,426]. 1-85075-228-1.

3120 **Graham** Matt P., The utilization of 1 and 2 Chronicles in the re-construction of Israelite history in the nineteenth century: SBL diss 116 [Emory 1983, ᴰ*Hayes* J. ⇒ 64,2869]. Atlanta 1990, Scholars. xi-268 p. 1-55540-354-9 [ZAW 103,297, H.-C. *Schmitt*].

3121 *Harris* R. Laird, Chronicles and the canon in NT times: JEvTS 33 (1990) 75-84 [< NTAbs 34,284].

3122 **Japhet** Sara, The ideology of Chr 1989 ➤ 5,2884: RHelmantica 41 (1990) 428s (L. *Amigo*); RHPR 70 (1990) 256 (P. *de Robert*).

3123 *Johnstone* William, Which is the best commentary? II. The Chronicler's work [JAPHET S.; anyway Chr cannot be understood except as the last word in the Hebrew Bible]: ExpTim 102 (1990s) 6-11.

3124 **Kalimi** Isaac, The Books of Chronicles, a classified bibliography. J 1990, Simor. xvi-230 p. 965-242-008-5 [OTAbs 14,112, C.T. *Begg*: first in a projected series of Bible Bibliographies].

3125 **Mason** Rex, Preaching the tradition; homily and hermeneutics after the Exile; based on the 'addresses' in Chronicles, the 'speeches' in the books of Ezra and Nehemiah and the post-exilic prophetic books. C 1990, Univ. ix-325 p. $49.50. 0-521-38304-8 [TDig 38,176]. – RExpTim 102 (1990s) 244s (W. *Johnstone*: critique of von Rad 1934, queried).

3126 *Moda* Aldo, Libri delle Cronache [...formano un'unità con EsdN]: BbbOr 32 (1990) 231-244.

3127 **Then** R., 'Gibt es denn keinen mehr unter den Propheten?' Zum Fortgang der alttestamentlichen Prophetie in frühjüdischer Zeit [< Diss. Rg. 1987s]: BeitErfAJ 22. Fra 1990, Lang. 321 p. Fs 36. 3-631-40360-7 [BL 91,97, A.G. *Auld*: at heart Chr attitude to prophecy].

3128 *Weinberg* I.P., ✆ Royal biography [Chr] in the Near East in the middle of the first millenium B.C.: VDI 195 (1990) 81-97; Eng. 97.

3129 *Zipor* M.A., On the presentation of the synoptic accounts of the monarchies (Samuel, Kings and Chronicles): AbrNahr 28 (1990) 127-135.

3130 **Kartveit** Magnar, Motive und Schichten der Landtheologie in I Chronik 1-9: ConBib OT 28, 1989 ➤ 5,2895: RTLZ 115 (1990) 760s (A.H.J. *Gunneweg*).

3131 **Oeming** Manfred, Das wahre Israel; die 'genealogische Vorhalle' 1 Chronik 1-9 [ev. Diss. Bonn 1988s ➤ 5,2896]: BW 128. Stu 1990, Kohlhammer. 237 p. DM 79. 3-17-010771-2. – ROTAbs 13 (1990) 313s (C.T. *Begg*).

3133 *Anbar* Moshe, [1 Chr 5,26] Poul roi d'Assyrie et Tiglath-Pilnéser roi d'Assyrie: BibNot 48 (1989) 7 seule.

3134 *Galil* Gerson, ✆ The pre-Davidic period in Chronicles: Zion 55 (1990) 1-26; Eng. I.

3135 **Gabriel** Ingeborg, Friede über Israel; eine Untersuchung zur Friedenstheologie in Chronik I 10 - II 36 [*šalom, menûhâ, šeqet* ...; Diss. Wien 1988 ➤ 5,2898: ÖsBSt 10. Klosterneuburg 1990, ÖsKBW. ix-226 p. Sch. 284. 3-85396-080-4 [BL 91,74, R.J. *Coggins*].

3136 *Scippa* Vincenzo, Davide e la conquista di Gerusalemme; la teologia del Cronista in 1 Cr 11,4-9: Asprenas 37 (1990) 59-73.

3137 **Aradie** Philippe, La figure de David dans les livres des Chroniques; de la figure historique à la figure symbolique: diss. Inst. Cath. & Sorbonne, DMeslin M. P 1990. 415 p. – RICathP 37,231-233; RTLv 22, p. 587.

3138 *Knoppers* Gary N., Rehoboam in Chronicles; villain or victim?: JBL 109 (1990) 423-440.

3139 *Snyman* Gerrie, Fictionality and the writing of history in 1 Chronicles 13: OTEssays 3 (1990) 171-190.

3140 *Wright* John W., Guarding the gates; 1 Chronicles 26.1-19 and the roles of gatekeepers in Chronicles: JStOT 48 (1990) 69-81.

3141 **Shaver** Judson R.,   *a*) Torah and the Chronicler's history work; an inquiry into the Chronicler's references to laws, festivals, and cultic institutions in relationship to Pentateuchal legislation [< diss. ND 1983, ᴰ*Blenkinsopp* J.]: BrownJudSt 196. Atlanta 1989, Scholars. xi-160 p. [JBL 110,718, E. *Ben Zvi*]. – *b*) Passover legislation and the identity of the Chronicler's law book: ➤ 334, ᴱ*Flesher* P., New Perspectives 5 (1990) 135-149.

3142 *Lorenzin* Tiziano,   2 Cr 2,12-13; un derash del Cronista?: BbbOr 32 (1990) 156-161.

3143 *Deboys* David G., [2 Chr 13] History and theology in the Chronicler's portrayal of Abijah: Biblica 71 (1990) 48-62.

3144 **Strübind** Kim, Tradition und Interpretation; die Josaphat-Rezeption in den Chronikbüchern als Beitrag zur Theologie des Chronisten: Diss. Berlin Kirchl. Hochschule 1989s, ᴰ*Welten*. – TR 86 (1990) 512.

3145 *Erder* Yoram, ❻ [2 Chr 29s] The date of the paschal sacrifice in the light of the 'Hezekiah Paschal' in the early Karaite *halakha*: Tarbiz 59 (1989s) 443-456; Eng. V.

3145* *Lorenz* Wolfgang, 'For we are strangers before thee and sojourners' – 2 Chron. 29:13: AmBapQ 9,4 (Human Rights, 1990) 268-280.

E5.4   *Esdrae libri,* **Ezra-Nehemiah.**

3146 *Auneau* Joseph, Les livres d'Esdras-Néhémie et des Chroniques: ➤ 323, Psaumes/Écrits 1990, 221-289.

3147 **Becker** Joachim, Ezra / Nehemiah: NEchter. Wü 1990, Echter. 124 p. DM 28. 3-429-01282-1. – ᴿZAW 102 (1990) 439 (O. *Kaiser*).

3148 **Blenkinsopp** Joseph, Ezra-Nehemiah, a commentary: OTLibrary 198 ➤ 4,3032: ᴿAndrUnS 28 (1990) 87s (G. *Wheeler*); Biblica 71 (1990) 100-2 (S. E. *McEvenue*); CBQ 52 (1990) 509s (R. W. *Klein*: best available; retains Chronicler authorship); HebSt 31 (1990) 106-8 (R. B. *Dillard*, also on ᴇsᴋᴇɴᴀᴢɪ T.); Interpretation 44 (1990) 310 (M. A. *Throntveit*); JBL 109 (1990) 525-7 (T. C. *Eskenazi*); JSS 35 (1990) 140-2 (H. G. M. *Williamson*, against whom 'Chronicler' authorship is defended); NorTTs 90 (1989) 229s (A. S. *Kapelrud*); SWJT 33,2 (1990s) 52 (D. G. *Kent*); VT 40 (1980) 500 (H. G. M. *Williamson*); ZAW 102 (1990) 143 (H.-C. *Schmitt*).

3149 *Dionisio* Francesco, E Dario disse, 'Che sia ricostruito il Tempio ...!'; storie di profeti, di funzionari regi, di mafia, di appalti e di 'lupara': BbbOr 32 (1990) 81-94.

3150 **Eskenazi** Tamara C., In an age of prose; SBL Mg 36, 1988 ➤ 4,3036; 5,2913: ᴿCritRR 3 (1990) 121-3 (J. *Blenkinsopp*); Interpretation 44 (1990) 422.424 (D. G. *Hagstrom*: furthers the demise of Chronicler authorship); VT 40 (1990) 127 (H. G. M. *Williamson*).

3151 *Eskenazi* Tamara C., Exile and the dreams of return: CurrTMiss 17 (1990) 192-200.

3152 *Fang* Mark, ❻ History and theology of Esdras: ColcFuJen 77 (1988) 399-410 [385-398 Daniel].

3153 **Hausmann** Jutta, Israels Rest ...: BW 124, ᴰ1987 ➤ 3,2869 ... 5,2915: ᴿCBQ 52 (1990) 122s (J. M. *Berridge*) ➤ 9356.

3154 *Moda* Aldo, Libri di Esdra e Neemia [... un'unità con i due libri delle Cronache ➤ 3126]: BbbOr 32 (1990) 129-139.

3155 *Morgan* Donn F., [Ezra-Neh/Chr] The beginnings of biblical theology: ➤ 82, ᶠHᴜɴᴛ J., Psalms 1990, 172-7.

3157 **Neusner** Jacob, Self-fulfilling prophecy; exile and return in the history of Judaism. SFlorida StHistJudaism 3. Atlanta 1990, Scholars. xxx-230 p. $65 [TR 87,426].

3158 *Halpern* Baruch, A historiographic commentary on Ezra 1-6; achronological narrative and dual chronology in Israelite historiography: ➤ 550, Hebrew Bible SD 1986/90, 81-142.

3159 *Williamson* H. G. M., *eben gelāl* (Ezra 5:8, 6:4) again: BASOR [260 (1985) 1-35, *Stager* L.] 280 (1990) 83-88.

3160 *Grol* H. W. M. van, Ezra 7,1-10; een literair-stilistische analyse: Bijdragen 51 (1990) 21-37; Eng. 37.

3161 *Rubinkiewicz* Ryszard, The book of Noah (1 Enoch 6-11) and Ezra's reform: ➤ 539*, DSS 25 (1989) 151-5.

3162 *Blenkinsopp* Joseph, [Is 66,5 ḥārēd(îm); Ezra 9s] A Jewish sect of the Persian period: CBQ 52 (1990) 5-20.

3163 **Gunneweg** A. H. J., Nehemia 1987 ➤ 3,2889 ... 5,2932: RNorTTs 90 (1989) 178s (A. S. *Kapelrud*).

3164 *Bishop* John, [Neh 4,9] The victory of the Spirit: ExpTim 102 (1990s) 19s.

3165 *Chrostowski* Waldemar, An examination of conscience by God's people as exemplified in Neh 9,6-37: BZ 34 (1990) 253-261.

3166 *Eshel* Hanan, *Kloner* Amos, ⊕ A Late Iron Age tomb between Bet Hanina and Nebi Samwil, and the identification of Hazor in Nehemiah 11:33: ➤ 4, FAMIRAN Ruth, Eretz-Israel 21 (1990) 37-40; 5 fig.; Eng. 102*.

3167 **Bergren** T. A., Fifth Ezra [4 Ezra 1-2] the text, origin and early history [diss. Ph 1988 ➤ 5,2939]: SeptCog 25. Atlanta 1990, Scholars. xvii-479 p. $41; sb./pa $27. 1-55540-348-4; -9-2 [BL 91,42].

3168 **Stone** Michael E., *a*) Fourth Ezra; a commentary: Hermeneia. Mp 1990, Fortress. xxii-496 p. 0-8006-6026-9. – *b*) A textual commentary on the Armenian version of IV Ezra: SBL SeptCog 34. xxvii-353 p. $35; $23. 1-55540-496-0.

3169 *Wittlieb* Marian, [4 Esra 7,28; 2 Bar 29,3 ...] Die theologische Bedeutung der Erwähnung von 'Māšîaḥ / Christós' in den Pseudepigraphen des Alten Testaments palästinischen Ursprungs: BibNot 50 (1989) 26-33.

E5.5 Libri Tobiae, Judith, Esther.

3170 *Auneau* Joseph, Écrits didactiques (Tobie – Judith – Baruch): ➤ 323, Psaumes/Écrits 1990, 353-387 [Esther ➤ 2930].

3171 **Goodspeed** E. J., [Tob Jud Mcb etc.] The Apocrypha, an American translation [1938]. NY 1989, Vintage. xxiv-493 p. $9 pa. 0-679-72452-4 [NTAbs 34,407].

3172 **Gross** H., Tobit, Judit: NEchter 1987 ➤ 3,2900 ... 5,2942: RBO 47 (1990) 203s (P. van der *Horst*); CBQ 52 (1990) 119 (J. W. *Klein*).

3173 *Grzybek* Stanisław, ℗ Problematic of family life in the book of Tobias: RuBi 42 (1989) 119-124.

_____

3173* *Bogaert* Pierre-M., Le 'rouleau' de Judith; Hanukka et le vingt-quatre du mois d'Ab: ➤ 618, Commémoration 1986/8, 163-171.
3174 *Heltzer* Michael, The Persepolis documents [*Hallock* R. 1978], the Lindos Chronicle and the book of Judith: ParPass 4,245 (1989) 81-101.
 Jensen H. J. L., [Judith] T-Nybrud 1990 ➤ 332.
3175 *Moda* Aldo, Libro di Giuditta: BbbOr 32 (1990) 21-26.
3176 *Moore* Carey A., Judith – the case of the pious killer: BR 6,1 (1990) 26-36; color. ill.
3177 *Schreyl* K. H., [Hans] Schäufeleins Judith-Wandbild im Nördlinger Rathaus: 7. Kulturtag 1988 [Nördlingen 1990] 183-239 [ZAW 103,169].
3178 *Virgulin* S., Due eroine della liberazione, Giuditta e Ester: ➤ 542*, Laici 1988/90, 65-88.

_____

3179 *Adler* Joshua J., The book of Esther – some questions and responses: JBQ 19 (1990s) 186-190.
3180 **Clines** David J. A., The Esther Scroll 1984 ➤ 65,2575 ... 3,2908: ᴿRExp 87 (1990) 490s (T. G. *Smothers*).
3181 *Clines* D. J. A., Reading Esther from left to right [in English with its cultural context]; contemporary strategies for reading a biblical text: ➤ 166, ᶠSheffield 1990, 31-52.
3182 *Edwards* Russel K., Reply to 'Ahasuerus is the villain': JBQ [18 (1989s), *Portnoy* M.] 19 (1990s) 34-39.
3183 **Gallazzi** Sandro, Ester: Comm. Biblico [ᵀ*Pistocchi* B., ᴱ*Borgonovo* G.] 1987 ➤ 4,3074: ᴿCC 141 (1990,1) 617s (P. *Bovati*, menzione anche di Aggeo, Zaccaria, Rut).
3184 *Goldman* Stan, Narrative and ethical ironies in Esther: JStOT 47 (1990) 15-31.
3185 *Harrelson* Walter, Textual and translation problems in the Book of Esther: PerspRelSt 17 (1990) 197-208.
3186 *Kasher* Rimon, *Klein* Michael, New fragments of Targum to Esther from the Cairo Genizah: HUCA 61 (1990) 89-112 + 12 pl.
3187 **Neusner** Jacob, Esther Rabbah I., [➤ a219] an analytical translation: BrownJudSt 182. Atlanta 1989, Scholars. xiii-193 p. $50. 1-55540-382-4 [NTAbs 34,272].
3188 *Russell* James R., Zoroastrian elements in the book of Esther: ➤ 555, Irano-Judaica 2 (1987/90) 33-40.
3189 *Segal* Eliezer, Human anger and divine intervention in Esther: Proof-texts 9 (1989) 247-256.
3190 *Snijders* L. A., Ester, en wijze satire: NedTTs 44 (1990) 109-120.
 Wills L. M., The Jew in the court of the foreign king 1990 ➤ 2518.
3191 **Wynn** Kerry H., The sociohistorical contexts of the recensions of Esther: diss. Southern Baptist Theol. Sem. ᴰ*Smothers* T. 1990. 340 p. 91-12511. – DissA 51 (1990s) 3785-A.

3192 *Vattioni* Francesco, Ester 1,10 (LXX): Tharabá: Aion 50,2 (1990) 217-225.
3193 *a) Berman* Joshua, Aggadah and anti-semitism; the midrashim to Esther 3:8; – *b) Fox* Michael V., The religion of the Book of Esther: Judaism 38 (1989) 185-196 / 39 (1990) 135-147.

3194 *Kessler* Rainer, Die Juden als Kindes- und Frauenmörder?; zu Est 8,11: ➤ 147, ᶠRENDTORFF R., Hebr. Bibel 1990, 337-345.

E5.8   *Machabaeorum libri,* 1-2 Maccabees.

3195 *Alonso Schökel* Luis, Il fallimento della violenza nei Maccabei: ➤ 514*c*, Violenza 1990, 83-106.

3196 *a) Applebaum* S., ✪ Hasmonean internal colonization; problems and motives; – *b) Rappaport* U., ✪ The land issue as a factor in inter-ethnic relations in Erets Israel during the Second Temple period: ➤ 348, Man and law 1986, 75-79 / 80-86.

3197 **Bar-Kochva** Bezalel, Judas Maccabeus; the Jewish struggle against the Seleucids [1980 ✪],ᵀ but expanded to twice the size, 1989 ➤ 5, 2960: ᴿBSO 53 (1990) 325s (M. *Goodman*); CBQ 52 (1990) 507s (D. J. *Harrington*: exciting); ClasR 40 (1990) 371-3 (Margaret H. *Williams*: 600 pages on the 8 major battles); JStJud 21 (1990) 87-91 (A. C. van der *Woude*: a monument of erudition and perspicacity); VT 40 (1990) 382s (W. *Horbury*); ZAW 102 (1990) 141 (O. *Kaiser*: monumental).

3198 **Derfler** Steven L., The Hasmonean revolt; rebellion or revolution? 1989 ➤ 5,2962; 0-88946-258-6: ᴿJStJud 21 (1990) 258s (F. *Garcia Martinez*: the student could learn more for $40 less from HARRINGTON's Maccabean Revolt); Paradigma 6,2 (1990s) 46s (K. H. *Wynn*, fierce against the misprints of 'Mellon Press').

3199 **Efron** Joshua, Studies in the Hasmonean period 1987 ➤ 4,3088; 5,2964: ᴿCritRR 3 (1990) 338-340 (D. J. *Harrington*).

3200 **Enermalm-Ogawa** Agneta, Un langage de prière... Mcb 1987 ➤ 3,2918 ... 5,2965: ᴿCritRR 2 (1989) 369s (R. *Doran*); NedTTs 43 (1989) 151s (J. W. van *Henten*).

3201 **Fischer** Thomas, Seleukiden und Makkabäer 1980 ➤ 61,3960 ... 3,2919: ᴿJQR 81 (1990s) 206 (M. *Smith*: sorry for the delay); RBgPg 68 (1990) 204 (P. *Salmon*).

3202 **Fischer** Thomas, Hasmoneans and Seleucids; aspects of war and policy in the second and first centuries [< ᴱ*Kasher* E., Greece and Rome in Eretz Israel 1990]. Bochum 1990, auct. 19 p. [ZAW 103,296].

3203 **Harrington** Daniel J., The Maccabean revolt 1988 ➤ 4,3092; 5,2967: ᴿCBQ 52 (1990) 120s (E. S. *Gruen*: skilful but sometimes strained); ExpTim 101 (1989s) 28s (R. *Mason*).

3204 *Healey* Joseph P., The Maccabean revolution: ➤ 334, ᴱ*Flesher* P., New perspectives 5 (1990) 151-171.

3205 *a) Hyldahl* Niels, The Maccabean rebellion and the question of 'Hellenization'; – *b) Cohen* Shaye D., Religion, ethnicity and 'Hellenism' in the emergence of Jewish identity in Maccabean Palestine: ➤ 325*, *Bilde*/Seleucid 1990, 188-203 / 204-223.

3206 **Kampen** John, The Hasideans and the origin of Pharisaism; a study in 1 and 2 Maccabees: SBL SeptCog 24, 1988 ➤ 4,3093; 5,2969: ᴿCBQ 52 (1990) 518s (E. S. *Gruen*); CritRR 3 (1990) 348s (D. J. *Harrington*); ETL 66 (1990) 182s (J. *Lust*); IrBSt 12 (1990) 98-100 (E. A. *Russell*: a welter of interesting suggestions); JBL 109 (1990) 528-530 (A. J. *Saldarini*); JStJud 21 (1990) 118-121 (F. *Garcia Martinez*: unconvinced); TLZ 115 (1990) 425s (K.-D. *Schunck*).

3207 *Rothschild* J.-P., Une pièce tardive à verser au dossier médiéval des Livres des Maccabées: ➤ 154, ᶠSACCHI P. 1990, 545-574.

3208 **Saulnier** Christiane, A revolta dos Macabeus: [T]*Ferreira* I.F.L.: Cadernos bíblicos 41. São Paulo 1987, Paulinas. 76 p. 85-05-00526-0. – [R]PerspT 22 (1990) 245-7 (J. *Vitório*).

3209 *Saulnier* Christiane, Livres historiques deutérocanoniques (1 et 2 Maccabées): ➤ 323, Psaumes/Écrits 1990, 389-439.

3210 **Sievers** Joseph, The Hasmoneans and their supporters, from Mattathias to the death of John Hyrcanus I: SFloridaStHistJudaism 6. Atlanta 1990, Scholars. x-171 p.; map. $50. 1-55540-449-9 [NTAbs 35,133].

3211 *a*) *Troiani* L., I profeti e la tradizione nell'età greco-romana; – *b*) *Sierra* S., Le condizioni spirituali degli Ebrei prima della distruzione del II° santuario: ➤ 154, [F]SACCHI P. 1990, 245-255 / 257-270.

3212 *VanderKam* James C., People and High Priesthood in early Maccabean times: ➤ 550, Hebrew Studies SD 1986/90, 205-225.

3213 *Doran* Robert, [1 Mcb 1,13ss] Jason's gymnasion: ➤ 173, [F]STRUGNELL J., Of scribes 1990, 99-109.

3214 *Wise* Michael O., A note on the 'three days' of 1 Maccabees X 34: VT 40 (1990) 116-122.

3215 *Rajak* Tessa, [1 Mcb 13,41...] The Hasmoneans and the uses of Hellenism: ➤ 183, [F]VERMES G. 1990, 263-280.

3216 *a*) *Dehandschutter* Boudewijn, Martyrium und agon; über die Wurzeln der Vorstellung vom *agōn* im Vierten Makkabäerbuch; – *b*) *Versnel* H.S., Quid Athenis et Hierosolymis? Bemerkungen über die Herkunft von Aspekten des 'effective death': ➤ 533, Martyrologie 1984/9, 215-9 / 162-196.

3217 **Heard** Warren J., Maccabean martyr theology; its genesis, antecedents and significance for the early soteriological interpretation of the death of Jesus: diss. Aberdeen 1987. 602 p. BRDX-91622. – DissA 51 (1990s) 3788-A; RTLv 22, p. 593 'earliest'.

3218 *Klauck* Hans-Josef, Brotherly love in Plutarch and in 4 Maccabees, [T]*Balch* David L.: ➤ 122, [F]MALHERBE A., Greeks 1990, 144-156.

3219 *Nauroy* Gérard, Du combat de la piété à la confession du sang; AMBROISE de Milan lecteur critique du IVe Livre des Maccabées: RHPR 70 (1990) 49-68; Eng. 145.

3220 *Perler* Othmar, Das vierte Makkabäerbuch, IGNATIUS von Antiochien und die ältesten Märtyrerberichte [< RivArchCr 25 (1949) 47-72]: ➤ 283, Sapientia 1990, 141-166.

3221 *Rordorf* Willy, Wie steht es um den jüdischen Einfluss auf den christlichen Märtyrerkult?: ➤ 506, Juden/Christen 1989/90, 61-71.

3222 **Weiner** E. & A., The martyr's conviction [... Maccabees]; a sociological analysis: BrownJudSt 203. Atlanta 1990, Scholars. x-159 p. $30. 1-55540-435-9 [NTAbs 35,134].

VII. Libri didactici VT

E6 *Poesis* .1 *metrica*, **Biblical versification**.

3223 **Alonso Schökel** Luis, A manual of Hebrew poetics, [T]*Graffy* Adrian: SubsBPont 11, 1988 ➤ 4,3103; 5,2981: [R]CBQ 52 (1990) 503-5 (J.F.A.

Sawyer: though this is a translation of 1987 Interpretación literaria de textos bíblicos, it is really the substance of his 1963 dissertation, not like the German 1971 but more practically related to users and to his own quarter-century of experience); CritRR 3 (1990) 101-3 (Adele *Berlin*: sensitive); OTAbs 13 (1990) 197 (T. P. *McCreesh*); VT 40 (1990) 379 (R. P. *Gordon*).

3224 **Alonso Schökel** Luis, Manuale di poetica ebraica 1989 → 5,2982: ᴿRivB 38 (1990) 241-6 (G. *Ravasi*).

3225 **Alter** Robert, The art of biblical poetry 1985 → 1,2978 ... 4,3105; also E 1990, Clark; 228 p. £10; 0-567-29176-6: ᴿExpTim 102 (1990s) 21 (C. S. *Rodd*).

3226 **Avishur** Yitshak, ⊕ Studies in Hebrew and Ugaritic Psalms: Perry Foundation, Hebrew Univ. J 1989, Magnes. 265 p. 965-223-704-2 [OIAc S90].

3227 *Baldacci* Massimo, Studi ugaritici e poesia biblica [MICHEL W. 1987; ZORRO E. 1987]: BbbOr 32 (1990) 95-101.

3228 *a)* *Buccellati* Giorgio, On poetry – theirs and ours; – *b)* *Renger* Johannes, 'Versstrukturen' als Stilmittel in den Inschriften Sargons II. von Assyrien: → 124, ᶠMORAN W., Lingering 1990, 105-134 / 425-437.

3229 *Cloete* W. T. W., The colometry of Hebrew verse: JNWS 15 (1989) 15-29.

3230 *Cooper* Alan, Two recent books on the structure of biblical Hebrew poetry [PARDEE D.; MEER W. van der & MOOR J. de; both 1988]: JAOS 110 (1990) 687-690.

3231 **Dion** Paul E., Hebrew poetics, a student's guide. Mississauga ON 1988, Benben. 50 p. – ᴿSR 19 (1990) 125 (Danna *Runnalls*).

3232 **Fecht** Gerhard, Metrik des Hebräischen und Phönikischen: ÄgAT 19. Wsb 1990, Harrassowitz. 211 p. 3-447-03026-7 [OIAc S90].

3233 **Fisch** Harold, Poetry with a purpose; biblical poetics and interpretation 1988 → 4,3115 (index!) 5,2984: ᴿJAAR 58 (1990) 708-710 (E. W. *Amend*); JRel 70 (1990) 135s (T. R. *Wright*), Judaism 39 (1990) 119-121 (E. L. *Greenstein*); TTod 47 (1990s) 107. 109 (P. D. *Miller*).

3234 *Floyd* Michael H., Falling flat on our Ars Poetica [< *Nemerov* H., satirizing *MacLeish* A.]; or, Some problems in recent studies of biblical poetry: → 82, ᶠHUNT J., Psalms 1990, 118-131.

3235 ᴱ**Follis** Elaine R., Directions in Hebrew poetry; JStOT 40, 1987 → 3,540 ... 5,2987: ᴿBZ 34 (1990) 315s (N. *Lohfink*).

3236 *Gammie* John [after *Shanks* H., pungent survey of KUGEL's JRel review of ALTER → 3,2930], Alter vs. Kugel; taking the heat in struggle over biblical poetry: BR 5,1 (1989) [26-29] 30-33: both needed, both have lacks; Alter sometimes better. – *Neusner* J., BR 5,3 (1989) 8s claims that Gammie condemns not only Kugel but also Journal of Religion: 'their book review columns in general are malicious and ugly!'; BR 5,4 (1989) 6s (H. D. *Schaffer* on parallelism).

3237 *Greenfield* Jonas C., The 'cluster' in biblical poetry: → 164, ᶠSEGERT S., *Sopher* 1990, 159-168.

3238 **Grossberg** D., Centripetal and centrifugal structures in biblical poetry: SBL Mg 39, 1989 → 5,2990: ᴿBL (1990) 76 (W. G. E. *Watson*).

3239 *Halle* Morris, Syllable-counting meters and pattern poetry in the OT: → 23, Mem. BLANC H. 1989, 110-120.

3240 **Lara Peinado** F., Himnos sumerios: Clásicos del pensamiento 50. M 1988, Tecnos. L-220 p. – ᴿCommSev 22 (1989) 266 (F. *Sánchez-Hermosilla*).

3241 **Meer** W. van der, *Moor* J.C. de, Structural analysis of biblical and Canaanite poetry: JStOT supp 74, 1988 ⇥ 5,410: RÉTRel 65 (1990) 264 (Françoise *Smyth*).
3242 **O'Connor** M., Hebrew verse structure 1980 ⇥ 61,3909 ... 1,2994: RRoczOr 46,1 (1988s) 135-7 (W. *Tyloch*).
3243 **Rousseau** F., La poétique fondamentale du texte biblique; le fait littéraire d'un parallélisme élargi et omniprésent: Recherches NS 20, 1989 ⇥ 5,2995: RArTGran 53 (1990) 313 (A. S. *Muñoz*); NRT 112 (1990) 893 (X. *Jacques*).
3244 *Soden* Wolfram von, Rhythmische Gestaltung und intendierte Aussage im Alten Testament und in babylonischen Dichtungen: ZAHeb 3 (1990) 179-206.
   Wagner Ewald, Grundzüge der klassischen arabischen Dichtung 1987s ⇥ 9495.
3245 *Zevit* Ziony, Roman JAKOBSON, psycholinguistics, and biblical poetry: JBL 109 (1990) 385-401.
3246 **Zurro** E., Procedimientos iterativos en la poesía ugarítica y hebrea [diss. R 1985]: BibOrPont 43. 1987 ⇥ 3,2947 ... 5,3000: RRivB 38 (1990) 531 (Cecilia *Carniti*).

E6.2 Psalmi, textus.

3247 *Ammassari* Antonio, Il Salterio latino di Pietro [1987 ⇥ 3,2949; 5,3001; OssRom 15.VII.1987 p. 5, *Federici* Tommaso]: BbbOr 32 (1990) 141-6.
3248 **Brandt** Leslie F., Psalms/Now. St. Louis 1986 = 1973, Concordia. 222 p.; ill. (*Kent* Corita). 0-570-03230-X.
3248* *Castel* Chrysostom, A feminist Psalter? The new Grail translation dechristianizes the Psalms: HomPast 90,7 (1989s) 21-30.
3249 EDeuchler Florenz, Ingeborg-Psalter [MS 9 1695 Conde-Chantilly] Faksimile: Codices Selecti 80. Graz 1985, Akad.-DV. 218 p.; 64 pl. DM 5500. – RTrierTZ 98 (1989) 235s (E. *Sauser*).
3250 *Farrell Shannon* Elizabeth, Le rouleau 11 Q Psa et le Psautier biblique: LavalTP 46 (1990) 353-8.
3251 *Guillo* Laurent, Le Psautier de Paris et le Psautier de Lyon: BProtF 136 (1990) 363-420 [< ZIT 90,698].
3252 TMowvley H., The Psalms 1989 ⇥ 5,3007: RExpTim 101 (1989s) 27 (J. *Eaton*).
3252* *Pietersma* A., Ra 2110 (P. Bodmer XXIV) and the text of the Greek Psalter: ⇥ 70, FHANHART R., 1990, 262-286.
3253 *Rogers* Nicholas, The original owner of the Fitzwarin Psalter: AntiqJ 69 (1989) 257-260; pl. XLI.
3254 ETescaroli Livio, I salmi nella tradizione ebraica; nuova traduzione dal testo masoretico: Commenti ebraici antichi alla Scrittura. R 1985, Città Nuova. 127 p. [KirSef 62 (1988s) p. 485].
3255 *Walter* Christopher, The aristocratic psalters and ode illustration in Byzantium: BySlav 51 (1990) 43-52; 8 fig.

E6.3 Psalmi, introductio.

3256 **Bellinger** W. H., Psalms; reading and studying the Book of Praises. Peabody MA 1990, Hendrickson. ix-166 p. 0-943575-35-4.
3257 **Day** J., Psalms: OT Guides. Sheffield 1990, Academic. 159 p. £6. 1-85075-703-8 [BL 91,70, J. C. L. *Gibson*].

3258 **Gerstenberger** Erhard S., Psalms I (1-60): FOTLit 14, 1988 → 4,3117; 5,3017: ᴿBiblica 71 (1990) 418-421 (J.W. *Rogerson*: challenging despite some eisegesis; 'shows how little we really know about the psalms'); BibTB 20 (1990) 38s (K.C. *Hanson*); HebSt 31 (1990) 154-6 (R.E. *Murphy*); CriswT 4 (1989s) 395s (L.R. *Bush*); JBL 109 (1990) 519-521 (J.C. *McCann*); Vidyajyoti 53 (1989) 518s (P.M. *Meagher*).

3259 *Howard* David M., Editorial activity in the Psalter; a state-of-the-field survey: WWorld 9 (1989) 274-285 [< OTAbs 13,69].

3260 *Monloubou* Louis, Les Psaumes: → 323, Psaumes/Écrits 1990, 15-87.

3261 **Seybold** Klaus, Introducing the Psalms [Die Psalmen 1986 → 2,2257], ᵀ*Dumphy* R.G., E 1990, Clark. xii-260 p. £10. 0-567-21974-X. – ᴿExpTim 102 (1990s) 181 (J. *Eaton*: a heavier work than its informal title suggests; Dumphy adds 10 p. on some Scots and English versions).

3262 **Watts** James W., [Ex 15,1-18; Dt 22,1-43; Jg 5,2-14; 1 Sam 2,1-20 ...] Psalms in narrative contexts of the Hebrew Bible: diss. Yale, ᴰ*Wilson* R. NHv 1990. 331 p. 90-34259. – DissA 51 (1990s) 2429s-A.

3263 **Westermann** Claus, Salmi, generi ed esegesi [Ausgewählte Psalmen 1984]ᵀ, pref. *Alonso Schökel* Luis. CasM 1990, Piemme. 290 p. Lit. 45.000 [NRT 113,909 J.-L. *Ska*].

E6.4 **Psalmi, commentarii.**

3264 *a)* **Allen** L.C. Ps 101-150, Word Comm. 21, 1983 → 64,2976 ... 5,3023: ᴿJTS 41 (1990) 565: (G.W. *Anderson*); Vidyajyoti 53 (1989) 104-6 (R.J. *Raja*, also on Craigie); – *b)* **Tate** Marvin E., Psalms 51-100: Word Comm. 20. Dallas 1990, Word. xxvii-579 p. 0-8499-0219-3.

3265 **Curti** Carmelo, Eusebiana I., Commentarii in Psalmos 1987 → 5,249; ²ʳᵉᵛ1989: ᴿGitFg 42 (1990) 158s (M. *Donnini*); Helmantica 41 (1990) 363s (S. *García Jalón*); RFgIC 118 (1990) 476-480 (G.M. *Vian*).

3266 ᴱ**Daur** Klaus-D., Arnobius junior, Commentarii in Psalmos: CCLat 25. Turnhout 1990, Brepols. xl-259 p.

3267 *Davey* William, The commentary of the Regius Psalter, its main source and influence on the Old English Gloss: Medieval Studies 49 (1987) 335-351 [< BTAM 14 (1990) 794].

3268 *Davis* Avrohom, The Metsudah Tehillim; a new linear Tehillim with English translation and notes. NY 1983, Metsudah. xii-297 p.; 16 fig. [KirSef 62 (1988s) p. 17].

3269 **Kinzig** W., In search of Asterius; studies on the authorship of the homilies on the Psalms [diss. Heidelberg 1988]: ForKDg 47. Gö 1990, Vandenhoeck & R. 317 p. DM 98 [RHE 85, p. 213*]. 3-525-55154-1.

3270 **Kraus** H.-J., Psalms 1-59 / 60-150, ᵀ*Oswald* H.C., 1988s → 5,2026 [BL 91,57, W.J. *Houston*: cites 'salvific' as a sample of the 'stilted and clumsy' English]. – ᴿOTEssays 2,3 (1989) 111s (E.J. *Smit*, 1); Vidyajyoti 53 (1989) 106s (R.J. *Raja*, 1).

3271 **Nielsen** E., 31 udvalgte salmer fra Det gamle testamente fortolket. Fredriksberg 1990, Ania. 135 p. Dk 148. 87-7457-098-6 [BL 91,59, K. *Jeppesen*: follow-up on Hammershaimb 1948, including one of his 15].

3273 **Ringgren** Helmer, Psaltaren 1-41, 1987 → 4,3161; 5,3031: ᴿSvEx 55 (1990) 106-111 (F. *Lindström*); TsTKi 60 (1989) 140s (Solfrid *Storøy*).

3274 **Sabourin** Léopold, Le livre des Psaumes, traduit et interprété; Recherches NS 18, 1988 → 4,3165; 5,3033: ᴿCBQ 52 (1990) 334s (C. *Stuhlmueller*: his 18th book); LavalTP 46 (1990) 410s (J. *Duhaime*); StMon 31 (1989) 460s (R. *Ribera-Mariné*).

3275 ᴱSimonetti Manlio, AGOSTINO, Commento ai Salmi 1988 ⇒ 5,3034:
ᴿSalesianum 52 (1990) 163s (O. *Pasquato*).

3276 **Tsai Lee-Chen** A., The development of LUTHER's hermeneutics in his
commentaries on the Psalms: diss. Aberdeen 1989. BRDX-94548. —
DissA 52,3324-A; RTLv 22, p. 586.

3277 **Villegas** M. Beltrán, El Libro de los Salmos. Santiago c. 1990, Univ.
Cat. Chile. – ᴿTVida 31 (1990) 201-4 (*ipse*).

3278 ᵀᴱWalsh P. G., CASSIODORUS, Explanation of the Psalms: Ancient
Christian Writers 51. NY 1990, Paulist. I. Ps 1-50, 618 p. 0-8091-0441-5
[II. Ps 51-100, 1991].

3279 *Wasserstein* A., Greek (and Christian?) sources in IBN EZRA's commentary on Psalms: ScrClasIsr 7 (1984) 101-112.

3280 **Westermann** Claus, The living Psalms, ᵀ*Porter* J. R. GR c. 1989, Eerd-
mans. $28; pa. $18. – ᴿBL (1990) 96 (J. *Sawyer*); IrBSt 12 (1990) 96-98
(T. D. *Alexander*: overhastily dismisses the titles); TS 51 (1990) 366s
(M. D. *Guinan*).

3280* **Williams** D., Psalms 1-72/73-150: Communicator's Comm. 13s [not
Word Comm. as ⇒ 5,3038, though published by Word]. Dallas 1989.
493 p.; 543 p. [CBQ 52,783]. 0-8499-0419-6; -20-X [ETRel 65,662 gives
Ogilvie L. J. as author].

E6.5 **Psalmi, themata.**

3281 **Allen** Leslie C., Psalms: Word *themes* 1987 ⇒ 3,2971; 4,3142: ᴿCritRR
2 (1989) 149-152 (Denise D. *Hopkins*).

3282 **Anyanwu** Akannamdi G. S., The Christological anthropology in St.
HILARY of Poitiers' Tractates on the Psalms: diss. Pont. Univ. Salesiana,
ᴰ*Riggi* Caligero. R 1983. 258 p.

3283 *Bianchi* Enzo, I Salmi imprecatori: ⇒ 325a, ParSpV 21 (1990) 83-100.

3284 ᴱ**Bitter** Gottfried, *Mette* Herbert, Leben mit Psalmen; Entdeckungen
und Vermittlungen 1983 ⇒ 65,2685: ᴿRivLtg 77 (1990) 347s (G. *Crocetti*:
originale).

3285 *Brown* Virginia, Flores psalmorum and Orationes psalmodicae in Be-
neventan script: MedvSt 51 (1989) 424-466; 4 pl.

3286 **Broyles** Craig C., The conflict of faith and experience in the Psalms
[< diss.] 1989 ⇒ 5,3042: ᴿExpTim 102 (1990s) 84s (J. *Eaton*).

3287 *a) Brzegowy* Tadeusz, ❷ Jerusalem, city of peace; contribution to
salvation-history in the Psalms: ⇒ 546, RuBi 42 (1989) 10-21. – *b)* ❷
Wybranie... The choice of Jerusalem in the light of the Psalms: RuBi 43
(1990) 94-104.

3288 *a) Burger* J. A., The law of Yahweh, the fear of Yahweh, and retribution in the wisdom psalms; – *b) Salters* R. B., Scepticism in the OT:
OTEssays 2,3 (1989) 75-95 / 96-105.

3289 *Colker* Marvin L., A Christianized Latin psalter in rhythmic verse
[Dublin Trinity MS 600, fol. 1-36]: SacrEr 30 (1987s) 329-408.

3289* *Cook* Johann, On the relationship between 11QPsª and the Septuagint
on the basis of the computerized data base (CAQP): ⇒ 519, Sep-
tuagint-Scrolls 1990, 107-130.

3290 *Costacurta* Bruna, La violenza nei Salmi: ⇒ 514c, Violenza 1990, 43-61.

3291 *a) Hamman* Adalbert G., L'utilisation des Psaumes dans les deux
premiers siècles chrétiens; – *b) Pfaff* R. W., Psalter collects as an aid to
the classification of Psalters: ⇒ 643, StPatr 18,2 (1983/9) 363-374 /
397-402.

3292 *a) Houk* Cornelius B., Acrostic Psalms and syllables; – *b) Kaufman* Ivan
T., Undercut by joy; the Sunday lectionaries and the psalms of lament; –
c) McMichael Ralph N.ᴶ, Psalmody in the Anglican rites of marriage; a
theological essay; – *d) Caldwell* Charles F., A pastoral perspective of
Psalms; – *e) Janecko* Benedict, Ecology, nature, and the Psalms: ↦ 82,
ᶠHᴜɴᴛ J., Psalms 1990, 54-60 / 66-78 / 79-85 / 86-95 / 96-108.

3293 *Hung* Celestino, ⊜ Eternal life in the Psalms: ColcFuJen 84 (1990)
203-212.

3293* **Jansen** Henry, The righteousness (SDQ) of God and humanity in the
Psalter: diss. ᴰ*Stek* J., Calvin Theol. Sem. v-155 p. + bibliog. – CalvinT
25 (GR 1990; no other date assigned) 331s.

3294 **Jeremias** Jörg, Das Königtum Gottes in den Psalmen 1987 ↦ 3,3009 ...
5,3059: ᴿScripTPamp 22 (1990) 246-8 (K. *Limburg*).

3295 *Kiernan* J.P., The Canticles of Zion: JRelAf 20 (1990) 188-204 [< ᴢɪᴛ
90,729].

3296 **Kramer** Samuel N., Distant echoes in the book of Psalms; gleanings
from Sumerian literature: Tarih 1 (WL 1990) ... [JQR 81,74 adv.].

3297 *Lamp* Erich, *Tilly* Michael, Öffentlichkeit als Bedrohung — ein Beitrag
zur Deutung des 'Feindes' im Klagepsalm des Einzelnen: BibNot 50
(1989) 46-57.

3298 *a) Leeuwen* C. van, Traditie en ervaring in de Psalmen; – *b) Vriezen* K.,
Psalmen en archeologie; inscripties met psalmcitaten in kerken uit de
Byzantijnse tijd in Palaestina en Arabia: ↦ 180*, ᶠTʀᴏᴍᴘ N., Gelukkig
c. 1990, 86-98 / 99-106; Eng. 257.

3299 **Lenhard** Doris, Vom Ende der Erde rufe ich zu Dir; eine rabbinische
Psalmenhomilie (PesR 9): FraJudSt 8. Fra 1990, Ges. Forderung Jud.
St. [viii-] 181 p.

3300 *Le Roux* J.H., W.S. PRINSLOO se immanente lees van die Psalms:
NduitsGT 30 (1989) 383-391 [focus on final form rather than on tra-
dition-history: OTAbs 13,169].

3301 **Lohfink** Norbert, Lobgesänge der Armen; Studien zum Magnifikat, den
Hodajot von Qumran und einigen späten Psalmen; mit Hodajot-Bibliog
1948-89 [*Dahmen* U.]: SBS 143. Stu 1990, KBW. 138 p. DM 29,80 [TR
87,426].

3301* **Mathies** D., Die Geschichtstheologie der Geschichtssummarien in den
Psalmen: Diss. ᴰ*Wagner*. Lp 1989s. – TR 86 (1990) 510.

3302 **Mathys** Hans-Peter, Dichter und Beter; die Theologen aus spätalt-
testamentlicher Zeit: Heb.-Diss. ᴰ*Klopfenstein*. Bern 1990. – TR 86
(1990) 509.

3303 **Meier** Janice K., An investigation of forgiveness in the penitential
psalms: diss. Baptist Theol. Sem., ᴰ*Smith* B. New Orleans 1989. 219 p.
90-20103. – DissA 51 (1990s) 890-A.

3304 **Nasuti** Harry P., Tradition history and the Psalms of Asaph [73-83;
50+96; 105s]: SBL diss. 88 (Yale 1983) 1988 ↦ 4,3191; 5,3065: ᴿCBQ 52
(1990) 532-4 (W.A. *Young*); ETL 66 (1990) 403s (W.A.M. *Beuken*); JBL
109 (1990) 522s (C.M. *Foley*); JRel 70 (1990) 451s (B. *Kaiser*); JStOT 47
(1990) 117s (R.S. *Hess*); TLZ 115 (1990) 102s (K. *Seybold*).

Oden A., ... Aᴜɢᴜsᴛɪɴᴇ's Enarrationes in Psalmos ... ecclesiology ᴰ1990
↦ 7229*.

3305 *Ostertag* Danielle, Les Psaumes en 'son et lumière': Tychique 82 (1989)
53-56 [77 (1989) 35-37; 79 (1989) 33-36].

3305* *Raja* R.J., Eco-spirituality in the Psalms: Vidyajyoti 53 (1989) 637-
650.

3306 **Rendsburg** G. A., Linguistic evidence for the northern origin of [36] selected psalms: SBL Mg 43. Atlanta 1990, Scholars. xiii-143 p. $25; pa. $15 [ZAW 103, 456, H. *Wahl*]; 1-55540-565-7; -6-5.

3307 *Rochettes* Jacqueline des, Psaumes et communication: BLitEc 91 (1990) 101-111; Eng. 111.

3308 **Spieckermann** Hermann, Heilsgegenwart; eine Theologie der Psalmen: FRL 148, ᴰ1989 ➤ 5,3072: ᴿBiblica 71 (1990) 421-5 (J. *Becker*); CBQ 52 (1990) 731s (R. E. *Murphy*: 'a theology' and 'presence of Heil' as opposed to Heilsgeschichte significant in title); TsTKi 61 (1990) 292-4 (Klara *Myhre*); ZAW 102 (1990) 314 (H. C. *Schmitt*).

3309 *Velema* W. H., Preekmotieven in de Psalmen: TRef 33 (Woerden 1990) 214-227 [< ZIT 90,751].

3310 **Vosberg** Lothar, Studien zum Reden vom Schöpfer in den Psalmen: Diss. Berlin Kirchl. Hochschule [1972: TR 86 (1990) 512].

3311 **Walker-Jones** Arthur W., Alternative cosmogonies in the Psalms: diss. ᴰ*Miller* P. Princeton Theol. Sem. 1990. – RelStR 17,193.

3312 *Wanke* Günther, Korach, Korachiten [-psalmen]: ➤ 857, TRE 19 (1990) 608s.

3313 *Youngblood* Ronald, Divine names in the Book of Psalms; literary structures and number patterns: ➤ 75, Mem. HELD M., JANES 19 (1989) 171-181.

3314 *Zegarra* R. Felipe, Salmos; el don de la vida: Páginas 14,95 (1989) 7-20.

E6.6　*Psalmi: oratio, liturgia;*　**Psalms as prayer.**

3315 **Arminjon** Blaise, Sur la lyre à dix cordes; à l'écoute des Psaumes au rythme des Exercices de saint IGNACE: Coll. Christus 73. P/Montréal 1990, D-Brouwer/Bellarmin. 602 p. 2-220-03176-5 / 2-89007-020-4.

3316 **Baldermann** Ingo, Ich werde nicht sterben, sondern leben; Psalmen als Gebrauchstexte: Wege des Lernens 7. Neuk 1990, Neuk-V. 146 p. 3-7887-1318-6.

3317 **Beaucamp** Évode, Israele in preghiera; dai Salmi al Padre nostro [1985 ➤ 1,3071], ᵀ*de Rosa* Elena: Le spighe. R 1986, Borla. 230 p. Lit. 15.000. – ᴿBenedictina 36 (1989) 219s (L. *De Lorenzi*).

3318 **Bonhoeffer** Dietrich, Gemeinsames Leben [&] Das Gebetbuch der Bibel, ᴱ*Müller* Gerhard L., *Schönherr* Albrecht: Werke 5. Mü 1987, Kaiser. 203 p. – ᴿRTPhil 122 (1990) 291 (H. *Mottu*).

3319 **Brueggemann** W., Israel's praise 1988 ➤ 4,3205; 5,3078: ᴿCritRR 3 (1990) 109-112 (M. J. *Haar*); Interpretation 44 (1990) 200 . 202 (W. A. *Young*); Pacifica 3 (1990) 341-4 (H. *Wallace*); Vidyajyoti 54 (1990) 315 (R. J. *Raja*).

3320 **Dyer** Joseph, *a*) Monastic psalmody of the Middle Ages: RBén 99 (1989) 41-74 [RHE 85 (1990) 479, H. *Silvestre*, détaillé]; – *b*) The singing of psalms in the early-medieval office: Speculum 64 (1989) 535-578.

3321 *Fischer* Balthasar, Christological interpretation of the Psalms seen in the mirror of the liturgy; QLtg 71 (1990) 227-235.

3322 **Goulder** Michael, The prayers of David (Psalms 51-72): JStOT supp 102. Sheffield 1990, Academic. 266 p. £35. 1-85075-258-3. – ᴿExpTim 102 (1990s) 212 (R. *Coggins*: enjoyable).

3323 **Huonder** Vitus, Die Psalmen der 'Liturgia Horarum' Papst PAULS VI.; Entstehung und Bewegung der Psalmenordnung im Vierwochenzyklus der

römischen Stundenliturgie: Hab.-Diss. ᴰ*Baumgartner*. Fribourg/S 1989s.
– TR 86 (1990) 509.

3324 *Łach* Jan, ✿ Les Psaumes – prière d'Israël et de l'adepte de Jésus:
AtKap 114 (1990) 42-50.

3325 *a) Luyten* J., David and the Psalms; – *b) Van den Berghe* P., Les
psaumes dans la langue de base de la prière liturgique; – *c) Vermeylen* J.,
L'usage liturgique des psaumes dans la société israélite antique: QLtg 71
(1990) 207-226 / 252-260 / 191-206.

3326 **Moore-Kochlacs** Emma C., The Psalms in the worship of the Church
today: diss. ᴰ*Rogers* C. Claremont 1990. 198 p. 90-34160. – DissA 51
(1990s) 2411-A.

3327 **Moriconi** Bruno, Uomini davanti a Dio; spiritualità dei Salmi 1989
➤ 5,3086: ᴿTeresianum 40 (1989) 625s (V. *Pasquetto*).

3328 *Neveu* Louis, Au pas des psaumes; lecture organique à trois voix [1.
1988 ➤ 4,3215] 2: CahLingLitRel 6. Angers 1990, Univ. cath. 139 p.
F 145 [NRT 113,908, J.-L. *Ska*]. – ᴿLavalTP 46 (1990) 408-410 (J.-J.
Lavoie, 1); RevSR 64 (1990) 87s (B. *Renaud*, 1).

3329 *Pasquetto* Virgilio, I salmi, scuola di preghiera e di vita: RivVSp 43
(1989) 123-140 [44 (1990) 55s].

3330 *Rodenberg* Otto, Gottes Gnade unter seinem Zorn; Anmerkungen zu
den Busspsalmen im Anschluss an M. Lᴜᴛʜᴇʀs Auslegungen: TBei 21
(Wu 1990) 307-318 [< ᴢɪᴛ 91,20].

3331 *Sevrugian* P., Zwei Beiträge zur Beziehung von Chludov-Psalter und
Jerusalemer Liturgie: RömQ 85 (1990) 80-97; 1 facsim.

3332 **Smith** Mark S., Psalms, the divine journey 1987 ➤ 3,2039 ... [4,3219!]
5,3091: ᴿCBQ 52 (1990) 111s (E. *Hensell*).

3333 **Stanislawski** M., Psalms for the Tsar 1988 ➤ 5,3091: ᴿJJS 41 (1990)
135s (H.-D. *Löwe*).

Stevens T., John Dᴏɴɴᴇ's sermons on the penitential psalms ᴰ1990,
➤ 1679.

3334 **Stoop** François [Prière des Psaumes], *Emery* Pierre-Yves, Méditation de
l'Écriture... Prière des Psaumes² [trois ouvrages de 1960-75 dans un
volume]: Vie monastique 6. Bellefontaine 1989 [Turnhout, Brepols].
120 p. F 60. – ᴿEsprVie 100 (1990) 382 (É. *Ricaud*: œuvre de Taizé).

3335 **Tournay** Raymond J., Voir et entendre Dieu avec les Psaumes ou la
liturgie prophétique du second Temple à Jérusalem: CahRB 24, 1988
➤ 4,3222; 5,3092: ᴿCBQ 52 (1990) 336s (D. *Launderville*).

3336 **Valles** Carlos G., Praying together; psalms for contemplation [onc
prayer for each psalm; 1989 ➤ 5,3093], ᵀ. Anand 1989, Gujarat-SP.
xii-332 p. $10; pa. $8 [TDig 37,389].

3337 *Vanek* Elizabeth Anne, The Psalms; praying from where one is: Emmanuel 96 (1990) 434-7; 447s.

3338 **Vincent** Monique, Saint Aᴜɢᴜsᴛɪɴ maître de prière d'après les Enarrationes in Psalmos [préf. *Neusch* Marcel: THist 84. P 1990, Beauchesne.
x-456 p. F 240 [TR 87,77]. 2-7010-1213-9.

3339 ᴱ**Walsh** Marcus, Christopher Sᴍᴀʀᴛ, A translation of the Psalms of
David, attempted in the spirit of Christianity and adapted to the divine
service [1755]: Poetical works of CS 3. Ox 1987, Clarendon. xxxix-440 p.
[KirSef 62 (1988s), p. 500].

3340 *Willems* Gerard F., Les Psaumes dans la liturgie juive: Bijdragen 51
(1990) 397-417.

3341 *Woolfenden* Graham, The Psalms in Jewish and early Christian worship:
PrPeo 4 (1990) 309-314.

3342 **Zim** Rivkah, English metrical psalms... prayer 1535-1601: 1987 ➤ 3,
3044 ... 5,3096: ᴿJEH 40 (1989) 121-3 (P. *Hatton*); JTS 41 (1990) 290-2
(J. *Shepherd*: modern psalm-translators are banal).

_____

3343 **Trigo** P., Salmos [modernos!] de vida y de fidelidad (oraciones desde
el compromiso por la liberación). M 1989, Paulinas. 168 p. [Cartha-
ginensia 6,251].

E6.7   *Psalmi: versiculi* – **Psalms by number and verse.**

3344 *Beentjes* P., De functie van Psalm 1 in een vergeten wijsheidsgeschrift
[Wis 3,15-4,5]: ➤ 180*, ᶠTʀᴏᴍᴘ N., c. 1990, 11-23; Eng. 255.
3345 *Wierenga* Lambert, 'Les deux routes'; le Psaume 1: RRef 41,1 (1990)
36-... [< ᴢɪᴛ 90,242].
3346 *a*) *Watts* James W., Psalm 2 in the context of biblical theology: HorBT
12,1 (1990) 73-91; – *b*) *Willis* John T., A cry of defiance – Psalm 2:
JStOT 47 (1990) 33-50; – *c*) *Becking* Bob, 'Wie Töpfe sollst du sie
zerschmeissen'; mesopotamische Parallelen zu Psalm 2,9b: ZAW 102
(1990) 59-79.
3347 **Lifschitz** Daniel, Dall'angoscia mi hai liberato, Salmi 3-6: TradEb-
Comm 1/2. T-Leumann 1990, Elle Di Ci. 259 p. Lit. 14.000 [TR 87,74].
3348 *Prinsloo* W.S., Psalm 3; die Here alleen bewerk die verlossing:
NduitsGT 30 (1989) 392-402 [< OTAbs 13,170].
3349 *Zenger* Erich, 'Gib mir Antwort, Gott meiner Gerechtigkeit' (Ps 4,2);
zur Theologie des 4. Psalms: ➤ 146, ᶠRᴇɪɴᴇʟᴛ H. 1990, 377-403.
3350 **Kinzig** Wolfram, Erbin Kirche; die Auslegung von Psalm 5,1 in den
Psalmenhomilien des Asᴛᴇʀɪᴜs und in der Alten Kirche: AbhHeid ph/h
1990/2. Heid 1990, Winter. 144 p. DM 38 [TR 87,76]. 3-533-04321-5;
pa. -0-7.
3351 *Loretz* Oswald, Adaption ugaritisch-kanaanäischen Literatur in Psalm
6; zu H. Gᴜɴᴋᴇʟs funktionalistischer Sicht der Psalmengattungen und zur
Ideologie der 'kanonischen' Auslegung bei N. Lᴏʜꜰɪɴᴋ [1987 ➤ 4,3229
(= ?) 3,3051]: UF 22 (1990) 195-220.
3351* *Nicole* Émile, [Ps 6,6 (30,10; 88,11s; 115,17)] 'Qui te célébrera dans le
séjour des morts?': Hokhma 41 (1989) 12-20.
3352 *Lohfink* Norbert, Ps 7,2-6 – vom Löwen gejagt: ➤ 7*, ᶠKɴᴏᴄʜ O.,
Freude 1991, 60-67.
3353 *a*) *Fang* M., ☉ Ps 8: ColcFuJen 82 (1989) 463-470; – *b*) *Gelabert Ballester*
Martín, [Ps 8] Lo hiciste casi como un Dios: TEspir 33 (1989) 291-312.
3354 *a*) *Holman* J., Een Griekse vertaling van Psalm 8 semiotisch belicht; – *b*)
Lukken G., De receptie van de Greimassiaanse semiotiek bij theologen;
weerstanden en misverstanden; – *c*) *Searle* M., Tusser énoncé et enunciatie; naar een semiotiek van gebedsteksten; – *d*) *Panier* L., Over figuren
in het discours; enkele overwegingen over de discursieve semiotiek: ➤ 97*,
ᶠTʀᴏᴍᴘ N., Gelukkig c. 1990, 136-146 / 121-135 / 193-211 / 182-192; Eng.
258-260.
3355 *a*) *North* Robert, Psalm 8 as a miniature of Psalm 104: ➤ 82, ᶠHᴜɴᴛ J.,
Psalms 1990, 2-10; – *b*) *Parys* Michel Van, Création et nature; le Messie
et le roi déchu; une lecture chrétienne du Psaume 8: Irénikon 63 (1990)
5-19; Eng. 19.
3356 *Ringgren* Helmer, [Ps 8,2; 1,7; 10s; 30,6] Some observations on the text of
the Psalms: ➤ 164, ᶠSᴇɢᴇʀᴛ S., *Sopher* 1990, 307-9.

3357 *Auffret* Pierre, 'Il exultera, mon cœur, dans ton salut'; étude structurelle du Psaume 11: BibNot 53 (1990) 7-13.

3358 *a) Hossfeld* Frank-Lothar, Nachlese zu neueren Studien der Einzugsliturgie von Ps 15; – *b) Conrad* Diethelm, Predigt über Psalm 22; – *c) Diedrich* Friedrich, Lehre mich, Jahwe!' Überlegungen zu einer Gebetsbitte in den Psalmen: ➤ 146, ᶠREISELT H., At. Botschaft 1990, 135-156 / 37-42 / 59-74.

3359 *a) Rose* A., Ps 15,10 et Ps 30,6 dans la tradition chrétienne; – *b) Fauquet* Y., Un type d'homme selon les Psaumes, le 'ḥasîd' (éléments d'un portrait): ➤ 589, Liturgie/anthrop. 1989/90, 229-244 / 91-107.

3360 *a) Barr* James, Do we perceive the speech of the heavens? A question in Ps 19 (Greek and Latin 18): ➤ 82, ᶠHUNT J., Psalms 1990, 11-17; – *b) Sedgwick* Colin J., The God who speaks; Ps 19: ExpTim 102 (1990s) 239s; – *c) Zazzu* G.N., La glossa al Salmo XIX nel salterio ottaplo di A[gostino] GIUSTINIANI [1470-1536; O.P.]: ➤ 154, ᶠSACCHI P. 1990, 575-582.

3361 *Zevit* Ziony, The common origin of the Aramaicized prayer to Horus [Papyrus Amherst 63] and of Psalm 20: JAOS 110 (1990) 213-228.

3362 *a)* Auffret Pierre, 'Dans ta force se réjouit le roi'; étude structurelle du Psaume XXI: VT 40 (1990) 385-410; – *b) Ludwig* Karl Josef, 'Bleib mir nicht fern, denn die Not dringt an!' (Ps 21,12); Über den Zusammenhang von Glaube und Krise in der Krankheit: ➤ 158*, ᶠSCHMITZ J. 1990, 188-195.

3363 *a) Heinemann* Mark H., An exposition of Psalm 22: BS 147 (1990) 286-308; – *b) Henshaw* Richard A., [Ps 22,1] My God, my God, why hast thou forsaken me?: ➤ 82, ᶠHUNT J., Psalms 1990, 61-65.

3364 *a) Pardee* Dennis, Structure and meaning in Hebrew poetry; the example of Psalm 23: ➤ 164, ᶠSEGERT S., Sopher 1990, 239-280; – *b) Dumon* Jan, [Ps 23,1] Als herder bidden; 'de Heer is mijn herder': CollatVL 20 (1990) 131-150; – *c) Sylva* Dennis D., The changing of images in Ps 23,5.6: ZAW 102 (1990) 111-6; – *d) Bailey* Kenneth E., Psalm 23 and Luke 15, a vision expanded: IrBSt 12 (1990) 54-71.

3365 *a) Auffret* Pierre, 'Qui est ce roi de la gloire?' Étude structurelle du Ps 24: RThom 90 (1990) 101-108; – *b) Pintaudi* Rosario, LXX Ps 24,15; 49,1-2 in un papiro di Vienna (P. Vindob. G. 29435): ➤ 25, ᶠBOGAERT/VAN LOOY 1989s, 357s.

3366 *Sedgwick* Colin J., [Ps 26] The strange case of the self-righteous psalmist: ExpTim 101 (1989s) 306s.

3367 *Basevi* Claudio, El salmo 29; algunas observaciones filológicas sobre el texto hebreo y griego: ScripTPamp 22 (1990) 13-47; lat. Eng. 47.

3368 **Kloos** Carola, [Ps 29, Ex 15] Yhwh's combat 1986 ➤ 2,2333 ... 5,3113: ᴿHenoch 12 (1990) 110s (B. *Chiesa*); JAOS 110 (1990) 343s (D. *Marcus*: many Baal traits rightly noted, but Ugarit sea-drying parallel dubious); VT 40 (1990) 245 (J.A. *Emerton*).

3369 *Gaebelein* Paul W.ᴶ, Psalms 34 and other biblical acrostics; evidence from the Aleppo Codex: ➤ 164, ᶠSEGERT S., Sopher 1990, 127-143.

3370 **Lifschitz** D., Salmo 34, 'Benedirò il Signore in ogni tempo', 1989 ➤ 5,3117: ᴿRivB 38 (1990) 263s (P. *Stefani*: una scommessa, un paradosso; ingenuo, affastellato).

3371 *Lohfink* Norbert, Das Böse im Herzen und Gottes Gerechtigkeit in der weiten Welt; Gedanken zu Psalm 36: ➤ 174, ᶠSUDBRACK J., Gottes Nähe 1990, 327-341.

3372 *Auffret* Pierre, *a*) 'Aie confiance en lui, et lui, il agira'; étude structurelle du Psaume 37: ScandJOT (1990,2) 13-43; – *b*) 'Car toi, tu as agi'; étude structurelle du Psaume 39: Bijdragen 51 (1990) 118-138; Eng. 138.

3373 *Stuhlmueller* Carroll, Psalm 46 and the prophecy of Isaiah: ➤ 82, ᶠHUNT J., Psalms 1990, 18-27.

3374 *Auffret* Pierre, *a*) 'Il est monté, Dieu'; étude structurelle du Psaume 47: ScEsp 42 (1990) 61-75; – *b*) Dans la ville de notre Dieu; étude structurelle du Psaume 48: ScEsp 42 (1990) 305-324.

3375 *Hunter* J. H., [Ps 50; 68; 97; 144] The literary composition of theophany passages in the Hebrew Psalms: JNWS 15 (1989) 97-107.

3376 *a*) *Dellazari* Romano, Salmo 51: Teocomunicação 19,86 (1989) 401-420; – *b*) *Wever* Tamis (co-red.) Schuld en boete in Jerusalem; Psalm 51 en Jeremia: ➤ 180*, ᶠTROMP N., c. 1990, 24-36; Eng. 255.

3377 *Doignon* Jean, [Ps 51; 103] Sur la 'descente' du Christ en ce monde chez HILAIRE de Poitiers: RHR 207 (1990) 65-75.

3378 *Lubetski* Meir, The utterance from the East; the sense of HWT in Psalms 52: 4,9: Religion 20 (L 1990) 217-232 [< ZIT 90,658].

3379 *Auffret* P., [Ps 63] 'Ma bouche s'adonnera à ta louange'; étude structurelle du Psaume 63: ÉglT 20 (1989) 359-386.

3380 *Schroer* Silvia, Psalm 65 – Zeugnis eines integrativen JHWH-Glaubens?: UF 22 (1990) 285-301.

3381 *Fokkelman* J. P., The structure of Psalm LXVIII: ➤ 563, OTS 26 (1988/90) 72-83.

3382 *Bauer* Johannes B., Exegesegeschichte und Textkritik Ps 68(69),32: ZAW 102 (1990) 414-7.

3383 *Mędala* Stanisław, ❷ Sitz im Leben des citations du Ps 69 dans le quatrième Évangile: ➤ 64, ᶠGRZYBEK S. 1990, 181-190; franç. 190s.

3384 *Sedgwick* Colin J., An old man's prayer; Ps 71: ExpTim 101 (1989s) 340s.

3385 *Brown* Margaret H., Psalm 72; the giftedness of the anointed king: ➤ 82, ᶠHUNT J., Psalms 1990, 28-33.

3386 *a*) *Krašovec* Jože, Antitetična [not 'antična' as cover] zgradba ... Antithetic structure of Ps 73: BogVest 49 (1989) 275-288; Eng. 286; – *b*) *Sedgwick* Colin J., [Ps 73] 'Lord, it's not fair!': ExpTim 101 (1989s) 371s.

3387 *a*) *Greenstein* Edward L., Mixing memory and design; reading Psalm 78: Prooftexts 10 (1990) 197-218; – *b*) *Lee* Archie C. C., The context and function of the plagues tradition in Psalm 78: JStOT 48 (1990) 83-89.

3388 *a*) *Schreiner* Josef, Geschichte als Wegweisung; Psalm 78; – *b*) *Ruppert* Lothar, Dürsten nach Gott; ein psalmistisches Motiv [42,3; 63,2] im religionsphänomenologischen Vergleich: ➤ 146, ᶠREINELT H. 1990, 307-328 / 237-251.

3389 *Toker* Naftali, [Ps 78] ❸ Reciprocal enrichment of an image and its referent: BethMikra 35 (1989s) 353-8 [< OTAbs 14,186].

3390 *Handy* Lowell K., Sounds, word and meaning in Psalm 82: JStOT 47 (1990) 51-66.

3391 *Meynet* Roland, L'enfant de l'amour (Ps 85): NRT 112 (1990) 843-858.

3392 *Virgulin* S., (Salmi 85 e 126) 'Ritorna... e noi ritorneremo!': ➤ 325*b*, ParSpV 22 (1990) 73-84.

3393 *Schmitt* John J., Psalm 87; Zion, the city of God's love: ➤ 82, ᶠHUNT P. Psalms 1990, 34-44.

3394 *a*) *Sedgwick* Colin J., Darkness amid the light; Ps 88: ExpTim 101 (1989s) 273s; – *b*) *Tate* Marvin E., Psalm 88, expository: RExp 87 (1990) 91-95.

3395 **Beer** S. De, [Ps 89; 132; 2 Sam 7] The Davidic covenant in the Psalms; a methodological investigation: diss. Unisa, ^D*Burden* J., Pretoria 1989. – OTEssays 2,3 (1989) 107.

3396 *Puech* Émile, [Ps 91] 11Q Ps Ap^a, un rituel d'exorcismes, essai de reconstruction: ➤ 527, RQum 14,55 (1989s) 377-403 + 5 facsimiles.

3397 *a*) *Dellazari* R., Salmo 95: Teocomunicação 18 (1988) 425-437 [< Stromata 45,498: 'noventa y cinco']; – *b*) *Svoboda* Joseph A., In psalmum [95] 'Venite' antiphonae seu invitatoria breviarii Vitoniani (1777) et breviarii Maurini (1787): EphLtg 104 (1990) 462-500.

3398 **Scoralick** Ruth, Trishagion... Ps 99, 1989 ➤ 5,3144: ^RTZBas 46 (1990) 370s (B. *Weber*).

3399 *Lohfink* Norbert, Die Universalisierung der 'Bundesformel' in Ps 100,3: TPhil 65 (1990) 172-183.

3400 **Brüning** Christoph, Mitten im Leben vom Tod umfangen; Ps 102 als Vergänglichkeitsklage und Vertrauenslied: Diss. ^D*Füglister* N. Salzburg 1990. 303 p. – RTLv 22, p. 587.

3401 *a*) *Steck* Odil H., Zu Eigenart und Herkunft von Ps 102: ZAW 102 (1990) 357-372; – *b*) *Childs* Brevard S., [Ps 102,19..] Analysis of a canonical formula, 'It shall be recorded for a future generation': ➤ 147, ^FRENDTORFF R., Hebr. Bibel 1990, 357-364.

3402 *Sedgwick* Colin J., What kind of God?: Ps 103: ExpTim 102 (1990s) 177s.

3403 *Parrish* V. Steven, Psalm 104 as a perspective on creation thought in the worship and reflection of preexilic Israel: diss. Vanderbilt, ^D*Harrelson* W. Nv 1989. 383 p. 90-17636. – DissA 51 (1990s) 530-A; RelStR 17,193.

3404 *Uehlinger* Christoph, Leviathan und die Schiffe in Ps 104,25-26 [... Dab'a Rollsiegel]: Biblica 71 (1990) 499-526; 3 fig.; franç. 526.

3405 *a*) *Burden* J.J., Psalm 105; maak vrede met die verlede (make peace with the past): NduitsGT 31 (1990) 147-153 [< OTAbs 14,67]; – *b*) *Lee* Archie C.C., Genesis I and the plagues tradition in Psalm CV: VT 40 (1990) 257-263; – *c*) *Brooke* George J., Psalms 105 and 106 at Qumran: ➤ 563, RQum 14,54 (1989s) 267-292.

3406 **Markert** Francis J., A critical edition of Richard ROLLE's 'English Psalter', Psalms 106-120, with glossary, notes, appendices and an introductory essay on his spirituality: diss. Fordham, ^D*Grennen* J. NY 1990. 508 p. 90-25021. – DissA 51 (1990s) 1607-A.

3407 *Oberholzer* J.P., Opmerkings oor die teologie van Psalm 106: HervTS 44 (1988) 380-7.

3408 *Kilian* Rudolf, Der 'Tau' in Ps 110,3 – ein Missverständnis?: ZAW 102 (1990) 417-9.

3409 *Bezeq* Ya'aqob, ❽ [Ps 113-118] The six *peraqim* of the Hallel... numerologies: BethM 36,124 (1990s) 91-93.

3410 *a*) *Geller* Stephen A., The language of imagery in Psalm 114: ➤ 124, ^FMORAN W., Lingering 1990, 179-194; – *b*) *Rossel* Wilfried, Eens en voorgoed werd ontzag geboren; exegetische en bijbeltheologische beschouwingen bij Psalm 114: CollatVL 20 (1990) 243-255.

3411 *Barré* Michael J., Psalm 116; its structure and its enigmas: JBL 109 (1990) 61-78.

3412 *Durst* Michael, Der Kölner Hilarius-Codex (Dombibliothek 29 [Darmstadt 20251]) und seine Lesarten; eine Beschreibung und Neukollationierung der Handschrift nebst einigen Überlegungen zu ihrer Situierung in der handschriftlichen Überlieferung von HILARIUS zu Ps 118: ➤ 100*, ^FKÖTTING B., JbAC 33 (1990) 55-80.

3413 **Milhau** Marc, HILAIRE, comm. sur le Ps 118[G]: SChr 344.347, 1988
→ 4,3309; 5,3155:   RAntClas 59 (1990) 403-5 (H. *Savon*); BLitEc 91
(1990) 235-7 (H. *Crouzel*); ETL 66 (1990) 199s (A. de *Halleux*); JbAC
33 (1990) 260-9 (M. *Durst*); JTS 41 (1990) 250-2 (C.P. *Bammel*);
PrOrChr 40 (1990) 203s (P. *Thiriez*); RHPR 70 (1990) 350s (D.A.
Bertrand).

3414 *Curti* Carmelo, La catena palestinese sui salmi graduali [119-133]: → 62,
FGRILLI A., Paideia 45 (1990) 93-101.

3415 *White* R.E.O., [Ps 119] The student's psalm?: ExpTim 102 (1990s)
71-74.

3416 *Willis* John T., An attempt to decipher Psalm 121:1b: CBQ 52 (1990)
241-251.

3417 *Mosis* Rudolf, 'Mit Jauchzen werden sie ernten'; Beobachtungen zu
Psalm 126: → 146, FREINELT H. 1990, 181-201.

3418 a) *Luyten* J., Psalm 130, reminiscenties en connotaties; – b) *Grol* H. van,
Psalm 131, een labyrint van verlangens: → 180*, FTROMP N., Gelukkig
c. 1990, 48-61 / 62-73; Eng. 256.

3419 *Pettey* Richard J., Psalm 130, a song of sorrow: → 82, FHUNT J.,
Psalms 1990, 45-53.

3420 *Rusche* Helga, Das letzte gemeinsame Gebet Jesu mit seinen Jüngern
[Mk 14,26], der Psalm 136: WissWeish 51 (1988) 210-212.

3421 **Hartberger** Brigit, 'An den Wassern von Babylonien' Ps 137 / Jer 51:
BoBB 63, D1986 → 4,3319; 5,3166: RVT 40 (1990) 241 (H.G.M. *Williamson*).

3422 *Bock* Martin, [Ps 137s] Rückblick und Danklied: ErbAuf 66 (1990) 143s.

3423 a) *Díaz Mateos* Manuel, [Ps 137] ¿Cómo cantar al Señor en tierra
extranjera?: RTLim 23 (1989) 83-97; – b) *Geiger* Joseph, ❶ [Ps 137,1]
'By the rivers of Babylon' [influenced by classical *topos* from Homer
through Hellenistic and Catullus]: Tarbiz 59 (1989s) 507s; Eng. VII; – c)
Kirschner Robert, Two responses to epochal change; AUGUSTINE and the
Rabbis on Ps. 137 (136): VigChr 44 (1990) 242-262.

3424 *Holman* J., A semiotic analysis of Psalm CXXXVIII (LXX); → 563,
OTS 26 (1988/90) 84-100.

3425 *Lin* Agnes, ❷ Psalm 139, a poem full of dynamism: ColcFuJen 83
(1990) 41-49.

3426 *Becking* B., 'Gij weet van de verborgen strik' [snare]; enkele opmer-
kingen bij Ps. 142.4: → 180*, FTROMP N., c. 1990, 74-85; Eng. 257.

3427 *Auffret* Pierre, 'Il règne, YHWH, pour toujours'; étude structurelle du
Psaume CXLVI: RThom 90 (1990) 623-633.

3428 *Warzecha* Julian, ❸ Sending of the Word in Ps 147: RuBi 42 (1989)
329-334.

3429 *Schiemenz* Günter P., Die Sintflut, das Jüngste Gericht und der 148.
Psalm: CahArch 40 (1990) 159-194; 28 fig.

E7.1 **Job,** *textus, commentarii.*

3430 **Clines** David J.A., Job 1-20: Word Comm. 17, 1989 → 5,3173: RIrBSt
12 (1990) 198s (T.D. *Alexander*: immense erudition); IrTQ 56 (1990)
306-8 (D. O'*Connor*).

3430* **Cox** Dermot, Man's anger and God's silence; the book of Job. Slough
1990, St. Paul. 144 p. £6 [HeythJ 32,390, J. *Eaton*].

3431 TEGillet Robert, GRÉGOIRE le Grand, Morales sur Job I (livres I-II)3rev
[11952 21975]: SChr 32 bis. P 1989, Cerf. 414 p. 3-204-04068-1.

3432 **Good** Edwin M.,   In turns of tempest; a reading of Job, with a translation.   Stanford 1990, Univ.   xiv-496 p. $45 [RelStR 17,254, J. L. *Crenshaw*: new, exciting].   0-8047-1785-0.

3433 ^{TE}**Goodman** L. E.,   SAADIEH b. J.   Fayyumī, The book of theodicy; translation and commentary on the book of Job: Yale Judaica 25, 1988 → 5,3178: ^RBL (1990) 142 (S. C. *Reif*); JQR 81 (1990s) 195-8 (D. *Novak*).

3434 **Gross** Heinrich, Ijob: NEchter 1986 → 2,2389... 3,3140: ^RScripTPamp 22 (1990) 1007 (K. *Limburg*).

3435 *a*) ^{TE}**Hagedorn** Ursula & Dieter,   J. CHRYSOSTOMOS Kommentar zu Hiob: PatrTStud 35. B 1990, de Gruyter.   xlii-323 (double) p.   DM 284. 3-11-012540-4. – ^RÉtClas 58 (1990) 399 (F.-X. *Druet*); RSPT 74 (1990) 633s (G.-M. de *Durand*); – *b*) Neue Fragmente des Hiobkommentars DIDYMOS' des Blinden: → 160, ^FSCHOW N., Charta Borgiana 1990, (I) 245-254.

3436 **Hartley** John E.,   The Book of Job: NICOT, 1988 → 4,3327; 5,3179: ^RRTLv 21 (1990) 90s (J. *Vermeylen*); Vidyajyoti 54 (1990) 268 (R. P. *Raja*); VT 40 (1990) 241s (J. A. *Emerton*); ZAW 102 (1990) 149 (O. *Kaiser*).

3437 *Lévêque* J.,   L'enseignement des Sages (Job – Les Proverbes): → 323, Psaumes/Écrits 1990, 89-155.

3438 **Rodd** Cyril R.,   The book of Job: Epworth Comm. L 1990, Epworth. xviii-142 p.   £7.   0-7162-0468-1. – ^RExpTim 102 (1990s) 151s (R. J. *Coggins*: based on REB text).

3439 ^E**Sorlin** Henri, (*Neyrand* Louis), CHRYSOSTOME sur Job: SChr 346.348, 1988 → 4,3337; 5,3184: ^RBLitEc 91 (1990) 237 (H. *Crouzel*); EsprVie 100 (1990) 477s (Y.-M. *Duval*); ETL 66 (1990) 201 (A. de *Halleux*); JTS 41 (1990) 255s (L. R. *Wickham*, 1); RHE 85 (1990) 210 (A. de *Halleux*); RHE 85 (1990) 526 (R. *Gryson*); RHPR 70 (1990) 354s (D. A. *Bertrand*); RivStoLR 26 (1990) 196-9 (J. *Mallet*).

3440 **Taylor** David B.,   Job, a rational exposition.   L 1990, Merlin.   309 p. £17.   0-86303-508-6. – ^RExpTim 102 (1990s) 85 (C. S. *Rodd*).

3441 **Thiele** Edwin & Margaret,   Job and the devil.   Boise ID 1988, Pacific. 137 p. $17. – ^RAndrUnS 28 (1990) 186s (G. *Christo*: the devil is scarcely mentioned, but the 'traditional' view that Moses wrote Job is defended, though without disposing of alternatives).

3442 **Vogels** W.,   Job: Belichting van het Bijbelboek.   Boxtel/Lv/Brugge 1989, KBS/VBS/Tabor.   215 p.   90-6173-455-X / 90-6597-284-3/-. – ^RTsTNijm 30 (1990) 306 (N. *Tromp*).

3443 *a*) **Wiesel** E., *Eisenberg* J.,   Job of God in storm en wind 1989 → 5,3185*a*;   90-304 0498-1:   ^RTsTNijm 30 (1990) 88 (L. *Grollenberg*); – *b*) **Eisenberg** Josy, *Wiesel* Élie,   Giobbe o Dio nella tempesta, ^T*Pagani* Chiara, 1989 → 5,3185*b*; Lit. 30.000: ^RLetture 45 (1990) 369s (G. *Ravasi*).

E7.2   *Job: themata*, Topics... *Versiculi*, Verse-numbers.

3444 *Assmann* Jan,   Der 'leidende Gerechte' im alten Ägypten – zum Konflikt-potential der ägyptischen Religion: → 38*, ^FCOLPE C. 1991, 203-224.

3445 ^E**Aufrecht** Walter E.,   Studies in the book of Job 1981/5 → 1,453:   ^RBO 47 (1990) 456-8 (H.-P. *Müller*).

3446 **Baskin** Judith R.,   Pharaoh's counsellors; Job, Jethro and Balaam in rabbinic and patristic tradition: BrownJudSt 47, 1983 → 64,3170... 1,3207:   ^RAbrNahr 28 (1990) 116s (S. P. *Brock*).

3447 *Blumenthal* Elke, Hiob und die Harfnerlieder: TLZ 115 (1990) 721-730.
3448 *Chow See-Wing,* ☉ Job; a believer searching for deeper conversion:
ColcFuJen 85 (1990) 349-356.
3448* *Fohrer* Georg, Man and disease according to the Book of Job: ⇥ 540*,
Koroth 9 (3d symposium 1987/8) 43-48.
3449 *Freedman* David N., The book of Job [> BR 4 (1988)]: ⇥ 550, Hebrew
Bible SD 1986/90, 33-51.
3450 **García-Moreno** A., Sentido del dolor en Job [com. Juan de PINEDA, 16°
siglo; diss. Pont. Univ. Gregoriana, ᴰ*Asensio* F.], Toledo 1990, S. Ildefonso. 192 p. 84-600-3783-1. – ᴿScripTPamp 22 (1990) 962-4 (S. *Ausín*).
3451 *Genuyt* François, Job et la condition humaine [groupe Arbresie 26-
30.VII.1989]: SémBib 56 (1989) 37-41.
3452 *a)* **Girard** R., Job 1987 ⇥ 3,3161; 5,3195: ᴿCritRR 3 (1990) 383-5 (P.
Domouchel: translation far from perfect); RelSt 25 (1989) 139s (U. *Simon*:
Job seen as finally a Christ-figure); – *b)* *Bonora* Antonio, Giobbe, capro
espiatorio secondo R. Girard: TItSett 14 (1989) 138-142; 140 il biblista
'sbaglierebbe a non prendere sul serio ...; il disinvolto *outsider* può scopri-
re cose per le quali il competente ... è diventato cieco', *Lohfink* N.).
3453 **Gutierrez** G., On Job ⇥ 3,3165; 5,3197: ᴿVidyajyoti 54 (1990) 96-101
(G. V. *Lobo*).
3454 **Heater** Homer ᴶ, A Septuagint translation technique in the Book of Job
[diss. Wsh 1976]: CBQ Mg 11, 1982 ⇥ 63,3233 ... 1,3215: ᴿBZ 34 (1990)
127s (E. *Kutsch*).
3455 **Horne** M. P., Theodicy and the problem of human surrender in Job:
Diss. Oxford 1989. – RTLv 22, p. 588.
3456 **Huber** P., Hiob Dulder ...? Miniaturen 1986 ⇥ 2,2411 ... 5,3200: ᴿByZ
82 (1989) 318s (Stella *Papadaki-Oakland*).
ᴱ**Jagersma** H., Job, studies 1989/90 ⇥ 538.
3457 **Jong** Aad T. H. M. de, Weerklank van Job; over geloofstaal in bij-
bellessen [diss. Nijmegen 1990, ᴰ*Ven* J. van der; RTLv 22, p. 587]:
Theologie en Empirie 8. Kampen 1990, Kok. 352 p. ƒ52.50. 90-242-
6504-5 [Bijdragen 51,466].
3457* *a)* *Maas* Jeannette P., A psychological assessment of Job; – *b)* *Weber*
Hans-Ruedi, The Bible and oral tradition [... African story-telling]:
Pacific JT 1s,2 (Fiji 1989) 55-68 / 1-13 [< TContext 8/2, p. 75].
3458 **Martini** Carlo M., Avete perseverato con me nelle mie prove (Riflessioni su Giobbe): Centro Ambrosiano. CasM 1990, Piemme. 158 p.
Lit. 22.000. – ᴿLetture 45 (1990) 370 (G. *Ravasi*).
3459 **Mickel** Tobias, Seelsorgerliche Aspekte im Hiobbuch; ein Beitrag zur
biblischen Dimension der Poimenik [Diss. Halle-Wittenberg]: TArb 48. B
1990, Ev.-V. 155 p. DM 17,50 [TR 87,338].
3460 *a)* *Miller* Ward S., The structure and meaning of Job; – *b)* *Mitchell*
Christopher, Job and the theology of the Cross; – *c)* *Raabe* Paul R.,
Human suffering in biblical context; – *d)* *Hulme* William, Pastoral
counseling in the book of Job: ConcordiaJ 15 (1989) 103-120 / 156-180 /
139-155 / 121-138 [< OTAbs 13, p. 172s].
3461 *Nielsen* Eduard, *Shadday* in the book of Job [31 times, 65% of OT
occurrences]: ⇥ 117*, ᶠLØKKEGAARD F., 1990, 249-258.
3462 **Oorschot** Jürgen van, Gott als Grenze ... Gottesreden des Hiobbuches:
BZAW 170, 1987 ⇥ 3,3175; 5,3205: ᴿBZ 34 (1990) 311s (E. *Kutsch*);
OLZ 85 (1990) 431s (H.-J. *Zobel*).
3463 **Penchansky** David, The betrayal of God; ideological conflict in Job:
Literary Currents in Biblical Interpretation 1. Louisville 1990, West-

minster/Knox. 124 p. $12 pa. 0-664-25123-4 [OTAbs 14,114, R. E. *Murphy*; BL 91,90: -32-3].

3464 *Rensburg* J. F. J. van, Characterizing a poetic line in Young Babylonian [Ludlul 2,44]; a metrical and grammatical approach: JSem 2,1 (1990) 90-99.

3465 *Ruppert* Lothar, Der leidende Gerechte: → 533, Martyrologie 1984/9, 76-87.

3466 *Strolz* Walter, Schöpfungsweisheit im Buch Ijob: Diakonia 21 (1990) 314-322.

3466* *a) Terrien* S., Job as a sage; – *b) Albertz* R., The sage and pious wisdom in the book of Job; the friends' perspective; – *c) Ceresko* A. R., The sage in the Psalms; – *d) Frymer-Kensky* Tikva, The sage in the Pentateuch; soundings; – *e) Perdue* L. G., Cosmology and social order in the wisdom tradition; – *f) Gammie* J. G., From prudentialism to apocalypticism; the houses of the sages and the varying forms of wisdom: → 336, Sage 1990, 231-242 / 243-261 / 217-230 / 275-287 / 457-478 / 479-497.

3467 *a) Thijs* L., Het verhaal van Job in het pastoraat; – *b) Knippenberg* M. van, Preken over Job; pastoraaltheologische reflekties: PrakT 17 (Zwolle 1990) 251-271 / 272-283 [< ZIT 90,646].

3468 *Verdejo Sánchez* M. Dolores, Los adverbios en las notas marginales del libro de Job de la Vetus Latina: → 761, Helmantica 40 (1987/9) 463-473.

3469 *Whedbee* J. William, The comedy of Job [< Semeia 7 (1977)]: → 367, ᴱ*Radday*, Humour 1990, 217-247.

3470 **Wilcox** John T., The bitterness of Job 1989 → 5,3219: ᴿ*AsbTJ* 45,2 (1990) 92s (J. B. *Burns*); BbbOr 32 (1990) 248-250 (also J. B. *Burns*, Eng.).

3471 *Wolfers* David, Science in the book of Job: JBQ 19 (1990s) 18-21.

3472 *Clines* D. J. A., False naivety in the prologue to Job: HebAnR 9 (1985) 127 136 [189 202, *Gordis* R., ecology, Job 40,15; < OTAbs 13, p. 281].

3473 *Cooper* Alan, Reading and misreading the prologue to Job [CLINES breakthrough, HebAnR 9 (1985) 127-136]: JStOT 46 (1990) 67-79.

Day Peggy L., An adversary in heaven, *śaṭan* ᴰ1988 → 2295.

3474 *Ebach* Jürgen, 'Ist es "umsonst", dass Hiob gottesfürchtig ist?'; lexikographische und methodologische Marginalien zu *ḥinnām* in Hi 1,9: → 147, ᶠRENDTORFF R., Hebr. Bibel 1990, 319-335.

3475 *Coogan* Michael D., Job's children: → 124, ᶠMORAN W., Lingering 1990, 135-147.

Job's daughters: *Chittister* J. 1990 → 8921; *Goričeva* T. (deutsch français español) → 8956-8958.

3476 *Rohan-Chabot* Claude de, Exégèse de Job 2:6 dans une homélie inédite de BASILE de Séleucie: → 643, StPatr 18,2 (1988/9) 197-201.

3477 **Course** John E., Speech and response; a rhetorical analysis of the introductions to the speeches of the book of Job (chs. 4-24): diss. St. Michael, ᴰ*Sheppard* G. Toronto 1990. 277 p. – RTLv 22, p. 587.

3478 **Cotter** David W., A study of Job 4-5 in the light of contemporary literary theory; diss. Pont. Univ. Gregoriana, ᴰ*Cox* D. R 1989. [xiii-] 396 p.

3479 *Smith* Gary V., Job IV 12-21; is it Eliphaz's vision?: VT 40 (1990) 453-463.

3480 *Burns* John B., The chastening of the just in Job 5:17-23; four strikes of Erra: ProcGLM 10 (1990) 18-30.

3481 *Wyatt* Nicolas, The expression *b^ekôr māwet* in Job XVIII 13 and its mythological background: VT 40 (1990) 207-216.

3482 *Ratner* Robert, The 'feminine takes precedence' syntagm and Job 19,15: ZAW 102 (1990) 238-251.

3483 *Mende* Theresia, 'Ich weiss, dass mein Erlöser lebt' (Ijob 19,25); Ijobs Hoffnung und Vertrauen in der Prüfung des Leidens: TrierTZ 99 (1990) 15-35.

3484 *Gross* Heinrich, Die Allmacht des Schöpfergottes; Erwägungen zu Ijob 26,5-14: → 146, ᶠREINELT H., At. Botschaft 1990, 75-83.

3485 *a*) *Hung* Celestine, ☯ An independent poem in the Book of Job [ch. 28]: ColcFuJen 85 (1990) 357-360 [< TContext 8/2, 34]; – *b*) *Wolfers* David, The volcano in Job 28: JBQ 18 (1989s) 234-240.

3486 *Malchow* Bruce V., A royal prototype in Job 29: → 82, ᶠHUNT J., Psalms 1990, 178-184.

3487 *Wehrle* Josef, Zur syntaktisch-semantischen Funktion der PV *k^e = m^e'aṭ* in Ijob 32,22: BibNot 55 (1990) 77-95 [n. 4, 'PV' nicht erklärt].

3488 *Gevirtz* Stanley, Phoenician *wšbrt mlṣm* and Job 33:23: → 164, ᶠSEGERT S., *Sopher* 1990, 145-158.

3489 *Vermeylen* Jacques, 'Connais-tu les lois des cieux?'; une lecture de Job 38-41: FoiTemps 20 (1990) 197-210.

3490 *Wolfers* David, *a*) [Job 40s... Behemoth, Leviathan] The Lord's second speech in the Book of Job: VT 40 (1990) 474-499; – *b*) [Job 40,26] Bulrush and bramble: JBQ 19 (1990s) 170-5.

3491 *Wolters* Al, 'A child of dust and ashes' (Job 42,6b): ZAW 102 (1990) 116-9.

E7.3   *Canticum Canticorum*, **Song of Songs,** *Das Hohelied, textus, comm.*

3492 **Alonso Schökel** Luis, El Cantar de los Cantares o la dignidad del amor. Estella 1990, VDivino. 94 p. – 84-7151-628-4. – ᴿEfMex 8 (1990) 277s (E. *Serraima Cirici*); HumT 11 (1990) 251s (D. *Augusto*); RelCu 36 (1990) 683 (M. A. *Martín Juárez*).

3493 **Alonso Schökel** Luis, Il Cantico dei Cantici; la dignità dell'amore. CasM 1990, Piemme. 94 p. Lit. 30.000 [Asprenas 38,393, S. *Cipriani*].

3494 APPONIUS: *a*) **König** Hildegard, Apponius – die Auslegung zum Lied der Lieder; die einführenden Bücher I-III und das christologisch bedeutsame Buch IX: kath. Diss. ᴰ*Vogt.* Tübingen 1990. – TR 96 (1989s) 520; – *b*) **Vregille** B. de, *Neyrand* L., Apponius in Ct: CCLat 19, 1986 → 2,2445... 5,3252: ᴿBijdragen 51 (1990) 88 (M. *Schneiders*); RB 97 (1990) 300s (M.-J. *Pierre*); Scriptorium 43 (1989) 313-323 (P. *Hamblenne*); – *c*) *Hamblenne* Pierre, Peut-on dater Apponius [Ct]?: RTAM 57 (1990) 5-33.

3495 ᵀᴱ**Danieli** Maria-Ignazia, ORIGENE, Omelie sul Cantico: TestP 82. R 1990, Città Nuova. 105 p. 88-311-3083-8. – ᴿAsprenas 37 (1990) 514s (L. *Fatica*).

3496 *Dünzl* Franz, GREGOR von Nyssa's Homilien zum Canticum auf dem Hintergrund seiner Vita Moysis: VigChr 44 (1990) 371-381.

3497 *Dziuba* Andrzej F., ☯ Commentary of Juan AZORA S.J. (1536-1603) on the Canticle: RuBi 42 (1989) 269-275.

3498 *Engammare* Max, François LAMBERT et son commentaire du Cantique des Cantiques [1524]; une lecture ecclésiale nouvelle pour un temps ecclésial nouveau: RHPR 70 (1990) 285-309.

3498* **Falk** Marcia, The Song of Songs, a new translation and interpretation [but it is a revised edition of her Love Lyrics from the Bible 1982

➤ 63,3292]. SF 1990, Harper. xviii-213 p. $19. 0-06-062339-X [TDig 38,263].

3499 **Goulder** Michael D., The song of fourteen songs: JStOT supp 36, 1987 ➤ 2,3436... 5,3242: ᴿJAOS 110 (1990) 338-340 (M. H. *Pope*).

3500 **Heinevetter** Hans-Josef, 'Komm nun, mein Liebster, dein Garten ruft dich!' Das Hohelied als programmatische Komposition [Diss. Münster 1987, ᴰ*Zenger* E.]: BoBB 69, 1988 ➤ 5,3242*: ᴿJTS 41 (1990) 807 (J. *Snaith*); RTLv 21 (1990) 91 (P.-M. *Bogaert*: sa 'théologie pour l'après-Tchernobyl'); TPQ 138 (1990) 399 (H. *Madl*); ZAW 102 (1990) 149 (H.-C. *Schmitt*); ZkT 112 (1990) 102 (G. *Fischer*: reich, musisch).

3501 **Kamin** S., *Saltman* A., Secundum Salomonem 1989 ➤ 5,3243: ᴿEstB 48 (1990) 138s (L. *Diez Moreno*); RÉJ 149 (1990) 168-170 (G. *Dahan*).

3502 **Keel** Othmar, Das Hohelied 1986 ➤ 2,2438; 3,3199: ᴿTLZ 115 (1990) 422s (W. *Herrmann*); TR 86 (1990) 287-292 (R. *Kampling*, auch über ᴴEINEVETTER H.); ZkT 112 (1990) 94-96 (J. M. *Oesch*).

3503 **Knight** George A. F., Revelation of God; a commentary on Song of Songs [with *Golka* F. W. on Jonah] 1988 ➤ 4,3405; 5,3245: ᴿTLZ 115 (1990) 190s (S. *Hidal*).

3504 **La Puente** Luis de. Expositio moralis in Canticum Canticorum. Siegburg 1987 = 1622, Schmitt. – ᴿDivinitas 34 (1990) 90s (R. M. *Schmitz*).

3505 **Matter** E. Ann, The voice of my beloved; the Song of Songs in western medieval Christianity: Middle Ages Series. Ph 1990, Univ. Pennsylvania. xiv-227 p. £28.50. 0-8122-8231-0 [BL 91,85, C. S. *Rodd*: allegories of Church/soul/Mary, alien to 20th century].

3506 *Moraldi* Luigi, Il 'Cantico dei Cantici' nella testimonianza di codici biblici della Biblioteca Ambrosiana: IstLombR 121 (1987) 87-96.

3507 ᴱ**Moreschini** C., GREGORIO di Nissa, Omelie sul Cantico 1988 ➤ 5,3246: ᴿSalesianum 52 (1990) 750 (S. *Felici*).

3508 **Murphy** Roland E., The Song of Songs; a commentary on the Book of Canticles or the Song of Songs: Hermeneia comm. Minneapolis 1990, Fortress. xxii-237 p. $22. 0-8006-6024-2 [BL 91,58, P. *Coxon*].

3509 *Neusner* Jacob, Song of Songs Rabbah [➤ k65] I [ch. 1-3], II. [ch. 4-8]: BrownJudSt 197s. Atlanta 1989, Scholars. xii-260 p.; xvi-257 p. $57 + 55. 1-55540-418-9; -9-7 [NTAbs 34,274].

3509* **Piattelli** A. A., Targum Shir ha-shirim (Parafrasi aramaica del Cantico dei Cantici). R 1987, Carucci. 172 p. Lit. 20.000 [NTAbs 34,138].

3510 **Tournay** Raymond J., Word of God, Song of love 1988 ➤ 4,3411; 5,3251*: ᴿBibTB 20 (1990) 175 (Chris A. *Franke*); BL (1990) 62s (P. W. *Coxon*); PerspRelSt 17 (1990) 188 (K. M. *Craig*: his thesis of double entendre throughout is compelling; but the numerous informative details lack a clear focus); RivB 38 (1990) 256 (A. *Bonora*); ScEsp 42 (1990) 111-3 (G. R. *Labonté*).

3511 *a*) *Ventura* Milka, *Fintoni* Luciano, Una versione del Cantico dei Cantici; – *b*) *Cosi* Giovanni, Verso il paese di Inanna: Anima 3 (F 1990) 107-114 / 106-116.

3512 **Weihrauch** Winfried, Das Hohelied in der Glaubensverkündigung des heiligen AMBROSIUS von Mailand: diss. Pont. Univ. Gregoriana, ᴰ*Pelland* G. R 1990; 408 p.; Extr. 3705, 145 p. – RTLv 22,590.

E7.4   **Canticum,** *themata, versiculi*.

3513 **Astell** Ann W., The Song of Songs in the Middle Ages. Ithaca NY 1990, Cornell Univ. x-193 p. $28 [TR 87,429].

3514 **Brenner** Athalya,   The Song of Songs: OT Guides, 1989 → 5,3253:   ᴿBL (1990) 68 (P. W. *Coxon*: admirably succinct).

3515 *a) Ch'en* Luke, ☉ The Canticles; a song of vocation: ColcFuJen 77 (1988) 373-384 [321-372 *al.* on Ct.]; – *b) Chan Yee-Yuen,* ☉ Song of Songs seen with association of ideas: ColcFuJen 84 (1990) 213-228.

3516 *Cottini* Valentino,   Linguaggio erotico nel Cantico dei Cantici e in Proverbi: LA 40 (1990) 25-45; Eng. 445.

3517 *Deckers-Dijs* M.,   Enunciatie in het Hooglied: → 180*, ᶠTᴿOMP N., Gelukkig c. 1990, 147-158; Eng. 259.

3518 **Deere** Jack S.,   The meaning of the Song of Songs; an historical and exegetical inquiry: diss. Dallas Theol. Sem. 1984.   335 p. – KirSef 62 (1988s) p. 25.

3519 *Dorsey* David A.,   Literary structuring in the Song of Songs: JStOT 46 (1990) 81-96.

3520 **Elliott** Sr. M. Timothea,   The literary unity of the Canticle ᴰ1989 → 5,3259:   ᴿLA 40 (1990) 508-513 (V. *Cottini*).

3521 *Engammare* Max,   Les colombes de tes yeux; l'utilisation réformée et contemporaine du Cantique des Cantiques: Hokhma 42 (1989) 1-16.

3522 *a) Garbini* Giovanni,   Il significato del Cantico dei Cantici [sovente assurdità logiche e linguistiche]; – *b) Meloni* Pietro,   Amore e immortalità nel Ct alla luce dell'interpretazione patristica; – *c) Pittaluga* Stefano,   Il Ct fra amor sacro e amor profano nella poesia latina medievale; – *d) Tibiletti* Carlo,   Celibato, matrimonio e antropologia delle origini: Realtà e allegoria nel Ct: D.AR.FI.CL.ET 128. Genova 1989.   9-23 / 45-62 / 63-83 / 25-43.

3523 *Harl* Marguerite,   Références philosophiques et références bibliques du langage de GRÉGOIRE de Nysse dans ses Orationes in Canticum Canticorum: → 80, ᶠHÖRNER Hadwig 1990, 117-131.

3524 *Lanczkowski* Johanna,   Einfluss der Hohe-Lied-Predigten BERNARDs auf die drei Helftaer Mystikerinnen: ErbAuf 66 (1990) 17-28.

3525 *Manns* Frédéric,   Une tradition juive dans les commentaires du Cantique des Cantiques d'ORIGÈNE: Antonianum 65 (1990) 3-22; Eng. 3.

3526 **Mariaselvam** Abraham,   The Song of Songs and ancient Tamil love poems...: AnBib 118, 1988 → 4,3425; 5,3261:   ᴿArTGran 53 (1990) 307-9 (A. *Torres*); CBQ 52 (1990) 526s (R. E. *Murphy*: many of the 'parallels' universal; supports only cautiously C. RABIN's 'direct influence' against P. *Craigie*); RB 97 (1990) 122 (R. J. *Tournay*; une dizaine de mots hébreux paraissent dériver du tamil ou du dravidien, p. 284s); Vidyajyoti 53 (1989) 574s (R. J. *Raja*).

3527 *Mateo-Seco* L. F.,   La cristología del In Canticum Canticorum de GREGORIO de Nisa: → 603, Stud/Nyss 1990, 173-190.

3528 **Matter** E. Ann,   The voice of my beloved; the Song of Songs in western medieval Christianity. Ph 1990, Univ. Pennsylvania. xxxv-227 p. $30 [RelStR 17,365, Lynda L. *Coon*].

3529 *a) Matter* E. Ann,   The Song of Songs in the 'Exercitia Spiritualia' of GERTRUDE the Great of Helfta; – *b) Raurell* Frederic,   La lettura del 'Cantico dei Cantici' al tempo di CHIARA e la 'IV lettera ad Agnese di Praga': Laurentianum 31 (1990) 39-49 / 198-309.

3530 *Mazor* Yair,   The Song of Songs or the Story of Stories? 'The Song of Songs' between genre and unity: ScandJOT (1990,1) 1-29 [1990,2, p. 115 clarifies that she attributed to M. FOX denial of structural unity only, not of other forms of unity].

3530* *Moye* Jerry,   Song of songs; back to allegory? Some hermeneutical considerations: AsiaJT 4,1 (Singapore 1990) 120-5 [< ZIT 91,203].

3531 *Ogden* Graham S.,   Some translational issues in the Song of Songs: BTrans 41 (1990) 222-8.

3532 **Pelletier** Anne-Marie,   Lectures du Cantique...: AnBib 121, 1989 ➤ 5,3264: [R]RB 97 (1990) 122-4 (R. J. *Tournay*); RBén 100 (1990) 557s (R.-F. *Poswick*); RTLv 21 (1990) 361s (P.-M. *Bogaert*).

3533 — *Beauchamp* Paul,   Typologie et 'figures du lecteur' [sous-titre de PELLETIER A., Ct]; RechSR 78 (1990) 221-232, aussi sur LARCHER C., Sagesse.

3534 [F]POPE M.,   Love and death in the Ancient Near East, [E]**Marks** J. 1987 ➤ 3,132: [R]OLZ 85 (1990) 142-6 (W. *Thiel*).

3535 **Raurell** Frederic,   El Càntic dels Càntics en els segles XII-XIII; lectura de Clara d'Assis: *a)* Santa Eulàlia de Rançana 1990, Facultat de Teologia de Catalunya.   158 p. – *b)* EstFranc 91 (1990) 421-559.

3536 *Sánchez Prieto* N.,   El Cantar de los Cantares para María: Cistercium 40 (1988) 433-447 [415-557, *al.*, María, la mujer invadida por Dios; < RET 50,124].

3537 *Sefati* Yitschak,   An oath of chastity in a Sumerian love song (SRT 31)?: ➤ 7, [F]ARTZI P., Bar-Ilan Studies 1990, 45-63.

3538 *Thompson* Yaakov,   The Song of Songs, the Bible's celebration of love: JBQ 19 (1990s) 199-203.

3539 *Villiers* D. W. de,   Not for sale! Solomon [as anti-hero] and sexual perversion in the Song of Songs: OTEssays 3 (1990) 317-324.

3540 *Wirt* S. E.,   Some new thoughts about the Song of Solomon [without allegory]: JEvTS 33 (1990) 433-6 [< ZAW 103,434].

3541 *Viviers* H.,   Die besweringsrefrein in Hooglied 2:7, 3:5 en 8:4 — 'Moenie die liefde rypdruk nie' of 'steur ons nie in one liefde nie': SkrifK 10 (Pretoria 1989) 80-89 [< OTAbs 14 (1991; wrongly 13,1990 at top of page; 72: 'The refrain of adjuration'... 'Don't arouse young love prematurely' or 'don't interrupt our love'].

3542 *Görg* M.,   [Ct 2,13; Gn 50 *bnt*] Ein biblischer Begriff im Licht seines ägyptischen Äquivalents: ➤ 114, [F]LICHTHEIM M. 1990, 241-256.

3543 *Feuillet* André,   Perspectives nouvelles à propos de l'interprétation du Cantique des Cantiques; les formules de possession mutuelle de 2,16; 6,3-4; 7,11:   Divinitas 34 (1990) 203-219.

3544 *Garbini* Giovanni,   Turris davidica (Cantico 4,4):   ParPass 252 (1990) 188-191.

E7.5   *Libri sapientiales* – **Wisdom literature.**

3545 *Alster* Bendt,   Shuruppak's instructions — additional lines identified in the Early Dynastic version: ZAss 80 (1990) 15-19.

3546 **Berger** Klaus,   *a)* Die Weisheitsschrift aus der Kairoer Geniza, Erstedition, Kommentar und Übersetzung: TArbNZ 1, 1989 ➤ 5,3274: [R]SNTU A-15 (1990) 214s (G. *Langer*); ZAW 102 (1990) 439s (O. *Kaiser*). – *b)* Die Bedeutung der wiederentdeckten Weisheitsschrift aus der Kairoer Geniza für das Neue Testament [... Qumran Serek]: NTS 36 (1990) 415-430.

3547 **Brunner-Traut** Emma,   Lebensweisheit der Alten Ägypter: Herderbü 1236, 1985 ➤ 1,3802; 2,2468: [R]CdÉ 65 (1990) 67s (J. G. *Griffiths*).

3548 **Clements** Ronald E.,   Wisdom for a changing world: Bailey Lectures 2. Berkeley 1990, BIBAL.   77 p. $8 [RelStR 17,353, J. L. *Crenshaw*].   0-941037-13-4.

3549 *Cox* Dermot, Human dignity in the OT wisdom: StMiss 39 (1990) 1-19.

3550 **Davidson** Robert,   Wisdom and worship [Cadbury Lectures 1989]. L/Ph 1990, SCM/Trinity.   148 p.   £9.50.   0-334-02461-7. – ᴿExpTim 102 (1990s) 116s (C. S. *Rodd*).

3550* **Eaton** John,   The contemplative face of OT Wisdom in the context of world religions.   Ph 1990, Trinity. $13.   0-334-01913-3. – ᴿTLond 93 (1990) 243 (R. N. *Whybray*).

ᴱ**Gammie** John G., *Perdue* Leo G.,   The sage in Israel and the Ancient Near East 1990 → 336.

3551 ᴱ**Gilbert** Maurice,   La Sagesse de l'Ancien Testament²ʳᵉᵛ [399-406, Une décennie sur les livres sapientiaux, 1979-1989]: BiblETL 51.   Lv 1990, Univ./Peeters.   460 p.   Fb 1500.   90-6186-399-6 / 90-6831-263-4. → 530.

3552 *Gilbert* Maurice, *a*) L'enseignement des Sages (Le Siracide, la Sagesse de Salomon): → 323, Psaumes/Écrits 1990, 295-351. [Proverbes → 3437; Qohéleth → 2930]; – *b*) Sabiduria: → 852, *Rossano* P., Nuevo Diccionario de Teología Bíblica. M 1990, Paulinas.   1711-1728.

3553 **Goldsworthy** Graeme,   Gospel and wisdom; Israel's wisdom literature in the Christian life 1987 → 3,2326 ... 5,3282:   ᴿSTEv 1 (1989) 87s (E. *Beriti*).

3554 *Gottlieb* Isaac B.,   Pirqe Abot and biblical wisdom: VT 40 (1990) 152-164.

3555 **Guter** Josef,   Ägyptische Weisheiten.   Bayreuth 1990, Hestia.   256 p. 3-88199-714-8 [OIAc Ja91].

3556 **Hall** David P.,   The seven pillories of wisdom.   Macon GA / Lv 1990, Mercer Univ. / Peeters.   viii-137 p. $19 [CBQ 53,357; PerspRelSt 18,187, J. *Durham*: really on NT interpreters].

3557 *a*) *Hallo* William W.,   Proverbs quoted in epic; – *b*) *Greenfield* Jonas C., Two proverbs of Aḥiqar: → 124, ꟳMORAN W., Lingering 1990, 203-217 / 195-201.

3558 *a*) *Hasan-Rokem* Galit,   And God created the proverb; inter-generic and inter-textual aspects of biblical paremiology — or the longest way to the shortest text; – *b*) *Murphy* Roland E., Proverbs in Genesis 2?; – *c*) *Camp* Claudia V., *Fontaine* Carole R.,   The words of the wise and their riddles [response *Slotkin* Edgar]: → 547, ᴱ*Niditch* Susan, Folklore 1990, 107-120 / 121-5 / 127-151 [153-160].

3559 *Hernando* Eusebio,   La sabiduría yahvista frente a la sabiduría pagana: TEspir 33 (1989) 343-361.

3560 *a*) *Jacobson* Arland D.,   Proverbs and social control; a new paradigm for wisdom studies; – *b*) *Wimbush* Vincent L.,   Sophrosyne; Greco-Roman origins of a type of ascetic behavior: → 152, ꟳROBINSON J. M., Gnosticism 2 (1990) 75-88 / 89-102.

3561 **Jones** G. L.,   Doethineb Israel: Cyfres Beibl a Chrefydd 9.   Cardiff 1990, Univ. Wales.   231 p.   £9.   0-7083-1069-9 [BL 91,81, G. H. *Jones*: on Wisdom; series Bible and Religion].

3562 *Koch* Ernst,   Die 'Himlische philosophia des heiligen Geistes'; zur Bedeutung alttestamentlichen Spruchweisheit im Luthertum des 16. und 17. Jahrhunderts: TLZ 115 (1990) 705-720.

3563 **Kottsieper** Ingo,   Die Sprache der Aḥiqarsprüche: BZAW 194.   B 1990, de Gruyter.   xi-302 p.; ill.   3-11-012331-2.

3563* *Lee* Archie, The 'critique of foundations' in the Hebrew wisdom tradition: AsiaJT 4,1 (1990) 126-135 [< ZIT 91,203].

3564 **Lips** Hermann von, Weisheitliche Traditionen im Neuen Testament: WM 64. Neuk 1990, Neuk-V. viii-512 p. DM 84.

3564* *Loader* J.A., Natuur en wysheid; een en ander oor die vraag of die wiel herontdek word: OTEssays 3 (1980) 159-170; Eng. 159.

3565 **Lunde** Paul, *Wintle* Justin, A dictionary of Arabic and Islamic proverbs 1984 → 1,3316: ᴿOLZ 85 (1990) 441s (W. *Reuschel*).

Morgan D.F., Between text and community; the 'writings' in canonical interpretation 1990 → 1564*.

3566 *Morgan* R., 'Wisdom', the preacher and the theologian: Anvil 7,1 (Nottingham 1990) 49-59 [< NTAbs 34,350].

3567 **Murphy** Roland E., The tree of life; an exploration of biblical Wisdom literature: Anchor Bible Reference Library. NY 1990, Doubleday. xi-194 p. 0-385-26244-2.

3568 **O'Connor** Kathleen M., The wisdom literature: MessageBSp 5, 1988 → 4,3459; 5,3295: ᴿCBQ 52 (1990) 331s (Camilla *Burns*: 'ch. 7 inculturates wisdom to the world of Hellenism'); Horizons 17 (1990) 147s (Mary C. *Conway*); Interpretation 44 (1990) 420.422 (Claudia V. *Camp*: fresh unapologetic feminism).

3569 *Ravasi* Gianfranco, 'Il nato di donna ... essere nauseante e inquinato'; la radicalità peccatrice dell'uomo negli scritti sapienziali ebraici: ScuolC 117 (1989) 603-620.

Römer W.H.P., *Soden* W. von, Weisheitstexte: TUmAT 3/1, 1990 → 858.

3570 **Sandelin** Karl Gustav, Wisdom as nourisher 1986 → 2,2488*... 5,3299: ᴿBO 47 (1990) 770-3 (J.W. van *Henten*); StPhilonAn 2 (1990) 220-3 (P. *Borgen*); TR 86 (1990) 15s (G. *Schimanowski*).

3571 *Shupak* Nili, Egyptian 'prophetic' writings and biblical wisdom literature: BibNot 54 (1990) 81-102.

3572 **Sirot** I.M., ⊕ Russian proverbs of biblical origin. Bru 1985, Žizn s Bogom xiv-112 p. [KirSef 62 (1988s) p. 42].

3573 **Stelert** F.J., Die Weisheit Israels [Diss. 1988s → 5,3303] — ein Fremdkörper im Alten Testament?: FreibTSt 143. FrB 1990, Herder. xii-324 p. DM 48. 3-451-22070-9 [BL 91,96, R.J. *Coggins*: ambitiously aims to answer No; with lines running into Catholic theology].

3574 **Synowiec** Juliusz, Mędrcy Izraela, ich pisma i nauka ... The sages of Israel, their writings and teaching. Kraków 1990, Sem. Franciszkanów. 286 p. 83-00-02587-4.

3575 *Virgulin* Stefano, Vita e lavoro come fonte di benedizione [nell'esistenza terrena, normalmente, nei libri sapienziali]: → 325a, ParSpV 21 (1990) 101-114.

3575* a) *Williams* R.J., The sage in Egyptian literature; — The functions of the sage in the Egyptian royal court; – b) *Kramer* S.N., The sage in Sumerian literature; a composite portrait; – c) *Sweet* R.F.G., The sage in Akkadian literature; a philological study; — The sage in Mesopotamian palaces and royal courts; – d) *Russell* J.R., The sage in ancient Iranian literature; — Sages and scribes at the court of ancient Iran; – e) *Mack-Fisher* L.R., A survey and reading-guide to the didactic literature of Ugarit; — The scribe (and sage) in the royal court at Ugarit: → 336, Sage 1990, 19-30.95-98 / 31-44 / 45-65.99-107 / 81-92.141-6 / 67-80.109-115.

3576 a) *Wills* Lawrence M., Observations on the 'wisdom narratives' in early biblical literature; – b) *Tobin* Thomas H., 4Q185 and Jewish

Wisdom literature: ➤ 173, ᶠSTRUGNELL J., Of scribes 1990, 57-66 /
145-152.

E7.6 **Proverbiorum liber,** *themata, versiculi.*

3577 **Bonora** Antonio, Proverbi-Sapienza; sapere e felicità: LoB 1.14. Brescia 1990, Queriniana. 134 p. Lit. 15.000. 88-399-1564-8 [NRT 113,910,
J.-L. *Ska*].

3578 **Boström** Lennart, The God of the sages; the portrayal of God in the
Book of Proverbs [Diss. Lund]: ConBibOT 29. Sto 1990, Almqvist & W.
x-260 p. Sk 172. 91-22-01340-7 [BL 91,105, W. *McKane*].

3579 *Burden* J. J., The wisdom of many; recent changes in Old Testament
Proverb interpretation: OTEssays 3 (1990) 341-359.

3580 **Camp** Claudia V., Wisdom and the feminine in Prov: BLit 11, 1985
➤ 1,3335... 5,3308: ᴿBZ 34 (1990) 117-120 (H. *Irsigler*); CritRR 2 (1989)
155-7 (Diane *Bergant*).

3581 *Cavalcanti* Elena, Dall'etica classica all'etica cristiana; il commento al
prologo del libro dei Proverbi, di BASILIO di Cesarea: SMSR 56 (1990)
353-378.

3581* *Crenshaw* J. L., The sage in Proverbs: ➤ 336, Sage 1990, 205-216.

3582 *Dick* Michael B., The ethics of the Old Greek Book of Proverbs:
StPhilonAn 2 (1990) 20-50.

3583 ᵀᴱ**Géhin** Paul, ÉVAGRE, Scholies aux Proverbes, SChr 348, 1987
➤ 3,3254... 5,3310: ᴿETL 66 (1990) 200s (A. de *Halleux*); JbÖstByz 40
(1990) 446-8 (W. *Lackner*); JTS 41 (1990) 686 (A. *Louth*); RBgPg 68
(1990) 179-181 (J. *Schamp*).

3584 **Kim See Nam,** The renderings of ancient versions of the Hebrew book
of Proverbs: diss. UCLA 1990, ᴰ*Segert* S. 90-33977. – DissA 51 (1990s)
2363-A.

3585 **Krispenz-Pichler** Jutta, Spruchkompositionen im Buch Proverbia: Eur-
HS 23/349, ᴰ1989 ➤ 5,3315: ᴿLA 40 (1990) 506s (A. *Niccacci*); TsTKi 61
(1990) 69s (S.*Storøy*).

3586 *a) Lang* Bernhard, Weisheit als Ethos; 'common sense' und einfache
Sittlichkeit in Buch der Sprichwörter; – *b) Michel* Diethelm, Zur Krise
der Weisheit in Israel: RUntHö 33 (1990) 281-8 / 289-297.

3587 **Ogilvie** L. J., Proverbs: Communicator's comm. Irving TX 1989, Word
[ÉTRel 65,662]. 0-8499-0421-8.

3588 *Paper* Herbert H., Proverbs [7,5 to end; full text] in Judeo-Persian:
➤ 555, Irano-Judaica 1 (1975/82) 122-147.

3589 *Tov* Emanuel, Recensional differences between the Masoretic text and
the Septuagint of Proverbs: ➤ 173, ᶠSTRUGNELL J., Of scribes 1990,
43-56.

3590 **Rosendal** B., Orsprogenes bog fortolket. K 1990, Dansk. Bibelselsk.
163 p. Dk 140. 87-7523-271-5 [BL 91,59, W. *Houston*: linked with Danish
proverb tradition].

3591 **Whybray** R. N., Wealth and poverty in the Book of Proverbs: JStOT
supp 99. Sheffield 1990. 132 p. £14.50. 1-85075-264-8 [BL 91,102,
W. G. E. *Watson*].

3592 **Burns** Camilla, The heroine with a thousand faces; woman wisdom in
Proverbs 1-9: diss. Graduate Theological Union, ᴰ*Morgan* D. Berkeley
1990. 204 p. 91-12328. – DissA 51 (1990s) 4155-A; RelStR 17,192.

3593 *a) Van Leeuwen* Raymond, Liminality and worldview in Proverbs 1-9; – *b) Reese* James M., A semiotic critique, with emphasis on locating the Wisdom of Solomon in the literature of persuasion; – *c) Perdue* Leo G., The death of the sage and moral exhortation; from Ancient Near Eastern instructions to Graeco-Roman paraenesis: ➤ 464, Semeia 50 (1990) 111-144 / 229-242 / 81-109.

3594 *Gargano* Guido I., L'immagine dell'ape laboriosa di Prov. 6,8 abc e la didascalia trasmessa dai Padri cristiani: ➤ 700, Tradizione 1989/90, 265-282.

3595 **Pardee** D., Ugaritic and ... Prov. 2 1988 ➤ 4,3490; 5,3324: ᴿBO 47 (1990) 446-9 (K. *Spronk*); JBL 109 (1990) 503s (S. B. *Parker*); ZAW 102 (1990) 455 (J. *Kottsieper*).

3596 *Garrett* Duane A., Votive prostitution again; a comparison of Proverbs 7:13-14 and 21:28-29: JBL 109 (1990) 681s.

3597 **Westermann** Claus, [Prov 10-21; 25-29] Wurzeln der Weisheit: die ältesten Sprüche Israels und anderer Völker. Gö 1990, Vandenhoeck & R. 186 p. DM 29,80. 3-525-51673-8 [BL 91,102, K. J. *Cathcart*: what he learned from his father, professor of African Studies at Berlin].

3598 *Gorgulho* Gilberto, [Prov 10-15; GIRARD R.] Sabedoria e desejo mimético: REB 50 (1990) 618-628.

3599 *Soden* Wolfram von, Kränkung, nicht Schläge in Spräche 20,30: ZAW 102 (1990) 120s.

3600 *Hocherman* Yaakov, Ⓗ Etymological studies in biblical language [Dt 24,6; Prov. 20,26; 22,8]: BethM 34 (1989) 131-7 [< OTAbs 14,35].

3600ᵃ **Römheld** Diethard, Wege der Weisheit; die Lehren Amenemopes und Proverbien 22,17-24,22 [Diss. Marburg ➤ 5,3298]: BZAW 184. B 1989, de Gruyter. x-223 p. DM 86 [JBL 110,521s, J. A. *Gladson*].

3601 *Barker* Kenneth L., Proverbs 23:7 – 'to think' or 'to serve food'?: ➤ 75, Mem. HELD M., JANES 19 (1989) 3-8.

3602 **Van Leeuwen** Raymond C., Context and meaning in Proverbs 25-27: SBL diss 96 (Toronto St. Michael's), 1988 ➤ 4,3905; 5,3330. ᴿCBQ 52 (1990) 140-2 (J. A. *Gladson*: good; some weaknesses); ETL 66 (1990) 404 (W. A. M. *Beuken*); HebSt 31 (1990) 249-252 (R. N. *Whybray*); JBL 109 (1990) 524s (A. J. *Saldarini*); JRel 70 (1990) 248 (C. *Camp*); ZAW 102 (1990) 165-7 (C. *Westermann*, long and critical).

3602* *Iwry* Samuel, [Prov 25,26] The curse of water pollution in Israel and in the Ancient Near East: ➤ 540*, Koroth 9 sp. (3d symposium 1987/8) 228-234.

E7.7 *Ecclesiastes* – **Qohelet,** *themata, versiculi.*

3603 *Bartelmus* Rüdiger, Haben oder Sein – Anmerkungen zur Anthropologie des Buches Kohelet [< Vortrag Giessen 1985]: BibNot 53 (1990) 38-67.

3604 *Ben-David* Israel, Ⓗ Some notes on the text of Midraš Ecclesiastes Rabba: Lešonenu 53 (1988s) 135-140.

3605 **Bonora** A., Qohelet: LoB 1.15, 1987 ➤ 3,3281: ᴿStPatav 37 (1990) 392-4 (M. *Milani*).

3606 *Brown* Stephen G., The structure of Ecclesiastes: ERT 14 (1990) 195-208 [< OTAbs 14,189; the list after p. 239 indicates 'Evangelical Review of Theology' as distinct from EvQ, though both are published by Paternoster].

3607 **Ceronetti** Guido, L'Ecclésiaste Qohélet, [T]*Devolto* Anna: L'Étranger 1. P 1987, EST. 125 p. [KirSef 62 (1988s) p. 489].

3608 *Cervera* Jordí, Una lectura postmoderna de l''Eclesiastès' [catalán]: EstFranc 91 (1990) 297-340.

3609 **Crenshaw** James L., Ecclesiastes: OTLibrary 1987 → 3,3282... 5,3333: [R]CriswT 4 (1989s) 175s (D. A. *Garrett*); NedTTs 43 (1989) 333s (P. B. *Dirksen*); SWJT 33,2 (1990s) 54 (H. B. *Hunt*).

3610 *a) Crenshaw* James L., Odd book in, Ecclesiastes; characterized by futility and cynicism, it stands alone; – *b) Pawley* Daniel, Reaching out to the 20th century; for modern writers, Ecclesiastes speaks with special power to the human condition: BR 6,5 (1990) 28-33 / 34-36.

3611 *Davila* James R., Qoheleth and Northern Hebrew: → 164, [F]SEGERT S., *Sopher* 1990, 69-87.

3612 **De Gregorio** Domenico, mons., Gli insegnamenti teologici di S. GREGORIO di Agrigento nel suo 'Commento all'Ecclesiaste'. R 1989, auct. 168 p. – [R]RasT 31 (1990) 411 (E. *Cattaneo*).

3613 **Diego Sánchez** Manuel, *a)* El 'Comentario al Eclesiastés' de DÍDIMO Alejandrino: diss. Augustinianum, [D]*Simonetti* M. R 1990. 117 p. extr.; – *b)* El 'comentario al Eclesiastés' de DÍDIMO Alejandrino: Teresianum 41 (1990) 231-242.

3614 **Díez Merino** Luis, Targum de Qohelet 1987 → 3,3284... 5,3334: [R]BZ 34 (1990) 301 (J. *Maier*); CBQ 52 (1990) 109s (Z. *Gerber*).

3615 **Durandeaux** Jacques, Une foi sans névrose? oui, l'actualité de Qohéleth: Parole présente. P 1987, Cerf. 287 p. [KirSef 62 (1988s) p. 498].

3616 **Ellul** Jacques, *a)* Reason for being; a meditation on Ecclesiastes [1987 → 3,3285], [T]*Hanks* J. GR 1990, Eerdmans. viii-306 p. $18.75 pa. [RelStR 17,355, J. L. *Crenshaw*: rhetoric, vanity... and insights; without consulting any sources; intended as the culmination of his career, but four later works have already been published]. – *b)* La razón de ser; meditación sobre el Eclesiastés 1989 → 5,3335: [R]CiTom 117 (1990) 147 (A. *Osuna*).

3617 *Fernández* Víctor M., El valor de la vida presente en Qohelet: RBibArg 52,38 (1990) 99-113.

3618 **Fox** M. V., Qohelet and his contradictions [overall interpretation differing from some of the parts already published]: JStOT Sup 71, BLit 18, 1985 → 5,1337: [R]BL (1990) 75 (R. B. *Salters*); ETL 66 (1990) 406s (A. *Schoors*); ÉTRel 65 (1990) 438s (D. *Lys*); JBL 109 (1990) 712-5 (J. L. *Crenshaw*); JTS 41 (1990) 566-8 (J. G. *Snaith*); OTEssays 3 (1990) 370-2 (J. *Spangenberg*); TLZ 115 (1990) 887s (G. *Sauer*).

3619 **Fredericks** Daniel C., Qoheleth's language... date: 1988 → 4,3520; 5,3338: [R]HebSt 31 (1990) 144-154 (A. *Hurvitz*); JTS 41 (1990) 153-5 (J. G. *Snaith*); ZAW 102 (1990) 148s (I. *Kottsieper* antwortet: 700 oder vor 550 unmöglich).

3620 *Gammie* John G., Stoicism and anti-stoicism in Qohelet: HebAnR 9 (1985) 169-187 [< OTAbs 13,282].

3621 *Hirshman* M., The Greek Fathers and the Aggada on Ecclesiastes; formats of exegesis in late antiquity: HUCA 49 (1988) 137-165 [< ZAW 102,275].

3622 *Ho Kit-Ching,* © Koheleth and 'futility' [*habel*]: ColcFuJen 84 (1990) 229-236.

3623 **Isaksson** Bo, Studies in the language of Qohelet 1987 → 3,3288... 5,3339: [R]ÉTRel 65 (1990) 271s (D. *Lys*); OrLovPer 20 (1989) 256s (A. *Schoors*); TLZ 115 (1990) 583s (S. *Holm-Nielsen*); TsTKi 60 (1989) 214s (Solfrid *Storøy*).

3624 **Jarick** John, GREGORY Thaumaturgus' paraphrase of Ecclesiastes [diss. Melbourne]: SeptCog 29. Atlanta 1990, Scholars. vii-375 p. $30; pa. $20. 1-55540-484-7; -5-5 [NTAbs 35,136].

3625 *Kaiser* Otto, Determination und Freiheit beim Kohelet/Prediger Salomo und in der frühen Stoa: NSys 31 (1989) 251-270; Eng. 270.

3626 **Kreeft** Peter, Three philosophies of life; Ecclesiastes, life as vanity; Job, life as suffering; Song of Songs, life as love. SF 1989, Ignatius. 140 p. $8. 0-89870-262-3 [TDig 37,272].

3627 **Krüger** Thomas, Theologische Gegenwartsdeutung im Kohelet-Buch: ev. Hab.-Diss. DBaltzer K. München 1990s. – RTLv 22, p. 588.

3628 *Labate* Antonio, Sulla catena all'Ecclesiaste di POLICRONIO: → 643, StPatr 18,2 (1983/9) 21-35.

3629 *a)* TELeanza Sandro, GREGORIO di Nissa, Omelie sull'Ecclesiaste: TPatr 86. R 1990, Città Nuova. 196 p. 88-311-3086-2; – *b)* ESiclari Alberto, TRinaldi Serena, GREGORIO di Nissa, Omelie sull'Ecclesiaste: Univ. Parma, Sc. Rel., Saggi e Testi. Parma 1987, Zara. 168 p. – ROrChrPer 56 (1990) 239s (J. D. *Baggarly*).

3630 *Levine* Etan, Qohelet's fool; a composite portrait: → 367, ERadday, Humour 1990, 277-294.

3631 *Mastnak* Wolfgang, Klangszenimprovisation Kohelet: RUntHö 33 (1990) 314-321 [< ZIT 90,852].

3631* **Michaud** Robert, Qohélet et l'hellénisme 1987 → 3,3295 ... 5,3348: RCrNSt 11 (1990) 617s (P. C. *Bori*).

3632 **Michel** Diethelm, Qohelet: ErtFor 258, 1988 → 4,2527: RHebSt 31 (1990) 210-3 (A. *Schoors*); ZAW 102 (1990) 156 (O. *Kaiser*).

3633 **Michel** Diethelm, Untersuchungen zur Eigenart des Buches Qohelet: BZAW 183 → 5,3350: RJBL 109 (1990) 711s (R. E. *Murphy*); RHPR 70 (1990) 257s (J.-G. *Heintz*: original et solide); ZAW 102 (1990) 452 (H.-C. *Schmitt*).

3634 *Michel* Diethelm, Koheletbuch: → 857, TRE 19 (1990) 345-356.

3635 **Mopsik** Charles, L'Ecclésiaste et son double araméen; Qohélet et son Targoum: Les Dix Paroles. Lagrasse 1990, Verdier. 147 p. 2-86432-079-7.

3635* *Murphy* Roland E., The sage in Ecclesiastes and Qoheleth the sage: → 336, Sage 1990, 263-271.

3636 **Ogden** Graham, Qohelet: Readings comm. 1987 → 4,3528; 5,3353: RBiblica 71 (1990) 425-9 (R. *Lauha*); CritRR 2 (1989) 175s (R. E. *Murphy*); ÉTRel 65 (1990) 112s (D. *Lys*); JTS 41 (1990) 149-152 (J. L. *Crenshaw*); TLZ 115 (1990) 262-4 (G. *Sauer*).

3637 *Pazera* Wojciech, ℗ De sanctione morali in Qohelet: → 64, FGRZYBEK S. 1990, 218-224.

3638 **Ravasi** Gianfranco, Qohelet 1988 → 4,3531; 5,3355: RBL (1990) 59s (J. R. *Porter*: novel and lively); RivB 38 (1990) 98-102 (G. L. *Prato*).

3639 *Rayak* Rachel, ℍ Lexical concatenation in Qohelet: BethM 36,124 (1990s) 94-96.

3640 *Schoors* Antoon, The pronouns in Qoheleth: HebSt 30 (1989) 71-87.

3641 **Schubert** Mathias, Schöpfungstheologie bei Kohelet [Diss. Leipzig 1986, DWagner S.]: BeitErfAT 15, 1989 → 5,3356: RBL (1990) 113 (R. N. *Whybray*); ZAW 102 (1990) 458 (A. *Fischer*).

Schwarzschild Roger, The syntax of 'šr in biblical Hebrew with special reference to Qohelet 1990 → 9230.

3643 *Sims* S., Problems with Ecclesiastes [Targum]...?: KingsTR 12,2 (1989) 49-51 [< NTAbs 34,224].

3644 **Sneed** Mark R., The social location of Qoheleth's thought; anomie and alienation in Ptolemaic Jerusalem: diss. Drew. Madison NJ 1990, 107 p. 91-12370. – DissA 51 (1990s) 4155-A.

3645 **Whybray** R. N., *a)* Ecclesiastes **comm.**: NCent 1989 → 5,3364: ᴿBL (1990) 63s (A. P. *Hayman*); HebSt 31 (1990) 262-4 (Elizabeth *Huwiler*); JBL 109 (1990) 709-711 (H. C. *Washington*); BTrans 41 (1990) 142s (G. S. *Ogden*); – *b)* Ecclesiastes: OT **Guides** 1989 → 5,3365.

3646 *Wyk* W. C. vanᴶ, Die relevansie van die boek Prediker: HervTS 45 (1989) 557-572 [< OTAbs 14,71].

3647 **Zafrani** Haïm, *Caquot* André, L'Ecclésiaste et son commentaire, 'le livre de l'ascèse'; la version arabe de la Bible de Saʿadya Gaon: Judaïsme en Terre d'Islam 4. P 1989, Maisonneuve & L. 132 p. F 150. 2-7068-0987-6 [BO 47,265]. – ᴿÉTRel 65 (1990) 437s (D. *Bourguet*: caractères hébraïques transcrits en arabe).

3647* *Ziegler* J., Der Gebrauch des Artikels in der Septuaginta des Ecclesiastes: → 70, ᶠHANHART R., 1990, 83-120.

3648 **Zlotowitz** Meir, Kohélet, l'Ecclésiaste, intr. *Scherman* Nosson, ᵀ*Gugenheim* Jean-J.: La Bible commentée. P 1987, Colbo. xlvii-241 p. [KirSef 62 (1988s) p. 486].

3649 *Lux* Rüdiger, 'Ich, Kohelet, bin König...' Die Fiktion als Schlüssel der Wirklichkeit in Kohelet 1,12 - 2,26: EvT 50 (1990) 331-342.

3650 *Ebach* J., '... and a time for exposition of Qoh 3 on the links between exegesis and time': → 330, Einwürfe 7 (1990)...

3650* *Lohfink* Norbert, Qoheleth 5:17-19 – revelation by joy: CBQ 52 (1990) 625-635.

3651 *Wise* Michael O., A calque from Aramaic in Qoheleth 6:12; 7:12; and 8:13: JBL 109 (1990) 249-257.

3652 *Dell'Aversano* C., Mišpaṭ in Qoh. 11:9c: → 154, ᶠSACCHI P. 1990, 121-134.

3653 *Salvaneschi* Enrica, Memento vivere (Qohélet 12,1-8): RaMIsr 56,1s (1990) 31-59.

3654 *a)* *Jarick* John, An 'allegory of age' as apocalypse (Ecclesiastes 12:1-7); – *b)* *Olley* John W., 'Righteous' and wealthy? The description of the ṣaddîq in wisdom literature: Colloquium 22,2 (Sydney 1990) 19-27 / 38-45 [< ZIT 90,665].

E7.8   *Liber Sapientiae* – **Wisdom of Solomon.**

3655 ᵀᴱ**Albert** K., Meister ECKHART, Kommentar zum Buch der Weisheit: Texte zur Philosophie 7, 1988 → 4,3549: ᴿTLZ 115 (1990) 840 (P. *Heidrich*).

3656 **Bizzeti** Paolo, Il libro della Sapienza; struttura e genere letterario: RivB supp. 11, 1984 → 65,2954: ᴿRTLv 21 (1990) 493 (J. *Vermeylen*: méthode de VANHOYE A., en faveur de la 'syncrisis' de BEAUCHAMP P., GILBERT M., contre le 'logos protrepticos' de REESE J., HAEFFNER G.).

3657 *Kolarcik* Michael, The wisdom of Ben Sira [SKEHAN-DI LELLA, SANDERS J.], the wisdom of Solomon [mostly not in English; since D. WINSTON 1979]: TorJT 6 (1990) 298-300.

3658 *Long* Eliza, ☉ God's attributes in the Book of Wisdom: ColcFuJen 24 (1990) 237-244.

3659 **Schmitt** Armin,   Weisheit: NEchter 23, 1989 ➤ 5,3379:   ᴿBL (1990) 61
(R. N. *Whybray*: judicious rather than innovative); TLZ 115 (1990) 19s
(W. *Herrmann*); ZAW 102 (1990) 161 (O. *Kaiser*).

3660 ᴱ**Thiele** Walter,   Sapientia Salomonis: VLat Beuron 11/1, 1977-85
➤ 1,3387 ... 3,3317:   ᴿCBQ 52 (1990) 142s (A. *Cody*).

3661 **Vílchez Líndez** José,   *a*) Sabiduría: Sapienciales 5, Nueva Biblia Española. Estella 1990, VDivino.   569 p.   84-7151-665-1; – *b*) Sapienza,
ᵀ*Tosatti* Teodora, *Chiecchi* Carlo: Commenti biblici.   R 1990, Borla.
653 p.   88-263-0736-9.

3661* *Winston* D.,   The sage as mystic in the Wisdom of Solomon: ➤ 336,
Sage 1990, 399-415.

3662 *a*) *Kraus Reggiani* C.,   Il sorite di Sapienza 6,17-20; – *b*) *Boccaccini* G.,
La Sapienza dello Pseudo-Aristea: ➤ 154, ᶠSᴀᴄᴄʜɪ P. 1990, 135-141 /
143-176.

3662* *Genuyt* François,   La sortie d'Égypte – lecture de Sagesse 10-11 / 12-
15 / 16-18,4: SémBib 57 (1990) 1-13 / 58,1-17 / 59,1-8.

3663 *a*) *Görg* Manfred,   Der Eine oder die Vielen; Beobachtungen zur
Religionskritik in Weish 13,1 f; – *b*) *Scharbert* Josef,   Die Alters-
beschwerden in der ägyptischen, babylonischen und biblischen Weisheit:
➤ 8*, ᶠAssꜰᴀʟɢ J. 1990, 119-128 / 289-298.

3664 *Berder* Michel, [Sg 11s] Théologie d'une libération et leçons de pédagogie
divine: VieChr 342 (mai 1990) 27-32 [Sg 3-5: 338,23-28; Sg 6-8:
339,28-32; Sg 9: 340,27-32; Sg 10: 341,26-31 etc.].

3665 **Dumoulin** Pierre,   La manne dans le livre de la Sagesse; synthèse de
traditions et préparation au mystère eucharistique; étude de Sg
16,15-17,1: diss. Pont. Univ. Gregoriana, ᴰ*Gilbert* M. Roma 1990.
409 p. – RTLv 22, p. 587.

3666 **Priotto** Michelangelo,   La prima Pasqua in Sap 18,5-25 [diss. PIB,
Roma]: RivB supp. 15, 1987 ➤ 3,3319; 5,3384:   ᴿBenedictina 36 (1989)
220-2 (S. *Spera*); CBQ 52 (1990) 131s (D. *Winston*).

E7.9   *Ecclesiasticus, Siracides;* **Wisdom of Jesus Sirach.**

3667 *Di Lella* Alexander A.,   The search for wisdom in Ben Sira: ➤ 82,
ᶠHᴜɴᴛ J., Psalms 1990, 185-196.

3668 *Engberg-Pedersen* T.,   [place of Ecclesiasticus in history]: T-Nybrud 1990
➤ 332.

3668* *a*) *Gammie* J. G.,   The sage in Sirach; – *b*) *Newsom* Carol A.,   The sage
in the literature of Qumran; the functions of the *maśkîl*: ➤ 336, Sage
1990, 355-372 / 373-382.

3669 **Kister** Menahem, ❿ *a*) A contribution to the interpretation of Ben Sira:
Tarbiz 59 (1989s) 303-378; Eng. II-s; – *b*) ❿ Additions to the article [on]
Sirach: Lešonenu [47 (1982s) 125-146] 53 (1988s) 38-53.

3670 **Minissale** Antonio,   Siracide: LoB 1.17, 1988 ➤ 4,3563; 5,3390:   ᴿSt-
Patav 37 (1990) 391s (M. *Milani*).

3671 **Nelson** Milward D.,   The Syriac version of the Wisdom of Ben Sira
compared to the Greek and Hebrew materials: SBL diss 107 [California
LA 1981] 1988 ➤ 4,3564; $18; pa. $12: ᴿCBQ 52 (1990) 329-331 (A. A. *Di
Lella*: lacks precision); ETL 66 (1990) 194 (A. de *Halleux*); JBL 109 (1990)
720s (B. G. *Wright*); JQR 81 (1990s) 189-191 (T. H. *Lim*); TLZ 115 (1990)
189s (G. *Sauer*).

3672 *Reiterer* Friedrich V., Deutung und Wertung des Todes durch Ben Sira:
➤ 146, ᶠReinelt H. 1990, 203-236.
3673 **Samaan** Kamil, Sept traductions arabes de Ben Sira: diss. Pont. Ist.
Biblico, ᴰ*Gilbert* M. R 1990. – AcPIB 9/7,578.
3674 **Skehan** P. W., *Di Lella* A. A., Wisdom of Ben Sira, AnchorB 39, 1987
➤ 3,3329 ... 5,3393: ᴿAfER 12 (1990) 118s (V. *Zinkuratire*); Claretianum
30 (1990) 489s (B. *Proietti*); EstB 48 (1990) 139-141 (Víctor *Morla*); JSS 35
(1990) 142-5 (R. J. *Owens*: excellent; stronger on textual-literary, less on
theological-social); LavalTP 46 (1990) 117s (Elizabeth *Farrell*).
3675 *Wlosiński* Marian, ⊘ Historisch-kritische Frage des Buches Jesus Sirach:
➤ 64, ᶠGrzybek S. 1990, 348-354; deutsch 354s.
3676 **Wright** Benjamin G., No small difference; Sirach's relationship to its
Hebrew parent text: SBL Cog 26, 1989 ➤ 5,3395: ᴿETL 66 (1990) 190-2
(J. *Lust*); JBL 109 (1990) 718s (M. D. *Nelson*); JStJud 21 (1990) 302-5
(P. C. *Beentjes*).
3677 *Zappella* Marco, Criteri antologici e questioni testuali del manoscritto
ebraico C di Siracide: RivB 38 (1990) 273-299; Eng. 300.

3678 *Peri* Israel, Steinhaufen im Wadi (zu Sirach 21,8): ZAW 102 (1990)
420s.
3679 *Prockter* L. J., 'His yesterday and yours today' (Sir 38:22); reflections
on Ben Sira's view of death: JSem 2,1 (1990) 44-56.
3680 *Margalit* Baruch, Two Hebrew cruxes [Sira 41,18: *yd* 'outhouse' as Dt
23,13; Qumran *'bdn* 'invent']: ZAHeb 3 (1990) 95-97.
3681 *Greenfield* Jonas C., Ben Sira 42.9-10 and its Talmudic paraphrase:
➤ 183, ᶠVermes G. 1990, 167-173.
3682 *Puech* Émile, Ben Sira 48:11 et la Résurrection: ➤ 173, ᶠStrugnell J.,
Of scribes 1990, 81-89; p. 90, place for a facsimile to be pasted in.
3683 *Beentjes* Pancratius C., 'Sweet is his memory, like honey to the palate';
King Josiah in Ben Sira 49,1-4: BZ 34 (1990) 262-6.

VIII. Libri prophetici VT

E8.1 **Prophetismus.**

3684 ᴱ**Armerding** Carl E., *Gasque* W. Ward, A guide to biblical prophecy.
Peabody MA 1989, Hendrickson. 288 p. 0-943575-11-7. 7 new art.
3685 **Asurmendi** Jesús, Il profetismo dalle origini ai giorni nostri 1987
➤ 4,3780; 5,3407: ᴿSalesianum 52 (1990) 165 (M. *Cimosa*).
3686 *Barstad* Hans M., Profetene i det gamle testamente, fakta eller
fiksjon?: NorTTs 91 (1990) 149-156.
3687 **Barton** John, Oracles of God ... after exile 1986 ➤ 2,2577 ... 5,3408:
ᴿAnglTR 71 (1989) 433s (D. F. *Morgan*); CBQ 52 (1990) 707-9 (D. L.
Petersen); IrTQ 56 (1990) 64s (T. *Stone*).
3688 **Beaucamp** Évode, Los profetas de Israel (o el drama de una alianza),
ᵀ*Ortiz García* Alfonso 1988 (= 1956), ➤ 5,3410: ᴿHumT 10 (1989)
110s (J. *Godinho de Lima*); Iter 1 (Caracas 1990) 166s (E. *Frades*);
RTLim 24 (1990) 293s (U. *Berges*).
3689 **Bennett** Boyce M., An anatomy of revelation; prophetic visions in the
light of scientific research. Harrisburg 1990, Morehouse. xiv-118 p.
[CBQ 53,169].

3690 *Berges* Ulrich, La profecía desde la Sagrada Escritura: RTLim 24 (1990) 383-404.

3691 *a) Berten* Ignace, Prophétisme et institution; – *b) Tihon* Marie-Alice, Prophétisme et histoire; – *c) Wénin* André, Prophétisme et institution dans la Bible; – *d) Reding* José, Pour une Église prophétique aujourd'hui: FoiTemps 20 (1990) (486-490) 546-565 / 491-507 / 508-524 / 525-545.

3692 *Bobzin* H., F. RÜCKERT und die Propheten des ATs: ➤ 766, Colloquium 1990, 47-63.

3693 **Bretón** Santiago, Vocación y misión, formulario profético [D1984]: AnBib 111, 1987 ➤ 3,3350; 5,3415: ᴿBZ 34 (1990) 307 (J. *Becker*); CBQ 52 (1990) 314-6 (L. *Laberge* blames him only for evaluating his achievement too modestly, but hopes that he may go on to add what the non-Hebrew texts have to say); RivB 38 (1990) 97s (A. *Rolla*).

3694 **Brueggemann** Walter, Hopeful imagination; prophetic voices in exile [Jer Ezek 2-Isa] 1986 ➤ 4,3585: ᴿCritRR 2 (1989) 152-4 (R. R. *Hutton*; also on his Hope within history).

3695 *Carroll* R. P., Is humour also among the prophets?: ➤ 367, ᴱ*Radday*, Humour 1990, 169-189.

3696 *Chappaz* Jean-Luc, Un nouveau prophète en Abydos: BSocÉg 14 (Genève 1990) 23-31; 1 fig.

3697 *Clements* R. E., The prophet and his editors: ➤ 166, ᶠSheffield 1990, 205-220.

3698 **Colpe** Carsten [➤ 214], Das Siegel der Propheten; historische Beziehungen zwischen Judentum, Judenchristentum, Heidentum und frühem Islam: ArbNZ 3. B 1990, Inst. Kirche und Judentum. 271 p. 3-923095-83-X.

3699 *Couturier* Guy, L'esprit de Yahweh et la fonction prophétique en Israël: ScEsp 42 (1990) 129-165.

3700 **Dearman** J. A., Property rights in the eighth-century prophets: SBL diss 106, 1988 ➤ 4,3595; 5,3420: ᴿBiblica 71 (1990) 264-6 (J. L. *Sicre*: objetivo, agradable); CBQ 52 (1990) 316s (L. *Boadt*: solid); ETL 66 (1990) 183s (J. *Lust*).

3701 *Deist* F. E., Profete in Israel; 'n Probleemstelling: HervTS 46 (1990) 71-84 [< OTAbs 14,73].

3702 *Dolbeau* François, 'De uita et obitu Prophetarum'; une traduction médiolatine des Vies grecques des Prophètes: RBén 100 (1990) 507-531.

3703 **Goff** James, Prophetie und Politik in Israel und im alten Ägypten: BeitÄg 7. Wien ... 112 p. – ᴿRTPhil 122 (1990) 559s (M. *Patané*).

3704 *Gonçalves* Francolino J., Prophètes: ➤ m408, ᴱ*Vesco* J.-L., L'AT ... École Biblique 1990, 119-153.

3705 **Hammerstaedt** Jürgen, Die Orakelkritik des Kynikers OENOMAUS: MgAltHW 188. Fra 1988, Athenäum. 328 p. DM 84. 3-610-09013-8. – ᴿAntClas 59 (1990) 340s (O. *Ballériaux*).

3706 *Heintz* Jean-Georges, Chronique d'Ancien Tetament; oracles et métaphores prophétiques en Israël antique [Ésaïe, Jérémie et le Second Ésaïe]: RHPR 70 (1990) 209-239.

3706* *Ibáñez Arana* Andrés, Los criterios de profecía: LumenVr 39 (1990) 193-250.

3707 *a) Kalluveettil* Paul, Social criticism as the prophetic role; a biblical prolegomenon; – *b) Walle* R. Vande, The Minor Prophets as conscientizers; – *c) Joseph* T. A., Social and political perestroika in Proto- Isaiah; – *d) Kaniarakath* G., Praying the Psalms as an experience of prophetic solidarity: Jeevadhara 19 (1989) 133-160 / 118-132 / 89-104 / 105-117.

3708 **Koch** Klaus, Die Propheten II 1983 ➤ 64,3387... 3,3373; ²1988: ᴿTPQ 138 (1990) 182s (Borghild *Baldauf*).

3709 *Laney* J. Carl, The Prophets and social concern: BS 147 (1990) 32-43.

3710 ᴱ**Loerzer** Sven, Visionen und Prophezeiungen; die berühmtesten [apokryphen] Weissagungen der Weltgeschichte. Augsburg 1988, Pattloch. 416 p. – ᴿLebZeug 44 (1989) 306 (A. *Weiser*).

3711 *McHatten* Mary T., The prophetic call to women; Isaiah, Jeremiah and Ezekiel: Emmanuel 96 (1990) 398-403 [< OTAbs 14,73].

3712 *Millard* Alan, The Old Testament in its ancient world; aspects of prophetic writings: ScotBEv 7 (1989) 88-99.

3713 *Miller* James E., Dreams and prophetic visions: Biblica 71 (1990) 401-4.

3714 **Miller** John W., Meet the prophets 1987 ➤ 3,378... 5,3436: ᴿCBQ 52 (1990) 326s (K. M. *Craig*: lucid).

3715 *Mottu* Henry, La parole et le geste; les actes symboliques des prophètes et la théologie pratique aujourd'hui: RTPhil 121 (1989) 291-306.

3716 **Niditch** Susan, The symbolic vision in biblical tradition [diss. Harvard 1979, ᴰ*Cross* F.] 1983 ➤ 64,3403... 1,3437: ᴿVT 40 (1990) 255 (R. P. *Gordon*).

3717 **Overholt** Thomas W., Channels of prophecy; the social dynamics of prophetic activity 1989 ➤ 5,3438; 0-8006-2411-4: ᴿExpTim 102 (1990s) 150 (H. *Mowvley*); TS 51 (1990) 780 (W. J. *Fulco*).

3718 *a*) *Overholt* Thomas W.; Prophecy in history, the social reality of interpretation; – *b*) (responses) *Auld* A. Graeme, Prophecy in books; – *c*) *Carroll* R. P., Whose prophet?...: JStOT 48 (1990) 3-29 . 51-54 / 31s / 33-49.

3719 *Parker* Margaret, Exploring four persistent prophetic images [Covenant – People rebel – Punishment – Restoration]: BR 6,5 (1990) 38-45.

3720 *a*) *Petuchowski* Jakob J., Faith and works in the biblical confrontation of prophets and priests; – *b*) *Goodman* Martin, Identity and authority in ancient Judaism: Judaism 39 (1990) 184-191 / 192-201.

3721 *a*) **Pongutá H.** Silvestre, Por medio de los Profetas, una presentación en el centenario de la presencia de la obra salesiana en Colombia [monografía, no compilación]: CuadB 1; – *b*) Escuela de Catequistas, Un pueblo, un libro; introducción a la Biblia / La Biblia en la catequesis. Bogotá 1990, Asociación Bíblica Salesiana. vi-156 p., 980-6035-32-1 / 48 p.; 32 p.

3722 *Randall* C. Corydon, An approach to biblical satire: ➤ 82, ᶠHUNT J., Psalms 1990, 132-144.

3723 **Renker** Alwin, Propheten – das Gewissen Israels; Anregungen für Unterricht und Verkündigung. FrB 1990, Herder. 125 p. DM 19,80. 3-451-21841-0 [BL 91,92, C. S. *Rodd*: essays on five prophets].

3724 **Rižskij** Moisej I., ⊕ Bibleyskie proroki... Biblical prophets and prophecy. Moskva 1987, Polit. Lit. 163 p. [KirSef 62 (1988s) p. 37].

3725 **Rofé** Alexander, The prophetical stories [⊕ 1982], ᵀ*Levy* D. 1988 ➤ 4,3629 [!]; 5,3440: ᴿRB 97 (1990) 102-111 (F. *Langlamet*).

3726 **Schneider** Christoph, Die innerprophetische Auseinandersetzung im AT als Krise des Jahweglaubens; zur Frage der sogenannten falschen Prophetie: Diss. ᴰ*Herrmann*, Kirchl. Hochschule Leipzig [1977 DDR; anerkannt 1990; TR 86 (1990) 516].

3728 **Schultz** Richard L., Prophecy and quotation, a methodological study: diss. Yale, ᴰ*Childs* B. NHv 1990. iv-459 p. 90-12323. – OIAc Oc90.

3729 *Shupak* Nili, Egyptian 'prophecy' and biblical prophecy; did the phenomenon of prophecy, in the biblical sense, exist in ancient Egypt?: JbEOL 31 (1989s) 5-40.

3730 **Sicre** J.-L., *al.*, La Iglesia y los profetas 1989 → 5,3447: ᴿBibFe 16 (1990) 308 (M. *Sáenz de Santa María*); CommSev 23 (1990) 297s (F. *Sánchez-Hermosilla Peña*).

3731 *Simian-Yofre* Horacio, La critica profetica nei confronti del sacerdozio: → 542*, Laici 1990, 89-112.

3732 **Sklba** Richard J., Pre-exilic prophecy; words of warning, dreams of hope; spirituality of pre-exilic prophets: MessageBSpir 3. Collegeville MN 1990, Liturgical. [vi-] 183 p. $14; pa. $10. 0-8146-5569-6 pa.

3733 *Soares-Prabhu* George M., The prophet as theologian; biblical prophetism as a paradigm for doing theology today: AsiaJT 2 (1988) 3-11.

3734 *Spreafico* Ambrogio, La violenza nei Profeti: → 514c, Violenza 1990, 65-81.

3735 **Stacey** W. D., Prophetic drama in the OT. L 1990, Epworth. x-310 p. £12.50. 0-7162-0470-3. – ᴿExpTim 102,7 top choice (1990s) 193s (C. S. *Rodd*).

3736 *a) Stiglmair* Arnold, '... So spricht Jahwe...' – Prophetenwort als Wort Gottes; – *b) Thiel* Winfried, Sprachliche und thematische Gemeinsamkeiten nordisraelitischer Propheten-Überlieferungen: → 146, ᶠRᴇɪɴᴇʟᴛ H., At. Botschaft 1990, 345-357 / 359-376.

3737 **Tångberg** K. Arvid, Die prophetische Mahnrede...: FRL 143, 1987 → 3,3393... 5,3454: ᴿCBQ 52 (1990) 542s (W. W. *Frerichs*); JBL 109 (1990) 514s (G. M. *Tucker*); TsTKi 60 (1989) 215-7 (Solfrid *Storøy*).

3738 **Tubbs** Fred C., The nature and function of humor and wit in the OT literary prophets: diss. SW Baptist Theol. Sem. 1990. 226 p. 90-33452. – DissA 51 (1990s) 2412-A.

3739 **Van Gemeren** Willem A., *a)* Interpreting the prophetic word. GR 1990, Zondervan. 545 p. $22. 0-310-21120-4 [BL 91,98, R. F. *Clements*: clear well-informed conservative]; – *b)* Prophets, the freedom of God, and hermeneutics: WestTJ 52 (1990) 79-99.

3740 ᴱ**Wallis** Gerhard, Zwischen Gericht und Heil; Studien zur alttestamentlichen Prophetie im 7./6. Jht. – 1987 → 4,328: ᴿTLZ 115 (1990) 18s (O. *Kaiser*).

3741 **Westermann** Claus, Prophetische Heilsworte...: FRL 145, 1987 → 3,3398 ... 5,3458: ᴿTR 86 (1990) 363s (J. *Scharbert*).

E8.2 **Proto-Isaias,** *textus, commentarii.*

3742 *Andersen* Knud T., Die Berufung Jesaias und seine Sendung: → 117*, ᶠLøᴋᴋᴇɢᴀᴀʀᴅ F. 1990, 17-23.

3743 **Brock** S. P., Isaiah: Peshiṭta 3/1, 1987 → 3,3399; 4,3649: ᴿJTS 41 (1990) 222-6 (M. *Weitzman*).

3744 *a) Bundy* David D., Eᴘʜʀᴇᴍ's exegesis of Isaiah; – *b) Yousif* P., Exegetical principles of St. Eᴘʜʀᴀᴇᴍ of Nisibis; → 643, StPatr 18,4 (1983/90) 234-9 / 296-302.

3745 **Chilton** Bruce D., The Isaiah targum: Aramaic Bible 11, 1987 → 3,3400; 4,3651: ᴿWestTJ 52 (1990) 368-370 (M. *Silva*: sometimes barely English).

3746 *Coggins* Richard J., Which is the best commentary? 12. Isaiah: ExpTim 102 (1990s) 99-102.

3747 **Croatto** J.S., Isaias I (1-39), ᵀ*Clasen* Jaime A.; ComB AT. Petrópolis 1989, Vozes/Metodista/Sinodal. 247 p. – ᴿPerspT 22 (1990) 250s (J. *Vitório* também sobre Col. Ef.).

3748 *Gevaryahu* Haim, Isaiah; how the book entered Holy Writ: JBQ = Dor 18 (1989s) 206-212.

3749 ᴱ**Gryson** Roger, Esaias 7,14-10,19: Vetus Latina Beuron 12 [Lfg. 4, 1989 → 5,3462]. Lfg. 5, Is 10,20 - 14,13. FrB 1990, Herder. p. 321-400. – ᴿJTS 41 (1990) 579-581 (J. K. *Elliott*, Lfg. 1).

3750 *Gryson* Roger, *Deproost* Paul-Augustin, La tradition manuscrite du commentaire de JÉRÔME sur Isaïe (livres I et II): Scriptorium 43 (1989) 175-222.

3751 *Gryson* Roger, *Szmatula* Dominique, Les commentaires patristiques sur Isaïe d'ORIGÈNE à JÉRÔME: RÉAug 36 (1990) 3-41.

3752 **Hayes** J. H., *Irvine* Stuart A., Isaiah, the eighth century prophet 1987 → 4,3656; 5,3465: ᴿBiblica 71 (1990) 103-6 (C. *Dohmen*); ETL 66 (1990) 184s (J. *Lust*, also on JOHNSON D. 1988); ÉTRel 65 (1990) 269 (D. *Lys*); Henoch 12 (1990) 237-9 (J. A. *Soggin*: sconcertante); Interpretation 44 (1990) 306s (W. *Janzen*); JTS 41 (1990) 561s (W. D. *Stacey*).

3753 **Helfmeyer** Franz-Josef, Isaia; il Santo d'Israele tuo redentore 1989 → 5,3466: ᴿSalesianum 52 (1990) 431 (M. *Cimosa*: su Protoisaia malgrado il sottotitolo).

3754 **Jacob** Edmond, Ésaïe 1-12: CommAT 8a, 1987 → 3,3403 ... 5,3467: ᴿBiblica 71 (1990) 415-8 (R. *Rendtorff*: praises distinction of 2-Is yet brings it well into his purview); TZBas 46 (1990) 282s (K. *Seybold*).

3755 **Kilian** R. Jesaja 1-12: 1986 → 2,2627 ... 5,3472: ᴿBLtg 63 (1990) 120s (B. M. *Zapff*).

3755* *Kooij* Arie van der, The Old Greek of Isaiah in relation to the Qumran texts of Isaiah; some general comments: → 519, Septuagint, Scrolls 1990, 195-213.

3756 **Montagnini** Felice, Isaia 1-39; l'occhio del profeta sugli eventi della storia: LoB 1.18. Brescia 1990, Queriniana. 134 p. Lit. 15.000. 88-399-1568-0. – ᴿAsprenas 37 (1990) 511s (A. *Rolla*).

3757 **Oswalt** John N., The book of Isaiah, chapters 1-39: NICOT, 1986 → 2,2628 ... 5,3476: ᴿRTLv 21 (1990) 88-90 (J. *Vermeylen*).
Owens John J., Analytical key to Is-Mal 1989 → 2038.

3758 *Pelletier* Anne-Marie, Le livre d'Isaïe et le temps de l'histoire: NRT 112 (1990) 30-43.

3759 **Ribera Florit** Josep, El Targum de Isaías: Biblioteca Midrásica 6, 1988 → 4,3663: ᴿWestTJ 52 (1990) 368-390 (M. *Silva*: somewhat more readable than CHILTON).

3760 *Vrame* Anton C., THEODORET, bishop of Kyros as an exegete of Isaiah, 1. A translation of his commentary, with an introduction: GrOrTR 34 (1989) 127-147.

3761 *Webb* Barry G., Zion in transformation; a literary approach to Isaiah: → 166, ᶠSheffield 1990, 65-84.

3762 **Widyapranawa** S. H., The Lord is Savior; faith in national crisis, a commentary on the Book of Isaiah 1-39: IntTComm. GR/E 1990, Eerdmans/Handsel. xiv-266 p. $15 pa. 0-8028-0338-5 / 1-871828-02-3 [OTAbs 14,119, L. *Boadt*].

E8.3 [Proto-]**Isaias 1-39,** *themata, versiculi.*

3763 *Ferrari* Leo C., Isaiah and the early AUGUSTINE: → 13, ᶠBAVEL T. van, AugLv 41 (1990s) 739-756.

3764 *Gitay* Y., Oratorical rhetoric; the question of prophetic language with special attention to Isaiah: AmstCah 10 (1989) 72-83 [< ZAW 103,125].

3765 **Høgenhaven** Jesper, Gott und Volk bei Jesaja ... 1988 → 4,3673; 5,3488: ᴿCBQ 52 (1990) 512s (P. L. *Redditt*); CritRR 3 (1990) 135-7 (W. E. *Lemke*); JTS 41 (1990) 559-561 (R. E. *Clements*); RHPR 70 (1990) 214s (J.-G. *Heintz*); TZBas 96 (1990) 283s (K. *Seybold*).

3766 **Høgenhaven** Jesper, The prophet Isaiah and Judaean foreign policy under Ahaz and Hezekiah: JNES 49 (1990) 351-4.

3766* **Jones** Ray C.ᴶ, Yahweh's judgment and kingship in the oracles of Isaiah ben Amoz: diss. Union Theol. Sem. Richmond 1990. 229 p. 01-11541. – DissA 51 (1990s) 3793-A.

3767 *Koch* Klaus, Damnation and salvation – prophetic metahistory and the rise of eschatology in the book of Isaiah: → 531, ExAud 6 (1990) 5-13.

3768 **Nielsen** Kirsten, There is hope for a tree ... Isaiah: JStOT supp 65, 1989 → 5,3491: ᴿBiblica 71 (1990) 262-4 (L. *Alonso Schökel*); CritRR 3 (1990) 167-9 (W. *Irwin*); ExpTim 101 (1989s) 28 (H. *Mowvley*); Interpretation 44 (1990) 416 . 418 (P. J. *Redditt*, also on FEWELL's Daniel); SvEx 55 (1990) 111-5 (Inger *Ljung*); TLZ 115 (1990) 736-8 (E.-J. *Waschke*); TsTKi 61 (1990) 68s (Terje *Stordalen*).

3769 *Torrell* Jean-Pierre, *Bouthillier* Denise, Quand saint THOMAS méditait sur le prophète Isaïe: RThom 90 (1990) 5-47.

3770 *Venter* P. M., Jesaja en die kanonvormingsproses vanaf die agste eeu voor Christus: HervTS 45 (1989) 527-553 [< OTAbs 14 (wrongly 13 at top of page), 74].

3771 ᴱ**Vermeylen** J., Livre d'Isaïe, Colloq.Bib.Lv 1987/9 → 5,614: ᴿComm-Sev 23 (1990) 99s (M. de *Burgos*); ETL 66 (1990) 399 (A. *Schoors*); NRT 112 (1990) 420-4 (J.-L. *Ska*); RHPR 70 (1990) 211-3 (J.-G. *Heintz*); RivB 38 (1990) 257s (A. *Bonora*).

3772 *Watts* John D. W., Is 1-33: Word **comm.** 24, 1985 → 2,2632 [Isaiah, Word–themes 1989 > 5,3481]: ᴿf.glT 20 (1989) 474-7 (L. *Laberge*); Themelios 15 (1989s) 29s (P. D. *Wegner*).

3773 *Willis* John R. [*šebet, matteh*] 'Rod' and 'staff' in Isaiah 1-39: OTEssays 3 (1990) 93-106.

3774 *Fang* Mark, ☉ Isaiah I-XII: ColcFuJen 85 (1990) 325-348.

3775 **Friesen** Ivan D., Composition and continuity in Isaiah 1-12: diss. St. Michael, ᴰ*Peckham* B. Toronto 1989. – RTLv 22, p. 588.

3776 **Sweeney** Marvin A., Isaiah 1-4 and the post-exilic understanding of the Isaianic tradition: BZAW 171, 1988 → 4,3679; 5,3498: ᴿArTGran 53 (1990) 317s (J. L. *Sicre*); Bijdragen 51 (1990) 85 (W. *Beuken*); BO 47 (1990) 755-763 (R. *Bickert*); CBQ 52 (1990) 137s (C. R. *Seitz*); RHPR 70 (1990) 215-7 (J.-G. *Heintz*); VT 40 (1990) 376 (H. G. M. *Williamson*).

3777 *Cholewiński* Alfred †, ☉ 'Postępujmy w światłości Jahwe' (Iz 2,5) ... on true disarmament: RuBi 42 (1989) 321-8 [394-6, memorial and bibliog., J. *Sulowski*).

3778 *Marx* Alfred, Ésaïe II 20, une signature Karaïte?: VT 40 (1990) 232-7.

3779 *Brown* William P., The so-called refrain in Isaiah 5:25-30 and 9:7-10:4: CBQ 52 (1990) 432-443.

3780 *Bühring* Gernot, *Uhlig* Siegbert, Der eliminierte 'Himmel'; zur ökumenischen Relevanz des Wortlautes des 'Sanctus': OstkSt 38 (1989) 43-56.

3781 *Diu* Isabelle, [Is 6,1] ÉRASME traducteur de St. Jean CHRYSOSTOME d'après les 'Homélies sur Ozias': Positions de thèses [P 1989, École des Chartes] 51-59 [< RHE 85,853].

3782 *Clements* R. E., The Immanuel prophecy of Isa. 7:10-17 and its messianic interpretation: ➤ 147, FRENDTORFF R., Hebr. Bibel 1990, 225-240.

3783 **Irvine** Stuart A., Isaiah, Ahaz, and the Syro-Ephraimitic crisis: SBL diss. 123 [Emory 1989, DHayes J.]. Atlanta 1990, Scholars. $32; sb./pa. $21. 1-55540-447-2.

3784 **Kamesar** Adam, The virgin of Isaiah 7:14; the philological argument from the second to the fifth century [< diss. Oxford 1987]: JTS 41 (1990) 51-75.

3785 **Laato** Antti, Who is Immanuel? [diss. Åbo] 1988 ➤ 4,3687; 5,3518: RCBQ 52 (1990) 521s (J. *Limburg*); JTS 41 (1990) 140s (R. E. *Clements*); VT 40 (1990) 247 (H. G. M. *Williamson*).

3786 *Eshel* Hanon, Isaiah VIII 23; an historical-geographical analogy: VT 40 (1990) 104-9.

3787 *Gregor* Barbara, Das '*galul* der Völker'– Jes 8,23: BibNot 51 (1990) 11s.

3788 *Auret* Adrian [5,3515!] Another look at û-mᵉśôś [rejoice 'despite' not 'for'] in Isaiah 8:6: OTEssays 3 (1990) 107-114.

3789 *Kruger* Paul A., Another look at Isa 9:7-20: JNWS 15 (1989) 127-141.

3790 *Gryson* Roger, Les six dons du Saint-Esprit; la version hiéronymienne d'Isaïe 11,2.3: Biblica 71 (1990) 395-400.

3791 *a)* *Sonnet* Jean-Pierre, 'Tu diras ce jour-là' (Is 12,1); *b)* *Pelletier* Anne-Marie, L'écriture du Livre d'Isaïe et l'élaboration théologique du temps de l'histoire: ➤ 541*, L'Écriture âme 1989/90, 163-187 / 189-206.

3792 *Gosse* Bernard, Oracles contre les nations et structures comparées des livres d'Isaïe [13-23 ...] d'Ézéchiel [25-32 ...]: BibNot 54 (1990) 19-21.

3793 **Gosse** B., Isaïe 13,1-14,23 ... oracles contre les nations: OBO 78, 1988 ➤ 4,3691; 5,3525: RBO 47 (1990) 196-8 (P. *Höffken* gives 8-line title); ExpTim 101 (1989s) 26 (R. *Coggins*); JBL 109 (1990) 124-6 (M. A. *Sweeney*); TR 86 (1990) 364-8 (J. *Vermeylen*, franç.).

3794 **Bertoluci** José M., [Is 14,12-15; Ezek 28,12-19] The son of the morning and the guardian cherub in the context of the controversy between good and evil: diss. Andrews, DShea W. – Berrien Springs MI 1985. – AndrUnS 28 (1990) 149.

3795 *Gosse* Bernard, Isaïe 21,11-12 et Isaïe 60-62: BibNot 53 (1990) 21s.

3796 **Johnson** Dan G., From chaos to restoration; an integrative reading of Isaiah 24-27 ['Integrative reading' seems to mean: against the four interpreters who lop off portions to fit the pattern; against *Wachstumsprozess* (but he also claims a part is added later)]: JStOT supp. 61, 1988 ➤ 4,3696; 5,3529: RCBQ 52 (1990) 540-2 (M. A. *Sweeney*); Interpretation 44 (1990) 418 . 420 (B. C. *Ollenburger*); JBL 109 (1990) 334s (C. R. *Seitz*); Themelios 16 (1990s) 24 (H. G. M. *Williamson*); TLZ 115 (1990) 498s (E. *Bosshard*).

3797 *Wodecki* Bernard, ❷ Das messianisch-eschatologische Gastmahl der Völker auf dem Sion (Jes 25,6-9): STWsz 27,2 (1989) 31-52; deutsch 53.

3798 **O'Kane** M. J., Isaiah 28-33; a literary and contextual analysis: diss. Edinburgh 1989. 496 p. BRD-90368. – DissA 51 (1990s) 2035-A.

3799 *Floss* Johannes P., Biblische Theologie als Sprecherin der 'gefährlichen Erinnerung' dargestellt an Jes 28,7-12?: BibNot 54 (1990) 60-80.

3800 *Baez Ortega* Silvio J., Un texto de Adviento; Is. 29,15-24: Teresianum 41 (1990) 161-180.

3801 *Gosse* Bernard, Isaïe 34-35; le châtiment d'Édom et des nations, salut pour Sion: ZAW 102 (1990) 396-404.

3802 *Donner* Herbert, 'Forscht in der Schrift Jahwes und lest!' [Is 34,16]; ein Beitrag zum Verständnis der israelitischen Prophetie: ZTK 87 (1990) 285-298.

3803 *a) Coetzee* J.H., The 'song of Hezekiah' (Is 38:9-20); a doxology of judgement from the exilic period; – *b) Venter* P.M., Isaiah and Jerusalem: OTEssays 2/3 (1989) 13-26 / 27-35.

E8.4   **Deutero-Isaias 40-52:** *commentarii, themata, versiculi.*

3804 **Barstad** H.M., A way in the wilderness; the 'second Exodus' in the message of Second Isaiah: JSS Mg 12. Manchester 1989, Univ. xii-148 p. 0-9057-8858-9 [BL 91,63, J. *Sawyer*).

3805 **Berquist** Jon L., The social setting of early postexilic prophecy: diss. Vanderbilt, ^D*Harrelson* W. Nv 1989. 344 p. 90-17608. – DissA 51 (1990s) 528s-A; RelStR 17,193.

3806 **Birch** Bruce C., Singing the Lord's song; a study of Isaiah 40-55: Lay Bible Studies. Nv 1990, Abingdon. vi-137 p. $5 pa. 0-687-38551-2 [OTAbs 14,429, J.W. *Wright*].

3807 *Currie* John B., Elihu and Deutero-Isaiah; a study in literary dependence: ProcGLM 10 (1990) 31-38.

3808 **Grimm** Werner, 'Fürchte dich nicht'; ein exegetischer Zugang zum Seelsorgepotential einer deuterojesajanischen Gattung: Fur HS 23/298, 1986 → 3,3467: ^RRHPR 70 (1990) 236s (J.-G. *Heintz*).

3809 ^{TE}**Grimm** Werner, *Dittert* Kurt, Jesaja 40-55; das Trostbuch Gottes; Deutero-Jesaja, Deutung – Wirkung – Gegenwart: Calwer BK. Stu 1990, Calwer. 96 + 146 p. DM 78. 3-7668-3051-1; -0-3 [BL 91,56, A. *Gelston*].

3810 **Hermisson** Hans-Jürgen, Deuterojesaja; BK AT 11/7 [Jes 45,8-25]. Neuk 1987, Neuk-V. 80 p. 3-7887-1258-9.

3811 **Hessler** Eva, Das Heilsdrama; der Weg zur Weltherrschaft Jahwes (Jes 40-55): RelWTSt 2, 1988 → 5,3541: ^RTLZ 115 (1990) 16-18 (R.G. *Kratz*: problem of her 1960 dissertation).

3812 *Jeppesen* Knud, From 'you, my servant' to 'the hand of the Lord is with my servants'; a discussion of Is 40-66: ScandJOT (1990,1) 113-129.

3813 **Kraus** Hans-Joachim, Das Evangelium der unbekannten Propheten, Jesaja 40-66: KleinBiblB. Neuk 1990. vii-263 p. DM 39 [TR 87,249]. 3-7887-1346-1.

3814 **Leene** H., De vroegere en de nieuwe dingen bij Deuterojesaja ^D1987 → 5,3544: ^RCBQ 52 (1990) 127s (W.A. *Vogels*); JBL 109 (1990) 129s (J.C. *VanderKam*).

3815 *Merendino* Rosario P., La novità operata da Dio; meditazione sul tema del ritorno in Is 40-53: → 325*b*, ParSpV 22 (1990) 35-49.

3816 **Schuller** Eileen, Post-exilic prophets: MessageBSp 4. Wilmington 1988, Glazier. 192 p. 0-89453-554-4; pa. -70-6. – ^RBibTB 20 (1990) 174s (Chris A. *Franke*); CBQ 52 (1990) 729-731 (P.J. *Griffin*).

3817 *Watts* Rikki E., Consolation or confrontation ? Isaiah 40-55 and the delay of the new Exodus: TyndB 41 (1990) 31-59.

3818 **Wilson** A., The nations in Deutero-Isaiah; a study on composition and structure ^D1986 → 3,3478: ^RZAW 102 (1990) 167s (H.-C. *Schmitt*: 'über Nationalismus und Universalismus bei Dt-Jes').

3819 *Zobel* H.-J., 'Alt' und 'neu' in der Verkundigung des Propheten Deuterojesaja: Greifswalder Universitätsreden NF 57 (1990) 18-27 [< ZAW 103,277].

3820 *a) Seitz* Christopher R., The divine council; temporal transition and new prophecy in the book of Isaiah [40,1-11]; – *b) Laato* Antti, The composition of Isaiah 40-55: JBL 109 (1990) 239-247 / 207-228.
3821 *Wieringen* Archibald van, Jesaja 40,1-11; eine drama-linguistische Lesung von Jesaja 6 her: BibNot 49 (1989) 82-93.
3822 *Silva* A.A. da, Jesaja 40:1-2 – suiwer evangelie!: HervTS 46 (1990) 656-671 [< OTAbs 14,194 'pure gospel'].
3823 *Cazelles* Henri, Sur *mdl* à Ugarit, en Is 40,15 et Hab 3,4: → 164, FSEGERT S., *Sopher* 1990, 49-52.
3823* *Kiesow* Klaus, [Is 41,1-4.21-29] Deuterojesajas Prozess gegen die Götter – oder Durchbruch zum Ein-Gott-Glauben: BLtg 63 (1990) 96-99.
3824 *Helewa* Giovanni, 'Per la mia gloria li ho creati' (Is 42,7): Teresianum 40 (1989) 435-478.
3825 *Willmes* Bernd, Gott erlöst sein Volk; Gedanken zum Gottesbild Deuterojesajas nach Jes 43,1-7: BibNot 51 (1990) 61-93.
3826 *Steck* Odil H., Beobachtungen zu Jesaja 49,14-26: BibNot 55 (1990) 36-46.
3827 *Avishur* Yitshaq, ⊕ Is 50,8: Lešonenu 52 (1987s) 18-25.
3828 *Steck* Odil H., Beobachtungen zu den Zion-Texten in Jesaja 51-54; ein redaktionsgeschichtlicher Versuch: BibNot 46 (1989) 58-90.
3829 *a) Steck* Odil H., Zions Tröstung; Beobachtungen und Fragen zu Jesaja 51,1-11; – *b) Albertz* Rainer, Das Deuterojesajabuch als Fortschreibung der Jesaja-Prophetie: → 147, FRENDTORFF R., Hebr. Bibel 1990, 251-276 / 241-250.
3830 *Marböck* Johannes, Exodus zum Zion; zum Glaubensweg der Gemeinde nach einigen Texten des Jesajabuches [52,7-12; 60ss; 35]: → 146, FREINELT H., At. Botschaft 1990, 163-179.
3831 *Watts* R.E., The meaning of *'alāw yiqpᵉsu mᵉlākîm pîhem* in Isaiah LII 15: VT 40 (1990) 327-335.

E8.5 *Isaiae 53ss, Carmina Servi YHWH:* **Servant-Songs.**

3831* *a) Collins* John J., Nebuchadnezzar and the Kingdom of God – deferred eschatology in the Jewish diaspora; – *b) Kippenberg* Hans G., Geheime Offenbarungsbücher und Loyalitätskonflikt im Antiken Judentum; – *c) Assmann* J., Der 'leidende Gerechte' im alten Ägypten: → 38*, Loyalitätskonflikte 1990, 252-7 / 258-268 / 203-224.
3832 *Haag* E., Der Gottesknecht als Jünger Jahwes; Tradition und Redaktion in Jes 50,4-9: → 176, FTHOMA A., Der menschenfreundliche Gott 1990, 11-35.
3833 *Renaud* B., La mission du Serviteur en Is 42,1-4; RevSR 64 (1990) 101-113.
3834 *Betz* Otto, Die Übersetzungen von Jes 53 (LXX, Targum) und die Theologia Crucis des Paulus [ineditum]: → 200, Jesus II (1990) 197-216 [→ 6140, *Kleinknecht* K.-T., Paulus als 'der leidende Gerechtfertigte' ²1988].
3835 *Gelston* A., Isaiah 52:13 - 53:12; an eclectic text and a supplementary note on the Hebrew manuscript Kennicott 96: JSS 35 (1990) 187-211.

3836 **Haag** Herbert, Der Gottesknecht bei Deuterojesaja: ErtFor 233, 1985
→ 1,3537 ... 4,3722: ᴿBLtg 63 (1990) 186s (L. *Schwienhorst-Schönberger*).

3837 *Kiesow* Klaus, Die Gottesknechtlieder – Israels Auftrag für die
Menschheit: BLtg 63 (1990) 156-9.

3838 **Koenig** Jean, Oracles et liturgies de l'exil 1988 → 4,3713; 5,3562:
ᴿBLitEc 91 (1990) 141 (M. *Delcor*: fragile); CBQ 52 (1990) 324-6 (C.
Stuhlmueller); ÉTRel 65 (1990) 270s (D. *Lys*: passionnant); JBL 109
(1990) 333s (W.A. *Vogels*); JSS 35 (1990) 501-3 (H.-M. *Barstad*); RHPR
70 (1990) 229-235 (J.-G. *Heintz*); RivB 38 (1990) 250-2 (A. *Bonora*).

3839 *McLain* Charles E., A comparison of ancient and medieval Jewish interpretations of the Suffering Servant in Isaiah: CalvaryB 6 (1990) 2-31.

3840 **Matheus** F., Singt dem Herrn ein neues Lied; die Hymnen Deuterojesajas [Diss. Heidelberg 1987, ᴰ*Rendtorff* R.]: SBS 141. Stu 1990,
KBW. 192 p.; foldout. DM 38 [ZAW 103,159, H.-C. *Schmitt*].

3841 **Pákozdy** László M., Ⓜ *Az Ebed Jahweh* [... Deuterojesaja teologiája
kortörténeti és vallastörténeti háttérben]. (in) Is 40-55 [2 ed. with
epilogue]. Budapest 1989, Ráday Kollegium. – ᴿTSzem 33 (1990) 122-5 (S.
Szathmáry).

3842 *Varo* Francisco, El cuarto canto del Siervo; balance de diez años de
investigación: ScripTPamp 22 (1990) 517-533 [W(H)YBRAY R., CLINES
D., BEAUCHAMP P.; bibliografía 533-8].

3843 **Glassner** Paul A., Jesaja 54, Vision eines auf Verheissung gegründeten
Jerusalem: Diss. ᴰ*Füglister* N. Salzburg 1990. 340 p. – RTLv 22, p. 588.

3844 *Davis* Ellen F., A strategy of delayed comprehension; Isaiah LIV 15:
VT 40 (1990) 217-221.

3845 *Boyce* Richard N., Isaiah 55:6-13, expository: Interpretation 44 (1990)
56-60.

E8.6   [Trito-] Isaias 56-66.

3846 **Beuken** W.A.M., Jesaia Deel III A (56,1-63,6) – B (63,7-66,24, with
Index also for I-II): PredikOT. Nijkerk 1989, Callenbach. 282 p.; 178 p.
ƒ72 + 65; sb. ƒ59,50 (? each). 90-266-0204-7; -5-7 [BL 91,53, P.R.
Ackroyd]. – ᴿTsTNijm 30 (1990) 306 (A. *Schoors*).

3847 **Koenen** Klaus, Ethik und Eschatologie im Tritojesajabuch; eine
literarkritische und redaktionsgeschichtliche Studie [ev. Diss. Tübingen
1987s, ᴰ*Hermisson* H.]: WM 62. Neuk 1990, Neuk-V. viii-275 p. [ZAW
103,299, H.-C. *Schmitt*]. 3-7887-1308-9.

3848 **Sekine** S., Die tritojesajanische Sammlung (Jes 56-66) redaktions-
geschichtlich untersucht [ev. Diss. München 1984, ᴰ*Jeremias* Jörg]: BZAW
175, 1989 → 5,3574: ᴿExpTim 102 (1990s) 24s (R. *Coggins*: against K.
ELLIGER's substantial unity); ZAW 102 (1990) 162 (H.-C. *Schmitt*).

3849 *Ackerman* Susan, [Is 57,3-13] Sacred sex, sacrifice and death; understanding a prophetic poem: BR 6,1 (1990) 38-44; color. ill.

3850 **Yoder-Neufeld** Thomas R., God and saints at war [→ 5,3579]; the
transformation and democratization of the divine warrior in Isaiah 59,
Wisdom of Solomon 5, 1 Thessalonians 5, and Ephesians 6: diss. Harvard.
– HarvTR 82 (1989) 481s.

3851 *Burghardt* Walter J., Isaiah 60:1-7, expository: Interpretation 44 (1990)
306-400.

3852 **Langer** Birgit, Gott als 'Licht' in Israel und Mesopotamien; eine Studie
zu Jes 60,1-3.19: ÖBSt 7, 1989 → 5,3580: ᴿBL (1990) 83 (G.I. *Davies*);
NRT 111 (1989) 932s (J.-L. *Ska*); ZMissRW 74 (1990) 310s (H. *Niehr*).

3853 *Grelot* Pierre, Sur Isaïe LXI; la première consécration d'un grand-prêtre: RB 97 (1990) 414-431; Eng. 414.

3854 *Gosse* Bernard, Détournement de la vengeance du Seigneur contre Édom et les nations en Isa 63,1-6: ZAW 102 (1990) 105-110.

3855 *a) Webster* Edwin C., The rhetoric of Isaiah 63-65; – *b) Beuken* W. A. M., The main theme of Trito-Isaiah, 'the Servants of YHWH': JStOT 47 (1990) 89-102 / 67-87.

3856 *Williamson* H. G. M., Isaiah 63,7-64,11, exilic lament or post-exilic protest?: ZAW 102 (1990) 48-58.

3857 **Fischer** Irmtraud, Wo ist Jahwe? Jes 63,7-...: SBB 19, 1989 ↠ 5,3583: ᴿTR 86 (1990) 451s (E. *Zenger*).

3858 **Ruiten** Jacobus van, Een begin zonder einde; de doorwerking van Jesaja 65,17 in de intertestamentaire literatuur en in het Nieuwe Testament [diss. ᴰ*Beuken* 1990, Amst KU. 247 p. – TsTNijm 31,88; RTLv 22,590]. Sliedrecht 1990, Merweboek. viii-247 p. *f* 35.

3859 *Buchheit* Vinzenz, [Is 65,25] Tierfriede bei HIERONYMUS und seinen Vorgängern: ↠ 100*, ᶠKÖTTING B., JbAC 33 (1990) 21-35.

3860 *Goergen* A., Das grosse Sammeln, das es noch nie gab; der Ausgang einer prophetischen Vision (Jesaja Kapitel 66): TGegw 33 (1990) 98-106.

E8.7 Jeremias.

3861 **Alba Cecilia** Amparo, Jeremías: Biblia babilónica, TEstCisn 41, 1987 ↠ 3,3510; 5,3585: ᴿHebSt 31 (1990) 119-122 (E. J. *Revell*, also on DIEZ-MACHO Salmos-Prov).

3862 **Brueggemann** Walter, To pluck... Jer 1-25: IntTComm 1988 ↠ 4,3746; 5,3586: ᴿAnglTR 71 (1989) 434-6 (D. F. *Morgan*); BibTB 20 (1990) 169s (L. A. *Sinclair*); BL (1990) 52s (R. P. *Carroll*: praise); HebSt 31 (1990) 113-6 (A. R. *Diamond*); Interpretation 44 (1990) 85s (A. J. *Everson*); TLZ 115 (1990) 103s (G. *Wanke*).

3863 **Carroll** Robert P., [↠ 3879] Jeremiah: OTLibrary, 1986 ↠ 2,7118... 5,3587: ᴿJBL 109 (1990) 126-9 (J. G. *Janzen*).

3864 **Clements** R. E., Jeremiah: Interpretation comm. 1988 ↠ 4,3749; 0-8042- 3127-3: ᴿBL (1990) 53 (R. J. *Coggins*); TS 51 (1990) 172 (M. D. *Guinan*).

3865 **Goldman** Amir P., Origines littéraires de la forme massorétique du livre de Jérémie: Diss. FrS 1989. – BZ 34,156.

3866 **Herrmann** Siegfried [↠ 3880], Jeremia: BK AT 12/1, 1986 ↠ 4,3754; 5,3590: ᴿRTPhil 122 (1990) 272 (G. *Lasserre*).

3867 **Holladay** W. L., Jeremias II (ch. 26-52): Hermeneia Comm. 1989 ↠ 5,3591: ᴿBL (1990) 55 (R. P. *Carroll*); CurrTMiss 17 (1990) 313s (S. A. *Knapp*); Interpretation 44 (1990) 410-412 (W. *Brueggemann*: well done, though his historical approach is open to some challenges); SWJT 33,2 (1990s) 52 (H. B. *Hunt*, 1); TS 51 (1990) 733-6 (L. *Boadt*).

3868 **Liwak** R., Der Prophet und die Geschichte... Jer: BW 121, 1987 ↠ 3,3828; 4,3760: ᴿNedTTs 44 (1990) 159s (B. *Becking*).

3869 **McKane** W., ICC Jeremiah I, 1986 ↠ 2,2728... 5,3592: ᴿNorTTs 90 (1989) 240-2 (H. M. *Barstad*).

3870 **Oosterhoff** B. J., Jeremia I (cap. 1-10): CommOT. Kampen 1990, Kok. 335 p. *f* 79,50. 90-242-0837-8. – ᴿOTAbs 13 (1990) 315 (C. T. *Begg*).

3871 **Pérez Castro** F., 'realizada por **Muñoz Abad** Carmen & 3 *al*.', Jeremias: CodProfCairo 5, 1987 ↠ 3,3533: ᴿJQR 81 (1990s) 159s (P. *Cassuto*).

3872 **Reynolds** B., Jean CALVIN, Sermons on Jeremiah: TStRel 46. Lewiston NY 1990, Mellen. viii-299 p. $70 [RHE 85,391*].

3873 **Soderlund** S., Greek text of Jeremiah 1985 → 2,2741 ... 5,3595: ᴿBSept-
Cog 22 (1989) 16-47 (J.G. *Janzen* defends himself and Tov against
Greenspoon).

3874 **Strobel** A., Geremia Lam. Bar.; cordoglio per Gerusalemme 1989
→ 5,3596: ᴿLaurentianum 31 (1990) 603s (F. *Raurell*); Salesianum 52
(1990) 434 (M. *Cimosa*).

3875 *Tov* Emanuel, The Jeremiah scrolls from Cave 4; → 527, RQum 14,54
(1989s) 189-206.

3876 **Bak Dong Hyun,** Klagender Gott – klagende Menschen; Studien zur
Klage im Jeremiabuch [Diss. B 1989, Kirchliche Hochschule, ᴰ*Welten* P.]:
BZAW 193. B 1990, de Gruyter. xiii-273 p. [ZAW 103,292, H.-C.
Schmitt]. 3-11-012341-X.

3877 **Bourguet** Daniel, Des métaphores de Jérémie: ÉtBN 9, 1987 → 3,3512 ...
5,3601: ᴿBiblica 71 (1990) 106-8 (P. *Bovati*); CBQ 52 (1990) 311-3 (J.G.
Williams: 'Confessions' understandably but regrettably bypassed); RHPR
70 (1990) 218-225 (J.-G. *Heintz*, avec longue bibliographie supplémentaire
225-9).

3878 *Bovati* Pietro, Dio protagonista del ritorno in Geremia: → 325*b*,
ParSpV 22 (1990) 17-34.

3879 **Carroll** Robert P., Jeremiah [comm. 1986 → 3863 supra]; OT **guides** 1989
→ 5,3602: ᴿETL 66 (1990) 187 (J. *Lust*: learned ignorance; frequently 'we
do not know': for scholars 'absolutely refreshing'; 'for the beginner it will
be rather confusing').

3880 **Herrmann** Siegfried, [→ 3866] Jeremias; der Prophet und das Buch:
ErtFor 271. Da 1990, Wiss. xiii-233 p. 3-534-09047-0.

3881 **Holladay** William L., [→ 3867] Jeremiah, a fresh reading [completely new
reconstruction of Jeremiah's life and work from his 1974 volume]. NY
1990, Pilgrim. xi-177 p. $13 pa. 0-8298-0848-5 [TDig 38,66]. – ᴿSWJT
33,2 (1990s) 54s (D.G. *Kent*).

3882 *Ibáñez Arana* Andrés, Jeremías y el Deuteronomio: ScripV 37 (1990)
266-341.

3883 **Kilpp** Nelson, Niederreissen und Aufbauen [Diss. 1987, → 4,3759]: BTSt
13. Neuk 1990. Neuk-V. 195 p. DM 38. 3-7887-1294-5. – ᴿExpTim 102
(1990s) 181 (R. *Coggins*: the author was born and teaches in South
America, but this is not liberation theology); ZAW 102 (1990) 447 (G.
Wenke).

3884 **Odashima** Taro, Heilsworte im Jeremiabuch; Untersuchungen zu ihrer
vordeuteronomistischen Bearbeitung [Diss. Bochum 1984, ᴰ*Herrmann* S.]:
BW 125, 1989 → 5,3616: ᴿBL (1990) 88 (R.P. *Carroll*); JBL 109 (1990)
703-5 (J.M. *Berridge*); TLZ 115 (1990) 258s (D. *Vieweger*); TüTQ 170
(1990) 224s (W. *Gross*).

3885 *Reynolds* Blair, God's power in Calvin's sermons on Jeremiah and
Micah; classical theism versus prophetic exegesis: ProcGLM 10 (1990)
66-78.

3886 **Seitz** Christopher R., Theology in conflict; reactions to the exile in Jer:
BZAW 176, 1989 → 5,1622: ᴿNBL (1990) 91 (R. *Davidson*); RHPR 70
(1990) 256s (P. de *Robert*); ZAW 102 (1990) 313 (H.-C. *Schmitt*); ZkT 112
(1990) 101 (G. *Fischer*).

3887 *Seitz* Christopher R., Mose als Prophet; Redaktionsthemen und
Gesamtstruktur des Jeremiabuches [Gastvortrag Marburg 1988]: BZ 34
(1990) 234-245.

3888 **Unterman** Jeremiah, From repentance to redemption; Jeremiah's thought in transition [relation to Dt]: JStOT supp. 54, 1987 → 3,3543... 5,3628*: ᴿCBQ 52 (1990) 138-40 (J. R. *Lundbom*: thesis unacceptable; not worth the trouble); JQR 81 (1990s) 213-5 (M. A. *Sweeney*).
3889 *Weippert* Helga, Vier neue Arbeiten zum Jeremiabuch [RIDOUARD A. 1983; POLK T. 1984; MOTTU H. 1985; DIAMOND A. 1987]: BZ 34 (1990) 95-104.

3890 **Biddle** Mark E., A redaction history of Jeremiah 2:1-4:2 [Inaug.-Diss. Zürich 1987, ᴰ*Schmid* H.]: ATANT 77. Z 1990, Theol.-V. xii-244 p. Fs 38. 3-290-10078-2 [BL 91,55, R. P. *Carroll*: excellent].
3891 **Cloete** Walter T. W., Versification and syntax in Jeremiah 2-25; syntactical constraints in Hebrew colometry: SBL diss. 117, 1989 → 5,3634: ᴿExpTim 102 (1990s) 23s (C. S. *Rodd*); TüTQ 170 (1990) 226s (W. *Gross*); ZAW 102 (1990) 441 (G. *Wenke*).
3892 **Althann** Robert, Philological... Jer 4-6; BibOrPont 38, 1983 → 64,3571 ... 3,3549: ᴿAulaO 8 (1990) 270s (G. del *Olmo Lete*); JNES 49 (1990) 365s (D. *Pardee*: some notable errors).
3893 *Stachel* Günter, 'Sta in porta domus Domini et loquere verbum'; die Predigt 19 Eckharts und der Spruch Jeremia 7,2: GeistL 63 (1990) 405-426.
3894 *Delcor* Mathias, Le culte de la 'Reine du Ciel' selon Jer 7,18; 44, 17-19.25 et ses survivances; aspects de la religion populaire féminine aux alentours de l'Exil en Juda et dans les communautés juives d'Égypte [< ᶠJ. van der *Ploeg*, AOAT 211 (1982) 101-122]: → 219*, Environnement 1990, 138-159.
3895 *Haag* Ernst, Zion und Schilo; traditionsgeschichtliche Parallelen in Jeremia 7 und Psalm 78: → 146, ᶠREINELT H., At. Botschaft 1990, 85-115.
3896 *O'Day* Gail R., Jeremiah 9:22-23 and 1 Corinthians 1:26-31; a study in intertextuality: JBL 109 (1990) 259-267.
3897 *Althann* Robert, The inverse construct chain and Jer 10:13; 51:16: JNWS 15 (1989) 7-13.
3898 **Baumgartner** Walter, Jeremiah's poems of lament [11; 15; 17; 18; 20...; Klagegedichte → 4,3742*! (not Lam) BZAW 32, 1917], ᵀ*Orton* David E., 1988: ᴿCBQ 52 (1990) 709s (K. M. *O'Connor*); JTS 41 (1990) 563s (R. E. *Clements*).
3899 **Diamond** A. R., [Jer 11-20] *a*) The confessions of Jeremiah in context: JStOT supp. 45, 1987 → 3,3521... 5,3644: ᴿWestJT 52 (1990) 370-2 (R. S. *Hess*); – *b*) Jeremiah's Confessions in the LXX and MT: VT 40 (1990) 33-50.
3900 **Mottu** Henry, Geremia; una protesta contro la sofferenza; lettura delle 'Confessioni' [Confessions de Jr 1985 → 3,3553] ᵀ*Davite* Franco: Parola per l'uomo d'oggi 7. T 1990, Claudiana. 197 p. Lit. 23.000. 88-7016-106-4.
3901 **O'Connor** Kathleen M., The confessions of Jeremiah: SBL diss 84, 1988 → 4,3784; 5,3646: ᴿCBQ 52 (1990) 129-131 (L. *Stulman*: serious even if not convincing); HebSt 31 (1990) 226-8 (W. *Brueggemann*); Interpretation 44 (1990) 203s (G. *Gerbrandt*); JRel 70 (1990) 85-87 (M. L. *Barre*).
3902 **Pohlmann** K. F., Die Ferne Gottes – Studien zum Jeremiabuch; Beiträge zu den 'Konfessionen' im Jeremiabuch und ein Versuch zur Frage nach den Anfängen der Jeremiatradition: BZAW 179, 1989 → 5,3647: ᴿBL (1990) 89 (R. P. *Carroll*); CBQ 52 (1990) 536-8 (C. T. *Begg*: a challenge);

ETL 66 (1990) 186 (J. *Lust*); JBL 109 (1990) 705-7 (Kathleen M. *O'Connor*); TPQ 138 (1990) 181s (F. *Hubmann*).

3903 **Smith** Mark S., The laments of Jeremiah and their contexts; a literary and redactional study of Jeremiah 11-20: SBL Mg 42. Atlanta 1990, Scholars. xxi-92 p. 1-55540-460-X; pa. -1-8 [BL 91,160].

3904 *Lerner* Meron B., ☉ *š'wr* [read *ma'or* in Lam. Rabba Proem 2, on Jer 16,11]: Lešonenu 53 (1988s) 287-290; Eng. IVs.

3905 *Davies* Philip R., Joking in Jeremiah 18: → 367, E*Radday*, Humour 1990, 191-201.

3906 *Bezuidenhout* L.C., 'Sing to Jahweh!... Cursed be the day on which I was born!'; a paradoxical harmony in Jeremiah 20:7-18: HervTS 46 (1990) 359-366 [< OTAbs 14,76].

3907 *Bakon* Shimon, [Jer 20,7] Jeremiah, a tragedy; thou hast enticed me, and I was enticed: JBQ 19 (1990s) 176-185.

3909 a) *Hermisson* Hans-Jürgen, [Jer 21ss] Die 'Königsspruch'-Sammlung im Jeremiabuch — von der Anfangs- zur Endgestalt; – b) *Hardmeier* Christoff, Jer 29,24-32 — 'eine geradezu unüberbietbare Konfusion' [*Duhm* B.]?; Vorurteil und Methode in der exegetischen Forschung: → 147, F*RENDTORFF* R., Hebr. Bibel 1990, 277-299 / 301-317.

3910 *Schweizer* Harald, Jeremias Attacke gegen die Berufskollegen (Jer 23,9-32): → 8*, F*ASSFALG* J. 1990, 321-334.

3911 *Alonso Schökel* Luis M., [Ger 22,13-19; 7,7-11...]: La coscienza dell'obiezione; considerazioni bibliche: CC 141 (1990,3) 45-51.

3912 *Christensen* Duane L., In quest of the autograph of the Book of Jeremiah; a study of Jeremiah 25 in relation to Jer. 46-51: JEvTS 33 (1990) 145-153 [< ZAW 103,434].

3913 *Hirth* Volkmar, [Jer 35, Rekabiter] Der Wandel des Arbeitsverständnisses in Altisrael beim Übergang zur Königszeit: BibNot 54 (1990) 9-13.

3914 *Dearman* J. Andrew, My servants the scribes; composition and context in Jeremiah 36: JBL 109 (1990) 403-421.

3915 *Smelik* K.A.D., Ostracon, schrijftafel of bockrol? Jeremia 36, Jesaja 30:8 en twee ostraca uit Saqqara: NedTTs 44 (1990) 198-207; Eng. 245; p. 287, correction for Text A, p. 203.

3916 **Hardmeier** Christof, [→ 3097] Prophetie im Streit vor dem Untergang Judas; erzählkommunikative Studien zur Entstehungssituation der Jesaja- und Jeremiaerzählungen in II Reg 18-20 und Jer 37-40 [Diss. 1987s → 4,2974; 5,3664]: BZAW 197. B 1990, de Gruyter. xvii-506 p. 3-11-011735-5. – R*TüTQ* 170 (1990) 148-150 (II.-J. *Stipp*).

3916* *Bogaert* P.-M., [Jér 40,4; 41,2 ∥ 2 R 25,25] La libération de Jérémie et le meurtre de Godolias; le texte court (LXX) et la rédaction longue (TM): → 70, F*HANHART* R. 1990, 312-322.

3917 *Gosse* Bernard, Jérémie XLV et la place du recueil d'oracles contre les nations dans le livre de Jérémie: VT 40 (1990) 145-151.

3918 **Abrego** José M., Jeremías [36-45] y el final del reino 1983 → 64,3599 ... 4,3804: R*TR* 86 (1990) 15 (E.S. *Gerstenberger*).

3919 *Dicou* A., De structuur van de versameling Profetieën over de volken in Jeremia 46-51: AmstCah 12,84-87 [< ZAW 103,126].

E8.8 **Lamentationes,** *Threni;* **Baruch.**

Bonora Antonio, Lamentazioni 1989 → 4134.

3920 *Helberg* J.L., Land in the book of Lamentations: ZAW 102 (1990) 372-385.

3921 *Krupp* Michael, Die jemenitische Version des 'Midrasch Echa': ➤ 147, ᶠRENDTORFF R., Hebr. Bibel 1990, 479-487.
3922 **Neusner** Jacob, Lamentations Rabbah, [➤ a219] an analytical translation: BrownJudSt 193. Atlanta 1989, Scholars. xvi-370 p. $70. 1-55540-412-X [NTAbs 34,273].
3923 *Wanke* Gunther, Klagelieder (Threni): ➤ 857, TRE 19 (1990) 227-230.
3924 **Westermann** Claus, Die Klagelieder; Forschungsgeschichte und Auslegung. Neuk 1990, Neuk.-V. 192 p. DM 29,80. 3-7887-1307-0 [BL 91, 101, I. W. *Provan*: essential, though claiming 'not literature, not theological'].
3925 *Zlotowitz* Meir, Eikha, les lamentations, commentaire rabbinique, intr. *Scherman* Nosson, ᵀ*Gugenheim* Jean-J.: La Bible commentée. P 1987, Colbo. (xlviii-) 141 + 31 p. [KirSef 62 (1988s) p. 486].
3926 *Provan* Iain W., *a*) Reading texts against an historical background; the case of Lamentations 1: ScandJOT (1990,1) 130-143; – *b*) Feasts, booths and gardens (Thr 2,6a). ZAW 102 (1990) 254s.
3927 *Gous* I. G. P., Lamentations 5 and the translation of verse 22: OTEssays 3 (1990) 287-302.

3928 *Fernández Marcos* N., Apocalipsis griego de Baruc; introducción, traducción [primera en español] y notas; Sefarad 50 (1990) 191-209.
3929 *a*) *Klijn* A. F. J., Recent developments in the study of the Syriac Apocalypse of Baruch; – *b*) *Leemhuis* Fred, The Arabic version of the Apocalypse of Baruch; a Christian text?: JPseud 4 (1989) 3-17 / 19-26 [< TR 87,74].
3930 **Willett** Tom W., Eschatology in the theodicies of 2 Baruch and 4 Ezra: JPseud supp 4, 1989 ➤ 5,3677: ᴿJStJud 21 (1990) 138-141 (S. *Mędala*).
3931 *Riaud* Jean, Paralipomena Jeremiae Prophetae: FolOr 27 (1990) 25-41.

E8.9 **Ezechiel**: *textus, commentarii; themata, versiculi.*

3932 **Allen** Leslie C., Ezekiel 20-48: Word comm. 29. Dallas 1990, Word. xxviii-301 p.; 7 fig. 0-8499-0228-2.
3933 **Becker** K., Ezechiele, Daniele; il profeta sacerdote e il servo del Dio vivente. Assisi 1989, Cittadella. 245 p. – ᴿSalesianum 52 (1990) 430s (M. *Cimosa*).
3934 **Blenkinsopp** Joseph, Ezekiel: Interpretation comm. Louisville 1990, W-Knox. x-242 p. $20. 0-8042-3118-4. – ᴿAsbTJ 45,2 (1990) 83-85 (D. L. *Thompson*); SWJT 33,2 (1990s) 55 (D. G. *Kent*: high quality though not very detailed); TS 51 (1990) 779s (W. T. *Miller*).
3935 ᴱ**Borret** Marcel, ORIGÈNE, Homélies sur Ezéchiel: SChr 352, 1989 ➤ 5,3680: ᴿGregorianum 71 (1990) 602 (G. *Pelland*); NRT 112 (1990) 264s (A. *Harvengt*); RÉG 103 (1990) 351s (P. *Nautin*).
3936 **Brownlee** W. H., Ezekiel 1-19: Word Comm. 28, 1986 ➤ 2,2777 ... 5,3681: ᴿBL (1990) 52 (R. E. *Clements* '1989').
3937 **Eichrodt** Walther, Der Prophet Hesekiel übersetzt und erklärt: ATD 22. Gö 1986 = 1966., Vandenhoeck & R. 41*-421 p. 3-525-51214-7.
3938 **Fuhs** H. F., Ezechiel II (25-48): NEchter 22, 1988 ➤ 4,3824; 5,3682: ᴿNedTTs 43 (1989) 332s (M. *Dijkstra*).

3939 **Maarsingh** B., Ezechiël II: PredikOT 1988 → 4,3832; 5,3684: 90-266-0742-3: RTsTNijm 30 (1990) 87s (J. *Lust*).

3940 TEMorel Charles, GRÉGOIRE, Homélies sur Ézéchiel [I, livre 1, 1986 → 2,2789a] II (Livre 2): SChr [327] 360. P 1990, Cerf. 563 p. 0-204-04116-5. – RRPg 63 (1989) 143s (M. *Reydellet*, 1); Studium 86 (R 1990) 309s (Vera *Paronetto*, 2).

3941 **Pérez Castro** F. (dir.) Ezequiel: CodProfC 6, 1988 → 3,3603; 5,3687: RJQR 81 (1990) 201s (E. J. *Revell*).

3941* **Stuart** Douglas, Ezekiel: Communicator's commentary 18. Waco 1986, Word. 426 p. 0-8499-0424-2.

3942 **Bodi** Daniel, The book of Ezekiel and the poem of Erra [< 1988 diss. NY Union Theol. Sem.]: OBO 104. FrS/Gö 1990, Univ./VR. ii-321 p. 3-7278-0731-8 / VR 3-525-53736-0. – RRHPR 70 (1990) 279s (J.-G. *Heintz*).

3943 **Davis** Ellen F., Swallowing the scroll D1989 → 5,3692: RBL (1990) 71s (R. E. *Clements*); ETL 66 (1990) 187s (J. *Lust*); ÉTRel 65 (1990) 615s (D. *Lys*); OTAbs 13 (1990) 107s (L. *Boadt*); TLZ 115 (1990) 675-7 (H. *Reventlow*).

3944 *Garfinkel* Stephen, Another model for Ezekiel's abnormalities: → 75, Mem. HELD M., JANES 19 (1989) 39-50.

3945 *Gosse* Bernard, La beauté qui égare Israel; l'emploi des racines YPH, YPY, YPḤ dans le livre d'Ézéchiel: BibNot 46 (1989) 13-16.

3946 **Joyce** Paul, Divine initiative and human response in Ezekiel: JStOT supp. 51, 1989 → 5,3694: RCritRR 3 (1990) 139-141 (W. *Brueggemann*); ETL 66 (1990) 188s (J. *Lust*); ExpTim 101 (1989s) 48s (R. *Carroll*); JTS 41 (1990) 141-3 (R. N. *Whybray*); TLZ 115 (1990) 420-2 (H. *Reventlow*); ZAW 102 (1990) 151s [H. C. (not listed p. 121; ? = *Schmitt*)].

3947 **Klein** Ralph W., Ezekiel; the prophet and his message: Studies on Personalities OT 1988 → 5,3695: RCBQ 52 (1990) 716s (H. V. *Parunak*); CritRR 3 (1990) 148-150 (D. J. *Block*); HebSt 31 (1990) 190-2 (L. C. *Allen*), Interpretation 44 (1990) 185 (M. *Hillmer*).

3948 **Krüger** Thomas, Geschichtskonzepte im Ezechielbuch [Diss. Mü 1986, DBaltzer K.]: BZAW 180, 1989 → 5,3696: RBL (1990) 82 (R. E. *Clements*); JBL 109 (1990) 707-9 (R. W. *Klein*).

3949 *Neṣer* Nissan, ⊕ Biblical language in the light of Ezekiel; r. Shlomo PARḤON: Lešonenu 52 (1987s) 36-65.

3950 **Rooker** Mark F., Biblical Hebrew in transition; the language of the book of Ezekiel [diss. Brandeis 1988 → 4,3840]: JStOT supp 90. Sheffield 1990, Academic. x-222 p. £25. 1-85075-230-3 [TDig 38,186].

3951 **Swanson** Phillip J., The role of covenant in Ezekiel's program of restoration: diss. Baptist Theol. Sem., DBailey D. New Orleans 1989. 209 p. 90-20104. – DissA 51 (1990s) 901s-A.

3952 *Dimant* J., *Strugnell* J., The Merkabah vision in Second Ezekiel (4Q385 4): → 527, RQum 14,55 (1989s) 331-348.

3953 *Elmen* Paul, [Ezek 1,16] The merkabah wheels and their work: AnglTR 71 (1989) 366-376.

3954 **Halperin** David, The faces of the chariot; early Jewish responses to Ezekiel's vision: TStAJ 16, 1988 → 4,3825: RCritRR 3 (1990) 340-2 (M. *Himmelfarb*); JStJud 21 (1990) 236-252 (M. *Mach*); JTS 41 (1990) 585-9

(C. *Murray-Jones*); NedTTs 44 (1990) 167s (A. *Kuyt*); Numen 37 (1990) 233-249 (Rachel *Elior*); RechSR 78 (1990) 466-8 (A. *Paul*).

3955 *Hoeps* Reinhard, [Ezech 1] Ezechiels Thronwagenvision: LingBib 63 (1989) 86-105; Eng. 105.

3956 *Adler* Joshua J. [Ezek 3-5] The symbolic acts of Ezekiel: JBQ 19 (1990s) 120-2.

3957 *Hengel* Martin, Zwischen Leben und Tod (Hes 3,16-21): TBeit 21 (1990) 225-9 [< ZIT 90,753].

3958 *Manns* Frédéric, [Ez 9,4.6] Il simbolo del Tau: TerraS 66 (1990) 54-67.

3959 **Ohnesorge** Stefan, Jahwe gestaltet sein Volk neu; zur Sicht der Zukunft Israels nach Ez 11.14-21; 20.1-44; 36,16-38; 37.1-14, 15-28: kath. Diss. ᴰ*Schreiner* J. Wü 1989s. – TR 86 (1990) 520.

3960 *Rooy* H. F. Van, *Smit* E. J., [Ezek 12,22.27; 18,2] The vox populi and structural elements of the Book of Ezekiel: OTEssays 3 (1990) 275-285.

3961 *Mosis* Rudolf, ❷ Krisenzeit und falsche Prophetie nach Ez 13, ᵀ*Bartnicki* Roman: ColcT 59,1 (1989) 53-64.

3962 *a)* *Propp* William H., The meaning of *tāpel* in Ezekiel [13, six times; 'folly', not 'plaster']; – *b)* *Allen* Leslie C., Annotation clusters in Ezekiel: ZAW 102 (1990) 404-8 / 408-413.

3963 *Malul* Meir, Adoption of foundlings in the Bible and Mesopotamian documents; a study of some legal metaphors in Ezekiel 16.1-7: JStOT 46 (1990) 97-126.

3964 *Gosse* Bernard, [Ézéch, 18,8-26...] L'emploi de *ʾwl(h)* dans le livre d'Ézéchiel, et quelques problèmes concernant la rédaction de ce livre: BibNot 53 (1990) 23-25.

3965 **Matties** Gordon H., Ezekiel 18 and the rhetoric of moral discourse [diss. Vanderbilt, ᴰ*Knight* D., Nv 1989]: SBL Diss 126. Atlanta 1990, Scholars. xi-244 p. 1-55540-458-8.

3966 **Sedlmeier** Franz, Studien zu Komposition und Theologie von Ezechiel 20 [kath. Diss. ᴰ*Mosis* R., Mainz 1989s – TR 86 (1990) 516]: SBB 21. Stu 1990, KBW. 444 p. DM 39 [TR 87,74].

3966* *Lieber* Elinor, 'He looked in the liver' (Ezekiel 21:26) [H; RSV 21,21]; the medical origins of liver divination: ➤ 540*, Koroth 9 sp. (3d symposium 1987/8) 235-245.

3967 **Swanepoel** M. G., Die teologie van Esegiël 33-39 [< diss. Pretoria 1987, ᴰ*Prinsloo* W. S.]: NduitsGT 31 (1990) 5-22 [< OTAbs 14,79].

3968 **Mills** Timothy J., [Ezek 38s] The Gog pericope and the Book of Ezekiel: diss. ᴰ*Riemann* P., Drew. Madison NJ 1989. 177 p. 90-14370. – DissA 51 (1990s) 192-A; RelStR 17,193.

3968* *Barthélemy* Dominique, Les relations de la Complutensis avec le papyrus 967 pour Ez 40,42 à 46,24: ➤ 70, ᶠHANHART R., 1990, 253-261.

3969 *Monari* Luciano, Il ritorno del Signore Ez 43,1-9: ➤ 325b, ParSpV 22 (1990) 51-59.

E9.1 Apocalyptica VT.

3970 **Aalen** S., Heilsverlangen und Heilsverwirklichung; Studien zur Erwartung des Heils in der apokalyptischen Literatur des antiken Judentums und im ältesten Christentum [Münster 1974 Delitzsch lectures]: ArbLGJ 21. Leiden 1990, Brill. xxi-70 p. *f* 55. 90-04-09257-9 [NTAbs 35,261].

3971 *Allen* Leslie C., Some prophetic antecedents of apocalyptic eschatology and their hermeneutical value: ➤ 531, ExAud 6 (1990) 15-28.

3972 *Bie* H. J. de,   Wat is apocalyptiek?:   TRef 33,2 (1990) 103-122 [< GerefTTs 90,255].

3973 **Collins** J. J.,   The apocalyptic imagination; an introduction to the Jewish matrix of Christianity 1984 ➤ 65,3262... 4,3860:   RSvEx 55 (1990) 120s (L. *Hartman*).

3974 *Gignoux* P., L'apocalyptique iranienne est-elle vraiment la source d'autres apocalypses?:   ➤ 488, From Alexander 1990, 77-88.

3975 *Grabbe* Lester L.,   The social setting of early Jewish apocalypticism: JPseud 4 (1989) 27-47 [< TR 87,74].

3976 *a*) *Hanson* Paul D.,   The matrix of apocalyptic; – *b*) *Delcor* Mathias, Jewish literature in Hebrew and Aramaic in the Greek era [... Apocrypha and Pseudepigrapha]; – *c*) *Walter* Nikolaus,   Jewish-Greek literature of the Greek period; – *d*) *Barr* James,   Hebrew, Aramaic and Greek in the Hellenistic age: ➤ 835, CHJud 2 (1989) 524-533 / 352-384 [409-503] / 385-408 / 79-114.

3977 E**Hellholm** David,   Apocalypticism 1979/83, ²1989 ➤ 5,3723:   RNorTTs 90 (1989) 237s (H. M. *Barstad*); SNTU-A 14 (1989) 280-2 (F. *Weissengruber*).

3978 **Körtner** U. H. J.,   Weltangst... Apokalyptik D1988 ➤ 4,3867; 5,3725: RActuBbg 27 (1990) 77s (J. *Boada*).

3979 *Licht* Jakob, *a*) ✜ The attitude to past events in the Bible and in apocalyptic literature: Tarbiz 60 (1990s) 1-18; Eng. I. – *b*) Biblisches Geschichtsdenken und apokalyptische Spekulation: Judaica 46 (1990) 208-224.

3980 **Marconcini** B., Apocalittica 1985 ➤ 3,3627: RDivThom 92 (1989) 430s (C. *Riccardi*).

3981 *Otzen* Benedikt,   Crisis and religious reaction; Jewish apocalypticism: ➤ 325*, *Bilde*/Seleucid 1990, 224-236.

3982 E**Reddish** Mitchell G.,   Apocalyptic literature, a reader.   Nv 1990, Abingdon.   352 p. $25 pa.   0-687-01566-9 [TDig 38,46; RelStR 17,256, J. J. *Collins*].

3983 **Rowland** C.,   The open heaven 1982 ➤ 63,3757... 1,3681:   RHenoch 12 (1990) 241 (J. A. *Soggin*).

3984 *Sacchi* Paolo,   L'apocalittica giudaica e la sua storia: BiblCuRel 55. Brescia 1990, Paideia.   374 p. Lit. 47.000.   88-394-0446-5.

3985 **Terry** Milton S.,   Biblical apocalyptics.   GR 1988 = c. 1890, Zondervan.   512 p. $17. – RCriswT 4 (1989s) 189s (T. D. *Lea*).

3986 *a*) *Webb* Robert L.,   'Apocalyptic'; observations on a slippery term; – *b*) *Davies* P. R.,   Qumran and apocalyptic, or obscurum per obscurius; – *c*) *Newsom* Carol A.,   Apocalyptic and the discourse of the Qumran community; – *d*) *Wolters* A., Apocalyptic and the Copper Scroll: ➤ 562, JNES 49 (1990) 115-126 / 127-134 / 135-144 / 145-155; ➤ a67.

3987 **Zager** W.,   Begriff und Wertung der Apokalyptik in der neutestamentlichen Forschung [ev. Diss. Mainz 1988, DBrandenburger E.]: EurHS 23/358. Fra 1989, Lang.   xvi-517 p.   3-631-40885-4 [NTAbs 34,105].

E9.2   **Daniel:** *textus, commentarii; themata, versiculi.*

3988 *Casey* Maurice,   PORPHYRY and Syrian exegesis of the book of Daniel: ZNW [73 (1982) 141-7, *Ferch* A. J.] 81 (1990) 139-142.

3989 *Chazan* Robert,   Le commentaire de RASHI sur le livre de Daniel: ➤ 521, RÉJ 149 (1990) 481s.

3989* **Ferguson** Sinclair D., Daniel: Communicator's Commentary 19. Waco 1986, Word. 252 p. 0-8499-0425-0.

3990 **Goldingay** J. E., Daniel: Word Comm. 30, 1989 ➤ 4,3880; 0-8499-0210-X: ᴿBL (1990) 54 (P. W. *Coxon*); CritRR 3 (1990) 127-9 (J. J. *Collins*).

3991 **Koch** K., Daniel: BK, 1986 ➤ 2,2831; 4,3882: ᴿRBibArg 52 (1990) 124-6 (J. S. *Croatto*).

3992 *Maina* Ernest, Le livre de Daniel en Judéo-Persan: ➤ 555, Irano-Judaica 1 (1975/82) 148-180.

3993 **Taylor** Richard A., An analysis of the Syriac text of the Book of Daniel: diss. Catholic Univ., ᴰ*Griffith* S. Wsh 1990. 434 p. 90-27650. – DissA 51 (1990s) 1594-A.

3994 *Berg* M. A. van den, De troost der profetie; LUTHERs voorrede van de profeet Daniël: TRef 33,1 (Woerden 1990) 28-44 [< ZIT 90,325].

3995 *Collins* John J., Inspiration or illusion; biblical theology and the Book of Daniel: ➤ 531, ExAud 6 (1990) 29-38.

3996 *Ginsberg* H. L., The book of Daniel: ➤ 835, CHJud 2 (1989) 504-523.

3997 **Goldingay** John E., [➤ 3990] Daniel: Word **Themes**. Dallas 1989, Word. 113 p. $10. – ᴿBS 147 (1990) 498s (R. A. *Taylor*).

3998 *Grelot* Pierre, Daniel: ➤ 323, Psaumes/Écrits 1990, 195-220.

3999 *Miller* James E., The redaction of Daniel: ProcGLM 10 (1990) 52-65.

4000 **Lacocque** André, Daniel: SPersOT 1988 ➤ 4,3884; 5,3750: ᴿInterpretation 44 (1990) 184 (M. *Hillmer*).

4001 **Pfandl** Gerhard, The latter days and the time of the end in the Book of Daniel: diss. Andrews, ᴰ*Hasel* G. Berrien Springs MI 1990. 531 p. 91-06812. – DissA 51 (1990s) 3442s-A.

4002 **Reid** Stephen B., Enoch and Daniel; a form critical and sociological study of the historical apocalypses [diss. Emory, ᴰ*Tucker* G.]: Mg 2. Berkeley 1989, BIBAL. xiii-147 p. $13 pa. 0-941037-07-8 [NTAbs 34,138].

4002* **Schlossberg** Eliezer, Concepts and methods in the commentary of R. SAADIA Gaon on the Book of Daniel: diss. Bar-Ilan. Ramat Gan 1988. – REJ 150, 509-512.

4003 **Fewell** Danna N., Circles of sovereignty... Dan 1-6: JStOT supp 72, 1988 ➤ 4,3887; 5,3756: ᴿETL 66 (1990) 401 (J. *Lust*).

4004 *Soesilo* Daud, Translating the poetic sections of Daniel 1-6: BTrans 41 (1990) 432-5.

4005 **Tidball** Derek, A world without windows [... secularized; Dan 1-6; Heb 11]. L 1987, Scripture Union. 160 p. £2.50 pa. 0-86201-382-8. – ᴿEvangel 7,1 (1989) 22s (D. *Prime*).

4006 *Henten* J. W. van, Het verhaal over Susanna als een pre-rabbijnse midrasj bij Dan 1:1-2: NedTTs 43 (1989) 278-293; Eng. 330.

4007 *Schwartz* Jacques, La Septante de Daniel (1,2-10): ZPapEp 81 (1990) 275-7.

ᴱ**Holbrook** Frank B., Symposium on Daniel 2 & 8 1980/6 ➤ 535.

4008 *Kevane* Eugene, [Dan 2,24...] Rome and the millennium in universal history: Divinitas 33 (1989) 245-268.

4009 *Dyer* Charles H., The musical instruments in Daniel 3: BS 147 (1990) 426-436.

4010 *a)* *Haag* Ernst, Die drei Männer im Feuer nach Dan. 3:1-30; – *b)* *Kellermann* Ulrich, Das Danielbuch und die Märtyrertheologie der Auferstehung: ➤ 533, Martyrologie 1984/9, 20-50 / 51-75.

4011 *Daube* D., [Dan 5,13] HEINE's Belsatzar: JJS 41 (1990) 254-8.

4012 *Croatto* J. Severino, Desmesura y fin del opresor en la perspectiva apocalíptica (estudio de Daniel 7-12): RBArg 52,39 (1990) 129-144.

4013 [Pace] **Jeansonne** Sharon, The Old Greek translations of Daniel 7-12 : CBQ Mg 19, 1988 ➤ 4,3900; 5,3770: ᴿBZ 34 (1990) 128s (W. *Schenk*).

4014 **Lucas** Ernest C., *a)* Akkadian prophecies, omens and myths as background for Daniel ch. 7-12: diss. Liverpool 1989. – TyndB 41 (1990) 161. – *b)* [Dan 7s] The source of Daniel's animal imagery [... Mesopotamian]: TyndB 41 (1990) 161-185.

4015 *Collins* Adela Y., Daniel 7 and Jesus: Journal of Theology 93 (Dayton 1989) 5-19 [< NTAbs 34,344].

4016 *a)* *Collins* Adela Y., Daniel 7 and the historical Jesus; – *b)* Collins John J., The meaning of 'the End' in the book of Daniel; – *c)* *Ulrich* Eugene, Orthography and text in 4QDanᵃ and 4QDanᵇ and in the received Masoretic text: ➤ 173, ᶠSTRUGNELL J., Of scribes 1990, 187-193 / 91-98 / 29-42.

4017 **Porter** Paul A., Miracles and monsters Dan 7s 1985 ➤ 1,3715... 5,3769: ᴿJQR 80 (1990) 133s (Adele *Berlin*).

4018 *Græsholt* G., [Daniel as unity around ch. 7]; *Høgenhaven* J., [Greek of Daniel]: ➤ 332, TNybrud 1990.

4019 *a)* *Raabe* Paul R., Daniel 7; its structure and role in the book; *b)* *Wilson* Gerald H., Wisdom in Daniel and the origin of apocalyptic: HebAnR 9 (1985) 267-275 / 373-381 [< OTAbs 13, p. 287].

4020 **Nuñez** Samuel, The vision of Daniel 8; interpretations from 1700 to 1800 [for 1900]: diss. Andrews 14. Berrien Springs MI 1987, Andrews Univ. x-451 p. $15 pa. – ᴿAndrUnS 28 (1990) 179-181 (P. G. *Damsteegt*).

4021 *Hauge* Martin R., [Dan 8,18; Neh 13,11; 2 Chr 30,16...] On the sacred spot; the concept of the proper localization before God: ScandJOT (1990,1) 30-60.

4022 *Seidl* Theodor, Die 70 Jahrwochen des Daniel in der Deutung der Peschitta; Dan 9,24-27, Analyse – Vergleich – Bewertung: ➤ 8*, ᶠASSFALG J. 1990, 335-347.

4023 *Wilson* Gerald H., The prayer of Daniel 9; reflection on Jeremiah 29: JStOT 48 (1990) 91-99.

4024 **Bodemann** [➤ 5,3745!] Reinhard, [Dan 9,24-27] Naissance d'une exégèse; Daniel dans l'Église ancienne...: BeiGBEx 28, 1986: ➤ 2,2823... 4,3876: ᴿJStJud 21 (1990) 95s (A. *Hilhorst*); RTPhil 122 (1990) 280 (Françoise *Morard*); TLZ 115 (1990) 600s (H.-G. *Thümmel*).

4025 **Farris** Michael, The formative interpretations of the seventy weeks of Daniel: diss. ᴰ*Walters* S. Toronto 1990. – RelStR 17,193.

4026 *Laato* Antti, The seventy yearweeks in the book of Daniel [9,24s]: ZAW 102 (1990) 212-225.

4027 *Lurie* David H., A new interpretation of Daniel's 'sevens' and the chronology of the seventy 'sevens': JEvTS 33 (1990) 303-9 [< ZAW 103,434].

E9.3   *Prophetae minores,* **Dōdekaprophētōn ... Hosea, Joel.**

4028 **Chisholm** R. B., Interpreting the Minor Prophets. GR 1990, Zondervan. 317 p. $3. 0-310-30801-1 [BL 91,68, R. N. *Whybray*: defensive but well informed].

4029 **Gelston** A.,   The Peshitta of the Twelve Prophets 1987 → 3,3674...
5,3781:   ᴿNedTTs 43 (1989) 241s (M. J. *Mulder*).
4030 **House** P. R.,   The unity of the Twelve: JStOT supp 97, BLit 27.
Sheffield 1990, Academic. 262 p. £27.50.   1-85075-250-8 [BL 91,78, A.
Gelston: nowhere asks whether the broad 'unifying' lines he traces are
applicable also to the major prophets]. – ᴿExpTim 102 (1990s) 150 (R.
Coggins).
4031 *Muraoka* Takamitsu,   In defense of the unity of the Septuagint Minor
Prophets: AnJapB 15 (1989) 27-36.
4032 *Muraoka* Takamitsu, *Shavitsky* Ziva,   Abraham Iʙɴ-Eᴢʀᴀ's biblical
Hebrew lexicon; the minor prophets, I: AbrNahr 28 (1990) 53-75.
4033 **Tov** E., (*Kraft* R. A., *al.*)   The Minor Prophets scroll from Nahal Ḥever
(8HevXIIgr) (The Seiyâl collection, 1): DJD 8 [the same (or similar!)
material as Bᴀʀᴛʜᴇ́ʟᴇᴍʏ D., Les devanciers d'Aquila 1963].   Ox 1990,
Clarendon. xi-171 p.; 20 pl. £50.   0-19-826327-9 [NTAbs 35,272]. – ᴿJJS
41 (1990) 260s (G. *Vermes*); Muséon 103 (1990) 369-372 (P.-M. *Bogaert*);
ZAW 102 (1990) 461s (O. *Kaiser*).

4034 **Beck** Eleonore,   Osea – Amos – Michea; il sogno divino [→ 5,3785 'di
Dio']; un mondo umano 1989:   ᴿSalesianum 52 (1990) 429s (M. *Cimosa*).
4035 **Beeby** H. D.,   Hosea, Grace abounding 1989 → 5,3786:   ᴿCalvaryB 6
(1990) 71-73 (B. K. *Heldt*); SWJT 33,2 (1990s) 55s (D. G. *Kent*).
4036 **Borbone** Pier Giorgio,   Il libro del Profeta Osea, edizione del testo
ebraico [< ᴰ1989, ᴰ*Sacchi* P.]: Henoch Quad 2.   T 1990, Zamorani.
ix-236 p. Lit. 50.000.   88-7158-004-4 [BL 91,44, G. I. *Davies*: by 'critical'
means 'reconstructed' text, as commonly nowadays; but of a book
perhaps unduly under Septuagint-Vorlage influence].
4037 **Borbone** P. G., *Mandracci* F., Concordanze... sir. Osea 1987 → 3,3677;
4,3916:   ᴿJSS 35 (1980) 158-160 (A. *Gelston*: fine despite computer p. 65).
4038 **Daniele** Dwight R.,   Hosea and salvation-history; the early traditions of
Israel in the prophecy of Hosea [Diss. Hamburg 1987, ᴰ*Koch* K.]: BZAW
191.   B 1990, de Gruyter. ix-148 p.   3-11012143-3 [ZAW 103,294, H.-C.
Schmitt].
4039 **Israel** Richard D.,   Prophecies of judgement; a study in the pro-
tasis-apodosis text structures in Hosea, Amos and Micah: diss. ᴰ*Knierim*
R.   Claremont 1989 vii-422 p.   90-00160. – OIAc Ja91.
4040 *Köckert* Matthias,   Verbindliches Reden von Gott in der Verkündigung
des Propheten Hosea: → 103, ꜰKʀᴏᴛᴋᴇ W., Wahrzeichen 1988, 238-277.
4041 **Limburg** James.   Hosea-Micah: Interpretation comm. 1988 → 4,3922:
ᴿCritRR 3 (1990) 153s (P. L. *Redditt*); JAOS 110 (1990) 160 (P. J. *King*).
4042 **Lipshitz** Abe,   Iʙɴ Eᴢʀᴀ on Hosea 1988 → 4,3923:   ᴿBL (1990) 57s
(R. B. *Salters*); HebSt 31 (1990) 195-7 (F. E. *Greenspahn*: also on Kᴀʟʟᴜs
M., Aʙᴜʟᴀꜰɪᴀ); JJS 41 (1990) 134s (D. *Frank*); Speculum 65 (1990) 596s
(S. D. *Benin*).
4043 *Muszyński* Henryk, ☉ Der Begriff der Sünde beim Propheten Hosea:
→ 64, ꜰGʀᴢʏʙᴇᴋ S. 1990, 201-216; deutsch 217.
4044 **Neef** Hans-Dieter,   Die Heilstraditionen... Hosea: BZAW 169, 1987
→ 3,3683... 5,3794:   ᴿBiblica 71 (1989) 113-6 (H. *Simian-Yofre*); BO 47
(1990) 763-7 (W. *Dietrich*); BZ 34 (1990) 291-3 (Jutta *Hausmann*); CBQ 52
(1990) 328s (M. J. *Buss*: challenging, though he often asserts rather than
proves); GerefTTs 90 (1990) 186-8 (A. van der *Wal*); NedTTs 43 (1989)
57 (C. van *Leeuwen*).

4045 *Rocha* José E., *al.*, La idolatría en el mensaje de Oseas: Xilotl 6,3 (Nicaragua 1990) 41 ...

4046 **Simon** Uriel, ✪ Abraham IBN EZRA's two commentaries on the minor prophets; I. Hosea, Joel, Amos. Ramat-Gan 1989, Bar-Ilan Univ. 965-226-103-3. – RE stB 48 (1990) 141s (L. *Díez Merino*); RÉJ 149 (1990) 207s (J.-C. *Attias*, aussi sur LIPSHITZ A., IBN EZRA on Hosea).

4047 **Yee** Gale A., Composition and tradition in the book of Hosea ...: SBL Diss 102, 1987 ➤ 3,3684 ... 5,3797: RBiblica 71 (1990) 109-112 (H. *Simian-Yofre*).

4048 *Plum* K.F., [Ps 45; Hos 1-3 ...] Der himmelske favntag; bibelsk ægteskabs- og seksualmetaforik: DaTTs 53 (1990) 161-182 [< NTAbs 35,201, The heavenly embrace ...; ZAW 103,276].

4049 *Lohfink* Norbert, Israels Ethos und der Bestand der Schöpfung; zu Hos 4,1-3: Entschluss 45,1 (1990) 8-11.

4050 *Raurell* Frederic, Hos 4,7; from 'dóxa' to 'atimía'; EstFranc 91 (1990) 177-190.

4051 **Pryce** Bertrand C., The resurrection motif in Hos 5:8 - 6:6; an exegetical study: diss. Andrews, DDavidson R. Berrien Springs MI 1989. – AndrUnS 28 (1990) 154.

4052 *McComiskey* T.E., Hos 9:13 and the integrity of the Masoretic tradition in the prophecy of Hosea: JEvTS 33 (1990) 155-160 [< ZAW 103,434].

4053 *Borbone* Pier Giorgio, [Os 10,10] 'Desiderio' o 'rimprovero'? Un errore congiuntivo nella tradizione di Osea: ➤ 154, FSACCHI P., 1990, 85-90.

4054 *Kreuzer* Siegfried, God as mother in Hosea 11? [< TüTQ 169 (1989) 123-132], TEAsen B.: TDig 37 (1990) 221-6 [correcting 34 (1987), *Schüngel-Straumann* H.: masculine forms are used for God].

4055 **Lee Dong Soo,** Studies in the text and structure of Hosea 12-14; diss. DAuld A. Edinburgh 1990. 367 p. – RTLv 22, p. 588.

4056 *Grün-Rath* Harald, 'Ich wirke wie Tau für Israel'; Theologie als Poesie am Beispiel von Hosea 14,5-9: ➤ 26, FBOHREN R., 1990, 61-68.

4057 **Meer** W. van der, Oude woorden worden nieuw; de opbouw van het boek Joël [diss. DNoort E.] 1989, ➤ 5,3821: RBiblica 71 (1990) 429-432 (W.S. *Prinsloo*); BL (1990) 84 (J.A. *Emerton*).

4058 **Prinsloo** W.S., Theology of ... Joel: BZAW 163, 1985 ➤ 1,3757 ... 5,3823: RBO 47 (1990) 767-9 (A.S. van der *Woude*); BZ 34 (1990) 116s (H. *Engel*); OLZ 85 (1990) 429s (B. *Johnson*).

Wahl Otto, Joel, Jona 1991 ➤ 4160.

4059 *Kapelrud* Arvid S., Fra virkelighet til metafor [Joel Is; Gn 3,1-19]: ➤ 21*, Mem. BJØRNDALEN A., TsTKi 60,4 (1989) 255-262; Eng. 262.

4060 *Brodsky* Harold, [Joel 1,4] 'An enormous horde arrayed for battle'; locusts in the book of Joel: BR 6,4 (1990) 32-39.

4061 **Simkins** Ronald A., The day of the locusts; the history of creation in the book of Joel: diss. Harvard, DCross F. CM 1990. 393 p. 91-13249. – DissA 51 (1990s) 4154-A.

4062 *a)* *Bonora* A., La liturgia del ritorno (Gioele 2); – *b)* *Ravasi* G.F., Osea; 'torniamo al Signore'; – *c)* *Rochettes* Jacqueline des, 'Šûbâ, Jiśrāēl'

(Os 14,2); la via del ritorno: → 325*b*, ParSpV 22 (1990) 61-71 / 9-16 / 85-98.

4063 *Park Cheol Woo,* Ⓚ The prophet Joel [ch. 4], a study: Sinhak Sasang 67 (Seoul 1989) 813-845 [< TContext 8,70].

E9.4 **Amos.**

4064 **Andersen** F. I., *Freedman* D. N., Amos: AnchorB 1989 → 5,3827: ᴿTS 51 (1990) 325s (W. *Brueggemann*); UF 22 (1990) 506s (O. *Loretz*); VT 40 (1990) 379 (J. A. *Emerton*).

4065 **Asurmendi** Jésus, *a*) Amos et Osée; CahÉv 64. P 1988, Cerf. 59 p. F 24. 0222-9714; – *b*) Amos y Oseas: CuadBib 64. Estella 1989, VDivino. 60 p. – ᴿIter 1 (1990) 141 (E. *Frades*).

4066 *Bechmann* Ulrike, Amos – das Wichtigste auf den Punkt gebracht: KatBlätt 115 (Mü 1990) 387-390 [< ZIT 90,495].

4067 *a*) *Deissler* Alfons, Die Propheten Amos und Hosea als 'Wegweiser' für das Gottesvolk; – *b*) *Becker* Joachim, Historischer Prophetismus und biblisches Prophetenbild: → 146, ᶠREINELT H., At. Botschaft 1990, 43-57 / 11-23.

4068 **Hayes** John H., Amos 1988 → 4,3954: ᴿCritRR 3 (1990) 132-4 (H. *Gossai*; also on G. SMITH 1989); ÉTRel 65 (1990) 613s (D. *Lys*); SWJT 33,2 (1990s) 56 (D. G. *Kent*: his 'updating' means sometimes 'disagree without replacing').

4069 **Heyns** M., Amos – advocate for freedom and justice; a socio-historical investigation: diss. Unisa, ᴰ*Deist* F. Pretoria 1989. – OTEssays 2,3 (1989) 108.

4070 *Kim Young-Il,* Ⓚ Language of Jewish worship in the book Amos: Sinhak Sasang 65 (Seoul 1989) 259-290 [< TContext 7/2, 59].

4071 **King** Philip J., Amos, Hosea, Micah 1988 → 4,3956; 5,3838: ᴿCBQ 52 (1990) 125-7 (R. S. *Boraas*); CritRR 3 (1990) 141-3 (W. E. *Rast*); RelStR 16 (1990) 256 (M. A. *Sweeney*).

4072 **Martin-Achard** Robert, L'homme de Teqoa; message et commentaire du livre d'Amos. Aubonne 1990, Moulin. 105 p. [BL 91,58, J. *Barton*: abridgment of his 1984 Amos].

4073 **Polley** Max E., Amos and the Davidic empire 1989 → 5,3841: ᴿAngl-TR 72 (1990) 459s (I. T. *Kaufman*); CritRR 3 (1990) 169-172 (R. *Gnuse*); JTS 41 (1990) 564 (H. *Mowvley*).

4074 *Richardson* H. Neil, † 19.III.1988: Amos's four visions of judgment and hope: BR 5,2 (1989) 16-21.

4075 **Rösel** Hartmut N., The book of Amos / Nahum. Haifa 1990, Univ. (TA, Reem). 315 p. 965-267-038-3.

4076 **Rosenbaum** Stanley N., Amos of Israel; a new interpretation. Macon GA 1990, Mercer Univ. xii-129 p. $25. 0-86554-355-0 [TDig 38,186].

4077 ᵀᴱ**Ruiz Gonzalez** Gregorio, Comentarios medievales... Amós 1987 → 3,3711 ... 5,3842: ᴿSefarad 50 (1990) 219s (M. J. de *Azcárraga*).

4078 **Schwantes** Milton, Amos. São Leopoldo/Petrópolis 1988. Sinodal/ Vozes. 124 p. 85-233-0102-X/-. – ᴿIter 1 (Caracas 1990) 167s (J.-P. *Wyssenbach*).

4079 **Smith** Gary V., Amos, a comm. 1989 → 5,3844: ᴿBS 147 (1990) 248s (E. H. *Merrill*).

4080 **Soggin** J. Alberto, The prophet Amos 1987 → 3,3712 ... 5,3845: ᴿNed-TTs 43 (1989) 142s (A. van der *Wal*).

4081 *Witaszek* Gabriel, ❷ Israelite society in the light of social criticism of the prophet Amos: RuBi 43 (1990) 105-111.

4082 *Giles* Terry, [Am 5,2; 8,14] The dual occurrence of *qûm* in the Book of Amos: IrBSt 12 (1990) 106-116.

4083 *Soden* Wolfram von, Zu einigen Ortsbenennungen bei Amos und Micha [Am 6,1 Şiyon?; Mi 1,10ss]: ZAHeb 3 (1990) 214-220.

4084 *Williamson* H. G. M., The prophet and the plumb-line; a redaction-critical study of Amos vii: → 563, OTS 26 (1988/90) 101-121.

4085 **Beyerlin** Walter, [Amos 7,7-9], Bleilot ... OBO 81, 1989 → 4,3975; 5,3853: ᴿBO 47 (1990) 769s (C. van *Leeuwen*); ETL 66 (1990) 189s (J. *Lust*).

4086 *Uehlinger* Christoph, Der Herr auf der Zinnmauer; zur dritten Amos-Vision (Am VII,7-8): BibNot 48 (1989) 89-104; 1 fig.

4087 *Heyns* Dalene, [Am 7,10-17] A social historical perspective on Amos's prophecies against Israel: OTEssays 3 (1990) 303-316.

E.5 Jonas.

Adam A. K. M., The sign of Jonah; a [Stanley] FISH-eye view 1990 → 4935.

4089 [**Baker** D., Obadiah [→ 4127] *Alexander* T. Desmond, Jonah: Tyndale OT. Leicester 1988, Inter-Varsity.

4090 *Band* Arnold J., Swallowing Jonah; the eclipse of parody: Prooftexts 10 (1990) 177-195.

4091 **Cuomo** Luisa, Una traduzione giudeo romanesca del libro di Giona: Zts romanische Philologie Beih 215. Tü 1988, Niemeyer. 153 p. DM 76. – ᴿTR 86 (1990) 287 (G. *Vanoni*).

4092 *Day* John, Problems in the interpretation of the book of Jonah: → 563, OTS 26 (1988/90) 32-47.

4093 *Dyck* F., Jonah among the prophets; a study in canonical context: JEvTS 33 (1990) 63-73 [< ZAW 103,434].

4094 *Ebach* Jürgen, Kassandra und Jona 1987 → 3,3729 ... 5,3864: ᴿTGL 80 (1990) 342s (J. *Gamberoni*).

4095 *Giroud* Jean-Claude [et groupe de Bordeaux 23.I.1988], Le Livre de Jonas: SémBib 57 (1990) 14-39.

4096 **Lacocque** André & Pierre-Emmanuel, Jonah, a psycho-religious approach to the prophet: StPersOT. Columbia 1990, Univ. S. Carolina. xxv-264 p. $30. 0-87249-674-0 [TDig 38,171, W. C. *Heiser*: 'A. LaCocque, P.-E. Lacocque' (his son)].

4097 **Miles** John R., Laughing at the Bible; Jonah as parody [< JQR 65 (1975) 168-181]: → 367, ᴱ*Radday*, Humour 1990, 203-215.

4098 *Nicol* George G., Neglected books, 1. Jonah: ExpTim 102 (1990s) 238s.

4099 *Paper* Herbert H., Jonah in Judeo-Persian [square-Hebrew text]: → 23, Mem. BLANC H., 1989, 252-5.

4100 *a) Potgieter* J. H., Jonah – a semio-structuralistic reading of a narrative; – *b) Heerden* S. W. van, Naive realism and the historicity of the book of Jonah: OTEssays 3 (1990) 61-69 / 71-91.

4101 **Ratner** Robert J., Jonah, the runaway servant: → 164, ᶠSEGERT S., *Sopher* 1990, 281-305.

4102 **Sasson** Jack M., Jonah: AnchorB 24B. NY 1990, Doubleday. xvi-368 p. $28 [TS 52,140, F. L. *Moriarty*]. 0-385-23525-9.

4103 *Wineman* Aryeh, The Zohar on Jonah; radical retelling or tradition?: HebSt 31 (Madison 1930) 57-69.

Thimmes Pamela, Convention and invention... studies in the biblical sea-storm type scenes ᴰ1989 ⇒ 4958.
4105 *Traina* Alfonso, La figlia del vento (Carmen de Iona, 29) [attribuita a TERTULLIANO o a CIPRIANO]: RFgIC 118 (1990) 200-2.
4106 *Craig* Kenneth M.ᴶ, [Jon 2,3-10; LANDES G. 1987] Jonah and the reading process: JStOT 47 (1990) 103-114.
4107 *a) Limburg* James, Jonah and the whale through the eyes of artists; – *b) Freedman* David N., Did God play a dirty trick on Jonah at the end?: BR 6,4 (1990) 18-25; color. ill. / 26-31.
4108 *Couffignal* Robert, Le Psaume de Jonas (Jonas 2,2-10); une catabase biblique, sa structure et sa fonction: Biblica 71 (1990) 540-552.
4109 *Halleux* André de, [Jon 3,10] À propos du sermon éphrémien sur Jonas et la pénitence des Ninivites: ⇒ 8*, ᶠASSFALG J. 1990, 155-160.

E9.6 *Michaeas,* **Micah.**

4110 **Alfaro** Juan I. [O.S.B.] Justice and loyalty... Micah 1989 ⇒ 5,3880: ᴿVidyajyoti 54 (1990) 545s (R. J. *Raja*).
4111 **Hagstrom** David G., The coherence of the book of Micah...: SBL diss 89, 1988 ⇒ 4,4002: ᴿBiblica 71 (1990) 122-6 (J. T. *Willis*); CriswT 4 (1989s) 393s (D. A. *Garrett*); CritRR 3 (1990) 131s (W. E. *March*); Interpretation 44 (1990) 81s (J. C. *McCann*).
4112 **Jeppesen** K., Grœder ikke... Mika ᴰ1987 ⇒ 4,4004: ᴿVT 40 (1990) 123s (P. *Wernberg-Møller*).
Limburg J., Micah 1988 ⇒ 4041.
4113 *Renaud* B., Michée... Sophonie Nahum 1987 ⇒ 3,3740... 5,3884: ᴿRevSR 64 (1990) 329-331 (R. *Kuntzmann*).
4114 **Reynolds** B., Jean CALVIN, Sermons on Micah: TStRel 47. Lewiston NY 1990, Mellen. x-449 p. $80 [RHE 85,391*].
4115 **Schibler** Daniel, Le livre de Michée: CommÉv 1989 ⇒ 5,3885: ᴿExpTim 102 (1990s) 181 (R. *Coggins*).
4116 **Shaw** Charles S., The speeches of Micah; a rhetorical-historical analysis: diss. Emory, ᴰHayes J. Atlanta 1990. 414 p. 91-06736. – DissA 51 (1990s) 3436s-A.
4117 **Smith** Ralph L., Micah- [and five others up through] Malachi: Word **Themes.** Waco 1990, Word. 123 p. $23. – ᴿSWJT 33,1 (1990s) 55s (T. V. *Brisco*).
4118 **Stansell** Gary, Micah and Isaiah; a form and tradition historical comparison; SBL diss. 85 [Heidelberg 1981, ᴰWolff H. W.], 1988 ⇒ 4,4010: ᴿBL (1990) 93 (B. P. *Robinson*); CBQ 52 (1990) 540s (M. A. *Sweeney*: aims to reverse current view that Micah is a pale reflection of his famous contemporary Isaiah); Interpretation 44 (1990) 420 (B. C. *Ollenburger*); JBL 109 (1990) 516s (J. T. *Willis*); TLZ 115 (1990) 735s (R. *Stahl*).
4119 *Strydom* J.G., Miga in konfrontasie met die Leiers van die volk; 'n kritiese ondersoek na A. S. van der WOUDE se Miga-analise: SkrifK 10 (1989) 168-182 (933-947) [< OTAbs 14,81s].
4120 **Wahl** Otto, Die Bücher Micha, Obadja und Haggai: Geistliche Schriftlesung 12. Dü 1990, Patmos. 3-491-77168-4. Mi p. 8-122 . 223-6 (Ob 124-158 . 226s; Hag. 160-222 . 227-30). 3-491-77168-4.

4121 **Wal** Adri van der, Micah, a classified bibliography: Applicatio 8. Amst 1990, Free Univ. [xii-] 207 p. £21.50. 90-6256-814-9.

4122 **[Baker** D. Obadiah ➤ 4127] *Waltke* Bruce K., Micah: Tyndale OT. Leicester 1988, Inter-Varsity.

4123 **Wolff** Hans W., Micah, a commentary [BK AT 14/4], ᵀ*Stansell* Gary. Mp 1990, Augsburg. ix-258 p. 0-8066-2449-3 [BL 91,62, W. *Houston*].

4124 *López Amar y León* Rolando, [Mi 3,1-12] La ruina de Jerusalén y el fin de la violencia: RTLim 23 (1989) 98-113.

4125 *Pannell* R., Mi 4,14-5,3: PerspRelSt 15 (1988) 131-143 [OTAbs 13, p. 184].

4126 *Hanhart* Robert [Micha 6,8; LXX 'Bereit sein mit Gott zu wandeln'] Der Prophet, die Septuaginta und PLATON: NSys 32 (1990) 113s.

E9.7 *Abdias, Sophonias...* **Obadiah, Zephaniah, Nahum.**

4127 **Baker** David W., Obadiah [Jonah & Micah]: Tyndale OT. Leicester 1988, Inter-Varsity. [207 p. £5.50 whole book]. – ᴿIrBSt 12 (1990) 50s (Gilian *Keys*).

4128 **Deissler** A., Zwölfpropheten III; Zefanja, Hag Sach Mal: NEchter 21, 1988 ➤ 4,4025: ᴿBLtg 63 (1990) 249s (R. *Oberforcher*).

4129 **House** Paul R., Zephaniah, a prophetic drama: JStOT supp 69 / BLit 16, 1988 ➤ 4,4026; 5,3904: ᴿCBQ 52 (1990) 313s (H. *Gossai*); ETL 66 (1990) 402s (J. *Lust*); JBL 109 (1990) 517-9 (B. *Glazier-McDonald*); JQR 81 (1990s) 175-8 (T. *Hiebert*); NorTTs 91 (1990) 162s (A. S. *Kapelrud*).

4130 *Nel* P. J., Structural and conceptual strategy in Zephaniah, chapter 1: JNWS 15 (1989) 155-167.

4131 *Steck* Odil H., Zu Zef 3,9-10: BZ 34 (1990) 90-95.

4132 **Achtemeier** Elizabeth, Nahum [through] Malachi 1986 ➤ 3,3761; 4,4027: ᴿTLZ 115 (1990) 261s (H. *Reventlow*).

4133 **Baker** David W., Nahum, Habakkuk and Zephaniah: Tyndale OT 1988 ➤ 4,4028: ᴿIrBSt 12 (1990) 95s (Gilian *Keys*).

4134 **Bonora** Antonio, Nahum-Sofonia-Abacuc-Lamentazioni; dolore, protesta e speranza: LoB 1.25, 1989 ➤ 5,3910: ᴿAsprenas 37 (1990) 109s (G. *Castello*); RivB 38 (1990) 529s (B. *Marconcini*).

4135 *Carrez* Maurice, Naoum Septante: RHPR 70 (1990) 35-48; Eng. 146.

4136 **Clark** David J., *Hatton* Howard A., A translator's handbook on the books of Nahum, Habakkuk, and Zephaniah; 1989 ➤ 5,3912: ᴿSalesianum 52 (1990) 737s (C. *Buzzetti*).

4137 *Patterson* R. D., *Travers* M. E., Nahum, poet laureate of the minor prophets [... newer literary theory]: JEvTS 33 (1990) 437-444 [< ZAW 103,434].

4138 **Robertson** O., The books of Nahum, Habakkuk, and Zephaniah: NICOT. GR 1990, Eerdmans. x-357 p. $29. 0-8028-2374-2 [BL 91,59, H. *Williamson*: reserves].

4139 **Seybold** Klaus, Profane Prophetie... Nahum: SBS 135, 1989 ➤ 5,3914: ᴿCritRR 3 (1990) 179s (J. *Limburg*, also on SCHELLING P., Ob); MüTZ 41 (1990) 395s (J. *Wehrle*).

4140 **Wal** Adri van der, Nahum, Habakkuk, a classified bibliography, with a special paragraph ... Qumran: Applicatio 6, 1988 → 4,4029: ᴿETL 66 (1990) 190 (J. *Lust*).

E9.8   *Habacuc,* **Habakkuk.**

4141 **Prinsloo** Gert T. M., A literary-exegetical analysis of the book of Habakkuk [Afrikaans]: diss. Pretoria 1989, ᴰ*Prinsloo* W. S. – DissA 51 (1990s) 2049-A.
Robertson O., Habakkuk NICOT 1990 → 4138.
4142 **Szeles** Maria, Wrath and mercy; a commentary on the books of Habakkuk and Zephaniah: IntTComm 1987 → 4,4037; 5,3921: ᴿEvangel 8,1 (1990) 23 (H. *Uprichard*); SWJT 33,1 (1990s) 56s (D. G. *Kent*).
4143 **Hiebert** T., [Hab 3] God of my victory 1986 → 2,2945 ... 5,3923: ᴿJTS 41 (1990) 144-7 (D. R. *Jones*).

E9.9   *Aggaeus,* **Haggai** – *Zacharias,* **Zechariah** – *Malachias,* **Malachi.**

4144 **Bentley** Michael, Building for God's glory; Haggai and Zechariah simply explained. Darlington 1989, Evangelical. 229 p. 0-85234-259-4. – ᴿEvangel 8,4 (1990) 22s (C. M. *Cameron*).
Deissler A., Haggai Sacharja Maleachi: NEchter 21, 1988 → 4128.
4145 **Meyers** Carol L. & Eric M., Haggai, Zechariah 1-8: AnchorB 25B, 1987 → 3,3781 ... 5,3928: ᴿClaretianum 30 (1990) 472-4 (B. *Proietti*); HeythJ 31 (1990) 213s (R. *Mason*).
4146 **Stuhlmueller** Carroll, Rebuilding with hope; a commentary on the books of Haggai and Zechariah: IntTComm 1988 → 4,4048; 5,3931: ᴿBTrans 41 (1990) 145 (D. J. *Clark*: 'translators will not normally turn to a theological commentary as a source of help'); Evangel 7,4 (1989) 22 (Joyce *Baldwin*); SWJT 33,2 (1990s) 56s (D. G. *Kent*); TLZ 115 (1990) 337s (H. *Reventlow*: 'Carol').
Wahl Otto, Haggai 1990 → 4120, p. 160-223. 227-230.
4147 **Wolff** Hans W., Haggai 1988 → 2,2954 ... 4,4052: ᴿCBQ 52 (1990) 145-7 (E. M. *Meyers*: among the best, despite two disturbing aspects); CriswT 4 (1989s) 399s (E. R. *Clendenin*: based on a literary theory repeatedly shown to be bankrupt); Interpretation 44 (1990) 307 (R. L. *Braun*); JBL 109 (1990) 130-2 (D. L. *Petersen*).

4148 **Ayre** James, In that day; an exposition of the final destiny of Israel according to Zechariah. Cheadle, Cheshire 1986, Myrtle Vale. 292 p. [KirSef 62 (1988s) p. 37].
4149 **Butterworth** George M., The structure of the book of Zechariah: diss. London 1989. – RTLv 22, p. 587.
4150 **Hanhart** Robert, Sacharja: BK AT 14/7/1. Neuk 1990, Neuk.-V. 80 p. (bis 1,17). 3-7887-1345-3.
4151 *Luria* Ben-Zion, Ⓗ [Zech ...] Book of remembrance: BethM 36,124 (1990s) 74-79.
4151* *Kline* Meredith G., [Zech 1:8] The rider of the red horse: Kerux 5,2 (1990) 2-20; 5,3 (1990) 9-28.
4152 *Fuller* Russell, Early emendations of the scribes; the tiqqun sopherim in Zechariah 2:12: → 173, ᶠSTRUGNELL J., Of scribes 1990, 21-28.

4153 *Bartelink* G.J.M., [Zach 3,1] *Antikeímenos* (Widersacher) als Teufels- und Dämonenbezeichnung: SacrEr 30 (1987s) 205-224.

4154 **Black** Mark C., The rejected and slain Messiah who is coming with his angels; the messianic exegesis of Zechariah 9-14 in the Passion narratives: diss. Emory, D*Holladay* C. Atlanta 1990. 281 p. 91-06713. – DissA 51 (1990s) 3423-A; RTLv 22,591 title 'The Christological use of Zech 9-14 in the NT'.

4155 *Bosshard* Erich, *Kratz* Reinhard G., Maleachi im Zwölfprophetenbuch: BibNot 52 (1990) 27-46.

4156 **Clendenin** Ewell R., The interpretation of biblical Hebrew hortatory texts; a textlinguistic approach to the book of Malachi: diss. Texas, D*Longacre* R. Arlington 1989. 226 p. 90-23444. – DissA 51 (1990s) 834-A.

4157 *Lescow* Theodor, Dialogische Strukturen in den Streitreden des Buches Maleachi: ZAW 102 (1990) 194-212.

4158 **O'Brien** Julia M., Priest and Levite in Malachi: SBL diss. 121 (Duke Univ. 1989, E*Meyers* E.). Atlanta 1990, Scholars. xiv-164 p. $23; sb./pa. $15 [TR 87,338]. 1-55540-438-3.

4159 *Ribera* Josep, El Targum de Malaquías [texto y traducción]: EstB 48 (1990) 171-197.

4160 **Wahl** Otto, Die Bücher Maleachi, Joel und Jona: Geistliche Schriftlesung 13. Dü 1991, Patmos. Mal. p. 22-65 . 146-8; Joel p. 68-107 . 149-152; Jona p. 110-143 . 152-5. 3-491-77169-2.

4161 *Habets* Goswin, Vorbild und Zerrbild; eine Exegese von Mal 1,6 - 2,9: Teresianum 41 (1990) 5-58.

4162 *Jones* David C., A note on the LXX of Malachi 2:16 ['if you hate, divorce'? (MT 'for he hates divorce')]: JBL 109 (1990) 683-5.

IX. NT Exegesis generalis

F1.1 New Testament Introduction.

4163 *Achtemeier* Paul J., Omne verbum sonat; the New Testament and the oral environment of late western antiquity: JBL 109 (1990) 3-27.

4164 **Aune** David E., The New Testament in its literary environment 1987 → 3,3801 ... 5,3951: RBR 5,6 (1989) 13 (H.W. *Attridge*); CriswT 4 (1989s) 391 (D.S. *Dockery*); JSS 35 (1990) 316s (M. *Goodman*); JTS 41 (1990) 204-6 (J. *Drury*).

4165 E**Baarlink** H., Inleiding tot het Nieuwe Testament. Kampen 1989, Kok. 350 p. ƒ47,50. – RGerefTTs 90 (1990) 118s (J. *Helderman*).

4166 **Bammel** Ernst, Jesu Nachfolger 1988 → 4,4072; 5,3952: RCBQ 52 (1990) 735-7 (B. *Fiore*: early Christian assertions of superiority derive from neither family link with, nor designation by, Jesus – if we can have as much confidence as Bammel in ipsissima verba Jesu).

4167 **(Ely Éser) Barreto** Cesar, A fé como ação na história; hermenêutica do Novo Testamento no contexto da América Latina [diss. Atlanta]: Libertação e teologia. São Paulo 1988, Paulinas. 347 p. 85-06-00810-3. – RPerspT 21 (1989) 237s (J. *Konings*: pastor metodista).

4168 **Berger** Klaus, *Colpe* Carsten, Religionsgeschichtliches Textbuch zum NT: NTD Texte 1, 1987 → 3,3805; 4,4075: ᴿTR 86 (1990) 110s (R. *Kampling*).

4169 *a*) *Berger* Klaus, Loyalität als Problem neutestamentlicher Hermeneutik; – *b*) *Betz* Hans-Dieter, Neues Testament und griechisch-hellenistische Überlieferung; → 38*, ᶠCOLPE C., Löyalitätskonflikte 1990, 121-131 / 225-231.

4170 **Blaiklock** E. M., The compact handbook of New Testament life [= ²The world of the NT 1983]. Minneapolis 1989, Bethany. 144 p. $6. 1-55661-061-0. – ᴿCriswT 4 (1989s) 388s (T. D. *Lea*).

4171 *Blomberg* Craig L., New Teatament genre criticism for the 1990s: Themelios 15 (1989s) 40-49.

4172 *Botha* J. E., Style, stylistics and the study of the New Testament: Neotestamentica 24 (1990) 173-184.

4173 **Carmichael** J., The birth of Christianity; reality and myth. NY 1989, Hippocrene. xii-228 p. $18. 0-87052-754-1 [NTAbs 34,374].

4174 **Conzelmann** H., *Lindemann* A., Interpreting the New Testament; an introduction to the principles and methods of NT exegesis [Arbeitsbuch zum NT⁸ʳᵉᵛ 1985], ᵀ*Schatzmann* S. Peabody MA 1988, Hendrickson. xix-389 p. $20. 0-913573-80-9 [with commendation of Helmut *Koester* and others].

4175 **Court** John M. & Kathleen M., The New Testament World. C 1990, Univ. 384 p. £19.50. 0-521-34007-1. – ᴿExpTim 102 (1990s) 119 (H. *Guite*); Month 251 (1990) 376 (Mary E. *Mills*: '£39.50').

4176 **Davies** Stevan L., The NT, a contemporary introduction 1988 → 4,4081; 5,3961: ᴿCBQ 52 (1990) 344s (J. J. *O'Rourke*: claimed neutral but rather liberal); CurrTMiss 17 (1990) 230 (J. L. *Bailey*).

4177 **Dicharry** Warren, Human authors of the New Testament 1. Mark, Matthew, Luke. Collegeville MN 1990, Liturgical. 223 p.; ill.; 3 maps. 0-8146-1956-8 [NTAbs 35,239: 'marvelous Mark', 'masterful Matthew', 'luminous Luke'].

4178 *a*) *Ebeling* Gerhard, Heiliger Geist und Zeitgeist; Identität und Wandel in der Kirchengeschichte; – *b*) *Wagner* Falk, Christentum und Moderne: ZTK 87 (1990) 185-205 / 124-143.

4179 **Edwards** O. C.ᴶ, How Holy Writ was written; the story of the NT. Nv 1990, Abingdon. 160 p. $9 [JAAR 58,745]. – ᴿAnglTR 72 (1990) 460s (C. *Bryan*).

4180 ᴱ**Epp** E., *MacRae* G., The NT and its modern interpreters 1989 → 5,394: ᴿCriswT 4 (1989s) 389-391 (C. C. *Newman*); Horizons 17 (1990) 148-150 (R. *Gnuse*: 'interpretations' in title); TS 51 (1990) 510-3 (R. J. *Dillon*: to non-initiates, 'chaos reigns').

4181 **Ferguson** Everett, Backgrounds of early Christianity 1987 → 3,3817 ... 5,3962: ᴿBR 5,6 (1989) 12s (H. C. *Kee*).

4182 **Fernández Ramos** Felipe, El Nuevo Testamento [I. 1988 → 5,3963]; II. Presentación y contenido: Síntesis 1. M 1989, Atenas. 446 p. – ᴿCarthaginensia 6 (1990) 207s (J. F. *Cuenca*); RelCu 36 (1990) 685 (A. *Moraldi*, 1s); Salmanticensis 37 (1990) 364-6 (G. *Pérez*); ScripTPamp 22 (1990) 1008s (J. M. *Casciaro*, 1); StLeg 30 (1989) 305s (C. De *Villapadierna*, 1s).

4183 *Fuller* Reginald H., Jesus, Paul and apocalyptic: AnglTR 71 (1989) 134-142.

4184 **Galloway** Kathy, Imagining [ten stories of] the gospels. NY 1990, Crossroad. 104 p.; ill. *Maule* Graham. $9 pa. 0-8245-0982-X [TDig 38,59].

4185 **Grant** Patrick, Reading the New Testament 1989 → 5,3966: RTLond 93 (1990) 157-9 (J. *Drury*: lively and sensitive).

4186 **Guenther** Heinz O., The footprints of Jesus' Twelve in early Christian traditions; a study in the meaning of religious [... number-] symbolism. NY 1985, Lang. vii-148 p. Fs 48.10 [RelStR 17,260, R. H. *Fuller*].

4187 **Guijarro Oporto** Santiago, La buena noticia de Jesús; introducción a los evangelios sinópticos y a los Hechos de los Apóstoles: Biblioteca Básica del Creyente, 1987 → 3,3823 ... 5,3968: RActuBBg 27 (1990) 57 (X. *Alegre* S.).

4187* **Guthrie** D., NT Introduction⁴ [³c. 1970]. DG/Leicester 1990, Inter-Varsity/Apollos. 1161 p. $40. 0-8308-2443-2 / 0-85111-761-9 [NTAbs 35,93]. **Hall** David, The seven pillories of wisdom [on NT interpreters] 1990 → 3556.

4188 **Harris** S. L., The New Testament, a student's introduction. Mountain View CA 1988, Mayfield. xvi-343 p.; 8 pl. $25. 0-87484-746-x [NTAbs 34,377].

4189 *Hedrick* Charles W., Toward a code of ethics for NT scholars; 'heavenly labials in a world of gutturals' [from a poem of W. STEVENS]: PerspRelSt 17 (1990) 101-115.

4190 **Hock** Ronald F., *O'Neil* E. N., The chreia 1986 → 1,3863* ... 3,3826: RCritRR 2 (1989) 292-4 (V. K. *Robbins*).

4191 **Horst** Pieter W. van der, *Mussies* Gerard, Studies on the Hellenistic background of the NT: Utrechtse Theologische Reeks 10. Utrecht 1990, Wever. [vi-] 242 p. ƒ30 [CBQ 53,171]. 90-72235-10-X.

4192 **Jantsch** J., Die Entstehung des Christentums bei A. v. HARNACK und E. MEYER [Diss. DChrist K.]: Diss AltG 28. Bonn 1990, Habelt. vii-448 p. DM 54. 3-7749-2403-1 [NTAbs 35,127].

4193 *a)* Jesus and his times. Pleasantville NY 1987, Reader's Digest. $25. – RBA 53 (1990) 41 (J. A. *King*); – *b)* Gesù e il suo tempo [1987], consulente italiano *Ravasi* G. Mi 1989, Reader's Digest. 335 p.; 400 fig. Lit. 20.000. – RCC 141 (1990.1) 304s (G. *Giachi*).

4194 **Johnson** Luke T., The writings of the NT, an interpretation 1986 → 3,3828 ... 5,3974: RCriswT 4 (1989s) 188s (D. S. *Dockery*); Vidyajyoti 53 (1989) 454s (P. M. *Meagher*).

4195 *Kampling* Rainer, Kontrastgesellschaft; zur Brauchbarkeit eines Begriffes für die neutestamentliche Wissenschaft: BibNot 52 (1990) 13-18.

4196 **Kemmer** A., Das Neue Testament; Einleitung für Laien.² FrB 1990, Herder. 270 p. [RTPhil 122, 577].

4197 **Kirchschläger** Walter, Kleiner Grundkurs Bibel; im Blick, das Neue Testament. StuTb 2. Stu 1990, KBW. 128 p. 3-460-11002-3.

4198 **Köster** H., Introducción al NT 1988 → 5,3977: RCiTom 117 (1990) 150s (J. L. *Espinel*); Iter 1 (1990) 139 (J.-P. *Wyssenbach*); QVidCr 146 (1989) 122s (P.-R. *Tragan*).

4199 **Kurz** William S., Farewell addresses in the New Testament: Zacchaeus. Collegeville MN 1990, Liturgical. 134 p.

4200 **Lemcio** Eugene E., The unifying kerygma of the New Testament [1. God who; 2. sent or raised; 3. Jesus; 4. A response; 5. towards God; 6. brings benefits: found in 10 of the 27 NT writings] II: JStNT 38 (1990) 3-11.

4201 **Lips** H. von, Weisheitliche Traditionen im NT [ev. Hab.-Diss. München 1989 → 5,3975]: WM 64. Neuk 1990. xii-512 p. DM 84. 3-7887-1340-2 [NRT 113,755, X. *Jacques*]. – RSUNT-A 15 (1990) 207 (A. *Fuchs*).

4202 **Lövestam** Evald, Axplock; nytestamentliga studier 1987 → 4,221: RSvEx 55 (1990) 160-3 (P. *Block*).

4203 **Luke** K.,   The TPI companion to the Bible [I. 1987 → 4,1078], II. New
Testament.   Bangalore 1988, Theol. Publ. – x-187 p. rs 25. – RVidyajyoti
54 (1990) 266 (P. M. *Meagher*).

4204 **McGonigle** Thomas D., *Quigley* James F.,   A history of the Christian
tradition [... high-school text]. NY 1988, Paulist. 218 p. $11. – RPrPeo 4
(1990) 76 (M. Cecily *Boulding*).

E**McKnight** Scot, Introducing New Testament interpretation 1989 → 357.

4206 *Manns* Frédéric,   La technique du *al tiqra* ['ne lis pas (ceci... mais)']
dans les Évangiles: RevSR 64 (1990) 1-7.

4207 **Martin** Francis,   Narrative parallels to the New Testament [294 brief
stories; from OT, rabbis, Hellenism]: SBL Resources 22.   Atlanta 1988,
Scholars. $32; pa. $21 [RB 98,307s, J. *Murphy-O'Connor*].

4209 **Mason** Steve, *Robinson* Tom,   An early Christian reader.   Toronto 1990,
Canadian Scholars. xiii-600 p.; maps. 0-921627-56-4.

4210 **Mertes** Klaus,   Jüngerprofile; die Gefährten Jesu und ihr Weg zum
Glauben. Fra 1989, Knecht. 155 p. DM 26. – RZkT 112 (1990) 371s (A.
Batlogg).

4211 **Morgen** M., Le NT: Parcours.   P 1989, Centurion.   106 p. – REsprVie
100 (1990) 539s (L. *Walter*).

4212 **Neill** S., [2]*Wright* T., Interpretation of the NT 1861-1986:   1988 → 4,
4103; 5,3987: RTorJT 6 (1990) 128s (S. *Brown*).

4213 E**Niemann** Franz J.,   Jesus der Offenbarer, Texte I; Altertum bis
Mittelalter; II. Frühe Neuzeit bis Gegenwart: Texte zur T. Fund 5/1s.
Graz 1990, Styria. 151 p.; 216 p. [TPhil 65,631].

4213* *a*) *Paissac* Maurice, Critique évangélique et philosophie; – *b*) *Léonard*
André, L'Évangile de Jésus et l'histoire: → 542, Év. Venasque 1989/90,
103-128 / 129-146.

4214 **Partridge** E.,   The book of New Testament word studies: Bible Reference Library.   Westwood NJ 1987, Barbour.   iv-215 p. $7 pa.   1-
55748-031-1 [NTAbs 34,102].

4215 **Patte** Daniel,   Structural exegesis for New Testament critics. Mp 1900,
Fortress. x-134 p. $8. 0-8006-2196-7. – RExpTim 102 (1990s) 182s (R.
Morgan: a lonely furrow; less fruitful than other literary approaches).

4216 **Penna** Romano, Letture evangeliche; saggi esegetici sui quattro Vangeli:
StudRBib, 1989 → 5,3992: RLateranum 56 (1990) 416 (*ipse*, con indizio
dei brani trattati).

4217 **Perkins** Pheme,   Reading the NT[2] 1988 → 4,4104; also L, Chapman:
RFurrow 40 (1989) 377 (J. *Byrne*); Vidyajyoti 53 (1989) 223 (P. M.
Meagher).

4218 **Piettre** Monique, Le parole 'dure' del Vangelo [1988 [2]1989], T*Crespi*
Pietro: Universale teologica 29.   Brescia 1990, Queriniana.   131 p. Lit.
15.000. 88-399-1229-0.

4219 **Puskas** Charles B.,   An introduction to the New Testament. Peabody
MA 1989, Hendrickson.   xxii-297 p. $20. 0-913573-45-0 [R. *O'Toole*
(blurb): 'teachers will delight in his imaginative presentation'... thorough
acquaintance with secondary literature... non-sectarian]. – RCommSev 23
(1990) 432s (M. de *Burgos*).

4221 **Russell** D. S.,   Poles apart; the Gospel in creative tension. E 1900, St.
Andrew. viii-171 p. £6.50. 0-7152-0646-X [NTAbs 35,260: binomia like
Scripture/tradition, faith/works, male/female are not contradictory but
complementary].

4222 *a*) *Schenk* Richard,   Omnis Christi actio nostra est instructio; the deeds
and sayings of Jesus as revelation in the view of AQUINAS; – *b*) *McGregor*

Bede, Revelation, creeds, and salvific mission; – *c*) *Cottier* Georges, Les motifs de crédibilité de la révélation selon Saint Thomas: ➤ 608, Révélation/Aquin 1989/90, 104-131 / 196-211 / 212-229.

4223 *a*) *Schenke* Martin, 'Er muss wachsen, ich aber muss abnehmen' – der Konflikt zwischen Jesusjüngern und Täufergemeinde im Spiegel des Johannes-Evangeliums; – *b*) *Betz* Hans-Dieter, Neues Testament und griechisch-hellenistische Überlieferung; ➤ 38*, FCOLPE C., Loyalitätskonflikte 1990, 301-313 / 225-231.

4224 **Schierse** F. J., Introduzione al NT: GdT 173, 1987 ➤ 3,3849: RProtestantesimo 45 (1990) 325 (B. *Corsani*).

4225 **Schweizer** E., Theologische Einleitung in das NT 1989 ➤ 5,3997: RNeotestamentica 29 (1990) 368s (H. A. *Lombard*); RHPR 70 (1990) 260 (M.-A. *Chevallier*); SNTU-A 14 (1989) 221-3 (M. *Hasitschka*).

4226 **Segalla** Giuseppe, Panoramas del Nuevo Testamento 1989 ➤ 5,3999: REfMex 8 (1990) 119-122 (R. H. *Lugo Rodríguez*); RelCu 36 (1990) 688s (A. *Moral*); RTLim 24 (1990) 294s (U. *Berger*).

4227 ESevrin Jean-Marie, The NT in early Christianity — La réception des Écrits néotestamentaires 1986/9 ➤ 5,606: RCollatVL 20 (1990) 115 (A. *Denaux*); RHE 85 (1990) 364-7 (C. *Focant*); RHPR 70 (1990) 261s (C. *Grappe*).

4228 **Shank** Robert, Harmony of the Gospels: Complete biblical [i.e. NT] library, 1 [out of 16 volumes, of which 11-16 are a Greek-English dictionary; the others commentaries on the single books]. Springfield MO 1986-1991, World Library (2274 E. Sunshine, 65804). 0-882343-361-X [to -376-X: TDig 38,155; no pp. or other authors].

4229 **Strecker** J., Neues Testament – [*Maier* J., hellenistisches und späteres, S. 137-184] Antikes Judentum: Grundkurs Theologie 2 [aus 10], Urban-Tb 422. Stu 1989, Kohlhammer. 192 p. DM 22. – RKIsr 5 (1990) 75s (Julie *Kirchberg*); TLZ 115 (1990) 276s (T. *Holtz*); TPQ 138 (1990) 274 (C. *Niemand*); ZAW 102 (1990) 164 (H.-C. *Schmitt*).

4230 **Sumrall** David L., A study of parent-child relationships among first-century Christians [ii. Synoptics; iii Paul; iv. other NT]: diss. Baptist Theol. Sem., DStevens G. New Orleans 1989. 233 p. 90-22330. – DissA 51 (1990s) 891-A.

4231 *Tarjányi* Béla, Ⓜ Die Geburt der christlichen Religion: ➤ 133, FNYÍRI T., 1990, 408-414.

4232 **Tilliette** Xavier, Filosofi davanti a Cristo, TESansonetti: Testi 5. Brescia 1989, Queriniana. 534 p. Lit. 55.000. RETL 66 (1990) 441s (E. *Brito*).

4233 **Tuñi Vancells** J. O., Jesús en comunitat; el Nou Testament un accés a Jesús: Horitzons 18, 1988 ➤ 5,4007: RQVidCr 145 (1989) 146 (D. *Roure*).

F1.2 *Origo Evangeliorum;* the Origin of the Gospels.

Aletti Jean-Noël, L'art de raconter Jésus-Christ 1989 ➤ 5355.

4234 **Aune** David E., The Gospels; biography or theology?: BR 6,1 (1990) 14-21.37; ill.

4235 **Amphoux** Christian-B., Histoire des Évangiles. P 1989, Kerux. 32 p. + 2 cassettes. – RÉTRel 65 (1990) 308 (*ipse*).

4236 **Burridge** Richard A., Gospels, genre and Graeco-Roman biography: diss. Nottingham 1989. 375 p. BRD-88607. – DissA 51 (1990s) 156s-A.

4237 **Dormeyer** D., Evangelium als literarische und theologische Gattung: ErtFor 263. Da 1989, Wiss. viii-200 p. DM 40. 3-534-02804-X [NTAbs 34,108].

ᴱ**Dungan** D. L., The interrelations of the Gospels, symposium BOISMARD M.-É., *al.*, ➤ 524, BiblETL 95, 1984/90.

4239 **Farmer** W. R., Jesus and the Gospel; tradition, Scripture, and canon 1982 ➤ 63,3968 ... 3,3867: ᴿSNTU A-15 (1990) 151-3 (A. *Fuchs*).

4240 *Faschian* Konstanz, Neue Studien zur Frage der Entstehung der neu-testamentlichen Schriften [ROBINSON J., Redating; CARMIGNAC, Naissance; THIEDE Mk 6,52s]: WissWeis 53 (1990) 66-72.

4241 **Frankemölle** Hubert, Evangelium – Begriff und Gattung: SBB 15, 1988 ➤ 4,4125: ᴿJBL 109 (1990) 345s (C. H. *Talbert*); StPatav 37 (1990) 702-4 (G. *Segalla*).

4242 **Fredriksen** Paula, From Jesus to Christ; the origins of the NT images of Jesus 1988 ➤ 4,4126; 5,4053: ᴿAmHR 95 (1990) 465s (A. J. *Hultgren*); CritRR 3 (1990) 200-2 (J. *Reumann*); Horizons 17 (1990) 325s (Mary Ann *Hinsdale*); JAAR 58 (1990) 496-8 (R. H. *Fuller*); JEH 41 (1990) 136s (C. J. A. *Hickling*); JJS 41 (1990) 122-5 (E. P. *Sanders*); JTS 41 (1990) 203s (J. D. G. *Dunn*: not Christology but Christian beginnings); Interpretation 44 (1990) 311s (A. *Terian*).

4242* *Galizzi* Mario, I quattro Vangeli: ➤ 1160, ᴱ*Cimosa* M., Parola e vita 1988, 212-297.

4243 **Funk** Robert W., New Gospel parallels²ʳᵉᵛ; Foundations and facets. Sonoma CA 1990, Polebridge. xvi-272 p. $22; pa. $16. – ᴿSNTU-A 14 (1989) 220s (A. *Fuchs*, 1 ed.).

4244 **Grelot** Pierre, L'origine des évangiles 1986 ➤ 2,3029 ... 5,4011: ᴿSvEx 55 (1990) 133-7 (A. *Ekenberg*, also on GERHARDSSON B. 1986).

4245 **Grelot** P., L'origine dei vangeli ... [CARMIGNAC 1986]ᵀ: SScr 1. Vaticano 1989, Editrice. 166 p. Lit. 24.000. – ᴿRasT 31 (1990) 408s (V. *Fusco*: importanza della tradizione, nemmeno menzionata da CARMIGNAC).

4246 **Koester** Helmut, Ancient Christian gospels; their history and development [canonical and others which contributed to the early stages of the history of Gospel literature [... Synoptic plus Q, 2 Clement, Diatess.]. L/Ph 1990, SCM/Trinity. xxxii-448 p. $30. 0-334-02459-5 [NTAbs 35,243].

4246* *a) Mare* W. Harold, Genre criticism and the Gospels; – *b) Silva* Moisés, The language and style of the Gospels: ➤ 370, Gospels Today 1990, 82-101 / 27-37.

4247 **O'Grady** John F., The four Gospels and the Jesus tradition 1989 ➤ 5,4015: ᴿBibTB 20 (1990) 172s (E. L. *Bode*: smooth but leaves some questions).

4248 *Packer* James I., Cos'è l'evangelizzazione? Evangelizzazione e teologia [*Green* M. 'La maggior parte degli evangelisti non è molto interessata alla teologia e la maggior parte dei teologi non è molto interessata al-l'evangelizzazione': purtroppo vero] ᵀ*Grottoli* C.: STEv NS 1 (1989) 41-60.

4249 **Ralph** Margaret N., Discovering the Gospels; four accounts of the Good News: Discovering the living Word. NY 1990, Paulist. vi-283 p. $12 pa. 0-8091-3200-1 [NTAbs 35,245: 72 questions that come up in the minds of high school juniors].

ᴱ**Robertson** M. J., *Lane* W., The Gospels today; a guide to some recent developments: NTStudent 6, 1990 ➤ 370.

4250 *a) Shuler* P. L., The genre(s) of the Gospels; – *b) Gerhardsson* Birger, The gospel tradition; – *c) Mayer* B. F., Objectivity and subjectivity in historical criticism of the Gospels: ➤ 524, Interrelations 1984/90, 459-483 (-494, *Stuhlmacher* P., response) / 497-545 / 546-560 (-564, *Fuller* R. H.).

4252 **Stanton** G. N.,   The Gospels and Jesus: Bible Studies 1989 ➤ 5,4016:
ᴿIrBSt 12 (1990) 200-2 (V. *Parkin*); RivStoLR 26 (1990) 178-180 (V.
Fusco); TLond 93 (1990) 244s (J. *Muddiman*, also on SANDERS-DAVIES
1989).
4253 *Vos* C. J. A.,   Die Evangelie as pragmatic-kommunikatiewe gebeure; 'n
Perspektief op Evangelistiek: SkrifK 10 (1989) 183-190 [< NTAbs
34,313].

F1.3   **Historicitas,** *chronologia* **Evangeliorum.**

4254 **Barnett** Paul,   Is the New Testament history? 1987 ➤ 3,3885:   ᴿClasW
83 (1989) 119s (A. M. *Devine*).
4255 **Blomberg** Craig L.,   The historical reliability of the Gospels 1987
➤ 3,3886 ... 5,4018:   ᴿCriswT 4 (1989s) 185s (G. *Davis*); IrTQ 56 (1990)
236s (M. *Mullins*); TLZ 115 (1990) 203s (N. *Walter*).
4256 *Botha* J.,   Kom ons stem; wat het Jesus regtig gesé? [Let us vote; what
did Jesus really say: R. FUNK 1985 enterprise situated in the 'myth of the
American West']: HervTS 46 (1990) 15-35 [< NTAbs 35,152].
4257 *Evans* C. A.,   Authenticity criteria in Life of Jesus research: ChrSchR
19,1 (GR 1989) 6-31 [< NTAbs 34,157].
4258 *García-Moreno* Antonio,   La historicidad de los Evangelios; boletín
bibliográfico (1980-1990) [... GRELOT P., TRESMONTANT C., CARMIGNAC
J.]: ScripTPamp 22 (1990) 927-955.
4259 **Grelot** Pierre,   Los Evangelios y la historia: BiblHerder SEscr 179, 1979
➤ 4,4147; 5,4023:   ᴿCommSev 22 (1989) 89s (M. de *Burgos*).
4260 **Grelot** P.,   Las palabras de Jesucristo: SEscr 183, 1988 ➤ 4,4140; 5,4026:
ᴿLumenVr 39 (1990) 341s (J. M. *Arroniz*); PerspT 22 (1990) 250s (J.
Vitório).
4261 **Grelot** P.,   Vangeli e storia / Le parole di Gesù Cristo: IntrNT 6s, 1988
➤ 5,4027:   ᴿRivB 38 (1990) 125s (A. *Bonora*).
4262 *Hinz* W.,   Chronologie des Lebens Jesu: ZDMG 139 (1989) 301-9
[< NTAbs 34,157: born Dec. 1, 7 B.C.; died Apr. 30, 28 A.D. (and yet)
lived 30 years and 5 months!: Hinz has 33 years].
4262* **Kee** Howard C.,   What can we know about Jesus?: Understanding
Jesus today 1.   NY 1990, Cambridge-UP. v-122 p. $22.50; pa. $7. 0-
521-36057-9; -915-0 [TDig 37,389].
4263 **Latourelle** René,   Jesus existiu? São Paulo 1989, Santuario. 232 p.
[REB 50,263].
4264 *a*) *Léonard* André,   L'Évangile de Jésus et l'histoire; – *b*) *Paissac*
Maurice,   Critique évangélique et philosophie: ➤ 542, Évangile 1989/90,
129-146 / 103-128.
4265 *a*) *Sánchez Mielgo* Gerardo,   La historicidad de los evangelios en la 'Dei
Verbum'; – *b*) *Gelabert Ballester* Martín,   Revelación, signos de los
tiempos y magisterio de la Iglesia: TEspir 34,101s ('Temas conciliares 25
años después' 1990) 197-230 / 231-255.
4266 **Wilson** Ian,   Are these the words of Jesus? Dramatic evidence from
beyond the NT. ... 1990, Lennard. x-182 p. £15 pa. – ᴿTablet 244 (1990)
860s (R. *Murray*); TLond 93 (1990) 486s (A. H. B. *Logan*).

F1.4   *Jesus historicus* – **The human Jesus.**

4267 **Alt** Franz,   Jesus, der erste neue Mann. Mü 1989, Piper.   160 p.
DM 19,80. – ᴿEvKomm 22,12 (1989) 47-49 (Susanne *Heine*); KIsr 5
(1990) 77s (M. *Brocke*); TR 87 (1991) 59s (Andrea *Tafferner*: richtig

Hilberath Bernd J., StiZt 1990, 180-192, 'reiht sich ein in die unheilvolle Geschichte antijüdischer Polemik im Christentum').

4268 *a)* **Boers** Hendrikus, Who was Jesus? 1989 ➔ 5,4037: ᴿRelStR 16 (1990) 261 (M.G. *Reddish*); RExp 87 (1990) 135s (J.E. *Jones*); – *b)* **Rosenberg** Roy A., Who was Jesus? 1986 ➔ 4,4265; 0-8191-5177-7; pa. -8-5: ᴿScripTPamp 22 (1990) 646s (J.M. *Casciaro*).

4269 **Bordoni** Marcello, Gesù di Nazaret; presenza, memoria, attesa 1988 ➔ 5,4038: ᴿCC 141 (1990,2) 507s (F. *Lambiasi*).

4270 **Borg** Marcus, Jesus, a new vision; spirit, culture, and the life of discipleship 1987 ➔ 4,4155; 5,4038: ᴿBR 5,5 (1989) 12.17 (Adela Y. *Collins*: some weaknesses); CritRR 2 (1989) 182-6 (R.G. *Hamerton-Kelly*); TorJT 6 (1990) 119-123 (R. *Cameron*).

4271 — *Borg* Marcus, What did Jesus really say?: BR 5,5 (1989) 18-25.

4272 **Bowden** John, Jesus; the unanswered questions 1988 ➔ 4,4157; 5,4040: ᴿAnglTR 72 (1990) 105-8 (D.F. *Winslow*); Interpretation 44 (1990) 424s (A.J. *Hultgren*); ScotBEv 8 (1990) 137 (D.J. *Graham*); Themelios 15 (1989s) 34 (R. *Bauckham*).

4273 **Bravo** Carlos, Jesús, hombre en conflicto [diss. Barc / S.Cugat, ᴰ*González Faus* J.I.]. México 1988, C.R.T. 282 p. – ᴿEfMex 8 (1990) 379-387 (V. *Girardi*).

4274 **Brown** Colin, Jesus in European Protestant thought, 1778-1860. GR 1988, Baker. xxiv-359 p. $19 pa. – ᴿCurrTMiss 17 (1990) 153s (D.R. *Ruppe*).

4275 **Bruggen** J. van, Christus op aarde; zijn levensbeschrijving door leerlingen en tijdgenoten: CommNT, 1987 ➔ 4,4160; 5,4043: ƒ49,50: ᴿNedTTs 44 (1990) 255-7 (M. de *Jonge*).

ᴱ**Collet** Giancarlo, Der Christus der Armen; das Christuszeugnis der lateinamerikanischen Befreiungstheologen 1988 ➔ 8516.

4276 **Cottin** Jérôme, Jésus-Christ en écriture d'images; premières représentations chrétiennes: Essais Bibliques 17. Genève 1990, Labor et Fides. 158 p.; 40 fig. 2-8309-0604-7.

4277 **Coulot** C., Jésus et le disciple ᴰ1987 ➔ 3,3917... 5,4045: ᴿSNTU-A 14 (1989) 227s (H. *Giesen*).

4278 *a)* *Cullom* Barbara A., By what authority? New Testament perspectives on the authority and leadership of Jesus; – *b)* *Hamilton* Andrew, The authoritative sinner [...Peter Mt 16]: Way 29 (1989) 277-286 / 287-295.

4279 *Davis* Charles, Is the maleness of Jesus a sacred sign? [...on occasion of ordination of first Anglican woman bishop]: Tablet 243 (1989) 190.192 (220s, response, *McDade* J.); comments 253, 317, 357.

4280 **Cunningham** Philip A., Jesus and the evangelists 1988 ➔ 4,4166; 5,4046: ᴿPerspRelSt 17 (1990) 284s (C.C. *Black*).

4281 **Dione** Hyacinthe, Jésus et le sabbat; contribution à la recherche historique sur Jésus de Nazareth: diss. Strasbourg 1988s. – BZ 34 (1990) 158.

4282 **Fabris** Rinaldo, Jesús de Nazaret 1985 ➔ 1,3955*b*... 3,3923: ᴿScripT-Pamp 22 (1990) 645s (J.M. *Casciaro*).

4283 **Feneberg** Wolfgang, Jesus, der nahe Unbekannte. Mü 1990, Kösel. 139 p. DM 24,80 [BZ 35,129, F. *Mussner*].

4284 **Fischer** Irmtraud, Wo ist Jesus? [ᴰGraz 1988 ᴰ*Marböck* J.]: SBB 19. Stu 1989, KBW [ZAW 103,296, H.-C. *Schmitt*].

4285 **Floris** Ennio, Sous le Christ, Jésus, 1987 ➔ 4,4171; 5,4050: ᴿFoiVie 89,2 (1990) 89s (G. *Vahanian*).

4287 *Georgi* Dieter, Leben-Jesu-Forschung: ➔ 857, TRE 20 (1990) 566-575.

Gisel P., Le Christ de Calvin 1990 ➔ k661*.

4288 *Gladstone* J.W., Three Bible studies; Jesus, the crowds and the King-dom: Religion and Society 36,1 (Bangalore 1989) 44-51 [< TContext 7/2, 40].

4289 **Gnilka** Joachim, Jesus von Nazaret, Botschaft und Geschichte: HerdT-KommNT Supp 3. FrB 1990, Herder. 131 p.; 8 fig. DM 70 [NRT 113, 754, X. *Jacques*]. 3-451-21989-1.

4290 **Gourgues** Michel, La sfida della fedeltà; l'esperienza di Gesù [1985 ➤ 1,1048], T: Letture bibliche. R 1987, Borla. 143 p. Lit. 10.000. – RBenedictina 36 (1989) 224 (E. *Tuccimei*).

4291 **Guthrie** D., Jesus the Messiah; an illustrated life of Christ. GR 1990 = 1972, Zondervan. xiv-386 p. $17 pa. 0-310-25431-0 [NTAbs 35,241].

4292 **Hamaide** J. Jésus... que dis-tu de toi-même 1988 ➤ 4,4175: RSpiritus 31 (1990) 226s (E. *Desmarescaux*).

4293 *Hernán Cubillos* Robert, HERRMANN's Communion of the Christian with God: contributions to an Evangelical perspective on the importance of experience of the 'inner life' of Jesus?: JEvTS 33 (1990) 179-188 [< ZIT 90,805].

4294 **Hoeffner** Kent, Jesus as eschatological prophet; biblical, historical and theological perspectives with special reference to E. SCHILLEBEECKX: diss. Southern Baptist Theol. Sem. 1990, DHendricks W. 326 p. 91-07136. – DissA 51 (1990s) 3113-A.

4295 **Hurth** Elizabeth, In His name, comparative studies in the quest for the historical Jesus: Life of Jesus Research in Germany and America, EurHS 23/367, 1989 ➤ 5,4062; 3-631-41955-4: RSNTU A-15 (1990) 202-4 (F. *Weissengruber*).

4297 *Kümmel* Werner G., Jesusforschung seit 1981, III. Die Lehre Jesu: TRu 55 (1990) 21-45.

4298 **Leclerc** E., De verborgen wegen van Gods Koninkrijk. Aver-bode/Kampen 1990, Altiora/Kok. 180 p. Fb 495. RCollatVL 20 (1990) 443s (J. De *Kesel*).

4299 **Legaut** Marcel, Meditación de un cristiano del siglo XX, TCuerva Francisco: Pedal 203. S 1989, Sígueme. 304 p. – RLumenVr 39 (1990) 348s (U. *Gil Ortega*: aspectos muy positivos, pero la misión de Jesús reducida al llamamiento de Dios).

4300 **Leivestad** Ragnar, Jesus in his own perspective; an examination of his sayings, actions, and eschatological titles, TAune D. 1987 ➤ 3,3938 ... 5,4067: RCritRR 3 (1990) 215-7 (M.J. *Borg*); PerspRelSt 17 (1990) 73-77 (R.B. *Vinson* compares with BORG M. 1987 and CHARLESWORTH J. 1988).

4301 *Levoratti* Armando J., La sombra del Galileo [THEISSEN G., Sígueme 1988]; un comentario: RBibArg 52,40 (1990) 193-233.

4302 **MacArthur** John F.J, The Gospel according to Jesus 1988 ➤ 5,4067*: RAndrUnS 28 (1990) 98s (J. *Paulien*); CriswT 4 (1989s) 198-200 (W.E. *Bell*).

4303 **Martín Descalzo** José L., Vida y misterio de Jesús de Nazaret [ed. 8, tres volúmenes in uno]: Nueva Alianza 114, 1989 ➤ 5,4069; 84-301-1047-7: RActuBbg 27 (1990) 60 (J. *Boada*).

4304 **Mateos** Juan, La utopía de Jesús: En torno al NT 8. Córdoba 1990, Almendro. 173 p. 84-86077-82-6.

4305 *Meier* John P., The historical Jesus; rethinking some concepts [distinc-tion from the 'historic' Christ no longer serviceable]: TS 51 (1990) 3-24.

4306 *a) Meyer* Ben F., How Jesus charged language with meaning; a study in rhetoric [Canadian Society of Biblical Studies presidential address, Quebec

May 29, 1989]: SR 19 (1990) 273-285; – b) How Jesus charged language with meaning [by phanopoeia, melopoeia, and logopoeia]; a study in rhetoric: CanadBib 49 (1989) 5-20 [< NTAbs 34,298].

4307 *Montagna* Davide M., Simboli dell'amicizia nelle Scritture [... Gesù]: PalCl 68 (1989) 279-286.

4308 **Morgan** G. Campbell, The crises of the Christ; the seven greatest events of his life. GR 1989 = 1903, Kregel. 324 p. $10. 0-8254-3258-8. – ᴿRExp 87 (1990) 514s (C. *Bugg*).

4309 **Morin** Émile, Non-lieu pour Jésus: Présence, 1989 → 5,4072; 2-08-066089-6: ᴿÉTRel 65 (1990) 116s (E. *Cuvillier*: catholique, pessimiste face à THEISSEN); FoiTemps 19 (1989) 395s (H. *Thomas*); Masses Ouvrières 432 (1990) 89s (G. *Sindt*: confus); NRT 112 (1990) 912s (X. *Jacques*).

4310 *Navone* John, Reflexões teológicas sobre a beleza [... de Jesucristo]: Brotéria 130 (1990) 419-428.

4311 *Okure* Teresa, Leadership in the NT [*Edet* Rosemary, ... Resurrection/feminist perspective]: NigerianJT 5 (1990) 71-93 [94-101].

4312 *Panimolle* Salvatore A., Storicità e umanità del Cristo nelle apologie di S. GIUSTINO Martire: RivB 38 (1990) 191-223; Eng. 223.

4313 *Pasquato* Ottorino, Sangue e umanità di Cristo nei concili ecumenici del medioevo, tra teologia, devozione e pietà popolare: Salesianum 52 (1990) 277-308.

4314 **Pelikan** Jaroslav, Jesus through the centuries 1985 → 1,3075 ... 5,4076: ᴿCathHR 75 (1989) 110s (W. P. *Loewe*); Manresa 61 (1989) 414 (J. M.); NatGrac 37 (1990) 132 (A. *Villalmonte*); Studium 30 (M 1990) 553 (L. *López de las Heras*).

4315 **Perkins** Pheme, Jesus as teacher: Understanding Jesus today 2. NY 1990, Cambridge-UP. v-177 p. $22.50; pa. $7. 0-521-36624-0; pa. -95-X [TDig 37,389].

4316 **Pikaza** Xabier, El Evangelio, I. Vida y pascua de Jesús: BiblEstB 75. S 1990, Sígueme. 440 p. 84-301-1105-0. – ᴿActuBbg 27 (1990) 200 (X. *Alegre S.*).

4317 ᴱ**Pirola** Giuseppe, *Cappellotti* Francesco, Il 'Gesù storico'; problema della modernità [seminario Torino 1985/6] 1988 → 4,495*; 5,4079: ᴿActuBbg 27 (1990) 78s (J. *Boada*).

4318 a) *Provencher* Normand, Singularité de Jésus et universalité du Christ; – b) *Langevin* Gilles, Singularité et universalité du Christ-Jésus; – c) *Lemieux* Raymond, Jésus, un produit culturel contemporain? réflexions sur le christianisme et l'art d'aujourd'hui: → 669, ᴱ*Petit* J., J.-C. universel 1989/90, 9-24 / 47-54 / 79-102.

4319 *Pyc* Marek, ❷ L'obbedienza di Cristo nelle opere di Hans Urs von BALTHASAR: STWsz 28,1 (1990) 41-65; ital. 65.

4320 **Riesner** Rainer, Jesus als Lehrer; eine Untersuchung zum Ursprung der Evangelienüberlieferung³ʳᵉᵛ 1984 → 62,4080 ... 5,4081: ᴿCarthaginensia 6 (1990) 373s (R. *Sanz Valdivieso*).

4320* **Romaniuk** Kazimierz, ❷ Sprawa Jezusa z Nazaretu. Wrocław 1988, Archidiec. 197 p. [ZNW 79,298].

4321 *Ross* J. M., Jesus's knowledge of Greek: IrBSt 12 (1990) 41-47.

4322 **Roux** Jean-Paul, Jésus. P 1989, Fayard. 528 p. F 140. – ᴿÉtudes 372 (1990) 856s (P. *Vallin*: rapprochements peu rigoureux).

4323 *Ruh* Ulrich, a) Die Schwierigkeiten mit dem 'wirklichen' Jesus; Bemerkungen zu einigen neueren Jesusbüchern: HerdKorr 44 (1990) 287-291; – b) Le difficoltà col Gesù 'reale', ᵀ*Colombi* Giulio: HumBr 45 (1990) 851-860.

4324 **Schnell** Christoph W., Basic assumptions in Jesus research; an evaluation of five different approaches: diss. ᴰ*Forster* W. Pretoria 1990. 168 p. – RTLv 22, p. 595.

4324* *a) Scott* B. B., Jesus as sage; an innovative voice in the common wisdom; – *b) Kerferd* G. B., The sage in Hellenistic philosophical literature (399 B.C.E. - 199 C.E.); – *c) Fiore* B., The sage in select Hellenistic and Roman literary genres; – *d) Collins* J. J., The sage in the apocalyptic and pseudepigraphic literature: ➤ 336, Sage 1990, 399-415 / 319-328 / 329-341 / 343-354.

4325 **Schweitzer** Albert, Storia della ricerca sulla vita di Gesù 1986 ➤ 2, 3103 ... 5,4085: ᴿHelmantica 41 (1990) 433-5 (L. *Amigò*).

4326 **Sauer** Jürgen R., Rückkehr des Heils; eine Untersuchung zum Problem des 'ethischen Radikalismus' des historischen Jesus: Diss. ᴰ*Stegemann*. Göttingen 1990. – RTLv 22, p. 595.

4327 **Secondin** Bruno, Alla luce del suo volto, 1. Lo splendore: Cammini dello Spirito 1989 ➤ 5,4087: 88-10-50713-4: ᴿAntonianum 65 (1990) 107s (V. *Battaglia*: odierno rinnovato interesse per la persona di Gesù).

4329 *Strecker* Georg, The historical and theological problem of the Jesus question [= EvT 20 (1969) 453-476 = Eschaton (1979) 159-182], ᵀ*Parker* N.: TorJT 6 (1990) 201-223.

4330 **Theissen** Gerd, *a)* The shadow of the Galilaean 1987 ➤ 4,3969; 5,4091: ᴿCritRR 2 (1989) 251s (B. F. *Meyer*); – *b)* L'ombre du Galiléen 1989 ➤ 5,4092: ᴿRHPR 70 (1990) 263s (R. *Prigent*); Telema 16,2 (1990) 81 (Madeleine *Lafue-Veron*); – *c)* L'ombra del Galileo 1990 ➤ 5,4093: ᴿStPatav 37 (1990) 704-6 (G. *Segalla*); *d)* A sombra do Galileu; pesquise histórica sobre Jesus em forma narrativa 1989 ➤ 5,4094: ᴿPerspT 21 (1989) 393-5 (J. *Konings*).

4330* **Wojciechowski** Michał: comments that his dissertation entitled Czynności symbologiczne (Les actions symboliques de Jésus à la lumière de l'AT, 1986) was wrongly classed [➤ 3,3532; 5,4727] under F43; it should be F14: it focuses a historical reconstruction, with exegesis of 10 Marcan and 4 Johannine texts, and some Christological conclusions.

4331 **Zahrnt** Heinz, Jesus von Nazareth. Mü 1987, Piper. 320 p. DM 38. – ᴿEvKomm 22,6 (1989) 55s (K. *Rieth*).

4332 *Zeitlin* J. M., Understanding the man Jesus; a historical-sociological approach: URM 13 (Toronto 1990) 164-176 [< NTAbs 35,154].

F1.5 *Jesus et Israel* – **Jesus the Jew.**

4333 *Barbaglio* Giuseppe, Gesù e il problema della violenza: ➤ 514c, Violenza 1990, 109-128.

4334 **Barnard** W. J., *Riet* P. van 't, De slip van een joodse man vastgrijpen; christelijke eredienst in het spoor van de joodse Jezus. Kampen 1989, Kok. 136 p. Fb 598. – ᴿCollatVL 20 (1990) 447s (A. *Goossens*).

4335 **Berlin** George L., Defending the faith – Jewish ... on Jesus 1989 ➤ 5,4104: ᴿJScStR 29 (1990) 127s (H. H. *Hiller*).

4336 *a) Cerbelaud* Dominique, Les Juifs dans le NT; – *b) Lauret* Bernard, Christologie et Messianisme; – *c) Blancy* Alain, Le conseil œcuménique des Églises et les Juifs; – *d) Dupuy* Bernard, Exégèse juive, exégèse chrétienne; – *e) Moingt* Joseph, Le chrétien, le juif et le grec: LumièreV 39, 196 (1990) 96-105 / 107-122 / 33-38 / 73-93 / 25-32.

4337 **Charlesworth** James H., Jesus within Judaism 1988 ➤ 4,4225; 5,4108: ᴿCiTom 117 (1990) 380s (J. L. *Espinel*); EvQ 62 (1990) 186s (I. H.

Marshall: shows 'BULTMANN moratorium' unperceptive and invalid); JJS 41 (1990) 126s (M. *Goodman*); TorJT 6 (1990) 110s (E. G. *Clarke*); Vidyajyoti 54 (1990) 610s (P. M. *Meagher*).

4338 **Charlier** Jean-Pierre, Jésus au milieu de son peuple [I-2 1987s ➤ 3,3979; 5,4109] 3. Les jours et la vie: Lire la Bible 85. P 1989, Cerf. 180 p. F 90. – ᴿEsprVie 100 (1990) 237s (E. *Cothenet*).

4339 **Collin** Matthieu, *Lenhardt* Pierre, Évangile et tradition d'Israël: CahÉv 73. P 1990, Cerf. 67 p. F 25 pa. 0222-9714 [NTAbs 35,239].

4340 *a*) *Cothenet* Édouard, L'arrière-plan vétéro-testamentaire du IVᵉ évangile; – *b*) *Dutheil* Jacques, L'évangile de Jean et le judaïsme; le Temple et la Torah; – *c*) *Légasse* Simon, Jésus roi et la politique du IVᵉ évangile: ➤ 545*, Jean, ACFEB 1989/90, 43-69 / 71-85 / 143-159.

4341 *a*) *Czajkowski* Michał, ❷ Qu'est-ce que cela veut dire que Jésus est Juif?; – *b*) *Langkammer* Hugolin, ❷ Les Juifs dans le NT: AtKap 114 (1990) 31-41 / 183-191.

4342 **Di Sante** C., *al.*, Ebrei ed ebraismo nel NT 1: Ascolta Israele. R 1989, Dehoniane. 173 p. Lit. 16.000. – ᴿProtestantesimo 45 (1990) 219s (M. *Abbà*: prezioso).

4343 *Eichmann-Leutenegger* Beatrice, '... was wäre die Kirche ohne Israel?' [F. WERFEL 1890-1945, 100. Gb.]: Orientierung 54 (1990) 168-171.

4344 **Falk** Harvey, Jesus the Pharisee; a new look at the Jewishness of Jesus 1985 ➤ 1,4003 ... 3,3986: ᴿHeythJ 31 (1990) 75s (J. K. *Riches*); IrTQ 56 (1990) 155s (E. *Mangan*).

4345 **Flusser** David, Das Christentum, eine jüdische Religion; Vorw. *Feneberg* Wolfgang. Mü 1990, Kösel. 168 p. 3-466-20327-9.

4346 **Freyne** Sean, Galilee, Jesus and the Gospels 1988 ➤ 4,4238; 5,4115: ᴿCBQ 52 (1990) 555-7 (S. P. *Kealy*); Furrow 40 (1989) 505s (J. D. G. *Dunn*: Galilean dimension weak); Horizons 17 (1990) 327s (Marie-Eloise *Rosenblatt*); JJS 41 (1990) 125s (M. *Goodman*); Pacifica 3 (1990) 240-2 (F. J. *Moloney*: stimulating); TS 51 (1990) 130-2 (L. J. *Topel*).

4347 **Gabriel** Sidney, The Nazarenes. NY 1987, auct. 223 p.; ill. [KirSef 62 (1988s), p. 504].

4348 *a*) *Gargano* Innocenzo, Rapporto tra Chiesa primitiva e Israele; – *b*) *Molari* Carlo, L'ebraicità di Gesù nella vita della Chiesa: ➤ 506, Ebraismo/NT 3 (1990) 97-112 / 113-133.

4349 *a*) *Guillet* Jacques, La Bibbia alle origini della Chiesa; – *b*) *Rordorf* Willy, La Bibbia nell'insegnamento e nella liturgia delle prime comunità; – *c*) *Lamarche* Paul, I settanta; – *d*) *Arnaldez* Roger, La Bibbia di FILONE d'Alessandria: ➤ 353 (< k147), Bibbia alle origini 1990, 63-81 / 83-119 / 13-36 / 37-62.

4350 **Hagner** Donald A., The Jewish reclamation of Jesus 1984 ➤ 65,3605 ... 5,4120: ᴿCurrTMiss 17 (1990) 301s (W. C. *Linss*).

4351 *Hengel* Martin, *Markschies* Christoph, The 'Hellenization' of Judaea in the first century after Christ [supplement to Judaism and Hellenism c. 1970]. L/Ph 1989, SCM/Trinity. 114 p. $10 pa. 0-334-00602-3 [TDig 38,64].

4352 **Hilton** Michael, *Marshall* Gordian, The Gospels and rabbinic Judaism 1988 ➤ 4,4243; 5,4125: ᴿCBQ 52 (1990) 558s (H. G. *Perelmuter*); RExp 87 (1990) 130-2 (D. E. *Garland* reacts); Themelios 15 (1989s) 32s (R. *France*).

4353 **Hooker** Morna D., Continuity and discontinuity; early Christianity in its Jewish setting 1986 ➤ 2,2138; 4,3994: ᴿJEH 40 (1989) 305 (E. P. *Sanders*).

4354 **Imbach** Josef,   a) Wem gehört Jesus? Seine Bedeutung für Juden, Christen und Moslems. Mü 1989, Kösel.   176 p. DM 26,80. – ᴿActuBbg 27 (1990) 73s (J. *Boada*); KIsr 5 (1990) 78s (Julie *Kirchberg*). – b) A chi appartiene Gesù? L'uomo di Nazaret nell'ebraismo contemporaneo: Studium 85 (R 1989) 7-18.

4355 *Kee* Howard C.,   The transformation of the Synagogue after 70 C.E.; its import for early Christianity: NTS 36 (1990) 1-24.

4356 **Kippenberg** H. G., *Wewers* G. A.,   Temi giudaici per lo studio del NT 1987 → 4,4248; 5,4129:   ᴿProtestantesimo 45 (1990) 325 (B. *Corsani*).

4357 *Klener* J.,   Messiaanse tijdgenoten van Jezus uit Nazareth in het werk van Flavius Josephus (een overzicht): Ter Herkenning 18,1 (1990) 1-21 [< GerefTTs 90,190].

4358 *Kotzé* P. P. A.,   Die Jesusbeweging as charismatiese waarderewolusie [Cullmann O.; Theissen G.: Jesus not political revolutionary]: Skrif-Kerk 10,1 (Pretoria 1989) 36-43 [< NTAbs 34,157].

4359 *Lamirande* Émilien,   Reliquit et matrem synagogam: → 13, ᶠBavel T. van, AugLv 41 (1990s) 677-688.

4360 *Lapide* Pinchas,   Jesus — ein gekreuzigter Pharisäer? Siebenstern 1427. Gü 1990, Mohn.   121 p. 3-579-01427-7 [NTAbs 34,400].

4361 *Lee* Bernard J.,   Conversation on the road not taken, 1. The Galilean Jewishness of Jesus 1988 → 4,4250:   ᴿCBQ 52 (1990) 753s (L. W. *Hurtado*: 'a kind of report of his [conscientious] readings in [an area fringing] his own competence'); CritRR 3 (1990) 213-5 (R. D. *Chesnutt*); LvSt 15 (1990) 83s (R. F. *Collins*); PerspRelSt 17 (1990) 285s (C. C. *Black*); Tablet 243 (1989) 946 (N. *King*, also on Charlesworth).

4362 ᴱ**Lenhardt** Pierre, *Collin* Matthieu,   La Torah orale des Pharisiens; textes de la tradition d'Israël: CahEv 73 supp. P 1990, Cerf.   115 p. F 45. 0222-9706.

4363 *Lewis* I.,   The pharisaic character: Contact 99,2 (St. Andrews UK 1989) 23-29 [< NTAbs 34,15].

Lichtenberger H., *Zenger* E. → 335, ᶠ**Flothkötter** H., Das Judentum — eine Wurzel des Christlichen 1990.

4364 **Lightfoot** John,   Commentary on the NT from the Talmud and Hebraica [1859 → Lat. 1658-74]: 1. Place names in the Gospels; 2. Mt-Mk; 3. Lk-Jn; 4. Acts-1 Cor. Peabody MA 1989, Hendrickson.   x-1664 p. $60 [RelStR 17, 269, M. S. *Jaffee*: cui bono?].

4365 **Lindsey** Robert L.,   Jesus Rabbi and Lord; the Hebrew story of Jesus behind our Gospels.   Oak Creek WI 1990, Cornerstone.   227 p. $11 [JPersp 4/3, 13, R. *Buth*]

4365* **Lohfink** Norbert,   Das Jüdische am Christentum; die verlorene Dimension 1987 → 3,4003 ... 5,4132:   ᴿCritRR 2 (1989) 443-5 (W. W. *Frerichs*: problems).

4366 *McRay* John,   a) Christianity; Judaism internationalized: RestQ 32,1 (1990) 1-10 [< NTAbs 34,349]; – b) Le juif Jésus et la *Torah*/Loi [< RestQ]: Praxis Juridique et Religion 7,2 (Strasbourg 1990) 111-123 [< NTAbs 35,199].

4367 **Mamlak** Gershon F.,   Jesus and the apostolic community; Jewish messianism or Hellenistic soteriology?: diss. NYU 1990, ᴰSinnigen W. 324 p. 90-20781. – DissA 51 (1990s) 962-A.

4368 **Montserrat Torrents** J.,   La sinagoga cristiana; el gran conflicto religioso del siglo I. Barc 1989, Muchnik.   346 p. – ᴿRelCu 36 (1990) 353 (M. A. *Martín Juárez*).

4369 **Mussner** Franz, Die Kraft der Wurzel 1987 ➤ 3,4010; 4,4254: ᴿFranz-St 70 (1988) 118s (Helga *Rusche*); ZRGg 42 (1990) 279-281 (S. Ben-*Chorin*).

4370 *Mussner* Franz, Methodisches Vorgehen beim 'religionsgeschichtlichen Vergleich' mit dem antiken Judentum [K. MÜLLER in ᶠ*Schnackenburg* 1989 richtig warnt vor STRACK-BILLERBECK]: BZ 34 (1990) 246s.

4371 **Neusner** Jacob, Judaism and Christianity in the age of Constantine 1987 ➤ 3,4011; 4,4260: ᴿJEH 40 (1989) 617 (N. de *Lange*); TLond 92 (1989) 54-56 (G. *Bonner*).

4372 **Neusner** Jacob, Il giudaismo nei primi secoli del cristianesimo [1984] 1989 ➤ 5,4140: ᴿHumBr 45 (1990) 105 (A. *Bodrato*); StPatav 37 (1990) 197s (G. *Segalla*).

4373 **Neusner** Jacob, Jødedomen i den første kristne tid [1984],ᵀ. Trondheim 1987, Tapir. 109 p. – ᴿSvEx 55 (1990) 123s (Kay *Svensson*).

4374 *Neusner* Jacob, *a)* Judaism and Christianity in the first century; how shall we perceive their relationship [lecture at Rome Lateran Univ. Jan. 1989]: ➤ 183, ᶠVERMES G. 1990, 247-259; – *b)* The Jewish-Christian argument in the first century — different people talking about different things to different people: ➤ 560, Law 1988/90, 173-186.

4375 *Paul* A., Les faux jumeaux [it is incorrect to say that Christianity is a fruit of Judaism]: Esprit 58,6 (P 1990) 125-134 [< NTAbs 35,63].

4376 **Pawlikowski** John, Jesus and the theology of Israel. Wilmington 1989, Glazier. 90 p. $7. – ᴿNewTR 32 (1990) 103s (Mary C. *Athans*).

4377 **Pelletier** Marcel, Les Pharisiens; histoire d'un parti méconnu: Lire la Bible 86. P 1990, Cerf. 372 p. F 110. 2-204-04007-X [NTAbs 34, 412]. – ᴿMondeB 66 (1990) 63 (F. *Brossier*).

4378 **Perelmuter** Hayim G., Siblings 1989 ➤ 5,4146: ᴿExpTim 102 (1990s) 185s (F. *Morgan*).

4379 **Riches** John, The world of Jesus; first-century Judaism in crisis: Understanding Jesus today. C 1990, Univ. v-151 p. $22.50; pa. $7. 0-521-38505-9; -676-4 [NTAbs 35,107]. – ᴿExpTim 102 (1990s) 245 (C. S. *Rodd*: by far the most impressive of the first four volumes in the inadequately planned/trimmed new series).

   Rosenberg Roy A., Who was Jesus? 1986 ➤ 4268*b*.

4380 **Russell** D. S., From early Judaism to early Church 1986 ➤ 2,3149 ... 4,4266: ᴿScotBEv 7 (1989) 126s (I. H. *Marshall*).

4382 **Sanders** E. P., Jesus and Judaism 1985 ➤ 1,4028 ... 5,4150: ᴿNedTTs 43 (1989) 148-150 (J. S. *Vos*).

4383 *a) Simeone* Renato, Ebraicità di Gesù; – *b) Soggin* J. Alberto, Gesù e i Farisei: ➤ 506, Ebraismo/NT 2 (1989) 5-24 / 75-92.

4383* *a) Sorani* G., Le radici ebraiche del cristianesimo; – *b) Kopciowski* E., Il patriarca Abramo; – *c) Caro* L., Mosè e la morte dell'egiziano: Amicizia Ebraico-Cristiana NS 25,1s (F 1990) 3-12 / 23-26 / 26-33 [< Judaica 46,188].

4384 **Stegmann** Dirk, Jüdische Wurzeln des Christentums; Grundstrukturen des alttestamentlichen und nachalttestamentlichen Glaubens bis zur Zeit Jesu: Rel.-Päd. 2. Essen 1990, Blaue Eule. 407 p. DM 66. – ᴿKIsr 5 (1990) 185 (Julie *Kirchberg*).

4385 **Swidler** Leonard, Yeshua 1988 ➤ 4,4273; 5,4153: ᴿHorizons 17 (1990) 166s (Mary T. *Rattigan*).

4386 *Swidler* L., Yeshua and his followers were not Christians — they were Jews; implications for Christians today: Religious Traditions 12 (Montreal-Sydney 1989) 65-90 [< NTAbs 34,200].

4387 **Vogler** Werner, Jüdische Jesusinterpretationen in christlicher Sicht: ArbKG 11, 1988 → 5,4157; DM 28. 3-7400-0081-3 [NTAbs 34,389]: RÉTRel 65 (1990) 276s (Jeanne-Marie *Léonard*).

4388 **Weinreb** F., Innenwelt des Wortes im NT; eine Deutung aus den Quellen des Judentums. Weiter/Allgau 1988, Thauros. 257 p. DM 38. 3-88411-034-9 [NTAbs 34,116].

4389 **Wilson** Marvin R., Our father Abraham; Jewish roots of the Christian faith 1989 → 5,4160: RCarthaginensia 6 (1990) 199s (R. *Sanz Valdivieso*); JRel 70 (1990) 465s (D. J. *Harrington*).

4390 **Zeitlin** Irving M., Jesus and the Judaism of his time 1988 → 4,4278; 5,4162: RSR 19 (1990) 111-3 (L. *Hurtado*).

F1.6 *Jesus in Ecclesia* – **The Church Jesus.**

4391 **Barlow** Philip L., The Bible in Mormonism: diss. Harvard. – HarvTR 82 (1989) 477.

4392 BONAVENTURE, Le Christ maître. P 1990, Vrin. 147 p. [RTPhil 122,576].

4393 **Booth** B., Contrasts — Gospel evidence and Christian beliefs. W. Sussex 1990, Pagel. 256 p. [TS 52,190].

4394 **Carol** Juniper B., Why Jesus Christ? Manassas 1986, Trinity. 531 p. 0-937495-03-4. – RAntonianum 65 (1990) 108s (V. *Battaglia*: heated defense of Scotist 'motive of the Incarnation')

4395 **Glebe-Møller** Jens, Jesus and theology — critique of a tradition [... beliefs like predestination have legitimated oppression]. Mp 1989, Fortress. 196 p. 0-8006-2334-7. – RExpTim 102 (1990s) 92 (T. J. *Gorringe*: 19th-century a-theology, inelegantly translated); TS 51 (1990) 766-8 (Stephen *Schäfer*).

4396 **Sesboüé** Bernard, Gesù Cristo nella tradizione della Chiesa 1987 → 4,4295: RCarthaginensia 6 (1990) 222 (F. *Martínez Fresneda*).

Wéber Édouard-Henri, Le Christ selon S. Thomas d'AQUIN: JJC 35, 1988 → 7485.

F1.7 *Jesus 'anormalis':* **to atheists, psychoanalysts, romance ...**

4397 **Aitmatov** Chingiz, The place of the skull [**❶** The scaffold; Muslim background novel], TWard Natasha. L 1989, Faber. 310 p. – RIslamochristiana 16 (1990) 301-4 (H. *Goddard*).

4398 **Arnaldez** Roger, Jésus dans la pensée musulmane: JJC 32, 1988 → 4,4298; 5,4173: RFoiVie 89,2 (1990) 92s (J.-D. *Dubois*); RHR 207 (1990) 98s (G. *Monnot*); Spıritus 31 (1990) 222s (M. *Borrmans*).

4399 *Aune* David E., Heracles and Christ; Heracles imagery in the Christology of early Christianity: → 122, FMALHERBE A., Greeks 1990, 3-19.

4400 *Benson* P. H., Model for Jesus' teachings about altruistic living in relation to personal well-being: JPsy&C 9,1 (Blue Jay CA 1990) 56-69 [< NTAbs 34,297].

4401 **Borghesi** M., La figura di Cristo in HEGEL 1983 → 64,6663; 1,6919: RProtestantesimo 45 (1990) 158s (S. *Rostagno*).

4402 **Bowman** Frank P., Le Christ des barricades 1987 → 3,4045: RJEH 40 (1989) 469s (C. *Lucas*).

4402* **Bruce** F. F., Gesù visto dai contemporanei; le testimonianze non bibliche [1974 ²1984 → 65,3654],T: PBT 19. T 1989, Claudiana. 204 p. Lit. 18.000. – RProtestantesimo 45 (1990) 72 (L. *Baratto*); Servitium 67 (1990) 100 (M. *Abbà*).

4403 **Carzedda** Salvatore,   The Quranic Jesus in the light of the Gospel; exploring a way to dialogue: Dialogue Forum 3.   Zamboanga 1990, Silsilah. 151 p. [TContext 8/2, 140, G. *Evers*].

4404 Der schwarze Christus; Wege afrikanischer Christologie [Le Christ noir, préf. *Luneau* René (not = **Chenu** Bruno, Le Christ noir américain: JJC 21, 1984 → 1,4067)], ᵀ*Faymonville* Ursula: Theologie der dritten Welt 17. FrB 1989, Herder. 205 p. DM 34. 3-451-21477-6. – ᴿActuBbg 27 (1990) 207s (J. *Boada*); TGL 80 (1990) 94-96 (K. J. *Tossou*); TsTNijm 30 (1990) 105 (J. *Heijke*); TPQ 138 (1990) 287s (K. J. *Tossou*); ZMissRW 74 (1990) 304s (W. *Löser*).

4405 *Clouse* B.,   Jesus' law of love and KOHLBERG's stages of moral reasoning: JPsy&Chr 9,3 (Blue Jay CA 1990) 5-15 [< NTAbs 35, 160].

4406 **Cottret** Bernard,   Le Christ des Lumières; Jésus de Nazareth de NEWTON à VOLTAIRE (1660-1760). P 1990, Cerf. 186 p. F 152. 2-204-04098-3. – ᴿÉtudes 373 (1990) 138 (P. *Vallin*); ExpTim 102 (1990s) 120s (J. *Kent*); FoiVie 89,6 (1990) 112-4 (J. *Blondel*).

4407 *Delobel* Joël,   Extra-canonical sayings of Jesus; MARCION and some 'non-received' logia: → 549, Gospel 1989, 106-116.

4408 **di Nola** A. M., [71 agrapha] Gesù segreto; ascesi e rivoluzione sessuale nel Cristianesimo nascente.   Universale Tasc. 70.   R 1989, Newton Compton. 157 p.; ill. Lit. 8.000 [NTAbs 34,406].

4409 **Downing** F. Gerald,   Christ and the Cynics 1988 → 4,4306; 5,4180: ᴿCBQ 52 (1990) 553-5 (R. J. *Miller*); ClasR 40 (1990) 175s (M. B. *Trapp*); JJS 41 (1990) 127s (M. *Goodman*).

4410 **Ellul** Jacques,   Jesus and Marx; from gospel to ideology 1988 → 4,4307: ᴿJRel 70 (1990) 655s (B. W. *Ballard*: against liberation theology); Nor-TTs 90 (1989) 174s (Ola *Tjørhom*: same problem as in Subversion of Christianity).

4411 **Epalza** Michel de,   Jésus otage 1987 → 3,4055 ... 5,4184: ᴿScEsp 42 (1990) 373s (G. *Novotny*).

4412 **Fleg** Edmond,   Gesù raccontato dall'Ebreo errante [1953], ᵀ*Lo Piccolo* Salvatore: Ascolta Israele. R 1989, Dehoniane. 359 p.

4413 **Forsyth** James,   FREUD, JUNG, and Christianity. Ottawa 1989, Univ. 189 p. $20 [RelStR 17, 46, R. R. *Crocker*: the question is not 'Does God exist?' but 'Why are humans religious?'].

4414 **Fox** Matthew,   The coming of the cosmic Christ 1988 → 4,8510; 5,4185: ᴿAnglTR 72 (1990) 342-4 (D. R. *McDonald*).

4415 **Galipeau** S. A.,   Transforming body and soul; therapeutic wisdom in the Gospel healing stories: JUNG and Spirituality. NY 1990, Paulist. x-155 p. $11. 0-8091-0442-3 [NTAbs 35,241: the author is an Episcopal priest and practicing psychotherapist].

4416 *a) Görges* Helmut,   'Der Narr' — ein Titel für Jesus? Von der Möglichkeit, Jesus als Narren zu verstehen: RUntHö 33 (1990) 170-8. – *b) Heymel* Michael,   Der Pfarrer als Komödiant: TPrac 25 (Mü 1990) 89-103 [< ZIT 90,567s].

 Grant Robert M.,   Jesus after the Gospels; the Christ of the second century 1990 → k25.

4417 *Guillaume* Baudouin,   La dernière tentation du Christ [film], ou le blasphème intégral: PenséeC 249 (1990) 44-65.

4418 **Healy** Kathleen,   Christ as the common ground; a study of Christianity and Hinduism. Pittsburgh 1990, Duquesne Univ. xiv-218 p. $25 [TS 52, 383-5, F. X. *Clooney*].

4419 **Keenan** John P., The meaning of Christ; a Mahāyana theology: Faith meets faith. Mkn 1989, Orbis. viii-312 p. $17. 0-88344-640-5 [TDig 37,370].

4420 **Keller** C., al., Jesus ausserhalb der Kirche; das Jesusverständnis in neuen religiösen Bewegungen. Z 1989, Theol.-V. 160 p. – RLebZeug 44 (1989) 309s (W. *Hering*).

4421 *Khalidi* Tarif, The Arab Jesus: NesTR 10,1s (1989) 3-20 [< ZIT 91,19].

4422 *Kottukapally* J., Christ in [KAZANTZAKIS N. 1950, Eng. 1961] The last temptation; a theological critique: Vidyajyoti 53 (1989) 29-49 . 109-124.

4423 *Mack* Burton L., All the extra Jesuses; Christian origins in the light of the extra-canonical Gospels: ➤ 326, Semeia 49 (1990) 169-176.

4424 **Malone** Peter, Movie Christs and antichrists. NY 1990, Crossroad. 167 p. $11 pa. 0-8245-1003-8 [TDig 38,72].

4425 **Messadié** Gerald, Ein Mensch namens Jesus; Roman [1988s ➤ 5,4199], TRuhland Kirsten. Mü 1989, Droemer Knaur. 752 p. DM 44. – REv-Komm 23 (1990) 303 (W. *Wunderlich*).

4426 — **Grelot** Pierre, Un Jésus de comédie, 'l'homme qui devint Dieu' [MESSADIÉ G. 1988s] 1989 ➤ 5,4188; 2-204-03195-X: RFoiVie 89,2 (1990) 91 (J.-D. *Dubois*).

4427 **Nientiedt** Klaus, Der 'wilde Mann' Jesus; Denys ARCANDS [Film] 'Jesus von Montréal': HerdKor 34 (1990) 135-8.

4428 **Pashan** Tobias, Jesus in Islam [diss.]: Scvartham 12 (1987) 127-139 (146).

4429 **Risse** Günter, 'Gott ist Christus, der Sohn der Maria'... im Koran D1989 ➤ 5,4204: RÖkRu 39 (1990) 375s (H. *Klautke*); RHE 85 (1990) 787s (E. *Platti*); TGl 80 (1990) 212-4 (H. *Jorissen*); ZMissRW 74 (1990) 314s (P. *Antes*).

4430 **Rizzardi** Giuseppe, Il fascino di Cristo nell'Islam 1989 ➤ 5,4205: RIslamochristiana 16 (1990) 335s (M. *Borrmans*).

4431 *Robinson* James M., Very Goddess and very man; Jesus' better self: ➤ 5,481a, EKing Karen L., Images of the feminine in Gnosticism 1985/8, 113-127 [128-135, *Hedrick* Charles W., response].

4432 a) *Ros* Salvador, Jesús en el marxismo humanista; – b) *Guerra* Augusto, Resucitar a los crucificados de este mundo; cristología de la liberación: REspir 47 (1988) 121-166 / 91-119 (207-231, Jesús, la pobreza y los pobres).

4432* *Ruh* Ulrich, Die Schwierigkeiten mit dem 'wirklichen' Jesus; Bemerkungen zu einigen neueren Jesusbüchern [... vor allem als Psychotherapeut geschätzt; DREWERMANN E.; WOLFF H. 1978; WEDEL E. v. 1990; ALT F. ...]: HerdKor 44 (1990) 287-291.

4433 **Schumann** Olaf H., Der Christus der Muslime; christologische Aspekte in der arabisch-islamischen Literatur²rev [¹1972D ev.]: Kölner Veröff. Rel-G 13, 1988 ➤ 5,4208: RRHR 207 (1990) 208s (G. *Monnot*).

4434 ESegal R. A., In quest of the hero; [birth-] mythos [A. *Dundes* on Jesus hero-pattern; also O. *Rank* on birth of hero, Lord RAGLAN's The Hero, a study in tradition, myth, and drama]. Princeton 1990, Univ. xli-223 p. $11 pa. 0-691-02062-0 [NTAbs 35,233].

4435 **Slusser** Gerald H., From JUNG to Jesus; myth and consciousness in the NT 1986 ➤ 2,3201: RCritRR 3 (1990) 236-9 (W. *Wink*).

Tilliette Xavier, Le Christ de la philosophie; prolégomènes à une christologie philosophique: CogF 155, 1990 ➤ 7548.

4436 **Vitz** Paul C., Sigmund FREUD's Christian unconscious 1988 ➤ 4,1602: RCalvinT 25 (1990) 122-5 (E. L. *Johnson*).

4437 **Wolff** Hanna, Jesus the therapist [⁶1978], ᵀ*Barr* R.R. Oak Park IL 1987, Meyer-Stone. xiii-178 p. $30; pa. $13. – ᴿCritRR 3 (1990) 246-8 (W. *Wink*).

4438 *Yarbrough* R.W., NT Christology and the Jesus of Islam: EvRT 14,2 (Exeter 1990) 113-125 [< NTAbs 35,57].

F2.1   *Exegesis creativa* – **innovative methods.**

4439 *Black* C.C., Rhetorical questions; the NT, classical rhetoric, and current interpretation [five books]: Dialog 29,1 (1990) 62-70 [< NTAbs 34,145].

4440 *Botha* J., On the 'reinvention' of rhetoric: Scriptura 31 (Stellenbosch 1989) 14-31 [< NTAbs 34,145].

4441 ᴱ**Corley** B., Colloquy on NT studies; a time for reappraisal and fresh approaches 1980/3 ➤ 3,530: ᴿSNTU A-15 (1990) 153-5 (A. *Fuchs*).

4442 **Egger** Wilhelm, Methodenlehre zum NT 1987 ➤ 3,4096; ... 5,4218: ᴿAtKap 115 (1990) 144-8 (J. *Warzecha*); FranzSt 71 (1989) 368-370 (J.-M. *Nützel*); RB 97 (1990) 126 (J. *Murphy-O'Connor*).

4443 **Egger** W., Metodologia del Nuovo Testamento 1989 ➤ 5,4219: ᴿLaurentianum 31 (1990) 597-9 (F. *Raurell*); RivB 38 (1990) 91-94 (V. *Fusco*).

4444 **Jasper** David, The New Testament and the literary imagination; pref. *McFague* Sallie, 1986 ➤ 3,3827.4103 ... 5,4220: ᴿRelStR 16 (1990) 63 (D. *Jobling*).

4445 **Kenny** Anthony, A stylometric study of the NT 1986 ➤ 2,3222... 4,4345: ᴿCritRR 2 (1989) 208-210 (P. *Sellow*).

4446 **Mack** Burton L., Rhetoric and the New Testament: Guides to Biblical Scholarship NT. Mp 1990, Fortress. 110 p. 0-8006-2395-9.

Meynet Roland, Rhétorique biblique ➤ 1731; 5349.

4447 **Moore** Stephen D., Literary criticism and the Gospels; the theoretical challenge 1989 ➤ 5,4229; $30. 0-300-04525-5: ᴿExpTim 101 (1989s) 347 (R. *Morgan*); TTod 47 (1990s) 337s. 340 (R.C. *Tannehill*).

4448 **Müller** Paul-Gerhard, Einführung in praktische Bibelarbeit: Stu KLK NT 20. Stu 1990, KBW. 214 p. 3-460-15501-9.

4449 ᴱ**Pfammatter** Josef, *Furger* Franz, Methoden der Evangelien-Exegese: TBer 13, 1985 ➤ 4,4353; DM 38: ᴿFranzSt 71 (1989) 99-101 (J. *Nützel*).

4450 *Quinn* W.W., R. BULTMANN's 'demythologization' hermeneutic as applied to NT and [U.S.] constitutional exegesis: Journal of Law and Religion 6 (St. Paul 1988) 297-316 [NTAbs 34,289].

4451 *Resseguie* James L., Defamiliarization [SHKLOVSKY V.] and the Gospels: BibTB 20 (1990) 147-153.

4452 *Schille* Gottfried, Zur Relation von Linguistik und Formgeschichte: TLZ 115 (1990) 87-93.

4453 **Stegner** William R., Narrative theology [... not 'narrative criticism'; 4 NT items] in early Jewish Christianity 1989 ➤ 5,1331: ᴿJJS 41 (1990) 272s (A.E. *Harvey*).

4454 **Stenger** Werner, Strukturale Beobachtungen zum NT: NTTools 12. Leiden 1990, Brill. 320 p. ƒ135 [TR 87,75]. 90-04-09113-0.

Non adhibetur hoc anno – Nᵒ 4455-4554 & 6792-6999 – not used this year.

F2.2   *Unitas VT-NT:* **The Unity of the Two Testaments.**

4555 **Beauchamp** Paul, L'un et l'autre Testament [1. 1976 ➤ 58,993] / 2. Accomplir les Écritures: Parole de Dieu. P 1990, Seuil. 410 p. F 180. –

REsprVie 100 (1990) 383s (É. *Ricaud*); Études 373 (1990) 135s (G. *Petitdemange*); OTAbs 13 (1990) 317 (R. E. *Murphy*: his norms of allegory vague and not universally shared); NRT 112 (1990) 888-891 (Y. *Simoens*); RTLv 21 (1990) 484s (C. *Focant*).

4556 **Buchanan** George W., Typology and the Gospel 1987 → 3,4124; 5,4327: RCritRR 3 (1990) 191-3 (R. M. *Davidson*).

4557 **Elderenbosch** P. A., Het evangelie als uitlegging van het Oude Testament 1986 → 3,4129: RNedTTs 43 (1989) 61s (C. H. *Lindijer*).

4558 EFriis **Plum** Karin, *Hallbäck* Gert, Det gamle Testamente og den kristne fortolkning: Forum for Bibelsk Exegese 1. K 1988, Mus. Tusculanum. 137 p. Dk 160. 87-7289-034-7. – RSvEx 55 (1990) 117-9 (L. *Eriksson*).

4559 *Göckeritz* Götz, Das Gesetz in der Unterscheidung von Gesetz und Evangelium: NSys 32 (1990) 181-193; Eng. 193s.

4560 **Grollenberg** Lucas, Unexpected Messiah [Onverwachte Messias ('prophesied' in Mt) 1987 → 4,4370], TBowden J. L 1988, SCM. £7 pa. 0-334-02402-1. – RThemelios 15 (1989s) 34s (R. *France* also did not know in what area to classify it); Vidyajyoti 54 (1990) 655s (P. M. *Meagher*).

4561 a) *Heymel* Michael, Warum gehört die Hebräische Bibel in den christlichen Kanon?; – b) *Soosten* Joachim von, Gottes Versprechen und des Menschen Bitte; gläubige Existenz nach Auschwitz: BTZ 7 (1990) 2-20 / 21-35.

4562 **Juel** Donald, Messianic exegesis 1988 → 3,4136... 5,4250: RJBL 109 (1990) 135-7 (D. M. *Hay*).

4563 **Koch** D. A., Die Schrift als Zeuge des Evangeliums: BeiHistT 69, 1986 → 5,4254: RBSeptCog 21 (1988) 3-9 (C. D. *Stanley*) [< NTAbs 34,49: 'Paul actively and consciously modified the wording of his Vorlage'].

4564 FLINDARS Barnabas, It is written; Scripture citing Scripture, ECarson D. ... 1988 → 4,97; 5,4255: RBZ 34 (1990) 272-4 (I. *Broer*); HebSt 31 (1990) 116-9 (J. *Blenkinsopp*: it would have been better to choose topics for selective probing); RExp 87 (1990) 136s (D. S. *Dockery*); ScotJT 43 (1990) 415-7 (R. A. *Piper*).

4565 *Muszyński* Henryk bp., ❷ 'Dieu d'Abraham, d'Isaak et de Jacob, Dieu de nos pères'; l'unité et la continuité de l'économie de salut, en example de l'Idée de Dieu: AtKap 114 (1990) 6-16.

4566 *Odendaal* D. H., The indispensability and significance of the Old Testament for the presentation of the Gospel among the nations: NDuitsGT 31 (1990) 298-309 [< OTAbs 14, p. 208].

4567 [EPapandreou Damaskinos], L'Ancien Testament dans l'Église [7. Seminar 1986]: ÉtThéol 8. Chambésy 1988, Centre Orthodoxe. 234 p. – ROstkSt 38 (1989) 215s (E. C. *Suttner*, mit 3 früheren Heften).

4568 *Piret* Pierre, L'intelligence chrétienne de l'Écriture Sainte: → 541*, L'Écriture âme 1989/90, 13-36.

4569 *Preus* Robert D., The unity of Scripture: ConcordTQ 54,1 (1990) 1-23 [< NTAbs 35,142].

4570 *Ramshaw* Gail, The First Testament [OT] in Christian lectionaries: Worship 64 (1990) 494-510.

4571 *Roloff* Jürgen, Die Geschichtlichkeit der Schrift und die Bezeugung des einen Evangeliums [< EVajta V., Ev. als Geschichte 1974, 126-158]: → 289, Verantwortung 1990, 11-43.

4572 a) *Rossi de Gasperis* Francesco, Lettura ebraica e lettura cristiana dell'AT; – b) *Carnucci Viterbi* Benedetto, Messianismo ebraico e Gesù: → 506, Ebraismo/NT 1 (1989) 47-117 / 119-144.

4573 *a) Van Buren* Paul M.,   On reading someone else's mail; the Church and Israel's Scriptures; – *b) Brocke* Edna,   Von den 'Schriften' zum 'Alten Testament' — und zurück? Jüdische Fragen zur christlichen Suche einer 'Mitte der Schrift': ➤ 147, ᶠRENDTORFF R., Hebr. Bibel 1990, 595-606 / 581-594.

4574 *Watt* J.G. van der,   Die verhouding tussen die Ou Testament en Nuwe Testament heilshistories oorweeg: SkrifKerk 10,1 (1989) 61-79 [< NTAbs 34,207].

4575 *a) Zenger* Erich,   Unser erstes Testament; von der Bedeuting des ATs für die Christen; – *b) Dohmen* Christoph,   Die Leidenschaft des lieben Gottes; zur Bedeutung des ATs für ein christliches Gottesbild; – *c) Fischer* Irmtraud,   Steht JHWH auf Seiten der Männer?; – *d) Schwienhorst-Schönberger* Ludger, 'Auge um Auge, Zahn um Zahn'; zu einem antijüdischen Klischée; – *e) Nübold* Elmar,   Die alttestamentliche Lesung in der Messfeier: BLtg 63 (1990) 130-141 / 141-9 / 149-155 / 163-175 / 176-182.

4576 *a) Zmijewski* Josef,   Zu unserer Belehrung geschrieben; Das AT und die urkirchliche Christusverkündigung; – *b) Beyse* Karl-Martin,   Lingua hebraica et revelatio Dei; eine didaktisch-theologische Skizze: ➤ 146, ᶠREINELT H., At. Botschaft 1990, 405-442; Bibliog. 443-7 / 25-36.

F2.3   *Unitas interna* – NT – **Internal unity.**

4577 **Dunn** James D.G.,   Unity and diversity in the New Testament² [¹1977 ➤ 58,9448]. L/Ph 1990, SCM/Trinity. 482 p. £17.50. 0-334-02436-6. – ᴿExpTim 102 (1990s) 222 [C.S. *Rodd*: new preface and chapter-introductions but pagination retained].

F2.5   *Commentarii* – **Commentaries on the whole NT.**

4578 *a)* ᵀᴱ**Delègue** Yves, (*Gillet* J.P.), ÉRASME, Les Préfaces au Novum Testamentum (1516), avec des textes d'accompagnement: Histoire et Société 20. Genève 1990, Labor et Fides. 251 p. [NTAbs 35,230]. 2-8309-0605-5. – *b)* ᴱ**Reeve** A., *Screech* M.A.,   ERASMUS' Annotations on the NT; Acts-Rom–1-2 Cor; facsimile of the final Latin text with all earlier variants: Studies in the History of Christian Thought 42. Leiden 1990, Brill. xxxiv-p. 271-564; 2 pl. *f* 140. 90-04-09124-6 [NTAbs 34,379].

4579 *Juel* D.,   New Testament commentaries: Dialog 29 (St. Paul 1990) 227s. 230s [< NTAbs 35,17].

4580 **Lachs** Samuel T.,   A rabbinic commentary ... MtMkLk 1987 ➤ 3,4156 ... 5,4278: ᴿRelStT 8,3 (1988) 57s (E. *Segal*).

4581 *a) Tripp* David,   'Observe the gradation'; John WESLEY's Notes on the New Testament; – *b) Martin* A.W.ᴶ,   'Then as now'; Wesley's Notes as a model for United Methodists today: QRMin 10 (1990) 49-64 / 25-47.

╔══════════════════╗
║   **X. Evangelia** ║
╚══════════════════╝

F2.6   **Evangelia Synoptica;** *textus, synopses, commentarii.*

4582 **Boismard** M.-E., *Lamouille* A.,   Synopsis graeca quattuor evangeliorum 1986 ➤ 2,3253 ... 5,4285: ᴿSvEx 55 (1990) 132s (T. *Fornbérg*).

4583 *a*) *Dungan* D. L., Synopses of the future; – *b*) *Elliott* J. K., The relevance of textual criticism to the Synoptic problem: ➤ 524, Interrelations 1984/90, 317-347 / 348-359.

4584 *Elliott* J. K., Which is the best synopsis?: ExpTim 102 (1990s) 200-4.

4585 *Jonge* H. J. de, XVIth-century Gospel harmonies, CHEMNITZ and MER-CATOR: ➤ 511, Théorie/pratique 1988/90, 155-166.

4586 **Kloppenborg** John S., Q parallels; synopsis, critical notes, and concordance: Facets 1988 ➤ 4,4395; 5,4286: ᴿCBQ 52 (1990) 559-561 (J. G. *Lodge*: no advertence to contributions by adversaries of Q-hypothesis); NT 32 (1990) 191s (J. K. *Elliott* compares this 'major reference work' with NEIRYNCK's 'modest vade mecum').

4587 *Koester* Helmut, The text of the Synoptic Gospels in the second century: ➤ 549, Gospel 1989, 19-37.

4588 **Neirynck** Frans, Q-Synopsis 1988 ➤ 4,4397: ᴿCBQ 52 (1990) 567 (E. C. *Maloney*: for rationale of the groupments we must await forthcoming continuation).

4589 **Poppi** Angelico, Sinossi dei quattro Vangeli [I. 1983 ➤ 64,4156] II. Introduzione e commento 1988 ➤ 4,4400; 5,4388: ᴿBenedictina 37 (1990) 215s (P. M. *Pierini*); Teresianum 40 (1989) 272s (V. *Pasquetto*).

4590 **Poppi** Angelico, Sinossi dei Quattro Vangeli² (Duplice e triplice tradizione in evidenza), I. Testo; II. Introduzione generale e ai singoli vangeli; commento. Padova 1990, Messaggero. 333 p.; 558 p. Lit. 28.000 + 35.000. 88-250-0009-X / 88-7026-969-8.

4591 **Sanders** E. P., *Davies* M., Studying the Synoptic Gospels 1989 ➤ 5,4289: ᴿLvSt 15 (1990) 71-73 (R. F. *Collins*); NT 32 (1990) 278s (J. K. *Elliott*, also on MCKNIGHT S.); Vidyajyoti 54 (1990) 546s (P. M. *Meagher*).

4592 ᴱ**Thomas** Robert L., *Gundry* Stanley N. [¹*Broadus* J. A., *Robertson* A. T.] The NIV harmony of the Gospels with explanations and essays. SF 1988, Harper & R. 341 p.; maps. 0-06-063523-1.

F2.7 *Problema synopticum:* The Synoptic Problem.

4593 *Bartnicki* Roman, ❷ *a*) Latest solutions to the Synoptic Problem [... ROLLAND, ORCHARD]: ➤ 546, RuBi 42 (1989) 28-41; – *b*) ❷ The formation of the Synoptic Gospels according to the Two-Gospel hypothesis of Bernard ORCHARD: ColcT 59,3 (1989) 5-35; Eng. 35; – *c*) ❷ Das synoptische Problem ehemals und heute: STWsz 27,1 (1989) 15-72; deutsch 72s.

4594 *Black* Matthew, The Aramaic dimension in Q, with notes on Luke 17.22 and Matthew 24.26 (Luke 17.23): JStNT 40 (1990) 23-41.

4594* **Crossan** John D., Sayings parallels; a workbook for the Jesus tradition 1986 ➤ 2,3255 ... 4,4404: ᴿNeotestamentica 24 (1990) 143s (W. S. *Vorster*).

4595 **Ennulat** Andreas, Die 'minor agreements' — ein Diskussionsbeitrag zur Erklärung einer offenen Frage des synoptischen Problems: Diss. ᴰ*Luz* U. Bern 1989s. 421 p. – TR 86 (1990) 511; RTLv 22, p. 592; ᴿETL 67 (1991) 372-385 (T. A. *Friedrichsen*) & 369 (F. *Neirynck*).

4596 *a*) *Farmer* W. R., The Two-Gospel hypothesis; – *b*) *McNicol* A. J., The composition of the Synoptic eschatological discourse: ➤ 524, Interrelations 1984/90, 125-156 (201-216, *Dungan* David, response) / 157-200.

4597 **Johnson** Sherman E., The Griesbach hypothesis and redaction criticism: SBL Mg 41. Atlanta 1990, Scholars. vii-172 p. $40; pa. $25.

4598 **Kim** Myung-Soo, Die Trägergruppe von Q; sozialgeschichtliche For-schung zur Q-Überlieferung in den synoptischen Evangelien [Diss. Ham-burg 1990, ᴰ*Paulsen* H.: RTLv 22, p. 593; TR 86,515]: WBEurHS 1/1. Ammersbek 1990, Lottbek-J. 389 p. 3-926987-34-0 [NTAbs 35,243: re-lates his theme to Korean Minjung].

4599 ᴱ**Kloppenborg** J. S., *al.*, Q-Thomas reader. Sonoma CA 1990, Pole-bridge. x-166 p. $15. 0-944344-11-9 [NTAbs 35,103].

4600 *Kloppenborg* John S., *a*) City and wasteland; narrative world and the beginning of the Sayings Gospel (Q): ➤ 375, Semeia 52 (1990) 145-160; – *b*) 'Easter faith' and the Sayings Gospel Q: ➤ 326, Semeia 49 (1990) 71-99.

4601 *a*) *Koester* Helmut, Q and its relatives; – *b*) *Kloppenborg* John S., Nomos and ethos in Q: ➤ 152, ᶠRobinson J. M., Gnosticism 1 (1990) 49-63 / 35-48.

4602 **Kosch** Daniel, Die eschatologische Tora des Menschensohnes; Unter-suchungen zur Rezeption der Stellung Jesu zu Tora in Q [Diss. FrS 1987s ➤ 4,4426]: NTOrb 12. FrS 1989, Univ. 544 p. Fs 98. 3-7278-0650-8. – ᴿSNTU A-15 (1990) 205s (A. *Fuchs*).

4603 *a*) *Levine* Amy-Jill, Who's catering the Q affair? Feminist observations on Q paraenesis; – *b*) *Camp* Claudia V., A feminist response [to all the papers]; paraenesis; method, form, and act: ➤ 464, Semeia 50 (1990) 145-161 / 243-260.

4604 **Longstaff** Thomas R. W., *Thomas* Page A., The Synoptic Problem, a bibliography 1716-1988: New Gospel Studies 4, 1988 ➤ 4,4408: also (Lv) Peeters: ᴿCBQ 52 (1990) 757s (R. L. *Mowery*: the 'keywords' are a problem); NT 32 (1990) 279-281 (J. K. *Elliott*: cautions); TorJT 6 (1990) 360s (J. S. *Kloppenborg*).

4605 — *Scholer* David M., Q bibliography supplement I, 1990: ➤ 544, SBL sem. 1990, 11-13.

4606 *Neirynck* Frans, Qᴹᵗ and Qᴸᵏ and the reconstruction of Q: ETL 66 (1990) 385-390.

4607 *Neirynck* F., *a*) The Two-Source hypothesis; – *b*) Mt 4,23-5,2: ➤ 524, Interrelations 1984/90, 3-22 (81-124) / 23-46 [47-80, *Tuckett* C. M. response].

4608 *Orchard* Bernard, Dei Verbum and the Synoptic Gospels: DowR 108 (1990) 199-214.

4609 *Robinson* James M., The international Q project; Work session 17 Nov. 1989: JBL 109 (1990) 499-501.

4610 *Sanz Valdivieso* Rafael, La fuente Q; publicaciones recientes [Polag A., Neyrinck F., Zeller D., Ruso R.]: Carthaginensia 6 (1990) 183-194.

4611 **Sato** Migaku, Q und Prophetie...: WUNT 2/29, 1988 ➤ 4,4412; 5,4301: ᴿCBQ 52 (1990) 362-4 (J. S. *Kloppenborg*); EstE 65 (1990) 98s (E. *Barón*); JBL 109 (1990) 137-9 (J. S. *Kloppenborg*); SNTU-A 14 (1989) 239-241 (A. *Fuchs*).

4612 *Schweizer* Eduard, What Q could have learned from Reginald Fuller: ➤ 52, ᶠFuller R., AnglTR supp. 11 (1990) 55-67.

4613 **Stein** Robert H., The Synoptic Problem; an introduction 1987 ➤ 3, 4189 ... 5,4303: ᴿBS 147 (1990) 120s (H. W. *Hoehner*: good but partial to Marcan priority); CurrTMiss 17 (1990) 155s (W. C. *Linss*); Evangel 7,2 (1989) 22 (H. C. *Bigg*: valuable); EvQ 62 (1990) 189-191 (*Akio Ito*).

4614 *Uro* Risto, Profeettakirja... Prophetische Schrift oder Weisheitssamm-lung? Die neuen Fragen der Q-Forschung [Kloppenborg J., Sato M.]: Teologinen Aikakauskirja 95,2 (Helsinki 1990) 121-5 [< IZBG 36, p. 149].

4615 **Wilson** Craig R., The Synoptic Problem; a case study in the control of knowledge: diss. Columbia Teachers' College, DSloan D. NY 1990. 466 p. 90-33913. — DissA 51 (1990s) 2419-A.

F2.8 *Synoptica:* **themata.**

4616 *Abugunrin* S.O., The Synoptic Gospel debate; a re-examination in the African context: AfrJ BSt 2,1s (Ibadan 1987) 25-51 [< NTAbs 34,159].

4617 **Baarlink** Heinrich, Die Eschatologie der synoptischen Evangelien [< Vervulling en voleinding 1984 → 1,264*] BW 120, 1986 → 2,7141 ... 4,a53: RCritRR 2 (1989) 178-180 (J. T. *Carroll*).

4618 *Buzzetti* C., La folla nei Sinottici: → 542*, Laici 1988/90, 151-171.

4619 **Chilton** Bruce, Profiles of a rabbi; synoptic opportunities in reading about Jesus [an alternative approach to the Synoptic problem: all depend upon the catechetical material itself, not upon one another]: Brown-JudaicSt 177. Atlanta 1989, Scholars. x-225 p. $40; sb. $25. 1-55540-362-X [TDig 37,352].

4620 **Hermant** Dominique, Jésus disait ... Allons ailleurs; présentation des paroles de Jésus conservées dans les Évangiles de Matthieu, Marc et Luc. P 1989, de Brouwer. 256 p. F 99. - RNRT 112 (1990) 138s (P. G.).

4621 **Lindsey** Robert L., The Jesus sources; understanding the Gospels [Jerusalem lectures 1982s]. Tulsa 1990, Ha-Kesher. 111 p. $7 [J Persp 4/3, 14, J. *Frankovic*].

4622 **McKnight** Scot, Interpreting the Synoptic Gospels. GR 1988, Baker. 141 p. - REvQ 62 (1990) 365 (D. *Wenham*).

4623 **Melbourne** Bertram L., Slow to understand; the disciples in Synoptic perspective D1988 → 5,4312: RAndrUnS 28 (1990) 173-5 (E. J. *Bursey*: against claim of KELBER W. and WEEDEN T. that Mark discredits the disciples, raises questions it does not treat adequately); CBQ 52 (1990) 759s (F. J. *Matera*); JTS 42 (1990) 596-9 (E. *Best*); PerspRelSt 17 (1990) 286s (C. C. *Black*).

4625 *Murray* Gregory, Five Gospel miracles [against 2-Source; Mk knew both Mt and Lk]: DowR 108 (1990) 79-89.

4626 **Orchard** B., *Riley* H., The order of the Synoptics 1987 → 3,4198 ... 5,4314: RNT 32 (1990) 383s (J. K. *Elliott*).

4627 **Piper** Ronald A., Wisdom in the Q tradition; aphoristic teaching of Jesus [... Lk 6; 11s]: SNTS Mg 61, 1989 → 5,4518: RBiblica 71 (1990) 432-6 (J. S. *Kloppenborg*); JTS 41 (1990) 608-610 (C. M. *Tuckett*).

4628 *a) Reicke* Bo, The history of the Synoptic discussion; – *b) Borgen* P., John and the Synoptics; – *c) Merkel* H., Die Überlieferungen der Alten Kirche über das Verhältnis der Evangelien: → 524, Interrelations 1984/90, 291-316 / 408-437 (-450, *Neirynck* Frans, response) / 566-590 (-604, *Orchard* Bernard, response).

4629 *Scaer* D.P., The two sacraments doctrine as a factor in Synoptic relationships: Philosophy & Theology 3 (Milwaukee 1989) 205-222 [< NTAbs 34,73].

4630 **Schmidt** Thomas E., Hostility to wealth in the Synoptic Gospels [diss. Cambridge, DBammel E.] 1987 → 3,4204; 4,4432: RRB 97 (1990) 610s (B. *Viviano*); Themelios 15 (1989s) 32 (R. *Willoughby*).

4631 **Stalter-Fouilloy** D., Histoire et violence; essai sur la liberté humaine dans les premiers écrits chrétiens [i. Synoptiques ...]: ÉtHPR 70. P 1990, PUF. 160 p. F 150 [NRT 113, 916, X. *Jacques*).

4632 **Theissen** Gerd, Lokalkolorit und Zeitgeschichte in den Evangelien; ein Beitrag zur Geschichte der synoptischen Tradition: NTOrb 8, 1989 ➤ 5,4317; FrS 3-7278-0605-2 / VR 3-525-53908-8: ᴿBZ 34 (1990) 132-4 (R. *Schnackenburg*); MüTZ 41 (1990) 295-7 (J. *Gnilka*); SNTU A-15 (1990) 198-200 (A. *Fuchs*); ZkT 112 (1990) 211 (R. *Oberforcher*).

4633 **Toritto** Joseph, Exploring the gospels of Matthew, Mark, and Luke; a manual for teachers: Christian Brothers Publications. Winona MN 1990, St. Mary's. 158 p. $20. 0-88489-239-5 [TDig 38,192].

4634 ᴱ**Tuckett** C. M., Synoptic studies, Ampleforth, 1982/4 ➤ 65,441 ... 3,4206: ᴿSNTU A-15 (1990) 156-8 (A. *Fuchs*).

4636 **Vouga** François, Jésus et la loi selon la tradition synoptique ᴰ1988 ➤ 5,4320: ᴿJBL 109 (1990) 535s (L. *Gaston*: 'the reader may not always think just that which the author so confidently states'); RB 97 (1990) 612s (B. T. *Viviano*: unsatisfactory); RBibArg 52,37 (1990) 60s (R. *Krüger*); ZevEth 34 (1990) 155s (W. *Rebell*).

4637 *Weiss* Herold, The sabbath in the synoptic gospels: JStNT 38 (1990) 13-27.

F3.1   **Matthaei evangelium:** *textus, commentarii.*

4638 **Banning** J. van, Opus imperfectum in Matthaeum, Praefatio. CCL 87B. Turnhout 1988, Brepols. ccclxvii p. [RHE 86,348s, R. *Gryson*: rare écrit arien attribué à Cʜʀʏsostoмᴇ]. – ᴿRHPR 70 (1990) 355 (J. *Doignon*).

4639 — **Mali** Franz, Das Verhältnis des Opus imperfectum in Matthäum zu den Matthäuskommentaren des Hɪᴇʀᴏɴʏᴍᴜs und des Oʀɪɢᴇɴᴇs: Diss. ᴰ*Bauer*. Graz 1989s. – TR 86 (1990) 510; RTLv 22, p. 597 'ᴰ*Schwendenwein* H.'.

4640 ᵀᴱ**Banterle** Gabriele, San Cʀᴏᴍᴀᴢɪᴏ di Aquileia, Commento a Matteo: Scriptores circa Ambrosium 3/2. Mi/R 1990, Biblioteca Ambrosiana / Città Nuova. 438 p. 88-311-9197-7.

4641 **Bruner** Frederick D., The churchbook, Mt 13-28: Matthew comm. 2. Dallas 1990, Word. xx + p. 477-1127. $25. 0-8499-0617-2 [TDig 37,350 sans date].

4642 **Davies** W. D., **Allison** Dale C., ICC Mt I (1-7) 1988 ➤ 4,4439; 5,4325: ᴿBR 6,6 (1990) 10s (M. *Borg*); CriswT 4 (1989s) 192-4 (J. A. *Burns*); EstE 65 (1990) 93s (A. *Vargas-Machuca*); Pacifica 3 (1990) 112-4 (N. *Watson*); SNTU A-15 (1990) 158-161 (A. *Fuchs*); TorJT 6 (1990) 129-131 (M. G. *Steinhauser*); Vidyajyoti 53 (1989) 629-631 (P. M. *Meagher*).

4643 **Foucauld** Charles de, Lecture du saint Évangile; St. Matthieu: Œuvres 5. P 1989, Nouvelle Cité. 378 p. F 150. – ᴿEsprVie 100 (1990) 77s (É. *Ricaud*).

4644 **Galizzi** Mario, Oltre ogni frontiera; Vangelo secondo Matteo I: Commenti al NT. T 1990, Elle Di Ci. 256 p. 88-01-14408-3.

4645 **Gnilka** J., Das Matthäusevangelium: HerdTK 2, 1988 ➤ 4,4440; 5,4326: ᴿAnnTh 4 (1990) 435-440 (B. *Estrada*); CBQ 52 (1990) 155s (D. J. *Harrington*, 1s: best in any language); EstE 65 (1990) 94s (A. *Vargas-Machuca*); SNTU-A 14 (1989) 244s (A. *Fuchs*); TPhil 65 (1990) 590s (J. *Beutler*); TPQ 138 (1990) 186s (O. *Knoch*); ZMissRW 74 (1990) 83s (J. *Kuhl*).

4646 **Gnilka** Joachim, Il Vangelo di Matteo [con] testo greco; ᵀ*Cavallini* Stefano: CommTeolNT 1/1. Brescia 1990, Paideia. I. 755 p. Lit. 100.000. – ᴿLetture 45 (1990) 762s (G. *Ravasi*).

4646* **Green** M., Matthew for today; expository study of NT. Irving 1989, Word. 304 p. 0-8499-3181-9 [ÉTRel 65,661].

4647 **Kilgallen** John, A brief commentary on the Gospel of Matthew. NY 1990, Paulist.

4648 ᴱ**Löfstedt** B., SEDULIUS Scottus, Komm. Mt 1,1-11,1: VLatG 14, 1989 ➤ 5,4331: ᴿJTS 41 (1990) 729-731 (M. *Winterbottom*); NRT 112 (1990) 594 (X. *Jacques*); RÉLat 68 (1990) 195s (J.-P. *Bouhot*); RHE 85 (1990) 735-9 (R. *Étaix*: nombreux compléments).

4649 **Luz** Ulrich, Mt 1-7 ᵀ*Linss* W. C. ➤ 5,4333; also E 1990, Clark [NTAbs 35,103 'incorporates minor changes that the author communicated to the translator'].

4650 **Meier** J. P., Matthew: NTMessage 3. Collegeville 1990, Ltg. xii-372 p. $13. 0-8146-65126 [NTAbs 35,104: reprint with bibliographical inserts].

4651 **Montague** George T., Companion God... comm. Mt 1989 ➤ 5,4334*: ᴿTS 51 (1990) 736s (Karen A. *Barta*).

4652 **Nepper-Christensen** Poul, Matthæus evangeliet; en kommentar. Århus 1988, Anis. – ᴿTsTKi 60 (1989) 58 (H. *Kvalbein*).

4653 **Patte** Daniel, The Gospel according to Matthew, a structural commentary on Matthew's faith 1987 ➤ 3,4222; 5,4335: ᴿCritRR 3 (1990) 230-2 (D. *Senior*); Neotestamentica 29 (1990) 373-6 (W. R. *Domeris*); TorJT 6 (1990) 353-5 (J. D. *Evers*).

4654 **Schmidt** Bernhard, ALBERTI Magni Super Matthaeum, cap. I-XIV [➤ 3, 4225]; XV-XXVIII: Opera 21. Münster 1987, Aschendorff. lxxvii-437 p.; p. 439-775. DM 512, pa. 472. – ᴿTrierTZ 99 (1990) 157s (K. *Reinhardt*).

4655 **Sheridan** J. Mark, The [Sahidic] homilies of RUFUS of Shotep on the Gospels of Matthew and Luke: diss. Catholic Univ., ᴰ*Johnson* D. Wsh 1990. 487 p. 90-27966. – DissA 51 (1990s) 1593s-A.

4656 **Smith** R. H., Matthew: Augsburg Comm. 1989 ➤ 5,4338: ᴿNeotestamentica 29 (1990) 386-9 (J. *Bohnen*).

4657 **Stutts** David H., A textual history of the Gospel of Matthew as found in the papyri, uncials, and principal third and fourth century Fathers: diss. Baptist Theol. Sem., ᴰ*Winbery* C. New Orleans 1989. 122 p. 90-20110. – DissA 51 (1990s) 896s-A.

4658 ᴱ**Vogt** Hermann, ORIGENES, Der Kommentar zum Evangelium nach Matthäus 2: BGL 30. Stu 1990, Hiersemann. x-371 p. [TR 87,76].

F3.2 **Themata** *de Matthaeo*.

4659 *Aarde* A. G. van, Immanuel as die geinkarneerde tora; funksionele Jesusbenaminge in die Matteusevangelie as vertelling: HervTSt 43,1s (1987) 242-7 [< NTAbs 34,22].

4660 *Backus* I., Deux cas d'évolution théologique dans les Paraphrases d'ÉRASME; la version inédite du fragment de la Paraphrase sur Matthieu (1521) et de l'Épître à Ferdinand (1522): ➤ 725, Érasme 1986/90, 141-151.

4661 **Bauer** David R., The structure of Matthew's Gospel...: JStNT supp. 31, ᴰ1988 ➤ 4,4456; 5,4342: ᴿBiblica 71 (1990) 126-9 (R. H. *Gundry*); CBQ 52 (1990) 338s (M. A. *Powell*); Interpretation 44 (1990) 89.92 (D. E. *Garland*); JBL 109 (1990) 536-8 (J. S. *Siker*); JTS 41 (1990) 175-8 (H. B. *Green*); RB 97 (1990) 616s (B. T. *Viviano*).

4662 *Brändle* Francisco, La oración en San Mateo; acogida de la voluntad de Dios: REspir 49 (1990) 9-25.

4663 **Brooks** Stephenson H., Matthew's community [diss. Columbia, ᴰ*Brown* R. E.] 1987 ➤ 3,4233; 5,4347: ᴿRB 97 (1990) 615s (B. T. *Viviano*).

4664 **Casalini** Nello, Il Vangelo di Matteo come racconto teologico; analisi
delle sequenze narrative: SBF 30. J 1990, Franciscan. 115 p. $10 pa.
[NTAbs 34,382]. – RLetture 45 (1990) 934-6 (G. *Ravasi*, anche su
Metafore di una vita 1990).

4665 **Chouinard** Larry E., A literary study of Christology in Matthew: diss.
Fuller Theol. Sem., DHagner D. Pasadena 1988. 476 p. 90-21824. —
DissA 51 (1990s) 898-A.

4666 *Comblin* José, *al.*, O evangelho de Mateus: Estudos B 26 (1990) 72 p.

4667 **Crosby** Michael H., House of disciples; Church, economics, and justice in Matthew 1988 ➤ 4,4458; 5,4353: RCBQ 52 (1990) 552s (R. L.
Rohrbaugh); CritRR 3 (1990) 193-5 (J. G. *Williams*); RelStR 16 (1990)
333 (J. S. *Kloppenborg*).

4668 *Deutsch* Celia, Wisdom in Matthew; transformation of a symbol: NT 32
(1990) 13-47.

4669 **Douglas** Rees C., Family, power, religion; a discussion of the background and functions of references to God as Father in the Gospel of
Matthew: diss. DMack B. Claremont 1989. – RelStR 17,194.

4670 **Edwards** Richard A., *a)* Narrative implications of *gár* in Matthew:
CBQ 52 (1990) 636-655; – *b)* Reading Matthew; the Gospel as narrative:
Listening 24,3 (now Romeoville IL 1989) 251-261 [< NTAbs 34,160].

4671 *Engelbrecht* J., *a)* The language of the Gospel of Matthew: Neotestamentica 29 (1990) 199-213; – *b)* 'n Nuwe benadering tot die styl van
Matteus: Scriptura 35 (1990) 26-34 [< NTAbs 35,157].

4672 **Fischer** B., Varianten zu Mt: VLatGesch 13, 1988 ➤ 4,4460; 5,4357:
RJBL 109 (1990) 530-3 (W. J. *Gochee*, † 6.VIII.1989); JTS 41 (1990) 637-
640 (J. K. *Elliott*); VigChr 44 (1990) 303 (G. M. *Bartelink*: auch Mk).

4673 *a) Fortuna* Mariola, ❷ The Hebrew Gospel of St. Matthew from a
medieval Jewish treatise: – *b) Mędala* Stanisław, ❷ New source for
investigations of the transmission of Matthew's Gospel [*Howard* G. 1987]:
RuBi 42 (1989) 241-9 / 249-259.

4673* **Geist** Heinz, Menschensohn und Gemeinde... Mt: ForBi 57, 1986
➤ 2,5791; 3,7209: RNorTTs 90 (1989) 180s (R. *Leivestad*).

4674 **Howell** David B., Matthew's inclusive story; a study in the narrative
rhetoric of the first Gospel [diss. Oxford 1988, DMorgan R.]: JStNT supp.
42. Sheffield 1990, JStOT. 292 p. £25. 1-85075-236-2 [NTAbs 35,102:
'inclusive' seems to refer to the 'implied reader' (not identified with the
disciples) without relevance to sex-language].

4675 **Kingsbury** J. D. *a)* Matthew as story[2rev] 1988 ([1]1986) ➤ 5,4362:
RCritRR 3 (1990) 211-3 (D. *Senior*, [1]1986): Vidyajyoti 53 (1989) 631s
(P. M. *Meagher*, [1]1986); – *b)* Reflections on the readers of Mt. 1988. –
RDeltioVM 18,2 (1989) 109s (S. *Agourides*).

4676 **Köhler** Wolf-Dietrich, Die Rezeption des Mt... vor Irenäus: WUNT
2/24, 1987 ➤ 3,4241; 5,4366: RBijdragen 51 (1990) 85s (M. *Parmentier*);
CritRR 2 (1989) 213-5 (J. D. *Kingsbury*); CrNSt 11 (1990) 376-8 (P.
Grech); SvEx 55 (1990) 172s (T. *Fornberg*).

4677 *Kopas* Jane, Jesus and women in Matthew: TTod 47 (1990s) 13-21.

4678 **Kowalczyk** Mirosław, ❷ Historyczny sens narodu... Mateusza... Historical significance of the nation in the light of the biblical and dogmatical
sources, with a special regard to Matthew's Gospel: diss. DBartnik C.
Lublin 1990. 328 p. – RTLv 22, p. 620.

4679 **Kunkel** Fritz [surgeon-therapist 1889-1956], Creation continues; a
psychological interpretation of the Gospel of Matthew[3] ([1]1946, [2]1973].
NY 1987, Paulist. 286 p. $9 pa. – RRB 97 (1990) 615 (B. T. *Viviano*).

4680 **McTernan** D. J., A call to witness; reflections on the Gospel of St. Matthew. Collegeville MN 1989, Liturgical. 104 p. $5. 0-8146-1838-3 [NTAbs 34,112: 13 pregnant passages].

4681 **Malina** Bruce J., *Neyrey* Jerome H., Calling Jesus names; the social value of labels in Matthew 1988 → 4,4471: RBibTB 20 (1990) 171s (R. *Hodgson*); CBQ 52 (1990) 165s (F. W. *Burnett*: admirable though combining incompatible methods).

4682 E**Mandruzzato** Enzo, Il buon messaggio seguendo Matteo 1989 → 5,4370; Biblioteca dell'Immagine: RRasT 31 (1990) 525s (B. *Marra* lo chiama 'ed.' ma non indica nessun collaboratore; RENAN 'centrale'; testo greco impeccabile).

4683 *Martin* François, Sortir du livre [Mt: accomplissement des Écritures]: SémBib 54 (1989) 1-18.

4684 *Mowery* Robert L., Subtle differences; the [30] Matthean 'Son of God' references: NT 32 (1990) 193-200.

4685 *Okeke* G. E., The after-life in St. Matthew as an aspect of Matthean ethic: Melanesian Journal of Theology 42,2 (Papua-NG 1988) 35-44 [→ 5,4373] = CommViat 31 (1988) 159-168 [< NTAbs 34,21].

4686 **Orton** D. E., The understanding scribe; Matthew and the apocalyptic ideal: JStNT supp 25, 1989 → 5,4374: RÉTRel 65 (1990) 450 (E. *Cuvillier*); RExp 87 (1990) 648 (D. E. *Garland*); TLond 93 (1990) 159s (L. *Houlden*); TLZ 115 (1990) 812s (Ingo *Broer*).

4687 **Overman** J. Andrew, Matthew's Gospel and formative Judaism; the social world of the Matthean community [diss. 1989 → 5,4375]. Mp 1990, Fortress. ix-174 p. $12 pa. 0-8006-2451-3 [JBL 110,725, F. W. *Burnett*].

4688 **Penn** Richard W., The call to discipleship; a Matthean model for contemporary evangelism: diss. Southern Baptist Theol. Sem., D*Poe* H. 1989. 281 p. 90-15972. — DissA 51 (1990s) 198-A.

4689 **Perlewitz** Miriam, The Gospel of Matthew: Message of Biblical Spirituality 8. Wilmington 1988, Glazier. 191 p. 0-89453-558-7; pa. -74-9. — RCBQ 52 (1990) 358s (P. *Rogers*).

4690 **Pettem** Michael, The question; what is the Sitz im Leben of the Gospel of Matthew?: [so RclStR 17,194; but DissA 51 (1990s) 3107-A gives as title 'Matthew: Jewish Christian or Gentile Christian']: diss. McGill, D*Wisse* F. Montreal 1989.

4691 **Powell** Mark A., The religious leaders in Matthew; a literary-critical approach: diss. Union Theol. Sem. Richmond 1988. 178 p. 90-17567. — DissA 51 (1990s) 534-A.

4692 **Richards** C., According to Matthew [for GCSE exams]. Glasgow 1989, Blackie. v-122 p. £5.25. 0-216-92619-X [NTAbs 34,387].

4692* *Robertson* Malcolm J.III, The present state of Matthaean studies in consequence of fresh perspectives: → 370, Gospels 1990, 38-50.

4693 *Sand* Alexander, Die Gemeinde zwischen 'jenen Tagen Jesu' und 'dem Tag des Gerichts'; zum Geschichtsverständnis des Matthäusevangeliums: TrierTZ 99 (1990) 49-71.

4694 **Schenk** W., Die Sprache des Mt 1987 → 3,4253 ... 5,4384: RBijdragen 51 (1990) 326 (W. *Weren*); JTS 41 (1990) 181s (G. *Stanton*: an invaluable reference tool); StPatav 37 (1990) 195s (G. *Segalla*).

4695 **Schweizer** E., Matteo e la sua comunità 1987 → 4,4480: RProtestantesimo 45 (1990) 220s (G. *Conte*).

4696 *Senior* Donald, The Jesus of Matthew; compassionate teacher, faithful son: Church 5,4 (NY 1989) 10-13 [< NTAbs 34,161].

4697 *Shuler* Philip L., PHILO's Moses and Matthew's Jesus; a comparative study in ancient literature: StPhilonAn 2 (1990) 86-103.

4698 **Strong** David K., The contribution of structural semantics to theological contextualization; a case study on 'righteousness' [in Mt]: diss. Fuller, ᴰ*Hiebert* P. Pasadena 1990. 459 p. 90-30669. — DissA 51 (1990s) 2062-A.

4699 *Suh Joong-Suk*, Ⓚ Community in the Gospel of Matthew: Sinhak Sasang 67 (Seoul 1989) 901-926 [< TContext 8/1,70].

4700 *Swanson* T. N., The ministry of Jesus as pictured in the Gospel of Matthew; a Bible study: Bangalore Theological Forum 24,3 (1989) 65-75 [< NTAbs 34,304].

4701 *Syreeni* Kari, Between heaven and earth; on the structure of Matthew's symbolic universe: JStNT 40 (1990) 3-13.

4702 *Trimaille* M., Citations d'accomplissement et architecture de l'Évangile selon S. Matthieu: EstB 48 (1990) 47-70; Eng., español 47.

4703 **Wilkins** Michael J., The concept of disciple in Mt... [diss. Fuller 1986]: NT supp 59, 1988 ⮞ 4,4485; 5,4388: ᴿCBQ 52 (1990) 769-771 (M. A. *Powell*: improves on RENGSTORF but no real surprises); JBL 109 (1990) 534s (R. H. *Gundry*); JTS 41 (1990) 179s (G. *Stanton*).

4704 **Wouters** Armin, 'Wer den Willen meines Vaters tut'; eine Untersuchung zum Verständnis vom Handeln im Matthäusevangelium; kath. Diss. ᴰ*Gnilka*. München 1989s. – TR 86 (1990) 517.

F3.3   *Mt 1s (Lc 1s ⮞ F7.5) Infantia Jesu* – **Infancy Gospels.**

4705 **Aus** Roger D., Weihnachtsgeschichte – Barmherziger Samariter – Verlorener Sohn; Studien zu ihrem jüdischen Hintergrund 1988 ⮞ 4,4220: ᴿTLZ 115 (1990) 510 (W. *Wiefel*).

4706 **Casalini** Nello, Libro sull'origine di Gesù Cristo; analisi letteraria e teologica di Matt 1-2: SBF Anal 28. J 1990, Franciscan. 173 p. $12. – ᴿLetture 45 (1990) 934-6 (G. *Ravasi*).

4706* a) *Cazelles* Henri, Sur l'histoire de Bethléhem; – b) *Calkins* Arthur B., The justice of Joseph revisited; – c) *Haudebert* Pierre, Les bergers en Luc 2,8-20; – d) *Jeanne d'Arc,* sr., 'Ce n'était pas une place pour eux' (Lc 2,7) [Miettes d'évangile]: ⮞ 109*, ᶠLAURENTIN R., *Kecharitōménē* 1990, 145-152 / 165-177 / 178-185 / 158s [153-164].

4707 *Corpuz* Ruben, The validity of the virginal conception language in the ecumenical dialogue: PhilipSa 24 (1989) 91-111.

4708 **Cullmann** Oscar, Die Entstehung des Weihnachtsfestes und die Herkunft des Weihnachtsbaumes²ʳᵉᵛ. [¹1947]. Stu 1990, Quell. 71 p. DM 9,80. 3-7918-2326-4 [NTAbs 35,256].

4709 **Feuillet** André, Le Sauveur messianique et sa mère dans les récits de l'enfance de s. Matthieu et de s. Luc: a) Teologica 4. Vaticano 1990, ed. 88 p. Lit. 10.000. – ᴿAsprenas 37 (1990) 513s (A. *Rolla*); EsprVie 100 (1990) 671 (É. *Ricaud*); Salmanticensis 37 (1990) 366s (G. *Pérez*); – b) Divinitas 34 (1990) 17-52. 103-150.

4710 **Fuller** R. H., He that cometh; the birth of Jesus in the New Testament. Wilton CT 1990, Morehouse. x-117 p. $9 pa. 0-8192-1544-9 [NTAbs 35,240].

4711 **Horsley** R. A., The liberation of Christmas 1989 ⮞ 4,4500; 5,4394: ᴿAnglTR 71 (1989) 209-211 (R. *Pelly*); CBQ 52 (1990) 347s (J. J. *Pilch*: intuitive-dynamic view of Magi as Persian Empire's opposition to Herod);

BibTB 20 (1990) 170s (P. *Hollenbach*); WestTJ 52 (1990) 373-5 (C. L. *Blomberg*).

4712 **Kremer** Jacob, Das Erfassen der bildsprachlichen Dimension als Hilfe für das rechte Verstehen der biblischen 'Kindheitsevangelien' und ihre Vermittlung als lebendiges Wort Gottes: ➤ 350, Metaphorik 1990, 78-109.

4713 *Miyoshi* Michi, Die Theologie der Spaltung und Einigung Israels in der Geburts- und Leidensgeschichte nach Matthäus: AnJap 15 (1989) 37-52.

4714 **Muñoz Iglesias** Salvador, Nacimiento e infancia de Jesús en San Mateo: Los Evangelios de la Infancia 4 [1-3, ➤ 64,4929... 5,5106]: BAC 509. M 1990, Católica. xvi-443 p. 84-7914-006-2.

4715 *Stevens* Maryanne, Paternity and maternity [cover 'Maternity and paternity'] in the Mediterranean; foundations for patriarchy: BibTB 20,2 ('Mary – woman of the Mediterranean' 1990) 47-53.

4716 **Tomić** Celestin, Isus iz Nazareta, Bog z nama: Evandelje po Mateju (1-2), po Luki (1-2), po Ivanu (1,1-18): Povijest Spasenja Svezak 10. Zagreb 1990.

4717 *Viviano* Benedict T., The genres of Matthew 1-2; light from 1 Timothy 1-4: RB 97 (1990) 31-53; franç. 31.

4718 *Wlodarczyk* Stanisław, ❷ The birth of Jesus as a sign of the on-coming of the fullness of [this] time: ➤ 64, [F]GRZYBEK S. 1990, 340-7; Eng. 347.

4719 *Hempelmann* Heinzpeter, 'Das dürre Blatt im Heiligen Buch', Mt 1,1-17 und der Kampf wider die Erniedrigung Gottes: TBeit 21,1 (1990) 6-23 [NTAbs 34,305: aesthetic, historical-hermeneutical, moral, and philosophical objections].

4720 *Bauer* David R., The literary function of the genealogy in Matthew's Gospel. ➤ 544, SBL seminars 1990, 451-468.

4721 *a) Asmussen* Hans-Georg, Der Zensus des Quirinius; – *b) Heymel* Michael, Seligspriesen von allen Geschlechtern; zur ökumenischen Bedeutung Mariens: Deutsches Pfarrerblatt 90 (Essen 1990) 531-3 / 528-530 [< ZIT 91,58].

4722 **Segalla** G., Una storia annunciata 1987 ➤ 4,4509; 5,4401: [R]ScripT-Pamp 22 (1990) 1009s (C. *Basevi*).

4723 *Gnuse* Robert, Dream genre in the Matthean infancy narratives: NT 32 (1990) 97-120.

4724 *a) Scott* Bernard B., The birth of the reader in Matthew; – *b) Plank* Karl A., The human face of otherness; reflections on Joseph and Mary (Matthew 1:18-25): ➤ 123*, [F]MEYER P., Faith 1990, 35-54 / 55-73.

4725 *Tronina* Antoni, ❷ More on the name of Maria[m]: RuBi 23 (1990) 127-130 (final -m omitted by and after JEROME).

4726 [E]**Fatica** L., ILDEFONSO di Toledo, La perpetua verginità di Maria: TestPatr 84. R 1990, Città Nuova. 160 p. Lit. 13.000. – [R]Asprenas 37 (1990) 515 (L. *Longobardo*).

4727 **Müller** Gerhard L., Was heisst: Geboren von der Jungfrau Maria? Eine theologische Deutung: QDisp 119, 1989 ➤ 5,4413: [R]GeistL 63 (1990) 226-231 (F.-J. *Steinmetz*); HerdKor 44 (1990) 590 (U. *Ruh*); TLZ 115 (1990) 297s (W. *Beinert*); TsTNijm 30 (1990) 105s (M. van *Tente*).

4728 Letters mostly defending Virgin Birth; BR [4,5 (1988) 10, *Barrett* J.] 5,1 (1989) 6-9 . 34-37; 5,3 (1989) 36-39.

4729 *Brawley* R.L., [Mt 1,18-25] Joseph in Matthew's birth narrative and the irony of good intentions: Cumberland Seminarian 28,2s (Memphis 1990) 69-76 [< NTAbs 35,158].

4730 *Oury* G.-M., L'exhortation apostolique Redemptoris custos [1989, 'se présente comme un simple commentaire spirituel de l'Évangile; considérations sur la 'dévotion populaire' et 'une certaine iconographie en Amérique et ailleurs']; la figure et la mission de saint Joseph: EsprVie 100 (1990) 11-15.

4731 **Schaberg** Jane, The illegitimacy of Jesus 1987 → 3,4273 ... 5,4415: ᴿCBQ 52 (1990) 364s (Barbara E. *Reid*: admits largely conjectural but can help toward feminist Mariology).

4732 *Longenecker* R.N., [Mt 1,18-25] Whose child is this?: ChrTod 34,18 (1990) 25-28 [< NTAbs 35,158].

4733 *Petrotta* A.J., An even closer look at Matt 2:6 and its OT sources: JEvTS 33 (1990) 311-5 [< NTAbs 35,158].

4734 *Good* Deirdre, [Mt 2,12 + 6 times] The verb *anachōréō* in Matthew's Gospel: NT 32 (1990) 1-12.

4734* *Álvarez Calderón* Jorge, [Mt 2,22] Nazaret; su significado para Jesús y para la Iglesia: Páginas 15,105 (Lima 1990) 15-31.

4735 ᵀ**Dubois** Joseph, ᴱ*Hoste* Anselme, Aelred de RIEVAULX, Quand Jésus eut douze ans: SChr 60, 1987 = 1958 → 3,5002; 4,4530: ᴿRÉAug 35 (1989) 202 (J. *Longère*).

F3.4 *Mt 3 ... Baptismus Jesu,* **Beginning of the Public Life.**

4736 **Backhaus** Knut, *Álloi kekopiákasín*; die 'Jüngerkreise' des Täufers Johannes unter besonderer Berücksichtigung ihres religionsgeschichtlichen Verhältnisses zu Jesus von Nazareth und dem frühen Christentum: Diss. Pd 1989. – BZ 34,157.

4737 *Badke* William B., Was Jesus a disciple of John?: EvQ 62 (1990) 195-204.

4738 *Betz* Otto, Was John the Baptist an Essene? [yes]: BR 6,6 (1990) 18-25; ill.

4739 **Dobbeler** Stephanie von, Das Gericht und das Erbarmen Gottes; die Botschaft Johannes des Täufers im Rahmen der Theologiegeschichte des Frühjudentums, ᴰ1988 → 5,4432: ᴿSNTU-A 14 (1989) 236s (A. *Fuchs*).

4740 **Ernst** Josef, Johannes der Täufer...: BZNW 53, 1989 → 5,4433: ᴿBZ 34 (1990) 274-8 (I. *Broer*); ÉTRel 65 (1990) 117s (E. *Cuvillier*: deux-sources, autrement semblable à LUPIERI); TGL 80 (1990) 343s (F.A. v. *Metzsch*); TPQ 138 (1990) 402 (A. *Fuchs*).

4741 *Infante* Lorenzo, Il Battista chiama al ritorno: → 325*b*, ParSpV 22 (1990) 127-140.

4742 **Lupieri** Edmondo, Giovanni Battista nella tradizione sinottica 1988 → 4,4536; 5,4436: ᴿOrpheus 10 (1989) 492-4 (Amalia *Tuccillo*); RTPhil 122 (1990) 275s (R. *Petraglio*).

4743 **Lupieri** Edmondo, Giovanni Battista fra storia e leggenda 1988 → 4,4537: ᴿGregorianum 71 (1990) 190 (A. *Orbe*: good on NT, but 200 pages on Mandean legends, 'doctrinalmente archipobres'); Helmantica 41 (1990) 432s (Rosa M. *Herrera*); RivB 38 (1990) 106-110 (G. *Segalla*).

4744 *Merklein* Helmut, Gericht und Heil; zur heilsamen Funktion des Gerichts bei Johannes dem Täufer, Jesus und Paulus: JbBT 5 (→ 2140, 1990) 71-92.

4745 *Murphy-O'Connor* Jerome, John the Baptist and Jesus; history and hypotheses [... why did he baptize in such an unsuitable place?... Elijah... Ephesus...]: NTS 36 (1990) 359-374.

4746 *Munier* C., *a*) [Mt 3,13-17] Rites d'onction, baptême chrétien et baptême de Jésus; – *b*) Initiation chrétienne et rites d'onction (IIe-IIIe siècles): RevSR 64 (1990) 217-234. 115-125.

4747 *Quesnel* Michel, Le baptême de Jésus: MondeB 65 (1990) 29-31. 37-40 [*al.* 23-28. 33-36. 41-47].

4748 *Vigne* Daniel, Le baptême du Christ, onction paradisiaque: NRT 112 (1990) 801-820.

4749 *Wessel* Daisy, Jordantaufe auf dem Schlangenstein: ➤ 5,210, Mem. WESSEL K. 1988, 375-384; pl. 453.

4750 *Charles* J.D., The 'Coming one'/'Stronger one' and his baptism; Matt 3:11-12; Mark 1:8; Luke 3:16-17: Pneuma 11,1 (Gaithersburg MD 1989) 37-50 [< NTAbs 35,23].

4751 *Dąbek* Tomasz M., [Mt 4,2] ❷ Fasting in the life of Jesus: RuBi 42 (1989) 125-131.

4752 **Chase** Keith W., [Mt 4,1-11] The Synoptic *peirasmoi* of Jesus; their Christological significance: diss. Baptist Theol. Sem. ᴰ*Simmons* B. New Orleans 1990. 317 p. 90-26807. – DissA 51 (1990s) 1647s-A.

4753 *Légasse* Simon, Tentation dans la Bible [*Lamarche* Paul, La tentation messianique]: ➤ 837, DictSpir 15,96ss (1990) 193-212 [-216].

4754 *Moloney* Raymond, The temptations of Christ; what do we mean when we say Christ was tempted?: PrPeo 4 (1990) 54-56.

4755 *Stegner* William R., [Mt 4,1-11...] The Temptation narrative; a study in the use of Scripture by early Jewish Christians: BiRes 35 (1990) 5-17.

4756 *Yang Seoung-Aeh*, Historical investigation on the temptation of Jesus according to Matthew 4:1-11 and Luke 4:1-13: Sinhak Jonmang 91 (1990) [< TContext 8/2, p. 67: ? ❸; pp. not indicated].

4757 *Macholz* Christian, [Mt 4,4-9] Das 'passivum divinum', seine Anfänge im Alten Testament und der 'Hofstil': ZNW 81 (1990) 247-253.

4758 *Martini* Carlo M., Wonen in het Galilea van de Heidenen (Mt 4,13); de hoop versterken en het kwaad weerstaan in het hedendaags Europa: CollatVL 20 (1990) 73-89.

F3.5 Mt 5... Sermon on the Mount [... plain, Lk 6,17].

4759 **Betz** Hans D., Essays on the Sermon on the Mount 1985 ➤ 1,4323... 5,4447*: ᴿTsTKi 60 (1989) 142s (H. *Kvalbein*).

4760 *Betz* Hans Dieter, The Sermon on the Mount and Q; some aspects of the problem; – *b*) *Mack* Burton L., Lord of the logia, savior or sage?: ➤ 152, ᶠROBINSON J.M., Gnosticism I (1990) 19-34 / 3-18.

4761 **Bouterse** Johannes, De boom en zijn vruchten; Bergrede en Bergredechristendom bij Reformatoren, Anabaptisten en Spiritualisten in de zestiende eeuw: diss. Leiden 1986. Kempen 1986, Kok. 460 p. *f* 69. 90-242-2194-3. – ᴿBijdragen 51 (1990) 446 (J. *Lambrecht*).

4762 **Derrett** J.D.M., The ascetic discourse 1989 ➤ 5,4451: ᴿTLZ 115 (1990) 268 (U. *Schnelle*); TR 86 (1990) 201 (J. *Fisch*).

4763 **Harvey** Anthony E., [Mt 5-7] Strenuous commands; the ethic of Jesus. L/Ph 1990, SCM/Trinity. viii-248 p. $18 pa. 0-334-02471-4 [TDig 38,268].

4764 **Lambrecht** Jan, Ich aber sage euch 1984 ➤ 65,3919... 3,4346: ᴿTsTKi 60 (1989) 143s (H. *Kvalbein*).

4765 **Lohfink** Gerhard, El sermón de la montaña, ¿para quién? [1988
→ 4,4564], ᵀ*Martínez de Lapera* V.A. Barc 1989, Herder. 274 p. –
ᴿActuBbg 27 (1990) 197s (X. *Alegre* S.); CiTom 117 (1990) 383s (J.L.
Espinel); NatGrac 37 (1990) 317 (F.F. *Ramos*); PerspT 22 (1990) 400-2
(J. *Vitório*); RTLim 24 (1990) 295s (U. *Berges*).

4766 — *Oberlinner* Lorenz, Wem gilt die Bergpredigt? [*Lohfink* G.]: BZ 34
(1990) 104-8.

4767 **Mabaka ma Mbumba,** La spécificité de l'agir chrétien selon le Sermon
sur la Montagne (Mt 5-7]: problème des critères et des fondements: diss.
(ᴰ*Alvarez-Verdes* L., Alfonsianum): Pont. Univ. Lateranensis. R 1990.
v-137 p.

4768 *McEleney* N.J., The sermon on the mount – then and now: Living
Light 27,1 (Wsh 1990) 30-35 [< NTAbs 35,158].

4769 **Schweizer** Eduard, El sermón de la montaña, ᵀ*Martínez de Lapera*
Victor A.: Biblia y Catequesis 12. S 1990, Sígueme. 154 p. 84-301-
1100-X. – ᴿActuBbg 27 (1990) 203s (X. *Alegre* S.).

4770 **Speyr** Adrienne von, Le Sermon sur la montagne [1948], ᵀ*Lépine* Madi,
Capol Cornélia: Sycomore. P 1989, Lethielleux. 256 p. F 125. –
ᴿEsprVie 100 (1990) 240 (L. *Barbey*).

4771 **Stoll** Brigitta, De virtute in virtutem... Bergpredigt bis 1200: BeiGBEx
30, ᴰ1988 → 4,4570; 5,4461: ᴿSvEx 55 (1990) 173-6 (A. *Hardelin*).

4772 **Strecker** Georg, The sermon on the mount, an exegetical commentary
[²1985 → 65,3929], ᵀ*Dean* O.C., 1988 → 4,4571; 5,4462: ᴿEstE 65 (1990)
480s (A. *Rodríguez Carmona*); JBL 109 (1990) 347-9 (D.R. *Bauer*);
Neotestamentica 29 (1990) 379-381 (P.J. *Hartin*).

4773 *a) Strecker* Georg, Das Gesetz in der Bergpredigt – die Bergpredigt als
Gesetz; – *b) Syreeni* Kari, Matthew, Luke, and the Law; a study in
hermeneutical exegesis: → 560, Law 1988/90, 109-125 / 126-155.

4774 **Tilborg** Sjef van, The Sermon on the Mount as an ideological intervention 1986 → 5,4464: ᴿNedTTs 44 (1990) 160s (P.J. *Farla*).

4775 **Vaught** Carl G., The sermon on the mount; a theological interpretation
1986 → 3,4362; 4,4573: ᴿCritRR 2 (1989) 253-5 (E. *McMahon*); Themelios 15 (1989s) 20s (D.J. *Falk* compares with LAPIDE P.).

4776 **Ward** Keith, The rule of love; reflections on the Sermon on the Mount.
L 1989, Darton-LT. 134 p. – ᴿSalesianum 52 (1990) 174s (G. *Abbá*).

4777 *a) Weder* Hans, 'But I say to you...'; concerning the foundations of
Jesus' interpretation of the Law in the 'Sermon on the Mount'; – *b) Patte*
Daniel, [Mt 5,44s; 23,13] 'Love your enemies' – 'Woe to you, scribes and
Pharisees'; the need for a semiotic approach to New Testament studies; –
c) Betz Hans-Dieter, The problem of Christology in the Sermon on the
Mount: → 24, ꟳBOERS H., Text 1990, 211-28 / 81-96 / 191-209.

4778 *a) Williams* James G., Paraenesis, ethics, and excess; Matthew's rhetoric
in the Sermon on the Mount; – *b) Gammie* John G., Paraenetic literature;
toward the morphology of a secondary genre: → 464, Semeia 50 (1990)
163-187 / 41-77.

4779 **Zerbe** Gordon M., Non-retaliation in early Jewish and New Testament
texts; ethical themes in social contexts: diss. ᴰ*Charlesworth* J. Princeton
Theol. Sem. 1990. – RelStR 17,194.

F3.6   **Mt 5,3-11 (Lc 6,20-22) Beatitudines.**

4780 *Bravo* Carlos, Pueblo de las bienaventuranzas [< Christus Mex (1989,
Is) 33-42], ᴱ*Pericas* R.M.: SelT 29 (1990) 199-206.

4781 **Devulder** Gérard, *a*) L'évangile du bonheur; les béatitudes: Petite enc. chr. P 1988, D-Brouwer. 48 p. F 36. – ᴿÉglT 30 (1989) 479s (M. *Dumais*); – *b*) Il vangelo della felicità; le beatitudini. ᵀ*Tosatti* Teodora; ᴱ*Scotti* Giuliana. Brescia 1990, Queriniana. 78 p. Lit. 10.000. 88-399-3068-X.

4782 **Hamm** M. Dennis, The Beatitudes in context; what Luke and Matthew meant: Zacchaeus. Wilmington 1990, Glazier. vii-120 p. $6. 0-89453-676-1 [NTAbs 34,384].

4783 *Harris* Julie A., The Beatitudes casket in Madrid; Museo Arqueológico; its iconography in context: ZKunstG 53 (1990) 134-9; 3 fig.

4784 **López-Melús** F.-M., Las bienaventuranzas 1988 ➤ 4,4583; 5,4471: ᴿAngelicum 67 (1990) 138-140 (J. *Salguero*); ScripTPamp 22 (1990) 273-5 (J. M. *Casciaro*); Teresianum 40 (1989) 624s (V. *Pasquetto*).

4785 *Meier* John P., Matthew 5:3-12, expository: Interpretation 44 (1990) 281-5.

4786 *a*) *Meloni* Pietro, Le Beatitudini nei padri della Chiesa; – *b*) *Panimolle* S. A., Beati ...! Guai ...! (Lc 6,20ss): ➤ 325*a*, ParSpV 21 (1990) 221-240 / 117-151.

4787 *Montero* D., Las bienaventuranzas: Nuevo Mundo 139 (Caracas 1988) 447-456 [< Stromata 45,500].

4788 **Weber** Christian L., Blessings; a womanchrist reflection on the beatitudes. SF 1989, Harper & R. 199 p. $14 [JAAR 58,164].

4789 *Ambrozić* A. M., [Mt 5,3] Reflections on the first beatitude: CommND 17,1 (1990) 95-104.

4790 *Andia* Ysabel de, L'interprétation irénéenne de la béatitude des doux; 'bienheureux les doux, ils recevront la terre en héritage' (Mt 5:5); ➤ 643, StPatr 18,3 (1983/9) 85-102 [43-70, *Bentivegna* J., The charismatic dossier of Saint IRENAEUS].

4791 *Cramer* Winfrid, Die Seligpreisung der Friedensstifter; zur Rezeption der Bergpredigt bei AFRAHAT: ➤ 8*, ꜰASSFALG J. 1990, 68-78.

4792 *Helewa* Giovanni, 'Beati gli operatori di pace', I. 'Cristo la nostra pace'; II. 'Le opere della pace'; [III.] La preghiera; pace del Cristo nel cuore; [IV.] 'Beati gli afflitti': RivVSp 44 (1990) 9-24 / 123-137 / 374-388 / 561-577.

4793 *Hellestam* Sigvard, Mysteriet met saltet [Mt 5,13; GERHARDSSON B., ꜰANDRÉN C. 1987]: SvEx 55 (1990) 59-63.

4794 *Fernández-Ramos* Felipe, [Mt 5,13] La sal de la tierra: StLeg 31 (1990) 63-85.

4795 *Kampen* John, A reexamination of the relationship between Matthew 5: 21-48 and the Dead Sea Scrolls: ➤ 544, SBL seminars 1990, 34-59.

4796 *Holmes* Michael W., [Mt 5,31; 19,9] The text of the Matthean divorce passages; a comment on the appeal to harmonization in textual decisions: JBL 109 (1990) 651-664.

4797 **Labosier** Brian C., [Mt 5,31s; 19,1-12] Matthew's exception clause in the light of canonical criticism; a case study in hermeneutics: diss. Westminster Theol. Sem., ᴰ*Silva* M. 1990. 339 p. 90-26393. – DissD 51 (1990s) 1661-A.

4798 *Marucci* Corrado, Clausole matteane e matrimoni misti; osservazioni critiche ad un saggio di T. STRAMARE [1986]: RasT 31 (1990) 74-85.

4799 *Smith* Don T., The Matthean exception clauses in the light of Matthew's theology and community: StudiaBT 17 (1989) 55-82.

4800 **Ito** Akio, [Mt 5,33-37] Matthew's understanding of the law with special reference to the Fourth Antithesis: diss. UK Council for Academic Awards 1989. 361 p. BRDX-88587. – DissA 51 (1990s) 192-A.

4801 *Blank* Josef, [Mt 5,34] No juréis en absoluto [< Orientierung 53 (1989) 97-99], ᵀᴱ*Boada* J.: SelT 29 (1990) 196-8.

4802 **Lo Ping-cheung**, [Mt 5,38-48; Lk 6,27-38 ...] Love and imitation in the NT and recent Christian ethics: diss, Yale, ᴰ*Outka* G. NHv 1990. 477 p. 91-01284. – DissA 51 (1990s) 2784-A; RelStR 17,192, ᴰ*Fern* R.

4803 *Krieger* Klaus-Stefan, Fordert Mt 5,39b das passive Erdulden von Gewalt? Ein kleiner Beitrag zur Redaktionskritik der 5. Antithese: BibNot 54 (1990) 28-32.

4804 *Łach* Jan, ❷ 'Wenn dich einer auf die rechte Wange schlägt, dann haft ihm auch die andere hin' (Mt 5,39): ➤ 64, ᶠGRZYBEK S. 1990, 167-174; deutsch 174.

4805 *Straw* Carole E., CYPRIAN and Mt 5:45; the evolution of Christian patronage: StPatr 18,3 (1983/9) 329-339.

4806 *Schwarz* Günther, *Ho blépōn en tō kryptō (kryphaiō)* (Matthaus 6,4b,6c.18b): BibNot 54 (1990) 38-40.

4807 *Stubblefield* Jon M., Matthew 6:5-15: RExp 87 (1990) 303-7.

4808 *Łach* Jan, ❷ 'Nul ne peut servir deux maîtres' (Mt 6,24): STWsz 28,2 (1990) 38-49; franç. 49s.

4809 *Lejeune* Charles, Les oiseaux et les lis; lecture – écologique – de Matthieu 6,25-34: Hokhma 44 (1990) 3-20.

F3.7 *Mt 6,9-13 (Lc 11,2-4)* **Oratio Jesu,** Pater Noster, **Lord's Prayer** [➤ H1.4].

4810 *Baarda* T., De korte texst van het Onze Vader in Lucas 11:2-4; een Marcionitische corruptie?: NedTTs 44 (1990) 273-287; Eng. 332.

4811 **Aquinas,** The three greatest prayers; commentaries on the Lord's Prayer, the Hail Mary, and the Apostles' Creed. 1990, Sophia. 190 p. $17 [JAAR 58,737].

4812 *Banning* Joop van, Il Padre Nostro nell'Opus imperfectum in Matthaeum [5° sec., di una persona di grande erudizione]: Gregorianum 71 (1990) 293-312; franç. 313.

4813 *a) Barth* Hans-M., Das Vaterunser als ökumenisches Gebet; – *b) Schroer* Silvia, Konkretionen; – *c)* Auslegung des AUGUSTINUS; – *d) Brandt* Henry G., 'Wie im Himmel so auf Erden', jüdische Predigt; – *e) Berger* Teresa, ... Mittelamerika; UnSa 45 (1990) 99-109 . 113 / 110-113 / 114-121 / 122-4 / 125-131.

4814 *Baumgardt* David [for the centenary of his birth], Kaddish and the Lord's Prayer [similarities denied by Jesuit Josef STAUDINGER]: JBQ 19 (1990s) 164-9.

4815 *Cruz Hernández* Miguel, El 'Padrenuestro' de Jesús de Nazaret: Religión y Cultura 36,172 (M 1990) 61-66 [< NTAbs 35,23].

4816 **Douglas-Klotz** N., Prayers of the cosmos; meditations on the Aramaic words of Jesus [Our Father, beatitudes...]. SF 1990, Harper & R. xi-90 p. $15. 0-06-061994-5 [NTAbs 35,100].

4817 **Guardini** Romano, Gebet und Wahrheit; Meditationen über das Vaterunser: Werke. Mainz/Pd 1988, Grünewald/Schöningh. 208 p. DM 32. – ᴿTPQ 138 (1990) 277 (J. Singer).

4818 ᴱ**Heer** Josef, Vater unser im Himmel; Anregungen für das Bibelgespräch zum Gebet des Herrn: StuTb 3. Stu 1990, KBW. 128 p. 3-460-11003-1.

4819 **Lochman** Jan M., The Lord's prayer [1988 ➤ 5,4495], [T]*Bromiley* Geoffrey W., GR 1990, Eerdmans. x-180 p. $12 pa. 0-8028-0440-3 [TDig 38,277].

4820 **Pronzato** Alessandro, Il Padre Nostro preghiera dei figli: Le preghiere del cristiano. T 1989, Gribaudi. 298 p. – [R]StMon 32 (1990) 255s (L. *Fossas Colet*).

4821 **Sabugal** Santos, Il Padrenostro nella catechesi antica e moderna, [TE]*Nicolosi* M.: Cristianesimo 2, 1985 ➤ 4,4610; 5,4500: [R]Asprenas 37 (1990) 122s (L. *Fatica*); Gregorianum 71 (1990) 599s (M. *Ruiz Jurado*).

4822 *Heinen* Heinz, [Mt 6,11] Göttliche Sitometrie; Beobachtungen zur Brotbitte des Vaterunsers: TrierTZ 99 (1990) 72-79.

4823 *Hultgren* Arland J., The bread petition of the Lord's Prayer: ➤ 52, [F]FULLER R., AnglTR supp 11 (1990) 41-54.

4824 *Locher* G., 'Wie auch wir ...' Die Unser-Vater-Bitte um Vergebung (Mt vi,12) bei LUTHER, ZWINGLI und CALVIN: ➤ 511, Théorie/pratique 1988/90, 287-301.

4825 *Moore* Ernest, [Mt 6,13] 'Lead us not into temptation': ExpTim [101 (1989s) 299-301 *Cameron* P.; 359-362 *Porter* S.] 102 (1990s) 171s: Cameron says it is the longest chapter in any book on the Lord's Prayer; but in LOHMEYER's 1965 it is the shortest; BONHOEFFER says all temptation is temptation of Jesus and is conquered in him.

4826 *Popkes* Wiard, Die letzte Bitte des Vater-Unser; formgeschichtliche Beobachtungen zum Gebet Jesu: ZNW 81 (1990) 1-20.

4827 *Black* Matthew, The doxology to the Pater noster with a note on Matthew 6.13B: ➤ 183, [F]VERMES G. 1990, 327-338.

4828 *Ricœur* Paul, [Mt 7,12; last half of 1988 Princeton lecture] The golden rule; exegetical and theological perplexities: NTS 36 (1990) 392-397.

4829 *a) Horsley* G. H. R., *Tí* at Matthew 7:14, 'because' not 'how'; – *b) Maggi* Alberto, Nota sull'uso di *tô sô onómati* e *anomía* in Mt 7,21-23; – *c) O'Callaghan* José, Discusión crítica en Mt 17,25: FgNt 3 (1990) 141-3 / 145-9 / 151-3.

4830 **Wegner** U., Der Hauptmann Mt 7,28: WUNT 2/14, 1985 ➤ 1,4401... 4,4622: [R]NedTTs 44 (1990) 65-67 (G. *Mussies*).

4831 **Carson** D. A., When Jesus confronts ... Mt 8-10, 1987 ➤ 4,4652; 5,4521: [R]AndrUnS 28 (1990) 90s (K. A. *Strand*).

4832 *Alonso* [*Díaz*] José, [Mt 8,18-27; 14,22s] Función de los pasajes evangélicos de la 'Calma de la tormenta' y el 'Andar sobre las aguas' en el plan de los Ejercicios de san IGNACIO: Manresa 61 (1989) 387-404.

4833 **Hengel** Martin, Sequela e carisma; studio esegetico e di storia delle religioni su Mt. 8,21 s. e la chiamata di Gesù alla sequela: 1968, [T]*Jacopino* Giuliana. StBPaid 90. Brescia 1990. 177 p. Lit. 21.000. 88-394-0439-2.

4834 *McCane* Byron R., 'Let the dead bury their own dead'; secondary burial and Matt 8:21-22: HarvTR 83 (1990) 31-43.

4835 *Blessing* Kamila, [Mt 8,30] Call not unclean; the pigs in the story of the legion of demons: ProcGLM 10 (1990) 90-106.

4836 *Vattuone* C., El endemoniado de Gerasa: Gladius 15 (BA 1989) 121-130 [< Stromata 45,500].

F4.1 *Mt 9-12; Miracula Jesu* – **The Gospel miracles.**

4837 **Beckwith** Francis J., David HUME's argument against miracles; a critical analysis. Lanham MD 1989, UPA. vii-152 p. $27. 0-8191-7487-4 [TDig 38,251].

4838 *Busse* Ulrich,   Metaphorik in neutestamentlichen Wundergeschichten?
Mk 1,21-28; Joh 9,1-41: ➤ 350, Metaphorik 1990, 110-134.

4839 *Buzzetti* Carlo,   Lo sfondo per comprendere i miracoli del NY; visione
scientifica o visione biblica? Un esempio di ermeneutica: Salesianum 52
(1990) 871-891.

4840 *Cirillo* Antonio,   Il valore rivelativo dei miracoli di Cristo in San Tommaso: AnnTh 4 (1990) 151-173.

4841 *Clopper* Laurence M.,   Miracula and The tretise of miraclis pleyinge
[... Jerome's Vulgate; Jeremiah commentaries]: Speculum 65 (1990)
878-905.

4842 **Cousin** Hugues,   *a*) Récits de miracles en milieux juif et païen: CahEv 66
supp. P 1988, Cerf. 83 p. F 41. 0222-9706; – *b*) Relatos de milagros en
los textos judíos y paganos, ᵀ*Darrical* Nicolas: Documentos en torno a
la Bibbia 17. Estella 1989, VDivino. 83 p. pt. 745. 84-7151-625-X. –
ᴿActuBbg 27 (1990) 193 (X. *Alegre* S.).

4843 **Drewermann** Eugen,   Tiefenpsychologie und Exegese [➤ 1694-1704] 2.
Die Wahrheit der Werke und der Worte; Wunder, Vision, Weissagung,
Apokalypse, Geschichte, Gleichnis⁵. Olten 1989, Walter. 851 p. DM 79.
– ᴿZkT 112 (1990) 209-211 (R. *Oberforcher*).

4844 — **Fehrenbacher** Gregor,   Heilung als Erlösung? Strukturen der theologischen Hermeneutik E. Drewermanns: kath. Diss. Bamberg, ᴰ*Fuchs*
O. 1990. – TR 86 (1990) 512; RTLv 22, p. 586.

4845 **Exum** J. Cheryl,   Signs and wonders; biblical texts in literary focus 1989
➤ 5,395: ᴿJRel 70 (1990) 302s (B. *Britt*).

4846 **Fabula** Nathaniel M.,   The power and method of healing; a description
and comparative study of the healings in the Philippines and in the New
Testament: ev. Diss. Tübingen 1990, ᴰ*Betz* O. 299 p. – RTLv 22, p. 592;
TLZ 116,774; TR 86, p. 519.

4847 **Fiederlein** Friedrich M.,   Die Wunder Jesu und die Wundererzählungen
der Urkirche 1988 ➤ 4,4636; 5,4542: ᴿLebZeug 44 (1989) 308s (M.
Gebel); ZkT 112 (1990) 219s (M. *Hasitschka*).

4848 *Gilman* James E.,   Reconceiving miracles: RelSt 25 (1989) 477-487.

4849 **Goldingway** John,   Signs, wonders and healing: When Christians disagree. Leicester 1989, Inter-Varsity. 192 p. £5.50. – ᴿEvangel 7,2 (1989)
23s (G. *Bray*).

4850 *a*) *Gowan* Donald E.,   Salvation as healing; – *b*) *Hammer* Paul L., God's
health for the world; some biblical understandings of salvation: ExAud 5
(1989) 1-19 / 77-98.

4851 **Greer** Rowen A.,   The fear of freedom; a study of miracles in the
Roman-Imperial church [... Fathers] 1989 ➤ 5,4546: ᴿAmerica 162
(1990) 130s (C. *Stinson*); AnglTR 72 (1990) 463-6 (R. D. *Young*); JTS 41
(1990) 662-4 (W. H. C. *Frend*); TTod 47 (1990s) 226 . 228 (R. H. *Weaver*).

4852 **Hergesel** Tomasz, ❷ Jesus cudotwórca: Attende Lectioni 14, 1987
➤ 3,4427: ᴿColcT 59,3 (1989) 190s (J. *Królikowski*).

4853 **Jenkins** David,   God, miracles, and the Church of England 1987
➤ 3,4429; 4,4645: ᴿEvangel 7,4 (1989) 24 (H. P. *Jansma*).

4854 **Kee** Howard C.,   Medicine, miracle and magic in New Testament times
1986 ➤ 2,3468 ... 4,4646: ᴿHenoch 12 (1990) 245-7 (F. *Lelli*); HeythJ 31
(1990) 71s (Mary E. *Mills*); JRS 80 (1990) 240 (R. *Lane Fox*).

4855 **Latourelle** René, *a*) Miracles of Jesus 1988 ➤ 4,4652; 5,4556: ᴿCalvinT
25 (1990) 109-111 (S. *Greidanus*: copes with the fact of p. 23, 'miracle stories belong to another age, another mentality ... fairies or ghosts'); CBQ
52 (1990) 562-4 (M. E. *Boring*: much that is good; but 28 of the 28

survive scrutiny; and his own thought structures are imposed e.g. in making the Good Samaritan's beneficiary also a Samaritan); ExpTim 102 (1990s) 118 (J. K. *Riches*: distances itself from earlier Catholic apologetic, but with loose criteria bypassing objections); PerspRelSt 17 (1990) 88-90 (N. E. *Parrish*, on his favor for inaugurated eschatology); SR 19 (1990) 253s (T. *Sinclair-Faulkner*: safe; not up to the ecumenical Paulist Press standard); TLZ 115 (1990) 595-7 (W. *Bindemann*: 'Erstaunlich, wieviel wissenschaftlichen Aufwand man treiben kann, um alte Apologetik zu re-etablieren. Das Ergebnis: eine Abhandlung, die dogmatische Vorentscheidungen als wissenschaftliche Analyse maskiert'); TorJT 6 (1990) 115-9 (Wendy J. *Cotter*); – *b*) Milagros de Jesús y teología del milagro [1986 ➤ 2,3471], [T]: Verdad e Imagen 112. S 1990, Sígueme. 382 p. – [R]QVidCr 154 (1990) 128 (C. *Pifarré*); RelCu 36 (1990) 690 (C. *Martín*).

4856 **McCaslin** Keith, What the Bible says about miracles 1988 ➤ 4,4654: [R]BS 147 (1990) 374 (R. P. *Lightner*).

4857 **McCready** William D., Signs of sanctity; miracles in the thought of GREGORY the Great: ST 91, 1989 ➤ 5,4558: [R]RHE 85 (1990) 371-7 (A. de *Vogüé*).

4858 **Maillot** Alphonse, I miracoli di Gesù [Ces miracles qui nous dérangent 1986 ➤ 3,4439], [T]*Revel* Delia B.: Parola per l'uomo d'oggi 8. T 1990, Claudiana. 173 p. 88-7016-129-3.

4859 **Mann** Ulrich, Zeit und Wunder: ➤ 675, Eranos-Jb 57 (1988) 1-47.

4860 **Mills** Mary E., Human agents of cosmic power in Hellenistic Judaism and the Synoptic tradition: JStNT supp 41. Sheffield 1990, JStOT. 184 p. £25; sb. £18.75. 1-85075-235-4 [NTAbs 35,104].

4860* **Mills** Mary E., [Mk 1,27] Agents of cosmic power in Hellenistic Judaism and the Synoptic tradition. Sheffield 1990, Academic. 184 p. £25. 1-85075-235-4. – [R]ExpTim 102 (1990s) 118s (W. G. *Morrice*).

4861 **Mosetto** Francesco, I miracoli evangelici...Celso/ORIGENE 1986 ➤ 2, 3474... 5,4559: [R]Teresianum 41 (1990) 701s (M. *Diego Sánchez*).

4862 *Nichols* Terence L., Miracles, the supernatural, and the problem of extrinsicism: Gregorianum 71 (1990) 23-40; franç. 41.

4863 **Nielsen** Helge K., Heilung und Verkündigung 1987 ➤ 3,4443... 5,4561: [R]Bijdragen 51 (1990) 329s (J. C. *Delbeek*); TLZ 115 (1990) 270-2 (G. *Schille*).

4864 *Onwu* Nienanya, [NT] Miracles, medicine and healing; theological perspective: TCNN Research Bulletin 21 (N. Nigeria 1990) 21-36 [< TContext 8/2, 29].

Prete B. & [Angelicum diss. 1987] *Scaglioni* A., I miracoli degli apostoli nella Chiesa delle origini; studi sui racconti dei miracoli negli Atti. 1989 ➤ 5556.

4865 **Rusecki** Marian, *a*) ❷ *Wierzcie* ...Believe my works; the motivation-function of the miracle in 20th century theology, 1988 ➤ 5,4567: [R]ColcT 59,3 (1989) 189s (J. *Królikowski*); – *b*) ❷ L'importance du sujet dans la confirmation du miracle dans l'apologétique de M. BLONDEL: AtKap 115 (1990) 48-57.

4866 **Shorter** Aylward, Jesus and the witchdoctor; an approach to healing and wholeness 1985 ➤ 1,4442; 4,4671: [R]RelStT 8,1s (1988) 108s (I. *Hexham*).

4867 *Silva* S., Los milagros de Jesús, ¿sólo signos literarios?: Revista Católica Cile 89 (1989) 8-15 . 185-9 [< Stromata 45,500].

4868 *a*) *Soares-Prabhu* George, Signs not wonders; understanding the miracles of Jesus as Jesus understood them; – *b*) *Tilby* Angela, Why the

need for signs and wonders?; – c) *Lyons* Adrian,   The God behind the signs: Way 30 (1990) 307-317 / 279-287 / 298-306.
4869 *Tassin* Claude,   Jesús, exorciste et guérisseur: Spiritus 15,120 ('Guérison et exorcisme'... Brésil/Afrique 1990) 285-303.
4870 **Williams** T. C.,   The idea of the miraculous; the challenge to science and religion.   L 1990, Macmillan.   269 p.   £35.   0-333-51194-8. – ᴿExpTim 102 (1990s) 252s (J. *Polkinghorne*: odd).

4871 **Fuchs** Albert,   [Mt 9,1-8] Offene Probleme der Synoptikerforschung; zur Geschichte der Perikope Mk 2,1-12 par: SNTU A-15 (1990) 73-99.
4872 *Kilpatrick* G. D.,   [Mt 9,9; 10,3] Matthew on Matthew [< ᴱ*Tuckett* C. M., Synoptic Studies 1984, 177-185]: ► 257, Principles 1990, 250-9.
4873 **Herrenbrück** Fritz,   [Mt 9,10] Jesus und die Zöllner; historische und neutestamentlich-exegetische Untersuchungen [< Diss. 1979 Tübingen, ᴰ*Hengel* M.]: WUNT 2/41.   Tü 1990, Mohr.   xii-380 p.   DM 114.   3-16-145553-3 [NTAbs 35,242]. – ᴿSNTU A-15 (1990) 200-2 (F. *Weissengruber*).
4874 *Vanhetloo* Warren,   [Mt 9,36...] The incarnate shepherd: CalvaryB 6 (1990) 33-48 [49-62, Two ninety and nines, Lk 15,3-6; Mt 18,12s; – 141-148, Pastors and their chief shepherd].
4875 *Charette* Blaine,   A harvest for the people? An interpretation of Matthew 9.37f: JStNT 38 (1990) 29-35.
4876 **Weaver** Dorothy J.,   [Mt 10] Matthew's missionary discourse; a literary critical analysis: JStNT supp 18,   Sheffield 1990, JStOT.   250 p.   £25. 1-85075-232-X. – ᴿExpTim 102 (1990s) 21s (G. *Stanton*: well-written).
4877 *Osei-Bonsu* Joseph,   [Mt 10:1-12; 1 Cor 7,10-15; Acts 17...] The contextualization of Christianity; some NT antecedents: IrBSt 12 (1990) 129-142.
4878 **Levine** Amy-Jill,   Social and ethnic... Mt 10:5b: StBEc 14, 1988 ► 4, 4682:   ᴿBibTS 20 (1990) 129s (B. J. *Malina*: pre-set agenda bypasses some fundamental data); CBQ 52 (1990) 754s (B. T. *Viviano*: too tidy); JBL 109 (1990) 723-5 (T. L. *Donaldson*); RExp 87 (1990) 646-8 (D. E. *Garland*).
4879 *Scott* J. Julius ᴶ,   Gentiles and the ministry of Jesus; further observations on Matt 10:5-6; 15:21-28:   JEvTS 33 (1990) 161-9 [< NTAbs 35,25].
4880 *MacDonald* D.,   [Mt 10,29] The worth of the assarion: Historia 38 (Stu 1989) 120-3 [< NTAbs 34,308: varied, sometimes one-sixteenth denarius].
4881 *Hirunuma* Toshio,   [Mt 10,29] *áneu toû patrós* 'without (of) the father' [< Studia Textus Novi Testamenti ❶ 252 (Aug. 1987) 2089-2100; FgNt 1,2 (1988) 237,77]: FgNt 3,5 (1990) 53-60; castellano 60-62.
4882 *Vogels* Walter,   Performers and receivers of the Kingdom; a semiotic analysis of Matthew 11,2-15:   ScEsp 42 (1990) 325-336.
4883 *Lambrecht* Jan,   [Mt 11,2-6] ❷ 'Are you the one who is to come...?'; contemporary interpretations of the Gospel proclamation of Jesus, ᵀ*Kantor* Maria [conference Kraków 5.XI.1987]: RuBi 42 (1989) 85-97; 141s, interview with J. *Chmiel*.
4884 *Papone* Paolo,   Il Regno dei Cieli soffre violenza? (Mt 11,12): RivB 38 (1990) 375s [rather 'forces itself on'].
4885 *Pregeant* Russell,   [Mt 11,19; Suggs M., Christ F., both 1970] The wisdom passages in Matthew's story: ► 544, SBL seminars 1990, 469-491.
4886 **Deutsch** sr. Celia,   [Mt 11,25-30] Hidden wisdom and the easy yoke [diss. Toronto, ᴰ*Longenecker* R.] 1987 ► 3,4488... 5,4593:   ᴿRB 97 (1990) 613s (B. T. *Viviano*); RExp 87 (1990) 645s (D. E. *Garland*).

4887 *Tassin* Claude, Matthieu 'targumiste'? L'exemple de Mt 12,18 (= Is 42,1): EstB 48 (1990) 190-214; Eng. 190 (Christological interpretation of the Servant).

4888 *Chico* Gabriel, [Mt 12,24...] Jesús y Beelzebul; la presencia del Reino en un cuadro polémico [→ 5,4596]: CommSev 22 (1989) 41-52.

4889 **Gilles** Jean, [Mt 12,46] I 'fratelli e sorelle' di Gesù 1985 → 1,4512... 4,4692: RProtestantesimo 45 (1990) 222s (A. *Adamo*).

F4.3 Mt 13... *Parabolae Jesu* – the Parables.

4890 **Aerts** Lode, Gottesherrschaft als Gleichnis? Eine Untersuchung zur Auslegung der Gleichnisse Jesu nach Eberhard JÜNGEL [Diss. Pont. Univ. Gregoriana D*Lentzen-Deis* F., R 1989 → 5,4603]: EurHS 23/403. Fra 1990, Lang. 346 p. 3-631-42965-7.

4891 *Aichele* GeorgJ, The fantastic in the parabolic language of Jesus: Neotestamentica 24,1 (1990) 93-105.

4892 **Baudler** Georg, Jesus im Spiegel seiner Gleichnisse 1986 → 2,3504... 5,4606: REstE 65 (1990) 107s (J. J. *Alemany*).

4893 *Beavis* Mary Ann, Parable and fable [JÜLICHER A. 1976 = 1919]: CBQ 52 (1990) 473-498.

4894 **Blomberg** Craig L., Interpreting the parables [extra chorum allegorically]. Leicester/DG 1990, Apollos/Inter-Varsity. 333 p. $20. 0-85111-411-3/0-8308-1271-7 [TDig 37,347]. – RExpTim 102 (1990s) 152s (B. G. *Powley*: 'parables are allegories'; he makes them too accessible).

4895 **Borsch** Frederick H., bp., Many things in parables 1988 → 4,4697; 5,4607: RAnglTR 71 (1989) 212-4 (R. A. *Whitacre*); CritRR 2 (1989) 186s (C. E. *Carlston*).

4896 *Bottani* Livio, Metafora, parabola e verità in RICŒUR: StPatav 37 (1990) 119-135; Eng. 135.

4897 **Breech** J., Jesus and postmodernism ['If Jesus is the answer, what is the question?'; we should bring to Jesus' parables questions from our postmodern situation; sequel to his 1983 Silence of Jesus]. Mp 1989, Fortress. 96 p. $8. 0-8006-2043-7 [NTAbs 34,106].

4898 **Bucher** A. A., Gleichnisse verstehen lernen; strukturgenetische Untersuchungen zur Rezeption synoptischer Parabeln: Praktische Theologie im Dialog 5. FrS 1990, Univ. x-192 p. Fs 28. 3-7278-0667-2 [NTAbs 35,238].

4899 [EButts J. R. → 5,4608] EFunk Robert W., The parables of Jesus: red [also pink, gray...] letter edition. Sonoma 1988, Polebridge. xx-107 p. $15. – RCBQ 52 (1990) 557s (C. C. *Carlston*: many diverse competent people have expressed their views in a way that tends to balance out idiosyncrasies).

4900 **Capon** Robert F., The parables of judgment 1989 → 5,4609: RTTod 47 (1990s) 484 (L. A. *Wagley*).

4901 EDelorme Jean, Les paraboles 1987/9 → 5,576: RAnnTh 4 (1990) 440-2 (B. *Estrada*); BZ 34 (1990) 136-8 (H.-J. *Klauck*); NRT 112 (1990) 907s (X. *Jacques*); ScEsp 42 (1990) 351-4 (J.-Y. *Thériault*).

4902 **Donahue** John R., The Gospel in parable 1988 → 4,4700; 5,4613: RCBQ 52 (1990) 743s (Karen A. *Barta*); Interpretation 44 (1990) 295s (S. *Brown*); JBL 109 (1990) 139-141 (J. D. *Crossan*); JRel 90 (1990) 87s (K. A. *Plank*); QRMin 10 (1990) 98-100 (J. A. *Darr*).

4903 **Dschulnigg** Peter, Rabbinische Gleichnisse und das NT D1988 → 4,4702; 5,4615: RJStJud 21 (1990) 108-111 (J. D. M. *Derrett*); TLZ 115 (1990) 344-6 (W. *Wiefel*).

4904 **Dutzmann** Martin, Gleichniserzählungen Jesu als Texts evangelischer Predigt [Diss. DWintzer F., Bonn 1988]: ArbPastT 23. Gö 1990, Vandenhoeck & R. 232 p. DM 58. 3-525-62323-2 [NTAbs 35,101].

4905 **Erlemann** Kurt, Das Bild Gottes in den synoptischen Gleichnissen: BW 126, 1988 ➤ 4,4704; 5,4617: RCarthaginensia 6 (1990) 208 (R. Sanz Valdivieso); JBL 109 (1990) 346s (L. T. Johnson); SNTU-A 14 (1989) 237s (A. Fuchs); WissWeis 51 (1988) 223s (B. Heininger).

4906 **Fisher** N. F., The parables of Jesus; glimpses of God's reign[2] [11979 Glimpses of the New Age]. NY 1990, Crossroad. xiv-178 p. $10 pa. 0-8245-1039-9 [NTAbs 35,240].

4907 **Harnisch** Wolfgang, Las parábolas de Jesús; una introducción hermenéutica, TOlasagasti Manuel: BiblEstB 66, 1989 ➤ 5,4621; 84-301-1075-5: RActuBbg 27 (1990) 57s (X. Alegre S.); CiTom 117 (1990) 382s (J. L. Espinel); EstAg 25 (1990) 454 (C. Mielgo); QVidCr 148s (1989) 229 (P. R. Tragan).

Iersel B. van, al., Parabelverhalen in Lukas 1987 ➤ 5365.

4908 **Kemmer** Alfons, Le parabole di Gesù; come leggerle, come comprenderle [1981, 21983], TGiombini Patricia: StBPaid 93. Brescia 1990, Paideia. 158 p. Lit. 16.000. 88-394-0451-1.

4909 *Kiehl* E. H., Why Jesus spoke in parables: ConcordJ 16,3 (1990) 245-257 [< NTAbs 35,21].

4910 **McArthur** H. K., Johnston R. M., They also taught in parables; [115 pre-220 C.E.] rabbinic parables from the first centuries of the Christian era. GR 1990, Zondervan. 221 p. $11. 0-310-51581-5 [NTAbs 34,411].

4911 *Martis* Douglas, Prophets, poets, parables; a study of Jesus as prophet: Way 29 (1989) 240-254.

4912 **Mateos** Juan, Camacho Fernando, Evangelio, figuras y símbolos; en torno al NT 4, 1989 ➤ 5,4630: RCommSev 23 (1990) 278s (M. de Burgos); RBibArg 52 (1990) 251s (R. Krüger).

4913 **Pérez-Cotapos** Eduardo, El método parabólico de Jesús según Dom Jacques DUPONT: diss. Pont. Univ. Gregoriana, DRasco E. R 1990, 628 p. – RTLv 22, p. 594.

4914 **Rau** Eckhard, Reden in Vollmacht; Hintergrund, Form und Anliegen der Gleichnisse Jesu [Hab.-Diss. Hamburg 1987, DWilckens U.]: FRL 149. Gö 1990, Vandenhoeck & R. 434 p. – 3-525-53831-6. – RSNTU A-15 (1990) 204s (A. Fuchs).

4915 **Scott** Brendan B., 'Hear then the parable' 1989 ➤ 5,4632: RIrBSt 12 (1990) 202-6 (D. Campbell); LvSt 15 (1990) 70s (J. Lambrecht); TS 51 (1990) 328-330 (J. R. Donahue); TTod 47 (1990s) 98s (J. T. Tucker).

4916 TESiman Emmanuel P., NARSAÏ, Cinq homélies sur les paraboles évangéliques 1984 ➤ 1,4497; 3,4513: RRHPR 70 (1990) 358s (P. Maraval).

4917 **Thoma** Clemens, Lauer Simon, Die Gleichnisse der Rabbinen 1, 1986 ➤ 2,3529 ... 4,4721: RZkT 112 (1990) 106 (R. Oberforcher).

4918 **Vonck** Pol, Understanding 42 Gospel parables[2] [11981]. Eldoret c. 1989, AMECEA. xii-128 p. $5. – RAfER 12 (1990) 119s (B. K. Zabajungu).

4919 *Vorster* William S., The function of metaphorical and apocalyptic language about the unobservable in the teaching of Jesus: ➤ 24, FBOERS H., Text 1990, 33-51.

4920 **Wailes** Stephen L., Medieval allegories of Jesus' parables: Center Med. Ren. St. 23, UCLA 1987 [➤ 5,4636 'Berkeley']: RManuscripta 34 (1990)

69s (R. F. *O'Toole*: the Holy Spirit guides, even today); Speculum 65 (1990) 1074-6 (Margaret R. *Miles*).

4921 **Wenham** David, The parables of Jesus, pictures of revolution: Jesus Library. L 1989, Hodder & S. 256 p. £7. 0-340-48811-5. – [R]ExpTim 101 (1989s) 49 (S. *Fowl*).

4922 **Westermann** Claus, The parables of Jesus in the light of the Old Testament [Vergleiche 1984 → 65,4071], [TE]*Golka* Friedmann W., *Logan* Alistair H. B. E/Mp 1990, Clark/Fortress. 211 p. $13. 0-567-29162-6 / 0-8006-2440-0. – [R]ExpTim 102 (1990s) 183 (W. G. *Morrice*).

4923 **Winton** A. P., The proverbs of Jesus; issues of history and rhetoric [diss. 1987, [D]*Chilton* B., Sheffield]: JStNT supp. 35. Sheffield 1990, Academic. 236 p. £25. 1-85075-219-2 [NTAbs 34,390]. – [E]ExpTim 101 (1989s) 377 (W. G. *Morrice*).

4924 **Young** Brad H., Jesus and his Jewish parables; rediscovering the roots of Jesus' teaching: Theological Inquiries, 1989 → 5,4639: [R]Interpretation 44 (1990) 425 (J. R. *Donahue*); JStJud 21 (1990) 305-9 (J. *Neusner*: in a crude and clumsy way, 'dust in the eyes of scholars', shows us how Jerusalem scholarship works, as of ten years ago ...); Themelios 15 (1989s) 71 [D. *Deboys*].

4925 *Bovon* François, [Mt 12,46-50; 13,1-23] Parabole d'Évangile, parabole du Royaume [> *Weder* H., Sprache der Bilder 1989]: RTPhil 122 (1990) 33-41; Eng. 41.

4926 *Harrington* Daniel J., The mixed reception of the Gospel; interpreting the parables in Matt 13:1-52: → 173, [F]STRUGNELL J., Of scribes 1990, 195-201.

Dautzenberg Gerhard, Mk 4 ... Gleichniskapitel 1990 → 5242.

4927 **Achtemeier** P. Mark, Matthew 13:1-23, expository: Interpretation 44 (1990) 61-65.

4928 *O'Callaghan* José, Dos variantes en la parábola del sembrador (Mt 13,4.7): EstB 48 (1990) 267-270.

4929 **Kogler** Franz, [Mt 13,31s...] Das Doppelgleichnis vom Senfkorn und vom Sauerteig...: ForBi 59, 1988 → 4,4733; 5,4644: [R]Biblica 71 (1990) 134-7 (A. *Puig i Tàrrech*); CBQ 52 (1990) 751s (M. L. *Soards*: a strong push for a Deutero-Markus); RivB 38 (1990) 532-4 (V. *Fusco*); SNTU-A 14 (1989) 277s (U. *Schnelle*); TLZ 115 (1990) 810-2 (G. *Strecker*); TR 86 (1990) 201-3 (G. *Nebe*).

4930 **Israel** Martin, [Mt 13,45] The pearl of great price 1988 → 5,4645: [R]Month 250 (1989) 695 (Claire *Elliott*).

4931 **Quacquarelli** A., Il triplice frutto della vita cristiana: 100, 60 e 30 (Matteo XIII,8 nelle diverse interpretazioni)[2] [[1]1953]. Bari 1989, Edipuglia. 127 p. → 5,4641 [NTAbs 35,106: 30 = married people; virgins = 60 or 100].

4932 *Seethaler* Angelika, [Mt 14,13 ...] Die Brotvermehrung – ein Kirchenspiegel?: BZ 34 (1990) 108-112.

4933 *Boismard* M.-E., *a)* Théorie des niveaux multiples; – *b*) Mt. 14,13s; – *c*) Mc. 1,40-44: → 524, Interrelations 1984/90, 231-243 (259-288) / 244-253 / 254-8.

4934 *Perrin* Louis, [Mt 16,1-20] La révélation et la filiation: SémBib 55 (1989) 19-27.

4935 *Adam* A. K. M., [Mt 16,1-4] The sign of Jonah; a [Stanley] FISH-eye view: ➤ 365, Semeia 51 (1990) 177-191.

F4.5 **Mt 16 ...** *Primatus promissus* – **The promise to Peter.**

4936 *Basser* Herbert W., [Joel] MARCUS's 'gates'; a response: CBQ [50 (1988) 443-455] 52 (1990) 307s; 308, Marcus admits and regrets that he attributed to Basser a defense rather than a rejection of J. EMERTON [in relation to DERRETT, JBL 104 (1985) 297-300].

4937 **Bessière** Gérard, Pierre, pape malgré lui: Présence, 1989 ➤ 5,4652: ᴿNRT 112 (1990) 787 (L.-J. *Renard*).

4938 ᴱ**Brown** Raymond E., *al.*, Pietro nel Nuovo Testamento; un'indagine ricognitiva fatta in collaborazione da studiosi protestanti e cattolici [Minneapolis 1973], ᵀ*Lugato* Sabina: Bibbia e rinnovamento. R 1988, Borla. 206 p. Lit. 20.000. 88-263-0446-7. – ᴿBenedictina 36 (1989) 581-3 (L. *De Lorenzi*); Laurentianum 31 (1990) 602s (L. *Martignani*).

4939 **Caragounis** Chrys C., Peter and the Rock: BZNW 58, 1990 [➤ 5,4654 '1989']: ᴿBiblica 71 (1990) 570-6 (G. *Claudel*: detailed objections); DeltioVM 19,2 (1990) 76-78 (I. A. *Karavidopoulos*); ExpTim 102 (1990s) 54s (D. *Hill*: confirms the consensus that the 'rock' is 'the just-mentioned Messiahship of Jesus').

4940 **Claudel** Gérard, La confession de Pierre; trajectoire d'une péricope évangélique: EtBN 10, 1988: ᴿBiblica 71 (1990) 129-133 (S. B. *Marrow*); CBQ 52 (1990) 740s (G. T. *Montague*: Peter's role 'symbolic souvenir'); EsprVie (1990) 232-5 (L. *Walter*: séduisant).

4941 **Deladrière** Valentin, Tu es Pierre; tous, soyez frères: Libre parole 12. Bru 1989, auct. (150, rue Portaels). 95 p. [RTLv 21,123].

4942 *Eno* Robert B., Forma Petri – Petrus, figura Ecclesiae; the uses of Peter [in AUGUSTINE]: ➤ 13, ᶠBAVEL T. van, AugLv 41 (1990s) 659-676.

4943 **Falbo** Giovanni., Il primato della chiesa di Roma alla luce dei primi quattro secoli. R 1989, Coletti. 434 p. Lit. 42.000 [TR 87,430].

4944 *Hester* Marcus, Foundationalism and Peter's confession: RelSt 26 (1990) 403-413.

4945 *Miller* David L., Prometheus, St. Peter and the Rock; identity and difference in modern literature: Eranos 57 (Fra 1988) 75-124 [< ZIT 91,195].

4946 **Sakkos** S. N., Ⓖ Ho Pétros kai hē Rōmē I. Hē martyría (testimony of the NT). Thessaloniki 1989, auct. 133 p. [NTAbs 35,253].

4947 **Schatz** Klaus, Der päpstliche Primat; seine Geschichte von den Ur-sprüngen bis zur Gegenwart. Wü 1990, Echter. 231 p. DM 26. – ᴿActuBbg 27 (1990) 183-7 (V. *Fábrega*); TGL 80 (1990) 348 (W. *Beinert*: hat seit dem Anfang Widerspruch hervorgerufen).

4948 **Thiede** Carsten P., Simon Peter, from Galilee to Rome 1986 ➤ 2,3557 ... 5,4664: ᴿJEH 41 (1990) 137s (W. H. C. *Frend*).

4949 ᴱ**Thiede** C. P., Das Petrusbild in der neueren Forschung 1987 ➤ 3,4546: ᴿSNTU A-15 (1990) 211 (A. *Fuchs*).

4950 *Farmer* H. R., [Mt 16,21s; 17,22s; 20,17s] The Passion prediction passages and the Synoptic Problem: a test case: NTS 36 (1990) 558-570.

4951 *Alonso* [*Díaz*] José, El misterio de la Transfiguración en el plan de los Ejercicios (paralelismo entre los discípulos y el ejercitante respecto de la 'Cruz'): Manresa 62 (1990) 325-336.

4952 *a) Andia* Ysabel de, [Mt 17,1-9] Le mystère de la Transfiguration; – *b) Lévêque* Jean,   La gloire du Fils dans l'Évangile de Jean: → 542, Évangile 1989/90, 45-78 / 79-101.

4953 *a) Chilton* B.D.,   A coin of three realms (Matthew 17.24-27); – *b) Lincoln* Andrew T.,   Matthew – a story for teachers?: → 166, FSheffield 1990, 269-282 / 105-125.

4954 *Patte* Daniel,   Bringing out of the Gospel-treasure what is new and what is old; two parables in Matthew 18 [and] 23:   QRMin 10 (1990) 79-108.

4955 *Dąbek* Tomasz M., ❷ [Mt 18,3] The child in the Bible: RuBi 42 (1989) 359-362.

4956 *Buscemi* A.M., [Mt 18,12s...] La parabola della 'pecorella smarrita': TerraS 65 (1989) 50-61.

4957 *Zyl* H.C. van,   Matteus 18:15-20; 'n Diachroniese en sinchroniese ondersoek met besondere verwysing na kerklike discipline: SkrifKerk 9,1 (1988) 75-92 [< NTAbs 34,165].

4958 **Thimmes** Pamela,   *a)* Convention and invention; studies in the biblical sea-storm type scene: diss. Vanderbilt, ᴰ*Tolbert* M.   Nashville 1989. – RelStR 17,194; – *b)* The biblical sea-storm type-scene [Mt 18,23; 14,22... comparing Homeric type-scenes, W. AREND 1933]: ProcGLM 10 (1990) 107-122.

4959 *Ellis* Robert A., [Mt 19,6-26 attractively modernized and continued] The rich young man remembers: ExpTim 102 (1990s) 240-2.

4960 *Marucci* Corrado,   Clausole matteane e critica testuale; in merito alla teoria di H. CROUZEL sul testo originale di Mt 19,9 [ORIGEN's text not authentic]: RivB 38 (1990) 301-323; Eng. 324s.

4961 *Wiebe* P.H., [Mt 19,9] Jesus' divorce exception: JEvTS 32 (1989) 327-333 [< NTAbs 34,165].

4962 *Kloppenborg* John S.,   Alms, debt and divorce; Jesus' ethics in their Mediterranean context: TorJT 6 (1990) 182-200.

4963 *Dinter* P.E., [Mt 19,12] Disabled for the Kingdom; celibacy, Scripture and tradition: Commonweal 117 (NY 1990) 571-7 [< NTAbs 35,160].
  Niemand Christoph, Studien ... [Mt 17] Abweichung des Mt & Lk von Mk 9,2-10, ᴰ1988 → 5266*.

4964 ᴱ**Pizzolato** Luigi F., [Mt 19,16-22] Per foramen acus 1986 → 2,3572 ... 5,4678*: ᴿLatomus 49 (1990) 228s (G. *Scarpat*).

4965 *O'Callaghan* José,   Nota crítica sobre Mt 19,30:   EstB 48 (1990) 271-3.

F4.8   **Mt 20 ...** *Regnum eschatologicum* – **Kingdom eschatology.**

4966 *Cóbreces* Ignacio R.,   Los obreros de la viña; elementos midráshicos en la parábola de Mt. 20,1-16:   Studium 30 (M 1990) 485-505.

4967 *Fortna* Robert T.,   You have made them equal to us (Mt 20:1-16): JTSAf 72 (1990) 66-72 [< NTAbs 35,160].

4968 **Gragg** Douglas L., [Mt 20,1-15] The parable of the workers in the vineyard and its interpreters; a text-linguistic analysis: diss. Emory, ᴰ*Boers* H.   Atlanta 1990. 222 p.   91-06722. – DissA 51 (1990s) 3434-A; RTLv 22, p. 593.

4969 **Hezser** Catherine, Lohnmetaphorik und Arbeitswelt in Mt 20,1-16; das Gleichnis von den Arbeitern im Weinberg im Rahmen rabbinischer Lohngleichnisse [Diss. Heid 1985, ᴰ*Theissen* G.]: NOrb 15.   FrS 1990, Univ. [x-]342 p. Fs 88 [NRT 113,761, X. *Jacques*]. 3-7278-06990 / VR 3-525-0699-0.

4970 *Mühlenberg* Ekkehard, Das Gleichnis von den Arbeitern im Weinberg (Matthäus 20,1-16) bei den Vätern: ➤ 80, ᶠHÖRNER H., Hermeneumata 1990, 11-26.

4971 *Gregorios* Paulos Mar, Ⓜ [Mt 20,20-28] *A diakonia...* Meaning and nature [< Risk Book, Geneva 1988], ᵀ*Pásztor* Jánosné: TSzem 33 (1990) 129-140.

4972 *O'Callaghan* José, Fluctuación textual en Mt 20,21.26.27: Biblica 71 (1990) 553-8.

4973 *Brandscheidt* Renate, Messias und Tempel; die alttestamentlichen Zitate in Mt 21,1-17: TrierTZ 99 (1990) 36-48.

4974 *Lentzen-Deis* Fritzleo, [Mt 21,1-11] Alcuni aspetti dell' 'ingresso di Gesù a Gerusalemme' secondo gli evangeli sinottici alla luce dello sfondo giudaico: ➤ 529*, Giudaismo 1990, 53-68.

4975 *Schibler* Hans-Jacob, Der Einzug in Jerusalem oder 'Warum nahm er ausgerechnet meinen Esel?' Erzählung zu Mt 21,1-11: CLehre 43 (1990) U-161s [< ZIT 91,53].

4975* *La Maisonneuve* sr. Dominique de, [Mt 21,7] Le Messie et son âne à la lumière de la tradition rabbinique: ➤ 109*, ᶠLAURENTIN R., 1990, 139-144.

4976 *Meyer* Ben F., [Mt 22,4] Many (= all) are called, but few (= not all) are chosen: NTS 36 (1990) 89-97.

4977 *Sim* David C., The man without the wedding garment (Matthew 22:11-13): HeythJ 31 (1990) 165-178.

4978 *Donaldson* Terence L., The law that 'hangs' (Mt. 22:40); rabbinic formulation and Matthean social world: ➤ 544, SBL seminars 1990, 14-33.

4979 **Saunders** Stanley P., [Mt 22,46] No one dared ask him anything more; contextual readings of the controversy stories in Matthew: diss. ᴰ*Kraftchik* S., Princeton Theol. Sem. 1990. 530 p. 90-30372. – DissA 51 (1990s) 2054-A; RelStR 17,194.

4980 **Newport** Kenneth G.C., The sources and Sitz im Leben of Matthew 23: diss. Oxford 1988. 458 p. BRD-91745. – DissA 51 (1990s) 3783-A.

4981 *Fusco* Vittorio, La invettiva e il lamento (Mt 23,1-39): ➤ 325a, ParSpV 21 (1990) 153-172.

4982 **Becker** Hans-Jürgen, Auf der Katedra des Mose; rabbinisch-theologisches Denken und antirabbinische Polemik in Matthäus 23,1-12 [Diss. Kirchliche Hochschule, B 1988, ᴰ*Osten-Sacken* P. von der]: ANTZ 4. B 1990, Inst. Kirche und Judentum. 267 p. DM 29,80. 3-923095-84-8 [NTAbs 35,99]. – ᴿKIsr 5 (1990) 183 (Julie *Kirchberg*).

4983 *Viviano* Benedict T., Social world and community leadership; the case of Matthew 23,1-12,34: JStNT 39 (1990) 3-21: i. Mt was in living dialogue with rabbinic Judaism; ii. his criticism of religious leaders' arrogance is aimed also at Christians; iii. the community remains true to Torah but not to halacha; iv. the leaders (servants) operated under stern eschatological proviso.

4984 *Newport* Kenneth G.C., A note on the 'Seat of Moses' (Matthew 23:2): AndrUnS 28 (1990) 53-58.

4985 **Del Verme** Marcello, [Mt 23,23] Giudaismo e Nuovo Testamento; il caso delle decime 1989 ➤ 5,4687*: ᴿHumBr 45 (1990) 864s (F. *Montagnini*).

4986 **Wenham** David, [Mt 24,1-36] The rediscovery of Jesus' eschatological discourse 1984 ➤ 65,4126 ... 5,4691: ᴿTZBas 46 (1990) 82s (R. *Riesner*).

4987 **Majernik** Jan, The parable of the servant left in charge in Mt 24,45-51; the exegesis and history of interpretation: diss. SBF, ᴰ*Bissoli* G. J 1990. vi-281 p. – LA 40 (1990) 533.

4988 **Reiser** Marius, [Mt 24s] Die Gerichtspredigt Jesu; eine Untersuchung zur eschatologischen Verkündigung Jesu und ihrem frühjüdischen Hintergrund [kath. Hab.-Diss. ^D*Gross*. Tübingen 1989s. – TR 86 (1990) 510]: NT Abh NF 23. Münster 1990, Aschendorff. viii-359 p.

4989 *Bockmuehl* M. N. A., [Mt 24,1s] Why did Jesus predict the destruction of the Temple?:   Crux 25,3 (Vancouver 1989) 11-18 [< NTAbs 34,156].

4990 **Tiede** David,   Jesus and the future: Understanding Jesus today.   C 1990, Univ.   v-103 p.   0521-38552-0; pa. -81-4.

4991 *Brown* Schuyler,   Faith, the poor, and the Gentiles; a tradition-historical reflection on Matthew 25:31-46:   TorJT 6 (1990) 171-181.

4992 *Lapoorta* Japie,   [Mt 25,31-46] Exegesis and proclamation, '... whatever you did for one of the least of these ... you did for me':   JTSAf 68 (Rondebosch 1989) 103-9 [< TContext 7/2, 18].

4993 *Jensen* Gordon,   [Mt 25,31-46] Left-handed theology and inclusiveness [why should we not have a theology favoring the left-handed as for hitherto underprivileged groups?]: Horizons 17 (1990) 207-218.

4994 *Thiede* C. P.,   Papyrus Bodmer 50, das neutestamentliche Papyrusfragment P⁷³ = Mt 25,43 / 26,2-3:   MusHelv 47 (1990) 35-40; pl. 3.

4995 *a) Brekelmans* F. H., De werkwijze van een evangelist; exegese van Mattheüs 26:1-2; – *b) Hemelsoet* B. P. M., De Zoon des Mensen, die niet heeft dar Hij zijn hoofd neerlegge, die macht heeft op de aarde om zonden te vergeven, volgens Mathcüs: AmstCah 10 (1989) 103-119 / 88-102 [< ZAW 103,126].

4996 **Hampel** V.,   Menschensohn und historischer Jesus; ein Rätselwort als Schüssel zum messianischen Selbstverständnis Jesu [kontinuiert Diss. Tü 1982, ^D*Betz* O.]. Neuk 1990. xiv-418 p. DM 68. – ^RSNTU A-15 (1990) 208s (A. *Fuchs*).

F5.1   *Redemptio,* Mt 26, *Ultima coena;*   **The Eucharist** [➤ H7.4].

4997 **Alonso Schökel** Luis,   Celebrating the Eucharist [1996 ➤ 2,3601], ^T*Deehan* John, *Fitzgerald-Lombard* Patrick.   NY 1989, Crossroad.   154 p. $15. – ^RWorship 64 (1990) 179s (T. J. *Fisch*).

4998 **Barth** Markus,   *a)* Das Mahl des Herren 1987 ➤ 3,4598... 5,4705: ^RCritRR 2 (1989) 180-2 (P. J. *Cahill*). – *b)* Riscopriamo la Cena del Signore; Comunione con Israele, con Cristo, e fra i suoi ospiti [Eng. 1988 ➤ 4,4801], ^T*Tomasetto* Domenico: Picc. C. Moderna 64.   T 1990, Claudiana.   144 p. Lit. 15.000.   88-7016-122-6.

4999 **Basurco** X.,   Compartir el pan; de la misa a la eucaristía.   San Sebastián 1987, Idatz.   381 p. – ^RStLeg 30 (1989) 311s (C. *Rodríguez del Curto*).

5000 **Bermejo** Luis M.,   Body broken and blood shed 1986 ➤ 3,4600... 5,4707:   ^RVidyajyoti 53 (1989) 07s (V. *Piovesan*).

5001 *Bermejo* Luis M.,   The private Mass; development or deviation?: Vidyajyoti 53 (1989) 139-156. 187-198 [509-512 *De Melo* C. M., Daily Mass and Mass stipends].

5002 *Biffi* Inos,   Il trattato teologico sull'Eucaristia; principi e progetto: ScuolC 117 (1989) 341-365.

5003 **Boguniowski** József,   Domus ecclesia; der Ort der Eucharistiefeier 1987 ➤ 4,9222:   ^RRuBi 42 (1989) 74s (W. *Bomba*); TR 86 (1990) 229-232 (S. *Rau*).

5004 *Brawley* Robert L.,   *Anamnesis* and absence in the Lord's Supper: BibTB 20 (1990) 139-146.

5005 *Cabié* Robert, La communion des fidèles au sang du Christ; pourquoi a-t-elle disparu en Occident et persisté en Orient?: BLitEc 91 (1990) 175-188; Eng. 188.

5006 **Crockett** William R., Eucharist, symbol of transformation 1989 ↠ 5, 4710: ᴿCalvinT 25 (1990) 129-131 (H. *Boonstra*); ETL 66 (1990) 227s (A. de *Halleux*: apparently Protestant; ecumenical); TS 51 (1990) 377 (Susan *Wood*).

5007 **Deiss** Lucien, La Messe; sa célébration expliquée: Petite enc. mod. chr. P 1989, De Brouwer. 156 p. F 45. – ᴿEsprVie 100 (1990) 361 (P. *Rouillard* commence: 'Le Père Deiss connaît bien la Bible').

5008 **Farnetani** Bernardino, Alla cena del Signore. Siena 1989, Tesoro Euc. 150 p. – ᴿCiVit 45 (1990) 285 (Duccia *Camiciotti*).

5009 *Galot* Jean, a) Il pasto pasquale II; – b) Pasto animato dalla fede; – c) Pasto escatologico; – d) Pasto spirituale: VConsacr 26 (1990) 103-119 / 595-611 / 783-799 / 875-888.

5010 **Garijo-Guembe** Miguel, *al.*, Mahl des Herrn 1988 ↠ 5,4713: ᴿTsTKi 60 (1989) 155s (Ola *Tjørhom*).

5011 **Giraudo** Cesare, Eucaristia per la Chiesa; prospettive sull'eucaristia a partire dalla 'lex orandi': Aloisiana 22, 1989 ↠ 5,4714: ᴿArTGran 53 (1990) 369 (A. *Segovia*); Asprenas 37 (1990) 484-492 (A. *Petti*); Carthaginensia 6 (1990) 386s (J. M. *Lozano Pérez*); EsprVie 100 (1990) 25s (P. *Rouillard*); ETL 66 (1990) 225-7 (A. de *Halleux*); NRT 112 (1990) 425s (L. *Volpe*); RivB 38 (1990) 391-6 (E. *Lodi*); StPatav 37 (1990) 162-6 (E. R. *Tura*); TLZ 115 (1990) 543-5 (R. *Biewald*); Worship 64 (1990) 464-6 (D. N. *Power*); ZkT 112 (1990) 73-81 (H. B. *Meyer*).

5012 *Giraudo* Cesare, Vers un traité de l'Eucharistie à la fois ancien et nouveau; la théologie de l'Eucharistie à l'école de la 'lex orandi': NRT 112 (1990) 870-877.

5013 *Joncas* J. M., Eucharist among the Marcosians; a study of IRENAEUS' Adversus Haereses 1,13-2: QLtg 71 (1990) 99-111.

5014 **Jounel** P., La Messe hier et aujourd'hui. P 1986, O.E.I.L. 173 p. – ᴿRuBi 42 (1989) 77s (A. *Dziuba*).

5015 *Kaufmann* Thomas, Zwei unbekannte Schriften BUCERs und CAPITOs zur Abendmahlsfrage aus dem Herbst 1525: ArRefG 81 (1990) 158-187; Eng. 187s.

5016 **Keller** Erwin, Eucharistie und Parusie; Liturgie- und theologiegeschichtliche Untersuchungen zur eschatologischen Dimension der Eucharistie anhand ausgewählter Zeugnisse aus frühchristlicher und patristischer Zeit [Diss. FrS]: StFrib 70. FrS 1989, Univ. xv-260 p. Fs 48. – ᴿZkT 112 (1990) 373s (H. B. *Meyer*).

5017 **Kodell** Jerome, The Eucharist in the NT: Zacchaeus, 1988 ↠ 5,4724: ᴿInterpretation 44 (1990) 314s (Frances T. *Gench*); RExp 87 (1990) 129s (D. E. *Garland*: excellent though sometimes taking rabbinic sources naively); RelStR 16 (1990) 262 ('Krodel').

5018 *Kollmann* Bernd, Ursprung und Gestalten der frühchristlichen Mahlfeier [diss. Göttingen 1989, ᴰ*Stegemann* H. ↠ 5,4725]: GöTArb 43. Gö 1990, Vandenhoeck & R. 296 p. DM 62. 3-525-87397-2 [NTAbs 35,119].

5018* *Le Boulluec* A., 'Mémorial' biblique et réflexion des pères grecs sur l'Eucharistie comme anamnèse: ↠ 618, Commémoration 1986/8, 181-190.

5019 **Léon-Dufour** Xavier, Sharing the Eucharistic bread 1987 ↠ 3,4620... 5,4727: ᴿCritRR 2 (1989) 217s (P. J. *Cahill*); RelStR 16 (1990) 262s (R. H. *Fuller*: also on KODELL: both a theology equally congenial to classical Protestantism); Vidyajyoti 53 (1989) 64s (V. *Piovesan*).

5020 **McAdoo** H. R., The Eucharistic theology of Jeremy TAYLOR today 1988 ➤ 5,4729: RAnglTR 72 (1990) 223-6 (P. V. *Marshall*).

5021 *McGrath* Alister, The Eucharist; reassessing ZWINGLI: TLond 93 (1990) 13-19.

5022 **Margerie** Bertrand de, Vous ferez ceci en mémorial de moi; annonce et souvenir de la mort du Ressuscité; préf. *Manaranche* A.: THist 80, 1989 ➤ 5,4730: RDoctCom 43 (1990) 297-9 (Dominique *Vibrac*); EsprVie 100 (1990) 204-6 (P. *Jay*).

5023 *Marinelli* Francesco, Matrimonio ed eucaristia: Lateranum 56 (1990) 117-142.

5024 **Messner** Reinhard, Die Messreform Martin LUTHERs und die Eucharistie der Alten Kirche; ein Beitrag zur systematischen Liturgiewissenschaft [Diss. Graz 1987]: InnsbTSt 25. Innsbruck 1989, Tyrolia. 240 p. DM 52. – RZkT 112 (1990) 81-87 (H. B. *Meyer*: 'K. Rahner-Preis').

5025 **Meyer** Hans B., Eucharistie; Geschichte, Theologie, Pastoral: HbLtgW 4. Rg 1989, Pustet. 602 p. DM 68 [TS 52,149, E. J. *Kilmartin*].

5026 *Moreton* Michael J., From the sacrifice of Christ to the sacrifice of the Church: ➤ 643, StPatr 18,2 (1983/9) 385-390.

5027 **Navarro Girón** María Ángeles, La carne de Cristo; el misterio eucarístico a la luz de la controversia entre Pascasio RADBERTO, RATRAMNO, RABANO Mauro y GODESCALCO. M 1989, UPC[omillas]. 269 p. – RCarthaginensia 6 (1990) 230 (F. *Martínez Fresneda*); RET 50 (1990) 465s (F. de *Carlos Otto*: diss. Comillas, DGesteira Garza M.).

5028 **O'Carroll** Michael, Corpus Christi, an encyclopedia of the Eucharist 1988 ➤ 4,4832: RHorizons 17 (1990) 345s (G. *Macy*: learned, rambling, idiosyncratic).

5029 **O'Connor** James T., The hidden manna, a theology of the Eucharist 1988 ➤ 5,4735: RAnnTh 4 (1990) 463-5 (T. J. *McGovern*).

5030 *a) Penner* E., *Wall* J., The Lord's Supper and the Church [NT; baptism requirement not absolute]; – *b) Toews* J. E., The nature of the Church: Direction 18,2 (Fresno 1989) 33-43 / 3-26 [< NTAbs 34,202].

5031 **Porro** C., L'Eucaristia, tra storia e teologia. CasM 1989, Piemme. 230 p. Lit. 27.000. – RStPatav 37 (1990) 410s (E. R. *Tura*).

5032 **Power** David N., The sacrifice we offer 1987 ➤ 3,4625 ... 5,4737: RJEH 40 (1989) 461s (R. *Rex*); JRel 70 (1990) 115s (Susan A. *Ross*).

5033 **Primavesi** Anne, *Henderson* Jennifer, Our God has no favourites; a liberation theology of the Eucharist. L 1990, Burns Oates. £5. – RTablet 244 (1990) 1167s (J. *Todd*).

5034 *Scales* D. A., Thomas CRANMER's 'True and Catholick doctrine of the Sacrament': Churchman 104 (1990) 102-131.

5035 *Schluchter* A., Sainte Cène et mort du Christ; quelques considérations bibliques: RRef 41,1 (1990) 49-52 [< NTAbs 34,351].

5036 **Schmemann** Alexander, The Eucharist, TKachur P., 1988 ➤ 5,4738: RNewTR 3,2 (1990) 107s (A. *Chirovsky*); TS 51 (1990) 182s (S. *Pope*).

5036* *Schmidt-Lauber* Hans-C., LUTHER — Chance oder Hindernis im ökumenischen Dialog über die Eucharistie: LtgJb 39 (1989) 89-104.

5037 **Smith** Dennis E., *Taussig* Hal E., Many tables; the Eucharist in the New Testament and the liturgy today. L/Ph 1990, SCM/Trinity. 144 p. $10. 0-334-02443-9 [NTAbs 35,121]. – RExpTim 102 (1990s) 189 (K. *Stevenson*).

5038 **Snoek** G. J. C., De eucharistie- en relieksverering in de Middeleeuwen; die middeleeuwse eucharistie-devotie en relieksverering in onderlinge

samenhang [Proefschrift Amst VU, ᴰ*Bredero* A.].   Amst 1989, Vrije
Univ. 434 p. ƒ49,50.   90-6256-854-8. – ᴿTsTNijm 30 (1990) 408s (J. van
Laarhoven).
5039 **Teigen** Bjarne W.,   The Lord's Supper in the theology of Martin
CHEMNITZ 1986 ➤ 3,4639;   0-9616252-0-1. – ᴿLuthTKi 13 (1989) 179s
(M. *Roensch*).
5040 *a*) *Therukattil* George,   The Eucharist, 1. The prophetic energizer for
Christian living; 2. A powerful prophetic symbol and memorial; – *b*)
Madtha William,   Gastro-semiotics of the Eucharist: Vidyajyoti 54
(1990) 189-194. 251-7 / 195-220.
5041 *Yule* Valerie,   The Eucharist as sacrament of the mission of the Church:
PrPeo 4 (1990) 44-53.

5042 *Casey* Maurice,   [Mt 26,28] The original Aramaic form of Jesus' interpretation of the Cup: JTS 41 (1990) 1-12.
5043 *Martín Ramos* Nicasio,   [Mt 26,28; 1 Cor 11,23-29] La Eucaristía,
misterio de reconciliación: CommSev 23 (1990) 31-73. 209-248. 333-354.
5044 *Mara* Maria Grazia,   COLET et ÉRASME au sujet de l'exégèse de Mt
26,39: ➤ 511, Théorie/pratique 1988/90, 259-272.

F5.3   **Mt 26,30 ...** ‖   *Passio Christi;* **Passion-narrative.**

5045 *Agourides* S., ⊖ Why Christ died: II. according to the evangelist John;
III. according to the apostle Paul; IV. according to Heb, 1 Jn, 1 Pt, Apc.:
DeltioVM 19,1 (1990) 13-35; 19,2, 22-61.
5046 **Bader** Günther,   Symbolik des Todes Jesu: HermUntT 25, 1988 ➤ 4,
4847: ᴿNorTTs 91 (1990) 157s (T. *Wyller*).
5047 **Barton** J.,   Love unknown; meditations on the death and resurrection
of Jesus. L 1990, SPCK. xiii-79 p. £5 pa.   0-281-04440-6 [NTAbs
34,397]. – ᴿTLond 93 (1990) 425 (H. *Dawes*).
5048 **Beardslee** W. A.,   Biblical preaching on the death of Jesus 1989 ➤ 5,4752;
0-687-03446-9:   ᴿExpTim 102 (1990s) 93s (D. W. *Cleverley Ford*: aims
between fundamentalist and liberal); TTod 47 (1990s) 226 (F. J. *Matera*:
well-conceived).
Black Mark C., Zech 9-14 in the Passion narratives ᴰ1990 ➤ 4154.
5049 **Blumenberg** Hans,   Matthäuspassion: Bibl. Suhrkamp 998.   Fra 1988,
Suhrkamp.   306 p. – ᴿTPhil 65 (1990) 464-6 (A. *Kreuzer*, als 'systematische Philosophie'; unerhört provokante eigenwillige Bibelauslegung);
TRu 55 (1990) 348-356 (M. *Petzoldt*).
5050 **Cilia** Lucia,   La morte di Gesù e l'unità degli uomini: diss. Angelicum,
ᴰ*de Santis* L. – R 1990. – RTLv 22,592.
5051 **Garland** D. E.,   One hundred years of study on the Passion narratives:
NABPR 3.   Macon GA 1989, Mercer Univ. xviii-174 p. $19.   0-
86554-371-2 [NTAbs 34,383: 2154 items in English, French, German; in
chronological order, with author index].
5052 **Goergen** Donald,   The death and resurrection of Jesus: A theology of
Jesus 2, 1988 ➤ 4,4855; 5,4758: ᴿCBQ 52 (1990) 157s (L. J. *Topel*:
repetitive, superficial; mistaken methodology).
5053 **Grayston** Kenneth,   Dying, we live; a new inquiry into the death of
Christ in the NT. NY 1990, Oxford-UP. viii-496 p. $40.   0-19-520789-0
[TDig 38,266]. – ᴿExpTim 102,8 top choice (1990s) 225-7 (C. S. *Rodd*).

5054 **Green** Joel B., The death of Jesus ...: [ᴰAberdeen]: WUNT 2/33, 1988
➤ 4,4856; 5,4760: ᴿCarthaginensia 6 (1990) 211s (R. *Sanz Valdivieso*);
EstE 65 (1990) 97s (A. *Vargas-Machuca*); Interpretation 44 (1990) 206s
(F.J. *Matera*); JTS 41 (1990) 182s (K. *Grayston*); SNTU-A 14 (1989) 229s
(A. *Fuchs*); TR 86 (1990) 111s (G. *Schneider*).

5055 **Kiehl** Erich H., The Passion of our Lord. GR 1990, Baker. 224 p.; ill.;
maps. $15. 0-8010-5286-6 [TDig 38,275].

5056 *La Delfa* Rosario, The suffering of Christ and its relationship to the
individual according to J.H. card. NEWMAN: Ho Theológos 7 (1989)
5-76.

5057 *Lunn* A.J., Christ's Passion as tragedy: ScotJT 43 (1990) 308-320.

5058 **Martin** Ernest L., Secrets of Golgotha; the forgotten history of Christ's
crucifixion [on Mount of Olives] 1988 ➤ 4,4864; 5, 4770: ᴿEvQ 62 (1990)
361-4 (I.H. *Marshall*); JEH 40 (1989) 449 (W.H.C. *Frend*: useful but too
prolix).

5059 *Martin* François, Mourir: Matthieu 26-27: SémBib 53 (1989) 18-47.

5060 **Matera** Frank J., Passion narratives and Gospel theologies 1986
➤ 2,3669 ... 5,4771: ᴿCritRR 2 (1989) 220-2 (M.L. *Soards*); HeythJ 31
(1990) 76 (J. *Coventry*).

5061 *a) Overman* J. Andrew, Heroes and villains in Palestinian lore;
Matthew's use of traditional Jewish polemic in the Passion narrative; – *b)*
Powell Mark A., The plot to kill Jesus from three different perspectives:
➤ 544, SBL seminars 1990, 592-600 / 601-613.

5062 *Roloff* Jürgen, Anfänge der soteriologischen Deutung des Todes Jesu
(Mk X.45 und Lk XXII.27) [< NTS 19 (1972s) 38-64]: ➤ 289,
Verantwortung 1990, 117-143.

5064 *Schenk* Wolfgang, Leidensgeschichte Jesu: ➤ 857, TRE 20 (1990)
714-721.

5065 *a) Soggin* J. Alberto, La morte di Gesù, aspetto storico; – *b) Simeo-*
ne Renato, ... aspetto teologico: ➤ 506, Ebraismo/NT 3 (1990) 5-21 /
25-37.

5066 *a) Stuhlmacher* Peter, Pourquoi Jésus a-t-il dû mourir? [< Jesus 1988],
ᵀ*Bolay* B., *al.*: – *b) Locoge* Bernard, Dire le sens de la croix aujourd'hui:
Hokhma 40 (1989) 17-36 / 37-49 (-62, *al.*).

5067 **Thurston** B.B., Wait here and watch; a Eucharistic commentary on the
Passion according to St. Matthew. St. Louis 1989, 'CBP'. 96 p. $7.
0-8272-4225-5 [NTAbs 34,115].

5068 **Feldmeier** Reinhard [Mt 26,36-46 ...] Die Krisis des Gottessohnes, die
Gethsemaneerzählung ... Mk [14,34-42]: WUNT 2/21, ᴰ1987 ➤ 4,4882;
5,5012: ᴿSNTU-A 14 (1989) 246-8 (A. *Fuchs*).

5069 *Roy* Louis, God's providence for Jesus [... Gethsemani]; comfort or no
comfort?: ScEsp 42 (1990) 293-303.

5070 **Spencer** William D. & Aída B., The prayer life of Jesus; shout of agony,
revelation of love; a commentary. Lanham MD 1990, UPA. xii-296 p.
$30 pa. 0-8191-7779-2 [NTAbs 35,246].

5071 **Del Rio** Domenico, [Mt 26,14] E Gesù disse: Giuda, chi sei? CinB 1989,
Paoline. 144 p. Lit. 16.000. – ᴿCC 141 (1990,2) 561-7 (F. *Castelli*:
romanzo dignitoso).

5072 **Klauck** H.-J., Judas 1987 ➤ 3,4683 ... 5,4777: ᴿSalesianum 52 (1990)
741 (C. *Bissoli*).

5073 **Pazzi** Roberto, Vangelo di Giuda. Mi 1989, Garzanti. 270 p. Lit. 26.000. – ᴿCC 141 (1990,2) 561-7 (F. *Castelli*: confuso e deludente; Gesù adora 'un dio che è in ognuno' e ama gli animali).

5074 *Perraymond* Myla, L'iconografia di Giuda Iscariota ed i suoi risvolti evangelici: SMSR 56 (1990) 67-93; 7 fig.

5075 **Castello** Gaetano, [Mt 26,59-66] L'interrogatorio di Gesù davanti al Sinedrio; contributo esegetico-storico alla cristologia neotestamentaria: diss. 6910 Pont. Univ. Gregoriana, ᴰ*Grech* P. R 1990s. – InfPUG 23/119, 14.

5076 **Foreman** D., Crucify him; a lawyer looks at the trial of Jesus. GR 1990, Zondervan. 222 p. $9 pa. 0-310-51211-5 [NTAbs 34,383].

5077 **Fricke** Weddig, [deutsch 1988 ⇒ 2,3658] *a*) Standrechtelijk gekruisigd; het proces van Jezus; persoon en proces van Jezus uit Galilea. Antwerpen/Rotterdam 1988, de Vries/Broutwerd. 185 p. ƒ39,50. 90-6174-490-3. – ᴿTsTNijm 30 (1990) 202 (W. *Weren*); – *b*) The court-martial of Jesus; a Christian defends the Jews against the charge of deicide [Standrechtlich gekreuzigt 1988 ⇒ 2,3658], ᵀ*Attanasio* S. NY 1990, Grove-W. viii-296 p. $22. 0-8021-1094-0 [NTAbs 35,101].

5078 ᴱ**Kertelge** K., Der Prozess gegen Jesus; QDisp 112, 1987/98 ⇒ 4,491*: ᴿKIsr 5 (1990) 183s (Julie *Kirchberg*); RuBi 42 (1989) 79s (J. *Woźniak*).

5078* *Rosen* Klaus, Der Prozess Jesu und die römische Provinzialverwaltung; zur historischen Methode und Glaubenswürdigkeit der Evangelien: ⇒ 61, ᶠHÜRTEN H. 1988, 121-143.

5079 *Kupiszewski* Henryk, Das Neue Testament und Rechtsgeschichte [... Pilatus]: ⇒ 86*, ᶠIGLESIAS Juan, 2 (1988) 809-821.

5080 *Maier* P. L., Who killed Jesus: ChrT 34,6 (1990) 16-19 [NTAbs 34,299: Pilate ultimately, but subject to 'Jewish pressures'].

5081 *Majsai* Tamás, Ⓜ Crucifixus sub Pontio Pilato: TSzem 33 (1990) 93-108.

5082 *Mamlak* G., The two trials of Jesus: Midstream 35,5 (NY 1989) 29-32 [< NTAbs 34,17].

5983 **Nardoni** D., Sotto Ponzio Pilato [juicio de los más variados autores]. R 1987, Ed. Letteratura e Scienze. 206 p. Lit. 20.000. – ᴿHelmantica 40 (1989) 499s (J. *Oroz Reta*: curioso).

5084 *Millar* Fergus, Reflections on the trials of Jesus: ⇒ 183, ᶠVERMES G. 1990, 355-381.

5085 *Deproost* Paul-Augustin [Mt 27,5] La mort de Judas dans l'Historia apostolica d'ARATOR (I,83-102): RÉAug 35 (1989) 135-150.

5086 **Mora** V., Le refus d'Israël, Mt 27,25: 1986 ⇒ 2,3692 ... 5,4787: ᴿCritRR 2 (1989) 299s (R. H. *Fuller*); RevSR 63 (1989) 150s (Michèle *Morgen*).

5087 *Smith* Robert H., Matthew 27:25, the hardest verse in Matthew's gospel ['his blood be upon us': 'has done more than any other sentence in the NT to feed the fires of anti-Semitism' (G. *O'Collins*)]: ⇒ 41, ᶠDANKER F., CurrTMiss 17 (1990) 421-8.

5088 *Weiss* Hans-Friedrich, Der Prozess Jesu; zur Frage der Schuld am Tod Jesu, I: Christenlehre 43 (1990) 131-6 [< ZIT 90,492].

5089 *McEleney* Neil J., Peter's denials – how many? to whom?: CBQ 52 (1990) 467-472 [three and as in Mark, despite Mt/Lk redactional details].

5090 *Louw* J. P., Die uur van die kruisiging en dagrekening in die antieke: Scriptura 29 (Stellenbosch 1989) 13-18 [< NTAbs 34,17].

5091 *Starowieyski* Marek, ❷ The Passion according to TATIAN's Syriac Diatessaron: RuBi 42 (1989) 259-268.

5092 **Magnolfi** Maria, [Mc 15,34] Elôi Elôi lema sabachthani; indagine esegetica e contributo all'interpretazione del grido di abbandono di Gesù: diss. Pont. Ist. Biblico, ᴰ*Grech* P.   R 1990. – AcPIB 9/7, 578.623-5.

5093 **Rossé** Gérard, [Mt 27,46; Mc 15,34] The cry of Jesus on the cross 1987 ➔ 4,4899; 5,4791:   ᴿRTLv 21 (1990) 229s (C. *Focant*); Themelios 16 (1990s) 28 (R. *Bauckham*); Vidyajyoti 53 (1989) 396s (P. *Meagher*).

5094 **Wells** Paul,   Entre ciel et terre; les dernières paroles de Jésus = RRéf 61,4s (1990). 179 p. [ZIT 90,819].

5095 *Zugibe* Frederick T.,   Two questions about crucifixion; does the victim die of asphyxiation? [no]; would nails in the hand hold the weight of the body? [yes]:   BR 5,2 (1989) 35-43.

5096 *Price* R.M.,   Jesus' burial in a garden; the strange growth of the tradition [rather the tradition that his body was stolen by gardener]: Religious traditions 12 (1989) 17-30 [< NTAbs 34,158, locating the periodical in Montreal-Sydney].

5097 *Herzog* Markwart, *Hagen* Markus von,   'Hinabgestiegen in das Reich des Todes'; Kunstgeschichtliche Überlegungen zur Höllenfahrt Jesu Christi: GeistL 62 (1989) 139-142 [> Eng. TDig 37,123-5, 1 fig., ᴱ*Asen* B.].

5098 *Otto* Randall E., [Mt 27,52; 1 Pt 3,18] Descendit in inferna; a Reformed review of a creedal conundrum: WestTJ 52 (1990) 143-150.

F5.6   Mt 28 || :   Resurrectio.

5099 **Balthasar** Hans Urs von, Mysterium paschale; the mystery of Easter, ᵀ*Nichols* Aidan.   E 1990, Clark. xii-297 p. $40.   0-567-09534-7 [TDig 38,251].

5100 *Berkhof* H.,   Het Nieuws en het Nieuwe van Jezus' Opstanding: KerkT 41 (1990) 1-9.

5101 **Brown** Raymond E.,   A risen Christ in Eastertime; essays on the Gospel narrative of the Resurrection [< Worship 1990].   Collegeville MN 1990, Liturgical.   95 p.   0-8146-2014-0.

5102 **Caba** José,   *a)* Resucitó Cristo, mi esperanza 1986 ➔ 2,3698 ... 4,4905: ᴾCritRR 2 (1989) 187-9 (A. *Casurella*), – *b)* Cristo, mia speranza, è risorto; studio esegetico dei 'vangeli' pasquali 1988 ➔ 4,4906:   ᴿLaurentianum 31 (1990) 599s (L. *Martignani*).

5103 **Carnley** Peter,   The structure of Resurrection belief 1987 ➔ 3,4702 ... 5,4806:   ᴿColloquium 22,1 (Auckland 1989) 45-50 (W.R.G. *Loader*) [< NTAbs 34,300]; JAAR 58 (1990) 115s (R.H. *Fuller*); LvSt 14 (1989) 193s (J. *Lambrecht*); St. Mark's Review 140 (Canberra 1990) 32-35 (F. *Rees*) [< NTAbs 35,19].

5104 *Contreras* E.,   Cristo ha resucitado; notas para leer la reflexión de los Padres de la Iglesia sobre el misterio de Cristo: NVZam 14,1 (1989) 3-43 [< RET 50,139].

5105 *Frei* H.W.,   How it all began; on the resurrection of Christ: Anglican and Episcopal History 58,2 (Austin TX 1989) 139-145 [< NTAbs 34,18].

5106 **Gennep** F.O. van, *Zuurmond* R., *al.*,   Waarlijk opgestaan? Een discussie over de opstanding van Jezus Christus.   Baarn 1989, Ten Have.   83 p. *f* 14,90. – ᴿCollatVL 20 (1990) 440s (E. Vanden *Berghe*).

5107 *Giraldo* N.,   ¿Es la resurrección de Cristo un hecho histórico?: CuestTeolMed (1990) 127-152 [REB 50,1030].

5108 **Guilbert** Pierre,   Il ressuscita le troisième jour 1988 ➔ 5,4818:   ᴿTéléma 15,3s (1989) 102-4 (Maryvonne *Duclaux*).

5109 **Harris** Murray J.,   From grave to glory; Resurrection in the NT, including a response to Norman L. GEISLER.   GR 1990, Zondervan.

192 p. $11.   0-310-51991-8. – RJEvTS 33 (1990) 369-373 (F. J. *Beckwith* also on GEISLER N.) [< NTAbs 35,155].

5110 **Ide** A. F., *al.*,   Resurrection, sex and God; essays on the foundations of faith.   Dallas 1990, Minuteman.   101 p. $10 pa.   0-926899-01-5 [NTAbs 34,399: the resurrection was an initiation-rite; Jesus was sexual and probably gay; God does not exist].

5111 *Jones* P. T.,   Not restored but resurrected: ExpTim 102 (1990s) 146-8.

5112 **Kartsonis** Anna D.,   Anastasis; the making of an image 1986 ⇒ 4,4921; xviii-264 p.; 89 fig. – RByZ 81 (1988) 327-9 (K. *Onasch*); JEH 40 (1989) 405-7 (J. *Shepard*).

5113 **Kessler** Hans,   La Resurrección de Jesús [1985] 1989 ⇒ 5,4824:   REstAg 25 (1990) 160 (C. *Mielgo*); RET 50 (1990) 98-101 (M. *Gesteira*).

5114 **Leblond** Germain,   L'Agneau de la Pâque éternelle.   P 1987, Desclée. 215 p.   2-7189-0333-3.

5115 **Lunny** William J.,   The sociology of the Resurrection 1989 ⇒ 5,4831: RVidyajyoti 54 (1990) 316 (R. J. *Raja*).

5116 **McDonald** J. I. H.,   The Resurrection; narrative and belief 1989 ⇒ 5,4832:   RJTS 41 (1990) 594-6 (C. F. D. *Moule*); TLond 93 (1990) 69s (W. G. *Jeanrond*: excellent, holistic).

5117 *McKnight* Scot,   The nature of resurrection; a debatable issue: JEvTS 33 (1990) 379 ... [< ZIT 90,806]; 369-375-378, *Beckwith* Francis J., *Habermas* Gary B., review articles.

5118 **Marxsen** Willi,   Jesus and Easter; did God raise the historical Jesus from the dead? [US lectures Oct. 1988], TFurnish Victor P.   Nv 1990, Abingdon.   92 p. $9.   0-687-19929-8 [TDig 37,373].

5119 EMiethe T. L. (*Habermas* G., *Flew* A.) Did Jesus rise from the dead? 1987 ⇒ 3,4710 ... 5,4833:   RCriswT 4 (1989s) 200s (D. L. *Akin*); Hist-Theor 28 (1989) 215-224 (B. L. *Mack*).

5120 *Moiser* J.,   The Resurrection – a new essay in biblical theology: KingsTR 13,1 (1990) 16-19 [< NTAbs 35,20].

5121 *Moloney* Francis J.,   Jesus of Nazareth and the Resurrection: PrPeo 4 (1990) 125-9 [141-3 *Selman* Francis J.].

5122 **Neyrey** Jerome,   The resurrection stories 1988 ⇒ 4,4927:   RBibTB 20 (1990) 130s (R. L. *Mowery*); Horizons 17 (1990) 322s (M. D. *Hamm*, also on the three other first 'Zacchaeus Studies'); RelStR 16 (1990) 73 (L. *Cope*); Vidyajyoti 54 (1990) 268 . 257 (R. J. *Raja*).

5123 **Nicolas** Marie-Joseph,   Teologia della Risurrezione.   Vaticano 1989, Editrice.   274 p. Lit. 32.000. – REsprVie 100 (1990) 413 (G. *Viard*: malgré CLAUDEL, 'connaître = naître avec' douteux).

5124 **O'Collins** G.,   *a*) Jesus risen 1987 ⇒ 3,4718 ... 5,4835:   RIrTQ 56 (1990) 340 (T. *Corbett*); ScotBEv 7 (1989) 134s (D. J. *Graham*: a mixed bag, even though it does not follow up the claim that we can learn about the first Easter also by suffering in a slum); – *b*) Jesús resucitado 1988 ⇒ 4,4931; 5,4836:   RIter 1 (1990) 170 (A. *Guerrero*); PerspT 22 (1990) 133s (C. *Palácio*).

5125 **O'Collins** G.,   Interpreting the Resurrection; examining the major problems in the stories of Jesus' Resurrection.   NY 1989, Paulist.   88 p. $9 [RB 98,466, J. *Murphy-O'Connor*].

5126 **Palumbieri** Sabino,   Cristo risorto leva della storia 1988, ²1989 ⇒ 5,4841: RAntonianum 65 (1990) 393s (C. *Teklak*); Teresianum 40 (1989) 617s (P. *Boyce*).

5127 *Peel* Malcolm L.,   The Resurrection in recent scholarly research: BR 5,4 (1989) 14-21 . 42s.

5128 *Rothert* Paula, Auferstanden ist der gute Hirt; die frühchristliche Darstellung des guten Hirten als Osterbild: ErbAuf 66 (1990) 129-137.

5129 *Surin* Kenneth, 'The sign that something else is always possible'; hearing and saying 'Jesus is risen' and hearing the voices of those who suffer; some textual/political reflections: LitTOx 4 (1990) 263-277 [< ZIT 91,10].

5130 *Winling* Raymond, La résurrection du Christ dans l'Antirrheticus adversus Apollinarem de GRÉGOIRE de Nysse: RÉAug 35 (1989) 12-43.

5131 **Wolfe** R. E., How the Easter story grew from Gospel to Gospel. Lewiston NY 1989, Mellen. vii-244 p. $80. 0-88946-003-5 [NTAbs 34,390].

5132 *Brown* R. E., The resurrection in Matthew (27:62-28:20): Worship 64 (1990) 157-170 [194-206, in John 20; 433-445, in John 21].

5133 *Eckardt* A. R., [Lk 24,5] Why do you search among the dead?: Encounter 51,1 (Indianapolis 1990) 1-17 [< NTAbs 34,300].

5134 *Heitz* Carol, [Mt 28,1] Sepulcrum Domini; le sépulcre visité par les saintes femmes (IXe-XIe siècle): ➤ 149, FRiché P., Haut Moyen-Âge 1990, 389-400 + VIII pl.

5135 *O'Collins* Gerald, [Mt 28,6] The empty tomb [opposes trend to stress it less than the apparitions]: Tablet 244 (1990) 479s.

5136 **Barlone** Sandro, Le apparizioni del Risorto agli Undici; natura e funzione secondo tre recenti disegni cristologici: diss. 6914 Pont. Univ. Gregoriana, DO'Collins G. R 1990s. – InfPUG 23/119, 14.

5137 **Muñoz León** Domingo, 'Iré delante de vosotros a Galilea' (Mt 26,32 y par); sentido mesiánico y posible sustrato arameo del lógion: EstB 48 (1990) 215-241; Eng. 215.

5137* *Arias* Mortimer [Mt 28,16-20], Church in the world; rethinking the great commission: TTod 47 (1990s) 410-8.

5138 *Bolognesi* Pietro, Matteo 28,16-20 e il suo contenuto: STEv NS 1 (1989) 25-39.

5139 *a) Perkins* Pheme, Christology and mission; Matthew 28:16-20; – *b) O'Day* G. R., Surprised by faith; Jesus and the Canaanite woman: Listening 24 (1989) 302-9 / 290-301 [< NTAbs 34,164s].

5140 *Ferrando* Miguel A., [Mt 28,18-20 ...] La misión de los discípulos de Jesús: TVida 31 (1980) 121-131.

5141 *Green* H. Benedict, Matthew 28:19, EUSEBIUS, and the *lex orandi*: ➤ 5,38*, FCHADWICK H., Making of orthodoxy 1989, 124-141.

5142 **Rzepkowski** Horst, [Mt 28,19] 'Make disciples of all nations'; a task entrusted to all God's people, TWalsh Dermot: VerbumSVD 30 (1989) 21-40 [5-10, *Musinsky* John].

5143 *Hre Kio* Stephen, Understanding and translating 'nations' in Mt 28.19: BTrans 41 (1990) 230-8.

5144 *Wagner* M. A., Christian education as making disciples: LuthTJ 24,2 (Adelaide 1990) 69-80 [< NTAbs 35,65].

5144* *Clerck* P. De, Les origines de la formule baptismale: ➤ 68*, FGY P.-M., Rituels 1990, 199-213.

F6.1   **Evangelium Marci** – *Textus, commentarii*.

5145 **Aranda Pérez** Gonzalo, El Evangelio de San Marcos en copto sahídico 1988 ➤ 4,4954; 5,4855: RScripTPamp 22 (1990) 597s (P. *Mond*); Sefarad 50 (1990) 481 (María V. *Spottorno*).

5146 **Bianchi** Enzo, Evangelo secondo Marco; commento esegetico-spirituale. Magnano vc 1990 = 1984 ➤ 3,4742, Qiqajon. [vi-] 342 p.; maps.
5147 **Bruggen** J. Van, Marcus CommNT 3/2. Kampen 1988, Kok. 436 p. ƒ69,50. 90-24207-78-9. – RNedTTs 44 (1990) 341s (H. *Welzen*).
5148 **Drewermann** E., *a*) Das Markusevangelium [I. 1987 ➤4,4956] II. 9,14-16,20. Olten 1988, Walter. 796 p.; 4 pl. DM 69. 3-530-16872-6 [NTAbs 34,245]. – RSNTU A-15 (1990) 161-3 (A. *Fuchs*: ⁵1989); WissWeis 51 (1988) 225 (H.-J. *Klauck*). – *b*) Das Markusevangelium [seine Übersetzung]. Olten 1989, Walter. 75 p. – RSalesianum 52 (1990) 431s (C. *Buzzetti*); ZkT 112 (1990) 208s (K. *Stock*: extract from his 1987s commentary; favors BUBER and STIER over 'Einheit' and 'everyday language'; but fails to use same German always for a single Greek term).
5149 **Galizzi** Mario, Voi l'avete ucciso!; Vangelo secondo Marco II [cap. 9,30-10,52]: Commenti al NT. T-Leumann 1988 = 1976, Elle Di Ci. 160 p. Lit. 6000. 88-01-16749-0.
5150 **Georgeot** J.-M., Évangile selon saint Marc...: Spiritualité 2, 1988-90 ➤ 5,4859: RRTLv 21 (1990) 227-9 (E. *Manning*).
5151 **Gnilka** J., Marco 1987 ➤ 3,4744... 5,4860: RBenedictina 36 (1989) 222s (S. *Spera*).
5152 **Guelich** Robert A., Mark 1-8,26: Word Comm. 34a, 1989 ➤ 5,4863: RInterpretation 44 (1990) 412-4 (E. *Best*).
5153 **Hughes** R. Kent, Mark; Jesus, servant and savior, I-II: Preaching the Word. Westchester IL 1989, Crossway. 240 p., $12 each. 0-89107-537-2; -22-4. – RRExp 87 (1990) 513s (C. *Bugg*).
5154 **Hurtado** Larry W., Mark²: New International [Version] Bible Comm. 2. Peabody MA 1989 [= ¹1983], Hendrickson. xiii-306 p. 0-943575-16-8.
5155 **Iersel** B. van, Marcus: Belichting 1986 / Reading Mark 1989 ➤ 5,4865: RNRT 112 (1990) 593s (X. *Jacques*); TsTNijm 30 (1990) 88s (S. *Noorda*).
5156 **Karavidopoulos** Ioannis, ⊕ To katà Markon evangelio. Thessaloniki 1988, Pournara. 520 p. – RDeltioVM 18,1 (1989) 77-79 (S. *Agouridis*).
5157 **Kilgallen** John J., Brief commentary on the Gospel of Mark. NY 1989, Paulist. – RExpTim 102 (1990s) 127 (C. S. *Rodd*: shows 5 goals; useful not only for Catholics).
5158 **Lührmann** Dieter, Das Mk-Ev: HbNT 3, 1987 ➤ 3,4750... 5,4869: RCBQ 52 (1990) 351-3 (J. *Marcus*: puts everything where it belongs, but sometimes swallowed up); TPhil 65 (1990) 256s (J. *Beutler*).
5159 ᵀMiłosz Czesław, Ewangelia według Marka; Apokalipsa. Lublin 1989, KUL. 140 p.; ill. zł 700 [AtKap 114 (1990) 331].
5159* **Monshouwer** D., Markus en drie jaar Torah; het evangelie gelezen als drie jaargangen schriftuitleg. Kampen 1989, Kok. 336 p. ƒ65 [JBL 110, 531, Sara J. *Denning-Bolle*].
5160 [ᴱ**Casciaro** J.M., ᵀᴱ*Gavigan* J. & B.] Navarre Bible St. Mark's Gospel [with] RSV/NeoV. Dublin 1989, Four Courts. 201 p.; map. 0-906127-93-9.
5161 **Ravasi** G. F., Il Vangelo di Marco: Conversazioni Bibliche S. Fedele. Bo 1990, Dehoniane. 136 p. Lit. 12.000. 88-10-70918-7 [NTAbs 35,107].
5162 ᴱ**Rummel** Erika, ERASMUS, Paraphrase on Mark: Collected Works 49, 1988 ➤ 5,4877: RHeythJ 31 (1990) 342-4 (G. R. *Dunstan*).
5163 ᴱ**Sabbe** M., L'Évangile selon Marc² [Lv 1971, ¹1974]: BiblETL 34. Lv 1988, Univ. 600 p. Fb 2400. 90-6186-280-9 / Peeters 90-6831-129-8. – RÉTRel 65 (1990) 451 (E. *Cuvillier*: risque réussi).
5164 **Thiede** C. P., ¿El manuscrito mas antiguo...? Mc en Qumran ➤ 5,a39: RActuBbg 27 (1990) 204 (X. *Alegre S.*).

5165 ᵀTorró J. Pascual, ᴱGuerrero Martínez F., S. JERÓNIMO, Marcos (10 homilías) 1988 → 4,4962: ᴿScripTPamp 22 (1990) 284 (M. Merino).
Zuurmond R., NT aethiopice.. Edition of the Gospel of Mark 1989 → 1906.

F6.2 Evangelium Marci, Themata.

5166 Ambrozić A. M., Jesus as the ultimate reality in St. Mark's Gospel: URM 12 (1989) 169-176 [< NTAbs 34,167].
5167 **Apicella** Raymond, Journeys into Mark; 16 lessons of exploration and discovery. Cincinnati 1990, St. Anthony. 60 p. $5. 0-86716-112-4 [TDig 37,248].
5168 **Balaguer** Vicente, Testimonio y tradición en San Marcos; narratología del segundo evangelio: Col. Teológica 73. Pamplona 1990, Univ. Navarra. 250 p. pt. 2500. 84-313-1102-9.
5169 **Barta** Karen A., The Gospel of Mark: MessageBSp 9, 1988 → 4,4963: ᴿCBQ 52 (1990) 547s (P. Zilonka).
5170 **Best** E., Disciples and discipleship in the Gospel according to Mark 1986 → 2,132*... 5,4882*: ᴿCritRR 3 (1990) 188s (D. M. Rhoads).
5171 **Biguzzi** G., 'Io distruggerò ...' il Tempio 1987 → 3,4759... 5,4884: ᴿFg-Nt 3,5 (1990) 83s (J. Peláez).
5172 **Bilo** Carl, Stervend verrijzen; met Markus op de weg van Jezus. Haarlem 1988, Gottmer. 171 p.; ill. ƒ23,50. 90-257-2149-4. – ᴿBijdragen 51 (1990) 441s (Kitty Mul).
5173 **Black** Clifton C., The disciple... Markan redaction: JStNT supp 27, ᴰ1989 → 5,4885: ᴿÉTRel 65 (1990) 272s (E. Cuvillier: not on the disciples but on Redaktionsgeschichte); PerspRelSt 17 (1990) 83-87 (E. K. Broadhead); TLZ 115 (1990) 589s (J.-W. Taeger); TS 51 (1990) 513-5 (W. R. Herzog).
5174 Botha P. J. J., [Mk...] The task of understanding the Gospel traditions; Werner KELLER's contribution to NT research: HervTS 46 (1990) 47-70 [< NTAbs 35,150].
5175 Breytenbach C., The Gospel of Mark as episodical narrative; reflections on the 'composition' of the Second Gospel: Scriptura spec. 4 (1989) 1-26 [< NTAbs 34,167].
5176 **Burdon** Christopher, Stumbling on God; faith and vision in Mark's Gospel. L 1990, SPCK. xii-110 p. £6. 0-281-04434-1 [NTAbs 35,100]. – ᴿTLond 93 (1990) 425s (Ruth R. Edwards).
5177 Castro Secundino, El sorprendente Jesús de Marcos: REspir 47 (1988) 9-48.
5178 **Collins** Adela Y., Is Mark's Gospel a life of Jesus? The question of genre: Père Marquette lecture 21. Milwaukee 1990, Marquette Univ. v-77 p. 0-87462-545-9 [NTAbs 35,109: 'history in an apocalyptic mode'].
5179 **Cuvillier** E., La tragédie de Jésus; Marc 1989 → 5,4888: ᴿProtestantesimo 45 (1990) 324 (B. Subilia).
5180 **Dahm** Christof, Israel im Markusevangelium: kath. Diss. Mainz 1990, ᴰSchenke L. – RTLv 22,592.
5181 **Dillmann** Rainer, Christlich handeln in der Nachfolge Jesu; Beispiele aus dem Mk-ev. Mainz 1989, Grünewald. 147 p. DM 22,80. – ᴿTGL 80 (1990) 513 (J. Ernst).
5182 **Doohan** Leonard, Mark, visionary of early Christianity 1986 → 3,4771 ... 5,4892: ᴿRelStT 8,3 (1988) 53s (E. L. Segal).
5183 **Dwyer** Timothy R., The motif of wonder in the Gospel of Mark: diss. Aberdeen 1990. – RTLv 22, p. 592.

5184 **Ernst** Josef, Marco, un ritratto teologico [1987 ➤ 4,4976], ᵀ*Dequal* Margherita & Bruno. Brescia 1990, Morcelliana. 182 p. Lit. 20.000. 88-372-1397-2.

5185 *Farmer* William R., *al.*, Narrative outline of the Markan composition according to the Two Gospel hypothesis: ➤ 544, SBL seminars 1990, 212-239.

5186 **Fendler** Folkert, Studien zum Markusevangelium; zur Gattung, Chronologie, Messiasgeheimnistheorie und Überlieferung des zweiten Evangeliums: ev. Diss. Giessen, ᴰ*Strecker*. – TR 86,515.

5187 **France** R. T., Divine government; God's Kingship in the Gospel of Mark [Moore lectures, Sydney 1989]. L 1990, SPCK. 135 p. £7. 0-281-04471-6. – ᴿExpTim 102 (1990s) 182 (E. *Franklin*: 'persuasive, not convincing').

5187* **Funk** Robert W., New Gospel parallels², I/2 Mark: Foundations and Facets. Sonoma CA 1990, Polebridge. xvi-272 p.; map. 0-944344-12-7 [ETL 67,165s, F. *Neirynck*: uses a not-yet-published 'Scholars' English translation].

5188 **Gargano** I., 'Lectio divina' su il Vangelo di Marco: Conversazioni Bibliche. Bo 1989, Dehoniane. 150 p. Lit. 15.000. 88-10-70915-2 [NTAbs 34,245].

5189 **Garland** Frances, Reading Mark in groups. L 1989, Bible Reading Fellowship. 122 p. £3.50. 0-900164-83-2 [ExpTim 102,31].

5190 **Hengel** M., Studies in... Mk 1985 ➤ 1,4779... 3,4900: ᴿTR 86 (1990) 369-371 (G. D. *Kilpatrick*, comparing to ᴱCANCIK H.).

5191 *Hubai* Peter, The legend of St. Mark; Coptic fragments: ➤ 49, Mém. FÓTI L. 1989, 165-233.

5192 *Hurtado* Larry W., The Gospel of Mark; evolutionary or revolutionary document?: JStNT 40 (1990) 15-32.

5193 *a) Jasper* D., St. Mark's Gospel and the interpretative community; – *b) Johnson* W. A., 'The Jews' in Saint Mark's Gospel: Religion and Intellectual Life 6,3s (New Rochelle 1989) 173-181 / 182-192 [< NTAbs 34,26].

5194 **Kingsbury** Jack D., Conflict in Mark; Jesus, authorities, disciples 1989 ➤ 5,4908: ᴿAnglTR 72 (1990) 461-3 (N. *Elliott*); FgNt 3,5 (1990) 75s (S. E. *Porter*); HorBT 12,1 (1990) 97s (H. C. *Kee*); Interpretation 44 (1990) 297s (C. C. *Black*); TTod 47 (1990s) 354 (C. J. *Roetzel*).

5195 *Kingsbury* Jack D., The religious authorities in the Gospel of Mark: NTS 36 (1990) 42-65.

5196 *Lahutsky* Nadia M., Paris and Jerusalem; Alfred LOISY and Père LAGRANGE on the Gospel of Mark: CBQ 52 (1990) 444-466 [p. 445, 'By today's standards Loisy's critical work sounds eerily contemporary and Lagrange's quaint and traditional'; p. 466, despite 1910 criticisms by P. OJETTI and others ('insufficiently respectful to magisterium'...) Lagrange was well in the center of options].

5196* *Lane* William L., The present state of Markan studies: ➤ 370, Gospels 1990, 51-81.

5197 *Lim* Bonaventure, Ⓖ Christian profession of faith seen from St. Mark's Gospel: ColcFuJen 81 (1989) 319-329.

5198 **Maas** W. J., Volmacht als predikaat van het Heil; een exegetisch-hermeneutisch onderzoek in het Markusevangelie 1987 ➤ 4,4987*; 90-6495-145-4. – ᴿNedTTs 44 (1990) 339s (H. *Welzen*).

5199 **Mack** Burton L., A myth of innocence; Mark and Christian origins 1988 ➤ 4,4988; 5,4913: ᴿAnglTR 71 (1989) 314-6 (F. W. *Hughes*); CBQ

52 (1990) 161-3 (W. H. *Kelber*: penetrating); Interpretation 44 (1990) 193-5 (J. A. *Overman*).

5200 **Malbon** Elizabeth S., Narrative space ... Mk 1986 → 2,3769 ... 5,4916: RCritRR 3 (1990) 220-2 (D. O. *Via*).

5201 **Marín** Javier J., The Christology of Mark; does [it] support the Chalcedonian formula 'truly man and truly God'?: Diss. D*Weder*. Zürich 1989s. – TR 86 (1990) 512.

5202 **Marshall** C. D., Faith ... Mk: SNTS Mg 64, D1989 → 5,4920: RJTS 41 (1990) 599-602 (E. *Best*).

5203 *a) Matera* Frank J., Jesus in the Gospel of Mark; the crucified Messiah; – *b) Navone* John, Divine and human conflict; the way of the Cross is the good news of the Kingdom of God: PrPeo 4 (1990) 87-90 / 91-95.

5204 *a) Mazzucco* Clementina, Satana e la morte nel Vangelo di Marco; – *b) Léon-Dufour* Xavier, Satana e il demoniaco nei vangeli: → 593, Diavolo 1 (1988/90) 155-179 / 143-154.

5205 **Miller** Dale & Patricia, The Gospel of Mark as midrash on earlier Jewish and New Testament literature: StBEC 21. Lewiston NY 1990, Mellen. x-394 p. $80. 0-88946-621-1 [TDig 38,73s; W. C. *Heiser*: father-daughter team].

5206 *Minette de Tillesse* Caetano, O segredo messiânico em Marcos: RBBras 7,1 (1990) 5-40 [< IZBG 36, p. 170].

5207 **Myers** Ched, Binding the strong man ... Mk 1988 → 4,4994. RDibTB 20 (1990) 42s (D. C. *Benjamin*); CritRR 3 (1990) 227-231 (W. M. *Swartley*); Pacifica 3 (1990) 242-7 (B. *Byrne*: Marxist, challenging); PerspRelSt 17 (1990) 189-192 (C. H. *Talbert*, also on HOORNAERT and L. BOFF); TS 51 (1990) 339-2 (Elizabeth S. *Malbon*).

5208 **Peabody** David B., Mark as composer [his favorite expressions; diss. Southern Methodist, D*Farmer* W.]: New Gospel Studies 1, 1987 → 3,4801 ... 5,4928: RJBL 109 (1990) 539-542 (P. *Sellew*).

5209 **Pieter** Johannes J., The disciples in the Gospel of Mark [Afrikaans]: diss. Pretoria 1990. – DissA 51 (1990s) 3111-A.

5210 **Räisänen** Heikki, The 'Messianic Secret' in Mark: StNW. E 1990, Clark. xvii-289 p. 0-567-09529-0.

5211 *Reid* Barbara E., Recent work on the Gospel of Mark [8 books]: NewTR 3,3 (1990) 98-103.

5212 **Riley** Harold, The making of Mark, an exploration 1989 → 5,4930; $25: RDowR 108 (1990) 225-9 (A. G. *Murray*); ETL 66 (1990) 419-3 (T. A. *Friedrichsen*).

5213 *Rodríguez* Leandro, El mesianismo secreto [CUENCA, sobre Luis de LEÓN; CILLERUELO L.]: EstAg 25 (1990) 371-8.

5214 **Roth** Wolfgang, Hebrew gospel ... Mk 1988 → 4,5007; 5,4932: RJBL 109 (1990) 538s (H. C. *Kee*); LingBib 62 (1989) 123s (W. *Schenk*).

5215 **Sariola** Heikki, Markus und das Gesetz, eine redaktionskritische Untersuchung [Diss. D*Veijola* T. Helsinki 1990. – RTLv 22, p. 895]: AnAc DissHumLit 56. Helsinki 1990, Acad. 277 p.

5216 *Schlarb* Robert, Die Suche nach dem Messiah; *zētéō* als terminus technicus der markinischen Messianologie: ZNW 81 (1990) 155-170.

5217 **Scholtissek** Klaus, Exousia; traditions- und redaktionsgeschichtliche Analysen zu einem Leitmotiv markinischer Christologie: kath. Diss. D*Kertelge* K. Münster 1989s. – TR 86 (1990) 618.

5218 **Stock** Augustine, The method and message of Mark 1989 → 5,4939: RBibTB 20 (1990) 132s (M. *McVann*); Interpretation 44 (1990) 425 . 428 (R. M. *Johnson*); TS 51 (1990) 132-4 (F. *Connolly-Weinert*).

5219 **Stock** Klemens, *a*) Gesù, la buona notizia; il messaggio di Marco [Jesus, die frohe Botschaft 1983 ➤ 64,4716][T]: Bibbia e Preghiera 6. R 1990, Apost. Pregh. 186 p. [AcPIB 9/7, 553]. – 88-7355-086-0. – *b*) La 'metánoia' in Marco: ➤ 325*b*, ParSpV 22 (1990) 101-125.
    Markus in Qumran? (O'CALLAGHAN J.) ➤ a73, *Aland* K.; *Rohrhirsch* F. ➤ a76.

5220 **Trakatellis** Demetrios, Authority and passion... Mk, [T]*Duvall* G. E., *Vulopas* H. Brookline MA 1987, Holy Cross Orthodox. xii-245 p. $24; pa. $16. – [R]JBL 109 (1990) 542-4 (J. S. *Siker*).

5221 [E]**Tuckett** C., The messianic secret: IssuesRT 1, 1983 ➤ 64,303; 2,3784*: [R]RivLtg 77 (1990) 219-221 (G. *Crocetti*, also on the next 3 'Issues').

5222 *Twelftree* G., Discipleship in Mark's Gospel: St. Mark's Review 141 (Canberra 1990) 5-11 [< NTAbs 35,162].

5223 **Via** Dan O., The ethics of Mark's Gospel 1985 ➤ 1,4808 ... 5,4946: [R]RExp 87 (1990) 640 (J. L. *Blevins*).

5224 *Vorster* W. S., Bilingualism and the Greek of the New Testament; Semitic interference in the Gospel of Mark: Neotestamentica 29 (1990) 215-228.

5225 **Waetjen** H. C., A reordering of power 1989 ➤ 5,4948: [R]Neotestamentica 29 (1990) 367s (P. J. J. *Botha*); TorJT 6 (1990) 364-7 (Wendy J. *Cotter*).

5226 **Weiss** Wolfgang, 'Eine neue Lehre in Vollmacht'; die Streit- und Schulgespräche des Markus-Evangeliums [*Albertz* M. 1919; Diss. Mainz]: BZNW 52, 1989 ➤ 5,4951; DM 136: [R]TLZ 115 (1990) 105-7 (P. *Pokorný*); TR 86 (1990) 371-3 (E. *Lohse*).

5226* **Zwick** Reinhold, Montage im Markusevangelium; Studien zur narrativen Organisation der ältesten Jesuserzählung: SBB 18. Stu 1989, KBW. xvi-652 p. DM 39 pa. [JBL 110,529-531, M. E. *Boring*: motto 'those who see films read narratives differently', BRECHT]. – [R]ArTGran 53 (1990) 319s (A. S. *Muñoz*).

F6.3 Evangelii Marci versiculi 1,1 ...

5227 *Boring* M. Eugene, Mark 1:1-15 and the beginning of the Gospel: ➤ 375, Semeia 52 (1990) 43-81.

5228 **Darù** Jean, Principio del Vangelo di Gesù Cristo secondo Marco: StBDeh 17. Bo 1990, Dehoniane. 140 p. 88-10-40718-0.

5229 *Delorme* J., 'Commencement de l'Évangile' et commencement de Marc: ➤ 180*, [F]TROMP N., Gelukkig c. 1990, 159-168; Eng. 259.

5230 **Oyen** G. van, De summaria in Marcus en de compositie van Mc 1,14-8,26: StNTAux 12, 1987 ➤ 3,4824 ... 5,4955: [R]GerefTTs 90 (1990) 186 (J. S. *Vos*).

5231 **Kuthirakkattel** Scaria, The beginning of Jesus' ministry according to Mark's Gospel (1,14-3,6), a redaction critical study [diss. 1987, Pont. Univ. Gregoriana, [D]*La Potterie* I. de ➤ 3,4820*]: AnBib 123. R 1990, Pont. Ist. Biblico. xxvi-300 p. Lit. 37.000. 88-7653-123-8.

5232 *a*) *Delorme* Jean, Text and context; 'the Gospel' according to Mark 1:14-18, [T]*Creech* James; – *b*) *Jennings* Theodore W.[J], [Mk] The martyrdom of the Son of Man: ➤ 24, [F]BOERS H., Text 1990, 273-287 / 229-243.

5233 *Schwarz* Günther, Kaì euthùs ekálesen autoús? (Markus 1,20a): BibNot 48 (1989) 19s.

5234 *Dillmann* Rainer, Die Bedeutung neuerer exegetischer Methoden für eine biblisch orientierte Pastoral aufgezeigt an Mk 1,39-45 – der Heilung eines Aussätzigen: TGL 80 (1990) 116-130.

5235 *Wojciechowski* Michał, ℗ The touching of the leper (Mk 1,40-45): RuBi 42 (1989) 362-8.

5236 **Kiilunen** Jermo, Die Vollmacht im Widerstreit ... Mk 2,1: diss. Helsinki ᴰ*Räisänen* H. 1985 ➤ 1,4822: ᴿSNTU A-15 (1990) 163-5 (A. *Fuchs*).

5237 *Schwarz* Günther, *Apestégasan tēn stegēn?* (Markus 2,4c): BibNot 54 (1990) nur 41.

5238 **Roure** Damià [➤ 5,4966, **Roure Muntada** Juan: diss. Pont. Ist. Biblico, ᴰ*Lentzen-Deis* F.], Jesús y la figura de David en Mc 2,23-26; trasfondo bíblico, intertestamentario y rabínico: AnBib 124. R 1990, Pont. Ist. Biblico. x-172 p. Lit. 33.000. 88-7653-124-6.

5239 **Orlando** Luigi, Marco 3,1-7a: diss. Angelicum, ᴰ*De Santis* L. R 1990. 187 p. (extr.). – RTLv 22, p. 594.

5240 *Dormeyer* D., Dialogue with the text (Mk 3:20f, 31-35); interactional Bible interpretation: Scriptura 33 (1990) 55-64 [< NTAbs 35,28].

5241 **Humphries** Michael L., [Mk 3,22s] The language of the Kingdom of God in the Beelzebul discourse: diss. Claremont 1990, ᴰ*Mack* Burton L. 394 p. 90-32579. – DissA 51 (1990s) 2048-A.

5242 **Dautzenberg** Gerhard, Mk 4,1-34 als Belehrung über das Reich Gottes; Beobachtungen zum Gleichniskapitel: BZ 34 (1990) 38-62.

5243 *Sellew* Philip, Oral and written sources in Mark 4.1-34: NTS 36 (1990) 234-267.

5244 *Herzog* W. R., [Mk 4,1-9 . 26-29 . 30-32] Biblical perspectives on 'Grow by caring': AmBapQ 8,3 (1989) 180-6 [< NTAbs 34,205].

5245 **Goan** Seán, To see or not to see ... Mark 4:10-12 revisited: MilltSt 25 (1990) 5-18.

5246 **Rauscher** Johann, [Mc 4.10-12] Vom Messiasgeheimnis zur Lehre der Kirche; die Entwicklung der sogenannten Parabeltheorie in der synoptischen Tradition (Mk 4,10-12 par Mt 13,10-17 par Lk 8,9-10: diss. Linz, ᴰ*Fuchs* [TR 86,511]. – ᴿETL 67 (1990) 385-390 (T. *Friedrichsen*).

5247 *Mateos* Juan, Mc 4,13.25; 8,31; 10,41 y 14,19.33 *ērxato* (Algunas notas II): FgNt 3 (1990) 159-166.

5248 *Fuchs* Albert, Die 'Seesturmperikope' Mk 4,35-41 parr im Wandel der urkirchlichen Verkündigung [< ᶠ*Stöger* A. 1989, 59-86]: SNTU A-15 (1990) 101-133.

5249 *Obeng* E. A., ⓖ *Tò thaûma* ... The miracle of the stilling of the storm and its implications for the Church in Africa: DeltVM 18,1 (1989) 43-52 [< NTAbs 34,310: formally magical meteorology, but with historical kernel since traditions rarely arise out of nothing].

5250 ᴱ**Detweiler** Robert, *Doty* William G., The daemonic imagination; biblical text [Mark 5,1-20] and secular story [ATWOOD Margaret, 'The sin eater' here in full; AAR colloquium]: AAR StRel 60. Atlanta 1990, Scholars. x-232 p. $25; sb./pa. $16. 1-55540-530-4; -21-2 [TDig 38,258]. 15 art.

5251 *Setti* Maurizio, Marco 5,1-20, esegesi e teologia: diss. Angelicum, ᴰ*Salguero* J. Roma 1990. – RTLv 22, p. 595.

5252 *LaHurd* Carol S., Reader response to ritual elements in Mark 5:1-20: BibTB 20 (1990) 120-160.

5253 *Fatum* L., [Mk 5,21-43] En kvindehistorie om tro og køn [a woman's story about faith and gender]: DanTTs 53 (1990) 278-299 [< NTAbs 35,163].

5254 **Selvidge** Maria J.,   Woman, cult, and miracle recital; a redactional critical investigation on Mark 5:24-34. Cranbury NJ 1990, Bucknell Univ.
159 p. $29.50. 0-8387-5143-1 [NTAbs 34,388].

5255 *Nestle* Dieter, 'Tochter, du hast dich getraut!' – zum Umgang mit
Evangelium nach Markus 5,25-34: EvErz 42 (Fra 1990) 396-401 [< ZIT
90,711].

5256 *LaVerdiere* E., [Mk 6...] 'Jesus among the Gentiles' / 'Do you still not
understand?' / 'Who do you say that I am?' etc.: Emmanuel 96 (1990)
338-345 / 382-389 / 454-463 ... [< NTAbs 35,28s].

5257 *Byrne* Brendan, [Mk 6,1-6] Failure; a New Testament reflection: Way
29 (1989) 117-126.

5258 *La Verdiere* E., [Mk 6,17-29] The death of John the Baptizer: Emmanuel 95 (NY 1989) 274-381.402 [< NTAbs 34,28].

5259 *La Potterie* Ignace de, [Mk 6,30-7,37 ...] The multiplication of the loaves
in the life of Jesus, ᵀ*Matthews* Edward G.: CommND 16 (1989) 499-516.

5260 *LaVerdiere* E., *a*) [Mk 6,31-44] The breaking of bread; – *b*) [Mk 6,45-56]
Resisting the mission to the nations: Emmanuel 95 (1989) 554-560. 577 /
96 (1990) 22-28 [< NTAbs 34,169].

5261 *LaVerdiere* Eugene, [Mk 7,1-23] Tradition, traditions, and the Word of
God: Emmanuel 96 (1990) 206-9. 212-6 [< NTAbs 34,310].

5262 *Skeat* T.C., A note on *pygmê* in Mark 7,3 [totally otiose]: JTS 41
(1990) 525-7.

5263 *Klamer* Willem, Het verhaal van een exorcisme; Marcus 7,24-31: TsT-
Nijm 30 (1990) 117-145; Eng. 145.

5264 *Gibson* Jeffrey, Jesus' refusal to produce a 'sign' (Mk 8.11-13): JStNT
38 (1990) 37-66.

5265 *Meye* Robert P., Mark 8:15 – a misunderstood warning: ⇒ 60,181,
ᶠOUDERSLUYS R., Saved by hope, ᴱ*Cook* J. 1978, 79-95.

5266 *LaVerdiere* E., [Mk 8,22-30 (31-33)], Jesus Christ, the Son of God:
Emmanuel 96 (1990) 606-9. 524-6 (574-9) [< NTAbs 35,163].

5266* **Niemand** Christoph, Studien zu den Minor Agreements der
synoptischen Verklärungsperikopen... Abweichungen des Mt & Lk von
Mk 9,2-10, ᴰ1988 ⇒ 5,4668: ᴿTPQ 138 (1990) 187-9 (F. *Fendler*).

5267 *Derrett* J.D. M., [Mk 9,5-7] Peter and the tabernacles: DowR 108
(1990) 37-48.

5268 *Viviano* Benedict T., Rabbouni and Mark 9:5 ['Lord' not 'teacher']:
RB 97 (1990) 207-218; franç. 207.

5269 *Mette* Norbert, Das Kind in der Mitte (Mk 9,36); eine Herausforderung
für die katholische Schule: Rel-Pädagog. Beiträge 25 (1990) 126-144
[< ZIT 90,360].

5270 *Deming* Will, Mark 9.42 - 10.12, Matthew 5.27-32, and B.Nid. 13b: a
first century discussion of male sexuality: NTS 36 (1990) 130-141.

5271 **Iersel** B. M. F., van Mark 9,43-48 in a martyrological perspective:
⇒ 5,17, ᶠBARTELINK G., Fructus 1989, 333-341.

5272 *Green* Barbara, [Mk 10,2] Jesus' teaching on divorce in the Gospel of
Mark: JStNT 38 (1990) 67-75.

   ᴱ**Pizzolato** L., [Mc 10,25] Per foramen acus 1986 ⇒ 4964.

5273 *May* David M., Leaving and receiving; a social-scientific exegesis of
Mark 10:29-31: PerspRelSt 17 (1990) 141-154.

5274 *Mattern* Liselotte, Welcher Dienst zählt? Bibelarbeit über Markus
10,35-45: Diakonie 17 (Stu 1990) 83-85 [< ZIT 90,423].

5275 *Làconi* Mauro, 'Ma tra voi non è così' (cf. Mc 10,43): Presbyteri 24
(1990) 655-666.

5276 *Sinclair* S. G., [Mk 10,46-52] The healing of Bartimaeus and the gaps in Mark's messianic secret: StLuke 33 (1990) 249-257 [< NTAbs 33,164].

5277 **Roemer** Carl E., Giving the vineyard to others; a form and redactional critical analysis of Mark 11 and 12: diss. Lutheran School of Theology, ᴰ*Rhoads* D. 543 p. 90-33111. – DissA 51 (1990s) 2054-A.

5278 **Stock** Klemens, L'attività di Gesù a Gerusalemme, Marco 11-12². R 1990s, Pont. Ist. Biblico. vii-136 p.

5279 *Fredriksen* Paula, [Mk 11,15-18] Jesus and the Temple, Mark and the war: ➤ 544, SBL seminars 1990, 293-310.

5280 **Dowd** Sharyn E., Prayer, power, and the problem of suffering... Mk 11,22-25: SBL diss. 105 (Emory 1986) 1988 ➤ 4,5059; 5,4997: ᴿCBQ 52 (1990) 153-5 (J. P. *Heil*: valuable); Interpretation 44 (1990) 312.314 (Joanna *Dewey*); PerspRelSt 17 (1990) 287s (C. C. *Black*); RelStR 16 (1990) 74 (L. *Cope*); TLZ 115 (1990) 891s (P. *Pokorný*).

5281 *Eck* E. van, *Aarde* A. G. van, A narratological analysis of Mark 12:1-12; the plot of the Gospel of Mark in a nutshell: HervTS 45 (1989) 778-800 [< NTAbs 35,30].

5282 *Milavec* Aaron, [Mk 12,1-12] The identity of 'the Son' and 'the others'; Mark's parable of the wicked husbandmen reconsidered: BibTB 20 (1990) 30-37.

5283 *Maillot* A., Le dénier à César, Marc 12.13-17: Tychique 82 (1989) 57-60.

5284 **Schwankl** Otto, Die Sadduzäerfrage (Mk 12,18-27) ᴰ1987 ➤ 3,4864; 4,5061: ᴿJBL 109 (1990) 144s (H. C. *Kee*); NedTTs 43 (1989) 335s (P. W. van der *Horst*).

5285 *Beasley-Murray* George, The vision on the mount; the eschatological discourse of Mark 13: ➤ 531, ExAud 6 (1990) 39-52.

5286 **Brandenburger** E., Markus 13 und die Apokalyptik: FRL 134, 1984: ➤ 65,4413 ... 2,3837: ᴿSvEx 55 (1990) 140-2 (L. *Hartman*).

F6.8   Passio secundum Marcum, 14,1 ... [➤ F5,3].

5287 **Best** Ernest, The temptation and the Passion; the Markan soteriology² [= ¹1975 + 65 p. pref.]. C 1990, Univ. lxxx-222 p. $49.50. 0-521-38360-9 [NTAbs 35,99].

5288 *Dowling* J., *a*) [Mk 14] Dining and discipleship by Mark: Emmanuel 95 (NY 1989) 364-9 [< NTAbs 34,29]. – *b*) Remote preparation for a meal by Mark [6,32-44; 8,1-10; 10,38s; 14,36]: Emmanuel 95 (NY 1989) 344s [< NTAbs 34,26]

Feldmeier Reinhard, Die Krise... Schlüssel der Markuspassion ᴰ1987 ➤ 5068.

5289 *Heil* John P., Mark 14,1-52; narrative structure and reader-response: Biblica 71 (1990) 305-331; franç. 332.

5290 *Barton* Stephen C., Mark as narrative; the story of the anointing woman (Mk 14:3-9): ExpTim 102 (1990s) 230-4.

5291 *Marín Heredia* Francisco, Un enigma en el arresto de Jesús (Mc 14,51-52): Carthaginensia 6 (1990) 269-281 [the courageous naked boy represents Jesus naked on the cross].

5292 *Meyer* Marvin W., [Mk 14,51s] The youth in the Secret Gospel of Mark: ➤ 326, Semeia 49 (1990) 129-153.

5293 *Petraglio* Renzo, La profezia di Gesù sul Tempio (Mc 14,58 e paralleli), tradizione a livello di stile profetico e narrativo: ➤ 700, Tradizione 1989/90, 151-184.

5294 *Bailey* Kenneth E. [Mk 15,30-39] The fall of Jerusalem and Mark's account of the Cross: ExpTim 102 (1990s) 102-5.

5295 **Schreiber** Johannes, Der Kreuzigungsbericht des Mk 15: BZNW 47, ᴰ1986 → 2,3852 ... 4,5074: ᴿBijdragen 51 (1990) 442 (J. *Lambrecht*).

Rossé Gérard, [Mk 15,34] The cry of Jesus on the cross [1982] 1987 → 5093.

5296 *Strijdom* J. M., *Aarde* A. G. van, Marcus 16,1-8 in die konteks van 'n konstruksie van die Markaanse gemeente: HervTS 46 (1990) 153-189 [< NTAbs 35,165: premising 12 theses about the time, place, and situation of the Markan community].

5297 *Combet-Galland* Corina, Qui roulera la peur? Finales d'évangile et figures du lecteur (à partir du chapitre 16 de l'évangile de Marc): ÉTRel 65 (1990) 171-189.

5298 *Vignolo* Roberto, Una finale reticente; interpretazione narrativa di Mc 16,8: RivB 38 (1990) 129-188; Eng. 188s.

XII. Opus Lucanum

F7.1   *Opus Lucanum* – **Luke-Acts.**

5299 *Au* Joseph, ⊜ The Exodus / Way motif in the Lucan writings: Colc-FuJen 81 (1989) 331-346.

5300 *a*) *Balch* David J., The genre of Luke-Acts; – *b*) *Marshall* I. Howard, Luke's view of Paul: SWJT 33,1 (1990s) 5-19 / 41-51.

5301 **Bock** Darrell L., Proclamation ... Lucan OT Christology 1987 → 3,4898 ... 5,5024: ᴿThemelios 15 (1989s) 21s (M. *Turner*).

5302 *a*) *Bock* Darrell L., The use of the Old Testament in Luke-Acts; Christology and mission; – *b*) *Carroll* John T., The use of Scripture in Acts; – *c*) *Plymale* Steven F., Luke's theology of prayer: → 544, SBL seminars 1990, 494-511 / 512-528 / 529-551.

5303 **Bovon** F., Luc le théologien² 1988 [¹1987] → 3,195 ... 5,5025: ᴿRBib-Arg 52 (1990) 61-63 (R. *Krüger*).

5304 **Brawley** R. L., Centering on God; method and message in Luke-Acts: Literary Currents in Biblical Interpretation. Louisville 1990, W-Knox. 256 p. $12 pa. 0-664-25133-1 [NTAbs 35,238].

5305 **Brawley** Robert L., Luke-Acts and the Jews 1987 → 3,4902 ... 5,5027: ᴿWestTJ 52 (1990) 156-8 (F. S. *Spencer*: favor for Pharisees overplayed).

5306 **Chance** J. Bradley, Jerusalem, the Temple, and the New Age in Luke-Acts [ᴰ1984] 1988 → 4,5087; 5,5020: ᴿCBQ 52 (1990) 149-151 (J. A. *Darr*: disappointing); CurrTMiss 17 (1990) 147; JAAR 58 (1990) 695-8 (N. *Elliott*); JBL 109 (1990) 350-2 (L. T. *Johnson*); PerspRelSt 17 (1990) 71-73 (M. L. *Soards* compares with MICHAELS J. 1 Pt 1988; TALBERT C. 1-2 Cor 1987); RelStR 16 (1990) 74 (L. *Cope*).

5307 *D'Angelo* Mary Rose, Women in Luke-Acts; a redactional view: JBL 109 (1990) 441-461.

5308 **Dauer** Anton, Beobachtungen zur literarischen Arbeitstechnik des Lukas: Athenäum Mg/BoBB 79. Fra 1990, Hain. 171 p. DM 54 [TR 87,75].

5309 **Decock** Paul B., Inculturation and 'communism' in Luke-Acts: Grace and Truth 2,2 (Hilton SAf 1989) 54-64 [< TContext 7/2, 17].

5310 **Ernst** J., Lukas, ein theologisches Portrait 1985 → 3,4907 (ital. → 4, 5089): ᴿSNTU-A 14 (1989) 276s (F. *Kogler*).

5311 **Esler** Philip E., Community and Gospel in Luke-Acts; the social and political motivations of Lucan theology: SNTS Mg 57, 1987 → 3,4908 ...

5,5033: ᴿBijdragen 51 (1990) 203s (B.J. *Koet*); CBQ 52 (1990) 744s (J.H. *Neyrey*: it reads like a dissertation, which Neyrey defines 'a series of discrete studies which do not interact'); EvQ 62 (1990) 365-8 (M.M.B. *Turner*); NedTTs 44 (1990) 163s (S.J. *Noorda*).

5312 **Fitzmyer** Joseph A., Luke the theologian; aspects of his teaching [Oxford D'Arcy lectures 1987] 1989 → 5,5034: ᴿExpTim 102 (1990s) 22 (N.O. *Richardson*: the essay 'Satan and demons' warns against letting a secondary theme dominate); JTS 41 (1990) 610 (I.H. *Marshall*); Month 251 (1990) 22s (P. *Edmonds*, also on STANTON G.); TLond 93 (1990) 245s (B.E. *Beck*); TS 51 (1990) 367s (C.H. *Talbert*); TTod 47 (1990s) 109 (Sharon H. *Ringe*).

5313 *Galizia* Ugo, *Pace* Giuseppe, Il più grande dei medici scrittori: PalCl 68 (1989) 619-626.

Garrett Susan R., The demise of the devil; magic and the demonic in Luke's writings 1989 → 2303*.

5314 *Gen* R.M., The phenomenon of miracles and divine infliction in Luke-Acts; their theological significance: Pneuma 11,1 (1989) 3-19 [< NTAbs 35,31: Lk 1,5-25; Acts 5,1-14; 9,1-21; 12,20-23; 13,4-12 all involve also a 'malignant' miracle equally sign of God's call].

5315 *Green* Joel B., 'The message of salvation' in Luke-Acts: ExAud 5 (1989) 21-34.

5316 *Kilgallen* John J., Social development and Lukan works: StMiss 39 (1990) 21-47.

5317 **Klinghardt** Matthias, Gesetz und Volk Gottes; das lukanische Verständnis des Gesetzes nach Herkunft, Funktion und seinem Ort in der Geschichte des Urchristentums [diss. Heid 1987, ᴰ*Berger* K.]: WUNT 2/32, 1988 → 4,5098; 5,5042: ᴿBZ 34 (1990) 140-3 (K. *Müller*); CBQ 52 (1990) 158s (C.H. *Talbert*).

5318 **Koet** B.J., Five studies... Lk/A ᴰ1989 → 5,5043; Fb 1000: ᴿCollatVL 20 (1990) 450s (H. *Hoet*); ExpTim 102 (1990s) 118 (A. *Hanson*).

5319 *Kurz* William S., Narrative models for imitation in Luke Acts: → 122, ᶠMALHERBE A., Greeks 1990, 171-189.

5320 *Larsson* Edvin, Lukas och pentateuken: → 21, Mem. BJØRNDALEN A., TsTKi 60,4 (1989) 293-9; Eng. 299.

5321 **Lindeboom** G.A., Dokter Lukas. Amst 1988. 123 p. ƒ19.50. – ᴿKerkT 41 (1990) 164 (G. de *Ru*: ontspanningslectuur).

5322 *Llamas* Román, La oración desde san Lucas: REspir 49 (1990) 27-61.

5323 **Marshall** I. Howard, a) Luke, historian and theologian²ʳᵉᵛ [= 1970 + 13 p. postscript-updating]. GR 1989, Zondervan. 252 p. $14. 0-310-28761-8 [NTAbs 34,248]. – b) The present state of Lucan studies: → 370, Gospels 1990, 102-114.

5324 **Menzies** Robert P., The development of early Christian pneumatology with special reference to Luke-Acts: diss. Aberdeen 1989. 390 p. BRDX-94246. – DissA 52,2956-A; RTLv 22, p. 594.

5325 *Moessner* David P., 'The Christ must suffer', the Church must suffer; rethinking the theology of the Cross in Luke-Acts: → 544, SBL seminars 1990, 165-195.

5326 ᴱ**Morris** Thomas V., Philosophy and Christian faith [*Adams* Marilyn, Separation and reversal in Luke-Acts (compared with apocalyptic); *Kretzmann* Norman, Romans 7 especially in AQUINAS]. ND 1988, Univ. 300 p. 0-268-01570-8. – ᴿAsbTJ 45,2 (1990) 94s (J.L. *Walls*).

5327 *O'Toole* Robert F., The [Luke-Acts] parallels between Jesus and Moses: BibTB 20 (1990) 22-29.

5328 *a) Parrott* Douglas M., [Luke-Acts] First Jesus is present, then the Spirit; an early Christian dogma and its effects; – *b) Pokorný* Petr, Strategies of social formation in the Gospel of Luke: ➤ 152, [F]ROBINSON J. M., Gnosticism 1 (1990) 119-133 / 106-118.

5329 *Plooy* G. P. V. du, The author in Luke-Acts: Scriptura 12 (1990) 102-107 [< IZBG 36, p. 198].

5330 *Powell* M. A., Are the sands still shifting? An update on Lukan scholarship: Trinity Seminary Review 11,1 (Columbus 1989) 15-22 [< NTAbs 34,170].

5331 *a) Richard* Earl, Luke, author and thinker; – *b) Soards* Marion L., The historical and cultural setting of Luke-Acts; – *c) Sweetland* Dennis M., Luke the Christian/Following Jesus; discipleship in Luke-Acts; – *d) Mowery* Robert L., God the Father in Luke-Acts: ➤ 551*, New views 1990, 15-32 (notes 163-5) / 33-47 (165-8) / 48-63.109-123 (168-171. 178-180) / 124-132 (180s).

5332 **Sanders** Jack T., The Jews in Luke-Acts 1987 ➤ 3,4930... 5,5050: [R]Bijdragen 51 (1990) 327s (B. J. *Koet*, also on TANNEHILL); NedTTs 43 (1989) 348s (P. W. van der *Horst*).

5333 **Seim** Turid K., Det doble budskap; avhengighet og avstand mellom kvinner og menn i Lukas-Acta: first woman's theology doctorate in Norway 1990. – NorTTs 91 (1990) 65; 248; assessment, *Larsson* Edvin, 66-83.

5334 **Sterling** Gregory E., Historiography and self-definition; JOSEPHOS, Luke-Acts and apologetic historiography: diss. Graduate Theological Union. Berkeley 1989. 697 p. 91-00374. – DissA 51 (1990s) 2487-A.

5335 **Sweetland** Dennis M., Our journey with Jesus; discipleship according to Luke-Acts: Good News 23. Collegeville MN 1990, Liturgical. 261 p. $15. 0-8146-5688-9.

Tannehill Robert C., The narrative unity of Luke-Acts 2, 1990 ➤ 5499.

5336 **Thornton** Hans-Jürgen, Der Zeuge Lukas; Studien zum Werk eines Paulusbegleiters: Ev. Diss. [D]*Hengel.* Tübingen 1989s. TLZ 116,774; TR 86 (1990) 519; RTLv 22,596 'Thronton Claus-Jürgen'.

5337 [E]**Tyson** J. B., Luke-Acts and the Jewish people 1988 ➤ 4,5112: [R]FgNt 3,5 (1990) 82s (J. *Mateos*); Neotestamentica 25 (1991) 433-5 (J. A. *Draper*); Vidyajyoti 54 (1990) 103s (R. J. *Raja*).

5338 *Vassiliadis* Petros, The legacy of St. Luke for the Church's mission: DeltioVM 19,2 (1990) 5-9.

5339 *Walaskay* Paul W., 'In our own language'; working with the NRSV of Luke-Acts: RelEdn 85 (Ch 1990) 222-8 [< ZIT 90,647].

F7.3   **Evangelium Lucae** – *Textus, commentarii.*

5340 **Bovon** François, Das Evangelium nach Lukas I (-9,50): EkK 3/1, 1989 ➤ 5,5057: [R]BZ 34 (1990) 278-281 (A. *Weiser*); SNTU-A 14 (1989) 248-250 (A. *Fuchs*); TLZ 115 (1990) 591-3 (J. *Ernst*).

5341 **Craddock** Fred B., Luke: Interpretation Comm. Louisville 1990, Knox. xi-298 p. $22 [CBQ 53,356].

5342 **Danker** Frederick W., Jesus and the New Age; a commentary on St. Luke's gospel[2rev] 1988 ➤ 5,5059: [R]CritRR 33 (1990) 197-9 (M. C. *Parsons*); Interpretation 44 (1990) 88s (J. A. *Darr*).

5343 [E]**Elliott** J. K., Luke: NT in Greek, Ox 1984-7 ➤ 3,4941... 5,5060: [R]BS 147 (1990) 121-3 (D. B. *Wallace*).

5344 **Evans** C. F., Saint Luke: TPI NT comm. L/Ph (Wynnewood) 1990, SCM/Trinity. xxi-933 p. £35; pa. £19.50. 0-334-00951-0; -0-2 [NTAbs

34,383]. – RExpTim 101 (1989s) 374 (C. S. *Rodd*); SWJT 33,3 (1990s) 43s (E. E. *Ellis*); TLond 93 (1990) 316s (L. *Houlden*).

5345 **Evans** Craig A., Luke: New International [Version] Biblical Commentary 3. Peabody MA 1990, Hendrickson. xvii-397 p. [NTAbs 35,101].

5346 **Gooding** David, According to Luke; a new exposition of the Third Gospel 1987 → 5,5065; 0-8028-0316-4: RKerkT 40 (1989) 345s (P. W. van der *Horst*); Mid-Stream 29 (1990) 100s (R. W. *Graham*: not exegetical).

5347 **Goulder** Michael D., Luke, a new paradigm I-II, 1989 → 5,5066: RCurrTMiss 17 (1990) 230s (F. W. *Danker*); ScotJT 43 (1990) 269-272 (J. *Nolland*); TLond 93 (1990) 67s (J. *Fenton*).

5347* **Kremer** J. Lukasev.: NEchter 3. Wü 1988, Echter. 264 p. DM 46. 3-429-01178-7. – RSNTU-A 14 (1989) 250s (M. *Hasitschka*).

5348 **Masini** Mario, Luca, il vangelo del discepolo: LoB 2.3, 1988 → 4,5125; 5,5068: RGregorianum 71 (1990) 587s (E. *Farahian*).

5349 **Meynet** Roland, L'évangile selon saint Luc, analyse rhétorique I-II, 1989 → 4,5126; 5,5069: REglT 20 (1989) 480-2 (W. *Vogels*); FoiTemps 19 (1989) 390s (C. *Focant*); MaisD 182 (1990) 146s (J. *Auneau*).

5350 **Morris** Leon, Luke, an introduction and commentary[2rev]: Tyndale NT comm. Leicester 1989, Inter-Varsity. 382 p.

5351 **Nolland** John, Luke 1-9:20: Word Comm. 35a, 1989 → 5,5071: RAsbTJ 45,2 (1990) 86-88 (J. R. *Dongell*: not up to FITZMYER); CurrTMiss 17 (1990) 302s (Sarah S. *Henrich*).

5352 **Tiede** David L., Luke: Augsburg Comm. 1988 → 4,5130; 5,5076: RBibTB 20 (1990) 133 (J. F. *O'Grady*); CBQ 52 (1990) 575-7 (Judette M. *Kolasny* praises; notes 'what went wrong in Nazareth?'); CriswT 4 (1989s) 392s (T. D. *Lea*); Interpretation 44 (1990) 92s (M. A. *Powell*).

5352* **Vesco** Jean-Luc, Jérusalem et son prophète... Luc 1988 → 4,5131; 5,5077: RJBL 109 (1990) 349s (F. A. *Niedner*).

5353 **Wiefel** [not as → 4,5133 & ind.] Wolfgang, Das Evangelium nach Lukas[2rev] (10 Auflagen seit 1961): THK 3. B 1988, Ev.-V. xviii-418 p. DM 27. 3-374-00040-1. – RTLZ 115 (1990) 739-741 (A. *Strobel*).

5354 **Wojcik** Jan, The road to Emmaus; reading Luke's gospel [as 'narrative gnosticism... a silent arrangement of scenes intended to provoke the reader into personal insights']. West Lafayette IN 1989, Purdue Univ. xi-168 p. $21.50. 1-55753-000-9 [TDig 37,391].

F7.4 *Lucae themata* – **Luke's Gospel, topics.**

5355 **Aletti** Jean-Noël, L'art de raconter Jésus-Christ; l'écriture narrative de l'évangile de Luc: Parole de Dieu, 1989 → 5,5080: RÉTRel 65 (1990) 626 (Danielle *Ellul*: parfois décevant); Études 372 (1990) 137 (R. *Marlé*); MondeB 64 (1990) 72 (M. *Quesnel*); NRT 112 (1990) 906 (X. *Jacques*); SémBib 60 (1990) 33-41 (L. *Panier*).

5356 **Beck** Brian E., Christian character in the Gospel of Luke 1989 → 5, 5082: RTLond 93 (1990) 485s (R. A. *Burridge*).

5357 *Bosch* D. J., Mission in Jesus' way; a perspective from Luke's Gospel: Missionalia 17,1 (Pretoria 1989) 3-21 [< NTAbs 34,31].

5358 *Buckley* F. J., Healing and reconciliation in the Gospel according to Luke: Emmanuel 96 (1990) 74-80 [< NTAbs 34,312].

5359 **Burigana** R. [Lc 8,1-3], *Fiorini* R. [Lc 22s], *Scarpat* S. [Lc 24,1-11], Dalla Galilea a Gerusalemme; l'itinerario delle donne nel Vangelo di Luca:

Esperienze e Analisi 6. Vicenza 1988, LIEF. 97p. Lit. 13.000 pa. [NTAbs 34,381].

5360 *D'Sa* Thomas, La salvación de los ricos según el evangelio de Lucas [< Vidyajyoti 52 (1988) 170-180], ᵀᴱ*Aute* Germán: SelT 29 (1990) 13-16.

5361 *Farmer* W.R., Luke's use of Matthew; a literary inquiry: AfrJBSt 2,1 (Ibadan 1987) 7-24 [< NTAbs 34,170].

5362 **Fischer** Bonifatius, Varianten zu Lukas: Die lateinischen Evangelien bis zum 10. Jht., / VLat, Reste der altlateinischen Bibel 17. FrB 1990, Herder. 48*-580 p. 3-451-21931-X [NRT 113,429, X. *Jacques*].

5363 *Fitzmyer* Joseph A., Luke's portrait of Jesus; the bearer of God's Spirit: Church 6,1 (NY 1990) 24-28 [< NTAbs 34,312].

5364 **Gueuret** Agnès La mise en discours... Lc: Thèses, ᴰ1987 ➤ 3,4967; 4,5139: ᴿÉglT 20 (1989) 483s (W. *Vogels*); RTLv 21 (1990) 93s (A. *Fossion*).

5365 **Iersel** Bas van, *al.*, Parabelverhalen in Lucas; van semiotiek naar pragmatiek: TFT-St 8, 1987 ➤ 3,4968 [! 4,5139*]; 90-361-9911-5. – ᴿBijdragen 51 (1990) 442s (J. *Lambrecht*).

5366 *Kingsbury* Jack D., Observations on 'the Son of Man' in the Gospel according to Luke: ➤ 41, ᶠDANKER F., CurrTMiss 17 (1990) 283-290.

5367 **Martini** Carlo M., Ministers of the Gospel; meditations on St. Luke's Gospel [L'evangelizzatore in S. Luca c.1980], ᵀ*Leslie* S. NY 1989, Crossroad. 104 p. $7. 0-8245-0959-5 [NTAbs 34,248].

5368 **Meynet** Roland, [➤ 5349] Avez-vous lu saint Luc? Guide pour la rencontre: Lire la Bible 88. P 1990, Cerf. 284 p. F 120. 2-204-04115-7.

5368* **Morris** Leon, Luke, an introduction and commentary²ʳᵉᵛ [¹1980]: Tyndale NT comm. Leicester/GR 1989, Inter-Varsity/Eerdmans. 382 p. 0-89111-634-5 / GR 0-8028-1423-0.

5369 **Moxnes** Halvor, The economy of the Kingdom; social conflict and economic relations in Luke's Gospel: OvBT, 1988 ➤ 4,5141* ['1989']; 5,5097: ᴿBibTB 20 (1990) 172 (D.E. *Oakman*); JBL 109 (1990) 725s (J.T. *Carroll*); Horizons 17 (1990) 150 (J.S. *Siker*); TLond 93 (1990) 160-2 (P.F. *Esler*); TorJT 6 (1990) 123-5 (J.S. *Kloppenborg*); TS 51 (1990) 172s (D. *Hamm*).

5370 **Nebe** G., Prophetische Züge im Bilde Jesu bei Lukas: BW 127, ᴰ1989 ➤ 5,5098: ᴿCommSev 23 (1990) 101s (M. de *Burgos*).

5371 ᴱ**Neirynck** Frans, L'Évangile de Luc²ʳᵉᵛ [¹1968/73]: BiblETL 32, 1989 ➤ 5,5099: ᴿETL 66 (1990) 413s (C.M. *Tuckett*: enormous amount of new material added p. 331-565) [TPQ 139,321, A. *Fuchs* notiert 35 Druckfehler].

5372 **Paglia** V., Colloqui su Gesù; letture dal Vangelo secondo Luca [67 brevi riflessioni]: Supersaggi 15. Mi 1989, Rizzoli. viii-269 p. Lit. 18.000. 88-17-11515-0 [NTAbs 35,245: the author is *parroco* of Santa Maria in Trastevere].

5373 **Petzke** Gerd, Das Sondergut [40%] des Evangeliums nach Lukas: Z Werkkomm. Z 1990, Theol.-V. 257 p. Fs 42. 3-290-10090-1 [NTAbs 35,245].

5374 **Pourciau** Chuck A., The use of explicit commentary in the Gospels of Luke and John: diss. Baptist Theol. Sem., ᴰ*Simmons* B. New Orleans 1990. 156 p. 90-26805. – DissA 51 (1990s) 1649-A.

5375 *Powell* Mark A., The religious leaders in Luke; a literary-critical study: JBL 109 (1990) 93-110.

5376 **Rius-Camps** Josep, L'èxode de l'home lliure; catequesi de Reixac sobre l'Evangeli de Lluc: Eines 3. Barc 1989, Claret. 198 p. 84-7263-627-5.

5377 *Schneider* Gerhard, Neuere Literatur zum dritten Evangelium (1987-1989) [SEGBROECK F. van, bibliog.; RADL W., WIEFEL W., BOVON F., KRAMER J.... comm.; KLEIN H., SOARDS M., NEBE G., ALETTI J.-N.]: TR 86 (1990) 353-360.

5378 **Segbroeck** Frans Van, The Gospel of Luke, a cumulative bibliography 1973-1988: BiblETL 88, 1989 ➤ 5,5102: ᴿETL 66 (1990) 414 (F. *Neirynck*: no book-reviews, unlike Van BELLE's Jn; but gives renvois to NTAbs); NT 32 (1990) 281s (J. K. *Elliott*); RThom 90 (1990) 348 (H. *Ponsot*).

5379 *a) Steyn* G. J., Intertextual similarities between Septuagint pre[-]texts and Luke's Gospel; – *b) Villiers* P. G. R. de, The medium is the message; Luke and the language of the NT against a Graeco-Roman background: Neotestamentica 24 (1990) 229-246 / 247-256.

5380 *Steyn* G. J., Die manifestering van Septuaginta-invloed in die Sondergut-Lukas: HervTS 45 (1989) 854-873 [< NTAbs 35,31].

F7.5   *Infantia, cantica* – **Magnificat, Benedictus: Luc. 1-3.**

Feuillet A., Le Sauveur messianique et sa mère dans le récit de l'enfance de Saint Luc: Coll. Teol. 4, 1990 ➤ 4709.

5382 **Panier** Louis, Une Écriture à lire; l'Évangile de l'enfance selon saint Luc; la cause des humains dans la naissance du Fils de Dieu; approche sémiotique et lecture théologique: diss. Lyon 1990, ᴰ*Duquoc* C. 542 p. – RTLv 22, p. 618; SémB 59 (1990) 30-43.

5383 *Tyson* Joseph B., The birth narratives and the beginning of Luke's Gospel: ➤ 375, Semeia 52 (1990) 103-120.

5384 *Merritt* H. Wayne, The angel's announcement; a structuralist study: ➤ 24, ᶠBOERS H., 1990, 97-108.

5385 *Schwarz* Günther, *Ex ephēmerías Abia*?: BibNot 53 (1990) 30s.

5386 *Kozar* Joseph V., The function of the character of Elizabeth as the omniscient narrator's reliable vehicle in the first chapter of the Gospel of Luke: ProcGLM 10 (1990) 214-235.

5387 ᴱ**Barkhuizen** J. H., [NT] Hymni christiani: HervTSt supp 1. Pretoria 1989, Herv. Kerk. xii-198 p. 0-620-14608-7 [NTAbs 34,396].

5388 **Bianchi** Enzo, Magnificat Lc 1.39-56; Benedictus Lc 1.67-80; Nunc dimittis Lc 2.22-38: Commento esegetico-spirituale. Magnano VC 1989 Qiqajon. 140 p.

5389 *Burger* C., LUTHERs Predigten über das Magnifikat (Lk 1,46-55): ➤ 511, Théorie/pratique 1988/90, 273-286.

5390 *Carmignac* Jean, Théologie du Magnificat: FolOr 27 (1990) 13-24.

5391 *Delorme* J., Le monde, la logique et le sens du Magnificat: SémBib 53 (1989) 1-17.

5392 **Kaut** Thomas, Befreier und befreites Volk; traditions- und redaktionsgeschichtliche Untersuchung zu Magnifikat und Benediktus im Kontext der vorlukanischen Theologie [Diss. Bonn 1988, ᴰ*Merklein* H., *Lohfink* N.]: BoBB 75. Fra 1990, Hain/Athenäum Mg. 350 p. DM 86 [TR 87,75]. 3-445-09133-1. – ᴿSNTU A-15 (1990) 166s (A. *Fuchs*).

Lohfink Norbert, Lobgesänge der Armen; Studien zum Magnifikat ... 1990 ➤ 3301.

5395 **Zeilinger** Franz, Zum Lobpreis seiner Herrlichkeit; exegetische Erschliessung der neutestamentlichen Cantica im Stundenbuch. W 1989, Herder. 256 p. DM 36,80 pa. – ᴿTPhil 65 (1990) 263s (J. *Beutler*); TR 86 (1990) 293-5 (O. B. *Knoch*).

5396 *Betori* G., Zaccaria e Gesù; dall'antica alla nuova benedizione nell'opera lucana: → 325*a*: ParSpV 21 (1990) 173-189.
5397 *Brock* S. P., The lost Old Syriac at Luke 1,35 and the earliest Syriac terms for the Incarnation: → 549, Gospel traditions 1988/90, 117-131.
5398 *Trudinger* L. Paul, [Lk 2,7] 'No room in the inn': ExpTim 102 (1990s) 172s.
5399 *Romaniuk* Kazimierz, ℗ 'A na ziemi pokój ludziom jego upodobania' (Łk 2,14): RuBi 42 (1989) 81-85.
5400 *Reicke* Bo, Jesus, Simeon, and Anna (Luke 2:21-40): → 60,181, ᶠOUDERSLUYS R., Saved by hope, ᴱCook J. 1978, 96-108.
5401 *Robert* René, Comment comprendre 'leur purification' en Luc II,22?: RThom 90 (1990) 449-455.
5402 *Soards* Marion L., Luke 2:22-40. expository: Interpretation 44 (1990) 400-405.
5403 *Buth* Randall, [Lk 2,34s] What kind of blessing is that?: Jerusalem Perspective 3/3 (1990) 7-10.
5404 *Gryglewicz* Feliks, [Lk 2,41-52] ℗ Jésus à douze ans: → 64, ᶠGRZYBEK S. 1990, 64-79.
5405 *Scheffler* E. H., The social ethics of the Lucan Baptist (Luke 3:10-14): Neotestamentica 24,1 (1990) 21-36.

F7.6   **Evangelium Lucae 4,1 ...**

5406 *d'Ornellas* Pierre, 'Jésus rempli de l'Esprit Saint' Lc 4,1: → 542, Év. Venasque 1989/90, 179-208.
5407 *Davidson* J. A., [Lk 4,14-21] The primacy of worship [as well as other prayer in Jesus' life]: ExpTim 101 (1989s) 44s.
5408 *Kolasny* Judette, An example of rhetorical criticism, Luke 4,16-30: → 551*, New views 1990, 67-77.171s.
   Monshouwer Dirk, The reading of the Bible [... Lk 4] in the first century [C.E.] 1990 → 142.
5409 **Schreck** Christopher, Luke 4,16-30, the Nazareth pericope in modern exegesis; a history of interpretation: diss. ᴰ*Neirynck* F. Leuven 1990. 490 p. – RTLv 22, p. 595.
5410 **Shin Kyo-Seon** Gabriel, *a*) Die Ausrufung des endgültigen Jubeljahres durch Jesus in Nazareth; eine historisch-kritische Studie zu Lk 4,16-30 [Diss. Luzern 1989, ᴰ*Kirchschläger* W. → 5,5135]: EurHS 23/378. Bern 1989, Lang. viii-391 p. Fs 69. 3-261-04137-4 [NTAbs 34,388]. – *b*) ◉ A comparative study of Luke 4:18-19 ['messiah'] and the OT and the Jewish tradition; Sinhak Jonmang 88 (Kwangju 1990) 13-23 [< TContext 8,69].
5411 **Noorda** Sijbolt J., [Lc 4,16-30] Historia vitae magistra 1989 → 5,5136; 90-6256-790-8: ᴿTsTNijm 30 (1990) 308 (P. *Farla*).
5412 *Schwarz* Günther, [Lk 4,25-27] Versuch einer Wiederherstellung des geistigen Eigentums Jesu: BibNot 53 (1990) 32-37.
5413 *Meynet* Roland, [Lc 5,12-14; 7,18-28] Pierre et le lépreux/ Jean-Baptiste et la prostituée: VieChr 346 (oct. 1990) 4-8; 347 (nov.) 23-28.
5414 *Safrai* Shmiel [Lk 6,1s] Sabbath breakers?: Jerusalem Perspective 3,4 (1990) 3-5 [< NTAbs 35,167: 'Unfamiliar with halakic details, Luke added plucking to rubbing']; Jesus never violated written or oral torahs, but did his disciples?
5415 *a*) *Frankfurter* David T. M., [Lk 7,22 ...] The origin of the miracle-list tradition and its medium of circulation; – *b*) *Hills* Julian V., Tradition,

redaction, and intertextuality; miracle lists in apocryphal acts as a test
case: ➤ 544, SBL seminars 1990, 344-374 / 375-390.

5416 **Thibeaux** Evelyn R., The narrative rhetoric of Luke 7:36-50; a study
of context, text, and interpretation: diss. Graduate Theological Union,
D*Donahue* J. R. Berkeley 1990. 541 p. 91-00363. – DissA 51 (1990s)
2411s-A; RelStR 17,194.

5417 *Geerard* Maurice, [Lc 7,36 *al.* – les trois réunies en Occident par GRÉ-
GOIRE] Marie-Madeleine, denonciatrice de Pilate [Ev. Nicodemi / Acta
Pilati]: ➤ 25*, FBOGAERT/VAN LOOY 1989s, 139-148.

5418 *Hofius* Otfried, Fusswaschung als Erweis der Liebe; sprachliche und
sachliche Anmerkungen zu Lk 7,44b: ZNW 81 (1990) 171-7.

5419 *Garrett* Susan R., Exodus from bondage; Luke 9:31 and Acts 12:1-24:
CBQ 52 (1990) 656-680.

5420 *Ravens* D. A. S., Luke 9.7-62 and the prophetic role of Jesus: NTS 36
(1990) 119-129.

F7.7   *Iter hierosolymitanum* – *Lc 9,51* ... – **Jerusalem journey.**

5421 **Moessner** D. P., Lord of the banquet ... Lukan travel narrative 1989
➤ 5,5153: RFgNt 3,5 (1990) 81s (J. *Mateos*); HorBT 12,1 (1990) 99-101
(Carol S. *LaHurd*); RExp 87 (1990) 492 (J. E. *Jones*); TS 51 (1990) 515-7
(D. *Hamm*); TTod 47 (1990s) 208s (J. M. *Hamilton*).

5422 **Schnackenburg** Rudolf, Der Jesusweg; Meditationen zum lukanischen
'Reisebericht': StuTb 4. Stu 1990, KBW. 96 p. 4-460-11004-X.

5423 *LaVerdiere* E., [Lk 9,51-55] Calling down fire from Heaven: Emmanuel
95 (NY 1989) 322-9 [NTAbs 34,32].

5424 **Uro** Risto, [Lk 10,3] Sheep among the wolves; a study of the mission
instructions of Q: AcFenn 47, 1987 ➤ 3,4207 ... 5,5156*: RSNTU-A 14
(1989) 241-4 (A. *Fuchs*); TR 86 (1990) 373s (R. *Pesch*).

5425 **Légasse** Simon, 'Et qui est mon prochain?' Étude sur l'objet de l'aga-
pé dans le NT: LDiv 136, 1989 ➤ 5,5160: RÉTRel 65 (1990) 274s (J.-D.
Causse); ScEsp 42 (1990) 357s (G. *Novotny*).

5426 **Mazamisa** I. W., Beatific comradeship; an exegetical hermeneutical
study on Lk 10:25-37 [diss. Kampen Calvijns-Acad.]. Kampen 1987, Kok.
212 p. ƒ42,50. 90-242-3192-2. – RNedTTs 44 (1990) 259 (S. *Noorda*).

5427 *Van Elderen* Bastiaan, [Lk 10,25-37] Another look at the parable of the
Good Samaritan: ➤ 60,181, FOUDERSLUYS R., Saved by hope, ECook J.
1978, 109-119.

5428 *Meynet* Roland, [Lc 10] Le prêtre et l'hérétique: VieChr 348 (déc. 1990)
25-30.

5429 *Linss* William C., [Lk 10,30-37; 12,16-20; 16,19-31; 18,9-34; JÜLICHER A.
1910] Example stories?: ➤ 41, FDANKER F., CurrTMiss 17 (1990)
447-453 [yes, against SCOTT B., CROSSAN J.D.].

5430 *Amjad-Ali* Christine M., [Lk 10,38-42] Martha and Mary: Al-Mushir
32 (Rawalpindi 1990) 59-67 [< TContext 8/2, 68].

5431 *Venetz* Hermann-J., [Lk 10,38-42] Die Suche nach dem 'einen Notwendigen': Orientierung 54 (1990) 185-9.

5432 *Schutter* William L., Luke 12:11-2 (sic) / 21:12-5 (sic) [in Contents 11-12
/ 12-15] and the composition of Luke-Acts: ProcGLM 10 (1990) 236-250.

5433 **Jolliffe** Ronald L., The woes on the Pharisees; a critical text and
commentary of Q [Lk] 11:46,53, 42,39-40, 44,47-48: diss. D*Robinson* J. M.
Claremont 1990. 203 p. 90-16085. – DissA 51 (1990s) 188-A; RTLv
22,591 '1989'.

5434 *Kollmann* Bernd, Lk 12,35-38 – ein Gleichnis der Logienquelle: ZNW 81 (1990) 254-261.

5435 **Visonà** Giuseppe, Citazioni patristiche e critica testuale neotestamentaria; il caso di Lc 12,49 [ignem super terram]: AnBib 125. R 1990, Pont. Ist. Biblico. vii-79 p. Lit. 18.500. 88-7653-125-4.

5436 *Schoenborn* Ulrich, El jardinero audaz; aspectos semánticos en Lucas 13,6-9: RBibArg 52,38 (1990) 65-84.

5437 *Wulf* Friedrich †, Die Heilung der gekrümmten Frau in Lk 13,10-17: GeistL 63 (1990) 312s.

5438 *Sandnes* Karl Olav, Jesus som profet [Lk 13,34s; 19,41-44]: TsTKi 60 (1989) 95-109; Eng. 109.

5439 *Schlosser* Jacques [Lc 13,35 par.] La parole de Jésus sur la fin du temple: NTS 36 (1990) 398-414.

5440 *Ramsey* George W., Plots, gaps, repetitions, and ambiguity in Luke 15: PerspRelSt 17 (1990) 33-42.

5441 **Welzen** H., Lucas evangelist van gemeenschap; een onderzoek naar de pragmatische effecten in Lc 15,1-17,30: diss. Nijmegen 1986. – ᴿNeotestamentica 24 (1990) 186s (W. S. *Vorster*).

5442 *Panimolle* Salvatore A., 'Mi alzerò e andrò da mio padre!'; il ritorno del figlio peccatore, Lc 15,11-32: ➤ 325*b*, ParSpV 22 (1990) 141-172.

5443 **Poensgen** H., Die Befreiung einer verlorenen Beziehung; eine biblisch-homiletische Untersuchung zu Lk 15,11-32 unter besonderer Berücksichtigung familientherapeutischer Erkenntnisse: EurHS 23/330. Fra 1989, Lang. ii-432 p. 3-8204-1259-X [NTAbs 34,251].

5444 *Vogler* Werner, Die Parabel von der grenzlosen Güte eines Vaters (Lk 15,11-32); Auslegungsmuster – Auslegung – Katechetischer Umgang: CLehre 43 (1990) 324-333.

5445 *a) Plessis* I. J. du, Philanthropy or sarcasm? – another look at the parable of the dishonest manager (Luke 16:1-13): Neotestamentica 24,1 (1990) 1-20; – *b) Porter* Stanley E., The parable of the unjust steward (Luke 16.1-13); irony is the key: ➤ 166, ᶠSheffield 1990, 127-153; – *c) Mann* C. S., [Lk 16,1-9] Unjust steward or prudent manager?: ExpTim 102 (1990s) 234s; – *d) Simonetti* Manlio, Un'antica interpretazione di Luca 16.1-8 [si riferisce a Paolo non universalmente accetto, secondo Girolamo]: ➤ 135, ᶠORBE A., Compostellanum 34 (1989) 41-49.

5446 *Flusser* David, [Lk 16,8] Jesus and the Essenes: Jerusalem Perspective, a bimonthly report on research into the words of Jesus 3/3 (1990) 3-5.13; 3/4 (1990) 6-8.

5446* *Pauly* D., [Lk 16,13] God or mammon; the reinstatement of the economy: ➤ 330, Einwürfe 7 (1990)...

5447 *a) Amjad-Ali* Charles M., [Lk 16,19-31] No name for the rich; the parable of Lazarus: Al-Mushir 32 (Rawalpindi 1990) 22-27 [17-29 in Urdu on Lk 10; < TContext 8/1,72]; – *b) O'Gorman* Richard, [Lk 16,19-31] L'histoire du mauvais riche homme; the text of the Old French Dives and Lazarus according to the Paris and Cambridge manuscripts: Manuscripta 34 (1990) 91-113; – *c) Palma Becerra* Juan, El rico y el pobre llamado Lázaro (Análisis narrativo de Lc 16,19-31): ➤ 125, ᶠMORENO/VILLEGAS 1990, 105-113.

5448 **Westra** A., De gelijkenis van de Rijke Man en de Arme Lazarus (Lk 16:19-31) bij de vroeg-christelijke Griekse schrijvers tot en met J. CHRYSOSTOMUS [diss. Leiden]. Assen 1987, Van Gorcum. 174 p. *f* 35. – ᴿKerkT 40 (1989) 169s (A. *Noordegraaf*).

5449 *Mitchell* Alan C., Zacchaeus revisited; Luke 19,8 as a defense: Biblica 71 (1990) 153-176; franç. 176.

5450 *Linden* Amnon, [Lc 19,41-47; 10,25-37] The Destruction of Jerusalem Sunday: SacrEr 30 (1987s) 253-292.

5451 *Amjad-Ali* Charles M., [Lk 19,47-20,8] The power of the people versus the power of the power-brokers: Al-Mushir 32 (Rawalpindi 1990) 79-91 [< TContext 8/2, p. 68].

F7.8 **Passio** – *Lc 22*...

5452 **Senior** Donald, The Passion... in Luke 1989 ➤ 5,5202: [R]Interpretation 44 (1990) 207s (Beverly R. *Gaventa*); NewTR 3,3 (1990) 107-9 (J. A. *Mindling*).

5453 **Soards** Marion L., *a*) The Passion according to Luke; the special material of Luke 22: JStOT supp. 14, 1987 ➤ 3,5063... 5,5202*: [R]TLZ 115 (1990) 196-8 (M. *Rese*). – *b*) [Lk 22,63-65] A literary analysis of the origin and purpose of Luke's account of the mockery of Jesus: ➤ 551*, New views 1990, 96-93. 174-7.

5454 *Bianchi* Enzo, [Lc 22,32...] Il ritorno di Pietro: ➤ 325*b*, ParSpV 22 (1990) 173-197.

5455 **Ochenbauer** Franz, Jesu Angst am Ölberg; eine exegetisch-bibeltheologische Untersuchung zu Lk 22,43-44: kath. Diss. [D]*Kremer* J. Wien 1989s. – TR 86,511; RTLv 22, p. 594.

[E]**Sylva** Dennis, Reimaging the death of the Lukan Jesus 1990 ➤ 378.

5456 **Tyson** Joseph B., The death of Jesus in Luke-Acts 1986 ➤ 2,4007; 5,5203: [R]SecC 7 (1989s) 190s (R. J. *Karris*).

5457 *Fleddermann* Harry, The end of Q [Lk 22,28 throne saying, 'key to genre of Q', BAMMEL E.]: ➤ 544, SBL Seminars 1990, 1-10.

5458 **Just** Arthur A., Table fellowship and the eschatological kingdom in the Emmaus narrative of Luke 24: diss. Durham 1990. 279 p. – RTLv 22, p. 593.

5459 *Warma* Susanne J., Christ, first fruits, and the Resurrection; observations on the fruit basket in Caravaggio's London 'Supper at Emmaus': ZKunstG 53 (1990) 584-6; 1 fig.

5460 *Schwarz* Günther, *Hoi dè ophthalmoì autôn ekratoûnto?* (Lukas 24,16a): BibNot 55 (1990) 16s.

XII. Actus Apostolorum

F8.1 **Acts** – *text, commentary, topics.*

5461 Acts of the Apostles: Navarre Bible, [T]*Adams* M. Dublin 1989, Four Courts. 272 p. £12.50; pa. £8. 1-85182-045-0; -4-2 [NTAbs 34,113].

5462 **Ancion** Jean, Actes des Apôtres hier, pratiques des chrétiens aujourd'hui. Grâce-Hollogne 1989, auct. (r. Vinâve 18). 128 p. Fb 150. – [R]FoiTemps 20 (1990) 283s (H. *Thomas*).

5464 *Baugh* Steven M., Phraseology and the reliability of Acts [speeches...]: NTS 36 (1990) 290-4.

5465 **Benéitez** Manuel, 'Esta salvación de Dios'... (Hech 28,28) estructuralista 1986 ➤ 2,4023. 4127... 5,5213: [R]TR 86 (1990) 112-4 (A. de *Oliveira*).

5466 **Boismard** Marie-Émile, *Lamouille* Arnaud, Les Actes des deux Apôtres: I. Introduction et textes; II. Le sens des récits; III. Analyses littéraires:

ÉtBN 12-14. P 1990, Gabalda. xi-186 p.; 409 p.; 344 p. F 88 + 155 +
150. 2-85021-038-2; -40-4; -41-2. – ᴿLA 39 (1989!) 365-8 (V. *Mora*);
PrOrChr 40 (1990) 200-2 (P. *Ternant*); RThom 90 (1990) 505s (H. *Ponsot*); Spiritus 31 (1990) 451s (J.-M. *Guillaume*).

5467 **Boismard** M.-E., *Lamouille* A., Texte occidental des Actes I-II, 1984
➤ 65,4597* ... 4,5226: ᴿSvEx 55 (1990) 130-2 (R. *Kieffer*); TLZ 115
(1990) 198-200 (H.-M. *Schenke*).

5468 **Bruce** F.F., Commentary on the Book of Acts: NICNT 1987 = 1954
➤ 4,5227; 5,5215: ᴿCBQ 52 (1990) 341-3 (R.F. *O'Toole*: remains a
classic despite weaknesses and no updating); CriswT 4 (1989s) 397s (T.D.
Lea); EvQ 62 (1990) 273s (A. *Campbell*); JEH 41 (1990) 138 (C.J.A.
Hickling); JTS 41 (1990) 197s (C.K. *Barrett*).

5469 **Bruce** Frederick F., The Acts of the Apostles; the Greek text with
introduction and commentary²ʳᵉᵛ [¹1951] GR 1990, Eerdmans. xxvii-
569 p. $40.

5470 *Bruce* F.F. / *Brehm* Alan, The significance of speeches / summaries for
interpreting Acts: SWJT 33,1 (1990s) 20-28 / 29-40.

5471 **Cassidy** Richard J., Society and politics in Acts 1987 ➤ 3,5088 ...
5,5218: ᴿCritRR 2 (1989) 189-192 (C.R. *Matthews*); CrNSt 11 (1990)
618-621 (G. *Betori*); NedTTs 43 (1989) 334s (J. van *Eck*); TPhil 65 (1990)
259s (J. *Beutler*); TR 86 (1990) 456 (R. *Pesch*).

5473 *Cothenet* Édouard, Les deux Actes des Apôtres [DELEBECQUE E. 1986]
ou Les Actes des deux Apôtres [BOISMARD M., LAMOUILLE A., 1990]:
EsprVie 100 (1990) 425-430.

5474 *Gasque* W. Ward, Actes des Apôtres; bilan de la recherche récente [=
Interpretation 42 (1988) 117-131], ᵀ*Desplanque* Christophe: Hokhma 42
(1989) 17-34.

5475 *Geer* Thomas C.ᴶ, The presence and significance of Lucanisms in the
'Western' text of Acts: JStNT 39 (1990) 59-76.

5476 **Gooding** D., True to the faith; a fresh approach to the Acts of the
Apostles. L 1990, Hodder & S. viii-440 p. £9. 0-340-52563-0 [NTAbs
35,241].

5477 **Hargreaves** J., A guide to Acts: TEF 27. L 1990, SPCK. xiv-253 p.;
ill. £7.50. 0-281-04367-1 [NTAbs 34,384].

5478 *House* P.R., Suffering and the purpose of Acts: JEvTS 33 (1990)
317-330 [< NTAbs 35,175].

5479 **Hemer** Colin J. [† 1987], ᴱ*Gempf* C.H., The Book of Acts in the setting
of Hellenistic history, pref. *Marshall* I.H. [from Gempf only introd. and
brief concluding chapter]: WUNT 49, 1990 ➤ 5,5231: ᴿInterpretation
44 (1990) 429s (L.T. *Johnson*); JBL 109 (1990) 726-9 (C.R. *Matthews*:
'passionate, protracted, and predictable' defense of historicity); TLZ 115
(1990) 813-5 (G. *Schille*).

5480 **Kee** Howard C., Good news to the ends of the earth; the theology of
Acts. L/Ph 1990, SCM/Trinity. vi-122 p. $11. 0-334-02486-2 [NTAbs
35,242].

5481 **Larsson** Edvin, *a*) Apostlagärningarna II. 13-20: KommNyaT. U
1987, EFS. 196 p. – ᴿTsTKi 60 (1989) 58-60 (O. *Myklebust*); – *b*) Från
Acta-forskningens fält: TsTKi 61 (1990) 49-66.

5482 **L'Éplattenier** Charles, Gli Atti degli Apostoli; quadro delle origini
cristiane: Lettura Pastorale della Bibbia. Bo 1990, Dehoniane. 218 p.
Lit. 24.000. – ᴿRivB 38 (1990) 536-9 (G. *Betori*).

5483 **Lüdemann** Gerd, *a*) Das frühe Christentum nach den Traditionen der
Apostelgeschichte; ein Kommentar 1987 ➤ 3,5103 ... 5,5236: ᴿRB 97

(1990) 276-283 (J. *Taylor*); – *b*) Early Christianity according to the traditions in Acts 1989 ⇥ 3,5103; 5,5237: ᴿCurrTMiss 17 (1990) 232s (E. *Krentz*); Neotestamentica 29 (1990) 384-6 (I. J. du *Plessis*).

5484 **Marconcini** Benito, Atti degli Apostoli, 1. Una comunità in comunione; 2. (13-28) Dalla comunione alla missione; contenuto e metodo dell'annuncio paolino: Commenti al NT. T-Leumann 1983-6, Elle Di Ci. 223 p.; 176 p. 88-01-10968-7 / -70-5.

5485 **Méhat** A., Simon dit Képhas; la vie clandestine de l'Apôtre Pierre [... ActAp]; essai historique: BibleVC. P 1989, Lethielleux. 184 p. F 90. – ᴿNRT 112 (1990) 904-6 (X. *Jacques*).

5485* *Monaci Castagno* Adele, Gli apostoli retori; interpretazioni dei discorsi degli Atti in Giovanni CRISOSTOMO: AnStoEseg 7 (1990) 631-646.

5486 *Mowery* Robert L., Direct statements concerning God's activity in Acts: ⇥ 544, SBL seminars 1990, 196-211.

5487 **Neudorfer** H.-W., Apg II: BKomm 9. Stu-Neuhausen 1990, Hänssler. 379 p. DM 40. – ᴿSNTU A-15 (1990) 182 (A. *Fuchs*).

5488 **O'Reilly** Leo, Word and sign in the Acts of the Apostles [diss. Gregorian, ᴰRasco E.]: AnGreg 243, theol. B/82, 1987 ⇥ 3,5106 ... 5,5242: ᴿCBQ 52 (1990) 357s (D. *Hamm*, whose 1975 dissertation is acknowledged but left unexploited).

5489 *Pascutto* Luigi, Attività di apostolato negli Atti degli Apostoli: PalCl 69 (1990) 743-8.

5490 **Pervo** Richard I., Profit with delight ᴰ1987 ⇥ 3,5108 ... 5,5244: ᴿCriswT 4 (1989s) 182s (C. *Blomberg*); JAAR 58 (1990) 307-310 (M. L. *Soards*: profit and delight yes; conviction no); TR 86 (1990) 456-8 (A. *Weiser*); WestTJ 52 (1990) 378-381 (D. E. *Johnson*: good despite his presuppositions).

5491 **Pesch** Rudolf. Die Apostelgeschichte 1986 ⇥ 2,4037 ... 5,5245: ᴿSNTU-A 14 (1989) 258s (A. *Fuchs*).

5492 *Piscopiello* Luigi, L'esegesi di san Giovanni CRISOSTOMO nelle omelie sugli Atti degli Apostoli: RivScR 4 (Molfetta 1990) 113-130.

5493 *a*) Polhill John B., Introduction to the study of Acts, – *b*) *Parsons* Mikeal C., Christian origins and narrative openings; the sense of a beginning in Acts 1-5; – *c*) *Dockery* David S., Acts 6-12; the Christian mission beyond Jerusalem; – *d*) *Blevins* James L., Acts 13-19; the tale of three cities; – *e*) *Songer* Harold S., Acts 20-28, From Ephesus to Rome; – *f*) *Richardson* Paul A., Worship materials for use with Acts; – *g*) *Carver* Gary L., Acts 2:42-47; – *h*) *Bailey* Raymond H., Acts 17:16-34: RExp 87,3 (1990) 385-401 / 403-422 / 423-437 / 439-450 / 451-463 / 465-471 / 475-480 / 481-5.

5494 *Porter* Stanley E., THUCYDIDES 1.22.1 and speeches in Acts; is there a Thucydidean view?: NT 32 (1990) 121-142.

5496 *Rodríguez Carmona* Antonio, Los semitismos de los Hechos de los Apóstoles, estado de la cuestión: EstE 65 (1990) 385-401.

5497 **Rius-Camps** Josep, De Jerusalén a Antioquía; génesis de la Iglesia cristiana, comentario lingüístico y exegético a Hch 1-12, 1989 ⇥ 5,5246: ᴿFgNt [already 2 (1989) 213] 3 (1990) 169s (D. A. *Black*: thorough and refreshing).

5498 **Stott** John R. W., The message of Acts; to the ends of the earth: The Bible speaks today. Leicester 1990, Inter-Varsity. 405 p. 0-85110-684-6.

5499 **Tannehill** Robert C., *a*) The narrative unity of Luke-Acts, a literary interpretation [1. 1986 ⇥ 2,3901], 2. The Acts of the Apostles. Mp 1990, Fortress. x-298 p. $27. 0-8006-2414-9 [NTAbs 34,389]. – ᴿTTod 47

(1990s) 452.454s (R. L. *Brawley*, 1s); – *b*) Mission in the 1990s; reflections on the Easter lections from Acts: QRMin 10 (1990) 84-97.

5500 *Taylor* Justin, The making of Acts; a new account [BOISMARD M., LAMOUILLE A. 1990]: RB 97 (1990) 504-524.

5501 *Verzan* Sabin, Les Actes des Apôtres – un livre des prototypes, en roumain: STBuc 42/1 (1990) 38-76, franç. 150; 42/2, 42-79, franç. 143; 80-83, conclusions (Eng.).

5502 **Wildhaber** Bruno, Paganisme populaire et prédication apostolique [8 textes des Actes; diss. Fribourg]: MondeB, 1987 → 3,5120; 2-8309-0045-6. – ᴿEstB 48 (1990) 282-6 (J. *Fernández Sangrador*).

F8.3   *Ecclesia primaeva Actuum:*   **Die Urgemeinde.**

5503 **Achtenmeier** Paul J., The quest for unity in the NT church 1987 → 3,5121 ... 5,5255: ᴿJBL 109 (1990) 149-151 (Beverly R. *Gaventa*); Neotestamentica 24 (1990) 155s (M. C. *Dippenaar*: the book holds that Paul's dispute with Peter in Gal 2,11-14 occurred after the council of Acts 15); ScotJT 43 (1990) 119s (J. D. G. *Dunn*).

5504 **Birkey** Del, The house church; a model for renewing the Church. Scottdale PA 1988, Herald.   180 p. $19. – ᴿEvQ 62 (1990) 277-9 (B. B. *Blue*: too uneven to be convincing).

5505 **Blue** Bradley B., In public and in private; the role of the House Church in early Christianity: diss. Aberdeen 1989.   312 p.   BRDX-94581. – DissA 52,3321-A; RTLv 22, p. 597.

Boguniowski Józef W., Domus ecclesiae; der Ort der Eucharistiefeier in den ersten Jahrhunderten ᴰ1986 → 5003.

5506 *a*) **Brown** R. E., *Meier* J. P., Antioche et Rome, berceaux du christianisme: LDiv 131, 1988 → 4,5274: ᴿBLitEc 91 (1990) 303-305 (S. *Légasse*); ÉTRel 65 (1990) 457s (M. *Bouttier*); – *b*) Antiochia e Roma; chiese-madri della cattolicità antica 1987 → 3,5131 ... 5,5264: ᴿClaretianum 30 (1990) 455-8 (B. *Proietti*).

5507 *Casalini* Nello, Democrazia e partecipazione nella Chiesa; modelli di comportamento della generazione apostolica: LA 40 (1990) 159-181; Eng. 447.

5508 *Collins* R. F., House churches in early Christianity: Tripod 55 (Hong Kong 1990) 38-44, Ⓒ 3-6 [NTAbs 34,345].

5509 *Cuvillier* Elian, Luc et les chistianismes primitifs: ÉTRel [59 (1984) 141-9, *Vouga* F.] 65 (1990) 93-99.

5510 **Cwiekowski** Frederick J., The beginnings of the Church 1988 → 4,5279; 5,5267: ᴿCBQ 52 (1990) 151s (J. J. *Pilch*: fair succinct survey, but uses 'Church' elusively, and his claimed 'objectivity' is sometimes dubious); ÉglT 20 (1989) 496-8 (N. *Bonneau*); Interpretation 44 (1990) 215s (Dorothy J. *Weaver*: delivers what it promises).

5511 **Dudley** Carl S., *Hilgert* Earle, New Testament tensions and the contemporary Church 1987 → 3,5134*; 5,5268: ᴿAndrUnS 28 (1990) 155s (P. *Follett*).

5512 *Dunn* James D. G., *a*) Die Instrumente kirchlicher Gemeinschaft in der frühen Kirche: UnSa 44 (1989) 2-14; – *b*) Gli strumenti della Koinonia nella Chiesa primitiva, ᵀ*Vetrali* T.: StEcum 7 (1989) 113-136; Eng. 136.

5513 *Faivre* Alexandre, Les premiers Chrétiens interpellent le Synode des évêques: RevSR 63 (1989) 17-46.

5514 *Fowler* B. G., The New Testament basis for the small church: AmBapQ 9,2 (1990) 91-96 [< NTAbs 35,57].

5515 **Hadot** Jean, Les origines du christianisme 1988 ➤ 4,5285: [R]FoiTemps 19 (1989) 393s (C. *Focant*); RTLv 21 (1990) 494s (J. *Ponthot*: tendance).

5516 *Hanssen* Ove C., Den urkristne gudstjeneste – en 'tjeneste ved Guds Ånd': TsTKi 61 (1990) 241-254; Eng. 254 'Early Christian worship – a worship by [or 'in presence of'?] the Spirit'.

5517 **Harrison** Everett F., Interpreting Acts; the expanding Church 1986 ➤ 3,5097: [R]GraceTJ 10 (1989) 88s (P. A. *Beals*).

5518 **Iori** R., La solidarietà nelle prime comunità cristiane; la dottrina degli Atti e di Paolo [diss. R 1987, Pont. Univ. Gregoriana]: Collana Scritturistica. R 1989, Città Nuova. 187 p. – [R]RivB 38 (1990) 113-5 (G. *De Virgilio*).

5519 **Jankowski** Augustyn, ℗ Kerygmat... The kerygma in the apostolic Church; NT theology of the proclaiming of the Word of God. Częstochowa 1989, Diecez. 190 p.

5520 *Kapliński* Piotr, ℗ Does Acts terminology show the pastoral authority of St. Peter?: RuBi 42 (1989) 368-372.

5521 **Kirchschläger** Walter, Die Anfänge der Kirche; eine biblische Rückbesinnung. Graz 1990, Styria. 207 p. DM 29,80. 3-22-11963-5.

5522 *a) Kretschmar* Georg, Die Kirche aus Juden und Heiden; – *b) Vos* Johannes S., Legem statuimus; rhetorische Aspekte der Gesetzesdebatte zwischen Juden und Christen, i. Paulus; ii. Apg.; iii. Justin; ➤ 506*, Juden/Christen 1989/90, 9-43 / 44-60.

5523 **Lavallée** François, L'Esprit Saint et l'Église; une analyse des Actes des Apôtres pour aujourd'hui. Montréal/P 1987, Paulines/Médiaspaul. 254 p. $16.50. – [R]ÉglT 20 (1989) 484s (M. *Dumais*).

5524 **MacDonald** Margaret Y., The Pauline churches...: SNTS Mg 60, [D]1988 ➤ 4,5296; 5,5281: [R]CBQ 52 (1990) 565-7 (G. W. *Buchanan*); JAAR 58 (1990) 716-9 (L. T. *Johnson*); JBL 109 (1990) 151-4 (Susan R. *Garrett*); JTS 41 (1990) 191-4 (F. *Watson*); RTLv 21 (1990) 231 (C. *Focant*).

5525 **Maloney** Linda, 'All that God had done with them'; the narration of the works of God in the early Christian community as described in the Acts of the Apostles: diss. Tübingen 1990. – BZ 34 (1990) 158.

5526 **Montserrat Torrens** J., La sinagoga cristiana; el gran conflicto religioso del siglo I. Barc 1989, Muchnik. 349 p. – [R]BibFe 16 (1990) 306 (A. *Salas*).

5527 **Schenke** L., Die Urgemeinde; Geschichtliche und theologische Entwicklung. Stu 1990, Kohlhammer. 358 p. DM 36 pa. 3-17-011076-4 [NTAbs 35,120].

5528 **Schneemelcher** W., Il cristianesimo delle origini [➤ 3,5155], [T]*Morato* G.: Universale pa. 201. Bo 1987, Mulino. 260 p. Lit. 18.000. – [R]StPatav 37 (1990) 198s (G. *Segalla*).

5529 *Taylor* Joan E., The phenomenon of early Jewish-Christianity; reality or scholarly invention? [DANIÉLOU J. 1958...]: VigChr 44 (1990) 313-334.

5530 *Vanhetloo* Warren, Church meetingplaces: CalvaryB 6 (1990) 32-43.

5531 **Volz** C. A., Pastoral life and practice in the Early Church. Mp 1990, Augsburg. 240 p. 0-8066-2446-9 [NTAbs 35,121].

5532 *Weiser* Alfons, Evangelisierung im Haus [*oîkos*... Jesus, Haustafel, Paulus]: BZ 34 (1990) 63-86.

5533 *Werners* Hans, Church communities then and now [< Diakonia 19 (1988) 6-14], [TE]*Asen* B.: TDig 37 (1990) 120-2.

F8.5 Ascensio, Pentecostes; ministerium Petri – *Act 1*...

5534 *Newman* Robert C., [Acts 1.1-12; 9,1-19; 10s] Parallel narratives in Acts; a case study for synoptic harmonization: ➤ 370, Gospels 1990, 150-165.

5535 *Cantalamessa* Raniero, [At 1,14] 'Perseveranti nella preghiera con Maria, la madre di Gesù', VConsacr 26 (1990) 403-427.
5536 *Stockhausen* Carol L., Luke's stories of the Ascension; the background and function of a dual narration: ProcGLM 10 (1990) 251-262.
5537 *Omanson* Roger L., How does it all fit together? Thoughts on translating Acts 1.15-22 and 15.19-21: BTrans 41 (1990) 416-421.
5538 *Kruijf* T. de, 'Bij monde van David' (Hand 1,16); Psalm 110 in het Nieuwe Testament: → 180*, FTromp N., Gelukkig c. 1990, 37-47; Eng. 256.
5539 *Jones* E., The origins of 'Ascension' terminology: Churchman 104,2 (1990) 156-161 [< NTAbs 35,61].
5540 **Parsons** Mikeal C., The departure of Jesus in Luke-Acts...: JStNT supp 21, 1987 → 4,5321; 5,4299: RVidyajyoti 53 (1989) 519 (R. J. *Raja*); WestTJ 52 (1990) 376-8 (F. S. *Spencer*: balance is hard to achieve).
5541 *Fernández Ramos* Felipe, [Act 2-5], La vida cristiana original: StLeg 30 (1989) 11-55.
5542 *Angel* Gervais, Sermons in Acts: Acts 2; the first Christian Pentecost: Evangel 7,3 (1989) 6-10 / 7,4 (1989) 5-7.
5543 *Beutler* Johannes, [Apg 2,1-12] Vielvölkerstadt [... Kinder aus aller Welt malen Jerusalem]: GeistL 63 (1990) 161-5.
5544 *Lemopoulos* George, The icon of Pentecost; a liturgical Bible study on Acts 2:1-4: EcuR 42 (1990) 92-97; 1 fig.
5545 *Newton* John A., Pentecost; power to be Christ's witnesses: ExpTim 102 (1990s) 208-210.
5546 a) *Vanhetloo* Warren, [Acts 2,1-4; 11,15s; 19,1-7] Spirit baptism [... occurs at time of conversion, not of water, p. 109]: CalvaryB 6 (1990) 90-119; – b) **McDonnell** Kilian, *Montague* George T., Christian initiation and baptism in the Holy Spirit; evidence from the first eight centuries. Collegeville MN 1990, Liturgical/Glazier. xiv-354 p. $13.
5547 *Grappe* Christian, À la jonction entre Inter et Nouveau Testament – le récit de la Pentecôte: FoiVie 89,5 = Cahier Biblique 29 (1990) 19-27.
5548 *Zuurmond* R., Glossolalie op Pinksteren? Notitics bij Handelingen 2,4: AmstCah 10 (1989) 120-8 [< ZAW 103,126].
5549 *Sandt* Huub van de, The fate of the Gentiles in Joel and Acts 2, an intertextual study: ETL 60 (1990) 56-77.
5550 *Matera* Frank J., [Acts 2,23s...] Responsibility for the death of Jesus according to the Acts of the Apostles: JStNT 39 (1990) 77-93.
5551 *Mainville* Odette, Jésus et l'esprit dans l'œuvre de Luc; éclairage à partir d'Ac 2,33: ScEsp 42 (1990) 183-208.
5552 *Tanton* L. T., The Gospel and water baptism; a study of Acts 2:38: JGrace 3,1 (1990) 27-52 [< NTAbs 35,40].
5553 *Ukachukwu Manus* C., The community of love in Luke's Acts; a sociological exegesis of Acts 2:41-47 in the African context: WAfJEc 2,1 (Ile-Ife 1990) 11-37 [< NTAbs 35,176].
5554 *Joubert* S., [Acts 2,42-47] Die gesigpunt van die verteller en die funksie van die Jerusalemgemeente hinne die 'opsommings' in Handelinge: Skrif-Kerk 10,1 (1989) 21-35 [< NTAbs 34,181].
5555 **Pattison** Stephen E., [Acts 2,42-47; 4,32-35; 5,12-16] A study of the apologetic function of the summaries of Acts: diss. Emory, DHolladay C. Atlanta 1990. 434 p. 90-27934. – DissA 51 (1990s) 1654-A; RelStR 17,194; RTLv 22, p. 594.
5556 a) **Prete** B., *Scaglioni* A., I miracoli degli apostoli nella Chiesa delle origini; studi sui racconti dei miracoli negli Atti [diss. *Scaglioni* → 4,5250;

5,5247) Roma, Angelicum]. T-Leumann 1989, LDC. 272 p. Lit. 28.000.
88-01-13966-7 [NTAbs 35,105]. – ᴿRasT 31 (1990) 410s (V. *Fusco*); – *b*)
Sampathkumar Antoni Raj, Les récits de miracle dans les Actes des
Apôtres: cath. diss. ᴰ*Schlosser* J. Strasbourg 1990. 286 p. – RTLv 22,
p. 595.
5557 **Co** Maria A., The composite summaries in Acts 3-5; a study of Luke's
use of summary as a narrative technique: diss. Leuven 1990, ᴰ*Delobel* J.
liv-420 p. – RTLv 22, p. 592.
5558 *Baxter* S. Edward, [Acts 3,21] A historical study of the doctrine of
apokatástasis: diss. Mid-America Baptist Theol. Sem. 1988. 316 p. 91-
12523. – DissA 51 (1990s) 4160-A.
5559 *a*) *Adinolfi* Marco, Il Socrate dell'Apologia platonica e il Pietro di Atti
4-5 di fronte alla libertà religiosa; – *b*) *Battaglia* Vincenzo, Cristo nostra
pace; libertà, pace e salvezza nella predicazione cristiana (... Col 1,15-20;
Ef 2,14s): ➤ a642*, Libertà, Antonianum 65 (1990) 422-441 / 442-466.
5560 *Sabugal* Santos, *a*) Los kérygmas de Pedro ante el Sanedrin judaico
(Act 4,8-12; 5,29-32); análisis histórico-tradicional; – *b*) Dios lo hizo Señor
y Mesías (Act 2,14-41); el primer kérygma anastasiológico de Pedro:
EstAg 25 (1990) 3-14 / 199-213.
5561 *a*) *Boismard* M.-E., Actes des Apôtres et Évangile de Pierre (Act
4,24b-30); – *b*) *Jiménez Berguecio* Julio, Accipietis donum Spiritus Sancti
(Act 2,38): ➤ 125, ᶠMORENO/VILLEGAS 1990, 163-7 / 225-247.
5562 *Bernhard* Ludger, [Apg 4,27 ...] Das frühchristliche Verständnis der
Formel *Iēsous paîs theoû* aufgrund der alten Bibelübersetzungen: ➤ 8*,
ᶠASSFALG J., Lingua restituta 1990, 21-29.
5563 *Fabris* Rinaldo, Anania e Saffira (At 5,1-11): ➤ 325a, ParSpV 21 (1990)
191-204.
5564 *Roosen* A., Service de la Parole et service des pauvres dans Actes 6,1-7
et 20,32-35: StMor 27 (R 1989) 43-76 [< NTAbs 34,44].
5565 *Kaczmarek* Tomasz, ☻ Atti 6,1-6 nell'interpretazione patristica: VoxPa
17 ('Diakonat w kościele starożytnym' 1989) 599-603; ital. 603.
5566 *Hill* C. C., Hellenists and Hebraists; a reappraisal: Diss. Oxford 1989.
– RTLv 22,591.
5567 *Hughes* J. J., [Acts 7] Life out of death: America 162 (NY 1990)
380s . 388.
5568 *Arai* Sasagu, [Acts 7,2-53] Stephanusrede — gelesen vom Standpunkt
ihrer Leser: AnJap 15 (1989) 53-85 [< NTAbs 34,323, C. R. *Matthews*].
5569 *deSilva* David A., The stoning of Stephen; purging and consolidating an
endangered institution: StudiaBT 17 (Pasadena 1989) 165-184.
5570 *Légasse* S., Encore *estôta* en Actes 7,55-56: FgNt 3,5 (1990) 63-66.
5571 *Karasszon* István, [Act 7,58] ☻ *Pál apostol*... murderer of Stephen the
martyr?: TSzem 33 (1990) 171s.
5572 *Schwartz* Joshua, [Acts 9,32-35; Sanh 7,2] Ben Stada and Peter in Lydia:
JStJud 21 (1990) 1-18.
5573 *Hamm* Dennis, Paul's blindness and its healing; clues to symbolic intent
(Acts 9; 22 and 26): Biblica 71 (1990) 63-72.
5574 *Frankfurter* David T. M., [Act 9,36] Tabitha in the Apocalypse of Elijah
[not same]: JTS 41 (1990) 13-25.
5575 *Angel* Gervais, The first Gentile convert; the speech at the home of
Cornelius, Acts 10: Evangel 8,1 (1990) 2-4.
5576 *Friesen* Abraham, Acts 10; the baptism of Cornelius as interpreted by
Thomas MÜNTZER and Felix MANZ: MennQR 64,1 (1990) 5-22 [< ZIT
90,289].

5577 **Rostkowski** Zbigniew, ⊕ Universality of salvation in Peter's speech in Caesarea, Acts 10,24-43: diss. Lublin 1990, ᴰ*Szlaga* J. xxxvi-280 p. – RTLv 22, p. 595.

5578 *Villiers* F. de, 'God raised him on the third day and made him manifest ... and he commanded us to preach to the people ...' (Acts 10: 34-40): JTSAf 70 (1990) 55-63 [< NTAbs 35,41].

5579 *Kilgallen* John J., Did Peter actually fail to get a word in? (Acts 11,15): Biblica 71 (1990) 405-410.

5580 *Jones* F. Stanley, The martyrdom of James in HEGESIPPUS, CLEMENT of Alexandria, and Christian apocrypha, including Nag Hammadi; a study of the textual relations: → 544, SBL seminars 1990, 322-335 [death of 'James the brother of Jesus' source is Hegesippus; nothing is said of Acts 12,2, death of 'James the brother of John'].

F8.7   **Act 13 ...** *Itinera Pauli,* **Paul's Journeys.**

5581 **Gourgues** Michel, L'Évangile aux païens (Actes des Apôtres 13-28): CahÉv 67. P 1989, Cerf. 67 p. F 25. 0222-9714.

5582 *Gempf* Conrad H., Historical and literary appropriateness in the mission speeches of Paul in Acts: diss. Aberdeen 1989. – RTLv 22, p. 592.

5583 *Pastore* Corrado, De la primera a la Nueva Evangelización: Iter 1 (Caracas 1990) 7-22 [-143, *al.*].

5584 **Pervo** R. L., Luke's story of Paul. Mp 1990, Fortress. 96 p. $6 pa. 0-8006-2405-X [NTAbs 34,387].

5585 *a*) *Schwartz* Daniel R., The end of the line; Paul in the canonical book of Acts; – *b*) *MacDonald* Dennis R., Apocryphal and canonical narratives about Paul: → 510, SMU Paul 1987/90, 3-24 / 55-70 [-77, *Stowers* S., comment].

5586 *Angel* Gervais, Partnership in the Gospel; Acts 13:16-47: Evangel 8,2 (1990) 2-3.

5587 *Johnson* Dennis E., [Acts 13,47 ...] Jesus against the idols; the use of Isaianic servant songs in the missiology of Acts: WestTJ 52 (1990) 343-353.

5588 *Haacker* Klaus, Gott und die Wege der Völker (Apg 14,16): TBeit 21 (Wu 1990) 281-5.

5590 *Burgos* Miguel de, Asamblea de Jerusalén (Hch XV) y Gal 2,1-14 en la obra Les Actes des deux Apôtres de BOISMARD M.-E., LAMOUILLE A.: CommSev 23 (1990) 405-428.

5591 *Dickinson* Royceᴶ, The theology of the Jerusalem conference, Acts 15,1-35: RestQ 32,2 (Abilene 1990) 65-83 [< NTAbs 34,323].

5592 *Jefford* Clayton N., An ancient witness to the apostolic decree of Acts 15? [Didache 6]: ProcGLM 10 (1990) 204-212.

5593 **Dubis** Kevin M., The use of Amos 9:11-12 in Acts 15: diss. Calvin Theol. Sem., ᴰ*Holwerda* D. v-114 p. + bibliog.

5594 *Jørgensen* Torstein, Acta 15:22-29, historiske og eksegetiske problemer: NorTTs 90 (1989) 31-45.

5595 **Wehnert** Jürgen, [Apg 16] Die Wir-Passagen ...: GöTheolArb 40, ᴰ1989 → 5,5333: ᴿCBQ 52 (1990) 577s (W. S. *Kurz*: important but Septuagint-imitation unconvincing); Neotestamentica 24 (1990) 154s (J. L. de *Villiers*); SNTU-A 14 (1989) 259-261 (A. *Fuchs*).

5596 *Martin* François, [Actes 16,6-40] Le geôlier et la marchande de pourpre: SémBib 59 (1990) 9-29; 60, 1-17.

5597 *a*) *Neyrey* Jerome H., Acts 17, Epicureans and theodicy; a study in stereotypes; – *b*) *Balch* David L., The Areopagus speech; an appeal to the Stoic historian Posidonius against later Stoics and the Epicureans: ⇒ 122, ᶠMALHERBE A., Greeks 1990, 118-134 / 52-79.

5597* *a*) [*Ukachuckwu*] *Manus* Chris, Luke's account of Paul in Thessalonica (Acts 17,1-9); – *b*) *Morgan-Gillman* Florence, Jason of Thessalonica (Acts 17,5-9); – *c*) *Donfried* K.P., 1 Thessalonians, Acts and the early Paul; – *d*) *Plevnik* Joseph, Pauline presuppositions: ⇒ 521, Thes. correspondence 1988/90, 27-38 / 39-49 / 3-26 / 50-61.

5598 *Meester* Paul de, Inculturation de la foi et salut des cultures; Paul de Tarse à l'Aréopage d'Athènes (Ac 17,22-32): Téléma 62,2 (1990) 59-80 [8-10, Maryknoll superior about the Chinese Church right to autonomy: TContext 8/1,33].

5599 **Tajra** Harry W., The trial of Paul [diss. Geneva, ᴰ*Bovon* F.]: WUNT 2/35, 1989 ⇒ 5,5341: ᴿEcuR 42 (1990) 357s (J. *Reumann*).

5600 *Slingerland* Dixon, Acts 18:1-17 and LUEDEMANN's Pauline chronology: JBL 109 (1990) 686-690.

5601 *Leary* T.J., The 'aprons' of St. Paul, Acts 19:12 [*semikínthia* is rather 'belts']: JTS 41 (1990) 527-9.

5601* *Crocker* P.T., Ephesus [Hermeias inscription mentioning silversmith-guild (Acts 19,24)]; its silversmiths, its tradesmen, and its riots: BurHist 23,4 (Melbourne 1987) 76-78 [< NTAbs 35,177].

5602 *Schulmeister* Paul, [Apg 20,9] Ⓜ Elalusznak a templomban... [Vom Schlafen in der Kirche... Massenmedien und der Marketing des Glaubens], ᵀ*Bánhegyi* Miksa B.: TBud 24 (1990) 71-76.

5603 **Alexander** Thomas C., Paul's final exhortation to the elders from Ephesus; the rhetoric of Acts 20:17-38: diss. Emory, ᴰ*Robbins* V. Atlanta 1990. 387 p. 90-37890. – DissΛ 51 (1990s) 1645s-A; RelStR 17,193; RTLv 22,591.

5604 *Angel* Gervais, Farewell to friends [1] 2, Exposition of Acts 20:17-38: Evangel [8,3] 8,4 (1990) 7-9.

5605 *Hüffmeier* Wilhelm, Predigt über Apostelgeschichte 20,35: Die Evangelische Diaspora 59 (Kassel 1990) 109-114 [< ZIT 91,126].

5606 *Dolfe* Karl G., The Greek word of 'blood' and the interpretation of Acts 20:28: SvEx 55 (1990) 64-70.

5607 *a*) *Rosenblatt* Marie-Eloise, Recurrent narration as a Lukan literary convention in Acts; Paul's Jerusalem speech in Acts 22:1-21; – *b*) *Cassidy* Richard J., The non-Roman opponents of Paul; – *c*) *Richard* Earl, Pentecost as a recurrent theme in Luke-Acts: ⇒ 551*, New Views 1990, 94-105 . 177s / 150-162 . 183-5 / 133-149 . 181-3.

5608 *Daube* David, On Acts 23; Sadducees and angels: JBL 109 (1990) 493-7.

5609 *a*) *Hirschfeld* Nicolle, The ship of St. Paul, I. Historical background; – *b*) *Fitzgerald* Michael, II. Comparative archaeology: BA 53 (1990) 25-30 / 31-39; ill.; ⇒ d287; *Vinson*.

5610 *a*) *Wehnert* Jürgen, Gestrandet; zu einer neuen These [SEPPELFRICKE A., Paulus war nie auf Malta: Die Zeit 52 (23.XII.1988) 33] über den Schiffbruch des Apostels Paulus auf dem Wege nach Rom (Apg 27-28): ZTK 87 (1990) 67-99; – *b*) *Sant* C., *Sammut* J., [Apg 27s] Paulus war doch auf Malta! [WARNECKE H. ᴰBremen]: TGL 80 (1990) 327-332.

5611 **Warnecke** Heinz, Die tatsächliche Romfahrt; SBS 127, ᴰ1987 ⇒ 3,5226; 5,5345: ᴿCurrTMiss 17 (1990) 145 (W.C. *Linss*: hesitant).

5612 *Tannehill* Robert C., [Acts 27...] Paul outside the Christian ghetto; stories of intercultural conflict and cooperation in Acts [Boers, Theology out of the ghetto 1971 ...]: ⇾ 24, [F]BOERS H., Text 1990, 247-263.
5613 *Schwank* Benedikt, 'Als wir schon die vierzehnte Nacht auf der Adria trieben' (Apg 27,27): ErbAuf 66 (1990) 44-49.
5614 *Mealand* D. L., [Acts 28,30s] The close of Acts and its Hellenistic Greek vocabulary: NTS 36 (1990) 583-597.

XIV. Johannes

G1 *Corpus Johanneum* .1 **John and his community.**

5615 *Barreto* J., Dios en las comunidades joaneas: EstTrin 21 (1987) 369-391 [345-67 paulinas, *Trevijano* R.].
5616 *a*) *Beutler* Johannes, Méthodes et problèmes de la recherche johannique aujourd'hui; – *b*) *Zumstein* Jean, La communuaté johannique et son histoire: ⇾ 538*, Communauté johannique 1988/90, 15-32 (-38, bibliog.) / 359-375.
5617 **Burge** Gary M., The anointed community; the Holy Spirit in the Johannine tradition 1987 ⇾ 3,5230 ... 5,5349: [R]EvQ 62 (1990) 253-264 (M. *Turner*; 264-268, Burge's invited response); STEv 1 (1989) 91 (E. *Beriti*).
5618 **Costa** Vincent, História e fé na comunidade joanina segundo Raymond E. BROWN: diss. 6904 Pont. Univ. Gregoriana, [D]*Pastor* F.-A. R 1990s. – InfPUG 23/119,14.
5619 **Ellis** E. Earle, The world of St. John, the gospels and epistles[2rev] [[1]1965] 1984 ⇾ 65,4737; 1,5179: [R]Neotestamentica 24 (1990) 152 (J.C. *Coetzee*).
5620 *Flusser* David, Hystaspes and John of Patmos: ⇾ 555, Irano-Judaica 1 (1975/82) 12-75.
5621 *Hawkin* David J., Johannine Christianity and ideological commitment: ExpTim 102 (1990s) 74-77.
 [E]**Kaestli** Jean-Daniel, *al.*, La communauté johannique et son histoire 1990 ⇾ 538*.
5622 *Kilpatrick* G. D., What John tells us about John [< [F]*Sevenster* J. 1970, 75-87]: ⇾ 257, Principles 1990, 333-344.
5623 *Lombard* H. A., Ondersoek na 'n Johannese kerk/skool: HervTSt 45 (1989) 59-78 [< NTAbs 34,38].
5624 **Quast** Kevin, *a*) Peter and the Beloved Disciple; figures for a community in crisis: JStNT supp 32, 1989 ⇾ 5,5354: [R]ÉTRel 65 (1990) 451s (E. *Cuvillier*); TLZ 115 (1990) 347-9 (H.-J. *Klauck*); – *b*) Reexamining Johannine community [MINEAR P. 1984; BURGE G. 1987; RENSBERGER D. 1988]: TorJT 5 (1989) 293-5.
5625 **Rensberger** David, Johannine faith and liberating community 1988 ⇾ 4,5400; 5,5355: [R]CBQ 52 (1990) 361s (J. *Winkler*); HorBT 11,2 (1989) 112s (F. F. *Segovia*); Interpretation 44 (1990) 93s (Gail R. *O'Day*); RelStR 16 (1990) 262 (D. M. *Smith*).
5626 *Rigato* Maria-Luisa, L'apostolo ed evangelista Giovanni', 'sacerdote' levitico [Eus. HE 3,31,3; 5,24,3]: RivB 38 (1990) 451-483; Eng. 483, 'acceptable'.
5627 **Riley** Gregory J., Doubting Thomas; controversy between the communities of Thomas and John: diss. Harvard, [D]*Koester* H. CM 1990. 199 p. 91-13248. – DissA 51 (1990) 4155-A.

5628 **Schnelle** Udo,   Antidoketische Christologie... in der johanneischen
   Schule: FRL 144, 1987 ➤ 3,5237; 5,5357:   ᴿSNTU A-15 (1990) 179
   (A. *Fuchs*).
5629 **Smith** D. Moody,   Johannine Christianity 1984 ➤ 65,4745... 3,5238:
   ᴿNeotestamentica 24 (1990) 148-150 (W. R. *Domeris*).
5630 **Stowasser** Martin,   Johannes der Täufer im Vierten Evangelium; eine
   Untersuchung zu seiner Bedeutung für die johanneische Gemeinde: kath
   Diss. ᴰ*Kremer* J.   Wien 1990. – RTLv 22,596.
5631 **Taeger** Jens-W.,   Johannesapokalypse und... Kreis ᴰ1988 ➤ 5,5359:
   ᴿSNTU A-15 (1990) 197s (U. *Schnelle*).
5632 **Tuñi** J. O.,   Las comunidades joánicas: Iglesia del NT 1988 ➤ 4,5404;
   5,5361:   ᴿActuBbg 27 (1990) 63 (X. *Alegre* S.).
5633 **Wahlde** Urban C. von,   The Johannine commandments; 1 John and
   the struggle for the Johannine tradition: Theological Inquiries.   NY
   1990, Paulist.   xii-294 p. $14 pa.   0-8091-3061-0 [NTAbs 35,116]. –
   ᴿExpTim 102 (1990s) 182 (S. S. *Smalley*); JTS 41 (1990) 611-3 (also S. S.
   Smalley).
5634 **Wengst** K.,   Bedrängte Gemeinde... Joh ³1990 [¹1981; ²1983 ➤ 1,5186;
   español 4,5407]:   ᴿSNTU A-15 (1990) 175 (A. *Fuchs*: von 142 auf 267
   Seiten).
5635 *Zumstein* Jean,   Visages de la communauté johannique: ➤ 545*, Jean,
   ACFÉB 1989/90, 87-106.

G1.2   **Evangelium Johannis:** *textus, commentarii.*

5635* *Aland* Kurt,   Der Text des Johannesevangeliums im 2. Jht. [< ᶠ*Greeven*
   H., 1986, 1-10]: ➤ 193, Supplementa 1990, 62-71.
5636 ᴱ**Backus** Irena,   Martin BUCER, Enarratio in Evangelion Johannis (1528,
   1530, 1536): Opera Latina 2 / StMedRefT 40.   Leiden 1988, Brill.
   lxvii 619 p.   ᴿRHPR 70 (1990) 373-5 (R. *Bodenmann*).
5637 **Barrett** C. K.,   Das Evangelium nach Johannes [1955, ²1978 ➤ 60,7086],
   ᵀ*Bald* Hans: Ke K Sondb.   Gö 1990, Vandenhoeck & R.   608 p.   3-525-
   51623-1. – ᴿSNTU A-15 (1990) 169s (A. *Fuchs*); WissWeis 53 (1990) 234s
   (H.-J. *Klauck*).
5638 ᵀᴱ**Berrouard** M.-F.,   S. AUGUSTIN, Homélies sur l'Évangile de saint
   Jean [XXXIV-XLII: Œuvres 73A, 1988 ➤ 4,5411*; 5,5363]; XLIV-LIV:
   Œuvres 73B.   P 1989, Ét. Aug.   556 p. – ᴿRHPR 70 (1990) 355s (J.
   Doignon, 73A); RSPT 74 (1990) 647s (G.-M. de *Durand*); RThom 90
   (1990) 307-311 (L. *Devillers*, AB).
5639 **Bianchi** Enzo,   Evangelio secondo Giovanni, commento esegetico-spirituale.   Magnano VC 1988, Qiqajon.   126 p.
5640 *Comfort* P. W.,   An analysis of five modern translations of the Gospel of
   John: Notes on Translation 3,3 (Dallas 1989) 30-55 [< NTAbs 35,146].
5641 **Delebecque** Édouard,   Év. de Jean 1987 ➤ 3,5250; 4,5415:   ᴿRÉG 103
   (1990) 350s (A. *Wartelle*).
5642 **Fatica** Luigi,   I Commentari a 'Giovanni' di TEODORO M./CIRILLO A.
   1988 ➤ 4,5418; 5,5366:   ᴿArTGran 53 (1990) 322s (A. *Segovia*); Teresianum 41 (1990) 299s (M. *Diego Sánchez*).
5643 **Fredrikson** Roger L.,   John: Communicator's Comm. 4.   Waco 1985,
   Word.   299 p. 0-8499-0156-X.
5644 **Godet** F.,   Das Evangelium des Johannes [¹1864, ⁴1903]. Giessen 1987,
   Brunnen.   vii-872 p. DM 88.   3-7655-9222-6 [NTAbs 34,384]. – ᴿSNTU
   A-15 (1990) 170s (A. *Fuchs*).

5645 **Grayston** Kenneth, The Gospel of John: Epworth Comm. L 1990, Epworth. 177 p. £7.50. 0-7162-0467-3 ['Narrative comm.', Ph 1990, Trinity, xxv-177 p. $15. 0-334-02474-9: NTAbs 35,101]. – RExpTim 102 (1990s) 151s (J. L. *Houlden*: courageous); StPatav 37 (1990) 394 (G. *Segalla*).

5646 TE**Heine** Ronald E., ORIGEN, commentary on the Gospel of John, books 1-10: Fathers 80, 1989 ➤ 5,5367: RRelStR 16 (1990) 346 (J. W. *Trigg*).

5647 TE**Jeanne d'Arc** sr., Évangile selon Jean, texte grec, tr. notes: Nouvelle Collection de Textes et Doc. P 1990, BLettres/D-Brouwer. xiii-151 p. 2-251-32023-7 / DB 2-220- 09174-8.

5648 **Kieffer** René, Johannesevangeliet 1-10 / 11-21: Kommentar till Nya Testamentet, 4AB 1987s ➤ 3,5257; 5,5369: RSvEx 55 (1990) 142-5 (J. *Sveinbjörnsson*).

5649 **Làconi** Mauro, Il racconto di Giovanni 1989 ➤ 5,5371: RCC 141 (1990, 4) 302s (G. *Giachi*); ScripTPamp 22 (1990) 598-600 (A. *García- Moreno*).

5650 **Léon-Dufour** Xavier, *a*) Lecture de l'Évangile selon Jean [I,1-4, 1987 ➤ 3,5259]; II, ch. 5-12: Parole de Dieu. P 1990, Seuil. 500 p. F 180. 2-02-012649-4 [NTAbs 35,244]. – RGregorianum 71 (1990) 382-4 (E. *Rasco*, 1); QVidCr 150 (1990) 207 (P.-R. *Tragan*, 1); RTLv 21 (1990) 214s (J. *Ponthot*, 1); Téléma 15,2 (1989) 71-73 (R. *Capoen*, 1); ZkT 112 (1990) 219 (M. *Hasitschka*, 1); – *b*) Lectura del Evangelio de Juan 1-4, TOrtiz García Alfonso: BiblEstB 68. S 1989, Sígueme. 348 p. 84-301-1095-X. – RActuBbg 27 (1990) 197 (X. *Alegre* S.); NatGrac 37 (1990) 316s (F. F. *Ramos*); – *c*) Lettura dell'evangelo secondo Giovanni, TGirlanda Antonio: Parola di Dio. CinB 1990, Paoline. I (cap. 1-4) 554 p.

Libera Alain de, *al.*, M. ECKHART, Le commentaire de l'Évangile selon Jean; le prologue 1989 ➤ k513.

5651 E**Livrea** Enrico, NONNO di Panopoli, Parafrasi del Vangelo di S. Giovanni, canto XVIII (... Jn 18): Speculum. N 1989, D'Auria. 213 p. – RNRT 112 (1990) 270 (A. *Harvengt*).

5652 **Parker** D. C., The International Greek New Testament project; the Gospel of John [after some resignations, the other editors are now J. K. *Elliott*, W. J. *Elliott*, J. L. *North*, and T. S. *Pattie*; with a Steering Committee replacing W. Elliott, North, and Pattie with E. J. *Epp* and C. D. *Osburn*]: NTS 36 (1990) 157-160.

5653 **Porsch** Felix, Johannes-Evangelium: StuKLK 4, 1988 ➤ 4,5443; 5,5378: RLebZeug 44 (1989) 155s (M. *Gebel*).

5654 TE**Rettig** John W., St. AUGUSTINE, Tractates on the Gospel of John 1-10 [out of 124]: Fathers 78, Wsh 1988 ➤ 4,5436; 5,5381: RJEH 40 (1989) 399s (G. *Bonner*); RelSt R 16 (1990) 347 (R. L. *Wilken*).

5655 **Ridderbos** H. N., Het evangelie naar Johannes, proeve van een theologische exegese I (1-10) 1987 ➤ 4,5437: RCritRR 2 (1989) 239-241 (H. *Boers*: maybe historically uncritical, but guides to a highly sympathetic reading).

5656 **Schnackenburg** Rudolf, Il vangelo di Giovanni IV. Esegesi ed excursus integrativi, TGatti Vincenzo: Comm. Teol. NT 4/4, 1987 ➤ 3,5262: RProtestantesimo 45 (1990) 143s (G. *Scuderi*); RivStoLR 26 (1990) 361-7 (Giuliana *Jacopino*); Salesianum 52 (1990) 744 (C. *Bissoli*).

5657 *Vogt* Hermann J., Beobachtungen zum Johannes-Kommentar des ORIGENES: TüTQ 170 (1990) 191-209.

5658 *Wartenberg* G., Zum Kommentar des Alexander ALESIUS zum Johannesevangelium: ➤ 511, Théorie/pratique 1988/90, 329-342.

5659 **Zevini** Giorgio, Vangelo secondo Giovanni 11-21: CommSpir 1987
➤ [65,4782...] 5,5386: ᴿSalesianum 52 (1990) 745 (C. *Bissoli*).

G1.3 **Introductio** *in Evangelium Johannis.*

5660 **Belle** Gilbert Van, Johannine [Gospel] bibliography 1966-1985: 1988
➤ 4,876; 5,5390: ᴿCommSev 23 (1990) 103s (M. de *Burgos*); RThom 90
(1990) 146s (L. *Devillers*); TLZ 115 (1990) 809s (T. *Holtz*); TPhil 65 (1990)
592s (J. *Beutler*).

5661 **Bittner** Wolfgang J., Jesu Zeichen im Joh.-Ev.: WUNT 2/26, 1987
➤ 3,5274... 5,5391: ᴿStPatav 37 (1990) 700-2 (G. *Segalla*).

5662 **Botha** Johannes E., A study in Johannine style, history, theory and
practice: diss. Pretoria 1990, ᴰ*Vorster* W. 260 p. – RTLv 22,591.

5663 *Braun* Willi, Resisting John; ambivalent redactor and defensive reader
of the Fourth Gospel: SR 19 (1990) 59-71.

5664 **Countryman** L.W., The mystical way in the Fourth Gospel 1987
➤ 3,5276... 5,5393: ᴿCritRR 2 (1989) 193-5 (K. B. *Quast*).

5665 **Dokka** Trond S., Å gjenkenne den ukjente... To recognise the unknown; on the possibility of human knowledge of God; a study based on
the signs material in the Gospel of John: diss. Oslo 1990. Oslo 1989, Fac.
Theol. – NorTTs 91 (1990) 248; assessments 129-139 (R. *Kieffer*) & 141-7
(H. *Deuser*); ST 44 (1990) 153s.

5666 **Fenton** John, Finding the way through John. L 1988, Mowbray. vi-
105 p. £6. 0-264-67142-2 [NTAbs 34,383].

5667 **Fortna** Robert T., The Fourth Gospel and its predecessor 1988
➤ 4,5454; 5,5395: ᴿCBQ 52 (1990) 748s (F. F. *Segovia*); CurrTMiss
17 (1990) 149 (D.W. *Kuck*); ExpTim 101 (1989s) 30 (S. S. *Smalley*); JBL
109 (1990) 352-5 (D.M. *Smith*); Pacifica 3 (1990) 344-6 (J. *Painter*); Rel-
StR 16 (1990) 261 (D.M. *Smith*); SNTU A-15 (1990) 176-8 (C. *Niemand*).

5668 *Giblin* Charles H., The tripartite narrative structure of John's Gospel:
Biblica 71 (1990) 449-467; franç. 468.

5669 **Grob** F., Faire l'œuvre de Dieu... Jean 1986 ➤ 3,5280... 5,5397: ᴿCrit-
RR 2 (1989) 197-9 (P. J. *Cahill*).

5670 **Harrington** Daniel J., John's thought and theology; an introduction:
Good News 33. Collegeville ᴹN 1990, Glazier/Liturgical. 120 p. $9 pa.
0-89453-796-2 [TDig 38,63].

5671 **Hengel** Martin, The Johannine question 1989 ➤ 5,5397*: ᴿCurrTMiss
17 (1990) 314 (E. *Krentz*); ExpTim 102 (1990s) 88 (Ruth B. *Edwards*, also
on his 1989 'Hellenization'); TLond 93 (1990) 480s (L. *Houlden*).

5672 **Hinrichs** Boy, 'Ich bin': SBS 133, 1988 ➤ 4,5456; 5,5398: ᴿTLZ 115
(1990) 346s (N. *Walter*).

5673 **Kügler** Joachim, Der Jünger, den Jesus liebte [Diss. Bamberg 1987,
ᴰ*Hoffmann* P.]: SBB 16, 1988 ➤ 5,5399: ᴿBiblica 71 (1990) 766-9 (C. A.
Evans); BZ 34 (1990) 138-140 (M. *Theobald*); CBQ 52 (1990) 350s (J. E.
Bruns); RTLv 21 (1990) 350-4 (J.-P. *Kaefer*: caractère non individuel,
difficil d'accepter); SNTU-A 14 (1989) 255s (U. *Schnelle*); TPhil 65
(1990) 258s (J. *Beutler*).

5674 *a) Lacoste* Munn, Una introducción al Evangelio de Juan; – *b) Lea*
T. D., La exégesis de textos significativos en Juan: DialT 32 (Colombia
1988) 7-16 / 17-39 [< Stromata 45,499].

5676 **Lindars** Barnabas, John: NTGuides. Sheffield 1990, JStOT. 106 p.
£5 pa. 1-85075-255-9 [TDig 38,173]. – ᴿExpTim 102 (1990s) 117s (C. S.
Rodd: splendid).

5677 **McGann** Diarmuid,   Journeying within transcendence; the Gospel of John through a Jungian perspective 1988 ➤ 4,5461:   RIrTQ 56 (1990) 247s (sr. Jo *O'Donovan*); Neotestamentica 29 (1990) 371s (J. C. *Latham*: sequel to his The journeying self ... Mark/Jung).

5678 *a) Marguerat* Daniel, La 'source des signes' existe-t-elle? Réception des récits de miracle dans l'évangile de Jean; – *b) Léon-Dufour* Xavier, Spécificité symbolique du langage de Jean: ➤ 538*, Communauté johannique 1988/90, 69-93 / 121-134.

5679 *a) Meyer* Marvin W.,   The youth in secret Mark and the beloved disciple in John; – *b) Hedrick* Charles W.,   Authorial presence and narrator in John; commentary and story: ➤ 152, FROBINSON J. M.,   Gnosticism 1 (1990) 94-105 / 74-93.

5680 **Mlakhuzhyl** George,   The Christocentric literary structure of the Fourth Gospel: AnBib 117, D1987 ➤ 3,5286 ... 5,5402:   RBibTB 20 (1990) 41s (U. C. von *Wahlde*); CritRR 2 (1989) 227-9 (R. A. *Culpepper*); HeythJ 31 (1990) 215-8 (J. *Ashton*: entertaining but implausible chiasms).

5681 *Morrison* sr. Lynn Marie,   John's Gospel in Chinese perspective: VerbumSVD 30 (1989) 272-4 [< BToday Sept. 1983].

5682 *Nepper-Christensen* Poul,   Hvem var den discipel, som Jesus elskede?: DanTTs 53 (1990) 81-105 [< ZIT 90,450].

5683 **Peterson** R. A.,   Getting to know John's Gospel; a fresh look at its main ideas.   Phillipsburg NJ 1989, Presbyterian & R.   xi-147 p. $8 pa.   0-87552-370-6 [NTAbs 34,113].

5684 **Rábanos Espinosa** Ricardo, *Muñoz León* Domingo,   Bibliografía joánica; evangelio, cartas y Apocalipsis 1960-1986: Bibliotheca Hispana Biblica 14. M 1990, Cons. Sup. Inv.   572 p. – RETL 66 (1990) 415-7 (F. *Neirynck*: adds to Van BELLE 1-3 Jn and Apc, and the years 1960-65 and 1986; but has only a fourth as many items on specific passages).

5685 **Röhl** Wolfgang,   Studien zur Frage nach der Rezeption des Johannesevangeliums in christlich-gnostichen Schriften aus Nag Hammadi: Diss. DOsten-Sacken v.d. Berlin 1990s. – RTLv 22, p. 597.

5686 **Ruckstuhl** Eugen,   Die literarische Einheit des Johannesevangeliums; der gegenwärtige Stand ...: NTOrb 5, 1987 ➤ 3,5292 ... 5,5404:   RSNTU-A 14 (1989) 253s (U. *Schnelle*).

5687 *a) Silva* Moisés,   The present state of Johannine studies; – *b) Robertson* Malcolm J.,   Historical tradition in the Fourth Gospel; after CARSON, an alternative; – *c) Johnson* Dennis E., 'I am'; intimations of eternity in John's Gospel: ➤ 370, Gospels 1990, 114-122 / 123-131 / 132-149.

5688 *Silva Santos* B.,   A fórmula 'ego eimi' no Quarto Evangelho: Liturgia e Vida 210 (Rio 1989) 12-23 [< Stromata 45,499].

5689 **Staley** Jeffrey L.,   The print's first kiss; a rhetorical investigation of the implied reader in the Fourth Gospel: SBL diss. 82, 1988 ➤ 4,5470: RCBQ 52 (1990) 173-5 (Elizabeth S. *Malbon* thinks that the playful title can be taken to mean or suggest that moderns encounter John through the print medium); CritRR 2 (1989) 246-8 (R. M. *Fowler*); Interpretation 44 (1990) 208.210 (Linda M. *Bridges*); RB 97 (1990) 617s (F. J. *Moloney*).

5690 **Tuñi Vancells** José O.,   O testemunho do Evangelho de João. Petrópolis 1989, Vozes.   184 p. [REB 50,258].

5691 **Turoldo** D. M.,   Il Vangelo di Giovanni; nessuno ha mai visto Dio ...: Problemi Attuali.   Mi 1988, Rusconi.   194 p. Lit. 22.000.   88-18-01029-8 [NTAbs 34,253].

5692 **Wahlde** Urban C. von,   The earliest version of John's Gospel; recovering the gospel of signs 1989 ↠ 5,5410:   ᴿRExp 87 (1990) 337s (R. A. *Culpepper*: readable, cogent).

5693 **Wengst** Klaus [↠ 5,5411!]   Interpretación del evangelio de Juan 1988: ᴿEstTrin 22 (1988) 325s (J. L. *Aurrekoetzea*); TVida 31 (1990) 357 (M. A. *Ferrando*).

G1.4   *Johannis themata*, topics.

5694 *Adamo* D. T.,   Sin in John's Gospel: EvRT 13 (Exeter 1989) 216-227 [< NTAbs 34,36].

5695 **Adkisson** Randall L.,   An examination of the concept of believing as a dominant motif in the Gospel of John: diss. Baptist Theol. Sem., ᴰ*Dukes* J.   New Orleans 1990.   184 p. 90-26806. – DissA 51 (1990s) 1645-A.

5696 **Anderson** Charles M.,   Sending formulas in John's Gospel; a linguistic analysis in the light of their background: diss. Southern Baptist Theol. Sem., ᴰ*Polhill* J.   1989. 235 p.   90-15968. – DissA 51 (1990s) 194-A.

5697 *Black* C. Clifton,   Christian ministry in Johannine perspective: Interpretation 44 (1990) 29-41.

5698 **Boismard** M.,   Moïse ou Jésus 1988 ↠ 5,5416: ᴿBiblica 71 (1990) 576-581 (G. *Segalla*: stimolante, soluzioni spesso fragili); CommSev 23 (1990) 102s (M. de *Burgos*); EsprVie 100 (1990) 286-8 (E. *Cothenet*); PrPeo 4 (1990) 458s (J. *McHugh*: unlike BULTMANN, finds John steeped in OT); RevSR 64 (1990) 88s (M. *Morgen*); RThom 90 (1990) 142-4 (L. *Devillers*); StPatav 37 (1990) 655-8 (L. *Cilia*).

5699 **Castellarin** Tomás A.,   El didáskein de Jesús; estudio exegético-teológico del termino en el cuarto evangelio: diss. Pont. Univ. Gregoriana, ᴰ*Caba* José. Roma 1990, Nᵒ 6894. – InfPUG 23/119 (1990s) 14.

5700 *a) Castro* Secundino,   Orar desde la sensibilidad del evangelio de Juan; – *b) Vaz* Armindo,   Lo específico de la oración de Jesús: REspir 49 (1990) 63-94 / 121-147.

5701 *Chang Sang,* ⓚ The role of women in the Gospel of John: Sinhak Sasang 67 (Seoul 1989) 816-859 [< TContext 8/1,70].

5702 ᴱ**Charlesworth** J. H.,   John and the Dead Sea Scrolls [= 1972; 9 art.].   NY 1990, Crossroad.   xvi-233 p. $17.   0-8245-1001-1 [NTAbs 35,100]. ↠ a75.

5703 **Choi Jongtae** Jonathan,   The Son of Man in the Fourth Gospel: diss. Calvin Theol. Sem., ᴰ*Holwerda* D.   vii-204 p. + bibliog. – CalvinT 25 (GR 1990; no other date assigned) 327.

5704 **Cirillo** A.,   Cristo rivelatore... Gv / T. AQUINO ᴰ1988 ↠ 4,3479; 5,5420: ᴿScripTPamp 22 (1990) 658-660 (J. L. *González Alió*).

5706 *Doohan* Leonhard,   Portraits of God in John: MilltSt 25 (1990) 37-62.

5707 **Dorado Guillermo** D.,   Moral y existencia cristianas en el IV evangelio y en las cartas de Juan: Est.ÉticaTeol 8, 1989 ↠ 5,5424: ᴿStPatavina 37 (1990) 196s (G. *Segalla*).

5708 *Dowell* Thomas M.,   Jews and Christians in conflict; why the fourth Gospel changed the Synoptic tradition: LvSt 15 (1990) 19-37.

5709 *Erdozain* Luis,   La fe, adhesión personal a Cristo, según el cuarto evangelio: EstE 65 (1990) 443-455.

5710 **Ferraro** Giuseppe,   La gioia di Cristo nel quarto vangelo: StBPaid 83, 1988 ↠ 4,5488; 5,5426:   ᴿÉTRel 65 (1990) 119s (E. *Cuvillier*: point de départ original); Helmantica 41 (1990) 431s (Rosa M. *Herrera*); RasT 31 (1990) 101s (D. *Marzotto*); ScuolC 117 (1989) 397s (N. *Spaccapelo*).

5711 **Groot** Marie de, Messianse ikonen [the seven 'I am' sayings are metaphorical icons], een vrouwenstudie van het Evangelie naar Johannes. Kampen 1988. Kok. 353 p. ƒ50. 90-242-2284-2 [NTAbs 34, 244]. – ᴿEcuR 42 (1990) 359s (Anneke *Geense-Ravestein*: asks not 'what does the text *mean*?' but 'what does it *do*?').

5712 **Harrington** D. J., John's thought and theology, an introduction: Good News 33. Wilmington 1990, Glazier. 120 p. $9. 0-89453-796-2 [NTAbs 34,364].

5713 *Hartin* P. J., The role of Peter in the Fourth Gospel: Neotestamentica 24,1 (1990) 49-61.

5714 **Hasitschka** Martin, Befreiung von Sünde nach dem Johannesevangelium; eine bibeltheologische Untersuchung: Innsb TSt 27, ᴰ1989 ⟶ 5,5437: ᴿTGL 80 (1990) 515s (J. *Ernst*).

5715 *a) Hasler* Victor, Glauben und Erkennen im Johannesevangelium; – *b) Lips* Hermann von, Anthropologie und Wunder im Johannesevangelium: EvT 50 (1990) 279-296 / 296-311.

5716 *Hengel* Martin, The Old Testament in the Fourth Gospel: HorBT 12,1 (1990) 19-41.

5717 *Herlong* T. H., The covenant in John: Emmanuel 95 (1989) 594-600 [< NTAbs 34,27].

5718 **Holleman** C. P. T.ᴶ, Descent and ascent in the Fourth Gospel; the Johannine deconstruction of the heavenly ascent revelatory paradigm: diss. Rice, ᴰ*Kelber* W. 1990. 349 p. 91-10979. – DissA 51 (1990s) 3784-A.

Ingram Kristen J., Good news for modern women; the Gospel of John 1989 ⟶ 8859.

5719 **Karris** Robert J., Jesus and the marginalized in John's Gospel: Zacchaeus Studies. Collegeville MN 1990, Liturgical. 119 p. $8 [NewTR 4/3, 98, D. J. *Harrington*].

5720 **Kelleher** Sean B., Praying with John. Bangalore 1988, Good Tidings. xvi-181 p. – ᴿVidyajyoti 54 (1990) 45s (G. *Mlakhuzhyil*).

5721 **Kieffer** René, Le monde symbolique de saint Jean: LDiv 137, 1989 ⟶ 5,5440: ᴿEsprVie 100 (1990) 238 (E. *Cothenet*: accès à son commentaire en suédois); Gregorianum 71 (1990) 613 (J. *Galot*); MondeB 64 (1990) 72 (F. *Brossier*); RThom 90 (1990) 145s (L. *Devillers*).

5722 *Koester* C. R., The Fourth Gospel in a three-year lectionary: WWorld 10,1 (1990) 21-26 [< NTAbs 34,174].

5723 *Kooy* Vernon H., The transfiguration motif in the Gospel of John: ⟶ 60,181, ᶠOUDERSLUYS R., Saved by hope, ᴱCook J. 1978, 64-78 [15-63 also on John: *Ridderbos* H., *Morris* L., *Jonge* Marinus de].

5724 **Koranda** Christian, Die johanneischen Wunder in der frühchristlichen Kunst; Diss. Wien Inst. Klas. Arch. 1989. – ArchAnz (B 1990) 145.

5725 **Kotila** Markku, Umstrittener Zeuge... Gesetz in Joh...: 1988 ⟶ 4,5496: ᴿCBQ 52 (1990) 561s (D. R. *Bauer*).

5726 *Kuśmirek* Anna, ❷ Theological function of the topographical data in the Fourth Gospel: RuBi 42 (1989) 342-8.

5727 *Léon-Dufour* Xavier, *a)* Où en est la recherche johannique? Bilan et ouvertures; – *b)* Quelques textes de portée mystique: ⟶ 545*, Jean, ACFÉB 1989/90, 17-41 / 255-263.

5728 *Lévêque* Jean, La gloire du Fils dans l'Évangile de Jean: ⟶ 542, Év. Venasque 1989/90, 79-101.

5729 *Lindars* Barnabas, Some recent trends in the study of John [HAENCHEN E.; ROBINSON J. A. T.; ᴱASHTON J. ....]: Way 30 (1990) 329-338.

5730 **Loader** William, The Christology of the Fourth Gospel; structure and issues: BeitBExT 23, 1989 ➤ 5,5446: ᴿSNTU A-15 (1990) 180s (F. *Weissengruber*).

5731 **Manns** Frédéric, John and Jamnia 1988 ➤ 4,5503: ᴿEstB 48 (1990) 142s (M. *Pérez Fernández*).

5732 **Neyrey** Jerome, An ideology of revolt; John's Christology in social science perspective. Ph 1989, Fortress. 272 p. $30. 0-8006-0895-X. – ᴿInterpretation 44 (1990) 187s (R. *Kysar*).

5733 **Norris** John M., The theological structure of St. AUGUSTINE's exegesis in his 'Tractatus in Iohannis Euangelium': diss. Marquette, ᴰ*Lienhard* J. Milwaukee 1990. [xiv-] 333 p. AA 91-17355.

5734 **O'Day** Gail, Revelation in the Fourth Gospel; narrative mode and theological claim ᴰ1986 ➤ 2,4203 ... 5,5451: ᴿNeotestamentica 29 (1990) 372s (D. B. *Pass* under surname Gail).

5735 *Oñate* Juan A., La mujer en el Evangelio según san Juan: AnVal 16,32 (1990) 35-

5737 *Osiek* Carolyn, The Jesus of John's Gospel, a breed apart: Church 5,3 (NY 1989) 119-123 [< NTAbs 34,38].

5738 *Pack* F., The Holy Spirit in the Fourth Gospel: RestQ 31 (1989) 139-149 [< NTAbs 34,175].

5739 **Panimolle** Salvatore A., Gesù di Nazaret nell'ultimo evangelo e nei primi scritti dei Padri: StRicB. R 1990, Borla. 451 p. Lit. 50.000 [TR 87,339]. 88-263-0757-1.

5740 **Parmentier** Roger, L'Évangile selon Jean actualisé et réécrit, résonances actuelles. Montpellier 1989, A.C.T.U.E.L. 150 p. 2-904558-47-6. – ᴿÉTRel 65 (1990) 627 (C.-B. *Amphoux*).

5741 *a) Pasquetto* Virgilio, Incarnazione come 'ascolto del Padre' nella visuale del IV Vangelo; – *b) Moriconi* Bruno, 'Segreto messianico' e sequela silenziosa: RivVSp 43 (1989) 375-394 / 515-533.

5742 *Perkins* Pheme, John's Gospel and Gnostic Christologies; the Nag Hammadi evidence: ➤ 52, ᶠFᴜʟʟᴇʀ R., AnglTR Supp. 11 (1990) 68-76.

5743 **Pidyarto Gunawan** Henricus, Jesus the new Elijah according to the Fourth Gospel: diss. Angelicum, ᴰ*Agius* J. R 1990. 182 p. – ETLv 22, p. 594.

5744 **Rhea** Robert, The Johannine son of man: ATANT 76. Z 1990, Theol.V. 79 p. Fs 24. 3-290-10061-8 [NTAbs 34,387]. – ᴿCarthaginensia 6 (1990) 372s (R. *Sanz Valdivieso*).

5745 *Rigato* Maria Luisa, Le figure femminili nel Vangelo secondo Giovanni ➤ 542*, Laici 1988/90, 173-233.

5746 **Rodríguez Ruiz** Miguel, Der Missionsgedanke des Joh.-Evs 1986 ➤ 3,5329 ... 5,5459: ᴿJBL 109 (1990) 146-9 (H. *Boers*).

5746* *Schenke* Hans M., 'Er muss wachsen, ich aber muss abnehmen'; der Konflikt zwischen Jesusjüngern und Täufergemeinde im Spiegel des Johannesevangeliums: ➤ 38*, ᶠCOLPE C., 1990, 301-313.

5747 *Schnelle* Udo, Perspektiven der Johannesexegese: SNTU A-15 (1990) 59-72.

5748 *Schwankl* Otto, Die Metaphorik von Licht und Finsternis im johanneischen Schrifttum: ➤ 350, Metaphorik 1990, 135-167.

5749 **Scott** James M.C., Sophia and the Johannine Jesus: Diss. Durham 1990. 389 p. BRD-93619. – DissA 52,2175-A; RTLv 22, p. 595.

5750 *Sellin* Gerhard, 'Gattung' und 'Sitz im Leben' auf dem Hintergrund der Problematik von Mündlichkeit und Schriftlichkeit im Johannesevangelium: EvT 50 (1990) 311-331.

5751 *a*) *Sevrin* Jean-Marie, Le quatrième évangile et le gnosticisme; questions de méthode; – *b*) *Kaestli* Jean-Daniel, L'exégèse valentinienne du quatrième évangile / Remarque sur le rapport du quatrième évangile avec la gnose et sa réception au IIᵉ siècle; – *c*) *Poffet* Jean-Michel, Indices de réception de l'évangile de Jean au IIᵉ siècle, avant IRÉNÉE: → 538*, Communauté johannique 1988/90, 251-268 / 323-350. 351-6 / 305-321.

5752 **Smith** D. Moody, Judaism and the Gospel of John: → 396, ᴰ*Charlesworth* J., Jews and Christians 1988/90, 76-96 (-99, discussion).

5753 **Stimpfle** Alois, Blinde sehen; die Eschatologie im traditionsgeschichtlichen Prozess des Johannesevangeliums [kath. Diss. Augsburg 1988, ᴰ*Leroy* H. → 4,5521]: BZNW 57. B 1990, de Gruyter. x-324 p. DM 112. 3-11-012017-8 [NTAbs 35,107]. – ᴿStPatav 37 (1990) 658-667 (L. *Sartori*).

5754 *Thiessen* K. H., Jesus and women in the Gospel of John: Direction 19,2 (1990) 52-64 [< NTAbs 35,35].

5755 **[Meye] Thompson** Marianne, *a*) The humanity of Jesus in the Fourth Gospel 1988 → 4,5523; 5,5465: ᴿCBQ 52 (1990) 366-8 (M. C. de *Boer*); Interpretation 44 (1990) 185 (R. *Kysar*, also on FORTNA); – *b*) Eternal life in the Gospel of John: ExAud 5 (1989) 35-55.

5756 **Tobler** Eva, Vom Missverstehen zum Glauben; ein theologisch-literarischer Versuch zum vierten Evangelium und zu Zeugnissen seiner Wirkung: EurHS 23/395. Bern 1990, Lang. iv-203 p. DM 48. 3-261-04243-5 [NTAbs 35,247: with a little help from Baroque poet Catharina-Regina von Greiffenberg].

5757 **Tong** Far-Dung, Gathering into one – a study of the oneness motif in the Fourth Gospel with special reference to Johannine soteriology: diss. Seminex, ᴰ*Smith* R. St. Louis 1983. 167 p. 90-30836. – DissA 51 (1990s) 2062s-A.

5758 *a*) *Vouga* François, Jean et la gnose; – *b*) *Vernette* Jean, L'utilisation de l'évangile de Jean dans les nouveaux mouvements religieux gnostiques; → 545*, Jean, ACFÉB 1989/90, 107-125 / 185-201.

5759 **Waldstein** Michael M., The mission of Jesus in John; probes into the 'Apocryphon of John' and the Gospel of John: diss. Harvard, ᴰ*Koester* H. CM 1990. 214 p. 90-22366. – DissA 51 (1990s) 896-A; RelStR 17,194.

5760 **Weber** Josef, Kreuzestheologie und Nachfolge im Johannesevangelium: Diss. Pont. Univ. Salesiana; ᴰ*Kothgasser* A. R 1989. 115 p. [Extr.].

5761 *Werner* E., Johannesevangelium und mittelalterlicher Dualismus: Heresis 12 (1989) 13-26 [< RHE 85, p. 268*].

5762 **Wijngaards** John. *a*) The Spirit in John: Zacchaeus Studies NT 1988 → 4,5527: ᴿCBQ 52 (1990) 348-50 (Mary C. *Boys* compares with KODELL J., NEYREY J., PRAEDER S. in same series); – *b*) The Gospel of John and his letters: MessageBSpir 11, 1986 → 2,4159; 3,5268: ᴿVidyajyoti 54 (1990) 46 (G. *Mlakuzhyil*).

5763 **Yee** Gale A., Jewish feasts and the Gospel of John 1989 → 5,5470: ᴿWorship 64 (1990) 276-8 (V. M. *Smiles*).

5764 *Young* Abigail A., Accessus ad Alexandrum; the praefatio to the Postilla in Iohannis Evangelium of ALEXANDER of Hales (1186?-1245): MedvSt 52 (1990) 1-23.

G1.5 Johannis Prologus 1,1 ...

5765 *Carter* Warren, The Prologue and John's Gospel; function, symbol, and the definitive word: JStNT 39 (1990) 35-58.

5766 *Dettwiler* Andreas, Le prologue johannique (Jean 1,1-18): → 538*, Communauté johannique 1988/90, 185-203.

5767 **Hofrichter** Peter [→ 5776], Im Anfang war der 'Joh-Prol' 1986 → 2,4217 ... 5,5481: RTLZ 115 (1990) 504s (W. *Vogler*).

5768 *Jesudass* A., Jesus the logos: Living Word 96 (Kerala 1990) 367-374 [< TContext 8/2, p. 46].

5769 TE**Klünker** Wolf-Ulrich, Thomas von AQUIN, Der Prolog des Johannes-Evangeliums [Super Ev. I,i-xi]: Hardenbeg-Goetheanum. Stu 1986, Freies Geistesleben. 206 p. DM 48 [TR 87,388s, L. *Hödl*].

5770 *Mortley* R., From word to silence, I. The rise and fall of Logos; II. The way of negation, Christian and Greek 1986 → 4,5535: RNedTTs 44 (1990) 169s (R. van der *Broek*).

5771 *a) Robinson* Gesine, The Trimorphic Protennoia and the prologue of the Fourth Gospel; – *b) Sanders* Jack T., Nag Hammadi, Odes of Solomon, and NT Christological hymns [Jn 1; Protennoia ...]: → 152, FROBINSON J. M., Gnosticism 2 (1990) 37-50 / 51-66.

5772 *Simoens* Yves, Le Prologue de saint Jean; une théologie qui est une exégèse: → 541*, L'écriture âme 1989/90, 61-80 [213-222, conclusion].

5773 **Theobald** Michael, Die Fleischwerdung des Logos ...: NTAbh NS 20, 1988 → 4,5536; 5,5487: RCBQ 52 (1990) 574s (J. T. *Forestell*); SNTU A-15 (1990) 171-3 (U. *Schnelle*); TPQ 138 (1990) 400s (A. *Fuchs*).

5774 *Tobin* Thomas H., The prologue of John and Hellenistic Jewish speculation: CBQ 52 (1990) 252-269.

5775 **Miller** E. L., Salvation-history in the prologue of John ... 1:3/4: NT supp. 60, 1989 → 5,5490: RNeotestamentica 29 (1990) 381-3 (J. G. van der *Watt*).

5776 **Hofrichter** Peter, Wer ist der 'Mensch, von Gott gesandt' in Joh 1,6 [gegen THEOBALD M.]: BibUnt 21 (Ergänzungsheft zu 17). Rg 1990, Pustet. 109 p.; Eng. summary p. 75-85. 3-7917-1244-4. – RArTGran 53 (1990) 302s (A. S. *Muñoz*); Salmanticensis 37 (1990) 367s (F. F. *Ramos*); StPatav 37 (1990) 394s (G. *Segalla*); TPQ 138 (1990) 401s (M. *Hutter*); TsTNijm 30 (1990) 309 (S. van *Tilborg*).

5777 *Pryor* John W., Jesus and Israel in the Fourth Gospel – John 1:11: NT 32 (1990) 201-218.

5778 *a) Kotzé* P. P. A., Die betekenis en konteks van genade en waarheid in Johannes 1:14-18; – *b) Watt* J. G. van der, Die strukturele komposisie van die Johannesevangelie heroorweg: SkrifKerk 8,1 (1987) 38-51 / 68-84 [< NTAbs 34,177].

5779 *Rochais* Gérard, 'Et le Verbe s'est fait chair', Jn 1,14: → 669, EPetit J., J.-C. Universel 1989/90, 25-48.

5780 *Letis* T. P., The Gnostic influences on the text of the Fourth Gospel: John 1:18 in the Egyptian manuscripts: BRefB 1,1 (Fort Wayne 1989) 4-7 [< NTAbs 34,218].

5781 *Coulot* Claude, Le témoignage de Jean-Baptiste et la rencontre de Jésus et de ses premiers disciples Jn 1,19-51; approches diachroniques et synchronie: → 545*, Jean, ACFÉB 1989/90, 225-238.

5782 *Robert* René, Un précédent platonicien à l'équivoque de Jean 1,18: RThom 90 (1990) 634-9.

5783 *Schenke* Ludger, Die literarische Entstehungsgeschichte von Joh 1, 19-51: BibNot 46 (1989) 24-57.

5784 *Castellano F.*, Antonio, [Jn 1,24-31] La exégesis de ORÍGENES y de HERACLEÓN en el Libro VI del 'Comentario a Juan': TVida 31 (1990) 309-330.

5785 *Odaka* Takeshi, ❶ 'Among you stands one you do not know' (John 1,26); the inseparable relation between man and God according to ORIGEN: Katorikku Kenkyu 29/58 (1990) 129-152.

5786 *Nortjé* S., [Jn 1,28] Johannes die Doper in Betanië oorkant die Jordaan: HervTSt 45 (Pretoria 1989) 573-585 [< NTAbs 34,177].

5787 **Kühn** Hans-Jürgen, Christologie und Wunder... Joh 1,35-51, ᴰ1988 ➤ 4,5547; 5,5497: ᴿBLitEc 91 (1990) 70s (S. *Légasse*); CBQ 52 (1990) 160s (P.J. *Cahill*); JBL 109 (1990) 145s (D.E. *Aune*); RB 97 (1990) 618s (F.J. *Moloney*).

5788 **Lobell** Leona M., [Jn 1,35] The Lamb of God; the sacred made visible, diss. ᴰ*Balakian* Ann. NYU 1989. 211 p. 90-16288. – DissA 51 (1990s) 1604.

5789 *Neirynck* F., The anonymous disciple of John 1 [,35: not the Beloved Disciple of 13,23; 21,20]: ETL 66 (1990) 5-37.

5790 **Hinnebusch** F., [Jn 1,39 ...] 'Come and you will see!'; St. John's course in contemplation. NY 1990, Alba. ix-91 p. $6 pa. 0-8189-0580-8 [NTAbs 34,385].

5791 *Ehrman* Bart D., Cephas and Peter [ancient tradition of two different persons, despite Jn 1,42]. JBL 109 (1990) 463-474.

5792 **Stichel** Rainer, [Jn 1,48] Nathanael... 1985 ➤ 1,5292... 3,5365: ᴿByZ 81 (1988) 305-8 (F.J. *Thomson*).

5793 *Koester* Craig R., Messianic exegesis and the call of Nathanael (John 1.45-51): JStNT 39 (1990) 23-34.

5794 *Baer* Bill, Il y eut des noces à Cana en Galilée (Jean 2,1-11), méditation biblique, ᵀ*Lepine* Josiane: Tychique 79 (1989) 37-43.

5794* *a) Colson* Jean, [Jn 2,1] Les noces du septième jour; – *b) Collin* Louis, À propos des traductions françaises de Jean 10,17-18; questions d'un théologien; – *c) Goedt* Michel de, La mère de Jésus en Jean 19,25-27: ➤ 109*, ᶠLAURENTIN René 1990, 187-193 / 195-205 / 207-216.

5795 **Gourgues** M., Mary, the mother of our faith, I. Mary, the 'woman' and the 'mother' in John [< NRT], Eng. ᵀ*Fedrigotti* L.M.: Theology Annual 2 (Hong Kong 1987) 93-117 (119-143, response by the translator) [145-154 *al*.; NTAbs 35,169.171].

5796 **Lütgehetmann** Walter, Die Hochzeit von Kana (Joh 2,1-11); zu Ursprung und Deutung einer Wundererzählung im Rahmen johanneischer Redaktionsgeschichte [Diss. Fra 1988s ➤ 4,5547*]: BibUnt 20. Rg 1990, Pustet. ix-402 p. DM 48. 3-7917-1243-8. – ᴿAntonianum 65 (1990) 668-670 (D. *Aračić*); ArTGran 53 (1990) 305s (A.S. *Muñoz*); ErbAuf 66 (1990) 314 (B. *Schwank*); RivB 38 (1990) 534-6 (P. *Grech*); Salmanticensis 37 (1990) 368s (F.F. *Ramos*); TsTNijm 30 (1990) 309 (A. van *Diemen*).

5797 *Manns* Frédéric, Un matrimonio diverso dagli altri: TerraS 65 (1989) 8-12 [98-100 Gv 1,48].

5798 *Muñoz* Jesús M., ❺ The wedding at Cana of Galilee: ColcFuJen 81 (1989) 347-367.

5799 **Serra** A.M., [Gv 2,1] E c'era... esegesi biblico-mariana 1989 ➤ 5,5505: ᴿPhilipSa 25 (1990) 307-9 (B. *Pena*).

5800 *Moloney* Francis J., Reading John 2:13-22; the purification of the Temple: RB 97 (1990) 432-452; franç. 432.

5801 *Stegemann* Ekkehard W., [Jn 2,13s] Zur Tempelreinigung im Johannesevangelium: ➤ 147, ᶠRENDTORFF R., Hebr. Bibel 1990, 503-516.

5802 **Letourneau** Pierre, Jn 2,23-3,36; un exposé sommaire de la double christologie johannique: diss. Laval 1990. 560 p. – RTLv 22, p. 593.

G1.6 Jn 3ss... Nicodemus, Samaritana.

5803 *Retoré* François, Nicodème, la Samaritaine, deux témoins privilégiés de la Bonne Nouvelle: ➤ 542, Évangile 1989/90, 23-43.

5804 **Orr** W., *Guy* W., [Jn 3,1-21...] Living hope; a study of the NT theme of birth from above. Santa Fe 1989, Sunstone 197 p. $13 pa. 0-86534-132-X [NTAbs 34,265].

5805 *Söding* Thomas, Wiedergeburt aus Wasser und Geist; Anmerkungen zur Symbolsprache des Johannesevangeliums am Beispiel des Nikodemus-sprache Joh 3,1-21: ➤ 350, Metaphorik 1990, 168-219.

5806 *Rothfuchs* Eckart, [Joh 3,1-16 Nikodemus] Narrative Schriftauslegung: LuthTKi 14 (1990) 28-33.

5807 *Auwers* Jean-Marie, La nuit de Nicodème (Jean 3,2; 19,39) ou l'ombre du langage: RB 97 (1990) 481-503; Eng. 481.

5808 *Alonso Schökel* Luis, [Jn 3,5: AMONIO] 'Lo engendra el espíritu fecundando el agua': ➤ 125, FMORENO/VILLEGAS 1990, 115-127.

5809 *Weder* Hans, L'asymétrie du salut; réflexions sur Jean 3,14-21 dans le cadre de la théologie johannique: ➤ 538*, Communauté johannique 1988/90, 155-185.

5810 *Plaga* Ulrich J., Licht und Wahrheit – eine Auslegung von Joh 3,21: ErbAuf 66 (1990) 56-58.

5811 *Klaiber* Walter, Der irdische und der himmlische Zeuge; eine Auslegung von Joh 3,22-36: NTS 36 (1990) 205-233.

5812 **Boers** Hendrikus, Neither on this mountain... Jn 4: SBL Mg 35,1988 ➤ 4,5560: RCBQ 52 (1990) 738s (G. A. *Phillips*); TLZ 115 (1990) 428s (K. *Wengst*).

5813 *Beck* Edmund, Der syrische Diatessaronkommentar zu der Perikope von der Samariterin am Brunnen: OrChr 74 (1990) 1-24.

5814 *Nielsen* E., [Jn 4,1-42, meeting at the well] Mødet ved brønden; nogle betragtninger: ➤ 85, FHYLDAHL N., DanTTs 53 (1990) 243-259 [< NTAbs 35,172].

5815 **Poffet** Jean-Michel, La méthode exégétique d'HÉRACLÉON et d'ORIGÈNE... Jean 4, 1985 ➤ 1,5308 ... 5,5524: RRB 97 (1990) 298s (M.-J. *Pierre*).

5816 **Okure** Teresa, The Johannine approach to mission... Jn 4,1-42: WUNT 2/31, 1988 ➤ 4,5564; 5,5525: RInterpretation 44 (1990) 314 (F. *Segovia*); JBL 109 (1990) 146-9 (H. *Boers*); Pacifica 3 (1990) 347-9 (J. *Painter*: some weaknesses); StPatav 37 (1990) 149-157 (G. *Segalla*); TLZ 115 (1990) 268-270 (K. *Wengst*).

5817 **Carmona** Paul, The Jewish Scriptures in the background of John 4:4-42, the Samaritan Woman narrative: diss. Leuven 1990, DCollins R. xlv-290 p. – RTLv 22,592.

5818 *Botha* J. E., a) Reader 'entrapment' as literary device in John 4:1-42: Neotestamentica 24,1 (1990) 37-47; – b) John 4:15; a difficult text speech act theoretically revisited: Scripture 35 (1990) 1-9 [< NTAbs 35,172].

5819 **Schwab** C., Une femme en Samarie; le récit d'une rencontre bouleversante. Lausanne 1990, Moulin. 85 p. [ÉTRel 65,483].

5820 a) *Crouzel* Henri, L'évangile de Jean et la patristique; l'exégèse origénienne de Jn 4,13-15; – b) *Amphoux* Christian-B., À propos de l'histoire du texte de Jean avant 300; quelques lieux variants significatifs: ➤ 545*, Jean, ACFÉB 1989/90, 163-171 / 205-223.

5821 *Koester* Craig R., 'The savior of the world' (John 4,42): JBL 109 (1990) 665-680.

5822 *Henaut* Barry W., John 4:43-54 and the ambivalent narrator; a response to CULPEPPER's Anatomy of the Fourth Gospel [1983]: SR 19 (1990) 287-304.

5823 *Culpepper* R. Alan, *a*) Un exemple de commentaire fondé sur la critique narrative; Jean 5,1-18; – *b*) L'application de la narratologie à l'étude de l'évangile de Jean: ➤ 538*, Communauté johannique 1988/90, 135-151 / 97-120.

5825 *a*) *Wallace* Daniel B., John 5,2 and the date of the Fourth Gospel: Biblica 71 (1990) 177-205; franç. 205; – *b*) *Görg* Manfred, [Joh 5,2] Betesda – 'Beckenhausen' ['basin-house']: BibNot 49 (1989) 7-10.

5826 *Klappert* Bertold, 'Mose hat von mir geschrieben', Leitlinien einer Christologie im Kontext des Judentums, Joh 5,39-47: ➤ 147, ᶠRENDTORFF R., Hebr. Bibel 1990, 619-640.

G1.7 Panis Vitae – *Jn 6 ...*

5827 *a*) *Roulet* Philippe, *Ruegg* Ulrich, Étude de Jean 6; la narration et l'histoire de la rédaction; – *b*) *Riniker* Christian, Jean 6,1-21 et les évangiles synoptiques: ➤ 538*, Communauté johannique 1988/90, 231-247 / 41-67.

5828 *Segalla* Giuseppe, La complessa struttura letteraria di Giovanni 6: TItSett 15 (1990) 68-89; Eng. 89.

5829 *Witkamp* L.T., Some specific Johannine features in John 6.1-21: JStNT 40 (1990) 43-60.

5830 *Martini* Carlo M., [Gv 6,14-69] Comprendere Gesù a Cafarnao: TerraS 66 (1990) 218-220 [221-4 *Ravasi* G.: 225-8, *Fabbretti* N.].

5831 **Kuzenzama** K.P.M., La structure bipartite de Jn 6,26-71; nouvelle approche: Recherches Africaines de Théologie 9, 1987 ➤ 4,5575: ᴿGregorianum 71 (1990) 214 (G. *Ferraro*); Salesianum 52 (1990) 741s (C. *Bissoli*).

5832 *Bienaimé* Germain, L'annonce des fleuves d'eau vive en Jean 7,37-39: RTLv 21 (1990) 281-310.417-454; Eng. 415.

5833 *Nugent* Andrew, What did Jesus write? (John 7,53-8,11): DowR 108 (1990) 193-8: a 'sign' (for Torah).

5834 *Romaniuk* Kazimierz, ❷ Jésus et la pécheresse publique (Jn 7,53-8,11): ColcT 59,4 (1989) 5-14; franç. 14.

5835 *Gourgues* Michel, 'Moi non plus je ne te condamne pas'; les mots et la théologie de Luc en Jean 8,1-11 (la femme adultère): SR 19 (1990) 305-318.

5836 *Lührmann* Dieter, Die Geschichte von einer Sünderin und andere apokryphe Jesusüberlieferungen bei DIDYMOS von Alexandrien [Tura]: NT 32 (1990) 289-316.

5837 *Ruf* Karl-Friedrich, Jesus und die Ehebrecherin (Joh 8,1-11); zu einem Bild von Gisela Harupa: CLehre 43 (1990) U-186-9 [< ZIT 91,116].

5838 *a*) *Cazeaux* Jacques, Concept ou mémoire?; la rhétorique de Jean chap. 8, v.12-59; – *b*) *Boismard* Marie-Émile, Approche du mystère trinitaire par le biais du IVᵉ évangile: ➤ 545*, Jean, ACFÉB 1989/90, 277-308 / 127-142.

5839 *Muñoz León* Domingo, La liberación por la Verdad; sustrato bíblicotargúmico y Derás de traspaso en Jn 8,31-36: ► 125, ᶠMORENO/VILLEGAS 1990, 129-146.

5840 *Kinghorn* Johann, John 8:32 – the freedom of truth: IntRMiss 79 (1990) 314-9.

5841 *Probst* A., [Jn 8,58] Jésus et Yahvé: RRéf 41,1 (1990) 44s [< NTAbs 34,320].

5842 *Engemann* Josef, Hirt: ► 853, RAC 15,116 (1990) 577-607; 8 fig.

5843 *VanderKam* James C., John 10 and the feast of the Dedication: ► 173, ᶠSTRUGNELL J., Of scribes 1990, 203-214.

5844 *Regopoulos* G., Ⓖ [Jn 10] Jesus Christ, 'the good shepherd' (interpretative approach): DeltioVM 18,2 (1989) 5-48.

5845 *Rodríguez Ruiz* Miguel, El discurso del Buen Pastor (Jn 10,1-18): coherencia teológico-literaria e interpretación: EstB 48 (1990) 5-45; Eng. 5.

5846 *Berrouard* Marie-F., Deux peuples, un seul troupeau, un unique Pasteur; ecclésiologie de saint AUGUSTIN et citations de Jean 10:16: ► 688*a, Collectanea 1986/90, 275-301.

5847 *Frend* W.H.C., 'And I have other sheep' – John 10:16: ► 5,38*, ᴱCHADWICK H., Making of orthodoxy 1989, 24-39.

5848 *Mateo-Seco* Lucas F., La exégesis de GREGORIO de Nisa a Jn 10:18: ► 643, StPatr 18,3 (1983/9) 495-506.

5849 *Calleja* Joseph, John 11, author's stylistic devices and church vocabulary: MeliT 41 (1990) 1-14.

5850 *Maas* J., De structuur van de geloofscommunicatie in Johannes 11,1-46: ► 180, ᶠTROMP N., Gelukkig c. 1990, 169-181; Eng. 260.

5851 **Marchadour** A., Lazare 1988 ► 4,5592; 5,5363: ᴿMasses Ouvrières 432 (1990) 81-83 (E. *Fudji*); RevSR 63 (1989) 151s (Michèle *Morgen*); RuBi 42 (1989) 76s (T. M. *Dąbek*).

5852 **Wagner** Josef, Auferstehung und Leben, Joh 11,1-12,19...: ᴰ1988 ► 4,5588b; 5,5568: ᴿBLitEc 91 (1990) 233s (S. *Légasse*); CBQ 52 (1990) 766-8 (G. *Rochais*); TPhil 65 (1990) 591s (J. *Beutler*); TR 86 (1990) 453-5 (R. *Kühschelm*); TsTNijm 30 (1990) 89 (A. van *Diemen*: 33 discrepancies found in Jn text).

5853 *Wolbert* Werner, 'Besser, dass ein Mensch für das Volk stirbt, als dass das ganze Volk zugrunde geht' (Joh 11,50); Überlegungen zur Devise des Kajaphas: TGL 80 (1990) 478-494.

5854 *Calduch Benages* Nuria, La fragrancia del perfume en Jn 12,3: EstB 48 (1990) 243-265; Eng. 243.

5855 *Beutler* Johannes, Greeks come to see Jesus (John 12,20f): Biblica 71 (1990) 333-347; franç. 347.

5856 **Kühschelm** Roman, [Jn 12,35-50] Verstockung, Gericht und Heil; exegetische und bibeltheologische Untersuchungen zum sogenannten 'Dualismus' und 'Determinismus' in Joh 12,35-50 [Hab.-Diss. Wien 1990, ᴰKremer]: BoBB 76. Fra 1990, Hain. 320 p. DM 88 pa. [BZ 35,272-4, R. *Schnackenburg*]; 3-445-09132-3. – ᴿSNTU A-15 (1990) 173s (A. *Fuchs*).

G1.8 Jn 13 ... Sermo sacerdotalis et Passio.

5857 **Landier** J., *al.*, Voici l'homme; pour accompagner une lecture de l'Évangile de Jean, ch. 13-21. P 1990, Ouvrières. 259 p.; 2 maps. F 98. 2-7080-2747-5 [NTAbs 35,244]. – ᴿEsprVie 100 (1990) 540 (L. *Walter*).

5858 *Fourie* S., *Rousseau* J., 'Eenheid' in Johannes 13-17: Scriptura 29 (Stellenbosch 1989) 19-35 [< NTAbs 34,42].

5859 *Jeffrey* Peter, Do you mind of I wash your feet? John 13 as a pattern for ecumenism: Pacific Journal of Theology 2,3 (Fiji 1990) 17-22.

5860 *Rand* J. A. du, Narratological perspectives on John 13:1-38: HervTS 46 (1990) 367-389 [< NTAbs 35,173].

5861 *Monaghan* F. J., [Jn 13,1] The love gospel: HomP 89,11 (1989) 26-29.

5862 *Wojciechowski* Michał, **℗** Umycie nóg uczniom, The washing of the disciples' feet (Jn 13,1-20): RuBi 43 (1990) 136-144.

5863 *Menken* M. J. J., The translation of Psalm 41.10 in John 13.18: JStNT 40 (1990) 61-79.

5864 *Schwank* Benedikt, 'Ein neues Gebot gebe ich euch' (Joh 13,34): Erb-Auf 66 (1990) 295-304.

5865 *Stepien* Jan, [Jn 13,34] **℗** De amore inimicorum sicut signo singulari spiritualitatis Novi Testamenti: → 64, ᶠGʀᴢʏʙᴇᴋ S. 1990, 302-310.

5866 **Beutler** J., Habt keine Angst, Joh 14: SBS 16, 1984 → 65,4921 ... 3,5422: ᴿSNTU-A 14 (1989) 256-8 (M. *Theobald*).

5867 *a) Koester* Helmut, Les discours d'adieu de l'évangile de Jean; leur trajectoire au premier et au deuxième siècle; – *b) Zumstein* Jean, La rédaction finale de l'évangile de Jean (à l'exemple du chapitre 21): → 538, Communauté johannique 1988/90, 269-280 / 207-230.

5868 *Blanco* Arturo, Word and truth in divine revelation; a study of the commentary of St. Tʜᴏᴍᴀs on John 14,6: → 608, Révélation/Aquin 1989/90, 27-48.

5869 *Feuillet* André, [Jn 14,15 ... 16.11] Les promesses johanniques de l'Esprit Paraclet; leur importance et la lumière projetée sur elles par le reste du NT: Divinitas 33 (1989) 16-43 . 107-130 . 216-244.

5870 *Beutler* Johannes, [Joh 14,27; 20,19s] Friede nicht von dieser Welt? Zum Friedensbegriff des Johannesevangeliums: GeistL 63 (1990) 165-175.

5871 *Dillow* Joseph C., Abiding is remaining in fellowship; another look at John 15:1-6: BS 147 (1990) 44-53.

5872 **Schneider** Paul G., [Jn 17s] The mystery of the Acts of John; an interpretation of the hymn and the dance in light of the Acts [94-96] theology: diss. Columbia, ᴰ*Hendrix* H. NY 1990. 274 p. 91-02457. – DissA 51 (1990s) 2781-A.

5873 **Brownson** James V., The first farewell; a redaction-critical reconstruction of the first edition of the farewell discourse in the Gospel of John: diss. Princeton Theol. Sem. 1990. 440 p. 90-30365. – DissA 51 (1990s) 2057-A.

5874 **Lloyd-Jones** Martyn, ᴱ*Catherwood* Christopher, Growing in the Spirit; the assurance of our salvation: Studies in Jesus' prayer for his own; John 17:17-24. Westchester ɪʟ 1989, Crossway. 158 p. $11. 0-89107-535-6 [TDig 37,273].

5875 **Rossé** Gerard, L'ultima preghiera di Gesù [Gv 17] 1988 → 5,5594: ᴿScripTPamp 22 (1990) 965-9 (A. *García-Moreno*).

5876 **Lloyd-Jones** Martyn †, [Jn 17:17-19] Sanctified through the truth; the assurance of our salvation. Westchester ɪʟ 1989, Crossway. 153 p. $11 pa. – ᴿBS 147 (1990) 239s (K. L. *Sarles*: one of the finest British expositors of the 20th century).

5877 **La Potterie** Ignace de, *a)* La Passione di Gesù secondo il vangelo di Giovanni, Testo e Spirito 1988 → 4,5617; 5,5597: ᴿEstTrin 24 (1990) 324 (J. M. de *Miguel*); Laurentianum 51 (1990) 601 (L. *Martignani*); – *b)* The hour of Jesus 1989 → 5,5598: ᴿPacifica 3 (1990) 97-99 (F. J. *Moloney*: a delight; modifies some of his overreactions).

5878 *Turner* Max,   Atonement and the death of Jesus in John – some questions to BULTMANN and [J. T.] FORESTELL: EvQ 62 (1990) 99-122.

5879 *Chang* Aloysius B., ☉ Judas, money and sin in St. John's gospel: ColcFuJen 84 (1990) 245-8.

5880 *Veldhuizen* Piet van, ☉ The right ear of Malchus (Jn 18,1-11):   RuBi 42 (1989) 276-8.

5881 *Derrett* J. D. M., *a)* [Jn 18,11] Peter's sword and biblical methodology; – *b)* Ecce homo ruber (John 19,5 with Isaiah 1,18; 63,1-2):   BbbOr 32 (1990) 180-191 / 215-229.

5882 *Droge* Arthur J.,   The status of Peter in the Fourth Gospel; a note on John 18:10-11:   JBL 109 (1990) 307-311.

5883 *Matera* Frank J.,   Jesus before Annas, John 18,13-14.19-24:   ETL 66 (1990) 38-55.

5884 *Michaels* J. Ramsey,   John 18.31 and the 'trial' of Jesus: NTS 36 (1990) 474-9.

5885 *Forster* Christian,   Théologie et histoire dans le récit johannique de la Passion à partir de deux exemples, comparution devant le grand prêtre et comparution devant Pilate: ↠ 545*, Jean, ACFÉB 1989/90, 239-254.

5886 *Lacan* Marc François,   Qu'est-ce que la vérité? (Jean 18,28-19,22): SémBib 60 (1990) 18-32.

5887 **Panackel** Charles,   Idou ho anthropos (Jn 19,5b)... [ᴰ1987]: AnGreg 25, 1988 ↠ 4,5621; 5,5603:   ᴿCBQ 52 (1990) 169s (B. D. *Ehrman*: citation bordering on plagiarism); RThom 90 (1990) 144s (L. *Devillers*).

5888 **Urban** Ángel,   El orígen divino del poder ... Jn 19,11a: ᴰ1989 ↠ 5,5602: ᴿQVidCr 154 (1990) 124 (E. *Vilanova*); REB 50 (1990) 490-2 (L. *Boff*).

5889 **Huerta Pasten** Eduardo,   'He aquí vuestro Rey' (Jn 19,14); estudio exegético-teológico de la realeza de Jesús en el Evagelio de Juan: diss. Pont. Univ. Gregoriana, ᴰ*Caba* J.   R 1990. 454 p.; extr. Nº 1990, 188 p. – RTLv 22, p. 593.

5890 *Witkamp* L. T.,   Jesus' laatste woorden volgens Johannes 19:28-30: NedTTs 43 (1989) 11-20; Eng. 52.

5891 *Bonora* Adalberto,   'E subito ne uscí sangue ed acqua' (Gv 19,34): Presbyteri 23 (1989) 263-272.

5892 *La Potterie* Ignace de,   Le côté transpercé de Jésus: Carmel 57 (1990) 17-27.

5893 *Nagel* Peter,   Der Lanzenstich Joh 19,34 im Triadon (Vers 487): ↠ 46*h*, ꟳELANSKAJA Alla I. = JCopt 1 (1990) 29-36.

5894 **Drewermann** Eugen, 'Ich steige'; Alt-Ägyptische Meditationen zu Tod und Auferstehung in Bezug auf Joh 20/21. Olten 1989, Walter. 322 p.; ill. 3-530-16901-3. – ᴿActuBbg 27 (1990) 66s (J. *Boada*).

5895 **Gangemi** A.,   I racconti post-pasquali nel Vangelo di Giovanni I [...-IV] 1990 ↠ 5,5607:   ᴿAsprenas 37 (1990) 373s (S. *Cipriani*).

5896 *Adamo* David T.,   Jesus' Resurrection and his disciples' acceptance (an exegetical study of John chapter 20): DeltioVM 19,2 (1990) 13-21.

5897 *Wyatt* Nicolas,   'Supposing him to be the gardener' (John 20,15); a study of the paradise motif in John: ZNW 81 (1990) 21-38.

5898 *D'Angelo* Mary Rose,   A critical note; John 20:17 and Apocalypse of Moses 31:   JTS 41 (1990) 529-536.

5899 *Neirynck* Frans,   John 21 [SNTS presidential address, Dublin July 25, 1989]: NTS 36 (1990) 321-336.

5900 *Napole* Gabriel M.,   Pedro y el discípulo amado en Juan 21,1-25: RBibArg 52,39 (1990) 153-177.

5901 *Pitta* Antonio, Ichthys ed opsarion in Gv 21,1-14; semplice variazione lessicale o differenza con valore simbolico?: Biblica 71 (1990) 349-363; Eng. 364.

5902 *Schwarz* Günther, *Blépousin*... ['sie sahen brennende Feuerkohlen'] (Joh 21,9b): BibNot 55 (1990) 14s.

5903 *a*) *Trudinger* Paul, [Jn 21,11] The 153 fishes; a response and a further suggestion; – *b*) *Cardwell* Kenneth, The fish on the fire, Jn 21:9: ExpTim 102 (1990s) 11s / 12-14.

5904 *Vischer* Georg, 'Das unbeschreibliche Geschehen'; Anmerkungen zu Predigtweise und Predigtlehre K. H. MISKOTTES anhand seiner Predigt über Joh 21,25: ➤ 96, ᶠBOHREN R. 1990, 52-60.

G2.1   Epistulae Johannis.

5905 ᵀᴱ**Delebecque** É., Épîtres de Jean 1988 ➤ 4,5640: ᴿÉtClas 58 (1990) 183s (X. *Jacques*); RÉG 103 (1990) 350 (A. *Wartelle*).

5906 *Klauck* Hans-Josef, *a*) Zur rhetorischen Analyse der Johannesbriefe; – *b*) *Kyría ekklēsía* in BAUERs Wörterbuch und die Exegese des zweiten Johannesbriefes: ZNW 81 (1990) 205-224 / 135-8.

5907 *Olsson* B., [1-3] Johannes och den s k framgångsteologin [success-gospel]: Religion och Bibel 45ss (Lund 1986ss) 3-15 [< NTAbs 35,192].

5908 **Smalley** S. S., 1,2,3 John: Word Comm. 51, 1984 ➤ 65,4968... 4,5454: ᴿVidyajyoti 54 (1990) 611s (G. *Mlakuzhyil*).

5909 **Strecker** G., Die Joh.-Briefe 1989 ➤ 5,5623: ᴿCommSev 23 (1990) 281s (M. de *Burgos*); SNTU-A 14 (1989) 273s (A. *Fuchs*); TR 86 (1989) 205-7 (J. *Becker*).

5910 **Vouga** François, Die Johannesbriefe: HbNT 15/3. Tü 1990, Mohr. ix-92 p. DM 27. 3-16-145650-5 [NTAbs 35,254].

5911 **Barsotti** Divo, Meditazione sulla Prima Lettera di Giovanni: Bibbia e Liturgia 33. Brescia 1990, Queriniana. 163 p. Lit. 15.000. 88-399-1633-4. – ᴿNRT 112 (1990) 943s (L.-J. *Renard*); StPatav 37 (1990) 395s (G. *Segalla*).

5912 **Dalbesio** Anselmo, Quello che abbiamo udito e veduto; l'esperienza cristiana nella Prima Lettera di Giovanni: RivB supp 22. Bo 1990, Dehoniane. 267 p. Lit. 35.000. 88-10-30210-9.

5913 *Kuntzmann* Raymond, *Morgen* Michèle, Un exemple de réception de la tradition johannique; 1 Jn 1,1-5 et l'Évangile de Vérité NH I, p. 30: ➤ 545*, Jean, ACFÉB 1989/90, 265-276.

5914 *Kügler* Joachim, In Tat und Wahrheit [aber das Problem ist 1 Joh 1,3f; WENGST K. 1976]: zur Problemanlage des ersten Johannesbriefes: BibNot 48 (1989) 61-88.

5915 *Hiebert* D. Edmond, An exposition of 1 John (continued): 8. 4:7-21; 9. 5:1-12; 10. 5:13-21: Bibliotheca Sacra 147 (1990) 69-88 / 216-230 / 309-328.

5916 *Scholer* David M., 1 John 4:7-21: RExp 87 (1990) 309-314.

5917 *Kölbel* Mathias, Vom Geliebtwerden und Lebenkönnen; Unterrichtsentwurf zu 1. Joh 4,7-12: CLehre 42,1 (1990) U-1-4 [5-9, *Walter* Elisabeth, zu Joh 4,1-26; < ZIT 90,272].

5918 *Busenitz* Irwin A., [1 Jn 5,16] The sin unto death: MastJ 1,1 (1990) 17-31 [... not an adumbration of the Roman Catholic doctrine].

5919 *Wendland* E. R., What is truth? Semitic density and the language of the Johannine epistles (with special reference to 2 John): Neotestamentica 29 (1990) 301-333.

G2.3 *Apocalypsis Johannis* – **Revelation: text, introduction.**

5920 *Baloira Bertolo* Manuel A., Originalidad y apropiaciones en el Comentario al Apocalipsis de BEATO de Liébana: → 761, Helmantica 40 (1987/9) 173-181.

5921 **Bianchi** Enzo, L'Apocalisse di Giovanni, commento esegetico-spirituale. Magnano VC 1990 [= 1982/8], Qiqajon. 205 p.

5922 **Boring** M. Eugene, Revelation: Interpretation comm. 1989 → 5,5643: ᴿBS 147 (1990) 250s (J. F. *Walvoord*); HorBT 12,1 (1990) 104s (J. A. *Walther*).

5923 ᵀᴱ**Courreau** J., L'Apocalypse expliquée par CÉSAIRE d'Arles; [+] Scholies [de sources diverses, IRÉNÉE, CLÉMENT...] attribués à ORIGÈNE: Les Pères dans la foi, 1989 → 5,5646: ᴿNRT 112 (1990) 147 (L.-J. *Renard*).

5924 **Foulkes** Ricardo, El Apocalipsis desde América latina 1989 → 5,5648: ᴿActuBbg 27 (1990) 55s (R. de *Sivatte*); RTLim 24 (1990) 297 (U. *Berges*).

5925 **Giesen** Heinz, Johannes-Apokalypse, ²*Müller* Paul: Stu KLKomm NT 18. Stu 1989, KBW. 192 p. DM 19,80. 3-460-15481-0. – ᴿTPQ 138 (1990) 402s (F. *Kogler*).

5926 **Hendriksen** W., *a)* Plus que vainqueurs... Apc. Mulhouse 1987, Grâce et Vérité. 199 p. – ᴿSTEv 1 (1989) 89s (R. *Montanari*); – *b)* Visioenen der Voleinding; een verklaring van het Boek der Openbaring [GR 1939], ᵀ. Kampen 1988 = 1952, Kok. 227 p. ƒ35 [KerkT 41,69].

5927 **Hughes** Philip E. † 1990, The book of Revelation, a commentary. $18. 0-8028-3684-4 [TDig 38,270].

5928 *Larson* Stan, The earliest Syriac commentary on the Apocalypse [BL Ms. Add. 17.127]: → 643, StPatr 18,4 (1983/90) 249-254.

5929 **Mulholland** M. Robert, Revelation; holy living in an unholy world: Asbury Comm. GR 1990, Zondervan. 376 p. $21. 0-310-51740-0 [NTAbs 34,394]. – ᴿBS 147 (1990) 500s (J. F. *Walvoord*: amillennial, ignores alternatives).

5930 ᴱ**Romero** Posé Eugenio, *a)* S. BEATI a Liebana, Commentarius in Apocalypsim 1985 → 1,5427... 5,5650: ᴿRHE 85 (1990) 878 (D. *Verhelst*); Salmanticensis 37 (1990) 250s (R. *Trevijano*); – *b)* El Comentario al Apocalipsis de TICONIO [STEINHAUSER R. 1987]: CrNSt 11 (1990) 179-185; Eng. 186.

5931 **Schroten** H. [† 1978; Cursus 1945s, ᴱ*Bijlsma* R.], Openbaring van Johannes voor de Gemeente verklaard. Haag 1988, Boeken-C. 312 p. ƒ50 pa. – ᴿKerkT 41 (1990) 69 (M. H. *Bolkestein*).

5932 **Steinhauser** Kenneth B., The Apocalypse commentary of TYCONIUS; a history of its reception and influence: EurHS 23/301, 1987 → 4,5675; 5,5651: ᴿBijdragen 51 (1990) 89 (M. *Parmentier*).

5933 **Still** William, A vision of glory – an exposition of the Book of Revelation: Didasko, 1987 → 5,5652; £4: ᴿEvangel 7,2 (1989) 22 (D. *Prime*).

5934 **Sweet** John, Revelation: TPI NT Comm. L/Ph 1990, SCM/TPI (Trinity Press International). xvii-361 p. 0-334-02311-4; pa. -2-2.

5935 **Thompson** Leonard L., The book of Revelation; apocalypse and empire. NY 1990, Oxford-UP. xiv-265 p., map. $30. 0-19-505551-9 [NTAbs 34,259].

5936 **Vanni** Ugo, L'Apocalisse; ermeneutica, esegesi, teologia: RivB Supp 17, 1988 ➤ 4,5676; 5,5653: ᴿCBQ 52 (1990) 763s (W. J. *Harrington*: theology too much based on 'Johannine school'); EstB 48 (1990) 279s (J. J. *Bartolomé Lafuente*); ÉTRel 65 (1990) 455s (E. *Cuvillier*: 'professeur à l'Institut Biblique Pontifical', mais surtout à l'Université Grégorienne); FgNt 3 (1990) 173s (J. *Peláez*); RBibArg 52 (1990) 63s (R. *Krüger*); Stromata 45 (1989) 240; Teresianum 40 (1989) 621s (V. *Pasquetto*); TLZ 115 (1990) 109s (M. *Karrer*).

5937 *Vian P., a*) I codici Vaticani della Lectura super Apocalipsim di Pietro di Giovanni OLIVI: ➤ 475, ᴱ*Buonocore* M., Miscellanea I, 329, 1987, 229-257; – *b*) I codici fiorentini e romano della Lectura super Apocalipsim di Pietro di Giovanni Olivi (con un codice di Tedaldo della Casa ritrovato): ArFrancHist 83 (1990) 463-489 [< RHE 86,19*].

G2.4 *Apocalypsis,* Revelation, topics.

5938 **Alonso Merino** P.-J., 'El cántico nuevo' en el Apocalypsis; perspectiva bíblico-teológica [diss. 1989 ➤ 5,5655]. R 1990, Pont. Univ. Gregoriana. xv-429 p. – ᴿStudium 30 (M 1990) 552 (L. *López de las Heras*).

5939 *Andreicut* Ioan, Interprétations erronées de certains textes de l'Apocalypse et la manière de les combattre (en roumain): STBuc 42,2 (1990) 81-98; franç. 143.

5940 *Barr* David L., The reader of/in the Apocalypse; exploring a method: ProcGLM 10 (1990) 79-91.

5941 *Bost* Hubert, La révocation [1685], apocalypse des Protestants? [actualisation de Pierre JURIEU]: ÉTRel 65 (1990) 205-219.

ᴱ**Botha** E. J., Reading Revelation 1987/8 ➤ 516.

5942 *a) Collins* Adela Y., Eschatology in the Book of Revelation; – *b) Rowland* Christopher, The Apocalypse; hope, resistance and the revelation of reality [< Radical Christianity 1988, 66-81]: ExAud 6 (1990) 63-72 / 129-144.

5943 *Collins* T., Moral guidance in the Apocalypse: Emmanuel 95 (1989) 502-9 [< NTAbs 34,197].

5944 *Corsini* Eugenio, Angelologia e demonologia nell'Apocalisse di Giovanni: ➤ 593, Diavolo 1 (1988/90) 189-198.

Dougherty Edward C. A., The syntax of the Apocalypse ᴰ1990 ➤ 9656.

5945 **Dughi** Thomas A., The breath of Christ's mouth; Apocalypse and prophecy in early Reformation ideology: diss. Johns Hopkins. Baltimore 1990. 420 p. 90-30187. – DissA 51 (1990s) 1652-A.

5946 *Filippini* Roberto, La forza della verità; sul concetto di testimonianza nell'Apocalisse: RivB 38 (1990) 398-448; Eng. 448s.

5947 **Fleck** Jude C., Eschatological poetics in [MILTON J.] 'Paradise lost', two seventeenth-century commentaries on Revelation, and selected sermons: diss. California. Berkeley 1990. 786 p. 91-03684. – DissA 51 (1990s) 3081-A.

5948 **Gamber** Klaus, Das Geheimnis der Sieben Sterne; zur Symbolik der Apokalypse: StPatrLtgBeih 17. Rg 1987, Pustet. 109 p.; 29 fig. DM 14,80 [NTAbs 35,111]. 3-7917-1140-7.

5949 *a)* **Giesen** Heinz, Symbole und mythische Aussagen in der Johannesapokalypse und ihre theologische Bedeutung; – *b) Trummer* Peter,

Einige Aspekte zur Bildersprache der Johannesapokalypse: ➤ 350, Metaphorik 1990, 255-277 / 278-290.

5950 **Guthrie** Donald, The relevance of John's Apocalypse 1987 ➤ 4,5634; 5,5671: ᴿBS 147 (1990) 251 (J. F. *Walvoord*); Themelios 16 (1990s) 25s (G. K. *Beale*).

5951 *Haręzga* Stanisław, ❷ L'importance du Verbe de Dieu et de l'Eucharistie dans la vie chrétienne selon l'Apocalypse de saint Jean: AtKap 115 (1990) 17-24.

5952 **Kamp** Hendrik R. van de, Israel in Openbaring, een onderzoek naar de plaats van het Joodse volk in het toekomstbeeld van de Openbaring aan Johannes: diss. ᴰ*Bruggen* J. van. Kampen 1990. – RTLv 22, p. 596.

5953 **Kealy** Seán P., The Apocalypse of John: MessageBSp 15, 1987 ➤ 3,5481; 5,5669: ᴿBibTB 20 (1990) 129 (D. L. *Barr*).

5954 *Kreitzer* Larry, Sibylline Oracles 8; the Roman imperial adventus coinage and the Apocalypse of John: JPseud 4 (1989) 69-85 [< TR 87,74].

5955 **Kretschmar** Georg, Die Offenbarung des Joh., die Geschichte ihrer Auslegung 1985 ➤ 1,5418 ... 4,5699: ᴿCrNSt 11 (1990) 208-210 (F. *Bovon*).

5956 **Krey** Philip D., Nicholas of Lʏʀᴀ; Apocalypse commentary as historiography: diss. ᴰ*McGinn* B. Chicago 1990. – RelStR 17,194; RTLv 22, p. 598.

5957 **La Rocca** Tommaso, Es ist Zeit; Apocalisse... Müɴᴛᴢᴇʀ 1988 ➤ 5, 5680: ᴿHumBr 45 (1990) 249 (P. *Grassi*).

5957* *Lupieri* Edmondo, Esegesi e simbologie apocalittiche [Apc < Henoch]: AnStoEseg 7 (1990) 379-396.

5958 **Marcato** Giorgio, La chiesa dell'Apocalisse; storia e teologia: diss. Angelicum, ᴰ*Salguero* J. R 1990. – RTLv 22, p. 594.

5959 **Mazzaferri** Frederick D., The genre of the Book of Revelation from a source-critical perspective: diss. 1989 ➤ 5,5683: ᴿCritRR 3 (1990) 222-4 (J. J. *Collins*: '1969, originated as ᴰ1986'); ÉTRel 65 (1990) 273s (E. *Cuvillier*: travail universitaire qui force l'admiration).

5960 **Moore** Hamilton, Revelation as an 'apocalypse' in the context of Jewish and Christian apocalyptic thought: diss. Belfast. – RTLv 22, p. 618 sans date.

5961 *Pilgrim* W. E., Universalism in the Apocalypse: WWorld 9 (1989) 235-243 [< NTAbs 34,63].

5961* **Pousseur** Robert, *Montalembert* Jean de, Le cri de l'Apocalypse. P 1990, Centurion. 164 p. F 90 [RTLv 22,84, J. *Ponthot*].

5962 *Rand* J. A. du, A socio-psychological view of the effect of the language (parole) of the Apocalypse of John: Neotestamentica 29 (1990) 351-365.

5963 *Rogers* Cornish, Images of Christian victory; notes for preaching from the Book of Revelation: QRMin 10 (1990) 69-78.

5964 *Roloff* Jürgen, Neuschöpfung in der Offenbarung des Johannes: JbBT 5 (➤ 2140: 1990) 119-138.

5965 *a) Rowland* Christopher, Revelation; mirror of our passion, goal of our longing; – *b) Pipkin* H. Wayne, Reading the signs of the times; the legacy of apocalyptic in Church history: Way 30 (1990) 124-134 / 318-328.

5966 *Selge* Kurt-Victor, Eine Einführung Joachims von Fɪᴏʀᴇ in die Johannesapokalypse: Deutsches Archiv für Erforschung des Mittelalters 46,1 (Köln 1990) 85-131 [< zɪᴛ 91,168].

5967 *Testa* Emmanuele, L'apocalittica giudeo-cristiana e il problema della salvezza: LA 40 (1990) 183-210; pl. 63-68; Eng. 447.

5968 **Thompson** Steven, The Apocalypse and Semitic syntax: SNTS Mg 52, 1985 ⮞ 1,5469 ... 5,5696: ᴿNedTTs 44 (1990) 67s (G. *Mussies*).

5969 *Vahanian* Gabriel, L'Apocalypse, l'Utopie, l'Occident: FoiVie 89,6 ('Europe-Protestantisme-Occident' 1990) 65-79.

5970 **Van Burkalow** James T., ᴱAnastasia, A study of St. John's Revelation. Pittsburgh 1990, Dorrance. 270 p. $13 [JBL 110,566].

5971 **Van Daalen** David H., A guide to the Revelation: ISPCK Study Guide 20, 1988. xii-205 p. rs 35. – ᴿVidyajyoti 53 (1989) 676 (R. J. *Raja*, also on KEALY S., BLEVINS J.).

5972 *Vanni* Ugo, Benedizioni e maledizioni nell'Apocalisse: ⮞ 325a, ParSpV 21 (1990) 205-217.

5973 *a) Weiser* Alfons, Ermutigung statt Bedrohung; zum Verständnis der Offenbarung des Johannes; – *b) Kehl* Medard, [Offb 22,20; 1 Kor 16,22 ...] 'Bis du kommst in Herrlichkeit ...'; die 'Wiederkunft' Jesu zum Gericht; – *c) Splett* Jörg, Leben im Lichte des Todes: LebZeug 44 (1989) 257-268 / 245-256 / 276-284.

G2.5 *Apocalypsis,* **Revelation** 1,1 ...

5974 *Blevins* James L., Revelation 1-3: RExp 87 (1990) 615-621.

5975 **Woschitz** Karl M., Erneuerung... Offb 1-3, 1987 ⮞ 3,5588 ... 5,5706: ᴿTPhil 65 (1990) 261s (J. *Beutler*).

5976 *Hellholm* David, The visions he saw or: To encode the future in writing; an analysis of the prologue of John's apocalyptic letter: ⮞ 24, ꟳBOERS H., Text and Logos 1990, 109-146.

5977 *Morton* R., The 'one like a Son of Man' in Daniel 7:8-13 reconsidered in Revelation 1:13-18: Kardia 5,1 (Portland OR 1990) 23-27 [< NTAbs 35,193].

5978 *Aune* D. E., The form and function of the proclamation to the seven churches (Revelation 2-3): NTS 36 (1990) 182-204.

5979 *Manns* Frédéric, [Apc 2s] L'évêque, ange de l'Église: EphLtg 104 (1990) 176-181; lat. 176.

5980 *Enroth* Anne-Marit, [Rev 2,7 ... 13,9] The hearing formula in the Book of Revelation: NTS 36 (1990) 598-608.

5981 *Martin* François [Cadir, préparation de la rencontre Brest 27-31.VIII. 1990], Apocalypse 4-6: SémBib 57 (1990) 40-56; 58,45-57, *Lombard* Denis, Apc 6s].

5982 *Viaud* Gérard, [Apc 4,4...] Les 24 presbytres de l'Apocalypse dans la tradition copte: BSACopte 29 (1990) 123-145; phot.

5983 *Hall* Robert G., Living creatures in the midst of the throne; another look at Revelation 4.6: NTS 36 (1990) 609-613.

5984 **Håkan** Ulfgard [⮞ 5,5713 Ulfgard H.], Feast and future; Rev 7: 1989: ᴿÉTRel 65 (1990) 122s (E. *Cuvillier*); RHPR 70 (1990) 276-8 (P. *Prigent*); TsTKi 61 (1990) 297-9 (M. *Synnes*).

5985 *Smith* Christopher R., The portrayal of the Church as the New Israel in the names and order of the tribes in Revelation 7.5-8: JStNT 39 (1990) 111-8.

5986 *Seng* Helmut, Apk 11,1-14 im Zusammenhang der Johannesapokalypse; Aufschluss aus LACTANTIUS und HIPPOLYTUS: VetChr 27 (1990) 111-121.

5987 *Keller* Catherine, Die Frau in der Wüste; ein feministisch-theologischer Midrasch zu Offb 12: EvT 50 (1990) 414-432.

5988 *Quispel* Gilles, The Holy Spirit as woman in Apocalypse 12: ⮞ 135, ꟳORBE A., Compostellanum 34 (1989) 37-39.

5989 *Soccorso* Vicente, Lo demoníaco según Apocalipsis 13,1-10; el Estado que tiende a autodivinizarse; expresión privilegiada de lo demoníaco en la historia: → 125, ᶠMORENO/VILLEGAS 1990, 169-207.

5990 *Fekkes* Jan[III], 'The bride has prepared herself'; Revelation 19-21 and Isaiah nuptial imagery: JBL 109 (1990) 269-287.

5991 *Zegwaart* H., [Rev 20:1-10] Apocalyptic eschatology and Pentecostalism; the relevance of John's millennium for today: Pneuma 10,1 (Gaithersburg MD 1988) 3-25 [< NTAbs 34,199].

G2.7 Millenniarismus, *Apc 21* ...

5992 *Arteaga* LL. José, Temas apocalípticos y lacunzismo, 1880-1918 [Manuel de LACUNZA Y DÍAZ S.J. 1731-1801; milenarismo en Chile]: → 125, ᶠMORENO/VILLEGAS 1990, 209-224.

5993 **Bacchiocchi** Samuele, The Advent hope for human hopelessness. Berrien Springs MI 1986, Biblical Perspectives. 424 p. $15. – ᴿBS 147 (1990) 244 (J. F. *Walvoord*, whose dispensationalism is attacked in the book).

5994 **Bahnsen** Greg L., *Gentry* Kenneth L., House divided. Tyler TX 1989, Inst. Christian Economics. 410 p. $10. – ᴿBS 147 (1990) 370-2 (J. F. *Walvoord*: full of errors and abuse, and confuses premillennialism with dispensationalism, in attacking HOUSE-ICE 1988 'Dominion theology' i.e. postmillennialism).

5995 *Bonner* Gerald, AUGUSTINE and millenarianism: → 5,38*, ᶠCHADWICK H., Making of orthodoxy 1989, 235-254.

5996 **Chilton** David, The Great Tribulation [of Apc occurred in God's past punishment of Israel and is not to be awaited today]. Fort Worth 1987, Dominion. 195 p. $6 pa. – ᴿCriswT 4 (1989s) 205s (T. D. *Lea*: significant example of postmillennialism).

5997 **Dumbrell** William J., The end of the beginning; Revelation 21-22 and the OT 1985 → 2,4403 ... 5,5730: ᴿThemelios 15 (1989s) 69s (G. K. *Beale*).

5998 *Karlberg* Mark W., Israel and the eschaton [FEINBERG's 'six distinctives of dispensationalism' and W. VAN GEMEREN's regrettably unfair presentation of covenant doctrine, in ᶠJOHNSON S., Continuity 1988]: WestTJ 52 (1990) 117-130.

5999 **Lubbers** G. C., The Bible versus millennial teachings. GR 1989, auct. 424 p. – ᴿCalvinT 25 (1990) 295-7 (D. E. *Holwerda*).

6000 **Poythress** Vern S., Understanding dispensationalists 1987 → 4,5761; 5,5726: ᴿGraceTJ 10 (1989) 102-5 (D. L. *Turner*) & 139-147 (R. L. *Saucy*; 123-138, *al.*; 147-159, Poythress response).

6001 *Shepherd* William H.[J], Revelation and the hermeneutics of dispensationalism: AnglTR 71 (1989) 281-299.

6001* *a) Witakowski* Witold, The idea of *septimana mundi* and the millenarian typology of the creation week in Syriac tradition; – *b) Ri Su-Min*, La caverne des trésors et le Testament d'Adam: → 779*, Symposium 5, 1988/90, 93-109 / 111-122.

6002 *Tabbernee* W., Revelation 21 and the Montanist 'New Jerusalem' [Pepouza-Tymion in Phrygia according to QUINTILLA c. 300]: AustralBR 37 (1989) 52-60 [< NTAbs 35,55].

6003 *Thomas* R. L., The spiritual gift of prophecy in Rev 22:18: JEvTS 32 (1989) 201-216 [< NTAbs 34,64].

6004 **Turner** Helen L., Fundamentalism in the Southern Baptist Movement; the crystalization of a millennialist movement: diss. Virginia, ᴰ*Fogarty* G. Charlottesville 1990. – RelStR 14,195.

| XIII. Paulus |

G3.1 **Pauli vita, stylus, chronologia.**

6005 **Barbaglio** Giuseppe, *a*) Paolo di Tarso e le origini cristiane 1985 ➤ 1,5511 ... 5,5736: ᴿTLZ 115 (1990) 816s (C. *Wolff*); – *b*) Pablo de Tarso y los orígenes cristianos [1985 ➤ 1,5511], ᵀ*Ortíz García* Alfonso: BiblEstB 65. S 1989, Sígueme. 391 p. 84-301-1089-5. – ᴿActuBbg 27 (1990) 54s (X. *Alegre*); Carthaginensia 6 (1990) 217 (J. F. *Cuenca*); CommSev 23 (1990) 279s (M. de *Burgos*); Iter 1 (Caracas 1990) 136s (J.-P. *Wyssenbach*); NatGrac 37 (1990) 313s (F. F. *Ramos*); RelCu 36 (1990) 684 (A. *Moral*); Studium 30 (M 1990) 552 (L. *López de las Heras*).

6006 *Barrett* Charles K., Pablo, misionero y teólogo [< ZTK 86 (1989) 18-32 ➤ 5,5737], ᵀᴱ*Aleu* J.: SelT 29 (1990) 335-342.

6007 **Bea** Fernando, Saulo, Saulo ... un testimone di Cristo 1988 ➤ 4,5768: ᴿTeresianum 40 (1989) 276s (V. *Pasquetto*).

6008 **Becker** Jürgen, Paulus, der Apostel der Völker 1989 ➤ 5,5739: ᴿEv-Komm 23 (1990) 299s (G. *Lüdemann*); RHPR 70 (1990) 207s (E. *Trocmé*).

6009 **Beker** J. Christiaan, The triumph of God; the essence of Paul's thought [= 1980 ➤ 61,6997 abridged and defended], ᵀ*Stuckenbruck* Loren T. Mp 1990, Fortress. xvi-132 p. $9 pa. 0-8006-2438-6 [TDig 38,48].

6010 *Best* Ernest, Paul and his converts 1988 ➤ 4,5770; 5,5741: ᴿEvQ 62 (1990) 270s (Ruth B. *Edwards*: delightful); Interpretation 44 (1990) 430.432 (M. H. *Hoops*); IrBSt 11 (1989) 142-5 (J. C. *McCullough*); Pro-testantesimo 45 (1990) 326 (B. *Corsani*); TS 51 (1990) 368 (B. *Fiore*) [CriswT 2 (1987s) 169s gives title 'Paul and his converts' for F. BRUCE].

6011 *Brändle* Francisco, El Jesús que transformó a Pablo: REspir 47 (1988) 49-64.

6012 **Breton** Stanislas, San Paolo, un ritratto filosofico [1988 ➤ 4,5773], ᵀ. Brescia 1990, Morcelliana. 142 p. Lit. 16.000. 88-372-1406-5.

Bristow John T., What Paul really said about women 1988 ➤ 8836; **Brownrigg** R., Pauline places 1989 ➤ g174; **Byrne** Brendan, Paul and the Christian woman 1989 ➤ 8839; *Guillemette* N., Saint Paul and women 1989 ➤ 8853.

6013 *Callan* Terrance, Psychological perspectives on the life of Paul; an application of the methodology of Gerd THEISSEN: SBEC 22. Lewiston 1990, Mellen. viii-161 p. $50. 0-88946-622-X [NTAbs 35,109].

6014 *Campbell* W. S., Paul's missionary practice and policy: IrBSt 12 (1990) 2-25.

6015 *Charlot* Cristiano M., L'imitazione di S. Paolo, III: Renovatio 24 (1989) 31-67.

6016 **Cianantoni** Luigi, La paternità apostolica di Paolo in rapporto al kerygma e alla paraklesi: diss. Pont. Univ. Gregoriana, ᴰ*Rasco* E. nᵒ 6874. R 1990s. – InfPUG 23,119 (1990s) 15.

6017 *Cipriani* Settimio, I 'collaboratori' di S. Paolo: ➤ 542*, Laici 1988/90, 279-301.

6018 **Dassmann** Ernst, Der Stachel im Fleisch; Paulus in der frühchristlichen Literatur bis Irenäus 1979 ➤ 60,7534; 61,7011 ...: ᴿZkT 112 (1990) 362-4 (L. *Lies*: hohe Qualität, zu wenig rezipiert).

6019 **Dreyfus** Paul, Saint Paul, un grand reporter sur les traces de l'Apôtre. P 1990, Centurion. 390 p. F 145. – [R]EsprVie 100 (1990) 608 (card.
P. *Poupard*).

6020 **Elliger** W., Paulus in Griechenland 1987 ➤ 3,5209; 4,5373: [R]TR 86
(1990) 204s (J. *Roloff*).

6021 *Engberg-Pedersen* Troels, Paulus livsfornægteren?: DanTTs 53 (1990)
1-18 [< ZIT 90,377].

6022 **Fitzpatrick** Joseph P., Paul, saint of the inner city. NY 1990, Paulist.
109 p. $6 pa. 0-8091-3129-3 [TDig 38,58].

6023 *a*) *Fonrobert* C., Paul; how can we understand him? how do we
understand our understanding? reflections in search of clarification; – *b*)
Krieger L., Paul and Torah; – *c*) *Louis* A. F., The psychological wisdom
of Pauline theology; – *d*) *Papworth* C., Paul, the olive tree and the wild
olive brach; – *e*) *Otto* J., Paul's inclusive Gospel: CentHermProt 60 (1990)
48-53 / 41-47 (34-40. 1-20 *al.*) / 29-34 / 54-59 / 60-72 [NTAbs 34,326ss].

6023* *Goldsmith* Martin, The genius of Roland ALLEN [on Paul's missionary
policies]: Evangel 7,3 (1989) 11-13.

6024 *Harrington* Daniel J., Paul and collaborative ministry [... not a solitary
trailblazer]: NewTR 3,1 (1990) 62-71.

6025 *Hay* David M., Job and the problem of doubt in Paul: ➤ 123*,
[F]MEYER P., Faith 1990, 208-222.

6026 *Hengel* Martin, Der vorchristliche Paulus: TBeit 21 (Wu 1990) 174-195
[< NTAbs 35,43].

6028 **Hildebrandt** Dieter, Saulus-Paulus; ein Doppelleben. Mü 1989, Hanser.
447 p. DM 48. [R]EvKomm 23 (1990) 300s (O. *Merk*).

6029 *Hubaut* Michel A., Paul de Tarse 1989 ➤ 5,5757: [R]NRT 112 (1990)
601s (X. *Jacques*); ScEsp 42 (1990) 355-357 (P.-É. *Langevin*: agréable,
insuffisant).

6030 **Hyldahl** N., Die paulinische Chronologie 1986 ➤ 2,4427 ... 4,5785: [R]St-
Patav 37 (1990) 398-400 (A. *Moda*).

6030* *Klessmann* Michael, Zum Problem der Identität des Paulus; psychologische Aspekte zu theologischen und biographischen Fragen: Wege
zum Menschen 41 (1989) 156-172 [< TLZ 116,228].

6031 *La Serna* Eduardo de, ¿'Ver – juzgar – actuar' en san Pablo?: RBib-
Arg 52,38 (1990) 85-98.

6032 *Legrand* Lucien, L'itinéraire spirituel de saint Paul: Spiritus 31,121
('Spiritualité missionnaire, aujourd'hui' 1990) 415-435.

6033 **Limbeck** Meinrad, Mit Paulus Christ sein; Sachbuch zur Person und
Theologie des Apostels Paulus. Stu 1989, KBW. 155 p.; 2 maps.
DM 35. 3-460-32811-8 [NTAbs 34,256]. – [R]EvKomm 23 (1990) 376 (R.
Linssen).

6034 **Lüdemann** Gerd, Opposition to Paul in Jewish Christianity 1989
➤ 5,5765: [R]CommSev 23 (1990) 280s (M. de *Burgos*); ExpTim 102
(1990s) (K. *Grayston*: favors BAUR); TorJT 6 (1990) 370s (M. O.
Steinhauser).

6035 **Maccoby** Hyam, Paul et l'invention du christianisme [The mythmaker
1986 ➤ 3,4437], [T]. P 1987, Lieu commun. 320 p. F 125. – [R]RBgPg 68
(1990) 214-7 (J. *Klener*, Eng.: holds Paul was never a Pharisee, Jesus and
his disciples *were*; worth studying).

6036 *Malherbe* Abraham, Paul and the popular philosophers 1989 ➤ 5,5768:
[R]CurrTMiss 17 (1990) 228 (E. *Krentz*).

6037 **Martini** Carlo M., *a*) The testimony of Paul; meditation on the life
and letters of St. Paul [Le confessioni di Paolo 1981], [T]*Leslie* S. NY

1989, Crossroad [Eng. already L 1983, St. Paul]. 102 p. $7 pa. 0-8245-0958-7 [NTAbs 34,257]; – *b*) ✪ Wyznania Pawła [the Confessions of Paul], medytacje. Kraków 1987, Apostolstwo Modlitwy. 113 p. – ᴿAt-Kap 114 (1990) 153s A.*Panasiuk*).

6037* **Martini** Carlo M., *a*) Paolo nel vivo del ministero. Mi 1989, Àncora; – *b*) In the thick of his ministry, ᵀ*Livingstone* Dinah. Middlegreen 1990, St. Paul. 91 p. 0-85439-336-6.

6038 **Pak Yeong Sik** James, Paul as missionary: diss. Pont. Ist. Biblico, ᴰ*Vanhoye* A. R 1990. 517 p. – AcPIB 9, p. 517; RTLv 22, p. 594; Biblica 71,145.

6039 *Pellicia* Flora, San Pablo evangelizador; hombre realista y creativo: RBibArg 52,40 (1990) 235-248.

6040 ᴱ**Penna** Romano, Antipaolinismo 1987/9 ⮞ 5,597: ᴿProtestantesimo 45 (1990) 327 (P. *Ribet*).

Perelmuter H., *Wuellner* W., Paul the Jew 1990 ⮞ a430.

6041 **Regner** Friedemann, 'Paulus und Jesus' im neunzehnten Jahrhundert... in der neutestamentlichen Theologie: StTNeunz 30, 1977 ⮞ 58,6846: ᴿTLZ 115 (1990) 350s (O. *Merk*).

6042 *Reid* D.G., The misunderstood apostle [steps toward rectifying in *Sanders* E., *Dunn* J., *Westerholm* S.]: ChrTod 34,10 (1990) 25-27 [< NTAbs 35,44].

6043 *Rivkin* Ellis, Paul's Jewish odyssey [against Maccoby H. 1986]: Judaism 38 (1989) 225-234.

6044 *Ródenas* Ángel, San Pablo, hombre y maestro de oración: REspir 49 (1990) 95-119.

6045 **Sanders** E.P., Paolo e il giudaismo palestinese 1986 ⮞ 2,4451... 4,5803: ᴿProtestantesimo 45 (1990) 144s (P. *Ribet*).

6046 **Sandnes** Karl Olov, Paul – one of the prophets? A contribution to the apostle's self-understanding: diss. Oslo 1988. – NorTTs 90 (1989) 50 ['First opponent' *Moxnes* H.; no (other) indication of Doktorvater].

6047 **Schelke** Karl H., Paolo; vita, lettere, teologia: BiblCuRel 56. Brescia 1990, Paideia. 276 p. 3-7278-0307-X / VR 3-525-53677-1.

6048 **Schnelle** Udo, Wandlungen im paulinischen Denken: SBS 137, 1989 ⮞ 5,5799: ᴿTLZ 115 (1990) 349 (E. *Reinmuth*); TZBas 46 (1990) 374s (P. *Dschulnigg*).

6049 **Segal** Alan F., Paul the convert; the apostolate and apostasy of Saul the Pharisee. NHv 1990, Yale Univ. xvi-368 p. $30. 0-300-04527-1 [NTAbs 34,395]. – ᴿTS 51 (1990) 737s (D.J. *Harrington*: partly earlier studies revised).

6050 **Thompson** W.G., Paul and his message for life's journey 1986 ⮞ 2,4457; 3,5606: ᴿVidyajyoti 54 (1990) 353-6 (P.M. *Meagher*).

6051 *Trudinger* P., St. Paul; a unitarian universalist Christian?: Faith and Freedom 43,1 (Oxford 1990) 55-58 [< NTAbs 34,329].

6052 *Vanhoye* Albert, *a*) L'apôtre Paul maître et guide pour la vie morale: ⮞ 672*b*, Mission 1990, 81-102; – *b*) The Apostle Paul as moral teacher and guide: ⮞ 672*a*, Catholic Priest 1990, 21-38 [AcPIB 89/7, 555].

6053 **Vos** J.S., Nieuw licht op de apostel Paulus; tendenties in het huidige onderzoek II: GerefTTs 90 (1990) 30-44.

6054 ᴱ*Wedderburn* A.J.M., Paul and Jesus 1989 ⮞ 5,615: ᴿIrBSt 12 (1990) 206s (E. *Best*).

6055 *White* Reginald,   Meet St Paul.   L 1989, Bible reading fellowship. 143 p.
£5.   0-900164-82-4 [ExpTim 102,31].

G3.2   **Corpus paulinum;** *introductio, commentarii.*

6056 *Aland* Kurt,   Methodische Bemerkungen zum Corpus Paulinum bei den
Kirchenvätern des zweiten Jahrhunderts [< ᶠ*Andresen* C., Kerygma 1979,
29-48]: ⮞ 193, Supplementa 1990, 97-116.

6057 *Aletti* Jean-Noël,   Saint Paul, exégète de l'Écriture: ⮞ 541*, L'Écriture
âme 1989/90, 37-59.

6058 **Carena** Carlo (*Luzi* Mario), San Paolo, le lettere; testo a fronte: I
millenni. T 1990, Einaudi. xlvi-331 p.; 24 color. fig. 88-06-11877-3.

6059 **Clabeaux** John J., A lost edition of the letters of Paul... Marcion: CBQ
Mg 21, 1989 ⮞ 5,5788: ᴿJTS 41 (1990) 631-4 (J. N. *Birdsall*: far-reaching
errors); TLZ 115 (1990) 594s (A. *Lindemann*).

6060 *a) Gamble* Harry Y.,   The Pauline corpus and the early Christian book;
– *b) Dassmann* Ernst,   Archaeological traces of early Christian veneration
of Paul: ⮞ 510, SMU Paul 1987/90, 265-280 / 281-306; 10 pl.

6061 **Hays** Richard B.,   Echoes of Scripture in the letters of Paul 1989
⮞ 5,5795: ᴿTTod 47 (1990s) 202s (E. E. *Ellis*).

6062 **Locke** John, ᴱ*Wainwright* Arthur W., A paraphrase and notes on
the Epistles... 1987 ⮞ 3,5634; 5,5799: ᴿCritRR 3 (1990) 239-241 (W.
Baird); JTS 41 (1990) 299s (R. *Morgan*); RB 97 (1990) 130s (J. *Murphy-
O'Connor*).

6063 **Malherbe** Abraham J.,   Ancient epistolary theorists 1988 ⮞ 4,5820;
5,5801: ᴿCBQ 52 (1990) 163-5 (S. K. *Stowers*: a landmark).

6064 *Munro* Winsome,   Interpolation in the epistles; weighing probability ['a
Pastoral stratum' (Pastoral-type redaction) in the other epistles]: NTS 36
(1990) 431-443.

6065 **Neumann** Kenneth J.,   The authenticity of the Pauline Epistles in the
light of stylostatistical analysis [diss. Toronto 1988 ᴰ*Hurd* J.]: SBL diss.
120. Atlanta 1990, Scholars. x-267 p. $30; pa. $17. 1-55540-428-6; -9-4.

6066 **Neyrey** Jerome H.,   Paul in other words; a cultural [anthropology,
psychology] reading of his letters. Louisville 1990, W-Knox. 263 p. $20.
0-664-21925-X [NTAbs 35,251].

6067 *Omanson* Roger L.,   Commentaries on Paul's letters: BTrans 41 (1990)
122-131.

6068 **Pardee** Dennis,   Handbook of ancient Hebrew letters: SBL Sourc 15,
1982 ⮞ 63,5647... 2,4474: ᴿOLZ 85 (1990) 313-5 (J. *Körner*).

6069 **Pitassi** Maria Cristina,   Le philosophe et l'Écriture; John Locke exégète
de Saint Paul: RTPhil Cah 14. Genève 1990, RTPhil. 99 p. 0250-6971.

6070 *Ramos Martín* Mariano J.,   La interpretación de las epístolas de S.
Pablo en las obras antipelagianas de S. Agustín: diss. ᴰ*Basevi* C. Pamplona 1990. 516 p. – RTLv 22, p. 595.

6071 **Richard** L.-A.,   Lettres de l'apôtre Paul traduites du grec. Lyon 1989,
Art et Histoire. 192 p. F 100 [NRT 113,441, X. *Jacques*].

6072 **Ries** J., *al.*,   Le epistole paoline nei Manichei, i Donatisti e il primo
Agostino: Sussidi patristici 5. R 1989, Augustinianum. 168 p. – ᴿVigChr
44 (1990) 401-4 (G. *Quispel*, Eng.).

6073 **Schmeller** Thomas,   Paulus und die 'Diatribe'; eine vergleichende Stilin-
terpretation ᴰ1987 ⮞ 3,5628... 5,5806: ᴿRB 97 (1990) 293s (J. *Murphy-
O'Connor*); RBibArg 52,38 (1990) 121s (R. *Krüger*); RTPhil 122 (1990)
277s (R. *Petraglio*); SNTU A-15 (1990) 185-8 (F. *Weissengruber*).

6074 **Schnider** Franz, *Stenger* Werner,   Studien zum nt. Briefformular 1987
→ 3,5629 ... 5,5807:   ᴿÉTRel 65 (1990) 629s (M. *Bouttier*); JBL 109 (1990)
156-8 (G. S. *Holland*).

6075 **Schreiner** T. R.,   Interpreting the Pauline epistles [9 steps]. GR 1990,
Baker.   167 p. $9 pa. 0-8010-8302-8 [NTAbs 35,116].

6076 *Simonetti* Manlio,   Paolo nell'Asia cristiana del II secolo: VetChr 27
(1990) 123-144.

6077 **Soards** Marion L.,   The Apostle Paul; an introduction to his writings
and teaching 1987 → 3,5630 ... 5,5807*: ᴿRelStT 8,1s (Edmonton 1988) 82
(T. A. *Robinson*); TLZ 115 (1990) 505-7 (H. *Hübner*).

6078 **Stanley** Christopher D.,   *a*) Citation technique in the Pauline epistles and
contemporary [to them] literature: diss. Duke, ᴰ*Smith* D. M.   Durham NC
1990. 443 p. 91-06624. – DissA 51 (1990s) 3437-A; RelStR 17,194; – *b*)
Paul and Homer; Greco-Roman citation practice in the first century C.E.:
NT 32 (1990) 48-78.

6079 **Stowers** Stanley K.,   Letter writing in Greco-Roman antiquity 1986
→ 2,4482 ... 5,5809:   ᴿDialog 27 (1988) 232-4 (D. E. *Fredrickson*, also on
MALHERBE A., MEEKS W.); HeythJ 31 (1990) 73s (A. *Louth*); JAAR 58
(1990) 154-6 (Kathleen O. *Wicker*: important); TsTKi 61 (1990) 70 (R.
Hvalvik, also on KUGEL-GREER).

6080 **Theekkara** Mathew, The face of early Christianity; a study of the Pauline
letters. Bangalore 1988, KJC.   xviii-259 p. rs 50. – ᴿVidyajyoti 54 (1990)
353s (P. M. *Meagher*).

6081 **Trobisch** David,   Die Entstehung der Paulusbriefsammlung...: NTOrb
10, 1989 → 5,5810:   ᴿBiblica 71 (1990) 581-3 (R. *Penna*: utile per la storia
ma non per la prima origine della collezione); NRT 112 (1990) 598s (X.
Jacques); TLZ 115 (1990) 682s (A. *Lindemann*); TPQ 138 (1990) 404s (A.
Fuchs).

6082 **Viciano** Alberto,   Cristo, el autor de nuestra salvación; estudio sobre el
comentario de TEODORETO de Ciro a las epístolas paulinas.   Pamplona
1990, EUNSA.   251 p. [Carthaginensia 7,522, F. *Martínez Fresneda*].

6082* *Viciano* Alberto,   THEODORET von Kyros als Interpret des Apostels
Paulus: TGL 80 (1990) 279-315.

6083 *Vogüé* A. de,   Fragments d'un texte monastique inconnu et du commentaire de PÉLAGE sur saint Paul dans le manuscrit de Paris n.a.1. 2199:
RBén 100 (1990) 482-492.

6084 *Vorster* J. N.,   Toward an interactional model for the analysis of letters
[... must take into account conversation-patterns]:   Neotestamentica 24,1
(1990) 107-130.

6085 ᴱ**Wente** Edward,   Letters from ancient Egypt: SBL Writings from the
Ancient World 1.   Atlanta 1990, Scholars.   xii-271 p. $26; pa./sb. $17.

G3.3 **Pauli theologia.**

6086 *Ballard* Paul,   The Pauline names for God: Churchman 104 (1990)
35-37 [< ZIT 90,447].

6087 **Bermudez** Catalina,   Aspectos de la doctrina de la gracia en los comentarios de santo TOMÁS a las epístolas paulinas: diss. Santa Croce,
ᴰ*Miralles* A.   Roma 1989.   265 p. – RTLv 22, p. 618.

6088 **Breytenbach** Cilliers,   Versöhnung... paulin.: WM 60, ᴰ1989 → 5,5814:
ᴿTLZ 115 (1990) 741-5 (O. *Hofius*: nicht überzeugend).

6089 *Buchanan* George W.,   The Day of Atonement and Paul's doctrine of
redemption: NT 32 (1990) 236-249.

6090 *Buscemi* A. Marcello, La fede in S. Paolo: TerraS 66 (1990) 177-184.

6091 **Capes** David B., Paul's use of Old Testament Yahweh-texts [7 for God, 7 for Christ] and its implication for his Christology: diss. SW Baptist Theol. Sem. 1990. 352 p. 90-26795. – DissA 51 (1990s) 1657s-A.

6092 *Cavina* Adriana, Etica e battesimo nella teologia paolina: Protestantesimo 45 (1990) 162-172.

6093 *Cook* James I., The concept of adoption in the theology of Paul: → 60,181, [F]OUDERSLUYS R., Saved by hope, [E]*Cook* 1978, 133-144.

6094 **Cousar** C.B., A theology of the Cross; the death of Jesus in the Pauline letters: OvBT 24. Mp 1990, Fortress. xiv-195 p. $12. 0-8006-1558-1 [NTAbs 35,110].

6095 **Crockett** William V., Universalism and the theology of Paul [his relevant texts do not indicate that all will be saved]: diss. Glasgow 1986. 380 p. BRDX-90294. – DissA 51 (1990s) 2058-A.

6096 **Dobbeler** A. von, Glaube als Teilhabe... paulinisch. 1987 → 3,5641... 5,5816: [R]CrNSt 11 (1990) 207s (M. *Carrez*).

6097 **Doohan** Helen, Paul's vision of the Church 1989 → 5,5817: [R]Horizons 17 (1990) 323s (Mary C. *Boys*); Interpretation 44 (1990) 432.434 (R. *Hielm*).

6098 **Eckstein** Hans-Joachim, Der Begriff syneidesis bei Paulus...: WUNT 2/10, 1983 → 64,5622...3,5674: [R]Gregorianum 71 (1990) 386-9 (U. *Vanni*).

6099 **Ellis** E. Earle, Pauline theology; ministry and society [i. ministry for the coming age; ii. the Spirit and the gifts; iii. Paul and the eschatological woman; iv. ministry and Church order; v. Pauline Christianity and the world order; < lectures, not specified p. x]. GR/Exeter 1989, Eerdmans/ Paternoster. xv-182 p. 0-8028-0451-9 / 0-85364-503-5. – [R]SWJT 33,1 (1990s) 53s (G. *Greenfield*).

6100 **Enos** Ralph G., To die is gain; the Christian's intermediate state in Pauline theology: diss. Dallas Theol. Sem. 1989. 212 p. 90-20888. – DissA 51 (1990s) 898-A.

6101 **Fitzmyer** Joseph A., Paul and his theology[2] [< NJBC] 1989 → 4,5820: [R]Gregorianum 71 (1990) 385s (J.M. *McDermott*); IrBSt 12 (1990) 152s (V. *Parkin*); RB 97 (1990) 128-130 (J. *Murphy-O'Connor*); RHPR 70 (1990) 268s (M.-A. *Chevallier*).

6102 **Gaffin** R.B., Resurrection and redemption; a study in Paul's soteriology[2] [= [1]1979]. Phillipsburg NJ 1987, Presbyterian & R. 155 p. $8 pa. 0-87552-271-8 [NTAbs 35,111].

6103 **Kreitzer** L. Joseph, Jesus and God in Paul's eschatology: JStNT supp 19, [D]1987 → 3,5648... 5,5824: [R]EvQ 62 (1990) 370s (N.T. *Wright*); RB 97 (1990) 291s (J. *Murphy-O'Connor*).

6104 **Lee Han-Soo,** Divine grace and the Christian life; a study on Paul's teaching on the tension between grace and human responsibility: diss. Aberdeen 1990. 487 p. BRDX-94547. – DissA 52,3319-A; RTLv 22, p. 593.

6105 *Mauser* Ulrich, Paul the theologian: HorBT 11,2 (1989) 80-106.

6106 **Mehl** Ulrich, Neue Schöpfung; eine traditionsgeschichtliche und exegetische Studie zu einem soteriologischen Grundsatz paulinischer Theologie: BZNW 56, 1989 → 5,5826; xv-436 p. DM 148: [R]ExpTim 102 (1990s) 25s (E. *Best*).

6107 *Millás* José M., *a*) Justicia de Dios; Rudolf BULTMANN intérprete de la teología paulina de la justificación: Gregorianum 71 (1990) 259-290; franç. 291; – *b*) La concepción paulina de la fe y la existencia cristiana según la interpretación de Rudolf Bultmann: EstE 65 (1990) 193-214.

6108 **Muller** Earl C., Trinity and marriage in Paul; the establishment of a communitarian analogy of the Trinity grounded in the theological shape of Pauline thought: AmerUnivSt 7/60. NY 1990, Lang. xv-550 p. 0-8204-0914-6.

6109 **Oechslen** R., Kronzeuge Paulus; Paulinische Theologie im Spiegel katholischer und evangelischer Exegese und die Möglichkeit ökumenischer Verständigung [Diss. Erlangen 1987, ᴰ*Roloff* J.]: BeitEvT 108. Mü 1990, Kaiser. 265 p. DM 79. 3-459-01863-1 [NTAbs 35,251].

6110 *a*) *Pastor Ramos* Federico, Cristo imagen del Padre [... corpus paulinum]; – *b*) *Fuster* Sebastián, (también) Cristo imagen del Padre: EstTrin 22 (1988) 383-398 / 399-412.

6111 *Penna* Romano, *a*) Aspetti originali della pneumatologia di S. Paolo: RivScR 4 (Molfetta 1990) 323-333; – *b*) Cristianesimo e laicità nella teologia di S. Paolo: → 542*, I laici 1988, 265-278.

6112 *Plevnik* Joseph, *a*) The center of Pauline theology [CBQ 31 (1989) 461-478 → 5,5828]: BS 147 (1990) 106s (J. D. *Grassnick* lengthy summary: 'an adequate answer to the issue discussed'); – *b*) Paul's eschatology: TorJT 6 (1990) 86-99.

6113 **Reid** J. B., Jesus; God's emptiness [Phil 2,5-8], God's fullness [Col 1,19; 2,9]; the Christology of St. Paul. NY 1990, Paulist. iv-145 p. 8. 0-8091-3165-X [NTAbs 35,115].

6114 **Röhser** Günther, Metaphorik und Personifikation der Sünde; antike Sündenvorstellungen und paulinische Hamartia [Diss. Heid 1985, ᴰ*Berger* K.]: WUNT 2/25, 1987 → 5,5830: ᴿNedTTs 43 (1989) 337s (P. W. van der *Horst*); TR 86 (1990) 203s (D. *Zeller*).

6115 **Schäfer** K., Gemeinde als 'Bruderschaft'; ein Beitrag zum Kirchenverständnis des Paulus [ev. Diss. Hamburg 1987, ᴰ*Schramm* T.]: EurHS 23/333. Fra 1989, Lang. 800 p. $83.80 pa. 3-8204-0210-1 [NTAbs 35, 115]. – ᴿSNTU A-15 (1990) 183 (A. *Fuchs*).

6116 **Seeley** David, The noble death; Graeco-Roman martyrology and Paul's concept of salvation [diss. Claremont 1987, ᴰ*Mack* B.]: JStNT supp 28. Sheffield 1990, JStOT. 370 p. $37.50. 1-85075-185-4 [TDig 38,187]. – ᴿExpTim 102 (1990s) 86s (A. J. M. *Wedderburn*); TLZ 115 (1990) 895s (E. *Lohse*).

6117 **Seifrid** Mark A., Justification by faith; the origin and development of a central Pauline theme: diss. ᴰ*Beker* J. C. Princeton Theol. Sem. 1990. 365 p. 90-30373. – DissA 51 (1990s) 2054s-A; RelStR 17.194.

6118 *a*) *Stolle* Volker, Rechtfertigung und [paulinische] Schriftauslegung; zum Schriftgebrauch im Rechtfertigungskapitel der ökumenischen Studie 'Lehrverurteilungen – kirchentrennend?': LuthTKi 14 (1990) 1-18; – *b*) 13 (1989) 81-99, *Hoffmann* Gottfried, Glaube und Liebe; zur Auseinandersetzung mit den Rechtfertigungsaussagen in 'Lehrverurteilungen – kirchentrennend?': weiter 166-174 (und 175s zu BAUR J.), *Martens* Gottfried; Hoffmanns Antwort 14 (1990) 63-84; Martens 85].

6119 **Theissen** Gerd, Psychological aspects of Pauline theology 1987 → 3, 5658 ... 5,5837: ᴿJBL 109 (1990) 154-6 (W. G. *Rollins*); JRel 70 (1990) 88s (also W. *Rollins*); Neotestamentica 29 (1990) 376-9 (W. R. *Domeris*); Themelios 15 (1989s) 102-4 (N. T. *Wright*).

6120 **Wedderburn** A. J. M., Baptism and resurrection ... in Pauline theology [Rom 6...] ᴰ1987 → 3,5661 ... 5,5838: ᴿInterpretation 44 (1990) 94.96 (R. P. *Carlson*); JTS 41 (1990) 183-7 (I. H. *Jones*); Protestantesimo 45 (1990) 145s (F. *Ferrario*); RB 97 (1990) 289-291 (J. *Murphy-O'Connor*); SvEx 55 (1990) 154-6 (L. *Hardman*); Themelios 15 (1989s) 33s (I. H. *Marshall*); TLZ 115 (1990) 25-30 (H. *Hübner*).

6121 *a*) *Wilken* Robert L., Free choice and the divine will in Greek Christian commentaries on Paul; – *b*) *Greer* Rowan A., The man from heaven; Paul's last Adam and APOLLINARIS' Christ: ➤ 510, SMU Paul 1987/90, 123-140 / 165-182.

G3.4 Themata paulina [Israel et Lex ➤ G4.6].

6122 *Bermúdez* Catalina, Predestinazione, grazia e libertà nei commenti di San TOMMASO alle lettere di San Paolo: AnnTh 4 (1990) 399-421.

6123 **Brauch** M. T., [48] Hard sayings of Paul. DG 1989, Inter-Varsity. 278 p. $9. 0-8308-1282-2.

6124 *Caraza* Ioan, *Indreptarea şi indumnezeirea...* La justification et la déification de l'homme en J.-C. selon S. Paul: OrtBuc 40,4 (1988) 125-136.

6125 **Carras** G. P., Paul and common denominator Judaism; the use of the letters of Paul and JOSEPHUS' 'Contra Apionem' as sources for reconstructing common denominators within Second Temple Judaism: diss. Oxford 1990. – RTLv 22,590.

6126 **Cruz** Hieronymus, Christological motives and motivated actions in Pauline paraenesis [Diss. 1982 R, Pont. Univ. Gregoriana, ᴰ*Rasco* E.]: EurHS 23/396. Fra 1990, Lang. 484 p. $81. 3-461-42857-X [NTAbs 35,110].

6127 **Dattoli** Michele, Genesi ed evoluzione della visione paolina sulla sofferenza di Cristo: diss. Angelicum, ᴰ*García Trapiello* J. Roma 1990. – RTLv 22, p. 619. iii-482 p.

6129 **Gebauer** R., Das Gebet bei Paulus; forschungsgeschichtliche und exegetische Studien [< Diss. Erlangen 1988, ᴰ*Merk* O.]: TVG-Mg 349, 1989 ➤ 5,5854; DM 39: ᴿSNTU A-15 (1990) 183-5 (R. *Oberforcher*).

6130 *Gräbe* P. J., De verhouding tussen indikatief en imperatief in die pauliniese etiek; enkele aksente uit die diskussie sedert 1924 [BULTMANN]: Scriptura 32 (1990) 54-66 [< NTAbs 35,42].

6131 **Gundry Volf** Judith M., Paul and perseverance; staying in and falling away [diss. Tübingen 1988, ᴰ*Hofius* O.]: WUNT 2/37. Tü 1990, Mohr. 325 p. DM 69. 3-16-145527-4. – ᴿExpTim 102 (1990s) 87 (J. *Proctor*); TsTNijm 30 (1990) 407s (J. *Smit*).

6132 **Hanson** Anthony T., The paradox of the Cross in the thought of St. Paul: JStNT supp. 17, 1987 ➤ 3,5681 ... 5,5856: ᴿCritRR 2 (1989) 200-2 (C. T. *Rhyne*).

6133 *a*) *Helewa* Giovanni, Lasciarsi esortare da Dio nell'intimo; spiritualità dell'ascolto secondo Paolo Apostolo; – *b*) *Forte* Bruno, 'Alta silentia'; il silenzio nella comunione trinitaria alla luce del silenzio della croce: RivVSp 43 (1990) 411-424 / 395-410.

6134 **Hofius** O., Paulusstudien 1989 ➤ 5,280: ᴿDeltioVM 19,1 (1990) 70-77 (S. *Agourides*); NRT 112 (1990) 597 (X. *Jacques*).

6135 **Holloway** Joseph O.ᴵᴵᴵ, *peripateō* as a thematic marker for Pauline ethics: diss. SW Baptist Theol. Sem. 1990. 388 p. 90-26797. – DissA 51 (1990s) 1660s-A.

Hooker Morna, From Adam to Christ, [14] essays on Paul 1990 ➤ 249.

6136 **Iovino** Paolo, Chiesa e... *thlípsis* in Paolo 1985 ➤ 1,5634 ... 3,5685: ᴿAngelicum 67 (1990) 136s (J. M. *Viejo*).

6137 **Jones** F. S., 'Freiheit'... Paulus ᴰ1987 ➤ 3,5688 ... 5,5857: ᴿCrNSt 11 (1990) 378-381 (G. *Barbaglio*); NedTTs 44 (1990) 259s (H. W. *Hollander*).

6138 *Kaitholil* George, Poverty and riches according to Paul: LivingWord 96 (Kerala 1990) 375-381 [< TContext 8/2, p. 46].

6139 **Kitzberger** Ingrid, Bau der Gemeinde; paulin. *oikodomē* 1986 ⇥ 4,a682; 5,5860: ᴿTLZ 115 (1990) 431-3 (H. *Hübner*); TPhil 65 (1990) 260s (N. *Baumert*).

6140 **Kleinknecht** K.-T., Der leidende Gerechtfertigte[2] (... Paulus) [¹1984 < Diss. Tü 1981]: WUNT 2/13. Tü 1988, Mohr. x-438 p. DM 89. – ᴿTGegw 33 (1990) 215-7 (H. *Giesen*: it has corrections and bibliographical update).

6141 **Koch** Dietrich-Alex, Die Schrift als Zeuge des Evangeliums ...bei Paulus: BHistT 69,1986 ⇥ 2,4525 ... 5,5862: ᴿNedTTs 43 (1989) 339 (J. S. *Vos*); ZkT 112 (1990) 212s (R. *Oberforcher*).

6142 *Kowalski* Alexander, ❷ Testi paolini sul diaconato nell'interpretazione dei Padri della Chiesa: VoxPa 17 (1989) 605-635; ital. 635.

6143 **Lincoln** Andrew T., Paradiso ora e non ancora; cielo e prospettiva escatologica nel pensiero di Paolo, ᵀᴱ*Zani* A. 1985 ⇥ 1,5598 ... 4,5848: ᴿHelmantica 41 (1990) 429-431 (H.-B. *Riesco Alvarez*).

6144 *a) Lindemann* A., Paul in the writings of the Apostolic Fathers; – *b) Norris* R. A.ᴶ, IRENAEUS' use of Paul in his polemic against the Gnostics: ⇥ 510, ᴱ*Babcock* W., Paul 1987/90, 25-45 / 79-98.

6145 *Lona* Horacio, La comprensión paulina de libertad en el marco de la cultura antigua [no 'compresión' como p. 3 e cubierta]: Proyecto CSE 2,3s (Buenos Aires 1990) 63-90.

6146 *López de Las Heras* Luis, El optimismo paulino: Studium 30 (M 1990) 195-229.

6147 *Lupo* Tiburzio, La castità nelle lettere di S. Paolo: PalCl 68 (1989) 139-151.

6148 **Maccise** C., Palabra y comunidad en San Pablo y en las comunidades de base en América Latina. Mex/R 1989, CEVHAC/Teresianum. 320 p. – ᴿSalmanticensis 37 (1990) 379s (J. M. *Sánchez Caro*).

6149 *Martín* Leonard M., Moral sexual missionária de Paulo (Subsidios para uma moral do matrimônio no Brasil): REB 50 (1990) 515-536 [537-555, *Dutra* C.].

6150 **Meeks** Wayne A., *a)* The first urban Christians; the social world of the apostle Paul 1983 ⇥ 64,5641 ... 4,5883: ᴿTEdn 26,1 (1989s) 111-3 (V. L. *Wimbush*: not Weeks as title); – *b)* Los primeros cristianos urbanos; el mundo social del apóstol Pablo: BiblEstB 64, 1988 ⇥ 4,5884; 5,5868: ᴿEfMex 8 (1990) 111s (S. *Vidal García*); EstTrin 24 (1990) 505-8 (J. L. *Aurrecoechea*).

6151 *a) Meeks* Wayne A., The circle of reference in Pauline morality; – *b) Stowers* Stanley K., Paul on the use and abuse of reason: ⇥ 122, ᶠMALHERBE A., Greeks 1990, 305-317 / 253-286.

6152 **Ménard** Camille, L'esprit de la nouvelle alliance chez Saint Paul 1987 ⇥ 3,5697 ... 5,5870: ᴿEstE 65 (1990) 378-380 (A. María *Artola*); RHPR 70 (1990) 272 (M.-A. *Chevallier*: essai d'herméneutique style RICŒUR/ GREIMAS); SR 19 (1990) 249s (L. *Painchaud*).

6153 *Monloubou* L., San Paolo e la preghiera ; preghiera ed evangelizzazione [1986], ᵀ*Galizzi*. T-Leumann 1988, LDC. 124 p. – ᴿRivB 38 (1990) 115-7 (G. *De Virgilio*).

6154 *Mowery* Robert L., The articular prepositional attributes in the Pauline corpus: Biblica 71 (1990) 85-92.

6155 *Müller* Paul-Gerhard, Tradition und Geist bei Paulus: TBer 18 (Z 1989) 31-60 [< ZIT 90,174].

6156 ᴱ**Murphy-O'Connor** J., *Charlesworth* J., Paul and the Dead Sea Scrolls. NY 1990 = 1968, Crossroad. 262 p. $19 [TS 51,572].

6157 **Myre** André, Un souffle subversif; l'Esprit dans les lettres pauliniennes 1987 → 4,5887: ᴿRHPR 70 (1990) 273 (M.-A. *Chevallier*); RTPhil 122 (1990) 278 (Aline *Lasserre*); Téléma 16,3s (1990) 85-87 (R. *Capoen*).

6158 **O'Toole** Robert, Who is a Christian? A study in Pauline ethics: Zacchaeus Studies. Collegeville MN 1990, Liturgical. 168 p. $10. 0-8146-5678-1 [TS 52,191]. For homilists and others, on the relevance of Paul's moral directives for today.

6159 *Pikaza* Xabier, La autoridad de Jesús en la tradición de Pablo: EstTrin 23 (1989) 85-127.

6160 *Porter* S.E., Wittgensteins classes of utterances and Pauline ethical texts: JEvTS 32 (1989) 85-97 [< NTAbs 34,50].

6161 **Reck** Reinhold, Kommunikation und Gemeindeaufbau; eine Studie zu Entstehung, Leben und Wachstum paulinischer Gemeinden in den Kommunikationsstrukturen der Antike: kath. Diss. ᴰ*Klauck*. Würzburg 1989s. – TR 86 (1990) 520.

6162 *Roberts* J.H., Aspekte van die kerk by Paulus: TEv 22,1 (Pretoria 1989) 6-12 [< NTAbs 34,50].

6163 *Roetzel* Calvin J., Election/calling in certain Pauline letters; an experimental construction: → 544, SBL seminars 1990, 552-569.

6164 **Schiefer Ferrari** Markus M., Die Sprache des Leids in den paulinischen Peristasenkatalogen: kath. Diss. ᴰ*Gnilka* J. München 1990. 501 p. – RTLv 22, p. 595.

6165 **Schruers** P., Christen worden met Paulus: Schrift en liturgie 16. Bonheiden/Brugge 1989, Bethlehem/Tabor. 93 p. Fb 280. – ᴿCollatVL 20 (1990) 346s (R. *Hoet*).

6166 **Siegert** Folker, Argumentation bei Paulus 1985 → 1,5766... 4,5977: ᴿZkT 112 (1990) 217s (E. *Ruschitska*).

6167 **Stuhlmacher** P., Adolf Schlatter als Paulusausleger – ein Versuch: TBeit 20,4 (Wu 1989) 176-190 [NTAbs 34,50].

6169 **Via** Dan O., [Gal 6,3; Phlp 3,6-10; Rom 9,30...; Mt 23-25s] Self-deception and wholeness in Paul and Matthew. Mp 1990, Fortress. viii-173 p. $11. 0-8006-2435-1 [NTAbs 35,261].

6170 **Vollenweider** Samuel, Freiheit als neue Schöpfung... *eleutheria*/Paulus: FRL 147, ᴰ1989 → 5,5880: ᴿNRT 112 (1990) 599-601 (X. *Jacques*); TsTKi 61 (1990) 225s (K.O. *Sandnes*); TZBas 46 (1990) 373s (U. *Gerber*).

6171 *Wolter* Michael, Der Apostel und seine Gemeinden als Teilhaber am Leidensgeschick Jesu Christi; Beobachtungen zur paulinischen Leidenstheologie: NTS 36 (1990) 535-557.

6172 **Yoder** John H., The fullness of Christ; Paul's vision of universal ministry. 1987, Brethren. 96 p. $9. – ᴿSWJT 33,2 (1990s) 58s (D. *Sansom*).

6173 **Zdziarstek** Roman S., *a*) ❷ Chrystianologia [what it means to be a Christian to] St. Paul, I. Aspekt ontyczny. Kraków 1989, P. Tow. Teologiczne. 270 p. – ᴿAngelicum 67 (1990) 426-9 (E. *Kaczyński*); RuBi 43 (1990) 177s (J. *Królikowski*); – *b*) ❷ Chrystonomiczność egzystencji chrześcijańskiej według św. Pawła: RuBi 42 (1989) 98-110.

6174 **Zeller** Dieter, *Charis* bei Philon und Paulus: SBS 142. Stu 1990, KBW. 215 p. 3-460-04421-7.

G4 **Ad Romanos** .1 *Textus, commentarii.*

6175 **Achtemeier** P., Romans: Interpretation comm. 1985 → 1,5663... 3,5719: ᴿVidyajyoti 54 (1990) 368.363 (P.M. *Meagher*).

6176 **Briscoe** D. Stuart, Romans: Communicator's Comm. 6. Waco 1982, Word. 264 p. 0-8499-0159-6.

6177 [ᴱ**Casciaro**], St. Paul's Epistles to the Romans and Galatians: RSV, NeoV, Navarre B. ᵀ*Adams* M. Dublin 1990, Four Courts. 212 p.; map. £12,50; pa. £8. 1-85182-056-6; -5-8 [NTAbs 34,394].

6178 **Dunn** James D. G., Romans: Word Comm. 38A-B, 1988 ➤ 4,5904; 5,5885: ᴿRB 97 (1990) 286s (J. *Murphy-O'Connor*); RExp 87 (1990) 644s (D. *Dockery*).

6179 ᴱ**Fraenkel** P., *Perrotet* L., Théodore de BÈZE [notes de *Widler* Marcus] Cours sur les Épîtres aux Romains et aux Hébreux (1564-66): Trav-HumRen 226, 1988 ➤ 4,5905; 5,5887: ᴿCrNSt 11 (1990) 413s (R. *Letham*, Eng.).

6180 **Galizzi** Mario, La storia ha un senso; lettera di Paolo ai Romani II [cap. 9-16]. Commenti al NT. T 1987, ElleDiCi. 126 p. 88-01-15674-X.

6181 **Grenholm** Christina, Romans interpreted; a comparative analysis of the commentaries of BARTH, NYGREN, CRANFIELD and WILCKENS on Paul's Epistle to the Romans [diss. Uppsala 1990]: AcU, StDocChr 30. 154 p. Sk 127. 91-554-2529-1 [NTAbs 35,112]. – ᴿLuthTKi 14 (1990) 124s (V. *Stolle*).

6182 ᴱ**Hamman** A., Jean CHRYSOSTOME commente saint Paul; homélies choisies sur l'Épître aux Romains (ᵀ*Legée* J.); homélies sur la 1ʳᵉ lettre aux Corinthiens (ᵀ*Winling* R.): Les Pères dans la foi. P 1988, D-Brouwer. 360 p. – ᴿEsprVie 100 (1990) 474s (Y.-M. *Duval*).

6183 **Hammond Bammel** Caroline P., Der Römerbriefkommentar des ORI-GENES, kritische Ausgabe der Übersetzung RUFINs, Buch 1-3: VLatGesch 16. FrB 1990, Herder. 264 p. DM 164. 3-451-21932-8.

6184 **Heil** John P., Paul's letter to the Romans; a reader-response commentary 1987 ➤ 3,5729 ... 5,5888: ᴿEstB 48 (1990) 277s (F. *Pastor-Ramos*: reserves); ScripTPamp 22 (1990) 1011 (C. *Basevi*).

6185 **Hendriksen** William, Romans 1-8, 1980s ➤ 62,6439 ... 65,5208: ᴿEvQ 62 (1990) 371s (N. T. *Wright*: nothing on why now; 'H's massive labours on the NT continue unabated').

6186 **Kruijf** T. C. de, De Brief ... aan de Romeinen 1986 ➤ 2,4559; 4,5909: ᴿCritRR 2 (1989) 215-7 (H. *Boers*); NedTTs 43 (1989) 59s (H. W. *Hollander*).

6187 ᵀᴱ**Mara** Maria Grazia, *a*) D. ERASMO, Parafrasi della Lettera ai Romani: Testi Storici 19. L'Aquila 1990, Japadre. 364 p. 88-7006-226-0; – *b*) Erasmo; dall'esegesi dotta alla parafrasi [Rom 1516]: AnStoEseg 7 (1990) 685-703.

6188 **Morris** Leon, The epistle to the Romans 1988 ➤ 4,5911: ᴿEvangel 8,2 (1990) 20s (H. C. *Bigg*); EvQ 62 (1990) 271-3 (G. *Houston*); Interpretation 44 (1990) 315s (R. L. *Tyler*); MastJ 1,1 (1990) 91-93 (J. E. *Rosscup*: mature).

6189 **Parker** T. H. L., Commentaries on Romans 1532-1542: 1986 ➤ 2,4564 ... 5,5896: ᴿHeythJ 31 (1990) 76s (F. F. *Bruce*).

6191 ᴱ**Rieger** Reinhold, Johann Adam MÖHLER, Vorlesung zum Römerbrief: Wewelbuch 169. Mü 1990, Wewel. 308 p. DM 58. 3-87904-169-5.

6192 **Ring** Thomas G., Aurelius AUGUSTINUS, Die Auslegung einiger Fragen aus dem Brief an die Römer, eingeleitet, übertragen und erläutert: Antipelag. Gesamtausgabe, Prolegomena 1. Wü 1989, Augustinus. 148 p. – ᴿTPhil 65 (1990) 600s (H. J. *Sieben*).

6193 **Schmithals** Walter, *a*) Römerbrief 1988 ➤ 4,5913; 5,5899: ᴿActuBbg 27 (1990) 201 (X. *Alegre* S.); EvKomm 22,10 (1989) 53s (P. *Stuhlmacher*:

'Umstrittener Paulus'); SNTU A-15 (1990) 188s (A. *Fuchs*); ZkT 112 (1990) 215s (E. *Ruschitska*); – *b*) Paolo, Lettera ai Romani, ᵀ*Antelli* Filippo: Le Opere 1. T 1990, Lindau. 160 p. Lit. 36.800. 88-7180-001-X.

6194 **Verdeyen** Paul, GUILLELMUS a Sancto Theodorico, Expositio super Epistolam ad Romanos: CCMed 56. Turnhout 1990, Brepols. 60 p. 6 microfiches CETEDOC. 2-503-63862-7.

6195 **Wilckens** Ulrich, La carta a los Romanos I (1-5), ᵀ*Martínez de Lapera* Victor A.: BiblEstB 61. S 1989, Sígueme. 410 p. 84-301-1092-5. – ᴿActuBbg 27 (1990) 64 (X. *Alegre* S.); HumT 2 (1990) 371s (A. *Couto*); NatGrac 37 (1990) 319 (F. F. *Ramos*).

6196 **Ziesler** John, Paul's letter to the Romans: TPI NT comm. 1989 ➤ 5,5903: ᴿBTrans 41 (1990) 351s (R. L. *Omanson*: aims to be concrete and social rather than theoretical); TLond 93 (1990) 318s (J. D. G. *Dunn*).

G4.2 *Ad Romanos: themata*, **topics.**

6197 **Aletti** Jean-Noël, *a*) Comment Dieu est-il juste? Clefs pour interpréter l'épître aux Romains: Parole de Dieu. P 1989, Cerf. 285 p. [AcPIB 9/7, 546; Études 375, 282 '1991']; – *b*) La présence d'un modèle rhétorique en Romains; son rôle et son importance [BETZ H., ...]: Biblica 71 (1990) 1-24; Eng. 25.

6198 *Alison* James N. F., O tema da justificação nas cartas aos Romanos e aos Galatas [< New Blackf]: PerspTeol 22 (1990) 221-233.

6199 **Byrne** Brendan, Reckoning with Romans 1986 ➤ 2,4551... 4,5918: ᴿVidyajyoti 54 (1990) 367s (P. M. *Meagher*).

6200 *Craffert* P. F., Die gesprek tussen A. B. du TOIT en E. P. SANDERS oor Paulus [Rom] en die Palestynse Judaisme; die pad vorentoe [road ahead]: HervTS 45 (1989) 843-863 [< NTAbs 35,42].

6201 *Crafton* Jeffrey A., Paul's rhetorical vision and the purpose of Romans; toward a new understanding. NT 32 (1990) 317-339.

6202 **Elliott** Neil, The rhetoric of Romans; argumentative constraint and strategy and Paul's dialogue with Judaism [diss. 1989 ᴰ*Beker* J. ➤ 5,5908]: JStNT supp. 45. Sheffield 1990, Academic. 332 p. 1-85075-261-3.

6203 *Fiore* Benjamin, Invective in Romans and Philippians: ProcGLM 10 (1990) 181-9.

6204 *Greinacher* Norbert, 'Ihr seid auf das Fundament der Apostel und Propheten gebaut' (Eph 2,20): Diakonia 21 (1990) 145-8 [> TDig 38,241-3, ᵀᴱ*Asen* B.].

6205 *Haacker* Klaus, *a*) Der Römerbrief als Friedensmemorandum: NTS 36 (1990) 25-41; – *b*) Reformation aus dem Römerbrief – bei M. LUTHER und heute: TBeit 21 (Wu 1990) 264... [< ZIT 90,753].

6206 **Heither** Theresia, 'Translatio religionis'; die Paulusdeutung des ORIGENES in seinem Kommentar zum Römerbrief [Diss. Bonn, ᴰ*Dassmann* E.]: BoBKG 10. Köln 1990, Böhlau. xii-330 p. [RHE 86,179, A. de *Halleux*]. – ᴿArTGran 53 (1990) 324s (A. *Segovia*).

6207 **Hicks** H. Beecher, Correspondence with a cripple from Tarsus; Romans in dialogue with the 20th century. GR 1990, Zondervan. 218 p. 0-310-52201-3.

6208 *Jeffers* James S., Pluralism in early Roman Christianity: Fides et Historia 22 (1990) 4-17 [< ZIT 90,479].

6209 **Jewett** Robert, Sin and salvation; Amedeus [film: Mozart; Salieri] in the light of Romans: ExAud 5 (1989) 159-169.

6210 **Lyonnet** Stanislas, Études sur l'Épître aux Romains: AnBib 120, 1989
  ⮕ 5,307: ᴿArTGran 53 (1990) 306s (A. *Segovia*); CC 141 (1990,4) 197s
  (L. *De Lorenzi*); FoiVie 89,5 (1990) 99s (R. J. *Seckel*); NRT 112 (1990)
  595s (X. *Jacques*); RivB 38 (1990) 382-4 (R. *Penna*); ScEspr 42 (1990) 354s
  (P.-E. *Langevin*).
6211 **Perrot** Charles, *a*) L'épître aux Romains: CahÉv 65. P 1988, Cerf.
  67 p. F 25. 0222-9714; – *b*) La carta a los Romanos: CuadB 65. Estella
  1989, VDivino. – ᴿEfMex 8 (1990) 122-4 (E. *Serraima Cirici*).
6212 **Ravasi** Gian Franco, Lettera ai Romani: Conversazioni Bibliche, Mi S.
  Fedele. Bo 1990, Dehoniane. 115 p. 88-10-70920-1.
6213 *Ringleben* Joachim, Die Einheit von Gotteserkenntnis und Selbster-
  kenntnis; Beobachtungen anhand von LUTHERs Römerbrief-Vorlesung:
  NSys 32 (1990) 125-133; Eng. 133.
6214 *Rossano* Pietro, La lettera ai Romani e il suo influsso sulla cultura
  europea: StDocHI 55 (1989) 1-12 [13-27, testo Neo-Vulgata].
6215 **Roukema** Riemer, The diversity of laws in ORIGEN's Commentary on
  Romans 1988 ⮕ 5,5915: ᴿNedTTs 44 (1990) 344s (P. *Wansink*).
6216 **Simonis** Walter, Der gefangene Paulus; die Entstehung des sogenannten
  Römerbriefs und anderer urchristlicher Schriften in Rom. Fra 1990,
  Lang. 156 p. Fs 41 pa. 3-631-42024-2 [NTAbs 34,396]. – ᴿSNTU A-15
  (1990) 190s (A. *Fuchs*); TLZ 115 (1990) 815s (C. *Kähler*).
6217 **Wedderburn** A. J. M., The reasons for Romans: StNTW, 1988 ⮕ 4,
  5926; 5,5920: ᴿCBQ 52 (1990) 768s (J. L. *White*); ExpTim 101 (1989s) 30
  (J. A. *Ziesler*); IrBSt 11 (1989) 145-7 (W. S. *Campbell*); Neotestamentica
  24 (1990) 152-4 (M. A. *Kruger*); NRT 112 (1990) 596s (X. *Jacques*); Pacifica 3 (1990) 224-6 (Wendy *Dabourne*); ScotJT 43 (1990) 417-9 (J. D. G.
  Dunn: case well made).

G4.3 *Naturalis cognitio Dei ...* **Rom 1-4.**

6218 **Longenecker** Bruce W., Eschatology and the Covenant; a comparison of
  4 Ezra and Romans 1-11: diss. ᴰ*Dunn* J. Durham 1990. 304 p. – RTLv
  22, p. 593.
6219 **Davies** Glenn N., Faith and obedience in Romans; a study in Romans
  1-4 [diss. 1987 ⮕ 5,5997]: JStNT Supp. 39. Sheffield 1990, JStOT. 232 p.
  £22.50. 1-85075-233-8 [NTAbs 35,111]. – ᴿExpTim 102 (1990s) 246 (J.
  Proctor).
6220 *Wetmore* H., The Gospel [Rom 1,1-17 and five other Pauline passages]:
  EvRT 14 (1990) 225-235 [< NTAbs 35,65].
6221 *Garlington* D. B., *a*) The obedience of faith in the letter to the Romans,
  I. The meaning of *hypakoē písteōs* (Rom 1:5; 16:26): WestTJ 52 (1990)
  201-224;– *b*) *Hierosylein* and the idolatry of Israel (Romans 2,22): NTS
  36 (1990) 142-151.
6222 *Hvalvik* Reidar, 'For jøde først og så for greker'; til betydningen av
  Rom 1,16*b*: TsTKi 60 (1989) 189-196; Eng. 196.
6223 *Delhaye* Philippe, *a*) Morale révélée et morale naturelle dans l'Épître aux
  Romains: ⮕ 608, Révélation/Aquin 1989-90, 69-103; – *b*) Éthique
  humaine et morale révélée dans l'Épître aux Romains: EsprVie 100
  (1990) 65-76 . 81-92.
6224 ᴱ**Kremer** Klaus, Um Möglichkeit oder Unmöglichkeit natürlicher
  Gotteserkenntnis heute 1982/5 ⮕ 2,453: ᴿNorTTs 91 (1990) 140 (T. S.
  Dokka).

6225 *Arroniz* José M., *a*) La manifestación del Creador y la seducción de la nada (Rom 1,18-23); – *b*) Rom 1,18-23 en los Comentarios patrísticos a la Carta a los Romanos: ScripV 37 (1990) 5-42 / 233-265.

6226 *Krentz* Edgar, The name of God in disrepute; Romans 2:17-29 [22-23]: ➤ 41, ᶠDANKER F., CurrTMiss 17 (1990) 429-439.

6227 *Weima* Jeffrey A. D., [Rom 3-7] The function of the Law in relation to sin; an evaluation of the view of H. RÄISÄNEN: NT 32 (1990) 219-235.

6228 *Achtemeier* P. J., Romans 3:1-8; structure and argument: ➤ 52, ᶠFULLER R., AnglTR supp 11 (1990) 77-87 [< NTAbs 34,230].

6229 **Kraus** Wolfgang, Der Tod Jesu als Heiligtumsweihe; Untersuchungen zum Umfeld der Sühnevorstellung in Röm 3,25-26a: Diss. ᴰ*Roloff* J. Erlangen 1989s. – TR 86 (1990) 514; RTLv 22, p. 593.

6230 **Lambrecht** Jan, ᴰ*Thompson* Richard W., Justification... Rom 3:27-31, 1989 ➤ 5,5934: ᴿJTS 41 (1990) 617s (J. D. G. *Dunn*).

6231 *a*) *Silberman* Lou H., Paul's midrash; reflections on Romans 4; – *b*) *Beker* J. Christiaan, Conversations with a friend about Romans; – *c*) *Johnson* E. Elizabeth, The wisdom of God as apocalyptic power: ➤ 123*, ᶠMEYER P., Faith 1990, 99-104 / 90-98 / 137-148.

6232 *Pines* Shlomo, [Rom 4,15; 5,9; 9,22...] Wrath and creatures of wrath in Pahlavi, Jewish and New Testament sources: ➤ 555, Irano-Judaica 1 (1975/82) 76-82.

G4.4 *Peccatum originale; redemptio cosmica:* **Rom 5-8.**

6233 *McDonald* Patricia M., Romans 5.1-11 as a rhetorical bridge [< ᴰ1989 ➤ 5,5939]: JStNT 40 (1990) 81-96.

6234 *a*) *Porter* Stanley E., The Pauline concept of original sin in light of rabbinic background; – *b*) *Clarke* Andrew D., The good and the just in Romans 5:7: TyndB 41 (1990) 3-30 / 128-142.

6235 **Sapp** David A., An introduction to Adam Christianity in Paul; a history of interpretation, the Jewish background, and an exegesis of Romans 5:12-21: diss. SW Baptist Theol. Sem. 1990. 392 p. 90-33451. – DissA 51 (1990s) 2427-A.

6236 *Biju-Duval* Denis, La traduzione di Rm 5,12-14: RivB 38 (1990) 353-373; Eng. 373.

Schottroff Luise, [Rom 5,12...] The seduction of Eve and Adam's sin 1990 ➤ 2344.

6237 *Cuvillier* Elian, Évangile et traditions chez Paul; lecture de Romains 6,1-14: Hokhma 45 (1990) 3-16.

6238 **Bryant** Rees O., [Rom 6,1-4; Gal 3,26s; Col 2,11-14] The role of baptism in the Pauline theology of conversion: diss. Fuller Theol. Sem., ᴰ*Gilliland* D. Pasadena 1990. 288 p. 90-26686. – DissA 51 (1990s) 1657-A.

6239 **Schlarb** Robert, Wir sind mit Christus begraben; die Auslegung von Römer 6,1-11 im Frühchristentum bis Origenes [ev. Diss. Wien 1987, ᴰ*Niederwimmer* K.]: BeitGbEx 31. Tü 1990, Mohr. x-291 p. 3-16-145546-0 [NTAbs 35,115].

6240 *Dunn* James D. G., Romans 7:14-25 in the theology of Paul: ➤ 2,28, ᶠERVIN H., Essays on apostolic themes, ᴱ**Elbert** P. 1985, 49-70.

6241 *Rosenau* Hartmut, Der Mensch zwischen Wollen und Können; theologische Reflexionen im Anschluss an Röm 7,14-25: TPhil 65 (1990) 1-30.

6242 *Voorwinde* S., Who is the 'wretched man' in Romans 7:24?: VoxRef 54 (1990) 11-25 [< NTAbs 35,46].

6243 *a) Froehlich* Karlfried, Romans 8:1-11; Pauline theology in medieval interpretation; – *b) Sampley* J. Paul, Faith and its moral life; individuation in the thought world of the Apostle Paul: ➤ 123*, [F]MEYER P., Faith 1990, 239-260 / 223-238.
6244 *Houston* Graham R., What to expect from Christian experience; Romans 8 revisited: Evangel 7,1 (1989) 9-12.
6245 *Breytenbach* C., Oor die vertaling van *perì hamartías* in Romeine 8:3: HervTSt 45,1 (Pretoria 1989) 30-33 [< NTAbs 34,51].
6246 *Lambrecht* Jan, The groaning creation; a study of Rom 8:18-30: LvSt 15 (1990) 3-18.
6247 **Christoffersson** Olle, The earnest expectation of the creature; the flood-tradition as matrix of Romans 8,18-27: ConBibNT 23. Sto 1990, Almqvist & W. 74 p. Sk 160. 91-22-00988-4 [BL 91,134, C. *Hickling*].
6248 *Grässer* Erich, Das Seufzen der Kreatur (Röm 8,19-22); auf der Suche nach einer 'biblischen Tierschutzethik': JbBT 5 (➤ 2140, 1990) 93-117.
6249 *Viciano* Alberto, Christologische Deutung von Röm 8,19-22 bei GREGOR von Nyssa: ➤ 603, Nyssa 1990, 191-204.
6250 *a) Obeng* E. A., An exegetical study of Rom. 8,26 and its implication for the Church in Africa: DeltioVM 18,2 (1989) 88-98; – *b) Simon* Werner, 'Denn um was wir in der rechten Weise bitten sollen, wissen wir nicht' (Röm 8,26): WissWeis 53 (1990) 1-18.

G4.6   *Israel et Lex;*   **The Law and the Jews,** *Rom 9-11.*

6252 *Bandstra* Andrew J., Paul and the law; some recent developments and an extraordinary book [WESTERHOLM S. 1988, 'fantastically good', but also SANDERS E. 1977]: CalvinT 25 (1990) 249-261.
6253 *Betz* Otto, Der fleischliche Mensch und das geistliche Gesetz; zum biblischen Hintergrund der paulinischen Gesetzeslehre [ineditum]: ➤ 200, Jesus II (1990) 129-196.
6254 *Brooten* Bernadette J., Paul and the Law; how complete was the departure?: PrincSemB supp 1 (1990) 71-89 [< NTAbs 34,325].
6255 **Cassirer** Heinz W. [son of Ernst], Grace and law; St. Paul, Kant, and the Hebrew prophets 1989 ➤ 5,5959 [also 4,5959!, dated 1988]: [R]BL (1990) 98 (F. F. *Bruce*); RelSt 26 (1990) 346-8 (C. *Gunton*).
6256 *Cohen* K. I., Paul the Benjaminite; mystery, motives and midrash: CHermProt 60 (1990) 21-28 [< NTAbs 34,332].
6257 *Cranfield* C. E. B., Giving a dog a bad name; a note on H. RÄISÄNEN's Paul and the Law ['has he been fair to St. Paul?']: JStNT 38 (1990) 77-85.
6258 **Diprose** Rinaldo, [Gal 3; Rom 9-11; Apc 20,1-6] Passato, presente e futuro nell'opera di Dio. Lux Biblica 1/1. R 1990, Ist.B.Ev. xv-156 p. Lit. 10.000 [NTAbs 35,118].
Dunn James D. G., Jesus, Paul and the Law 1990 ➤ 226.
6259 *Federici* Tommaso, Ebrei ed Ebraismo nelle lettere di S. Paolo: ➤ 506, Ebraismo/NT 3 (1990) 43-89.
6260 **Frank** Susan, The unbelieving Jews in Rom 9-11; a study of selected Latin commentaries from ATTO of Vercelli (886-961) to GILES of Rome (1274-1316): diss. Temple, [D]*Sloyan* G. Ph 1990. 247 p. 91-00272. – DissA 51 (1990s) 2782-A.
6261 **Fuchs-Kreimer** Nancy, The 'essential heresy'; Paul's view of the Law according to Jewish writers, 1886-1986: diss. Temple. Ph 1990. 361 p. 91-00273. – DissA 51 (1990s) 2780-A.

6262 **García Aviles** Rafael J., Llamados a ser libres; 'no la Ley, sino el hombre': En torno al NT (ciclo B). Córdoba 1990, Almendro. 282 p. 84-86077-83-4.

6263 **Gaston** Lloyd, Paul and the Torah 1987 → 4,196; 5,5961: ᴿCriswT 4 (1989s) 398s (D. S. *Dockery*); JTS 41 (1990) 188-190 (Morna D. *Hooker*); MastJ 1,1 (1990) 82-85 (I. A. *Busenitz*: ill-compatible with Jn 14,6); Pacifica 3 (1990) 95-97 (W. J. *Dalton*: similar to VAN BUREN's Theology 2 p. 277-283); RB 97 (1990) 287-9 (J. *Murphy-O'Connor*); RelStT 8,1s (1988) 80s (A. E. *Milton*).

6264 *Geer* T. C., Paul and the law in recent discussion [→ 5,5962; HÜBNER H. 1984; RÄISÄNEN H. 1986; SANDERS E. 1983; GASTON L. 1987]: RestQ 31,2 (1989) 93-107 [< NTAbs 34,47].

6265 **Gorday** Peter, Principles of patristic exegesis .. Rom 9-11, 1983 → 65, 5256 ... 4,5963: ᴿScripTPamp 22 (1990) 644s (A. *Viciano*).

6266 *Guerra* Anthony J., Romans; Paul's purpose and audience, with special attention to Romans 9-11: RB 97 (1990) 219-237; franç. 219s.

6267 *a) Hofius* O., 'All Israel will be saved'; divine salvation and Israel's deliverance in Romans 9-11; – *b) Satran* D., Paul among the rabbis and the Fathers; exegetical reflections; – *c) Beker* J. C., Romans 9-11 in the context of the early Church: PrincSemB supp. 1 (1990) 19-39 / 90-105 / 40-55 [< NTAbs 34,331].

6268 *Holland* Glenn S., 'Anti-Judaism' in Paul; the case of Romans: ProcGLM 10 (1990) 190-203.

6269 *Hyldahl* Niels, Paulus og loven [*lov* = law (*love* = promise)]: DanTTs 53 (1990) 183-192 [< ZIT 90,736].

6270 **Johnson** E. Elizabeth, The function of apocalyptic and wisdom traditions in Romans 9-11, ᴰ1989 → 5,5965: ᴿSalmanticensis 37 (1990) 371-3 (R. *Trevijano*).

6271 **Kaylor** R. David, Paul's covenant community... Rom 1988 → 5,5966: ᴿParadigms 6,2 (1990s) 52s (T. *Meyer*).

6272 ᴱ**Kertelge** Karl, Das Gesetz im [Tagung Brixen 1985]: QDisp 108, 1986 → 2,382 ... 4,5966: ᴿTLZ 115 (1990) 427s (T. *Holtz*).

6273 *Laurenzi* M. Cristina, 'Sola fide' o 'regno di Dio'? Su Israele e cristianesimo in Leonhard RAGAZ: Protestantesimo 45 (1990) 95-102.

6274 **Liebers** Reinhold, Das Gesetz als Evangelium: ATANT 75, ᴰ1989 → 5,5967: ᴿTLZ 115 (1990) 273s (H. *Räisänen*).

6275 **Lim Ah Kam,** Paul, Judaism and the Law: diss. Drew, ᴰ*Doughty* D. Madison NJ 1990. 250 p. 91-00090. – DissA 51 (1990s) 2425-A; RelStR 17,194.

6276 **Martin** Brice L., Christ and the law in Paul [→ 5,5960 < diss. McMasters]: NT supp 62. Leiden 1989, Brill. xi-186 p. $57.50. – ᴿSWJT 33,3 (1990s) 48 (E. E. *Ellis*).

6277 *Meeks* Wayne A., On trusting an unpredictable God; a hermeneutical meditation on Romans 9-11: → 123*, ᶠMEYER P., Faith 1990, 105-124.

6278 *Moltmann* Jürgen, [Rom 9-11] Israel's No; Jews and Jesus in an unredeemed world: ChrCent 107 (1990) 1021-4 [< NTAbs 35,194].

6279 **Osten-Sacken** Peter von der, Die Heiligkeit der Tora; [5 neuere] Studien zum Gesetz bei Paulus 1989 → 5,5973: ᴿKIsr 5 (1990) 183 (Julie *Kirchberg*); SNTU-A 14 (1989) 263s (H. *Giesen*).

6280 **Panimolle** Salvatore A., La libertà cristiana; la libertà dalla legge nel NT e nei primi Padri della Chiesa: Teologia sapienziale 8. Vaticano 1988, Editrice. 228 p. Lit. 20.000. – ᴿCC 141 (1990,4) 519s (A. *Vanhoye*: stesura un po' frettolosa).

6281 *a) Payne* John B.,   ERASMUS on Romans 9:6-24; – *b) Margolin* Jean-Claude,   The epistle to the Romans (ch. 11) according to the versions and/or commentaries of VALLA, COLET, LEFÈVRE, and Erasmus; T*Farthing* John L.; – *c) Hobbs* R. Gerald, Hebraica veritas and traditio apostolica; St. Paul and the interpretation of the Psalms in the 16th c.; – *d) Bland* Kalman P., Issues in 16th-c. Jewish exegesis; – *e) Bedouelle* Guy, The consultations of the universities and scholars concerning the 'great matter' of King Henry VIII: ➤ 556*b*, Bible 16th c. 1982/90, 119-135.235-241 / 136-166.241-8 / 83-99.221-231 / 50-67.210-221 / 21-36.200-2.

6281* **Penna** Romano, Il problema della Legge nelle lettere di S. Paolo; alcuni aspetti [< RClerIt 71 (1990) 324-334.419-427, ritoccato]: RivB 38 (1990) 327-352; Eng. 352.

6282 **Räisänen** Heikki, Paul and the Law² [¹1983 ➤ 64,5532...]... 1987 ➤ 5,5976: RJTS 41 (1990) 187s (Morna D. *Hooker*).

6283 **Räisänen** Heikki, The Torah and Christ 1986 ➤ 2,209... 4,5972: RRHE 85 (1990) 362-4 (P.-T. *Camelot*).

6284 *Räisänen* Heikki, Der Bruch des Paulus mit Israels Bund: ➤ 560, Law 1988/90, 156-172.

6285 **Sanders** E.P., Paolo, la legge e il popolo giudaico [1983 ➤ 64,5532]: StBPaid 86. Brescia 1989, Paideia. – RRivB 38 (1990) 539-541 (M. *Làconi*).

6286 *Sanders* E.P., When is a law a law? The case of Jesus and Paul: ➤ 526, Religion & Law 1985/90, 139-158.

6287 *Sonderegger* Katherine A., Karl BARTH's dogmatic interpretation of Israel [firmly anti-Judaic, never anti-Semitic]: diss. Brown, D*Dietrich* W. Providence 1990. 370 p. 91-01835. – DissA 51 (1990s) 2785-A.

6288 *Stolle* Volker, Die Juden zuerst – das Anliegen des Römerbriefs: LuthTKi 14 (1990) 154-165.

Thielman Frank, ... Paul's view of the law 1989 ➤ 6500.

6289 *Trocmé* Étienne, Comment le Dieu d'Abraham, d'Isaac et de Jacob peut-il être à la fois fidèle et libre? (Épître aux Romains, chap. 9 à 11): FoiVie 89,1 (1990) 7-10.

6290 *a) Van Buren* Paul M., The Church and Israel; Romans 9-11; – *b) Segal* A.F., Paul's experience and Romans 9-11; – *c) Welker* M., Righteousness and God's righteousness: PrincSemB supp. 1 (1990) 5-18 / 56-70 / 124-139.

6291 **Watson** F., Paul, Judaism, and the Gentiles... sociological 1986 ➤ 2,4634*... 5,5982: RCritRR 3 (1990) 241s (S.G. *Wilson*); NedTTs 43 (1989) 58s (P.W. *van der Horst*).

6292 **Westerholm** Stephen, Israel's law and the Church's faith 1988 ➤ 4,3981; 5,5983: RBiblica 71 (1990) 269-272 (H. *Räisänen*); CBQ 52 (1990) 177s (G.T. *Montague*); Interpretation 44 (1990) 96 (R.G. *Hall*); JBL 109 (1990) 729-731 (F. *Thielman*); JRel 70 (1990) 249s (R.B. *Hays*); JTS 41 (1990) 613-5 (N.T. *Wright*); Pacifica 3 (1990) 349-351 (B. *Byrne*); RExp 87 (1990) 491s (D.S. *Dockery*); RHPR 70 (1990) 270s (C. *Grappe*); Themelios 16 (1990s) 27s (D. *Moo*).

6293 *Parmentier* Martin, Greek Church fathers on Romans 9, part II: Bijdragen 51 (1990) 2-20.

6294 *Dettori* L., [Rom 9,5; 1 Jn 5,20] La divinità di Gesù Cristo: Lux Biblica 1,2 (R 1990) 81-85 [< NTAbs 35,46].

6294* *Aletti* Jean-Noël, Saint Paul, exégète de l'Écriture, Rm 10s: ➤ 541*, L'Écriture âme de la théologie 1990, 37-50.

6295 *Dewey* Arthur J., A re-hearing of Romans 10:1-15: ➤ 544, SBL seminars 1990, 273-282.

6296 *Mussner* Franz, Fehl- und Falschübersetzungen von Röm 11 in der 'Einheitsübersetzung': TüTQ 170 (1990) 137-139.

6297 *Hvalvik* Reidar, A 'Sonderweg' for Israel; a critical examination of a current interpretation of Romans 11.25-27: JStNT 38 (1990) 87-107.

6298 *Osborne* William L., The Old Testament background of Paul's 'All Israel' in Romans 11:26*a*: AsiaJT 2 (1988) 282-293.

6299 **Carbone** Sandro P., La misericordia universale di Dio in Romani 11,30-32 [diss. Antonianum/Gerusalemme, bib. 310, ᴰ*Buscemi* A.]. Genova 1990. xxxiv-42 p.

G4.8 Rom 12...

6300 *Moiser* Jeremy, Rethinking Romans 12-15: NTS 36 (1990) 571-582.

6301 **Martin** Robert S., [Rom 13,1-7] Exegesis or expediency; an analysis of the New Christian Right's interpretation of the relationship of the believer and the state in Paul: diss. SW Baptist Theol. Sem. 1990. 270 p. 90-33449. – DissA 51 (1990s) 2425-A.

6302 *Munro* Winsome, Romans 13:1-7, Apartheid's last biblical refuge: BibTB 20 (1990) 161-8.

6303 *Porter* Stanley E., Romans 13:1-7 as Pauline political rhetoric: FgNt 3 (1990) 115-139.

6304 *Thorkildsen* Dag, Fra Martin LUTHER til Eivind BERGGRAV; fortolkning og bruk av Rom. 13.1-7 [Prøveforelesning Oslo 1989]: NorTTs 90 (1989) 105-123.

6305 *Torti* Giovanni, Romani 13,1-7 nell'esegesi di ORIGENE: Renovatio 24 (1989) 227-233.

6306 *Ellul* J., Petite note complémentaire sur Romains 13,1 [à propos de PENA Marc, Le stoïcisme et l'Empire Romain; BRUN J., Le Stoïcisme; tous deux 1980; Néron, soi-disant 'choisi pour le rôle des dieux' (SÉ NÈQUE)]: FoiVie 89,6 (1990) 81-83.

6307 *Klaiber* Walter, Von Christus angenommen (Röm 13,7): TBeit 21,1 (Wu 1990) 1-5 [< ZIT 90,174].

6308 *Keck* Leander E., Romans 15:4, an interpolation?: ➤ 123*, ᶠMEYER P., Faith 1990, 125-136.

6309 *a)* *Hoffmann* R.J., Women in the Marcionite churches of the second century; an inquiry into the provenance of Romans 16; – *b)* *Cocchini* Francesca, Il linguaggio di Paolo 'servo fedele e prudente' nel commento di ORIGENE alla Lettera ai Romani; – *c)* *Gorday* Peter J., The justus arbiter; Origen on Paul's role in the epistle to the Romans: ➤ 643, St. Patr 18,3 (1983/9) 161-181 / 355-364 / 393-403.

6310 *Romaniuk* Kazimierz, Was Phoebe in Romans 16,1 a deaconess?: ZNW 81 (1990) 132-4: no; a courteous exaggeration.

6311 *Schulz* R.R., A case for 'president' Phoebe in Romans 16:2: LuthTJ 24 (1990) 124-7 [< NTAbs 35,182].

6312 *Refoulé* François, À contre-courant; Romains 16,3-16 [list fitting Ephesus better than Rome, despite recent dissents]: RHPR 70 (1990) 409-420; Eng. 509.

6313 *Scholer* David N., 'The God of peace will shortly crush Satan under your feet' (Romans 16:20a); the function of apocalyptic eschatology in Paul: ➤ 531, ExAud 6 (1990) 53-61.

G5.1	**Epistulae ad Corinthios** (I vel I-II) – *textus, commentarii.*

6314 **Barbaglio** G., 1-2 Corinzi: LoB 2.7, 1989 ➤ 5,6005: RAsprenas 37 (1990) 111s (A. *Rolla*); NRT 112 (1990) 909s (X. *Jacques*); RivB 38 (1990) 117s (L. *De Lorenzi*).

6315 **Carrez** Maurice, *a)* La première épître aux Corinthiens: CahÉv 66. P 1988, Cerf. 67 p. F 25. 0222-9714; – *b)* La primera carta a los Corintios, T*Darrical* N.: CuadB 66. Estella 1989, VDivino. 63 p. 84-7151-627-6. – RActuBbg 27 (1990) 192s (X. *Alegre* S.).

6316 **Fabris** Rinaldo, Identità cristiana; Prima lettera di Paolo ai Corinzi: Commenti NT. T-Leumann 1986, Elle Di Ci. 214 p. 88-01-13177-1.

6317 **Chafin** Kenneth L., 1,2 Corinthians: Communicator's Comm. 7. Waco 1985, Word. 298 p. 0-8499-0347-5.

6318 EFatica Luigi, AMBROSIASTER, Commento alla Prima [➤ 5,6007]/ Seconda Lettera ai Corinzi: StPatr 78s. R 1989, Città Nuova. 255 p.; 168 p. Lit. 20.000; 13.000. – RAsprenas 37 (1990) 499-501 (L. *Longobardo*); EstTrin 24 (1990) 303s (N. *Silanes*).

6319 **Fee** Gordon D., 1 Cor NICNT 1987 ➤ 3,5842 ... 5,6008: RRHPR 70 (1990) 271 (M.-A. *Chevallier*); Vidyajyoti 54 (1990) 360 (P. M. *Meagher*).

6319* **Harrisville** Roy A., 1 Corinthians: Augsburg Comm. 1987 ➤ 3,5843; 5,6009: RCritRR 2 (1989) 202-5 (S. *Hafermann*).

6320 **Kilgallen** John J., First Corinthians; an introduction and study guide 1987 ➤ 3,5845; 4,6012: RRelStT 8,1s (1988) 99s (T. A. *Robinson*); Vidyajyoti 54 (1990) 359 (P. M. *Meagher*).

6320* *Pesce* Mauro, Il commento dell'AMBROSIASTER alla Prima lettera ai Corinzi: AnStoEseg 7 (1990) 593-629.

6321 *Schenk* Wolfgang, Korintherbriefe: ➤ 857, TRE 19 (1990) 620-640.

6322 **Senft** Christophe, La Première Épître de Saint Paul aux Corinthiens[2rev] [[1]1979 ➤ 60,7821]: CommNT 2/7. Genève 1990, Labor et Fides. 231 p. [NTAbs 34,395]. 2-8309-0584-9. – RCommSev 23 (1990) 433s (M. de *Burgos*).

6323 **Talbert** Charles H., Reading Cor 1-2, 1987 ➤ 3,5851 ... 5,6014: RCritRR 2 (1989) 249-251 (K. A. *Plank*).

G5.2	*1 & 1-2 ad Corinthios* – *themata,* **topics.**

6324 **Fitzgerald** John T., Cracks in an earthen vessel ... hardships/Cor: SBL diss. 199 [Yale 1984, D*Malherbe* A.] 1988 ➤ 4,6019; 5, also 6019: RCBQ 52 (1990) 746-8 (G. D. *Fee*); RB 97 (1990) 133s (J. *Murphy-O'Connor*); Salmanticensis 37 (1990) 369-371 (R. *Trevijano*).

6325 *McGraw* L., The city of Corinth: SWJT 32,1 (Fort Worth 1989) 5-10 [< NTAbs 34,53].

6326 **Marshall** Peter, Enmity in Corinth D1987 ➤ 3,5860 ... 5,6023: RNed-TTs 43 (1989) 245 (G. *Bouwman*).

6327 **Stonebury** Harry A.III, Corinthian honor, Corinthian conflict; a social history of early Roman Corinth and its Pauline community: diss. California, D*Frank* R. Irvine 1990. 570 p. 90-30047. – DissA 51 (1990s) 2127-A.

6328 **Theissen** Gerd,   The social setting of Pauline Christianity; essay on Corinth, ^{TE}*Schütz* John R. E 1990, Clark. xiii-210 p. £17.

6329 **Wire** Antoinette C.,   The Corinthian women prophets; a reconstruction through Paul's rhetoric. Mp 1990, Fortress. 316 p. $25 [TTod 48,506, Virginia *Burrus*].

G5.3   **1 Cor 1-7:**   *sapientia crucis ... abusus matrimonii.*

6330 **Theis** Joachim,   Paulus als Weisheitslehrer; der Gekreuzigte und die Weisheit Gottes in 1 Kor 1-4: Diss. ^D*Eckert.* Trier 1989s. – TR 86 (1990) 519; RTLv 22, p. 596.

6331 *a) Lampe* Peter,   Theological wisdom and the 'Word about the Cross'; the rhetorical scheme in 1 Cor 1-4; – *b*) 1 Cor 2,1-13 (*Cousar* Charles B.); 3,1-9 (*Rhyne* C. Thomas); 4,1-5 (*Bassler* Jouette M.), expository; – *c*) *Ellis* E. Earle,   *Sōma* in First Corinthians; – *d*) *Furnish* Victor P., Belonging to Christ; a paradigm for ethics in 1 Cor; – *e*) *Craddock* Fred B.,   Preaching to Corinthians: Interpretation 44 (1990) 117-31 / 169-173 . 174-9 . 179-183 / 132-144 / 145-157 / 158-168.

6332 *Gerlin* Andrea [1 Cor 1,10s ... 7,1.25 ...] Community and ascesis; Paul's directives to the Corinthians interpreted in the Rule of AUGUSTINE: → 688*a, Collectanea 1986/90, 303-311.

6333 *a) Gillespie* Thomas W.,   Interpreting the kerygma; early Christian prophecy according to 1 Cor. 2:6-16; – *b*) *Wire* Antoinette C.,   Prophecy and women prophets in Corinth; – *c*) *Wisse* Frederik W.,   Textual limits to redactional theory in the Pauline corpus: → 152, ^FROBINSON J.M., Gnosticism 1 (1990) 151-166 / 134-150 / 167-178.

6334 **Bockmuehl** M. N. A., [1 Cor 2,7-10] Revelation and mystery in ancient Judaism and Pauline Christianity: WUNT 2/36. Tü 1990, Mohr. xvi-310 p. DM 98. 3-16-145339-5 [BL 91,104, F. F. *Bruce*].

6335 *Crouzel* Henri,   L'exégèse origénienne de 1 Cor 3,11-15 [< ^F*Daniélou* J., Epektasis 1972, 273-283]: → 217, Fins dernières 1990, II (273-283).

6336 *Rosscup* James E.,   A new look at 1 Corinthians 3:12 – 'Gold, silver, precious stones': MastJ 1,1 (1990) 33-51 [< NTAbs 34,334].

6337 *Wolff* Christian,   'Nicht über das hinaus, was geschrieben ist'; 1 Kor 4,6 in der neueren Auslegungsgeschichte: → 76, ^FHENKYS J. 1989, 187-194.

6338 *Spencer* W. D.,   The power in Paul's teaching (1 Cor 4:9-20): JEvTS 32,1 (1989) 51-61 [< NTAbs 34,54].

6339 **Plank** Karl A.,   Paul and the irony of affliction, 1 Cor 4,9-13: ^D1987 → 3,5887 ... 5,6037: ^RCritRR 2 (1989) 237-9 (A. K. M. *Adam*).

6340 *Starowieyski* Marek, [1 Kor 4,13] ❷ *Perikátharma* and *perípsēma*; contribution to the history of patristic exegesis: Eos 78 (1990) 281-294; français 295.

6341 *Fiore* Benjamin,   Passion in Paul and Plutarch; 1 Corinthians 5-6 and the polemic against Epicureans: → 122, ^FMALHERBE A., Greeks 1990, 135-143.

6342 *a) Lewis* L. A., [1 Cor 6,1-11] The law courts in Corinth; an experiment in the power of baptism; – *b*) *Koenig* J.,   Christ and the Hierarchies in First Corinthians; – *c*) *Cope* L.,   First Corinthians 8-10; continuity or contradiction?: → 52, ^FFULLER R., AnglTR supp 11 (1990) 88-98 / 99-113 / 114-123 [< NTAbs 34,333].

6343 *Tiede* D. L.,   Will idolaters, sodomizers, or the greedy inherit the kingdom of God? A pastoral exposition of 1 Cor 6,9-10: WWorld 10,2 (1990) 147-155 [< NTAbs 34,334].

6344 **Kim Youn Tae,** Ethos and tradition in Pauline ethics; a study of 1 Corinthians 6:12-20: diss. Drew, ᴰ*Doughty* D. Madison NJ 1990. 191 p. 91-00089. – DissA 51 (1990s) 2423s-A; RelStR 17,194.

6345 **Muller** E. C., [1 Cor 6,16s; 11,2-16; 14,33-36; Gal 3,28] Trinity and marriage in Paul; the establishment of a communitarian analogy of the Trinity grounded in the theological shape of Pauline thought [diss. Marquette]: AmerUnivSt 7/60. xv-550 p. $81.50. 0-8204-0914-6 [NTAbs 35,114].

6346 *Kaye* B., [1 Cor 6,16; Mk 10,6-8; Eph 5,31] 'One flesh' and marriage: Colloquium 22,2 (1990) 46-57 [< NTAbs 35,29].

6347 *MacDonald* Margaret Y., [D capitalized in footnote 10 (like D. R. MacDonald frequently cited) but not on cover], Women holy in body and spirit; the social setting of 1 Corinthians 7: NTS 36 (1990) 161-181.

6348 *Ward* Roy B., [1 Cor 7,7s] Musonius [Rufus] and Paul on marriage: NTS 36 (1990) 281-9.

6349 *Best* Ernest, 1 Corinthians 7:14 and children in the church: IrBSt 12 (1990) 158-166.

6350 *Dawes* Gregory W., 'But if you can gain your freedom' (1 Corinthians 7:17-24): CBQ 52 (1990) 681-697.

6351 *Papadopoulos* K. N., Ⓖ Note on 1 Cor. 7,36-38: DeltioVM 19,2 (1990) 10-12.

G5.4 *Idolothyta ... Eucharistia:* **1 Cor 8-11.**

6352 *Winter* Bruce W., Theological and ethical responses to religious pluralism – 1 Corinthians 8-10: TyndB 41 (1990) 209-226.

6352* **Willis** Wendell L., Idol meat 1 C. 8.10 ᴰ1985 ➤ 1,5833 ... 3,5001: ᴿCritRR 3 (1990) 243-8 (L. L. *Welborn*).

6353 *Thompson* William G., 1 Corinthians 8:1-13, expository: Interpretation 44 (1990) 406-9.

6354 *Hwang Hyon-Sook*, Ⓚ Freedom in 1 Cor 9:15-19: Sinhak Sasang 68 (1989) 30-46 [< TContext 8/1,70 'No. 67'].

6354* **Martin** Dale B., [1 Cor 9,16-23] Slavery as salvation; the metaphor of slavery in Pauline Christianity. NHv 1990, Yale Univ. xxiii-245 p. $25 [TS 52,587, Carol L. *Stockhausen*].

6355 **Saez Gonzálvez** Ramón, El problema de las carnes inmoladas a los ídolos y las soluciones propuestas; un estudio teológico-bíblico sobre la unidad y la diversidad en el NT: diss. Pont. Univ. Gregoriana, ᴰ*Vanni* U. R 1990s. – InfPUG 23,119 (1990s) 16.

6355* *Vidman* Ladislav, Verkauf von Opferfleisch [1 Cor 10,25; Plinius]: ➤ 780, Schmidt-Kolloquium 1988/90, 147-155.

6356 *Callan* Terrance, [1 Cor 10,1-22] Paul and the Golden Calf [presidential address, Pittsburgh Apr. 20, 1990]: ProcGLM 10 (1990) 1-17.

6357 *Sebothoma* Wilfried A., a) *Koinōnia* in 1 Corinthians 10:16: Neotestamentica 24,1 (1990) 63-69; – b) *Koinōnia* in 1 Cor 10,16; its significance for liturgy and sacrament: QLtg 70 (1989) 243-249; franç. 250.

6358 *Templeton* David J., [1 Cor 11] Bread and body; semantics and infrastructure: IrBSt 12 (1990) 184-194.

6359 *Gill* David W. J., The importance of Roman portraiture for head-coverings in 1 Corinthians 11:2-16: TyndB 41 (1990) 245-260.

6360 *Amjad-Ali* Christine [1 Cor 11,2-16] The equality of women; form or substance?: Al-Mushir 31,4 (Rawalpindi 1989) 140-8.

6361 *MacDonald* Dennis R., [1 Cor 11,2-16] Corinthian veils and Gnostic androgynes: ➤ 5,481*a*, ᴱ**King** Karen L., Images of the feminine in Gnosticism 1985/8, 276-292 [293-6, *Brooten* Bernadette J., response].

6362 *Hall* David R., [1 Cor 11,10] A problem of authority: ExpTim 102 (1990s) 39-42.

6362* *Karrer* Martin, Der Kelch des Neuen Bundes; Erwägungen zum Verständnis des Herrenmahls nach 1 Kor 11,23b-25: BZ 34 (1990) 198-221.

6363 *Betz* Otto, Das Mahl des Herrn bei Paulus [ineditum]: ➤ 200, Jesus II (1990) 217-251.

6364 *Pesce* Mauro, [1 Cor 11,29] Mangiare e bere il proprio giudizio, una concezione culturale comune a 1 Cor e a Soṭa?: RivB 38 (1990) 495-513.

G5.5 1 Cor 12s... Glossolalia, charismata.

6365 *Balasundaram* Franklyn J., The voice and the voices, or the history and development of the charismatic movement; a theological critique: *a*) AsiaJT 4,1 (1990) 225-252; – *b*) Bangalore Theological Forum 21s (1989s) 94-139; summary TContext 8/1, 118.

6366 **Bentivegna** G., Effusione dello Spirito Santo e doni carismatici; la testimonianza di S. Aɢᴏsᴛɪɴᴏ. Messina 1990, Ignatianum. 124 p. Lit. 12.500 [NRT 113,311, B. C.].

6367 *Biffi* Inos, La teologia medioevale dei 'carismi', I: TItSett 15 (1990) 198-225...; Eng. 225.

6368 ᴱ**Burgess** Stanley M., *al.*, Dictionary of Pentecostal and charismatic movements 1988 ➤ 5,6069: ᴿRExp 87 (1990) 143 (D. S. *Dockery*: superb).

6369 **Carson** D. A., Showing the Spirit... 1 Cor 12-14, 1987 ➤ 3,5921... 5,6070: ᴿNedTTs 44 (1990) 68 (H. W. *Hollander*); ScotBEv 8 (1990) 62s (G. *Houston*); STEv 1 (1989) 212s (P. *Finch*); Themelios 15 (1989s) 71 (P. D. *Gardner*); Vidyajyoti 54 (1990) 361-3 (P. M. *Meagher*).

6370 *Connelly* James T., Not in reputable churches? The reception of the charismatic movement in the mainline churches in America: ➤ 2,28, ᶠEʀᴠɪɴ II., Essays on apostolic themes, ᴱ**Elbert** P., 1985, 184-192.

6371 **Czakański** Tadeusz, The Christian prophets and charism of prophecy in the New Testament and the origins of the Church: diss. Pont. Univ. Lateranensis, ᴰ*Manza* Sergio. R 1987. xxxviii-209 p.

6372 **Espinel Marcos** José Luis, Profetismo cristiano; una espiritualidad evangélica: Glosas 13. S 1990, San Esteban. 199 p. pt 1200. – ᴿCarthaginensia 6 (1990) 250 (J. F. *Cuenca*); CommSev 23 (1990) 297 (M. de *Burgos*).

6373 **Giesriegl** Richard, Die Sprengkraft des Geistes; Charismen und apostolischer Dienst nach dem 1. Korintherbrief 1989 ➤ 5,6075: ᴿTGL 80 (1990) 516s (J. *Ernst*); TPQ 138 (1990) 403s (C.-P. *März*).

6374 *a*) *Giglioni* Paolo, Perché una 'nuova' evangelizzazione?; – *b*) *Esquerda Bifet* Juan, Valor evangelizador y desafios actuales de la 'experiencia' religiosa: EuntDoc 43 (1990) 5-36 / 37-56.

6375 **Grudem** Wayne, The gift of prophecy in the NT and today ᴰ1988 ➤ 4,6082; 5,6078: ᴿAndrUnS 28 (1990) 96-98 (W. *Richardson*).

6376 *Grundman* Christoffer, Die missionstheologische Herausforderung von Heilungserfahrungen, ZMissRW 74 (1990) 54-59 [> TDig 38, 245-8, ᵀᴱ*Asen* B.].

6377 *Henau* Ernest, Geestelijke vernieuwingsbewegingen in de Kerk: Collat-Vʟ 20 (1990) 41-58.

6378 **Labuschagne** Gideon J.J., [Charismatic] miracle healing: diss. ᴰ*Dreyer* T. Pretoria 1990. – DissA 51 (1990s) 3113-A.

6379 *Lang* Bernhard, Charisma and the disruption of the family in early Christianity: ➤ 127, ᶠMÜLLER E.W., Die Vielfalt der Kultur 1990, 278-287.

6380 **Lederle** Henry I., Treasures... 'Spirit-baptism' [ᴰ1986 ➤ 3,5935] 1988 ➤ 5,6089: ᴿMissiology 18 (1990) 483s (F.H. *Morgan*).

6381 *Lohfink* Norbert, Where are today's prophets? [< StiZt 206 (1988) 183-192], ᵀᴱ*Asen* B.A.: TDig 37 (1990) 103-7.

6382 **Lowry** David, The prophetic element in the Church as conceived in the theology of Karl RAHNER. Lanham MD 1990, UPA. 258 p. $41.75 [JAAR 58,740].

6383 *Luz* Ulrich, Carisma e institución a la luz del NT [< EvT 49 (1989) 76-94], ᵀᴱ*Puig Massana* R.: SelT 29 (1990) 17-28.

6384 **McConnell** D.R., A different Gospel; a historical and biblical analysis of the modern faith movement. Peabody MA 1988, Hendrickson. 195 p. $8 pa. – ᴿCriswT 4 (1989s) 406-8 (C.O. *Brand*: what makes the charismatic movement offensive to many Baptists and others).

6385 *a) Moltmann* Jürgen, The scope of renewal in the Spirit; – *b) Bittlinger* Arnold, A 'charismatic' approach to the theme; – *c) Breck* John, 'The Lord is the Spirit', an essay in Christological pneumatology: EcuR 42 (1990) 98-106 / 107-113 / 114-121 [-174. 197-328, *al.*].

6386 *Nethöfel* Wolfgang, Genese und Struktur pneumatologischer Erkenntnis [... Paulus < Gn 2s; 22; Jos 2 ...]: NSys 31 (1989) 230-249; Eng. 249.

6387 *Ogrodzki* Jan, ❷ Prophetic service of the Church in the light of the biblical concept of the Word of God: RuBi 42 (1989) 132-9.

6388 *Oppenheimer* Helen, Spirit and body; prophecy, diversity and Christian identity: TLond 93 (1990) 133-141.

6389 *Osiek* Carolyn, Christian prophecy; once upon a time?: ➤ 41, ᶠDAN-KER F., CurrTMiss 17 (1990) 291-7.

6390 **Poloma** Margaret M., The Assemblies of God at the crossroads; charisma and institutional dilemmas. Knoxville 1989, Univ. Tennessee. xxi-309 p. $40; pa. $18. 0-87049-604-2; -7-7. – ᴿTDig 37 (1990) 380 (W.C. *Heiser*: by a Catholic, from questionnaires with Assemblies approval).

6391 *Pottmeyer* Hermann J., Die pneumatologische Dimension der Kirche; Geistbegabung aller Kirchenglieder, nicht Geistmonopol der Kirchen-leitung: Diakonia 21 (1990) 170-4.

6392 *Price* R.M., Confirmation and charisma: StLuke 33 (1990) 173-182 [< NTAbs 35,31].

6393 **Rey** Bernard, *al.*, Jésus vivant au cœur du renouveau charismatique: JJC 43. P 1990, Desclée. 285 p. – ᴿEsprVie 100 (1990) 413 (G. *Viard*).

6394 **Robeck** Cecil M., Charismatic experience in history. Peabody MA 1985, Hendrickson. 180 p. $9 pa. – ᴿCriswT 4 (1989s) 207-9 (C.O. *Brand*).

6395 *Rozman* Francè, [in Slovene] Charismas and ministries in the early Church: BogVest 49 (1989) 121-134; Eng. 133.

6396 **Schatzmann** Siegfried, A Pauline theology of charismata [< ᴰ1981 SW Sem.]. Peabody MA 1989 [= 1987], Hendrickson. x-117 p. $8. 0-913573-45-0. – ᴿCritRR 3 (1990) 232s W.E. *Mills*).

6397 *Suurmond* J.J., *a)* The meaning and purpose of Spirit-baptism and the charisms: Bijdragen 51 (1990) 172-193; 194 Eng. summ.; – *b)* Een introductie tot de charismatische vernieuwing: KerkT 40 (1989) 33-50.

6398 *Wenz* Gunther, Charisma und Amt: TBeit 21 (1990) 116-135 [< ZIT 90,465].
6399 *Whitehead* James & Evelyn, The gift of prophecy: SpTod 41 (1989) 292-304.

6400 *Jackson* T. A., Concerning spiritual gifts; a study of 1 Corinthians 12: Faith and Mission 7,1 [Wake Forest NC 1989] 61-69 [< NTAbs 34,187].
6401 *Charles* Gary W., 1 Corinthians 12:1-13, expository: Interpretation 44 (1990) 65-70.
6402 *Díaz Rodelas* J. Miguel, La pretendida fórmula subyacente a 1 Cor 12,13; Gal 3,28 y Col 3,11: ➤ 182, FVALLS I. 1990, 109-122.
6403 *Perriman* Andrew, [1 Cor 12,27; Eph 1,22s] 'His body, which is the church ...'; coming to terms with metaphor: EvQ 62 (1990) 123-142.
6404 *Cereti* Giovanni, Membra di Cristo, ciascuno per la sua parte (cf. 1 Cor 12,27): Presbyteri 23 (1989) 505-516.
6405 *Holladay* Carl R., 1 Corinthians 13; Paul as apostolic paradigm: ➤ 122, FMALHERBE A., Greeks 1990, 80-98.
6406 *Smit* J., 1 Korinte 13; hooglied of spotrede?: 180*, FTROMP N., Gelukkig c. 1990, 107-118; Eng. 258.
6407 *Rowe* Arthur, Silence and the Christian women of Corinth; an examination of 1 Corinthians 14:33b-36: ComViat 33 (1990) 41-84.

G5.6 **Resurrectio;** *1 Cor 15* ... [➤ F5.6; H9].

6408 **Barth** K. [1 Cor 15] La resurrezione dei morti 1984 ➤ 4,6112: RPro- testantesimo 45 (1990) 73s (P. *Ribet*).
6409 **Boer** Martinus C. de, The defeat of death ... 1 Cor 15, Rom 5: JStNT supp 22, 1988 ➤ 4,6115; 5,6116: RCBQ 52 (1990) 741-3 (Beverly R. *Gaventa*); EvQ 62 (1990) 368 (L. J. *Kreitzer*); ExpTim 101 (1989s) 31 (J. D. G. *Dunn*); JTS 41 (1990) 194-6 (J. A. *Ziesler*); TLZ 115 (1990) 817s (C. *Wolff*); TTod 47 (1990s) 109s (K. P. *Donfried*).
6410 Ede **Lorenzi** Lorenzo, Résurrection du Christ et des Chrétiens (1 Cor. 15) 1983/5 ➤ 1,466 ... 5,6122: RRelStT 8,1s (1988) 83s (B. F. *Meyer*).
6411 **Kim Kwangsoo,** The social function of 1 Corinthians 15; resurrection as an ideology of purity: diss. Southern Baptist Theol. Sem., DBorchert G. 1990, 272 p. 91-12508. – DissA 51 (1990s) 3793-A.
6412 **Sellin** G., Der Streit um ... 1 Kor 15 [< ev. Hab. Diss. Münster 1981]: FRL 138, 1986 ➤ 3,5975; 4,6114: RSNTU A-15 (1990) 191-3 (F. *Weissen- gruber*).
6413 *Villegas M.* Beltrán, [1 Cor 15 ...] Los dos Adanes y el hombre nuevo; avatares de un tema paulino: TVida 31 (1990) 47-53.
6414 *Sabugal* Santos, ¡ Cristo 'fue resucitado el tercer día ...' ! (1 Cor 15,4-8): EstAg 25 (1990) 487-503.
6415 *Christensen* Jens, [1 Cor 15,4; from Hosea 6,2 'possible but hardly evident'; likelier Gn 1,11s 'third day']: ScandJOT (1990,2) 101-113.
6416 *Habermas* Gary R., [1 Cor 15,12-20 ...] Jesus' Resurrection and con- temporary criticism; an apologetic: CriswT 4 (1989s) 159-174. 373-385.
6417 *Binder* Hermann, Zum geschichtlichen Hintergrund von 1 Kor 15,12: TZBas 46 (1990) 193-201.
6418 *Schweizer* Eduard, 1 Corinthians 15:20-28 as evidence of Pauline eschatology and its relation to the preaching of Jesus: ➤ 60,181, FOU- DERSLUYS R., Saved by hope, ECook J. 1978, 120-132.

6419 *Lambrecht* Jan, Structure and line of thought in 1 Cor. 15:23-28: NT 32 (1990) 143-151.
6420 *Macky* Peter W., [1 Cor 15,23-26] Paul's four windows on the eschaton: ProcGLM 10 (1990) 136-150.
6421 *Pelland* Gilles, La théologie et l'exégèse de MARCEL d'Ancyre sur 1 Cor 15:24-28: Gregorianum 71 (1990) 679-695; Eng. 695.
6422 *Alfeche* Mamerto, The rising of the dead in the works of AUGUSTINE (1 Cor. 15,35-57): AugLv 39 (1989) 54-98.
6423 *Painchaud* Louis, Le sommaire anthropogonique de L'écrit sans titre (NH II,117:27 - 118:2) à la lumière de 1 Co 15:45-57: VigChr 44 (1990) 382-393.
6424 **Olson** Mark J., IRENAEUS, the Valentinian Gnostics, and the Kingdom of God (A.H. Book V); the debate about I Corinthians 15:50: diss. Virginia, DGamble H. Charlottesville 1990. 199 p. 90-29898. – DissA 51 (1990s) 3108-A; RelStR 17,194.
6425 *a) Harrelson* Walter J., Death and victory in 1 Corinthians 15:51-57; the transformation of a prophetic theme; – *b) Martyn* Louis J., The covenants of Hagar and Sarah: ⇒ 123*, FMEYER P., Faith 1990, 149-159 / 160-192.

G5.9 **Secunda epistula ad Corinthios.**

6426 **Barnett** Paul, The message of II Corinthians: The Bible speaks today 1988 ⇒ 5,6122: RCriswT 4 (1989s) 184s (D. L. *Akin*).
6427 *Cheong Yang-Mo,* ❂ 2 Corinthians, exegetical introduction: Samok 138 (Seoul 1990) 106-117 [< TContext 8/1,69].
6428 **Danker** F. W., II Cor: Augsburg Comm. 1989 ⇒ 5,6131: RLvSt 15 (1990) 84s (J. *Lambrecht*); TorTJ 6 (1990) 358-360 (K. B. *Quast*); Vidyajyoti 54 (1990) 366s (P. M. *Meagher*).
6429 *a) Duduit* Michael, Preaching ['in' omitted on cover] 2 Corinthians; – *b) Dockery* David S., Commenting on commentaries on 2 Corinthians: CriswT 4 (1989s) 145-152 / 153-7.
6430 **Fabris** Rinaldo, Al servizio della comunità; seconda lettera di Paolo ai Corinzi: CommNT. T-Leumann 1984, Elle Di Ci. 160 p. 88-01- 10050-7.
6431 *Hafemann* Scott, 'Self-commendation' and apostolic legitimacy in 2 Corinthians; a Pauline dialectic?: NTS 36 (1990) 66-88.
6432 *a) Hay* David M., The shaping of theology in 2 Corinthians; convictions, doubts, and warrants; – *b) Martin* Ralph P., Theological perspectives in 2 Corinthians; some notes: ⇒ 544, SBL seminars 1990, 257-272 / 240-256.
6433 **Kremer** Jacob, 2. Korintherbrief: StuKLK NT 8. Stu 1990, KBW. 127 p. 3-460-15381-4.
6434 **Kruse** Colin, II Corinthians: Tyndale NT 1987 ⇒ 3,5993; 4,6128: REvangel 7,2 (1989) 21 (S. *Motyer*); Pacifica 3 (1990) 94s (C. *Monaghan*).
6435 **Martin** R. P., 2 Cor. Word Comm. 40, 1986 ⇒ 5,6136: RVidyajyoti 54 (1990) 364-6 (P. M. *Meagher*).
6436 *Rolland* Philippe, La structure littéraire de la Deuxième Épître aux Corinthiens: Biblica 71 (1990) 73-84.
6437 **Spencer** A. B. & W. D., 2 Corinthians: Bible Study Comm. GR 1989, Zondervan. 144 p. $7 pa. 0-310-36101-X [NTAbs 34,259].
6438 **Voigt** G., Die Kraft des Schwachen; Paulus an die Korinther II: Biblisch-theologische Schwerpunkte 5. Gö 1990, Vandenhoeck & R. 134 p. DM 19,80 pa. 3-525-61286-9 [NTAbs 35,254].

6439 **Wolff** Christian, Der zweite Brief des Paulus an die Korinther: ThHk NT 8. B 1989, Ev.-V. xxi-270 p. DM 32. 3-374-00857-7 [RB 98,467, J. *Murphy-O'Connor*].

6440 **Young** Frances, *Ford* David F., Meaning and truth in 2 Corinthians 1988 → 3,5999; 5,6140: ᴿCriswT 4 (1989s) 187s (D. J. *Akin*); ScotBEv 8 (1990) 59s (D. J. *Graham*); ScotJT 43 (1990) 273-5 (N. T. *Wright*); WestTJ 52 (1990) 158-160 (M. *Silva*: 'the authors appear to have slight regard for the unity of the Bible').

6441 *a) Blomberg* Craig, The structure of 2 Corinthians 1-7; – *b) Garland* David E., The sufficiency of Paul, minister of the New Covenant; – *c) Wells* C. Richard, The crisis in pastoral ministry: CriswT 4 (1989s) 3-20 / 21-37 / 39-55.

6442 *Perriman* Andrew, Between Troas and Macedonia; 2 Cor 2:13-14: ExpTim 101 (1989s) 39-41.

6443 **Oliveira** Anacleto de, Die Diakonie der Gerechtigkeit und der Versöhnung in der Apologie des 2. Korintherbriefes; Analyse und Auslegung von 2 Kor 2,14 - 4,6; 5,11 - 6,10 [kath. Diss. Münster 1988, ᴰ*Kertelge* K.]: NTAbh 21. Münster 1990, Aschendorff. vii-456 p. DM 128. 3-402-03643-6 [NTAbs 35,111].

6444 *Breytenbach* J. C., Paul's proclamation and God's thriambos (notes on 2 Corinthians 2:14-16b): Neotestamentica 29 (1990) 257-272.

6445 **Trevijano Etcheverría** Ramón, La idoneidad del Apóstol (2 Cor 2-14 - 4,6): Salmanticensis 37 (1990) 149-175; Eng. 175.

6446 [Masumbuko] **Renju** Peter, A semantic analysis of 2 Corinthians 2:14-3:18 [diss.]. Haarlem 1986, Ned. Bijb.-G. x-122 p. – ᴿNedTTs 43 (1989) 147s (W. *Weren*).

6447 **Hafemann** Scott J., Suffering and ministry in the Spirit; Paul's defense of his ministry in II Corinthians 2:14 - 3:3 [= WUNT 2/19, 1986 → 2,4475]. GR 1990, Eerdmans. xiv-261 p. $22. 0-8028-0442-X.

6448 **Kromer** Michael L., Word [? World], metaphor, text; contributions to the interpretation of 2 Corinthians 3: diss. Edinburgh 1989. 377 p. – RTLv 22, p. 593 'World'.

6449 **Stockhausen** Carol K., Moses' veil... 2 Cor 3s: AnBib 116, ᴰ1989 → 5,6148: ᴿBiblica 71 (1990) 436-9 (M. *Carrez*); CBQ 52 (1990) 572s (J. P. *Heil*: plausible); RivB 38 (1990) 119-122 (L. *De Lorenzi*); SvEx 55 (1990) 146-9 (H. *Johansson*).

6450 **Srampickal** T., The ministry of the New Covenant; an exegetical study of 2 Cor. 3:6.7-18: diss. ᴰ*Lambrecht* J. Lv 1989. xiv-402 p. – TsTNijm 30 (1990) 190; LvSt 15 (1990) 420s.

6451 *Kayama* H., The doxa of Moses and Jesus (2 Cor. 3:7-18 and Luke 9:28-32): BMeijiG 23 (1990) 23-48 [< NTAbs 35,185].

6452 *De Lorenzi* Lorenzo, [2 Cor 3,16] Il ritorno del popolo al Signore: → 325b, ParSpV 22 (1990) 199-228.

6453 **Green** William P.ᴵᴵᴵ, Suffering and eschatology; a critical study of 2 Corinthians 4 with particular emphasis on the relationship of suffering and eschatology in Paul: diss. ᴰ*Bandstra* A., Calvin Theol. Sem. vi-239 p. + bibliog. – CalvinT 25 (GR 1990; no other date assigned) 330.

6454 *Garrett* Susan R., The God of this world and the affliction of Paul: 2 Cor 4:1-12: → 122, ᶠMALHERBE A., Greeks 1990, 99-117.

6455 **Martin** Ralph P., [2 Cor 4,7] Paradoxes of ministry: ExpTim 102 (1990s) 82-84.

6456 *Romaniuk* Kazimierz, Résurrection existentielle ou eschatologique en 2 Co 4,13-14? [*Murphy-O'Connor* J. 1988]: BZ 34 (1990) 248-252.

6457 **Tolksdorf** Roland A., Bedachte Rede; Bedeutung und Handlung in adressierter Rede, gezeigt am Beispiel von 2. Korinther 5: Diss. ᴰ*Baarlink* H. Kampen 1990. xviii-326 p. – TsTNijm 30, p. 303; RTLv 22, p. 596.

6458 *Glasson* T. Francis, 2 Corinthians v. 1-10 versus Platonism: ScotJT 43 (1990) 145-155.

6459 *a*) *Metts* Roy, Death, discipleship and discourse strategies; 2 Cor 5:1-10 – once again; – *b*) *Turner* David L., Paul and the ministry of reconciliation in 2 Cor 5:11 - 6:2: CriswT 4 (1989s) 57-76 / 77-95.

6460 ᴱ*Lewis* Jack F., Interpreting 2 Cor 5:14-21 [also by *Danker* F., *Mead* R., *Stagg* F.], an exercise in hermeneutics: StBEC 17. Lewiston NY 1989, Mellen. x-194 p. $50. 0-88946-617-3 [NTAbs 34,393; JBL 110, 367, tit. pp.].

6461 **Mell** Ulrich, Neue Schöpfung... 2 Cor 5,14-17: BZNW 56. B 1989, de Gruyter [RB 98,150, J. *Murphy-O'Connor*].

6462 *Jezierska* Ewa J., [2 Cor 5,15; R 14,7s] ❷ St. Paul, de la préexistence du chrétien: ColcT 59,3 (1989) 27-33; franç. 33.

6463 *Waller* Elizabeth, The rhetorical structure of II Cor. 6:14 - 7:1; is the so-called 'non-Pauline interpolation' a clue to the redactor of II Corinthians?: ProcGLM 10 (1990) 151-165.

6464 *a*) *Melick* Richard R.ᴶ, Collection for the saints; 2 Corinthians 8-9; – *b*) *Akin* Daniel L., Triumphalism, suffering, and spiritual maturity; an exposition of 2 Corinthians 12:1-10 in its literary, theological, and historical context: CriswT 4 (1989s) 97-117 / 119-144.

6465 *Stowers* Stanley R., Perì mèn gár and the integrity of 2 Cor. 8 and 9: NT 32 (1990) 340-8.

6466 **Betz** H. D., 2 Cor 8: 1985 ➤ 1,5922 ... 4,6349: ᴿTR 86 (1990) 374s (D. *Zeller*).

6467 *Chevallier* Max-Alain †, L'argumentation de Paul dans II Corinthiens 10 à 13: RHPR 70 (1990) 3-15; Eng. 145.

6468 *Penna* Romano, La presenza degli avversari di Paolo in 2 Cor 10-13; esame letterario: Lateranum 56 (1990) 83-116.

6469 **Sumney** Jerry L., Identifying Paul's opponents; the question of method in 2 Corinthians [diss. Southern Methodist 1987, ᴰ*Furnish* V.]: JStNT supp. 40. Sheffield 1990, JStOT. 256 p. $30 [NTAbs 34,396]. 1-85075-234-6. – ᴿExpTim 102 (1990s) 86 (A. J. M. *Wedderburn*).

6470 **Georgi** Dieter, Opponents in 2 Cor 1986 ➤ 2,4763 ... 5,6134: ᴿCritRR 2 (1989) 195-7 (W. *Baird*); IrTQ 56 (1990) 76-78 (S. W. *Need*); RBibArg 52 (1990) 122-4 (U. *Schoenborn*).

6471 *Fitzgerald* John T., Paul, the ancient epistolary theorists, and 2 Corinthians 10-13; the purpose and literary genre of a Pauline letter: ➤ 122, ᶠMALHERBE A., Greeks 1990, 190-200.

6472 *Ward* Richard F., *a*) 2 Corinthians 10:7-12: RExp 87 (1990) 605-9; – *b*) [2 Cor 10,10; 11,6] Pauline voice and presence as strategic communication: ➤ 544, SBL seminars 1990, 283-292.

6473 *Murphy-O'Connor* Jerome, Another Jesus (2 Cor 11:4): RB 97 (1990) 238-251; franç. 238.

6474 *Gallas* Sven, 'Fünfmal vierzig weniger einen ...'; die an Paulus vollzogenen Synagogalstrafen nach 2 Kor 11,24: ZNW 81 (1990) 178-191.

6474* *a*) *Ten Napel* Erik, 'Third heaven' and 'paradise'; some remarks on the exegesis of 2 Cor. 12,2-4 in Syriac; – *b*) *Reller* Jobst, Der Text des

Kommentars Mose BAR KEPHAS zu den paulinischen Briefen: ➤ 779*, Symposium 5, 1988/90, 53-65 / 67-69.

6475 **Ott** Rudi, 'Wenn ich schwach bin, dann bin ich stark' (2 Cor 12,10), Auslegung der Korintherbriefe im Religionsunterricht...: kath. Diss. ᴰ*Neuenzeit*. Würzburg 1989s. – TR 86 (1990) 520.

G6.1   Ad Galatas.

6476 **Barclay** John M.G., Obeying the truth... Gal 1988 ➤ 4,6165; 5,6161: ᴿCBQ 52 (1990) 737s (P. *Rogers*); JTS 41 (1990) 619-624 (F. *Watson*); ScotBEv 8 (1990) 131s (R. *Higginson*); WestTJ 52 (1990) 160-2 (M. *Silva*: great merit).

6477 **Betz** H.D., Der Galaterbrief [1979], ᵀ*Sibylle* Ann 1988 ➤ 4,6166; 5,6162: ᴿSNTU-A 14 (1989) 264s (A. *Fuchs*).

6478 **Borse** Udo, Der Brief an die Galater: RgNT, 1984 ➤ 65,5437... 2,4795: ᴿZkT 112 (1990) 218s (E. *Ruschitska*).

6479 *Bruce* F.F., The Spirit in the letter to the Galatians: ➤ 2,88, ᶠERVIN H., Essays on Apostolic Themes, ᴱ**Elbert** P. 1985, 36-48.

6480 **Corsani** Bruno, Lettera ai Galati: CommStoEseg 9. Genova 1990, Marietti. 493 p. 88-211-6715-1.

6481 **Cosgrove** Charles H., The Cross and the Spirit... Gal 1988 ➤ 4,6170: ᴿParadigms 6,2 (1990s) 53s (D.J. *Dittman*).

6482 **Daalen** D.H. van, A guide to Galatians: TEF Study Guide 28. L 1990, SPCK. x-102 p. £7.50 pa. 0-281-04502-X [NTAbs 35,253].

6483 *Dolamo* R.T.H., Rhetorical speech in Galatians: TViat 17 (Sovenga SAf 1989) 30-37 [< NTAbs 35,186].

6484 *Elliott* John H., Paul, Galatians, and the Evil Eye: ➤ 41, ᶠDANKER F., CurrTMiss 17 (1990) 262-273.

6485 **Fung** R.Y.K., The epistle of Paul to the churches of Galatia: NICNT 1988 ➤ 4,6173; 5,6167: ᴿAndrUnS 28 (1990) 161s (S. *Kubo*); Biblica 71 (1990) 439s (R. *Penna*); CBQ 52 (1990) 750s (E. *Hensell*: informed and cautious, though firmly assuming South-Galatian theory, and Gal Paul's earliest letter); EvQ 62 (1990) 274s (A. *Campbell*: replaces H. RIDDERBOS; excellent, though not adventurous or questioning); JBL 109 (1990) 731-3 (C.H. *Cosgrove*); JTS 41 (1990) 618 (J. *Barclay*); TLZ 115 (1990) 107s (D. *Lührmann*).

6486 *Hansen* G.W., Paul's three-dimensional application of Genesis 15:6 in Galatians: Trinity Theological Journal 1 (Singapore 1989) 59-77 [< NTAbs 34,56].

6487 **Howard** G., Paul, crisis in Galatia; a study in early Christian theology² = ¹c. 1979 + 21 p. intr.]: SNTS Mg 35. C 1990, Univ. xxxvi-114 p. 0-521-38230-0 [NTAbs 35,113].

6488 *a)* *Howard* J.K., The new Eve; Paul and the role of women; – *b*) *Trebilco* P., Women as co-workers and leaders in Paul's letters: Journal of the Christian Brethren research fellowship 122 (Wellington ᴺᶻ 1990) 19-26 / 27-36 [< NTAbs 35,179].

6489 *Kraftchick* Steven J., [Gal] Why do the rhetoricians rage?: ➤ 24, ᶠBOERS H., Text 1990, 55-79.

6490 *Lategan* Bernard C., Is Paul developing a specifically Christian ethics in Galatians?: ➤ 122, ᶠMALHERBE A., Greeks 1990, 318-328.

6491 *Levinsohn* S.H., Phrase order and the article in Galatians; a functional sentence perspective approach: OPTAT 3,2 (Dallas 1989) 44-64 [< NTAbs 34,189].

6492 **Longenecker** Richard N., Galatians: Word comm. 41. Dallas 1990, Word. cxix-323 p. $19.25 [NTAbs 35,250]. 0-8499-0240-1.

6493 *Marín Heredia* Francisco, Evangelio de la gracia; carta de San Pablo a los Gálatas; traducción y comentario: Carthaginensia 6 (1990) 3-137.

6494 *Panier* Louis, Parcours pour lire l'Épître aux Galates: SémBib 53 (1989) 48-53; 54, 36-41; 55, 29-33.

6494* **Rogers** Elinor M., Semantic structure analysis of Galatians [ᴱ*Callow* J. (? series, with Col and 2 Thes)]. Dallas 1989, Summer Institute of Linguistics. vii-215 p. – ᴿWestTJ 52 (1990) 381-3 (M. *Silva*: different).

6495 *Russell* Walt, Who were Paul's opponents in Galatia?: BS 147 (1990) 329-350: Jewish-Christians, rather than (Antinomian) 'Judaizers'.

6496 **Salvador** Miguel, San Pablo, Cartas a los Gálatas, Romanos, Filipenses y Filemón: Mensaje NT 7. S 1990, Sígueme [al.]. 214 p. 84-301-1103-4.

6497 *Silva* Moisés, Text and language in the Pauline corpus; with special reference to the use of conjunctions in Galatians: Neotestamentica 29 (1990) 273-281.

6498 *Smit* Joop, Opbouw en gedankengang van de brief aan de Galaten; vier [reeds gepubliceerde] studies: Diss. Nijmegen 1987. Franckcr 1988, Wever. 128 p. ƒ 39,50. – ᴿBijdragen 51 (1990) 444 (J. *Lambrecht*).

6499 **Smit** J., Brief aan de Galaten: BelichtingBb 1989 ➤ 5,6183: ᴿCollatVʟ 20 (1990) 115s (R. *Hoet*).

6500 **Thielman** Frank, From plight to solution; a Jewish framework for understanding Paul's view of the law in Galatians and Romans: VT supp 61, 1989 ➤ 5,5979: 90-04-09176-9.

6501 *Ukpong* J. S., *Asahu-Ejere*, La carta a los Gálatas y el problema del pluralismo cultural en el cristianismo [< RAfT 12 (1988) 66-77], ᵀᴱ*Angles* Jaime: SelT 29 (1990) 97-102.

6502 *Wagner* Guy, Les motifs de la rédaction de l'Épître aux Galates: ÉTRel 65 (1990) 321-332.

6503 **Zahn** T., Der Brief des Paulus an die Galater [³1922], ᴱ*Hengel* M. Wu 1990, Brockhaus. vii-301 p. DM 68. 3-417-29217-4 [NTAbs 35,116]. – ᴿSNTU A-15 (1990) 193s (A. *Fuchs*).

6504 *Buscemi* Alfio M., Gal 1,1-5; struttura e linea di pensiero: LA 40 (1990) 71-103; Eng. 446.

6505 *Koptak* Paul E., Rhetorical identification in Paul's autobiographical narrative, Galatians 1.13-2.14: JStNT 40 (1990) 97-113.

6506 *Craffert* P. F., Paul's Damascus experience as reflected in Galatians 1; call or conversion: Scriptura 29 (Stellenbosch 1989) 36-47 [< NTAbs 34,56].

6507 *Schmidt* Andreas, [Gal 1,18; 2,1 ...] Das historische Datum des Apostelkonzils [46: weder 43s (*Hahn* F., *al.*) noch 47s [*Lüdemann* G., *al.*]: ZNW 81 (1990) 122-131.

6508 *Ulrichs* Karl F., Grave verbum, ut de re magna [BᴇɴɢᴇL J.]; nochmals Gal 1,18, *historêsai Kēphân*: ZNW 81 (1990) 262-9.

6509 *Hallbäck* Geert, Jerusalem og Antiokia i Gal. 2; en historisk hypotese: DanTTs 53 (1990) 300-316 [NTAbs 35,188].

6510 **Bartolomé** Juan J., El evangelio y su verdad... Gal 2,5, 1988 ➤ 4,6188; 5,6191: ᴿActuBbg 27 (1990) 192 (X. *Alegre* S.); BLitEc 91 (1990) 234 (S. *Légasse*); CBQ 52 (1990) 548s (S. B. *Marrow*); Claretianum 30 (1990) 453s (B. *Proietti*).

6511 *Jegher-Bucher* Vreni,   Formgeschichtliche Betrachtung zu Galater 2,11-16; Antwort an James D. HESTER: TZBas [42 (1986) 386-408] 46 (1990) 305-321.

6512 *Bietenholz* P. G.,   'Simulatio'; ÉRASME et les interprétations controverses de Galates 2,11-14: → 725, Érasme 1986/90, 161-9.

6513 *Holmberg* Bengt,   Sociologiska perspektiv på Gal 2:11-14 (21) [THEISSEN G., Kairos 17 (1975) 284-299]: SvEx 55 (1990) 71-92.

6514 *Hamerton-Kelly* R. G.,   *a)* Sacred violence and 'works of law'; 'is Christ then an agent of sin?' (Galatians 2:17):   CBQ 52 (1990) 55-75; – *b)* Sacred violence and the curse of the law (Galatians 3.13); the death of Christ as a sacrificial travesty: NTS 36 (1990) 98-118 [p. 102s, Religion as sacred violence (*Girard* R.)].

6515 **Farahian** Edmond,   Le 'je' paulinien ... Gal. 2,19-21: AnGreg 253, 1988 → 4,6191; 5,6194:   ᴿBLitEc 91 (1990) 232s (S. *Légasse*); CBQ 52 (1990) 745s (J. J. *O'Rourke*); ETRel 65 (1990) 453 (G. *Wagner*: tant d'efforts au service d'un a priori contestable: Gal la dernière lettre de Paul).

6516 **Gilthvedt** Gary E.,   Dying 'through the law to the law' (Gal 2.19): diss. St. Andrews 1989.   BRDX-92165. – DissA 51 (1990s) 4152-A; RTLv 22, p. 593.

6517 **Hansen** G. W.,   [Gal 3; 4,21-31] Abraham in Galatians ᴰ1989 → 5,6170: ᴿExpTim 102 (1990s) 23 (C. J. A. *Hickling*: somewhat laboured middle way between current 'formal constraints' and the 'real Paul' unpremeditated cascade of invective).

6518 *Stanley* Christopher D.,   'Under a curse'; a fresh reading of Galatians 3.10-14 [contradicts Dt (27,26)? LUTHER, LAGRANGE]: NTS 36 (1990) 481-511.

6519 *Wallace* Daniel B.,   Galatians 3:19-20, a crux interpretum for Paul's view of the law: WestTJ 52 (1990) 225-245.

6520 *Young* Norman H.,   [Gal 3,24s] The figure of the *paidagōgos* in art and literature: BA 53 (1990) 80-86; ill.

6521 *Bruce* F. F.,   One in Christ Jesus; thoughts on Galatians 3:25-29: JChrB 122 (1990) 7-10 [< NTAbs 35,187].

6522 *Wire* A. C.,   [Gal 3,28] Not male and female: Pacific Theol. R. 19,2 (SF 1986) 37-43 [< NTAbs 34,190].

6523 *Blank* J.,   [Gal 5,1] Zu welcher Freiheit hat uns Christus befreit? Die theologische Dimension der Freiheit: StiZt 207 (1989) 460-472.

G6.2   Ad Ephesios.

6524 **Arnold** Clinton E.,   Ephesians; power and magic: SNTS 63, 1989 → 5,6213:   ᴿBZ 34 (1990) 282s (R. *Schnackenburg*); RelStR 16 (1990) 154 (Susan R. *Garrett*); TsTNijm 30 (1990) 90 (L. *Visschers*).

6525 **Attinger** Daniel,   La lettera agli Efesini; commento esegetico-spirituale. Magnano VC 1988, Qiqajon.   106 p.

6526 **Baugh** Steven M.,   Paul and Ephesus; the Apostle among his contemporaries: diss. California, ᴰ*Frank* R. Irvine 1990. 234 p. 90-30023. – DissA 51 (1990s) 2127-A.

6527 *Cameron* P. S.,   The structure of Ephesians: FgNt 3,5 (1990) 3-18; castellano 17s.

6528 *Daoust* J.,   L'épître aux Éphésiens [QUESNEL M.], la tradition johannique à Éphése [E. COTHENET: MondeB 64,1990]: EsprVie 100 (1990) 519-521.

6529 **Hoppe** Rudolf, Epheserbrief, Kolosserbrief 1987 → 3,6077: ᴿTLZ 115 (1990) 272s (P. *Pokorny*, auch über WRIGHT N., Col.).

6530 **Lincoln** Andrew T., Ephesians: Word Comm. 42. Dallas 1990, Word. xcvii-494 p.
6531 *Marcheselli* Cesare C., Le lettere dalla prigionia / pastorali: ➤ 1160, E*Cimosa* M., Parola e vita 1988, 289-304.
6532 *Packer* J. I., Godliness in Ephesians: Crux 25,1 (Vancouver 1989) 8-16 [< NTAbs 34,58].
6532* **Pérez** Gabriel [*Rubio* Luis, Heb p. 145-233], San Pablo, cartas a los Efesios y Colosenses; cartas pastorales; escrito a los Hebreos: Mensaje NT 8. S 1990, Sígueme [y tres otras editoriales]. 233 p. 84-301-1109-3.
6533 **Powell** Ivor, Exciting epistle to the Ephesians. GR 1989, Kregel. 302 p. $15 pa. – RBS 147 (1990) 379 (R. P. *Lightner*: brief praise); CalvinT 25 (1990) 149 (V. D. *Verbrugge*: for preacher, not scholar; uses King James version).
6534 *Rese* Martin, Church and Israel in the deuteropauline letters [Eph, Col, Past]: ScotJT 43 (1990) 19-32.
6535 *Rumble* D., The Ephesian connection [of Paul with God]. Shippenburg PA 1990, Destiny. xv-190 p. $7 pa. 1-56043-016-8 [NTAbs 35,115].
6536 **Schnackenburg** Rudolf, Der Brief an die Epheser: EkK NT 10, 1982 ➤ 63,6040... 1,5981: RTsTKi 61 (1990) 223-5 (M. *Synnes*).

6537 *a) Barkhuizen* J. H., The strophic structure of the eulogy of Ephesians 1:3-14; – *b) Lemmer* H. R., A multifarious understanding of eschatology in Ephesians; a possible solution to a vexing issue: HervTS 46 (1990) 390-413 / 102-119 [< NTAbs 35,187s].
6538 **Kitchen** Martin, [Eph 1,10] The *anakephalaiōsis* of all things in Christ; theology and purpose in the Epistle to the Ephesians: diss. Manchester 1988. 393 p. BRD-88728. – DissA 51 (1990s) 197-A.
6539 **Eaton** Michael A., Baptism with the Spirit [Eph 1,13]; the teaching of Dr. Martyn LLOYD-JONES. Leicester 1989, Inter-Varsity. 253 p. £7. 0-85110-663-3. – RExpTim 101 (1989s) 125s (G. *McFarlane*).
6540 *Doignon* Jean, Variations inspirées d'ORIGÈNE sur le 'prince de l'air' (Eph 2,2) chez HILAIRE de Poitiers: ZNW 81 (1990) 143-8.
6541 **Eke** Lawrence, The unity of the Church; study of Eph 2,11-22; 4,1-6: diss. 'Pontifical Urban University', D*Virgulin* S. R 1990. iv-98 p. extr.
6542 **Steinmetz** Franz-Josef, Wie weit ist es bis Ephesus? [Christus hat den Zaun niedergerissen, Eph 2,11-15]; Kirche im Prozess. Salzburg 1989, Müller. 154 p. DM 29,80. – RGeistL 63 (1990) 153s (F. *Lentzen-Deis*).
6543 *Resner* André[J], Maintain the broken wall; Ephesians 2:14-18: RestQ 32 (1990) 121... [< ZIT 90,462].
6544 *a) Greinacher* Norbert, 'Ihr seid auf das Fundament der Apostel und Propheten gebaut' (Eph 2,20); – *b) Mette* Norbert, 'Und prophetisch reden werden eure Söhne und Töchter' (Apg 2,17); Firmung als Herausforderung der Gemeinde und Kirche: Diakonia 21 (1990) 145-8 / 187-9 [< ZIT 90,493].
6545 *Basevi* Claudio, La missione di Cristo e dei cristiani nella lettera agli Efesini; una lettura di Ef 4,1-25: RivB 38 (1990) 27-54; Eng. 55.
6546 **Miletic** Stephen F., 'One flesh', Eph 5...: AnBib 115, 1988 ➤ 4,6221; 5,6247: RCBQ 52 (1990) 760-2 (Mary Ann *Getty*: sensitive); RB 97 (1990) 128 (J. *Murphy-O'Connor*).
6547 *Kaye* Bruce, 'One flesh' and marriage: Colloquium 22,2 (Sydney 1990) 46... [< ZIT 90,665].

6548 *Porter* Stanley E., *iste ginōskontes* in Ephesians 5,5; does chiasm solve a problem? : ZNW 81 (1990) 270-6.

6549 *Theobald* Michael, Heilige Hochzeit; Motive des Mythos im Horizont von Eph 5,21-33: → 350, Metaphorik 1990, 220-254.

6550 *Toews* J. E., [Eph 5,21-33] Paul's radical vision for the family: Direction 19,1 (Fresno 1990) 29-38 [< NTAbs 34,337].

6551 *Beck* J. R., [Eph 5:22-33] Is there a head of the house in the home? Reflections on Ephesians 5: Journal of Biblical Equality 1 (Lakewood CO 1989) 61-70 [< NTAbs 35,49].

6552 *Rodgers* Peter R., The allusion to Genesis 2:23 at Ephesians 5:30: JTS 41 (1990) 92-94.

6553 **Peretti** Frank E., [Eph 6,12] The present darkness. Westchester IL 1986, Crossway. 376 p. $9. – ᴿBS 147 (1990) 240-2 (J. L. *Burns*: entertaining but oversimplified).

6554 *Arnold* C. E., [Eph 6,10-20] Giving the devil his due: ChrTod 34,11 (1990) 16-18 [< NTAbs 35,49].

G6.3   Ad Philippenses.

6555 **Aspan** Paul F., Toward a new reading of Paul's letter to the Philippians in light of a Kuhnian analysis of New Testament criticism: diss. Vanderbilt, ᴰ*Tolbert* M. Nv 1990. – RelStR 17,193; RTLv 23, p. 542.

6556 **Portefaix** Lilian, Sisters rejoice ...; ConBib NT 20, 1988 → 4,6228; 5,6256. – ᴿCBQ 52 (1990) 359s (Carolyn *Osiek*: welcome replacement to defunct 'roles of women' approach); ClasW 83 (1989s) 536s (Catherine S. *Hamilton*: unconvincing); NedTTs 44 (1990) 257s (P. W. van der *Horst*); RTPhil 122 (1990) 279 (Françoise *Morard*); RB 97 (1990) 132s (J. *Murphy-O'Connor*); SvEx 55 (1990) 149-152 (Ingvild S. *Gilhus*).

6557 *Rolland* Philippe, La structure littéraire et l'unité de l'Épître aux Philippiens: RevSR 64 (1990) 213-6.

6558 **Schenk** W., Die Philipperbriefe 1984 → 65,5504 ... 4,6229: ᴿSemeia 48 (1989) 135-146 . 161-9 (H. *Combrink*; J. *Voelz*).

6559 **Silva** Moisés, Philippians: Wycliffe comm. 1988 → 4,6230; ᴿBS 147 (1990) 249s (S. D. *Toussaint*); GraceTJ 10 (1989) 246-8 (J. *Williams*: not atomistic); RExp 87 (1990) 641s (D. E. *Garland*); Themelios 16 (1990s) 26s (G. F. *Hawthorne*).

6560 *White* L. Michael, Morality between two worlds; a paradigm of friendship in Philippians: → 122, ᶠMALHERBE A., Greeks 1990, 201-215.

6561 *Dailey* Thomas F., To live or die; Paul's eschatological dilemma in Philippians 1:19-26: Interpretation 44 (1990) 18-28.

6562 *Droge* Arthur J., Did Paul commit suicide?: [contemplated in Phlp 1,21-26; 2 Cor 5,1-8 ...]: BR 5,6 (1989) 14-21 . 42; 6,2 (1990) 6-8 letters, reply; and p. 10, ᴱ*Shanks*, 'Do we deliberately try to provoke and irritate?'; further 6,3 p. 7, *Blenkinsopp* J.

6563 *Sartorius* W., [Phil 2,1-4] Disponibles en Jésus-Christ comme tout à nouveau; liberté — égalité — fraternité: RRéf 61,2 (1990) 3-8.

6564 **Fowl** Stephen E., The story of Christ in the ethics of Paul; an analysis of the function of the hymnic material in the Pauline corpus [Phil 2,6-11; Col 1,15-20, 1 Tim 3,16 not used for Christology]; diss. Sheffield, ᴰ*Thiselton* A.; JStNT supp 36. Sheffield 1990, JStOT. 235 p. $43.50. 1-85075-220-6 [TDig 38,264]. – ᴿExpTim 102 (1990s) 183 (R. P. *Martin*).

6565 *Steenburg* D., [Phlp 2,6-11; Col 1,15-20, 'Adam Christology'] The worship of Adam and Christ as the image of God: JStNT 39 (1990) 95-109.

6566 **Stolte** Klaus, Ph 2,6-11; Entäusserung Christi; Studien zu Johann GERHARDS Lehre von der Person Jesu Christi: Diss. 1967 [DDR; Berlin Kirchl. Hochschule; jetzt als Doktortitel: TR 86 (1990) 512].

6567 *Verwilghen* Albert, Le Christ médiateur selon Ph 2,6-7 dans l'œuvre de saint AUGUSTIN: ↠ 13, FBAVEL T. van, AugLv 41 (1990s) 469-482.

6568 *Buscemi* A. Marcello, [Flp 2,6-11 ...] Aspetti cristologici negli inni delle lettere paoline: TerraS 65 (1989) 196-202. 246-9.

6569 *Cavalcanti* Elena, Filip. 2,6-11 nel De Trin. di ILARIO (De Trin. VIII, 45-47; X, 23-26: ↠ 135, FORBE A., Compostellanum 35 (1990) 123-143.

6570 *Cizewski* Wanda, Forma Dei – forma servi; a study of Thomas AQUINAS' use of Philippians 2;6-7: DivThom 92 (1989) 3-32.

6571 *Engberg-Pedersen* T., Paulus livsfornægteren? For og imod Vilhelm GRØNBECHS [1940] Paulustolkning: DanTTs 53 (1990) 1-18 [< NTAbs 34,326: Paul was rightly represented as denying the value of human life and action in the world, though Phlp 3 and 1 Cor 6s show how this was to direct attention toward Christ and fellow-men].

6572 **Leonarda** S., 'Mia gioia e mia corona' (Fil 4,1); ricerca biblico-teologica [diss. 1988, DFederici T.]. R 1988, Pont. Univ. Urbaniana. 198 p. Lit. 19,500 [NTAbs 34,393].

6573 **Leonarda** Salvatore, 'Mia gioia ...' Fil 4,1; La gioia nelle lettere di san Paolo 1988 ↠ 4,6241: RCC 141 (1990,1) 403 (G. *Ferraro*).

G6.4   Ad Colossenses.

6574 **Attinger** Daniel, La lettera ai Colossesi; commento esegetico-spirituale. Magnano VC 1989, Qiqajon. 118 p.

6575 **De Maris** Richard E., The reconstruction of the Colossian philosophy: diss. Columbia, DBrown R. E. NY 1990. 91-18551.

6576 *Ernst* Josef, Kolosserbrief: ↠ 857, TRE 19 (1990) 370-8.

6577 **Furter** Daniel, Les Épîtres de Paul aux Colossiens et à Philémon: CommÉv 8, 1987 ↠ 5,6271: RRTPhil 122 (1990) 276s (F. *Amsler*).

6578 **Ghini** Emanuela, Lettera ai Colossesi; commento pastorale: LPastB 21. Bo 1990, Dehoniane. 256 p. Lit. 22.000. 88-10-20548-0 [NTAbs 35,112].

6579 TEParker David C., Philip MELANCHTHON, Paul's letter to the Colossians [1527 lecture notes]: Historic Texts and Interpreters. Sheffield 1989, Almond. 126 p. £21.50. 1-85075-210-9 [NTAbs 34,120]. – RExpTim 102 (1990s) 27 (R. *Morgan*).

6580 **Wright** N. T., Colossians and Philemon: Tyndale NT 1986 ↠ 3,6135 ... 5,6277: RSTEv 1 (1989) 88s (M. *Clemente*).

6581 *Wright* N.T., Poetry and theology in Colossians 1.15-20: NTS 36 (1990) 444-468.

6582 *Marcheselli Casale* Cesare, Der christologische Hymnus; Kol 1,15-20 im Dienste der Versöhnung und des Friedens: Teresianum 40 (1989) 3-21.

6583 *Schweizer* Eduard, Colossians 1:15-20, expository: RExp 87 (1990) 97-104.

6584 **Eller** Vernard, [Col 1,16] Christian anarchy; Jesus' primacy over the powers 1987 ↠ 3,6126; 5,6282: RThemelios 16 (1990s) 26 (A. *Kirk*).

6585 **Wink** Walter, [Col 1,16] Unmasking the powers 1986 → 2,4869; 4,6252: ^RTLZ 115 (1990) 534s (M. J. *Suda*).

6586 *a*) *Moriconi* Bruno, Prolungare Cristo; Col. 1,24 e la 'elevazione' di Elisabetta della Trintiá; – *b*) *Pasquetto* Virgilio, La vita cristiana come 'peregrinazione' nel NT: RivVSp 44 (1990) 262-275 / 251-261.

6587 *Reumann* John, Colossians 1:24 ('what is lacking in the afflictions of Christ'); history of exegesis and ecumenical advance: → 41, ^FDANKER F., CurrTMiss 17 (1990) 454-461.

6588 *Allen* W., The English for *agôna* at Colossians 2:1: BRefB 1,2 (Fort Wayne 1990) 10-12 [< NTAbs 35,189].

6589 *Hunt* J.P.T., Colossians 2:11-12, the circumcision/baptism analogy, and infant baptism: TyndB 41 (1990) 227-244.

6590 *Yates* Roy, Colossians 2,14; metaphor of forgiveness: Biblica 71 (1990) 248-259.

6591 *Owanikin* R. M., Colossians 2:18, a challenge to some doctrines of certain Aladura churches in Nigeria: AfrJBSt 2,1 (Ibadan 1987) 89-95 [< NTAbs 34,192].

6592 **Gielen** Marlis, [Col 3 ...] Tradition und Theologie neutestamentlicher Haustafelethik; ein Beitrag zur Frage einer christlichen Auseinandersetzung mit gesellschaftlichen Normen [< Diss. Bonn 1988 ^D*Merklein* H.]: Fra 1990, Hain XV-600 p. DM 138 [BZ 35, 140, A. *Weiser*]. 3-445-09131-5. – ^RSNTU A-15 (1990) 194s (A. *Fuchs*).

G6.5 *Ad Philemonem* – **Slavery in NT background.**

6593 **Binder** Hermann, (*Rohde* Joachim), Der Brief des Paulus an Philemon: THk NT 8/2. B 1990, Ev.-V. 71 p. DM 15 [TR 87,251]. 3-374-00975-1.

6594 **Bradley** Keith R., Slavery and rebellion in the Roman world, 140 B.C. – 70 B.C., 1989 → 5,6293: ^RRÉLat 68 (1990) 11-18 (J. C. *Dumont*, aussi sur M. MAZZA 1986).

6595 **Carandini** A., Schiavi in Italia; gli strumenti pensanti dei Romani fra tarda Repubblica e medio Impero; Stud Arch 8. R 1988, Nuova It. Scientifica. 387 p.; ill. – ^RJRS 80 (1990) 195s (D. W. *Rathbone*).

6596 **Collange** Jean-François, L'épître de s. Paul à Philémon: Comm. NT XIc 1987 → 3,6147 ... 5,6293: ^RRB 97 (1990) 131 (J. *Murphy-O'Connor*).

6597 *Díaz Mateos* Manuel, 'La solidaridad de la fe'; eclesiología de la Carta a Filemón: Páginas 101 (Lima 1990) 23-39 [< TContext 8/2, p. 97].

6598 **Dumont** Jean C., Servus; Rome et l'esclavage sous la République 1987 → 5,6296: ^RLatomus 49 (1990) 208-211 (P. *Salmon*); RBgPg 68 (1990) 205-211 (R. *Chevallier*).

6599 **Garlan** Yvon, Slavery in ancient Greece 2^{rev} 1988 → 4,6266; 5,6299: ^RJIntdis 20 (1989s) 278-281 (S. W. *Hirsch*).

6600 **Klein** Richard, Die Sklaverei in der Sicht der Bischöfe AMBROSIUS und AUGUSTINUS 1988 → 4,6269; 5,6302: ^RActuBbg 27 (1990) 41-43 (V. *Fábrega*); Athenaeum 78 (1990) 583 (A. *Marcone*); HZ 250 (1990) 678s (W. *Backhaus*); JRS 80 (1990) 258s (R. *Lizzi*).

6601 **Lyall** Francis, Slaves, citizens, sons; legal metaphors in the epistles 1984 → 65,5546 ... 3,6156: SecC 7 (1989s) 243s (J. L. *Jaquette*).

6602 **Martin** Dale B., Slavery as salvation; the metaphor of slavery in Pauline Christianity [diss. Yale, ^D*Meeks* W.]. NHv 1990, Yale Univ. xxiii-245 p. $25. 0-300-04735-5 [NTAbs 35,114].

6603 *Roberts* J. H., Navorsingsberig; 'n kommentaar, Filemon en Kolossense: TEv 22,3 (Pretoria 1989) 14-20 [< NTAbs 34,194].

6604 **Scholl** Reinhold, Corpus der ptolemäischen Sklaventexte: ForAntSklav Beih 1, Stu 1990, Steiner. x-1127 p. (3 vol.) DM 190. – ᴿCdÉ 65 (1990) 166-8 (J. A. *Straus*).

6605 *Soards* Marion L., Some neglected theological dimensions of Paul's letter to Philemon: PerspRelSt 17 (1990) 209-219.

G6.6   **Ad Thessalonicenses.**

6606 **Adinolfi** Marco, La prima lettera ai Tessalonicesi nel mondo greco-romano: Bibliotheca Pont. Athenaei Antoniani 31. R 1990, Antonianum. 311 p. Lit. 30.000.

6607 *Bercovitz* J. Peter, Paul and Thessalonica: ProcGLM 10 (1990) 123-135.

6608 *a)* *Binder* Hermann, Paulus und die Thessalonicherbriefe; – *b)* *Marshall* I. Howard, Election and calling to salvation in 1 and 2 Thessalonians; – *c)* *Getty* Mary Ann, The imitation of Paul in the letters to the Thessalonians; – *d)* *Aarde* A. van, The struggle against heresy in the Thessalonian correspondence and the origin of the apostolic tradition; – *e)* *Stichele* Caroline Vander, The concept of tradition and 1 and 2 Thessalonians: ➤ 521, Thes. Correspondence 1988/90, 87-93 / 259-276 / 277-283 / 418-425 / 499-504.

6609 **Hill** Judith L., Establishing the Church in Thessalonica: diss. Duke, ᴰ*Smith* D. M. Durham ɴᴄ 1990. 300 p. 90-28215. – DissA 51 (1990s) 1648s-A.; RelStR 17,194.

6610 **Johanson** Bruce C., To all the brethren.. 1 Thes: ConBib NT 16, ᴿCritRR 3 (1990) 208-211 (D. D. *Schmidt*); JBL 109 (1990) 158-160 (S. *Kraftchick*); RB 97 (1990) 131s (J. *Murphy-O'Connor*).

6611 **Malherbe** Abraham, *a)* Paul and the Thessalonians 1987 ➤ 3,6178 ... 5,6319: ᴿVidyajyoti 54 (1990) 358s (P. M. *Meagher*); – *b)* 'Pastoral care' in the Thessalonian church: NTS 36 (1990) 375-391.

6612 **Marxsen** Willi, La prima lettera ai Tessalonicesi, ᵀ*Leibbrandt* Mirella A., ᴱ*Rostagno* Bruno, 1988 ➤ 4,6293; 5,6320: ᴿProtestantesimo 45 (1990) 72s (G. *Conte*).

6613 **Mendoza** Jaime, Christian vocation in 1 and 2 Thessalonians: diss. Pamplona 1990, ᴰ*Basevi* C. 342 p. – RTLv 22, p. 594.

6614 *a)* *Olbricht* Thomas H., An Aristotelian rhetorical analysis of 1 Thessalonians; – *b)* *Lührmann* Dieter, The beginnings of the Church at Thessalonica: ➤ 122, ᶠMᴀʟʜᴇʀʙᴇ A., Greeks 1990, 216-236 / 237-249.

6615 **Plevnik** J., *a)* The ultimate reality in 1 Thessalonians: *a)* URM 12 (1989) 256-271 [< NTAbs 34,193]; – *b)* [in Slovene] BogVest 49 (1989) 307-314; Eng. 313.

6616 *Richard* Earl, Contemporary research on 1 (& 2) Thessalonians: BibTB 20 (1990) 107-115.

6617 **Salvador** Miguel, San Pablo, Cartas a los Tesalonicenses y a los Corintios, comentario: El Mensaje del Nuevo Testamento 6. S 1990, Sígueme [+ 3 *al.*, + 'Texto bíblico: La Casa de la Biblia']. 230 p.; map. 84-301-1102-6.

6618 **Smith** Abraham, The social and ethical implications of the Pauline rhetoric in 1 Thessalonians: diss. Vanderbilt, ᴰ*Tolbert* M. – Nashville 1989. 251 p. 90-17644, – DissA 51 (1990s) 531-A. RelStR 14,194.

6619 *a) Vanhoye* Albert, La composition de 1 Thess.; – *b) Hughes* F. W., The rhetoric of 1 Thess,; – *c) Tuckett* C. M., Synoptic tradition in 1 Thess. ?; – *d) Kieffer* René, L'eschatologie en 1 Thessaloniciens dans une perspective rhétorique; – *e) Schnelle* Udo, Die Ethik des 1. Thessalonicherbriefes; – *f) Watt* J. G. van der, The use of *záō* in 1 Thessalonians; a comparison with *záō/zōē* in the Gospel of John: ➤ 521, Thess. correspondence 1988/90, 73-86 / 94-116 / 160-182 / 206-219 / 295-305 / 356-369.

6620 **Ubieta** José A., La Iglesia de Tesalónica: Iglesia del NT, 1988 ➤ 4,6298: ᴿActuBbg 27 (1990) 63 (X. *Alegre* S.).

6621 **Wanamaker** C. A., The Epistles to the Thessalonians, a commentary on the Greek text: NIGT. GR/Exeter 1990, Eerdmans/Paternoster. xxviii-316 p. $30. 0-8028-2394-7 / [NTAbs 35,254].

6622 **Weiss** N. E., 1 & 2 Thessalonians: Chi Rho comm. Adelaide 1988, Lutheran. 176 p.; map. $13. 0-85910-484-2 [NTAbs 34,123].

6623 *a) Lambrecht* Jan, Thanksgivings in 1 Thes 1-3; – *b) Wuellner* Wilhelm, [1 Thes 1,1-10 ...] The argumentative structure of 1 Thessalonians as paradoxical encomium: ➤ 521, Thes. correspondence 1988/90, 183-205 / 117-136.

6624 *Wallace* Daniel B., A textual problem in 1 Thessalonians 1:10, *ek tês orgês* vs. *apò tês orgês*: BS 147 (1990) 470-479: originally *apò*.

6626 *Okeke* G. E., The context and function of 1 Thess. 2:1-12 and its significance for African Christianity: AfrJBSt 2,1 (Ibadan 1987) 77-88 [< NTAbs 34,193].

6627 *Fowl* Stephen, A metaphor in distress; a reading of *nēpioi* in 1 Thessalonians 2.7: NTS 36 (1990) 469-473.

6628 *Gaventa* Beverly R., Apostles as babes and nurses in 1 Thessalonians 2:7: ➤ 123*, ᶠMEYER P., Faith 1990, 193-207.

6629 *a) Gilman* John, Paul's *eisodos*; the proclaimed and the proclaimer (1 Thes 2,8); – *b) Broer* Ingo, 'Der ganze Zorn ist schon über sie gekommen'; Bemerkungen zur Interpolationshypothese und zur Interpretation von 1 Thes 2,14-16; – *c) Holtz* Traugott, The judgment on the Jews and the salvation of all Israel; 1 Thes 2,15-16 and Rom 11,25-26: ➤ 521, Thes. correspondence 1988/90, 62-70 / 137-159 / 284-294.

6630 *Stegemann* Ekkehard, Zur antijüdischen Polemik in 1 Thess 2,14-16: KIsr 5 (1990) 54-64.

6631 *Söding* Thomas, [1 Thess 2,16 ...] Widerspruch und Leidensnachfolge; neutestamentliche Gemeinden im Konflikt mit der paganen Gesellschaft: MüTZ 41 (1990) 137-155.

6632 *Simpson* John W.ᴶ, The problems posed by 1 Thessalonians 2,15-16 and a solution: HorBT 12,1 (1990) 42-72.

6633 *Meyer* Ben F. [1 Thess 4; 1 Cor 15; 2 Cor 5,2-4] Did Paul's view of the resurrection of the dead undergo development? [< his Critical Realism 1989]: ExAud 5 (1989) 57-76.

6634 **Míguez** N. P., [1 Thes 4,1-12] *a)* La ética cristiana; una opción contra 'Hegemónica': CuadT 10,2 (1989) 15-25 [< NTAbs 34,339]; – *b)* Pablo y la revolución cristiana en el primer siglo: Cuadernos de Teología 10,1 (Buenos Aires 1989) 67-80 [< NTAbs 34,193].

6635 *a) Baumert* Norbert, Brautwerbung — das einheitliche Thema von 1 Thess 4,3-8; – *b) Carras* George P., Jewish ethics and Gentile converts;

remarks on 1 Thes 4,3-8; – *c*) *Chapa* Juan, Consolatory patterns? 1 Thes
4,13.18; 5,11: ➤ 521, Thes. correspondence 1988/90, 316-339 / 306-315 /
220-8.

6636 **Xavier** Aloysius, A study of *theodídaktoi* (1 Thes 4,9), source and
theology: diss. Pont. Univ. Gregoriana, ᴰ*Rasco* E. R 1990s. – InfPUG
23,119 (1990s) 17.

6637 **Aejmelaeus** Lars, Wachen vor dem Ende; die traditionsgeschichtlichen
Wurzeln von 1. Thess 5:1-11 und Luk 21:34-36: Ekseg 44, 1985 ➤ 2,4903:
ᴿSvEx 55 (1990) 152s (C. *Cavallin*).

6638 *a*) *Focant* Camille, Les fils du jour (1 Thes 5,5); – *b*) *Jonge* H. J. de, [1
Thes 5,10] The original setting of the *Christòs apéthanen hypér* formula; –
c) *Langevin* Paul-Émile, L'intervention de Dieu selon 1 Thes 5,23-24:
➤ 521, Thes. correspondence 1988/90, 348-355 / 229-235 / 236-256.

6639 *Lautenschlager* Markus, *Eíte grēgorōmen eíte katheúdomen*; zum
Verhältnis von Heiligung und Heil in 1 Thess 5,10: ZNW 81 (1990)
39-59.

6640 *Buscemi* A. M., Pregate incessantemente (1 Tess. 5,17): TerraS 65 (1989)
2-7.101-7.

6641 *Dirscherl* Erwin, 'Löscht den Geist nicht aus!' (1 Thess 5,19); zum
Problem der Geisterfahrung in der Kirche: TGL 80 (1990) 74-88.

6642 *a*) *Hartman* Lars, The eschatology of 2 Thess. as included in a communication; – *b*) *Schmidt* Daryl D., The syntactical style of 2 Thessalonians; how Pauline is it?; – *c*) *Holland* Glenn S., 'A letter supposedly
from us'; a contribution to the discussion about the authorship of 2
Thessalonians; – *d*) *Laub* Franz, Paulinische Autorität in nachpau-
linischer Zeit (2 Thes); – *e*) *Koester* Helmut, From Paul's eschatology to
the apocalyptic schemata of 2 Thessalonians; – *f*) *Menken* M. J. J., The
structure of 2 Thessalonians: ➤ 521, Thes.correspondence 1988/90, 470-
485 / 383-393 / 394-402 / 403-417 / 441-458 / 373-382.

6643 **Holland** Glenn S., The tradition ... 2 Thes ᴰ1988 ➤ 4,6302; 5,6330:
ᴿTLZ 115 (1990) 683s (T. *Holtz*).

6644 **Hughes** Frank W., Early Christian rhetoric and 2 Thes: JStNT supp 30,
1989 ➤ 5,6331: ᴿJTS 41 (1990) 196s (I. H. *Marshall*).

6645 *Neri* P., 2 Ts, ovverosia, prima [sic] lettera ai Tessalonicesi: BbbOr 32
(1990) 230 . 246.

6646 *Sumney* Jerry L., The bearing of a Pauline rhetorical pattern on the
integrity of 2 Thessalonians: ZNW 81 (1990) 192-204.

6647 *a*) *Collins* Raymond F., 'The Gospel of our Lord Jesus' (2 Thes 1,8); a
symbolic shift of paradigm; – *b*) *Giblin* Charles H., 2 Thessalonians 2
re-read as pseudipigraphal; a revised reaffirmation of the threat to faith; –
c) *Danker* Frederick, *Jewett* Robert, Jesus as the apocalyptic benefactor
in Second Thessalonians; – *d*) *Krentz* Edgar, Traditions held fast;
theology and fidelity in 2 Thessalonians: ➤ 521, Thes.correspondence
1988/90, 426-440 / 459-469 / 486-498 / 506-515.

6648 *LaRondelle* H. K., [2 Thess 2] The Middle Ages within the scope of
apocalyptic prophecy: JEvTS 32 (1989) 345-354 [< NTAbs 34,194].

6648* *Farrow* D., Showdown; the message of Second Thessalonians 2:1-12
and the riddle of the 'Restrainer': Crux 25,1 (Vancouver 1989) 23-26
[< NTAbs 34,59].

6649 *Krodel* Gerhard, The 'religious power of lawlessness' (*katéchon*) as precursor of the 'lawless one' (*ánomos*), 2 Thess 2:6-7: → 41, [F]DANKER W., CurrTMiss 17 (1990) 440-6.

G7 Epistulae pastorales.

6650 *Beker* J. Christiaan, The pastoral epistles — Paul and we: → 24, [F]BOERS H., Text 1990, 265-272.

6651 *Cothenet* E., Les épîtres pastorales: CahEv 72. P 1990, Cerf. 62 p.; map. F 25. [NTAbs 35,110] 0222-9714.

6652 **Donelson** Lewis R., Pseudepigraphy and ethical argument in the pastoral epistles: HermUntT 22, 1986 → 2,4909 ... 5,6335: [R]TLZ 115 (1990) 507s (E. *Reinmuth*).

6653 **Fee** Gordon D., 1-2 Timothy, Titus: NICNT 1984 [Good News comm. slightly revised] → 2,4912: [R]CriswT 4 (1989s) 401s (T. D. *Lea*).

6654 **Fiore** Benjamin, The function of personal example in the Socratic and Pastoral Epistles [diss. Yale 1982, [D]*Malherbe* A.; Socrates epistles: 1-7 in name of Socrates, 8-29 of a sort of community of his disciples (TLZ 116,279)]: AnBib 105, 1986 → 2,4913; 4,6310: [R]RB 97 (1990) 292s (J. *Murphy-O'Connor*).

6655 **Guthrie** Donald, The pastoral epistles, an introduction and commentary[2rev] [[1]1957]: Tyndale NT Comm. Leicester 1990, Inter-Varsity. 240 p. 0-85111-883-6 [NTAbs 35,113].

6656 **Kidd** Reggie M., Wealth and beneficence in the Pastoral Epistles; a 'bourgeois' form of early Christianity?: SBL diss. 123 [Duke Univ. [D]*Young* F., → 5,6338]. Atlanta 1990, Scholars. x-227 p. $25; pa. $15 [TR 87,340]. 1-55540-445-6.

6657 **Knoch** Otto, 1-2 Tim Tit 1988 → 4,6311; 5,6339: [R]BLtg 63 (1990) 61s (K. *Löning*).

6658 **Maestrl** W. F., Paul's pastoral vision; pastoral letters for a pastoral church today. NY 1989, Alba. xx-220 p. $13 pa. 0-8189-0556-5 [NTAbs 34,119].

6659 **Marcheselli-Casale** Cesare, Chiesa in fermento; le due lettere a Timoteo, la lettera a Tito: Commenti al NT. T-Leumann 1985, Elle Di Ci. 199 p. 88-01-11031-6.

6660 **Oden** Thomas, 1-2 Tim Tit 1989 → 5,6343: – [R]HorBT 12,1 (1990) 95s (L. T. *Johnson*).

6661 *a) Quinn* Jerome D., Paraenesis and the Pastoral Epistles; lexical observations bearing on the nature of the sub-genre and soundings in its role in socialization and liturgies; – *b) Perdue* Leo C., The social character of paraenesis and paraenetic literature; – *c) Robbins* Vernon K., A socio-rhetorical response [to all the papers]: → 464, Semeia 50 (1990) 189-210 / 5-39 / 261-271.

6662 *Rozman* Francè, [in Slovene] Pastoral letters and necessary virtues of bearers of ecclesiastical offices: BogVest 49 (1989) 289-306; Eng. 304.

6663 **Schlarb** Egbert, Die gesunde Lehre; Häresie und Wahrheit im Spiegel der Pastoralbriefe [ev. diss. [D]*Lührmann* D. 1989 → 5,6345]: Marburger Theol. St. 28. Marburg 1990, Elwert. 387 p. 3-7708-0932-7.

6664 **Sweeney** Michael L., From God's household to the heavenly chorus; a comparison of the Church in the Pastoral Epistles with the Church in the letters of IGNATIUS of Antioch: diss. Union Theol. Sem. Richmond 1989. 188 p. 91-11542. – DissA 51 (1990s) 3784s-A.

6665 **Towner** Philip H.,   The goal of our instruction; the structure of theology and ethics in the Pastoral Epistles: JStNT supp 34, 1989 ➤ 5,6346: ᴿBZ 34 (1990) 284s (R. *Schnackenburg*).

6666 **Wolter** Michael,   Die Pastoralbriefe als Paulustradition: FRL 146, ᴰ1988 ➤ 4,6316; 5,6350: ᴿCBQ 52 (1990) 180s (M. *Kiley*); JBL 109 (1990) 160-2 (B. *Fiore*); SNTU-A 14 (1989) 267-9 (A. *Fuchs*).

G7.2 1-2 ad Timotheum.

6667 **Grünzweig** Fritz,   Erster Timotheus-Brief: Edition C B-18.   Stu-Neuhausen 1990, Hänssler. 292 p. DM 35 [TR 87,339].

6668 **Roloff** Jürgen,   Der erste Brief an Timotheus: EkK 15, 1988 ➤ 4,6318: ᴿSNTU-A 14 (1989) 269s (A. *Fuchs*); TLZ 115 (1990) 684-6 (V. *Hasler*); TsTKi 61 (1990) 295-7 (M. *Synnes*).

6669 *Verzan* Sabin (en roumain, diss.), La première Épître du saint Apôtre Paul à Timothée; introduction, traduction et commentaire: STBuc 40 (1988) 2,9-122; 3,10-101; 4,10-115; 5,14-85; 6,30-108; ...

6670 *Bush* Peter G.,   A note on the structure of 1 Timothy: NTS 36 (1990) 152-6.

6671 **Harris** Timothy J.,   Why did Paul mention Eve's deception? A critique of P.W. BARNETT's interpretation of 1 Timothy 2: EvQ [61 (1989) 225-238] 62 (1990) 335-352.

6672 *Grossi* Vittorino, [1 Tim 2,4...] Il porsi della questione della 'voluntas salvifica' negli ultimi scritti di AGOSTINO (a.420-427) I.: ➤ 688*a, Collectanea 1986/90, 315-328.

6673 *Danet* Anne-Laure, 1 Timothée 2,8-15 et le ministère pastoral féminin: Hokhma 44 (1990) 23-44 (45-58, *Coninck* Frédéric de).

6674 *Fee* G.D.,   *a*) Women in ministry; the meaning of 1 Timothy 2:8-15 in light of the purpose of 1 Timothy: JChrB 122 (1990) 11-18 [< NTAbs 35,190]; – *b*) Issues in evangelical hermeneutics 3. The great watershed; intentionality and particularity/eternality, 1 Timothy 2:8-15 as a test case: Crux 26,4 (Vancouver 1990) 31-37 [< NTAbs 35,190].

6675 *Redekop* Gloria N.,   Let the women learn; 1 Timothy 2: 8-15 reconsidered: SR 19 (1990) 235-245.

6676 *Scholer* D.M.,   Women in the Church's ministry; does 1 Timothy 2:9-15 help or hinder?: Daughters of Sarah 16,4 (Ch 1990) 7-12 [< NTAbs 35,51].

6677 *Kroeger* C.C.,   Women in the Church; a classicist's view of 1 Tim 2:11-15 [against *one* woman who was in error]: Journal of Biblical Equality 1 (Lakewood CO 1989) 3-31 [32-39-44-49, responses by *Emig* E., *Hubbard* R., *Blomberg* C.: < NTAbs 35,51].

6678 *Zachman* Randall C., [1 Tim 3,16...] Jesus Christ as the image of God in CALVIN's theology: CalvinT 25 (1990) 45-62.

6679 *Brenk* Frederick E.,   Old wineskins recycled; *autarkeia* in 1 Timothy 6.5-10: FgNt 3,5 (1990) 39-50; castellano 50s.

6680 **Prior** Michael,   Paul the letter-writer & 2 Tim: JStNT supp 23, 1989 ➤ 5,6356: ᴿBiblica 71 (1990) 583-6 (J.L. *White*: clear interesting superstructure with shaky underpinnings); ÉTRel 65 (1990) 121 (E. *Cuvillier*); EvQ 62 (1990) 372-4 (R.A. *Campbell*); ExpTim 101 (1989s) 30s (A.

Hanson; entirely unconvincing that Paul wrote 2 Tim); JTS 41 (1990) 206s (J. L. *Houlden*: successfully overturns everything); RB 97 (1990) 294s (J. *Murphy-O'Connor*); RExp 87 (1990) 643s (E. G. *Hinson*); TLZ 115 (1990) 430s (A. *Weiser*).

6681 *De Virgilio* Giuseppe, Ispirazione ed efficacia della Scrittura in 2 Tm 3,14-17: RivB 38 (1990) 485-494.

Reck Reinhold, 2 Tim 3,16 in der altkirchlichen Literatur; eine wirkungs-geschichtliche Untersuchung zum Locus classicus der Inspirationslehre 1990 → 1523.

G8 Epistula ad Hebraeos.

6682 *Alomía* B. M., La singularidad de Jesús en la epístola a los Hebreos: Theologika 4,1 (Lima 1989) 2-33 [< NTAbs 34,60].

6683 **Attridge** Harold W., The epistle to the Hebrews: Hermeneia comm. 1989 → 5,6362: ᴿCurrTMiss 17 (1990) 394s (E. *Krentz*); ÉTRel 65 (1990) 121s (E. *Cuvillier*: fera date dans la recherche); FgNt 3,5 (1990) 76s (D. A. *Black*); Horizons 17 (1990) 324s (Mary Ann *Getty*); JTS 41 (1990) 625-7 (F. F. *Bruce*); Neotestamentica 29 (1990) 383s (S. W. *Theron*); ScotJT 43 (1990) 275-7 (R. M. *Wilson*); TorJT 6 (1990) 356s (R. N. *Longenecker*); TS 51 (1990) 332-4 (R. *Brown*).

6684 *Attridge* Harold W., Paraencsis in a homily (lógos parakléseōs); the possible location of, and socialization in, the 'Epistle to the Hebrews': → 464, Semeia 50 (1990) 211-226.

6685 *Auneau* Joseph, Le sacerdoce au 1ᵉʳ siécle; du grand-prêtre juif à Jésus le grand-prêtre: Masses Ouvrières 430 (1990) 64-75.

6687 **Baylis** Charles P., The author of Hebrews' use of Melchizedek from the context of Genesis: diss. Dallas Theol. Sem. 1989. 213 p. 90-20887. – DissA 51 (1990s) 887-A.

6688 **Bénétreau** S., L'épître aux Hébreux I. Comm.év. 10. Vaux/Scine 1989, EDIFAC. 270 p. F 120 pa. 2-804407-09-X [NTAbs 34,254].

6689 **Bruce** Frederick F., The Epistle to the Hebrews 2ʳᵉᵛ [¹1964]: NICNT. GR 1990, Eerdmans. xxii-426 p. $28. 0-8028-2316-5 [TDig 38,254: additions especially from Vanhoye].

6690 *Charles* Daryl, The Angels, sonship and birthright in the letter to the Hebrews: JEvTS 33 (1990) 171-8 [< NTAbs 35,52].

6691 **Collins** Raymond E., Letters that Paul did not write ... Heb...: Good News Studies 28, 1988 → 4,6331; 5,6367: ᴿCBQ 52 (1990) 551s (T. H. *Tobin*: Hebrews is no part of the problem).

6692 *Fernández* Víctor M., La vida sacerdotal de los cristianos según la carta a los Hebreos: RBibArg 52,39 (1990) 145-152.

6693 **Frede** H. J., Vetus Latina 25/2, Lfg. 7, Hbr 7,10 – 9,12; Lfg 8, Hbr 9,12 – 10,28. FrB 1990. Herder. p. 1317-1396. 1397-1475 [NRT 113, 421, X. *Jacques*].

6694 **Grässer** Erich, An die Hebräer I (1-6): EkK NT 17/1. Z/Neuk 1990, Benziger/Neuk. x-388 p. DM 132. 3-545-23120-8 / 3-7887-1335-6 [NTAbs 35,112]. – ᴿSNTU A-15 (1990) 195s (A. *Fuchs*).

6695 **Hagner** Donald A., Hebrews: New International [Version] Biblical Comm 14. Peabody MA 1990 [comm. = ? 1983], Hendrickson. xv-278 p. 0-943575-17-6 [NTAbs 35,113].

6696 *Hamm* Dennis, Faith in the Epistle to the Hebrews; the Jesus factor: CBQ 52 (1990) 270-291.

6697 **Hewitt** Thomas, L'epistola agli Ebrei [1960], ᵀ1986 ➤ 2,4938: ᴿProtestantesimo 45 (1990) 146s (Milena *Beux*).
6698 ᴱ**Holbrook** F. B., Issues in the Book of Hebrews: Daniel and Revelation
Committee Series 4.   Silver Spring MD, Seventh-Day Adventist Biblical
Research.   xiii-237 p.   0-925675-03-2 [NTAbs 34,255].
6699 *Horak* Tomasz, ❷ Eschatologia Listu do Hebrajczyków: ColcT 59,2
(1989) 5-18; 19, De eschatologia ep. ad Hebr.
6700 **Hurst** L. D., The Epistle to the Hebrews; its background of thought
[< diss. Oxford 1982, ᴰ*Caird* G]: SNTS Mg 65. C 1990, Univ. xiv-
209 p. $39.50. 0-521-37097-3 [NTAbs 35,151].
6701 *Kelly* Douglas F., Prayer and union with Christ [... Hebrews; 1988
Rutherford Lecture]: ScotBEv 8 (1990) 109-127.
6702 **Lehne** Susanne, The New Covenant in Hebrews [diss. Columbia 1989
➤ 5,6380]: JStNT supp. 44. Sheffield 1990, JStOT. 183 p. £27.50. 1-
85075-238-9 [TDig 38,276]. – ᴿExpTim 102 (1990s) 247 (R. *Williamson*).
6703 **Loader** William R. G., *al.*, Glaube in der Bewährung; Hebräer- und
Jakobusbrief: Bibelauslegung für die Praxis 25. Stu 1990, KBW. 159 p.
3-460-25251-0.
6704 **Madsen** N. P., Ask and you will receive; prayer and the letter to the
Hebrews.   St. Louis 1989, 'CBP'. 136 p. $10 pa. 0-8272-0018-8 [NTAbs
34,119].
6705 **März** Claus-Peter, Hebräerbrief: NEchter 1989 ➤ 5,6383: ᴿActuBbg
27 (1990) 59 (X. *Alegre* S.); ArTGran 53 (1990) 309s (A. *Segovia*); TPQ
138 (1990) 404 (K. M. *Woschitz*).
6706 *Schlosser* Jacques, La médiation du Christ d'après l'épître aux Hébreux:
RevSR 63 (1989) 169-181.
6708 *Swetnam* James, The structure of Hebrews; a fresh look [ATTRIDGE H.
1989, 'a typographical tour de force']: MeliT 41,1 (1990) 25-46.
6709 *Vanhoye* Albert, Il sacerdozio di Cristo e il laicato nell'epistola agli
Ebrei: ➤ 592*, Laici 1990, 125-150.

6710 **Übelacker** Walter G., Der Hebräerbrief als Appell; Untersuchungen zu
exordium, narratio und postscriptum (Hebr 1-2 und 13,22-25): ConBib
NT 21, 1989 ➤ 5,6397: ᴿÉTRel 65 (1990) 628 (P. *Magne de la Croix*);
SvEx 55 (1990) 156-160 (B. *Holmberg*); TLZ 115 (1990) 201s (C.-P. *März*).
6711 *Aldridge* Marion D., Hebrews 1:1a; Exodus 35:30-36:3: RExp 87
(1990) 611-3.
6712 *Bachmann* Michael, '... gesprochen durch den Herrn' (Hebr 2,3); Erwägungen zum Reden Gottes und Jesu im Hebräerbrief: Biblica 71
(1990) 265-294; franç. 294.
6713 *Lategan* Bernard C., Some implications of Hebrews 2:5-18 for a
contextual anthropology: ➤ 24, ᶠBOERS H., Text 1990, 149-163.
6714 *Chopineau* Jacques, [Héb 3,7] Midrache sur aujourd'hui: FoiVie 89,6
(1990) 85-89.
6715 **Zesati Estrada** Carlos, Hebreos 5,7-8; estudio histórico-exegético [diss.
Pont. Ist. Biblico, AcPIB 9,6 (1989s) 481]: AnBib 113. R 1990, Pontificio
Istituto Biblico. xxv-392 p. Lit. 48.000. 88-7653-113-0.
6716 *Allen* W., The translation of *apò tês eulabeías* at Hebrews 5,7: BRefB
1,1 (Fort Wayne 1989) 9s [< NTAbs 34,339].
6717 **Lee Jun Dug**, The understanding of Melchizedek in Hebrews 7: 1-3:
diss. ᴰ*Bandstra* A., Calvin Theol. Sem. vii-102 p. + bibliog. – CalvinT 25
(GR 1990; no other date assigned) 334.

6718 **Casalini** Nello, Dal simbolo alla realtà; l'espiazione dall'Antica alla Nuova Alleanza secondo Ebr 9,1-14; una proposta exegetica: SBF Anal 26, 1989 ➤ 5,6408: ᴿGregorianum 71 (1990) 588s (J. *Galot*); TLZ 115 (1990) 890s (C.-P. *März*).

6719 *a) Smith* R. E., Hebrews 10:29, By which was sanctified; – *b) Greenlee* J. H., Hebrews 11:11 — Sarah's faith or Abraham's?: NoTr 4,1 (Dallas 1990) 32-37 / 37-42 [< NTAbs 35,191].

6720 **Rose** Christian, Die Wolke der Zeugen; eine exegetisch-traditions-geschichtliche Untersuchung zu Hebräer 10,32-12,3: ev. Diss. Tübingen 1989, 398 p. RTLv 22,595.

6721 **Cosby** Michael R., The rhetorical composition and function of Hebrews 11... [diss. Emory 1985] 1988 ➤ 4,6362: ᴿCBQ 52 (1990) 343s (D. F. *Watson*); PerspRelSt 17 (1990) 186-8 (K. M. *Craig*).

6722 *Swetnam* James, Hebrews 11; an interpretation; MeliT 41 (1990) 97-114.

6723 *Estes* Daniel J., [Heb 11,9s; Gn 11s; 23] Looking for Abraham's city: BS 147 (1990) 399-413.

6724 *Horst* Pieter W. van der, Sarah's seminal emission; Hebrews 11:11 in the light of ancient embryology: ➤ 122, ᶠMALHERBE A., Greeks 1990, 287-302.

6725 *Smith* T. C., An exegesis of Hebrews 13: 1-17: Faith and Mission 7,1 (Wake Forest NC 1989) 70-78 [< NTAbs 34,195].

6725* *Basevi* Claudio, La teologia del matrimonio nell'epistola agli Ebrei (Eb 13,4): AnnTh 4 (1990) 349-368.

6726 *Ruager* Søren, 'Wir haben einen Altar' (Hebr. 13.10); einige Überlegungen zum Thema: Gottesdienst/Abendmahl im Hebräerbrief: KerDo 36 (1990) 72-77; Eng. 77.

G9.1   1-2 Petri.

6727 **Bosetti** Elena, Il pastore; Cristo e la Chiesa nella prima lettera di Pietro: RivB supp 21. Bo 1990, Dehoniane. 344 p. Lit. 40.000. 88-10-30209-5 [NTAbs 35,109: diss. Gregoriana 1988, ᴰ*Vanni* U.].

6728 **Clowney** Edmund P., The message of 1 Peter; the way of the Cross: The Bible Speaks today. Leicester/DG 1989, InterVarsity. 234 p. $10 pa. 0-85110-789-3 / DG 0-8308-1227-X [NTAbs 34,118]. – ᴿEvangel 7,4 (1989) 23 (H. *Uprichard*).

6729 **Davids** Peter H., The first epistle of Peter [replacing first half of *Stonehouse* N. B.]; NICNT. GR 1990, Eerdmans. xxii-266 p. $25. 0-8028-2347-5. [NTAbs 35,110].

6730 *Drăgusin* Valeriu, (en roumain) Eschatologie des épîtres catholiques; OrtBuc 40,2 (1988) 114-123.

6731 *Ellul* Danielle, Un exemple de cheminement rhétorique; 1 Pierre: RHPR 70 (1990) 17-34; Eng. 146.

6732 **Frankemölle** Hubert, 1-2 Petrusbrief, Judasbrief: NEchter 18/20, 1987 ➤ 3,6269 ... 5,6418: ᴿCBQ 52 (1990) 345-7 (A. D. *Jacobson*: fine despite avoidance of *Sachkritik*).

6733 *Green* Gene L., The use of the Old Testament for Christian ethics in 1 Peter: TyndB 41 (1990) 276-289.

6734 **Grudem** Wayne A., 1 Peter 1988 ➤ 4,6369; 5,6420: ᴿCalvinT 25 (1990) 102-5 (J. A. D. *Weima*: replaces 1959 STIBBS A., WALLS A.); CriswT 4 (1989s) 397 (D. S. *Dockery*).

6735 *Janse van Rensburg* J. J., The use of intersentence relational particles and asyndeton in First Peter: Neotestamentica 29 (1990) 283-300.

6736 **Knoch** Otto, Der erste und zweite Petrusbrief; der Judasbrief: RgNT. Rg 1990, Pustet. 333 p. DM 78 [NRT 113,763, X. *Jacques*]. 3-7917-1257-8.

6737 **Lamau** Marie-Louise, Des chrétiens dans le monde; communautés pétriniennes: LDiv 134, 1988 → 5,6423: REsprVic 100 (1990) 29-31 (L. *Walter*); RB 97 (1990) 134-6 (J. *Taylor*); RHPR 70 (1990) 275s (C. *Grappe*).

6738 *a*) *Langkammer* Hugolin, ❷ Die wichtigsten theologischen Themen des 1. Petrusbriefes: – *b*) *Suski* Andrzej, ❷ L'idea della rinascita nella prima lettera di Pietro: → 64, FGRZYBEK S. 1990, 157-166; deutsch 166 / 311-327; ital. 328.

6739 **Martin** Troy W., Metaphor and composition in 1 Peter: diss. D*Betz* H. Chicago 1990. – RelStR 17,194.

6740 **Michaels** J. Ramsey, 1 Peter: Word **comm.** 49, 1988 → 4,6375; 5,6425: RCalvinT 25 (1990) 272-4 (D. *Deppe*); CBQ 52 (1990) 353-5 (S. *McKnight*; maybe finest available); CritRR 3 (1990) 224-7 (J. H. *Elliott*); CurrTMiss 17 (1990) 233 (E. *Krentz,* also on MARTIN R., James); RExp 87 (1990) 644 (D. *Dockery*).

6741 **Michaels** J. Ramsey, 1 Peter: Word **themes.** Dallas 1989, Word. xiv-114 p. $10. 0-8499-0788-8 [NTAbs 34,258].

6742 **Mudendeli** Martin, L'utilisation de l'Ancien Testament dans la Première Épître de Pierre; unité dynamique des Écritures: diss. Pont. Univ. Gregoriana 1987, D*Vanni* U. R 1990. Extr. 108 p.

6743 **Prostmeier** Ferdinand-R., Handlungsmodelle im ersten Petrusbrief [kath. Diss. D*Brox* N., Regensburg 1989]: ForBi 63. Wü 1990, Echter. 590 p. DM 64. 3-429-01313-5 [NTAbs 35,252].

6745 *Rousseau* J. [1 Pt] 'n multidimensionele benadering tot die kommunikasie van ou gekanoniseerde tekste: SkrifKerk 9,1 (Pretoria 1988) 33-56 [< NTAbs 34,149].

6746 **Thurén** Lauri, The rhetorical strategy of 1 Peter, with special regard to ambiguous expressions [diss. Åbo 1990]. Åbo 1990, Acad. viii-213 p. 951-9498-63-X [NTAbs 35,116].

6747 *Vanni* Ugo, La pratica del sacerdozio dei cristiani alla luce della Prima Lettera di Pietro; spunti e riflessioni: → 542*, Laici 1990, 235-264.

6748 **Vaughan** Curtis, *Lea* Thomas D., 1-2 Peter, Jude. GR 1988, Zondervan. 240 p. $9 pa. – RGraceTJ 10 (1989) 248s (A. B. *Luter*).

6749 *Villagrá Saura* Lucia, Análisis sintáctico y estilístico de las cartas de san Pedro: Veleia 5 (Vitoria 1988) 245-256.

6750 *Rigato* Maria-Luisa, Quali i profeti di cui nella 1 Pt 1,10?: RivB 38 (1990) 73-90: profeti cristiani.

6751 *Oancea* Constantin I., 1 Petru 2,9 (en roumain): OrtBuc 40,4 (1988) 136-146.

6752 *Seim* Turid K., Hustavlen 1 Pet 3,1-7 og dens tradisjonshistoriske sammenheng: NorTTs 91 (1990) 101-114.

6753 **Dalton** William J., Christ's proclamation to the spirits[2] ... 1 Peter 3,18 - 4,6: AnBib 23, 1989 → 5,6436: RJStNT 40 (1990) 121 (R. L. *Webb*: of widely recognized importance); Vidyajyoti 54 (1990) 654s (P. M. *Meagher*).

6754 *Scharlemann* M. H., He descended into hell; an interpretation of 1 Peter 3:1-20: ConcordJ 15 (1989) 311-322 [< NTAbs 34,61].

6755 *a*) *Attridge* Harold W., [1 Pt 3,18s...] Liberating death's captives; reconsideration of an early Christian myth; – *b*) *Pearson* Birger A., The

Apocalypse of Peter and canonical 2 Peter: ➤ 152, ᶠRoBINSON J. M., Gnosticism 2 (1990) 103-115 / 67-74.

6756 *Bastian* Bernard, [1 Pierre 5,1-4] Être berger selon le cœur de Dieu: Tychique 77 (1989) 17-19; 79 (1989) aussi 17-19; 82 (1989) 39s.

6757 *Aletti* Jean-Noël, La seconde épître de Pierre et le Canon du NT: ➤ 379, Canon 1990, 239-253.

6758 *Harvey* A. P., [2Pt, Jud, Test. XII ...] The testament of Simeon Peter: ➤ 183, ᶠVERMES G. 1990, 339-354.

6759 *Vena* Osvaldo T., [2 Pt] La lucha por la ortodoxía en las comunidades cristianas del 2º siglo: RBibArg 52,37 (1990) 1-28.

6760 **Allchin** A. M., [2 Pt 1,4] Participation in God; a forgotten strand in Anglican tradition. L 1988, Darton-LT. 85 p. £3.50. – ᴿScotJT 43 (1990) 140s (D. J. *Kennedy*).

6761 *Wolters* Al, 'Partners of the deity'; a covenantal reading of 2 Peter 1:4: CalvinT 25 (1990) 28-44.

6762 *Pisarek* Stanisław, ❷ *Hypomonē* im zweiten Petrusbrief (1,6): ➤ 64, ᶠGRZYBEK S. 1990, 237-247; deutsch 247.

6763 *Ramos* Felipe F., [2 Pt 3,13: Configuración] Desfiguración de la vida cristiana: NatGrac 37 (1990) [7-80] 167-273.

G9.4   **Epistula Jacobi ...** data on both apostles James.

6764 **Adamson** James B., James; the man and his message ➤ 5,6442: GR/ Exeter 1989, Eerdmans/Paternoster. xxii-553 p; $30. 0-8028-0167-6/. ᴿÉTRel 65 (1990) 454 (E. *Cuvillier*); ExpTim 102 (1990s) 23 (C. E. B. *Granfield*: complements his 1976 NICNT).

6765 **Aland** Barbara, Das NT in syrischer Übersetzung 1 (kath. B.), 1986 ➤ 2,1246 ... 4,6396: ᴿBO 47 (1990) 458-460 (S. *Brock*).

6766 **Attinger** Daniel, La lettera di Giacomo; commento esegetico-spirituale. Magnano VC 1988, Qiqajon. 69 p.

6767 **Barsotti** Divo, Meditazione sulla lettera di Giacomo: Bibbia e Liturgia 30. Brescia 1986, Queriniana. 89 p. Lit. 8000.

6768 **Church** Christopher L., A Forschungsgeschichte on the literary character of the Epistle of James: diss. Southern Baptist Theol. Sem., ᴰBorchard G. 1990. 300 p. 91-12505. – DissA 51 (1990s) 3791-A.

6769 *Frankemölle* Hubert, *a*) Das semantische Netz des Jakobusbriefes; zur Einheit eines umstrittenen Briefes: BZ 34 (1990) 161-197; foldout; – *b*) Der Jakobusbrief als Weisheitsschrift im Kontext frühjüdischer Weisheit: RUntHöh 33 (1990) 305-313 [< ZIT 90,852].

6770 *Fry* Euan, Commentaries on James, 1 and 2 Peter, and Jude: BTrans 41 (1990) 326-336.

6771 *Kinowaki* E., ERASMUS' Paraphrasis in Epistolam Jacobi and his anthropology: ➤ 725, Érasme 1986/90, 153-160.

6771* *Manns* F., Jacob le Min, tos. Hulin 2,22-24: CrNSt 10 (1989) 449-465.

6772 **Martin** Ralph P., James: Word comm. 48, 1988 ➤ 4,6404: ᴿAndrUnS 28 (1990) 171-3 (P. I. *Maynard-Reid*: a masterpiece).

6773 **Pratscher** Wilhelm, Der Herrenbruder Jakobus ...: FRL 139, 1987 ➤ 3, 6305; 5,6460: ᴿCurrTMiss 17 (1990) 234 (W. C. *Linss*); JBL 109 (1990) 162-4 (S. K. *Brown*); NedTTs 43 (1989) 336s (P. W. van der *Horst*); RHPR 70 (1990) 274s (C. *Grappe*); SNTU-A 14 (1989) 234s (A. *Fuchs*).

6774 *Pratscher* Wilhelm, Der Standort des Herrenbruders Jakobus im theologischen Spektrum der frühen Kirche: SNTU A-15 (1990) 41-58.

6775 **Schnider** Franz, Der Jakobusbrief 1987 → 3,6309 ... 5,6461: ᴿAntonianum 65 (1990) 386s (M. *Nobile*).
6776 *Wall* Robert W., James as apocalyptic paraenesis: RestQ 32,1 (1990) 11-22 [< NTAbs 34,340].

6777 *Porter* Stanley E., Is *dipsuchos* (James 1,8; 4,8) a 'Christian' word?: Biblica 71 (1990) 469-498; franç. 498.
6778 *Frankemölle* Hubert, [Jak 1,12-15] Zum Thema des Jakobusbriefes im Kontext der Rezeption von Sir 2,1-18 und 15,11-20 [Vortrag Tübingen kath. Fak. 21,I.1989]: BibNot 48 (1989) 21-49.
6779 *Johnson* Luke T., Taciturnity and true religion; James 1:26-27: → 122, ᶠMALHERBE A., Greeks 1990, 329-339.
6780 *Smith* Dirkie J., Exegesis and proclamation; 'show no partiality ...' (James 2:1-13): JTSAf 71 (1990) 59-68 [< TContext 8/1,24].
6781 *Burchard* Christoph, Nächstenliebegebot, Dekalog und Gesetz in Jak 2,8-11: → 147, ᶠRENDTORFF R., Hebr. Bibel 1990, 517-533.
6782 **Tamez** Elsa, [James 2,17-26] The scandalous message of James; faith without works is dead [Santiago, lectura latinoamericana 1985 → 2,5001], ᵀ*Eagleson* J. NY 1990, Crossroad. viii-102 p. $9 pa. 0-940989-56-5 [NTAbs 35,253].
6783 *McKnight* Scot, James 2:18a; the unidentifiable interlocutor: WestTJ 52 (1990) 355-364.
6783* *MacArthur* John F.ᴶ, Faith according to the apostle James: JEvTS 33 (1990) 35-42 (43-49-62, responses, *Radmacher* Earl D., *Saucy* Robert L.) [< ZIT 90,516].
6784 *Lautenschlager* Markus, Der Gegenstand des Glaubens im Jakobusbrief: ZTK 87 (1990) 163-184.
6785 *Diprose* R., [Gc 2,21-23] Fede e opere: Lux biblica 1,2 (R 1990) 75-79.
6786 *Marconi* Gilberto, La malattia come 'punto di vista'; esegesi di Gc 5,13-20: RivB 38 (1990) 57-72: mediazioni offerte per la situazione umana di estrema debolezza.

G9.6 Epistula Judae.

6787 **Bauckham** R. J., Jude, 2 Peter: Word **Themes**. Dallas 1990, Word. xiii-114 p. $10. 0-8499-0792-6 [NTAbs 34,390].
6788 *Bauckham* Richard, Jude and the relatives of Jesus in the early Church. E 1990, Clark. 459 p. £20 [NTAbs 35,248].
6789 *Charles* J. Daryl, 'Those' and 'these'; the use of the Old Testament in the Epistle of Jude: JStNT 38 (1990) 109-124.
6790 *Joubert* S., Language, ideology and the social context of the letter of Jude: Neotestamentica 29 (1990) 335-349.
6791 **Watson** Duane F., Invention, arrangement, and style ... Jude, 2Pt: SBL diss 104, 1988 → 5,6477: ᴿBiblica 71 (1990) 273-6 (F.W. *Hughes*); CBQ 52 (1990) 175-7 (C.C. *Black*); JBL 109 (1990) 164-6 (B.A. *Pearson*).

Non adhibentur hoc anno – Nº 4455-4554 & 6792-6999 – **not used this year.**

XV. Theologia Biblica

H1 **Biblical Theology** .1 [OT] **God.**

7000 *Bakon* Shimon, Biblical monotheism; some of its implications [creator; judge; covenanter ...]: JBQ 19 (1990s) 83-91.

7001 **Birnbaum** David, God and evil [➤ 5,7001]; a unified theodicy/theology/philosophy. Hoboken 1989, KTAV. xxi-260 p. $20. 0-88125-307-3 [TDig 38,49]. – RJJS 41 (1990) 286s (L. *Jacobs*: subtitle 'a Jewish perspective'); TS 51 (1990) 374s (S. *Bevans*).

7002 *Boshoff* Willem, Early Yahwism; the quest for a new paradigm [*Moor* J. de 1990]: OTEssays 3 (1990) 361-7.

7003 **Bouyer** Louis, Gnosis; la connaissance de Dieu dans l'Écriture 1988 ➤ 4,a662; 5,7002*: REsprVie 100 (1990) 687 (M. *Carrez*): EstTrin 23 (1989) 331s (N. *Silanes*); ÉTRel 64 (1989) 464 (J. *Ansaldi*: très dur contre les epithètes pour les Protestants dans l'intr.); Gregorianum 71 (1990) 183s (J. *Galot*: 'Graff'-WELLHAUSEN et DUHM paralysent l'exégèse ...); NRT 112 (1990) 417 (Y. de *Andia*: Écriture-Tradition).

7004 **Buckley** Michael J., At the origins of modern atheism 1987 ➤ 4,8010; 5,7007: RPerspRelSt 17 (1990) 272-6 (J. *Sykes*: atheism inevitably results from divorcing God from religious experience; also on LAMPERT's NIETZSCHE and SPRINTZEN's CAMUS).

7005 **Cazelles** H., La Bible et son Dieu: JJC 40, 1989 ➤ 5,7010: REsprVie 100 (1990) 284-6 (É. *Cothenet*); RivB 38 (1990) 377-9 (G. *Ravasi*); Téléma 16,3 (1990) 103-5 (C. *Delher*).

7006 **Dore** Clement, God, suffering and solipsism. Basingstoke 1989, Macmillan. x-120 p. £22.50. – RJTS 41 (1990) 788-790 (P. *Sherry*).

7007 **Farley** Wendy, Tragic vision and divine compassion; a contemporary theodicy. Louisville 1990, Westminster/Knox. 150 p. $14. – RTTod 47 (1990s) 478-480 (J. S. *Munday*).

7007* **Frame** John M., The doctrine of the knowledge of God; a theology of lordship. Phillipsburg 1987, Presbyterian & R. 437 p. $25. – RMastJ 1,1 (1990) 79-82 (C. *Good*).

7008 *Gianto* Agustinus, Allah pencipta ... God the creator and his people; a biblical theological essay: Orientasi Baru 4 (1990) 9-26 [AcPIB 9/7, 548].

7008* **Gutiérrez** G., El Dios de la vida. Lima 1989, CEP. 368 p. – RPerspTcol 22 (1990) 380-2 (F. *Taborda*); RTLim 24 (1990) 306-8 (J. M. *Carreras*).

7009 EHaag Ernst, Gott der Einzige: QDisp 104, 1984/5 ➤ 1,288 ... 4,8018: RBL (1989) 106 (J. W. *Rogerson*: six Catholics importantly refute B. LANG's claim that Israelite religion was polytheistic until 8th century prophets began to move it; N. *Lohfink* 'pre-monarchy if not yet monotheistic was no longer polytheistic').

7010 **Hebblethwaite** Brian, The ocean of truth; a defense of objective theism 1988 ➤ 4,8020: RJAAR 58 (1990) 500-3 (M. L. *Wallace*, also on *Haymes* B.).

7011 *Heering* H. J., LEVINAS' Godconceptie [14 geschriften] en de God der filosofen: TsTNijm 30 (1990) 159-172; Eng. 172.

7012 **Hodgson** Peter C., God in history; shapes of freedom [... HEGEL]. Nv 1989, Abingdon. 287 p. $22. – RInterpretation 44 (1990) 434.435 (R. P. *Roth*); TS 41 (1990) 142s (C. *O'Regan*).

7012* **Köckert** Matthias, Vätergott und Väterverheissungen ... ALT: FRL 142, 1988 ➤ 4,8023; 5,7017: RÉTRel 65 (1990) 110s (T. *Römer*: phase 'destructive'; 'maintenant il est temps de reconstruire'); JBL 109 (1990) 320-2 (T. L. *Thompson*); Salesianum 52 (1990) 169 (R. *Vicent*).

7013 **Konowitz** Israel, The God idea in Jewish tradition [1906] THimelstein Shmuel. J 1989; (Hoboken, Ktav). xx-485 p.; ❸ 29 p. $39,50 [RelStR 17, 80, M. S. *Jaffee*].

7014 **Levenson** Jon D., Creation and the persistence of evil; the Jewish dogma of divine omnipotence 1988 ➤ 4,8026; 5,7021: RDialog 28 (1989) 152-4 (J. K. *Robbins*); Interpretation 44 (1990) 196 (J. *Van Seters*).

7015 **L'Heureux** John, Comedians. NY 1990, Viking Penguin. 209 p. $18. –
ᴿAmerica 162 (1990) 588s (J. A. *Appleyard*); TTod 47 (1990s) 319s. 321
(Frances *Stefano*: Flannery O'CONNOR style stories, 'Life is chaos and
God is a comedian').

7016 **Lønning** Per, bp. Zum Thema 'Verborgenheit Gottes'; Bemerkungen zu
Eberhard JÜNGEL: KerDo 36 (1990) 285-299; Eng. 299.

7017 **McFague** Sallie, Models of God 1987 ⮞ 3,6354 ... 5,7023: ᴿDialog 27
(1988) 131-140 (T. *Peters*: 'McFague's metaphors'); RelStR 16 (1990)
36-40 (Sheila G. *Davaney*) & 40-42 (J. B. *Cobb*); ScotBEv 8 (1990) 55-57
(B. *McCormack*: 'It is difficult to believe that liberating existence will be
promoted on such transparently shaky grounds').

7018 **McLelland** Joseph C., Prometheus rebound; the irony of atheism
[... really antitheism: conceives God as tyrannical obstacle to human
freedom]. Waterloo ON 1988, W. Laurier Univ. xvi-306 p. – ᴿSR 19
(1990) 118s (R. *Forsman*).

7019 **Mayer** R., Jüdische Gotteserfahrung gemäss der Tora: KlBücherei 118.
Meitingen 1989, Kyrios. 56 p. DM 6. 3-7838-2118-5 [NTAbs 34,254].

7020 *Metz* Johann B., Der biblische Monotheismus und die neuen My-
thologien: ⮞ 133, ꟻNYÍRI T., 1990, 272-280.

7021 *Moltmann* Jürgen, Lässt Gott das Leiden zu ? Perspektiven der
Theodizeefrage heute: ⮞ 132, ꟻNIPKOW K., Bildung 1989, 270-4.

7022 **Moor** J. C. de, The rise of Yahwism; the roots of Israelite monotheism:
BiblETL 91. Lv 1990, Univ./Peeters. xxi-315 p. Fb 1250. 90-6186-358-9
/ 90-6831-203-0 [BL 91, 116, J. C. L. *Gibson*: an ALBRIGHT redivivus?]. –
ᴿZAW 102 (1990) 452s (H.-C. *Schmitt*).

7023 **Neusner** Jacob, ⮞ 4,8033] The incarnation of God; the character of
divinity in formative Judaism. Mp 1988, Fortress. 256 p. $25. 0-8006-
2086-0. – ᴿJQR 81 (1990s) 219-227 (E. R. *Wolfson*).

7023* **Niehr** Herbert, JHWH als Arzt; Herkunft und Bedeutung einer alttestamentlichen Gottesprädikation: kath. Hab.-Diss. ᴰ*Schreiner*. Würzburg
1989. – TR 86 (1990) 510.

7024 *Perelmuter* Hayim G., Judaism and transcendence; from Abraham to
the late Middle Ages: SpTod 41 (1989) 18-29.

7025 **Ruff** Pierre-Jean, Un seul Dieu ? ou le problème du mal. Lillois 1989,
Alliance. 158 p. F 100. 2-87300-000-7. – ᴿÉTRel 65 (1990) 643 (A.
Gounelle: non-conformiste, serein).

7025* a) *Schoen* Edward L., Anthropomorphic concepts of God; – b)
Steglich David, A God by any other name; – c) *McKim* Robert, The
hiddenness of God: RelSt 26 (1990) 123-139 / 117-121 / 141-161.

7026 **Spieckermann** Hermann, 'Barmherzig und gnädig ist der Herr...':
ZAW 102 (1990) 1-18.

7027 **Surin** Kenneth, Theology and the problem of evil 1986 ⮞ 2,5060 ...
4,8042: ᴿHeythJ 31 (1990) 79s (K. *Ward*: unconvinced); TorJT 6 (1990)
323s (A. H. *Khan*).

7028 **Thompson** Alden, Who's afraid of the OT God? 1988 ⮞ 5,7035;
176 p.; £6.50; Exeter 0-85364-440-3: ᴿÉTRel 65 (1990) 113s (D. *Lys*).

7029 **Vicchio** Stephen J., The voice from the whirlwind; the problem of evil
in the modern world. Westminster MD c. 1990: Christian Classics.
vi-326 p. $20 pa. [NewTR 4,1, 84-87, S. *Bevans*, also on WHITNEY B.].

ʜ1.3 *Immutabilitas* – **God's suffering; process theology.**

7030 **Bube** Paul C., Ethics in John COBB's process theology [diss.]. Atlanta
1988, Scholars. xiv-184 p. [RelStR 17, 242, N. F. *Gier*].

7031 *a*) *Cobb* John B.,   Two types of postmodernism; deconstruction and process; – *b*) *Sweet* Leonard I.,   Straddling modernism and postmodernism: TTod 47 (1990s) 149-158 / 159-164.

7032 *Cook* Robert R.,   God, middle knowledge [SUÁREZ] and alternative worlds: EvQ 62 (1990) 293-310.

7032* **Dodds** Michael J.,   The unchanging God of love ... AQUINAS 1986 → 2,5074 ... 4,8049: RETL 66 (1990) 208-210 (R. *Wielockx*: intéressant ... à reformuler sinon à resoudre).

7033 *Duncan* J. Ligon[III],   Divine passibility and impassibility in nineteenth century American confessional Presbyterian theologians: ScotBEv 8 (1990) 1-15.

7034 **Fiddes** Paul S.,   The creative suffering of God 1988 → 4,8051; 5,7043: RCalvinT 25 (1990) 93-95 (C. *Minnema*); JAAR 58 (1990) 705-7 (W. *McWilliams*); JRel 70 (1990) 471s (J. B. *Pool*); JTS 41 (1990) 316-8 (D. F. *Ford*); NewTR 3,2 (1990) 101s (Z. *Hayes*); ScotJT 43 (1990) 114s (R. E. *Olson*).

7035 *a*) *Forster* Peter R.,   Divine passibility and the early Christian doctrine of God; – *b*) *Blocher* Henri,   Divine immutability; – *c*) *Wells* Paul,   God and change; Moltmann in the light of the Reformed tradition; – *d*) *Helm* Paul,   The impossibility of divine passibility; – *e*) *Bauckham* Richard,   In defence of [MOLTMANN Eng. 1974] The crucified God; – *f*) *Cook* E. David,   Weak Church, weak God; the charge of anthropomorphism: → 586, Impassibility 1989/90, 23-51 / 1-22 / 53-68 / 119-140 / 93-118 / 69-92.

7036 **Franklin** Stephen T.,   Speaking from the depths; Alfred N. WHITEHEAD's hermeneutical metaphysics of propositions, experience, symbolism, language, and religion. GR 1990, Eerdmans. xiv-410 p. $27.50. 0-8028-0370-9 [TDig 37,362].

7037 *Fretheim* Terence E.,   *a*) Suffering God and sovereign God in Exodus; a collision of images; – *b*) The repentance of God; a key to evaluating OT God-talk: HorBT 11,2 (1989) 31-56 / 10,1 (1988) 47-70.

7038 *Galot* Jean,   *a*) Dio soffre?: CC 141 (1990,1) 535-545; – *b*) Le mystère de la souffrance de Dieu; le problème: EsprVie 100 (1990) 261-8.

7039 **Gonnet** Dominique,   Dieu aussi connaît la souffrance: Théologie. P 1990, Cerf. 120 p. F 72 [ÉTRel 65,661: 'Dieu connaît aussi]. – REsprVie 100 (1990) 399 (G. M. *Oury*).

7040 *a*) *González Montes* Adolfo,   Pasibilidad divina e historia trinitaria; el misterio de Dios en la obra de Jürgen MOLTMANN; – *b*) *Martínez Camino* Juan A.,   'Más cercano' y 'humano'; Dios en la teología de E. JÜNGEL: EstTrin 23 (1989) 191-243 / 249-297.

7040* *Gounelle* André,   Théologie du process et création: RHPR 70 (1990) 181-197; Eng. 284, 'Process theology and suffering'!

7041 **Helm** Paul,   Eternal God; a study of God without time. Ox 1988, Clarendon, xv-230 p. £20. – RJTS 41 (1990) 790-2 (B. *Hebblethwaite*); Salesianum 52 (1990) 447s (C. *Cantone*); ScotBEv 8 (1990) 63s (G. *Bray*); TTod 47 (1990s) 77s. 80 (Kathryn *Tanner*).

7042 **Jaeckel** Theodor,   Anything but a quiet life; ideas of God in the Bible 1989 → 5,7049: RBL (1990) 103 (R. *Davidson*); Vidyajyoti 54 (1990) 103 (R. J. *Raja*).

7042* *Kunzler* Michael,   Die dogmatische Lehre von der göttlichen Unveränderlichkeit und die trinitarischen Doxologien im liturgischen Gebet der byzantinischen Kirche — eine Gegenüberstellung: TGL 80 (1990) 22-35.

7043 *Kuramatsu* Isao,   Die gegenwärtige Kreuzestheologie und LUTHER, besonders in Rücksicht auf die Theologie des Schmerzes Gottes von Kazo KITAMORI: KerDo 36 (1990) 273-283; Eng. 283.

7044 *a) Livezey* Lois G., Women, power, and politics; feminist theology in process perspective; – *b) Howell* Nancy R., The promise of a process feminist theology of relations; – *c) McDaniel* Jay, Land ethics, animal rights, and process theology; – *d) Hallman* Joseph M., How is process theology theological ? ProcSt 17 (1988) 67-77 / 78-87 / 88-102 / 112-7 [< ZIT 89,672].

7045 *McDonald* H. D., Process Christology [p. 43; 'Process Theology' p. 5; PITTENGER N. 1944, 1959, 1970]: VoxEvca 20 (1990) 43-55.

7046 **Meland** Bernard E., Essays in constructive theology; a process perspective. Ch 1988, Exploration. 329 p. $15. [RelStR 17, 242, J. A. *Stone*: friendly critic of S. OGDEN].

7046* ᴱ**Nash** Ronald H., Process theology. GR 1987, Baker. 388 p. $17. 0-8010-6782-0. – ᴿCritRR 2 (1987) 448-451 (L. S. *Ford*).

7047 **Oden** Thomas C., The living God 1987 → 3,6362; 5,7055: ᴿPerspRelSt 17 (1990) 253-260 (R. C. *Wood*).

7048 **O'Hanlon** G. F., The immutability of God in the theology of H. U. v. BALTHASAR. C 1990, Univ. 229 p. £30 [JAAR 58,741]. 0-521-36649-6.

7048* *a) Padgett* Alan G., God and time; toward a new doctrine of divine timeless eternity; – *b) Taliaferro* Charles, The passibility of God; – *c) Burns* Robert M., The divine simplicity in St. THOMAS: RelSt 25 (1989) 209-215 / 217-224 / 271-293.

7049 **Pailin** David, God and the processes of reality 1989 → 5,7055*: ᴿExpTim 101 (1989s) 53 (P. A. *Byrne*); ModT 7 (1990s) 1993 (T. E. *Burke*); TS 51 (1990) 354s (J. A. *Bracken*).

7049* *Pendergast* R. J., A thomistic-process theory of the Trinity: ScEsp 42 (1990) 35-59.

7050 **Philipps** Winfred G., Schubert OGDEN's transcendental strategy against secularism [... though he is often considered a process theologian]: HarvTR 82 (1989) 447-466.

7051 **Reynolds** Blair, Towards a process pneumatology [diss.]. L / Cranbury NJ 1990, Selinsgrove / Susquehanna Univ. 214 p. $34.50 [TS 52, 171, B. J. *Lee*].

7051* *Sacchi* Mario E., El Dios inmutable de la filosofía perenne y de la fe católica: DoctCom 42 (1989) 242-278.

7052 *Sarot* Marcel, *a)* Het lijden van God ? Enkele terminologische notities bij een hedendaagse theologische discussie: NedTTs 44 (1990) 35-50: Eng. 56; – *b)* Patripassianism, Theopaschitism and the suffering of God; some historical and systematic considerations: RelSt 26 (1990) 363-375.

7053 *Sarot* Marcel, *a)* De Passibilitas Dei in de hedendaagse westerse theologie; een literatuuroverzicht: KerkT 40 (1989) 196-206 [< ZIT 89, 581]; – *b)* Auschwitz, morality, and the suffering of God: ModT 7 (1990s) 135-152.

7054 ᴱ**Sia** Santiago, Charles HARTSHORNE's concept of God; philosophical and theological responses [of Hartshorne to 14 contributors]: Studies in philosophy and religion 12. Boston 1990, Kluwer. xiii-331 p. $99. 0-7923-0290-7 [TDig 37,352].

7055 **Suchocki** Marjorie H., The end of evil; process eschatology in historical context [ᴰ1973] 1988 → 5,7061: ᴿJAAR 58 (1990) 729-731 (B. *Whitney*).

7056 **Suchocki** Marjorie H., God-Christ-Church; a practical guide to process theology²ʳᵉᵛ. NY 1989, Crossroad. 281 p. $17 [JAAR 58,164].

7057 **Varillon** François, La sofferenza di Dio; note teologiche e spirituali; intr. *Galot* Jean. R 1989, Città Nuova. 103 p. – ᴿTVida 31 (1990) 218s (M. *Arias*).

7058 ᴱVeken J. van der, God en wereld; basisteksten uit de proces-theologie:
Sleutelteksten GT 7.   Haag 1989, Meinema ➤ 5,7067;   143 p. ƒ26,50.
90-211-6106-0. – ᴿTsTNijm 30 (1990) 101 (R. *Munnik*).

7059 **Weinandy** Thomas G., Does God change ? [ᴰ1975] 1985 ➤ 1,6993 ...
5,7068: ᴿIrTQ 56 (1990) 63s (G. *O'Hanlon*).

7060 **Zoppoli** Enrico, 'Mistero della sofferenza di Dio' ? Il pensiero di
S. Tᴏᴍᴍᴀsᴏ: Studi Tomistici 34.   Vaticano 1988, Editrice.   85 p.
Lit. 10.000. – ᴿGregorianum 71 (1990) 184s (J. *Galot*: non prende in
considerazione la rivelazione biblica né, sembra, la Commissione Teologica Internazionale del 1982).

H1.4   *Femininum in Deo* – **God as father and as mother** [➤ F3.7; H8.8s].

7060* *Baudler* Georg, Grosse Mutter — erhabener Vater; die Stellung der
Frau in der Kirche aus dem Blickpunkt der Religionsgeschichte [i. Die
Abrahams-Religion als Gegenbewegung zur (verkommenen) Religion
der Grossen Mutter ... iii. Die Abwertung der Frau durch die mön-
chisch-asketische Religiosität; iv. die Frau im Lebensfeld der Gottes-
erschliessung Jesu ...]: ZkT 112 (1990) 257-270.

7061 **Boff** L., The maternal face of God [... in Mary; 1979], ᵀ1987 ➤ 3,6430
... 5,7075; also L 1989, Collins: 0-00-599197-8: ᴿAnglTR 72 (1990)
114-6 (W. E. *Limbrick*); ExpTim 101 (1989s) 351 (Elaine *Graham*).

7062 ᴿ**Brown** Joanne C., *Bohn* Carole R., Christianity, patriarchy, and abuse;
a feminist critique.   NY 1989, Pilgrim.   viii-173 p. – ᴿRelStR 16 (1990)
327 (Heidi M. *Ravven*).

Douglas R. C., Family, power ... God as father in Mt, ᴰ1989 ➤ 4669.

7063 **Dourley** John P., The goddess, mother of the Trinity; [... Eᴄᴋʜᴀʀᴛ] a
Jᴜɴɢɪᴀɴ implication: St. Psych. Rel. 4.   Lewiston ɴʏ 1990, Mellen.
112 p. $50.   0-88946-244-5.

7064 **Durrwell** François-X., Nuestro Padre; Dios en su misterio [Le Père 1987
➤ 3,6436], ᵀ*Ortiz García* Alfonso: Verdad e Imagen 110.   S 1990,
Sígueme.   249 p.   84-301-1101-8. – ᴿActuBbg 27 (1990) 217s (J. *Vives*);
HumT 11 (1990) 383-5 (J. *Cunha*); TVida 31 (1990) 219s (M. *Arias*).

7065 *Ferrando* Miguel Ángel, Apuntes para una teología del Padre en el
Evangelio según san Juan: ➤ 125, ᶠMᴏʀᴇɴᴏ/Vɪʟʟᴇɢᴀs 1990, 147-161.

7066 **Galot** Jean, *a*) Abba, Père! cri du plus ardent amour.   Lv 1990,
Sursum.   133 p. Fb 490. – ᴿGregorianum 71 (1990) 808 (ipse); NRT 112
(1990) 945 (G. N.); – *b*) Sens et valeur d'une fête du Père: EsprVie 100
(1990) 97-103.

7067 *Gerl* Hanna-Barbara, Gott – Vater und Mutter?: ErbAuf 66 (1990)
5-16, 81-95.

7068 **Gerstenberger** E., Jahwe ein patriarchaler Gott? 1988 ➤ 4,8084; 5,7081:
ᴿCritRR 3 (1990) 123-6 (Phyllis A. *Bird*); LebZeug 44 (1989) 71s (F.
Courth).

7069 *Grossmann* Sigrid, Befreiung vom Vater–Gott; Grundströmungen feministischer Theologie; EvKomm 22,4 (1989) 20-22.

7069* *Hauke* Manfred, 'Mutter unsere', 'Heilige Geistin' und 'Jesu Christa';
Bemerkungen zum feministischen Gottes- und Christusbild: ForumKT 6
(1990) 22-37.

7070 **Horie** Michiaki & Hildegard, Auf der Suche nach dem verlorenen
Vater; über die Wiedergewinnung des Vaterbildes Wu 1988, Brockhaus.
141 p. DM 16,80. – ᴿKerkT 40 (1989) 259s (G. *de Ru*).

7071 **Kinsley** David,   The goddesses' mirror; visions of the divine from East and West. Albany 1988, SUNY. xx-320 p. – RSR 19 (1990) 259s (Manabu *Waida*).

7071* *Lafontaine* René,   La personne du Père dans la théologie de saint Thomas: ➤ 541*, L'Écriture âme 1989/90, 81-108.

7072 **Leonard** Graham, *al.*,   Let God be God; thinking theologically about inclusive language L 1990, Morehouse. 112 p. $7. 0-8192-1517-1. – RTLond 93 (1990) 305 (P. *Avis*: response to feminism).

7073 **Marriage** Alwyn,   Life-giving Spirit; responding to the feminine in God. L 1989, SPCK. ix-133 p. £8 pa. – RTLond 93 (1990) 423s (Susan F. *Parsons*).

7074 *a*) *Martín Velasco* Juan,   Dios como padre | en la historia de las religiones; – *b*) *García López* Félix,   ... en el AT a la luz de las interpretaciones recientes de la historia de Israel; – *c*) *Ladaria* Luis F.,   ... en HILARIO de Poitiers; – *d*) *Schneider* Gerhard,   El Padre de Jesús, visión bíblica; – *e*) *Sesboüé* Bernard,   Dios Padre en la reflexión teológica actual: EstTrin 24 (1990) 359-383 / 385-399 / 443-479 / 401-441 / 481-503.

7075 *Mattison* Robin D.,   God/Father; tradition and interpretation: RefR 42 (1989) 189-206 [< ZIT 89,447].

7075* **Miller** John W.,   Biblical faith and fathering; why we call God 'Father' 1989 ➤ 5,7087; 0-8091-3107-2: RTS 51 (1990) 556s (P. M. *Arnold*); TTod 47 (1990s) 486.488 (Kathleen A. *Farmer*: anti-inclusive grasping at straws).

7076 **Mollenkott** Virginia R. [The divine feminine[3] 1983 ➤ 1,6337] *a*) Gott eine Frau? Vergessene Gottesbilder der Bibel, TKnirck C. M. [1985 ➤ 1,6338]: B-Reihe 295. Mü 1990, Beck. 3-404-34783-5 [BL 91,159]. – *b*) Dieu au féminin; images féminines de Dieu dans la Bible, TSherman Paule (*Bazinet* Lise); préf. *Hébrard* Monique. Montréal/P 1990, Paulines/ Centurion. 139 p. F 85 [RTLv 21,404].

7076* *Newman* Barbara,   Some mediaeval theologians and the Sophia tradition [feminine image of God's activity in creation]: DowR 108 (1990) 111-130.

7077 **Nzuzi** Bibaki,   Le Dieu-Mère chez les Yombe (l'inculturation et le discours 'proverbial' sur Dieu); diss. Pont. Univ Gregoriana, DRoest Crollius A. Roma 1990, No 6890. – InfPUG 23,119 (1990s) 16.

7077* *Pouilly* Jean,   Dieu notre Père; la révélation de Dieu Père et le 'Notre Père': CahÉv 68. P 1989, Cerf. 67 p. F 25. 0222-9714.

7078 **Rae** Eleanor, [Marie-] *Daly* Bernice,   Created in her image; models of the feminine divine. NY c. 1990, Crossroad. $16 [TTod 47,91 adv.].

7079 **Raurell** Frederic,   Der Mythos vom männlichen Gott 1989 ➤ 5,7092: RLaurentianum 31 (1990) 616-9 (E. M. *Kraft*); MüTZ 41 (1990) 188s (A. *Loichinger*); NatGrac 37 (1990) 134-6 (A. *Villalmonte*); RivB 38 (1990) 105s (A. *Minissale*); TPQ 138 (1990) 389s (J. *Janda*); TZBas 46 (1990) 186s (H. *Reventlow*).

7080 *Robson* Jill,   Dieu au foyer; images féminines de Dieu et de la prière: ÉTRel 65 (1990) 573-586.

7081 **Ruether** Rosemary R.,   Frauenbilder — Gottesbilder; feministische Erfahrungen in religionsgeschichtlichen Texten, TKeune B. (*Baumotte* M.): Siebenstern 490. Gü 1987, Mohn. 411 p.; ill. DM 28,80. – RTLZ 115 (1990) 226-8 (K. *Lüthi*).

7082 *Rupprecht* Konrad,   Zu Herkunft und Alter der Vater-Anrede Gottes im Gebet des vorchristlichen Judentums; nicht durchgehend wissenschaftliche

Erlebnisse, Beobachtungen, Überlegungen und Spekulationen: → 147, ᶠRENDTORFF R., Hebr. Bibel 1990, 347-355.

7083 *Schroer* Silvia, Gott Sophia und Jesus Sophia; Biblische Grundlageneiner christlichen und feministischen Spiritualität: BLtg 62 (1989) 20-25.

7084 *Schüngel-Straumann* Helen, Pfingstliche Geistkraft/Lebenskraft (*rûaḥ*); alttestamentliche Wurzeln einer verdrängten weiblichen Vorstellung: Diakonia 21 (1990) 149-157.

7085 *a*) *Starhawk* Catherine M. & 4 others, 'If God is God she is not nice'; – *b*) *Weaver* Mary Jo, Who is the goddess and where does she get us?; – *c*) *Hackett* Jo Ann, Can a sexist model liberate us?; Ancient Near East 'fertility' goddesses; – *d*) *Eilberg-Schwartz* Howard, Witches of the west; neopaganism and goddess worship as enlightenment religions: JFemStRel 5,1 (1989) 103-118 / 49-64 / 65-76 / 77-96 [< ZIT 89,566].

7085* **Strotman** Angelika, 'Mein Vater bist du' (Sir 51,10); zur Bedeutung der Vaterschaft Gottes in kanonischen und nichtkanonischen frühjüdischen Schriften: Diss. St. Georgen, ᴰ*Beutler* J. Fra 1989s. – TR 86 (1990) 514; RTLv 22, p. 596.

7086 **Trible** Phyllis, God en sekse-gebonden taalgebruik [God and the rhetoric 1978] 1988 → 5,7095; 90-304-0417-5: ᴿTsTNijm 30 (1990) 99 (Annelies de *Bont*).

7087 *Wacker* Marie-Thérèse, Gott als Mutter? Zur Bedeutung eines biblischen Gottes-Symbols für feministische Theologie: IZT 25 (1989) 523-8 – [→ 5,7096] Concilium 226 (P 1989) 125-133, ᵀ*Guého* Marie-T.

7088 **Wedel** E. von, Als Jesus sich Gott ausdachte; die unerwiderte Liebe zum Vater: Tabus des Christentums. Stu 1990, Kreuz. 141 p. DM 24,80. 3-7831-1011-4 [NTAbs 35,108; the drama between a son and his father; Jesus adopted God as his ideal father].

7088* **Wren** Brian, What language shall I borrow? God-talk in worship; a male response to feminist theology 1989 → 4,a864; 5,7098: ᴿExpTim 101 (1989s) 218s (Mary *Barr*); Tablet 344 (1990) 453s (D. *Crystal*); TS 51 (1990) 375 (J.S. *Nelson*: after 'how thought and reality interrelate through language', on the whole accepts feminism for hymn-revision, perhaps overlooking how religious experience has been nurtured for so many even by inadequate language).

H1.7   Revelatio.

7089 **Bekye** Paul Kuusegme, Divine revelation and traditional religions, with particular reference to the Dagaaba of West Africa: diss. 6897 Pont. Univ. Gregoriana, ᴰ*Dupuis* J. R 1990s. – InfPUG 23/119,14.

7089* **Bockmuehl** Markus N.A., Revelation and mystery in ancient Judaism and Pauline Christianity [diss. C 1987, ᴰ*Horbury* W.]: WUNT 2/36. Tü 1990, Mohr. xvi-310 p. DM 98 pa. 3-16-145339-5 [NTAbs 34,391].

7090 *Caragounis* Chrys, L'universalisme moderne; perspectives bibliques sur la révélation de Dieu: Hokhma 45 (1990) 17-45.

7091 *Devillers* Luc, De Léon XIII à Vatican II; note sur 'Dei Verbum' vingt-cinq ans après: RThom 90 (1990) 271-4.

7092 *Dulles* Avery, From images to truth; NEWMAN on revelation and faith: TS 51 (1990) 252-267 [434-9, ... on infallibility].

7093 **Fisichella** Rino, La Révélation et sa crédibilité 1989 → 5,7108; ᵀ*Duverne* Didier, *Cuenot* Daniel; ᴿArTGran 53 (1990) 345s (E. *Barón*); RThom 90 (1990) 275-7 (G. *Narcisse*).

7094 *Gaboriau* Florent, Sur le concept de Révélation: RThom 90 (1990) 533-569.

7094* *a*) *Geffré* Claude, Révélation et expérience historique des hommes; – *b*) *Richard* Jean, Le champ herméneutique de la Révélation d'après C. Geffré: LavalTP 46 (1990) 3-16 / 17-30.

7095 *a*) **Kuhn** Peter, Offenbarungsstimmen im Antiken Judentum ... Bat Qol 1989 ➤ 5,7113*a*; Hab.D. Fra: ᴿActuBbg 27 (1990) 196 (J. *Boada*).

— *b*) **Gorringe** T.J., Discerning Spirit — a theology of revelation. L/Ph 1990, SCM/Trinity. 144 p. £9. 0-334-02462-5. – ᴿExpTim 102 (1990s) 250 (G. *Newlands*).

— *c*) **Hinrichs** Maurus, ᴱ*Dettloff* Werner, Christliche Offenbarung und religiöse Erfahrung im Dialog. 1984. – ᴿWissWeis 51 (1988) 228-233 (N. *Hartmann*).

Hoeps Reinhard, ... Schöpfung als Offenbarung 1990 ➤ 9892.

7095* **Jong** Jacobus de, Accommodatio Dei, a theme of Klaas SCHILDER's theology of revelation: diss. ᴰ*Kumphuis* J. Kampen 1990. 305 p. – TsT-Nijm 30 (1990) 188; RTLv 22,586.

7096 *Lutz* Theodor, Wort und Bild in der Offenbarung; Überlegungen zur alttestamentlich-jüdischen Überlieferung: GeistL 62 (1989) 19-30.

7097 *Meis W.*, Anneliese, El concepto de 'Revelación' en la Constitución Dogmática Dei Verbum: TVida 31 (1990) 5-15.

7098 *Nash* Ronald, Southern Baptists and the notion of revealed truth: CriswT 2 (1987s) 371-384.

7099 **Perlman** Lawrence, Abraham HESCHEL's idea of revelation: Brown-JudSt 171. Atlanta 1989, Scholars. ix-171 p. [RelStR 17, 173, E.N. *Dorff*].

7100 *Ramos* Felipe F., Revelación divina y Iglesia; reflexiones sobre la Dei Verbum; Salmanticensis 37 (1990) 265-300; Eng. 300.

7101 **Ruiz Arenas** Octavio, Jesús, epifanía ... Revelación 1987 ➤ 4,8115: ᴿFranBog 30 (1988) 238s [< OssRom 20. VIII. 1988 p. 23]; ScripT-Pamp 22 (1990) 1022s (C. *Izquierdo*).

7102 *Saarinen* Risto, Offenbarung und Evidenz bei Hermann LOTZE und Wilhelm HERRMANN: KerDo 36 (1990) 301-312; Eng. 312, 'Revelation and its self-evidence'.

7102* *a*) *Schaeffler* Richard, Die religiöse Erfahrung und das Zeugnis von ihr; Erkundung eines Problemfeldes; – *b*) *Schneider* Theodor, Selbst-mitteilung Gottes und Lehramt der Kirche; – *c*) *Splett* Jörg, Die Bedingung der Möglichkeit; zum transzendentalphilosophischen Ansatz der Theologie K. RAHNERS; – *d*) *Hilberath* Bernd J., Ist der christliche Absolutheitsanspruch heute noch vertretbar?: ➤ 158*, ᶠSCHMITZ J. 1990, 13-34 / 35-67 / 68-87 / 105-131.

7103 *Scharbert* Josef, 'Gesicht', 'Wort' und 'Traum' als Offenbarungsmittel im AT: ➤ 64, ᶠGRZYBEK S. 1990, 260-290.

7103* *a*) *Scheffczyk* Leo, Der neuscholastische Traktat De revelatione divina, die dogmatische Konstitution Dei Verbum und die Lehre des hl. THOMAS; – *b*) *Hödl* Ludwig, Die veritates fidei catholicae und die Analogie der Wahrheit im mittelalterlichen Streit der Fakultäten; – *c*) *Elders* Leo, Aquinas on Holy Scripture as the medium of divine revelation; – *d*) *Nicolas* Jean-Hervé, Aspects épistémologiques de la révélation; – *e*) *Torrell* Jean-Pierre, Le traité de la prophétie de S. Thomas d'Aquin et la théologie de la révélation: ➤ 607, Révélation/Aquin 1989/90, 12-26 / 49-68 / 132-152 / 153-170 / 171-195.

7104 **Schelling** F. W. J., Philosophie de la Révélation, I. Introduction, ᵀᴱ*M-arquet* J.-E., *Courtine* J.-F.: Épiméthée. P 1989, PUF. 203 p. F 120. 2-13-04249-1. – ᴿÉTRel 65 (1990) 647s (J.-P. *Gabus*).
7105 **Schmitz** Josef, Offenbarung: Leitfaden Theologie 19, 1989 ➤ 4,8116; 5,7119: ᴿTLZ 115 (1990) 540s (M. *Petzoldt*: deserved an even sooner review).
7106 **Segundo** Juan Luis, El dogma que libera; fe, revelación y Magisterio 1989 ➤ 5,7120: ᴿEfMex 8 (1990) 276s (J. M. *Crespo* G.); EstTrin 23 (1989) 342 (J. M. de *Miguel*); PerspTeol 22 (1990) 382-5 (A. T. *Murad*).
7107 **Shorter** Aylward, La Revelación y su interpretación [1983] 1986 ➤ 3, 6493: ᴿStudium 29 (M 1989) 557s (P. *Blázquez*).
7108 **Steinheim** Salomon L. [1789-1866 ➤ 4,b293], Die Offenbarung nach dem Lehrbegriffe der Synagoge. Hildesheim 1986 = 1835, Olms. 4 vol. I. xxiv-362 p.; II. xvi-468 p.; III. xvi-420 p.; IV. xi-598 p. 3-487-07753-1; -4-X; -5-8; -6-6.
7109 *Thoma* Clemens, Auffrischung und Neugestaltung der Offenbarung in biblischer und nachbiblischer Zeit: TBer 18 (Z 1989) 15-30 [< ZIT 90,174].
7109* **Torres Queiruga** Andrés, A revelación de Dios na realización do homem 1985 ➤ 3,6497 [español 1987 ➤ 3,6498; 5,7124*]: ᴿPerspT 21 (1989) 249-252 (J. B. *Libânio*: en galego, excelente tratado).

H1.8 **Theologia fundamentalis.**

7110 **Abraham** William, The logic of evangelism. L 1989, Hodder & S. x-245 p. £8 pa. – ᴿTLond 93 (1990) 497 (P. *Cotterell*: he means the theology of evangelising).
7111 *Andonegui* Javier, Teología como ciencia; aspectos peculiares del piantamiento escotista: ScripV 36 (1989) 379-430.
7112 a) *Ansaldi* Jean, La théologie comme science; – b) *Houziaux* Alain, Sciences et théologie; problèmes et schèmes transdisciplinaires; – c) *Müller* Denis, La résistance du réel comme principe épistémologique d'une éthique incarnée: ÉTRel 65 (1990) 385-400 / 363-384 [401-410, Gen 1,1-2,4] / 353-361.415-9.
7112* *Arens* Edmund, Zur Struktur theologischer Wahrheit; Überlegungen aus wahrheitstheoretischer, biblischer und fundamentaltheologischer Sicht: ZkT 112 (1990) 1-17.
7113 **Bouillard** Henri, Vérité du christianisme [c. 1948, never published because of the attacks on 'nouvelle théologie' in his first volume of the series Théologie in 1944], ᴱ*Neufeld* K.-H.: Théologie. P 1989, D-Brouwer. 416 p. F 148. – ᴿZkT 112 (1990) 324-6 (Neufeld).
7113* **Brown** David, a) Invitation to theology. Ox 1989, Blackwell. vii-182 p. $30; pa. $9. 0-631-16474-X [TDig 37,349]. – ᴿExpTim 101 (1989s) 290 (C. S. *Rodd*). – b) Continental philosophy and modern theology 1987 ➤ 5,7129: ᴿHeythJ 31 (1990) 369s (B. R. *Brinkman*).
7114 **Caillot** Joseph, L'Évangile de la communication; pour une nouvelle approche du Salut chrétienne: CogF 152. P 1988, Cerf. 374 p. F 149. – ᴿArTGran 53 (1990) 340s (R. *Franco*: teol. fund.); RTLv 21 (1990) 363 (C. *Focant*: théologie fondamentale).
7114* *Clayton* John, Piety and the proofs: RelSt 26 (1990) 19-42.
7115 **Dalferth** Ingolf U., Theology and philosophy: Signposts in Theology, 1988 ➤ 4,8136; 5,7134: ᴿTPhil 65 (1990) 288-290 (F. *Ricken*).

7115* a) **Davis** Caroline F.,   The evidential force of religious experience.   Ox 1989, Clarendon. 268 p. £27.50. – ᴿRelSt 26 (1990) 544-6 (H. P. *Owen*); – b) *Levine* Michael P.,   'If there is a God, any experience which seems to be of God, will be genuine' [*Swinburne* R.]: RelSt 26 (1990) 207-217.

7116 *Doré* Joseph,   Bulletin de théologie fondamentale [*Kern* W. *al.*; *Wagner* F.; *Van Beeck* F.; *Forte* B.; *Pié i Ninot* S.; *Latourelle-O'Collins; Maddox* R. ...]:   RechSR 78 (1990) 269-292.

7117 **Drehsen** Volker,   Neuzeitliche Konstitutionsbedingungen der Praktischen Theologie; Aspekte der theologischen Wende zur soziokulturellen Lebenswelt christlicher Religion.   Gü 1988, Mohn. xvi-622 p.; 602 p. – ᴿTRu 55 (1990) 228-241 (F. *Wagner*).

7118 **Farley** Edward,   Ecclesial reflection; an anatomy of theological method 1982 ⋙ 63,1388 ... 3,6522:   ᴿTLZ 115 (1990) 453-7 (S. *Hübner*).

7119 **Farley** Edward,   The fragility of knowledge; theological education in the Church and the university.   Ph 1988, Fortress.   191 p. – ᴿInterpretation 44 (1990) 436.438 (R. R. *Osmer*: continues his much-discussed Theologia 1983 ⋙ 65,5814).

7119* **Forte** Bruno,   Gedächtnis, Prophetie und Begleitung; eine Einführung in die Theologie. ᵀ*Bertz* August. Z 1989, Benziger.   266 p. DM 38. – ᴿTGL 80 (1990) 96 (W. *Beinert*: keineswegs 'Einführung'; 'Bertz').

7120 *Frame* John M.,   Christianity and contemporary epistemology [*Pollock* L., 1986; the (1963 Edmund) 'GETTIER problem': Is justified belief true knowledge?]:   WestTJ 52 (1990) 131-141.

7121 **Fries** Heinrich,   Teologia fondamentale [1985], ᵀ: BiblTeolContemporanea 53, 1987 ⋙ 4,8144; 88-399-0353-4:   ᴿGregorianum 71 (1990) 589s (R. *Fisichella*).

7122 **Gravem** Peder,   Gudstro og virkelighetservaring; den metafysiske gudstanke som problem i kristen gudslære, belyst ut fra G. EBELING, E. JÜNGEL og W. PANNENBERG: diss. Oslo 1988. – NorTTs 90 (1989) 50; judicia censorum 129-153 ⋙ 7155.

7123 *Gunton* Colin,   Using and being used; Scripture and systematic theology: TTod 47 (1990s) 248-259.

7124 **Hofmann** Peter,   Glaubensbegründung; die Transzendentalphilosophie der Kommunikationsgemeinschaft in fundamentaltheologischer Sicht [cf. ᴰ1987s ⋙ 4,8147*]: FraTSt 36. Fra 1988, Knecht.   352 p. – ᴿTPhil 65 (1990) 296s (H.-J. *Höhn*).

7125 **Huyssteen** Wentzel van,   Theology and the justification of faith; constructing theories in systematic theology, ᵀ*Snijders* H. F.   GR 1989, Eerdmans.   205 p. $19 pa. – ᴿInterpretation 44 (1990) 439-441 (G. R. *Lilburne*: philosophy-of-science methods).

7126 *Jiménez Ortiz* Antonio,   La teología fundamental frente al pensamiento de Karl JASPERS, en la obra de Heinrich FRIES: EstE 65 (1990) 299-315.

7127 **Kasper** Walter,   Teologia e Chiesa [1987]ᵀ: BTContemporanea 60.   Brescia 1989, Queriniana.   341 p. Lit. 38.000. – ᴿRivScR 3 (1989) 528-530 (M. *Semeraro*).

ᴱ**Kern** Walter,   Handbuch der Fundamentaltheologie 1985s ⋙ 846.

7128 **Krop** H. A.,   De status van de theologie volgens Johannes Duns SCOTUS; de verhouding tussen theologie en metafysica [Diss. Leiden, ᴰ*Adriaanse* H.]. Amst 1987, Rodopi. x-279 p. ƒ48. – ᴿTLZ 115 (1990) 45-47 (J. B. M. *Wissink*).

ᴱ**Küng** H., *Tracy* D.,   Paradigm change in theology 1980/9 ⋙ 637*.

7130 **Lash** Nicholas,   Easter in ordinary 1988 ⋙ 5,7019:   ᴿExpTim 101 (1989s) 88 (D. F. *Ford*: superb on role of experience in knowing God); JTS 41

(1990) 784-6 (G. M. *Jantzen*: splendid deconstruction of W. JAMES; good on BUBER; not looking to some extraordinary realm but finding the risen Christ in ordinary); Month 250 (1989) 30s (P. *Endean*).

7131 *a) Laurenzi* Maria Cristina, Aspetti della funzione teologica del paradosso; – *b) Staglianò* Antonio, Il compito della teologia tra cultura e saperi; riflessione sul problema epistemologico: RasT 31 (1990) 163-191 / 139-162.

7132 **Léonard** André, Cohérence de la foi; essai de théologie fondamentale. P 1989, Desclée. 162 p. – ᴿNRT 112 (1990) 255 (R. *Escol*).

7132* **Lightner** Robert P., Evangelical theology 1986 ➤ 3,6557: ᴿWestTJ 50 (1988) 222-6 (J. M. *Frame*: not quite right).

7133 **Maddox** Randy L., Toward an ecumenical fundamental theology [ᴰ1982]: [J]AAR 47, 1984 ➤ 1,6411; 4,9089: ᴿCalvinT 25 (1990) 74s (J. *Bolt*: a superb introduction).

7134 *Maddox* Randy L., The recovery of theology as a practical discipline: TS 51 (1990) 650-672.

7135 *a) Marlé* René, La question du pluralisme en théologie; – *b) Dumont* Camille, Enseignement de la théologie et méthode scientifique: Gregorianum 71 (1990) 465-486; Eng. 486 / 441-463; Eng. 463: 'science' cannot be applied univocally to theology, but neither can 'teach'.

7136 *Marlé* René, Il problema del pluralismo in teologia: CC 141 (1990,2) 521-534.

7137 **Marquardt** F. W., Vom Elend und Heimsuchung der Theologie 1988 ➤ 5,7148: ᴿComViat 33 (1990) 117s (J. *Smolik*); Orientierung 54 (1990) 78-80 (P. *Petzel*); Stromata 45 (1989) 237s.

7138 **Miranda** José Porfirio, Apelo a la razón; teoría de la ciencia y crítica del positivismo. S 1988, Sígueme. 508 p. – ᴿEfMex 8 (1990) 108-110 (J. F. *Gómez Hinojosa*).

7139 **Moltmann** Jürgen, Was ist heute Theologie? 1988 ➤ 4,8160 [Eng. ➤ 4,8161]: ᴿColcT 59,1 (1989) 178-180 (I.. *Balter*); TLZ 115 (1990) 53s (U. *Kühn*).

7140 **Mondin** Battista, Scienze umane e teologia 1988 ➤ 5,7150: ᴿHumBr 44 (1989) 905 (G. *Penati*); Salesianum 52 (1990) 179-181 (S. *Palumbieri*).

7141 *Mousse* Jean, Dogme et vérité, quelle conciliation: MélSR 47 (1990) 123-132; Eng. 133.

7142 ᴱNeufeld K., Problemas y perspectivas de teología dogmática [1983]: Verdad e Imagen 92, 1987 ➤ 5,7157: ᴿEfMex 8 (1990) 243-255 (J. J. *Herrera Aceves*); TVida 31 (1990) 69-76 (S. *Silva G.*).

7142* *O'Collins* Gerald, Catholic theology (1965-90): America 162 (1990) 86s. 104s (86-s, *Wister* R., USA; 79s, *O'Meara* T., doctoral programs).

7143 **Pauly** Wolfgang, Wahrheit und Konsens; die Erkenntnistheorie von Jürgen HABERMAS und ihre theologische Relevanz: Saarbrücker Theol. Forschungen 1. Fra 1989, Lang. v-385 p. Fs 80. – ᴿTLZ 115 (1990) 910-2 (W. *Pfüller*).

7144 **Pié i Ninot** Salvador, Tratado de Teología Fundamental 1989 ➤ 5,7162: ᴿBurgense 31 (1990) 268-270 (A. *Álvarez-Suárez*); EstE 65 (1990) 376s (J. J. *Alemany*); Salmanticensis 36 (1989) 235-7 (A. *González Montes*); ZkT 112 (1990) 110s (K. H. *Neufeld*).

7145 **Poythress** Vern S., Symphonic theology; the validity of multiple perspectives in theology 1987 ➤ 4,8170: ᴿSTEv NS 1 (1989) 214 (P. *Bolognesi*).

7146 **Ratzinger** J., Principles ... for a fundamental theology 1987 ➤ 3,281; 4,8173: ᴿJRel 69 (1989) 432s (E. *Borgman*).

7147 *Rossano* Pietro,   Compito e responsabilità della teologia [in occasione della sua laurea honoris causa, P Institut Catholique 23.III.1990]:   Lateranum 56 (1990) 1-9.

ᴱ**Ruggicri** Giuseppe,   Enciclopedia di Teologia Fondamentale 1987 ➤ 843.

7148 *Sauter* Gerhard,   Fundamentaltheologie — Grundlagenforschung oder Symptom einer Orientierungskrise?:   VerkFor 35,1 (1990) 30-40.

7149 *Scolas* Paul,   Pour une apologétique: RTLv 21 (1990) 55-69; Eng. 144, Defence of an Apologetics.

7150 **Seckler** Max,   Teologia, scienza, chiesa; saggi di teologia fondamenta le, ᵀᴱ*Coffele* Gianfranco 1988 ➤ 5,354: ᴿCC 141 (1990,1) 609s (J. *O'Donnell*); RivScR 3 (1989) 533 (G. *Ancona*).

7151 *a) Seckler* Max,   Die ekklesiologische Bedeutung des Systems der 'loci theologici'; erkenntnistheoretische Katholizität und strukturale Weisheit; *b) Lehmann* Karl,   Dogmengeschichte als Topologie des Glaubens; Programmskizze für einen Neuanfang: TJb (1989) 97-125 / 126-139 [140-177, *Pesch* O.].

7152 *Stavenga* G. J.,   Theologie als wetenschap: KcrkT 40 (1989) 268-279 [< ZIT 89,770].

7153 **Waldenfels** H.,   Kontextuelle Fundamentaltheologie 1985 ➤ 1,6448 ... 4,8190: ᴿNZMissW 44 (1988) 60-62 (F. *Frei*).

7154 **Waldenfels** H.,   Teologia fondamentale nel contesto del mondo contemporaneo. T 1987, Paoline,   742 p. – ᴿComm Sev 22 (1989) 267 (J. *Duque*); QVidCr 148s (1989) 231 (A. *Ferrer*).

7155 *a) Widmann* Peter,   Om teologiens teoretiske fundament; første officielle opposition ved Peder Gʀᴀᴠᴇᴍꜱ doktordisputation [➤ 7122]; – *b) Hafstad* Kjetil,   Skarpsindig spekulasjon i rasjonalitetens gevanter; andre opposisjon...: NorTTs 90 (1989) 129-142 / 143-153; cf. 50.

H2.1 **Anthropologia theologica – VT & NT.**

7156 **Álvarez Turienzo** Saturnino,   Regio media salutis; Imagen del hombre y su puesto en la creación, S. Aɢᴜꜱᴛíɴ: BibSalm Est. 108, 1988 ➤ 5,7173: ᴿSalmanticensis 37 (1990) 136s (J. L. *Ruiz de la Peña*).

7157 *Álvarez Turienzo* S.,   San Agustín; imagen de la Trinidad en su concepción antropológica: EstTrin 23 (1989) 31-56.

7157* **Badger** Carlton M.ᴶ,   The new man created in God; Christianity, congregation and asceticism in Aᴛʜᴀɴᴀꜱɪᴜꜱ of Alexandria: diss. Duke, ᴰ*Gregg* R. Durham ɴᴄ 1990. 305 p. 91-00092. – DissA 51 (1990s) 2781-A; RelStR 17,194.

7158 *Balducci* Ernesto,   La imagen del hombre que emerge del Concilio [Vat. II]; AnCalas 31 (1989) 477-482 [379-402, *Torres Queiruga* A.].

7159 *Barreto Betancort* J.,   Para una antropología bíblica; anotaciones sobre el ambito del 'Logos': Almogaren 1,2 (1988) 81-96 [< RET 50,119].

7159* **Bucher** Gérard,   La vision et l'énigme; éléments pour une Analytique du lógos [... principe explicatif de l'origine et de l'histoire humaine], préf. *Serres* Michel: La nuit surveillée. P 1989, Cerf. 474 p. F 146 [RTLv 22, 539, P. *Weber*].

7160 ᴱ**Bühler** Pierre,   Humain à l'image de Dieu 1985/9 ➤ 5,447: ᴱÉTRel 65 (1990) 200 (J. *Ansaldi*); Études 372 (1990) 570 (R. *Marlé*); Gregorianum 71 (1990) 591s (L. F. *Ladaria*); ZkT 112 (1990) 342s (K. H. *Neufeld*).

7161 *Cappelletti* Vincenzo,   Origini ᴄᴀʀᴛᴇꜱɪᴀɴᴇ dell'antropologia moderna: Clio 25 (R 1989) 559-570.

7162 **Cerutti** Maria Vittoria, Antropologia e Apocalittica: Storia delle Religioni 7. R 1990, Bretschneider. 194 p. 88-7062-706-3.

7163 *Ciola* Nicola, Un 'cantico' per l'uomo immagine di Dio; presentazione sistematica del pensiero del cardinale Pietro PAVAN ad opera di Mons. Franco BIFFI: Lateranum 56 (1990) 11-82.

7164 **Colombo** G., Conoscenza di Dio e antropologia. Mi 1988, Massimo. 159 p. Lit. 15.000. – ᴿRasT 31 (1990) 629s (L. *Borriello*).

7165 **Colzani** Gianni, *a*) Antropologia teologica; l'uomo paradosso e mistero 1989 → 5,7178: ᴿCarthaginensia 6 (1990) 221s (F. *Martínez Fresneda*); – *b*) Antropologia cristiana [1985 → 3,6614],ᵀ Assisi 1987, Cittadella. 267 p. – ᴿTeresianum 40 (1989) 594-6 (F. *Di Giacomo*).

7166 **Comblin** José, *a*) Retrieving the human; a Christian anthropology [1985 → 3,6614]. ᵀ*Barr* Robert R.: Theology and Liberation. Mkn 1990, Orbis. ix-259 p. [NewTR 4/3, 100, A. *Furnasari*]. $30; pa. $15. 0-88344-678-2; -57-X.

7167 **Conn** Walter, Christian conversion; a developmental interpretation of autonomy and surrender 1986 → 3,6616: ᴿCCurr 38 (1988s) 354-7 (Rosemary C. *Barciauskas*).

7167* *Cothenet* É., Corps psychique, corps spirituel: → 589, Liturgie et anthropologie 1989/90, 47-61.

7168 ᶠDEISSLER Alfons, Der Weg zum Menschen; Zur philosophischen und theologischen Anthropologie, ᴱ**Mosis** R., *al.*, 1989 → 5,45: ᴿTPhil 65 (1990) 589s (H.-W. *Jüngling*, unter 'Biblische Theologie').

7169 **Eruch** Anthony O., Vatican II; image of God in man; an inquiry into the theological foundations and significance of human dignity in the pastoral constitution on the Church in the modern world 'Gaudium et spes'. R 1987, Urbaniana. xxiv-324 p. – ᴿNRT 112 (1990) 262 (R. *Escol*).

7170 **Focant** Camille, La famille, de Jésus à saint Paul: Horizons de la Foi 26. Bru 1989, Connaître la Bible. 48 p. Fb 100. – ᴿRTLv 21 (1990) 95s (H. *Wattiaux*).

7171 *Fuchs* Stephen, The importance of anthropology for evangelisation: Indian Missiological Review 12,1 (Shillong 1990) 5-16 (17-28, *Godwin* C.); summary TContext 8/1,124.

7172 *Gesché* Adolphe, Dieu, preuve de l'homme [... l'homme, pour se comprendre, est toujours allé frapper à la porte des dieux]: NRT 112 (1990) 3-29.

7173 **Holscher** Ludger, The reality of the mind; AUGUSTINE's philosophical arguments for the human soul as a spiritual substance. L 1987, Routledge-KP. 342 p. $51. – ᴿJAAR 58 (1990) 287 (R. *Penaskovic*).

7174 **Hughes** P.E., The true image 1989 → 5,1984*.7190: ᴿEvangel 8,4 (1900) 21s (W.S. *Campbell-Jack*); KerkT 41 (1990) 155 (G. de *Ru*); ScotBEv 8 (1990) 148 (J.L. *McPake*).

7175 **Iammarrone** Giovanni, L'uomo immagine di Dio; antropologia e cristologia: RicTeol. R 1989, Borla. – ᴿQVidCr 154 (1990) 127 (J.-A. *Rocha*).

7175* **Kijas** Zdzisław, Dieu mesure de l'homme selon Paul A. FLORENSKY; esquisse d'une anthropologie théandrique orthodoxe: diss. ᴰ*Halleux* A. de. Louvain-la-Neuve 1990. 645-xxxiv p. (3 vol.) – RTLv 22, p. 147.619 & Travaux de doctorat 15/3.

7176 *Köhler* Theodor W., 'Dicendum est eum non esse hominem'; ein mögliches frühes Zeugnis für die anthropologische Gewichtung des Phänomens des reflexiven Selbstverhältnisses [... SCOTUS, AQUINAS; DESCARTES]: FreibZ 37 (1990) 30-50.

7177 **Johnson** Mark, The body in the mind; the bodily basis of meaning, imagination, and reason. Ch 1987, Univ. 233 p. $27.50. – ᴿJAAR 58 (1990) 503-6 (Susan E. *Henking*: co-author of Metaphors we live by 1980).

7178 **Langemeyer** Georg, Menschsein im Wendekreis des Nichts; Entwurf einer theologischen Anthropologie auf der Basis des alltäglichen Bewusstseins 1988 → 3,8224: ᴿBijdragen 51 (1990) 333 (U. *Hemel*).

7178* **Lee Sang Hoon,** The theological anthropology in the Second Council of Orange: diss. Drew, ᴰ*Pain* J. Madison NJ 1990. – RelStR 17,192.

7179 **Linke** D. B., *Kurten* M., Parallelität von Gehirn und Seele; Neurowissenschaft und Leib-Seele-Problem. Stu 1988, Enke. 108 p. – ᴿTPhil 65 (1990) 138-140 (H. *Goller*).

7180 *Lobato* Abelardo, La dignidad del hombre en santo Tomás de AQUINO: Carthaginensia 6 (1990) 139-153.

7181 **Nellas** Panayotis, Le vivant divinisé, anthropologie des Pères de l'Église, ᵀ*Palierne* Jean-Louis: Théologies, 1989 → 4,8230; 5,7195: ᴿArTGran 53 (1990) 327s (A. *Segovia*); Contacts 32 (1990) 226-231 [J. *Monchanin*]; NRT 112 (1990) 140s (B. P.); RTPhil 122 (1990) 565 (J. *Borel*); ScripTPamp 22 (1990) 623-5 (J. *Alviar*).

7182 *Onoh* Torty O., A critical analysis of the Old Testament doctrine of man and traditional religion: Theol. College of N. Nigeria Research Bulletin 20 (1989) 22-33 [< TContext 8/1,28].

7183 **Pannenberg** Wolfhart, Anthropologie 1983 → 64,6259 ... 5,7197: ᴿBijdragen 51 (1990) 92s (U. *Hemel*, deutsch).

7184 *Porter* Stanley E., Two myths; corporate personality and language/mentality determinism: ScotJT 43 (1990) 289-307.

7184* *Pröpper* Thomas, Das Faktum der Sünde und die Konstitution menschlicher Identität; ein Beitrag zur kritischen Aneignung der Anthropologie W. PANNENBERGS: TüTQ 170 (1990) 267-289; 289-298, Pannenbergs Antwort.

7185 *Richard* Jean, Anthropologie religieuse et theologie [*Meslin* M. 1988]: LavalTP 46 (1990) 383-402.

7185* *a) Rubin* Nissan, Body and soul in talmudic and mishnaic sources; – *b) Young* Allan, Psychiatry and self in Bible and Talmud; the example of posttraumatic stress disorder and enemy ḥerem [p. 200: *Press*: Talmud uses *moaḥ* for both brain and marrow; therefore both Bible and Talmud see the brain as fundamentally similar to the narrow within the long bones]: → 540*, Koroth 9 sp. (3d symposium 1987/8) 151-164 / 194-210.

7186 **Ruiz de la Peña** Juan L., Imagen de Dios, antropología teológica fundamental 1988 → 4,8243; 5,7202: ᴿAngelicum 67 (1990) 260s (A. *Lobato*); EfMex 8 (1990) 273-6 (M. *Ramirez* A.); EstE 65 (1990) 351-4 (L. *Vela*); ForumKT 6 (1990) 238s (A. *Ziegenaus*); RET 50 (1990) 95-97 (C. *García Andrade*); Salmanticensis 36 (1989) 238-240 (J. R. *Flecha*).

7187 *Ruiz de la Peña* J. L., Antropología cristiana: EstTrin 22 (1988) 413-426.

7188 **Sahagún Lucas** Juan de, El hombre, ¿quién es? 1988 → 4,8745: ᴿBurgense 31 (1990) 275s (E. *Bueno*); Salmanticensis 36 (1989) 241-3 (J. L. *Ruiz de la Peña*).

7189 **Sanna** Ignazio, Immagine di Dio e libertà umana; per un'antropologia a misura d'uomo. R 1990, Città Nuova. 312 p. Lit. 30.000. 88-311-3219-9. – ᴿGregorianum 71 (1990) 783s (L. F. *Ladaria*).

7189* **Schenk** Richard, Die Gnade vollendeter Endlichkeit; zur tranzendentaltheologischen Auslegung der thomanischen Anthropologie [Diss. Mü]: FreibTSt 135. FrB 1989, Herder. 538 p. DM 98. – ᴿZkT 112 (1990) 202-5 (K. H. *Neufeld*).

7190 **Schillebeeckx** Edward, Mensen als verhaal van God [Eng. → 7944]. Baarn 1989, Nelissen. 288 p. Fb 1900. – RCollatVL 20 (1990) 215-222 (J. De *Kesel*); TsTNijm 30 (1990) 417s (F. *Haarsma*) [+ 259-275, *ipse*].

7191 *Schmidt* Werner H., 'Was ist der Mensch?'; anthropologische Einsichten des Alten Testaments: GLern 4 (Gö 1989) 111-129 [< ZIT 90,62].

7191* *a) Schrey* Heinz-Horst, Leib, Leiblichkeit; - *b) Gloy* Karen, Leib und Seele: → 857, TRE 20 (1990) 638-643 / 643-9.

7192 *Théophane* père, Le mystère de la liberté dans l'homme déifié, selon Saint MAXIME le Confesseur: Contacts 32 (1990) 4-15.

7193 *Tornós* Andrés, Dimensión antropológica de la teología: MiscCom 48 (1990) 305-321.

7194 *Wolbert* Werner, Wann ist der Mensch ein Mensch? Zur Frage nach Beginn und Ende personalen Lebens: MoralThJb 1 (Mainz 1989) 15-33 [< ZIT 90,192].

7195 **Zincone** Sergio, Studi sulla visione dell'uomo in ambito antiocheno 1985 → 5,7207: RScripTPamp 22 (1990) 248-252 (A. *Viciano*).

H2.8 Oecologia VT & NT – saecularitas.

7196 **Albertz** R., Der Mensch als Hüter seiner Welt; alttestamentliche Bibelarbeiten zu den Themen des konziliaren Prozesses [acht (seine?) Aufsätze: Gn 1; 20; 25; Lv 25; 1 K 21; Is 2,2-5...]: Tb 16. Stu 1990 Calwert. 144 p. DM 16,80 3-7668-3081-3 [BL 91,103, C. S. *Rodd*: OT for Christians].

7197 EAltner Günter G., Ökologische Theologie; Perspektiven zur Orientierung 1989 → 5,429*: RÖkRu 39 (1990) 252s (H. *Zillasser*; Rubrik 'Konziliarer Prozess'); TsTNijm 30 (1990) 315s (T. J. van *Bavel*).

7198 *Álvarez* Andrés S., Respuesta ética al desafio ecológico: NatGrac 37 (1990) 81-104.

7199 **Barros** M., *Caravias* J. L., Teología de la tierra 1989 → 5,7214: RCarthaginensia 6 (1990) 232s (F. *Martínez Fresneda*).

7200 *Bartl* Klaus, Schwerpunkte der Säkularisierungsdebatte seit F. GOGARTEN; [cf. D1989 → 5,7214*]; ein Literaturbericht: VerkF 35,1 (1990) 41-61.

7201 **Bateson** Gregory [1904-1980], Ökologie des Geistes; anthropologische, psychologische, biologische und epistemologische Perspektiven, THoll Hans G.: TbWiss 571. Fra 1985, Suhrkamp. 675 p. DM 24. 3-518-28171-2. – RBijdragen 51 (1990) 104s (U. *Hemel*, deutsch).

7201* *Beek* A. van de, Descriptief en prescriptief in de ecologische discussie: NedTTs 43 (1989) 21-30; Eng. 52.

7202 **Berry** Thomas, The dream of the earth. SF 1988, Sierra. 241 p. $19. – RCCurr 38 (1988s) (P. *Heinegg*).

7203 *a) Berthouzoz* Roger, Pour une éthique de l'environnement; la responsabilité des chrétiens dans la sauvegarde de la crèation; – *b) Siegwalt* Gérard, La crise écologique, un défi pour la pensée, pour la foi et pour la praxis: → 677, Environnement, 1988, SuppVSp 169 (1989) 43-87 / 88-100.

7204 **Binns** Emily, The world as creation: Zacchaeus. Wilmington c. 1990, Glazier. 104 p. $5 pa.

7205 **Bradley** Ian, God is green. L 1990, Darton-LT. 118 p. £7. 0-232-51870-X. – RExpTim 101, 11 top choice (1989s) 321s (C. S. *Rodd*: weak on Hebrew and OT, but makes an urgent case against the claim that Christianity led to ecological disaster).

7206 *Breytenbach* Cilliers,   Glaube an den Schöpfer und Tierschütz: EvT 50 (1990) 343-356 [> NSys 33,93].

7207 **Carpenter** James A.,   Nature and grace; toward an integral perspective. NY 1988, Crossroad. 224 p. $22.50. 0 8245-0858-0. – ᴿInterpretation 44 (1990) 212.214 (G. *Fackre*); JPsy&T 17 (1989) 183s (J. D. *Carter*).

7208 *Caviglia* Giovanni,   Gesù Cristo centro del cosmo e della storia; in lui trova vera luce il mistero dell'uomo: Salesianum 52 (1990) 333-401.

7208* **Chalier** Catherine,   L'alliance avec la nature. P 1989, Cerf. 212 p. F 146. – ᴿEsprVie 100 (1990) 80 (J. *Crépin*).

7209 *Christiansen* Drew,   Ecology, social justice, and development: TS 51 (1990) 64-81.

7210 *Coleman* John A.,   The secular; a sociological view: Way 30 (1990) 16-25.

7212 **Coste** René,   Paix, justice, gérance de la création. P 1989, Nouvelle Cité. 168 p. F 85. – ᴿEsprVie 100 (1990) 78s (L. *Barbey*).

7213 *Daecke* Sigurd M.,   Missbrauch der Natur als Missbrauch Gottes; Überlegungen zu einer ökologischen Theologie: EvKomm 23 (1990) 653-6 [-8, *Glüder* D., 5 Bücher].

7214 **Dombrowski** Daniel A.,   HARTSHORNE and the metaphysics of animal rights.   Albany 1988, SUNY. 159 p. – ᴿJRel 69 (1989) 430s (P. E. *Devenish*).

7215 *a*) *Dreitcer* Andrew D.,   A new creation; – *b*) *Blewett* Jane,   Social justice and creation spirituality; – *c*) *Clarke* Thomas E.,   Creational spirituality: Way 29 (1989) 4-12 / 13-25 / 68-80.

7218 *Falcke* Heino,   Die theologischen Leitworte im konziliaren Prozess: Umkehr, Schalom und Bund: Diakonia 20 (1989) 297-305 [289-296, *Blasberg-Kuhnke* Martina].

7219 *Fantino* Jacques,   El hombre verdadero según san IRENEO: EstTrin 23 (1989) 3-30.

7219* *Fernández del Riesgo* Manuel,   Secularización y postmodernidad (secularidad versus secularismo y la crisis de la ética civil):   EstAg 25 (1990) 525-574.

7220 *a*) *Gläser* Bernhard,   Ganzheitlichkeit im Umweltschutz — mehr als nur ein Schlagwort?; – *b*) *Bierter* Willy,   Vom Umweltschutz zur Naturpolitik: Universitas 45 (1990) 105-113 / 114-132.

7221 *Gómez Hinojosa* José F.,   De la ecología a la ecofilía: EfMex 8 (1990) 25-56.

7222 *Gradl* Felix,   Alttestamentlicher Schöpfungsglaube und seine Konsequenz für die Beziehung zwischen Mensch und Natur: FranzSt 71 (1989) 42-57.

7223 **Halkes** C. J. M.,   *a*) ... en alles zal werden herschapen; gedachten over de heelswording van de schepping in het spanningsveld tussen natuur en cultuur. Baarn 1989, Ten Have. 192 p. *f* 27.50. – ᴿTsTNijm 30 (1990) 104 (T. J. van *Bavel*); – *b*) Das Antlitz der Erde erneuern: Siebenstern. Gü 1990. – ᴿOrientierung 54 (1990) 151 (Johanna *Jäger-Sommer*).

7224 *Hay* Donald A.,   Christians in the global greenhouse [release of CO_2 in cars and sprays; ... a biblical ethic for the environment]: TyndB 41 (1990) 109-127.

7225 *Hilpert* Konrad,   Verantwortung für die Erhaltung der natürlichen Umwelt?: TGegw 33 (1990) 37-54 [-64, Tierethik (... STEFFAHN Harald 1987) *Spiegel* Egon].

7226 *Hoeckman* Remi,   The ecological degradation; a challenge to religious: Angelicum 67 (1990) 57-72 [69s, OT; 71s, NT].

7227 *Honings* Bonifacio, L'ecologia nel pensiero di GIOVANNI PAOLO II: Lateranum 56 (1990) 355-363.

7228 **Hyland** J. R., The slaughter of terrified beasts; a biblical basis for the humane treatment of animals. Sarasota 1988, Viatoris. 74 p. $8.50. – ᴿBibTB 20 (1990) 40s (K. L. *Eades*).

7229 *a) Ignatios* IV., Patriarch von Antiochien, Die Schöpfung bewahren; – *b) Lemmel* Monika [dazu], 'Alles Vergängliche ist nur ein Gleichnis'; – *c) Pfürtner* Stephen H., Bevölkerungswachstum und die Zukunft der Erde; – *d) Geldbach* Erich, Wider die Resignation im konziliaren Prozess; – *e) Planer-Friedrich* Götz, Ekklesiologische Desiderata des Konziliaren Prozesses: UnSa 45 (1990) 194-210 / 211-8 / 225-237 / 238-258 / 259-261.

7230 *Kasper* Walter, Natur-Gnade-Kultur; zur Bedeutung der modernen Säkularisierung: TüTQ 170 (1990) 87-97.

7231 *Keler* Hans von, 'Machet euch die Erde untertan'; Schöpfungsethik in der Krise: Zeitwende 60 (1989) 143-7 [< ZIT 89,597].

7232 *Kelly* Tony, Wholeness; ecological and catholic?: Pacifica 3 (1990) 201-223.

7233 **Kirchoff** Hermann, Sympathie für die Kreatur; Mensch und Tier in biblischer Sicht. Mü 1987, Kösel. 98 p. DM 19,80. – ᴿTGegw 33 (1990) 55-58 (E. *Spiegel*).

7233* **Kleckley** Russell, Omnes creaturae sacramenta; creation, nature, and world view in LUTHER's theology of the Lord's Supper: ev. Diss. ᴰ*Schwarz*. München 1989s. – TR 86 (1990) 517.

7234 **Krolzik** Udo, Säkularisierung der Natur; Providentia-Dei-Lehre und Naturverständnis der Frühaufklärung 1988 → 5,7233: ᴿHerdKor 43 (1989) 338 (A. S.).

7235 *a) Labuschagne* C. J., Het bijbelsc scheppingsgeloof in ecologisch perpectief; – *b) Bavel* T. J. van, De kerkvaders over de schepping; aanzet tot christelijke uitbuiting van de natuur?; – *c) Houtepen* Anton, 'Integrity of creation'; naar een ecologische scheppingstheologie: TsTNijm 30 (1990) 5-17; Eng. 17 / 18-33 / 51-75; Eng. 75 [34-50, *Laarhoven* Jan van, Visics van HILDEGARD].

7236 **Linzey** Andrew, *Regan* Tom, Animals and Christianity. L 1989, SPCK. 210 p. £13. 0-281-04373-6. – ᴿExpTim 101 (1989s) 57 (C. S. *Rodd* praises though noting use of Bible without hermeneutics or evolution).

7237 **Lønning** Per, Creation — an ecumenical challenge? Reflections issuing from a study by the Institute for Ecumenical Research, Strasbourg, France. Macon GA / Lv 1989, Mercer Univ. / Peeters. viii-272 p. $32 [CBQ 52,590].

7238 *Love* Janice, Der konziliare Prozess, der ÖRK und die Zukunft der ökumenischen Bewegung: ÖkRu 39 (1990) 396-414 [389-396, *Hempel* Johannes].

7239 **McDonagh** Sean, The greening of the Church. L/Mkn 1990, Chapman/ Orbis. x-227 p. $17. 0-225-66586-7 / Mkn 0-88344-694-4. – ᴿExpTim 102,1 2d-top choice (1990s) 2s (C. S. *Rodd*).

7240 *Maldamé* Jean-Michel, Place de l'homme dans l'univers: RThom 90 (1990) 109-131.

7241 *Mayer* Rainer, Was bedeutet das: 'konziliarer Prozess'? Zeitwende 61,1 (Karlsruhe 1990) 1-9 (-19) [< ZIT 90,330].

7242 *Meyer* Ben F., In tune with a world that is good; variations on the theme of authenticity: TorJT 6 (1990) 3-14.

7243 *Modler* Peter, Pierre TEILHARD de Chardin und die ökologische Frage [... America 78s (1947s)]: TPhil 65 (1990) 234-245.

7244 **Moltmann** J., Gott in der Schöpfung 1985 ➤ 1,6536...5,7241: ᴿFranz-
St 71 (1989) 229s (J. *Schlageter*).

7245 **Moltmann** J., Dieu dans la création 1988 ➤ 4,8282; 5,7242: ᴿÉglT 20
(1989) 489-491 (J. R. *Pambrun*); EstE 65 (1990) 112s (R. *Franco*); Foi-
Temps 19 (1989) 398s (H. *Thomas*); NRT 112 (1990) 610s (B. *Pottier*);
Téléma 15,2 (1989) 81s (R. De *Haes*); TVida 30 (1989) 150s (C. *Casale
Rolle*).

7246 **Moltmann** J., Dios en la creación 1987 ➤ 4,8283; 5,7243; ᴿCiTom 117
(1990) 155s (E. *García*).

7247 **Moltmann** Jürgen, La giustizia crea futuro; una politica ispirata alla
pace e un'etica fondata sulla creazione in un mondo minacciato [Ge-
rechtigkeit schafft Zukunft, Mü/Mainz 1989, Kaiser/Grünewald],ᵀ: GdT
193. Brescia 1990, Queriniana. 142 p. Lit. 12.000. 88-399-0693-2. – ᴿGregorianum 71 (1990) 790s (J. *Joblin*).

7248 **Moltmann** Jürgen, Creating a just future; the politics of peace and
the ethics of creation in a threatened world. L/Ph 1989, SCM/Trin-
ity. 104 p. £4.50. 0-334-01909-5. – ᴿExpTim 101 (1989s) 349s (K. W.
Clements).

7249 *Moltmann* Jürgen, Para una reforma ecológica [< EvKomm 21,1 (1988)
35-38], ᵀᴱ*Aleu* J.: SelT 29 (1990) 207-211.

7250 *Mortensen* Viggo, Naturen som utfordring til etikken; fra naturviden-
skabelig etik til økologisk etik: NorTTs 91 (1990) 23-39.

7251 **Murphy** Charles M., At home on earth; foundations for a Catholic ethic
of the environment. NY 1989, Crossroad. xx-180 p. $16. 0-8245-0966-8
[TDig 37,279].

7252 *Murray* R., The Bible on God's world and our place in it: Christian
Jewish Relations 22,2 (L 1989) 50-59 [< NTAbs 34 p. 207 = 33 n. 366];
7-25 *Solomon* N.; 26-36, *Ariarajah* S.

7255 *Newbigin* Lesslie, Evangelisatie in de context van secularisatie, ᵀ*Spij-
kerboer-Mons* A. C. M.: KerkT 41 (1990) 269-277.

7256 **Osborn** L., Stewards of creation; environmentalism in the light of
biblical teaching: Latimer Studies 34. Ox 1990, Latimer. 60 p. £1.75. 0-
946307-33-4 [BL 91, 119, R. *Hammer*].

7257 **Pannenberg** Wolfhart, *a*) Christentum in einer säkularisierten Welt. FrB
1988, Herder. 79 p. DM 10,80. 3-451-21244-7. – ᴿColcT 59,1 (1989)
180s (L. *Balter*); LebZeug 44 (1989) 149s (U. *Lück*); Tablet 244 (1990) 424
(M. P. *Gallagher*); TR 86 (1990) 7-9 (G.-L. *Müller*). – *b*) Christianity in a
secularized world 1989 ➤ 5,7247; $12: ᴿWestTJ 52 (1990) 383-5 (R.
Letham: 25 c per page of text; some ideas seeming weak in comparison
with others on offer today turn out worth considering).

7258 ᴱ**Peters** T., Cosmos as creation; theology and science in consonance.
Nv 1989, Abingdon. 288 p. 0-687-09655-3. – ᴿExpTim 101 (1989s) 317
(J. *Polkinghorne*).

7259 *Raiser* Konrad, 'Eine Hoffnung lernt gehen'; Zwischenbilanz des konziliaren Prozesses für Gerechtigkeit, Frieden und Bewahrung der Schöpfung: ÖkRu 39 (1990) 77-94.

7260 *a*) *Rajotte* Freda, Justice, peace, and the integrity of creation: RelEdn
85,1 ('Religious education and the integrity of creation' 1990) 5-14 (-50,
al.) [< ZIT 90,360]; – *b*) Justice, peace and the integrity of creation
resource materials 1988: ᴿCurrTMiss 17 (1990) 311s (R. *Fernández-
Callenes*).

7261 **Ringeling** Hermann, Leben im Anspruch der Schöpfung [teils neue
Aufsätze] 1988 ➤ 5,7251: ᴿMüTZ 41 (1990) 107-9 (B. *Irrgang*); TPhil 65
(1990) 475s (K. *Schanné*).

7262 *a*) *Robert* Philippe de, Perception de la nature et confession du créateur selon la Bible hébraïque; – *b*) *Gabu* Jean-Paul, Pour une nouvelle doctrine du Dieu créateur et de la création; – *c*) *Tavardon* Paul, La doctrine de la création selon ORIGÈNE dans la mouvance platonicienne: ÉTRel 65 (1990) 49-57 / 77-91 / 59-76.

7263 *Roshwald* Mordecai, Man and universe in Greek and Hebrew perception: Judaism 38 (1989) 63-73.

7264 *Ross-Bryant* Lynn, The land in American religious experience: JAAR 58 (1990) 333-355.

7264* *a*) *Salas* Antonio, La ecología; perspectiva sociológica — perspectiva religiosa; – *b*) *Folgado Flórez* Segundo, Ecología y teología; desde la fe en la (re-) creación; – *c*) *Cañellas* Gabriel, Ecología; creación y 'tierra prometida'; – *d*) *Gallego* Epifanio, Ecología; evangelio y 'nueva creación'; – *e*) *Bennassar* Bartomeu, Ecoética; la ecología, desafío a la moral; la ética, salvación de la ecología: BibFe 16,47 (1990) 160-191 / 192-215 / 216-240 / 241-264 / 265-300.

7265 *Salvati* Giuseppe M., Crisi ecologica e concezione cristiana di Dio: Sapienza 43 (1990) 145-160.

7266 *Salvoldi* Valentino, 'Gli hai dato potere sull'opera delle tue mani': Presbyteri 23 (1989) 179-190.

7266* *a*) *Schaeffer* Jill, The liberation of creation: EcuR 42 (1990) 61-67. – *b*) *Schümmer* Léopold, Justice, paix et sauvegarde de la création chez CALVIN: Irénikon 63 (1990) 47-62. 186-198; Eng. 62.198.

7267 **Schupp** Franz, Schöpfung und Sünde; von der Verheissung der wahren und gerechten Welt, vom Versagen der Menschen und vom Widerstand gegen die Zerstörung. Dü 1990, Patmos. xiv-608 p. DM 50. – ᴿTGL 80 (1990) 522s (W. *Beinert*: 'not just another book on ecology' — but rather that than Gn 1-3).

7267* *Selling* Joseph A., Reflections on the 'conciliar process' from Basel to Seoul ... and back: Bijdragen 51 (1990) 290-313; p. 311 n. 4, 'The use of the term "conciliar process" [nowhere here defined, though loosely equated with ('Movement for) Peace with Justice for the whole creation'] has been controversial ... The RC and Orthodox traditions have particular problems ... because of the ecclesial and juridical connotations of the term "conciliar"; [Basel document itself states] some "churches taking part in the assembly prefer not to use 'conciliar process,'" ... but it has gained much acceptance, even within the RC community, "informally"'.

7268 *Silva* G. Sergio, La naturaleza en los Evangelios: → 125, ᶠMORENO/ VILLEGAS 1990, 67-104.

7269 *Streithofen* Heinrich B., Vom Umgang mit Tieren und Menschen; zum Verhältnis von Jägern und Tierschützern: Neue Ordnung 44,1 (Walberberg 1990) 67- ... [< ZIT 90,269].

7270 **Tanner** Kathryn, God and creation in Christian theology; tyranny or empowerment 1988 → 4,8298; ᴿRelStR 16 (1990) 246 (P. C. *Hodgson*: on God-talk).

7271 **Thiele** Johannes, Die mystische Liebe zur Erde; Fühlen und Denken mit der Natur: Wege der Mystik. Stu 1989, Kreuz. 269 p. 3-7831-0976-0. – ᴿActuBbg 27 (1990) 212s (J. *Boada*).

7272 **Toolan** David, Facing west from California's shores; a Jesuit's journey into New Age consciousness. NY 1987, Crossroad. xii-337 p. $20. [RelStR 17/2, 215, Mary F. *Bednarowski*, also on M. FOX and 12 other New Age or ecology books].

7273 *a*) *Vischer* Lukas, 'Rechte künftiger Generationen — Rechte der Natur'; – *b*) *Moltmann* Jürgen, *Giesser* Elisabeth, Menschenrechte, Rechte der

Menschheit und Rechte der Natur: EvT 50 (1990) 433-6 (468-471) [al. 444-468] / 437-444.

7274 **Werner** Hans Joachim, Eins mit der Natur; Mensch und Natur bei FRANZ von Assisi, Jakob BÖHME, Albert SCHWEITZER und Pierre TEILHARD de Chardin: Schwarze Reihe 309. Mü 1986, Beck. 164 p.; 4 fig. DM 19,80. – ᴿTLZ 115 (1990) 842s (H. H. *Jenssen*: klar, lesbar).

7275 *Williams* M. D., Regeneration in cosmic context: EvJ 7,2 (Myerstown PA 1989) 68-80 [< NTAbs 34,298].

7275* **Wybrow** C., The Bible, Baconianism, and mastery over nature: diss. McMaster, ᴰ*Greenspan* L. Hamilton ON 1990. – RelStR 17,191.

7276 *Zils* Diethard, Die Kirche als Raum der Sorge für Gerechtigkeit, Frieden und Bewahrung der Schöpfung: WAntw 31,1 (Mainz 1990) 5-13 [< ZIT 90,248].

7277 **Zwillenberg** Lutz O., Zwischen Bit und Bibel [die Natur — ein Brückenschlag im Zeitalter der Informatik]. Bern 1986, Hallwag. 225 p. [KirSef 62 (1988s) p. 42].

H3.1 *Foedus* – **the Covenant;** the Chosen People.

7277* **Adler** Elaine J., The background for the metaphor of covenant as marriage in the Hebrew Bible, diss. California, ᴰ*Milgrom* J. Berkeley 1990. 471 p. 91-03623. – DissA 51 (1990s) 3094-A.

7278 *Au* Joseph, ☻ The ambivalence of Jews and Gentiles in salvation history: ColcFuJen 84 (1990) 171-201.

7279 a) *Cook* Robert R., Divine foreknowledge; some philosophical issues: VoxEvca 20 (1990) 57-72; – b) *Viney* Donald W., Does omniscience imply foreknowledge? CRAIG on HARTSHORNE: ProcSt 18 (1989) 30-37 [< ZIT 90,191].

7280 **Damrosch** David, The narrative covenant 1987 ➤ 3,6734 ... 5,7266: ᴿCritRR 2 (1989) 157-160 (R. C. *Culley*: largely Mesopotamian); JAOS 110 (1990) 340-3 (J. *Van Seters*: aim commendable, result disheartening); JRel 70 (1990) 251s (H. *Marks*); PerspRelSt 17 (1990) 183-6 (L. M. *Bridges*, also on *Hanson* D., 'People called').

7281 a) *Gołębiewski* Marian, ☻ L'unité et la continuité de l'idée d'alliance; – b) *Muszyński* Henryk, ☻ La permanence de la première alliance: AtKap 114 (1990) 17-30 / 171-182.

7282 **Graafland** C., Van CALVIJN tot BARTH; oorsprong en ontwikkeling van de leer der verkiezing in het Gereformeerd Protestantisme 1987 ➤ 5,7269: ᴿKerkT 41 (1990) 131-141 (E. *Dekker*, H. *Veldhuis*: 'Van Calvijn tot BERKHOF'); NedTTs 43 (1989) 158s (N. T. *Bakker*).

7283 **Høgenhaven** J., Den gamle pagt; en introduktion til den nyere debat om pagten i Det gamle Testamente: Tekst og Tolkning 8. K 1990, Akademisk. 98 p. Dk 98. 87-500-2883-9 [BL 91,112, K. *Jeppesen*]. – ᴿNorTTs 91 (1990) 253s (A. S. *Kapelrud*).

7284 **Kaufman** Y., Christianity and Judaism, two covenants [1929s] ᵀ*Efroymson* C. W. J 1988, Magnes. xi-230 p. $20. – ᴿRB 97 (1990) 141 (B. T. *Viviano*).

7285 a) *Klenicki* Léon, Peuple choisi; une perspective juive contemporaine [réponse *Fisher* E. J.]; – b) *McDade* John, L'alliance juive garde sa validité; – c) *Kessler* Colette, L'alliance; une lecture juive: Sidic 23,3 (1990) 8-14 [15-17] / 18-23 / 2-7.

7287 **Lohfink** Norbert, Der niemals gekündigte Bund; exegetische Gedanken zum christlich-jüdischen Dialog 1989 ➤ 5,7274: ᴿGeistL 63 (1990) 154

(P. *Imhof*); KIsr 5 (1990) 182s (Julie *Kirchberg*); TLZ 115 (1990) 669s (L. *Wächter*: Titel aus einer Äusserung von JOHANNES PAUL II. 1980); TPQ 138 (1990) 180s (J. *Marböck*); TsTNijm 30 (1990) 200 (L. *Grollenberg*); ZAW 102 (1990) 154s (H.-C. *Schmitt*, auch über 'Unsere neuen Fragen' 1989); ZMissRW 74 (1990) 156s (G. *Steins*).

7288 *Lohfink* Norbert, Bundestheologie im Alten Testament; zum gleichnamigen Buch von Lothar PERLITT [1973, [R]unveröffentlicht]: → 265, Studien zum Dt 1990, 325-361.

7289 **McComiskey** Thomas E., The covenants of promise 1985 → 1,6578 ... 4,8316: [R]JStOT 17 (1990) 116s (R. S. *Hess*).

7290 *a) Mooney* Christopher F., Cybernation, responsibility, and providential design: TS 51 (1990) 286-309; – *b) Talbott* Thomas, Providence, freedom, and human destiny: RelSt 26 (1990) 227-245.

7291 *a) Newman* Murray L., The continuing quest for the historical covenant: → 82, [F]HUNT J., Psalms 1990, 158-171; – *b) Ska* Jean-Louis, Popolo sacerdotale e popolo dell'alleanza nell'Antico e Nuovo Testamento: → 607, Laici 1988/90, 19-38.

7292 **Nicholson** Ernest W., God and his people; covenant... 1986 → 2,5342 ... 5,8318 (pa. 1988): [R]BZ 34 (1990) 296-8 (N. *Lohfink*); JRel 69 (1989) 233s (E. F. *Campbell*).

7293 **Poole** David, De foedere Dei; the history of the covenant concept from the Bible to Johannes CLOPPENBURG: Diss. [D]*Heron*. Erlangen 1989s. 393 p. – TR 86 (1990) 514; RTLv 22, p. 599.

7293* **Stüben** Joachim, Das Heidentum im Spiegel von Heilsgeschichte und Gesetz; ein Versuch über die Paganitas im Werk des AMBROSIASTER: Diss. Hamburg 1990. – RTLv 22, p. 598.

H3.3 *Fides in VT* – **Old Testament faith.**

7294 **Dumbrell** W. J., The faith of Israel 1988 → 4,8328; 5,7286*: [R]Andr-UmS 28 (1990) 94s (W. H. *Shea*); GraceTJ 10 (1989) 243s (M. *Grisanti*); Themelios 16 (1990s) 22 (R. L. *Hubbard*).

7295 *Goldstein* J. A., Even the righteous can perish by his faith: ConsJud 41,3 (NY 1989) 57-70 [< NTAbs 34,69].

H3.5 *Liturgia, spiritualitas VT* – **OT prayer.**

7296 *Adler* R. J., The rabbinic development of Rosh Hashanah: ConsJud 41,2 (1988s) 34-41 [< NTAbs 34,218].

7297 [E]**Avril** Anne-Catherine, *La Maisonneuve* Dominique de, Prières juives: CahÉv 68 supp. P 1989, Cerf. 75 p. F 40. 0222-9706.

7298 [E]**Bonora** A., La spiritualità dell'AT [StSp → 854] 1987 → 5,7293: [R]RivB 38 (1990) 231-4 (F. *Festorazzi*: preferisce all'omonimo [E]*Fanuli* A., StSpG, salvo per alcune parti).

7299 [E]**Cattani** Luigi, La preghiera quotidiana d'Israele. T 1990, Gribaudi. 219 p. Lit. 22.000. – [R]PalCl 69 (1990) 608 (G. *Lavarda*: Cattani p. 608; Cattanei p. 1000).

7299* *Cazelles* Henri, L'homme devant Dieu: → 589, Liturgie 1989/90, 25-31.

7300 *Chmiel* Jerzy, ❷ Les racines juives de la liturgie chrétienne: AtKap 114 (1990) 51-62.

7301 **Cohn-Sherbok** Dan, Jewish petitionary prayer; a theological exploration: TorontoStT 35. Lewiston NY 1989, Mellen. 165 p. $50 [TDig 37,152].

7302 **Di Sante** Carmine, La preghiera di Israele 1985 ➤ 2,5358 ... 4,8335:
ᴿHumT 10 (1989) 133s (J. *da Silva Peixoto*).

7302* ᴱ**Fanuli** A., La Spiritualità dell'AT: StSpG [➤ 855] 1, 1989 ➤ 5,7295*:
ᴿAsprenas 37 (1990) 231-4 (A. *Rolla*).

7303 ᴱ**Fisher** E. J., The Jewish roots of Christian liturgy [15 art., all < SIDIC].
NY 1990, Paulist, v-202 p. $10. 0-8091-3132-3 [NTAbs 35,255].

7304 *Fleischer* Ezra, ❺ On the beginnings of obligatory Jewish prayer [not
early Maccabean as I. ELBOGEN 1913, nor through Second Temple times]:
Tarbiz 59 (1989s) 397-441; Eng. III-V.

7305 **Gammie** J. G., Holiness in Israel: OvBT 1989 ➤ 5,7297: ᴿBL (1990)
101 (R. E. *Clements*); Horizons 17 (1990) 321s (T. F. *Dailey*); HorBT 11,2
(1989) 107s (S. E. *Balentine*); NewTR 3,3 (1990) 105s (L. *Boadt*); TS 51
(1990) 366 (A. L. *Laffey*).

7306 *Gerstenberger* Erhard S., Riten zur persönlichen Lebensbegleitung im
Alten Testament: BLtg 62 (1989) 170-8.

7307 ᴱ**Green** Arthur, Jewish spirituality 1986 ➤ 2,5361 ... 5,7298; also L
1989, SCM; £17.50; 0-334-02427-7: ᴿExpTim 101 (1989s) 156s (F.
Morgan); HeythJ 31 (1990) 94s (L. *Jacobs*); TLond 93 (1990) 85s (B.
Ettlinger).

7308 *Hoffman* J., The ancient Torah service in light of the Realia of the
Talmudic era: ConsJud 42,2 (1989s) 41-48 [< NTAbs 34,361].

7309 **Hoffman** Lawrence [HUC rabbi], *a)* The art of public prayer; not for
clergy only. Wsh 1988, Pastoral. xiv-290 p. $20. – ᴿTS 51 (1990) 147s
(J. L. *Empereur*). – *b)* Beyond the text; a holistic approach to liturgy.
... 1987, Midland. $35. 0-253-31199-3 (pa. 10, Indiana Univ.). – ᴿCritRR
2 (1989) 396-8 (J. L. *Empereur*).

7309* *a)* *Hoffman* Lawrence A., The Jewish lectionary, the Great Sabbath,
and the Lenten calendar; liturgical links between Christians and Jews in
the first Christian centuries; – *b)* *Taft* Robert, A tale of two cities; the
Byzantine Holy Week Triduum as a paradigm of liturgical history:
➤ 175*, ꟳTALLEY T., Time 1990, 3-20 / 21-41.

7310 *Hoffmann* Daniel, Das Fest als Emphase der religiösen Existenz — die
Emphase als Wesensmerkmal der jüdischen Festtage: MüTZ 41 (1990)
119-136.

7311 **Jarach** Paola, Shemà Israel; l'ebreo orante 1988 ➤ 5,7802: ᴱCC 141
(1990,3) 326 (S. M. *Katunarich*); HumBr 44 (1989) 600s (M. *Orsatti*);
StEcum 7 (1989) 494 (L. *Pietrobelli*).

7312 **Kaplan** A., Las aguas del Eden; el misterio de la 'mikvah'. Bilbao 1988,
D-Brouwer. 108 p. – ᴿEstAgust 24 (1989) 255 (A. *Crespo*.

7313 *Külling* Samuel R., Manches steht in der Bibel — ohne (direkte) Worte
[... posture in prayer]: Fundamentum (Schweiz 1990,3) 4-7 [< OTAbs
14,135].

7314 *Maher* Michael, The *meturgemanim* and prayer [220 Pentateuch (targum)
versions; Sifre Dt gives 13 synonyms of 'prayer']: JJS 41 (1990) 226-246.

7315 **Manns** Frédéric, La prière d'Israël 1986 ➤ 2,5370 ... 5,7105: ᴿJQR 81
(1990s) 203-5 (R. S. *Sarason*).

7316 *Muchowski* P., ❻ The characteristics of Nazireat: Euhemer 152 (1989)
59-66 [< NTAbs 34,363].

7317 *Rabello* O. M., L'osservanza delle feste ebraiche nell'impero romano:
ScrClasIsr 6 (1982) 57-84.

7318 **Sestieri** Lea, La spiritualità ebraica: StNCr 4, 1987 ➤ 3,6782 ... 5,7310:
ᴿDivThom 92 (1989) 407s (M. *Belda*); HumT 11 (1990) 251 (H. *Alves*);
RThom 90 (1990) 162 (P.-M. *Fourcade*).

7318* a) Sestieri Lea, Le feste ebraiche; lo shabat; – b) Garrone Daniele, Attualità delle feste bibliche; – c) Alonso Schökel Luis, La teologia della festa nell'Antico Testamento; – d) Corsani Bruno, Le feste ebraiche nel Nuovo Testamento: ➔ 575*, Riscoperta 1990, 41-53. 55-67 / 77-88 / 67-76 / 89-101.

7319 Vigée Claude, La manna e la rugiada, feste della Torah 1988 ➔ 5,7312: ᴿCC 141 (1990,1) 204s (S. M. Katunarich).

7320 Wachs S. P., Aleinu [prayer]; rabbinic theology in biblical language: ConsJud 42,1 (1989) 46-49 [< NTAbs 34,226].

7321 Walter Wolfgang, Meinen Bund habe ich mit dir geschlossen; Jüdische Religion in Fest, Gebet und Brauch. Mü 1989, Kösel. 223 p. – ᴿZRGg 42 (1990) 187s (S. Ben-Chorin).

7322 a) Westermann Claus, Sacré et Sainteté de Dieu dans la Bible, ᵀLauret B.; – b) Buit M. du, La sainteté du peuple dans l'AT: VSp 143 (1989) 13-24 / 25-37.

7323 Williamson Hugh G. M., Laments at the destroyed temple... ancient Jewish prayers: BR 6,4 (1990) 12-17. 44; ill.

7324 Zahavy Tzvee, Studies in Jewish prayer. Lanham MD 1990, UPA. 192 p. $31.50 [JAAR 58,743].

H3.7 Theologia moralis VT – OT moral theology.

7325 Bleich J. David, Contemporary halakhic problems: Library of Jewish Law 4.10.16. NY 1983-9, KTAV. I. 1977, xviii-406 p.; II. 1983, xvii-423 p.; III. 1989, xv-415 p. 0-87068-450-7 [I.III.], -1-5 [II.]; pa. 0-88125-064-3. – ᴿExpTim 102 (1990s) 95 (F. Morgan, 3).

7326 a) Borowitz Eugene B., The Torah, written and oral, and human rights; foundations and deficiencies; – b) Walf Knut, Gospel, Church law, and human rights; – c) Garaudy Roger / Na'im Abdullahi A. an-, Islam...; – d) Mukerji Bithka, ... Hindu understanding: ➔ 402, Concilium (1990,2) 25-33 / 34-45 / 46-60. 61-69 / 70-78...

7327 Freund R. A., Some aspects of Jewish sexual ethics and Hellenism: JRefJud 36,4 (1989) 55-69 [< NTAbs 34,220].

7328 Goldstein Sidney, Suicide in rabbinic literature. Hoboken 1989, KTAV. xvi-128 p. $17. 0-88125-147-X. – ᴿExpTim 102 (1990s) 61 (Julia Neuberger).

7328* Gottlieb Claire, Varieties of marriage in the Bible and their analogues in the ancient world: diss. NYU 1989, ᴰGordon C. 238 p. 90-16265. – DissA 51 (1990s) 608-A.

7329 Hammer Reuven, The biblical perception of the origin of evil: Judaism 39 (1990) 318-325.

7330 Henriksen Jan-Olav, Ansvar som etisk prinsipp; tanker fra og omkring Hans JONAS' etikk: NorTTs 90 (1989) 155-169.

7331 Jakobovitz I., Los experimentos médicos con seres humanos en la legislación judía: Ética y ciencia 2 (BA 1988) 19-22 [< Stromata 45,498].

7332 Loewenstein Mark J., Jewish divorce and the secular law: Judaism 39 (1990) 7-13.

7333 a) Maier Johann, Torah und Pentateuch, Gesetz und Moral; Beobachtungen zum jüdischen und christlich-theologischen Befund: ➔ 154, ᶠSACCHI P. 1990, 1-54; – b) Sellès J.-M. Péché mortel et discipline juive de l'excommunication: ➔ 65*, ᶠGY P., Rituels 1990, 455-464.

7334 Oberforcher Robert, Alttestamentliche Ethik: ➔ 923, NLexMor 1990, 24-37.

7335 *a)* **Petsonk** Judy, *Remsen* Jim,   The intermarriage handbook; a guide for
Jews and Christians.   NY c. 1990, Morrow.   416 p. – *b)* **Rosenberg** Roy
A., *Meehan* Peter, *Payne* John,   Happily intermarried; authoritative
advice for a joyous Jewish-Christian marriage.   NY 1989, Macmillan.
246 p. – ᴿJudaism 39 (1990) 121-5 (G. *Hirschberg*).

7335* **Sanders** E. P.,   Jewish law from Jesus to the Mishnah.   L/Ph 1990,
SCM/Trinity.   404 p. £17.50.   0-334-02102-2. – ᴿExpTim 102 (1990s) 120
(C. *Middleburgh*).

7336 **Soete** A.,   Ethos der Rettung, Ethos der Gerechtigkeit; Studien zur
Struktur von Normbegründung und Urteilsfindung im AT und ihrer
Relevanz für die ethische Diskussion der Gegenwart [Diss. Bonn 1986,
ᴰ*Böckle* F.].   Wü 1987, Echter.   160 p. – ᴿStPatav 37 (1990) 166-171 (G.
Segalla).

7337 **Wright** C. J. H.,   Living as the people of God; the relevance of Old
Testament ethics.   Leicester 1989, Inter-Varsity.   224 p. £7. – ᴿOTEssays
3 (1990) 375s (P. J. *Nel*).

H3.8   *Bellum et pax VT-NT*   –   War and peace in the whole Bible.

7338 *Amalorpavadass* D. S.,   Towards a theology of peace; an Indian approach, understanding and experience of peace: IndTSt 26 (1989)
195-218.

7339 *Anna Maria* sr.,   Peace and justice in Scripture: RelLife 28,139 (Dublin
1989) 284-291 [< NTAbs 34,203].

7340 **Barbé** Dominique,   A theology of conflict and other writings on
nonviolence [24-47, a non-violent reading of the Bible; Cain and Abel...;
5-15, scapegoat, GIRARD R.].   Mkn 1989, Orbis.   xvii-181 p.; portr.
0-88344-546-8.

7340* **Beaude** Jean-F.,   Pour une théologie de la non-violence.   Montréal 1989,
Fides.   110 p. – ᴿLavalTP 46 (1990) 425s (M. *Dion*).

7341 ᴱ**Biffi** F.,   La pace sfida 1986/8 ⇒ 4,526:   ᴿNRT 112 (1990) 102s (L.
Volpe).

7342 **Budzik** Stanisław,   Doctor pacis... AUGUSTINUS 1988 ⇒ 5,7325:   ᴿTR
86 (1990) 212s (C. *Müller*).

7343 **Charalampidis** Kōstas P., ⊕ *Symbolikes parastaseis* of peace and hope in
the early Christian art.   Thessaloniki 1990, Pournaras.   267 p.; ill.

7344 *Cole* Penny J.,   JOHN of Abbeyville and a theology of war: TorJT 6
(1990) 56-62.

7345 *Coppenger* Mark,   The golden rule and war [peace has been more lethal
than war... war can be a mercy the enemy himself should wish for if he
were to become the lethal instrument of a wicked cause]: CriswT 4 (1989s)
295-312.

7346 **Dear** John,   Our God is nonviolent; witnesses in the struggle for peace
and justice.   NY 1990, Pilgrim.   xv-133 p. $11 pa.   0-8298-0853-3 [TDig
38,54].

7347 *Downing* F. Gerald,   Jesus of Nazareth in a nuclear age [*Wengst* K. ...]:
ScotJT 43 (1990) 207-223.

7348 *Drewermann* Eugen, *a)* Gewalt — und wie man damit umgeht; – *b)* Die
Denkmäler der Propheten oder Worum geht es eigentlich?:   RUntHö 33
(Dü 1990) 71-78 / 116-... [< ZIT 90,429s].

7349 **Guicherd** C.,   L'Église catholique et la politique de défense au début des
années 1960 [< diss. Genève].   Genève 1988, Inst. Hautes Études Internationales. – ᴿNRT 112 (1990) 93-97 (É. *Herr*).

7350 **Häring** Bernhard, La no violencia [1986 ➤ 5,7355],ᵀ. Barc 1989,
Herder. 230 p. – ᴿCarthaginensia 6 (1990) 340s (A. *Puigcerber*).

7351 *Helgeland* John, Civil religion, military religion, Roman and American:
Forum 5,1 (1989) 22-44.

7352 **Hobbs** T.R., A time for war; a study of warfare in the OT: OT studies
3. Wilmington 1989, Glazier. 248 p. $16 pa. 0-89453-656-7. – ᴿNewTR
3,3 (1990) 106s (L.J. *Hoppe*).

7353 **Johnson** James T., The quest for peace; three moral traditions in
western culture 1987 ➤ 4,8371: ᴿJRel 69 (1989) 131s (J. *Kelsay*).

7354 **Kang Sa-Moon,** Divine war: BZAW 177, 1989 ➤ 5,7339*: ᴿAndrUnS
28 (1990) 165-7 (H. K. *LaRondelle*); ArTGran 53 (1990) 303s (J. L. *Sicre*);
BLitEc 91 (1990) 288s (M. *Delcor*); ÉTRel 65 (1990) 266s (Françoise
Smyth); WestTJ 52 (1990) 372s (T. *Longman*).

7355 **Kaufman** Gordon D., Una teologia per l'era nucleare [1985],ᵀ: GdT 179.
Brescia 1988, Queriniana. 113 p. Lit. 11.000. 88-399-0679-7. – ᴿGregorianum 71 (1990) 380-2 (R. *Fisichella*: 'Non è facile tradurre un libro ...
suscita l'ilarità ... forse avremmo fatto bene a non continuare').

7356 **Küng** Hans, Projekt Weltethos. Mü 1990, Piper. 191 p. DM 19,80. –
ᴿUniversitas 45 (1990) 1215s (G. *Kleinschmidt*).

7357 **Labouérie** Guy, Dio di violenza o Dio di misericordia? Una lettura della
Bibbia [1982 ➤ 63,6270], ᵀ*Caré* Mario. T-Leumann 1984, Elle Di Ci.
238 p. Lit. 9000. 88-01-11653-5.

7358 **Lana** Italo, Studi sull'idea della pace nel mondo antico [Grecia, Roma,
mondo cristiano]: AcT, Mem mor/st/fg 5/13/1s (1989). 88 p. – ᴿHelmantica 41 (1990) 419s (J. *Oroz Reta*); Orpheus 11 (1990) 135s (F.
Corsaro); RÉLat 68 (1990) 238s (Antoinette *Novara*).

7358* *Lenihan* David A., The just war theory in the work of Saint
Augustine: AugSt 19 (1988) 37-70.

7359 **Lingen** Anton van de, Les guerres de Yahvé; l'implication de ʏʜᴡʜ
dans les guerres d'Israël selon les livres historiques de l'Ancien Testament:
LDiv 139. P 1990, Cerf. 280 p. F 185. 2-204-04069-X. – ᴿEsprVic 100
(1990) 686 (L. *Monloubou*); MondeB 66 (1990) 62 (M. *Berder*); RBibArg
52 (1990) 249-251 (J. P. *Martín*).

7360 **Lohfink** Norbert, Il Dio della Bibbia e la violenza [Gewalt und
Gewaltlosigkeit im AT: QDisp 96, 1983 ➤ 64,407*, solo contributi di
Lohfink] 1985 ➤ 3,6845: ᴿProtestantesimo 44 (1989) 225 (J. A. *Soggin*:
truncated part of QDisp 96, 'follows "the sociologist" Girard for the part
referring to sociology; then develops his own view, in two parts, Violenza
come tema nella ricerca vta. / Gli strati del Pent. e la guerra').

7361 *Lohfink* Norbert, Der gewalttätige Gott des Alten Testaments und die
Suche nach einer gewaltfreien Gesellschaft [adaptiert < Il Dio violento
dell'AT e la ricerca della società non-violenta: CC 155,3211 (1984,2)
30-48]: JbBT 2 (1987) 106-136.

7362 **McSorley** Richard, New Testament basis of peacemaking [¹1979] ³1985
➤ 1,6691: ᴿCriswT 3 (1989) 377s (C. L. *Blomberg*).

7363 **Maier** J., Krieg und Frieden sowie das Verhältnis zum Staat in der
Literatur des frühen Judentums: Beit. Friedensethik 9. Barsbüttel 1990,
Inst. Theol. & Frieden. 116 p. [ZAW 103, 303, H.-C. *Schmitt*].

7364 **Mantovani** Mauro, Bellum Iustum; die Idee des gerechten Krieges in
der römischen Kaiserzeit [Z hist. Seminar]: Geist und Werk der Zeiten
77. Fra 1990, Lang. xii-149 p. Fs 35. 3-261-04222-2.

7365 **Mayhew** Peter, A theology of force and violence. L/Ph 1989, SCM/
Trinity. xii-112 p. £6. – ᴿFurrow 40 (1989) 629-631 (M. K. *Duffy*: fa-

vors cautious use of violence); Month 250 (1989) 391 (M. *Lovell*: readably but too briefly treats a real problem).

7366 **Moltmann** J.,   Gerechtigkeit schafft Zukunft; Friedenspolitik in einer bedrohten Welt.   Mü/Mainz 1989, Kaiser/Grünewald.   130 p. DM 12. – ᴿMüTZ 41 (1990) 109-111 (B. *Irrgang*).

7366* *Oberforcher* Robert,   Verkundet das Alte Testament einen gewalttätigen Gott? Fundamentalistische Relikte im Umgang mit gewalttätigen Zügen im biblischen Gottesbild: ➤ 1416, Eindeutige Antworten? ²1988, 133-158.

7367 *Pinthus* E.I.,   The roots of the peace testimony in the message of the Bible: Friends' Quarterly 26,2 (Kent 1990) 54-63 [< NTAbs 34,350].

7368 ᴱ**Planer-Friedrich** Götz,   Frieden und Gerechtigkeit; auf dem Weg zu einer ökumenischen Friedensethik 1987/9 ➤ 5,723*: ᴿTLZ 115 (1990) 234s (G. *Krusche*).

7369 **Ramsey** Paul †,   Speak up for just war or pacifism, a critique of the United Methodist bishops' letter 'In defense of creation' 1988 ➤ 5,7349: ᴿJTS 41 (1990) 328-330 (O. *O'Donovan*: so good that it may give the bishops' undisciplined moralizing longer life than it deserves).

7370 *Reents* Christine,   'Schalom' und 'Heiliger Krieg'; neuzeitliche Verwendung und Ursprung in der hebräischen Bibel: CLehre 42 (1989) 132-140 [< zit 89,551].

7371 **Reuver** Marc,   Christians as peacemakers; peace movements in Europe and the USA. Geneva 1988, WCC. x-84 p. Fs 10.   2-8254-0928-6. – ᴿBijdragen 51 (1990) 447s (H. *Goddijn*).

7372 **Rousseau** Félicien,   Courage or resignation and violence; a return to the sources of ethics.   Montréal 1987, Bellarmin. 265 p. – ᴿTLZ 115 (1990) 139s (H. *Kress*).

7373 *a*) *Snyman* S. D.,   Geweld — 'n onopgeloste teologiese probleem vir die Ou Testament: NederduitsGT 11 (1990) 319-24 [< OTAbs 14,144]. – *b*) *Spanneut* Michel,   Saint Augustin et la violence: ➤ 182*, ᶠVEREECKE L., StMor 28 (1990) 79-113.

7374 *Soggin* J. Alberto, *a*) Krieg AT (*Hegermann* Harald NT): ➤ 857, TRE 20 (1990) 19-25 (25-28) [11-19. 28-55 *al.*]; – *b*) *Soggin,* Guerra 'santa' o 'guerra di* YHWH' nella Bibbia ebraica: ➤ 514*c*, Violenza 1990, 29-40.

7374* **Spiegel** E.,   Gewaltsverzicht 1987 ➤ 3,6859 ... 5,7351: ᴿVT 40 (1990) 375s (H. G. M. *Williamson*).

7375 **Stalter-Fouilloy** Danielle;   Histoire et violence; essai sur la liberté humaine dans les premiers écrits chrétiens: HPR Ét 70. P 1990, PUF. 160 p. [TPhil 65,632].

7375* **Stern** Philip D.,   A window on ancient Israel's religious experience; the *ḥerem* re-investigated and re-interpreted [Near Eastern 'order versus chaos' myth]: diss. NYU 1989, ᴰ*Levine* B.   299 p. 90-16309. – DissA 51 (1990s) 535-A; OIAc Oc90.

7376 **Tambasco** A. J.,   Blessed are the peacemakers 1989 ➤ 5,609: ᴿHorizons 17 (1990) 151s (W. H. *Osterle*); TS 51 (1990) 173 (L. T. *Johnson*).

7377 *Villiers* E. de,   Peace conceptions in South Africa in the light of the biblical concept of peace: Scriptura 28 (Stellenbosch 1989) 24-40 [< NTAbs 34,68].

7378 **Weigel** George,   Tranquillitas ordinis 1989 ➤ 3,6866 ... 5,7355: ᴿMonth 251 (1990) 72s (G. W. *Hughes*).

7379 **Wengst** Klaus,   Pax romana, ᵀ*Bowden* J.   1987 ➤ 3,6869 ... 5,7357: ᴿCritRR 2 (1989) 255-7 (E. G. *Weltin*); JEH 40 (1989) 253 (S. G. *Hall*: stimulating though conclusion is wrong; the title is wrongly given as

'Morality and ethics in early Christianity' p. 253, from *Womer* J. on same page); SecC 7 (1989s) 188-190 (C. A. *Bobertz*: reserves).

7380 **Will** James E., A Christology of peace 1989 → 5,7359: RHorBT 11,2 (1989) 109s (Carol F. *Jegen*); TS 51 (1990) 375s (M. L. *Cook*: better title 'Christ is our peace', Eph 2,14).

7381 *a*) *Wink* Walter, Is there an ethic of violence?; – *b*) *Haughton* Rosemary, Godly anger and beyond: Way 30 (1990) 103-113 / 114-123.

H4.1 – Messianismus.

7382 **Bauckham** Richard J., MOLTMANN, Messianic theology in the making 1987 → 4,k512: RScotBEv 8 (1990) 128s (C. M. *Cameron*).

7383 **Coppens** J., Le Messianisme ... ²1989 → 5,7363: RTLZ 115 (1990) 673s (R. *Martin-Achard,* franç.).

7384 *Cornițescu* Emilien, Messie — le Seigneur de la paix et de la justice, en roumain: STBuc 42/2 (1990) 5-19; franç. 142.

7385 **Kaut** Thomas, Befreier und befreites Volk: BoBB 77. Fra 1990, Hain. 360 p. DM 88.

7386 **Neusner** J., *al.,* Judaisms and their Messiahs 1987 → 4,494; 5,7368: RJSS 35 (1990) 152s (M. D. *Goodman*).

7387 **Neusner** J., Messiah in context 1984 → 65,6109 ... 3,6880: RAbrNahr 28 (1990) 139-142 (J. *Painter*).

7388 **Van Groningen** G., Messianic revelation in the Old Testament. GR 1990, Baker. 1018 p. $40. 0-8010-9307-4 [BL 91, 121, R. *Hammer*: exhaustive erudition, but most experts now would attribute to the later writer what he attributes to the characters portrayed].

7389 *Wiesel* Élie, Abenddämmerumg in der Ferne. FrB 1988, Herder. 260 p. DM 30. – REvKomm 23 (1990) 53s (R. *Boschert*: 'Messias in der Heilanstalt').

7390 *Wodecki* Bernard, ℗ The gradation of the messianic idea in the Bible: → 64, FGRZYBEK S. 1990, 356-367; Eng. 365.

H4.3 *Eschatologia VT* – OT hope of future life.

7391 *Bauckham* Richard, Early Jewish visions of hell [*Himmelfarb* M. 1983]: JTS 41 (1990) 355-385.

7392 **Blue** Lionel [Jewish radio talks] & *Magonet* Jonathan, The guide to the here and hereafter. L 1989, Collins Fount. 226 p. £3.50. 0-00-627043-3 [ExpTim 101,62].

7393 *Cortese* Enzo, Escatología del Antiguo Testamento [*Fohrer* G., *Von Rad* G. ...] y teología de la liberación: RBíbArg 51 (1989) 129-141.

7394 *Dillon* R. J., Death's sting; the Bible [... OT] and the funeral rite: Church 6,2 (1990) 13-17 [< NTAbs 34,348].

Ego Beate, Im Himmel wie auf Erden D1989 → a128.

7395 **Gowan** Donald E., Eschatology in the OT 1986 → 2,5445 ... 5,7371: RCriswT 3 (1988s) 210-2 (D. C. *Baker*).

7396 **Krieg** M., Todesbilder im AT: ATANT 73, 1988 → 4,8411; 5,7373: RBL (1990) 104s (J. R. *Porter*); ZAW 102 (1990) 153 (W. *Heinicke*).

7397 **Martin-Achard** Robert, La mort en face ... 1988 → 4,8414; 5,7374: RCBQ 52 (1990) 527s (M. *Kolarcik*: explicit belief in life after death appears mostly with apocalyptic: Is 65,20; 26,19, Job 19,25s; Dan 12,1s); ETL 66 (1990) 178 (J. *Lust*).

7398 **Mayer-Hirsch** Nechamah, Het huis van de levenden — Beth haChajem; joodse gebruiken bij de dood. Baarn 1989, Ten Have. 111 p., Fb. 398. – RCollatVL 20 (1990) 439s (E. Vanden *Berghe*).

7399 *Moor* Johannes C. de, Lovable death in the Ancient Near East: UF 22 (1990) 233-245.

7400 *Schmidt* Werner H., 'Denkt nicht mehr an das Frühere!'; eschatologische Erwartung — Aspekte des Alten Testaments: GLern 4,1 (Gö 1989) 17-32 [< ZIT 89,553].

H4.5   *Theologia totius VT* – **General Old Testament theology.**

7400* **Barthélemy** Dominique, Dieu et son image; ébauche d'une théologie biblique: Foi Vivante. P 1990, Cerf. 224 p. – REsprVie 100(1990) 622 (P. *Jay*).

7401 **EBen-Chorin** Schalom, *Lenzen* Verena, Lust an der Erkenntnis; jüdische Theologie im 20. Jahrhundert; ein Lesebuch. Mü 1988, Piper 879. 502 p. DM 29,80. – RTLZ 115 (1990) 195s (C. *Hinz*).

7402 *Cazelles* Henri, Théodicée et théologie bibliques: → 64, FGRZYBEK S. 1990, 33-44, en français.

7403 **Childs** Brevard S., OT theology in a canonical context 1988 → 3,6759 ... 5,7376: RHorizons 17 (1990) 320 (Mary C. *Callaway*); ZkT 112 (1990) 89s (R. *Oberforcher*).

7404 **Childs** Brevard S., Teologia dell'AT in un contesto canonico 1989 → 5,7377: RTItSett 15 (1990) 283-8 (P. *Rota Scalabrini*).

7405 *Cohen* Samuel S., Essays in Jewish theology. Cincinnati 1987, HUC. 366 p. – RRÉJ 149 (1990) 257s (M. R. *Hayoun*).

7406 *Collins* John J., Is a critical biblical theology possible?: → 550, Hebrew Bible SD 1986/90, 1-17.

7406* **Cornelius** Forrest C., The theological significance of darkness in the OT: diss. Southern Baptist Theol. Sem. DSmothers T. 1990. 217 p. 91-12507. – DissA 51 (1990s) 2792-A.

7407 *Dirksen* Peter, Israelite religion and OT theology: ScandJOT (1990,2) 96-100.

7408 **Goldy** Robert G., The emergence of Jewish theology in America. Bloomington 1990, Indiana Univ. 149 p. $25 [JAAR 58,326].

7409 *Gossai* Hemchand, The Old Testament among Christian theologians [an essential part, not mere pre-understanding or contrast to NT]: BR 6,1 (1990) 22-25. 36 [< NTAbs 34,205].

7410 **Haacker** Klaus, *Hempelmann* Heinzpeter, Hebraica veritas; die hebräische Grundlage der biblischen Theologie als exegetische und systematische Aufgabe. Wu 1989, Brockhaus. 80 p. DM 22. – RKIsr 5 (1990) 182 (Julie *Kirchberg*).

7410* *a) Heerden* S. W. van, Validity in Old Testament and biblical theology; – *b) Bosman* H. L., The validity of biblical theology; historical description or hermeneutical 'CHILDS' play'?; – *c) Wessels* W. J., The validity of OT theology; EICHRODT, a forerunner of the modern era: OTEssays 3 (1990) 121-131 / 133-146 / 147-157.

7411 *Henry* Carl F. H., Canonical theology; an evangelical appraisal: ScotBEv 8 (1990) 76-108.

7411* **Høgenhaven** Jesper, Problems and prospects of OT theology 1988 → 5,7385: RCritRR 3 (1990) 137-9 (S. *Terrien*); Interpretation 44 (1990) 82.84s (L. G. *Perdue*).

7412 **Legrand** Lucien, *a*) Le Dieu qui vient 1988 → 4,8427: ᴿMasses Ouvrières 432 (1989) 84-86 (G. *Sindt*); RevSR 63 (1989) 148-150 (B. *Renaud*). – *b*) Il Dio che viene; la missione nella Bibbia [1988 → 4,8427]. R 1989, Borla. 231 p. Lit. 20.000. – ᴿCC 141 (1990,4) 407s (A. *Wolanin*); StPatav 37 (1990) 722 (L. *Sartori*). – *c*) Unity and plurality; mission in the Bible [Le Dieu qui vient 1988 → 4,8427], ᵀ*Barr* R. R. Mkn 1990, Orbis. xv-189 p. $17. 0-88344-692-8 [NTAbs 35,258].

7413 *a*) *Lemke* Werner E., Is Old Testament theology an essentially Christian theological discipline? – *b*) *Walker-Jones* Arthur W., The role of theological imagination in biblical theology: HorBT 11,1 (1989) 59-72 / 73-... [< ᴢɪᴛ 90,334].

7413* **McDermott** John M., La sofferenza umana nella Bibbia; saggio di teologia biblica, ᵀ*Martorena* Hilva: PiccBiblT 9. R 1990, Dehoniane. 200 p. Lit. 18.000. 88-396-0316-6.

7414 *Marquardt* F. W., [on Frans BREUKELMAN's Biblical Theology as 'a biblical way of reading the Bible']: → 330, Einwürfe 7 (1990)...

7414* ᵀᴱ**Neusner** Jacob, Scriptures of the Oral Torah; sanctification and salvation in the sacred books of Judaism, an anthology. SF 1987, Harper & R. [iv-] 396 p. 0-06-066106-2.

7415 **Raurell** Frederic, Teologia biblica, a l'encalç d'una dificil identitat. Barc 1989, Fac. Teol. Fil. Catalunya. 87 p. – ᴿLaurentianum 31 (1990) 619-621 (A. *Bosch*).

7416 *Rogerson* J. W., 'What does it mean to be human?'; the central question of Old Testament theology: → 166, ᶠSHEFFIELD 1990, 285-298.

7416* *a*) *Scharbert* Josef, Leiden AT; *Lauer* Simon, Judentum; *Wolter* Michael NT: → 857, TRE 20 (1990) 670-672-677-688 [-713 *al.*]; – *b*) *Seebass* Horst, Leben: AT; *Wewers* Gerd A., Judentum; *Dautzenberg* Gerhard, NT: → 857, TRE 20 (1990) 520-524-526-530 [-566; 514-520, *al.*].

7417 *Terino* Jonathan, Il popolo dell'Antico Testamento; presenza e testimonianza: STEv NS 1 (1989) 7-24.

7418 **Van Buren** Paul M., Theology of the Jewish-Christian reality 3. Christ in context [1980 → 61,k176] 1988 → 4,8436.8555; 5,7401: ᴿAnglTR 71 (1989) 216-8 (J. A. *Carpenter*: Christianity like Judaism is a continuation of Israel, each in its own way); Missiology 18 (1990) 363 (H. M. *Goodpasture*); RelStR 16 (1990) 316-8 (P. *Haas*) & 320-3 (Rosemary R. *Ruether*: 'philo-Semitic sycophancy').

7418* **Van Roo** William A., Telling about God 1-3, 1986s → 2,3248... 5,7415: ᴿEsprVie 100 (1990) 346s (P. *Jay*: difficile de juger sans avoir lu ses ouvrages précédents cités).

7419 **Vogel** Manfred H., A quest for a theology of Judaism [14 essays] 1987 → 4,278: ᴿCritRR 2 (1989) 466-8 (M. *Friedman*); JRel 69 (1989) 584-6 (M. *Sokol*).

7419* **Werner** Wolfgang, Studien zur alttestamentlichen Vorstellung vom Plan Jahwes: BZAW 173, 1988: → 5,7403: ᴿBLitEc 90 (1989) 128s (M. *Delcor*); BO 47 (1990) 747-9 (M. *Dijkstra*); BZ 34 (1990) 290s (H. D. *Preuss*); JBL 109 (1990) 512-4 (M. E. *Biddle*).

7420 **Westermann** Claus, *a*) Elements of OT theology [1978], ᵀ*Stott* Douglas W., 1982 → 63,6488 *c*...1,6788: ᴿRelStT 8,3 (1988) 45s (D. B. *MacKay*); – *b*) Teologia do Antigo Testamento, ᵀ*Dattier* Frederico. São Paulo 1987, Paulinas. 205 p. 85-06-00721-2. – ᴿPerspT 21 (1989) 391s (J. *Vitório*).

7421 **Zimmerli** Walther, Esquisse d'une théologie de l'Ancien Testament:

LDiv 141.   P/Genève 1990, Cerf./Fides.   296 p. 2-204-04164-5 / Fides
2-7621-1483-7.

H5.1   *Deus* – **NT** – **God** [as Father ➤ H 1.4].

7422 *a) Fabris* Rinaldo, Il Dio di Gesù Cristo nella teologia di Matteo; – *b)*
Fusco Vittorio, Rivelazione di Gesù — rivelazione di Dio; il problema
del 'Dio di Gesù Cristo' nella prospettiva marciana; – *c) Barbi* Augusto,
Il Dio di Gesù nell'opera lucana; – *d) Segalla* Giuseppe, Dio Padre di
Gesù nel Quarto Vangelo: ScuolC 117,2 ('La teo-logia di Gesù' 1989)
121-148 / 149-166 / 167-195 / 196-224 [fasc. 3s, p. 251-286, *De Lorenzi*
Lorenzo, Il Dio di Paolo].

7423 **Hurtado** Larry W., One God, one Lord 1988 ➤ 4,8021, non 8842;
5,7405: ᴿCBQ 52 (1990) 123-5 (J. C. *Kesterson*); CriswT 4 (1989s)
408-410 (D. B. *Capes*); Dialog 28 (1989) 238s (D. H. *Juel*); EvQ 62 (1990)
374s (R. T. *France*); Month 250 (1989) 393 (Margaret *Barker*: when and
how did Jesus first come to be worshiped as divine?).

7424 **Joest** Wilfried, Die Wirklichkeit Gottes / Der Weg Gottes mit dem
Menschen: Dogmatik 1s, 1984/6 ➤ 5,7406: ᴿNedTTs 44 (1990) 82s (J. P.
Boendermaker).

7425 **Kasper** Walter, The God of Jesus ᵀ1984 ➤ 65,6176... 3,6943: ᴿDialog
27 (1988) 235.238 (T. J. *Martin*).

7425* **Kellenberger** J., God relationships with and without God [... KIER-
KEGAARD; Judaeo-Christian perspective]. L 1989, Macmillan. 176 p. £35.
0-333-49135-1. – ᴿExpTim 102 (1990s) 89s (P. *Vardy*).

7426 **Marguerat** Daniel, Le Dieu des premiers chrétiens: Essais Bibliques 16.
Genève 1990, Labor et Fides. 223 p. 2-8309-0607-1 [NTAbs 35,119].

7427 **Muñoz** Ronaldo, Dios de los cristianos 1987 ➤ 5,7411: ᴿScripTPamp
22 (1990) 295s (J. L. *Lorda*).

7428 **Neuhaus** Gerd, Atheismus oder anonymes Christentum? Ein Versuch
transzendentaler Hermeneutik des Gottesglaubens in Auseinandersetzung
mit FEUERBACH, MARX, HORKHEIMER und BENJAMIN 1985 ➤ 1,6804:
ᴿZkT 112 (1990) 111-3 (K. H. *Neufeld*).

7429 **Nicholls** David, Deity and domination; images of God and the State in
the nineteenth and twentieth centuries. NY 1989, Routledge. xiv-321 p.
$30. – ᴿTS 51 (1990) 754s (P. *Lakeland*: images of God drawn from the
political arena in turn affect it).

7430 **Schlosser** Jacques, Le Dieu de Jésus: LDiv 129, 1987 ➤ 3,6952...
5,7413: ᴿRevSR 64 (1990) 85s (M. *Morgen*); SNTU-A 14 (1989) 226s (H.
Giesen).

7431 **Simonis** Walter, Gott in Welt; Umrisse christlicher Gotteslehre 1988
➤ 5,7414: ᴿMüTZ 41 (1990) 303s (E. *Zwick*).

7432 **Vorgrimler** H., Dottrina teologica su Dio [Theologische Gotteslehre],ᵀ:
GdT 188. Brescia 1989, Queriniana. 242 p. Lit. 22.000. – ᴿNRT 112
(1990) 256 (R. *Escol*); RivScR 3 (1989) 531 (G. *Ancona*).

H5.2   **Christologia ipsius NT.**

7432* ᴱ**Dupont** J., Jésus aux origines² 1973/89 ➤ 5,7423: ᴿNRT 112 (1990)
592s (X. *Jacques*).

7433 [*Fitzmyer* J. A.] ᵀᴱ**Müller** P. G., Bibel und Christologie 1987 ➤ 3,6961;
4,8452: ᴿTR 86 (1990) 223-5 (O. B. *Knoch*).

      Fredriksen Paula, From Jesus to Christ 1988 ➤ 4242.

7434 **Habermann** Jürgen, Präexistenzaussagen im NT [ev. Diss. München 1989, ᴰ*Hahn* F.]: EurHS 23/362. Fra 1990, Lang. 645 p. Fs 105. 3-631-41769-1 [NTAbs 34,399].

7435 **Jonge** Marinus de, Christology in context; the earliest Christian responses to Jesus 1988 → 4,8455*; 5,7428: ᴿInterpretation 44 (1990) 69-71 (M. E. *Boring*).

7436 **Jossa** Giorgio, Dal Messia al Cristo; le origini della cristologia: StBPaid 88, 1989 → 5,7429: ᴿAsprenas 37 (1990) 354-7 (A. *Rolla*); Helmantica 41 (1990) 433 (L. *Amigo*); StPatav 37 (1990) 396s (G. *Segalla*).

Klappert Bertold, Leitlinien einer Christologie... Joh 5,39-47: 1990 → 5826.

7437 *La Potterie* Ignace de, 'Le problème formidable de la conscience de Jésus' (M. BLONDEL): → 542, Evangile, Venasque 1989/90, 147-177 [non 'le problème fondamental', ActaPIB 9,6 (1989s) 459].

7438 **Marquardt** F.-W., Das christliche Bekenntnis zu Jesus, dem Juden; eine Christologie 1. Mü 1990, Kaiser. 308 p. DM 79. 3-459-01837-2 [NTAbs 35,120]. – ᴿSNTU A-15 (1990) 221 (A. *Fuchs*).

7439 **Moltmann** Jürgen, Der Weg Jesu Christi; Christologie in neutestamentlichen Dimensionen. Mü 1989, Kaiser. 379 p. – ᴿCommSev 23 (1990) 107s (M. de *Burgos*).

7440 **Müller** U. B., Die Menschwerdung des Gottessohnes; frühchristliche Inkarnationsvorstellungen und die Anfänge des Doketismus: SBS 140. Stu 1990, KBW. 136 p. DM 29,80. 3-460-04401-2 [NTAbs 35,259]. – ᴿArTGran 53 (1990) 311s (A. *Segovia*).

7441 **Pokorny** Petr, The genesis of Christology; foundations for a theology of the New Testament, ᵀ*Lefébure* Marcus. E 1987, Clark. xvi-266. £15. – ᴿPacifica 3 (1990) 229s (N. *Young*); RB 97 (1990) 138 (J. *Murphy-O'Connor* cannot understand why it was translated, and wishes it 'the success it deserves').

7442 **Richard** Earl, Jesus, one and many; the Christological concept of NT authors 1988 → 4,8459; 5,7434: ᴿBibTR 20 (1990) 131s (D. M. *Sweetland*); CBQ 52 (1990) 170s (M. *Cahill*); Horizons 17 (1990) 326s (G. S. *Sloyan*).

7443 **Scroggs** Robin, The reality and revelation of God; Christology in Paul and John...: Proclamation comm. 1988 → 4,8461; 5,7436. – ᴿCBQ 52 (1990) 172s (D. M. *Stanley*: a thoughtful pointer for Protestants; curiously omits 1 Cor 12,12-27; Rom 12,4-8 on the body of Christ); RB 97 (1990) 137s (J. *Murphy-O'Connor*).

7444 **Segundo** Juan Luis, *a*) Jesus of Nazareth I-V, 1984-8 → 65,6339...: ᴿTorJT 6 (1990) 106-9 (R. *Haight*). – *b*) The humanist Christology of Paul 1986 → 2,5542 ... 5,7439: ᴿCritRR 2 (1989) 244-6 (R. H. *Fuller*); Vidyajyoti 54 (1990) 104 (P. J. *James*). – *c*) The Christ of the Ignatian Exercises: JNYT 4,1988 → 3,4039; 4,4294: ᴿMonth 250 (1989) 148-150 (P. *Endean*: agreeably outrageous).

7445 **Segundo** Juan Luis, *a*) Jésus devant la conscience moderne 1988 → 5,7442: ᴿBLitEc 91 (1990) 77s (S. *Légasse*); EsprVie 100 (1990) 331-3 (J. *Milet*); RBgPg 68 (1990) 217 (P. *Salmon*). – *b*) Le christianisme de Paul; l'histoire retrouvée 1988 → 5,5876.7443: ᴿLavalTP 46 (1990) 118 (G. *Chénard*).

7446 **Sinclair** Seatt G., Jesus Christ according to Paul; the Christologies of Paul's undisputed epistles and the Christology of Paul [→ 5,5834]: BIBAL Mg. 1, 1988. 150 p. $13. 0-941037-08-8.

7447 **Stegner** William R., Narrative theology in early Jewish Christology [i.e. Judeo-Christian]. Louisville 1989, Westminster-Knox. 141 p. $12 pa. – ᴿCalvinT 25 (1990) 149s (J. A. D. *Weims*).

7447* **Vives** Josep, 'Si oyerais su Voz...'; exploración cristiana del misterio de Dios: PresTeol 48, 1988 ➤ 5,7417:   ᴿTVida 30 (1989) 239s (M. *Arias Reyero*).
7448 **Witherington** Ben, The Christology of Jesus. Mp 1990, Fortress. x-310 p. $25.   0-8006-2430-0 [NTAbs 35,261].
7449 *Wong* Teresa, ☉ An introduction to the Christology of the NT: ColcFuJen 83 (1990) 51-63.

H5.3   *Christologia praemoderna* – **patristic through Reformation.**

7450 **Bartos** Jan F., Gesù Cristo rivelazione di Dio nel pensiero di S. Bᴏɴᴀᴠᴇɴᴛᴜʀᴀ: diss. Seraphicum 76, ᴰ*Iammarrone* L. R 1990, Misc. Francescana.
7450* **Böhm** Thomas, Die Christologie des Aʀɪᴜs; dogmengeschchtliche Überlegungen unter besonderer Berücksichtigung der Hellenisierungs-frage: kath. Diss. ᴰ*Müller* G. L. Münchcn 1990. – RTLv 22, p. 618.
7451 *Boersma* Hans, Alexandrian or Antiochian? a dilemma in Bᴀʀᴛʜ's Christology: WestTJ 52 (1990) 263-280.
7452 **Brennecke** Hanns Christoph, Studien zur Geschichte der Homöer: BHistT 73, 1988 ➤ 5,7449:   ᴿJbAC 33 (1990) 256-260 (H. J. *Vogt*); RTLv 21 (1990) 74-78 (A. de *Halleux*).
7453 *Brox* Norbert, Wer ist Jesus? – oder: die ersten Konzilien; worüber der Streit unvermeidbar und wie er zu führen ist: Orientierung 54 (1990) 52-56.
7453* **Casteel** Robert L., The Wisdom Christology of Hᴜɢʜ of St. Victor: diss. St. Louis, ᴰ*Hellmann* W. 179 p. 91-15493. – DissA 52, 190-A; RTLv 22, p. 619 sans date.
7454 *Chryssavgis* John, Patristic Christology; through the looking glass of the heretics: Pacifica 3 (1990) 187-200.
7455 **Denis** Philippe, Le Christ étendard; l'Homme-Dieu au temps des Réformes, 1500-1565: Jésus depuis Jésus, 1987 ➤ 4,8469; F 123:   ᴿRHE 84 (1989) 152-4 (J.-F. *Gilmont*: brillant).
7456 *Derycke* Hugues, Le Christ universel selon saint Aᴜɢᴜsᴛɪɴ: BLitEc 91 (1990) 163-173; Eng. 174.
7456* **Dowling** Maurice J., Mᴀʀᴄᴇʟʟᴜs of Ancyra, Problems of Christology and the doctrine of the Trinity: diss. Queen's Univ. Belfast 1987. 394 p. BRDX-91895. – DissA 51 (1990s) 4161-A.
7457 *Drobner* Hubertus R., *a*) Outlines of the Christology of St. Aᴜɢᴜsᴛɪɴᴇ III: MeliT [40 (1989)] 41 (1990) 53-68; – *b*) Grammatical excgesis and Christology in St. Augustine: ➤ 643, StPatr 18,4 (1983/90) 49-63.
7458 **Drobner** Hubertus R., Person-Exegese und Christologie bei Augustinus; zur Herkunft der Formel una persona: Philosophia Patrum 8, 1986 ➤ 4,8470; 5,7452:   ᴿJTS 41 (1990) 264-6 (R. *Williams*).
7459 *Duggan* George H., Christologies, ancient and modern: HomPast 90,10 (1989s) 10-18.
7460 ᵀ**Fernández Sahelices** José C., ᴱ*Guerrero Martínez* Fernando, San Aᴛᴀɴᴀsɪᴏ, La Encarnación del Verbo: Bibl. Patr. 6. M 1989, Ciudad Nueva. 115 p. 84-86987-11-3. – ᴿActuBbg 27 (1990) 231 (J. *Vives*): ScripTPamp 22 (1990) 647s (A. *Viciano*).
7461 *Gisel* Pierre, Le Christ de Cᴀʟᴠɪɴ: JJC 44. P 1990, Desclée. 208 p. – ᴿÉtudes 373 (1990) 712 (R. *Marlé*).
7462 *González* Carlos I., *a*) Antecedentes de la cristología arriana en el siglo III: Medellín 16 (1990) 315-361 [< TContext 8/2, p. 81]. – *b*) La

tradición de la cristología apostólica en el siglo II: Medellín 15 (1989) 15-69 [< TR 86,524]. – c) Postnicea; la atormentada recepción de la cristología nicena I: RTLim 24 (1990) 343-382.

7463 **Grillmeier** Alois, (*Hainthaler* Theresia), Jesus der Christus 2/2, Die Kirche von Konstantinopel im 6. Jahrhundert 1989 ➤ 5,7459: ᴿTGL 80 (1990) 359 (W. *Beinert*); TLZ 115 (1990) 694-8 (B. *Lohse*); TS 51 (1990) 741-3 (B. E. *Daley*).

7463* **Grillmeier** A., Jesus der Christus im Glaube der Kirche, 2/4 (mit *Hainthaler* T.), Die Kirche von Alexandrien mit Nubien und Äthiopien nach 451. FrB 1990, Herder. xxiv-436 p. DM 84 [NRT 113,886, L. *Renwart*].

7464 **Grillmeier** Alois, Christ in Christian tradition 2/1,1987 ➤ 3,7001; 4,8474: ᴿRHE 85 (1990) 724-9 (A. Van *Roey*).

7465 **Grillmeier** Alois, Le Christ dans la tradition chrétienne 2/1, Le concile de Chalcédon (451), réception et opposition (451-513), ᵀ*Pascale-Dominique* sr.: CogF 154. P 1990, Cerf. 505 p. F 180. – ᴿEsprVie 100 (1990) 170-3 (P. *Jay*); Études 372 (1989) 714 (R. *Marlé*); QVidCr 152 (1990) 172s (J. *Bosch*); RHE 85 (1990) 531 (P. H. *Daly*); RHPR 70 (1990) 349s (P. *Maraval*); RTLv 21 (1990) 496s (A. de *Halleux*: ajoute des index à l'édition allemande; pour '451-513' lire 518).

7466 *Grillmeier* Aloys [sic], Die anthropologisch-christologische Sprache des LEONTIUS von Byzanz und ihre Beziehung zu den Symmikta Zetemata des Neoplatonikers Porphyríos: ➤ 80, ᶠHÖRNER Hadwig 1990, 61-72.

7468 **Hanson** Richard P. C., The search for the Christian doctrine of God; the Arian controversy 1988 ➤ 4,8475: ᴿBLitEc 91 (1990) 227-230 (H. *Crouzel*); CathHR 76 (1990) 579-583 (C. *Kannengiesser*); ÉTRel 65 (1990) 126 (A. *Gounelle*: savant, clair); Gregorianum 71 (1990) 782s (C. I. *González*); JTS 41 (1990) 668-673 (C. *Stead*); RHPR 70 (1990) 348s (P. *Maraval*); Themelios 16 (1990s) 31 (G. *Keith*); TS 51 (1990) 334-7 (J. T. *Lienhard*).

7469 *a)* **Hanson** Richard, The achievement of orthodoxy in the fourth century A.D.; – *b)* *Williams* Rowan, Does it make sense to speak of pre-Nicene orthodoxy?: ➤ 5,38*, ᶠCHADWICK H., Making of orthodoxy 1989, 142-156 / 1-23.

7470 *Henne* Philippe, La véritable christologie de la Cinquième Similitude du Pasteur d'HERMAS: RSPT 74 (1990) 182-203; Eng. 204.

7470* **Jensen** Oddvar J., Kristi person; til betydningen av læren om Kristi person i Martin LUTHERS teologi 1520-1546: diss. Oslo 1988. – NorTTs 90 (1989) 50 ['First opponent, *Hägglund* B.'].

7471 **Ladaria** Luis F., La cristología de HILARIO: AnGreg 255, 1989 ➤ 5,7466: ᴿArTGran 53 (1990) 362s (A. *Segovia*); CommSev 23 (1990) 262 (M. *Sánchez*); ETL 66 (1990) 426 (A. de *Halleux*); Gregorianum 71 (1990) 427 (*ipse*); PerspTeol 22 (1990) 391-3 (C. *Palacio*); RasT 31 (1990) 96-98 (A. *Orazzo*); RÉAug 36 (1990) 192s (J. *Doignon*); RSPT 74 (1990) 637-9 (G.-M. de *Durand*); TLZ 115 (1990) 896-8 (G. *Wendelborn*).

7472 *Leclercq* Jean, La christologie clunisienne au siècle de S. HUGUES: StMonast 31 (1989) 267-278 [< ZIT 90,264].

7472* *McGuckin* John, Did AUGUSTINE's Christology depend on THEODORE of Mopsuestia?: HeythJ 31 (1990) 39-52.

7473 **Macquarrie** John, Jesus Christ in modern thought [i ... rise of classical Christology ... Chalcedon ... Reformation ... his own proposals], L/Ph 1990, SCM/Trinity. 454 p. £17.50. 0-334-02446-3. – ᴿExpTim 102,5 top choice (1990s) 129-131 (C. S. *Rodd*).

7473* *Malaty* Tadros Y., La christologie de l'Église copte, *mía phûsis toû theoû lógou sesarkōménē*: Istina 35 (1990) 147-158.
7474 *May* Georg, Das Lehrverfahren gegen Eutyches im November des Jahres 448; zur Vorgeschichte des Konzils von Chalkedon: AnHConc 21 (1989) 1-61.
7475 ᴱMeijering E.P., [*Winden* J.C.M. Van), ATHANASIUS, De incarnatione Verbi. Amst 1989, Gieben. 431 p. *f* 120. 90-5063-023-5. – ᴿAntClas 59 (1990) 391-3 (J. *Schamp*).
7476 ᴱOhlig Karl-Heinz, Christologie [Texte] I-II. Graz 1989, Styria. 227 p.; 239 p. Sch je 198. – ᴿTLZ 115 (1990) 298s (R. M.); TPQ 138 (1990) 281s (W. *Raberger*).
7477 *a*) *Olivar* A., Sobre la Cristología de San Pedro CRISÓLOGO: Bessarion (1985,4) 95-116 [< BTAM 14 (1990) p. 776]; – *b*) *Carreras* José M., La cristología de San IGNACIO: RTLim 24 (1990) 46-68.
7478 *Orbe* Antonio, En torno al modalismo de Marción: Gregorianum 71 (1990) 43-64; franç. 64s.
7479 **Pifarré** Cebrià, ARNOBIO el Joven y la cristología del 'conflictus' 1988 ➤ 35,7473: ᴿBurgense 31 (1990) 576s (E. *Bueno*); EstFranc 91 (1990) 605s (J. *Ferrer*); JTS 41 (1990) 703-711 (W. *Kinzig*); StMon 31 (1989) 188s (A. *Olivar*).
7480 **Posset** Franz, LUTHER's Catholic Christology according to his Johannine lectures of 1527 [diss. Marquette, ᴰ*Hagen* K.] 1988 ➤ 4,8485: ᴿSixtC 20 (1989) 526s (D. H. *Shantz*).
7481 **Ruello** Francis, La Christologie de T. d'AQUIN: THist 76, 1987 ➤ 2,7013; 4,8486: ᴿSalesianum 52 (1990) 907s (P.T. *Stella*).
7481* **Schmidt** Axel, Die Christologie in M. LUTHERS späten Disputationen: Diss. ᴰ*Bäumer*. FrB 1990. 405 p. – RTLv 22, p. 601.
7482 *Slusser* Michael, The issues in the definition of the Council of Chalcedon: TorJT 6 (1990) 63-69.
7483 *Stewart* Alistair C., Persona in the Christology of LEO I, a note: BJRyL 71,1 (1989) 3-5.
7483* *Tacelli* R. K., Of one substance; Saint ATHANASIUS and the meaning of Christian doctrine: DowR 108 (1990) 91-110.
7484 **Torrance** Iain R., Christology after Chalcedon; SEVERUS... Sergius 1988 ➤ 4,8490*; 5,7477*: ᴿJEH 40 (1989) 400s (W. H. C. *Frend*).
7485 **Weber** Édouard-Henri, Le Christ selon saint Thomas d'AQUIN: JJC 35. P 1988, Desclée. 336 p. F 165. 2-7189-0403-8. – ᴿBijdragen 51 (1990) 445s (H. J. M. *Schoot*, Eng.); EsprVie 100 (1990) 343-5 (P. *Jay*); Gregorianum 71 (1990) 397s (P. *Gilbert*); MélSR 47 (1990) 163-5 (B. *Rey*); RechSR 78 (1990) 149-155 (F. *Ruello*, aussi sur son propre livre); RevSR 64 (1990) 204s (P. *Gauthier*); RTPhil 122 (1990) 437s (J. *Borel*); TS 51 (1990) 135-7 (R. *Cessario*).

H5.4 (*Commentationes de*) *Christologia* **moderna.**

7486 *Alemany* José J., Cristología narrativa: MiscCom 48 (1990) 495-513.
7487 **Amato** Angelo, Gesù il Signore 1988 ➤ 5,7481: ᴿAngelicum 67 (1990) 266s (G. M. *Salvati*); CC 141 (1990,2) 611s (F. *Lambiasi*); Iter 1 (Caracas 1990) 164-6 (J. C. *Ayestarán*); Lateranum 56 (1990) 365-370 (M. *Bordoni*); RTLim 24 (1990) 302s (A. *Saavedra*); TR 86 (1990) 224s (H. *Vorgrimler*).
7488 *Antinucci* Lucia, Gesù, il volto umano di Dio; la proposta cristologica di Christian DUQUOC; Asprenas 37 (1990) 406-430.

7489 *Athappily* Sebastian, The *scandalon* of the uniqueness of Jesus Christ; some critical reflections [... RAHNER K.]: Christian Orient 11 (Kerala 1990) 103-119 [< TContext 8/2, p. 39].

7490 **Auer** Johann, Jesuscristo hijo de Dios e hijo de María [1986 ➤ 2,5582],[T] Barc 1989, Herder. 546 p. – [R]Carthaginensia 6 (1990) 223s (F. *Martínez Fresneda*: for a Summa Theologica originally projected with J. RATZINGER); PerspT 22 (1990) 388-391 (C. *Palácio*); RelCu 36 (1990) 689 (R. de la *Torre*); RTLim 24 (1990) 299-302 (F. *Interdonato*).

7491 **Balthasar** Hans Urs von, Mysterium paschale [German 1969], Eng. [T]*Nichols* A. E 1990, Clark. xii-297 p. $40. (TS 52, 162, J. R. *Sachs*: incarnation and soteriology, not just Easter; but chiefly original is the SPEYR-inspired view that *descendit ad inferos* means not triumph with souls of the just, but solidarity of the 'crucified as sinner' with all who died in sin). ➤ 7541.

[E]**Ban** Joseph D., Christological foundation 1988 ➤ 385*.

7492 **Bellet** Maurice, Christ: JJC 42. P 1990, Desclée. 216 p. – [R]Études 373 (1990) 136s (J. *Thomas*).

7493 **Biagi** Ruggero †, Cristo profeta sacerdote e re; dottrina di S. TOMMASO e sviluppi della teologia moderna. Bo 1988, Studio Domenicano. 192 p. – [R]Angelicum 67 (1990) 135s (E. de *Cea*).

7494 **Blocher** Henri, Christologie. Vaux/Seine 1986, Fac.Év. 374 p. (3 vol.). – [R]ScotBEv 8 (1990) 136 (G. *Bray*).

7495 **Brambilla** Franco G., La Cristologia di SCHILLEBEECKX; la singolarità di Gesù come problema ermeneutico [[D]1985] 1989 ➤ 5,7487: [R]Lateranum 56 (1990) 380-2 (G. *Ancona*, anche su *Iammarrone* L. 1985); QVidCr 152 (1990) 173 (J.-A. *Rocha*).

7496 *Brito* Emilio, Le Médiateur; chronique de christologie: RTLv 21 (1990) 329-342 [*Ruello* F., *Weber* E., *Sesboüé* B.; al. infra].

7497 **Cardó** C., Emmanuel; estudios sobre Jesucristo: Patmos 195. M 1989, Rialp. 368 p. [R]RET 50 (1990) 352 (M. *Gesteria*: canto de cisne preconciliar).

7498 **Carreira das Neves** Joaquim, Jesus Cristo, História e fe 1988 ➤ 5,4044: [R]HumT 2 (1990) 282s (J. *Monteiro*).

7499 **Chesnut** Glenn F., Images of Christ 1984 ➤ 65,6279 ... 5,7491: [R]IrTQ 56 (1990) 153s (W. G. *Jeanrond*).

Coakley Sarah, Christ without absolutes ... TROELTSCH 1988 ➤ m223.

7500 **Daniels** Richard W., 'Great is the mystery of godliness'; the Christology of John OWEN [Puritan]: diss. Westminster Theol. Sem., [D]*Davis* D. 494 p. 90-26391. – DissA 51 (1990s) 2058-A.

7501 **De Marco** Donald, The Incarnation in a divided world. Front Royal VA 1988, Christendom College. 200 p. $9. – [R]HomPast 90,1 (1989s) 75-77 (S. *Donnelly*).

7502 *De Virgilio* Giuseppe, La cristologia di H. Urs von BALTHASAR; missione e persona di Cristo: Studium 86 (R 1990) 183-203.

7504 **Gertler** Thomas, Jesus Christus — die Antwort der Kirche auf die Frage nach dem Menschsein: Erfurter TSt 52, 1986 ➤ 2,5611 ... 5,7497: [R]RTLv 21 (1990) 340-2 (E. *Brito*).

7505 *González de Cardedal* Olegario, Boletín de cristología I [*Amato* A. 1989; *Mateos* A., *Sesboüé* B. 1988]: Salmanticensis 37 (1990) 212-236.

7506 **Gounelle** André, Le Christ et Jésus, trois christologies américaines; TILLICH, COBB, ALTIZER. P 1990, Desclée. 215 p. – [R]EsprVie 100 (1990) 465-471 (P. *Jay*); Études 373 (1990) 282s (R. *Marlé*); RHPR 70 (1990) 490s (G. *Siegwalt*).

7507 *Gounelle* André, Trois christologies [i. parole; ii. changement; iii. personne-événement]: ÉTRel 65 (1990) 247-259.
7508 *Grandis* Giancarlo, Questioni di cristologia rosminiana: ScuolC 117 (1989) 1-26.
7509 *Halleux* André de, Actualité du Néochalcédonisme; un accord christologique récent entre Orthodoxes [Aarhus 1964... Addis Abeba 1971]|: RTLv 21 (1990) 32-54; Eng. 144.
7510 *Hatem* Jad, La christologie gnostique de HINDIYYÉ [A. 'Ujaymi 1720-1798]: NESTR 11,1 (1990) 45-57.
7511 **Hattrup** Dieter, Die Bewegung der Zeit... christologische Vermittlung 1988 → 5,7500: ᴿEstE 65 (1990) 481s (A. *Tornos*).
7512 **Hebblethwaite** Brian L., The Incarnation 1987 → 3,235; 5,7502: ᴿAnglTR 71 (1989) 107-9 (D. F. *Winslow*: vigorous against The Myth); ScotJT 43 (1990) 111-4 (T. *Hart*).
7513 *Herman* Wayne R., MOLTMANN's Christology: StudiaBT 17 (1989) 3-31.
7513* **Hodges** Larry M., Hope and history; a critical examination of the Christologies of W. PANNENBERG and J. MOLTMANN: diss. Baylor 1980. 196 p. 91-07961. – DissA 51 (1990s) 3434-A.
7514 *Iammarrone* Luigi, Un nuovo saggio di cristologia [*Bordoni* M. 1982-2-6]: DivThom 92 (1989) 317-389 e continua.
7515 *Jaki* Stanley, Christology and the birth of modern science: AsbTJ 45,2 (1990) 61-72.
7516 **Johnson** Elizabeth A., Consider Jesus; waves of renewal in Christology. NY 1990, Crossroad. xii-149 p. $15. 0-8245-0990-0 [NTAbs 34,400; RelStR 17,143, B. O. *McDermott*: largely Roman Catholic since 1950]. – ᴿExpTim 102 (1990s) 153 (J. *Quinn*: 'A more dogmatic stance would make it a more helpful guide'); Tablet 244 (1990) 1132s (D. *Edwards*, also on J. MACQUARRIE).
7517 **Kerk** Arina Van de, Introduction aux lectures féministes de la Christologie [exposition USA, 'Jésa Christa' crucifiée]: ÉTRel 65 (1990) 593-607.
7518 **Krieg** Robert A., Story-shaped Christology 1988 → 4,8456; 5,7430: ᴿCBQ 52 (1990) 159s (D. M. *Rhoads*: helpful on a self-outdating topic); RivB 38 (1990) 111s (V. *Fusco*).
7519 **Küng** Hans, The incarnation of God... HEGEL [1970], ᵀ1988 → 3,7061 ... 5,7507*: ᴿInterpretation 44 (1990) 75-78 (R. *Burke*); JAAR 58 (1990) 128-130 (J. A. *Bracken*); JRel 70 (1990) 267-9 (P. C. *Hodgson*); Themelios 16 (1990s) 30 (M. *Alsford*).
7519* **Kuschel** Karl-Josef, Christus — geboren vor aller Zeit? Die systematischtheologische Diskussion um die Präexistenz Christi im 20. Jahrhundert: Kath. Hab.–Diss. ᴰ*Gross*. Tübingen 1989s. – TR 86 (1990) 510.
7520 *Lacoste* Jean-Yves, Théologie anonyme et christologie pseudonyme; C. S. LEWIS, les Chroniques de Narnia: NRT 112 (1990) 381-393.
7521 **Lapide** Pinchas, Wurde Gott Jude? Vom Menschsein Jesu. Mü 1987, Kösel. 96 p. DM 16,80. 3-466-20293-0. – ᴿZRGg 42 (1990) 84-86 (S. *Ben-Chorin*).
7522 **Lefebure** Leo D., Toward a contemporary Wisdom Christology... RAHNER, PITTENGER ᴰ1988 → 5,7511: ᴿTS 51 (1990) 376s (R. *Masson*).
7523 *Lohaus* Gerd, Die Lebensereignisse Jesu in der Christologie Karl RAHNERS: TPhil 65 (1990) 349-386.
7524 **Madonia** N., Ermeneutica e cristologia in W. KASPER. Palermo 1990, Augustinus, 307 p. – ᴿEuntDoc 43 (1990) 555s (P. *Miccoli*).

7524* *Maniecki* Kazimierz, ❷ L'aspect christologique de la théologie de l'icône d'áprès Léonide OUSPENSKY: STWsz 27,1 (1989) 74-95; franç. 95s.

7525 *Marchesi* Giovanni, Il mistero dell'Incarnazione del Verbo; mito o realtà storica e salvifica?: CC 141 (1990,4) 434-447.

7526 **Marshall** Bruce, Christology in conflict... RAHNER, BARTH 1987 ➤ 3,7069; 5,7613: ᴿAnglTR 71 (1989) 445-7 (L. *Richard*); JRel 70 (1990) 470s (C. A. *Wilson*).

7526* **Menacherry** Cheriyan, History, symbol and myth in the Christology of Raymond PANIKKAR: diss. Pont. Univ. Gregoriana, ᴰ*Dupuis* J. Roma 1990. 440 p.; Extr. Nº 3617, 133 p. – RTLv 22, p. 620.

7527 *Mennekes* Friedhelm, Das Christusbild im Wandel; Theologie in Bildern: TGegw 33 (1990) 227-235.

7528 *Michel* O., Christologische Überlegungen: TBeit 21,1 (1990) 32-34 [< NTAbs 34,344].

7529 **Moltmann** Jürgen, *a*) Der Weg Jesu Christi; Christologie in messianischen Dimensionen 1989 ➤ 5,7515: ᴿEvT 50 (1990) 574-586 (B. *Klappert*); TR 86 (1990) 485s (E. *Arens*); TsTKi 61 (1990) 232s (J.-O. *Henriksen*). – *b*) The Way of Jesus Christ; Christology in messianic dimensions. L 1990, SCM. xx-388 p.

7530 —**Fernández García** Bonifacio, Cristo de esperanza; la cristología escatológica de J. MOLTMANN: BSalmEst 105, 1988 ➤ 5,7516: ᴿRTLv 21 (1990) 333-5 (J. *Brito*).

7530* **Morris** Thomas V., The logic of God incarnate 1986 ➤ 2,5634... 5,7517a: ᴿRelSt 25 (1989) 409-423 (J. *Hick*).

7531 *Nichol* Frank, Towards a Christology of grace: Pacifica 3 (1990) 323-334.

7532 **Nicoletti** Michele, La dialettica dell'incarnazione... KIERKEGAARD 1983 ➤ 64,6707... 2,5636*: ᴿZkT 112 (1990) 118s (J. *Feiderer*).

7533 *a*) *Ocáriz* Fernando, La personne du Verbe, source de vérité; – *b*) *Blanco* Arturo, Parola, persona e storia nella rivelazione divina: AnnTh 4 (1990) 249-262 / 263-282.

7534 **Oden** Thomas, The word of life: [Methodist Christology] Systematic theology 2. SF 1989, Harper & R. xxi-583 p. $40 [RelStR 17, 143, J. J. *Buckley*]. – ᴿParadigms 6,2 (1990s) 49s (K. *Barron*); TTod 47 (1990s) 215s. 217 (B. *Cooke*: a basis for discussion).

7534* **Ols** Daniel, Le cristologie contemporanee e loro posizioni fondamentali al vaglio della dottrina di S. TOMMASO: diss. Angelicum, ᴰ*Duroux* B. Roma 1990. – RTLv 22, p. 620.

7535 *Osten-Sacken* Peter von der, Christologie im Gespräch mit jüdischer Theologie: BTZ 7 (1990) 157-176.

7536 **Ottati** Douglas F., Jesus Christ and Christian vision [... how he affects behavior; 'theology of the heart']. Minneapolis 1989, Augsburg-F. 163 p. $11. – ᴿTTod 47 (1990s) 69s (S. C. *Guthrie*).

7537 *Pals* Daniel L., Several Christologies of the Great Awakening: AnglTR 72 (1990) 412-427.

7538 *Popescu* Dumitru (en roumain), Tendances dans la christologie catholique contemporaine: OrtBuc 40,4 (1988) 9-14.

7539 *Rapczak* Kimberly A., Metaphorical Christology; Jesus as parable and sacrament of God to the world [*McFague* S.]: Paradigms 6,1 (1990) 39-51.

7540 *Renwart* Léon, 'Jésus un et multiple'; chronique de Christologie [*Grillmeier* A. 1990; *Hadot* J.; *Gisel* P., *Gounelle* A., *Madonia* N. 1990 ...]: NRT 112 (1990) 718-730.

7541 **Saward** John, The mysteries of March; H. U. von BALTHASAR on the Incarnation and Easter [supra → 7491]. Wsh 1990, Catholic Univ. XXI-186 p. $23; pa. $13. [TS 52, 155, E. T. *Oakes*]. – ᴿPrPeo 4 (1990) 381s (J. *Tolhurst*).

7542 *Schoonenberg* Piet, Der Christus 'von oben' und die Christologie 'von unten': TrierTZ 99 (1990) 95-124.

7543 *Schreiter* Robert J., Jesus Christ and mission; the cruciality of Christology: Missiology 18 (1990) 429-437.

7544 **Schweizer** E., Jesus Christ, the man from Nazareth and the exalted Lord 1989 → 3,3962; 4,8544: ᴿVidyajyoti 53 (1989) 628s (P. M. *Meagher*).

7545 *Semeraro* Marcello, Rassegna; Sulla cristologia: RivScR 3 (1989) 515-522.

7546 **Snyder** Mary H., The Christology of Rosemary R. RUETHER, a critical introduction. Mystic CT 1988, Twenty-third. xv-152 p. £10 [JTS 41,349]. – ᴿFurrow 40 (1989) 761 (Linda *Hogan*); Horizons 17 (1990) 352s (Mary *Tardiff*).

7546* *Sugirtharajah* R. S., Wisdom, Q, and a proposal for a Christology: ExpTim 102 (1990s) 42-46.

7547 [Teixeira da] **Cunha** Jorge, O evento do Filho; Advento do Homem, a relação do homem à Cristo pascal, fonte da ética na obra de F. X. DURRWELL: BibHumT 1. Porto 1989, HumT. 275 p. – ᴿHumT 2 (1990) 365-371 (J. E. *Borges de Pinho*); Salesianum 52 (1990) 748 (*Cafs*: maturità straordinaria); Salmanticensis 37 (1990) 256s (J.-R. *Flecha Andrés*).

7547* **Thatcher** Adrian, Truly a person, truly God. L 1990, SPCK. 151 p. £10. 0-281-04446-5. – ᴿExpTim 102 (1990s) 186 (T. J. *Gorringe*).

7548 **Tilliette** Xavier, Le Christ de la philosophie; prolégomènes à une christologie philosophique: CogF 155. P 1990, Cerf. 293 p. F 145. 2-204-04088-6 [NRT 113,888, L. *Renwart*].

7548* **Vitalini** Sandro, Christologie: GdT 1990, Fac. Théol. ... 143 p. – ᴿEsprVie 100 (1990) 206s (P. *Jay*: je ne sais ce que signifie 'section pastorale' ... dans le sous-titre).

7549 *Wenz* Günther, Christologische Paralipomena: TRu 55 (1990) 46-88.

7550 **Willers** Ulrich, Friedrich NIETZSCHES antichristliche Christologie; eine theologische Rekonstruktion: InnsTSt 23, 1988 → 5,7540: ᴿTPhil 65 (1990) 305-8 (J. *Splett*); TR 86 (1990) 421-3 (P. *Köster*).

7550* **Won Bae Son,** The self-limited Christ; a kenotic theology of the Incarnation [THOMASIUS G., GORE C. ...]: diss. ᴰ*Klooster* F., Calvin Theol. Sem. iv-155 p. + bibliog. – CalvinT 25 (GR 1990; no other date assigned) 336.

7551 ᴱ**Zeller** Dieter, Menschwerdung Gottes — Vergöttlichung von Menschen: NTOrb 7, 1988 → 5,769: ᴿOLZ 85 (1990) 522-4 (H.-M. *Schenke*).

H5.5 *Spiritus Sanctus; pneumatologia* – **The Holy Spirit.**

7552 **Anderson** James B., A Vatican II pneumatology of the paschal mystery; the historical doctrinal genesis of Ad Gentes 1,2-5, ᴰ1988 → 4,8558; 5,7541*: ᴿAnHConc 21 (1989) 228-230 (J. *Schumacher*); CC 141 (1990,2) 99s (G. *Ferraro*); VerbumSVD 30 (1989) 94-97 (H. *Scholz*).

7553 **Asciutto** L., Rapsodia spirituale; il Nuovo Testamento ci parla dello Spirito. Brescia 1989, Morcelliana, 208 p. Lit. 20.000 – ᴿStPatav 37 (1990) 212s (B. *Belletti*).

7553* **Berkhof** Hendrik, Theologie des Heiligen Geistes[2] [Nachtrag: Diskussion mit *Gerber* U.]. Neuk 1988, Neuk.–V. xi-182 p. DM 19,80. – [R]TGL 80 (1990) 102s (W. *Beinert*).

7554 **Burgess** Stanley M., The Holy Spirit; Eastern Christian traditions. Peabody MA 1989, Hendrickson. xii-260 p. $12. 0-913573-81-7 [RelStR 17, 167, Susan A. *Harvey*].

7555 *Caprioli* Mario, Lo Spirito Santo e il sacerdote: Teresianum 41 (1990) 589-616.

7556 **Chevallier** Max-Alain, Souffle de Dieu; le Saint-Esprit dans le Nouveau Testament [1. 1978 → 58,8329; 60,9030 ...] 2s. PoinT 54. P 1990s, Beauchesne. II. (Paul, Jean) p. 265-663; III. (Études) v-197 p. F 165 + 90. 2-7010-1166-3; -219-8.

7557 *Coffey* David, The Holy Spirit as the mutual love of the Father and the Son [... AUGUSTINE]: TS 51 (1990) 193-229.

7558 *Colwell* Gary, Speaking of the Holy Spirit [not 'Script' as on cover]: two misconceptions: RelStT 8,1s (1988) 55-65.

7559 **Comblin** José, The Holy Spirit and Liberation 1989 → 5,7547; also Burns-Oates £9; 0-86012-163-1: [R]ExpTim 101 (1989s) 52 (K.W. *Clements*); JRel 70 (1990) 473s (R. E. *Otto*).

7559* **Crosby** Daniel E., A critique of the pneumatological paradigm in the theologies of James D. G. DUNN and Gustavo GUTIÉRREZ; a question of eschatology: diss. SWBaptist Theol. Sem. 1990. 251 p. 90-33444. – DissA 51 (1990s) 2422-A.

7560 **Dabney** D. Lyle, Die Kenosis des Geistes; Kontinuität zwischen Schöpfung und Erlösung im Werk des Heiligen Geistes: Diss. Tübingen 1989 → 5,7548*: TLZ 115 (1990) 555.

7561 **Dirscherl** Erwin, Der Heilige Geist und das menschliche Bewusstsein; eine theologiegeschichtlich-systematische Untersuchung [Diss. Bonn. [D]*Breuning* W.]: Bonner Dogmatische St. 4. Wü 1989, Echter. 790 p. – [R]MüTZ 41 (1990) 186s (W. *Müller*); TPhil 65 (1990) 616-8 (M. *Kehl*).

Eaton Michael A., Baptism with the spirit ... LLOYD-JONES ... [Eph 1,13] 1989 → 6539.

7562 **Ervin** Howard M., Conversion-initiation and the baptism in the Holy Spirit; a critique of James D. G. DUNN, Baptism in the Holy Spirit. Peabody MA 1984, Hendrickson. viii-172 p. 0-913573-12-4.

7562* **Hilberath** Bernd J., Heiliger Geist — heilender Geist. Mainz 1988, Grünewald. 120 p. DM 16,80. – [R]TR 86 (1990) 186s (K. J. *Lesch*).

7563 *Hübner* Hans, Der Heilige Geist in der Heiligen Schrift: KerDo 36 (1990) 181-207; Eng. 207.

7563* **Kim Sung Soo**, Creator Spiritus; the Holy Spirit in the theology of Karl BARTH: diss. Southern Baptist Theol. Sem. [D]*Ward* W. 1990. 342 p. 91-12509. – DissA 51 (1990s) 3793-A.

7564 **Lambiasi** F., Lo Spirito Santo, memoria e presenza 1987 → 4,8574; 5,7555: [R]Divinitas 33 (1989) 195 (A. *Pedrini*); Salesianum 52 (1990) 442s (A. *Amato*).

7564* *Langemeyer* Georg B., Grundlegende Aspekte einer systematischen Pneumatologie: TGL 80 (1990) 3-21.

7565 **Lavatori** Renzo, *a*) Lo Spirito Santo ... BASILIO 1986 → 2,5705; 5,7556: [R]ÉglT 20 (1989) 502-6 (G. *Hudon*). – *b*) Lo Spirito Santo dono del Padre e del Figlio. Bo 1987, Dehoniane. 304 p. Lit. 30.000. 88-10-40906-X. – [R]DoctCom 42 (1989) 201s (A. *Pedrini*).

7565* **Lin Hong-Hsin,** Die Person des Heiligen Geistes als Thema der Pneumatologie in der Reformierten Kirche: ev. Diss. ᴰ*Moltmann* J. Tübingen 1989s. – TR 86 (1990) 519.
7566 *Magnoli* Claudio, Quarant'anni di letteratura liturgica attorno al tema pneumatologico: ScuolC 117 (1989) 77-103.
7567 a) *Miguel González* José M. de, Presencia del Espíritu Santo en la celebración eucarística; – b) *Garijo Güembe* M. M., Epíclesis y Trinidad; rememoración y presencia de Cristo: EstTrin 24 (1990) 141-159 / 107-139.
7568 **Navarro Girón** María Ángeles, La acción del Espíritu Santo en la transformación eucarística según la tradición patrística: RET 50 (1990) 29-54.
7569 ᵀᴱ**Noce** Celestino, DIDIMO, il Cieco, Lo Spirito Santo: TPatr 89. R 1990, Città Nuova. 173 p. Lit. 15.000. 88-311-3089-7.
7570 **Packer** James L. Auf den Spuren des Heiligen Geistes [1984 → 1,7026],ᵀ. Giessen 1989, Brunnen. 287 p. – ᴿTGL 79 (1989) 627 (W. *Beinert*).
7571 *Remy* Gérard, Une théologie pascale de l'Esprit Saint [DURRWELL F. 1989]: NRT 112 (1990) 731-741.
7572 **Rodenberg** O., Gott redet noch; das Zeugnis der Bibel vom Heiligen Geist: Theologie & Dienst 58. Giessen 1989, Brunnen. 44 p. DM 6,80. 3-7655-9058-4 [NTAbs 35,260].
7573 **Santos Ferreira** J. M. dos, Teologia do Espírito Santo em AGOSTINHO ᴰ1987 → 5,7562: ᴿSalmanticensis 37 (1990) 249s (R. *Trevijano*).
7574 **Vermeulen** C., Het hart van de kerk; de plaats van de Heilige Geest in de theologie van Karl BARTH [< ᴰ1986 → 2,6148]. Nijkerk 1986, Callenbach. 340 p. *f* 39,50. – ᴿKerkT 40 (1989) 164s (H. *Vreekamp*).

H5.6 *Spiritus et Filius*; 'Spirit-Christology'.

7575 *Brito* Emilio, Le rapport du Christ et du Saint-Esprit dans la 'Glaubenslehre' de SCHLEIERMACHER: ETL 66 (1990) 319-354.
7576 *Cerbelaud* Dominique, Questions et réponses sur le 'Filioque' [*Bobrinskoy* B., *Meyer* H., *Sesboüé* B., *al.*]: BLitEc 91 (1990) 243-250.
7577 **Congar** Yves, The Word and the Spirit [1984 → 65,6402], ᵀ*Smith* David, 1986 → 2,5726 ... 4,8586: ᴿScripB 20 (1989s) 17 (M. *King*).
7577* **Gamillscheg** Maria H. A., Die Kontroverse um das Filioque; Möglichkeiten einer Problemlösung auf Grund der Forschungen und Gespräche der letzten hundert Jahre: kath. Diss. ᴰ*Suttner* E. Wien 1990. – RTLv 22, p.516.
7578 *Ladaria* Luis F., La unción de Jesús y el don del Espíritu: Gregorianum 71 (1990) 547-570; franç. 571.
7578* **Riaud** Alexis, Le Filioque; origine et rôle de la troisième Personne de la Trinité. P 1989, Fraternités S-Esprit. 71 p. – ᴿArTGran 53 (1990) 361s (A. *Segovia*).
7579 *Theobald* Michael, Geist- und Inkarnationschristologie; zur Pragmatik des Johannesprologs (Joh 1,1-18): ZkT 112 (1990) 129-149.

H5.7 *Ssma Trinitas* – The Holy Trinity.

7580 *Arias Reyero* Maximino, Teología de la Trinidad (desde el concilio Vaticano II): → 125, ᶠMORENO/VILLEGAS 1990, 249-293.
7581 **Boff** Leonardo, Trinity and society 1988 → 5,7584: ᴿAnglTR 72 (1990) 112-4 (J. E. *Skinner*); GrOrTR 34 (1989) 180-2 (J. *Gros*); JPsy&T 17

(1989) 185s (M.K. *Mayers*); Salesianum 52 (1990) 747 (L.A. *Gallo*); Tablet 243 (1989) 1213s (J. *O'Donnell*: basically acceptable, more precision needed); TS 51 (1990) 143-5 (R.T. *Sears*).

7582 *Braaten* Carl E., The triune God; the source and model of Christian unity and mission: Missiology 18 (1990) 415-427.

7583 **Bradshaw** Timothy, Trinity and ontology; a comparative study of the theologies of Karl BARTH and Wolfhart PANNENBERG. E 1988, Rutherford. 460 p. £27. 0-946068-31-3. – RÉTRel 65 (1990) 472s (D. *Müller*).

7584 *Ciola* Nicola, La crisi del teocentrismo trinitario e il suo 'superamento' nella odierna teologia trinitaria; riflessoni storico-sistematiche: Lateranum 56 (1990) 183-218 [219-249, Maria e la SS. Trinità, *Sciattella* Marco].

7585 **Courth** Franz, Trinität in der Schrift und Patristik: HbDG 2/1a, 1988 ➤ 4,8605: RTR 86 (1990) 458-464 (B. *Studer*) [1b, 1985 ➤ 1,7058, in der Scholastik, 464-6 V. *Marcolino*].

7586 *Daubercies* P., Réflexions sur nature et personne: EsprVie 100 (1990) 17-24. 33-39.

7587 **Elorriaga** Carlos, Revelación y Trinidad en Karl BARTH: EstTrin 23 (1989) 173-189.

7588 **Forte** Bruno, La Trinité comme histoire 1989 ➤ 5,7590: RFoiTemps 20 (1990) 375s (G. *Harpigny*); NRT 112 (1990) 608s (L. *Renwart*).

7589 *Forte* Bruno, Trinität als Geschichte; der lebendige Gott — Gott der Lebenden. Mainz 1989, Grünewald. – RRHPR 70 (1990) 484 (G. *Siegwalt*: needed in French); TPhil 65 (1990) 309s (W. *Löser*).

7590 *Forte* Bruno, Trinità e rivelazione; un dialogo teologico con HEGEL, SCHELLING e BARTH: Asprenas 37 (1990) 5-26.

7591 *Galot* Jean, La génération éternelle du Fils: Gregorianum 71 (1990) 657-678; Eng. 678.

7592 *Grey* Mary, The core of our desire; [feminist] re-imaging the Trinity: TLond 93 (1990) 363-372.

7593 **Grözinger** Albrecht, Erzählen und Handeln; Studien zu einer trinitarischen Grundlegung der Praktischen Theologie [i. 'Geschichte' als Mitte der Trinitätslehre ...]. Mü 1989, Kaiser. 130 p. DM 14,80. – RBTZ 7 (1990) 286-290 (C. *Grethlein*); TLZ 115 (1990) 541-3 (E. *Hühner*).

7594 **Hilberath** Bernd J., Der Personbegriff der Trinitätstheologie ... D1986 ➤ 2,5753 ... 5,7592: RNedTTs 44 (1990) 83s (A. van de *Beek*).

7595 **Kelly** Anthony, The Trinity of love; a theology of the Christian God. Mp/L 1989, Glazier/Fowler Wright. xiv-272 p. £13. 0-89453-743-1. – RExpTim 101 (1989s) 316 (R. *Butterworth*).

7595* **Leslie** Benjamin, Trinitarian hermeneutics ... K. BARTH: diss. DGeisser. Zürich 1989s. – TR 86,512.

7596 *McGrath* Alister E., Understanding the Trinity. GR 1988, Zondervan. 154 p. [RelStR 17, 143, G. *Charter*].

7597 *Martínez Fernández* Francisco J., El pensamiento trinitario de JUAN PABLO II: EstTrin 22 (1988) 265-315.

7598 **Milano** Andrea, La Trinità dei teologi e dei filosofi; l'intelligenza della persona in Dio 1987 ➤ 4,8624: REsprVie 100 (1990) 207s (P. *Jay*).

7599 **Navone** John J., Self-giving and sharing; the Trinity and human fulfillment. Collegeville MN 1989, Liturgical. x-161 p.; $12 pa. 0-8146-1774-3 [TDig 37,278], – RHomPast 90,11s (1989s) 88s (J.V. *Schall,* grace and wisdom).

7600 **O'Donnell** J.J., The mystery of the Triune God 1988 ➤ 4,8626; 5,7598: RTVida 31 (1990) 217s (M. *Arias*).

7601 **O'Donnell** John J.,   Il mistero della Trinità 1989 → 5,7599:   ᴿCC 141
(1990,3) 301s (M. *Simone*); NRT 112 (1990) 609s (L. *Renwart*); Protestantesimo 45 (1990) 327s (B. *Rostagno*).
7601* *a) Olson* R.,   Wolfhartᴘᴀɴɴᴇɴʙᴇʀɢ's doctrine of the Trinity; – *b)*
Spence Alan,   John Oᴡᴇɴ and trinitarian agency: ScotJT 43 (1990)
175-206 / 157-173.
7602 *Osborne* Kenan B.,   Trinitarian doctrine: → 837*, DMA 12 (1989)
189-198.
7603 *Panikkar* Raimon,   La Trinidad y la experiencia religiosa: Aguas Vivas.
Barc 1989, Obelisco. – ᴿQVidCr 150 (1990) 213s L. *Duch*).
7604 **Panikkar** Raimundo,   Trinità ed esperienza religiosa del'uomo.   Assisi
1989, Cittadella.   127 p. Lit. 16.000. – ᴿHumBr 45 (1990) 866 (T. *Goffi*:
not a theological treatise, but threads of a real insight).
7604* **Pauw** Amy,   The supreme harmony of all; the Trinity in the thought of
Jonathan Eᴅᴡᴀʀᴅs: Diss. Yale, ᴰ*Kelsey* D.   NHv 1990. – RelStR 17,192.
7605 **Peñamaría de Llano** Antonio,   El Dios de los cristianos; estructura
introductoria a la teología de la Trinidad (tratado de Dios uno y trino):
Síntesis 2/2. M 1990. Atenas.   292 p.
7606 **Pikaza** Xabier,   Dios como Espíritu y Persona; razón humana y misterio
trinitario: Koinonia 24.   S 1989, Secr. Trin. – ᴿLumenVr 39 (1990) 344s
(F. *Ortiz de Urtaran*); QVidCr 150 (1990) 213s (J. *Bosch*); TVida 31 (1990)
220s (M. *Arias*).
7607 **Radlbeck** Regina,   Der Personbegriff in der Trinitätstheologie der Gegenwart, untersucht am Beispiel der Entwürfe J. Mᴏʟᴛᴍᴀɴɴs und W.
Kᴀsᴘᴇʀs [Diss. ...] Rg 1989, Pustet.   232 p. – ᴿArTGran 53 (1990) 360s
(R. *Franco*); Carthaginensia 6 (1990) 382s (F. *Martínez Fresneda*); CiTom
117 (1990) 393-5 (L. *Lago*).
7607* **Rhee Jung Suck**,   A history of the doctrine of the eternal generation of
the Son and its significance in the doctrine of the Trinity: diss. ᴰ*Plantinga*
C., Calvin Theol. Sem. vi-225 p. + bibliog. – CalvinT 25 (GR 1990; no
other date assigned) 335s.
7608 **Sesé Alegre** F. J.,   Trinidad, Escritura, historia; la Trinidad y el Espíritu
Santo en la teología de Rᴜᴘᴇʀᴛᴏ de Deutz.   Pamplona 1988, Eunsa,
278 p. – ᴿAnnTh 4 (1990) 175-7 (A. C. *Chacón*).
7609 *Silanes* Nereo,   La Trinidad en la reflexión teológica hodierna, boletín
bibliográfico: EstTrin 23 (1989) 299-313.
7610 **Simonet** André,   Éléments pour une spiritualité trinitaire; I. La source;
II. Le jaillissment; III. La gerbe.   Namur 1989, Centre diocésain; I. 144 p.;
IIs, 1990, 150 p.; III. 144 p. – ᴿPrOrChr 40 (1990) 202s (P. *Ternant*).
7611 **Smalbrugge** Matthias,   La nature trinitaire de l'intelligence ᴀᴜɢᴜs-
ᴛɪɴɪᴇɴɴᴇ de la foi: Amst. StTheology 6.   Amst 1988, Rodopi. x-205 p. –
ᴿTLZ 115 (1990) 129 (K.-H. *Kandler*).
7612 **Spada** Domenico,   Le formule trinitarie, da Nicea a Costantinopoli:
Subsidia Urb. 32.   R 1988, Pont. Univ. Urbaniana.   417 p. Lit. 45.000. –
ᴿArTGran 52 (1989) 288s (A. *Segovia*); Gregorianum 71 (1990) 185s (C. I.
González).
7613 *Stăniloae* Dumitru, [en roumain] La Sainte Trinité — créatrice, salvatrice
et but éternel de tous les croyants: OrtBuc 38,2 (1986) 14-63.
7614 **Tavard** Georges,   La vision de la Trinité [1981]: Théologies. P/Mon-
tréal 1989, Cerf/Bellarmin.   168 p. F 95. – ᴿRTLv 21 (1990) 365s (A. de
Halleux).
7615 **Torrance** Thomas F.,   The Trinitarian faith 1988 → 4,8640; 5,7606:
ᴿCalvinT 25 (1990) 119-123 (J. D. *Morrison*); ExpTim 102 (1990s) 186

(R. *Butterworth*); ScotJT 43 (1990) 263-7 (D. F. *Ford*); Themelios 16 (1990s) 32 (J. *Webster*); TS 51 (1990) 522-4 (J. A. *Bracken*).

7616 *Torrance* Thomas F., *a*) CALVIN's doctrine of the Trinity: CalvinT 25 (1990) 165-193. – *b*) The doctrine of the Holy Trinity according to St. ATHANASIUS: AnglTR 71 (1989) 395-405.

7617 *Vives* Josep, Trinitat, creació i salvació en la història: RCatalT 15 (1990) 155-180; Eng. 180.

7618 **Willis** W. Waite^J, Theism, atheism and the doctrine of the Trinity 1987 ➤ 3,7191; 5,7607: ^RAnglTR 71 (1989) 328-330 (D. *Scott*: very ambitious); JRel 70 (1990) 114s (Catherine M. *La Cugna*).

H5.8 *Regnum messianicum, Filius hominis* - **Messianic kingdom, Son of Man.**

7619 *Baumann* Rolf, 'Gottesherrschaft' oder 'Reich Gottes': Orientierung 54 (1990) 74-78.

7619* **Bejick** Urte, Basileia; Vorstellungen vom Königtum Gottes im Umfeld des Neuen Testaments: diss. Heidelberg 1990s, ^DBerger. – RTLv 22,591.

7620 *Blei* K., Koninkryk Gods en geschiedenis, in gesprek met W. PANNENBERG: KerkT 41 (1990) 103-116.

7621 *Botha* C. J., What is the Kingdom of God?: TEv 22,3 (Pretoria 1989) 30-35 [< NTAbs 34,204].

7621* **Cantalamessa** Raniero, La vie dans la Seigneurie du Christ, ^TBurkard Ginette, *al.*: Théologies. P 1990, Cerf. 292 p. F 148. – ^REsprVie 100 (1990) 335 (E. *Vauthier*); Études 373 (1990) 570 (R. *Marlé*).

7622 **Findeis** Jürgen, Die Dynamik der Gottesherrschaft; exegetisch-theologische Studie zur Vergegenwärtigung der Gottesherrschaft in der Partizipation der Völker am eschatologischen Gottesheil: Hab.-Diss. ^DKertelge. Münster 1989. – TR 86 (1990) 510.

7622* *Focant* Camille, La famille en perspective du Royaume; Jésus et les familles: LVitae 44 (1989) 7-20.

7623 *Glasson* T. Francis, The temporary Messianic kingdom and the Kingdom of God: JTS 41 (1990) 517-525.

7624 **Hampel** Volker, Menschensohn und historischer Jesus; ein Rätselwort als Schlüssel zum messianischen Selbstverständnis Jesu. Neuk 1990, Neuk-V. xiv-418 p. DM 68. 3-7887-1287-2 [NTAbs 35,102].

7625 **Hare** Douglas R. A., The Son of Man tradition. Mp 1990, Fortress. xiv-316 p. $25. 0-8006-2448-3 [NTAbs 35,257].

7626 **Kearns** Rollin, Die Entchristologisierung des Menschensohn 1988 ➤ 4, 8657, 5,7624: ^REstE 65 (1990) 365-7 (A. *Vargas Machuca*); JBL 109 (1990) 721-3 (R. H. *Fuller*); JTS 41 (1990) 171-5 (M. *Casey*: his fifth learned and ingenious book on the subject); Salesianum 52 (1990) 740s (C. *Bissoli*).

7627 **Khamor** Levi [= *Opisso* A. M.], The revelation of the Son of Man. Petersham MA 1989, St. Bede's. xvi-326 p. $16 pa. 0-932506-51-8 [NTAbs 34,125].

7627* **Kim Jae Sung**, CALVIN's doctrine of the Kingdom of God: diss. ^DGamble R., Calvin Theol. Sem. v-162 p. + bibliog. – CalvinT 25 (GR 1990; no other date assigned) 332.

Kingsbury J. D., 'Son of Man' in Lk 1990 ➤ 5366.

7628 *Lewellen* Thomas C., Has lordship salvation been taught throughout church history?: BS 147 (1990) 54-68.

7629 *McCarthy* Brian R., Jesus, the Kingdom, and theopolitics: ➤ 544, SBL seminars 1990, 311-321.

7630 **Margerie** B. de, Liberté religieuse et Règne du Christ 1988 ➤ 4,8662; 5,7630: ^RAntonianum 65 (1990) 677s (P. G. *Pesce*); ScEspr 42 (1990) 115 (G. *Pelland*: valable contre LEFÈVRE; mais il y a encore l'Église du siècle dernier); ScripTPamp 22 (1990) 293 (J. L. *Illanes*).

7631 *Moltmann* Jürgen, Zuerst das Reich Gottes: Gottes Herrschaft im Himmel oder auf Erden?: EvKomm 22,8 (1989) 10-15.

7632 **Müller** Mogens, Der Ausdruck 'Menschensohn' in den Evangelien; Voraussetzungen und Bedeutung 1984 ➤ 65,6456 ... 3,7228: ^RSvEx 55 (1990) 137s (C. C. *Caragounis* presents without critical judgments a book with which he radically disagrees).

7633 *Oreng* E. A., The 'Son of Man' motif and the intercession of Jesus: AfTJ 19,2 (1990) 155-167 [< NTAbs 35,195].

7634 *Ramos Guerreira* Julio A., Cristo, Reino y mundo, tres referencias obligadas para la acción pastoral de la Iglesia: Salmanticensis 37 (1990) 177-200; Eng. 200.

7635 *Rászlai* Tibor, Ⓜ Rabbi, and/or Lord; toward God's sole lordship: TSzem 33 (1990) 182-8.

7635* **Schnackenburg** Rudolf, Signoria e Regno di Dio, uno studio di teologia biblica [Gottes Herrschaft und Reich 1965], ^T*Mastandrea* A., al.: Studi Religiosi. Bo 1990, Dehoniane. xxxvii-430 p. 88-10-40774-1.

7636 **Schütz** Georg, Plädoyer für eine optimistische Theologie; Entwürfe einer narrativen Basileiologie: Diss. Theol. 60. St. Ottilien 1985, EOS. 665 p. 3-88096-806-3. – ^REstE 65 (1990) 267s (J. J. *Alemany*).

7637 **Schwarz** G., Jesus 'der Menschensohn'; aram.... 1986 ➤ 2,3808 ... 4, 8666: ^RKerkT 41 (1990) 143s (G. *Mussies*).

7638 **Sheehan** Thomas, The first coming; how the Kingdom of God became Christianity 1986 ➤ 2,3178 ... 5,7677: ^RCurrTMiss 17 (1990) 303s (J. C. *Rochelle*); JEH 41 (1990) 275s (B. *Hebblethwaite*: bad history, but shows that historical methods alone do not suffice); JStNT 38 (1990) 128 (S. E. *Porter*: promises much, delivers little); LvSt 15 (1990) 73-76 (R. *Michiels*); TR 86 (1990) 375s (R. *Kampling*: US-mix with Belletristik).

7639 **Viviano** Benedict T., The Kingdom of God in history 1988 ➤ 4,8671; 5,7640: ^RBibTB 20 (1990) 135 (A. J. *Tambasco*).

7639* *Walther* Christian, Königsherrschaft Christi: ➤ 857, TRE 19 (1990) 311-323.

H6.1 *Creatio, sabbatum NT* [➤ E3.5]; **The Creation** [➤ E1.6; H2.8].

7640 *Artola* José M., Consideraciones sobre la doctrina de Santo TOMÁS acerca de la creación: CiTom 117 (1990) 213-229.

7641 **Bacchiocchi** Samuele, Du sabbat au dimanche [^D1977] ^T*Sébire* D. 1984 ➤ 1,7135 ... 4,8673: ^RRThom 90 (1990) 349s (J.-M.F.).

7642 *a*) *Bettiolo* Paolo, 'Avec la charité comme but'; Dieu et création dans la méditation d'ISAAC de Ninive; – *b*) *Joos* André, La nouvelle création; rencontre du divin et de l'humain dans la Sophia; Pavel FLORENSKIJ: Irénikon 63 (1990) 323-345, Eng. 345 / 346-358. 463-482; Eng. 358.482.

7643 *Blandino* Giovanni, The motive for creation and incarnation: Teresianum 41 (1990) 255-260.

7644 **Daly** Gabriel, Creation and redemption: Theology for a pilgrim people. Dublin 1989, Gill & M. 230 p. £8 pa. – ^RAugSt 19 (1988!) 207-212 (F. Van *Fleteren*: imprecisions); DocLife 39 (1989) 444s (J. *Paterson*: Irish names once again in theological writing); MilltSt 25 (1990) 114-6 (J. *Macken*).

7645 **Dawn** Marva J., Keeping the sabbath ['] wholly[']; ceasing, resting, embracing, feasting. GR 1989, Eerdmans. xvii-217 p. $11 pa. [AndrUnS 28,189].

7646 **Ganoczy** A., Doctrina de la creación [1983], T1986 → 3,7247: RTVida 29 (1988) 309s (C. *Casale*).

7647 EGerardi Renzo, La creazione, Dio, il cosmo, l'uomo [con saggi di *Bonora* A., *Salvati* G., *Mosso* S., *Salmona* B.; Movimento ecclesiale di impegno culturale, S. Lussurgiu, Oristano, sett. 1988]: Coscienza 19. R 1990, Studium. 162 p. – RLateranum 56 (1990) 414 (*ipse*).

7648 **Katz** David S., Sabbath and sectarianism 1988 → 5,7645: RJTS 41 (1990) 295s (B. *White*).

7649 *Lemmens* Leon, De zondag in het licht van de paasverschijningen: CollatVL 20 (1990) 257-271.

7649* **Lonchamp** Jean-Pierre, La création du monde: Petite enc.mod.chr. P 1990, D-Brouwer. 136 p. F 43. – REsprVie 100 (1990) 509s & 328-*jaune* (P. *Jay*).

7650 **Manaranche** André, En séparant le sable de l'eau; la Création [en forme de lettres à un jeune homme]: Lumière et Vérité. 292 p. F 65. – REsprVie 100 (1990) 344s (P. *Jay*).

7651 *Melendo Granados* Tomás, Creación divina y trabajo humano: Burgense 31 (1990) 47-65.

7652 *Molnar* Paul L., The function of the Trinity in MOLTMANN's ecological doctrine of creation: TS 51 (1990) 673-697.

7653 **Parker** K. L., The English Sabbath 1988 → 5,7648. RIstina 35 (1990) 231 (B. *Dupuy*); JEH 41 (1990) 491-5 (A. *Milton,* also on KATZ D.).

7654 **Primus** John H., Holy time; moderate Puritanism and the Sabbath. Macon GA 1990, Mercer Univ. $25; pa. $17. 0-86554-30-2;-50-X. [RelStR 17, 77, D. A. *Sweeney*].

7655 *Richard* Jean, Le traité de la création dans la dogmatique allemande de Paul TILLICH: RHPR 70 (1990) 108-124; Eng. 145.

7656 **Ruiz de la Peña** José L., Teología de la creación 1986 → 2,5820... 5,7650; ²1987, 84-293-0736-2: REstE 65 (1990) 231s (P. *Ferrer Pi*).

7657 **Ruiz de la Peña** J. L., Teologia della creazione. R 1988, Borla. 158 p. Lit. 25.000. – RStPatav 37 (1990) 205s (L. *Sartori*).

7658 *Scharbert* Josef, Biblischer Sabbat und modernes Wochenende: → 146, FREINELT H., AT-Botschaft 1990, 285-306.

7659 *a) Siefer* Gregor, Verschwindet der Sonntag im Wochenende?; – *b) Mette* Norbert, Sonntag ohne Samstag? Ein Diskussionsbeitrag zu kirchlichen Stellunghahme: Diakonia 21,1 (Mainz 1990) 13-20 / 39-41 [< ZIT 90,197].

7660 **Tanner** Kathryn, God and creation in Christian theology; tyranny or empowerment? 1988 → 5,7652: RRelSt 26 (1990) 550-2 (D. F. *Ford*); TS 41 (1990) 140s (J. E. *Thiel*); TTod 47 (1990s) 66.68s (J. M. *Incandela*).

H6.3 *Fides, veritas in NT* – **Faith and truth.**

7661 **Akhtar** Shabbir, Reason and the radical crisis of faith: AmerUnivSt 7/30. NY 1987, P. Lang. 281 p. $40. 0-8204-0451-9. – RJAAR 58 (1990) 111-3 (Arvind *Sharma*).

7661* **Arens** Edmund, Bezeugen und bekennen, elementare Handlungen des Glaubens [Hab.-Diss. Münster, DMetz J.-B.]: BeitTRelW. Dü 1989, Patmos. 464 p. DM 40. – RTGL 80 (1990) 211 (W. *Beinert*).

7662 **Badia** L. F., Basic Catholic beliefs for today; the Creed explained. NY 1984, Alba, 170 p. $9. 0-8189-8469-0. – ᴿRelStT 8,1s (1988) 91-93 (E. J. *McCullough*).

7663 [Die belgischen Bischöfe] Unser Glaube; wie wir ihn bekennen, feiern und leben, ᵀ*Schütz* Ulrich, 1988 ➤ 5,7656: ᴿTR 86 (1990) 52-54 (D. *Emeis*).

7664 [Belgium bishops' Livre de la foi] Believing and belonging; living and celebrating the faith. Collegeville 1990, Liturgical. x-218 p. $12. 0-8146-1598-8 [TDig 37,345].

7665 *Bodem* Anton, Hierarchie der Wahrheiten: Salesianum 52 (1990) 857-869.

7666 [Vicente] *Burgoa* Lorenzo, Información y credibilidad; un análisis crítico del testimonio y de la creencia: Studium 29 (M 1989) 415-460.

7667 **Charlton** William, Philosophy and Christian belief. L 1988, Sheed & W. 244 p. £12.50. 0-7220-6630-9. – ᴿGregorianum 71 (1990) 389s (J. M. *McDermott*).

7668 ᴱ**Colombo** G., L'evidenza e la fede. Mi 1988, Glossa. 479 p. – ᴿAnnTh 4 (1990) 447-454 (A. *Blanco*); Burgense 31 (1990) 273s (R. *Berzosa Martínez*).

7669 *Duran* Alain, No hay fe sin relación con los pobres [< VSp 142 (1988) 273-290], ᵀᴱ*Pou* Eduard: SelT 29 (1990) 3-12.

7670 **Ellul** Jacques, Ce que je crois. P 1987, Grasset. 292 p. F 88. – ᴿDiv-Thom 92 (1989) 432 (Y. *Poutet*).

7671 **Fischer** Johannes, Glaube als Erkenntnis; zum Wahrnehmungscharakter des christlichen Glaubens: BeitEvT 105. Mü 1989, Kaiser. 202 p. DM 56. – ᴿActuBbg 27 (1990) 69s (J. *Boada*); TGL 80 (1990) 354 (W. *Beinert*); TLZ 115 (1990) 537-540 (B. *Hildebrandt*).

7672 **Freyburger** Gérard, Fides 1986 ➤ 3,7221; 4,8697: ᴿAntClas 59 (1990) 439-441 (B. *Rochette*).

7672* *Gagey* Henri-J., La foi chez Bᴜʟᴛᴍᴀɴɴ et après lui ➤ 404, Identité 1990, 129-170.

7673 *García Trapiello* J., La fe bíblica, sometida a prueba: Angelicum 67 (1990) 509-537.

7673* **Gau** James V., The theological and psychological foundations of adult faith, as seen in Hans Urs von Bᴀʟᴛʜᴀsᴀʀ, Melanie Kʟᴇɪɴ, and D. W. Wɪɴɴɪᴄᴏᴛᴛ: diss. ᴰ*Schurman* P. Claremont 1990. 240 p. 90-34149. – DissA 51 (1990s) 2422-A.

7674 *Hodges* Z. C., We believe in: Assurance of salvation: JGrace 3,2 (1990) 3-17 [< NTAbs 35,198].

7675 **Holloway** Richard, Crossfire; faith and doubt in an age of certainty. GR 1988, Eerdmans. 175 p. $11 pa. – ᴿAnglTR 72 (1990) 344-6 (E. G. *Adams*).

7676 **Jossua** Jean-Pierre, La foi en question: Présence. P 1989, Flammarion. 147 p. – ᴿLavalTP 46 (1990) 426s (J. C. *Breton*, aussi sur 'Le Dieu de la foi chr.').

7677 **Kasper** Walter, La foi au défi [1985s],ᵀ. P 1989, Nouvelle Cité. – ᴿQVidCr 152s (1990) 171s (B. *Ubach*).

Kee Howard C., Knowing the truth; a sociological approach 1989 ➤ g644.

7678 *Kiesow* Klaus, Wege aus der Glaubenskrise — drei biblische Modelle: WAntw 31 (Mainz 1990) 83-87 [< zɪᴛ 90,398].

7679 **Lagarde** Claude & Jacqueline, L'adolescent et la foi de l'Église; animer une équipe en catéchèse: Ephéta 2. P 1990, Centurion/Privat. 244 p. F 79. – ᴿEsprVie 100 (1990) 222s (L. *Barbey*).

7679* *La Potterie* Ignace de,   Verità: ➤ 838, DizTF 1990, 5-19.

7680 **Lochman** Jan M.,   The faith we confess 1984 ➤ 1,7178 ... 4,8701:   ᴿIr-TQ 56 (1990) 150s (A. P. F. *Sell*).

7681 **Lønning** Per,   Kristen tro; tradisjon og oppbrudd.   Oslo 1989, Univ. 310 p. Nk 275. – ᴿNorTTs 91 (1990) 168-170 (P. W. *Böckman*).

7682 **Miller** David L.,   Hells and Holy Ghosts, a theopoetics of Christian belief.   Nv 1989, Abingdon. – ᴿRHPR 70 (1990) 482s (G. *Vahanian*: the author of 'Christs' and 'Three faces of God' shows that fundamentalism and paganism cohabit).

7683 **Müller** Alois,   Der dritte Weg zum Glauben; Christsein zwischen Rückzug und Auszug: G-Reihe.   Mainz 1990, Grünewald.   106 p. DM 19,80. – ᴿZkT 112 (1990) 343s (K. H. *Neufeld*).

7684 **Nadeau** Marie-Thérèse,   Foi de l'Église; évolution et sens d'une formule: THist 78.   P 1988, Beauchesne.   341 p. F 135. – ᴿEsprVie 100 (1990) 202-4 (P. *Jay*: 'locution employée... à propos du baptême des petits enfants': mais p. 223 donne une récension de Lᴀɢᴀʀᴅᴇ ➤ 7679).

7685 **Niebuhr** H. R.,   ᴱ*Niebuhr* R. R.,   Faith on earth; an inquiry into the structure of human faith.   NHv 1989, Yale Univ.   123 p. $18. – ᴿTTod 47 (1990s) 308-310 (G. *Green*).

7685* **Pojman** Louis P.,   Religious belief and the will.   L 1886, Routledge. xiii-258 p. £20. – ᴿRelSt 25 (1989) 131-4 (J. *Harrison*).

7686 **Rebell** Walter (Psycholog),   Alles ist möglich dem, der glaubt; Glaubensvollmacht im frühen Christentum.   Mü 1989, Kaiser.   167 p. DM 29,80. 3-459-01789-9.   ᴿActuBbg 27 (1990) 211s (J. *Boada*); TLZ 115 (1990) 31-33 (K. T. *Kleinknecht*).

7687 **Sabugal** S.,   Io credo; la fede della Chiesa; il simbolo della fede, storia e interpretazione.   R 1990, Dehoniane.   1294 p. Lit. 100.000. – ᴿAsprenas 37 (1990) 250s (B. *Forte*); StPatav 37 (1990) 385-7 (E. R. *Tura*).

7687* *Schlüter* Richard,   Die Gemeinde als Lernort des Glaubens; Überlegungen zu einer Dimension der Gemeindepädagogik heute: TGʟ 80 (1990) 165-179.

7688 **Schneider** Theodor,   La nostra fede; una spiegazione del simbolo apostolico.   R 1989, Queriniana.   532 p. Lit. 60.000. – ᴿRivScR 4 (1990) 603-9 (A. *Restu*).

7689 **Sheard** Robert B.,   Let God be God; the historical dimension of religious truth: RelStT 8,1s (1988) 45-53.

7689* **Theissen** Gerd,   Biblical faith, an evolutionary approach 1984 ➤ 65, 6510 ... 3,7300:   ᴿRHPR 70 (1990) 242s (G. *Vahanian*).

7690 **Zielinski** Vladimir,   Afin que le monde croie; méditation d'un croyant orthodoxe à propos du livre du Cardinal Rᴀᴛᴢɪɴɢᴇʀ, Entretiens sur la foi.   P 1989, Nouvelle Cité.   159 p. F 78. – ᴿNRT 112 (1990) 932 (L.-J. *Renard*).

H6.6   *Peccatum NT* – Sin, Evil [➤ E1.9].

7691 *Bracchi* Remo,   Il concetto di 'peccato' nei nomi che lo definiscono: EphLtg 103 (1990) 221-268. 368-405; lat. 221,368.

7692 *Brown* S.,   Sin and atonement; biblical imagery and the experience of evil: UnSemQ 44,1s (1990) 151-6 [< NTAbs 35,59].

7693 **Delumeau** Jean,   Il peccato e la paura; l'idea di colpa in Occidente dal XIII al XVII secolo: Le occasioni 11, 1987 ➤ 5,7677; Lit. 60.000: ᴿAsprenas 37 (1990) 87-92 (P. *Pifano*).

7694 — *Basset* Lytta, Le péché à l'heure de la déculpabilisation [*Delumeau* J., Le péché et la peur 1983]: RTPhil 121 (1989) 423-439.

7695 **Gestrich** Christof, Die Wiederkehr des Glanzes in der Welt; die christliche Lehre von der Sünde und ihrer Vergebung in gegenwärtiger Verantwortung. Tü 1989, Mohr. x-394 p. DM 64. – ᴿTR 86 (1990) 481s (G. *Wenz*).

7696 — *Haas* Hanns-Stephan, Diagnose und Therapie der Überlebenskrise; Überlegungen zu Christoph GESTRICHS Lehre von der Sünde und ihrer Vergebung [Wiederkehr des Glanzes 1989]: VerkF 35,1 (1990) 84-94.

7697 **Görres** Albert, Karl RAHNER, Das Böse; Wege zu seiner Bewältigung in Psychotherapie und Christentum: Tb 1631. FrB 1989, Herder. 253 p. DM 14,90. – ᴿZkT 112 (1990) 122s (K. H. *Neufeld*).

7698 **Hatem** Jed, *a*) L'Écharde du mal dans la chair de Dieu; – *b*) Mal et transfiguration. P 1987, Cariscript. 244 p.; 187 p. – ᴿTR 86 (1990) 414-9 (J. *Clam*).

7699 **Highfield** Ron, BARTH and RAHNER in dialogue; towards an ecumenical understanding of sin and evil. NY 1989, Lang. 187 p. [JAAR 58,327].

7700 **Israel** Martin, *a*) The dark face of reality; a study of emergent awareness. L 1989, Collins Fount. 158 p. £ 3. 0-00-627150-2. – *b*) The quest for wholeness. L 1989, Darton-LT. 133 p. £7. 0-232-51756-8. – ᴿExpTim 101 (1989s) 57 (G. T. *Eddy*: a physician's wise but sometimes mythic reflections on evil) & 61 (E. H. *Robertson*).

7701 **Journet** Charles, Le mal, essai théologique. S.-Maurice 1988, S.-Augustin. 336 p. – ᴿNVFr 64 (1989) 75-77 (G. *Brazzola*).

7701* **Kulisz** Józef, ❷ TEILHARDOWSKIE rozumienie grzechu. Wsz 1989, Akad. Katol. Teol. 224 p. zł 900 [ColcT 59/4,176].

7702 **Millás** José M., Die Sünde in der Theologie R. BULTMANNS: FraTheolSt 34, 1987 → 3,7324; 5,7687: ᴿRTLv 21 (1990) 101s (E. *Brito*).

7703 **Millás** José M., Pecado y existencia cristiana; origen, desarrollo y función de la concepción del pecado en la teología de R. BULTMANN [→ 4,8718]. Barc 1989, Herder. 376 p. 84-254-1636-1. – ᴿActuBbg 27 (1990) 89 (J. *Boada*); Angelicum 67 (1990) 261-3 (S. *Jurić*); CommSev 23 (1990) 105-7 (M. de *Burgos*); EfMex 8 (1990) 263-7 (C. *Zesati*); EstE 65 (1990) 469s (J. *Iturriaga*); LumenVr 39 (1990) 78s (U. *Gil Ortega*); Salmanticensis 37 (1990) 255s (J.-R. *Flecha Andrés*).

7704 **Ohly** Friedrich, Metaphern für die Sündenstufen und die Gegenwirkungen der Gnade: Rh/Wf Akad Vorträge G 302. Opladen 1990, Westdeutscher-V. 169 p. DM 38. 3-531-07302-8.

7705 **O'Keefe** Mark, What are they saying about social sin? NY 1990, Paulist. 118 p. [NewTR 4/3, 130, G. D. *Coleman*].

7706 **Spaemann** Heinrich, Macht und Überwindung des Bösen in biblischer Sicht. Ostfildern 1988, Schwaben-V. 46 p. DM 9,80. – ᴿZkT 112 (1990) 221 (M. *Hasitschka*).

7707 **Vicchio** Stephen J., The voice from the whirlwind; the problem of evil and the modern world [diss]. Westminster MD 1989, Christian Classics. vi-326 p. $20. – ᴿTS 51 (1990) 763s (M. R. *Tripole*).

7708 *Visotzky* B. L., Mortal sins: UnSemQ 44,1s (1990) 31-53 [< NTAbs 35,83].

7709 *Wilkin* R. N., Repentance and salvation, 4. NT — Gospels, Acts: JGrace 3,1 (Roanoke TX 1990) 11-25 [< NTAbs 35, p. 18]; – 5. NT repentance ... epistles and Revelation: JGrace 3,2 (1990) 19-32 [< NTAbs 35, p. 203].

H7 Soteriologia NT.

Aalen S., Heilsverlangen ... ín der Apokalyptik 1990 ➤ 3970.

7710 *Akin* Daniel L., BERNARD of Clairvaux, evangelical of the 12th century (an analysis of his soteriology): CriswT 4 (1989s) 327-350.

7710* *Alonso Schökel* Luis, La simbolica biblica della salvezza: ➤ 671* Ragione/simboli 1988/90, 39-66.

7711 *Bayer* Oswald, Was ist Rechtfertigung? Grund und Grenze der Theologie: EvKomm 23 (1990) 659-662.

7712 *Blackburn* R., Salvation in the New Testament experience: Friends' Q 25,8 (Kent 1989) 370-7 [< NTAbs 34,203].

7713 *a) Bosch* David J., Salvation; a missiological perspective; – *b) Weborg* John, Be not far; a reflection on the lifework of Jesus Christ ['Cur Deus homo?' to ATHANASIUS!]: ExAud 5 (1989) 139-157 / 123-137.

7714 **Braaten** Carl E., Justification, the article by which the Church stands or falls. Minneapolis 1990. vii-191 p. $13. 0-8006-2403-3 [TDig 37,348].

7715 *Cottier* Georges M.M., Le salut dans le monde de la secularité. NVFr 64 (1989) 1-19.

7716 **Edwards** Denis, What are they saying about salvation? 1986 ➤ 2,5891*; 3,7349: RIrTQ 56 (1990) 237s (B. *Cosgrave*).

7717 *Espezel* Alberto, Quelques aspects de la sotériologie de Hans Urs von BALTHASAR: NRT 112 (1990) 80-92.

7718 **Fiddes** Paul S., Past event and present salvation; the Christian idea of atonement. L 1989, Darton-LT. 243 p. £11. 0-232-51807-6. – RExpTim 101,1 2d-top choice (1989s) 2-4 (C.S. *Rodd*); Month 250 (1989) 391 (P. *Gallagher*).

7719 **Gäde** Gerhard, Eine andere Barmherzigkeit; zum Verständnis der Erlösungslehre ANSELMS von Canterbury: BonnDogmSt 3. Wü 1989, Echter. 324 p. DM 48. – RTR 86 (1990) 215-8 (G.L. *Müller*).

7719* **Garrison** Roman, Redemptive almsgiving in early Christianity: diss. DRichardson G. Toronto 1989. – RelStR 17,194.

7720 **Gunton** Colin E., The actuality of atonement; a study of metaphor, rationality and the Christian tradition 1989 ➤ 5,7707; also E, Clark, £12: RExpTim 101,1 top choice (1989s) 1s (C.S. *Rodd*); JTS 41 (1990) 318-320 (V. *White*), ScotJT 43 (1990) 401-3 (T. *Williams*); TLond 93 (1990) 400s (K. *Surin*, also on FIDDES P.).

7720* **Hart** Trevor A., Two models of salvation in relation to Christological understanding in the Patristic East: diss. Aberdeen 1989. – RTLv 22, p. 597.

7721 *Hernández Rodríguez* A.S., La otra historia de la Salvación: Almogaren 2,1 (1989) 55-79.

7722 **Hodges** Zane C., Absolutely free. Dallas/GR 1989, Redención Viva / Zondervan. 238 p. $15. – RCriswT 4 (1989s) 420-2 (D. L. *Akin*: harsh but important biblical reply to 'Lordship salvation').

7723 **Hoekema** Anthony A. † 17.X.1988, Saved by grace. GR 1989, Eerdmans. 277 p. $23. – RBS 147 (1990) 488 (J. A. *Witmer*: praise, reserves).

7724 **Hultgren** Arland J., Christ and his benefits 1987 ➤ 3,7364 ... 5,7711: RScotJT 43 (1990) 272s (N. T. *Wright*).

7725 *Kandler* Karl-Hermann, Rechtfertigung – kirchentrennend? Bemerkungen zu dem Arbeitsergebnis 'Lehrverurteilungen – kirchentrennend?': KerDo 36 (1990) 209-217; Eng. 217.

7726 **Kimme** August, Rechtfertigung und Heiligung in christologischer Sicht; eine dogmatische Untersuchung. Erlangen 1989, Luther. 223 p. – ᴿTLZ 115 (1990) 765s (F. *Jacob*).

7727 *Lull* Timothy F., (*al.*) The doctrine of justification today: Dialog 27 (St. Paul 1988) 250-9 (-290).

7728 **McGrath** Alister E., Iustitia Dei 1986 → 3,7373 … 5,7216: ᴿDialog 27 (1988) 308-316 (S. S. *Ickert*); HeythJ 31 (1990) 78s (A. *Hamilton*); JEH 41 (1990) 470-4 (F. *Clark*); TLond 93 (1990) 222s (A. *Louth*); TsTKi 61 (1990) 76s (T. *Austad*).

7729 **McGrath** Alister E., Justification by faith; what it means to us today 1988 → 5,8754: ᴿBS 147 (1990) 238s (K. L. *Sarles*).

7730 *Maimela* Simon S., Salvation as a socio-historical reality: JBlackT 4 (1990) 43-56; summary TContext 8/1,119.

7731 *Malan* F. S., Salvation in the New Testament emphases of the different writers: Theologia Viatorum 17 (Sovenga, SAf 1989) 1-20 [< NTAbs 35,199].

7732 **Mannermaa** Tuomo, Der im Glauben gegenwärtige Christus; Rechtfertigung und Vergöttung; zum ökumenischen Dialog: AGTLuth 8. Hannover 1989, Luther-VH. 200 p. DM 19,80. – ᴿTLZ 115 (1990) 766-8 (M. *Plathow*); TR 86 (1990) 469-473 (G. *Wenz,* auch über SAARINEN R. 1989).

7733 *Mannermaa* Tuomo, *Pfnür* Vinzenz, Einig in Sachen Rechtfertigung? Eine lutherische und eine katholische Stellungnahme zu Jörg BAUR: TRu 55 (1990) 325-335 / 336-347.

7734 *Marrow* Stanley B., Principles for interpreting the New Testament soteriological terms: NTS 36 (1990) 268-280.

7734* **Martens** Gottfried, Die Rechtfertigung des Sünders – Rettungshandeln Gottes oder historisches Interpretament? Grundentscheidungen lutherischer Theologie und Kirche bei der Behandlung des Thema 'Rechtfertigung' im ökumenischen Kontext: Diss. ᴰ*Slenczka.* Erlangen 1989s. – TR 86 (1990) 514; RTLv 22, p. 617.

7735 *Matthews* Melvyn, 'Who told you that you were naked?' A metaphor for a Christian theology of atonement: TLond 93 (1990) 212-220.

7736 ᴱ**Meyer** H., *Grossmann* G., Rechtfertigung im ökumenischen Dialog: ÖkPersp 12. Fra 1987, Knecht. 280 p. DM 36. 3-7820-0527-9. – ᴿNorTTs 90 (1989) 126-8 (Ola *Tjørhom*: 3-87476-230-0).

7737 **Muller** Richard A., Christ and the decree; Christology and predestination … 1986 → 3,7378; 4,8756: ᴿJRel 69 (1989) 405s (B. G. *Armstrong*); ScotJT 43 (1990) 127-9 (M. *Jinkins*).

7738 *Pandit* Moti Lal, Freedom versus redemption: Living Word 96,2 (1990) 74-86; summary TContext 8/1,120.

7738* **Pemsel** Sabine, Ecclesia justificans? Das Verhältnis von Kirche und Rechtfertigung in Entwürfen der neueren katholischen und protestantischen Theologie: Diss Freiburg/Br 1989s, ᴰ*Greshake.* – TR 86 (1990) 515.

7739 *Radu* Dumitru, (en roumain) La justification et la déification de l'homme en Jésus-Christ: OrtBuc 40,2 (1988) 27-75 [7-27, évêque Vasile *Coman*].

7740 *a) Rodger* Symeon, The soteriology of ANSELM of Canterbury; an Orthodox perspective; – *b) Harrison* Vera, Some aspects of Saint

GREGORY [Nazianzen] the Theologian's soteriology: GrOrTR 34 (1989) 19-43 / 11-18.

7741 **Ryre** Charles, So great salvation. Wheaton IL 1989, Victor. 166 p. $13. – RCriswT 4 (1989s) 403-6 (D. L. *Akin*: in the evangelicals' current 'lordship debate', gravely neglects Z. HODGES).

7742 **Schwager** Raymund, Jesus im Heilsdrama; Entwurf einer biblischen Erlösungslehre: Innsbrucker Theologische Studien 29. Innsbruck 1990, Tyrolia. 307 p. 3-7022-1746-0; p. 226-232 Opfer im AT. – RHerdKor 44 (1990) 393s (H. B.); KerkT 41 (1990) 343s (R. *Kaptein*: belangrijk); NedTTs 43 (1989) 69s (R. *Kaptein*); TGL 80 (1990) 520-522 (B. *Dieckmann*).

7743 *Sedgwick* Peter, 'Justification by faith'; one doctrine, many debates?: TLond 93 (1990) 5-13.

7744 *Seim* Turid K., Smerte [pain] og forløsning; nytestamentlige fødselsbilder [portrayals of birth] i spenningen mellom virkelighet og ritualisert utopi: NorTTs 91 (1990) 85-99.

7745 **Sesboüé** Bernard, Jésus-Christ l'unique médiateur...: JJC 33, 1988 → 4, 8765; 5,7726: RFoiTemps 19 (1989) 394s (G. *Harpigny*); Gregorianum 71 (1990) 397 (J. *Dupuis*); Month 250 (1989) 69s (P. *Gallagher*); TS 51 (1990) 526s (J. L. *Heft*).

7746 **Smeaton** George, The doctrine of the atonement according to the Apostles. Peabody MA 1988 = 1870, Hendrickson. xii-548 p. 0-913573-98-1.

7747 **Steindl** H., Genugtuung... ANSELM D1989 → 5,7729: RTR 86 (1990) 214s (H. *Verweyen*).

7748 **Studer** Basil, Dieu sauveur; la rédemption dans la foi de l'Église ancienne, THoffmann Joseph, 1989 → 5,7731: REstTrin 23 (1989) 139s (N. *Silanes*); LavalTP 46 (1990) 411-4 (R.-M. *Roberge*); QVidCr 146 (1989) 127 (M. *Nin*); RTPhil 122 (1990) 283s (J. *Borel*).

7749 **Swinburne** Richard, Responsibility and atonement. NY 1989, Oxford UP. 213 p. $50, pa. $15. RRelSt 26 (1990) 431-3 (P. *Helm*); TS 51 (1990) 770s (J. F. *Keenan*).

Turner Max, Atonement... in John, BULTMANN, FORESTELL 1990 → 5878.

7750 **VanGemeren** Willem, The progress of redemption 1988 → 5,7732: RThemelios 16 (1990s) 28s (D. L. *Bock*).

7751 **Viciano** Alberto, Cristo salvador... TERTULIANO 1986 → 3,7404; 4,8772: RAngelicum 67 (1990) 431s (Nella *Filippi*).

7752 **Vidal Taléns** José, El Mediador y la mediación; la cristología de W. KASPER en su génesis y estructura: Valentina 21. Valencia 1988, Fac. Ferrer. 498 p. – RActuBbg 27 (1990) 219s (J. *Boada*); RTLv 21 (1990) 335s (E. *Brito*).

7753 **Vitoria Cormenzana** F. Javier, ¿Todavía la salvación cristiana? Los diseños soteriológicos de cuatro cristologías actuales 1986 → 3,7406; 5,7735: RRTLv 21 (1990) 338-340 (E. *Brito*).

7754 **Von Rohr** John, The covenant of grace in Puritan thought 1986 → 3,7403; 5,7739: RWestTJ 52 (1990) 169-171 (D. A. *Weir*).

7755 **Wenz** Günther, Geschichte der Versöhnungslehre in der evangelischen Theologie der Neuzeit 1s, 1984-6 → 2,5932; 3,7410: RTsTKi 60 (1989) 238 (J.-O. *Henriksen*); ZkT 112 (1990) 315-321 (R. *Schwager*).

7756 **Wheeler** David I., *a*) A relational view of the atonement; prolegomenon to a reconstruction of the doctrine. NY 1989, Lang. 289 p. [JAAR 58,328]. – *b*) Toward a process-relational Christian soteriology: Process Studies 18 (Claremont 1989) 102-114 (-117, *Basinger* David, response).

7757 *Zimmermann* Gunter, Rechtfertigungslehre und Säkularisation: ZRGg 42 (1990) 299-315.

H7.2 *Crux, sacrificium;* **The Cross; the nature of sacrifice.**

7758 *Albertine* Richard, Selected survey of the theme 'spiritual sacrifice' to AUGUSTINE: EphLtg 104 (1990) 35-50; lat. 35.

7759 *Alessi* Adriano, L'essere e la croce; dibattito sull'onto-teologia': Salesianum 52 (1990) 53-111.

7760 *Argaud* Jacky, Réchauffer Prajāpati; analyse du sacrifice védique dans son fonctionnement de référence à l'acte fondateur: ÉTRel 65 (1990) 5-14.

7761 **Ashby** Godfrey, Sacrifice, its nature and purpose 1988 → 5,7743: RTLond 93 (1990) 57 (R.J. *Halliburton*).

7762 *Bonora* A., La violenza e il sacro [GIRARD R.]: → 514c, Violenza 1990, 7-26.

7763 *Bottani* Livio, Mondo sociale e mimesi della natura umana; la violenza in René GIRARD tra imitazione e resistenza: Sapienza 43 (1990) 197-206.

7763* *Cernokrak* N., L'homme et le sacrifice cultuel de la Nouvelle Alliance: → 589, Ltg/Anthroplogie 1989/90, 33-45.

7764 *Coleman* K.M., Fatal charades; Roman executions staged as mythological enactments [... as in R. GIRARD, not mentioned]: JRS 80 (1990) 44-73.

7765 **Cousar** Charles B., A theology of the Cross: OvBT. Mp 1990, Fortress. xiv-194 p. [CBQ 53,170]. – RExpTim 102 (1990s) 246 (D. *Hill*).

7766 **Deneken** Michel, Le salut par la croix dans la théologie catholique contemporaine (1930-1985) [... GIRARD R.]: Thèses. P 1988, Cerf. 419 p. – RSR 19 (1990) 388 (Anne *Fortin-Melkevik*).

7767 EDetienne M., *Vernant* J.-P., The cuisine of sacrifice among the Greeks [1979 → 61,465], T*Wissing* P. Ch 1989, Univ. vii-276 p. $17.25. 0-226-14353-8 [BL 91, 125, N. *Wyatt*: steaming offal and the stench of death].

7768 **Ehler** Bernhard, Die Herrschaft des Gekreuzigten... KÄSEMANN: BZNW 46, 1986 → 2,5790...5,7617: RHeythJ 30 (1989) 226s (D.V. *Way*).

7768* **Ferlay** Philippe, Dieu sacrifice éternel. P 1990, Nouvelle Cité. 235 p. F 190. – REsprVie 100 (1990) 493s (P. *Jay*: more to come).

7769 *a*) *Girard* Marc, Le symbolisme de la Croix; de l'archetype universel au symbole clef de la foi chrétienne [... champ plus vaste du symbolisme du bois]; – *b*) *Gourgues* Michel, La foi chrétienne primitive face à la Croix; le témoignage des formulaires pré-pauliniens: ScEspr 41 (1989) 5-31 / 49-69.

7770 **Girard** René, Das Heilige und die Gewalt, T*Maiberger-Ruh* Elisabeth, 1987 → 5,8782: RLebZeug 43 (1989) 70s (J. *Splett*).

7771 **Girard** R., Things hidden 1987 → 3,7420: RJAAR 57 (1989) 640-2 (T.V. *Peterson*: 'survival of the human species depended on the invention of social structures to solve the mimetic crisis that began to tear apart communities' i.e. imitators challenge the authority of those being imitated).

7772 **Gourgues** Miguel, Le crucifié: du scandale à l'exaltation: JJC 38, 1989 → 5,7758; F 125: RÉTRel 65 (1990) 453s (E. *Cuvillier*: maîtrise; mais on voudrait plus sur les particularités de chaque auteur du NT, et du niveau théologique).

7773 EGrottanelli C., Sacrificio e società nel mondo antico 1983/8 → 5,790*: RAufidus 7 (1989) 229-235 (G. *Cipriani*); Helmantica 41 (1990) 380s (H.B. *Riesco Alvarez*).

7774 *Grottanelli* Cristiano, Appunti sulla fine dei sacrifici [cruenti, col cristianesimo;... GIRARD R.]: EgVO 12 (1989) 175-192; 175 'filone di pensiero antisacrificale nel Cristianesimo antico' – distinct from the 'main line'.

7775 ᴱHamerton-Kelly Robert G., Violent origins 1983/7 ⇥ 3,639.7423; 4,8784: ᴿClasW 83 (1989s) 113 (J. *Rubenstein*).
Hamerton Kelly R. G., Sacred violence (... GIRARD R.) 1990 ⇥ 6514.

7776 *Harl* K. W., Sacrifice and pagan belief in 6th and 7th-century Byzantium: Past and Present 128 (1990) 7-27 [< RHE 85,387*].

7777 **Hönig** Elisabeth, Die Eucharistie als Opfer nach den neueren ökumenischen Erklärungen 1988 ⇥ 5,4721 [ᴿJTS 41 (1990) by E. J. *Yarnold* noted there p. 804; the documents show reluctance to reflect on the meaning of sacrifice, though all follow the NT in applying the term to Christ's saving work].

7778 **Hoffmann** Norbert, Kreuz und Trinität; zur Theologie der Sühne 1982 ⇥ 64,6971: ᴿEstTrin 24 (1990) 287s (X. *Pikaza*).

7779 *a) Humphreys* Fischer, Christ died for our sins according to the Scriptures; *b) Patterson* Paige, Reflections on the Atonement [*Humphreys*, Death of Christ 1978]: CriswT 3,2 (1989) 295-305 / 307-320.

7780 *Jamros* Daniel P., Satisfaction for sin; AQUINAS on the Passion of Christ: IrTQ 56 (1990) 307-328.

7780* ᴱ**Jüngel** Eberhard, Heilsbedeutung das Kreuzes für Glaube und Hoffnung des Christen. Tü 1990, Mohr. 93 p. – *a) Ebeling* Gerhard, Der Sühnetod Christi als Glaubensaussage; eine hermeneutische Rechenschaft; – *b) Becker* Jürgen, Die neutestamentliche Rede vom Sühnetod Jesu; – *c) Jörns* Klaus-Peter, Der Sühnetod Jesu Christi in Frömmigkeit und Predigt; ein praktisch-theologischer Diskurs; – *d) Härle* Wilfried, Die Rede von der Liebe und vom Zorn Gottes: ZkT Beih 8 (1990) 3-28 / 29-49 / 70-93 / 50-69.

7781 *Kruse* Heinz, ❹ The rationale of the [postexilic] Old Testament sacrifice: Katorikku Kenkyu 29,58 (1990) 1-24.

7782 *Kuhn* Heinz-Wolfgang, Kreuz NT: ⇥ 857, TRE 19 (1990) 713-725 [-779 al.; 16 pl.].

7783 **McGrath** Alister, The enigma of the Cross 1987 ⇥ 3,7431 [4,8795; 5,7762 the mystery... 1988]: ᴿScotBEv 7 (1989) 135-7 (T. *Hart*).
McKenna Andrew, Biblical structuralism; testing the victimary hypothesis: 1990 ⇥ 3040.

7784 *McLean* Bradley, On the revision of scapegoat terminology: Numen 37 (1990) 168-173 (in FRAZER, BURKERT etc.) 'scapeman' would diminish unwanted influence of Jewish ritual.

7785 *a) Morrow* Duncan, For God and... ourselves alone; René GIRARD on violence, conflict and culture [... dangers of mimesis, agreed; so also D. *Stevens* in Studies 77 (1988) ⇥ 7792; cf. G. O'*Hanlon's* response there]; – *b) Murphy* Seamus, response: Studies 78 (1989) 177-185 / 186-190.

7786 **Morris** Leon, The cross of Jesus 1988 ⇥ 4,8797; 5,7767: ᴿWestTJ 52 (1990) 155s (A. J. *Bandstra*).

7787 **Palaver** Wolfgang, Politik und Religion bei Thomas HOBBES; eine Kritik aus der Sicht der Theorie René GIRARDS: kath. Diss. Innsbruck 1989s. – TR 86 (1990) 510.
Pattison George, Violence [GIRARD], kingship and cultus 1990s ⇥ 2976.

7787* **Redman** Robert R., The Christ of the Cross; the Christology and soteriology of H. R. MACKINTOSH: Diss. ᴰ*Heron*. Erlangen 1989s. – TR 86 (1990) 514.

7788 **Rey** B., Nous prêchons un Messie crucifié 1989 ➤ 5,7769: ᴿÉTRel 65 (1990) 135s (J. *Ansaldi*: un degré supérieur à son Jésus 1988).

7789 *Segal* Charles, Sacrifice and violence in the myth of Meleager and Heracles; HOMER, Bacchylides, SOPHOCLES: Helios 17,1 ('René GIRARD and western literature, 1990) 7-24 [-155, al.; ➤ 3040].

7790 *Sequeri* P., 'Dare la vita' ed 'essere sacrificato'... TItSett 14 (1989) 143-153; p. 147: provocazione alla teologia, GIRARD, Choses 202: Rien dans les Evangiles pour suggérer que la mort de Jésus est un sacrifice.

7791 **Solié** Pierre, Le sacrifice — fondateur de civilisation et d'individuation. P 1988, Michel. 256 p. – ᴿBrotéria 129 (1989) 337-340 (F. *Pires Lopes* mentions JUNG and FREUD but not Girard).

7792 *Stevens* David, Unmasking the gods of violence; the work of René GIRARD: Studies 77 (Dublin 1988) 309-320 (321-7 response by G. *O'Hanlon*, on the whole favorable).

7793 **Stott** John R. W., The Cross of Christ 1986 ➤ 2,5957... 5,7772: ᴿCriswT 4 (1989s) 210s (D. L. *Akin*: already a classic).

7794 *a) Trabucco* Giovanni, La violenza e il sacro in René GIRARD; – *b) Cavedo* Romeo, La violenza del Dio liberatore [Esodo]: Servitium 67 (Bergamo 1990) 32-41 / 9-18 [5-8. 19-31. 42-76, *al.*].

H7.4 **Sacramenta**, *Gratia*.

7795 **Bardy** Gustave, Menschen werden Christen; das Drama der Bekehrung in den ersten Jahrhunderten, ᴱ*Blank* Josef. FrB 1988, Herder. 364 p. DM 42. – ᴿZkT 112 (1990) 234s (K. H. *Neufeld*).

7796 **Barth** Gerhard, El bautismo en el tiempo del cristianismo primitivo 1986 ➤ 2,5967; 3,7448: ᴿEstE 65 (1990) 364s (J. A. *Goenaga*).

7797 **Béguerie** Philipp, *Duchesneau* Claude, Pour vivre les sacrements. P 1989, Cerf. 220 p. F 98. – ᴿEsprVie 100 (1990) 27s (P. *Rouillard*); Spiritus 31 (1990) 454s (R. *Desmarescaux*).

7798 **Bernardo** Bonifácio, Simbolismo e tipologia do baptismo em TERTU-LIANO e Santo AMBROSIO; estudio litúrgico-teológico = Didaskalia 18 (1988). 453 p. 0253-1674.

7799 **Blanchette** Claude, Pénitence et Eucharistie; dossier d'une question con-troversée: Recherches 21,1989 ➤ 5,7783; F 140: ᴿEsprVie 100 (1990) 26s (P. *Rouillard*); ETL 66 (1990) 228s (A. de *Halleux*); NRT 112 (1990) 426s (L. *Volpe*).

7800 *Calvo Espiga* Arturo, El Bautismo signo productor de la pertenencia a la Iglesia-una: ScripV 37 (1990) 117-154.

7801 **Chauvet** Louis-M., Symbole et sacrement 1987 ➤ 4,8813; 5,7789: ᴿMaisD 182 (1990) 156-163 (I. H. *Dalmais*).

7802 **Cipriani** Settimio, Evangelizzare i sacramenti; riflessioni biblico-liturgi-che per la celebrazione dei sacramenti 1988 ➤ 5,7790: ᴿCC 141 (1990,2) 616 (A. *Elberti*).

7803 *a) Colwell* John, Alternative approaches to believer's baptism (from the Anabaptists to BARTH); – *b) Letham* Robert, Baptism in the writings of the Reformers: ScotBEv 7,1 (1989) 3-20 / 21-64.

7804 **Cottrell** Jack, Baptism, a biblical study. Joplin MO 1989, College Press. 170 p. $6 pa. – ᴿBS 147 (1990) 375 (R. P. *Lightner*: argues from too few texts, against the 150 which make faith the sole condition of salvation).

7805 *a) Crouzel* Henri, Le baptême selon les Pères Anténicéens; – *b) Mar-tínez-Sierra* Alejandro, El poder de perdonar los pecados postbautismales en el libro 'De poenitentia' de S. AMBROSIO: → 135, ᶠORBE A., Compostellanum 35 (1990) 181-205 / 277-291.

7806 **Dacquino** Pietro, Storia del matrimonio cristiano alla luce della Bibbia [1.1984 → 65,6629]; 2. Inseparabilità e monogamia. T-Leumann 1988, Elle Di Ci. 413 p. Lit. 24.000. 88-01-15849-1. – ᴿGregorianum 71 (1990) 186s (M. *Zalba*).

7807 *Dattrino* Lorenzo, Il battesimo e l'iniziazione cristiana in OTTATO di Milevì; → 175, Mem. TESTINI P., RivArchCr 66 (1990) 81-100.

7807* *Dienst* Karl, Konfirmation [erst Reformationszeit]: → 857, TRE 19 (1990) 437-445.

7808 *Driscoll* Michael S., Sacramental symbols in a technical age: Listening 25,1 (1990) 61-70 [< ZIT 90,208].

Dudley M., *Rowell* G., Confession and absolution 1990 → 404*.

7809 **Elliott** Peter J., What God has joined ... the sacramentality of marriage. Staten Island 1990, Alba. xxxv-287 p. $16. 0-8189-0568-9 [TDig 37,358].

7810 **Espeja** Jesús, Sacramentos y seguimiento de Jesús 1989 → 5,7796: ᴿCarthaginensia 6 (1990) 228s (F. *Martínez Fresneda*).

7811 **Espeja** J., Para comprender los sacramentos. Estella 1990, VDivino. 170 p. – ᴿCiTom 117 (1990) 386s (D. *Salado*).

7812 **Fernández** Domiciano, Dios ama y perdona sin condiciones; posibilidad dogmática y conveniencia pastoral de la absolución general sin confesión privada. Bilbao 1989, D-Brouwer. 101 p. – ᴿNatGrac 37 (1990) 124s (A. *Villalmonte*).

7813 **Ferraro** Giuseppe, Dottrina della liturgia sui sacramenti della fede. R 1990, Dehoniane. 224 p. Lit. 20.000. 88-396-0285-2. – ᴿCC 141 (1990,2) 403s (U. *Burroni*); Gregorianum 71 (1990) 811 (*ipse*).

7814 **Ferraro** Giuseppe, I sacramenti e l'identità cristiana 1986 → 4,8815*; 5,7797: ᴿEphLtg 104 (1990) 341s (A. *Pistoia*).

7815 **Fourez** G., Les sept sacrements: Parcours. P/Québec 1989, Centurion/Paulines. 122 p. F 59. – ᴿNRT 112 (1990) 261 (L. *Renwart*).

7816 **Fugel** Adolf, Tauflehre und Taufliturgie bei H. ZWINGLI [Diss. → 5, 7797*, aber:] Goldach 1989, Schmid-Fehr. ᴿETL 66 (1990) 224s (A. de *Halleux*).

7817 **Ganoczy** Alexandre, Aus seiner Fülle haben wir alle empfangen; Grundriss der Gnadenlehre 1989 → 5,7799: ᴿTGegw 33 (1990) 365-7 (B. *Hidber*); TLZ 115 (1990) 58-62 (G. *Wenz*).

7818 **Gondal** M.-L., La voie du baptême; des adultes entrent dans la foi: Racines. P 1990, Nouvelle Cité. 191 p. F 79. – ᴿNRT 112 (1990) 941 (G. N.).

7819 **González Dorado** Antonio, Los sacramentos del Evangelio: Textos Básicos Sem. Lat.-Am. 9/1. México 1989, CEM. 604 p. – ᴿEfMex 8 (1990) 103s (J. M. *Hernández* R.).

7820 *Gounelle* André, Protestantismes et sacrements: LavalTP 46 (1990) 197-207.

7821 *Gy* Pierre-Marie, Du baptême pascal des petits enfants au baptême *quamprimum*: → 149, ᶠRICHÉ P., Haut Moyen-Âge 1990, 353-365.

7822 *Haquin* André, Vers une nouvelle théologie des sacrements: ETL 66 (1990) 355-367.

7823 *Hart* Mark D., Reconciliation of body and soul; GREGORY of Nyssa's deeper theology of marriage [... tragic search for gratifying companionship]: TS 51 (1990) 450-478.

7824 **Hassab Alla** Waheed, Le baptême des enfants dans la tradition de l'église copte d'Alexandrie 1986 ➤ 1,7367 ... 3,7475: ᴿRechSR 78 (1990) 621 (H. *Bourgeois,* aussi sur de titres semblables).

7825 *Hauser* Martin, Heute unzeitgemäss: BASILIUS' des Grossen Aufruf zur heiligen Taufe?: FreibZ 37 (1990) 499-514.

7826 **Heiser** Lothar, Die Taufe in der Orthodoxen Kirche; Spendung und Symbolik nach der Lehre der Väter: Sophia Quellen 25. Trier 1987, Paulinus. 335 p.; 32 fig. DM 60. 3-7902-1411-6. – ᴿTrierTZ 98 (1989) 230s (E. *Sauser*).

7827 *Hickling* C.J.A., Baptism in the first-century churches; a case for caution: ➤ 166, ᶠSheffield 1990, 249-267.

7827* **Hillier** Richard, Baptismal exegesis in ARATOR's 'Historia apostolica': diss. Durham 1990. – RTLv 22, p. 597.

7828 **Hudson** Henry T., Baptism in the Bible. GR 1987, Bible Doctrines. 157 p. $8. – ᴿBS 147 (1990) 111 (R. P. *Lightner*).

7829 *a) Kasper* Walter, The Church as a place of forgiveness, ᵀ*Wimmer* Albert K., – *b) Bürkle* Horst, Guilt and its resolution ontside of the Christian tradition, ᵀ*Dodds* Michael J., – *c) Cessario* Romanus, Christian satisfaction and sacramental reconciliation: CommND 16 (1989) 160-171 / 172-185 / 186-196.

7829* **Kisimba** Nyemko, La parole comme manifestation personnelle de Dieu dans les sacrements selon M. LUTHER (1483-1546) [diss.], préf. *Vanneste* A.: RechAfrThéol 10. Kinshasa 1988, Fac.Théol.Cath. xiv-238 p. – ᴿScEsp 42 (1990) 365s (J.-M. *Dufort*).

7830 **Klauck** Hans-Josef, Gemeinde – Amt – Sakrament; neutestamentliche Perspektiven [22 art] 1989 ➤ 5,292: ᴿTPQ 138 (1990) 173-5 (C.-P. *März*).

7831 **Kranemann** Benedikt, Die Krankensalbung in der Zeit der Aufklärung; Ritualien und pastoralliturgische Studien im deutschen Sprachgebiet [kath. Diss. Münster 1989, ᴰ*Richter* K.] LtgWQFor 72. Münster 1990, Aschendorff. xxxix-440 p. 3-402-03858-7.

7831* **Lauriot-Prévost** Alex et Maud, Le mariage, mystère trinitaire. P 1988, Fayard. 150 p. F 78. – ᴿSpiritus 31 (1990) 455s (M. *Oger*).

7832 **Lawler** Michael G., Symbol and sacrament; a contemporary sacramental theology 1987 ➤ 4,8827*; 5,7813: ᴿTLZ 115 (1990) 136s (G. *Wainwright,* deutsch).

7833 **Lies** Lothar, Sakramenten-Theologie, eine personale Sicht. Graz 1990, Styria. 375 p. Sch 420. – ᴿAsprenas 37 (1990) 377s (B. *Forte*); TLZ 115 (1990) 915-7 (G. *Wenz*).

7834 ᴱ**Limouris** G., *Vaporis* N. M., Orthodox perspectives on BEM 1985 ➤ 2,5989: ᴿNedTTs 44 (1990) 80s (K. *Blei*).

7835 *a) Lohfink* Norbert, Aus der Taufe leben — Taufvergessenheit, Taufsymbolik, Tauferneuerung; – *b) Mühlen* Heribert, Die Firmung als geschichtliche Fortdauer der urkirchlichen Geisterfahrung: RUntHö 33,1 (Dü 1990) 4-12 / 13-24 [< ZIT 90,281].

7836 **López-González** Pedro, Penitencia y reconciliación; estudio histórico-teológico de la 'res et sacramentum': Col.Teol. 64. Pamplona 1990, EUNSA. 357 p. – ᴿBurgense 31 (1990) 567s (N. *López Martínez*); NRT 112 (1990) 747 (R. *Escol*).

7836* *Lülsdorff* Raimund, Das Zusammenwirken von Weihe- und Ehesakrament im Neuen Testament: TGL 80 (1990) 333-340.

7837 **Magne** Jean, Logique des sacrements [➤ 5,7814] / des dogmes; préf. *Tardieu* M.: Orig. Chr. 3s. P 1989, auct. 247 p.; 249 p. F 148 chaque. – ᴿTLZ 115 (1990) 799-801 (K.-H. *Kandler*); TsTNijm 30 (1990) 420 (T. J.

van *Bavel*: 'voor de weerlegging van deze ideeën zou de samenwerking nodig zijn van verschillende specialisten').

7838 *Mandouze* A., Sacramentum et sacramenta chez AUGUSTIN: BBudé (1989) 367-375.

7839 *Mattam* J., Towards a theology of the sacrament of reconciliation: Vidyajyoti 53 (1989) 421-434. 489-500.

7840 *Mazza* Enrico, La formula battesimale nelle omelie catechetiche di TEODORO di Mopsuestia: EphLtg 104 (1990) 23-34; lat. 23.

7841 *Meis W.* Anneliese, La gracia, ¿ verdad teológica en crisis?: TVida 31 (1990) 227-255.

7842 *Millás* José M., Fe y sacramento del matrimonio; reflexiones acerca del reciente libro de Francisco ALARCÓN, 'El matrimonio celebrado sin fe' [Almería 1988; diss. Pont. Univ. Gregoriana]: Gregorianum 71 (1990) 141-151.

7842* **Nocent** A., *al.*, Os sacramentos; teologia e história da celebração ᵀ*Vidigal* Raimundo. São Paulo 1989, Paulinas. 458 p. 85-05-00941-X. ᴿPerspT 21 (1990) 402-4 (F. *Taborda*).

7843 **Osborne** Kenan B., Reconciliation and justification; the sacrament and its theology. NY 1990, Paulist. vi-304 p. $15. 0-6091-3143-9 [TDig 38,77].

7844 **Osborne** Kenan B., Teología sacramental, introducción general [NY 1988 ► 4,8837],ᵀ. Valencia 1990, Edicep. 171 p.: ᴿEstE 65 (1990) 477-9 (J. L. *Larrabe*); RET 50 (1990) 348-350 (también J. L. *Larrabe*).

7845 **Philips** Gérard, L'union personnelle avec le Dieu vivant... la grâce² 1989 – 1974 ► 5,7821: ᴿRTLv [5 (1975) 223-5, J. *Coppens*] 21 (1990) 239s (G. *Thils*).

7846 **Piolanti** Antonio, I sacramenti. Vaticano 1990, Editrice. 606 p. – ᴿEuntDoc 43 (1990) 233-7 (D. *Composta*).

7847 **Price** C. P., Mysteries and sacraments: ► 52, FULLER R., AnglTR supp 11 (1990) 124-138 [< NTAbs 34,350].

7848 **Probst** Manfred, *Lüdicke* Klaus, Eheschliessung — mehr als ein rechtliches Ding?: TR 86 (1990) 265-280.

7849 **Rocchetta** Carlo, Sacramentaria fondamentale; dal 'mysterion' al 'sacramentum': Corso Teol. Sist. 8. Bo 1989, Dehoniane. 598 p. Lit. 45.000. 88-10-50308-2. – ᴿGregorianum 71 (1990) 809 (*ipse*); NRT 112 (1990) 745s (L. *Renwart*); StPatav 37 (1990) 387-390 (E. R. *Tura*); Teresianum 41 (1990) 279s (M. *Caprioli*).

7850 *Rosier* Irène, Signes et sacrements; Thomas d'AQUIN et la grammaire spéculative: RSPT 74 (1990) 392-435; Eng. 436.

7851 *Rovira Belloso* Josep M., El sagrament de la penitència en el concili de Trento: RCatalT 15 (1990) 67-136; Eng. 137.

7852 **Ruffini** E., *Lodi* E., 'Mysterion' e 'sacramentum'; la sacramentalità negli scritti dei Padri e nei testi liturgici primitivi: Nuovi Saggi Teologici 24. Bo 1987, Dehoniane. 318 p. Lit. 27.000 – ᴿNRT 112 (1990) 433s (L. *Renwart*: 'la théologie récente a tendance à étendre l'usage du mot sacramentum au-delà des sept rites classiques').

7853 **Salachas** Demetrios, Ⓖ *Ta mystēria...* Les sacrements d'initiation chrétienne (Baptême – Confirmation – Eucharistie) dans le nouveau Code de Droit canonique de l'Église catholique: Dialogos 2. Thessaloniki 1989, Kyriakidis. 214 p. – ᴿRTLv 21 (1990) 354-7 (A. de *Halleux*).

7854 *Saldanza* Giuseppe, La grazia matrimoniale nella fase conciliare; cambiamento di prospettiva rispetto alla fase preparatoria: EphLtg 104 (1990) 368-414; lat. 368 [103 (1989) 281-308, fase prep.; 113-160, tra Casti Connubii e Vat. II].

7855 **Saraiva Martins** J., I sacramenti della Nuova Alleanza 1987 → 3,7498; 5,7826*: ᴿAnnTh 4 (1990) 184-6 (A. *Blanco*).

7856 **Saxer** Victor, Les rites d'initiation chrétienne du IIᵉ au VIᵉ siècle; esquisse historique et signification d'après leurs principaux témoins. Spoleto 1988, Centro Alto Medioevo. 700 p. Lit. 95.000. – ᴿEsprVie 100 (1990) 360s (P. *Rouillard*); RevSR 63 (1989) 159s (C. *Munier*); RTPhil 122 (1990) 562s (J. *Borel*).

7857 **Sequeira** John B., Tout mariage... sacramentel? ᴰ1985 → 3,7502: ᴿMaisD 179 (1989) 151-6 (F. *Deniau*).

7858 **Steffen** Uwe, Taufe; Ursprung und Sinn des christlichen Einweihungsritus 1988 → 5,7830: ᴿKerkT 41 (1990) 70 (G. de *Ru*).

7859 **Stevick** Daniel B., Baptismal moments, baptismal meanings: Prayer Book Studies 26. NY 1987, Church Hymnal. xxii-215 p. $15. – ᴿAnglTR 71 (1989) 88-94 (L. *Weil*).

7860 **Taborda** Francisco, a) Sacramentos, práxis e festa; para uma teologia latino-americana dos sacramentos: Teologia e libertação 4/5. Petrópolis 1987, Vozes. 191 p. – ᴿPerspT 20 (1988) 115-9 (A. Tadeu *Murad*). – b) Sacramentos, práxis e festa [Petrópolis 1987; M 1987; Dü 1988]; crítica e autocrítica: PerspTeol 21 (1989) 85-99.

7861 **Taborda** Francisco, Sacramentos, praxis y fiesta; para una teología latinoamericana de los sacramentos, ᴿ*Ortiz García* A.: Cristianismo y Sociedad 10, 1987 → 4,8848: ᴿLumenVr 38 (1989) 441s (U. *Gil Ortega*).

7862 **Taborda** Francisco, Sakramente; Praxis und Fest, ᵀ*Goldstein* H.: BiblBefreiung. Dü 1988, Patmos. 182 p. DM 40. – ᴿTLZ 115 (1990) 291-3 (J. *Althausen*); ZkT 112 (1990) 67-73 (L. *Lies*).

7863 **Vorgrimler** Herbert, Teología de los sacramentos [1987 → 3,7509], ᵀ*Villanueva* Marciano: BiblT 13. Barc 1989, Herder. 414 p. – ᴿCiTom 117 (1990) 157-9 (D. *Salado*); EstAg 25 (1990) 180 (Z. *Herrero*); RTLim 24 (1990) 303-5 (L. *Almonte Cruz*).

7863* *Vorgrimler* Herbert, Krankensalbung: → 857, TRE 19 (1990) 664-9.

7864 *Zalba* Marcelino, Normas de la Iglesia sobre el valor y la licitud de la absolución general con manifestación genérica de los pecados mortales: Gregorianum 71 (1990) 229-256; Eng. 257.

7865 a) *Zauner* Wilhelm, Sakramente in einer säkularisierten Gesellschaft; – b) *Baumgartner* Jakob, Zur Frage der Generalabsolution: TPQ 138 (1990) 99-107 / 108-119.

7866 **Zerndl** Josef, Die Theologie der Firmung in der Vorbereitung und in den Akten des Zweiten Vatikanischen Konzils [LG 11; diss. Pont. Univ. Gregoriana]. Pd 1986. 64+456 p. – ᴿAtKap 114 (1990) 305s (B. *Nadolski*).

7867 *Zorzin* Alejandro, Kᴀʀʟsᴛᴀᴅᴛs 'Dialogus vom Tauff der Kinder' ... : ArRefG 79 (1988) 27-57; Eng. 58.

H7.6 *Ecclesiologia, theologia missionis, laici* - **The Church.**

7868 **Aarflot** Andreas [bp. Oslo], Let the Church be the Church; the voice and mission of the people of God. Mp 1988, Augsburg Fortress. 128 p. $7. – ᴿCurrTMiss 17 (1990) 74 (L. A. *Kauppi*); TsTKi 60 (1989) 69-71 (Ola *Tjørhom*).

7869 **Abruzzese** S., Comunione e liberazione; identité catholique e disqualification du monde: Sciences humaines et religions. P 1989, Cerf. 253 p. – ᴿNRT 112 (1990) 776s (B. *Joassart*).

7870 **Alegre** X., Iglesia, ¿de dónde vienes, a dónde vas?: Cristianisme i Justicia 2. Barc 1989. 157 p.; pt 920. – ᴿNRT 112 (1990) 742s (A. *Toubeau*).

7871 **Antón** Ángel, El misterio de la Iglesia 1986s ➤ 3,7517; 4,8859; 5,7837: ᴿDivinitas 33 (1989) 311s (B. *Gherardini*); EstE 65 (1990) 228-231 (J. A. *Estrada*, 2).

7872 **Auer** Johann, La Iglesia, sacramento universal de salvación [1983] 1986 ➤ 2,6019; 3,7521: ᴿFranBog 31 (1989) 211s (*Hernán Fonseca* R.).

7873 **Barbaglio** Giuseppe, Le sens biblique de la laïcité [La laicità ... interpretazione biblica 1987 ➤ 5,7840], ᵀ*Vulliez* Hyacinthe. P 1989, Cerf. 172 p. F 90. – ᴿBLitEc 91 (1990) 289 (Jacqueline des *Rochettes*: résoument 'laïc' – mot ambigu; 'pourra séduire par son originalité'); MélSR 47 (1990) 63 (L. *Debarge*); NRT 112 (1990) 104s (A. *Toubeau*); QVidCr 150 (1990) 209 (J.-A. *Rocha*).

7874 **Barrett** C. K., Kerk, ambt en sacramenten in het Nieuwe Testament [Manchester lectures 1983 ➤ 2,6023],ᵀ. Haag 1988, Boeken-C. 111 p. ƒ 19,50. 90-2390-099-5. – ᴿNedTTs 44 (1990) 258s (R. A. *Bitter*).

7874* *a*) **Beaulac** Jules, L'Église de chez nous; réflexions spirituelles et pastorales. Montréal 1989, Paulines. 373 p. – ᴿScEsp 42 (1990) 119s (J. C. *Breton*). – *b*) **Blanc** Philippe, L'Église, mystère trinitaire et sacrement de salut; étude de l'ecclésiologie de Charles JOURNET: diss. 6891 Pont. Univ. Gregoriana, ᴰAntón Á. – R 1990s. – InfPUG 23/119, 14.

7875 **Biser** Eugen, Glaubenskonflikte; Strukturanalyse der Kirchenkrise ['Kölner Erklärung' 1989]: Tb 1687. FrB 1989, Herder. 127 p. DM 9.80. – ᴿTGL 80 (1990) 208s (W. *Beinert*).

7875* **Blázquez** Ricardo, La Iglesia del Concilio Vaticano II, 1988 ➤ 5,7842: ᴿScripTPamp 22 (1990) 627-635 (J. R. *Villar*).

7876 **Bojorge** Horacio, El fiel laico en el horizonte de su pertenencia; aspectos bíblicos de la teología del laicado II; Stromata 45 (1989) 191-233.

7877 ᴱ**Camps** A., *al.,* Oecumenische inleiding in de missiologie 1988. – ᴿNedTTs 44 (1990) 346s (K. H. *Enklaar*).

7878 *Cavallin* C., Folkkyrkotankar i nytestamentlig belysning: Religion och Bibel 45ss (Lund 1986ss) 17-27 [< NTAbs 35,195 'People-ecclesiologies']. ᴱ**Cazelles** Henri, Commission biblique pontificale, Unité et diversité dans l'Église 1989 ➤ 520.

7879 *Chevallier* Max-Alain †, Jésus a-t-il voulu l'Église?: ÉTRel 65 (1990) 489-503.

7880 *Dussmann* Ernst, Identifikation mit der Kirche; ekklesiale Bilder in frühchristlicher Zeit: MüTZ 40 (1989) 323-335.

7881 ᵀᴱ**Dattrino** Lorenzo, OTTATO di Milevì, La vera Chiesa: CollTPatr 71, 1988 ➤ 4,8894; 5,7885: ᴿSalesianum 52 (1990) 753 (S. *Felici*).

7882 **Dianich** Severino, La Chiesa mistero di comunione⁵ [– ¹1975] 1987 ➤ 4,8997; 190 p. Lit. 15.000: ᴿRasT 30 (1989) 89s (Lorena *Corradino*).

7883 *Échappé* Olivier, L'ecclésiologie du Vatican II à travers le Code de droit canonique de 1983: RICathP 33 (1990) 109-124.

7884 *Eitel* Keith E., 'The way'; Christ's uniqueness and its bearing on modern missions: CriswT 4 (1989s) 279-293.

7885 **Elberti** Arturo, Il sacerdozio regale dei fedeli nei prodromi del Concilio Ecumenico Vaticano II (1903-1962): AnGreg 254, 1989 ➤ 5,7864: ᴿETL 66 (1990) 234s (A. de *Halleux*); Gregorianum 71 (1990) 230s (*ipse*); NRT 112 (1990) 430s (A. *Toubeau*).

7886 **Espeja** Jesús, L'Église, mémoire et prophétie: Théologies 1987 ➤ 3,7585 ... 5,7865: ᴿLVitae 45 (1990) 114s (P. *Tihon*).

7886* **Estrada** J.,   Del misterio de la Iglesia al pueblo de Dios 1988 ➤ 4,8903; 5,7866: ᴿTVida 30 (1989) 318s (C. *Casale*).

7887 **Faivre** Alexandre,   The emergence of the laity in the early Church [Les laïcs aux origines 1984 ➤ 65,6725], ᵀ*Smith* D. NY 1990, Paulist. iii-242 p. $12 pa.   0-8091-3123-4 [NTAbs 34,397: Until 3d century all Christians were considered *klêros* 'people set apart'].

7888 **Forte** B.,   L'Église icône de la Trinité; brève ecclésiologie 1985 ➤ 2,6055; 4,8910: 110 p.: ᴿAtKap 114 (1990) 498-502 (A. *Nowicki*).

7889 *Fürst* Walter,   Von innen heraus bauen; zur Aktualität der Frage J.-B. HIRSCHERS, 'Wie soll das Christentum in der Gegenwart unter uns lebendig werden?': TGegw 33 (1990) 82-97 [368s, ᴿSTÖBENER M., FÜRST 1968 Glaube (über HIRSCHER)].

7890 *George* Timothy, [fiery reactions to 1986 Southern Baptist Convention resolution on] The Priesthood of all believers and the quest for theological integrity: CriswT 3,2 (1989) 283-294.

7891 *Gerosa* Libero,   Le 'charisme originaire'; pour une justification théologique du droit des associations dans l'Église: NRT 112 (1990) 224-235.

7892 **Gnanakan** Ken R.,   Kingdom concerns; biblical... theology of mission. Bangalore 1989, Theol. Book.   208 p. – ᴿMissiology 18 (1990) 488s (R. E. *Hedlund*).

7893 *a) Goebel* Hans-Theodor,   Notae ecclesiae; zum Problem der Unterscheidung der wahren Kirche von der falschen Kirche; – *b) Weinrich* Michael,   Die Weltlichkeit der Kirche; systematische Zugänge zu einem Grundproblem der Ekklesiologie: EvT 50 (1990) 222-241 / 206-222.

7894 *a) Greinacher* Norbert,   ¿Invierno en la Iglesia? [< TüTQ 167 (1987) 182-193], ᵀᴱ*Giménez* J.; – *b) Biser* Eugen,   ¿Qué futuro hay para la Iglesia? [< StiZt 205 (1987) 3-14], ᵀ*Puig Massana* R.; – *c) Chevallier* Max-Alain,   La Iglesia, tensión entre unidad y pluralidad [< RHPR 66 (1986) 1-20], ᵀᴱ*Rocafiguera* J.; – *d) Valentini* Donato,   Iglesia universal y Iglesia local [< Credere Oggi 7,41 (1987) 5-25], ᵀ*Melloni Ribas* J.; – *e) Lorscheider* Aloisio,   La comunidad eclesial, sacramento de liberación [< Orientierung 51 (1987) 110-117], ᵀ*Torres* M.:   SelT 28 (1989) 3-10 / 11-18 / 19-28 / 29-35 / 36-40.

7895 **Grootaers** Jan,   Le chantier reste ouvert; les laïcs dans l'Église et dans le monde 1988 ➤ 5,7877: ᴿScEsp 42 (1990) 230-3 (G. *Raymond*: un laïc qui enseigne depuis 20 ans à Louvain).

7895* **Guillet** Charles-Marie,   La Iglesia.   Bilbao 1989, Mensajero.   135 p. 84-271-1559-8. – ᴿEstE 65 (1990) 471s (J. *Iturriaga*).

7896 ᴱ**Gunton** Colin, *Hardy* Daniel [and 4 others] On being the Church; essays on the Christian community 1989 ➤ 5,468: ᴿExpTim 101 (1989s) 218 (R. *Butterworth*); TLond 93 (1990) 311s (D. L. *Horne*).

7897 **Hanson** A. & R.,   The identity of the Church. L 1987, SCM.   276 p. £10.50. – ᴿThemelios 16 (1990s) 32s (D. F. *Wright*: robustly Anglican).

7898 **Hanson** Paul D.,   The people called 1986 ➤ 2,6072... 5,7878: ᴿHebSt 31 (1990) 172s (L. J. *Hoppe*); JAAR 58 (1990) 283-5 (W. *Harrelson*).

7899 **Hauerwas** Stanley, *Willimon* William H.,   Resident aliens; life in the Christian colony [the Constantinian era is over]; a provocative Christian assessment of culture and ministry for people who know that something is wrong.   Nv 1989, Abingdon.   175 p. $10. 0-687-36159-1 [TDig 37,367].

7900 **Henau** E.,   De kerk; instrument en teken van heil: Nikè.   Lv 1989, Akko.   241 p. ƒ39,25.   90-334-2101-1. – ᴿCollatVL 20 (1990) 337 (J. *Bonny*); TsTNijm 30 (1990) 216 (F. *Haarsma*).

7901 *Himes* Kenneth R., Mixed reactions; the reception of Gaudium et spes [Vatican II on the Church in the modern world]: NewTR 3,1 (1990) 5-17.

7902 *Homeyer* Josef, Die Kirche und Europa aus katholischer Sicht: UnSa 44 (1989) 266-274; > The Church and Europe, a Catholic view, ᵀᴱ*Asen* B. A., TDig 37,203-7.

7903 **Hünermann** Peter, *Schaeffler* Richard, Theorie der Sprachhandlungen und heutige Ekklesiologie: QDisp 109, 1987 → 3,644: ᴿTPQ 138 (1990) 286s (H. *Puchberger*).

7904 *a) Illanes* José Luis, La discusión teológica sobre la noción de laico; – *b) Borda* Enrique, Reflexiones sobre la teología de la misión en el XXV aniversario del decreto 'ad Gentes': ScripTPamp 22 (1990) 771-789 / 843-861 [791-842 *al.*, aniv. Vat. II].

7905 *Jones* L. Gregory, Why there is no one debate between 'communitarians' and 'liberals'; an essay on the importance of community; a review article [*Nisbet* R. 1953; *Bellah* R. 1985; *Sandel* M. 1982; *Bernstein* R. 1983; *Neuhaus* R. 1984; *Hauerwas* S. 1981; *Boff* L. 1986, 1985]: PerspRelSt 17 (1990) 53. 56-70.

7906 **Karrer** Leo, Aufbruch der Christen; das Ende der klerikalen Kirche 1989 → 5,7884: ᴿBurgense 31 (1990) 262s (E. *Bueno*); ForumKT 5 (1989) 229-231 (F. *Reckinger*); LebZeug 44 (1989) 156s (A. *Weiser*); TsTKI 61 (1990) 230s (Ola *Tjørhom*).

7907 **Kasper** Walter, Theology and Church [→ 255*a*]. L 1989, SCM. £12.50 pa. – ᴿTLond 93 (1990) 53 (R. M. *Burns*: now bishop over his and KÜNG's Tübingen, acceptable to Rome and markedly circumspect, judicious, irenic; but critical, for RAHNER against neo-scholasticism ...).

7908 **Kasper** Walter, Teología y Iglesia [1987 → 3,7622],ᵀ: Biblioteca Herder 187. Barc 1989, Herder. 448 p. – ᴿCiTom 117 (1990) 389s (L. *Lago*); CommSev 23 (1990) 110s (M. *Sánchez*); QVidCr 148s (1989) 232s (E. *Vilanova*).

7909 *Kasper* Walter, Vocación y misión de los laicos en la Iglesia y en el mundo [< StiZt 205 (1987) 579-593], ᵀᴱ*Priego* Juan J.: SelT 28 (1989) 101-110.

7910 *Kealy* Séan P., Jesus' approach to mission: AfER 39 (1989) 27-36.

7911 **Kent** John, The unacceptable face 1987 → 3,7628; 4,8933*: ᴿEngHR 105 (1990) 278s (E. *Norman*); ScotBEv 8 (1990) 61s (D. W. *Bebbington*).

7912 **Köster** F., Kirche im Koma? Der Mut zu einer ganz anderen. Fra 1989, Knecht. 199 p. DM 26. 3-7820-0589-9. – ᴿTsTNijm 30 (1990) 106s (W. *Boelens*).

7913 **Lakeland** Paul, Theology and critical theory; the discourse of the Church [... with a little help from HABERMAS]. Nv 1990, Abingdon. 271 p. $18.85 [TS 52, 368, C. O'*Regan*].

7913* **Lange** Maurice F. F. de, L'ecclésiologie de Jean DANIÉLOU, diss. ᴰ*Pagé* J.-G. Laval 1990. 471 p. – RTLv 22, p. 615.

7914 *La Soujeole* Benoît-D. de, 'Société' et 'Communion' chez S. Thomas d'AQUIN; étude d'ecclésiologie: RThom 90 (1990) 587-622.

7915 *Leitmaier* Charlotte, Morphologie der kirchlichen Strukturen; Divinisierung des kirchlichen Amtes als Gefahr für den Glauben: Diakonia 21 (1990) 100-106.

7915* *a) Lehmann* Karl, Wer ist Kirche? Plädoyer für ein erneuertes Laientum; – *b) Härle* Wilfried, Sichtbare und verborgene Kirche; – *c) Kässmann* Margot, Kirche im konziliaren Prozess [Ökologie]; – *d) Schottroff* Luise, Botschafterinnen an Christi Statt: → 93, ᶠJUNG H., Vernünftiger Gottesdienst 1990, 164-177 / 243-255 / 210-224 / 271-294.

7916 ᴱ**Limouris** Gennadios, Church, Kingdom, world 1985/6 ➤ 3,665; 5,7893:
ᴿJeevadhara 19 (1989) 308s (R. *Rao*).

7916* **Lindquist** Curtis G., The Church as a Christian community of hope;
a comparative study of MOLTMANN and HAUERWAS using a cul-
tural-linguistic style of thinking: diss. Emory, ᴰ*Saliers* D. Atlanta 1990.
359 p. 90-27925. – DissA 51 (1990s) 1661-A; RelStR 17,192.

7917 **Lods** Marc, Protestantisme et tradition de l'Église, ᴱ*Pérès* J.-N., *Dubois*
J.-D.: Patrimoines Christianisme 1988 ➤ 5,299: – ᴿEsprVie 99 (1989) 43s
[É. *Cothenet*].

7918 **Lutz** Jürgen, Unio und Kommunio; zum Verhältnis von Rechtfertigungslehre und Kirchenverständnis bei M. LUTHER; eine Untersuchung
zu ekklesiologisch relevanten Texten der Jahre 1519 bis 1528 [Diss.
Freiburg/Br 1989s, ᴰ*Greshake*. – TR 86,515]: KkKSt 55. Pd 1990, Bonifatius. 311 p. [TPhil 65,632].

7919 *März* Claus-Peter, Neutestamentliche und patristische Anmerkungen zum kirchlichen Sprachgebrauch von 'Laien': TJb (1989) 235-244
[-314, *al.*].

7920 *Marcelli* Piergiorgio, La simbologia delle doti della Chiesa in OTTATO
di Milevì; problemi e significato: SMSR 56 (1990) 219-244.

7921 **Meier** Bertram, Die Kirche der wahren Christen; J.M. SAILERS Kirchenverständnis zwischen Unmittelbarkeit und Vermittlung: MüKHistSt
4. Stu 1990, Kohlhammer. 425 p. [TPhil 65,632].

7922 *Mesters* Carlos, The Bible and the new evangelization: EAPast 27,1
(1990) 4-39 [< TContext 8/1,73].

7922* **Miller** E. J., J. H., NEWMAN on the idea of the Church 1987 ➤ 3,7653;
5,7899*: ᴿCritRR 2 (1989) 324-6 (Anne *Carr*).

7923 **Möller** Christian, Lehre von Gemeindeaufbau, I. Konzepte – Programme – Wege 1987 ➤ 3,7654: ᴿTZBas 46 (1990) 87s (W. *Neidhart*).

7924 **Monsegú** Bernardo, *a*) La Iglesia que Cristo quiso 1986 ➤ 3,7657;
4,8960 ['C. P. Barbado']: ᴿEstE 65 (1990) 82s (J. *Iturriaga*).

7925 *a*) *Müller* Hans M., Gemeindeaufbau: TRu 55 (1990) 308-324; – *b*)
Landau Peter, Kirchenverfassungen [... Urkirche; Vorkonstantinisch ...]
➤ 857, TRE 19 (1990) 110-165.

7926 **Muschalek** Georg, Kirche — noch heilsnotwendig? Über das Gewissen,
die Empörung und das Verlangen²: Bild und Gleichnis 5. Tü 1989, von
Seth. 91 p. DM 14,80. – ᴿZkT 112 (1990) 344s (K. H. *Neufeld*).

7927 *a*) *Nagy* Stanisław, ℗ Laïques dans la communauté communale de
l'Église; – *b*) *Wistuba* Halina, ℗ La femme dans l'Église et dans le monde:
AtKap 114,3 ('Christifideles laici' 1990) 377-387 / 407-418.

7928 *a*) *Neuner* Peter, The Church as *koinonia*, a central theme of Vatican II,
ᵀ*Endean* Philip; – *b*) *Cosstick* Vicky, Formation and the *koinonia* Church;
– *c*) *Elvey* Frank, Koinonia for people of the Exodus: Way 30 (1990)
176-187 / 188-198 / 199-209.

7929 *Nossol* Alfons, Pilgernde Kirche – Ecclesia peregrinans – im Strom der
Zeit: LebZeug 44 (1989) 98-107.

7929* **Oden** Amy G., Dominant images for the Church in AUGUSTINE's
'Enarrationes in Psalmos'; a study in Augustine's ecclesiology: diss.
Southern Methodist, ᴰ*Babcock* W. 1990. 296 p. 90-27826. – DissA 51
(1990s) 1062s-A; RelStR 17,194.

7930 **Parent** Rémi, *a*) Une Église de baptisés; pour surmonter l'opposition
clercs/laïcs 1987 ➤ 3,7667: ᴿRTLv 21 (1990) 373s (M. *Simon*); SR 19
(1990) 371s (R. *Lemieux*); – *b*) Una Iglesia de bautizados: Presencia

teológica 37. Sdr 1987, SalTerrae. 219 p. 84-293-0777-X. – REstE 65 (1990) 80s (J. *Iturriaga*).

7931 E**Pastore** Corrado, La inculturación del evangelio: Estudios Teológicos [para Religiosos] 3. Caracas 1988, ITER. 166 p. 980-300-220-1. – P.35-57, *Renaud* Bruno; 59-69, *Santos de Villamañán* Adolfo; 99-123, *Bazarra* Carlos; 125-149, *Rodríguez V.* Julián; 151-166, *Pérez-Esclarín* Antonio.

7931* a) *Pathil* Kuncheria, Catholic ecclesiology and changes it faces today; – b) *Abraham* K.C., C.S.I. [Church of South India] ecclesiology; some issues and challenges; – c) *Jesudoss* D.M., The concept of the Church; a Lutheran perspective: Jeevadhara 19 (1989) 282-306 / 249-266 / 267-281.

7932 **Peña** Braulio, Laymen in the Church; Jesus and his people: PhilipSa 24 (1989) 171-248.

7933 [da Silva] *Pereira* Antônio, Participação dos leigos nas decisões da Igreja à luz do Vaticano I e II: REB 50 (1990) 93-116.

7934 *Persaud* Winston D., Boldly embracing humanity; toward a theology of mission: CurrTMiss 17 (1990) 201-6.

7935 *Quacquarelli* Antonio, Le origini patristiche del sacerdozio dei fedeli nella concezione della teologia battesimale di Antonio ROSMINI: VetChr 27 (1990) 5-19.

7936 *Quinzá Lleó* Xavier, Signa temporum; la semiótica de lo temporal en el proceso de redacción de la 'Gaudium et spes': MiscCom 48 (1990) 323-369.

7938 **Rebell** W., Zum neuen Leben berufen; kommunikative Gemeindepraxis im frühen Christentum: Tb 88. Mü 1990, Kaiser. 223 p. DM 19,80. 3-459-01869-0 [NTAbs 35,259: varying NT models of Church].

7939 *Rigal* Jean, L'ecclésiologie tridentine: BLitEc 91 (1990) 251-273; Eng. 273.

7940 a) *Ritter* Adolf M., Grundlagen und Grundfragen der Kirchengemein-schaft in vorkonstantinischer Zeit; – b) *Dassmann* Ernst, Hirtentheologie und Hirtenbild vor Nicäa; → 135, FORBE A., Compostellanum 35 (1990) 223-245 / 207-222.

7941 *Ritter* Adolf M. [*al.*], Laie: → 857, TRE 20 (1990) 378-385 [-399; 404-9 Laizismus, *Mehl* Roger].

7942 *Rossum* J. van, De ecclesiologie van A.S. CHOMJAKOV (1804-1860): KerkT 40 (1989) 19-32.

7943 **Sales** Michel, Le corps de l'Église; études sur l'Église une, sainte, ca-tholique et apostolique: Communio. P 1989, Fayard. 282 p. F 98. – RSpiritus 31 (1990) 337s (M. *Oger*); TR 86 (1990) 315 (W. *Beinert*); ZkT 112 (1990) 326 8 (K.H. *Neufeld*: eine bunte Sammlung über die kon-stitutive Verbindung zu Israel).

7944 **Schillebeeckx** Edward, Church; the human story of God [→ 7190; planned as a successor to Jesus 1974, Eng. 1979; and Christ 1977, Eng. 1980; but modified because we are in a period of church po-larization]. NY 1990, Crossroad. xix-268 p. $23. 0-8245-1050-X [TDig 38,85]. – RExpTim 102 (1990s) 213s (R. *Butterworth*: maybe all we will ever see of that awaited third volume).

7945 *Semeraro* Marcello, Il Cristiano laico nel testo conciliare di Lumen Gentium 30-31: Lateranum 56 (1990) 143-181.

7946 **Senn** Felix, Orthopraktische Ekklesiologie? K. RAHNERS Offenba-rungsverständnis und seine ekklesiologischen Konsequenzen im Kon-text der neueren katholischen Theologiegeschichte [Diss. Fr]: FreibZ ÖkBeih 19. FrS 1989, Univ. 816 p. Fs 68. – RTLZ 115 (1990) 853-5 (M. *Plathow*); ZkT 112 (1990) 355-7 (K.H. *Neufeld*).

7946* ᴱSeybold M., Fragen in der Kirche und an die Kirche 1987/8 ➤ 5,517: ᴿTPQ 138 (1990) 190s (S. *Birngruber*).

7947 *a*) *Solberg* Mary M., Some thoughts on Church, ministry, and mission; – *b*) *Wi Jo Kang*, Sending and receiving in Christian mission: CurrT-Miss 17 (1990) 128-132 / 133-9.

7948 *Spijker* H. van de, Das Schiff der Kirche – die Arche Noachs – das Jonas-boot; drei maritime Kirchenbilder: TGegw 33 (1990) 172-8.

7948* *Spindler* Marc, Regards partagés sur les missions protestantes? Émiettement détestable ou pluralisme enviable?: Spiritus 31 (1990) 186-201.

7949 **Sullivan** Francis A., The Church we believe in; one, holy, catholic and apostolic 1988 ➤ 5,7920; Gill 0-7171-1636-0; £9: ᴿAmerica 162 (1990) 509s (R.P. *Imbelli*); CalvinT 25 (1990) 116-8 (R.R. *Recker*: proper Eucharist is the most crucial mark of the Church); ExpTim 101 (1989s) 217s (R. *Butterworth*); HomPast 90,10 (1989s) 76s (J.R. *Sheets*: good); Month 250 (1989) 438 (A. *Meredith*); NRT 112 (1990) 258s (A. *Toubeau*); TLZ 115 (1990) 637s (H. *Kirchner*); Worship 64 (1990) 254s (K. *McDonnell*).

7950 **Thaler** Anton, Gemeinde und Eucharistie; Grundlegung einer eucharistischen Ekklesiologie: PrakT im Dialog 2, 1988 ➤ 5,7922: ᴿTGl. 80 (1990) 229 (M. *Kunzler*); TPQ 138 (1990) 192 (H. *Hollerweger*).

7951 *Tourneux* André, Église et Eucharistie à Vatican II: NRT 112 (1990) 338-355.

7952 **Valadier** P., L'Église en procès; catholicisme et société moderne (Calmann-Lévy) 1987 ➤ 3,7713; 4,9002; aussi coll. Champs 199: P 1989, Flammarion. 241 p. – ᴿNRT 112 (1990) 259 (D. *Dideberg*).

7953 **Valadier** P., La Iglesia en proceso; catolicismo y sociedad moderna: Presencia teológica 58. Santander 1990, Sal Terrae. 244 p. – ᴿCommSev 23 (1990) 435s (M. *Sánchez*).

7954 *Valentini* Donato, Iglesia universal e Iglesia local [< Credere Oggi 7,41 (1987) 5-25], ᵀᴱ*Melloni Ribas* Javier: SelT 28 (1989) 29-35.

7955 *Vanhoye* Albert, Le origini della missione apostolica nel Nuovo Testamento: CC 141 (1990,4) 544-558.

7956 *Vellanical* Mathew, Local Church; New Testament perspectives: Bible-Bhashyam 15 (1989) 5-24.

7957 *Vernette* Jean, Église et sectes: Spiritus 30 (1989) 119-149.

7958 **Villar** J.R., Teología de la Iglesia particular, ... en francés: Col. Teol. 63. Pamplona 1989, EUNSA. xix-578 p. – ᴿBurgense 31 (1990) 597-9 (E. *Bueno*); NRT 112 (1990) 743s (R. *Escol*).

7959 *Vogt* Hermann, Die totale Mission der Mormonen; Aufstieg und Expansion einer amerikanischen Grosssekte: ZkT 112 (1990) 406-426.

7960 **Webber** Robert E., The Church in the world; opposition? tension? or transformation? 1986 ➤ 3,7724: ᴿRelStT 8,1s (1988) 93s (D. *Skoyles*).

7960* **Wee** Daniel D., LUTHER's understanding of the universal priesthood as it relates to ministry in daily life in the twentieth century: diss. Princeton Theol. Sem. 1990. 170 p. 91-02158. – DissA 51 (1990s) 3443s-A..

7961 *Williams* Michael D., Where's the Church? The Church as the unfinished business of dispensational theology: GraceTJ 10 (1989) 165-182.

7962 **Wostyn** Lode L., Doing ecclesiology; Church and mission today. Manila 1990, Claretian. 146 p. [TContext 8/1, 133, G. *Evers*].

H7.7 *Œcumenismus* – The ecumenical movement.

7963 *Aarde* A.G. van, 'n Nuwe-Testamentiese begronding van die eenheid van die kerk en die eis ['demand'] om kerkeenheid vandag: HervTSt 45 (1989) 461-475 [< NTAbs 34,66, 'quest'].

7964 **Alberigo** Giuseppe, Nostalgie di unità; saggi 1989 ➤ 5,224: ᴿGregorianum 71 (1990) 606s (J. E. *Vercruysse*); JEH 41 (1990) 341 (H. *Chadwick*: a grand master); TPhil 65 (1990) 279s (K. *Schatz*) [& 277, H. *Sieben* über La chiesa nella storia 1988].

7965 *Andel* Cornelis P. van, Intercommunie en Ambt; laatste gespreksronde aan de hand van liturgische teksten: KerkT 41 (1990) 10-25.

7966 *Arnold* Matthieu, À propos de la seconde édition [1991!] de Einheit durch Vielfalt, d'Oscar CULLMANN: RHPR 70 (1990) 461-5.

7967 **Avis** Paul, Anglicanism and the Christian Church; theological resources in historical perspective. Mp 1989, Fortress. 335 p. $35. – ᴿAnglTR 72 (1990) 469-471 (F. M. *McClain*).

7968 *Barreda* Jesús-Ángel, El 'espíritu ecuménico' y la misión: Studium 29 (M 1989) 389-414.

7969 **Barth** Hans-M., Einander Priester sein; allgemeines Priestertum in ökumenischer Perspektive: Kirche und Konfession 29. Gö 1990, Vandenhoeck & R. 257 p. DM 38 pa. – ᴿÖkRu 39 (1990) 493s G. *Schütz*).

7970 **Baur** Jörg, Einig in Sachen Rechtfertigung? Zur Prüfung des Rechtfertigungskapitels der Studie des Ökumenischen Arbeitskreises evangelischer und katholischer Theologen 'Lehrverteilungen – kirchentrennend?'. Tü 1989, Mohr. ix-111 p. DM 29 pa. – ᴿTLZ 115 (1990) 461-3 (T. *Mahlmann*).

7971 *Bavaud* Georges, L'Église Catholique pourrait-elle entrer au Conseil œcuménique? : NVFr 65 (1990) 99-110 [> TDig 38,9-14, R. *Jermann*]: not dogma but pastoral and structural considerations still prevent.

7972 **Bilheimer** Robert S., Breakthrough; the emergence of the ecumenical tradition. GR/Geneva 1989, Eerdmans/WCC. x-235 p. Fs 27.50 pa. – ᴿTLZ 115 (1990) 636s (K. *Raiser*).

7973 *Birmelé* André, Les dialogues entre Églises chrétiennes; bilan et perspectives: Études 373 (1990) 679-690.

7974 *Blaser* K., Une Église des confessions. Genève 1990, Labor et Fides. 120 p. F 99. 2-8309-0602-0 [ÉTRel 65,659].

7975 *Boyd* Robin, A BARTHian theology of interfaith dialogue: Pacifica 3 (1990) 288-303.

7976 *Brent* Allen, Ecumenical reconciliation and cultural episcopates [threefold order in IGNATIUS A., ...]: AnglTR 72 (1990) 255-279.

7977 *Briard* J., Le rassemblement œcuménique européen de Bâle 1989, chance et interpellation pour les Églises, les chrétiens: FoiTemps 20 (1990) 5-25.

7978 **Brun** Maria, Orthodoxe Stimmen zum II. Vatikanum; ein Beitrag zur Überwindung der Trennung: FreibZ ÖkBeıh 18, 1988 ➤ 5,7954: ᴿOstkSt 38 (1989) 212s (E. C. *Suttner*).

7979 ᴱ**Bsteh** Andreas, Dialog aus der Mitte christlicher Theologie [St. Gabriel Tagungen 1986]: Beit.Rel.-Theol. 5. Mödling 1987 ➤ 4,535: ᴿTPQ 137 (1989) 305s (J. *Janda*).

7980 ᴱ**Burgess** J. A., *Gros* J., Building unity...: Documents 4, 1989 ➤ 5,643: ᴿTS 51 (1990) 355-7 (J. T. *Ford*).

7981 **Carile** Sergio, I Metodisti, nell'Inghilterra della rivoluzione industriale. T 1989, Claudiana. 365 p. Lit. 33.000. 88-7016-096-3. – ᴿEcuR 42 (1990) 364s (A. *Comba*: approach to union with Italian Waldensians).

7982 **Chrysostomos** bp., *Auxentios* hieromonk, The Roman West and the Byzantine East. Etna CA 1988, Center for Traditionalist Orthodox Studies. 59 p. $5.50 pa. – ᴿGrOrTR 34 (1989) 178-180 (J. E. *Rexine*).

7983 *Ciobotea* Daniel, Ökumene als Metanoia der getrennten Konfessionen in ihrer Kritik und ihrer Hoffnung: UnSa 45 (1990) 287-290 [274-326, *al.*; 291-6, *Sanders* Wilm, Oberammergau].

7984 *Corbon* Jean, Une catéchèse orthodoxe-catholique est-elle possible dans les églises d'Antioche?: PrOrChr 40 (1990) 56-78.

7985 *Cottret* Bernard, Tolérance ou liberté de conscience? [... dichotomie paulinienne Grâce/Loi années 1680]: ÉTRcl 65 (1990) 333-350.

7986 *a*) *Craddock* Fred B., Christian unity and the NT; a conversation between Luke and John; – *b*) *Willebrands* Johannes card. The Catholic Church and the ecumenical movement; Mid-Stream 27 (1988) 1-12 / 13-34 (35-44, *Crumley* James R., response).

7987 **Cullmann** Oscar, L'unità attraverso la diversità; il suo fondamento e il problema della sua realizzazione [1986], ᵀ*Capra* Gianni: GdT 178, 1987 → 3,7769; 4,9035: ᴿETL 66 (1990) 217s (J. E. *Vercruysse*, franç.); Dial-Ecum 24 (1989) 334-7 (A. *González-Montes*).

7988 *Cullmann* Oscar, Unidad en la diversidad a la luz de la 'jerarquía de verdades': Diálogo Ecuménico 24 (1989) 237-247 [< RET 50,131].

7989 **Damaskinos** metr., Ⓖ Theologische Dialoge, eine orthodoxe Perspektive. Thessaloniki 1986, Kyriakidis. 355 p. – ᴿTLZ 115 (1990) 310-2 (G. *Larentzakis*).

7990 **Dick** J. A., The Malines conversations [1921-5] revisited [< diss. Lv]: BiblETL 85. Leuven 1989, Univ./Peeters. 278 p. Fb 1500. – ᴿCathHR 76 (1990) 392s (J. J. *Hughes*); ETL 66 (1990) 233s (A. de *Halleux*); ExpTim 102 (1990s) 59 (J. *Kent*); JEH 41 (1990) 323s (H. *Chadwick*); JTS 41 (1990) 772-6 (R. J. *Lahey*); NRT 112 (1990) 931s (N. *Plumat*); Tablet 244 (1990) 217s (O. *Chadwick*); TLZ 115 (1990) 831s (N. P. *Moritzen*); TS 51 (1990) 564 (H. J. *Ryan*: complements AUBERT).

7991 **Dick** Ignace, Sens et vicissitudes de l'"uniatisme'; l'écartèlement de la double fidélité. Beyrouth 1984, S.-Paul. 127 p. – ᴿIstina 35 (1990) 125 (B. *Dupuy*).

7992 **Dionne** J. Robert, The papacy and the Church, a study of praxis and reception in ecumenical perspective 1987 → 3,7776 ... 5,7963: ᴿMélSR 47 (1990) 52s (F. *Frost*); NRT 112 (1990) 273s (R. *Escol*).

7993 *Döring* Heinrich, Einheit durch Vielfalt?: UnSa 44 (1989) 101-114. 145 [*al.* 98-131].

7994 *Dürrenmatt* Friedrich, Sur la tolérance [1977], ᵀ*Bühler* Pierre: RTPhil 122 (1990) 449-465; Eng. 578.

7995 **Dulles** Avery, The catholicity of the Church 1985 → 1,7443 ... 5,7967: ᴿHeythJ 31 (1990) 88s (M. *Santer*).

7996 *a*) *Dumoulin* Jean, Tolérance et intolérance dans l'histoire de l'Église; – *b*) *Scolas* Paul, Vérité et tolérance; éléments pour une réflexion théologique: FoiTemps 20 (1990) 407-424 / 389-406 [425-434, *Lobet* Benoît, cours de religion].

7997 *Dunn* James D. G., Unity and diversity in the Church; a New Testament perspective: Gregorianum 71 (1990) 629-655; franç. 656.

7998 *Dura* Nicolae V. (en roumain), *a*) La théologie orthodoxe et les théologies confessionnelles dans l'œcuménisme contemporain; – *b*) La théologie et les théologies; la théologie orthodoxe et les nouveaux courants théologiques; – *c*) Document de Lima (B.E.M.): OrtBuc 38 (1986) 3,61-89 / 4,46-77 / 2,119-147.

7999 *Dyck* M. J. van, Worden Rome en Canterbury een?; Receptie van het ARCIC-Eindrapport: CollatVL 20 (1990) 193-213.

7999* **Eber** Jochen, Einheit der Kirche als dogmatisches Problem bei Edmund SCHLINK: Diss. Erlangen 1990, ᴰ*Slenczka* R. 320 p. – STLv 22, p. 616.

8000 **Eham** Markus, Gemeinschaft im Sakrament; die Frage nach der Möglichkeit sakramentaler Gemeinschaft zwischen katholischen und nichtkatholischen Christen; zur ekklesiologischen Dimension der ökumenischen Frage: EurHS 23/293, 1986 → 2,6191; 4,9047: ᴿBijdragen 51 (1990) 93s (A. van Eijk).

8001 *Falconer* Alan D., Celebrating twenty-five years of the decree on ecumenism (24th Nov., 1964): MilltSt 26 (1990) 9-22.

Farmer W., *Kereszty* R., Peter and Paul in the Church of Rome; the ecumenical potential ... 1990 → g52.

8003 *a) Frieling* Reinhard, Wozu Ökumene?: – *b) Ganoczy* Alexandre / *Honecker* Martin, Rechtfertigung und Gerechtigkeit in der Perspektive katholischer / evangelischer Theologie; – *c) Maron* Gottfried / *Spengler* Helmut, Allgemeines Priestertum im Protestantismus / in der Kirche: Im Lichte der Reformation 33 (Gö 1990) 5-24 / 25-40.41-60 / 67-79.80-91 [< ᴢɪᴛ 90,285].

8004 **Fries** H., Leiden an der Kirche [< Christ in der Gegenwart 1989, 159,000 copies sold]. FrB 1989, Herder. 79 p. DM 10,80. 3-4512-1595-0. – ᴿTPQ 138 (1990) 190 (R. *Zinnhobler*); TsTNijm 30 (1990) 106 (W. *Boelens*).

8005 **Fries** H., *Pesch* O.H., Streiten für die eine Kirche 1987 → 3,7794; 4,9054: ᴿBurgense 31 (1990) 261s (E. *Bueno*).

8006 **Fries** H., *Rahner* K., La unión de las Iglesias, una posibilidad reale [1983] 1987 → 3,7797: ᴿHumT 10 (1989) 267s (A. de *Pinho*).

8007 *a) Fries* Heinrich, Einigung der Kirchen – reale Möglichkeit; – *b) Pesch* Otto H., Die Lehrverurteilungen des 16. Jhdts. und die ökumenische Situation der Gegenwart ... Risiken und Chancen; – *c) Kasper* Walter, Grundkonsens und Kirchengemeinschaft; – *d) Houtepen* Anton, Kirche im Werden; fundamentaltheologische Beiträge zu einer ökumenischen Ekklesiologie: TJb (1989) 319-373 / 374-416 / 417-438 / 439-459.

8008 *Frost* Francis, Le monde anglo-saxon et l'œcuménisme: Ensemble 3 (Lille 1989) [< EsprVie 100 (1990) 177-180, J. *Daoust*].

8008* **Fu-Long Lien**, Die Ekklesiologie in der Theologie Karl RAHNERs, mit besonderem Hinblick auf das Problem der interkulturellen und interreligiösen Vermittlung des Christentums: Diss. ᴰ*Pesch* O. Hamburg 1990. – RTLv 22, p. 615.

8009 **Garijo-Guembe** M.M., *al.*, Mahl des Herrn 1988 → 4,362: ᴿArTGran 52 (1989) 282s (A. *Segovia*).

8010 **Grès-Gayer** Jacques, Paris-Cantorbéry (1717-1720); le dossier d'un premier œcuménisme: Textes, dossiers, documents 13. P 1989, Beauchesne. 561 p. F 255. 2-7010-1196-5. – ᴿÉTRel 65 (1990) 638s (H. *Bost*: source précieuse, malgré l'omission de RABAUT 1806); Études 372 (1990) 425s (J. *Thomas*); NRT 112 (1990) 930s (A. *Harvengt*); TS 51 (1990) 563s (G.H. *Tavard*).

8011 *Grislis* Egil, Eucharistic convergence in ecumenical debate; an intimation of the future of Christianity: TorJT 6 (1990) 247-265.

8012 *Gros* Jeffrey, Ecumenism and the identity of U.S. Catholics: NewTR 3,1 (1990) 46-61.

8013 *Hall* Thor. Paul KNITTER's presuppositions for interfaith dialogue; a critique: PerspRelSt 17 (1990) 43-52.

8014 *Halleux* A. de, Tradition liturgique et unité chrétienne: RICathP 36 (1990) 181-190 [157-170, *Zizioulas* J.; 171-9, *Kretschmar* G.: tous trois pour le doctorat d'honneur].

8015 *Hanc* Wojciech, ❷ Signification de la hiérarchie des vérités dans le dialogue œcuménique: AtKap 112 (1989) 66-79.

8015* **Han-Rhinow Jeong Ae**, Die frühchristlichen Kirchenordnungen und ihr Amtsverständnis als Beitrag zur ökumenischen Diskussion um das Lima Document: ev. Diss. ᴰ*Kretschmar* O. München 1990s. – RTLv p. 597.

8016 *Harnoncourt* Philipp, Die vielen Kirchen und die eine Kirche; zu den Zielvorstellungen der ökumenischen Bewegung: ➤ 76, ᶠHENKYS J., 1989, 341-9.

8016* **Harrison** Brian W., Le développement de la doctrine catholique sur la liberté religieuse: ᵀᴱ*Morin* Dominique M. ... Chémeré. 205 p. 2-85652-107-X. – ᴿPenséeC 239 (1989) 21-40 (F. *Argad*: questionne 'l'incompétence radicale de l'État en matière religieuse').

8017 *Hauerwas* Stanley, The importance of being Catholic; unsolicited advice from a Protestant bystander: Listening 25,1 (1990) 27-46 [< ZIT 90,308].

8018 *Henn* William, The hierarchy of truths and Christian unity [Edmond *Dublanchy*'s 79 columns on Infallibility in Dictionnaire de Théologie Catholique end with only 13 likeliest examples of its exercise, and show that very fallible means must be used to ascertain whether any really are such]: ETL 66 (1990) 111-142.

8019 *Heubach* Joachim, Amt und Volk Gottes nach LUTHER; ein Beitrag zum ökumenischen Dialog: Lutherische Kirche in der Welt 35 (1988) 53-63 [< TLZ 115,158].

8020 *Houtepen* Anton, Ökumenische Hermeneutik; auf der Suche nach Kriterien der Kohärenz im Christentum: ÖkRu 39 (1990) 279-296.

8021 *Kallis* Anastasios, Ferrara-Florenz (1438-1439); 'Räubersynode' oder 'Modell eines kommenden Unionskonzils'?: ÖkRu 39 (1990) 182-200.

8022 **Kinnamon** Michael, Truth and community; diversity and its limits in the ecumenical movement. Genève 1988, WCC. x-118 p. Fs 13,50. 2-8254-0935-9. – ᴿÉTRel 65 (1990) 425-7 (J.-M. *Prieur*, aussi sur six autres publications WCC); TLZ 115 (1990) 308s (H. *Krüger*); TorJT 6 (1990) 321-3 (J. M. *Laporte*); TsTKi 60 (1989) 153s (Ola *Tjørhom*).

8023 **Klausnitzer** Wolfgang, Das Papstamt im Disput 1987 ➤ 3,7831 ... 5,7989: ᴿEstE 65 (1990) 121s (A. *Navas*); HeythJ 31 (1990) 347s (J. *Wicks*); RHPR 70 (1990) 487s (M. *Lienhard*); TsTNijm 30 (1990) 208 (H. *Witte*).

8024 *Küng* Hans, Ecumenism and truth; the wider dialogue: Tablet 243 (1989) 92s [introduction to his new Paradigm Change with D. *Tracy*].

8025 *Lanne* Emmanuel, Les Catholiques orientaux; liberté religieuse et œcuménisme: Irénikon 63 (1990) 20-46; Eng. 46.

8026 ᴱ**Lehmann** K., *Pannenberg* W., Lehrverurteilung — kirchentrennend? [I. 1986 ➤ 3,661] II. Materialien zu den Lehrverurteilungen und zur Theologie der Rechtfertigung; III. Materialien zur Lehre von den Sakramenten und vom kirchlichen Amt: Dialog der Kirchen 5s. FrB / Gö 1989s, Herder / Vandenhoeck & R. 374 p.; 352 p. je DM 48. 3-451-20850-4; -1-2 / VR 3-525-56926-4; -7-0. – ᴿNRT 112 (1990) 744s (R. *Escol*); TsTNijm 30 (1990) 317s (G. P. *Hartvelt*; G. *Lukken*); TGL 80 (1990) 223 (W. *Beinert*, 2).

8027 ᴱ**Lehmann** Karl, *Pannenberg* Wolfhart, The condemnations of the Reformation era; do they still divide? ᵀ*Kohl* Margaret, 1989 ➤ 5,7993: ᴿCathHR 76 (1990) 845s (C. J. *Peter*); ExpTim 102 (1990s) 124s (G. W. P. *McFarlane*); TS 51 (1990) 790 (T. P. *Rausch*).

8028 *Lévy* Antoine, Un dialogue entre croyants et athées; le premier volume de la collection Amen [< Amen ❷]: Istina 35 (1990) 268-276.

8029 **Lochhead** David, The dialogical imperative 1988 → 5,7996: ᴿAnglTR 71 (1989) 330s (R. M. *Kawano*); SR 19 (1990) 372s (R. B. *Sheard*); TLond 93 (1990) 60-63 (A. *Race*, also on ᴱD'COSTA G. 1986/8).

8030 **Luttenberger** Albrecht P., Johannes ECK und die Religionsgespräche: → 5,k177, Eck-Symposium 1986/8, 192-222.

8031 *a) Marinos* Anastasios N., Religiöser Pluralismus und seine Grenzen ... Verfassungsrechtliche Perspektiven, ᵀ*Glauser* Adelheid; – *b) Klautke* Heinz, Anmerkungen und Fragen; – *c) Suttner* Ernst C., Dialog und Uniatismus [... schliessen einander aus]: UnSa 45 (1990) 70-75,95 / 76-83 / 87-95.

8032 **Maron** Gottfried, Zum Gespräch mit Rom; Beiträge aus evangelischer Sicht; Bensheimer Hefte 69, 1988 → 5,312: ᴿEvKomm 22,3 (1989) 52 (H. *Vorster*).

8033 *Marshall* I. H., Inter-faith dialogue in the NT: EvRT 13 (Exeter 1989) 196-215 [< NTAbs 34,70].

8034 *Martínez Camino* Juan A., De las guerras de religión al ateismo; una tesis de W. PANNENBERG: MiscCom 47 (1989) 157-179 (397-425).

8035 *a) Mejía* Jorge, Giustizia, pace, integrità della creazione nei rapporti attuali tra le Chiese; – *b) Sullivan* Francis A., Il Decreto sull'ecumenismo [1964]; presupposti ecclesiologici e conseguenze; – *c) Miccoli* Paolo, Tolleranza e intolleranza: RasT 31 (1990) 223-230 / 231-246 / 269-284.

8036 *Metz* Johann-B., Die eine Welt als Herausforderung an das westliche Christentum: UnSa 44 (1989) 314-322 [dazu 45 (1990) 281-6. 290, *Tesfai Yacob*].

8037 *Mitri* Tarek, Église, nation et culture; l'expérience des chrétiens orthodoxes d'Antioche; une approche socio-historique: Irénikon 63 (1990) 451-461; Eng. 461.

8037* **Moro** D., Il 'munus' del vescovo di Roma nel confronto ecumenico-dottrinale di I. MARKOVIĆ e N. MILAŠ [diss. Antonianum 1984]: R 1986, Pont. Athenaeum Antonianum. 127 p. – ᴿNRT 112 (1990) 274s (R. *Escol*).

8038 **Newbigin** Lesslie, The Gospel in a pluralist society [Glasgow Univ. Robertson Lectures 1988]. GR 1989, Eerdmans. xl-244 p. 2-8254-0971-5. – ᴿProtestantesimo 45 (1990) 233s (G. *Girardet*); QRMin 10 (1990) 97-103 (E. A. *Percell*).

8039 *Østnor* Lors, *a)* Kirkens enhet; et bidrag til forståelsen av norske teologers oppfatning av det økumeniske problem i mellomkrigstiden: diss. Oslo 1988. – NorTTs 90 (1989) 49; – *b)* Ortodoksi og ortopraksi; stillningtagen til politiske spørsmål som økumenisk problem [prøveforelesning Oslo 1988]: NorTTs 90 (1989) 87-104; cf. 49.

8040 *Oeyen* Christian, Hundert Jahre nach DÖLLINGER [† 24.IX.1890]; die Utrechter Union heute: ÖkRu 39 (1990) 66-76.

8041 *Ottlyk* Ernő, ⓜ Ukran katolikusok és ortodoxok: TSzem 33 (1990) 87-92.

8042 *Pannenberg* Wolfhart, Das Christentum als ökumenische Religion: → 133, ᶠNYÍRI T. 1990, 309-318.

8043 **Pickering** W. S. F., Anglo-Catholicism; a study in religious ambiguity. L 1989, Routledge. xiii-286 p. £35. 0-415-01343-7. – ᴿExpTim 101 (1989s) 84s (J. *Kent*); TLond 93 (1990) 72-74 (A. *Wilkinson*: powerful critique).

8044 *Planer-Friedrich* Götz, Kirchenrecht und Evangelium; zur Begründung eines ökumenischen Kirchenrechts: TVers 17 (1989) 129-140.

8045 *Pool* Jeff B.,   Baptist infidelity to the principle of religious liberty: PerspRelSt 17 (1990) 13-30.

8046 *Quéré* France,   Difficile tolérance: RTPhil 121 (1989) 195-209.

8047 **Raiser** Konrad,   Ökumene im Übergang; Paradigmcnwechsel in der Ökumenischen Bewegung?   Mü 1989, Kaiser.   205 p. DM 20. – ᴿÖkRu 39 (1990) 357s (J. *Brosseder*).

8047* *Rordorf* Willy,   Le problème de la tradition dans la discussion œcuménique des dernières décennies: ➤ 700, Tradizione 1989/90, 7-30.

8048 **Runcie** Robert,   The unity we seek, ᴱ*Pawley* Margaret.   L 1989 Darton-LT.   VIII-161 p. £8. – ᴿExpTim 102 (1990s) 30 (R. G. *Lunt*); Tablet 243 (1989) 1370s (E. *Yarnold*).

8049 *Runcie* Robert [Anglican primate, Heythrop lecture after his visit to the Pope],   Anglican-Roman Catholic relations today: Month 251 (1990) 4-11.

8050 *Russell* John M.,   PANNENBERG on Eucharist and unity: CurrTMiss 17 (1990) 118-121.

8051 **Ryan** Thomas,   A survival guide for ecumenically-minded Christians. Ottawa 1989, Novalis; *al.*   163 p. $10 pa. [RelStR 17, 50, J. T. *Ford*].

8052 *a*) *Samartha* Stanley J.,   The Holy Spirit and people of other faiths; – *b*) *Chapman* Mark E.,   The Spirit and the Magisterium; authority in the community of freedom; – *c*) *Tillard* J.-M. R.,   Spirit, reconciliation, Church: EcuR 42 (1990) 250-263 / 268-278 / 237-249 [also 92-174 and 197-236.279-328, papers prepared for Canbèrra WCC meeting].

8053 **Santa Ana** Julio de,   Ecumenismo e liberazione; riflessioni sulla relazione tra unità cristiana e regno di Dio [1987 ➤ 3,7889]: La Chiesa sacramento di liberazione 14.   Assisi 1989, Cittadella.   327 p. – ᴿSalesianum 52 (1990) 184 (L. A. *Gallo*: uruguaiano metodista).

8054 **Sartori** Luigi,   L'unità della Chiesa; un dibattito e un progetto: GdT 191.   Brescia 1989, Queriniana.   229 p. Lit. 18.000. – ᴿCC 141 (1990,3) 318s (G. *Blandino*); NRT 112 (1990) 929s (A. *Harvengt*); StPatav 37 (1990) 157-161 (E. R. *Tura*).

8055 ᶠSCHEELE Werner,   Communio Sanctorum; Einheit der Christen — Einheit der Kirche, ᴱ**Schreiner** J. 1988 ➤ 4,129; 5,8021: ᴿTRu 55 (1990) 242s (R. *Slenczka*).

8056 **Schenk** Wolfgang,   Lima — Ökumene als Gegenaufklärung und Gegenreformation; exegetische Einsprüche gegen die kategoriale Unterordnung von Taufe und Herrenmahl unter einem Amtsbegriff: Forum Theologiae Linguisticae 19.   Bonn 1990, Linguistica Biblica.   [iv-] 121 p. 3-87797-029-X.

8057 *Schillebeeckx* Edward,   Identiteit, eigenheid en universaliteit van Gods heil in Jezus [to queries from students of his latest book, Mensen als verhaal van God; 8 points: i. 'Religion' covers an entirety of disparate phenomena; ii. Jesus' election is an extension of Israel's; iii. Christianity is tied down to a historical particularity; iv. 'imitation' (sequela) of Jesus is essential in relation to Jesus' unique universality; v. in today's context; vi. as part of the general human quest for the meaning of history; vii. there remains a tension between Jesus' identification of God and God's own identity; viii. mission must be dialogue]: TsTNijm 30 (1990) 259-275; Eng. 275.

8058 *Schneider* Theodor,   Römisch (und) Katholisch? Eine ökumenische Situationsbeschreibung aus römisch-katholischer Sicht: ÖkRu 39 (1990) 29-45 (-65, Anfragen: *Dantine* Johannes, *Lønning* Per); 318-320, *Ratzinger* J., Entgegnung zu Schneider; 321, Antwort.

8059 **Seckler** Max, Die schiefen Wände des Lehrhauses; Katholizität 1988 ➤ 5,353: ᴿBurgense 31 (1990) 263-5 (E. *Bueno*); TPQ 138 (1990) 277 (J. *Singer*).

8059* *a*) *Sheppard* David, bp., The decade of evangelism I. Evangelism with a good heart [witness and understanding, not fundamentalism]; – *b*) II. *Braybrooke* Marcus, Dialogue or evangelism?: ExpTim 102 (1990s) 131-5 / 164-6.

8060 **Skublics** Ernest, How Eastern Orthodoxy can contribute to Roman Catholic renewal. Lewiston NY 1989, Mellen. viii-231 p. – ᴿSR 19 (1990) 387s (J. M. *Flynn*).

8061 *Skublics* Ernst, Ekklesiologie im Dialog mit der orthodoxen Kirche: TrierTZ 99 (1990) 125-135; 136-141, Stellungnahme, *Weier* Reinhold.

8062 *Smith* Joanmarie, Ecumenism, commitment, and evangelism: QRMin 9,1 (1989) 3-18.

8063 **Stăniloae** Dumitru, Le génie de l'Orthodoxie [1978], ᵀ*Ciobotea* Dan-Ilie: Théophanie, 1985 ➤ 1,7564: ᴿOrtBuc 38,2 (1986) 154s (I. *Tulcan*).

8064 ᵀᴱ**Stormon** E. J., Towards the healing of schism. NY 1988, Paulist. vii-559, A$13. – ᴿPacifica 3 (1990) 105s (P. *Knowles*: documents of tranquil diplomacy; there is also a more heated arena).

8065 *Stuart* E. B., Unjustly condemned?: Roman Catholic involvement in the APUC [Association for the Promotion of the Unity of Christendom] 1857-64: JEH 41 (1990) 44-63.

8066 **Tavard** George H., A review of Anglican orders; the problem and the solution. Collegeville MN 1990, Liturgical. 167 p. $13 [TS 52, 183, J. J. *Hughes*].

8067 ᴱ**Thurian** Max, Churches respond to BEM 1988 ➤ 5,8035: ᴿOstkSt 38 (1989) 194s (H. M. *Biedermann*, 4).

8068 **Tillard** Jean-Marie R., Église d'églises 1987 ➤ 3,7911 ... 5,8036: ᴿNor-TTs 90 (1989) 255s (Ola *Tjørhom*); Salesianum 52 (1990) 186-8 (D. *Valentini*).

8069 **Tillard** J. M. R., Chiesa di chiese, l'ecclesiologia di comunione, 1989 ➤ 5,8037: ᴿAnnTh 4 (1990) 177-184 (E. *Juliá*: commenta AGOSTINO Sermo 138 come dice, ma ben più); StPatav 37 (1990) 667-672 (L. *Sartori*, anche su Il vescovo di Roma ital. 1985).

8070 *Tillard* J.-M. R., *a*) Canterbury et Rome, proches et loin: FreibZ 37 (1990) 137-153; – *b*) Corps du Christ et Esprit Saint; les exigences de la communion: Irénikon 63 (1990) 163-184; Eng. 185.

8071 *a*) *Tillard* Jean-M. R., The Eucharist and the visibility of the Church's Koinonia; – *b*) *Thompson* David M., A Disciples view of the Lord's Supper and the unity of the Church: Mid-Stream 27,4 (1986 Catholic/Disciples meeting, 1988) 337-351 (352-6, *Lahutsky* Nadia, response) / 337-372 (373-4, *Meier* John P., response).

8072 ᴱ**Urban** H., *Wagner* H., Handbuch der Ökumenik 2s, 1986s ➤ 3,7918; 4,9137: ᴿNorTTs 90 (1989) 170-3 (Ola *Tjørhom*); TLZ 115 (1990) 151-8 (M. *Sens*, 1-3).

8073 *Vigil* José M., Kairós; fenómeno, género, oportunidade: REB 50 (1990) 675-685.

8074 *a*) *Vischer* Lukas, Ⓜ Divisions among our Reformed churches, ᵀ*Karasszon* István; – *b*) *Pásztor* János, Ⓜ The commission Faith and Order met in Hungary (August 9-21, 1989): TSzem 33 (1990) 76-81 / 82-86.

8075 ᴱ**Voicu** S., *Cereti* G., Enchiridion oecumenicum 1986-8 ➤ 3,7920; 5,8043: ᴿÉTRel 65 (1990) 204s (J. *Cottin*).

8076 *Wagner* Harald, Konziliarität und Kontinuität: UnSa 44 (1989) 14-28 [29-44, *Houtepen* Anton].
8077 *Wenz* Gunther, Lima und das Luthertum; ein Buch [*Seils* M., Lutherische Konvergenz? (BEM)]: TLZ 115 (1990) 81-88.
8078 **Wessels** A., En allen die geloven zijn Abrahams geslacht. Baarn 1989, Ten Have. 167 p. *f* 23,50. – ᴿCollatVL 20 (1990) 122 (R. *Hoet*). ᴱ**Willaime** J.-P., Vers de nouveaux œcuménismes 1989 ➤ 707.
8079 **Willebrands** Johannes Kard., Mandatum unitatis; Beiträge zur Ökumene 1989 ➤ 5,373: ᴿAtKap 115 (1990) 346-8 (L. *Górka*); TPhil 65 (1990) 618s (W. *Löser*).

H7.8   **Amt** – *Ministerium ecclesiasticum.*

8080 *Almeida* Antônio J. de, O celibato dos presbíteros e dos bispos; uma análise com interesse pastoral [...no abolir a lei geral do celibato, mas dispensar a determinadas pessoas (*Grelot* P.)]: REB 50,197 (1990) 138-172 [437-451, *Veloso* Reginaldo, Celibato e carisma].
8081 **Antón** Ángel, Conferencias episcopales 1989 ➤ 5,8050: ᴿEfMex 8 (1990) 105-8 (C. *Rossell*); QVidCr 147 (1989) 135s (P. *Busquets*); RivScR 3 (1989) 525-8 (M. *Semeraro*).
8082 *Aranda Lomeña* Antonio, El sacerdocio de Jesucristo en los ministros y en los fieles; estudio teológico sobre la distinción 'essentia et non gradu tantum': ScripTPamp 22 (1990) 365-404 [323-363. 405-514, *al.*, 'formación de los sacerdotes'].
8083 **Arrieta** Juan Ignacio, El Sínodo de los Obispos: Coll. Canónica. Pamplona 1987, Univ. Navarra. 256 p. pt. 2100. – ᴿRTLv 21 (1990) 103s (A. de *Halleux*).
8084 **Auneau** Joseph, Le sacerdoce dans la Bible: CahÉv 70. P 1990, Cerf. 66 p. F 24. 0222-9714 [NTAbs 34,396]. – ᴿMondeB 66 (1990) 62 (F. *Brossier*).
8084* **Bacchi** Lee F., The theology of ordained ministry in the letters of AUGUSTINE of Hippo: diss. Marquette. Milwaukee 1990. 333 p. 91-01409. – DissA 51 (1990s) 2778-A.
8085 **Becker** Hans-Jürgen, Die Appellation vom Papst an ein allgemeines Konzil: For.KRecht, 17. Köln 1988, Böhlau. ix-511 p. DM 118. 3-412-00787-0. – ᴿSpeculum 65 (1990) 607-610 (C. M. D. *Crowder*).
8085* *Bevans* Stephen, The biblical-theological understanding of stewardship; an ecclesiastical view: VerbumSVD 30 (1989) 103-114.
8086 *Blaser* Klauspeter, Le synode en régime protestant: RTPhil 122 (1990) 67-84; Eng. 142.
8087 **Bourgeois** Henri, *al.*, Les Évêques et l'Église; un problème. P 1989, Cerf. 126 p. F 70. – ᴿEsprVie 100 (1990) 44-46 (P. *Jay*).
8088 **Bradshaw** Paul F., Ordination rites of the ancient churches of East and West. NY 1990, Pueblo. xi-288 p. $17.50. – ᴿTS 51 (1990) 782 (J. F. *Baldovin*); Worship 64 (1990) 555-8 (K. B. *Osborne*).
8089 *Brock* Raymond T., *Lukens* Horace C., [Extramarital] Affair-prevention in the ministry: JPsy&Chr 8 (1989) 44-55 [< BS 147 (1990) 367].
8090 **Cancouet** Michel, *Violle* Bernard, Les diacres. P 1990, Desclée. 132 p. – ᴿEsprVie 100 (1990) 412s (G. *Viard*).
8091 **Caprioli** Mario, Il decreto conciliare 'Presbyterorum ordinis'; storia – analisi – dottrina, Is. R 1989, Teresianum. 390 p., 430 p. – ᴿBurgense 31 (1990) 571s (N. *López Martínez*).

8092 **Card** Terence, Priesthood and ministry in crisis 1988 → 4,9154; 5,8055: ᴿScotBEv 8 (1990) 57 (C. *Bulley*).

8093 **Carpin** A., Il Sacramento dell'Ordine; dalla teologia ISIDORIANA alla teologia TOMISTA. Bo 1988, S. Ruffillo. 206 p. – ᴿRasT 31 (1990) 310 (E. *Cattaneo*).

8093* *a) Chantraine* Georges, Le prêtre au service de la vie dans le Christ; – *b) Haas* John, Le caractère sacral du prêtre comme fondement de sa vie et son enseignement moraux, ᵀ*Renard* Louis: → 672*b*, Mission 1990, 25-49 / 51-80.

8094 **Cholij** Roman, Clerical celibacy in East and West [< Gregorian Univ. diss. 'Married clergy and ecclesiastical continence in the light of the Council of Trullo (691)' → 5,8059]. Leominster 1989, Fowler Wright. xiv-226 p. £10. 0-85244-154-1. – ᴿExpTim 101 (1989s) 318s (R. *Butterworth*); HomP 90,7 (1989s) 72-74 (G. W. *Rutler*); JTS 41 (1990) 725-9 (D. *Callam*); ScripTPamp 22 (1990) 670s (J. R. *Villar*); Tablet 244 (1990) 14 (C. H. *Lawrence*: an unconvincing defense).

8095 *Cipriani* Gustavo, Il prete fra tradizione e novità [*Thils* Gustave, Prêtres de toujours 1990]: Asprenas 37 (1990) 224-230.

8096 *Correa* Peter, The identity of the ministerial priest according to JOHN PAUL II: PhilipSa 25 (1990) 5-27.

8097 *Costigan* Richard F., The consensus of the Church [Vatican I definition of infallibility]; differing classical views: TS 51 (1990) 25-48.

8097* **Crichton** J. D., Servants of the people. Slough 1990, St. Paul. 164 p. £6. 0-85439-318-8. – ᴿExpTim 102 (1990s) 156s (A. *Lovegrove*: experienced advice to priests on the Church's mission).

8098 *Demmer* Klaus, Kann der Zölibat heute gelebt werden?: HerdKor 44 (1990) 473-8.

8099 *Donfried* Karl P., A New Testament scholar looks at the issue of ministry: Dialog 27 (St. Paul 1988) 8-16 [17-23(-47), *Chapman* Mark E., *al.*].

8100 *a) Dowd* Mary, In the midst of the community; mission and ministry; – *b) Dunning* James B., What kind of Church does the rite want?: Way 29 (1989) 182-196 / 197-206.

8101 **Drewermann** Eugen, Kleriker; Psychogramm eines Ideals. Olten 1989, Walter. 900 p. DM 88. – ᴿHerdKorr 44 (1990) 85-89 (U. *Ruh*); TGL 80 (1990) 214-6 (W. *Beinert*); TPQ 138 (1990) 256-9 (M. *Scheuer*); TR 86 (1990) 497-501 (K. *Thomas*); TsTNijm 30 (1990) 323 (P. *Vandermeersch*).

8102 *Dulles* Avery, Episcopal conferences; their teaching authority [their influence depends rather on the persuasiveness and relevance of their statements]: America 162 (1990) 7-9 (10-13. 21 *Novak* M., social teaching).

8103 **Dunn** Patrick J., Priesthood; a reexamination of the Roman Catholic theology of the presbyterate. Staten Island 1990, Alba. xii-232 p. $13 pa. 0-8189-0581-6 [TDig 38,56].

8104 *Dură* Nicolae V., (en roumain) Le primat dans l'Église orthodoxe: STBuc 40,1 (1988) 15-50.

8105 *Evans* Gillian, The Anglican doctrine of primacy: AnglTR 72 (1990) 363-378.

8106 **Favale** Agostino, Il ministero presbiterale 1989 → 5,8064*: ᴿAngelicum 67 (1990) 133-5 (E. *de Cea*); Asprenas 37 (1990) 99-102 (P. *Russo*); CC 141 (1990,4) 95s (G. *Mucci*); Claretianum 30 (1990) 464-6 (B. *Proietti*); Gregorianum 71 (1990) 508s (J. *Galot*); Teresianum 40 (1989) 584s (M. *Caprioli*); VConsacr 26 (1990) 397-401 (A. *Lipari*).

8107 *a) Favale* Agostino, Identità teologica del presbitero; – *b) Ambrosiano* Antonio, 'Pro eis sanctifico meipsum' (Gv 17,19); consacrazione e missione dei presbiteri: Lateranum 56 ('Formazione teologica e formazione al presbiterato' 1990) 441-483 / 503-524 [-782, *al.*; 761-782, indicazioni bibliografiche].

8108 *Fee* G. D., *Laos* and leadership under the New Covenant: Crux 25,4 (1989) 3-13 [< NTAbs 34,200].

8109 *Fernández* Pitter,   El presbiterado en América Latina; apuntes para conocer la problemática vocacional en tiempos de la Colonia: Tiusi 3 (Caracas 1989) 149-173.

8110 *Ferraro* Giuseppe,   La nuova preghiera di ordinazione presbiterale [... accentua la dimensione trinitaria]: CC 141 (1990,3) 26-39.

8111 **Fichter** Joseph,   Pastoral provisions: married Catholic priests.   KC 1989, Sheed & W.   160 p. $14.   1-55612-306-X. – ᴿAmerica 162 (1990) 18s (J. J. *Hughes*).

8112 *Flórez García* Gonzalo,   Sobre la teología del ministerio ordenado: StLeg 30 (1989) 57-93.

8113 *Galot* Jean,   L'État de vie des Apôtres [... célibat]: EsprVie 100 (1990) 417-425.

8114 **González Faus** J. I.,   Hombres de la comunidad... ministerio 1989 → 5,8070:   ᴿEstAg 25 (1990) 459s (T. *Marcos*); PerspT 21 (1990) 405s (F. *Taborda*).

8115 *Grego* Igino,   San GIROLAMO e la controversia sul sacerdozio presbiterale: Asprenas 37 (1990) 278-292.

8116 **Grelot** Pierre,   Les Ministères dans le peuple de Dieu 1988 → 4,9164; 5,8075:   ᴿTLZ 115 (1990) 447-9 (A. *Greiner*).

8117 *Grelot* Pierre,   Le ministère chrétien dans sa dimension sacerdotale: NRT 112 (1990) 161-182.

8118 **Greshake** Gisbert,   The meaning of Christian priesthood.   Westminster MD 1989, Christian Classics.   173 p. $11 pa. – ᴿHomPast 90,8 (1989s) 77s (T. W. *Case*).

8119 **Grootaers** Jan,   Primauté et collégialité... G. PHILIPS: BiblETL 72, 1986 → 3,7969 ... 5,8076:   ᴿSalesianum 52 (1990) 181-3 (D. *Valentini*).

8120 *Guarino* Thomas,   The priesthood and analogy; a note on the formation and redaction of Lumen gentium, 10:   Angelicum 67 (1990) 309-327.

8121 *Guillet* Jacques,   Le ministère dans l'Église; ministère apostolique — ministère évangélique: NRT 112 (1990) 481-502.

8121* [Borges] **Hackmann** Geraldo L.,   Servir a Cristo na comunidade; o ministerio presbiteral em E. SCHILLEBEECKX: diss. Pont. Univ. Gregoriana, ᴰ*Pastor* F. A.   Roma 1990, 370 p.; extr. Nº 3626, 125 p. – RTLv 22, p. 603.

8122 *Halliburton* John,   The authority of a bishop [Anglican] 1987 → 3,7971*; 4,9167:   ᴿJEH 40 (1989) 152s (J. R. H. *Moorman*).

8123 **Hill** Edmund,   Ministry and authority in the Catholic Church 1988 → 4,9171; 5,8080:   ᴿMonth 250 (1989) 147 (Elizabeth *Lord*).

8124 *Hoffmann* Paul,   Das Erbe Jesu und die Macht in der Kirche; neutestamentliche Kriterien für den Dienst in der Gemeinde: Diakonia 21 (1990) 246-252.

8125 **Houssiau** A., *Mondat* J.,   Le sacerdoce du Christ et des serviteurs selon les Pères de l'Église: Coll. Cerfaux-Lefort 8.   LvN 1990, Centre Hist. Rel. 268 p. – ᴿVetChr 27 (1990) 451s (C. *Colafemmina*).

8125* **Jeffcoat** James B., Martin LUTHER's Doctrine of ministry: diss. Drew; ᴰ*Rowe* K. Madison NJ 1989. 280 p. 90-14368. – DissA 51 (1990s) 190s-A; RelStR 17,192.

8126 *Karrer* Martin, Das urchristliche Ältestenamt: NT 32 (1990) 152-188.

8127 ꟻKINGDON Robert M.: Regnum, religio et ratio, 60th b., ᴱ**Friedman** Jerome: Sixteenth Century Essays 8, 1987 ➤ 4,82: ᴿChH 58 (1989) 235s (L. H. *Zuck*, 'Regum' in title and no date: R. RICHGELS treats BEL-LARMINE on celibacy).

8128 **Klinken** Jaap van, Diakonia, mutual helping with justice and compassion. GR 1989, Eerdmans. 144 p. $11 pa. [TTod 47, 189 adv.]. 0-8028-0470-5.

8129 *Landersdorfer* Anton, Die Bestellung der Bischöfe in der Geschichte der katholischen Kirche: MüTZ 41 (1990) 271-290.

8129* *La Potterie* Ignace de, La struttura di alleanza del sacerdozio ministeriale: Communio NS 13 (1990) 102-114.

8130 **Laurance** John D., Priest as type of Christ... CYPRIAN 1984 ➤ 65, 6881... 5,8087: ᴿMaisD 178 (1989) 166s (P. de *Clerck*).

8131 **Lawler** Michael G., A theology of ministry. KC 1990, Sheed & W. xiii-130 p. $11 pa. 1-55612-310-8 [TDig 38,71].

8132 ᴱ**Legrand** Hervé, *al.*, Les conférences épiscopales 1988/8 ➤ 5,691: ᴿÉglT 20 (1989) 499-501 (M. *Lefebvre*); LavalTP 46 (1990) 103-5 (R.-M. *Roberge*); RevSR 63 (1989) 161s (J. *Hoffmann*); RThom 90 (1990) 134-9 (B. D. de *La Soujeole*).

8133 *Linnan* John E., Ministry since Vatican II; a time of change and growth: NewTR 3,1 (1990) 33-45.

8134 *a) Linss* Wilhelm C., Ministry in the NT; 'in the beginning'; – *b) Rorem* Paul, Mission and ministry in the early Church; bishops, presbyters and deacons, but... [with 4th century growth, bishop came to have supervision over a *cluster* of churches]; – *c) Hendel* Kurt K., The doctrine of the ministry; the Reformation heritage: CurrTMiss 17 (1990) 6-14 / 15-22 / 23-33 [-73, *al.*].

8135 **Llin Cháfer** A., Sacerdocio y ministerio... T. de VILLANUEVA. Valencia 1988, Fac. Ferrer. 284 p. ᴿBurgense 31 (1990) 569-571 (N. *López Martínez*).

8136 **Lodi** Enzo, Infondi lo Spirito degli apostoli; teologia liturgica-ecumenica del ministero ordinato: Caro Salutis Cardo 6, 1987 ➤ 3,7978*: ᴿTR 85 (1989) 314s (R. *Kaczynski*).

8137 **Loppa** L., 'In persona Christi' – 'nomine Ecclesiae'; linee per una teologia del ministero nel Concilio Ecumenico Vaticano II e nel magistero post-conciliare (1962-1985). R 1985, Pont. Univ. Lateranense. 197 p. – ᴿDivThom 92 (1989) 391-3 (L. *Iammarrone*).

8138 *Lorenz* Heinz, Diakonie; VerkF 35,2 (1990) 36-58.

8138* **McDonnell** John J., Communio, collegiality, conciliarity; a comparative analysis of these concepts drawn from certain Catholic and Orthodox theologians: diss. Pont. Univ. Gregoriana, ᴰ*Sullivan* F. A. Roma 1990, 510 p.; extr. nº 3663, 125 p. – RTLv 22, p. 615.

8139 **McKee** Elsie A., Diakonia in the classical Reformed tradition and today. GR 1989, Eerdmans. 160 p. $13 pa. [TTod 47, 189 adv.]. 0-8028-0352-0. – ᴿTTod 47 (1990s) 330s (D. *Foxgrover*).

8140 *a) Marczewski* Marek, ❷ Kirche und der Diakon; – *b) Colson* Jean, ❷ Diakonia und Bischof in den ersten drei Jahrhunderten der Kirche [< ᴱ*Rahner* K., Diaconia 1962, 23-30, ᵀ*Marczewski*]: VoxPa 17 (1989) 581-6; deutsch 586 / 587-597.

8141 **Martelet** Gustave,   Deux mille ans d'Église en question [I. 1984
➤ 65,6768]; II. des martyrs à l'Inquisition; III. Du schisme d'Occident à
Vatican II: Théologie du Sacerdoce 2s.   P 1990, Cerf. 436 p., F 150;
368 p., F 143. – (III) 2-204-04127-0. – ᴿArTGran 53 (1990) 355s (E. *López
Azpitarte*, 2) & 356s (A. *Segovia*, 3); Études 372 (1990) 716 & 373 (1990)
713s (R. *Marlé*).

8142 **Martini** Carlo M.,   Gottes Wort uns aufgetragen; vom geistlichen Dienst
[Exerzitien 1987].   FrB 1989, Herder.   152 p.   DM 19,80. – ᴿTPQ 138
(1990) 300 (M. *Scheuer*).

8143 **Marzotto** D.,   Celibato 1987 ➤ 4,230; 5,8098:   ᴿScripTPamp 22 (1990)
300 (E. *Molina*).

8144 **Mayer** Bernhard, *Seybold* Michael,   Die Kirche als Mysterium in ihren
Ämtern und Diensten 1987 ➤ 5,8098*:   ᴿTR 86 (1990) 312-5 (H.
Hoping).

8145 **Messer** Dionald E.,   Contemporary images of Christian ministry. Nv
1989, Abingdon.   192 p. $13 pa. – ᴿCalvinT 25 (1990) 131s (L. M.
Tamminga).

8145* **Möbs** Ulrich,   Das kirchliche Amt bei K. RAHNER — eine Untersuchung der Amtsstufen und ihrer Ausgestaltung: Diss. Giessen 1989s,
ᴰ*Mayer*. – TR 86 (1990) 515.

8146 ᴱ**Müller** Hubert, *Pottmeyer* Hermann J.,   Die Bischofskonferenz; theologischer und juridischer Status 1989 ➤ 5,494:   ᴿRTLv 21 (1990) 104s
(K. H. *Calles*); TPQ 138 (1990) 75s (P. *Gradauer*).

8147 *Murray* Robert,   Profecía, política y sacerdocio [< Month 248 (1987)
354-360], ᵀᴱ*Marcet* Carles: SelT 28 (1989) 93-100.

8148 *Neuner* J.,   Authority in the Church: Vidyajyoti 54 (1990) 133-145.

8149 **Osborne** Kenan,   Priesthood; a history... 1989 ➤ 5,8107:   ᴿCathHR 76
(1990) 318s (D. N. *Power*); HomPast 90,5 (1989s) 75s (J. R. *Sheets*:
diminishes AQUINAS); Horizons 17 (1990) 154s (P. *Chirico*); TS 51 (1990)
378 (L. *Örsy*); Worship 64 (1990) 92-94 (J. M. *Huels*).

8150 **Pagé** Jean-Guy,   Prêtre, un métier sans avenir?:   Brèches Théologiques
4.   Montréal / P 1989, Paulines/Médiaspaul.   393 p. – ᴿScEsp 42 (1990)
117s (G. *Pelland*).

8151 *Pfürtner* Stephan H.,   Der Zölibat — ein Instrument 'heiliger Herrschaft'?:   Diakonia 20 (1989) 89-100.

8152 *Ramallo* Valentin,   A propósito de la naturaleza y futuro de las
Conferencias Episcopales: EstE 65 (1990) 56-69.

Ratzinger Joseph card., *al.*,   Mission et formation du prêtre 1990 ➤ 672*b*.

8154 **Rausch** Thomas P.,   Authority and leadership in the Church 1989
➤ 5,8112:   ᴿHorizons 17 (1990) 348s (R. *Kress*); NewTR 3,2 (1990) 104s
(R. *Marzheuser*).

ᴱ**Reese** Thomas J.,   Episcopal conferences 1989 ➤ 445.

8155 **Runcie** R.,   Authority in crisis? 1988 ➤ 4,9195:   ᴿFurrow 40 (1989) 182
(G. *Woodman*).

8156 **Sabourin** Léopold,   Early Catholicism and ministries; bibliographical
commentary. Burlington ON 1989, Trinity.   126 p.   1-55011-078-0 [NTAbs
34,265].

8157 **Sabourin** Léopold,   Protocatholicisme et ministères; commentaire bibliographique. Montréal 1989, Bellarmin.   121 p. – ᴿLavalTP 46 (1990) 249s
(P.-H. *Poirier*); ZkT 112 (1990) 121s (K. H. *Neufeld*).

8158 **Schillebeeckx** Edward,   The Church with a human face 1987 (1985
➤ 1,7682) 4,9198*b*:   ᴿJRel 69 (1989) 565s (B. *Hinze*: a recasting of the
articles published in 1981 as Ministry, Leadership).

8158* **Schillebeeckx** Edward, Por uma Igreja mais humana, [T]*Leal Ferreira* Isabel F.: Teologia hoje. São Paulo 1989, Paulinas. 377 p. 85-08-00962-5 [PerspT 22, 118-121, F. *Taborda*].

8159 *Schöllgen* Georg, Sportulae; zur Frühgeschichte des Unterhaltsanspruchs der Kleriker: ZKG 101 (1990) 1-20.

8160 **Schwartz** Robert M., Servant leaders of the People of God; an ecclesial spirituality for American priests. NY 1989, Paulist. x-265 p. $13. – [R]TS 51 (1990) 530-2 (R. *Kress* claims 'American prosperity is not a blessing, it is an achievement').

8161 *Tavard* George A., The ordained ministry in historical ambiguity; where does it fit?: DocLife 38 (1988) 466-477. 518-529.

8162 **Thils** Gustave, Prêtres de toujours et prêtres d'aujourd'hui; à l'occasion du Synode de 1990: RTLv Cah. LvN 1990, Univ. 78 p. F 180. – [R]Asprenas 37 (1990) 224-230 (S. *Cipriani*).

8163 *a) Tita* Michael (en roumain), La Prêtrise dans l'œcuménisme actuel et le point de vue orthodoxe; – *b) Farchat* Kamal, Le mystère du sacerdoce dans la structure sacramentelle de l'Église; – *c) Broscăreanu* René [*Stan* Alexandre I.], Le sacerdoce dans les dialogues œcuméniques: OrtBuc 38,4 (1986) 79-94 / 40,1 (1988) 31-46 / 47-63.

8164 **Vanhoye** Albert, Old Testament priests and the new priest according to the New Testament 1986 ⇒ 2,6343 ... 4,9207: [R]HeythJ 31 (1990) 77s (J. *Coventry*: some dissents).

8164* *Vanhoye* Albert, Sacerdoti ad immagine di Cristo buon pastore: Vocazioni 7 (1990) 7-10 [AcPIB 9/7,554].

8165 *Volz* C.A., The pastoral office in the early Church: WWorld 9 (St. Paul 1989) 359-366 [NTAbs 34,66].

8166 *Whitehead* Evelyn E. & James D., Legitimacy and the religious leader: NewTR 3,2 (1990) 5-17.

8167 *Wood* Susan, The sacramentality of episcopal consecration: TS 51 (1990) 479-496.

H8 *Liturgia; oratio, vita spiritualis*   NT – **Prayer.**

8167* **Allchin** A.M., Participation in God; a forgotten strand in Anglican tradition. Wilton CT 1988, Morehouse-Barlow. ix-85 p. $8 pa. – [R]AnglTR 71 (1989) 105-7 (J.E. *Booty*).

8168 *Álvarez-Suárez* Aniano, Dimensión teológica y existencial de la 'sequela Christi': Burgense 31 (1990) 9-38.

8169 *Andia* Ysabel de, Purity of heart [... biblical data], [T]*Rousseau* Mary F.: CommND 16 (1989) 32-53.

8170 **Baldovin** John, The urban character of Christian worship ... stational liturgy: OrChrAnal 228, 1987 ⇒ 3,8037 ... 5,8129: [R]ByZ 83 (1990) 106 (P. Van *Deun*); OstkSt 38 (1989) 302-4 (F. van de *Paverd*); Speculum 65 (1990) 605-7 (Annabel J. *Wharton*); ZkT 112 (1990) 374s (H.B. *Meyer*).

8171 *Barnes* Michael, The body in the Spiritual Exercises of Ignatius of Loyola [and (*al.*) in various religions of India]: Religion 19,3 (L 1989) 263-274 [197-285; < ZIT 89,827].

8172 *Beeck* Frans J. van, A note on two liturgical greetings and the people's reply [Dominus/Pax vobiscum, grounded in OT/NT]: EphLtg 103 (1989) 519-522.

8173 **Behr-Sigel** Élisabeth, Le lieu du cœur, initiation à la spiritualité de l'Église orthodoxe: Théologies. P 1989, Cerf. 158 p. F 85. – [R]EsprVie 100 (1990) 323s (G.M. *Oury*); RHPR 70 (1990) 139s (J.C. *Larchet*).

8174 **Beulay** Robert,   La Lumière sans forme; introduction à l'étude de la
mystique chrétienne syro-orientale: L'Esprit et le Feu.   Chevetogne 1988.
365 p. Fb 980. – ᴿRTLv 21 (1990) 216-8 (A. de *Halleux*); RTPhil 122
(1990) 284s (J. *Borel*).

8175 *Bockmuehl* M.,   Should we kneel to pray? [standing was normal in the
Bible]: Crux 26,3 (1990) 14-17 [< NTAbs 35,59].

8176 *Borchers* Deena,   Dance in Christian worship [... 'one of the first forms
of Christian worship, inherited from the Jews']: CurrTMiss 17 (1990)
207-213.

8177 *Borobio* Dionisio,   Leitourgía y Diakonía; la liturgía como expresión de
las cuatro dimensiones de la misión: Salmanticensis 36 (1989) 135-158.

8178 *Bowden* John,   'This is the word of the Lord' [Bible and church
power-politics in liturgy, notably the 1980 Alternative Service Book]:
TLond 93 (1990) 266-282.

8179 ᵀᴱ**Brock** S., The Syriac Fathers on prayer 1987 ➤ 3,8047... 5,8135:
ᴿGrOrTR 34 (1989) 175-8 (bp. *Chrysostomos*: admirable, but over-
distinguishes Latin/Hellenic/Syriac traditions); JEH 41 (1990) 333s (S. G.
Hall); JRS 80 (1990) 259 (Maggie *Ross*).

8180 **Burini** Clara, *Cavalcanti* Elena,   La spiritualità della vita quotidiana negli scritti dei Padri: ➤ 854, StSp 3c, 1988   ➤ 4,9226; 5,8136:
ᴿBenedictina 36 (1989) 227-9 (M. *Spinelli*); Salesianum 52 (1990) 766s
(S. *Felici*).

8181 **Carmody** John,   Toward a male spirituality.   Mystic 1989, Twenty-
Third.   vii-117 p. $8 pa. – ᴿHorizons 17 (1990) 357s (T. *Dunne*).

8182 **Cavarnos** Constantine,   Paths and means to holiness, ᵀbp. *Chrysostomos*.
Etna CA 1986, Centre for Traditionalist Orthodox Studies.   57 p. – ᴿRel-
StT 8,1s (1988) 95s (G. C. *Papademetriou*).

8183 *a) Chauvet* Louis-Marie,   Ritualité et théologie; – *b) Gagnebin* Lawrent,
Rite et contre-rite?:   RechSR 78 (1990) 535-564 / 565-579.

8184 **Chinnici** Joseph P.,   Living stones; the history and structure of Catholic
spiritual life in the United States; Centennial [➤ 5,477d].   NY 1989,
Macmillan.   xxiv-258 p. – ᴿNewTR 3,1 (1990) 97s (J. M. *Lozano*).

8185 **Cipriani** Settimio,   La preghiera nel Nuovo Testamento; spunti di esegesi
e di spiritualità⁴ [²1973]: Meditazioni bibliche 3.   Mi 1989, OR.   400 p.
Lit. 20.000. – ᴿAsprenas 37 (1990) 234-6 (F. *Bindella*); CC 141 (1990,3)
323 (G. *Giachi*).

8185* **Codina** Víctor,   Seguir a Jesús hoy 1988 ➤ 4,9555:   ᴿTVida 30 (1989)
319 (A. *Bravo Retamal*).

8186 ᵀᴱ**Congourdeau** Marie-Hélène,   Nicolas CABASILAS [1320-1363], La vie
en Christ: SChr 355.361.   P 1989s, Cerf.   247 p. (vol. 2), 2-204-04113-0. –
ᴿPrOrChr 40 (1990) 204-6 (P. *Leduc*); StMon 32 (1990) 242s (M. *Nin*).

8187 **Cothenet** Édouard,   Exégèse et liturgie [14 art.]: LDiv 133, 1988
➤ 4,9233; 5,247:   ᴿEphLtg 103 (1989) 110s (A. *Pistoia*); RTLv 21 (1990)
363s (A. *Haquin*); TorJT 6 (1990) 362-4 (M. *Gourgues*).

8187* *a) Cusson* Gilles,   Ascèse et mystique; tradition chrétienne, Bible et
Exercices; – *b) Lever* Denise,   Le regard de Jésus, un regard qui sauve; –
c) Boilard Pauline,   Incarnation de la Parole et examen spirituel du
conscient: CahSpirIg 13 (1989) 123-135 / 43-53 / 205-216.

8188 *Decloux* Simon,   L'actualité de la spiritualité ignatienne: NRT 112
(1990) 641-659.

8189 **Dicharry** Warren,   To live the Word, inspired and incarnate; an integral biblical spirituality 1985 ➤ 1,7733:   ᴿVidyajyoti 54 (1990) 313
(R. H. *Lesser*).

8190 *Doohan* L.,   Scripture and contemporary spirituality: SpTod 42,1 (Ch 1990) 62-74.

8191 **Dubay** Thomas,   Fire within; St. TERESA of Avila, St. JOHN of the Cross, and the Gospel – on prayer.   SF 1989, Ignatius.   vii-358. $18. – ᴿTS 51 (1990) 539s (S. *Payne* says nothing of any third-place 'Gospel' contribution, and considers 'perhaps wise' the omission of 20 years Teresa-John research).

8192 **Dumm** Demetrius,   Flowers in the desert; a spirituality of the Bible 1987 ➤ 3,8058: ᴿCBQ 52 (1990) 111 (E. *Hensell*).

8193 ᴱ**Dupré** Louis, *Saliers* Don E.,   Christian spirituality 3. Post-reformation and modern: EWSp 18, 1989 ➤ 5,8151: ᴿExpTim 102 (1990s) 216 (A. *Louth*); TS 51 (1990) 747-9 (Sandra M. *Schneiders*: balanced).

8193* *Dupré* Louis,   The Christian experience of mystical union [...with sources in Paul/John]: JRel 69 (1989) 1-13.

8194 **Faricy** Robert, *a*) Seeking Jesus in contemplation and discernment. L / Westminster MD 1988, Collins / Christian Classics. 111 p. 0-87061-142-9. – *b*) Camminare nello Spirito. R 1985, Città Nuova. 109 p. Lit. 6000. 88-311-4750-6. – ᴿGregorianum 71 (1990) 430s (*ipse*).

8195 *Favale* Agostino,   Spiritualità e scuole di spiritualità: Salesianum 52 (1990) 819-856.

8195* ᴱ**Felici** Sergio,   Spiritualità del lavoro 1985/6 ➤ 2,5432: ᴿDivThom 92 (1989) 434s (C. *Riccardi*).

8196 *Fournier* Marie-Hélène,   Des rites chrétiens pour nos familles; redécouvrir la richesse de nos traditions judéo-chrétiennes: LVitae 44 (1989) 87-97.

8197 *a*) *Fox* Matthew,   Creation spirituality; a personal retrospective; – *b*) *Goizueta* Robert S.,   Liberating creation spirituality: Listening 24,2 (1989) 116-.... / 85-115 [and 5 other articles on Fox: < ZIT 89,516].

8198 **Galot** Jean,   The eucharistic heart, ᵀ*Hayde* sr. Aine.   Dublin/SF 1990, Veritas/Ignatius. 143 p. $13. 1-85390-160-1 [TDig 37,363].

8199 *Goffi* Tullo,   La spiritualità contemporanea: ➤ 854, StSp (Dehoniane) 1976. 490 p. – ᴿDivThom 92 (1989) 399-403 (E. *Julià*).

8200 **Green** Thomas H.,   Gebete — Türen zu Gott; Anleitung zum Beten. W-Mödling 1990, St. Gabriel.   108 p. DM 22,80.

8201 **Grethlein** Christian,   Abriss der Liturgik; ein Studienbuch zur Gottesdienstgestaltung. Gü 1989. 278 p. DM 48. – ᴿBTZ 7 (1990) 291-6 (A. *Grözinger*: 'Plädoyer für den Reichtum der Sinne').

8202 **Griffiths** Bede,   A new vision of reality; Western science, Eastern mysticism and Christian faith.   Springfield IL 1989, Templegate.   304 p. $15. 0-87243-180-0 [TDig 37,367].

8203 *Grossi* V., *Siniscalco* P.,   La vita cristiana nei primi secoli: SpCr, Storia e Testi 2, 1988 ➤ 5,8167: ᴿJEH 41 (1990) 139 (W. H. C. *Frend*).

8204 **Hamman** Adalbert G.,   Das Gebet in der alten Kirche, ᵀ*Spoerri* Annemarie: Traditio Christiana 7, 1989 ➤ 5,8170*: ᴿTPhil 65 (1990) 270s (H. J. *Sieben*).

8205 *Hamman* A.-G.,   Saint IRÉNÉE et la prière: ➤ 135, ᶠORBE A. Compostellanum 35,1s (1990) 9-21.

8206 **Hausherr** Irénée,   Spiritual direction in the early Christian East [1955], ᵀ*Gythiel* Anthony P. Kalamazoo 1990, Cistercian.   XXXIII-434 p. [TS 52,352, G. A. *Maloney*].

8207 **Herlyn** Okko,   Beten; welchen Sinn hat es, mit Gott zu reden: Tb 451. Wu 1990, Brockhaus.   91 p. – ᴿTZBas 46 (1990) 382s (J. *Fangmeier*).

8208 **Hunt** T. W., The doctrine of prayer [Southern Baptist...]. Nv 1986, Convention Press. 158 p. $4 pa. – RCriswT 4 (1989s) 212s (A. L. *Reid*).

8209 **Johnson** Arthur L., Faith misguided; exposing the dangers of mysticism 1988 → 5,8173: RCriswT 4 (1989s) 196-98 (K. A. *Richardson*: regrettably leaves open no category for legitimate 'evangelical' mysticism).

8210 **Johnson** L. T., Faith's freedom; a classic spirituality for contemporary Christians. Mp 1990, Fortress. xi-188 p. $11 pa. 0-8006-2428-9 [NTAbs 35,119].

8210* **Jungmann** Josef, The place of Christ in liturgical prayer [¹1925], EFischer Balthasar. L 1989 (centenary of Jungmann's birth), Chapman. 300 p. £12.50. 0-225-66528-X. – RExpTim 102 (1990s) 30 (K. *Stevenson*: Rolls-Royce of liturgiology).

8211 **Keller** Carl A., Approche de la mystique, I: Théologie et Spiritualité. Le-Mont-sur-Lausanne 1989. 229 p. – RRTPhil 122 (1990) 289s (J. *Schouwey*).

8212 **King** Thomas M., Enchantments [... conversion is not enough]; religion and the power of the word. KC 1989, Sheed & Ward. xiv-232 p. $23; pa. $15. – RTS 51 (1990) 567s (J. A. *Wiseman*).

8213 *Knijff* M. W. de, ⓜ The 'coram Deo' as condition of human existence, TCzánik Peter: TSzem 33 (1990) 68-71 (fasc. 2; wrongly indicated also in fasc. 1 German and English summary of contents).

8214 **Kolvenbach** P. H., In cammino verso la Pasqua; esercizi spirituali. R 1989, CC. 238 p. Lit. 20.000. – RPalCl 68 (1989) 1511 (A. *Pedrini*).

8215 **Kolvenbach** Peter-Hans, Le chemin de Pâques; exercices spirituels pour changer de vie [1987s deutsch → 5,8177], TGuervel Michel. P 1990, Seuil. 224 p. F 110. – RÉtudes 372 (1990) 571s (J. *Thomas*).

8216 **La Potterie** Ignace de, La prière de Jésus, le Messie, le Serviteur de Dieu, le Fils du Père [Het gebed 1985/7; ital. 1989 → 5,8179], TPasselecq G. P 1990, Desclée. 151 p. [NRT 113,617, L. J. *Renard*]. – REsprVie 100 (1990) 677 (É. *Cothenet*); Divinitas 33 (1989) 316 (A. *Pedrini*, ital.).

8217 *La Potterie* Ignace de, Para una renovación de la espiritualidad del Corazón de Jesús: Tierra Nueva 74 (Santiago, Chile 1990) 91-96.

8218 *a) Legrand* Lucien, Gospel spirituality; – *b) Martin* M. S., Liberating spirituality: IndTSt 26 (1989) 231-243 / 244-253.

8218* O leitura orante da Biblia: Tua palavra e vida 1. São Paulo/Rio 1990, Loyola/CRB. 79 p. – RPerspT 21 (1990) 411s (J. *Vitório*).

8219 **Lonsdale** David, Eyes to see, ears to hear. L 1990, Darton-LT. 184 p. £9. 0-232-51792-4. – RExpTim 102 (1990s) 156 (G. S. *Wakefield*: Ignatian spirituality: excellent, sensitive, highly recommended).

8220 **McGinn** B., *al.*, Christian spirituality 1985 → 1,271*... 5,8181; also L 1989, SCM; £17.50: RTLond 93 (1990) 165s (D. *Nineham*).

8221 *McNamara* Martin, A new heart for a new world; a new approach to theology of Sacred Heart devotion; some biblical evidence [symbol of intellect and will]: IrTQ 56 (1990) 201-228.

8222 **Martini** Carlo M., Pan para un pueblo [Il pane], TGarcía-Abril Jesús: Servidores y Testigos 38. Sd 1988, SalTerrae. 103 p. 84-293-0827-X. – RActuBbg 27 (1990) 99 (F. *de P. Solá*).

8223 **Martini** Carlo M., *a)* Es ist der Herr; Christus begegnen [Exerzitien für Theologiestudenten 1982]; – *b)* Gottes Wort uns aufgetragen; vom geistlichen Dienst [... für junge Priester]. FrB 1988s, Herder. 96 p.; 150 p. DM 11,50; 19,80. – RZkT 112 (1990) 221 (M. *Hasitschka*).

8224 EMarx Jacques, Sainteté et martyre 1980/9 → 5,490: AnBoll 108 (1990) 423-5 (B. *Joassart*).

8225 **Miles** Margaret R., a) The image and practice of holiness; a critique of the classic manuals of devotion. L 1989, SCM. xi-207 p. £10.50 pa. – ᴿTLond 93 (1990) 167s (Grace *Jantzen*: splendid). – [= ?] b) Practicing Christianity; critical perspectives for an embodied spirituality [... profit of ascetical practices]. NY 1988, Crossroad. 207 p. $20. – ᴿTTod 47 (1990s) 85s (Janet K. *Ruffing*).

8226 **Miquel** P., Cinq mille ans de prière 1989 → 5,8183: ᴿNRT 112 (1990) 455 (J. *Masson*).

8227 *Mitchell* Curtis C., The practice of fasting in the New Testament: BS 147 (1990) 455-469.

8228 *Mataji* Vandana, sr., Ashram; visage indienne de la vie religieuse et de prière chrétienne: Spiritus 31 (1990) 12-24.

8229 *Moore* Sebastian, Jesus the liberator of desire [1989 → 5,8184]: DowR 108 (1990) 1-19.

8229* **Nguyen Van Si** Ambrosius, La théologie de l'imitation du Christ chez saint BONAVENTURE: diss. Pont. Univ. Gregoriana, ᴰ*Adnès* P. Roma 1990. 331 p. Extr. Nº 3631, 79 p. – RTLv 22, p. 598.

8230 [Aghiorita] **Nicodemo**, MACARIO di Corinto, Filocalia, IV., ᵀ*Artioli* M. Benedetta, *Lovato* M. Francesca. T 1987, Gribaudi. lvi-580 p. Lit. 65.000. – ᴿDivThom 92 (1989) 215-231 (G. *Perini*).

8231 **Papademetriou** George C., An introduction to Orthodox spirituality. Brookline MA 1988, Holy Cross. 24 p. $1.50 pa. – ᴿGrOrTR 34 (1989) 401s (J. D. *Mummert*).

8232 **Pennington** M. Basil, Call to the center; the Gospel's invitation to deeper prayer: Image. NY 1990, Doubleday. 207 p. $9 [CBQ 52,781].

8233 **Pikaza** Xabier, Para vivir la oración cristiana. Estella 1989, VDivino. 222 p. – ᴿEfMex 8 (1990) 281s (J. *Martínez Z.*).

8234 **Pinckaers** Servais T., La prière chrétienne [NT ...]. FrS 1989, Univ. XIV-316 p. Fs 35. – ᴿAngelicum 67 (1990) 449-451 (G. *Phan tan Thanh*); NRT 112 (1990) 454 (L.-J. *Renard*); RBén 100 (1990) 592 (L. *Wankenne*); RThom 90 (1990) 166-8 (H.-F. *Rovarino*).

8235 **Rizzi** Armido, Dieu cherche l'homme; refondre la spiritualité, ᵀ. P 1989, Centurion. 150 p. F 78. – ᴿRTLv 21 (1990) 222-5 (G. *Thils*).

8236 **Rizzi** Armido, El mesianismo en la vida cotidiana 1986 → 3,3108: ᴿTArg 26,2 (1989) 118s (F. *Hubeňák*).

8237 **Rock** Judith, *Mealy* Norman, Performer as priest and prophet; restoring the intuitive in worship through music and dance. SF 1988, Harper & R. xxi-138 p. $14 pa. – ᴿAnglTR 71 (1989) 338-340 (Lisa *Thompson*).

8238 **Rossetti** S., Fire on the earth; daily living in the Kingdom of God. Mystic CT 1989, Twenty-Third. x-118 p. $8 pa. 0-89662-291-4 [NTAbs 34,126].

8239 *Russell* Kenneth C., Spirituality; searching the past, moving into the future: ÉglT 20 (1989) 167s [-351, al., special issue].

8239* **Salzman** Jörg Christian, Lehren und Ermahnen; zur Geschichte des christlichen Wortgottesdienstes in den ersten drei Jahrhunderten: ev. Diss. ᴰ*Hengel* M. Tübingen 1990. 230 p. – RTLv 22, p. 595.

8240 **Schütz** Christian, Praktisches Lexikon der Spiritualität 1988 → 5,967; 3-451-21063-0: ᴿEstE 65 (1990) 484s (J. *García Pérez*); NRT 112 (1990) 131 (L.-J. *Renard*).

8241 **Scotto** Dominic F., The liturgy of the hours; its history and its importance as the communal prayer of the Church after the liturgical reform of Vatican II. Petersham MA 1987, St. Bede. 213 p. – ᴿHumT 10 (1989) 129s (J. *da Silva Peixoto*).

8242 *Siemerink* Hans, Prayer and our image of God: JEmpirT 2 (1989) 27-43 [< ZIT 89,746].
8242* **Smith** G. M., Dance of the Graces; ritual in early Christianity [Ac-John/Thomas]: Epochē 16 (LA 1988) 69-100 [< NTAbs 35,88].
8243 *a*) *Soares-Prabhu* George M., Speaking to 'Abba'; prayer as petition and thanksgiving in the teaching of Jesus; – *b*) *Hoffmann* Lawrence A., Rabbinic *berakhah* and Jewish spirituality; – *c*) *Martín Velasco* Juan, Petitionary prayer and thanksgiving in the world religions: ➤ 402, Concilium (1990,3) 31-43 / 18-30 / 7-17 [44-108, *al.*].
8244 **Špidlík** Tomáš, La spiritualité de l'Orient chrétien, II. La prière: OrChrAnal 230, 1988 ➤ 4,9288; 5,8203: ᴿCC 141 (1990,4) 196s (E. G. *Farrugia*); RTPhil 122 (1990) 566s J. *Borel*).
8245 *a*) *Špidlík* Tomáš, La preghiera nella Chiesa Orientale; – *b*) *Canopi* Anna Maria, La preghiera nella vita monastica benedettina: ViPe 73 (1990) 439-447 / 530-542.
8247 ᴱ**Sponheim** Paul R., A primer on prayer [i. OT/NT...]. Ph 1988, Fortress. 152 p. – ᴿInterpretation 44 (1990) 107 (D. N. *Mosser*).
8248 **Taft** Robert J., The liturgy of the hours in East and West 1986 ➤ 2,6444 ... 5,8205: ᴿHumT 10 (1989) 128s (J. *da Silva Peixoto*).
8249 **Taft** Robert, La liturgia delle Ore in oriente e in occidente: Testi di Teologia 4, 1988 ➤ 5,8206 ('Tesi'): ᴿScuolC 117 (1989) 393-7 (M. *Navoni*).
8250 *Teani* Maurizio, Mitezza e vita ecclesiale: CC 141 (1990,1) 35-40.
8251 **Vaz** Armindo, Jesus, o orante e mestre de oração, 1987 ➤ 5,8213: ᴿTeresianum 41 (1990) 691s (M. *da Graça*).
8252 *Wénin* André, Repères bibliques pour un chemin de vie spirituelle: FoiTemps 19 (1989) 291-303.
8253 **Whitehead** Evelyn E. & James D., Les étapes de l'âge adulte; évolution psychologique et religieuse, ᵀ*Chambert* Jules, *Comte* Robert: Chemins spirituels. P 1990, Centurion. 288 p. F 140. – ᴿEsprVie 100 (1990) 672 (L. *Barbey*).
8254 *Wieczorek* A., The God of the Scriptures; an invitation to passionate prayer: RRel 48 (1989) 643-652.
8255 **Wybrew** Hugh, The Orthodox liturgy; the development of the Eucharistic liturgy in the Byzantine rite. L 1989, SPCK. x-189 p. £9. 0-281-04416-3. – ᴿExpTim 101 (1989s) 156 (Diane K. *Tripp*).

H8.1 **Vocatio**, *vita religiosa communitatis* – *Sancti*; **the Saints.**

8256 *Asiain* Miguel Ángel, La elaboración del capítulo VI de la Lumen Gentium, sobre los religiosos, en el Vaticano II: AnCalas 32 (1990) 11-69 [337-482].
8257 **Augé** Matías, *al.*, Storia della vida religiosa 1988 ➤ 5,8216: ᴿStMon 31 (1989) 426 (J. A. *Rocha*); Teresianum 40 (1989) 590-4 (C. *Pérez Milla*).
8258 **Boisvert** Laurent, Le célibat religieux. P 1990, Cerf. 136 p. F 70. – ᴿEsprVie 100 (1990) 400 (M. *Trémeau*).
8259 **Bondì** Roberta C., To love as God loves [... early monasticism] 1987 ➤ 4,9305: ᴿQRMin 9,1 (1989) 100-4 (G. *Lee*).
8260 **Bossard** Robert, Das Erlebnis der Berufung; Darstellung und Analyse: ZRGg 42 (1990) 50-69.
8261 **Brown** Peter, The body and society; men, women, and sexual renunciation in early Christianity 1988 ➤ 4,9307; 5,8221: ᴿAmHR 95 (1990) 791s (Jo Ann *McNamara*); HistRel 30 (1990s) 100-2 (G. G. *Stroumsa*);

Horizons 17 (1990) 152s (K.J. *Egan*); JAAR 58 (1990) 483-6 (R.M. *Grant*: vivid; among errors, 'George MacRae is called MacRae'); JEH 41 (1990) 76s (J.A. *Brundage*); JTS 41 (1990) 231-5 (A. *Louth*: enormous insight); Tablet 243 (1989) 458 (A. *Cameron*); WestTJ 52 (1990) 163-5 (P.J. *Leithart*).

8262 **Carroll** Michael F., Catholic cults and devotions; a psychological inquiry. Montreal 1989, McGill-Queen's Univ. xxi-230 p. $30. – ᴿTS 51 (1990) 148-150 (W.W. *Meissner*).

8263 [García] **Colombás** María, La tradición benedictina [i. monaquismo hindú, jain, hebreo, maniqueo; ii. orígenes en el cristianismo...]. Zamora 1989, Montecasino. 411 p. – ᴿRHE 84 (1989) 567s (T. *Moral*: d'un grand expert, mais écrit il y a plusieurs années; et avec documentation trop réduit).

8264 **Criswell** W.A., Prayer/angelology, ᴱ*Patterson* P.: Great doctrines of the Bible 7 [sermons; series apart from 40 volumes of his sermons published by Zondervan]. GR 1987, Zondervan. 144 p. $13. – ᴿCriswT 3 (1988) 201s (C.E. *Colton*).

8265 **Dattrino** Lorenzo, Il primo monachesimo: SpCr 3, 1984 → 1,7729: ᴿBenedictina 37 (1990) 217-9 (L. *Crippa*).

8266 *Dunn* Marilyn, Eastern influence on western monasticism in the eleventh and twelfth centuries: ByzF 13 (1988) 245-259.

8267 **Elliott** Alison G., Roads to paradise; reading the lives of the early saints. Hanover 1987, UP NEng (for Brown Univ.). xvi-244 p. $25. – ᴿClasR 39 (1989) 43-45 (M. *Whitby*); JRel 69 (1989) 400-2 (G.G. *Stroumsa*).

8268 *Ferguson* J., Hymns in the Early Church: Bulletin of the Hymn Society 12,7 (Surrey UK 1989) 114-123 [< NTAbs 34,94].

8268* **Fischer** Linda K., The geography of Protestant monasticism [... Sweden, Germany]: diss. Minnesota. Minneapolis 1990. 337 p. 91-07424. – DissA 51 (1990s) 3488-A.

8269 *Galot* Jean, Vivre ensemble un grand amour. Lv 1988, Sursum. 168 p. – ᴿRThom 90 (1990) 168 (G.-H. *Masson*).

8270 *Gavazzi* Paolo, La povertà religiosa; progetti di riforma alla metà del '800 [the 1800s]: StPatav 37 (1990) 361-383; Eng. 383.

8271 **Gozier** A., L'expérience bénédictine dans le miroir de la Bible; une lecture de la Règle de saint Benoît. P 1988, S. Paul. 237 p. F 100. – ᴿFoiTemps 20 (1990) 93 (H. *Thomas*).

8272 *Guerra* Augusto, Hago voto de clase media; en torno a la pobreza religiosa [< REspir 47 (1988) 295-326], ᴱ*Rocafiguera* J.M.: SclT 29 (1990) 151-160.

8273 ᴱ**Hilhorst** A., De heiligenverering in de eerste eeuwen van het christendom 1988 → 5,675: ᴿTLZ 115 (1990) 287s (U. *Gäbler*).

8274 **Holze** Heinrich, Erfahrung und Theologie im frühen Mönchtum; Untersuchungen zu einer Theologie des monastischen Lebens bei den ägyptischen Mönchsvätern, Johannes CASSIAN und BENEDIKT von Nursia: Hab-Diss. Bethel, ᴰ*Ruhbach*. Bielefeld 1989. – RHE 85 (1990) 470.

8275 **Hourcade** Janine, L'Église est-elle misogyne? Une vocation antique et nouvelle [les vierges consacrées, y compris vivant seules]; pref. *Raffin* mgr. Pierre. P 1990, Téqui. 100 p. F 62. – ᴿEsprVie 100 (1990) 368 (G.-M. *Oury*).

8276 *Ihnatowicz* Janusz A., ❷ Profession of the evangelical counsels as consecration in the documents of Vatican II: STWsz 27,2 (1989) 63-78; Eng. 79.

8277 *Jossua* J.-P., Sociologie des canonisations: VSp 143,2 ('Pourquoi des saints?' 1989) 165-171.
8278 *Kellermann* Diether, Heilig, Heiligung im Alten und Neuen Testament [... Archäologische Funde belegen die Bedeutung der Wurzel QDŠ]: ➤ 403, Heiligenverehrung 1990, 27-47.
8279 **Kolb** Robert, For all the saints; changing perception of martyrdom and sainthood in the Lutheran Reformation. Macon GA 1987, Mercer Univ. 186 p. $30. – ᴿJAAR 58 (1990) 295-7 (M. U. *Edwards*).
8279* *a*) *Kolvenbach* Peter-Hans, Le rôle du supérieur dans la communauté ignatienne; – *b*) *Le Pichon* Xavier, Jésus et [... le danger des techniques de] la communication [son Communication et communion 1987, 22-37]; – *c*) *Renwart* Léon, Théologie de la vie religieuse; chronique bibliographique: VieCons 61 (1989) 7-22 / 335-348 / 32-53 [aussi 62 (1990) 53-65].
8280 **Léthel** M., Connaître l'amour du Christ qui surpasse toute connaissance; la théologie des saints. Venasque 1989, Carmel. 600 p. – ᴿEspr-Vie 100 (1990) 145-9 (C. *Schönborn*: 'Seuls les saints sont théologiens' pose une grande interrogation à la théologie d'aujourd'hui).
8281 *Maldari* Donald C., The identity of religious life; the contributions of Jean-Marie TILLARD critically examined: LvSt 14 (1989) 325-345.
8281* **Manz-van der Meer** A. E. G., Op zoek naar loutering; oorsprong en ontwikkeling van de enkratitische ascese tot in de dertiende eeuw n. Chr.[... het judese christendom was niet overwegend ascetisch]: diss. ᴰ*Quispel* G., Utrecht 1989. – TsTNijm 30 (1990) 85.
8282 *Mara* Maria Grazia, Bibbia e storia nel fenomeno monastico; la Vita Antonii: ➤ 135, ᶠORBE A., Compostellanum 35 (1990) 263-275.
8283 **Munier** Charles, Matrimonio e verginità nella Chiesa antica, ᵀᴱ*Ramella* Giovanni: Traditio cristiana 4. T 1990, SEI. lv-300 p. Lit. 50.000. – ᴿCivClasCr 11 (1990) 329s (Clementine *Mazzucco*).
8284 **Nürnberg** Rosemarie, Askese als sozialer Impuls; monastisch-asketische Spiritualität als Wurzel und Triebfeder sozialer Ideen und Aktivitäten der Kirche in Südgallien im 5. Jht. [Diss. Bonn, ᴰ*Deissmann* E.]: Hereditas 2. Bonn 1988, Borengässer. xxx-354 p. DM 60. – ᴿJTS 41 (1990) 711-4 (G. *Gould*); RTLv 21 (1990) 368s (A. de *Halleux*); ZkT 112 (1990) 228s (S. *Renoldner*).
8285 *Olajuba* Oyeronke (f.), Celibacy and the Bible: JosSt 1 (Jos, Nigeria 1990) 50-63 [< TContext 8/2, 28].
8286 *Panikkar* Raimon, [*al.*], Espiritualitat i mitjans de comunicació: QVidCr 154 ('L'eclipsi de la comunicació' 1990) 66-72 [7-79].
8286* **Petersen-Szemeredy** Griet, Römische Asketinnen der Spätantike; eine Studie zu Motivation und Gestaltung der Askese christlicher Frauen Roms auf dem Hintergrund ihrer Zeit: Diss. ᴰ*Fabry*. Erlangen 1989s. – TR 86 (1990) 514; RTLv 22, p. 597 '*D Felmy* K. C.'
8287 **Rousselle** A., Der Ursprung der Keuschheit, ᵀ*Voullié* R. Stu 1989, Kreuz. 298 p. DM 32. – ᴿGymnasium 97 (1990) 184s (Ines *Stahlmann*).
8288 *Rowdon* Harold H., The Brethren concept of sainthood: VoxEvca 20 (1990) 91-102.
8289 *Seeliger* Hans R., ℗ Die Entstehung des Heiligenbildes in der Alten Kirche, ᵀ*Myszor* Wincenty: STWsz 27,2 (1989) 21-29; deutsch 29.
8290 *Széll* Margit, Ⓜ Im Bannkreis Jesu: TBud 24 (1990) 31-36.
8291 *Takács* Nándor (bp., interview), Ⓜ Will the religious orders come to life again in Hungary?: TBud 24 (1990) 25-30 (1-24. 35-62, *al.*, on religious life today).

8292 **Walsh** Michael, The secret world of Opus Dei; an investigation into the controversial sect at the heart of the Roman Catholic Church. L 1989, Grafton. 219 p. £16. – ᴿTLond 93 (1990) 312 (R. *Kollar*: prejudiced: e.g. BALAGUER was vain and extravagant; members are alienated from their family as in a cult).

8293 *Wire* Antoinette C., The social functions of women's asceticism in the Roman East: → 5,481*a*, ᴱ**King** Karen L., Images of the feminine in Gnosticism 1985/8, 308-323 [324-8, *Schüssler Fiorenza* Elisabeth, response].

8294 *Young* R. D., Recent interpretations of early Christian ascetism [... *Brown* P.; *Pagels* E.]: Thomist 54 (1990) 123-140 [< NTAbs 34,370].

H8.2 Theologia moralis NT.

8294* **Abrams** S. P., Do justice or suffer fury: diss. Amst. 1990. – RTLv 22, p. 585; TsTNijm 31,88.

8295 *Allsopp* Michael E., Joseph FLETCHER's Situation ethics; twenty-five years after the storm: IrTQ 56 (1990) 170-190.

8296 *Álvarez Verdes* Lorenzo, Las éticas bíblicas del Nuevo Testamento: EstB 48 (1990) 112-136 [bibliographical survey].

8297 **Arraj** James, Is there a solution to the Catholic debate on contraception? Chiloquin 1989, Inner Growth. 128 p. $10. – ᴿRTLv 21 (1990) 85 (H. *Wattiaux*).

8298 **Aubert** J.-M., Compendio della morale cattolica: Compendi 3. CinB 1989, Paoline. 446 p. Lit. 24.000. – ᴿAsprenas 37 (1990) 240-2 (L. *Medusa*).

8299 *Beardslee* William A., Ethics and hermeneutics [... SCHÜSSLER FIORENZA E.]: → 24, ᶠBOERS H., Text 1990, 15-32.

8299* **Beilner** Wolfgang, El evangelio regla de vida, ᵀ*Ruiz-Garrido* Constantino. Barc 1989, Herder. 258 p. 84-254-1659-0. – ᴿPerspT 22 (1990) 264-6 (J. *Vitório*).

8300 *Belmans* Théo G., Le paradoxe de la conscience erronée d'ABÉLARD à Karl RAHNER: RThom 90 (1990) 570-586.

8301 ᴱ**Bernos** Marcel, Sexualité et religions; textes [modernes] réunis: Cerf-Histoire. P 1988, Cerf. 306 p. F 124. – ᴿRTLv 21 (1990) 109 (H. *Wattiaux*).

8302 **Blum** William, Forms of marriage; monogamy reconsidered: Spearhead 105ss. Eldoret 1989, Gaba. XXIV-320 p. $15. – ᴿAfER 39 (1989) 121-8 (J. T. *Agbasiere*, B. *Zabajungu*).

8303 *Bonandi* Alberto, Allargando il panorama; sui manuali di teologia morale fondamentale (1970-1987): ScuolC 117 (1989) 27-76.

8304 *Borges de Pinho* José E., Elementos para uma teologia de fraternidade humana: HumT 10 (1989) 315-344.

8305 *Boyd* George N. [*al.*], SCHLEIERMACHER's 'Über den Unterschied zwischen Naturgesetz und Sittengesetz': JRelEth 17,2 ('New perspectives on Schleiermacher's ethics' 1989) 41-50 [1-76; < ZIT 90,268].

8306 *Bradley* James, Alasdair MACINTYRE [Whose justice? 1988] on the good life and the 'narrative model': HeythJ 31 (1990) 324-6.

8307 **Cahill** Lisa S., Between the sexes.. ethics of sexuality 1985 → 1,7838... 4,9348: ᴿBijdragen 51 (1990) 215s (J. J. *Suurmond*, Eng.).

8308 *Cahill* Lisa S., The New Testament and ethics; communities of social change: Interpretation 44 (1990) 383-395.

8309 **Carlotti** P.,   Storicità e morale; un'indagine nel pensiero di Alfons AUER: BiblScR 86. R 1989, LAS. 162 p. Lit. 20.000. – ᴿRasT 31 (1990) 526 (G. *Mattai*).

8310 **Carter** Charles W., *Thompson* R. Duane, The biblical ethic of love: AmerUnivSt 7/79. NY 1990, Lang. xix-245 p. 0-8204-1365-8.

8311 *Chethimattam* John B., [*al.*] Christian moral theology: Jeevadhara 19 (1989) 317-332 [-386].

8312 **Chilton** Bruce, *McDonald* J. I. H.,   Jesus and the ethics of the Kingdom 1988 ➤ 3,8176... 5,8265: ᴿAndrUnS 28 (1990) 92-94 (H. *Weiss*).

8313 *Churruca* Juan de, Der gerechte Lohn im Neuen Testament: RIDA 36 (1989) 131-149.

8314 **Clemons** James T.,   What does the Bible say about suicide? Mp 1990, Fortress. ix-126 p. $8. 0-8006-2399-1 [TDig 38,53: W. C. *Heiser*: eighth leading cause of death in the US].

8315 **Coda** Piero, '... J'étais un étranger ...' — réflexion théologique [Congresso Caritas Europa, Strasburgo 8-10 marzo 1990]: Lateranum 56 (1990) 241-260.

8316 **Coleman** Gerald D.,   Divorce and remarriage in the Catholic Church. NY 1988, Paulist. $6. 0-8091-3016-5. – ᴿGregorianum 71 (1990) 596s (P. C. *Beltrão*); HomP 90,8 (1989s) 76s (J. J. *Farraher*: should not have been granted an Imprimatur); Horizons 17 (1990) 158s (W. P. *Roberts*); NewTR 3,1 (1990) 111s (C. F. *O'Connor*: nothing new).

8317 **Collange** J. F.,   Théologie des droits de l'homme. P 1989, Cerf. 363 p. 2-204-03065-1. – ᴿÉTRel 65 (1990) 101-4 (J. *Ansaldi*).

8318 *a*) *Collange* Jean-François, Freiheit und Menschenrechte zwischen Liberalismus und Marxismus, ᵀ*Hüffemeier* W., *al.*; – *b*) *Fergusson* David, Das Konzept der Freiheit in der heutigen britischen Theologie, ᵀ*Berger* Ullrike: BTZ 7 (1990) 217-229 / 230-242.

8319 **Countryman** L. William, Dirt, greed and sex; sexual ethics in the NT and their implications for today 1988 ➤ 4,9356; 5,8267: ᴿAnglTR 72 (1990) 95-103 (M. H. *Floyd*); JTS 41 (1990) 627-9 (K. *Grayston*); PrPeo 4 (1990) 204 (J. *Parr*); ScotJT 43 (1990) 277-9 (S. *Fowl*).

8320 **Curran** Charles E.,   Tensions in moral theology 1988 ➤ 4,175: ᴿHorizons 17 (1990) 178s (R. M. *Gula*); JRel 70 (1990) 481s (R. J. *Feenstra*).

8321 **Curran** Charles, Sexualität und Ethik, Nachwort *Pfürtner* Stephan. Fra 1988, Athenäum. 228 p. DM 38. – ᴿEvKomm 22,2 (1989) 40 (D. *Stollberg*, mit 5 anderen Büchern über katholische Sexualmoral).

8322 **Dacquino** Pietro,   Storia del matrimonio cristiano alla luce della Bibbia [1. 1984 ➤ 65,6629] 2. Inseparabilità 1988 ➤ 5,8270: ᴿAnnTh 4 (1990) 191-9 (A. *Miralles*).

8323 **Demmer** Klaus, Gebet, der zur Tat wird; Praxis der Versöhnung [... Verbote und Gebote sind nicht alles]. FrB 1989, Herder. 93 p. DM 12,80. – ᴿErbAuf 66 (1990) 237 (B. *Schwank*).

8324 **Demmer** K.,   Interpretare e agire; fondamenti della morale cristiana [1985 ➤ 2,6477]: TMor, StT 2. CinB 1989, Paoline. 236 p. Lit. 18.000. – ᴿRasT 31 (1990) 215s (Donatella *Abignente*).

8325 *De Young* James B.,   A critique of prohomosexual interpretations of the Old Testament Apocrypha [... Sirach] and Pseudepigrapha: BS 147 (1990) 437-453.

8326 **Dominian** Jack, *Montefiore* Hugh, God, sex and love. L/Th 1989. SCM/T. 112 p. $9 pa. 0-334-00533-7. – ᴿExpTim 102 (1990s) 62s (K. G. *Greet*, under Montefiore); TLond 93 (1990) 417s (J. S. *Spong*: important).

8327 *Engammare* Max, Liturgies protestantes du mariage au XVIe siècle; de l'engagement mutuel à la cléricalisation: RTPhil 122 (1990) 42-65, Eng. 141.

8328 **Enichlmayr** Johann, Wiederverheiratet nach Scheidung; Kirche im Dilemma; Versuch einer pastoralen Aufarbeitung 1986 ⮕ 3,8198: ^RSTWsz 27,2 (1989) 274-6 (A. J. *Nowak*).

8328* **Ford** S. Dennis, Sins of omission; a primer on moral indifference. Mp 1990, Fortress. 128 p. 0-8006-2401-7. – ^RExpTim 102 (1990s) 161-3 (C. S. *Rodd* puts this in first place of this fasc. 6, but stresses Ogden Nash's contribution more than Scripture's).

8329 *Fuček* Ivan, Christologic-Trinitary aspects of the human body and the marriage act: ObnŽiv 44 (1989) 214-232 (Croatian; Eng. 232).

8330 *Fuchs* Josef, Innovative morality [in a new concrete situation, we must give an already existing norm the meaning and content it does not have in its abstract formulation: 34th Bellarmine Lecture, St. Louis University Oct. 10, 1990; unabridged]: TDig 37 (1990) 303-312.

8331 **Fuchs** J., Für eine menschliche Moral I, 1988 ⮕ 5,263: ^RZkT 112 (1990) 223s (H. *Rotter*).

8332 **Gaudemet** Jean, Le mariage en Occident 1987 ⮕ 3,8206 ... 5,8290: ^RMaisD 179 (1989) 145-150 (F. *Deniau*); RHE 85 (1990) 211 (P. H. *Daly*).

8333 **Gaudemet** Jean, Il matrimonio in Occidente, ^TPistocchi Bruno. T 1989, SEI. 434 p. Lit. 36.000. – ^RBenedictina 37 (1990) 537-9 (Filena *Patroni Griffi*).

8334 **George** Martin, Die Ehe in der Antike; die Entwicklung in der philosophischen Ethik und ihre Konfrontationen mit dem christlichen Vollkommenheitsideal bei Johannes CHRYSOSTOMOS auf dem Hintergrund der asketischen Theologie des 4. Jahrhunderts: ev. Hab.-Diss. ^DLilienfeld. Erlangen 1989. – RHE 85 (1990) 470.

8334* **Grube** Dirk M., A narrative on the is/ought problem and its ramifications for NT ethics; the relationship between belief systems and morality in the case of Paul and the historical Jesus: diss. Temple, ^DDean T. Ph 1990. – DissA 52 (1991s) 573-A. RelStR 17,191.

8335 *Gubler* Marie-Louise, Eine biblisch orientierte Pastoral: Diakonia 20 (1989) 11-15.

8336 **Guroian** Vigen, Incarnate love; essays in Orthodox ethics 1989 ⮕ 5, 8297: ^RPerspRelSt 17 (1990) 261-4 (P. *Lewis*, also on RAMSEY P. 1988 and MCELROY's MURRAY).

8337 **Häring** Bernhard, Ausweglos? Zur Pastoral bei Scheidung und Wiederverheiratung; ein Plädoyer. FrB 1989, Herder. 96 p. DM 14,80. – ^RNRT 112 (1990) 100 (L. *Volpe*); ZkT 112 (1990) 225s (H. *Rotter*, auch über Härings 'Erfahrung mit der Kirche').

8338 **Häring** Bernhard, ¿Hay una salida? Pastoral para divorciados. Barc 1990, Herder. 148 p. – ^RRTLim 24 (1990) 449-451 (F. *Interdonato*).

8339 **Häring** Bernhard, Teologia morale verso il terzo millennio. Brescia 1990, Morcelliana. 144 p. Lit. 18.000. – ^RRasT 31 (1990) 98s (B. *Marra*).

8340 **Hanigan** James P., Homosexuality, the test case for Christian sexual ethics: Theological Inquiries 1988 ⮕ 4,9383; 5,8301: ^RNRT 112 (1990) 101s (L. *Volpe*).

8341 *Hays* Richard B., Scripture-shaped community; the problem of method in New Testament ethics: Interpretation 44 (1990) 42-55 [*Meeks* W.: the term 'NT ethics' confuses historical and normative categories].

8342 **Heth** William, *Wenham* G. J., Jesus and divorce 1984 ⮕ 65,3952 ... 2,3430: ^RCriswT 3 (1988s) 212-4 (J. E. *White*).

8343 **Heyward** Carter,   Touching our strength; the erotic as power and love of
      God.   SF 1989, Harper.   x-195 p. $13 pa. – ᴿAnglTR 72 (1990) 346-351
      (J. *Lassen-Willems*: God = 'our power in mutual relation').
8343* **Jaw Jin-Yuan** Paul,   The roles of Jesus Christ in the ethics of James M.
      GUSTAFSON: diss. Drew.   Madison NJ 1989.   483 p. 90-14366. – DissA 51
      (1990s) 197-A.
8344 *Johnston* Mark D.,   Affatus; natural science as moral theology: EstLul
      30 (1990) 3-30. 139-150; summary (Eng.) 75. 211.
8345 *Juel* D. H.,   Homosexuality and Christian traditions: WWorld 10,2
      (1990) 166-9 [< NTAbs 34,349].
8346 **Kammer** Charles L.,   Ethics and liberation; an introduction 1988
      ↠ 5,8312: ᴿSalesianum 52 (1990) 177s (G. *Abbá*).
8347 **Kirchschläger** Walter,   Ehe und Ehescheidung im NT 1987 ↠ 3,8232;
      5,8314: ᴿTR 86 (1990) 295s (N. *Bäumert*).
8348 **Knijff** H. W. de,   Venus aan de leiband 1987 ↠ 5,8315:   ᴿBijdragen 51
      (1990) 90s (M. *Parmentier*, also on BRUNDAGE).
8349 *Kotva* J. J.,   Scripture, ethics, and the local church; homosexuality as
      a case study: Conrad Grebel Review 7,1 (Waterloo ON 1989) 41-61
      [< NTAbs 34,69].
8349* **Lachner** Gabriele,   Die Kirchen und die Wiederheirat Geschiedener;
      eine ökumenisch-theologische Studie: kath. Diss, ᴰ*Döring*.   München
      1989s. – TR 86 (1990) 517; RTLv 22, p. 617.
8350 *Lance* H. D.,   The Bible and homosexuality: AmBapQ 8,2 (King of
      Prussia PA 1989) 140-151 [< NTAbs 34,70: Lev 18:22 and 20:13 clearly
      against, though 1 Cor 6,9 and 1 Tim 1,10 are ambiguous and Gen 19 and
      Jg 19 irrelevant].
8351 *Leonardi* Giovanni,   Un'introduzione all'etica del Nuovo Testamento
      [*Segalla* G. 1989 ↠ 300]: StPatav 37 (1990) 602-625.
8352 **Lohse** Eduard,   Theologische Ethik des Neuen Testaments: TWiss 5/2,
      1988 ↠ 4,9394; 5,8322:   ᴿCritRR 3 (1990) 217-220 (W. M. *Swartley*);
      EvKomm 22,3 (1989) 53 (K. T. *Kleinknecht*); RTLv 21 (1990) 242s (J.
      Étienne); TLZ 115 (1990) 597-600 (G. *Strecker*).
8353 **Longenecker** Richard N.,   New Testament social ethics for today 1984
      ↠ 65,7080 ... 3,8238: ᴿGraceTJ 10 (1989) 115-7 (D. L. *Turner*).
8354 **MacIntyre** Alasdair,   Three rival versions of moral inquiry; encyclo-
      paedia, genealogy, and tradition: Edinburgh Gifford Lectures 1988.   ND
      1990, Univ.   x-236 p.   0-268-01871-5. – ᴿSalesianum 52 (1990) 915-7 (G.
      Abbá).
8355 **MacIntyre** Alisdair,   Whose justice? Which rationality?   ND 1988,
      Univ.   432 p. $23.   0-268-01942-8. – ᴿJRel 69 (1989) 220-232 (J. *Stout*).
8356 *Magesa* Laurenti C.,   Sexual orientation and preference; recent de-
      velopments in Christian thought on homosexuality: Chiea 5,4 (Nairobi
      1989) 3-45 [< TContext 8/1, 19].
8357 **Mahoney** John,   The making of moral theology 1987 ↠ 3,8247 ... 5,8330:
      ᴿCritRR 2 (1989) 277-9 (R. *Hindery*); EcuR 42 (1990) 74-76 (J. M.
      Gustafson).
8358 **Malherbe** Abraham J.,   Moral exhortation; a Greco-Roman sourcebook
      1986 ↠ 2,6525 ... 5,8331:   ᴿSecC 7 (1989s) 182-4 (J. H. *Elliott*, also on
      MEEKS and STOWERS in the series).
8359 *Marra* Bruno,   Etica della vita coniugale; pref. *Mattai* G.   N 1988,
      Dehoniane.   228 p. – ᴿSalesianum 52 (1990) 178s (G.. *Gatti*).
8360 **Marxsen** Willi,   'Christliche' und christliche Ethik im NT 1989 ↠ 5,
      8334: ᴿTLZ 115 (1990) 746-8 (G. *Strecker*).

8361 **Mattheeuws** Alain, Union et procréation; développement de la doctrine des lois du mariage: préf. *Danneels* Card. G. et *Hennaux* J.-M.: Recherches morales; positions. P 1989, Cerf. 288 p. F 109. – ᴿRTLv 21 (1990) 85-87 (H. *Wattiaux*: témérité, ... à vouloir tout prouver).

8362 **Mattioli** Anselmo, Le realtà sessuali nella Bibbia; storia e dottrina 1987 → 5,8335: ᴿTeresianum 40 (1989) 278s (P. *Mantovani*).

8363 **Miegge** Mario, Vocation et travail; essai sur l'éthique puritain: Histoire et société 16. Genève 1989, Labor et Fides. 171 p. – ᴿRTPhil 122 (1990) 139s (D. *Müller*).

8364 **Mikat** Paul, Die Polygamiefrage in der frühen Neuzeit: Rh/W Vorträge G 394. Opladen 1988, Westd.-V. – ᴿTZBas 46 (1990) 185s (U. *Gerber*).

8365 **Moltmann** J., La giustizia crea futuro ... : GdT 193. Brescia 1990, Queriniana. 160 p. Lit. 17.000. – ᴿStPatav 37 (1990) 723 (L. *Sartori*).

Montefiore Hugh, *Dominian* Jack, God, sex and love 1989 → 8326.

8366 **Moser** A., *Leers* B., Teologia morale; conflitti ed alternative, ᵀᴱ*Pompei* G. Assisi 1988, Cittadella. 318 p. Lit. 20.000. – ᴿRasT 31 (1990) 99s (G. *Mattai*).

8367 **Neuner** Peter, Geeint im Leben — getrennt im Bekenntnis? Die konfessionsverschiedene Ehe; Lehre – Probleme – Chancen. Dü 1989, Patmos. 111 p. DM 19,80. 3-491-77773-9. – ᴿÖkRu 39 (1990) 136-8 (M. *Schmitt*); TLZ 115 (1990) 380-2 (C. *Bäumler*).

8368 *Nowak* Kurt, Das Faktum und seine Deutung; Interpretationsmodelle zu Sterilisation und Euthanasie im Dritten Reich: TLZ 115 (1990) 241-254.

8369 **O'Donovan** Oliver, Resurrection and moral order 1986 → 2,6540 ... 5,8348: ᴿRelStR 16 (1990) 105-110 (D. F. *Ottati*, also on McCLENDON J., RENDTORFF T., SEDGWICK T.).

8370 **Ogletree** Thomas W., Hospitality to the stranger 1985 → 1,7908; 3,8260: ᴿNeotestamentica 24,1 (1990) 147s (K. *Nürnberger*).

8371 **Olejnik** Stanisław, ⓟ Teologia moralna. Wsz 1988, Akad. Teol. Katolickiej. 378 p.; 191 p.; 278 p. – ᴿTR 86 (1990) 395-401 (Γ. *Scholz*: amplissimum compendium).

8371* **Oppenheimer** Helen, Marriage. L 1990, Mowbray. 129 p. £6. 0-264-67193-7. – ᴿExpTim 102 (1990s) 33s (C. S. *Rodd*'s top choice for this fasc. 2 for its excellent writing, but with no word as to whether or how it fits the rubric 'Expository').

Panimolle S. A., La libertà ... dalla legge nel NT 1988 → 6280.

8372 **Pignan** Pidalani, Le mariage chrétien et le mariage traditionnel kabiye [Togo] à la lumière de l'enseignement du concile Vatican II [diss. Alfonsiana, Roma]. P 1987, Sogico. 180 p.; 6 pl. – ᴿDivThom 92 (1989) 435s (Y. *Poutet*: mariage déclaré indissoluble après plusieurs semaines).

8373 **Pinckaers** Servais, Les sources de la morale chrétienne 1985 → 2,6548 ... 4,9414: ᴿSuppVSp 169 (1989) 177-192 (R. *Simon*), 193-202 réponse.

8374 *Pinto* Gilberte, Couples sans enfants; l'Évangile donne-t-il un sens à notre vie? Étude biblique (diss. Toulouse): EsprVie 100 (1990) 602-7 (L. *Monloubou*, résumé).

8375 *Platten* S., The biblical critic and the moral theologians: KingsTR 12,1 (1989) 11-17 [< NTAbs 34,72].

8376 *Pokorný* Petr, Neutestamentliche Ethik und die Probleme ihrer Darstellung [SCHNACKENBURG R. 1986; SCHULZ S. 1987; LOHSE E. 1988; SCHRAGE W. 1989]: EvT 50 (1990) 357-371.

8377 *Price* Richard M., The distinctiveness of early Christian social ethics: HeythJ 31 (1990) 257-276.

8378 *Puszkar* Bogdan, Die Scheidungspraxis in der Russisch-Orthodoxen Kirche: OstkSt 38 (1989) 136-165.

8379 *Ratzinger* card. Joseph, Man between reproduction and creation; theological questions on the origin of human life, T*Caldwell* Thomas A.; CommND 16 (1989) 197-211.

8380 **Rawls** John, Théorie de la justice [1971], T*Audard* Catherine. P 1987, Seuil. – RRTPhil 122 (1990) 253-260 (É. *Fuchs*), cf. 119 (1987) 279-290 (G. *Küng*).

8381 *Reilly* Martin, James M. GUSTAFSON's framework for theocentric ethics: IrTQ 56 (1990) 114-123.

8382 *Renner* J.T.E., *Pfitzner* V.C., Justice and human rights; some biblical perspectives: LuthTJ 24,1 (Adelaide 1990) 3-6.7-10 [< NTAbs 34,351].

8383 **Richard** Lucien, Is there a Christian ethics? 1988 → 5,8356: RAnglTR 71 (1989) 455s (T. F. *Sedgwick*); RTLv 21 (1990) 244s (J. *Étienne*).

8384 *Roberts* J.H., De vraagstuk van 'n Nuwe-Testamentiese etiek: Scriptura 32 (1990) 36-53 [< NTAbs 35,64].

8385 *Robertson* O.P., Reflections on NT testimony concerning civil disobedience [in relation to abortion]: JEvTS 33 (1990) 331-351 [< NTAbs 35,201].

8386 **Rousselle** Aline, Porneia; on desire and the body in antiquity, T*Pheasant* Felicia: Family, Sexuality, and Social Relations in past times 1988 → 4,b794: RClasR 39 (1989) 329s (Jane F. *Gardner*: stated aim is to trace the origins of the obsession with chastity evident in early Christianity: bleak view of classical society, sex bad for male training); TS 50 (1989) 362-5 (D.G. *Hunter*).

8387 *Scaer* D.P., The Christian family in today's society viewed in a biblical perspective: ConcordTQ 54,2s (1990) 81-97 [< NTAbs 35,202].

8388 **Schnackenburg** Rudolf, Die sittliche Botschaft des NTs, I. 1986 → 2, 6533 ...; 2, 1988 → 4,9422; 5,8360: RActuBbg 27 (1990) 62 (X. *Alegre S.*, 2); EstE 65 (1990) 94s (A.V. *Gutiérrez*); RTLv 21 (1990) 95 (C. *Focant*, 2); Salesianum 52 (1990) 173s (G. *Abbá*, 2); TLZ 115 (1990) 686-9 (G. *Strecker*); TPhil 65 (1990) 262s (J. *Beutler*); TR 86 (1990) 20s (H. *Frankemölle*).

8389 **Schnackenburg** R., Il messaggio morale del NT, 1. Da Gesù alla Chiesa primitiva: CommNT supp 1, 1989 → 5,8361: RRivB 38 (1990) 544-6 (A. *Gelardi*).

8390 **Schnackenburg** R., El mensaje moral del NT I, T*Villanueva* Marciano: BiblH 185. Barc 1989, Herder. 323 p. 84-254-1642-6. – RActuBbg 27 (1990) 201-3 (J. *Boada*); CommSev 23 (1990) 104s (M. de *Burgos*); RTLim 24 (1990) 445s (V. *Ferrer Meyer*).

8391 **Schrage** Wolfgang, Ethics of NT 1988 → 4,9423; 5,8363: RCritRR 2 (1989) 241-4 (R.W. *Wall*); CurrTMiss 17 (1990) 395s (E. *Krentz*); Interpretation 44 (1990) 188-190 (R. *Scroggs*); Pacifica 3 (1990) 335-9 (M. *Coleridge*); Vidyajyoti 54 (1990) 495s (S. *Arokiasamy*).

Schürmann H., Studien zur neutestamentlichen Ethik 1990 → 299.

8392 **Schurr** Victor, *Vidal* Marciano, Bernhard HÄRING y su nueva Teología moral católica. M 1989, Perpetuo Socorro. 108 p. – RRET 50 (1990) 111-8 (J.L. *Larrabe*).

Segalla G., Introduzione all'etica biblica del Nuovo Testamento; problemi e storia 1989 → 300.

8392* *Selb* Walter, Die Christianisierung der Ehe in der Kirche (nach Quellen der alten westsyrischen Kirche): → 54, ᶠ*Gampl* I., ArKR 39,1s (1990) 266-275.

8393 **Sernau** Scott, Please don't squeeze the Christian into the world's mold 1987 → 4,9428: MastJ 1 (1990) 96-99 (D. C. *Deuel*).

8394 *Slattery* Maureen, The history of love and marriage in Western culture [*Flandrin* J. 1981; *Arts* H. 1990]: Pastoral-Sciences 9 (1990) 199-206.

8395 **Sloyan** Gerard S., Catholic morality revisited; origins and contemporary challenges. Mystic CT 1990, Twenty-Third. vi-168 p. $10 pa. 0-89622-418-X. – ᴿNewTR 3,4 (1990) 112-4 (G. D. *Coleman*).

8396 **Soete** Annette, Ethos der Rettung, Ethos der Gerechtigkeit. Wü 1987, Echter. 359 p. 3-429-01104-3. – ᴿÉTRel 65 (1990) 525s (J. *Rennes*).

8397 *Šolić* Petar, The anthropology of homosexuality (in Croatian): ObnŽiv 44 (1989) 578-607; Eng. 608.

8398 **Spong** J. S., Living in sin? 1988 → 5,8367: ᴿAmerica 162 (1990) 507s (E. F. *Flynn*); AnglTR 71 (1989) 114-6 (Anne C. *Garrison*, H. C. *McGehee*); Interpretation 44 (1990) 324.326 (Lisa S. *Cahill*); TLond 93 (1990) 418s (D. *Field*: defends morality by redefining sin).

8399 ᴱ**Stemmeler** M. L., *Clark* J. M., Homophobia [disapproval of homosexuality; *Thurston* T. M., Lv 18,22; *Eron* L. J., Test. Naphtali] and the Judaeo-Christian tradition: GayRel 1. Dallas 1990, Monument. vi-217 p.; 3 pl. $20 pa. 0-930383-18-4 [NTAbs 35,121].

8400 **Stout** Jeffrey, Ethics after Babel; the languages of morals and their discontents 1988 → 5,8368: ᴿCalvinT 25 (1990) 262-6 (A. D. *Verhey*, also on Stout's Flight from authority).

8400* **Strom** Paul R., Christ in the margins ['much of what Christianity has to say about Christ is unethical'?]; elements for an ethical Christology derived from the works of R. R. RUETHER, J. L. SEGUNDO, and M. ABE: diss. Iliff, ᴰ*Wilbanks* D. Denver 1990. 91-06647. – DissA 51 (1990s) 3437-A.

8401 *Stylianopoulos* Theodore, The indissolubility of marriage in the New Testament; principle and practice: GrOrTR 34 (1989) 335-345.

8402 **Sutton** Ray, Second chance; biblical principles of divorce and remarriage. Fort Worth 1988, Dominion. 253 p. $9 pa. – ᴿCriswT 4 (1989s) 439-441 (B. *Mitchell*: useful apart from the premises).

8403 *Viana* Mikel de, Revelación y moral fundamental: Iter 2 (Caracas 1990) 9-29.

8404 **Vidal** Marciano, Para conocer la ética cristiana. Estella 1989, VDivino. 375 p. – ᴿEfMex 8 (1990) 125-8 (U. *Sánchez*).

8404* **Voyles** Richard J., Christian practice as Halakhah; introducing a halakhic paradigm into Christian thinking: diss. Emory, ᴰ*Blumenthal* D. Atlanta 1990. 182 p. 91-06738. – DissA 51 (1990s) 3438-A.

8405 **Washington** Joseph R.ᴶ, Race and religion in early nineteenth century America, 1800-1850; constitution, conscience, and Calvinist compromise. Lewiston NY 1988, Mellen. 996 p. (2 vol.) $100. – ᴿPerspRelSt 17 (1990) 265-7 (Terry *Matthews*: 'can only be described as an embarrassment').

8406 *Weber* Philippe, La morale du chrétien, hier et aujourd'hui: FoiTemps 20 (1990) 101-121.

8407 *Williams* Robert, Toward a theology for Lesbian and gay marriage: AnglTR 72 (1990) 134-157 [158-174, 'interested' comments; p. 129 ed. 'to adjust our thoughts on... ministry of reconciliation in a world gone berserk, we provide a forum for some of Williams' ideas'].

8408 *Wogaman* J. Philip, Paternalism and autonomy: Studies in Christian Ethics 2,1 (E 1989) 66-78 [-81 response, *Wilson* Kenneth].
8409 *Yearley* Lee H., Recent work on virtue: RelStR 16 (1990) 1-9.

H8.4 *NT ipsum de reformatione sociali* – **Political action in Scripture.**

8410 *Aichele* George ᴶ, Poverty and the hermeneutics of repentance: CCurr 38 (1988s) 458-467.
8411 **Ambrosio** G., *al.*, La dottrina sociale della Chiesa: Disputatio 1. Mi 1989, Glossa. 250 p. Lit. 30.000. – ᴿNRT 112 (1990) 934 (C. *Mertens*).
8412 **Bandow** Doug, Beyond good intentions; a biblical view of politics 1988 → 5,8387: ᴿCalvinT 25 (1990) 86-89 (J. B. *Hulst*: does not get beyond good intentions).
8413 *a) Barclay* Oliver R., *Sugden* Chris, Biblical social ethics in a mixed society; – *b) Stanley* Brian, Evangelical social and political ethics; an historical perspective; – *c) Schluter* Michael, *Clements* Roy, Jubilee institutional norms; a middle way between creation ethics and kingdom ethics as the basis for Christian political action: EvQ 62 (1990) 5-18 [63-86, current positions] / 19-36 / 37-63.
8414 **Bassler** Jouette M., God and mammon; asking for money in the New Testament. Nv c. 1990, Abingdon. $10 pa. 0-687-14952-2 [RelStR 17, 133 adv.].
8415 **Bauckham** R., The Bible in politics; how to read the Bible politically: Third Way Book. L 1989, SPCK. x-166 p. £7. 0-281-04402-3. – ᴿBL (1990) 97 (C. S. *Rodd*); IrBSt 11 (1989) 147-9 (J. H. *McCormack*: '1979'); Vidyajyoti 54 (1990) 544s (R. J. *Raja*).
8416 **Baum** Gregory, Compassion and solidarity; the Church for others [5 Radio Canada lectures]. NY 1990, Paulist. 107 p. $6 pa. 0-8091-3141-2 [TDig 38,47].
8417 *Bayer* Richard C., Do we want a Christian economics? The U.S. bishops' pastoral letter: TS 51 (1980) 627-649.
8418 **Beisner** E. Calvin, Prosperity and poverty; the compassionate use of resources in a world of scarcity. Westchester IL 1988, Crossway. xv-304 p. $10 pa. – ᴿWestTJ 52 (1990) 175-7 (P. J. *Liethart*).
8419 **Berten** Ignace, Christ pour les pauvres 1989 → 5,8391: ᴿÉTRel 65 (1990) 137s (C. *Izard*: l'auteur est provincial dominicain de Belgique-Sud); FoiTemps 19 (1989) 277 (P. *Weber*); Masses Ouvrières 432 (1990) 91 (J. *Landier*).
8420 *Blanco* Severiano, El Dios de los pobres en la revelación bíblica: EphMar 40,1s ('María y la opción por los pobres' 1990) 7-24.
8421 **Calvez** Jean-Yves, L'économie, l'homme, la société (L'enseignement social de l'Église). P 1989, D-Brouwer. 362 p. – ᴿBLitEc 91 (1990) 207s (R. *Coste*); CC 141 (1990, 2) 297 (G. *Salvini*); Salesianum 52 (1990) 437s (M. *Toso*).
8421* **Clark** Stanley D., The political Jesus; a study of the Gospels and a comparison with selected liberation Christologies: diss. Baptist Theol. Sem., ᴰ*Dukes* J. New Orleans 1990. 168 p. 90-26808. – DissA 51 (1990s) 1647-A.
8422 *Cone* J. H., Christian theology and Scripture as the expression of God's liberating activity for the poor: BangaloreTF 22,2 (1990) 26-39 [< NTAbs 35,60].
 Coote Robert B. & Mary P., Power, politics, and the making of the Bible 1990 → g608.

8423* **Cotterell** Peter, Mission and meaninglessness; the good news in a world of suffering and disorder. L 1990, SPCK. 112 p. £13. 0-281-04449-X. – ᴿExpTim 102,4 top choice (1990s) 97-99 (C. S. *Rodd*).

8424 **Coulie** B., Les richesses... GREG. NAZ.: 1985 ➤ 3,8325; 4,9446*: ᴿByzantina 15 (1989) 479-481 (P. A. *Vannopoulos* ⓖ); EpeterisByz 47 (1987-9) 454-6 (D. C. *Kalamakis,* ⓖ).

8425 *Dawsey* James M., The biblical authority of the poor: ExpTim 101 (1989s) 295-8.

8426 **Dorrien** Gary J., Reconstructing the common good; theology and the social order. Mkn 1990, Orbis. vii-222 p. $20. 0-88344-659-6 [TDig 38,56].

8427 **Duchrow** Ulrich, Global economy; a confessional issue for the churches? Geneva 1987, WCC. 231 p. $9.50. – ᴿNorTTs 90 (1989) 182s (K. *Nordstokke*); TsTKi 60 (1989) 154s (Axel *Smith*).

8428 **Ellul** Jacques, Jesus and MARX; from Gospel to ideology. GR 1988, Eerdmans. xvi-187 p. $13 pa. – ᴿAndrUnS 28 (1990) 159-161 (A. *Dupertuis*); ExpTim 101 (1989s) 60 (E. H. *Robertson*).

8429 **Fabris** R., La scelta dei poveri nella Bibbia: Le Spighe. R 1989, Borla. 252 p. Lit. 20.000 pa. 88-263-0496-3 [NTAbs 34,397].

8430 **Farina** Marcella, Chiesa di poveri e chiesa dei poveri [II.] La memoria della Chiesa: Prisma 7, 1988 ➤ 4,9456; 5,8400: ᴿNRT 112 (1990) 108s (A. *Toubeau*); Teresianum 40 (1989) 597-9 (F. *Di Giacomo*).

8431 **Geremek** Bronisław, Geschichte der Armut; Elend und Barmherzigkeit in Europa (ⓟ), ᵀ*Griese* Friedrich. Mü 1988, Artemis. 328 p. DM 48. – ᴿEvKomm 22,6 (1989) 53.55 (W. *Hartmann*).

8432 **Gerten** I., Christ pour les pauvres; Dieu à la marge de l'histoire: Théologies. P 1989, Cerf. 128 p. F 69. 2-204-03018-X. – ᴿTsTNijm 30 (1990) 316s (H. *Häring*).

8433 **Getz** G. A., A biblical theology of material possessions. Ch 1990, Moody. 438 p.; 2 fig.: 9 maps. $25. 0-8024-0891-6 [NTAbs 35,118].

8434 **Getz** G. A., Real prosperity [sequel to A biblical theology of material possessions]. Ch 1990, Moody. 188 p. 0-8024-0892-3 [NTAbs 35,256: 126 principles under 12 themes].

8435 **González** Carlos I., Pobreza y riqueza, en obras selectas del cristianismo primitivo; 'Sepan cuantos' 564, 1988 ➤ 5,8406: ᴿEstE 65 (1990) 475s (P. *Castón*).

8435* *González* Carlos I., Cimentación cristológica de los derechos humanos en el Documento de Puebla: StMiss 39 ('Human Rights' 1990) 79-109.

8436 **González** Justo L., Faith and wealth; a history of early Christian ideas on the origin, significance, and use of money. SF 1990, Harper & R. xvi-240 p. $20. 0-06-063317-4. – ᴿExpTim 101 (1989s) 378s (L. *Houlden*); TS 51 (1990) 517s (L. T. *Johnson*); TTod 47 (1990s) 324-6 (L. T. *Johnson*, also on BOFF-PIXLEY).

8437 *Grácio das Neves* Rui M., El dios del Sistema frente al Dios de la Sociedad Alternativa, II: CiTom 117 (1990) 43-66 (517-533).

8438 *Grünfeld* Joseph, Pre-rational power play [risk-taking is the link between power and play (NIETZSCHE, HEIDEGGER)]: ScEsp 42 (1990) 337-350.

8439 **Haan** Roelf, The economics of honour; biblical reflections on money and property 1988 ➤ 5,8410; 2-8254-0934-0: ᴿVidyajyoti 54 (1990) 48s (S. *Raj*).

8440 *Harrington* W., Property and wealth in the New Testament: Scripture in Church 29,78 (Dublin 1990) 230-240 [< NTAbs 34,348].

8441 *Haustein* Manfred, Personale oder strukturelle Diakonie [CAMPBELL A., Nächstenliebe mit Mass; Helferberufc christlich gesehen 1086]: TLZ 115 (1990) 401-410.

8442 **Hay** Donald A., Economics today; a Christian critique [... Bible core]. Leicester 1989, Inter-Varsity. 336 p. £11. − ᴿJTS 41 (1990) 792-800 (R. *Preston*).

8442* **Janssen** Heinrich, Die Bibel als Grundlage der politischen Theorie des Joh. ALTHUSIUS: ev. Diss. ᴰ*Dahm*. Münster 1989s. − TR 86 (1990) 517.

8443 *Jennings* Theodore W.ᴶ, WESLEY's preferential option for the poor: QRMin 9,3 (1989) 10-29.

8444 *Johnson* Sherman E., The message of Jesus to the poor and the powerful: ➤ 52, FULLER R., AnglTR supp 11 (1990) 16-28.

8444* **Journet** Charles, Théologie de la politique; intr. *Cabanne* Marie-Agnès: Prémices 8. FrS 1987, Univ. 164 p. Fs 22 [RTLv 22, 539, P. *Weber*].

8445 **Kammer** Charles L.ᴵᴵᴵ, Ethics and liberation; an introduction [college text]. Mkn 1988, Orbis. 243 p. $12 pa. − ᴿInterpretation 44 (1990) 214s (E. *Mount*).

8446 **Kealy** Seán P., Jesus and politics: ZacSt. Collegeville MN 1990, Liturgical. 96 p. 0-8146-5668-4.

8447 **Kellner** Wendelin, O Filho do Homem [1985 ➤ 1,7114]: São Paulo 1987, Paulinas. 150 p. 85-05-00740-9. − ᴿPerspT 21 (1989) 292s (J. *Vitório*).

8448 *Klein* Ralph W., The God of the Bible confronts the politics of hunger: CurrTMiss 17 (1990) 110-7.

8449 *Knight* Christopher, Christians and the politics of liberty ['new right' monopoly of the rhetoric of liberty: recent solutions of social problems result in a 'dependency culture' inhibiting individual dignity through responsibility]: TLond 93 (1990) 191-7.

8450 *Langan* John, The ethics of business: TS 51 (1990) 81-100.

8451 ᴱ**Lawrence** Fred, Communicating a dangerous memory; soundings in political theology: Lonergan Workshop Supp. 6, 1987 ➤ 3,659: ᴿÉglT 20 (1989) 144-152 (J. R. *Pambrun*, also on MELCHIN K. 1987).

8452 **Lebacqz** Karen, Six theories of justice 1986 ➤ 3,8344: ᴿTLond 93 (1990) 124-133 (A. M. *MacKinnon*).

8453 **Lebacqz** Karen, Justice in an unjust world; foundations for a Christian approach to justice. Mp 1987, Augsburg. 192 p. $13 pa. − ᴿInterpretation 44 (1990) 78-80 (H. R. *Beckley*).

8454 a) *Legrand* Lucien, Power in the Bible; − b) *Amaladass* Anand, Towards a theology of power; an Indian perspective: Jeevadhara 19,109 ('The human problem; power and its ambiguities' 1989) 43-56 / 33-42 [... al.].

8455 **Levi** Werner, From alms to liberation; the Catholic Church, the theologians, poverty, and politics. NY 1989, Praeger. vi-175 p. $36. − ᴿTS 51 (1990) 184 (J. P. *Hogan*).

8456 **Lohfink** Norbert F., Option for the poor 1987 ➤ 3,8348 ... 5,8424: ᴿCritRR 2 (1989) 139-142 (W. E. *Pilgrim*, also on HOPPE L.); VT 40 (1990) 251 (H. G. M. *Williamson*).

8457 *Losada* J., El servicio de los pobres en la Iglesia; reflexión y eclesiología: 'Corintios XIII' [título de la revista, de contenido no especialmente bíblico] 46 (1988) 33-66 [< RET 50,128].

8458 **Martini** Carlo M., Per dare un'anima alla città; sette conversazioni sulla politica come servizio. Mi 1990, In Dialogo. 132 p.; ill. Lit. 14.000. – RCC 141 (1990,3) 100s (J. *Joblin*).

8459 **Meeks** M. Douglas, God the economist 1989 ↝ 5,8429: RTTod 47 (1990s) 198.200 (J. P. *Wogaman*).

8460 **Minnerath** Roland, Jésus et le pouvoir: PoinT 46, 1987 ↝ 3,8362... 5,8430: RRTLv 21 (1990) 108s (H. *Wattiaux*).

8461 **Miranda** José Porfirio, Apelo a la razón; teoría de la ciencia y crítica del positivismo [... capitalismo]: Hermeneia 27, 1988 ↝ 5,8549; 84-301-1065-8: RPerspT 22 (1990) 259-261 (J. A. *Guerrero*).

8462 *Mitchell* M. M., Social teaching and social history; learning from the early Church [G. THEISSEN Zenos lectures, McCormick Theol. Sem. Ch 1989]: ChrCent 106 (1989) 724s [< NTAbs 34,75].

8462* **Montefiore** Hugh, Christianity and politics. L 1990, Macmillan. 119 p. £29.50. 0-333-51774-1; pa. -2391-1. – RExpTim 102 (1990s) 93 (A. *Kee*: inadequate brevity).

8463 *Mott* S. C., How should Christian economists use the Bible? A study in hermeneutics: BAsnChr Economists 13 (Wenham MA 1989) 7-19 [< NTAbs 34,71].

8464 **Naudet** Jean-Yves, Dominez la terre; pour une économie au service de la personne: Cité vivante 1. P 1989, Fleurus. 192 p. – RRThom 90 (1990) 499-502 (G.-M. *Marty*: sage, serein).

8465 **Novak** Michael, Free persons and the common good. Lanham MD 1989, Madison. xii-233 p. – RCC 141 (1990,4) 519s (J. *Joblin*).

8466 **Nyce** Dorothy Y., Jesus' clear call to justice: Peace & Justice 11. Scottdale PA 1990, Herald. 95 p. $6. 0-8361-3533-4.

8467 **Oakman** Douglas E., Jesus and the economic questions of his day 1986 ↝ 2,6627... 6,8437: RCritRR 2 (1989) 230-2 (T. E. *Schmidt*); HeythJ 31 (1990) 74s (R. J. *Taylor*); JEH 40 (1989) 135s (F. *Watson*); JJS 41 (1990) 270 (M. *Goodman*); Neotestamentica 24 (1990) 150s (W. R. *Domeris*).

8468 *Pawlas* Andreas, Evangelische politische Theologie: KerDo 36 (1990) 314-332; Eng. 332.

8469 *Pougin* Erwin, Einige biblische Regeln zur Wirtschafts- und Managementethik: JbChr Socialwissenschaften 31 (Münster 1990) 213-221 [< ZIT 90,350].

8470 **Rasmussen** L., Land is life; towards a just sharing of land; biblical reflections: LWF Documentation 27 (Geneva 1990) 15-21 [< NTAbs 34,351].

8471 **Ratzinger** J., Iglesia, ecumenismo y política 1987 ↝ 3,280*b... 5,8441: RScripTPamp 22 (1990) 255-8 (J. L. *Illanes*).

8472 **Ratzinger** Joseph, Church, ecumenism and politics 1988 ↝ 5,8442: RCritRR 2 (1989) 454s (L. S. *Cunningham*); ScotJT 43 (1990) 136s (M. *Santer*).

8473 **Rebello** Cedric, The social activist's Bible. Bangalore 1988, Claretian. 148 p. [Vidyajyoti 54,474].

8474 **Rowland** Christopher, Radical Christianity [from Jesus, Paul, John, through MÜNTZER and liberation theology], 1988 ↝ 5,8445: RJTS 41 (1990) 777-781 (J. K. *Riches*).

8475 **Schillebeeckx** Edward, La politique n'est pas tout [↝ 4,9509s], TPasselecq Georges; Apologique. P 1988, Cerf. 98 p. F 75. – RVSp 143 (1989) 134s (sr. *Pascale-Dominique*).

8476 **Schmidt** Thomas E., Hostility to wealth in the Synoptic Gospels 1987 ↝ 3,8383... 5,8449: RJBL 109 (1990) 142-4 (W. E. *Pilgrim*).

8477 **Schottroff** Luise, *Stegemann* Wolfgang, Jesus von Nazareth — Hoffnung der Armen[3] [[1]1978 ➤ 60,6692]: Urban-Tb 639. Stu 1990, Kohlhammer. 164 p. 3-17-011196-5. — Eng. 1986 ➤ 2,6636: [R]CritRR 2 (1989) 233s (D. *Goldsmith*, also on PALLARES).

8478 *Segalla* J., El Nuevo Testamento y el Estado: Didascalia-Arg. 420 (1989) 4-9 [➤ Stromata 45, 499].

8479 *a) Sens* Matthias, Menschliche Wirtschaft — Auf der Suche nach biblischen Kriterien für menschenwürdige Wirtschaftssysteme; – *b) Planer-Friedrich* Götz, Theologische 'Reflexionen über die Schuldenkrise'; – *c) Kiss* Igor, Luthers Stellung zum Wucher: ZeichZt 44 (1990) 53-55 / 65s / 67-70 [< ZIT 90,399].

8480 *Serra* J. L., Lucha por la tierra, lucha de Dios: Christus 528 (Méx. 1989) 58-64 [< Stromata 45, 500].

8480* **Sheedy** Patrick D., Justice and human need; an investigation of scriptural and Roman Catholic sources: diss. Marquette, [D]*Maguire* D. Milwaukee 1989. 484 p. 90-14063. – DissA 51 (1990s) 537-A.

8481 *Sleeper* C. F., The use of Scripture in Church social policy statements: Theology and Public Policy 2,2 (Wsh 1990) 47-60 [< NTAbs 35,202].

8482 *Stegner* William R., Recent religious/political developments [end of communism] in a New Testament theological perspective: AsbTJ 45,2 (1990) 73-81.

8483 *Susin* L. C., Jesus, o 'Cristo' e seu projeto político: Teocomunicação 80 (1988) 135-147 [< Stromata 45, 500].

8484 **Tinder** Glenn, The political meaning of Christianity; an interpretation. Baton Rouge 1989, Louisiana State Univ. 257 p. $30. – [R]TTod 47 (1990s) 436. 438. 440 (W. *Brueggemann*: comfort to status quo).

8485 *Vanni* Ugo, Carità e politica nel Nuovo Testamento: CC 141 (1990,1) 15-28; ➤ 651.

8486 *Waetjen* H. C., Using the Bible for liberation and justice: JIntden 15,1 (Atlanta 1987s) 91-101 [< NTAbs 35,11].

8487 **Walsh** J. P. M., The mighty from their thrones 1987 ➤ 3,2608 ... 5,9534: [R]AnglTR 71 (1989) 312-4 (R. A. *Henshaw*).

8488 *Waterman* A. M. C., Denys MUNBY on economics and Christianity [God and the rich society 1961 ...]: TLond 93 (1990) 108-116.

8489 **Weber** H.-R., Power; focus for a biblical theology 1989 ➤ 5,8463: [E]ExpTim 102 (1990s) 63 [C. S. *Rodd*]; Missiology 18 (1990) 352 (W. C. *Stumme*); NRT 112 (1990) 137s (L.-J. *Renard*); ÖkRu 39 (1990) 127s (G. *Fritz*); Vidyajyoti 54 (1990) 218s (G. V. *Lobo*).

8490 *a) Wright* N. T., The New Testament and the 'state'; – *b) Austad* Torleiv, Attitudes toward the state in Western theological thinking; – *c) Wright* Christopher J. H., The people of God and the State in the Old Testament: Themelios 16 (1990s) 11-17 / 18-22 / 4-10.

8491 **Yoder** John H., A política de Jesus [1984 ➤ 1,262]: [T]*Sander* Luis M.: Estudos bíblico-t. São Leopoldo 1988, Sinodal. 172 p. 85-233-0129-1. – [R]PerspT 22 (1990) 247-9 (J. *Vitório*).

H8.5   **Theologia liberationis latino-americana.**

8492 *a) Agostini* Nilo, Consciência e conscientização; – *b) Anjos Márcio* F. dos, Optar pelos pobres e fazer teologia moral; – *c) Comblin* José, O ressurgimento do tradicionalismo na teologia latino-americana; – *d) Boff* Leonardo, A implosão do socialismo autoritário e a Teologia da Libertação: REB 50,197 (1990) 5-24 / 25-43 / 44-75 / 76-92.

8493 *Álvarez-Suárez* Aniano,   Repensamiento teológico de 'la teología de la liberación':   Teresianum 40 (1989) 23-43.

8494 **Anton** Peter,   Befreiungstheologie und Transzendentaltheologie; DUSSEL, RAHNER: FreibTSt 137.   FrB 1988, Herder.   625 p.   DM 89. – [R]TPQ 138 (1990) 409s (F. *Gruber*).

8495 **Baldwin** Deborah,   Protestants and the Mexican revolution; missionaries, ministers, and social change.   Urbana 1990, Univ. Illinois.   203 p. $27 [JAAR 58,157].

8495* **Baske** Klemens,   Versuch eines konstruktiven Dialogs zwischen der lateinamerikanischen Theologie der Befreiung und der Theologie Karl RAHNERs: kath. Diss., [D]*Jorissen*.   Bonn 1989s. – TR 86 (1990) 513.

8496 *Betto* frei o.p.,   A teologia da libertação ruiu com o muro de Berlim? REB 50 (1990) 922-9.

8497 [Lucchetti] *Bingemer* Maria Clara,   Solidariedade ou conflito — possibilidades de diálogo entre a Doutrina Social da Igreja e a Teologia da Libertação: REB 50 (1990) 844-857.

8498 *Blue* J. Ronald,   Major flaws in liberation theology: BS 147 (1990) 89-103.

8499 *a)* **Boff** Clodovis,   Theology and praxis; epistemological foundations 1987 → 3,8410; 4,9537:   [R]TGL 80 (1990) 353s (K. J. *Tossou*); – *b)* Théorie et pratique; la méthode des théologies de la libération: CogF.   P 1990, Cerf.   408 p.   F 239.   2-204-04093-2 [ÉTRel 65,659].

8500 **Boff** Clodovis, **Pixley** Jorge, Les pauvres; choix prioritaire [Opção pelos pobres].   P 1990, Cerf. – [R]REB 50 (1990) 975s (–: inaugurates new 'Collection Libération').

8501 **Boff** L.   Jesus Christus, der Befreier, [T]*Goldstein* H., *Hermans* K. 1986, [2]1987 → 3,8413; 4,9539:   [R]LebZeug 43 (1988) 71-73 (T. *Herr*); NZMissW 44 (1988) 77-79 (J. G. *Piepke*).

8502 **Boff** Leonardo,   Nova evangelização (Perspectiva dos oprimidos).   Petrópolis 1990, Vozes.   126 p. – [R]REB 50 (1990) 1005-1016 (E. F. *Alves*, also on companion-volumes by KLOPPENBURG B., AGOSTINI N.).

8503 **Boff** Leonardo,   Faith on the edge; religion and marginalized existence [< O caminhar 1980 + Fe na periferia 1978], [T]*Barr* Robert B. SF 1989, Harper & R.   212 p. $20 [JAAR 58,157]. – [R]America 163 (1990) 164 (J. P. *Fitzpatrick*: 'Underdevelopment is the direct consequence of development').

8504 **Boff** Leonardo.   When theology listens to the poor 1988 → 4,9540: [R]SpTod 41 (1989) 71s (R. G. *Weakland*: arc the 'experiences' of the poor sometimes manipulated?).

8505 [E]**Boff** L., *Kern* B., *Müller* A.,   Werkbuch Theologie der Befreiung.   Dü 1988, Patmos.   192 p.; ill.   DM 28. – [R]TLZ 115 (1990) 472s (J. *Althausen*).

8506 *a)* *Boff* Leonardo,   La originalidad de la Teología de la Liberación en G. GUTIÉRREZ [< REB 48 (1989) 531-543], [E]*Suñol* M.; – *b)* Metz J. B.,   La pugna de la teologia para la integración de la historia y de la sociedad [< Cristianismo y Sociedad 26/98 (1988) 61-67], [E]*Messa* J.:   SelT 29 (1990) 273-280 / 268-272.

8506* **Borgman** E. P. N. M.,   Sporen van de bevrijdende God; universitaire theologie in aansluiting op latijnsamerikaanse bevrijdingstheologie, zwarte theologie en feministische theologie: diss. [D]*Häring* H.   Nijmegen 1990.   360 p. – TsTNijm 31, p. 92; RTLv 22, p. 618.

8507 *Brandt* Hermann,   Die Benutzung des Judentums in der Befreiungstheologie: ÖkRu 39 (1990) 424-439 [page omitted from p. 429 supplied separately].

8508 **Cadorette** Curt, From the heart of the people; the theology of Gustavo GUTIÉRREZ 1988 → 5,8486: ᴿScotJT 43 (1990) 133s (J. L. *Wilkinson*).

8509 **Calvez** Jean-Yves, Tiers monde; un monde dans le monde; Portes ouvertes. P 1989, Ouvrières. 200 p. – ᴿRICathP 34 (1990) 179s (L. de *Vaucelles*).

8509* **Campbell** Margaret M., Critical theory and liberation theology; a comparison of Jürgen HABERMAS and Gustavo GUTIÉRREZ: diss. Graduate Theological Union, ᴰ*Osborne* K. Berkeley 1990. 243 p. 91-18153. – DissA 52 (1991s) 189-A; RelStR 17, p. 192.

8510 **Casaldáliga** Pedro, Kampf und Prophetie; Aufzeichnungen einer Reise durch Nicaragua. W-Mödling 1990, St. Gabriel. 160 p.

8511 **Castillo** F., *al.*, Teología de la liberación y realidad chilena. Santiago 1989, Rehue. 96 p. – ᴿPáginas 14,100 (Lima 1989) 187s (Ana *Gispert-Sauch*).

8512 ᴱ**Castillo** Fernando, Die Kirche der Armen in Lateinamerika, eine theologische Hinführung. FrS 1987, Exodus. 231 p. – ᴿTPhil 65 (1990) 628 (M. *Sievernich*).

8513 **Chenu** Bruno, Teologías cristianas de los terceros mundos; teologías latinoamericana, negra norteamericana, negra sudafricana, africana y asiática, ᵀ*Medrano* Luiza. Barc 1989, Herder. 244 p. 84-254-1643-4. – ᴿActuBbg 26 (1989) 203s (J. *Boada*).

8514 **Ching** Theresa L., Efficacious love; its meaning and function in the theology of Juan L. SEGUNDO. Lanham 1989, UPA. x-157 p. $26.50. 0-8191-7561-7 [TDig 37,254].

8515 **Codina** Victor, Vorwärts zu Jesus zurück; von der modernen Theologie zur solidarischen Nachfolge [1984 → 65,7216], ᵀ. Salzburg 1990, O. Müller. 272 p. DM 35. – ᴿTGL 80 (1990) 354s (K. *Hollmann*).

8516 **Collet** Giancarlo, Der Christus der Armen; das Christuszeugnis der lateinamerikanischen Befreiungstheologen 1988 → 5,452: ᴿLebZeug 43 (1988) 73s (B. *Neumann*); TPQ 138 (1990) 410s (E. *Gruber*).

8517 *Composta* Dario, Le difficoltà della teologia della liberazione [SEGUNDO J.]: PalCl 68 (1989) 1463-1475.

8517* **Costa** Ruy O., Toward a Latin American Protestant ethic of liberation; a comparative study of the writings of Rubem ALVES and José MIGUEZ BONINO from the perspective of the sources and substance of their social ethics: diss. Boston Univ. 1990, ᴰ*Deats* P. 725 p. (2 vol.) 89-24725. – DissA 50 (1989s) 2111-A.

8518 **Cox** Harvey, The silencing of L. BOFF 1988 → 5,8494: ᴿAnglTR 71 (1989) 441-3 (R. E. *Hood*); PrPeo 4 (1990) 157 (S. E. *Hall*: useful despite journalese); Tablet 243 (1989) 1274 (Carol *Pimento-Pinto*).

8519 *Crawford* Robert G., Black liberation theology in South Africa and liberation theology in Latin America: ExpTim 101 (1989s) 329-334.

8520 *Croatto* J. Severino, Die Bibel gehört den Armen; Perspektiven einer befreiungstheologischen Hermeneutik [Hermeneutica biblica 1984 → 3, 1251], ᵀ*Schöder* Christoph: ÖkExistH 5. Mü 1989, Kaiser. 101 p. DM 19,80 pa. [TR 86,347].

8521 a) *Crüsemann* Frank, Anstösse; Befreiungstheologische Hermeneutik und die Exegese in Deutschland; – b) *Sundermeier* Theo, 'Fremde Theologien': EvT 50 (1990) 535-545 / 524-534.

8522 **Damico** Linda H., The anarchist dimension of liberation theology 1987 → 3,8448: ᴿJAAR 58 (1990) 277s (C. *Cadorette*).

8523 **Dammert** José, *al.*, Irrupción y caminar de la Iglesia de los pobres; presencia de Medellín. Lima 1989, Inst. B. Las Casas/CEP. 336 p. – ᴿPerspT 21 (1990) 236-8 (J.-B. *Libânio*).

8524 *Dawsey* James M., The lost front door into Scripture; Carlos MESTERS, Latin American liberation theology, and the Church Fathers: AnglTR 72 (1990) 292-305.

8525 **Dri** Rubén, A Utopia de Jesus, [T]*Alves* José B. São Paulo 1986, Icone. 264 p. [REB 50,501].

8525* **Dupertuis** Atilio R., Liberation theology; a study in its soteriology: diss. Andrews 9, 1982. Berrien Springs MI 1987, Andrews Univ. xviii-361 p. $15 pa. – [R]AndrUnS 28 (1990) 157-9 (E. J. *Hernandez*).

8526 **Duquoc** Christian, Liberación y progresismo; un diálogo teológico entre América Latina y Europa 1989 → 5,8499: [R]ActuBbg 27 (1990) 67 (J. *Vives*); EstFranc 91 (1990) 341-4 (M. *Boero*); Iter 1 (Caracas 1990) 161-4 (J. de la *Torre*).

8526* **Dussel** Enrique, Die Geschichte der Kirche in Lateinamerika [1967 [2]1971], [T]*Goldstein* Horst. Mainz 1988, Grünewald. 435 p. DM 48. – [R]ZkT 112 (1990) 251 (J. *Wicki*).

8527 [E]**Fornet-Betancourt** R., Positionen Lateinamerikas: Solidarität 1. Fra 1989, Materialis. 146 p. 3-88535-096-3. – [R]TsTNijm 30 (1990) 425 (G. van *Rossum*).

8528 *Gaillardetz* Richard R., Can Orthodox ethics liberate? A test case for the adequacy of an Eastern ethic: Horizons 17 (1990) 60-75.

8529 *Galli* Carlos M., Teología de la liberación y doctrina social de la Iglesia hoy: Stromata 46 (1990) 187-203 [175-186, *Rubiolo* Eugenio].

8530 **Garcia** Ismael, Justice in Latin American theology of liberation [D]1987 → 3,8468 ... 5,8508: [R]Interpretation 44 (1990) 78-80 (H. R. *Beckley*).

8531 **González** Justo L., Mañana; Christian theology from a Hispanic perspective. Nv 1990, Abingdon. $14. 0-687-23067-5 [RelStR 16,355].

8532 *González Dorado* Antonio, Inculturación y endoculturación de la Iglesia en América Latina (anotaciones para una investigación del proceso): EstE 65 (1990) 403-442.

8533 *González Faus* José I., La Teología de la Liberación como segunda reforma de la Iglesia: RCatalT 15 (1990) 139-152; Eng. 152.

8534 *González Montes* Adolfo, España en America; evangelización y defensa de la dignidad humana: Salmanticensis 36 (1989) 209-231; Eng. 232 'against distortions of indigenist ideology'.

8535 **Goodpasture** H. McKennie, Cross and sword; an eyewitness history of Christianity in Latin America. Mkn 1989, Orbis. xix-314 p. $30; pa. $14. – [R]NewTR 3,3 (1990) 109s (L. *Nemer*: 'fresh, informative, interesting' — and pre-ecumenical items); NRT 112 (1990) 764 (J. *Masson*); TS 51 (1990) 540-2 (E. S. *Sweeney*); TTod 47 (1990s) 228.230 (J. *Gros*).

8536 *Greinacher* Norbert, Der Schrei nach Gerechtigkeit in Lateinamerika; die prophetische Dimension der Theologie der Befreiung: TüTQ 170 (1990) 104-119.

8537 **Gutiérrez** Gustavo, Dios o el oro en las Indias 1989 → 5,8515: [R]Nat-Grac 37 (1990) 128 (E. *Rivera*); Páginas 14,98 (Lima 1989) 110 (J. J. *Tamayo Acosta* < Vida Nueva 1.VII.1989); PerspT 21 (1989) 258-260 (F. *Taborda*).

8538 **Gutiérrez** Gustavo, Gott oder das Gold; der befreiende Weg des Bartolomé de LAS CASAS, [T]. FrB 1990, Herder. 217 p. DM 38. – [R]HerdKor 44 (1990) 493 (U. *Ruh*).

8539 **Gutiérrez** Gustavo, Drinken uit de eigen bron; de geestelijke reis van een volk 1988 → 5,8516: [R]Bijdragen 51 (1990) 211s (B. *Höfte*).

8540 *Gutiérrez* Gustavo, God-talk during Ayacucho [Peruvian for 'corner of the dead'], [TE]*Bonness* Mary Kay: TDig 37 (1990) 227-231, title and text contrasting 'after Auschwitz' and 'during Ayacucho' (nowhere really explained) though *desde* of the Spanish title could imply either.

8541 **Gutiérrez** Gustavo, The truth shall make you free; confrontations, ᵀ*O'Connell* Matthew J. Mkn 1990, Orbis. xii-204 p. $20; pa. $13. 0-88344-679-0; -63-4 [TDig 38,62].

8542 *Gutiérrez* Gustavo, L'option pour les pauvres [Eng.],ᵀ: Études 367-377.

8543 *Hawks* James, Juan Luis SEGUNDO's critique of David TRACY: HeythJ 31 (1990) 277-294.

8543* **Hellenstein** Pius, Evangelikale Theologie der Befreiung: Diss. ᴰ*Lochman(n)*. Basel 1989s. – TR 86,511.

8544 ᴱ**Hennelly** Alfred T., Liberation theology; a documentary history. Mkn 1989, Orbis. xxvi-547 p. $35; pa. $20. 0-88344-593-X. – ᴿNRT 112 (1990) 770s (A. *Harvengt*); Tablet 244 (1990) 866s (Elizabeth *Lord*); Vidyajyoti 54 (1990) 615s (G. *Lobo*).

8545 **Hennelly** Alfred, Theology for a liberating church; the new praxis of freedom. Wsh 1989, Georgetown Univ. 207 p. $11 pa. – ᴿAmerica 161 (1989) 168s (B. *Cooke*); Horizons 17 (1990) 350s (J. R. *Connolly*); TS 51 (1990) 379 (J. *Zimbelman*).

8546 **Hernández Pico** Juan, Un cristianismo vivo; reflexiones teológicas desde Centroamérica. S 1987, Sígueme. 195 p. – ᴿTPhil 65 (1990) 627 (M. *Sievernich*).

8547 **Herzog** Frederick, God-walk; liberation shaping dogmatics 1988 ➤ 5, 8520: ᴿTR 86 (1990) 40s (E. *Arens*).

8547* **Hewitt** Marsha A., From theology to social theology; J. L. SEGUNDO and the theology of liberation. NY 1990, Lang. xii-184 p. $42 [TS 52, 395, K. P. *O'Higgins*: final defense against Vatican overlooks earlier admissions].

8548 **Höfte** B. J., Bekering en bevrijding; de betekenis van de latijnsamerikaanse theologie van de bevrijding voor een praktisch-theologische basistheorie: diss. ᴰ*Kessel* R. van. Utrecht 1990. Hilversum 1990, Gooi & S. 90-304-0531-7. – TsTNijm 30 (1990) 191.

8548* **Hoy** Michael C., The faith that works; J. L. SEGUNDO's theology of liberation in comparison with some contemporary Catholic and Protestant theologies and the theologies of Paul and LUTHER on the relationship of faith and works: diss. Lutheran School of Theology, ᴰ*Braaten* C. 1990. – 371 p. 90-33109. – DissA 51 (1990s) 2059-A.

8549 **Hundley** Raymond C., Radical liberation theology; an evangelical response. Wilmore KY 1987, Bristol. 141 p. $13. – ᴿCriswT 4 (1989s) 209s (K. E. *Eitel*).

8550 **Ibáñez Langlois** J. M., Teología de la liberación y libertad cristiana. Santiago 1989, Univ. Católica. 126 p. – ᴿAnnTh 4 (1990) 474-8 (E. *Colom Costa*).

8550* *a) Ibarrázaval* Diego, Inculturación latinoamericana de la catequesis; – *b) Barrios Valdes* Marciano, La Iglesia en América Latina durante el siglo XX: TVida 30 (1989) 271-297 / 299-300.

8551 *Jobling* David, Writing the wrongs of the world; the deconstruction of the biblical text in the context of liberation theologies: ➤ 365, Semeia 51 (1990) 81-118.

8552 **Kee** Alistair, MARX and the failure of liberation theology. L 1990, SCM/TPI. XII-303 p. £15. 0-334-02437-4. – ᴿExpTim 101,12 top choice (1989s) 353s (C. S. *Rodd*: achieves very little); Month 251 (1990) 444s (S. *Loughlin*).

8552* **Kendrick** Peter W., Christian freedom and liberation; a biblical and theological critique of the concept of salvation in the theology of G. GUTIÉRREZ: diss. Baptist Theol. Sem. New Orleans 1990. 142 p. 90-27418. – DissA 51 (1990s) 1661-A.

8553 **Kessler** Hans, Reduzierte Erlösung? Zum Erlösungsverständnis der Befreiungstheologie. FrB 1987, Herder. 63 p. – ᴿTPhil 65 (1990) 626 (H. *Sievernich*).

8554 **Koopmans** Joop, Das Leben umarmen; Befreiungstheologie in der Praxis. W/Mödling 1990, Südwind/S. Gabriel. 224 p. DM 26,80.

8555 **Kruip** Gerhard, Entwicklung oder Befreiung? Elemente einer Ethik sozialer Strukturen am Beispiel ausgewählter Stellungnahmen aus der katholischen Kirche Mexikos (1982-7): Forschungen zu Lateinamerika 19. Saarbrücken 1988, Breitenbach. 597 p. – ᴿTPhil 65 (1990) 627s (M. *Sievernich*); TR 86 (1990) 402-5 (W. *Kroh*).

8556 *Laboa* Juan M., Planteamiento social de la evangelización en la historia de la Iglesia: MiscCom 48 (1990) 99-126.

8557 **Lois** Julio, Teología de la liberación; opción por los pobres: HistIglT. San José CR 1988, 'DEI'. 506 p. 84-245-0445-3. – ᴿActuBbg 26 (1989) 233 (R. de *Sivatte*).

8558 *López-Gay* Jesús, Boletín de publicaciones sobre la historia de la Iglesia en America Latina (1984-8): Burgense 31 (1990) 524-564 [29 items].

8559 **Lutte** Gérard, De la religion à l'Évangile — jeunes chrétiens révolutionnaires au Nicaragua. Bru 1989, Vie ouvrière. – ᴿRNouv 46,3 (1990) 100 (A. *Linard*) [45,7s (1989) numéro sur Nicaragua].

8560 **McGovern** A.T., Liberation theology and its critics; toward an assessment. Mkn 1989, Orbis. xxi-281 p. $15. – ᴿNRT 112 (1990) 771s (L. *Volpe*).

8561 *Maimela* S.S., Christian socialism as precursor of liberation theology: JBlackT 3,2 (Atteridgeville SAf 1989) 14-27 [3/3, 52-70, *Muzorewa* G.: < TContext 8/1,22s].

8562 **Marlé** René, Introduction à la théologie de la libération 1988 → 4,9603; 5,8533: ᴿScEsp 42 (1990) 362s (G. *Novotny*).

8563 *Martínez Díez* Felicísimo, Teología latinoamericana y teología europea; el debate en torno a la liberación: Teología y Pastoral. M 1989, Paulinas. 230 p. – ᴿScripTPamp 22 (1990) 294 (J.L. *Illanes*).

8564 *Martínez Díez* Felicísimo, La 'nueva' evangelización; ¿restauración o alternativa?: CiTom 117,383 ('Pastoral indígena y nueva evangelización' 1990) 571-591.

8565 *Mateo-Seco* Lucas F., El futuro de la teología de la liberación: ScripTPamp 22 (1990) 195-211.

8566 **Mertens** H.-E., Niet het kruis, maar de Gekruisigde; schets van een christelijke bevrijdingsleer: Nikè. Lv 1990. 185 p. – ᴿCollatVL 20 (1990) 451s (J. De *Kesel*).

Mesters Carlos, Defenseless flower; a new reading of the Bible, ᵀ*McDonagh* Francis 1989 → 1215.

8568 ᴱ**Metz** Johann-B., *Rottländer* Peter, Lateinamerika und Europa, Dialog der Theologen [Münster 28. Sept. – 2. Okt. 1988]: Forum Politische Theologie 8, 1988 → 4,611; 5,8538: ᴿTPhil 65 (1990) 630 (M. *Sievernich*).

8569 **Min Kyongsuk** Anselm, Dialectic of salvation, issues in theologies of liberation. Albany 1989, SUNY. x-207 p. $39.50; pa. $13. – ᴿNewTR 3,2 (1990) 105s (A. *Fornassari*: much needed); TS 51 (1990) 184s (A.J. *Tambasco*).

8570 **Moreno Rejón** F., Teologia moral a partir dos pobres; a moral na reflexão teológica da América Latina. Aparecida-SP 1987, Santuario. 238 p. – ᴿHumT 2 (1990) 385s (J. *Cunha*).

8571 *Moseley* Romney M., Decolonizing theology in the Caribbean; prospects for hermeneutical reconstruction: TorJT 6 (1990) 235-246.

8572 *Müller* Gerhard L., Recht und Notwendigkeit einer Befreiungstheologie: MüTZ 41 (1990) 327-346.

8573 *Murphy* Seamus, Epistemological issues in liberation theology and feminist philosophy: MilltSt 26 (1990) 61-76.

8574 **Nessan** Craig L., Orthopraxis or heresy; the North American response to Latin American liberation theology. Atlanta 1989, Scholars. vii-455 p. $33; pa. $22. – ᴿTS 51 (1990) 551s (M. J. *Schuck*).

8575 **Nordstokke** Kjell, De fattiges kirke; basismenigheter og frigjørings-teologi i Latin-Amerika. Oslo 1987, Kirkelig Kulturverksted. 189 p. Nk 130. – ᴿNorTTs 90 (1989) 53-57 (K. W. *Ruyter*).

8576 *Oguogho* J.M., South African liberation theologies versus racism and the apartheid system [Tᴜᴛᴜ and Bᴏᴇsᴀᴋ lack critical analysis of their own ideological substructures]: AfER 39 (1989) 168-182.

8576* **Ojoy** Virgilio, Traces of humanistic Marxism in Gustavo Gᴜᴛɪ́ᴇ́ʀʀᴇᴢ's theology of liberation; an attempt at positing the compatibility of Marxist views with religion: diss. ᴰ*Schrijver* G. de. Leuven 1990. xxxiv-284 p. – LvSt 15 (1990) 428s; RTLv 22, p. 620.

8577 *a)* *Ojoy* Virgilio, Gustavo Gᴜᴛɪ́ᴇ́ʀʀᴇᴢ's God-talk from the perspective of the poor; – *b)* *Gomez* Fausto, Meaning of justice, peace and the preferential option for the poor: PhilipSa 25 (1990) 325-351 / 353-366.

8578 **O'Neill** Michael, God hears the cry of the poor [Perú 'ᴄᴇʙs' 1965-86]; diss. Pont. Univ. Gregoriana. R 1990. 320 p. - REB 50 (1990) 759 [930-940, *Ribeiro de Oliveira* P., sobre ᴄᴇʙs].

8579 *a)* *Pannenberg* Wolfhart, Christianity, Marxism, and liberation theology [... responses]; – *b)* *Elliot* Mark, Hammer and Sickle as Cross; Marxism as faith: ChrSchR 18,3 ('Christianity and Marxism' 1989) 215-226 [-237] / 267-280.

8580 **Pasquetto** V., Mai più schiavi 1988 → 4,9613; 5,8543: ᴿAngelicum 67 (1990) 131s (A. *Lobato*); DivThom 92 (1989) 431 (M. *Tábet*); Teresianum 40 (1989) 266-9 (B. *Moriconi*).

8581 **Peter** Anton, Befreiungstheologie und Transzendentaltheologie; Enrique Dᴜssᴇʟ und Karl Rᴀʜɴᴇʀ im Vergleich: FreibTSt 137. FrB 1988, Herder. 625 p. DM 89. – ᴿTR 86 (1990) 483-5 (A. *Tafferner*).

8582 *Piepke* Joachim, Die Frage der Menschenrechte im Amerika des 16. Jahrhunderts: TGegw 33 (1990) 20-36.

8583 **Pixley** George V., *Boff* Clodovis, The Bible, the Church and the poor: Theology and liberation. L 1989, Burns Oates / Mkn 1990, Orbis. 266 p. $30; pa. $15. / Mkn. 0-88344-614-6; -599-9 [TDig 38,80]. – ᴿEcuR 42 (1990) 362s (W. *Kinne*); ExpTim 102 (1990s) 88s (D. B. *Forrester*).

8584 *Possenti* Vittorio, Struttura dell'azione e compito pubblico del cristianesimo; dottrina sociale della Chiesa e teologia della liberazione a confronto: Sapienza 43 (1990) 21-39.

8585 **Pottenger** John R., The political theory of liberation theology; toward a reconvergence of social values and social science. Albany 1989, SUNY. 264 p. $44.50; pa. $17. – ᴿMonth 251 (1990) 201s (B. B. *McClory*); TTod 47 (1990s) 326.328 (P. E. *Sigmund*).

8586 *Prien* Hans-Jürgen, Lateinamerika: → 857, TRE 20 (1990) 451-480.

8587 *Rodríguez* Gabriel I., Relação entre as Comunidades Eclesiais de Base e a hierarquia; estudo do tema na eclesiologia de Leonardo BOFF: PerspTeol 21 (1989) 51-70.

8588 **Rowland** Christopher, Radical Christianity; a reading of recovery [... early apocalyptic; MÜNTZER; liberation theology]. Mkn 1988, Orbis. 199 p. $15. – ᴿTTod 47 (1990s) 182s (V. L. *Wimbush*).

8589 **Rowland** Christopher, *Corner* Mark, Liberating exegesis; the challenge of liberation theology in biblical studies: Biblical Foundations in Theology. L/Louisville 1990, SPCK/W-Knox. 205 p. £11. 0-281-04437-6/. – ᴿExpTim 101 (1989s) 314 (L. *Houlden*).

8590 *Russell* Anthony J., Theology in context and 'the right to think' in three contemporary theologians; GUTIÉRREZ, DUSSEL, and BOFF: Pacifica 2 (1989) 282-322.

8590* *Sanders* David, The power of the Bible [perceived in a four-month visit to Brazil]: Tablet 244 (1990) 412s.

8591 *Saranyana* Josep-Ignasi, La evangelización americana (siglo XVI), historia e historiografía: ScripTPamp 22 (1990) 899-905.

8592 *Sayés* José A., El problema del sobrenatural; síntesis histórica y su incidencia en las teologías de la secularización y de la liberación: Burgense 31 (1990) 309-388.

8593 **Scannone** Juan Carlos, Teología de la liberación y doctrina social de la Iglesia. M / Buenos Aires 1987, Cristiandad/Guadalupe. 285 p. – ᴿStromata 45 (1989) 461-4 (G. T. *Farrell*); TPhil 65 (1990) 629s (M. *Sievernich*).

8594 *Schwantes* Milton, [Gespräch: Die Bibel] Mit den Augen der Armen: EvKomm 23 (1990) 137-141.

8595 **Segundo** J. L., Theology / RATZINGER → 1,8184... 4,9627: ᴿCCurr 38 (1988s) 485s (J. P. *Vrana*).

8595* *Seibold* Jorge R., Palabra de Dios y pueblo de Dios; la actualización de la Sagrada Escritura en la evangelización de América Latina: Stromata 46 (1990) 3-63...

8596 **Shaull** Richard, Naming the idols; biblical [Exodus...] alternatives for U.S. foreign policy. Oak Park IL 1988, Meyer-Stone. 176 p. $10. – ᴿTTod 47 (1990s) 703.706.708 (P. E. *Sigmund*: shrill, self-righteous).

8597 **Sigmund** Paul E., Liberation theology at the crossroads; democracy or revolution? NY 1990, Oxford-UP. viii-257 p. $30. 0-19-506064-4 [TDig 38,87]. – ᴿAmerica 163 (1990) 43s (P. J. *Williams*, also on *McGovern*).

8598 *Silva* Airton J. da, Notas sobre alguns aspectos da leitura da Bíblia no Brasil hoje [p. 137 '*dābār* significa 'palavra' e 'acontecimento'... Ora, a sociedade capitalista possui enorme habilidade para transformar discursos instituintes e históricos em discursos instituídos e competentes... dissimiladores das relações de dominação']: REB 50 (1990) 117-137.

8599 **Sobrino** Jon, Gesù in America latina; suo significato per la fede e la cristologia: Ricerche teologiche. R 1986, Borla. 258 p. Lit. 20.000. – ᴿBenedictina 36 (1989) 246s (E. *Tuccimei*).

8600 *Sobrino* Jon, The crucified peoples; Yahweh's suffering servant today: → 402, Concilium (1990,6) 120-9.

8601 *Sobrino* Jon, Liberation from sin [< SalT 76 (1988) 15-28 = RLatAmT 13 (1988) 13-31], ᵀᴱ*Bonness* Mary Kay: TDig 37 (1990) 141-5.

8601* **Stemmeler** Michael, Theology of liberation and political theology; L. BOFF and G. GUTIÉRREZ in conversation with J.-B. METZ and J. MOLTMANN: diss. Temple, ᴰ*Raines* J. Ph 1989. – RelStR 17,193.

8602 **Stoll** David, Is Latin America turning Protestant? The politics of evangelical growth. Berkeley 1990, Univ. California. xxi-424 p. $25. 0-520-06499-2 [TDig 38,89].

8603 **Tamayo-Acosta** J. J., Para comprender la teología de la liberación 1989 → 5,8569: REfMex 8 (1990) 278-280 (E. *Bonnín*); NRT 112 (1990) 185 (L. V).

8603* **Waschenfelder** J., Johann B. METZ's critique of bourgeois Christianity: diss. McMaster, DRobertson J. Hamilton ON 1990. – RelStR 17,192.

8604 *Wicks* Robert J., Entering the cave of the tiger; a psychological analysis of North American middle class resistance to liberation theology's call to conversion to the neighbor: Pastoral Sciences 7 (1988) 69-80.

H8.6   *Theologiae emergentes* – 'Theologies of' emergent groups.

8605 **Alberich** Emilio, Le catéchisme universel, obstacle ou catalysateur dans le processus d'inculturation? TDumont Jacqueline; Concilium 224 (P 1989) 97-106 = Der Weltkatechismus, Hindernis oder Katalysator, TDrasen-Seghers Victoria M.: IZT 25 (1989) 343-8.

8605* **Alphonse** Martin P., The Gospel and Hindu *bhakti*; Indian Christian responses from 1900 to 1985 — a study in contextual communication: diss. Fuller Theol. Sem., DHiebert P. Pasadena 1990. 344 p. 90-20673. – DissA 51 (1990s) 887-A.

8606 *Amalorpavadass* Duraismy S., Theological reflections on inculturation: IndTSt 27 (1990) 217-272 [< TContext 8/2, 115, *Evers* G., long summary].

8607 *a) Amalorpavadass* D. S., Réflexions théologiques sur l'inculturation; – *b) Hastings* Adrian, Le christianisme occidental et la confrontation des autres cultures: MaisD 179 (1989) 57-66 / 31-44.

8607* **Anyaka** Godfrey, A reexamination of African traditional religion: diss. Fordham, DCousins E. NY 1990. – RelStR 17,191.

8608 *Baldridge* William E., Toward a native American theology: AmBapQ 8,4 (Rochester 1989) 227-238 [< ZIT 90,223].

8609 **Basave Fernandez del Valle** Agustín, Vocación y estilo de México; fundamentos de la Mexicanidad. Méx 1989, Limusa. 1050 p. 968-18-3112-8. – RActuBbg 27 (1990) 161-6 (E. *Forment*).

8610 *Baum* Gregory, La théologie contextuelle [canadienne] de Douglas HALL: LavalTP 46 (1990) 149-166.

8611 **Baur** John, *al.*, The Catholic Church in Kenya, a centenary history. Nairobi 1990, St. Paul Publications, Africa. 256 p. [TContext 8/1, 137, H. *Janssen*].

8611* **Bennett** David W., Perspectives of biblical pastoral leadership; a case study of ten churches in Pune, India: diss. Fuller Theol. Sem., DElliston E. Pasadena 1990. 373 p. 90-29100. – DissA 51 (1990s) 1650-A.

8612 *Berranger* Olivier de, Une poignée de cendres; foi chrétienne, agnosticisme coréen; pour une théologie critique de l'inculturation [document C. T. J. ...]: NRT 112 (1990) 183-201.

8613 **Büscher Martin** E. H., Afrikanische Weltanschauung: Wirtschaft 29. Freiburg 1988, Haufe. 100 p. DM 48. – RTR 86 (1990) 243s (B. *Doppelfeld*).

8614 **Bujo** Bénézet, Teologia africana nel suo contesto sociale [1986 → 3, 8587] → 5,8581: TZappieri B.: GdT 185. Brescia 1988, Queriniana. 216 p. Lit. 18.000. – RETL 66 (1990) 219s (A. *Vanneste*).

8615 **Bujo** Bénézet, African Christian morality at the age of inculturation. Nairobi 1990, St. Paul. 137 p. [TContext 8/2, 138, H. *Janssen*].

8616 *Bujo* Bénézet, Eucharist in Black African perspective [The two sources of life; the Eucharist and the cult of ancestors in Africa: ChAfC 2,1 (1986) 67-85], E*Jermann* Rosemary: TDig 37 (1990) 127-131.

8616* *Campbell* M.G., Inculturation; some New Testament perspectives: JosStudies 1,1 (Jos, Nigeria 1990) 4-14 [< TContext 8/1,27].

8617 **Caplan** Lionel, Religion and power; essays on the Christian community in Madras. Madras 1989, Christian Literature. 170 p. rs 30. – RecuR 42 (1990) 360-2 (P.J. *Gallup*).

8618 *Carr* Dhyanchandi, [India lower-caste] Dalit theology is biblical and it makes the Gospel relevant: South India Churchman (Madras, Nov. 1990) 3-7 [< TContext 8/2, 114].

8619 **Carrier** Hervé, Gospel message and human cultures from Leo XIII to John Paul II [1987 ➤ 5,8585],T. Pittsburgh 1989, Duquesne Univ. xiii-178 p. $30. – RMissiology 18 (1990) 373 (D.J. *Hesselgrave*).

8619* **Casalegno** Ugo, Antropologi e missionari a confronto. R 1988, LAS. 128 p. 88-213-0176-1. – RClaretianum 30 (1990) 449s (S.M. *González Silva*); ZkT 112 (1990) 253 (J. *Wicki*).

8620 *Caspersz* Paul, The role of the Christian Church in contemporary Sri Lanka: Vidyajyoti 53 (1989) 289-298.

8621 *Chaos* Samuel H., John L. Nevius (1829-1893) and the contextualization of the Gospel in 19th century China: AsiaJT 2 (1988) 294-311.

8622 *Charbonnier* J., Towards a theology of the Chinese church: IndTSt 26 (1989) 171-180.

8623 **Chenu** Bruno, Teologías cristianas de los terceros mundos 1989 ➤ 5, 8589: RPerspT 22 (1990) 105-8 (J.B. *Libânio*).
  Chenu Bruno, Le Christ noir américain: JJC 21, 1984 ➤ 1,4067...; Der Schwarze Christus... afrikanischer Theologie 1989 ➤ 5,516: supra ➤ 4404.

8624 *Chmiel* Jerzy, ❷ Inculturation and biblical theology: ➤ 64, FGrzybek S. 1990, 45-48; Eng. 49.

8625 *Christensen* Thomas, 'Tisser une nouvelle natte par-dessus les vieilles...'. Quelques réflexions relatives à la contextualisation de l'Évangile dans l'Église évangélique luthérienne de Cameroun: PosLuth 37,1 (P 1989) 20-40 [< ZIT 89,378].

8626 **Clark** Francis X., An introduction to the Catholic Church in Asia 1987 ➤ 3,8599: RVidyajyoti 53 (1989) 98s (G.V. *Lobo*).

8627 *a) Clooney* Francis X., Robert DE Nobili, adaptation and the reasonable interpretation of religion; – *b) Thomas* Norman E., Globalization and the teaching of mission: Missiology 18 (Scottdale 1990) 25-36 / 13.23.
  ECollet G., Theologien der Dritten Welt 1990 ➤ 399.

8628 *Collins* Raymond, *Ukachukwu Manus* Chris, Contemporary New Testament scholarship; outlining its relevance for African Christianity: Bodija 1,1 (Ibadan 1989s) 8-22 [< TContext 8/2, p. 24].

8629 *Colombo* Giuseppe, La fede e l'inculturazione: TItSett 15 (1990) 172-182; Eng. 182.

8630 **Cone** James H., La noirceur de Dieu, TKea M., *Philibert* J.; préf. *Mottu* H. Genève 1989, Labor et Fides. 294 p. – RÉtudes 372 (1990) 857 (R. *Marlé*).

8631 *Conn* Harvie M., Contextual theologies [and the question of 'syncretism']; the problem of agendas: WestTJ 52 (1990) 51-63.

8632 Cooperazione missionaria tra sviluppo e vangelo: SUMA (Segretariato unitario di animazione missionaria) Sussidi 11. Bo 1990, EMI. 87 p. Lit. 4000.

8633 ᴱ**Costa** Ruy O., One faith, many cultures 1986/8 ➤ 4,542: ᴿPacifica 3 (1990) 114-6 (S. *McNulty*).
ᴱ**David** M., Western colonialism in Asia and Christianity 1988 ➤ 597.

8634 **Davis** Cyprian [O.S.B.] The history of black Catholics in the United States. NY 1990, Crossroad. xvii-347 p. $25. 0-8245-1010-0 [TDig 38,54].

8635 *de Gruchy* John W., South African theology comes of ago: RelStR 17 (1991) 217-223.

8636 *Diatta* Nazaire, *a*) Et si Jésus-Christ, premier-né d'entre les morts, était l'initié? La personnalité de l'initié joola face au Christ: Téléma 15,1 (1989) 49-73; – *b*) Évangélisation et pastorale d'inculturation: Téléma 16,3s (1990) 5-23 (-65, *al.*).

8637 *Dulles* Avery, Cattolicesimo e cultura americana; un dialogo difficile: CC 141 (1990,3) 16-25.

8638 **Eckardt** A. Roy, Black, woman, Jew; three wars for human liberation. Bloomington 1989, Indiana Univ. ix-229 p. $35. – ᴿAmerica 163 (1990) 67-69 (Judith R. *Baskin*); Horizons 17 (1990) 353s (Susannah *Heschel*: splendid).

8639 **Eilers** Franz-J. Communication between cultures. Manila 1987, Divine Word. 137 p. – ᴿVerbumSVD 30 (1989) 93s (E. *Zeitler*).

8640 **Eitel** Keith, Transforming culture; developing a biblical ethic in an African context. Nairobi 1986, Evangel. 185 p. $6 pa. – ᴿCriswT 3 (1988s) 199s (Ebbie *Smith*).

8641 *Eitel* Keith E., Contextualization; contrasting African voices: CriswT 2 (1987s) 323-334.

8642 **Ellis** Carl F.ᴶ, Beyond liberation; the Gospel in the Black American experience 1983 ➤ 1,8261: ᴿRelStR 16 (1990) 248 (J. H. *Evans*).

8643 **End** T. van den, *al.*, Indonesische Geloofsbelijdenissen: IIMO 20. Leiden 1986, IIMO. iii-231 p. 90-71387-19-4. – ᴿNedTTs 44 (1990) 81s (L. A. *Hoedemaker*).

8644 *Evans* James H.ᴶ, African-American Christianity and the postmodern condition: JAAR 58 (1990) 207-220.

8645 *Exem* A. van, Religious faith, belief and practices; a case study: Word and Worship 23,2 (Bangalore 1990) 67-73; Eng. summary TContext 8/1, 116.

8646 *Fragoso* Hugo, O etnocentrismo na primeira evangelização do Brasil: Convergência 25,233 (RJ 1990) 289-303; Eng. summary TContext 8/1, 120.

8647 **Franklin** Robert M., Liberating visions; human fulfilment and social justice in African-American thought. Mp 1990, Fortress. ix-174 p. $10. 0-8006-2392-4 [TDig 37,362].

8648 **Frostin** Per, Liberation theology in Tanzania and South Africa; a First World interpretation: StTLund. Malmö 1988, Lund Univ. x-284 p. 91-7966-159-9 [Chartwell-Bratt 0-86238-159-9]. – ᴿCalvinT 25 (1990) 95-98 (P. G. *Schrotenboer*: he is not interested in its truth claims; it must be evaluated in terms of its internal logic); ETRel 65 (1990) 293s (Anne-Marie *Goguel*: remarquable); ExpTim 101 (1989s) 51s (A. C. *Ross*: 'one of the most important theological works of the '80s'; 26-p. introd. 'best and clearest exposition of Lib. Theol. available in English'); NorTTs 91 (1990) 187s (N. E. *Bloch-Hoell*); TsTKi 61 (1990) 234s (T. H. *Hovland*).

8649 **Gernet** Jacques, China and the Christian impact; a conflict of cultures [cf. ➤ 2,6804], ᵀ*Lloyd* Janet. C 1985, Univ. $49.50; pa. $18. – ᴿAnglTR 71 (1989) 95-98 (T. J. *Kodera*).

8650 **Gilliland** Dean S., The Word among us; contextualizing theology for mission today. Dallas 1989, Word. 344 p. $16. – ^RNorTTs 91 (1990) 179s (K. *Nordstokke*).

8651 **Gittins** A., Gifts and strangers; meeting the challenge of inculturation. NY 1989, Paulist. 144 p. $10 [TS 51,382].

8652 **Govender** S.P., In search of tomorrow; the dialogue between Black Theology and Marxism in South Africa 1987 ➤ 5,8608: ^RKerkT 40 (1989) 160s (L. A. *Hoedemaker*).

8653 **Grayson** J. Huntley, Korea, a religious history. Ox 1989, Clarendon. xii-319 p.; 20 fig. £37.50. – ^RNRT 112 (1990) 279s (J. *Scheuer*).

8654 *Hahn* Eberhard, Anmerkungen zur Lektüre der Heiligen Schrift in Brasilien: KerDo 36 (1990) 111-154; Eng. 155: predetermined by experience of oppression as a dogma, reducing exegesis to the attempt of providing biblical verification; the Gospel loses its critical potential.

8655 **Hall** Douglas J., Thinking the faith; Christian theology in a North American context 1989 ➤ 5,8611: ^RTS 51 (1990) 166s (R. L. *Maddox*).

8656 *Hamilton* Andrew, What has Asia to do with Australia? Reflection on the theology of Aloysius PIERIS: Pacifica 3 (1990) 304-322.

8657 *Harris* Max, Indigenismo y catolicidad; folk dramatizations of evangelism and conquest in central Mexico: JAAR 58 (1990) 55-68.

8658 **Hastings** Adrian, African Catholicism; essays in discovery [11 reprints + 1 ineditum] 1989 ➤ 5,276: ^RExpTim 101 (1989s) 251s (A. C. *Ross*: good); Furrow 40 (1989) 758s (S. P. *Kealy*); Gregorianum 71 (1990) 605s (A. *Wolanin*); TS 51 (1990) 570 (J. C. *McKenna*).

8659 *Hayes* Diana L., Tracings of an American theology: LvSt 14 (1989) 365-376.

8660 *Heim* S. Mark, [al.] Mapping globalization for theological education: TEdn 26,1 supp. (1990) 7-34 [-112].

8661 *Hesselgrave* David J., *Rommen* Edward, Contextualization; meanings, methods, and models. ➤ 5,8612; also GR 1989, Baker. xii-281 p. $15. 0-8010-4338-7 [TDig 37,367]. – ^RMissiology 18 (1990) 494 (P. A. *Beals*).

8662 *Hillman* Eugene, An evaluation of inculturation [*Schineller* P.; *Gittins* A. J.; *Shorter* A.]: AfER 32,6 (1990) 368-374 [< TContext 8/2, 120: more pluriformity and subsidiarity needed].

8663 *Honings* Bonifacio, Adattamento missionario ed etica cristiana; una teologia morale di nuovi rapporti umani: RivScR 4 (Molfetta 1990) 47-64.

8663* **Hopkins** Dwight N., Black theology, U.S.A. and South Africa [diss.]. Mkn 1989, Orbis. 249 p. $15. 0-88344-639-1. – ^RExpTim 102 (1990s) 124s (A. C. *Ross*).

8664 [Ikenga] **Metuh** Emefie, African religions in western conceptual schemes [➤ 4,9691]; the problem of interpretation: Studies in Igbo Religion. Ibadan 1985, Pastoral Institute Bodija. 176 p. – ^RZRGg 42 (1990) 181s (H.-J. *Greschat*).

8665 *Jean-Nesmy* Claude, En commun à l'Orient et à l'Occident; l'homme [écrits récents Japon-Chine]: EsprVie 100 (1990) 161-170.

8666 **Jesudasan** Ignatius, A Gandhian theology of liberation 1984/7 ➤ 65, 7339; 5,8615: ^RIrTQ 56 (1990) 238-241 (G. *Flynn*).

8667 *Kagabo* Liboire, L'état des mœurs sociales au Burundi: Au cœur de l'Afrique (1990,1) 71-84; Eng. summary TContext 8/1, 123.

8668 *Kakichi* Kadowaki, 'Nô'; dramma sacro giapponese e cristianesimo: EphLtg 104 (1990) 291-8; lat. 291.

8669 ᴱKalu Ogbu U.,   African Church historiography, an ecumenical perspective [Nairobi Aug. 2-8, 1986] 1988 ➤ 5,682: ᴿTLZ 115 (1990) 551-3 (J. *Althausen*).

8670 *Kumugisha* Joseph,   Evaluating approaches to evangelization: AfER 39 (1989) 12-26.

8671 **Kavunkal** Jacob,   To gather them into one; evangelization in India today, a process of building community [Diss. Pont. Univ. Gregoriana 1985]: Stud. Miss. Verbi Divini 17.   Nettetal/Indore 1985, Steyler/Satprakashan-SK. xviii-226 p. − ᴿTLZ 115 (1990) 857-9 (K. *Roeber*).

8672 **Kim Kwang-Won**,   Zur Theologie der Negation; Versuch einer koreanischen kontextuellen Theologie im Gespräch mit dem 'Hwaom' Buddhismus Uisangs: Prot. author's diss. at kath. Fak. Bonn, 1990. − TContext 8/2, 130.

8673 **Kinne** Warren, A people's Church? The Mindanao-Sulu church debacle [diss. Birmingham]: Studien zur intellektuellen Geschichte des Christentums 64. Fra 1990, Lang. 324 p. [TContext 8/2, 131, G. *Evers*; cf. p. 134].

8674 *Kitagawa* Joseph M., The Asian Christian tradition, I. The younger churches of Asia from the perspective of Christian history; II. (Japan) An Asian perspective in global revolution: AnglTR 71 (1989) [226-231] 241-260.406-424; − IIIs. The emergence of the Christian dilemma: AnglTR 72 (1990) 62-84. 175-198.

8674* **Kunnie** Julian E.,   Bridges across the Atlantic; relating Black theologies in the United States and South Africa, focussing on social analytical methodology with James CONE and Desmond TUTU as respective symbolic figures: diss. Graduate Theological Union, ᴰ*Song* C. Berkeley 1990. − RelStR 17,192.

8675 **Kwon Jin-Kwan**,   The emergence of Minjung as the subjects of history; a Christian political ethic in the perspective of Minjung theology: diss. Drew, ᴰ*Ogletree* T. Madison NJ 1990. − RelStR 17,193.

8675* **Leeuwen** Gerwin van,   Fully Indian, authentically Christian; a study on the first fifteen years of the National Biblical Catechetical and Liturgical Centre (1967-1982) Bangalore, India, in the light of the theology of its founder, D.S. AMALORPAVADASS. Bangalore/Utrecht 1990. 357 p. [TContext 8/1, 131, G. *Evers*].

8676 **Luzbetak** Louis J.,   The Church and cultures; new perspectives on missiological anthropology 1988 ➤ 5,8627: ᴿTéléma 15,3s (1989) 97s (Maryvonne *Duclaux*); TS 51 (1990) 185s (M. H. *Kelleher*); VerbumSVD 30 (1989) 385-7 (E. *Nunnenmacher*).

8677 ᴱ*Madey* Johannes,   Der römische apostolische Stuhl, die Kongregation für die Ostkirchen und die Schicksale der syro-malabarischen Kirche: OstkSt 38 (1989) 166-184.

8678 ᴱ**Malone** Peter,   Discovering an Australian theology 1988 ➤ 5,8631: ᴿEcuR 42 (1990) 175 (sr. M. Leonora *Moorhead*: 40,000 years of faith experience by aborigines, 200 by Europeans).

8679 **May** John D.,   Christus initiator; Theologie im Pazifik: Theologie Interkulturell 4. Dü 1990, Patmos. 151 p. [TContext 8/1, 132, H. *Janssen*].

8680 **Mbiti** John S.,   Bibel und Theologie im afrikanischen Christentum 1987 ➤ 3,8664; 4,9717: ᴿEvKomm 2,1 (1989) 53 (K. *Nürnberger*); TR 86 (1990) 222s (K. J. *Tossou*).

8681 **Mbiti** John S.,   Bible and theology in African Christianity 1986 ➤ 3, 8661 ... 5,8615: ᴿHeythJ 31 (1990) 96s (G. *Parrinder*).

8682 *a) Michael* Sebastian M., Beyond inculturation; – *b) Amaladoss* M., Mission: from Vatican II into the coming decade; – *c) Onwura* Emeka, Mission: Christian converts in traditional Igbo society in Nigeria: Vidyajyoti 54 (1990) 6-18 / 269-280 / 281-8.

8683 **Milingo** Emmanuel, The world in between; Christian healing and the struggle for spiritual survival, E*Macmillan* Mona, 1984 ➤ 1,8309; 2,6870: RRelStT 8,1s (1988) 106s (I. *Hexham*: more truly African than MBITI).

8684 **Miranda** Dionisio, Pagkamakatao; reflections on the theological virtues in the Philippine context 1987 ➤ 4,9718: RPhilipSa 24 (1989) 155s (G. *Gregory*).

8685 **Mitchell** Henry H., *Lewter* Nicholas C., Soul theology; the heart of American Black culture 1986 ➤ 2,6872; 3,8666: RHeythJ 31 (1990) 118.

8686 *Mkhatshwa* Smangaliso, The role of contextual theology in a changing South Africa: JTSAfr 72 (1990) 3-8 [< TContext 8/2, 113].

8687 *Moloney* Raymond, The lay pastors of Kinshasa — a challenge from Africa: Furrow 40 (1989) 215-221.

8688 *Moroney* Patrick, Some dangers of inculturation [lip-service with too little understanding]: VerbumSVD 31 (1990) 327-338.

8689 **Mosala** Itumeleng J., Biblical hermeneutics and Black theology in South Africa. GR 1989, Eerdmans. xiv-218 p. $16 pa. [TTod 47,71 adv.]. 0-8028-0372-5. – RCalvinT 25 (1990) 292-5 (P. G. *Schrotenboer*); TTod 47 (1990s) 482s (T. L. *Wimbush*).

8690 *Mosha* Raymond S., An African response to post-Vatican II spirituality: Chiea 5,2 (Nairobi 1989) 3-10 [< TContext 7/1, 19].

8691 *Mozia* M.I., Education of the African Christian conscience: Bodija Journal 1,1 (Ibadan 1989s) 30-43 [< TContext 8/2, 120].

8692 **Mugambi** J.N., African Christian theology; an introduction. Nairobi 1989, Heinemann. 152 p. [TContext 8/2, 128, H. *Janssen*].

8693 **Mugambi** Jesse N.K., The biblical basis for evangelization; theological reflections based on an African experience. Nairobi 1989, Oxford-UP. 147 p. [TContext 8/1, 137, H. *Janssen*].

8694 EMugambi J.N.K., *Magesa* Laurenti, Jesus in African Christianity; experimentation and diversity in African Christology. Nairobi 1989, Initiatives. 164 p. [TContext 8/1, 133, H. *Janssen*].

8695 **Muzorewa** Gwinyai H., The origins and development of African theology 1985 ➤ 1,8316 ... 3,8680: RTLZ 115 (1990) 859-861 (J. *Althausen*).

8696 **Neckebrouck** Valeer, La Terza Chiesa e il problema della cultura [La Tierce Église devant le problème de la culture 1987 ➤ 4,9723], T*Vendrame* Giancarlo: Problemi e dibattiti 13. R 1990, Paoline. 129 p. – RSalesianum 52 (1990) 769 (P. *Carlotti*).

8697 EMyers Kenneth A., Aspiring to freedom; JOHN PAUL II's encyclical Social concerns. GR/Exeter 1988, Eerdmans/Paternoster. 169 p. £8.50. 0-8028-0412-8. Essays by P. *Berger*, M. *Novak*, G. *Weigel*, al. – RExpTim 101 (1989s) 124 (J. *Mahoney*: mixed reception).

8698 *Nedungatt* George, Syro-Malabar liturgical reform in focus: Vidyajyoti 53 (1989) 173-185. 249-263 [451-3, letter of bishop Abraham *Mattam*: sometimes unfair].

8699 **Newbigin** Lesslie, Foolishness to the Greeks; the Gospel and western culture 1986 ➤ 2,6890 ... 5,8644: RBijdragen 51 (1990) 210 (J.-J. *Suurmond*: expansion of his 'The other side of 1984'); CriswT 4 (1989s) 218s (K. E. *Eitel*).

8699* **Nicolson** Ronald, A black future? Jesus and salvation in South Africa. L/Ph 1990, SCM/Trinity. 255 p. £9.50. 0-334-00120-X. – RExp-

Tim 102 (1990s) 155 (A.C. *Ross*: Natal professor, adds a bit on Latin America).

8700 **Nolan** Albert, God in South Africa; the challenge of the Gospel. GR 1988, Eerdmans. xiii-241 p. A$19. – RPacifica 3 (1990) 353-5 (C. *Murray* doubts that the author would agree to publishers' claim of 'contextual theology').

8701 **Nothomb** Dominique, Lettres à Noji; devenir chrétien sans cesser d'être Africain. Kinshasa 1989, St. Paul Afrique. 79 p. [TContext 8/1, 130, M. *Moerschbacher*].

8702 *Osei-Bonsu* Joseph, Biblically/theologically based inculturation: AfER 32,6 (1990) 346-358 [< TContext 8/2, 116].

8703 E**Parratt** John, A reader in African Christian theology 1987 ➤ 4,9735; 5,8653: RPacifica 3 (1990) 107-9 (G.W. *Trompf*).

Pastore C., *al.*, La inculturación del evangelio 1988 ➤ 362.

8704 **Peelman** Achiel, L'inculturation; l'Église et les cultures: Horizon du Croyant 8, 1989 ➤ 5,8654*: REsprVie 100 (1990) 96 (L. *Debarge*); Pastoral Sciences 8 (1989) 119s (J. *Gauthier*).

8704* *a) Peelman* Achiel, Le Christ est amérindien; perspectives anthropologiques et théologiques; – *b) Melançon* Louise, Quelle figure du Christ pour une théologie non sexiste?; – *c) Ménard* Camil, Jésus le Christ est l'unique sauveur? Le salut chrétien confronté aux autres religions du salut: ➤ 669, E*Petit* J., J.-C. universel? 1989/90, 175-196 / 197-218 / 55-78.

8705 **Pieris** Aloysius, An Asian theology of liberation 1988 ➤ 5,8655: RPacifica 3 (1990) 359-361 (J. *Haire*).

8706 **Pieris** Aloysius, Une théologie asiatique de la libération [1988 ➤ 5, 8655], T*Feisthauer* J. P 1990, Centurion. 232 p. F 140. – REsprVie 100 (1990) 494s (P. *Jay*: la proclamation des Mages n'était pas pour leur Asie); Études 373 (1990) 137s (R. *Marlé*).

8707 **Pirotte** Jean, *Soetens* Claude, Évangélisation et cultures non européennes; guide du chercheur en Belgique francophone: RTLv Cah 27. LvN 1989, Fac. Théol. 179 p. Fb 780. – RGregorianum 71 (1990) 786s (J.E. *Vercruysse*).

8708 E**Pobee** John S., *Hallencreutz* Carl F., Variations in Christian theology in Africa. Nairobi 1986, Uzima. viii-113 p. – RJRel 69 (1989) 268s (T. *Walker*).

8709 **Poupard** Paul, L'Église au défi des cultures; inculturation et évangélisation. P 1989, Desclée. 180 p. F 125. – REsprVie 100 (1990) 351 (L. *Debarge*).

8710 Pour une théologie contemporaine du Moyen-Orient 1987/8 ➤ 5,724: RScEsp 42 (1990) 363s (G. *Novotny*).

8711 **Priest** Doug, Doing theology with the Maasai. Pasadena 1990, Carey. viii-240 p. $11. 0-87808-441-X [TDig 38,81].

8712 **Pulsfort** Ernst, Christliche Ashrams in Indien: MünstTAbh 7. Altenberge 1989, Telos. xxii-235 p. DM 34,80. 3-89375-016-9. – RVidyajyoti 54 (1990) 657s (G. *Gispert-Sauch*).

8713 **Recinos** Harold J., Hear the cry! A [U.S.] Latino pastor challenges the church. Louisville 1989, W/Knox. 156 p. $12 [RelStR 17,145, J.T. *Ford*].

8714 **Rehbein** Franziska C., Heil in Christentum und Afro-Brasilianischen Kulten; ein Vergleich am Beispiel des Candomblé: Stimmen der kommenden Kirche 3. Bonn 1989, Borengässer. xxiii-214 p. DM 28. – RTLZ 115 (1990) 802-4 (W. *Hüffmeier*); TPQ 138 (1990) 411s (J. *Janda*); ZkT 112 (1990) 346-8 (K.H. *Neufeld*).

8715 *a) Reinhard* Wolfgang, Christliche Mission und Dialektik des Kolonialismus; – *b) Gründer* Horst, Mission, Kolonialismus und Emanzipation in Schwarzafrika: HistJb 109 (1989) 353-370 / 371-386 [387-420, *Rivinius* K., China; 421-451, *Volz* A., Kamerun].

8715* **Rennstich** Karl, Die zwei Symbole des Kreuzes; Handel und Mission in China und Südostasien. Stu 1988. 280 p. – ᴿVerbumSVD 30 (1989) 194-7 (H. *Rzepkowski*).

8716 *Rivinius* Karl Josef, Evangelisierung und innerweltliche Strukturen [... Neokolonialismus]: VerbumSVD 30 (1989) 129-152 [gekürzt in StiZt 296 (1988) 651-663].

8716* *Robinson* Gnana, Kontextuelle Theologie am Beispiel Indien: BTZ 7 (1990) 51-65.

8717 O rosto indio de Deus 1/7, Desafios da religião do povo. São Paulo 1989, Vozes. 357 p. – ᴿCC 141 (1990,3) 545s (F. A. *Pastor*).

8718 **Rücker** Heribert, 'Afrikanische Theologie', Darstellung und Dialog: InnsbTSt 14, 1985 ➤ 1,8342 ... 5,8662: ᴿZkT 112 (1990) 125s (A. *Darlap*).

8719 *Samy* Ama, Inculturation, the case of Zen meditation [*Dinh Duc Dao* Joseph, OmnisTerra 188 (1988) 257-273]: Vidyajyoti 53 (1989) 56-61.

8720 **Sanneh** Lamin, Translating the message; the missionary impact on culture: Amer. Soc. Missiology 13, 1989 ➤ 5,8669: ᴿCalvinT 25 (1990) 139-142 (R. R. *Recker*).

8721 *Sanon* Anselme T., Initiation à la théologie africaine: Écoute, Afrique 2 (Burkina Faso 1989) 5-20 [< TContext 8/2, 112].

8722 **Schaaf** Y., Hij ging zijn weg met blijdschap; over de geschiedenis en de rol van de Bijbel in Afrika. Kampen 1990, Kok. 300 p. *f* 42,50. 90-242-4997-X. – ᴿTsTNijm 30 (1990) 408 (J. *Heijke*).

8723 **Schineller** Peter, A handbook on inculturation. NY 1990, Paulist. iv-141 p. $9. 0-8091-3124-2 [TDig 38,85].

8724 *Schmidt-Leukel* Perry, Die Relevanz der Theologie; zwei neue deutschsprachige Veröffentlichungen zur Theologie der EATWOT [1990]: MüTZ 41 (1990) 389-394.

8725 *Schreiter* Robert J., Teaching theology from an intercultural perspective: TEdn 26,1 (1989s) 13-34 (35-42, response, *Matsuoka* Fumitaka).

8726 *Scott* William H., Visayan religion at the time of Spanish advent: PhilipSa 25 (1990) 397-415 [24 (1989) 120-153, *Fernandez* Pedro on evangelization of Nueva Vizcaya].

8727 *Bogaert* Michael van den, Communication, community and tribals: Sevartham 15 (1990) 43-55; summary TContext 8/1, 121.

8728 *Semporé* Sidbe, L'Afro-Christianisme, un courant irréversible: Spiritus 30 (1989) 193-205.

8729 **Shorter** Aylward, Toward a theology of inculturation [in a papal document first 1979] 1988 ➤ 4,9749; 5,8673: ᴿCalvinT 25 (1990) 113-6 (R. R. *Recker*: a book on contextualization); Horizons 17 (1990) 170s (Kathleen *Dugan*); TLond 93 (1990) 62-64 (W. J. *Hollenweger*); TTod 47 (1990s) 80-82 (W. *Brueggemann*).

8730 *Spindler* Marc R., *a)* Writing African Church history (1969-1989), a survey of recent studies: Exchange 19,1 (1990) 70-87 [< TContext 8/1, 125]; – *b)* Afrikaanse kerkgeschiedenis (1969-1989); quot terrae incognitae!: NedTTs 44 (1990) 1-14; Eng. 56.

8731 **Stackhouse** Max L., Apologia; contextualization, globalization and mission in theological education 1988 ➤ 4,9753; 5,8676: ᴿOTEssays 2,3 (1989) 109s (J. H. Le *Roux*).

8732 **Stewart** Carlyle F.[III], God, being and liberation; a comparative analysis of the theologies and ethics of James H. CONE and Howard THURMAN [< diss. Northwestern 1982]. Lanham MD 1989, UPA. xvii-306 p. $37.50. 0-8181-7521-8 [TDig 38,88].

8733 *Sugirtharajah* R. S., Jesus research and Third World Christologies: TLond 93 (1990) 387-391.

8734 **Sundermeier** Theo, Nur gemeinsam können wir leben; das Menschenbild schwarzafrikanischer Religionen: Siebenstern 784. Gü 1988, Mohn. 304 p. DM 24,80. – [R]EvKomm 22,1 (1989) 53s (K. *Nürnberger*); TLZ 115 (1990) 578-580 (S. *Krügel*); VerbumSVD 30 (1989) 391-3 (A. *Quack*).

8735 *Sundermeier* Theo, Begegnung mit den Fremden; Plädoyer für eine verstehende Missionswissenschaft: EvT 50 (1990) 390-400.

8736 **Takenaka** Masao, God is rice — Asian culture and Christian faith: Risk. Geneva 1986, WCC. – [R]AsiaJT 2 (1988) 586s (D. J. *Elwood*: symbol of life for Asia, as bread is for Jesus and the West).

8736* *Tan Xing*, Culture-Christians on the China mainland: Tripod 60,6 (Hong Kong 1990) 47-58 [< TContext 8/2, 114].

8737 *Tienou* Tite, The right to difference; the common roots of African theology and African philosophy: AfrJEvT 9,1 (1990) 24-34 [< TContext 8/2, 112].

8738 [E]**Trompf** Garry W., The Gospel is not western; Black Theology from the Southwest Pacific 1987 → 3,734... 5,8684: [R]JPsy&T 16 (1988) 299s (S. G. *Lingenfelter*); TGL 80 (1990) 356s (K. J. *Tossou*).

8739 **Udoh** Enyi Ben, Guest Christology; an interpretative view of the Christological problem in Africa [diss. Princeton 1983]: Studien zur interkulturellen Geschichte des Christentums 59. Fra 1988, Lang. v-284 p. [RelStR 17, 51, Nancy M. *Victorin-Vangerud*].

8740 **Wan-Tatah** Victor, Emancipation in African theology; an inquiry into the relevance of Latin American liberation theology to Africa [diss.]: AmerUnivSt ... 14. NY 1989, Lang. 225 p. [TContext 8/2, 128, M. *Moerschbacher*].

8741 *Westerlund* David, African religion in African scholarship. Sto 1985 [Pacifica 3,109].

8742 **Whyte** Bob, Unfinished encounter; China and Christianity. L 1988, Collins. 537 p. $11. – [R]TS 51 (1990) 170s (P. *Fleming*).

8743 *Wilfred* Felix, *a*) Dogma and inculturation: Vidyajyoti 53 (1989) 345-353; – *b*) Towards on anthropologically and culturally founded ecclesiology; reflections from an Asian perspective: Vidyajyoti 54 (1990) 501-511.

8744 *Wilfred* Felix, Pluralismo religioso e inculturación cristiana [< IndTSt 25 (1988) 5-26], [TE]*García-Nieto* S.: SelT 29 (1990) 119-123.

8745 **Wuthnow** Robert, The struggle for America's soul. GR c.1989, Eerdmans. 189 p. $23. – [R]America 163 (1990) 21 (J. *Gros*: ecumenical Presbyterian).

8746 **Yewangoe** Andreas A., Theologia crucis in Asia; Asian Christian views on suffering in the face of overwhelming poverty and multifaceted religiosity in Asia [diss.]: AmstStT 6. Amst 1987, Rodopi. xii-352 p. *f* 70. – [R]ZkT 112 (1990) 250s (J. *Wicki*).

H8.7   *Mariologia* – **The mother of Jesus in the NT.**

[E]**Bäumer** Remigius, *Scheffczyk* Leo, Marienlexikon 1989 → 5,917*.

8747 *Balasuriya* Tissa, Mary and human liberation: Logos 29,1s (Colombo 1990) 1-192 [< TContext 8/2, 121: his reflections].

8748 **Balthasar** Hans Urs von, Maryja na dziś [1987], [T]*Waloszek* Joachim. Wrocław 1989, Archidiecez. – [R]AtKap 115 (1990) 340s (J. *Królikowski*).

8749 *Barriola* Miguel A., 'Bendita tú entre las mujeres; una femineidad insólita al servicio de la fe común [i. ¿María 'opio' del feminismo?]: TArg 26,1 (1989) 5-71.

8750 **Beinert** Wolfgang, Unsere liebe Frau und die Frauen 1989 → 5,8697: [R]EphMar 40 (1990) 164 (D. *Fernández*, sotto cognome Wolfgang, ma p. 362 e 167 giusto).

8751 *Beyers* Rita, De nativitate Mariae; problèmes d'origine [Paschase RADBERT c. 868 (C. LAMBOT 1934) non prouvé; guère attesté avant 1000]: RTPhil 122 (1990) 171-188; Eng. 295.

8752 **Brennan** Walter, The sacred memory of Mary 1988 → 5,9780: [E]Dialog 25 (1989) 66. 68 (F. C. *Senn*).

8753 *Cadegan* U. M., *Heft* J. L., Mary of Nazareth, feminism, and the tradition: Thought 65 (1990) 169-189 [< RHE 85,420*].

8754 **Cantalamessa** Raniero, Maria, uno specchio per la Chiesa. Mi 1989, Àncora. 270 p. Lit. 17.000. 88-7610-290-6. – [R]Benedictina 37 (1990) 248-250 (L. *Crippa*); Gregorianum 71 (1990) 787 (J. *Galot*); PalCl 68 (1989) 1324 (A. *Pedrini*).

8755 **Carroll** Michael P., The cult of the Virgin Mary, psychological origins 1986 → 2,6953... 5,9782: [R]CathHR 76 (1990) 814-6 (E. R. *Carroll*); HeythJ 31 (1990) 97s (M. J. *Walsh*: not as good as his 1973 'Visions of the Virgin Mary; the effect of family structures', on Medjugorje); JRelHist 15 (1988s) 255s (J. *Moorhead*: not sensitive enough to history); JScStR 27 (1988) 653 (W. J. *Bildstein*).

8756 **Casale** Umberto, Benedetta fra le donne; saggio teologico sulla mariologia e la questione femminile. T-Leumann 1989, Elle Di Ci. 192 p. Lit. 13.000. 88-01-10439-1. – [R]Gregorianum 71 (1990) 789 (C. I. *González*).

8757 *Dasnabedian* Thamar, La figure de Marie dans le panégyrique de la Sainte Mère de Dieu de Grigor NAREKATSI: PrOrChr 40 (1990) 3-26.

8758 *Denaux* Adelbert, L'Œcuménisme et Marie [= CollatVL 18 (1988) 59-85], [T]*Gertrude-Marie* sr.: FoiTemps 19 (1989) 411-441.

8759 *a) Díez Merino* L., Interpretación mariológica de citas bíblicas en San ISIDORO de Sevilla; – *b) Muñoz León* D., El uso de la Biblia en el tratado 'De virginitate perpetua S. Mariae' de San ILDEFONSO de Toledo: → 644, Llamas E., EstMar 55 (1990) 125-173 / 251-285.

[E]**Donnelly** Doris, Mary, woman of Nazareth; biblical and theological perspectives 1990 → 523.

8761 **Dumas** André & Francine, Marie de Nazareth; Entrée libre 3, 1989 → 5,8907: [R]RTLv 21 (1990) 249s (R. *Guelluy*: soulignent la condition humaine commune).

8762 **Durrwell** François-Xavier, Marie; méditation devant l'Icône. P/Montréal 1990, Médiaspaul/Paulines. 125 p. F 57. 2-7122-0367-X / 2-89039-415-8.

8763 [TE]**Fatica** Luigi, ILDEFONSO di Toledo, La perpetua verginità di Maria: TPatr 84. R 1990, Città Nuova. 160 p. Lit. 15.000. 88-311-3084-6.

8764 [E]**Felici** S., La mariologia nella catechesi dei Padri 1988/9 → 5,8711: [R]Carthaginensia 6 (1990) 229s (F. *Martínez Fresneda*).

8765 *Fiddes* Paul S., Mary in the theology of Karl BARTH: Month 250 (1989) 300-9.

8766 **Forte** Bruno, *a)* Maria, la donna icona del Mistero; saggio di mariologia simbolico-narrativa 1989 → 5,8712: [R]Lateranum 56 (1990) 383-6

(P. *Coda*); RivScR 4 (1990) 584-7 (M. *Semeraro*). – *b*) Maria — Mutter und Schwester des Glaubens [Maria la donna icona], [T]*Huber* Mara. Z 1990, Benziger. 291 p. DM 38. – [R]TGL 80 (1990) 523s (W. *Beinert*).

8767 *Galot* Jean, Presencia de Maria en la vida consagrada [< Vida consagrada desde 1980]. Bogotá 1989, Paulinas. 172 p. – [R]TVida 31 (1990) 217 (T. K. M.).

8767* *Garofalo* S., Maria di Nazareth pellegrina della fede: ➤ 607, Laici 1988/90, 303-321.

8768 **Gebara** I., *Bingemer* María Clara, María, mujer profética 1988 ➤ 5,8720: [R]RET 50 (1990) 343-5 (E. *Tourón*).

8769 **Gebara** I., *Bingemer* M., Mary, mother of God, mother of the poor [deutsch 1988 ➤ 5,8721]. Mkn 1989, Orbis. 96 p. $27; pa. $14. – [R]EcuR 42 (1990) 363s (Bette J. *Ekeya*); ExpTim 102 (1990s) 57s (Deborah F. *Middleton*: can appeal to both Protestants and Catholics: Christianity has moved from being christocentric to being a religion based on christology and mariology); LebZeug 44 (1989) 72s (F. *Courth*); Pacifica 3 (1990) 361-3 (J. *Wilcken*: mixed reaction).

8770 **Gharib** Georges, Testi mariani II. Padri... 1989 ➤ 5,8723: [R]EphMar 40 (1990) 335 (D. *Fernández*).

8771 **Gherardini** Brunero, La Madre; Maria in una sintesi storico-teologica. Frigento AV 1989, Casa Mariana. 492 p. – [R]EuntDoc 43 (1990) 175-7 (D. D. *Composta*); Lateranum 56 (1990) 416 (*ipse*).

8772 **Gironés [-Guillem]** Gonzalo, La humanidad salvada y salvadora; tratado dogmático de la madre de Cristo 1987 ➤ 5,8724: [R]ScripTPamp 22 (1990) 663s (J. L. *Bastero*).

8773 [E]**Gössmann** Elisabeth, *Bauer* Dieter R., Maria — für alle Frauen oder über alle Frauen 1987/9 ➤ 5,669: [R]TGL 80 (1990) 98s (W. *Beinert*).

8774 *Gray* Mary C., Reclaiming Mary; a task for feminist theology: Way 29 (1989) 334-340.

8775 **Gubler** M.-L., Der Name der Jungfrau war Maria; Rückbesinnung auf die biblische Botschaft: Topos-Tb 193. Mainz 1989, Grünewald. 102 p. DM 8,80. 3-7867-1448-7 [NTAbs 34,263].

8776 **Guella** Elói O., As raízes mariológicas em INÁCIO de Antióquia: Teocomunicação 20,87 (1990) 25-32 [< TContext 8/1, 91].

8777 *Herrmann* Teofil, ❷ Pneumatologisches Fundament Mariens Mittlerschaft der Gnaden: ➤ 64, [F]GRZYBEK S. 1990, 94-102; deutsch 102.

8778 [E]**Jegen** Carol F., Mary according to women [Chicago-Mundelein festival 1983; seven women's contemporary interpretation of traditional titles]. KC 1985, Sheed & W. 183 p. $8 [RelStR 17,146, Annabelle S. *Wenzke*].

8779 [E]**Kania** Wojciech, ❷ Ojcowie wspólnej wiary; teksty o Matce Bożej (w. VIII-XI): Beatam me dicent 3. Niepokalanów 1986. 231 p. – [R]AtKap 114 (1990) 502s (J. *Królikowski*).

8780 **Kinsley** David, The goddesses' mirror; visions of the divine from East and West [10 including Mary]. Albany 1989, SUNY. xix-320 p. [RelStR 17,42, Denise L. *Carmody*].

8781 **Kniazeff** Alexis, La Mère de Dieu dans l'Église Orthodoxe: Théologies. P 1990, Cerf. 219 p. – [R]Contacts 32 (1990) 308-312 [J. *M(onchanin)*].

8782 **La Potterie** I. de, Maria in het mysterie van het Verbond[2rev] [[1]1985 Het Mariamysterie ...]: Schrift en Liturgie 8. Bonheiden 1990, Abdij Bethlehem. 301 p.

8783 **La Potterie** I. de, Marie dans le mystère de l'Alliance: JJC 34, 1988
→ 4,9853; 5,8739: REphMar 40 (1990) 163s (S. *Blanco*); MélSR 47 (1990)
166s (M. *Huftier*).

8784 **La Potterie** Ignace de, Maria nel mistero dell'alleanza 1988 → 4,9834;
5,8740: RCC 141 (1990,2) 405s (S. *De Fiores*); Teresianum 40 (1989) 247s
(M. *Caprioli*).

8785 **Laurentin** René, ❷ Matka Pana; krótki traktat teologii maryjnej [1987
→ 5,8741*a* ital.], TProczek Z.: Theotokos 1. Wsz 1989, Marianów. 386 p.
– RAtKap 115 (1990) 341-6 (J. *Królikowski*).

8786 **Laurentin** René, Maryja Matka Odkupiciela [cf. ital. 1988 → 5,8741*b*],
TZeleźnik Tadeusz. Wsz 1988, PAX. 162 p. – RAtKap 114 (1990) 506-8
(J. *Królikowski*).

8787 *Leczkowski* Jerzy, ❷ Mariologia św. Tomasza z AKWINU: STWsz 28,1
(1990) 223-242.

8788 **López Melús** F. M., Maria de Nazareth en el Evangelio 1989 → 5,8745:
RAngelicum 67 (1990) 425s (J. *Salguero*); QVidCr 148s (1989) 233s (P.
Puig).

8789 *López Melús* Francisco M., Los textos bíblicos y el 'Magnificat' en la
encíclica 'Redemptoris Mater': → 644*, *Llamas* E., EstMar 54 (1989)
87-97.

8790 *McHugh* John, The doctrine of the Immaculate Conception; reflections on a problem in ecumenical dialogue [p. 335: 'what I am suggesting
is this: that Mary did in fact truly die ... but because of her Immaculate
Conception, that is because of her holiness and righteousness, this
medical death was not the dreaded visitant...']: Month 250 (1989)
330-336.

8791 **Maggi** Alberto, Nostra Signora degli eretici 1988 → 5,8746: RCC 141
(1990,2) 518 (P. *Vanzan*).

8792 **Maggi** Alberto, Notre Dame des Hérétiques, TMalnoy Marie-Catherine:
Mariologie. P/Montréal 1990, Médiaspaul/Paulines. 206 p.; map. F 99.
2-1122-0357-7 / Canada 2-89039-409-3.

8793 **Maggi** Alberto, Nuestra Señora de los herejes; María y Nazaret: En
torno al NT. Córdoba 1990, Almendro. 189 p.

8794 *a) Malina* Bruce J., Mother and son / 'From Isis to Medjugorje; why
apparitions?'; – *b) Neyrey* Jerome H., Maid and mother in art and
literature; – *c) Pilch* John, Marian devotion and wellness spirituality;
bridging cultures: BibTB 20 (1990) 54-64.76-84 / 65-75 / 85-94.

8795 *a) Malone* Mary T., Mary, mother of God; an educational problem?; –
b) Smith Joanmarie, Feminist spirituality, the way of wisdom; – *c)
Trevett* Christine, Patriarchal structures and religious education: BrJ-
RelEd 12,1 (1989) 15-19 / 11-14 / 6-10 [< ZIT 89,743].

8796 Maria madre di Dio e madre della Chiesa; Cattolici e Testimoni di
Geova [< convegno Roma 1987]. T-Leumann 1989, L.D.C. 200 p. Lit.
15.000. – RPalCl 68 (1989) 511 (G. P. *De Paoli*).

8797 Marie Mère de Dieu, rencontre spirituelle et théologique. Venasque 1988,
Carmel. 327 p.; p. 11-28, *Ponnau* D., Maria von Nazareth; 32-46, *Goedy*
M. de, Es war angebracht, dass die Mutter der Erlöserin eine Jüdin war;
39-72, *La Potterie* I. de, Die Heimsuchung Mariens als Beginn des Neuen
Bundes; 75-99, *Quacquarelli* A., Theologie der Gemeinschaft und Ma-
rienikonologie; 135-145, *Garrigues* J. M., Maria als Eschatologie der
Kirche... [TR 86 (1990) 393s, S. *Napiórkowski*].

8799 **Menvielle** Louis, Marie mère de vie... IRÉNÉE 1986 → 2,6972... 4,9845:
RÉglT 20 (1989) 137-140 (G. *Hudon*).

8800 *Milet* Jean, Étude philosophique; la dévotion à Marie: EsprVie 100 (1990) 129-143 . 150-4.
8801 **Molette** Ch., Maric mémoire de l'Église: Radio ND 1987s. P 1989, Cerf. 325 p. F 119. – ᴿNRT 112 (1990) 260s (L.-J. *Renard*).
8802 **Moltmann-Wendel** Elisabeth, *al.*, Was geht uns Maria an? [< Concilium] 1983/8 → 4,388; 5,8752: ᴿTLZ 115 (1990) 842s (H.-J. *Kühne*).
8803 *Moorhead* John, Mary and the Incarnation: GrOrTR 34 (1989) 347-355.
8804 **Mourophidis** S., ☻ The mother of Jesus in the NT. Athena 1989, Parartima. 207 p. – ᴿDeltio VM 18,2 (1989) 111-4 (S. *Agourides*).
8805 **Napiórkowski** Stanisław C., ☻ Spór o matkę; mariologia jako problem ekumeniczny: diss. Lublin 1988. 188 p. – ᴿAtKap 114 (1990) 312-4 (bp. J. *Wojtkowski*).
8806 *Napolillo* Pasquale, Maria nell'Antico Testamento [... Gn 3,15; Is 7,14]: PalCl 68 (1989) 153-162.
8807 **O'Donnell** Christopher, At worship with Mary; a pastoral and theological study. Dublin 1989, Dominican. 230 p. £13. – ᴿDocLife 39 (1989) 275s (D. *Flanagan*).
8808 *Pascual Torró* Joaquín, La antítesis Eva-María en PRUDENCIO: → 135, ᶠORBE A., Compostellanum 35 (1990) 292-308.
8809 **Perry** N., *Echeverria* L., Under the heel of Mary 1989 → 5,8760; 0-415-01296-1: ᴿExpTim 101 (1989s) 90s (G. *Huelin*: politicized excesses).
8810 **Pikaza** Xabier, La madre de Jesús; introducción a la Mariología: Nueva Alianza 111. S 1989, Sígueme. 411 p. 84-301-1077-1. – ᴿActuBbg 27 (1990) 90s (F. *de P. Solá*); CiTom 117 (1990) 391s (M. *Iribertegui*); CommSev 23 (1990) 298 (J. M. *López*); EstTrin 24 (1990) 309s (J. M. de *Miguel*); Gregorianum 71 (1990) 789s (J. *Galot*); LumenVr 39 (1990) 86-88 (U. *Gil Ortega*); NRT 112 (1990) 428 (R. *Escol*); RET 50 (1990) 341-3 (E. *Tourón*); REspir 49 (1990) 162s (S. *Guerra*).
8811 *Pinho* Arnaldo de, A propósito de tres obras recentes de Mariología [*Ratzinger-Balthasar*, ᵀ1987; *La Potterie* I. de, 1988; *Forte* B. 1989]: HumT 11 (1990) 241-8.
8812 **Räisänen** H., Die Mutter Jesu im NT² [¹1969]: AnFenn B247, 1989 → 5,8766: ᴿSvEx 55 (1990) 139s (A. *Ekenberg*).
8813 *Raineri* Osvaldo, L'effigie di Maria 'Patto di misericordia'; note per un 'Mariale aethiopicum': EphLtg 103 (1989) 92-109.
8814 *Ratzinger* card. Joseph, 'You are full of grace'; elements of biblical devotion to Mary, ᵀ*Koeppel* Josephine: CommND 16 (1989) 54-68.
8815 *Restrepo Posada* J., La virginidad de María; a propósito del libro 'El rostro materno de Dios' del teólogo Leonardo BOFF: Cuestiones Teológicas 1,43s (Medellín 1989) 269-282.
8816 [**Rostagno** S., *al.*] Maria nostra sorella 1988 → 4,9862; 5,8747: ᴿCC 141 (1990,2) 617 (V. *Caporale*); Divinitas 33 (1989) 312s (B. *Gherardini*); TLZ 115 (1990) 615-7 (W. *Nagel*).
8817 — *Fortarel* Marco, La Madonna nella Bibbia in un libro che rifà la gente [Maria nostra sorella 1988 ... delusione e amarezza]: PalCl 69 (1990) 381-5.
8818 *Schümmer* L., Un Réformé parle de Marie: RRéf 61,3 (1990) 1-20 [< NTAbs 35,64].
8819 *Schumacher* Joseph, Das mariologische Konzept in der Theologie der 'römischen Schule' [*Schauf* H. 1938 für *Passaglia* C. und seine Kollegen und Studenten in der Gregoriana c. 1850]: TrierTZ 98 (1989) 207-226.

8819* **Shirley** Edward, The relationship between Christology and Mariology in the writings of Karl RAHNER: diss. Fordham, [D]*Heaney* J. NY 1990. – RelStR 17,192.

8820 *Spencer* M. D., The apparition of Mary [Guadalupe...] in the light of the theology of the Bible [Gn 3,15; Lk 1s; Jn 19,25s; Rev 12]: RRel 48 (1989) 760-773.

8821 **Stirnimann** Heinrich, Marjam; Marienrede an einer Wende. FrS 1989, Univ. xvi-327 p. DM 58. – [R]TGL 80 (1990) 361s (W. *Beinert*).

8822 *Teuma* Edmund, The Blessed Virgin's genealogy in the Qur'ān, an exegetical problem: MeliT 41,1 (1990) 47-52.

8823 *Tourón del Pie* Eliseo, María, oyente y discípula de la palabra: RET 50 (1990) 435-467.

8824 *Yarnold* Edward, Mary and the work of ARCIC: Month 250 (1989) 58-62.

H8.8 *Feminae NT* – **Women in the NT and early Church.**

8825 **Agostinucci** Gianna, *Campanini* Giorgio, La questione femminile; chiesa e storia. CasM c.1989, Piemme. 95 p. Lit. 12.000. – [R]HumBr 45 (1990) 246s (Tina *Leonzi*).

8826 *a) Alexandre* Monique, Immagini di donne ai primi tempi della cristianità; – *b) Georgoudi* Stella, BACHOFEN, il matriarcato e il mondo antico; riflessioni sulla creazione di un mito; [T]*Zaidman* Louise B., ➤ 498, Storia delle donne 1990, 465-513 / 518-536.

8827 **Aspegren** Kerstin, The male woman; a feminine ideal in the early Church: AcU Women in Religion 4. Sto 1990, Almqvist & W. 189 p. 91-554-2598-4.

8827* **Atwood** Richard A., Mary Magdalene in the New Testament gospel and early tradition: diss. [P]*Stegemann*. Basel 1988s. – TR 86,511.

8828 **Avis** Paul, Eros and the sacred. L 1989, SPCK. 166 p. £8. 0-281-04424-4. – [R]ExpTim 102 (1990s) 28 (N. *Slee*: powerful critique of Christianity's attitude to women); TLond 93 (1990) 231 (P. *Baelz*: feminist but not merely; powerful despite a certain breathlessness).

8829 **Aynard** Laure, La Bible au féminin; de l'ancienne tradition à un christianisme hellénisé: LDiv 138. P 1990, Cerf. 326 p. F 170. 2-204-04022-3. – [R]EsprVie 100 (1990) 347-350 (sr. Marie-Geneviève *Missègue*: overgeneralizes); FoiTemps 20 (1990) 475s (Alice *Dermience*); MondeB 65 (1990) 70 (F. *Culdaut*).

8830 [E]**Bader** D., Maria Magdalena; zu einem Bild der Frau in der christlichen Verkündigung: Erzd.Fr. Mü 1990, Schnell & S. 88 p.; 23 pl. 3-7954-0288-3 [< NTAbs 35,256: *Schüngel-Straumann* A., *Jensen* A., *Gössmann* E., *Hofstätter* H. H., *Dirks* M.].

8831 *a) Bernard* Jacques, Quelques notes sur la femme dans la Bible; – *b) Beaurent* Jean-Marie, Femme et homme dans le cœur de Dieu: MélSR 47 (1990) 67-104; Eng. 104 / 105-114; Eng. 114.

8832 **Bonnet** Jacques, Marie-Madeleine et son mystère. Roanne 1988, auct. 149 p. 2-9500-3154-4. – [R]ÉTRel 65 (1990) 277s (D. *Lys*).

8833 *Borsch* Frederick H., Jesus and women exemplars: ➤ 52, [F]FULLER R., AnglTR supp 11 (1990) 29-40.

8834 **Bouyer** Louis, Figures mystiques féminines: Épiphanie. P 1989, Cerf. 186 p. F 74. – [R]RTLv 21 (1990) 250 (R. *Guelluy*: verve parfois agressive).

8835 *Bremmer* J., Why did early Christianity attract upper-class women?: ➤ 5,17, [F]BARTELINK G., Fructus 1989, 37-48.

8836 **Bristow** John T., [Eph 5,22; 1 Tim 2,9-15; 1 Cor 14,33-36] What Paul really said about women 1988 ⇢ 4,9889: ᴿBR 5,3 (1989) 33 (R. B. *Ward*); RExp 87 (1990) 134s (Molly *Marshall-Green*).

8837 ᵀᴱ**Brock** Sebastian P., *Harvey* Susan A., Holy women of the Syrian Orient 1987 ⇢ 3,g352 ... 5,8789: ᴿClasW 83 (1989s) 255s (Gail P. *Corrington*: admirable).

8838 *Burggraf* Jutta, Una contemplazione essenziale dell'immagine cristiana della donna; AnnT 3 (1989) 3-33.

8839 **Byrne** Brendan, Paul and the Christian women 1989 ⇢ 5,8791: ᴿFurrow 40 (1989) 378s (Eleanor *Cunney*); Pacifica 3 (1990) 109-112 (Morna D. *Hooker*: moderate); Tablet 244 (1990) 560 (E. *Flood* is disappointed, ultimately with Catholic living of Scripture).

8840 *Centore* F. F., Thomism and the female body as seen in the Summa Theologiae: Angelicum 67 (1990) 37-56.

8841 *Corrington* Gail P., The milk of salvation; redemption by the mother in late antiquity and early Christianity: HarvTR 82 (1989) 393-413 + 7 pl.

8842 ᴱ**Dautzenberg** G., *al.*, Die Frau im Urchristentum 1983/6 ⇢ 64,393 ... 2,7000: ᴿVoxPa 17 (1989) 949-957 (M. *Marczewski*).

8842* **Davis** Margaret H., [Ct., N.T.] 'Thy maker is thy husband'; the espousal metaphor in seventeenth century New England: diss. Alabama, ᴰ*Johnson* Claudia. 1990. 90-28299. – DissA 51 (1990s) 1612-A.

8843 *Dermience* Alice, *a*) The Bible and feminism [< La foi et le temps 19,6 (1989) 544-570], ᵀᴱ*Jermann* Rosemary: TDig 37 (1990) 215-220; – *b*) Église et féminisme; 1975-1987: FoiTemps 19 (1989) 99-116.

8844 *Dewey* J., Teaching the NT from a feminist perspective: TEdn 26,1 (Vandalia OH 1989) 86-105 [< NTAbs 34,146].

8845 **Donovan** Mary Ann, Sisterhood as power; the past and passion of ecclesial women. NY 1990, Crossroad. 136 p. $17. – ᴿHorizons 17 (1990) 329s (M. Augusta *Neal*: subtitle as above, also in JAAR; but in BIP 'women religious as catalysts of the future').

8846 **Dunfee** Susan N., Beyond servanthood; Christianity and the liberation of women. Lanham MD 1989, UPA. 192 p. $24.75; pa. $14.25. 0-8191-7223-5; -4-3 [RelStR 17, 236, A. *Loades*].

ᴱ**Duperray** Ève, Marie-Madeleine dans la mystique, les arts ... 1988/9 ⇢ 525.

8847 **Fabris** Rinaldo, La femme dans l'Église primitive [1982 ⇢ 64,7588], ᵀ*Garoche* Sylvie, 1987 ⇢ 4,9897; 5,8803: ᴿRTPhil 122 (1990) 433 (Aline *Lasserre*).

8848 **Faricy** Robert, The Lord's dealing; the primacy of the feminine in Christian spirituality 1988 ⇢ 5,8805: ᴿGregorianum 71 (1990) 430 (*ipse*); Horizons 17 (1990) 355s (Joanmarie *Smith*).

8849 *a*) *Farrell* Gerardo T., La mujer en la Iglesia; aspectos pastorales; – *b*) *Marino* Antonio. María, la mujer y la Iglesia; los tres nombres de la humanidad redimida: TArg 26,2 (1989) 55-73 / 35-54.

8850 ᴱ**Gössmann** Elisabeth, Il tempo della donna [GIOVANNI PAOLO II, Mulieris dignitatem]: GdT 195. Brescia 1990, Queriniana. Lit. 8500. – ᴿAsprenas 37 (1990) 379s (G. *Mattai*).

8851 **Grey** Mary, Redeeming the dream; feminism, redemption and Christian tradition. L 1989, SPCK. 209 p. £12. 0-281-04410-4. – ᴿExpTim 102 (1990s) 28 (N. *Slee*).

8852 **Guerra Gómez** Manuel, El sacerdocio femenino (en las religiones greco-romanas y en el cristianismo de los primeros siglos). Toledo 1987, Aldecoa. 619 p. – ᴿEmerita 58 (1990) 167-9 (M. J. *López de Ayala*).

8853 *Guillemette* N., Saint Paul and women: EAPast 26,2 (Manila 1989) 121-133 [< NTAbs 34,48].

8854 *Harrison* Verna E. F., Male and female in Cappadocian theology: JTS 41 (1990) 441-471.

8855 **Heeney** Brian, The women's movement in the Church of England 1850-1930: 1988 ➤ 5,8810: ᴿJEH 40 (1989) 629 (Sheila *Fletcher*).

8856 **Heine** Susanne, Frauen der frühen Christenheit 1986 ➤ 2,7007... 5,8812: ᴿActuBbg 27 (1990) 71-73 (J. *Boada*).

8857 **Heine** Susanne, Women and early Christianity; are the feminist scholars right? 1987 ➤ 4,9902*: ᴿBijdragen 51 (1990) 205s (J. J. *Suurmond*); CritRR 2 (1989) 205-7 (B. *Witherington*); HeythJ 31 (1990) 334-6 (J. *Murphy-O'Connor*: not really a weapon for anti-feminists); Interpretation 44 (1990) 101s (Frances T. *Gench*).

8858 **Hourcade** Janine, La femme dans l'Église 1986 ➤ 2,7069b... 4,9904*: ᴿRTPhil 121 (1989) 233s (Francine *Carrillo*); Téléma 15,3s (1989) 95s (Maryvonne *Duclaux*).

8859 *Ingram* K. J., Good news for modern women; the Gospel of John: SpTod 41 (1989) 305-318.

8860 **Kenneally** James K., The history of American Catholic women. NY 1990, Crossroad. x-286 p. $25 [TS 52, 379, Karen *Kennelly*].

8861 ᴱ**Kennelly** Karen, American Catholic women; a historical exploration: Bicentennial. NY 1989, Macmillan. xviii-231 p. $25. – ᴿNewTR 3,1 (1990) 90-92 (Ann O. *Graff*); TS 51 (1990) 155s (Patricia *Byrne*).

8862 **Kruse** I., Mädchen, wach auf! Frauengeschichten aus dem Neuen Testament [und einer Modern-Israel-Reise]. Stu 1989, Kreuz. 223 p. DM 19,80. 3-7831-0964-7 [NTAbs 34,264].

8863 **Lang** Judith, Ministers of grace; women in the early Church 1989 ➤ 5,8816: ᴿExpTim 101 (1989s) 86s (R. *Butterworth*: not helped by JOHN PAUL II's strained exegesis).

8864 **Lindboe** I. M., Women in the NT, a select bibliography: Bibliog 1. Oslo 1990, Univ. Fac. Theol. 90 p. 82-9919131-9 [NTAbs 35,258].

8865 *MacDonald* Margaret Y., Early Christian women married to unbelievers: SR 19 (1990) 221-234.

8866 **Maillot** A., Marie, ma sœur; la femme dans le Nouveau Testament (et au début du christianisme). P 1990, Letouzey et Âné. 176 p. F 120. 2-7063-0179-1 [NTAbs 35,258].

8867 **Martínez Díez** F., Las mujeres en la Iglesia; iguales en dignidad y corresponsables en la misión. Caracas 1990, Paulinas. 114 p. – ᴿStudium 30 (M 1990) 558s (M. *Fernández*).

8868 **Martini** C. M., Women in the Gospels [La donna nel suo popolo 1987]. NY 1990, Crossroad. 136 p. $10. 0-8245-0986-2 [NTAbs 34,385].

8869 **Mayeski** Marie Anne, Women, models of liberation. KC 1989, Sheed & W. xii-240 p. $13 pa. – ᴿHorizons 17 (1990) 330s (Georgia M. *Keightley*).

8870 **Mazzucco** Clementina, 'E fui fatta maschia' [Perpetua]; la donna nel cristianesimo primitivo; pref. *Corsini* Eugenio: Univ. Torino Fondo Parini-Chirio Lett. 1. F 1989, Lettere. 196 p. – ᴿCivClasCr 11 (1990) 105s (Adriana *Della Casa*); RivStoLR 26 (1990) 180-6 (P. A. *Gramaglia*); SicGymn 43 (1990) 353-5 (F. *Corsaro*).

8870* *Mello* C. M. de, Mary of Bethany — the silent contemplative: RRel 48 (1989) 690-7.

8871 *a) Militello* Cettina, CHIARA e il 'femminile'; – *b) Covi* Ettore, Il femminile nel linguaggio morale di Chiara d'Assisi; – *c) Godet* Jean-François,   Claire et la vie au féminin; symboles de femme dans ses écrits: Laurentianum 31,1s ('Chiara; Francescanesimo al femminilc' 1990) 62-105 / 106-147 / 148-175.

8872 **Moltmann-Wendel** Elisabeth,   Le donne che Gesù incontrò [5]T. Brescia 1989, Queriniana.   166 p.; 18 fig. – RHumT 11 (1990) 372s (A. *Couto*).

8873 **Morosi** E.,   Pagine femminili del Vangelo; donne di fronte a Cristo: Nuovi Sentieri di Emmaus. R 1989, Borla.   147 p. Lit. 15.000.   88-263-0240-7 [NTAbs 35,104].

8874 **Parazzoli** Ferruccio,   Gesù e le donne: Letteratura Biblica 1.   T 1989, Paoline.   119 p.; sketches. Lit. 25.000.   88-315-0196-8 [NTAbs 34,386]. – RPalCl 68 (1988) 1455s, ripetuta 69 (1990) 285 (A. *Pedrini*).

8876 **Pellegrini** Letizia,   Specchio di donna; l'immagine femminile nel XIII secolo; gli 'exempla' di STEFANO di Borbone: Religione e Società 14.   R 1989, Studium.   xxxv-177 p. – RRivStoLR 26 (1990) 385-8 (R. *Valabrega*).

8877 **Pernoud** Régine,   Vrouwen in de middelecuwen; haar politieke en sociale betekenis, TMarez Oyens Eric de.   Baarn 1986, Ambo.   224 p. – RBTAM 14 (1990) 793s (G. H.).

8878 **Pirot** Jean,   Trois amies de Jésus...: Lire la Bible 74, 1986 → 2,7021 ... 5,8826:   RGregorianum 71 (1990) 384s (E. *Farahian*: le débat n'est pas clos).

8879 *Price* R. M.,   Mary Magdalene; Gnostic apostle?:   Grail 6,2 (Waterloo 1990) 54-76 [< NTAbs 35,89].

8880 **Rapley** Elizabeth,   The devotees; women and church in seventeenth-century France.   Montreal 1990, McGill-Queen's Univ.   xxvii-283 p. C$30 [TS 52, 152, J. B. *Collins*].

8881 *Reineke* Martha J.,   'This is my body'; reflections on abjection, anorexia, and medieval women mystics: JAAR 58 (1990) 245-265.

Rigato Maria Luisa,   Le figure femminili Gv 1990 → 5745.

8882 **Russell** Letty M.,   Befreien wir das Wort; feministische Bibelauslegung [1985 → 3,1515], TSchneck Hildegard; Vorw. *Schottroff* Luise.   Mü 1989, Kaiser.   196 p. DM 28.   3-459-01788-0. – RActuBbg 27 (1990) 80s (J. *Boada*).

8883 **Schmidt** Alvin J.,   Veiled and silenced; how culture shaped sexist theology [Jesus taught an equality of women contrary to patriarchal/agrarian culture].   Macon GA 1989, Mercer Univ.   xvii-238 p. $35; pa. $20 [RelStR 17, 139, Frances B. *Sullivan*].

8884 ESchmidt E. R.,   *al.*,   Feministisch gelesen; ausgewählte Bibeltexte für Gruppen und Gemeinden; Gebete für den Gottesdienst.   Stu 1988s, Kreuz.   296; 297 p. je DM 29,80.   3-7831-0909-4; -3 [NTAbs 34,240].

8885 *Schottroff* Luise,   Die mutigen Frauen aus Galiläa und der Auferstehungsglaube: Diakonia 20 (1989) 221-6.

8886 **Schüssler Fiorenza** E.,   En mémoire d'elle 1986 → 2,7025 ... 4,9925: RLVitae 44 (1989) 235s (A. *Godin*).

8887 **Schüssler Fiorenza** E.,   Zu ihrem Gedächtnis 1988 → 5,8836:   RÖkRu 39 (1990) 138-140 (Ruth *Albrecht*).

8888 **Schüssler Fiorenza** Elisabeth,   In memoria di lei; una ricostruzione femminista delle origini cristiane [1985 → 64,7405]: Sola Scriptura 14.   T 1990, Claudiana.   x-397 p. Lit. 45.000.

8889 **Sorge** Elga,   Religion und Frau; weibliche Spiritualität im Christentum.   Stu 1985. – RBTZ 7 (1990) 44-50 (Helga *Kuhlmann*).

8889* **Synek** Eva Maria,   Heilige Frauen in der frühen Christenheit; zu den Frauenbildern in hagiographischen Texten des christlichen Ostens: kath. Diss. DSuttner.   Wien 1989s. – TR 86,511.

8890 *Szafrański* A. Ludwik, ❷ Le diaconesse ed il loro ruolo nella Chiesa primitiva: VoxPa 17 ('Diakonat' 1989) 737-754; ital 755.

8891 **Tepedino** Ana Maria, As discípulas de Jesus. Petrópolis 1990, Vozes. 134 p. [REB 50,495].

8892 *Thraede* K., Zwischen Eva und Maria, das Bild der Frau bei AMBROSIUS und AUGUSTIN auf dem Hintergrund der Zeit: ➤ 715, Frauen 1987/90, 129-139.

8893 *Thraede* K., Ärger mit der Freiheit; die Bedeutung von Frauen in Theorie und Praxis der alten Kirche, ᴱ*Schaffenorth* G., Freunde 1977 [< *Heinen* Heinz, 'Sollte das Christentum in Spanien tatsächlich von Frauen eingeführt worden sein', TrierTZ 98 (1989) 227-9].

8894 **Thurston** Bonnie B., Widows; a women's ministry in the early Church. Mp 1989, Fortress. 96 p. $9. 0-8006-2317-7. – ᴿExpTim 101 (1989s) 313 (S. C. *Barton*); Horizons 17 (1990) 328s (Rea *McDonnell*); Interpretation 44 (1990) 428s (B. *Crawford*: perhaps not so structured an organization); SecC 7 (1989s) 241s (P. F. *Bradshaw*); TS 51 (1990) 368s (Jo Ann *Heaney-Hunter*); TTod 47 (1990s) 106s (B. *Witherington*).

8895 **Wahlberg** Rachel L., Jesus according to a woman 1986 = 1975 ➤ 2,3114: ᴿAsiaJT 2 (1988) 186s (Grisana *Sae Lee*).

8896 **Weinmann** U., Mittelalterliche Frauenbewegungen; ihre Beziehungen zur Orthodoxie und Häresie: Frauen in Geschichte und Gesellschaft 9. Pfaffenweiler 1990, Centaurus. 308 p. DM 38 [RHE 85, p. 269*].

8897 **Witherington** Ben, Women and the genesis of Christianity. C 1990, Univ. xv-273 p. $44.50; pa. $15 [TS 52, 390, Dolores L. *Greeley*: condensation of his W-Ministry and W-Earliest]. – ᴿExpTim 102 (1990s) 184 (Ruth B. *Edwards*: popular condensation by his wife Ann).

8898 **Witherington** Benᴵᴵᴵ, Women in the earliest churches: SNTS Mg 59, 1988 ➤ 4,9939: ᴿCBQ 52 (1990) 368s (S. L. *Davies*: like Paul's letters, 'written in response to one or several opposing parties, but it is never very clear who those parties are or what they believe'); EstB 48 (1990) 281s (F. *Pastor-Ramos*); EvQ 62 (1990) 275-7 (A. G. *Padgett*: good, some reserves); HZ 250 (1990) 386s (W. *Schuller*: völlig ohne Kenntnis der Sachverhalte; RAC 'Frau' unerwähnt...); JBL 109 (1990) 359s (C. *Osiek*); JEH 40 (1989) 586-9 (A. *Cameron*: distinguished, scholarly, fair); JTS 41 (1990) 629-631 (Frances M. *Young*); RB 97 (1990) 127s (J. *Murphy-O'Connor*).

H8.9 *Theologia feminae* – Feminist theology.

8899 *a)* *Amaladoss* M., Women and the future of humanity; – *b)* *Agira* Benedicta L., Communion; role of women: Vidyajyoti 54 (1990) 233-243 / 245-250.

8900 **Aubert** Jean-Marie, L'exil féminin 1988 ➤ 5,8847: ᴿActuBbg 26 (1989) 64 (H. *Vall*).

8901 **Behr-Sigel** Élisabeth, Le ministère de la femme dans l'Église [varia] 1987 ➤ 4,9947; 5,8852: ᴿEcuR 42 (1990) 177s (Janet *Crawford*).

8902 *Behr-Sigel* Elisabeth, L'ordination des femmes; un problème œcuménique: Contacts 32 (1990) 101-127 [224, lettres; 299-303, réponse].

8903 ᴱ**Beinert** Wolfgang, Frauenbefreiung und Kirche; Darstellung — Analyse — Dokumentation 1987 ➤ 4,9948; 5,8853: ᴿTLZ 115 (1990) 134s (U. *Gerber*).

8904 **Bélanger** Sarah, Les soutanes roses; portrait du personnel pastoral féminin au Québec. Montréal 1988, Bellarmin. 296 p. – ᴿSR 19 (1990) 370s (Denise *Beillette*).

8905 **Bennett** Anne M., From woman-pain to woman-vision. Mp 1989, Fortress. 180 p. – ᴿRelStR 16 (1990) 328 (Dawn *De Vries*).

8905* **Benson** Patricia N., Surrender to God; a feminist critique and reinterpretation: diss. Graduate Theological Union, ᴰ*Schneiders* S. Berkeley 1990. 299 p. 91-00261. – DissA 51 (1990s) 2421-A; RelStR 17,192.

8906 *a) Bergin* Helen, *al.*, Sexism ancient and modern; turning a male world upside down; – *b) Field* Barbara L., Betty is a prime number; matching metaphors of priesthood and womanhood: Pacifica 3 (1990) 157-171 / 172-186.

8907 *a)* [Lucchetti] *Bingemer* Maria Clara, 'Como o pai me enviou, eu também vos envio' (a mulher na evangelização); – *b) Taborda* Francisco, Feminismo e teologia feminista no primeiro mundo; breve panorámica para uma primeira informação: PerspTeol 22 (1990) 289-309 / 311-337.

8908 *Blasberg-Kuhnke* Martina, Feministische Theologie; zur Entwicklung und Zukunft der Frauenfrage in Diakonia: Diakonia 20 (1989) 30-35.

8909 *Blomberg* Craig L., Not beyond what is written; a review of Aida SPENCER's Beyond the curse [1985]: CriswTJ 2 (1987s) 403-421.

8910 *Boschman* E., Women's role in ministry in the Church: Direction 18,2 (Fresno 1989) 44-53 [1 Cor 11,3-16; 14,33-40; 1 Tim 2,11-15; Tit 2,3-5; 1 Pt 3,1-7: NTAbs 34,200].

8911 *Brown* Kelly D., God is as Christ does; toward a womanist theology: JRelTht 46,1 (1989) 7-16 [< ZIT 89,708].

8912 *Bruland* Esther B., Evangelical and feminist ethics; complex solidarities: JRelEth 17,2 (1989) 139-160 [< ZIT 90,269].

8913 **Bührig** Marga, Spät habe ich gelernt, gerne Frau zu sein; eine feministische Autobiographie. Stu 1987, Kreuz. 258 p. – ᴿEcuR 42 (1990) 71s (A. J. van der *Bent*) & 72-74 (Susanne *Heine*).

8914 **Byrne** Lavinia, Women before God ➤ 4,9955; 5,8862: ᴿTablet 243 (1989) 1030 (Renée *Haynes*).

8915 *Cahill* Lisa S., Feminist ethics: TS 51 (1990) 49-64.

8916 *Camp* Richard L., From passive subordination to complementary partnership; the papal conception of a woman's place in Church and society since 1878: CathHR 76 (1990) 506-525.

8917 **Cannon** Katie G., Black womanist ethics 1988 ➤ 4,9956; 5,8863: ᴿAnglTR 71 (1989) 333-5 (Anne E. *Patrick*).

8918 **Carr** Anne E., Transforming grace... women's experience 1988 ➤ 4, 9957; 5,8865: ᴿCritRR 2 (1989) 436-8 (S. H. *Ringe*); CurrTMiss 17 (1990) 154 (Faye E. *Schott*); Interpretation 44 (1990) 97s (Marcia *Bunge*).

8919 **Carr** Anne E., Frauen Verändern die Kirche; christliche Tradition und feministische Erfahrung,ᵀ. Gü 1990, Mohn, 320 p. DM 29,80. – ᴿHerdKor 44 (1990) 442s (K. *Nientiedt*).

8920 *a) Carr* Anne, Women, justice, and the Church – *b) Gillis* Chester, Teaching feminist theology; a male perspective: Horizons 17 (1990) 269-279 / 244-255.

8921 **Chittister** Joan, Job's daughters; women and power: Madeleva lectures. NY 1990, Paulist. vi-83 p. $4. 0-8091-3180-3 [TDig 38,51].

8922 **Chopp** Rebecca S., The power to speak; feminism, language, God 1989 ➤ 5,8866: ᴿTTod 47 (1990s) 440. 442. 444 (Cleo M. *Kearns*).

8923 **Christ** Carol P., Laughter of Aphrodite 1987 ➤ 4,9959: ᴿAnglTR 71 (1989) 335-8 (Flora A. *Keshgegian*); Horizons 17 (1990) 175 (Margaret *Brennan*).

8924 *Chrysostomos* bp., Women in the Church; some current issues in perspective: GrOrTR 34 (1989) 119-125.

8925 **Condren** Mary, The serpent and the goddess. SF 1990, Harper & R. 268 p. $14. – ᴿAmerica 162 (1990) 330s (Marie Anne *Mayeski*).

8926 ᴱ**Conn** Joann W., Women's spirituality; resources for Christian development 1986 ➤ 2,289; 3,8930: ᴿHeythJ 31 (1990) 101 (Margaret *Barker*).

8927 *Craig* Kerry M., *Kristjansson* Margret A., Women reading as men / men reading as women; a structural analysis for the historical project: ➤ 365, Semeia 51 (1990) 119-136.

8927* **Culp** Kristine A., Ecclesial connections; ecclesiological construction and a feminist theology of critical vision: diss. ᴰ*Carr* A. Ch 1990. – RelStR 17,192.

8928 *Da Gangi* Bonaventura, Il sacerdozio alle donne: PalCl 68 (1989) 711-724.

8929 *D'Angelo* M.R., Women partners [with each other] in the New Testament: JFemRel 6,1 (Atlanta 1990) 65-86 [< NTAbs 35,57].

8929* **Deifelt** Wanda, Toward a Latin American feminist hermeneutics; a dialogue with the biblical methodologies of E. SCHÜSSLER FIORENZA, P. TRIBLE, C. MESTERS, and P. RICHARD: diss. Northwestern, ᴰ*Ruether* R. Evanston IL 1990. 343 p. 91-14542. – DissA 51 (1990s) 4161-A.

8930 *Delfor Mandrioni* Hector, Para una antropología de la femineidad: TArg 26,1 (1989) 73-110.

8931 *Derroitte* Henri, Le 11ᵉ colloque du CERDIC [Centre d'échanges et de recherches sur la diffusion et l'inculturation du christianisme, 27-31 août 1990]; La femme en mission: RTLv 21 (1990) 514-6.

8932 *DeVries* Dawn, SCHLEIERMACHER's Christmas Eve dialogue [on the Incarnation: *Massey* Marilyn, Feminine soul 1985 p. 136]; bourgeois ideology or feminist theology?: JRel 69 (1989) 169-183.

8933 *Dietrich* Gabriele, On doing feminist theology in South Asia: Kristu Jyoti 6,2 (Bangalore 1990) 26-65 [72-89, *Shanti* Margaret: < TContext 8/2, 118].

8934 *Dijk-Hemmes* Fokkelien van / *Wacker* Marie-Theres, Feministische Theologie und Antijudaismus in den Niederlanden / in der BR: KIsr 5 (1990) 160-7 / 168-178 [➤ a415].

8935 *Donaldson* Mara E., From Womanspririt to Weaving; women and theology, 1979-1989: AnglTR 72 (1990) 240-6.

8936 **Dresen** G., Onschuldfantasieën; Offerzin en heilsverlangen in feminisme en mystiek [kath. diss. Nijmegen 1990, ᴰ*Brinkgreve* C.] Nijmegen 1990, SUN. 335 p. *f*39,50. 90-6168-325-5. – ᴿTsTNijm 30 (1990) [303] 323s (R. *Pattijn*).

8938 *Dunfee* Susan N., Women in ministry; estrangement from ourselves: QRMin 9,2 (1989) 52-74.

8939 **Duquoc** Christian, La femme, le clerc et le laïc; œcuménisme et ministère: Entrée libre 4, 1989 ➤ 5,8879: ᴿRHPR 70 (1990) 493 (A. *Birmelé*: idéologie romaine menace non seulement tout dialogue mais la pérennité même de l'Église catholique); TüTQ 170 (1990) 223s (R. *Puza*).

8940 ᴱ**Eck** Diana L., *Jain* Devaki, Speaking of faith ... women, social change 1983/6 ➤ 4,556: ᴿModT 7 (1990s) 201s (Mary M. *Fulkerson*).

Eckardt A. Roy, Black – woman – Jew; three wars for human liberation 1989 ➤ 8639.

8942 *a*) *Edgar* William, Le ministère pastoral de la femme; – *b*) *Barilier* Roger, Ordination pastorale et autorité du ministère: RRéf 41,1 (1990) 29-35 / 13-28 [< ZIT 90,242].

8943 **Edwards** Ruth B., The case for women's ministry. L 1989, SPCK. ᴿExpTim 101,6 top choice (1989s) 161-3 (C.S. *Rodd*).

8944 *Edwards* Ruth B., ¿Sacerdocio de la mujer? [< What is the theology of women's ministry?: ScotJT 40 (1987) 421-436], ᵀᴱ*Pericas* Rafael M.: SelT 28 (1989) 83-92.

8945 *a) Elizondo* Felisa, La dignidad de la mujer — una reflexión existencial sobre 'Mulieris dignitatem'; – *b) Pintos* Margarita, Mujer y teología feminista: Moralia 11,3 (M 1989) 205-220 / 221-232 [151-272, *al.* < ZIT 89,616].

8946 **Evdokimov** Paul, Die Frau und das Heil der Welt [La femme et le salut du monde 1958; deutsch 1960 unverändert], ᵀ*Flotow* E. von. Moers/ Aschaffenburg 1989, Brendow/Kaffke. 128 p. – ᴿTG1 80 (1990) 97s (W. *Beinert*).

8947 **Ferder** Fran, **Heagle** John, Partnership; women and men in ministry. ND 1989, Ave Maria. 189 p. $7. – ᴿNewTR 3,2 (1990) 116s (M. E. *Hines*); cf. 3/3, 63-70 (K. *Himes*);

8947* **Field** Anne T., Integrating the shadow; a contribution of JUNGIAN psychology to feminist theology: diss. Graduate Theological Union. Berkeley 1990. 248 p. 91-00368. – DissA 51 (1990s) 2422-A.

8948 *Field-Bibb* Jacqueline, Women and ministry; the Presbyterian Church of England: HeythJ 31 (1990) 150-164.

8949 **Fischer** Kathleen, Women at the well; feminist perspectives on spiritual direction. L 1989, SPCK. vi-215 p. £8 pa. – ᴿRelStR 16 (1990) 527 (Frances B. *Sullivan*); TLond 93 (1990) 232 (Elaine *Graham*).

8950 **Flax** Jane, Thinking fragments; psychoanalysis, feminism, and post-modernism in the contemporary west. Berkeley 1990, Univ. California. 272 p. $25. [RelStR 17, 137, Kathryn A. *Rabuzzi:* 'splendid, jargon-free'].

8951 *a) Freitas* Maria Carmelita de, Potencial profético da mulher la-tino-americana na Igreja e na sociedade; – *b) Weiler* Lúcia, Uma leitura feminista da Bíblia; perspectivas hermenêuticas: Convergência 25,230 (RJ 1990) 95-105 / 25,233 (1990) 272-288; Eng. summary TContext 8/1, 121s.

8952 *Gadille* J., Mission chrétienne et cultures: RHE 85 (1990) 705-719.

8953 **Gerl** Hanna-Barbara, Die bekannte Unbekannte; Frauenbilder in der Kultur und Geistesgeschichte 1988 → 5,8887: ᴿLebZeug 44 (1989) 73s (Lina *Börsig-Hover*).

8954 *Giardini* Fabio, The 'femininity' [cover and p. 615 'feminility'] of Christian holiness according to 'Mulieris dignitatem' of JOHN PAUL II: Angelicum 67 (1990) 539-554.

8955 **Goldenburg** Naomi R., Returning words to flesh; feminism, psycho-analysis, and the resurrection of the body. Boston 1990, Beacon. viii-255 p. $20. [RelStR 17, 234, Susanne *Pangerl*]. 0-8070-6738-5.

8956 **Goričeva** T., Hiobs Töchter, ᵀ*Butz* B. 1988 → 5,8890: ᴿOstkSt 38 (1989) 57 (H. M. *Biedermann*).

8957 **Goritcheva** Tatiana, Filles de Job; les féministes de 'Maria' [1988 deutsch], ᵀ: Vie des hommes. P 1989, Nouvelle Cité. 156 p. F 79. – ᴿÉtudes 372 (1990) 428 (Agnès *Auschitzka*).

8958 **Góricheva** Tatiana, Hijas de Job. Barc 1989, Herder. 154 p. – ᴿLu-menVr 39 (1990) 344 (F. *Ortiz de Urtaran*); PerspT 22 (1990) 261-3 (F. *Taborda*); RTLim 24 (1990) 314s (Hanni *Rolfes*).

8959 **Halkes** Catharina J. M., Gott hat nicht nur starke Söhne; Grundzüge einer feministischen Theologie, ᵀ*Krattiger-van Grinsven* U. B 1988, Ev.-V. [Mohn]. 140 p. – ᴿTLZ [109 (1984) 561-3] 115,58.

8960 **Hampson** Daphne, Theology and feminism. Ox 1990, Blackwell. 188 p. £35; pa. £10. 0-631-14934-0; 4-9. – ᴿExpTim 102,2, 2d-top choice (1990s) 34s (C. S. *Rodd*: self-styled 'post-Christian feminist' but not strident).

8961 **Hardesty** Nancy A., Inclusive language in the Church 1987 ➤ 3,8960: RPacifica 3 (1990) 103-5 (Pauline *Smith*).

8962 **Haughton** Rosemary, A libertação da mulher, T. Petrópolis 1990, Vozes. 166 p. [REB 50,495].

8963 **Hauke** Manfred, Women in the priesthood? [D1981, ²1986] T1988 ➤ 5,8896: RScEsp 42 (1990) 366-8 (B. de *Margerie*: capital, exhaustif).

8964 **Heine** Susanne, *a*) Christianity and the Goddess; systematic criticism of a feminist theology, T*Bowden* J. L c. 1989, SCM. £7. – RTablet 243 (1989) 1030 (Renée *Haynes*). – [= ?] *b*) Women and early Christianity; are the feminist scholars right? T*Bowden* John. SCM £7. – RTablet 243 (1989) 726-8 (Jennifer *Dines*: clumsy).

8965 *Heine* S., Brille der Parteilichkeit [*Schüssler Fiorenza* E.]; zu einer feministischen Hermeneutik: EvKomm 23 (1990) 354-7 [< NTAbs 35,10].

8966 *Hendrickx* Marie, Un autre féminisme?: NRT 112 (1990) 67-79.

8967 **Heyward** Carter, E*Davis* Ellen C., Speaking of Christ; a Lesbian feminist voice. NY 1989, Pilgrim. 93 p. – RRelStR 16 (1990) 327s (Heidi M. *Ravven*).

8968 E**Hogan** June S., Gender matters; women's studies for the Christian community. GR 1990, Zondervan Academic. 304 p. [RelStR 17, 139, Frances B. *Sullivan*].

8969 *Horne* Brian, L'ordination des femmes à la prêtrise; réponse théologique au second Rapport de la Chambre des évêques: Istina 34 (1989) 129-132 (–181, *al.*).

8970 **Janetzky** Birgit, *al.*, Aufbruch der Frauen; Herausforderung und Perspektiven feministischer Theologie. Münster 1989, Liberación. 188 p. DM 24,80. – REvKomm 23 (1990) 349 (Reinhild *Traitler*); TGL 80 (1990) 362 (W. *Beinert*).

8971 *a*) *Jantzen* Grace M., Who needs feminism?; – *b*) *Coakley* Sarah, Creaturehood before God, male and female; – *c*) *Primavesi* Anne, The part for the whole? an ecofeminist inquiry; – *d*) *Hampson* Daphne, Where do we go from here?: TLond 93 (1990) 339-343 / 343-354 / 355-362 / 373-380.

8972 **Kamphaus** Franz, Bischof, Mutter Kirche und ihre Töchter. FrB 1989, Herder. 127 p. – RNatGrac 37 (1990) 129s (A. *Villalmonte*).

E**Keay** Kathy, Men, women and God 1985/7 ➤ 1613.

8973 *Kimel* Alvin F.J, The Holy Trinity meets Ashtoreth; a critique of the Episcopal 'inclusive' liturgies: AnglTR 71 (1989) 25-47 [< ZIT 89,433].

8974 *Kinder* Donald, CLEMENT of Alexandria; conflicting views on women: SecC 7 (1989s) 213-220.

8975 **King** Ursula, Women and spirituality; voices of protest and promise 1989 ➤ 5,8908*; RTLond 93 (1990) 169s (Monica *Furlong*).

8975* **Lacocque** André, The feminine unconventional: OvBT. Mp 1990, Fortress. xvi-144 p. [CBQ 53,358].

8976 *Lagerwerf* Leny, African women doing theology; a survey: Exchange 19,1 (1990) 1-69; summary TContext 84, 122 (no address p. 10).

8977 *Latham* Jackie, Male and female he created them... not masculine and feminine [distinction (unexplained) presumably in reference to JOHN PAUL II's (translator's) 'personal resources of femininity are not inferior to personal resources of masculinity']: Month 250 (1989) 384-7.

8977* *Legrand* H., 'Traditio perpetuo servata?' La non-ordination des femmes; tradition ou simple fait historique?: ➤ 65*, FGy P., Rituels 1990, 393-416.

8978 *Leonard* Ellen, *a*) Experience as a sources for theology; a Canadian and feminist perspective: SR 19 (1990) 143-162; – *b*) Women and Christ; toward inclusive Christologies: TorJT 6 (1990) 266-285.

8979 *Letham* Robert, The man-woman debate; theological comment [Gn 1,26; 'the feminist movement within the Church is incompatible with the historic Christian doctrines of God and man']: WestTJ 52 (1990) 65-78.

8980 *Liefeld* W., Women and the nature of ministry: JBibEq 2 (Lakewood CO 1990) 1-15 [< NTAbs 35,198].

8980* **Lindsey** Judy Ann, Preaching through the eyes of Eve; feminine experience and biblical hermeneutics: diss. ᴰ*Trotter* J. Claremont 1990. 127 p. 90-34158. – DissA 51 (1990s) 2410-A.

8981 **Loades** Ann, Searching for lost coins 1987 ➔ 4,a13; 5,8914: ᴿRelSt 25 (1989) 538s (R. H. *Bell*: a gentle voice); ScotJT 43 (1990) 134-6 (Mary *Hayter*).

8981* **Lorentzen** Lois Ann, The production of life; a feminist theology of work: diss. Univ. S. California, ᴰ*Briggs* Sheila. – DissA 51 (1990s) 198-A.

8982 *Luamba* Nkebi, Le ministère des femmes dans l'Église kimbanguiste: MélSR 47 (1990) 171-188; Eng. 189.

8983 **McDannell** Colleen, The Christian home in Victorian America, 1840-1900. Bloomington 1986, Indiana Univ. xvii-193 p. $25. – ᴿJRel 69 (1989) 251s (Ann *Braude*: follow-up to the home-centered ideology that linked motherhood and morality in Barbara WELTER's 'Cult of true womanhood', American Quarterly 1966).

8984 **MacKinnon** Catharine A., Toward a feminist theory of the State. CM 1989, Harvard. xvii-330 p. $25 [RelStR 17, 134, Kathryn A. *Rabuzzi*: rightly: 'objectivity' is a misleading construct masking male-centeredness as aperspectivalism].

8985 **Martin** Faith, Call me blessed; the emerging Christian woman. GR 1988, Eerdmans. 180 p. 0-8028-0302-4. – ᴿScotBEv 7 (1989) 66s (Shirley A. *Fraser*: better than the cover and title).

8986 *Meier* John P., On the veiling of hermeneutics (1Cor 11:2-16) [< CBQ 40 (1978) 212-226; really on the 1977 Vatican document on ordination of women; afterword p. 312]: ➔ 271, Mission of Christ 1990, 291-314.

8987 **Meyer-Wilmes** Hedwig, Rebellion auf der Grenze; Ortsbestimmung feministischer Theologie [Diss. ᴰ*Häring* H. – TsTNijm 30, 191]: Frauenforum. FrB 1990, Herder. 288 p. DM 32. 3-451-21821-6. – ᴿNRT 112 (1990) 777s (L. *Renwart*); Salesianum 52 (1990) 751s (M. *Midali*).

8987* **Michael** Magali C., Feminism and the postmodern impulse; Doris LESSING, Marge PIERCY, Margaret ATWOOD, and Angela CARTER: diss. Emory, ᴰ*Johnston* J. Atlanta 1990. 132 p. 90-27929. – DissA 51 (1990s) 1609-A.

8988 **Migoras** José L., Mujer, ensayo teológico: Nuevos Horizontes 1. Lima 1990, Paulinas. 334 p. – ᴿRTLim 24 (1990) 447s (M. *Díaz Mateos*).

8989 **Miles** Margaret M., Carnal knowing; female nakedness and religious meaning in the Christian West. Boston 1989, Beacon. xx-259 p.; ill. $25. – ᴿRelStR 16 (1990) 328 (Kathryn A. *Rabuzzi*).

8990 **Minh-ha Trinh** T., Woman, native, other; writing postcoloniality and feminism. Bloomington 1989, Indiana Univ. viii-173 p.; ill. [RelStR 17, 134, Kathryn A. *Rabuzzi*: lucid, jargon-free, poststructuralist].

8991 ᴱ**Moll** Helmut, The Church and women, a compendium [reprints] 1988 ➔ 5,492: ᴿAnnTh 4 (1990) 217-221 (E. *Juliá*).

8992 **Moltmann-Wendel** Elisabeth, Wenn Gott und Körper sich begegnen; feministische Perspektiven zur Leiblichkeit. Gü 1989, Mohn. 158 p. DM 24,80. – ᴿEvKomm 23 (1990) 351 (Reinhild *Traitler*).

8993 *Moltmann-Wendel* Elisabeth, Zur Kreuzestheologie heute; gibt es eine feministische Kreuzestheologie?: EvT 50 (1990) 546-557.

8993* **Mourao** Maria M. M., Nuns' stories, nuns' voices; resistance at the margins of patriarchal ideology: diss. Illinois, ^D*Smarr* Janet. Urbana 1990. 329 p. 91-14353. – DissA 51 (1990s) 4112-A.

8994 *Nasimyu-Wascke* sr. Anne, La polygamie devant une critique féministe; pour une profonde transformation des mentalités et des structures, ^T*Duclaux* Maryvonne: Téléma 15, 3s (1989) 60-72.

8995 **Noddings** Nel, Women and evil. Berkeley 1989, Univ. California. 293 p. $25. – ^RTS 51 (1990) 361-3 (Karen *Lebacqz*).

8996 *Okure* Teresa, A theological view of women's role in promoting cultural / human development: AfER 39 (1989) 362-7.

8997 **O'Neill** M., Women speaking — women listening; women in inter-religious dialogue. Mkn 1990, Orbis. 131 p.

8998 **Pascoe** Peggy, Relations of rescue; the search for female moral authority in the American West, 1874-1939. NY 1990, Oxford-UP. 301 p. $30 [(JAAR 58,327)].

8999 *Phan* Peter C., Gender roles in the history of salvation; man and woman in the thought of Paul EVDOKIMOV: HeythJ 31 (1990) 53-66.

9000 *Pintos* Margarita [*al.*]., Mujer y teología feminista: Moralia 11,3 ('La mujer, realidad y promesa' 1989) 221-232 [151-272].

9001 *Pires Lopes* F., Igreja também feminina: Brotéria 130 (1990) 408-418.

9002 *Podles* Mary E. & Leon J., The feminine and universal salvation [advocated by BALTHASAR against AUGUSTINE]: America 163 (1990) 294-6.

9003 **Procter-Smith** Marjorie, In her own rite; constructing feminist liturgical tradition. Nv 1990, Abingdon. 189 p. $12. – ^RTTod 47 (1990s) 486 (Christine M. *Smith*); Worship 64 (1990) 551s (Gail *Ramshaw*).

9004 **Raming** Ida, Frauenbewegung und Kirche; Bilanz eines 25-jährigen Kampfes für die Gleichberechtigung und Befreiung der Frau seit dem 2. Vatikanischen Konzil. Weinheim 1989, Deutscher Studien-V. 179 p. DM 24. – ^RTGL 80 (1990) 216s (W. *Beinert*: all but p. 15-37 on ordaining women, her 1973 diss.).

9005 Reading the Bible as black women. 198.../6. 12 art. – ^RAsiaJT 2 (1988) 192s (Lydia N. *Niguidula* names no woman or other as author of any of the articles discussed).

9006 **Rinaldi** B., Femministe nordiche e vescovi romani. Clusone 1989, C. Ferrari. 191 p.; 10 fig. Lit. 15.000 [NRT 112, 937, A. *Toubeau*].

9007 *Rousseau* Mary F., Pope JOHN PAUL II's Letter on the dignity and vocation of women; the call to *communio*: CommND 16 (1989) 212-232.

9008 *Ruether* Rosemary R., Feminist theology in global context: In God's Image (Hong Kong, Dec. 1990) 4-7 [< TContext 8/2, 118].

9009 **Ruether** Rosemary R., Unsere Wunden heilen, unsere Befreiung feiern; Rituale in der Frauenkirche. Stu 1988, Kreuz. 319 p. DM 29,80 pa. – ^RBLtg 62 (1989) 123s (Birgit *Jeggle-Merz*).

9010 ^E**Schaumberger** C., *Schottroff* Luise, Schuld und Macht; Studien zu einer feministischen Befreiungstheologie 1987/8 → 5,738*: ^RBTZ 7 (1990) 39-44 (Helga *Kuhlmann* zu Schottroff über Gn 3).

9011 **Schmetterer** Eva, 'Was ist die Frau, dass du ihrer gedenkst?' Eine systematisch-dogmatische Untersuchung zum hermeneutischen Ansatz feministischer Theologie [Diss. Wien, ^D*Schulte* R.]. Fra 1989, Athenäum. 261 p. – ^RTGL 80 (1990) 363 (W. *Beinert*).

9013 *Schottroff* Luise, Die Herren wahren den theologischen Besitzstand; zur Situation feministisch-theologischer Wissenschaft [MOHR Wilma 1987]:

EvKomm 23 (1990) 347s [-354, *Traitler* Reinhild (10 Bücher), 354-6 (SCHÜSSLER–FIORENZA E.)].

9014 **Schüssler Fiorenza** Elisabeth, *a*) Bread not stone; the challenge of feminist biblical interpretation 1986 → 1,8622...3,9023; now also E 1990, Clark. xxv-182 p. £10. 0-567-29184-7. – ᴿExpTim 102 (1990s) 184 (Ruth B. *Edwards*). – *b*) Changing the paradigms: ChrCent 107 (1990) 796-800 [< NTAbs 35,10].

9015 *Scorsone* Suzanne, In the image of God; male, female, and the language of the liturgy: CommND 16 (1989) 139-151.

9016 **Scott** Joan W., Gender and the politics of history. NY 1988, Columbia. xii-242 p. – ᴿHistTheor 29 (1990) 71-82 (W. H. *Sewell*).

9017 *Segalla* Giuseppe, L'ermeneutica biblica femminista di E. SCHÜSSLER FIORENZA [In memoria di lei, ᵀ*Corsani Comba* M. 1990 → 8888: originalità, forza retorica, contraddizioni]: StPatav 37 (1990) 385-399.

9017* **Siegele-Wenschkewitz** Leonore, Studien zur protestantischen Universitätstheologie und zur feministischer Theologie im 20. Jh.: Hab.-Diss. ᴰ*Stoodt*. Fra 1989s. – TR 86 (1990) 509.

9018 **Soberal** José Dimas, O ministério ordenado da mulher, ᵀ*Luiz Schmitz* Ilton: Mulher. São Paulo 1989, Paulinas. 370 p. – ᴿPerspT 21 (1990) 406-410 (F. *Taborda*).

9019 *a*) *Stenger* Mary-Ann, Feminism and pluralism in contemporary theology; – *b*) *Bouchard* Guy, L'homme n'est pas l'humain: LavalTP 46 (1990) 291-305 / 307-315.

9020 **Thistlewaite** Susan, Sex, race, and God; Christian feminism in black and white. NY 1989, Crossroad. vii-184 p. $20. – ᴿTS 51 (1990) 792s (Diana L. *Hayes*).

9021 *Tolbert* M. A., Protestant feminists and the Bible; on the horns of a dilemma: UnSemQ 43 (1989) 1-17 [< NTAbs 34,150].

9022 ᴱ**Tolhurst** James, Man, woman, and priesthood. 1989, Gracewing. xvi-225 p. £8. 0-85244-162-2. – ᴿExpTim 102 (1990s) 190 (Ruth B. *Edwards*: 7 crude articles against priesthood of women); TLond 93 (1990) 420s (A. *Webster*: God writes straight even with women ministers).

9023 *Umeagudosu* Margaret A., Women in Igbo [Nigeria] Christian churches: AfTJ 18 (Tanzania 1989) 209-223.

9024 **Van Buren** Jane S., The modernist madonna; semiotics of the maternal metaphor. Bloomington 1989, Indiana Univ. xvii-215 p. – [RelStR 17, 135, Kathryn A. *Rabuzzi*: 'enormously' helpful].

9025 *a*) *Vesely* Etna, – *b*) *Fuček* Ivan, Mulieris dignitatem, significance / theological accents. ObnŽiv 44 (1989) 45-57. 58-66 in Croatian; Eng. 57,66. [294-307, *Gruenfelder* Anna-M., deutsch 307s].

9026 *Walter* Tony, Why are most churchgoers women? [the fact is undeniable, but the percentages are slight, some 55 to 45 in Anglican and Roman Catholic England, where the overall percentage of women to men is 51-49 (notably more both in Scotland/Wales churches and in nonconformist churches); the sociologists ought to try to answer but don't]: VoxEvca 20 (1990) 73-90.

9027 *Weaver* Mary Jo, Empowered by an alternative tradition; women's options in an uncongenial Church: Listening 25,1 (1990) 86-100 [< ᴢɪᴛ 90,308].

9028 **Welch** Sharon D., A feminist ethic of risk. Ph 1990, Fortress. 216 p. $10 [JAAR 58,539]. – ᴿTTod 47 (1990s) 458-460 (Lisa S. *Cahill*).

9029 *Wojciechowski* Tadeusz, Könnte eine Frau katholischer Priester werden?: AnCracov 20 (1988) 299-308 [< ᴢɪᴛ 89,431].

9030 **Young** Pamela D., Feminist theology / Christian theology; in search of method. Mp 1990, Fortress. 132 p. – RNRT 112 (1990) 937 (A. *Toubeau*: pas réussie).

H9 **Eschatologia NT,** *spes,* **hope.**

9031 **Aliquò** Pietro, Nati per essere felici; elementi di escatologia cristiana. Messina 1989, Ignatianum. 216 p. Lit. 14.000. – RCC 141 (1990,4) 513 (G. *Mucci*: fresca spontaneità di un inno alla vita; riserve sull'inferno).
9031* **Alves** Rubem, Je crois en la résurrection du corps; méditations: Épiphanie. P 1990, Cerf. 91 p. F 57. – REsprVie 100 (1990) 622s (P. *Jay*: psychanalyste Réformé).
9032 **Ancona** Giovanni, Il significato cristiano escatologico della morte [diss. Pont. Univ. Lateran., DBordoni M.]: Corona Lateranensis 38. R 1990, Univ. Lateranense. 204 p. Lit. 25.000. – RAsprenas 37 (1990) 504-6 (S. *Cipriani*); RivScR 4 (1990) 577-9 (M. *Semeraro*).
9033 **Badham** P. & L., Death and immortality in the religions of the world 1987 → 3,377; 4,a54: RJRel 69 (1989) 142s (P. *Knecht*).
9034 EBecker Hansjakob, *al.*, Im Angesicht des Todes, ein interdisziplinäres Kompendium 1s: Pietas Liturgica 3s, 1982/7 → 4,523: 3-88096-283-9; -4-7: RBijdragen 51 (1990) 331s (G. *Rouwhorst*); TR 86 (1990) 488-491 (B. *Kranemann*).
9035 *Birou* Alain, Histoire et eschatologie; propos pour notre temps: RThom 90 (1990) 409-435.
9036 **Blamires** Harry, Knowing the truth about heaven and hell. AA 1988, Servant. 160 p. $8. – RHomPast 90,2 (1989s) 77-79 (S. *Donnelly*).
9037 **Bordoni** M., *Ciola* N., Gesù nostra esperanza, saggio di escatologia 1988 → 4,a62; 5,8977: RCarthaginensia 6 (1990) 220s (P. *Martínez Fresneda*); Salmanticensis 36 (1989) 251s (J. L. *Ruiz de la Peña*).
9038 **Bourgeois** Henri, La mort, sa signification chrétienne: L'horizon du croyant. P 1988, Desclée. 182 p. – RMélSR 47 (1990) 117s (M. *Huftier*).
9038* *Bourgeois* H., Purgatoire: → 833, Catholicisme 13, 55 (1989) 304-314 (-315, *David-Danel* M. L., iconographie).
9039 *Bridger* Francis, Ecology and eschatology; a neglected dimension [... the greening of eschatology]: TyndB 41 (1990) 290-301.
9040 *Brom* L. J. van den, Eschatologie als theologisch laboratorium — een illustratie: KerkT 40 (1989) 102-125.
9041 *Bruce* F. F., Eschatology; understanding the End of Days: BR 5,6 (1989) 43s.
9042 **Bultmann** Rudolf, Storia ed escatologia [Gifford Lectures 1957],T; post-fazione *Rizzi* Armido: GdT 190. Brescia 1989, Queriniana. 220 p. – RLateranum 56 (1990) 382s (G. *Ancona*).
9043 — **Boschini** P., Escatologia senza storia; storicismo e antistoricismo nel pensiero di R. BULTMANN: Ermeneutica e fenomenologia 4. Bo 1988, Coop. Libr. Univ. 179 p. Lit. 20.000 [NTAbs 33,375].
9044 — *Pelser* G.M.M., R. Bultmann se ontmitologisering van die Nuwe-Testamentiese eskatologie: HervTS 45 (1989) 815-842 [< NTAbs 35,9].
9045 *Campbell-Jack* W. C., Common grace and eschatology: ScotBEv 7 (1989) 100-115.
9046 **Ciccarese** Maria Pia, Visioni dell'aldilà in Occidente: BiblPatr 8, 1987 → 3,9064: RSalesianum 52 (1990) 756 (S. *Felici*).
9047 **Cooper** John W., Body, soul, and life everlasting 1989 → 5,8984: RBS 147 (1990) 489s (F. R. *Howe*); TTod 47 (1990s) 228 (R. A. *Muller*).

9048 *Crouzel* Henri, *a*) Mort et immortalité chez Origène; – *b*) L'apocatastase chez Origène: ➤ 217, Fins dernières 1990, I [< BLitEc 79 (1978)] 19-38. 91-96. 181-196] / XII [< ᴱ*Lies* L., Origeniana Quarta 1985/7] 282-290.

9049 *a*) *Cunningham* Agnes, From strangers to citizens; eschatology in the patristic era; – *b*) *Fackre* Gabriel, Eschatology and systematics; – *c*) *Yoder* John H., Ethics and eschatology; – *d*) *Weber* Timothy, Happily at the edge of the abyss; popular premillennialism in America: ➤ 531, ExAud 6 (1990) 73-85 / 101-117 / 119-127 / 87-100.

9050 *Di Sante* Carmine, Il messianismo [come sinonimo di speranza, p. 421]; tra l'attesa e la realizzazione: RasT 31 (1990) 421-432.

9051 *Downing* V. K., The doctrine of regeneration in the second century: EvRT 14,2 (1990) 99-112 [< NTAbs 35,88: glorification after death is one stage in a process already begun].

9052 **Druet** F.-X., Language, images et visages de la mort chez Jean CHRY-SOSTOME: Fac.ph/ʟ Namur 74; ÉtClas Coll. 3. Namur 1990, ÉtClas/Univ. xxiii-474 p. Fb 2600; pa. 2200. 2-87037-170-5. – ᴿMuséon 103 (1990) 383 (J. *Mossay*); NRT 112 (1990) 926s (S. *Hilaire*); RSPT 74 (1990) 634-6 (G.-M. de *Durand*); RTAM 57 (1990) 285s (Anne-Marie *Guillaume*).

9053 **Durst** Michael, Die Eschatologie des HILARIUS 1987 ➤ 3,9069 ... 5,8992: ᴿColcT 59,1 (1989) 177s (J. *Gliściński*); TLZ 115 (1990) 757 (H.-G. *Thümmel*).

9054 **Duval** Yvette, Auprès des saints corps et âme; l'inhumation 'ad sanctos' dans la chrétienté d'Orient et d'Occident du IIIᵉ au VIIᵉ siècle. P 1988, Ét. Aug. XV-230 p.; 3 pl. – ᴿJTS 41 (1990) 257s (G. *Gould*).

9055 **Escribano-Alberca** Ignacio, Eschatologie, von der Aufklärung bis zur Gegenwart: HbDg 4/7d, 1987 ➤ 3,9073; 4,a76: ᴿTPhil 65 (1990) 280-3 (M. *Kehl*); TR 86 (1990) 38-40 (G. *Greshake*: Reserven).

9055* **Fairchild** Mark R., Eschatology in the Q source: diss. Drew, ᴰ*Doughty* D. Madison ɴᴊ 1989. 249 p. 90-14363. – DissA 51 (1990s) 196-A; RelStR 17,194.

9056 *Fernández Ardanaz* Santiago, El problema de la muerte en el diálogo cristianismo-helenismo del s. II: ScripV 37 (1990) 43-116.

9057 **Fernández García** Bonifacio, Cristo de esperanza; la cristología esca-tologica de J. MOLTMANN. S 1988, Univ. 323 p. 84-7299-208-X. – ᴿCla-retianum 30 (1990) 466s (J. *Rovira*); EstE 65 (1990) 472-4 (A. *Tornos*).

9058 **Finger** Thomas N., Christian theology, an eschatological approach [I. 1985 ➤ 2,7164]; II. Scottdale ᴘᴀ 1989, Herald. 544 p. $30 [CBQ 52,588].

9059 ᴱ**Gardiner** Eileen, Visions of heaven and hell before Dante. NY 1989, Italica. xxix-286 p.; ill. $17.50. – ᴿSpeculum 65 (1990) 986-8 (S. *Botterill*).

9060 **Gourgues** Michel, A vida futura segundo o Novo Testamento, ᵀ*Ferreira* I.F.L.: Cadernos bíblicos 43. São Paulo 1986, Paulinas. 82 p. 85-05-00549-X. – ᴿPerspT 20 (1988) 258-260 (J. B. *Libânio*).

9061 **Greshake** G., *Kremer* J., Resurrectio 1986 ➤ 2,7167 ... 5,9003: ᴿPerspT 22 (1990) 256-9 (J. B. *Libânio*).

9061* **Grayson** Bobby K., Is reincarnation compatible with Christianity? A historical, biblical, and theological evaluation: diss. SW Baptist Theol. Sem. 1989. 2328 p. [? DissA 51 (1990s) 188-A]. 90-14715.

9062 *Gurjewitsch* Aaron J., Die Darstellung von Persönlichkeit und Zeit in der mittelalterlichen Kunst und Literatur (in Verbindung mit der Auffassung vom Tode und des Jenseits): ArKulturG 71 (1989) 1-44.

9063 **Hällström** Gunnar af, Carnis resurrectio 1988 ➤ 5,9003: ᴿSecC 7 (1989s) 237-9 (W. S. *Babcock*).

9064 *Hannah* Vern A., Death, immortality and resurrection; a response to John YATES, 'The origin of the soul': EvQ [61 (1989) 121-140] 62 (1990) 241-251.

9065 *Hatcher* Brian A., Eternal punishment and Christian missions; the response of the Church Missionary Society to broad church theology: AnglTR 72 (1990) 39-61.

9066 **Hayes** Zachary, Visions of a future; a study of Christian eschatology: New Theology 8. Collegeville MN 1989, Glazier. 213 p. $15 pa. 0-89453-742-3. – ᴿExpTim 102 (1990s) 57 (D. *Fergusson*); TS 51 (1990) 568s (B.T. *Viviano* says that what makes this an ideal textbook is its 'perfect theological poise', but does not spell out what 'perfect theological poise' is).

9067 **Hellemo** Geir, Adventus Domini; eschatological thought in 4th-century apses and catecheses [diss. Oslo 1985], ᵀ*Waaler* Elinor R.: VigChr supp. 5.   Leiden 1989, Brill.   xxiv-309 p.; 47 fig. $75.   90-04-08836-9. – ᴿRelStR 16 (1990) 347 (J. J. *Yiannias*).

9068 *Herms* Eilert, SCHLEIERMACHERS Eschatologie nach der zweiten Auflage der 'Glaubenslehre': TZBas 46 (1990) 97-123.

9069 **Hummel** Reinhart, Reinkarnation; Weltbilder des Reinkarnationsglaubens und das Christentum 1988 ➤ 5,9005: ᴿTPhil 65 (1990) 293s (M. *Kehl*).

9070 *Jankowski* Augustyn, ❷ Continuum eschatologicum — notio utilis in theologia Novi Testamenti: ➤ 64, ᶠGRZYBEK S. 1990, 126-139; lat. 139.

9071 *Kees* R., Unsterblichkeit und Tod; zur Spannung zweier anthropologischer Grundaussagen in GREGOR von Nyssa, Oratio Catechetica: ➤ 603, Stud./Nyss. 1990, 211-231.

9072 **Kehl** Medard, Eschatologie 1988; ¹1986 ➤ 2,7179 ... 5,9007: ᴿCarthaginensia 6 (1990) 227 (F. *Martínez Fresneda*); Orientierung 54 (1990) 220-3 (G. *Bachl*: 'von der Rechenschaft unserer Hoffnung').

9073 **Kenel** Sally A., Mortal gods; Ernest BECKER [on our denial of death] and fundamental theology. Lanham MD 1988, UPA. 226 p.   ᴿJRel 69 (1989) 419s (Bonnie *Miller-McLemore*).

9074 **König** Adrio, The eclipse of Christ in eschatology 1989 ➤ 5,9008: ᴿCriswT 4 (1989s) 415-7 (D. E. *Lanier*); HorBT 12,1 (1990) 92-94 (D. A. *Hagner*); TS 51 (1990) 277 (Z. *Hayes*).

9075 **Kramer** K.P., The sacred art of dying; how world religions understand death 1988 ➤ 5,9009: ᴿNRT 112 (1990) 285 (J. *Masson*); TLZ 115 (1990) 801s (P. *Heidrich*).

9076 **Kugelmann** L., Antizipation [eschatologische Predigt Jesu ...], eine begriffsgeschichtliche Untersuchung [ᴰ*Pannenberg* W.]: ForSystÖ 50. Gö 1986, Vandenhoeck & R. 374 p. DM 74, 3-525-56257-8. – ᴿTsTNijm 30 (1990) 213s (H. *Häring*).

9077 *Link* Christian, Auferstehung der Toten; gibt es ein Leben nach dem Tod?: EvKomm 22,11 (1989) 28-31.

9078 *Logister* W., Reïncarnatie; de vele kanten van een oud en nieuw geloof. Tielt 1990, Lannoo. 168 p. Fb 545. – ᴿCollatVL 20 (1990) 439 (E. *Vanden Berghe*).

9079 **Lohmann** Hans, Drohung und Verheissung; exegetische Untersuchungen zur Eschatologie bei den Apostolischen Vätern [ev. Diss. Bonn 1987, ᴰ*Grässer* E.]: BZNW 55, 1989 ➤ 5,9016: ᴿExpTim 102 (1990s) 25 (E. *Best*).

9080 *Lona* Horacio E., Die dem Apologeten ATHENAGORAS zugeschriebene Schrift 'De resurrectione mortuorum' und die altchristliche Auferstehungsapologetik: Salesianum 52 (1990) 525-578.

9081 **Lorizio** Giuseppe, Eschaton e storia nel pensiero di A. ROSMINI...:
Aloisiana 21, 1988 ➤ 4,k345; 5, k398:   ᴿVetChr 27 (1990) 207-211 (A.
Quacquarelli); ZkT 112 (1990) 109s (K. H. *Neufeld*).

9082 **McDannell** C., *Lang* B., Heaven, a history 1988 ➤ 4,a106; 5,9019:
ᴿCathHR 76 (1990) 813s (C. J. *Peter*: good, but more on SWEDENBORG
than on Jesus-Paul-John combined); CritRR 3 (1990) 305-8 (Carol
Zaleski).

9083 — **Lang** Bernhard, *McDannell* Colleen, Der Himmel; eine Kulturgeschichte des ewigen Lebens Ed. 586. Fra 1990, Suhrkamp. 578 p. DM 26.
– ᴿHerdKorr 44 (1990) 346 (D. *Seeber*; Titel irreführend).

9084 **McGill** Arthur C., Death and life, an American theology 1987 ➤ 4,a108:
ᴿJRel 69 (1989) 422-4 (G. D. *Kaufman*).

9085 *MacIntosh* J. J., Reincarnation and relativized identity: RelSt 25 (1989)
153-165.

9086 **Marcheselli-Casale** Cesare, Risorgeremo, ma come?: RivB supp. 18,
1988 ➤ 4,a110; 5,9023; ᴿAsprenas 37 (1990) 93-96 (V. *Fusco*); Carthaginensia 6 (1990) 385s (F. *Martínez Fresneda*); ExpTim 101 (1989s)
59 (B. L. *Horne*: good even without W. RALEIGH's serene evocation of
heaven); NedTTs 44 (1990) 342s (P. W. van der *Horst*, Eng.: an impressive knowledge).

9087 ᵀᴱ**Micaelli** Claudio, TERTULLIANO, La resurrezione dei morti: Collana
TestPatr 87. R 1990, Città Nuova. 217 p. Lit. 20.000. 88-311-3087-0.

9088 **Mondin** Battista, Preesistenza, sopravvivenza, reincarnazione. Mi 1989,
Àncora. 235 p. Lit. 19.000. – ᴿHumBr 45 (1990) 391 (B. *Belletti*).

9089 **Murphy** Marie, New images of the last things; Karl RAHNER on death
and life after death 1988 ➤ 5,9028: ᴿTLZ 115 (1990) 852s (M. *Ulrich*).

9090 ᴱ**Musschenga** A. W., *Vroom* H. M., Houdt het op met de dood? Over
zin en onzin van het geloof in een eeuwig leven. Kampen 1989, Kok.
150 p. Fb 565. – ᴿCollatVL 20 (1990) 440s (E. Vanden *Berghe*).

9090* **Ngayihembako** Mutahinga, *Télos* dans l'eschatologie du Nouveau
Testament: diss. ᴰ*Bovon* F. Genève 1990. – RTLv 22, p. 594.

9091 **Nigg** Walter, La morte dei giusti; dalla paura alla speranza [descrizione
della morte di una ventina di persone]. R 1990, Città Nuova. 166 p.
Lit. 15.000. – ᴿCC 141 (1990,4) 514 (G. *Mucci* raccomanda).

9092 *Noonan* Harold W., The possibility of reincarnation: RelSt 26 (1990)
483-491 (493-500, *Stoeber* Michael; 501-4, *Daniels* Charles B.).

9093 *O'Donoghue* N. D., The awakening of the dead: IrTQ 56 (1990) 49-59.

9094 *Okeke* George E., Eschatology in Jewish Christianity: Living Word 95
(Kerala 1989) 306-320 [< TContext 8/2, p. 45].

9095 **Oppenheimer** Brian, The hope of heaven; what happens when we die?;
pref. Abp. *Runcie*. C/Cincinnati 1988, Cowley/Forward. 160 p. $8 pa. –
ᴿAnglTR 71 (1989) 110 (H. B. *Porter*).

9096 **Ott** Ludwig †, Eschatologie in der Scholastik, ᴱ*Naab* Erich: HbDg 4/7b.
FrB 1990, Herder. 258 p. 3-451-00748-7 [TPhil 65, 631].

9097 *Packer* J. I., The problem of eternal punishment: Crux 26,3 (1990) 18-25
[< NTAbs 35,63].

9098 *Pattison* George, From KIERKEGAARD to CUPITT; subjectivity, the body
and eternal life: HeythJ 31 (1990) 295-308.

9099 **Phan** Peter C., Eternity in time, a study of K. RAHNER's eschatology
1988 ➤ 5,9035: ᴿJAAR 58 (1990) 517-9 (S. J. *Duffy*); JRel 70 (1990) 469s
(O. *Hentz*);JTS 41 (1990) 776s (J. *Macquarrie*).

9100 *a*) *Pinnock* Clark H., The destruction of the finally impenitent; – *b*)
Brown Harold O. J., Will the lost suffer forever?: CriswT 4 (1989s) 243-
259 / 261-278.

Plum Karin F., Der himmelske favntag, [embrace]: bibelsk ægtes-kabs- og seksualmetaforik: DanTTs 33 (1990) 161-182 [< ZAW 103, 276] ➤ 4048.

9102 *Pouderon* Bernard, ATHÉNAGORE et TERTULLIEN sur la résurrection: RÉAug 35 (1989) 209-230.

9103 *Race* Alan, Creation from the nuclear end [...'nuclear eschatology']: TLond 92 (1989) 503-510; 511-3, response, *Wiles* Maurice.

9104 **Ratzinger** J., 'Eschatologie', Tod und ewiges Leben [cf. Eng. 1988 ➤ 4,a132]. Rg 1990, Pustet. 238 p. – ᴿStudium 30 (M 1990) 554 (L. *López de las Heras*).

9105 **Reiser** Marius, Die Gerichtspredigt Jesu; eine Untersuchung zur eschatologischen Verkündigung Jesu und ihrem frühjüdischen Hintergrund [kath. Hab.-Diss. Tübingen 1989]: NTAbh NF 23. Münster 1990, Aschendorff. ix-359 p. 3-402-04771-3.

9106 *Reymond* R.L., Dr. John STOTT on Hell [Evangelical Essentials 1988: annihilation, perhaps]: Presbyterion 16,1 (St. Louis 1990) 41-59 [< NTAbs 35,64].

9107 ᴱ**Rigobello** Armando, L'immortalità dell'anima 1987 ➤ 3,9133: ᴿSalesianum 52 (1990) 198s (S. *Palumbieri*).

9108 **Roberts** Richard H., Hope and its hieroglyph; a critical decipherment of Ernst BLOCH's Principle of Hope. [J]AAR StR 57. Atlanta 1990, Scholars. xvi-248 p. $21; pa. $14 [TS 52, 160, J.J. *Godfrey*].

9108* **Robison** Jay P., Personal eschatology; an analysis of contemporary Christian interpretations [...CULLMANN O.; HICK J....]: diss. Southern Baptist theol. sem. 1990, ᴰ*Hendricks* W. 214 p. 91-07138. – DissA 51 (1990s) 3114-A.

9109 **Scheffczyk** Leo, 'Unsterblichkeit' bei Thomas von AQUIN auf dem Hintergrund der neueren Diskussion: Bayer. Akad. 1988. Mü 1989, Beck. 51 p. [TR 86,525].

9110 *Scherer* James A., Why mission theology cannot do without eschatological urgency; the significance of the end: Missiology 18 (1990) 396-413.

9111 *Schönborn* C., 'Auferstehung des Fleisches' im Glauben der Kirche: IkaZ 19 (1990) 13-29 = 'Resurrection of the Flesh' in the faith of the Church: CommND 17 (1990) 8-26.

9112 **Sesboüé** B., La résurrection et la vie; petite catéchèse sur les choses de la fin. P 1990, D-Brouwer. 167 p. [RTPhil 122,577].

9113 **Shedd** W.G.T., The doctrine of endless punishment [1885]. E 1986, Banner of Truth. 201 p.£5. 0-85151-491-X. – ᴿScotBEv 7 (1989) 51 (S. *Travis*).

9114 *a)* *Steenberghen* Fernand Van, Notre vie future; – *b)* *Vermeylen* Jacques, Quel salut pour l'homme la Bible fait-elle entrevoir?; – *c)* *Scolas* Paul, 'Je crois è la résurrection de la chair': FoiTemps 19 (1989) 58-82/ 195-216/475-495.

9115 **Sullivan** Clayton, Rethinking realized eschatology 1988 ➤ 5,9054: ᴿCriswT 3 (1989) 397-9 (C.L. *Blomberg*: should never have been published); CurrTMiss 17 (1990) 75 (Faye E. *Schott*); JBL 109 (1990) 343-5 (R.H. *Hiers*); PerspRelSt 17 (1990) 88-90 (N.E. *Parrish*).

9116 ᴱ**Sullivan** Lawrence E., Death, after life, and the soul [< 14 EncRel articles]. NY 1989, Macmillan. xii-282 p. $13 pa. [RelStR 17, 42, J. *Price*; also on his Hidden truths; magic, alchemy, and the occult < EncRel: xii-284 p. $13].

9116* **Sung Kee Ho** The doctrine of the Second Advent of Jesus Christ in the writings of Albert B. SIMPSON: diss. Drew, ᴰ*Pain* J. Madison NJ 1990. – RelStR 17,192.

9117 **Thiede** Werner, Auferstehung der Toten — Hoffnung ohne Attraktivität? Das christliche Bekenntnis zur eschatologischen Heilserwartung und seine unterschätzte religionsdidaktische Relevanz; Analysen und Rekonstruktionen: ev. Diss. ᴰ*Sturm* W. München 1989s. – TR 86 (1990) 517; RTLv 22, p. 621.

9118 **Thomas** Pascal [pseudonyme pour équipe lyonnaise], *a)* La réincarnation, oui ou non? 1987 ⇒ 4,a142: ᴿScEsp 42 (1990) 229s (A. *Couture*). – *b)* Reincarnazione, si o no? [La Réincarnation], ᵀ*Pistocchi* Bruno. Mi 1990, Paoline. 118 p. Lit. 9.000. – ᴿLetture 45 (1990) 661s (G. *Sommavilla*).

9119 **Thomas** Louis-V., *al.*, Réincarnation, immortalité, résurrection: Pub. 45. Bru 1988, Fac. St-Louis. xiv-262 p. – ᴿETL 66 (1990) 221-3 (E. *Brito*). LavalTP 46 (1990) 111-3 (A. *Couture*).

9120 **Tiede** David, Jesus and the future: Understanding Jesus today. C 1990, Univ. v-103 p. $22.50; pa $7. 0-521-38552-0; –81-4 [NTAbs 35, 107].

9121 **Tornos** Andrés, Escatología I, 1989 ⇒ 5,9057: ᴿMiscCom 47 (1989) 595s (Esperanza *Bautista*).

9122 *Tornos* Andrés, Publicaciones sobre escatología 1979-1989: MiscCom 47 (1989) 301-317.

9123 **Tugwell** Simon, Human immortality and the redemption of death. L 1990, Darton-LT. xii-196 p. £13 [TS 52, 359, J. M. *Dittenberger*].

9124 *a) Vanhoutte* Koen, Reïncarnatieleer; een eerste terreinverkenning; – *b) Cruyenaere* Leo de, Reïncarnatie en christelijke ethiek; – *c) Berghe* Eric Vanden, Reïncarnatie — hoeft het wel?; – *d) Henau* Ernest, Preken over dood en eeuwig leven; – *e) Bulckens* Jef, *Verbestel* Willy, Reïncarnatie in beeld: CollatVL 20 (1990) 357-378 / 379-398 / 399-416 / 417-431 / 433-8.

9125 ᴱ**Verbeke** Werner, *al.*, The use and abuse of eschatology in the Middle Ages 1984/8 ⇒ 4,426; 5,9059: ᴿCathHR 75 (1989) 151s (D. C. *West*: some titles, sans pp.).

9126 **Vernette** J., Réincarnation, résurrection; communiquer avec l'au-delà; les mystères de la Vie après la vie: Mulhouse 1988 ⇒ 5,9060: ᴿNRT 112 (1990) 791s (J. *Scheuer*).

9127 *Vicente Arregui* Jorge, Sobre la muerte y el morir: ScripTPamp 22 (1990) 113-143.

9128 *Vogler* Werner, 'Tod' nach dem Neuen Testament: CLehre 42 (B 1989) 324-331 [< ZIT 90, 126].

9129 *Wohlmuth* Josef, Zur Bedeutung der 'Geschichtsthesen' Walter BENJAMINS für die christliche Eschatologie: EvT 50 (1990) 2-20 (-26, Antwort, *Jones* Gareth; 26-39, ... und Arme, G*orringe* T.; 40-56, ... und Zivilreligion, *Honecker* Martin).

H9.5 *Theologia totius [V-] NT* – **General [O-] NT theology.**

9130 *Adam* A.K.M., Biblical theology and the problem of modernity; from Wredestrasse zu Sackgasse: HorBT 12,1 (1990) 1-18.

9131 **Beeck** Frans J. van, God encountered I, 1989 ⇒ 5,9067: ᴿTS 51 (1990) 145-7 (R. P. *Imbelli*).

9132 *Donahue* J. R., The changing shape of NT theology [= 5,8070]: HorBT 11,2 (1989) 1-27.

9133 *Dowd* S. E., New Testament theology and the spirituality of early Christianity; relationships and implications: LexTQ 24 (1989) 69-80 [< NTAbs 34,64].

9134 **Dunn** James D. G., *Mackey* James P., New Testament theology in dialogue; Christology and ministry 1988 ⇒ 3,9161 ... 5,9071: ᴿInterpretation 44 (1990) 210s (J. *Gros*); Vidyajyoti 53 (1989) 456-8 (P. M. *Meagher*).

9134* **García Aviles** Rafael J., Llamados a ser libres; 'no la Ley, sino el hombre' – ciclo B: En Torno al NT 9. Córdoba 1990, Almendro. 282 p.

9135 **Gnilka** Joachim, Neutestamentliche Theologie, ein Überblick 1989 ➤ 5,9073: ᴿActuBbg 27 (1990) 56s (X. *Alegre*); ArTGran 53 (1990) 301 (A. *Segovia*); StPatav 37 (1990) 400s (G. *Segalla*); TLZ 115 (1990) 745s (E. *Schweizer*); TPQ 138 (1990) 400 (K. M. *Woschitz*).

9136 *Gräbe* P. J., Ansatzpunkte für eine Theologie des Neuen Testaments bei Oscar CULLMANN und Leonhard GOPPELT: HervTSt 46 (1990) 85-101 [< NTAbs 35,194].

9137 *Hartman* Lars, Is the crucified Christ the center of a New Testament theology?: ➤ 24, ᶠBOERS H., Text 1990, 175-188.

9138 **Hübner** H., Biblische Theologie des NTs, I. Prolegomena. Gö 1990, Vandenhoeck & R. 307 p. DM 62. 3-525-53586-4 [NTAbs 35,258].

9139 **Kieffer** René, Die Bibel deuten — das Leben deuten; Einführung in die Theologie des NTs 1987 ➤ 3,9167: ᴿRHPR 70 (1990) 259 (M.-A. *Chevallier*); ZkT 112 (1990) 213 (R. *Oberforcher*).

9140 **Kittel** Gisela, Der Name über alle Namen I. AT 1989: II. Biblische Theologie / NT: BibTSchwerpunkte 2s. Gö 1990, Vandenhoeck & R. 250 p. 243 p. je DM 30. 3-525-61283-4; -4-2 [NTAbs 35,119].

9140* *Lamarche* Paul, Hypothèses à propos des divergences théologiques dans le Nouveau Testament: ➤ 557*, Canon 1990, 441-491.

9141 **Langkammer** Hugolin, ⓟ Teologia Nowego Testamentu I-II 1984s ➤ 3,8774s; 5,9078: ᴿSTWsz 27,2 (1989) 247-259 (J. *Łach*).

9142 **Léon-Dufour** Xavier, Słownik teologii biblijnej [Vocabulaire], ᵀRomaniuk Kazimierz³. Poznań 1985, Pallottinum. 1168 p. [KirSef 62 (1988s), p. 506].

9143 **Lohse** Eduard, Théologie du NT [1974], ᵀ*Jundt* Pierre: MondeB. Genève 1987, Labor et Fides. 285 p. 2-8309-0094-4. – ᴿGregorianum 71 (1990) 382 (E. *Rasco*); Masses Ouvrières 432 (1990) 88 (P. *Cazau*), 'Lhose' 3 fois).

9144 *Lohse* Eduard, Theologie als Schriftauslegung [zum Gedenken an H. CONZELMANN]: TLZ 115 (1990) 865-876.

9145 **Malmede** Hans H., Die Lichtsymbolik im NT 1986 [< Diss. Bonn 1959] ➤ 3,9171; 5,9082: ᴿCritRR 2 (1989) 219s (J. R. *Michaels*); TLZ 115 (1990) 110-2 (O. *Böcher*).

9146 *Panier* Louis, Une lecture sémiotique des textes; questions de théologie biblique: SémBib 56 (1989) 19-36.

9147 **Pannenberg** Wolfhart, Systematische Theologie I, 1988 ➤ 5,9087: ᴿTR 86 (1990) 1-8 (G.-L. *Müller*).

9148 **Pregeant** Russell, Mystery without magic. Oak Park IL 1988, Meyer-Stone. xii-179 p. $13 pa. – ᴿAnglTR 71 (1989) 110-2 (D. N. *Mosser*: as a college theology text, good but tough).

9149 **Räisänen** Heikki, Beyond New Testament theology; a story and a programme [... since Bultmann's cannot be surpassed] L/Ph 1990, SCM/ Trinity. xviii-206 p. $15 pa. 0-334-01907-9 [TDig 38,62]. – ᴿExpTim 101,10 top choice (1989s) 289s (C. S. *Rodd:* a gap exists between NT theology and studies of individual NT problems); TLond 93 (1990) 484s (R. *Morgan*).

9150 **Sasse** Hermann, We confess | Jesus Christ / the sacraments / the Church; ᵀ*Nagel* Norman. St. Louis 1985/5/6, Concordia. 104 p.; 157 p.; 136 p. [LuJb 56, p. 162].

9151 **Siegwalt** Gérard, Dogmatique pour la catholicité évangélique I 1986
➤ 3,6581 ... 5,9091: ᴿJRel 69 (1989) 264s (W. *McCoy*); RevSR 63 (1989)
283s (G. *Wackenheim*).

9152 **Vanhoye** Albert, La nuova alleanza nel Nuovo Testamento [¹1988,
ristampa con aggiunte e correzioni]. R 1990, Pont. Ist. Biblico. 183 p.

9152* **Yarbrough** Robert W., The *Heilsgeschichtliche* perspective in modern
NT theology [HOFMANN J. von; SCHLATTER A.]: diss. Aberdeen 1985.
541 p. BRDX-89544. – DissA 51 (1990s) 902-A.

XVI. Philologia biblica

J1 **Hebraica** .1 *grammatica.*

9153 *a)* *Avinun* Sarah, ⊕ Syntactic, logical and semantic aspects of Masoretic accentuation signs: – *b)* *Breuer* Mordekhai, ⊕ On the emergence
of the accentual system: Lešonenu 53 (1988s) 157-192; Eng. I. / 203-213;
Eng. III.

9154 **Barr** James, [➤ 3976*d*] The variable spellings of the Hebrew Bible
(Schweich Lectures 1986) 1989 ➤ 5,9095: ᴿBL (1990) 145 (J.C.L. *Gibson*:
his limpid and elegant but deadly style); JSS 35 (1990) 503-516 (E. *Tov*);
JTS 41 (1990) 571-5 (A.R. *Millard*); RÉJ 149 (1990) 191s (C. *Aslanoff*).

9154* *Charlesworth* J.H., The Beth Essentiae and the permissive meaning of
the Hiphil (Aphel): ➤ 173, ᶠSTRUGNELL J., Of scribes 1990, 67-78.

9155 *Cohen* Dalia, *Weil* Daniel, ⊕ The original realization of the Tiberian
Masoretic accents; a deductive approach: Lešonenu 53 (1988s) 7-30,
Eng. Is.

9156 **Deiana** Giovanni, *Spreafico* Ambrogio, Guida allo studio dell'ebraico
biblico. R 1990, Libreria S. Scritture. 206 p. 88-237-6005-5. – ᴿLA 40
(1990) 497-501 (M. *Pazzini*).

9157 **Döhmer** Klaus, Die Affixe des Hebräischen 1988 ➤ 4,a180; 5,9098:
ᴿLingB 62 (1989) 127 (W. *Schenk*).

9158 **Eskhult** M., Studies in verbal aspect and narrative technique in biblical
Hebrew prose: StSemUps 12. Sto 1990, Almqvist & W. 142 p. 91-
554-2518-6 [BL 91, 152, W.G.E. *Watson*]. – ᴿTüTQ 170 (1990) 307s (W.
Gross).

9159 *Garr* W. Randall, Interpreting orthography: ➤ 550, Hebrew Bible SD
1986/90, 53-80.

9160 *a)* *Goerwitz* Richard L., Tiberian Hebrew segol — a reappraisal; – *b)*
Rieger Reinhold, Überlegung zum 'Passiv' im Hebräischen: ZAHeb 3
(1990) 3-10 / 54-72.

9162 **Hoftijzer** Jacob, Function ... of nun paragogicum 1985 ➤ 1,8794 ...
4,a189: ᴿHebSt 31 (1990) 173-6 (A.F. *Rainey*); TLZ 115 (1990) 21s (J.
Körner).

9163 **Hunter** A. Vanlier, Biblical Hebrew workbook; an inductive study for
beginners. Lanham MD 1988, UPA. xii-234 p. $15.25. – ᴿCBQ 52 (1990)
320s (S. *Segert*: rather technical comments for a manual which he says is
to be used by students with a teacher).

9163* **Jamieson-Drake** David W., Scribes and schools in monarchic Judah; a
socio-archaeological approach: diss. Duke, ᴰ*Meyers* Carol L. Durham NC
1988. 88-22019 – OIAc JuJ89.

9164 **Kittel** Bonnie P., Biblical Hebrew 1989 ➤ 5,9103: ᴿCriswT 4 (1989s)
179s (D.A. *Garrett*: commended); ExpTim 102 (1990s) 84 (C.S. *Rodd*);

JAOS 110 (1990) 584-6 (W. S. *LaSor*: excellent; some criticism); JRel 70 (1990) 310 (D. *Pardee* tries to be fair).

9165 *Knauf* Ernst A., War 'Biblisch-Hebräisch' eine Sprache?: Empirische Gesichtspunkte zur linguistischen Annäherung an die Sprache der althebräischen Literatur: ZAHeb 3 (1990) 11-23.

9166 **Körner** Jutta, Hebräische Studiengrammatik[4]. Lp 1990, VEB. 412 p. 3-324-00099-8 [OIAc Oc90] – [R]ZDMG 139 (1989) 228s (H. *Bobzin*).

9167 **Lambdin** Thomas O., Lehrbuch Bibel-Hebräisch, [Introduction 1971], [TE]*Siebenthal* Heinrich von. Giessen / Ba 1990, Brunnen/Hänssler. xxviii-349 p. 3-7665-9361-3 / Ba 3-7751-1562-5 [ZAW 103,301, H. W. *Hoffmann*].

9168 — **Williamson** H.G.M., Annotated key to LAMBDIN's... biblical Hebrew: JStOT Manual 3, 1987 (reprinted 1989) ➤ 3,9231: [R]TLZ 115 (1990) 807 (G. *Begrich*).

9168* **Leonard** Jeanne-Marie, Enquête sur l'émergence du Hiphil en hébreu biblique: diss. Montpellier 1990. – RTLv 22, p. 588.

9169 *Malone* Joseph L., Pretonic lengthening; an early Hebrew sound change: JAOS 110 (1990) 460-471.

9170 *Merwe* C.H.J. van der, *a*) An adequate linguistic framework for an Old Hebrew linguistic database; an attempt to formulate some criteria: JSem 2,1 (1990) 72-89; – *b*) Recent trends in the linguistic description of Old Hebrew: JNWS 15 (1989) 217-241.

9171 **Meyer** Rudolf, Gramática de la lengua hebrea, [T]*Sáenz-Badillos* Ángel. Barc 1989, Riopedras. 490 p. – [R]ScripTPamp 22 (1990) 639 (P. *Monod*).

9172 *Minkoff* Harvey, The man who wasn't there [Masek, Calney, Adam, Malachi ...]; textual mysteries created by Hebrew spelling: BR 6,6 (1990) 26-31.

9173 **Niccacci** Alviero, The syntax of the verb in classical Hebrew prose [1986 ➤ 2,7260], [T]*Watson* W.G.E.: JStOT supp 86. Sheffield 1990, Academic. 218 p. £27.50. 1-85075-226-5 [BL 91, 154, J.C.L. *Gibson*].

9173* **Qimron** Elisha, The Hebrew of the Dead Sea Scrolls: HarvSemSt 29, 1986 ➤ 2,7262 ... 5,9111: [R]TLZ 115 (1990) 426s (S. *Holm-Nielsen*).

9174 **Seow** C.L., A grammar for biblical Hebrew 1987 ➤ 3,9224; 5,9115: [R]JAOS 110 (1990) 337-8 (E. M. *Cook*: some complaints).

9175 **Specht** Günther, Wissensbasierte Analyse althebräischer Morpho-syntax; das Expertensystem AMOS: Mü Univ AOtt 35. St. Ottilien 1990, EOS. ix-136 p. DM 42. 3-88096-535-8 [BL 91, 155, J. *Barr*].

9176 **Verheij** A.J.C., Verbs and numbers; a study of the frequencies of the Hebrew verbal tense forms in the books of Samuel, Kings, and Chronicles, 1: StSemNeer 28. Assen 1990, Van Gorcum. iv-135 p. *f* 35. 90-232-2572-4.

9177 **Waldman** Nahum M., The recent study of Hebrew; a survey of the literature ... 1989 ➤ 5,9117; $35: [R]CBQ 52 (1990) 733s (M. D. *Guinan*: superbly printed); LA 40 (1990) 495-7 (A. *Niccacci*); JStJud 21 (1990) 299s (A. S. van der *Woude*: invaluable i.e. valuable).

9178 **Waltke** Bruce K., *O'Connor* M., An introduction to biblical Hebrew syntax. WL 1990, Eisenbrauns. xiii-265 p. $37.50. 0-931-46431-5. – [R]AulaO 8 (1990) 285s (W.G.E. *Watson*); BL (1990) 149s (J.C.L. *Gibson*); HebSt 31 (1990) 253-9 (W. R. *Bodine*: two gifted and creative scholars); JStJud 21 (1990) 300s (A. van der *Woude*: conspicuous value); LA 39 (1989!) 310-327 (A. *Niccacci*); SWJT 32,3 (1989s) 57 (F. B. *Huey*); TLZ 115 (1990) 733s (G. *Begrich*); TüTQ 170 (1990) 308-310 (W. *Gross*).

9179 *Weippert* Manfred, Die Petition eines Erntearbeiters aus Meṣad Ḥašavyāhū und die Syntax althebräischer erzählender Prosa: → 147, FRENDTORFF R., Hebr. Bibel 1990, 449-466.

9180 *Weisenberger* Aṣila T., ❶ *Harbeh 'arbeh*: BethM 66,124 (1991s) 80-83.

9181 *a) Wernberg-Møller* P.C.H., Observations on the old accusative ending in Masoretic Hebrew; – *b) Revell* E.J., Conjunctive *dagesh*; a preliminary study; – *c) Christensen* Duane I., The Masoretic accentual system and repeated metrical refrains in Nahum, Song of Songs, and Deuteronomy: → 551, 8th Masor. 1988/90, 121-138 / 95-101 / 31-36.

J1.2 Lexica et inscriptiones hebraicae; later Hebrew.

9182 EAlonso Schökel Luis, Diccionario bíblico hebreo-español. Valencia 1990s, Institución San Jerónimo. Fasc. 1 *a-ašērâ*; 2. – *damam*; 3. – *ḥāmēš*; 4. (1991) – *k'f*; 5. – *miktab*; 6. – *nepeš*; 7. – *'āqar*...80 p. pt. 1000 each. 84-86067-36-7; – 42-1; – 43-X [igual para los demás fascículos]; obra completa 84-86067-37-5. No hay etimologías; las palabras están en orden estrictamente alfabético, no bajo la raiz verbal [BL 91,151, D.J.A. *Clines*, 1: 'nowhere near so technical as Gesenius, but a full generation ahead of it methodologically speaking...: Philology is dead, long live linguistics!']. ROTAbs 13 (1990) 301 (R.E. *Murphy*, 1: a handsome, artistic production).

9184 **Andersen** Francis I., *Forbes* A. Dean, The vocabulary of the OT 1989 → 5,9120*; RBL (1990) 144 (D.J.A. *Clines*: handsome and easily usable counterpart of R. *Morgenthaler* NT); LA 40 (1990) 492-5 (A. *Niccacci*: tanta fatica ne valeva la pena?).

9185 *Bar-Asher* Moshé, *a)* L'hébreu mishnique; esquisse d'une description: CRAI (1990) 199-237; – *b)* Quelques phénomènes grammaticaux en hébreu mishnique: RÉJ 149 (1990) 351-367.

9186 *Bazaq* Ya'aqob, ❶ The collective noun as literary ornament in biblical *taqbolet*: Lešonenu 52 (1987s) 106-111.

9187 EBen-Ḥayyim Z., The historical dictionary of the Hebrew language, Materials I. 200 B.C.E. – 300 C.E. J 1988, Academy of the Hebrew Language. 121.613 p. microfiches in binder. [OIAc F89].

9187* **Betzer-Bistritzer** Zvi, ❶ A morphology of the Responsa Hebrew of the 19th century (verb and pronouns): diss. Bar-Ilan. Ramat-Gan 1989. 504 p. – RTLv 22,590.

9188 *Blau* Joshua, ❶ On the multilayered structure of biblical Hebrew in the light of modern Hebrew: → 515, Lešonenu 54 (1989s) 103-115 (–150, 301-325 *al*.]; Eng. II.

9189 *Borokovsky* Esther, ❶ A theory of locative-symmetrical verbs: Lešonenu 52 (1987s) 75-80.

9190 **Brenner** Athalya, Colour terms in the OT: JStOT supp. 21, 1982 → 63,7827 ... 1,8829: RLešonenu 52 (1987s) 191-3 (J. *Blau*).

9191 *a) Clines* David J.A., The [Sheffield] dictionary of classical Hebrew; – *b) Reymond* Philippe, Vers la publication d'un dictionnaire hébreu-français; – *c) Roberts* J.J.M., The Princeton classical Hebrew dictionary project: ZAHeb 3 (1990) 73-80 / 81-83 / 84-89.

9191* *Dijkstra* Meindert, The so-called 'Aḥitūb-inscription from Kahun (Egypt) [Hyksos (or) Late Bronze, not first-millennium Aramaic]: ZDPV 106 (1990) 51-56.

9192 *Dinah* Joseph, ❶ Hebrew-Arabic lexicography problems: Lešonenu 52 (1987s) 94-105.

9193 *a) Dotan* Aron, ❺ From Masora to grammar — the beginnings of grammatical thought in [medieval] Hebrew; – *b) Eldar* Ilan, ❺ ḤAYYŪJ's grammatical analysis; – *c) Goldenberg* Esther, ❺ Medieval linguistics and good Hebrew; – *d) Sáenz-Badillos* Ángel, ❺ Principles in editing medieval texts: ➤ 515, Lešonenu 54 (1989s) 155-168 / 169-181 / 183-216 / 217-230; Eng. Vs. VIIs.VIII.IXs.

9194 **Fowler** Jeaneane D., Theophoric personal names in ancient Hebrew; a comparative stody: JStOT supp 49, ᴰ1988 ➤ 4,a221; 5,9130: ᴿCBQ 52 (1990) 115-18 (Ziony *Zevit*); ÉTRel 65 (1990) 263s (Françoise *Smyth*: un peu gauchi par intérêt 'jeu de noms' théologique); HebSt 31 (1990) 141-4 (D. *Pardee*); JBL 109 (1990) 316s (J.J.M. *Roberts*); JSS 35 (1990) 135-8 (P. *Wernberg-Møller*); JTS 41 (1990) 137-9 (J. *Barr*: philological competence with strong religious bias, as often nowadays); TLZ 115 (1990) 264s (V. *Hirth*).

9195 **Glinert** Lewis, The grammar of modern Hebrew 1989 ➤ 5,9132: ᴿBSO 53 (1990) 506-8 (S. *Morag*); HebSt 31 (1990) 156-170 (S. *Bolozky*, Gabriella *Hermon*).

9196 *Ilan* T., ❺ Kethiv changes of names C.E.: Lešonenu 52 (1987s) 1-7.

9197 ᶠIWRY Samuel, Biblical and related studies, ᴱKort A. ... 1985 ➤ 1,71: ᴿJNES 49 (1990) 88-94 (D. *Pardee*, all on F. CROSS re-reading of Pardee's 1982 Lachish inscription).

9198 *Jenni* Ernst, Zur Semantik der hebräischen Personen, Tier- und Ding-vergleiche: ZAHeb 3 (1990) 133-166.

9199 **Klein** Ernst, Comprehensive etymological dictionary 1987 ➤ 5,9141: ᴿHebSt 31 (1990) 188-190 (D. *Grossberg*).

9200 ᴱ[*Koehler* J., *Baumgartner* W.] **Stamm** J.J., Hebräisches und Aramäisches Lexikon zum AT³ [Lfg. 3, 1983 ➤ 64,7851 ... 3,9261], Lfg. 4, *r'h – tš'*. Leiden 1990, Brill. p. 1081-1659. 90-04-09256-0 [BL 91,159; RHPR 71,184, J.-G. *Heintz*].

9201 **Krauss** S., Griechische und lateinische Lehnwörter im Talmud, Midrasch und Targum [I 1898; II 1899]. Hildesheim 1987, Olms. xli-349 p.; x-687 p. ᴿArTGran 52 (1989) 360s (A. *Torres*).

9202 **Layton** Scott C., Archaic features of Canaanite personal names in the Hebrew Bible [Diss. Chicago 1987]: HarvSemMg 47. Atlanta 1990, Scholars. xiii-299 p. $17. 1-55540-513-4.

9203 *Lübbe* J.C., Hebrew lexicography; a new approach [semantic domains: e.g. PQD]: JSem 2,1 (1990) 1-15.

9203* **Masson** Michel, Langue et idéologie; les mots étrangers en hébreu moderne 1986 ➤ 4,a231; 2-222-03867-7: ᴿZDMG 140 (1990) 154-6 (H. *List*).

9204 [*Gesenius* W.] ¹⁸**Meyer** R., *Donner* H., Hebräisches und aramäisches Handwörterbuch zum AT, Lfg. 1, 1987 ➤ 4,a232; 5,9143: ᴿHenoch 17 (1990) 104-6 (J.A. *Soggin*); NorTTs 90 (1989) 61s (H.M. *Barstad*).

9205 *a) Miletto* G., Il Kethib-Qere nella tradizione babilonese; – *b) Capelli* P., L'epistola greca di Bar Kokhba e la questione del vernacolo giudaico nel II secolo: ➤ 154, ᶠSACCHI P. 1990, 91-104 / 271-8.

9206 *a) Mishor* Mordechay, ❺ A new edition of ... – *b) Engel* Edna, ❺ A palaeographic study of Oxford Ms. Heb d. 69 [dated near 500 C.E., published c. 1910]: Lešonenu 53 (1988s) 215-264 (phot. 247) / 265-276 + 10 fig.; Eng. IIIs/IV.

ᶠMORESHET Menahem, Studies in the Hebrew language 1989 ➤ 125*.

9207 **Murtonen** A., Hebrew in its West-Semitic setting I-A, 1986 ➤ 2,7306 ... 5,9145: ᴿHenoch 12 (1990) 106-8 (B. *Chiesa*, anche su

HOFTIJZER J. 1981, scusando il ritardo); OLZ 85 (1990) 322s (W. *Herrmann*).

9208 — **Murtonen** A., Hebrew / non-Masoretic I. Ba, Root system, Hebrew Material: StScmLangLing 13. Leiden 1988, Brill. 90-04-68064-3 [BL 91,159].

9209 — **Murtonen** A., Hebrew / non-Masoretic I. Bb, Root system; comparative material and discussion. – C, D, & E: Numerals under 100, Pronouns, Particles: StSemLangLing 13. Leiden 1989, Brill. 90-04-08899-7 [BL 91,159].

9210 — **Murtonen** A., Hebrew in its West-Semitic setting; a comparative survey of non-Masoretic dialects and traditions, II. Phonetics and Phonology; III, Morphosyntactics: StSemLangLing 16. Leiden 1990, Brill. 90-04-09309-5 [BL 91,159].

9210* *a*) *Naveh* Joseph, Miscellanea onomastica hebraica; – *b*) *Masson* Émilia, Les premiers noms sémitiques à Chypre: ➤ 125, ᶠSZNYCER M., Semitica 39 (1990) 59-62 / 41s.

9211 *a*) *Ornan* Uzzi, Ⓗ The basic factors of a Hebrew word; – *b*) *Ben-David* Israel, Ⓗ The capacity of grammatical patterns to generate contextual and pausal forms in biblical Hebrew: ➤ 515, Lešonenu 54 (1989s) 247-268 / 279-299; Eng. XI; XIIs.

9211* *Poulter* A.J., *Davies* G.I., The Samaria ostraca; two onomastic notes ['*dn 'm; šmyd*']: VT 40 (1990) 237-240.

9212 **Rabin** Chaim, Die Entwicklung der hebräischen Sprache: Veröffentlichungen der Hochschule für jüdische Studien Heidelberg 2. Wsb 1988, Reichert. 59 p. 3-88226-439-X.

9212* **Ratzhabi** Yehudah, Ⓗ Biblical euphemisms for human genitals: BethM 34 (1989s) 192-6 [< OTAbs 14,37].

9213 **Sappen** Raphael, The rhetorical-logical classification of semantic changes Ⓗ, ᵀ. Braunton, Devonshire 1987, Merlin. 91 p. [HebSt 31,269].

9214 *Scagliarini* Fiorella, Precisazioni sull'uso delle matres lectionis nelle iscrizioni ebraiche antiche: Henoch 12 (1990) 131-145; Eng. 146.

9215 *Segal* Peretz, Ⓗ The Hebrew IOU note from the time of the Bar Kochba period [ErIsr 20,256]: Tarbiz 60 (1990s) 113-8; Eng. IV.

9216 *Wasserstein* A., A marriage contract [c. 230 C.E.] from the province of Arabia Nova; notes on Papyrus Yadin 18: JQR 80 (1990) 93-130.

9217 **Wilson** William, Old Testament Word Studies. Peabody MA 1990 [= ? pre-1900]. xvi-566 p. 0-917006-27-5.

9218 **Wolf** George, Some lexicographical comments on the Hebrew Bible. Brooklyn 1990, Moriah. v-198 p.

9219 **Yadin** Y., *Naveh* J., *Meshorer* Y., Masada I., The Aramaic and Hebrew ostraca and jar inscriptions; the coins of Masada: Masada I. J 1989, Israel Exploration Soc. xv-68 p., 60 pl.; p. 69-132, pl. 61-81. 965-221-010-2 [BL 91, 33, A. R. *Millard*: 4699 coins].

9220 *Yaḥalom* Joseph, Ⓗ Israeli pointing: Lešonenu 52 (1987s) 112-143.

9221 **Sirat** Colette, Les papyrus en caractères hébraïques trouvés en Égypte 1985 ➤ 1,8858 ... 3,9286*: ᴿJSS 35 (1990) 153-6 (S. *Hopkins*).

9221* ᴱ**Katz** David, The origins of the Yiddish language: Winter symposium 15-17 Dec. 1985. Oxford 1987. – ᴿBSO 52 (1989) 304 (L. *Glinert*).

9222 **Simon** Bettina, Jiddische Sprachgeschichte [Deutschland 16. & 18. Jdt.); Versuch einer neuen Grundlegung. Fra 1988, Athenäum. 227 p. – ᴿEv-

Komm 22,8 (1989) 53s (W. O. *Dreessen*); OLZ 85 (1990) 182-4 (J. *Schildt*); Salesianum 52 (1990) 232 (R. *Sabin*).

J1.3 Voces ordine alphabetico *consonantium* hebraicarum.

9223 *Brauer* Bernd, *al.*, Lexikalisches Material [91 Hebrew words from b to t (then beginning again with) – *b*) in Hebrew-alphabet order, as here, but with three or four articles cited under each (thus not only articles dealing explicitly with that term, as here)]: ZAHeb 3 (1990) 221-231.

9224 *agmon, aggan: Rubiato Díaz* M. Teresa, Recipientes bíblicos 1: Sefarad 50 (1990) 167-180 + 7 fig.; Eng. 184.

9225 *agarṭel* (Ezra 1,9): Sefarad 50 (1990) 425-453; 6 fig.; Eng. 454 (*Rubiato Díaz, al.*).

9226 *ûrîm: Houtman* C., The Urim and Thummim; a new suggestion: VT 40 (1990) 229-232 [Hendiadys for a single object, 'charged' by being brought near the divine presence].

9227 *'ôt:* JBQ 18 (1989s) 241-250 (S. *Baron*).

9227* *El: Hvidberg-Hansen* Finn O., Fra El til Allah: → 117*, ᶠLøKKEGAARD F. 1990, 113-127.

9228 *îm: Elwolde* John, Non-biblical supplements to classical Hebrew *'im*: VT 40 (1990) 221-3.

9228* *Ross* J. M., *Amen:* ExpTim 102 (1990s) 166-171.

9229 *'āmar: Eskhult* Mats, Über einige hebräische Verben des Sprechens — Etymologie und Metapher: → 184, ᶠVITESTAM G., OrSuec 38s (1989s) 31-35.

9230 *ašer: Schwarzschild* Roger, The syntax of *ᵃšer* in biblical Hebrew with special reference to Qoheleth: HebSt 31 (Madison 1990) 7-39.

9231 *el: Sivan* Daniel, *a*) Tšt *'el* and *yšt 'al* in Ugaritic; problems in methodology; – *b*) Is there vowel harmony in verbal forms with aleph in Ugaritic?: UF 22 (1990) 311s / 313-5.

9232 *'lp:* 'to be an abecedarian': JAOS 110 (1990) 122 (M. D. *Coogan*).

9233 *ēš:* **Morla Asensio** Víctor, El fuego en el AT 1988 → 4,a249; 5,9168: ᴿBZ 34 (1990) 294s (E. *Gerstenberger*); RHR 207 (1990) 93s (A. *Caquot*, 'Morala').

9233* *Pytel* Jan K., ❷ Symbolism of fire in Holy Scripture: RuBi 42 (1989) 115-9.

9234 *aš* 'concubine' (akkad.): RAss 84 (1990) 41-43 (H. *Sauren*).

9235 *Ašera: Margalit* Baruch, The meaning and significance of Ashcrah ['consort', √ 'follow'; at Ajrûd and Qôm, 'YHWH's consort']: VT 40 (1990) 264-297; 1 fig.

9236 *Cooper* Alan, A note on the vocalization of *'aštoret:* ZAW 102 (1990) 98-100.

9237 *Márquez Rowe* I., Acerca de la etimología de Tarteso; variación sobre un tema del Marqués de Mondéjar [... *ašteret*]: AulaO 8 (1990) 255s.

9238 *et: Lerner* Joel, ❸ Evolution of the use of *'et* in biblical Hebrew: Lešonenu 52 (1987s) 81-93.

9239 *bayit: Layton* Scott C., The steward in ancient Israel; a study of Hebrew (*'ašer*) *'al-habbayit* in its Near Eastern setting: JBL 109 (1990) 633-649.

9240 *bā'ar: Dietrich* M., *Loretz* O., Ugaritisch *b'r* I 'anzünden' und *b'r* II 'verlassen': UF 22 (1990) 51-54.

9241 *bārak: Müller* Hans-Peter, Segen im AT; theologische Implikationen eines halb vergessenen Themas: ZTK 87 (1990) 1-32.

9241* **gag** (G *doma, stegē*): **Ellington** John,   Up on the housetop [in many rainy areas flat roofs like those of Palestine are not familiar]: BTrans 41 (1990) 238-243 [*Naden* T., Another stoɪ(e)y, on 39 (1988) 246, Acts 20].

9242 **gam:** **Merwe** C.H.J. Van der, The Old Hebrew particle *gam*; a syntactic-semantic description of *gam* in Gn-2Kg [diss. Stellenbosch 1968]: AOtt 34. St. Ottilien 1990, EOS. 228 p. DM 45. 3-88096-534-X. – ᴿOT-Essays 3 (1990) 376-8 (J. A. *Naudé*).

9243 **damqu:** *Garelli* Paul, La conception de la beauté en Assyrie: ➤ 124, ᶠMORAN W., Lingering 1990, 173-7.

   daq ➤ 9273.

9243* **derek ereṣ:** Tarbiz 60 (1990s) 147-162; Eng. I (S. *Safrai* ❹).

9244 **derôr:** **Charpin** Dominique, L'*andurārum* à Mari: MARI 6 (1990) 253-270.

9244* **hāyā:** *Niccacci* Alviero, Sullo stato sintattico del verbo *hāyā*: LA 40 (1990) 9-23; Eng. 445.

9245 **hālak aḥᵃrê:** *Vanoni* Gottfried, Zur konnotativen Bedeutung; am Beispiel des althebräischen HLK *'aḥarē* ('nachfolgen') und seinen Übersetzungen: ➤ 8*, ᶠASSFALG J. 1990, 379-387.

9245* **ḥlf:** *Ribera* J., El doble significado de la partícula aramea *ḥlf*: AulaO 8 (1990) 136-8.

9246 **zā'aq:** **Boyce** Richard N., The cry to God in the OT: SBL diss 103, ᴰ1988 ➤ 4,8009; 5,9175: ᴿCBQ 52 (1990) 313s (M. D. *Futato*); HebSt 31 (1990) 108s (J. G. *Harris*); Interpretation 44 (1990) 81s (J. C. *McCann*); JBL 109 (1990) 119-121 (S. E. *Balentine*); JStOT 48 (1990) 123s (R. S. *Hess*).

9246* **zākar:** *Fabry* H.-J., Gedenken und Gedächtnis im Alten Testament: ➤ 618, Commémoration ÉPHÉR 1988, 141-154.

9247 **ḥāyâ:** *Woźniak* Jerzy, ❾ Die Vorgeschichte der Schwurformel *ḥaj Jahwe*: ➤ 64, ᶠGRZYBEK S. 1990, 368-372; deutsch 373.

9248 **ḥsr:** *Bronznick* Norman N., An unrecognized denotation of the verb *ḥsr* in Ben-Sira and rabbinic Hebrew: HebAnR 9 (1985) 91-105 [277-300, *Revell* E.J., Waw consecutive; < OTAbs 13, p. 250s].

9249 **ḥesed:** *Romerowski* S., Que signifie le mot *ḥesed*?: VT 40 (1990) 89-103 [not vol. 60 as p. 89 top].

9250 **Sakenfeld** Katharine D., Faithfulness...*ḥesed* 1985 ➤ 1,8893...5,9175*: ᴿVidyajyoti 54 (1990) 267s (R. J. *Raja*).

9251 **ṭbl:** *Dietrich* M., *Loretz* O., Hurritisch-ugaritisch-hebräisch *ṭbl* 'Schmied': UF 22 (1990) 87s.

9252 **yārā':** **Costacurta** Bruna, La vita minacciata: AnBib 119, ᴰ1988 ➤ 4, a264; 5,9178: ᴿCBQ 52 (1990) 710s (C. *Bernas*: results of a word-theme study inevitably meager or banal; appeal to NT out of place); JTS 41 (1990) 806 (K. J. *Cathcart*); RivB 38 (1990) 102-5 (R. P. *Merendino*); Salmanticensis 37 (1990) 363s (M. *García Cordero*); TLZ 115 (1990) 499s (H. *Reventlow*).

9253 **Gruber** Mayer I., Fear, anxiety and reverence in Akkadian, biblical Hebrew and other North-West Semitic languages: VT 40 (1990) 411-422.

9254 **yāśar:** *Margalith* Othniel, On the origin and antiquity of the name 'Israel' [besides Meša and Meneptaḥ, also Ugarit and Shalmanesser III]: ZAW 102 (1990) 225-237 ['gerecht', *yašar*], 103,274: note added.

9255 **yāšēn:** **McAlpine** Thomas H., Sleep...: JStOT Sup 38, 1987 ➤ 3,9138*; 5,9178*: ᴿBZ 34 (1990) 307s (H. D. *Preuss*); TLZ 115 (1990) 806s (W. *Herrmann*).

9256 **kēn:** *Greenstein* Edward L., [*kēn, hēn, kôh*...]. The syntax of saying 'yes' in biblical Hebrew: ➤ 75, Mem. HELD M., JANES 19 (1989) 51-59.

9257 *l(w'):* **Ognibeni** B., Tradizioni orali ... *l'/lw* 1989 ➤ 4,2547; 5,9185: ᴿRivB 38 (1990) 381s (G. *Ravasi*).

9257* *Lieberman* S., *Lo/Lo*; an analysis of a Kethib-Qere phenomenon: ➤ 551, ᴱ*Revell* E., 8. Kongress 1988/90, 79-86.

9258 *me'ôd: Wernberg-Möller* P., Two biblical Hebrew adverbs in the dialect of the Dead Sea Scrolls: ➤ 183, ꜰVERMES G., Essays 1990, 21-26 [-35, *šam*].

9259 *mabbûl* (Ps 29,10), a new interpretation: Lešonenu 53 (1988s) 193-201 (C. *Cohen*, ❹; Eng. I-III).

9260 *mišārum: Olmo Lete* G. del, Ug. *mšr* (KTU 1.40:1) y el edicto *Mišarum* [no 'canto' sino 'rectificación', una especie de año jubilar]: AulaD 8 (1990) 130-133.

9261 *mt: Dietrich* M., *Loretz* O., *mt* 'Môt, Tod' und *mt* 'Krieger, Held' im Ugaritischen: UF 22 (1990) 57-65.

9261* *nūbalum* 'dry land, Festland': *Groneberg* Brigitte, La culture matérielle à Mari; der Nūbalum und seine Objekte: MARI 6 (1990) 161-180.

9262 *nûp: Dietrich* M., *Loretz* O., Die Wurzel *nûp* 'hoch sein' im Ugaritischen: UF 22 (1990) 67-74.

9263 *nepeš: Zevit* Ziony, Phoenician *nbš/npš* and its Hebrew semantic equivalents: ➤ 164, ꜰSEGERT S., *Sopher* 1990, 337-344.

9264 *Barré* Michael L., Mesopotamian light on the idiom *nāšā' nepeš* [not always 'desire'; sometimes 'flee for refuge']: CBQ 52 (1990) 46-54.

9265 *naša', maśśa: Kessler* Rainer, Das hebräische Schuldanwesen; Terminologie und Metaphorik: WDienst 20 (Bielefeld 1989) 181-196 [< ZIT 89, 721].

9266 *Garbini* Giovanni, SYS, 'campo salato' in ebraico: EgVO 13 (1990) 139-141.

9266* *ebbum, ebbūtum:* MARI 6 (1990) 181-218: prud'homme, expert (Cécile *Michel*).

9267 *'ēber:* **Loretz** O., Habiru-Hebräer BZAW 160, 1984 ➤ 65,7843 ... 5,9197: ᴿVT 40 (1990) 251s (G. I. *Davies*).

9268 *'ed: Schenker* Adrian, Zeuge, Bürge, Garant des Rechts; die drei Funktionen des 'Zeugen' im AT: BZ 34 (1990) 87-90.

9269 *ᵃdayin: Buth* Randall, *a)* [Aram.] *'edayin/tóte* — anatomy of a Semitism in Jewish Greek: ➤ 164 ꜰSEGERT S., Sopher 1990, 33-48; – *b)* Matthew's Aramaic glue: Jerusalem Perspective 3,5 (1990) 10-12 [< NTAbs 35,157].

9269* *'attâ; hēn, hinneh:* NduitsGT 31 (1990) 134-146 (C. van der *Merwe*) [< OTAbs 14,36; but 'particles' not 'participles' in English title].

9270 *'ayin: Hurowitz* Victor (Avigdor), The etymology of biblical Hebrew *'ayin* 'appearance' in light of Akkadian *šiknu:* ZAHeb 3 (1990) 90-94.

9271 *'elītum: Márquez Rowe* I., Ac. *elītum u wirittum,* 'ida y vuelta': AulaO 8 (1990) 134s.

9272 *'ll: Kedar-Kopfstein* Benjamin, Glossen zur traditionellen biblischen Philologie (2) [*ta'ᵃlûlîm* Jes 3,4; 66,4; *daq/doq* Jes 40,15.22]: ZAHeb 3 (1990) 207-209 / 209-211.

9273 *'lm: Layton* Scott C., The Semitic root **ǵlm* and the Hebrew name 'Ālæmæt [1 Chr 6,45 ... 8,36]: ZAW 102 (1990) 80-94.

9273* *'arš: Vitestam* Gösta, *'arsh* and *kursī*; an essay on the throne traditions in Islam: ➤ 117*, ꜰLØKKEGAARD F. 1990, 369-378.

9274 *pa'î > p'ûi:* Lešonenu 53 (1988s) 54-59 (S. *Sharvit*).

9275 *mpqd* on ostraca: Lešonenu 52 (1987s) 68-74 (J. *Garfinkel*).

9276 *ṣbw: Dietrich* M., *Loretz* O., Die ugaritischen Zeitangaben *ṣbu špš* ‖ *'rb špš* und *špšm:* UF 22 (1990) 75-77.

9277 *ṣedeq:* ➤ 9731 **Baumann** R., 'Gottes Gerechtigkeit' Verheissung und Herausforderung für diese Welt [< Diss. Tübingen 1968]: Tb 1643. FrB 1989, Herder. 252 p. DM 16. 3-451-08653-3. – ᴿTsTNijm 30 (1990) 405 (L. *Grollenberg*).

9278 **Krašovec** Jože, La justice...: OBO 76, 1988 ➤ 4,a307; 5,9205: ᴿBO 47 (1990) 749s (K. *Koch*); CBQ 52 (1990) 519s (M. B. *Dick*: his encyclopedic coverage more helpful than his restricted thesis); ÉTRel 65 (1990) 624s (D. *Bourguet*).

9279 *ṣûr:* **Olofsson** Staffan, God is my rock; a study of translation technique and theological exegesis in the Septuagint [diss. Uppsala 1988 – ST 44 (1990) 154s]: ConBib OT 31. Sto 1990, Almqvist & W. ix-208 p. Sk 178. 91-22-01394-6. – ᴿBL (1991) 48 (B. *Lindars*).

9280 *ṣarrāpu:* 'goldsmith', ᴸᵁSIMUG.KUG.GI: SAAB 2 (1988) 77-80 (S. *Parpola*).

9281 *ṣrrt: Dietrich* M., *Loretz* O., Ugaritisch *ṣrrt ṣpn, ṣrry* und hebräisch *jrktj ṣpwn:* UF 22 (1990) 79-88.

9282 *qdš: Barkay* Gabriel, A bowl with the Hebrew inscription QDŠ: IsrEJ 40 (1990) 124-9; 1 fig.; pl. 14.

9283 *qôṣ* 'Dornen': ➤ 859, TWAT 7, 1s (1990) (J. *Hausmann*).

9284 *qāṭôn* 'klein': ➤ 859, TWAT 7,1s (1990) 3-10 (R. E. *Clements*).

9285 *qînâh* 'Klagelied': ➤ 859, TWAT 7,1s (1990) 21-25 (G. *Fleischer*).

9286 *qayiṣ* 'Sommer': ➤ 859, TWAT 7,1s (1990) 26-29 (J. *Hausmann*).

9287 *qîr* 'Mauer': ➤ 859, TWAT 7,1s (1990) 29-34 (M. J. *Mulder*).

9288 *qālāh* 'gering schätzen': ➤ 859, TWAT 7,1 (1990) 34-40 (J. *Marböck*).

9289 *qālal* 'Fluch': ➤ 859, TWAT 7,1s (1990) 40-49 (J. *Scharbert*).

9290 *qlʿ: Eichler* Barry L., On weaving etymological and semantic threads; the Semitic root qlʿ: ➤ 124, ꟳMORAN W., Lingering 1990, 163-9.

9291 *qen* 'Nest': ➤ 859, TWAT 7,1s (1990) 49-51 (P. *Mommer*).

9292 *qin'āh* 'Eifersucht': ➤ 859, TWAT 7,1s (1990) 51-62 (*Reuter*).

9293 *qānāh* 'Erwerben': ➤ 859, TWAT 7,1s (1990) 63-71 (E. *Lipiński*).

9294 *qæsæm,* 'Wahrsagerei': ➤ 859, TWAT 7,1s (1990) 78-84 (L. *Ruppert*).

9295 *qēṣ* 'Ende': ➤ 859, TWAT 7,1s (1990) 84-92 (S. *Talmon*).

9296 *qāṣîn* 'Vorgesetzter': ➤ 859, TWAT 7,1s (1990) 93-95 (K. *Nielsen*).

9297 *qāṣap* 'Zorn': ➤ 859, TWAT 7,1s (1990) 93-104 (F. *Reiterer*).

9298 *qāṣîr* 'Ernte': ➤ 859, TWAT 7,1s (1990) 106-112 (J. *Hausmann*).

9299 *qāṣēr* 'kurz': ➤ 859, TWAT 7,1s (1990) 112-7 (J. *Marböck*).

9300 *qārā'* 'rufen': ➤ 859, TWAT 7,1s (1990) 117-147 (*Schauerte, al.*).

9301 *qārôb* 'nahe': ➤ 859, TWAT 7,1s (1990) 147-161 (R. *Gane*, J. *Milgrom*).

9302 *qæræb* 'Innenseite': ➤ 859, TWAT 7,1s (1990) 161-5 (*Rattray,* J. *Milgrom*).

9303 *qorban* 'Opfergabe': ➤ 859, TWAT 7,1s (1990) 165-171 (H.-J. *Fabry*).

9304 *qārāh* 'begegnen': ➤ 859, TWAT 7,1s (1990) 172-5 (H. *Ringgren*).

9305 *qirjah* 'Stadt': ➤ 859, TWAT 7,1s (1990) 177-180 (M. J. *Mulder*).

9306 *qæræn* 'Horn': ➤ 859, TWAT 7,1s (1990) 181-9 (B. *Kedar-Kopfstein*).

9307 *qārā'* 'zerreissen': ➤ 859, TWAT 7,1s (1990) 189-195 (W. *Thiel*).

9308 *qāšab* 'aufmerken': ➤ 859, TWAT 7,1s (1990) 197-205 (R. *Mosis*).

9309 *qāšæh* 'hart': ➤ 859, TWAT 7,1s (1990) 205-211 (M. *Zipor*).

9310 *qāšar* 'binden': ➤ 859, TWAT 7,1s (1990) 211-7 (J. *Conrad*).

9311 *rā'āh* 'sehen': ➤ 859, TWAT 7,1ss (1990) 225-266 (H. *Fuhs*).

9312 *rô'š* 'Kopf': ➤ 859, TWAT 7,3s (1990) 271-282 (*Beuken;* 282-4 U. *Dahmen*); 'Gift, poison' 284-7 (G. *Fleischer*).

9313 *rī'šôn* 'erster': ➤ 859, TWAT 7,3s (1990) 287-291 (H. D. *Preuss*).

9314 *re'šīt* 'Anfang': → 859, TWAT 7,3s (1990) 291-4 (*Rattray*, J. *Milgrom*).

9315 *rab* 'gross (viele) sein': → 859, TWAT 7,3s (1990) 294-320 (*Blum, al.*).

9316 *rābaṣ* '(sich) lagern': → 859, TWAT 7,3s (1990) 320-330 (G. *Vanoni*).

9317 *ræg̱æl* 'Fuss': → 859, TWAT 7,3s (1990) 330-345 (F. J. *Stendebach*).

9318 *rāgam* 'steinigen, stoning': → 859, TWAT 7,3s (1990) 345-7 (*Schunck*).

9319 *ræga'* 'Augenblick' : → 859, TWAT 7,3s (1990) 347-350 (T. *Kronholm*).

9320 *rādāh* 'herrschen': → 859, TWAT 7,3s (1990) 351-8 (H.-J. *Zobel*).

9321 RDM, *tardemāh* 'Tiefschlaf': → 859, TWAT 7,3s (1990) 358-361 (M. *Oeming*).

9322 *rādap* 'folgen, verfolgen': → 859, TWAT 7,3s (1990) 362-372 (*Frevel*).

9323 *rāwāh* 'tränken': → 859, TWAT 7,3s (1990) 378-381 (P. *Maiberger*).

9324 *rûaḥ* 'Geist': → 859, TWAT 7,3s (1990) 385-418 (*Tengström*; 419-425, H.-J. *Fabry*; 382-5 *reaḥ* 'riechen, smell', T. *Kronholm*).

9326 *rûm* 'hoch sein': → 859, TWAT 7,3s (1990) 425-434 (U. *Dahmen*).

9327 *terû'āh* 'Kampfgeschrei': → 859, TWAT 7,3s (1990) 434-8 (H. *Ringgren*).

9328 *rûṣ* 'laufen': → 859, TWAT 7,3s (1990) 438-445 (P. *Maiberger*).

9329 *rôš* 'arm/poor': → 859, TWAT 7,3s (1990) 445-8 (M. *Sæbø*).

9330 *rāḥāb* 'breit': → 859, TWAT 7,3s (1990) 449-460 (R. *Bartelmus*).

9331 *raḥamîm* 'Barmherzigkeit': → 859, TWAT 7,3s (1990) 465-476 (H. *Simian-Yofre*; 476s U. *Dahmen*).

9332 *ræḥæm*, 'Mutterleib, womb': → 859, TWAT 7,3s (1990) 477-482 (T. *Kronholm*).

9333 *Sperling* S. David, Biblical *rḥm* I and *rḥm* II: → 75, Mem. HELD M., JANES 19 (1989) 149-159.

9334 *rāḥaṣ* 'waschen': → 859, TWAT 7,3s (1990) 482-490 (H.-J. *Zobel*).

9335 *rāḥôq* 'fern': → 859, TWAT 7,3s (1990) 490-7 (L. *Wächter*).

9336 *rîb* '(Recht) Streit' : → 859, TWAT 7,3s (1990) 496-501 (H. *Ringgren*).

9336* **Laytner** Anson, Arguing with God; a Jewish tradition. Northvale NJ 1990, Aronson. 226 p. $22.50 [RelStR 17, 267, S. D. *Breslauer*].

9337 *rêq* 'leer': → 859, TWAT 7,3s (1990) 502-8 (B. *Kedar-Kopfstein*).

9338 *rākab* 'reiten': → 859, TWAT 7,3s (1990) 508-515 (*Barrick/Ringgren*).

9339 *rekûš* 'Besitz': → 859, TWAT 7,3s (1990) 515-9 (W. *Thiel*).

9340 *rākak* 'zart': → 859, TWAT 7,3s (1990) 519-521 (D. *Kellermann*).

9341 *rôkel* 'Händler': → 859, TWAT 7,3s (1990) 521-3 (E. *Lipiński*).

9342 *mirmāh* 'Betrug': → 859, TWAT 7,3s (1990) 523-7 (*Kartveit*).

9343 *rāmas* 'treten': → 859, TWAT 7,3s (1990) 532-4 (G. *Waschke*).

9344 *rānan* 'jubeln': → 859, TWAT 7,3s (1990) 538-545 (J. *Hausmann*).

9345 *rea'* 'Nächster': → 859, TWAT 7,3s (1990) 545-555 (D. *Kellermann*)

9346 *rā'eb* 'hungern': → 859, TWAT 7,3s (1990) 555-566 (T. *Seidl*).

9347 *rô'eh* 'Hirte': → 859, TWAT 7,3s (1990) 566-576 (*Wallis*) → 5842s.

9348 *rā'am* 'lärmen, Donner; thunder': → 859, TWAT 7,3s (1990) 576-9 (I. *Fischer*).

9349 *ra'anān* 'grün (Baum)': → 859, TWAT 7,3s (1990) 580-2 (P. *Mommer*).

9350 *rā'āh* 'Böse': → 859, TWAT 7,3s (1990) 582-611 (C. *Dohmen*; 611s, *Rick*).

9351 *rā'aš* '(Erd)beben': → 859, TWAT 7,3s (1990) 612-6 (H. *Schmoldt*).

9352 *rāpā'* 'Heilen': → 859, TWAT 7,3s (1990) 617-625 (*Brown*; → *repā'îm* a997).

9353 *rāpāh* 'schlaff, soft': → 859, TWAT 7,3s (1990) 636-9 (K.-M. *Beyse*).

9354 *Toorn* Karel van der, The nature of the biblical Teraphim in the light of the cuneiform evidence': CBQ 52 (1990) 203-222.

9355 *šʾl*: Lemaire André, 'BŠ'L [*Bordreuil* P. sceau d'Abisha'al 'mon père est renard']; anthroponyme hébreu fantôme?: ZAHeb 3 (1990) 212s.

9356 *še'erit:* **Carena** O., Il resto d'Israële 1986 ➤ 4,a322: [R]NRT 111 (1989) 582 (A. *Wénin*). ➤ 3153.

9357 *šb'* I: UF 22 (1990) 149-168 (I. *Kottsieper*).

9358 *šēgal* – ša ckalli = SAL.É.GAL: Lešonenu 52 (1987s) 8-17 (Shoshana *Arbeli-Raweth*).

9359 *Parpola* Simo, The Neo-Assyrian word for 'queen' [read E. GAL '*segallu*', biblical *šegal* Neh 2,6; Ps 45,10]: SAAB 2 (1988) 73-76.

9360 *šēlôm:* **Stendebach** Franz J., 'Ganzheit' oder 'Genüge'? Vorarbeiten zum Artikel *šālôm* im ThWAT: ➤ 146, [F]REINELT H. 1990, 329-344.

9361 *šālîš:* **Schley** Donald G., The *šālîšîm*; officers or special three-man squads?: VT 40 (1990) 321-8.

šam ➤ 9258.

9362 *šāma':* **Arambarri Echaniz** Jesús, [[D]1988 ➤ 5,9247] Der Wortstamm 'hören' im AT; Semantik und Syntax eines hebräischen Verbs: SBB 20. Stu 1990, KBW. 350 p. 3-460-00201-8 [OIAc Oc90].

9363 *šānâ:* **Behnstedt** Peter, Zum Gebrauch von '*am* und *sana* im Arabischen: ➤ 23, Mem. BLANC H. 1989, 27-44.

9364 *šāpuṭ, mišpat ṣdq:* **Bazak** J., The meaning of the term 'justice and righteousness' in the Bible: ➤ 537, Jewish Law 1986/9 ...

9365 *šākam:* **Janowski** Bernd, Rettungsgewissheit/Morgen: WM 59, 1989 ➤ 5,9245: [R]ZAW 102 (1990) 445 (H.-C. *Schmitt*).

J1.5 *Phoenicia, ugaritica* – North-West Semitic [➤ T5.4].

9365* **Aitken** K. T., The Aqhat narrative; a study in the narrative structure and composition of a Ugaritic tale [➤ 1978 diss. updated only to 1984]: JSS Mg 13. Manchester 1990, Univ. ix-213 p. 0-950-78859-7 [BL 91, 123, N. *Wyatt*: welcome despite jargon; his translation of Aqhat is competent].

9366 *Amadasi Guzzo* Maria Giulia, Two Phoenician inscriptions carved in ivory; again the Ur box and the Sarepta plaque: Orientalia 59 (1990) 58-66; 3 fig.

9366* *a*) *Amadasi Guzzo* M. Giulia, Noms de vases [p. 15; ailleurs vase] en phénicien; – *b*) *Greenfield* Jonas C., Some Phoenician words [*ḥmd, šb', nsr, gzl, grl; kšm' ql ybrk*]: ➤ 175, [F]SZNYCER M., Semitica 38 (1989s) 15-25 / 155-8.

9367 **Aufrecht** W. E., A corpus of Ammonite inscriptions: AncNE TSt 4. Lewiston NY 1989, Mellen. 0-88946-089-2 [BL 91,157]. – [R]AulaO 8 (1990) 271-4 (M. *Heltzer*).

9368 **Bordreuil** P., *Pardee* D., La trouvaille épigraphique de l'Ougarit I. Concordance: Mem 86. P 1989, RCiv. 457 p. – [R]AulaO 8 (1990) 142 (G. del *Olmo Lete*).

9369 *Branden* Albert Van den, L'inscription Sabratha 2 [*Garbini* G., Epigrafia 45 (1983) 104-7]: BbbOr 32 (1990) 147-155.

9369* *a*) *Caquot* André, Notes philologiques sur la légende ougaritique de Danel et d'Aqhat; – *b*) *Caubet* Annie, Note sur les chars d'Ougarit: ➤ 175, [F]SZNYCER M., Semitica 38 (1990) 73-79 / 81-85; 2 fig.

9370 **Cunchillos-Ilarri** J. L., Estudios de epistolografía ugarítica: Fuentes de la Ciencia Bíblica 3, 1989 ➤ 5,9254: [R]BL (1990) 119 (W. *Watson*).

9371 *Cunchillos* J.-L., *a*) Las inscripciones fenicias del Tell de Doña Blanca (III) TDB 89001 y 89003 [I. Actas Cartagena 1990; II. Sefarad 51 (1991)]: AulaO 8 (1990) 175-9; 5 fig.; – *b*) Polaridades vocálicas en el verbo ugarítico: Sefarad 50 (1990) 185-9.

9372 [dedicated to MORTON W. H.] Studies in the Mesha inscription and
Moab, ᴱ**Dearman** A.: Archaeology and Biblical Studies 2, 1989 ➤ 5,
392.9256*; $20; sb. pa. $13. 1-55540-556-5; 357-3: ᴿBL (1990) 30 (J.C.L.
Gibson); ETL 66 (1990) 193s (J. *Lust*); VT 40 (1990) 507s (J. A. *Emerton*).

9373 *Dietrich* M., *Loretz* O., The syntax of omens in Ugaritic, ᵀ*White*
Richard: ➤ 164, ᶠSEGERT S., *Sopher* 1990, 89-109.

9374 *Fensham* Frank C. †, *a*) Remarks on Keret II: 15:1-8; a poem on the
excellence of Hariya; – *b*) The term *'dn* in Keret (KTU 1.14: II: 32-34) and
a few other occurrences in Ugaritic reconsidered: JNWS 15 (1989) 91-
96 / 87-90.

9375 *Garbini* Giovanni, *a*) Sull'iscrizione cartaginese Res 776: OrAnt 28
(1989) 213-6; – *b*) L'ancella del Signore [iscrizione fenicia di Ur: *Amadasi
Guzzo* M. G., Orientalia 59 (1990) 58-66]: RStFen 18 (1990) 207s.

9376 *Hettema* Theo L., 'That it be repeated'; a narrative analysis of KTU
1.23: JbEOL 31 (1989s) 77-94.

9377 **Huehnergard** John, Ugaritic vocabulary in syllabic transcription: Harv-
SemSt 32, 1987 ➤ 3,9468; 5,9263: ᴿBO 47 (1990) 728-736 (W. H. van
Soldt); OLZ 85 (1990) 37s (W. *Herrmann*); RB 97 (1990) 479 (J. M. de
Tarragon).

9378 *a*) *Isaksson* Bo, The position of Ugaritic among the Semitic languages; –
b) *Eksell* Kerstin, Remarks on poetical functions of the genitive in some
Northwestern Semitic poetry: ➤ 184, ᶠVITESTAM G., OrSuec 38s (1989s)
54-70 / 21-30.

9379 *Lipiński* Edward, Epigraphy in crisis [CROSS F. M. upside-down tracing
in ᶠLAMBDIN claimed to be 'oldest Semitic inscription']: BAR-W 16,4
(1990) 42s.49.57.

9379* *Mack-Fisher* L. R., The scribe (and sage) in the royal court at Ugarit:
➤ 336, Sage 1990, 133-9; bibliog. 67-80.

9380 **Margalit** B., The Ugaritic poem of Aqht; text tr. comm.: BZAW 182,
1989 ➤ 5,9267*: ᴿArTGran 53 (1990) 417-9 (A. *Torres*); BL (1990) 124
(W.G.E. *Watson*); ExpTim 101 (1989s) 278 (J.C.L. *Gibson*).

9381 *Olmo Lete* G. del., Textos ugaríticos y su crítica literaria; a propósito
de [*Caquot* A. *al.*, Textes II 1989; *Parker* S. 1989]: AulaO 8 (1990)
183-195.

9382 **Pardee** Dennis, Les textes para-mythologiques de la 24ᵉ campagne
(1961) [8 from Ugaritica V (1968) and 1 from Ugaritica VII (1978)]: Ras
Shamra-Ougarit [0291-1655] 1988; ➤ 4,a349; 5,9268*: 2-86538-185-4.–
ᴿBL (1990) 35 (J. F. *Healey*); UF 22 (1990) 1-4 (M. *Dietrich*, O. *Loretz*
on insinuation against first-hand reliability of KTU, propagated in the
review of W. WATSON, *Orientalia* 58 (1989) 559 [60 (1991) 135, Watson's
retractation); UF 23,1-7, Pardee & Dietrich-Loretz 'reconciliation'].

9382* *Pardée* Dennis, Troisième réassemblage du RS 1.0199: Syria 65 (1988)
173-191; 2 fig.; facsimile.

9383 **Parker** Simon B., The pre-biblical narrative tradition ... Keret, Aqhat:
SBS 24, 1989 ➤ 5,9270: ᴿJBL 109 (1990) 696-9 (M. S. *Smith*); TLZ 115
(1990) 338-340 (O. *Loretz*).

9384 *Parker* Simon B., Toward literary translations of Ugaritic poetry: UF
22 (1990) 257-270.

9385 *Rainey* Anson F., The prefix conjugation patterns of early Northwest
Semitic: ➤ 124, ᶠMORAN W., Lingering 1990, 407-420.

9386 **Renfroe** Fred Hilton, *a*) Arabic and Ugaritic lexicography; diss. Yale.
NHv 1989. 268 p. 90-11384. – OIAc S90. – *b*) The foibles of a feeble
monarch (KTU 1.16.VI: 41-54): UF 22 (1990) 279-284.

9386* **Roshwalb** Esther H., 'Build-up' and 'climax' in Ugaritic literature with biblical parallels and its bearing on biblical studies: diss. ᴰ*Gordon* C. NYU 1988. 88-25051. – OIAc JuJ 89.

9387 *Smelik* K.A.D., The literary structure of King Mesha's inscription: JStOT 46 (1990) 21-30.

9388 *a) Smith* Mark S., Poetic structure in KTU 1.3 I 4-21; – *b) Watson* W.G.E., Abrupt speech in Ugaritic narrative verse; – *c) Voigt* R., Probleme der Ugaritistik: UF 22 (1990) 317-9 / 415-420 (-423) / 399-414.

9389 **Tropper** Josef, Der ugaritische Kausativstamm und die Kausativbildungen des Semitischen; eine morphologisch-semantische Untersuchung zum S-Stamm und zu den umstrittenen nichtsibilantischen Kausativstämmen des Ugaritischen: Abh. Lit. Alt. Syr 2. Münster 1990, Ugarit-V. xi-229 p. 3-927120-06-5 [OIAc S90; ZAW 103,312, I. *Kottsieper*].

9390 *Tropper* Josef, *a)* Silbenschliessendes Aleph im Ugaritischen — ein neuer Versuch. – *b)* Zur Vokalisierung des ugaritischen Gt-Stammes; – *c)* Zur Morphologie der Verben *primae h* im Ugaritischen und in den anderen nordwestsemitischen Sprachen; – *d)* Die ugaritischen Verben *tertiae'* und ihre Modi: UF 22 (1990) 359-369; Eng. 359 / 371-3 / 375-382 / 383-396.

9391 **Verreet** E., Modi ugaritici; eine morpho-syntaktische Abhandlung über das Modalsystem im Ugaritischen: OrLovAnal 27, 1988 ↠ 4,a357; 5,9277: ᴿOrLovPer 20 (1989) 255s (A. *Schoors*).

9391* **Verreet** E., Ugaritische Lexicographie ↠ 9855, ᴱ**Swiggers** P., Langage 1990, 76-93.

9392 *Watson* W.G.E., *a)* Ugaritic onomastic (1s) [personal names, updating *Gröndahl* F. 1967]: AulaO 8 (1990) 113-127 . 243-250: – *b)* Comments on KTU 1.114.29'-31': AulaO 8 (1990) 265-7.

9393 *West* David R., The Semitic origins of Ariadne [Ug. = 'light of lord'] and Atalanta [Gk. *atal-* 'young' + *anta* / *anat*]: UF 22 (1990) 425-432.

9393* *Xella* P., Transmission orale et composition formulaire dans les poèmes mythologiques d'Ugarit: ↠ 762*, Phoinikeia grammata 1982, 62-72.

J1.6 Aramaica.

9393* **Arnold** Werner, Das Neuwestaramäische I. Texte aus Baxʼa: Semitica Viva 4/1, 1989 ↠ 5,9284*b*; X-368 p. DM 88 [BL 91, J. F. *Healey*]. – ᴿZDMG 140 (1990) 380s (C. *Correll*).

9394 **Beyer** K., Die aramäischen Texte ... 1984 ↠ 65.7925 ... 5,9287: ᴿLešonenu 52 (1987s) 180-190 (J. *Blau*, ☉).

9394* *Beyer* Klaus, *Livingstone* Alasdair, Eine neue reichsaramäische Inschrift aus Taima: ZDMG 140 (1990) 1s; 2 fig.

9395 *a) Brock* Sebastian P., Three thousand years of Aramaic literature: – *b) Healey* John F., Ancient Aramaic culture and the Bible / Were the Nabataeans Arabs?: Aram 1,1 (1989) 11-23 / 31-37 / 38-44.

9396 *a) Cook* Edward M., The orthography of final unstressed long vowels in old and imperial Aramaic; – *b) Macuch* Rudolf, Some orthographico-phonetic problems of ancient Aramaic and the living Aramaic pronunciation: ↠ 164, ᶠ**SEGERT** S., *Sopher* 1990, 53-67 / 221-237.

9397 **Fassberg** Steven E., A grammar of the Palestinian Targum fragments from the Cairo Genizah: HarvSemSt 38. Atlanta 1990, Scholars. [x–] 322 p. $40; pa. $25. 1-55540-569-X.

9398 *Garr* W. Randall, On the alternation between construct and *dī* phrases in biblical Aramaic: JSS 35 (1990) 213-251.

9399 *a) Gawlikowski* M., Une coupe magique araméenne; – *b) Lozachmeur* Hélène, Un ostracon araméen inédit d'Éléphantine (Collection Clermont-Ganneau n⁰ 125?); – *c) Röllig* Wolfgang, Zwei aramäische Inschriften vom Tall Šeḫ Ḥasan/Syrien: → 125, ᶠSZNYCER M., Semitica 38 (1989s) 137-143; 3 fig.; pl. XXIV-XXV/39 (1990) 29-36; 2 fig.; pl. III./ 149-154; 1 fig.; pl. VI.

9399* *Greenfield* Jonas C., Some notes on the Arsham letters: → 555, Irano-Judaica 1 (1975/82) 4-11. – *b) Greenfield* Jonas C., *Stone* Michael E., Two notes on the [Cairo Geniza; Qumran fragments] Aramaic Levi document: → 173, ᶠSTRUGNELL J., Of scribes 1990, 153-161.

9400 *Gropp* Douglas M., The language of the Samaria papyri; a preliminary study: → 164, ᶠSEGERT S., *Sopher* 1990, 169-187.

9401 ᴱ**Heinrichs** Wolfhart, Studies in Neo-Aramaic: HarvSemSt 36. Atlanta 1990, Scholars. 207 p. $21, pa. $14. 1-55540-430-8. 14 art. [CBQ 53,521, tit. pp.], → 2921: ᴿJJR 41 (1990) 274s (A. *Salvesen*).

9401* *Hillmann* Reinhard, Zu den Scheidungsklauseln im Ehevertrag zwischen 'Ananyah bar 'Azaryah und der Sklavin Tamut, Papyrus Kraeling BMAP 2 [Elephantine]: → 147, ᶠRENDTORFF R., Hebr. Bibel 1990, 469-478.

9402 *Hoberman* Robert D., Emphasis harmony in a modern Aramaic dialect [Jews of Azerbaijan]: Language 64 (1988) 1-26.

9402* *Israel* Felice, La datazione del proverbio n⁰ 110 di Aḥiqar [Elephantine]: → 125, ᶠSZNYCER M., Semitica 38 (1989s) 175-8.

9403 **Jastrow** O., Der neuaramäische Dialekt von Hertevin (Provinz Sürt) [Türkei; Jahr 1970]: Semitica Viva 3, 1988 → 4,a369; DM 132: ᴿBL (1990) 146 (J. F. *Healey*).

9403* *a) Jobling* William J., Some new Nabataean and North Arabian inscriptions of the Hisma in southern Jordan; – *b) Qozi* Youssif, Remarques sur une inscription nabatéenne de Mada'in in Salih/AlHigr; – *c) Wenning* Robert, Two forgotten Nabataean inscriptions; – *d) Healey* John F., The Nabataean contribution to the development of the Arabic script: → 783, Aram 2 (1989/90) 99-111/113-122/143-150/93-98.

9404 *a) Lipiński* E., Araméen d'Empire: → 9855, *Swiggers* P., Le langage 1990, 94-133; – *b) Macuch* Rudolf, Recent studies in Neo-Aramaic dialects [JASTROW O., SABAR Y.]: BSO 53 (1990) 214-223.

9404* **Maraqten** Mohammed, Die semitischen Personennamen in den alt- und reichsaramäischen Inschriften aus Vorderasien: TStOrientalistik 5, 1988 → 4,a371*: ᴿRSO 63 (1989) 357s (G. *Garbini*: mancanze).

9405 **Morag** Shelomo, Babylonian Aramaic; the Yemenite tradition. J 1988, Ben Zvi. – ᴿBSO 53 (1990) 585 (L. *Glinert*).

9405* *Morag* Shlomo, ❸ On ᴴᴴᴮ YHB and NTN in Babylonian Talmudic Aramaic: Lešonenu 53 (1989s) 291s.

9406 *Naudé* J. A., Die teopasbaarheid van GB ['government-binding', CHOMSKY] – teorie op nie-lewende tale; evidensie oor die interpretasie van klitiekverskynsels in Bybelse Aramees: JSem 2,1 (1990) 22-43.

9407 **Odisho** Edward Y., The sound system of modern Assyrian (Neo-Aramaic) 1988 → 5,9306*: ᴿJSS 35 (1990) 177-181 (R. D. *Hoberman*); ZDMG 140 (1990) 157 (G. *Krotkoff*).

9408 *Pennacchietti* F. A., Due pagine da un manoscritto inedito di una poesia religiosa neoaramaica di Yawsip Ğemdānī (XVII sec.): → 154, ᶠSACCHI P. 1990, 691-709 + 2 fot.

9409 **Porten** Bezalel, *Yardeni* Ada, Textbook of Aramaic documents from ancient Egypt, I. 1986; II. 1989 → 2,7529; 5,9307: ᴿArPapF 36 (1990) 93s

(J. *Oelsner* 1); Orientalia 59 (1990) 552-4 (E. *Lipiński*); RB 97 (1990) 270-6 (P. *Grelot*, 2).

9410 *Porten* Bezalel, The calendar of Aramaic texts from Achaemenid and Ptolemaic Egypt: ➤ 555, Irano-Judaica 2 (1987/90) 13-32.

9410* a) *Sanders* J.C.J., Atlas of Christian Aramaic civilisation; – b) *Hage* Wolfgang, Early Christianity in Mesopotamia; some remarks concerning authenticity of the chronicle of Arbela: The Harp 1,2s (Kottayam 1987s) 31-37 / 39-46 [< TContext 7/2, 29].

9411 *Shaked* Saul, 'Do not buy anything from an Aramaean'; a [Cairo Genizah] fragment of Aramaic proverbs with a Judaeo-Iranian version: ➤ 192, ᶠYARSHATER E., 1990, 230-9.

9412 *Smit* E.J., The Saqqara letter [of King Adon, 1942]; historical implications: JSem 2,1 (1990) 57-71.

9413 ᴱ**Sokoloff** M., Arameans, Aramaic... 1980/3 ➤ 64,8094; 65,437... 2,7534: ᴿAulaO 8 (1990) 282s (G. del *Olmo Lete*); JNES 49 (1990) 366s (D. *Pardee*).

9414 **Sokoloff** Michael, A dictionary of Jewish Palestinian Aramaic of the Byzantine period: Dictionaries of Talmud, Midrash and Targum 2. Ramat-Gan 1990, Bar-Ilan Univ. [viii–] 823 p. 965-226-101-7. – ᴿTarbiz 66 (1990s) 272-287 (A. *Tal*).

9415 *Stuckenbruck* Loren T., Revision of Aramaic-Greek and Greek-Aramaic in... Qumran Cave 4 by J.T. MILIK [1976]: JJS 41 (1990) 13-48.

9416 *Svedlund* Gerhard, Alexander outwitted by the Amazons [(Cairo) Geniza fragment in Galilean Aramaic]: ➤ 184, ᶠVITESTAM G., OrSuec 38s (1989s) 158-162.

9417 *Takashina* Yoshiyuki, Two residual notes on the modern Aramaic of Hertevin: Orient-Japan 26 (1990) 105-122.

9418 a) *Toll* Christopher, Die aramaischen Ideogramme im Mittelpersischen; – b) *Müller-Kessler* Christa, Die Überlieferungsstufen des christlich-palästinischen Aramaisch: ➤ 777, Or.-Tag. 1988/90, 25-45 / 55-60.

9419 *Wacholder* B.Z., The ancient Judaeo-Aramaic literature (500-165 B.C.E.); a classification of pre-Qumran texts: ➤ 554, ArchHist DSS 1985/90, 257-281.

9420 *Woudhuizen* Fred C., The [1912 Lydian-Aramaic] Sardis bilingue reconsidered: Orpheus-Thrac 1 (1990) 90-106.

9421 [*Lewis* N., Greek Papyri], **Yadin** Y., *Greenfield* J.C., Aramaic and Nabatean signatures and subscriptions: The documents from the Bar Kochba period in the [Nahal Hever] cave of letters. J 1989, Israel Expl. Soc. xxii-164 p.; 40 pl. 965-221-009-9 [BL 91,29, L.L. *Grabbe*: the Aramaic and Nabatean *texts* will be published in a further volume].

9422 *Yardeni* Ada, New Jewish Aramaic ostraca: IsrEJ 40 (1990) 130-152; 6 fig.; pl. 15-7: provenance unknown.

J1.7 Syriaca.

9422* *Attridge* Harold W., The original language of the [Syriac] Acts of Thomas: ➤ 173, ᶠSTRUGNELL J., Of scribes 1990, 241-250.

9423 *Bauer* G.M., *al.*, ❻ New epigraphical finds from Hadramauth [on palm-leaves grafts, 1989]: VDI 193 (1990) 168-173; 4 fig.

9423* *Briquel-Chatonnet* F., Rôle de la langue et de l'écriture syriaques dans l'affirmation de l'identité chrétienne au Proche-Orient: ➤ 762*, Phoinikeia grammata 1989, 165-9.

9424 *Brock* Sebastian, *a*) Syrian manuscripts copied on the Black Mountain, near Antioch: → 8. ^FAssfalg J. 1990, 59-67 [described in Assfalg's Syrische Handschriften 1963, n° 105]; – *b*) Some further East Syrian liturgical fragments from the Cairo Genizah: OrChr 74 (1990) 44-61; – *c*) The dispute between soul and body; an example of a long-lived Mesopotanian literary genre: Aram 1,1 (1989) 53-64.

9425 **Gignoux** Philippe, Incantations magiques syriaques: RÉJ Coll., 1987 → 3,9543 ... 5,9319: ^RBijdragen 51 (1990) 89s (M. *Parmentier*); JSS 35 (1990) 324-6 (A. P. *Hayman*: no discussion of the religious issues involved).

9425* *Hunter* Erica C. D., Syriac inscriptions from a Melkite monastery on the Middle Euphrates: BSO 52 (1989) 1-17; pl. I-IV.

9426 **Kaufhold** H., Syrische Handschriften juristischen Inhalts in südindischen Bibliotheken: Szb ph/h 535. W 1989, Österr. Akademie. 56 p. [RHE 85,352*].

9427 **Kiraz** G. A., Syriac Primer: JStOT Manuals 5, 1989 → 5,9322: ^RExpTim 101 (1989s) 50 (J. G. *Snaith*: encouraging); JSS 35 (1980) 162 (S. *Brock*: can be helpfully used alongside more standard works); JTS 41 (1990) 221s (A. *Gelston*: not for scholars).

9428 **Muraoka** Takamitsu, Classical Syriac for Hebraists 1987 → 3,9550 ... 5,9323: ^RCBQ 52 (1990) 128s (E. G. *Mathews*); ZDMG 139 (1989) 426s (R. M. *Voigt*).

9429 **Nouro** Abrohom, Suloko [Syriac manual] I. Glane/Losser 1989, Syro. 136 p. – ^RETL 66 (1990) 195 (A. de *Halleux*: apparently in Syriac only without any explanations in a European language; otherwise like Kiraz, 'adapte la langue classique au dialecte syro-occidental' pour l'héritage national-chrétien des communautés en Europe et Amérique).

9430 *Rodrigues Pereira* A. S., Two Syriac verse homilies on Joseph: JbEOL 31 (1989s) 95-120.

9431 *Seidel* Ulrich, Studien zum Vokabular der Landwirtschaft im Syrischen II: AltOrF 16 (1989) 89-139.

9432 ^E**Strothmann** Werner, Syrische Passionslieder: GöOrF 1/32. Wsb 1989, Harrassowitz. xiii-172 p. 3-447-02934-X.

9432* *Suermann* Harald, Die Übersetzungen des Probus und eine Theorie zur Geschichte der syrischen Übersetzung griechischer Texte: OrChr 74 (1990) 103-114.

9433 *Teixidor* Javier, Deux documents syriaques du IIIe siècle après J.-C., provenant du Moyen Euphrate: CRAI (1990) 144-163; 3 fig. (163-6, *Guillaumont* A.).

9433* *a*) *Wickham* Lionel, Translation techniques, Greek/Syriac and Syriac/English; – *b*) *Goldenberg* Gideon, On some niceties of Syriac syntax: → 779, Symposium 5 1988/90, 345-353 / 335-344.

J2.1 **Akkadica** (sumerica).

9434 *a*) *Alster* Bendt, Sumerian literary dialogues and debates and their place in ancient Near Eastern literature; – *b*) *Weitemeyer* Mogens, Babylonian and Assyrian catalogues; – *c*) *Knudsen* Ebbe E., On Akkadian texts in Greek orthography: → 117*, ^FLøkkegaard F. 1990, 1-16 / 379-390 / 147-161.

9434* **Archi** Alfonso, *Pomponio* Francesco, Testi cuneiformi neo-sumerici da Drehem N. 0001-0412: Museo egizio di Torino, Catalogo 2/7. Mi 1990, Cisalpino. 215 p.; 412 facsimiles. 88-205-0663-7.

9435 *a*) *Artzi* P., Studies in the library of the Amarna archive; – *b*) *Rainey* Anson F., Genitive *ana* in the Canaanite el-Amarna tablets; – *c*) *Yargon* Shmuel, El-Amarna *mu'rašt* and biblical *Moreshet*; – *d*) *Demsky* Aaron, The education of Canaanite scribes in the Mesopotamian cuneiform tradition: ➤ 7, ᶠARTZI P. 1990, 139-156 / 171-6 / 207-212 / 157-170.

9436 *Black* J. A., *a*) A recent study of Babylonian grammar [*Groneberg* Brigitte, Syntax, Morphologie und Stil der jungbabylonischen 'hymnischen' Literatur 1987 ➤ 9449]: JRAS (1990) 95-104; – *b*) The alleged 'extra' [non-Akkadian, 'edited out' by scribes] phonemes of Sumerian: RAss 84 (1990) 107-120.

9437 *Borger* Rykle, Schlüssel zu M. E. COHEN, Canonical Lamentations of Ancient Mesopotamia [= Potomac MD 1988, auct. (11903 Reynolds Ave. -20854) $90]: BO 17 (1990) 5-39.

9437* *Bottéro* Jean, Akkadien; écriture et culture: ➤ 762*, Phoinikeia grammata 1989, 113-117.

9438 *Bruschweiler* Françoise, La plainte du roseau, eršemma de Dumuzi [Musée d'Art de Genève] MAH 16014: RAss 84 (1990) 119-124; 2 phot. avec facsim.

9439 **CAD** 13 'Q', ᴱ**Reiner** E. (*Brinkman* J.) 1982 ➤ 62,784 ... 5,9329: ᴿOLZ 85 (1990) 29-32 (W. *Sommerfeld*).

9440 **Caplice** Richard, Introduction to Akkadian (³ʳᵉᵛ with *Snell* Daniel), 1988 ➤ 4,a395: ᴿAION 49,4 (1989) 457-9 (L. *Cagni*); Salesianum 52 (1990) 477 (R. *Sabin*).

9441 *Casini* Marinella, 'Carcere' nella terminologia accadica: EgVO 13 (1990) 127-134.

9442 **Cavigneaux** Antoine, *al.*, The series Erim-huš = *anantu* and An-ta-gál = *šaqú*: MSL 17, 1985 ➤ 1,9087; 5,9330: ᴿWZKM 80 (1990) 262-4 (H. *Hirsch*).

9443 *Cochavi-Rainey* Zipora, *a*) Egyptian influence in the Akkadian texts written by Egyptian scribes in the fourteenth and thirteenth centuries B.C.: JNES 49 (1990) 57-65; – *b*) Tenses and modes in cuneiform texts written by Egyptian scribes in the Late Bronze Age: UF 22 (1990) 5-23.

9443* **D'Agostino** Franco, Il sistema verbale sumerico nei testi lessicali di Ebla: StSemit 7. R 1990, Univ. x-189 p. [OIAc Ja 91].

9444 *Dietrich* M., Die akkadischen Texte der Archive und Bibliotheken von Emar: UF 22 (1990) 25-48.

9445 *Edzard* Dietz O., Indusschrift aus der Sicht des Assyriologen: ZAss 80 (1990) 124-134.

9446 *a*) *Edzard* Dietz O., Selbstgespräch und Monolog in der akkadischen Literatur; – *b*) *Kramer* Samuel N., BM 96927; a prime example of ancient scribal redaction; – *c*) *Wilcke* Claus, Orthographie, Grammatik und literarische Form; Beobachtungen zu der Vaseninschrift Lugalzaggesis (SAKI 152-156); – *d*) *Reiner* Erica, Nocturnal talk: ➤ 124, ᶠMORAN W., Lingering 1990, 149-162 / 251-267 + 2 phot. / 455-504 / 421-4.

9447 *a*) *Farber* Walter, *Mannam lušpur ana Enkidu*; some new thoughts about an old motif: JNES 49 (1990) 299-321. – *b*) *Görg* Manfred, Die Eigennamen in der Grossen Inschrift Tukulti-Ninurtas I. vom 'Neuen Palast' in Assur: BibNot 47 (1989) 10-12.

9447* *a*) **Freydank** H., *Saporetti* C., Babu-Ahha-Iddina, die Texte: Analisi elettronica per cuneiforme, Corpus Medio-Assiro. R 1989, Denicola. 94 p. – *b*) **Gelb** Ignace J., *Kienast* B., Die altakkadischen Königsinschriften des dritten Jahrtausends v. Chr.: FreibOrSt 7. Stu 1990, Steiner. xvi-435 p.; 30 fig.; XX pl. 3-515-04248-2.

9448 **Gianto** Agustinus, Word order variation in the Akkadian of Byblos [diss. Harvard 1987]: StPohl 15. R 1990, Pontificio Istituto Biblico. x-190 p. Lit. 20.000. 88-7653-576-4.

9448* **Gomi** Tohru, *Hirose* Yoko & Kazutaka, Neo-Sumerian administrative texts of the Hirose collection. Potomac MD 1990, Capital Decisions. x-163 p. [OIAc Ja91].

9449 **Groneberg** Brigitte, Syntax, Morphologie und Stil der jungbabylonischen 'hymnischen' Literatur, 1. Grammatik; 2. Belegsammlung und Textkatalog: FreibAltorSt 14, 1987 ➤ 4,a400; 5,9335: ᴿBSO 52 (1989) 334 (A. R. *George*); JAOS 110 (1990) 568-571 (W. L. *Moran*: merit despite some disagreements).

9449* **Hayes** John L., A manual of Sumerian grammar and texts: Aids RANE 5. Malibu 1990, Undena. vii-311 p. 0-89003-198-3 [OIAc S90].

9450 ᴱ**Hecker** K. *Sommerfeld* W., Keilschriftliche Literaturen [XXXII. Rencontre 1985] 1986 ➤ 2,543: ᴿZAss 80 (1990) 144s (D. O. *Edzard*).

9450* **Hecker** Karl, Rückläufiges Wörterbuch des Akkadischen: SANTAG, Arbeiten und Untersuchungen zur Keilschriftkunde 1. Wsb 1990, Harrassowitz. xii-316 p. DM 112. 3-447-02868-8 [BL 92,136, W. *Lambert*].

9451 *Hess* Richard S., Rhetorical forms in EA[marna] 162: UF 22 (1990) 137-148.

9452 *Høyrup* Jens, Algebra and naive geometry; an investigation of some basic aspects of Old Babylonian mathematical thought: AltOrF 17 (1990) 27-69.262-354.

9453 **Huehnergard** John, The Akkadian of Ugarit: HarvSemSt 34, 1989 ➤ 5,5240: ᴿJBL 109 (1990) 695s (D. *Marcus*).

9454 **Jacobsen** Thorkild, The harps that once... Sumerian poetry in translation 1987 ➤ 3,9580: ᴿBO 95 (1990) 375-394; 5 phot. (W.H.P. *Römer*); JAOS 110 (1990) 119-122 (D. O. *Edzard*, deutsch).

9455 *Kataja* Laura, A [computer] reverse list of Neo-Assyrian signs: SAAB 2 (1988) 125-8.

9456 *a)* *Klein* Jacob, The 'bane' of humanity, a lifespan of one hundred twenty years [*Civil* M., Enlil and Namzitarra 1974]; – *b)* *Vanstiphout* H.L.J., The Mesopotamian debate poems; a general presentation (I): AcSum 12 (1990) 57-70 / 271-318.

9457 *a)* *Knudsen* Ebbe E., Akkadian in Greek orthography; evidence of sound change in an ancient traditional pronunciation; – *b)* *Pedersén* Olof, Written and oral traditions; Mesopotamia compared with other cultures: ➤ 184, ᶠVITESTAM G., OrSuec 38s (1989s) 71-80 / 120-4.

9458 *a)* *Kramer* Samuel N., The 'Barnett' Enmerkar tablet; a new Sumerian dialect (?); – *b)* *Sollberger* Edmond, Deux inscriptions royales: ➤ 107, ᶠKUPPER J.-R. 1990, 7-25; 3 pl. / 1-5; 2 pl.

9459 **Kraus** F. R., Sonderformen akkadischer Parataxe; die Koppelungen: Akad. Med. lett. 50/1, 1987 ➤ 3,9583: ᴿWZKM 80 (1990) 264s (H. *Hirsch*).

9460 *a)* *Lieberman* Stephen J., Canonical and official cuneiform texts; towards an understanding of Assurbanipal's personal tablet collection; – *b)* *Leichty* Erle, A *tamītu* from Nippur; – *c)* *Watkins* Calvert, A Celtic-Latin-Hittite etymology [*duno-* ('fort') / *funis* / *Tuḫḫuštu*]: ➤ 124, ᶠMORAN W., Lingering 1990, 305-336 / 301-4 / 451-3.

9461 *Michalowski* Piotr, The shekel and the vizier: ZAss 80 (1990) 1-8.

9462 **Oberhuber** Karl, Sumerisches Lexikon zu REISNER G., Sumerisch-babylonische Hymnen 1896: Innsbrucker Sumerisches Lexikon. Innsbruck 1990, Univ. Inst. Spr. W. 583 p. 3-85124-144-4.

9463 ᶠOTTEN Heinrich, Documentum Asiae Minoris antiquae, ᴱNeu E. *al.*
1988 ➤ 4,112*: ᴿZAss 80 (1990) 151-4 (H. *Klengel*).

9464 **Polentz** Bernhard, Die Eigenbegrifflichkeit babylonischer Redeformen
dargestellt am Musterbeispiel des Erra-Epos [Diss. Mü 1988]: Theorie und
Forschung 99, Orientalistik 1. Rg 1989, Roderer. xxi-270 p. 3-89073-
454-5 [OIAc S90].

9465 **Schrotter** Manfred K., Emesal-Studien; Sprach- und Literaturgeschicht-
liche Untersuchungen zur sogenannten Frauensprache des Sumerischen:
BeitKuW 69. Innsbruck 1990, Univ. Inst. Spr. W. ix-297 p. 3-85124-
142-8.

9466 *Selz* Gebhard J., Ein neuer altsumerischer Brief aus dem Vorderasiatischen Museum, zu Berlin [*Deimel* A., Or 16 (1925) 51 'Tempelwirt-
schaft']: AltOrF 16 (1989) 380-2.

9466* **Sigrist** Marcel, *a)* Messenger texts from the British Museum. Potomac
MD 1990, Capital Decisions. 44 p. + 337 transliterated texts. 0-962001-
33-3. – *b)* Larsa Year Names / Old Babylonian Account Texts in the Horn
Museum: Andrews Univ. Cuneiform Texts 3s. Berrien Springs 1990,
Andrews Univ. 87 p. / v-138 p. [101 facsimiles]. 0-943872-53-7; -4-5 [OIAc
Ja91].

9467 **Soden** W. von, Introduzione all'orientalismo antico, ᵀᴱ*Mora* C: Studi
VO Antico 1, 1989 ➤ 5,9357: ᴿAsprenas 37 (1990) 371s (A. *Rolla*).

9468 *Vogelzang* Marianna E., Patterns introducing direct speech in Akkadian
literary texts: JCS 48 (1990) 50-70.

9469 *Yoshikawa* Mamoru, The origin of Sumerian verbal preformatives:
AcSum 11 (1989) 293-304 [< ◐ The Minato 5 (1964) 8-19].

9470 *a) Yoshikawa* Mamoru, Some remarks on Sumerian phonology (I); – *b)*
Steiner Gerd, Sumerisch und Elamisch; typologische Parallelen: AcSum
12 (1990) 339-347 / 143-176.

J2.7 **Arabica.**

9471 ᴱ**Ashtiany** Julia, *al.*, 'Abbasid Belles-Lettres: Cambridge History of
Arabic Literature. C 1990, Univ. xv-517 p. 0-521-24016-6.

9471* BEDWELL: **Hamilton** Alastair, William Bedwell, the Arabist 1985
➤ 2,7576*; 3,9622: ᴿOLZ 85 (1990) 695-7 (D. *Bellmann*); ZDMG 140
(1989) 240s (H. *Bobzin*).

9472 **Beeston** A.F.L., *al.*, Sabaic dictionary 1982 ➤ 63,8166 ... 3,9607: ᴿRSO
63 (1989) 312-5 (L. *Ricci*).

9473 *Bellamy* James A., Arabic verses from the first/second century; the
inscription of 'En 'Avdat: JSS 35 (1990) 73-79.

9474 *Bobzin* Hartmut, Agostino GIUSTINIANI (1470-1536) und seine Bedeutung für die Geschichte der Arabistik: ➤ 777, Or.-Tag. 1988/90, 131-9.

9475 *Branca* Paolo, Il contributo di Ǧurǧī ZAYDĀN agli studi linguistici arabi:
IstLombR 121 (1987) 109-117.

9476 *Carter* M.G., Arab linguistics and Arabic linguistics ['Arab' = their
own; 'Arabic' ours]: Zts Gesch. der Arabisch-Islamischen Wissenschaften
4 (1987s) 205-218 [< OLZ 85, 636].

9477 **Corriente** F., Gramática árabe⁶ 1988 ➤ 5,9371: ᴿStromata 45 (1989) 474.

9477* **Corriente** F., Nuevo diccionario español-árabe. M 1988, Inst. Hispano-Árabe. 1213 p. – ᴿBSO 53 (1990) 516s (J.A. *Abu-Haidar*).

9478 **Fischer** Wolfdietrich, Grammatik des klassischen Arabisch²ʳᵉᵛ [¹1972]:
Porta Linguarum Orientalium 11. Wsb 1987, Harrassowitz. 272 p. – ᴿAr-
Or 58 (1990) 406 (P. *Zemánek*).

9478* **Herzallah** Rukayyah S., Aspects of Palestinian Arabic phonology: diss. Cornell, [D]*Clements* G. Ithaca NY 1990. 275 p. 91-06315. – DissA 51 (1990s) 3056-A.

9479 *a) Kästner* Hartmut, Gibt es im Arabischen doppelt transitive Verben?: – *b) Blohm* Dieter, Semantische und syntaktische Reflexivität im Arabischen; – *c) Waldmann* Albert, Zur Appositions-struktur im Arabischen; – *d) Schulz* Eckehart, Computer in der Arabistik; Stand und Perspektiven: HalleB 13s (1990) 117-123 / 131-9 / 149-155 / 85-94.

9479* **Nakishbendy** Abdullatif M. al-, Language factors that may cause difficulties for American adults in learning Arabic: diss. [D]*Sartain* H. Pittsburgh 1990. 175 p. 91-06800. – DissA 51 (1990s) 2722-A.

9480 **Nebes** N., Funktionsanalyse von *kāna yaf'alu* 1982 → 64,8169 ... 3,9632: [R]OLZ 82 (1991) 54-56 (D. *Blohm*).

9480* *Nevo* Yehuda D., A new Negev Arabic inscription [Rubeibe]: BSO 52 (1989) 18-23; facsim.; 2 pl. [24-37, The estates of 'Amr b. al-'As in Palestine, *Lecker* Michael].

9481 *Orsatti* Paola, Gli studi di paleografia araba oggi; problemi e metodi: ScrCiv 14 (1990) 281-331.

9482 **Owens** Jonathan, The foundations of grammar; an introduction to medieval Arabic grammatical theory: AmstStLangSc 3/45. Amst/Ph 1988, Benjamins. xii-371 p. $45. – [R]BSO 53 (1990) 508-510 (G. *Khan*); JSS 35 (1990) 174-8 (A. *Shivtiel*: an alarming number of errors); Language 65 (1989) 824-7 (Karin C: *Ryding*); ZDMG 139 (1989) 431s (E. *Wagner*).

9482* *Peled* Yishai, Non-referential pronouns in topic position in medieval Arabic grammatical theory and in modern usage: ZDMG 140 (1990) 3-27.

9483 *Renfroe* Fred, South Arabian inscriptions in the Yale Babylonian collection: Muséon 103 (1990) 155-165; 12 fig.

9484 **Ricks** S. D., Lexicon of inscriptional Qatabanian: StPohl 14, 1989 → [65,8032] 5,9385: [R]AulaO 8 (1990) 280-2 (F. *Bron*).

9485 **Rosenhouse** Judith, The [North-Israel] bedouin Arabic dialects 1984 → 2,7585: [R]OLZ 85 (1990) 183-5 (H.-R. *Singer*).

9486 **Rosenthal** Franz, *a)* Nineteen [as 'mystic' number < AnBib 12 (1959)]; – *b)* al-KINDĪ als Literat [< Orientalia 11 (1942)]: → 290, Muslim history 1990, I p. 304-318 / VI p. 262-288.

9487 **Sabuni** Abdulghafur, Wörterbuch des arabischen Grundwortschatzes; die 2000 häufigsten Wörter. Ha 1988, Buske. 272 p. DM 42. – [R]WZKM 80 (1990) 240-2 (A. A. *Ambros*).

9488 **Schall** Anton, Elementa arabica; Einführung in die klassische arabische Sprache 1988 → 4,a443: [R]Biblica 71 (1990) 588s (A. *Gianto*: could be useful, though dubiously all in transliteration); JAOS 110 (1990) 171s (A. S. *Kaye*); ZDMG 139 (1989) 432s (E. *Wagner*).

9489 **Sellheim** Rudolf, Arabische Handschriften, Materialien zur arabischen Literaturgeschichte [1.1976]; 2: Verzeichnis der orientalischen Handschriften in Deutschland A17. Stu 1987, Steiner. 416 p.; 24 pl. DM 280. – [R]Mundus 25 (1989) 40s (H. *Müller*).

9490 **Sibai** Mohamed M., Mosque libraries; an historical study: Libraries and Librarianship in the Muslim world [< diss. Indiana Univ. 1984] L 1987, Mansell. x-174 p. £27. – [R]JSS 35 (1990) 376-8 (P. *Auchterlonie*; weak on accuracy and original research; seems never to have examined a *waqf* document or visited any of the libraries cited).

9491 *a) Suleiman* M. Y., SĪBAWAIHĪ's 'parts of speech' according to SAJJĀJĪ; a new interpretation; – *b) Matar* Zeina, *Kahl* Oliver, A treatise on the amicable numbers 220 and 284 attributed to Abū Ma'shar al-BALKHĪ: JSS 35 (1990) 245-263 / 233-243.

9492 **Ullmann** Manfred, Adminiculum zur Grammatik des klassischen Arabisch [zu 15 grammatischen Phänomenen, 803 Belegstellen]. Wsb 1989, Harrassowitz. viii-96 p. DM 24,80. – ᴿWZKM 80 (1990) 244s (A. A. *Ambros*).

9493 **Ullmann** Manfred, Aufs Wasser schreiben; Beiträge zur Lexikographie des klassischen Arabisch 7: Szb Bayerische Akad. p/h 1989/1. Mü 1989. 29 p. – ᴿWZKM 80 (1990) 245s (A. A. *Ambros*).

9494 **Voigt** Rainer M., Die infirmen Verbaltypen des Arabischen und das Biradikalismus-Problem: MainzAkad OrKomm Veröff 39, 1988 ➤ 4,a448; 5,9393: ᴿAcOrK 50 (1989) 202-6 (J. *Hämeen-Anttila*); JRAS (1990) 141-4 (C. *Holes*). Kratylos 35 (1990) 179-184 (Frithiof *Rundgren*).

9495 **Wagner** Ewald, Grundzüge der klassischen arabischen Dichtung I-II: Grundzüge 68-70. Da 1987s, Wiss. xii-220 p.; x-213 p. je DM 45 ➤ 5, 2996; 3-534-01896-6; 3874-6: ᴿBO 45 (1990) 499-501 (G. van *Gelder*).

9496 ᴱ**Witkam** Jan J., Manuscripts of the Middle East; a journal devoted to the study of [mostly Arabic, some Turkish] handwritten materials of the Middle East 1; 2 (Leiden 1987) 159 p. *f* 107. – ᴿJSS [33 (1988) 314-7] 35 (1990) 375s: (C. E. *Bosworth*: excellent value; vol. 3 is about to appear).

9497 *Zemánek* Petr, À propos de la pharyngalisation et de la glottalisation en arabe: ArOr 58 (1990) 125-134.

J3 Ægyptia.

9498 **Andrews** Carol A. R., Catalogue of demotic papyri in the British Museum 4. Ptolemaic legal texts from the Teban area. L 1990, British Museum. 129 p.; 96 pl. 0-7141-0952-5.

9499 *Baines* John, Interpreting the story of the shipwrecked sailor: JEA 76 (1990) 55-72 [168-170, *Berg* David, his fire].

9500 **Barguet** Paul, Textes des sarcophages 1986 ➤ 3,9652; 4,a451*: ᴿOLZ 85 (1990) 19-21 (W. *Barta*).

9501 *Barta* Winfried, Das Demonstrativpronomen *nw* als kongruierendes Subjekt im *pw*-Satz nach Beispielen der Pyramidentexte: GöMiszÄg 114 (1990) 31-34.

9502 *Barta* Winfried, a) Der Palasthorustiel und seine Vorläufer in der Frühzeit: GöMiszÄg 117s (1990) 55-58; 8 fig.; – b) Zur Konstruktion ägyptischer Personennamen mit einem Königsnamen als Komponente: ZägSpr 117 (1990) 2ss.

9504 a) *Barta* Winfried, Zur sekundären Wortstellung eines nominalen Subjekts; – b) *Gessler-Löhr* Beatrix, Zur Schreibung von *m3'-ḫrw* mit der Blume; – c) *Banna* E. el–, Un titre nouveau, 'Le gardien de volailles du temple de Rê', *Miniw-3pdw n pr-r'*: GöMiszÄg 116 (1990) 21-24 / 25-43; 5 fig. / 7-17 + 2 pl.; plan.

9505 **Bierbrier** M. L., Hieroglyphic texts from Egyptian stelae etc. 11. L 1987, British Museum. 50 p.; 96 pl. £70. 0-7141-0935-5. – ᴿAJA 76 (1990) 220-3 (J. H. *Taylor*); BO 47 (1990) 351-8 (P. *Munro*).

9506 **Blackman** A. M., The story of King Kheops and the magicians, transcribed from Papyrus Westcar (Berlin 3033). Reading, Berks 1988, J. V. Books. v-18 p.; 12 pl. [VarAeg 5,8].

9507 *Bogoslovsky* Ye. S., ⊕ Statuette of a court attendant of the time of Tutankhamun [from Memphis; inscription]: VDI 193 (1990) 70-78; 4 fig.; Eng. 78.

9508 **Bonhême** Marie-Ange, Les noms royaux... Eg. 3ᶜ int. 1987 ➤ 3,9659; 5,9402: ᴿBO 17 (1990) 85-88 (K. *Jansen-Winkeln*). JEA 76 (1990) 245s (M. L. *Bierbrier*).

9510 **Bresciani** Edda, Letteratura e poesia dell'antico Egitto, introduzione, traduzioni originali e note. T 1990, Einaudi. xv-1027 p.; 17 (foldout/color.) fig. 88-06-12215-0.

9511 **Brunner** Hellmut, Grundzüge einer Geschichte der altägyptischen Literatur ⁴ʳᵉᵛ [1986] ➤ 5,9405; 3-534-04100-3: ᴿJEA 76 (1990) 209s (J. *Baines*).

9512 *Cannuyer* Christian, Recherches sur l'onomasiologie du feu en Ancien Égyptien: ZägSpr 117 (1990) 103-111.

9513 **Černy** Jaroslav, ᴱ*Koenig* Yvan, Papyrus hiératiques de Deir el-Medineh II (18-34) 1986 ➤ 5,9408: ᴿCdÉ 65 (1990) 71s (B. van de *Walle* †); JEA 76 (1990) 240-2 (S. *Quirke*).

9513* *a) Chappaz* Jean-Luc, Remarque sur un exercice scolaire [une des innombrables copies de Kemit, seul texte dont nous possédons le titre]; – *b) Doret* Éric, Sur une caractéristique grammaticale de quelques sarcophages d'el-Bersheh; – *c) Kasser* Rodolphe, Le grand-groupe dialectal copte de Basse-Égypte et son extension véhiculaire panégyptienne: ➤ 70*: BSocÉg 13 (Mém. HARI R. Genève 1989) 33-43 / 45-50 / 73-82.

9514 *Chetverukhin* Alexandr S., *a)* Old Egyptian introductory particles of the base *m(j)* and the verb 'see, behold, look': ArOr 58 (1990) 135-146; – *b)* Some theoretical aspects of Old Egyptian nominal sentence; structure and semantics: AltOrF 17 (1990) 3-17.

9514* **Clagett** Marshall, Ancient Egyptian science, I. Knowledge and order; a source book; II: JAPS Mem. 184. Ph 1989, Amer. Ph. Soc. I. xv-406 p.; map; II. p. 407-736 + 739-862 plates. 0-87169-184-1.

9515 **Clère** Jacques J., Le papyrus de Nesmin; un Livre des Morts hiéroglyphique de l'époque ptolemaïque; IFAO 661, 1987 ➤ 4,a465: ᴿBO 47 (1990) 310-2 (S. *Pernigotti*).

9516 *Collier* Mark, The circumstantial *sḏm(.f) / sḏm.n(.f)* as verbal verbforms in Middle Egyptian: JEA 76 (1990) 73-85.

9517 **Davies** W. V., Egyptian hieroglyphs 1987 ➤ 3,9672; 5,9410: ᴿAncHRes 20 (1990) 179s (J. *Walker*).

9518 *Derchain* Philippe, *a)* L'auteur du papyrus Jumilhac: RÉgp 41 (1990) 9-28; 29, sa photo, avec? et sans nom; – *b)* Les hiéroglyphes à l'époque ptolémaïque: ➤ 762*, Phoinikeia grammata 1989, 129-149.

9519 *Diego Muñiz* José M. de, Reconsideración de unos ejemplos iniciales de la construcción pseudoverbal *sin jw* I: BAsocEspEg 2 (1990) 22-60.

9520 **Doret** E., Narrative verbal system 1986 ➤ 2,7603 ... 5,9413: ᴿAcOrK 50 (1989) 180-5 (R. *Pierce*); JAmEg 27 (1990) 223s (E. S. *Meltzer*).

9521 *Doret* Éric, Phrase nominale, identité et substitution dans les textes des sarcophages II: RÉgp 41 (1990) 39-56...

9522 ᵀ**Faulkner** R. O. [1972], ᴱ**Andrews** Carol, The ancient Egyptian Book of the Dead 1985 ➤ 2,7605; 5,6416: ᴿCdÉ 65 (1990) 68-71 (H. *Milde*).

9523 ᵀᴱ**Fischer-Elfert** Hans-Werner, Die satirische Streitschrift des Papyrus Anastasi I: ÄgAbh 44. Wsb 1986, Harrassowitz. xi-309 p. DM 74. – ᴿWeltOr 20s (1989s) 252-6 (Waltraud *Guglielmi*).

9524 *Gaboda* Péter, A P-prefix in Egyptian: ➤ 49, Mém. FÓTI L. 1989, 93-117.

9525 *Gabolde* Marc, Le droit d'aînesse d'Ankhesenpaaton; à propos de [KRAUSS R., ALLEN J.] sur la stèle UC 410 [regravure]: BSocÉg 14 (Genève 1990) 33-47; 10 fig.

9525* **Giblin** James C., The riddle of the Rosetta Stone, key to ancient Egypt. NY 1990, Crowell. 85 p. 0-690-04797-5 [OIAc F91].

9526 **Goedicke** Hans, Old Hieratic paleography. Baltimore 1988, Helgo. xxiv p.; 72 pl. [VarAeg 5,8].

9527 *Goedicke* Hans, Sinuhe's self-realization (Sinuhe B 113-127): ZägSpr 117 (1990) 129-139.

9528 **Graefe** Erhart, Mittelägyptische Grammatik für Anfänger³*rev* [¹1987 → 3,9677; ²1988 → 5,9424]. Wsb 1990, Harrassowitz. xxi-253 p. 3-447-02934-3 [OIAc F91,11]. – ᴿWeltOr 20s (1989s) 241-3 (R. *Hannig-Hildesheim*, 2).

9529 **Grandet** Pierre, *Mathieu* Bernard, Cours d'égyptien hiéroglyphique. P 1990–, Khéops. I. xxi-426 p.; 32 fig.; map. 2-9504-3681-1.

9529* **Greig** Gary S., The influence of the semantic categories of Egyptian verbs of perception and cognition on grammatical structure in Late Egyptian: diss. Chicago 1990. xv-233 p. [OIAc JJ90].

9530 *a) Hallof* Jochen, Codierungslisten und Analyse ägyptischer Hieroglyphen; – *b) Plas* Kirk van der, Eine internationale ägyptologische Datenbank zwischen Traum und Wirklichkeit; – *c) Thelwall* Robin, Micro-computer dictionary making; – *d) Strudwick* Nigel, The micro-computer and the Egyptian stela: → 78, ᶠHINTZE F., Meroitica 12 (1990) 135-142 / 237-242 / 313-325 / 301-312.

9530* **Hollis** Susan T., The ancient Egyptian 'Tale of two brothers', the oldest fairy tale in the world [< diss. Harvard 1982]; pref. *Leprohon* Ronald J. Norman 1990, Univ. Oklahoma. xii-276 p. 0-8061-2269-2.

9531 ᴱ**Hornung** Erik, Texte zum Amduat I. **Spycher** Lotty, Kurzfassung und Langfassung, 1. bis 3. Stunde: AegHelv 3. Basel/Genève 1987, Univ. xviii-342 p.

9532 *Jansen-Winkeln* Karl, Vermerke [nicht-Satzhafte, objektgebundene Texte]; zum Verständnis kurzer und formelhafter Inschriften auf ägyptischen Denkmälern: MiDAI-K 46 (1990) 127-156.

9533 *Kammerzell* Frank, Funktion und Form; zur Opposition von Perfekt und Pseudopartizip im Alt- und Mittelägyptischen: GöMiszÄg 117s (1990) 181-202; correction in 119 (1990) 39.

9534 **Koch** Roland, Die Erzählung des Sinuhe: Bibliotheca Aegyptiaca 17. Bru 1990, Fond. Reine Élisabeth. vi-81a double p. (B left, facsimile; 'a' right, comment); no translation.

9535 *Kondō* Jirō, Hieratic inscriptions from the tomb of Amenophis III: Orient-Japan 26 (1990) 94-101 + 3 fig.

9535* **Kroeber** Burkhart, Die Neuägyptismen vor der Amarnazeit; Studien zur Entwicklung der ägyptischen Sprache vom Mittleren zum Neuen Reich: Diss. Tübingen 1970, ᴰ*Brunner* H. xxvi-220 p. [OIAc Ja91].

9536 *Meyer* Gudrun, Das Hirtenlied in den Privatgräbern des Alten Reiches: StAltÄgK 17 (1990) 235-284.

9537 *Moftah* R., Der Laubbaum als Schriftzeichen: GöMiszÄg 119 (1990) 61-64.

9538 **Munro** Irmtraut, Untersuchungen zu den Totenbuch-Papyri der 18. Dynastie; Kriterien ihrer Datierung. L 1988, Kegan Paul. xxi-369 p.; 23 pl. £45. – ᴿOLZ 85 (1990) 655s (L. *Kákosy*).

9539 *Munro* Irmtraut, Der Totenbuch-Papyrus des Veziers Wsr-Jmn: GöMiszÄg 116 (1990) 73-78; 79-89 facsimiles; 90-95 photos.

9540 *Nibbi* Alessandra, A contribution to our understanding of *kmt* [not simply 'Egypt']: DiscEg 16 (1990) 63-72.

9541 ᶠPOLOTSKY H. J.: Essays on Egyptian grammar 1986 ⇒ 4,711: ᴿOLZ 82 (1991) 14-18 (K. *Jansen-Winkeln*).

9541* *a*) *Polotsky* Hans J., 'Perfekt' und 'Imperfekt' von SETHE zu GARDINER; – *b*) *Thissen* Heinz-J., Bemerkungen zum demotischen Harfner-Gedicht; – *c*) *Vernus* Pascal, La date du Paysan Éloquent; – *d*) *Sweeney* Deborah, Involvement category in Late Egyptian: ⇒ 114, ᶠLICHTHEIM M. 1990, (II) 768-772 / 980-993 / 1033-1047 / 943-979.

9542 *Polz* Daniel, Die śnᶜ-Vorsteher des Neuen Reiches: ZägSpr 117 (1990) 43-60.

9543 *Quaegebeur* Jan, La stèle Brooklyn 71.37.2 reconsidérée [... une des pièces vedettes]: GöMiszÄg 119 (1990) 73-87 + 2 fig.

9544 **Rachewiltz** Boris de, Il libro dei Morti degli Antichi Egizi, papiro di Torino. R 1986, Mediterranee. 179 p.; 40 pl. Lit. 40.000. – ᴿBO 17 (1990) 66s (A. De *Caluwe*).

9545 *Roccati* Alessandro, Lo scriba: ⇒ 483, L'uomo egiziano 1990, 63-88.

9546 *Röbler-Köhler* Ursula, Die formale Aufteilung des Papyrus Jumilhac [Louvre E. 17110]: CdÉ 65 (1990) 21-40.

9546* **Roehrig** Catharine H., The Eighteenth Dynasty titles royal nurse (*mn't nswt*), royal tutor (*mn' nswt*) and foster brother/sister of the Lord of the Two Lands (*sn/snt mn' n nb t3wy*): diss. California. Berkeley 1990. 454 p. 91-03856. – DissA 51 (1990s) 3447-A.

9547 **Sadek** Abdul-Aziz F., Contribution à l'étude de l'Amdouat: OBO 65, 1985 ⇒ 1,a647* ... 5,9445: ᴿOLZ 85 (1990) 148-150 (C. *Jacq*); WeltOr 20s (1989s) 256-9 (U. *Luft*).

9548 **Schenkel** Wolfgang, Einführung in die altägyptische Sprachwissenschaft: Orient. Einf. Da 1990, Wiss. xii-206 p. 3-534-03506-2.

9549 **Schenkel** Wolfgang, Materialien zur Vorlesung; Einführung in die klassisch-ägyptische Sprache und Schrift ¹1987, ²1989 ⇒ 3,8694; ²264 p.: ᴿDiscEg 16 (1990) 81-88 (M. *Collier*: needed tool for replacing GARDINER with POLOTSKY approach); 18 (1990) 83-90, ed. 2.

9550 **Smith** M., Catalogue of demotic papyri in the British Museum III. The mortuary texts of Papyrus BM 10507 [companion-papyrus to 2, Glanville's 1955 Instructions of 'Onkhsheshonqy]. L 1987, British Museum. 216 p.; 11 pl. £95. 0-7141-0937-1. – ᴿJEA 76 (1990) 246-8 (J. D. *Ray*).

9551 **Spiegelberg** Wilhelm, Der demotische Text der Priesterdekrete von Kanopus und Memphis (Rosettana), mit hieroglyphischen und griechischen Fassungen und deutscher Übersetzung nebst demotischem Glossar. Hildesheim 1990 = 1922, Olms. 222 p. 3-487-09309-X.

9552 *Thissen* Heinz-Josef, Demotistik und Ägyptologie: ZägSpr 117 (1990) 63-69 [79-88, ein religiöser Text, *Vittman* Günter].

9553 *Thompson* Stephen E., The origin of the pyramid texts found on Middle Kingdom Saqqâra coffins [querying *Altenmüller* H., *Barta* W.]: JEA 76 (1990) 17-25.

9554 *Vernus* Pascal, Les espaces de l'écrit dans l'Égypte pharaonique: BSocFrEg 119 (1990) 35-53; 1 fig.; 3 pl.

9555 *Vleeming* S. P., Transliterating Old Egyptian in demotic: GöMiszÄg 117s (1990) 219-223.

9556 **Vycichl** Werner, La vocalisation de la langue égyptienne I. La phonétique: BÉt 16. Le Caire 1990, IFAO. xi-260 p. 2-7247-0097-X.

9557 *Wallet-Lebrun* C., *Rwyt* et *s3tw* dans la biographie d'Ouni: VarAeg 5 (1989) 27-58. 155.

9558 **Ward** William A., Essays on feminine titles ... 1986 ⇒ 2,7633 ... 5,9455*: ᴿJEA 76 (1990) 228-232 (D. *Franke* excuses the shortcomings).

9559 ᵀWente E., ᴱMeltzer E. S., Letters from ancient Egypt: SBL Writings from the Ancient World 1. Atlanta 1990, Scholars. xii-271 p. $27; sb./pa. $17. 1-55540-472-3; -3-1 [BL 91, 132, K. A. Kitchen: 'pleasant'].

9560 ᶠWestendorf Wolfhart, Studien zu Sprache und Religion Ägyptens 1984 ➤ 65,148: ᴿOLZ 85 (1990) 13-19 (J. Assmann: detaillierte Analysen).

9561 **Winand** Jean, Le voyage d'Ounamon... concordance 1987 ➤ 3,9703; 5,9458: ᴿBO 17 (1990) 64-66 (D. van der Plas).

9562 **Browne** Gerald M., Studies in Old Nubian 1988 ➤ 4,a456: ᴿBO 17 (1990) 122-4 (W. Vycichl: beaucoup sur la linguistique).

9563 — Satzinger Helmut, Relativsatz und Thematisierung im Altnubischen [Browne G., Studies in Old Nubian 1988, p. 28-52]: WZKM 80 (1990) 185-205.

9564 **Browne** Gerald M., Chrysostomus Nubianus: PapyrCastroct 10, 1984 ➤ 65,d578; 2,7640b: ᴿCdÉ 65 (1990) 185s (W. Vycichl).

9565 **Khalil** Mokhtar, Studien zum Altnubischen; Nubisch-Ägyptische Beziehungen [Diss. Bonn 1985s]: EurHS 27/19. iv-194 p. Fs 44. 3-8204-8980-0. – ᴿBO 17 (1990) 124-133 (G. M. Browne).

J3.4 Coptica.

9566 **Atiya** Aziz S. †, The Coptic encyclopedia. NY 1990, Macmillan. 8 vol.; 500 ill. $900. 0-02-897025-X [JAAR 58,690 adv. calls Atiya 'the author' but says 'all articles signed'].

9566* a) Barta Winfried, Versuch einer Grobgliederung der ägyptisch-koptischen Syntax; – b) Gomaà Farouk, Die Orte mit Namen ihrit; – c) Kolta Kamal S., Ärztenamen der kopto-arabischen Epoche: ➤ 8*, ᶠAssfalg J., Lingua restituta 1990, 9-16 / 114-8 / 190-4; 1 fig.

9567 **Bouvarel-Boud'hors** Anne, Catalogue des fragments coptes, I. bibliques 1987 ➤ 4,a524: ᴿArPapF 36 (1990) 91s (P. Nagel).

9568 Dembska Albertyna, A note on the meaning of the Coptic verb tōoue 'arise', 'rise': RoczOr 46,1 (1988s) 105-110.

9569 **Hasitzka** Monika R. M., Koptische Texte: Corpus Papyrorum Raineri 12, 1987 ➤ 3,9714: ᴿWZKM 80 (1990) 233-6 (W. Brunsch).

9570 **Green** Michael, The Coptic Share pattern [aorist...] and its ancient Egyptian ancestors 1987 ➤ 3,9713: ᴿCdÉ 65 (1990) 186-192 (L. Depuydt, unconvinced); OLZ 85 (1990) 408-410 (H.-M. Schenke).

9571 **Layton** Bentley, Catalogue of Coptic literary manuscripts in the British Library acquired since the year 1906: 1987 ➤ 4,a533; 5,9471: ᴿOLZ 85 (1990) 154-8 (H.-M. Schenke).

9572 **MacCoull** Leslie S. B., Coptic documentary papyri... Beinecke/Yale 1986 ➤ 2,7647: ᴿWZKM 80 (1990) 236-8 (W. Brunsch).

9573 MacCoull Leslie S. B., Missing pieces of the Dioscorus archive: CdÉ 65 (1990) 107-110.

9574 a) MacCoull Leslie S. B., More Coptic Papyri from the Beinecke collection; – b) Nagel Peter, Editionen koptischer Bibeltexte seit Till 1960: ArPapF 35 (1989) 25-35; fig. 2-8 [others 37-42, al.] / 43-100.

9575 Miller C. D. G., Arabisch wird zur Sprache der Kopten: Nubica 1s (1990) 277-290.

9576 Müller Caspar D. G., Gab es ein koptisches Theater?: BSACopte 29 (1990) 9-22.

9577 *Orlandi* Tito, Due fogli papiracei da Medinet Madi (Fayum); l'historia horsiesi: EgVO 13 (1990) 109-126.
9578 *Orlandi* Tito, Egyptian monasticism and the beginnings of the Coptic literature: ➤ 780, Schmidt-Kolloquium 1988/90, 129-142.
9579 *Pelsmaekers* J., *Mekyra* of *kyra*? Vragen rond enkele koptische grafplaten: Bulletin de l'Institut Historique Belge de Rome 60 (1990) 35-42; 2 pl.
9579* **Polotsky** H. J., Grundlagen des koptischen Satzbaus, erste Hälfte; Amer. Stud. Papyrol. 28, 1984 ➤ 4,a536; 5,9475: ᴿArPapF 36 (1990) 89-91 (H.-M. *Schenke*); BO 17 (1990) 140s (A. I. *Elanskaya*); JEA 76 (1990) 255-8 (M. *Green*); JSS 35 (1990) 184s (M. *Smith*).
9580 *a*) *Quecke* Hans, Zur direkten und indirekten Rede im Koptischen; – *b*) *Shisha-Halevy* Ariel, The 'tautological infinitive' in Coptic; a structural examination; – *c*) *Layton* Bentley, The Coptic determinator syntagm and its constituents; – *d*) *Schenke* Hans-Martin, Ein Brief als Textzeuge für den mittelägyptischen Dialekt des Koptischen [P. Mich. inv. 525]; – *e*) *Kasser* Rodolphe, Marius CHAÎNE et la thèse d'une relation phonologique privilégiée entre les langues coptes saïdique et bohaïrique [+ A standard system of sigla for referring to the dialects of Coptic]: ➤ 46*b*, ᶠELANSKAJA Alla I. = JCopt 1 (1990) 129-135 / 99-127 / 79-97 / 59-72; pl. 17 / 73-77 [141-151].
9580* **Sidarus** Adel Y., *a*) IBN AR-RĀHIBS Leben und Werk; ein koptisch-arabischer Enzyklopädist des 7./13. Jahrhunderts: Islamkund. Unters. 36. FrB 1975, Schwarz. DM 42. – ᴿOrChr 74 (1990) 257-260 (C.D.G. *Müller*). – *b*) Les lexiques onomasiologiques gréco-copto-arabes du Moyen Âge et leurs origines anciennes: ➤ 8*, ᶠASSFALG J. 1990, 348-359.
9581 *a*) *Weima* Jeffrey A. D., The second tense in the Gospel of Thomas; the 'sleeping beauty' of the Coptic verbal system: Orientalia 59 (1990) 491-510; – *b*) *Worp* Klaas A., Der Berliner Ostrakon P. 14735; koptisch oder griechisch?: ArPapF 36 (1990) 75-77 [Beides].

J3.8 Æthiopica.

9582 **Haile** Getatchew, A catalogue of Ethiopian manuscripts 8, Collegeville MN, 1985 ➤ 3,9732: ᴿOLZ 85 (1990) 324s (B. M. *Weischer*).
9583 **Kapeliuk** Olga, Nominalization in Amharic: ÄthF 23, 1988 ➤ 5,9483*: ᴿWZKM 80 (1990) 300-2 (Renate *Richter*).
9584 **Leslau** Wolf, Concise dictionary of Ge'ez (classical Ethiopic). Wsb 1989, Harrassowitz. xi-247 p. DM 88. 3-447-02873-4 [BL 91, 152, M. A. *Knibb*: abridgment of his 1987 Comparative Dictionary ➤ 3,9734). – ᴿWZKM 80 (1990) 290s (A. A. *Ambros*).
9585 **Leslau** Wolf, Comparative dictionary of Ge'ez 1987 ➤ 3,9734; 4,a456: ᴿOrChr 74 (1990) 270-5 (M. *Kropp*); ZDMG 139 (1989) 430s (E. *Wagner*).
9585* *Leslau* Wolf, The Ge'ez and the Arabic vocabulary: ➤ 117, ᶠLÖFGREN O., On both sides 1989, 23-38.
9586 **Six** Veronica, Äthiopische Handschriften, 2... bayerische Staatsbibliothek. Wsb 1989, Steiner, 200 p. – ᴿOrChrPer 56 (1990) 496s (O. *Raineri*).
9586* *Six* Veronika, Kategorien der äthiopischen Zaubertexte: ZDMG 139 (1989) 310-7.
9587 **Uhlig** S., Introduction to Ethiopian palaeography: ÄthFor 28. Stu 1990, Steiner. 118 p. DM 58. 3-515-05401-4 [BL 91, 155, M. A. *Knibb*: Addis Ababa lectures dedicated to E. ULLENDORFF].

9588 **Uhlig** Siegbert, Äthiopische Paläographie: ÄthF 22, 1988 ➤ 4,a550: RAnBoll 108 (1990) 224-6 (U. *Zanetti*); OrChrPer 56 (1990) 497-502 (O. *Raineri*).

9589 **Ullendorff** Edward, A Tigrinya chrestomathy 1985 ➤ 1,9523...4,a551: RJAOS 110 (1990) 355s (G. *Hudson*).

9589* **Ullendorff** Edward, [➤ 313] The two Zions; reminiscences of Jerusalem and Ethiopia 1988 ➤ 4,a552: RBSO 52 (1989) 551s (M. A. *Knibb*); JSS 35 (1990) 185s (G. M. *Wickens*). – *b*) Some further material from the Eugen MITTWOCH Nachlass: BSO 53 (1990) 64-76.

9590 *Voigt* Rainer, The gemination of the present-imperfect forms in Old Ethiopic: JSS 35 (1990) 1-17.

9591 *Zanetti* Ugo, Les manuscrits éthiopiens de la Bibliothèque des Bollandistes: AnBoll 108 (1990) 5-28.

J4 Anatolica.

9592 *Álvarez-Pedrosa* Juan A., La heteróclisis en hetita: Emerita 58 (1990) 185-204; Eng. 185.

9593 *Arbeitman* Yoël L., Hittite *pái-*, why no *wái-*? an Anatolian-Indo-European heterogloss: ➤ 79, FHOENIGSWALD...

9594 **Archi** Alfonso, Hethitische Briefe: KaB 57, 1987 ➤ 3,9743; 4,a553: RBO 47 (1990) 423-432 (T. van den *Hout*).

9594* *a*) *Badalì* Enrico, Il significato del verbo ittito *palwae-*; – *b*) *Nowicki* Helmut, Zur Etymologie von heth. *paluae*: ➤ 160*, Mem. SCHULER E.v., Orientalia 59 (1990) 130-142 / 239-242.

9595 *a*) *Carruba* Onofrio, Zur Erforschung der anatolischen Sprachen [ROSENKRANZ B. 1978]: OLZ 85 (1990) 5-13; – *b*) *Faucounau* J., Les signes homophones existent-ils véritablement dans l'écriture 'hittite hiéroglyphique'?: Belleten 53,206ss (1989) 487-496.

9595* **Friedrich** J., *Kammenhuber* A., Hittite dictionary [3/3 1986 ➤ 4,a559], 2 E². Heid 1988, Winter. 3-533-03999-4. – RZDMG 140 (1990) 376-380 (J. *Tischler*).

9596 **Garrett** Andrew J., The syntax of Anatolian pronominal clitics [Hittite, Luvian, Lycian...]: diss. Harvard. CM 1990, 310 p. 91-13159. – DissA 51 (1990s) 4104-A.

9597 *Girbal* Christian, *a*) Der Pluralisator /t/ in hurritischen Verbformen: AltOrF 16 (1989) 78-83; – *b*) Zur Grammatik des Mittani-Hurritischen: ZAss 80 (1990) 93-101 [Mittani with two *t*'s and one *n* throughout].

9598 FGÜTERBOCK Hans G., Kaniššuwar, EHoffner H. A., *al.*, 1986 ➤ 3,42; 4,a558: RJAOS 110 (1990) 352s (A. *Archi*).

9599 **Güterbock** Hans G., *Hoffner* Harry A., Hittite Dictionary 3/2s, 1983 ➤ 2,7664: ROLZ 85 (1990) 22-36 (V. *Haas, J. Klinger*).

9600 **Hagenbuchner** Albertine, Die Korrespondenz der Hethiter I. Die Briefe unter ihren sprachlichen und thematischen Gesichtspunkten [➤ 5,8498]; II.,...Transkription, Übersetzung und Kommentar: Texte der Hethiter 15s. Heid 1989, Winter. xxix-175 p.; xxviii-483 p. DM 125 + 260; pa. 98 + 230: RZAss 80 (1990) 308-313 (H. *Freydank*).

9600* *Harmatta* J., Hethitisch-Luwisch: ➤ 170*, FSZABÓ A., AcAntH 31,3s (1985-8) 251-265.

9601 **Held** Warren G.J, *al.*, Beginning Hittite. Columbus 1988, Slavica. 0-89357-184-9 [OIAc Ap89].

9602 **Hout** Theodorus P. J. van den, Studien zum spätjunghethitischen Texte der Zeit Tuthalijas IV., KBö IV-10 + (CTH 106): Diss. DCate P. ten. Amst 1989. – OIAc Ap89.

9603 **Kronasser** Heinz, Etymologie der hethitischen Sprache (2. Indices, **Neu** E.) 1987 ➤ 3,9775; 5,9503: ᴿBO 47 (1990) 158s (T. van den *Hout*).

9603* *Lebrun* R., Les langues anatoliennes, leur répartition et leur fonction de 2000 à 500 av. J.-C.: ➤ 9855, ᴱ*Swiggers* P., Language 1990, 56-75.

9604 **Luraghi** Silvia, Old Hittite sentence structure [< diss. 1987]: Theoretical Linguistics. L 1990, Routledge. x-188 p. 0-415-04735-8 [OIAc Oc90].

9605 **Marazzi** Massimiliano, *al.*, Il geroglifico anatolico; problemi di analisi e prospettive di ricerca: RicLingFg 24. R 1990, Univ. ix-483 p. 88-85134-23-8.

9606 **Neu** Erich, Das Hurritische; eine altorientalische Sprache in neuem Licht [bilingual tablets from 1983 and 1985 Boğazköy, first examples of Hittite wisdom literature]: Akad Mainz Abh 1988 ➤ 5,9505*; 3-315-05179-1: ᴿBL (1990) 35 (W. *Watson*).

9606* *a*) *Neu* Erich, Zur Grammatik des Hurritischen auf der Grundlage der hurritisch-hethitischen Bilingue aus der Boğazköy-Grabungskampagne 1983; – *b*) *Plank* Frans, Das Hurritische und die Sprachwissenschaft: ➤ 801*, Hurriter 1988, 91-115 / 69-93.

9607 *a*) *Neu* Erich, Das hethitische Wort für 'Frau'; – *b*) *Neumann* Günter, Hethitisch *purusiyala*- 'Kranz, Gebinde': HistSprF 103 (1990) 208-217/218s.

9607* *a*) *Neu* Erich, Zum hurritischen Verbum; – *b*) *Neumann* Günter, Hethitisch *widul*(i) 'Wagenkorb'; – *c*) *Salvini* Mirjo, Ein Beitrag zur hurritisch-urartäischen Morphologie; – *d*) *Wegner* Ilse, Phonotaktischer n-Verlust in Jussivformen des Boğazköy-Hurritischen: ➤ 160*, Mem. Sᴄʜᴜʟᴇʀ F.v., Orientalia 59 (1990) 223-233/234-8/243-250/298-305.

9608 **Oettinger** Norbert, 'Indo-Hittite'-Hypothese und Wortbildung 1986 ➤ 4,a566: ᴿZDMG 139 (1989) 231-3 (J. *Tischler*).

9608* *Oettinger* Norbert, Die 'dunkle Erde' im Hethitischen und Griechischen: WeltOr 20s (1989s) 83-98.

9609 *Oshiro* Terumasa, On kinship terms in hieroglyphic Luwian: Orient-Jap 26 (1990) 86-93.

9610 **Otten** Heinrich, *Rüster* Christel, Die hurritisch-hethitische Bilingue und weitere Texte aus der Oberstadt: KaB 32. B 1990, Mann. xv-56 p. 3-7861-1560-5.

9611 *a*) *Poetto* Massimo, Luvio geroglifico *ku-ma-ya-la* 'animali da sacrificio'; – *b*) *Del Monte* Giuseppe F., Licio *kumali*- 'vittima sacrificale'; – *c*) *Raggi Braglia* Maria Stella, IE. *per*- 'volare' nelle lingue anatoliche: OrAnt 28 (1989) 193-6/197-200/201-211.

9612 **Rüster** Christel, *Neu* Erich, Hethitisches Zeichenlexikon — Inventar und Interpretation der Keilschriftzeichen aus den Boğazköy-Texten: StudBoğT Beih 2, 1989 ➤ 5,9510: ᴿRHPR 70 (1990) 245 (J.-G. *Heintz*).

9613 **Starke** Frank, Untersuchung zur Stammbildung des keilschrift-luwischen Nomens: StBoğT 31. Wsb 1990, Harrassowitz. xxvi-705 p. 3-447-02879-3.

9614 **Tischler** Johann, Hethitisch-Deutsches Wörterverzeichnis 1982 ➤ 63, 8263...2,7672: ᴿJNES 49 (1990) 355-360 (A. *Ünal*).

9615 *a*) *Villar* F., On the 2d person singular pronoun in Hittite and in Indo-European: – *b*) *Hamp* Eric P., **sor* 'woman' and 'Indo-Hittite'; – *c*) *Oshiro* Terumasa, The relative conjunctions in hieroglyphic Luwian: JIndEur 16 (1988) 1-8/121s/9-21.

9616 *Watanabe* Kazuko, Mit Gottessiegeln versehene hethitische 'Staatsverträge': AcSum 11 (1989) 261-276.

9617 **Yoshida** Daisuke, Die Syntax des althethitischen substantivischen Genitivs: Texte der Hethiter 13, 1987 ➤ 3,9764; 5,9516: ᴿJAOS 110 (1990) 124s (Sara E. *Kimball*).
9618 **Yoshida** Kazuhiko, The Hittite mediopassive endings in –*ri*: StIndE 5. B/NY 1990, de Gruyter. xi-216 p. DM 136. 3-11-012346-0 / US 0-80925-701-1.

───────

9619 **Tezcan** Nuran, Elementarwortschatz Türkisch-Deutsch: Turcologie 1. Wsb 1988, Harrassowitz. xv-206 p. DM 40. – ᴿOLZ 85 (1990) 456-8 (A. *Bassarak*: 'Gut!').
9619* *Stachowski* Marek, Ergänzungen zu [Kᴀʜᴀɴᴇ Henry & Renée, *Tietze* Andreas, Urbana 1958] The lingua franca in the Levant; Turkish nautical terms of Italian and Greek origin: FolOr 25 (1989) 195-225.

J4.4 **Phrygia, Lydia, Lycia.**

9620 **Brixhe** Claude, Essai sur le grec anatolien au début de notre ère ²ʳᵉᵛ 1987 ➤ 5,9518: ᴿKratylos 35 (1990) 207s (A. *López Eire*).
9621 **Melchert** H. Craig, Lycian lexicon; Lexica anatolica 1. Chapel Hill NC 1989, auct. [OIAc Ap89].
9622 *a*) *Ray* John D., An outline of Carian grammar [A text ...]; – *b*) *Adiego* Ignacio J., Deux notes sur l'écriture et la langue cariennes; – *c*) *Bayun* Lilia S., *Orel* Vladimir E., Die neuphrygischen Inschriften mit dem Partizip *gegreimeno-;* – *d*) *Gusmani* Roberto, Karische Beiträge II: Kadmos 29 (1990) 54-83 [126...] / 133... / 35-37 / 47-53.

J4.8 **Armena, georgica.**

9623 *Bolognesi* G., Rapporti lessicali tra l'armeno e l'iranico [< IstLombR 96 (1962) 235-258]: ➤ 202, Studi 1990, 197-224 (-364, simili).
9624 *Greppin* John A. C., Armenian and the theory of etymology: JIndEur 17 (1989) 165-170.
9625 **Kévorkian** Raymond H., Catalogue des 'incunables' arméniens 1986 ➤ 3,9774... 5,9530: ᴿAcOrH 51 (1990) 277-9 (A. *Hultgård*).
9626 **Minassian** Martiros, Répertoire des verbes de l'arménien ancien: Pub. 4. Genève 1985, Fond. Ghoukassiantz. 294 p.
9626* *Salvini* Mirjo, Les inscriptions commémoratives urartéennes: ➤ 618, Commémoration 1986/8, 21-34; 7 fig.
9627 *Zanetti* Ugo, Les 'manuscrits arméniens' des Bollandistes: AnBoll 108 (1990) 48-50.

───────

9627* *a*) *Esbroeck* Michel van, Ein georgischer liturgischer Kanon für Maria [sic] Himmelfahrt; – *b*) *Outtier* Bernard, Nouveaux fragments onciaux du lectionnaire géorgien ancien; – *c*) *Müller* C.D.G., Der Weg des Georgischen zur Literatursprache: ➤ 8*, ᶠAssfᴀʟɢ J. 1990, 89-101 / 269-271 / 240-4.
9628 *Fähnrich* Heinz, *a*) Altgeorgische Kasusrelationen; – *b*) Die Funktionen der georgischen Präverben: RGéorg 5 (1989) 63-65 / 67-77.
9628* *a*) *Danelia* Korneli, Fremdsprachige grammatische Elemente in den altgeorgischen Schriften: Georgica 11 (1988) 7-10; – *b*) *Dshorbenadse* Bearion, Die Vokalpräfixe des georgischen Verbs: Georgica 12 (1989) 9-13.

9629 *Harris* Alice C., Reply to B. George HEWITT: RGéorg [3 (1987) 173-213] 5 (1989) 203-225: defense of her 1985 Diachronic syntax; the Kartvelian case.

9629* **Marchev** Yolanda, Die Morpheme der georgischen Sprache, Versuch einer Strukturanalyse. Z 1986, Amirani. 124 p. – RGeorgica 11 (1988) 100-2 (H. *Fähnrich*).

J5 **Graeca** .1 *grammatica, onomastica, inscriptiones.*

9630 *Abbenes* J.G.J., The middle imperative plural, type *pherésthō* in Greek: HistSprF 103 (1990) 236-244.

9631 E**Adorno** Francesco, Corpus dei papiri filosofici greci e latini I/1, 1989 RParPass 252 (1990) 232-8 (Margherita *Isnardi Parente*).

9632 *Adrados* Francisco R., La oposición aspectual griega presente/aoristo, examinada de nuevo: Emerita 58 (1990) 1-20; Eng. 1.

9633 [*Bauer* Walter], **Aland** Kurt & Barbara, Griechisch-deutsches Wörterbuch ... NT 1988 ➤ 4,a459 ... 5,9536: RCarthaginensia 6 (1990) 506s (R. *Sanz Valdivieso*); ÉTRel 65 (1990) 631 (E. *Cuvillier*); JBL 109 (1990) 340-3 (F. W. *Danker*: high standard but not yet the end of the road); Protestantesimo 45 (1990) 63s (B. *Corsani*); ScripTPamp 22 (1990) 1001s (K. *Limburg*); TZBas 46 (1990) 372s (K. *Haaker*).

9634 **Allen** W. S., Vox graeca ... pronunciation³ 1987 ➤ 5,9537: RGymnasium 97 (1990) 260-2 (T. G. *Heinze*).

9635 *a) Austefjord* Anders, On the oldest types of aorists in Indo-European; – *b) Shields* Kenneth, Tense, linguistic universals, and the reconstruction of Indo-European: JIndEur 16 (1988) 23-32 / 241-251.

9635* **Bagnall** Roger S., *al.*, Columbia Papyri 8: AmerStPapyrol 28. Atlanta 1990, Scholars. 238 p.; 57 pl. 1-55540-396-4 [OIAc Ja91].

9636 **Bécares Botas** V., Diccionario de terminología gramatical griega. S 1985, Univ. – RHelmantica 38 (1987) 420-2 (M. A. *Marcos Casquero*).

9637 **Bernand** André, De Thèbes à Syène [sans Thèbes mais avec Philae depuis 1969; inscriptions en continuation du volume 1972 De Koptos à Kosseir, qui ne contenait ni Koptos ni Kosseir]. P 1989, CNRS. xi-397 p.; 163 pl. – RCdÈ 65 (1990) 129-159! (J. *Bingen*).

9637* **Bernand** Étienne, Inscriptions grecques et latines d'Akôris: IFAO BÉt 103, 1988 ➤ 4,a582: RJAOS 110 (1990) 753s (R. S. *Bagnall*).

9638 E**Betz** Hans D., The Greek magical papyri in translation, 1. Texts 1986 ➤ 2,7692 ... 4,a583: RHeythJ 31 (1990) 52s (Mary E. *Mills*); RIIR 207 (1990) 326s (A. *Bernand*); SecC 7 (1989s) 180-2 (D. C. *Duling*).

9639 **Bingen** Jean, *Clarysse* Willy, Les ostraca grecs (O. Elkab gr.): Elkab 3. Bru 1989, Fond. Ég. R. Élisabeth. 154 p.; 20 pl. [OIAc Ja91].

9639* *Bingen* Jean, L'épigraphie grecque d'Hermonthis à Philae [*Bernand* A., De Thèbes à Syène 1989 ➤ 9637]: CdÉ 65 (1990) 129-159.

9640 **Blümel** Wolfgang, Die Inschriften von Mylasa I. Stadt; II. Umgebung: Österr./Wf Akad. Bonn 1987s, Habelt. xii-271 p., DM 272 / ix-230 p.; 24 pl.; 2 maps. – RClasR 40 (1990) 438-441 (S. *Mitchell*).

9640* **Boyaval** Bernard, Album de papyrus documentaires de Lille: CahPapÉg Supp 2. Lille 1990, Univ. XII pl. 2-9504764-0-6.

9641 *Brixhe* Claude, Bulletin de dialectologie grecque [... koiné]: RÉG 103 (1990) 201-230.

9641* *Brooten* Bernadette J., The gender of *Isēl* in the Jewish inscription from Aphrodisias: ➤ 173, FSTRUGNELL J., Of scribes 1990, 163-173.

9642 **Buonocore** Marco, Le iscrizioni latine e greche, Vatican 1987 ➤ 4,g823; 5,9546 ('l.g.'); ᴿLatomus 49 (1990) 500s (Monique *Dondin-Payne*).

9643 **Cervin** Richard S., Word-order in ancient Greek; VSO, SVO, SOV, or all of the above?: diss. Illinois, ᴰ*Hook* H. Urbana 1990. 91-14192. – DissA 51 (1990s) 4104-A.

9644 **Chastagnol** A. *al.*, L'Année Épigraphique 1986: ᴿLatomus 49 (1990) 927-9 (R. *Chevallier*).

9645 *Cignelli* Lino, *Bottini* G. Claudio, La concordanza del pronome relativo nel greco biblico: LA 40 (1990) 47-69; Eng. 445s.

9646 **Clarysse** W., *al.*, Berichtigungsliste der griechischen Papyrusurkunden aus Ägypten; Konkordanz und Supplement zu Band I-VII. Lv 1989, Peeters. xii-302 p. Fb 5000. – ᴿCdÉ 65 (1990) 169s (J. A. *Straus*).

9647 ᴱ**Coles** R. A. *al.*, Oxyrhynchus Papyri **54**, Mem 71, 1987 ➤ 4,a501; 5,9550: ᴿRÉG 103 (1990) 293-5 (A. *Blanchard*).

9648 ᴱ**Cotton** Hannah M., *Geiger* J., Masada II ... Latin and Greek documents 1989 ➤ 5,9552: ᴿRÉLat 68 (1990) 254s (R. *Adam*).

9649 ᴱ**Cuvigny** H., *Wagner* G., Les ostraca grecs de Douch I (1-57) 1986 ➤ 2,7705 ... 4,a594 [II. 1988 ➤ 4,a595; 5,9553]: ᴿBO 17 (1990) 137-9 (M. Lauretta *Moioli*); JEA 76 (1990) 254 (R. S. *Bagnall*).

9650 **Dagron** Gilbert, *Feissel* Denis, Inscriptions de Cilicie: Centre Byzance, Collège de France Mg 4. P 1987. 297 p. – ᴿTyche 5 (1990) 204-6 (P. *Siewert*).

9651 **Delaunois** Marcel, Essai de syntaxe grecque classique; réflexions et recherches 1988 ➤ 4,a596: ᴿSalesianum 52 (1990) 218s (R. *Della Casa*).

9652 *Di Benedetto* Vincenzo, At the origins of Greek grammar: Glotta 68 (1990) 19-39.

9653 **Dicharry** Warren F., Greek without grief, an outline guide to NT Greek³ [¹1980, ²1981 ➤ 63,8286]. Ch 1989, Loyola. xii-195 p. $16. 0-8294-0629-8 [NTAbs 34,375].

9654 ᴱ**Diethart** Johannes M., *Worp* Klaas A., Notarunterschriften im by-zantinischen Ägypten: Papyrussammlung Rainer 16. W 1986, Hollinek. 104 p.; vol. of 59 pl. 3-85119-221-4. – ᴿBO 17 (1990) 135-7 (J. G. *Keenan*).

9655 **Dobson** J. H., Learn New Testament Greek; [➤ 5,9555] begin reading the Greek text in 10 days! GR 1988, Baker. 306 p. 0-564-07872-7. – ᴿFgNt 3 (1990) 174 (J. *Peláez*); Vidyajyoti 53 (1989) 635s (P.M. *Meagher*).

9656 **Dougherty** Edward C. A., The syntax of the Apocalypse: diss. Catholic Univ., ᴰ*Gignac* F. Wsh 1990. 653 p. 90-27611. – DissA 51 (1990s) 1658-A; RTLv 22, p. 592.

9657 **Dubois** Laurent, Recherches sur le dialecte arcadien 1986 ➤ 5,9556: ᴿZSavR 106 (1989) 604s (G. *Thür*).

9658 **Efird** James M., A grammar for New Testament Greek. Nv 1990, Abingdon. xvii-168 p. 0-687-15678-5.

9659 **Fanning** Buist M., Verbal aspect in New Testament Greek [diss. Oxford 1987, ᴰ*Caird* G.]: TheolMg. Ox 1990, Clarendon. xiv-471 p. £48. 0-19-826729-0.

9660 **Fraser** Peter M., *Matthews* Elaine, Lexicon of Greek personal names I, 1987 ➤ 3,9805 ... 5,9561: ᴿAntClas 59 (1990) 412-5 (A. *Martin*); Gnomon 62 (1990) 97-103 (O. *Masson*, franç); HZ 250 (1990) 662s (F. *Gschnitzer*); JEH 40 (1989) 135 (J. *Shepard*); Mnemosyne 43 (1990) 185-7 (C. J. *Ruijgh*).

9661 *García-Ramón* J. L., Proportionale Analogie im Griechischen; der Dativ Pluralis der 3. Deklination in den aiolischen und westgriechischen Dialekten: Glotta 68 (1990) 133-156.

9662 **Gauthier** Philippe, Nouvelles inscriptions de Sardes II. Genève 1989, Droz. 207 p.; 14 pl. – ᴿClasR 40 (1990) 437s (A. *Erskine*).

9663 **Giacomelli** Roberto, Achaea Magno-Graecia [primo corpus completo dei testi epigrafici in alfabeto acheo di Magna Graecia]: Studi grammaticali e linguistici 17. Brescia 1988, Paideia. 105 p. – ᴿSalesianum 52 (1990) 150s (R. *Gottlieb*).

9664 **Gronewald** Michael, *al.*, Kölner Papyri 5, 1985 → 2,7720 (not 'Grönewald'): ᴿCdÉ 65 (1990) 160-5 (J. *Lenaerts*).

9665 **Guarducci** Margherita, L'epigrafia greca dalle origini al tardo impero 1987 → 3,9809: ᴿArchClasR 41 (1990) 488-491 (Maria Letizia *Lazzarini*).

9666 **Guillemette** P., Le Nouveau Testament grec analysé [21,014 formes, y comprises les variantes de Nestle-Aland[26]]. Scottdale 1986, Herald [also Eng. 1986 → 5,9564]. 456 p. 0-8361-3418-4. – ᴿÉTRel 65 (1990) 445 (C.B. *Amphoux*: intérêt pratique et deux dangers).

9667 **Guillemette** Pierre, Analyse des griechischen Neuen Testaments [Greek NT 1986]. Stu-Neuhausen 1988, Hänssler. – ᴿEstE 65 (1990) 236 (A. *Vargas-Machuca*: ignora GUERRA M. 1978 ²1988).

9668 *Hägg* Tomas, Titles and honorific epithets in Nubian Greek texts: Symbolae 65 (Oslo 1990) 147-177.

9669 **Hagedorn** U. & D., *al.*, Griechische Urkundenpapyri Mü 1. Stu 1986, Teubner. xiii 298 p. ᴿGnomon 62 (1990) 404-8 (Herwig *Maehler*)

9670 **Harrauer** H./**Hasitzka** Monika, *al.*, Griechische Texte III/VII: Corpus Papyrorum Raineri 1978/1986 → 2,7722/4,a610: ᴿRÉG 103 (1990) 300s. 297-9 (Hélène *Cuvigny*).

9670* *Helioudes* Giannis N., Ⓖ The Greek scholars' conception of the rhythm and metcr of the Greek language during the 18th and 19th centuries: TAth 61 (1990) 298-310; Eng. 904.

9671 **Hermann**..., Tituli Lydiae 2: As.Min. 5. W 1989, Österr. Akad. p. 295-532: ᴿAmJPg 111 (1990) 279-281 (T.R.S. *Broughton*).

9671* *Horsley* G. R. H., *a)* The fiction of 'Jewish Greek'; – *b) Koine* or Atticism — a misleading dichotomy: → 5,401, New Documents 5 (1989) 5-40 / 41-48.

9672 **Kastner** Wolfgang, Sprachgeschichtliche Erläuterungen zur griechischen Grammatik. Fra 1988, Diesterweg. 98 p. – ᴿSalesianum 52 (1990) 485 (R. *Bracchi*).

9673 *Kilpatrick* G.D. †, The articular infinitive in the NT/The imperfect in indirect speech: JTS 41 (1990) 94-98.

9674 **Kramer** Barbel, *Hagedorn* Dieter, Griechische Texte der Heidelberger Papyrus-Sammlung 1986 → 2,7734; 5,9570*: ᴿRÉG 103 (1990) 202s (A. *Blanchard*).

9675 *Lange* N.R.M. de, Greek and Byzantine fragments in the Cairo Genizah, review article: BJG 5 (1989) 13-17 [< ByZ 83,141].

9678 ᴱ**Lewis** Naphtali, The documents from the Bar Kokhba period in the Cave of Letters [→ 5,9571]; Greek papyri: Judean Desert Studies 2. J 1989, Israel Exploration Soc./Hebrew Univ. 176 p.; 40 pl. $60. 965-221-009-9. – ᴿBAR-W 16,3 (1990) 66 (J. *Fitzmyer*); BASP 27 (1990) 69-75 (J. G. *Keenan*).

9679 *Lewis* Naphtali, A Jewish landowner in Provincia Arabia [Dead Sea shore: Greek papyrus]: ScrClasIsr 8s (1988) 132-7.

9680 **Louw** J.P., *Nida* E.A., Greek... semantic domains 1988 → 4,a617; 5,9572: ᴿEvQ 62 (1990) 183-6 (I. H. *Marshall* praises except for its sweeping criticisms of BAUER-DANKER); Language 65 (1989) 900s (B. M. *Siet-*

sema); Protestantesimo 45 (1990) 64-67 (B. *Corsani*); RelStR 16 (1990) 64 (B. D. *Ehrman*).

9681 *Louw* J. P., New Testament Greek; the present state of the art: Neotestamentica 29 (1990) 159-172.

9682 *Luppe* Wolfgang, Der Anfang der 'Busiris'-Hypothesis (P. Oxy. 3651) [*Cockle* H. 1984]: ZPapEp 80 (1990) 13-15.

9683 *Lust* Johan, J. F. SCHLEUSNER and the [*Kraft-Tov ... Jacques*] lexicon of the Septuagint: ZAW 102 (1990) 256-262.

9684 **Maresch** Klaus, *Packman* Zola M., Papyri from the Washington University collection, St. Louis MO, [I. Chico, Am.St.Papyr.] II: Papyrol-Colon 18. Opladen 1990, Westdeutscher-V. xv-247 p.; XXXIII (foldout) pl. 3-531-09928-0.

9685 **Marshall** M.H.B., Verbs, nouns and postpositives in Attic prose: Scottish Classical Studies 3, 1987 ⟶ 4,a618; £12.50: RMnemosyne 43 (1990) 178-182 (C. J. *Ruijgh*).

9686 *Masson* Olivier, Remarques sur les noms des femmes en grec: MusHelv 47 (1990) 129-138.

9687 **Martin** R. A., Syntax criticism of Johannine literature, the Catholic Epistles, and the Gospel Passion accounts [... criteria for determining whether a text was composed originally in Greek]: StBEC 18. Lewiston NY 1989, Mellen. x-185 p. 0-88946-618-1 [NTAbs 34,374: completes trilogy].

9688 **Metzger** Bruce, Lexical aids for students of New Testament Greek. E 1990, Clark. xi-100 p. £5.

9688* **Orrieux** Claude, Zénon de Caunos 1985 ⟶ 4,a627: RAnÉCS 45 (1990) 865-7 (A. *Gara*).

9689 **Perschbacher** W. J., Refresh your Greek; practical helps for reading the NT. Ch 1989, Moody. xli-1274 p. $30. [NTAbs 34, 240: after 315 words occurring 50 times, Greek text at top of page and grammatical analyses below; 104-p. summary of Greek grammar and other appendices].

9690 EPleket H. W., *Stroud* R. S., Supplementum epigraphicum graecum ⟶ 4,a633: **SEG** 34 (1984), 35 (1985) 1988: RAntClas 59 (1990) 459s (A. *Martin*, 34s); ClasR 40 (1990) 432-6 (P. M. *Fraser*); Salesianum 52 (1990) 161 (R. *Della Casa*).

9691 *Porath* Pinhas, *a*) [Six] Newly discovered Greek inscriptions: ScrClasIsr 8s (1988) 166-8+6 fig.; – *b*) A new [Greek] boundary stone from the southern Golan: ScrClasIsr 10 (1989s) 130-3; phot.

9692 **Porter** Stanley E., Verbal aspect 1989 ⟶ 5,9581; Fs 134; 0-8204-0847-6; RExpTim 101 (1989s) 346s (H. F. *Guite*).

9693 **Rea** J. R.; Oxyrhynchus Papyri **55,** Mem. 75, 1988 ⟶ 5,9583: REikasmós 1 (Bo 1990) 257-260 (Rosa *Giannattasio Andria*); RÉG 103 (1990) 295-7 (H. *Cuvigny*).

9694 **Rehkopf** Friedrich, Septuaginta-Vokabular 1989 ⟶ 5,9584: RSalesianum 52 (1990) 171s (R. *Sabin*).

9695 **Robert** Louis, Documents d'Asie Mineure. BÉF 239bis. P 1987, de Boccard. VII-568 p. – RHZ 250 (1990) 383s (P. *Herrmann*).

9696 **Robinson** T. A., Mastering Greek vocabulary. Peabody MA 1990, Hendrickson. xi-176 p. $8. 0-943575-45-1 [NTAbs 35,97].

9697 **Roslon** Józef W. L., Ⓟ Gramatyka języka greckiego ... with OT and especially NT texts. Wsz 1990, Akad. Teol. Kat. 384 p.

9698 **Roth-Gerson** L., Ⓗ The Greek inscriptions from the synagogues in Eretz-Israel. J 1987, Yad Ben Zvi. 216 p. – RJStJud 21 (1990) 277 (M. *Mach*).

9699 **Schehr** Timothy P., Syntax of the moods and tenses of the Greek verb in Septuagint Genesis 1-15: diss. HUC. Cincinnati 1990. 346 p. 90-25830. – DissA 51 (1990s) 1599-A.

9700 **Sijpesteijn** P., *al.*, Papyri in the collection of the Erasmus Univ. (Rotterdam). Bru 1986, Fond.Ég.R.Élis. 64 p.; 8 pl. – RRÉG 103 (1990) 299s (H. *Cuvigny*).

9700* ESirivianou M., *al.*, The Oxyrhynchus papyri **56**: Greco-Roman Memoir 76. L 1989, Egypt Expl. Soc. (British Academy). xii-200 p.; 8 pl. 0-85698-105-2 [OIAc JJ 90].

9701 **Soisalon-Soininen** Ilmari, [seine] Studien zur Septuaginta-Syntax 1987 ➤ 3,305: RTR 86 (1990) 103s (H.-P. *Müller*).

9702 **Spicq** Ceslas, Note di lessicografia neotestamentaria I, 1988 ➤ 4,a640; 5,9589: RProtestantesimo 45 (1990) 67s (B. *Corsani*); STEv 1 (1989) 212 (P. *Bolognesi*); StPatav 37 (1990) 698s (G. *Leonardi*).

9703 *Stephens* Laurence D., Initial *r(h)* in Attic; new evidence for the effect of lexical status and syntactic configuration of *r-* after final short vowels: ILCL 15 (1990) 55-75.

9704 **Taylor** Ann, Clitics and configurationality in ancient Greek [changes from Homeric through *koinē*]: diss. Pennsylvania, DRinge D. Ph 1990. 217 p. 91-12632. – DissA 51 (1990) 4104-A.

9705 *Treu* Kurt, Christliche Papyri XV [2 Cor-Gal-Eph; Mani...]: ArPapF 36 (1990) 95-98.

9706 **Tucker** Elizabeth F., The creation of morphological regularity; early Greek verbs in *-éō, -áō, -óō, -úō* and *-íō*: HistSprF Erg.-H. 35. Gö 1990, Vandenhoeck & R. xiii-542 p. DM 178. – RHistSprF 103 (1990) 301-4 (Rüdiger *Schmitt*).

9707 **Turner** E.G., 2revParsons P.J., Greek manuscripts of the ancient world 1987 ➤ 4,a642; 5,9593: RJEA 76 (1990) 250s (J.D. *Thomas*).

9707* **Van Voorst** Robert E., Building your New Testament Greek vocabulary. GR 1990, Eerdmans. xii-110 p. $8. 0-8028-0486-1.

9708 **Vincent** Marvin R., Word studies in the New Testament. Peabody MA c. 1990 = 1886, Hendrickson. I. Mt-Lk, xxiv-822 p.; II. Jn vii-607 p.; III. Paul xl-565 p.; IV. 624 p. 0-917006-30-5 all 4.

9708* MVoigt Eva Maria [Lfg. 10s], **Meier-Brügger** Michael [12s], Lexikon des frühgriechischen Epos [I: A. 1955] II. *bádēn -kapnós* Lfg. 10, 1982; 11, 1984; 12, 1987; 13, 1989. Gö (1979), Vandenhoeck & R. [Gnomon 63, 97-106, O. *Szemerényi*].

9709 **Wagenaar** Christofoor, Thesaurus graecitatis monasticae [12,500 fiches on 179 microfiches; many words in no existing dictionary, others re-evaluated from context]. Doetinchem c. 1989, St. Willibrordsabdij. ƒ 337. – RBijdragen 51 (1990) 87 (M. *Parmentier*).

9710 *Wagner* Guy, *al.*, Documents grecs découverts dans la Vallée des Reines: BIFAO 90 (1990) 365-380; pl. XXVIII.

9711 **Wessel** K. † [bozze lasciate c. 1946]; EFerrua A., Inscriptiones graecae christianae veteres Occidentis. Bari 1989, Edipuglia. vi-345 p. – RVetChr 27 (1990) 231s (L. *Moretti*).

9712 **Woodard** Roger D., On interpreting morphological change; the Greek reflexive pronoun. Amst 1990, Gieben. viii-134 p. 90-5063-049-9.

9713 *Wong* H., The nature of the Greek of the New Testament — its past and present: Scriptura 32 (Stellenbosch 1990) 1-27 [< NTAbs 35,15].

9714 **Wong Sek-Muk** Simon, A classification of semantic case-relations in the Pauline epistles: diss. Pretoria 1990. – DissA 51 (1990s) 3053-A.

9715 **Wouters** Alfons, The Chester Beatty codex AC 1499, a Graeco-Latin lexicon on the Pauline epistles and a Greek grammar 1988 → 4,2657; 5,9595: ᴿClasR 40 (1990) 152s (J. N. *Birdsall*); RÉG 103 (1990) 304-6 (A. *Blanchard*).

J5.2 **Voces graecae** (*ordine alphabetico* **graeco**).

9716 *agapáō* (LXX): → 546, ᴱ*Muraoka* T., Melbourne symposium 1990 (S. P. *Swinn*).

9717 *Nuchelmans* J., À propos de **hágios** avant l'époque hellénistique: → 5,17, ᶠBARTELINK G., Fructus 1989, 239-258.

9718 *Martin* Alain, *Athénaioi* et **Athēnaîoi** [ainsi p. 291; accents ajoutés à main p. 169 faux] en Égypte gréco-romaine: AncSoc 20 (1989) 169-184.

9719 *Rodríguez Somolinos* Juan, **anabrýzō** (addendum lexicis), *brýzō* (Archil. Fr. 28 D) y el epitafio del rey Midas: Emerita 58 (1990) 225-230.

9719* *anaginóskō: Svenbro* J., La lecture à haute voix; le témoignage des verbes grecs signifiant 'lire': → 762*, Phoinikeia grammata 1989, 105-108.

9720 **Ostwald** M., *anánkē* in THUCYDIDES 1988 → 5,9601: ᴿGnomon 62 (1990) 458s (O. *Wenskus*).

9721 *anakephalaíōsis: Osborn* Eric, The logic of recapitulation [Jonas; mostly Fathers (IRENAEUS)]: → 135, ᶠORBE A., Compostellanum 35,1s (1990) 23-37.

9722 **Ginn** Richard J., The present and the past; a study of **anámnēsis:** PittsbTMg 20. Allison Park PA 1989, Pickwick. [xi-] 92 p. $12 pa. [CBQ 52,589].

9723 *Sznol* Shifra, Compounds with **anti-** in Hellenistic-Jewish sources: FgNt 3 (1990) 109-114.

9724 *Padilla* Carmen, Sobre el verbo **apokrínomai** en el Nuevo Testamento: FgNt 3,5 (1990) 67-74.

9725 *arēn* 'lamb': HistSprF 103 (1990) 26-29 (M. *Meier-Brügger*; 20s, F. O. *Lindeman*).

9726 *La Villa* Jesús de, El concepto de **aristeîa** y la interpretación de SÓFOCLES, Phil. 1428-33: Emerita 58 (1990) 205-216.

Bouyer L., *Gnosis* → 7003.

9727 *daímōn: Brenk* Frederick, I veri demoni greci 'nella nebbia ammantellati'? ESIODO e PLUTARCO: → 693, Diabolos 1988/90, 1, 23-25.

9728 *diakonía: Collange* Jean-François, Évangile, vie quotidienne et diaconie ['ābad, écrit 'habad']; enquête biblique et réflexion ecclésiologique: ÉTRel 65 (1990) 221-233.

9729 **Collins** J. N., Diakonia; re-interpreting the ancient sources [diss. King's College London 1976, ᴰ*Evans* C. F.]. Oxford 1990, UP. xv-368 p. 0-19-506067-9 [NTAbs 35,117]. – ᴿExpTim 102 (1990s) 213 (L. *Houlden*: it has become a slogan).

9730 **Klinken** Jaap van, Diakonia. GR/Kampen 1989, Eerdmans/Kok. 134 p. 0-8028-0470-5/90-242-0948-X. – ᴿExpTim 102 (1990s) 215s (W. D. *Horton*).

9731 *dikaiosýne: Baumann* R., 'Gottes Gerechtigkeit' [... klassisches Griechentum] — Verheissung und Herausforderung für diese Welt: Tb 1643. FrB 1989, Herder. 253 p. DM 15,90. – ᴿZAW 102 (1990) 438 (H.-C. *Schmitt*).

9731* *dîos:* RPg 64 (1990) 163-171 (P. A. *Perotti*).

9732 **Banyard** Maureen L., The concept of glory [*dóxa* < *dokéō*] and the nature of man; a study of Jewish, Christian, Buddhist and Zoroastrian thought: diss. Leicester 1989. 323 p. BRD-89520. – DissA 51 (1990s) 897-A.

dýnamis: ᴱNicolet Claude, Du pouvoir dans l'antiquité; mots et réalités: ÉPHÉ Cah.Glotz 1, 1990 ➤ 760.

9732* *empázomai* et la racine **pa*-: RPg 64 (1990) 143-150 (A. *Blanc*).

9733 **Parker** James F., *euangélion-euangelízō*; a contextual analysis of their meaning in the NT and the Apostolic Fathers: diss. Baptist Theol Sem., ᴰ*Simmons* B. New Orleans 1990. 217 p. 90-26809. – DissA 51 (1990s) 1663-A.

9734 *thélō:* **Heitsch** Ernst, Wollen und verwirklichen, von Homer zu Paulus. Abh Mainz, g/soz 12. Mainz 1989, Akad. Wiss. 54 p.

9735 *Theodótous* [as nominative, with final *-s* in the following line]: JQR 80 (1990) 87-91 (S. *Schwartz*).

9736 *thrikē:* **Adams** Douglas Q., The Indo-European words for 'hair'; reconstructing a semantic field: JIndEur 16 (1988) 69-93.

9737 *hierós:* **Brenk** Frederick E., Plus saint que chez Homère; sanctus chez Vergile: ➤ 5,786, Écrivains 1988/9, 305-7. ➤ 9750*.

9737* *hiketeía:* **Szlezák** Thomas A., Hikesie und Bitte in EURIPIDES' 'Medea': ➤ 160*, Mem. SCHULER E.v., Orientalia 59 (1990) 280-297.

9738 *Ioudaîos:* **Pritz** R., Who is a Jew in the Gospels? Jerusalem Perspective 3,5 (1990) 5s [< NTAbs 35, 151].

9738* *hístōr* 'judge, witness': Glotta 68 (1990) 157-166 (E. D. *Floyd*).

9739 *kaí:* **Hoopert** D. A. [1 Cor 2,1-5; 3,1-3; Eph 2,1-7; Heb 12,1-13,17] The Greek conjuction *kaì* used with a personal pronoun [to introduce application of something just discussed]: OPTAT 3,2 (Dallas 1989) 83-89 [< NTAbs 34,152].

9740 *Lossau* Manfred, *Kaí* initial et quelques prolongements littéraires: ÉtClas 58 (1990) 247-257.

9741 *Mourlon Beernaert* Pierre, Le verbe grec **katéchein** dans le N. T. [...rapport à la catéchèse]: LVitae 44 (1989) 377-387 [401-412, *Fossion* André, 'Entre théologie et catéchèse, la catéchétique'].

Cozzo Andrea, *Kérdos* 1988 ➤ g730.

9742 *Kramer* Johannes, Was bedeutet **koimētērion** in den Papyri [burial-place, not sleeping-place]: ZPapEp 80 (1990) 269-272.

9743 *koinōnía:* **Karwacki** Roman, ℗ Communio: ColcT 59,3 (1989) 34-42; deutsch 43.

9744 *kólymbos:* HistSprF 103 (1990) 261-3 (W. B. *Lockwood*).

9745 **Luter** A. Boydᴶ, 'Worship' as service; the New Testament usage of *latreúō:* CriswT 2 (1987s) 335-344.

9746 *Drexhage* Hans-Joachim, *Láchanon* und *lachanopôlai* im römischen Ägypten (1.-3.Jh.n.Chr.): MünstHand 9,2 (1990) 88-116; Eng. franç. 117.

9747 *lichanos,* (epi-) lígdēn, lat. pollex, pollingere: Glotta 68 (1990) 1-3 (M. *Meier-Brügger*).

9748 *Sulyok* Elemér, ℳ Biblische Bedeutungsnuancen der **Metánoia:** ➤ 133, ᶠNyíri T. 1990, 378-383.

9749 *Serça* Pierre, Les noms en *-mós* et en *-mē* [*logismós, gnōmē* ...] dans les périphrases avec *poieîn/poieîsthai, tithénai/títhesthai*: Pallas 34 (1988) 147-157.

9750 *mystērion:* **Bouyer** Louis, The Christian mystery; from pagan myth to Christian mysticism, ᵀ*Trethowan* Illtyd. E 1990, Clark. 312 p. £20. 0-567-00514-2. – ᴿExpTim 102 (1990s) 216 (A. *Louth*).

9750* *Sieg* Franciszek, ✪ Sense of the terms *hierón* [71 times] and *naós* [45 times] in the NT: RuBi 42 (1989) 335-341.

9751 *nóos* (HESIOD, PINDAR): Glotta 68 (1990) 68-85. 179-202 (Shirley D. *Sullivan*).

9752 *nósos / noûsos*: HistSprF 103 (1990) 245-8 (M. *Meier-Brügger*).

9753 *Elliott* J. K., The position of causal *hóti* clauses in the New Testament: FgNt 3 (1990) 155-7.

9753* *parádosis:*   *a) Irmscher* J., Der Terminus *paradosis*; – *b) Tábet* Michelangelo, I testi paolini sulla *parádosis* nei commenti patristici (secoli I-III): ➤ 700, Tradizione 1989/90, 55-61 / 39-53.

9754 *Levinskaya* Irinia, A Jewish or Gentile prayer house? The meaning of *proseuchē:* TyndB 41 (1990) 154-9.

9754* *ptýō, chréptomai:*   *Perpillou* Jean-Louis, Sur deux verbes signifiant 'cracher'; from 'cough' to 'spit' in ancient Greek: RPg 64 (1990) 9-31.

9755 *Schiappa* Edward, Did PLATO coin *rhētorikē*? (probably): AmJPg 111 (1990) 457-470.

9756 *rhís:* MüStSprW 51 (1990) 125-8 (M. *Meier-Brügger*).

9757 *sábbaton: Devos* Paul, 'Méga sábbaton' chez saint ÉPIPHANE: AnBoll 108 (1990) 293-306.

9758 *Mateos* Juan, Sabbata, sabbaton, prosabbaton, *paraskeuē:* FgNt 3,5 (1990) 19-37; Eng. 37s.

9759 *Cheyns* André, Le verbe *sébō* dans l'œuvre de PLATON I: RBgPg 68 (1990) 54-73.

9760 *Kearns* John M., *Semnótēs* and dialect gloss in the Odussia of Livius Andronicus: AmJPg 111 (1990) 40-52.

9761 *Botteri* Paula, *Stásis;* le mot grec, la chose romaine: Métis 4 (1989) 87-100.

9762 *Battisti* Daniela, *Synetós* as aristocratic self-definition: GrRByz 31 (1990) 5-25.

9763 *synistēmi,* 'a sample lexical entry': ➤ 546, ᴱ*Muraoka* T., Melbourne symposium 1990 ... (J.A.L. *Lee*).

9764 *Boano* Attilio G., Note etimologiche su *stoicheîon:* IstLombR 124 (1990) 353-372; 1 fig.

9765* *sŷrinx:* HistSprF 103 (1990) 35-37 (J. *Greppin*).

9766 *sōtēría:* **Cowen** G., Salvation; word studies from the Greek NT. Nv 1990, Broadman. 159 p. $8. 0-8054-1035-X [NTAbs 35,117].

9767 *te:* Notes on PIE *k^we:* MüStSprW 51 (1990) 129-145 (S. *Nigron*).

9768 *Elliott* J. K., *te* in the NT: TZBas 46 (1990) 202-4.

9769 *Mayerson* Philip, The words *tonáchion* and *gonáchion* in the Egyptian papyri: ZPapEp 83 (1990) 241s.

9770 *hypokritēs: Barr* James, The Hebrew-Aramaic background of 'hypocrisy' in the Gospels: ➤ 183, ᴱVERMES G. 1990, 307-326.

9770* *Hiltbrunner* Otto, Warum wollten sie nicht *philánthrōpoi* heissen?: ➤ 100*, ꟳKÖTTING B., JbAC 33 (1990) 7-20.

9771 **Sullivan** Shirley D. [➤ 9751; 9773], Psychological activity in HOMER; a study of *phren.* Ottawa 1988, Carleton Univ. ix-303 p. – ᴿRÉG 103 (1990) 312s (G. *Liberman*).

9772 *Baumert* Norbert, Zur Begriffsgeschichte von *chárisma* im greichischen Sprachraum: TPhil 65 (1990) 79-100; 395-415, Das Fremdwort 'Charisma' in der westlichen Theologie.

9773 *psyche, nóos: Sullivan* Shirley D., *a)* A multi-faceted term; *psyche* in Homer, the Homeric Hynms, and Hesiod; – *b)* The psychic term noos in

Homer and the Homeric Hymns: StItFgC 81 (1988) 151-180 / 82 (1989) 152-195.

J5.5 Cypro-Minoa [➤ т9. 1-4].

9773* *Best* Jan, Thrakische Namen in mykenischer Schrift: ➤ 891, Thracians 1984/90, 135-142.

9774 **Bile** Monique, Le dialecte crétois ancien; étude de la langue des inscriptions; recueil des inscriptions posterieures aux IC: ÉcFrAth ÉtCrét 27, 1988 ➤ 5,9648; F 750; 2-86958-018-5: ᴿAntClas 59 (1990) 419s (G. *Purnelle*); Gnomon 62 (1990) 74-76 (M. *Meier-Brügger*); RPg 64 (1990) 201-3 (J.-L. *Perpillou*).

9775 *Freeman* Philip M., New evidence for pre-Greek labiovelars: JIndEur 17 (1989) 171-180.

9776 a) *García-Ramón* J. L., Mykenisch *e-qi-ti-wo-e* [... gr. *ephthien*]; – b) *Hajnal* Ivo, Die mykenische Verbalform *e-eto*; – c) *Plath* Robert, Mykenisch *e-re-e*: MüStSprW 51 (1990) 7-20 / 21-26 / 169-182.

9777 *Hallager* Erik, *al.*, The first Linear B tablets from Khania: Kadmos 29 (1990) 24-34.

9777* *Lamberterie* Charles de, Grec mycénien *po-ro-e-ko-to*; les nodules de Thèbes et les taureaux de Nestor: RPg 64 (1990) 111-125.

9778 *Meier-Brügger* M., Zu griech. *klisié* und myk. *ki-ri-ta*: Glotta 68 (1990) nur 167.

9779 *Milani* Celestina, I toponimi micenei e il catalogo delle navi: IstLombR 121 (1987) 151-188.

9780 *Piteros* Christos, *Olivier* Jean-Pierre, *Melena* José L., Les inscriptions en Linéaire B des nodules de Thèbes (1982); la fouille, les documents, les possibilités d'interprétation: BCH 114 (1990) 103-184.

9781 *Schwink* Frederick W., A reconsideration of the Mycenaean medio-passive finite ending: JIndEur 17 (1989) 127-154.

J6 Indo-Iranica.

9782 **Alavi** Bozorg, *Lorenz* Manfred, Lehrbuch der persischen Sprache⁵ʳᵉᵛ. Lp 1988, VEB. 308 p. – ᴿSalesianum 62 (1990) 470 (R. *Bracchi*).

9783 ᶠASMUSSEN Jes P., A green leaf: Acta Iranica 28, 1988 ➤ 4,6: ᴿWZKM 80 (1990) 302-7 (Rüdiger *Schmitt*: detaillierte Analysen).

9784 ᴰ**Camps** A., *Muller* J.-C., ROTII Heinrich (1620-68) Sanskrit grammar and manuscripts 1988 ➤ 4,a709; 5,9678: ᴿOLZ 85 (1990) 206-8 (S. *Kratzsch*).

9785 **Damerow** Peter, The proto-Elamite texts from Tepe Yahya: AmSchPreh 39. CM 1989, Harvard Peabody Museum. xiv-81 p. 0-87365-542-7.

9786 **Davari** G. Djelani, Baktrisch, ein Wörterbuch 1982 ➤ 5,9679: ᴿJIndEur 17 (1989) 187.

9787 **Gignoux** Philippe, Noms propres sassanides en moyen perse épigraphique: Iranisches Personennamenbuch 2/2, 1986 ➤ 5,9681: ᴿArOr 58 (1990) 183s (O. *Klíma*).

9788 **Grillot-Susini** Françoise, Éléments de grammaire élamite 1987 ➤ 5,9682 ('1989'): ᴿAcOrK 51 (1990) 279-284 (Rüdiger *Schmitt*); JRAS (1989) 149-151 (J. A. *Black*).

9789 **Hinz** W., *Koch* H., Elamisches Wörterbuch 1987 ➤ 3,9960: ᴿMünst-Hand 9,1 (1990) 114-6 (J. *Wiesehöfer*).

9789* *a)* *Lecoq* Pierre, Paradis en vieux perse?; – *b)* *Stronach* Daniel, On the genesis of the Old Persian cuneiform script: ➤ 138, [F]PERROT J., Iran 1990, 209-211 / 195-202 + 2 fig.

9790 **Mylius** Klaus, Wörterbuch Deutsch-Sanskrit. Lp 1988, Enzyklopädie. 322 p. M 92. – [R]OLZ 85 (1990) 462s (M. *Balk*: good).

9791 *Parpola* Asko, The coming of the Aryans to Iran and India and the cultural and ethnic identity of the Dasas: StOr 64 (1988) 196-302 [IndEurJ 17 (1989) 188s (E. C. *Polomé*)].

9791* *Sims-Williams* Nicholas, New studies on the verbal system of Old and Middle Iranian [KELLENS J. 1984; SAMADI M. 1986]: BSO 52 (1989) 255-264.

9792 *Winters* C. A., The Dravidian language and the Harappan script: ArOr 58 (1990) 301-9.

9792* [E]**Yarshater** Ehsan, Persian literature: Columbia Lectures on Iranian Studies 3. NY 1988, Bibliotheca Persica. xi-562 p. $49.50; pa. $19.50. – [R]BSO 52 (1989) 365s (Julie S. *Meisami*).

J6.5 **Latina.**

9793 *Haffter* Heinz, LEUMANNS [Manu, geb. 1889] Herkunft und Mitarbeit beim Thesaurus Linguae Latinae: MusHelv 47 (1990) 3-8 [–29, *al.*].

9793* **Jory** J., Corpus Inscriptionum Latinarum 6/7 fasc. 7. B 1989, de Gruyter. IX + p. 7315-7746. [Gnomon 63, 139-143, H. *Chantraine*].

9794 [E]**Mariner** S., Diccionario latino I. p. 65-112. M 1988, Cons. Sup. Inst. Fg. – [R]Salesianum 52 (1990) 490 (A. *Gottlieb*).

9795 **Salomies** Olli, Die römischen Vornamen 1987 ➤ 5,9685*: [R]Latomus 49 (1990) 192-5 (M. *Lejeune*).

9796 Thesaurus linguae latinae XI, 1 fasc. 4 [➤ 5,9686]: (col. 481-640) pars-pastor. Lp 1988, Thesaurus-VG. – [R]BBudé (1989) 92 (G. *Serbat*).

9797 **Walser** Gerold, Römische Inschrift-Kunst; römische Inschriften für den akademischen Unterricht und als Einführung in die lateinische Epigraphik. Stu 1988, Steiner. 296 p. – [R]Salesianum 52 (1990) 162s (R. *Della Casa*).

J8.1 **Philologia generalis.**

9798 **Boeckh** August, La filologia come scienza storica [1877]: Micromegas 14, 1987 ➤ 4,a731: [R]RÉG 103 (1990) 270s (J. *Schneider*).

9799 [E]**Campanile** Enrico, *Cardona* Giorgio R., *Lazzeroni* Romano, Bilinguismo e biculturalismo nel mondo antico: Atti Pisa 28s. IX. 1987: Testi linguistici 13, 1988 ➤ 5,779: [R]Salesianum 52 (1990) 476s (R. *Della Casa*).

9800 *a)* *Clarysse* W., Abbreviations and lexicography: AncSoc 21 (1990) 33-44; – *b)* *Dohmen* Christoph, 'naphar mātāti šūt šunnâ lišānu'; zur Frage der Semantik in der Semitistik: BibNot 47 (1989) 13-34.

9801 [E]**Cohen** David, Les langues chamito-sémitiques: Les langues dans le monde ancien et moderne 2. P 1988, CNRS. 318 p. – [R]Salesianum 52 (1990) 479s (R. *Sabin*: I. 1988 era sulle lingue africane).

9802 **Dauses** August, Grundbegriffe der Lexematik; Methoden und Probleme der Wortschatzbetrachtung in Synchronie und Diachronie. Stu 1989, Steiner. 102 p. – [R]Salesianum 52 (1990) 481 (R. *Gottlieb*).

9802* **Doerfer** Gerhard, Grundwort und Sprachmischung... Körperbezeichnungen 1988 ➤ 4,a753: [R]ZDMG 140 (1990) 145-7 (N. *Boretzky*).

9803 *Mollova* M., Les problèmes de constitution d'un dictionnaire étymologique d'une langue particulaire [sic]: Problemi, Čeboksari 1986: ArOr 58 (1990) 158-164.

9804 *Naumann* Horst, Soziolinguistische Aspekte der Eigennamen: → 737, Kolloq. Frings T. 1990, 150-8.

9804* **Olender** Maurice, Les langues du Paradis; Aryens et Sémites, un couple providentiel; préf. *Vernant* Jean-Pierre. P 1989, Seuil. 312 p. 2-02-010883-6 [OIAc F91,17].

9805 *a)* **Salvadore** Marcello, Il nome, la persona; saggio sull'etimologia antica: Pubbl. 110. Genova 1987, Univ. dip. Arch-Fg. [Gnomon 63, 1-4, M. *Kraus*]. – *b)* Il foedus e la nascita della lingua: Sileno 16 (1990) 5-39.

9806 *Shimomiya* Tadao, Indogermanistik in Japan: Kratylos 35 (1990) 1-17; Bibliog. 18-31.

9807 **Strasser** Gerhard F., Lingua universalis; Kryptologie und Theorie der Universalsprachen im 16. und 17. Jahrhundert: Wolfenbüttler Forschungen 38. Wsb 1988, Harrassowitz. 291 p. – [R]BibHumRen 51 (1989) 689-692 (O. *Pot*).

9808 [E]**Wasserman** Julian N., *Roney* Lois, Sign, sentence, discourse; language in medieval thought and literature. Syracuse NY 1989, Univ. xxii-318 p. $40; pa. $19. – [R]Speculum 65 (1990) 514 (tit. pp.).

J8.2 Grammatica comparata.

9809 [E]**Bammesberger** Alfred [Mem. COWGILL W. nicht = 4,675]. Die Laryngaltheorie und die Rekonstruktion des indogermanischen Laut- und Formensystems: IndGBib. Heid 1988, Winter. 385 p. – [R]Salesianum 52 (1990) 215-7 (R. *Bracchi*).

9810 *a)* *Best* Jan, Comparative Indo-European linguistics and archaeology; towards a historical integration; – *b)* *Barber* E.J.W., Archaeolinguistics and the borrowing of Old European technology; – *c)* *Paliga* Sorin, Proto-/Pre-Indo-European...: → 735, JIndEur 17 (1989) 335-340 / 239-249 / 309-334.

9811 **Buck** Carl D., A dictionary of selected synonyms in the principal Indo-European languages; a contribution to the history of ideas. Ch 1988 = 1949, Univ. xix-1515 p. 0-226-07937-6.

9812 **Childe** V. Gordon, The Aryans, a study of Indo-European origins. NY 1987, Dorset. xii-221. – [R]ArGlotIt 74 (1988) 213 (G. *Bonfante*: brutto scritto non toccato dall'autore dopo 1956 perché non menziona il deciframento del miceneo).

9813 *Cohen* Chaim, The 'Held method' for comparative Semitic philology: → 75, Mem. HELD M., JANES 19 (1989) 9-23.

9813* [E]**Cohen** David, Les langues chamito-sémitiques: [F]*Perrot* Jean,] Les langues dans le monde ancien et moderne 3. P 1988, CNRS. 318 p.; 2 foldout maps. 2-222-04057-4. [OIAc Ja91].

9814 **Collinge** N.E., The laws of Indo-European: Pa.2. Amst 1985, Benjamins. xviii-308 p. – [R]RBgPg 68 (1990) 164s (M. *Leroy*).

9814* COWGILL Warren, [Indo-European] Studies in memory of ∼ 1985/7 → 4,675: [R]ZDMG 140 (1990) 144s (D. *Maur*).

9815 **Doerfer** Gerhard, Grundwort und Sprachmischung; eine Untersuchung an Hand von Körperteilbezeichnungen: MüOstasSt 47, 1988 → 4,a753: [R]Salesianum 52 (1990) 482 (R. *Gottlieb*).

9816 **Drinka** Bridget A., The sigmatic aorist in Indo-European; evidence for the space-time hypothesis: Diss. Texas, [D]*Polome* E. Austin 1990. 320 p. 90-31558. – DissA 51 (1990s) 2003-A.

9817 *Durand* Olivier, Une réflexion sur les begadkefat en chamito-sémitique: OrAnt 28 (1989) 217-225.
9817* *a) Freu* Jacques, L'arrivée des Indo-Européens en Europe; – *b) Haudry* Jean, Aspects de la tradition indo-européenne en Grèce; panthéon, mythologie, philosophie: BBudé (1989) 3-41 / 42-55.
9818 **Gamkrelidze** T. V., *Ivanon* V. V., ❸ The Indo-European language and the Indo-Europeans. Tbilisi 1984, Univ. 2 vol. – ᴿGeorgica 11 (1988) 97-100 (R. *Eckert*).
9818* *a) Gamkrelidze* Thomas V., On the problem of an Asiatic original homeland of the Proto-Indo-Europeans; – *b) Greppin* John A. C., The make-up of the Armenian unclassified substratum; – *c) Bolognesi* Giancarlo, Arménien et Iranien; une théorie linguistique passée inaperçue: ➤ 754, Worlds 1988/90, 5-14 / 203-210 / 227-336.
9819 **Khan** Geoffrey, Studies in Semitic syntax: London Or. Ser. 38, 1988 ➤ 4,a757: ᴿBO 47 (1990) 292-9 (J. W. *Dyk*); BSO 52 (1989) 546s (J. C.L. *Gibson*); Kratylos 35 (1990) 176-9 (H. B. *Rosén*).
9820 *a) Kortlandt* Frederik, The spread of the Indo-Europeans; – *b) Zimmer* Stefan, On Indo-Europeanization; – *c) Steiner* Gerd, The immigration of the first Indo-Europeans into Anatolia reconsidered: ➤ 735, JIndEur 18 (1990) 131-140 / 141-155 / 185-214.
9821 **Mallory** J. P., In search of the Indo-Europeans 1989 ➤ 5,9719; 0-500-05052-X: ᴿAntiqJ 69 (1989) 338s (Susan *Sherratt*): JField 17 (1990) 89-93 (A. *Sherratt*).
9822 **Martinet** André, L'Indoeuropeo; lingue, popoli e culture 1987 ➤ 5,9721: [Des steppes aux océans 1986], ᵀ*Barba* Mario; Lit. 25.000: ᴿAevum 64 (1990) 111s (G. *Bonfante*); Latomus 49 (1990) 201s (F. *Mawet*).
9823 **Mayrhofer** Manfred, Etymologisches Wörterbuch des Altindoarischen 1/3; 1/4 usastá- -ᴋᴀʀᴛ²: IndGB. Heid 1988, Winter. p. 167-236 / 237-316. – ᴿBSO 53 (1990) 534-6 (J. C. *Wright*); Salesianum 52 (1990) 491s. 225s (R. *Gottlieb*).
9824 **Renfrew** Colin, Archaeology and language; the puzzle of Indo-European origins 1987 ➤ 5,9730: ᴿAmHR 95 (1990) 125-7 (Marija *Gimbutas*); ClasW 83 (1989s) 359 (B. *Vine*); JIntdis 20 (1989s) 257-262 (Miriam S. *Balmuth*); Language 64 (1988) 800s (J. H. *Jasanoff*).
9824* **Retső** Jan, Diathesis 1989 ➤ 5,9731: ᴿZDMG 140 (1990) 428 (E. *Wagner*).
9825 *Yang Dawu*, [Vowel/Consonant] Length in Proto-Semitic: RCiv 3 (Chang-chun 1988) 22-34 [< OTAbs 14,34].
9825* *Yoffee* Norman, Before Babel; a review article [*Renfrew*, Archaeology and Language 1987; *Mallory*, In search of the Indo-Europeans 1989]: PrPrehSoc 56 (1990) 299-313.
9826 *a) Zanotti* David G., The [*Gimbutas* M.]. Kurgan model of Proto-Indo-European expansion; a review and revision: Orpheus-Thrac 1 (1990) 7-17 (18-23 Gimbutas reply). – *b) Schlerath* Bernfried, Indoiranisch *vástra*-ntr. 'Gewand, Kleidung': ➤ 160*, Mem. Sᴄʜᴜʟᴇʀ E.v., Orientalia 59 (1990) 251-4. – *c) Hart* Gillian R., 'Class I present'; subjunctive and middle voice in Indo-European: BSO 53 (1990) 446-468.

ȷ8.3 Linguistica generalis.

9827 ᴱ**Aarsleff** Hans, *al.*, Papers on the history of linguistics; proceedings of the 3d Int. Conference 1984/7 ➤ 3,746: ᴿRBgPg 68 (1990) 758-761 (R. *Schreyer*).

9828 ᴱ**Bátori** István S., *al.*, Computational linguistics; an international handbook of computer-oriented language research and applications: Handbooks of Linguistics 4. B 1989, de Gruyter. xxxii-933 p. DM 728. – ᴿDLZ 111 (1990) 525-9 (K. *Albrecht*).

9829 **Belardi** Walter, Linguistica generale, filologia e critica dell'espressione. R 1990, Bonacci. 557 p. 88-7573-220-5.

9830 *Ben-Hayyim* Ze'ev, ❻ Remarks on Phil[1]ippi's Law: Lešonenu 53 (1988s) 113-120; Eng. VIII (Philippi).

9831 *Bologna* Maria Patrizia, Storia della linguistica e teoria linguistica; A. F. Pᴏᴛᴛ [1871] e la ricostruzione: StClasOr 40 (1990) 43-64.

9832 **Bühler** Karl, Theory of language; the representational function of language, ᵀ*Goodwin* Donald F.: Foundations of Semiotics 25. Amst/Ph 1990, Benjamins. lxii-508 p. 90-272-3297-0 / Ph 1-55619-200-2.

9833 **Cardona** Giorgio R., Dizionario di linguistica² [meno strutturalista di ¹1969]. R 1988, Armando, 320 p. – ᴿSalesianum 52 (1990) 217s (R. *Gottlieb*).

9834 *Cartlidge* David R., Combien d'unités avez-vous de trois à quatre? [Ionesco]; what do we mean by intertextuality in early Church studies? ['Linguistic studies has (sic) recently challenged basic understandings about texts'; not 'Is?' but 'How is' a frog a text? (apart from the bird, mouse, arrows in Herodotus 4,131s)]: ➙ 544, SBL seminars 1990, 400-411.

9835 **Chomsky** Noam, The logical structure of linguistic theory. Ch 1985 = 1975, Univ. [vi–] 592 p. 0-226-10436-2 pa.

9836 *Collinge* N. E., Thoughts on the [linguistic] pragmatics of ancient Greece: PrPgS 34 (1988) 1-13.

9837 **Cotterell** Peter, *Turner* Max, Linguistics and biblical interpretation 1989 ➙ 5,9746: ᴿBL (1990) 99 (J. *Sawyer*); CriswT 4 (1989s) 417-9 (E. R. *Clendenin*: clear, forceful, important); EvQ 62 (1990) 188s (P. *Ellingworth*); JStNT 40 (1990) 124 (SFP = ? SF Stephen *Fowl*, or SEP Stanley *Porter*, p. 127: fascinating, but on hermeneutics rather than linguistics); ScotBEv 8 (1990) 144s (B. *Mitchell*).

9838 ᴰ**Davis** Hayley G., *Taylor* Talbot J., Redefining linguistics. I, 1990, Routledge. vii-172 p. 0-415-05495-8; pa. –6-6. 3 other art.

9839 *Gueunier* Nicole, Où va la linguistique?: Études 373 (1990) 181-191.

9840 **Hagège** Claude, La structure des langues³ [¹1982]: Que sais-je? 2006. P 1990, PUF. 128 p. 2-13-043217-4.

9841 **Harris** Roy, *Taylor* Talbot J., Landmarks in linguistic thought; the western tradition from Socrates to Sᴀᴜssᴜʀᴇ [Biblc p. 35-45]. L 1989, Routledge. $42.50; pa. $15. xviii-199 p. – ᴿLanguage 66 (1990) 581-4 (W. P. *Lehmann*).

9842 **Hock** Hans H., Principles of historical linguistics 1986 ➙ 2,7858: ᴿKratylos 35 (1990) 190s (Theodora *Bynon*).

9843 **Hudson** R. A., Sociolinguistics: TextbLing. C 1990, Univ. xii-250 p. 0-521-22833-6; pa. -9668-4.

9844 **Kuryłowicz** Jerzy, ❼ Studia językoznawcze ... Sprachwissenschaftliche Studien. Wsz 1987, Państwowe. 512 p. – ᴿDLZ 111 (1990) 529-532 (K. *Günther*).

9845 *LaSor* William S., Proto-Semitic; is the concept no longer valid?: ➙ 164, ᶠSᴇɢᴇʀᴛ S., *Sopher* 1990, 189-205.

9846 **Lindeman** Frederik O., Introduction to the 'Laryngeal Theory' [= ²ʳᵉᵛEinführung in die Laryngaltheorie 1970] 1988 ➙ 4,a781: ᴿBO 17 (1990) 52-55 (Birgit A. *Olsen*).

9846* *Merz* Michael B., Linguistische Methoden in der Liturgiewissenschaft; zum Stand der Entwicklung: ArLtgW 32 (1990) 1-8.
9847 **Milner** Jean-Claude, Introduction à une science du langage: Des Travaux. P 1989, Seuil. 714 p. F 200.   ᴿÉtudes 372 (1990) 558s (Nicole *Gueunier*).
9848 **Muñiz Rodríguez** Vicente, Introducción a la filosofia del lenguaje; problemas ontológicos. Barc 1989, Anthropos. 237 p. – ᴿBurgense 31 (1990) 286s (J. de *Sahagún Lucas*).
9849 ᴱ**Newmeyer** Frederick J., Linguistics; the Cambridge survey. C 1988, Univ. x-500 p., $49.50; viii-320 p., $39.50; ix-350 p., $39.50; x-291 p., $39.50. – ᴿLanguage 65 (1989) 812-9 (R. *Hudson*).
9850 *Nicolet* Daniel, Langage et raison; philosophie, linguistique et ce qui leur ressemble: RTPhil 121 (1989) 353-375.
9851 **Rastier** François [→ 9932], Sémantique interprétative: Formes sémiotiques. P 1987, PUF. 277 p. 2-13-039833-2. – ᴿÉTRel 65 (1990) 448 (C.-B. *Amphoux*).
9852 **Resweber** Jean-Paul, La philosophie du language³ʳᵉᵛ [¹1979]: Que sais-je? 1765. P 1990, PUF. 128 p. 2-13-043137-2.
9853 *Schenkeveld* D.M., Studies in the history of ancient linguistics, III. The Stoic *téchnē perì phōnês*: Mnemosyne 43 (1990) 86-108.
9854 **Silva** Moises, God, language and Scripture; reading the Bible in the light of general linguistics: Foundations of Contemporary Interpretation 4. GR 1990, Zondervan. 0-310-40951-9.
9855 ᴱ**Swiggers** Pierre, *Wouters* Alfons, *al.*, Le langage dans l'antiquité: La Pensée linguistique 3. Lv 1990, Peeters. 212 p. 90-6831-272-3. – 9 art.
9856 ᴱ**Taylor** Daniel J., The history of linguistics in the classical period: St. Hist. Language Sciences 46. Amst 1987, Benjamins. xii-298 p. ƒ100. – ᴿClasR 40 (1990) 334s (Gillian R. *Hart*).
9857 *Visagie* F.J., The beginning of the word; introduction to a theory of archaeological grammar: Neotestamentica 24,1 (1990) 131-142.
9857* **Waterson** Natalie, Prosodic phonology; the theory and its application to language acquisition and speech processing. Newcastle 1987, Grevatt. xii-162 p. £15. – ᴿBSO 52 (1989) 203s (J. *Kelly*).

J8.4 *Origines artis scribendi* – **The origin of writing.**

9858 *Amiet* Pierre, La naissance de l'écriture ou la vraie 'révolution' [Sumer/Égypte]: RB 97 (1990) 525-541; Eng. 525.
9859 **Bernal** Martin, Cadmean letters; the transmission of the alphabet to the Aegean and further west before 1400 B.C. WL 1990, Eisenbrauns. xiii-156 p.; ill., maps. 0-931464-47-1. – ᴿUF 22 (1990) 507 (O. *Loretz*).
9860 *Coldstream* J.N., The beginnings of Greek literacy; an archaeologist's view [... how the Greeks acquired their alphabet]: AncHRes 20 (1990) 144-159.
9861 *Colless* Brian E., The proto-alphabetic inscriptions of Sinai: AbrNahr 28 (1990) 1-52.
9862 **Coulmas** Florian, The writing systems of the world. Ox 1989, Blackwell. 0-631-16513-4 [OIAc JuJ89].
9863 *Daniels* Peter T., Fundamentals of grammatology [escape from I. Gᴇʟʙ claim that Phoenician letters are really syllables]: JAOS 110 (1990) 727-731.
9864 ᴱ**Detienne** Marcel, Les savoirs de l'écriture en Grèce ancienne 1988 → 5,9779: RHR 207 (1990) 77-82 (Catherine *Darbo-Peschanski*).

9865 **Dietrich** M., *Loretz* O., Die Keilalphabete 1988 ⇸ 4,a801; 5,9780: ᴿZAW 102 (1990) 145 (I. *Kottsieper*).

9865* **Godart** Louis, Le pouvoir de l'écrit aux pays des premières écritures: Néréides [ISSN 1147-4904]. P 1990, Errance. 240 p. 2-87772-039-X [OIAc F91,10].

9866 **Goody** Jack, La logica della scrittura e l'organizzazione della società. T 1988, Einaudi. xiv-233 p. Lit. 25.000. – ᴿCC 141 (1990,1) 615 (E. *Baragli*).

9867 **Green** Margaret W., *Nissen* Hans J., *al.*, Zeichenliste der archaischen Texte aus Uruk 1987 ⇸ 3,a49: ᴿJAOS 110 (1990) 351s (M. A. *Powell*); Mundus 25 (1989) 108-110 (Gertrud *Farber*).

9868 *Haarmann* Harald, Writing from Old Europe to ancient Crete; a case of cultural continuity: ⇸ 735, JIndEur 17 (1989) 251-274.

9869 **Harris** William V., Ancient literacy [... Greeks first provably able to write a non-syllabic script after 700 B.C.]. CM 1989, Harvard Univ. xv-385 p.; 8 fig. $35. 0-674-03380-9 [NTAbs 34,269]. – ᴿAntiqJ 69 (1989) 344s (H. *Bowden*: literacy is not just schooling).

9870 **Healey** John F., The early alphabet: Reading the Past. L 1990, British Museum. 64 p. 0-7141-8073-4 [OIAc Oc90].

9871 ᴱ**Hooker** J. T., Reading the past; ancient writing from cuneiform to the alphabet [197-257, *Healey* J. F., The early alphabet; *Walker* C. on cuneiform, *Davies* W. Egyptian...]. L 1990, Guild. 384 p. £18. 0-520-07431-9 [BL 91, 127, W.G.E. *Watson*].

9872 **Immerwahr** Henry R., Attic script; a survey: MgClasArch. Ox 1990, Clarendon. xxiii-214 p.; 42 pl. £65. 0-19-813223-9. – ᴿAntiqJ 70 (1990) 124-6 (R. *Osborne*).

9872* *Isserlin* B.D.J., The 'pseudo-hieroglyphic' inscriptions from Byblos and their relation to early alphabetic writing: ⇸ 125, ᶠSZNYCER M., Scmitica 38 (1989s) 179-185.

9873 **Jeffery** L. H., ²ʳᵉᵛ*Johnston* A. W., The local scripts of archaic Greece; a study of the origin of the Greek alphabet and its development from the eighth to the fifth centuries B.C.: MgClasArch. Ox 1990, Clarendon. xx-482 p.; 80 pl. 0-19-814061-4.

9873* *a) Loretz* O., Phönizisches Alphabet und die Keilalphabete aus Ugarit; – *b) Röllig* W., The spread of the Phoenician alphabet in the Mediterranean area; – *c) Millard* A. R., The uses of the early alphabets — Phoenician; – *d) Amadasi Guzzo* M. G., 'The shadow line'; réflexions sur l'introduction de l'alphabet en Grèce; – *e) Brixhe* C., De la phonologie à l'écriture; quelques aspects de l'adaptation de l'alphabet cananéen au grec; – *f) Isserlin* B. S. J., The transfer of the alphabet to the Greeks; the state of documentation: ⇸ 762*, Phoinikeia grammata 1989, 6-19 / 20-24 / 25-36 / 37-50 / 51-58 / 59-60.

9874 **Naveh** J., Early history of the alphabet 1982 ⇸ 64,8514...5,9787: ᴿRSO 62 (1988) 172s (F. *Israel*).

9875 ᴱ**Senner** Wayne M., The origins of writing [12 Arizona State Univ. lectures 1984] 1989 ⇸ 5,9790: ᴿPhoenix 44 (Toronto 1990) 385-8 (Haruo *Konishi* draws a hypothetical conclusion favoring the Semiticists).

9876 **Steensberg** Axel, Hard grains, irrigation, numerals and script. K 1989, Acad. Sc./Let., Comm. Agr. 147 p.; 56 fig. [OIAc JuJ89].

9877 **Vachek** Josef, ᴱ*Luelsdorff* Philipp A., Written language revisited. Amst 1989, Benjamins. xiv-221 p. 90-272-2064-6.

9878 *a) Vanstiphout* H.L.J., *Miḫiltum*, or the image of cuneiform writing; – *b) Velde* Herman te, Egyptian hieroglyphs as linguistic signs and metalinguistic informants: Visible Religion 6 ('The image in writing'

1988) 152-164/169-179 [< JAOS 110 (1990) 333s, P.T. *Daniels*, with criticism of the 'strange definition of iconography'].

J9.1 *Analysis linguistica loquelae de Deo* – **God-talk.**

9879 **Albano** Franz J., Freedom, truth and hope; the relationship of philosophy and religion in the thought of Paul RICŒUR [diss. Claremont 1986]. Lanham MD 1987, UPA. xvi-252 p. $13.50. – ᴿLvSt 15 (1990) 79-81 (F.D. *Vanzina*).

9880 *Alfocea* Antonio, *Fuster* Sebastián, Dios como metáfora (Hermann HESSE o la búsqueda de la consistencia de ser individual) II: EscrVedat 19 (1989) 85-105.

9881 **Almeida Lucas** Maria Clara de, *a*) Ho Flos Sanctorum em linguagê; os santos extravagantes. Lisboa 1988, Inst. Nac. Inv. 179 p. – *b*) Le discours hagiographique; un jeu de destinateurs: SémBib 58 (1990) 18-44.

9882 **Alston** William P., Divine nature and human language. Ithaca NY 1989, Cornell Univ. 273 p. – ᴿRelSt 26 (1990) 433-5 (Gabrielle *Garthwaite*).

9882* *Brümmer* Vincent, Metaphorical thinking and systematic theology: NedTTs 43 (1989) 213-228.

9883 *Clarkson* Shannon, Language about God: StRTo 18,1 (1989) 37-50 [< ZIT 89,636].

9884 **Cooke** Bernard J., The distancing of God; the ambiguity of symbol in history and theology [➔ 5,9802] Mp 1990, Fortress. viii-381 p. $25. 0-8006-2415-7 [TDig 38,53]. – ᴿHorizons 17 (1990) 128-132 (R.A. *Duffy*) & 132-8 (J. *Carmody*) & 138-140 (Monika K. *Hellwig*) & 140-3 (G. *Macy*); 143-6 (Cooke response).

9885 **Dillistone** F.W., Power of symbols 1986 ➔ 3,a77 ... 5,9803: ᴿAnglTR 72 (1990) 476-8 (J.W. *Dixon*).

9886 **Franklin** Stephen T., Speaking from the depths; A.N. WHITEHEAD's hermeneutical metaphysics of propositions, experience, symbolism, language and religion. GR 1990, Eerdmans. xiv-410 p. $27.50. 0-8028-0370-9. – ᴿExpTim 102 (1990s) 252 (D.A. *Pailin*: significant).

9887 *García-Murga* José R., Teología como realismo hermenéutico: Misc-Com 47 (1989) 345-369.

9888 **Geffré** Claude, The risk of interpretation 1987 ➔ 3,a85; 4,a826: ᴿJRel 70 (1990) 112 (R. *Schreiter*); LvSt 15 (1990) 434-6 (R. *Michiels*).

9889 *Gerber* Uwe, Auf welche Adressaten trifft religiöse Sprache heute?: TZBas 46 (1990) 351-360.

9890 **Green** Garrett, Imagining God; theology and the religious imagination. SF 1989, Harper & R. x-179 p. $23. – ᴿWestTJ 52 (1990) 162s (R.E. *Otto*).

9891 *Harvey* Michael G., WITTGENSTEIN's notion of 'theology as grammar': RelSt 25 (1989) 89-103.

9892 *Hoeps* Reinhard, Das Wort Gottes und die Sprache der Dinge; Versuch über die Betrachtung der Schöpfung als Offenbarung: ZkT 112 (1990) 178-193.

9893 ᴱ**Hünermann** Peter, *Schaeffler* Richard, Theorie der Sprachhandlungen und heutige Ekklesiologie: QDisp 109, 1987 ➔ 3,644: ᴿLebZeug 43 (1988) 80s (J. *Kreiml*).

9894 **Jeanrond** W.G., Text and interpretation 1988 ➔ 2,7910 ... 5,9814: ᴿInterpretation 44 (1990) 106s (D.B. *McKim*).

9895 *Jiménez Sánchez-Mariscal* J.D., Lenguaje, ética y religión en L. WITTGENSTEIN: RelCu 36 (1990) 591-612.

9896 *Joy* Morna, Hermeneutics and *mimēsis* [... RICŒUR P.]: SR 19 (1990) 73-86.

9896* *Lønning* Per, Der begreiflich Unergreifbare; 'Sein Gottes' und modern-theologische Denkstrukturen: ForSysÖk 49, 1986 → 3,a96: ᴿTsTKi 60 (1989) 66-69 (P. *Gravem*).

9897 *McWilliams* Warren M., God the friend, a test case in metaphorical theology: PerspRelSt 16 (1989) 109-120 [< ᴢɪᴛ 90,163].

9898 *Maurer* Ernstpeter, Biblisches Reden von Gott — ein Sprachspiel?:... BARTH, WITTGENSTEIN: EvT 50 (1990) 71-82.

9899 *Meyer zu Schlochtern* Josef, Die Bedeutung der Metapher für die religiöse Sprache [ᴱNOPPEN J.-P. van, Erinnern 1989]: TR 86 (1990) 441-450.

9900 **Moore** Gareth, Believing in God; a philosophic essay ['People do not discover religious truths; they make them']. E 1989, Clark. 288 p. £15. 0-567-09498-7. – ᴿExpTim 101 (1989s) 89 (P. *Vardy*: a Roman Catholic Cupitt's non-theistic Catholicism).

9901 ᴱNOPPEN J.-P. van, Erinnern... Metapher/religiöse Sprache 1988 → 4, a848; 5,9826: ᴿTPQ 138 (1990) 81 (C. *Schacherreiter*).

9902 **Oberhammer** Gerhard, Versuch einer transzendentalen Hermeneutik religiöser Traditionen: Univ. Wien Inst. Indologie. Leiden 1987, Brill. 48 p. – ᴿRTLv 21 (1990) 102 (E. *Brito*).

9903 *Pieterse* Hendrik J.C., A dialogical theory of communication from a practical theological perspective: EvQ 62 (1990) 223-240.

9904 **Prichard** Rebecca B., Genre, metaphor, and theory; the interpretation of form and content in theological texts; diss. Graduate Theological Union, ᴰ*Reist* B. Berkeley 1990. – RelStR 17,192.

9905 **Raden** Matthias J., Das relative Absolute; die theologische Hermeneutik Paul RICŒURS: EurHS 23/323. Fra 1988, Lang. 352 p. 3-8204-1136-4. ᴿEstE 65 (1990) 369 (J.J. *Alemany*).

9906 **Renck** Günther, Contextualization of Christianity and Christianization of language; a case study from the highlands of Papua New Guinea [Luth. Diss. Erlangen]: MgMission Ök 5. Erlangen 1990. 316 p. [TContext 8/1, 136, H. *Janssen*].

9907 *Rohls* Jan, Sprachanalyse und Theologie bei I.U. DALFERTH: TRu 55 (1990) 200-217.

9908 *a) Rubio Ferreres*, Lenguaje religioso y hermenéutica filosófica en Paul RICŒUR; – *b) Pérez Tapias* José A.,... Utopía y escatologia en PR; – *c) Avila Crespo* Remedios, El ocaso de los ídolos y la aurora de los símbolos: CommSev 22 (1989) 3-20 / 21-30 / 31-39.

9909 *Santos* Emil M., Theology of pastoral communication; themes and bibliographical sketch: Salesianum 52 (1990) 621-675.

9910 **Schaeffler** R., Das Gebet und das Argument; zwei Weisen des Sprechens von Gott — eine Einführung in die Theorie der religiösen Sprache: BeitTRelW. Dü 1989, Patmos. xii-346 p. DM 44,80. 3-491-71086-3. – ᴿTsTNijm 30 (1990) 212s (H. *Rikhof*).

9911 **Shupe** David, A grammar of dissent; a critical inquiry into language, deliterality, and religion: diss. ᴰ*Wiggins* J. Syracuse NY 1989. – RelStR 17,191.

9912 *Tessier* Robert, La métaphore religieuse dans la presse écrite; indice de sécularisation ou de déplacement du sacré?: SR 19 (1990) 87-105.

9913 **Tracy** David, Plurality and ambiguity 1997 → 3,a117.a997... 5,9833: ᴿPacifica 3 (1990) 363-5 (J.M. *Richard*; has much to offer, though soaked in elitism and interruptions).

9914 **Vahanian** G., Dieu anonyme 1989 → 5,9815; 2-220-03078-4: ᴿRevSR 64 (1990) 331s (R. *Sublon*); TsTNijm 30 (1990) 214 (H.J. *Heering*).

9915 *Verst* Ludger, Analogie und Metapher; zur Hermeneutik metaphorisch-praktischer Rede von Gott: LingBib 63 (1989) 58-84; Eng. 84s.

9916 *Vissers* John A., Interpreting the classic; the hermeneutical character of David TRACY's theology in The analogical imagination [1981; as in Blessed Rage 1975 and Plurality 1987, he aims to reappropriate SCHLEIERMACHER, incorporating LONERGAN, RAHNER, RICŒUR along the way]: CalvinT 25 (1990) 194-206.

9917 *a*) *Williams* Rowan, Language, reality and desire in AUGUSTINE's De doctrina; – *b*) *Louth* Andrew, Augustine on language; – *c*) *Burrell* David B., GHAZALI and AQUINAS on the names of God; – *d*) *White* Graham, LUTHER's views on language: LitTOx 3 (1989) 138-150 / 151-8 / 173-180 / 188-218 [< ZIT 89, 582].

9918 *Zimmer* Christoph, *a*) Definierbarkeit und Definition des Ausdrucks 'Gott': LingBib 62 (1989) 5-47; 63 (1989) 5-31; Eng. 47s. 32. – *h*) Negation und via negationis: LingBib 64 (1990) 53-87; Eng. 91; bibliog. 88-91.

9919 **Zimmermann** Joyce A., Liturgy as language of faith; a liturgical methodology in the mode of Paul RICŒUR's textual hermeneutics 1988 → 5,9837: ᴿJAAR 58 (1990) 733-5 (M. B. *Aune*).

J9.2 *Hermeneutica paratheologica* – **Wider linguistic analysis.**

9920 **Biehl** Peter, Symbole... Hand, Haus, Weg 1989 → 5,9842: ᴿTZBas 46 (1990) 189s (W. *Neidhart*).

9921 **Courtes** Joseph, Sémantique de l'énoncé; applications pratiques. P 1989, Hachette. 286 p. – ᴿSémBib 56 (1989) 42.

9922 **Eco** Umberto, Signo [1973, 1976], ᵀ*Serra Cantarell* F. Barc 1988, Labor. 216 p. – ᴿNatGrac 37 (1990) 139 (V. *Muñiz*).

9923 **Edwards** Viv, *Sienkewicz* Thomas J. Oral cultures past and present; rappin' and Homer: Language Library. Ox 1990, Blackwell. xii-244 p.; map. 0-631-16569-X.

9924 *Grondin* J., L'herméneutique comme science rigoureuse selon Emilio BETTI (1890-1968): Archives de philosophie 53 (1990) 177-199 [< RSPT 74, 650].

9925 **Honneth** Axel, *Joas* Hans, Kommunikatives Handeln [HABERMAS]: Tb-Wiss 625, Fra 1988, Suhrkamp. 420 p. DM 24. – ᴿDLZ 111 (1990) 772-7 (H. *Metzler*).

9926 **Illgner** Susanne, Verkündigende Sprache und automatische Sprachverarbeitung; Überlegungen zur Semantik: diss. Heidelberg 1990s, ᴰ*Eisinger*. – RTLv 22, p. 586.

9927 **Jauss** Hans Robert, Pour une herméneutique littéraire [Ästhetische Erfahrung 1982], ᵀ*Jacob* M.: Bibliothèque des Idées. P 1988, Gallimard. 457 p. – ᴿRHPR 70 (1990) 249-251 (J.-G. *Heintz*).

9928 **Kaulen** Heinrich, Rettung und Destruktion; Untersuchungen zur Hermeneutik Walter BENJAMINS: Studien zur deutschen Literatur 94. Tü 1987, Niemeyer. vi-289 p. – ᴿDLZ 111 (1990) 522-5 (Daniela *Assenowa*).

9929 *Kissling* Christian, Die Theorie des kommunikativen Handelns in Diskussion [HABERMAS J.: ᴱ*Honneth* A. 1989; ᴱ*Arens* E. 1989]: FreibZ 37 (1990) 233-252.

9930 **Kühn** R., Deuten als Entwerden; eine Synthese des Werkes Simone WEILS in hermeneutisch-religionsgeschichtlicher Sicht: FreibTSt 136. FrB

1989, Herder. xiv-457 p. DM 58. 3-451-21385-0. – ᴿTsTNijm 30 (1990) 96 (H. *Berger*).

9931 *Masiá Clavel* Juan, Deseo, tiempo y narración; la filosofía de P. Rɪcœᴜʀ como hermenéutica de la experiencia crítica: MiscCom 47 (1989) 371-389.

9932 **Rastier** François [→ 9852], Sens et textualité. P 1989, Hachette. 286 p. – ᴿSémBib 56 (1989) 43.

9933 *Ricken* Friedo, Hermeneutik und Metaphysik [Vortrag Innsbruck, Emerich Cᴏʀᴇᴛʜ zu ehren, 70. Gb.]: TPhil 65 (1990) 69-73; 74-78, Coreths Antwort.

9934 **Rieger** Reinhold, Interpretation und Wissen; zur philosophischen Begründung der Hermeneutik bei F. Sᴄʜʟᴇɪᴇʀᴍᴀᴄʜᴇʀ und ihrem geschichtlichen Hintergrund: S-Archiv 6. B 1988, de Gruyter. ix-361 p. DM 105. – ᴿTLZ 115 (1990) 218s (H. *Peiter*).

9935 **Warnke** Georgia, Gᴀᴅᴀᴍᴇʀ; hermeneutics, tradition and reason 1987 → 3,a162; 5,9868: ᴿHeythJ 31 (1990) 330s (A. *Louth*).

9936 **Webb** Eugene, Philosophers of consciousness; Pᴏʟᴀɴʏɪ, Lᴏɴᴇʀɢᴀɴ, Vᴏᴇɢᴇʟɪɴ, Rɪcœᴜʀ, Gɪʀᴀʀᴅ, Kɪᴇʀᴋᴇɢᴀᴀʀᴅ. Seattle 1988, Univ. Washington. ix-342 p. $30. – ᴿTS 51 (1990) 150s (Merold *Westphal*).

9937 *Zak* Adam, Die Zeit der Sprache — die Sprache der Zeit [Rᴏsᴇɴ-sᴛᴏᴄᴋ-Hᴜᴇssʏ E.]: Orientierung 54 (1990) 2-7.

J9.4 **Structuralismus,** deconstructio.

9938 **Gall** Robert S., Of/From theology and deconstruction [loosely = Dᴇʀʀɪᴅᴀ-style post-structuralism]: JAAR 58 (1990) 413-437.

9939 **Hart** Kevin, The trespass of the sign; deconstruction, theology and philosophy. C 1990, Univ. xii-292 p. £37.50. 0-521-35481-1. – ᴿExpTim 102 (1990s) 158 (I. *Markham*: interdisciplinary, competent).

9940 *Jespers* F.F.M., Sporen van Dᴇʀʀɪᴅᴀ [...deconstructie] bij nordamerikaanse theologen [Tʀᴀᴄʏ D., Aʟᴛɪᴢᴇʀ T., Sᴄʜᴀʀʟᴇᴍᴀɴɴ R.]: TsTNijm 30 (1990) 172-183; Eng. 183.

9941 *a*) *Jobling* David, Writing the wrongs of the world; the deconstruction of the biblical text in the context of liberation theologies; – *b*) *Taylor* Mark C., The eventuality of texts [Dᴇʀʀɪᴅᴀ and Lᴇᴠɪɴᴀs poststructural alternatives]: → 365, Semeia 51 (1990) 81-118 / 215-240.

9942 *Moeshammer* A.A., Disclosing but not disclosed; Gʀᴇɢᴏʀʏ of Nyssa as deconstructionist: → 695, Stud./Nyss. 1990, 99-123.

9943 **Southwell** Samuel B., Kenneth Bᴜʀᴋᴇ and Martin Hᴇɪᴅᴇɢɢᴇʀ, with a note against deconstructionism. Gainesville. 1987, Univ. Florida. 157 p. $15. – ᴿJAAR 58 (1990) 152-4 (R. S. *Gall*).

9944 **Taylor** Mark C., Erring... Dᴇʀʀɪᴅᴀ 1984 → 1,g323...4,a907: ᴿCCurr 38 (1988s) 468-474 (D. R. *Blumenthal*).

J9.6 *Analysis narrationis* – **Narrative-analysis.**

9945 ᴱ**Bühler** P., *Habermacher* J.-F., La narration; quand le récit devient communication 1988 → 4,a911: ᴿTLZ 115 (1990) 56s (M. *Heymel*).

9946 **Calame** C., Le récit en Grece ancienne 1986 → 5,9875: ᴿAnÉCS 45 (1990) 868-871 (Catherine *Peschanski*); Mnemosyne 43 (1990) 166-8 (Irene J. F. de *Jong*).

9947 *Hinze* Bradford, Narrative contexts, doctrinal reform: TS 51 (1990) 407-433.

9948 ᴱKemp J. Peter, *Rasmussen* David, The narrative path; the later works of Paul Rɪᴄœᴜʀ. CM 1989, MIT. viii-121 p. $11 [RelStR 17, 141, M.J. *Wallace*].

9949 **Ledbetter** Mark, Virtuous intentions; the religious dimension of narrative: AAR 66. ᴹAtlanta 1989, Scholars. 100 p. $13 [JAAR 58,162; RelStR 17, 246, J. *Smith*].

9950 **Ricœur** Paul, Zeit und Erzählung [1978], ᵀ*Rochlitz* Rainer: Übergange 18. Mü 1988s. 2 vol. – ᴿGrazBei 17 (1990) 323-332 (Barbara *Feichtinger*).

J9.8 *Theologia narrativa* – Story-theology.

9951 **Ben-Chorin** Schalom, Narrative Theologie des Judentums anhand der Pessach–Haggada; Jerusalem Vorlesungen. Tü 1985, Mohr. 165 p. DM 28. – ᴿJEcuSt 24 (1987) 129s (J. M. *Oesterreicher*).

9952 *Grethlein* Christian, Bezieht sich Theologie nur auf 'Geschichten' [Gʀö-ᴢɪɴɢᴇʀ A. 1989]: BTZ 7 (1990) 286-290.

Hauerwas S., *Jones* L. G., Why narrative? Readings in narrative theology 1990 → 416*.

9953 **Nelson** Paul, Narrative and morality; a theological inquiry 1987 → 3, a204 ... 5,9281: ᴿRelSt 25 (1989) 393-6 (J. *Milbank*).

9954 *Spohn* William C., Parable and narrative in Christian ethics [... promises and problems of narrative theology ...]: TS 51 (1990) 100-114.

Stegner William R., Narrative theology in ... [Christianity → 5,9882] Christology 1989 → 7447.

(IV.) Postbiblica

ᴋ1 **Pseudepigrapha** [= catholicis 'Apocrypha'] .1 *VT, generalia.*

9955 *Bar-Ilan* Meir, The date of the words of *Gad the Seer* [ms. in Hebrew copied at Cochin, c. 1750]: JBL 109 (1990) 475-492.

9956 **Charlesworth** James H., Gli pseudepigrafi dell'Antico Testamento e il Nuovo Testamento; prolegomena allo studio delle origini cristiane [1985 → 1,9649], ᵀ*Boccaccini* Gabriele: StBPaid 91. Brescia 1990, Paideia. 307 p. Lit. 34.000. 88-394-0440-6.

Delcor M., Apocrypha and pseudepigrapha 1989 → 3976*b*.

9957 **Denis** Albert-Marie, Concordance grecque des pseudépigraphes d'AT 1987 → 3,a212; 5,9885: ᴿBiblica 71 (1990) 587s (S. *Pisano*: accompanied by four exhaustive indices in microfiche); BZ 34 (1990) 303 (J. *Schreiner*); JBL 109 (1990) 132s (J.J. *Collins*); JTS 41 (1990) 155-7 (D.R. *de Lacey*); NedTTs 44 (1990) 261s (T. *Baarda*); TLZ 115 (1990) 676-8 (T. *Holtz*).

9957* *Denis* Albert-Marie, Les genres littéraires des pseudépigraphes d'Ancien Testament; essai de classification: → 539*, DSS FolOr 25 (1989) 99-112.

9958 **Díez Macho** A., Apócrifos del AT 5, 1987 → 3,335; 5,9887: ᴿGregorianum 71 (1990) 375s (G. L. *Prato*).

9958* ᴱ**Dupont-Sommer** A., *Philonenko* M., La Bible, écrits intertestamentaires 1987 → 3,a214 ... 5,9888: ᴿRÉJ 149 (1990) 189-191 (Mireille *Hadas-Lebel*).

9959 **McNamara** Martin, Les écrits de la période intertestamentaire [1983 → 64,8597], ᵀ*Desjardins* Maurice. Montréal 1986, Fides. 252 p. $20. – ᴿÉglT 20 (1989) 125s (L. *Laberge*).

9960 **Migne** J.-P., Dictionnaire des Apocryphes [1856-8]. Turnhout 1989,

Brepols. lxxii-1296 p.; 1324 p. Fb 5000 [RelStR 17, 175, J. R. *Mueller*: best of 19th century scholarship].

9961 **Russell** D. S., OT Pseudepigrapha 1987 ➤ 3,a221 ... 5,9892: RAnglTR 72 (1990) 220s (J. I. *Hunt*: excellent); ScripTPamp 22 (1990) 1007s (P. *Monod*: título 'Russel', texto 'Rusell').

9962 ESacchi Paolo, Apocrifi dell'AT II, 1989 ➤ 5,9893: RCC 141 (1990,3) 299s (G. L. *Prato*); StPatav 37 (1990) 194s (G. *Segalla*).

9963 *Stuhlmacher* Peter, Die Bedeutung der Apokryphen und Pseudepigraphen des Alten Testaments für das Verständnis Jesu und der Christologie: BiWelt 22 (1989) 13-25 [< ZIT 90,400].

к1.2 Henoch.

9964 **Böttrich** Christfried, Weltweisheit — Menschheitsethik — Urkult; Studien zum slavischen Henochbuch: Diss. DKähler C. Lp 1990. – RTLv 22,590 'Bàttrich'; TLZ 116,771 'Böttrich'.

9965 **Kvanvig** Helge S., Roots of apocalyptic; the Mesopotamian background of the Enoch figure and of the Son of Man: WM 61, 1988 ➤ 5,3727: RJBL 109 (1990) 715-8 (J. J. *Collins*); NorTTs 90 (1989) 232-5 (H. M. *Barstad*).

9966 **Mopsik** Charles, Le livre hébreu d'Hénoch ou livre des palais [de plusieurs siècles postérieur à Hénoch éth. ou slave] 1989 ➤ 5,9901: RÉTRel 65 (1990) 443 (D. *Bourguet*).

9966* *Nickelsburg* George W. E., Two Enochic manuscripts; unstudied evidence for Egyptian Christianity: ➤ 173, FSTRUGNELL J., Of scribes 1990, 251-260.

9967 **Peters** Ulrike, Wie der biblische Prophet Henoch zum Buddha wurde; die jüdische Henochtradition als frühes Beispiel interkultureller und interreligiöser Vermittlung zwischen Ost und West: TheolTSt 5. Sinzig 1989, St. Meinrad. 212 p. DM 48. – RKIsr 4 (1990) 75 (Julie *Kirchberg*: störende Druckfehler).

9968 **Reddish** M. G., Apocalyptic literature [mostly Enoch and other apocrypha], a reader. Nv 1990, Abingdon. 352 p. $25. 0-687-01566-9. [NTAbs 35,131].

9968* *Uhlig* Siegbert, Bemerkungen zur Textkritik des äthiopischen Henoch und insbesondere der Epistel Henochs: ZDMG 139 (1989) 21-42.

к1.3 Testamenta.

9969 *Jonge* Marinus de, Testaments des douze Patriarches: ➤ 837, DictSpir 15, 96ss (1990) 300-8.

9969* *Jonge* M. de, Test. Benjamin 3:8 and the picture of Joseph as 'a good and holy man': ➤ 533, Martyrologie 1984/9, 204-214.

9970 **Schmidt** Francis, Le Testament grec d'Abraham: TStAJ 11, 1986 ➤ 2,8055 ... 5,9907: RBO 47 (1990) 204-6 (P. *Höffken*); NedTTs 44 (1990) 72s (C. E. *Donker*).

9971 EKnibb Michael A., Studies on the Testament of Job; SNTS Mg 66, 1989 ➤ 5,9908; £25: RTR 86,338, tit. pp.

к1.4 Salomonis psalmi et odae.

9972 **Lattke** Michael, Die Oden Salomos ... für NT 3. Forschungsgeschichtliche Bibliographie 1799-1984 mit kritischen Anmerkungen: OBO 25/3, 1986 ➤ 2,8069 ... 5,9915: RCBQ 52 (1990) 523s (D. *Bundy*).

9972* *Morgan-Wynne* J. E.,   The experience of the Spirit in the Odes of
Solomon: ➤ 643, StPatr 18,3 (1983/9) 173-181.
9973 *Kruse* Heinz, Die 24. Ode Salomos: OrChr 74 (1990) 25-43.

K1.6 Jubilaea, Adam, Aḥiqar, Asenet.

9973* **Bertrand** Daniel A., La vie grecque d'Adam et Ève 1987 ➤ 3,a265;
5,9927: ᴿCritRR 3 (1990) 333-6 (M. E. *Stone*); RTPhil 122 (1990) 135 (É.
Junod).
9974 **Lipscomb** William L., The Armenian apocryphal Adam literature [diss.
Columbia 1982]: UPenn ArmenianStT 8. Atlanta 1990, Scholars. x-288 p.
$30. 1-55540-455-3 [NTAbs 35,128].
9975 ᵀᴱ**VanderKam** James C., Book of Jubilees: CSCOr 510s, 1989 ➤ 5,
9919 [BL 91,43, M. *Knibb*; haplography of 'Tānāsee' in paragraph
defending Pontifical Biblical Institute's Ethiopian A 2.12 manuscript,
corrected in BL 92,6].

K1.7 Apocalypses, ascensiones.

9976 **Himmelfarb** Martha, *a*) Tours of Hell [pseudepigraphic apocalypses]
1983 ➤ 64,6474 ... 4,8410*: ᴿJTS 41 (1990) 355-385 (R. *Bauckham* as
'Jewish visions'); – *b*) Heavenly ascent and the relationship of the apocalypses and the Hekhalot literature: HUCA 49 (1988) 73-100 [< ZAW
102,275].
9977 **Kappler** Claude, Apocalypses et voyages dans l'Au-Delà 1987 ➤ 3,3625,
4,3866: ᴿWeltOr 20s (1989s) 296-9 (M. *Hutter*).
9978 ᴱ**Termolen** Rosel, Apokalypsen, das Buch der geheimen Offenbarungen [Abraham, Sophonias, 4 Ezra ...]. Augsburg 1990, Pattloch. 328 p.
3-629-00549-7.
9979 **Rubinkiewcz** R., L'Apocalypse d'Abraham en vieux slave [diss. R 1978]
1987 ➤ 3,a262: ᴿBL (1989) 142 (M. A. *Knibb*).
9980 *Netzer* Amnon, A midrash on the Ascension of Moses in Judeo-
Persian: ➤ 555, Irano-Judaica (1987/90) 105-143.
9981 **Rosso Ubigli** L., Considerazioni sulla datazione dell'Apocalisse di
Mosè (o Vita greca di Adamo ed Eva): ➤ 154, ᶠSACCHI P. 1990,
232-333.
9982 **Schalit** Abraham, Untersuchungen zur Assumptio Mosis [I. to 1,17; II.
awaited to 4,9, both posthumous], ᴱ*Schreckenberg* H.: ArbLGJ 17.
Leiden 1989, Brill. *f* 140. 90-04-08120-8. [NTAbs 34,276].
9983 *Tromp* Joh., Taxo [AssMos 9: name corrupt therefore left unexplained],
the messenger of the Lord: JStJud 21 (1990) 200-9.
9984 **Acerbi** Antonio, L'Ascensione di Isaia 1989 ➤ 5,9929: ᴿRSPT 74 (1990)
623s (G.-M. de *Durand*).
9984* *Hall* Robert G., The Ascension of Isaiah; community situation, date,
and place in early Christianity: JBL 109 (1990) 289-306.
9985 **Frankfurter** David T. M., Elijah in Upper Egypt; studies in the history
and composition of the Coptic Elijah Apocalypse: diss. Princeton 1990,
ᴰ*Himmelfarb* M. 407 p. 90-27546. – DissA 51 (1990s) 1652-A; RelStR
17,194.

K2.1 Philo judaeus alexandrinus.

9986 *Belletti* Bruno, Il Logos come immagine di Dio in Filone d'Alessandria:
Sapienza 43 (1990) 311-320.

9987 **Burkhardt** Helmut, Inspiration ... bei Philo 1988 → 4,1405; 5,9934: RTLZ 115 (1990) 444s (H. M. *Schenke*); TR 96 (1990) 197-201 (F. G. *Untergassmair*); VT 40 (1990) 503s (W. *Horbury*).
Cazeaux J., La trame et la chaîne 2. Le cycle de Noé dans Philon 1989 → 5,2217,

9987* **Conley** T. M., Philo's rhetoric 1987 → 3,a270: RCritRR 2 (1989) 367s (S. *Isser*).

9988 *Decharneux* Baudouin, Mantique et oracles dans l'œuvre de Philon d'Alexandrie: → 757, Oracles = Kernos 3 (1990) 123-133.

9989 *Downing* F. Gerald, Ontological asymmetry in Philo and Christological realism in Paul, Hebrews and John: JTS 41 (1990) 423-440.

9990 *García Martínez* Florentino, Entorno literario del NT [apócrifos, Qumran, Filón, JOSEFO (AT, *Asurmendi* J.)]: → 370*, Introd. I, 1990, 391-409 (383-390).

9991 **Grabbe** Lester L., Etymology in early Jewish interpretation; the Hebrew names in Philo: BrownJudSt 115, 1988 → 5,9938: RJBL 109 (1990) 527s (A. *Mendelson*); RÉJ 149 (1990) 303s (Madeleine *Petit*); StPhilonAn 2 (1990) 187-194 (R. *Goulet*).

9992 *Guerra* Anthony J., The One God topos in Spec. Leg. 1.52 → 544, SBL seminars 1990, 148-164.

9993 TEKraus **Reggiani** Clara, Filone di A., L'uomo e Dio: Univ. S. Cuore. Mi 1986, Rusconi. 674 p. Lit. 42.000. – RDivThom 92 (1989) 455-7 (G. *Visconti*).

9994 *Levoratti* Armando J., La lectura 'espiritual' de la Biblia [Filón ... hoy]: RBibArg 52,37 (1990) 29 54.

9995 [Pablo] *Martín* José, Filón Hebreo y Teófilo cristiano; la continuidad de una teología natural: Salmanticensis 37 (1990) 301-317; Eng. 317.

9996 **Ménard** J., Gnose de Philon 1987 → 3,a277 ... 5,9946: RRB 97 (1990) 297 (M.-J. *Pierre*).

9997 **Pepin** Jean, La tradition de l'allégorie de Philon à Dante 1987 → 3,a282: RSalesianum 52 (1990) 907 (P. *Canaccini*: half revised reprints).

9998 **Radice** Roberto, Platonismo e creazionismo in Filone 1989 → 5,9951: RGregorianum 71 (1990) 604 (G. *Pelland*); RET 50 (1990) 104-6 (M. *Gesteira*).

9999 **Radice** R., *Runia* D. T., Philo bibliography 1937-86; 1988 → 4,a933; 5,9951: RJTS 41 (1990) 642s (R. *Williamson*); VigChr 44 (1990) 85s (J. den *Boeft*).

a1 **Runia** D. T., Philo ... and the Timaeus of PLATO 1986 → 3,a285; 4,a995: RCritRR 2 (1989) 378-381 (T. H. *Tobin*); VigChr 44 (1990) 83-85 (J. den *Boeft*).

a2 *Runia* David T., *a*) Philo, Alexandrian and Jew [→ 5,9953] (ineditum); – *b*) Mosaic and Platonist exegesis; Philo on 'finding' and 'refinding' [< VigChr 40 (1986)]: → 293, Exegesis 1990, I, 1-18 / VI, 209-217.

a3 **Siegert** Folker, Philon ... 'Feuer' (De Deo): WUNT 46, 1988 → 3,a987; 5,9957: RCBQ 52 (1990) 569s (Earle *Hilgert*); CritRR 3 (1990) 358-360 (J. R. *Royse*); JStJud 21 (1990) 136-8 (M. E. *Stone*); JTS 41 (1990) 169-171 (R. *Williamson*); NedTTs 44 (1990) 263s (P. W. van der *Horst*).

a4 *Siegert* F., Der armenische Philon ...: ZKG 100 (1989) 353-369 [< ByZ 83,150].

a5 *a*) *Sterling* Gregory E., Philo and the logic of apologetics; an analysis of the Hypothetica; – *b*) *Carras* George P., Philo's Hypothetica, JOSEPHUS' Contra Apionem and the question of sources: → 544, SBL seminars 1990, 412-430 / 431-450.

Philon, Alexander ... bruta animalia, ETerian A. 1988 → g327.

a6 **Williamson** Ronald, Jews in the Hellenistic world; Philo: CamCW. C 1989, Univ. xii-314 p. £35; pa. £13. 0-521-30511-X; 1548-4: RBL (1990) 144 (F. F. *Bruce*); EvQ 62 (1990) 279s (P. *Ellingworth*); Henoch 12 (1990) 242-5 (Clara *Kraus Reggiani*).

a6* *a*) *Winston* David, Judaism and Hellenism; hidden tensions in Philo's thought; – *b*) *Helleman* Wendy E., Philo of Alexandria on deification and assimilation to God; – *c*) *Cohen* Naomi G., Agrippa I and De specialibus legibus IV 151-159; – *d*) *Runia* David T., *al.*, How to search Philo; Annotated bibliography 1986-7, provisional 1988-90: StPhilonAn 2 (1990) 1-19 / 51-71 / 72-85 / 105-140, 10 fig.; 141-169. 170-5.

K2.4 *Evangelia apocrypha* [sic etiam acatholici] – **Apocryphal Gospels.**

a7 **Burrus** Virginia, *a*) Chastity as autonomy; women in the stories of apocryphal Acts 1987 ➤ 3,8853; 5,8790*: RCritRR 2 (1989) 300s (R. I. *Perno*); – *b*) Canonical references to extra-canonical 'texts'; PRISCILLIAN's defense of the Apocrypha ['why should I condemn what I have not read?'; but he was put to death for it]: ➤ 544, SBL seminars 1990, 60-67.

a8 ᴱ**Hedrick** C. W., The historical Jesus and the rejected Gospels 1988 ➤ 4,309: RSalmanticensis 37 (1990) 373-7 (R. *Trevijano*).

a9 **Santos Otero** Aurelio de, Los Evangelios Apócrifos; colección de textos griegos y latinos⁶ [¹1956]: BAC 148. M 1988, Católica. xxvi-781 p. RArTGran 53 (1990) 314s (A. *Segovia*); ETL 66 (1990) 417 (F. *Neirynck*: bibliography still stops with ³1975, except for added NH Thomas & Philip).

a10 ᴱ**Schneemelcher** W., Neutestamentliche Apokryphen in deutscher Übersetzung I⁶ [correcting minor errors of I⁵ 1987 ➤ 3,a298*; 5,9961]. Tü 1990, Mohr. x-442 p.; DM 98. 3-16-145606-8 [NTAbs 35,132]. – RBZ 34 (1990) 267-9 (R. *Schnackenburg*, 2⁵); Muséon 103 (1990) 181-4 (A. M. *Denis*, 2⁵); NT 32 (1990) 379-381 (J. K. *Elliott*, 2⁵); OrChrPer 56 (1990) 504s (V. *Poggi*, 2⁵); RB 97 (1990) 139s (J. *Murphy-O'Connor* compares with Charlesworth, and puts in a class apart the 'magnificent' and 'majestic' OT volumes of DÍEZ MACHO); SNTU-A 15 (1990) 215-7 (A. *Fuchs*, I⁶); SvEx 55 (1990) 167-171 (E. *Thomassen*); VigChr 44 (1990) 298s (A.F.J. *Klijn*, 2⁵).

a11 *Perler* Othmar, Das Protevangelium des Jakobus nach dem Papyrus Bodmer V [< FreibZ 6 (1959) 23-35]: ➤ 283, Sapientia 1990, 505-517.

a12 *Shanzer* Danuta, 'Asino vectore virgo regia fugiens captivitatem'; APULEIUS and the tradition of Protevangelium Jacobi [though D. *Massé*'s 1934 claims of Apocalypse/Gospels reflected in Apuleius are wild and unaccepted]: ZPapEp 84 (1990) 221-9.

a13 *Pilhofer* Peter, JUSTIN und [d.h. zitiert] das Petrusevangelium [Promotionsvorlesung]: ZNW 81 (1990) 60-78.

a14 *Treat* Jay C., The two manuscript witnesses to the Gospel of Peter: ➤ 544, SBL seminars 1990, 391-9.

a15 **Crossan** John D., [EvPt] The cross that spoke 1988 ➤ 5,9983: RJBL 109 (1990) 356-8 (J. B. *Green*: not a convincing treatment of origins of the Passion narrative); NewTR 2,1 (1989) 106s (D. *Senior*).

a16 *a*) *Hills* Julian, Proverbs as sayings of Jesus in the Epistula Apostolorum; – *b*) *Crossan* John D., Thoughts on two extracanonical gospels [Peter, Secret Mark]; – *c*) *Dewey* Arthur J, 'Time to murder and create'; visions and revisions in the Gospel of Peter: ➤ 326, Semeia 49 (1990) 7-34 / 155-168 / 101-127.

a17 *Despineux* Myriam, Une version latine palimpseste du Ve siècle de l'Évangile de Nicodème (Vienne, ÖNB MS 563): Scriptorium 42 (Bru 1988) 176-183.

a18 *Izydorczyk* Zbigniew, The unfamiliar Evangelium Nicodemi: Manuscripta 33 (St. Louis 1989) 169-191.

a19 *Broek* Roelof van den, Der Bericht des koptischen Kyrillos von Jerusalem über das Hebräerevangelium: ➤ 661, Schmidt-Kolloquium 1988/90, 165-180.

K2.7 Alia apocrypha NT.

a20 **Kampen** Lieuwe van, Apostelverhalen; doel en compositie van de oudste apokriefe Handelingen der Apostelen: diss. ᴰ*Broek* R. van den. Utrecht 1990 [Sliedrecht, Merweboek; 90-71864-17-0] 338 p. – TsTNijm 30, p. 304; RTLv 22, p. 596.

a21 ᴱ**Prieur** Jean-Marc, Acta Andreae: CCApocr 5s, 1989 ➤ 5,9975; Fb 11.100; ᴿÉTRel 65 (1990) 655-7 (*ipse*); RHE 85 (1990) 359-362 (L. *Leloir*); SNTU-A 15 (1990) 217s (A. *Fuchs*); VigChr 44 (1990) 404-7 (G. *Quispel*, Eng.).

a22 *MacDonald* Dennis R., Intertextuality in Simon's 'redemption' of Helen the whore; Homer, heresiologists, and The Acts of Andrew: ➤ 544, SBL seminars 1990, 136-143.

a23 *Bauer* Johannes B., Die Korruptel Acta Johannis 52: VigChr 44 (1990) 295-7.

a24 *Drijvers* Han J. W., Der getaufte Löwe und die Theologie der Acta Pauli: ➤ 661, Schmidt-Kolloquium 1988/90, 181-190.

a25 *a) Rosenstiehl* Jean-Marc, L'itinéraire de Paul dans l'au-delà; contribution à l'etude de l'Apocalypse apocryphe de Paul; – *b) Göltz* Hermann, Beobachtungen zur Gestalt der apostelgleichen Protomärtyrerin Thekla: ➤ 661, Schmidt-Kolloquium 1988/90, 197-212 / 191-6.

a26 **Van Voorst** Robert E., The ascents of James; history and theology of a Jewish-Christian community: SBL Diss 112 (NY Union), 1989 ➤ 5,9976: ᴿETL 66 (1990) 417s (J. *Verheyden*).

a26* *Wischmeyer* Wolfgang, Die Epistula Anne ad Senecam, eine jüdische Missionsschrift des lateinischen Bereichs: ➤ 506*, Juden/Christen 1989/90, 72-93.

Veilleux Armand, 1-2 Apocryphe de Jacques 1987 ➤ a560.

a27 **Buchholz** Dennis D., Your eyes will be opened; a study of the Greek (Ethiopic) Apocalypse of Peter: SBL diss. 97 (Claremont 1984), 1988 ➤ 4,b20; 5,9982: ᴿCBQ 52 (1990) 549s (Martha *Himmelfarb*).

a27* *Redmond* Sheila A., The date of the fourth Sibylline oracle: SecC 7 (1989s) 129-1: near 200 rather than 80 A.D.

a28 **Herbert** Maire, *McNamara* Martin, Irish biblical apocrypha — selected texts in translation. E 1989, Clark. 196 p. £20. 0-567-09524-6. – ᴿExpTim 102 (1990s) 55 (J. G. *Snaith*: 9 OT, 20 NT, selected from a larger work); NT 32 (1990) 381-3 (J. K. *Elliott*).

a29 — *Schneiders* Marc, On the use of the label *apocryphon* in recent studies of medieval Irish texts [DUMVILLE D.; MCNAMARA M.]: Bijdragen 51 (1990) 314-323.

K3 **Qumran** .1 *generalia.*

a30 **Amusin** Iosif D., Ⓜ The Dead Sea scrolls and the Qumran community [< Ⓔ], ᵀ*Biró* Daniel, *Kalmár* Éva. Budapest 1986, Gondolat. 406 p.; 16 pl.; bibliog. p. 356-401 [KirSef 62 (1988s), p. 500].

a31 ᶠCARMIGNAC Jean, Études qumraniennes, RQum 13 (1988) → 4,22: ᴿFolOr 27 (1990) 223-235 (Z. *Kapera*); JStJud 21 (1990) 113-8 (M. A. *Knibb*).

a32 *Cross* Frank M., Père de VAUX was a Dead Sea Scroll hero: BAR-W 16, 1 (1990) 18.62 [amid other letters challenging Dead Sea Scrolls 'team' p. 10s. 16s].

a32* *a)* *Delcor* Mathias, La recherche qumrânienne pendant le dernière décennie 1976-1987; – *b)* *Fröhlich* Ida, Recherches sur Qumrân en Hongrie [bibliog.]: → 539*, DSS, FolOr 25 (1989) 5-31 / 75-78 [79-83].

a33 *Fitzmyer* J. A., The Dead Sea Scrolls; major publications and tools for study²*rev* [¹1975]: SBL Resources 20. Atlanta 1990, Scholars. $30; sb./pa. $17. 1-55540-510-X; –1-8 [BL 91, 136, P. S. *Alexander*].

a34 *Golb* Norman, Khirbet Qumran and the manuscripts of the Judaean wilderness; observations on the logic of their investigation: → 562, JNES 49 (1990) 103-114.

a35 *Isaac* E., The Dead Sea Scrolls controversy: MeditQ 1,3 (Durham NC 1990) 75-86 [< NTAbs 35,72].

a35* *a)* ᴱ*Kapera* Zdzisław J., Ⓟ Rękopisy z Qumran I-II: Filomata [0015-1615] 391 (Kraków 1989) 183-280; 395 (1990) 3-90. – ᴿFolOr 27 (1990) 272 (E. *Lipiński*). – *b)* *Kapera* Zdzisław J., 1989; the third battle of the scrolls begins [first, their antiquity; second, 1955-60, E. WILSON's 'essenizing Christianity']: FolOr 27 (1990) 291-7.

a36 **Knibb** Michael A., The Qumran community: CamCW 2, 1987 → 3, a314...5,9998: ᴿCritRR 2 (1989) 376-8 (C. *Newsom*); JNES 49 (1990) 200-2 (M. O. *Wise*); Vidyajyoti 54 (1990) 543s (P. M. *Meagher*).

a37 **Moraldi** Luigi, I manoscritti di Qumran² [¹1971 + Temple Scroll, Job Targum etc.]: Classici delle Religioni 1986 → 3,a315: ᴿBL (1989) 138 (P. R. *Davies*: despite typographical errors, compares favorably with similar works in any language).

a38 *Nebe* G.-Wilhelm, Die Bedeutung der Materials for the Dictionary Series I der Academy of the Hebrew Language für die Qumranforschung: → 527, RQum 14,56 (1989s) 651-676.

a39 *a)* *Qimron* E., The need for a comprehensive critical edition of the Dead Sea Scrolls; – *b)* *Stegemann* H., Methods for the reconstruction of scrolls from scattered fragments: → 554, ArchHistDSS 1985/90, 121-131 / 189-220.

a39* **Reed** S., Qumran Cave 1; documents and photographs: DSS Inventory Project, 1. Claremont CA 1990, Ancient Biblical Manuscript Center. 42 p. $10 [NTAbs 35,269].

a40 *Schiffman* Lawrence H., The significance of the Scrolls: BR 6,5 (1990) 18-27.52; ill.

a41 *Schuller* Eileen, The 40th anniversary of the Dead Sea Scrolls: StRTo 18,1 (1989) 61-66 [< ZIT 89,636].

a42 *a) Shanks* Hershel, The Dead Sea Scroll monopoly must be broken [... spurns $100,000 offer to publish still-secret photos; interview with *Milik* J.]; – *b) Wiseman* Donald J., The bottleneck of archaeological publication: BAR-W 16,5 (1990) 60-63 [64s Shanks, Scholarly concealment of *miqsat ma'aseh ha-tôrâ* from Qumran Cave 4].

a43 *Tomitanul* Lucian (en roumain), Khirbet Qumran et les onze grottes à manuscrits esséniens: STBuc 40,1 (1988) 8-14.

a44 *a) Shanks* Hershel, Dead Sea Scroll variation on 'show and tell' — it's called 'tell, but no show' [*Baumgarten* J., 'I'll describe these DSS texts I've got here in my hand, but I won't let you see them'; (cover) *Strugnell* J., 'It seems we've acquired a bunch of fleas who are in the business of annoying us']; – *b)* [on *Fitzmyer* Joseph A.], Leading DSS scholar denounces delay: BAR-W 16.2 (1990) 18-21 / 22-00.

a45 **Vermes** Geza, The Dead Sea Scrolls in English[3] 1987 ➤ 3,a118 ... 5,a6: ᴱBR 4,6 (1988) 9; JNES 49 (1990) 199s (M. O. *Wise*); JSS 35 (1990) 146s (F. F. *Bruce*: a resource non-Hebraists can rely on); RB 97 (1990) 15s (J. *Murphy-O'Connor*: the individual introductions seldom reflect current progress even of Vermes himself).

a46 *Woude* Adam S. van der, Fünfzehn Jahre Qumranforschung (1974-1988), 3. Die Lieder für das Sabbatopfer; 4s. DJD 6s; Nicht-kanonische Psalmen usw. Höhle 4; – B. Biblische texte: TRu 55 (1990) 245-307 ...

a47 *Woude* A. S. van der, De rollen van de Dode Zee; ontcijferingsmethoden en nieuwe teksten: KerkT 41 (1990) 92-102.

K3.4 *Qumran,* **Libri biblici** [➤ singuli] et pseudo-biblici; **commentarii.**

a48 *a) Ulrich* Eugene, The biblical scrolls from Qumran Cave 4; a progress report of their publication; – *b) Cook* Johann, Orthographical peculiarities in the Dead Sea biblical scrolls: ➤ 527, RQum 14,54 (1989s) 207-228 / 293-306.

a49 *Kister* Menahem, Barnabas 12:1; 4:3 [*Dimant* D., *Strugnell* J., RQum 13 (1988) 49] and 4Q Second Ezekiel: RB 97 (1990) 63-67; franç. 63.

a50 *a) Newsom* C., 'He has established for himself priests'; human and angelic priesthood in the Qumran Sabbath Shirot; – *b) Smith* M., Ascent to the heavens and deification in 4QM^a [denies BAILLET's attribution to Michael]: ➤ 554, ArchHistDSS 1985 / 90, 101-120 / 181-8.

a50* *a) Newsom* Carol A., Kenneth BURKE meets the Teacher of Righteousness; rhetorical strategies in the Hodayot and the Serek ha-Yahad; – *b) Schuller* Eileen, Some observations on blessings of God in texts from Qumran: ➤ 173, ꟳSTRUGNELL J., Of scribes 1990, 121-131 / 133-143.

a51 *Qimron* Elisha, Times for praising God; a fragment of a scroll from Qumran (4Q409): JQR 80 (1989s) 341-6 + 2 phot.

a52 **Schuller** Eileen M., Non-canonical psalms from Qumran 1986 ➤ 2,8145 ... 5,a13: ᴿIsrEJ 40 (1990) 232-4 (Esther G. *Chazon*); JAOS 110 (1990) 771s (P. R. *Davies*); JNES 49 (1990) 197-9 (M. O. *Wise*).

a53 *Sinclair* Lawrence A., 11QPs^a; a Psalms scroll from Qumran; text and canon: ➤ 82, ꟳHUNT J., Psalms 1990, 109-115.

a54 *a) Piñero* A., Sobre las concepciones de la inspiración en los Hodayot de Qumran y en el Pseudo-Filón (LAB); – *b) García Martínez* F., Tradiciones apocalípticas en Qumran; 4QSecondEzekiel: ➤ 154, ꟳSACCHI P. 1990, 279-302 / 303-321.

a55 *Steudel* Annette, Eschatological interpretation of Scripture in 4Q177 (4Q catena[a]): ➤ 527, RQum 14,55 (1989s) 473-481.

a56 **Brooke** George J., Exegesis at Qumran; 2QFlorilegium in its Jewish context: JStOT supp 29, 1985 ➤ 1,9789 ... 5,a14: [R]JAOS 110 (1990) 157s (L. H. *Schiffman*: a solid basis, despite some recommendations).

a56* *White* Sidnie Ann, 4QDt[Fl], biblical manuscript or excerpted text?: ➤ 173, [F]STRUGNELL J., Of scribes 1990, 13-20; 1 phot.

a57 *a)* *Schiffman* Lawrence H., The new halakhic letter (4QMMT) and the origins of the Dead Sea sect: BA 53 (1990) 64-73; ill. – *b)* *Burgmann* Hans, 4Q MMT, Versuch einer historisch begründbaren Datierung [Schiffman L., BA 1990]: FolOr 27 (1990) 43-62.

a57* *Kapera* Zdzisław J., *a)* Appendix A; an anonymously received pre-publication of the 4QMMT [... MILIK edition awaited early 1991 in Harvard Semitic Studies; Kapera's publication was discussed at a conference in Madrid and he was prevailed upon to withhold and destroy his text: H. *Shanks* in BAR-W 17/5,14]; – *b)* Qumran cave 4, special report p. 3-4 explains this step, and mentions that Oxford claims the right to publish 4QMMT: The Qumran Chronicle 1,2 (Kraków Apr. 1991 for Dec. 1990) 12 p. / p. 5-53 (–67 with 4 phot.); p. 69-117, further by *Muchowski* P., *Schiffman* L., *Eisenman* R., al.

K3.5 *Rotulus Templi* – **The Temple Scroll**, *al.*

a58 [E]**Brooke** George J., Temple scroll studies 1987/9 ➤ 5,568: [R]ETL 66 (1990) 192s (J. *Lust*); JStJud 21 (1990) 99-102 (F. *García Martínez*); VT 40 (1990) 502s (J. A. *Emerton*).

a59 **Jacobs** Steven L., The biblical Masorah and the Temple Scroll (11Q Torah); some problems and solutions: diss. HUC, [D]*Weisberg* D. Cincinnati 1990, 134 p. 90-31838. — DissA 51 (1990s) 2053-A; OIAc Ja91.

a60 *a)* *Maier* J., The Temple Scroll and tendencies in the cultic architecture of the Second Commonwealth; – *b)* *Levine* B. A., A further look at the Mo'adim of the Temple Scroll; – *c)* *Milgrom* J., The Scriptural foundations and deviations in the laws of purity of the Temple Scroll; – *d)* *Schiffman* L. H., The impurity of the dead in the Temple Scroll: ➤ 554, ArchHistDSS 1985/90, 67-82 / 53-66 / 83-99 / 135-156.

a61 *Schiffman* L., The King, his guard, and the royal council in the Temple Scroll: PAAR 54 (1987) 237-259 [< NTAbs 34,216].

a62 *Schiffman* Lawrence H., *a)* Exclusion from the sanctuary and the city of the sanctuary in the Temple Scroll: HebAnR 9 (1985) 301-320 [< OTAbs 13, p. 299]; *b)* Miqṣat Ma'aseh ha-Torah and the Temple Scroll: ➤ 527, RQum 14,55 (1989s) 435-457.

a62* *a)* *Schiffman* Lawrence H., The Septuagint and the Temple Scroll; shared 'halakhic' variants; – *b)* *Brooke* George J., The Temple Scroll and LXX Exodus 35-40; – *c)* *Tov* Emanuel, The contribution of the Qumran scrolls to the understanding of the LXX: ➤ 519, Septuagint, Scrolls 1990/2, 277-297 / 81-106 / 11-47.

a63 *Scippa* Vincenzo, Il rotolo del Tempio: Asprenas 37 (1990) 474-483 [p. 481: col. 64, la crocifissione].

a64 **Swanson** Dwight D., The Temple Scroll and the Bible; methodology of 11QT: diss. Manchester 1990. – RTLv 22,591.

a64* *a)* *Tyloch* Witold, La provenance et la date du Rouleau du Temple; – *b)* *Eisenman* Robert, The historical provenance of the 'Three Nets of Belial' allusion in the Zadokite document and *balla'/bela'* in the Temple Scroll; –

c) Schiffman Lawrence H., The Law of the Temple Scroll and its provenance: ➤ 539*, DSS FolOr 25 (1989) 33-39 / 51-66 / 89-98.

a65 ᴱVivian Angelo, Rotolo del Tempio: Testi del Vicino Oriente Antico 6/1. Brescia 1990, Paideia. 302 p. Lit. 42.000. 88-394-0442-2. – ᴿSalesianum 52 (1990) 898 (M. *Cimosa*).

a66 **Wise** M. O., A critical study of the Temple Scroll from Qumran Cave 11 [diss. Ch 1988, ᴰ*Golb* N.]: SAOC 49. Ch 1990, Univ. xvii-292 p.; 10 fig. 0-918986-63-X [NTAbs 35,135].

a67 *a) Wise* Michael O., The eschatological vision of the Temple Scroll; – *b) Eisenman* Robert, Eschatological 'rain' imagery in the War Scroll from Qumran and in the letter of James; – *c) Lim* Timothy H., Eschatological orientation and the alteration of Scripture in the Hakakkuk Pesher: ➤ 562, JNES 49 (1990) 155-172 / 173-184 / 185-194.

a68 **Yadin** Y., The Temple Scroll 1983-7 ➤ 65,8615 ... 5,a28: ᴿSefarad 50 (1990) 220-2 (F. *Sen*).

a69 **Schiffman** Lawrence H., The eschatological community of the Dead Sea Scrolls: SBL Mg 38, 1989 ➤ 5,a30: ᴿJStJud 21 (1990) 281-4 (F. *García Martínez*: first monograph dedicated wholly to 1QSᵃ).

a70 *Duhaime* Jean, Étude comparative de 4QMᵃ fgg. 1-3 et 1QM: ➤ 527, RQum 14,55 (1989s) 459-472.

a71 *Eshel* Hanan, ❿ The historical background of 4QTest in the light of archaeological discoveries: Zion 55 (1990) 141-150; Eng. VII.

a72 *Wolters* Al, The Copper Scroll and the vocabulary of Mishnaic Hebrew: ➤ 527, RQum 14,55 (1989s) 483-495.

κ3.6 **Qumran et NT.**

a73 *Aland* Kurt, Die Papyri aus Höhle 7 von Qumran und ihre Zuschreibung zum Neuen Testament durch J. O'Callaghan [< NTS 20 (1974) 358-376]: ➤ 193, Supplementa 1990, 142-157.

a74 **Casciaro Ramírez** José M., Qumrān y el NT, aspectos eclesiológicos [5 art. 1969-76] 1982 ➤ 53,8680 ... 1,9810: ᴿAngelicum 67 (1990) 129s (J. M. *Viejo*).

a75 ᴰ**Charlesworth** James H., John and the Dead Sea Scrolls; / (with *Murphy-O'Connor* J.) Paul and the Dead Sea Scrolls [reissues of original essays 1972 / 1968]: Christian Origins Library. NY 1990, Crossroad. xvi-233 p.; xvi-262 p. $17 each, pa. 0-8245-1001-1; -0-3 [TDig 37,353].

a75* *Lichtenberger* Hermann, Reflections on the history of John the Baptist's communities: ➤ 539*, DSS FolOr 25 (1989) 45-49.

a76 **Rohrhirsch** Ferdinand, Markus in Qumran? Eine Auseinandersetzung mit den Argumenten für und gegen das Fragment 7Q5 mit Hilfe des methodischen Fallibilismusprinzips: MgStB. Wu 1990, Brockhaus. [viii-] 152 p. 3-417-29362-6.

a77 *Socci* Antonio, 7Q5; eppur coincide; una scoperta silenziata; se quello ritrovato in Palestina è un frammento evangelico, san Marco avrebbe scritto tutto prima del 50 [coperta: 'e Marco subito scrisse']; sempre più studiosi ci credono; e in autunno [1991] un simposio decisivo ... 'É già una vittoria per il padre José O'Callaghan ... più agguerrito difensore è Thiede': Trenta Giorni 9,6 (1991) 10-14 [15s, *Paci* Stefano M., su Tʀᴇsᴍᴏɴᴛᴀɴᴛ e il contrario giudizio di P. Gʀᴇʟᴏᴛ; 17-19 su Sʜᴀɴᴋs contro Sᴛʀᴜɢɴᴇʟʟ].

a78 *Stegemann* H., Jesucristo y el Maestro de Justicia de Qumrân: ComSev 22 (1990) 343-354.

a79 **Thiede** Carsten P., Die älteste Evangelien-Handschrift?[2] [[1]1986 ➤ 2, 8168]. 1989. [R]ErbAuf 66 (1990) 482 (B. *Schwank*: wichtig; Neuerscheinungen 1986-9).

κ3.8 **Historia et doctrinae Qumran.**

a80 *a) Baumgarten* J.M., The Qumran-Essene restraints on marriage; – *b) Collins* J.J., Was the Dead Sea sect an apocalyptic community? – *c) Schwartz* D.R., On two aspects of a priestly view of descent at Qumran: ➤ 554, ArchHistDSS 1985/90, 13-24 / 25-51 / 157-179.

a81 *Brooke* George J., History and hermeneutics at Qumran: Bulletin of the Institute for Antiquity and Christianity 16,3 (Claremont 1989) 8-11 [< JStJud 21,153].

a81* *a) Burgmann* Hans, Who was the 'Wicked Priest'? [Jonathan Maccabeus]; – *b) Chmiel* Jerzy, La conscience de communauté et l'attitude sectaire à Qumran; remarques herméneutiques: ➤ 539*, DSS, FolOr 25 (1989) 41-44 / 137-142.

a82 **Callaway** Phillip R., The history of the Qumran community [D]1988 ➤ 4,b64; 5,a42: [R]BL (1989) 35 (G. *Vermes*); CBQ 52 (1990) 148s (D.J. *Harrington*); JQR 81 (1990s) 192-4 (F.J. *Murphy*); JTS 41 (1990) 160-4 (G.J. *Brooke*); Themelios 16 (1990s) 25 (F.F. *Bruce* †).

a83 **Davies** P.R., Behind the Essenes; history and ideology in the Dead Sea Scrolls: BrownJudSt 94, 1987 ➤ 3,a367; 4,b65*: [R]BL (1989) 132 (C.T.R. *Hayward*).

a84 *Davies* Philip R., Halakhah at Qumran [... *Schiffman* L.]: ➤ 183, [F]VERMES G., Essays 1990, 37-50.

a84* *Delcor* Mathias, Commémorer à Qumran; l'historicisation des fêtes: ➤ 618, Commémoration 1986/8, 155-162.

a85 *Fernández-Ardanaz* Santiago, El problema del hombre en los textos de Qumrân; semántica de los principales términos antropológicos: RCatalT 15 (1990) 1-65; Eng. 65.

a86 **Flusser** David, The spiritual history of the Dead Sea Sect, [T]*Glucker* Carol. TA 1989, MOD. 97 p. [OIAc Oc90]. 965-05-0480-X.

a87 *a) García Martínez* Florentino, *Woude*. A S. van der, A 'Groningen' hypothesis of Qumran origins and early history; – *b) Callaway* P.R., Qumran origins; from the Doresh to the Moreh: ➤ 527, RQum 14,56 (1989s) 521-542 [= García ➤ 539* FolOr 25 (1989) 113-136] / 637-650 [cf. FolOr 25,143-150].

a88 **Jefford** Clayton N., Some observations on the concept of sin at Qumran: OccP 16. Claremont 1989, Inst. Antiquity & Christianity. 15. p.

a88* *Kapera* Zdzisław J., Bibliography of Norman GOLB's hypothesis of the Jerusalem origin of the Dead Sea Scrolls: FolOr 27 (1990) 217-221.

a89 *Knibb* Michael A., The teacher of righteousness — a messianic title?: ➤ 183, [F]VERMES G., Essays 1990, 51-65.

a90 *a) Maier* Johann, Zu Kult und Liturgie der Qumrangemeinde; – *b) Wise* Michael O., The Teacher of Righteousness and the High Priest of the intersacerdotium; two approaches: ➤ 527, RQum 14,56 (1989s) 543-586 / 587-613.

a91 *Newsom* Carol A., 'Sectually explicit' literature from Qumran [... insufficiently]: ➤ 550, Hebrew Bible SD 1986/90, 167-187.

a92 **Talmon** Shemaryahu, The world of Qumran from within 1989 ➤ 5,365: RJStJud 21 (1990) 292-5 (F. *García Martínez*).

a93 **Weinfeld** Moshe, Organizational pattern: NTOrb 2, 1986 ➤ 2,8188... 5,a56: RHebSt 31 (1990) 259-262 (Shaye *Cohen*).

a94 *White* Richard T., The house of Peleg in the Dead Sea Scrolls: ➤ 183, FVERMES G., Essays 1990, 67-98.

FYADIN Y., Archaeology and history in the Dead Sea Scrolls, ESchiffman L. 1989 ➤ 554.

K4.1 Esseni, Zelotae.

a95 **Beall** Todd S., JOSEPHUS' description of the Essenes...DSS: SNTS Mg 58, D1988 ➤ 4,b72; 5,a57: RCBQ 52 (1990) 339s (C. *Bernas*: an engaging package); ClasW 83 (1989s) 525s (Shaye *Cohen*: competent but dull); Interpretation 44 (1990) 206 (J. A. *Overman*: the Essenes were hardly a 'major' Jewish sect); JNES 49 (1990) 202-4 (M. O. *Wise*); JTS 41 (1990) 164-9 (P. R. *Davies*); OLZ 85 (1990) 435s (G. *Baumbach*); VT 40 (1990) 124 (J. A. *Emerton*).

a96 **Burgmann** H., Die essenischen Gemeinden von Qumrân und Damaskus in der Zeit der Hasmonäer und Herodier (130 ante- 68 post): ArbNTJ [cf. 7, 1987 ➤ 3,a363] 8. Bern 1988, Lang. 541 p. Fs 82. 3-8204-9905-9. – RBL (1990) 130 (G. *Vermes*: highly imaginative; O'CALLAGHAN's NT fragments 'überzeugend').

a96* *Davies* P. R., The birthplace of the Essenes; where is 'Damascus'?: RQum 14 (1990) 503-519: the almost identical title 'The Damascus of Qumran geography', PEQ 87 (1955) 34-48, by R. *North*, not cited, possibly because it was omitted from the cumulative index of PEQ (1911-63) p. 13.

a97 **Hengel** M., The Zealots [1961] T1989 ➤ 5,a59: REstE 65 (1990) 479s (A. *Vargas-Machuca*); ÉTRel 65 (1990) 275s (E. *Cuvillier*); JJS 41 (1990) 268s (M. *Goodman*); JSS 35 (1990) 148-151 (F. F. *Bruce*: some minutiae in the good translation); JTS 41 (1990) 593s (N. de *Lange*); Pacifica 3 (1990) 340s (F. J. *Moloney*).

a98 *Mędala* Stanisław, Le camp des Esséniens de Jérusalem à la lumière des récentes recherches archéologiques: ➤ 539*, DSS FolOr 25 (1989) 67-74.

a99 *Pileggi* David, Who were the Essenes?: Jerusalem Perspective 3/4 (1990) 9s.15.

a100 EVermes G., *Goodman* M., The Essenes 1989 ➤ 5,a63: RCritRR 3 (1990) 360s (J. J. *Collins*); JJS 41 (1990) 139s (T. *Rajak*); JSS 35 (1990) 147s (A. *Salvesen*); JTS 41 (1990) 582-5 (G. J. *Brooke*); TLZ 115 (1990) 265s (C. *Burchard*).

K4.3 Samaritani.

a101 **Ben-Hayyim** Z. ⊕ *Tībāt Marqe*, a collection of Samaritan Midrashim 1988 ➤ 5,a64: RBO 47 (1990) 736-9 (I.R.M. *Bóid*); Sefarad 50 (1990) 481-3 (L. F. *Girón-Blanc*).

a102 **Bóid** I.R.M., Principles of Samaritan Halakhah: StJudLA 38, 1989 ➤ 5,a65: RJStJud 21 (1990) 233s (G. D. *Sixdenier*); RHPR 70 (1990) 254 (P. de *Robert*).

a103 ECrown Alan D., The Samaritans 1989 ➤ 5,389: RBLitEc 91 (1990) 287s (M. *Delcor*); ExpTim 101,2 2d-top choice (1989s) 354 (C. S. *Rodd*:

repetitious); JStJud 21 (1990) 102-4 (F. *García Martínez*); JTS 41 (1990) 157-160 (R. J. *Coggins*); Protestantesimo 45 (1990) 138s (J. A. *Soggin*).

a104 **Dexinger** F., Der Taheb, ein 'messianischer' Heilsbringer der Samaritaner: Kairos Stud. 3. Salzburg 1986, Müller. 202 p. – ᴿJQR 80 (1989s) 139-141 (A. D. *Crown*).

a105 *Dexinger* Ferdinand, Die Taheb-Vorstellung als politische Utopie: Numen 37 (1990) 1-23.

a106 **Egger** Rita, JOSEPHUS Flavius und die Samaritaner...: NTOrb 4, 1986 → 2,8195 ... 5,a66: ᴿOLZ 85 (1990) 47-49 (W. *Wiefel*).

a107 *Powels* Sylvia, Samaritan proverbs: AbrNahr 28 (1990) 76-95.

a108 **Pummer** Reinhard, The Samaritans: IconRel 23, Judaism 5, 1987 → 3, a399 ... 5,a72: ᴿCBQ 52 (1990) 361 (Marilyn F. *Collins* does not aim to locate it in its series); CritRR 2 (1989) 147-9 (J. D. *Purvis*: it treats today's Nablus-Holon); JRelHist 15 (1988s) 145s (A. D. *Crown*); OLZ 85 (1990) 434-6 (R. *Macuch*).

a109 **Rabello** Alfredo M., Giustiniano, ebrei e samaritani, alla luce delle fonti storico-letterarie, ecclesiastiche e giuridiche 2: VocabGiust Mg 2, 1990 → 4,b89; 5,a73; p. 493-975. Lit. 42.000: ᴿJQR 81 (1990s) 216-8 (A. *Wasserstein*); JStJud 21 (1990) 269-271 (G. *Stemberger*: worthily replaces JUSTER).

a109* *Rappaport* Uriel, ⊕ The Samaritans in the Hellenistic period: Zion 55 (1990) 371-396; Eng. XVs.

a110 ᴱ**Rothschild** J.-P., *al.*, Études samaritaines 1985/8 → 4,497: ᴿBL (1990) 142 (R. J. *Coggins*); BO 47 (1990) 739-743 (I.R.M. *Bóid*).

a111 **Schur** Nathan, History of the Samaritans: BeiErfAJ 18, 1989 → 5,a75: ᴿRHPR 70 (1990) 252s (P. de *Robert*).

κ4.5 *Ṣadoqitae, Qaraitae* – **Cairo Genizah; Zadokites, Karaites.**

Berger K., Die Weisheitsschrift aus der Kairoer Geniza: TArbNZ 1, 1989 → 3546.

a112 **Boyce** Mark, The poetry of the Damascus Document: diss. ᴰ*Gibson*. Edinburgh 1990. vi-421 p. D88442. – OIAc Oc90.

a113 *a)* *Davies* P. R., The birthplace of the Essenes; where is 'Damascus'?: – *b)* *Boyce* J. Mark, The poetry of the Damascus Document and its bearing on the history of the Qumran sect: RQum 14,56 (1989s) 503-520 / 615-628.

a114 **Goitein** S. D., A Mediterranean society 1978-88 → 60,y369 ... 4,b95: ᴿBSO 52 (1989) 337s (J. *Wansbrough*, 4s); JQR 80 (1989s) 172-5 (L. *Nemoy*, 5); Speculum 65 (1990) 677s (J. *Neusner*, 5).

a115 *Harviainen* Tapani, De Karaitis Lithuaniae; transcription of recited biblical texts, description of the pronunciation tradition, and peculiarities of shewa: → 184, ᶠVITESTAM G., OrSuec 38s (1989s) 36-44.

a116 **Khan** Geoffrey, Karaite Bible manuscripts from the Cairo Genizah: Genizah series 9. C 1990, Univ. xv-186 p.; 17 pl. $85. 0-521-39227-6 [TDig 38,69].

a117 *Khan* Geoffrey, Al-QIRQISĀNĪ's opinions concerning the text of the Bible and parallel Muslim attitudes towards the text of the Qurʾān: JQR 81 (1990s) 59-73.

a118 *Nemoy* Leon, Isaac BEN SOLOMON (1755-1826) on the Karaite creed: JQR 80 (1989s) 49-85.

a119 *Paul* A., Quaraïtes [sic]: → 833, Catholicisme 13,55 (1989) 240s.

a120 *Qimron* E., *Šabu'ot ha-banim* [so unmistakably in title and table of contents; but the early lines of the text have twice *ha-bᵉrît*: in Damascus Doc. 15,1-2]: JQR 81 (1990s) 115-8.

a121 ᴱ**Reif** S.C., Published material from the Cambridge Genizah collections. C 1989, Univ. xvi-608 p. £125 [or? pa.] £75. – ᴿVT 40 (1990) 372 (J.A. *Emerton*).

a122 *Stegemann* Hartmut, Das Gesetzeskorpus der 'Damaskusschrift' (CD IX-XVI): → 527, RQum 14,55 (1989s) 409-434.

к5 Judaismus prior vel totus.

a123 *Beer* Moshe, [Avot 4,13: 3 crowns] ⊕ The term 'crown of Torah' in rabbinic literature and its social significance: Zion 55 (1990) 307-417; Eng. XVs.

a124 *a*) *Brody* Robert, Judaism in the Sasanian empire; a case study in religious coexistence; – *b*) *Shaked* Saul, Zoroastrian polemics against Jews in the Sasanian and early Islamic period: → 555, Irano-Judaica (1987/90) 52-62 / 85-104.

a125 *Bulka* Reuven P., As a tree by the waters; Pirkey Avoth, psychological and philosophical insights. J 1980, Feldheim. 279 p. 0-87306-237-X.

a126 **Chouraqui** André, Il pensiero ebraico [³1975], ᵀ1989 → 5,a36: ᴿAsprenas 37 (1990) 246s (R. *Forte*); CC 141 (1990,4) 428s (... M. *Katunarich*); NRT 112 (1990) 140 (L.-J. *Renard*); QVidCr 152s (1990) 169 (J.A. *Rocha*).

a126* **Cohen** Shaye J.D., From the Maccabees to the Mishnah 1987 → 3,a413; 4,b109: ᴿRB 97 (1990) 124s (J. *Taylor*).

a127 **Cohen** Stuart A., The three crowns; structures of communal politics in early rabbinic Jewry. C 1990, Univ. xii-294 p. £30. 0-521-37290-9 [BL 91, 134, L.L. *Grabbe*].

a128 **Ego** Beate, Im Himmel wie auf Erden; Studien zum Verhältnis von himmlischer und irdischer Welt im rabbinischen Judentum [ev. Diss Tübingen 1987, ᴰ*Rüger* H.]: WUNT 2/34, 1989 → 5,a90: ᴿHenoch 12 (1990) 248s (B. *Chiesa*); KIsr 5 (1990) 180 (Julie *Kirchberg*); NorTTs 90 (1989) 235-7 (H.M. *Barstad*).

a129 **Flesher** Paul V.M., New perspectives on ancient Judaism 5. Society and literature in analysis. Lanham MD 1990, UPA. 204 p. $30 [JAAR 58,533].

a130 *Flusser* David, ⊕ 'Which is the right way that a man should choose for himself?' [Abot 2,1]: Tarbiz 60 (1990s) 163-178; Eng. II.

a130* *a*) *Fraade* S.D., The early rabbinic sage; – *b*) *Fishbane* M., From scribalism to rabbinism; perspectives on the emergence of classical Judaism: → 336, Sage 1990, 417-436 / 439-456.

a131 *Goldberg* Arnold, Formen und Funktionen von Schriftauslegung in der frührabbinischen Literatur (1 Jh. v. Chr. bis 8. Jh. n. Chr.): LingBib 64 (1990) 5-21; Eng. 21.

a132 *Goldberg* Arnold, The rabbinic view of Scripture [< FraJüdBeit 15 (1987) 1-15], ᵀ*Samely* Alexander: → 183, ᶠVERMES G., Essays 1990, 153-166.

a133 **Hayman** Peter E., ⊕ Development and change in the teachings of Rabbi Yohanan BEN NAFHA: diss. Yeshiva, ᴰ*Feldblum* M. NY 1990. 483 p. 91-11428. – DissA 51 (1990s) 3782-A.

a133* **Hayoun** M.-R., La littérature rabbinique: Que sais-je? 2526. P 1990, PUF. 128 p. 2-13-042999-8 [ÉTRel 65,661].

a134 **Illman** Carl-Johan, *Harviainen* Tapani, Judisk historia [70-1980 A.D.]: Religionsvetenskapliga Skrifter 14. Åbo 1986, Akademi. 145 p. – ᴿSvEx 55 (1990) 124s (J. *Bergman*).

a135 *Jospe* Raphael, Hillel's rule [bShab 31a *regel* 'foot' may be pun for Latin *regula*]: JQR 31 (1990s) 45-57.

a135* *Kippenberg* Hans G., Geheime Offenbarungsbücher und Loyalitäts-konflikt im antiken Judentum: ➤ 38*, ꜰCOLPE C., 1990, 258-268.

Lightstone Jack N., Society...in Judaism; a sociology of knowledge 1988 ➤ g655.

a136 *Lightstone* Jack N., Names without 'lives'; why no 'lives of the rabbis' in early rabbinic Judaism?: SR 19 (1990) 43-57.

a137 **Loth** Heinz-Jürgen, Judentum: Religionen 4, 1989 ➤ 5,a104; DM 14,80: ᴿKIsr 5 (1990) 74 (Julie *Kirchberg*).

a138 **Maccoby** Hyam, Early rabbinic writings: CamCW 3, 1988 ➤ 4,b122; 5,a105: ᴿHebSt 31 (1990) 204-7 (Tz. *Zahavy*).

a139 **Maccoby** Hyam, Judaism in the first century: Issues RelSt, 1989 ➤ 5, a106: ᴿEvQ 62 (1990) 360s (I. H. *Marshall*: tendentious, but no more than Christians have often been); ExpTim 102 (1990s) 119s (L. *Alexander*: PHILO influenced Judaism so little because Alexandrian Jewry was wiped out; readable but flip in comparison with serious LEE B. J.).

a140 *a*) *Maier* J., Rivelazione, tradizione e autorità religiosa nel giudaismo palestinese e babilonese; – *b*) *Kraus Reggiani* Clara, Tradizione e inno-vazione nel giudaismo ellenistico: ➤ 700, Tradizione 1989/90, 73-92 / 93-117.

a141 *Manns* Frédéric, La polémique contre les judéo-chrétiens en Pesiqta de Rab KAHANA 15: LA 40 (1990) 211-266; Eng. 447.

a142 *Monshouwer* Dirk, The reading of the Bible in the synagogue in the first century [C.E: PERROT C. in Mikra]: Bijdragen 51 (1990) 68-83; Eng. 83.

a143 *Morris* P., The embodied text; covenant and Torah: Religion 20,1 (1990) 77-87 [< NTAbs 34,363].

a144 *Murmelstein* Benjamin, Spuren altorientalischer Einflüsse im rabbini-schen und frühchristlichen Schrifttum. R 1990. [iv–] 47 p. [4 art. < ZAW 1932-69].

a145 **Navarro Peiró** María A., Abot de r. NATAN 1987 ➤ 3,a432...5,a109: ᴿJStJud 21 (1990) 130-2 (L. F. *Girón*); NRT 112 (1990) 423s (V. *Roisel*).

a146 **Ness** Lester J., Astrology and Judaism in late antiquity: diss. Miami Univ. 1990. 377 p. 91-10462. – DissA 51 (1990) 3867-A.

a147 **Neusner** Jacob, The ecology of religion; from writing to religion in the study of Judaism ['his first and only book on his own methods']. Nv 1989, Abingdon. 315 p. $28. 0-687-11512-4 [TDig 37,375].

a148 ᴱNeusner J. *al.*, Judaic perspectives on ancient Israel 1987 ➤ 3,355; 5,a115: ᴿGregorianum 71 (1990) 169-173 (G. L. *Prato*).

a149 **Neusner** Jacob, Judaism and its social metaphors; Israel in the history of Jewish thought [the metaphor is 'Israel'] 1989 ➤ 5,a114: ᴿBL (1990) 140 (P. R. *Davies*); TLond 93 (1990) 408-410 (W. R. *Telford*).

a149* **Neusner** Jacob, Judaism in the matrix of Christianity 1986 ➤ 2,8239: ᴿIrBSt 11 (1989) 153-5 (E. A. *Russell*).

a150 **Neusner** Jacob, Torah through the ages; a short history of Juda-ism. L/Ph 1990, SCM/Trinity. xiii-178 p. $22. 0-334-02456-0; pa. -40-4 [NTAbs 35, 130].

a151 **Neusner** Jacob, The Fathers according to Rabbi NATHAN...: Brown-JudSt 114. Atlanta 1986, Scholars. 274 p. $42. 1-55540-051-5. – ᴿJQR 80 (1989s) 185s (A. J. *Saldarini*).

a152 *Neusner* Jacob, URBACH's Hazal revisited [The Sages, T*Abrahams* I. 1975, reprinted 1987 ➤ 3,a452]: RelStT 8,1s (1988) 66-74.

a153 **Neusner** J., *Green* W.S., Writing with Scripture 1989 ➤ 5,118: RExpTim 102 (1990s) 91 (F. *Morgan*).

a154 **Niebuhr** Karl-W., Gesetz und Paränese; katechismusartige Weisungsreihen in der frühjüdischen Literatur: WUNT 2/28, D1987 ➤ 3,3242 ... 5,a119: RNedTTs 44 (1990) 166s (J. W. van *Henten*).

a155 **Otzen** Benedikt, Judaism in antiquity; political development and religious currents from Alexander to Hadrian [1984], T*Cryer* Frederick H.: Bib.Sem. Sheffield 1990, JStOT. 243 p. – RETL 66 (1990) 408 (J. *Lust*); ExpTim 102 (1990s) 86 (R. *Mason*: useful and enjoyable, though overlooking FISHBANE M., COGGINS R., BARTON J.).

Plaskow Judith, Standing again at Sinai; Judaism from a feminist perspective 1988 ➤ 1625.

a156 **Prigent** Pierre, Le Judaïsme et l'image: TStAJ 24. Tü 1990, Mohr. xviii-381 p.; ill. 3-16-145599-1.

a158 **Roper** Roy D., Factors contributing to the origin and success of the pre-Christian Jewish missionary movement: diss. D*Freedman* D., Michigan Univ. AA 1988. 88-21644. – OIAc JuJ89 ['Coy Dee'].

a159 *Rosenfeld* Ben-Zion, ❸ The standing and activities of Rabban GAMALIEL prior to his move to Yavneh: Zion 55 (1990) 151-169; Eng. VIIs.

a160 E**Safrai** S., The literature of the sages 1, 1987 ➤ 3,a449 ... 5,a127: RAntonianum 65 (1990) 104s (M. *Nobile*); TLZ 115 (1990) 22-25 (S. *Schreiner*); ZkT 112 (1990) 107s (R. *Oberforcher*).

a161 **Segal** Alan F., The other Judaisms of late antiquity [7 reprints] 1987 ➤ 4,260: RJQR 80 (1989s) 199 (G. G. *Stroumsa*).

a162 E**Seltzer** Robert M., Judaism, a people and its history [< 1987 EncRel]. NY 1989, Macmillan. xiv-338 p. $13. 0-02-897374-7 [TDig 37,270]. – RExpTim 102 (1990s) 221s (P. D. *Bishop*).

a163 **Shmueli** Efraim [1908-1985], Seven Jewish cultures; a reinterpretation of Jewish history and thought, pref. *Shmueli* Gila (his daughter). C 1990, Univ. xvii-293 p. £30. 0-521-37381-6.

a164 **Sigal** Philip, E*Sigal* Lillian, Judaism, the evolution of a faith 1988 ➤ 5,a131: RCarthaginensia 6 (1990) 198 (R. *Sanz Valdivieso*).

a165 TE**Smilévitch** Éric, Pirqé Avot, commentaires: entier, Moïse MAÏMONIDE; partiels, RACHI, Rabbénou YONA, Le Maharal de Prague, r.Hayim de VOLOZYNE: Les Dix Paroles. Lagrasse 1990, Verdier. 299 p. – RHokhma 45 (1990) 66s (J.-J. *Hugé*).

a166 E**Stemberger** G., Die Juden [60 extracts, none biblical]: Beck'sche Reihe 410. Mü 1990, Beck. 348 p. DM 9,80. 3-406-34002-4 [BL 91,23].

a167 *a)* *Stemberger* G., Das Fortleben der Apokalyptik in der rabbinischen Literatur; – *b)* *Neusner* Jacob, Why Judaism won the fourth century [C.E.] as the true first century in the history of the Judaic and Christian west: ➤ 154, F*SACCHI* P. 1990, 335-347 / 349-362.

a168 *Strobel* Karl, Aspekte des politischen und sozialen Scheinbildes der rabbinischen Tradition; das spätere 2. und das 3. Jh. n. Chr.; Anhang, Zur Münzprägung von Diocaesarea–Sepphoris in severischer Zeit: Klio 72 (1990) 478-497.

a169 T**Toaff** Gadiel, Sefer Yezirah (Il libro della creazione) [anteriore al 6° sec.]. R 1988, Carucci. 105 p. Lit. 12.000. – RBAsEspOr 26 (1990) 344s (C. del *Valle*).

a170 *Visotsky* B.L., Prolegomenon to the study of Jewish-Christianities in rabbinic literature: AJS 14,1 (CM 1989) 47-70 [< NTAbs 34,225].

a171 **Wylen** Stephen M.,   Settings of silver; an introduction to Judaism. Mahwah NJ 1989, Paulist. x-397 p. $11. 0-8091-3071-8 [TDig 37,296].

κ6 **Mišna,** *tosepta; Tannaim.*

a172 *Cohen* Martini S., The names of biblical verses: JBQ 18 (1989s) 251-258.

a173 **Correns** D.,   Mischna 2/9 Taanijot Fastentage 1989 ➤ 4,b161; 5,a140: ᴿArTGran 53 (1990) 420s (A. *Torres*); NRT 112 (1990) 603s (X. *Jacques*); TLZ 115 (1990) 808s (S. *Schreiner*); ZAW 102 (1990) 298 (I. *Kottsieper*).

a174 **Destro** Adriana, The law of jealousy; anthropology of Sotah: Brown-JudSt 181. Atlanta 1989, Scholars. xii-189 p. $45 [TR 86,522].

a175 **Eilbert-Schwartz** Howard, The human will in Judaism; the Mishnah's philosophy of intention: BrownJudSt 103, 1986 ➤ 2,8266 ... 5,a141: ᴿJQR 81 (1990s) 179-188 (B. S. *Jackson*).

a176 **Goldberg** Abraham, The Mishna treatise Eruvin 1986 ➤ 4,b164; 5,a142: ᴿBO 45 (1990) 460-6 (W. *Zuidema*).

a176* **Halivni** David W.,   Midrash, Mishnah and Gemarah 1986 ➤ 2,8269 ... 4,b165:   ᴿCritRR 2 (1989) 372-6 (B. M. *Bokser*).

a177 *Jaffee* Martin S., The *taqqanah* in Tannaitic literature; jurisprudence and the construction of rabbinic memory: JJS 41 (1990) 204-225.

a178 **Manns** F., Leggere la Mišnah [1984], ᵀ*Busi* Giulio: StBPaid 78, 1987 ➤ 3,a460; Lit. 22.000: ᴿBL (1989) 137 (N. de *Lange*: fluent and readable; in some ways up to date; somewhat slanted).

a179 ᵀ*Muchowski* P., ❽ Traktat Miszny Kidduszin: Euhemer 31,3 (Wsz 1988) 35-45 [< NTAbs 34,222].

a180 **Neusner** Jacob, A history of the Mishnaic law of damages 1-5, 1983-5 ➤ 64,8899; 65,8694: ᴿCBQ 52 (1990) 355-7 (Tzvee *Zahavy*).

a181 **Neusner** J., The philosophical Mishnah [1s, 1988s ➤ 5,a150]; 3. The tractates' agenda, from Nazir to Zebaḥim; 4. The Repertoire: BrownJudSt 158.172. Atlanta 1989, Scholars. xv-344 p.; xv-200 p. $60; $50. 1-55540-336-0; -8-7 [NTAbs 34,136].

a182 **Neusner** Jacob, Uniting the dual Torah; Sifra and the problem of the Mishnah. C 1990, Univ. xii-233 p. 0-521-38125-8.

a183 *Neusner* Jacob, Physics in an odd idiom; the Stoic theory of mixtures in the applied reason of the Mishnah: BSO 52 (1989) 419-429.

a184 *Neusner* Jacob, *a*) The Mishnah's generative mode of thought; Literaturwissenschaft and analogical-constrastive reasoning: JAOS 110 (1990) 317-321; – *b*) The Mishnah's philosophical method; the Judaism of hierarchical classification in Greco-Roman context: SecC 7 (1989s) 193-211; – *c*) La méthode philosophique de la Mishna; le judaïsme hiérarchique, classement dans le contexte gréco-romain: SR 19 (1990) 27-42; – *d*) Judaism's politics of hierarchization; the results of comparison in the study of religion: ➤ 38*, ꟳCOLPE C., 1990, 58-67.

a185 *Pesce* Mauro, Trasmissione culturale e tradizione di gruppo; la caratteristica della Mishnah; il caso del trattato Joma: ➤ 700, Tradizione 1989/90, 120-134.

a186 *a*) *Principe* S., L'immagine della terra di Israele nella Mishnah; – *b*) *Vivian* Angelo, Il trattato mishnico Berakhot e la sua concettualizzazione [ind. per] Il lessico concettuale del trattato mishnico Berakhot (mBer): ➤ 154, ꟳSACCHI P. 1990, 363-374 / 383-534.

Sanders E., Jesus to Mishnah ➤ 437.

a187 *Schwartz* Joshua, Gallus, Julian and anti-Christian polemic in Pesikta Rabbati: TZBas 46 (1990) 1-19.

κ6.5 Talmud; midraš.

a187* ᴱ**Abramson** S., ⊖ Selections from Samuel BEN CHOFNI (Ḥofni), Introduction to Talmud. ⊘ ⊖ intr. not. J 1990, Mekize Nirdamim. [xii-] 237 p. 0334-1313.

a188 **Alba Cecilia** Amparo, Midrás de los Diez Mandamientos y libro precioso de la salvación: Biblioteca Midrásica 7. Valencia 1990, S. Jerónimo. vii-311 p. 84-86067-39-1.

a189 *Alexander* Philip S., Quid Athenis et Hierosolymis? Rabbinic Midrash and hermeneutics in the Graeco-Roman world: ⇒ 183, ᶠVERMES G., Essays 1990, 101-134.

a190 ᴱ**Avery-Peck** A., The literature of early rabbinic Judaism; issues in Talmudic redaction and interpretation [symposium]: New Perspectives in Ancient Judaism 4, 1989 ⇒ 5,378: – ᴿJJS 41 (1990) 275s (L. *Jacobs*).

a191 *a) Becker* H.J., 'Sirillo-Handschriften' des Talmud Yerushalmi; – *b) Goldberg* A., Stereotype Diskurse in den frühen Auslegungsmidraschim: FraJudBei 16 (1988) 53-73 / 23-51 [< JStJud 21,112].

a192 *Becker* H.J., Zwei neue Yerushalmi-Handschriften und die 'Gemara' zu Eduyot mit dem Kommentar des Shlome SIRILLO: FraJudBei 17 (1989) 57-66 [< JStJud 21,260].

a193 ᴱ**Bokser** Ben Zion & Baruch M., The Talmud, selected writings: Classics of Western Spirituality. NY 1989, Paulist. ix-247 p. $18; pa. $13. 0-8091-0430-X; -3114-5 [TDig 38,89].

a194 **Boyarin** Daniel, Intertextuality and the reading of midrash: Indiana Studies in Bib.Lit. Bloomington 1990, Indiana Univ. xiii-161 p. $27.50. 0-253-31251-5. – ᴿJStJud 21 (1990) 254-8 (J. *Neusner*: alarming ignorance of scholarship of the Mekhilta, to which he devotes his entire book).

a195 *Cohen* Shaye J.D., The rabbinic conversion ceremony [bYeb 47; Gerim 1,1]: JJS 41 (1990) 177-203.

a196 *Cutter* William, Citing and translating a context; the Talmud in its 'Post Modern' setting: Judaism 39 (1990) 104-111.

a197 **Diamond** Eliezer B., ⊘ A model for a scientific edition and commentary for 'Bavli Ta'anit' I, with a methodological introduction: diss. Jewish Theol. Sem. NY 1990. 367 p. 91-08043. – DissA 51 (1990s) 3736s-A.

a198 *Gibbs* R., *al.*, [bŠabb 116s] Empty margins? [debate about saving the margins of a Torah scroll on Sabbath from a fire related to Christians]: ConsJud 42,2 (1989s) 21-33 [< NTAbs 34,360].

a199 *Goldberg* A., *a)* Midrashsatz; Vorschläge für die descriptive Terminologic der Formanalyse rabbinischer Texte; – *b)* Pesiqta Rabbati 26, ein singulärer Text in der frühen rabbinischen Literatur: FraJud Bei 17 (1989) 45-56 / 1-44 [< JStJud 21,259].

a200 **Gordis** Robert, The dynamics of Judaism; a study in Jewish law [halakhah]. Bloomington 1990, Indiana Univ. x-244 p. $30. 0-253-32602-8 – ᴿJJS 41 (1990) 281-3 (L. *Jacobs*).

a201 *Green* W.S., Will success [...*Steinsaltz* A.] spoil the Talmud: Moment 15,3 (Wsh 1990) 22-27. 54-56 [< NTAbs 34,360].

a202 **Hoah** Aminoah, The redaction of the tractate Sukkah and Moed-Katan in the Babylonian Talmud. Ramat Aviv 1988, Rosenberg School of Jewish Studies. 420 p. 965-372-004-X [BO 47,264].

a203 ᵀᴱ**Hüttenmeister** F. G., Scheqalim-Scheqelsteuer: Yerushalmi 2/5. Tü 1990, Mohr. xviii-186 p. DM 128. 3-16-145607-6 [BL 91,148, P. S. *Alexander*].

a204 *Jacobs* Louis, The story of r. Phinehas BEN YAIR and his donkey in B. Hullin 72-b: → 183, ᶠVERMES G. 1990, 193-205.

a205 **Kalmin** Richard, The redaction of the Babylonian Talmud; Amoraic or Saboraic? HUC Mg 12. Cincinnati 1989, HUC. xviii-215 p. – ᴿHebSt 31 (1990) 182-8 (J. *Neusner*: useless result); JStJud 21 (1990) 261-3 (J. *Neusner*: arbitrary, disorganized, trivial).

a206 *Kalmin* Richard, *a*) Friends and colleagues, or barely acquainted? relations between fourth-generation masters in the Babylonian Talmud: HUCA 61 (1990) 125-158; – *b*) Quotation forms in the Babylonian Talmud; authentically Amoraic, or a later editorial construct?: HUCA 49 (1988) 167-187 [< ZAW 102,275]; – *c*) Saints or sinners; scholars or ignoramuses? Stories about the Rabbis as evidence for the composite nature of the Babylonian Talmud: AJS 15,2 (CM 1990) 179-205 [< NTAbs 35,217].

a207 **Kensky** Allan D., ⊕ 'Midrash Tanhuma Shmot', critical edition, through Beshallah ...: diss. Jewish Theol. Sem., ᴰ*Dimitrovsky* H. – NY 1990. – 91-09397. – DissA 51 (1990s) 3736-A.

a208 *Kister* Menahem, ⊕ Metamorphoses of aggadic traditions: Tarbiz 60 (1990s) 179-224; Eng. IIs.

a209 *Klein* M. L., Targum manuscripts in Leningrad [Inst. Or. St.; Antonin 13-38, Firkovitch I-II 39-91]: Studies in Bibliography and Booklore 17 (Cincinnati 1989) 1-18 [< NTAbs 34,362].

a209* **Kosovsky** Moshe, Concordance to the Talmud Yerushalmi [1-3, 1979-84 Onomasticon; thesaurus of proper names] → 1,9931: ᴿZDMG 139 (1989) 229-231 (P. *Schäfer*).

a210 *Kraemer* D., Scripture commentary in the Babylonian Talmud, primary or secondary ['significant' in J. NEUSNER 1986, dubiously holding Sota and Sanhedrin more typical than Sukka]: AJS 14,1 (CM 1989) 1-15 [< NTAbs 34,222].

a211 *Laytner* A., Suffering in the Sifrei [1,12]; AKIBA's lesson on Menasheh: JRefJud 37,2 (1990) 47-51 [< NTAbs 34,362].

a212 **Levinas** Emmanuel, Nine Talmudic readings [Quatre 1968 + Du sacré 1977], ᵀ*Aronowicz* Annette. Bloomington 1990, Indiana Univ. xxxix-197 p. 0-253-33379-2 [TDig 38,277].

a213 **Loewe** R., Rylands Haggada ... Sephardi 1988 → 5,a176: ᴿJTS 41 (1990) 227s (N. de *Lange*: balances 1985 Ashkenazi); Sefarad 50 (1990) 486-9 (Ana M. *López Álvarez*).

Manns F. Jacob le Min 1989 → 6771*.

a213* *Meir* O., ⊕ The story of the rabbi's death [Judah ha-Naśî', jKilay 9,3; jKetub 12,3]; a study of modes of traditions' redaction: JerStHLit 12 (1990) 147-177 [< NTAbs 35,218].

a214 *Moscovitz* Leib, ⊕ *Sugyot muhlafot* in the Talmud Yerushalmi [... produced by hundreds of Amoraim during more than 150 years]: Tarbiz 60 (1990s) 19-66; Eng. Is.

a215 **Neusner** Jacob, The Bavli and its sources; the question of tradition in the case of Tractate Sukkah: BrownJudSt 85, 1987 → 3,a494; 4,b190: ᴿJQR 80 (1989s) 249-261 (H. *Fox*).

a216 **Neusner** Jacob, The canonical history of ideas; the place of the so-called Tannaite Midrashim; Mekhilta attributed to R. ISHMAEL, Sifra, Sifré to

Numbers, and Sifré to Deuteronomy: SFlorida Judaism 4. Atlanta 1990, Scholars. xvi-224 p. $55. 1-55540-436-7 [NTAbs 35,129].

a217 **Neusner** J., Invitation to midrash; a teaching book. SF 1989, Harper & R. 400 p. $36; pa. $13. 0-06-066112-7. – ᴿCalvinT 25 (1990) 299-303 (K. *Pomykala*: 'hypothesis', not introduction); TS 51 (1990) 173s (A. J. *Saldarini*).

a218 **Neusner** Jacob, *a*) The Midrash, an introduction. Northvale NJ 1990, Aronson. xii-234 p. $25; 0-87668-814-8. – *b*) A Midrash reader. Mp 1990, Fortress. vii-176 p. $10. 0-8006-2433-5 [NTAbs 35,130: companion to 1987 What is Midrash?].

a219 **Neusner** Jacob, The Midrash compilations of the sixth and seventh centuries, an introduction to the rhetorical, logical, and topical program; I. Lamentations Rabbah [➤ 3922]; II. Esther Rabbah I [➤ 3187]; III. Ruth Rabbah [➤ 2929]; IV. Song of Songs Rabbah [➤ 3509]: BrownJudSt 187-190. Atlanta 1989, Scholars. xvii-193 p.; xvi-150 p.; xix-157 p.; xxi-218 p. $48 + 45 + 46 + 53. 1-55540-404-9; -5-7; -6-5; -7-3. [NTAbs 34,273].

a220 ᵀ**Neusner** Jacob, Tractate Bava Mesia ch. 1-10: Talmud of Babylonia American translation 21a-d / BrownJudSt 213-216. Atlanta 1990, Scholars. A = I. ch. 1-2, xvi-241 p.; B-II, ch. 3-4; xvi-171 p.; C-III, ch. 5-6; xvi-201 p.; D-IV, ch. 7-10; xvi-213 p. 1-55540-504-5; -5-3; -6-1; 7-X.

a221 *Neusner* Jacob, From Mishnaic philosophy to Talmudic religion; the transformation of Judaism between 200 and 400 A.D.: JAAR 58 (1990) 633-651.

a222 *Peli* Pinchas H., Responses to Jew-hatred; midrashic texts reveal how the Jewish community faced antagonistic neighbors: BR 5,5 (1989) 36 41.

a223 *Reich* Walter, Bringing the Talmud into the 20th century [*Steinsaltz* A. 1990]: BR 63 (1990) 11s.

a223* *Rosenzweig* M. L., *Silberman* L. H., A Sukkot midrash; Pesikta de Rav Kahana 27:3: JRefJud 37,4 (NY 1990) 31-36 [< NTAbs 35,220].

a224 *Schwartz* Larry, Talmudic approaches to the distribution of the tax burden: JQR 81 (1990s) 93-113.

a225 **Shinan** Avigdor, The world of the Aggadah. TA 1990, MOD. 148 p. 965-05-0497-4.

a226 *Silberman* Lou, 'Dionysian revelers?' [AbZara, *Neusner* tr. 33,64 'medicinal drink prepared from the phallus of Dionysian revelers' (*Jastrow* I, 400b) should be rather 'a drink from a fountain with herm-shaped spout']: HebSt 30 (Madison 1990) 41-45.

a227 **Steinsaltz** Adin, Talmud I. [➤ 5,a190] Tractate Bava Metzia 1. NY 1989, Random. 252 p. $40. 0-394-57666-7. – ᴿCommentary 90,1 (NY 1990) 27 31 (E. *Alexander*, 'a Talmud for Americans') [NTAbs 35,74]; JStJud 21 (1990) 295-9 (J. *Neusner*: perspicacious and creative distillation of what he thinks important, but without a cogency like RASHI's). – RelStR 17 (1991) 225-9 (J. *Neusner*, also on EHRMAN A. 1969).

a228 **Steinsaltz** Adin, Talmud Bava Metzia 2s. NY 1990, Random House. xi-365 p.; xii-256 p. 0-394-58233-0; -4-9 [OIAc Oc90].

a229 **Stemberger** Günter, Midrasch 1989 ➤ 5,a193: ᴿKIsr 5 (1990) 76 (Julie *Kirchberg*).

a230 **Stemberger** G., Il Talmud; introduzione, testi, commenti: Studi Religiosi, 1989 ➤ 5,a192: ᴿRivB 38 (1990) 384-7 (M. *Perani*).

a231 **Taradach** Madeleine, El midrash; introdució a la literatura midráshica, als targumim i als midrashim: Col·lectanea Sant Pacià 38, 1989 ➤ 5,a195: ᴿEstFranc 91 (1990) 356-8 (J. *Ferrer i Costa*); RCatalT 15 (1990) 225s (R. de *Sivatte*).

a232 **Taradach** Madeleine, Le Midrash; introduction à la littérature midrashique — *drš* dans la Bible, les Targumim, les Midrašim: MondeB 22. Genève 1990, Labor et Fides. 283 p. – ᴿHokhma 45 (1990) 64-66 (J.-J. *Hugé*).

a233 ᵀᴱ**Tilly** Heinz-Pctcr, Moed Qatan – Halbfeiertage: Übersetzung des Talmud Yerushalmi 2/12. Tü 1988, Mohr. DM 89. 3-16-745069-X. – ᴿGregorianum 71 (1990) 173-5 (G. L. *Prato*, anche su 2/10, HÜT-TENMEISTER F.).

a234 ᵀᴱ**Townsend** John T., Midrash Tanhuma. Hoboken 1989, KTAV. xvii-334 p. $39.50 [JTS 41,826]. – ᴿBibTB 20 (1990) 133s (E. *Unger*).

a235 *Visotzky* B. L., Two types of midrash study [J. *Goldin* far better than J. *Neusner*]: ConsJud 41,4 (1989) 65-71 [< NTAbs 34,223].

a236 *a) Wieseltier* L., Unlocking the rabbis' secrets [STEINSALTZ devoid of critical spirit]: NY Times Book Review (17. XII. 1989) 3.31; – *b) Green* J. M., Backstage at the Steinsaltz Talmud factory: Midstream 35,9 (NY 1989) 19-22 [< NTAbs 34,226.221].

a237 *Yassif* E., ❸ The cycle of tales in rabbinic literature: JerStHLit 12 (1990) 103-145 [< NTAbs 35,221: some 300 stories in 30 cycles of 3-40 each show four redactional principles: a single narrative framework, specific perception of genre, biography, relation to a biblical verse].

K7.1 **Judaismus mediaevalis,** *generalia.*

a238 **Biale** David, Power and powerlessness in Jewish history 1986 ⇒ 3, a516... 5,a200: ᴿJudaism 39 (1990) 379-381 (A. *Eisen*).

a239 *Brague* R., Athènes, Jérusalem, La Mecque; l'interprétation 'musulmane' [née de l'étude de la pensée médiévale] de la philosophie grecque chez Léo STRAUSS: Revue de Métaphysique et de Morale 94,2 (1989) 309-336 [353-367, *Malherbe* M., sur Strauss et HOBBES: < RSPT 74 (1990) 138].

a240 **Davidson** Herbert A., Proofs for eternity; creation and the existence of God in medieval Islamic and Jewish philosophy 1987 ⇒ 3,a519: ᴿJAOS 110 (1990) 366s (D. H. *Frank*: a towering achievement; Davidson at the height of his powers; best since seminal WOLFSON).

a241 *Díez Merino* Luis, Los fundadores de la escuela targúmica de la Universidad de Barcelona: Henoch 12 (1990) 77-97.

a242 *Faur* José, Four classes of conversos [Spain, c. 1400]: RÉJ 149 (1990) 113-124.

a243 **Giller** Pinchas, The Tiqqunim; symbolization and theurgy: diss. Graduate Theol. Union, ᴰ*Matt* D. Berkeley 1990. 238 p. – DissA 51 (1990s) 4160-A; RelStR 17,195.

a244 **Graboïs** Arieh, Les sources hébraïques médiévales, 1. Chroniques, lettres et 'responsa': Typologie des Sources du Moyen-Âge occidental. Turnhout 1987, Brepols. 96 p. – ᴿSpeculum 65 (1990) 990s (R. *Chazan*).

a245 **Navarro Peiro** Ángeles, Narrativa hispanohebrea (siglos XII-XV; introducción y selección de relatos y cuentos): EstCuHeb 11. Córdoba 1989, Almendro. 233 p.; ill. 84-86077-67-2.

a246 *Richler* Benjamin J., Translation and translators, Jewish: ⇒ 837*, DMA 12 (1989) 133-6.

a247 *Romero* Elena, La crianza del hombre; otra versión judeoespañola del midráš hebreo Yesirat ha-Valad: Sefarad 50 (1990) 413-423.

a248 **Saperstein** Marc, Jewish preaching, 1200-1800, an anthology 1989 ⇒ 5,a214: ᴿZion 55 (1990) 463-5 (J. *Dan*). — ⇒ a326.

a250 *Schäfer* Peter, Jewish magic literature in late antiquity and early Middle Ages: JJS 41 (1990) 75-91.

a251 **Shmuelevitz** Aryeh, The Jews of the Ottoman Empire [c.1500] 1984 → 2,d187: RRHR 207 (1990) 447 (S. *Schwarzfuchs*).

a252 **Simon** Heinrich & Marie, Filozofia żydowska [1984 → 65,8738], TPszczólkowski Tomasz G. Wsz 1990, Wiedza Powszechna. 195 p. − RAt-Kap 115 (1990) 336s (Z. *Pawlak*).

a253 **Sirat** Colette, A history of Jewish philosophy in the Middle Ages [1983] 1985 → 1,9960; 5,a218: RRelStT 8,3 (1988) 41-43 (F. *Landy*).

a254 **Sperber** D., A commentary on Derech Erez Zuta [also called Ze'ira], ch. 5-8. J 1990, Bar-Ilan. 190 p. 965-226-109-2 [NTAbs 34,277 without indication of date or genre; two volumes awaited on ch. 1-4 and 9].

a255 *a) Suárez Fernández* L., Iglesia y Judíos en España durante la Edad Media; − *b) Beinart* H., La Diaspora safardi en Europa y especialmente en la Cuenca del Mediterraneo; − *c) Fiey* J.-M., Juifs et chrétiens dans l'orient syriaque; − *d) Romano* D., El papel judío en la transmisión de la cultura; − *e) Cohen* R. Amran, La situación moral y social de las comunidades judías españolas, la judería toledana en tiempos de Rabi Asher BEN YEYIEL [c.1300]: Hispania Sacra 40 (Congreso internacional Hist.Ecl., Salamanca 1987: 1988) 893-909/911-931 / 933-953 / 955-978 / 1007-1013 [< RHE 85,513].

a256 *a) Todeschini* Giacomo, Familles juives et chrétiennes en Italie à la fin du Moyen Âge; deux modèles de développement économique; − *b) Genot-Bismuth* Jacqueline, Le mythe de l'Orient dans l'eschatologie des Juifs d'Espagne à l'époque des conversions forcées et de l'expulsion: AnÉCS 45 (1990) 787-817/819-838.

a257 *Zonta* Mauro, L'Iḥṣa' al-'Ulūm in ambiente ebraico, 1. Il Ṭabb al-Nufūs di IBN 'AQNĪN: Henoch 12 (1990) 53-75; Eng. 75.

K7.2 Maimonides.

a258 **Fenton** Paul B., Deux traités de mystique juive [one by Maimonides' grandson Obadiah, the other by his last descendant David II], préf. *Vajada* Georges. Lagrasse 1987, Verdier. 202+132 P. − RJQR 80 (1989s) 135-8 (M. *Blaustein*).

a259 **Fox** Marvin, Interpreting Maimonides; studies in methodology, metaphysics and moral philosophy: StHistJud. Ch 1990, Univ. 400 p. $27 [JAAR 58,739]. 0-226-25941-2.

a260 **Goldfield** Lea N., Maimonides' treatise on resurrection 1986 → 2,8326 ... 5,a223: Speculum 64 (1989) 957s (N. *Roth*).

a261 *Halbertal* Moshe, ❶ *Sefer ha-Mizwot* of Maimonides — his architecture of *halakha* and theory of interpretation: Tarbiz 59 (1989s) 457-480; Eng. V.

a262 EHyman Arthur, Maimonidean studies [: I, 1989] II: Scharf Trust. NY 1990, Yeshiva Univ. 222 p + ❶ 42. 0-88125-398-8.

a263 **Leaman** Olivier, Moses Maimonides: Arabic thought and culture. L 1990, Routledge. 190 p. £10. 0-415-03608-9. − RExpTim 102 (1990s) 255 (C. H. *Middleburgh*).

a264 **Levinger** Jacob S., ❶ Maimonides as philosopher and codifier. J 1989, Bialik. 286 p. − RRelStR 16 (1990) 361 (A. *Melamed*).

a265 **Shwarz** Zvi, The social and political ideas of Maimonides, 1988. RRÉJ 149 (1990) 208s (J.-P. *Rothschild*).

a266 **Smilévitch** Eric, Moïse Maimonide, *al.*, Commentaires du Traité des Pères, Pirqé Avot: Les dix paroles. Lagrasse 1990, Verdier. 299 p. 3-86432-117-3.

K7.3 Alii magistri Judaismi mediaevalis.

a267 RASHI: *a) Ahrend* Moshé, L'adaptation des commentaires du Midrash par Rashi et ses disciples à leur exégèse biblique; – *b) Gelles* Benjamin, Solidarité du *peshat* et du *derash* dans l'exégèse de Rashi; – *c) Goetschel* Roland, Rashi et le Hizzeqûni sur la 'Aqedah et les sacrifices: – *d) Salters* Robert B., L'exégèse de Rashi et de Rashbam sur l'Ecclésiaste; – *e) Signer* Michael, Rashi narrateur: ➤ 529, RÉJ 149 (1990) 473s / 491s / 493s / 507 / 517-9.

a268 *a) Banitt* Menahem, Le commentaire biblique de Raschi, l'œuvre d'un humaniste; – *b) Touitou* Elazar, L'œuvre de Rashi; exégèse biblique et éthique juive; – *c) Touati* Charles, Rashi commentateur du Talmud; – *d) Nahon* Gérard, Les Tosafistes: CRAI (1990) 590-596 / 597-603 / 604-607 / 608-617.

a269 *Dahan* Gilbert, Le colloque sur 'Rachi, l'homme, son œuvre et son temps' (7-9 mars 1988) [Univ. Bar-Ilan]: RÉJ 149 (1990) 299-301 [325s, Inst. Universitaire Rachi, Troyes, *Chazelas* Geneviève].

Doron Pinchas, Interpretation of difficult passages in Rashi 3. Numbers 1990 ➤ 2765.

a270 **Greenberg** Joseph A., ⊕ Foreign words in the Bible commentary of Rashi. J 1988, Meḥabber. 360 p.; 24 fig. [KirSef 62 (1988s) p. 20].

a271 *Grossman* Avraham, ⊕ Marginal notes and addenda of R. SHEMAIAH and the text of Rashi's biblical commentary: Tarbiz 60 (1990s) 67-98; 4 fig.; Eng. IIs.

a272 **Pearl** Chaim, Rashi; Jewish Thinkers, 1988 ➤ 5,a238: ᴿBAsEspOr 26 (1990) 350s (C. del *Valle*: 'Pearl' como texto, no 'Peart' como título).

a273 *Sonnet* Jean-Pierre, S. KAMIN [1938-89], lectrice de Rashi; de la cohérence et de la pertinence d'un projet exégétique; présent. *Dubois* Marcel: NRT 112 (1990) 237-249 [236].

a274 *Walton* Michael T. & Phyllis J., In defense of the Church Militant; the censorship of the Rashi Commentary in the Magna Biblia Rabbinica: SixtC 21 (1990) 385-400.

a275 SAADIA: *Dotan* Aron, A new fragment of Saadiah's *Sab'īn Lafẓah* [lexicography and Karaite controversy]: JQR 80 (1989s) 1-14.

a276 *Jospe* Raphael, Early philosophical commentaries on the Sefer Yeẓirah; some comments [Saadia c. 900, *al.*]: RÉJ 149 (1990) 369-415.

a277 *Lasker* Arnold A. & Daniel J., ⊕ 642 parts [relevant to postponement of Roš Ha-Šanâ in 921 C.E.]; more concerning the Saadya – BEN MEIR controversy: Tarbiz 60 (1990s) 119-128; Eng. IVs.

a278 **Ratzaby** Yehuda, ⊕ *Oṣar*... A dictionary of Judaeo-Arabic in R. Saadya's Tafsir. Ramat Gan 1985, Bar-Ilan Univ. 151 p. – ᴿLešonenu 52 (1987s) 200-3 (M. *Shwartz*).

a279 *Netzer* Nissan, ⊕ The contribution of Rabbi David KIMCHI to the solution of absolute hapax legomena by reference to rabbinic Hebrew: HUCA 59 (1988) ⊕ 1-11 [< OTAbs 13, p. 124].

a280 GERSONIDES: *Couteau* Élisabeth, Le colloque international Gersonide; Science et philosophie médiévales; Gersonide en son temps (1288-1344): RÉJ 149 (1990) 339-344.

a281 NAHMANIDES: TEPerani Mauro, Nahmanide (Ramban), La legge del Signore è perfetta. R 1989, Carucci. 154 p. Lit. 16.000. – RBAsEspOr 26 (1990) 348 (C. del *Valle*).

a282 BEN EZRA: [Abumalham] **Mas Montserrat,** Et *Kitāb al-Muhādara wal-Mudakara* (Libro de la rememoración y del recuerdo) de Moshe ben Ezra [c. 1055-1140]. M 1985s, Cons.Sup. I. Arabic text; II. castellano. – RRÉJ 149 (1990) 158-162 (C. del *Valle Rodríguez*).

a283 *Wolfson* Elliot R., God, the demiurge and the intellect; on the use of the word kol ['all'] in Abraham ibn Ezra [c. 1092-1167]: RÉJ 149 (1990) 77-111.

a284 *David* Abraham, An unknown letter of Rabbi SAMUEL son of Hoshana the Third [Jerusalem 1000] in the John Rylands University Library of Manchester: BJRyL 72,1 (1990) 33-36.

a285 *Goldfeld-Vogelman* L. N., Yehudah BEN SHEMARYAH, a 13th century scholar, as reflected by a Genizah manuscript: → 154, FSACCHI P. 1990, 665-674.

a286 FALAQUERA [c. 1223-91]: **Jospe** R., Torah and Sophia; the life and thought of Shem Tov ibn Falaquera 1988 → 5,a282: RHenoch 12 (1990) 207-226 (M. *Zonta*); RÉJ 149 (1990) 216-9 (Colette *Sirat*).

a286* **Harvey** Steven, FALAQUERA's Epistle of the debate, an introduction to Jewish philosophy 1987 → 5,a282*b*: RRelStR 16 (1990) 167 (M. *Kellner*).

a287 *Chiesa* B., Una fonte sconosciuta dell'Etica di Shem Tob ibn Falaquera [c. 1223-1291]; la Summa Alexandrinorum [*Jospe* R. 1988, 417-438]: → 154, FSACCHI P. 1990, 583-612.

a288 ECattani L., Jehudah HALEVI, Liriche religiose e canti di Sion: Tradizione d'Israele 2, 1987 → 4,b236; 5,a244: RHenoch 12 (1990) 117s (G. *Tamani*).

a288* — **Lasker** Daniel J., Proselyte Judaism, Christianity, and Islam in the thought of Judah HALEVI [Kuzari 2,1]: JQR 81 (1990s) 75-91.

a289 EAlsina Trias Teresa, *Olmo Lete* Gregorio del, El Diwán de Yosef IBN ṢADDĪQ [1070-1149] según la edición crítica de *Yonah David* [1982]. Sabadell 1987, AUSA. 116 p.; 23 pl. – RJQR 80 (1989s) 426s (R. P. *Scheindlin*); Sefarad 50 (1990) 215-7 (C. del *Valle*).

a290 **Loewe** Raphael, IBN GABIROL. Jewish Thinkers. L 1989, Weidenfeld & N. 196 p. £11; pa. £6. – RJJS 41 (1990) 276s (Adena *Tanenbaum*).

a291 TEChouraqui André, Bahya IBN PAQUDA, I doveri del cuore [arab., ⊕ T1161, *ibn-Tibbon* Y.]T: Classici del Pensiero Religioso I. CinB 1988, Paoline. 536 p. – RRivB 38 (1990) 387s (M. *Perani* non indica traduttore italiano se non S. *Sierra* di 1983).

a292 EBusi Giulio, BERTINORO 1988/9 → 5,570: RRivB 38 (1990) 389-391 (M. *Perani*).

a293 **Wolfson** Elliot R., The book of the pomegranate, M. De LEÓN [diss. Brandeis 1987 → 3,a569]: BrownJudSt 144. Atlanta 1988, Scholars. XV-124 p. + ⊕ 409 p. 1-55540-213-5. – RRÉJ 149 (1990) 210s (C. *Mopsik*).

a294 **Calders i Artís** Tessa, El princep i el monjo, d'Abraham ben Šemuel ha-Levi IBN HASDAY [judío catalán c. 1200]: OrBarc 2. Sabadell 1987, AUSA. 278 p. 84-86329-21-3. – RBO 47 (1990) 206s (F. *García Martínez*).

a295 **Hayoun** Maurice-Reuven, La philosophie et la théologie de MOÏSE de Narbonne (1300-1362): Texts and Studies in Medieval and Early Modern Judaism 4. Tü 1989, Mohr. xxi-320 p. – RRÉJ 149 (1990) 162-5 (F. *Kaplan*).

a296 **Fontaine** T.A.M., In defense of Judaism; Abraham IBN DAUD, sources and structures of *ha-Emunah ha-Ramah* [diss. VU Amst 1986]: StSemNeer 26. Assen 1990, Van Gorcum. 334 p. 90-232-2404-3.

a297 **Cohen** Martin S., The Shi'ur Qomah 1985 → 64,8941 ... 5,a269: ᴿJAOS 110 (1990) 582-4 (M. D. *Swartz*).

K7.4 *Qabbalâ, Zohar, Merkabâ* — Jewish mysticism.

a298 **Brin** Gershon, Studies in the biblical exegesis of Rabbi R. Joseph QARA: Rosenberg Publ. TA 1990, Univ. 179 p. 965-372-008-2.

a298* *Chaze* M., De la signification des fêtes dans la Bible et le Talmud selon quelques kabbalistes des XIIIᵉ et XIVᵉ siècles: → 618, Commémoration 1986/8, 255-273.

ᴱ**Dan** J., The age of the Zohar 1986-8/9 → 522.

a299 **Dan** Joseph, Jewish mysticism and Jewish ethics 1986 → 2,8352; 4,b243: ᴿRÉJ 149 (1990) 213s (M.-R. *Hayoun*).

a300 *Elior* Rachel, Merkabah mysticism (*Halperin* D. 1988): Numen 37 (1990) 233-249.

a301 **Ginsburg** Elliot K., The sabbath in the classical Kabbalah: Judaica. Albany 1989, SUNY. xx-341 p. $44.50; pa. $15. – ᴿJJS 41 (1990) 278s (L. *Jacobs*).

a302 **Ginsburg** Elliot K., Sod ha-Shabbat... MEIR IBN GABBAI: Judaica. Albany 1989, SUNY. xvi-264 p. $49.50. – ᴿJJS 41 (1990) 278s (L. *Jacobs*).

a303 *Horst* P. W. van der, Het onderzoek van de vroege joodse mystiek sinds SCHOLEM; de 'major trends' na Major Trends: NedTTs 44 (1990) 121-138.

a304 **Idel** M., Kabbalah; new perspectives 1988 → 4,b248; 5,a256: ᴿAmHR 95 (1990) 127s (D. R. *Blumenthal*); BL (1989) 136 (A. P. *Hayman*); HistRel 30 (1990) 215-7 (I. *Culianu*); JAAR 58 (1990) 287-290 (S. R. *Isenberg*); RTPhil 122 (1990) 436s (J. *Borel*, aussi sur son Aboulafia).

a305 **Idel** Moshe, Language, torah, and hermeneutics in Abraham ABULA-FIA ⊕, ᵀ*Kallus* Menahem 1988 → 5,a257: ᴿRÉJ 149 (1990) 211-3 (J.-P. *Rothschild*: exégèse radicale et audacieuse).

a306 **Janowitz** Naomi, The poetics of ascent [...SCHOLEM] 1989 → 5,a205; 0-88706-636-4; -7-2 [RelStR 17, 44, D. R. *Blumenthal*].

a307 ᴱ**Lachower** F., *Tishby* I., *al.*, The wisdom of the Zohar, an anthology 1989 → 5,a259; I. xxxi-443 p.; II. xi + p. 447-863; III. ix + p. 865-1596. 0-19-710043-0 all. [BL 91, 149, A. P. *Hayman*].

a308 **Langer** Georg, Die Erotik der Kabbala: Symbolon. Mü 1989, Diederichs. 149 p. 3-424-01001-4.

a309 *Mach* Michael, Das Rätsel der *Hekhalot* im Rahmen der jüdischen Geistesgeschichte [*Halperin* D., Faces of the chariot 1988]: JStJud 21 (1990) 236-252.

a310 **Mopsik** Charles, La Cabale. P 1988, Grancher. 150 p. – ᴿRTPhil 122 (1990) 138 (J. *Borel*).

a311 *a) Reichmann* R., Die 'Wasser-Episode' in der Hekhalot-Literatur; – *b) Hermann* Klaus, *Rohrbacher-Sticker* Claudia, Die magischen Traditionen der New Yorker Hekhalot-Handschrift JTS 8128 im Kontext ihrer Gesamtredaktion: FraJudBei 17 (1989) 67-100 / 101-149 [< JStJud 21,260].

a312 **Safran** Alexandre, Sagesse de la Kabbale [I.], II. P 1987, Stock. 271 p. ᴿRTPhil 122 (1990) 435s (Esther *Starobinski*).

a313 **Safran** Alexandre, Die Weisheit der Kabbala [rum.], ᵀ*Jonas* Ingrid. Bern 1988, Francke. 252 p. – ᴿSalesianum 52 (1990) 172 (R. *Vicent*).

a314 **Schäfer** Peter, Geniza-fragmente zur Hekhalot-Literatur 1984 ➤ 65, 8770 ... 4,b252: ᴿJQR 80 (1989s) 142-5 (Rachel *Elior*).

a315 **Schäfer** Peter, Hekhalot-Studien 1988; ➤ 4,b255; 5,a266: DM 158; 3-16-145388-3: ᴿGregorianum 71 (1990) 376-8 (G.L. *Prato*, anche su Übersetzüng 2, 1987); JAOS 110 (1990) 580-2 (L. *Schiffman*: 'a paean', also for Übersetzung and Konkordanz); JSS 35 (1990) 521-4 (A.F. *Hayman*); JStJud 21 (1990) 278-281 (F. *García Martínez*); OLZ 85 (1990) 682-4 (L. *Wächter*).

a316 ᴱ**Schäfer** Peter, *al.*, Konkordanz zur Hekhalot-Literatur I (A-K), II (L-T) 1986-8 ➤ 2,8361 ... 5,a267: ᴿJStJud 21 (1990) 133-6 (H. *Gaylord*); RHR 207 (1990) 206s (N. *Séd*).

a317 **Schäfer** Peter, *al.,* Übersetzung der Hekhalot-Literatur II: 1987 ➤ 3, a594; 4,b254: ᴿJQR 80 (1989s) 200-2 (M. *Verman*); NedTTs 44 (1990) 168s (P.W. van der *Horst*).

a318 **Wald** Stephen G., The doctrine of the divine name [Zohar]; an introduction to classical kabbalistic theology: BrownJudSt 149, 1988 ➤ 5,a274: ᴿRÉJ 149 (1990) 209 (C. *Mopsik*).

a319 **Wirszubski** C. [1915-77], ᴱ*Schneider* C., *Idel* M., Pico della MIRAN-DOLA's encounter with Jewish mysticism. J 1989, Israel Academy. xi-292 p. – ᴿHenoch 12 (1990) 250-2 (F. *Lelli*).

K7.5 Judaismus saec. 14-18.

a320 *Blasco Martínez* Asunción, Instituciones sociorreligiosas judías de Za-ragoza (siglos XIV-XV); sinagogas, cofradías, hospitales: Sefarad [49 (1989) 227-236] 50 (1990) 1-46. 265-288; Eng. 288.

a321 **Bowman** Steven B., The Jews of Byzantium (1204-1453) 1987 ➤ 2,8731 ... 5,a279: ᴿBSO 52 (1989) 124-6 (D. *Frank*).

a322 ᴱ**Carmel** Alex, *al.*, The Jewish settlement in Palestine 634-1881: TAVO B-88. Wsb 1990, Reichert. 181 p.; p. 22-38, *Schein* Sylvia, Crusader period; + 5 other periods. 3-88226-479-9.

a323 *Esposito* Anna, Le 'comunità' ebraiche di Roma [dopo l'espulsione da Spagna 1492] prima del sacco (1527); problemi di identificazione: Henoch 12 (1990) 165-188; Eng. 189.

a324 **Harshav** Benjamin, The meaning of yiddish. Berkeley 1990, Univ. California. xix-205 p. 0-520-05947-6.

a326 **Horowitz** Carmi, The Jewish sermon in 14th century Spain; the Derashot of R. Joshua IBN SHU'EIB: HarvJudMg 6. CM 1989, Harvard Univ. ix-206 p. 0-674-47455-4; pa. -6-2.

a327 **Jordan** William C., The French monarchy and the Jews; from Philip Augustus to the last Capetians. Ph 1989, Univ. Pennsylvania. 370 p. – ᴿRHist 383 (1990) 357-360 (A. *Graboïs*).

a327* *a*) *Lehram* J.C.H., Jüdische Martyrologie und Weisheitsüberlieferung; – *b*) *Henten* J.W. van, Das jüdische Selbstverständnis in den ältesten Martyrien: ➤ 533, Martyrologie 1984/9, 88-126 / 127-161.

a328 **Moreen** Vera B., Iranian Jewry's hour of peril and heroism [Babai IBN-LUTF, Book of a forced convert 1617-1662; diss.]. NY/J 1987, [P]AAR. xv-247 p. $25. – ᴿEngHR 105 (1990) 470s (D.S. *Katz*: defects of a dissertation).

a329 **Ruderman** David B., Kabbalah, magic and science; the cultural uni-verse of a sixteenth-century Jewish physician [YAGEL Abraham, 1553-1623]. CM 1988, Harvard Univ. 234 p. – ᴿHenoch 12 (1990) 252-4 (F. *Lelli*).

a330 ᵀᴱ**Rudermann** David B., A valley of vision [*Gê Hizzayôn*]; the heavenly journey of Abraham ben Hananiah YAGEL [1553-1624] Ph 1990, Univ. Pennsylvania. xii-365 p. $35 [RelStR 17, 266, H. E. *Adelman*].

a331 **Schwartz** Dan, The religious philosophy of Samuel IBN ZARRA [Spain c. 1370]: diss. Bar-Ilan. Ramat-Gan 1989. – RÉJ 149 (1990) 262-4.

a332 VOLOZHINER: *a*) ᵀᴱ**Gross** Benjamin, r. Hayyim de Volozhyn, L'ame de la vie, *nefesh hahayyim*: Les Dix Paroles. Lagrasse 1986, Verdier. lxxii-404 p. – *b*) **Lamm** Norman, *Tora lishmah*; Torah for Torah's sake in the works of Rabbi Hayyim of Volozhin and his contemporaries. Hoboken 1989, KTAV. xvii-3689 p. $25; pa. $15 [JTS 41,823].

K7.7 Hasidismus et Judaismus saeculi XIX.

a333 *Gutwein* Daniel, ⊕ MARX's ideas on the relationship between Jews and capitalism; from SOMBART to WEBER: Zion 55 (1990) 419-447; Eng. XVIs.

a334 **Heschel** Abraham J., The circle of the Baal Shem Tob 1985 ⇒ 5,a301*: ᴿJudaism 39 (1990) 250s (M. M. *Faierstein*).

a335 **Heschel** A. J., La terra è del Signore; il mondo interiore dell'ebreo in Europa Orientale [yiddish 1946; Eng. 1950], ᵀ*Poli* E.: Il Ponte. Genova 1989, Marietti. xviii-135 p. Lit. 19.000. – ᴿLetture 45 (1990) 370-2 (Susanna *Invernizzi*); RivB 38 (1990) 388s (M. *Perani*).

a336 **Jacobson** Yoran, La pensée hassidique [⊕], ᵀ*Chalier* Catherine: La nuit survenue. P 1989, Cerf. 184 p. F 164. – ᴿÉtudes 372 (1990) 140 (G. *Petitdemange*).

a337 *Katz* David S., The Chinese Jews and the problem of religious authority in eighteenth- and nineteenth-century England: EngHR 105 (1990) 893-919.

a338 *Klorman* Bat-Zion E., The Messiah Shukr Kuḥayl II (1868-75) [Yemen] and his tithe (*ma'sér*); ideology and practice as a means to hasten redemption: JQR 79 (1988s) 199-217.

a339 **Mendelssohn** Moses, Schriften über Religion und Aufklärung, ᴱ*Thom* M. B 1989, Union. 528 p. M 36. – ᴿTLZ 115 (1990) 432s (W. *Gericke*).

a340 *Oevermann* Susanne, Der Traum im Sefer Hasidim (Ms. Parma) [*Harris* M. 1963]: Henoch 12 (1990) 19-51; Eng. 51.

a341 *Rapoport-Albert* Ada, ⊕ The Hasidic movement after 1772; continuity and change: Zion 55 (1990) 183-245; Eng. VIIIs.

a342 ᴱ**Ratner** Dov B. [1852-1917], Midrash Seder Olam, published by his daughter Sarah Slonimsky, ᴱ*Misrsky* Samuel K. Brooklyn 1988 Moznaim. 160 double p.

a342* **Robberechts** Édouard, Les Hassidim: Fils d'Abraham. Turnhout 1990, Brepols. 306 p.; ill.; map. 3-503-50002-1.

a343 ᴱ**Safran** Bezalel, Hasidism, continuity or innovation? 1985/9 ⇒ 5,a104: ᴿJJS 41 (1990) 279s (L. *Jacobs*); JTS 41 (1990) 812 (S. C. *Reif*).

K7.8 Judaismus contemporaneus.

a343* **Abitbol** Michel, Les deux terres promises; les Juifs de France et le Sionisme. P 1989, O. Orban. 298 p. – ᴿRHist 283 (1990) 142-4 (Esther *Benbassa*); Zion 55 (1990) 130-3 (S. *Almog*).

a344 **Baeck** Leo, L'essenza dell'ebraismo ᵀ*Danna* Carlo: Radici 8. Genova 1988, Marietti. xii-267 p. – ᴿSalesianum 52 (1990) 165s (R. *Vicent*).

a345 ᴱCohen Arthur A., *Mendes-Flohr* Paul, Contemporary Jewish religious thought 1987 → 2,242... 4,b271: ᴿRelStR 16 (1990) 112-4 (P. *Van Buren*) & 114-7 (M. *Vogel*).

a346 **Ellis** Marc H., Toward a Jewish theology of liberation 1987 → 3,a620; 4,b275: ᴿAsiaJT 2 (1988) 589s (R. *Deutsch*); IrTQ 56 (1990) 68s (D. *O'Connor*).

a347 ᴱ**Endelman** Todd M., Jewish apostasy in the modern world 1987 → 4,356: ᴿZion 55 (1990) 127-9 (M. *Meir*, ❸).

a348 **Fackenheim** E. L., What is Judaism? An interpretation for the present age. NY 1987, Summit. – ᴿRaMIsr 56 (1989) 369-375 (Irene *Kajon*).

a349 **Goldberg** Davis J., *Rayner* John D., The Jewish people; their history and their religion. Hmw 1989, Penguin. xiv-409 p.; 23 fig. £6. [JTS 41,352].

a350 **Gottlieb** Freema, The lamp of God; a Jewish book of light. Northvale NJ 1989, J. Aronson. xxi-498 p. 0-87668-898-9.

a351 *Greenberg* S., KADUSHIN [M., Theology of Seder Eliahu 1932] as explorer of the rabbinic universe of discourse and discoverer of organic thinking (I): ConsJud 42,1 (1989s) 5-19; 42,2 (1989s) 3-11 [< NTAbs 34,221.361].

a352 **Hartman** David, A living covenant; the innovative spirit in traditional Judaism 1985 → 2,8390; 0-02-914140-0: ᴿJRel 70 (1990) 663-5 (J. *Stern*); Judaism 39 (1990) 243-8 (N. *Gillman*: 'the exciting future of Jewish theology').

a353 **Hayoun** Maurice R., Le judaïsme moderne [... Europe, surtout Allemagne]: Que sais-je? P 1989, PUF. 126 p. – ᴿREJ 149 (1990) 241-3 (G. *Nahon*: réussite de concision, de science et de courage; réserves mineures).

a354 **Heller** Alfred, ᴱ*Benz* Wolfgang, Dr. SELIGMANNS Auswanderung; der schwierige Weg nach Israel: Beck'sche Reihe 414. Mü 1990, Beck. 354 p. DM 24. 3-406-34006-7.

a356 *Holtz* Barry W., Finding our way; Jewish texts and the lives we lead today. NY 1990, Schocken. 257 p. $23 [JAAR 58, 739].

a357 **Isenberg** Shirley B., India's Bene Israel, a comprehensive inquiry and sourcebook. Bombay 1988, Popular Prakashan. xxii-443 p. £24.50. – ᴿBSO 53 (1990) 170s (J. B. *Segal*).

a358 **Lau** Israel M., Wie Juden leben; Glaube — Alltag — Feste, ᴿ*Meislisch* S., ᵀ*Magall* M. Gü 1988, Mohn. xviii-384 p. DM 48. – ᴿTLZ 115 (1990) 266s (S. *Schreiner*).

a359 **Liebman** Charles S., *Cohen* Steven M., Two worlds of Judaism; the Israeli and American experiences. NHv 1990, Yale Univ. 202 p. $25 [JAAR 58,327].

a360 **Meyer** Michael A., Response to modernity 1988 → 4,b286; 5,a327: ᴿAmHR 95 (1990) 128-130 (D. *Vital*).

a361 *Migliau* Bice, Nuove prospettive di studio sulle Cinque Scole del Ghetto di Roma [distrutte 1908-10 per fare la 'Via del Progresso']; l'identificazione ed il recupero dell'Arōn di Scola Catalana: Henoch 12 (1990) 191-202 + 5 fig.; Eng. 205.

a362 **Mittleman** Alan L., Between KANT and Kabbalah; an introduction to Isaac BREUER's philosophy of Judaism. Albany 1990, SUNY. 227 p. [JAAR 58,327].

a363 *Nehorai* Michael Z., ❸ Remarks on the rabbinic rulings of Rabbi KOOK [A. I., 1865-1935, chief rabbi of Eretz-Israel]: Tarbiz 59 (1989s) 481-505; Eng. VI.

a364 **Neusner** Jacob, The religious world of contemporary Judaism; observations and convictions [... How many Judaisms?]: BrownJudSt 191. Atlanta 1989, Scholars. xxiii-201 p. $55. 1-55540-410-3 [NTAbs 34,273].

a364* *Neusner* J., Getting a Jewish education [his experiences 1954-60]: Midstream 36,6 (NY 1990) 29-31 [< NTAbs 35,219].

a365 **Prijs** Leo, Worte zum Sabbat; über die jüdische Religion: Beck'sche Reihe 419. 117 p. DM 16,80. 3-406-34011-3.

a366 ᴱ**Proctor** Samuel, *Schmier* Louis, Jews of the South: selected essays. Macon GA 1982, Mercer Univ. viii-131 p. $13. – ᴿRelStR 16 (1990) 205-210 (C. R. *Wilson*, with 7 books on U. S. South Christians).

a367 *Salvarani* Brunetto, Le motivazioni religiose della narrativa ebraica [moderna: AGNON S., YEHOUSHUA A., GROSSMAN D.]: HumBr 44 (1989) 526-547.

a368 **Schine** Robert S., Jewish thought in flux; Max WIENER (1882-1950) [Jüdische Religion im Zeitalter der Emanzipation 1935]: diss. Jewish Theol. Sem. NY 1990. 286 p. 90-30001. – DissA 51 (1990s) 2056-A.

a369 *Shulman* Harvey, The theo-political thought of Emil FACKENHEIM: Judaism 39 (1990) 221-23.

a370 **Stillman** Norman A., The language and culture of the Jews of Sefrou, Morocco; an ethnolinguistic study: JSS Mg 11. Manchester 1988, Univ. xv-171 p.; 8 pl., 3 maps. £15. – ᴿJSS 35 (1990) 157s (D. *Schroeter*).

a371 **Unterman** Alan, ℗ The Jews, faith and life. Łódź 1989, Wyd. Łódzkie. 312 p. – ᴱAtKap 114 (1990) 304s (J. *Bagrowicz*).

a372 **Wyschogrod** Michael, The body of faith; God in the people Israel. SF 1989, Harper & R. xviii-320 p. $15 pa. 0-06-069706-7 [OTAbs 14, 232, W. T. *Miller*].

　　　K8　*Philosemitismus* – **Judeo-Christian rapprochement.**

a373 ᴱ**Almog** Shmuel, Antisemitism through the ages 1987 ➤ 5,a347: ᴿSpeculum 64 (1989) 1056.

a373* ᴱ**Amersfoort** J. van, *Oort* J. van, Juden und Christen in der Antike. Kampen 1990, Kok. 150 p.

a374 **Andel** C. P. van, Rome en Jerusalem... na Auschwitz 1988 ➤ 5,a348: ᴿKerkT 41 (1990) 73-75 (W. *Nijenhuis*).

a375 **Beeck** Franz J. van, Loving the Torah more than God? [LEVINAS 1955 title] towards a Catholic appreciation of Judaism [Ch 1988 Cody lecture]. Ch 1989, Loyola. xvii-105 p. $10. 0-8294-0620-4 [TDig 37,250]. – ᴿHorizons 17 (1990) 354s (J. A. *Colombo*).

a376 *a)* *Beker* J. Christiaan, The NT view of Judaism; – *b)* *Smith* D. Moody, [in John]; – *c)* *Hillerbrand* Hans J., M. LUTHER and the Jews: 587*, ᴱCHARLESWORTH J. H., Jews and Christians; exploring the past, present and future: Shared ground among Jews and Christians; a series of explorations, 1, 1990...

a377 ᴱ**Brakelmann** Günter, *Rosowski* Martin, antisemitismus; von religiöser Judenfeindschaft zur Rassenideologie: Kleine Reihe 1547. Gö 1989, Vandenhoeck & R. 150 p. DM 17,80: 3-525-33560-1. – ᴿTLZ 115 (1990) 833s (K. *Nowak*).

a378 **Braybrooke** Marcus, Time to meet; towards a deeper relationship between Jews and Christians. L/Ph 1990, SCM/Trinity. 180 p. £8.50. 0-334-02447-1. – ᴿExpTim 1st choice 102,1 (1990s) 1s (C. S. *Rodd*).

a379 ᴱ**Brockway** Allan, *Van Buren* Paul, *Rendtorff* Rolf, *Schoon* Sijon, The theology of the churches and the Jewish people 1988 ➤ 5,a359: ᴿRHPR 70 (1990) 136s (E. *Jacob*).

a380 *Charlesworth* J. H., David FLUSSER's vision: Explorations 4,1 (Ph 1990) 1.4. [< NTAbs 35,137].

a381 **Chazan** Robert, Daggers of faith; thirteenth-century Christian missionizing and Jewish response 1989 ➤ 5,a363: ᴿCathHR 76 (1990) 119-121 (N. *Roth*); TS 51 (1990) 176 (J. T. *Pawlikowski*).

a382 *Chazan* Robert T., In the wake of the Barcelona disputation [ex-Jew Dominican friar Paul 1263 against Moses BEN-NAHMAN]: HUCA 61 (1990) 185-201.

a383 **Chevallier** Yves, L'antisémitisme; le Juif comme bouc émissaire 1988 ➤ 5,a364: ᴿCC 141 (1990,3) 98 (S. M. *Katunarich*).

a384 ᴱ**Chrostowski** Waldemar, *Rubinkiewicz* Ryszard, ❷ Żydzi i Judaizm w dokumentach Kościoła i nauczaniu Jana Pawła II (1965-1989): Kościół a Żydzi i Judaizm 1. Wsz 1990, Akad. Teol. Katolickiej. 254 p.

a385 *Coggan* Donals, Jews and Christians: TLond 93 (1990) 261-6.

a386 ᴱ**Cohen** Susan S., Antisemitism; an annotated bibliography, I: Heb. Univ. Sassoon Center 1987 ➤ 4,940: ᴿJQR 80 (1989s) 169-171 (T. *Kushner*).

Colpe Carsten, Das Siegel der Propheten; historische Beziehungen zwischen Judentum, Judenchristentum ... 1990 ➤ 214.

a386* *Conway* John S., Christian-Jewish relations during the fifties: Kirchliche Zeitgeschichte 3,1 (Gö 1990) 11-26 [< ZIT 90,481].

a387 **Cutler** A. & H., The Jew as ally of the Muslim 1985 ➤ 2,8429 ... 5,a367: ᴿRelStT 8,3 (1988) 33-35 (R. *Firestone*).

a388 *Dewey* Arthur J., Pauline marginalia; a response to the work of George SAIGA [Antisemitism and the New Testament, awaited from Paulist Press]: ProcGLM 10 (1990) 166-180.

a389 *Dundes* Alan, The ritual murder or blood libel legend; a study of anti-Semitic victimization through projective inversion: Temenos 25 (Helsinki 1989) 7-32 [< ZIT 90,217].

a390 **Dupuy** B., *al.,* Juifs et chrétiens; un vis-à-vis permanent. Bru 1986/8, Fac. Univ. S. Louis. 190 p. F 120. – ᴿNRT 112 (1990) 422s (M. J. *Horowitz*).

a391 **Edwards** John, The Jews in Christian Europe 1400-1700: 1988 ➤ 5,a377: ᴿCathHR 76 (1990) 567s (J. *Friedman*); ModT 7 (1990s) 196s (H. J. *Hillerbrand*).

a392 *Endreffy* Zoltán, ⓜ Ist ein christlich-jüdischer Dialog möglich?: ➤ 133, ᶠNYÍRI T. 1990, 81-85.

a393 *Engelsviken* Tormod, The Willowbank declaration on the Christian Gospel and the Jewish people: Mishkan 11 (1989) 71-84 [< BS 147 (1990) 480s].

a394 **Epperson** Steven, Gathering and restoration; Mormon ways of understanding the Jewish people: diss. Temple, ᴰ*Samuelson* N. Ph 1990. – RelStR 17,190.

a395 *Faber* D. J., Vreemdelingen in de staat Gods; de Joden in historiografische teksten uit de XIde en XIIde eeuw: Tijdschrift voor Geschiedenis 103 (Groningen 1990) 395-411 [< RHE 85,348*].

a396 *Feldman* L., Is the New Testament antisemitic? [on the whole no; anti-Jewish theological statements are not against Jews]: Moment 15,6 (Wsh 1990) 32-35 . 50-52 [< NTAbs 35,198].

a397 **Fornberg** Tord, Jewish-Christian dialogue and biblical exegesis: StMission 47, 1988 ➤ 4,b328; 5,a383: RSvEx 55 (1990) 128-130 (L. *Eriksson*); TsTKi 61 (1990) 310 (Terje *Stordalen*).

a398 *Gossmann* Hans-Christoph, Die Verbindung von jüdischer Kultur und hebräischer Sprache und ihre Rezeption in der antijüdischen Literatur: LingBib 64 (1990) 96-99.

a399 **Grayzel** Solomon [1896-1980], The Church and the Jews in the XIIIth century [I (1198-1254), 1966 = 1933], II (1254-1314), E*Stow* Kenneth R. NY/Detroit 1989, Jewish Theol.Sem./Wayne State Univ. xxiii-357 p. $30. 0-8143-2254-9 [TDig 37,366].

a400 **Gutwirth** Jacques, Les judéo-chrétiens d'aujourd'hui: Sciences humaines et religions 1987 ➤ 4,b338; F 125: RLVitae 45 (1990) 117s (L. *Partos*).

a401 *Hank* Elisabeth, Wir Christen nach Auschwitz — eine Skizze: Orientierung 17 (1988) 181-186 > 'Christians after Auschwitz', TE*Asen* B.: TDig 37 (1990) 241-5.

a402 **Haynes** Stephen R., Prospects for post-Holocaust theology; 'Israel' in the theologies of Karl BARTH, Jürgen MOLTMANN, and Paul VAN BUREN: diss. Emory, D*Detweiler* R. Atlanta 1989. 368 p. 90-15649. – DissA 51 (1990s) 196s-A.

a403 *Henrix* Hans H., Der nie gekündigte Bund [nicht über *Lohfink* N.] – Basis des christlich-jüdischen Verhaltnisses: ErbAuf 66 (1990) 193-208.

a404 **Hoffmann** Christhard, Juden und Judentum im Werk deutscher Althistoriker 1988 ➤ 5,a389: RHZ 251 (1990) 655s (K. *Christ*).

a405 **Hortzitz** Nicoline, 'Früh-Antisemitismus' in Deutschland (1789-1871/2); strukturelle Untersuchungen zu Wortschatz, Text und Argumentation: Germanistische Linguistik 83. Tü 1988, Niemeyer. xi-347 p. DM 124. – RDLZ 111 (1990) 439-442 (U. *Schröter*).

a406 **Hsia Po-Chia** R., *a*) The myth of ritual murder; Jews and magic in Reformation Germany. NHv 1988, pa.1990, Yale Univ. 256 p. $27.50/ $12. 0-300-04120-9; -746-0. – RSixtC 20 (1989) 141s (J. *Friedman*); – *b*) Printing, censorship, and anti-Semitism in Reformation Germany: ➤ 37*, FCHRISMAN M., Process of change 1988, 135-148.

a407 **Iber** Harald, Christlicher Glaube oder rassischer Mythus; die Auseinandersetzung der Bekennenden Kirche mit Alfred ROSENBERGS 'Der Mythus des 20. Jahrhunderts' [Diss. B]: EurHS 23/286. Fra 1987, Lang. 374 p. Fs 71. – RTLZ 115 (1990) 122-4 (K. *Nowak*: schwach).

a408 **John Paul II,** On the holocaust [parts of 13 discourses 1979-88], E*Fischer* Eugene J. Wsh 1988, Catholic Bishops Conference. – RCC 141 (1990,3) 101s (S. M. *Katunarich*).

a409 *Jordan* William C., The erosion of the stereotype of the last tormentor of Christ [sponge-bearer, the depraved Stephaton]: JQR 81 (1990s) 13-44.

a410 **Juden:** LuJb 57 (1990) 350 (Bibliog. No 723-742].

a411 **Katunarich** S. M., Breve storia dell'ebraismo e dei suoi rapporti con la cristianità 1987 ➤ 3,a679 ... 5,a394: RHenoch 12 (1990) 123s (Sergio *Sierra*).

a412 **Kellenbach** Katharina von, Anti-Judaism im Christian-rooted feminist writings; an analysis of major U.S. American and West German feminist theologians: diss. Temple, D*Eilberg-Schwartz* H. Ph 1990. 261 p. 91-00297. – DissA 51 (1990s) 2778-A; RelStR 17,191.

a413 *a*) [*Keller* Hermann present.], Wir und die Juden — Israel und die Kirche; Leitsätze in der Begegnung von Juden und Christen; Hauptversammlung des Reformierten Bundes [Siegen,] 12. Mai 1990; – *b*)

Erklärung zur Begegnung zwischen lutherischen Christen und Juden; Driebergen ND 8.V.1990: KIsr 5 (1990) 88-91 / 177-180.

a414 **Kohler-Spiegel** Helge, Juden und Christen, Geschwister im Glauben; ein Beitrag zur Lehrplantheorie am Beispiel Verhältnis Christentum-Judentum: Diss. D*Riesinger*. Salzburg 1989s. – TR 86,511.

a415 *Kohn-Roelin* Johanna, Weil wir uns erinnern wollen; Perspektiven feministischer Theologie zur Überwindung des Antijudaismus: Orientierung 54 (1990) 189-191.

a416 E**Kremers** Heinz, Die Juden und M. LUTHER 1985 → 1,602*... 5,a401: RJRelHist 15 (1988s) 151-3 (M. *Schild*).

a417 *Krop* Henri A., Duns SCOTUS and the Jews; scholastic theology and enforced conversion in the thirteenth century: Nederlands Archief voor Kerkgeschiedenis 69 (Leiden 1989) 161-175 [< ZIT 90,411].

a418 *Laga* Carl, Judaism and the Jews in MAXIMUS Confessor's works; theoretical controversy and practical attitudes: BySlav 51 (1990) 177-188.

a419 *Lange* N.R.M. de, A fragment of Byzantine anti-Christian polemic: JJS 41 (1990) 92-190.

a420 **Langmuir** Gavin I., History, religion, and antisemitism. Berkeley 1990, Univ. California. 391 p. $37.50 [JAAR 58,535].

a421 *Leingruber* Stephan, Von der Verketzerung zum Dialog; Darstellung und Behandlung der Juden im christlichen Religionsunterricht: ZkT 112 (1990) 288-303.

a422 **Levison** Frederick, Christian and Jew; Leon LEVISON 1881-1936. ... 1989, Pentland. 352 p. £12.50. 0-946270-69-4. – RExpTim 101 (1989s) 224 [C. S. *Rodd*: not to be missed].

a423 **Lindblad** Diane M., Louis-Ferdinand CÉLINE; an aesthetics of anti-Semitism: diss. Washington, D*Collins* D. Seattle 1989. 179 p. 90-20936. – DissA 51 (1990s) 875s-A.

a424 **Lindeskog** Gösta † (E*Illman* Karl-Johan, *Martola* Nils), Das jüdisch-christliche Problem; Randglossen zu einer Forschungsepoche: AcU, HistRel 9, 1986 → 2,8481 ... 5,a407: RJTS 41 (1990) 201-3 (W. *Horbury*); RHR 207 (1990) 317-320 (M. *Carrez*); SvEx 55 (1990) 125-8 (K.-G. *Sandelin*).

a425 **Litvinoff** Barnet, Il roveto ardente; storia dell'antisemitismo. Mi 1989, Mondadori. 525 p. Lit. 36.000. – RCC 141 (1990,3) 538s (F. *Molinari*).

a426 *Lodahl* Michael, Anti-Judaism in Christian theology; a critical response to H. Ray DUNNING's Grace, faith, and holiness [KC 1988, Beacon]: AsbTJ 45,2 (1990) 5-17 [19-28 response, *Spross* Daniel].

a427 **Lubac** Henri de, Résistance chrétienne à l'antisémitisme 1940-1944: 1988 → 4,b363; 5,a408: RArHistPont 27 (1989) 462-4 (G. *Martina*).

a428 **Lubac** Henri de, Resistenza cristiana all'antisemitismo, ricordi 1940-1944, T*Gozzi* Cristiana. Mi 1990, Jaca. 217 p. Lit. 23.000. – RLetture 45 (1990) 764s (Susanna *Invernizzi*).

a428* E**McInnes** Val A., Renewing the Judeo-Christian wellsprings 1987 → 3,553; 4,b366: RCritRR 2 (1989) 476-8 (C. *Williamson*).

a429 **MacLennan** R. S., Early Christian texts on ['against'] Jews and Judaism [diss. Minnesota 1988, D*Kraabel* A.]: Brown JudSt 194. Atlanta 1990, Scholars. xxvi-203 p.; 2 fig.; map. $56. 1-55540-414-6 [NTAbs 34,411].

a430 *Malchow* Bruce V., Causes of tolerance and intolerance toward Gentiles in the First Testament: BibTB 20 (1990) 3-9.

a431 *Mamlak* G., Christian missionaries — Jewish scholars: Midstream 36,7 (NY 1990) 36-42 [< NTAbs 35, 199].

a432 **Markish** Shimon,   Erasmus and the Jews 1986 ➤ 2,8488; 3,a698: ᴿHeythJ 31 (1990) 242s (Margaret M. *Phillips*).

a433 *Marmur* Dow, Christians, Jews and antisemitism now: TorJT 6 (1990) 224-234.

a434 **Miller** Ronald H., Dialogue and disagreement; Franz ROSENZWEIG's relevance to contemporary Jewish-Christian understanding 1989 ➤ 5,a414: ᴿTS 51 (1990) 564s (D. J. *Moore*).

a435 **Neudecker** Reinhard, Die vielen Gesichter des einen Gottes; Christen und Juden im Gespräch: ÖkExH 6. Mü 1989, Kaiser. 132 p. DM 19,80. – ᴿKIsr 5 (1990) 79 (Julie *Kirchberg*).

a436 **Neudecker** Reinhard, I vari volti del Dio unico, cristiani ed ebrei in dialogo; pref. *Toaff* Elio: Ponte. Genova 1990, Marietti, xiv-141 p. [Acta PIB 9,457]. 88-211-8365-3.

a437 **Neuenzeit** Paul, Juden und Christen auf neuen Wegen zum Gespräch; Ziele, Themen, Lernprozesse; *Fiedler* Peter, Beitrag. Wü 1990, Echter. 216 p. DM 24,80. – ᴿKIsr 5 (1990) 79s (Julie *Kirchberg*).

a438 *Neuman* Matthias, Confessions of a 20th century Christian Judaizer: America 163 (1990) 323-6.

a439 **Neusner** Jacob, *a*) with *Greeley* Andrew, The Bible and us; a priest and a rabbi read Scripture together. ... 1990, Warner. – *b*) How Judaism and Christianity can talk to each other; the basis for an interreligious dialogue: BR 6,6 (1990) 32-36.40s45 (39, Greeley reply).

a440 *Niewiadomski* Józef, Die katholische Kirche in Polen und die Juden: KIsr 5 (1990) 65-73.

a441 **Novak** David, Jewish-Christian dialogue 1989 ➤ 5,a419: ᴿTS 51 (1990) 186 (D. J. *Harrington*); TTod 47 (1990s) 222.224 (P. M. *Van Buren*: rich, except conclusions).

a442 **Oesterreicher** John M., The new encounter between Christians and Jews. NY 1988, Philosophical. 472 p. $25. 0-8022-2496-2. – ᴿJAAR 58 (1990) 135s (R. W. *Ross*).

a443 **Orfale** Moisés, El tratado 'De iudaicis erroribus ex Talmut' de JERÓNIMO de Santa Fe: Controversia 10. M 1987, Cons. Sup. xiv-322 p. – ᴿSefarad 50 (1990) 217s (C. *Carrete Parrondo*; importante).

a444 *Papp* Vilmos [*Karasszon* István], Ⓜ Antiszemitizmus a Bibliában? [KÁLVINNÁL?]: TSzem 33 (1990) 109-113 [–115].

a445 **Perelmuter** Hayim, *Wuellner* Wilhelm, Paul the Jew; Jewish/Christian dialogue: CHH 60. Berkeley 1990, Univ. California. 89 p.

a446 **Petuchowski** J.J., *Thoma* C., Lexikon der jüdisch-christlichen Begegnung 1989 ➤ 5,a421: ᴿNRT 112 (1990) 422 (L.-J. *Renard*); TLZ 115 (1990) 738s (C. *Hinz*); TPhil 65 (1990) 619s (H.-W. *Jüngling*); TPQ 138 (1990) 75 (G. *Stemberger*).

a447 *Petuchowski* Jakob J., Looking beyond the Scriptures [Cincinnati Xavier Univ. Ecumenical lecture 1989]: AnglTR 72 (1990) 26-38.

a448 ᴱ**Reinharz** Jehuda, Living with antisemitism; modern Jewish responses 1987 ➤ 3,452: ᴿCahHist 34 (1989) 86s (A. *Gueslin*).

a449 *Remaud* Michel, Mystère d'Israël et unité de l'Eglise: Tychique 78 (1989) 30-34.

a450 **Rendtorff** Rolf, Hat denn Gott sein Volk verstossen? 1989 ➤ 5,a426: ᴿTLZ 115 (1990) 469s (K. *Meier*).

a451 **Rengstorf** Karl H., *Kortz-Fleisch* Siegfried von, Kirche und Synagoge; Handbuch zur Geschichte von Christen und Juden; Darstellung mit Quellen. Mü 1988 = 1968/70, dtv. 504 p.; 745 p. DM 68. – ᴿHZ 251 (1990) 653-5 (F. *Lotter*).

a452 *a) Ritter* Adolf M., Chrysostomus und die Juden — neu überlegt; – *b) Wyschogrod* Michael, Die Auswirkungen des Dialogs mit dem Christentum auf mein Selbstverständnis als Jude; – *c) Metz* Johann-B., Kirche nach Auschwitz: KIsr 5 (1990) 109-122 / 135-147 / 99-108.

a453 ᴱ**Rudin** A. James, *Wilson* Marvin R., A time to speak; the Evangelical-Jewish encounter 1987 ⇒ 4,638: ᴿRHPR 70 (1990) 137 (E. *Jacob*).

a454 **Saperstein** Marc, Moments of crisis in Jewish-Christian relations [5 Chautauqua lectures 1988]. Ph 1989, Trinity. xii-84 p. $7 pa. – ᴿCurrTMiss 17 (1990) 227 (J. C. *Rochelle*) & 393 (F. *Sherman*); PerspRelSt 17 (1990) 180-3 (K. S. *Ford*, also on Novak D.; Williamson C.).

a455 *Schmied* A., Ein Aussen, das zuinnerst betrifft; kirchliches Selbstverständnis im Blick auf das Judentum: TGegw 33 (1990) 107-119.

a456 **Schreckenberg** Heinz, Die christlichen Adversus-Judaeos-Texte und ihr literarisches Umfeld (1.-11. Jh.)²ʳᵉᵛ mit Ikonographie [¹1982]: EurHS 23/172. Fra 1990, Lang. 750 p. DM 145. 3-631-42603-8. – ᴿDLZ 111 (1990) 484-6 (G. *Haendler*); TGL 80 (1990) 348s (H. R. *Drobner*). TS 51 (1990) 369s (J. T. *Pawlikowski*).

a457 ᴱ**Sell** Allan P. F., Reformed theology and the Jewish people. Geneva 1986, WCC. – ᴿTorJT 6 (1990) 100-2 (R. *Humphries*, also touching six cognate works).

a458 *a) Siegele-Wenschkewitz* Leonore, Die Diskussion um Antijudaismus in der feministischen Theologie — ein neues Feld des jüdisch-christlichen Gesprächs; – *b) Plaskow* Judith, Feministischer Antijudaismus und der christliche Gott; – *c) Stegemann* Wolfgang, Das Verhältnis Rudolf Bultmanns zum Judentum; ein Beitrag zur Pathologie des strukturellen theologischen Antijudaismus: KIsr 5 (1990) 5-8 / 9-25 / 26-44.

a459 **Simonsohn** Shlomo, The Apostolic See and the Jews 492-1404 / 1394-1464: 1988s ⇒ 4,b392; 5,a439: ᴿJEH 41 (1990) 279s (P.N.R. *Zutshi*: first stages of a vast project); Speculum 65 (1990) 493s (Mary *Stroll*).

a460 *a) Suárez Fernández* Luis, Iglesia y Judíos en España durante la Edad Media; – *b) Beinart* Haim, La Diáspora sefardí en Europa y especialmente en la cuenca del Mediterráneo; – *c) Fiey* Jean Maurice, Juifs et Chrétiens dans l'Orient Syriaque; – *d) David* Romano, El papel judío en la transmisión de la cultura: Hispania Sacra 40 (1988) 893-910 / 911-932 / 933-954 / 955-980 [–1010 *al.* < zit 90,47].

a461 **Swidler** L. [& *Eron* L. J. on Jesus; *Sloyan* G. & *Dean* L. on Paul], Bursting the bonds? A Jewish-Christian dialogue on Jesus and Paul: Faith meets Faith. Mkn 1990, Orbis. viii-224 p. $35; pa. $17. 0-88344-713-4; -2-6 [NTAbs 35,260].

a462 *a) Theissen* Gerd, Aporien im Umgang mit den Antijudaismen des Neuen Testaments; – *b) Thyen* Hartwig, Juden und Christen — Kinder eines Vaters?; – *c) Wyschogrod* Michael [⇒ a452*b*], The impact of dialogue with Christianity on my self-understanding as a Jew: ⇒ 147, ꟳRendtorff R., Hebr.Bibel 1990, 535-553 / 689-705 / 725-736 [607-617, *Hüber* Wolfgang; 707-715, *Tödt* Heinz E.; 717-723, *Wiesel* E. 1975].

a463 **Thoma** Clemens, Theologische Beziehungen zwischen Christentum und Judentum² [= ¹1982]: WB-Forum 35 [= Grundzüge 44]. Da 1989, Wiss. 174 p. DM 19,80. – ᴿTGegw 33 (1990) 71s (E. *Grunert*).

a464 *Tomson* P. J., K. H. Miskotte und das heutige jüdisch-christliche Gespräch: NedTTs 44 (1990) 15-34: Eng. 56.

a465 **Torm** Axel, Israelsmission og Israels mission. Århus 1990, okay. 271 p. Dk 250. ᴿNorTTs 91 (1990) 189 (N. E. *Bloch-Hoell*).

a466 *Torrekens* Michel, Antisionisme et/ou antisémitisme: RNouv 44,10 (1988) 91-95.

a467 *a*) *Van Buren* Paul M., L'Église et le peuple juif, ᵀ*Carra de Vaux* Bruno; – *b*) *Dujardin* Jean, L'enseignement de l'Église catholique sur le judaïsme depuis 'Nostra aetate': LumièreV 39, 196 ('De la question juive à la question chrétienne', 1990) 59-71 / 39-57.

a468 *Walzer* Michael, A particularism of my own [...'Judaism is often described by Christian writers ... as a particularist, even a tribal, religion' p. 195]: RelStR 16 (1990) 193-7 (–201-3, *Meilaender* Gilbert, *Johnson* James).

a469 *a*) *Warzecha* Julian, ℗ Les documents de l'Église sur les Juifs; – *b*) *Turowicz* Jerzy, ℗ Les Juifs dans l'enseignement de JEAN PAUL II; – *c*) *Chrostowski* Waldemar, ℗ La responsabilité pour la mort du Christ; – *d*) *Gebert* Konstanty, ℗ Envers Dieu et l'extermination (la vie religieuse juive du temps Shoah): AtKap 114 ('Żydowskie korzenie chrześcijaństwa' 1990) 192-202 / 203-221 / 222-241 / 242-255.

a470 **Zuidema** Willem, Partenaire de Dieu BibleVC 1987 ➤ 5,a452*: ᴿFoi-Temps 19 (1989) 83s (J. *Michel*).

XVII,3 Religiones parabiblicae

M1.1 **Gnosticismus classicus.**

a470* *Bertrand* M., Gnose et tradition chrétienne: Connaissance des Religions 5 (1989s) 177-188 [< ETL 66, p. 131*].

a471 **Brox** N., Erleuchtung und Wiedergeburt; Aktualität der Gnosis. Mü 1989, Kösel. 105 p. DM 24,80. 3-466-20311-2. – ᴿActuBbg 27 (1990) 206 (J. *Boada*); TGL 80 (1990) 210s (R. *Geisen*); TsTNijm 30 (1990) 313 (F. van de *Paverd*).

a472 **Couvert** Étienne, La Gnose contre la foi. ... 1989, Chiré. 252 p. F 115. – ᴿEsprVie 100 (1990) 365 (L. *Barbey*).

a472* *a*) *Culianu* Ioan P., Loyal to history — the system of Gnosticism and a vision of history; – *b*) *Elsas* Christoph, Argumente zur Ablehnung des Herrscherkults in jüdischer und gnostischer Tradition; – *c*) *Nagel* Peter, Die Typologie des Leidens im Manichäismus; – *d*) *Rudolph* Kurt, Zum Problem von Loyalitätskonflikten in der Gnosis: ➤ 38*, Der 'leidende Gerechte' / Loyalitätskonflikten 1990, 232-6 / 269-281 / 282-291 / 292-300.

a473 *Edwards* M. J., Neglected text in the study of Gnosticism [*Plotinus* ...]: JTS 41 (1990) 36-50.

a474 **Filoramo** Giovanni, A history of Gnosticism [L'attesa della fine 1983 ➤ 64,9102], ᵀ*Alcock* Anthony. Ox 1990, Blackwell. xxii-269 p. $45. 0-631-15756-5 [NTAbs 35,125].

a474* *Filoramo* Giovanni, Aspetti della demonologia gnostica: ➤ 693, Diavolo 1 (1988/90) 199-213.

a475 *Fischer-Mueller* E., Aydeet, Yaldabaoth; the Gnostic female principle in its fallenness: NT 32 (1990) 79-95.

a476 ᴱ**Gianotto** Claudio, La testimonianza veritiera: Testi del Vicino Oriente Antico 8, letteratura egiziana gnostica e cristiana 1. Brescia 1990, Paideia. 206 p. Lit. 30.000. 88-394-0453-8.

a477 ᵀᴱ**Guillaumont** Antoine & Claire, ÉVAGRE, Le Gnostique ... SChr 356, 1989 ➤ 5,a459: ᴿGregorianum 71 (1990) 601s (G. *Pelland*); JbAC 33 (1990) 269-271 (H. M. *Schenke*); JTS 41 (1990) 687-690 (G. *Gould*);

Muséon 103 (1990) 379s (B. *Coulie*); NRT 112 (1990) 266s (V. *Roisel*); OrChrPer 56 (1990) 238 (V. *Ruggieri*); RÉG 103 (1990) 263-7 (P. *Gérin*); RHR 207 (1990) 210s (Madeleine *Petit*); RivStoLR 26 (1990) 188-190 (J. *Mallet*); RPg 63 (1989) 305s (É. des *Places*); VigChr 44 (1990) 301s (G.J.M. *Bartelink*).

Hatem Jad,   La christologie gnostique de HINDIYYÉ 1990 → 7510.

a479 *Hinlicky* Ellen & Paul,   Gnosticism; old and new [... 'New Age']:   Dialog 28 (1989) 12-17 [18-29, *Peters* T.; 236, letter of Sylvia *Rand*].

a480 ᴱ**King** Karen L.,   Images of the feminine in Gnosticism 1988 → 5,481*a*: ᴿCurrTMiss 17 (1990) 305s (Sarah S. *Henrich*); JEH 41 (1990) 515s (S. G. *Hall*).

a481 **Lacarrière** J.,   The Gnostics [1973],   ᵀ*Rootes* N. [1977].   SF 1989, City Lights.   136 p. $7 pa. 087286-243-7 [NTAbs 34,610].

a482 **Layton** Bentley,   The Gnostic scriptures 1987 → 3,a759... 5,a465:   ᴿBO 47 (1990) 143-7 (J. *Helderman*); HeythJ 31 (1990) 333s (A. *Louth*); JEH 40 (1989) 617s (S. G. *Hall*); Vidyajyoti 53 (1989) 165s (P. M. *Meagher*).

a483 **Leisegang** Hans,   Die Gnosis⁵ 1985 → 1,a165:   ᴿOLZ 85 (1990) 49-51 (H.-M. *Schenke*).

a484 **Marcovich** Miroslav,   Studies in Graeco-Roman religions and Gnosticism: Studies in Greek and Roman religions 4, 1988 → 4,228; ᴿClasR 40 (1990) 83s (J. G. *Griffiths*).

a485 **Meyer** Marvin W.,   ROSSI's 'Gnostic' tractate: OccP 13.   Claremont 1988, Inst. for Antiquity and Christianity. 29 p.

a486 **Moraldi** Luigi,   Le apocalissi gnostiche 1987 → 3,a762; 4,b416:   ᴿAthenaeum 78 (1990) 207-9 (F. *Jucci*).

a487 **Onuki** Takashi,   Gnosis und Stoa ... Apocryphon des Johannes: NTOrb 9, 1989 → 5,a469:   ᴿBZ 34 (1990) 146s (H.-J. *Klauck*); VigChr 44 (1990) 99-101 (G. *Quispel*).

a487* *Pearson* Birger A.,   *a*) Gnosticism in early Egyptian Christianity [ineditum < Boston 1987 SBL]; — *b*) [Moritz] FRIEDLÄNDER [1989] revisited; Alexandrian Judaism and Gnostic origins [< Studia Philonica 1973]; – *c*) Gnosticism as Platonism [< HarvTR 77 (1984) 55-72]: → 281, Gnosticism 1990, 194-213 / 10-28 / 148-164.

a488 **Perkins** Pheme,   The Gnostic dialogue; the early Church and the crisis of Gnosticism: Theological Inquiries, NY 1990, Paulist.   xi-239 p. $8. 0-8091-2320-7.

a489 *Rudolph* Kurt,   Die Gnosis; Texte und Übersetzungen: TRu 55 (1990) 113-152.

a490 *Schmithals* Walter,   NT und Gnosis: ErtFor 208, 1984 → 65,8904... 5,a474:   ᴿZkT 112 (1990) 214s (E. *Ruschitska*).

a491 *Scholz* Piotr O.,   Gnostische Elemente in nubischen Wandmalereien; das Christusbild: → 781, Uppsala 1986 = Nubica 1s (1990) 565-584; 10 fig.

a492 **Tardieu** Michel,   *Dubois* Jean-Daniel,   Introduction à la littérature gnostique I, 1986 → 2,8562... 5,a479:   ᴿRPg 63 (1989) 144-6 (J.-C. *Fredouille*).

a492* *Tardieu* Michel,   Commémoration gnostique de Sem: → 618, Commémoration 1986/8, 219-223.

a493 *a*) *Trevijano* Ramón,   Las cuestiones fundamentales gnósticas; – *b*) *Montserrat-Torrens* Joseph,   Le pérates: → 135, ᶠORBE A., Compostellanum 34 (1989) 199-212 / 185-198.

a494 *Turner* John D.,   The figure of Hecate and dynamic emanationism in the Chaldean Oracles, Sethian Gnosticism, and Neoplatonism: SecC 7 (1989s) 221-232.

a495 **Wilson** R. M., Gnosis and the New Testament. Ox 1968, Blackwell
→ 49,8209 n: ᴿDeltioVM 18,1 (1989) 65-76 (S. *Agouridis*).

M1.2 **Valentinus** – *Pistis sophia,* Elchasai.

a496 **Desjardins** Michael R., Sin in Valentinianism: SBL diss. 108. Atlanta
1990, Scholars. ix-157 p.; 9 fig. $20; pa. $13. 1-5540-225-9. – ᴿExpTim
102 (1990s) 123 (C. S. *Rodd*).
a497 **Good** Deirdre J., Reconstructing the tradition of Sophia in Gnostic
literature: SBL Mg 32, 1987 → 3,a785: ᴿCritRR 3 (1990) 267-271 (D. M.
Parrott); JAOS 110 (1990) 118 (Jorunn J. *Buckley*).
a498 *Leeper* Elizabeth A., From Alexandria to Rome; the Valentinian
connection to the incorporation of exorcism as a prebaptismal rite: Vig-
Chr 44 (1990) 6-24.
a499 **Markschies** Christoph, Valentinus gnosticus? Untersuchungen zur va-
lentinischen Gnosis mit einem Kommentar zu den Fragmenten Valentins:
ev. Diss. Tübingen 1990. 546 p. – RTLv 22, p. 597.
a500 *Pasquier* Anne, Étude de la théologie du Nom dans le traité gnostique
d'Eugnoste à partir d'un fragment de Valentin: Muséon 103 (1990)
205-214.
a501 *Trofimovac* M. K., Ⓖ The first penitent hymn of Sophia; from the
Gnostic interpretation: VDI 195 (1990) 105-116; Eng. 116.

M1.3 **Corpus hermeticum; Orphismus.**

a502 *Bader* Françoise, La langue des dieux; hermétisme et autobiographie:
ÉtClas 58 (1990) 3-28 . 221-246.
a503 **Büchli** Jörg, Der Poimandres, ein paganisiertes Evangelium ...: WUNT
2/27, 1987 → 3,a793 ... 5,a491: ᴿBZ 34 (1990) 144-6 (R. *Schnackenburg*);
NedTTs 44 (1990) 246s (R. van den *Broek*).
a503* **Fowden** Garth, The Egyptian Hermes 1986 → 3,a797 ... 5,a493: ᴿÉch-
MClas 34 (1990) 96-100 (G. *Leroux*); JRS 80 (1990) 237-240 (R. *Lane
Fox*); OLZ 85 (1990) 403-8 (L. *Kákosy*, Eng.: a landmark).
a504 *Lelli* Fabrizio, Le versioni ebraiche di un testo ermetico, il Sefer
ha-Levanah [< arab. Libro della Luna]: Henoch 12 (1990) 147-163;
Eng. 164.
a505 *Pinnoy* Maurits, PLUTARQUE et l'Orphisme: AncSoc 21 (1990) 201-214.
a505* **Scarpi** P., Ermete Trismegisto, Poimandres, Il convivio: ClasGr-
Lat. Venezia 1987, Marsilio. 105 p. Lit. 12.000. 88-317-4956-0 [NTAbs
35,270].

M1.5 **Mani,** *dualismus;* **Mandaei.**

a506 *Baconsky* Teodor, Originile, doctrina, raspîndirea [diffusion] și influența
Maniheismului: STBuc 40,2 (1988) 102-125.
a507 ᵀᴱ**Böhlig** Alexander, [*Asmussen* Jes P.; anthology] Die Gnosis, 3. Der
Manichäismus 1980 → 61,k315: ᴿRelStR 16 (1990) 155 (B. A. *Pearson*).
a508 *a*) Böhlig Alexander, Die Bedeutung des CMC für den Manichäismus; –
b) *Koenen* Ludwig [→ a521], How dualistic is Mani's dualism: → 590,
CodManCol II 1988, 35-56 / 1-34.
a509 **Brenon** Anne, Le vrai visage du Catharisme. Potret-sur-Garonne 1988,
Loubatières. 321 p. – ᴿCathHR 75 (1980) 143s (W. L. *Wakefield*: merits
translation).

a510 *Casadio* Giovanni, Manicheismo e storia della religione in Germania: SMSR 56 (1990) 393-402.

a511 *a) Chadwick* Henry, The attraction of Mani; – *b) Bianchi* Ugo, Essenza ed esistenza (o Logos e Mythos) nel pensiero gnostico manicheo: ➤ 135, ᶠOʀʙᴇ A., Compostellanum 34 (1989) 159-178 / 179-183.

a512 *Decret* François, *a)* Les Manichéens d'Afrique: ➤ 552, Epistole 1989, 79-83; *b)* Du bon usage du mensonge et du parjure; Manichéens et Priscillianistes face à la persécution dans l'Empire chrétien (IVᵉ-Vᵉ): ➤ 111, ᶠLÉVÊQUE P., 4 (1990) 141-9.

a512* **Duvernoy** J., Le catharisme; 1. la religion des cathares; 2. l'histoire des cathares. Toulouse 1989, Privat. vi-410 p.; 392 p. – ᴿRHist 281 (1989) 528s (M. *Pacaut*).

a513 *Fonkič* B. L., *Poljakov* F. B., Paläographische Grundlagen der Datierung des Kölner Mani-Kodex: ByZ 83 (1990) 22-28; 3 fig.

a514 **Fontaine** P. F. M., The light and the dark; a cultural history of dualism, 3. Dualism in Greek literature and philosophy 5-4 c. B.C., 1988 ➤ 5,a508: ᴿRBgPg 68 (1990) 224 (R. *Hoven*).

a515 *Geng* S., *Klimkeit* H. J., Zerstörung manichäischer Klöster in Turfan [Berliner Frag. M 112]: Zentralasiatische Studien 18 (1985) 7-11 [< OLZ 90,124].

a515* — *Shimin* Geng, *Klimkeit* H.-J., *Laut* J. P., Die Geschichte der drei Prinzen; Weitere neue manichäisch-türkische Fragmente aus Turfan: ZDMG 139 (1989) 328-345.

a516 ᴱ**Giversen** Søren, The Manichaean Coptic papyri in the Chester Beatty library I-IV, 1986-8 ➤ 2,7643; 5,a510: ᴿOLZ 85 (1990) 291-5 (H.-M. *Schenke*); Orientalia 59 (1990) 524-541 (W.-P. *Funk*); RHR 207 (1990) 82-85 (A. *Guillaumont*).

a516* *Giversen* Søren, Manichaean literature and the writings of Augustine: ➤ 117*, ᶠLøKKEGAARD F. 1990, 63-74.

a517 **Hutter** Manfred, Mani und die Sassaniden; der iranisch-gnostische Synkretismus einer Weltreligion: Scientia 12, ➤ 4,b449: ᴿOLZ 85 (1990) 203 (W. *Sundermann*).

a518 **Hutter** Manfred, Studien zum iranischen Manichäismus; eine gnostische Religion zwischen Zoroastrismus und Christentum: Hab.-Diss. ᴿ*Bauer* J. Graz 1989s. – TR 86 (1990) 509.

a519 *Kasser* Rodolphe, *a)* Le cheminement de l'âme, second chant de Thom le Manichéen: RTPhil 122 (1990) 505-515; – *b)* Le sixième et le septième chants de Thôm le Manichéen [out of 2000 pages of (Chester Beatty ...) Coptic Manichaean inedita]: RHPR 70 (1990) 421-432; – *c)* L'enfant captif et libéré; les traquenards évités; quatrième et cinquième chants [coptes de Médinét Madi 1930] de Thôm le Manichéen: StClasOr 40 (1990) 221-236.

a520 **Klimkeit** H.-J., Manichaean art and calligraphy: IconRel 20, 1982 ➤ 63,8986 ... 2,8592: ᴿStIran 18 (1989) 133s (P. *Gignoux*).

a521 *a) Koenen* Ludwig, Wie dualistisch ist Manis Dualismus?; – *b) Oerter* Wolf B., Die 'Vorzüge der manichäischen Religion'; Betrachtungen zu Kephalaia cap. 154: ➤ 780, Schmidt-Kolloquium 1988/90, 241-258 / 259-271.

a522 *Lim* Richard, Unity and diversity among western Manichaeans; a reconsideration of Mani's *sancta ecclesia*: RÉAug 35 (1989) 231-250.

a523 **Ménard** Jacques, De la gnose au manichéisme 1986 ➤ 2,8596 ... 5,a515: ᴿRB 97 (1990) 297 (M.-J. *Pierre*).

a524 *Poupin* Roland, La spécificité occidentale du catharisme et les relations bogomilo-cathares: RHPR 70 (1990) 149-164; Eng. 283.

a525 **Ries** J., *a*) Les études manichéennes 1988 → 4,b456: RScripTPamp 22 (1990) 651s (A. *Viciano*); – *b*) Paul et Mani → 552, Le epistole paoline nei manichei 1988/9, 7-27.

a526 *a*) *Ries* Julien, Dieux cosmiques et Dieu biblique dans la religion de Mani; – *b*) *Markus* Robert A., AUGUSTINE's Confessions and the controversy with JULIAN of Eclanum; Manichaeism revisited: → 13, FBAVEL T. van, AugLv 41 (1990s) 757-772 / 913-925.

a527 **Roll** Eugen, Mani, der Gesandte des Lichts² [¹1976]. Stu 1989, Mellinger. 145 p.; (color.) ill. DM 39. – ROLZ 85 (1990) 591-3 (W. *Sundermann*: kein Mani-Spezialist).

a528 **Runciman** Steven, Häresie und Christentum; der mittelalterliche Manichäismus [1947], TJatho Heinz. Mü 1988, Fink. 255 p. DM 48. 3-7705-2498-5. – RDLZ 111 (1990) 513-5 (N. *Winkler*); WissWeis 53 (1990) 80 (W. *Dettloff*).

a529 *Russel* James R., Kartīr and Mānī; a shamanistic model of their conflict: → 192, FYARSHATER E., 1990, 180-193.

a530 *Scott* D. A., Manichaean responses to Zoroastrianism (politico-religious controversies in Iran, past to present: 3): RelSt 25 (1989) 435-457.

Shimin Geng → a515s.

a531 *Sundermann* Werner, La passion de Mani — calendrier liturgique ou événement historique?: → 618, Commémoration 1986/8, 225-231.

a532 **Villey** André, ALEXANDRE de Lycopolis, Contre la doctrine de Mani 1985 → 1,a218 ... 3,a823: RRÉAug 35 (1989) 186-8 (Aline *Pourkier*).

M2.1 **Nag⁺ Ḥammadi,** *generalia.*

a533 ERobinson James M. (*Smith* Richard), The Nag Hammadi library in English³ʳᵉᵛ 1988 → 4,b460: RBR 6,1 (1990) 10s (J. *Brashler*); JTS 41 (1990) 217s (R. M. *Wilson*); VigChr 44 (1990) 203s (R. van den *Broek*).

a534 EHedrick C. W., Nag Hammadi Codices XI, XII, XIII: NHS 28. Leiden 1990, Brill. xxxiv-566 p. $190. 90-04-07825-8 [NTAbs 35,126]. XI. EPagels E., Turner J., Wire A., p. 3-285; – XII. EWisse F., p. 289-355; – XIII. ETurner J., p. 359-457.

a535 **Arthur** Rose H., The wisdom goddess; feminine motifs in eight Nag Hammadi documents 1984 → 1,a220 ... 3,a825: RSecC 7 (1989s) 60s (M. *Desjardins*).

a535* **Broek** R. van den, De taal van de Gnosis; gnostische teksten uit Nag Hammadi, 1986 → 3,a827; 4,b461: RNedTTs 43 (1989) 253s (J. *Helderman*).

a536 **Dart** John, The Jesus of heresy and history; the discovery and meaning of the Nag Hammadi Gnostic library 1988 → 4,4305; 5,a524: RBR 6,1 (1990) 11.13 (J. *Brashler*).

a537 EDietzfelbinger Konrad, Apokryphe Evangelien aus Nag Hammadi: Argo 7. ... 1988, Dingfelder. 262 p. DM 27,80. 3-926-253-12-6. – Schöpfungsberichte aus NH, 1989. 360 p. DM 40. 3-926-253-17-7. – Erlöser und Erlösung, Texte NH: Argo 1990, Dingfelder. 380 p. DM 40; pa. 35. 3-926-253-19-3; -8-5. – REvKomm 22,10 (1989) 54s (R. *Linssen*).

a538 TEEdwards Richard A., Wild Robert A., The sentences of Sextus 1981 → 62,9358 ... 64,9171: RZKG 100 (1989) 413s (G. *May*).

a538* *Emmel* Stephen, Reconstructing a dismembered Coptic library: ➤ 152, FRoBINSON J. M., Gnosticism 2 (1990) 145-161.
a539 E**Hedrick** C. W., *Hodgson* R., Nag Hammadi, Gnosticism, and early Christianity 1983/6 ➤ 2,374...5,a525: RPacifica 3 (1990) 226-9 (J. *Painter*).
a540 *a*) *Kuntzmann* Raymond, La découverte des manuscrits gnostiques de Nag Hammadi; – *b*) *Mahé* Jean-Pierre, Au delà des Écritures, la Gnose: MondeB 63 (1990) 3-6 (26s) / 7-9.
a541 *Schoenborn* Ulrich, Nag Hammadi en castellano; informe sobre publicaciones recientes: RBibArg 52,38 (1990) 115-120.
a542 **Scholten** Clemens, Martyrium und Sophia-mythos im Gnostizismus... NH: JbAC Egbd 14, 1987 ➤ 4,b463: RJEH 40 (1989) 263s (W. H. C. *Frend*); OLZ 85 (1990) 439-441 (D. *Kirchner*); ScripTPamp 22 (1990) 660s (A. *Viciano*); TLZ 115 (1990) 729-731 (H.-M. *Schenke*); TR 86 (1990) 114-6 (T. *Baumeister*).
a543 *Troger* Karl-W., 'Sie haben ihn nicht getötet...' Koptische Schriften von Nag Hammadi als Auslegungshintergrund von Sure 4.157 (156): ➤ 780, Schmidt-Kolloquium 1988/90, 221-234.
a544 **Williams** Michael A., The immovable race; a Gnostic designation [some 24 times in NH texts]...: NHSt 29, D1985 ➤ 2,8564: RJAOS 110 (1990) 133s (G. G. *Stroumsa*); SecC 7 (1989s) 61-63 (Pheme *Perkins*).

M2.2 *Evangelium etc. Thomae* – **The Gospel (etc.) of Thomas.**

a545 **Alcalá** Manuel, El Evangelio copto de Tomás, palabras ocultas de Jesús: BiblEstB 67, 1989 ➤ 5,a530: RCarthaginensia 6 (1990) 214s (J. F. *Cuenca*).
a546 *Conick* April D. de, The yoke saying in the Gospel of Thomas 90: VigChr 44 (1990) 280-294.
a546* *Fieger* Michael, Die Frau im Thomasevangelium: ➤ 8*, FASSFALG J. 1990, 102-7.
a547 **Jackson** Howard M., The lion becomes man 1985 ➤ 1,a162... 5,a533: RTLZ 115 (1990) 434s (H.-G. *Bethge*).
a548 *Jackson* Howard M., The seer Nikotheos and his lost apocalypse in the light of Sethian apocalypses from Nag Hammadi and the Apocalypse of Elchasai: NT 32 (1990) 250-277.
a549 **Kloppenborg** John S., *al.* [named but part not specified], Q Thomas reader. Sonoma CA 1990, Polebridge. x-166 p. 0-944344-11-9.
a550 *Koester* Helmut, *Patterson* Stephen J., The Gospel of Thomas; does it contain authentic sayings of Jesus?: BR 6,2 (1990) 28-39.
a551 E**Layton** Bentley, Nag Hammadi Codex II, 2-7, together with XIII, 2e Brit.Lib.Or 4926(1) and P. Oxy. 1,654-655: I. Gospel According to Thomas, ... to Philip, Hypostasis of the Archons; indexes; II. Origin of the World, Expository Treatise, On the Soul, Book of Thomas the Contender: NHS 20s. Leiden 1989, Brill. xv-336 p.; xiv-281 p. ƒ320 both [NRT 112,604, X. *Jacques*]. 90-04-08131-3; -9019-5.
a552 *Menard* Jacques-E., L'evangile selon Thomas / Philippe: MondeB 63 (1990) 13s / 15s [*al.*, 16-33].
a553 *a*) *Neller* Kenneth V., Diversity in the Gospel of Thomas; clues for a new direction?; – *b*) *Snodgrass* Klyne R., The Gospel of Thomas; a secondary Gospel; – *c*) *Hedrick* Charles W., Thomas and the Synoptics; aiming at a consensus: SecC 7 (1989s) 1-18 / 19-38 / 39-56.
a554 *Patterson* Stephen J., The Gospel of Thomas and the historical Jesus; retrospectus and prospectus: ➤ 544, SBL seminars 1990, 614-636.

a554* *a*) *Pokorny* Petr,   Die Herrenworte im Thomasevangelium und bei Paulus; ein Bericht zur Überlieferungsgeschichte der Sprüche Jesu; – *b*) *Malich* Burkhard,   Die Stellung der Liturgen in den koptisch-gnostischen Schriften: ➤ 780, Schmidt-Kolloquium 1989/90, 157-164 / 213-220.

a555 *Shanks* Hershel,   How to break a scholarly monopoly; the case of the Gospel of Thomas: BAR-W 16,6 (1990) 55.

a555* *Sieber* John H.,   The Gospel of Thomas and the New Testament: ➤ 152, FROBINSON J. M.,   Gnosticism 1 (1990) 64-73.

a556 **Kuntzmann** Raymond,   Le livre de Thomas [Athl. NH II,7] 1986 ➤ 2,8614...4,b480:   RBO 95 (1990) 368-370 (J. van *Amersfoort*); TLZ 115 (1990) 893-5 (H.-M. *Schenke*).

a557 *Beyer* Klaus,   Das syrische Perlenlied; ein Erslösungsmythos als Märchengedicht: ZDMG 140 (1990) 234-259.

a558 *Noja* S.,   L'Évangile arabe apocryphe de Thomas, de la 'Biblioteca Ambrosiana' de Milan (G 11 sup): ➤ 154, FSACCHI P., 1990, 681-690.

M2.3   *Singula scripta* – **Nag' Ḥammadi, various titles.**

a559 **Rouleau** Donald,   L'Épître apocryphe de Jacques (NH 1,2); *Roy* Louise, L'acte de Pierre (BG4): BCNH 18, 1987 ➤ 3,a855...5,a557:   RBO 47 (1990) 277-289 (J. *Zandee*); OrChrPer 56 (1990) 211s (E. J. *Kilmartin*); TLZ 115 (1990) 575-7 (H.-M. *Schenke*).

a560 *Veilleux* Armand,   1-2 Apocalypse de Jacques: NH V 3s, 1986 ➤ 3,a856; 4,b487: RBO 47 (1990) 670s (G. G. *Stroumsa*).

a561 *Vliet* J. van der,   Spirit and prophecy in the Epistula Iacobi Apocrypha (NHC I,2):   VigChr 44 (1990) 25-53.

a562 ELayton B.,   [Apocryphon of John] NHC II,2-7... 1989 ➤ a551 supra: RJTS 41 (1990) 218-220 (R. M. *Wilson*).

a563 *Buckley* Jorunn J.,   'The Holy Spirit is a double name'; Holy Spirit, Mary, and Sophia in the Gospel of Philip: ➤ 5,a481*a*, EKing Karen L., Images of the feminine in Gnosticism 1985/8, 211-227 [228-238, *Rudolph* Kurt, response].

a564 *Stroud* William J.,   New Testament citations in the NH Gospel of Philip: ➤ 544, SBL seminars 1990, 68-79.

a565 *Carroll* Scott T.,   The 'Apocalypse of Adam' and pre-Christian gnosticism: VigChr 44 (1990) 263-279.

a566 **Morard** Françoise,   L'apocalypse d'Adam (NH V,5): BCNH-T 15, 1985 ➤ 1,a249...5,a555:   RTLZ 115 (1990) 495-7 (H.-M. *Schenke*).

a566* *Martin* Luther H.,   Genealogy and sociology in the Apocalypse of Adam: ➤ 152, FROBINSON J. M., Gnosticism 2 (1990) 25-36.

a567 *Brown* Schuyler,   The scriptural reading of Scripture ['the *historical* reading of Scripture is *pre*-Scriptural', W. C. SMITH] and the Coptic Gospel of Truth: ➤ 544, SBL seminars 1990, 637-644.

a568 **Williams** Jacqueline A.,   Biblical interpretation in the Gnostic Gospel of Truth...: SBL diss. 79 (Yale 1983) 1988 ➤ 4,b494; 5,a563:   RCBQ 52 (1990) 178-180 (Janet *Timbie*); JAOS 110 (1990) 118s (Deirdre *Good*).

a569 ᵀ**Painchaud** Louis, ᴱ*Thomassen* Einar, Le traité tripartite (NH I,5): BCNH-T 19. Québec 1989, Univ. Laval. xviii-535 p. – ᴿETL 66 (1990) 195s (A. de *Halleux*); NRT 112 (1990) 918 (X. *Jacques*); TR 86 (1990) 211s (H. J. *Klauck*); TorJT 6 (1990) 944-6 (M. *Desjardins*, also on VEILLEUX A. 17, ROULEAU D. 18).

a570 **Gilhus** Ingvild S., The nature of the archons (CC II,4): StOrRel 12, 1985 → 1,a242 ... 5,a552: ᴿVigChr 44 (1990) 205s (R. van den *Brock*).

a570* *King* Karen L., Ridicule and rape, rule and rebellion; the Hypostasis of the Archons: → 152, ᶠROBINSON J. M., Gnosticism 2 (1990) 3-24.

a571 **Painchaud** Louis, Le deuxième traité du Grand Seth (NH VII,2): BCNH-T 6, 1982 → 63,9042: ᴿTLZ 115 (1990) 181-5 (W. P. *Funk*, auch über T 4s).

a572 **Sevrin** Jean-Marie, Le dossier baptismal séthien; études sur la sacramentaire gnostique: BCNH Ét 2, 1986 → 1,a256 ... 5,a559: ᴿTLZ 115 (1990) 577s (D. *Kirchner*).

a572* *a*) *Sotto* Nicole, 'The treatise on resurrection'; an attempt at a synchronic analysis: → 114, ᶠLICHTHEIM M. 1990, 877-888.

M3.1 *Quid est religio? Inquisitiones speculativae* – **What is religion?**

a573 **Aldanov** Doris, The human predicament, I. The secular ideologies; II. Theory of religion. ... 1988, Vikas. 618 p.; 550 p. [JAAR 58,533].

a574 **Barnes** Michael H., In the presence of mystery; an introduction to the story of human religiousness²*ʳᵉᵛ* [¹1984]. Mystic CT 1990, Twenty-Third. viii-330 p. $15. 0-89622-425-2 [TDig 38,47].

a575 **Barz** Helmut, Die zwei Gesichter der Wirklichkeit, oder Auf die Suche nach den Göttern. Z 1989, Artemis. 166 p. DM 28 [TR 86,345].

a576 **Beckford** James A., Religion and advanced industrial society. L 1989, Unwin Hyman. 189 p. £22; pa. £9. 0-04-301228-0; -9-9. – ᴿExpTim 101,5 2d-top choice (1989s) 130s (C. S. *Rodd*).

a577 *Bianchi* Ugo, Diffusione, proselitismo, missione; tre esempi di fenomenologia religiosa: Ricerche storico-bibliche 2 (1990) 13-24.

a578 **Bourgeois** Patrick L., The religious within experience and existence. Pittsburgh 1990, Duquesne Univ. 132 p. $24 [JAAR 58,325].

a579 **Brown** L. B., The psychology of religious belief 1987 → 4,b512; 5,a581: ᴿRelSt 25 (1989) 543s (Kate *Loewenthal*).

a580 **Bryant** David J., Faith and the play of imagination; on the role of imagination in religion. Macon GA 1989, Mercer Univ. 217 p. $17. – ᴿTTod 47 (1990s) 460. 462s (G. *Green*).

a581 **Bucaro** Giuseppe, Filosofia della religione; forme e figure². R 1988, Città Nuova. – ᴿEuntDoc 43 (1990) 173s (L. *Clavell*).

a582 **Byrne** Peter, Natural religion and the nature of religion; the legacy of Deism. L 1989, Routledge. xv-271 p. £35. 0-415-04104-X. – ᴿExpTim 102 (1990s) 92s (R. M. *Burns*); TLond 93 (1990) 394 (I. *Markham*).

a583 **Christian** William A., Doctrines of religious communities; a philosophical study 1987 → 5,a586: ᴿHeythJ 31 (1990) 368s (G. *D'Costa*).

a584 **Dawson** Lorne L., Reason, freedom and religion; closing the gap between the humanistic and scientific study of religion. NY 1988, P. Lang. x-250 p. – ᴿSR 19 (1990) 376s (L. D. *Kliever*).

a585 *Debarge* Louis, Le syncrétisme religieux: EsprVie 100 (1990) 635-9.

a586 *Donovan* Peter, Neutrality in religious studies: RelSt 26 (1990) 103-115.

a587 **French** Hal W., A study of religious fanaticism and responses to it; adversary identity. Studies in Religion and Society 26. Lewiston NY 1990, Mellen. 184 p. $50. 0-88946-238-0.

a588 *Geffré* Claude, Diversités et convergences de l'expérience religieuse: RICathP 35 (1990) 17-22 [*al.* 3-16. 23-50].

a589 **Geisler** Norman, *Corduan* Winfried, Philosophy of religion² 1988 ↠ 4,b537; 5,a617: RCurrTMiss 17 (1990) 235s (T. *Peters*).

a589* **Haught** John F., What is religion? An introduction. NY 1990, Paulist. v-273 p. $11. 0-8091-3117-X [TDig 38,64].

a590 **Hill** Brennan R., *Knitter* Paul, *Madges* William, Faith, religion and theology; a contemporary introduction [college text by Xavier Univ. professors]. Mystic CT 1990, Twenty-Third. xii-388 p. $20 pa. – RHorizons 17 (1990) 297-302 (Denise L. *Carmody*) & 302-5 (M. *Barnes*) & 305-8 (L. S. *Cunningham*) & 308-312 (Mary Ann *Hinsdale*); 312-9 response.

a591 **Hubbeling** H. G., Principles of the philosophy of religion: PhilRel 25, 1987 ↠ 5,a637; 90-232-2272-5: RTsTNijm 30 (1990) 113 (A. van *Dijk*).

a592 *Knitter* Paul, Grundfragen zu einer Theologie der Religionen: EvKomm 23 (1990) 606s. 609s.

a593 *Kühn* Ulrich, Grundprobleme einer Theologie der Religionen: UnSa 45 (1990) 48-62.

a593* **Meissner** W. W., Life and faith; psychological perspectives on religious experience 1987 ↠ 3,a851: RCritRR 2 (1989) 418-420 (J. D. *Driskill* & L. J. *Bryant*).

a594 **Pieper** Josef, ¿Que significa 'sagrado'? Un intento de clarificación, TYanguas J. M.: Bolsillo 127. M 1990, Rialp. 116 p. – RScripTPamp 22 (1990) 959-962 (J. L. *Lorda*: un pequeño tesoro).

a595 **Rusecki** Martin, ❷ *Istota...* Essence and origin of religion. Wsz 1989, Verbinum. 268 p. – RAtKap 114 (1990) 159-161 (Z. *Pawlak*).

a596 *Sánchez Meca* Diego, Filosofía de la religión; anotaciones al diseño de un ámbito disciplinar: Carthaginensia 6 (1990) 155-167.

a597 **Schmitz** Joseph, Filosofia della religione, TEBartolomei M. C. 1988 ↠ 5,a694: RRasT 31 (1990) 217s (Giuseppina De Simone).

a598 **Sell** Alan P. E., The philosophy of religion 1975-1980: 1988 ↠ 4,b596; 5,a700: RJAAR 58 (1990) 524-6 (H. A. *Durfee*); RelSt 25 (1989) 402s (H. P. *Owen*); Themelios 16 (1990s) 30s (R. *Sturch*).

a599 EVieillard-Baron J. L., *Kaplan* F., [ETL 66,119* puts Kaplan first] Introduction à la philosophie de la religion [30 études]. P 1989, Cerf. 507 p. F 189. – RCarthaginensia 6 (1990) 389s (D. *Sánchez Meca*: 'Kaplam' en título, 'Kaplan' en texto).

a600 **Wagner** Falk, Was ist Religion? 1986 ↠ 2,8773; 3,b2: REstE 65 (1990) 381s (J. A. *Martínez Camino*); TsTKi 60 (1989) 232s (J. O. *Henriksen*).

a601 **Watts** Fraser, *Williams* Mark, The psychology of religious knowing 1988 ↠ 5,a721: RTS 51 (1990) 566s (W. J. *Sneck*).

M3.2 **Historia comparationis religionum:** *centra, scholae.*

a602 *Adriaanse* H. J., Godsdienstwijsgerig onderzoek in Nederland 1980-1990; een overzicht: NedTTs 44 (1990) 308-331: Eng. 332, philosophy of religion.

a603 **Godlove** Terry F., Religion, interpretation and diversity of belief; the framework model from KANT to DURKHEIM to [Donald] DAVIDSON. C 1989, Univ. vii-207 p. £25. 0-521-36179-6. – RExpTim 102 (1990s) 126

(W. D. *Hudson*); TLond 93 (1990) 396s (D. *Brown*); TS 51 (1990) 567 (J. *Reuscher*).

a604 *Gold* Daniel,   The paradox in writing on religion: HarvTR 83 (1990) 321-332.

a605 **Greschat** Hans-Jürgen,   Was ist Religionswissenschaft? 1988 → 4,b542; 5,a626:   ᴿEvKomm 22,2 (1989) 34s (H.-V. *Findeisen*).

a606 **Johnstone** Ronald L.,   Religion in society³. ENJ 1988, Prentice-Hall. vii-296 p. – ᴿRelStT 8,1s (1988) 75-77 (Rachael *Kohn*).

a607 **Jordan** Louis H.,   Comparative religion; its genesis and growth 1986 = 1905 → 3,a929:   ᴿRelSt 25 (1989) 134-6 (T. *Fitzgerald*).

a608 **Kurtz** Paul,   The transcendental temptation; a critique of religion and the paranormal. NY 1986, Prometheus.   500 p. $20. – ᴿJAAR 58 (1990) 130s (T. *Peters*: important).

a609 **Lapointe** Roger,   Socio-anthropologie du religieux; la religion populaire au péril de la modernité.   Genève 1988, Droz.   258 p. – ᴿRTPhil 122 (1990) 442s (G. *Berthold*).

a610 ᴱ**Linders** Tullia, *Nordquist* Gullög, Gifts to the gods 1985/7 → 3,666; 5,a658:   ᴿJPrehRel 3s (1989s) 60-65 (H. G. *Buchholz*).

a611 **Ménard** Jacques,   Introduction à l'histoire des religions: Gnostica 1987 → 3,a952; 5,a665:   ᴿBO 17 (1990) 141s (J. van *Amersfoort*).

a612 *Minear* Paul S.,   The holy and the sacred [holy = wherever God is found; sacred = wherever religion is found (Random H. dict.)]: TTod 47 (1990s) 5-12.

a613 *a) Oliviéro* Philippe, *Orel* Tufan,   L'expérience rituelle; – *b) Rivière* Claude,   Rites profanes, bribes du sacré: RchSR 78 (1990) 329-369; bibliog. 369-372; Eng. 115 / 373-395; Eng. 116.

a614 **Penner** Hans H.,   Impasse and resolution; a critique of the study of religion: Toronto StRel 8.   NY 1989, Lang.   x-239 p. $39.   0-8204-0976-6 [TDig 38,79].

a615 *Pfüller* Wolfgang,   Das Problem der 'religiösen Erfahrung': TVers 17 (1989) 79-90.

a616 ᴱ**Plas** Dirk van der,   Effigies Dei; essays on the history of religions [40th anniv. Dutch branch of IAHR] 1987 → 4,402:   ᴿBO 47 (1990) 303-5 (M. *Hutter*).

a617 **Preus** J. Samuel,   Explaining religion 1987 ► 3,a971 ... 5,a680:   ᴿBijdragen 51 (1990) 103s (U. *Hemel*, Eng.).

a618 *Ries* J.,   Historia religionum: ETL Elenchus bibliographicus 66 (1990) p. 113*-137* [Islam 100 items, Hinduism 50, Buddhism 45].

a619 *Schlette* Heinz R.,   Zum Universalitätsanspruch von Religionen: Orientierung 54 (1990) 99-102.

a620 **Smart** Ninian,   Religion and the western mind [Stirling Univ. Drummond lectures 1985 + essays] 1987 → 3,301:   ᴿJRel 69 (1989) 560-2 (Laurie L. *Patton*).

a621 *a) Smith* Houston,   Postmodernism's impact on the study of religion; – *b) Raschke* Carl A.,   Fire and roses [ᴱᴄᴏ U.]; toward authentic post-modern religious thinking: JAAR 58 (1990) 653-670 / 671-689.

a622 *Smith* Wilfred C.,   Thoughts on transcendence [... through history there has been a general human tendency to perceive it]: ZRGg 42 (1990) 32-49.

a623 *Stephenson* Gunther,   Religionsgeschichte und religiöses Weltbild in der späten Aufklärung: ZRGg 42 (1990) 289-298.

a624 *Tjeltveit* Alan C.,   The impossibility of a psychology of the Christian religion; a theological perspective: JPsy&T 17 (1989) 205-212 [327-393 *al.*, relating theology to psychology].

a625 **Vidal** Jacques (étudiants de), ᴱ*Ries* Julien, Symboles et religions, cours de l'année 1986s: Homo Religiosus Cah. 1, 1989 ➤ 5,a717; Fb 900: ᴿRTLv 21 (1990) 218-22 (J. *Étienne*).

a626 **Vroom** Hendrik M., Religions and the truth; philosophical reflections and perspectives [1988 ➤ 5,a718], ᵀ*Rebel* J. W.: Currents of Encounter. GR/Amst 1989, Eerdmans/Rodopi. 388 p. $24 pa. 0-8028-0502-7 / [TDig 38,92]. – ᴿNRT 112 (1990) 631s (J. *Masson*).

a627 *a) Ward* Keith, Truth and the diversity of religions; – *b) Clark* Stephen R. L., World religions and world orders; – *c) Jantzen* Grace M., Could there be a mystical core of religion?; – *d) Vroom* Hendrik M., Do all religious traditions worship the same God?: RelSt 26 (1990) 1-18 / 43-57 / 59-71 / 73-90.

a628 *Werblowsky* R. J. W., Book survey: Numen 37 (1990) 250-277.

a629 ᶠ**Werblowsky** R. J. Z., Gilgul 1987 ➤ 4,149: ᴿRHR 207 (1990) 416-9 (P. *Gignoux*).

a630 ᴱ**Zinser** Hartmut, Der Untergang von Religionen. B 1986, Reimer. 340 p., 20 fig. DM 58. 3-496-00842-3. – ᴿTR 86 (1990) 158s (R. *Seiwert*).

a631 **Zirker** H., Critica della religione: GdT 187, 1989 ➤ 5,a728: ᴿNRT 112 (1990) 284 (R. *Escol*).

M3.3 **Individui conspicui** *in investigatione religionum.*

a632 **Ahern** Annett, BERGER's dual-citizenship approach to religion: diss. McMaster, ᴰ*Greenspan* L. 1989. – RelStR 17,191.

a633 **Aziz** Robert, C. G. JUNG's psychology of religion and synchronicity. Albany 1990, SUNY. 269 p. $44.50 [JAAR 58,325].

a634 **Cox** Harvey, Many mansions 1988 ➤ 4,b518; 5,248: ᴿMissiology 18 (1990) 88 (E. L. *Copeland*).
   Cox Harvey, Göttliche Spiele; meine Erfahrungen mit den Religionen 1989 ➤ 216*.

a635 **D'Costa** Gavin, John HICK's theology of religions 1987 ➤ 5,a595: ᴿTLond 93 (1990) 59s (M. *Barnes*).

a636 *a) Fernández Fernández* José L., Experiencia religiosa y experiencia jurídica; – *b) Tornos* Andrés, Experiencia, lógica y lenguaje en las filosofías de la religión; dos lecturas de WITTGENSTEIN: MiscCom 47 (1989) 415-426 / 391-413.

a637 **Forsyth** James, FREUD, JUNG and Christianity [the question is no longer 'Does God exist?' but 'Why is the human person religious?']. Ottawa 1989, Univ. 189 p. £20. 0-7766-0212-8. – ᴿExpTim 102 (1990s) 127 (D. *Atkinson*: clear).

a638 **Gillis** C., Question of final belief, John HICK. L 1989, Macmillan. 186 p. £29.50. 0-333-45173-2. – ᴿExpTim 101 (1989s) 56 (G. *D'Costa*); RelStR 16 (1990) 331 (J. *Carlson*).

a639 **Hibino** Eiji, The sacred and the holy; an investigation of Thomas J. J. ALTIZER's dialectic of the sacred: diss. Drew. Madison NJ 1989. 187 p. 90-14365. – DissA 51 (1990s) 193-A.

a640 **Hick** John, An interpretation of religion; human responses to the transcendent (Gifford Lectures 1986s) 1989 ➤ 5,a631: ᴿJAAR 58 (1990) 710-4 (C. R. *Mesle*); Month 250 (1989) 490s (M. A. *Barnes*); RelStR 16 (1990) 139 (P. C. *Hodgson*); TorJT 6 (1990) 330-4 (D. *Wiebe*); TS 41 (1990) 137-9 (T. W. *Tilley*).

a641 **Jaeschke** Walter, Reason in religion; the foundations of HEGEL's philosophy of religion [essays 1986 ➤ 3,a925], ᵀ*Stewart* J. Michael,

Hodgson Peter C.   Berkeley 1990, Univ. California.   xvii-464 p. $50 [TS 52,355, P. *Lakeland*].

a642 *a) Loughlin* Gerard,   Prefacing pluralism; John HICK and the mastery of religion [Hick response]; – *b) Foerster* John,   Paul TILLICH and inter-religious dialogue; – *c) Surin* Kenneth,   A certain 'politics of speech'; religious pluralism...; – *d) Barnes* L. Philip,   Relativism, ineffability, and the appeal to experience; a reply to the myth-makers [*Cupitt* D.]: ModT 7,1 ('Aspects of Christian uniqueness' 1990s) 29-55 [57-66] / 1-27 / 67-100 / 101-114.

a643 *Merkur* Daniel,   FREUD's atheism, object relations and the theory of religion [PRUYSER P. 1974 & 1983; RIZZUTO A. 1979; GAY P. 1987...]: RelStR 16 (1990) 11-16.

a644 *Miller* Glenn T.,   The pedagogy of religion; a study in the thought of Joseph KITAGAWA: PerspRelSt 17 (1990) 117-127.

a645 **Oppenheim** Frank M.,   [J.] ROYCE's mature philosophy of religions 1987 → 3,a960 ... 5,a671: RAmerica 162 (1990) 16-18 (D. J. *Casey*); JAAR 58 (1990) 513-7 (Eric von der *Luft*).

a646 **Plantinga** Richard,   Gerardus van der LEEUW on religion and theology: diss. McMaster, D*Vallee* G.   Hamilton ON 1990. – RelStR 17,192.

a647 *a) Plantinga* Richard J.,   In the beginning; P. D. CHANTEPIE DE LA SAUSSAYE on Religionswissenschaft and theology; – *b) Webb* Eugene,   Recent French psychoanalytic thought and the psychology of religion [GIRARD R., LACAN J....]: RelStI 8,1s (1988) 24-30 / 31-44.

a648 **Pradés** José A.,   Persistance et métamorphose du sacré; actualiser DURKHEIM et repenser la modernité: Sociologie d'aujourd'hui, 1987 → 4,b582; 5,a679: RLavalTP 46 (1990) 105-7 (C. *Ménard*).

a649 *Prades* José A.,   *Benoît* Denis,   OTTO et DURKHEIM; intérêt heuristique de la problématique de la substantivité du sacré: SR 19 (1990) 339-350.

a650 **Raposa** Michael L.,   PEIRCE's philosophy of religion: Peirce studies 5. Bloomington 1989, Indiana Univ.   x-180 p. $25.   0-253-34833-1 [TDig 37,381].

a651 *Rogers* William R.,   *Barnard* David,   Paul PRUYSER and the psychology of religion: RelStR 16 (1990) 124s / 125-9.

a651* **Sharpe** Eric J.,   Nathan SÖDERBLOM and the study of religion.   Chapel Hill 1990, Univ.NC 258 p. – RHistRel 30 (1990) 424-6 (J. M. *Kitagawa*: 'a giant in the history of religions').

a652 **Soneson** Jerome,   Religious pluralism and theological method; a constructive development of the thought of John DEWEY: diss. Harvard, D*Kaufman* G.   CM 1990.   261 p.   90-35619. – DissA 51 (1990s) 2428-A.

a653 *Tan* Wyle,   Religious pluralism revisited [HICK J.]: AsiaJT 2 (1988) 342-9.

a654 **Yandell** Keith E.,   HUME's 'inexplicable mystery'; his views on religion. Ph 1990, Temple Univ.   360 p. $40 [JAAR 58,329].

M3.4   **Religiones praeter judaeo-christianam** *inter se comparatae.*

a655 *Ahrens* Theodor,   Heilsverkündigung in einer Welt vieler Religionen; Überlegungen zu Dialog und Mission: UnSa 45 (1990) 20-27.38.

a656 *Alemany* José J.,   Experiencia religiosa; panorama bibliográfico reciente: MiscCom 48 (1990) 257-272.

a657 **Barkan** Leonard,   The gods made flesh; metamorphosis and the pursuit of paganism.   NHv 1990, Yale Univ.   413 p. $18 pa.   0-300-04742-8. – RSpeculum 64 (1989) 655 (M. U. *Sowell*).

a658 *Biallas* Leonard J., Teaching world religions through their Scriptures: Horizons 17 (1990) 92-102.

a659 **Carmody** Denise & John, Peace and justice in the Scriptures of the world religions. NY 1988, Paulist. 191 p. $10. 0-8091-3014-9. – ᴿExpTim 101 (1989s) 222 (P. D. *Bishop*); TorJT 6 (1990) 337-9 (J. T. *O'Connell*).

a660 **Carmody** Denise L. & John T., Prayer in world religions. Mkn 1990, Orbis. viii-168 p. $10. 0-88344-644-8 [TDig 37,352].

a661 ᴱ**Coward** Harold, Sacred word and sacred text ... 1988 → 4,b517; 5,a590: ᴿPacifica 3 (1990) 101-3 (P. *Rule*); Vidyajyoti 53 (1989) 339s (G. *Gispert-Sauch*).

a662 ᴱ**Dhavamony** Mariasusai, La meditazione nelle grandi religioni [Eng. franç. 1976]. Assisi 1989, Cittadella. 278 p. Lit. 20.000. – ᴿCC 141 (1990,3) 306s (A. *Barruffo*).

a663 *Flórez* Gonzalo, Bien y mal en las religiones no cristianas: StLeg 31 (1990) 13-49.

a664 **Graham** William A., Beyond the written word 1988 → 3,a912 ... 5,a623: ᴿJTS 41 (1990) 325-8 (M. *Warner*).

a665 *Lanternari* Vittorio, Dalla salute alla salvezza; dall'osservanza religiosa alla fede mistica nelle società tradizionali: SMSR 56 (1990) 43-65.

a666 *Mondin* Battista, *a*) La religione e le sue funzioni; – *b*) La salvezza nelle religioni non cristiane: CiVit 45 (1990) 103-118 (301-310) / 5-14.

a667 **Parrinder** Geoffrey, Encounters in world religions. NY 1987, Crossroad. 224 p. $16. 0-8245-0826-2. – ᴿPacifica 3 (1990) 230s (R. *McKinney*).

a668 ᴱ**Ries** H., *Limet* H., Les rites d'initiation 1984/6 → 2,494; 3,702; 4,b590: ᴿSalmanticensis 36 (1989) 247-250 (D. *Borobio*); TLZ 115 (1990) 15s (G. *Lanczkowski*).

a669 **Roheim** Géza, L'animisme, la magie et le roi divin [1930],ᵀ (reprint): Science de l'homme. P 1988, Payot. 420 p. F 195. 2-228-88080-9. – ᴿÉTRel 65 (1990) 105 (J. *Argaud*).

a670 **Ruiz Ayucar** Miguel, El Evangelio y los Santos de las grandes religiones. M 1989, Alpuerto. 1413 p. 84-381-0133-X. – ᴿActuBbg 27 (1990) 237s (J. *Boada*); EstFranc 91 (1990) 360s (J. *Ferrer i Costa*); Manresa 62 (1990) 466s (J. I. *Macua* P.).

a671 ᴱ**Seltzer** Robert M., Religions of antiquity [selections from EncRel]. L 1989, Collier-Macmillan. 306 p. 0-02-897373-9. – ᴿExpTim 102 (1990s) 221s (P. D. *Bishop*).

a671* **Sutherland** Stewart, *al.*, The world's religions 1988 → 4,418: ᴿRelSt 26 (1990) 163-6 (G. *Parrinder*).

a672 *Wipf* Karl A., Phänomena des Göttlichen in urgeschichtlicher Zeit: JPrehR 2 (1988) 35-50, 30 fig. ...

M3.5 **Religiones mundi cum christianismo comparatae.**

a673 *Aleaz* K. P., Religious pluralism and Christian witness; a biblical-theological analysis: BangaloreTF 21,4 (1989) ... 22,1 (1990) 48-67 [< NTAbs 35,58].

a674 *Amaladoss* M., The pluralism of religions and the significance of Christ: Vidyajyoti 53 (1989) 401-420.

a675 **Ariarajah** S. W., The Bible and people of other faiths 1989 → 1,a264 ... 5,a569: ᴿDeltioVM 19,2 (1990) 72-76 (S. *Agourides*).

a676 **Barnes** Michael, Religions in conversation; Christian identity and religious pluralism. L 1989, SPCK. 200 p. £10. 0-281-04418-X. – ᴿExp-

Tim 101 (1989s) 255 (G. *D'Costa*); RelSt 26 (1990) 299-301 (G. *Chryssides*).

a677 **Berger** Peter L., Der Zwang zur Häresie; Religion in der pluralistischen Gesellschaft [1980 → 61,y256], ᵀ*Köhler* Willi; auch 1980, Fischer. 224 p. DM 24. 3-10-007104-2. – ᴿTLZ 115 (1990) 185s (H. *Moritz*).

a678 *a) Bürkle* Horst, Die Theologie der Religionen und die Christologie; – *b) Kreiner* Amin, Die Relevanz der Wahrheitsfrage für die Theologie der Religionen; – *c) Schmidt-Leukel* Perry, Der Immanenzgedanke in der Theologie der Religionen; – *d) Döring* Heinrich, Der universale Anspruch der Kirche und die nichtchristlichen Religionen: MüTZ 41 (1990) 3-19 / 21-42 / 43-71 / 73-97.

a679 *Chimirri* Giovanni, La pluralità delle religioni: CiVit 45 (1990) 555-562.

a680 *Clooney* Francis X., When the religions become context: TTod 47 (1990s) 30-38.

a681 **Cragg** Kenneth, The Christ and the faiths 1986 → 2,8665 ... 5,a592: ᴿHeythJ 31 (1990) 113s (J. *Coventry*: Resurrection played down).

a682 *Dajczer* Tadeusz, ❷ Le status théologique des religions non-chrétiennes: STWsz 27,2 (1989) 167-187; franç. 187s.

a683 **D'Costa** G., Theology and religious pluralism 1986 → 2,8667 ... 5,a596: ᴿVidyajyoti 53 (1989) 166s (S. *Painadath*, also on PARRINDER G.).

a683* *a) Duch* Lluís, El cristianismo y las religiones, ayer y hoy; – *b) Torres Queiruga* Andrés, El encuentro actual de las religiones; *c) Gil* Eusebio, Cristianismo y tipologías religiosas, – *d) Pikaza* Xabier, Cultura [... egipcia, mesopotámica, iránica] y religión bíblico-cristiana; – *e) Alemany* José J., Religión y fe: BibFe 16,48 ('La religión biblica' 1990) 406-430 / 431-471 / 378-405 / 324-377 / 311-323..

a684 **Dupuis** Jacques, *a)* Jésus-Christ à la rencontre des religions: JJC 39. P 1989, Desclée. 345 p. F 175. 2-7189-0433-X. – ᴿÉtudes 372 (1990) 569s (R. *Marlé*). – *b)* Gesù Cristo incontro alle religioni. Assisi 1989, Cittadella. 376 p. Lit. 28.000. – ᴿAsprenas 37 (1990) 96-99 (G. *Ragozzino*); Gregorianum 71 (1990) 428 (*ipse*); HumBr 45 (1990) 863s (Caterina *Conio*); StPatav 37 (1990) 724s (L. *Sartori*, 'il migliore testo oggi disponibile').

a685 *Elders* Leo J., The theological meaning of non-Christian religions: *a)* HomPast 90,2 (1989s) 9-17; – *b)* DoctComm 42 (1989) 31-41.

a686 **Fernando** Antony, Christianity made intelligible (as ONE of the world's religions). Kadawata, Sri Lanka 1990, Inter-cultural. 222 p. £2.75. – ᴿMüTZ 41 (1990) 401-3 (P. *Schmidt-Leukel*).

a686* *Friedli* Richard, Le Christ dans les cultures; carnets de route et de déroutes; un essai de théologie des religions. FrS/P 1989, Univ./Cerf. 162 p. Fs 28 [RTLv 21,402].

a687 *Gesché* Adolphe, El cristianismo y las demás religiones [< RTLv 19 (1988) 315-341], ᵀᴱ*Ribas Padros* P.: SelT 29 (1990) 103-118.

a688 **Grant** Robert, Gods and the one God; Christian theology in the Graeco-Roman world 1986 → 2,8683 ... 5,a625: ᴿTR 86 (1990) 21s (D. *Zeller*).

a689 **Griffiths** Paul G., Christianity through non-Christian eyes. Mkn 1990, Orbis. xiv-286 p. – ᴿIslamochristiana 16 (1990) 325 (M. L. *Fitzgerald*).

a690 ᴱ**Hick** J., *Knitter* P., The myth of Christian uniqueness 1987 → 4,b546; 5,a632: ᴿPacifica 3 (1990) 116-8 (S. *McNulty*: a brave attempt).

a691 **Hillman** Eugene, Many paths; a Catholic approach to religious pluralism. Mkn 1989, Orbis. xi-95 p. $15. – ᴿNewTR 3,2 (1990) 114s (J. *Carlson*).

a692 *Hunt* Anne, No other name? A critique of religious pluralism: Pacifica 3,1 (1990) 45-60 [< ZIT 90,312].

a693 **Kellenberger** J., God-relationships with and without God. NY 1990, St. Martin's. xi-176 p. $40. – ᴿTS 51 (1990) 761-3 (Stephen *Duffy*).

a694 *Martinson* Paul V., Dynamic pluralism: Dialog 28 (1989) 6-11.

a695 *a*) *Ménard* Camil, Jésus le Christ est-il l'unique sauveur? Le salut chrétien confronté aux autres religions de salut; – *b*) *Provencher* Normand, Singularité de Jésus et universalité du Christ; – *c*) *Langevin* Gilles, Singularité et universalité du Christ-Jésus: ↠ 669, J.-C. universel? 1989/90, 55-78 / 9-24 / 47-54.

a696 ᴱ**Neusner** Jacob, *al.*, Religious writings and religious systems; systemic analysis of holy books in Christianity, Islam, Buddhism, Greco-Roman religions, ancient Israel, and Judaism [two Brown Univ. seminars 1988]: Brown Studies in Religion 2, 1989 ↠ 5,592: ᴿBL (1990) 109 (J. F. A. *Sawyer*).

a697 **Newbigin** Lesslie, The Gospel in a pluralist society. L 1989, SPCK / GR 1990, Eerdmans. $15 pa. /0-8028-0426-8. – ᴿExpTim 102 (1990s) 90 (G. *D'Costa*); Pacifica 3 (1990) 356-8 (B. L. *Barber*); TLond 93 (1990) 395s (C. *Lewis*: 'Christ-uniqueness not arrogance' oversimplified).

a698 **Panikkar** R., Der neue religiöse Weg; im Dialog der Religionen leben. Mü 1990, Kösel. 189 p. DM 36 [NRT 113,278, J. *Masson*].

a699 **Placher** William C., Unapologetic theology; a Christian voice in a pluralistic conversation. Louisville 1989, Westminster/Knox. 178 p. $14. – ᴿTTod 47 (1990s) 65s (G. A. *Lindbeck*).

a700 **Poupard** Paul, Las religiones 1989 ↠ 5,a678: ᴿCiTom 117 (1990) 156s (J. *Díaz Murugarren*).

a701 **Richards** Glyn, Towards a theology of religions. L 1989, Routledge. xii-179 p. £30. – ᴿRelSt 26 (1990) 175-7 (J. *Hick*); TLond 93 (1990) 163s (A. *Race*, also on *Gillis'* HICK); TS 51 (1990) 373s (P. J. *Griffiths*).

a702 **Ries** Julien, Les chrétiens parmi les religions, des Actes des Apôtres à Vatican II 1987 ↠ 3,a977 ... 5,a683: ᴿGregorianum 71 (1990) 395s (J. *Dupuis*).

a702* ᴱ**Ries** J., *Limet* H., Les rites d'initiation: Homo Religiosus 13, 1984/6 ↠ 2,494 ... 4,b590: ᴿRHist 280 (1988) 541-4 (Nicole *Belayche*).

a703 **Rossano** Pietro, Il perché dell'uomo e le risposte delle grandi religioni 1988 ↠ 5,a687: ᴿHumBr 44 (1989) 606s (G. *Colombi*).

a704 *Rossano* P., Unicité du Christ et rencontre des religions: RICathP 36 (1990) 145-155 (221-9).

a705 **Smart** Ninian, The world's religions; old traditions and modern transformations 1989 ↠ 5,a703: ᴿExpTim 101 (1989s) 91 (P. D. *Bishop*: beautifully produced; seems splendid in the parts you don't know about); NRT 112 (1990) 283s (J. *Masson*); TLond 93 (1990) 58 (G. *Parrinder*).

a706 **Smith** Jonathan Z., Drudgery divine; on the comparison of early Christianities and the religions of Late Antiquity [Jordan lectures in comparative religion 14]: Studies in the History of Judaism. Ch 1990, Univ. xiii-145 p. 0-226-76362-5; pa. -3-3.

a707 *Smith* Joseph J., Christianity and world religions; Paul KNITTER's pluralistic perspective: Landas 4,1 (1990) 15-69 [< TContext 8,74: 'non-normative Christology'].

a707* **Strolz** Walter, Heilswege der Weltreligionen 1-3, 1984-7 ↠ 3,a993 ... 5,a707: ᴿWissWeish 52 (1989) 87-89 (W. *Dettloff*).

a708 **Swidler** L., *al.*, Death or dialogue; from the age of monologue to the age of dialogue. L/Ph 1990, SCM/Trinity. 151 p. £10.50. 0-334-02445-5. – ᴿExpTim 102 (1990s) 317s (G. *D'Costa*).

a709 ᴱSwidler Leonard,   Toward a universal theology of religion 1987
→ 3,a994 ... 5,a710:   ᴿDialog 28 (1989) 154 (M. C. *Fonner*); Vidyajyoti 53
(1989) 169s (S. *Painadath*).

a710 **Veliath** Dominic,   Theological approach and understanding of religions
[diss. R., Pont. Gregorian Univ.].   Bangalore 1988, Kristu Jyoti College.
xvi-407 p. rs 100. – ᴿVidyajyoti 53 (1989) 170s (G. *Gispert-Sauch*).

a711 **Waldenfels** H.,   Begegnung der Religionen: TVers 1/1. Bonn 1990,
Borengässer.   xi-377 p. DM 44 [NRT 113,310, J. *Masson*].

a712 *Wong* Joseph,   Christ and non-Christian religions: PhilipSa 25 (1990)
157-193.

M3.6   **Sectae.**

a713 **Binder** Andreas,   Wie christlich ist die Anthroposophie? Standort-
bestimmung aus der Sicht eines evangelischen Theologen.   Stu 1989,
Urachhaus.   277 p. DM 26. – ᴿTGL 80 (1990) 350-3 (R. *Geisen*).

a714 **Bowker** John,   Licensed insanities; religions and belief in God ... 1987
→ 3,a879 ... 5,a579:   ᴿHeythJ 31 (1990) 331s (E. *Hulmes*).

a715 **Gramaglia** P. A.,   Spiritismo; dimensioni occulte della realtà?[2]   CasM
1990, Piemme.   328 p. Lit. 33.000 [NRT 113,280, L. *Volpe*].

a716 **Grom** Bernhard,   Anthroposophie und Christentum.   Mü 1989, Kösel.
198 p. – ᴿTGL 80 (1990) 99-101 (R. *Geisen*).

a717 **Hogan** Barbara,   The limits of religious pluralism; an investigation of the
concept of pluralism in selected syntheses of American religious history:
diss. Temple, ᴰ*Raines* J.   Ph 1990. – RelStR 17,193.

a718 **Mayer** J.-F.,   Confessions d'un chasseur de sectes [expériences des
enquêtes pour ses volumes (Sectes nouvelles, un regard neuf 1981; Les
Sectes; Les sectes et nous)]: L'histoire à vif. P 1990, Cerf. 157 p. F 75
[NRT 113,280, A. *Toubeau*: parcours pittoresque; l'auteur était catholique,
de l'Opus Dei à 15 ans; ensuite de LEFEBVRE; rebaptisé 1976 dans l'Église
orthodoxe russe].

a719 **Samuel** Albert,   Para comprender las religiones de nuestro tiempo.
Estella 1990, VDivino.   218 p. – ᴿCommSev 23 (1990) 467s (M. *Sánchez*);
EfMex 8 (1990) 397s (A. *Cardenas*); RelCu 36 (1990) 691 (C. *Martín*).

a720 **Vernette** J.,   Les sectes: Que sais-je? 2519. P 1990, PUF.   128 p. –
ᴿEsprVie 100 (1990) 538s (L. *Walter*).

a721 *Wild* Maria,   The New Age; challenge to the churches [< BiKi 44 (1989)
22-27], ᵀᴱ*Asen* B.: TDig 37 (1990) 137-9.

M3.8   **Mythologia.**

a722 **Austin** Norman,   Meaning and being in myth [... LACAN J.; ... Job].
University Park PA 1990, Penn State Univ.   xiii-239 p. $28.50 [RelStR
17,157, J. S. *Pendergast*].

a723 **Baum** Klaus,   Die Transzendierung des Mythos [SCHELLING, ADORNO]:
Epistemata 38.   Wü 1988, Königshausen & N. 438 p. DM 78. – ᴿDLZ
111 (1990) 712-4 (G. *Kleinstück*).

a724 **Belier** W.,   Feiten, fouten en fabels; ontstaan en ontwikkeling van
George DUMÉZILS 'Idéologie tripartite' [17.000 pagina's]: diss. ᴰ*Leer-
touwer* L. Leiden 1989.   411 p. – TsTNijm 30 (1990) 84.

a725 **Birenbaum** Harvey,   Myth and mind 1988 → 4,b624:   ᴿRelStR 16 (1990)
234 (D. M. *Doyle*).

Bouyer Louis,   The Christian mystery; from pagan myth to Christian mysticism 1990 → 9750.

a726 **Buchholz** René, Zwischen Mythos und Bilderverbot; die Philosophie ADORNOS als Anstoss zu einer kritischen Fundamentaltheologie im Kontext der späten Moderne: kath. Diss. ᴰ*Waldenfels*. Bonn 1989s. – TR 86 (1990) 513.

a727 **Casey** T., Meaning in myth. KC 1989, Sheed & W. 150 p. $15 [TS 51,382].

a728 **Deforge** Bernard, Le commencement est un Dieu; un itinéraire mythologique: Vérité des mythes. P 1990, BLettres. 189 p. 2-251-32416-X [Kernos 4,336, J. *Desautels*].

a728* *Deifel* Elisabeth, Wahrheit und Wert von Symbol und Mythos: ZkT 112 (1990) 30-48.

a729 **Dexter** Miriam R., Whence the goddesses? A source book: Athene Series. NY 1990, Pergamon. xvi-280 p. 0-08-037281-3 [OIAc JJ90].

a729* **D'jakonov** I. M., ⊕ Arhaičskie mify vostoka i zapada [Archaische Mythen des Ostens und des Westens]: Issledovanija po fol'kloru. Moskva 1990, Nauka. 247 p.

a730 **Evers** Tilman, Mythos und Emanzipation; eine kritische Annäherung an C. G. JUNG. Ha 1987, Junius. 318 p. DM 29,80. – ᴿTLZ 115 (1990) 457-461 (J. *Scharfenberg*).

a730* *Fuchs* Ottmar, Die mythisch-symbolische Dimension religiöser Geschichte: → 350, Metaphorik 1990 11-77.

a731 *Fuhrmann* Manfred, Die antiken Mythen im christlich-heidnischen Weltanschauungskampf der Spätantike: AntAb 36 (1990) 138-151.

a732 **Gärtner** Hannelore, Kleines Lexikon der griechischen und römischen Mythologie. Lp 1989, VEB. 399 p.; ill.

a733 **Ganowicz** Jacek, 'Ideology', 'meaning', and 'myths'; MARX, WEBER, and DURKHEIM on the three dimensions of sacred symbolism and their uses in society: diss. Syracuse NY 1990. 388 p. 91-11880. – DissA 51 (1990s) 4152-A.

a734 **Grabner-Haider** Anton, Strukturen des Mythos; Theorie einer Lebenswelt. Fra 1989, Lang. 511 p. – ᴿVerbumSVD 31 (1990) 459-463 (H. *Rzepkowski*).

a735 *Güttgemanns* Erhardt, Der Mythos als Ort des Paradigmenwechsels [*Kuhn* T.]: LingBib 62 (1989) 49-95; Eng. 95s ['confronts BULTMANN'].

a736 **Highwater** Jamaka, Myth and sexuality. NY 1990, Penguin-NAL. $19. 0-453-00708-2 [ClasW 83,234 adv.].

a737 **Hübner** Kurt, Die Wahrheit des Mythos 1985 → 1,a412 ... 5,a736: ᴿGnomon 62 (1990) 1-7 (D. *Bremer*).

a738 **Kerényi** Karl, Goddesses of sun and moon [1943-6], ᵀ*Stein* Murray: Dunquin Series, 2. Dallas 1988 = 1979, Spring. 84 p.

a739 **Lincoln** Bruce, Discourse and the construction of society; comparative studies of myth, ritual, and classification. NY 1989, Oxford-UP. ix-238 p. $22 [RelStR 17,42, J. *Strong*].

a740 **Lurker** Manfred, Die Botschaft der Symbole, in Mythen, Kulturen und Religionen. Mü 1990, Kösel. 344 p.; 124 fig. DM 48. – ᴿTGl 80 (1990) 364 (K. *Hollmann*); ZkT 112 (1990) 491s (H. B. *Meyer*).

a741 **Muhawi** Ibrahim, *Kanaana* Sharif, Speak, bird; speak again; Palestinian Arab folktales. LA 1988, Univ. California. xvii-420 p. $40; pa. $15. – ᴿJAOS 110 (1990) 784 (P. *Heath*).

a742 ᴱ**Noel** Daniel C., Paths to the power of myth; Joseph CAMPBELL and the study of religion. NY 1990, Crossroad. xiv-214 p.; ill. 0-8245-1024-0. Karen *King*, Wendy *Doniger*, and 10 others on Campbell.

a743 **Pannenberg** Wolfhart, Cristianesimo e miti; nuove prospettive del mito nella tradizione biblica e cristiana[2]: StBPaid 57. Brescia 1989, Paideia. 112 p. Lit. 13.000. – [R]HumBr 45 (1990) 341s (F. *Della Vecchia*).

a744 **Rue** Loyal D., Amythia, crisis in the natural history of western culture. Tuscaloosa 1989, Univ. Alabama. xiv-207 p. $30 [JTS 41,349].

a745 **Schlatter** Gerhard, Mythos, Streifzüge durch Tradition und Gegenwart. Mü 1989, Trickster. 237 p. DM 36. – [R]ZkT 112 (1990) 194-7 (G. *Baudler*).

a746 **Strenski** Ivan, Four theories of myth in twentieth century history; CASSIRER, ELIADE, LÉVI-STRAUSS and MALINOWSKI 1987 ➤ 4,b651: [R]ÉTRel 65 (1990) 421-4 (M. *Despland*); HistRel 30 (1990) 199-203 (C. *Grottanelli*); JScStR 29 (1990) 537s (R. A. *Segal*); RelSt 26 (1990) 548-550 (R. M. *Burns*).

a747 **Triomphe** Robert, Le lion, la vierge et le miel: Vérité des Mythes 3. P 1989, BLettres. 391 p.; 41 pl. F 175. 2-251-32415-1. – [R]AntClas 59 (1990) 437-9 (A. *Touwaide*).

M4 Religio romana.

a748 **Argetsinger** Kathryn, Dies natales; self, patron, and city in Roman religion: diss. Princeton 1990. 170 p. 90-12718. – DissA 50 (1989s) 3707-A.

a749 *Armisen-Marchetti* Mireille, L'expression du sacré chez SÉNÈQUE: Pallas 36 (1990) 89-99.

a750 *Baena de Alcázar* Luis, La iconografía de Diana en Hispania: BSAΛ 55 (1989) 79-105 + 7 pl.

a750* *a) Beard* Mary, Priesthood in the Roman Republic; – *b) North* John, Diviners and divination at Rome: ➤ 389, Pagan priests 1990, 17-48 / 49-71.

a751 **Bremmer** J. N., *Horsfall* N. M., Roman myth and mythography 1987 ➤ 3,b48* ... 5,a757; [R]AntClas 59 (1990) 441-3 (J. *Poucet*).

a752 **Brouwer** H. H. J., Bona dea; the sources and description of the cult: ÉPR 110, 1989 ➤ 5,a758: [R]Tyche 5 (1990) 192s (G. *Dobesch*).

a753 *Cancik-Lindemaier* Hildegard, Kultische Priviligierung und gesellschaftliche Realität; ein Beitrag zur Sozialgeschichte der Virgines Vestae: Saeculum 41,1 (1990) 1-16.

a753* **Carozzi** Claude, Le voyage de l'âme dans l'au-delà, d'après la littérature latine (Ve-VIIIe siècles): diss. Aix 1989, [D]*Duby* G. – [R]RIist 283 (1990) 157-171 (D. *Le Blevec*).

a754 *Celluprica* Vincenza, DIOCLE di Magnesia fonte della dossografia stoica di Diogene LAERZIO: Orpheus 10 (1989) 58-79.

a755 **Champeaux** Jacqueline, Fortuna... le culte II. 1987 ➤ 5,a760: [R]Latomus 49 (1990) 907s (D. *Briquel*).

a756 *Champeaux* Jacqueline, *a)* Sors oraculi; les oracles en Italie sous la République et l'Empire / 'Sorts' et divination inspirée; pour une préhistoire des oracles italiques: MÉF 102 (1990) 271-302 / 801-828. – *b)* 'Pietas'; piété personnelle et piété collective à Rome: BBudé (1989) 263-279.

a757 **Coarelli** Filippo, I santuari del Lazio 1987 ➤ 5,a762: [R]Latomus 49 (1990) 716s (M. *Torelli*).

a757* **Colish** Marcia J., The Stoic tradition ... in Latin I-II 1985 ➤ 3,b52 ... 5,a763: [R]Speculum 65 (1990) 633-6 (Jill *Kraye*).

a758 *Codoñer* Carmen, Lexique du 'sacré' et réalités religieuses chez PÉTRONE: RPg 63 (1989) 47-59.

a758* *Corciulo di Giandomenico* Marisa, LUCREZIO; una proposta didattica tra l'antico e il moderno: Aufidus 8 (1989) 135-160.

a759 **Dionigi** Ivano, LUCREZIO; le parole e le cose. Bo 1988, Pàtron. 186 p. – ᴿRPg 63 (1989) 131-3 (J. *Dangel*).

a760 *Feldman* Louis H., The enigma of HORACE's thirtieth sabbath [Sat 1,69: better than the six other proposed solutions, 'the thirtieth, a sabbath' related to the New Moon and to Apollo]: ScrClasIsr 10 (1989s) 87-112.

a761 **Fishwick** Duncan, The imperial cult in the Latin West: ÉPR 108, 1987 → 3,b57; 5,a768: ᴿClasW 83 (1989s) 235 (C. R. *Phillips*); CritRR 3 (1990) 265-7 (H. D. *Betz*).

a762 *Fishwick* Duncan, *a*) DIO [Cassius 52.35] and Maecenas; the emperor and the ruler cult: Phoenix 44 (Toronto 1990) 267-275; – *b*) PRUDENTIUS and the cult of Divus Augustus: Historia 39 (1990) 475-486; – *c*) Dated inscriptions and the *feriale duranum* [calendar of rites prescribed for the Roman army everywhere]: Syria 65 (1988) 349-361.

a763 *Forsyth* P. Y., Call for Cybele: AncHB 4,4 (1990) 75-78.

a764 *Fredouille* Jean-Claude, Les écrivains et le sacré à Rome: → 5,786, Écrivains 1988/9, 85-115.

a765 *Giannantoni* Gabriele, *Vegetti* Mario, L'etica degli antichi: Elenchos 11 (1990) 335-347 / 349-352.

a766 ᵀᴱ**Godwin** J., LUCRETIUS, De rerum natura IV. Wmr 1986, Aris & P. xii-170 p. £8.25. – ᴿLatomus 49 (1990) 163s (F. *Desbordes*).

a767 *Guillaumont* François, CICÉRON et le sacré dans la religion des philosophes: BBudé (1989) 56-71.

a768 **Haudry** Jean, La religion cosmique des Indo-Européens [reprints] 1987 → 5,a771: ᴿRBgPg 68 (1990) 218-221 (Dominique *Briquel*: analyses nouvelles, suggestives); Salesianum 52 (1990) 151s (R. *Bracchi*).

a769 **Heck** E., *Mē theomacheîn* oder, Die Bestrafung des Gottesverächters ... römischer Religion: StudKlasPg 24, 1987 → 4,b672; 5,g731: ᴿGymnasium 97 (1990) 52s (R. *Klein*).

a770 *Hellegouarc'h* J., *Parce, precor* ... ou TIBULLE et la prière [à sa maîtresse; aux dieux]; étude stylistique: ILCL 14 (1989) 49-68.

a771 **Johnston** Sarah I., Hekate soteira; a study of Hecate's roles in the Chaldaean Oracles and related literature: AmClasSt 21. Atlanta 1990, Scholars. viii-192 p. – ᴿRÉLat 68 (1990) 242s (R. *Turcan*).

a772 *Kreitzer* Larry, Apotheosis of the Roman Emperor: BA 53 (1990) 210-7; ill. (coins).

a773 **Lane** E. N., Corpus cultus Iovis Sabazii 3. Conclusions: ÉPR 100. Leiden 1989, Brill. 68 p. – ᴿKernos 3 (1990) 391s (F. *Mora*).

a773* *a*) *Le Glay* Marcel, La place des affranchis dans la vie municipale et dans la vie religieuse [importante sous Octave, moins sous Tibère; ... Carthage]; – *b*) *Beschaouch* Azedine, Qu'est-ce qu'un 'idurio'? spiritualité punique et culture latine en Afrique romaine; – *c*) *Khanoussi* Mustapha, Mercure psychopompe en Afrique romaine; – *d*) *Sebaï* Leïla L., À propos du flaminat féminin dans les provinces africaines: MÉF 102 (1990) 621-638 / 639-646 / 647-9 / 651-686.

a774 *a*) *Loraux* Nicole, Che cos'è una dea? ᵀ*Marogna* Giorgia V.; – *b*) *Scheid* John, Indispensabili 'straniere'; ruoli religiosi delle donne a Roma, ᵀ*Zaidman* Louise B. → 498, Storia delle donne 1990, 13-55 / 424-464.

a775 **Mastandrea** Paolo, Lettori cristiani di SENECA filosofo: AntClasCr 28. Brescia 1988, Paideia. 99 p. Lit. 15.000. – ᴿGnomon 62 (1990) 649s (J. *Doignon*).

a776 **Meer** L. van der, The bronze liver of Piacenza 1987 ⮕ 4,b682; 5,a781: RArGlotIt 73 (1988) 162-4 (G. *Bonfante*: lode, suggerimenti); ClasPg 85 (1990) 67-71; 1 fig. (J. *Linderski*).

a777 **Momigliano** Arnaldo, Saggi di storia della religione romana; studi e lezioni 1983-86, EDi Donato Riccardo: Le Scienze Umane. Brescia 1988, Morcelliana. 203 p. 88-372-1336-0.

a778 **Moore** Timothy J., Artistry and ideology: LIVY's vocabulary of virtue: MgAltWiss 192. Fra 1989, Athenaeum. xii-248 p. DM 68. 3-610-09018-9. – RAntClas 59 (1990) 370s (J. *Wankenne*).

a779 **Mora** Fabio, Prosopografia Isiaca: ÉPR 113. Leiden 1990, Brill. xxii-526 p.; xi-162 p., 2 maps. *f* 240 + 90. – RCdÉ 65 (1990) 177s (G. *Nachtergael*).

a779* **Mynors** R. A. B., VIRGIL, Georgics. Ox 1990, Clarendon. xci-345 p. 0-19-814445-8.

a780 *Negri* Angela Maria, Sunt lacrimae rerum et mentem mortalia tangunt [Verg. Aen. 1,462]: StItFgC 81 (1988) 240-258.

a781 *Orr* David G., Learning from Lararia; notes on the household shrines of Pompeii: ⮕ 89, FJASHEMSKI Wilhelmina (1988) I, 293-9 + 8 fig.

a782 *Ozanam* Anne-Marie, Le mystère et le sacré dans le stoïcisme romain à l'époque néronienne: BBudé (1990) 275-288 [-316, al.].

a783 **Pailler** Jean-Marie, Bacchanalia; la répression de 186 av. J.-C.: 1988 ⮕ 5,a784: RAnÉCS 45 (1990) 919-921 (J. *Scheid*); RHR 207 (1990) 419-422 (Annie *Dubourdieu*).

a784 **Parke** H. W. (1903-1986), Sibyls and Sibylline prophecy in classical antiquity, EMcGing Brian C.: Croom Helm Clas. St., 1988 ⮕ 4,b685: RClasR 40 (1990) 174s (N. *Horsfall*: distressing); ÉchMClas 34 (1990) 459-462 (R. J. *Clark*).

a785 *Pekáry* Thomas, Das Opfer vor dem Kaiserbild: BonnJbb 186 (1986) 91-103.

a786 **Porte** Danielle, Les donneurs du sacré; le prêtre à Rome 1989 ⮕ 5,a787: RAntClas 59 (1990) 443-7 (J. *Poucet*).

a787 **Radke** Gerhard, Zur Entwicklung der Gottesvorstellung und der Gottesverehrung in Rom: ImpulsFor 50, 1987 ⮕ 5,a789: RGymnasium 97 (1990) 357-360 (W. *Fauth*); Latomus 49 (1990) 226-8 (G. *Freyburger*).

a788 ERoncali Renata, SENECA, Apokolokuntōsis. Lp 1990, Teubner. xxxiv-60 p. 3-322-00670-0.

a789 **Rutherford** R. B., The meditations of Marcus AURELIUS, a study: ClasMg. Ox 1989, Clarendon. xviii-282 p. 0-19-814879-8.

a790 [Hanlein] **Schäfer** Heidi, Veneratio Augusti; eine Studie zu den Tempeln des ersten römischen Kaisers. R 1985, Bretschneider. xviii-304 p.; 70 pl. – RLatomus 49 (1990) 218-220 (Christiane *Delplace*).

a791 *a) Scheid* John, La parole des dieux; l'originalité du dialogue des Romains avec leurs dieux; – *b) Garnsey* Peter, Propitiation et prosperité; religion et survivance de la cité: Opus 6ss (1987ss) 125-136 / 137-145.

a792 *Schmidt* Joël, Textes sacrés et textes mystiques du paganisme romain: RICathP 30 (1989) 91-105.

a793 **Segal** Charles, LUCRETIUS on death and anxiety; poetry and philosophy in De rerum natura. Princeton 1990, Univ. xii-279 p. 0-691-06826-7.

a794 **Sfameni Gasparro** Giulia, Soteriology... Cybele: ÉPR 103, 1985 [ital. 1979] ⮕ 1,a522; 3,b79*: RRÉLat 68 (1990) 243s (J. *Beaujeu*).

a795 **Turcan** Robert, Les cultes orientaux dans le monde romain 1989 ⮕ 5,a797: RJbAC 33 (1990) 248-250 (W. *Burkert*).

a796 **Turcan** R., Religion romaine, 1. les dieux; 2. le culte: IconRel 17/1s, 1988 ⇢ 4,b694; 5,a796: ᴿNRT 112 (1990) 629 (A. *Harvengt*).

a797 **Vanggaard** Jens H., The Flamen, a study in the history and sociology of Roman religion ᴰ1988 ⇢ 5,a797*; 87-7289-059-2: ᴿAntClas 59 (1990) 447-451 (J. *Poucet*); RHR 207 (1990) 94s (R. *Turcan*).

a798 **Vermeule** C., The cult images of imperial Rome 1987 ⇢ 3,b83: ᴿRBg-Pg 68 (1990) 231-3 (R. *Turcan*: repose sur la numismatique).

a799 *Veyne* Paul, *a)* La nouvelle piété sous l'Empire; s'asseoir auprès des dieux, fréquenter les temples: RPg 63 (1989) 175-194; – *b)* La Providence stoïcienne intervient-elle dans l'Histoire? [... CICÉRON, SÉNÈQUE]: Latomus 49 (1990) 553-574.

M4.5 **Mithraismus.**

a800 **Beck** Roger, Planetary gods... Mithras: ÉPR 109, 1988 ⇢ 4,b698; 5,a804: ᴿClasR 40 (1990) 328-330 (J. *Liebeschuetz*); JRS 80 (1990) 236s (J. R. *Hinnells*).

a801 *Callieri* Pierfrancesco, On the diffusion of Mithra images in Sasanian Iran; new evidence from a seal in the British Museum: EWest 40 (1990) 79-97; 9 fig.

a802 **Clauss** Manfred, Mithras; Kult und Mysterien. Mü 1990, Beck. 215 p.; 124 fig.; map. 3-406-34325-2.

a803 *Clauss* Manfred, Die sieben Grade des Mithras-Kultes: ZPapEp 82 (1990) 183-194 (dazu 195-7, *Merkelbach* R., Priestergrade?).

a804 *Clauss* Manfred, Sol invictus Mithras [auf deutsch]: Athenaeum 78 (1990) 423-450; 1 pl.

a805 *Duchesne-Guillemin* Jacques, Sur l'origine des mystères de Mithra: CRAI (1990) 281-5.

a806 *Edwards* M. J., HERODOTUS and Mithras; Histories 1,131: AmJPg 111 (1990) 1-4.

a807 **Geden** A. S., Mithraic sources in English [= ²Select passages illustrating Mithraism 1925]. Hastings UK 1990, Chthonios. vi-87 p. £15. 0-948366-20-6 [NTAbs 34,407].

a808 *Gordon* Richard, Authority, salvation and mystery in the mysteries of Mithras: ⇢ 179, Mem. TOYNBEE J. 1988, 45-80 + 11 pl.

a808* *a)* Hopfe Lewis M., Mithraism in Syria; – *b)* Ries Julien, Le culte de Mithra en Iran: ⇢ 828, ANRW 2/18/4 (1990) 2214-35 / 2728-75.

a809 *Kocsis* L., Inschriften aus dem Mithras-Heiligtum des Hauses des Tribunus Laticlavius im Legionslager von Aquincum aus dem 2.-3. Jahrhundert: AcArchH 41 (1989) 81-92; 10 fig. [94-98, *Fitz* J., proso-pographisch].

a810 **Merkelbach** Reinhold, Mithras 1984 ⇢ 65,9155 ... 4,b699: ᴿArKulturG 71 (1989) 230s (M. *Clauss*); Helmantica 40 (1989) 504-6 (L. *Amigo*).

a811 **Ulansey** David, The origins of the Mithraic mysteries; cosmology and salvation in the ancient world 1989 ⇢ 5,a808: ᴿBA 53 (1990) 174s (E. N. *Lane*); Times Lit.Supp. (L 27.VII.1990) 807s (J. D. *North*: 'star qualities') [< NTAbs 35,57].

a812 **Wauters** C. A., Mithras. Deventer 1985, Ankh-Hermes. 58 p. ƒ17,50. – ᴿKerkT 40 (1989) 160 (C. F. van *Andel*).

M5.1 *Divinitates Graeciae* – **Greek gods and goddesses.**

a813 **Alroth** Brita, Greek gods and figurines; aspects of the anthropomorphic dedications [diss. Uppsala]: Boreas 18, 1989 ⇢ 5,a812; 60 fig.: ᴿAJA 94 (1990) 505s (C. W. *Hedrick*); ClasR 40 (1990) 185s (Lucille *Burn*).

a814 **Arafat** K. W., Classical Zeus, a study in art and literature: MgClasArch. Ox 1990, Clarendon. xvii-225 p.; 40 pl.

a815 **Aubriot** Mme Danièle, Recherches sur la prière dans les conceptions religieuses de la Grèce ancienne, jusqu'à la fin du Vᵉ s. av. J.-C.: diss. d'État, P-Sorbonne 1989. – Kernos 3 (1990) 410.

a816 *Bader* Françoise, Pan [et Pūṣán]: RPg 63 (1989) 1-46.

a817 *a) Bader* Françoise, La langue des dieux en grec; – *b) Cheyns* André, La notion de *sébas* dans la poésie homérique: ➤ 5,786, Écrivains 1988/9, 247s / 245s [243s, *Aubriot* D., *thámbos*].

a818 *Ballabriga* Alain, Le dernier adversaire de Zeus; le mythe de Typhon dans l'épopée grecque archaïque: RHR 207 (1990) 4-30; Eng. 3.

a819 **Blundell** Mary Whitlock, Helping friends and harming enemies, a study in SOPHOCLES and Greek ethics 1989 ➤ 5,a818: ᴿRPg 63 (1989) 292-4 (A. *Machin*).

a820 *Brashear* William, A further note on an Argive votive relief of Selene: HarvTR [78 (1985) 439-443, *Patterson* S.] 83 (1990) 333-339; 340s, Patterson admits he had overlooked the 1855 comment and *Delatte* A. 1913, but has nothing to change.

a821 ᴱ**Bremmer** Ian, Interpretations of Greek mythology 1987 ➤ 3,b99; 5,a821: ᴿAthenaeum 78 (1990) 553-6 (Anna Lucia *D'Agata*); JHS 110 (1990) 246 (Helen *King*).

a822 *a) Brenk* Frederick E., I veri demoni greci 'nella nebbia ammantellati'? Esiodo e Plutarco; – *b) Bianchi* Ugo, Sulla demonologia del medio- e neoplatonismo: ➤ 693, Diavolo 1 (1988/90) 23-35 / 51-62.

a823 **Bruit-Zaidman** Louise, *Schmitt-Pantel* Pauline, La religion grecque: Cursus. P 1989, Colin. 190 p.; 23 fig.; map. 2-200-33038-3. – ᴿAntClas 59 (1990) 432s (Vinciane *Pirenne-Delforge*); ClasR 40 (1990) 501s (B. C. *Dietrich*: admirably clear).

a824 **Burkert** Walter, ❾ Apollo of Didyma and Olbia: VDI [1986/1, 25-64, *Rusajeva* A. S.] 193 (1990) 155-160; Eng. 160.

a825 **Caldwell** Richard, The origin of the gods; a psychoanalytic study of Greek theogonic myth. Ox 1989, Univ. Press. xvi-206 p.; 2 fig. £22.50. – ᴿClasR 40 (1990) 502s (P. *Walcot*: not for the serious student).

a826 *Camps i Gasct* Montserrat, Dona, ciutadania i religió a l'Atenes del s. V a.C.: Laurentianum 31 (1990) 19-26.

a827 *Chaniotis* Angelos, Drei kleinasiatische Inschriften zur griechischen Religion: EpAnat 15 (1990) 127-133; ❶ 134.

a828 **Clay** Jenny S., The politics of Olympus; form and meaning in the major Homeric hymns. Princeton 1989, Univ. xii-291 p. 0-691-06775-9.

a829 *a) Davies* J. K., The Greek states; religion and the state; – *b) Kirk* G. S., The development of ideas, 750 to 500 B.C.: ➤ 831, CAH² 4 (1988) 368-388 / 389-413.

a830 *De Fidio* Pia, Potere politico e funzione del sacro nelle società micenee: 111, ᶠLÉVÊQUE P., 4 (1990) 151-171.

a831 **Desautels** Jacques, Dieux et mythes de la Grèce ancienne; la mythologie gréco-romaine. Québec 1988, Univ. Laval. xii-652 p.; 129 fig.; 2 maps. C$45. 2-7637-7153-X. – ᴿAntClas 59 (1990) 436s (S. *Byl*); ClasR 40 (1990) 173 (M. *Grant*); Kernos 3 (1990) 388s (A. *Motte*); SR 19 (1990) 364s (G. *Berthiaume*).

a832 **Detienne** Marcel, Dionysos at large [à ciel ouvert, P 1986, Hachette, 2-01-011954-1; ital. 1987 ➤ 4,b726], ᵀ*Goldhammer* Arthur: Revealing Antiquity. CM 1989, Harvard Univ. 90 p. £13.50 [RelStR 17,159, Sarah I. *Johnston*: good]. – ᴿClasR 40 (1990) 173s (R. *Seaford*).

a833 **Edlund** Ingrid E. M.,   The gods and the place [Etruria, Magna Graecia] 1987 ➤ 5,a839: ᴿLatomus 49 (1990) 713-6 (M. *Torelli*).

a834 ᴱ**Edmunds** Lowell, Approaches to Greek myth. Baltimore 1990, Johns Hopkins Univ. vii-448 p.; ill. 0-8018-3863-0. 8 art.; p. 23-90, *Versnel* H. S., Myth and ritual.

a835 *Faraone* C. A., Aphrodite's *kestos* and apples for Atalanta; aphrodisiacs in early Greek myth and ritual: Phoenix 44 (Toronto 1990) 219-243.

a836 **Ferguson** John, Among the gods; an archaeological exploration of ancient Greek religion. L 1989, Routledge. xviii-249 p. £35. 0-415-02953-2. – ᴿClasR 40 (1990) 503s (B. C. *Dietrich*: subtitle unrealized).

a837 *a*) *Fol* Alexander, The Thracian Dionysos, I. Zagreus; – *b*) *Beschi* Luigi, Bendis, the great goddess of the Thracians, in Athens: Orpheus-Thrac 1 (1990) 37-45 / 29-36; 5 fig.

a838 *Fowden* Elizabeth, The early Minoan goddess; images of provision: JPrehRel 3s (1989s) 15-18; 5 fig.

a839 **Goodison** Lucy, Death, women and the sun; symbolism of regeneration in early Aegean religion: BInstClas supp. 53. L 1989, Institute of Classical Studies. 124 p. £40. 0-900587-56-3. – ᴿAntiquity 64 (1990) 969s (C. *Renfrew*).

a840 **Graf** Fritz, Griechische Mythologie; eine Einführung 1985 ➤ 2,8884; 3,b130: ᴿGrazBei 17 (1990) 273-7 (W. *Potscher*).

a841 ᴱ**Hägg** R., *Marinatos* N., Early Greek cult practice 1986/8 ➤ 5,792: ᴿAJA 94 (1990) 348s (Carla M. *Antonaccio*).

a842 *a*) *Hägg* Robin, Mycenaean religion in perspective; cult practices and beliefs; – *b*) *Marinatos* Nanno, A puberty rite at Thera; evidence from new frescoes: [abstracts of Rome Swedish Institute lectures] JPrehRel 3s (1989s) 48-51.

a842* *Hegyi* D., Prehellenic roots of the Greek cult of Apollo: ➤ 67, Mem. HAHN I., AcAntH 32 (1989) 5-21.

a843 **Henrichs** Albert, Die Götter Griechenlands; ihr Bild im Wandel der Religionswissenschaft; Thyssen-Auseinandersetzungen aus der Antike 49. Bamberg 1987, Buchner. – ᴿEos 78 (1990) 409-412 (M. *Winiarczyk* ❷).

a844 *Jouan* François, Les écrivains et le sacré en Grèce: ➤ 5,786, Écrivains 1988/9, 51-84.

a845 **Kerényi** Karl, *a*) Apollo; the wind, the spirit, and the god; four studies, ᵀ*Solomon* Jon: Dunquin Series 16. Dallas 1983, Spring. 76 p. – *b*) Athene, virgin and mother; a study of Pallas Athene, ᵀ*Stein* Murray. Z 1978, Spring. [iv-] 106 p. 0-88214-216-X; -09-7.

a846 *Kurke* Leslie, Pouring prayers; a formula of IE sacral poetry: JIndEur 17 (1989) 113-125.

a847 **Long** Charlotte R., The twelve gods of Greece and Rome: ÉPR 107, 1987 ➤ 3,b143: ᴿHZ 249 (1989) 131-3 (F. *Graf*).

a848 *Loucas-Durie* Éveline, Kinyras et la sacralisation de la fonction technique à Chypre; – *b*) *Malkin* Irad, Delphoi and the founding of social order in ancient Grace: Métis 4,1 (1989) 117-127 / 129-153.

a849 **Luck** Georg, Arcana mundi... texts 1985 ➤ 2,8901 ... 4,a862: ᴿHelios 15 (1988) 151-170 (C. R. *Phillips*).

a850 **Malkin** Irad, Religion and colonization in ancient Greece ᴰ1987 ➤ 4,b762; 5,a866: ᴿAthenaeum 78 (1990) 557-9 (G. *Maddoli*); Mnemosyne 43 (1990) 259s (J. H. *Croon*).

a851 *Marazov* Ivan, Aspects of the royal Hestia, I. Hestia and the idea of autochthonicity: Orpheus-Thrac 1 (1990) 73-89.

a852 **Marinatos** Nanno, Minoan sacrificial ritual 1986 ➤ 4,b763: ᴿAntClas 59 (1990) 562s (R. *Laffineur*); Gnomon 62 (1990) 140-144 (W.-D. *Niemeier*); JPrehRel 3s (1989s) 65-68 (Gisela *Walberg*: interesting, conjectural).

a853 **Muth** Robert, Einführung in die griechische und die römische Religion 1988 ➤ 5,a878: ᴿGymnasium 97 (1990) 48-52 (G. *Radke*).

a854 **O'Connor** E. M., Symbolum salacitatis; a study of the god Priapus as a literary character [< diss. Univ. California S. Barbara 1984]: StKlasPg 40. Fra 1989, Lang. 214 p. Fs 47. 3-8204-1078-3 [NTAbs 34,275].

a855 **Otto** Walter F., Dionysus, myth and cult: Dunquin series, 14. Dallas 1989, Spring. xxi-243 p.; 13 pl. 0-88214-214-3.

a856 **Paris** Ginette, *a*) Pagan grace; Dionysos, Hermes, and goddess memory in daily life. Dallas 1990, Spring. 152 p. $15 [JAAR 58,163]. – *b*) Pagan meditations; the worlds of Aphrodite, Artemis, and Hestia; ᵀ*Moore* Gwendolyn. Dallas 1986, Spring. 204 p. 0-88214-330-1.

a857 **Parker** W. H., Priapea, poems for a phallic god 1988 ➤ 4,b785: ᴿClasR 40 (1990) 31-33 (P. *Howell*: unfavoring); Gymnasium 97 (1990) 580-2 (H. *Gärtner*); Latomus 49 (1990) 681s (R. *Verdière*).

a858 *Riedweg* Christoph, The 'atheistic' fragment from Euripides' Bellerophontes (286N²): ILCL 15 (1990) 39-53.

a859 *Robertson* Noel, Some recent work in Greek religion and mythology [BURKERT W.; PUHVEL J. ...]: ÉchMClas 34 (1990) 419-442; 435, GIRARD in explaining everything explains nothing, least of all the origins of animal sacrifice.

a860 **Rudhardt** Jean, Le rôle d'Eros et d'Aphrodite dans les cosmogonies grecques 1986 ➤ 3,b178: ᴿRHR 207 (1990) 434s (C. *Jacob*).

a861 *Rudhardt* Jean, De la maternité chez les déesses grecques: RHR 207 (1990) 367-388.

a862 **Salmona** Bruno, La spiritualità dell'antica Grecia. R 1986, Studium. 256 p. Lit. 16.000. ᴿViPe 73 (1990) 148s (R. *Quintino*).

a862* **Sergent** Bernard, Homosexuality in Greek myth, ᵀ*Goldhammer* A. 1986 ➤ 3,b188: ᴿHistRel 30 (1990s) 311-3 (D. H. *Garrison*).

a863 ᴱ**Siems** A. K., Sexualität und Erotik in der Antike: WegFor 605, 1988 ➤ 5,556; DM 87, sb. 67: ᴿGymnasium 97 (1990) 86s (Ines *Stahlman*).

a864 **Simon** Erika, Eirene und Pax; Friedensgöttinnen in der Antike: Szb Fra 24/3, 1988 ➤ 4,b797: ᴿAnzAltW 43 (1990) 257-260 (Gerda *Schwarz*); Gymnasium 97 (1990) 470-2 (G. *Radke*).

Sissa Giulia, *Detienne* Marcel, La vie quotidienne des dieux grecs 1989 ➤ d205.

a865 **Sobel** Hildegard, Hygieia, die Göttin der Gesundheit. Da 1990, Wiss. 136 p.; 20 pl.

a866 **Vernant** Jean-Pierre, *Vidal-Naquet* Pierre, Myth and tragedy in ancient Greece [ch. 1-7, 1972; ch. 8-17, 1986 ➤ 4,b807], ᵀ*Lloyd* Janet. ... 1988, Zone. 527 p. $33; pa. $19. 0-942299-18-3; -9-1. – ᴿJRel 70 (1990) 677s (M. N. *Nagler*, also on Myth and society 1988); RelStR 16 (1990) 339s (R. A. *Swanson*).

a867 **Versnel** H. S., Ter unus, Isis, Dionysos, Hermes: Inconsistencies in Greek and Roman religion 1. Leiden 1990, Brill. xiv-268 p. ƒ120 [TR 86,346].

a868 **Veyne** Paul, Did the Greeks believe in their myths? [1983 ➤ 64,9464], ᵀ*Wissing* Paula. Ch 1988, Univ. xii-161 p. £20; pa. £8.75. – ᴿClasR 40 (1990) 172 (S. *Goldhill*: cites HUSSERL and HEIDEGGER instead of SYME and FINLEY); JHS 110 (1990) 246 (Helen *King*).

a869 **Warren** Peter, Minoan religion as ritual action: SIMA pocket 72, 1988
➤ 5,a915: ᴿJPrehRel 3s (1989s) 68s (Nanno *Marinatos*).

a870 *Winiarczyk* Marek, Methodisches zum antiken Atheismus: RheinMus
133 (1990) 1-15 [Bibliographie in Elenchos 10 (1989) 103-192].

M5.2   *Philosophorum critica religionis;*   **Greek philosopher-religion.**

a871 **Alsina Clota** José, El Neoplatonismo; síntesis del espiritualismo antiguo: Auctores, textos y temas, filosofía 27. Barc 1989, Anthropos.
159 p. 84-7658-178-5.

a872 *Aujoulat* Noël, De la phantasia et du pneuma stoïciens, d'après SEXTUS
Empiricus, au corps lumineux néo-platonicien: Pallas 34 (1988) 123-146.

a873 [*Dörrie* Heinrich], **Baltes** Matthias, (*Mann* Friedhelm), Der Platonis-
mus in der Antike; Grundlagen — System — Entwicklung. Stu-Bad
Cannstatt 1987-90, Frommann-Holzboog. I. xvii-557 p.; II. xvi-531 p.
3-7728-1153-1; -4-X.

a874 *Banu* Ion, La philosophie de Gorgias, une ontologie du lógos: RPg 61
(1987) 234-244; 63 (1989) 195-212.

a875 **Barimah-Apau** Michael, The God of PLATO in the dialogues. R 1989,
Pont. Univ. Urbaniana. xvi-202 p.

a876 *Becchi* Francesco, A proposito degli studi sugli scritti etici di PLU-
TARCO: AtenRom 35 (1990) 1-16.

a877 ᵀᴱ**Behr** Charles A., P. Aelius ARISTIDES, the complete works, I.
Orations I-XVI. Leiden 1986, Brill. 536 p. *f*220. – ᴿSecC 7 (1989s)
185-7 (R. J. *Wilken*).

a878 **Bostock** David, PLATO's Theaetetus. Ox 1988, Clarendon. 296 p.
£17.50. 0-19-824489-4. - ᴿGnomon 62 (1990) 107-113 (E. *Heitsch*).

a879 ᴱ**Boudouris** K. J., Ionian philosophy [meeting in Samos 1988]. Athens
1989, International Asn. for Greek Philosophy. 454 p. – ᴿScrClasIsr 10
(1989s) 140-6 (S. *Scolnicov*).

a880 ᴱ**Calame** Claude, Métamorphoses du mythe en Grèce antique 1987/8
➤ 4,b719; 5,a831: ᴿClasR 40 (1990) 324-6 (R. G. A. *Buxton*); MélSR 47
(1990) 163 (L. *Debarge*); RBgPg 68 (1990) 198s (L. *Jerphagnon*); ScEsp 42
(1990) 127s (J. *Harvey*).

a881 **Capasso** Mario, Comunità senza rivolta; quattro saggi sull'epicureismo;
préf. *Gigante* Marcello: Saggi 26. N 1988, Bibliopolis. 177 p. – ᴿRPg 63
(1989) 130s (Antoinette *Novara*).

a882 **Capizzi** Antonio, The cosmic republic; notes for a non-peripatetic
history of the birth of philosophy in Greece: Philosophica 3. Amst 1990,
Gieben. [x-] 521 p. 90-70265-55-9.

a883 **Casey** John, Pagan virtues; an essay in ethic. Ox 1990, Clarendon.
242 p. £27.50. 0-19-82958-6. – ᴿExpTim 102 (1990s) 154 (G. J. *Warnock*
hints that the gulf is not so much between pagan/NT as between
Catholic/Protestant).

a884 **Combès** Joseph, Études néoplatoniciennes: Krisis. Grenoble 1989,
Millon. 315 p. – ᴿParPass 253 (1990) 313-320 (A. *Lingutti*).

a885 *Cook* Albert, Equanimity and danger; distribution of questions and
style of confrontation in the four dialogues around Socrates' trial:
Arethusa 23 (1990) 255-279.

a886 **Copleston** Frederick, Storia della filosofia I. Grecia e Roma [1946,
ʳᵉᵛ1956], ᵀʳᵉᵛ*Grilli* Alberto. Brescia 1988, Paideia. 655 p. Lit. 60.000.
88-394-0406-6. – ᴿAntClas 59 (1990) 420s (O. *Ballériaux*: unique en son
genre); Latomus 49 (1990) 906s (L. *Jerphagnon*).

a887 **Daiber** H., Aᴇᴛɪᴜs Arabus; die Vorsokratiker in arabischer Über-lieferung: Wsb 1980, Akad. Wiss. 33. – ᴿOrientalia 59 (1990) 333s (G. M. *Browne*).

a888 **Engberg-Pedersen** Troels, The Stoic theory of oikeiosis; moral development and social interaction in early Stoic philosophy: Studies in Hellenistic Civilization 2. Aarhus 1990, University. 278 p. 87-7288-323-5.

a889 **Ferber** R., Pʟᴀᴛᴏs Idee des Guten²ʳᵉᵛ [¹1984]. St-Augustin 1989, Richarz. 388 p. – ᴿElenchos 11 (1990) 360-4 (B. *Centrone*).

a890 **Ferguson** John, Morals and values in ancient Greece: Classical World. Bristol 1989, Classical. viii-103 p.; 9 fig. £5. – ᴿClasR 40 (1990) 498s (P. *Walcot*).

a891 **Ferrari** G. R. F., Listening to the cicadas; a study of Pʟᴀᴛᴏ's Phaedrus 1987 → 4,b738: ᴿAmJPg 111 (1990) 403-8 (N. D. *Smith*); HeythJ 31 (1990) 374s (J. *Ferguson* †).

a892 *Fischer* Norbert, *a*) Menschsein als Möglichsein; Pʟᴀᴛᴏɴs Menschenbild angesichts der Paradigmendiskussion in der Platonforschung: TüTQ 170 (1990) 23-41; – *b*) Philosophieren als Sein zum Tode; zum Interpretation von Platons 'Phaidon': FreibZ 37 (1990) 1-30.

a892* *Freyer-Schauenburg* Brigitte, Zum Bildnis des Demokrit: MiDAI-R 96 (1989) 313-331; pl. 62-77.

a893 **Gadamer** Hans-G., The idea of the good in Platonic-Aristotelian philosophy 1986 → 5,a845· ᴿHeythJ 31 (1990) 105s (J. *Ferguson* †).

a894 *Gaudin* Claude, Lectio difficilior; le système dans la théorie platonicienne de l'âme selon l'interprétation de M. Gᴜᴇʀᴏᴜʟᴛ: Phronesis 25,1 (1990) 47-82.

a895 **Griswold** Charles L.ᴶ, Self-knowledge in Pʟᴀᴛᴏ's 'Phaedrus'. NHv 1986, Yale Univ. xii-315 p. £28.50. – ᴿHeythJ 31 (1990) 103s (J. *Ferguson* †).

a896 **Heidegger** Martin, Vom Wesen der Weisheit; zu Pʟᴀᴛᴏɴs Höhlengleichnis und Theätet, ᴱ*Mörchen* Hermann: Gesamtausgabe 34. Fra 1988, Klostermann. 338 p. – ᴿTPhil 65 (1990) 445-7 (J. *Cesar das Neves*).

a897 *a*) *Hock* Ronald F., A dog in the manger; the Cynic Cynulcus among Athenaeus's deipnosophists; – *b*) *Vorster* Willem S., Stoics and early Christians on blessedness: → 122, ꜰMᴀʟʜᴇʀʙᴇ A., Greeks 1990, 20-37 / 38-51.

a898 **Hülser** Karlheinz, Die Fragmente zur Dialektik der Stoiker [1. ...] 2.-3, 1987; 4. 1988. Stu, Fromman-Holzboog. p. 406-1919. – ᴿTPhil [63 (1988) 398-400] 65 (1990) 106-110 (F. *Ricken*).

a899 ᵀᴱ**Inwood** Brad, *Gerson* L. P., Hellenistic philosophy; introductory readings. Indianapolis 1988, Hackett. xvi-266 p. $26.50; pa. $7. – ᴿClasR 40 (1990) 71s (G. B. *Kerferd*).

a900 **Irwin** Terence, Classical thought. Ox 1989, UP. 206 p. $A60. 0-1921-9196-9. – ᴿAncHRes 20 (1990) 127-130 (K. R. *Jackson*: a masterpiece; first of a projected Oxford History of Philosophy).

a901 **Isnardi Parente** M., L'eredità di Pʟᴀᴛᴏɴᴇ nell'Accademia antica. Mi 1989, Guerini. 94 p. – ᴿElenchos 11 (1990) 384s (B. *Centrone*).

a901* **Ivanka** Endre von, Plato christianus; la réception du platonisme chez les Pères de l'Église: [reprints, Einsiedeln 1984]ᵀ: Théologiques. P 1990, PUF. 469 p. F 265 [NRT 113,772, B. *Pottier*: admirable].

a902 *Lafrance* Yvon, La théorie platonicienne de la *doxa*. P/Montréal 1981, BLettres/Bellarmin. 2-89007-271-6 / P 2-251-22607-3. – ᴿRHPR 70 (1990) 131s (J. *Frère*).

a903 *Lévy* Carlos, Cɪᴄᴇ́ʀᴏɴ et le Moyen Platonisme; le problème du souverain bien selon Pʟᴀᴛᴏɴ: RÉLat 68 (1990) 50-65.

a904 **Lloyd** Anthony C.,   The anatomy of Neoplatonism.   Ox 1990, Clarendon.   ix-198 p.   0-19-824229-8.

a905 **Long** A. A., *Sedley* D. N.,   The Hellenistic philosophers 2, 1987 ➤ 3, b142 ... 5,a861:   ᴿAntClas 59 (1990) 422-4 (O. *Balleriaux*); Biblica 71 (1990) 137-141 (F. E. *Brenk*); HeythJ 31 (1990) 230-2 (A. H. *Armstrong*); JHS 110 (1990) 199-202 (R. W. *Sharples*); Latomus 49 (1990) 225s (A. *Grilli*, ital.); Phoenix 44 (Toronto 1990) 186-9 (J. *Brunschwig*, franç.).

a906 **Mansfeld** J.,   Studies in later Greek philosophy and Gnosticism: CS 292, 1989 ➤ 5,311:   ᴿClasR 40 (1990) 75-77 (J. *Dillon*).

a907 **Miller** Mitchell H.ᴶ,   PLATO's 'Parmenides'; the conversion of the soul.   Princeton 1986, Univ.   xiii-299 p.   £20.10. – ᴿHeythJ 31 (1990) 104s (J. *Ferguson*).

a908 **Morgan** Michael L.,   Platonic piety; philosophy and ritual in fourth-century Athens.   NHv 1990, Yale Univ.   x-273 p.   0-300-04517-4.

a909 *Morris* T. F.,   PLATO's Euthyphro: HeythJ 31 (1990) 309-323.

a910 *Noël* Marie-Pierre,   La persuasion et le sacré chez Gorgias: BBudé (1989) 139-151.

a911 ᴱ**Patzer** Andreas,   Der historische Sokrates: WegFo 585, 1986 ➤ 4,456; DM 79.   3-534-08380-6:   ᴿEos 77 (1989) 357-361 (M. *Winiarczyk*).

a912 **Places** Édouard des,   JAMBLIQUE, Protreptique: Coll. Budé.   P 1989, BLettres.   viii-172 (doubles) p.   2-251-00397-5. – ᴿAntClas 59 (1990) 346-9 (O. *Balleriaux*).

a913 *Places* Édouard des,   Chronique de la philosophie religieuse des Grecs (1988-1990): BBudé (1990) 410-427.

a914 *Places* Édouard des,   Ellenismo: ➤ 838, DizTF 1990, 379-381 (850-2, Platonismo cristiano).

a915 **Reesor** Margaret E.,   The nature of man in early Stoic philosophy 1989 ➤ 5,a891; also NY 1989, St. Martin's.   vii-179 p. $45 [RelStR 17,158, G. E. *Kessler*: on *télos*, *dóxa*, and other narrowly linguistic concerns].

a916 **Richard** Marie-Dominique,   L'enseignement oral de PLATON; une nouvelle interprétation du platonisme 1986 ➤ 3,b175; F 149:   ᴿAntClas 59 (1990) 308 (M. *Meulder*).

a917 **Romilly** J. de,   Les grands sophistes dans l'Athènes de Périclès 1988 ➤ 5,a892; F 100:   ᴿJHS 110 (1990) 238s (G. B. *Kerferd*); NVFr 64 (1989) 155s (F. X. *Putallaz*).

a918 ᵀᴱ**Rowe** C. J.,   PLATO, Phaedrus.   Wmr 1986, Aris & P.   viii-224 p.   £18.75; pa. £8.25. – ᴿClasR 40 (1990) 232-4 (D. B. *Robinson*).

a919 *a*) *Rudhardt* Jean,   Dans quelle mesure et par quelles images les mythes des grecs ont-ils symbolisé le néant? ; – *b*) *Létoublon* Françoise,   La notion de non-être dans l'histoire de la langue grecque archaïque; – *c*) *Couloubaritsis* Lambros,   La logique du mythe et la question du non-être: RTPhil 122 (1990) 303-312 / 313-322 / 323-340 [-430, *al.*].

a920 *Rundgren* Frithiof,   Arabische Beiträge zur Geschichte des Stoizismus: ➤ 184, ᶠVITESTAM G.,   OrSuec 38s (1989s) 149-157.

a921 ᴱ**Saffrey** H. D., *Westerink* L. G.,   PROCLUS, Théologie platonicienne 1987 ➤ 5,a895:   ᴿEmerita 58 (1990) 153s (E. A. *Ramos Jurado*); Gymnasium 97 (1990) 54-56 (M. *Erler*).

a921* **Saffrey** H. D.,   Recherches sur le néoplatonisme après Plotin: HistDoctAntClas 14.   P 1990, Vrin.   317 p.   2-7116-1024-1.

a922 *Seeck* Gustav A.,   Die Frage nach der Tugend (PLATON, CICERO, HABERMAS, JONAS): Gymnasium 97 (1990) 289-304.

a923 **Stone** I. F.,   The trial of Socrates.   L 1988, Cape.   xi-282 p.   £13. – ᴿClasR 40 (1990) 60s (Elizabeth *Telfer*); JHS 110 (1990) 239s (K. J. *Dover*).

a924 *Thesleff* Holger, Divine and human law in early Platonism: ➤ 560, Law 1988/90, 91-108.

a925 *a) Thesleff* Holger, Theaitetos and Theodoros; – *b) Jatakari* Tuija, Der jüngere Sokrates [... vermutlicher Lehrer des Aristoteles: wirklich PLATON selbst]: Arctos 24 (1990) 147-159 / 29-45.

a926 **Vogel** Cornelia J., Rethinking PLATO and Platonism: Mnemosyne supp. 92, 1986 ➤ 3,b197: ᴿAntClas 59 (1990) 307 (M. *Meulder*); Elenchos 11 (1990) 114-8 (B. *Centrone*).

a927 ᴱ**Westerink** L. G., Prolégomènes à la philosophie de PLATON, ᵀ*Trouillard* J. (*Segonds* A. P.): Coll. Budé. P 1990, BLettres. xcix-103 (doubles) p. 2-251-00412-2.

M5.3 *Mysteria Eleusinia; Hellenistica;* **Mysteries, Hellenistic cults.**

a928 *Åström* Paul, *Reese* David S., Triton shells in East Mediterranean [... Cyprus] cults: JPrehRel 3s (1989s) 5-14; 7 fig.

a929 *a) Åström* Paul, A Cypriote cult scene; – *b) Dietrich* B. C., A Minoan symbol of renewal; – *c) Loucas* Ioannis & Eveline, The Megaron of Lykosoura and some prehistoric telesteria, ᵀ*Leuren* J. van: JPrehR 2 (Göteborg 1988) 5-11; 5 fig. / 12-24 / 25-34; 2 fig.

a929* *Aubert* J.-J., Threatened wombs; aspects of ancient uterine magic: GrRByz 30 (1990) 421-449.

a930 *Berardi* Elisabetta, PLUTARCO e la religione; l'*eusébeia* come giusto mezzo fra *deisidaimonía* e *atheótēs*: CivClasCr 11,2 (1990) 141-170.

ᴱ**Bilde** Per, *al.*, Religion and religious practice in the Seleucid kingdom 1990 ➤ 325*.

a931 *Brashear* William, Zauberformular [P. Berol 11734]: ArPapF 36 (1990) 49-74.

a932 ᴱ**Brenk** F., Miscellanea Plutarchea 1985/6 ➤ 2,521; 3,b101: ᴿEmerita 57 (1989) 376-8 (Manuela *García Valdes*).

a933 *Briquel* Dominique, Divination étrusque et mantique grecque; la recherche d'une origine hellénique de l'Etrusca disciplina: Latomus 49 (1990) 321-342.

a934 **Burkert** Walter, Antike Mysterien; Funktion und Gehalt. Mü 1990, Beck. 153 p.; 12 fig. – ᴿWissWeis 53 (1990) 231s (C. *Auffarth*); ZMissRW 74 (1990) 305-7 (W. *Blümer*).

a934* **Burkert** W., Ancient mystery cults 1987 ➤ 3,b103 ... 5,a827: ᴿAmHR 95 (1990) 140s (Emily *Vermeule*); CritRR 2 (1989) 288-290 (L. H. *Martin*).

a935 *a) Burkert* W., Antike Mysterien; eine Einführung; – *b) März* C.-P., 'Selig, wer jenes geschaut ...'. Initiation und Initiationsriten bei den Mysterien; – *c) Zeller* D., Sterbende Götter als Identifikationsfiguren: BiKi 45 (1990) 118-124 / 125-131 / 132-9.

Daszewski Wiktor A., Dionysos der Erlöser 1985 ➤ e927.

a936 *a) Dentzer* Jean-Marie, Le Sanctuaire syrien; – *b) Gawlikowski* Michel, Les temples dans la Syrie à l'époque hellénistique et romaine; – *c) Teixidor* Javier, Sur quelques aspects de la vie religieuse en Syrie à l'époque hellénistique et romaine: ➤ 481, Syrie II (1989) 297-322; fig. 61-70 / 323-346; fig. 71-83 / 81-95.

a937 **Dowden** Ken, Death and the maiden; girl's initiation rites in Greek mythology. L 1989, Routledge. x-257 p.; 8 maps. 0-415-01263-5 [Kernos 4,338, P. *Bonnechère*].

a938 **Frey** Martin, Untersuchungen zur Religion und zur Religionspolitik des Kaisers Elagabal: Historia Einz 62. Stu 1989, Steiner. iv-125 p.

DM 36. 3-515-05370-0. – ᴿAntClas 59 (1990) 451s (Cécile *Bertrand-Dagenbach*).

a939 **Freyburger-Galland** M. & *Freyburger* G., *al.*, Sectes religieuses en Grèce et à Rome dans l'antiquité païenne 1986 ➤ 2,8877 ... 5,a843: ᴿAntClas 59 (1990) 435s (B. *Rochette*).

a940 **Giebel** Marion, Das Geheimnis der Mysterien; antike Kulte in Griechenland, Rom und Ägypten. Z 1990, Artemis. 250 p. 3-7608-1027-6 [OIAc S90].

a941 **Graf** Fritz, Nordionische Kulte; religionsgeschichtliche und epigraphische Untersuchungen zu den Kulten von Chios, Erythrai, Klazomenai und Phokaia: BHelvRom 21, 1985 ➤ 2,8885; 5,a848: ᴿAntClas 59 (1990) 462s (A. *Martin*).

a941* **Harrauer** Christine, Meliuchos... in Zaubertexten 1987 ➤ 3,b133: ᴿBO 47 (1990) 366-8 (L. *Kákosy*).

a942 **Horst** Pieter W. van der, De onbekende God... de joodse en hellenistische achtergrond 1988 ➤ 4,207 (not 'Der...'): ᴿNedTTs 44 (1990) 69-71 (H. J. W. *Drijvers*).

Horst Pieter W. van der, *Mussies* Gerard, Studies on the Hellenistic background of the NT 1990 ➤ 4191.

a943 **Johnston** S., Hekate soteira; a study of Hekate's roles in the Chaldean Oracles and related literature [diss. Cornell, ᴰ*Clinton* K.] AmClasSt 21. Atlanta 1990, Scholars. viii-192 p. $18; pa. $14. 1-55540-426-X; -7-8 [NTAbs 34,409].

a944 *Kákosy* László, From fertility to cosmic symbolism; outlines of the history of the cult of Apis: AcClasDebrecen 26 (1990) 3-7.

a945 ᴱ**Merkelbach** Reinhold, *Totti* Maria, Abrasax; ausgewählte Papyri religiösen und magischen Inhalts, 1. Gebete: Rh/Wf Akad, Abh.Papyr-Colon 17. Opladen 1990, Westdeutscher-V. xii-252 p.; 3 pl. 3-531-09927-2 [OIAc S90].

a945* **Schröder** Stephen, PLUTARCHS Schrift De Pythiae oraculis; Text, Einleitung und Kommentar: Beiträge zur Altertumskunde 8. Stu 1990, Teubner. xxvii-474 p. 3-519-07457-5.

a946 **Schwarz** Gerda, Triptolemos; Ikonographie einer Agrar- und Mysteriengottheit: GrazBei supp. 2. Graz-Horn 1987, Berger. xiii-260 p.; 25 pl. – ᴿAJA 94 (1990) 351s (Susan G. *Cole*: detailed, careful).

a947 **Sissa** Giulia, Greek virginity [Le corps virginal 1987], ᵀ*Goldhammer* Arthur: Revealing Antiquity 3. CM 1990, Harvard. [viii-] 240 p. 0-674-36320-5.

a948 ᴱ**Sørensen** J. Podemann, Rethinking religion... Hellenistic (K April 1984) 1989 ➤ 5,a902: ᴿClasR 40 (1990) 327s (J. G. *Griffiths*); RHR 207 (1990) 205s (R. *Turcan*).

a949 *Sourvinou-Inwood* Christiane, What is *polis* religion?: ➤ 759, Greek city 1986/90, 295-322.

a950 *Świderek* Anna, La cité grecque et l'évolution de la mentalité religieuse dans les premiers temps de l'époque hellénistique: Eos 78 (1990) 259-272.

a951 **Valglio** Ernesto, Divinità e religione in Plutarco. Genova 1988, Comp.Librai. 292 p. – ᴿOrpheus 10 (1989) 495-8 (C. *Bevegni*).

a952 ᴱ**Wimbush** V. L., Ascetic behaviour in Greco-Roman antiquity, a sourcebook: StAntChr. Mp 1990, Fortress. 0-8006-3105-6 [BL 91,161].

M5.5 **Religiones anatolicae.**

Alp Sedat, Beiträge zur Erforschung des hethitischen Tempels 1983 ➤ d791.

a953 *Archi* Alfonso, The names of the primeval gods [Hurrian]: ➤ 160*, Mem. SCHULER E. v., Orientalia 59 (1990) 114-129.

a954 *Beckman* Gary, The Hittite 'Ritual of the Ox' (CTH 760.1.2-3): Orientalia 59 (1990) 34-55.

a955 **Borghouts** J. F., 'Duizend goden van Chatti en duizend goden van Egypte'; de relaties tussen Egypte en de Hettieten: Schatten uit Turkije. Leiden 1986, Ned.Inst.Nab. Oosten. 30 p. [OIAc S90].

a956 **Buffo** L., I re ellenistici e i centri religiosi dell'Asia Minore. F 1985, Nuova Italia. 364 p. [Mnemosyne 44, 267-9, H. W. *Pleket*].

a957 *Güterbock* Hans G., A religious text from Maşat: ➤ 3, Mem. ALKIM U., 1986, 205-214.

a957* *Dinçol* Ali M., Ein Hurro-Hethitisches Festritual *(Ḫ)išuwaš*: Belleten 53,206ss (1989) 1-30.

a958 *Haas* Volkert, *Šeḫur* 'Horn' und *šeḫuriya* 'harnen' in hethitischen Ritualanweisungen: AltOrF 16 (1989) 182-4.

a958* *a) Haas* Volkert, Die hurritisch-hethitischen Rituale der Beschwörerin Allaituraḫ(ḫ)i und ihr literarhistorischer Hintergrund; – *b) Wegner* Ilse, Grammatikalische und lexikalische Untersuchungen hurritischer Beschwörungsformeln aus Boğazköy: ➤ 801*, Hurriter 1988, 117-143 / 145-155.

a959 *Hoffmann* Inge, Die Schlange im Bett; Anlässe für Rituale bei den Hethitern. AltOrF 17 (1990) 186-8.

a960 ᵀ**Hoffner** Harry A., Hittite myths, ᴱ*Beckman* Gary M.: SBL WritAW 2. Atlanta 1990, Scholars. xi-92 p.; map. 1-55540-481-2.

a961 **Hutter** Manfred, Behexung, Entsühnung und Heilung... Tunnawiya 1988 ➤ 4,b815; 5,a925: ᴿBO 47 (1990) 159-162 (G. *Beckman*); CBQ 52 (1990) 516-8 (M. S. *Moore*); OLZ 85 (1990) 667s (I. *Hoffmann*); ZDMG 140 (1990) 152-4 (O. *Soysal*).

a962 *a) Imparati* Fiorella, Obligations et manquements envers la divinité Pirwa; – *b) Kammenhuber* Annelies, Marduk und Santa in der hethitischen Überlieferung des 2. Jt.s v. Chr.: ➤ 160*, Mcm. SCHULER E. v., Orientalia 59 (1990) 166-187 / 188-195.

a963 **Jakob-Rost** Liane, Hethitische Rituale und Festbeschreibungen: KaB 59, 1989 ➤ 5,a926: ᴿOLZ 85 (1990) 546-9 (V. *Haas*).

a964 *Orel* Vladimir E., Phrygian religion and rituals; Indo-European and non-Indo-European components: Orpheus-Thrac 1 (1990) 107-9.

a964* *a) Oster* R. E., Ephesus as a religious center under the Principate; I. Paganism before Constantine; – *b) MacKay* Theodora S., The major sanctuaries of Pamphylia and Cilicia; – *c) Frei* Peter, Die Götterkulte Lykiens in der Kaiserzeit: ➤ 828, ANRW 2/18/3 (1990) 1661-1728 / 2045-2129 / 1729-1864.

a965 ᴱ**Pecchioli Daddi** Franca, *Polvani* Anna Maria, La mitologia ittita: TestiVOA 4, Asia Minore 1. Brescia 1990, Paideia. 185 p. Lit. 30.000.

a966 **Popko** M., Hethitische Rituale: KaB 58, 1988 ➤ 4,b824: ᴿOLZ 85 (1990) 416-8 (V. *Haas*: Verbesserungen); ZAss 80 (1990) 146-151 (S. *Košak*).

a967 **Wagner** Jörg, Kommagene, Heimat der Götter. Dortmund 1987, Harenberg. 184 p. DM 24,80. – ᴿHZ 251 (1990) 663s (E. *Olshausen*).

---

a967* *a) Russell* J. R., Pre-Christian Armenian religion; – *b) Esbroeck* M.

van, La religion géorgienne pre-chrétienne: ➤ 828, ANRW 2/18/4 (1990) 2679-2692/2694-2725.

M6   Religio canaanaea, syra.

a968 *Ahlström* Gösta W., The bull figurine from Dhahrat et-Tawileh [8k S Jenin]: BASOR 280 (1990) 77-82; 2 fig.

a969 **Amir** David, ❿ *Elim vegiborim; alilot kᵉnaʿaniyot bᵉUgarit...* [1986 ➤ 2,8953; 4,b829]. Dan 1987, Bet Usiškin. xvi-243 p. – ᴿBO 47 (1990) 180-3 (G. del *Olmo Lete*); Syria 65 (1988) 457s (A. *Caquot*: remplace Z. RIN 1968, superficiel).

a970 **Barker** Margaret, The older testament... royal cult 1987 ➤ 3,b237... 5,a937: ᴿJBL 109 (1990) 335-7 (G. W. E. *Nickelsburg*: self-destructing tissue of speculation).

a971 **Baudler** Georg, Erlösung vom Stiergott; christliche Gotteserfahrung im Dialog mit Mythos und Religionen. Mü 1989, Kösel. 436 p. DM 48. 3-7668-0864-8. – ᴿActuBbg 27 (1990) 238s (J. *Boada*); ArTGran 53 (1990) 338s (E. *Barón*); EvKomm 23 (1990) 567s (Udo *Tworuschka*); TGegw 33 (1990) 215 (B. *Häring*); TGL 80 (1990) 209s (R. *Dieckmann*); TPhil 65 (1990) 294-6 (K. *Mertes*); TsTNijm 30 (1990) 327 (P. A. van *Gennip*); ZkT 112 (1990) 197-9 (R. *Schwager*).

a971* *a) Bilde* Per, Atargatis/Dea Syria; Hellenization of her cult in the Hellenistic-Roman period?; – *b) Zahle* Jan, Religious motifs on Seleucid coins; – *c) Teixidor* Javier, Interpretations and misinterpretations of the East in Hellenistic times: ➤ 325*, *Bilde*/Seleucid 1990, 151-187 / 125-136 + 2 pl. / 66-78.

a972 *Bird* Phyllis, Women's religion in ancient Israel: ➤ 4,851, ᴱ**Lesko** Barbara S., Women's earliest records 1987/9, 283-298 (-302, responses).

a973 **Block** Daniel J., The gods of the nations; studies in ancient Near Eastern national theology 1988 ➤ 5,a939: ᴿExpTim 102 (1990s) 245 (J. *Day*: Yahweh compared to Chemosh, Milkom, Qaus, about whom we know very little).

a974 **Bonnet** Corinne, Melqart, cultes...: StPhoen 8, 1988 ➤ 4,b839; 5,a940: ᴿBiblica 71 (1990) 276-9 (F. *Israel*); BO 47 (1990) 184-8 (H. M. *Barstad*); JAOS 110 (1990) 590-2 (M. S. *Smith*); OrLovPer 20 (1989) 259s (E. *Lipiński*); RStFen 18 (1990) 227-9 (S. *Ribichini*); ZAW 102 (1990) 144 (I. *Kottsieper*).

a975 *Bordreuil* Pierre, À propos de Milkou, Milkart et Milkʿashtart: ➤ 164, ᶠSEGERT S., *Sopher* 1990, 11-21.

a975* *Bordreuil* Pierre, *Pardee* Dennis, Le papyrus du *marzeaḥ*: ➤ 175, ᶠSZNYCER M., Semitica 38 (1990) 49-68; phot. p. 48 et VII-X après 68.

a976 *Bovati* Pietro, La missione nella religione dell'antico Israele: ➤ 529, RicStoB 2 (1990) 25-44.

a978 *Branden* A. Van den, Les dieux des Patriarches: BbbOr 32 (1990) 27-56.

a979 **Caquot** A. *al.*, Textes ougaritiques [I. mythes et légendes 1974] II. Religieux et rituels 1989 ➤ 5,a944: ᴿPEQ 121 (1989) 157s (J. F. *Healey*).

a980 *Clifford* Richard J., *a)* Phoenician religion: BASOR 279 (1990) 55-64; – *b)* Pantheons of [Phoenician] gods: Archaeology 43,2 (1990) 29.

a981 ᶠCROSS Frank M., Ancient Israelite religion, ᴱ**Miller** P. D.... 1987 ➤ 3,42; 4,b842: ᴿBSO 52 (1989) 334s (J. *Wansbrough*); Gregorianum 71 (1990) 379-381 (G. L. *Prato*); HebSt 31 (1990) 213-6 (W. *Vogels*); JAOS 110 (1990) 131 (J. A. *Soggin*; also on ᶠPOPE M. 1987); VT 40 (1990) 253s (J. A. *Emerton*).

a982 *Curtis* A. H. W., Some observations on 'bull' [god] terminology in the Ugaritic texts and the OT: ➤ 563, OTS 26 (1988/90) 17-29.

a983 *Dalley* Stephanie, Yahweh in Hamath in the 8th century BC; cuneiform material and historical deduction: VT 40 (1990) 21-32.

a983* *Delcor* Matthias, *a)* Le personnel du Temple d'Astarté à Kition d'après une tablette phénicienne (CIS 86 A et B) [< UF 11 (1979) 147-164]; – *b)* De l'Astarté cananéenne des textes bibliques à l'Aphrodite de Gaza [< FolOr 21 (1980) 83-92] – *c)* Les trônes d'Astarté [< Congresso Studi Fenici I/3 (1983) 777-787]; ➤ 219*, Environnement 1990, 1-18 / 19-27 / 28-38.

a984 **Dietrich** Manfred, *Loretz* Oswald, Mantik in Ugarit; keilalphabetische Texte der Opferschau — Omensammlungen — Nekromantie: AbhLitAlt-Syr 3. Münster 1990, Ugarit-V. ix-307 p. 3-927120-05-7. – OIAc Oc90.

a984* *Dombrowski* B. W. W., [Jos 3,11 ...] On the background of the formula *adōn kol ha-areṣ*; Near Eastern deities and their epithets: 174*, FSZABÓ Árpád AcAntH 31,3s (1985-8) 179-250.

a985 **Eilberg-Schwartz** Howard, The savage in Judaism; an anthropology of Israelite religion and ancient Judaism. Bloomington 1990, Indiana Univ. xiii-289 p. $35; pa. $18 [JBL 109,755]. 0-253-31946-3; -20591-3.

a986 *Fauth* Wolfgang, Das Kasion-Gebirge und Zeus Kasios; die antike Tradition und ihre vorderorientalischen Grundlagen: UF 22 (1990) 105-118.

a987 *a) Ferguson* Ian, Malta, builders of temples, builders of dolmens; – *b) Everson* Michael, The neolithic goddess of Old Europe preserved in a non-Indo-European setting [Basque/Mari]: ➤ 735, JIndEur 17 (1989) 214-237; 4 fig. / 277-295.

a988 **Finegan** Jack, Myth and mystery; an introduction to the pagan religions of the biblical world. GR 1989, Baker. 335 p. $25 [JAAR 58,326].

a988* **Fleming** Daniel E., The installation of Baal's high priests at Emar; a window on ancient Syrian religion: diss. Harvard. CM 1990. 458 p. 90-35607. – DissA 51 (1990s) 2363-A.

a989 *a) Fronzaroli* Pelio, Il culto degli Angubbu a Ebla; – *b) Bonechi* Marco, Un atto di culto a Ebla: QuadSemit 16 / MiscEbl 2 (1989) 1-26 / 131-147.

a989* **Graman** Robert M. [**Braman** in RTLv 23, p. 538], The problem of magic in ancient Israel; a century of studies: diss. Drew. Madison NJ 1990. iii-247 p. 90-14262. – DissA 51 (1990s) 195-A; OIAc Oc90: RelStR 17,193.

a990 **Gutmann** Joseph, The Jewish life cycle: IconRel 23/4, 1987 ➤ 3,b252: ᴿOLZ 85 (1990) 181s (Ina *Willi-Plein*).

a990* **Hammerstaedt** Jürgen, Die Orakelkritik des Kynikers Oenomaus [< EUSEBIUS Praep.; Diss.]: BeitKlasPg 188. Fra 1988, Athenaeum. 328 p. DM 84. – ᴿClasR 40 (1990) 18s (M. B. *Trapp*).

a991 *Handy* Lowell K., [Ps 29; 82; Gn 6,2-4; Job 1 ...] Dissenting deities or obedient angels; divine hierarchies in Ugarit and the Bible: BiRes 35 (1990) 18-35.

a992 **Heider** G. C., The cult of Molek 1985 ➤ 1,a572 ... 5,a955: ᴿJNES 49 (1990) 370-2 (D. *Pardee*); NedTTs 44 (1990) 248s (K. A. D. *Smelik*).

a993 *Israel* Felice, *a)* Materiali per 'Moloch': RStFen 18 (1990) 151-5; – *b)* Note ammonite II; la religione degli Ammoniti attraverso le fonti epigrafiche: SMSR 56 (1990) 307-337.

a994 *Kippenberg* H. G., Pseudikonographie; Orpheus auf jüdischen Bildern: VisRel 7 (1986/90) 233-243 + 11 fig.

a994* *Knauf* Ernst A., 'O Gott ein Tau vom Himmel gies'; kanaanäische Mythologie im Kirchenlied: BibNot 50 (1989) 34-45.

a995 **Korpel** M. Christina Annette, A rift in the clouds; Ugaritic and Hebrew descriptions of the divine [diss. ᴰ*Moor* J. de. Kampen 1990. 721 p. – TsTNijm 31,90; RTLv 22, p. 588]: Ug.-B.Lit. 8 Münster 1990, Ugarit-V. xii-721 p. 3-927120-07-3. – ᴿUF 22 (1990) 497-502 (M. *Pope*).

a996 **Lewis** Theodore H., Cults of the dead in ancient Israel and Ugarit 1989 ↠ 5,a961: ᴿBA 53 (1990) 178s (R. E. *Cooley*); ZAW 102 (1990) 448s (O. *Kaiser*).

a997 *Liwak –., Rᵉpā'îm*: ↠ 859, TWAT 7,3s (1990) 625-636.

a998 **Loretz** O., Ugarit und die Bibel; Kanaanäische Götter und Religionen im Alten Testament. Da 1990, Wiss. ix-272 p. DM 64; sb. 49. 3-534-08778-X [BL 91,128, J. A. *Emerton*].

a999 *a*) *Loon* Maurits van, The naked rain goddess; – *b*) *Dentzer* Jean-Marie, Édicules d'époque hellénistico-romaine et tradition des pierres cultuelles en Syrie et en Arabie: ↠ 28, ꟻBOUNNI A., 1990, 363-368 + pl. 120-129 / 65-79 + pl. 14-17.

a999* **Maier** Walter A., Ašerah 1986 ↠ 2,8974 ... 5,a963: ᴿSyria 65 (1988) 464s (A. *Caquot*: réserves).

b1 **Moor** Johannes C. De, An anthology of religious texts from Ugarit 1987 ↠ 3,b265*a* ... 5,a965: ᴿRB 97 (1990) 477s (J. M. de *Tarragon*).

b2 **Moor** Johannes C. De, *Spronk* Klaas, A cuneiform anthology of religious texts from Ugarit 1987 ↠ 3,b265 ... 5,a965: ᴿJAOS 110 (1990) 761 (D. *Marcus*).

Moor J. C. de, The rise of Yahwism; the roots of Israelite monotheism 1990 ↠ 7022.

b3 **Niehr** Herbert, Der höchste Gott; alttestamentlicher ᴊʜᴡʜ-Glaube im Kontext syrisch-kanaanäischer Religion ... BZAW 190. B 1990, de Gruyter. x-268 p. DM 98. 3-11-012342-8 [RB 98,141s, J.-M. de *Tarragon*].

b4 *a*) *Olmo* Lete G. del, Pervivencias cananeas (ugaríticas) en el culto fenicio, II. El culto 'mlk'; – *b*) *Picard* Colette, Les sacrifices Molk chez les puniques; certitudes et hypothèses; – *c*) *Ribichini* Sergio, Qualche osservazione sull'antropomorfismo delle divinità fenicie e puniche; – *d*) *Xella* Paolo, 'Divinités doubles' dans le monde phénico-punique: ↠ 175, ꟻSZNYCER M., Semitica 39 (1990) 67-76 / 77-88 / 127-133 / 167-175.

b4* *Olmo Lete* G. del, Dos rituales regios hurritas de Ugarit (KTU 1.132/1.111): AulaO 8 (1990) 21-31.

b5 **Olyan** Saul M., Asherah ...: SBL Mg 34, 1988 ↠ 4,b871; 5,a969: ᴿBA 53 (1990) 116s (M. P. *Matheney*); CBQ 52 (1990) 332-4 (J. W. *Betlyon*); JAOS 110 (1990) 578-580 (G. W. *Ahlström*: misinterprets Dan-Bethel; too dependent on Cross); JBL 109 (1990) 504-6 (E. T. *Mullen*); JQR 81 (1990s) 207-212 (S. D. *Sperling*); JRel 70 (1990) 449 (D. *Edelman*); JStOT 46 (1990) 127s (R. S. *Hess*).

b6 *Rüterswörden* U., Rahab: ↠ 859, TWAT 7,3s (1990) 372-8.

b7 *Sanmartín* J., El ordo litúrgico KTU 4.14 [una lista de comestibles; commonly called economic, likelier cultic]: AulaO 8 (1990) 89-99.

b8 (*Schroer*) **Ammann** Silvia, Die Göttin auf den Stempelsiegeln aus Palästina: Hab.-Diss. FrS 1989. – BZ 34,156.

b9 *Shea* William H., The Khirbet el-Qom tomb inscription again: VT [37 (1987) 50-62, Judith *Hadley*] 40 (1990) 110-6, 1 fig.

b10 *Smick* Elmer B., Old Testament cross-culturalism; paradigmatic or enigmatic?: JEvTS 32 (1989) 3-16 [< ᴢɪᴛ 89,509].

b11 **Smith** Mark S., The early history of God; Yahweh and the other deities in Ancient Israel. SF 1990, Harper & R. 197 p. [JAAR 58,535]. 0-06-067416-4. – ᴿUF 22 (1990) 514 (O. *Loretz*).

b12 *Smith* Mark S.,   The Near Eastern background of solar language for Yahweh: JBL 109 (1990) 29-39.

b13 *Soggin* J. Alberto,   Appunti per lo studio della religione d'Israele in epoca pre-esilica: → 154, FSACCHI P., 1990, 55-63; – RBASOR 277s (1990) 131s (K. P. *Jackson*).

b14 **Tigay** Jeffrey H.,   You shall have no other gods 1986 → 3,b276 ... 5,a981: RBASOR 277s (1990) 131s (K. P. *Jackson*); Syria 65 (1988) 465s (A. *Caquot*).

b15 *Vuk* Tomislav,   Religione, nazione e stato nel Vicino Oriente Antico e nella Bibbia: LA 40 (1990) 105-158; Eng. 446.

b15* **Weltman** Sheldon J.,   The biblical polemic against the foreign divine images: diss. Drew, DHuffmon H. Madison NJ 1990. v-260 p. 90-32134. – DissA 51 (1990s) 2055-A; OIAc F91,21.

b16 *a*) *Zayadine* Fawzi,   The pantheon of the Nabataean inscriptions in Egypt and the Sinai; – *b*) *Tarrier* Dominique,   Baalshamin dans le monde nabatéen; à propos de découvertes récentes; – *c*) *Knauf* Ernst A.,   Dushara und Shai Al-Qaum: → 783, Aram 2 (1989/90) 151-174 / 197-203; 3 fig. / 175-183.

M6.5   Religio aegyptia.

b17 *Alfi* Mostafa El-,   Ramesside divinities of Nubia: VarÆg 6 (1990) 161-4 = DiscEg 18 (1990) 21-26.

b18 **Allen** James P. [p. 1-28; also 89-101, The natural philosophy of Akhenaten], *al.* [...*Assmann* J., p. 85-88 and 135-159]: Religion and philosophy in ancient Egypt: Yale Egyptological Studies 3.   NHv 1989, Yale Univ. vii-159 p. 0-912532-18-1.

b19 EArmstrong A.H.,   Classical Mediterranean spirituality; Egypt ... 1986 → 2,234 ... 4,b888: RJRel 69 (1989) 100s (J. D. *Tabor*).

b20 **Assmann** Jan,   Ma'at; Gerechtigkeit und Unsterblichkeit im Alten Ägypten [für H.-G. GADAMERS 90. Geburtstag, aber nicht eine Festschrift (-Kompilation)].   München 1990, Beck.   319 p.; 13 fig.   3-406-34667-7 [ZAW 103,292, O. *Kaiser*].

b20* *Assmann* Jan,   Der 'leidende Gerechte' im Alten Ägypten; zum Konfliktpotential der ägyptischen Religion: → 38*, FCOLPE C., Loyalitätskonflikte 1990, 203-224.

b21 *a*) *Assmann* Jan,   Egyptian mortuary liturgies; – *b*) *Malaise* Michel,   Bes et les croyances solaires; – *c*) *Redford* Donald B.,   The sea and the goddess; – *d*) *Shirun-Grumach* Irene,   Bedeutet 'in der Hand des Gottes' Gottesfurcht?: → 114, FLICHTHEIM M. 1990, 1-45 / (II) 680-729 / 824-835 / 836-852.

b21* *Bács* Tamás A.,   Two calendars of lucky and unlucky days: StAltÄgK 17 (1990) 41-64.

b22 *Baines* John R.,   Trône et Dieu; aspects du symbolisme royal et divin des temps archaïques: BSocFrÉg 118 (1990) 5-37; 13 fig.

b23 **Barta** Winfried,   Komparative Untersuchungen zu vier Unterweltsbüchern: [0936-2762] MüÄgUnt 1.   Fra 1990, Lang.   190 p.   3-631-42143-5 [OIAc Ja91].

b23* *Barta* Winfried,   Zum Wesen des Gottes Osiris nach Zeugnissen der älteren Totenliteratur: ZägSpr 117 (1990) 89-93.

b24 *a*) *Barta* Winfried,   Der 'Vorwurf an Gott' in der Lebensgeschichte des Sinuhe; – *b*) *Hannig* Rainer,   Die Schwangerschaft der Isis; – *c*)

Westendorf Wolfhart, Eine Königstitulatur des Osiris: ⇒ 16, ᶠBECKE-RATH J. v. 1990, 21-27 / 91-95 / 253-261.

b25 *Bauval* Robert G., The seeding of the star gods; a fertility rite inside Cheops's pyramid?: DiscEg 16 (1990) 21-27 + 1 fig.

b26 **Becker-Colonna** Andrcina L., *al.*, Akhenaton, la caduta degli dèi, testi. R 1990. 176 p.; ill. – p. 59-64, *Piccirillo* Michele; p. 65-82, *Sturtewagen* Christian.

b27 *Bianchi* R. S., New light on the Aton: GöMiszÄg 114 (1990) 35-40 + phot.

b28 **Bietak** Manfred, *a*) The concept of eternity in ancient Egypt and the Bronze Age world; an archaeological approach: ⇒ 4, ᶠAMIRAN R., Eretz-Israel 21 (1990) 10*-18*; 4 fig.; – *b*) Zur Herkunft des Seth von Avaris: ÄgLev 1 (1990) 9-16; 5 fig.

b29 **Bilolo** Mubabinge, [⇒ 2170] Les cosmo-théologies philosophiques d'Héliopolis et d'Hermopolis; essai de thématisation et de systématisation; préf. *Thausing* G.: Acad. Pensée Africaine 1, Égypte 2. Kinshasa 1986, Univ. [OIAc JuJ89].

b30 *Boochs* Wolfgang, Der ehebrecherische Sohn; Anmerkungen zu H.-W. FISCHER: GöMiszÄg [112 (1989) 23] 114 (1990) 43-45.

b31 *Borghouts* J. F., Martyria; some correspondent motifs in Egyptian religion: ⇒ 533, Martyrologie 1984/9, 197-203.

b32 *Castel Ronda* Elisa, Algunos aspectos de dioses felinos en el antiguo Egipto: BAsocEspEg 2 (1990) 5-21.

b33 **Cauville** Sylvie, Essai sur la théologie du temple d'Horus à Edfou: IFAO BÉt 102, 1987 ⇒ 3,b296*ab*: ᴿBO 47 (1990) 312-6 (M.-Theresia *Derchain-Urtel*); JAOS 110 (1990) 754-7 (R. K. *Ritner*: some 20 suggestions).

b34 ᴱ**Daniel** Robert W., *Maltomini* Franco, Supplementum magicum: PapyrolColon 16. Opladen 1990, Westd.-V. I. xxvi-213 p.; VIII pl. 3-531-00926-4.

b35 ᴱ**Donadoni Roveri** Anna Maria, Egyptian civilization; religious beliefs [ital. 1988 ⇒ 5,b1]. Mi 1988, Electa. 261 p.; 343 fig. 88-435-2681-2 [OIAc F91,6: 17 titles; including several rather on excavations or funerary practices].

b35* ᴱ**Eggebrecht** Arne, Suche nach Unsterblichkeit; Totenkult und Jenseitsglaube im Alten Ägypten. Hildesheim 1990, Roemer- und Pelizaeus-Museum. 114 p.; 38 color. pl. 3-8053-1224-5 / Mus. -92-X.

b36 **Ellis** Normandie, Awakening Osiris; a new translation of the Egyptian book of the dead. GR 1988, Phanes. 0-933-999-74-7 [OIAc JuJ89].

b36* *a*) *Englund* Gertie, Gods as a frame of reference; – *b*) *Sørensen* Jørgen P., Ancient Egyptian religious thought and the XVIth Hermetic treatise: ⇒ 5,842, Uppsala 1987/9, 7-28 / 41-57.

b37 **Fazzini** Richard A., Egypt, Dynasty XXII-XXV: IconRel 16/10, 1988 ⇒ 4,b901; 5,b3: ᴿBO 47 (1990) 305-9 (A. *Niwiński*).

b38 *a*) *Fóti* László, Hermes Trismégiste et la mythologie égyptienne; – *b*) *Kákosy* László, Hermetić obelisks: ⇒ 49, Mém. FÓTI 1989, 9-27 / 235-257; phot.

b39 *Glaser* Susanne, Le jugement et la justification de l'homme après sa mort d'après le papyrus d'Any: ⇒ 49, Mém. FÓTI L. 1989, 119-128.

b40 **Godron** Gérard, Études sur l'Horus Den et quelques problèmes de l'Égypte archaïque: CahOrientalisme 19. Genève 1990, Cramer. 241 p.; XVIII pl.

b41 **Hart** George, Egyptian myths; the legendary past. L 1990, British Museum. 80 p. 0-7141-2064-2 [OIAc Oc90].

b42 *Hasenfratz* Hans-Peter, Zur 'Seelenvorstellung' der alten Ägypter: ZRGg 42 (1990) 193-216.

b43 ᴱ**Helck** Wolfgang, Tempel und Kult 1986/7 → 3,818.b313 ... 5,b13: ᴿDiscEg 16 (1990) 97-102 (Alison *Roberts*); OLZ 85 (1990) 658s (J. *Hallof*).

b44 **Hoffmeier** James K., 'Sacred' ... *dsr*: OBO 59, 1985 → 1,a623 ... 5,b15: ᴿCdÉ 65 (1990) 62-67 (M. *Malaise*).

b45 **Hommema-van Eik** M., Toetsing voor de toegang; Dodenboek spreuk 125c: diss. ᴰ*Heerma van Voss* M. Amst 1990. 99 p. – TsTNijm 30 (1990) 188; RTLv 22, p. 613.

b46 **Hopfner** Theodor, Griechisch-ägyptischer Offenbarungszauber; seine Methoden II,1s: StPalaeogPap 23. Amst 1983-90 = 1924, Hakkert. 344 p.; p. 345-667. 90-256-0838-8; -996-1.

b47 **Horst** P. W. van der, Chaeremon²: ÉPR 101, 1987 (¹1984) → 65,9333 ... 5,b17: ᴿBO 47 (1990) 364s (M. *Malaise*).

b48 *Jansen-Winkel* Karl, a) Zum Zölibat der Gottesgemahlin: VarAeg 5 (1989) 203s; – b) Amun fesselt die Fremdländer: BibNot 49 (1989) 11-24.

b49 **Johnson** Sally B., The cobra goddess of ancient Egypt; predynastic, early dynastic, and Old Kingdom periods: Studies in Egyptology. L 1990, Kegan Paul. xxv-276 p.; 655 fig. 0-7103-0212-6.

b50 *Jürgens* Peter, Der Tote als Mittler zwischen Mensch und Göttern im Berliner Sargtexte-Papyrus; ein Zeugnis inoffizieller Religion aus dem Mittleren Reich: GöMiszÄg 116 (1990) 51-63.

b51 **Kákosy** László, Zauberei im alten Ägypten, ᵀ*Szóbel* Eszter, *Derzsi* Ildikó. Lp 1989, Koehler & A. 267 p.; 31 fig. 3-7338-0062-1.

b52 *Kákosy* László, Fragmente eines unpublizierten magischen Textes in Budapest: ZägSpr 117 (1990) 140-157; pl. VI.

b53 **Keller** Sharon R., Egyptian letters to the dead in relation to the Old Testament and other Near Eastern sources: diss. NYU, ᴰ*Gordon* C. NY 1990. vii-237 p. 90-16277. – OIAc Oc90.

b54 **Koch** Klaus, Das Wesen altägyptischer Religion im Spiegel ägyptologischer Forschung 1989 → 5,h21; DM 25: ᴿZAW 102 (1990) 447s (H.-C. *Schmitt*).

b55 *Koenig* Yvan, Les textes d'envoûtement de Mirgissa: RÉgp 41 (1990) 101-117; facsim. 118-125.

b56 *Kormyschewa* Eleonora, Local gods of Egypt in Cush and problems of Egyptian settlers: → 78, ᶠ*HINTZE* F., Meroitica 12 (1990) 199-223.

b56* a) *Krauss* Rolf, Vorläufige Bemerkungen zu Seth und Horus/Horusauge im Kairener Tagewählkalender nebst Notizen zum Anfang des Kalendertages; – b) *Loeben* Christian E., Bemerkungen zum Horustempel des Neuen Reiches in Edfu; – c) *Patané* Massimo, Quelques remarques sur la présence de Seth dans les Textes des Pyramides à la Basse Époque: BSocÉg 14 (Genève 1990) 49-56 / 57-68; 5 fig. / 69-71.

b57 **Kruchten** J.-M., Le grand texte oraculaire de Djéhoutymose 1986 → 2,9032: ᴿBO 47 (1990) 620-8 (M. *Römer*).

b58 **Kurth** Dieter, Der Sarg der Teuris; eine Studie zum Totenglauben im römerzeitlichen Ägypten: ÄgTreverensia 6. Mainz 1990, von Zabern. ix-73 p.; 10 pl. + 4 color. 3-8053-1080-3.

b59 *Lorton* David, Observations on the birth and name of Horus in Coffin Texts spell 148: VarAeg 5 (1989) 205-212.

b60 *Morkot* Robert G., Nb-m3't-R' — united-with-Ptah: JNES 49 (1990) 323-337.

b61 *Munro* Irmtraut, Der Totenbuch-Papyrus des Veziers Wsr-Jmn: Gö-MiszÄg 116 (1990) 73-78 + 11 facsimiles; VI pl.

b62 *a) Neveu* François, À propos du P.DM. 28; un conseil royal consacré aux affaires de 'La tombe'; – *b) Vernus* Pascal, Entre Néo-Égyptien et démotique; la langue utilisée dans la traduction du rituel de repousser l'agressif (étude sur la diglossie I): RÉgp 41 (1990) 143-152 / 153-208.

b63 **O'Callaghan** José, Las raíces religiosas del hombre; el alma del antiguo Egipto: Biblioteca Básica del Creyente. M 1990, Atenas. 152 p. [ActaPIB 9,487].

b64 *Onasch* Christian, Die kuschitische Religion [KORMYSCHEWA E.]: Nubica 1s (1990) 47-75.

b65 *Pernigotti* Sergio, Il sacerdote: → 483, L'uomo egiziano 1990, 127-160.

b66 *Piccione* Peter A., Mehen, mysteries, and resurrection from the coiled serpent: JAmEg 27 (1990) 43-52; 4 fig.

b67 **Plas** Dirk van der, '... uw liefelijk aangezicht te aanschouwen ...!'; over plaats en functie van de zintuigen [sense-organs] in de cultus en volksvroomheid van het Oude Egypte: Rede 9 nov.: Opuscula Niliaca Noviomagensia 2. Nijmegen 1989, Katholieke Univ. 63 p.; ill.

b68 *Quaegebeur* Jan, The Egyptian clergy and the cult of the Ptolemaic dynasty: AncSoc 20 (1989) 93-113 + 6 fig.

b69 *Ritner* Robert K., O[stracon] Gardiner 363; a spell against night terrors: JAmEg 27 (1990) 25-41.

b70 *Rondot* Vincent, Le Naos de Domitien; Toutou et le sept flèches [jardin du musée du Caire]: BIFAO 90 (1990) 303-337; 8 fig.; pl. XVII-XXIII.

b70* **Seipel** Wilfried, Ägypten; Götter, Gräber und die Kunst; 4000 Jahre Jenseitsglaube, I. Linz 1989, Landesmuseum. 368 p.; 529 (color.) fig. 3-900746-14-1.

b71 *Sternberg* Heike, Mythische Motiven und Mythenbildung in den ägyptischen Tempeln und Papyri der griechisch-römischen Zeit: GöOrF 4/14, 1986 → 1,a656 ... 5,b43: ᴿOLZ 85 (1990) 158-160 (J. *Hallof*).

b73 **Teeter** Emily, The presentation of Maat; the iconography and theology of an ancient Egyptian offering ritual: diss. ᴰ*Wente* E. Ch 1990. xx-632 p. (23 pl.); bibliog. p. 305-334. – OIAc Oc90.

b73* *Thompson* Dorothy J., The high priests of Memphis under Ptolemaic rule: → 389, Pagan priests 1990, 97-116.

b74 *Youssef* Youhanna N., La Christianisation des fêtes d'Osiris: BSACopte 29 (1990) 147-152.

b75 **Zabkar** Louis V., Hymns to Isis ... Philae 1988 → 4,b940: ᴿJAmEg 27 (1990) 229 (R. S. *Bianchi*).

M7 **Religio mesopotamica.**

b76 *a) Alster* Bendt, *Jeyes* Ulla, Two Utu hymns and a copy of a royal inscription; – *b) Selz* Gebhard J., Studies in early syncretism; the development of the pantheon in Legaš; – *c) Watanabe* Kazuko, *abbūta(m)/abbuttu ṣabātu(m)* — zur immanenten und transzendenten Interzession: AcSum 12 (1990) 1-10 + 4 facsim. / 111-142 / 319-338.

b76* **Badali** Enrico, *Zinko* Christian, Der 16. Tag des AN.TAH.ŠUM–Festes; Text, Übersetzung, Kommentar, Glossar: Scientia 20. Innsbruck 1989, Scientia. 128 p. 1010-612X [OIAc Ap91,4].

b77 *a) Charpin* Dominique, Les divinités familiales des Babyloniens d'après les légendes de leurs sceaux-cylindres; – *b) Spycket* Agnès, Ex voto mésopotamiens du IIᵉ millénaire av. J.-C.; – *c) Tunca* Önhan, 'Temple' ou 'bâtiment de prestige'? À propos des temples des périodes d'el-Obed et d'Uruk, et des données ethnoarchéologiques: ➤ 107, ᶠKUPPER J.-R. 1990, 59-78 / 79-86, 6 fig. + III pl. / 263-269, 2 fig. + II pl.

b77* **Charpin** Dominique, Le clergé d'Ur au siècle d'Hammurabi 1986 ➤ 2,9061 ... 5,b67: ᴿJESHO 32 (1989) 229-236 (W. F. *Leemans*: la fonction de *šandabakku*).

b78 *Cola Alberich* Julio, Números simbólicos y rituales en el Asia del Indo al Mediterráneo: BAsEspOr 25 (1989) 199-215.

b79 **Cooper** Jerrold S., The curse of Agade 1983 ➤ 64,9627 ... 1,a681: ᴿOLZ 85 (1990) 308-310 (W. G. *Lambert*, Eng.).

b79* *Farber* G., *me* (*gârza*, *parçu*) [?... divine power, functions]: ➤ 853*, RLA 7,7s (1990) 610-3.

b80 **Farber** Walter, Schlaf, Kindlein, schlaf! Mesopotamische Babybeschwörungen und Rituale: Mesopotamian Civilizations 2, 1989 ➤ 5, b69: ᴿZAss 80 (1990) 136-8 (W. von *Soden*).

b81 **Geller** Markham J., Forerunners to Udud-Hul; Sumerian exorcistic incantations: FreibAltorSt 12, 1985 ➤ 5,b74; DM 56: ᴿWZKM 80 (1990) 269-272 (H. *Hirsch*).

b82 *Groneberg* Brigitte, Zu den mesopotamischen Unterweltsvorstellungen; das Jenseits als Fortsetzung des Diesseits: AltOrF 17 (1990) 244-261.

b83 *a)* *Guinan* Ann K., The human behavioral omens; on the threshold of psychological inquiry; – *b)* *George* Lynne, Mesopotamian extipicy; explorations in ethics and metaphysics; – *c)* *Rochberg-Halton* F., Astrology, astronomy, and the birth of scientific inquiry: BCanadMesop 19 (1990) 9-14 / 15-24 / 25-33.

b85 *Horowitz* Wayne, Two notes on Etana's flight to heaven: Orientalia 59 (1990) 511-517; 1 fig.

Hutter Manfred, Altor.... Unterwelt... 'Nergal und Ereškigal': OBO 63, 1985 ➤ 2178.

b85* *Kuhrt* Amélie, Nabonidus and the Babylonian priesthood: ➤ 389, Pagan priests 1990, 117-155; fig. 15-19; map.

b86 *Kupper* J.-R., Les formules de malédiction dans les inscriptions royales de l'époque paléo-babylonienne: RAss 84 (1990) 157-163.

b87 *a)* *Kutscher* Raphael, The cult of Dumuzi/Tammuz; – *b)* *Klein* Jacob, Šulgi and Išmedagan; originality and dependence in Sumerian royal hymnology: ➤ 7, ᶠARTZI P. 1990, 29-44 / 65-136; pl. II.

b88 **Lambert** W. G., *a)* Ancient Mesopotamian gods; superstition, philosophy, theology: RHR 207 (1990) 115-130; franç. 105; – *b)* The name of Nergal again: ZAss [77 (1987) 161-8, *Steinkeller* P.] 80 (1990) 40-52 [53-59, Steinkeller].

b89 *a)* *Lambert* W.G., A new Babylonian descent to the netherworld [Inanna]; – *b)* *Abusch* Tzvi, An early form of the witchcraft ritual *Maqlû* and the origin of a Babylonian magical ceremony; – *c)* *Ferry* David [versification of Moran's translation] Prayer to the gods of the night: ➤ 124, ᶠMORAN W., Lingering 1990, 289-300 / 1-57 / 171 only.

b89* *a)* ᴱ**Lara Peinado** Federico, Himnos babilónicos: Clásicos del Pensamiento. M 1990, Tecnos. ix-174 p. 84-309-1820-5 [OIAc Ja91].

— *b)* **Ludwig** Marie-Christine, Untersuchungen zu den Hymnen des Išme-Dagan von Isin: Santag, Arbeiten und Untersuchungen zur Keilschriftkunde 2. Wsb 1990, Harrassowitz. xviii-255 p.; ill.

b90 **McCall** Henrietta, Mesopotamian myths: The Legendary Past. L 1990, British Museum. 80 p. 0-7141-2063-4 [OIAc Oc90].

b91 **Maul** Stefan M., Herzberuhigungsklagen; die sumerisch-akkadischen Eršahunga-Gebete. Wsb 1988, Harrassowitz. 538 p. – ᴿJAOS 110 (1990) 571s (M. E. *Cohen*).

b92 **Mayer** Werner, Untersuchungen zur Formensprache der babylonischen 'Gebetsbeschwörungen' [Diss. Münster 1975, ᴰ*Soden* W. v.]: StPohl 5, 1976 ➤ 58,c884: ᴿOLZ 85 (1990) 38-40 (D. O. *Edzard*).

b93 *Mayer* Werner R., *a*) Ein Ritual gegen Feindschaft im Museo Nazionale d'Arte Orientale zu Rom: Orientalia 59 (1990) 14-33; 1 fig.; pl. V-VI; – *b*) Sechs Šu-ila-Gebete: Orientalia 59 (1990) 449-477; facsimiles 478-490.

b94 *Moreno Garrido* Jaime, Elementos del pensamiento mesopotámico antiguo: ➤ 125, ᶠMORENO/VILLEGAS 1990, 35-66.

b95 *Pailler* Jean Marie, Les religions orientales [histoire de leur étude: CUMONT F.], III: Pallas 35 (1989) 95-112 + 1 fig.

b96 **Parpola** Asko, The sky-garment; a study of the Harappan religion and its relation to the Mesopotamian and later Indian religions: StOrFinn 57, 1985 ➤ 1,a702; 3,b386: ᴿJRAS (1989) 165s (W. C. *Brice*).

b97 **Pomponio** Francesco, Formule di maledizione della Mesopotamia preclassica: Testi... mesop. 1. Brescia 1990, Paideia. 125 p. Lit. 17.000. 88-394-0434-1 [BL 91,129, W. G. *Lambert*].

b98 ᶠPORADA Edith, Monsters and demons 1987 ➤ 3,133: ᴿBSO 52 (1989) 121s (Dominique *Collon*).

b99 **Reiner** Erica, Your thwarts in pieces, your mooring rope cut [citation from the elegy of a woman who died in childbirth]; poetry from Babylonia and Assyria 1985 ➤ 2,6076: ᴿJAOS 110 (1990) 132s (B. *Alster*: of most benefit to Assyriologists).

b100 *Rawi* F. N. H. al-, Tablets from the Sippar library; I. The 'Weidner Chronicle', a supposititious royal letter concerning a vision: Iraq 52 (1990) 1-10; 11-13, transcribed text; pl. I.

b102 **Starr** Ivan, Queries to the Sungod; divination and politics in Sargonid Assyria: State Archives of Assyria 4. Helsinki 1990, Univ. lxxix-409 p. DM 200; pa. 145 [ZAW 103,310, O. *Kaiser*]. 951-570-059-0; 8-2.

b103 *Vanstiphout* H. L. J., The man from Elam, a reconsideration of Ishbi-Erra 'hymn B' [*Van Dijk* J. 1978]: JbEOL 31 (1989s) 53-62.

b104 *Vogelzang* M. E., The cunning of Ea and the threat to order: JbEOL 31 (1989s) 66-76.

b105 *Wright* G. R. H., Of fishes and men; fish symbols in ancient religion: JPrehRel 3s (1989s) 30-44; 3 fig.

b106 *Zaccagnini* Carlo, Golden cups offered to the gods at Emar: Orientalia 59 (1990) 518-520.

M7.4 **Religio persiana,** *Iran.*

b107 ᶠASMUSSEN Jes P., A green leaf, ᴱ**Duchesne-Guillemin** J. 1988 ➤ 4,6: ᴿBSO 53 (1990) 351s (P. C. *Kreyenbroek*).

b108 **Boyce** Mary, A Persian stronghold of Zoroastrianism 1989 = 1977 ➤ 58,d238*b*; 61,m515: ᴿStIran 19 (1990) 271-3 (P. *Gignoux*).

b109 *a*) *Boyce* Mary, Some further reflections on Zurvanism; – *b*) *Irani* Kaikhusrow D., Understanding Zarathustra — a philosophic perspective: ➤ 192, ᶠYARSHATER E., 1990, 20-29 / 104-109.

b110 *Boyd* James W., *Williams* Ron G., Ritual spaces; an application of aesthetic theory to Zoroastrian ritual: JRit 3,1 (Pittsburgh 1989) 1-44 [< ZIT 89,497].

b111 **Choksy** Jamsheed K., Purity and pollution in Zoroastrianism; triumph over evil 1989 ➤ 5,b100; xxvii-185 p.: ᴿBSO 53 (1990) 352-4 (P. G. *Kreyenbroek*); JScStR 29 (1990) 268s (A. L. *Greil*).

b112 **Colledge** M. A. R., The Parthian period: IconRel 14/3, 1986 ➤ 2,9083; 3,b399: ᴿBSO 53 (1990) 349-351 (M. *Boyce*).

b113 **Dandamaev** M. A., *Lukonin* V. G., The culture and social institutions of ancient Iran, ᵀ*Kohl* P. L. (*Dadson* D. J.). C 1989, Univ. 400 p. $90. 0-521-32107-7. – ᴿClasR 40 (1990) 368s (S. *Hornblower*: SYME's 'dullness unredeemed by exactitude' only a bit too strong).

b113* *a*) *Gnoli* G., Cyrus et Zoroastre; une hypothèse; – *b*) *Bianchi* Ugo, Dieu créateur et vision universaliste; le cas de l'empire achéménide; – *c*) *Shaked* Saul, Mythes d'origine comme actes de commémoration et de différenciation en Iran sasanide: ➤ 618, Commémoration 1986/8, 201-210 / 191-200 /211-8.

b114 ᵀᴱ**Hempel** Jürgen, Die Kopenhagener Handschrift Cod. 27, eine Sammlung von zoroastrischen Gebeten, Beschwörungsformeln, Vorschriften und wissenschaftlichen Überlieferungen: GöOrF 3/2. Wsb 1974, Harrassowitz. 242 p.

b114* *Hjerrild* Bodil, The survival and modification of Zoroastrianism in Seleucid times: ➤ 325*, *Bilde*/Seleucid 1990, 140-150.

b115 *Kingsley* Peter, The Greek origin of the sixth-century dating of Zoroaster. DSO 53 (1990) 245-265.

b116 *Kotwal* Dastur P. M., A brief history of the Parsi priesthhood: Ind-IranJ 33 (1990) 165-175.

b117 *Škoda* V. G., ⊕ Toward the reconstruction of a ritual in the Sogdian temple: ArOr 58 (1990) 147-151; Eng. 151.

M8.1 *Religio proto-arabica* – **Early Arabic religious graffiti.**

b118 *Blichfeldt* Jan-Olav, *Khāṣṣa* and *'āmma*; on slogans, concepts and social settings in Islamic history; – *b*) *Retsö* Jan, The earliest Arabs: ➤ 184, ꟳVITESTAM G., OrSuec 38s (1989s) 14-20 / 131-9.

b119 *Jamme* A., A new Qatabanian dedicatory inscription to the god Bašamum, Ja 3198 [NAM 224, correcting BEESTON A.]: ➤ 117, ꟳLÖFGREN O., On both sides 1989, 13-16.

b120 *Ryckmans* Jacques, Une table à libations avec inscription sabéenne provenant du Ǧawf du Yémen: ➤ 117, ꟳLÖFGREN O., 1989, 69-81.

b121 *Westenholz* Aage, A note on the pre-Islamic Arabic dialect of Syria on the basis of Greek inscriptions: ➤ 117*, ꟳLØKKEGAARD F. 1990, 391-6.

M8.2 *Muḥammad et asseclae* – **Qur'ān and early diffusion of Islam.**

b122 **Almond** Philip C., Heretic and hero; Muḥammad and the Victorians: Studies in Oriental Religions 18. Wsb 1989, Harrassowitz. ix-107 p. DM 48 [RelStR 17,181, A. *Zahniser*].

b123 **Assiouty** Sarwat A. al-, Recherches comparées sur le christianisme primitif et l'Islam premier: I. Sources ... forgées; II. Jésus le non-Juif; III. Origines égyptiennes 1987-9 ➤ 5,b117: ᴿIslamochristiana 16 (1990) 304-7 (P. *Ternant*); PrOrChr 40 (1990) 210s (aussi P. *Ternant*: fantastique); Salesianum 52 (1990) 735s (C. *Bissoli*: esaggerato, non inutile).

b124 **Bamyeh** Mohammed A., The origins of Islam; a study in historical sociology: diss. Wisconsin, ᴰ*Elder* J. Madison 1990. 776 p. 90-33758. — DissA 51 (1990s) 3196-A.

b125 **Bencheikh** Jamel Eddine, Le voyage nocturne de Mahomet. P 1988, Imprimerie Nat. 305 p. 68 fig. F 320; pa. 245. 2-11-080958-2; -40-X. – ᴿÉTRel 65 (1990) 107s (J. *Argaud*).

b126 ᵀᴱ**Cooper** J., Ṭabari, Commentary on the Qur'ān [abridged] 1. Ox 1987, UP. 492 p. £45. – ᴿBSO 53 (1990) 331-4 (A. A. M. *Shereef*); CritRR 2 (1989) 363-5 (L. T. *Librande*).

b127 **Crone** Patricia, Meccan trade and the rise of Islam. Princeton 1987, Univ. 300 p. $32.50. – ᴿBSO 52 (1989) 339s (J. *Wansbrough*); JAOS 110 (1990) 472-486 (R. B. *Serjeant*: 'misconceptions and flawed polemics').

b128 **Crone** Patricia, Roman, provincial and Islamic law; the origins of the Islamic patronate 1987 → 5,b134; vii-178 p.; $39.50: ᴿBSO 53 (1990) 128s (A. A. M. *Shereef*); JSS 35 (1990) 326-330 (D. S. *Powers*); RelStR 16 (1990) 364 (N. *Haram*).

b129 — *Hallaq* Wael B., The use and abuse of evidence; the question of provincial and Roman influences on early Islamic law [CRONE P. 1987]: JAOS 110 (1990) 79-91.

b130 **Delcambre** Anne-Marie, L'Islam: Repères 82. P 1990, Découverte. 128 p. – ᴿRThom 90 (1990) 532 (J. *Jomier*).

b131 **Eaton** Charles L., Der Islam und die Bestimmung des Menschen, ᵀ*Schmid* E.-L.; Vorw. *Schimmel* A., 1987 → 5,b134*: ᴿOLZ 85 (1990) 325-330 (E. *Serauky*).

b132 ᵀᴱ**Eddé-Terrasse** Anne Marie, 'Izz al-din IBN SHADDAD, Al-A'laq al-Khatira. Damas 1984, Institut Français. 381 p.; 4 maps. – ᴿRHE 85 (1990) 901s (J. M. *Fiey*).

b133 **Endress** Gerhard, An introduction to Islam [1982], ᵀ*Hillenbrand* Carole, 1988 → 4,b994; 5,b135; 0-85224-496-7; -524-6: ᴿBO [40 (1983) 780s] 47 (1990) 230s (G. H. A. *Juynboll*).

b134 *Erder* Yoram, The origin of the name Idris in the Qur'ān; a study of the influence of Qumran literature in early Islam: JNES 49 (1990) 339-350.

b135 **Fattal** Michel, Pour un nouveau langage de la raison; convergences entre l'Orient et l'Occident [l'Islam et le *lógos* grec], préf. *Aubenque* Pierre. P 1988, Beauchesne. 112 p. F 120. – ᴿRHP 207 (1990) 209s (L. *Brisson*).

b136 **Gimaret** Daniel, Les noms divins en Islam; exégèse lexicographique et théologique 1988 → 3,b997; 5,b145: ᴿJAOS 110 (1990) 779s (Marie *Bernand*); JRAS (1990) 150s (J. *Baldick*); RHR 207 (1990) 88s (R. *Deladrière*).

b137 **Gisel** Pierre, *Waardenburg* Jacques, L'Islam, une religion; suivi d'un débat, Quels types d'approches requiert le phénomène religieux. Genève 1989, Labor et Fides. 154 p. 2-8309-0134-7. – ᴿÉTRel 65 (1990) 295s (J.-P. *Gabus*).

b138 **Glassé** Cyril, The concise encyclopedia of Islam 1989 → 5,b146: ᴿHorizons 17 (1990) 185 (J. *Renard*); JRel 70 (1990) 305s (J. W. *Morris*: only partly factual).

b139 ᴱ**Hagemann** Ludwig, *Glei* Reinhold, Nikolaus von KUES, Cribratio Alcorani, Sichtung des Korans: Schriften 20a... 1989, Philos.Bibl. 420a. xx-160 p. DM 28. 3-7873-0934-9. – ᴿTLZ 115 (1990) 446s (K.-H. *Kandler*); TR 86 (1990) 121s (H. *Zirker*); ZMissRW 74 (1990) 151-3 (H. *Busse*).

b140 **Havenith** Alfred, Les Arabes chrétiens nomades au temps de Mohammed: Coll. Cerfaux-Lafort 7, 1988 → 5,b154: ᴿFoiTemps 20 (1990) 378s (G. *Harpigny*).

b141 **James** David, Qur'ans of the Mamluks. L 1988, Alexandria/Thames & H. 270 p.; 90 pl. + 80 color; map. £35. – ᴿJRAS (1989) 328s (R. *Irwin*).

b142 **Jomier** Jacques, How to understand Islam [Pour connaître 1988 → 5,b162], [T]*Bowden* John → 5,b163; 0-334-02070-0; also NY 1989, Crossroad. 168 p.; ill.: maps. $15 pa. 0-8245-0981-1 [RelStR 17,180, Jane D. *McAuliffe*]. – [R]ExpTim 101 (1989s) 222 (S. *Wilding*).

b143 **Jomier** Jacques, Para conocer l'Islam, [T]*Ortiz García* Alfonso. Estella 1989, VDivino. 165 p.; ill. 84-7151-641-1. – [R]ActuBbg 27 (1990) 342 (J. *Boada*).

b144 **Kassis** Hanna E., *Kobbervig* Karl I., Las concordancias del Coran. M 1987, Inst. Hispano-Árabe. xxxviii-882 p. 84-7472-076-1. – [R]BO 47 (1990) 232s (J. *Burton*: excellent).

b145 **Kennedy** Hugh, The Prophet and the age of the Caliphates; the Islamic Near East from the sixth to the fifteenth century: History of the Near East [first to appear] 1986 → 5,b167: [R]JRAS (1989) 131-4 (L. J. *Conrad*); Speculum 65 (1990) 182-4 (F. M. *Donner*).

b146 **Khalidi** Tarif, Classical Arab Islam; the culture and heritage of the golden age 1985 → 1,a785 ... 5,b169: [R]JNES 49 (1990) 360-2 (D. A. *Agius*).

b147 [T]**Khoury** A. T., (*Abdullah* M. S.), Der Koran 1987 → 4,d8: [R]TLZ 115 (1990) 256-8 (H. *Preissler*).

b147* The march of Islam A.D. 600-800. Richmond 1988, Time-Life. 176 p. 0-8094-6420-9 [OIAc F91,20].

b148 **Masson** Denise, L'eau, le feu, la lumière d'après la Bible, le Coran et les traditions monothéistes. P 1985, D-Brouwer. 186 p. – [R]RechSR 78 (1990) 606 (H. *Bourgeois*).

b148* *Monnot* G., Le *dhikr* dans le Coran et la commémoration dans l'Islam: → 618, Commémoration 1986/8, 247-253.

b149 [E]**Nasr** Seyyed H., Islamic spirituality, [I.] Foundations: EWSp 19, 1987 → 3,b460 ... 5,b189: [R]CritRR 2 (1989) 361-3 (A. A. *Asani*); JAOS 110 (1990) 368s (C. W. *Ernst*: admirable); StIran 18 (1989) 139s (G. *Monnot*).

b151 **Netton** Ian R., Allah transcendent; studies in the structure and semiotics of Islamic theology and cosmology: Exeter Arabic and Islamic Studies 5. L 1989, Routledge. xiii-383 p. £40. – [R]JSS 35 (1990) 357-9 (C. *Genequand*).

b152 **Peters** Francis E., Judaism, Christianity, and Islam; the classical texts and their interpretation, I. From covenant to community; II. The word and the law and the people of God; III. The works of the spirit. Princeton 1990, Univ. In one vol., $75. Paperback: xxv-408 p.; xxv-395 p.; xxv-408 p.; $15 each. 0-691-07356-2; -2044-2; -54-X; -55-8 [TDig 38,80].

b153 **Rippin** Andrew, Muslims, their religious beliefs and practices, I. The formative period: Library of Religious Beliefs. NY 1990, Routledge. xviii-155 p. $47.50; pa. $15. 0-415-04518-5; -9-3 [TDig 38,84].

b154 **Talbi** Mohammad, *Bucaille* Maurice, Réflexions sur le Coran 1989 → 5,b218: [R]RThom 89 (1989) 674 (J. *Jomier*) + 90 (1990) 339, objection de Bucaille; 340, rétractation de Jomier.

b155 **Wadud-Muhsin** A., Women in the Qur'ān; the absence of sex-role stereotyping in the text: diss. Michigan, [D]*Mir* M. AA 1988. 212 p. – DissA 50 (1989s) 463-A; ETL 66, p. 126*.

b156 *Ward* Seth, A fragment from an unknown work by al-ṬABARĪ on the tradition 'expel the Jews and Christians from the Arabian peninsula (and the lands of Islam)': BSO 53 (1990) 407-420.

b157 **Watt** W. Montgomery, Muhammad's Mecca; history in the Qur'ān 1988 → 5,b225: [R]JRAS (1989) 322s (W. L. *Treadwell*); JSS 35 (1990) 330-3 (L. J. *Conrad*); WZKM 80 (1990) 243s (A. A. *Ambros*).

b158 ᴱWatt W. M., *McDonald* M. V., ṬABARI 6, Muḥammad at Mecca 1989 → 5,b225: ᴿBSO 53 (1990) 328-330 (J. *Burton*).

b159 *Watt* W. Montgomery, Thoughts on the present state of Islamic studies: ExpTim 101 (1989s) 263-5 [+255 on EWSp].

b160 ᵀWilliams John A., Al-ṬABARI, The early ʿAbbāsī empire, I. The reign of Abū Jaʿfar al-Munṣūr, AD 754-775; II. The sons and grandsons of al-Manṣūr; the reigns of al-Mahdī, al-Hadī and Hārūn al-Rashīd. C 1988s, Univ. xx-263 p., £30 / xviii-342 p. £55. – ᴿJSS 35 (1990) 340-356 (A. *Elad*: vol. II is partially parallel to C. E. BOSWORTH's vol. 30 in the independent SUNY series, 1989: far more accurate).

M8.3   **Islam,** *evolutio recentior* – **later history and practice.**

b161 **Adriani** Maurilio, Islam tradizione e destino. F 1989, Nardini. 132 p. Lit. 25.000. – ᴿCiVit 45 (1990) 185 (B. *Farnetani*).

b162 **Amanat** Abbas, Resurrection and renewal; the making of the Babi movement in Iran, 1844-1850. Ithaca NY 1989, Cornell Univ. 461 p. $34.50. – ᴿJAAR 58 (1990) 691-7 (S. A. *Arjomand*).

b163 **Asin Palacios** Miguel, Amor humano, amor divino; IBN ARABI: Andalucía universal, tres culturas. Córdoba 1990, Almendro. 144 p. 84-86077-84-2.

b164 **Ayalon** David, Outsiders in the lands of Islam 1988 → 5,228: ᴿJRAS (1989) 327s (P. *Jackson*).

b165 ꟳAYALON David, Studies in Islamic history and civilization, ᴱSharon M. 1986 → 3,14: ᴿOLZ 85 (1990) 686-690 (D. *Sturm*).

b166 **Bannerman** Patrick, Islam in perspective; a guide to Islamic society, politics and law. L 1988, Routledge. viii-278 p. – ᴿBSO 53 (1990) 513-6 (A. K. S. *Lambton*).

b167 **Biegman** Niek, Egypte; derwisjen, heiligen, kermissen. Haag 1990, SDU. 176 p.; ill. ƒ125. 90-6179-075-1 [Bijdragen 51,465].

b168 *Borrmans* Maurice, Les droits de l'homme en milieu musulman: StMiss 39 (1990) 253-276 (-302, déclaration du Conseil Islamique de l'Europe).

b169 **Bürgel** Johann C., The feather of Simurgh; the 'licit magic' of the arts in medieval Islam 1988 → 4,b989: ᴿJAOS 110 (1990) 785-7 (J. *Renard*).

b170 *Çağatay* Neşet, The development of theological studies in Turkey: Belleten 54,209 (1990) 355-363 (❶ 347-354).

b171 ᵀᴱCelentano G., al-GHAZALI, Il libro della meditazione (*kitāb al-tefakkur*). Trieste 1988, Soc. Testi Islamici. 109 p. Lit. 16.000. – ᴿAsprenas 37 (1990) 366-8 (O. *Marra*).

b172 **Cilardo** Agostino, Studies on the Islamic law of inheritance: AION 50/2 Supp. 63. N 1990, Ist. Univ. Orientale. 63 p.

b173 *Corbin* Henry † 1978, Temple and contemplation [Eranos-Jb lectures]: Islamic texts and contexts. L 1986, Kegan Paul. xii-413 p. £9. – ᴿHeythJ 31 (1990) 95s (I. R. *Netton*: highly esoteric).

b174 **Deftery** Ferhad, The Isma'ilis, their history and development. C 1990, Univ. xviii-804 p. £60 [TR 86,345].

b175 *a) Denny* Frederick M., Ethical dimensions of Islamic ritual law [response *Gillen* Lois A.]; – *b) Ayoub* Mahmoud, Law and grace in Islam [response *Alishan* Leonardo P.]: → 526, Religion & Law 1985/90, 199-210 [211-220] / 221-9 [231-241].

b176 ᴱEsposito John L., Voices of resurgent Islam. Oxford 1983, UP. viii-294 p. $25. – ᴿRelStT 8,1s (1988) 97s (A. *Rippin*).

b177 **Esposito** John L., Islam, the straight path. NY 1988, Oxford-UP. x-230 p. $30; pa. $11. – ᴿRelStR 16 (1990) 363 (S. E. *Brown*: severe).

b178 ᵀᴱ**Gimaret** Daniel, *Monnot* Guy, SHAHRASTANI, Livre des religions et des sectes: Unesco Œuvres Représentatives. Lv 1986, Peeters. xxv-727 p. 90-6831-065-8. – ᴿBO 47 (1990) 503-5 (R. G. *Khoury*); JAOS 110 (1990) 139s (R. M. *Frank*).

b179 **Gramlich** Richard, Die Wunder der Freunde Gottes; Theologien und Erscheinungsformen des islamischen Heiligenwunders: FreibIslamSt 11,1987 → 5,b147: ᴿJAOS 110 (1990) 523s (Annemarie *Schimmel*).

b180 **Grunebaum** Gustav E. von, L'identité culturelle de l'Islam [1973, Eng.] ᵀ*Stuvéras* Roger: 'Tel'. P 1989, Gallimard. xvi-304 p. – ᴿRThom 90 (1990) 516s (J. *Jomier*).

b181 **Hartmann** Karl, Die Geschichte des Islam: Atlas-Tafel-Werk zur Geschichte der Weltreligionen 2. Stu 1989, Quell. ii-184 p. DM 56. – ᴿTLZ 115 (1990) 334-6 (C. *Kehnscherper*).

b182 ᵀ**Hillenbrand** Carole, The history of al-ṬABARI 26, The waning of the Umayyad caliphate. Albany 1989, SUNY. xiv-300 p. $49.50; pa. $20. – ᴿJSS 35 (1990) 337-340 (Patricia *Crone*).

b183 **Hiro** Dilip, Holy Wars; the rise of Islamic fundamentalism. NY 1989, Routledge. xiv-334. $15. ᴿTS 51 (1990) 793 (P. M. *Arnold*: Islamic fundamentalism thoroughly documented).

b184 *Homerin* T. Emil, A bird ascends in the night; elegy and immortality in Islam: JAAR 58 (1990) 541-568; bibliog. 568-573.

b185 ᴱ**Hovannisian** Richard G., Ethics in Islam; 9th G. LEVI DELLA VIDA biennial conference. Malibu CA 1985, Undena. 127 p. – ᴿOLZ 85 (1990) 448s (H. *Preissler*).

b186 ᴱ**Jackson** Paul, The Muslims of India; beliefs and practices. Bangalore 1988, Theol. Publ. xxix-297 p. rs 62. – ᴿVidyajyoti 53 (1989) 573s (M. *Talib*).

b187 *Khoury* Adel T., Islam, Theokratie und Toleranz: UnSa 45 (1990) 14-19.38.

b188 *Kimmel* Michael, *al.*, Religion and revolution in Iranian society: Social Compass 36,4 (Lv 1989) 411-4 [-550; < zɪᴛ 90,124].

b189 **Lane** Edward W., Arabian society in the Middle Ages; Studies from his [severely expurgated 1859 translation of] the Thousand and One Nights, ᴱ*Lane-Poole* Stanley 1883; new intr. *Bosworth* C. E. L/NJ 1987. Curzon/Humanities. xviii-283 p. – ᴿRBgPg 68 (1990) 954 (J. *Thiry*).

b190 **Lapidus** Ira M., A history of Islamic societies. C 1988, Univ. 1002 p.; 36 pl. $42.50. – ᴿJAAR 58 (1990) 297-301 (I. K. *Poonawala*); JAOS 110 (1990) 365s (M. G. *Morony*); JRAS (1990) 145-7 (R. I. *Moore*).

b191 *Lewis* Archibald R. †, The Islamic world and the Latin West, 1350-1500: Speculum 65 (1990) 833-844.

b192 *Mahdi* Muhsin, Al-FĀRĀBĪ's imperfect state [ᵀᴱ*Walzer* R. 1985]: JAOS 110 (1990) 691-726.

b193 ᴱ**Mantran** Robert, Les grandes dates de l'Islam. P 1990, Larousse. 288-xvi p. [RelStR 17,180, D. P. *Little*].

b194 *Melichar* Erwin, Zum Erkenntnis des Verfassungsgerichthofes über das Islamgesetz: → 54, ᶠGAMPL I., ArKR 39,1s (1990) 194-204.

b195 **Metzger** Henri, La correspondance passive d'Osman Hamdi Bey [1842-1910]: AIBL Mémoire NS 11. P 1990, de Boccard. 99 p.

b196 *Michel* Thomas F., Appunti sui musulmani sovietici e la 'glasnost': CC 141 (1990,4) 28-41.

b197 **Morony** Michael G., Iraq after the Muslim conquest. Princeton 1984, Univ. 689 p.; 8 fig. £65. – ᴿWeltOr 20s (1989s) 343-5 (H. *Halm*).

b198 **Nagel** Tilman, Die Festung des Glaubens; Triumph und Scheitern des islamischen Rationalismus im 11. Jahrhundert 1988 ➤ 5,b487: ᴿBSO 53 (1990) 130s (W. *Madelung*).

b198* *Nwyia* Paul †, Langage figuratif et figures bibliques dans l'exégèse coranique de ḤARRĀLĪ: MUSJ 51 (1990) 197-238 (239-255 ❹ 3 textes).

b199 **Rahman** Fazlur, Health and medicine in the Islamic tradition; change and identity, ᴱ*Marty* Martin, *Vaux* Kenneth. NY 1987, Crossroad. 149 p. $19. – ᴿJAAR 58 (1990) 141-3 (D. G. *Shaw*).

b199* *Reinhart* A. Kevin, Impurity; no danger [Islamic purity rules; E. GELLNER on KHOMEINI; Mary DOUGLAS]: HistRel 30 (1990s) 1-24.

b200 **Rodinson** Maxime, Europe and the mystique of Islam, [1980], ᵀ*Veinus* Roger. L 1988, Tauris. xx-163 p. £7. – ᴿJRAS (1989) 140-2 (C. F. *Beckingham*).

b201 **Salame** D. D. A., Faith and reason in the Islamic tradition and particularly in GHAZALI: diss. ᴰ*Ermatinger* C. St. Louis Univ. 1988. 250 p. – DissA 50 (1989s) 713-A; ETL 66, p. 125*.

b202 *Scheiber* Gottfried W., Theologischer Fundamentalismus im Islam: ➤ 1416, Eindeutige Antworten?², 1988, 63-88.

b203 **Sellam** Sadek, Être musulman aujourd'hui: Rencontres. P 1989, Nouvelle Cité. 184 p. – ᴿRThom 90 (1990) 512s (J. *Jomier*).

b204 *Thorau* Peter, Zur Geschichte der Mamluken und ihrer Erforschung [MUIR W. 1968 = 1986; *Irwin* R. 1986]: WeltOr 20s (1989s) 227-240.

b205 *Wasserstrom* Steven M., Recent works on the 'creative symbiosis' of Judaism and Islam [GOITEIN S. 1988; LEWIS B. 1984; NEWBY G. 1988...]: RelStR 16 (1990) 43-47.

b206 **Watt** W. M., Islamic fundamentalism and modernity 1989 ➤ 5,b223: ᴿSpiritus 31 (1990) 340 (M. *Borrmans*).

M8.4   *Alter philosemitismus* – **Islamic-Christian rapprochement.**

b207 **Anderson** Norman, Islam in the modern world; a Christian perspective. Leicester 1990, Apollos. 288 p. £12. 0-85111-141-8. – ᴿScotBEv 8 (1990) 130s (R. W. *Thomas*).

b208 **Arkoun** Mohammed, Ouverture sur l'Islam 1989 ➤ 5,b112; 0993-5754: ᴿÉTRel 65 (1990) 431 (Françoise *Smyth*); RThom 90 (1990) 513s (J. *Jomier*).

b209 *Arkoun* Mohammed, New perspectives for a Jewish-Christian-Muslim dialogue: ComViat 33 (1990) 19-25.

b210 **Arnaldez** Roger, Réflexions chrétiennes sur la mystique musulmane. P 1989, O.E.I.L. 248 p. – ᴿRThom 90 (1990) 677s (J. *Jomier*).

b211 **Bayly** Susan, Saints, goddesses and kings; Muslims and Christians in south Indian society, 1790-1900: S. Asian Studies 43. C 1989, Univ. xv-504 p. $59.50. 0-521-37201-1 [TDig 38,47; RelStR 17,333, S. P. *Brock*].

b212 *Borrmans* Maurice, L'Académie royale de Jordanie et le dialogue islamo-chrétien: PrOrChr 40 (1990) 79-92.

b213 **Busse** Heribert, Die theologischen Beziehungen des Islams zu Judentum und Christentum; Grundlagen des Dialogs im Koran und die gegenwärtige Situation: Grundzüge 72. Da 1988, Wiss. vi-193 p. DM 36. – ᴿTGegw 33 (1990) 72s (E. *Grunert*); WZKM 80 (1990) 248s (A. A. *Ambros*).

b214 **Caspar** Robert, Pour un regard chrétien sur l'Islam; Religions en Dialogue. P 1990, Centurion. 206 p. – ᴿÉtudes 373 (1990) 139 (L.

Pouzet, aussi p. 227-238); Islamochristiana 16 (1990) 316s (M. *Borrmans*); RThom 90 (1990) 675s (J. *Jomier*).

b215 The challenge of the Scripture; the Bible and the Qur'ān [Ces Écritures qui nous questionnent 1987], ᵀ*Brown* S. E.: Faith Meets Faith [➤ 5,b151]. Mkn 1989, Orbis. vii-104 p. $27; pa. $14. 0-88344-651-0; -0-2 [NTAbs 38,235]. – ᴿExpTim 102 (1990s) 95 (M. *Forward*: challenging but dull, and J. *Gabus* shows Reformed assumptions).

b216 *Chapman* Colin, Going soft on Islam? [... hesitant answers to 'is there any salvation or revelation in it?' 'is it inspired by the Devil?']: VoxEvca 19 (1989) 7-31.

b217 **Colpe** Carsten, Problem Islam. Fra 1989, Athenäum. 160 p. DM 28. – ᴿEvKomm 23 (1990) 763s (H. *Klautke*).

b218 **Étienne** Bruno, La France et l'Islam. P 1989, Hachette. 321 p. – ᴿSpiritus 31 (1990) 340s (M. *Borrmans*).

b219 *a)* *Ferré* André, Muḥammad a-t-il exclu de l'Arabie les Juifs et les Chrétiens?; – *b)* *Puel* Hugues, Les droits économiques et sociaux en Islam; un point de vue chrétien; – *c)* *Didier* Hugues, Interférences islamochrétiennes dans les représentations du Bouddhisme: Islamochristiana 16 (1990) 43-65 / 15-23 / 115-138,

b220 *Gilliot* Claude, Bulletin d'islamologie et d'études arabes: RSPT 74 (1990) 477-505.

b221 **Khoury** Paul, Matériaux pour servir à l'étude de la controverse théologique islamo-chrétienne de langue arabe du VIIIᵉ au XIIᵉ siècle 1989 ➤ 5,b174: ᴿIslamochristiana 16 (1990) 328s (J.-M. *Gaudeul*); OrChrPer 56 (1990) 199 (V. *Poggi*).

b222 *Lawrence* Bruce B., Current problematics in the study of Islam: RelStR 16 (1990) 293-300 [ARKOUN M. 1987; ASAD T. 1986; ᴱMARTIN R. 1985].

b223 **Longton** Joseph, Fils d'Abraham; panorama des communautés juives, chrétiennes et musulmanes 1987 ➤ 5,b178: ᴿHokhma 45 (1990) 67-69 (J.-J. *Hugé*, aussi sur ROBBERECHTS E., Hassidim 1990; KAPLAN S., Falashas 1990).

b224 **Moucarry** Chawkat G., Islam and Christianity at the crossroads, ᵀ*Monkcom* David. ..., Lion. £5. – ᴿTablet 243 (1989) 258 (E. *Hulmes*).

b225 **Riccardi** Andrea, *al.*, Cristianesimo e Islam; l'amicizia possibile. Brescia 1989, Morcelliana. 166 p. Lit. 16.000. – ᴿSapienza 43 (1990) 343s (B. *Belletti*).

b226 *Rizzardi* Giuseppe, [➤ 5,b203] Islam, errore o eresia? VII-VIII: Renovatio 24 (1989) 9-30, 187-225, fine.

b227 **Rotter** Ekkehart, Abendland und Sarazener; das okzidentale Araberbild und seine Entstehung im Frühmittelalter: Der Islam Beih. 11, 1986 ➤ 3,b471; 5,b204: ᴿGrazBei 17 (1990) 296-8 (S. *Olms*).

b227* ᵀᴱ*Samir Khalil*, Un traité du Cheikh Abū ʿAlī NAẒĪF ibn Yumn sur l'accord des Chrétiens entre eux malgré leur désaccord dans l'expression: MUSJ 51 (1990) 327-343.

b228 **Sanson** Henri, [Christianisme au miroir de l'Islam; 1984]; Dialogue intérieur avec l'Islam: Religions en dialogue. P 1990, Centurion. 214 p. F 135. – ᴿÉtudes 373 (1990) 571s (J. *Thomas*); RThom [85 (1985) 323] 90 (1990) 676s (J. *Jomier*).

b229 *Tessaro* Elisa, Gli studi islamici a Padova: StPatav 37 (1990) 375-382.

b230 **Thomson** Ahmad, Blood on the Cross; Islam in Spain in the light of Christian persecution through the ages. L 1989, Taha. 351 p. – ᴿIslamochristiana 16 (1990) 345s (J. *Lacunza Balda*).

b231 **Zirker** Hans, Christentum und Islam 1989 → 5,b2271: ᴿLebZeug 44 (1989) 310 (W. *Hering*).

M8.5 **Religiones Indiae** *et variae.*

b232 **Ahir** Diwan Chand, Heritage of Buddhism. Delhi 1989, 'B.R.' $34. 81-7018-552-1 [TDig 37,341 sans pp.].

b233 ᴱ**Alger** Harvey P., Understanding mantras: Rel.St. Albany 1989, SUNY. 530 p. $59.50. – ᴿRHR 207 (1990) 189-192 (G. *Colas*).

b234 *Burford* Grace G., Believing and seeing; the roles of faith, reason, and experience in Theravāda Buddhism: Horizons 17 (1990) 217-227.

b235 **Carruthers** Michael, *al.*, Founders of faith; the Buddha [*Dawson* Raymond, Confucius ...]. Ox 1989, Univ.-P. 376 p. £9 [JTS 41,823].

b236 *Chang* Aloysius B., Liberative elements in the Confucian tradition: Japanese Religions 16,2 (Kyoto 1990) 24-42; summary TContext 8/1, 127.

b237 *Coccioli* Carlo, Budda e il suo glorioso mondo. Mi 1990, Rusconi. 240 p. Lit. 35.000. – ᴿCiVit 45 (1990) 634 (Duccia *Camiciotti*).

b238 *a*) *Dhavamony* Mariasusai, Hindu hospitality and tolerance (Hindu attitude to foreigners, strangers and immigrants); – *b*) *Raj* Sebasti L., Human rights movements within Hinduism (... Dravidian); – *c*) *Fuss* Michael, Der Buddha und die Menschenrechte nach dem Dhammapada: StMiss 39 (1990) 303-320 / 321-339 (341-358, *Wayman* A.) / 359-376.

b239 *Dhavamony* Mariasusai, L'Induismo, via di salvezza oggi?: CC 141 (1990,1) 128-141.

b240 **Dumoulin** Heinrich, Zen Buddhism, a history² [1959, Eng. ¹1963], ᵀ*Heisig* James W., *Knitter* Paul: I. India and China, xxiii-349 p.; II. Japan, x-509 p. NY 1988-90, Macmillan. $55 each; pa. $15. 0-02-908230-7; pa. -60-9 [TDig 37,367].

b241 ᴱ**Ellwood** Robert S., Eastern spirituality in America; selected writings. NY 1987, Paulist. vi-246 p. – ᴿTLZ 115 (1990) 336s (N.-P. *Moritzen*).

b242 **Goyal** S. R., A history of Indian Buddhism. Meerut 1987, Kusumanjali. 532 p.; 8 pl. rs 350. – ᴿJRAS (1989) 168s (L. S. *Cousins*).

b243 *Griffiths* Paul J., Encountering Buddha theologically: TTod 47 (1990s) 39-51.

b244 *Grimes* John, Two paradigms of religious language [K. Stchidananda *Murty*, Revelation and reason in Advaita Vedānta 1974]: SR 19 (1990) 331-8.

b245 **Kamstra** Jacques H., De Japanse religie, een fenomenale godsdienst. Hilversum 1988, Gooi & S. 157 p. *f* 29,50. 90-3040-448-5. – ᴿNedTTs 44 (1990) 247s (B. C. A. *Walraven*).

b246 **Karow** O., Symbolik des Buddhismus; Tafelband: Symbolik der Religionen 22. Stu 1989, Hiersemann. 376 p.; 220 fig. DM 190. – ᴿNRT 112 (1990) 278 (J. *Masson*).

b247 *King* Winston L., Motivated goodness and unmotivated perfection in Buddhist ethics: AnglTR 71 (1989) 143-152.

b248 **Kinsley** David, Hindu goddesses; visions of the divine feminine in the Hindu religious tradition 1986 → 4,d61: ᴿJRel 69 (1989) 289s (R. L. *Brubaker*).

b249 **Klimkeit** Hans-J., Der Buddha, Leben und Lehre: Urban-Tb 428. Stu 1990, Kohlhammer. 244 p., 1 fig. DM 22 [OLZ 86,98, A. v. *Gabain*].

b250 **Klostermaier** Klaus K., A survey of Hinduism. Albany 1989, SUNY. xvi-649 p.; 40 fig.; 35 phot. $56.50; pa. $19 [RelStR 17,90, G. *Yocum*]. – ᴿTLZ 115 (1990) 14s (H. W. *Gensichen*).

b251 *Lorenz* Günther, Seelenwanderungslehre und Lebensführung in Oberschichten; Griechenland und Indien: TLZ 115 (1990) 409-416.

b256 **Mbiti** John S., African religions and philosophy²ʳᵉᵛ [¹1968]. Ox 1990,
Heinemann. xv-288 p. 0-435-89591-5. → H8.6, where many items deal
with African religions.

b257 **Morgan** Kenneth W., Reaching for the moon; on Asian religious paths.
Chambersburg PA c. 1990, Anima. $21 [RelStR 17,62 adv.].

b258 **Morrinis** E. Alan, Pilgrimage in the Hindu tradition; a case study of
West Bengal. New Delhi 1984, Oxford-UP. $48. – ᴿRelStT 8,1s (1988)
88-91 (L. *Anderson*: spells Morinis in text, with appropriate apostrophe;
Morrinis in title, with inexplicable apostrophe).

b259 **Oberhammer** Gerhard, Philosophy of religion in Hindu thought. Delhi
1989, Sri Satguru. xxii-149 p. rs 75. 81-7030-204-8. – ᴿVidyajyoti 54
(1990) 429s (G. *Gispert-Sauch*).

b260 **Omodeo-Salé** Marino, Il Buddhismo; dalla filosofia alla religione. Mi
1990, Àncora. 174 p. Lit. 16.000. – ᴿCiVit 45 (1990) 387 (B. *Farnetani*).

b261 **Panikkar** Raimundo, The silence of God; the answer of the Buddha
1989 → 5,b269: ᴿCalvinT 25 (1990) 137-9 (R. R. *DeRidder*: Buddhists
admit they have no written records from within some centuries after the
founder's death); Missiology 18 (1990) 364 (C. A. J. *Pillai*).

b262 **Preston** D. L., The social organization of Zen practice [California;
compared with Jonestown] C 1988, Univ. 171 p. £25. 0-5213-5000-X. –
ᴿNcdTTs 44 (1990) 335s (J. H. *Kamstra*).

b263 **Ruegg** David S., Buddha-nature... [Jordan Lectures 13]. L 1989, School
of Oriental and African Studies. 220 p. F 200. – ᴿRHR 207 (1990) 422-4
(A. *Bareau*).

b264 *Scott* David A., The Iranian face of Buddhism: EWest 40 (1990) 43-77;
8 fig.

b265 *Smith* Brian K., Eaters, food, and social hierarchy in ancient India; a
dietary guide to a revolution of values: JAAR 58 (1990) 177-205.

M8.8   *Interactio cum religione orientali;* **Christian dialogue with the East.**

b266 **Alldritt** Leslie D., Ontology of love; the religio-philosophical thought of
Paul TILLICH and Zen Buddhism: diss. Temple, ᴰ*De Martino* R. Ph
1990. – RelStR 17,190.

b267 *Barnes* Michael, The Buddhist-Christian dialogue: Way 30 (1990) 55-64.

b268 **Ching** Julia, Konfuzianismus und Christentum, ᵀ*Köhn* Detlef: Dialog
der Religionen. Mainz 1989, Grünewald. 230 p. DM 39,80. 3-7867-
1442-8. – ᴿActuBbg 27 (1990) 240 (J. *Boada*); MüTZ 41 (1990) 307s (E.
Gössmann).

b269 *Citraro* Gloria, Il confucianesimo di Matteo RICCI: SMSR 56 (1990)
279-284.

b270 *Clooney* Francis X., Vedānta, theology, and modernity; theology's new
conversation with the world's religions: TS 51 (1990) 268-285.

b271 **Cobb** J. B., Bouddhisme-christianisme 1988 → 5,b238: ᴿActuBbg 26
(1989) 50s (J. *Boada*); LavalTP 46 (1990) 120 (J.-C. *Breton*); NRT 112
(1990) 277 (J. *Masson*); Spiritus 31 (1990) 224 (D. *Regan*).

ᴱ**Creed** A., *Natavarian* V., Monastic life in the Christian and Hindu
tradition 1985/90 → 776*.

b272 **Delahoutre** M., Textes sacrés de l'Inde et prière chrétienne des Heures:
BibVC. P 1989, Lethielleux. 261 p. F 96 [NRT 113,286, J. *Masson*:
douteux].

b273 *Fernhout* R., BARTHS kritiek op de analogia entis toegepast op de hymne op Puruṣa; achtergrondbijdrage voor een kritische dialog tussen christenen en hindoes: KerkT 41 (1990) 206-226,

b274 *a) Florida* Robert E., What does comparative religion compare? The Buddhist-Christian example; – *b) Petit* Gaston, Quelques réflexions sur l'iconographie symbolique hindoue et chrétienne: SR 19 (1990) 163-171 / 171-190.

b275 *Fritsch-Oppermann* Sybille, Der Tod, Ende oder Übergang? Über Zeit und Ewigkeit in Christentum und Buddhismus: Zeitschrift für Mission 16,4 (1990) 214-223 [< TContext 8/2, p. 106].

b276 **Gira** Dennis, Comprendre le bouddhisme: Religions en dialogue. P 1989, Centurion. 205 p. F 115. – ᴿNRT 112 (1990) 277s (J. *Masson*); RICathP 33 (1990) 199s (P. *Massein*); ScEsp 42 (1990) 121s (A. *Couture*); Spiritus 31 (1990) 458s (E. *Pezet*).

b277 **Gozier** André, Le père Henri LE SAUX à la rencontre de l'Hindouisme: Religions en dialogue. P 1989, Centurion. 167 p. F 89. – ᴿNRT 112 (1990) 625s (J. *Masson*).

b278 **Griffiths** Bede, A new vision of reality; Western science, Eastern mysticism and Christian faith. L 1989, Collins. £16. – ᴿTablet 243 (1989) 1516s (J. *Todd*).

b279 ᴱ**Hiltebeitel** Alf, Criminal gods and demon devotees; essays on the guardians of popular Hinduism [< 3 1985s meetings]. Albany 1989, SUNY. xii-491 p. $74.50; pa. $24.50. 0-88706-981-9; -2-7 [TDig 37,256].

b280 **Hooker** Roger, Thomas in Hinduism and Christianity. Fra 1989, Lang, 396 p. Fs 74. 3-631-40416-6. – ᴿExpTim 101 (1989s) (P. D. *Bishop*).

b281 **Huber** Friedrich, Die Bhagavad-Gita in der neueren indischen Auslegung und in der Begegnung mit dem christlichen Glauben: Hab.-Diss. ᴰ*Moritzen*. Erlangen 1989s. – TR 86 (1990) 509.

b282 *Keenan* John P., Mahāyāna theology; how to reclaim an ancient Christian tradition: AnglTR 71 (1989) 377-394.

b283 *Kristiansen* Roald E., Den tomme Gud; Kristen gudstro og buddhistisk tomhetslære: NorTTs 90 (1989) 19-30.

b284 **Krüger** J. S. (Kobus), Metatheism; early Buddhism and traditional Christian theism. Pretoria c. 1990, Unisa. 152 p. $13. 0-86981-620-9.

b285 **Küng** Hans, *Bechert* Heinz, Buddhismus: Christentum und Weltreligionen 3, GTB Sachbuch 18. Gü 1988, Mohn. 234 p. DM 12,80. – ᴿTLZ 115 (1990) 491-5 (K.-W. *Tröger*, auch über 1-2).

b286 **Malieckal** Louis, Yajna and Eucharist; an inter-religious approach to the theology of sacrifice [diss. LvN]. Bangalore 1989, Dharmaran. 368 p. [TContext 8/1, 141, G. *Evers*].

b287 *Marrion* Malachy, The Hindu Code of Manu and the Regula Benedicti; forest dweller, wandering ascetic and monk: StMon 32 (1990) 7-58.

b288 *Neu* Rainer, Die Analogie von buddhistischem und christlichem Mönchtum; eine sozialgeschichtliche und religionswissenschaftliche Untersuchung: ZRGg 42 (1990) 97-121.

b289 **Nguyen van Tot** Pierre, Le Bouddha et le Christ ᴰ1987 → 5,b265: ᴿTeresianum 40 (1989) 234s (E. *Pacho*).

b290 **Pieris** Aloysius, Love meets wisdom; a Christian experience of Buddhism 1988 → 5,b272: ᴿIntRMiss 79 (1990) 230-2 (D. *Nicholl*, also on HOOKER R., *al.*); Missiology 18 (1990) 89s (M. G. *Fonner*).

b291 **Pieris** Aloysius, Liebe und Weisheit; Begegnung von Christentum und Buddhismus 1989 → 5,b273: ᴿActuBbg 27 (1990) 243s (J. *Boada*); EvKomm 23 (1990) 54 (W. *Kröger*: 'Dialog statt Befreiungstheologie?');

MüTZ 41 (1990) 14s (P. *Schmidt-Leukel*); ÖkRu 39 (1990) 376s (A. *Rössler*); TContext 7 (1980) 133 (G. *Evers*); ZkT 112 (1990) 114s (K. H. *Neufeld*).

b292 **Pulsfort** Ernst, Christliche Ashrams in Indien; zwischen dem religiösen Erbe Indiens und der christlichen Tradition des Abendlandes [Diss. Münster]; MünsteranerTAbh 7. Altenberge 1989. 235 p. [TContext 8/1, 139, G. *Evers*]. – ᴿZMissRW 74 (1990) 313s (R. *Hummel*).

b293 **Roth** Nancy, A new Christian yoga. L 1989, Cowley. 118 p. $20 with tape. 0-936384-96-4. – ᴿExpTim 102 (1990s) 94s (N. *Slee*).

b294 **Sahay** K. N., Christianity and culture change in India. New Delhi 1986, Inter-India. 332 p. rs 245. – ᴿSevartham 13 (1988) 138s (F. *Matthijs*).

b295 ᴱ**Sharma** Arvind, Neo-Hindu views of Christianity 1988 → 5,518: ᴿJAOS 110 (1990) 737s (P. *Olivelle*).

b296 **Spink** Kathryn, A sense of the sacred ... Bede GRIFFITHS 1989 → 5,b279: ᴿTS 51 (1990) 179s (D. *Toolan*).

b297 **Staffner** Hans, Jesus Christ and the Hindu community; is a synthesis of Hinduism and Christianity possible? 1988 → 5,b280: ᴿMissiology 18 (1990) 489 (R. E. *Hedlund*); TS 51 (1990) 570s (J. D. *Redington*).

b298 *a) Taylor* Richard W., Ashrams and the Kingdom of God; – *b) Samy* Ama, The way of Zen; – *c) Anand* Subhash, The light-bearing dark night: Vidyajyoti 54 (1990) 19-27 / 73-86; 10 fig. / 53-71.

b299 **Thelle** Notto B., Buddhism and Christianity in Japan; from conflict to dialogue, 1854-1899: 1987 → 3,b551: ᴿJRel 69 (1989) 146 (J. *Heisig*).

b300 **Thomas** M. M., Christus im neuen Indien; Reform-Hinduismus und Christentum [The acknowledged Christ of the Indian renaissance 1969, minus three chapters], ᵀᴱ*Gensichen* A, & H.-W. Gö 1989, Vandenhoeck & R. 204 p. DM 39,80. 3-525-56327-2. – ᴿTsTNijm 30 (1990) 318 (J. van *Lin*).

b301 *Tweed* Thomas A., 'The seeming anomaly of Buddhist negation'; American encounters with Buddhist distinctiveness, 1858-1887: HarvTR 83 (1990) 65-92.

b302 **Vempeny** Ishanand, Kṛṣṇa and Christ, in the light of some of the fundamental themes and concepts of the Bhagavad Gītā and the New Testament 1988 → 5,b284: ᴿNRT 112 (1990) 626s (J. *Masson*); TS 51 (1990) 554-6 (F. X. *Clooney*); Vidyajyoti 53 (1989) 96s (J. T. *Matheikal*).

b303 *Waldenfels* Hans, Buddhism and Christianity in dialogue, ᵀ*Arndt* Stephen W.: CommND 15 (1988) 411-422 [-467, *al.*].

b304 *Wijngaards* J., Learning [religious thought] from the East: Tablet 243 (1989) 1461s: new Vatican document too cautious (see unsigned analysis p. 1479s).

XVII,1 Historia Medii Orientis Biblici

Q1 *Syria, Canaan,* **Israel Veteris Testamenti.**

b305 *a) Ackroyd* Peter, The written evidence for Palestine; – *b) Stern* Ephraim, New evidence for the administrative divisions of Palestine in the Persian period; – *c) Elayi* Josette, The Phoenician cities of the Achaemenid period: → 822, Achaemenid 4 (1986/90) 207-220 / 221-6 / 227-237.

b306 **Ahlström** Gösta W., Who were the Israelites? 1986 → 2,9202.b811 ... 5,b287: ᴿBASOR 277s (1990) 135s (D. C. *Hopkins*); JNES 49 (1990) 81-83 (E. A. *Knauf*).

b307 **Arasola** K., The end of historicism; Millerite hermeneutic of time prophecies in the OT. U 1990, Univ. x-226 p. 91-630-0105-5 [NTAbs 35,136].

b308 *Asurmendi* Jesús, *García Martínez* Florentino, Historia e instituciones del pueblo bíblico: → 370*, Introd. I, 1990, 119-365.

b309 [Martins] **Balancin** Euclides, História do Povo de Deus. São Paulo 1990, Paulinas. 166 p. 85-05-01091-4. – ᴿPerspT 21 (1990) 415s (J. *Vitório*).

b310 *Barr* James, LUTHER and biblical chronology [sometimes sensibly critical, sometimes wildly inventive]: BJRyL 72,1 (1990) 51-67.

b311 **Bock** Sebastian, Kleine [→ 5,b291!] Geschichte des Volkes Israel, von den Anfängen bis in die Zeit des NTs; Einl. *Lohfink* Norbert 1989; 3-451-08642-5: ᴿTPQ 138 (1990) 274 (Irmtraud *Fischer*).

b312 **Carceles** M. A., Historia bíblica. M 1990, Palabra. 166 p. [RelCu 36,515].

b313 **Cazelles** Henri, Storia politica di Israele dalle origini ad Alessandro Magno [1981] ᵀ1985 → 2,9209 ... 4,d92: ᴿBenedictina 35 (1988) 218s (L. De *Lorenzi*).

b314 **Clauss** Manfred, Geschichte Israels 1986 → 2,9210 ... 5,b294: ᴿOLZ 85 (1990) 432-4 (S. *Herrmann*: unzureichend).

b315 **Daniel-Rops** H., El pueblo de la Biblia [1942], ᵀ*Correa Veglison* Antonio F. de: Arcaduz. M 1989, Palabra. 374 p. pt 1651. 84-7118-639-X. – ᴿActuBbg 27 (1990) 60s (R. de *Sivatte*).

b316 **Donner** Herbert, Geschichte des Volkes Israel 2, 1986 → 4,d94; 5,b295: ᴿOLZ 85 (1990) 176-8 (R. *Stahl*).

b316* *Durand* Jean-Marie, L'assemblée en Syrie à l'époque pré-amorite: QuadSemit 16 / MiscEbl 2 (1989) 27-44.

b317 **Elgavish** David, ⊕ *Ha-šalîḥ* ... The emissary and his mission; the diplomatic service in the cuneiform sources and in the Bible: diss. Bar-Ilan, ᴰ*Artzi* P. Ramat-Gan 1989. v-348 p. + Eng. summ. 175 p. – OIAc S90; RTLv 27, p. 587 ['523 p., 1990'].

b318 **Görg** Manfred, Beiträge zur Zeitgeschichte der Anfänge Israels: ÄgAT 22, 1989 → 5,b297: ᴿLA 40 (1990) 492 (A. *Niccacci*).

b319 *a*) *Graf* David F., The origin of the Nabataeans; – *b*) *Bartlett* John R., From Edomites to Nabataeans; the problem of continuity; – *c*) *Abdul-Karim* Mohammed A., The Nabataeans in the Arab tradition: → 783, Aram 2 (1989/90) 45-75 / 25-34 / 421-4.

b320 ᴱ**Hayes** J. H., *Miller* J. M., Israelite and Judaean history. L/Ph 1990 pa. = 1977, SCM/Trinity. xxxi-236 p. £20. 0-334-02435-8 [BL 91,36, G. H. *Jones*: invaluable, but bibliographies not updated after 13 years; only some errors corrected (DEVER!)]. – ᴿCarthaginensia 6 (1990) 367s (R. *Sanz Valdivieso*).

b321 **Herrmann** Siegfried, Historia de Israel en la época del Antiguo Testamento²ʳᵉᵛ [1973],ᵀ: BtEstB 23. S 1985, Sígueme. 554 p. – ᴿCiTom 117 (1990) 148-150 (J. A. M.).

b322 **Hughes** Jeremy, Secrets of the times; myth and history in biblical chronology [schematic and mythical but based on historically retrievable material; < diss.]: JStOT supp 66. Sheffield 1990, Academic. xiv-515 p. £35. 1-85075-178-1 [BL 91,18, G. H. *Jones*]. – ᴿExpTim 102 (1990s) 21

(B. *Coggins*: schematic; co-regencies irrelevant); JJS 41 (1990) 261-3 (J. *Barton*: clarity and common sense).

b324 **Jagersma** Hendrik,   Israels Geschichte zur alttestamentlichen Zeit [1979 → 61,m976], ᵀ*Thiele* Friedrich.   Konstanz 1982, Christliche-VA.   319 p. – ᴿZSavR 106 (1989) 739-741 (B. *Diamant*, Eng.).

b325 ᴱ**Jepsen** Alfred,   *Schunck* Klaus-Dietrich,   Von Sinuhe bis Nebukadnezar; Dokumente aus der Umwelt des Alten Testaments⁴ʳᵉᵛ [¹1975 → 56, 7276]. B 1988, Ev.-V.   255 p.; 89 fig. M 19,80. – ᴿTLZ [104 (1979)] 115 (1990) 423-5 (G. W. *Ahlström*); ZkT 112 (1990) 93s (J. M. *Oesch*).

b326 *King* Philip J.,   The great 8th century: BR 6,4 (1989) 22-33.44; ill. [best BR 1989 article: BA 7,3 p. 13].

b327 **Knauf** Ernst A.,   Ismael²: AbhDPV, 1989 [= ¹1985 → 1,a924 + Addenda 135-163] → 4,d97; 5,b303:   ᴿOrAnt 28 (1989) 275-7 (G. *Garbini*); RHPR 70 (1990) 247s (J.-G. *Heintz*).

b328 **Kreuzer** Siegfried,   Die Frühgeschichte Israels…:   BZAW 178, ᴰ1989 → 5,b304:   ᴿÉTRel 65 (1990) 618s (T. *Römer*); JBL 109 (1990) 699-701 (J. S. *Rogers*); TR 86 (1990) 195-7 (H. *Reventlow*).

b329 **Lemche** Niels P.,   Ancient Israel; a new history of Israelite society: Biblical Seminar 1988 → 4,d98; 5,b306:   ᴿBA 53 (1990) 177s (F. S. *Frick*); Biblica 71 (1990) 559-561 (T. L. *Thompson*: a sound and recommended textbook, though not as exciting as his 1985 Early Israel, and 'not yet… independent of the biblical historiography'); BO 47 (1990) 449-453 (M. J. *Mulder*); BZ 34 (1990) 312-5 (H. *Engel*); Carthaginensia 6 (1990) 195 (R. *Sanz Valdivieso*); CBQ 52 (1990) 722-4 (A. J. *Hauser*: replete with bare 'possibilities'); Henoch 12 (1990) 108-110 (J. A. *Soggin*: ottimo); Interpretation 44 (1990) 202s (R. *Gnuse*); JBL 109 (1990) 317-320 (D. C. *Hopkins*); JSS 35 (1990) 133s (R. N. *Whybray*); RB 97 (1990) 604s (J.-M. de *Tarragon*); VT 46 (1990) 247-9 (J. A. *Emerton*).

b329* **Malamat** A.,   Mari and the early Israelite experience (Schweich Lectures 1984) 1989 → 5,b307:   ᴿBL (1990) 33s (W. G. *Lambert*); Henoch 12 (1990) 232s (J. A. *Soggin*); Orientalia 59 (1990) 550-2 (M. *Liverani*); ZAW 102 (1990) 450 (O. *Kaiser*).

b330 **Merrill** Eugene H.,   Kingdom of priests; a history of Old Testament Israel 1987 → 4,2101:   ᴿEvQ 62 (1990) 356s (D. G. *Deboys*).

b331 *Millard* A. R.,   a) Israelite and Aramean history in the light of inscriptions: TyndB 41 (1990) 261-275; – b) The homeland of Zakkur [formerly read Zakir; stela found 1903 at Afis, 40 k SW Aleppo]: → 125, ᶠSᴢɴʏᴄᴇʀ M., Semitica 39 (1990) 47-52.

b332 **Miller** J. M., *Hayes* J. H.,   A history of ancient Israel and Judah 1986 → 2,9232… 5,b311: ᴿJJS 41 (1990) 117-9 (J. *Hughes*); Vidyajyoti 53 (1989) 516s (P. M. *Meagher*).

b333 **Neher** André & Renée.   **⊕** Biblical history of the people of Israel.   J 1985s.   2 vol., 24 fig., maps.   965-09-0048-9 [KirSef 62 (1988s) p. 21].

b333* **Nibbi** Alessandra,   Canaan and Canaanite in ancient Egypt 1989 → 5,b114:   ᴿMuséon 103 (1990) 367-9 (C. *Vandersleyen*).

b334 **Nordheim** Eckhard von,   Die Selbstbehauptung Israels in der Welt des Alten Orients: Hab.-Diss. ᴰ*Georgi*.   Fra 1989s. – TR 86 (1990) 509.

b335 **Reinhold** G. G. G.,   Die Beziehungen Altisraels zu den aramäischen Staaten in der israelitisch-jüdischen Königszeit [ev. Diss. Frankfurt 1989, ᴰ*Schottroff* W.]: EurHS 23/368.   xv-370 p.; 17 pl. Fs 98. – ZAW 103,455 (H.-C. *Schmitt*).

b336 ᴱ**Rosenthal** Franz, ṬABARI, history [SUNY]; introduction; creation to flood: → 5, 1974; on SUNY vol. 18 (*Morony* M.) and 32 (*Bosworth* C.):

RCritRR 2 (1989) 357-360 (L. T. *Librando*); cf. EYarshater E., TABARI, History in 38 vol. → 3,b782; RBSO 52 (1989) 402 (A. *Rippin*).

b336* **Said** S. S., *Stephenson* F. R., *Rada* W., Records of solar eclipses in Arabic chronicles: BSO 52 (1989) 38-64.

b337 **Schäfer** Peter, Histoire des Juifs dans l'antiquité 1989 → 5,b320; TSchulte Pascale: RMondeB 65 (1990) 71 (I. H. *Dalmais*); RHPR 70 (1990) 134 (F. *Blanchetière*: traduction souvent laborieuse; titre plutôt 'Histoire de la Palestine d'Alexandre à la conquête arabe'); Salesianum 52 (1990) 743 (R. *Vicent*).

b338 EShanks Hershel, Ancient Israel, a short history... → 4,326; Wsh 1988, BA[R]Soc. [→ 5,b322, 1989 SPCK]: RBA 53 (1990) 45 (C. P. *Mariottini*); CBQ 52 (1990) 538-540 (W. H. *Shea*); CritRR 3 (1990) 93-96 (Diana *Edelman* would not use it as a classroom text).

b339 **Sigrist** Christian, *Neu* Rainer, Ethnologische Texte zum AT. 1. Vor- und Frühgeschichte Israels 1989 → 5,b323; DM 48: RZAW 102 (1990) 300 (tit. pp.).

b340 **Smelik** Klaas A. D., Historische Dokumente aus dem alten Israel 1987 → 3,b592... 5,b324: RCBQ 52 (1990) 135-7 (W. H. *Shea*); TR 86 (1990) 105s (D. *Conrad*).

b341 [*Soggin* J. A., *al.*] Le origini di Israele 1986/7 → 3,564... 5,b330: RCBQ 52 (1990) 583s (J. J. *Sullivan*); Gregorianum 71 (1990) 175-8 (G. L. *Prato*).

b341* **Soggin** J. Alberto, A history of ancient Israel 1984 → 65,9573... 5,b329: RCritRR 3 (1990) 96-98 (H. D. *Lance*).

b342 *a)* *Tadmor* Hayim, Alleanza e dipendenza nell'antica Mesopotamia e in Israele; terminologia e prassi; – *b)* *Zaccagnini* Carlo, The forms of alliance and subjugation in the Near East of the Late Bronze Age; – *c)* *Weinfeld* Moshe, The common heritage of covenantal traditions in the ancient world: → 724, Trattati 1986/90, 17-36 / 37-79 / 175-191.

b343 **Vogt** Klaus, Piccola storia d'Israele; quando arriverete in quella terra. Assisi 1989, Cittadella. 128 p. Lit. 12.000. – RBenedictina 37 (1990) 517-521 (P. M. *Pierini*, also on four cognate volumetti).

Q2 **Historiographia** – theologia historiae.

b344 **Adler** William, Time immemorial; ancient history and its sources in Christian chronography from Junilius AFRICANUS to George SYNCELLUS: DumbO St 26. Wsh 1989. vii-263 p.

b345 *Ankersmit* F. R., Historiography and postmodernism: History and Theory 28 (1989) 137-153.

b346 TEArnaud-Lindet Marie-Pierre: Paul OROSIUS, Histoires (Contre les païens): Coll. Budé. P 1990, BLettres. I. 301 (doub.) p. 2-251-01347-0.

b347 **Bartlett** John R., The Bible; faith and evidence; a critical enquiry into the nature of biblical history. L 1990, British Museum. [viii-] 272 p.; maps. [OIAc F91]. 0-7141-1717-X.

b348 **Bellomi** Lorenzo, Con Dio dentro la storia; la presenza attiva del cristiano nella storia. T-Leumann 1990, LDC. 180 p. Lit. 13.000. – RHum-Br 45 (1990) 862s (P. *Zovatto*).

b349 *Berranger* Olivier de, Pour une lecture théologique de l'histoire chez NEWMAN: NRT 112 (1990) 821-842.

b350 *Bonnaud* R., Le système de l'histoire. P 1989, Fayard. 334 p. F 140 [RHE 85, p. 183*].

b351 **Boschi** Bernardo G., Le origini di Israele nella Bibbia fra storia e teologia; la questione del metodo e la sfida storiografica 1989 → 5,b337: RAsprenas 37 (1990) 351-4 (V. *Scippa*).

b352 *Boshoff* W., Geskiedskrywing, godsdiensgeskiedenis en die Ou Testament: TEv 23,2 (1990) 12-21 [< OTAbs 14,164, Historiography, history of religions and the OT].

b353 *Burgess* R.W., History vs. historiography in late antiquity: AncHB 4 (1998) 116-124.

b353* ᴱ**Calder** William M.ᴵᴵᴵ, *Demandt* Alexander, Eduard MEYER, Leben und Leistung eines Universalhistorikers: Mnemosyne Supp. 112. Leiden 1990, Brill. x-537 p. 90-04091-31-9 [OIAc Ja91].

b354 *Cecolin* Romano, Le nuove concezioni del tempo e la Bibbia: RivLtg 77 (1990) 387-413.

b355 **Cesana** Andreas, Johann J. BACHOFENs Geschichtsdeutung; eine Untersuchung ihrer geschichtsphilosophischen Voraussetzungen. Ba 1983, Birkhäuser. 240 p. – ᴿRTPhil 122 (1990) 558s (J. *Schouwey*).

b356 **Colliot-Thelène** C., Max WEBER et l'histoire: Philosophies. P 1990, PUF. 121 p. F 24. 2-13-043133-X [ÉTRel 65,660].

b357 **Conyers** A.J., God, hope, and history... MOLTMANN 1988 → 5,b343 [< diss.]: ᴿTTod 47 (1990s) 230.232 (B.A. *Harvey*).

b358 **Dean** William, History making history; the new historicism in American religious thought. Albany 1988, SUNY. 175 p. $39.50; pa. $13. – ᴿJAAR 58 (1990) 698-700 (D. *Brown*).

b359 *a*) *Deist* F.E., Biblical and modern historiography; on presuppositions and hermeneutics; – *b*) *Le Roux* J.H., Biblical and modern historiography; the widest horizon; – *c*) *Gräbe* Ina, Theory of literature and OT studies – narrative conventions as exegetic reading strategies: OTEssays 3 (1990) 7-22 / 23-42 / 43-59.

b360 **Dihle** Albrecht, Die Entstehung der historischen Biographie: Szb Heid p/h 1986/3, 1987 → 5,b347; ᴿAnzAltW 43 (1990) 155-9 (D. *Flach*).

b361 **Doran** Robert M., Theology and the dialectics of history. Toronto 1990, Univ. xvi-732. $105. 0-8020-2713-X. – ᴿExpTim 102 (1990s) 187s (R. *Butterworth*: a massive and meticulously articulated work on LONERGAN).

b362 **Dunkel** A., Christlicher Glaube und historische Vernunft; eine interdisziplinäre Untersuchung über die Notwendigkeit eines theologischen Geschichtsverständnisses [Diss. ᴰ*Pannenberg* W.]: ForSystÖk 57. Gö 1989, Vandenhoeck & R. 344 p. DM 98. 3-525-56264-0. – ᴿTsTNijm 30 (1990) 213 (A. *Brants*).

b363 **Espinoza Becerra** Carlos, La tensión escatológica en la teología de la historia de Oscar CULLMANN: diss. Pont. Univ. Gregoriana, ᴰ*Ladaria* L. Roma 1990. xxxviii-432 p. – RTLv 22, p. 602.

b364 *Fernández Fernández* Gerardo, Dios ¿el sentido de la historia?: StLeg 30 (1989) 95-116.

b364* *Fritz* Volkmar, Weltalter und Lebenszeit; mythische Elemente in der Geschichtsschreibung Israels und bei HESIOD: ZTK 87 (1990) 145-162.

b365 **Garbini** G., Storia e ideologia nell'Israele antico 1986 → 2,9256... 5,b349: ᴿRBgPg 68 (1990) 213s (P. *Salmon*); RTPhil 122 (1990) 272s (A. *Moda*: avec une ardeur iconoclaste, œuvre des portes souvent déjà bien connues).

b366 **Garbini** Giovanni, History and ideology in ancient Israel 1988 → 4, d131; 5,b350: ᴿAmHR 95 (1990) 1500 (M. *Smith*: largely absurd but not wholly useless); CBQ 52 (1990) 118s (J.J. *Sullivan*); Interpretation 44 (1990) 301-3 (W. *Brueggemann*: some value despite 'shrillness and pretentiousness' and failure to define 'ideology' or admit that his own is 19th-century); JRel 70 (1990) 245s (S.W. *Holloway*: saccharin-free); JTS

41 (1990) 124-9 (P. R. *Davies*: sense-cum-nonsense); VT 40 (1990) 510s (G. I. *Davies*).

b367 *Geiger* Joseph,   Form and content in Jewish-Hellenistic historiography: ScrClasIsr 8s (1988) 120-9.

b368 **Gellner** Ernest,   Plough, sword and book; the structure of human history.   Ch 1988, Univ.   288 p. – ᴿHistTheor 29 (1990) 234-240 (W. H. *McNeill*); JIntdis 21 (1990s) 117s (J. J. *Sheehan*).

b369 **Gentili** Bruno, *Cervi* Giovanni,   History and biography in ancient thought: London Studies in Classical Philology.   Amst 1988 ↠ 4,d132: ᴿRBgPg 68 (1990) 196s (M. *Delaunois*).

b369* *a*) *Godsey* John D.,   Christian faith's partnership with history; – *b*) *Smith* D. Moody,   John and the Synoptics in light of the question of faith and history; – *c*) *Cosgrove* Charles H.,   The salvation of Jesus; a theological reflection on the destiny of the Kingdom in history; – *d*) *Schweizer* Eduard,   What do we really mean when we say 'God sent his Son'?: ↠ 123*, ᶠMEYER P., Faith and history 1990, 261-278 / 74-89 / 279-297 / 298-312.

Gibert Pierre,   Vérité historique et esprit historien; ... Gédéon face à HÉRODOTE 1990 ↠ e42.

b370 **Góźdź** K.,   Jesus Christus als Sinn der Geschichte ... PANNENBERG 1988 ↠ 5,b355: ᴿArTGran 53 (1990) 246s (R. *Franco*); CiTom 117 (1990) 387s (L. *Lago*).

b371 **Graf** Joseph,   Die Suche nach der 'Einheit in der Theologie' Gottlieb SÖHNGENS (1892-1971); Beitrag zum Durchbruch des heilsgeschichtlichen Denkens: Diss. Pont. Univ. Gregoriana, ᴰO'Collins G.   Roma 1990. 545 p. – RTLv 22, p. 603.

b372 *Grandazzi* A.,   L'avenir du passé; de l'histoire de l'historiographie à l'historiologie: Diogène 151 (1990) 56-78 [< RHE 85,347*].

b373 *Hammann* Gottfried,   L'histoire de l'Église à l'écoute de la 'Nouvelle Histoire'; esquisse pour l'enseignement de l'histoire du christianisme: RTPhil 121 (1989) 27-56.

b373* *Havas* L.,   [1 Cor 12,15 (not cited)] Fable and historical concept in ancient times [Menenius Agrippa (Livy 2,329), Once upon a time each organ of the body had its own volition]: ↠ 67, Mem. HAHN I., AcAntH 32 (1989) 63-73.

b374 *Hölscher* Lucian,   Geschichte und Vergessen: HZ 249 (1989) 1-17.

b375 **Hogan** John P.,   COLLINGWOOD and theological hermeneutics.   Lanham MD 1989, UPA/College Theol. Soc.   viii-238 p. $27.50; pa. $14.75. – ᴿTS 51 (1990) 177s (J. A. *Colombo*).

b376 **Hoornaert** Eduardo,   The memory of the Christian people: Theology and Liberation 5.   L 1989, Burns & O.   xii-304 p. £10.   0-86012-164-X. – ᴿExpTim 101 (1989s) 252 (T. *Hart*: to understand the first three centuries of Christianity, we must unlearn much of what later Christian historians ingrained into us).

b377 *Ingram* David,   BLUMENBERG [Hans, 1976] and the philosophical grounds of historiography: HistTheor 29 (1990) 1-15.

b378 *Klengel* Horst,   Kontinuität und Diskontinuität in der Geschichte des alten Vorderasien; zu einer neuen historischen Synthese [LIVERANI M. 1988]: OLZ 85 (1990) 389-398.

b379 **Koch** Kurt,   Der Gott der Geschichte ... PANNENBERG ᴰ1988/9 ↠ 5, b360: ᴿActuBbg 27 (1990) 75s (J. *Boada*); ÉTRel 65 (1990) 471s (D. *Müller*: un monument); TLZ 115 (1990) 763-5 (F. *Wagner*); TR 86 (1990) 11-13 (G.-L. *Müller*); TsTKi 61 (1990) 305s (J.-O. *Henrikssen*).

b380 *Kraus* Hans-Christof, Aktualität und Grenzen der Fachtradition; neue Veröffentlichungen zur Geschichte der deutschen Geschichtswissenschaft: ZRGg 42 (1990) 72-79.

b381 **Krois** John M., CASSIRER; symbolic forms and history.   NHv 1987, Yale Univ. xvii-262 p. £30. – RHeythJ 31 (1990) 329s (F. C. *Copleston*).

b382 *McGrath* John A., The rights and limits of history: DowR 108 (1990) 20-36.

b383 **Manno** A. G., Lo storicismo di W. DILTHEY. N 1990, Loffredo. 350 p. Lit. 40.000. – RAsprenas 37 (1990) 368-370 (P. *Orlando*).

b384 *Mendels* D., Preliminary thoughts on 'creative' history in the Hellenistic Near East in the third and second centuries B.C.: ScrClasIsr 10 (1989s) 78-86.

b385 **Merkley** Paul, The Greek and Hebrew origins of our idea of history: Toronto Studies in Theology 32, 1987 ➤ 3,b628: REvQ 62 (1990) 357-361 (Ruth B. *Edwards*: an ambitious but disappointing book); HistTheor 28 (1989) 134s [P. *Munz*].

b386 **Momigliano** Arnaldo, The classical foundations of modern historiography: Sather Classical Lectures 54. Berkeley 1990, Univ. California. xiv-162 p. 0-520-06890-4.

b387 **Monsegú** Bernardo, Clave teológica de la Historia según Donoso CORTÉS³ʳᵉᵛ. M 1988, Pasionario. 313 p. 84-85638-02-6. – RActuBbg 27 (1990) 46-48 (J. A. *Yoldi*).

b388 *Murphey* Rhoads, Bigots or informed observers? A periodization of pre-colonial English and European writing on the Middle East [*Beck* B., 1987; *Damiani* A., 1979; *Haynes* J., 1986; *Schiffer* R., 1982]: JAOS 110 (1990) 291-303.

b389 ENeusner Jacob, The Christian and Judaic invention of history: AAR StRel 55. Atlanta 1990, Scholars. ix-256 p. (7 reprints + 5 of Neusner). 1-55540-331-2.

b390 *Patterson* Lee, On the margin; postmodernism, ironic history, and medieval studies: Speculum 65 (1990) 87-108.

b391 *Peters* Ted, [† 19.I.1985 Eric] VOEGELIN for the theologian: Dialog 28 (1989) 210-222 [219, his attack against LUTHER and justification]

b392 **Plass** Paul, Wit and the writing of history [TACITUS unmasks insincere politicians by putting incongruous words into their mouths]; the rhetoric of historiography in imperial Rome 1988 ➤ 5,b373: RGreeceR 37 (1990) 117 (T. *Wiedemann*); Helmantica 41 (1990) 408 (J. *Oroz Reta*); Phoenix 44 (Toronto 1990) 393-7 (J. *Griffin*); RPg 63 (1989) 333s (J.-M. *André*).

b393 *Potworowski* Christophe, History and incarnation in the theology of Marie-Dominique CHENU: ScEsp 42 (1990) 237-265.

b394 *Quinza Lleo* Xavier, Los signos de los tiempos como tópico teológico: EstE 65 (1990) 457-468.

b395 *Ratzinger* J., La théologie de l'histoire de saint BONAVENTURE [D1957], T1988 ➤ 5,b374: RNRT 112 (1990) 257s (P. *Gilbert*).

b396 *Ruggieri* Giuseppe, Glaube und Geschichte: TJb (1989) 178-201.

b397 **Salmon** Pierre, Histoire et critique³ʳᵉᵛ. Bru 1987, Univ. 234 p. Fb 1060. – RRHE 85 (1990) 796 (J.-P. *Hendricks*).

b398 **Schlaudraff** Karl-Heinz, 'Heil als Geschichte'... CULLMANNs 1988 ➤ 4,d161: RActuBbg 26 (1989) 238s (J. *Boada*); CritRR 3 (1990) 234-6 (R. W. *Yarbrough*); TLZ 115 (1990) 54-56 (J. *Fangmeier*).

b399 *Scholtz* Gunter, Das Historismusproblem und die Geisteswissenschaften im 20. Jahrhundert: ArKulturG 71 (1989) 463-486.

b400 **Schryver** R. de, Historiografie; vijfentwintig eeuwen geschiedschrijving van West-Europa. Assen 1990, Van Gorcum. 404 p. ƒ 59,50 [RHE 85,347*].

b401 *Starr* Chester G., Ancient history in the twentieth century: ClasW 84 (1990s) 177-187.

b402 **Verschaffel** T., Het lezen van geschiedenis; de traditionele theorie van de XVIIde en XVIIIde eeuw: Theoretische Geschiedenis 17 (1990) 243-255 [< RHE 85,347*].

b403 **Wells** Ronald A., History through the eyes of faith. SF 1989, Harper & R. x-262 p. $19 pa. – ᴿBS 147 (1990) 251s (J. D. *Hannah*); CalvinT 25 (1990) 142-5 (J. P. *Ellens*).

b404 **Younger** K. Lawsonᴶ, Ancient conquest accounts; a study in ancient Near Eastern and biblical history writing: JStOT supp 98. Sheffield 1990, Academic. 392 p. £35. 1-85075-352-4 [BL 91,42, A. D. H. *Mayes*: many interesting parallels, but their significance inadequately set forth].

b405 *a) Zuev* V. Yu., ❺ M. I. ROSTOVTZEFF's creative path when writing 'Studies in the history of Scythia and the Bosphorus Kingdoms'; – *b)* ❺ *Frolov* E. D., The fate of a scholar, Rostovtzeff and his place in Russian studies of ancient history: VDI 195 (1990) 148-153 / 194 (1990) 143-164; 3 fig.; Eng. 164s.

Q3 *Historia Ægypti* – **Egypt.**

b406 *Alfi* Mostafa El-, The rivalry between Thebes and Heliopolis, BM Stela 8462: DiscEg 17 (1990) 7-14.

b407 *a) Altenmüller* Hertwig, Bemerkungen zür Gründung der 6. Dynastie; – *b) Helck* Wolfgang, Gedanken zur Entstehung des altägyptischen Staates; – *c) Raduan* Ali, Zur Stellung des Königs in der Zweiten Zwischenzeit: ➤ 16, ꜰBECKERATH J. v. 1990, 1-20 / 97-117 / 223-233; 3 fig.; pl. 14-15.

b408 *a) Andressy* Petra, Zur Verwaltung des Alten Reiches; – *b) Apelt* Dietlind, Bemerkungen zur Thronfolge in der 25. Dynastie; – *c) Wenig* Steffen, Pabatma – Pekereslo – Pekar-tror; ein Beitrag zur Frühgeschichte der Kuschiten: ➤ 78, ꜰHINTZE F., Meroitica 12 (1990) 13-21 / 23-31 / 333-352.

b409 **Arborio Mella** Federico A., L'Egitto dei Faraoni; storia, civiltà, cultura: Storia e documenti 24. Mi 1989, Mursia. 477 p.; 103 fig.; 107 (color.) pl.; 4 maps.

b410 *Awadalla* Ataf, Un document prouvant la corégence d'Amenemhat et de Sesostris I: GöMiszÄg 115 (1990) 7-11; 3 pl.

b411 *Baines* John R., Restricted knowledge, hierarchy, and decorum; modern perceptions and ancient institutions: JAmEg 27 (1990) 1-23.

b412 *Beckerath* Jürgen von, Nochmals zur Regierung Tuthmosis' I: StAlt-ÄgK 17 (1990) 65-74.

b413 *Bentley* Juliette, Akencheres [MANETHO; JOSEPHUS F., Apion 1,96]: DiscEg 16 (1990) 29s.

b413* **Bongard-Levin** C. M., ❺ Perednjaja Azija, Egipet: Istorija Drevnego Vostoka 2. Moskva 1988, Nauka. 624 p. 186 fig.; 12 color. pl.; 3 maps; r 4.60. – ᴿFolOr 27 (1990) 264-6 (E. *Lipiński*).

b414 **Boorn** G. P. F. van den, The duties of the vizier; civil administration in the early New Kingdom 1988 ➤ 4,d177: ᴿOLZ 85 (1990) 527-530 (W. *Helck*); Orientalia 59 (1990) 73s (A. R. *Schulman*).

b415 **Bowman** Alan K., Egypt after the Pharaos 1986 ➤ 2,9302 ... 5,b391: ᴿBO 17 (1990) 133-5 (R. *Scholl*); JEA 76 (1990) 249s (W. *Clarysse*).

b416 **Brunner-Traut** Emma, Frühformen des Erkennens, am Beispiel Ägyptens. Da 1990, Wiss. xii-210 p.; ill. DM 59 [OLZ 86, 747, W. *Reineke*].

b417 *Brunt* P. A., *a*) The administrators of Roman Egypt [< JRS 64 (1975) 124-147]; – *b*) The Romanization of the local ruling classes in the Roman Empire [< Assimilation 1974/6, 161-173]: → 206, Roman imperial 1990, 215-254.514 / 267-281; addendum 515-531.

b418 *Burkhalter* Fabienne, Archives locales et archives centrales en Égypte romaine: Chiron 20 (1990) 191-216.

b418* *Cameron* Alex, Two mistresses of Ptolemy Philadelphus: GrRByz 31 (1990) 287-311.

b419 **Carcenac Pujol** Claude-Brigitte, Jesús; 3,000 años antes de Cristo, un faraón llamado Jesús. Barc 1987, Plaza & J. 272 p.; 16 pl. 84-01-37278-X [OIAc S90].

b420 **Cimmino** Franco, *a*) Hatshepsowe e Tuthmosis III, una regina ambiziosa e un gran faraone; – *b*) Ramesses II il grande: La Storia. Mi 1981/4, Rusconi. 249 p. / 423 p. [OIAc S90].

b421 **Clarysse** Willy, *Vandorpe* Katelijn, Zenon, een Grieks manager in de schaduw van de piramiden. Lv 1990, auct. (Univ.) 112 p.; ill. Fb 300. – ᴿCdÉ 65 (1990) 170s (G. *Nachtergael*).

b421* *a*) *Criscuolo* Lucia, 'Philadelphos' nella dinastia lagide; – *b*) *Huss* Werner, Die Herkunft der Kleopatra Philopator: Aegyptus 70 (1990) 89-96 / 191-203.

b422 *Deineka* T. A., ❸ The ideological foundations of Egypt's foreign policy in the period between XVI and XIV centuries B.C.: VDI 193 (1990) 135-155; Eng. 155.

b423 *Derchain-Urtel* Maria-Theresia, Ägypten in griechisch-römischer Zeit: ZägSpr 117 (1990) 111-9.

b423* **Der Manuelian** P., Studies in the reign of Amenophis II 1987 → 3, b667: ᴿNikephoros 1 (1988) 269-272 (W. *Decker*).

b424 *Dijk* Jacobus van, The overseer of the treasury Maya, a biographical sketch: OMRO 70 (1990) 23-27; 28, 2 fig.

b425 *Dodson* Aidan, Crown Prince Djhutmose and the royal sons of the eighteenth dynasty: JEA 76 (1990) 87-96; pl. V.

b426 *a*) *Dziobek* Eberhard, *Dorman* Peter F., Additional name stones of Senenmut; – *b*) *Fischer-Elfert* Hans-W., Drei Personalnotizen: GöMisz-Äg 119 (1990) 7-9 + 3 fig. / 13-18.

b427 *Endesfelder* Erika, Noch einmal zum Feudalismus im alten Ägypten: Klio 72 (1990) 188-194.

b427* **Fischer** Henry G., Egyptian women of the Old Kingdom and of the Heracleopolitan period. NY 1989, Metropolitan Museum of Art. viii-52 p.; 25 fig. 0-87099-565-0.

b428 *Franke* Detlef, Erste und Zweite Zwischenzeit — ein Vergleich: ZägSpr 117 (1990) 119-129.

b429 *Gabolde* Luc, Nerkarê a-t-il existé?: BIFAO 90 (1990) 213-222.

b430 **Goudriaan** Koen, Ethnicity in Ptolemaic Egypt: Dutch Mg. AncH 5. Amst 1988, Gieben. 175 p. – ᴿClasR 40 (1990) 370s (J. L. *Rowlandson*); Gnomon 62 (1990) 652-4 (A. E. *Samuel*).

b431 *Grandet* Pierre, Un texte historique de Ramsès III à El-Kāb (et autres textes ramessides): RÉgp 41 (1990) 95-99; 2 fig.; pl. 5-6.

b431* *a*) *Griffiths* J. Gwyn, Royal renewal rites in ancient Egypt; – *b*) *Assmann* Jan, Égypt ancienne; la mémoire monumentale: → 618, Commémoration 1986/8, 35-47 / 48-56.

b432 *Hauben* Hans, L'expédition de Ptolémée III en Orient et la sédition domestique de 245 av. J.-C.: ArPapF 36 (1990) 29-37.

b432* **Heinsohn** Gunnar [author of 'Die Sumerer gab es nicht'], *Illig* Heribert, Wann lebten die Pharaonen? Archäologische und technologische Grundlagen für eine Neuschreibung der Geschichte Ägyptens und der übrigen Welt. Fra 1990, Eichborn. 406 p. 3-8218-0422-X [OIAc Ja91].

b433 **Helck** W., Politische Gegensätze... 1986 ⇒ 2,9382... 5,b403: ᴿBO 47 (1990) 635s (U. *Luft*).

b434 **Helck** Wolfgang, Untersuchungen zur Thinitenzeit: ÄgAbh 45, 1987 ⇒ 3,b681: ᴿWeltOr 20s (1989s) 243-8 (Eva *Martin-Pardey*); ZDMG 140 (1990) 150-2 (J. v. *Beckerath*).

b435 *Jansen-Winkeln* Karl, Zu den biographischen Texten der 3. Zwischenzeit: GöMiszÄg 117s (1990) 165-180.

b436 **Kitchen** K.A., Ramesside inscriptions; [7,b986 ⇒ 5,b410]; historical and biographical 8, fasc. 6s, Indexes C, Publications and manuscript sources [p.13-64 ⇒ 5,b412; p. 161-224, books cited]. Ox 1990, Blackwell. 0-946344-39-5; -40-X [OIAc S90]. – ᴿBO 47 (1990) 618-620 (W. *Helck*, 7,9-15; 8,1s); OLZ 85 (1990) 656-8 (J. v. *Beckerath*, 7,9-6; 8,1s).

b437 **Lalouette** Claire, L'empire des Ramsès 1985 ⇒ 3,b60: ᴿCdÉ 65 (1990) 72-74 (A.R. *Schulman*).

b437* *Lasken* Jesse E., Towards a new chronology of ancient Egypt: DiscEg 17 (1990) 87-141; editor's apologia p. 5.

b438 *Leclant* Jean, Une nouvelle reine d'Égypte: Noub-Ounet: CRAI (1990) 516-520; 3 fig. (porte de Saqqara).

b439 **Lesko** Barbara S., The remarkable women of ancient Egypt. Providence ʀɪ 1987, ʙᴄ-Scribe. 36 p.; 8 color. pl. 0-930548-01-9.

b440 **Lewis** N., Greeks in Ptolemaic Egypt 1986 ⇒ 3,b692... 5,b418: ᴿMeditHistR 5 (1990) 222s (W.Z. *Rubinsohn*); RÉG 103 (1990) 291s (A. *Blanchard*).

b441 **Lewis** Naphtali, La mémoire des sables; la vie en Égypte sous la domination romaine [1983 ⇒ 64,a39], ᵀ*Chuvin* P. P 1988, Colin. 222 p.; ill. – ᴿCaesarodunum 22-CR (1989) 138 [R. *Chevallier*]; CahHist 34 (1989) 149s (J. *Rougé*).

b442 **Lichtheim** Miriam, Ancient Egyptian autobiographies chiefly of the Middle Kingdom; a study and an anthology: OBO 84, 1988 ⇒ 4,d210*: ᴿBL (1990) 123 (K.A. *Kitchen*).

b442* ᴱ**Lloyd** Alan B., ᴇʀᴏᴅᴏᴛᴏ II. L'Egitto ⇒ 5,b422; ᵀ*Fraschetti* Augusto, 1989: ᴿAegyptus 70 (1990) 299s (F. *Muccioli*).

b443 *Luft* Ulrich, Mythes historisés dans l'Égypte ptolémaïque; ⇒ 49, Mem. Fóᴛɪ L. 1989, 289-318.

b444 **Manniche** Lise, Sexual life in ancient Egypt 1987 ⇒ 3,b697... 5,b426: ᴿJAOS 110 (1990) 757s (M.V. *Fox*).

b445 *Monnet Saleh* Janine, Interprétation globale des documents concernant l'unification dÉgypte (suite) [... palette de Merynar]: BIFAO 90 (1990) 259-279; 4 fig.

b446 *O'Mara* Patrick F., Toward a multi-modeled chronology of the 18th dynasty: DiscEg 17 (1990) 29-44.

b447 *Oosterhout* G.W. van, The astronomical data from the Illahun papyri: DiscEg 17 (1990) 75-84.

b448 *Perdu* Olivier, Neshor à Mendès sous Apriès: BSocFrÉg 118 (1990) 38-49; 3 fig.

b449 *Pérez Largacha* Antonio, La política exterior egipcia a principios de la XVIII dinastia: BAsEspOr 25 (1989) 129-136.

b450 **Quirke** Stephen, The administration of Egypt in the Late Middle Kingdom; the hieratic documents. New Malden, Surrey 1990, 'SIA'. ix-253 p. 1-872561-01-2.

b451 **Quirke** Stephen, Who were the Pharaohs? A history of their names with a list of cartouches [*Parkinson* Richard, drawings]. L 1990, British Museum. 80 p.; ill. 0-7141-0955-X.

b452 *Rainey* Anson F. and Zippora *Cochavi*-, Comparative grammatical notes on the treaty between Ramses II and Hattusili III: → 114, FLICHTHEIM M. 1990 (II) 796-823.

b453 *Raubitschek* Antony E., Überlegungen zu einigen Beiträgen der Konferenz 'Ideologische und methodologische Grundprobleme der antitiken Geschichtsschreibung': Klio [66 (1984) 338-478] 72 (1990) 568-575.

b454 **Redford** D. B. [Ben-Gurion univ. lectures 1986, EAhituv S.] Egypt and Canaan in the New Kingdom: Beer-Sheva 4. Beer-Sheva 1990, BG-Univ. vii-121 p. $12. 0334-2255 [BL 91,129, K. A. *Kitchen*: useful despite misprints].

b455 **Redford** Donald B., Pharaonic king-lists, annals, and day-books; a contribution to the study of the Egyptian sense of history 1986 → 4,d219*; 5,b436: RJEA 76 (1990) 210s (C. *Vandersleyen*, franç.).

b456 **Rice** Michael, Egypt's making; the origins of ancient Egypt, 5000-2000 B.C. L 1990, Routledge. xxii-322 p.; 111 fig.; 12 color. pl.; p. 291-6, 8 fig., The Egyptian hound. 0-415-05092-8.

b456* *Ritner* Robert K., The end of the Libyan anarchy in Egypt; p. Rylands IX, cols. 11-12: Enchoria 17 (1990) 101-9.

b457 *Römer* Malte, Varia zu Psusennes 'II.' und zur 21. Dynastie: Gö-MiszÄg 114 (1990) 93-99.

b458 *Rubio Campos* Jorge, Damnatio memoriae de Senenmut: BAsocEspEg 2 (1990) 61-74.

b459 *Ryboli* K. S. B., A reconsideration of some royal nomens of the thirteenth dynasty: GöMiszÄg 119 (1990) 101-113.

b460 **Samuel** Alan E., The shifting sands of history; interpretations of Ptolemaic Egypt: Asn. Ancient Historians 2. Lanham MD 1989, UPA. xiii-85 p. $17.50; pa. $8.25. – RClasR 40 (1990) 507s (Dorothy J. *Thompson*: good); GreeceR 37 (1990) 243 (P. J. *Rhodes*).

b461 *Schulman* Alan R., The royal butler Ramessessami'on, an addendum: CdÉ 65 (1990) 12-20.

b462 **Seton-Williams** M. V., A short history of Egypt. L 1989, Rubicon. x-86 p. 0-948694-12-9 [OIAc F91,19].

b463 *Sonnabend* Holger, Fremdenbild und Politik D1986 → 2,9619 ... 5,b440: RBO 47 (1990) 658-665 (H. *Heinen*).

b464 *Sturtewagen* Christian, Studies in Ramesside administrative documents: → 114, FLICHTHEIM M. 1990, (II) 933-942.

b465 *Taylor* John H., The vizier Ankhefenkhonsu: GöMiszÄg 116 (1990) 97-99 + 4 fig.

b466 **Troy** Lana, Patterns of queenship in ancient Egyptian myth and history: Boreas 14, 1986 → 2,9360 ... 5,b444: RJEA 76 (1990) 214-220 (G. *Robins*: brilliant).

b467 *Vercoutter* Jean, L'Égypte ancienne[13rev]: Que sais-je? 247. P 1990, PUF. 127 p.; map.

b468 **Vernus** Pascal, *Yoyotte* Jean, Les Pharaons 1988 → 4,d228: RBO 17 (1990) 73s (P. *Dils*).

b469 *a)* *Weggelaar* N., *Kort* C., The calendar reforms of ancient Egypt: DiscEg 13 (1989) 79-86; – *b)* *Oosterhout* G. W. van, Solar eclipses and Sothic dating: DiscEg ... 16 (1990) 73.
b470 **Zibelius-Chen** Karola, Die ägyptische Expansion nach Nubien: TAVO Beih B-78, 1988 ⇥ 4,g472; DM 108: ᴿBO 47 (1990) 641-3 (J. *Vercoutter*).
b471 *Zibelius-Chen* K., Politische Opposition im Alten Ägypten: StAäK 17 (1990) 339-360.

b472 **Griggs** C. W., Early Egyptian Christianity, from its origins to 451 C.E.: Coptic Studies 2. NY 1990, Brill. vii-276 p.; 2 maps. *f* 140. 90-04-09159-9 [NTAbs 34,407].

Q4 Historia Mesopotamiae.

b473 *Boncquet* Jan, CTESIAS' Assyrian king-list and his chronology of Mesopotamian history: AncSoc 21 (1990) 5-16.
b474 **Bottéro** Jean, Mésopotamie 1987 ⇥ 3,194: ᴿRTPhil 121 (1989) 97 (T. *Römer*).
b475 *a)* **Brinkman** J. A., The Babylonian Chronicle revisited; – *b)* *Na'aman* Nadav, Praises to the Pharaoh in response to his plans for a campaign to Canaan; – *c)* *Alster* Bendt, Lugalbanda and the early epic tradition in Mesopotamia; – *d)* *Wilhelm* Gernot, Marginalia zu HERODOT, Klio 199: ⇥ 124, ꜰMORAN W., Lingering 1990, 73-104 / 397-405 / 59-72 / 505-524.
b476 *a)* **Brinkman** John A., Political covenants, treaties, and loyalty oaths in Babylonia and between Assyria and Babylonia; – *b)* *Liverani* Mario, Terminologia e ideologia del patto nelle iscrizioni reali assire; – *c)* *Fales* Frederick M., Istituzioni a confronto tra mondo semitico occidentale e Assiria nel I millennio a. C.; il trattato di Sefire: ⇥ 724, Trattati 1986/90, 81-111 / 113-147 / 149-173.
b477 ᴱ**Cannadine** David, *Price* Simon, Rituals of royalty; power and ceremonial in traditional societies: Past and Present 1987 ⇥ 3,487; 4,d233: ᴿHeythJ 31 (1990) 227s (Ruth *Finnegan*).
b478 **Capomacchia** A. M. G., Semiramis 1986 ⇥ 2,9366... 5,b456: ᴿAevum 64 (1990) 115-7 (D. M. *Cosi*).
b478* *a)* *Charpin* Dominique, Les Édits de 'restauration' des rois babyloniens et leur application; – *b)* *Lafforgue* Gilbert, Les zones de dissidence en Asie Occidentale du 2ᵉ millénaire avant J.-C. [... Ḫabiru]: ⇥ 760, Pouvoir 1983/90, 13-24 / 25-36.
b479 *Conradie* A. F., The Calah wall inscriptions [thought to show Ashurnasirpal II conquering westward only to Carchemish, with no mention of Lebanon or Mediterranean]: JNWS 15 (1989) 31-38; a detached booklet gives in transliteration six different versions for each of the 60 lines.
b480 **Cooper** Jerrold S., Reconstructing... the Lagash-Umma border conflict 1983 ⇥ 1,b93: ᴿBO 47 (1990) 398-401 (G. *Steiner*).
b481 *Córdoba* J. M., Presencia internacional de una gran potencia en la segunda mitad del II milenio; el caso de Mitanni, arqueología e historia: BAsEspOr 25 (1989) 77-116 + 3 fig.; 26 (1990) 129-158; fig. 6-8.
b482 *Cwik-Rosenbach* Marita, Zeitverständnis und Geschichtsschreibung in Mesopotamien: ZRGg 42 (1990) 1-20.
b483 **Dandamayev** M. A., Slavery in Babylonia [1974] ᵀ1984 ⇥ 65,9687; 1,2531: ᴿMnemosyne 43 (1990) 247-252 (B. J. van der *Spek*).

b483* **Diakonoff** I. M., ⊕ Mesopotamija: Istorija Drevnego Vostoka 1. Moskva 1983, Nauka. 536 p.; 134 fig.; 32 color. pl.; 4 maps. r 3,40. – ᴿFolOr 27 (1990) 266s (E. *Lipiński*).

b484 *Dietrich* Manfried, Semiramis; oder, War die Frau im alten Orient nur schön: → 768, Waren sie 1985/9, 117-182; fig. 44-76.

b485 *a)* *Durand* Jean-Marie, Documents pour l'histoire du royaume de Haute-Mésopotamie II; – *b)* *Villard* Pierre, III: MARI 6 (1990) 271-302 / 559-584.

b486 *Fales* Frederick M., Prosopography of the Neo-Assyrian empire; the many faces of Nabú-sarru-usur: SAAB 2 (1988) 105-124.

b487 *Foster* Benjamin R., Naram-Sin in Martu and Magan: AnRIM 8 (1990) 25-44.

b488 *a)* *Garelli* Paul, L'influence de Samsi-Addu sur les titulatures royales assyriennes; – *b)* *Klengel* Horst, Halab - Mari-Babylon; Aspekte syrisch-mesopotamischer Beziehungen in altbabylonischer Zeit; – *c)* *Buccellati* Giorgio, From Khana to Laqê; the end of Syro-Mesopotamia: → 107, ᶠKUPPER J.-R., De la Babylonie 1990, 97-102 / 183-195 / 229-253.

b489 **Gelb** I. J., Die altakkadischen Königsinschriften des dritten Jahrtausends v. Chr. [Text, Übersetzung, Kommentar]: FrAltorSt 7. Stu 1990, Steiner. xvi-434 p. DM 120. 3-515-04248-2 [BL 91, 29, W. G. *Lambert*: text-collection up to date, comments not].

b490 *Glombiowski* Krzysztof, Die Eroberung Babylons durch Kyros in orientalischer und griechischer Überlieferung: Altertum 36 (1990) 49-55.

b491 **Gonnick** Larry, The cartoon history of the universe; 1-7; from the Big Bang to Alexander the Great. NY 1990, Doubleday. 0-385-26520-4 [< Pirradziš → 3,12].

b492 **Grayson** A. Kirk, Assyrian rulers [3000-]1115 BC, 1987 → 3,b736; 5,b483: ᴿBO 47 (1990) 686-707 (O. *Pedersén*); Orientalia 59 (1990) 544-9 (W. *Farrer*).

b493 **Harrak** Amir, Assyria and Hanigalbat [14th-12th cent. B.C.] 1987 → 3,b738; 4,b243: ᴿOLZ 85 (1990) 539-544 (H. *Freydank*); ZAss 80 (1990) 139s (J. N. *Postgate*).

b494 **Huot** Jean-Louis, Les sumériens; entre le Tigre et l'Euphrate: Néréides. P 1989, Errance. 259 p.; ill.; maps. 2 903442-96-7. – ᴿBCanadMesop 20 (1990) 37 (M. *Fortin*).

b495 *Hurowitz* Victor, *Westenholz* Jean G., LKA 63, a heroic poem in celebration of Tiglath-Pileser I's Musru-Qumanu campaign: JCS 48 (1990) 1-49 [before *Livingstone* A., Court poetry 1989].

b496 *Kienast* Burkhart, Narāmsīn mut ᵈINANNA: → 160*, Mem. SCHULER E. v., Orientalia 59 (1990) 196-203.

b497 *Klein* Jacob, Šeleppūtum, a hitherto unknown Ur III princess: ZAss 80 (1990) 20-40; 1 pl.; 1 facsim.

b498 ᴱ**Klengel** Horst, *al.*, Kulturgeschichte des alten Vorderasien: DDR Ak. Wiss. AltG [0138-3914] 18. B 1989, Akademie. 564 p.; 220 (color.) phot. 3-05-000577-7.

b498* *a)* *Klinger* Jörg, Überlegungen zu den Anfängen des Mittani-Staates; – *b)* *Wilhelm* Gernot, Gedanken zur Frühgeschichte der Hurriter und zum hurritisch-urartäischen Sprachvergleich: → 801*, Hurriter 1988, 27-42/ 43-67; 1 fig.

b499 **Kristensen** Anne K. G., Who were the Cimmerians, and where did they come from? Sargon II, the Cimmerians, and Rusa I: Vid.Selskab.Med 57. K 1988, Munksgaard. 141 p. 87-7304-191-2.

b500 *Lafforgue* Gilbert, Les zones de dissidence en Asie Occidentale du 2ᵉ millénaire avant J.-C.: ➤ 760, Du pouvoir 1983/90, 25-36.

b501 *Lambert* W. G., Samsu-Iluna in later tradition: ➤ 107, ᶠKUPPER J.-R. 1990, 27-34; 2 facsim.

b502 *Lanfranchi* Giovanni B., Sargon's letter to Aššur-šarru-usur; an interpretation [*Parpola* S., SAA 1, 1987]: SAAB 2 (1988) 59-64.

b503 *a) Lanfranchi* Giovanni B., Scholars and scholarly tradition in Neo-Assyrian times; a case study; – *b) Ponchia* Simonetta, Royal decisions and courtiers' compliance; on some formulae in Neo-Assyrian and Neo-Babylonian letters: SAAB 3 (1989) 99-114 / 115-128.

b504 ᴱ**Lévêque** Pierre, Les premières civilisations: 1. Des despotismes orientaux à la cité grecque²: Peuples et civilisations, 1987 ➤ 5,b474: ᴿCahHist 34 (1989) 71s (P. *Cabanes*: rajeunissement de la série que des générations d'étudiants ont utilisée); Syria 65 (1988) 461-4 (Emilia *Masson*: sévère).

b505 *Ling-Israel* Pnina, The Sennacherib prism in the Israel museum — Jerusalem: ➤ 7, ᶠARTZI P. 1990, 213-248; pl. IV-XVI.

b506 **Liverani** Mario, Prestige and interest; international relations in the Near East ca. 1600-1100 B.C. Padova 1990, Sargon. 313 p. Lit. 40.000 [ZAW 103, 453, J. A. *Soggin*].

b507 *Liverani* Mario, The growth of the Assyrian empire in the Habur/Middle Euphrates area; a new paradigm: SAAB 2 (1988) 81-92 + 7 maps.

b508 *Maeda* Tohru, Father of Akalla and Dalaga, governors of Umma: AcSum 12 (1990) 71-78.

b508* *Malul* Meir, Susapinnu, the Mesopotamian paranymph and his role [named from the stained cloth *šušippu* which he kept as proof of bride's virginity]: JESHO 32 (1989) 241-278.

b509 *Neumann* Hans, Überlegungen zu Ursprung, Wesen und Entwicklung des frühen Staates im alten Mesopotamien: OLZ 85 (1990) 645-655.

b510 **Nissen** Hans J., The early history of the ANE [1983 ➤ 64,a95], ᵀ*Lutzeier* Elizabeth, *Northcott* Kenneth J., 1988 ➤ 5,b480: ᴿAmHR 95 (1990) 790 (C. W. *Meade*); JRel 70 (1990) 82 (T. L. *Thompson*).

b511 **Nissen** Hans J., Mesopotamia before 5000 years: Sc. Storiche, Sussidi didattici 1. R 1987, Univ. 188 p.; 2 pl. [OIAc Oc90].

b511* *a) Nissen* Hans J., Die Frühgeschichte (Mesopotamiens) als Forschungsproblem; – *b) Renger* Johannes, Probleme und Perspektiven einer Wirtschaftsgeschichte Mesopotamiens: Saeculum 40 (1989) 179-187 / 166-178.

b512 *a) Postgate* Nicholas, Ancient Assyria — a multiracial state; – *b) Millard* Alan R., Mesopotamia and the Bible [Heythrop College Lecture 1987]: Aram 1,1 (1989) 1-9; map p. 10 / 24-30.

b513 **Questa** C., Semiramide redenta. Urbino 1989, Quattro Venti. 406 p. – ᴿGitFg 42 (1990) 129-131 (N. *Scivoletto*).

b514 *Reade* Julian, Shalmaneser or Ashurnasirpal in Ararat? [*Lambert* W., AnSt 11 (1961) 144-158]: SAAB 3 (1989) 93-97.

b515 ᶠREINER Erica, Language, literature, and history, ᴱ**Rochberg-Halton** F. 1987 ➤ 3,136; 45,b486: ᴿOLZ 85 (1990) 160-3 (J. *Oelsner*, titles; some lengthy analyses).

b516 **Roux** G., La Mésopotamie, essai d'histoire politique, économique et culturelle 1985 ➤ 1,b116 ... 4,d260*: ᴿBO 47 (1990) 147-151 (H. W. F. *Saggs*).

b517 *a*) TABARI 1, 18, 27, 38: ᴿBO 47 (1990) 812-4 (P. *Chalmeta*). – *b*) **Perlmann** Moshe, TABARI 4 (SUNY), The ancient kingdoms 1987 ➤ 5,b481: ᴿJSS 35 (1990) 163s (Carole *Hillenbrand*). ➤ b336.

b518 *Tadmor* Hayim, *Landsberger* Benno [1890-1968], *Parpola* Simo, The sin of Sargon and Sennacherib's last will: SAAB 3 (1989) 3-51; 2 pl.; 2 facsim.

b519 **Uhlig** Helmut, Die Sumerer, ein Volk am Anfang der Geschichte. Bergisch Gladbach 1989, Lübbe. 272 p.; 26 pl. in center. 3-7857-0560-3.

b520 *Vermaak* P. S., Die rol van die groot families in die Ur III-tydperk: JSem 2,1 (1990) 112-124.

b521 **Watanabe** Kazuko, Die *adê*-Vereidigung anlässlich der Thronfolgeregelung Asarhaddons ᴰ1987 ➤ 3,b760; 5,b495: ᴿOLZ 85 (1990) 543-6 (Stephanie *Dalley*: basically re-edits Esarhaddon Vassal-Treaties); ZAss 80 (1990) 160-4 (W. *Farber*).

b521* **Wilhelm** Gernot, The Hurrians [1922], ᵀ*Barnes* Jennifer, 1989 ➤ 5, b497; pa. £8.75. 0-85668-489-9: ᴿAntiquity 64 (1990) 169s (D. *Oates*).

b522 ᶠWOLSKI Jósef: Near Eastern Studies, 1987 ➤ 3,170: ᴿWeltOr 20s (1989s) 336-341 (E. *Kettenhofen*: very detailed summaries, many but not all on history).

b523 *Wu Yuhong, Dalley* Stephanie, The origins of the Manana dynasty at Kiuh, and the Assyrian king list: Iraq 52 (1990) 159-165.

b524 ᴱ**Yoffee** Norman, *Cowgill* George L., The collapse of ancient states and civilizations [Mesopotamia...] 1982/8 ➤ 4,467: ᴿBO 47 (1990) 607-9 (H. *Freydank*); JField 16 (1989) 461-7 (C. E. *Lincoln*).

b525 **Zawadzki** S., The fall of Assyria and Median-Babylonian relations in light of the Nabupolassar Chronicle: Historia 143, 1988 ➤ 5,b498: ᴿArOr 58 (1990) 404s (Jana *Pečírková*); BO 47 (1990) 708-710 (Stephanie *Dalley*).

b526 *Zawadzki* Stefan, Ein wichtiger Fehler in der neubabylonischen Chronik BM 21946 und seine Folgen; das Krönungsdatum Nebukadnezars II [*Wiseman* D., *Vogt* E. ... nach 32 nicht 22 Tagen, 15. Sept. 605]: AltOrF 17 (1990) 100-6.

Q4.5   *Historia Persiae* – Iran.

b527 *a*) *Ackroyd* Peter B., The biblical portrayal of Achaemenid rulers; – *b*) *Kuhrt* Amélie, Alexander and Babylon: ➤ 822, Achaemenid 5 (1987/90) 1-16 / 121-130.

b528 **Balcer** Jack M., HERODOTUS and Bisitun 1987 ➤ 3,b765... 5,h501*: ᴿGnomon 62 (1990) 605-9 (J. *Wiesehöfer*).

b529 *a*) *Boucharlat* Rémy, Suse et la Susiane à l'époque achéménide; données archéologiques; – *b*) *Kuhrt* Amélie, Achaemenid Babylonia; sources and problems: ➤ 822, Achaemenid 4 (1986/90) 149-175 / 177-194.

b530 *Brown* S. C., Medien [Eng.]: ➤ 853* RLA 7,7 (1990) 619-622 [617s Medisch, *Schmitt* R.].

b531 *a*) *Charpin* Dominique, Une alliance contre l'Élam et le rituel du *lipit napištim*; – *b*) *Vallat* François, Réflexions sur l'époque des *sukkalmah*: ➤ 138, ᶠPERROT J., Iran 1990, 109-118 / 119-126 + 1 fig.

b532 **Dąbrowa** Edward, La politique de l'état parthe à l'égard de Rome 1983 ➤ 1,b141: ᴿWeltOr 20s (1989s) 332-6 (E. *Kettenhofen*).

b533 *Daniel* Elton L., Manuscripts and editions of BAL'AMĪ's *Tarjamah-i Tārīkh-i ṬABARĪ*: JRAS (1990) 282-321.

b534 *Funk* Bernd, ❷ Early relations between the Greeks and the empire of the Achaemenians in the light of Old Persian and classical sources: VDI 193 (1990) 3-22; Eng. 23.

b534* ᴱ**Gignoux** Philippe, Transition periods in Iranian history; Actcs du Symposium de Fribourg-en-Brisgau (22-24 Mai 1985): StIran Cah 5, 1987 → 4,738*: ᴿBSO 52 (1989) 362s (A. D. H. *Bivar*).

b535 *Herrenschmidt* Clarisse, Manipulations religieuses de Darius Iᵉʳ: → 111, ᶠLÉVÊQUE P., 4 (1990) 195-207.

b535* **Klíma** Otakar, Ruhm und Untergang des alten Iran [Sláva a pád, 1977],ᵀ. Lp 1988, VEB-Brockhaus. 231 p. 3-325-00161-0 [OIAc F91,14].

b536 **Koch** Heidemarie, Verwaltung und Wirtschaft im persischen Kernland zur Zeit der Achämeniden: TAVO B-89. Wsb 1990, Reichert. 428 p. 3-88226-468-3 [OIAc Oc90].

b537 ᴱ**Kuhrt** Amélie, *al.*, Achaemenid history 3. Method and theory 1985/8 → 4,713: ᴿJAOS 110 (1990) 773-5 (R. N. *Frye*).

b538 *Kuhrt* Amélie, The Achaemenid empire; a Babylonian perspective: PrPgS 34 (1988) 69-76.

b539 *Luria* B. Z., ❶ Concerning the history of the Jews in Adiabene [rabbinic addenda to JOSEPHUS]: Sinai 103,2 (1988) 61-75 [< JStJud 21,338].

b540 *Miroschedji* P. de, La fin de l'Elam; essai d'analyse et d'interprétation: IrAnt 25 (1990) 47-95.

b541 **Nowak** Thomas J., Darius' invasion into Scythia; geographical and logistical perspectives: diss. Miami Univ. 1989, ᴰ*Yamauchi* E. – OIAc JuJ 89 gives AA order as 1333649.

b542 *Panitschek* Peter, Zur Darstellung der Alexander- und Achaeme-nidennachfolge als politische Programme in kaiserzeitlichen Quellen: Klio 72 (1990) 457-473.

b543 **Podany** Amada H., The chronology of the Hana period: diss. UCLA 1989, ᴰ*Buccellati* Giorgio. 88-22883. – OIAc JuJ 89.

b544 **Sancisi-Weerdenburg** Heleen, Achaemenid history I-III, 1987s → 3,787 ... 5,b513: ᴿClasR 40 (1990) 89-95 (S. *Hornblower*).

b545 *Sartre* Maurice, La Syrie sous la domination achéménide: → 481, Syrie II (1989) 9-18.

b546 **Schmitt** Rüdiger, *a)* Epigraphisch-exegetische Noten zu Dareios' Bīsutūn-Inschriften: Szb ph/h 561. W 1990, Österr. Akad. 88 p. 3-7001- 1770-1. – *b)* The name of Darius: → 192, ᶠYARSHATER E. 1990, 194-9.

b546* **Schön** Dorit, Laristan — eine südpersische Küstenprovinz; ein Beitrag zu seiner Geschichte: Szb ph/h 553. W 1990, Österr. Akad. 94 p. 3-7001-1801-5.

b547 *Scurlock* J. A., HERODOTOS' Median [i.e. 'of the Medes'] chronology again (*sýn* 'including' or 'excluding'): IrAnt 25 (1990) 149-163.

b548 ᶠSTÈVE M.-J., Fragmenta historiae elamicae ᴱ**Meyer** L. De... 1986 → 3,153: ᴿOLZ 85 (1990) 198-203 (R. *Schmitt*).

b549 **Weiskopf** Michael, The so-called 'great satraps' revolt' 366-360 B.C.; concerning local instability in the Achaemenid Far West: Historia Einz. 63, 1989 → 5,b519; DM 34: ᴿClasR 40 (1990) 363-5 (S. *Hornblower*: a myth; DIODORUS all wrong).

b550 **Winter** Engelbert, Die sāsānidisch-römischen Friedensverträge des 3. Jh. n. Chr. — ein Beitrag zum Verständnis der aussenpolitischen Beziehungen zwischen beiden Grossmächten: EurHS 3/350, 1988 → 4,287; 5,b520; Fs 68. 3-8204-1368-5: ᴿBO 47 (1990) 163-178 (E. *Kettenhofen*).

b551 *Wolski* Józef, *a*) Die gesellschaftliche und politische Stellung der grossen parthischen Familien: Tyche 4 (1989) 221-7; – *b*) Alexandre le Grand et l'Iran ➤ 488, From Alexander 1990, 1-10.

b552 *Wylie* Graham, How did Trajan succeed in subduing Parthia where Mark Antony failed?: AncHB 4 (1990) 37-43.

b553 **Yamauchi** Edwin M., Persia and the Bible; pref. *Wiseman* Donald J. GR 1990, Baker. 578 p.; ill.; maps; bibliog. p. 525-547. 0-8010-9899-8. – ᴿAulaO 8 (1990) 283-5 (M. *Heltzer*); ExpTim 102 (1990s) 212s (J. F. *Healey*).

b554 *a*) *Young* T. Cuyler, The Persian empire [... to Xerxes]; – *b*) *Kuhrt* Amélie, Babylonia from Cyrus to Xerxes; – *c*) *Eph'al* I., Syria-Palestine under Achaemenid rule; – *d*) *Mellink* Machteld, Anatolia; ➤ 831, CAH² 4 (1988) 1-111 / 112-138 / 139-164 / 211-233.

Q5 *Historia Anatoliae:* **Asia Minor, Hittites** [➤ T8.2], **Armenia** [➤ T8.9].

b555 *Altman* Amnon, On the legal meaning of some of the assertions in the 'historical prologue' of the Kizzuwatnu treaty (KBo I,5): ➤ 7, ᶠARTZI P. 1990, 177-206.

b556 **Desideri** Paolo, *Jasink* Anna Margherita, Cilicia, dall'età di Kizzuwatna alla conquista macedona: Univ. Fond. Parini-Chirio. Storia 1. T 1990, Le Lettere. xvii-246 p.; 16 pl. 88-7166-012-9 [OIAc Ap91,6].

b557 *Dijkstra* M., On the identity of the Hittite princess mentioned in label KTU 6.24 (RS 17.72): UF 22 (1990) 97-101.

b558 *Giorgieri* Mauro, Magia e intrighi alla corte di Labarna-Hattusili: IstLombR 124 (1990) 247-277.

b559 *Güterbock* Hans G., Wer war Tawagalawa?: ➤ 160*, Mem. SCHULER E.v., Orientalia 59 (1990) 156-165.

b560 *Klengel* Horst, Nerikkaili; zum Problem der Homonymie im hethitischen Anatolien: AltOrF 16 (1989) 185-8.

b561 *a*) *Liverani* Mario, Hattušili alle prese con la propaganda ramesside; – *b*) *Soysal* Oğuz, Noch einmal zur Šukziya-Episode im Erlass Telepinus: ➤ 160*, Mem. SCHULER E. v., Orientalia 59 (1990) 207-217 / 271-9.

b562 **McGing** B., The foreign policy of Mithridates VI 1986 ➤ 3,b794... 5,b528: ᴿVDI 193 (1990) 204-9 (S. Yu. *Saprykin* ☉).

b563 *Mellaart* J., Some reflections on the history and geography of Western Anatolia in the late fourteenth and thirteenth centuries B.C.: ➤ 3, Mem. ALKIM U. 1986, 215-230.

b564 *Mora* Clelia, Una probabile testimonianza di coreggenza tra due sovrani ittiti [Hattušili III e Tuthalja IV]: IstLombR 121 (1987) 97-108.

b565 *Uchitel* A., Post Hittite historiography in Asia Minor: ScrClasIsr 10 (1989s) 1-11.

b566 *Westbrook* Raymond, *Woodard* Roger D., The edict of Tudhaliya IV: JAOS 110 (1990) 641-659.

Q6.1 **Historia Graeciae classicae.**

b567 **Allison** June W., Power and preparedness in THUCYDIDES [diss. 1974] AmJPgMg 5. Baltimore 1989, Johns Hopkins Univ. viii-168 p. £14.50. – ᴿClasR 40 (1990) 228s (R. *Osborne*); GreeceR 37 (1990) 243s (P. J. *Rhodes*).

b568 **Amit** Moshe, ☉ *Toledot Yavan haqalqalît*, economic history of Greece. J 1984, Magnes. 555 p. – ᴿQadmoniot 23 (1990) 127 (G. *Herman*, ☉).

b569 **Asheri** David; E*Medaglia* Silvio M., T*Fraschetti* Augusto, ERODOTO, Le storie 3. La Persia: Fond. Valla. Mi 1990, Mondadori. lxviii-396 p.; 24 pl.; 19 maps. 88-04-32760-X [OIAc Ap91,4].

b570 **Bengtson** Hermann, History of Greece from the beginnings to the Byzantine cra [⁴1969 rev, 1977], T*Bloedow* Edmund F. (updated): Classical Texts and Studies 3, 1988; ⇒ 5,b543; $90; pa. $40. 0-7766-0210-1; -111-3: RAntClas 59 (1990) 473-5 (D. *Viviers*); Gymnasium 97 (1990) 366 (K. *Brodersen*).

b570* **Bernal** Martin, Black Athena I, 1987 ⇒ 3,b809: RJMeditArch 3 (1990) 57-66 (Sarah *Morris*) & 67-75 (Patricia M. *Bikai*) & 77-81 (J. D. *Ray*) & 83-110 (J. D. *Muhly*); 111-137 (*Bernal* response).

b571 **Bluestone** Natalie H., Women and the ideal society; Plato's 'Republic' and modern myths of gender. Amherst 1988, Univ. Massachusetts. 248 p. $25; pa. $12. 0-87023-580-X; -1-8. – EClasW 83 (1989s) 246s (S. D. *Olson*).

b572 **Blundell** Sue, The origins of civilization in Greek and Roman thought 1986 ⇒ 2,9421; 3,b812: RAncHRes 20 (1990) 69s (R. *Mortley*).

b573 *Burke* Edmund M., Athens after the Peloponnesian War; restoration efforts and the role of maritime commerce: ClasAnt 9 (1990) 1-13.

b574 **Burkert** Walter, al., HÉRODOTE et les peuples non grecs [août 1988]: Entretiens AntClas 35. Genève 1990, Fond. Hardt. [viii-] 350 p.

b574* *Cartledge* Paul, HERODOTUS and 'the other'; a meditation on empire: ÉchMClas 34 (1990) 27-40.

b575 **Cataldi** Silvio, La democrazia ateniese e gli alleati (Ps.-SENOFONTE, Athenaion Politeia, I, 14-18): SaggiMatUniv. Padova 1984, Programma. 181 p. Lit. 16.000. – RAntClas 59 (1990) 488-490 (H. *Verdin*).

b576 **Darbo-Peschanski** Catherine, Le discours du particulier; essai sur l'enquête HÉRODOTÉENNE; préf. *Veyne* Paul. P 1987, Seuil. 254 p. F 99. 2-02-009524-6. – RAntClas 59 (1990) 298-300 (H. *Verdin*).

b577 **Davies** John K., Das klassische Griechenland und die Demokratie [Democracy and... 1978], T. Mü 1983, dtv. 299 p. – RArKulturG 71 (1989) 227-230 (B. *Smarczyk*).

b578 *Donlan* Walter, The pre-state community in Greece; Symbolae 64 (Oslo 1989) 5-29.

Dover Kenneth, The Greeks and their legacy 1988 ⇒ 223.

b579 **Drews** Robert, The coming of the Greeks; Indo-European conquests in the Aegean and the Near East 1988 ⇒ 4,d330; 5,b553*: RAJA 94 (1990) 155s (Susan N. *Skomal*); AmJPg 111 (1990) 264-8 (R. D. *Woodard*); Gnomon 62 (1990) 703-6 (F. *Kiechle*); HZ 251 (1990) 662s (B. *Patzek*).

b580 **Du Bois** Page, Sowing the body 1988 ⇒ 4,d331; 5,b555: RAmHR 95 (1990) 142s (Eva C. *Keuls*); ClasR 40 (1990) 124s (Gillian *Clark*); Gnomon 62 (1990) 458 (H. *Zinser*); Phoenix 44 (Toronto 1990) 184-186 (Rosemary M. *Nielsen*).

b581 *Evans* J. A. S., Six new studies on HERODOTUS [FLORY S., BALCER J., ...]: AmJPg 111 (1990) 92-104.

b582 **Fehling** Detlev, HERODOTUS and his 'sources'; citation, invention and narrative art [Quellenangaben 1971 updated], T*Howie* J. G.: ARCA classical and medieval 21. Leeds 1989, Cairns. 277 p. A$90. 0-905205-70-7. – RAncHRes 20 (1990) 180-3 (R. *Nyland*); AnzAltW 43 (1990) 49-55 (R. *Bichler*).

b583 **Flory** Stewart, The archaic smile of HERODOTUS 1987 ⇒ 4,d335; 5,b558: RClasPg 85 (1990) 60-64 (Carolyn *Dewald*).

b584 **Garland** Robert, The Greek way of life; from conception to old age. L 1990, Duckworth. xiii-376 p.; 45 fig. 0-7156-2261-7.

b585 **Gilli** G., Origini dell'eguaglianza; ricerche sociologiche sull'antica Grecia. T 1988, Einaudi. 569 p. – [R]AntÉCS 45 (1990) 876s (C. *Mossé*).

b586 **Gould** John, HERODOTUS. NY 1989, St. Martin's. 164 p.; 2 maps. $25 [RelStR 17, 158, C. F. *Aling*: good, on story].

b587 [E]**Grant** M., *Ritzinger* Rachel, Civilization of the ancient Mediterranean, Greece and Rome I-III, 1988 → 4,444: [R]AmHR 95 (1990) 466-8 (W. *Donlan*).

b588 **Grimal** Pierre, Les erreurs de la liberté. P 1989, BLettres. 201 p. – [R]RivCuClasM 31 (1989) 85-87 (E. *Paratore*).

b589 **Halperin** David M., One hundred years of homosexuality [... David and Jonathan] and other essays on Greek love. L 1990, Routledge. x-229; ill. £10 pa. – [R]GreeceR 37 (1990) 255s (P. *Walcot*).

b590 **Hammond** N. G. L., A history of Greece to 322 B.C.[3] [[1]1959 [2]1967] 1986 → 2,9445: [R]Ellinika 40 (1989) 439 (I. *Touloumakos*, deutsch: unsatisfactory).

b591 **Hansen** Mogens H., Was Athens a democracy? 1989 → 5,b573: [R]AntClas 59 (1990) 485s (D. *Viviers*: yes); ClasR 40 (1990) 177s (R. A. *Knox*).

b592 **Hartog** François, The mirror of HERODOTUS: the representation of the other in the writing of history, [T]*Lloyd* Janet: The New Historicism 5. Berkeley 1988, Univ. California. xxv-386 p. – [R]AmHR 95 (1990) 460s (S. *Flory*).

b593 *a) Heath* Malcolm, Justice in THUCYDIDES' Athenian speeches; – *b) Barceló* Pedro, Thukydides und die Tyrannis: Historia 39 (1990) 385-400 / 401-425.

b594 **Hornblower** Simon, THUCYDIDES 1987 → 4,d352; 5,b579: [R]ClasR 40 (1990) 227s (R. *Osborne* praises); Gnomon 62 (1990) 177-9 (O. *Wenskus*).

b595 **Iriarte** Ana, Las redes del enigma; voces femininas en el pensamiento griego; pref. *Loraux* Nicole. M 1990, Taurus. 161 p.; 11 fig. [Kernos 4, 340, E. *Suárez de la Torre*].

b596 **Jones** Nicholas F., Public organization in ancient Greece: AmPhSocMem 176, 1987 → 5,b584: [R]ClasR 40 (1990) 95s (K. H. *Kinzl*); RHist 232 (1989) 213-6 (J. *Haillet*); RPg 63 (1989) 263-271 (E. *Will*).

b597 **Just** Roger, Women in Athenian law and life. L 1989, Routledge. x-317 p. 0-415-00346-6.

b598 **Kearns** Emily, The heroes of Attica: Bulletin Supp 57. L 1989, Univ. Inst. Clas. xiv-212 p.; 6 pl. 0-900587-60-1.

b599 **Keuls** Eva C., Il regno della fallocrazia 1988 → 5,b585: [R]RFgIC 118 (1990) 73-77 (Franca *Perusino*).

b600 **Lateiner** Donald, The historical method of HERODOTUS: Phoenix Supp 23. Toronto 1989, Univ. 319 p. 0-8020-5793-4.

b601 *Lateiner* Donald, Deceptions and delusions in HERODOTUS [not 'of': sham priests and prophets]: ClasAnt 9 (1990) 230-246.

b602 **Lehmann** Gustav A., Die mykenisch-frühgriechische Welt ... 1985 → 2, b850; 3,f686: [R]Athenaeum 78 (1990) 197-201 (C. *Mora*).

b603 **Leimbach** Rüdiger, Militärische Musterrhetorik ... THUKYDIDES 1985 → 2,9459; 4,d361: [R]Eos 78 (1990) 402-4 (R. *Turasiewicz* ❷).

b604 **Long** T., Repetition and variation in the short stories of HERODOTUS 1987 → 5,b590: [R]Helmantica 41 (1990) 274s (P. *Orosio*).

b605 **McGregor** Malcolm F., The Athenians and their empire 1987 → 4,d366; 5,b592: 0-7748-0279-0; pa. -69-3: [R]ÉchMClas 34 (1990) 450-3 (E. *Badian*).

b606 **Massey** Michael, Women in ancient Greece and Rome. C 1988, Univ. iv-36 p.; 20 pl. $5 pa. 0-521-31807-6. – RClasW 83 (1989s) 254s (F. *Mensch*: good high-school text).

b606* **Mossè** C., La vita quotidiana della donna nella Grecia antica 1988 → 5,b597: RMaia 42 (1990) 87s (Nicoletta *Marini*).

b607 **Ober** Josiah, Mass and elite in democratic Athens; rhetoric, ideology, and the power of the people. Princeton 1989, Univ. xviii-390 p. $39,50. – RClasR 40 (1990) 348-356 (M. H. *Hansen*); GreeceR 37 (1990) 242s (P. J. *Rhodes*).

b608 **Osborne** Robin, Demos 1985 → 2,9464; 4,d370: RAntClas 59 (1990) 486s (H. *Verdin*).

b609 *Payen* Pascal, Discours historique et structures narratives chez HÉRODOTE: AnÉCS 45 (1990) 527-550.

b610 *Petzold* Karl-Ernst, Zur Entstehungsphase der athenischen Demokratie: RFgIC 118 (1990) 145-178.

b611 **Piccirilli** Luigi, Storie dello storico TUCIDIDE; edizione critica, traduzione e commento delle Vite tucididee [... A. MÁRCELLINUS, *al.*]. Genova 1985, Melangolo. xlvi-205 p. Lit. 25.000. 88-7018-067-0. – RAntClas 59 (1990) 305 (H. *Verdin*).

b612 FRAUBITSCHEK Anton E., The Greek historians 1985 → 2,92: RAnzAltW 43 (1990) 45-49 (R. *Bichler*).

b613 **Reeve** C. D. C., Philosopher-kings; the argument of PLATO's Republic. Princeton 1988, Univ. – RAmJPg 111 (1990) 105-9 (G. R. F. *Ferrari*: lively).

b614 **Reinsberg** Carola, Ehe, Hetärentum und Knabenliebe im antiken Griechentum: Archäol. Bibliothek. Mü 1989, Beck. 262 p.; 120 fig.

b615 *Romilly* Jacqueline de, La mémoire du passé dans la Grèce antique: RHist 283 (1990) 3-12.

b616 **Rosén** Haiim B., HERODOTI historiae I, libri I-IV, 1987 → 3,b854; 5,b609: RScrClasIsr 10 (1989s) 134-140 (R. *Freundlich*).

b617 **Sassi** Maria M., La scienza dell'uomo nella Grecia antica [né medicina né religione, pare]. T 1988, Boringhieri. 250 p. – RRFgIC 118 (1990) 323-7 (Caterina *Licciardi*).

b618 **Sealey** Raphael, The Athenian republic; democracy or the rule of law? 1987 → 4,d390: REchMClas 34 (1990) 74-77 (C. *Mossé*); Gnomon 61 (1989) 744-6 (Mogens H. *Hansen*).

b619 **Shaw** Clara S., Aspects of the narrating voice in HERODOTUS: diss. Brown. Providence 1990. 131 p. 91-01831. – DissA 51 (1990s) 2733-A.

b620 **Shimron** Binyamin, Politics and belief in HERODOTUS: Historia Einz. 58. Stu 1989, Steiner. x-126 p. DM 40. – RClasR 40 (1990) 473s (R. *Osborne*); GreeceR 37 (1990) 245 (P. J. *Rhodes*).

b621 **Sinclair** R. K., Democracy and participation in Athens 1988 → 5,b613: RAntClas 59 (1990) 482s (J.-M. *Hannick*); ClasJ 85 (1989s) 359s (D. *Lateiner*); Mnemosyne 43 (1990) 264-7 (P. J. J. *Vanderbroeck*).

b622 **Snyder** Jane M., The woman and the lyre; women writers in classical Greece and Rome. Carbondale 1989, Southern Illinois Univ. xvi-199 p.; map. $25. – RClasR 40 (1990) 294s (Maria *Wyke*).

b623 **Strauss** Barry, Athens after the Peloponnesian War 1987 → 4,d397; 5,b617: RRÉG 103 (1990) 278-280 (C. *Vial*).

b624 **Tatum** James, XENOPHON's imperial fiction; on 'The education of Cyrus'. Princeton 1989, Univ. 288 p. $32.50. 0-691-06757-0. – RClasR 40 (1990) 229-231 (Rosemary *Stevenson*).

b625 **Thomas** Rosalind, Oral tradition and written record in classical Athens 1989 ➤ 5,b618: ᴿAntClas 59 (1990) 478s (J. *Labarbe*); ClasR 40 (1990) 297s (D. *Fehling*); Gnomon 62 (1990) 673-7 (Ø. *Andersen*).

b626 **Toynbee** Arnold, Los griegos [1981], ᵀ*Calderón* José E. ... 1988, Fondo de Cultura Económica. – ᴿEfMex 8 (1990) 254-262 (P. M. *Gasparotto*: ... apostasía di Toynbee ... ignorancia del catolicismo).

b627 **Vandiver** Blanche E., Heroes in HERODOTUS; the interaction of myth and history: diss. Texas, ᴰ*Green* P. Austin 1990. 415 p. 90-31735. – DissA 51 (1990s) 2009-A; OIAc F91,20.

b628 *Vilatte* Sylvie, L'insularité dans la pensée grecque; au carrefour de la Géographie, de l'Ethnographie, de l'Histoire: RHist 281 (1989) 3-13.

b629 *Virgilio* Biagio, Atene; democrazia e potere personale; aspetti della grecità come modello: AtenRom 35 (1990) 49-70.

b630 **Wallace** Robert W., The Areopagus council to 307 B.C. Baltimore 1989, Johns Hopkins Univ. xvii-294 p. £22.50. – ᴿClasR 40 (1990) 356-8 (D. M. *Lewis*); GreeceR 37 (1990) 242 (P. J. *Rhodes*).

b631 **Waters** K. H., HERODOTUS, the historian; his problems, methods, and originality 1985 ➤ 1,b218 ... 4,d405: ᴿAntClas 59 (1990) 296s (H. *Verdin*).

b632 *a) Wilson* J. R., Sophrosyne in THUCYDIDES; – *b) Develin* Robert, Thucydides on speeches: AncHB 4 (1990) 51-57 / 58-60.

b633 *Winterling* Aloys, Die Männergesellschaften im archaischen Griechenland: Universitas 45 (1990) 717-727; 5 fig.

b633* *Wolski* J., Thémistocle était-il promoteur de la démocratie athénienne?: ➤ 67, Mem. HAHN I., AcAntH 32 (1989) 43-49.

b634 **Wood** Ellen M., Peasant-citizen and slave; the foundations of Athenian democracy. NY 1988, Verso. 210 p. $40. – ᴿJIntdis 20 (1989s) 281-3 (H. A. T. *Reiche*).

Q6.5   Alexander, Seleucidae; historia Hellenismi.

b635 *Ambaglio* Delfino, STRABONE e la storiografia greca frammentaria: ➤ 53, ᶠGABBA E., Storia 1988, 73-83.

b636 **Bengtson** H., Die Diadochen 1987 ➤ 4,d311; 5,b541: ᴿHZ 251 (1990) 665-7 (E. *Olshausen*).

b637 **Bengtson** Herrmann, Die hellenistische Weltkultur 1988 ➤ 5,b542: ᴿHZ 250 (1990) 663-6 (K. *Bringmann*).

b638 *Bernard* Paul, Nouvelle contribution de l'épigraphie cunéiforme à l'histoire hellénistique [≅ CRAI (1989) 294-307]: BCH 114 (1990) 513-541.

b639 *Bilde* P., Begrebet 'hellenisme': DanTTs 52,3 (1989) 204-215 [< ZNW 81,149].

b640 *Bloedow* Edmond F., Alexander the Great and Bactria [HOLT F. 1988]: ParPass 46,256 (1991) 44-80.

b641 **Bohm** Claudia, Imitatio Alexandri im Hellenismus; Untersuchungen zum politischen Nachwirken Alexanders des Grossen in hoch- und späthellenistischen Monarchien [Diss. Köln 1986]: QForschAntW 3. Mü 1989, Florentz. 232 p.; 17 pl. [OIAc Ap91,4].

b642 **Borza** Eugene N., In the shadow of Olympus; the emergence of Macedon. Princeton 1990, Univ. viii-333 p. [AncHB 5,179, Elizabeth *Carney*].

b643 **Bosworth** A.B., Conquest and empire / Alexander 1988 ➤ 5,b546: ᴿAmJPg 111 (1990) 558-561 (Elizabeth D. *Carney*); Gymnasium 97 (1990) 173-5 (F. F. *Schwarz*); JHS 110 (1990) 254s (F. W. *Walbank*).

b644 **Bosworth** A. B., From ARRIAN to Alexander 1988 ➤ 5,b545; RClasPg 85 (1990) 320-4 (A. M. *Devine*).

b645 **Bowersock** Glen W., Hellenism in late antiquity [Rome American Academy T. S. Jerome lectures]. C 1990, Univ. xii-109 p.

b645* *a*) *Briant* Pierre, The Seleucid Kingdom, the Achaemenid Empire and the history of the Near East in the first millennium B. C.; – *b*) *Friedman* Jonathan, Notes on culture and identity in imperial worlds: ➤ 325*, *Bilde*/Seleucid 1990, 40-65 / 14-39.

b646 **Cartledge** Paul, *Spawforth* Antony, Hellenistic and Roman Sparta, a tale of two cities: States and cities of ancient Greece. L 1989, Routledge. xiii-304 p.; 2 maps. £35. – RGreeceR 37 (1990) 244 (P. J. *Rhodes*).

b647 **Cunliffe** Barry, Greeks, Romans, and barbarians 1988 ➤ 4,d580; 5,b552: RAmHR 95 (1990) 1171s (J. F. *Drinkwater*); ClasR 40 (1990) 343-5 (O. *Murray*); ClasW 84 (1990s) 77s (R. B. *Hitchner*); Phoenix 44 (Toronto 1990) 196-8 (A. A. *Barrett*).

b648 *Deremetz* Alain, PLUTARQUE; histoire de l'origine et genèse du récit: RÉG 103 (1990) 54-78.

b649 **Errington** R. Malcolm, A history of Macedonia [1986 ➤ 3,d333], TErrington Mrs. Catherine, with some footnote updating. Berkeley 1990, Univ. California. x-320 p. $35. 0-520-06310-8 [AncHB 5,183, Elizabeth *Carney*].

b650 *Fredericksmeyer* E. A., Alexander and Philip; emulation and resentment: ClasJ 85 (1989s) 300-315.

b651 **Golan** David, ❾ History of the Hellenistic world. J 1983, Magnes. 888 p.; 45 fig.; 8 maps. – RQadmoniot 23 (1990) 127s (G. *Herman* ❾).

b651* *a*) *Goldstein* Jonathan A., The Hasmonean revolt and the Hasmonean dynasty; – *b*) *Hegermann* Harald, The Diaspora in the Hellenistic age; – *c*) *Finkelsteim* Louis, The Pharisaic leadership after the Great Synagogue; – *d*) *Mørkholm* Otto †, Antiochus IV; – *e*) *Gabba* Emilio, The growth of anti-Semitism or the Greek attitude towards Jews: ➤ 835, CHJud 2 (1989) 292-351 / 115-166 / (229-) 245-277 / 278-291 / 614-656.

b652 **Grant** Michael, From Alexander to Cleopatra; the Hellenistic world. NY 1990 = 1982, Collier-Macmillan. xv-319 p. $15 pa. [RelStR 17,158, D. N. *Wigtil*].

b653 **Green** Peter, Alexander to Actium; the historical evolution of the Hellenistic age: Hellenistic Culture and Society 1. Berkeley 1990, Univ. California. xxiii-970 p.; 217 fig.; 30 maps. $65. 0-520-05611-6 [NTAbs 35,126].

b654 *Habicht* C., The Seleucids and their rivals; ➤ 832, CAH² 8 (1989) 124-387.

b655 *Hamilton* Jim, Recent work on ARRIAN [BOSWORTH A., 1988]: AncHRes 20 (1990) 51-59.

b656 **Hammond** N. G. L., Three historians of Alexander 1985 ➤ 64,a159 ... 3,b826: RVDI 192 (1990) 202-8 (L. P. *Marinovich*).

b657 **Hammond** N., *Walbank* F., History of Macedonia 3, 1988 ➤ 5,b569: RRPg 63 (1989) 282-6 (J. *Tréheux*).

b657* *a*) *Hengel* Martin, The political and social history of Palestine from Alexander to Antiochus III (333-187 B.C.E.); – *b*) The interpretation of Judaism and Hellenism in the pre-Maccabean period: ➤ 835, CHJud 2 (1989) 35-78 / 167-228.

b658 *a*) **Högemann** Peter, Alexander und Arabien 1985 ➤ 2,9450; 3,b831: RAnzAltW 43 (1990) 200-5 (P. W. *Haider*). – *b*) **Holt** Frank L., Alexander the Great and Bactria 1988 ➤ 5,b576: RAJA 94 (1990) 162s (E. N.

Borza); AmHR 95 (1990) 794s (Janice J. *Garbert*); JHS 110 (1990) 256-8
(A. B. *Bosworth*); StIran 19 (1990) 21-35; 4 fig., map (P. *Bernard*); VDI
195 (1990) 165-172 (I. R. *Pichikyan* ❸).

b659 **Kagan** Donald, The fall of the Athenian empire 1987 ➤ 4,d355:
ᴿClasJ 85 (1989s) 360-4 (H. E. *Yunis*).

b660 ᴱ**Kuhrt** Amélie, *Sherwin-White* Susan, Hellenism in the East 1984/7
➤ 4,d358; 5,b588: ᴿBO 47 (1990) 710-6 (B. *Scholz*); JAOS 110 (1990)
117s (R. H. *Sack*).

b661 *Loreto* Luigi, Per la storia del protoellenismo [BENGTSON H. 1987]:
AtenR 34 (1989) 194-202.

b662 *Martin* Luther H., The *Encyclopedia Hellenistica* [not a book but the
sum of knowledge] and Christian origins: BibTB 20 (1990) 123-7.

b663 *Podes* Stephan, Handlungserklärung bei POLYBIOS; intellectualisme
historique? ein Beitrag zur hellenistischen Historiographie: AncSoc 21
(1990) 215-240.

b664 *Possehl* Gregory L., Alexander in India; the last great battle: ➤ 728,
World 1990.

b665 **Samuel** Alan E., The promise of the west 1988 ➤ 4,d384; 5,b511: ᴿBO
45 (1990) 522s (G. *Mussies*).

b666 *Schepens* Guido, Zum Problem der 'Unbesiegbarkeit' Alexanders des
Grossen: AncSoc 20 (1989) 15-53.

Schmitt Hatto H., *Vogt* Ernst, Kleines Wörterbuch des Hellenismus 1988
➤ 937.

b667 **Schwenk** Cynthia J., Athens in the age of Alexander; the dated laws
and decrees of 'the Lykourgan Era', 338-332 B.C., 1985 ➤ 1,b211;
4,d389: ᴿRFgIC 118 (1990) 78-82 (M. *Faraguna*).

b668 **Walbank** F. W., El mundo helenístico. M 1985, Taurus. 265 p.; 8 fig.;
4 maps. – ᴿFaventia 11,1 (1989) 175s (G. *Carrasco Serrano*).

b669 *Winnicki* J. K., Militäroperationen von Ptolemaios I. und Seleukos I. in
Syrien in den Jahren 312-311 v.Chr. (II): AncSoc 20 (1989) 55-90; 2
maps.

b670 **Wiśniewski** Bohdan, PHILON von Larissa, Testimonia und Kommentar.
Wrocław 1987, Soc. Scient. Łódź. 46 p. zł 35. – ᴿScrClasIsr 8s (1988)
192-5 (J. *Glucker*: severe; unfortunately the only edition available).

Q7   Josephus Flavius.

b671 **Bailey** Arthur A., Josephus' use of *Heimarménē*; an interpretation of his
philosophy of Jewish history related to the destruction of Jerusalem: diss.
Brigham Young Univ., ᴰ*Mackay* T. 1990. 217 p. 90-22870. – DissA 51
(1990s) 961s-A.

b672 **Basnage** J. [1653-1723], Vervolg op Flavius Josephus; Of algemene
historie der jootsche naatsie [Histoire des Juifs 1707; ned. 1726]. Utrecht
1988, De Banier. xxvi-1940 p. – ᴿNedTTs 44 (1990) 265s (P. W. van der
Horst).

b673 *Begg* Christopher, 'Josephus's portrayal of the disappearance of Enoch,
Elijah, and Moses'; some observations: JBL [108 (1989) 225-238, *Tabor*
J. D.] 109 (1990) 691-3.

b674 **Bilde** Per, Flavius Josephus between Jerusalem and Rome — his life, his
works and their importance 1988 ➤ 4,4412; 5,b627: ᴿBAR-W 16,5
(1990) 8 (M. *Broshi*); CBQ 52 (1990) 340s (D. J. *Harrington*: rightly claims
that scholars use bits and pieces of Josephus without sufficient familiarity
with his whole work and life); CritRR 3 (1990) 336-8 (Shaye *Cohen*); JJS

41 (1990) 270-2 (Tessa *Rajak*); JSS 35 (1990) 151s (M. D. *Goodman*); JSt-Jud 21 (1990) 98s (W. S. *Vorster*); TLZ 115 (1990) 587s (G. *Baumbach*).

b675 **Bohrmann** Monette, Flavius Josèphe, les Zélotes et Yavné; pour une relecture de la 'Guerre des Juifs' 1989 ➤ 5,b628: ᴿRHPR 70 (1990) 136 (E. *Trocmé*: plutôt sur la mentalité juive/talmudique).

b676 **Briley** Terry R., Josephus the historian and the man; an analysis of Josephus as historian of the Jewish War against the Romans: diss. HUC. – Cincinnati 1990. 197 p. 91-07140. – DissA 51 (1990s) 3491-A.

b677 *Brunt* P. A., Josephus on social conflicts in Roman Judaea [< Klio 55 (1977) 149-153]: ➤ 206, Roman imperial 1990, 282-7. 517ss.

b678 **Deutsch** Guy N., Iconographie... Josephus/Fouquet 1986 ➤ 3,b881; 4,d415*: ᴿSpeculum 64 (1989) 695 (A. H. van *Buren*).

b679 *Eckstein* A. M., Josephus and Polybius; a reconsideration [of Cohen S., HistTheor 21 (1982)]: ClasAnt 9 (1990) 175-208.

b680 **Feldman** Louis H., *Hata* Gohei, Josephus, Judaism and Christianity 1987 ➤ 3,338; 5,b629: ᴿClasR 40 (1990) 242s (Margaret H. *Williams*); JJS 41 (1990) 130s (G. *Vermès*).

b681 *Feldman* Louis H., Prophets and prophecy in Josephus: JTS 41 (1990) 386-422.

b682 *Frenschkowski* Marco, Iranische Königslegende in der Adiabene; zur Vorgeschichte von Josephus, Antiquitates XX,17-33: ZDMG 140 (1990) 213-233.

b683 *Fuks* Gideon, Josephus and the Hasmoneans: JJS 41 (1990) 166-176.

b683* *a)* *Gera* Dov, On the credibility of the history of the Tobiads (Josephus, Ant 12,156-222.228-236) [far from accurate]; – *b)* *Saulnier* Christiane, Flavius Josèphe; apologiste de Rome pour servir l'histoire juive: ➤ 540, Greece/Israel 1985/90, 21-38 / 84-91.

b684 *Gutmann* Joseph, Josephus' Jewish Antiquities in twelfth-century art; renovatio or creatio? [< ZtsKunstG 48 (1985) 434-441]: ➤ 5,272, Sacred images 1989, IX, 434-441.

b685 **Hadas-Lebel** Mireille, Flavius Josèphe, le Juif de Rome 1989 ➤ 5,b635: F 110; 2-213-02307-7: ᴿÉTRel 65 (1990) 458s (E. *Cuvillier*: excellent, mais les parallèles à Paul semblent tous d'Actes/Pastorales); RHPR 70 (1990) 135s (M. *Matter*: vision ni cohérente ni neuve); ZAW 102 (1990) 302 (L. *Kottsieper*).

b686 *Hadas-Lebel* Mireille, Une lettre en français de Menasseh ben Israël, à propos du Testimonium flavianum: RÉJ 149 (1950) 125-8.

b687 **Hardwick** Michael E., Josephus as an historical source in patristic literature through Eusebius: BrownJudSt 128. Atlanta 1989, Scholars. xi-137 p. $45 [RelStR 17, 176, R. M. *Grant*].

b688 *Kraft* Robert A., Tiberius Julius Alexander and the crisis in Alexandria according to Josephus: ➤ 173, ᶠStrugnell J., Of scribes 1990, 175-184.

b689 *Maas* Michael, Photius' treatment of Josephus and the high-priesthood: Byzantion 60 (1990) 183-194.

b690 *Main* Emmanuelle, Les Sadducéens vus par Flavius Josèphe: RB 97 (1990) 161-206; Eng. 161.

b691 *Meier* John P., Jesus in Josephus; a modest proposal [A 18,63s has more claim to authenticity if we start from the part about James; moreover every word in the whole passage (except *Christianōn*) occurs elsewhere in Josephus]: CBQ 52 (1990) 76-103.

b692 ᴱ**Nodet** É. (*Berceville* Gilles, *al.*), Flavius Josèphe, Les Antiquités Juives, livres I à III: I. Introduction et texte; II. Traduction et notes. P 1990, Cerf. xlv-155 p.; 190 p. F 185. 2-204-04051-7 [BL 91,39, Tessa *Rajak*:

high praise for a text greatly improving on NIESE]. – ᴿEsprVie 100 (1990) 472s (Y.-M. *Duval* dans 'bulletin de patrologie'); MondeB 65 (1990) 71 (J. *Potin*); NRT 112 (1990) 919s (V. *Roisel*); RBibArg 52 (1990) 181s (J.P. *Martin*).

b693 **Paul** André,   Le judaïsme ancien 1987 → 3,b893 ... 5,b640:   ᴿÉglT 20 (1989) 477s (L. *Laberge*: coquilles).

b693* *Ritoók* Zs.,   Josephus and Homer [Apion 1,12: Homer could not write]: → 67, Mem. HAHN I., AcAntH 32 (1989) 137-152.

b694 *Schwartz* Daniel R.,   *a*) On some papyri and Josephus' sources and chronology for the Persian period: JStJud 21 (1990) 175-199; – b) On drama and authenticity in Philo and Josephus [Antiquities less dramatic and more factual than Jewish War or PHILO]:   ScrClasIsr 10 (1989s) 113-129.

b695 **Schwartz** Seth,   Josephus and Judaean politics: Columbia Studies in the Classical Tradition 18.   Leiden 1990, Brill.   xl-257 p.   90-04-09230-7.

b696 *Schwartz* Seth,   The 'Judaism' of Samaria and Galilee in Josephus's version of the letter of Demetrius I to Jonathan (Antiquities 13,48-57): HarvTR 82 (1989) 377-391.

b697 *Swerdlow* N.M.,   Astronomical chronology and prophecy; Jean-Dominique CASSINI's discovery of Josephus's great lunisolar period of the Patriarchs: JWarb 53 (1990) 1-13.

b698 **Villalba i Varneda** Pere,   The historical method of Flavius Josephus [Catalán diss. 1981] 1986 → 3,b904 ... 5,b645:   ᴿCritRR 2 (1989) 383-5 (S.D. *Robertson*); Faventia 10 (1988) 214-6 (J. *Gómez Pallarès*); JAOS 110 (1990) 131s (D.R. *Schwartz*: valuable despite 'translationese').

Q8.1   *Roma Pompeii et Caesaris*   –   **Hyrcanus to Herod.**

b699 **Berti** Nadia,   La guerra di Cesare contro Pompeo; commento storico a Cassio DIONE, libri XLI-XLII,1-2.   Mi 1987, Jaca.   170 p. – ᴿTyche 4 (1989) 246 (G. *Dobesch*).

b700 **Bickerman** Elias J.,   The Jews in the Greek age 1988 → 4,d444:   ᴿAmHR 95 (1990) 464s (S. *Eddy*: 'How could so eminent a scholar turn out such poor work'); BR 5,1 (1989) 10s (L.H. *Feldman*); JAOS 110 (1990) 576s (A. *Kamesar*: lack of documentation frustrating); JBL 109 (1990) 338-340 (A. *LaCocque*); JHS 110 (1990) 158s (F. *Millar*); JStJud 21 (1990) 97s (F. *García Martínez*); RelStR 16 (1990) 149 (A.T. *Kraabel*).

b700* **Bonnefond-Coudry** Marianne,   Le Sénat de la république romaine de la guerre d'Hannibal à Auguste; pratiques délibératives et prise de décision: BÉF.   R 1989, Éc. Française.   v-837 + xl p.; 5 plans. – ᴿClasR 40 (1990) 377s (A. *Keaveney*).

b701 ᴱ**Braund** David C.,   The administration of the Roman Empire, 241 B.C.-A.D. 193: Exeter Studies in History 18,   1988 → 4,d573*:   ᴿClasR 40 (1990) 180s (J.S. *Richardson*: fine).

b702 *Broughton* T.R.S.,   L. Manlius Torquatus and the governors of Asia: AmJPg 111 (1990) 72-74.

b703 **Burckhardt** Leonhard A.,   Politische Strategien der Optimaten in der späten römischen Republik [< Diss. Basel 1985]: Historia Einz 57.   Stu 1988, Steiner.   296 p. DM 66.   3-515-05098-1. – ᴿAntClas 59 (1990) 510-2 (P. *Simelon*); AnzAltW 43 (1990) 211-3 (G. *Dobesch*).

b704 **Dack** E. Van 't, *al.*,   The Judean-Syrian-Egyptian conflict of 103-101 B.C.; a multilingual dossier concerning a 'war of scepters': Comité Klass./Hellenisme.   Bru 1989, Acad.   172 p.; 15 pl., foldout chart.   90-

6569-403-X [OIAc Oc90]. – ᴿAegyptus 70 (1990) 301-3 (Lucia *Criscuolo*).

b705 **Delling** G.,   Die Bewältigung der Diasporasituation 1987 ⮞ 3,b928 ... 5,b661: ᴿSNTU-A 14 (1989) 286s (C. *Niemand*); SvEx 55 (1990) 119s (L. *Hartman*).

b706 *Derow* F. S.,   Rome, the fall of Macedon and the sack of Corinth [c. 168 B.C.]: ⮞ 832, CAH² 8 (1989) 290-523 [*al.* Rome and Greece to 100 B.C. 81-289].

b707 *Dobesch* G.,   Europa in der Reichskonzeption bei Caesar, Augustus und Tiberius: AcArchH 41 (1989) 53-59.

b708 *Elbern* Stephan, Geiseln [hostages] in Rom: Athenaeum 78 (1990) 97-140.

b708* *a)* **Epstein** David F.,   Personal enmity in Roman politics, 218-43 BC 1987 ⮞ 5,b664: ᴿAnzAltW 43 (1990) 214-6 (G. *Dobesch*). – *b)* Ferenczy H. †,   Zur Vorgeschichte der Begründung des augusteischen Prinzipats: ⮞ 67, Mem. HAHN I., AcAntH 32 (1989) 111-127.

b709 *a)* *Ferrary* Jean-Louis,   Traités et domination romaine dans le monde hellénique; – *b)* *Grelle* Francesco, Città et trattati nel sistema romano imperiale; – *c)* *Canfora* Luciano, Trattati in TUCIDIDE: ⮞ 724, Trattati 1986/90, 217-235 / 237-256 / 193-216.

b709* *Gilboa* A.,   The intervention of Sextus Julius Caesar, governor of Syria, in the affair of Herod's trial: ScrClasIsr 5 (1980) 185-194.

b710 **Gruen** E. S.,   Studies in Greek culture and Roman policy [Cincinnati Univ. lectures 1985]: Cincinnati ClasSt NS 7.   Leiden 1990, Brill. x-209 p. $37.50.   90-04-09051-7 [NTAbs 35,126].

b711 *Hayne* Léonie, LIVY and Pompey: Latomus 49 (1990) 435-442.

b712 *Hillman* Thomas P.,   Pompeius and the Senate, 77-71:   Hermes 118 (1990) 444-454.

b713 **Hölkeskamp** Karl-Joachim,   Die Entstehung der Nobilität. Stu 1987, Steiner.   303 p. – ᴿAevum 64 (1990) 61-67 (G. *Zecchini*: prosopografia e storia politica).

b714 **Huzar** Eleanor G.,   Mark Antony, a biography [reprint (Univ. Minnesota 1978)] 1986 ⮞ 4,d482: ᴿAnzAltW 43 (1990) 219-221 (G. *Dobesch*).

b715 **Jehne** Martin,   Der Staat des Diktators Caesar 1987 ⮞ 4,d487; 5,b683: ᴿAnzAltW 43 (1990) 227s (R. *Friese*); Latomus 49 (1990) 704-6 (A. *Keaveney*).

b716 **Jerphagnon** Lucien,   Histoire de la Rome antique; les armes et les mots 1987 ⮞ 4,d488: ᴿRBgPg 68 (1990) 201 (P. *Fontaine*).

b717 **Kasher** Aryeh,   Jews and Hellenistic cities in Eretz-Israel; relations of the Jews in Eretz-Israel with the Hellenistic cities during the Second Temple period (332 BCE- 70 CE): TStAJ 21.   Tü 1990, Mohr.   xv-372 p.   3-16-145241-0 [BL 91,137, Tessa *Rajak*].

b718 **Kasher** A., Jews in Hellenistic-Roman Egypt 1985 ⮞ 1,b298 ... 5,b689: ᴿKerkT 40 (1989) 347 (G. *Mussies*).

b719 **Katzman** Yisrael, ❻ History of the Roman Republic.   J 1990, Magnes. 678 p.; 8 maps. – ᴿQadmoniot 23 (1990) 128s (G. *Herman*, ❻ p. 127 Šatzman).

b720 *a)* *Kearney* R. A.,   Asiarchs, archiereis, and archiereiai of Asia; new evidence from Amorium in Phrygia: EpAnat 16 (1990) 69-80; ❼ 80. – *b)* *Keppie* L. J. F.,   The history and diaspora of the Legion XXII Deiotariana [in Egypt 8 B.C.E.]: ⮞ 540, Greece/Israel 1985/90, 54-61.

b720* ᴱLewis N., *Reinhold* M.,   Roman civilization; selected readings, 1. The Republic and the Augustan age; 2. The Empire³.   NY 1990, Columbia Univ. v-674 p. $40 pa.   0-231-07131-0; -3-7 [NTAbs 35,267].

b721 *Lintott* Andrew, Electoral bribery in the Roman Republic: JRS 80 (1990) 1-16.

b722 *Loposzko* Tadeusz, ℗ Damio, wróg... the enemy of Pompey: ⇒ 108, ᶠLANOWSKI L., Eos 78,1 (1990) 195-202.

b723 **McLaren** J. S., Jewish involvement in the administration of Palestine, 100 BC-AD 70: diss. Oxford 1990. – RTLv 22,591.

b724 **Maier** J., Zwischen den Testamenten; Geschichte und Religion in der Zeit des Zweiten Tempels: NEchter Egb-AT 3. Wü 1990, Echter. 317 p. DM 48; sb. 44. 3-429-01282-9 [BL 91,38, L. *Grabbe*].

b725 *Mandell* S. R., The Isthmian proclamation and the early stages of Roman imperialism in the Near East: ClasB 65 (1989) 89-94 [< NTAbs 34,93].

b726 **Mastrocinque** Attilio, Lucio Giunio Bruto; ricerche di storia, religione e diritto sulle origini della repubblica romana: Univ. Trento. Trento 1988, La Reclame. 293 p. Lit. 70.000. – ᴿAntClas 59 (1990) 507-510 (J. *Poucet*); AtenRom 35 (1990) 122-4 (Monica *Affortunati*).

b727 *Mayer* Günter, Zur jüdischen Geschichte: TRu 55 (1990) 1-20.

b728 **Meier** Christian, *a)* Caesar. B 1982, Severin & S. 591 p. 67 fig. – ᴿGnomon 62 (1990) 22-39 (E. *Badian*, Eng.). – *b)* César. P 1989, Seuil. 492 p. – ᴿAnÉCS 45 (1990) 893-5 (J. *Andreau*).

b729 *Nardo* Dante, Antonio e ORAZIO: ⇒ 62, ᶠGRILLI A., Paideia 45 (1990) 321-336.

b730 **Nippel** Wilfried, Aufruhr und 'Polizei' in der römischen Republik 1988 ⇒ 5,b701: ᴿAmHR 95 (1990) 470s (A. *Lintott*); Athenaeum 78 (1990) 580s (A. *Marcone*); Latomus 49 (1990) 697-700 (R. *Combes*).

b731 *North* John, Politics and aristocracy in the Roman republic: ClasPg 85 (1990) 277-287 (*al.* 255-276. 288-298).

b732 **Ortmann** Ursula, Cicero, Brutus und Octavian – Republikaner und Caesarianer: ihr gegenseitiges Verhältnis im Krisenjahre 44/43 v. Chr.: Diss. Alte Geschichte 25. Bonn 1988, Habelt. vi-559 p. DM 64. – ᴿClasR 40 (1990) 178s (R. *Seager*: 'nothing new, much of value').

b733 **Otzen** Benedikt, *a)* Den antike jødedom, politisk 1984 ⇒ 65,1984: ᴿTsTKi 60 (1989) 56-8 (D. *Rian*); – *b)* Judaism in antiquity; political development and religious currents from Alexander to Hadrian, ᵀ*Cryer* F. H.: Biblical Seminar. Sheffield 1990, Academic. 243 p. £35; £50. 1-85075-197-8; -090-4 [BL 91,39, T. *Rajak*: clear and racy, evidently for theology students]. – ᴿOTAbs 13 (1990) 305 (L. *Greenspoon*).

b734 **Pelling** C.B.R., PLUTARCH, 'Life of Antony' 1988 ⇒ 5,b707: ᴿAthenaeum 78 (1990) 567s (Rita *Scuderi*); ClasPg 85 (1990) 329-332 (D. *Sansone*); Latomus 49 (1990) 706s (J.-L. *Fournet*).

b735 **Podes** Stephan, Die Dependenz des hellenistischen Ostens von Rom zur Zeit der römischen Weltreichsbildung... 1986 ⇒ 4,d517: ᴿLatomus 49 (1990) 212s (J. C. *Dumont*).

b736 **Prause** Gerhard, Herodes der Grosse; die Korrektur einer Legende[2] [¹1977]. Stu 1990, Deutsche VA. 375 p. – ᴿZRGg 42 (1990) 287s (W. *Jasper*).

b737 **Roberts** Alan, Mark Antony 1988 ⇒ 5,b714: ᴿClasR 40 (1990) 179s (J. *Geiger*: grievously deficient).

b738 *Saulnier* Christiane, L'aîné et le porphyrogenète; recherche chronologique sur Hyrkan II et Aristobule II: RB 97 (1990) 54-62; Eng. 54.

b739 **Schuller** Wolfgang, Frauen in der römischen Geschichte 1987 ⇒ 3,d16 ... 5,b721: ᴿRPg 63 (1989) 353s (M. *Ducos*).

b740 **Shchukin** Mark B.,   Rome and the barbarians in central and eastern Europe, 1st century B.C. - 1st century A.D.:   BAR-Int 542. Oxford 1989. I. End of La Tène period, v-246 p.; II. Beginnings of Early Roman period, p. 247-487; 42 fig.; maps. 0-86054-690-X.

b740* **Simon** Erika,   Augustus; Kunst und Leben 1986 → 3,d24... 5,b726: ᴿAnzAltW 43 (1990) 260-2 (Gerda *Schwarz*); Latomus 49 (1990) 910s (L. *Foucher*); Nubica 1s (1990) 362-7 (P. *Scholz*, auch über ZANKER P., *al.*).

b741 **Sullivan** Richard D.,   Near Eastern royalty and Rome, 100-30 BC: Phoenix Supp. 24.   Toronto 1990, Univ.   xx-523 p.; ill.; 5 maps.   0-8020-2682-6 [OIAc S90].

b742 *Swain* S. C. R.,   Hellenic culture and the Roman heroes of PLUTARCH: JHS 110 (1990) 126-145.

b742* **Thommen** Lukas,   Das Volkstribunat der [klassischen 1985] späten römischen Republik [< Diss. Basel 1987]: Historia Einz. 59.   Stu 1989, Steiner.   287 p. DM 66. – ᴿClasR 40 (1990) 379s (P. S. *Derow*).

b743 *Wet* B. X. de,   Contemporary sources in PLUTARCH's Life of Antony: Hermes 118 (1990) 80-90.

b744 *Wylie* Graham J.,   Pompey *megalopsychos*: Klio 72 (1990) 445-456.

Q8.4   **Zeitalter Jesu Christi**: particular/general.

b745 *Brunt* P. A.,   a) Publicans in the principate; – b) Roman imperial illusions [both inedita]: → 206, Roman imperial 1990, 354-432 / 433-480.

b746 **Christ** Karl,   Geschichte der römischen Kaiserzeit 1988 → 4,d456: ᴿAmHR 95 (1990) 1173s (B. *Baldwin*); Athenaeum 78 (1990) 227-9 (A. *Marcone*).

b747 *Ducos* Michèle,   La justice dans l'œuvre de TACITE: RÉLat 68 (1990) 99-111.

b748 **Freis** Helmut,   Historische Inschriften zur römischen Kaiserzeit von Augustus bis Konstantin 1984 → 3,b934:   ᴿGrazBei 17 (1990) 284-6 (M. *Hainzmann*).

b749 *Hengel* Martin, Der alte und der neue 'Schürer': JSS 35 (1990) 19-64 (-72 *Bloedhorn* Hanswulf, Korrekturen zu den Inschriften 3,1-86).

b750 **Horsley** G. H. R., New documents 1979: 1987 → 4,4987.a611*; 5,b679: ᴿGnomon 62 (1990) 645-7 (W. *Wischmeyer*); NT 32 (1990) 189s (P. *Elbert*).

b751 *Jal* P., TITE-LIVE et le métier d'historien dans la Rome d'Auguste: BBudé (1990) 32-48.

b752 **Jantsch** Johanna,   Die Entstehung des Christentums bei Adolf von HARNACK und Eduard MEYER: Diss. Marburg 1989. Ha 1989, Rowohlt Alt-G 28. – Chiron 20 (1990) 415.

b752* *Kákosy* L.,   Germanicus in Theben [19 A.D.; Tacitus Ann. 18.4.65]: → 67, Mem. HAHN I., AcAntH 32 (1989) 129-136.

b753 **Keresztes** Paul,   Imperial Rome and the Christians; [I.] From Herod the Great to about 200 A.D., II. to the death of Constantine.   Lanham MD 1989, UPA.   vii-216 p.; xiii-385 p. $29.75; $42.50.   0-8191-7469-6; -528-5 [TDig 38,69]. – ᴿExpTim 102 (1990s) 56 (W. H. C. *Frend*: one misses a 'critical thrust' amid some unimportant details).

b754 **Kolb** Frank, Untersuchungen zur Historia Augusta 1987 → 5,b691: ᴿAnt-Clas 59 (1990) 527s (R. *Delmaire*); RPg 63 (1989) 137-9 (A. *Chastagne*).

b755 **Künzl** Ernst, Der römische Triumph; Siegesfeier im antiken Rom [... Titus] 1988 → 5,b692: ᴿClasR 40 (1990) 181s (J. *Briscoe*); Helinium 30 (1990) 132 (J. *Bourgeois*).

b756 **Kuhnen** Hans-Peter, Palästina in griechisch-römischer Zeit: HbArch 2/2. Mü 1990, Beck. xxi-424 p.; ill.; maps. 3-406-32876-8.

b757 *Lana* Italo, Introspicere in TACITO: Orpheus 10 (1989) 26-57.

b758 ᵀᴱ**Le Bonniec** H., *Hellegouarc'h* J., TACITE Hist. Livres 2-3, 1989 → 5,b730*b*: ᴿClasR 40 (1990) 289-291 (K. *Wellesley*).

b759 ᴱ**Lebrun** François, Les grandes dates du christianisme. P 1989, Larousse. 232 p. F 95. 2-03-740007-1. − ᴿETRel 65 (1990) 460 (H. *Bost*).

b761 **Linder** Amnon, The Jews in Roman imperial legislation [❿ 1983] 1987 → 4,d504; 5,b693. − ᴿGnomon 62 (1990) 39-42 (F. *Millar*); JEH 40 (1989) 398s (D. E. L. *Johnston*); Latomus 49 (1990) 904s (R. *Delmaire*); Mnemosyne 43 (1990) 270-2 (P. W. van der *Horst*: important).

b762 *Lounsbury* Richard C., The arts of SUETONIUS 1987 → 5,b694: ᴿLatomus 49 (1990) 881s (O. *Devillers*).

b763 *Meulenberg* Leonardo, A Igreja diante do desafio do Império Romano: REB 50 (1990) 629-642.

b764 **Niswonger** Richard L., New Testament history. GR 1988, Zondervan Academie. 332 p. − ᴿCBQ 52 (1990) 344s (J.J. *O'Rourke*: rather an Introduction; conservative).

b765 **Potter** David S., Prophecy and history in the crisis of the Roman Empire; a historical commentary on the thirteenth Sibylline Oracle: ClasMg. Ox 1990, Clarendon. xix-443 p.; 22 fig. 0-19-814483-0.

b766 **Ramage** Edwin S., The nature and purpose of Augustus' 'Res gestae' 1987 → 4,d519; 5,b711: ᴿLatomus 49 (1990) 875s (J.-M. *André*).

b767 ᴱ**Reverdin** Olivier, *Grange* Bernard, [*Raaflaub* A., *al.*], Opposition et résistance à l'empire d'Auguste à Trajan: Entretiens 33. Genève 1987, Hardt. x-401 p. Fs 68. − ᴿClasR 40 (1990) 509s (D. *Braund*).

b768 *Rousselle* Aline, Vivre sous deux droits; la pratique familiale poly-juridique des citoyens romains juifs: AnÉCS 45 (1990) 839-859.

b769 **Saulnier** Christiane, Storia d'Israele 3, 1988 → 4,d531: ᴿAsprenas 37 (1990) 109 (V. *Scippa*); Benedictina 36 (1989) 576-8 (L. *De Lorenzi*).

b770 **Schäfer** Peter, Histoire des Juifs [en Palestine] dans l'antiquité, ᵀ*Schulte* Pascale 1989 → 5,b718: ᴿRTLv 21 (1990) 225 (P.-M. *Bogaert*).

b771 **Schrömbges** Paul, Tiberius und die res publica romana ᴰ1986 → 4,d532: ᴿAnzAltW 43 (1990) 73s (H. *Grassl*).

b772 *Schürer* E., ᴱ**Vermes** G., *al.*, *a*) History of the Jewish people in the age of Jesus Christ 1973-1986 → 55,6676 ... 4,d534: ᴿZkT 112 (1990) 104s (R. *Oberforcher*, 1-3). − *b*) Storia II 1987 → 4,d535: ᴿÉtClas 58 (1990) 183 (X. *Jacques*).

b773 **Schwartz** Daniel R., ❿ Agrippa I, the last king of Judaea. J 1987, Shazar Center. 238 p.; 23 fig. [KirSef 62 (1988s) p. 187], 3-16-145341-7. − ᴿBAngIsr 10 (1990s) 93s (D. M. *Jacobson*).

b774 ᴱ**Sherk** Robert K., The Roman Empire, Augustus to Hadrian: Translated Documents 6, 1988 → 4,d547; 5,b725: ᴿCBQ 52 (1990) 762s (L. L. *Thompson*: literal; inscriptions line-by-line).

b775 **Stahlmann** I., Imperator Caesar Augustus; Studien zur Geschichte des Principatsverständnisses in der deutschen Altertumswissenschaft bis 1945. Da 1988, Wiss. viii-277 p. DM 69; sb. 57. − ᴿGymnasium 97 (1990) 175-8 (M. *Wissemann*).

b776 **Vardiman** E. E., La grande svolta; la Giudea tra ellenismo e primo cristianesimo [Die grosse Zeitwende 1978], ᵀ1987 → 5,b733: ᴿBL (1990) 42 (F. F. *Bruce*: for readers who need to be told 'Diadochi means Alexander's successors').

b777 **Wendland** Paul [1864-1915], La cultura ellenistico-romana nei suoi rapporti con giudaismo e cristianesimo [⁴1972], ᵀᴱ*Firoi* G., 1986 ➤ 2,9635 ... 5,b737: ᴿRBgPg 68 (1990) 213 (P. *Salmon*).

b778 **Will** E., **Orrieux** C., Ioudaïsmos-Hellénismos 1986 ➤ 2,9639 ... 5,b738: ᴿCritRR 2 (1989) 385-8 (B. Z. *Wacholder*); Mnemosyne 43 (1990) 268-270 (P. W. van der *Horst*: original and intelligent).

b779 *Wittenburg* Andreas, Consensus universorum e versione greca delle Res gestae [divi Augusti]: Sileno 16 (1990) 41-49.

b780 *Zuckerman* Constantine, Hellenistic politeuma and the Jews; a reconsideration [*Kasher* A., Jews in ... Egypt 1985]: ScrClasIsr 8s (1988) 171-185.

Q8.7 *Roma et Oriens,* **prima decennia post Christum.**

b781 **Barrett** Anthony A., Caligula, the corruption of power. L 1989, Barrett. xxvi-334 p.; 31 fig.; 7 maps. £35. – ᴿGreeceR 37 (1990) 245 (T. *Wiedemann*).

b782 *Bell* A. A., PLINY the younger; the kinder, gentler Roman; ClasB 66,1 (Ch 1990) 37-41 [< NTAbs 34,367].

b783 *a) Beranger* Jean, L'expression du pouvoir suprême chez TACITE; – *b) Millar* Fergus, L'empereur romain comme décideur: ➤ 760, Du pouvoir 1983/90, 181-205 / 207-220.

b784 *Billerbeck* Margarethe, Philology at the imperial court: GreeceR 37 (1990) 191-203.

b785 *Borzsák* I., Zu TACITUS' hellenistisch-orientalischen Beziehungen: ➤ 488, From Alexander 1990, 47-54.

b786 *a) Bowersock* Glen W., Social and economic history of Syria under the Roman Empire; – *b) Sartre* Maurice, La Syrie à l'époque hellénistique; – *c) Rey-Coquais* Jean-Paul, La Syrie, de Pompée à Dioclétien; histoire politique et administrative; – *d) Will* Ernest, La Syrie à l'époque hellénistique et romaine; mille ans de vie intellectuelle et artistique: ➤ 481, Syrie II (1989) 63-80 / 31-44 / 45-61 / 567-579.

b787 *Edwards* M. J., Satire and verisimilitude; Christianity [counterfeit Cynics] in LUCIAN's Peregrinus: Historia 38 (1989) 89-98 [< NTAbs 34,367].

b788 **Ferrary** Jean-Louis, Philhellénisme et impérialisme; aspects idéologiques de la conquête romaine du monde hellénistique, de la seconde guerre de Macédoine à la guerre contre Mithridate [diss. d'État]: BÉF 271. R 1988, École Française. xvi-690 + 12 p. – ᴿClasPg 85 (1990) 324-9 (E. S. *Gruen*); ClasR 40 (1990) 373-7 (J. *Briscoe*).

b789 *Fishwick* D., *a)* PLINY and the Christians; the rites ad imaginem principis; – *b)* The temple of Caesar at Alexandria: AmJAncH 9,2 (CM 1984) 123-60 / 131-4 [< NTAbs 34,368].

ᴱ**French** D. H., *Lightfoot* C. S., The eastern frontier of the Roman Empire 1988/9 ➤ 734.

b789* *Geraci* Giovanni, Gli anni settimo e ottavo 'sacri' di Nerone in Egitto; un'ipotesi: Aegyptus 70 (1990) 97-111.

b790 *a) Giua* Maria A., Appunti per uno studio sull'incidenza storica dell'ambiente nell'opera di TACITO; – *b) Scuderi* Rita, Alcuni riferimenti alla vita politica di Roma nelle Quaestiones romanae di PLUTARCO: ➤ 53, ᶠGABBA E. 1988, 101-116 / 117-142.

b791 **Goodman** Martin, The ruling class of Judaea 1987 ➤ 4,d472; 5,b670: ᴿBibTB 20 (1990) 370 (B. J. *Malina*: excellent history despite some insensitivity to categories); ClasPg 85 (1990) 164-6 (Shaye *Cohen*); ÉchMClas 9 (1990) 90-93 (G. M. *Paul*); IsrEJ 40 (1990) 237-9 (D. J. *Schwartz*); JRelHist 15 (1988s) 352-4 (A. D. *Crown*); Vidyajyoti 54 (1990) 609s (P. M. *Meagher*).

b791* *a*) *Goodman* Martin, The origins of the great revolt; a conflict of status criteria; – *b*) *Piatelli* Daniella, The Jericho inscription concerning Theodotus, *apeleutheros* of the empress Agrippina: → 540, Greece/Israel 1985/90, 39-53 / 75-83.

b792 **Hadas-Lebel** Mireille, Jérusalem contre Rome: Patrimoines Judaïsme. P 1990, Cerf. 555 p.; map. 2-204-04141-6.

b793 ᴱ**Holladay** C. R., Poets —... Ezekiel trag.: Fragments from Hellenistic Jewish Authors 2, 1989 → 5,b678: ᴿBL (1990) 134 (J. R. *Porter*).

b794 **Jakob-Sonnabend** W., Untersuchungen zum Nero-Bild der Spätantike [Diss. München 1986, ᴰ*Schmidt* H.]: AltWTSt. Hildesheim 1990, Olms. viii-215 p. DM 39,80. 3-487-09297-2 [NTAbs 34,409].

b794* **Levick** Barbara, *a*) Claudius; the corruption of power. NHv 1990, Yale Univ. 272 p. $25. 0-300-04734-7. – ᴿNY Review of Books (6.XII. 1990) 49-52 (H. *Lloyd-Jones*: 'Life styles of the rich and famous' also on BARRETT A., Caligula) [< NTAbs 35,221; cf. 34,403.410], – *b*) 'I Claudius' revisited [*Graves* R. 1986; 1991 (1. Aug.) 2000th birthday]: AncHRes 20 (1990) 135-143.

b795 *Lightfoot* C. S., Trajan's Parthian war and the fourth-century perspective: JRS 80 (1990) 115-126; 2 maps.

b796 ᴱ**Martin** H. H., *Woodman* A. J., TACITUS, Annals, book IV: Greek and Latin Classics. C 1989, Univ. viii-283 p. – ᴿRÉLat 68 (1990) 200-2 (J. *Hellegouarc'h*).

b797 **Mastellano Iovane** Eugenia, Paura e angoscia in TACITO; implicazioni ideologiche e politiche: Studi latini 2. N 1989, Loffredo. 173 p. – ᴿRÉLat 68 (1990) 214s (J. *Hellegouarc'h*).

b798 *Menaut* Léon, Mémoires d'Hadrien: BInstC-Chr 91,2 (1990) 35-43.

b799 *Mendecki* Norbert, ⊘ Der Aufstand der jüdischen Diaspora (115-117) und der Bar-Kochba-Aufstand (132-135): → 64, ᶠGRZYBEK S. 1990, 192-200; deutsch 200.

b800 *a*) *Mor* M., ⊘ Bar Kochba revolt — was it a farmers' uprising [... JosF B 6,216], – *b*) *Isaac* B., ⊕ Jewish land in Judaea after the first revolt [Jo₃F B 6,216; Vita 422]; – *c*) *Jankelewitz* R., ⊘ The Gentiles' struggle for land-ownership in Eretz-Israel: → 348, Man and law 1986, 95-116 / 87-94 / 117-123.

b801 *Newbold* R.F., A belief dilemma in Claudian: AncHRes 20 (1990) 88-95.

b802 *Picard* Gilbert C., Le monument qui réconforta Néron: CRAI (1990) 659-665; 2 fig.

b803 *Pimentel Álvarez* J., Dos piezas del epistolario de PLINIO; documentos históricos: Analogía 4,2 (Xochimilco MÉX 1990) 183-7 [< NTAbs 35,223].

b804 *Pucci Ben Zeev* Miriam, New perspectives on the Jewish-Greek hostilities in Alexandria during the reign of emperor Caligula [38 C.E.; CRACCO-RUGGINI L.: POLAČEK A.]: JStJud 21 (1990) 227-235.

b805 **Raebel** Bernd, Die Krise der jüdischen Führungselite in Palästina und der Ausbruch des Jüdischen Krieges; eine Untersuchung zur sozialen und religiösen Unruhe in der Umwelt des frühen Christentums: Diss. ᴰ*Theissen* G. Heidelberg 1989s. – TR 86 (1990) 516.

b806 *Rokéah* David, ⊘ TACITUS [Hist. 5,2] and the God of Israel: Zion 55 (1990) 265-8; Eng. XI.

b807 *a*) *Sage* M. M., TACITUS' historical works; a survey and appraisal; – *b*) *Suerbaum* Werner, Zweiundvierzig Jahre Tacitus-Forschung; systematische Gesamtbibliographie zu Tacitus' Annalen 1939-1980 (1981-86, *Benario* H. W.); – *c*) *Morford* Mark, Tacitus' historical methods in the Neronian books of the 'Annals': → 828, ANRW 2/33/2 (1990) 851-1030 (index 1629-47) / 1032-1476 (-1498) / 1582-1627.

b808 *Schäfer* Peter, Hadrian's policy in Judaea and the Bar Kochba revolt; a reassessment: → 183, FVERMES G. 1990, 281-303.

b809 *Scherrer* Peter, Augustus, die Mission des Vedius Pollio und die Artemis Ephesia: JbÖsA 60-H (1990) 87-101; 6 fig.

b810 **Schwier** H., Tempel und Tempelzerstörung... im ersten jüdischen Krieg [Diss. Heid 1988]: NOrb 11, 1989 → 5,b723: RNRT 112 (1990) 915s (X. *Jacques*); RivB 38 (1990) 541-4 (R. *Penna*); TPQ 138 (1990) 399s (G. *Stemberger*).

b811 **Soverini** Paolo, Impero e imperatore nell'opera di PLINIO il Giovane; aspetti e problemi del rapporto con Domiziano e Traiano: → 828, ANRW 2/33/1 (1989) 515-554.

b812 *Veltri* G., Enteignung des Landes oder Pax Romana? Zur politischen Geschichte der Juden nach 70: FraJudBei 16 (1988) 1-22 [< JStJud 21,111].

b813 **Vielberg** Meinhold, Pflichten ... Wertvorstellungen des TACITUS 1987 → 5,b734: RLatomus 49 (1990) 85-8 (É. *Aubrion*).

b814 **Wiedemann** Thomas, The Julio-Claudian emperors: ClasWorld 5. Bristol 1989, Classical. xiii-94 p.; 22 fig.; map. £5. – RGreeceR 37 (1990) 229-231 (J. *McAuslan*, also on the 4 prior volumes).

b815 *a*) *Williams* Margaret H., Domitian, the Jews and the 'Judaizers' — a simple matter of cupiditas and maiestas?; – *b*) *Portmann* Werner, Zu den Motiven der diokletianischen Christenverfolgung: Historia 39 (1990) 196-211 / 212-248.

b816 TEWilliams Wynne, Pliny the Younger, correspondence with Trajan from Bithynia (Epistles X). Wmr 1990, Aris & P. x-159 p. – RRÉLat 68 (1990) 199s (J. *Hellegouarc'h*).

Q9.1 **Roma** *prae- et post-christiana.*

b817 **Alföldy** Géza, The social history of Rome [³1984], TBraund D., *Pollock* F. 1988 → 4,d569; 5,b742: RÉchMClas 34 (1990) 468-470 (H. W. *Bird*).

b818 **Birley** Anthony R., The African emperor, Septimius Severus²ʳᵉᵛ 1988 [¹1972] → 5,b747: RLatomus 49 (1990) 902-4 (Mireille *Corbier*).

b819 EBoeft J. den, *al.* Philological and historical commentary on AMMIANUS M. 1987 → 5,b751: RLatomus 49 (1990) 188-190 (J. *Rougé*).

b820 EBonamente G., *Nestori* A., I Cristiani e l'impero nel IV secolo 1987/8 → 5,633: RCC 141 (1990,1) 611s (A. *Ferrua*); ClasR 40 (1990) 394s (N. B. *McLynn*).

b822 *Chamoux* François, Un historien mal aimé. DIODORE de Sicile: BBudé (1990) 243-252.

b823 **Christ** K., Römische Geschichte 1980; – ... und Wissenschaftsgeschichte I-II, 1982 → 4,d578: RHelmantica 41 (1990) 414-6 (E. *Fernández Vallina*).

b824 *Christiansen* E. G., The great conflict revisited; recent work on Christianity and paganism [*Lane Fox* R. 1987; *Sordi* M. Eng. 1986; *MacMullen* R. 1984; *Rike* R. 1987]: Helios 15,2 (Lubbock TX 1988) 133-149 [< NTAbs 34,64].

b825 **Dal Covolo** Enrico, I Severi e il cristianesimo — ricerche sull'ambiente storico-istituzionale delle origini cristiane tra il secondo ed il terzo secolo: BiblScRel 87, 1989 ➤ 5,b659: ᴿAegyptus 70 (1990) 303-6 (G. *Casanova*); Aevum 64 (1990) 136s (A. *Barzanò*); JTS 41 (1990) 649-651 (W. H. C. *Frend*); Orpheus 11 (1990) 193s (A. *Ceresa-Gastaldo*); RÉAug 36 (1990) 185s (A. *Le Boulluec*); RivStoLR 26 (1990) 186-8 (M. *Simonetti*); Salesianum 52 (1990) 722-4 (Luvete J. *Kataka*); SMSR 56 (1990) 292-4 (Myla *Perraymond*).

b826 **Demandt** Alexander, Der Fall Roms 1984 ➤ 65,9953 ... 4,d584: ᴿArKulturG 71 (1989) 503-5 (F. *Kolb*).

b827 **Drexler** Hans, Politische Grundbegriffe der Römer.   Da 1988, Wiss. viii-255 p. – ᴿGnomon 61 (1989) 740-2 (J. *Hellegouarc'h*).

b828 *Elbern* Stephan, Das Verhältnis der Spätantiken Kaiser zur Stadt Rom: RömQ 85 (1990) 19-49.

b829 *Euzennat* Maurice, La frontière romaine d'Afrique: CRAI (1990) 565-580; 3 fig.

b830 ᵀᴱ**Foulon** Eric [X] / *Weil* Raymond [XI], POLYBE, Histoire livres X-XI Coll. Budé. P 1990, BLettres.   195 (doubles) p. – ᴿSalesianum 52 (1990) 783 (S. *Felici*).

b831 ᴱ**Jal** Paul, Tite-LIVE hist. XI (livre XXI) Coll. Budé. P 1988, BLettres. – ᴿAntClas 59 (1990) 368s (J. *Wankenne*); RÉLat 68 (1990) 190s (J.-C. *Richard*).

b832 **Frey** Martin, Untersuchungen zur Religion und Religionspolitik des Kaisers Elagabal: HistEinz 63. Wsb 1989, Steiner. iv-125 p. DM 36. 3-515-05370-0. – ᴿAnÉCS 45 (1990) 921-3 (J.-M. *Pailler*).

b833 **Grant** M., The fall of the Roman Empire²ʳᵉᵛ [¹1976]. NY 1990, Macmillan-Collier. xv-235 p.; 9 maps. $13. 0-02-028560-4 [NTAbs 35,125].

b834 **Grant** Robert M., Augustus to Constantine; the rise and triumph of Christianity in the Roman world [pa. = 1970]. SF 1990, Harper & R. xiv-334 p. $13. 0-06-250350-2 [NTAbs 35,126].

b835 **Grimal** Pierre, Rome, la littérature et l'histoire [98 art. 1938-1984]: Coll. Éc. Franç. 93, ➤ 4,202: ᴿGnomon 62 (1990) 76 (E. J. *Kenney*).

b836 **Haehling** Raban von, Zeitbezüge des T. LIVIUS in der ersten Dekade seines Geschichtswerkes: HistEinz 61. Stu 1989, Steiner. 248 p. – ᴿGGA 242 (1990) 182-197 (J. *Briscoe*).

b837 *Hartmann* B., Tod und Auferstehung der antiken Religionen [Diokletian 303, Galerius 311]: Numen 37 (1990) 220-232.

b838 **Kienast** D., Römische Kaisertabelle; Grundzüge einer römischen Kaiserchronologie. Da 1990, Wiss. xxvi-377 p. DM 65 [Gymnasium, 98, 93, R. *Klein*].

b839 *Koshelenko* G. A., *al.* / *Bolshakov* A. O., *al.*, ❸ The classical world; the rise of the [Roman] state: VDI 192 (1990) 93-106 / 193 (1990) 120-134 [194 (1990) 68-75].

b840 **Laudizi** G., SILIO Italico; il passato tra mito e restaurazione etica. Lecce 1989. 187 p. – ᴿRÉLat 68 (1990) 213s (J. P. *Callu*).

b841 **MacMullen** Ramsey, Corruption and the decline of Rome 1988 ➤ 4, d609; 5,b777: ᴿAntClas 59 (1990) 528s (J. *Wankenne*); AnzAltW 43 (1990) 237-241 (R. *Klein*); CritRR 3 (1990) 273-6 (E. G. *Weltin*); ÉchMClas 34 (1990) 473-5 (T. D. *Barnes*); JIntdis 20 (1989s) 463s (Callie *Williamson*).

b842 **Matthews** John, The Roman Empire of AMMIANUS. Baltimore 1989, Johns Hopkins Univ. xiv-608 p.; 4 fig.; 8 maps. $55 [RelStR 17, 258]. – ᴿRÉLat 68 (1990) 23-27 (J. *Fontaine*).

b843 ᴱ**Momigliano** Arnaldo, *Schiavone* Aldo, Storia di Roma I. Roma in Italia. T 1988, Einaudi. xlii-628 p. – ᴿAthenaeum 78 (1990) 223-7 (J.-C. *Richard*).

b844 *Newbold* R. F., Nonverbal communication in TACITUS and AMMIANUS: AncSoc 21 (1990) 189-199.

b845 *Noè* Eralda, Considerazioni sull'Impero Romano in STRABONE e CASSIO DIONE: IstLombR 122 (1988) 101-126.

b846 *Pallottino* Massimo, Quelques réflexions méthodologiques sur la protohistoire italienne: CRAI (1990) 346-350.

b847 **Rabello** Alfredo M., Giustiniano, Ebrei e Samaritani II: Mg.Vocab.G 2, 1988 ⇥ 5,b787; 88-14-01801-4: ᴿAntClas 59 (1990) 538-41 (J. *Schamp*).

b848 **Raepsaet-Charlier** Marie-Thérèse, Prosopographie des femmes de l'ordre sénatorial (Iᵉʳ-IIᵉ siècles) [< diss. Bru 1977]: Acad. Belg. lett. 4. Lv 1987, Peeters. x-810 p.; vol. of 72 tables. Fb 2980. 90-6831-086-0; -7-9. – ᴿAntClas 59 (1990) 517-520 (A. *Martin*).

b849 **Richardson** J. S., Hispaniae; Spain and the development of Roman imperialism, 218-82 B.C. C 1986, Univ. xi-218 p.; 4 maps. A$90. 0-521-32183-2. – ᴿAncHRes 20 (1990) 43-50 (B. D. *Hoyos*).

b850 **Salemme** Carmelo, Similitudini nella storia; un capitolo su AMMIANO Marcellino: StLat 1. N 1989, Loffredo. 144 p. – ᴿSicGymn 43 (1990) 369s (F. *Corsaro*).

b851 *Schulz* Udo W., Zur Erforschung des altrömischen Kalenders: ⇥ 160*, Mem. SCHULER E. v., Orientalia 59 (1990) 255-264.

b852 *Solin* N., Zu pannonischen Juden: AcArchH 41 (1989) 233-6.

b853 **Sordi** Marta, The Christians and the Roman Empire, ᵀ*Bedini* A. 1986 ⇥ 2,9621: ᴿVoxPa 17 (1989) 941-9 (Maria *Jaczynowska* ❷).

b854 *Sordi* Marta, Los cristianos y el imperio romano [1983 ⇥ 65,9921], ᵀ: Ensayos 49. M 1988, Encuentro. 189 p. – ᴿCarthaginensia 6 (1990) 392 (V. *Sánchez*: continuación de 'El cristianismo y Roma' 1965).

b855 **Sordi** Marta, Il mito troiano e l'eredità etrusca di Roma: Univ. Catt. Mg Stor. Ant. 4. Mi 1989, Jaca . 86 p. Lit. 15.000. 88-16-95051-X. – ᴿAntClas 59 (1990) 506s (J. *Poucet*).

b856 ᴱ**Walsh** P.G., Titi LIVI Ab urbe condita libri XXVIII-XXX ⇥ 3,d114: XX-156 p.: ᴿBBudé (1989) 211s (P. *François*).

b857 **Watt** W. S., Vellei PATERCULI Historiarum libri duo 1988 ⇥ 4,d623: ᴿRPg 63 (1989) 313-9 (A. *Vassileiou*).

b858 **Whittaker** C. R., Les frontières de l'Empire romain. P 1989, BLettres: 209 p. – ᴿAnÉCS 45 (1990) 896-8 (P. *Leveau*).

b859 *Wirth* Gerhard, Hannibalian; Anmerkungen zur Geschichte eines überflüssigen Königs: BonnJbb 190 (1990) 201-231.

b860 **Wistrand** Erik, Felicitas imperatoria: Acta Univ. gr./lat. 48. Göteborg 1987, Univ. 114 p. 91-7346-180-6. – ᴿAntClas 59 (1990) 516s (J. *Poucet*).

Q9.5 **Constantinus**, Julianus, **Imperium Byzantinum.**

b861 *Baglivi* Nicola, Costantino I nelle 'Historiae adversus paganos' di Paolo OROSIO: Orpheus 10 (1989) 311-334.

b862 *Buck* David F., Some distortions in EUNAPIUS' account of Julian the Apostate: AncHB 4 (1990) 113-5.

b863 **Burrurini** E., La croce e lo scettro; dalla nonviolenza evangelica alla chiesa costantiniana. Fiesole 1990, Cultura della Pace. 160 p. Lit. 18.000. – ᴿRasT 31 (1990) 523s (P. *Vanzan*).

b864 **Chuvin** Pierre, Chronique des derniers païens; la disparition du paganisme dans l'Empire romain, du règne de Constantin à celui de Justinien: Histoire. P 1990, BLettres/Fayard. 350 p. 2-251-38003-5.

b865 **Chuvin** Pierre, A chronicle of the last pagans [1990], ᵀ*Archer* B. A.: Revealing Antiquity 4. CM 1990, Harvard Univ. 188 p. – ᴿNorTTs 91 (1990) 189-191 (Øyvind *Norderval*).

b866 **Cosi** Dario M., Casta mater Idaea; Giuliano 1986 ➤ 5,b756: ᵀᴿAnÉCS 45 (1990) 923-5 (Aline *Rousselle*).

b867 *Crabbé* Inge, The Byzantine emperors from 610 to ca. 1400 A.D. in al-QALQAŠANDĪ's *Ṣubḥ al-A'ša*: OrLovPer 20 (1989) 213-229.

b868 *Criscuolo* Ugo, La difesa dell'ellenismo dopo Giuliano; LIBANIO e Teodosio: Koinonia 14,1 (1990) 5-28.

b869 **Demandt** Alexander, Die Spätantike; römische Geschichte von Diocletian bis Justinian...: HbAltW 3/6, 1989 ➤ 5,b757: ᴿDLZ 111 (1990) 68s (J. *Irmscher*); GGA 242 (1990) 15-23 (Ingemar *König*); Gnomon 62 (1990) 135-140 (H.-J. *Diesner*); Gymnasium 97 (1990) 180-2 (J. *Szidal*); JbAC 33 (1990) 244-8 (G. *Wirth*).

b870 **Ducellier** A., L'Église byzantine; entre pouvoir et esprit (313-1204): BtHistChr 21. P 1990, Desclée. 279 p.; 3 maps [NRT 113, 606, N. *Plumat*].

b871 *Frezza* Paolo, L'esperienza della tolleranza religiosa fra pagani e cristiani dal IV al V sec. d.C. nell'oriente ellenistico: StDocHI 55 (1989) 41-97.

b872 *Hall* Stuart G., Konstantin I. der Grosse (306-337), ᵀ*Schäferdiek* K.: ➤ 857, TRE 19 (1990) 488-499 (-503, -Zeitalter, *Schneemelcher* W.).

b873 **Herrin** Judith, The formation of Christendom 1987 ➤ 3,d81; 4,b770: ᴿByZ 82 (1989) 284-9 (L. *Perrone*, ital.); ClasW 83 (1989s) 64s (D. J. *Constantelos*); HcythJ 31 (1990) 89s (Pauline *Allen*); JEH 40 (1989) 101 (R. *Markus*); JRS 80 (1990) 261s (Mary *Whitby*); RHE 85 (1900) 203s (P. H. *Daly*).

Hunger Herbert, ... Die byzantinische Buchkultur 1989 ➤ 1790.

b874 *Irmscher* Johannes, The Jews under the reign of Justinian: ➤ 108, ᶠLANOWSKI J., Eos 78,1 (1990) 155-161.

b875 **Isaac** B., The limits of empire; the Roman [and Byzantine] army in the east. Ox 1990, Clarendon. 492 p.; 13 fig.; 5 maps. – ᴿBAngIsr 10 (1990s) 88-91 (S. *Dar*).

b876 **Jeffreys** E. & M., *Scott* R., *al.*, The Chronicle of John MALALAS 1986 ➤ 4,d598*; 5,b773: ᴿBySlav 51 (1990) 57s (S. *Ivanov*); JbÖstByz 40 (1990) 449-451 (J. *Haldon*).

b877 *a*) *Jeffreys* E. M., MALALAS' use of the past; –*b*) *Scott* R. D., Malalas' view of the classical past: ➤ 479, Reading 1990, 121-146 / 147-164.

b878 *Kajanto* I., Sopravvivenza dei nomi teoforici nell'età cristiana. AcArchH 41 (1989) 159-168.

b879 **Lane Fox** Robin, Pagans and Christians 1988 ➤ 3,d87... 5,b776: ᴿAncHRes 20 (1990) 67-69 (Alanna *Nobbs*); TsTNijm 30 (1990) 192-8 (A. *Davids*, 'Een nieuwe benadering').

b880 *Lemerle* Paul †, Présence de Byzance: JSav (1990) 247-268.

b881 *Levenson* David, Julian's attempt to rebuild the Temple; an inventory of ancient and medieval sources: ➤ 173, ᶠSTRUGNELL J., Of scribes 1990, 261-279.

b882 **Liebeschuetz** J., Barbarians and bishops; army, church and state in the age of Arcadius and Chrysostom. Ox 1990, Clarendon. XIV-312 p.; 7 pl.

b883 *Loverance* Rowena, Byzantium. L/CM 1988, British Museum/Harvard Univ. 72 p.; 54 fig. 34 color. pl., 1 map. – ᴿAJA 94 (1990) 169s (Olenka *Pevny*).

b883* *Luz* Menahem, MARINUS [485 C.E., biographer and successor of PRO-

CLUS], an Eretz Israel Neoplatonist at Athens: → 540, Greece/Israel 1985/90, 92-104.

b884 **McCormick** Michael, Eternal victory; triumphal rulership in late antiquity, Byzantium and the early medieval west [< diss. Victory and its celebration, Lv 1981]. C/P 1986 Univ./Sciences de l'Homme. xvi-453 p.; 13 fig. – ᴿBySlav 50 (1989) 79-81 (Ursula *Treu*).

b885 **MacMullen** R., Christianizing the Roman Empire 1984 → 65,9961 ... 4,d607: ᴿMnemosyne 43 (1990) 273-5 (J. *Bremmer*).

b886 **Mazal** Otto, Handbuch der Byzantinistik. Graz 1989, Akad. 279 p. Sch 420. – ᴿClasR 40 (1990) 412s (R. *Browning*); DLZ 111 (1990) 567s (K.-P. *Matschke*).

b887 **Meyendorff** John, Imperial unity and Christian divisions; the Church 450-680 A.D. Crestwood NY 1989, St. Vladimir. xv-402. $15. – ᴿTS 51 (1990) 743-5 (L. D. *Davis*).

b888 **Nörr** Dieter, Causa mortis; auf den Spuren einer [rechtshistorischen] Redewendung: MüBeitPapR 80. Mü 1986, Beck. vi-228 p. – ᴿGnomon 61 (1989) 685-702 (O. *Behrends*).

b889 **Prato** C., *Micalella* D., GIULIANO, Contro i Cinici 1988 → 5,b785: ᴿAnzAltW 43 (1990) 235-7 (R. *Klein*); Emerita 58 (1990) 336s (J. *García Blanco*); RÉAug 36 (1990) 191s (J. *Bouffartigue*).

b891 *a*) *Schneider* Wolfgang C., Victoria sive Angelus Victoriae; zur Gestalt des Sieges in der Zeit des Übergangs von der antiken Religion zum Christentum; – *b*) *Bringmann* Klaus, Tradition und Neuerung; Bemerkungen zur Religionsgesetzgebung der christlichen Kaiser des 4. Jh.s: → 61, ᶠGRAF ZU DOHNA L. 1989, 29-54 / 13-28.

b892 **Shahid** Irfan, Rome/Byzantium and the Arabs 1984 → 65,9974 ... 5,b794: ᴿBO 47 (1990) 224-230 (L. Van *Rompay*); EpeterisByz 47 (1987-9) 449-453 (A. G. C. *Savvides*).

b893 **Stemberger** Günther, Juden und Christen im hl. Land; Palästina unter Konstantin und Theodosius 1987 → 3,d110 ... 5,b796: ᴿAmHR 95 (1990) 790s (R. L. *Wilken*); JEH 41 (1990) 139s (W. H. C. *Frend*); RömQ 85 (1990) 124-6 (R. *Klein*); TRu 55 (1990) 109s (A. M. *Ritter*).

b893* *Szidat* Joachim, Constantin bei AUGUSTIN: RÉAug 36 (1990) 243-256.

b894 *a*) *Tate* George, La Syrie à l'époque byzantine, essai de synthèse; – *b*) *Canivet* Pierre, Le christianisme en Syrie des origines à l'avènement de l'Islam: → 481. Syrie II (1989) 97-116 / 117-148.

b895 **Vittinghoff** Friedrich [p. 1-28, Staat, Kirche und Dynastie beim Tode Konstantins], *al.*, L'Église et l'Empire au IVᵉ siècle; sept exposés suivis de discussions: Entretiens AntClas 34. Genève 1989, Fond. Hardt. [viii-] 365 p.

b895* *Wirth* Gerhard, Anastasius, Christen und Perser; zu den Problemen des Verhältnisses zwischen Staat und Kirche um die Wende zum 6. Jh.: → 100*, ᶠKÖTTING B., JbAC 33 (1990) 81-139.

b896 *Wischmeyer* Wolfgang, M. Iulius Eugenius; eine Fallstudie zum Thema 'Christen und Gesellschaft im 3. und 4. Jahrhundert': ZNW 81 (1990) 225-246.

XVIII. Archaeologia terrae biblicae

T1.1   **General biblical-area archeologies.**

b897 **Adam** Jean-Pierre, Le passé recomposé; chroniques d'archéologie fantasque [... inscription phénicienne du Brésil] 1988 → 5,b807; 2-02-

010363-X: ᴿAntClas 59 (1990) 553s (C. *Delvoye*: amusant, par l'auteur de L'archéologie devant l'imposture 1975).

b898 ᴱAmitai Janet, *al.*, Biblical archeology today 1984/5 ➤ 3,802:   ᴿJPreh-Rel 3s (1989s) 54-57 (K. A. *Kitchen*).

b899 ᴱÅström Paul, High, middle or low?... chronology colloquium 1987 ➤ 5,831*: ᴿAJA 94 (1990) 345s (W. *Rudolph*); PEQ 121 (1989) 152-4 (T. *Watkins*: SIMA-pocket 56s).

b900 ᴱAurenche Olivier, *al.*, Chronologies in the Near East [CNRS symposium, Lyon Nov. 1986]: BAR-Int 379. Ox 1987. 744 p. £45. – ᴿAJA 94 (1990) 683s (S. E. *Falconer*).

ᴱBapty Ian, *Yates* Tim, Archaeology after structuralism 1990 ➤ 470.

b901 Bartlett J. R., The Bible, faith and evidence; a critical inquiry into the nature of biblical history [intended to complement KENYON-MOOREY, The Bible and recent archaeology]. L 1990, British Museum. 272 p. £20. 0-7141-1717-X [BL 91,34, A. *Phillips*].

b902 Binford Lewis R., Preistoria dell'uomo; la nuova archeologia, ᵀ*Di Mario* Francesco. Mi 1990, Rusconi. 316 p.; ill. Lit. 45.000. – ᴿLetture 45 (1990) 563 (Carla *Castelli*).

b902* *Burger* J., Biblical archaeology — a misnomer? [only if taken to mean it proves the Bible true]: TEv 23 (Pretoria 1990] 2-6 [OTAbs 14,18].

b903 ᴱChampion T. C., Centre and periphery; comparative studies in archeology: One World Archeology 11, 1986/9 ➤ 5,537 [but not 'Campion'; Champion correct as in Index]. – ᴿAJA 94 (1990) 485s (P. S. *Wells*: one of 20 volumes from the 1986 Southampton congress).

b904 *Chapman* Rupert L., The three ages [Stone, Bronze, Iron] revisited; a critical study of Levantine usages, I. The critique: PEQ 121 (1989) 89-111.

b905 ᴱConkey Margaret W., *Hastorf* Christine A., The uses of style in archeology: New Directions. C 1990, Univ. ix-124 p. 0-521-35061-1 [OIAc F91,4 enumerates ten items, mostly theoretic aesthetics, without pages].

b906 Courbin Paul, What is archaeology? An essay on the nature of archaeological research [1982 ➤ 63,a13], ᵀ*Bahn* P. Ch 1988, Univ. 197 p.; 4 fig. $25. 0-226-11656-5. – ᴿClasW 84 (1990s) 76 (Susan J. *Rotroff*: too angry); JField 16 (1989) 245-8 (I. *Hodder*: excellent translation of a reactionary ill-informed book).

b907 Deichmann Friedrich W., Einführung in die christliche Archäologie 1983 ➤ 64,a388... 2,9709: ᴿGrazB 17 (1990) 269-273 (E. *Pochmarski*).

b908 Dever William G., Recent archaeological discoveries and biblical research [Stroum lectures]. Seattle 1990, Univ. Washington. 200 p.; 60 fig. $17.50. 0-295-96588-6. – ᴿBAR-W 16,3 (1990) 6.8 (M. D. *Coogan*) & 52-58.62 [lengthy citation].

b909 *Frevel* Christian, 'Dies ist der Ort, von dem geschrieben steht:...'; zum Verhältnis von Bibelwissenschaft und Palästinaarchäologie: BibNot 47 (1989) 35-89.

b910 Fritz Volkmar, Einführung in die biblische Archäologie 1985 ➤ 1,b421; 3,d134: ᴿBASOR 277s (1990) 132s (J. D. *Seger*); TLZ 115 (1990) 49s (K.-H. *Bernhardt*).

b911 Geltzer M., ❿ *Archeologiya Izrailia*; brief outline. J 1983, Aliya. 46 p.; ill. [KirSef 62 (1988s) p. 186].

b912 Grant M., The visible past; Greek and Roman history from archaeology 1960-1990 [30 excavated sites or projects]. NY 1990, Scribner's. xix-258 p.; 16 pl.; 9 maps. $27.50. 0-684-19124-5 [NTAbs 35,264].

b913 ᴱGrant M., *Kitzinger* R., Civilization of the ancient Mediterranean I-II, 1987 ➤ 4,444: ᴿClasW 83 (1989s) 60s (C. F. *Natunewicz*).

b914 *a) Hachmann* Rolf, Über Natur der Kultur; – *b) Girtler* Roland, Alltagskultur und Urgeschichte: ➤ 128, ᶠ*Narr* K., Saeculum 41 (1990) 216-243 / 244-254.

b915 **Hankey** Henry, Archaeology; artifacts and artification: SIMA pocket 37. Göteborg 1985, Åström. – ᴿAntClas 59 (1990) 554s (R. *Laffineur*: husband of Vronwy Hankey).

b916 **Harris** Edward, Principles of archaeological stratigraphy² [¹1979 ➤ 64,s23]. L 1989, Academic. xiv-170 p.; 68 fig. £17.50. 0-12-326651-3. – ᴿAntiquity 64 (1990) 971s (S. *Roskams*: basic problems survive the cosmetic-marketwise updating); IntJNaut 19 (1990) 255s (J. *Adams*).

b917 *Himmelmann* Nikolaus, Der Hellenismus in der Archäologie: ➤ 791*, KlasArch 13 (1988/90) 13-16.

b918 ᴱ**Hodder** Ian, Archaeology as long-term history 1987 ➤ 4,447: ᴿBInst-Arch 26 (1989) 272-4 (A. *Fridriksson*).

b919 ᴱ**Hodder** Ian, The archaeology of contextual meanings 1987 ➤ 3,499; 4,d642: ᴿBInstArch 26 (1989) 274-6 (G. *Lucas*).

b920 [Israel] 1990 excavation opportunities: BAR-W 16,1 (1990) 38-47.

b921 ᴱ**Koester** Helmut, *Hendrix* Holland L., Archaeological resources for NT studies ➤ 3,f314; Ph 1987, Fortress. I. 300 p. + 282 color-slides. $450. – ᴿCritRR 3 (1990) 87-89 (E. *Krentz*).

b922 ᴱ**Lamberg-Karlovsky** C. C., Archaeological thought in America. C 1989, Univ. viii-357 p.; ill. £35. 0-521-35452-8. – ᴿAntiqJ 69 (1989) 340s (N. *Hammond*: as monolithic and humourless as in Russia, but the study shows merits).

b923 **Lance** H. Darrell, Archéologie et Ancien Testament [1981 ➤ 62,a899], ᵀ*Römer* Thomas. Genève 1990, Labor et Fides. 132 p. [RTPhil 122,577]. 3-8309-0597-0.

b924 *Lemche* Niels P., On the use of 'system theory' in modern OT research and biblical archaeology: ScandJOT (1990,2) 73-88.

b925 *a) Maley* Willy, Undermining archaeology; from reconstruction to deconstruction; – *b) Walsh* Kevin, The post-modern threat to the past: ➤ 470, ᴱ*Bapty* I., Archaeology 1990, 61-77 / 294-310.

b925* **Malina** Jaroslav, *Vašiček* Zdenek, Archaeology yesterday and today; the development of archaeology in the sciences and humanities [1980], ᵀᴱ*Zvelebil* Marek. C 1990, Univ. xiv-320 p.; 50 fig. £40; pa. £15. 0-521-26621-1; -31977-3 [Antiquity 65.417, B. *Trigger*].

b926 *Matthews* Victor H., *Moyer* James C., The use and abuse of archaeology in current one-volume Bible commentaries: BA 53 (1990) 104-115 [New Jerome amplest, except Harpers for literary parallels; Collegeville has finest colored map collection].

b927 **Mazar** Amihai, Archaeology of the Land of the Bible, 10,000-586 B.C.E. NY 1990, Doubleday. 602 p.; 256 fig.; 11 maps. $30. 0-385-23970-X. – ᴿBAR-W 16,6 (1990) 10.70 (O. *Borowski*); ExpTim 102 (1990s) 149s (J. R. *Bartlett*).

b928 **Meyers** E., *Strange* J., Les Rabbins et les premiers chrétiens; archéologie et histoire [1981] 1984 ➤ 65,a17b... 4,d653: ᴿOLZ 85 (1990) 321s (P. *Schäfer*).

b928* **Michell** J., A little history of astro-archaeology² [¹1978]. L 1989, Thames & H. 128 p.; 97 fig. £5. 0-500-27557-2. – ᴿAntiquity 64 (1990) 597s (I. J. *Thorpe*).

b929 **Millard** Alan,   Archaeologia e Bibbia [Treasures 1985 ➤ 1,b433], ᵀᴱ*Ravasi* Gianfranco 1988 ➤ 4,d654; 5,b837: ᴿCC 141 (1990,2) 100s (S. *Votto*); STEv 1 (1989) 209-211 (D. *Valente*).

b930 **Millard** A.,   Trésors des temps [bibliques 1986 ➤ 3,d15] évangéliques. P/Méry-sur-Oise 1990, Cerf/Sator.   189 p.; ill. F 165 [NRT 113, 758, X. *Jacques*].

b931 ᴱ**Murphy** Edwin,   DIODORUS Siculus, The antiquities of Asia [Library Book II]. Ox 1989, Transaction.   xvii-130 p.; 18 pl.; map. £23. – ᴿClasR 40 (1990) 478 (S. *Hornblower*).

b932 *Oesch* Josef M.,   Fundamentalismus und fundamentalistische Versuchung im Spannungsfeld von Archäologie und Bibel: ➤ 1416, Eindeutige Antworten?² 1988, 111-124.

b932* **Paddayya** K.,   The new archaeology and aftermath; a view from outside the Anglo-American world.   Pune 1990, Ravish.   x-71 p. [Antiquity 65, 417, B. *Trigger*].

b933 *Podborský* Vladimír,   Grenzen der Möglichkeit einer Kulturhistorie der Urzeit: ➤ 4*, ᶠANGELI W., Mitt. Anthrop. Wien 118s (1988s) 15-25; Eng. 15.

b934 *Popham* Mervyn,   Reflections on [SNODGRASS A. 1988] 'An archaeology of Greece'; [relative merits of] surveys and excavations: OxJArch 9 (1990) 29-35.

b935 *Randsborg* Klavs, a) Archeology in the twentieth century, a Scandinavian view; – b) The metamorphosis of antiquity; centre and periphery in Europe from 1000 B.C. to A.D. 1000; – c) Between Italy and Afghanistan; archaeological surveys and ancient civilizations: AcArchK 60 (1989) 151-164; 5 fig. / 165-174; 2 fig. / 175-185; 8 fig.; all ᵀ*Davidson* Joan F.

b936 *Rautman* Marcus L.,   Archaeology and Byzantine studies: ByzF 15 (1990) 137-165.

b937 a) *Renfrew* Colin,   Archaeology and linguistics; some preliminary issues; – b) *Zvelebil* Marek & Kamil,   Agricultural transition, 'Indo-European origins', and the spread of farming [Renfrew]: ➤ 754, Worlds 1988/90, 15-24 / 237-264 + 2 maps.

b938 **Rogerson** J., *Davies* P., The OT world 1989 ➤ 5,b843: ᴿBA 53 (1990) 172-4 (D.C. *Browning* compares to van der WOUDE); BInstArch 26 (1989) 292-4 (B. *Levitan*: dissatisfied); JStJud 21 (1990) 276 (A.S. van der *Woude*); TLond 93 (1990) 65s (R. *Coggins*).

b939 ROSE D. Glenn mem.: Archaeology and biblical interpretation, ᴱ**Purdue** L.G., *al.*, 1987 ➤ 4,125: ᴿJAOS 110 (1990) 572s (K.N. *Schoville*).

b940 **Saggs** H.W.F.,   Civilization before Greece and Rome [Egypt, Mesopotamia; but also Indus, Arabia, Anatolia ...]. L 1989, Batsford.   322 p. £20.   0-7134-5277-3 [BL 90,24].

b941 **Sartre** Maurice,   *Tranoy* Alain,   La Méditerranée antique (Vᵉ siècle avant J.-C. / IIIᵉ siècle ap. J.-C.): Cursus. P 1990, A. Colin.   192 p.   2-200-33050-2 [OIAc Ja91]. – ᴿLA 40 (1990) 478s (M. *Piccirillo*).

b942 *Scheepers* C.L.,   A methodological debate in biblical archaeology [1960s American paradigm shift from inductive to deductive will revolutionize]: OTEssays 3 (1990) 325-339.

b943 **Shanks** Hershel,   Archaeology and the Bible; the best of BAR; I. Early Israel; II. Archaeology in the world of Herod, Jesus and Paul.   Wsh 1990, BAR. $19 each; both $36 [adv. 16/5].

b944 **Shanks** Michael, *Tilley* Christopher,   Social archaeology. Ox 1987, Polity = Albuquerque 1988, Univ. NM.   243 p.; 10 fig. $30; pa. $16. 0-7456-0183-9; -4-7 / NM 0-8263-1064-8; 5-6. – ᴿJField 17 (1990)

219-221 (Patty Jo *Watson*: overlaps their Re-Constructing 1987 ⟿ 4, d660).

b945 *Shay* Talia,   Israeli archaeology — theory and practice: Antiquity 63 (1989) 768-772.

b946 **Silberman** Neil A.,   Between past and present; archaeology, ideology, and nationalism in the modern Middle East.   NY 1989, Holt.   xii-285 p.; map. $25.   0-8050-0906-X. – ᴿAntiquity 64 (1990) 696 (P. *Gathercole*).

b947 *Silberman* Neil A., Lure of the Holy Land; a century of archaeology has radically altered our understanding of the world of the Bible ... and raised some difficult challenges for the century ahead: Archaeology 43,6 (1990) 28-35; ill.

b947* ᴱSteinsland Gro,   Words and objects; towards a dialogue between archaeology and history of religions 1986 ⟿ 3,465; 4,e774:   ᴿJPrehR 2 (1988) 66-68 (Hilda E. *Davidson*).

b948 ᴱStone P., *MacKenzie* R.,   The excluded past; archaeology in education [archaeologists pressured to support nationalistic claims; 7 papers from 1986 Southampton congress + 18 others].   L c. 1989, Unwin Hyman. 314 p. – ᴿAntiquity 64 (1990) 694s (J. *Alexander*).

b949 *Stutt* Arthur, *Shennan* Stephen,   The nature of archaeological arguments [we hear both sides, then (by illogical intuition) choose that which is more logical; computer can help]: Antiquity 64 (1990) 766-777.

b950 **Trigger** Bruce G.,   A history of archaeological thought 1989 ⟿ 5,b852: ᴿAntiquity 64 (1990) 958-960 (A. *Schnapp*: updates C. STARK 1880; extends WILLEY & SABLOFF 1974).

b951 **Tubb** Jonathan N., *Chapman* Rupert L.,   Archaeology and the Bible.   L 1990, British Museum.   112 p.   0-7141-1719-8 [OIAc Oc90].

b952 *Winkelmann* Friedhelm,   Zur Entstehung und Ausbreitung des Christentums: Altertum 36 (1990) 182-9; 6 fig. (maps).

b952* *Yamauchi* Edwin,   Archaeology and the Gospels; discoveries and publications of the decade (1978-87): ⟿ 370, Gospels Today 1990, 1-12.

T1.2   **Musea, organismi, expositiones.**

b953 *Adams* B., ❻ The Petrie Museum of Egyptian Archeology (University College, London): VDI 194 (1990) 217-223; 5 fig.

b954 Antike Welt: [*Priese* Karl-H., *al.*] Auf der Berliner Museumsinsel; Pergamon- und Bodemuseum; Ägyptisches Museum; Antikensammlung; Frühchristlich-Byzantinische Sammlung. Mainz 1990, von Zabern. 140 p.; (color.) ill.

b955 **Aufrère** Sydney,   Collections égyptiennes.   Rouen 1987, Musées Seine-Maritime.   243 p.; ill.   2-902093-05-5 [OIAc S90].

b956 Autun, les collections égyptiennes dans les musées de Saône-et-Loire [exposition]. Autun 1988, Ville.   388 p. [OIAc S90].

b957 **Avigad** Nahman,   The Herodian quarter in Jerusalem Wohl Archaeological Museum.   J 1989, Keter.   80 p.; ill. [BL 91,26, A. R. *Millard*].

b958 ᴱBianchi R. S.,   Cleopatra's Egypt; age of the Ptolemies [catalogue of exposition, Brooklyn/ Detroit/München] 1988 ⟿ 4,d671 (5,b855 deutsch): ᴿCdÉ 65 (1990) 182-4 (Dorothy J. *Thompson*).

b959 The Bible: 100 landmarks from the E.P. Prothro collection.   Dallas 1990, Southern Methodist Univ. Bridwell Library.   xxi-128 p.; 15 fig. – ᴿBS 147 (1990) 495s (R. D. *Ibach*: described in 14 chapters, author not named).

b960 ᴱBothmer Bernard V., al., Antiquities from the collection of C. G. Bastis [NY exhibition catalogue; Egypt, Cyclades ...] 1987, → 4,d674; DM 148: ᴿBO 17 (1990) 117s (K. Parlasca).

b961 ᴱBothmer Dietrich von, Glories of the past; ancient art from the Shelby White and Leon Levy collection. NY 1990, Met. x-280 p.; (color.) ill. 0-87099-593-6 [OIAc F91,2 names the 21 separate contributors].

b962 Bourriau Janine, Egyptian antiquities acquired in 1988 by museums in the United Kingdom: JEA 76 (1990) 157-9.

b963 Bulian Giovanni, Il nuovo Museo Archeologico di Roma e la mostra 'Archeologia a Roma; materia e tecnica dell'arte antica': BArteR 64 (1990) 73-76; 1 fig.; color. pl. VI.

b964 Caquot André (Vesco J.-L.), Rapport sur l'état et les activités de l'École Biblique et Archéologique Française de Jérusalem: CRAI (1990) 699-702.

b965 Caubet Annie, Aux sources du monde arabe; l'Arabie avant l'Islam; collections du Musée du Louvre (1990-3 dans l'Institut du Monde Arabe). P 1990, Réunion Musées. 111 p.; 59 fig.; F 100. 2-7118-2368-7 [RB 98,140].

b966 Caubet Annie, al., Le Louvre et la Bible: MondeB 67 (1990) 1-54; foldout maps.

b966* Delorenzi Enzo, Grilletto Renato, Mummie del Museo egizio di Torino (n. 13000-13025), indagine antropo-radiologica. Torino 1989, Cisalpino. 46 p.; ill. 88-205-0641-6.

b967 De Puma Richard D., Roman portraits [sculpture, Iowa Univ. exhibition Oct. 1988]. Iowa City 1988, Univ. Museum. 92 p.; 159 fig.; 3 color. pl. – ᴿAJA 94 (1990) 167s (Susan Wood).

b968 Dewachter Michel, La collection égyptienne du Musée Champollion. introd. Leclant Jean 1986→ 3,d184; cf. → 5,b859: ᴿBO 47 (1990) 646-8 (E. L. Ertman).

b968* Donadoni Roveri Anna Maria, Museo egizio. Torino c. 1989, Barisone. 72 p.; many (color.) phot.; (legends and) text ital. 3-48; deutsch 49-60; English 61-71. Lit. 10.000.

b969 Dorman Peter, al., Egypt and the Ancient Near East. NY 1987. Metropolitan Museum of Art. 159 p., 114 fig.; 2 maps. 0-87099-413-1 [OIAc Ja91]. → e612.

b970 Février P.-A., Leyge F., Catalogue de l'exposition sept. 1986 pour le congrès d'archéologie chrétienne à Lyon, ensuite à Paris. Lyon 1986, Sauvetage des sites archéologiques médiévaux. 201 p., ill. [RHE 85,555].

b971 Friedman Florence D., Beyond the Pharaohs; Egypt and the Copts in the 2nd to 7th centuries A.D. [1989 exhibition catalogue]. -/Baltimore 1989, Rhode Island School of Design/Walters Art Gallery. 296 p.; 212 fig. + 11 color; 5 plans; 2 maps. – ᴿBSACopte 29 (1990) 143-6 (W. Boutros-Ghali).

b972 Grimal Nicolas. Travaux de l'IFAO 1989-1990: BIFAO 90 (1990) 381-424.

b973 Homès-Fredericq Denise, Franken H. J., Pottery and potters — past and present; 7000 years of ceramic art in Jordan; Ausstellungskatalog Univ. Tü 20. Tü 1986, Verlag Tü. 263 p.; ill. – ᴿVT 40 (1990) 243 (Judith M. Hadley).

b974 Horváth Judit, The history of Egyptological studies at the arts faculty of L. Eötvös University, Budapest: → 49, Mem. FÓTI L. 1989, 143-163.

b975 ᴱJacobek Roman, al., Götter, Heroen, Herrscher in Lykien, Ausstellung [Wien]; Wien 1990, Schroll. 244 p. 3-7031-0662-X. 117-243, Katalog; 1-115, 20 spezializierte Artikel, Metzger Henri, al.

b976 Jahresbericht 1989 des Deutschen Archäologischen Instituts: ArchAnz (1990) 559-618; 619-629, personelle Gliederung.

b977 [*Humbert* J.-E., présent.] Jérusalem de la pierre à l'esprit, 1890-1990, centenaire de l'École Biblique et Archéologique Française de Jérusalem; exposition. J/Lyon 1990, École Biblique et Archéologique/Bibliothèque Municipale. 192 p.; ill. 2-9504381-3-3.

b978 ᴱJones Mark, *al.*, Fake? The art of deception. L 1990, British Museum. 112 p.; 335 (color). fig. 0-7141-2058-8; pa. -1703-X.

b979 Kaiser Augustus und die verlorene Republik [Ausstellung-Katalog 1986] (Staatliche Museen, Preussischer Kulturbesitz). Mainz 1988, von Zabern. 638 p.; 952 fig + 14 color. – ᴿAJA 94 (1990) 358s (Elizabeth *Bartman*: 455 items, several essays; the most important show of ancient art anywhere since 1946).

b980 [*Keenan* James G., opening lecture] Another Egypt; Coptic Christians at Thebes (7th-8th c. A.D.) Chicago Oriental Institute museum exhibit Oct. 1990 - June 1991: DiscEg 18 (1990) 103s.

b981 **Kitchen** K. A. (*Beltrão* M. da C.], Catalogue of the Egyptian collection in the National Museum, Rio de Janeiro [= ²Catálogo, *Childe* A., *Vanitzin* D. P., 1919]. Rio 1990, Museu/Univ. (Wmr, Aris & P). xxxii-276 p., text all in English and Portuguese; vol of vii-232 pl. £60. 0-85668-492-9; -514-3 [BL 91,127, N. *Wyatt*: rich material authoritatively translated].

b982 Der Königsweg, 9000 Jahre Kunst und Kultur in Jordanien und Palästina [Museum Köln 1987] 1987 → 3,d212: ᴿAulaO 8 (1990) 269s (G. del *Olmo Lete*, títulos sin pp.).

b983 **Krauspe** Renate, Ägyptisches Museum der Karl-Marx-Universität Leipzig; Führer durch die Ausstellung³ʳᵉᵛ. Lp 1987, Univ. Direktorat für Forschung. 75 p.; 93 fig. + 8 color. M 10.

b984 *Le Rider* Georges [*Heurgon* Jacques], Rapport sur l'état et l'activités de l'école française d'Athènes [de Rome]: CRAI (1990) 765-773 [775-789].

b985 **Maguire** Eunice D. & Henry P., *al.*, Art and holy powers in the early Christian house [1989 exhibition-catalogue, 150 items]: ILByzSt 11. Urbana 1989, Univ. Illinois. 251 p. $25 [RelStR 17, 262, Sarah G. *Bassett*]. – ᴿMakedonika 27 (1989s) 447 (Th. *Papazotos*, Ⓖ).

b986 **Mitchell** T. C., The Bible in the British Museum; interpreting the evidence 1988 → 4,d696: ᴿPEQ 121 (1989) 157 (Georgina *Herrman*).

b987 **(Morigi) Govi** Cristiana, *Curto* Silvio, *Pernigotti* Sergio, Il senso dell'arte nell'Antico Egitto: esposizione Museo Civico Bologna. Mi 1990, Electa. 263 p., 242 (color.) fig.; map. 88-435-3157-3 [OIAc F91,16].

b988 ᴱMottier Yvette, *Bosson* Nathalie, Les Kellia, ermitages coptes en Basse-Égypte: Musée d'Art 1989-90. Genève 1989, Fond. Kellia. 112 p. 2-8293-0094-7 [OIAc Oc90].

b989 *Murphy-O'Connor* Jerome, The École Biblique de Jérusalem; a century of scholarship (1890-1990): Scripture in Church 20 (Dublin 1990) 471-9 [< NTAbs 35,2]. → y8.

b990 ᴱNissen Hans J., *al.*, Frühe Schrift und Techniken der Wirtschaftsverwaltung im alten Vorderen Orient; Informationsspeicherung und -verarbeitung vor 5000 Jahren: Berliner Museen, Ausstellung Mai-Juli 1990, Katalog. B 1990, Franzbecker. xii-222 p. 3-88120-110-6 [OIAc JJ 90].

b991 *Pergola* Philippe, *al.*, Activités de l'École française de Rome, section antiquité: MÉF 102,1 (1990) 443-504.

b992 *Podvin* Jean-Louis, Aegyptiaca de Picardie [Amiens, Soissons ...]: CdÉ 65 (1990) 41-54; map.

b993 ᴱ**Raven** M. J., Wel moge het U bekomen; feestmal — godenmaal — dodenmaal in de oudheid: Tentoonstelling Rijksmuseum jun.-aug. 1987. Leiden 1987. 96 p. 90-71201-05-8 [OIAc Oc90].

b994 ᴱ**Robins** Gay, Beyond the pyramids; Egyptian regional art from the Museo Egizio, Turin; catalogue of 54 objects. Atlanta 1990, Emory Univ. 95 p. [OIAc Ja91 names Barry *Kemp* and the other four contributors].

b995 **Rosovsky** Nitza, *Ungerleider-Mayerson* Joy, The museums of Israel 1989 ➔ 5,b876; also J 1990, Steimatzky. – ᴿTerraS 66 (1990) 298 (P. S. *Colbi*).

b996 *Sadek* Ashraf I., La collection égyptienne du Musée de l'Évêché de Limoges (France); le sarcophage de Iret-Hor-erou: GöMiszÄg 115 (1990) 85-93; 2 phot.; facsimiles.

b997 ᴱ**Sagona** Antonio G., *Zimmer* J. K., Images of the ancient world; archeology at the University of Melbourne, Westpac Gallery, Oct.-Nov. 1988. Melbourne 1988, Univ. Clas. St. 167 p. ill.

b998 **Saleh** Mohamed, *Sourouzian* Hourig, *Liepe* Jürgen, Official catalogue of the Egyptian Museum Cairo: Egyptian Organization of Antiquities. Mainz 1987, von Zabern. 3-8053-0942-2; -52-X [OIAc JJ 90].

b999 **Samman** Tarif al-, *Mazal* Otto, Die arabische Welt und Europa; Ausstellung der Handschriften- und Inkunabelsammlung der Österreichischen Nationalbibliothek. Graz 1988, Akad. 486 p.; 96 pl. – ᴿWZKM 90 (1990) 251s (H. *Bobzin*).

d1 **Seipel** Wilfried, Ägypten; Götter, Gräber und die Kunst; 4000 Jahre Jenseitsglaube: Linz Schlossmuseum Ausstellung Apr.-Sept. 1989: Kataloge des Ö. Landesmuseums NF 22/1. 368 p. 3-900746-14-1 [OIAc JJ 90].

d2 **Selzer** Wolfgang, *al.*, Römische Steindenkmäler: Katalog, Landesmuseum Mainz. Mainz 1988, von Zabern. 267 p.; 351 fig. + 52 color. 3-8053-0993-7. – ᴿZDPV 106 (1990) 191s (E. *Knauf*, U. *Hübner*).

d3 *Will* Ernest, L'École Biblique et la découverte archéologique: CRAI (1990) 857-864.

d4 **Wilson** David, The British Museum; purpose and politics. L 1989, British Museum. 126 p.; 5 fig.; 20 pl. £5 pa. 0-7141-1714-5. – ᴿAntiquity 64 (1990) 439s (J. V. G. *Malley*); BInstArch 26 (1989) 305s (K. *Feldman*).

d5 **Ziegler** Christiane, Catalogue des stèles, peintures et reliefs égyptiens de l'Ancien Empire et de la Première Période Intermédiaire vers 2686-2040 av. J.-C. P 1990, Réunion Mus. Nat. 376 p. 2-7118-2228-1 [OIAc F91].

T1.3 *Methodi*, **Science in archeology.**

d6 **Adkins** Lesley & Roy A., Archaeological illustration: Manuals in Archaeology. C 1989, Univ. xv-259 p. £30. 0-521-35478-1. – ᴿAntiqJ 69 (1989) 342s (P. L. *Drewett*, also on DORRELL P., Photography).

d7 **Aitken** M. J., Science-based dating in archaeology. L 1990, Longman. xx-274 p.; 91 fig. £22; pa. £12. 0-582-05498-2; -49309-9. – ᴿAntiqJ 69 (1989!) 343s (G. *Bailey*); Antiquity 64 (1990) 963 (J. *Head*).

d8 *Aitken* M. J., Luminescence dating; a guide for non-specialists: Archaeometry 31 (1989) 147-159.

d9 **Alvisi** Giovanni, La fotografia aerea nell'indagine archeologica. R 1989, Nuova Italia Scientifica. 152 p.; 52 fig. – ᴿArchClasR 42 (1990) 517-520 (D. *Adamesteanu*).

d10 *Bagolini* Bernardino, *Biagi* Paolo, The radiocarbon chronology of the Neolithic and Copper Age of Northern Italy: OxJArch 9 (1990) 1-23.

d11 *Chalavoux* J., *al.*, De la fouille à l'expérimentation, en passant par les archéosciences; l'exemple de la micromorphologie: RArchéom 14 (1990) 17-22; 5 fig.

d12 **Clark** Anthony, Seeing beneath the soil; prospecting methods in archaeology. L 1990, Batsford. 176 p.; 117 fig., £30. 0-7134-5858-5. – ᴿAntiqJ 70 (1990) 122 (J. *Musty*).

d12* *a)* *Evin* J., *Aurenche* O., *Gasco* J., Techniques for the classification, selection and interpretation of a series of ¹⁴C dates from the Near East; – *b)* *Waterbolk* H. T., Quality differences between radiocarbon laboratories illustrated on material from SW Asia and Egypt; – *c)* *Bruins* H. J., *Mook* W. G., Radiocarbon dating in the NE Sinai desert, Ein el-Gudeirat, Kadesh-Barnea: ➤ 814*b*, PACT 29, 1987/90, 105-124; 4 fig. / 141-157; 12 fig. / 311-334; 13 fig.

d13 **Gersbach** Egon, Ausgrabungen heute; Methoden und Techniken der Feldgrabung; Beit. *Hahn* Joachim. Da 1990, Wiss. vii-167 p. 3-534-08329-6 [OIAc Ja91].

d14 *Glover* E. & I., *Vita-Finzi* C., First-order ¹⁴C dating of marine molluscs in archaeology: Antiquity 64 (1990) 562-7.

d15 *a)* *Guermandi* Maria Pia, ALADINO: verso un sistema computerizzato per lo studio e l'analisi dei dati archeologici; – *b)* *Eisner* Michael, The ARBOR information system for classical archaeology and history of art: Archeologia e calcolatori 1 (1990) 263-294 / 253-262.

d16 *Gunneweg* J., *Mommsen* H., Instrumental neutron activation analysis and the origin of some cult objects and Edomite vessels from the Ḥorvat Qitmit shrine: Archaeometry 32 (1990) 7-18.

d16* ᴱ**Henderson** Julian, Scientific analysis in archaeology and its interpretation: Oxford Committee / UCLA Institute, Archaeological Research Tools 5. Ox 1989. x-311 p.; 153 fig. £16 pa. 0-947816-19-4 [Antiquity 65,434, M. *Jones*].

d17 *Karmi* K., *Bar-Yosef* O., ⊕ Carbon-14 dating: Qadmoniot 23,1s (1990) 20-25.

d18 **Kelley** Jane H., *Hanen* Marsha P., Archaeology and the methodology of science. Albuquerque 1988, Univ. New Mexico. xiii-452 p. $30. 0-8263-1030-3. – ᴿAJA 94 (1990) 153 (Patty Jo *Watson*); JField 16 (1989) 467-9 (C. *Renfrew*).

d18* ᴱ**Mannoni** Tiziano, *Molinari* Alessandra, Scienze in archeologia: Ciclo Certosa di Pontignano 7-19.XI.1988: Univ. Siena. F 1990, Insegna del Giglio. 470 p. Lit. 70.000. 88-7814-082-1. 43-205 ceramica, monete; 209-422 fauna, flora; 425-466 computers.

d19 **Polach** Dilette, Radiocarbon dating literature; the first 21 years, 1947-1968, annotated bibliography (5 chapters by continent, 9 others by topic). L 1988, Academic. x-370 p. 0-12-559290-6.

Prodhomme Jean, La préparation des publications archéologiques 1987 ➤ 1151.

d20 *Reiss* Francis, An improved technique for photography of artefacts in the field: MeditArch 3 (1990) 47-54; pl. 24.

d21* ᴱ**Ross** Seamus, *al.*, Computing for archaeologists [Oxford lectures]. Ox 1990, Committee for Archaeology. 218 p.; (color.) ill. £16. 0-947816-18-6 [Antiquity 64,961 adv.).

d21 **Shennan** Stephen, Quantifying archaeology 1988 ➤ 4,d739: ᴿHelinium 30 (1990) 288-291 (F. *Verhaeghe*).

T1.4   *Exploratores* – **Excavators, pioneers.**

d22 **Ackerman** Robert, J. G. FRAZER, his life and work 1987 ➤ 3,d251: ᴿClasPg (1990) 80-83 (G. W. *Stocking*); ScotJT 43 (1990) 129-132 (Ursula *King*: standard).

d23 *Amiet* P., de MECQUENEM Roland [b. 1977 (for 1877!), d. 1957] (franç.): ➤ 853*, RLA 7,7s (1990) 614.

d24 *Blumenthal* Elke, Heinrich Leberecht FLEISCHER und die Leipziger Ägyptologie: ZägSpr 117 (1990) 93-103.

d25 *a) Bresciani* Edda, De Jean-François à Angelica, le 6 décembre 1827; une lettre retrouvée; – *b) Ray* M.J.D. (John), Thomas Young et CHAMPOLLION: BSocFrÉg 119 (1990) 15-24; 2 fig. / 25-34.

ᴱ**Christenson** Andrew L., Tracing archaeology's past; the historiography of archaeology 1989 ➤ 793*.

d27 *a) Cobet* Justus, Heinrich SCHLIEMANN nach hundert Jahren; die Historisierung von Mythos und Ärgernis / Troia vor Schliemann; – *b) Wohlleben* Joachim, Homer vor Schliemann [summary of awaited monograph]; – *c) Patzek* Barbara, Schliemann und die Geschichte der Archäologie im neunzehnten Jahrhundert; – *d) Calder* W., Apocolocyntosis; the biographers and the archaeologists: ➤ 792, Schliemann 1989/90, 12-26.118-151 / 27-30 / 31-56 / 360-378.

d28 *Conrad* Lawrence I., The dervish's disciple; on the personality and intellectual milieu of the young Ignaz GOLDZIHER [Tagebuch ᴱ*Scheiber* A. 1978]: JRAS (1990) 225-266.

d29 ᴱ**Daniel** Glyn, *Chippindale* Christopher, The pastmasters, eleven modern pioneers of archaeology. L 1989, Thames & H. 176p.; 22 pl. £18. 0-500-05051-1. – ᴿAntiquity 64 (1990) 163-5 (N. *Hammond*).

d30 *a) Dewachter* Michel, Un curieux bédouin; CHAMPOLLION l'Égyptien, les portraits du voyage en Orient; – *b) Leclant* Jean, L'expédition de l'Égypte, l'Institut d'Égypte, et la Description de l'Égypte; – *c) Humbert* Jean-Marcel, Napoléon et l'Égypte, ou l'osmose de deux mythes; – *d) Delmas* Jean, Un 'Égyptien' de l'Aveyon; le lieutenant-général Jean-J. TARAYRE (1770-1855): ➤ 34, ᶠCHAMPOLLION I, L'Égypte (1990) 41-49; 8 color. pl. (17-30.69-77) / 11-16 / 31-38 / 39s.

d31 *Fagan* Brian, Rethinking prehistory [Colin RENFREW]: Archaeology 43,4 (1990) 32-39; ill.

d31* **Eriksen** E.O., Holy Land explorers. J 1989, Franciscan [BL 91,158].

d32 ᴱ**Freier** Elke, *Reineke* Walter F., K.R. LEPSIUS Tagung 1984/8 ➤ 5,850: ᴿArOr 58 (1990) 409s (W.B. *Oerter*).

d33 *Graefe* Erhart, Eine Seite aus den Notizbüchern von Robert HAY: ➤ 16, ᶠBECKERATH J. v. 1990, 85-90; pl. 8a.

d34 **Gräslund** Bo, The birth of prehistoric chronology; dating methods and dating systems in nineteenth-century Scandinavian archaeology: New Studies in Archaeology. C 1987, Univ. ix-132p.; 36 pl. £22.50 [PraehZ 66, 236s, K.-H. *Willroth*].

d35 **Guérin** Victor, ⊕ Description géographique, historique et archéologique de la Palestine, 7: Galilée 2 [1880], ᵀ*Ben-Amram* Ḥayim. J 1987, Yad Ben Zvi. 339p. 965-217-097-0 [KirSef 62 (1988s) p. 625].

d36 **Hartleben** Hermine, Jean-François CHAMPOLLION, sa vie et son œuvre 1790-1832 [C. sein Leben 1906], ᵀ*Meunier* Denise. P 1990 = 1983, Pygmalion/Watelet. 623p.; ill.; map.

d37 **Kettel** Jeannot, Jean-François CHAMPOLLION le jeune; répertoire de bibliographie analytique 1806-1989: Mém. AIBL NS 10. P 1990, de Boccard. vii-293p.; 8pl. in center. F 165. 2-85074-317-1.

d38 *a) Lacouture* Jean, CHAMPOLLION, années d'apprentissage; – *b) Ziegler* Christiane, Les années Champollion; des signes sans secrets; – *c) De-*

wachter Michel, Champollion au bout de son rêve: ➤ 35, ^FCHAM-POLLION II, L'Europe 1990, 72-77 / 80-109 [-174, al.] / 172-199; color. ill.

d39 **Laurens** Henry, *al.*, L'expédition d'Égypte (1798-1801). P 1989, A. Colin. 520 p. – ^RÉtudes 372 (1990) 414s (P. *Vallin*).

d40 **Laurens** Henry, Kléber en Égypte 1798-1800 [➤ 5,b929]; Kléber et Bonaparte 1798-1799 [correspondance, carnet]: Voyageurs occidentaux en Égypte 25. Le Caire 1988, IFAO. viii-579 p.; 7 pl., 4 foldout maps. – ^RJRAS (1990) 158s (P. M. *Holt*: beautifully produced).

d41 *a)* *Leclant* Jean, Le mythe de Pharaon et Isis; – *b)* *Vercoutter* Jean, Le rêve oriental de Bonaparte; – *c)* *Bari* Hubert, La Description de l'Égypte: ➤ 35, ^FCHAMPOLLION II, L'Europe 1990, 12-21 / 22-43 / 44-59.

d42 *Lehmann* Hannes, Wolfgang HELBIG (1839-1915) [... Die Fibula Praenestina und ihre Präsentation]: MiDAI-R 96 (1989) 7-86.

d43 **Levine** P., The amateur and the professional; antiquarians, historians and archaeologists in Victorian England, 1838-1886. C 1986, Univ. 210 p. £25. – ^RRHist 280 (1988) 580s (W. *Findlay*).

d44 *Lock* Peter, D. G. HOGARTH (1862-1927) '... a specialist in the science of archaeology': AnBritAth 85 (1990) 175-200.

d45 *Piacentini* Patrizia, Le lettere di Ippolito ROSELLINI nella Biblioteca Estense di Modena = StEgPun 8 (1990), 111 p.; II pl.

d46 *Ramage* Nancy H., Sir William HAMILTON [c. 1770; in Naples for 37 years] as collector, exporter, and dealer; the acquisition and dispersal of his collections: AJA 94 (1990) 469-480; 11 fig.

d47 *Sack* Dorothee, *Schirmer* Wulf, Erinnerung an Karl WULZINGER [1886-1948]... in Damaskus: IstMitt 39 (1990) 463-481; pl. 46s.

d48 *a)* *Schindler* Wolfgang, Dichtung und Wahrheit; Schliemanns Selbstbiographie im Kontext; – *b)* *Scheuer* Helmut, H. S.s 'Selbstbiographie'; zur Gattungstypologie der Autobiographie in der zweiten Hälfte des neunzehnten Jhts.: ➤ 792, SCHLIEMANN 1989/90, 152-169 / 346-359.

d48* **Shepherd** Naomi, The zealous intruders 1987 ➤ 3,d280; 5,b944: ^RCathHR 75 (1989) 288s (R. T. *Handy*); Encounter 50 (Indianapolis 1989) 285-294 (T. A. *Idinopulos*); PEQ 121 (1989) 149 (M. *Hannam*: PEF a 'curious Victorian hybrid').

d49 **Smits** Jan, De Verenigde Nederlanden op zoek naar het Oude Egypte (1580-1780) — de traditie gevolgt en gewogen [diss. Groningen]. Culemborg 1988, Boldingh. 312 p. ƒ42.50. 90-9002156-6. – ^RBO 17 (1990) 58-61 (M. J. *Raven*: caution).

d50 *Traill* David A., *a)* The SCHLIEMANN controversy: AncHRes 20 (1990) 81-87; – *b)* The archaeological career of Sophia Schliemann: Antichthon 23 (1989) 99-107.

d51 *a)* *Turner* David, Heinrich SCHLIEMANN, the man behind the mask [... a complex genius]: Archaeology 43,6 (1990) 36-42; ill. – *b)* *Dyck* Andrew R., Schliemann on the excavation of Troy; three unpublished letters: GrRByz 31 (1990) 323-337.

d52 *a)* *Wildung* Dietrich, [Karl-Richard] LEPSIUS, le disciple inspiré; – *b)* *Corteggiani* Jean-Pierre, MARIETTE invente Aïda: ➤ 35, ^FCHAMPOLLION II, L'Europe (1990) 202-9 / 227-247; color. ill.

d53 **Winstone** H. V. F., Woolley of Ur; the life of Sir Leonard WOOLLEY. L 1990, Secker & W. 314 p.; 8 pl. 0-436-55790-9 [OIAc F91,22]. – ^RTablet 244 (1990) 763s (E. C. *Hodgkin*).

d54 *Witte* Reinhard, [*al.*] SCHLIEMANN und Berlin [100. Todestag 26.XII.

1990]: Altertum 36 (1990) 133-143 [-181; 197-253]; 189, Kongress Athen 14.-22.IV.1990.

T1.5   *Materiae primae* – **metals, glass.**

d55 **Herold** Karl, Konservierung von archäologischen Bodenfunden; Metall, Keramik, Glas: Szb ph/h 565. W 1990, Akad. Wiss. 235 p.; 42 color. pl. 3-7001-1789-2.

d56 **Limet** Henri, Textes administratifs relatifs aux métaux: ARMT 25, 1986 ⇥ 3,d287; 5,b954: ᴿMARI 6 (1990) 655-8 (M. *Anbar*); OLZ 85 (1990) 165-7 (Stephanie *Dalley*).

---

d57 *Aes*, BRONZE: *a*) *Sutherland* C. H. V., Procurement of *aes* for coinage of the early Empire; – *b*) *Kos* Peter, The Carthage aes nummi of the first tetrarchy: ⇥ 90, ᶠJELOČNIK A., 1988, 27-33 / 99-107; 10 pl.

d58 *Alabastrum:* *Harrell* James A., Misuse of the term 'alabaster' in Egyptology: GöMiszÄg 119 (1990) 37-42.

---

d59 *Argentum*, SILVER: ᴱ**Baratte** François, Argenterie romaine et byzantine 1983/8 ⇥ 1,720; 5,b959: ᴿRArchéol (1990) 187s (Catherine *Metzger*).

d60 **Roggenbuck** Petra, Untersuchungen zu den Edelmetallfunden der römischen Kaiserzeit zwischen Limes, Nord- und Ostsee [Diss. Hamburg 1988], BAR-Int. 449. Ox 1988. 332 p.; ill.; 49 maps. – ᴿBInstArch 26 (1989) 294s (P. *Guest*).

---

d61 *Aurum*, GOLD: *Lana* Italo, PLINIO il Vecchio; miniere d'oro e minatori (Nat. Hist. XXIII 70-73): Aufidus 10 (Bari 1990) 147-162.

d62 **Eluère** Christiane, Les secrets de l'or antique. P 1990, Bibliothèque des Arts. 239 p.; 260 (color.) fig. 2-85047-036-8 [OIAc JJ90].

---

d63 *Carbonium:* *Richardson* W. F., Carbon, mercury and nitre: Prudentia 22,2 (1990) 4-15.

---

d64 *Cuprum*, COPPER: **Knapp** A. Bernard, Copper production and divine protection... Cyprus: SIMA pocket 42, 1986 ⇥ 2,9859: ᴿAntClas 59 (1990) 580s (R. *Laffineur*); JPrehR 2 (1988) 63-66 (B. C. *Dietrich*).

d65 *a*) *Lerberghe* Karel van, Copper and bronze in Ebla and in Mesopotamia; – *b*) *Zaccagnini* Carlo, Terms for copper and bronze at Ebla; – *c*) *Amadasi Guzzo* Maria Giulia, Remboursement et passage de propriété d'objets en métal précieux: ⇥ e333*, Wirtschaft/Ebla 1986/8, 253-5 / 359 / 121-4.

d65* **Lo Schiavo** F., *al.*, Metallographic and statistical analyses of copper ingots from Sardinia [where oxhide form was first found in 1857, then not until 1903 in Crete]: Soprintendenza Sassari, Quad. 17. Ozieri 1990, Torchietto. 227 p.; 125 fig. [text and captions also in Italian: Antiquity 65,420, D. *Ridgway*].

---

d66 *Lapis lazuli:* *a*) **Rosen** Lessie von, Lapis lazuli in [geological 1988] archaeological contexts: SIMA pocket [65;] 93. Partille [1988] 1990, Åström. [47 p.] 56 p. – *b*) *Pinnock* Frances, Observations on the trade of lapis lazuli in the IIIʳᵈ millennium B.C.: → e333*, Wirtschaft/Ebla 1986/9, 107-110.

d66* **Marmor,** MARBLE: ᴱ**Fant** J. C., Ancient marble quarrying and trade 1986/8 → 5,843: ᴿJRS 80 (1990) 229 (Hazel *Dodge*). → 806, *Herz* N.

d67 OBSIDIAN: *Francaviglia* Vincenzo M., Les gisements d'obsidienne hypercaline dans l'ancien monde; étude comparative: RArchéom 14 (1990) 43-63.

d68 **Pigmenta:** *Rouchon* O., *al.*, Pigments d'Égypte; étude physique de matières colorantes bleue, rouge, blanche, verte et jaune, provenant de Karnak: RArchéom 14 (1990) 87-97; 6 fig.

d70 **Vitrum,** GLASS: **Grose** David F., Early ancient glass; core-formed, rod-formed, and cast vessels and objects from the Late Bronze Age to the early Roman Empire, 1600 B.C. to A.D. 50: Toledo Mus. NY 1989, Hudson Hills. 453 p.; 713 fig. + 677 color.

d71 *Müller* P., *Schvoerer* M., Les verres anciens; la question de la databilité par thermoluminescence: Archaeometry 32 (1990) 205-210.

d72 Check list of recently published articles and book on glass: JGlass 32 (1990) 212-263.

d73 *Painter* Kenneth, *al.*, The Portland vase [most famous glass object in the world, Roman cameo discovered c. 1582]: JGlass 32 (1990) 14-188; 131 fig.

d74 *Stern* Eva M., [500 some] Glass vessels exhibited in the Bölge Museum, Adana: Belleten 53, 206ss (1989) 583-593; 19 color. phot. (595-605 ✆, ᵀ*Yağci* Emel E.).

d75 ZINC: ᴱ**Craddock** P. T., 2000 years of zinc and brass: OccP 50. L 1990, British Museum. vii-266 p. 0-86159-050-3 [OIAc Ja91].

T1.6   *Silex, os:*   '**Prehistory**' — **flint and bone industries.**

d76 *Arensburg* B., *al.*, Mousterian and Aurignacian human remains from Hayonim Cave, Israel: Paléorient 16,1 (1990) 107-9.

d77 **Campana** Douglas V., Natufian and protoneolithic bone tools; the manufacture and use of bone implements in the Zagros and the Levant: BAR-Int 494. Ox 1989. xii-156 p.

d78 **Clark** Grahame, Prehistory at Cambridge and beyond [Dorothy GARROD from Palestine, but mostly South-Pacific oriented]. C 1989, Univ. x-176 p. £19.50. 0-521-35031-X. – ᴿAntiquity 64 (1990) 165-7 (N. *Hammond*).

d79 *Clermont* Norman, *Smith* Philip E. L., Prehistoric, prehistory, pre-historian; ... who invented the terms?: Antiquity 64 (1990) 97-102 [G. d'EICHTHAL 1843].

d80 **Coinman** Nancy R., Refiguring the Levantine Upper Paleolithic; a comparative examination of lithic assemblages from the southern Levant: diss. Arizona State, ᴰ*Clark* G. 1990. 471 p. 91-01867. – DissA 51 (1990s) 2790-A.

d81 *Crabtree* Pam J., *Campana* Douglas V., A note on the first season of excavation at the Late Natufian site of Salibiya I [20 k N Jericho], Jordan valley: Paléorient 16,1 (1990) 111-3; 3 fig.

d82 **Daniel** G., *Renfrew* C., The idea of prehistory[2] [[1]1957-62]. E 1988, Univ. 221 p.; ill. £19.50; pa. £6. – [R]BInstArch 26 (1989) 252s (T. *Watkins*).

d83 *Dennell* Robin, Progressive gradualism, imperialism and academic fashion; Lower Palaeolithic archaeology in the 20th century: Antiquity 64 (1990) 549-558; 2 fig.

d84 *Edwards* Phillip C. & W. Ian, Heat treatment of chert in the Natufian period: MeditArch 3 (A-NZ 1990) 1-5; pl. 1-6.

d85 **Ehrenberg** Margaret, Women in prehistory. L 1989, British Museum. 192 p.; 52 fig. £10. 0-7141-1388-3. – [R]Antiquity 64 (1990) 424s (Jacquetta *Hawkes*).

d86 **Goring-Morris** A. N., At the edge; terminal pleistocene hunter-gatherers in the Negev and Sinai: BAR-Int 361, 1987 → 3,d313; 4,d823: [R]PEQ 121 (1989) 151s (A. *Betts*).

d87 [E]**Henry** Donald O., *Odell* George H., Alternative approaches to lithic analysis [American Anthropological Asn Tulsa, June 1987]. Wsh 1989, Am.Anthr.Asn. xii-259 p.; 72 fig. 0-913167-30-4. – [R]Antiquity 64 (1990) 429-431 (Diane *Holmes*; one on Jordan Wadi Hasa).

d88 **Henry** Donald O., From foraging to agriculture; the Levant at the end of the Ice Age. Ph 1989, Univ. Pennsylvania. xx-277 p. $39. – [R]AJA 94 (1990) 489s (J. *Zarins*).

d89 *Holmes* Diane L., The flint axes of Nagada, Egypt; analysis and assessment of a distinctive predynastic tool type: Paléorient 16,1 (1990) 1-21.

d90 **Holmes** Diane L., Predynastic lithic industries of Upper Egypt; a comparative study of the lithic traditions of Badari, Nagada and Hierakonpolis: C Mg Afr.Arch. 33 / BAR-Int 469. Ox 1989. xiii-496 p.; ill.

d91 *Lechevallier* M., *al.*, Une occupation khiamienne et sultanienne à Hatoula (Israël)?: → 808, Colloque F. HOURS: Paléorient 15,1 (1989) 1-10.

d92 *Luu Tran Tieu*, Les plus anciennes industries sur galet et les problèmes du 'berceau de l'humanité': AcArchH 42 (1990) 3-11.

d92* [E]**Mellars** Paul, *Stringer* Chris, The human revolution; behavioural and biological perspectives on the origin of modern humans. E 1989, Univ. xiv-800 p.; 114 fig. £65; pa. £20. 0-85224-596-3; -646-3 [Antiquity 65,412, C. *Gamble*].

d93 **Mithen** Steven J., Thoughtful foragers; a study of prehistoric [mesolithic] decision making: NewStArch. C 1990, Univ. xii-289 p.; 57 fig. £35. 0-521-35570-2. – [R]AntiqJ 70 (1990) 122s (A. *Whittle*).

d94 *Nishiaki* Yoshiro, Corner-thinned blades; a new obsidian tool type from a pottery neolithic mound in the Khabur Basin, Syria [Kaškašok 2]: BASOR 280 (1990) 5-14; 6 fig.

d95 **Ohel** Milla Y., Lithic analysis of Acheulean assemblages from the Avivim sites, Israel: BAR-Int 562. Ox 1990. vi-158 p. 0-86054-710-8 [OIAc Ap91,10].

d96 **Ohel** Milla Y., The Acheulean of the Yiron plateau, [N.] Israel: BAR-Int 307, 1986 → 3,d314*a: [R]PEQ 121 (1989) 151 (L. *Copeland*).

d97 *Perlès* Catherine, Les industries lithiques taillées de Franchthi (Argolide, Grèce); présentation générale et industries paléolithiques: Excav. 3. Bloomington 1987, Indiana Univ. x-355 p.; 61 fig.; 4 pl. – [R]AJA 94 (1990) 490s (C. *Edens*: excavations 1967-76); Antiquity 64 (1990) 868s (Denise de *Sonneville-Bordès*, Eng.).

d98 *Perlès* Catherine, L'outillage de pierre taillée en Grèce; approvisionnement et exploitation des matières premières: BCH 114 (1990) 1-42.

d99 **Proverbio** Edoardo, Archeoastronomia [...megalitica, *cromlech* orientati astronomicamente]. R 1989, Teti. 250 p. – ᴿRivArch 14 (1990) 129s (G. *Romano*).

d100 *Rollefson* Gary O., Neolithic chipped stone technology at 'Ain Ghazal, Jordan; the status of the PPNC phase: Paléorient 16,1 (1990) 119-124.

d101 **Roodenberg** J.J., Le mobilier en pierre de Bouqras 1986 ⇥ 2,9888; 5,b978: ᴿOLZ 85 (1990) 422-4 (E. *Lindemeyer*).

Smith Philip E.L., Paleolithic archaeology in Iran 1986 ⇥ e543*.

d102 *Vishnyatsky* L.B., ❻ The origin of homo sapiens; traditional conceptions and new facts: SovArch (1990,2) 99-114; Eng. 114.

d102* **Wenke** Robert J., Patterns in prehistory; humankind's first three million years³ [¹1980]. NY 1990, Oxford-UP. [x-] 614 p. 0-19-505522-5.

d103 **Whittle** Alasdair, Problems in Neolithic Archaeology: New Studies, 1988 ⇥ 4,d839*: ᴿHelinium 30 (1990) 129s (D. *Cahen*).

T1.7 **Technologia antiqua.**

d104 *Avizur* S., ❻ How mankind's first engine, the water-wheel, was invented and developed in Eretz-Israel [2d century B.C.E.; not documented]: ⇥ 348, Man and law 1986, 209-222.

d105 **Balthazar** Judith W., Copper and bronze working in Early through Middle Bronze Age Cyprus: SIMA pocket 84. Jonsered 1990, Åström. xxxv-459 p.; 91 fig.; 38 pl. 81-85058-46-7 [Antiquity 65,168, A. B. *Knapp*].

d106 *Beit-Arieh* Itzhaq, to E.A. KNAUF on mirror mining tools: Levant [20 (1988) 244] 22 (1990) 163.

d107 *Belli* Oktay, Untersuchungen zur Eisenmetallurgie in Hubuşkia: ⇥ 3, Mem. ALKIM U. 1986, 271-299; 7 fig.; 3 maps; IX pl.

d108 *Bruto* M. Luisa, *Vannicola* Cinzia, *a*) Strumenti e tecniche di lavorazione dei marmi antichi; – *b*) Ricostruzione e tipologia delle *crustae* parietali in età imperiale: ArchClasR 42 (1990) 287-324; 38 fig. / 325-376; 43 fig.

d110 **Cotterell** Brian, *Kamminga* Johan, Mechanics of pre-industrial technology; an introduction to the mechanics of ancient and traditional material culture. C 1990, Univ. xv-325 p. 0-521-34194-9 [OIAc Ja91].

d111 **Fintzi** Yehuda, ❻ Woodcraft in the biblical period in the light of comparative material from the Ancient Near East and rabbinic literature: diss. Tel Aviv 1985. 455 p.; 24 fig. [KirSef 62 (1988s) p. 187].

d112 *Goedicke* Hans, Two mining records from the Wadi Hammamat: RÉgp 41 (1990) 65-93.

d113 *Greene* Kevin, Perspectives on Roman technology [WHITE K., WIKANDER O., OLESON J.]: OxJArch 9 (1990) 209-219.

d114 *a*) *Heilmeyer* W. D., Arte antica e produzione artistica; lo studio delle officine nell'archeologia classica; – *b*) *De Angeli* Stefano, Mimesis e Techne: QuadUrb 57,1 (1988) 7-26 / 27-45.

d115 *Houston* George W., The state of the art; current work in the technology of ancient Rome [WHITE K.; OLESON J.]: ClasJ 85 (1989s) 63-80.

d116 **McNutt** Paula M., The forging of Israel; iron technology, symbolism, and tradition in ancient society [diss. Vanderbilt 1989 ⇥ 5,b998]: JStOT supp 108. Sheffield 1990, Academic. 307 p. 1-85075-263-X.

d117 **Mieroop** Marc Van de, Crafts in the early Isin period [90 tablets, diss. Yale 1983] 1987 ⇥ 3,d328; 5,d2: ᴿBO 47 (1990) 152-7 (B. *Lafont*, aussi sur Sumerian documents 1987); JAOS 110 (1990) 566s (M.A. *Powell*: good); RAss 84 (1990) 89s (D. *Charpin*).

d118 **Moscati** Sabatino, Techne; studi sull'artigianato fenicio: StPunica 6. R 1990, Univ. 91 p.; XXIX pl.

d118* *Muscarella* Oscar W., Luristan; *Falsone* Gioacchino, Phoenicia; *Leahy* M., Egypt; *Tubb* J. N., Sea-peoples, Palestine; *Mitchell* T. C., textes: → 4,729, **Curtis** John, Bronze-working centres of western Asia 1986/8, 33-44 / 227-250 / 297-309 / 251-270 / 271-284.

d119 **Neesen** Lutz, Demiurgoi und Artifices; Studien zur Stellung freier Handwerker in antiken Städten: EurHS 3/403. Fra 1989, Lang. 331 p. – ᴿMünstHand 9,1 (1990) 116-8 (L. *Wierschowski*).

d120 *Negbi* Ora, ❸ Metalworking in the central Jordan valley at the transition from the Bronze Age to the Iron Age: → 4, ꟼAMIRAN Ruth, ErIsr 21 (1990) 212-225; 4 fig. (map); Eng. 108*s.

d121 **Neumann** Hans, Handwerk in Mesopotamien [Diss. B 1980] 1987 → 3,d330 ... 5,d4: ᴿArOr 58 (1990) 92s (B. *Hruška*); Orientalia 59 (1990) 81s (M. A. *Powell*).

d122 **Nylén** Erik, *Lamm* Jan Peder, Stones, ships and symbols [1978, deutsch 1981]; *Lamm*, Catalogue and bibliography. Sto 1988, Gidlunds. 210 p.; ill. Sk 135. 91-7844-116-1. – ᴿHelinium 30 (1990) 140s (S. De *Laet*).

d123 ᴱ**Powell** Anton, Classical Sparta; techniques behind her success 1989 → 5,d6: ᴿClasR 40 (1990) 345-7 (A. J. *Spawforth*).

d124 **Pusch** Edgar B., Metallverarbeitende Werkstätten der frühen Ramessidenzeit in Qantir-Piramesse/Nord, ein Zwischenbericht: Ägypten und Levante 1 (W 1990) 75-113; Eng. franç. 113; 12 fig.; VII (color.) pl.; foldout plan.

d125 ᴱ**Rolley** C., Techniques/bronze 1988 → 5,548: ᴿRArchéol (1990) 173 (F. *Baratte*).

d126 **Saladino** Vincenzo, Arte e artigianato in Grecia dall'età del Bronzo alla fine dell'età classica: StTAnt 9, 1988 → 5,d9; Lit. 30.000: ᴿAntClas 59 (1990) 556s (D. *Viviers*: 'bon mais sans images ni 'diachronie').

d127 **Schneider** Helmuth, Das griechische Technikverständnis, von den Epen HOMERS bis zu den Anfängen der technologischen Fachliteratur: ImpulsF 54. Da 1989, Wiss. 313 p. DM 54, sb. 42 [Gymnasium 98, 186s, F. X. *Herrmann*]

d128 *Stanley* Phillip V., The value of ergasteria [factories] in Attica; a reexamination: MünstHand 9,1 (1990) 1-13; deutsch/franç. 119.

d129 *Vandeput* Lutgarde, Splitting techniques in quarries in the Eastern Mediterranean: AcArchLov 26s (1987s) 81-99 + 8 pl.

d130 *a) Waelkens* Marc, al., Quarries and the marble trade in antiquity; – *b) Kozelj* Tony, Extraction of blocks in antiquity; special methods of analysis: → 806, Marble 1988, 11-24 + 14 fig. / 31-39; 16 fig.

T1.8 Architectura.

d131 *Altekamp* Stefan, Griechische Architekturornamentik; Fachterminologie im Bauhandwerk?: ZPapEp 80 (1990) 33-61 + 3 fig.

d133 *Arnold* Felix, A study of Egyptian domestic buildings: VarAeg 5 (1989) 75-93; 6 fig.

d134 *Aupert* Pierre, L'évolution des appareils en Grèce à l'époque impériale: BCH 114 (1990) 593-637; 18 fig.

d135 *Baldwin* Barry, *a)* The date, identity, and career of VITRUVIUS: Latomus 49 (1990) 425-434; – *b)* The non-architectural side of Vitruvius ['some topical frivolities have been excised', but not the rest]: Prudentia 21,2 (1989) 4-12.

d136 **Balty** Jean C.,   La maison urbaine en Syrie: ➤ 481, Syrie II (1989) 407-422; fig. 114-123 [décor architectural rom. p. 457-476, *Dentzer-Feyde* Jacqueline (-490 byz., *al.*)].

d137 *Barletta* Barbara A.,   An 'Ionian Sea' style in archaic Doric architecture: AJA 94 (1990) 45-72; 19 fig.

d138 ᴱ**Barton** J. M.,   Roman public buildings: History 20.   Exeter 1989, Univ. xii-177 p.; 51 fig.; 40 pl.; 2 maps. £2.50. – ᴿGreeceR 37 (1990) 252 (B. A. *Sparkes*); Phoenix 44 (Toronto 1990) 400s (Joann *Freed*).

d139 **Besenval** [sic, vol. 3 index] Roland,   Technologie de la voûte dans l'Orient ancien: Synthèse 15, 1984 ➤ 65,a204: ᴿRArtLv 21 (1988) 164-6 (R. *Donceel*).

d140 **Burdejewitz** Mariusz,   The Aegean Sea Peoples and religious architecture in the Eastern Mediterranean at the close of the Late Bronze Age: BAR-Int 558.   Ox 1990. ix-196 p. 0-86054-705-1. – OIAc Oc90.

d141 ᴱ**Callebat** L., *Fleury* P., VITRUVE, De l'architecture X 1986 ➤ 2,9913 ... 5,d22: ᴿHelmantica 41 (1990) 394 (Rosa M. *Herrera*).

d142 *De Laine* Janet,   Structural experimentation; the lintel arch, corbel and tie in western Roman architecture [... Rome, Ostia]:   WorldArch 21 (1989s) 407-424; 9 fig.

d143 **Endruweit** Albrecht,   Städtlicher Wohnbau in Ägypten; klimagerechte Lehmarchitektur in Amarna: Diss. ᴰ*Jungel* F. [OIAc Ap89] Gö sans date.

d144 *Eyice* Semavi,   Quelques observations sur l'habitat byzantin, en Turquie: ➤ 3, Mem. ALKIM U., 1986, 513-530; XII pl.

d145 **Fagerström** Kåre,   Greek Iron Age architecture; developments through changing times: SIMA 81, 1988 ➤ 4,d868: ᴿAJA 94 (1990) 348-351 (W. D. E. *Coulson*: errors on every page); JPrehRel 3s (1989s) 70s (J. van *Leuven*).

d146 *Fantar* M'hammed,   La maison punique: in ᴱ**Garcin** Jean-Claude,   L'habitat traditionnel dans les pays musulmans autour de la Méditerranée; rencontre d'Aix-en-Provence (6-8 juin 1984) [1. L'héritage architectural, formes et fonctions; xiv-321 p.; 117 pl.] 2. Histoire et le milieu, p. 325-645: Études Urbaines 1. Cairo 1988, IFAO. 2-7247-006 [1-9] 2-7 [OIAc F91,8, titres sans pp.].

d147 *Fischer* Moshe,   Figured capitals in Roman Palestine; marble imports and local stone; some aspects of 'imperial' and 'provincial' art: PEQ 121 (1989) 112-132; 20 fig.

d148 *Frey* Louis,   Médiétés et approximation chez VITRUVE: RArchéol (1990) 285-330; 27 fig.

d149 **Ganschow** Thomas,   Untersuchungen zur Baugeschichte in Herculaneum: Antiquitas 3/30.   Bonn 1989, Habelt. 345 p.; 33 fig.; 23 pl.

d150 *Gasché* H., Mauer, archäologisch (mur, franç.) [*Edzard* D., philologisch]: ➤ 853*, RLA 7,7s (1990) 590-5 [589s]; 596-601, in Anatolien (franç.) *Aurenche* O.

d151 **Grandjean** Yves,   Recherches sur l'habitat thasien à l'époque grecque: Études thasiennes 12. Athènes/P 1988, Éc. Française/de Boccard. xii-354 p.; p. 355-508, 120 pl., 12 foldout plans. – ᴿRArchéol (1990) 177-180 (Marie-Françoise *Billot*).

d152 **Günther** Hubertus,   Das Studium der antiken Architektur in den Zeichnungen der Hochrenaissance: RömFHertziana 14. Tü 1988, Wasmuth. 402 p. 519 fig.; 124 pl. [Gnomon 63, 157-166, G. *Brands*].

d153 ᴱ**Hägg** Robin, *Konsola* Dora,   Early Helladic architecture and urbanization 1985/6 ➤ 3,817 ... 5,d31: ᴿAntClas 59 (1990) 567-9 (R. *Laffineur*); ArchWroc 40 (1989) 169s (B. *Rutkowski* ☯).

d154 *Hannestad* Lise, *Potts* Daniel, Temple architecture in the Seleucid Kingdom: → 325*, *Bilde*/Seleucid 1990, 91-123; 24 fig.

d155 **Hersey** George, The lost meaning of classical architecture [survival of the column-capitals]; speculations on ornament from VITRUVIUS to Venturi. CM 1988, MIT. xii-204 p.; 83 fig. £9. – ᴿClasR 40 (1990) 186s (G. B. *Waywell*).

d156 **Herzog** Zeev, Das Stadtor... 1986 → 2,9923... 5,d34: ᴿOLZ 82 (1991) 53 (C. *Tietze*); TR 86 (1990) 106-110 (R. *Wenning*).

d157 **Hissel** Gerhard, Späthelladische Hausarchitektur; Studien zur Architekturgeschichte des griechischen Festlandes in der späten Bronzezeit. Mainz 1990, von Zabern. ix-269 p.

d158 *Klein* Jacob, Building and dedication hymns in Sumerian literature: AcSum 11 (1989) 27-63; 64-66, facsimiles; 67, photos.

d159 *Kleiss* Wolfram, Kastenmauern in der frühen iranischen Architektur: → 138, ᶠPERROT J., Iran 1990, 165-172; 4 fig.

d160 *a*) *Kozlowski* Stefan K., *Kempisty* Andrzej, Architecture of the pre-pottery neolithic settlement in Nemrik (55 k NW Mosul], Iraq; – *b*) *Schirmer* Wulf, Some aspects of building at the 'aceramic-neolithic' settlement at Çayönü Tepesi: WorldArch 21 (1989s) 348-362; 6 fig. / 363-387; 14 fig.

d161 *Kroes* Richard, Woodwork in the foundations of stone-built Roman bridges: Babesch 65 (1990) 97-105; 3 fig.

d162 **Kubba** Shamil A. A., Mesopotamian architecture and town planning from the Mesolithic to the end of the Protohistoric period ca. 10.000 - 3,500 B.C.; BAR-Int 367. Ox 1987. iv-236 p.; vol. of 307 pl. £30 each. 0-86054-476-1. – ᴿBO 47 (1990) 211s (O. *Aurenche*).

d163 *Leick* Gwendolyn, A dictionary of Ancient Near Eastern architecture. L 1988, Routledge. xix-261 p.; 68 fig.; 103 pl.; 5 maps. £35. 0-415- 00240-0. – ᴿAntiquity 64 (1990) 158-161 (I. M. E. *Shaw*: H. LOYN's Middle Ages better); BInstArch 26 (1989) 282s (H. *Crawford*); ClasW 84 (1990s) 247s (J. M. *Russell*: unreliable).

d164 ᴱ**Levy** E., Le système palatial en Orient, en Grèce et à Rome 1985/7 → 3,825... 5,d46: ᴿAnzAltW 43 (1990) 193-6 (P. W. *Haider*: völlig unverständlich ist das Fehlen aller 14 Palastanlagen Palästinas).

d165 ᴱ**Macready** Sarah, *Thompson* F. H., Roman architecture in the Greek world 1985/7 → 4,454; 5,d51: ᴿBonnJbb 190 (1990) 724-8 (W. K. *Kovacsovics*); Helinium 29 (1989) 262s (G. *Raepsaet*).

d166 *Margueron* Jean, La Salle aux Piliers du Palais de Mari de l'époque agadéenne: MARI 6 (1990) 385-399; 12 fig.

d167 **Martin** Roland, Architecture et urbanisme 1987 → 5,d54: ᴿGymnasium 97 (1990) 281 (Berthild *Goscel-Raeck*); JHS 110 (1990) 265s (J. *Carter*).

d168 *Medeksza* Stanisław, Remarks on structural engineering in Nubia, based upon a study of Christian houses 'A' and 'B' in Old Dongola: Nubica 1s (1990) 77-94; 15 fig.

d169 *Müller-Karpe* Michael, Der Guss in der verlorenen Sandform in Mesopotamien: MDOG 122 (1990) 173-192; 23 fig.

d170 **Müller-Wiener** Wolfram, Griechisches Bauwesen in der Antike 1988 → 5,d60: ᴿHZ 250 (1990) 123s (U. *Schädler*).

d171 *Netzer* Ehud, Architecture in Palestine prior to and during the days of Herod the Great: → 791*, KlasArch 13 (1988/90) 37-50; 15 fig.

d172 *a*) *Oates* David, Innovations in mud-brick; decorative and structural techniques in ancient Mesopotamia; – *b*) *Smith* Philip E. L., Architectural innovation and experimentation at Ganj Dareh, Iran: WorldArch 21 (1989s) 388-406; 6 fig. / 323-335; 6 fig.

d173 **Patrich** J., ❻ *Mi-beit ha-sᵉ'ar lᵉbeit ha-even*, From hair tent to stone house. J 1984, Ministry of Defense. 334 p.; 8 fig.; 37 pl. – ᴿQadmoniot 23,1s (1990) 65s (A. *Kempinski* ❻).

d174 **Pesando** Fabrizio, *Oikos* e *ktesis*, la casa greca in età classica 1987 → 4,d894; 5,d64: ᴿPhoenix 44 (Toronto 1990) 203s (Helena *Fracchia*); RPg 63 (1989) 367s (Marie-C. *Hellmann*).

d175 **Pietilä Castrén** Leena, Magnificentia publica; the victory monuments of the Roman generals in the era of the Punic wars. Helsinki 1987, Soc. Sc. Fenn. 178 p. – ᴿAevum 64 (1990) 132s (N. *Berti*).

d176 **Porta** Gabriella, L'architettura egizia delle origini in legno e materiali leggeri. Mi 1989, Cisalpino. 162 p.; 68 pl. Lit. 60.000. 88-205-0617-3 [BO 47,262].

d177 *Potts* D. T., Notes on some horned buildings in Iran, Mesopotamia and Arabia: RAss [81 (1987) 99-104, *Amiet* P.] 84 (1990) 33-40; 4 fig.; franç. 40.

d178 *Raven* Maarten J., A transom-window from Tuna el-Gebel: OMRO 69 (1989) 51-63; phot. 64.

Rette C., Lydian masonry ᴰ1990 → e907.

d179 *Richardson* P., Religion, architecture and ethics; some first century case studies: HorBT 10,2 (Pittsburgh 1988) 19-49 [< NTAbs 34,79].

d180 *a) Robins* Gay, The 14 to 11 proportion in Egyptian architecture; – *b) Legon* J. A. R., The 14:11 proportion at Meydum: DiscEg 16 (1990) 75-80 / 17 (1990) 15-22.

d181 **Romano** Elisa, La capanna e il tempio; VITRUVIO o dell'Architettura 1987 → 4,d900; 5,d67; Lit. 25.000: ᴿGnomon 62 (1990) 7-11 (L. *Callebat*); RFgIC 118 (1990) 352-5 (E. *Narducci*).

d182 **Ronig** Franz J., Architektur und Liturgie; wie man in frühchristlicher Zeit liturgisch umgestaltete — dargestellt an einigen Beispielen: TrierTZ 98 (1989) 124-146; 19 fig.

d183 *Sear* Frank B., VITRUVIUS and Roman theater design: AJA 94 (1990) 249-258; 18 fig.

d184 **Sheckler** Allyson E., Roman honorary arches in Iberia: diss. Boston Univ., ᴰKleiner F. 399 p. 91-05384. – DissA 51 (1990s) 3119-A.

De **Theatro**: → d300, *Boatwright* M.; d310, *Frézouls* E.; d316, *Golvin* J.; d320, *Hülsemann* M.

d185 **Thornton** M. K. & R. L., Julio-Claudian building programs; a quantitative study in political management. Wauconda IL 1989, Bolchazy-Carducci. xvii-156 p.; 25 fig. – ᴿAJA 94 (1990) 515 (J. C. *Anderson*: random-to-incomprehensible use of inadequate data; ClasW 84 (1990s) 246 (H. V. *Benden*: interesting approach, lacks coherence); MünstHand 9,2 (1990) 118s (C. *Schäfer*).

d186 *Vallet* Régis, Les habitations à salles hypostyles des débuts de l'époque d'Obeid: CRAI (1990) 867-874; 4 fig.

d187 *Vann* R. Lindley, Pre-cast gypsum as a building material: → 89, ᶠJASHEMSKI W. (1989) 241-7 + 12 fig.

d188 *Wallace-Hadrill* Andrew, Roman arches and Greek honours; the language of power at Rome: PrPgSoc 36 (1990) 143-181.

d189 **White** L. Michael, Building God's house in the Roman world; architectural adaptation among pagans, Jews, and Christians: ASOR library. Baltimore 1990, Johns Hopkins Univ. xvii-211 p.; 27 fig. $27.50 [BASOR 280, 92 adv.]. 0-8018-3906-8.

d190 **Wright** G. R. H., Ancient building in South Syria and Palestine: HbOr 1985 ➤ 1,b709 ... 5,d73: ᴿRArtLv 21 (1988) 170s (R. *Donceel*).

T1.9 *Supellex;* **furniture; objects of daily life.**

d191 *Ammerman* Albert J., Towards the study of neolithic households: ➤ 818*, Mem. PUGLISI S. 1988s, 73-82; ital. 82.

d192 **Bimson** John, [*Blaiklock* F. M.] The compact handbook of Old (➤ 5,d74) [New] Testament life. Minneapolis 1988/9, Bethany. 172 p. [185 p.] $6 each, pa. – ᴿBA 53 (1990) 179s (R. *Adams*).

ᴱ**Donadoni** Sergio, L'uomo egiziano 1990 ➤ 483; **Donadoni Roveri** Anna Maria, Egyptian daily life 1987 ➤ e567.

d193 **Gubel** E., Phoenician furniture 1987 ➤ 4,d915; 5,d77: ᴿBL (1990) 31s (A. R. *Millard*); OrLovPer 20 (1989) 261s (E. *Lipiński*).

d194 **Hamman** Adalbert G., La vita quotidiana nell'Africa di s. AGOSTINO 1989 ➤ 5,d78: ᴿCC 141 (1990,3) 310s (G. *Cremascoli*).

d195 **Jahn** Birgit, Bronzezeitliches Sitzmobiliar der griechischen Inseln und des griechischen Festlandes: Diss. Münster 1988; EurHS 38/31. Fra 1990, Lang. xiii-539 p.

d196 **Janssen** Rosalind M. & Jac J., Growing up in ancient Egypt. L 1990, Rubicon. xii-177 p. 0-948695-15-3 [OIAc Ja91].

d197 *Kessler* Dieter, Zur Bedeutung der Szenen des täglichen Lebens in den Privatgräbern (II); Schreiber und Schreiberstatue in den Gräbern des AR: ZägSpr 117 (1990) 21-43; 7 fig.

d198 *Köpstein* Silvia, Altägyptische Bezeichnungen für Tische, Sitz- und Liegemöbel vom Alten bis zum Neuen Reich: AltOrF 16 (1989) 2-35; 2 fig.

d199 **Mackie** George M., Bible manners and customs [1898]. Old Tappan NJ c. 1984, Revell. 175 p. [KirSef 62 (1988s) p. 40].

d200 **Matthews** Victor H., Manners and customs in the Bible 1988 ➤ 5,d83: ᴿInterpretation 44 (1990) 316s (J. W. *Aageson*).

Mossé Claude, La vita quotidiana della donna nella Grecia antica 1983/7 ➤ b606*.

d201 **Robert** Jean-Noël, Les modes à Rome. P 1988, BLettres. 324 p.; 12 fig. – ᴿCaesarodunum 22-CR (1989) 52 [R. *Chevallier*].

d202 **Romano** James F., Daily life of the ancient Egyptians. Pittsburgh 1990, Carnegie Museum. iv-52 p.; 28 fig. £5 pa. 0-911239-18-9 [Antiquity 64,675].

d203 *Schmitz* Bettina, Tochter – Ehefrau – Mutter; Frauenalltag im alten Ägypten: ➤ 768, Waren sie nur schön? 1985/9, 69-115; fig. 16-43.

d204 **Sissa** Giulia, *Detienne* Marcel, La vie quotidienne des dieux grecs. P 1989, Hachette. 301 p. 12 pl.; 2 maps. F 118. 2-01-01781-0. – ᴿÉTRel 65 (1990) 106 (Danielle *Ellul*); Kernos 3 (1990) 389s (Vinciane *Pirenne-Delforge* puts Detienne first).

d205 **Sissa** Giulia, *Detienne* Marcel, Vita quotidiana degli dei greci, ᵀ*Gasparri* Claudia. Bari 1989, Laterza. 283 p.; ill. Lit. 30.000. – ᴿLetture 45 (1990) 280s (Carla *Castelli*).

d207 **Thompson** J. A., Handbook of life in Bible times. DG 1986, Inter-Varsity. 384 p. $35. – ᴿCriswT 3 (1989) 385s (E. R. *Clendenen*).

T2.1 *Res militaris;* **weapons, army activities.**

d208 **Anlagan** Çetin, *Bilgi* Önder, ❶ (also) Weapons of the protohistoric age. İstanbul 1989, Sadberk Hanim Museum. 119 p. [OIAc F91,1].

d209 **Blois** L. de, The Roman army and politics 1987 ➤ 5,d85: ᴿRBgPg 68 (1990) 205 (J. P. *Callu*).

d210 *Cahn* David, Waffen und Zaumzeug. Basel 1989, Antikenmuseum / S. Ludwig. 107 p.; 52 fig.

d211 *Ciałowicz* Krzysztof M., L'étude des armes égyptiennes dans les époques prédynastique et archaïque; la typologie des pointes de flèches et des javelots: FolOr 27 (1990) 63-77; 78s = 11 fig.

d212 **Creveld** Martin van, Technology and war from 2000 B.C. to the present. NY 1989, Free Press. 352 p. $23. – ᴿJIntdis 20 (1989s) 641-3 (G. *Parker*).

d213 **Davies** R. W., Service in the Roman army, ᴱ*Maxfield* Valerie A. 1989 ➤ 5,252: ᴿClasR 40 (1990) 183 (L. *Keppie*).

d214 **Davison** David P., The barracks of the Roman army from the 1st to 3d centuries A.D. ...: BAR-Int 472. Ox 1989. xiv-562 p.; ill.

d215 *Devijver* Herbert, *Wonterghem* Frank Van, The funerary monuments of equestrian officers of the late republic and early empire in Italy (50 B.C.-100 A.D.): AncSoc 21 (1990) 59-98 + 37 fig.

d216 **Dintsis** Petros, Hellenistische Helme: Arch 43. R 1986, Bretschneider. xxii-394 p.; 83 pl.; 34 foldouts; 22 maps. 88-85007-71-6. – ᴿAntClas 59 (1990) 596s (R. *Laffineur*).

d217 *Driel-Murray* C. van, New light on old tents: Journal of Roman Military Equipment Studies 1 (Newcastle 1990) 109-136; 10 fig.

d218 **Dupuy** R. E., The encyclopedia of military history from 3500 B.C. to the present ²ʳᵉᵛ. NY 1986, Harper & R. xxi-1524 p.; ill.; maps. $40. – ᴿRBgPg 68 (1990) 517 (L. De *Vos*, vlaams).

d219 **Fortenberry** Cheryl D., Elements of Mycenaean warfare: diss. Cincinnati 1990, ᴰ*Walberg* Gisela. 603 p. 90-32620. – DissA 51 (1990s) 2066-A.

d220 **Foss** Clive, *Winfield* David, Byzantine fortifications 1986 ➤ 5,d91: ᴿSpeculum 65 (1990) 663-5 (R. P. *Lindner*).

d221 **Franzoni** C., Habitus atque habitudo militis; monumenti funerari: St. Archeol. 45, 1987 ➤ 5,d93: ᴿAevum 64 (1990) 121-3 (M. Vittoria *Antico Gallina*).

d222 **Gerolymatos** André, Espionage and treason 1986 ➤ 3,d390; 4,d938: ᴿAntClas 59 (1990) 479-481 (H. *Verdin*).

d223 *Haas* Volkert, Kompositbogen und Bogenschiessen als Wettkampf im Alten Orient: Nikephoros 2 (1989) 27-41; fig. 1s (p. 313).

d224 ᴱ**Hackett** John, Warfare in the ancient world. L 1989, Sidgwick & J. 256 p. 0-283-99591-2 [OIAc Ja91].

d225 **Hanson** Victor D., The western way of war; infantry battle in classical Greece. L/NY 1989, Hodder & S./Knopf. xxiv-244 p. $20. – ᴿJIntdis 21 (1990s) 122-5 (E. L. *Wheeler*).

d226 ᴱ**Ireland** Robert J., Sextus Iulius FRONTINUS, Strategemata. Lp 1990, Teubner. xxxiv-129 p. 3-322-00746-4.

d227 *Kayser* F., Les 'statores' [de l'armée romaine] en Égypte: BIFAO 90 (1990) 241-6.

d228 **Kolias** T. G., Byzantinische Waffen 1988 ➤ 5,d95*: ᴿAevum 64 (1990) 315-7 (C. M. *Mazzucchi*); Ellinika 40 (1989) 175s (G. T. *Dennis*, Eng.).

d229 *Kronholm* T., qǽšæt, 'Bogen': ➤ 859, TWAT 7,1s (1990) 218-225.

d230 *a*) *Leriche* Pierre, Les fortifications grecques et romaines en Syrie; – *b*) Ulbert Thilo, Villes et fortifications de l'Euphrate à l'époque paléo-chrétienne: ➤ 481, Syrie II (1989) 267-282; fig. 43-52.

d232 **Müller** Hans W., Der 'Armreif' des Königs Ahmose und der Handgelenkschutz des Bogenschützen im Alten Ägypten und Vorderasien:

DAI-K Sonderschrift 25, 1989 ➤ 5,d101; x-49 p.; 21 fig.; 6 pl. DM 60: ᴿNikephoros 2 (1989) 257s (W. *Decker*).

d233 *Müller* Hans W., Zwei weitere Sichelschwerter: ➤ 16, ᶠBECKERATH J. v. 1990, 215-222; pl. 13.

d234 *a) Noble* Duncan, Assyrian chariotry and cavalry; – *b) Fales* Frederick M., Grain reserves, daily rations, and the size of the Assyrian army; – *c) Postgate* J. Nicholas, The Assyrian Porsche? [chariot (-troops)]: SAAB 4,1 (1990) 61-68 / 23-34 / 35-38.

d235 *Olbrycht* Marcus, ❷ De Parthorum arte oppida muniendi: Meander 45 (1990) 273-8.

d236 *Scurlock* Jo Anne, Assyrian battering rams revisited [Neo-Assyrian palace reliefs]: SAAB 3 (1989) 129-131; 1 fig.

d237 *Smith* Frederick W., The fighting unit; an essay in structural military history: AntClas 59 (1990) 149-165.

d238 *Speidel* M. P., Work to be done on the organisation of the Roman army: BInstArch 26 (L 1989) 99-106.

d239 **Stillman** Nigel, *Tallis* Nigel, Armies of the ancient Near East, 3000 B.C. to 539 B.C.; organisation, tactics, dress and equipment. Worthing 1984, auct. 208 p.; 210 fig.

d240 *Taracha* Piotr, Dating the cheek-piece of a helmet from Ialysos, Rhodes: ArchWroc 40 (1989) 9-13; 5 fig.

d241 *a) Watkins* Trevor, The beginnings of warfare [... Megiddo, Qadesh]; – *b) Wiseman* D. J., The Assyrians; – *c) Sekunda* Nick, The Persians; – *d) Devine* Albert, Alexander the Great; – *e) Connolly* Peter, The Roman army in the age of POLYBIUS: ➤ 486,Warfare 1989, 15-35 / 36-53 / 82-103 / 104-129 / (136-) 149-168; (color) ill.

d242 **Wheeler** Everett L., Stratagem and the vocabulary of military trickery: Mnemosyne supp. 108, 1988 ➤ 5,d108; ƒ48. 90-04-08831-8: ᴿAntClas 59 (1990) 416s (J. *Labarbe*); ClasR 40 (1990) 403s (C. *Tuplin*).

d243 *Wyatt* N., A further weapon for Baal? [Ug. *qrdm* 'fenestrated axe', the *second* weapon held by 'Baal au Foudre']: UF 22 (1990) 459-465.

T2.2. *Vehicula,* transportation.

d244 **Bugh** Glenn R., The horsemen of Athens 1988 ➤ 5,d110: ᴿAmHR 95 (1990) 463s (J. *Ober*); AnÉCS 45 (1990) 890s (Pauline *Schmitt Pantel*); AntClas 59 (1990) 483-5 (D. *Viviers*); ClasR 40 (1990) 98-100 (J. F. *Lazenby*); Gnomon 62 (1990) 420-423 (I. G. *Spence*: 'cavalry'; diss. Maryland 1979).

d245 **Bulliet** Richard W., The camel and the wheel. NY 1990, Columbia Univ. xxiii 327 p.; 125 fig. $18 [OLZ 86, 263, B. *Brentjes*].

d246 **Liebowitz** Harold, Terra-cotta figurines and model vehicles: Ch. Or. Inst. Selenkahiye Excav.: BiblMesop 22, 1988 ➤ 5,d114: ᴿMesopT 25 (1990) 245-7 (A. *Invernizzi*).

d247 **Littauer** M. A., *Crouwel* J. H., Chariots and related equipment from the tomb of Tut'ankhamun 1985 ➤ 1,b764... 5,d115: ᴿDiscEg 18 (1990) 97-99 (Alessandra *Nibbi*); JEA 76 (1990) 232-6; 3 fig. (C. N. *Reeves*: stimulating); OLZ 85 (1990) 530-2 (M. *Eaton-Krauss*, Eng.).

d248 *Littauer* M. A., *Crouwel* J. H., A terracotta wagon model from Syria in Oxford: Levant 22 (1990) 160-162; 4 fig.

d249 *a) Olivová* Vera, Chariot racing in the ancient world; – *b) Ebert* Joachim, Neues zum Hippodrom und zu den hippischen Konkurrenzen in Olympia: Nikephoros 2 (1989) 65-88; fig. 4-11 / 89-107; fig. 12.

d250 *Ritter* Thomas, *ḏr.wt*, der Speichenkranz des Wagenrades: ZägSpr 117 (1990) 60-62.

d251 *Sorokin* Sergey, Horse-drawn vehicles of the Eurasian forest-steppe in pre-'Centaurian' times: IrAnt 25 (1990) 97-147; 15 fig.

d252 *Strommenger* Eva, Planwagen aus dem mittleren Euphrattal: → 28, ᶠBOUNNI A. 1990, 297-301 + pl. 98-102.

d253 *Toporov* V. N., The Thracian horseman in an Indo-European perspective: Orpheus-Thrac 1 (1990) 46-63.

T2.3 Nautica.

d254 *Amigues* Suzanne, Termes techniques de construction navale dans THÉO-PHRASTE, HP, V, 7,1-3: RArchéol (1990) 85-96.

d255 *Andiñach* Pablo, Una antigua barca del mar de Galilea: RBibArg 52,39 (1990) 179-184; 3 fig. p. 178.

d256 *Arnold* Béat, Some objections to the link between Gallo-Roman boats and the Roman foot (*pes monetalis*) [WEERD M. de]: IntJNaut 19 (1990) 273-7.

d257 *Bacilieri* Ottorino, *Guerreschi* Antonio, Anatomia di un naufragio [Comacchio Valle Ponti]: ArchViva 9,12 (1990) 10-23; ill.

d258 *Cannuyer* Christian, Encore le naufrage du Naufragé: BSocÉg 14 (Genève 1990) 15₋21.

d259 **Casson** Lionel L., The Periplus Maris Erythraei. Princeton 1989, Univ. 326 p. $50. 0-691-04060-5. – ᴿBSO 53 (1990) 126s (G. S. P. *Freeman-Grenville*); JRAS (1990) 127-131 (A. F. L. *Beeston*).

d260 *Casson* Lionel, Documentary evidence for Graeco-Egyptian shipbuilding: BASP 27 (1990) 15-19.

d261 *Dietrich* M., *Loretz* O., Schiffshandel und Schiffsmiete zwischen Byblos und Ugarit (KTU 4,338: 10-18): UF 22 (1990) 89-96.

d262 *Figueira* Thomas J., Aigina and the naval strategy of the late fifth and early fourth centuries: RheinMus 133 (1990) 15-52.

d262* *Frost* Frank J., *Hadjidaki* Elpida, Excavations at the harbor of Phalasarna in Crete; the 1988 season: Hesperia 59 (1990) 513-527; 11 fig.; pl. 79-82.

d263 **Garland** Robert, The Piraeus 1987 → 4,d973: ᴿGnomon 62 (1990) 706-710 (K. v. *Eickstedt*); Phoenix 44,1 (Toronto 1990) 102s (M. H. *Jameson*).

d263* a) *Gibbins* David, Analytical approaches in maritime archaeology; a Mediterranean perspective; – b) *Parker* A. J., Classical antiquity; the maritime dimension: Antiquity 64 (1990) 335-346; 9 fig. / 376-389; 3 fig.

d264 *Górski* Hubert J., La barque d'Amon dans la décoration du temple de Thoutmosis III à Deir el-Bahari: MiDAI-K 46 (1990) 99-112; 4 fig.; pl. 29-31.

d265 *Haldane* C., Egyptian hulls and the evidence for caulking: IntJNaut 19 (1990) 135s.

d266 *Hauben* Hans, Triérarques et triérarchie dans la marine des Ptolémées: AncSoc 21 (1990) 119-139.

Hirschfeld N., *Fitzgerald* M., The ship of St. Paul (Acts 27,6) 1990 → 5609.

d267 **Johnston** P. Forsythe, Ship and boat models in ancient Greece... → 1,b797; 3,d439: Annapolis 1985, Naval Institute. 216 p.; ill. $29. 0-87021-628-7. – ᴿIntJNaut 19 (1990) 171s (Honor *Frost*).

d268 **Jones** Dilwyn, A glossary of ancient Egyptian nautical titles and terms 1988 → 4,d142*: ᴿBO 47 (1990) 628-630 (H. De *Meulenaere*); IntJNaut 19 (1990) 177.

d269 **Jones** Dilwyn,   Model boats from the tomb of Tut'ankhamūn: T. Tomb series 9.   Ox 1990, Griffith Inst.   xii-67 p.; XXXVIII pl.   0-900416-49-1.

d270 *Kapitän* Gerhard,   Ancient two-armed stone-stocked wooden anchors — Chinese and Greek: IntJNaut 19 (1990) 243-5; 2 fig.

d271 *Kazianes* Demetrios, *al.*,   Three amphora wrecks from the Greek world: IntJNaut 19 (1990) 225-232.

d271* *Lavier* Marie-Christine,   Les formes d'écriture de la barque *nšmt*: ➤ 70*, Mém. HARI R., BSocÉg 13 (1989) 89-101; 4 pl.

d272 **Linder** Elisha,   The maritime texts of Ugarit; a study in Late Bronze Age shipping: diss. Brandeis, ᴰ*Gordon* C.   Boston 1970.   ii-238 p. [OIAc Oc90].

d273 **Meijer** Fik,   A history of seafaring in the classical world 1986 ➤ 4,d990; 5,d148:   ᴿMeditHR 4 (1989) 375s (P. F. *Johnson*).

d274 ᴱ**Miège** Jean-Louis,   Navigation et migrations en Méditerranée de la préhistoire à nos jours.   P 1990, CNRS.   422 p.   2-222-04296-8 [OIAc Oc90].

d275 *Mills* J. S., *White* R.,   The identity of the resins from the Late Bronze Age shipwreck at Ulu Burun (Kaş): Archaeometry 31 (1989) 37-44.

d276 **Morrison** John S., *Coates* John F.,   Die athenische Triere; Geschichte und Rekonstruktion eines Kriegsschiffs der griechischen Antike [1986 ➤ 2,a18], ᵀ*Felten* W.; KuGAW 44.   Mainz 1990, von Zabern. 380 p.; ill.

d277 *Nagel* Peter,   Seefahrt, Schiff und Hafen im manichäischen Psalmenbuch; Aufnahme und Wandlungen einer christlichen Bildgruppe im Manichäismus: ➤ 8*, ASSFALG J. 1990, 245-253.

d278 **Patch** Diana C., *Haldane* Cheryl W.,   The Pharaoh's boat at the Carnegie.   Pittsburgh 1990, Carnegie Museum.   iv-49 p.; 24 fig.   £5 pa.   0-911239-22-7 [Antiquity 64,675].

d279 **Pearson** Colin,   Conservation of marine archaeological objects.   L 1987, Butterworths.   iv-297 p.; ill.   £55.   0-408-10668-9. – ᴿAntiquity 64 (1990) 438s (Wendy *Robinson*).

d280 *Pekáry* L. & T.,   Artemon und Dolon; Vorarbeiten zum Corpus der hellenistisch-römischen Schiffdarstellungen: AcArchH 41 (1989) 477-487; 11 fig.

d281 *Raban* Avner,   Medieval anchors from the Red Sea: IntJNaut 19 (1990) 299-306; 6 fig.

d281* *Riville* Frédérique,   Apoculamus nos (Pétrone 62,3); une métaphore nautique en latin vulgaire impérial; contribution à l'étude des verbes signifiant 'partir' en latin: RPg 63 (1989) 85-99.

d282 *Rosen* Ralph M.,   Poetry and sailing in HESIOD's Works and Days: ClasAnt 9 (1990) 99-113.

d283 *Sidebotham* Steven E.,   Ship graffiti from Mons Porphyrites [Gebel Dukhan]:   BIFAO 90 (1990) 339-345; 4 fig.; map; photo.

d284 **Sperber** Daniel,   Nautica talmudica 1986 ➤ 4,e1*; 5,d162:   ᴿBSO 52 (1989) 336s (J. *Wansbrough*: meagre harvest).

d285 **Starr** Chester G.,   The influence of sea power on ancient history 1989 ➤ 5,d163:   ᴿAmHR 95 (1990) 1503 (L. *Casson*); ClasR 40 (1990) 506s (P. de *Souza*: against U.S. naval officer A. T. Mahan 1890 & 1918; disappointing).

d286 *Stone* G. R.,   *a)* A bronze dagger and the Ulu Burun shipwreck [parallels found by PETRIE, now in Jerusalem and Australia]: BurHist 26 (1990) 104-121 [< OTAbs 14,153]; – *b)* The Galilee boat; a fishing vessel of NT times: BurHist 25,2 (Melbourne 1989) 46-54 [< NTAbs 34,80].

d287 *a) Vinson* Steve, Ships in the ancient Mediterranean; – *b) Bass* George F., Nautical archaeology and biblical archaeology; – *c) Haldane* Douglas, Anchors of antiquity; – *d) Peachey* Claire, Model building in nautical archaeology; the Kinneret boat: BA 53 (1990) 13-18 / 4-10 / 19-24 / 46-53; ill.

d288 **Wachsmann** Shelley, The excavations of an ancient [65 C.E.] boat in the Sea of Galilee (Lake Kinneret): Atiqot-Eng. 19. J 1990, Israel Antiquities Authority. 138 p.; ill.; foldout.

d289 *Wachsmann* Shelley, ❶ *a)* On sea-going vessels depicted in Egyptian art: Qadmoniot 23,1s (1990) 2-20; 36 fig. + Eng. cover; – *b)* Una barca nel mare di Galilea: ArchViva 9,11 (1990) 10-17; ill.

d290 *a) Westendorf* Wolfhart, Die Insel des Schiffbrüchigen — keine Halbinsel!; – *b) Vandersleyen* Claude, En relisant le Naufragé: ➤ 114, ᶠLICHTHEIM M. 1990, (II) 1056-1064 / 1019-1024.

d291 *Williams-Thorpe* O., *Thorpe* R.S., Millstone provenancing used in tracing the route of a fourth-century BC Greek merchant ship [wrecked at Mallorca]: Archaeometry 32 (1990) 115-137.

d292 *Yalouris* N., The shipwreck of Antikythera; new evidence of its date after supplementary investigation [silver coins 85-67 BC, bronze 70-60]: ➤ 30, ᶠCAMBITOGLOU A. *Eumousia* 1990, 135s; pl. 31.

T2.4   *Athletica,* **sport, games.**

d293 *Aiger* Heribert, Zur gesellschaftlichen Stellung von Henkern, Gladiatoren und Berufsathleten: ➤ 773*, Randgruppen 201-220 [AnPg 59, 12674].

d294 *Alföldy* G., Ein Faustkampf um Faustinianus?: ZPapEp 80 (1990) 185-8.

d295 ᴱ**Angeli Bernardini** Paola, Lo sport in Grecia 1988 ➤ 5,d166: ᴿRFgIC 118 (1990) 203-6 (M. *Vetta*).

d296 **Bell** David J., A study of the *kelēs* event in ancient Greece, from the pre-classical period to the 1st century B.C.: diss. Edinburgh 1989. 268 p. BRD-89246. – DissA 51 (1990s) 962-A.

d297 *Bell* David, The horse race (*kélēs*) in ancient Greece from the pre-classical period to the first century B.C.: Stadion 15,2 (1989) 167-190.

d298 *Boardman* John, Sport: ➤ 831, CAH² Plates to vol. 4 (1988) 158-166.

d299 *Boardman* John, Chariot, trapeze or lyre? [Late Geometric fragment, fig. 1]: OxJArch 9 (1990) 367s.

d300 *Boatwright* Mary T., Theaters in the Roman Empire: BA 53 (1990) 184-192; ill.

d301 **Brettler** Marc Z., *Poliakoff* Michael, Rabbi Simeon ben Lakish at the gladiators['] banquet; rabbinic observations on the Roman arena: Harv-TR 83 (1990) 93-98.

d302 *Buhmann* Horst, Frauensport im alten Griechenland: Anregung [Zts. für Gymnasialpädagogik, Mü] 35 (1989) 107-114 [AnPg 60, p. 861].

d303 *Burkert* W., Heros, Tod und Sport — Ritual und Mythos der Olympischen Spiele in der Antike: ➤ 736, Körper 1988, 31-43 [< Nikephoros 2 (1989) 31-43].

d304 *Crowther* Nigel B., *a)* Recent trends in the study of Greek athletics (1982-1989); – *b)* A Spartan Olympic boxing champion: AntClas 59 (1990) 246-255 / 198-201.

d305 *Crowther* Nigel B., The evidence for kicking in Greek boxing [weak]: AmJPg 111 (1990) 176-181.

d306 **Decker** W., Sport und Spiel im alten Ägypten 1987 ⇒ 3,d463; 4,e16: RNikephoros 1 (1988) 273-8 (P. W. *Haider*); Nubica 1s (1990) 387-9 (P. *Scholz*).

d307 *Decker* Wolfgang, Bibliographie zum Sport im Alten Ägypten 1984-5: Nikephoros [Zts für Sport und Kultur im Altertum; Hildesheim] 1 (1988) 245-268, ⇒ 3,d463; 4,e16.

d308 **Di Donato** Michele, *Teja* Angela, Agonistica e ginnastica nella Grecia antica 1989 ⇒ 5,d175: RHumBr 45 (1990) 558s (G. E. *Manzoni*).

d309 *Eisenberg* Christiane, Sportgeschichte als Sozialgeschichte; Überlegungen zu einigen britischen Neuerscheinungen: Stadion 15,2 (1989) 277-287.

d310 *Frézouls* Edmond, Les edifices des spectacles en Syrie: ⇒ 481, Syrie II (1989) 385-406; fig. 105-115.

d311 *Gager* John G., Curse and competition in the ancient circus: ⇒ 173, FSTRUGNELL J., Of scribes 1990, 215-228 [curse = *katadesmoí, defixiones*].

d312 *Gandolfo* G. B., *a*) Il sacerdote nella pastorale dello sport; – *b*) Sport e donna; due problemi della società contemporanea: PalCl 69 (1990) 487-491 / 331-7.

d313 *Geominy* Wilfred, *Lehmann* Stefan, Zum Bronzebild des sitzenden Faustkämpfers im Museo Nazionale Romano: Stadion 15,2 (1989) 139-165; 9 pl.

d314 *Gisler-Huwiler* M., À propos des apobates et de quelques cavaliers de la frise nord du Parthénon: ⇒ 18, FBERGER E., Kanon 1988, 15-18.

d315 *Gnilda* Christian, *Palestra* bei PRUDENTIUS: ILCL 14 (1989) 365-382.

d316 **Golvin** Jean-Claude, L'amphithéâtre romain; essai de théorisation de sa forme et de ses fonctions 1988 ⇒ 5,d30: RArchClasR 42 (1990) 499-507 (L. *Polacco*).

d317 **Golvin** Jean-Claude, *Landes* Christian, Amphithéâtre et gladiateurs. P 1990, CNRS. 237 p.; (color.) ill.; maps. 2-87682-046-3.

d318 *Gori* Gigliola, Elementi greci, etruschi e lucani nelle pitture tombali a soggetto sportivo di Paestum: Stadion 16,1 (1990) 73-89.

d319 *a*) *Guiraud* Hélène, Images d'athlètes sur des vases attiques; – *b*) *Millon* Claude, *Schouler* Bernard, Les jeux olympiques d'Antioche; – *c*) *Moreau* Alain, Le discobole meurtrier; – *d*) *Dumont* Jacques, Les combats de coq furent-ils un sport?: Pallas 34 (1988) 77-98; 8 fig. / 61-76 / 1-18 / 33-44.

d320 **Hülsemann** Matthias, Theater, Kult und bürgerlicher Widerstand im antiken Rom; die Entstehung der architektonischen Struktur des römischen Theaters im Rahmen der gesellschaftlichen Auseinandersetzung zur Zeit der Republik: EurHS 3/307. Fra 1987, Lang. 248 p.; 13 foldout plans.

d321 *Kollmann* Roland, Gesundheit, Sport und Religion; eine religionspädagogisch wichtiger Zusammenhang: RelPBei 24 (1989) 126-144 [< ZIT 89,684].

d322 *Krüger* Julian, Die Badeanlagen von Oxyrhynchos — eine historisch-terminologische Untersuchung: Tyche 4 (1989) 109-118.

d323 **Kyle** Donald G., Athletics in ancient Athens: Mnemosyne supp. 95, 1987 ⇒ 3,d471 ... 5,d185: RNikephoros 2 (1989) 275-8 (Monika *Lavrencic*); QuadUrb 64 (1990) 139-141 (G. *Tedeschi*).

d324 *Lämmer* Manfred, Griechische Wettkämpfe in Jerusalem und ihre politische Hintergrunde: Kölner Beiträge zur Sportwissenschaft [Schorndof: Hofmann] 2 (1973) 182-227.

d325 **Laser** Siegfried: Sport und Spiel: Arch. Homerica T, 1987 ➤ 5,d188: ᴿNikephoros 1 (1988) 278-283 (W. *Decker*).

d326 *McGettigan* Mary R.,   The earliest depiction of an armed acrobatic dance; the [Louvre 750 B.C.] Lambros oinochoe: ➤ 784, AJA 94 (1990) 304 (summary).

d327 **Mandell** Richard D.,   Sport, a cultural history.   NY 1984, Columbia Univ. – ᴿNikephoros 2 (1989) 241-5 (C. *Ulf*).

d328 **Manderscheid** Hubertus,   Bibliographie zum römischen Badewesen unter besonderer Berücksichtigung der öffentlichen Thermen.   Mü/B 1988, Wasmuth.   243 p.; 431 plans. DM 88. – ᴿNikephoros 2 (1989) 288-290 (W. *Decker*).

d329 **Morgan** Catherine,   Athletes and oracles; the transformation of Olympia and Delphi in the eighth century B.C.   C 1990, Univ.   xii-324 p.; ill.; maps. £27.50.   0-521-37451-0. – ᴿAntiqJ 70 (1990) 123s (R. A. *Tomlinson*).

d330 *Morgan* M. Gwyn,   Politics, religion and the games in Rome, 200-150 B.C.: Philologus 134,1 (1990) 14-36.

d331 *Mouratidis* Ioannis,   Are there Minoan influences on Mycenaean sports, games and dances?:   Nikephoros 2 (1989) 43-64.

d332 **Nardoni** Davide,   I gladiatori romani.   R 1989, Ed. ital. lett. scienze.   254 p.; ill.

d333 *Northedge* Alastair,   The racecourses at Sāmarrā: BSO 53 (1990) 31-56; 11 fig. (map); pl. I-IV.

d334 *Peiser* Benny,   The crime of Hippias of Elis; zur Kontroverse um die Olympionikenliste [auf deutsch]:   Stadion 16,1 (1990) 37-65.

d334* *Perysinakis* I. N.,   The athlete as warrior; PINDAR's P. 9,97-103 and P. 10,55-59:   BInstClas 37 (1990) 43-49.

d335 *Pfister* Gertrud,   Die andere Perspektive; Frauenforschung und Sportgeschichte: Stadion 16,1 (1990) 143-169.

d336 **Poliakoff** Michael B.,   Studies in the terminology of the Greek combat sports²ʳᵉᵛ [< diss.]: BeitKlasPg 146. Fra 1986, Hain.   xiv-202 p.; 29 fig.; DM 74.   3-445-02487-1. – ᴿAntClas 59 (1990) 418s (J. *Lenaerts*); Helmantica 40 (1989) 480s (J. M. *García G.*).

d337 *Poliakoff* Michael,   Overlooked realities; sport myth and sport history: Stadion 16,1 (1990) 91-102.

d338 ᴱ**Raschke** Wendy,   The archaeology of the Olympics 1984/8 ➤ 4,767; 5,d195:   ᴿAJA 94 (1990) 506s (Nancy *Serwint*); ClasW 83 (1989s) 363s (D. G. *Romano*); RBgPg 68 (1990) 225-7 (R. *Chevallier*); RelStR 16 (1990) 70 (V. S. *Ruebel*: sport inseparable from cult).

d339 *Rauch* André,   Des jeux aux sports; pour une histoire des différences: CahHist 34 (1989) 41-53.

d340 **Sansone** David,   Greek athletics and the genesis of sport 1988 ➤ 4,e40; 0-520-06099-7:   ᴿClasW 83 (1989s) 542 (Barbara K. *Gold*).

d341 *Scobie* Alex,   Spectator security and comfort at gladiatorial games: Nikephoros 1 (1988) 191-243.

d342 *Sebrane* Michael, ❿ EB and MB I board games in Canaan and the origin of the Egyptian *senet* game: ➤ 4, ᶠAMIRAN Ruth, ErIsr 21 (1990) 233-8; 6 fig. (map); Eng. 109*.

d343 *Segal* Arthur, Theatres in ancient Palestine during the Roman-Byzantine period (an historical-archaeological survey): ScrClasIsr 8s (1988) 144-165; 8 fig. [abridged ❿ in ErIsr 19 (1987) 106-124].

d344 *Shelton* John,   New texts from the Oxyrhynchus racing archive: ZPapEp 81 (1990) 265s.

d345 *Stephanis* I.E., Ⓖ Athlētôn apología [inscriptions]: Elliniki 39 (1988) 270-290; franç. 485-7.

d346 **Sweet** Waldo E., Sport and recreation in ancient Greece; a sourcebook with translations; pref. *Segal* E. 1987 ➤ 3,d483*: ᴿClasPg 85 (1990) 160-3 (T.F. *Scanlon*); Nikephoros 2 (1989) 267-9 (Monika *Lavrencic*); RelStR 16 (1990) 258 (E.J. *Leland*).

d346* *Szilágyi* J.Gy., Etruskische Kommentare zur Geschichte eines griechischen Bildmotivs (Brettspiel, Würfelspiel): ➤ 67, Mem. HAHN I., AcAntH 32 (1989) 23-41; 8 fig.

d347 *a) Tatum* W. Jeffrey, Another look at the spectators at the Roman games; – *b) West* W.C., M. Oulpios Domestikos and the athletic synod at Ephesus: AncHB 4 (1990) 104-7 / 84-89.

d348 *Teja* Angela, Die Villa Hadriana in Tivoli; ein Gymnasion grossen Stils?: Stadion 16,1 (1990) 67-71.

d349 *Thuillier* Jean-Paul, La nudité athlétique (Grèce, Étrurie, Rome): Nikephoros 1 (Hildesheim 1988) 29-38 [AnPg 60, p.863].

d350 **Tzachou-Alexandri** Olga, Mind and body; athletic contests in ancient Greece [Athens Museum exhibition catalogue]. Athenai 1989, Ministry of Culture. 351 p.; 9 fig.; 274 color. pl.; 5 plans. – ᴿAJA 94 (1990) 507s (Nancy *Serwint*).

d351 **Weiler** Ingomar, Der Sport bei den Völkern der alten Welt; eine Einführung² [= ¹1981 + 31-item bibliog. Nachtrag]. Da 1988. 303 p. DM 41. – ᴿNikephoros 2 (1989) 246-9 (T.F. *Scanlon*).

d352 *a) Weiler* Ingomar, Langzeitperspektiven zur Genese des Sports; – *b) Giatsis* Sotiris G., The Byzantine views on the human body form the basis for physical activities in this period: Nikephoros 2 (1989) 7-26 / 157-173; fig. 30-36 (p. 327-330).

d353 *Weiler* Ingomar, Gedanken zur Wissenschaftsgeschichte der Agonistik und Gymnastik: ➤ 731*, Integration 1987/9, 183-9 [AnPg 60, p.861].

d354 *Wirkus* Bernd, 'Werden wie die Griechen'; Implikationen, Intentionen und Widersprüche im Olympismus Pierre de COUBERTINs; Stadion 16,1 (1990) 103-128.

d355 **Wörrle** Michael, Stadt und Fest im kaiserzeitlichen Kleinasien... Oinoanda 1988 ➤ 4,c48; 5,d204: ᴿGnomon 62 (1990) 432-5 (M. *Le Glay*); JRS 80 (1990) 183-193 (S. *Mitchell*, also on ZIEGLER R. 1985); Nikephoros 2 (1989) 279-283 (P. *Frisch*); Tyche 4 (1989) 245s (G. *Dobesch*).

d356 **Ziegler** Ruprecht, Städtische Prestige und kaiserliche Politik; Studien zum Festwesen in Ostkilikien im 2. und 3. Jh. n.Chr.: Ph. Fak. 2, 1985 ➤ 4,e50: ᴿNikephoros 1 (1988) 292s (H. *Grassl*).

T2.5   **Musica.**

d357 *Argyropoulou-Evelpidis* Réna [† 27.VIII.1990], Ⓖ Musical instruments in antiquity: Nomismatika Chronika 8 (1989) 31-34 [< RBgNum 135,255].

d358 *Boardman* John, The lyre player group of seals; an encore: ArchAnz (1990) 1-17; 23 fig.

d359 *Bower* Calvin M., BOETHIUS' De institutione musica; a handlist of manuscripts: Scriptorium 42 (Bru 1988) 205-251.

Dyer Charles H., The musical instruments in Daniel 3, 1990 ➤ 4009.

d360 *Castelo Ruano* Raquel, *López Grande* María José, Instrumentos musicales egipcios: BAsEspOr 25 (1989) 137-155 + 5 fig.

d361 *Ceci* Francesca, Ermetta fittile dalla Via Nomentana; un nuovo tipo di sonaglio di età romana [*crepitaculum*, rattle]: ArchClasR 42 (1990) 441-8; 5 fig.

d362 **Comotti** Giovanni, Music in Greek and Roman culture [La musica 1979 ⮞ 61,e519* (index wrongly Comolti), revised], T*Munson* Rosaria V. ⮞ 5,d213. Baltimore 1989, Johns Hopkins Univ. xii-186 p.; 13 fig. $23. 0-8018-3364-7. – RAmJPg 111 (1990) 109-112 (J. *Solomon*); ClasW 84 (1990s) 233s (Leona *Archer*); ClasR 40 (1990) 185 (E. K. *Borthwick*); JHS 110 (1990) 266s (P. *Walcot*).

d363 *Cortés García* Manuela, Organología oriental en el-Andalus [... música eg., mesop.]: BAsEspOr 26 (1990) 303-317 + 54 fig. [not entirely in sequence].

d363* **Flender** Reinhard, Die biblische Sprachgesang und seine mündliche Überlieferung in Synagoge und griechischer Kirche: Quellenkataloge zur Musikgeschichte 20, 1988 ⮞ 5,d217: RBZ 34 (1990) 317-9 (J. *Maier*).

d364 E**Gentili B.**, *Pretagostini* R., La musica in Grecia 1985/8 ⮞ 5,d218: RAufidus 7 (1989) 235s (O. *Imperio*); Maia 42 (1990) 193-5 (Ilaria *Tarzi*); Salesianum 52 (1990) 148s (C. *Semeraro*); Sileno 16 (1990) 353-7 (G. *Tedeschi*).

d365 *Goldberg* Geoffrey, Ḥazzan and Qahal; responsive chant in Minhag Ashkenaz: HUCA 61 (1990) 203-217.

d366 *Hameline* Jean-Yves, Éléments d'anthropologie, de sociologie historique et de musicologie du culte chrétien: RechSR 78 (1990) 397-424; Eng. 117s.

d367 *Kaden* Christian, 'Was hat Musik mit Klang zu tun?' Ideen zu einer Geschichte des Begriffs 'Musik' und zu einer musikalischen Begriffsgeschichte: ArBegrG 32 (1989) 34-75.

d368 *Karageorghis* Vassos, A Late Bronze Age musical instrument?: Levant 22 (1990) 159; fig. 3 [from Kition].

d369 **Knapp** Bettina L., Music, archetype, and the writer; a Jungian view. Univ. Park 1988, Penn State Univ. 234 p. $25. 0-271-00624-2. – RModT 7 (1990s) 115-120 (J. M. *Spencer*).

d370 *Lo Muzio* Ciro, Classificazione degli strumenti musicali raffigurati nell'arte Gandhārica: RSO 63 (1989) 257-284; 10 fig.

d371 **Moran** N. K., Singers in Late Byzantine and Slavonic painting: Byz. Neerlandica 2. Leiden 1986, Brill. xii-175 p.; 87 fig. + 10 color. – RByZ 82 (1989) 315-8 (P. L. *Vocotopoulos* Ⓖ).

d371* a) *Neubauer* E., Das Musikkapitel der Ǧumal al-Falsafa von Muḥammad ibn 'Ali al-HINDI (1135 n.Chr.); – b) *Neubauer* Eckhard & Elsbeth, Henry G. FARMER [† 1965] on oriental music; an annotated bibliography: ZtsGesch. Arabisch-Islamischen Wissenschaften 4 (1987s) 51-59 / 219-266 [< OLZ 85,636].

d372 E**Pizzani** Ubaldo, *Milanese* Guido, AGOSTINO d'Ippona, De Musica: Lectio Augustini 5. Palermo 1990, Augustinus. 89 p. Lit. 16.000. – RRSPT 74 (1990) 646s (G.-M. de *Durand*).

d373 **Pöhlmann** Egert, Beiträge zur antiken und neueren Musikgeschichte: Quellen Mus. 17. Fra 1988, Lang. 206 p.; 14 fig. 3-8204-1212-3. – RAnzAltW 43 (1990) 265s (W. *Salmen*).

d374 **Rashid** Subhi A., Musikgeschichte in Bildern, Mesopotamien 2/2, 1984 ⮞ 2,a77 ... 5,d227: RJAOS 110 (1990) 758-760 (Anne D. *Kilmer*: standard reference work).

d375 a) *Rashid* Subhi A., Die Musik der Keilschriftkulturen; – b) *Hickmann* Ellen, *Manniche* Lise, Altägyptische Musik; – c) *Werner* Erik, Die Musik

im alten Israel; – *d*) *Zaminer* Friedel, ... Griechenland; – *e*) *Riethmül-*
ler Albrecht, Musik zwischen Hellenismus und Spätantike: ➤ 5,d228,
ᴱ*Riethmüller*, Musik des Altertums 1989, 1-30 / 31-75 / 76-112 / 113-206
/ 207-325; ill.

d376 *Sallmann* Klaus, Aᴜɢᴜsᴛɪɴᴜs' Rettung der Musik und die antike
Mimesistheorie: ➤ 80, ꜰHÖRNER Hadwig 1990, 81-92.

d377 *Santosuosso* Alma C., Music in Bᴇᴅᴇ's De temporum ratione; an
11th-century addition to ms. London, British Library, Cotton Vespasian
B.VI: Scriptorium 43 (1989) 255-9; pl. 20.

d378 *Schmidt* Margot, Lydische Harmonie: ➤ 30, ꜰCᴀᴍʙɪᴛoɢʟoᴜ A., *Eumousia* 1990, 221-6; pl. 42.

d379 **Seidel** Hans, Musik in Altisrael; Untersuchungen zur Musikgeschichte
und Musikpraxis Altisraels anhand biblischer und ausserbiblischer Texte
[< Diss. 1970]: BErfAJ 12. Fra 1989, Lang. 352p. Fs36. 3-8204-
9867-2 [BL 91,41, J.H. *Eaton*]. – ᴿExpTim 102 (1990s) 85 (J. *Eaton*);
ZAW 102 (1990) 459 (H.-C. *Schmitt*).

d380 *Tokarczyk* Alicja, ❷ De arte musica Graecorum antiquorum notula:
Meander 45 (1990) 353-9.

d381 *Tumbarello* Giacomo, La musica e gli strumenti musicali nella Bibbia:
BbbOr 32 (1990) 73-79.

т2.6   **Textilia,** *vestis,* clothing.

d382 *a*) *Bergman* Ingrid, The triangular Nubian textiles; how were they
produced?; – *b*) *Fleury-Lemberg* Mechthild, A recent silk find from
Antinoë [... made in Iran]: ➤ 56, ꜰGᴇɪᴊᴇʀ Agnes 1988, 29-32; 6 fig. /
33-39; 12 (color.) fig.

d383 **Bezontákos** Nikolaos P., ❷ He archaia ellenikē mitra 1987 ➤ 5,d235:
ᴿWienerSt 103 (1990) 255 (H. *Schwabl*).

d384 **Brown** Kristine S., The question of Near Eastern textile decoration of
the early first millennium ʙ.C. as a source for Greek vase painting of the
orientalizing style: diss. Pennsylvania, ᴰDe Vries K. Ph 1981. xv-771 p.;
45 pl. 81-07720. – OIAc Ja91.

d385 **Carroll** Diane Lee, Looms and textiles of the Copts: Mem. 11. SF
1988, California Academy of Science. 201 p.; ill.

d386 *a*) *Dietrich* M., *Loretz* O., Die hurro-ugaritische Textilbezeichnung
ᴀʟʟ; – *b*) *Soldt* W.H. van, Fabrics and dyes at Ugarit; – *c*) *Xella* P.,
'Arsenic et vieilles dentelles' — encore sur la terminologie des textiles à
Ugarit: UF 22 (1990) 49s / 321-357 / 467-474.

d386* *Gatier* Pierre-Louis, Un témoignage [étoffe] sur des églises d'Antioche:
Syria 65 (1988) 383-8; 3 fig.

d387 **Goette** Hans R., Studien zu römischen Togadarstellungen: Beit. Skulp-
tur 10. Mainz 1990, von Zabern. x-207 p.; 94 pl.

d388 *Habermann* Wolfgang, Ägyptisches und Karthagisches Leder als antike
Sortenbezeichnungen: RheinMus 133 (1990) 138-143.

d389 *Janssen* Rosalind M., Gewänder für das Leben und den Tod im Alten
Ägypten: Altertum 36 (1990) 5-13; 8 fig. + color. pl.

d390 *Janssen* Rosalind M. & J.J., Candlewick coverlets: DiscEg 16 (1990)
53-60 + 2 fig.

d391 *a*) *La Follette* Laetitia, Costume and ritual initiation; the headdress
and hairstyle of the Roman bride; – *b*) *Roussin* Lucille A., Women's and
children's costume in the mosaics from Piazza Armerina; – *c*) *Stone*

Shelley C., The late Roman toga [summaries from colloquium on The Role of Costume in Roman Art]: ➤ 784, AJA 94 (1990) 332s.

d392 *McGing* Brian C., Lease of a linen-weaving shop in Panopolis: ZPapEp 82 (1990) 115-121.

d392* a) *Mottier* Yvette, À propos de l'interdiction du mélange de lin et laine (Lev. 19,19; Deut. 22,11); – b) *Staehelin* Elisabeth, Zum Ornat an Statuen regierender Königinnen: ➤ 70*, Mém. HARI R., BSocÉg 13 (1989) 117-120 / 145-156; 3 fig.

d393 **Neumann** Reingard, *Murza* Gerhard, Persische Seiden; die Gewebekunst der Safawiden und ihrer Nachfolger. Lp 1988, Seemann. 335 p.; 260 (color.) fig. DM 98. – ᴿWeltOr 20s (1989s) 349-352 (Johanna *Zick-Nissen*).

d394 *Oerter* Wolf B., Die Leder- und Flechtarbeiten des Koptischen Museums Kairo: BSACopte 29 (1990) 49-54.

d395 **Pionati Shams** Glorianne, Some minor textiles in antiquity [... amiante, could be 'washed' in fire... chanvre]: SIMA pocket 48. Göteborg 1987, Åström. 44 p. 91-86098-54-3. – ᴿAntClas 59 (1990) 604 (G. de *Pierpont*).

d396 **Ribichini** Sergio, *Xella* Paolo, La terminologia dei tessili nei testi di Ugarit: 1985 ➤ 3,d521 ... 5,d243: ᴿMARI 6 (1990) 659-664 (J.-M. *Durand*).

d397 *Ryder* M. L., Wool remains from Scythian burials in Siberia: OxJArch 9 (1990) 313-321; 6 fig.

d398 *Stager* Lawrence E., Painted pottery and its relationship to the weaving crafts in Canaan during the Early Bronze Age I: ➤ 4, ᶠAMIRAN Ruth, Eretz-Israel 21 (1990) 83*-88*; 1 fig.

d399 *Török* László, The costume of the ruler in Meroe; remarks on its origin and significance: ArNilM 4 (1990) 151-184 + 41 fig.; franç. 9.

d400 **Tolle-Kastenbein** Renate, Frühklassische Peplosfiguren 1986 ➤ 2,a106 ... 5,d247: ᴿBonnJbb 190 (1990) 631-6 (J. *Raeder*).

d401 a) *Vogelsang-Eastwood* G. M., The textiles from Quseir al-Qadim, Egypt; – b) *Barnett* J. C., The conservation of an Egyptian Fifth-Dynasty funerary dress; – c) *Hooft* Philomeen van 't, De datering van koptische weefsels en de interpretatie van de iconografie; – d) *Raven* M. J., The collection of Egyptian textiles in the RM[us]O: Proceedings of the archaeological textiles meeting 1989, OM[ed]RO 70 (1990) 195-200 / 205-8 / 208-211 / 193-5; ill.

d402 *Walters* Elizabeth J., Attic grave reliefs... women in the dress of Isis 1988 ➤ 5,d643: ᴿJAmEg 27 (1990) 232s (R. S. *Bianchi*).

d403 **Watson** Philip J., Costume of Old Testament peoples. L 1987, Batsford. 64 p., (colour.) ill. (*Cassin-Scott* J.) [KirSef 62 (1988s) p. 36].

T2.7 *Ornamenta corporis,* **jewelry, mirrors.**

d404 **Andrews** Carol, Ancient Egyptian jewellery. L 1990, British Museum. 208 p. 0-7141-0954-1 [OIAc Oc90].

d405 *Artzy* Michal, Pomegranate scepters and incense stand found in priest's grave [t. Nami, 12 k. S. Haifa]: BAR-W 16,1 (1990) 48-51.

d406 **Bechinger** Richard, *Schienierl* Peter W., Silberschmuck aus Ägypten, Ausstellung 1984. Fra 1984, Galerie Exler. 118 p.; incl. 92 pl. 2-924927-00-6 [OIAc S90].

d407 *Calmeyer* P., Meder, Tracht der: ➤ 853*, RLA 7,7 (1990) 615-7; 4 fig.

d408 **Davidson** Patricia F., *Oliver* Andrew, Ancient Greek and Roman gold jewelry in the Brooklyn Museum: Wilbour Mg 8. Brooklyn 1984, Museum. xxii-214 p.; 270 fig.

d409 **Dayagi-Mendels** Michal, Perfumes and cosmetics in the ancient world: Catalogues 305. J 1989, Israel Museum. 139 p. 965-278-058-8 [OIAc JJ90].

d410 *Durand* Jean-Marie, La culture matérielle à Mari (I); le bijou *húb-til-lá/ 'gur₇-me'*: MARI 6 (1990) 125-158 (159s *gur₇-me, Charpin* D.).

d411 *Grimm* Alfred, Das Königsornat mit dem Sonnenvogel; zu *s(j)3t* und *db.3* als Bezeichnungen königlicher Trachtelemente: GöMiszÄg 115 (1990) 33-37 + 7 pl.

d412 *Harrington* Spencer P. M., Royal treasures of Nimrud: Archaeology 43,4 (1990) 48-53; color. ill.

d413 **Hattatt** Richard, Ancient brooches and other artefacts... from the author's collection, 4. Ox 1989, Oxbow. 520 p.

d414 *Hegazy el-Sayed, Van Siclen* Charles C., A cache of jewelry from the edifice of Amenhotep II at Karnak: VarAeg 5 (1989) 227-239; 9 fig. [p. 173: Volume 5 was intended to inaugurate 4 issues annually, but the middle one was double and all were late, so three issues annually will again be the norm].

d415 **Hoffman** Gail L., Immigrants, imports, and problems in the study of influence; archaeological evidence for artistic transmission from the Near East to Crete, ca. 1100 - ca. 700 B.C., with special reference to the Tekke Jewelry: diss. Michigan, ᴰ*Pedley* J. AA 1990. 90-34439. – OIAc Ap91,8.

d417 **Lambrechts** Roger, Corpus speculorum etruscorum, Belgique 1. R 1987, Bretschneider. 180 p. dont 110 pl. [Gnomon 63, 182-5, I. *Jucker*].

d417* *Limper* Klaudia, Uruk Perlen – Ketten – Anhänger; Grabungen 1912-1985; Endbericht 2, 1988 ⇒ 5,d256: ᴿMesopT 25 (1990) 240-2 (A. *Invernizzi*).

d418 **Maaskant-Kleibrink** Marianne, The engraved gems, Roman and non-Roman: Nijmegen Rijksmuseum 10, 1986 ⇒ 5,d257; 90-71923-01-0: ᴿBabesch 65 (1990) 168s (J. P. *Guépin*).

d419 *Meer* L. B. van der, Dilemmas and antithetical deities on Etruscan mirrors: Babesch 65 (1990) 73-79; 3 fig.

d420 **Megow** Wolf-Rüdiger, Kameen von Augustus bis Alexander Severus: Antike Münzen 11, 1987 ⇒ 5,d259; DM 228, 3-11-010703-1: ᴿAnt-Clas 59 (1990) 629-632 (Jean-C. *Balty*).

d421 *Miroschedji* P. de, Note d'orfèvrerie néo-élamite [épingles]: ⇒ 138, ᶠPERROT J., Iran 1990, 181-192 + 2 pl.

d422 **Musche** Brigitte, Vorderasiatischer Schmuck zur Zeit der Arsakiden und der Sasaniden 1988 ⇒ 5,d261: ᴿOLZ 85 (1990) 459-461 (Monika *Dahneke-Roschanzamir*); StIran 18 (1989) 140-2 (Rika *Gyselen*); ZDMG 140 (1990) 177s (A. von *Gladiss*).

d423 *Naguib* Saphinaz-Amal, Hair in ancient Egypt: AcOrK 51 (1990) 7-26.

d424 **Paszthory** Emmerich, Salben, Schminken und Parfüme im Altertum; Herstellungsmethoden und Anwendungsbereiche im östlichen Mediterraneum: AntWelt Sondernummer 1990. 64 p.; 87 (color.) fig.

d425 **Pfrommer** Michael, Untersuchungen zur Chronologie früh- und hochhellenistischen Goldschmucks: IstFor 37. Tü 1990, Wasmuth. xxiv-470 p.; 31 pl. 3-8030-1758-0 [OIAc F91,18].

d426 **Philip** Hanna, Mira et magica; Gemmen im äg. Museum B 1987 ⇒ 3,d539; 4,e121: ᴿBSO 52 (1989) 123s (R. *Kotansky*).

d427 **Quillard** Brigitte, Bijoux carthaginois 2: Publ. 32. LvN 1987, Inst. Arch. Art. xviii-297 p.; 43 pl.

d428 **Schienerl** Peter W., Schmuck und Amulett im Antike und Islam: Acta Culturologica 4. Aachen 1988, Alano. 153 p.; 127 fig.

d429 **Speidel** M. Alexander, Die Friseure des ägyptischen Alten Reiches; eine historisch-prosopographische Untersuchung zu Amt und Titel *jr-šn*: Diss. Zürich 1989s. Konstanz 1990, Hartung-Gorre. v-246 p. 3-89191-343-5. – OIAc Oc90.

d430 *Stone* Michael E., An Armenian epitome of EPIPHANIUS's De gemmis: HarvTR 82 (1989) 467-476.

d431 *Troy* Lana, The dating of the glass bird pendants; material from the Scandinavian joint expedition to Sudanese Nubia: GöMiszÄg 114 (1990) 107-9.

d432 *Zouhdi* Bashir, Les bijoux antiques du Musée National de Damas: → 481, Syrie II (1989) 557-566; fig. 210-212.

T2.8   **Utensilia.**

d433 *a) Avigad* Nahman, The inscribed pomegranate from the 'House of the Lord': BA 53 (1990) 157-166; ill. – *b) Kempinski* A., ☻ queries N. Avigad pomegranate/macehead: Qadmoniot [22 (1989) 95-102] 23 (1990) 126.

d434 *Braun* Eliot, Basalt bowls of the EB I horizon in the southern Levant: Paléorient 16,1 (1990) 87-96; 4 fig.

d435 *Byvanck-Quarles van Ufford* L., À propos du trésor de Rogozen [Bulgaria, 165 chased silver vessels]: Babesch 65 (1990) 51-72; 34 fig.

d436 *Drummond* David C., *Janssen* Rosalind M. & J.J., An ancient Egyptian rat trap: MiDAI-K 46 (1990) 91-98; 3 fig.; pl. 28.

d437 **Gershuny** Lilly, Bronze vessels from Israel and Jordan: Präh. Bronzefunde 2/6, 1985 → 1,b933; 2,a129: ᴿBO 47 (1990) 487s (Gloria M. *Bellelli*).

d438 *Henne* Dr., Überlegungen zur altägyptischen Wasseruhr: GöMiszÄg 115 (1990) 45-56.

d439 *Hofmann* Inge, Brenn- oder Vergrösserungsgläser im meroitischen Reich: VarAeg 5 (1989) 133-7; 1 fig.

d440 **Kunisch** Norbert, Griechische Fischteller, Natur und Bild. ... 1989, Mann. DM 28. 3-7861-1562-1: ᴿAntClas 59 (1990) 589-591 (L. *Lacroix*).

d441 *Levy* Abraham, Small inventions; they changed how people lived in the Hellenistic age: BAR-W 16,4 (1990) 32-41.

d442 *Mengoli* Pierangelo, La clessidra di Karnak; l'orologio ad acqua di Amenophis III: OrAnt 28 (1989) 227-271; 6 fig.; pl. XXVIII-XXXVII.

d443 *Miller* Robert L., *Ds*-vessels, beer mugs, cirrhosis and casting slag: GöMiszÄg 115 (1990) 63-82.

d444 **Muscarella** Oscar W., Bronze and iron... in the Met 1988 → 5,d281*: ᴿJField 17 (1990) 488-490 (Georgina *Herrmann*).

d445 *Neve* Peter, Eine hethitische Bronzesäge aus Hattusa-Boğazköy: Ist-Mitt 39 (1989) 399-406; 1 fig.

d446 *Rubiato Díaz* María Teresa, al., Recipientes biblicos I-II (*agmon, agarṭel*): Sefarad 50 (1990) 167-180 + 7 fig.; 425-454; 6 fig.

d447 *Shaheen* Alaa el-din M., EB III - MB I axe in the Egyptian private middle kingdom tombs; an assessment: GöMiszÄg 117s (1990) 203-212 + 5 fig.

d448 **Sinn** Friederike, Stadtrömische Marmorurnen 1987 → 4,e152; 5,d287: ᴿAntClas 59 (1990) 618-622 (J.-C. *Balty*, aussi sur CAIN H., Kandelaber 1985).

d449 *Vanschoonwinkel* Jacques, Considérations nouvelles sur les assiettes dites mycéniennes découvertes en Syrie: RArtLv 21 (1988) 51-61; 4 fig.

d450 *Weyl* Robert, Le *yad*, main de lecture et boîte à senteurs: RÉJ 149 (1990) 137-146; 6 fig.

d451 *Zauzich* Karl-Theodor, *Röllig* Wolfgang, Ein ägyptischer Schreiberpalette in phönizischer Umgestaltung: → 160*, Mem. SCHULER E. v., Orientalia 59 (1990) 320-332; pl. XII.

T2.9 *Pondera et mensurae* – Weights and measures.

d452 *Edwards* W.T., Ancient weights and measurements: Biblical Illustrator 15,2 (Nv 1989) 70-72 [< OTAbs 13, p. 255; similar short items from there are cited p. 220.224.226.252.254.256-260.269.276.280.291s.296].

d452* *Hocquet* Jean-Claude, La métrologie, voie nouvelle de la recherche historique: CRAI (1990) 59-77; 4 fig.

d453 *Humphrey* John W., A note on *stádion* in CASSIUS Dio [7,5 to the Roman mile from Latin sources, but 8 from Greek sources]: AncHB 4 (1990) 17-22.

d454 *Kidson* Peter, A metrological investigation [... later ratios identical with Roman]: JWarb 53 (1990) 71-97; 5 fig.

d455 *Kloner* Amos, Lead weights of Bar Kokhba's administration: IsrEJ 40 (1990) 58-67; 2 fig. (map); pl. 6-7.

d456 *Kubba* Shamil, The Ubaid period; evidence of architectural planning and the use of a standard unit of measurement — the 'Ubaid cubit' — in Mesopotamia: Paléorient 16,1 (1990) 45-55; 28 fig.

d456* *Mathieu* Bernard, Études de métrique égyptienne II. Contraintes métriques et production textuelle dans l'Hymne à la crue du Nil: RÉgp 41 (1990) 127-141.

d457 *Meischner* Jutta, Zwei Gewichtbronzen in Form von Kaiserporträts: MiDAI-R 96 (1989) 407-418; pl. 109-111.

d458 *Naeh* Shlomo, ❽ 'Polishing measures and cleaning scales'; a chapter from the tractate of weights and measures [Baba Batra 5,10]: Tarbiz 59 (1989s) 379-395; Eng. III.

d459 *Potts* D.T., Lock [spelled 'locky' in title, page-heads, and contents, though not in text] and key in ancient Mesopotamia: MesopT 25 (1990) 185-192.

d460 *Powell* M.A., Masse und Gewichte [Eng.]: RLA 7,7s (1990) (457-) 465-517 (-527, bei den Hethitern; -530 Index).

d461 *Reineke* Walter F., Untersuchungen zur Länge der ägyptischen Elle: → 78, ᶠHINTZE F., Meroitica 12 (1990) 257-268 + 2 fig.

d462 *Rolk* Elke, Das Nbj-Masssystem, ein bisher unerforschtes altägyptisches Längenmasssystem: GöMiszÄg 119 (1990) 91-99; 3 fig.

d463 *Rottländer* Rolf C.A., Zweierlei Masseinheiten an e i n e m Bauwerk? [Ephesos Artemision; Rom Tiber-Tempel ...]: JhÖsA 60-H (1990) 19-41; 9 fig.

d464 *Şahin* Sencer, Ein Bleigewicht aus Nikomedeia unter Kaiser Philippus und seinem Statthalter M. Aurelius Artemidorus: EpAnat 16 (1990) 139-145; pl. 21; ❶ 146.

d465 *Vickers* Michael, Golden Greece; relative values, minae, and temple inventories: AJA 94 (1990) 613-625.

d466 *Zaccagnini* Carlo, The Nuzi wool measures once again: → 160*, Mem. SCHULER E. v., Orientalia 59 (1990) 312-9.

d467 *Zupko* Ronald E., Weights and measures, western European: ➤ 827*, DMA 12 (1989) 582-591; 592-6, tables for England and France.

T3.1 **Ars,** *motiva, pictura.*

d468 **Allag** C., *Barbet* A., *al.*, Mise en valeur des peintures murales romaines; relevés, prélèvements, techniques audio-visuelles et publications: Bulletin 10. P 1990. 47 p.

d469 **Allen** Terry, Five essays on Islamic art. Sebastopol CA 1988, Solipsist. ix-131 p.; 55 pl. $46. – ᴿBSO 53 (1990) 134s (N. F. *Safwat*).

d470 **Andrén** Arvid, Deeds and misdeeds in classical art and antiquities: SIMA pocket 36. Göteborg 1986, Åström. 176 p.; 21 fig. 91-86098-31-4. – ᴿAntClas 59 (1990) 555 (G. de *Pierpont*).

d471 **Arafat** K. W., Classical Zeus, a study in art and literature: Mg Clas-Arch. Ox 1990, Clarendon. xvii-225 p.; 40 pl. 0-19-814912-3.

d472 *Assmann* J., Die Macht der Bilder; Rahmenbedingungen ikonischen Handelns im alten Ägypten: Visible Religion 1986/90, 1-16 + 10 fig.

d473 **Bahn** Paul G., *Vertut* Jean, Images of the Ice Age. L 1988, Windward. 240 p.; 122 fig. £15. – ᴿAJA 94 (1990) 153s (W. *Davis*).

d474 *Bahn* Paul, Pigments of the imagination [human blood found in cave-art]: Nature 347 (Oct. 4, 1990) 426.

d475 ᴱ**Barbet** Alix, La peinture murale antique, restitution et iconographie 1985/7 ➤ 4,721: ᴿAJA 94 (1990) 701s (M. L. *Anderson*).

d476 **Barbet** Alix, La peinture murale romaine; les styles décoratifs pompéiens 1985 ➤ 1,b971 ... 4,e171: ᴿArchClasR 38ss (1986-8) 290-2 (Irene *Bragantini*).

d477 *Barnett* Richard D., Polydactylism in the ancient world [an extra finger or toe in paintings or statues]: BAR-W 16,3 (1990) 46-51.

d478 **Belting** Hans, Bild und Kult; eine Geschichte des Bildes vor dem Zeitalter der Kunst. Mü 1990, Beck. 700 p.; 296 fig. + 12 color. 3-406-34367-8. – ᴿWissWeis 53 (1990) 233s (C. *Auffarth*).

d479 **Bérard** Claude, *al.*, A city of images; iconography and society in ancient Greece [La cité; deutsch 1985 ➤ 5,d313], ᵀ*Lyons* Deborah. Princeton 1989, Univ. viii-178 p.; 168 phot. + 63 color. $32.50. – ᴿClasR 40 (1990) 513s (Elisabeth *Moignard*: infuriating but ...).

d480 *Bisconti* Fabrizio, Sulla concezione figurativa dell' 'habitat' paradisiaco; a proposito di un affresco romano poco noto [catacombe di Priscilla]: ➤ 175*, Mem. TESTINI P. = RivArchCr 66 (1990) 25-80; 31 fig.

d481 **Boardman** John, The Greek art of narrative: ➤ 30, ᶠCAMBITOGLOU A., Eumousia 1990, 57-62; pl. 10-11.

d482 **Bigham** Steven, L'attitude des chrétiens à l'égard des images pendant les trois premiers siècles de l'Église: diss. ᴰ*Petit* J. Montréal 1990. 370 p. – RTLv 22, p. 596.

d483 ᴱ**Boespflug** F., *Lossky* N., Nicée 2 (787-1987), douze siècles d'images religieuses 1986/7 ➤ 3,592 ... 5,d317: ᴿCahArch 37 (1989) 182s (T. *Velmans*); Téléma 15,2 (1989) 83-85 (R. De *Haes*).

d484 *Bolshakov* Andrey O., The ideology of the Old Kingdom portrait: GöMiszÄg 117s (1990) 89-134; 2 fig.; bibliog. p. 134-142.

d485 *Bonfante* Larissa, The naked Greek; how art and literature reflect the custom of civic nudity: Archaeology 43,5 (1990) 28-35.

b486 *a) Bothmer* Bernard V., Eyes and iconography in the splendid century; King Amenhotep III and his aftermath; – *b) Myśliwiec* Karol, The art of Amenhotep III, a link in a continuous evolution; – *c) Johnson* W.

Raymond,   Images of Amenhotep III in Thebes; styles and intentions: ➔ 790, Amenhotep III (1987/90) 84-90; pl. 20-27 / 16-25; pl. 2-9 / 26-46; 8 fig.; pl. 10-11.

b487 **Bourriau** Janine,   Pharaohs and mortals; Egyptian art in the Middle Kingdom 1988 ➔ 4,e177:   ᴿBO 17 (1990) 114-6 (R. E. *Freed*); ClasW 83 (1989s) 121s (Karen P. *Foster*).

b488 **Brendel** Otto J.,   Was ist römische Kunst? [Prolegomena to ...], ᵀ*Willinghöfer* Helga: Tb 228. Köln 1990, Du Mont. 158 p.; ill.

d489 **Brown** Frank B.,   Religious aesthetics; a theological study of making and meaning [... relevance of art to religion].   Princeton 1989, Univ. xvi-225 p. $27.50. – ᴿTS 51 (1990) 776s (Margaret R. *Miles*).

d490 **Buechner** Frederick,   The faces of Jesus.   SF 1989, Stearn / Harper & R. 256 p.; 150 color. photos from art (Boltin Lee). $20.   0-06-069269-3 [TDig 37,253].

d491 **Byrne** Michael,   The Greek geometric warrior figurine; interpretation and origin: diss. LvN 1987, ᴰ*Hackens* T. – RArtLv 21 (1988) 204s.

d492 **Charalampidēs** Kōstas P.,   ⓖ *Symbolikes parastaseis ...* Symbolic representations of peace and hope in early Christian art of the west. Thessaloniki 1990, Pournaras.   169 p.; 61 pl.

d493 **Chevrier** Jean-François,   Portrait de Jurgis BALTRUŠAITIS [p. 129-231; 56 fig.: his 1933]: Art sumérien, art roman.   P 1989, Flammarion.   271 p.; bibliog. p. 270s.   2-08-012038-7.

d494 *Codina* Victor,   Una teología más simbólica y popular [< PerspT 18 (1986) 149-173], ᵀᴱ*Rocafiguera* Josep M.: SelT 28 (1989) 69-80.

d495 **Cormack** R.,   Writing in gold 1985 ➔ 2,a166; 3,d591:   ᴿByZ 82 (1989) 309-313 (D. I. *Pallas*).

d496 **Crimi** Carmelo,   Michele SINCELLO, Per la restaurazione delle venerande e sacre immagini: BollClas supp. 7.   R 1990, Acc. Lincei.   67 p.

d497 **Croisille** Jean-Michel,   Poésie et art figuré de Néron aux Flaviens; recherches sur l'iconographie et la correspondance des arts à l'époque impériale: Coll. Latomus 179.   Bru 1982.   742 p.; 167 pl. Fb 4500. – ᴿAntClas 59 (1990) 622s (Janine *Balty*).

d498 **Crouan** D.,   L'art et la liturgie; essai sur les rapports constants unissant l'art et la liturgie au cours des siècles.   P 1988, Téqui.   208 p. – ᴿSalesianum 52 (1990) 767 (C. *Chenis*).

d499 *D'Angelo* M. Carmela,   Analisi morfologica di un motivo araldico vicino-orientale: EgVO 11 (1988) 155-166; 13 (1990) 135-8; 3 fig.

d500* **Dillenberger** John,   The visual arts and Christianity in America; from the colonial period to the present.   NY 1988, Crossroad.   290 p. $39.50. – ᴿJAAR 58 (1990) 700-3 (Lois M. *Faink*); TTod 47 (1990s) 93s.96.98 (J. W. *Cook*).

d501 ᴱ**Distante** Giovanni,   La legittimità del culto delle icone 1987/8 ➔ 4,552; 5,d325: ᴿStMon 32 (1990) 231-3 (M. *Nin*).

d502 *Dochniak* Craig C.,   The *ḥpš* hieroglyph as a module in Egyptian art and the subsequent implications of its use: VarAeg 5 (1989) 97-102; 3 fig.

d503 *Duhard* Jean-Pierre,   Le corps féminin et son langage dans l'art paléolithique: OxJArch 9 (1990) 241-256; 5 fig.

d504 **Ehrhardt** Wolfgang,   Stilgeschichtliche Untersuchungen an römischen Wandmalereien von der späten Republik zur Zeit Neros: DAI, 1987 ➔ 5,d327:   ᴿArchClasR 42 (1990) 477-480 (Irene *Bragantini*); Gymnasium 97 (1990) 375-7 (Agnes *Allrogen-Bedel*).

d505 *Engemann* Josef,   Künste, bildende, Frühchristentum: ➔ 857, TRE 20 (1990) 131-5 [-176, später]; 253-6, Kunst und Religion AT, *Welten* Peter [Religionsgeschichtlich, usw. *al.* 243-253. 256-337, 4 pl. + 4 color.).

d506 *Erickson* Kathleen P., Self-portraits [GAUGUIN P.: VAN GOGH V.] as Christ: BR 6,3 (1990) 24-31. 44; color. ill.

d507 **Filarska** Barbara, ❷ Początki sztuki chrześcijańskiej, Initia artis christianae: Źródła i mg. 113. Lublin 1986, KUL. 342 p.; 482 fig. – ᴿArchWroc 40 (1989) 195s (J. *Ziomecki*, ❷).

d508 *Finneiser* Klaus, Untersuchungen zur Königsikonographie im Erscheinungssaal des Chonsu-Tempels in Karnak mit Hilfe mathematisch-statistischer Verfahren: → 78, ᶠHINTZE F.,Meroitica 12 (1990) 119-130 + 3 fig.

d508* **Forman** Werner, *Kischkewitz* Hannelore, Die altägyptische Zeichnung^{2rev} [^{1}1971]. Hanau 1988, Dausien. 34 p. + 61 (color./foldout) photos, with explanation on left-hand page. 3-7684-1847-2.

d509 **Francis** E.D., Image and idea in Fifth-Century Greece [ᴱ*Vickers* Michael]: Art and Literature after the Persian Wars. L 1990, Routledge. x-156 p. 0-415-01914-1 [OIAc Oc90].

d510 **Giuliano** Antonio, Storia dell'arte greca. R 1989, Nuova Italia Scientifica. 425 p.; 413 fig.

d511 **Goldmann** Christoph, Message biblique de Marc Chagall; der Bildmidrasch eines jüdischen Malers zur hebräischen Bibel: diss. ᴰ*Rendtorff* R. Heidelberg 1990s. – RTLv 22,590: 'Message biblique de' *sic*, français.

d512 *Grabar* André, Dieu et les hommes; un thème d'iconographie chrétienne; CahArch 38 (1990) 5s.

d513 **Grabar** Oleg, The formation of Islamic art^{2rev} [^{1}1973]. NHv 1987, Yale Univ. xix-232 p.; 77 pl.; map. £40; pa. £15. – ᴿJRAS (1989) 144s (G. *Goodwin*).

d514 **Grinten** Franz Joseph van der, *Mennekes* Friedhelm, Menschenbild – Christusbild; Auseinandersetzung mit einem Thema der Gegenwartskunst^2 [^{1}1984 → 1,b996]. Stu 1985, KBW. 296 p.; ill. DM 58. 3-460-32281-0. – ᴿBijdragen 51 (1990) 98s (J. *Besemer*: successful formula of 'Menschenbild-Christusbild').

d515 *Gutmann* Joseph, Jüdische Kunst [< ᴱ*Rubenach* B., Begegnungen 1981, 167-179]: → 5,272, Sacred images 1989, I, 167-179.

d516 **Hachlili** Rachel, Ancient Jewish Art... HbOr 6/1/2B/4, 1988 → 4,e193: ᴿBAngIsr 10 (1990s) 84-88 (Claudine *Dauphin*); NedTTs 44 (1990) 264s (P. W. van der *Horst*); RÉJ 149 (1990) 200-2 (Gabrielle *Sed-Rajna*).

d517 **Harpur** Yvonne, Decoration in Egyptian tombs, Old Kingdom 1987 → 3,d607: ᴿBO 17 (1990) 90-97 (H. G. *Fischer*); JAOS 110 (1990) 592s (A. R. *Schulman*); OLZ 85 (1990) 23-28 (P. *Jánosi*).

d518 **d'Hulst** Roger-Adolf, (*Vandenven* Marc), The Old Testament: P. P. Rubens Corpus L. Burchard 3. L 1989, Harvey Miller. 402 p.; 178 pl. £62. – ᴿRHE 85 (1990) 866 (D. *Bradley*).

d519 **Immerwahr** Sara A., Aegean painting in the Bronze Age. Univ. Park 1990, Penn. State. Univ. xxiv-240 p.; 94 fig. + 23 color. 0-271-00628-5 [OIAc S90].

d520 **Ivanov** Vladimir, Das grosse Buch der russischen Ikonen. FrB 1988, Herder. 224 p.; 168 color. pl. 3-451-21258-7. – ᴿOstkSt 38 (1989) 211s (E. C. *Suttner*).

d521 *Iversen* Erik, Metrology and canon [defense of his Canon and proportions in Egyptian art^{1,2}]: MiDAI-K 46 (1990) 113-125; 5 fig.

d522 **Jacobs** Bruno, Griechische und persische Elemente in der Grabkunst Lykiens zur Zeit der Achämenidenherrschaft: SIMA 18. Göteborg 1987, Åström. 91-86098-683 [OIAc F89].

d523 *a) Junge* Friedrich, Versuch zu einer Ästhetik der ägyptischen Kunst; – *b) Müller* Maya, Die ägyptische Kunst aus kunsthistorischer Sicht; –

c) Wildung Dietrich,   Bilanz eines Defizits; Problemstellungen und Methoden in der ägyptologischen Kunstwissenschaft: → 799, Äg. Kunst 1987/90, 1-38; pl. 1-4 / 39-56; pl. 5s / 57-80; pl. 7-14.

d524 *Kakovkin* A. Y., **O** On two groups of Coptic art monuments with antique subjects [Leda and the swan; Judgment of Paris]: VDI 192 (1990) 80-92; 3 fig.; Eng. 92.

d525 **Karageorghis** Vassos,   Blacks in ancient Cypriot art.   Houston 1988, Menil.   62 p.; 52 fig.; 2 maps. – ᴿAJA 94 (1990) 161s (F. M. *Snowden*).

d526 *Kiilerich* Bente,   Physiognomics and the iconography of Alexander the Great: Symbolae 63 (Oslo 1988) 51-66.

d527 **Krauss** H., *Uthemann* E.,   Was Bilder erzählen; die klassischen Geschichten in der abendländischen Malerei. Mü 1987, Beck. 546 p. – ᴱEos 77 (1989) 337s (W. *Appell*).

d528 **Lafontaine-Dosogne** Jacqueline,   Histoire de l'art byzantin et chrétien d'Orient 1987 → 4,e204...5,d339: ᴿByZ 82 (1989) 291-3 (F. *Winckelmann*).

d529 **Lange** Günther, *al.*,   Kunst zur Bibel; 32 Bildinterpretationen 1988 → 5,d341: ᴿTGegw 33 (1990) 213s (H. *Schalk*); TPQ 138 (1990) 81s (J. *Janda*).

d530 **Lebeau** P.,   Aux origines de l'art chrétien: Le temps de lire, 3, 1988 → 5,d343: ᴿFoiTemps 19 (1989) 87s (A. *Haquin*).

d531 *Lepage* Claude,   Contribution de l'ancien art chrétien d'Éthiopie à la connaissance des autres arts chrétiens: CRAI (1990) 799-822; 9 fig.

d532 ᴱ**Limouris** G.,   Icons, windows on eternity; theology and spirituality in colour. Geneva 1990, WCC. 228 p.; ill. £10 pa. – ᴿExpTim 102 (1990s) 157 (J. *Frederick*: about dogma, not art); TLond 93 (1990) 505s (J. *Baggley*).

d533 **Loon** G. van,   The meaning of Old Testament scenes in the sanctuaries of medieval Coptic churches: diss. in progress: Newsletter, Centre of Non-Western Studies 3 (Leiden 1990) 62s.

d534 **Meer** F. van der,   Christus' oudste gewaald [attire]; over de oorspronkelijkheid van de oudchristelijke kunst². Baarn 1989, Ambo. 341 p.; ill. Fb 1090. – ᴿCollatVL 20 (1990) 117 (W. *Dumon*).

d535 **Milburn** Robert,   Early Christian art and architecture 1988 → 4,c213; 5,d352: ᴿAJA 94 (1990) 517s (Caroline J. *Hemans*: sadly out of date).

d536 **Miles** Margaret,   Image as insight; visual understanding in Western Christianity and secular culture. Boston 1985, Beacon. xii-200 p. $25. – ᴿJAAR 58 (1990) 267-276 (J. W. *Dixon*).

d537 *Millet* N. B.,   The Narmer macehead and related objects: JAmEg 27 (1990) 53-59; 2 fig.

d538 *Moorsel* Paul van,   Forerunners of the Lord: saints of the Old Testament in medieval Coptic church decoration: CahArch 37 (1989) 119-133; 16 fig.

d539 *Moret* Jean-Marc, *Iō apotaurōménē* [vase-painting]: RArchéol (1990) 3-28; 15 fig.

d540 **Morgan** Lyvia,   The miniature wall paintings of Thera 1988 → 5,d353; $90; 0-521-24727-6: ᴿAJA 94 (1990) 347s (Maria C. *Shaw*); ClasW 83 (1989s) 376 (Karen P. *Foster*); JHS 110 (1990) 261s (Sara A. *Immerwahr*).

d541 **Neils** Jenifer,   The youthful deeds of Theseus: Archaeologica 76. R 1987, Bretschneider. xii-190 p.; 85 fig.; 27 pl. 88-7689-006-8. – ᴿAJA 94 (1990) 352s (J. H. *Oakley*); AntClas 59 (1990) 559-561 (D. *Martens*); Babesch 65 (1990) 179s (W. van de *Put*).

d542 **Nichols** A.,   Le Christ et l'art divin; théologie de l'image dans la tradition chrétienne [The art of God incarnate 1980 → 61,s356],ᵀ:

Croire et savoir. P 1988, Téqui. 183 p. – ᴿSalesianum 52 (1990) 752 (C. *Chenis*).

d543 **Nunn** Astrid, Die Wandmalerei und die glasierte Wandschmuck im Alten Orient: HbOr 7/1/2/B6, 1988 ➤ 5,d356: ᴿMcsopT 25 (1990) 242-5 (A. *Invernizzi*).

d544 **Pelikan** Jaroslav, Imago Dei; the Byzantine apologia for icons: Bollingen 35/36. Princeton 1990, Univ. xii-196 p. $40 [TS 52, 390, J. L. *Empereur*].

d545 *Pemberton* Elizabeth, The beginning of monumental painting in mainland Greece: ➤ 89, ᶠJASHEMSKI W. (1989) II, 181-197.

d546 **Pfeiffer** Heinrich, Gottes Wort im Bild; Christusdarstellungen in der Kunst 1986 ➤ 2,a201 ... 4,e219: ᴿTrierTZ 98 (1989) 234s (E. *Sauser*).

d547 *Pierre-Muller* Béatrice, Une grande peinture des appartements royaux du palais de Mari (Salles 219-220): MARI 6 (1990) 463-558; XXXII pl.

d548 **Pomorska** Iréna, Les flabellifères à la droite du roi en Égypte ancienne 1987 ➤ 3,d636: ᴿJAOS 110 (1990) 157 (W. A. *Ward*); WeltOr 20s (1989s) 262-4 (D. *Kessler*).

d549 *Quacquarelli* Antonio, Scènes évangéliques dans l'iconographie des premiers siècles: ➤ 542, Év. Vénasque 1989/90, 209-219.

d550 *Robins* Gay, a) Problems in interpreting Egyptian art: DiscEg 17 (1990) 45-58; – b) Proportions of standing figures in the north-west palace of Aššurnaṣirpal at Nimrud: Iraq 52 (1990) 107-116 + 10 fig.; – c) Proportions in Persian and Egyptian art: BEgSem 9 (1987s) 53-56 + 7 fig.

d551 **Raw** Barbara C., Anglo-Saxon crucifixion iconography and the art of the monastic revival: Anglo-Saxon England 1. C 1990, Univ. xii-296 p. $55 [CBQ 52,781].

d552 **Rouveret** Agnès, Histoire et imaginaire de la peinture ancienne: BÉF 274. R 1989, Éc. Française de Rome. x-577 p.; 22 fig.; 25 pl. F 500. – ᴿAntClas 59 (1990) 599-604 (C. *Delvoye*).

d553 *Rutschowscaya* Marie-Hélène, L'art au temps de la gnose: MondeB 63 (1990) 34-39; (color.) ill.

d554 *Sauser* Ekkart, Ikonografische Besonderheiten am Bild des heiligen Nikolaus von Myra: TrierTZ 99 (1990) 161-9; 2 color. pl.

d555 **Schäfer** Heinrich, Principles of Egyptian art [1919], ᴱ*Brunner-Traut* Emma [1959], ᵀ*Baines* J. 1988 ➤ 4,e228: ᴿBO 47 (1990) 344-9 (K. *Mysliwiec*: unique, invaluable).

d556 **Schefold** Karl, *Jung* Franz, Die Urkönige, Perseus, Bellerophon, Herakles und Theseus in der klassischen und hellenistischen Kunst. Mü 1988, Hirmer. 384 p.; ill. [Bedeutung für das Evangelium 1983 ➤ 4,e231].

d556* **Schmidt** Heinrich & Margarethe, Il linguaggio delle immagini; iconografia cristiana [Bildersprache⁴ (1984; ¹1981)], ᵀ1988 ➤ 4,e232: ᴿSalesianum 52 (1990) 160s (R. *Sabin*).

d557 a) *Schwarz* Mario, Syro-palästinensischer Einfluss auf die nubische Wandmalerei und Kirchenarchitektur; – b) *Balicka-Witakowska* Ewa, Descente de croix sur peinture murale de la cathédrale de Faras; – c) *Gorecki* Tomasz, Archangel and Saint Mercurios — new iconographical interpretations of the two murals from Faras cathedral; – d) *Lewczuk* Jarosław, Studies on the iconography of Thoueris in the art of the kingdom of Kush: ➤ 781, Nubien/Uppsala 1986/90, 585-602 / 459-474 / 535-540 / 541-8.

d557* **Shedid** Abdel Ghaffar, Stil der Grabmalereien in der Zeit Amenophis, II., untersucht an den thebanischen Gräbern Nr. 104 und Nr. 80: DAI-K Veröff. 66, 1988 ➤ 4,e235: ᴿJAmEg 27 (1990) 220-3 (N. *Strudwick*).

d558 *Stansbury-O'Donnell* Mark D., Polygnotos's Nekyia [counterpart of Iliupersis in Delphi Knidian Lesche described by PAUSANIAS]; a reconstruction and analysis: AJA 94 (1990) 213-235; 5 fig.

d559 *Stein-Schneider* Herbert, Le retable d'Issenheim [de Matthias GRÜNEWALD] et son message dissident: ÉTRel 65 (1990) 27-47 . 191-204; 3 pl.

d559* *Tchao* Joseph, Le langage esthétique et l'œuvre d'art; essai de comparaison entre la philosophie de l'art en Occident et l'esthétique chinoise: ScEsp 42 (1990) 5-34.

d560 *Televantou* Christina, ❻ The rendering of the human figure in the Theran wall-paintings: ArchEph 127 (1988) 135-166; 10 fig.; Eng. p. 166.

d561 *Tézé* Jean-Marie, Théophanies du Christ: JJC Résonances 4, 1988 ↠ 4,8550; 5,d377: ᴿÉTRel 65 (1990) 302s (J. *Cottin*).

d562 **Thierry** Jean-Michel, *al.*, Armenische Kunst 1988 ↠ 5,d379: ᴿTrierTZ 98 (1989) 160 (E. *Sauser*).

d564 *a)* *Thümmel* Hans-Georg, Bild und Bilderstreit in der Dichtung; – *b)* *Heidenreid* Richard, Repräsentationsbilder und Frontalität; – *c)* *Weiss* Günter, Byzantinische Kunst als Kunst des Mittelmeerraumes: ↠ 5,210, Mem. WESSEL K. 1988, 283-301 / 135-7 / 369-373.

d565 *Turnheim* Yehudit, The bud-wreath, a local variation of a classical ornament: ZDPV 106 (1990) 162-171; 6 fig.; pl. 20-25.

d566 **Ugolnik** Anthony, The illuminating icon. GR 1989, Eerdmans. 273 p. $20. – ᴿTTod 47 (1990s) 100.102.104s (M. O. *Cartwright*).

d566* *Vogt* Hermann J., Der Streit um das Lamm; das Trullanum und die Bilder: AnHistCon 20 (1988) 134-149.

d567 *Walter* Christopher, The Thracian horseman; ancestor of the warrior saints?: ↠ 717, ByzF 14 (1989) 657-673; pl. 249-255.

d568 *Walter-Karydi* Elena, Die Entstehung der Grotteskenornamentik in der Antike: MiDAI-R 97 (1990) 137-152; 1 fig.; pl. 1 (color); 34-42.

d569 **Whale** Sheila, The family in the eighteenth dynasty of Egypt; a study of the representation of the family in [93] private tombs [diss. Auckland]. Sydney 1989, Australian Centre for Egyptology. x-308 p. £28. 0-85837-679-9. – ᴿDiscEg 18 (1990) 91s (A. *Dodson*).

d569* **Wheeler** Marion. His face; images of Christ in art: Chameleon Books. ... 1988, Equation/Thorsons. 128 p. £15. 0-915829-63-0. – ᴿTablet 243 (1989) 488 (P. *Reyntiens*).

d570 **Woodford** Susan, An introduction to Greek art 1986 ↠ 4,e249: ᴿAncHRes 20 (1990) 125-7 (Joanna *Savage-Slater*).

d571 **Zanker** Paul, Augustus und die Macht der Bilder 1987 ↠ 4,e251; 5,d385*: ᴿAmHR 95 (1990) 472s (M. *Reinhold*); AtenRom 35 (1990) 209-212 (V. *Saladino*); Latomus 49 (1990) 281s (L. *Foucher*).

d572 **Zanker** Paul, The power of images in the age of Augustus, ᵀ*Shapiro* Alan. AA 1988, Univ. Michigan. vii-385 p. $30. 0-472-10101-3. – ᴿClasW 83 (1989s) 546 (R. F. *Thomas*: impressive).

d573 *Zanker* Paul, Bilderzwang; Augustan political symbolism in the private sphere, ᵀ*Shapiro* H. A.: ↠ 179, Mem. TOYNBEE J. 1988, 1-13 + 8 pl.

T3.2 Sculptura.

d574 '*Amr* Abdel-Jalil, Four Ammonite sculptures from Jordan: ZDPV 106 (1990) 114-8; pl. 7-8.

d575 **Andreae** Bernard, Laokoon und die Gründung Roms 1988 ↠ 4,e254*: ᴿAJA 94 (1990) 164s (K. *Galinsky*).

d576 *Azarpay* Guitty, A photogrammetric study of three Gudea statues: JAOS 110 (1990) 660-5; 1 fig.

d577 *a*) *Azarpay* Guitty, Gudea's canon; on art and mensuration; – *b*) *Trichet* Jean, *Vallat* François, L'origine égyptienne de la statue de Darius [trouvée à Suse 1972]: → 138, ^FPerrot J., Iran 1990, 83-85 + 6 fig. / 205-8; 2 fig.

d578 **Baines** John, Fecundity figures; Egyptian personification and the iconology of a genre 1985 → 3,d661; 5,d389: ^RBO 47 (1990) 639-4 (Waltraud *Guglielmi*).

d579 *Balty* Jean C., Un portrait [buste] de Shahba-Philippopolis et l'iconographie de Philippe l'Arabe: → 28, ^FBounni A. 1990, 5-13; 8 fig.

d580 **Barr-Sharrar** Beryl, The Hellenistic and Early Imperial decorative bust 1987 → 3,d664: ^RBonnJbb 190 (1990) 672-680 (H.-U. *Cain*).

d581 *Bernard* Paul, Vicissitudes au gré de l'histoire d'une statue en bronze d'Héraclès entre Séleucie du Tigre et la Mésène: JSav (1990) 3-68; 26 fig.

d582 *Bol* Peter C., Polyklet, der Bildhauer der griechischen Klassik: Ant-Welt 21 (1990) 159-176; 35 fig.

d583 **Boschung** D., Die Bildnisse des Caligula. B 1989, Mann., 138 p.; 37 fig.; 47 pl. – ^RBonnJbb 190 (1990) 655-664 (D. *Hertel*).

d584 *Boube* Jean, Une statue-portrait de Ptolémée de Maurétanie à Sala (Maroc): RArchéol (1990) 331-380; 24 fig.

d585 *Burkhalter* Fabienne, Les statuettes en bronze d'Aphrodite en Égypte romaine d'après les documents papyrologiques: RArchéol (1990) 51-60; 3 fig.

d586 **Caillet** Jean-Pierre, *Loose* Helmuth N., La vie d'éternité; la sculpture funéraire dans l'antiquité chétienne. P/Genève 1990, Cerf-Tricorne. 150 p.; 113 fig.; 113 (color.) phot. F 490. 2-204-04090-8 / 2-8293-00971 [NRT 113, 926, A. *Toubeau*].

d587 *Capriotti* G., Ricerche sulla struttura di stele regali egiziane: RSO 63 (1989) 1-12.

d588 *Chappaz* Jean-Luc, Répertoire annuel des figurines funéraires 3: BSoc-Ég 14 (Genève 1990) 89-104.

d589 **Connelly** Joan B., Votive sculpture of Hellenistic Cyprus 1988 → 5, d398; $35: ^RClasR 40 (1990) 423s (Veronica *Tatton-Brown*).

d590 *Damaty* Mamdouh M., Squatting statues in the Cairo Museum: MiDAI-K 46 (1990) 1-13; 4 fig.; pl. 1-9.

De Puma Richard, Roman portraits [sculpture exhibition] 1988 → b967.

d591 **Donohue** Alice A., Xoana and the origins of Greek sculpture 1988 → 5, d401: ^RAJA 94 (1990) 158s (A. *Stewart*).

d592 **Droste zu Hülshoff** Vera von, *Schlick-Nolte* Brigit, Ushebtis I.: Corpus Antiquitatum Aeg., Rhein-Main 2. Mainz 1984, von Zabern. 79 loose leaves. DM 68. 3-8035-0786-1. – ^RBO 47 (1990) 358-362 (J. van *Dijk*: loose-leaf principle unjustified, though incidental defects are being improved).

d593 **Dunand** Françoise, Catalogue de terres cuites gréco-romaines d'Égypte. P 1990, Réunion Musées. 349 p. 2-7118-2227-3 [OIAc Ap91,6].

d594 *Filseck* Karin M. von, Noch einmal zum Strigilisreiniger Ephesos-Wien; Klassik oder Klassizismus?: JhÖsA 60-H (1990) 1-5; 2 fig.

d595 **Fıratlı** *Nezih* † 27.III.1979, *al.*, La sculpture byzantine figurée au Musée Archéologique d'Istanbul: BIF Ét. Anatol. 13. P 1990, Maisonneuve. X-268 p.; 128 pl. – ^RRömQ 85 (1990) 245-250 (Jutta *Dresken-Weiland*).

d596 *Fleischer* Robert, Ein Gemmenporträt des Antiochos III: ArchAnz (1990) 467-471; 6 fig.

d597 **Fullerton** Mark D.,   The archaistic style in Roman statuary: Mnemosyne supp. 110. Leiden 1990, Brill. xiv-215 p.; 91 fig. 90-04091-46-7.

d599 **Gimbutas** Marija, The language of the goddess. L 1989, Thames & H. xxii-388 p.; 492 fig.; 13 maps. £30. 0-599-01480-9. – ᴿAntiqJ 69 (1989) 345s (A. *Sherratt*: attractive artefacts tendentiously interpreted).

d600 **Giuliani** L., Bildnis und Botschaft; hermeneutische Untersuchungen zur Bildniskunst der römischen Republik 1986 → 4,e280; 5,d404: ᴿDialArch 7,2 (1988s) 104s; RArchéol (1990) 188-190 (F. *Queyrel*).

d601 *Giuliani* Luca, Zur spätrepublikanischen Bildniskunst; Wege und Abwege der Interpretation antiker Porträts: AntAb 36 (1990) 103-115; 10 fig.

d601* *Görler* Woldemar, Nochmals, PLINIUS und der Laokoon; zu einer neuen Deutung von N.H. 36,37 [ANDRAE B. 1986-8]: RheinMus 133 (1990) 176-180.

d602 *Harper* Prudence O., A bronze head of the Late Iron Age from the Levant [NY Met, parallel to 1982 Jordan Umm Udheinah find]: → 4, ᶠAMIRAN Ruth, Eretz-Israel 21 (1990) 35*-39*; 6 fig.

d602* *Hartswick* Kim J., The Ares Borghese reconsidered: RArchéol (1990) 227-283; 16 fig.

d603 *Harvey* Julia, Some notes on the wooden statues from the tomb of Nakht at Assiut [from Corpus of private wooden statuary, dissertation in progress at London Univ. College, ᴰ*Dixon* D.]. GöMiszÄg 116 (1990) 45-50.

d604 **Hauptmann** Ralf, Die sumerische Beterstatuette: Mg 12. Fra 1989, Liebieghaus [OIAc JJ 89].

d605 *Herrmann* Hans-Volkmar, Die Siegerstatuen von Olympia … : Nikephoros 1 (1988) 119-183.

d606 **Himmelman** Nikolaus, Herrscher und Athlet, die Bronzen vom Quirinal [one each, in expectation of their move from Terme Museum to Palazzo Massimo]. Mi 1989, Olivetti. 247 p.; 107 fig. – ᴿAJA 94 (1990) 696-8 (Ellen D. *Reeder*).

d607 **Hölzl** Regina, Die Giebelfelddekoration von Stelen des Mittleren Reichs: Univ. Inst. Afrikanistik 55 / BeitÄg 10. Wien 1990, AFRO. 183 p. 3-85043-055-3 [OIAc Ja91].

d607* *Kaiser* Werner, Zur Buste als einer Darstellungsform ägyptischer Rundplastik: MiDAI-K 46 (1990) 269-285; pl. 61-67.

d608 *Knauer* Elfriede R., Multa egit cum regibus et pacem confirmavit; the date of the equestrian statue of Marcus Aurelius [176 A.D.]: MiDAI-R 97 (1990) 277-306; pl. 82-90.

d609 ᴱ**Kozloff** Arielle P., **Mitten** David G., The gods delight; the human figure in classical bronze [exhibition catalogue]. Bloomington/ Cleveland 1988, Indiana Univ./Museum. xiii-173 p. $25 pa. 0-910386-93-5. – ᴿClasW 84 (1990s) 63s (W. *Rudolph*).

d610 **Krelöl** Barbara, Privatstatuen als Mittler [Magisterarbeit]. Mü 1989, Univ. viii-97 p.; 7 fig. [OIAc Ap91,9].

d611 *Langdon* Susan, From monkey to man; the evolution of a geometric sculptural type [8th century Greek sanctuaries]: AJA 94 (1990) 407-424; 17 fig.

d612 *Leach* Eleanor W., The politics of self-presentation; PLINY's letters and Roman portrait sculpture: ClasAnt 9 (1990) 14-39 + 14 fig.

d613 **(Leander) Touati** Anne-Marie, The great Trajanic frieze 1987 → 4,e290; 5,d410: ᴿRBgPg 68 (1990) 227-231 (R. *Turcan*).

d613* **Maderna** Caterina, Iuppiter, Diomedes und Merkur als Vorbilder für römische Bildnisstatuen; Untersuchungen zum römischen statuarischen Idealporträt: ArchGesch 1, 1988 ➤ 5,d421: ᴿGGA 242 (1990) 165-173 (J. *Bergemann*).

d614 *Maoz* Rivka, Les Vénus au village dormant [Shaar ha-Golan, 6000 B.C.E.]: MondeB 62 (1990) 62s; 1 fig.

d615 *Markoe* Glenn E., Egyptianizing male votive statuary from Cyprus; a reexamination: Levant 22 (1990) 111-122; 17 fig.

d616 **Martin** Geoffrey T., Corpus of reliefs of the New Kingdom from the Memphite necropolis and Lower Egypt 1987 ➤ 3,d692: ᴿJAOS 110 (1990) 122s (W. W. *Ward*); OLZ 85 (1990) 659-662 (C.-B. *Arnst*).

d617 **Massner** Anne-Kathryn, Bildnisausgleichung; Untersuchungen zur Entstehung- und Wirkungsgeschichte der Augustusporträts (43 v.Chr. - 68 n.Chr.): Röm. Herrscherbild 4. – B 1982, Mann. xiv-166 p.; 35 pl. – ᴿAntClas 59 (1990) 626-9 (Jean-C. *Balty*).

d618 **Mattusch** Carol M., Greek bronze statuary 1989 ➤ 5,d424: ᴿPhoenix 44 (Toronto 1990) 388-392 (M. F. *Kilmer*).

d619 **Moormann** Eric M., La pittura parietale romana come fonte di conoscenza per la scultura antica 1988 ➤ 5,d425: ᴿAJA 94 (1990) 702-4 (Elisabeth *Bartman*).

d620 **Naguib** Saphinaz-Amal, Funerary statuettes 1985 ➤ 3,d697: ᴿCdÉ 65 (1990) 82-84 (J.-L. *Chappaz*).

d621 a) *Noy* Tamar, ❽ New aspects of pottery figurines in the Yarmukian culture; – b) *Tadmor* Miriam, ❽ A group of figurines and miniature vessels of the chalcolithic period: ➤ 4, AMIRAN Ruth, ErIsr 21 (1990) 226-232; 6 fig.; Eng. 109* / 249-258; 8 fig.; Eng. (without provenance) 110*.

d622 *Parlasca* Klaus, La sculpture grecque et la sculpture d'époque romaine impériale en Syrie: ➤ 481, Syrie II (1989) 537-556; fig. 195-209.

d623 **Pfrommer** Michael, Studien zu alexandrischer und grossgriechischer Toreutik 1987 ➤ 5,d429: ᴿArchWroc 40 (1989) 176-8 (Barbara *Gąssowska* ❽); Gnomon 62 (1990) 625-632 (E. *Lippolis*, ital.); Latomus 49 (1990) 526-9 (F. *Baratte*: vaisselle d'argent).

d624 *Prag* A., Reconstructing King Philip II [statuary head]; the 'nice' version: AJA 94 (1990) 237-247; 6 fig.

d625 *Quaegebeur* Jan, La stèle Brooklyn 71.37.2 reconsidérée: GöMiszÄg 119 (1990) 73-87; 2 fig.

d626 *Queyrel* François, Portraits princiers hellénistiques; chronique bibliographique: RArchéol (1990) 97-172; 15 fig.

d627 *Quirke* Stephen, Kerem in the [Cambridge] Fitzwilliam Museum: JEA 76 (1990) 170-174; pl. XIV-XV.

d628 **Ridgway** Brunilde S., Hellenistic sculpture I. The styles of ca. 331-200 B.C.: WI StClas. Madison 1990, Univ. Wisconsin. xxvi-405 p.; 187 pl. 0-299-11820-7 [OIAc JJ90].

d629 *Rolley* Claude, Les bronzes grecs et romains; recherches récentes, X. statues: RArchéol (1990) 405-422; 7 fig.

d630 **Rose** Charles B., Julio-Claudian dynastic group monuments: diss. Columbia. NY 1987. 796 p. 90-20598. – DissA 51 (1990s) 906-A.

d631 **Schlögl** Hermann A., *Brodbeck* Andreas, Ägyptische Totenfiguren aus öffentlichen und privaten Sammlungen der Schweiz: OBO arch. 7. FrS/ Gö 1990, Univ./VR. 354 p. 3-7278-0675-3 / 3-525-53657-7 [BL 91,160].

d632 **Schneider** Rolf M., Bunte Barbaren 1986 ➤ 4,e311: ᴿArchClasR 41 (1989) 466-8 (P. *Pensabene*).

d633 *Schneider* Rolf M.,   Kolossale Dakerstatuen [Dacian] aus grünem Porphyr: MiDAI-R 97 (1990) 235-260; 3 fig.; pl. 2 (color.) + 67-74.

d634 *a) Schoske* Sylvie,   Kunst — Geschichte; Bemerkungen zu einem neuerworbenen Königskopf im ägyptischen Museum (SMPK) Berlin; – *b) Schulz* Regine, Eine neue Statue des Pn-R'w im Hildesheim Pelizaeus-Museum; Gedanken zur Formenvielfalt im kuboiden Typenkanon der 19. Dynastie: ➤ 799, Äg. Kunst 1987/90, 81-94, pl. 15-23 / 95-108; 5 fig.; pl. 24-26.

d634* **Schröder** Stephan F.,   Römische Bacchusbilder [surtout grande et petite plastique] in der Tradition des Apollon Lykeios; Studien zur Bildformulierung und Bildbedeutung in späthellenistisch-römischer Zeit: Arch 77. R 1988, Bretschneider.   xii-216 p.; 31 pl. – ᴿRPg 64 (1990) 225s (G. *Siebert*).

d635 **Schulman** Alan R.,   Ceremonial execution and public rewards [on NK] stelae: OBO 75, 1988 ➤ 4,e312; 5,d441:   ᴿWeltOr 20s (1989s) 249-252 (R. *Drenkhahn*).

d636 *Schulman* Alan R.,   The ubiquitous Senenmut [-statues]: BEgSem 9 (1987s) 61-70 + 6 fig.

d637 **Scott** Gary D.ᴵᴵᴵ,   The history and development of the ancient Egyptian scribal statue: diss. Yale, ᴰ*Simpson* W.   NHv 1990. I. text, xxvi-469 p.; II-IV catalogue, 1201 p.   90-11923. – OIAc S90.

d638 *Simon* Erika,   Triptolemos in Syrien [Bronzestatuen] (pl. XIII-XVII): ➤ 160*, Mem. SCHULER E. v., Orientalia 59 (1990) 265-270.

d639 **Smith** R. R. R.,   Hellenistic royal portraits: MgClas. Arch. 1988 ➤ 4, e315; 5,d444; $125:   ᴿAJA 94 (1990) 508s (A. *Stewart*); AntiqJ 69 (1989) 350s (Susan *Walker*); NumC 150 (1990) 243s (I. *Carradice*: chiefly sculpture, but coins for comparison).

d640 *Smith* R. R. R.,   Late Roman philosopher portraits from Aphrodisias: JRS 80 (1990) 127-155.177; XVI pl.

d641 *a) Szafranski* Zbigniew E.,   Observations on the Second Intermediate period relief; – *b) Moursi* Mohamed,   A masterpiece scribe-statue from the Old Kingdom: ➤ 16, ᶠBECKERATH J. v. 1990, 245-251; pl. 18-19 / 209-214; 1 fig.; pl. 11-12.

d642 *Touchette* Lori-Ann,   A new interpretation of the Orpheus relief: Arch-Anz (1990) 77-90; 4 fig.

d643 *Tracy* Stephen V.,   Hands [handwritings, i.e. letter-cutting in stone] in Samian inscriptions of the Hellenistic period: Chiron 20 (1990) 59-75 + 27 fig. (97-100, the grain decree).

d644 *Uçankuş* Hasan T.,   Die bronzene Siegerstatue eines Läufers aus dem Meer vor Kyme: Nikephoros 2 (1989) 135-155; fig. 21-29 (p. 322-6).

d645 *a) Vandersleyen* Claude,   The sculpture in the round of Amenhotep III; types and purposes; – *b) Strauss-Seeber* Christine,   Kriterien zur Erkennung der königliche Rundplastik Amenophis' III.; – *c) Bryan* Betsy M.,   Private relief sculpture outside Thebes and its relation to Theban relief sculpture: ➤ 790, Amenhotep III 1987/90, 1-8 / 9-15; 13 fig.; pl. 1 / 65-80; pl. 18-19.

d645* **Vermeule** Cornelius,   The cult images of imperial Rome 1987 ➤ 3,b83: ᴿLatomus 49 (1990) 908s (J. P. *Callu*: ... un charmant Castor de Kansas City).

d646 **Vierneisel-Schlörb** Barbara,   Klassische Denkmäler und Votivreliefs: Glyptothek München, Katalog der Skulpturen 3.   Mü 1988, Beck. 239 p. – ᴿGGA 242 (1990) 157-164 (B. *Schmaltz*).

d647 *Wäfler* Markus,   Nicht-Assyrer neuassyrischer Darstellungen [Diss. München 1971]: AOAT 26. Neuk/Kevelaer 1975, Neuk / Butzon & B. xiii-399 p.; 30 pl., 4 foldout plans. DM 245. – ᴿBO 47 (1990) 775-8 (Erika *Bleibtreu*: nothing on why now).

d648 *Wipf* Karl A.,   Phänomene des Göttlichen in urgeschichtlicher Zeit [fertility figurines]: JPrehRel 3s (1989s) 19-29; 55 fig.

d649 *Witt* Günter,   Der Körper als Thema in der bildenden Kunst der Renaissance: Stadion 15,2 (1989) 191-200; 21 fig.

d650 **Zagdoun** Mary Anne,   La sculpture archaïsante dans l'art hellénistique et dans l'art romain du Haut-Empire: BÉF 269.   P 1989, École Française d'Athènes. xiii-263 p.; vol. of 274 fig. – ᴿAJA 94 (1990) 509s (M. D. *Fullerton*).

T3.3   *Glyptica:* **stamp and cylinder seals,** scarabs, amulets.

d651 *a) Adams* Barbara,   An enigmatic sealing from Abydos: → 4, ᶠAMIRAN R.; – *b) Esse* Douglas J.,   Early Bronze Age cylinder seal impressions from Beth Yeraḥ: ErIsr 21 (1990) 1*-9*; 13 fig. / 27*-34*; 2 fig.

d652 *Amiet* Pierre,   [Sceaux de] Eretz-Israel Marlik et Tchoga-Zanbil: RAss 84 (1990) 44-47; 3 fig.

d653 **Avigad** Nahman, Hebrew bullae 1986 → 2,a264 ... 5,d453: ᴿJRelHist 15 (1988s) 351s (B. *Jobling*); OLZ 85 (1990) 316s (H.-J. *Zobel*).

d654 *Avigad* N.,   *a)* Two Hebrew 'fiscal' bullae: IsrEJ 40 (1990) 262-6; pl. 28; – *b)* The seal of Mefa'ah [provenance unknown; PICCIRILLO's mosaics at Umm Rasas claimed to confirm Jawa site 10 k. S Amman]: IsrEJ 40 (1990) 42s.

d655 *Balty* Janine,   La mosaïque de Sarrin: AnASyr 37s (1988s as on ❹ cover) 251-269 + VIII pl.

d656 *Baudot* Marie Paule,   The Ancient Near Eastern seals and gems in the Biblical Museum at the Catholic University of Louvain: AcArchLov 26s (1987s) 113-123 + 53 fig.

d657 *Beckman* Gary,   More Anatolian stamp seals in America [California private collection]: OrAnt 28 (1989) 177-9 + 8 fig.

d658 *Ben-Tor* Amnon,   ❺ A stamp-seal and a seal impression of the chalcolithic period from Tel Gerar: → 4, ᶠAMIRAN Ruth, ErIsr 21 (1990) 80-86; 12 fig.; Eng. 103*s.

d659 *Beyer* Dominique, *Charpin* Dominique,   *a)* Les sceaux de Yasīm-Sūmū, serviteur de Zimri-Lim; – *b)* Le sceau de Zazia, roi des Turukkéens: MARI 6 (1990) 619-623; 5 fig. / 625-8; 2 fig.

d660 **Buchanan** Briggs, *Moorey* P. R. S.,   Catalogue of Ancient Near Eastern Seals in the Ashmolean Museum 1. The Iron Age stamp seals 1988 → 5,d459: ᴿBSO 52 (1989) 543s (W. G. *Lambert*).

d661 **Collon** Dominique,   First impressions 1987 → 3,d739 ... 5,d460: ᴿAulaO 8 (1990) 274s (G. del *Olmo Lete*: 'firts'); Syria 65 (1988) 235-8 (P. *Amiet*).

d662 **Collon** Dominique,   Near Eastern Seals: Interpreting the Past. L 1990, British Museum. 64 p. 0-7141-2072-3 [OIAc Oc90].

d663 *Collon* Dominique,   The life and times of Teḥeš-atal [on a seal attributed to a Hurrian by SOLLBERGER]: RAss 84 (1990) 129-136; 4 fig.

d664 **Courtois** Jacques-C., *Webb* Jennifer M.,   Les cylindres-sceaux d'Enkomi 1987 → 3,d741; 4,e346: ᴿOrientalia 59 (1990) 443-5 (D. M. *Matthews*).

d665 *Crowley* Janice, *Adams* Anthony,   The seal scan project; a preliminary report: MeditArch 3 (1990) 55-73; 10 fig.

d666 *Dierichs* Angelika, Leda-Schwan-Gruppen in der Glyptik und ihre monumentalen Vorbilder: Boreas 13 (Münster 1990) 37-50; pl. 5.

d667 *Dinçol* Ali M. & Belkıs, Hethitische Hieroglyphensiegel in der Museen zu Samsun, Gaziantep und Kahramanmaraş: ⇒ 3, Mem. ALKIM U. 1986, 233-244 + VIII pl.

d668 *a) Dinçol* Ali M., Neue hethitische Hieroglyphensiegel ... İstanbul, Ereğli, Karaman...; – *b) Carruba* Onofrio, *Mora* Clelia, Il segno L 277 del geroglifico anatolico [titolo regale soprattutto in sigilli]: ⇒ 160*, Mem. SCHULER E. v., Orientalia 59 (1990) 150-6; pl. VIII-XI / 143-9.

d669 *Eidem* Jesper [the inscription], *Møller* Eva [the decoration], A royal seal from the ancient Zagros: MARI 6 (1990) 635-9; 2 fig.

d670 *Garfinkel* Yosef, The Eliakim Na'ar Yokan seal impression [three ALBRIGHT samples]; sixty years of confusion in biblical research: BA 53 (1990) 74-79; ill.

d671 *Garlan* Yvon, Remarques sur les timbres amphoriques de Sinope: CRAI (1990) 490-507; 13 fig.

d672 **Gignoux** P., *Gyselen* Rika, Bulles et sceaux sassanides 1987 ⇒ 3,d745; 5,d468: ᴿBSO 52 (1989) 361s (W. *Sundermann*); JRAS (1989) 151-3 (D. N. *MacKenzie*).

d673 *Gitler* Haim, Four magical and Christian amulets: LA 40 (1990) 365-374; pl. 61-62; summary 451.

d674 **Giveon** Raphael, Scarabs... Israel: OBO 83, 1988 ⇒ 4,e356; 5,d469: ᴿBO 47 (1990) 647s (Magdalena *Stoof*).

d675 *Goldwasser* Orly, A cartouche of Semenkhkare from Canaan (Yarqon Tell Jeriše): GöMiszÄg 115 (1990) 29-31; 1 fig.; 1 pl.

d676 *Gonnet* Hatice, ❶ Observations sur les sceaux de Mutawalli II: Belleten 54,209 (1990) 9-13 + 7 fig.

d677 *Gorelick* Leonard, *Gwinnett* A. John, The Ancient Near Eastern cylinder seal as social emblem and status symbol: JNES 49 (1990) 45-56.

d678 **Hallager** Erik, The master impression, a clay sealing from... Kastelli 1985: SIMA 69, 1985 ⇒ 2,a289; 3,d748: ᴿAntClas 59 (1990) 563s (R. *Laffineur*).

d679 **Helck** Wolfgang, Thinitische Topfmarken: ÄgAbh 50. Wsb 1990, Harrassowitz. [vi-]164 p. 3-447-02982-X. – ᴿLA 40 (1990) 488s (A. *Niccacci*).

d680 **Joshi** Jagat P., *Parpola* Asko, Corpus of Indus seals and inscriptions I. Collections in India: Memoir/India 86. Helsinki 1987, Academia Scientiarum Fennica. xxxii-392 p.; 39 phot. + 16 color. – ᴿWeltOr 20s (1989s) 294s (T. *Barthel*).

d681 **Keel** O., *al.*, Studien zu den Stempelsiegeln aus Palästina/Israel 2, OBO 88, 1989 ⇒ 5,d475: ᴿAcOrK 51 (1990) 265-8 (Ingolf *Thuesen*); BL (1990) 122 (A. R. *Millard*).

d682 **Keel** Othmar, *Shuval* Menakhem, *Uehlinger* Christoph, Studien zu den Stempelsiegeln aus Palästina/Israel [1. 1985 ⇒ 1,d152... 4,e362], 3. Die frühe Eisenzeit, ein Workshop: OBO 100, FrS/Gö 1990, Univ./VR. xiii-455 p.; 36 + 109 fig.; XXII pl. Fs 120. 3-7278-0692-3 / VR 3-525-53732-8. – ᴿUF 22 (1990) 509s (O. *Loretz*).

d683 **Keel** O., *Uehlinger* C., Altorientalische Miniaturkunst; die ältesten visuellen Massenkommunikationsmittel; ein Blick in die [R. & E. Schmidt] Sammlungen des Biblischen Instituts der Universität Freiburg Schweiz. Mainz 1990, von Zabern. 163 p.; 170 fig. + 12 color. DM 45. 3-8053-1152-4 [BL 91,30, A. R. *Millard*].

d684 *Keel* Othmar, Ptah auf Siegelamuletten aus Palästina/Israel; einige Gesetzmässigkeiten bei der Übernahme von Motiven der Grosskunst auf Miniaturbildträger: VisRel 7 (1986/90) 199-222 + X pl.

d685 *Klengel-Brandt* Evelyn, *a)* Altbabylonische Siegelabrollungen (VS VII-IX): AltOrF 16 (1989) 253-356; 101 fig.; pl. V-XIX; – *b)* Siegelabrollungen auf einer Ḫana-Tafel: Orientalia 59 (1990) 1-13; 5 fig.; pl. I-IV.

d686 **Matthews** Donald M., Principles of composition in Near Eastern glyptic of the later second millennium B.C. [diss. Cambridge 1988]: OBO arch 8. FrS/Gö 1990, Univ./VR. [x-]166 p.; 626 fig.; 16 pl. 3-7278-0698-2 / 3-525-53658-5 [OIAc Ja91].

d687 *Moortgat-Correns* Ursula, Zum Siegel der assyrischen Königin Rimeni: → 3, Mem. ALKIM U., 1986, 253-270; 10 fig.

d688 *Mora* Clelia, La datazione di 'Malnigal' [sigillo ittita]: OrAnt 28 (1989) 183-191; 1 fig.

d689 **Müller-Winkler** Claudia, Die ägyptischen Objekt-Amulette...: OBO arch 5, 1987 → 3,d767... 5,d480: ᴿArOr 58 (1990) 410s (B. *Vachala*).

d690 *Porada* Edith, More seals of the time of the Sukkalmaḫ: RAss 84 (1990) 171-8 + 3 planches.

d691 **Rashad** Mahmoud, Die Entwicklung der vor- und frühgeschichtlichen Stempelsiegel in Iran, im Vergleich mit Mesopotamien, Syrien und Kleinasien; von ihren Anfängen bis zum Beginn des 3. Jahrstausends v.Chr.: ArchMIran Egb 13. B 1990, Reimer. 303 p.; 48 pl. 3-456-00392-8 [OIAc Oc90].

d692 *Salvini* Mirjo, Considerazioni su alcuni sigilli reali ittiti: Sefarad 50 (1990) 455-463; 1 fig.; castellano/Eng. 464.

d693 *a) Seidl* Ursula, Altelamische Siegel; – *b) Bachelot* Luc, Les relations entre Suse et la Haute-Mésopotamie au IIIᵉ millénaire av. J.-C.; étude de sceaux et scellements trouvés à Kutan (région d'Eski-Mossoul); – *c) Gyselen* Rika, Note de glyptique sassanide; quelques éléments d'iconographie religieuse: → 138, ᶠPERROT J., Iran 1990, 129-135; 6 fig. / 67-78 + 3 fig. / 253-265 + 2 pl.

d694 *Śliwa* Joachim, ❷ Skarabeusz Zielnicki [Tuthmosis III... *Jaeger* M. 1982]: Meander 45 (1980) 187-192; 2 fig.; lat. 193.

d695 **Śliwa** Joachim, Egyptian scarabs and magical gems from the collection of Constantine Schmidt-Ciążyński: Zeszyty 917. Kraków 1989, Uniw. Jagielloński. 104 p.; 155 fig. on XXVII pl. zł 800. 83-01-09530-X.

d696 **Speck** P., Byzantinische Bleisiegel in Berlin 1986 → 4,e376: ᴿByZ 82 (1989) 321s (D. *Theodoridis*).

d697 *Taracha* Piotr, Götter mit Löwen und Symbolik dieses Tieres in der kappadokischen Glyptik-Ikonographie (19.-18. Jht. v.Chr.): RoczOr 46,1 (1988s) 111-121; 4 pl.

d698 *Teissier* Beatrice, The seal impression Alalakh 194; a new aspect of Egypto-Levantine relations in the Middle Kingdom: Levant 22 (1990) 65-73; 3 fig.

d699 **Teissier** M. B., Egyptian iconography on Syro-Palestinian cylinder seals of the Middle Bronze Age (c. 1920-1550 B.C.): diss. Oxford 1990. – BInstClas 37 (1990) 211.

d700 *Trokay* Madeleine, Renaissance de thématique accadienne dans la glyptique Kassite: → 107, ᶠKUPPER J.-R. 1990, 88-96; 17 fig. [→ m7 Charpin].

d701 **Wickede** Alwo von, Prähistorische Stempelglyptik in Vorderasien [Diss. München 1989]: MüVorderasSt 6. Mü 1990, Profil. xvii-334 p.; 60 pl.; 63 phot. 3-89019-249-1[OIAc S90].

d702 **Wiese** André, Zum Bild des Königs auf ägyptischen Siegelamuletten: OBO 96. FrS/Gö 1990. Univ./VR. xv-207 p.; 32 pl. Fs 64. 3-7278-0670-2 / VR 3-525-53726-3 [BL 91, 132, K. A. *Kitchen*].

d703 **Younger** J. G., The iconography of the Late Minoan and Mycenaean sealstones and finger-rings 1988 ➔ 4,e385*: ᴿPraehZts 65 (1990) 88s (W. *Schiering*).

d704 *Zwierlein-Diehl* Erika, Griechische Gemmenschneider und augusteische Glyptik: ArchAnz (1990) 539-557; 14 fig.

T3.4 **Mosaica.**

d705 *Balil* Alberto, Algunos mosaicos de tema mitológico: BSAA 55 (1989) 113-145 + 3 pl.

d706 *Balty* Janine, La mosaïque / peinture en Syrie: ➔ 481, Syrie II (1989) 491-523; fig. 171-187 / 525-536; fig. 188-194.

d707 **Ben Khader** Aïcha B., Corpus des mosaïques de Tunisie [2/2, 1985 ➔ 2,a324; 5,d495] 2/3, Thuburbo Majus, Ouest. Tunis 1987. – ᴿLatomus 49 (1990) 240 (L. *Foucher*); Speculum 64 (1989) 643s (R. E. *Kolarik*).

d708 ᴱ**Bertelli** Carlo, Die Mosaiken; ein Handbuch der musivischen Kunst von den Anfängen bis zur Gegenwart. FrB 1989, Herder. 360 p.; 253 color. phot. DM 168. – ᴿZkT 112 (1990) 488s (H. B. *Meyer*).

d709 **Bertoli** Bruno, *Niero* Antonio, I mosaici di San Marco; un itinerario biblico 1986 ➔ 5,d496: ᴿRivScR 4 (1990) 294s (S. *Palese*).

d710 *a) Berzobohaty* Peter, *Jobst* Werner, Mosaikenforschung 1988, Bericht über die Arbeiten am Palastmosaik von Konstantinopel; – *b) Koranda* Christian, Pedaturaangaben in frühchristlichen Mosaikinschriften; Bemerkungen zur Menora-Inschrift der neugefundenen Synagoge in Plovdiv: AnzW 126 (1989) 225-237; 15 (color.) fig. / 103-110; 1 fig.

d711 **Boeselager** Dela von, Antike Mosaiken in Sizilien; Hellenismus und römische Kaiserzeit, 3. Jh. v.Chr.-3. Jh. n.Chr.: Archaeologica 40, 1983 ➔ 1,d177; 2,a327: ᴿArchClasR 42 (1990) 453-6 (Simonetta *Angiolillo*).

d712 **Campbell** Sheila, The mosaics of Antioch: Subsidia mediaevalia 15, Corpus of Mosaic Pavements in Turkey 4, 1988 ➔ 5,d497: ᴿAJA 94 (1990) 516s (D. *Parrish*); BonnJbb 190 (1990) 718-720 (Janine *Balty*); Gnomon 62 (1990) 665s (F. *Baratte*).

d713 **Daszewski** Wiktor A., Corpus of mosaics from Egypt 1, 1985 ➔ 3,d788 ... 5,d499: ᴿCdÉ 65 (1990) 94-96 (J. *Balty*).

d714 **Demus** Otto, The mosaics of San Marco in Venice 1984 ➔ 1,d183: ᴿByZ 81 (1988) 321-7 (F. W. *Deichmann*); Speculum 65 (1990) 971s (Annabel J. *Wharton*).

d715 *Donderer* Michael, Römische Mosaiken des Mittelmeerraumes in öffentlichen Sammlungen der Bundesrepublik Deutschland: ArchAnz (1990) 157-180; 34 fig.

d716 *Foerster* G., Allegorical and symbolic motifs with Christian significance from mosaic pavements of sixth-century Palestinian synagogues: ➔ 39, ᶠCORBO V., Christian archaeology 1990, 545-552.

d717 *Loos-Dietz* E. P. de, Les mosaïques à Khirbat al-Mafjar près de Jéricho: Babesch 65 (1990) 123-138; 11 fig.

d718 **Ovadiah** Ruth & Asher, Hellenistic, Roman, and early Byzantine mosaic pavements in Israel 1987 ➔ 4,e396; 5,d507: ᴿArchClasR 41 (1989) 491s (M. Luisa *Morricone*).

d719 *Ovadiah* Asher, Mosaic pavements of the Herodian period in Israel: MeditHistR 5 (1990) 207-221; 5 pl.

d720 **Parrish** David,   Season mosaics of Roman North Africa 1984 ⇥ 65,a547 ... 3,d797:   ᴿGnomon 62 (1990) 637-641 (M. *Donderer*).

d722 **Russell** James,   The mosaic inscriptions of Anemurium 1987 ⇥ 4,e399; 5,d508:   ᴿByZ 83 (1990) 141 (C. *Mango*); Byzantion 60 (1990) 560s (Janine *Balty*).

d723 *Steiner* Richard C.,   A Syriac church [mosaic] inscription from 504 C.E. [now with Mar A. Samuel in Lodi NJ]: JSS 35 (1990) 99-107; 3 fig.

d724 **Wisskirchen** Rotraut,   Das Mosaikprogramm von S. Prassede in Rom; Ikonographie und Ikonologie: Diss. Bonn 1989. – ArchAnz (1990) 148, nur Titel.

T3.5   *Ceramica*, **pottery**   [⇥ *singuli situs*, infra].

d725 *Adams* William Y.,   Times, types, and sites; the interrelationship of ceramic chronology and typology: BEgSem 8 (1986s) 7-31 + 15 fig.

d726 ᴱ**Allan** James, *Roberts* Caroline,   Syria and Iran; three studies in medieval ceramics: Islamic Art 4.   Ox 1987, Univ.   220 p.; 28 pl. – ᴿBSO 53 (1990) 133s (A. *Northedge*).

d727 **Allen** Susan H.,   Northwest Anatolian grey wares in the Late Bronze Age; analysis and distribution in the Eastern Mediterranean: diss. Brown. Providence 1990.   478 p. 91-01726. – DissA 51 (1990s) 2789-A.

d728 *Amiet* P.,   Quelques épaves de la vaisselle royale perse de Suse: ⇥ 138, ᶠPERROT J., Iran 1990, 213-9 + 5 pl.

d729 **Amyx** D. A.,   Corinthian vase-painting of the archaic period 1988 ⇥ 5,d516; $225;   0-520-03166-0;   ᴿAJA 94 (1990) 691s (Mary B. *Moore*); Babesch 65 (1990) 180s (Maria *Stoop*).

d730 *Barlow* J. A., *Idziak* P.,   Selective use of clays at a Middle Bronze Age site in Cyprus: Archaeometry 31 (1989) 66-76 (54-65, *al.*, black-topped pottery).

d731 *Benyon* Diane E., *al.*, Tempering types and sources for EB ceramics from Bab edh-Dhra and Numeira, Jordan: JField 13 (1986) 297-305.

d732 **Bergoffen** Celia Jane,   A comparative study of the regional distribution of Cypriote pottery in Canaan and Egypt in the Late Bronze Age: diss. NYU 1989, ᴰ*Hansen* D. 753 p. 90-16245. – DissA 51 (1990s) 540-A; OIAc Oc90.

d733 **Berry** John David,   A preliminary study of ceramics from the Northern Negev; tracing pottery production with instrumental neutron activation analysis: diss. California-Fullerton 1985.   ix-262 p. AA microfilm 1327090 [OIAc F91,1].

d734 **Blakely** Jeffrey A.,   Historical geography and its impact on the analysis and publication of excavated ceramics in the British and American traditions of Palestinian archaeology: diss. Pennsylvania, ᴰ*Muhly* J.   Ph 1990. 334 p. 91-12537. – DissA 51 (1990s) 4166-A.

d735 **Boardman** John,   Athenian red figure vases: World of Art.   L 1989 [pa. = 1985], Thames & H.   252 p. £6 pa.   0-500-20244-3. – ᴿAntiqJ 69 (1989) 351 (Lucilla *Burn*).

d736 **Burn** Lucilla,   The Meidias painter 1987 ⇥ 4,e417; 5,d523:   ᴿAJA 94 (1990) 353s (Mary B. *Moore*); Babesch 65 (1990) 161-3 (J. M. *Hemelrijk*: 36 vases by him, 210 in his style); JHS 110 (1990) 269s (M. *Robertson*).

d737 **Burow** Johannes,   Die Antimenesmaler: Forschungen zur antiken Keramik 2/7.   Mainz 1989, von Zabern.   xii-126 p.; 160 pl.

d738 ᴱ**Christiansen** Jette, *Melander* Torben, Proceedings of the 3rd Symposium on ancient Greek and related pottery, Copenhagen 1987/8 ➤ 5,838: ᴿAJA 94 (1990) 690s (G. *Hedreen*).

d739 **Coulson** William D.E., The Dark Age pottery of Messenia: SIMA pocket 43, 1986 ➤ 2,a343; 5,d524: ᴿAntClas 53 (1990) 574s (R. *Laffineur*).

d740 **Ferrari** Gloria, I vasi attici a figure rosse del periodo arcaico. R 1988, Bretschneider. 196 p.; 99 pl. – ᴿAJA 94 (1990) 692s (J. *Neils*); DLZ 111 (1990) 96-98 (E. *Paul*).

d741 **Frank** Susanne, Attische Kelchkratere; eine Untersuchung zum Zusammenspiel von Gefässform und Bemalung: EurHS 38/24. Fra 1990, Lang. 326 p.; 18 pl.

d742 *Freyer-Schauenburg* Brigitte, Corpus vasorum antiquorum, Kiel 1. Mü 1988, Beck. 129 p.; 58 fig.; 56 pl. DM 142. – ᴿDLZ 111 (1990) 692-4 (E. *Paul*).

d743 *a) Goren* Yuval, ◉ Pottery from chalcolithic and Early Bronze Age I cemeteries in Israel; some aspects of the development of ceramic technology; – *b) Zevulun* Uzza, ◉ Tell el-Yahudiyah juglets from a potter's refuse pit at Afula: ➤ 4, ᶠAMIRAN Ruth, ErIsr 21 (1990) 119-126; Eng. 105* / 174-190; 10 fig.; Eng. 107*.

d744 *Guéry* Roger, Les marques de potiers sur *terra sigillata* découvertes en Algérie III: AntAfr 26 (1990) 87-111; 7 fig.

d745 **Hemelrijk** J.M., Corpus vasorum antiquorum, Netherlands I. Amst 1988, A. Pierson Museum. xi-138 p.; 89 fig.; 64 pl. *f* 198. – ᴿGnomon 62 (1990) 717-722 (Erika *Kunze-Götte*).

d746 **Holmberg** Erik J., The red-line painter and the workshop of the Acheloos painter: SIMA pocket 87. Jonsered 1990, Åström. 107 p.; ill.

d747 **Iacovou** Maria, Pictorial pottery... Cyprus [ᴰ1984]: SIMA 79 [wrongly 78 on cover], 1988 ➤ 4,g637: ᴿRArchéol (1990) 174 (A. *Hermary*).

d748 *a) Johnson* David J., Nabataean piriform ungucntaria; – *b) Mason* James R.B., *'Amr* Khairieh, A study of Nabataean pottery manufacturing techniques; an experiment for reconstructing the production of fine bowls; – *c) Villeneuve* François, The pottery from the oil-factory at Khirbet Edh-Dharih (2nd century AD: ➤ 783, Aram 2 (1989/90) 235-248; 4 fig. / 287-307; 9 fig. / 367-384; 1 fig.; VIII pl.

d749 ᴱ**Kolb** Charles C., Ceramic-ecology 1988; current research on ceramic materials; BAR-Int 513. Ox 1989. xiii-421 p.

d750 *Lebeau* Marc, *a)* La céramique du Tombeau IVR2-SE.T7 dc Mari (Chantier A, palais oriental); – *b)* La céramique du Tombeau 300 de Mari (Temple d'Ishtar): MARI 6 (1990) 375-383 / 349-364 + VIII pl.; 373s bibliog.

d751 **Lévêque** Pierre, *Morel* Jean-Paul, Céramiques hellénistiques et romaines: AnnLitt Besançon 331. P 1987, BLettres. 339 p.; ill. 2-251-60331-X. – ᴿAntClas 59 (1990) 598s (G. *Raepsaet*).

d752 **Lezzi-Hafter** Adrienne, Der Eretria-Maler, Werke und Weggefährten: Kerameus 6. Mainz 1988, von Zabern. xiv-383 p.; vol. of xxiv + 196 pl., 113 ill., 921 phot. DM 198. – ᴿClasR 40 (1990) 420s (J.H. *Oakley*); GreeceR 37 (1990) 119s (B.A. *Sparkes*).

d753 *McPhee* Ian M., *Trendall* A.D., Addenda to [1987 AntKunst Beih 14] Greek red-figured fish-plates: AntKunst 33 (1990) 31-51: 100 new samples, 30 new locations.

d754 **Magness** Jodi, A typology of the Late Roman and Byzantine pottery of Jerusalem: diss. Pennsylvania, ᴰ*De Vries* K. Ph 1989. 914 p. 90-15131. – DissA 51 (1990s) 541-A.

d755 **Mountjoy** Penelope A.,   Mycenean decorated pottery, a guide to its identification: SIMA 73, 1986 ➤ 2,a360; 3,d850 (not SIMA 71): ᴿAntClas 59 (1990) 573s (R. *Laffineur*).

d756 *Nadelmann* Yonatan, 'Chiselled' inscriptions and markings on pottery vessels from the Iron Age II (discussion and catalogue): IsrEJ 40 (1990) 31-41; 6 fig.; pl. 4-5.

d757 *a) Nicholson* Paul T., *Patterson* Helen I.,   Ceramic technology in Upper Egypt; a study of pottery firing; – *b) Tite* M. S., *Bimson* M.,   Glazed steatite; an investigation of the methods of glazing used in ancient Egypt: WorldArch 21 (1989s) 71-86; 8 fig. / 87-100; 8 fig.

d758 **Oakley** John H.,   The Phiale painter; Forschungen zur antiken Keramik 2/8.   Mainz 1990, von Zabern.   xii-121 p.; 151 pl.

d759 *Orton* C. R., *Tyers* P. A.,   Statistical analysis of ceramic assemblages: ArchCalc 1 (1990) 81-110; 3 fig.

d760 *Pascual Buyé* Ignacio,   La cerámica de cocina de Sagunto desde la fundación hasta el cambio de era: ➤ 33, ᶠCHABRET A. 1989, 93-142; 20 fig.

d761 *Payne* Joan C.,   The chronology of predynastic Egyptian decorated ware: ➤ 4, ᶠAMIRAN Ruth, Eretz-Israel 21 (1990) 77*-88*; 3 fig.

d762 *a) Pollard* Richard,   Quantification; towards a standard practice; – *b) Wallace* Colin,   Roman pottery studies in Britain, 1890-1919; – *c) Symonds* R. P.,   Roman pottery bibliography: JRomPot 3 (1990) 75-79 / 80-87 / 92-130.

d763 *Porat* Naomi,   Local industry of Egyptian pottery in Southern Palestine during Early Bronze I period: BEgSem 8 (1986s) 109-119 + 17 fig.; map.

d764 **Rombos** Theodora,   The iconography of Attic Late Geometric II pottery: SIMA pocket 68.   Jonsered 1988, Åström.   578 p.; 78 pl. – ᴿClasR 40 (1990) 418s (K. A. *Sheedy*).

d765 **Rova** Elena,   Distribution and chronology of the Nineveh 5 pottery and of its culture: CMatArch 2.   R 1988, Univ.   276 p.; XXXIII pl.

d766 *Schneider* Gerwulf,   A technological study of North Mesopotamian stone ware [pottery]: WorldArch 21 (1989s) 30-50; 11 fig.

d767 *a) Schöne* Angelika,   Die Hydria des Meidias-Malers im Kerameikos; zur Ikonographie der Bildnisfriese; – *b) Sheedy* Kenneth A., A prothesis scene from the Analatos painter: MiDAI-A 105 (1990) 163-178; pl. 25-30; foldout 7-9 / 117-115; 2 fig.; pl. 14-21.

d768 *Shapiro* H. A.,   Old and new heroes; narrative, composition, and subject in Attic black-figure: ClasAnt 9 (1990) 114-148 + 11 fig.

d768* *Small* David B.,   Handmade burnished ware and prehistoric Aegean economics; an argument for indigenous appearance: JMeditArch 3 (Sheffield 1990) 3-25.

d769 *a) Steinmann* Frank,   Klassifizierung von Tongefässen; – *b) Wolf* Pawel,   Eine Methode zur Auswertung qualitativer Merkmale; ➤ 78, ᶠHINTZE F., Meroitica 12 (1990) 293-296 + 4 fig. / 353-9.

d770 **Thompson** Homer A. & Dorothy B.,   Hellenistic pottery and terracottas ➤ 5,d556 [< Hesperia 1934 and 1952-66], ᴱ*Rotroff* Susan B. Princeton 1987, Amer. Sch. Athens.   459 p.; 64 pl.   0-87661-944-8. – ᴿBabesch 65 (1990) 164s (B. *Heldring*).

d771 *Turner* J. D., *al.*,   Drawing potsherds; a low-cost computer-based system: Archaeometry 32 (1990) 177-182.

d772 **Venit** Marjorie S.,   Greek painted pottery from Naukratis in Egyptian museums 1988 ➤ 4,e457:   ᴿGnomon 62 (1990) 473s (J. *Boardman*); ZDMG 140 (1990) 374-6 (H.-G. *Buchholz*).

d773 *Verner* Miroslav, Zu K. PREUSS 'Keramikfunde': ZägSpr [113 (1986) 69-76] 117 (1990) 69-76.

d774 ^E**Vickers** Michael, Pots and pans 1985/7 → 4,780; 5,d559: ^RBInstArch 26 (1989) 299-301 (P. *Craddock*).

d775 *Vitelli* Karen D., Were pots first made for foods? Doubts from Franchthi: WorldArch 21 (1989s) 17-29; 3 fig.

d776 *Walter* V., *Besnus* Y., Reconnaissance de traces de microorganismes dans des céramiques archéologiques à l'aide de restes de pyrite transformée: RArchéom 14 (1990) 29-35; 10 phot.

d777 **Wood** Bryant G., The sociology of pottery in ancient Palestine; the ceramic industry and the diffusion of ceramic style in the Bronze and Iron Ages [diss. Cambridge 1977]: ASOR Mg 4 / JStOT supp. 103. Sheffield 1990, Academic. 148 p.; 24 fig. 1-85075-269-9.

T3.6 Lampas.

d778 **Bailey** D. M., Catalogue... Roman provincial lamps. L 1988, British Museum. xv-560 p.; 162 fig.; 160 pl. 0-7141-1278-X. – ^RClasR 40 (1990) 187s (R. *Ling*); JRS 80 (1990) 230s (H. *Williams*).

d779 **Bonnet** Jacqueline, Lampes céramiques signées; définition critique d'ateliers du Haut Empire: Documents Arch. Française 13. P 1988, Sciences de l'Homme. 225 p.; 65 fig. – ^RAJA 94 (1990) 168s (Norma *Goldman*).

d780 *a*) *Bunimovitz* Shlomo, *Zimhoni* Orna, Ⓗ 'Lamp and Bowl' foundation deposits from the end of the Late Bronze Age – beginning of the Iron Age in Eretz-Israel; – *b*) *Sussman* Varda, Ⓗ Pottery vessels versus lamps; identity of fashioning: → 4, ^FAMIRAN Ruth, ErIsr 21 (1990) 41-53; 10 fig.; Eng. 102* / 191-6; 2 fig.; Eng. 107*s.

d781 *Bussière* Jean, Les lampes à entonnoir d'Algérie [... possiblement puniques]: AntAfr 26 (1990) 25-37; 26 fig.

d782 *Carretero Vaquero* Santiago, Lucernas romanas con paisaje de influencia alejandrina; temas pastoriles: BSAA 55 (1989) 149-165 + 3 pl.

d783 **Engle** A., Light, lamps and windows in antiquity: Readings in Glass History 20, 1987 → 4,e464; $16: ^RRArtLv 21 (1988) 175s (Veronique Van *Driessche*).

d784 *Gal* Z., Ⓗ A kernos from Horvat Rosh Zayit in Lower Galilee: Qadmoniot 23,1s (1990) 51s.

d785 *Haley* Evan W., The lamp manufacturer Gaius Iunius Draco: Münst-Hand 9,2 (1990) 1-12; deutsch 12s; franç. 13.

d786 *Hofmann* Inge, Eine römische Bildlampe und ihr Motiv im meroitischen Reich: VarAeg 5 (1989) 123-132; 3 fig.

d787 **Loffreda** Stanislao, Lucerne 1989 → 5,d571: ^ROrChr 74 (1990) 268s (W. *Gessel*).

d788 *Loffreda* Stanislao, *a*) The Greek inscriptions on the Byzantine lamps from the Holy Land: → 39, ^FCORBO V., Christian archaeology 1990, 475-500; – *b*) Nuovi tipi di iscrizioni su lucerne bizantine: LA 40 (1990) 357-363; 4 fig.; pl. 59-60; Eng. 451; – *c*) Le lucerne bizantine palestinesi espressione popolare della fede cristiana: TerraS 66 (1990) 116-122; 9 fig.

d789 **Michelucci** Maurizio, La collezione di lucerne del Museo Egizio di Firenze: Accad. Studi 39. F 1975, Olschki. 130 p. [OIAc Oc90].

d790 **Williams** H., The lamps: Kenchreai 5, 1981 ➤ 65,a596: ᴿArchClasR 38ss (1986-8) 221-3 (Liliana *Mercando*).

T3.7 **Cultica.**

d791 **Alp** Sedat, Beiträge zur Erforschung des hethitischen Tempels 1983 ➤ 64,b72... 2,a380; ᴿBO 47 (1990) 717-722 (J. de *Roos*).

d792 *Brooten* B.J., Were women and men segregated in ancient synagogues?: Moment 14,7 (Wsh 1989) 32-39 [< NTAbs 34,219].

d793 **Cattaneo di Ciaccia** G., Il luogo di culto nella storia: PiccBScR 8. Mi 1989, Àncora. 217 p. – ᴿSalesianum 52 (1990) 767 (C. *Chenis*).

d794 *Cree* F. de, Votive beds in the Rockefeller Museum, Jerusalem; a case of Mesopotamian influence in IIId millenium Palestine?; AcArchLov 26s (1987s) 109-111; 2 fig.

d794* *Fehérvári* G., Mihrab: ➤ 840, Encyclopaedia of Islam 7 (1990) 7-15; VIII pl. – *Masdjid* (mosque) 6 (1990) 644-677 (J. *Pedersen*); 677-688 (R. *Hillenbrand*, architecture) [707s, al-Aḳsa, *Grabar* O.].

d795 ᴱ**Fox** Michael V., Temple in Society 1986/8, ➤ 4,734: ᴿOLZ 85 (1990) 521s (B. *Brentjes*).

d796 *Godlewski* Włodzimierz, The northern church in Old Dongola: AnNilM 4 (1990) 37-56; 15 fig. + VI pl.

d797 *Huot* Jean-Louis, Des sanctuaires orientaux; à propos de quelques idées reçues (Çatal Hüyük, Obeid...): ➤ 111, ᶠLÉVEQUE P., 4 (1990) 209-219.

d798 **Kraus** F.R., The role of temples from the Third Dynasty of Ur to the First Dynasty of Babylon, ᵀ*Foster* Benjamin R. [unpublished original; French awaited in Journal of World History; not = ᵀ1974, *Serlin* S.] MgANE 2/4. Malibu 1990, Undena. [iv] 20 p. 0-89003-240-8.

d799 ᴱ**Levine** Lee I., The synagogue in Late Antiquity 1984/7 ➤ 3,551: ᴿBA 53 (1990) 40s (W. *Soll*); JAOS 110 (1990) 123s (J. *Neusner*: each paper is of high standard); RPg 63 (1989) 350s (Lyliane *Sznajder*).

d800 *a*) *Margalit* Shlomo, The bi-apsidal churches in Palestine, Jordan, Syria, Lebanon, and Cyprus; – *b*) *Peña* Ignacio, Bautisterios y martyria rurales en el norte de Siria (siglos V-VI); – *c*) *Chen* Doron, Dating synagogues in Galilee; on the evidence from Meroth and Caparnaum: LA 40 (1990) 321-334; pl. 45-48 / 335-348; pl. 49-54 / 349-355; pl. 55-58. – Eng. 450.

d801 **Martin** H.G., Römische Tempelkultbilder 1987 ➤ 4,e476: ᴿJRS 80 (1990) 233s (Valérie *Huet*, also on VERMEULE C. 1987).

d802 *Mostafa* Doha M., Réflexions sur la fonction cosmographique du temple égyptien: VarAeg 5 (1989) 103-118; 7 fig.

d802* **Negev** A., Tempel, Kirchen und Zisternen... Negev/Nabatäer 1983 ➤ 64,b101... 2,a393: ᴿTsTKi 60 (1989) 55 (D. *Rian*).

d803 *Rahmani* L.Y., Stone synagogue chairs; their identification, use and significance: IsrEJ 40 (1990) 192-214; pl. 19-21.

d804 **Rutkowski** Bogdan, The cult places of the Aegean 1986 ➤ 2,8923; 3,b179: ᴿAntiqJ 69 (1989) 340s (J.F. *Cherry*); CritRR 2 (1989) 294-6 (Jorunn J. *Buckley*).

d805 **Spencer** Patricia, The Egyptian temple; a lexicographical study 1984 ➤ 65,8083... 4,e481: ᴿJAOS 110 (1990) 116s (D.P. *Silverman*).

White I.M., Building God's house in the Roman world; architectural adaptation among pagans, Jews, and Christians 1990 ➤ d189.

Zwickel W., Räucherkult... archäolog. 1990 ➤ 2721.

T3.8 **Funeraria;** *Sindon,* **the Shroud.**

d807 *Adams* C.V.A., *a*) Shepensut, priestess of Thebes; her mummification and autopsy; – *b*) An investigation into the mummies presented to

H. R. H. the Prince of Wales in 1869:   DiscEg 16 (1990) 9-17 + 2 fig. /
18 (1990) 5-19.

d808 *a*) *Ambrogi* Annarena,   Sarcofagi e urne con ghirlande della prima età
imperiale;   – *b*) *Amedick* Rita,   Monatsbilder auf einem antiken
Sarkophag: MiDAI 97 (1990) 163-196; pl. 46-52 / 197-210; pl. 53-59.

d809 **Anson** Francisco,   Después del Carbono 14, la Sábana Santa: Arcaduz.
M 1989, Palabra.   162 p.; ill.   84-7118-648-9. – ᴿActuBbg 27 (1990) 235
(A. *Boada*: among 'Fakes' in British Museum exhibition); StCatt 34 (1990)
378 (L. *Fossati*).

d810 **Bachofen** J. J.,   Il simbolismo funerario degli antichi [1856], ᵀᴱ*Pezzella*
M.   N 1989, Guida.   727 p. – ᴿEuntDoc 43 (1990) 547s (P. *Miccoli*).

d811 **Baima Bollone** Pier Luigi,   Sindone o no?   T 1990, SEI.   335 p.; ill. Lit.
35.000. – ᴿCC 141 (1990,4) 618s (V. *Marcozzi*).

d812 **Bloch-Smith** Elizabeth,   Judahite burial practices and beliefs about the
dead: diss. ᴰ*Stager* L. Ch 1990, Univ.   xi-346 p.; bibliog. p. 297-346. –
OIAc JJ90.

d812* **Bonnet-Eymard** Bruno,   La vittoria della Santa Sindone acquisita dalla
scienza.   S.-Pierre-les-Vaudes 1990, Contre-Réforme.   80 p. Lit. 10.000
[StCatt 34,549].

d813 **Bruns-Özgan** Christine,   Lykische Grabreliefs 1987 ➤ 3,d903... 5,d604:
ᴿDLZ 111 (1990) 98-101 (M. *Oppermann*).

d814 **Bulst** Werner,   Betrug am Turiner Grabtuch;   der manipulierte Car-
bontest.   Fra 1990, Knecht.   64 p.; 35 fig. DM 18 pa.   3-7820-0609-7. –
ᴿZkT 112 (1990) 496s (A. *Batlogg*: hochemotional).

d815 *Casey* Michael T.,   The holy shroud of Turin: IrTQ 56 (1990) 60-62.

d816 **Chappaz** Jean-Luc,   Les figurines funéraires égyptiennes [Genève] 1984
➤ 65,a632 ... 5,d605:   ᴿCdÉ 65 (1990) 84-88 (Joyce L. *Haynes*).

d817 **Corsini de Ordeig** Manuela,   Historia del sudario de Cristo.   M 1988,
Rialp.   177 p. – ᴿScripTPamp 22 (1990) 653s (J. A. *Vázquez-Rodríguez*).

d818 Les cultes funéraires en Égypte et en Nubie (*Le Nouëne* Patrick, *al.*).
Calais/Béthune/Dunkerque 1988, Musées.   91 p.; ill.

d819 *Daoudel* Yves,   À propos du Saint Suaire: PenséeC 238 (1989) 88s.

d820 *a*) *Dothan* Moshe, ⊕ An infant jar-burial [t. Akko]; – *b*) *Garfinkel* Yosef,
Bonfil Ruhama, ⊕ Graves and burial customs of the MB IIA period in
Gesher [15 k S ḥ. Kerak]: ➤ 4, ᶠAMIRAN Ruth, ErIsr 21 (1990) 148-151;
7 fig.; Eng. 106* / 132-147; 6 fig.; Eng. 106*.

d821 *Fattovich* Rodolfo,   The stelae of Kassala; a new type of funerary
monuments in the Eastern Sudan: ArNilM 3 (1989) 55-63; 3 fig.; V pl.

d822 **Fedak** Janos,   Monumental tombs of the Hellenistic age; a study of
selected tombs from the pre-classical to the early imperial era: Phoenix
supp 27 [0079-1784]. Toronto 1990, Univ.   xiii-498 p.; 278 fig.   0-8020-
2694-X [OIAc S90].

d823 *Fossati* Luigi,   La Sindone; carbonio 14 squalificato: StCatt 34 (1990)
547-9.

d823* *Frieden* Lucius von,   La S. Sindone, un anno dopo, ᵀ*Pace* G.: TerraS
65 (1989) 207-210 [p. 207 (ed.) 'Nessuno infatti considera definitivi gli
studi, condotti nel 1988 con sconcertante superficialità giornalistica'].

d824 *Gallorini* Carla, *al.*,   Alcuni 'coni' e 'mattoni' funerari inediti: EgVO 13
(1990) 65-74 + 9 fig.

d825 **Green** Christine I.,   The temple furniture from the sacred animal
necropolis at North Saqqara 1964-1975: Memoir 53.   L 1987, Egypt
Exploration Soc. xiv-131 p.; 132 fig. – ᴿArOr 58 (1990) 291 (B. *Vachala*).

d826 *Haikal* G.,   Commentaire des textes du sarcophage no° 22-954 du Musée
Vatican: RSO 63 (1989) 13-24.

d827 *Hall* E. T., The Turin shroud, an editorial postscript: Archaeometry 31 (1989) 92-95 [1260-1380, consistent with the first historical mention in 1353]; p. 235-7, heated 'revised version' by H. E. *Gove*, participant rejected because he was not considered a 'true believer'.

d828 *Hall* Edward, interviewed by *Cornwell* John, Science and the Shroud: Tablet 243 (1989) 36-38 [31s, ed.].

d829 *Hrouda* Barthel, Die altbabylonischen Tumuli von Baġūz bei Mari; Begräbnisse der Ḫanäer?: ⇒ 107, ᶠKUPPER J.-R. 1990, 103-114; 7 fig. (map).

d830 *Jean-Marie* Marylou, Les tombeaux en pierres de Mari: MARI 6 (1990) 303-318 + XVIII pl.

d831 **Kleiner** Diana E. E., Roman imperial funerary altars with portraits 1987 ⇒ 3,d921 ... 5,d616: ᴿBonnJbb 190 (1990) 664-672 (Guntram *Koch*); Latomus 49 (1990) 765s (L. *Lerat*); RPg 63 (1989) 372s (J.-C. *Richard*).

d832 **Lapp** Günther, Sarge des Mittleren Reichs... Khashaba [jetzt in der Schweiz]: ÄgAbh 43, 1985 ⇒ 1,d309; 2,a423: ᴿCdÉ 65 (1990) 79-81 (O. *Berlev*).

d833 **Longerstay** Monique, Les tombes rupestres à auge du Maghreb antique: AION supp. 61 (per) 49 (1989). N 1989, Ist. Univ. Orientale. 53 p.

d834 *Lorenz* Bernd, Bestattung und Totenkult im Alten Testament: ZRGg 42 (1990) 21-31.

d835 **Lüscher** Barbara, Untersuchungen zu ägyptischen Kanopenkästen vom Alten Reich bis zum Ende der Zweiten Zwischenzeit [ᴰBa 1987]: Hild-ÄgBeit 31. Hildesheim 1990, Gerstenberg. xvi-147 p.; 9 fig.; 13 pl. 3-8067-8121-4.

d836 *McHugh* William P., Implications of a decorated predynastic terracotta model for Saharan neolithic influence in the Nile Valley: JNES 49 (1990) 265-280; 7 phot.; called only 'stable or storehouse' but strikingly resembling Palestine chalcolithic ossuaries (Azor etc.).

d837 *Meyer* Elizabeth A., Explaining the epigraphic habit in the Roman Empire; the evidence of epitaphs: JRS 80 (1990) 74-96; 6 fig.

d838 *a) Pedrini* Arnaldo, La Sindone... tra 'giallo' e 'falso'; – *b) Gandolfo* G. B., Appunti in margine alla Sacra Sindone; – *b) Lupo* Tiburzio, La Sindone al lupo di carbonio 14: PalCl 69 (1990) 827-9 / 68 (1989) 249-252 / 561-8.

d839 **Petrosillo** Orazio, *Marinelli* Emanuela, La Sindone, un enigma alla prova della scienza. Mi 1990, Rizzoli. 266 p. Lit. 34.000 [StCatt 34,549].

d839* *Petrosillo* Orazio, Sacra Sindone; contestato il radiocarbonio e riaperto il caso: ViPe 73 (1990) 680-691 [... limiti intrinseci del metodo].

d840 *a) Rouillard* Hedwige, Un détail menant de la déesse Astarté à la vierge Marie; permanence des formules de malédiction contre les violateurs de tombes et d'écrits; – *b) Yon* Marguerite, Les sarcophages 'sidoniens' de Kition: ⇒ 125, ᶠSZNYCER M., Semantica 39 (1990) 155-161 / 178-186; 1 fig.; pl. VII.

d841 *Sartre* Annie, Architecture funéraire de la Syrie: ⇒ 481, Syrie II (1989) 423-446; fig. 124-140 [441-456, Palmyre, *Schmidt-Colinet* Andreas].

d842 *Saxer* V., Le suaire de Turin aux prises avec l'histoire: RHÉgFrance 76,196 (P 1990) 21-55 [< NTAbs 35,154] = ⇒ 5,d635 ital.

d843 **Seidlmayer** Stephan J., Gräberfelder aus dem Übergang vom Alten zum Mittleren Reich: StArchGAltäg 1. Heid 1990, Orient-V. xiv-465 p.

d844 **Silberman** Neil A., Coffins in a human shape; a short history of anthropoid sarcophagi: BAR-W 16,4 (1990) 52-54.

d845 *Singer* Suzanne F., Has the shroud of Turin been dated — finally? [yes, medieval: though genesis of such an image is still unexplained]: BR 5,2 (1989) 38s.

d846 **Steele** Caroline S., Living with the dead; house burial at Abu Salabikh, Iraq: diss. ᴰ*Pollock* Susan. Binghamton 1990, SUNY. xv-274 p. 90-23944. – OIAc F91,20.

d846* **Stevenson** Kenneth E., *Habermas* Gary R., The Shroud and the controversy. Nv 1990, Nelson. 248 p. $16. 0-8407-7174-6 [TDig 37,385].

d847 **Stewart** H. M., Mummy-cases and inscribed funerary cones in the Petrie collection 1986 → 2,a442 ... 5,d638; £15: ᴿJEA 76 (1990) 223-5 (J. H. *Taylor*).

d848 *Testa* E., Legislazione funeraria greco-romana e le memorie degli eroi e dei martiri: LA 39 (1989) 77-104.

d849 *Testa* Pietro, Il cosiddetto 'naos' ligneo del museo del Cairo; una nuova interpretazione [per trasporto di mummia]: EgVO 13 (1990) 29-37 + 6 fig.

d850 *Walker* Susan, Aspects of Roman funerary art: → 179, Mem. TOYNBEE J. 1988, 23-36 + 18 pl.

d851 *Wąsowicz* Aleksandra, Les coutumes funéraires du Bosphore à l'époque de Mithridate VI Eupator er de ses successeurs: RArchéol (1990) 61-84; 28 fig.

d852 *Will* Ernest, La maison d'éternité et les conceptions funéraires des Palmyréniens: → 111, ᶠLÉVÊQUE P. 4 (1990) 433-440.

d853 *Yellin* Janice, The decorated pyramid chapels of Meroe and Meroitic funerary religion: → 70, ᶠHINTZE F., Meroitica 12 (1990) 361-374.

T3.9 *Numismatica,* **coins.**

d854 **Alram** Michael, Nomina propria iranica in nummis; Materialgrundlagen 1986 → 5,d649: ᴿStIran 18 (1989) 135-7 (Rika *Gyselen*); ZDMG 139 (1989) 249-252 (J. *Tischler*, auch über GIGNOUX P. 1986).

d855 *Augé* Christian, La monnaie en Syrie à l'époque hellénistique et romaine: → 481, Syrie II (1989) 149-190; fig. 11-14 [p. 191-204, en Syrie byzantine, *Morrisson* Cécile].

d856 *Baydur* Nezahat, ❶ Some Attalid coins: → 3, Mem. ALKIM U., 1986, 439-450; IV pl.

d857 **Beltrán Martínez** Antonio, La moneda romana 3. El imperio. M 1986, Fonumis. 272 p. – ᴿFaventia 11,1 (1989) 178s (G. *Carrasco Serrano*) [= 10 (1988) 186s].

d858 *Bianchi* Francesco, Monete giudaiche di età ellenistica: RSO 63 (1989) 213-229.

d859 *Bowsher* Julian M. C., Early Nabataean coinage: → 783, Aram 2 (1990) 221-8; 1 fig.

d860 **Broome** Michael, A handbook of Islamic coins: London 1985, Seaby. 230 p. £30. – ᴿRitNum 92 (1990) 362s (Lucia *Travaini*).

d861 **Bruun** P. M., Die spätrömische Münze als Gegenstand der Thesaurierung: Stud. Fundmünze 4. B 1987, Mann. vii-87 p. 3-7861-1380-7. – ᴿJRS 80 (1990) 254s (C. E. *King*).

d862 **Burnett** Andrew, Coinage in the Roman world 1987 → 4,e458; 5,d656: ᴿClasR 40 (1990) 429s (C. E. *King*).

d863 **Butcher** Kevin,   Roman provincial coins; an introduction to the Greek imperials. L 1988, Seaby. 128 p.; ill. £25.   1-85264-010-3. – RClasR 40 (1990) 429s (C. E. *King*).

d864 **Cahn** Herbert A., *al.*,   Griechische Münzen aus Grossgriechenland und Sizilien 1988 → 5,d658:   RJbNumG 39 (1989) 103s (D. O. Λ. *Klose*).

d865 *Callu* J. P., *Barrandon* J. N.,   'Médaillons' d'Hadrien à Probus; données analytiques: → 90, FJELOČNIK A. 1988, 35-42.

d866 **Carradice** Ian, *Price* M. J.,   Coinage in the Greek world 1988 → 4,e551; 5,d659:   RClasR 40 (1990) 427s (N. K. *Rutter*).

d867 **Carson** R. A. G.,   Coins of the Roman Empire. L 1990. 367 p.; 63 pl. £100 [RBgNum 137, 222, T. *Vermeeren*].

d868 ECasey John, Reece Richard,   Coins and the archaeologist^{2rev} [^{1}c. 1973]. L 1988, Seaby.   306 p.; 8 pl. £17.50. – RNumC 150 (1990) 241-3 (C. E. *King*).

d869 *Chaves Tristán* Francisca,   Los hallazgos numismáticos y el desarrollo de la segunda guerra púnica en el sur de la Península Ibérica [< Punic Wars, Ambères 23-26.XI.1988]: Latomus 49 (1990) 613-622.

d870 **Christiansen** Erik,   The Roman coins of Alexandria 1988 → 4,e554; 5,d660:   RGnomon 62 (1990) 753-5 (A. *Gara*); JRS 80 (1990) 231s (C. J. *Howgego*); NumC 150 (1990) 264-6 (R. *Reece*).

d871 *Cocchiaro* A., *al.*,   Monete [sin dal 3º sec. a.C.] dagli scavi di Brindisi (1984-8): AnItNum 37 (1990) 81-133.

d872 **Cooper** Denis R.,   The art and craft of coinmaking; a history of minting technology 1988 → 5,d661:   RNumC 150 (1990) 239s (D. *Sellwood*).

d873 *Cutroni Tusa* Aldina,   Monete macedoni ed ellenistiche nei ripostigli siciliani: AnItNum 37 (1990) 49-80; pl. X-XII.

d874 **Davesne** Alain, *Le Rider* Georges,   Le trésor de Meydancıkkale (Cilicie Trachée 1980) [5,315 pièces en argent, dès 342 av. J.-C.]: IFÉtAnat. P 1989, RCiv.   377 p.; vol. of 157 pl. F 592. – RRBgNum 136 (1990) 366s (P. *Naster*).

d875 *a) Dorcey* Peter F.,   The posthumous Alexander tetradrachms of Odessos; – *b*) *Meyer* Eckhard,   Die Bronzeprägung von Laodikeia in Syrien 194/217;   JbNumG 37s (1987s) 31-40 / 57-92; Eng. 131s.

d876 *Driessche* Véronique Van,   À propos du monnayage des Ptolémées au IIIᵉ s. av. J.-C.: RArtLv 21 (1988) 63-74.

d877 *Elayi* J. & G.,   Systems of abbreviation used by Byblos, Tyre and Arwad in their pre-Alexandrine coinages: JbNumG 37s (1987s) 11-22; pl. 3-4; Eng. 131.

d878 **Foss** Clive,   Roman historical coins. L 1990, Seaby. xxix-335 p.; ill. £29.50 [NumC 151, 251, K. *Butcher*].

d879 *Gibson* Shimon, *Urman* Dan,   Three coins of Alexander Jannaeus from El 'Al in the Golan Heights: BAnglsr 10 (1990s) 67-72; 2 fig.

d880 *Giove* Teresa,   Il ripostiglio di Sala Consilina [museo Napoli, 85 stateri d'argento di Magna Grecia]: AnItNum 37 (1990) 9-48; pl. I-IX.

d881 *Gyselen* Rika,   Note de métrologie sassanide; les drahms de Khusbō II: RBgNum 135 (1989) 5-23.

d882 *Hansman* John,   Coins and mints of ancient Elymais: Iran 28 (1990) 1-11; pl. I-VIII.

d883 **Hill** Philip V.,   The monuments of ancient Rome as coin types. L 1989, Seaby. 145 p.; 203 fig.; 2 maps. 1-85264-021-9.

d884 *Holloway* R. R.,   Early Roman coinage: Dédalo 24 (São Paulo 1990) 227-243.

d885 *a) Howgego* Christopher J., Why did ancient states strike coins?; – *b) Ashton* Richard H. J., The solar disk drachms of Caria; – *c) Bauslaugh* Robert, Cistophoric countermarks and the monetary system of Eumenes II: NumC 150 (1990) 1-25 / 27-38; pl. 1-3 / 39-65; pl. 4-6.

d886 **Kindler** Arie, *Stein* Alla, A bibliography of the city coinage of Palestine from the 2nd century B.C. to the 3rd century A.D.: BAR-Int 374. Ox 1987. viii-262 p. £17. 0-86054-482-6. – ᴿBO 47 (1990) 214 (J. P. A. van der *Vin*).

d887 **Klose** Dietrich A. O., Die Münzprägung von Smyrna in der römischen Kaiserzeit [diss. Saarbrücken, ᴰ*Franke* P.]: 'AMUGS' 10, 1987 ➤ 4,e577: ᴿAJA 94 (1990) 704s (W. E. *Metcalf*); NumC 150 (1990) 259-264 (C. J. *Howgego*: first-rate; 5536 Roman coins); RBgNum 136 (1990) 375-7 (T. *Hackens*).

d888 *Kraay* Colin, The Greek states; coinage: ➤ 831, CAH² 4 (1988) 431-445; plates (separate volume) 237-248 by M. Jessop *Price*.

d889 **Lahusen** G., Die Bildnismünzen der römischen Republik. Mü 1989, Hirmer. 112 p.; 94 pl. – ᴿNumC 150 (1990) 268s (M. H. *Crawford*).

d890 *Lendon* Jon E., The face on the coins and inflation in Roman Egypt: Klio 72 (1990) 106-134.

d891 *Le Rider* Georges, Un groupe de cistophores de l'époque attalide: BCH 114 (1990) 683-701; 3 fig. (map).

d892 *a) Levante* Edoardo, The coinage of Selinus in Cilicia; – *b) Lacam* Guy, A new consular solidus in the name of Valens from the mint of Antioch: NumC 150 (1990) 226-233; pl. 19-22 / 237 only; pl. 23A.

d893 **Manfredi** Lorenza-Illa, Riconiazioni ed errori di conio nel mondo punico: RStFen 18 supp. R 1990, Cons. Naz. 268 p. IX pl.

d894 **Mildenberg** Leo, The coinage of the Bar Kokhba war 1984 ➤ 1,d36 ... 5,d682: ᴿOLZ 85 (1990) 51-53 (H.-D. *Schultz*).

d895 *Mildenberg* Leo, Rebel coinage in the Roman Empire: ➤ 540, Greece/Israel 1985/90, 62-74; 26 fig.

d896 *a) Missere* Federica, Iconografia della Boule e del Demos nella monetazione greca imperiale dell'Asia Minor; – *b) Vanni* Franca Maria, La monetazione di Leptis Magna: RitNum 92 (1990) 75-128; II pl. / 33-73; 193 fig.

d897 **Pankiewicz** Ryszard, Fluctuations de valeur des métaux monétaires dans l'antiquité romaine: EurHS 3/384. Fra 1989, Lang. 196 p.

d898 *Picard* Olivier, Philippe II et le monnayage des cités grecques: RÉG 103 (1990) 1-15; 6 fig.

d899 *Póczy* K., Auf der Spur einer Münzstätte in Aquincum: AcArchH 41 (1989) 495-8; 7 fig. [508-520 *al.*, Fundmünzen].

d900 *a) Schmitt-Korte* Karl, Nabataean coinage II. New coin types and variants; – *b) Mattingly* Harold B., The beginning of Athenian new style silver coinage; – *c) Bopeararchchi* Osmund, Graeco-Bactrian issues of later Indo-Greek kings: NumC 150 (1990) 105-133; pl. 10-15 / 67-78 / 79-103; pl. 7-9.

d901 **Schönert-Geiss** Edith, Die Münzprägung von Maroneia [Thrakien]: B 1987, Griechisches Münzewerk. 253 p.; vol. of 93 pl. – ᴿJbNumG 37s (1987s) 134-6 (D. O. A. *Klose*).

d902 *Touratsoglou* Ioannis, Die Münzstätte von Thessaloniki in der römischen Kaiserzeit 132/31 v.Chr. bis 368 n.Chr.: DAI-Antike Münzen. B 1988. 353 p. 57 pl. – ᴿArchWroc 40 (1989) 190-3 (A. *Kunisz* ❷; 'v.Chr.'); JbNumG 39 (1989) 107-9 (D. O. A. *Klose*); RBgNum 135 (1989) 225-7 (T. *Hackens*).

d903 **Turcan** Robert, Nigra moneta; sceaux, jetons... plombs... Musée de Lyon. P 1987, Boccard. 213 p.; 36 pl.

d904 *a)* *Visonà* P., The Yale hoard of Punic bronze coins from Malta; – *b)* *Acquaro* E., *Viola* M. R., La collezione numismatica Viola; le monete puniche II: RStFen 18 (1990) 169-192; pl. XVI / 197-206; pl. XVIII-XXI.

d905 *Weiss* Peter, Mythen, Dichter und Münzen von Lykaonien [AULOCK H. v.]: Chiron 20 (1990) 221-237.

Yadin Y., *al.*, The [4699] coins of Masada 1989 ⇥ 9219.

d905* *a)* *Zehnacker* Hubert, Rome, une société archaïque au contact de la monnaie (Vᵉ-IVᵉ siècle); – *b)* *Parise* Nicola F., Moneta e società in Magna Grecia; l'esempio di Crotone: ⇥ 811, Crise 1987/90, 307-326 / 299-306.

d906 **Ziegler** Ruprecht, Münzen Kilikiens aus kleineren deutschen Sammlungen: Vestigia 42. Mü 1989, Beck. viii-196 p.; 72 pl.; map. – ᴿBonn-Jbb 1990) 720-4 (W. *Leschhorn*); JbNumG 37s (1987s) 133 (D. O.A. *Klose*); RBgNum 135 (1989) 215s (P. *Naster*).

T4   *Situs,* **excavation-sites**   .1   *Chronica,* **bulletins.**

d906* ᴱ*Aurenche* Olivier, Chronique archéologique: Syrie / Jordanie / index: Syria 66 (1988) 399-414 / 415-434 / 435s.

d907 Excavations: IsrEJ 40 (1990) 71-76; map; 219-228, signed; map; pl. 22-24.

d908 *González Echegaray* J., Investigaciones arqueológicas en Levante III: AulaO 8 (1990) 33-67; 3 maps, 40 + 36 + 34 sites.

d909 ᴱ**Kerner** S., The Near East antiquity; German contributions to the knowledge of Jordan, Palestine, Syria and Egypt, I. Amman 1990. 110 p. – ᴿLA 40 (1990) 478 (M. *Piccirillo*).

d910 ᴱ*Piccirillo* Michele, Ricerca storico-archeologica in Giordania 10: LA 40 (1990) 455-478; map 454; book-reviews 478-484.

d911 ᴱ*Pommerantz* Inna, *Roshwalb-Hurowitz* Ann, Excavations and surveys in Israel 9 (1989s) fasc. 1-2 together, 179 p.; 174 fig.; 2 maps.

T4.2   *Situs effossi,* **syntheses.**

d912 *Ahlström* Gösta W., [culture, pottery] Diffusion in Iron Age Palestine; some aspects: ScandJOT (1990,1) 81-105.

d913 *a)* *Bienkowski* Piotr, The division of Middle Bronze IIB-C in Palestine; – *b)* *Hoffmeier* James K., Reconsidering Egypt's part in the termination of the Middle Bronze Age in Palestine: Levant 21 (1989) 169-176 (-8, Jericho, *Chapman* R. L.); bibliog. p. 178s / 181-191; -193 bibliog.

d914 **Brug** J. F., A literary and archaeological study of the Philistines [diss Mp 1984 ⇥ 2,a515]: BAR-Int 265. Ox 1985. x-312 p. 0-86054-337-4. – ᴿNedTTs 44 (1990) 62 (K. A. D. *Smelik*).

d915 *Bunimovitz* Shlomo, Problems in the 'ethnic' identification of the Philistine material culture [pottery, cult, burial...]: TAJ 17 (1990) 210-222.

d916 *a)* *Cauvin* Jacques, La néolithisation au Levant et sa première diffusion; – *b)* *Dollfus* Geneviève, Les processus de néolithisation en Iran — bilan des connaissances; – *c)* *Le Brun* Alain, La néolithisation de Chypre; – *d)* *Perlès* Catherine, La néolithisation de la Grèce: Néolithisation 1984/9, 3-36; 4 fig. / 37-64; map / 95-104 + 3 fig. / 109-124 + 3 fig.

d916* *Chapman* Rupert L., Review article [MIROSCHEDJI P. de, Urbanisation 1986/9]; in pursuit of the Early Bronze Age: BAngIsr 10 (1990s) 73-83.

d917 *a) Chen* D., On planning of synagogues and churches in Palaestina; a comparison with Syria and Illyricum; – *b) Ben-Pechat* M., Baptism and monasticism in the Holy Land; archaeological and literary evidence (fourth to seventh centuries): ➤ 39, ᶠCORBO V., Christian archaeology 1990, 523-534 / 501-522.

d918 **Cohen** Rudolph, ❺ *Seqer...* Archaeological survey of Israel West 12-03 (167) [= ? ➤ 4,g913c]. J 1985, Dept. Antiq. xx-106 + 35 p.; XX pl. [KirSef 62 (1988s) p. 187].

d919 *Dever* William G., 'Hyksos', Egyptian destructions, and the end of the Palestinian Middle Bronze Age: Levant [21 (1989) 181-193, *Hoffmeier* J.] 22 (1990) 75-81; 83-89 rejoinder.

d920 *Dornemann* Rudolph H., The beginning of the Bronze Age in Syria in light of recent excavations: ➤ 28, ᶠBOUNNI A. 1990, 85-96 + pl. 18-21.

d920* *a) Dothan* Trude, The arrival of the Sea Peoples; cultural diversity in Iron Age Canaan; – *b) Dothan* Moshe, Archaeological evidence for movements of the early 'Sea Peoples' in Canaan: ➤ 5,543, AASOR 49 (1989) 1-14 / 59-70.

d921 **Finkelstein** Israel, The archaeology of the Israelite settlement 1988 ➤ 4,e629; 5,d715: ᴿBInstArch 26 (1989) 260-2 (R. *Chapman*); OLZ 85 (1990) 179 (G. *Pfeifer*); NorTTs 91 (1990) 175-7 (M. *Skjeggestad*); ZAW 102 (1990) 147s (U. *Schorn*).

d922 *Goedicke* Hans, Palestine in the early third century B.C.: VarAeg 5 (1989) 194-202.

d922* *Halpern-Zilberstein* Marie-Christine, The archaeology of Hellenistic Palestine: ➤ 835, CHJud 2 (1989) 1-34; 13 fig.

d923 **Kempinski** Aharon, Syrien und Palästina (Kanaan) in der letzten Phase der Mittelbronze IIB-Zeit [< Diss. J 1974, ᴰ*Mazar* B.]: ÄgAT 4, 1983 ➤ 64,b253... 4,e633: ᴿJAOS 110 (1990) 345-7 (W. G. *Dever*: archaeologically naive exercise in Kulturgeschichte).

d924 **Kempinski** Aharon, The Middle Bronze Age; *Gonen* Rivka, The Late Bronze Age: ArchIsrBiblP 6s. TA 1989, Open Univ. 171 p.; 88 fig.; 8 color. pl. 965-302-482-5.

d925 *Kerkhof* Vera L., Interaction; Middle and Late Bronze in Transjordan: Catastrophism and Ancient History 9 (1987) 118 [< OTAbs 13, p. 126.140s: 5-16.61-71, *Stiebing* W.; 81-90, *Sanders* M. on Jericho; 43-48, *Storck* H. on Ur].

d926 **Kuhnen** H.-P., Palästina in griechisch-römischer Zeit: HbArch, Vorderasien 2/2. Mü 1990, Beck. xxi-424 p.; 28 pl. DM 248. 3-406-32876-8 [BL 91,31, L. L. *Grabbe*].

d927 *Smith* Robert H., The southern Levant in the Hellenistic period: Levant 22 (1990) 123-130.

d928 **Taylor** Joan E., A critical investigation of material assigned [by BAGATTI B., TESTA E.] to Palestinian Jewish-Christians of the Roman and Byzantine periods; diss. Edinburgh 1989. 649 p. BRD-91710. – DissA 51 (1990s) 3790-A.

d929 **Weippert** Helga, Palästina in vorhellenistischer Zeit: HbArch Vorderasien 2/1, 1988 ➤ 4,e639; 5,d724: ᴿHenoch 12 (1990) 233s (J. A. *Soggin*); OLZ 85 (1990) 424-6 (E. *Klengel-Brandt*); PEQ 121 (1989) 155-7 (G. R. H. *Wright*); RHPR 70 (1990) 243-5 (J.-G. *Heintz*); ZDPV 106 (1990) 183-5 (O. *Kaiser*).

d930 *Zaccagnini* Carlo, The transition from bronze to iron in the Near East and in the Levant; marginal notes [KNAPP A. 1986]: JAOS 110 (1990) 493-502.

T4.3 **Jerusalem,** *archaeologia et historia.*

d931 *Andia* Ysabel de, Jérusalem, cité de Dieu, dans l'Adversus haereses d'IRÉNÉE de Lyon: ➤ 135, ᶠORBE A., Compostellanum 34 (1989) 237-254.

d932 **Ariel** D. T., Excavations at the City of David, [Y. SHILOH] 1978-1985, II. Imported stamped amphora handles, coins, worked bone and ivory, and glass: Qedem 30. J 1990, Hebrew Univ. xx-388 p.; 33 fig.; VI pl. 0333-5884 [ZAW 103, 291, V. *Fritz*].

d933 ᴱ**Asali** K. J., Jerusalem in history [... FRANKEN H., MENDENHALL G.]. Essex/NY 1989, Scorpion/Olive Branch. 295 p. £14. 0-905906-70-5 [BO 47,263; ExpTim 101, 345].

d934 **Bahat** Dan, *Rubinstein* Chaim, The illustrated atlas of Jerusalem [Atlas Karta ha-Gadol 1989], ᵀ. NY 1990, Simon & S. 192 p.; 400 fig. $95 [OIAc S90]. 0-13-451642-7.

d935 *Barkay* Gabriel, ❻ A Late Bronze Age Egyptian temple in Jerusalem: ➤ 4, ᶠAMIRAN Ruth, ErIsr 21 (1990) 94-106; 20 fig.; Eng. 104*.

d936 *Bashear* Suliman, Qur'ān 2:114 and Jerusalem [alternative: Mecca]: BSO 52 (1989) 215-238.

d937 *Bloedhorn* Hanswulf, Herodianische Architektur in Jerusalem: ➤ 791*, KlasArch 13 (1988/90) 437.

d938 **Burgoyne** M. H., *Richards* D. S., Mamluk Jerusalem 1987 ➤ 4,e649: ᴿBO 47 (1990) 826-831 (J. M. *Rogers*); JAmEg 27 (1990) 239-243 (G. T. *Scanlon*); Levant 22 (1990) 149-153 (U. W. *Haarmann*: 'on closer look, a highly political and sensitive subject').

d939 *Chambon* Alain, *al.*, Jerusalem (Emeq Refaim, etc.): ExcSIsr 9 (1989s) 145-156.

d940 **Cohen** Amnon, [➤ g945] Economic life in Ottoman Jerusalem: StIslam 13. C 1989, Univ. xiii-179 p.; 6 fig.; map. £27.50. – ᴿBSO 53 (1990) 511s (Caroline *Finkel*); JRAS (1990) 390s (Amy *Singer*).

d941 *Cohen* Amnon, Gold and silver crafting in Ottoman Jerusalem; the role played by the guild: Tarih 1 (WL 1990) ... [JQR 81,74 adv.].

d942 *Corbo* Virgilio, Gethsémani et ses sanctuaires de la Passion [< TerreS mars 1989]: EsprVie 100 (1990) 311s (-314; J. *Daoust*, annoncé prématurément p. 241].

d943 *Crocker* P. T., The Jerusalem *millo*; bone of contention: BurHist 26 (1990) 121-4 [< OTAbs 14,150].

d944 *Dalmais* I. H., Les liturgies chrétiennes dans le cadre de Jérusalem: MondeB 62 (1990) 51-59; 63 (1990) 49-52; 64, 55-57; 65, 55-59 (les Arméniens); 66 (1990) 45-47 (les Géorgiens).

d945 *Daoust* J., La vie à Jérusalem au temps de Jésus [< MondeB 60 (1989), *Carrez* M.]: EsprVie 100 (1990) 138s.

d946 **Drijvers** Jan W., Helena Augusta; waarheid en legende: Proefschrift Groningen 1989. 275 p. – ᴿJbAC 33 (1990) 253-6 (S. *Heid*: son of the Syriac scholar H. J. W. DRIJVERS; on the Finding of the Cross).

d947 ᴱ**Eckardt** Alice L., Jerusalem, city of the ages: American Academic Asn for Peace in the Middle East. Lanham MD 1987, UPA. 407 p.; maps [KirSef 62 (1988s), p. 617].

d948 **Fleckenstein** Karl-Heinz, *Müller* Wolfgang, Jérusalem, ville sainte des trois monothéismes [1988 ➤ 5,d739], ᵀ*Feisthauer* Joseph. P 1989, D-Brouwer. 238 p. – ᴿÉtudes 372 (1990) 572 (P. *Frison*).

d949 **Franken** H. J., *Steiner* M. I., Excavations in Jerusalem 1961-1967, II. The Iron Age extramural quarter on the south-east hill [using (also) Kathleen M. KENYON's notebooks]: British Academy Mg Archaeology 2. Ox 1990, UP. xiii-134 p. £30. 0-19-727001-8 [BL 91,29, A. G. *Auld*].

d949* *Gauger* J.-D., Überlegungen zum Programma Antiochos' III für den Tempel und die Stadt Jerusalem (Jos. Ant. Jud. 12,145-146) und zum Problem jüdischer Listen: Hermes 118 (1990) 150-164.

d950 *Hausherr* R., Spätgotische Ansichten der Stadt Jerusalem (oder, War der Hausbuchmeister in Jerusalem?): Jahrbuch der Berliner Museen 29s (1987s) 47-70; 30 fig. [< RHE 86,182*].

d950* *Hetherington* Paul, Who is this King of Glory? The Byzantine enamels of an icon frame and revetment in Jerusalem [Greek Patriarchate Museum]: ZKunstG 53 (1990) 25-38; 8 fig.

d951 **Jeremias** Joachim, Gerusalemme al tempo di Gesù [1923, ³1962], ᵀ1989 ➤ 5,d746: ᴿCC 141 (1990, 3) 196s (V. *Fusco*).

d952 *Koenen* Klaus, Zur Inschrift unter dem Robinson-Bogen: ZDPV 106 (1990) 180-2.

d953 **Kollek** Teddy [longtime mayor], *Eisner* Shulamith, My Jerusalem; twelve walks in the world's holiest city. NY 1990, Summit. 160 p. $25 [CBQ 52,779].

d954 ᴱ**Küchler** M., *Uehlinger* C., Jerusalem: NOrb 6, 1987 ➤ 3,a48 ... 5,d781: ᴿVT 40 (1990) 246 (Judith M. *Hadley*).

d955 **Kühnel** Bianca, From the earthly to the heavenly Jerusalem; representations of the Holy City in Christian art of the first millennium: RömQ 42 Supp. R 1987. 279 p.; 125 fig. – ᴿOstkSt 38 (1989) 66s (E. C. *Suttner*).

d956 *Laperrousaz* Ernest-Marie, De l'arche de Wilson à la piscine double du Strouthion; les abords souterrains du mur occidental du Temple de Jérusalem: RÉJ 149 (1990) 291-3 + 3 fig.

d957 **Lev** Marvin, The traveler's key to Jerusalem; a guide to the sacred places of Jerusalem. NY 1989, Knopf. vi-228 p. $19. 0-394-55635-6 [TDig 37,272].

d958 **Little** Donald P., A catalogue of the Islamic documents from al-Ḥaram al-Šarīf in Jerusalem 1984 ➤ 3,e54: ᴿJSS 35 (1990) 365-7 (L. *Kalus*, français: important).

d959 *Macir* Aren M., A possible bilingual Hebrew-Egyptian inscription from the 'Ophel', Jerusalem: GöMiszÄg 114 (1990) 63-69.

d960 **Mare** W. Harold, The archaeology of the Jerusalem area 1987 ➤ 3,e59 ... 5,d758: ᴿCriswT 3 (1989) 394s (R. M. *Ulrey*).

d961 *Mayer* Hans E., Die Hofkapelle der Könige von Jerusalem: Deutsches Archiv für Erforschung des Mittelalters 44 (Köln 1988) 489-509 [< ZIT 89,465].

d962 **Mazar** Eilat & Benjamin, Excavations in the south of the Temple mount; the Ophel of biblical Jerusalem: Qedem 29. J 1989, Univ. Inst. Archaeology. xvii-137 p.; 195 fig.; 33 pl.; 29 plans. 0333-5884. – ᴿPEQ 122 (1990) 146s (Margaret *Steiner*).

d963 **Oppermann** Ralf, Die Geschichte des Muristan bis zum Ende der römischen Zeit: Diss. ᴰ*Otto*. Osnabrück 1989s. – TR 86 (1990) 518.

d964 *Pellistrandi* Christine, Jérusalem, épouse et mère: Lire la Bible 87, 1989 ➤ 5,d766: ᴿÉTRel 65 (1990) 624 (D. *Lys*).

d964* **Peters** F.E., Jerusalem and Mecca 1986 → 2,a564...4,e678: ᴿCritRR 2 (1989) 265-7 (T.A. *Idinopulos*).

d965 *Pixner* Bargil, Church of the Apostles [cenacle Acts 1,1-13] found on Mt. Zion: BAR-W 16,3 (1990) 16-35.60; color. ill.

d966 ᴱ**Poirion** D., Jérusalem, Rome, Constantinople; l'image et le mythe de la ville au Moyen Âge [colloque Ét. Médiév., Sorbonne-IV]. P 1986, Univ. 252 p.; ill. F 150. 2-904315-41-1. – ᴿRevue de Synthèse (1989,1) 155s (Françoise *Bonney*) [ByZ 83,302].

d967 **Prag** Kay, Jerusalem: Blue Guide 1989 → 5,d768: ᴿRB 97 (1990) 144 (J. *Murphy-O'Connor*).

d968 **Prawer** Joshua, The history of the Jews in the Latin Kingdom of Jerusalem. Ox 1988, Clarendon. 245 p. $69. – ᴿJAAR 58 (1990) 519-521 (T.A. *Idinopulos*); JEH 40 (1989) 620 (P.W. *Edbury*); Speculum 65 (1990) 1036-8 (S. *Bowman*).

d969 **Purvis** James D., Jerusalem, the Holy City, a bibliography 1988 → 4,e680; 5,d771: ᴿRB 97 (1990) 143 (J. *Murphy-O'Connor*).

d970 *Recio Veganzones* A., La representación arquitectónica de la Rotonda del Santo Sepulcro en la escultura paleocristiana de occidente: → 39, ᶠCORBO V., Christian archaeology 1990, 571-589.

d971 **Rosen-Ayalon** Myriam, The early Islamic monuments of al-Haram al-Sharif, an iconographic study: Qedem 28, 1989 → 5,d777: ᴿRB 97 (1990) 619s (J. *Murphy-O'Connor*).

d972 *Rosen-Ayalon* Myriam, Art and architecture in Ayyūbid Jerusalem: IsrEJ 40 (1990) 305-314; pl. 29-32.

d973 **Rubin** Ze'ev, ❹ Jerusalem in the Byzantine Period. TA 1985, Everyman's Univ. 170 p. – ᴿByzantion 60 (1990) 577s (Rivkah *Fishman-Duker*).

d974 *Ruderman* Abraham, Was there a fourth Temple? [tunnel under Western Wall; *Bahat* D., Jerusalem Post Feb. 2, 1990]: JBQ 19 (1990s) 206-8.

d974* **Saulnier** Christiane, Jérusalem, guide historique et culturel. P 1989, Larousse. 240 p. F 155. – ᴿRICathP 32 (1989) 111 (F. *Brossier*).

d975 *Stone* Garry R., A four-chambered gate on Jerusalem's Ophel [similar to Megiddo IVA-IVB, but equated by Eilat MAZAR with the 'Water-Gate' Neh 3,26]: BurHist 25 (1989) 81-92 [< OTAbs 13, p. 24].

d976 **Thorau** Peter, Sultan Baibars I von Ägypten; ein Beitrag zur Geschichte des Vorderen Orients im 13. Jh.: TAVO-B63, ᴰ1987 → 3,e80: ᴿBSO 53 (1990) 135s (P. *Jackson*); Speculum 65 (1990) 504-6 (C.F. *Petry*).

d977 *Tsafrir* Yoram, The 'Massive Wall' [WARREN C. 1869] east of the Golden Gate, Jerusalem: IsrEJ 40 (1990) 280-6.

d978 **Tushingham** A.D., *al.*, Excavations in Jerusalem 1961-7, I. 1985 → 1,d470... 5,d787: ᴿIsrEJ 40 (1990) 229s (M. *Broshi*: erroneous conclusions).

d979 **Ussishkin** D., ❹ Village of Silwan, Necropolis 1986 → 2,a576; 3,e83: ᴿBASOR 277s (1990) 133-5 (Elisabeth *Bloch-Smith*).

d980 **Walker** P.W.L., Holy city, holy places? Christian attitudes to Jerusalem and the Holy Land in the fourth century: Early Christian Studies. Ox 1990, Clarendon. xix-438 p.; 10 fig. 0-19-814467-9.

d981 **Wightman** G.J., The Damascus Gate, Jerusalem; excavations by C.M. BENNETT and J.B. HENNESSY 1864-66: BAR-Int 519, 1989 → 5, d790; 0-86054-660-8. – ᴿBL (1990) 36 (A. *Auld*: not part of '3d north wall').

d982 *Wightman* Gregory J.,   Temple fortresses in Jerusalem II. The Hasmonean *Baris* and Herodian Antonia: BAngIsr 10 (1990s) 7-35; 9 fig. [36-66 Temple → 3046].

---

d983 *Arav* Rami, *al.*,   An eighth century monastery near Jerusalem [16825. 13654]:   LA 40 (1990) 313-320; 2 fig.; pl. 41-44; 10-line Greek inscription; summary 449.

d984 **Bethania:** *Taylor* Joan E.,   The Bethany cave; a Jewish-Christian cult site? [revising E. TESTA, LA 14 (1964) 128-131]: RB 97 (1990) 453-465; 2 fig.; franç. 453.

d985 **Dawwāra:** *Finkelstein* Israel,   Excavations at Khirbet ed-Dawwara, an Iron Age site northeast of Jerusalem [1.5 k SE Mukhmas]:   TAJ 17 (1990) 161-209; 23 fig.

d986 **En Yael:** *Edelstein* Gershon,   What's a Roman villa doing outside Jerusalem?:   BAR-W 16,6 (1990) 32-42; mosaic photos in color [44-49, *Rapuano* Yehudah,   Did Philip baptize the eunuch at En Yael?].

d987 **Geba':**   EMazar Benjamin, ❶ Gcva... Tell Abu-Shusha, Mishmar ha-'Emeq.   J 1988, Meuchad/IsrExpl.   236p.; 234 fig. š 30. 12 art. – RIsrEJ 40 (1990) 240 (Hannah *Katzenstein:* tit. pp.).

d988 **Arnold** P.M.,   Gibeah, the search for a biblical city [= Geba']: JStOT supp 79.   Sheffield 1990, Academic.   196 p. £25.   1-85075-223-0 [BL 91,34, A.G. *Auld*]. – RExpTim 102 (1990s) 116 (J.F. *Healey*).

d989 **Giloh:** *Mazar* Amihai,   Iron Age I and II towers at Giloh and the Israelite settlement: IsrEJ 40 (1990) 77-101; 11 fig.; pl. 9-13.

d990 **Nisya-Ramallah** 1979-86, 6 seasons' report: AndrUnS 28 (1990) 151 [diss. **Livingston** David P., Andrews 1989, DStorfjell J.].

d991 **Qaṣr 'Ali,** E. Olivet: *Hirschfeld* Yizhar,   A church and water reservoir built by Empress Eudocia: LA 40 (1990) 287-294; 4 fig.; pl. 33-34; summary 449.

d992 **Saṭaf** [W Jerusalem] 1988; chalco./Byz.:   IsrEJ 40 (1989) 223-6 (S. *Gibson*, A. *Kloner*).

d992* *Gibson* Shimon, *Kloner* Amos,   ❶ Saṭaf, an archaeological project of landscape and environment in the Judaean hills: Qadmoniot 23 (1990) 97-103; ill.

T4.4   *Situs alphabetice:*   **Judaea, Negeb.**

d993 **Schwartz** Joshua, ❶ Jewish settlement in Judea, after the Bar-Kochba war until the Arab conquest 1986 → 3,e90; 4,e693*:   RByzantion 60 (1990) 576s (Rivkah *Fishman-Duker*).

d994 *'Ajrud:* *Catastini* Alessandro,   Profeti tra epigrafia ed epistolografia [iscrizione Ajrud menziona 'congregazione' *dr*, 'capo' *sr*, YHWH, *ba'al* come 1 Re 18]: EgVO 13 (1990) 143-7.

d995 *Scagliarini* Fiorella,   Osservazioni sulle iscrizioni di Kuntillet 'Aǧrud: RSO 63 (1989) 199-212.

d996 *Tigay* Jeffrey H.,   A Second Temple parallel to the blessings from Kuntillet 'Ajrud (Suk 4,5 supports taking *ašerā* as cult-object):   IsrEJ 40 (1990) 218 only.

d997 **Arad:** *Govrin* Yehuda, ❶ The question of the origin of early Arad's population: → 4, FAMIRAN Ruth, ErIsr 21 (1990) 107-110; Eng. 104*.

d998 **Balaḥ:** *Yellin* Joseph, *al.*, The origin of Late Bronze white burnished slip wares from Deir el-Balaḥ: IsrEJ 40 (1990) 257-261; 2 fig.

d999 **Bataš** (Timna) 1987/9: ExcSIsr 9 (1989s) 61-63; fig. 56 (A. *Mazar*, G. *Kelm*).

c1 **Beersheba:** *Schoors* Antoon, The Bible on Beer-Sheba [9th World Congress paper, 8.VIII.1985]: TAJ 17,1 (1990) 100-109.

e2 **Beṣor:** *Gophna* Ram, *a*) The Early Bronze I settlement at ʿEn Besor oasis [his 1970-83 excavations]: IsrEJ 40 (1990) 1-11; 6 fig.; pl. 1 [= ErIsr 20 (1989) 37-43 ❿]; *b*) The Egyptian pottery of ʿEn Besor: TAJ 17 (1990) 144-162; 13 fig.

e3 **Beth-Shemesh:** *Wightman* G.J., The date of Bethshemesh stratum II; AbrNahr 28 (1990) 96-115 + 116-126 fig.

e4 **Deir,** Hirbet [10 k WNW En-Gedi]: TerraS 65 (1989) 22-25; map, 2 fot. (P. *Kaswalder*).

e5 **Eilat:** *Crocker* P.T., *a*) Ezion-Geber and Elath in the time of Solomon; – *b*) The tomb of Amenhotep I - no. 39 [Thebes; *Rose* J.]; – *c*) Isotopic and trace element analysis of Roman marble: BurHist 25 (1989) 119-125 / 26 (1990) 55-57 / 58-61 [< OTAbs 13,234s; others p. 243.245.248.255].

e6 **Ekron:** *Dothan* Trude, *Gitin* Seymour, Ekron of the Philistines; how they lived, worked and worshiped for five hundred years: BAR-W 16,1 (1990) 20-36; color. ill.; II. (Gitin) Olive-oil suppliers to the world; 16,2 (1990) 32-42.59.

e7 [*Gitin* S.], Cultic inscriptions [15] found in Ekron [Miqne]: BA 53 (1990) 232.

e8 **Eshtemoʿa:** *Yeivin* Zeʿev, ❿ The silver hoard from Eshtemoʿa: ʿAtiqot 10 (1990) 43-57; 24 fig.; Eng. 15*.

e9 **Gath:** *Görg* Manfred, Zu einem weiteren Träger des Ortsnamens Gat [äg. *kntw*]: BibNot 55 (1990) 3s.

e10 **Gerar:** *Gilead* Isaac, Grar [20 k SE Gaza], a chalcolithic site in the northern Negev, Israel: JField 16 (1989) 377-394; 10 fig.

e11 **Gesher** 223.202: Pre-pottery neo, MB cemetery: Qadmoniot 23,1s (1990) 26-30 (Y. *Garfinkel* ❿).

e12 **Gilat** [18 k NW Beersheba] *Alon* David, ❿ Cult artifacts from Gilat and relations with northern Edom in the chalcolithic period: ʿAtiqot 10 (1990) 1-12: Eng. 1*s.

e13 *Alon* David, *Levy* Thomas E., ❿ The Gilat sanctuary; its centrality and influence in the southern Levant during the late 5th-early 4th millennium BCE: → 4, ᶠAMIRAN Ruth, Eretz-Israel 21 (1990) 23-36; 12 fig.; Eng. 101*s.

e14 **Halif** 1983-7: → 500, ASOR Reports 1990, 1-32; 24 fig. (J.D. *Seger, al.*).

e15 **Herodium:** *Corbo* Virgilio C., Herodion I. Gli edifici della Reggia-Fortezza: SBF 20, 1989 → 5,d804: ᴿQadmoniot 23,1s (1990) 64s (J. *Patrich* ❿).

e16 **Netzer** Ehud, Herodium, an archaeological guide. J 1987, Carta. 48 p. $7 pa. – ᴿBA 53 (1990) 237 (J. *McRay*, also on KHOURI R., Umm Qais).

e17 **Hirschfeld** Yizhar, ❿ Map of Herodium. J 1985, Dept. Antiquities [KirSef 62 (1988s), p. 618].

e18 **Ḥeṣi:** *a*) *Toombs* Lawrence E., The Joint Archaeological Expedition to Tell el-Hesi and the results of earlier excavations; – *b*) *Drower* Margaret S., W.M. Flinders PETRIE, the Palestine Exploration Fund and Tell el-Hesi; – *c*) *King* Philip J., Frederick Jones BLISS at Tell el-Hesi and elsewhere; – *d*) *Gibson* Shimon, *Rajak* Tessa, Tell el-Hesi and the camera; the photographs of Petrie and Bliss: → 816, PEQ 122,2 (1990) 100-113; 10 fig. / 87-93; 3 fig. / 96-100 / 114-124 + 15 fig.

e19 ᴱ**Dahlberg** Bruce T., *O'Connell* Kevin G.,   Tell el-Hesi; the site and the expedition: ASOR Report, Hesi 4.   WL 1989, Eisenbrauns.   xix-214 p. $42.50.

e20 *Ira: a) Beit-Arieh* Itzhaq, ⊕ An Early Bronze Age III stratum at Tel 'Ira in the northern Negev; – *b) Beck* Pirhiya, ⊕ A figurine from Tel 'Ira: → 4, ᶠAMIRAN Ruth, ErIsr 21 (1990) 66-79; 11 fig.; Eng. 103* / 87-93; 13 fig.; Eng. 104*.

e21 *Izbet Ṣarṭa: Shea* William H.,   The 'Izbet Ṣarṭah ostracon [an alphabet in one line, preceded by four lines including Aphek, Shiloh, Ashdod, Gath, Kiriath-Jearim]: AndrUnS 28 (1990) 59-86; facsimile.

e22 *Jericho: Wood* Bryant G.,   Did the Israelites conquer Jericho? A new look at the archaeological evidence: BAR-W 16,2 (1990) 44-59 [... 'KENYON is on weak ground'; biblical data supported by archeology, but Israel was probably resident in Canaan throughout LB-II]. – Summary by R. *Ibach* in BS 147 (1990) 482.

e23 ᴱ**Franken** H.J., In search of the Jericho potters 1974 → 56,9092; 61,s537: ᴿRArtLv 21 (1988) 167s (R. *Donceel* excuse le retard).

e24 *Rudermann* Abraham,   Did the Israelites conquer Jericho?: JBQ 19 (1990s) 52-54.56.

e25 *a) Bienkowski* Piotr,   Jericho was destroyed in the Middle Bronze Age, not the Late Bronze Age; – *b) Wood* Bryant G.,   Dating Jericho's destruction; Bienkowski is wrong on all counts: BAR-W 16,5 (1990) 45s.69 / 45.47-49.68.

e26 *a) Netzer* E., *Birger* R.,   A Byzantine monastery at Nuṣeib 'Uweishira, west of Jericho [*Di Segni* L., inscription]; – *b) Netzer*,   The Byzantine churches of Herodion [*Di Segni*, inscription]; – *c) Magen* Y., *Talgam* R., The monastery of Martyrius at Ma'ale Adummim (Khirbet el-Muraṣṣaṣ) and its mosaics [*Di Segni*, inscriptions]; – *d) Hirschfeld* Y.,   List of the Byzantine monasteries in the Judean desert: → 39, ᶠCORBO V., Christian archaeology 1990, 191-200 [-204] / 165-176 [-190] / 91-152 [-164] / 1-90; ill.

e27 *Wright* G.R.H.,   The severed head in earliest Neolithic times [... Jericho]: JPrehR 2 (1988) 51-36.

e28 *Khan Aḥmar: Meimaris* Yannis E.,   The monastery of St. Euthymios the Great at Khan el-Ahmar... 1976-9. Athens 1989.   120 p. (of which 71 are 166 fig. and 8 color. pl.). – ᴿLA 40 (1990) 524-6 (E. *Alliata*).

e29 *Patrich* Joseph,   The Sabaite Laura of Jeremias in the Judean desert: LA 40 (1990) 295-311; 11 fig. (map); pl. 35-40; summary 449.

e30 *Lachish:* → 857, TRE 20 (1990) 365-8; plan (V. *Fritz*).

e31 **Kloner** Amos, *Tepper* Yigal, ⊕ *Ma'arakhot*... The hiding complexes in the Judaean Shephelah 1987 → 5,d836:   ᴿIsrEJ 40 (1990) 239s (Hannah *Katzenstein*).

e32 *a) Zimhoni* Orna,   Two ceramic assemblages from Lachish levels III and II; – *b) Ussishkin* David,   The Assyrian attack on Lachish; the archaeological evidence from the southwest corner of the site: TAJ 17,1 (1990) 3-52; 35 fig. / 53-86; 14 fig.

e33 *Luzit: a) Avni* G., *Dahari* U.,   [8 k N Beth Guvrin] Christian burial caves from the Byzantine period at Luzit [*Di Segni* L., the inscriptions]; – *b) Magen* Y., A Byzantine church at Beit 'Einun (Beth Anoth) in the Hebron hills; – *c) Frankel* R., *al.,* The oil press at Ḥorvath Beit Loya [1433.1080]; – *d) Patrich* J.,   The cells (ta kellia) of Choziba, Wadi el-Qilt; – *e) Goldfus* H., Khallat ed-Danabîya, a desert monastery [1807.1444]: → 39, ᶠCORBO V., Christian archaeology 1990, 301-314 [-320] / 275-286 / 287-300 / 205-226 / 227-244.

e34 *Mampsis:* Negev Avraham, The architecture of Mampsis I-II ...: Qedem 26s, 1988 ➤ 5,d838: ᴿCritRR 3 (1990) 90-93 (P. C. *Hammond*).

e35 *Negev* Avraham, Mampsis: the end of a Nabataean town: ➤ 783, Aram 2 (1989/90) 337-358 + 12 fig.

e36 *Ma'on* synagogue: Qadmoniot 23 (1990) 115-125; ill. (D. *Amit, Z. Ilan* ⊕).

e37 *Masada:* Cotton Hannah M., ⊕ Documents of the Tenth Legion Fretensis discovered at Masada: Qadmoniot 23,1s (1990) 54-58.

e38 *Cotton* Hannah M., *Price* Jonathan, ⊕ Who conquered Masada in 66 CE, and who lived there until the fortress fell?: Zion 55 (1990) 449-454; Eng. XVII.

e39 **Livneh** Mike, The last fortress; the story of Masada and its people, ᵀ*Chaver* Yael. TA 1989, Ministry of Defence. 304 p. 965-05-0410-9 [OIAc F91].

e40 *Small* David B., Phasing Masada's architecture: Levant 22 (1990) 139-147; 3 plans.

e41 *Mšaš:* Dever William G., Archaeology and Israelite origins; review article [FRITZ V., KEMPINSKI A., Ergebnisse Mšaš 1983]: BASOR 279 (1990) 89-95.

e42 *Negeb:* Borowski Oded, The Negev — the southern stage for biblical history: BR 5,3 (1989) 40-44.

e43 *Haiman* Mordechai, ⊕ The Early Bronze Age in the western Negev highlands: ➤ 4, ᶠAMIRAN Ruth, ErIsr 21 (1990) 152-166; 18 fig.; Eng. 106*s.

e44 **Hartmann-von Monakow** Lore, Durch die Negev-Wüste. Z 1985, Freunde Kirjath Jearim. 72 p.; (color.) phot. [Hartmann T.) [KirSef 62 (1988s), p. 617].

e48 *Qaṣra:* Kloner Amos, ⊕ The cave chapel of Ḥorvat Qaṣra [1431/1053]: 'Atiqot 10 (1990) 129-137; 17 fig.; Eng. 29* [Greek inscriptions 141-154, Eng. 31*-35*, *Di Segni* L., *Patrich* J.].

e50 *Qiriath-Yéarim:* ➤ 833, Catholicisme 13,55 (1989) 327 (M. *Du Buit*).

e51 *Radum* [1659.0665] 1989: IsrEJ 40 (1990) 315s; map (I. *Beit-Arieh*, B. *Cresson*).

e52 *Rafat:* Bagatti Bellarmino †, Le antichità di Rafat e dintorni: LA 40 (1990) 263-286; 12 fig.; pl. 25-32; Eng. 448.

e53 *Reḥovot:* Tsafrir Y., On the pre-planning of ancient churches and synagogues; a test case, the northern church at Rehovot in the Negev: ➤ 39, ᶠCORBO V., Christian archaeology 1990, 535-544.

e54 *Ṣataf* 3d 1988, chalco: PEQ 121 (1989) 158 (S. *Gibson*).

e55 *Se'ir:* Görg Manfred, Zur Identität der 'Šeir-Länder': BibNot 46 (1989) 7-12.

e56 *Šiqmim* 1989, chalco: IsrEJ 40 (1990) 226-8 (T. *Levy*, D. *Alon*).

e57 ᴱLevy T. E., Shiqmim I., studies concerning societies in the Northern Negev Desert, Israel (1982-1984): BAR-Int 356, 1987 ➤ 3,e148; 4,e741: ᴿOrLovPer 20 (1989) 257s (A. *Schoors*).

e57* *Subeita:* Segal A., Architectural decoration in Byzantine Shivta; BAR-Int 420. Ox 1988. 262 p. – ᴿMesopT 25 (1990) 247-250 (G. *Cantino Wataghin*).

e58 *Yarmut:* Miroschedji Pierre de, The Early Bronze Age fortifications at Tel Yarmut — an interim statement: ➤ 4, ᶠAMIRAN Ruth, Eretz-Israel 21 (1990) 48*-61*; 16 fig.

e59 **Miroschedji** P. de, Yarmout I 1988 ➤ 4,e744*; 5,d857: ᴿPaléorient 15,2 (1989) 153s (W. G. *Dever*).

e60 *Ziklag:* Fritz Volkmar, Der Beitrag der Archäologie zur historischen Topographie Palästinas am Beispiel von Ziklag: ZDPV 106 (1990) 78-85.

T4.5 **Samaria, Sharon.**

e61 *Gophna* Ram, *Zuk* Zvika, ◉ Chalcolithic settlements in western Samaria: ➤ 4, [F]AMIRAN Ruth, ErIsr 21 (1990) 111-8; 6 fig.; Eng. 105*.

e62 [E]Jacoby D., *Tsafrir* Y., ◉ Jews, Samaritans, and Christians in Byzantine Palestine. J 1988, Yad Ben-Zvi. 264 p. – [R]Byzantion 60 (1990) 578s (Rivkah *Fishman-Duker*).

e63 *Aphek:* **Kochavi** Moshe, Aphek in Canaan; the Egyptian governor's residence and its finds: catalogue 312 (◉ + Eng.). J 1990, Israel Museum. xxix-42 p. 965-278-081-2 [OIAc S90].

e64 *Apollonia:* *Birnbaum* Rahel, *Ovadiah* Asher, A Greek inscription from the early Byzantine church at Apollonia [1962, 1976]: IsrEJ 40 (1990) 182-191; pl. 18.

e65 *Burj/Aḥmar:* **Pringle** Denys, The red tower 1986 ➤ 2.a628 ... 4,e773: [R]BSO 52 (1989) 349s (A. *Northedge*); RB 97 (1990) 476s (J. *Murphy-O'Connor*).

e66 *Bethel:* *Jamme* A., The Bethel inscribed stamp again; a vindication of Mrs. Theodore Bent: BASOR [209 (1973) 33-36] 280 (1990) 89-91.

e67 *Caesarea* 1989: ExcSIsr 9 (1989s) 38-42; fig. 31-35 (K. *Holum*, A. *Rahan*).

e68 *Raban* A., *al.*, Caesarea and its harbours; a preliminary report on the 1988 season: IsrEJ 40 (1990) 241-256; 6 fig.; pl. 25-27.

e69 **Oleson** J. P., [? ➤ 5,d862] *Raban* A., The harbours of Caesarea 1989: [R]IntJNaut 19 (1990) 348s (A. *Flinder*).

e70 **Blakely** Jeffrey A., Caesarea Maritima; the pottery and dating of Vault I: Excav. Report 4, 1987 ➤ 3,e159; 5,d864 (not Blakeley): [R]AJA 94 (1990) 363s (S. E. *Sidebotham*, also on 'Herod's Dream'); IsrEJ 40 (1990) 317-9 (Kathleen W. *Slane*).

e71 **Gersht** Rivkah, ◉ *Ha-Pissul*... The sculpture of Caesarea. TA 1987, Kibbutz Movement. 78 p.; ill., maps [KirSef 62 (1988s), p. 618].

e72 *Hohlfelder* Robert L., The subsidence of Caesarea Maritima's harbor: ➤ 784, AJA 94 (1990) 330s (summary).

e73 *Holum* Kenneth, The end of classical urbanism at Caesarea Maritima, Israel: ➤ 89, [F]JASHEMSKI Wilhelmina (1989) II, 87-102 + phot.

e74 *a)* *Hopfe* Lewis M., Caesarea [Maritima] Palaestinae as a religious center; – *b)* *Mussies* Gerard, Marnas god of Gaza: ➤ 828, ANRW 2/18/4 (1990) 2380-2411 / 2412-57.

e75 *Porath* Yosef, ◉ Pipelines of the Caesarea water supply system: ʿAtiqot 10 (1990) 101-110; 12 fig.; Eng. 19*s.

e75* **Levine** Lee I., *Netzer* Ehud, Excavations at Caesarea M: Qedem 21, 1986 ➤ 2,a629 ... 5,d863: [R]Syria 65 (1988) 469-471 (J.-P. *Sodini*).

e76 *a)* *Ringel* J., Literary and numismatic evidence of maritime activity in Caesarea during the Roman period; – *b)* *Hohlfelder* R. L., PROCOPIUS, De aedificiis 1.11.18-20; Caesarea Maritima and the building of harbours in late antiquity: MeditHistR 3,1 (L 1988) 63-74 / 54-62 [< NTAbs 34,76s].

e77 *Dor* 1988: ExcSIsr 9 (1989s) 28-32; fig. 23-27 (E. *Stern, al.*); 114-8.

e78 *Stern* E., New evidence from Dor for the first appearance of the Phoenicians along the northern coast of Israel: BASOR 279 (1990) 27-34; 5 fig.

e79 **Ebal;** 8 seasons: Qadmoniot 23,1s (1990) 42-50 (A. *Zertal* **❶**).
e80 **Far'a N.:** **Mallet** Joël, Tell el-Far'ah II,1s, Le Bronze Moyen: RCivMém 66, 1987 ➤ 4,e763: ᴿPaléorient 15,2 (1989) 154-8 (W. G. *Dever*).
e81 **Gerizim:** *Magen* Yitshak, **❶** Mount Gerizim, a temple-city: Qadmoniot 23 (1990) 70-96; ill.
e82 *a*) *Magen* Y., The Church of Mary Theotokos on Mount Gerizim [the inscriptions, *Di Segni* L.] / A Roman fortress and a Byzantine monastery at Khirbet el-Kiliya [1826.1487]; – *b*) *Hizmi* H., The Byzantine church at Khirbet el-Beiyûdât [1945.1522]; preliminary report [*Di Segni*, The inscriptions]; ➤ ᶠCORBO V., Christian archaeology 1990, 333-42 [-50] / 321-332 / 245-264[-274].
e83 **Gezer:** *a*) *Finkelstein* Israel, On archaeological methods and historical considerations; Iron Age II Gezer and Samaria; – *b*) *Dever* William G., Of myths and methods [response, also to other articles in this issue]: BASOR 277s (1990) 109-119 / 120-130.
e84 **Seger** Joe D., Gezer, the Field I caves: Annual 5. J 1989, HUC. xv-243 p.; 82 pl.
e85 *a*) *Reich* Ronny, The 'boundary of Gezer' inscriptions again; – *b*) *Schwartz* Joshua, Once more on the 'boundary of Gezer' inscriptions and the history of Gezer and Lydda at the end of the Second Temple period: IsrEJ [38 (1985) 235-245, *Rosenfeld* B.] 40 (1990) 44-46; 1 fig. / 47-57.
e86 **Gitin** Seymour, Gezer III, a ceramic typology of the Late Iron II, Persian and Hellenistic periods at Tell Gezer: Glueck Annual 3. J 1990, HUC. 261 p.; p. 265-494 + 103 pl. and loose plans. 965-222-208-X [Gezer IV by *Dever* W. was 1986 ➤ 2,a598].
e87 *Holladay* John S.ᴶ, Red slip, burnish, and the Solomonic gateway at Gezer: BASOR 277s (1990) 23-70; 18 fig.
e88 **Jaffa-Tel Aviv:** *Applebaum* S., The status of Jaffa in the first century of the current era: ScrClasIsr 8s (1988) 138-144.
e89 *Radan* G.T., The strategic and commercial importance of Jaffa, 66-69 B.C.: MeditHistR 3,1 (L 1988) 74-86.
e90 **Mazar** Amihai, Excavations at Tel Qasile II. The Philistine sanctuary...: Qedem 20, 1985 ➤ 1,d544; 4,e765: ᴿJQR 80 (1989s) 411-4 (S. M. *Paley*).
e91 *Kebara* (Carmel): Paléorient 14,2 (1988) 123-6 (P. *Goldberg, al.*).
e91* **Lydda:** *Oppenheimer* A., Jewish Lydda in the Roman era: HUCA 49 (1988) 115-136 [< ZAW 102, 275].
e92 *Mirzbaneh,* dhahr, 1987: ➤ 4, ᶠAMIRAN R., ErIsr 21 (1990) 239-248; 11 fig.; (map); Eng. 109* (I. *Finkelstein*).
e93 *Nami* (Dor 1443.2296). 1985-8: IsrEJ 40 (1990) 73-76; 2 fig. (M. *Artzy*).
e94 **Sefinim:** **Ronen** Avraham, *al.*, Sefinim [Iraq al-Barul] prehistoric sites, Mt. Carmel, Israel: BAR-Int 230. Ox 1984. 290 p. p. 291-533. – ᴿBInstArch 26 (1989) 295s (L. *Copeland*: 'Sefunium').
e95 **Šekem,** Sichem: *Brodsky* Harold, Three capitals in the hills of Ephraim [Shechem, Samaria, Tirzah]: BR 5,1 (1990) 38-44.
e96 **Šiloh,** Shiloh: **Schley** Donald G., Shiloh [diss. Emory 1986] 1989 ➤ 5, d886: ᴿÉTRel 65 (1990) 439s (D. *Lys*); ExpTim 101 (1989s) 120s (A. H. W. *Curtis*); TLZ 115 (1990) 342-4 (E. *Otto*).
e97 **Šomron**-Sabastiya: **Tappy** Ron E., Studies in the archaeology and history of Israelite Samaria: diss. Harvard. CM 1990. 427 p. 90-35621. – DissA 51 (1990s) 2435-A.
e98 *Stager* Lawrence E., Shemer's estate: BASOR 277s (1990) 93-107; 2 fig.
e99 **Dar** Shimon, Landscape and pattern... Samaria [Diss. TA], BAR-Int 308, 1986 ➤ 3,e175; 4,e770: ᴿJJS 41 (1990) 266s (Fanny *Vitto*).

e100 **Stratonis Turris:** *Arav* Rami, Some notes on the foundation of Straton's Tower: PEQ 121 (1989) 144-8.

e101 **Sumaqa** [154.230], 950 animal bones; Byz. Carmel subsistence: IsrEJ 40 (1990) 287-304; 6 fig. (L. *Horwitz, al.*).

e102 **Šuni:** *Shenhav* Eli, *a*) Le théâtre romain de Shuni [NE Césarée], rival de celui de Césarée: MondeB 67 (1990) 58-60; – *b*) ❹ Shuni/Miamas: Qadmoniot 23,1s (1990) 58-62.

T4.6 **Galilaea;** pro tempore *Golan*.

e103 **Gal** Zvi, ❹ *Ha-Galîl ha-Taḥton* ... Lower Galilee, Historical geography in the biblical period. TA 1990, Kibbutz Meuḥad. 158 p.; 101 fig. [OIAc F91].

e104 **Aḥzib:** *Mazar* Eilat, ❹ A horsemen's tomb at Akhziv: Qadmoniot 23 (1990) 104-9; ill.

e105 **Smith** P., *Horwitz* L., *Zias* J., Human remains from the Iron Age cemeteries at Akhziv, I. The built tomb from the southern cemetery: RStFen 18 (1990) 137-150; 2 fig.; pl. XII-XV.

e106 '**Akko:** *Applebaum* Shimon, The Roman colony of Ptolemais-Akko: → 540, Greece/Israel 1985/90, 135-140.

e107 **Kashtan** N., 'Akko-Ptolemais, a maritime metropolis in Hellenistic and early Roman times, 332 BCE - 70 CE, as seen through the literary sources: MeditHistR 3,1 (L 1988) 37-53.

e108 **Anafa** (= Aḥdar 2105.2869): *Fuks* Gideon, Tel Anafa — a proposed identification [Arsinoe]: ScrClasIsr 5 (1980) 178-184.

e109 **Banias:** Qadmoniot 23 (1990) 110-4 (V. *Tzaferis*, R. *Avner*, ❹).

e110 Banias, Temple of Pan 1989: ExcSIsr 9 (1989s) 85s; fig. 71s (Z. *Ma'oz*); 3s (V. *Tzaferis*, R. *Avner*).

e111 **Tzaferis** Vassilios, Banias, la ville de Pan: MondeB 64 (1990) 50-53; ill.

e112 **Bethsaida:** *Crocker* P.T., Where is Bethsaida?: Buried History 25,3 (Melbourne 1989) 79-81 [< NTAbs 34,21].

e113 **Beth-Shean** 1989s: → 4, ᶠAMIRAN R., ErIsr 21 (1990) 197-211; 15 fig.; Eng. 108* (A. *Mazar*).

e114 Beth-Shean 1988/9: ExcSIsr 9 (1989s) 120-8; fig. 107-119 (Y. *Tsafrir*, G. *Foerster*).

e115 **Foerster** Gideon, *al.*, Beth-shân, fouilles: MondeB 66 (1990) 29-39 [*al.*, 18-28; 2-17, Beth-shân Biblique].

e116 Glorious Beth-Shean ... new excavation [no author indicated]: BAR-W 16,4 (1990) 16-31; ill.

e117 **Last** Rosa, *Stein* Alla, Ala Antiana in Scythopolis; a new inscription from Beth-Shan: ZPapEp 81 (1990) 224-8.

c118 **Colbi** Paul S., Une ville au riche passé; Beit-Shean [< TerreS 1989]: EsprVie 100 (1990) 186-8 (J. *Daoust*).

e119 **Beth-Shearim:** *Görg* Manfred, Bēsara [JosF Vita 118s] — Bet-Še'arim: BibNot 52 (1990) 7-10.

e120 **Capharnaum:** *a*) *Bottini* Giovanni C., La casa di San Pietro a Cafarnao; – *b*) *Loffreda* Stanislao, Il memoriale di San Pietro a Cafarnao: TerraS 65 (1989) 156-162 / 163-6.

e121 **Manns** Frédéric, Una chiesa ottogonale, ᵀ*Cisternino* Giuseppe: TerraS 66 (1990) 229-232 [238-241, *Bottini* Giovanni C., Casa di S. Pietro].

e122 **Tzaferis** Vasilios, *al.*, Excavations at [Greek Orthodox] Capernaum, I, 1978-1982 [with] Pepperdine Univ. WL 1989, Eisenbrauns. xx-234 p.; 14 plans. – ᴿBAR-W 17,3 (1991) 6,8 (J. D. *Seger*); LA 40 (1990) 517-524

(S. *Loffreda*); RB 97 (1990) 475s (J. *Murphy-O'Connor*: indispensable complement to the work of CORBO and Lof[f]reda).

e123 *Carmelus: Daoust* J., Au Carmel sur les pas d'Élie [couvent Stella Maris: < MondeB 58 (1989), *Berder* M.]: EsprVie 100 (1990) 123-5.

e124 **Dan:** Biran Avraham, ⊕ The Middle Bronze II ramparts of Tel Dan: → 4, ᶠAMIRAN Ruth, ErIsr 21 (1990) 56-65; 11 fig.; Eng. 103*.

e125 *Biran* Avraham, Le sanctuaire de Dan: MondeB 66 (1990) 52-54.

e126 *Schulman* Alan R., An enigmatic Egyptian presence at Tel Dan: → 16, ᶠBECKERATH J. v. 1990, 235-244; pl. 17.

e127 *Stone* G.R., Dan macehead Assyrian II: BurHist 26 (1990) 71-79 [< OTAbs 14,153].

e127* *Giscala:* **Meyers** E.M. & C.L., (*Strange* J.F.), Excavations at the ancient synagogue of Gush Ḥalav: Meiron Excavation Project 5. WL 1990, ASOR/Eisenbrauns. xx-292 p. $40. 0-931464-59-5 [NTAbs 35,267].

e128 **Golan** chalco 1988: IsrEJ 40 (1990) 71s (Claire *Epstein*).

e129 *Gopher* Avi, Mujahiya, an early pre-pottery neolithic B site in the Golan Heights: TAJ 17 (1990) 115-143; 17 fig.

e130 ᴱ**Hachlili** R., *al.*, Jewish art in the Golan. Haifa 1987, Museum. 47 p.; 24 fig. [KirSef 62 (1988s) p. 187].

e131 *Vinitzky* Lipaz, ⊕ The date of the dolmens in the Golan and Galilee — a reassessment [EB II]: → 4, ᶠAMIRAN Ruth, ErIsr 21 (1990) 167-173; map; Eng. 107*.

e132 **Hazor:** Geva Shulamit, Hazor, Israel; an urban community of the 8th century B.C.E.: BAR-Int. 543. Ox 1989. [viii-] 180 p.; c. 30 plans. 0-86054-689-6.

e133 *a) Beck* Pirhiya, A note on the 'schematic statues' from the stelae temple at Hazor; – *b) Lipschitz* Oded, The date of the 'Assyrian residence' at Ayyelet ha-Shahar: TAJ 17,1 (1990) 91-95; 2 fig. / 96-99; 2 fig.

e134 *Dunayevsky* I., *Kempinski* A., ⊕ The eastern rampart of Hazor: ʿAtiqot 10 (1990) 23-28; Eng. 13*.

e135 *Stern* Ephraim, Hazor, Dor and Megiddo in the time of Ahab and under Assyrian rule: IsrEJ 40 (1990) 12-30; 3 fig.; pl. 2-3.

e136 *Ussishkin* David, ⊕ Notes on the Middle Bronze Age fortifications at Hazor: → 4, ᶠAMIRAN Ruth, Eretz-Israel 21 (1990) 1-5; 5 fig.; Eng. 101*.

e137 **Hazorea:** Meyerhof Ezra L., The Bronze Age necropolis at Kibbutz Hazorea, Israel: BAR-Int 534. Ox 1989. vi-173 p.

e138 **Ḥešeq:** *a) Manns* F., Joseph de Tibériade, un judéo-chrétien du quatrième siècle [Épiphane: parenthèse entre les Ébionites; en rapport avec la construction des premières églises de Galilée]; – *b) Aviam* M., [1757.2619] Ḥorvat Ḥesheq — a unique church in Upper Galilee; preliminary report [*Di Segni* L., the inscriptions]: → 39, ᶠCORBO V., Christian archaeology 1990, 553-9 / 351-378 [-390].

e139 **Goranson** Stephen C., The Joseph of Tiberias [as Galilee church builder] episode in Epiphanius; studies in Jewish and Christian relations: diss. Duke, ᴰ*Meyer* E. Durham NJ 1990. 212 p. 91-06617. – DissA 51 (1990s) 3439-A [RelStR 17,195 title 'J. of T. as a source on JC rel.'].

e140 **Hula:** Greenberg Raphael, ⊕ The settlement of the Hula Valley in the urban phase of the Early Bronze Age: → 4, ᶠAMIRAN Ruth, ErIsr 21 (1990) 127-131; map; Eng. 105*s.

e141 **Greenberg** Raphael, ⊕ Ha-Yišub... The settlement of the Hula Valley in EB II-III [Master's diss.]. J 1987, Hebrew Univ. 109 + 6* p. – OIAc Ap91,7.

e142 *Jezreel: Portugali* Y., ⊕ The settlement pattern in the western Jezreel valley from the 6th century B.C.E. to the Arab conquest [as in two recent surveys]: ➤ 348, Man and law 1986, 7-19.

e143 **Kabri** [164.270], 4 seasons: Qadmoniot 23,1s (1990) 31-41 (A. *Kempinski, al.* ⊕).

e144 **Kempinski** Aharon, ⊕ Excavations at Kabri, 1987. TA 1988, Univ. xi-20 + 71 p. [KirSef 62 (1988s), p. 619].

e145 *Kinneret |* 'Urayma: **Fritz** Volkmar, Kinneret; Ergebnisse der Ausgrabungen auf dem Tell el-'Oreme am See Gennesaret 1982-1985: AbhDPV 15. Wsb 1990, Harrassowitz. xviii-395 p. 3-447-03049-6 [OIAc Oc90].

e146 *Megiddo:* **Kempinski** Aharon, Megiddo, a city-state 1989 ➤ 5,d927: RZDPV 106 (1990) 188-191 (H. *Weippert:* comparative table of his and LOUD's stratification/chronology, p. 189).

e147 *Stern* Ephraim, SCHUMACHER's shrine in Building 338 at Megiddo; a rejoinder: IsrEJ [39 (1989) 149-172, *Ussishkin* D.] 40 (1990) 102-7; 1 fig.

e148 *Ussishkin* David, Notes on Megiddo, Gezer, Ashdod, and Tell Batash in the tenth to ninth centuries B.C.: BASOR 277s (1990) 71-91; 12 fig.

e149 *'Miṣrefot Mayim'* ⊕ and northern Israel settlements: BethM 36,124 (1991s) 1-10 (B. Z. *Luria*).

e150 *Muntaḥa:* **Gopher** Avi, The flint assemblages of Muntaḥa, final report: Cah CNRS-J 4. P 1989, Paléorient. 162 p.; 8 pl. [OIAc F91].

e151 *Nahariya:* **Dauphin** Claudine, *Edelstein* G., L'église byzantine de Nahariya 1984 ➤ 3,e218 ... 5,d941: RPEQ 122 (1990) 144-6 (Fanny *Vitto*).

e152 *Nazareth:* *Álvarez Calderón* J., Nazaret; su significado para Jesús y para la Iglesia: Páginas 15,105 (Lima 1990) 15-31 [< NTAbs 35,152].

e153 *Feig* Nurit, ⊕ [Roman] Burial caves at [a ridge east of] Nazareth: 'Atiqot 10 (1990) 67-79; 11 fig.; Eng. 17*.

e154 **Folda** Jaroslav, The Nazareth capitals and the Crusader shrine of the annunciation 1986 ➤ 2,a689 ... 5,d942*: RIsrEJ 40 (1990) 234s (Nurith *Kenaan-Kedar*); Syria 65 (1988) 479 (L. *Pressouyre*).

e155 *Longstaff* T. R. W., Nazareth and Sepphoris; insights into Christian origins [from texts and excavation]: ➤ 52, FFULLER R., AnglTR supp 11 (1990) 8-15 [< NTAbs 34,353].

e156 *Pritz* R. A., Nazarene Jewish Christianity, from the end of the NT period until its disappearance in the fourth century 1988 ➤ 4,e781: RRÉJ 149 (1990) 147-150 (S. *Mimouni:* not on Ebionites or Elkasaites); Salmanticensis 37 (1990) 377-9 (M. *Sánchez Caro*).

e157 Wawiyat (Nazareth) 1987: IsrEJ 40 (1990) 72s (J. P. *Dessel, al.*).

e158 **Qedeš** [10 k NW Hazor]: *Magness* Jodi, Some observations on the Roman temple at Kedesh [excavated since 1981 ...]: IsrEJ 40 (1990) 173-181 [➤ 784, AJA 94 (1990) 300, summary).

e159 *Qiri:* **Ben-Tor** Amnon, *al.*, Tell Qiri ... in Jezreel valley 1975-7: Qedem 24, 1987 ➤ 4,e809; 5,d943: RBO 47 (1990) 801-5 (Margaret *Steiner*); JQR 80 (1989s) 179-182 (S. M. *Paley*).

e160 *Quneitra:* EGoren-Inbar N., Quneitra, a Mousterian site on the Gilan Heights: Qedem 31. J 1990, Hebrew Univ. xv-239 p. 0333-5844 [OIAc F91,11 gives titles and authors (sans pp.) of the 13 specialized articles).

e161 *Roš Zayit:* **Gal** Zvi, Khirbet Roš Zayit — biblical Cabul: a historical-geographical case: BA 53 (1990) 88-97; ill.

e162 *Šadûd:* **Braun** E., *al.*, En Shadud; salvage excavations at a farming community in the Jezreel valley, Israel: BAR-Int 249, 1985 ➤ 1,d573; 4,e810: RPEQ 122 (1990) 143 (Kay *Prag*).

e163 *Sepphoris* 1987s: IsrEJ 40 (1990) 219-222 (E. *Meyers, al.*).

e164 *Adan-Bayevitz* David, *Perlman* Isadore, The local trade of Sepphoris in the Roman period: IsrEJ 40 (1990) 153-172; 5 fig. (map).

e165 *Crocker* P.T., Sepphoris; past history and present discoveries; BurHist 23,4 (Melbourne 1987) 64-76 [< NTAbs 35,206].

c166 **Neʿeman** Yehuda, ⓪ Sepphoris in the period of the Second Temple, Mishna and Talmud. J 1987. 494 p.; ill.; maps [KirSef 62 (1988s), p. 619].

e167 *Šiqmîm* 1987/9: ExcSIsr 9 (1989s) 167-170; fig. 165-170 (T. *Levy*, D. *Alon*).

e168 **Sussita:** *Tzaferis* Vassilios, Sussita [Decapolis; 'largest archaeological site on the east bank of the Sea of Galilee'] awaits the spade: BAR-W 16,5 (1990) 50-58; ill.

e169 **Tiberias:** **Dudman** H., (*Ballhorn* E.), Tiberias. J 1988, Carta. 240 p. $24.25. 965-220-141-3 [NTAbs 35,263].

e170 **Ubeidiya:** Paléorient 14,2 (1988) 63-65 (E. *Tchernov*).

e171 **Yaquš** [S Beth-Shan, 2024.2244] 1989, EB: IsrEJ 40 (1990) 222s (D. *Esse*).

T4.8   *Transjordania:* **East-Jordan.**

e172 **Boling** Robert G., The early biblical community in Transjordan: SocWA 6, 1988 → 4,e823*; 5,d955: ᴿBZ 34 (1990) 128 (W. *Thiel*); CBQ 52 (1990) 108s (Carol *Meyers*: gains and suffers from the brevity of its summary of GLUECK's surveys); JAOS 110 (1990) 159 (W. E. *Aufrecht*); JBL 109 (1990) 324-7 (J. A. *Dearman*); JTS 41 (1990) 131-3 (J. *Day*); TLZ 115 (1990) 214s (S. *Timm*).

e173 ᴱ**Garrard** A., *Gebel* H., Prehistory of Jordan 1986/8 → 5,d958: ᴿBInst-Arch 26 (1989) 262s (T. *Watkins*).

e174 ᴱ**Hadidi** Adnan, Studies in the history and archaeology of Jordan III, 1987 → 3,816; 4,e824: ᴿBInstArch 26 (1989) 266-8 (T. *Watkins*).
ᴱ**Thompson** H.O., Archaeology in Jordan 1989 → 502.

e175 **Zwickel** W., Eisenzeitliche Ortslagen im Ostjordanland: TAVO B-81. Wsb 1990, Reichert. 416 p., 8 maps. DM 74 [ZAW 103,465, Ulrike *Schorn*]. 3-88226-502-7.

---

e176 *Abaṭa* deir ʿain; Ghor eṣ-Ṣafi) 2d, 1990: LA 40 (1990) 475s K.D. *Politis*); ADAJ 34 (1990) 377-385; 6 fig.; III pl. (K.D. *Politis*).

e177 *Abila* 6th 1990: LA 40 (1990) 468-475; pl. 76 (W.H. *Mare*).

e178 *Abu Hamid,* near Deir ʿAlla [Inst. Franç./Univ. Yarmouk] 1988: LA 40 (1990) 483; MondeB 65 (1990) 50-53; ill. (Geneviève *Dollfus*).

e179 **Dollfus** Geneviève, Fouilles dans la vallée [du Jourdain; Abu-Hamid...]: Fouilles. P 1990, Syros Alternatives. 46 p. F 69. – ᴿMondeB 65 (1990) 65 (F. *Comte*).

e180 *ʿAmman:* **Zayadine** Fawzi, La campagne d'Antiochos III le Grand en 219-217 et le siège de Rabbatamana: RB 97 (1990) 68-84; 5 fig.; IV pl.; Eng. 68.

e181 *ʿAqaba*-Maʿan survey 1990: LA 40 (1990) 455-7 (W.J. *Jobling*).

e182 *Whitcomb* Donald, Diocletian's *miṣr* at ʿAqaba: ZDPV 106 (1990) 156-163; 2 fig.

e183 *Azraq:* ᴱ**Copeland** Lorraine, *Hours* Francis, The hammer on the rock; studies in the early palaeolithic of Azraq, Jordan: CNRS, Univ. Lumière: BAR-Int 540. Ox/Lyon 1989. 482 p. 0-86054-686-1 [OIAc JJ90].

e184 *Balu,* 5 k E mt. Šihan, Moab; 1987, LB-Iron: ZDPV 106 (1990) 86-113; 11 fig.; pl. 1-6 (U. *Worschech*).

e185 *Baq'a:* **McGovern** Patrick E., *al.,* The Late Bronze Age and Early Iron Ages of Central Transjordan; the Baq'ah Valley project 1977-81: Museum Mg 65. Ph 1988, Univ. Museum. xxii-365 p.; 104 fig.; 80 pl. $95. – ᴿBASOR 280 (1990) 93s (W. E. *Rast*).

e186 *Deir 'Alla:* **Kooij** G. van der, *Ibrahim* M. M., Picking up the threads ... a continuing review of excavations at Deir Alla, Jordan [< exhibition Leiden 1989], ᵀ. Leiden 1990, Univ. 112 p. 90-72821-02-5 [OIAc Oc90].

e187 *Dharīḥ* (near Tannur, 30 k SE Dead Sea), Nabatean, ❹: ADAJ 34 (1990) ❹ 5-13; 4 fig. (map); 4 pl. (Z. al-*Muheisen*, F. *Villeneuve*).

e188 *a) Dentzer-Feydy* Jacqueline, Khirbet edh-Dharih; architectural decoration of the temple; – *b) Killick* Marie, Les Nabatéens à Idhruh [12 k E Petra]: – *c) Lindner* Manfred, A unique lithic Early Bronze Edomite-Nabataean site in southern Jordan [Sadeh 13 k S Petra-Harun]; both past and present: ➜ 783, Aram 2 (1989/90) 229-234 / 249-252 / 77-83 + 4 fig.; 7 pl.

e189 *Dibon: Hübner* Ulrich, *a)* Der erste moabitische Palast: BibNot 51 (1990) 13-18; 1 fig.; – *b)* Ein byzantinischer Brotstempel aus Dibon: ZDPV 106 (1990) 177-9; 1 fig.; pl. 13-B.

e190 *Tushingham* A. D., Dhībān reconsidered; King Mesha and his works: ADAJ 34 (1990) 183-192.

e191 ᴱ**Dearman** Andrew, Studies in the Mesha inscription and Moab 1989 ➜ 4,392.9256*: ᴿTLZ 115 (1990) 881-4 (H. M. *Niemann*).

e192 *Feinan* (tell wadi-), 1988, pottery-neolithic: ADAJ 34 (1990) 27-51; 13 fig. (M. *Najjar, al.*).

e193 *Gadara* – Umm Qeis; 1989: ADAJ 34 (1990) 321-336; 8 fig.; VI pl. (T. *Weber, al.*); 351-3, *Weber*, Decapolis sculpture.

e194 *Bol* P. C., *al.,* Gadara in der Dekapolis, deutsche Ausgrabungen ... 1986-8: ArchAnz (1990) 193-266; 40 fig. [< LA 40,479].

e195 *Gazal* ('ayn) 1989, pre- and pottery-neo: ADAJ 34 (1990) 11-23; 2 fig.; 2 pl. (Z. *Kafafi, al.*).

e196 *Kafafi* Zeidan A., Early pottery contexts from 'Ain Ghazal, Jordan: BASOR 280 (1990) 15-30; 12 fig.

e197 *Gerasa: Clark* Vincent A., The Bishop Isaiah church at Geraš — a brief note: ZDPV 106 (1990) 175s.

e198 *Zayadine* Fawzi, Visite du site, *al.,* La Pompéi de l'Orient, Jerash: MondeB 62 (1990) 19-26 (*al.* p. 1-43); plan 20; ill.

e199 *a) Manzano* Braulio, Gerasa o Gadara? ᵀ*Anguita* Luis A.; – *b) Manns* Frédéric, L'esorcismo di Gadara [... con foto di Kursi]: TerraS 65 (1989) 151-5 / 146-150.

e200 *Hešbon: Knauf* Ernst A., Hesbon, Sihons Stadt. ZDPV 106 (1990) 135-144.

e201 *Ḥumayma* 1989: ADAJ 34 (1990) 285-307; 9 fig.; pl. I-III (J. P. *Oleson*, field report) & 313-9 (Sylvie *Blétry-Sébé*, habitat et urbanisme).

e202 *Iktanu* 2d 1989 [EB-MB: ADAJ 34 (1990) 119-128; 7 fig.; II pl. (Kay *Prag*); – PEQ 121 (1989) 158s (Kay *Prag*).

e203 *Iskander* (24 k S Madaba) 1987: ➜ 500, ASOR reports 1990, 33-58; 29 fig. (Suzanne *Richard*).

e204 *Jawa:* **Helms** Svend, Early Islamic architecture of the desert; a bedouin station in Eastern Jordan. E 1990, Univ. xi-188 p. 0-85224-627-7 [OIAc S90].

e205 *Juwayda* Roman tomb, **Ⓐ**: ADAJ 34 (1990) **Ⓐ** 19-22: 3 fig.; 4 pl. (Kh. F. al-*Tarawnah*).

e206 **Kerak:** *Steele* Caroline S., Early Bronze Age socio-political organization in southwest Jordan [Kerak plateau]: ZDPV 106 (1990) 1-31; 9 fig.

e207 *a*) *Timm* Stefan, Einige Orte und Strassen auf dem Gebiet des alten Moabs bei EUSEBIUS; – *b*) *Olivier* J. P. J., The El-Kerak district of Jordan (ancient Moab) in nineteenth-century maps; a few preliminary remarks; – *c*) *Miller* J. Maxwell, Recent archaeological exploration on the El-Kerak plateau: JNWS 15 (1989) 179-215 / 169-177 / 143-153.

e208 **Worschech** Udo, Die Beziehungen Moabs zu Israel und Ägypten in der Eisenzeit; siedlungsarchäologische Untersuchungen im Kernland Moabs (Arḍ al-Kerak): ÄgAT 18. Wsb 1990, Harrassowtz. [viii-] 144 p.; 33 fig., X pl.; map; Eng. p. 129. 3-447-03001-1.

e209 **Lehun:** *Homès-Fredericq* Denyse, Les fouilles belges à Lehun (Jordanie): ➤ 107, ᶠKUPPER J.-R. 1990, 285-262; I pl.

e210 *Limes arabicus* 1989: ADAJ 34 (1990) 357-376; 20 fig. (S. T. *Parker*).

e211 Limes Arabicus 1987: ➤ 500, ASOR reports 1990, 89-136; 32 fig. (S. T. *Parker*).

e212 *Mayerson* Philip, Towards a comparative study of a frontier [east of wadi ʿAraba]: IsrEJ 40 (1990) 267-279.

e213 ᴱ**Parker** S. T., The Roman frontier in central Jordan...: BAR-Int 340, 1987 ➤ 3,506; 4,e829: ᴿPEQ 121 (1989) 150s (H. I. *Macadam*).

e214 *Madaba:* **Piccirillo** Michele, Madaba; le chiese e i mosaici. T 1989, Paoline. 174 p. Lit. 45.000. – ᴿCC 141 (1990,3) 536s (A. *Ferrua*); Letture 45 (1990) 87-89 (G. *Ravasi*); SMSR 56 (1990) 285-291 (Alessandra *Acconci*).

e215 **Piccirillo** Michele, Madaba, Mount Nebo, Umm er-Rasas; a brief guide to the antiquities. Amman 1990, al-Kutba. 44 p.; ill. – ᴿLA 40 (1990) 484 (P. *Kaswalder*).

e216 Madaba plains 1987: ➤ 500, ASOR reports 1990, 59-87; 30 fig. (L. T. *Geraty, al.*).

e217 *Mekawer,* Malechios church: LA 40 (1990) 466-8; pl. 83-85 (M. *Piccirillo*).

e218 *Nebo:* *Piccirillo* Michele, a) Dove va la ricerca sul Monte Nebo?; – *b*) P. Francesco QUARESMI, un caposcuola della Palestinologia moderna; – *c*) Una nuova cappella della diocesi di Philadelphia-Amman in Giordania [Kursi]: TerraS 65 (1989) 81-89 / 185-8 / 218-221.

e219 *a*) *Piccirillo* Michele, Il dayr del Diacono Tommaso alle ʿUyun Musa - Monte Nebo; – *b*) *Alliata* Eugenio, Ceramica bizantina e omayyade di ʿUyun Musa: LA 40 (1990) 227-246; 10 fig. (1 foldout); pl. 1-24 / 247-261; 10 fig. – Eng. 448.

e220 *Piccirillo* Michele, *a*) La chapelle du prêtre Jean au mont Nébo; – *b*) Une chapelle byzantine [Kursi] près d'Amman: MondeB 62 (1990) 60s / 65 (1990) 66s.

e221 *a*) *Piccirillo* M., *Alliata* E., L'eremitaggio di Procapis e l'ambiente funerario di Robebos al Monte Nebo-Siyagha; – *b*) *Alliata* E., Nuovo settore del monastero al Monte Nebo-Siyagha: ➤ 39, ᶠCORBO V., Christian archaeology 1990, 391-426 / 427-466, ill.

e221* *Arndt* Marian B., **Ⓟ** New archeological discoveries in the Mount Nebo region: ➤ 546, RuBi 42 (1989) 42-51 + 3 fig. (map).

e222 *Nimrin* 1st 1989: ADAJ 34 (1990) 131-150; 15 fig.; II pl. (J. W. *Flanagan*, D. W. *McCreery*) & 153-171; 8 fig.; X pl. (R. H. *Dornemann*, pottery).

e223 *Nisya:* **Livingston** David P.ᴶ, Khirbet Nisya 1979-1986; a report on six years of excavation: diss. Andrews, ᴰ*Storfjell* B. Berrien Springs MI 1990. vi-283 p. 90-07147. – OIAc Ap91.

e224 *Pella*-Faḥl 10th 1988: ADAJ 34 (1990) 57-86; 13 fig.; VII pl. (P. C. *Edwards, al.*).

e225 Yabis survey (between Pella and ʿAjlun) 1989: ADAJ 34 (1990) 95-118 (G. *Palumbo, al.*).

e226 Yabis, wadi, 1990: LA 40 (1990) 457-9 (G. *Palumbo*, J. *Mabry*).

e227 *Petra*-Zantur 1st 1988: ADAJ 34 (1990) 249-273; 8 fig.; X pl. (R. A. *Stucky*).

e228 *Bienkowski* Piotr, Umm el-Biyara, Tawilan and Buseira [excavated by Crystal-M. BENNETT, † 1987] in retrospect: Levant 22 (1990) 91-108; 18 fig. (map).

e229 *Blagg* Thomas F. C., Column capitals with elephant-head volutes at Petra: Levant 22 (1990) 131-7; 5 fig.

e230 **Byrd** Brian F., *al.*, Excavations at Beidha, 1. The Natufian encampment at Beidha; late pleistocene adaptation in the southern Levant; pref. *Kirkbride* Diana: Jutland Arch. Soc. 23/1. Aarhus 1989, Univ. 126 p.; 42 fig.; ❹ summary. £16. – ᴿPEQ 122 (1990) 143s (A. N. *Garrard*).

e231 *Fiema* Zbigniew T., *Jones* Richard N., The Nabataean king-list revised; further observations on the second Nabataean inscription from Tell esh-Shuqafiya, Egypt: ADAJ 34 (1990) 239-248; 2 fig.

e232 **Khairy** Nabil I., The 1981 Petra excavations: AbhDPV 13. Wsb 1990, Harrassowitz. xiii-162 p.; 54 fig.; 28 pl.; 4 maps. 3-447-02878-5 [OIAc F91,14]. – ᴿLA 40 (1990) 480s (E. *Alliata*).

e233 *a) Kirkbride* Diana, The Nabataeans, Trajan and the Periplus ['after' p. 259 largely autobiographical]; – *b) Hamarneh* Salih, The Nabataeans after the decline of their political power; from the Arabic Islamic sources, ᵀ*Johnstone* Penelope, *Shama'a* Najah: ⇴ 783, Aram 2 (1989/90) 253-265 / 425-436.

e234 *Lindner* Manfred, Ein nabatäisches Heiligtum oberhalb der Nischenklamm (*Sidd el-Ma'ağin*) von Petra (Jordanien): ZDPV 106 (1990) 145-155: 1 fig.; pl. 14-19.

e235 **McKenzie** Judith, The architecture of Petra: British Acad. Mg. Arch. 1. Ox 1990, UP. xxii-209 p.; 245 pl. 9 maps. 0-19-72700-X.

e236 *a) Parr* Peter, Sixty years of excavation in Petra; a critical assessment; – *b) Zeitler* John P., A private building from the first century BC in Petra: ⇴ 783, Aram 2 (1989/90) 7-23 / 385-402 + 14 fig.; 7 pl.

e237 **Stierlin** H., Städte in der Wüste; Petra, Palmyra und Hatra...: Ant-KunstVO, 1987 ⇴ 5,e10: ᴿNedTTs 44 (1990) 59s (K. A. D. *Smelik*).

e238 *Vannini* Guido, *al.*, Petra crociata: ArchViva 9,11 (1990) 34-49; ill.

e239 **Wenning** Robert, Die Nabatäer, Denkmäler und Geschichte: NOrb 3, 1987 ⇴ 3,e317... 5,e13: ᴿBonnJbb 190 (1990) 716s (T. *Weber*); CritRR 3 (1990) 98-101 (D. F. *Graf* adds many 1983-9 articles); PEQ 122 (1990) 150s (B. *Isserlin*).

e240 *Ram:* **Bienert** Hans-Dieter, The er-Ram stone mask at the Palestine Exploration Fund, London: OxJArch 9 (1990) 257-261.

e241 *Sadeh* (15 k SSW Petra) 2d 1988, lithic to Nabatean: ADAJ 34 (1990) 193-225; 15 fig.; XII pl. (M. *Lindner, al.*).

e242 *Sa'idiyeh* 4th 1989: Levant 22 (1990) 21-42; 27 fig. (J. N. *Tubb*).

e243 **Pritchard** James B., Tell es-Saʻidiyeh... 1964-6: 1985 ➤ 1,d713... 5,e16: ᴿCBQ 52 (1990) 132-4 (K. G. *Hoglund*).

e244 *Samra: Humbert* J.-B., Khirbet es-Samra du diocèse de Bosra: ➤ 39, ᶠCORBO V., Christian archaeology 1990, 467-474.

e245 *Humbert* Jean-Baptiste, *Desreumaux* Alain, Huit campagnes de fouilles au Khirbet es-Samra (1981-1989): RB 97 (1990) 252-269.

e246 *Tawilan: a) Bienkowski* Piotr, The chronology of Tawilan and the 'dark age' of Edom; – *b) Mattingly* Gerald L., Settlement on Jordan's Kerak plateau from Iron Age IIC through the early Roman period: ➤ 783, Aram 2 (1989/90) 35-44 / 309-330 + 5 maps.

e247 *Tišbe: Thiel* Winfried, Die Lage von Tischbe in Gilead: ZDPV 106 (1990) 119-134; 6 fig.; pl. 9-13: Iştib 12 k NW Jerash.

e248 *Umeiri* (Dreijat, Jawa: Madaba plains project) 3d 1989: AndrUnS 28 (1990) 5-25 + 25 pl. (R. W. *Younker, al.*).

e249 *Umm Raşaş* 5th 1990: LA 40 (1990) 463-6; pl. 80-82 (M. *Piccirillo*).

e250 *Piccirillo* Michele, L'identificazione storica delle rovine di Umm er-Rasas — *Kastron Mefaa* in Giordania: Biblica 71 (1990) 527-541; 2 fig.; 6 fot.; Eng. 541.

e251 *Yasileh* 3d, 1990: LA 40 (1990) 459-462; pl. 69-75 (Z. al-*Muheisen*, franç.).

e252 *Yutil: Olszewski* Deborah L., *al.*, WHS 784 X (Yutil al-Hasa), a Late Ahmarian site in the Wadi Hasa, West-Central Jordan: PrPrehSoc 56 (1990) 33-49; 3 fig.

т5.1 **Phoenicia** – *Libanus*, **Lebanon.**

e253 **Elay** Josette, Pénétration grecque en Phénicie 1988 ➤ 4,e911; 5,e28: ᴿBO 17 (1990) 56s (E. *Lipiński*); RArtLv 21 (1988) 166s (R. *Donceel*).

e254 **Elayi** J., Recherches sur les cités phéniciennes 1987 ➤ 3,e337: ᴿAulaO 8 (1990) 275s (M. *Heltzer*).

e255 **Jidejian** Nina, I love Lebanon; [also French] J'aime le Liban, ᵀ*Jalabert* Henri. Beirut 1984, Imprimerie Catholique. 64 p.; 95 fig. – ᴿBerytus 37 (1989) 189-191 (Hélène *Sader*; one of four books 'intended for children of the world', but not Lebanon — no Arabic).

e256 **Salibi** Kamal, A house of many mansions; the history of the Lebanon reconsidered 1988 ➤ 5,e30: ᴿBSO 52 (1989) 355 (M. E. *Yapp*).

e257 *a) Stieglitz* Robert R., The geopolitics of the Phoenician littoral in the Early Iron Age; – *b) Markoe* Glenn E., The emergence of Phoenician art; – *c) Anderson* William P., The beginnings of Phoenician pottery; vessel shape, style, and ceramic technology in the early phases of the Phoenician Iron Age; – *d) Bikai* Patricia M., Suggested readings: BASOR 279 (1990) 9-12; map / 13-26; 12 fig. / 35-54; 12 fig. / (7s) 65s.

e258 *Baʻalbek: Hajjar* Y., La triade de Heliopolis-Baalbek 1977 ➤ 58,d431; 61,s995: ᴿNumen 37 (1990) 280-3 (J. *Greenfield*).

e259 *Hajjar* Youssef, *a)* Baalbek, grand centre religieux sous l'Empire; – *b)* Dieux et cultes non héliopolitains de la Beqaʻ, de l'Hermon et de l'Abilène à l'époque romaine; – *c)* Divinités oraculaires et rites divinatoires en Syrie et en Phénicie à l'époque gréco-romaine: ➤ 828, ANRW 2/18/4 (1990) 2458-2508 / 2509-2604 / 2236-2320.

e260 *Byblos: Joukowsky* Martha S., The young archaeologist in the oldest port city of the world. Beirut 1988, Imprimerie Catholique. 141 p.; 30 fig.; 14 pl. + 4 color. – ᴿBerytus 37 (1989) 191-3 (Amélie *Beyhum*: some objections).

e261 **Salles** Jean-François, La Nécropole 'K' de Byblos: RCiv Mém 2, 1980 ⇥ b515: ᴿOLZ 85 (1990) 175s (E. *Lindemeyer*).

e261* *Davie* Michael F., *Salamé-Sarkis* Hassān, Le *Théouprosopon*-Ras aš-Šaq'a (Liban); étude géo-historique: MUSJ 51 (1990) 1-48; 5 fig.

e262 ***Kāmid/Lōz:*** *Hachmann* Rolf, Kāmid el-Lōz 1963-1981, German excavations in Lebanon, Part I: Berytus 37 (1989) 187 p.

e263 **Miron** Renate, Kamid el-Loz 10, das Schatzhaus im Palastbereich; die Funde: Saarb. Beit. 46. Bonn 1990, Habelt. 233 p. 83 (color.) fig., 87 pl. DM 102 [ZAW 103, 163, O. *Kaiser*].

e264 ***Sarafand:*** **Anderson** William P., Sarepta I [⇥ 5,e18]: the Late Bronze and Iron Age strata of Area II,Y. Beirut 1988, Univ. Libanaise. 446 p.; 52 pl. – ᴿAJA 94 (1990) 502 (Z. *Gal*).

e265 ***Sidon:*** **Elayi** Josette, Sidon, cité autonome de l'empire perse 1989 ⇥ 5,e40; 321 p.; 15 fig.: ᴿRBgNum 136 (1990) 363s (P. *Naster*).

e266 **Stucky** Rolf A., Tribune d'Echmoun 1984 ⇥ 65,b13 ... 5,e42: ᴿBabesch 65 (1990) 163s (E. M. *Moormann*).

e267 *Tyrus: Nitsche* Andreas, Bemerkungen zu Chronologie und Herkunft der protogeometrischen Importkeramik von Tyros: HaBeiArch 13s (1986s) 7-49; 11 fig.

e267* **Linant de Bellefonds** Pascale, Sarcophages antiques de la nécropole de Tyr; une étude iconographique: RCiv Mém 59, 1985 ⇥ 3,e356; 4,e939: ᴿSyria 65 (1988) 466-9 (F. *Baratte*).

e268 ᴱ**Schmeling** Gareth, Historia Apollonii regis Tyri 1988 ⇥ 4,e942; 5,e44: ᴿClasR 40 (1990) 291-4 (J. B. *Hall*: he did not know what exactly he was editing).

T5.2 *Situs mediterranei* **phoenicei et punici.**

e269 *Bartoloni* P., Aspetti precoloniali della colonizzazione fenicia in Occidente: RStFen 18 (1990) 157-167.

e269* *Bondì* Sandro F., I Fenici in Erodoto 1988/90: ⇥ b574, *Burkert* W., Hérodote, p. 255-286 (-300 discussion).

e270 **Ciafaloni** D., *Pisano* G., La collezione Torno; materiali fenicio-punici [49 ceramica + 43]: Studia Punica 1, 1987 ⇥ 3,e364: ᴿJNWS 15 (1989) 243 (F. C. *Fensham*).

e271 ᴱ**Delz** J., SILIUS Italicus, Punica 1987 ⇥ 5,e49: ᴿDLZ 111 (1990) 159-162 (W. *Hofmann*); Gymnasium 97 (1990) 270s (M. von *Albrecht*); Latomus 49 (1990) 169s (R. *Verdière*); RFgIC 118 (1990) 219-224 (P. *Fedeli*); RPg 63 (1989) 320s (G. *Liberman*).

e272 ᴱ**Gehrig** U., *Niemeyer* H. G., Die Phönizier im Zeitalter Homers; Kestner-Museum, Hanover, 14. Sept. - 25. Nov. 1990. Mainz 1990, von Zabern. 260 p.; 79 pl. – ᴿRStFen 18 (1990) 231 (E. *Acquaro*).

e273 **Gras** M., *al.*, L'univers phénicien 1989 ⇥ 5,e51: ᴿAulaO 8 (1990) 145-7 (G. del *Olmo Lete*).

e274 *Huss* Werner, Die Leiter als Symbol im punischen und neupunischen Bereich: ZDPV 106 (1990) 172-4; 1 fig.

e275 *Leighton* Robert, Antiquarianism and prehistory in West Mediterranean islands; AntiqJ 69 (1989) 183-204; pl. XXXVIII-XXXIX [giants].

e276 **Mazza** Federico, *Ribichini* Sergio, *Xella* Paolo, Fonti classiche per la civiltà fenicia e punica 1988 ⇥ 5,e55: ᴿRSO 63 (1989) 358 (J. A. *Soggin*).

e276* *Stampolidis* N., A funerary cippus at Eleutherna [Alphá-Peristerés] — evidence of Phoenician presence?: BInstClas 37 (1990) 99-106.

e277 **Hispania:** *a*) *Aubet Semmler* Maria E.,   Die Phönizier in Spanien; – *b*) *Apellaniz* Juan M.,   Zur paläolithischen Kunst in Spanien; – *c*) *Irmscher* Johannes, Sardinien im Altertum: Altertum 36 (1990) 95-104; 6 fig. / 113-8; 5 fig. / 118-122; 5 fig.

e278 **Harrison** Richard J.,   Spain at the dawn of history; Iberians, Phoenicians and Greeks: Ancient Peoples and Places 1988 ➤ 5,e66: ᴿAJA 94 (1990) 157s (Katina T. *Lillios*).

e279 *Martín de la Cruz* José C.,   Die erste mykenische Keramik von der Iberischen Halbinsel: PraehZts 65 (1990) 49-52 (-61, *al.*).

e280 **Perdigones Moreno** Lorenzo,   La necrópolis fenicio-púnica de Cádiz, siglos vi-iv a.c.: StPun 7. R 1990, Univ. 90 p.

e281 *a*) *Rouillard* Pierre,   Phéniciens et grecs à Toscanos; notes sur quelques vases d'inspiration gréco-géometrique de Toscanos (1967); – *b*) *Maass-Lindemann* Greta,   Die phönikische Keramik von Lixus im Vergleich mit südandalusischer Keramik: MadMit 31 (1990) 178-185; 1 fig. pl.; 20-21 + color. d. / 186-193; 6 fig.

e282 *Sardinia:* *Scheuer* Joan G.,   Searching for the Phoenicians in Sardinia: BAR-W 16,1 (1990) 53-60; color. ill.

e283 **Hölbl** Günther,   Ägyptisches Kulturgut im phönizischen und punischen Sardinien: ÉPR 102, 1986 ➤ 2,a793 ... 5,e86: ᴿZDMG 139 (1989) 228 (W. *Huss*).

e284 **Scandone Matthiae** Gabriella,   Egitto e Sardegna; contatti fra culture: Sardò 3. Sassari 1988, Cittadella. 49 p.

e285 ᴱ**Balmuth** Miriam S.,   Nuragic Sardinia and the Mycenaean world [Rome American Academy colloquium Sept. 1986]: BAR-Int 387. Ox 1987. 270 p.; 88 fig. 14 art. – ᴿAJA 94 (1990) 156s (G. S. *Webster*).

e286 *Tharros:* **Acquaro** E.,   Scavi al tofet di Tharros; le urne dello scavo Pesce - I: Coll. StFen 29, ➤ 5,e87 (1989!): ᴿRStFen 18 (1990) 233 (H.-G. *Niemeyer*).

e287 ᴱ**Barnett** R. D.,   *Mendleson* C., Tharros, British Museum catalogue 1987 ➤ 3,e391 ... 5,e89: ᴿBInstArch 26 (1989) 235s (B. *Isserlin*).

T5.3 **Carthago.**

e288 **Barceló** Pedro A.,   Karthago und die iberische Halbinsel vor den Barkiden 1988 ➤ 5,e91: ᴿHZ 251 (1990) 667s (H. G. *Niemeyer*).

e289 *Bateson* Donal, *al.*,   The early nineteenth-century Jackson collection of coins from Carthage: NumC 150 (1990) 145-177; pl. 17-18.

e290 **Ben Khader** Aïcha B., *Soren* D.,   Carthage, a mosaic of ancient Tunisia (exhibition catalogue). NY/L 1987, American Museum of Natural History/Norton. 238 p.; (color.) ill. $20. – ᴿClasR 40 (1990) 410s (H. *Hurst*).

e291 *a*) *Bron* François,   Notes sur quelques stèles provenant du tophet de Carthage; – *b*) *Desanges* Jehan,   Sur quelques erreurs de Strabon à propos de Carthage et de son territoire; – *c*) *Moscati* Sabatino, ± 550 a.C.; dai Fenici ai Cartaginesi: ➤ 175, ᶠSᴢɴʏᴄᴇʀ M. = Semitica 38 (69-72 + pl. XI-XV / 95-100 / 39 (1990) 53-57.

e292 ᴱ**Clover** F.-M., *Humphreys* R. S.,   Tradition and innovation in late antiquity 1984/9 ➤ 5,781 (p. 129-169 Clover, Felix Carthago). – ᴿRPg 63 (1989) 305 (E. des *Places*).

e293 **Elliger** W.,   Karthago; Stadt der Punier, Römer, Christen: Urban-Tb 412. Stu 1990, Kohlhammer. 224 p. DM 24,80 [ZAW 103, 152, H.-C. *Schmitt*].

e294 **Huss** W.,   Geschichte der Karthager 1985 ➤ 1,d789 ... 5,e99: ᴿVDI 194 (1990) 183-190 (I. S. *Shifman* †).

e295 *Huss* Werner,   Die Depositenbank von Karthago: JbNumG 39 (1989) 21-26; Eng. 100.

e296 ᴱ**Lipiński** E., Carthage: Studia Phoenicia 6, 1986/8 ➤ 4,752: ᴿJAOS 110 (1990) 588-590 (P. G. *Mosca*).

e297 **Niemeyer** Hans G.,   Das frühe Karthago und die phönizische Expansion im Mittelmeerraum: Ha-Jungius 60.   Gö 1989, VR. 34 p.; 3 pl.

e298 *a*) *Niemeyer* Hans G.,   Karthago, Stadt der Phönizier am Mittelmeer; – *b*) *Stieglitz* Robert R.,   Die Göttin Tanit im Orient: AntWelt 21 (1990) 89-105; 25 (color.) fig. (maps) / 106-9; 13 fig. (maps).

e299 **Prévot** Françoise,   Mactar V. 1984 ➤ 65,b708: ᴿRArchéol (1990) 437s (J.-C. *Picard*).

e300 **Rives** James B.,   Religion and authority in the territory of Roman Carthage from Augustus to Constantine: diss. Stanford 1990, ᴰ*Treggiari* Susan M. 290 p. 91-02341. – DissA 51 (1990s) 2842-A.

e301 *Scullard* H.H., The Carthaginians in Spain: ➤ 832, CAH² 8 (1989) 17-43.

e302 *Vegas* Mercedes,   Archaische Töpferöfen in Karthago: MiDAI-R 97 (1990) 33-54; 8 fig. (54-56, *Acquaro* Enrico).

e303 *Xella* Paolo,   KAI 78 e il pantheon di Cartagine: RStFen 18 (1990) 209-217.

T5.4   **Ugarit** – *Ras Šamra.*

e304 **Amico** Eleanor B.,   The status of women at Ugarit: diss. Wisconsin, ᴰ*Schoville* K.   Madison 1990.   584 p. 90-13332. – DissA 51 (1990s) 268-A; OIAc Oc90.

e304* *Courtois* J.-C.,   À propos des archives royales d'Ougarit; la correspondance diplomatique [accadienne syllabique] était conservée dans les locaux des Archives Est du palais royal [1951-3: correction de son SDB fasc. 52 (1979) 1223-1230, inexact]: Syria 65 (1988) 389-394; plan.

e305 **Cunchillos** Jesús-Luis,   La travaille épigraphique de l'Ougarit 2, bibliographie: RS-Ougarit 5 / Mém 87, 1990. P 1990, RCiv. 202 p. 2-86538-205-9. – ᴿUF 22 (1990) 508 (O. *Loretz* disapproves repeated fulness of citation).

e306 *Du Buit* M.,   Ras Shamra, Ougarit: ➤ 833, Catholicisme 13,55 (1989) 495-8.

e306* *Freu* Jacques,   La tablette RS 86.2230 et la phase finale du royaume d'Ugarit: Syria 66 (1988) 395-8.

e307 ᵀᴱ**Hvidberg-Hansen** Finn O.,   Kanaʿanæiske myter og legender; tekster fra Ras Shamra-Ugarit: Bibel og historie 13s. Aarhus 1990, Univ. Bind I. x-235 p.; II. xvi-247 p. 87-7288-266-2; -4-6.

e308 **Izre'el** Shlomo,   *Singer* Itamar, The general's letter from Ugarit; a linguistic and historical reevaluation of RS 20.33 (Ugaritica V, No. 20). TA 1990, Univ. 222 p.; 8 pl.; 2 maps.

e309 *a*) *Lagarce* Élisabeth & Jacques,   Un bâton magique égyptien en ivoire à Ras Shamra; – *b*) *Yon* Marguerite,   Ougarit et ses dieux (Travaux 1978-1988): ➤ 28, ᶠBOUNNI A. 1990, 171-188 + pl. 40-49 / 325-339 + pl. 108-111.

e310 *Mendecki* Norbert, ❷ Ugarit (Ras Szamra) — history of a half-century of excavations: RuBi 42 (1989) 111-4 [without use of ZDPV 1973s].

   Pardee Dennis,   Les textes para-mythologiques (de 1961) 1988 [and controversy over KTU reliability] ➤ 9382.

e310* **Shifman** I. S., Ⓚ Kultura drevnego Ugarita. Moskva 1987. – ᴿSyria 65 (1988) 458-461 (A. *Caquot*).

e311 *Soldt* W. H. van, De stad Ugarit: PhoenixEOL 36,2 (1990) 9-30; 3 fig.

e311* **Yon** M., *al.*, Ras Shamra - Ougarit III. Le centre de la ville, 38ᵉ-44ᵉ campagnes (1978-1984) 1987 ➤ 4,g3: ᴿArOr 58 (1990) 187 (P. *Charvát*); JPrehRel 3s (1989s) 69s (P. *Åström*).

T5.5 Ebla.

e312 *Archi* Alfonso, Données épigraphiques éblaïtes et production artistique: RAss 84 (1990) 101-105.

e313 *a) Archi* Alfonso, Imar au IIIᵉ millénaire d'après les archives d'Ébla; – *b) Bonechi* Mario, À propos des noms propres d'Ébla [*Krebernik* M. 1988]: MARI 6 (1990) 21-38 / 221-244.

e314 ᴱ**Bahnassi** Afif, Ebla Archaivs. Damascus 1989, Der Tlass. 152 p.

e315 *Bonechi* M., I 'regni' dei testi degli archivi di Ebla: AulaO 8 (1990) 157-174; Eng. 157.

e316 **Conti** Giovanni, *a)* Il sillabario della quarta fonte della lista lessicale bilingue eblaita: QuadSemit 17 / MiscEbl 3, ➤ 485*. F 1990, Univ. viii-220 p. – *b)* Le fonti del vocabolario bilingue eblaita: MiscEbl 2 (1989) 79-115.

e316* *a) Diakonoff* I. M., The importance of Ebla for history and linguistics; – *b) Kienast* Burkhardt, *Waetzoldt* Hartmut, Zwölf Jahre Ebla; Versuch einer Bestandsaufnahme; – *c) Stieglitz* Robert R., Ebla and the gods of Canaan; – *d) Gordon* Cyrus H., Eblaite and Northwest Semitic [+ response to W. G. *Lambert*]; – *e) Rendsburg* Gary A., Monophthongization of *aw/ay* > *ā* in Eblaite and Northwest Semitic: ➤ e319, Eblaitica 2 (1990) 3-29 / 31-77 / 79-89 / 127-139 [145s] / 91-126.

e317 *Fronzaroli* Pelio, Forms of the dual in the texts of Ebla, ᵀ*Jaffe* Matthew L.: ➤ 164, ᶠSEGERT S., *Sopher* 1990, 111-125.

e318 ᴱ**Gordon** C., Eblaitica 1, 1987 ➤ 3,491; 4,g10: ᴿBSO 52 (1989) 115s (W. G. *Lambert*); OLZ 85 (1990) 164-5 (H. *Klengel*).

e319 ᴱ**Gordon** Cyrus H., *Rendsburg* Gary A., Eblaitica, essays on the Ebla archives and Eblaite language, 2: NYU Ebla Center. WL 1990, Eisenbrauns. v-163 p. 0-931464-49-8. p. 147 corrigenda to Eblaitica 1; 149-163, indices to Eblaitica 1 & 2. 5 art., ➤ e316*.

e320 **Krebernik** Manfred, Die Personennamen der Ebla-Texte 1988 ➤ 4,g13; 5,e118: ᴿBO 47 (1990) 433-445 (J. G. *Dercksen*, also on ᴱCAGNI L. 1985/7).

e321 **Mander** Pietro, Administrative texts of the archive L. 2769: Materiali Epigrafici di Ebla 10. R 1990, Univ. xvii-245 p.

e322 **Matthiae** Paolo, Ebla, un impero ritrovato; dai primi scavi alle ultime scoperte². T 1989, Einaudi. xxvii-365 p.; 18 fig.; 177 pl. Lit. 55.000. – ᴿCC 141 (1990.1) 606s (A. *Ferrua*).

e323 *Matthiae* Paolo, Nouvelles fouilles à Ébla en 1987-1989: CRAI (1990) 384-431; 25 fig.

e324 *a) Matthiae* Paolo, The reception suites of the Old Syrian palaces; – *b) Archi* Alfonso, Tuttul-sur-Balih à l'âge d'Ebla: ➤ 107, ᶠKUPPER J.-R. 1990, 209-228; 9 fig. / 197-207.

e325 *a) Matthiae* Paolo, A class of Old Syrian bronze statuettes and the sanctuary B2 at Ebla; – *b) Mazzoni* Stefania, Observations about Iron Age glyptics from Tell Afis and Tell Mardikh: ➤ 28, ᶠBOUNNI A. 1990, 345-354 + pl. 112-9 / 215-223 + pl. 59-61.

e326 *Milano* Lucio, *é-duru₅ ki* = 'one score' (of people) in the Ebla accounting: ZAss 80 (1990) 9-14.

e327 **Pettinato** G., Ebla, nuovi orizzonti 1986 → 2,a841; 5,e121: ᴿOrientalia 59 (1990) 74-81 (A. *Alberti*).

e328 **Pettinato** Giovanni, The archives of Ebla. NY c. 1989, Doubleday. $18 [58 copies offered for sale at $9 in BR 6,3 (1990) 5].

e329 ᴱ**Pettinato** Giovanni, *al.*, Testi lessicali bilingui della biblioteca L.2769, I. traslitterazione: Materiali epigrafici di Ebla 4, 1982 → 64,b642*: ᴿOLZ 85 (1990) 296-9 (J. *Oelsner*, in sostituzione al recensente mancato).

e330 *Pomponio* Francesco, Exit Kiš dagli orizzonti di Ebla: MesopT 25 (1990) 175-184.

e330* *Sollberger* Edmond, Une tablette d'Ibla [PETTINATO G., texte 'historico-lexical' (sans pareil) de noms géographiques]: MARI 6 (1990) 647s; 2 fig.

e331 *a*) *Tonietti* Maria Vittoria, Le liste delle d a m e n; cronologia interna; criteri ed elementi per una datazione relativa dei testi economici di Ebla [Aggiornamento alla cronologia dei n a r]; – *b*) *Catagnoti* Amalia, I NE-DI dei testi amministrativi degli archivi di Ebla: QuadSemit 16 / → 485*, Miscellanea Eblaitica 2 (1989) 79-116 [119-129] / 149-201.

e332 *Viganò* L., Šu mu-takₓ and takₓ at Ebla: AulaO 8 (1990) 101-111.

e333 *Visicato* Giuseppe, Fara ed Ebla; nuove prospettive storico-politiche nel periodo protodinastico: OrAnt 28 (1989) 169-176.

e333* ᴱ**Waetzoldt** Hartmut, *Hauptmann* Harald, Wirtschaft und Gesellschaft von Ebla; Akten der Internationalen Tagung Heidelberg [4.-7. Nov.] 1986/8 → 4,707: p. 125-9, *Arcari* Elena, The administrative organization of the city of Ebla; – p. 139-148, *Astour* Michael C., The geographical and political structure of the Ebla empire; – 325-332, *Soden* W. von, Ebla, die früheste Schriftkultur Syriens; etc. mostly in vol. 4.

T5.8 **Situs effossi Syriae** *in ordine alphabetico.*

e334 *Frankfurter* David T. M., Stylites and phallobates; pillar religions in late antique Syria [at Hierapolis near the Euphrates are stone phalli '1800 ft. high' which 'a man' climbs twice each year and lives on top seven days: LUCIAN De dea Syria]: VigChr 44 (1990) 168-198: 2 fig.

e335 **Grainger** John D., The cities of Seleukid Syria. Ox 1990, Clarendon. xi-253 p.

e336 **Klengel** Horst, Syrien zwischen Alexander und Mohammed; Denkmale aus Antike und frühem Christentum. W 1987 [= 1986], Herold. 212 p. [RelStR 17, 71, R. *Ousterhout*]. – ᴿHZ 250 (1990) 384-6 (P. *Weiss*).

e337 **Meijer** Diederik J. W., A survey in northeastern Syria [< diss. Amst.]. İstanbul 1986, Ned.Inst. 58 p.; 34 fig.; map. – ᴿOLZ 85 (1990) 670-2 (E. *Lindemeyer*).

e338 *Moorey* P. R. S., From gulf to delta in the fourth millennium BCE; the Syrian connection: → 4, ᶠAMIRAN Ruth, Eretz-Israel 21 (1990) 62*-69*; 4 fig. (map.).

e339 *Oelsner* Joachim, Weitere Bemerkungen zu den Neirab–Urkunden (FALES F., EPH'AL I.): AltOrF 16 (1989) 68-77.

e340 *a*) *Sodini* Jean-Pierre, Les églises de Syrie du Nord; – *b*) *Restle* Marcell, Monuments chrétiens de la Syrie du Sud: → 481, Syrie II (1989) 347-372; fig. 84-98 / 373-384; fig. 99-104.

e341 *Weber* Thomas,   Etruskisches Bronzegerät in Syrien: ArchAnz (1990) 435-448; 13 fig.

---

e342 *A'la,* jabl: **Peña** Ignacio, Inventaire du Jebel El-A'la; recherches archéologiques dans la région des Villes Mortes de la Syrie du Nord: SBF min 31. J 1990, Franciscan. 267 p.; map.
e343 *Aleppo:* **Ohta** Keiko, The history of Aleppo, known as ad-Durr al-Muntakhab by IBN ASH-SHIḤNA: StCulturIslam 40. Tokyo 1990, InstAsiaAf. 420 p. (p. 19-420 in Arabic, numbered ❹ 1-375).
e344 *Lambert* W. G., Ḥalam, Il-Ḥalam and Aleppo: MARI 6 (1990) 641-4.
e345 *Amrit:* ➤ 481, Syrie II (1989) 19-30; 9 fig. (Nassib *Saliby*).
e346 *Antiochia* (➤ e858) *Kennedy* H., *Liebeschuetz* H. W. G., Antioch and the villages of northern Syria in the 5th and 6th centuries A.D.: Nottingham Medieval Studies 32 (1988) 65-90 [< ByZ 82,445].
e347 *Apameia:* ᴱ**Balty** Janine, Apamée de Syrie, bilan de recherches 1973-79. Bru 1984, Centre Recherches Archéol. 524 p. – ᴿArchaiognosia 4 (1985s) 196-8 (M. *Kreeb* ❺).
e347* *Atij* (Ḫabur) 1, 1986: Syria 65 (1988) 139-171; 33 fig. (M. *Fortin*).
e348 *Barîša:* **Peña** I., *al.*, Inventaire du Jébel Barîcha 1987 ➤ 3,e445; 4,g28: ᴿRHE 85 (1990) 875s (Jacqueline *Lafontaine-Dosogne*); Syria 65 (1988) 480 (J.-P. *Sodini*: utile).
e348* *Peña* I., Aspectos del monacato sirio: ➤ 39, ᶠCORBO V., Christian archaeology 1990, 561-570.
e349 *Barri:* *Pecorella* Paolo E., Tell Barri/Kahat durante il II millennio: ➤ 28, ᶠBOUNNI A. 1990, 259-263 + pl. 71-82.
e350 *Bassit:* *Courbin* Paul, Fragments d'amphores protogéometriques grecques à Bassit [N Ras Shamra]: ➤ 28, ᶠBOUNNI A. 1990, 49-58; 59 map; pl. 9-13.
e351 *Bïa* 1987: MDOG 121 (1989) 5-63; 39 fig. (Eva *Strommenger*, al.).
e352 *Krebernik* Manfred, Die Textfunde aus Tall Bïa: MDOG 122 (1990) 67-87; ill.
e353 *Boṣra:* *Mukdad* Riyad al-, *Dentzen* Jean-Marie, Les fouilles franco-syriennes à Bosra (1981-1987): AnASyr 37s (1988s as on ❹ cover) 224-230 + 11 pl.
e353* **Sartre** Maurice, Bostra, des originès... 1985 ➤ 2,a860: ᴿSyria 65 (1988) 249-253 (P. *Leriche*, J. *Teixidor*).
e354 *Damascus:* **Pitard** Wayne T., Ancient Damascus 1987 ➤ 3,e466... 5,e127: ᴿAmHR 95 (1990) 141 (G. *Buccellati*).
Davies P., Where is [Essene] 'Damascus'? 1990 ➤ a96*.
e355 **Pouzet** Louis, Damas au VIIᵉ-XIIᵉ siècle; vie et structures religieuses d'une métropole islamique: Recherches NS 15, 1985 ➤ 4,g37: ᴿBSO 53 (1990) 337-9 (P. M. *Hout*); JRAS (1990) 388s (H. *Kennedy*).
e356 **Sack** Dorothée, Damaskus; Entwicklung und Struktur einer orientalisch-islamischen Stadt: Damasc.For. 1, 1989 ➤ 5,e128*; DM 135: ᴿDLZ 111 (1990) 901s (E. *Badstübner*).
e357 **Sader** H. S., Les états araméens ᴰ1987 ➤ 3,e467... 5,e129: ᴿArOr 58 (1990) 187s (Jana *Pečirková*).
e358 *Dara* 'ayn: **Abu Assaf** 'Ali, Der Tempel von 'Ain Dara: DamFor 3. Mainz 1990, von Zabern. viii-66 p.; 18 (foldout) fig.; 62 pl. 3-8053-1108-7 [OIAc Ja91].
e359 *Denit* archaeological survey: AnASyr 37s (1988s as on ❹ cover) 14-34 (*Shawki Shaath* ❹).

a360 **Dura:** Goldman Bernard, Foreigners at Dura-Europos; pictorial graffiti and history: Muséon 103 (1990) 5-25.

a360* Leriche Pierre, Maḥmoud Asad, Bilan des campagnes de 1986 et 1987 de la Mission Franco-Syrienne à Doura-Europos: Syria 65 (1988) 261-281; 20 fig. (283s, Auge Christian, monnaies; 285-295, Geyer B., environnement; 297-313, Bessac J.-C., remparts; 315-321, Will E., population; 323-342, Allara Anny, maisons; 343-7, Downey Susan, citadel palace).

e361 Perler Othmar, Zu den Inschriften des Baptisteriums von Dura-Europos [< FDaniélou J. 1972, 175-185]: ➤ 283, Sapientia 1990, 437-447.

e361* Velud Christian, Contexte historique régional des fouilles de Doura-Europos entre les deux guerres mondiales: Syria 65 (1988) 363-382.

e362 **Emar:** **Arnaud** Daniel, Recherches au pays d'Aštata, Emar 6, 1985-7 ➤ 2,a870; 4,g40: RBSO 53 (1990) 323-5 (A. R. George); RAss [83 (1989)] 84 (1990) 49-85 (J.-M. Durand).

e363 a) Durand J.-M., La cité-État d'Imar à l'époque des rois de Mari; – b) Margueron J., Imar ou Emar; une recherche qui se prolonge; – c) Beyer D., Quelques vestiges de l'imagerie émariote du Bronze Moyen; – d) Geyer B., Une ville aujourd'hui engloutie, Émar; contribution géomorphologique à la localisation de la cité; – e) Joannès F., Une mention d'Émar dans un texte de Haradum: MARI 6 (1990) 39-92 / 103-6 / 93-102; 14 fig.; 7 phot. / 107-120 / 121s.

e364 Tsukimoto Emar: AnJap 15 (1989) 3-

e365 **Ḫabur:** a) Oates David & Joan, Aspects of Hellenistic and Roman settlement in the Khabur basin; – b) Tate Georges, Les paysages ruraux en Syrie du Nord à l'époque romano-byzantine: ➤ 28, FBOUNNI A. 1990, 227-243; 244 map; + pl. 62-66 / 379-383 + pl. 130-2.

e366 Halawa-A 1986s: AnASyr 37s (1988s) 242-250; 5 fig. (J. W. Meyer).

e367 **Orthmann** Winfried, Halawa 1980-6: SaarbBeiAltR 52. Bonn 1989, Habelt. 152p.; 70 fig.; 16 plans. – RBCanadMesop 19 (1990) 37s (M. Fortin).

e368 **Hama:** Riis P. J., Buhl Marie-Louise, Les objets de la période dite syro-hittite (âge du fer): Hama Fouilles 1931-8, 2/2 / Starre Beretninger 12. K 1990, Nationalmuseet. 324p. 87-89438-00-0 [OIAc F91,19].

e369 **Humīdīya:** **Eichler** Seyyare, Tall al-Hamīdīya [1. 1984 ➤ 1,d883], 2, Recent excavations in the Upper Khabur region [Berne Dec. 9-11, 1986] Vorbericht 1985-7: OBO arch 6. FrS/Gö 1990, Univ./VR. ii-472p. + ❹ 20p. Fs 170 [CBQ 53,170].

e370 **Ḥammam/Turkman:** ELoon Maurits N. van, Hammam et-Turkman I; report on the University of Amsterdam's 1981-4 excavations in Syria: Uitg 63, Leiden 1988, Ned. Hist.-Arch. Instituut te Istanbul. I. xxix-349p.; 110pl.; II. p.351-744; pl.111-208; map. 90-6258-063-7. – RBCanad-Mesop 19 (1990) 35s (M. Fortin).

e371 **Hauran:** EDentzer J.-M., Hauran I. Recherches archéologiques 1985s ➤ 2,a857; 3,e464: RAnÉCS 45 (1990) 904-6 (J.-P. Vallat); Syria 65 (1988) 246-9 (J. Teixidor).

e372 **Ory** Solange, Cimetières et inscriptions du Hawran et du Gabal al-Duruz: Mém. 85. P 1989, RCiv. 75p.; 45pl. 2-86538-200-8 [OIAc F91,17].

e373 **Hazna:** Bader N. O., al., Soviet investigations in NE Syria 1988: AnASyr 37s (1988s as on ❹ cover) 190-201 + 23 fig.

e373* Hrim [S Deir ez-Zor]: sauvetage 1986, 9e-12e siècle: Syria 65 (1988) 63-98; 18 fig. (Sophie Berthier, B. Geyer).

e374 *Ḥuwayra:* **Moortgat-Correns** Ursula, Tell Chuēra 1982-3: 1988 ➤ 4,g49: ᴿJAOS 110 (1990) 764-6 (G. M. *Schwartz*).

e375 *Orthmann* Winfried, Zu den monumentalen Steinbauten von Tell Chuera: ➤ 28, ᶠBOUNNI A. 1990, 249-254 + pl. 67-70.

e376 *Kowm: Cauvin* Jacques, L'occupation préhistorique du désert syrien; nouvelles recherches dans la cuvette d'El Kowm (1984-1989): AnASyr 37s (1988s, as on ❹ cover) 51-65 (-77, Umm et Tiel).

e376* **Dornemann** R. H., Neolithic... Kowm 1986 ➤ 2,a875...5,e147: ᴿSyria 65 (1988) 231-3 (H. de *Contenson*).

e377 *Leilan:* 1985; AJA 94 (1990) 528-581; 35 fig. (H. *Weiss*, al.).

e378 *Akkermans* Peter, *Weiss* Harvey, Tell Leilan 1987 operation 3; a preliminary report on the Lower Town Palace: AnASyr 37s (1988s, as on ❹ cover) 91-99 + 10 fig. (110-127, tablets, *Eidem* Jasper; 128-141, sceaux, *Parayre* Dominique.

e379 **Schwartz** Glenn M., A ceramic chronology from Tell Leilan, Operation I. NHv 1989, Yale Univ. xxv-200 p.; 69 fig.; 17 pl. $35. – ᴿAcOrK 51 (1990) 269-272 (Ingolf *Thuesen*); AJA 94 (1990) 684-6 (Sally *Dunham*).

e380 *Weiss* Harvey, 'Civilizing' the Habur plains; mid-third millennium state formation at Tell Leilan: ➤ 28, ᶠBOUNNI A. 1990, 387-399 + pl. 133-140.

e381 *Mari* 1985: MARI 6 (1990) 5-18 (J. *Margueron, al.*).

e382 *Abou Assaf* Ali, Zur Datierung des Wandgemäldes von Saal 132 im Palast von Mari: ➤ 28, ᶠBOUNNI A., Resurrecting 1990, 1s; 2 pl.

e383 **Durand** Jean-Marie, Archives épistolaires de Mari 1/1 (1/2 par *Charpin* D. *al.*): ARM 26, 1988 ➤ 4,g55: ᴿOLZ 85 (1990) 535-9 (H. *Klengel*); RB 97 (1990) 471-3 (H. *Cazelles*; in title dated 1968).

e384 **Heintz** Jean-Georges, Bibliographie de Mari, Archéologie et textes [1933-1988]: Strasbourg GRESA 2. Wsb 1990, Harrassowitz. x-128 p. 3-447-03009-7 [OIAc Oc90]. – ᴿRHPR 70 (1990) 278s (ipse).

Malamat A., Mari and the early Israelite experience 1984 ➤ b329*.

e385 *a)* *Margueron* Jean-Claude, La peinture de l'investiture et l'histoire de la Cour 106; – *b)* *Birot* M., La lettre de Yarīm-Līm Nᵒ 72-39 + 72-8; – *c)* *Finet* A., Homme à *sikkum* et *sikkānum* d'après ARM II 76 et I 113; – *d)* *Durand* Jean-Marie, ARM III, ARM VI, ARM XIII, ARM XXII: ➤ 107, ᶠKUPPER J.-R. 1990, 115-125 / 127-135 / 137-148 / 149-177.

e386 *Margueron* Jean, *a)* La ruine du palais de Mari; – *b)* Une tombe royale sous la salle du trône du palais des Shakkanakku: MARI 6 (1990) 423-431 / 400-422; 26 fig. (➤ e888) [433-451, palais de Zimri-Lim].

e387 *Nakata* Ichiro, A further look at the institution of *sugāgūtum* in Mari: ➤ 75, Mem. HELD M., JANES 19 (1989) 113-118: appointed head of a provincial, and not merely nomadic, locality.

e388 *Sasson* Jack M., Mari historiography and the Yakhdun-Lim disc inscription: ➤ 124, ᶠMORAN W., Lingering 1990, 439-449.

e389 *Mozan:* **Buccellati** G. & M. Kelly-, Mozan I BiblMesop 20, 1988 ➤ 4,g57: ᴿBCanadMesop 19 (1990) 36s (M. *Fortin*); RAss 84 (1990) 95s (P. *Amiet*).

e390 *Muḥammad Diyab* t.: **Durand** Jean-Marie, *al.*, Tell Mohammad Diyab, campagnes 1987 et 1988: Cah I. P 1990, Société pour l'Étude du Proche-Orient ancien. – ᴿBCanadMesop 20 (1990) 36 (M. *Fortin*).

e391 *Mullā Maṭar* 1989: MDOG 122 (1990) 125-152; 29 fig. (D. *Sürenhagen*).

e392 *Munbāqa* 1987/1988: MDOG 121 (1989) 65-94; 16 fig.; 122 (1990) 9-42; 22 fig. (D. *Machule*, al. (p. 43s, *Karstens* K., Rollsiegel; 45-66, *Meyer* Walter, Tafelfunde).

e393 *Machule* Dittmar, Tall Munbāqa; die spätbronzezeitliche Stadtanlage und die Häuser: ➔ 28, ᶠBOUNNI A. 1990, 199-205 + pl. 50-58,

e395 *Palmyra:* *Asa'ad* Khaled, ❹ The discovery of an Umayyad souq in Palmyra: AnASyr 37s (1988s ❹ cover) 121-140.

e396 *Bounni* Adnan, Palmyre et les Palmyréniens: ➔ 481, Syrie II (1989) 251-266; fig. 38-42.

e397 *a) Bounni* Adnan, Le sanctuaire de Nabû/Apollon à Palmyre, lieu de rencontre des caractéristiques syro-hellénistiques et romaines; – *b) Leriche* Pierre, La ville hellénistique d'Ibn Hani (Syrie du Nord): ➔ 791*, KlasArch 13 (1988/90) 359-362; 1 fig. / 354-8; 2 fig.

e398 **Degeorge** Gérard, Palmyre — métropole du désert. P 1987, Segher. 178 p.; (color.) ill.; bibliog. 166-172 [KirSef 62 (1988s), p. 620].

e399 *Drijvers* Han J. W., The Syrian cult relief: VisRel 7 (1986/90) 69-78 + 8 fig.

e400 *Gawlikowski* Michel, *a)* Le premier temple d'Allat: ➔ 28, ᶠBOUNNI A. 1990, 101-6; pl. 22-23; – *b)* Les dieux de Palmyre / des Nabatéens: ➔ 828, ANRW 2/18/4 (1990) 2605-2658 / 2659-77.

e401 *O'Connor* M., The etymologies of Tadmor and Palmyra [from Ḥurrian *tad* 'love', *pal* 'know'; no relation to palms]: ➔ 5,176, SCHWARTZ B. Mem. 1988, 235-254 [< OTAbs 13, p. 149].

e402 *Rompay* L. Van, Palmyra, Emesa en Edessa; semitische steden in het gehelleniseerde Nabije Oosten: PhoenixEOL 36,2 (1990) 73-84; 2 fig.

e403 *Qara Quzaq* [near new Euphrates bridge to Hasaka] 1989, MB: AulaO 8,1 (1990) 5-13 + 14-20, pl. (G. del *Olmo Lete*, E. *Olávarri Goicoechea, al.*).

e404 *Qumloq*, Abu: AnASyr 37s (1988s ❹) 15-40 (Ḥamīdo *Ḥamādeh* ❹).

e405 *Raqā'i:* AJA 94 (1990) 3-23; 24 fig. (Hans H. *Curvers*, Glenn M. *Schwartz*).

e406 *Resāfa:* **Ulbert** Thilo, Resafa 2, Basilika 1986 ➔ 2,a898 ... 5,e171: ᴿAntClas 59 (1990) 646s (C. *Delvoye*); Syria 65 (1988) 473-9; 2 plans (J.-P. *Sodini*); ZDPV 106 (1990) 192-4 (Claudia *Nauerth*).

e407 *a) Saliby* Nassib, Une maison arabe à Resafa; – *b) Ulbert* Thilo, Ein spätantikes Sigillata-Tablett aus Resafa: ➔ 28, ᶠBOUNNI A. 1990, 277-281 + pl. 83-97 / 317-321 + pl. 105-107.

e408 *Šeḫ Ḥamad:* *Kühne* Hartmut, Gedanken zur historischen und städtebaulichen Entwicklung der assyrischen Stadt Dūr-Katlimmu: ➔ 28, ᶠBOUNNI A. 1990, 153-164 + pl. 35-39.

e409 *Kühne* Hartmut, Report on the excavation at Tall Šeḫ Ḥamad / Dur-Katlimmu 1985: AnASyr 37s (1988s as on ❹ cover) 142-6 + 17 fig.

e410 *Šeḫ Ḥassan:* *Boese* Johannes, Excavations at Tell Sheikh Hassan; preliminary report on the 1988 campaign in the Euphrates valley: AnASyr 37s (1988s as on ❹ cover) 158-173 + 26 fig.

e411 *Terqa:* *Wilcke* Claus, Kudurmabuk in Terqa: ➔ 107, ᶠKUPPER J.-R. 1990, 179-181.

e412 *Tuneinir*/Khabur 1987-9 (St. Louis Community College): AnASyr 37s (1987s ❹) 279-283 + 7 fig.

e413 *Wastani:* *Khouri* Wedad, *Castellana* Pasquale, Frühchristliche Städte im nördlichen Jebel Wastani (Syrien): AntWelt 21 (1990) 14-25; 26 fig.

e414 *Yabrūd:* Solecki Ralph, Report of the summer 1987 Yabroud researches: AnASyr 37s (1988s as on ❹ cover) 9-32 + 33-49, fig.

T6.1 **Mesopotamia:** *generalia.*

e415 **Baffi Guardata** Francesca, *Dolce* Rita, Archeologia della Mesopotamia, l'età cassita e medio-assira: Archaeologica 88. R 1990, Bretschneider. xiv-296 p.; ill.; maps. 88-7689-037-8.

e416 *Brentjes* Burchard, Die 'dunklen Jahrhunderte' der frühen Eisenzeit und die Kulturgeschichte Mittelasiens: HalleB 12 (1988) 5-46 + 10 maps.

e417 *Dandamaeva* M. M., ❸ Aspects of the history of Hellenism in Babylonia: VDI 195 (1990) 3-25; Eng. 25s.

e418 *Geller* M. J., Babylonian astronomical diaries and corrections of DIODORUS: BSO 53 (1990) 1-7.

e419 *Hallo* William W., The limits of skepticism [in interpreting ancient Near East data; AOS presidential address, 199th meeting, New Orleans 14.III.1989]: JAOS 110 (1990) 187-199.

e420 **Hecker** K., *Sommerfeld* W., Assyriologisches Anschriftenverzeichnis: Akkadica supp. 4. Bru 1990, Fond. Dossin. 134 p. 90-6831-255-3 [OIAc Oc90].

e421 *Lebeau* Marc, Esquisse d'une histoire de la Haute Mésopotamie au début de l'Âge du Bronze: ZAss 80 (1990) 241-295; p. 296, 2 maps.

e422 *a) Liverani* Mario, La forma dei campi neosumerici; – *b) Johnson* Gregory A., Late Uruk in greater Mesopotamia; expansion or collapse? – *c) Frangipane* Marcella, *Palmieri* Alba, Aspects of centralization in the Late Uruk period in Mesopotamian periphery: ➤ 818*, Mem. PUGLISI S. 1988s, 289-328 / [II] 595-614 / 539-560.

e423 ᴱ*Nashef* Khaled, Archaeology in Iraq: AJA 94 (1990) 259-289; 33 fig.

e424 *Oppenheimer* Aharon, Das biblische Babylonien in der rabbinischen Literatur: JStJud 21 (1990) 76-86.

e425 *Sanlaville* P., Considérations sur l'evolution de la Basse Mésopotamie au cours des derniers millénaires: Paléorient 15,2 (1989) 5-27.

e426 **Thomsen** Marie-Louise, Europa og Babylon. K 1990, Det kongelige Bibliotek. 59 p. 87-7023-377-2 [OIAc JJ90].

e427 *Westenholz* Joan G., Towards a new conceptualization of the female role in Mesopotamian society [ᴱ*Durand* J.-M., 33ᵉ Rencontre 1986/7]: JAOS 110 (1990) 510-521.

T6.3 *Mesopotamia, scripta effossa* – **Excavated Tablets.**

e428 **Alberti** Amedeo, *Pomponio* Francesco, Pre-Sargonic and Sargonic texts from Ur edited in [*Burrows* E.] UET 2, supp.: StPohl 13, 1986 ➤ 2,a914; 3,e550: ᴿBO 47 (1990) 671-4 (B. *Jagerama*); JAOS 110 (1990) 128-130 (J.-J. *Glassner*: de valeur incontestable); OLZ 85 (1990) 299-308 (G. J. *Selz*).

e429 **Alster** Bendt, *Geller* Markham J., Sumerian literary texts: CunT 58. L 1990, British Museum. 28 p.; 91 pl. 0-7141-1129-5.

e430 **Arnaud** Daniel, Altbabylonische Rechts- und Verwaltungsurkunden aus dem Musée du Louvre: Berliner BeitVO Texte 1. B 1989, Reimer. 18 p.; 63 pl. 3-496-00990-X [OIAc F91,1].

e431 *a) Biggs* Robert D., *Zettler* Richard L., Cuneiform texts in Chicago collections; – *b) Tsukimoto* Akio, Akkadian tablets in the Hirayama collection I: AcSum 12 (1990) 15-32 + 33-49 facsim. / 177-211; 212-227 facsim.; 229-259 phot.

e432 *Damerow* Peter, *Nissen* Hans, *al.*, Zur rechnergestützten [computerized] Bearbeitung der archaischen Texte aus Mesopotamien (ca. 3200-3000 v. Chr.): MDOG 121 (1989) 139-152; 3 fig.

e433 **Dijk** Jan van (*Falkenstein* A., ᴱ*Mayer* W. R.) Literarische Texte aus Babylon 1987 ⇒ 3,e553; 5,e183:   ᴿZDMG 139 (1989) 278 (B. *Kölver*).

e434 **Donbaz** Veysel, [71 Kültepe] Keilschrifttexte in den Antikenmuseen zu Stamboul 2; FreibAltorSt Beih 2, 1989 ⇒ 5,e184; DM 44:   ᴿAulaO 8 (1990) 142-5 (W. *Farber*); WZKM 80 (1990) 277-9 (Renate *Wernisch*).

e435 *Donbaz* Veysel,   Some Neo-Assyrian contracts from Girnavaz and vicinity: SAAB 2 (1988) 3-19 + 20-26, facsimiles; 27-30, photos.

e436 *Driel* G. van, *Jas* R., A second Middle Assyrian text on gold: JbEOL 31 (1989s) 63-65; phot.; facsim.

e437 **Forde** Nels W.,   Neo-Sumerian texts from South Dakota Univ., ... 1987 ⇒ 5,e186:   ᴿJAOS 110 (1990) 762-4 (D. C. *Snell*).

e437* *Frame* Grant, *al.*,   Cuneiform texts in the collections of McGill University, Montreal: AnRIM 7 (1989) 1-52; ill.

e438 **Frayne** Douglas R.,   Old Babylonian period (2003-1595 B.C.): RIMA early 4. Toronto 1990, Univ. xxxi-853 p.   0-8020-5873-6.

e439 **Freydank** Helmut,   Mittelassyrische Rechtsurkunden 1982 ⇒ 63,2511; 2,a927:   ᴿOrientalia 59 (1990) 83-85 (J. N. *Postgate*).

e440 *Freydank* Helmut, Die Tontafelfunde der Grabungskampagne 1913-1914 aus Kār-Tukultī-Ninurta (Tulūl al-'Aqar): AltOrF 16 (1989) 61-67.

e441 *Friberg* J.,   Mathematik [Eng.: the main publications of mathematical cuneiform texts ... analyses]: ⇒ 853*, RLA 7,7s (1990) 531-585.

e442 **Garelli** P., *Collon* D.,   Cuneiform texts from Cappadocian tablets in the British Muscum 6. L 1975, British Museum.   34 p.; 58 pl.:   ᴿOLZ 85 (1990) 167-171 (B. *Kienast*).

e442* **Gehlken** Erlend,   Uruk, spätbabylonische Wirtschaftstexte aus dem Eanna-Archiv I. Texte verschiedenen Inhalts: Endberichte 5. Mainz 1990, von Zabern. [xii-] 215 p.; 155 facsimiles. 3-8053-1217-2.

e443 ᴱ**Gelb** I. J. †, *Kienast* B.,   Die altakkadischen Königsinschriften des dritten Jahrtausends v. Chr.: FreibOrSt 7. Stu 1990, Steiner.   xvi-434 p.; XX pl. 3-515-04248-2.

e443* **Gomi** Tohru, *Hirose* Y. & K.,   Neo-Sumerian administrative texts of the Hirose collection. Potomac MD 1990, Capital Decisions. 139 p.; XLV pl. 0-9620013-2-5.

e444 **Gurney** O. R.,   Literary and miscellaneous [Babylonian] texts in the Ashmolean Muscum: Cuneiform Texts 11, 1989 ⇒ 5,e188a: ᴿJRAS (1990) 377s (D. J. *Wiseman*); ZAss 80 (1990) 155-168 (A. R. *George*).

e445 **Hunger** H., *Pingree* D., MUL.APIN, an astronomical compendium in cuneiform: AfO Beih 24. W 1989, Harn. – ᴿBSO 53 (1990) 209-213 (M. J. *Geller*, also on REINER E.).

e446 *a) Jas* Remko,   A Neo-Assyrian letter without address [AJSL 1912s; not in ABL]; – *b) Mattila* Raija,   Balancing the accounts of the royal New Year's reception; seven administrative documents from Nineveh; – *c) Ponchia* Simonetta,   Neo-Assyrian corn-loans; preliminary notes: SAAB 4,1 (1990) 3s; facsim. 5 / 7-18 + 5 fig. / 39-60; 7 fig.

e447 **Joannès** Francis,   Archives de Borsippa; la famille Ea-ilūta-bāni: Hautes Études Orientales 25, 1989 ⇒ 5,e190:   ᴿOrAnt 28 (1989) 277-280 (F. *D'Agostino*).

e448 **Joannès** Francis, Les tablettes néo-babyloniennes de la Bodleian Library conservées à l'Ashmolean Museum: CuneifT 12. Ox 1990, Clarendon. [vi-] 47 p.; XLIX pl. 0-19-815467-4.

e449 **Klengel** Horst, Altbabylonische Texte aus Babylon 1983 ⇾ 64,b726 ... 2,a934: ᴿZAss 80 (1990) 297-306 (C. *Wilcke*).

e450 **Kraus** F. R., Briefe aus kleineren westeuropäischen Sammlungen 1985 ⇾ 2,a936; 3,e564: ᴿZAss 80 (1990) 141-3 (W. *Sommerfeld*).

e451 **Kraus** F. R. † 19.I.1991, Brieven uit Babylonië: JbEOL 31 (1989s) 41-52.

e452 **Kutscher** Raphael † 29.I.1989, Royal Inscriptions — the Brockman tablets in the University of Haifa 1989 ⇾ 5,e191: ᴿAcSum 12 (1990) 349-351 (M. *Yoshikawa*).

e453 **Kwasman** Theodore, Neo-Assyrian legal documents in the Kouyunjik collection of the British Museum: StPohl 14, 1988 ⇾ 4,g101: ᴿBSO 53 (1990) 123s (Sue *Rollin*); OLZ 85 (1990) 666s (Stephanie *Dalley*, Eng.).

e454 **Lanfranchi** Giovanni B., The correspondence of Sargon II, part [1. 1987 ⇾ 3,e574] 2. Letters from the northern and northeastern provinces: SAA 5. Helsinki 1990, Univ. xxxvii-272 p.; 40 fig.; 3 pl. 951-570-079-5; pa. -8-7.

e455 **Leichty** Erle, Catalogue of the Babylonian tablets in the British Museum 6-8, 1986-8 ⇾ 4,g103; 5,e196: ᴿBSO 53 (1990) 121-3 (M. J. *Geller*).

e456 **Livingstone** Alasdair, Mystical and mythological explanatory works of Assyrian and Babylonian scholars 1986 ⇾ 2,a939...4,g104: ᴿOLZ 85 (1990) 663s (A. R. *George*, Eng.).

e457 *Maidman* Maynard P., Joins to five published Nuzi texts: JCS 48 (1990) 71-85.

e458 *Molina Martos* M., [15] Tablillas neosumerias del Museo Bíblico del Seminario Diocesano de Palma de Mallorca [bought in Jerusalem in the 1930s]: AulaO 8 (1990) 69-81 + 82-87, fig.

e459 **Parpola** Simo, The correspondence of Sargon II, 1/1, 1987 ⇾ 3,e570; 4,g106: ᴿBSO 52 (1989) 118-120 (A. R. *George*); JAOS 110 (1990) 567s (Barbara N. *Porter*); RB 97 (1990) 118-120 (M. *Sigrist*); WeltOr 20s (1989s) 270-3 (W. von *Soden*); WZKM 80 (1990) 259-262 (Stephanie *Dalley*, Eng.).

e460 **Parpola** Simo, *Watanabe* Kazuko, Neo-Assyrian treaties and loyalty oaths: SAA 2. Helsinki 1988, Univ. lxii-123 p.; IX pl. – ᴿRB 97 (1990) 120s (M. *Sigrist*).

e461 **Postgate** J. N., The archive of Urad-Šerūa and his family; a Middle Assyrian household in government service: Analisi elettronica del cuneiforme. R 1988, Denicola (Herder). xxxiii-233 p. Lit. 48.000. – ᴿZAss 80 (1990) 306-8 (H. *Freydank*).

e462 **Sachs** Abraham J. †, ᴱ*Hunger* Hermann, Astronomical diaries and related texts from Babylonia [I. 1988 ⇾ 4,g110], II. Diaries from 261 B.C. to 165 B.C.: Denkschrift 210. W 1989, Österr. Akad.

e463 **Sigrist** Marcel, [⇾ g372] Tablettes du Princeton Theological Seminary, époque d'Ur III: Kramer OccPub 10. Ph 1990, Univ. Museum. vii-93 p.; 148 pl. (facsimiles). 0-9347-1897-0.

e464 *Snell* Daniel C., The [Ur-III, copyist Carl H.] LAGER texts; transliterations, translations and notes: AcSum 11 (1989) 155-224.

e465 ᵀᴱ**Soldt** W. H. van, Letters in the British Museum: AltbBriefe 12. Leiden 1990, Brill. x-155 p. 90-04-09208-0.

e466 ᴱ**Spar** Ira, Cuneiform texts in the Met I, 1988 ⇾ 4,g112; 5,e206: ᴿRAss 84 (1990) 90s (D. *Charpin*).

e467 **Steinkeller** Piotr,   Sale documents of the Ur III period [D1977] 1989
→ 5,e207: RBSO 53 (1990) 594 (M. A. *Powell*).

e468 **Wallenfels** Ronald,   Sealed cuneiform tablets from Hellenistic Uruk; an
iconographic and prosopographic analysis of the private business documents [= 'a study of the seals and sealing practices']: diss. Columbia
1989, D*Hallo* W.   NY 1989.   xi-1029 p.; 1079 seal drawings; 99 pl. 91-
02460. – DissA 51 (1990s) 2727-A; OIAc Oc90.

e470 **Westenholz** Aage,   Old Sumerian and Old Akkadian texts in Philadelphia
II. The 'Akkadian' texts...   1987 → 3,e585; 5,e212: RAcOrK 51 (1990)
272-5 (O. *Pedersén*); JAOS 110 (1990) 760s (J.-J. *Glassner*, franç.); ZAss
80 (1990) 135s (W. von *Soden*).

e471 **Whiting** Robert M.J,   Old Babylonian letters from Tell Asmar: As-
syriological Studies 22, 1987 → 4,g118; 5,e213: RRB 97 (1990) 600-3 (S.
Izre'el); WZKM 80 (1990) 266-8 (H. *Hirsch*).

e472 **Yıldız** Fatma, *Gomi* Tohru,   Die [Ur III] Puzriš-Dagan-Texte 2, 1988
→ 4,g119: RBSO 53 (1990) 125s (A. *Uchitel*); JCS 48 (1990) 118-122 (P.
Michalowski); Orientalia 59 (1990) 440-2 (M. *Sigrist*); WZKM 80 (1990)
272s (H. *Hirsch*).

e473 **Zhi** Yang,   Sargonic inscriptions from Adab: Publ. 1.   Changchun 1989,
Inst.Hist.Anc.Civilizations.   xii-449 p. (393-431 facsimiles).

T6.5   **Situs effossi Iraq** *in ordine alphabetico.*

e474 *Abu Qubûr* [10 k N Sippar, SW Baghdad] 1987s, Achaemenid residence:
→ c423, AJA 94 (1990) 264s (H. *Gasche*).

e475 *Agadé:* **Glassner** J.-J.,   La chute d'Akkadé, l'événement et sa mémoire, E*Kühne* H., *al.*, B 1987, Reimer.   132 p.   DM 32.   3-496-00878-4. –
RRAss 84 (1990) 88s (D. *Charpin*).

e476 *Wall-Romana* Christophe,   An areal location of Agade: JNES 49 (1990)
205-245; maps.

e477 *Aḫmar:* E**Bunnens** Guy,   [Melbourne Univ.] Tell Ahmar 1988 season:
AbrNahr supp. 2. Lv 1990, Orientaliste.   x-151 p.; 64 fig.   90-6831-322-3.

e478 *Aššur:* *Miglus* Peter A.,   Untersuchungen zum Alten Palast in Assur:
MDOG 121 (1989) 93-133; 23 fig. (135-8; 153-167, Texte, *Pedersén* O.).

e479 *Babylon:* *Bergamini* Giovanni,   Preliminary report on the 1988-1989
operations at Babylon, Shu-Anna: MesopT 25 (1990) 5-12.

c480 *Günbatti* Cahit, † Eski Babil devrinde timar ve devlet arazisinin tahsisi
hakkında bazi görüsler (fief and land allotment): Belleten 55/212 (1991)
1-12.

c481 **Koldewey** Robert, 5rev*Hrouda* Barthel,   Das wieder erstehende Babylon.
Mü 1990, Beck.   447 p.; loose map.   3-406-31674-3 [OIAc Oc90].

e482 *Lamirande* Émilien,   Babylon(ia): → 829, AugL 1,4 (1990) 566-9.

e482* **Oates** Joan, Babylon2rev [11979]: Ancient People and Places 94.   L
1988 [= 1986 → 2,a960], Thames & H.   216 p.; 137 fig.   0-400-27394-7.

e483 *Spek* R.J. van der,   'Is dit niet het grote Babylon, dat ik gebouwd
heb?': PhoenixEOL 36,2 (1990) 51-63; 3 fig.

e484 *Duwari* t. abu [100k E Babylon, N Nippur] 1987-9: → e423, AJA 94
(1990) 260-3; 2 fig. & JField 17 (1990) 141-162; 11 fig. (Elizabeth G. *Stone*).

e485 *Fara:* **Martin** Harriet P.,   Fara, a reconstruction of the ancient Mesopotamian city of Shuruppak.   Birmingham 1988, auct.   309 p.; 579 fig.;
28 pl.; 6 microfiches.

e486 *Gawra* tepe: **Rothmann** Mitchell S., Centralization, administration, and function at fourth millennium B.C. tepe Gawra, Northern Iraq, diss. Pennsylvania, ᴰ*Dyson* R. Ph 1988. 89-08410. – OIAc JJ89.

e487 *Ḥamad Āga aṣ-Ṣaġîr* 1988: MDOG 122 (1990) 89-123; 21 fig. (P. Z. *Spanos*).

e488 *Hamida* [Iraq N. Jazira between Uwainat and Rabiyah; none of these names on maps p. 259 or 283] 1987: ➤ e423, AJA 94 (1990) 270-2 (P. *Zimansky*).

e489 *Hatra:* *Venco Ricciardi* Roberta, Second preliminary report on the excavation at Hatra (Season 1988): MesopT 25 (1990) 37-45 [p. 27-35, *Salihi* W. I. *al.*, Shrine XIII].

e490 *Hawa:* Tell el- Hawa [100 k NW Mosul] 2d-3d, 1987s: MeditArch 3 (1990) 75-92; 15 fig.; pl. 25-29 (W. *Ball*).

e491 *Imlihîya:* **Boehmer** R. M., *Dämmer* H. W., T Imlihiye... 1985 ➤ 1,g1 ... 5,e224: ᴿBO 47 (1990) 774s (Ö. *Tunca*).

e492 *Iščali:* **Hill** Harold D., *Jacobsen* Thorkild, Excavations at Ishchali / *Delougaz* D. P., Khafajah mounds B, C, and D: Old Babylonian buildings in the Diyala region Is, OIP 98. Ch 1990, Univ. Or. Inst. xxxiii-235 p.; 31 fig.; 68 pl. 0-918986-62-1.

e493 *Isin:* **Ferwerda** G. T., A contribution to the early Isin craft archive 1985 ➤ 1,e4: ᴿOLZ 85 (1990) 412-6 (Maria D. *Ellis*).

e494 *Jemdet Nasr* 2d, 1989: Iraq 52 (1990) 25-39; 12 fig. (R. J. *Matthews*).

e495 *Kar-Tukultī-Ninurta* 1986-9: MDOG 122 (1990) 157-171; 12 fig. (R. *Dittmann*).

e496 *Lagaš:* **Bahrani** Zeinab, The administrative building at Tell Al Hiba, Lagash: diss. NYU, ᴰ*Hansen* D., NY 1989. 90-16242. – OIAc Oc90.

e497 *Larsa:* ᴱ**Huot** Jean-Louis, Larsa... 8s/10 et ʿOueli 1983: RCiv Mém 73, 1987 ➤ 4,g139: ᴿBO 47 (1990) 466-8 (B. *Hrouda*); JAOS 110 (1990) 349-351 (Sally *Dunham*); OLZ 85 (1990) 310-3 (G. R. H. *Wright*, Eng.).

e497* *Huot* J.-J., *Vallet* R., Les habitations à salles hypostyles d'époque Obeid O de Tell el-'Oueli: Paléorient 16,1 (1990) 125-9; 3 fig.

e498 *Nemrik* 9th, prepottery neolithic, 1985s (Wsz 1990, Uniw., 236 p. 83-230-0289-7: S. *Kozlowski*) [OIAc Oc90].

e499 *Nimrud* 1989, 20 kg of gold objects from tomb of Queen Yabaya: ➤ e423, AJA 94 (1990) 280-2; fig. 24-26 (< Watan Arabi June 2).

e500 *Crocker* P. T., An Assyrian royal tomb [Queen Taliya and another woman]: BurHist 25 (1989) 92-95 [< OTAbs 13, p. 16].

e501 *Harrak* Amir, The royal tombs of Nimrud and their jewellery: BCanadMesop 20 (1990) 5-13; 12 fig.

e502 **Herrmann** Georgina, Ivories 1986 ➤ 2,a973... 5,e231: ᴿBInstArch 26 (1989) 271s (O. H. *Krzyszkowska*).

e503 *Paley* Samuel M., The entranceway inscriptions of the 'Second House' in the northwest palace of Ashurnasirpal II at Nimrūd (Kalḫu): ➤ 75, Mem. HELD M., JANES 19 (1989) 135-142 + 9 fig.

e504 *Nineveh* 1989 [continuing 14 different excavators since 1840, with dates here noted]: Iraq 52 (1990) 63-73; pl. VI-XIII (M. Louise *Scott*, John *MacGinnis*).

e505 *Bleibtreu* Erika, Five ways to conquer a city [LAYARD's Nineveh-Kuyunjik, though P. BOTTA published his Khorsabad as Monuments de Ninive 1849s]: BAR-W 16,3 (1990) 36-44.

e506 *Scurlock* J. A., The Euphrates flood and the ashes of Nineveh (DIOD. II.27.1-28.7): Historia 39 (1990) 382-4.

e507 *Nippur:* *Brandt* Margaret C., Nippur; building an environmental model: JNES 49 (1990) 67-73.

e508 *Charpin* Dominique, Un quartier de Nippur et le problème des écoles à l'époque paléo-babylonienne: RAss [83 (1989)] 84 (1990) 1-15; Eng. 16.

e509 *Jacobsen* Thorkild, Notes on Ekur [Enlil temple in Nippur]: ➤ 4, F AMIRAN Ruth, Eretz-Israel 21 (1990) 40*-47*.

e510 **Stone** Elizabeth C., Nippur neighborhoods: SAOC 44, 1987 ➤ 3,e606: R BO 47 (1990) 559-571 (G. van *Driel*: 'Old Babylonian Nippur'); ZAss 80 (1990) 228-240 (J. N. *Postgate*: 'Archaeology and the texts — bridging the gap').

e511 *Yoshikawa* Mamoru, Looking for Tummal [locality near Nippur]: AcSum 11 (1989) 285-291; map.

e512 *Zettler* Richard L., Field plans from the Ur III temple of Inanna at Nippur: AcSum 11 (1989) 305-9; 5 fig.

e513 *Nuzi:* E **Owen** D. I. ..., Studies on the civilization and culture of Nuzi and the Hurrians 2, 1987 ➤ 3,505.e566: R OLZ 85 (1990) 419-421 (C. *Zaccagnini*, Eng.; also on BARRELET M. 1984).

e513* *a) Stein* Diana L., Mythologische Inhalte der Nuzi-Glyptik; – *b) Börker-Klähn* Jutta, Die archäologische Problematik der Hurriter-Frage und eine mögliche Lösung: ➤ 801*, Hurriter 1988, 173-209; 42 fig. / 211-247; 33 fig.

e514 *Sabra* 140 k NE Baghdad: **Tunca** Ö., Tell Sabra: Akkadica supp. 5. Lv 1987, Peeters. viii-109 p.; 110 pl. [OLZ 86, 168-171, D. *Sürenhagen*].

e515 *Salabiḫ,* tell abu 1988s / 'Uruk mound' 1987: Iraq 52 (1990) 95-106; 6 fig. / 85-93; 5 fig. [75-83, early channels, *Wilkinson* T. J.].

e516 **Moon** Jane, Catalogue of Early Dynastic pottery: Abu Salabikh 3, 1987 ➤ 5,e242: R JCS 48 (1990) 123-6 (S. *Pollock*).

e517 *Pollock* S., Political economy as viewed from the garbage dump; Jemdet Nasr occupation at the Uruk mound, Abu Salabikh: Paléorient 16,1 (1990) 57-75; 12 fig.

e518 *Sāmarrā'* 1989, canals, 10th cent.: Iraq 52 (1990) 121-147; 16 fig. (T. *Wilkinson, al.*).

e519 *Seleucia:* *Invernizzi* Antonio, ® Seleucia-on-the-Tigris, a Greek metropolis in Asia: VDI 193 (1990) 174-186; 15 fig.

e520 **Seman:** *Córdoba* Joaquín M., Tell es-Seman = Aḫunā? Stationen einer altbabylonischen Reiseroute durch das Baliḫ-Tal [bei Bia ➤ e351]: AltOrF 17 (1990) 360-378; 2 fig.; map.

e521 *Sippar:* *Zawadzki* Stefan, Great families of Sippar during the Chaldean and early Persian periods (626-482 BC): RAss 84 (1990) 17-25; franç. 25.

e521* *Umma:* *Lambert* W. G., The names of Umma: JNES 49 (1990) 75-80.

e522 *Ur:* **Diakonoff** I. M., ® Liudi goroda Ura... Men of Ur: Kultura Narodov Vostoka. Moskva 1990, Akademia Nauk. 429 p.; 5-p. Eng. r 2.20. 5-02-016568-9 [BL 91,125, T. C. *Mitchell*].

e523 **Luby** Edward M., Social variation in ancient Mesopotamia; an architectural and mortuary analysis of Ur in the early second millennium B.C.: diss. SUNY, D *Stone* Elizabeth. Stony Brook 1990. 536 p. 91-04068. – DissA 51 (1990s) 3119-A.

e524 *Hruška* Blahoslav, Ur, die Entstehung eines altmesopotamischen Stadtstaates: AltOrF 16 (1989) 36-41.

e525 *Warka:* **Boehmer** Rainer M., Uruk 38, 1985. Mainz 1987, v. Zabern. 99 p.; 39 fig.; III pl. – R MesopT 25 (1990) 253-5 (B. *Carruba*).

e526 **Eichmann** Ricardo, Uruk, die Stratigraphie, Grabungen 1912-1977 in den Bereichen 'Eanna' und 'Anu-Ziqqurrat': Endberichte 3. Mainz 1990, von Zabern. xi-235 p., 48 pl.; 106 plans apart. 3-8053-1032-3 [OIAc JJ90].

e527 **Szarzyńska** Krystyna, ℗ *Z badań* ... From research on the oldest Sumerian inscriptions from the city Uruk. Wsz 1986, Univ. 283 p. [OIAc F91,20].

T6.7 **Arabia.**

e528 [E]**Boucharlat** R., *Sarles* J. F., Arabie Orientale 1982/4 ➤ 3,804: [R]AulaO 8 (1990) 152-5 (M. *Molina Martos*).

e529 **Parker** S. Thomas, Romans and Saracens 1986 ➤ 2,a987 ... 5,e254: [R]Latomus 49 (1990) 743s (P. *Salmon*); RB 97 (1990) 142s (J. *Taylor*).

e530 *Zadok* Ran, On early Arabians in the Fertile Crescent: TAJ 17 (1998) 223-231.

---

e531 *Bahrain:* **Lombard** Pierre, *Salles* Jean-F., La nécropole de Janussan (Bahrain). Lyon 1984, Gis-Maison de l'Orient. 185 p.; 31 pl. 2-903264-35-X. – [R]BO 47 (1990) 789-793 (E. C. L. *During Caspers*).

e532 *Kuwait:* **Salles** Jean-François, Une église découverte au Koweit: MondeB 67 (1990) 63-65.

e533 *Faw* Qibli 1989: GöMiszÄg 114 (1990) 9-12; 6 (foldout) fig. (P. *Grossmann, G. Lease*).

e534 *Ḥayma:* [E]**Vogt** B., *Franke-Vogt* U., Shimal 1985s [Oman, Univ. Göttingen] Excavations of the German archaeological mission in Ras al-Khaimah: BBVO 8, 1987 ➤ 3,e645; 5,e260: [R]ArOr 58 (1990) 408s (P. *Charvát*).

e535 *San'a:* **Kopp** Horst, *Wirth* Eugen, Beiträge zur Stadtgeographie von San'a: TAVO B-95. Wsb 1990, Reichert. 97 p.; 30 pl.; 4 loose plans. 3-88226-486-1 [OIAc Oc90].

e536 [E]**Serjeant** R. B., *Lewcock* Ronald, San'ā' 1983 ➤ 64,b799: [R]BSO 53 (1990) 136-8 (A. K. *Irvine*).

T6.9 **Iran,** *Persia;* Asia centralis.

e537 **Amiet** P., L'âge des échanges inter-iraniens 1986 ➤ 4,g195: [R]VDI 192 (1990) 196-202 (E. V. *Antonova*).

e538 [F]**Berghe** Lows Van den, Archaeologia iranica, [E]**Meyer** L. de 1989 ➤ 5,28: [R]MesopT 25 (1990) 252-7 (A. *Invernizzi:* analisi dettagliate).

e539 **Brosius** Maria, Untersuchung zur Stellung der Frau in achaimenidischer Zeit: Staatsprüfung Münster 1986, [D]*Orth* W. vi-243 p. – OIAc Oc90.

e540 **Gnoli** Gherardo, The idea of Iran; an essay on its origins: Orientale Rome 52. R 1989, Ist. Med./Estr.Oriente. xvi-216 p.

e541 **Golombek** Lisa, *Wilbur* Donald, The Timurid architecture of Iran and Turan. Princeton 1988, Univ. xxvii-510 p.; vol. of. xviii p., XVI pl.; 482 fig.; 161 plans; 8 maps. – [R]AION 49,4 (1989) 459-462 (M. *Bernardini*).

e542 **Harper** Prudence, Silver vessels of the Sassanian period I. Royal imagery 1981 ➤ 65,a415: [R]BO 47 (1990) 786-9 (Carol *Bier*).

e543 **Kawami** Trudy S., Monumental art of the Parthian period in Iran: AcIran 26, 1987 ➤ 5,e269; $75: [R]JAOS 110 (1990) 772s (R. N. *Frye:* most of the 63 sculptures are in Khuzestan, not the Iranian homeland-plateau); StIran 18 (1989) 261s (P. *Gignoux*).

e543* **Smith** Philip E. L.,   Palaeolithic archaeology in Iran 1986 ➤ 2,a998; 3,e660:   ᴿBO 47 (1990) 486 (F. *Hole*).

---

e544 *Isfahan:*   **Grabar** Oleg,   The great mosque of Isfahan: Kevorkian Series. NY 1990, Univ.   x-141 p.; 52 fig.   0-8147-3027-2.

e545 *Khurha:*   *Hakemi* Ali,   The excavation of Khurha [40 k SW Qom; 1955, to verify HERZFELD's temple-theory]: EWest 40 (1990) 11-41; 31 fig.

e546 *Marlik:*   **Negahban** Ezzat O.,   Metal vessels from Marlik: PrähBronzF 2/3.   Mü 1983, Beck.   x-100 p.; 5 pl.   DM 110.   3-406-08068-5. – ᴿBO 47 (1990) 780-6 (Gloria M. *Bellelli*).

e547 *Naqš-i Rustam:*   **Seidl** Ursula,   Die elamischen Felsreliefs von Kurangun und Naqš-e Rustam 1986 ➤ 4,g206*; 5,e277:   ᴿJAOS 110 (1990) 773 (R. N. *Frye*).

e548 *Persepolis:*   **Stähler** Klaus,   Die Freiheit in Persepolis? Zum Statuentyp der sog. Penelope: Boreas 13 (Münster 1990) 5-12.

e549 **Wilber** Donald L.,   Persepolis; the archaeology of Parsa, seat of the Persian kings [< diss. 1969]. Princeton 1989, Univ.   x-129 p. $25. – ᴿBA 53 (1990) 236s (E. *Yamauchi*: superficial).

e550 *Susa:*   **Joannès** F.,   Textes babyloniens de Suse d'époque achéménide: ➤ 138, ᶠPERROT J., Iran 1990, 173-180; 2 facsimiles.

e551 *a)* **Stève** Marie-Joseph, *Gasche* Hermann,   Le tell de l'Apadana avant les Achéménides;   *b) Boucharlat* Rémy,   La fin des palais achéménides de Suse; une mort naturelle: ➤ 138, ᶠPERROT J., Iran 1990, 15-32; 14 pl.; 3 (foldout) plans / 225-232 + 1 fig.

e552 *Tchoga Zanbil:*   *Mousavi* Ali,   Tépé Horreye, le *bît akitu* de Tchogha Zanbil?: ➤ 138, ᶠPERROT J., Iran 1990, 143s + 1 pl.

e553 **Boucharlat** Remy, *Lecomte* Olivier,   Fouilles de Tureng Tepe... J. DESHAYES 1960-79: RCiv Mém 24, 1987 ➤ 4,g221; 5,e285:   ᴿJAOS 110 (1990) 347-9 (L. *Bier*).

---

e554 *Bernard* Paul, *al.*,   Fouilles de la mission franco-soviétique à l'ancienne *Samarkand* (Afrasia), première campagne, 1989: CRAI (1990) 356-380; 10 fig.

e555 **Derrett** J. Duncan M.: Ideology and law, ᴱ*Sontheimer* G.-D., *Althal* P. K. Univ.Heid: BeitSüdasien F 7.   Wsb 1982, Steiner.   xi-463 p.   DM 72. – ᴿOLZ 85 (1990) 76-78 (M. *Schetelich*).

e556 **Pollet** G., *al.*,   Archaeological sites of ancient India: Corpus topographicum Indiae antiquae 2 / OrLovAn 37.   Lv 1990; Univ. Dep. Oriëntalistiek.   127 p.; maps N° 34-83.   90-6831-259-6.

T7.1   Aegyptus, *generalia.*

e557 **Adams** Barbara,   Predynastic Egypt.   Shire 1988.   76 p.; ill. £2.50 pa. 0-85263-938-4. – ᴿFolOr 27 (1990) 263s (K. M. *Ciałowicz*).

e558 **Ägypten**, Dauer und Wandel: DAI-K 75. Jahr 1982/5 ➤ 1,834; 3,e688: ᴿCdÉ 65 (1990) 55-62 (C. *Cannuyer*).

e559 **Amiable** Louis, *Guieysse* Paul,   L'Égypte ancien et la Franc-Maçonnerie; textes *Lauzeray* Christian.   P 1988, Trédaniel.   87 p.   2-85707-267-8 [OIAc Ja91].

e560 **Aufrère** Sydney H.,   La momie et la tempête; Nicolas-Claude FABRI DE PEIRESC et la curiosité égyptienne en Provence au début du XVIIᵉ siècle. Avignon 1990, A. Barthélemy.   356 p.; 10 fig.; XXXII pl.   2-903044-78-3.

e561 **Beaucour** Ferdinand, *Laissus* Yves, *Orgogozo* Chantal, La découverte de l'Égypte. P 1989, Flammarion. 272 p.; (color.) ill. 2-08-010965-0 [OIAc JJ90].

e562 **Bellion** Madeleine, Égypte ancienne; catalogue des manuscrits hiéro-glyphiques et hiératiques et des dessins, sur papyrus, cuir ou tissu, publiés ou signalés. P 1987, auct. vi-501 p. 3-9502074-0-5. – ᴿBO 17 (1990) 63s (U. *Luft*).

e563 **Bonhême** Marie-Ange, *Forgeau* Annie, Pharao, Sohn der Sonne, die Symbolik des ägyptischen Herrschers [Pharaon, les secrets du pouvoir], ᵀ*Ris-Eberle* Susanne. Z 1988, Artemis. 299 p.; ill.

e564 **Bucaille** Maurice, Mummies of the Pharaohs; modern medical inves-tigations; what medical research tells us about the body of Pharaoh Meneptah [drowned according to Ex 14,28], ᵀwith *Pannell* Alastair A. D. NY 1990, St. Martin's. xx-236 p.; 158 fig.

e565 **Davis** Whitney, The canonical tradition in ancient Egyptian art: New art history and criticism. C 1989, Univ. xx-272 p.

ᴱ**Donadoni** Sergio, L'uomo egiziano 1990 → 483.

e566 ᴱ**Donadoni Roveri** Anna Maria, Civiltà degli Egizi; le arti della cele-brazione; Torino Museo Egizio. Mi 1989, Electa. 261 p. = ? Egyptian civilization; religious beliefs. Mi 1989, Electa. 261 p.; 377 fig. (index p. 251-7). 88-435-2681-2 [OIAc F91,6, tit. sans pp.; 17 art.].

e567 ᴱ**Donadoni Roveri** Anna Maria, Egyptian civilization; daily life. Mi 1987, Electa. 262 p.; 350 fig. 88-435-2556-5 [OIAc F91,6: titles of the 10 art.].

e568 ᴱ**Donadoni Roveri** Anna Maria, Egyptian civilization; monumental art. Mi 1989, Electa. 261 p.; 377 fig. 88-435-2991-9 [OIAc F91,7: titles of 4 art.].

e569 **Emmel** Stephen, An international directory of institutions holding col-lections of Coptic antiquities outside of Egypt: Int.Asn.Coptic Studies. R 1990, Centro Italiano Microfiches. [vi-] 122 p. 88-85354-00-9.

e570 **Endesfelder** Erika, Die Ägyptologie an der Berliner Universität; zur Geschichte eines Fachgebietes: Berichte B6. B 1988, Univ. 109 p. [OIAc Ja91].

e571 *a) Fischer* Henry G., Women in the Old Kingdom and the Heracleo-politan period; – *b) Lesko* Leonard H., The Middle/New Kingdom; – *c) Ward* William A., Non-royal women and their occupations in the Middle Kingdom; – *d) Robins* Gay, Some images of women in New Kingdom art and literature; – *e) Allam* Schafik, Women as owners of immovables in pharaonic Egypt: → 4,851, ᴱ**Lesko** Barbara, Women's earliest records 1987/9, 5-24 / 31s.101-3 / 33-43 / 105-116 / 123-135.

e572 **Goyon** Jean-Claude, *Josset* Patrice, Un corps pour l'éternité; autopsie d'une momie. P 1988, Léopard d'Or. 150 p. F 130. 2-86377-065-9. – ᴿÉTRel 65 (1990) 262 (J. *Argaud*).

e573 **Griggs** C. Wilfred, Early Egyptian Christianity from its origins to 451 C.E.: Coptic Studies 2. Leiden 1990, Brill. vii-276 p.

e574 **Hobson** Christine, Exploring the world of the Pharaohs 1987 → 3,e703; 4,g243: ᴿBA 53 (1990) 41-43 (J. K. *Hoffmeier*, also on ALDRED ²1987).

e575 ᴱ**Hornung** Erik, Zum Bild Ägyptens im Mittelalter und in der Re-naissance / Comment se représente-t-on l'Égypte au Moyen Âge et à la Renaissance: OBO 95. FrS/Gö 1990, Univ./VR. 241 p.; 11 pl. 3-7278-0669-9 / 3-525-53725-5 [OIAc JJ90].

e576 **Hornung** Erik, Geist der Pharaonenzeit. Z 1989, Artemis. 3-7608-1005-5 [OIAc JJ89].

e577 **Kamel** Ibrahim, *Girgis* Girgis D., Catalogue général des Antiquités du Musée Copte, Nos. 1-253, Coptic Funerary Stelae. Cairo 1987. 271 p.; ill. – ᴿGöMiszÄg 119 (1990) 115-7 (Sofia *Schaten*).

e578 **Kemp** Barry J., Ancient Egypt; anatomy of a civilization 1989 ➔ 5,e307; £35: ᴿAJA 94 (1990) 686-9 (W. *Davis*); Antiquity 64 (1990) 422s (R. B. *Parkinson*); ClasW 84 (1990s) 245 (A. R. *Schulman*); JField 17 (1990) 481-5 (Kathryn *Bard*).

e579 **Kurth** Dieter, *Rössler-Köhler* Ursula, Zur Archäologie des 12. oberäg. Gaues...: GöOrF 4/16, 1987 ➔ 3,e707: ᴿWeltOr 20s (1989s) 261s (D. *Kessler*).

e580 *Leclant* Jean, *Clerc* Gisèle, Fouilles et travaux en Égypte et au Soudan, 1988-1989: Orientalia 59 (1990) 335-439; pl. XVIII-LXXXIX.

e581 *Meltzer* Edmund S., Queens, goddesses and other women of ancient Egypt [WARD W., TROY Lana, both 1986]: JAOS 110 (1990) 503-9.

e582 ᴱ**Murphy** Edwin, *a*) Diodorus on Egypt; Book I of DIODORUS Siculus' Historical Library. Jefferson NC 1985, McFarland. xv-178 p. 0-89950-147-8. – *b*) The Antiquities of Egypt; a translation with notes of Book I of the Library of History of Diodorus Siculus; revised and expanded. New Brunswick 1990, Transaction. xiv-179 p.; 29 pl. 0-88738-303-3 [OIAc Ja90].

e583 *Naguib* Saphinaz-Amal, Egyptian collections; myth-makers and generators of culture: GöMiszÄg 114 (1990) 81-90.

e584 **O'Callaghan** José, Las raíces religiosas del hombre; el alma del Antiguo Egipto: Bibl.Básica del Creyente. M 1990, Atenas. 151 p. 84-7020-265-0.

e585 *Patanè* Massimo, Quelles leçons faut-il tirer de l'Égypte ancienne?: DiscEg 18 (1990) 37-42.

e586 *Quaegebeur* Jan, Textes bibliques et iconographie égyptienne: OrLov-Per 20 (1989) 49-73; 18 fig.

e587 **Rice** Michael, Egypt's making; the origins of ancient Egypt 5000-2000 BC. L 1990, Routledge. 416 p.; 200 fig. + 12 colour. £25. 0-415-05092-8 [Antiquity 64/1 adv.].

e588 **Roccati** Alessandro, Egitto, immagini di Fulvio Roiter. Ponzano TR 1988, Vianello. 110 fig.; legends interspersed in groups.

e589 **Romer** John, People of the Nile; a new light on the civilization of ancient Egypt. L 1989, M. Joseph. 224 p., half (color.) phot. 0-7181-3268-8.

e590 **Russmann** Edna R., Egyptian sculpture, Cairo and Luxor. L 1989, British Museum. xii-230 p. £25. 0-7141-0053-3 [BO 47,526].

e591 **Schott** Siegfried †, ᴱ*Schott* Erika, Bücher und Bibliotheken im alten Ägypten; Verzeichnis der Buch- und Spruchtitel und der Termini technici. Wsb 1990, Harrassowitz. 553 p.

e592 **Schulze** Peter H., Frauen im Alten Ägypten. Bergisch Gladbach 1987, G. Lübbe. 312 p.; 37 pl.; 2 maps. DM 40. 3-7857-0478-8 [BO 17,133].

e592* **Sourouzian** Hourig, Musée égyptien du Caire, catalogue officiel: Ég. Org.Ant. Mainz 1987, von Zabern. 268 p. F 360. 2-8053-0940-6.

e593 **Syndram** Dirk, Ägypten — Faszinationen; Untersuchungen zum Ägypterbild im europäischen Klassizismus bis 1800 [➔ Diss. Hamburg 1985]: EurHS 28/104. Fra 1990, Lang. 454 p.; 150 fig. 3-631-41901-5 [OIAc F91,20].

e594 **Syriani** Samuel al-, *Habib* Badri, Guide to ancient Coptic churches and monasteries in Upper Egypt. Cairo... Anba Rowes. 88 p. ◐; 191 phot. – ᴿBSACopte 29 (1990) 157s (D. G.).

e594* **Vercoutter** Jean, L'Égypte ancienne[13rev] [¹1946]: Que sais-je? 247. P 1990, PUF. 127 p.; maps. 2-1304-3516-5.
e595 *Yurco* Frank J. [Were the ancient Egyptians black or white? [BAR-W 15/5 (1989)], replies to heated letters: BAR-W 16,1 (1990) 14-16 [... like asking 'Are the Americans black or white?']; 16,2 (1990) 14.65.67.70-74.
e596 **Zivie-Coche** Christiane, Égypte: Points planète. P 1990, Seuil. 206 p. – ᴿMondeB 66 (1990) 63 (Isabelle *Briend*).

T7.2 **Luxor,** *Karnak* [East Bank] – **Thebae** [West Bank].

e597 *Caldecoat* David, Find of new statues in Egypt [22 in good condition, on west side of Luxor Amun temple]: BurHist 25 (1989) 76-78 [< OTAbs 13, p. 16].
e598 **Golvin** J.-C., *Goyon* J., Karnak, Ägypten; Anatomie eines Tempels [1987 ⇒ 3,e718], ᵀ*Wildung* D. Tü 1990, Wasmuth. 140 p. (color.) ill. [ZAW 103,154, O. *Kaiser*].
e599 *Golvin* Jean-Claude, *al.*, Essai d'explication des murs 'à assises courbes' à propos de l'étude de l'enceinte du grand temple d'Amon-Rê à Karnak: CRAI (1990) 905-939; 8 fig.; 7 pl.; 940-2, précisions chronologiques, *Gabolde* Marc; carbone-14, *Lefur* Daniel.
e600 *Leclant* J., *Clerc* Gisèle, Karnak, Louxor, rive gauche thébaine: ⇒ e580, Orientalia 59 (1990) 384-401.
e600* *Martinez* Philippe, À propos du sanctuaire d'Alexandre à Karnak; réflexions sur la politique architecturale et religieuse des premiers souverains lagides: ⇒ 70*, Mém. HARI R., BSocÉg 13 (1989) 107-116.
e601 [ᴱ**Murnane** W. J.], The road to Kadesh; a historical interpretation of the battle reliefs of King Sety I at Karnak[2rev] [¹1985]: SAOC 42. Ch 1990, Univ.Or.Inst. xvi-157 p. 0-918986-67-2. – ᴿBO 17 (1990) 74-85 (P. W. *Haider*); JEA 76 (1990) 237s (K. A. *Kitchen*).
e602 **Saghir** M. El-, *al.*, Le camp romain de Louqsor 1986 ⇒ 2,b52; 4,g270: ᴿJEA 76 (1990) 252-4 (R. S. *Bagnall*).
e603 **Sourouzian** H., Monuments du roi Meneptah: DAI-K Sonderschrift 22. Mainz 1989, von Zabern. ix-237 p.; 43 pl.
e604 *Yurco* Frank J., [Karnak 'Cour de la cachette' 1976] 3,200-year-old picture of Israelites found in Egypt: BAR-W 16,5 (1990) 20-38; ill. – 17,1 (1991) 18 (L. H. *Weiner*) queries; 17,6 (1991) 54-60.93 proposes a different panel, while praising Yurco; his response p. 1,21; 6,61.

---

e605 **Abitz** Friedrich, Ramses III. in den Gräbern seiner Söhne: OBO 72, 1986 ⇒ 5,e339: ᴿJEA 76 (1990) 239s (K. A. *Kitchen*); OLZ 85 (1990) 278s (W. *Barta*).
e606 **Abitz** F., Baugeschichte und Dekoration des Grabes Ramses' VI.: OBO 89, 1989 ⇒ 5,e338: ᴿZAW 102 (1990) 293 (Brigitte *Michallik*).
e607 *Abitz* Friedrich, Der Bauablauf und die Dekoration des Grabes Ramses' IX: StAltÄgK 17 (1990) 1-40; XII fig.
e608 *Arnst* Caris-Beatrice, Das Inselheiligtum im Gartenteich; zu einer Bestattungsszene in Privatgräbern des Neuen Reiches [Theben, Saqqara]: AltOrF 16 (1989) 203-215; pl. I-IV.
e609 *Bell* Martha R., An armchair excavation of KV 55 [DAVIS T., Tomb of Queen Tiyi 1910; his photos help to correct earlier plans]: JAmEg 27 (1990) 97-137; 12 fig.

e610 *Bell* Martha R.,   Notes on the exterior construction signs from Tutan-khamun's shrines: JEA 76 (1990) 107-124.

e611 ᴱCorzo Miguel Ángel, Wall paintings of the tomb of Nefertari, scientific studies for their conservation: ASAE; 1987 ➤ 3,e736 (index!):   ᴿFolOr 27 (1990) 265s (J. *Śliwa*).

e612 **Dorman** Peter F.,   The monuments of Senenmut; problems in historical methodology ➤ 4,d187; 5,a301: [Thebes 71 & 353: prove there was never a conflict between Hatšepsut and Thutmosis III; her memory was vandalized 20 years after her death by unknown persons] L 1988, Kegan Paul. 247 p.; 22 pl. £45. – ᴿBO 47 (1990) 636-641 (L. *Gabolde*); OLZ 85 (1990) 397-402 (W. *Helck*: serious but strained).

e613 **Dziobek** Eberhard, *Abdel Raziq* Mahmud, *al.*,   Das Grab des So-bekhotep Theben Nr. 63; DAI-K ArchVeröff 71.   Mainz 1990, von Zabern. 93 p.; 31 (color.) pl.; plans in pocket. 3-8053-0974-0.

e614 *Dziobek* Eberhard,   Reconstructing the wall scenes in Theban tomb 63: BEgSem 9 (1987s) 5-8 + 6 fig.

e615 **Graefe** Erhart,   Das Grab des Ibi, Obervermögenverwalters der Got-tesgemahlin des Amun (Thebanisches Grab Nr. 36); Beiträge: Fouilles Belges Ég. 1.   Bru 1990, Fond. R. Elisabeth. 86 p.; 70 fig.; 43 p. [OIAc F91,11].

e616 **Hari** Robert,   La tombe thébaine du père divin Neferhotep (TT 50) 1985 ➤ 1,e119:   ᴿCdÉ 65 (1990) 75-77 (A.-P. *Zivie*); JAOS 110 (1990) 160s (A. R. *Schulman*).

e617 **Hornung** Erik,   The Valley of the Kings, horizon of eternity [Tal der Könige 1982 ➤ 63,d426], ᵀ*Warburton* David. NY 1990, Timken. 221 p. £35. 0-943221-07-2 [OIAc S90].

e618 **Hornung** Erik,   Tal der Könige; die Ruhestätte der Pharaonen⁵ [¹1982 ➤ 63,d426]. Z 1990, Artemis. 224 p.; ill. 3-7608-0519-1.

e619 **Hornung** Erik, *al.*,   Zwei ramessidische Königsgräber, Ramses IV. und Ramses VII.: Theben 11. Mainz 1990, von Zabern. [vi-] 139 p.; 120 pl. + 12 color. 3-8053-1067-6 [OIAc Ja91].

e620 *Kákosy* L., Fourth preliminary report on the Hungarian excavation in Thebes, tomb Nº 32 (Season 1986-7): AcArchH 42 (1990) 293-301; 5 fig.

e621 **Leblanc** Christian,   *Ta set neferou*; une nécropole de Thèbes-Ouest et son histoire I. Géographie — Toponymie; Historique de l'exploration scientifique du site; préf. *Goyon* Jean-Claude. Cairo 1989, Nubar. xxx-117 p.; 215 pl. 2-9504385-1-X [OIAc Ap91,9].

e622 **Lipińska** Iadwiga,   The temple of Tuthmosis III; statuary and votive monuments: Deir el-Bahari H. Wsz 1984, PNN. 58 p.; 22 fig.; 58 pl.; plan. – ᴿArchClasR 41 (1989) 444s (Loredana *Sist*).

e623 **Manniche** Lise,   The wall decoration of three Theban tombs (TT 77,175, and 249): Niebuhr Publ. 4, 1988 ➤ 4,g278: ᴿAcOrK 51 (1990) 261-5 (R. H. *Pierce*); AntClas 59 (1990) 551s (R. *Tefnin*).

e624 **Manniche** Lise, [once known at Thebes but now] Lost tombs; a study of certain eighteenth dynasty monuments in the Theban necropolis. L 1988, Kegan Paul. 260 p.; 80 pl. £40. 0-7103-0200-2. – ᴿBO 17 (1990) 98-101 (E. *Dziobek*).

e625 **Niwiński** Andrzej,   Studies on the illustrated Theban funerary papyri of the 11th and 10th centuries B.C.: OBO 86. FrS/Gö 1989, Univ./VR. xlii-442 p.; 90 fig.; 78 pl. Fs 118. – ᴿOrientalia 59 (1990) 542-4 (F. *Tiradritti* compares with Madame Bovary).

e626 **Reeves** C. N.,   Valley of the Kings; the decline of a royal necropolis [< diss. Durham 1984]: Studies in Egyptology. L 1990, Kegan Paul. xiii-

376 p.; 15 pl. £55.   0-7103-0368-6 [OIAc S90]. – ᴿAntiquity 64 (1990) 964s (A. *Dodson*).

e627 **Reeves** Nicholas,   The complete Tutankhamun; the king, the tomb, the royal treasure [Thebes].   L 1990, Thames & H.   224 p.   0-500-05058-9 [OIAc Oc90].

e628 *Sijpesteijn* P. J.,   The oldest inscription on the [which?] Colossus of Memnon? [*Bernand* M. & E. 1960]: ZPapEp 82 (1990) 154 only.

e629 *Siliotti* Alberto,   Lassù nel cielo di Tebe [foto da mongolfiera (balloon)]: ArchViva 9,10 (1990) 10-25.

e630 *Wilfong* Terry G.,   Western Thebes in the seventh and eighth centuries [A.D.]; a bibliographic survey of Jême and its surroundings: BASP 26,1s (1989) 89-145.

e631 **Bierbrier** Morris,   Les bâtisseurs du Pharaon; la confrérie de Deir el-Médinah [Tomb-builders 1984 ➤ 1,2378], ᵀ*Couturier* Paul: Civilisation et Tradition. Monaco 1986, Rocher. 213 p.; 100 fig. 2-268-00399-X [OIAc Ja91].

e632 **Fornari** Annamaria, *Tosi* Mario,   Nella Sede della Verità; Deir el Medina e l'ipogeo di Thutmosi III.   Mi 1987, Ricci.   231 p.; 25 pl. – ᴿOrientalia 59 (1990) 555 (Franca M. *Vacante*).

e633 **McDowell** A. G.,   Jurisdiction in the [ancient] workmen's community of Deir El-Medîna [diss. Ph 1987, ᴰ*O'Connor* D. ➤ 3,e754]: EgUitgaven 5. Leiden 1990, Ned.Instituut Nab.Oosten.   xii-307 p.   90-6258-205-2.

e634 **Ventura** R.,   Living in a city of the dead...:   OBO 69, 1986 ➤ 3,e752 ... 5,e362: ᴿIsrEJ 40 (1990) 231s (S. *Ahituv*); OLZ 85 (1990) 396s (Renate *Müller-Wollermann*: far from the last word).

e635 *Wilfong* Terry G.,   A concordance of published Coptic and Greek ostraca from the Oriental Institute's excavation at Medinet Habu [*Stefanski* E. & *Lichtheim* M. 1952 = OHM; but the original Chicago numbering (HM) is used in CRUM's Coptic Dictionary]: Enchoria 17 (1990) 155-160.

e636 **Myśliwiec** K.,   Keramik und Kleinfunde aus der Grabung im Tempel Sethos' I in Gurna 1987 ➤ 3,e748: ᴿArOr 58 (1990) 293s (B. *Vachala*); BO 47 (1990) 341-4 (C. A. *Hope*).

e637 **Burkard** Günter,   Grabung in Asasif 1963-1970, 3. Die Papyrusfunde 1986 ➤ 2,b147: ᴿEnchoria 17 (1990) 169-171 (R. *Jasnow*).

т7.3 **Amarna.**

e638 **Aldred** Cyril,   Akhenaten, King of Egypt 1988 ➤ 4,g290; 5,e271: ᴿAncHRes 20 (1990) 176-8 (Juliette *Bentley*: more than an abridged updating of his 1968 A-Pharaoh).

e639 *Bentley* Juliette,   Tutankhamen; some problems with the interpretation of archaeological evidence: AncHRes 20 (1990) 26-34; 1 fig.

e640 *a*) *Bonnel* Roland G.,   The ethics of El-Amarna; – *b*) *Tobin* Vincent A.,   The bicameral mind as a rationale of Egyptian religion: ➤ 114, ᶠLICHTHEIM M. 1990, 71-97 / (II) 994-1018.

e641 *Bryce* Trevor B.,   The death of Niphururiya [in Hittite document, Tutankhamun not Akhenaten]: JEA 76 (1990) 97-105.

e642 *Eaton-Krauss* M.,   Akhenaten versus Akhenaten [REDFORD D., ALDRED C.: 'two books could not be more different']: BO 47 (1990) 541-550.

e643 *Griffiths* J. Gwyn, Two contexts of *3ḫ*: (1) with Isis; (2) with Akhenaten: DiscEg 18 (1990) 27-34.

e643* *Hornung* Erik, Echnaton und die Sonnenlitanei: → 70*, Mém. HARI R., BSocEg 13 (1989) 65-68.

e644 **Khouli** A. El-, *Kanawati* N., Quseir el-Amarna [across the river from Qis, modern Qusiya], The tombs of Pepy-ankh and Khewen-wekh: Australian Centre for Egyptology Reports 1. Sydney 1989. 57 p.; 46 (color.) pl. 0-85837-663-6.

e644* *Liverani* Mario, A seasonal pattern for the Amarna letters: → 124, ᶠMORAN W., Lingering 1990, 337-349.

e645 **Mangano** Mark J., Rhetorical content in the Amarna correspondence from the Levant: diss. HUC, ᴰ*Weinberg* D. Cincinnati 1990. 224 p. 90-28107. – DissA 51 (1990s) 1593-A.

e646 **Martin** Geoffrey T., The Royal Tomb at El 'Amarna; The Rock Tombs of El-'Amarna 7/2, The reliefs, inscriptions, and architecture. L 1989, Egypt Expl. Soc. xxii-72 p.; 91 pl. 0-85698-107-9 [BO 47,261].

e647 **Moran** W. L., *al.*, Les lettres d'El-Amarna, ᵀ*Collon* D., *Cazelles* H.: LAPO 13, 1987 → 3,e766 ...5,e381: ᴿBO 47 (1990) 577-601 (S. *Izre'el*); BSO 52 (1989) 117 (A. R. *Millard*: excellent); CBQ 52 (1990) 327s (A. *Fitzgerald*: so immensely serviceable that transcriptions on facing page would fill an ultimate need: hopefully in the publication of the original English manuscript which 'obviously exists'); ÉtClas 58 (1990) 92 (Corinne *Bonnet*); VT 40 (1990) 254s (J. N. *Postgate*); WZKM 80 (1990) 273-7 (H. *Hirsch*).

c648 *Na'aman* Nadav, On gods and scribal traditions in the Amarna letters: UF 22 (1990) 247-255.

e649 *O'Connor* David, Demarcating the boundaries; an interpretation of a scene in the tomb of Mahu, el-Amarna: BEgSem 9 (1987s) 41-49 + 2 fig.

e650 **Samson** Julia, Nefertiti and Cleopatra 1987 = 1985 → 3,e770: ᴿAJA 94 (1990) 346s (W. *Davis*).

e651 *a) Sturtewagen* Christian, La tomba di Tutu; – *b) Piccirillo* Michele, Le lettere di El-Amarna e l'impero egiziano in Siria-Palestina: → 470*, Akhenaton 1990, 65-82 / 59-64.

Tutankhamun → **Bell** M. e610; **Reeves** N. → e627.

c652 *Walsem* R. van, De stad Amarna; exponent van traditie, vernieuwing en ideologie: PhoenixEOL 36,2 (1990) 31-50; 8 fig.

e653 *Westendorf* Wolfhart, Bemerkungen zum Sonnenhymnus von Amarna: → 8*, ᶠASSFALG J. 1990, 405-9.

T7.4   **Memphis**, *Ṣaqqara* – **Pyramides**, *Giza* (Cairo).

e654 *Bourriau* Janine, Canaanite jars from New Kingdom deposits at Memphis, Kom Rabiʿa: → 4, ᶠAMIRAN Ruth, Eretz-Israel 21 (1990) 18*-26*; 10 fig.

e655 ᴱ**Bresciani** Edda, *al.*, Saqqara IV, tomba di Bakenrenef (L. 24), attività del cantiere scuola 1985-7. Pisa 1988, Giardini. 87 p. [OIAc S90].

e656 *Bresciani* Edda, *al.*, L'attività archeologica dell'Università di Pisa in Egitto, a Saqqara (1989) e a Medinet Madi (1990): EgVO 13 (1990) 1-22 + 5 pl.

e657 *a) Giddy* L. L., *al.*, Memphis 1989; – *b) Jones* Michael, The temple of Apis in Memphis: JEA 76 (1990) 1-15; 9 fig.; pl. I-IV / 141-147; pl. VI-VII.

e658 **Lauer** Jean-Philippe, Saqqara, une vie; entretiens avec Philippe FLAN-DRIN. P 1988, Rivages. 237 p.; 39 pl. 2-86390-136-7 [OIAc F91,15].

e659 **Lloyd** A. B., *Harpur* Y. M.,   Saqqâra tombs II: the mastabas of Meru, Semdenti, Khui and others: ArchSurvEg 40. L 1990, Egypt Expl. Soc. xvi-53 p.; 9 fig.; 36 pl. 0-85698-113-3.

e660 **Martin** Geoffrey T.,   The Memphite tomb of Horemheb I, 1989 → 5,e349: RVarAeg 6 (1990) 195-203; 5 fig. (C. C. *Van Siclen*).

e661 **Martin** Geoffrey T.,   The tomb-chapels of Paser and Ra'ia at Saqqara 1985 → 1,e163...5,e395: RArOr 58 (1990) 197 (B. *Vachala*).

e662 *Testa* Pietro, *a*) Il complesso funerario del re Scepses-ka.f in Saqqâra Sud; ricerca del progetto architettonico originario; – *b*) Il complesso funerario del re Ḥuny in Meidūm; ricerca... DiscEg 17 (1990) 59-72; 4 fig. / 18 (1990) 55-69; 4 fig.

e663 **Thompson** Dorothy J.,   Memphis under the Ptolemies 1988 → 4,g340; 5,e396: RAegyptus 70 (1990) 300s (Lucia *Criscuolo*); AmHR 95 (1990) 1501s (Sarah B. *Pomeroy*); AnÉCS 45 (1990) 863-5 (Annie *Forgeau*); ClasPg 85 (1990) 317-320 (J. G. *Manning*); Gnomon 62 (1990) 609-612 (R. *Bogaert*, franç.).

e664 *Thompson* Dorothy J.,   Ptolemaios and the 'lighthouse'; Greek culture in the Memphite Serapeum: PrPgS 33 (1987) 105-121.

e665 EZivie Alain-Pierre,   Memphis 1986/8 → 4,781 (index 'A'): RBO 47 (1990) 316-323 (J. *Malek*).

e666 **Zivie** Alain,   Découverte à Saqqarah; le vizir oublié [Apar-El → 5,e397]. P 1990, Seuil. 197 p.; 163 (color.) phot. (index p. 193-5). 2-02-012499-8.

———————

e667 *Abusir:*   **Verner** Miroslav, Abusir I, the mastaba of Ptahshepses, Reliefs 1/1.   Praha (1977) 1986, Univ. 286 p.; 134 fig.

———————

e668 *Bartel* Hans-G.,   Anmerkungen zum Zusammenhang zwischen Pyramiden und Rechtecken im ägyptischen Alten Reich: AltOrF 17 (1990) 223-243; 4 fig.

e669 *a*) *Baz* Farouk el-,   Finding a pharaoh's funeral bark; – *b*) *Miller* Peter, Riddle of the pyramid boats: NatGeog 173 (1988) 512-533 / 534-550; ill.

e670 **Cimmino** Franco,   Storia delle piramidi. Mi 1990, Rusconi. 488 p., ill. Lit. 42.000. – RLetture 45 (1990) 931-3 (G. *Ravasi*).

e671 *Deaton* John C.,   The post Old Kingdom evidence for the function of pyramids: VarAeg 5 (1989) 183-8.

e672 FEDWARDS I. E. S.:   Pyramid studies, R**Baines** J., *al.*, 1988 → 4,41: RBO 47 (1990) 609-613 (H. *Altenmüller*: tit. pp.; some comment).

e673 *Engles* Drew R.,   An Early Dynastic cemetery at Kafr Ghattati [near Mena House, cleared by G. A. REISNER in 1924]: JAmEg 27 (1990) 71-87; 28 fig.

e673* **Hawass** Zahi A.,   The pyramids of ancient Egypt. Pittsburgh 1990, Carnegie Museum. iv-52 p.; 26 fig. £5 pa. 0-911239-21-9.

e674 **Héry** François-X., *Enel* Thierry,   La Bible de pierre; l'alphabet sacré de la grande pyramide. P 1990, Laffont. 224 p. F 100. – RÉtudes 373 (1990) 560 (P. *Frison*).

e675 **Hodges** Peter,   How the pyramids were built, EKeable Julian. Longmead 1989, Element. xii-154 p. 1-85230-127-9.

e676 **Lauer** Jean-Philippe,   Le mystère des Pyramides[3rev] [¹1948, 'remanié' 1974]. P 1988, Cité. 290 p. F 150. 2-258-02368-8. – RÉTRel 65 (1990) 106s (J. *Argaud*).

e677 *Leclant* J., *Clerc* G., Giza, Abousir, Saqqara, Memphis: ⇒ e580, Orientalia 59 (1990) 354-367.

e678 **Lehner** Mark, The pyramid tomb of Hetep-heres and the satellite pyramid of Khufu 1985 ⇒ 2,b120; 5,e410: ᴿOLZ 85 (1990) 21-24 (E. *Martin-Pardey*).

e679 **Lepre** J. P., The Egyptian pyramids; a comprehensive, illustrated reference. Jefferson NC 1990, McFarland. xviii-341 p. 0-89950-461-2 [OIAc F91,15].

e680 *Moore* Carey A., How I almost climbed Cheops' pyramid: BAR-W 16,6 (1990) 56-61.

e681 **Petrie** William M. F., The pyramids and temples of Giza ²ʳᵉᵛ (update by *Hawass* Zahi, p. 97-136). L 1990, Histories & Mysteries of Man. xii-136 p.; VII pl. 1-85417-051 ...

e682 *Robins* Gay, Irrational numbers and pyramids: DiscEg 18 (1990) 43-53.

e683 *Selwitz* Charles, Deterioration of the Great Sphinx; an assessment of the literature: Antiquity 64 (1990) 853-9; 2 fig.

e684 *Shimron* B., HERODOTUS and the pyramid builders [2,24: 8th century]: Athenaeum 78 (1990) 191-5.

e685 **Stadelmann** Rainer, Die ägyptischen Pyramiden... 1985 ⇒ 1,e169; 2,b122: ᴿArOr 58 (1990) 196s (B. *Vachala*).

e686 **Stadelmann** Rainer, Die grossen Pyramiden von Giza: Welt der Wunder — Wunder der Welt. Graz 1990, Akad.DV. 285 p. 175 fig.; 163 (color.) pl. 3-201-01480-X.

e687 *Staehelin* Elisabeth, Zum Motiv der Pyramiden als Prüfungs- und Einweihungsstätten: ⇒ 114, ᶠLICHTHEIM M. 1990, (II) 889-932.

e688 *Trigger* B. G., Monumental architecture [... pyramids]; a thermodynamic explanation of symbolic behaviour: WorldArch 22 (1990s) 119-132.

e689 **Dahshur:** *Legon* John A. R., The geometry of the Bent Pyramid: GöMiszÄg 116 (1990) 65-72; 3 fig.

---

e690 **Kubiak** W., Al-Fusṭāṭ 1987 ⇒ 5,e419: ᴿJSS 35 (1990) 166s (F. M. *Donner*).

e691 *Banna* Essam cl-, Y aurait-il un temple d'Amenophis II dans le village d'Arab el-Hisn, au nord d'Héliopolis? (d'après une stèle inédite de ce roi): GöMiszÄg 114 (1990) 17-27; map; 1 pl.

e692 **Debono** Fernand, *Mortensen* Bodil, The predynastic cemetery at Heliopolis 1950: DAI-K ArchVeröff. 63. Mainz 1988, von Zabern. 58 p.; 20 pl.; I plan. DM 88. 3-8053-0945-7. – ᴿBO 47 (1990) 334-7 (Barbara *Adams*).

e693 *Banna* Essam el-, Une nécropole inédite d'époque archaïque découverte près de Hélouan, au sud du Caire: GöMiszÄg 117s (1990) 7-27 + XXII pl. (map).

e694 **Debono** Fernand, *Mortensen* Bodil, El Omari, a neolithic settlement and other sites in the vicinity of wadi Hof, Helwan: DAI-K ArchVeröff 82. Mainz 1990, von Zabern. 155 p.; 52 pl.; 2 foldout plans. 0-8053-1119-2.

T7.5 **Delta Nili.**

e695 ᴱ**Brink** E. C. M. van den, The archaeology of the Nile Delta, Egypt, problems and priorities (Cairo Netherlands Inst. Oct. 1986) 1988 ⇒ 4,724: ᴿDiscEg 16 (1990) 103-8 (S. *Snape*).

e696 **Alexandria:** ᶠADRIANI Achille, Alessandria e il mondo ellenistico-romano I-III, ᴱ**Bonacasa** N., *al.*, 1984 ➤ 1,3*: ᴿOLZ 85 (1990) 289-292 (K. *Parlasca*).

e697 **Canfora** Luciano, La véritable histoire de la bibliothèque d'Alexandrie [La biblioteca scomparsa], 1988 ➤ 5,e424; ᵀ*Manganaro* –, *Dubroco* –: ᴿRBgPg 68 (1990) 201-3 (M.-C. *Lambrechts-Baets*).

e698 **Canfora** Luciano, Het ware verhaal van de Alexandrijnse bibliothek, ᵀ*Pluym* Els. Nijmegen 1990, SUN. – ill. ƒ29,50. 90-6168-293-2 [PhoenixEOL 37/1, 65s, M. L. *Folmer*].

e699 *Daoust* J., La Bibliothèque d'Alexandrie va revivre: EsprVie 100 (1990) 182-4 [< Sources Unesco 9 (1989); histoire et grandiose projet pour l'avenir].

e700 *Doris* Sergio, Alessandria d'Egitto; un mito?: ➤ 62, ᶠGRILLI A. = Paideia 45 (1990) 105-120.

e701 **Haas** Christopher J., Late Roman Alexandria; social structure and intercommunal conflict in the entrepôt of the East: diss. Michigan, ᴰ*Eadie* J., AA 1989. 88-21578. – OIAc JJ89.

e702 *Siewert* Paul, Geschichte Alexandrias und seiner antiken Bibliothek: Biblos 39 (1990) 274-7.

e703 *Lukaszewicz* Adam, Fragmenta Alexandrina I; some inscriptions from the Roman baths at Kom el Dikka: ZPapEp 82 (1990) 133-6.

e704 **Behbeit:** Gallo Paolo, Quelques monuments royaux [... Ramsès II] provenant de Behbeit el-Hagar: BIFAO 90 (1990) 223-8; pl. VII-VIII.

e705 **Bubastis:** ᴱ**Frösén** Jaakko, *Hagedorn* Dieter, Die verkohlten Papyri aus Bubastos (Pap.Bub.): PapyrolColon 15. Opladen 1990, Westd.-V. I. 221 p.; 32 pl. 3-531-09925-6.

e706 **Kom/Ḥişn:** **Buck** Paul E., Structure and content of Old Kingdom archaeological deposits in the western Nile delta, Egypt; a geoarchaeological example from Kom el-Hisn: diss. Univ. Washington, ᴰ*Wenke* R. Seattle 1990. xiii-348 p. 90-25988. – OIAc Ja91.

e708 **Mashuṭa:** *Paice* Patricia, A preliminary analysis of some elements of the Saite and Persian pottery at Tell el-Maskhuta: BEgSem 8 (1986s) 95-103 + 8 fig.

e709 *Kettenhofen* Erich, Einige Beobachtungen zu Hērōōnpolis ['ero...', Stele aus Mashuṭa; identisch mit Pithom (wie) Gn 46,28G]: OrLovPer 20 (1989) 75-97; map.

e710 **Dabʿa,** Qanṭîr, Tanis: ➤ e580, Orientalia 59 (1990) 347-350 (J. *Leclant*, G. *Clerc*).

e711 *Herrmann* Christian, Weitere Formen für ägyptische Fayencen aus der Ramsesstadt: Ägypten und Levante 1 (Wien 1990) 17-73; ill.; 1 color. pl.

e712 **Tanis:** **Stierlin** Henri, *Ziegler* Christiane, Tanis, vergessene Schätze [➤ 3,e809, Grabschätze] der Pharaonen, ᵀ*Wildung* Dietrich. Mü 1987, Hirmer. 224 p.; 117 fig. – ᴿNubica 1s (1990) 393-5 (P. *Scholz*).

e713 *Bietak* Manfred, Zur Herkunft des Seth von Avaris [Tanis 400-Jahresstele]: ÄgLev 1 (1990) 9-16; 5 fig.; phot.

e714 ᴱ**Brissaud** P., Cahiers de Tanis I, 1987 ➤ 4,g380: ᴿJAmEg 27 (1990) 228 (R. S. *Bianchi*); WeltOr 20s (1989s) 259s (D. *Kessler*).

T7.6   *Alii situs Aegypti* **alphabetice.**

e714* **Abu Mina:** *Engemann* Josef, Das Ende der Wallfahrten nach Abu Mina und die Datierung früher islamischer glasierter Keramik in Ägypten: JbAC 32 (1989) 161-171 + 21 fig.; Nachtrag 33,240s.

e715 *Abydos: Haarlem* Willem M. van, Were the archaic kings buried in Sakkara or Abydos?: DiscEg 17 (1990) 73s.

e715* Umm el-Qaab 3d, 4th, Königsfriedhof: MiDAI-K 46 (1990) 53-90; 9 fig.; pl. 18-27 (G. *Dreyer*).

e716 *Dautzenberg* N., Zur Systematik der Abydosliste [76 Könige]: Gö-MiszÄg 114 (1990) 47-52.

e717 *Ahmim:* **Kanawati** Naguib, The rock tombs of El-Hawawish [3s, 1982s ➤ 2,b157... 5,g390], 7. 1987, 58 p.; 20 (color.) pl.; 9. 1989, 62 p.; 37 fig.; 11 pl. Sydney, Macquarie Univ. 0-85837-608-3; -62-8. – ᴱDiscEg 18 (1990) 93-95 (G. T. *Martin*).

e718 *Akoris: Kawanishi* Hiroyuki, *Tsujimura* Sumiyo, Akoris Ninth Season, preliminary report. Kyoto 1989, Paleological Asn. v-33 p.; 13 pl. [OIAc Oc90].

e718* *Alamein,* Marina 1987s: MiDAI-K 46 (1990) 15-51 (W. A. *Daszewski*).

e719 *Aswan: MacCoull* Leslie S. B., Christianity at Syene/Elephantine/Philae: BASP 27 (1990) 151-162.

e720 *Bernand* Étienne, À propos d'une inscription grecque d'Éléphantine: ZPapEp 82 (1990) 179-181.

e721 **Junge** Friedrich, Elephantine XI, Funde und Bauteile, 1.-7. Kampagne, 1969-1976; DAI-K Arch. Veröff. 49, 1987 ➤ 4,g396: ᴿBO 47 (1990) 338-342 (P. *Vernus*).

e722 Elephantine 17th-18th, Stadt und Tempel: MiDAI-K 46 (1990) 185-249; 18 fig.; pl. 37-53 (W. *Kaiser, al.*); p. 252-261, *Farid* A., demotisches Familienarchiv; p. 263-8, *Willerding* K. & *Wolf* Giscla, Pflanzreste [N.B. An enclosed tag warns that the ISBN is 3-8053-1167-2; not as printed].

e723 **Dreyer** Günther, Elephantine VIII. Der Tempel der Satet 1986 ➤ 2,h148; 4,g395: ᴿArOr 58 (1990) 197s (B. *Vachala*); JEA 76 (1990) 226 (A. J. *Spencer*).

e724 **Rösing** F. W., Qubbet el Hawa und Elephantine; zur Bevölkerungsgeschichte von Ägypten [Hab.-Diss. Ulm 1987]. Stu 1990, Fischer. viii-413 p.; 133 fig. 3-437-50325-1 [OIAc S90].

e725 **Vassilika** Eleni, Ptolemaic Philae. OrLovAn 34. Lv 1989, Univ. xxiv-403 p.; 44 pl. Fb 3800. 90-6831-200-6 [OLZ 86,152-4, J. *Hallof*].

e726 *Heilporn* Paul, La provenance de la dédicace I. Th. Sy 302 [attribuée à l'ilot Sehel à mi-chemin entre Eléphantine et Philae]: CdÉ 65 (1990) 116-121.

e727 *Van Siclen* Charles C.ᴵᴵᴵ, Remarks on the Tuthmosid temple of Khnum at Elephantine: VarAeg 6 (1990) 188-194.

e728 **Bernand** André, De Thèbes à Syène. P 1990, CNRS. xi-395 p.; 163 pl. 2-222-04305-0 [OIAc S90].

e729 *Dakhleh: Valloggia* Michel, Balat I, le mastaba de Medou-Nefer 1986 ➤ 2,b151: ᴿJEA 76 (1990) 227 (A. J. *Mills*).

e730 *Aufrère* Sydney, (*Ballet* Pascale), La nécropole sud de Qila al-Dabba (oasis de Dakhla, secteur de Balat), un palimpseste archéologique: BIFAO 90 (1990) 1-17 (-28).

e731 *Soukiassian* Georges, *al.*, La ville d'Ayn-Aṣil à Dakhla; état des recherches: BIFAO 90 (1990) 347-358; 2 fig., pl. XXIV-XXVII.

e732 Dakhleh-Khargeh, Duš: ➤ e580, Orientalia 59 (1990) 406-414 (J. *Leclant*, G. *Clerc*).

e733 *Deir/Ballas* [20 k S Dendera]: **Lacovara** Peter, Preliminary report on the Deir el-Ballas expedition, 1980-1986: AmResEg Reports 12. WL 1990, Eisenbrauns. x-67 p.; XVII pl.; 5 foldout plans. 0-936770-24-4.

e734 **Dendera:** *Cauville* Sylvie, Les inscriptions dédicatoires du temple d'Hathor à Dendera: BIFAO 90 (1990) 83-114; pl. I-IV.

e735 **Daumas** François, (*Lenthéric* Bernard), Le temple de Dendara 1987 ➤ 3,e827: ᴿBO 17 (1990) 109-114 (P. *Germond*).

e736 **Dûš:** *Reddé* Michel, *al.*, Quinze années de recherches françaises à Douch; vers un premier bilan: BIFAO 90 (1990) 281-301; ill.

e737 **Esna:** *Krause* Martin, Verlorene Inschriften der Eremitensiedlungen 3 und 4 bei Esna: ➤ 16, ᶠBECKERATH J. von, 1990, 147-170.

e738 Adaïma [8 k S Esna], prédynastique, 1989: BSocFrÉg 117 (1990) 7-22; 22 fig. (wavy ledge-handles), 5 maps.

e738* **Hierakonpolis:** **Adams** Barbara, The Fort cemetery at Hierakonpolis 1987 ➤ 3,835; 4,g413: ᴿBO 47 (1990) 643-6 (S. *Hendrickx*).

e739 **Idfu:** *Finnestad* Ragnhild B., Image of the world and symbol of the creator... Edfu: StOrRel 10, 1985 ➤ 1,e224... 5,e471: ᴿOLZ 85 (1990) 285-8 (L. *Kákosy*).

e740 **Götte** Karin, Die Weinopferszenen im Tempel von Edfu: Magisterarbeit ᴰ*Derchain* P. Köln 1986. – OIAc Ap89.

e741 **Kurth** Dieter, Die Dekoration der Säulen im Pronaos des Tempels von Edfu: GöOrF 4/11, 1983 ➤ 64,b893; 65,b419: ᴿOLZ 85 (1990) 279-285 (Maria-T. *Derchain*).

e742 ᴱ**Kurth** Dieter, Edfu, Studien zu Ikonographie, Textgestaltung, Schriftsystem, Grammatik und Baugeschichte: Inschriften/Edfu, Begleitheft 1. Wsb 1990, Harrassowitz. viii-83 p. 3-447-02999-4 [OIAc S90].

e743 **Rochemonteix** M., *Chassinat* E. [1894-7] ²ʳᵉᵛ*Cauville* Sylvie, *Devauchelle* Didier, Le temple d'Edfou I/14, 1984 ➤ 3,e836: ᴿBO 17 (1990) 102-108 (A. *Egberts*: 'sic' too often; some 120 further corrections offered); CdÉ 65 (1990) 77-79 (P. *Germond* 15, 1985); JAOS 110 (1990) 592 (R. S. *Bianchi*).

e744 **(El)Kab:** **Depuydt** Frans, Archaeological-topographical surveying of El-kab and surroundings, 1. Topography; – 2. (**Hendrickx** Stan, *Huyge* Dirk), Inventaire des sites archéologiques. Bru 1989, Fond.R.Élisabeth. 41 p., 2 plans; 25 p., 3 pl., 2 plans [OIAc Ja91].

e745 **Maadi: Rizkana** Ibrahim, *Seeher* Jürgen, Maadi [I. 1987 ➤ 3,e846; II. 1988 ➤ 4,g423; III. 1989 ➤ 5,e479] IV. The predynastic cemeteries of Maadi and Wadi Digla: DAI-K ArchVeröff 81. Mainz 1990, von Zabern. 179 p.; 54 + XXXVII pl. 3-8053-1156-7. – ᴿBO 47 (1990) 323-6 (M. *Chlodnicki*, 1) & 326-334 (Béatrix *Midant-Reynes*, 2).

e745* *Seeher* Jürgen, Maadi – eine prädynastische Kulturgruppe zwischen Oberägypten und Palästina: PraehZts 65 (1990) 123-156; 17 fig.

e746 **Best** Jan G. P., [Maadi] A timber-grave complex in Egypt around 3200 BC: Orpheus-Thrac 1 (1990) 24-28.

e747 **Merimde:** **Eiwanger** Josef, Merimde-Benisalame II 1988 ➤ 4,g424: ᴿJAmEg 27 (1990) 219s (B. *Williams*).

e748 **Naga'/Dêr:** **Podzorski** Patricia V., Their bones shall not perish; an examination of predynastic human skeletal remains from Naga-ed-Dêr in Egypt [< 1982 Berkeley Master's thesis]. New Malden, Surrey 1990, 'SIA'. xii-166 p.; ill. 1-872561-00-4.

e749 **Oxyrhynchus:** **Krüger** Julian, Oxyrhynchos in der Kaiserzeit; Studien zur Topographie und Literaturrezeption [Diss. Berlin Freie Univ. 1987]: EurHS 3/341. Fra 1990, Lang. xiii-377 p. 3-631-42935-5 [OIAc Ap91,9].

e750 **Kutzner** Edgar, Untersuchungen zur Stellung der Frau im römischen Oxyrhynchos: EurHS 3/392. Fra 1989, Lang. 167 p.

e751 *Siwa:* **Kuhlmann** Klaus P., Das Ammoneion; Archäologie, Geschichte und Kultpraxis des Orakels von Siwa [-Oasis]: ArchVeröff 75, 1988 ➤ 4,b820: ᴿJAmEg 27 (1990) 229s (R. S. *Bianchi*).

e752 *Egberts* A., The identity crisis of an Egyptian priest [Siwa oasis tomb]: VarAeg 5 (1989) 3-7.

e753 *Tebtunis: Hadji-Minaglou* Gisèle, Rapport préliminaire sur la deuxième campagne de fouilles à Tebtynis (octobre 1989): BIFAO 90 (1990) 229-234; 9 fig.

e754 *Tihna* [2 k E Minya]: *Alfi* Mostafa El-, The tomb of Nikaʿankh at Tihna (Fraser tomb nᵒ 2): DiscEg 16 (1990) 35-40 + 2 fig.

т7.7   **Antiquitates Nubiae et alibi.**

e755 **Alföldy** Géza, Der Obelisk auf dem Petersplatz in Rom; ein historisches Monument der Antike: SzbHeid ph/h 1990/2. Heid 1990, Winter. 115 p.; XVI color. phot. 3-553-04283-0.

e756 **Aufrère** Sydney, Collections égyptiennes... Musées départementaux de Seine-Maritime; catalogue. P 1987, Musées de France. 234 p., ill. 2-902093-05-[o-]5.

e758 *Gabra* Gawdat, Ein Block Ptolemaios' V. Epiphanes aus Babylon: ➤ 16, ꟳBECKERATH J. v. 1990, 49-51; pl. 2a.

e759 **Grenier** Jean-Claude, La décoration statuaire du 'Serapeum' du 'Canope' de la Villa Adriana; essai de reconstitution et d'interprétation: Monumenti, Musei e Gallerie Pontificie [= MÉF-Ant 101 (1989) 925-1019]. R 1990, École Française. vii-55 p.; ill.

e760 ᴱ**Hägg** Tomas, Nubian culture 1986/7 ➤ 4,740; 5,e486: ᴿOLZ 85 (1990) 28s (Inge *Hofmann*).

e761 **Hintze** Fritz, *Reineke* Walter F., Felsinschriften aus dem sudanesischen Nubien 1989 ➤ 5,e487: ᴿOLZ 85 (1990) 524-7 (H. S. *Smith*, Eng.); WZKM 80 (1990) 238-240 (Inge *Hofmann*).

e762 **Hölbl** Günther, Museo Archeologico Nazionale di Napoli, le stele funerarie della collezione egizia. R 1985, Poligrafico. xi-73 p., 14 pl., Lit. 5000· ᴿBO 17 (1990) 120-2 (M. L. *Bierbrier*).

e763 ᴱ**Krause** Martin, Nubische Studien 1982/6 ➤ 4,750 [Mem. DINKLER E.]: ᴿBO 47 (1990) 649-651 (J. *Desanges*).

e764 *Leclant* Jean, L'exploration archéologique de la zone de la IVᵉ Cataracte du Nil: CRAI (1990) 316-320; 4 fig.

e765 *Leclant* J., *Clerc* Gisèle, Soudan: ➤ e580, Orientalia 59 (1990) 417-434.

e766 ᴱ**Robertshaw** Peter, A history of African archaeology. L 1990, Currey. vii-278 p. 0-85255-065-0 [OIAc S90].

e767 **Scott** Gerry D.ᴵᴵᴵ, Ancient Egyptian art at Yale. NHv 1987, Yale Univ. Art Gallery. 232 p. 0-89467-038-7. – ᴿBO 17 (1990) 119s (E. *Feucht*).

e768 *Simon* Christian, Les populations Kerma; évolution interne et relations historiques dans le contexte égypto-nubien: ArNilM 3 (1989) 139-147.

e769 **Williams** Bruce B., Excavations between Abu Simbel and the Sudan frontier [4. 1989 ➤ 5,e495] 7. Twenty-Fifth Dynasty and Napatan remains at *Qustul*, cemeteries W and V. Ch 1990, Univ. Or. Inst. xxvii-83 p.; 15 pl. 0-918986-[46-X (I, 1980)]-60-5. – ᴿCdÉ 65 (1990) 88-93 (Brigitte *Gratien*, 5).

e770 **Williams** Bruce, [Adindan ➤ 5,e495] C-group ... OINE 5/5, 1983 ➤ 3, e878: ᴿJAmEg 27 (1990) 230-2 (K. *Grzymski*, also on OINE 3/1, 1986).

---

e771 *Aethiopia:* **Dombrowski** Franz A., Tanasee 106, eine Chronik der Herrscher Äthiopiens: ÄthF 12. Wsb 1983, Steiner. 133 p.; 230 p. DM 128. – ᴿJAOS 110 (1990) 353s (D. *Crummey*: 'Äthiopens').

e772 **Munro-Hay** S. C., Excavations at Aksum: Memoir 10. L 1989, British Institute in Eastern Africa. xvi-359 p.; 186 fig.; 72 pl. 0-500-97008-4. – ᴿAntiquity 64 (1990) 689s (P. L. *Shinnie*).

e773 *Fattovich* Rodolfo, The peopling of the Northern Ethiopian-Sudanese borderland between 7000 and 1000 BP; a preliminary model: Nubica 1s (1990) 3-45; 6 fig. (maps).

e773* *a)* **Knefelkamp** Ulrich, Die Suche nach dem Reich des Priesterkönigs Johannes [diss. Fr 1985]. Gelsenkirchen 1986, Müller. 269 p.; ill. – ᴿNubica 1s (1990) 381s (P. *Scholz*). – *b)* **Gumilev** L. N., Searches for an imaginary kingdom; the legend of the kingdom of Prester John: Past and Present. C 1988, Univ. 420 p.; ill. $59.50. 0-521-32214-6. – ᴿJRel 70 (1990) 130s (Elizabeth L. *Wilson*).

e774 *a)* *Török* László, Augustus and Meroe; – *b)* *Witakowski* Witold, Syrian influences in Ethiopian culture: ➤ 184, ᶠVITESTAM G., OrSuec 38s (1989s) 171-190; 14 fig. (map) / 191-202.

e775 *Barkal:* **Donadoni** Sergio, Italian excavations at the Jebel Barkal in 1987: Nubica 1s (1990) 149-152 (-160).

e778 *Bérénice:* **Vercoutter** Jean, Découverte [1880 ... 1990] de Bérénice Panchrysos: CRAI (1990) 899-903; 2 fig.

e779 *Cyrene:* *Maffre* Jean-J., La céramique du IVᵉ siècle avant notre ère à Apollonia de Cyrénaïque: BSocAntiquaires de France (1989) 55s.

e780 *Caputo* Giacomo, Il teatro augusteo di Leptis Magna: MgArchLibica 3. R 1987, Bretschneider. 148 p.; 188 pl. + 39 apart. – ᴿGnomon 62 (1990) 455-7 (A. *Di Vita*).

e781 **Laronde** André, Cyrène et la Libye hellénistique; Libykai historiai. P 1987, CNRS. 524 p.; 185 fig.; map. – ᴿAJA 94 (1990) 698s (G. W. M. *Harrison*).

e782 ᴱ**Mastino** Attilio, L'Africa romana, ➤ 5,856: Atti del 1-5 convegno di studio, Sassari 1983-7. Sassari 1984-8, Gallizzi. 221 p.; 286 p.; 457 p.; 743 p.; 527 p.; ill. Lit. 40.000 each. – ᴿAJA 94 (1990) 360-2 (R. J. *Rowland*: reverse inflation; 743 p. for the same price as 221 p.).

e783 **Schaus** Gerald P., The east Greek, island, and Laconian pottery: Cyrene extramural sanctuary of Demeter and Persephone 2, 1985 ➤ 4,g449: ᴿArchClasR 42 (1990) 460-7 (S. *Stucchi*).

e784 *Dongola:* **Gartkiewicz** Przemysław M., Dondola 2; the Cathedral in Old Dongola and its antecedents: Nubia 1. Wsz 1990, PWN. 326 p. 83-01-04459-4 [OIAc Oc90].

e785 *Faras:* *Vantini* Giovanni, The Faras Golgotha and the apocrypha: ➤ 781, Nubien/Uppsala 1986/90, 653-660.

e786 *Geili:* ᴱ**Caneva** I., El Geile, the history of a Middle Nile environment, 7000 B.C.-A.D. 1500: BAR-Int 424. Ox 1988. 411 p.; ill.

e787 *Hambukol* (Upper Nubia) 1987-8: JAmEg 27 (1990) 139-163; 26 fig. (K. *Grzymski*).

e788 *Meroe:* **Hinkel** Friedrich W. & † Marion, Das Priesterhaus Meroe 251; Gedanken zum Bau des Wadi Tarabil-Museums bei den Pyramiden von Meroe: AltOrF 17 (1990) 18-26.

e789 *Nag'/Fariq:* Strouhal Eugen, Rock tombs at Nag' el-Fariq (Egyptian Nubia): ArNilM 4 (1990) 107-135, 12 fig + XIV pl.

e790 *Nag'/Šeyma:* **Bietak** Manfred, *Schwarz* Mario, Nag' el-Scheima [Sayala-Nubien] I, 1987 → 3,e893; 5,e508: ᴿArOr 58 (1989) 292s (E. *Strouhal*); Nubica 1s (1990) 370s (P. *Scholz*).

e791 *Naqlun:* Godlewski Włodzimierz, *al.,* Deir el Naqlun (Nekloni) 1986-7, first preliminary report; appendix 1988, *Dobrowski* Jarosław: Nubica 1s (1990) 171-208.

e792 *Qaṣr Ibrim:* Driskell Boyce N., *al.,* A newly discovered temple at Qasr Ibrim, preliminary report: ArNilM 3 (1989) 11-34; 3 fig.; XVI (color.) pl.

e793 *Šaqadud:* Caneva Isabella, *Marks* Anthony, More on the Shaqadud pottery; evidence for Saharo-Nilotic connections during the 5th-4th millennium B.C.: ArNilM 4 (1990) 11-26 + IX pl.

e794 *Tabo:* **Maystre** Charles, Tabo I. statue 1986 → 4,g478; 5,e509: ᴿArOr 58 (1990) 402s (E. *Strouhal*); OLZ 85 (1990) 531-6 (Karola *Zibelius-Chen*).

T7.9 Sinai.

e796 **Anati** Emmanuel, I siti a plaza di Har Karkom: Mg Preistoria 9. Capo di Ponte 1987, Centro Camuno. 240 p.; 233 fig. [OIAc JJ 90].

e797 *Finkelstein* Israel, *Perevolotsky* Avi, Processes of sedentarization and nomadization in the history of Sinai and the Negev: BASOR 279 (1990) 67-81; bibliog. 81-88.

e798 **Gandolfo** Emilio, Egitto e Sinai; sulle orme dell'Esodo. Mi 1985, Ist. Propag.Libraria. 118 p.; color. ill.; map. [KirSef 62 (1988s), p. 621].

e799 *Gilead* Isaac, The neolithic-chalcolithic transition and the Qatifian of the northern Negev and Sinai: Levant 22 (1990) 47-63; 10 fig.

e800 *Görg* Manfred, Der Sinai, '(Der Berg) des Erzgebietes' [Dᴏssɪɴ G. 1948, si-En-ni; äg. *bj3*]: BibNot 54 (1990) 12-18.

e801 *Miziolek* Jerzy, Transfiguratio Domini in the apse at Mount Sinai and the symbolism of light: JWarb 53 (1990) 42-60.

e802 *Oren* E.D., *Yekutieli* Y., ⊕ North Sinai during the MB I period — pastoral nomadism and sedentary settlement: → 4, ᶠAMIRAN Ruth, Eretz-Israel 21 (1990) 6-22; 14 fig.; Eng. 101*.

e803 ᴱRainey A.F., Egypt, Israel, Sinai; archaeological and historical relationships in the biblical period 1982/7 → 3,834; 5,e519: ᴿIsrEJ 40 (1990) 236s (S. *Ahituv*); JNES 49 (1990) 367-9 (G.W. *Ahlström*: the 'Exodus and history' problem).

e804 *Wimmer* Stefan, Egyptian temples in Canada and Sinai: → 114, ᶠLICHTHEIM M. 1990, (II) 1065-1106.

T8.1 Anatolia, *generalia.*

e805 **Beck** Brandon H., From the rising of the sun; English images of the Ottoman Empire to 1715: AmUnivSt 9/20. NY 1987, Lang. x-151 p. – ᴿJAOS 110 (1990) 291-303 (R. *Murphey*).

e806 *Bittel* Kurt, Aus Isaurien [1952]: → 3, Mem. ALKIM U., 1986, 471-9; 2 fig.; III pl.

e807 ᴱBorchardt Jürgen, Götter, Heroen, Herrscher in Lykien. Wien 1990, Schroll. 240 p. 3-7031-0662-X [OIAc JJ90].

e808 **Brandes** Wolfram, Die Städte Kleinasiens im 7. und 8. Jahrhundert [< Diss. 1984]: Berliner Byzantinistische Arbeiten 56. B/Amst 1989,

Akademie/Gieben. 244 p. M 42. – ᴿDLZ 111 (1990) 569-571 (M. *Springer*) [ByZ 83,300].

e809 **Desideri** Paolo, *Jasink* Anna Margherita, Cilicia, dall'età di Kizzuwatna alla conquista macedone: Storia 1. T 1990, Lettere. xvii-246 p.; 16 (color.) pl.; 4 maps. 88-7166-012-9.

e810 **Edwards** Robert W., The fortifications of Armenian Cilicia 1987 ➤ 4,g491; 5,e526: ᴿBySlav 50 (1989) 87s (B. *Brentjes*); OrChrPer 56 (1990) 199s (V. *Ruggieri*); Syria 65 (1988) 472s (L. *Pressouyre*).

e811 **Eid** Volker, Ost-Türkei; Völker und Kulturen zwischen Taurus und Ararat: Kunst-Reiseführer. Köln 1990, DuMont. 438 p. 3-7701-1455-8 [OIAc Ja91].

e812 **Hellenkemper** Hansgerd, *Hild* Friedrich, Neue Forschungen in Kilikien: Tabula Imp. Byz. Veröff. 4/W Denkschr. ph/h 186 ➤ 4,g496: ᴿSpeculum 65 (1990) 170-2 (C. *Foss*, hesitant).

e813 **Hotz** Walter, Die Mittelmeerküsten Anatoliens; Handbuch der Kunstdenkmäler. Da 1989, Wiss. 3-534-03073-7 [OIAc JuJ89].

e814 ᴱ**Linders** Tullia, *Hellström* Pontus, Architecture and society in Hecatomnid Caria 1987/9 ➤ 5,852: ᴿClasR 40 (1990) 424-6 (R. A. *Tomlinson*).

e815 **Lloyd** Seton, Ancient Turkey; a traveller's history of Anatolia 1989 ➤ 5,e533: ᴿAncHRes 20 (1990) 191-3 (T. R. *Bryce*).

e816 ᶠMELLINK Machteld J., Ancient Anatolia, ᴱ**Canby** Jeanny V., *al.* 1986 ➤ 2,71; 4,g499: ᴿBO 47 (1990) 468-476 (J. *Yakar*).

e817 *Mellink* Machteld J., Archaeology in Anatolia: AJA 94 (1990) 125-151; 29 fig. (map).

e818 *Mileta* Christian, Zur Vorgeschichte und Entstehung der Gerichtsbezirke der Provinz Asia: Klio 72 (1990) 427-444.

e819 **Moscati** Sabatino, (*Bisi* Anna M.) Le civiltà periferiche del Vicino Oriente Antico; mondo anatolico e mondo siriano: Storia universale dell'arte, I. Le civiltà antiche e primitive. T 1989, UTET. 270 p.; (color.) ill.; 5 maps. 88-02-04238-1.

e820 **Önen** Ülgür, Karien; Südliche Westküste Anatoliens; Antike Städte, Geschichte, Kunstwerke. İzmir 1986, Akademia. viii-189 p.; 153 fig.

e821 **Özal** Turgut, La Turquie en Europe. P 1988, Plon. 276 p. – ᴿEpeterisByz 47 (1887-9) 457-462 (D. *Kalamakis*: falsification de l'histoire par le Président de la Turquie).

e822 *Özsait* Mehmet, ❶ New prehistoric sites in Pisidia [1982, Yeşilova SW Burdur: neo 5, chalco 6, EB 8 sites]: ➤ 3, Mem. ALKIM U. 1986, 73-87 + X pl.; franç. p. 87s.

e823 **Rankin** H. D., Celts and the classical world [... Galatia]. L 1987, Croom Helm. 319 p. – ᴿAnzAltW 43 (1990) 221-6 (G. *Dobesch*).

e824 **Roos** Paavo, Survey ... tombs ... Caria I 1985 ➤ 5,e538: ᴿBO 47 (1990) 805-8 (J. M. *Hemelrijk*).

e825 **Sinclair** T. A., Eastern Turkey I 1987 ➤ 3,e920; II. 1989 ➤ 5,e359: ᴿSpeculum 65 (1990) 1048-51 (C. *Foss*, 1).

e826 **Stierlin** Henri, Kleinasiatisches Griechenland; klassische Kunst und Kultur von Pergamon bis Nimrud Dagh. Stu 1986, Belser. 231 p.; 178 fig.

e827 *Thierry* Jean-Michel, Topographie et état actuel des monuments géorgiens de la Turquie orientale: RGéorg 5 (1989) 129-149 + 20 fig. (... maps).

e828 *Wickert* Ulrich, Kleinasien: ➤ 857, TRE 19 (1990) 244-265; foldout map.

e828* *Yakar* Jak, The chronology of the Transcaucasian – East Anatolian Early Bronze Age: → 4, AMIRAN Ruth, Eretz-Israel 21 (1990) 94*-100*; map.

т8.2 **Boğazköy,** *Hethaei* – **The Hittites.**

e829 **Bittel** Kurt, Gli Ittiti [Les Hittites 1976], ᵀ*Lenzini* Marcello, *De Luigi Rotondi* Maria C.: Il mondo della figura. Mi 1983 = 1977, Rizzoli. [vi-]335 p.; 340 fig. Lit. 16.000. 88-17-29523-X.

e830 **Eren** Mustafa, *Hoffner* Harry A.ᴶ [title also ❶] Boğazköy tablets in the archeological museum of İstanbul 4: Türk Tarih Kurumu Yayınları 6/27. Ankara 1988, Atatürk Kültür Kurumu. xlix-74 p.

e831 *Gindin* Leonid A., Keteioi (= Hittites) and Paiones (= Proto-Armenians) – allies of Troy [IL. 2,815-877; 10,428-441]: Orpheus-Thrac 1 (1990) 64-72.

e832 **Klengel** H., Texte verschiedenen Inhalts: KaB 60. B 1990, Akademie. x-50 p.; DM 78. 3-05-000944-6 [OLZ 86, 171-3, V. *Haas*, I. *Wegner*].

e833 *Neve* Peter, Die Ausgrabungen in Boğazköy-Ḫattuša 1989: ArchAnz (1990) 267-303, 29 fig.; 305-314, Südburg inscription, *Hawkins* John D.

e834 **Neve** Peter, Hattuscha Information: Ancient Anatolian Civilizations 2. İstanbul 1987, Archaeology and Art. [OIAc JJ90].

e835 **Otten** Heinrich, Die Bronzetafel aus Boğazköy, I. Staatsvertrag 1988 → 4,g514 (II. 1989 → 5,e351): ᴿKratylos 35 (1990) 204-6 (H.C. *Melchert*).

e835* *Roos* J. de, KBo 33-216; a votive text of Tuthalias IV: JACiv 4 (Chang-chun 1989) 39-48 [< OTAbs 14,31].

т8.3 **Ephesus.**

e836 **Bammer** Anton, Ephesus, Stadt an Fluss und Meer. Graz 1988, Akad.-DV. 250 p.; 43 fig.; 80 pl. – ᴿAcArchH 42 (1990) 42 (1990) 368 (M. *Szabó*).

e837 *Bammer* Anton, *al.*, *a)* Éphèse, la cité d'Artemis: MondeB 64 (1990) 8-15 (4-47), ill. – *b)* A peripteros of the geometric period in the Artemision of Ephesus. AnSt 40 (1990) 137-160; 30 (foldout) fig.

e838 *Engelmann* H., Ephesische Inschriften: ZPapEp 84 (1990) 89-94.

e839 **Friesen** Steve, Ephesus, twice *neokoros*: diss. Harvard, ᴰ*Koester* H. CM 1990. 352 p. 90-35608. – DissA 51 (1990s) 2417-A; RelStR 17,194.

e840 **Galvano** A., Artemis Efesia: Il Mondo dell'Arte 5. T 1989, Quadrante. 141 p.; 6 pl. Lit. 19.500. 88-381-0091-8 [NTAbs 35,125].

e841 *Gessel* Wilhelm M., Die Johannestradition auf dem Ayasoluk im Lichte der apokryphen Johannesakten: → 8*, ᶠASSFALG J. 1990, 108-113.

e842 *Jobst* Werner, Ein spätantikes Säulenmonument in Ephesos: IstMitt 39 (1989) 245-255; pl. 26, 6-28.

e842* **Oster** Richard E., A bibliography of ancient Ephesus: ATLA 19. Metuchen NJ 1987, Scarecrow. xxiv-155 p. – ᴿCritRR 2 (1989) 129-133 (E. J. *Epp*).

e843 **Thür** Hilke, Das Hadrianstor in Ephesos 1989: Forsch. Eph. 11,1. W 1989, Akad. 162 p.; 179 fig.; 16 plans.

e844 *Thür* Hilke, Arsinoe IV, eine Schwester Kleopatras VII, Grabinhaberin des Oktogons von Ephesos? Ein Vorschlag: JhÖsA 60-H (1990) 43-56; 11 fig. [57-85, Memmius-Monument, *Outschar* Ulriche].

т8.4 **Pergamum.**

e845 **Filgis** M. N., *Radt* W., Das Heroon: Altertümer von Pergamon 15/1, 1986 → 3,e951 ... 5,e560: ᴿAnzAltW 43 (1990) 85-89 (H. *Vetters*).

e846 *Habicht* Christian,   Athens and the Attalids in the second century B.C.: Hesperia 59 (1990) 561-577.

e847 *a) Klinkott* Manfred,   Die 'ambulationes pensiles' in der pergamenischen Stadtbaukunst; – *b) Radt* Wilfgang,   Ungewöhnliche Kapitelle von der Unteren Agora in Pergamon: IstMitt 39 (1989) 273-280; 2 fig.; pl. 30 / 455-463; 3 fig.; pl. 45.

e848 *a) Pairault-Massa* Françoise-Heline,   Die Magnésie du Méandre à Pergame; mythologie et politique dans le bas-relief des autels micro-asiastiques; – *b) Schwandner* E.-L., Hermogenes in Pergamon?: → 791*, Klas.Arch 13 (1988/90) 175/...

e849 *Mellink* M., *Radt* W., Pergamon 1988: AJA 94 (1990) 146-9: fig. 24-29.

e850 **Radt** W.,   Pergamon, Geschichte und Bauten 1988 → 5,e570:   ᴿBO 47 (1990) 491s (J. M. *Hemelrijk*); Gymnasium 97 (1990) 282s (A. *Gutsfeld*); JHS 110 (1990) 265 (S. *Mitchell*).

e851 *Radt* Wolfgang,   Pergamon, Vorbericht über die Kampagne 1989: ArchAnz (1990) 397-424; 18 (foldout) fig.

T8.6 *Situs Anatoliae,*   **Turkey sites** in alphabetical order.

e852 *Acem:* *Özgüç* Nimet,   An Early Bronze Age jar from Acemhöyük: → 4, ᶠAMIRAN Ruth, Eretz-Israel 21 (1990) 70*-73*; 3 fig.

e853 *Adıyaman* (Urfa highway) survey 1985-8: AnSt 40 (1990) 81-135; 33 fig. (S. *Blaylock*, *al.*).

e854 *Aizanoi:* *Naumann* Rudolf,   Zeustempel und Kybeleheiligtum in Aizanoi: → 3, Mem. ALKIM U., 1986, 503-9; III pl.

e855 *Alişar:* *Gorny* Ronald L.,   Alişar Höyük in the second millennium B.C.: diss. ᴰ*Kantor* H.   Chicago 1990.   xx-687 p. (3 vol.) – OIAc F91,11.

e856 *Amorium,* E. Phrygia, 2d 1989: AnSt 40 (1990) 205-218; 4 fig. (R. M. *Harrison*).

e857 *Antakya:* *Djobadze* Wachtang, *al.*,   Archeological investigations in the region west of Antioch-on-the-Orontes: ForKunstG 13.   Stu 1986, Steiner.   234 p.; 74 fig.; 100 pl.; 10 loose plans. – ᴿByZ 83 (1990) 131-4 (J. C. *Balty*); Byzantion 60 (1990) 561-5 (Jacqueline *Lafontaine-Dosogne*). **Kennedy** H., *Liebeschuetz* H., Antioch 1988 → e346.

e858 *Norris* Frederick W.,   Antioch-on-the-Orontes as a religious center; I. Paganism before Constantine: → 828, ANRW 2/18/4 (1990) 2322-79.

e859 *Apameia Phrygia:* **Christol** Michel, *Drew-Bear* Thomas,   Un castellum romain près d'Apamée de Phrygie: Tituli AsMin Egbd 12, 1987 → 5,e578: ᴿAntClas 59 (1990) 622 (G. *Raepsaet*).

e860 *Aphrodisias:* **Budde** Ludwig,   St. Pantaleon von Aphrodisias in Kilikien: Beiträge zur Kunst des Christlichen Ostens 9, 1987 → 5,e580:   ᴿByZ 83 (1990) 128-131 (G. *Mietke*).

a861 *Cormack* Robin,   Byzantine Aphrodisias; changing the symbolic map of a city: PrCPgSoc 36 (1990) 26-41.

e862 *Doruk* Seyhan, ⬤ Aphrodisias — recherches, fouilles, historique: Belleten 53,206ss (1989) 553-563.

e862* *Horst* P. W. van der,   Jews and Christians in Aphrodisias in the light of their relations in other cities of Asia Minor: NedTTs 43 (1989) 106-121; Eng. 141.

e863 ᴱ**La Genière** Juliette de, *Erim* Kenan,   Aphrodisias 1985/7 → 3,e971; 5,e582: ᴿRArchéol (1990) 427s (C. *Le Roy*).

a864 *Levinskaya* Irina, The inscription from Aphrodisias and the problem of God-fearers: TyndB 41 (1990) 312-8.

e865 *Nelton* Sharon, Master of Aphrodisias [for 20 years: Kenan T. ERIM, excavator]: Archaeology 43,1 (1990) 50-57; ill.

e866 *Assos:* **Wescoat** Bonna D., [cf. → 3,e976] The architecture and iconography of the temple of Athena at Assos: diss. Oxford 1983. 458 p. BRD-90100. – DissA 51 (1990s) 1669-A.

e867 *Balboura* (N. Lycia) 1987; AnSt 40 (1990) 29-54; 5 fig. (D. K. *Money*, lion sarcophagi) & 55-67 (A. *Farrington*, J. J. *Coulton*, bath-buildings spacer-pins) & 69-79; 5 fig. (L. *Bier*, lower theatre).

e868 *Çatal:* **Crépon** Pierre, **Dressler** Sophie, Un village d'agriculteurs en Asie Mineur il y a 8000 ans, Çatal Hüyük: Un lieu, des hommes, une histoire. P 1988, A. Michel. 57 (unnumbered) p. 2-226-03075-1 [OIAc F91,5].

e869 **Ducos** Pierre, Archéozoologie quantitative; les valeurs numériques immédiates à Çatal Hüyük: Cahiers du Quaternaire 12. P 1988, CNRS. 112 p.; 2 pl. 2-222-03975-4 [OIAc JJ90].

e869* *Claros:* La *Genière* Juliette de, Le sanctuaire d'Apollon à Claros: RÉG 103 (1990) 95-110; 3 fig.

e870 *Demirci:* **Korfmann** M., Demircihüyük 1975-8, I, 1983 → 65,b490; II.-III. 1987 → 5,e588: ᴿAcArchH 42 (1990) 355-8 (J. *Makkay*, 1); BO 47 (1990) 476-9 (J. *Yakar*, 2) & 478-485 (3s: *Seeher* J., *Turan* E.).

e871 *Deve:* **Klengel-Brandt** Evelyn, Kleinfunde aus Deve Hüyük bei Karkamisch im vorderasiatischen Museum Berlin: → 28, ᶠBOUNNI A. 1990, 133-146 + pl. 30-34.

e872 *Dikli*-Taş 1989: BCH 114 (1990) 877-880 (P. *Darcque, al.*).

e873 *Domuz:* Çambel Halet, ❶ Domuztepe → 3, Mem. ALKIM U. 1986, 31-44 + VI pl.

e873* *Eregli:* Stiernon D., Héraclée de Thrace [Ercğli]: → 836, DHGE 23 (1990) 1306-37.

e874 *Göreme:* a) Grishin A. D., The church of Yusuf Koç near Göreme village in Cappadocia; – b) Wallace Sue Ann, Liturgical planning in some Cappadocian churches; a re-evaluation following recent excavations in central Anatolia: MeditArch 3 (1990) 39-45; 1 fig.; (pl. 20-23) / 27-38; pl. 18-19.

e875 **Kostof** Spiro, Caves of God; Cappadocia and its churches. Ox 1990, UP. xxxi-308 p.; 25 fig.; 45 pl. £10 [JTS 41, 826].

e876 *Gordion:* DeVries Keith, The Gordion excavation seasons of 1959-1973 and subsequent research: AJA 94 (1990) 371-406; 40 fig.

e877 *Simpson* Elizabeth, 'Midas's bed' and a royal Phrygian funeral: JField 17 (1990) 69-87; 28 fig.

e878 *İstanbul:* **Harrison** Martin, A temple for Byzantium [Saraçhane]; the discovery and excavation of Anicia Juliana's palace-church in Istanbul. L/Austin 1989, H. Miller/Texas Univ. 160 p.; 136 fig. + 42 color. £30. 0-292-78109-1. – ᴿAntiquity 64 (1990) 693s M. *Vickers*); Byzantion 60 (1990) 565-8 (Jacqueline *Lafontaine-Dosogne*); RHE 85 (1990) 557 (D. *Bradley*).

e878* *Abel* Olivier, La cité de Constantin: FoiVie 89,3s ('Constantinople aux portes de l'Europe' 1990) 3-14 (-127, *al.*).

e879 **Mainstone** Rowland J., Hagia Sophia 1988 → 4,g579*; 5,e600: ᴿBySlav 51 (1990) 251s (Marie *Pardyová*).

e880 **Ousterhout** R. G., The architecture of the Kariye Camii in Istanbul: DumbO St 25. Wsh 1987. 292 p. $40. – ᴿByZ 83 (1990) 126-8 (C. *Mango*).

e881 *Schmalzbauer* Gudrun, Konstantinopel, ᵀ*Schaferdiek* K. [– Synoden, *al.*]: ➤ 857, TRE 19 (1990) 503-518 [-529].

e882 *Karakaya:* **Ökse** Tuba, Mitteleisenzeitliche Keramik Zentral-Ostanatoliens, mit dem Schwerpunkt Karakaya-Stauseegebiet am Euphrat: Berliner Beiträge VO 9. B 1988, Reimer. xx-301 p., 15 pl.; 6 maps. DM 88. – ᴿOLZ 85 (1990) 672-7 (J.-W. *Meyer*).

e883 *Karatepe: Darga* A. Muhibbe, ❶ Karatepe, pottery finds of Azatiwattaya's castle: ➤ 3, Mem. ALKIM U. 1986, 371-400; plan; XI pl.

e884 *Knidos* (Datça): *Berges* Dietrich, *Tuna* Numan, Ein Heiligtum bei Alt-Knidos: ArchAnz (1990) 19-35; 16 fig.

e885 *Kültepe:* **Özgüç** Tahsin, Kültepe-Kaniş II 1986 ➤ 3,e999: ᴿVDI 194 (1990) 171-7 (N. B. *Yankovskaya*).

e886 *Özgüç* Tahsin, A terracotta figurine from the city mound of Kanesh: ➤ 4, ꟼAMIRAN Ruth, Eretz-Israel 21 (1990) 74*-76*; 3 fig.

e887 *Günbattı Cahit,* ❶ Cinq tablettes de Kültepe sur la vente de maisons et quelques résultats tirés de celle-ci: Belleten 53, 206ss (1989) 51-59 + 4 facsimiles.

e888 *Teissier* Béatrice, A *Shakkanakku* seal impression from Kültepe: MARI 6 (1990) 649-653; 4 fig.

e889 *Kurban:* **Wilkinson** T. J., Town and country in southeastern Anatolia, 1. Settlement and land use at Kurban Höyük and other sites in the Lower Karababa Basin: OIP 109. Ch 1990, Univ. xviii-315 p. 0-918986-64-8.

e890 ᴱAlgaze Guillermo, Town and country in southeastern Anatolia, 2. The stratigraphic sequence at Kurban Höyük: OIP 110. Ch 1990, Univ. Or. Inst. xxxix-438 p.; volume of xiii-169 p. 0-918986-65-6 [OIAc Oc90].

e891 *Kyme:* İ*dil* Vedat, Neue Ausgrabungen im aeolischen Kyme: Belleten 53, 206ss (1989) 525-543; 45 phot. (545-8 Inschriften, *Holtheide* Bernard).

e892 *Limyris: Schweyer* Anne-Valérie, Observations sur une tombe sculptée de Limyris [Lycie-E]: RArchéol (1990) 367-386; 9 fig.

e893 *Miletus:* **Ehrhardt** Norbert, Milet und seine Kolonien 1983 ➤ 64,d64... 3,f10: ᴿAnzAltW 43 (1990) 118s (C. *Ulf*).

e894 *a) Parzinger* Hermann, Zur frühesten Besiedlung Milets; – *b) Pfrommer* Michael, Zum Fries des Dionysostempel von Milet: IstMitt 39 (1989) 415-431; 5 fig. / 433-439; pl. 42; map.

e895 *a) Altenhöfer* Erich, *Bol* Renate, Die Eroten-Jagdfries des Theaters in Milet; – *b) Günther* Wolfgang, Zu den Anfängen des Kaiserkults in Milet; – *c) Herrmann* Peter, Ein Tempel für Caligula in Milet?: IstMitt 39 (1989) 17-47; pl. 2-5 / 173-8; pl. 34,4 / 191-6.

e896 *Mina: Boardman* John, Al Mina [Orontes mouth, WOOLLEY L. 1930] and history: OxJArch 9 (1990) 109-190; 3 fig.

e897 *Nevalı Çori* [E of Lidar (Malatya), S of Çayönü]: AJA 94 (1990) 427; fig. 1-3 (M. *Mellink* < H. *Hauptmann*).

e898 *Nicaea:* **Atasöy** Nurhan, *Raby* Julian, İznik; the pottery of Ottoman Turkey: İstanbul univ. & Ekonomi Bankası. L 1989, Alexandra. 784 p.; 688 fig. + 303 colour. £120. – ᴿJRAS (1990) 162-4; 2 pl. (G. *Goodwin*).

e899 *Tite* M. S., İznik [Nicaea] pottery; an investigation of the methods of production: Archaeometry 31 (1989) 115-132.

e900 *Perge:* **Atik** Nese, Die Keramik aus den Südthermen von Perge [Diss. FrB 1989]: ArchAnz (1990) 143 (nur Titel).

e901 *İnan* Jale, Der Demetrios- und Apolloniosbogen in Perge: IstMitt 39 (1989) 237-244.

e902 **Sagalassos** (Pisidia) 5th 1989: AnSt 40 (1990) 185-198; 7 (foldout) fig.; pl. XXVII-XXIX (M. *Waelkens, al.*).

e903 **Sardis** 1987-9: ➤ 784, AJA 94 (1990) 310 (C. H. *Greenewalt*, summary).

e904 Sardis 1986: ➤ 500, ASOR reports 1990, 137-177, 37 fig. (C. H. *Greenewalt, al.*).

e905 *Bonz* Marianne P., The Jewish community of ancient Sardis; a reassessment of its rise to prominence: HarvClasPg 93 (1990) 343-359; 2 fig.

e906 *Botermann* Helga, Die Synagoge von Sardes; eine Synagoge aus dem 4. Jahrhundert?: ZNW 81 (1990) 103-121; 3 fig.

e907 **Ratte** Christopher, Lydian masonry and monumental architecture of Sardis: diss. Univ. California, [E]*Greenewalt* C. Berkeley 1990. iv-395 p. 90-06483. – OIAc JJ 90.

e908 **Seleucia:** *Faucouneau* J., L'inscription bilingue gréco-sidétique de Séleukia: AntClas 59 (1990) 166-171; 3 fig.

e909 **Toprakkale:** **Wartke** Ralf-Bernhard, Toprakkale; Untersuchungen zu den Metallobjekten im Vorderasiatischen Museum zu Berlin: Schriften zur Geschichte und Kultur des Alten Orients 22. B 1990, Akademie. 164 p.; 37 fig.; XLIII pl. 3-05-000921-7.

e910 **Troja:** *Easton* Donald F., *a)* Reconstructing SCHLIEMANN's Troy: ➤ 792, Schliemann 1989/90, 431-447; 13 fig.; – *b)* Schliemann's excavations at Troy: ➤ 891, Thracians 1984/90, 15-38; 14 fig.

e911 *Hrouda* Barthel, Noch einmal Troia: ➤ 3, Mem. ALKIM U. 1986, 197-202 + 1 pl.

e912 *Korfmann* Manfred, Zu Troias ältester 'Verteidigungsmauer': IstMitt 39 (1989) 307-313; 4 fig.

e913 **Sefériadès** Michel, Troie I; Matériaux pour l'étude des sociétés du Nord-Est Égéen au début du Bronze Ancien: RCiv 15, 1985 ➤ 1,e360 ... 4,g614: [R]BonnJbb 190 (1990) 608-610 (S. *Hiller*).

e914 *Tûr ʿAbdīn: Kettenhofen* Erich, Toponyme im Tûr ʿAbdīn: StClasOr 40 (1990) 441s.

e915 **Palmer** Andrew, Monk and mason on the Tigris frontier; the early history of Tur Abdin. C 1990, Univ. 265 p. $65 [JAAR 58, 535].

e916 *Xanthos:* **Childs** William A. P., *Demargne* Pierre, Le monument des néréides; le décor sculpté: Fouilles de Xanthos 8. P 1989, Klincksieck. xv-414 p.; 33 fig.; vol. of 161 phot., LXXIX dessins (14 foldout). 2-252-02594-8. – [R]AntClas 59 (1990) 591-4 (C. *Delvoye*).

e917 *Frézouls* Edmond, L'exploration du théâtre de Xanthos: CRAI (1990) 875-890; 5 fig.; 3 pl.

T8.9   *Armenia, Urarțu.*

e918 *Anson* E. M., Neoptolemus and Armenia: AncHB 4 (1990) 125-8.

e919 **Belli** Oktay, Van, die Hauptstadt der Urartäer (Ostanatolien)[3]. İstanbul 1988, NET Turist. 79 p.

e919* **Bock** Ulrich, Georgien und Armenien; zwei christliche Kulturlandschaften im Süden der Sowjetunion ➤ 5,e892: Köln 1988, DuMont. 352 p.; 131 fig.; 83 phot. + 36 color. – [R]IkiZ 80 (1990) 64 (B. *Spuler* †).

e920 [E]**Haas** Volkert, Das Reich Urartu 1984/6 ➤ 2,557 ... 4,g627*: [R]Klio 72 (1990) 575-9 (H. *Neumann*).

e921 *Işık* Cengiz, Urartäisch-griechischer religionsgeschichtlicher Gedankenaustausch, nach einer Darstellung: Belleten 54,209 (1990) 15-27; 2 fig.

e922 *Ivanchik* A. I., ❷ The Cimmerians and Urartu on the eve of Sargon II's eighth campaign: VDI 194 (1990) 3-19; Eng. 19.

e923 **Kleiss** Wolfram, Bastam II 1988 ➙ 4,g630: ᴿOLZ 85 (1990) 73-76 (G. R. H. *Wright*, Eng.).

e923* ᴱ**Sanders** Wilm, Armenien; kleines Volk mit grossem Erbe. Ha 1989, Kath. Akademie. 148 p. – ᴿIkiZ 80 (1990) 156 (B. *Spuler*).

e924 **Sisinni** Francesco, *al.*, ᴱ*Antonini* Chiara S., I tesori dei Kurgani del Caucaso settentrionale; nuove scoperte degli archeologi sovietici nell'Adygeja e nell'Ossezia settentrionale: R Museo Naz. Arti Popolari 1990s. R 1990, Leonardo-De Luca. I. 66 pp. + 67-199 (color. pl.); II. 62 p.; XX pl.; p. 85s. 88-7813-293-4; -338-8.

e925 **Uras** Esat, The Armenians in history and the Armenian question [1950;²]ᵀ, Ankara 1988, Documentary. xiv-1048 p. – ᴿJRAS (1990) 165-170 (C. J. *Walker*: Turkish viewpoint); REB 50 (1990) 252-6 (A. H. *Campolina Martins*: uma distorção).

e925* **Yıldırım** Recep, Urartu iğneleri [pins]: Yayınları 6/37. Ankara 1989, Türk Tarih Kurumu. xxi-133 p.; 38 pl. 975-16-0213-0.

e926 *Zimansky* Paul, Urartian geography and Sargon's eighth campaign: JNES 49 (1990) 1-21.

т9.1 **Cyprus.**

e927 **Daszewski** Wiktor A., Dionysos der Erlöser; Griechische Mythen im spätantiken Cypern: KulturGAW 2, 1985 ➙ 2,8870: ᴿRArtLv 21 (1988) 177s (Pauline *Donceel-Voûte*).

e928 **Hermary** Antoine, Catalogue des antiquités de Chypre, sculptures: Louvre. P 1989, Réunion Musées. 496 p.; 1000 fig. + 12 color. F 450. 2-7118-2279-6. – ᴿAntClas 59 (1990) 576-8 (R. *Laffineur*; p. 575 on SIMA 20/11s).

e929 *Knapp* A. Bernard, Cypriote archaeology; a review of [four] recent symposia: JAOS 110 (1990) 71-78.

e930 *Kosznicki* Michał, ❷ Greek and Persian policy in Cyprus 500-450 B.C.: Meander 44 (1989) 361-8.

e931 *Papageorghiou* Athanassios, Chronique des fouilles et découvertes archéologiques à Chypre en 1989: BCH 114 (1990) 941-985; ill.

e932 ᴱ**Peltenburg** E. J., Early society in Cyprus 1988/9 ➙ 5,861: ᴿAntiquity 64 (1990) 433s (A. B. *Knapp*).

e933 **Stewart** James R. † 1962, Corpus of Cypriote artefacts of the Early Bronze Age, 1. ᴱ*Stewart* Eve, *Åström* Paul: SIMA 3/1. Göteborg 1988, Åström. 197 p. 27 fig.; 29 pl. map. [Gnomon 63, 179; Diana L. *Bolger*].

e934 ᴱ**Tatton-Brown** Veronica, Cyprus and the East Mediterranean in the Iron Age 1988/9 ➙ 5,871: ᴿAntiqJ 70 (1990) 126 (D. J. *Symons*); ClasR 40 (1990) 415-7 (H. W. *Catling*).

─────────

e935 *Alasia:* *Charpin* Dominique, Une mention d'Alašiya dans une lettre de Mari [*une* ville de Chypre, plausiblement Enkomi]: RAss 84 (1990) 125-7; facsim.

e936 **Courtois** J. C., Alasia III. objets... d'Enkomi 1984 ➙ 2,b308: ᴿGnomon 62 (1990) 470-2 (K. *Kilian*).

e937 *Masson* Olivier, Un vieux problème: Alasia = Chypre? [ᴹᴱᴿᴿᴵᴸᴸᴱᴱˢ R. 1987]: RÉG 103 (1990) 231-5.

e938 **Merrillees** Robert S., Alashia revisited 1987 ➤ 3,f64; 4,g646: ᴿBO 47 (1990) 795-801 (A. B. *Knapp*: M. is by profession a diplomat).

e939 *Amathous:* Amathonte 1989: BCH 114 (1990) 987-1037 (A. *Hermary, al.*).

e940 *Aupert* Pierre, Progrès de l'archéologie et de l'histoire de l'étéochypriote Amathonte depuis OHNEFALSCH-RICHTER: FolOr 27 (1990) 81-88: 89-92 = 4 fig.; map.

e941 *Parayre* Dominique, Deux chapiteaux hathoriques à Amathonte; étude des disques solaires ailés: BCH 114 (1990) 215-240; 42 fig.

e942 **Queyrel** Anne, Les figurines hellénistiques...: Amathonte 4, 1988 ➤ 4,g648; 5,e643: ᴿAntClas 59 (1990) 597s (G. *Raepsaet*).

e943 *Episkopi:* **Swiny** Stuart, Episkopi Phaneromeni 2: SIMA 74,2, 1986 ➤ 2,b310; 5,e649: ᴿAntClas 59 (1990) 582s (R. *Laffineur*).

e944 *Kalavasos Tenta:* **Todd** I. A., Vasilikos Valley project 6, excavations at Kalavasos-Tenta I [1976-9, 1984]: SIMA 71/6. Göteborg 1987, Åström. 202 p.; 57 fig.; 41 pl. – ᴿPEQ 122 (1990) 149s (Carolyn *Elliott*).

e945 *Kazaphani:* **Nicolaou** Ino & Kyriacos, Kazaphani, a middle/late Cypriot tomb at Kazaphani-Ayios Andronikos, T. 2A.B. Nicosia 1989, Department of Antiquities. x-121 p.; 18 fig.; 39 pl. – ᴿClasR 40 (1990) 414s (H. W. *Catling*); RB 97 (1990) 474s (J.-B. *Humbert*).

e946 *Khirokitia:* ᴱ**Lebrun** Alain, Fouilles récentes à Khirokitia (Chypre) 1983-1986: Mém. 18. P 1989, RCiv. 288 p.; 71 fig.; 24 pl. F 178 pa. 2-86538-197-8 [Antiquity 64,676].

e947 *Kition:* **Yon** Marguerite, *Caubet* Annie, Kition-Bamboula III...: RCiv Mém. 56, 1985 ➤ 2,b316; 5,e654: ᴿAntClas 59 (1990) 581s (R. *Laffineur*); Syria 65 (1988) 239-241 (V. *Cook*).

e948 *Lemba* project 1988: Levant 22 (1990) 155 (E. *Peltenburg*).

e949 **Peltenburg** Edgar J., *al.*, Lemba... 1976-83: SIMA 70/1, 1985 ➤ 1,e398... 5,e656: ᴿAntClas 59 (1990) 583s (R. *Laffineur*).

e950 *Maa-Palaeokastro:* **Karageorghis** Vassos, *Demas* M., *al.*, Excavations at Maa-Palaeokastro 1979-1986. Nicosia 1988, Dept. Antiq./Nicolaou. x-498 p.; vi-254 pl.; vol. of 22 pl.; 9 plans. – ᴿRArchéol (1990) 428s (A. *Hermary*).

T9.3 *Graecia,* **Greece** – mainland sites in alphabetical order.

e951 **Lolos** Yannos B., The Late Helladic I pottery of the southwestern Peloponnesos and its local characteristics: SIMA pocket 56. Göteborg 1987, Åström. xiv-611 p.; vol. of 674 fig. $128. – ᴿAJA 94 (1990) 500s (L. P. *Day*).

e952 *a) Papachatzis* Nicolaus, *Loucas* Ioannis, Chronique des fouilles [grecques]; – *b) Motte* André, Chronique des rencontres scientifiques et des expositions: Kernos 3 (1990) 367-375 / 477-386 [vol. 4, 313-329].

e953 *Pariente* Anne, Chronique des fouilles et découvertes archéologique en Grèce en 1989: BCH 114 (1990) 703-850; ill.

e954 *Sherratt* E. S., 'Reading the texts'; archaeology and the Homeric question: Antiquity 64 (1990) 807-824.

e955 *Aegina:* *Johnston* Alan W., Aegina, Aphaia-Temple, XIII. The storage amphorae: ArchAnz (1990) 37-64; 18 fig.

e956 *Argos* 1989: BCH 114 (1990) 851-875 (Anne *Pariente, al.*).

e957 *Athenae:* **Aleshire** Sara B., The Athenian Asklepieion; the people, their dedications, and the inventories. Amst 1989, Gieben. 385 p.; 12 pl.

e958 **Frantz** A., *al.*, The Athenian agora 24. Princeton 1988, American School Athens. xxi-156 p.; 77 pl. 0-87661-224-9. – RJRS 80 (1990) 250s (B. *Ward-Perkins*).

e959 *Giovannini* Adalberto, Le Parthénon, le trésor d'Athéna et le tribut des alliés: Historia 39 (1990) 129-148.

e960 *Kuznetsov* V. D., *a)* ❻ The builders [not 'building' as p. 255] of the Erechtheion: VDI 195 (1990) 27-44: Eng. 44; – *b)* Some questions of public construction works in Athens: SovArch (1990,4) 45-50.

e961 **Moore** Mary, *Philippides* Mary, Attic black-figured pottery: Athenian agora 23, 1986 ➤ 3,f100 ... 5,e679: RGnomon 62 (1990) 663-5 (J. *Burow*); Phoenix 44,1 (Toronto 1990) 99-102 (M. F. *Kilmer*).

e962 *Oikonomides* A. I. N., The Athenian cults of the three Aglauroi and their sanctuaries below the Acropolis of Athens: AncW 21,1s (1990) 11-17 (-22).

e963 *Schädler* Ulrich, Ionisches und Attisches am sogenannten Erechtheion in Athen: ArchAnz (1990) 361-378; 10 fig.

e964 *Corinthus:* *Edwards* Charles M., [PAUSANIAS' temple of] Tyche at Corinth: Hesperia 59 (1990) 542; 2 fig.; pl. 83-88.

e965 **Risser** Martha K., Corinthian Conventionalizing pottery: diss. Pennsylvania, DDeVries K. Ph 1989. 205 p. 90-15158. – DissA 51 (1990s) 204-A.

e966 *Koester* Helmut, Melikertes at Isthmia; a Roman mystery cult: ➤ 122, FMALHERBE A., Greeks 1990, 355-366.

e967 **Sturgeon** Mary C., Isthmia 4, Sculpture 1, 1987 ➤ 5,e687: RAJA 94 (1990) 159s (Susan E. *Kane*); ClasR 40 (1990) 421s (C. A. *Picón*); Gnomon 62 (1990) 183-5 (H. R. *Goette*).

e968 *Williams* Charles K., *Zervos* Orestes H., Excavations at Corinth, 1989; the Temenos of Temple E: Hesperia 59 (1990) 325-369; 5 fig.; pl. 57-68.

e969 *Delphi:* *Laroche* Didier, *Nenna* Marie-Dominique, Le trésor de Sicyone et ses fondations: BCH 114 (1990) 241-284; 26 fig.

e970 **Roux** Georges, La terrasse d'Attale I, relevés et restaurations par Olivier *Callot*: Fouilles de Delphes 2. P 1987, de Boccard. 163 p.; 21 fig.; vol. of 213 pl. – RAntClas 59 (1990) 584s (G. *Raepsaet*).

e971 *Roux* Georges, Deux riches offrandes dans le sanctuaire de Delphes; Le stylidion de Cyzique [Anth. 6,342]; le lion d'or de Crésus [HEROD. 1,50]: JSav (1990) 221-245; 10 fig.

e972 *Khostia:* EFossey John M., *Morin* Jacques, Khostia 1983: 1986 ➤ 3, f112; 90-70265-60-5: RAntClas 59 (1990) 569 (R. *Laffineur*).

e973 *Locris:* **Katzonopoulou** Dora, Studies of the eastern cities of Opuntian Lokris: Halai, Kyrtones, Korseia, Bumiteleia: diss. Cornell. Ithaca NY 1990. 221 p. 91-06212. – DissA 51 (1990s) 3118-A.

e974 *Methon:* *Hatzopoulos* Miltiade, *al.*, Deux sites pour Méthone de Macédoine: BCH 114 (1990) 639-668.

e975 *Mycenae:* *French* Elizabeth, Possible northern intrusions at Mycenae [Handmade Burnished Ware, 'of course'] ➤ 891, Thracians 1984/90, 39-51; 10 fig.

e976 *Carlier* Pierre, La double face du pouvoir royal dans le monde mycénien: ➤ 760, Du pouvoir 1983/90, 37-52.

e977 *Cline* Eric, An unpublished Amenhotep III faience plaque from Mycenae: JAOS 110 (1990) 200-212; 4 fig.; 3 pl.

e978 ᴱ**Demakopoulou** Katie, The Mycenaean world; five centuries of early Greek culture, 1600-1100 B.C. Athenai 1988, Ministry of Culture. 280 p.; 235 color. pl.; 2 maps. – ᴿAJA 94 (1990) 499-500 (J. B. *Rutter*).

e979 *Mayer* Adele, Wallpaintings from the area of the prehistoric cemetery, Mycenae: AnBritAth 85 (1990) 213-223; 5 fig. [223-270, *al.*, on Mycenae].

e980 **Papadopoulos** Thanasis J., Mycenaean Achaia; SIMA 55/1, (ᴰ1972) 1979 ➤ 60,u243; 65,b612: ᴿBO 47 (1990) 808-810 (Susan *Sherratt*).

e981 **Schachermeyr** Fritz, Mykene und das Hethiterreich 1986 ➤ 2,b347; 4,g709: ᴿMeditHR 5 (1990) 82-85 (A. *Kempinski*).

e982 **Taylour** W. D., Well built Mycenae I. The excavations 1981 ➤ 63,d651: ᴿGnomon 62 (1990) 80s (S. *Hiller*).

e983 *Nemea: Wright* James C., *al.*, The Nemea Valley archaeological project; a preliminary report: Hesperia 59 (1990) 579-659; 27 fig.; pl. 93-97.

e984 *Olympia,* Neue Ausgrabungen: AntWelt 21 (1990) 177-188; 15 (color.) fig. (H. *Kyrieleis*).

e985 *Paradeisos:* **Hellström** Pontus, Paradeisos, a Late Neolithic settlement in Aegean Thrace: Memoir 7. Sto 1987, Medelhavsmuseet. 143 p. – ᴿAJA 94 (1990) 681s (M. *Fotiadis*).

e986 *Pylos:* **Coleman** John E., Excavations at Pylos...: Hesperia supp 21, 1986 ➤ 3,f126; 5,e702: ᴿAntClas 59 (1990) 572s (R. *Laffineur*); PraehZts 65 (1990) 84-86 (Maria *Sipsie-Eschbach*).

e987 **Stavrianopoulou** Eftychia, Untersuchungen zur Struktur des Reiches von Pylos; die Stellung der Ortschaften im Lichte der Linear B-Texte: SIMA pocket 77. Partille 1989, Åström. 252 p.

e988 *Sparta:* **Cartledge** Paul, **Spawforth** Anthony, Hellenistic and Roman Sparta; a tale of two cities: States and Cities of Ancient Greece. L 1989, Routledge. xii-304 p.; 2 maps [Kernos 4, 333, I. *Loucas*: subtitle 'a table of two cities'].

e989 *Lafranchis* Tristan, Mistra: Notre Histoire 65, mars 1990 [< EsprVie 100 (1990) 377-9, J. *Daoust*].

e990 *Torone* (Chalkidike) 1988: JMeditArch 3 (1990) 93-142; 31 fig.; pl. 30-34 (A. *Cambitoglou*, J. K. *Papadopoulos*).

e991 *Vergina: Andronikos* Manolis, ☉ The royal tombs in Vergina: VDI 192 (1990) 107-129; 15 fig. [161-6, *Neverov* O. Ya].

---

e992 **Rolle** Renate, The world of the Scythians. L 1989, Batsford. 141 p.; 97 fig.; 22 pl. £20. 0-7134-6109-8. – ᴿAntiquity 64 (1990) 174s (T. *Taylor*; also on HARTOG F., Herodotus 1988).

e992* **Mertens-Horn** M., Die Löwenkopf-Wasserspeier des griechischen Westens im 6. und 5. Jht. v.Chr. im Vergleich mit den Löwen des griechischen Mutterlandes: DAI-R Erg.-H. 28. Mainz 1988, von Zabern. 214 p.; 84 pl.; 3 foldouts. DM 128. – ᴿGymnasium 97 (1990) 279-281 (Helga *Herderjürgen*).

T9.4 Creta.

e993 *Bammer* Anton, Wien und Kreta; Jugendstil und minoische Kunst: JbÖsA 60-H (1990) 129-151; 27 fig.

e994 **Bernd** Carl A., Creta erfahren; zu Fuss und mit dem Fahrzeug zu Palästen, Klöstern und Kastellen. Salzburg 1989, O. Müller. 321 p.; 30 maps. DM 40. – ᴿErbAuf 66 (1990) 75 (A. B).

e995 **Castleden** Rodney, Minoans; life in Bronze Age Crete. L 1990, Routledge. xiii-210 p.; 65 fig.; 20 pl. 0-415-040'70-1.

e996 **Dabney** Mary K., A comparison of correlations in the spatial distribution of archaeological remains from prepalatial and palatial period settlements and tombs in central Crete: diss. Columbia. NY 1989. 253 p. 90-20514. – DissA 51 (1990s) 905-A.

e997 ᴱ**Darque** Pascal, *Poursat* Jean-Claude, L'iconographie minoënne 1983/5 ➤ 1,868; 2,b365: ᴿGnomon 62 (1990) 50-61 (W.-D. *Niemeier*).

e998 **Gondicas** Daphné, Recherches sur la Crète occidentale [➤ 5,e710] de l'époque géométrique à la conquête romaine; inventaire des sources archéologiques et textuelles, position du problème. Amst 1988, Hakkert. iii-427 p.; 28 pl.; 2 maps. 90-256-0942-2. – ᴿAntClas 59 (1990) 490-3 (D. *Viviers*).

e999 **Kofkou** Anna, Crète; tous les musées et les sites archéologiques, ᵀ*Tournay* B. de. Athenai 1989, Ekdotike. 288 p.; 358 (color.) ill.; 2 maps. – ᴿKernos 3 (1990) 390s (Éveline *Loucas-Durie*).

g1 **Krause** Siegfried, Vorpalastzeitliche minoische Plastik: Diss. FrB 1989. – ArchAnz (1990) 145, nur Titel.

g2 *Lebessi* Angeliki, *Muhly* Polymnia, Aspects of Minoan cult; sacred enclosures; the evidence from the Syme sanctuary (Crete): ArchAnz (1990) 314-336; 25 fig.

g3 **Raison** Jacques, (*Stürmer* Veit,) Bulletin des études égéo-anatoliennes; l'archéologie de la Crète et ses connexions (jusqu'à la fin du IIᵉ millénaire): RÉG 103 (1990) 111-200.

g4 **Walberg** Gisela, Tradition and innovation; essays in Minoan art 1986 ➤ 4,g743: ᴿAntClas 59 (1990) 561s (R. *Laffineur*).

---

g5 *Gortyna:* ᴱ**Di Vita** A., Gortina I: MgScuola Atene 3. R 1988, Bretschneider. 424 p.; 285 fig., 1 color.; 1 foldout. 88-7062-647-4. – ᴿAntClas 59 (1990) 585-7 (D. *Viviers*).

g6 *Knossos: Bennet* John, Knossos in context; comparative perspectives on the Linear B administration of LM II-III Crete: AJA 94 (1990) 193-211.

g7 **Castleden** Rodney, The Knossos labyrinth; a new view of the 'Palace of Minos' at Knossos. L 1990, Routledge. xii-205 p.; 54 fig.; 20 pl. £18. 0-415-03315-2. – ᴿAntiqJ 69 (1989!) 347s (K. *Branigan*: superficial, unconvincing); GreeceR 37 (1990) 252s (B. A. *Sparkes*).

g8 ᴱ**Hägg** Robin, *Marinatos* Nanno, The function of the Minoan palaces 1984/7 ➤ 4,739; 5,e709: ᴿGnomon 62 (1990) 435-441 (W. *Schiering*); JAOS 110 (1990) 126s (Gloria *London*); MeditHistR 5 (1990) 88-93 (R. B. *Koehl*).

g9 *Poblome* J., *Dumon* Catherine, A Minoan building program? Some comments on the unexplored mansion at Knossos: AcArchLov 26s (1987s) 69-73 + 12 fig.

g10 **Raison** Jacques, Le palais du second millénaire à Knossos I. Le quartier nord: ÉcFrÉtCrét 28, P 1988, Geuthner ➤ 5,e715: 310 p.; 8 fig.; vol. of 173 p., 154 pl.; 12 plans: ᴿAJA 94 (1990) 689s (J. *Bennet*); PraehZts 65 (1990) 86-88, 1 fig. (Imma *Kilian*).

g11 *Malia* 1989: BCH 114 (1990) 908-939 (J.-C. *Poursat, al.*).

g12 **Phovini:** *Sakellarakis* John, Death in Minoan Crete [Phovini excavations, 10 k from Knossos]: ILN 278,7093 (Spring 1990) 92s.

g13 *Giesecke* H.-E., Menschenopfer [... SAKELLARAKIS]: JPrehRel 3s (1989s) 45-47.

T9.5   Insulae graecae.

g14 **Åström** Paul, *al.*, Studies in Aegean chronology: SIMA pocket 25, 1984 ➤ 65,b643 ... 3,f148: ᴿBO 47 (1990) 214-6 (T. R. *Bryce*).

g15 ᴱ**Buchholz** Hans-Günter, Ägäische Bronzezeit. Da 1987, Wiss.   xii-555 p.; 126 fig.; 16 pl. DM 175. – ᴿOLZ 85 (1990) 271-4 (P. *Taracha*).

g16 *Cherry* J. F., The first colonization of the Mediterranean islands; a review of recent research [7000-4000 for Aegean, earlier than was supposed; 10000 for Cyprus Akrotiri; around 8000 for some large-island groups], JMeditArch 3 (1990) 145-221.

g17 **Friedrich** Horst, VELIKOVSKY, SPANUTH und die Seevölker-Diskussion; Argumente ... [German and English on facing pages] Velikovsky, Spanuth, and the Sea Peoples discussion; arguments for a migration of Atlanto-European Late Bronze Age megalithic peoples towards 700 B.C. to the Mediterranean. Worthsee 1988, auct. [OIAc JJ89].

g18 **Immerwahr** Sara A., Aegean painting in the Bronze Age. Univ. Park 1990, Penn, State Univ. 241 p.; 41 fig.; 92 pl. + 23 color. $75. 0-271-00628-5 [Antiquity 65,172, P. *Warren*].

g19 **Lambrou-Phillippson** C., Hellenorientalia; the Near Eastern presence in the Bronze Age Aegean, ca. 3000-1100 B.C.: interconnections based on the material record and the written evidence plus orientalia; a catalogue of Egyptian, Mesopotamian, Mitannian, Syro-Palestinian, Cypriot and Asia Minor objects from the Bronze Age Aegean [< diss. Athens] ᵀ; SIMA pocket 95. Göteborg 1990, Åström. 503 p.; 82 pl. 91-89098-87-X [OIAc F91,14].

g20 **Treuil** René, Le Néolithique et le Bronze ancien égéens 1983 ➤ 64,d190; 1,e490: ᴿÉtClas 58 (1990) 91 (C. *Baurain*).

g21 **Vanschoonwinkel** Jacques, L'Égée à la fin du IIᵉ millénaire (env. 1250-900 av. J.-C.); essai de synthèse fondé sur les témoignages archéologiques et les sources écrites: diss. LvN 1987, ᴰ*Hackens* T. – RArtLv 21 (1988) 201-4.

g22 **Warren** Peter, *Hankey* Vronwy, Aegean Bronze Age chronology 1989 ➤ 5,e723: ᴿAntiquity 64 (1990) 414s (Susan *Sherratt*).

g23 **Cyclades:** **Barber** R. L. N., The Cyclades in the Bronze Age 1987 ➤ 4,g768; 5,e227: ᴿAJA 94 (1990) 497-9 (J. L. *Davis*).

g24 *Gautier* J., Centres de production et échanges céramiques dans les Cyclades (apport de la microscopic optique): RArchéom 14 (1990) 65-85; 24 color. phot.

g25 *Rougemont* Georges, Géographie historique des Cyclades; l'homme et le milieu dans l'archipel: JSav (1990) 199-220; map.

g26 *Délos* 1989: BCH 114 (1990) 892-907 (A. *Farnoux, al.*).

g27 *Brunet* Michèle, Contribution à l'histoire rurale de Délos aux époques classique et hellénistique: BCH 114 (1990) 669-682.

g28 *Courbin* Paul, Les monuments aux hexagones du sanctuaire délien: RArchéol (1990) 361-6; 6 fig.

g28* **Kreeb** M., Untersuchungen zur figürlichen Anstaltung delischer Privathäuser. Ch 1988. 357 p.; 14 pl. [TopoiOO 1, 101, F. *Queyrel*].

g29 *Keos:* **Bikaki** Aliki H., Ayia Irini, the potters' marks: Keos 4, 1984 ➤ 1,e496*b*; 4,g764: ᴿGnomon 62 (1990) 181-3 (S. *Hiller*).

g30 **Caskey** Miriam E., The temple at Ayia Irini; the statues: Keos 2/1, 1986 ➤ 3,f146... 5,e731; ᴿArchWroc 40 (1989) 169 (B. *Rutkowski*); JPrehR 2 (1988) 61s (A. D. *Moore*).

g31 **Cummer** W. W., *Schofield* Elizabeth, *al.*, Ayia Irini, house A: Keos 3, 1984 ➤ 5,e732: ᴿGnomon 61 (1989) 724-7 (S. *Hiller*).

g32 **Davis** Jack L., Ayia Irini period V: Keos 5,1986 ➤ 2,b396; 3,f162; 3-8053-0841-8: ᴿAntClas 59 (1990) 564s (R. *Laffineur*; 565s, CASKEY M., Temple); JHS 110 (1990) 260s (G. *Cadogan*).

g33 **Georgiou** Hara S., Ayia Irini; specialized domestic and industrial pottery: Keos 6, 1986 ➤ 2,b395... 4,g763: ᴿRBgPg 68 (1990) 233s (J. *Vanschoonwinkel*).

g34 *Kos:* **Stambolidis** N. C., Ⓖ *Ho bōmos*... The altar of Dionysus on Cos, essays on Greek plastic and architecture. Athēnai 1987. 285 p.; 84 pl. [TopoiOO 1, 98-100, A. *Farnoux*].

g35 *Lemnos:* **Pernicka** E., *al.*, On the composition and provenance of metal artefacts from Poliochni on Lemnos: OxJArch 9 (1990) 263-298; 9 fig. (map).

g36 *Melos:* **Renfrew** C., Archaeology of cult – Phylakopi 1986 ➤ 2,b399... 4,g767; ᴿPraehZts 65 (1990) 89-94 (K. *Kilian*).

g37 *Rhodus:* **Luttrell** A., Rhodes and Jerusalem: 1291-1411: ByzFor 12 (1987) 187-207 [< ByZ 83,291].

g39 *Thasos* 1989: BCH 114 (1990) 881-891 (J.-Y. *Empereur, al.*).

g40 ᴱ**Wagner** Günther A., *Weisgerber* Gerd, Antike Edel- und Buntmetallgewinnung auf Thasos: 'Der Anschnitt' Beih 6 / Veröff. 42. Bochum 1988, Bergbau-Museum. 279 p.; 291 fig.; 2 foldout color. pl. 3-921533-40-6 [TopOO 1, 71-75, A. *Müller*].

g41 *Thera:* **McCoy** Floyd W., *Haiken* Grant, Anatomy of an eruption; how a terrifying series of explosions reshaped the Minoan island of Thera: Archaeology 43,3 (1990) 42-49; color. ill.

g42 *Manning* S. W., The Thera eruption; the third congress [3-9.IX.1982] and the problem of date: Archaeometry 32 (1990) 91-100.

g43 **Morgan** Lyvia, The miniature wall paintings of Thera; a study in Aegean culture and iconography. C 1988, Univ. xix-234 p.; 200 fig.; 3 colour. pl. $66. 0-521-24727-6. – ᴿClasW 83 (1989s) 376 (Karen P. *Foster*).

T9.6   **Urbs Roma.**

g44 *Ammerman* Albert J., On the origins of the Forum Romanum: AJA 94 (1990) 627-645; 6 fig.

g45 *Belloni* Gian Guido, La colonna traiana; qualche questione: Aevum 64 (1990) 95-102.

g46 **Boatwright** Mary T., Hadrian and the city of Rome 1987 ➤ 3,f178... 5,e750: ᴿAJA 94 (1990) 359s (J. C. *Anderson*); AmÉCS 45 (1990) 911-3 (Y. *Thébert*); Latomus 49 (1990) 283s (Christiane *Delplace*); RPg 63 (1989) 343s (J.-C. *Richard*).

g47 **Brucia** Margaret A., Tiber Island in ancient and medieval Rome: diss. Fordham, ᴰ*Evans* H. NY 1990. 183 p. 90-25914. – DissA 51 (1990s) 1601-A.

g48 ᴱBury E.,   Urbs Roma; lateinische Quellentexte zur Geschichte der Stadt und zu ihren Bauwerken: Altspr. TAbh.   Stu 1986, Klett.   134 p.; 20 fig.; 6 maps.   3-12-656200-0. – ᴿGrazBei 17 (1990) 283s (F. *Witek*).

g49 **Coarelli** Filippo,   Il Foro Boario 1988 ➔ 5,e753:   ᴿBabesch 65 (1990) 190-2 (T. L. *Heres*); GGA 242 (1990) 173-182 (R. *Neudecker*); Gnomon 62 (1990) 730-4; 3 fig. (T. P. *Wiseman*); Latomus 49 (1990) 230-4 (J. *Debergh*).

g50 *de Grummond* Nancy T.,   Pax Augusta and the horae on the Ara Pacis Augustae: AJA 94 (1990) 663-677.

g51 *Esch* Arnold,   Die Via Cassia in der Landschaft: AntWelt 21 (1990) 134-158; 34 color. fig.

g52 **Farmer** William R., *Kereszty* Roch,   Peter and Paul in the Church of Rome; the ecumenical potential of a forgotten perspective.   NY 1990, Paulist.   x-186 p. $12 [TR 87,76].   0-8091-3102-1.

g53 *Kleiner* Fred S.,   The arches of Vespasian in Rome: MiDAI-R 97 (1990) 127-136; pl. 32-33.

g54 *Koeppel* Gerhard M.,   Die historischen Reliefs der römischen Kaiserzeit VII. Der Bogen des Septimius Severus, die Decennalienbasis und der Konstantinsbogen: BonnJbb 190 (1990) 1-64; 29 fig. [186 (1986) 1-90, IV. varia].

g55 *Lange* Judith, *Vendittelli* Laura,   La cenerentola dei monumenti [piramide di Cestio]: ArchViva 9,13 (1990) 10-15; ill.

g56 *Lefèvre* Eckard,   Das Bild-Programm des Apollo-Tempels auf dem Palatin: Xenia 24.   Konstanz 1989, Univ.   57 p.; 29 fig. DM 26,80. – ᴿGrazBei 17 (1990) 261-4 (F. *Felten*).

g57 *Milella* Marina, *al.*,   Foro Traiano; contributi per una ricostruzione storica e architettonica: ArchClasR 41 (1989) 33-214; 117 fig.

g58 **Nardoni** D.,   La colonna Ulpia Traiana.   R 1986, Ed. Letteratura e Scienze.   190 p. Lit. 20.000. – ᴿHelmantica 40 (1989) 500s (J. *Oroz Reta*).

g59 *a*) *Pensabene* Patrizio, [Provenance determination:] The arch of Constantine; marble samples; – *b*) *Mello* Emilio, *al.*,   A computer-based pattern recognition approach to the provenance study of Mediterranean marbles through trace elements analysis: ➔ 806, Marble 1988, 411-8 (453-462; 5 fig.) / 283-291; 4 fig.

g60 *Rose* Charles B.,   'Princes' and barbarians on the Ara Pacis: AJA 94 (1990) 453-467; 12 fig.

g61 *Schütz* Michael,   Zur Sonnenuhr des Augustus auf dem Marsfeld [gegen Bᴜᴄʜɴᴇʀ E. 1982]: Gymnasium 97 (1990) 432-457; 7 fig.

g62 *Simonelli* Antonella,   La tradizione classica e l'origine del Capitolium: AtenRom 35 (1990) 71-77.

g63 **Vance** William L.,   America's Rome; I. Classical Rome; 2. Catholic and contemporary Rome.   NHv 1989, Yale Univ.   xxiv-454 p.; 155 pl. + 12 color.; xx-498 p.; 55 pl. + 8 color. $30 each. 0-300-03670-1; -4453-4. – ᴿClasW 84 (1990s) 58s (Susan F. *Wiltshire*).

g64 *Wegner* Max,   Römische Miszellen: JhÖsA 60-H (1990) 103-119; 8 fig.

T9.7   *Roma,* **Catacumbae.**

g65 **Baruffa** Antonio,   Le catacombe di San Callisto; storia, archaeologia, fede 1989 ➔ 4,g807; 5,e767:   ᴿGregorianum [70 (1989) 598s ➔ 5,e767 dated 1988] 71 (1990) 608 (J. *Janssens*); PalCl 69 (1990) 90 (G. *Del Col*).

g67 *Bergquist* Anders,   Bona fide? Gᴜᴀʀᴅᴜᴄᴄɪ on the bones of St. Peter [1989]: Antiquity 64 (1990) 412s.

g68 **Deckers** Johannes G., *al.*,   Die Katakombe 'Santi Marcellino e Pietro' 1987 ➤ 3,f211 ... 5,e772: ᴿRHE 85 (1990) 720-4 (Pauline *Donceel-Voûte*); RömQ 85 (1990) 236-245 (A. *Weiland*).

g69 *Falasca* Stefania,   *a*) Where are Peter's bones? [M. GUARDUCCI interview]: 30 Days 3,2 (SF 1990) 38-45 [< NTAbs 34,354]; – *b*) Dov'è finito Pietro? M. GUARDUCCI... 'c'è chi tenta di occultare le reliquie': 30 Giorni 8,2 (1990) 40-45.

g70 **Ferrua** Antonio,   Catacombe sconosciute; una pinacoteca del IV secolo sotto la Via Latina.² F 1990, Nardini.   156 p.; 150 (color.) fig. Lit. 70.000. – ᴿCC 141 (1990,4) 617s (C. *Capizzi*).

g71 **Guarducci** Margherita,   La tomba di san Pietro 1989 ➤ 5,e778:   ᴿCC 141 (1990,1) 460-7 (A. *Ferrua*).

g72 **Guyon** Jean,   Le cimètière Aux deux lauriers 1987 ➤ 4,g814; 5,e779: ᴿJEH 40 (1989) 589-591 (W. H. C. *Frend*).

g73 **Konikoff** Adia,   Sarcophagi from Jewish catacombs of ancient Rome 1986 ➤ 2,b437... 5,e381:   ᴿJQR 81 (1990s) 169 (R. *Hachlili*).

g74 *Lange* Ulrike, *Sörries* Reiner,   Die Procla-Platte; eine polychrome Loculusverschlussplatte aus der anonymen Katakombe an der Via Anapo in Rom: AntWelt 21 (1990) 45-56; 18 (color.) fig.

g75 *Pergola* Philippe,   Die Domitilla-Katakombe: Boreas 13 (Münster 1990) 103-112; pl. 20.

g76 *Rasch* Jürgen J.,   Zur Rekonstruktion der Andreasrotunde an Alt-St.-Peter: RömQ 85 (1990) 1-18; 7 fig.

g76* *Rordorf* W.,   La commémoration des martyrs dans le christianisme des premiers siècles: ➤ 618, Commémoration 1986/8, 173-180.

g77 *Rutgers* Leonard V.,   Überlegungen zu den jüdischen Katakomben Roms: ➤ 100*, ᶠKÖTTING B., JbAC 33 (1990) 140-157.

g78 **Sakkos** Stergios N., Ⓖ *Ho Pétros kaì hē Rōmē*... Peter and Rome, I. testimony of the NT.   Thessaloniki 1989.   135 p.; Eng. 103-5; deutsch 100-2.

g79 *Vismara* Cinzia,   Ancora sugli Ebrei di Roma [... Vigna Randanini]: ArchClasR 38s (1986ss) 150-161; 1 fig.; pl. LXXI.

T9.8   *Roma,* **Ars palaeochristiana.**

g80 **Arbeiter** Achim,   Alt-St. Peter 1988 ➤ 4,g822; 5,e785:   ᴿTR 86 (1990) 377-381 (H.-R. *Seeliger*).

g81 *Barcley Lloyd* Joan E.,   Das goldene Gewand der Muttergottes in der Bildersprache mittelalterlicher und frühchristlicher Mosaiken in Rom, ᵀ*Spath* Sigrid: RömQ 85 (1990) 66-85.

g81* *Bejaoui* Fethi,   Documents d'archéologie et d'épigraphie paléochrétiennes récemment découverts en Tunisie dans la région de Jilma: CRAI (1990) 256-277; 15 fig. (mosaïques...).

g82 **Blaauw** Sible de,   Cultus et decor, liturgie en architectuur in laat-antiek en middeleuws Rome, Basilica Salvatoris Sanctae Mariae Sancti Petri: diss. Delft 1987, Eburon.   670 p.; ill.   90-70879-80-8. – ᴿBijdragen 51 (1990) 330 (J. C. *Delbeek*).

g83 *Bratož* Rajko,   Die Geschichte des frühen Christentums im Gebiet zwischen Sirmium und Aquileia im Licht der neueren Forschung: Klio 72 (1990) 508-550.

g84 *Duval* Noël,   Les nouveautés de l'archéologie tunisienne; le site d'Hʳ [? Ḥajar] el Gousset [ou Goussa (ce toponyme indique le souvenir d'une église) p. 318] (Études d'archéologie chrétienne nord-africaine, XXI), à propos du Bulletin des Travaux de l'Institut National d'Archéologie et Arts (Tunis), comptes-rendus avril-juin 1988 (95 p.; résumé ❹): RÉAug 36 (1990) 315-327; 10 fig.

g85 **Ferrua** Antonio,   Note e giunte alle iscrizioni cristiane antiche della Sicilia.   Vaticano 1989, Pont. Ist. Archeologia Cristiana.   155 p.; ill. Lit. 35.000. – ᴿCC 141 (1990,2) 517s (J. *Janssens*).

g86 **Karol** Dieter,   Die frühchristliche [AT] Wandmalerei 1987 ➔ 3,f227... 5,e789:   ᴿScripTPamp 22 (1990) 652s (A. *Viciano*).

---

g87 [*Chaste* A., *Giacometti* M.] ᵀᴱSCHNIEPER Robert,   Die Sixtinische Kapelle.   Z 1986, Benziger.   271 p.; ill. DM 220. – ᴿZkT 112 (1990) 493-5 (M. *Illmer*).

g87* *Daltrop* Georg,   Die Rezeption des Konstantinsbogens im Quattrocentozyklus der Sistinischen Kapelle: 81*, ᶠHÜRTEN H. 1988, 167-176; 4 fig.

T9.9   *(Roma) Imperium occidentale,* **Europa.**

g88 *Archer* William C.,   The paintings in the alae of the Casa dei Vettii and a definition of the Fourth Pompeian style: AJA 94 (1990) 95-123; 19 fig.

g89 *a) Bernstein* Frances,   Pompeian women and the programmata; – *b) Dwyer* Eugene,   Decorum and the history of style in Pompeian sculpture: ➔ 89, ᶠJASHEMSKI W. (1988) I, 1-18 / 105-111 + 14 fig.

g90 **Bolla** M.,   Le necropoli romane di Milano. Mi 1988, Civico museo. 236 p.; XXI pl. – ᴿAevum 64 (1990) 123-6 (M. Vittoria *Antico Gallina*).

g91 **Gassner** V.,   Die Kaufläden in Pompeii.   W 1986. – ᴿVDI 192 (1990) 208-211 (B. C. *Lyapustin*).

g92 **Greco** E., *Theodorescu* D.,   Poseidonia - Paestum 3. Forum Nord 1987 ➔ 1,e550... 5,e799:   ᴿLatomus 49 (1990) 288s (J. *Debergh*).

g93 **Greenhalgh** Michael,   The survival of Roman antiquities in the Middle Ages.   L 1989, Duckworth.   288 p. £35.   0-7156-2129-7. – ᴿAntiquity 64 (1990) 190s (M. *Vickers*: full of learning and good sense).

g94 *Joyce* Hetty,   Hadrian's villa and the 'dome of Heaven':   MiDAI-R 97 (1990) 347-381; 8 fig.; pl. 103-112.

g95 **Kockel** Valentin,   Die Grabbauten vor dem Herkulaner Tor in Pompeji 1983 ➔ 2,b462:   ᴿDLZ 111 (1990) 130 (W. *Schindler*).

g96 **Maaskant-Kleibrink** Marianne, *al.*,   Settlement excavations at Borgo le Ferriére ('Satricum') [Iron Age to Roman Republican excavated already 1896], I. The campaigns 1979-81.   Groningen 1987, Forsten.   viii-356; map apart. *f* 135.   90-6980-013-6. – ᴿBO 47 (1990) 216-223 (R. R. *Knoop*: beautiful, sloppy).

g97 **Mertens** Dieter,   Die Mauern von Selinunt, Vorbericht: MiDAI-R 96 (1989) 87-154; 14 fig.; pl. 1-33 + 2 foldouts.

g98 **Posac** Carlos, *Puertas* Rafael,   La basílica paleocristiana de Vega del Mar.   Marbella 1989, Peralta.   139 p.; 9 fig.; XXVI pl.; 5 plans. – ᴿBAsEspOr 26 (1990) 357s (P. *Lavado*).

g99 *Rakob* Friedrich,   Die Rotunde in Palestrina: MiDAI-R 97 (1990) 61-92; 25 (foldout) fig.; pl. 12-22.

g100 **Richardson** L.ᴶ,   Pompeii, an architectural history 1988 ➔ 5,e804: ᴿAntiquity 64 (1990) 693 (Susan *Walker*); Gnomon 62 (1990) 152-161 (S. *De Caro*).

g101 *Sestieri Bertarelli* Maria, Statuette femminili arcaiche e del primo classicismo nelle stipi votive di Poseidonia [...Paestum]; i rinvenimenti presso il tempio di Nettuno: RINASA 12 (1989) 5-48; 31 fig.

g102 [ᴱ**Sirago** Vito, *Camodeca* Giuseppe], Puteoli; studi di storia antica [I. 1977] VIII, 1984 / IX-X, 1985s / XI, 1987: AntClas 57 (1988) 594s; 59 (1990) 610-4 (résumés de Franz de *Ruyt*).

XIX. Geographia biblica

Ul   **Geographies.**

g103 ᴱ**Ahrweiler** Hélène, Géographie historique du monde méditerranéen 1988 ➤ 5,e807: ᴿSpeculum 65 (1990) 109 (W. E. *Kaegi*).

g104 *González Echegaray* Joaquín, Geografía y arqueología bíblicas: ➤ 370*, Introd. I, 1990, 19-117.

g105 **Hanoon** Naʾil, Studies in the historical geography of northern Iraq during the Middle and Neo-Assyrian periods: diss. ᴰ*Grayson* A. K. Toronto 1986. – OIAc Ap89.

g106 **Huntingford** G. W. B. †, ᴱ*Pankhurst* Richard, The historical geography of Ethiopia from the first century A.D. to 1704. Ox 1989, UP for British Academy. xlix-311 p.; 20 maps. £60. – ᴿJRAS (1990) 136-8 (E. *Ullendorff*).

ᴱ**Kark** Ruth, The land that became Israel; studies in historical geography 1990 ➤ 347.

g107 *Laminger-Pascher* Gertrud, Lykaonien und die Ostgrenze Phrygiens: EpAnat 16 (1990) 1-13; ❶ 14.

g108 **Lane** Belden C., Landscapes of the sacred; geography and narrative in American spirituality: Hecker Studies, 1988 ➤ 4,g860*: ᴿNewTR 3,1 (1990) 107s (T. *McGonigle*); TLZ 115 (1990) 96s (F. W. *Graf*).

g109 **Miquel** André, La géographie humaine du monde musulman jusqu'au milieu du XIᵉ siècle [1. 1967; 2. 1975; 3. 1980] 4: Les travaux et les jours. P 1988, EHESS. – ᴿCahHist 34 (1989) 173-5 (T. *Bianquis*).

g110 **Richer** Jean, Geografia sacra del mondo greco, ᵀ*Anselmi* G. Mi 1989, Rusconi. 374 p.; 57 pl. Lit. 43.000: ᴿHumBr 45 (1990) 870 (Giulia *Carazzali*); Letture 45 (1990) 377 (Carlo *Castelli*).

g111 ᴱ**Wagstaff** I. M., Landscape and culture; geographical and archaeological perspectives 1987 ➤ 4,465 (not 'Wegstaff'). – ᴿBInstArch 26 (1989) 301-3 (M. *Bell*).

g112 *Scollar* Irwin, al., Grossmassstäbliche, digitale archäologische Kartographie auf der Basis von Luftbildern, geophykalischen Messungen und einer Datenbank: BonnJbb 186 (1986) 535-556 [Hou H. S., Digital document processing, NY 1983].

Ul.2   **Historia geographiae.**

g113 ᵀᴱ**Baladié** Raoul, STRABON, Géographie IV (livre 7) 1899 ➤ 5,e818*: ᴿRPg 63 (1989) 300s (P. *Pedech*).

g114 *Baud* Michel, La représentation de l'espace en Égypte ancienne [carte de Turin 'des mines d'or']; cartographie d'un itinéraire d'expédition: BIFAO 90 (1990) 51-63; 6 fig.

g115 **Bernecker** Annemarie, Die Feldzüge des Tiberius und die Darstellung der unterworfenen Gebiete in der 'Geographie des PTOLEMAEUS'. Bonn 1989, Habelt. 529 p.; maps.

g116 *Brincken* Anna-Dorothee von den,   Christen im Orient auf abend-ländischen Karten des 11. bis 14. Jahrhunderts: ➤ 777, Or.-Tag. 1988/90, 90-98.

g117 *Bultrighini* Umberto,   La Grecia descritta da PAUSANIA; trattazione diretta e trattazione indiretta: RFgIC 118 (1990) 282-305.

g118 **Campbell** Tony, The earliest printed maps, 1472-1500. Berkeley 1987, Univ. California. 244 p. $75. – ᴿSixtC 20 (1989) 301s (D. *Buisseret*).

g119 *Chevallier* R., Les cartes dans les sources historiques romaines [< Colloque 'Cartographie antique', Paris, sept. 1987]: Caesarodunum 22-CR (1989) 156-165.

g120 ᴱ**Dalché** Patrick G., HUGUES de Saint-Victor, La 'Descriptio mappe mundi' 1988 ➤ 5,e821: ᴿSpeculum 65 (1990) 701s (G. *Kish*).

g121 ᴱ**De Sandoli** S., Francesco QUARESMI, Elucidatio Terrae Sanctae [1639]: SBF maior 32. J 1989, Franciscan. – ᴿRHE 85 (1990) 568 (R. *Aubert*, 'Sandolsi').

ᴱ**Desreumaux** A., *Schmidt* F., Moïse géographe (➤ 5,e823); supra ➤ 329.

g122 *Ekschmitt* Werner, Weltmodelle; griechische Weltbilder von THALES bis PTOLEMÄUS. Mainz 1989, von Zabern. 191 p. – ᴿRTPhil 122 (1990) 549s (S. *Imhoof*: histoire de la philosophie).

g123 *Galán* José M., A remark on calculations of area in the Rhind mathematical papyrus: GöMiszÄg 117s (1990) 161-4.

g124 ᴱ**Harley** J.B., *Woodward* David, History of cartography I, 1987 ➤ 3,496... 5,e829: ᴿVDI 194 (1990) 205-216 (A. V. *Podosinov*, L. S. *Chekin*).

g125 *Hucker* Bernd U., Zur Datierung der Ebstorfer Weltkarte: Deutsches Archiv für Erforschung des Mittelalters 44 (Köln 1988) 510-538 [< ZIT 89,465].

g126 *Kunitzsch* Paul, Die Überlieferung des [PTOLEMAEUS] Almagest, grie-chisch-arabisch-lateinisch: ➤ 8*, ᶠASSFALG J. 1990, 203-210.

g127 *Leitz* Christian, Studien zur ägyptischen Astronomie: ÄgAbh 49, 1989 ➤ 5,e837: ᴿLA 40 (1990) 490s (A. *Niccacci*).

g128 ᴱ**Lestringant** Frank, André THÉVÉT, Cosmographie du Levant [1554]. Genève 1985, Droz. cxxi-374 p.   ᴿMeditHistR 5 (1990) 95-97 (B. *Arbel*).

g129 **Maguire** Henry, Earth and ocean ... Byzantine art 1987 ➤ 3,f276; 5,e839: ᴿOrChrPer 56 (1990) 201-3 (E. G. *Farrugia*).

g130 *Mannert* Konrad, 'Aethiopia, oder das Reich von Axum und von Meroe'; Auszüge aus seiner zehnbändigen Geographie der Griechen und Römer (1788-1825), Einführung, Anmerkungen, *Scholz* Piotr: Nubica 1s (1990) 125-148.

g131 *Marcotte* Didier, Le périple dit de SCYLAX; esquisse d'un commentaire épigraphique et archéologique: LinceiBClas 7 (1986) 166-182.

g132 *a)* *Mazzoni* Stefania, La cartografia archeologica nel Vicino Oriente; problemi, modelli, prospettive; – *b)* *Pecorella* Paolo E., Ricognizioni in Anatolia orientale e Persia occidentale; una esemplificazione; – *c)* *Ferri* Walter, Cartografia archeologica nel Fayum: ➤ 817, ᴱPASQUINUCCI Marinella, La cartografia archeologica 1988/9, 239-249 / 251-268; 4 maps / 269s + map.

g133 **Miller** Konrad, Mappae arabicae [1926-31], ᴱ*Gaube* H.; TAVO-B65, 1986 ➤ 2,b499; 5,e842: ᴿZDMG 140 (1990) 160s (G. D. *Davary*).

g134 **Nicolet** Claude, L'inventaire du monde 1988 ➤ 4,g892; 5,e843: ᴿAu-fidus 7 (1989) 241s (P. *Fedeli*); JRS 80 (1990) 178-182 (N. *Purcell*: 'maps, lists, money, order and power').

g135 **Sambursky** S.,   The physical world of the Greeks / of Late Antiquity /
Physics of the Stoics. L 1987 reprints, Routledge. xiv-255 p.; xii-189 p.;
xi-153 p. A$21; 14; 17.   0-7102-1304-0; -5-0; -6-9. – ᴿAncHRes 20 (1990)
60-62 (R. G. *Tanner*: epoch-making on physics and mathematics).

g136 *Schmidt* Francis, Jewish representations of the inhabited earth during
the Hellenistic and Roman periods: ➤ 540, Greece/Israel 1985/90, 119-
134; 3 fig.

g137 ᵀᴱ**Silberman** A., POMPONIUS MÉLA: Budé 1988 ➤ 4,g900:   ᴿClasR 40
(1990) 285-7 (O. A. W. *Dilke*).

g138 *Smith* C. D.,   Maps as art and science; maps in xvIth century Bibles:
Imago Mundi 42 (1990) 65-88; 12 fig. [< RHE 85,359*].

U1.4   Atlas – maps.

g139 **Beltrán Lloris** F., *Marco* Simón F., Atlas de historia antigua 1987
➤ 5,e857: ᴿLatomus 49 (1990) 273s (Y. *Perrin*).

g140 ᴱ**Blake** Gerald, *al.*, The Cambridge Atlas of the Middle East and North
Africa 1987 ➤ 5,e839; 124 p.; 9 fig.; 58 maps: ᴿJAOS 110 (1990) 142s
(J. R. *Clark*: only in small part an advance on the Oxford atlas).

g141 **Brossier** François, Atlante della storia biblica [1987 ➤ 3,f290], ᵀ1989
➤ 5,e860: ᴿNRT 112 (1990) 139 (L.-J. *Renard*).

g142 **Chadwick** H., *Evans* G. R., Atlas du Christianisme, ᵀ*Cannuyer* C.,
Poswick R., 1987 ➤ 4,g909*b*: ᴿStMon 31 (1989) 425s (J. A. *Rocha*).

g143 The Collegeville Bible Study atlas. Collegeville MN 1990, Liturgical.
20 p. $6. 0-8146-1976-2 [NTAbs 35,263]. ➤ b926.

g144 **Cornu** Georgette, Atlas du monde arabo-islamique à l'époque classique... répertoire des toponymes 1985 ➤ 5,e863: ᴿZDMG 140 (1990)
161-4 (H.-R. *Singer*).

g145 **Denk** Wolfgang, Atlaskartographie; theoretische und praktische Probleme dargestellt am Beispiel des TAVO: TAVO B-57. Wsb 1990,
Reichert. xvi-216 p.; 23 loose color. pl. 3-88226-478-0 [OIAc S90].

g146 **Fārūqī** Ismail R. & Lois L. al-, The cultural atlas of Islam. NY [L]
1986, [Collier-] Macmillan. xv-512 p.; ill.; 77 maps. £90. – ᴿOLZ 85
(1990) 57s (P. *Heine*).

g147 **Forlanini** M., Anatolia; l'impero Hittita: [ᴱ*Liverani* M., *al.*] Atlante
storico del Vicino Oriente Antico 4/3. R 1986, Univ. 20 pl.

g148 Hammond Atlas of the Bible Lands [ᴱ*Frank* Harry T. 1977], ²ʳᵉᵛ**Boraas**
Roger, 1984 ➤ 1,e616: ᴿBA 53 (1990) 229.

g149 ᴱ**Jedin** H., *Latourette* K. S., *Martin* J., Atlas d'Histoire de l'Église;
les églises chrétiennes hier et aujourd'hui [1970 ²1987 ➤ 3,f296; ᴿRoczTK
36,4 (1989) 147-150 (M. *Budziarek*)], ᵀMaredsous centre informatique.
Turnhout 1990, Brepols. 84*-152-xxxix p.; 152 pl. Fb 2695. – ᴿRBén 100
(1990) 570 (D. *Misonne*); Irénikon 63 (1990) 594 (E. Lt.); NRT 112 (1990)
761s (A. *Harvengt*); RThom 90 (1990) 652s (B. *Montagnes*).

g150 **Lender** Yeshaʿyahu, Map of Har Nafha (196): Archaeological Survey of
Israel. J 1990, Antiquities Authority. xxxviii-*117 + 20 + xxix p.; map
apart. 965-406-000-0 [OIAc S90].

g151 **Littell** F. H., Atlas zur Geschichte des Christentums, ᵀᴱ*Geldbach* E.,
1989 ➤ 5,e865 (Littell richtig); Karten *Hausmann* F., ᵀ*Schiffelbein* K.-D.:
ᴿTLZ 115 (1990) 115s (K. *Matthiae*).

g152 *Matthews* Victor H., *Moyer* James C., Biblical atlases; which ones are
best?: BA 53 (1990) 220-231; ill.

g152* *Pisarek* Stanisław, ❷ Survey of new biblical Atlases: RuBi 42 (1989) 309-313.

g153 **Pritchard** James B., Harper [Times] Atlas 1987 → 3,e869: ᴿBAR-W 16,4 (1990) 4 (B. J. *Beitzel*).

g154 ᴱ**Pritchard,** ᵀᴱ*Keel* O., *Küchler* M., Herders grosser Bibelatlas 1989 → 5,e870: ᴿBZ 34 (1990) 124s (J. *Schreiner*); NRT 112 (1990) 892s (X. *Jacques*); TPhil 65 (1990) 255s (H. *Engel*); TR 86 (1990) 361s (F. *Mussner*); TrierTZ 99 (1990) 79s (R. *Bohlen*); TRu 55 (1990) 109-111 (L. *Perlitt*).

g155 **Rasmussen** Carl G., NIV Atlas of the Bible 1989 → 5,e871: ᴿCurr-TMiss 17 (1990) 396 (R. W. *Klein*: 'literalistic e. g. 15th century Exodus').

g156 **Roaf** Michael, Cultural atlas of Mesopotamia and the Ancient Near East. NY/Oxford 1990, Facts on File. 238 p.; ill.; maps. 0-8160-2218-6 [OIAc F91,19].

g157 **Rogerson** John, Atlas of the Bible 1989 (1985 → 1,e623 ... 4,g923): ᴿExpTim 101 (1989s) 278 (C. S. *Rodd* dates 1989).

g157* **Strange** John, [*Bergquist* Ulla, Karten], *a*) Stuttgarter Bibelatlas [→ 5, e878]; historische Karten der biblischen Welt, ᵀᴱ*Lange* Joachim. Stu 1989, Deutsche Bibelgesellschaft. 64 p. DM 25. 3-438-06020-5. – ᴿLuth-TKi 14 (1990) 135s (V. *Stolle*). – *b*) Atlante biblico [Bibelatlas, K 1988, danese] ᵀ*Cignoni* Mario. R 1990, Libreria di Sacre Scritture. 64 p. Henoch 12 (1990) 367s (J. A. *Soggin* raccomanda 'caldamente, anche perché ha rinunciato alla ricostruzione, sempre fantasiosa e velleitaria, d'itinerari quali quello dell'Esodo').

g158 **Turner** Reuben, The popular Jewish Bible atlas from Abraham to Bar-Kochba. L 1986, Jewish Chronicle. 80 p.; (color.) ill., maps [KirSef 62 (1988s), p. 624].

g159 **Wamena** Poh M., *Waller* R., *Tidy* M., Atlante storico dell'Africa. T 1990, SEI. 160 p. Lit. 38.000. – ᴿHumBr 45 (1990) 712 (M. *Perrini*).

U1.5 **Photographiae.**

g160 **Brenner** Frederic, photos; text *Yehoshua* A. B., Israel, ᵀ*Simpson* Philip. NY 1988, Harper & R. 192 p. $40. – ᴿBS 147 (1990) 117 (F. D. *Lindsey*: high praise).

g161 **Folberg** Neil, *a*) In a desert land; photographs of Israel, Egypt and Jordan. NY 1987, Abbeville. 0-89659-759-8; – *b*) Die Wüste; Israel, Ägypten und Jordanien. Mü 1988, Hirmer. 3-7774-4860-5 [OIAc Ap89].

g162 **Halliday** Sonia, *Luchington* Laura, High above the Holy Land; unique aerial photographs of Israel, text *Dowley* Tim [→ 2,b531!; 3,f312], intr. *Bruce* F. F., 1986 (deutsch 1986 → 4,g932): ᴿBS 147 (1990) 117s (F. D. *Lindsey*, with four similar collections).

g163 **Jobbins** Jenney, The Red Sea coasts of Egypt; Sinai and the mainland. Cairo 1989, American University. x-115 p.; color. phot. Hartwell T. 977-424-206-8 [OIAc Oc90].

g164 **Kennedy** David, *Riley* Derrick, Rome's desert frontier from the air. L 1990, Batsford. 256 p.; 188 fig. 0-7134-6262-0 [OIAc S90]. – ᴿRÉLat 68 (1990) 241s (R. *Chevallier*).

g165 **Masum** Caroline, *Alexander* Pat, Picture archive of the Bible; *Millard* Alan, archaeological notes. Tring 1987, Lion. 192 p.; colour. ill.; maps [KirSef 62 (1988s) p. 191]; deutsch/ned. 1987 → 4,g934s.

g165* **Nur** Amos,   Earthquakes in the Holy Land, 55-minute video tape.
Stanford c. 1990, Univ. Geophysics Dept., C. MacAskill, $45 [BAR-W
17/5, 9, D. *Gill*].

g166 **Pankhurst** Richard, *Ingrams* Leila, Ethiopia engraved; an illustrated
catalogue of engravings by foreign travellers from 1681 to 1900. L 1988,
Kegan Paul. 214 p. £30. – ᴿJRAS (1990) 138-141 (E. *Ullendorff*).

g167 **Storper-Perez** Danielle, *Goldberg* Harvey E.,   Au pied du mur de
Jérusalem: Toledot-Judaïsmes. P 1989, Cerf. 224 p.; phot. Brenner F. –
ᴿSalesianum 52 (1990) 745 (R. *Vicent*).

g168 **Sturzebecker** Russell L.,   Photo-atlas, athletic-cultural... 1985 ➤ 3,d482:
ᴿNikephoros 2 (1989) 259-266 (P. *Roos*).

g169 **Taylor** Jane, *a*) High above Jordan [➤ 5,e891]: L 1989, Three's; – *b*)
Biblische Stätten im Luftbild; Jordanien, ᵀ*Puchtier* R. Giesen 1990,
Brunnen. 64 p. DM 39. 3-7655-5739-0 [BL 91,42, A. G. *Auld*: stunning].

g170 **Thompson** James, The East imagined, experienced, remembered; orientalist nineteenth century painting; with an essay by *Scott* David. Dublin
1988, National Gallery. vii-183 p. 0-903162-45-8 [OIAc S90].

g171 **Travlos** John,   Bildlexikon zur Topographie des antiken Attika 1988
➤ 5,e891:   ᴿGnomon 62 (1990) 442-5 (H. *Lauter*); HZ 250 (1990) 660s (J.
Bleicken).

g172 **Wolman** Baron, The Holy Land; Israel from the air. SF 1987, Chronicle. 144 p. $35. – ᴿBS 147 (1990) 117 (F. D. *Lindsey*).

U1.6   **Guide books,** *Führer*.

g173 **Bizzeti** Paolo,   La Turchia; guida per i cristiani: Bibbia e Testi Biblici.
Bo 1990, Dehoniane. 160 p. Lit. 30.000 [RivB 38,224 adv.].

g174 **Brownrigg** R.,   Pauline places; in the footsteps of Paul through Turkey
and Greece. L 1989, Hodder & S. xv-186 p. £8. 0-340-50401-3 [NTAbs
34,254].

g175 **Díez** F.,   Guía de TS.   Estella/M 1990, VDivino/Affinsa. 448 p. – ᴿSalmanticensis 37 (1990) 381 (J. M. *Sánchez Caro*).

g176 **Hughes** R.,   Travels in the Holy Land [a 10-day program]. L 1989. –
ᴿTerraS 65 (1989) 234 (L. A. *Anguita*).
Jerusalem guide: **Lev** M. ➤ d957; **Prag** K. ➤ d967; **Saulnier** C., ➤ d973*;
atlas **Bahat** D. ➤ d934.

g177 **Kilgallen** John J.,   A New Testament guide to the Holy Land 1987
➤ 3,f328:   ᴿBA 53 (1990) 116 (G. W. *Knight*: mixture of fact and
tradition); Vidyajyoti 53 (1989) 282 (P. M. *Meagher*).

g178 **Lumbreras** Juan M.,   E, el país de Jesús; viaje a Tierra Santa. M 1989,
Mensajero. 291 p. – ᴿManresa 62 (1990) 91 (J. C. *Macua Paternina*).

g179 **Lyk-Jensen** Per,   Jordan — en kulturhistorisk rejsefører. Espergærde
1988, Safra. 158 p. Dk 157. – ᴿNorTTs 90 (1989) 60s (H. M. *Barstad*).

g180 ᴱ**Mehling** Marianne,   Egypt: Phaidon Cultural Guide. Ox 1990,
Phaidon. 419 p.; ill.; maps. 0-7148-2508-5 [OIAc Ja91].

g181 **Murphy-O'Connor** Jerome, The Holy Land, an archaeological guide[2]
1986 ➤ 2,b546... 5,e900; reprinted 1988, £7; 0-19-285158-6:   ᴿBL (1990)
34 (A. G. *Auld*).

g182 **Vilnay** Zeev,   Guía de Israel[4]. J 1980, Semana. 592 p.; ill. – ᴿBAs-
EspOr 26 (1990) 355 (P. *Lavado*: ya ed. 5ª).

U1.7   **Onomastica.**

g183 *Beinlich* Horst,   Spätzeitquellen zu den Gauen Unterägyptens: GöMisz-
Äg 117s (1990) 59-88.

g184 **Bell** Robert E., Place-names in classical mythology; Greece 1989
➤ 5,e907; £34.75: ᴿClasR 40 (1990) 529s (A. R. *Burn*).

g185 *Darnell* John C., Articular *Km.t* / *Kmy* and partitive *Kēme* (including
an Isis of Memphis and Syria, and the *Kmy* of Setne I 5,11 west of
which lived Ta-Buhu): Enchoria 17 (1990) 69-81.

g186 *Dietrich* M., *Loretz* O., Die Ortsnamen *gt* '*ṯtrt* und '*ṯtrt* || *hdr'y*: UF
22 (1990) 55s.

g187 *Dziobek* Eberhard, Eine bislang übersehene topographische Bezeich-
nung für den Bereich Theben-Assiut?: GöMiszÄg 114 (1990) 53-58 +
2 fig.

g188 **Eilers** Wilhelm, Iranische Ortsnamenstudien 1987 ➤ 3,f345; 5,e908:
ᴿZDMG 140 (1990) 177 (J. *Tischler*).

g189 **Fadhil** Abdulillah, Studien zur Topographie und Prosopographie der
Provinzstädte des Königreichs Arrapḫe 1983 ➤ 1,e666: ᴿOLZ 85 (1990)
171-5 (K. *Kessler*); RAss 84 (1990) 94s (D. *Charpin*).

g190 *Gascou* Jean, Nabla / Labla: CdÉ 65 (1990) 111-5.

g191 **Hilou** Abdullah al-, Topographische Namen des Syro-Palästinischen
Raumes nach arabischen Geographen; historische und etymologische
Untersuchungen: Diss. Freie Univ. Berlin 1986. – OIAc Ap89.

g192 *Levine* Louis D., K. 4675+ — The Zamua itinerary: SAAB 3 (1989)
75-92; 5 fig.

g193 *Minnen* Peter van, Encore quelques toponymes du nome Hermopolite:
ZPapEp 82 (1990) 93-96.

g194 *Misgav* Haggai, Two notes on the ostraca from Ḥorvat Uza: IsrEJ
40 (1990) 215-7: *(m)rptm* (or *mrp'm*) may be an otherwise unknown
place-name; cf. Hab 3,17.

g195 **Müller** Dietram, Topographischer Bildkommentar zu ... HERODOTs
Griechenland 1987 ➤ 3,f357; 5,e912: ᴿGnomon 62 (1990) 385-393 (H.-J.
Gehrke).

g196 **Reeg** G., Die Ortsnamen Israels ... TAVO B51, 1989 ➤ 5,e915: ᴿCrit-
RR 3 (1990) 357 (J. *Neusner*: topography not of the real Palestine but of
what the rabbis thought).

g197 *Schwab* Eckart, Beobachtungen zur 'kanonischen' Reihenfolge der
Städte in Ortsnamen-Listen mit verbesserten Lesungen einiger frag-
mentarischen KTU-Tafeln: UF 22 (1990) 303-310.

g198 **Thompson** T. L., *al.*, Toponymie palestinienne... Acre/Jérusalem 1988
➤ 4,g963; 5,e916: ᴿJAOS 110 (1990) 766s (A. F. *Rainey* feels the lack of
the meaning of Arabic and modern Hebrew words used for toponyms);
WZKM 80 (1990) 242s (A. A. *Ambros*).

g198* *Wu-Yuhang*, The locality of the four cities [... west of Tigris] in ARM 1
138 and 131 and the date of the two letters: JACiv 4 (Chang-chun 1989)
49-53 [55-60, *Yang Zhi*, The king Lugal-Ane-Mundu: < OTAbs 14,33].

g199 *Ziv* Yehuda, ⊕ Naming places [in modern Israel from Arabic]: Lešonenu
53 (1988s) 126-131; Eng. IX.

U2.1 **Geologia**: soils, mountains, volcanoes, earthquakes.

g200 *Akurgal* Ekrem, Role of geomorphological features in Anatolian history: ➤ 3, Mem. ALKIM U. 1986, 21-30.

g200* **Andel** T. van, *Runnels* C., Beyond the acropolis; a rural [geological]
Greek past 1987 ➤ 4,g967; 5,e917: ᴿAmHR 95 (1990) 463 (C. G.
Thomas).

g201 *Andel* Tjeerd H. van, *al.*, Land use and soil erosion in prehistoric and
historical Greece: JField 17 (1990) 379-396; 10 fig.

g201* **Arad** V., *al.*, Mediterranean — Dead Sea project; bibliography, historical review: Geological Survey of Israel Report (0333-6069). J 1990, Ministry of Energy. 50 p. [OIAc Oc90].

g202 ᴱ**Bergier** J. F., Montagnes, flcuves, forêts dans l'histoire; barrières ou lignes de convergence? St. Katharinen 1989, Scripta Mercaturae. 240 p. – ᴿRevue Roumaine d'Histoire 28 (1989) 329-331 (C. *Zaharia*) [< ByZ 83,300].

g203 *Borowski* Oded, The Carmel; formidable barrier and wedge into the sea: BR 6,5 (1990) 46-53; color. ill.

g203* *Bruce* Graham A., From holy mountains to the new earth: TEv 23,2 (Pretoria 1990) 27-34 [< OTAbs 14,2].

g204 *Herz* Norman, Geology of Greece and Turkey; potential marble source regions: ➤ 806, Marble 1988, 7-10; 3 maps.

g205 **Inbar** M., *al.*, Hula Valley and Korazim region: Bibliography of geological research. J 1989, Ministry of Energy. 66 p. [OIAc Oc90].

g205* *Lana* Italo, PLINIO il Vecchio; miniere d'oro e minatori (Nat. Hist. XXIII 70-73): Aufidus 10 (1990) 147-162.

g206 *Soren* David, The day the world ended at Kourion; reconstructing an ancient earthquake: NatGeog 174 (1988) 30-53; color. ill.
Thera eruption ➤ g41s.

g207 **Tseren** Erich, Ⓑ *Biblejskie kholmi* [biblical heights ...], ᵀ*Šafranskiy* H. B. Moskva 1986, Pravda. 478 p. [KirSef 62 (1988s) p. 37].

g208 **Weiner** D., *al.*, *a*) Beer Sheva valley and Negev — Western foothills; – *b*) Northern Negev: Geological Survey. J 1990/89, Ministry of Energy. 72 p.; 115 p. 0333-6069 [OIAc Oc90].

υ2.2 *Hydrographia:* **rivers, seas, salt.**

g209 *Biernacka-Lubańska* Malgorzata, Ⓟ Les prises d'eau des aqueducs romains: ArchWsz 40 (1989) 29-40; 18 fig; Eng. 205.

g209* *Braemer* Frank, Prospections archéologiques dans le Hawran, II. Les réseaux de l'eau: Syria 65 (1988) 99-137; 25 fig.

g210 *Briend* Jacques, Regards sur le Jourdain et sa vallée... la geste d'Israël: MondeB 65 (1990) 8-22 (2-7, *al.*; ➤ 4747).

g211 *Buccellati* Giorgio, Salt at the dawn of history; the case of the bevelled-rim bowls: ➤ 28, ᶠBOUNNI A., Resurrecting 1990, 17-37; map, 5 fig.

g212 *Durand* Jean-Marie, Le sel à Mari (II); les salines sur les bords du Habur: MARI 7 (1990) 629-634.

g213 ᴱ**Edwards** Alasdair J., *Head* Stephen M., Red Sea. Ox 1987, Pergamon. x-441 p.; ill., maps [KirSef 62 (1988s) p. 200].

g214 *Erkut* Sedat, Ⓣ Le sel et son usage chez les Hittites: Belleten 54,209 (1990) 1-7.

g215 **Garbrecht** Günther, *Netzer* Ehud, Die Wasserversorgung des geschichtlichen Jericho und seiner königlichen Anlagen (Gut, Winterpaläste): Mitt. Braunschweig Univ. Leichtweiss Institut für Wasserbau. Braunschweig/J 1991. 137 p.; ill. 0343-1223.

g216 **Garbrecht** Günther, *al.*, Die Wasserversorgung antiker Städte [2. Pergamon 1987 ➤ 5,e561] 3. Mitteleuropa; Thermen, Baumaterialen, Hygiene: GeschWV 111. Mainz 1988, von Zabern. 223 p. DM 68. 3-8053-0984-8. – ᴿAntClas 59 (1990) 636s (G. *Raepsaet*); ArchWsz 40 (1989) 194s (Malgorzata *Biernacka-Lubańska*, 2-3; deutsch von P. *Taracha*); JRS 80 (1990) 230 (J.J. *Coulton*); RArchéol (1990) 184 (P. *Gros*, 3).

g217 *Heimpel* Wolfgang,   Ein zweiter Schritt zur Rehabilitierung der Rolle des Tigris in Sumer: ZAss 80 (1990) 204-213.

g218 *Hinkel* Marion,   Wasserbauten im alten Sudan: Altertum 36 (1990) 29-36; 7 fig.

g219 *Kappeler* Thomas,   Das 'Tote Meer' bei DIOGENES von Oinoanda (NF 40) [nicht Asphaltitis; vielmehr (ein) Nordsee]: EpAnat 15 (1990) 7-17; ❶ 18.

g220 **Kreiger** Barbara,   Living waters; myth, history, and politics of the Dead Sea.   NY 1988, Continuum.   226 p. $25. – ᴿCBQ 52 (1990) 719s (Marilyn M. *Schaub*: not the Dead Sea Scrolls but the geology and ecology of the Dead Sea area: literary and enjoyable).

g221 *Levy* Thomas E.,   How ancient man first utilized rivers in the desert: BAR-W 16,6 (1990) 20-31; ill.

g222 *Muheisin* Zeidoun al-,   Maîtrise de l'eau et agriculture en Nabatène; l'exemple de Pétra: ➤ 783, Aram 2 (1990) 205-220.

g223 **Nomachi** Kazuyochi,   Nil, Strom der Ströme [Le Nil 1989 ➤ 5,e937]. FrB 1989, Herder.   196 p.; 191 color. phot. DM 98. – ᴿErbAuf 66 (1990) 248 (V. A.).

g224 **Potts** Daniel T.,   The Arabian Gulf in antiquity, I. From prehistory to the fall of the Achaemenid empire; II. From Alexander the Great to the coming of Islam.   Ox 1990, Clarendon.   xxvii-419 p.; 44 fig.; XII pl. – xxi-369 p.; 25 fig.; XII pl.   0-39-814390 7; 1 5.

g225 *a*) *Renger* Johannes,   Rivers, water courses and irrigation ditches and other matters concerning irrigation based on Old Babylonian sources (2000-1600 B.C.); – *b*) *Waetzoldt* H.,   Zu den Bewässerungseinrichtungen in der Provinz Umma [+ Nachtrag zu 3,23-56]: BSumAgr 5 (1990) 31-46 / 1-29 [280-3].

g226 *Sartori* Marco,   Le piene del Nilo (Her. II, 13) ed i tempi delle Révolutions geologiques nel settecento: ➤ 53, ᶠGABBA E., 1988, 155-171.

g227 *Schiøler* Thorkild,   The watermills at the Crocodile River; a turbine mill dated to 345-380 A.D.:   PEQ 121 (1989) 133-143; 5 fig.

U2.3   **Clima, pluvia.**

g228 *Brewer* Douglas J.,   Temperatures in predynastic Egypt inferred from the remains of the Nile perch: WorldArch 22 (1990s) 288-303.

g229 *Croke* Brian,   Climatic changes in antiquity: AncHRes 20 (1990) 168-175.

g230 *Kelley* A. L.,   The current status of Egyptian prehistory, I. Paleogeographical and palaeoclimatological considerations: JACiv 4 (Chang-chun 1989) 1-27 [< OTAbs 14,22].

U2.5   *Fauna;*   **Animals.**

g231 *Adams* J. N.,   *a*) *Filocalus* as an epithet of horse-owners in Pelagonius; its origin and meaning ['attentive, careful', echoing Greek veterinaries]: ClasPg 85 (1990) 305-310; – *b*) The meaning and use of *subiugale* in veterinary Latin: RFgIC 118 (1990) 440-453.

g232 *Alcock* Anthony,   The ox and the donkey [treated kindly/roughly]: JEA 76 (1990) 188s.

g233 **Ali-Shtayeh** Mohammed S.,   The genus Pythium in the West Bank and Gaza Strip.   Nablus 1986, Univ. an-Najah.   76 p.; ill. [KirSef 62 (1988s) p. 200].

g234 *a*) *Altenmüller* Hartwig, Nilpferd und Papyrusdickicht in den Gräbern des Alten Reiches; – *b*) *Germond* Philippe, L'oryx, un mal-aimé du bestiaire égyptien: → 70, Mém. HARI R., BSocÉg 13 (1989) 9-21 / 51-55; 4 fig.

g234* *Amigues* Suzanne, Boúprēstis, nom d'animal et nom de plante: RPg 64 (1990) 89-97.

g235 *Asmussen* Jes P., Simurg ['a fabulous bird' but always for *nešer* 'eagle'] in Judeo-Persian translations of the Hebrew Bible: → 192, FYARSHATER E. 1990, 1-5.

g236 **Bacher** Ilona, Die Fliege in Kultur und Religion der alten Ägypter: Magisterarbeit. Mü 1989, Univ. 179 p.; 3 pl. [OIAc Ap91,4].

g237 *Balconi* Carla, Le dichiarazioni di bestiame ed il controllo del patrimonio zootecnico nell'Egitto romano: Aegyptus 70 (1990) 113-122.

g238 *Baratay* Éric, Les animaux du Christ; le bœuf et l'âne dans la Nativité du XVIIe siècle à nos jours: CahHist 34 (1989) 107-133; 2 fig.

g239 *Bastianini* Guido, Una dichiarazione di [proprietà di] un cammello; SPP XXII 97 riconsiderato: Tyche 5 (1990) 1-4; pl. 1.

g240 **Beavis** Ian C., Insects and other invertebrates in classical antiquity 1988 → 5,e951; 0-85989-284-0: RAntClas 59 (1990) 223-8 (Liliane *Bodson*, 'une contribution propice au renouveau de l'histoire de l'entomologie antique'); Salesianum 52 (1990) 473s (R. *Bracchi*).

g241 EBodson Liliane, L'animal dans l'alimentation humaine; les critères de choix 1986/8 → 4,123; 5,e954; 0761-3032-0-3: RAntClas 59 (1990) 427-9 (S. *Byl*); Latomus 49 (1990) 888-890 (Mireille *Corbier*).

g242 *Bodson* Liliane, Nature et fonction des serpents d'Athéna: → 111, FLÉVÊQUE P. 4 (1990) 45-62; 2 fig.

g243 **Bökönyi** S., Tierhaltung und Jagd; Tierknochenfunde der Ausgrabungen 1964 bis 1981: Kāmid el-Lōz 12. Bonn 1990, Habelt. 215 p.; 61 fig.; 40 pl. [ZAW 103,445, O. *Kaiser*].

g244 **Boessneck** Joachim, Die Tierwelt des Alten Ägyptens, untersucht anhand kulturgeschichtlicher und zoologischer Quellen 1988 → 4,h8; 5,e955: RZDMG 140 (1990) 191 (J. v. *Beckerath*).

g245 EBoessneck Joachim, Die Münchner Ochsenmumie 1987 → 3,f416; 4,h9: RBO 17 (1990) 70-72 (C. S. *Churcher*).

g246 [*Kessler* D. p. 1-36] **Boessneck** Joachim, *Driesch* Angela von den (p. 37-214), Tuna el-Gebel I., die Tiergalerien: ÄgBei 24, 1987 → 3,f417; 4,h10: RBO 17 (1990) 67-70 (C. S. *Churcher*).

g247 *a*) *Borthwick* E. Kerr, Bees and drones in ARISTOPHANES, AELIAN and EURIPIDES: – *b*) *Osborne* Catherine, Boundaries in nature; eating with animals in the 5th century B.C.: BInstClas 37 (1990) 57-62 / 15-29.

g247* **Bouchud** Jean, La faune du gisement natoufien de Mallaha (Eynan), Israel: Mém 4. J 1987, Centre de Recherche Français. 178 p.; 90 fig.; 6 pl. – RSyria 65 (1988) 231 (H. de *Contenson*).

g248 *Bresciani* Edda, La corazza di Inaro era fatta con la pelle del grifone del Mar Rosso: EgVO 13 (1990) 103-7.

g249 *Byl* Simon, *Schouls* Sarah, Quelques préjugés d'ARISTOTE en ichtyologie et leur survivance chez certains de ses successeurs jusqu'au XVIIIe siècle: RBgPg 68 (1990) 305-314.

g250 **Cahen** Daniel, *al.*, Les chats des Pharaons; 4000 ans de divinité féline (exposition). Bru 1989, Inst. Sc. Naturelles. 93 p. [OIAc S90].

g251 *Campana* Douglas V., *Crabtree* Pam J., Communal hunting in the Natufian of the Southern Levant; the social and economic implications: JMeditArch 3 (1990) 223-243.

g252 *Camps* Gabriel, Des incertitudes de l'art aux 'erreurs' d'HÉRODOTE; la faune des temps néolithiques et préhistoriques de l'Afrique du Nord: CRAI (1990) 35-57; 12 fig.

g252* **Charbonneau-Lassay** Louis, La bestiaire du Christ; la mystérieuse emblématique de J.-C. P 1975 Arché. 1000 p. F 1140.

g253 *Charron* Alain, Massacres d'animaux à la basse époque: RÉgp 41 (1990) 209-213.

g254 *Cholidis* Nadja, Tiere und Tierförmige Gefässe auf Rädern; Gedanken zum Spielzug im Alten Orient: MDOG 121 (1989) 197-220; 36 fig.

g255 **Chouliara-Raïos** Hélène, L'abeille et le miel en Égypte d'après les papyrus grecs. Ioannina 1989, Univ. 257 p. – ᴿCdÉ 65 (1990) 180s (Hélène *Cuvigny*).

g256 ᴱ**Clark** Willene B., *McMunn* Meradith T., Beasts and birds of the Middle Ages; the bestiary [... moral applications] and its legacy. Ph 1989, Univ. Pennsylvania. xii-224 p. $30. – ᴿManuscripta 34 (1990) 79.

g257 *Clements* R. E., *rœmœś* 'kriechende Tiere': ➤ 859, TWAT 7,3s (1990) 535-8.

g258 ᴱ**Clutton-Brock** Juliet, *Grigson* Caroline, Animals and archaeology 1-4: BAR-Int 163.183.202.227, 1983s ➤ 3,f425: ᴿBInstArch 26 (1989) 246-9 (R. *Hubbard*, 1.3.4).

g259 **Clutton-Brock** Juliet, A natural history of domesticated mammals 1987 ➤ 4,b19 (+ 'natural', 'mammals'): ᴿPraehZts 65 (1990) 73-76 (Cornelia *Becker*).

g260 *Compagnoni* Pia, L'asino nella Bibbia e nell'arte figurativa: TerraS 65 (1989) 62-66.

g261 *Cornelius* Izak, The lion in the art of the Ancient Near East; a study of selected motifs: JNWS 15 (1989) 53-70 + 14 fig.

g262 **Czernohaus** Karola, Delphindarstellungen von der minoischen bis zur geometrischen Zeit: SIMA pocket 67. Göteborg 1988, Åström. 111 p.; 121 pl.

g263 ᴱ**Davis** L. B., *Reeves* B. O. K., Hunters of the recent past [Southampton meeting 1986]: One World Archaeology. L 1990, Unwin Hyman. 415 p. 0-04-445029-X. – ᴿAntiquity 64 (1990) 433 (Marsha A. *Levine*: mostly on America; one on French cave art; and J. C. *Driver*, 'Meat in due season, the timing of communal hunts').

g264 **Davis** Simon J. M., The archaeology of animals 1987 ➤ 3,f431... 5,e965; $27.50. 0-300-04065-2: ᴿJField 17 (1990) 337-340 (L. C. *Todd*, also on HILLSON S., Teeth 1986).

g265 **Delorme** Jean, *Roux* Charles, Guide... faune aquatique 1987 ➤ 3,f433; 5,e966: ᴿRArchéol (1990) 175s (J. *Marcadé*).

g266 *a) Dils* Peter, Stucco heads of crocodiles; a new aspect of crocodile mummification; – *b) Criscuolo* Lucia, Un'epigrafe augurale su testa di coccodrillo; Aegyptus 70 (1990) 73-85; 10 pl. / 87s; 2 fig.

g267 *Dixon* D. M., A note on some scavengers of ancient Egypt: WorldArch 21 (1989s) 193-7.

g267* **Domagalski** Bernhard, Hirsch: ➤ 853, RAC 15,116 (1990) 551-577.

g268 **Driesch** Angela von den, Geschichte der Tiermedizin; 5000 Jahre Tierheilkunde. Mü 1989, Callwey. 295 p.; 458 fig. [AnPg 60, p. 854].

g269 *Edel* Elmar, Der Kanal der beiden Fische [Mugiliden(arte), W. Delta]: DiscEg 16 (1990) 31-33.

g270 **Eisenstein** Herbert, Einführung in die arabische Zoographie; das tierkundliche Wissen in der arabisch-islamischen Literatur. B 1990, Reimer. 306 p. 3-496-00383-9.

g271 **Englund** Robert K., Organisation und Verwaltung der Ur III-Fischerei: BBVO 10. B 1990, Reimer. xvii-253 p. 3-496-00389-8 [OIAc S90]. Fischteller, fish-plates → *Kunisch* N. d440; → *McPhee* I. d753.

g272 **Gautier** Achilles, La domestication; Et l'homme créa 'ses animaux' [alias... 'l'animal']: Jardin des Hesperides. P 1990, Errance. 281 p.; ill. 2-903442-89-4. – [R]Helinium 30 (1990) 297-300 (S. *De Laet*).

g273 *Goldsmith* Naomi F., *Gould* Edwin, Sumerian bats, lion-headed eagles, and iconographic evidence for the overthrow of a female-priest hegemony: BA 53 (1990) 142-156.

g274 *Grigson* Caroline, Size and sex; evidence for the domestication of cattle in the Near East: → 813, Beginnings of agriculture 1987/9, 77-109.

g275 *Haley* Evan W., The fish-sauce trader L. Junius Puteolanus: ZPapEp 80 (1990) 72-78. → g419.

g276 *Hamp* Eric P., The Indo-European horse: → 754, Worlds 1988/90, 211-226.

g277 *Harrauer* Hermann, Zwei ptolemäische Papyri zur Schafhaltung: → 160, [F]SCHOW N., Charta Borgiana 1990, (I) 285-295.

g278 *Hartosiewicz* L., Species interferences and the interpretation of neolithic animal explication: AcArchH 42 (1990) 287-292.

g279 *Hayward* Lorna G., The origin of the raw elephant ivory used in Greece and the Aegean during the Late Bronze Age: Antiquity 64 (1990) 103-9.

g280 *Heimpel* W., *a*) Maultier; *b*) Maus: → 853*, RLA 7,7s (1990) 602-5-9.

g281 **Herzog** Isaac, The royal purple and the biblical blue, argaman and tekhelet; on the dye industries in ancient Israel, [E]*Spanier* Ehud (*Ron* Moshe): Univ. Haifa Center for Maritime Studies, *al.* J 1987, Keter. 220 p.; (color.) ill. [KirSef 62 (1988s) p. 494].

g282 *Hofmann* Inge, Zum Motiv des traubennaschenden Vogels: Varia Aegyptiaca 5 (1989) 9-18; 3 fig.

g283 *Hofmann* Inge, *Tomandl* Herbert, Die Bedeutung des Tieres in der meroitischen Kultur 1987 → 3,f445; 5,e980: [R]ArOr 58 (1990) 403s (E. *Strouhal*).

g284 **Hofmann** Ulrich, Fuhrwesen und Pferdehaltung im Alten Ägypten: diss. Bonn 1989. 543 p.; 114 fig. DM 53. – [R]Nikephoros 2 (1989) 250-6 (W. *Decker*).

g285 **Hollom** P. A. D., *al.*, Birds of the Middle East and North Africa. Vermillion SD 1988, Butto. 280 p. $32.50. – [R]JAOS 110 (1990) 172s (J. A. C. *Greppin*).

g285* *Horsley* G. R. H., A fishing-cartel in first-century Ephesus: → 5,401, New Documents 5 (1989) 95-114.

g286 *Horwitz* Liora K. (→ g296), *Tchernov* Eitan, Cultural and environmental implications of hippopotamus bone remains in archaeological contexts in the Levant: BASOR 280 (1990) 67-76; 5 fig.

g287 **Houlihan** Patrick F., The birds of ancient Egypt 1986 → 2,b640 ... 5,e983: [R]JEA 76 (1990) 211-4 (Helen M. *Strudwick*).

g288 **Hovel** Haim, Check-list of the birds of Israel with Sinai. TA 1987, Univ./Society for the protection of nature. 196 p.; ill. 965-349-000-1 [KirSef 62 (1988s) p. 200].

g289 *a*) *Hrouda* Barthel, Zur Bedeutung des Fisches in der 'späthethitischen' Kunst; religiöse oder nur profane Darstellung?: – *b*) *Tefnin* Roland, Une figurine en plomb du 'maître des antilopes' découverte à Oumm el-Marra: → 28, [F]BOUNNI A. 1990, 109-113 + pl. 24-26 / 307-314 + pl. 103-104.

g290 **Hyland** Ann, Equus; the horse in the Roman world. NHv/L 1990, Yale Univ./Batsford. xii-285 p.; 16 pl. $28.50/£25. /0-7134-6260-4. – [R]AntiqJ

70 (1990) 137 (Annabel K. *Lawson*); Manuscripta 34 (1990) 241; RÉLat 68 (1990) 217s (J.-P. *Thuillier*).

g291 *Janssen* J.J., On the scent of a fox: DiscEg 16 (1990) 43-50 + 1 fig.

g292 *Jördens* Andrea, Ichthýos hypēresía; Bemerkungen zu CPR XIV 3 [not private enterprise as *Fantoni* Georgina 'Permission to sell fish']: ZPapEp 84 (1990) 47-52.

g293 *Kádár* Zoltán, Über die Tiere um Orpheus auf einem Mosaik der Villa bei Casale (Piazza Armerina): ➤ 5,210, Mem. WESSEL K. 1988, 139-145; pl. 419-421.

g294 **Kessler** Dieter, Die heiligen Tiere und der König, I., Beiträge zu Organisation, Kult und Theologie der spätzeitlichen Tierfriedhöfe: ÄgAT 16, 1989 ➤ 5,e989: ᴿZDMG 140 (1990) 425s (J. v. *Beckerath*).

g295 *Köhler Rollefson* Ilse, Changes in goat exploitation at ʿAin Ghazal between the Early and Late Neolithic; a metrical analysis: Paléorient 15,1 (1989) 141-6.

g296 (*Kolska*) *Horwitz* Liora, The origin of partially digested bones recovered from archaeological contexts in Israel: Paléorient 16,1 (1990) 97-106.

g297 *Kroll* Stephan, Chemische Analysen — neue Evidenz für Pferdeställe in Urartu und Palästina: IstMitt 39 (1989) 329-333; 1 fig.

g298 **Leiderer** Rosmarie, Anatomie der Schafsleber im babylonischen Leberorakel; eine makroskopisch-analytische Studie. Mü 1990, Zuckschwerdt. 198 p.; 62 (color.) fig. 3-88603-348-1.

g299 **Leone** Aurora, Gli animali da trasporto nell'Egitto ...: PapyrCastroct 12, 1988 ➤ 4,h54; 5,e991: ᴿBiblica 71 (1990) 141-4 (W. Van *Gucht*).

g300 *Levine* Marsha A., Dereivka [SE Kiev] and the problem of horse domestication [shows we know even less than we thought about this revolutionary event]: Antiquity 64 (1990) 717-740; 13 fig.

g300* **McDonald** Diana K., Serpent imagery on Ancient Near Eastern pottery: diss. Columbia, ᴰ*Porada* Edith. NY 1990. x-215 p. + 50 pl. 90-20572. – OIAc Oc90.

g301 *MacGregor* Alexander, Beast-lore; catuli and lioness at Tiberianus 2,14: AmJPg 111 (1990) 395-7.

g302 *Mack-Fischer* Loren R., From Ugarit to Gades; Mediterranean veterinary medicine: ➤ 164, ᶠSEGERT S., *Sopher* 1990, 207-220.

g303 *McLeod* G., Wild and tame animals and birds in Roman law: ➤ 130, ᶠNICHOLAS B., New Perspectives 1989, ... [< ClasR 40,331].

g304 *Maeda* Tohru, Bringing (mu-túm) livestock and the Puzurish-Dagan organization in the Ur III dynasty: AcSum 11 (1989) 69-111.

g305 *Manns* Frédéric, Il simbolo dell'agnello: TerraS 66 (1990) 270-280.

g306 a) *Marasco* Gabriele, Alessandro Magno e le cacce al leone; – b) *Adams* J.N., Some Latin veterinary terms: Sileno 16 (1990) 169-176 / 117-131.

g307 *Martin* Susan D., Servum meum mulionem conduxisti; mules, muleteers and transportation in classical Roman law: AmPgTr 120 (1990) 301-314.

g308 *Miller* Robert L., Hogs and hygiene ['the pig resembles the human in more ways than any other nonprimate mammalian', *Pond* W., *Houpt* K.]: JEA 76 (1990) 125-40.

g309 ᴱ**Morphy** Howard, Animals into art [1986 Southampton conference]: One World Archaeology 7. L 1989, Unwin Hyman. xxvi-265 p.; 160 fig.; 28 colour. pl. £50. 0-04-445030-3. – ᴿAntiquity 64 (1990) 426.428 (J.D. *Lewis-Williams*).

g310 *Moure Romanillo* Alfonso, Fauna y medio ambiente en el arte rupestre paleolítico: ➤ 9, Mem. BALIL A. = BSAA 56 (1990) 38-52.

g311 *Müller* H.-P. [ug. *Tropper* J.], *re'em* 'Wildstier' [unicorn]: → 859, TWAT 7,3s (1990) 267-271.

g312 *Olmo Lete* G. del, Sheep and goats in ancient Mesopotamia; 7th meeting of the Sumerian Agriculture Group [Barcelona 7-9 July]: AulaO 8 (1990) 129s.

g312* **Pardee** Dennis, Les textes hippiatriques RS II, 1985 → 2,b661 ... 5,g8: RSyria 65 (1988) 243-6 (G. del *Olmo Lete*).

g313 **Pilali-Papasteriou** A., Die bronzenen Tierfiguren aus Kreta: PrähBronz 1/3, 1985 → 2,b663 ... 5,g9: Mü 1985, Beck. 182 p.; 44 fig.; 26 pl. – RAcArchH 42 (1990) 361s (M. *Szabó*).

g314 *Reiter* Karim, *a)* Falknerei im Alten Orient? II. Die Quellen: MDOG 121 (1989) 169-196; 8 fig.; – *b)* Falknerei in Ugarit: UF 22 (1990) 271-276.

Rice Michael, The Egyptian hound 1990 → b456.

g315 *Ridgway* Brunilde S., Birds, 'meniskoi', and head attributes in archaic Greece: AJA 94 (1990) 583-612; 19 fig.

g316 *Rippinger* Léon, [poisson, fish] Latin (*mūrēna / mūraena*) *flūta / plauta*: RPg 63 (1989) 255-262.

g317 *Rowley-Conwy* Peter, Bird bones from the temple at Qasr Ibrim: Ar-NilM 3 (1989) 35-38; (color.) pl. VI-VII.

g318 **Sauneron** Serge, Un traité égyptien d'ophiologie, papyrus Brooklyn 47.218.48 & 85. Le Caire 1989, IFAO. xii-244 p.; 27 pl. 2-7247-077-5 ... [BO 47,526].

g319 *Schauer* Peter, Mittelbronzezeitliche Vogelplastik: → FANGELI W., Mitt. Anthrop. Wien 118s (1988s) 45-59; 5 fig.; Eng. 45.

g320 **Schöpf** Hans, Fabeltiere. Graz 1988, ADEVA. 167 p. – RSalesianum 52 (1990) 231 (R. *Bracchi*).

g321 *Schubert* Paul, Reçu pour le *phóros probátōn*: CdÉ 65 (1990) 97-102; 1 fig.

g322 **Shackleton** Judith C., Marine molluscan remains from Franchthi cave: Excav. 4. Bloomington 1988, Indiana Univ. x-194 p.; 30 fig.; 3 pl. $27.50. – RAJA 94 (1990) 682s (D. S. *Reese*).

g323 *Silkinson* Richard H., A possible origin for the 'shoulder ornaments' [rosettes] in Egyptian representations of lions: VarAeg 5 (1989) 59-71; 9 fig.

g324 **Snead** Stella, Animals in four worlds [photos; text *Doniger* Wendy, *Michell* George]. Ch 1989, Univ. ix-199 p. $46. – RBSO 53 (1990) 586s (Albertine *Gaur*).

g325 *Stephens* Viola G., Like a wolf on the fold; animal imagery in VERGIL: ILCL 15 (1990) 107-130.

g326 *Teffer* Y., ☯ The rise and fall of dove-raising ['columbaria' not for burial]: → 348, Man and law 1986, 170-196.

g327 TETerian A., PHILON, Alexander ... bruta animalia: Philon 36, 1988 → 4,h64; 5,g26: RRTPhil 122 (1990) 552 (S. *Imhoof*); ScEsp 42 (1990) 113s (G. *Pelland*); StPhilonAn 2 (1990) 184-6 (D. T. *Runia*).

g328 *Uerpmann* Hans-Peter, Die Domestikation des Pferdes im Chalkolithikum West- und Mitteleuropas: MadMit 31 (1990) 109-153; 10 fig.

g329 *Wälchli* Philipp, Hund und Katze im Abendmahl; ein Bildmotiv und sein biblischer Ursprung: TZBas 46 (1990) 322-332; 5 fig.

g330 *Weigel* Richard D., Gallienus' 'animal series' and Roman religion: NumC 150 (1990) 135-143; pl. 16.

g331 **Wheeler** Alwyne, *Jones* Andrew K. G., Fishes: Manuals in Archaeology 1989 → 5,g32*: RJField 17 (1990) 496-9 (H. Sorayya *Carr*).

g333 *Ziderman* I. Irving, Seashells and ancient purple dyeing: BA 53 (1990) 98-101.

U2.7 **Flora;** *plantae biblicae et antiquae.*

g334 *Ambros* Arne A., Gestaltung und Funktion der Biosphäre im Koran: ZDMG 140 (1990) 290-325 [... Tiere].

g335 ᵀᴱ**Amigues** Suzanne, Tʜᴇᴏᴘʜʀᴀsᴛᴇ, Recherches sur les plantes [I. 1988 ➤ 4,h91; 5,g35], II livres III-IV: Coll. Budé. P 1988s, BLettres. I (1-2) lviii-145 (doubles) p.; II (3-4), 304 (d.) p. 2-251-00403-7; -4-5. – ᴿClasR 40 (1990) 236-8 (R. W. *Sharples*).

g336 *Amigues* Suzanne, Un conte étymologique; Hélène et les serpents [*helénion* = six plantes différentes]: JSav (1990) 177-198; 8 fig.

g337 **Bauer** Thomas, Das Pflanzenbuch des Aʙū Ḥᴀɴīᴇᴀ ad-Dīnawarī, Inhalt, Aufbau, Quellen [ᴱ*Lewin* B., Handschriften erst nach 1918 gefunden]. Wsb 1988, Harrassowitz. viii-290 p. DM 58. – ᴿOLZ 85 (1990) 422-4 (M. *Ullmann*).

g338 *Baum* Nathalie, Le *kwnt* de l'Égypte ancienne et ses relations avec le figuier commun (Ficus carica L.): VarAeg 5 (1989) 175-181.

g339 **Beaux** Nathalie, Le cabinet de curiosités de Thoutmosis III; plantes et animaux du 'jardin botanique' de Karnak: OrLovAn 36. Lv 1990, Univ. Dept. Oriëntalistiek. x-349 p.; LXVII pl. + dessins. 90-6831-268-5.

g340 **Carroll-Spillecke** Maureen, *Kēpos*, der antike griechische Garten: Wohnen in der klassischen Polis 3. Mü 1989, Dt. Kunst.-V. 99 p.; 33 fig.

g341 *Dobias-Lalou* Catherine, Amandes de Cyrène et d'ailleurs: RPg 63 (1989) 213-219.

g342 a) *Felix* Yehuda, ⊙ *rôš* [hemlock], *laʿanâ* [wormwood]; – b) *Har-Even* Shulamith, ⊙ Verse and plant [Prov. 20,30; Gen 49,22]: Lešonenu 53 (1988s) 31s; 1 fig.; Eng. III / 34s; Eng. IVa.

g343 *Ferrari* Leo C., The tree in the works of St. Aᴜɢᴜsᴛɪɴᴇ: AugLv 38 (1988) 37-53.

g343* *Fine* Stephen, On the development of a symbol; the date palm in Roman Palestine and the Jews: JPseud 4 (1989) 105-118 [< TR 87,74].

g344 **Germer** Renate, Flora des pharaonischen Ägypten 1985 ➤ 1,e843... 4,h110: ᴿJAmEg 27 (1990) 225-7 (Nathalie *Baum*, also on Dɪᴛᴛᴍᴀʀ J. 1986).

g345 **Germer** Renate, Katalog der altägyptischen Pflanzenreste der Berliner Museen 1988 ➤ 1,e843... 4,h111: ᴿOLZ 85 (1990) 662s (W. *Barta*).

g346 **Germer** Renate, Die Pflanzenmaterialien ... Tutanchamun 1989 ➤ 5,g45: ᴿOLZ 82 (1991) 30-33 (M. *Eaton-Krauss*).

g347 a) *Greppin* John A. C., The various aloes in ancient times; – b) *Markey* T. L., Eurasian 'apple' as arboreal unit and item of culture: JIndEur 16 (1988) 33-48 / 49-68.

g348 *Haldane* Cheryl W., Shipwrecked plant remains: BA 53 (1990) 55-60; ill.

g349 ᴱ**Hastorf** Christine, *Popper* Virginia, Current paleoethnobotany; analytical methods and cultural interpretations of archaeological plant remains. Ch 1988, Univ. 236 p.; 38 fig. $10 pa. 0-226-31893-1. – ᴿJField 17 (1990) 334-7 (Julie *Hansen*).

g350 *Heimpel* W., Maulbeerbaum: ➤ 853*, RLA 7,7s (1990) 601.

g351 **Hepper** F. Nigel, Pharaoh's flowers, the botanical treasures of Tutankhamun: Kew Botanical Gardens. L 1990, Stationery Office. xii-80 p.; 40 (colour.) pl.; map. 0-11-250040-4 [OIAc F91,12: '870 p.'].

g352 **Hepper** F. Nigel, Planting a Bible garden; a practical reference guide for the home gardener, schools, colleges, and churches in all climates of the world: Kew Botanic Gardens. L 1987, Stationery Office. 104 p.; 16 (color.) pl. [KirSef 62 (1988s) p. 498].

g353 *Hepper* F. Nigel, Flax and linen in biblical times: BurHist 25 (1989) 105-116 [< OTAbs 13, p. 256; 20-23, gardens and parks, *Crocker* T.].

g354 *Herzhoff* Bernhard, *Phēgos*; zur Identifikation eines umstrittenen Baumnamens: Hermes 118 (1990) 257-272 . 385-404.

g355 **Hugonot** Jean-Claude, Le jardin dans l'Égypte ancienne: EurHS 38/27, 1989 ➤ 5,g46: ᴿHelmantica 41 (1990) 437-440 (J. *Oroz Reta*); LA 40 (1990) 489s (A. *Niccacci*).

g356 **Jacquat** Christiane, Les plantes de l'âge du Bronze; catalogue des fruits et grains. St-Blaise 1988, Busu. 162 p.; 47 pl.

g357 *Kruijf* T. C. de, Der Ölbaum und seine Frucht in der Kultur und im Kult des Altertums: Bijdragen 51 (1990) 246-255; Eng. 256 'in the cultural and religious experience of people in antiquity'.

g358 *Küster* Hansjörg, Bronzezeitliche Pflanzenreste aus Tall Munbāqa: MDOG 121 (1989) 85-91; 1 fig.

g359 *Lamberty-Zielinski* H., *qāneh* 'Schilf': ➤ 859, TWAT 7,1 (1990) 71-78.

g360 *a)* *Larew* Hiram G., Oak (quercus) galls preserved at Herculaneum in A.D. 79; – *b)* *Ricciardi* Massimo, *Aprile* Giuseppa G., Identification of some carbonized plant remains from the archaeological area of Oplontis [Torre Annunziata]: ➤ 89, ᶠJASHEMSKI W. (1988) I, 145-8; 1 fig. / 317-325 + 17 fig.

g361 **Larsen** Torben B., The butterflies of Egypt: Apollo Books. Cairo-Svendborg 1990, American Univ. 112 p.; 8 pl. 977-424-218-1 / 87-88757-14-5 [OIAc F91,15].

g362 *a)* *Linderski* J., Garden parlors; nobles and birds; – *b)* *McKay* Alexander G., Pleasure domes at Baiae: ➤ 89, ᶠJASHEMSKI W., (1989) II, 105-127 / 155-169 + 6 fig.

g363 **Manniche** Lise, An ancient Egyptian herbal. L 1989, British Museum. 176 p.; ill.

g364 *Moftah* Ramses, Der Laubbaum als Schriftzeichen: GöMiszÄg 119 (1990) 61-64.

g365 *Monbrun* P., Artémis et le palmier-dattier: Pallas 35 (1989) 69-91 + 8 fig.

g366 *a)* *Müller* Naomi F., Palm trees in paradise; Victorian views of the Ancient Near East landscape; – *b)* *Gleason* Kathryn L., The garden portico of Pompey the Great; an ancient public park preserved in the layers of Rome: Expedition 32,2 ('Gardens and landscapes of the past' 1990) 52-60 / 4-13; ill.

g367 *Mulder* M. J., *rimmôn* 'Granatsapfel': ➤ 859, TWAT 7,3s (1990) 528-532.

g368 *Nibbi* Alessandra, A note on the cedarwood from Maadi: DiscEg 17 (1990) 25-27.

g369 **Paszthory** Emmerich, Salben, Schminken und Parfüme im Altertum; Herstellungsmethoden und Anwendungsbereiche im östlichen Mediterraneum: AntWelt Sondernummer 21 (1990) 64 p.; 87 (color.) ill.

g370 **Pearsall** Deborah, Paleoethnobotany, a handbook of procedures. San Diego 1989, Academic. 470 p. 136 fig. $59. 0-12-548040-7. – ᴿJField 17 (1990) 334-7 (Julie Hansen, also on PIPERNO D. 1988).

g371 *Raven* Maarten J., Resin in Egyptian magic and symbolism: OMRO 70 (1990) 7-20; 10 fig.

g372 **Sigrist** R. Marcel, Les šattukku 1984 ➤ 65,b924: ᴿOLZ 85 (1990) 410-2 (M. *Krebernik*).

g373 *Stemler* Ann, A scanning electron microscopic analysis of plant impressions in pottery from the sites of Radero, el Zakiab, l. Um Direiwa and el Kadada: ArNilM 4 (1990) 87-98 + VII pl.

g374 *a) Wiesl* Y., *al.*, ❶ Flora in ancient Eretz-Israel [... has not changed much in 3000 years]: – *b) Kindler* A., ❶ Agricultural symbols on ancient Jewish coins in Eretz-Israel: ➤ 86, Man and law 1986, 231-243 / 223-230.

g375 *Wilson* Hilary, Sycamore and fig: DiscEg 18 (1990) 71-82; 11 fig.

U2.8 Agricultura, alimentatio.

g376 *Addabbo* Anna Maria, Ancora sul cap. 160 del De agricultura di CATONE: AtenRom 35 (1990) 102-112.

g377 *Agius* Dionisius A., Arab expertise in cultivation as reflected in the Siculo-Arabic agricultural terminology: Muséon 103 (1990) 167-176.

g378 ᵀᴱ**André** Jacques, COLUMELLE, De l'agriculture XII (De l'Intendante) 1988 ➤ 4,h144: ᴿAntClas 59 (1990) 382s (R. *Verdière*); Helmantica 41 (1990) 392 (Rosa M. *Herrera*).

g379 *Avner* Uzi, Ancient agricultural settlement [in severe climate] and religion in the Uvda valley in southern Israel: BA 53 (1990) 125-141; ill.

g380 **Battaglia** Emanuela, 'Artos'... papiri 1989 ➤ 5,g71: ᴿCC 141 (1990,4) 624s (A. *Ferrua*).

g381 **Borowski** Oded, Agriculture in Iron Age Israel 1987 ➤ 3,f535... 5,g77: ᴿBA 53 (1990) 43 (T. V. *Brisco*); BSO 52 (1989) 335s (J. F. *Healey*); OLZ 85 (1990) 560-2 (D. *Conrad*); TLZ 115 (1990) 584-7 (H. M. *Niemann*).

g382 *Broshi* Magen, ❶ Agriculture and economy in Roman Palestine according to Babatha's papyri [27 in Greek, ᴱ*Lewis* N.]: Zion 55 (1990) 269-281; Eng. XI.

g383 *Bruins* Hendrik J., ❶ Ancient agricultural terraces at Naḥal Mitnan [E Kadeshbarnea]: 'Atiqot 10 (1990) 127s; Eng. 22*-28*.

g384 *Brunsch* Wolfgang, P. Hamburg D 51; Liste über die Abgabe von Saatgut (recto) und Quittierung der Ernteabgabe (verso): ZägSpr 117 (1990) 11-20; pl. 1-2.

g384* ᵀᴱ**Carazzali** Giulia, APICIO, l'arte culinaria; manuale di gastronomia classica: Tb Bompiani. Mi 1990. 350 p. – ᴿAufidus 11s (1990) 261 (A. *Ramini*).

g385 **Charles** M., Agriculture in lowland Mesopotamia in the late Uruk / early Dynastic period: diss. London 1990. – BInstClas 37 (1990) 209.

g386 **Chernoff** Miriam C., The archaeobotanical material from Tel el Ifshar, Israel; a diachronic study of agricultural strategies during the third and second millennia B.C.E.: diss. Brandeis, ᴰ*Zeitlin* Judith F. Boston 1989. 88-25815. – OIAc JJ89.

g387 *a) Clark* Royston, Towards the integration of social and ecological approaches to the study of early agriculture; – *b) Edwards* Kevin J., The cereal pollen record and early agriculture: ➤ 813, Beginnings of agriculture 1987/9, 3-22 / 113-135.

g388 *Crawford* Gary W., *Takamiya* Hiroto, The origins and implications of late prehistoric plant husbandry in northern Japan: Antiquity 64 (1990) 889-911.

g389 *Cruz-Uribe* Eugene, A note on the Early Demotic grain formula: Enchoria 17 (1990) 55-68; pl. 3-4.

g390 **Cuvigny** Hélène, L'arpentage par espèces dans l'Égypte ptolémaïque 1985 ➤ 3,f542; 4,h155: ᴿRÉG 103 (1990) 302s (A. *Blanchard*).

g391 *a) Dar* S., ❶ Agriculture and agricultural produce in Eretz-Israel in the Roman-Byzantine period; a. structure of the agricultural unit; b. ... wine-press; – *b) Porat* J., ❶ Aspect of the development of ancient irrigation agriculture in Jericho and Ein-Gedi; – *c) Kloner* A., ❶ The structure at Hulda [not a synagogue] and its use as a wine-press: ➤ 348, Man and law 1986, 142-169 / 127-141 / 197-208.

g392 *Davis* Michael, Cannibalism and nature [ARISTOTLE 1253 a 31-37 ...]: Métis 4,1 (1989) 33-50.

g393 *De Martino* Francesco, *a)* Economia dell'oliveto nell'Italia romana: ParPass 254 (1990) 321-347; – *b)* Latifondo ed agricoltura a schiavi [ŠTAERMAN, KOLENDO, KUZIŠČIN]: ParPass 44,246 (1989) 217-231.

g394 **Dolce** Rita, *Zaccagnini* Carlo, Il pane del re 1989 ➤ 5,841.g91: ᴿMesopT 25 (1990) 251-3 (P. *Mollo*); Orientalia 59 (1990) 555s (Barbara *Cifola*); Protestantesimo 45 (1990) 218s (J. A. *Soggin*).

g395 *Evans* Edith, Dining with the ancients; what the literary and archaeological records tell us about Roman cooking: Archaeology 43,6 (1990) 55-61; ill.

g396 *Fales* Frederick M., A Middle Assyrian text concerning vineyards and fruit groves: SAAB 3 (1989) 53-59; Pl. III.

g397 **Forbes** Mrs L., Olives in the agriculture of classical antiquity: diss. Liverpool 1990. – BInstClas 37 (1990) 209.

g398 *a) Fouchard* Alain, L'éloge de l'agriculture et des agriculteurs en Grèce au IVᵉ siècle avant J.-C.; – *b) Doukellis* Panagiotis, *Pónos* et travail agricole dans les discours de Libanios: ➤ 111, ꜰLÉVEQUE P. 3 (1989) 133-147 / 125-132.

g398* *Gaál* E., [1 to 50 *parīsum*, amount of food given (? daily) to] Prisoners of war in Alalaḫ VII [querying M. TSEVAT, HUCA 29 (1958) 121]: ➤ 67, Mem. HAHN I., AcAntH 32 (1989) 1-3.

g399 **Garnsey** P., Famine and food supply 1988 ➤ 4,h164; 5,g96: ᴿClasPg 85 (1990) 238-244 (K. R. *Bradley*); ClasR 40 (1990) 103-6 (R. P. *Duncan-Jones*); ÉtClas 58 (1990) 407s (H. *Leclercq*).

g400 *Gil'ad* Haim, [Dt 11,10; 1 Kgs 21,2] A garden of vegetables: JBQ 19 (1990s) 123-6 [vegetables are nowhere named in the Bible except Num 11,5, and even there three of the five plants are rather pumpkin].

g401 *Goodman* Martin, Kosher olive oil in antiquity: ➤ 183, ꜰVERMES G. 1990, 227-245.

g402 **Gregg** Susan A., Foragers and farmers; population interaction and agricultural expansion in prehistoric Europe; Prehistoric Archeology and Ecology series. Ch 1989, Univ. 275 p.; 15 fig. $25; pa. $10. 0-226-30735-2; -6-0. – ᴿJField 16 (1989) 348-350 (A. *Sherratt*).

g403 *Greppin* J. A. C., The words for 'beet' in three interrelated systems; Greco-Roman, Armenian and Arabic: Byzantion 60 (1990) 145-163.

g404 *Grottanelli* Cristiano, La distribution de la viande dans la Cyropédie: Métis 4 (1989) 185-209.

g405 **Guidi** M., L'allevamento dei suini nelle tavolette micenee: Aevum 64 (1990) 17-32.

g406 *Halstead* Paul, Quantifying Sumerian agriculture — some seeds of doubt and hope [not on computerization, but on the high seed-yield ratios]: BSumAgr 5 (1990) 187-195.

g407 **Hamel** Gildas, Poverty and charity in Roman Palestine [... how much food was available?]: NE Studies 23. Berkeley 1990, Univ. California. xiv-290 p. [RB 98, 313s, J. *Murphy-O'Connor*].

g408 *Hancock* R.G.V., *al.*, The abuse of bone analysis for archaeological dietary studies: Archaeometry 31 (1989) 169-179.

g409 *Harrak* Amir, La liste de vaisselle et de nourriture VAT 18046: AltOrF 17 (1990) 70-75.

g410 **Heine** Peter, Kulinarische Studien; Untersuchungen zur Kochkunst im arabisch-islamischen Mittelalter, mit Rezepten. Wsb 1988, Harrassowitz. 137 p. DM 68. – ᴿWZKM 80 (1990) 247s (A.A. *Ambros*).

g411 *Heine* Peter, Kochen im Exil — zur Geschichte der arabischen Küche: ZDMG 139 (1989) 318-327.

g412 *Heltzer* Michael, Vineyards and wine in Ugarit (property and distribution): UF 22 (1990) 119-135.

g413 **Henry** Donald O., From foraging to agriculture; the Levant at the end of the Ice Age. Ph 1989, Univ. Pennsylvania. 0-8122-8137-3 [OIAc JJ89].

g414 **Herz** P., Studien... Lebensmittelversorgung 1988 → 5,g107; Hab.-D. Mainz 1985: ᴿAthenaeum 78 (1990) 581-3 (A. *Marcone*); DLZ 111 (1990) 65-67 (T. *Sternberg*); Tyche 4 (1989) 251 (G. *Dobesch*).

g415 *Højlund* Flemming, Date honey production in Dilmun in the mid 2d millennium B.C.; steps in the technological evolution of the *madbasa* [date honey room]: Paléorient 16,1 (1990) 77-86; 10 fig.

g416 *Hoffmann* Richard C., Tools, agricultural, European [*Hassan* Ahmad Y. el-, Islamic]: → 837*, DMA 12 (1989) 72-83 [-86].

g417 **Hopkins** David C., The highlands of Canaan... agricultural: SocWB 3, 1985 → 2,b773... 5,g110: ᴿTLZ 115 (1990) 340s (H.M. *Niemann*).

g418 **Hruška** Blahoslav, [Czech] Der traditionelle Ackerbau im alten Mesopotamien. Praha 1990, Orientalni ustav. 516 p.; deutsch 391-516. 80-900060-8-6 [OIAc Oc90].

g419 *Immerzeel* Mat, Profession, negotiator allecarius; fabrication et commerce de sauce de poissons dans le nord-ouest de l'empire romain: OMRO 70 (1990) 183-190 + 6 fig. → g275.

g420 **Kehoe** Dennis P., Economics of agriculture... N. Africa 1988 → 4,h176; 5,g113: ᴿClasR 40 (1990) 116-8 (R.P. *Duncan-Jones*); Gnomon 62 (1990) 468-470 (K.-P. *Johne*).

g421 **Kilianotis** A., A commentary on PHILO of Alexandria's De agricultura: diss. Trinity. Dublin 1990. – BInstClas 37 (1990) 208.

g421* *Kramer* Johannes, *Spanelaion* ['oil from unripe olives', not from a specific place]: ZPapEp 81 (1990) 261-4.

g422 *Lanciers* Eddy, Ägyptisches Brot (k′k′) in UPZ I 149 und die wirtschaftliche Lage zur Zeit Ptolemaios' IV. Philopator: ZPagEp 82 (1990) 89-92.

g423 *a)* *La Placa* P.J., *Powell* M.A., The agricultural cycle and the calendar at pre-Sargonic Girsu; – *b)* *Hruška* Blahoslav, Das landwirtschaftliche Jahr im alten Sumer; – *c)* *Maekawa* K., Cultivation methods in the Ur III period; – *d)* *Driel* G. van, Neo-Babylonian agriculture III. Cultivation; – *e)* *Zaccagnini* Carlo, Again on the yield of the fields at Nuzi; – *f)* *Liverani* Mario, The shape of Neo-Sumerian fields: BSumAgr 5 (1990) 65-104 / 105-114 / 115-145 / 219-266 / 201-217 / 147-186.

g424 **Lissarrague** François, The aesthetics of the Greek banquet; images of wine and ritual [Un flot d'images 1987 → 4,e446], ᵀ*Szegedy-Maszek* Andrew]. Princeton 1990, Univ. vii-150 p.; 111 fig. 0-691-03595-4.

g425 *Littauer* M.A., *Crouwel* J.H., Ceremonial threshing in the Ancient Near East, I. Archaeological evidence: Iraq 52 (1990) 15-19 [19-23, *Steinkeller* P., II. Threshing implements in ancient Mesopotamia; cuneiform sources]; pl. II-III.

g426 *Lloyd* J.B.,   The banquet theme in Ugaritic narrative: UF 22 (1990) 169-193.

g427 *Maekawa* Kazuya,   The agricultural texts of Ur III Lagash of the British Museum (VI):   AcSum 11 (1989) 113-128; 129-142 facsimiles; 143s appendix.

g428 *Maidman* M.P.,   A feast for the mind; liver, oil, and other divine delicacies: BCanadMesop 19 (1990) 5-8 [15-24, *George* L., extipicy].

g429 *Malagardis* Nassi,   Images du monde rural attique à l'epoque archaïque: ArchEph 127 (1988) 95-134.

g430 *Markle* Minor M.,   Participation of farmers in Athenian juries and assemblies: AncSoc 21 (1990) 149-165.

g431 *Mattingly* D.J.,   Paintings, presses and perfume production at Pompeii [an unusual type of olive (or ? perfume) -press is known from four Pompeii paintings]: OxJArch 9 (1990) 71-90; 12 fig.

g432 *a) Mayeske* Betty Jo,   A Pompeian bakery on the Via dell'Abbondanza: – *b) Meyer* Frederick G.,   Food plants identified from carbonized remains at Pompeii and other Vesuvian sites: ➤ 89, ᶠJASHEMSKI W. (1988) I, 149-158 + 13 fig. / 183-220 + 47 fig.

g433 *Meijer* Fik,   The financial aspects of the leges frumentariae of 123-58 BC: MünstHand 9,2 (1990) 14-22; français 22; deutsch 22s.

g434 *Migeotte* Léopold,   Distribution de grain à Samos à la période hellénistique; le 'pain gratuit' pour tous?: ➤ 25, ᶠBOGAERT/VAN LOOY 1989s, 297-308.

g435 **Milano** Lucio,   Testi amministrativi; assegnazione di prodotti alimentari (Archivio L.2712, parte 1): ARET 9.   R 1990, Univ. Missione Arch. Siria. xvii-419 p.; LXVIII pl.; 1 disc. Lit. 130.000.

g436 *Milano* Lucio,   Addition [12 photos only] to 'Barley for rations and barley for sowing', ASJ 9:   AcSum [9 (1987)] 12 (1990) 79-87.

g437 **Mrozek** Stanisław,   Les distributions d'argent et de nourriture... Haut-Empire romain 1987 ➤ 4,h184:   ᴿClasR 40 (1990) 181s (R.P. *Duncan-Jones*).

g438 *Neeve* Pieter W. de †,   A Roman landowner and his estates; PLINY the Younger: Athenaeum 78 (1990) 363-402.

g439 *Nielsen* Bruce E.,   An acknowledgment of a loan of wheat [Oxy P. Col. inv. 166]:   BASP 27 (1990) 95-100 + 1 pl.

g440 **Oehme** Marlis,   Die römische Villenwirtschaft; Untersuchungen zu den Agrarschriften CATOS und COLUMELLAS und ihrer Darstellung bei NIEBUHR und MOMMSEN [Diss. Marburg 1986]: Diss. Alte Geschichte 24. Bonn 1988, Habelt. xi-313 p.; DM 45. – ᴿAnzAltW 43 (1990) 266-9 (P. *Pantischek*); ClasR 40 (1990) 184 (K.D. *White*).

g441 ᴱ**Öhrnberg** Kaj,   *Miroueh* Sahban,   IBN-SAYYĀR el-Warrāq, Kitāb al-ṭabīkh [cuisine]: StudOr 60.   Helsinki 1987, Finnish Oriental Soc. x-343 p. Fm 200. – ᴿOLZ 85 (1990) 337-9 (P. *Heine*).

g442 **Palmer** Ruth,   Wine in the Mycenaean palace economy: diss. Cincinnati Univ. 1989, ᴰ*Palaima* T.   311 p. 90-19864. – DissA 51 (1990s) 491-A.

g443 *Paul* G.M.,   JOSEPHUS [B 2,883-6], the Epitome de Caesaribus and the grain-supply of Rome: AncHB 4 (1990) 79-83.

g444 *Piselli* Francesco,   Nel foco che li affina [(Dante Purg. 2.26.145)... cibi nell'AT, poi materiali di costruzione]: BbbOr 32 (1990) 3-20. 103-127.

g445 **Ponsich** M.,   Aceite de oliva y salazones de pescado; factores geo-económicos de Bética y Tingitania.   M 1988, Univ. Complutense.   253 p.; 115 fig.   84-7491-248-2. – ᴿJRS 80 (1990) 201s (D.J. *Mattingly*).

g446 ᴱ**Purnelle** Gérald, CATO, De agricultura... [1988 ➤ 5,g132] index verborum. Liège 1988, Centre Informatique. xxiii-192 p. – ᴿClasR 40 (1990) 282s (A. S. *Gratwick*); Latomus 49 (1990) 479-482 (P. *Hamblenne*).

g447 *Quaegebeur* Jan, Les rois saïtes amateurs de vin: AncSoc 21 (1990) 241-271.

g448 *Rowland* Robert J.ᴶ, The production of Sardinian grain in the Roman period: MeditHR 5 (1990) 14-20.

g449 *Rowley-Conwy* Peter, Nubia AD 0-550 and the 'Islamic' agricultural revolution; preliminary botanical evidence from Qasr Ibrim, Egyptian Nubia: ArNilM 3 (1989) 131-8; map.

g450 **Sandy** D. Brent, The production and use of vegetable oils in Ptolemaic Egypt: BASP supp. 6, 1989 ➤ 5,g136; $23: ᴿCdÉ 65 (1990) 178-180 (Hélène *Cuvigny*).

g451 *Scheidel* Walter, a) *Agricola, colonus, cultor, rusticus*; Beobachtungen zum rechtlichen und sozialen Status der 'Landwirte' in COLUMELLAS Schrift 'De re rustica': Maia 42 (1990) 257-265; – b) Feldarbeit von Frauen in der antiken Landwirtschaft: Gymnasium 97 (1990) 405-431.

g452 *Segarra* D., La ofrenda de alimentos en Ebla durante el reinado de Ibbi-Sipiš: AulaO 8 (1990) 219-241; Eng. 219.

Seidel Ulrich, Studien zum Vokabular der Landwirtschaft im Syrischen 1989 ➤ 9431.

g454 *Sijpesteijn* Pieter J., Liste mit Getreide-, Öl- und Geldzahlungen: Tyche 5 (1990) 171-4; pl. 20-21.

g456 **Spurr** M. S., Arable cultivation in Roman Italy c. 200 B.C. - c. A.D. 100: JRS Mg 3, 1986 ➤ 4,h197; 5,g139: ᴿParPass 44,246 (1989) 231-240 (F. *De Martino*).

g457 *Stärk* Ekkehard, Vindemia; drei Szenen zu den Römern auf dem Lande: Gymnasium 97 (1990) 193-211.

g458 **Steensberg** Axel, Hard grains, irrigation, numerals and script in the rise of civilisations: Research on agricultural implements 6. K/Brede 1989, Danish Acad./Museum. 147 p.; 56 fig. 87-98169-15. – ᴿAntiquity 64 (1990) 968s (N. *Yoffee*: numbering of hard grains developed into the first scripts; archaeologists are too concerned with religion, toys, linguistics).

g459 *Strubbe* J. H. M., A new inscription on sitonia (free distributions of grain, not only in years of shortage); EpAnat 16 (1990) 109-114.

g460 **Tchernia** André, Le vin de l'Italie romaine 1986 ➤ 2,b754... 5,g142: ᴿArchWsz 40 (1989) 178-181 (A. *Loś*, ❷).

g461 **Virlouvet** C., Famines et émeutes à Rome 1985 ➤ 2,9632... 5,g145: ᴿAevum 64 (1990) 131s (P. *Grattarola*).

g462 *Wagner* Guy, *Tiphágion* [not tophágion as he earlier proposed; a kind of *tiphē* or wheat-grain]: ZPapEp 80 (1990) 239-242.

g463 **Wilhelm** Gernot, Das Archiv des Silwa-teššup 3. Rationenlisten II. Wsb 1985, Harrassowitz. 213 p.; X pl. – ᴿOLZ 85 (1990) 40-43 (C. *Zaccagnini*); OrAnt 28 (1989) 273-5 (Paola *Negri Scafa*).

g464 a) *Wilkinson* T. J., Soil development and early land use in the Jazira region, Upper Mesopotamia; – b) *Wilshusen* Richard H., *Stone* Glenn D., An ethnoarchaeological perspective on soils: WorldArch 22 (1990s) 87-103 / 104-114.

g465 *Will* Elizabeth L., Celtic importation of Roman wine in the second and first centuries c.c.: ➤ 742*, Rome's Alpine frontier 1986, RArtLv 21 (1988) 25-30.

g466 **Zohary** D., *Hopf* M., The domestication of plants in the Old World 1988 ➤ 5,g151: ᴿIndEur 17 (1989) 189-192 (E. C. *Polomé*).

g467 *Zohary* Daniel,   Domestication of plants in the Old World; the emerging synthesis: ➤ 754, Worlds 1988/90, 35-42; 2 maps.

U2.9 **Medicina** *biblica et antiqua.*

g468 *Adamson* P.R.,   Some anatomical and pathological terms in Akkadian [*papām libbi, ra'ïbu, ruqqu, šaḫurru*]: RAss 84 (1990) 27-32.

g469 **Agelarakis** Anagnostis,   The paleopathological evidence; indicators of stress of the Shanidar proto-Neolithic and Ganj Dareh early Neolithic human skeletal collections: diss. Columbia, ᴰ*Solecki* R.   NY 1990. xvii-550 p. – OIAc Oc90.

g470 *Anastassiou* Anargyros, *Schmidt* Volkmar,   Zum 3. Kap. der ps.-hippokratischen Schrift De affectionibus: RheinMus 133 (1990) 259-263.

g471 *Arce* Agostino,   I Francescani di Terra Santa e la peste: TerraS 65 (1989) 123-8.

g472 *Arthur-Katz* Marilyn,   Sexuality and the body in ancient Greece: Métis 4 (1989) 155-179.

g473 *Barcia Goyanes* Juan J.,   La anatomía en la Biblia [*luz* Ps 34,21; *galîl* Ct 5,14; *yated* Dt 23,14]: EscrVedat [17 (1987) 61-74; 18 (1988) 33-42] 19 (1989) 127-132; 20 (1990) 227-235.

g474 **Bardinet** Thierry,   Dents et mâchoirs dans les représentations religieuses et la pratique médicale de l'Égypte ancienne: StPohl 15.   R 1990, Pontificio Istituto Biblico.   xxi-280 p.   88-7653-591-8 [OIAc S90].

g475 *Baumgarten* Joseph M.,   The 4Q Zadokite fragments on skin disease [without comment on Lv 13 three types]: JJS 41 (1990) 153-165; 2 pl.

g476 *Benedum* Christa,   Asklepios; der homerische Arzt und der Gott von Epidauros: RheinMus 133 (1990) 210-226.

g477 *Biggs* R.D.,   Medizin A. In Mesopotamien [Eng.]: ➤ 853*, RLA 7,7s (1990) 623-9 (-631, bei den Hethitern, *Beckman* G.).

g478 *a*) *Bürgel* J.C.,   Die Auferweckung vom Scheintod; ein Topos in der medizinischen Literatur des arabischen Mittelalters; – *b*) *Terzioğlu* A., Eine bisher unbekannte Handschrift über die Herstellung der Arzneien im Topkapi-Palast in Istanbul und ihre Bedeutung für die Geschichte der Pharmacie: Zts für Geschichte der Arabisch-Islamischen Wissenschaften 4 (1987s) 175-194 / 160-174 [< OLZ 85,626].

g479 ᴱ**Burguière** Paul, *al.*, SORANOS, Maladies des femmes I, 1988 ➤ 4,h215; 5,g159: ᴿAntClas 59 (1990) 337-9 (S. *Byl*); ClasR 40 (1990) 19s (Helen *King*); Gymnasium 97 (1990) 92s (V. *Langholf*).

g480 *Camoletto* Silvia,   Sul linguaggio traumatologico di CELSO [De medicina]: BStLat 20 (1990) 14-24.

g481 **Cohen** Mark N.,   Health and the rise of civilization.   NHv 1986, Yale Univ. 285 p. $24. 0-300-04006-7. – ᴿAJA 94 (1990) 486s (G.R. *Milner*: 'hunter-gatherer' theories either misleading or incorrect); Antiquity 64 (1990) 688 (G. *Lewis*).

g482 *Crocker* P.,   Apothecaries, confectionaries, and a new discovery at Qumran: BurHist 25,2 (1989) 36-46 [< NTAbs 34,76].

g483 *Dasen* Veronique,   Dwarfs in Athens: OxJArch 9 (1990) 191-207; 16 fig. (vase-paintings; one model may have served for several).

g484 *Degen* Rainer,   Das Verzeichnis der Schriften des HIPPOKRATES in der Überlieferung des BARHEBRAEUS; ein kritischer Bericht: ➤ 8*, ᶠ*Assfalg* J., Lingua restituta orientalis 1990, 79-88.

g485 *Dols* Michael W.,   Syriac into Arabic; the transmission of Greek medicine: Aram 1,1 (1989) 45-52.

g486 *Doucet* Dominique, Le thème du médecin dans les premiers dialogues philosophiques de S. AUGUSTIN: AugLv 39 (1989) 447-461.

g487 **Eggers Lan** Conrado, HIPÓCRATES; de la medicina antigua: BiblGr-RMex. México 1987, Univ. clxxxi-30 (double) p. 968-36-0121-9. – ᴿAnt-Clas 59 (1990) 302s (S. *Byl*: outdated).

g488 *Fawver* Jay D., *Overstreet* R. Larry, Moses and preventive medicine [... fatty foods to be avoided; circumcision diminishes cancer]: BS 147 (1990) 270-285.

g489 **Fischer** Peter M., Prehistoric Cypriot skulls...: SIMA 75, 1986 ⇒ 2,b770 ... 5,g170: ᴿAntClas 59 (1990) 578s (R. *Laffineur*).

g489* *Gerlitz* Peter, Krankheit, religionsgeschichtlich / *Scharbert* Josef, AT / *Müller* Ulrich B., NT: ⇒ 857, TRE 19 (1990) 675-680 / 680-3 / 684-6.

g490 *Gero* Stephen, GALEN on Christians; a reappraisal of the Arabic evidence: OrChrPer 56 (1990) 371-411.

g491 **Ghalioungui** Paul, The physicians of pharaonic Egypt 1983 ⇒ 1,e960... 4,h230: ᴿOLZ 85 (1990) 151-3 (W. *Westendorf*).

g492 *Gómez-Royo* E., *Buigues-Oliver* G., Die Haftung der Ärzte in den klassischen und nachklassischen Quellen: RIDA 37 (1990) 167-195.

g493 **Grand'Henry** Jacques, ʿAli B. RIḌWĀN, Le livre de la méthode du médecin: LvOr. Publ. 20.31, 1979/84 ⇒ 3,f608: ᴿOLZ 85 (1990) 335-7 (G. *Strohmaier*: unfavorable).

g494 *Greppin* J. A. J., Reference to physicians and to GALEN in the Armenian Fables of Mikhitar Gosh: ByZ 83 (1990) 91-97.

g496 **Grensemann** Hermann, Knidische Medizin II; Versuch einer weiteren Analyse der Schicht A in den pseudohippokratischen Schriften De natura muliebri und De mulieribus I und II: Hermes Einz 51, 1987 ⇒ 3,f610... 5,g177: ᴿGnomon 62 (1990) 579-583 (G. *Wöhrle*); RBgPg 68 (1990) 171s (S. *Byl*).

g497 *Griffiths* John G., Love as a disease [Beatty I, *Lichtheim* M. Ancient Egyptian Literature 2 (1976) 185; also Ct 2,5; 5,8 alludes to love as a disease; Greek parallels more abundant 'without great anatomical precision' (*Dover* K., Theocritus 1971, 175)]: ⇒ 114, ᶠLICHTHEIM M. 1990, 349-364.

g498 **Grmek** Mirko D., Diseases in the ancient Greek world 1988 ⇒ 4,h286; 5,g178: ᴿClasW 83 (1989s) 378 (P. *De Lacy*); RelStR 16 (1990) 258 (Madeleine M. *Henry*).

g499 *Gunasingam* S., Catalogus of Tamil manuscripts in the library of the Wellcome Institute for the History of Medicine: JRAS (1990) 359-369.

g500 **Harakas** Stanley S., Health and medicine in the Eastern Orthodox tradition. NY 1990, Crossroad. xii-190 p. $20. – ᴿTS 51 (1990) 790s (J. J. *Pilch*).

g501 *Harakas* Stanley S., Health and medicine in the Eastern Orthodox tradition; salvation as the context of healing: GrOrTR 34 (1989) 221-237.

g502 ᴱ**Hart** Gerald D., Disease in ancient man 1979/83 ⇒ 65,638*. b985; 1,e971: ᴿBInstArch 26 (1989) 270s (R. L. *Miller*).

g503 ᵀᴱ**Hersant** Yves, HIPPOCRATE, sur le rire et la folie 1989 ⇒ 5,g181*; F 35; 2-86930-235-5: ᴿAntClas 59 (1990) 304 (A. *Touwaide*); HumT 10 (1989) 403-6 (J. A. *Castro*).

g504 **Honda** Gisho, *al.*, Herb drugs and herbalists in Syria and North Yemen: Studia Culturae Islamicae 19. Tokyo 1990, Inst. AsAfrica. [ix-] 156 p.

g505 **Horstmanshoff** Hermann F. J., De pijlen van de pest; pestilenties in de Griekse wereld (800-400 v.C.) [diss. Leiden 1989]. Amst 1989. 299 p. –

ᴿAntClas 59 (1990) 425s (S. *Byl*); ClasR 40 (1990) 523s (P. *Potter*); Gymnasium 97 (1990) 91 (H. *Längin*).

g506 **Houzey** Dominique, Histoire de la médecine chinoise: Médecine et Société. P 1988, Payot. 295 p. F 140. 2-228-88090-6. – ᴿÉTRel 65 (1990) 109 (J. *Argaud*: amandes de pêches et de prunes, 'l'archéologie l'atteste').

g507 *Huyse* Philip, Die persische Medizin auf der Grundlage von HERODOTS Historien: AncSoc 21 (1990) 141-8: for an amateur, his symptoms are surprisingly accurate and enable a diagnosis.

g509 ᵀᴱ**Iskander** Albert Z., De optimo medico consulendo arabica versio, Ⓐ + Eng.: Corpus medicorum graecorum supp. or. 4, 1988 ➤ 5,g184: ᴿClasQ 40 = 84 (1990) 236-257 (V. *Nutton*: 30 years work but he doesn't know Greek).

g510 **Jackson** Ralph, Doctors and diseases in the Roman Empire 1988 ➤ 4,h242; 5,g185: ᴿAncHRes 20 (1990) 185-190 (J. *Walker*); AntClas 59 (1990) 429s (A, *Touwaide*); ClasW 83 (1989s) 247s (P. *De Lacy*); RArchéol (1990) 430-2 (G. *Sabbah*).

g511 *Jouan* François, L'oracle, thérapeutique de l'angoisse: ➤ 757, Oracles = Kernos 3 (1990) 11-26.

g512 ᵀᴱ**Jouanna** Jacques, HIPPOCRATE, Des vents; de l'art 1988 ➤ 5,g186: ᴿParPass 254 (1990) 397-400 (A. *Jori*).

g513 ᵀᴱ**Jouanna** Jacques, HIPPOCRATE II/1, De l'ancienne médecine: Coll. Budé. P 1990-, BLettres. 237 (doubles) p. 3-251-00417-3.

g514 *a) Koelbing* Huldrych M., Le médecin dans la cité grecque; – *b) Kollesch* Jutta, Knidos als Zentrum der frühen wissenschaftlichen Medizin im alten Griechenland: Gesnerus [Soc. Suisse d'Histoire de la Médecine, Aarau] 46 (1989) 29-43 / 11-28 [AnPg 60, p. 855].

g515 **Krug** Antje, Medicina nel mondo classico. F 1990, Giunti. 270 p.; 96 fig. Lit. 35.000. 88-09-20152-3.

g516 **Kudlien** Fridolf, Die Stellung des Arztes in der römischen Gesellschaft 1986 ➤ 2,b781... 5,g192: ᴿAnzAltW 43 (1990) 105-8 (D. *Nickel*).

g517 **Kühn** J.-H., *Fleischer* U., Index hippocraticus 1989 ➤ 5,g192*; DM 664: ᴿGymnasium 97 (1990) 361s (Rüdiger *Schmitt*).

g518 *Künzl* Ernst, Operationsräume in römischen Thermen; zu einem chirurgischen Instrumentarium aus der Colonia Ulpia Traiana, mit einem Auswahlkatalog römischer medizinischer Instrumente im römischen Landesmuseum Bonn: BonnJbb 186 (1986) 491-509; 19 fig.

g519 **Lloyd** Geoffrey E. R., The revolutions of wisdom; studies in the claims and practice of ancient Greek science [... Hippocratic corpus]: Sather Lectures 52, 1987 ➤ 5,g196: ᴿPhoenix 40,1 (Toronto 1990) 97s (A. *Jones*).

g520 *Löfstedt* Bengt, Notizen zu Sprache und Text von CELSUS, De medicina: MusHelv 47 (1990) 60-62.

g521 **Lorenz** Günther, Antike Krankenbehandlung in historisch-vergleichender Sicht; Studien zum konkret-anschaulichen Denken: Bibl KlAltW NF 2/81. Heid 1990, Winter. 362 p. 3-533-04140-9 [OIAc Oc90].

g521* *Manetti* Daniela, Doxographical deformation of medical tradition in the report of the Anonymus Londinensis on Philolaus: ZPapEp 83 (1990) 219-233.

g522 *Masson* Michael, Remarques étymologiques sur quelques mots grecs relatifs au vocabulaire médical: RPg 63 (1989) 195-208 [*arados, katias, storúnē, saura*].

g523 **Matthaeus** Hartmut, Der Arzt in römischer Zeit; medizinische Instrumente und Arzneien; archäologische Hinterlassenschaft in Siedlungen und Gräbern: Limesmuseum Aalen 43. Stu 1989, Württemberg. Landesmuseum. 108 p.; ill. [AnPg 60, p. 855].

g524 ᴱMeulenbeld G. Jan, *Wujastyk* Dominik, Studies on Indian medical history, Wellcome Institute 2-4 Sept. 1985. Groningen 1987, Forsten. vii-247 p. – ᴿOLZ 85 (1990) 716s (C. *Vogel*).

g524* **Nickel** Diethard, Untersuchungen zur Embryologie GALENS: Schriften zur Geschichte und Kultur der Antike 27. B 1989, Akademie. 116 p. 3-05-000697-8.

g525 **Nutton** Vivian, From Democedes to Harvey; studies in the history of medicine; Coll. Studies 277, 1988 ➤ 5,g203; £32: ᴿClasR 40 (1990) 443s (Helen *King*).

g526 *Ochoa* José A., La terminología técnica en la traducción latina del siglo XII del *Perì aérōn* HIPOCRÁTICO: Emerita 58 (1990) 255-271.

g527 **Pisi** Giordana, La peste in SENECA tra scienza e letteratura: Univ. Parma, Inst. lat. 10. R 1989, Bulzoni. 115 p. Lit. 15.000. – ᴿÉtClas 58 (1990) 291 (Thérèse *Ory*).

g529 *Pettinato* Giovanni, Nascita, matrimonio, malattia e morte ad Ebla: ➤ e333*, Wirtschaft/Ebla 1986/8, 299-316; p. 308, La malattia [sumerico *tu-ra*, non come da lui precedentemente interpretato] 'rivela la pietà degli Eblaiti e il loro legame con il mondo divino': 17 testi, nessuno con qualcosa sui rimedi.

g530 **Phillips** E. D., Aspects of Greek medicine. Ph/L 1987 = 1973, Charles/ Croom Helm. 240 p.; 15 fig. – ᴿAnÉCS 45 (1990) 889s (Aline *Rousselle*: 'Pillips').

g531 *Piétri* Luce, Les médecins dans la Gaule chrétienne du Vᵉ au VIIᵉ siècle; rôle et réputation: ➤ 111, ᶠLÉVÊQUE P. 3 (1989) 341-357.

g532 **Pigeaud** Jackie, Folies et cures 1987 ➤ 4,h262; 5,g211: ᴿAnÉCS 45 (1990) 884-6 (Aline *Rousselle*).

g533 **Potter** Paul, Hippocrates V-VI: Loeb 472s. CM/L 1988, Harvard/ Heinemann. xv-333 p.; xv-361 p. $18.50 each. 0-674-99520-8 / L 0-434-99472-3; -3-1. – ᴿAntClas 59 (1990) 301 (S. *Byl*: 50 years after I-IV 1923-31 by W. H. S. *Jones*); Athenaeum 78 (1990) 563-6 (D. *Fausti*).

g534 **Potter** Paul, Short [➤ 5,g213!] handbook of Hippocratic medicine. Québec 1988, Sphinx. 59 p.; 4 fig. $5. 2-920123-07-6. – ᴿAntClas 59 (1990) 303 (S. *Byl*); ClasR 40 (1990) 191 (J. T. *Vallance*, also on R. JACKSON).

g535 ᴱ**Price** T. Douglas, The chemistry of prehistoric human bone [Madison Wisconsin Univ. School of American Research 1986 Santa Fe seminar]. C 1989, Univ. £35. 0-521-362-16-4. – ᴿAJA 94 (1990) 680s (M. J. *Becker*); Antiquity 64 (1990) 962s (R. *Gillespie*).

g536 **Rahman** Fazlur, Health and medicine in the Islamic tradition; change and identity. NY 1987, Crossroad. viii-149 p. $20. – ᴿBSO 52 (1989) 129-131 (H. D. *Isaacs*).

g537 *Römer* Cornelia, Ehrung für den Arzt Themison [Alexandria]: ZPapEp 84 (1990) 81-88.

g538 *Romano* Roberto, Per l'edizione dei Libri medicinali di AEZIO Amideno (IV): Lincei-BClas 8 (1987) 69-78.

g539 *Rowland* J. Thompson, The rise and decline of surgery in dynastic Egypt: Antiquity 63 (1989) 312-9 [AnPg 60, p. 856].

g540 **Sabbah** Guy, *al.*, Bibliographie des textes médicaux latins 1987 ➤ 5,g215: ᴿPhoenix 44 (Toronto 1990) 399s (L. *Brisson*).

g541 *Schrenk* L. P., Byzantine evidence for GALEN's On medical experience: ByZ 82 (1989) 251-7.

g542 **Skoda** Françoise,   Médecine ancienne et métaphore; le vocabulaire de l'anatomie et de la pathologie en grec ancien. P 1988, Peeters/Selaf. xxii-341 p. – ᴿRÉG 103 (1990) 308s (Véronique *Boudon*).

g543 *Smith* Patricia, The trephined skull from the Early Bronze Age period at Arad: → 4, ᶠAMIRAN Ruth, Eretz-Israel 21 (1990) 89*-93*; 4 fig.

g544 ᵀᴱ**Staden** Heinrich von, Herophilus, the art of medicine in early Alexandria, 1989 → 5,g222: $140. 0-521-23646-0: ᴿAntClas 59 (1990) 333s (S. *Byl*); ClasR 40 (1990) 238-240 (J. *Longrigg*); ÉtClas 58 (1990) 412 (Thérèse *Ory*); Phronesis 35 (1990) 194-215 (R. J. *Hankinson*, 'Saying the phenomena').

g544* *Stöhr* Martin, 'Denn ich bin der Herr, dein Arzt': Gedanken zur Pathologie der Geschichte: Junge Kirche 51 (Bremen 1990) 479-488.

g545 ᴱ**Sullivan** Lawrence E., Healing and restoring; health and medicine in the world's religious traditions. NY 1989, Macmillan. xx-468 p. $35 [RelStR 17, 134, J. S. *Strong*].

g546 ᴱ**Tamani** Giuliano, Il Canon medicinae di AVICENNA nella tradizione ebraica; le miniature del manoscritto 2197 della Biblioteca Universitaria di Bologna: Dentro Veneto. Padova 1988, Programma. 93 p. – ᴿHenoch 12 (1990) 249s (G. *Busi*); RÉJ 149 (1990) 214-6 (J. *Shatzmiller*).

g547 *Teodorsson* Sven-Tage, A forgotten anatomical method traced? [PLUT. QNat 912 D-E commending tart foods]: Eranos 88 (1990) 64-66.

g548 *Tsekourakis* D., Die Ursachen von Krankheiten bei PLUTARCH: Ellinika 49 (1989) 257-269.

g549 **Ubelaker** Douglas H., Human skeletal remains; excavation, interpretation²ʳᵉᵛ [¹1978]: Manuals on Archaeology 2. Wsh 1989, Taraxacum. xi-172 p.; 164 fig. $20. – ᴿAJA 94 (1990) 487s (Marshall J. *Becker*).

g550 *Van Beek* Gus & Ora, The function of the bone spatula [32 found at Jemmeh: an ophthalmic instrument]: BA 53 (1990) 205-9.

g551 *Veldhuis* Niek, The new Assyrian [magical-medical] compendium for a woman in childbirth: AcSum 11 (1989) 239-260.

g552 **Vitrac** Bernard, Médecine et philosophie au temps d'HIPPOCRATE: Histoires des Sciences. P 1989, Presses Univ. de Vincennes. 187 p. – ᴿAnÉCS 45 (1990) 887s (Aline *Rousselle*).

g553 *Walker* Jim, Food, health and disease in ancient Egypt: AncHRes 20 (1990) 96-107.

g554 *Waltke* Bruce, Relating human personhood to the health sciences; an OT perspective [Gn. 1,26s...]: Crux 25,3 (1989) 2-10 [< OTAbs 13, p. 154].

u3   *Duodecim Tribus:* **Israel Tribes;** Land-Ideology.

g555 **Aldrich** Timothy W., The land promise in the New Testament: diss. Dallas Theol. Sem., 1985 (?) [KirSef 62 (1988s), p. 503].

g555* *Blancy* Alain, Israël et sa terre: FoiVie 89,1 (1990) 21-37.

g556 *Chrostowski* Waldemar, ❷ La terre d'Israël dans l'économie de salut et de [ou 'dans la'] conscience juive: AtKap 114 (1990) 63-76.

g557 *Engelken* Karen, Kanaan als nicht-territorialer Terminus: BibNot 52 (1990) 47-63.

g558 *Feldman* Louis H., Some observations on the name of Palestine: HUCA 61 (1990) 1-3.

g559 **Kallai** Zacharia, Historical geography ... tribal territories [1967] 1986 → 4,h284; 5,g233: ᴿBSO 52 (1989) 120s (J. D. *Martin*); IsrEJ 40 (1990) 230s (E. F. *Campbell*: impressive); JAOS 110 (1990) 335-7 (R. S. *Hess*:

ponderous; based on presuppositions; only 2 extrabiblical documents); OLZ 85 (1990) 45-47 (E. A. *Knauf*).

g559* **Mendels** Doron, The Land of Israel... Hasmonean 1987 ⇒ 3,f669... 5,g234: ᴿAntonianum 65 (1990) 384-6 (M. *Nobile*).

g560 **Na'aman** Nadav, Borders and districts in biblical historiography (1986 ⇒ 2,b824... 5,g236: ᴿJNES 49 (1990) 83-88 (Diana *Edelman*); JQR 80 (1989s) 163-8 (Z. *Kallai*); SvEx 55 (1990) 104-6 (M. *Ottosson*).

g560* **Niemann** H. M., Die Daniten 1985 ⇒ 1,f11... 5,g237: ᴿProtestantesimo 45 (1990) 140-2 (J. A. *Soggin*).

g561 **Rask** Phillip J., The lists of the twelve tribes of Israel [28; only Nm 2 repeated (in Nm 7 and 10)]: diss. Catholic Univ. of America, ᴰ*Meier* J. Wsh 1990. 668 p. 90-27648. – DissA 51 (1990s) 1662-A.

g562 *Rossi de Gasperis* Francesco, La terra promessa, un dono da condividere: RasT 31 (1990) 608-614.

g563 *Sarigiannis* George, ⓖ Tribal divisions and notions of urban planning [among] the ancient Hebrews according to the Hebrew original text and the translation of the Septuagint: DeltioVM 18,2 (1989) 49-87.

g564 **Wolff** K. E. [a Sister of Zion], 'Geh in das Land, das ich Dir zeigen werde...': Das Land Israel in der frühen rabbinischen Tradition und im Neuen Testament [Diss. ᴰ*Beutler* J.]: EurHS 23/340. Fra 1989, Lang. 393 p. Fs 34. 3-8204-1066-8 [BL 91, 150, P. S. *Alexander*].

u4 *Limitrophi*, adjacent lands.

g565 **Barrelet** Marie-Thrèse, Problèmes concernant les Hurrites 1984 ⇒ 65, d31; 3,f677: ᴿWeltOr 20s (1989s) 276-280 (D. L. *Stein*).

g566 **Bartlett** John R., Edom and the Edomites: JStOT Sup 84, 1989 ⇒ 5, g242: ᴿBAnglsr 10 (1990s) 91-93 (E. *Stern*); BL (1990) 30 (G. I. *Davies* says it inaugurates a new PEQ Mg series 'even if, unaccountably, practically all trace of its sponsorship is missing from the book itself'); ÉTRel 65 (1990) 619s (Françoise *Smyth*); ExpTim 101 (1989s) 310 (J. F. *Healey*: some unanswered questions); PEQ 122 (1990) 139-142 (P. *Bienkowski*); Qadmoniot 23 (1990) 127 (E. *Stern*, ⓖ); VT 40 (1990) 384 (J. A. *Emerton*).

g567 *Bonfante* Giuliano, I Pelasgi [...Dalmazia, Creta]: ArGlotIt 73 (1988) 50-52.

g568 ᴱ**Briend** Jacques, -*Seux* M.-J.), Israël et les nations d'après les textes du Proche-Orient ancien: CahÉv 69 supp. P 1989, Cerf. 115 p. F 45. 0222-9706.

g569 **Bryce** Trevor R., The Lycians I 1986 ⇒ 2,b839... 5,g243: ᴿAnzAltW 43 (1990) 184-6 (Edith *Specht*).

g570 **Fourgous** Denise, Les Dryopes; peuple sauvage ou divin?: Métis 4,1 (1989) 5...

g571 **Kasher** Aryeh, Jews, Idumeans and ancient Arabs: TStAntJ 18, 1988 ⇒ 4,h295: ᴿÉTRel 65 (1990) 617s (Danielle *Ellul*); JAOS 110 (1990) 574-6 (D. *Goodblatt*).

g572 **Rolle** Renate, The world of the Scythians [1980, ᵀ1989 ⇒ 5,g258]. Berkeley 1989. 141 p.; 100 fig. $25 [RelStR 17, 158, C. J. *Aling*].

g573 **Strange** John, Caphtor-Keftiu 1980 ⇒ 61,3591...65,d50: ᴿFolOr 27 (1990) 257-9 (L. *Hellbing*, Eng.).

g574 **Timm** S., Moab zwischen den Mächten; Studien zu historischen Denkmälern und Texten: ÄgAT 17. Wsb 1989, Harrassowitz. vii-

516 p. DM 128. 3-447-02940-4 [BL 91,130, J.R. *Bartlett*: solid evidence free of speculation].

g575 **Wilhelm** Gernot, The Hurrians [Grundzüge der... 1982 ➤ 63,9778*], T*Barnes* Jennifer. L 1989, Aris & P. $40. 0-85668-442-2. – RZAss 80 (1990) 145s (D.O. *Edzard*).

U4.5   *Viae* – **Routes, roads.**

g576 *Bauzou* Thomas, Les routes romaines de Syrie: ➤ 481, Syrie II (1989) 205-222.

g577 *Davidović* Vesna, Trade routes between northern Syria and central Anatolia in the middle of the III millennium B.C.: AcSum 11 (1989) 1-25 + 6 fig. (map).

g578 **Grassi** Paolo, *Biagi* Maria Cristina, present., Le vie mercantili tra Mediterraneo e Oriente nel mondo antico; catalogo mostra Roma 16.X.1985-2.III.1986. R 1986, Paleani. 285 p.; ill.; maps [JAOS 109,721].

g579 **Halfmann** Helmut, Itinera principum 1986 ➤ 4,h307; 5,g270: RAcArchH 42 (1990) 378s (B. *Lőrincz*); JRS 80 (1990) 219-222 (J.-L. *Mourgues*).

g580 **Jettmar** Karl, *Thewalt* Volker, Between Gandhara and the silk roads; rock-carvings along the Karakorum highway; discoveries by German-Pakistani expeditions 1979-1984. Mainz 1987, von Zabern. 3-8053-0954-6 [OIAc S89 sans pp.].

g581 **Klimkeit** Hans-Joachim, Die Seidenstrasse 1988 ➤ 5,g272: RZDMG 140 (1990) 172-4 (Annemarie von *Garain*).

g582 *Laut* Jens P., Die alte Seidenstrasse im Licht neuerer Publikationen [*Hopkirk* P., *Klimkeit* H. ...]: ZRGg 42 (1990) 367-370.

g583 **Nashef** Khaled, Rekonstruktion und Reiserouten zur Zeit der altassyrischen Handelsniederlassungen: TAVO B-83, 1987 ➤ 3,f706; 5,g275: RBO 47 (1990) 675-684 (P. *Villard*: de grand inetérêt).

g584 *Pekáry* T., Zu den römischen Reichsstrassen: AcArchH 41 (1989) 399-404.

g585 **Tardieu** Michel, Les paysages reliques; routes et haltes syriennes d'Isidore à Simplicius: ÉPHÉR Bt. 94. Lv 1990, Peeters. 211 p.; ill. 90-6831-296-0.

g586 *Tzedakis* Yannis, *al.*, Les routes minoennes: BCH 114 (1990) 43-62.

U5   *Ethnographia,* **Sociologia** [servitus ➤ E3.5; G6.5].

g586* *Alföldy* G., Das Heer in der Sozialstruktur des römischen Kaiserreichs: ➤ 67, Mem. HAHN I., AcAntH 32 (1989) 169-186.

g587 *Álvarez-Verdes* L., El método sociológico en la investigación bíblica actual; incidencia en el estudio de la ética bíblica: StMor 27,1 (R 1989) 5-41 [< NTAbs 34,3].

g588 *Arens* Eduardo, Los evangelios en la perspectiva sociológica: Páginas 104 (Lima 1990) 71-86 [< TContext 8/2, 116].

g589 *Baines* John, Restricted knowledge, hierarchy, and decorum; modern perceptions and ancient institutions: JAmEg 27 (1990) 1-23.

g591 *Bastomsky* S., Rich and poor; the great divide in ancient Rome and Victorian England: GreeceR 37,1 (1990) 37-43 [NTAbs 35,83: in

CICERO's time the rich had an income from 714 to 10,476 (later 17,142) times that of 'the' poor: no statistics for 'much better' England].

g592 *Behrens* Hermann, Das Sozialverhalten des Urmenschen (homo erectus): PraehZts 66 (1991) 10-13.

g593 **Blasi** A. J., Early Christianity as a social movement: TorStRel 5. NY 1988, Lang. v-240 p. $34.50. 0-8204-0581-7 [NTAbs 34,373]. – ᴿBibTB 20 (1990) 169 (B. J. *Malina*: anachronistic sociology of religion).

g594 *Blasi* A. J., On precision in studying ancient Palestine: Sociological Analysis 51 (Wsh 1990) 395-9 [G. LANG confuses data of two different populations]: 401-5, Lang's reply [< NTAbs 35,213].

g595 ᴱ**Blok** Josine, *Mason* Peter, Sexual asymmetry; studies in ancient society 1987 ➤ 5,g287: ᴿAntClas 59 (1990) 505 (G. *Raepsaet*: 'L'école féministe américaine n'en finit pas de faire des émules... perdre de leur originalité, sinon de leur crédibilité').

g596 *Blok* Josine, Patronage and the Pisistratidae: Babesch 65 (1990) 17-28.

g597 *Bobrova* Larisa V., *Koshurnikov* Sergej G., On some new works in the social history of the Old Babylonian period [STONE E. 1977, unsuccessful]: AltOrF 16 (1989) 51-60.

g598 *Bonete Perales* Enrique, P. L. BERGER, una teoría sociológica de la modernidad: RelCu 36 (1990) 557-590.

g599 **Bonhoeffer** Dietrich, Sanctorum communio, eine dogmatische Untersuchung zur Soziologie der Kirche, ᴱ*Soosten* Joachim von: Wcrkc 1. Mü 1986, Kaiser. 344 p. – ᴿRTPhil 122 (1990) 290s (H. *Mottu*).

g600 *a) Bruhns* Hinnerk, La cité antique de Max WEBER; – *b) Nippel* Wilfried, Moses I. FINLEY and Weber; some comments and theses: Opus 6ss (1987ss) 27-42 / 43-50.

g601 ᴱ**Buss** Andreas E., Max WEBER in Asian studies: Internat. Studies in Sociology 42, 1985 ➤ 2,b864; 94-04-07695-6: ᴿZDMG 139 (1989) 227 (H. *Bechert*).

g602 **Caillé** Alain, Splendeurs et misères des sciences sociales; esquisse d'une mythologie: Pratiques sociales et théories. Genève 1986, Droz. 412 p. F fr. 215. – ᴿRHE 85 (1990) 901 (J.-P. *Hendrickx*).

g603 *a) Cantarella* Eva, 'Neaniskoi'; classi di età e passaggi di 'status' nel diritto ateniese; – *b) Mactoux* Marie-Madeleine, Esclaves et rites de passage; – *c) Torelli* Mario, Riti di passaggio maschili di Roma arcaica: ➤ 748, MÉF 102,1 (1990) 37-51 / 53-81 / 93-106.

g604 *a) Capogrossi-Colognesi* Luigi, Max WEBER e i limiti della società antica; – *b) Perrin* Yves, Peinture et société à Rome; questions de sociologie; sociologie de l'art, sociologie de la perception; – *c) Keuls* Eva, New light on the social position of vase painters in late archaic Athens: ➤ 111, ᶠLÉVÊQUE P. 3 (1989) 55-65 / 311-342 / 149-167; 9 fig.

g605 *Carruba* Onofrio, Alle origini del matriarcato: IstLombR 124 (1990) 239-346.

g606 ᴱ**Casalegno** Ugo, Antropologi e missionari a confronto: Ieri, oggi, domani 4. R 1988, LASalesianum. 127 p. – ᴿTeresianum 40 (1989) 599s (F. *Di Giacomo*).

g607 ᴱ**Clements** R. E., The world of ancient Israel; anthropological... 1989 ➤ 5,387: ᴿExpTim 101,7 top choice (1989s) 193-6 (C. S. *Rodd*: GOTTWALD overemphasized); NorTTs 91 (1990) 255s (H. M. *Barstad*); VT 40 (1990) 506s (J. A. *Emerton*).

g608 **Coote** R. B. & M. P., Power, politics, and the making of the Bible; an introduction. Minneapolis 1990, Fortress. xi-191 p. $13. 0-8006-2441-6

[BL 91, 69, I. W. *Prován*: too assured to take into account that the Bible is a 'work' profoundly subversive of all human authority and power structures].

g609 **Dandameyev** M. A. (p. 4-16), ❻ Gosudarstvo (State) i socialnie struktury na Drevnom Vostoka. Moskva 1989, Nauka. 160 p. r 1,40. 5-02-016575-1 [p. 17-37, *Jacobson* V., & *Kozyrava* N., Mesopotamia; 53-85, *Schiffmann* I., Palestine; 86-108, *Berlev* O. & 109-126, *Bogoslovsky* Y., 109-126, Egypt]. – FFolOr 27 (1990) 268 (E. *Lipiński*).

g610 **Dekker** G., Godsdienst en samenleving; inleiding tot de studie van de godsdienstsociologie. Kampen 1987, Kok. 247 p. *f* 35. 90-2425-271-7. – RNedTTs 44 (1990) 357s (J. *Visser*).

g611 EDemarchi Franco, W. SCHMIDT etnologo 1986/9 ⟶ 5,804: RSalesianum 52 (1990) 732-5 (U. *Casalegno*).

g612 *Deniaux* Élisabeth, *Schmitt-Pantel* Pauline, La relation patron-client en Grèce et à Rome: Opus 6ss (1987ss) 147-163.

g613 *Dijkstra* K., State and steppe; the socio-political implications of Hatra inscription 79 [*Safar* F., Sumer 17 (1961) phot.]: JSS 35 (1990) 81-98: tribal oath of improved loyalty to Hatra dynasty.

g614 **Dixon** Suzanne, The Roman mother 1988 ⟶ 4,h340; 5, g294: RAmHR 95 (1990) 468 (Sarah B. *Pomeroy*); ClasJ 85 (1989s) 264-6 (Jane E. *Phillips*); ClasPg 85 (1990) 333-8 (Judith *Evans-Grubbs*); ClasW 83 (1989s) 127s (Larissa *Bonfante*); ÉchMClas 34 (1990) 470-3 (M. *Golden*); RPg 63 (1989) 384s (M. *Ducos*).

g615 *Donaldson* T. L., Rural bandits, city mobs and the Zealots [HORSLEY R. A., HANSON J. S. 1985]: JStJud 21 (1990) 19-40.

g616 **Dumortier** Francis, La patrie des premiers chrétiens [⟶ 4,d460]. P 1988, Ouvrières. 321 p. 2-7082-2564-2. – RÉTRel 65 (1990) 125s (G. *Balestier-Stengel*: situation socio-économique grecque-romaine).

g617 **Ebertz** M. N., Das Charisma des Gekreuzigten: WUNT 45, 1987 ⟶ 3,f773 ... 5,g397: RTGegw 31 (1988) 277s (H. *Giesen*); TR 86 (1990) 282s (N. *Mette*).

g618 **Eichenauer** Monika, Untersuchungen zur Arbeitswelt der Frau in der römischen Antike: EurHS 3/360, 1988 ⟶ 5,g298: RMünstHand 9,1 (1990) 111-4 (J. *Wiesehöfer*).

g619 *Eichler* Selke, Untersuchungen zu den Wasserträgern von Deir-el-Medineh I: StAäK 17 (1990) 135-175.

g620 **Eilberg-Schwartz** H., The savage in Judaism; an anthropology of Israelite religion and ancient Judaism. Bloomington 1990, Indiana Univ. xiii-290 p. $18 pa. [ZAW 103, 446, H.-C. *Schmitt*].

g621 *a)* *Endesfelder* Erika, Die Stellung der Frauen in der Gesellschaft des Alten Ägypten; – *b)* *Röwer-Döhl* Ruth, Die Frau im antiken Griechenland: ⟶ 768, Waren sie nur schön? 1985/9, 23-70; fig. 1-15 / 183-223; fig. 77-105.

g622 **Felder** Cain H., Troubling biblical waters; race, class, and family 1989 ⟶ 5,g300: RCurrTMiss 17 (1990) 226s (P. H. *Gundani*).

g623 *a)* *Feucht* Erika, Kinder fremder Völker in Ägypten I; – *b)* *Hodel-Hoenes* Sigrid, Betrachtungen zum Dank im Alten Ägypten; – *c)* *Gessler-Löhr* Beatrix, Zur Datierung einiger königlicher Truchsesse [stewards] unter Amenophis III.: ⟶ 16, FBECKERATH J. v. 1990, 29-48 / 119-138 / 53-73; pl. 2b-5.

g624 *Foxhall* Lin, The dependent tenant; land leasing and labour in Italy and Greece: JTS 80 (1990) 97-114; 2 fig. (map).

g625 **Franklin** Naomi P., The stranger within their gates (how the Israelite portrayed the non-Israelite in biblical literature) [6 episodes; *ḥesed* demanded]: diss. Duke, ᴰ*Bailey* L. Durham NC 1990. 174 p. 91-00095. – DissA 51 (1990s) 2775-A; RelStR 17,193.

g626 *a) Fuks* Alexander, The sharing of property by the rich with the poor in Greek theory and practice; – *b) Applebaum* Shim'on, Jewish urban communities and Greek influences: ScrClasIsr 5 (1980) 46-63 / 158-177.

g627 **Gardner** Jane F., Women in Roman law and society 1987 ⇒ 3,f740 ... 5,g302: ᴿAncHRes 20 (1990) 65-67 (R. A. *Bauman*).

g628 ᴱ**Gibson** M., *Biggs* R. D., The organization of power 1983/7 ⇒ 3,781; 5,g303: ᴿBO 47 (1990) 395-8 (J.-J. *Glassner*).

g629 ᴱ**Gill** Robin, Theology and sociology; a reader 1987 ⇒ 4,h358; 0-8091-2978-7: ᴿEcuR 42 (1990) 77s (A. W. *Black*); Gregorianum 71 (1990) 595s (M. *Chappin*); ScotBEv 8 (1990) 65s (H. H. *Davis*).

g630 *Glassner* Jean-J., L'hospitalité en Mésopotamie ancienne; aspect de la question de l'étranger: ZAss 80 (1990) 60-75.

g631 *a) Glassner* Jean-Jacques, Women, hospitality and the honor of the family; – *b) Harris* Rivkah, Independent women in ancient Mesopotamia?; – *c) Grosz* Katarzyna, Some aspects of the position of women in Nuzi; – *d) Kuhrt* Amélie, Non-royal women in the Late Babylonian period, a survey; – *e) Roth* Martha T., Marriage and matrimonial prestations in first millennium B.C. Babylonia: ⇒ 4,851, ᴱ**Lesko** Barbara, Women's earliest records 1987/9, 71-90 / 145-156 / 167-180 / 215-239 / 245-255 [plus shorter introductions and responses].

g632 **Grant** Robert M., Cristianesimo primitivo e società, ᵀᴱ*Firpo* G. 1987 ⇒ 3,f745; 5,g307: ᴿOrpheus 10 (1989) 217-9 (Amalia *Tuccillo*); Salesianum 52 (1990) 726 (S. *Felici*).

g633 *Greeley* Andrew, Sociology and the Catholic Church; four decades of bitter memories: Sociological Analysis 50,4 (Anniversary issue, 1989) 393-8 [351-362, *Kivisto* Peter: < ZIT 90,295].

g634 **Günther** Rosemarie, Frauenarbeit ... ᴰ1987 ⇒ 5,g308: ᴿGnomon 61 (1989) 102-8 (L. *Schumacher*); Klio 72 (1990) 601-3 (H. *Krummrey*); MünstHand 9,1 (1990) 11-4 (J. *Wiesehöfer*).

g635 *Hackett* David G., Sociology of religion and American religious history; retrospect and prospect: JScStR 27 (1988) 461-474.

g636 *Hall* Jonathan, Black Athena [BERNAL M. 1987]; a sheep in wolf's clothing?: JMeditArch 3 (1990) 247-254 [255-274, *Manning* Sturt W.; 275-9, 280-2, Bernal responses].

g637 *Hallett* J. P., Women as *same* and *other* in classical Roman elites: Helios 16,1 (Lubbock TX 1989) 59-78 [< NTAbs 34,92].

g637* *Henning* Irene, Sozialgeschichtliche Bibelauslegung: Junge Kirche 51 (Bremen 1990) 504s [*Ahrens* Matthias 502s: < ZIT 90,597].

g638 *Herr* Theodor, Zum Verhältnis von Sozialwissenschaft und Theologie; hermeneutische Überlegungen: TGL 80 (1990) 36-57 [49-54, Umgang mit der Heiligen Schrift].

g639 **Holmberg** B., Sociology and the New Testament; an appraisal. Mp 1990, Fortress. viii-173 p. $11. 0-8006-2443-2 [NTAbs 35,93].

g640 **Hopkins** K., Death and renewal 1983 ⇒ 65,d99 ... 4,h369: ᴿGnomon 62 (1990) 424-8 (J. v. *Ungern-Sternberg*).

g641 **Horsley** Richard A., Sociology in the Jesus movement. NY 1989, Crossroad. 178 p. $23. – ᴿTTod 47 (1990s) 464. 466-8 (R. K. *Fenn*).

g642 **Just** Roger, Women in Athenian law and life [and literature and mythology]. L 1989, Routledge. x-317 p. £30. – ᴿClasR 40 (1990) 361s (D. M. *MacDowell*: men regarded women as threatening savages).

g643 **Kaster** R., Guardians of language 1988 → 5,g321: ᴿAncHB 4 (1990) 95-100 (J. *Vanderspoel*); RPg 63 (1989) 351 (P. *Flobert*); Speculum 65 (1990) 1002-5 (E. A. *Meyer*).

g644 **Kee** Howard C., Knowing the truth; a sociological approach to NT interpretation 1989 → 5,g322: ᴿExpTim 101 (1989s) 313s (S. C. *Barton*: fails to ask 'What is NT theology?'); FgNt 3, (1990) 78s (J. H. *Elliott*: methodologically inadequate); Neotestamentica 24 (1990) 156s (P. P. *Craffert*); TTod 47 (1990s) 356 (R. K. *Fenn*).

g645 *a*) *Kehoe* Dennis P., Comparative approaches to the social history of Roman Egypt [Boston seminar Dec. 29, 1989, AmPgAsn]: – *b*) *Hobson* Deborah W., Naming practices in Roman Egypt; – *c*) *Keenan* James G., Pastoralism in Roman Egypt; – *d*) *Bagnall* Roger S., Official and private violence in Roman Egypt; – *e*) *Frier* Bruce W., A new papyrology?: BASP 26/3s (1989) 153-6 / 157-174 / 175-198 + 2 fig. / 201-216 / 217-226.

g646 ᴱ**Kocka** Jürgen, Max WEBER, der Historiker [Internationaler Historikertag 1985]: Kritische Studien zur Geschichtswissenschaft 73, 1986 → 4,688: ᴿEngHR (1990) 754s (N. *Johnson*); HistJb 109 (1989) 511-3 (W. *Weber*).

g647 *Koptev* A. V., ❹ The 'freedom' and 'slavery' of *coloni* in the late Roman Empire: VDI 193 (1990) 24-38; Eng. 39s.

g648 *Koshurnikov* S. G., ❹ City headmen, governors, and burgomasters; legal proceeding, king's administration, and community in the Old Babylonian Dilbat: VDI 194 (1990) 76-93; Eng. 93.

g649 *Krieger* David J., Conversion [in sociology of knowledge]; on the possibility of global thinking in an age of particularism: JAAR 58 (1990) 223-243.

g650 *a*) *Kühnert* Barbara, Zur sozialen Mobilität in der späten römischen Republik; *plebs* und *ordo equester*; – *b*) *Lotze* Detlef, Spielräume sozialer Mobilität in Athen und Sparta; Überlegungen zu verschiedenen Ausprägungen griechischer Gesellschaft in klassischer Zeit: Klio 72 (1990) 144-150 / 135-143.

g651 **Kyrtatas** Dimitris J., The social structure of the early Christian communities [ᴰ1980], pref. *Ste-Croix* B. de, 1987 → 4,h736; 5,g325: ᴿBibTB 20 (1990) 128s (B. J. *Malina*; thoroughly provoking; vapid claim to be Marxist); CritRR 3 (1990) 395-7 (J. T. *Fitzgerald*: outdated; GUELZOW bypassed).

g652 *Lamberg-Karlovsky* C. C., ❹ Patterns of interaction in the third millennium, from Mesopotamia to the Indus valley: VDI 192 (1990) 3-21; 5 maps; Eng. 21.

g653 ᴱ**Lang** Bernhard, Anthropological approaches to the OT 1985 → 1,295 ... 3,f760: ᴿBZ 34 (1990) 120s (J. *Scharbert*: 'anthropology' in Anglophone sense of 'ethnology plus prehistory'); Vidyajyoti 54 (1990) 266s (R. J. *Raja*).

g654 *Levine* Molly M., Anti-Black and Anti-Semitic? Have classical historians suppressed the Black and Semitic roots of Greek civilization? [BERNAL M.]: BR 6,3 (1990) 32-36. 40; ill.

g655 **Lightstone** Jack N., Society, the sacred, and scripture in ancient Judaism; a sociology of knowledge 1988 → 4,h384: ᴿCBQ 52 (1990) 564s (A. J. *Saldarini*); SR 19 (1990) 110s (W. O. *McCready*); VT 40 (1990) 250 (W. *Horbury*).

g656 **Liverani** Mario,   Antico Oriente; storia, società, economia 1988
→ 4,b385:   RAevum 64 (1990) 112s (M. *Guidi*); BO 47 (1990) 605s (M.
Stol).

g657 **Loprieno** Antonio,   Topos und Mimesis; zum Ausländer in der ägyptischen Literatur 1988 → 5,9440:   RDiscEg 16 (1990) 89-95 (S. *Quirke*).

MacDonald Margaret,   The Pauline churches; a socio-historical study of
institutionalization 1988 → 5524.

g659 **McKechnie** Paul,   Outsiders in the Greek cities in the fourth century
B.C. L 1989, Routledge. viii-231 p. £25. – RGreeceR 37 (1990) 114 (P. J.
Rhodes); JHS 110 (1990) 253s (R. A. *Knox*).

g660 **Malina** Bruce J.,   Christian origins and cultural anthropology 1986
→ 2,b901 ... 4,h390:   RSecC 7 (1989s) 239-241 (R. A. *Ramsaran*).

g661 *Marshall* Anthony J.,   Women on trial before the Roman Senate:
ÉchMClas 34 (1990) 333-366.

g662 **Meeks** Wayne A.,   The moral world of the first Christians 1987
→ 2,b908 ... 5,g340:   RCritRR 2 (1989) 223s (C. F. *Sleeper*); Vidyajyoti
53 (1989) 682s (G. V. *Lobo*).

g663 *Molendijk* Arie L.,   Wissenschaft und Weltanschauung; Max WEBER
und Eduard SPRANGER über 'voraussetzungslose Wissenschaft' und
Theologie: NSys 31 (1989) 82-108; Eng. 108.

g664 EMommsen Wolfgang J.,   *Schwentker* Wolfgang,   Max WEBER und
seine Zeitgenossen: London German Historical Institute 21, 1988
→ 5,546 ['Deutsches Hist. Inst.']:   RDLZ 111 (1990) 684-7 (F. *Hauer*).

g665 *Morris* Brian,   Anthropological studies of religion; an introductory text
1987 → 4,h397; 5,g344;   0-521-33991-X: RNedTTs 44 (1990) 58s (V. B.
Kuiper); RelSt 25 (1989) 255-7 (T. *Fitzgerald*).

g666 **Mrozek** Stanisław,   Lohnarbeit im klassischen Altertum; ein Beitrag
zur Sozial- und Wirtschaftsgeschichte.   Bonn 1989, Habelt.   171 p.

g667 *Müller-Wollermann* Renate,   *a*) Sanktionen zur Regelung staatlicher
Arbeiten im Ägypten des Neuen Reiches: JACiv 4 (Chang-chun 1989)
29-38 [< OTAbs 14,30]; – *b*) Das ägyptische Alte Reich als Beispiel einer
WEBERschen Patrimonialbürokratie: BEgSem 9 (1987s) 25-40.

g667* *Murphy* Nancey,   Theology and the Social Sciences — discipline and
antidiscipline: Zygon 25 (Ch 1990) 309-316 [< ZIT 90,798].

g668 *Neumann* Hans,   Bemerkungen zur Freilassung von Sklaven im alten
Mesopotamien gegen Ende des 3. Jahrtausends v.u.Z.:   AltOrF 16
(1989) 220-233.

g669 *Newbold* B. F.,   Patterns of anxiety [about death, loss, shame...] in
SALLUST, SUETONIUS and PROCOPIUS: AncHB 4 (1990) 44-50.

g670 *Noy* David,   Matchmakers and marriage-markets in antiquity: Éch-
MClas 34 (1990) 375-400.

g671 *Otto* Eckart,   ¿Tiene la racionalidad moderna raices bíblicas? [WEBER
M. < EvKomm 21 (1988) 85-88], TSerra F., FGiménez J.:   SelT 29
(1990) 63-66.

g672 **Peltenburg** Edgar,   Early society in Cyprus.   E 1989, Univ. xvi-404 p.; ill.

g672* *a*) *Pesce* Mauro,   Antropologia biblica; punto di riferimento o frutto
del pensiero moderno?; – *b*) *Sermoneta* J. B.,   L'antropologia biblica
nella Guida dei perplessi di Mosè MAIMONIDE e il suo capovolgimento
nel Trattato teologico-politico di Benedetto SPINOZA; – *c*) *Idel* Moshe,
The anthropology of Yohanan ALEMANNO; sources and influence [con-
temporary of Pico and Ficino 15 cent.; influenced by BATALYAWSI I.
1052-1127]; – *d*) *Cohen* Charles L.,   Biblical anthropology and Puritan
religious experience [BIANCHI Daniela]; – *e*) *Rutto* Giuseppe,   Re-

formkatholizismus [B. Bolzano 1781-1848] e antropologia religiosa: ⇒ 526*a, AnStoEseg 7,1 (1990) 45-78 / 79-91 / 93-112 / 205-223 [257-275] / 335-343.

g673 *Petrikovits* H. V., Altvölkerkunde (Archäologie und Völkerkunde): Ac-ArchH 41 (1989) 527-532.

g674 ᴱ**Raaflaub** Kurt A., Social struggles in archaic Rome; new perspectives on the conflict of the orders 1981/6 ⇒ 4,458; 5,g353: ᴿLatomus 49 (1990) 207s (D. *Briquel*); Veleia 5 (1988) 323-5 (Laura *Sancho Rocher*).

g675 ᴱ**Rawson** B., The family in ancient Rome 1986 ⇒ 3,507. f787... 5,g355: ᴿVeleia 5 (1988) 319-321 (Rosa *Mentxaka*).

g676 **Rilinger** R., Humiliores - honestiores; zu einer sozialen Dichtomie im Strafrecht der römischen Kaiserzeit. Mü 1988, Oldenburg. 336 p. – ᴿAthenaeum 78 (1990) 230 (A. *Marcone*).

g677 **Rogerson** J., Anthropology and the OT 1984 = 1978 ⇒ 60,6503... 4,h400: ᴿVidyajyoti 54 (1990) 267 (P. M. *Meagher*).

g678 *Romano* Alba, Women in ancient Rome; the Roman mother [Dixon Suzanne 1988]: AncHRes 20 (1990) 108-115.

g679 **Rossi** Pietro, Max Weber; oltre lo storicismo. Mi 1988, Saggiatore. 281 p. Lit. 35.000. – ᴿHumBr 44 (1989) 736s (P. *Grassi*).

g680 **Saldarini** Anthony J., Pharisees, scribes and Sadducees in Palestinian society; a sociological approach ⇒ 4,h410* (Glazier 1988; also E 1989, Clark): ᴿBibTB 20 (1990) 173s (N. *Elliott*); BZ 34 (1990) 270-2 (R. *Schnackenburg*); CurrTMiss 17 (1990) 393 (J. L. *Bailey*); ExpTim 101 (1989s) 279s (J. R. *Bartlett*); Interpretation 44 (1990) 310s (B. *Chilton*); JJS 41 (1990) 267s (M. *Goodman*); NRT 112 (1990) 602s (X. *Jacques*); RExp 87 (1990) 132s (D. E. *Garland*); TS 51 (1990) 128-130 (R. A. *Wild*).

g681 **Scaff** Lawrence A., Fleeing the iron cage; culture, politics, and modernity in the thought of Max Weber. Berkeley 1989, Univ. California. xiv-265 p. $37.50 [RelStR 17,234, W. R. *Garrett*].

g683 *Schäfer-Lichtenberger* Christa, Stadt und Eidgenossenschaft im AT... M. Weber; Diss. ᴰ*Rendtorff* R.; BZAW 156, 1983 ⇒ 64,2633.d735... 3,f794: ᴿBLitEc 91 (1990) 133-6 (J.-M. *Husser*).

g684 *Schäfer-Lichtenberger* Christa, Vom Nebensatz zum Idealtypus; zur Vorgeschichte des 'Antiken Judentums' von Max Weber: ⇒ 147, ᶠRendtorff R., Die hebräische Bibel und ihre zweifache Nachgeschichte 1990, 419-433.

g685 **Schmeller** Thomas, Brechungen; urchristliche Wandercharismatiker im Prisma soziologisch orientierter Exegese: SBS 136, 1989 ⇒ 5,g359: ᴿBZ 34 (1990) 134-6 (R. *Schnackenburg*); TLZ 115 (1990) 433s (W. *Vogler*).

g686 *Schmeller* Thomas, Sociological exegesis of the NT [BiKi 44 (1989) 103-110], ᵀᴱ*Asen* B.: TDig 37 (1990) 231-4.

g687 **Schöllgen** G., Ecclesia sordida? 1985 ⇒ 65,d154... 5,g361: ᴿCathHR 76 (1990) 99s (D. E. *Groh*).

g687* *Segal* Robert A., Victorian anthropology [Stocking W. 1987; also his Malinowski/Essays 1986]: JAAR 58 (1990) 469-477.

g688 **Serrano Delgado** José M., Status y promoción social de los libertos en Hispania romana: Publ. Fil/Let 106. Sevilla 1988, Univ. 240 p. 84-7405-405-2. – ᴿAntClas 59 (1990) 513s (J. A. *Straus*).

g688* *Sharot* Stephen, Israel; sociological analyses of religion in the Jewish state: Sociological Analysis 51-special (Wsh 1990) 561-570 [1-80; in Belgium, Italy, France, India...: < zIT 90,796].

g689 ᴱ**Sigrist** Christian, *Neu* Rainer, Ethnologische Texte zum AT, I, Vor- & Frühgeschichte Israels 1989 ⇒ 5,g365: ᴿZkT 112 (1990) 92 (R. *Oberforcher*).

g690 **Smith** D. L.,   Religion of the landless 1989 ➤ 5,g366:   ᴿExpTim 102 (1990s) 85s (R. *Mason*).

g691 *Snowden* F. M.,   Black-White relations in the ancient Greek and Roman worlds: MeditQ 1,2 (1990) 72-92 [< NTAbs 35,84].

g692 *Soldt* W. H. van [*Wilhelm* G.], Matrilinearität A. in Elam [B. bei den Hethitern]: ➤ 853*, RLA 7,7s (1990) 586-8 [-590].

g693 **Sourvinou-Inwood** Christiane,   Studies in girls' transitions [... pre-puberty ritual] in Attic iconography. Athens 1988, Kardamitsa. 159 p. – ᴿAJA 94 (1990) 694s (Eva C. *Keuls*).

g694 **Specht** Edith,   Schön zu sein und gut zu sein; Mädchenbildung und Frauensozialisation im antiken Griechenland: Frauenforschung 9. W 1989, Frauenverlag. 192 p.; 17 fig. DM 32. – ᴿClasR 40 (1990) 508s (G. *Clark*).

g695 **Stahl** John A.,   Power dynamics during the rise of the state; an application of the RASCH model to archaeological data [two Ur Burials, one Ur-III and one following]: diss. Northwestern. Evanston 1989. 635 p. 90-15411. – DissA 51 (1990s) 205-A.

g696 **Stambaugh** J., *Balch* D.,   The social world of the first Christians 1986 ➤ 3,f801a [= b: ➤ 4,h417]: ᴿIrTQ 56 (1990) 66s (T. *Finan*, also on GRANT R.).

g697 *Stanley* Farland H.ᴶ, Geographical mobility in Roman Lusitania: ZPapEp 82 (1990) 249-266 + 3 maps.

g698 a) *Tarragon* J.-M.,   Ethnographie; Philologie semitique; – b) *Murphy-O'Connor* J., Géographie: ➤ m408, ᴱ*Vesco* J. L., L'AT, École Biblique 1990, 19-28. 37-61 / 7-18.

g699 *Taylor* W. F.,   Sociological exegesis; introduction to a new way to study the Bible, I. History and theory; II. Results: Trinity Sem. Review 11,2 (Columbus 1989) 99-110; 12,1 (1990) 26-42 [< NTAbs 34,290; 35,11].

g700 **Theissen** Gerd, [➤ 4632] Sociologia do movimento de Jesus [1979 ➤ 60,y73], ᵀ*Fuchs* Werner, *Höhn* Annemarie. S. Leopoldo/Petrópolis 1989, Sinodal/Vozes. 172 p. – ᴿREB 50 (1990) 488-490 (L. *Garmus*).

g701 **Theissen** Gerd,   Sociologia del cristianesimo primitivo 1987 ➤ 5,g373: ᴿTeresianum 40 (1989) 270s (V. *Pasquetto*).

g702 *Theissen* Gerd,   Hacia una teoría de la historia social del cristianismo primitivo [< ÉTRel 63 (1988) 199-225], ᵀᴱ*Villanova* Gabriel: SelT 29 (1990) 50-62.

g703 **Thompson** Lloyd A.,   Romans and Blacks 1989 ➤ 5,g375: ᴿAmJPg 111 (1990) 543-557 (F. M. *Snowden*: nothing new, some distortions); ClasR 40 (1990) 395-7 (J. F. *Gardner*); RÉLat 68 (1990) 231-3 (J. *Desanges*).

g704 *Tidball* Derek,   The social context of the NT 1984 ➤ 65,d161a; 1,f150*: ᴿCriswT 3 (1988s) 217s (C. C. *Newman*).

g705 *Tyrell* Hartmann,   Worum geht es in der 'Protestantischen Ethik'? Ein Versuch zum besseren Verständnis Max WEBERs: Saeculum 41 (1990) 131-177.

g706 *Uchitel* Alexander,   Organization of manpower in Achaemenid Persia according to the fortification archive: AcSum 11 (1989) 225-238.

g707 *Vasojević* Andrej L.,   Soziale Gruppen Ägyptens zur Zeit der assyrischen Eroberung: ZägSpr 117 (1990) 171-8.

g708 *Vernant* Jean-Pierre,   De la psychologie historique à une anthropologie de la Grèce ancienne: Métis 4 (1989) 305-314.

g709 **Waldstein** Wolfgang,   Operae libertorum; Untersuchungen zur Dienstpflicht freigelassener Sklaven: ForAntSklaverei 19. Stu 1986, Steiner. 467 p. DM 118. 3-515-04699-2. – ᴿAntClas 59 (1990) 514s (J. A. *Straus*:

le monde romain 'fait moins d'esclaves que d'affranchis'); RÉLat 68 (1990) 224-6 (J. C. *Dumont*).

g710 ᴱ**Wallace-Hadrill** Andrew, Patronage in ancient society 1984/9 ➤ 5,808: ᴿClasR 40 (1990) 399-403 (Miriam *Griffin*); GreeceR 37 (1990) 117s (T. *Wiedemann*); RÉLat 68 (1990) 223s (J.-C. *Richard*).

g711 *a*) *Wallace-Hadrill* Andrew, PLINY the Elder and man's unnatural history; – *b*) *Hardwick* Lorna, Ancient Amazons — heroes, outsiders, or women?: GreeceR 37 (1990) 90-96 / 14-35.

g712 **Weber** Max, Ensayos sobre sociología de la religión 3, ᵀ*Almaraz* José: Ensayistas 238. M 1987, Taurus. 494 p.; map. – ᴿBAsEspOr 26 (1990) 362-5 (P. *Lavado*).

g713 **Wiedemann** Thomas, Adults and children in the Roman Empire 1989 ➤ 5,g383; £27.50: ᴿClasR 40 (1990) 397-9 (J. F. *Gardner*).

g714 **Willis** Timothy M., Elders in pre-exilic Israelite society; diss. Harvard, ᴰ*Cross* F. CM 1990. 282 p. 90-35625. – DissA 51 (1990s) 2412-A.

g715 **Wolff** Hans W., Anthropologie des Alten Testaments⁵ [paperback of ⁴1984; ¹c. 1973]: Tb 91. Mü 1990, Kaiser. 368 p. DM 26. 3-459-01872-0 [BL 91,122, J. W. *Rogerson*].

Wood Bryant G., The sociology [= industry, diffusion] of pottery in Bronze/Iron Age Palestine 1990 ➤ d777.

g716 *Wunder* H., Historische Frauenforschung, ein neuer Zugang zur Gesellschaftsgeschichte: ➤ 715, Frauen 1987/90, 31-41.

U5.3 **Commercium, oeconomica.**

g717 *Albeck* S., ❶ The laws of non-Jews and the financial laws in the Talmud: Sinai 103,2 (1988) 29-65 [< JStJud 21,338].

g718 **Andreau** Jean, La vie financière dans le monde romain 1987 ➤ 4,h437; 5,g387: ᴿAntClas 59 (1990) 522-4 (M.-T. *Raepsaet-Charlier*); SicGymn 43 (1990) 361-7 (G. *Puglisi*).

g719 *a*) *Andreau* Jean, Les financiers et commerçants constituaient-ils, à Rome, des groupes de pression économique? [BARLOW C. 1978]; – *b*) *Dekkers* E., Des prix et du commerce des livres à l'époque patristique; – *c*) *Nachtergael* Georges, La caricature d'un banquier à son comptoir [terre cuite Sieglin]; – *d*) *Bonneau* Danielle, L'or et l'argent des statues de culte [papyr. ég.]: – *e*) *Naster* Paul, L'or et l'argent dans les textes élamites des tablettes comptables de Persépolis: ➤ 25, ᶠBOGAERT/VAN LOOY 1989s, 9-22 / 99-115 / 314-322 / 35-47 / 323-335.

g720 *a*) *Andreau* Jean, La cité antique et la vie économique; – *b*) *Gauthier* Philippe, Grandes et petites cités; hégémonie et autarcie: Opus 6ss (1987ss) 175-185 / 187-202.

g721 *a*) *Bickel* Susanne, Les domaines funéraires [...fonction administrative et économique des temples] de Thoutmes IV; – *b*) *Kákosy* László, A strange form of the name Djehutimes [functionary of Ramesses II tomb]: ➤ 70*, Mém. HARI R., BSocÉg 13 (1989) 23-32 / 69s; 2 fig.

g722 *a*) *Bikai* Patricia M., The Phoenicians, rich and glorious traders of the Levant; – *b*) *Markoe* Glenn, A nation of artisans: Archaeology 43,2 (1990) 22-30 / 31-35.

g723 *Blitzer* Harriet, Korōneïka; storage-jar production and trade in the traditional Aegean: Hesperia 59 (1990) 675-711; 1 fig.; pl. 99-112.

g723* **Boochs** Wolfgang, Die Finanzverwaltung im Altertum 1985 ➤ 1,f181; ... 5,g393: ᴿSyria 65 (1988) 253 (H. de *Contenson*).

g724 **Briant** P., Rois, tributs et paysans [14 art. 1972-82] 1982 → 63,e125...
65,d230: ᴿBO 47 (1990) 300-3 (R. J. van der *Spek*).

g725 **Callatay** François de, Histoire économique et monétaire des guerres
mithridatiques: diss. LvN 1988, ᴰ*Hackens* T. – RArtLv 21 (1988) 207-9.

g726 *Carter* Elizabeth, Elamite exports: → 138, ꟳPᴇʀʀᴏᴛ J., Iran 1990,
89-100.

g727 *Clarysse* W., *Lanciers* E., Currency and the dating of demotic and
Greek papyri from the Ptolemaic period [prices doubled at change from
silver to copper standard in 210 B.C.]: AncSoc 20 (1989) 117-132.

g728 *Cohen* Edward E., Commercial lending by Athenian banks; cliometric
fallacies and forensic methodology: ClasPg 85 (1990) 177-190.

g729 *Cook* Margaret L., Timokrates' 50 talents and the cost of ancient
warfare: Eranos 88 (1990) 69-97.

g730 **Cozzo** Andrea, Kerdos 1988 → 4,h453; 5,g397: ᴿAtenRom 35 (1990)
37-39 (L. *Paganelli*).

g731 *a) Dolce* Rita, Some aspects of the primary economic structures of Ebla
[3-2 millen.]; stores and workplaces; – *b) Matthiae* Paolo, On the
economic foundations of the early Syrian culture of Ebla; – *c) Mazzoni*
Stefania, Economic features of the pottery equipment of Palace G; – *d)*
Klengel Horst, Ebla im Fernhandel des 3. Jahrtausends; – *e) Biga* Maria
G., Frauen in der Wirtschaft von Ebla: → e333*, Wirtschaft/Ebla 1986/8,
35-45; pl. VII-X / 75-80 / 81-92 + 9 fig. / 245-251 / 159-171.

g732 *Darnell* John C., A note on 'rb.t (and 'rb/arēb) [pledge, deposit of
money]: Enchoria 17 (1990) 83-87.

g733 **Drexhage** Raphaela, Untersuchungen zur römischen Osthandel 1988
→ 5,g403 [... Palmyra; Diss. Münster]: ᴿHZ 250 (1990) 129s (L. *Neesen*);
MünstHand 9,2 (1990) 127-130 (H. W. *Pleket*).

g733* *Driel* G. van, The Murašus in context [Sᴛᴏʟᴘᴇʀ M. W., Entrepreneurs
1985]: JESHO 32 (1989) 203-229.

g734 **Duncan-Jones** Richard, Structure and scale in the Roman economy. C
1990, Univ. xvi-245 p. 0-521-35477-3 [Tyche 6, 256-9, W. *Scheidel*].

g735 **Elayi** Josette, Économie des cités phéniciennes sous l'Empire perse:
AION supp. 62 a 50 (1989). N 1990, Ist. Univ. Orientale. viii-104 p.

g736 **Engelmann** H., *Knibbe* D., Das Zollgesetz der Provinz Asia; eine neue
Inschrift aus Ephesos; Beitrag, *Hueber* Friedmund: Epigraphica Anatolica 14 (1986). 206 p. – ᴿCRAI (1990) 675-698 (C. *Nicolet*).

g737 **Freyberg** Hans-Ulrich von, Kapitalverkehr und Handel im römischen
Kaiserreich (27 v.Chr. - 235 n.Chr.): Univ. FrB. FrB 1988, Haufe. 198 p.

g738 **Gabba** E., Del buon uso della ricchezza; saggi di storia economica e
sociale del mondo antico 1988 → 4,h469... 5,g403*: ᴿAthenaeum 78
(1990) 251-5 (G. *Salmeri*).

g739 *Gabba* Emilio, The finances of King Herod: → 540, Greece/Israel 1985/
90, 160-8.

g740 **Garlan** Yvon, Guerre et économie en Grèce ancienne 1989 → 5,g405:
ᴿAthenaeum 78 (1990) 209-212 (Laura *Boffo*); Gnomon 62 (1990) 464-6
(P. *Cartledge*); RPg 63 (1989) 149-153 (R. *Lonis*).

g741 **Garnsey** P., *Saller* R., The Roman empire; economy, society and culture
1987 → 3,d72; 5,b766: ᴿLatomus 49 (1990) 707s (J. *Rougé*).

g742 **Garnsey** Peter, *Saller* Richard, Das römische Kaiserreich; Wirtschaft,
Gesellschaft und Kultur, ᵀ*Maass* Hans-J.: Enzyklopädie 501. Ha 1989,
Rowohlt. 217 p. – ᴿTyche 5 (1990) 203 (W. *Scheidel*, auch über Famine
1988).

g743 *Garsoïan* Nina G., *al.*, Trade: → 837*, DMA 12 (1989) 96-123.

g744 *Goehring* James E., The world engaged; the social and economic world of early Egyptian monasticism: ➤ 152, ᶠROBINSON J. M., Gnosticism 2 (1990) 134-144.

g745 **Goldsmith** Raymond W., Premodern financial systems 1987 ➤ 5,g407: ᴿSpeculum 65 (1990) 160-2 (Julius *Kirshner*: choices unexplained, errors abound).

g746 **Green** H.A., Economic and social origins of Gnosticism ᴰ1985 ➤ 1,f212 ... 5,g410: ᴿNumen 37 (1990) 283 (I. *Gruenwald*).

g747 *Greengus* Samuel, Bridewealth in Sumerian sources: HUCA 61 (1990) 25-88.

g748 **Grosz** Katarzyna, The archive of the [Arrapḫe] Wully family: Niebuhr Publ. 5. K 1988, Mus. Tusc. 288 p. 87-7289-040-1. – ᴿBO 47 (1990) 402-423 (M. *Malul*: valuable despite weaknesses).

g749 *Hanson* K.C., The Herodians and Mediterranean kinship, III. Economics: BibTB 20 (1990) 10-21.

g750 *Hölkeskamp* Karl-J., City and territory, war and trade in the ancient Mediterranean [SHIPLEY G., History of Samos 1987]: MeditHistR 5 (1990) 72-81.

g751 *Isager* Signe, Kings and gods in the Seleucid Empire; a question of landed property in Asia Minor: ➤ 525*, *Bilde*/Seleucid 1990, 79-90.

g752 **Jongman** Wilhelm, The economy and society of Pompeii: Dutch Mg. Hist 4, 1988 ➤ 5,g416: ᴿAmHR 95 (1990) 469s (J. L. *Franklin*); ClasR 40 (1990) 111-6; 1 fig. (N. *Purcell*).

g753 *Kaplony-Heckel* Ursula, Soll und haben in Pathyris: ➤ 16, ᶠBECKERATH J. v. 1990, 139-146.

g754 *Katz* Jacob, ❺ Reflections on the relationship between religion and economics: Tarbiz 60 (1990s) 99-111; Eng. III.

g755 ᴱ**Kedar** B. Z., al., ❺ Commerce in Palestine through the ages. J 1990, Yad Ben Zvi. 337 p. 965-217-069-0 [OIAc Oc90].

g756 *Kelly-Buccellati* Marilyn, Trade in metals in the third millennium; northeastern Syria and eastern Anatolia: ➤ 28, ᶠBOUNNI A. 1990, 117-128; 129 map; + pl. 28-29.

g757 **Kirschenbaum** Aaron, Sons, slaves, and freedmen in Roman commerce [diss. Columbia 1969, ᴰ*Schiller* A.], pref. *Watson* A. Wsh/J 1987, Catholic U./Magnes. xii-229 p. – ᴿAmHR 95 (1990) 471s (B. D. *Shaw*); HZ 250 (1990) 128s (W. *Backhaus*).

g758 *Kitchen* Kenneth A., Early Canaanites [on a museum stela] in Rio de Janeiro and a 'corrupt' Ramesside land-sale: ➤ 114, ᶠLICHTHEIM M. 1990, (II) 635-645.

g759 *Knapp* A. Bernard, Ethnicity, entrepreneurship, and exchange; Mediterranean inter-island relations in the Late Bronze Age: AnBritAth 85 (1990) 115-153.

g760 **Koch** Heidemarie, Verwaltung und Wirtschaft im persischen Kernland zur Zeit der Achämeniden: TAVO B-89. Wsb 1990, Reichert. [viii-] 428 p. 3-88226-468-3.

g761 *Levick* Barbara, 'Caesar omnia habet'; property and politics under the Principate: ➤ b767, Opposition 1986/7, p. 187-212 (-218, discussion).

g762 *Ligt* L. de, Demand, supply, distribution; the Roman peasantry between town and countryside; rural monetization and peasant demand: Münst-Hand 9,2 (1990) 25-57; 10,1 ...

g763 **McCann** Anna M., al., The Roman port and fishery of Cosa; a center of ancient trade 1987 ➤ 3,f863; 4,h484: ᴿGnomon 62 (1990) 71-74 (P. *Arthur*).

g764 *McGinn* T. A. J., The taxation of Roman prostitutes [Caligula 40 A.D., along with much other information about them]: Helios 16,1 (Lubbock TX 1989) 79-110 [< NTAbs 34,93].

g765 *Maekava* Kazuya, Rations, wages and economic trends in the Ur III period: AltOrF 16 (1989) 42-50.

g766 *a*) *Meyers* Carol, Women and the domestic economy of early Israel; – *b*) *Mieroop* Marc Van de, Women in the economy of Sumer: ➤ 4,851, ᴱLesko Barbara, Women's earliest records 1987/9, 265-276 / 53-66.

g767 **Moxnes** Halvor, The economy of the Kingdom. Ph 1988, Fortress. xxii-183 p. $13 pa. – ᴿBA 53 (1990) 179 (S. *Sheeley*).

g768 **Neusner** Jacob, The economics of the Mishnah: StHistJudaism. Ch 1990, Univ. xvi-183 p. $45; pa. $15. 0-226-57655-8; -6-6 [NTAbs 35,129; BL 91,139, P. R. *Davies*].

g769 *Neusner* Jacob, ARISTOTLE's Economics and the Mishnah's economics; the matter of wealth and usury: JStJud 21 (1990) 41-59.

g770 **Nicolet** Claude, Rendre à César; économie et société dans la Rome antique 1988 ➤ 5,g429: ᴿAnÉCS 45 (1990) 914-6 (J. *Andreau*); RPg 63 (1989) 340s (F. *Flobert*).

g771 **Peacock** D. P. S., *Williams* D. F., Amphorae and the Roman economy 1986 ➤ 2,b999 ... 4,h495: ᴿLatomus 49 (1990) 890s (P. *Desy*).

g772 *Powell* Marvin A., Identification and interpretation of long term price fluctuations in Babylonia; more on the history of money in Mesopotamia: AltOrF 17 (1990) 76-99.

g773 *Radici Colace* Paola, Moneta, linguaggio e pensiero nei Padri della Chiesa fra tradizione pagana ed esegesi biblica: Koinonia 14,1 (1990) 47-64.

g774 *Renger* Johannes, Zur Rolle von Preisen und Löhnen im Wirtschafts-system des alten Mesopotamien an der Wende vom 3. zum 2. Jahrtausend v.Chr. — Grundsätzliche Fragen und Überlegungen: AltOrF 16 (1989) 234-252.

g775 *Rostovtzeff* Michel, Capitalisme et économie nationale dans l'antiquité [une certaine modernité: ❸ 1900], ᵀ*Depretto-Genty* C.: Pallas 33 (1987) 19-40; 7-17 présentation de Jean *Andreau*.

g776 **Rowlandson** Jane L., Landholding in the Oxyrhynchite nome, 30 B.C. - c. 300 A.D.: diss. Oxford 1983. 384 p. – BR 50111 [7 microfiches: OIAc Ja91].

g777 **Simon** Robert, Meccan trade and Islam; problems of origin and structure: BiblOrH 32,1. Budapest 1989, Akad. 206 p. – ᴿBSO 53 (1990) 510s (J. *Wansbrough*).

g778 *Skait* Aaron, The sale contracts from Khafajah: ➤ 7, ᶠARTZI P. 1990, 255-276; map.

g779 **Smith** Thyrza R., Mycenaean trade and interaction in the West Central Mediterranean 1600-1000 B.C.: BAR-Int 371. Ox 1987. £14. 0-86054-479-6. – ᴿAntiqJ 69 (1989) 348s (Lucia *Vagnetti*: born out of date, overlooks too much).

g780 *Stanley* Phillip V., The purpose of loans in ancient Athens; a reex-amination: MünstHand 9,2 (1990) 57-72; deutsch 72s; franç. 73.

g781 **Steinkeller** Piotr, Sale documents of the Ur-III period 1989 ➤ 5,e207: ᴿRAss 84 (1990) 91-94 (D. *Charpin*).

g782 **Stenger** Werner, 'Gebt dem Kaiser...' Besteuerung Palästinas: BoBB 68, 1988 ➤ 4,h510 ... 5,g446: ᴿCBQ 52 (1990) 570-2 (P. *Hollenbach*); TR 86 (1990) 202 (R. *Kampling*).

g783 **Vannier** François, Finances publiques et richesses privées dans le discours athénien aux Ve et IVe siècles: Ann Litt Besançon 362, 1988 → 5,g452; 2-251-60362-X: ^RAntClas 59 (1990) 488 (D. *Viviers*).

g784 *Wensky* Margret, Die Frau in Handel und Gewerbe, vom Mittelalter bis zur frühen Neuzeit: → 768, Waren sie nur schön? 1985/9, 267-298; fig. 136-150.

g785 *Whitehorne* John E. G., Soldiers and veterans in the local economy of first century Oxyrhynchus: → 160, ^FSCHOW J., Charta Borgiana 1990, (II) 543-557.

g786 **Wierschowski** Lothar, Heer und Wirtschaft ^D1984 → 1,f258... 4,h517: ^RBonnJbb 190 (1990) 641-4 (Hinnerk *Bruhns*).

U5.7 **Nomadismus;** ecology.

g787 *Cauvin* Jacques, Nomadisme néolithique en zone aride; l'oasis d'El Kowm (Syrie): → 28, ^FBOUNNI A. 1990, 41-47 [41: bc en minuscules: convention pour chronologie C 14 non calibrée].

 ^EClutton-Brock J., The walking larder; problems of domestication, pastoralism ... 1986/9 → 794.

g788 ^EKent Susan, Farmers as hunters; the implications of sedentism: New Directions in Archaeology. C 1989, Univ. 152 p. 0-521-36217-2. – ^RAntiquity 64 (1990) 432s (Marsha A. *Levine*).

g789 *Kramer* Samuel N., The marriage of Martu [-nomads, with the city-state Ninab]: → 7, ^FARTZI P. 1990, 11-27; pl. I.

g790 **LaBianca** Øystein S., Sedentarization and nomadization; food system cycles at Hesban and vicinity in Transjordan: Hesban 1. Berrien Springs MI 1990, Andrews Univ. xx-353 p. [0-94387-00-6 in OIAc S90].

g791 **Levi** Mario A., I nomadi alla frontiera; i popoli delle steppe e l'antico mondo greco-romano: Centro RicDAntClas Mg 13. R 1989, Bretschneider. 143 p.; 23 pl. 88-7062-663-6 [OIAc J91].

g792 **Mahasneh** Hamzeh M., The settlement patterns of the Levant during the neolithic period: diss. Pennsylvania, ^DMuhly J. Ph 1990. x-497 p. 90-15132. – DissA 51 (1990s) 204-A; OIAc Oc90.

g793 **Maisels** C. K., The emergence of civilisation; from hunting and gathering to agriculture, cities, and the state in the Near East. L 1990, Routledge. xx-395 p. £45. 0-415-00168-4 [BL 91,128, A. R. *Millard*].

g794 ^ENa'aman Nadav, *Finkelstein* Israel, ❸ From nomadism to monarchy; archaeological and historical aspects of early Israel. J 1990, Yad Ben-Zvi/ Israel Explor. Soc. 462 p. 965-217-073-9 [OIAc Oc90].

g795 *Sarao* K. T. S., Iron, urbanization and Buddhism: ArOr 58 (1990) 102-4.

g796 **Staubli** Thomas, Das Image der Nomaden im alten Israel und in der Ikonographie seiner sesshaften Umwelt: Diss. FrS 1989. – BZ 34,156.

g797 *Tangri* Daniel, *Wyncoll* Greg, Of mice and men; is the presence of commensal animals in archaeological sites a positive correlate of sedentism?: Paléorient 15,2 (1989) 85-94.

g798 *Ṭoḳer* Naphtali, ❸ Blame of shepherds ['šmt ha-rôʿîm] as a typical collection in shepherds' proverbs: BethM 66,124 (1990s) 29-41.

g799 ^EWhittaker C. R., Pastoral economies in classical antiquity: PgSoc supp. 14, 1985 → 5,809: ^RClasPg 85 (1990) 238-244 (K. R. *Bradley*).

g800 *Wilkinson* T. J., The development of settlement in the Jazira between the 7th and 1st Millennia B.C.: Iraq 52 (1990) 49-62; 8 fig.

g801 *Zarins* Juris,   Early pastoral nomadism and the settlement of lower Mesopotamia: BASOR 280 (1990) 31-56; bibliog. 57-65.

U5.8   Urbanismus.

g802 **Biggar** Nigel,   Theological politics; a critique of [Church of England report] Faith in the city: Latimer Studies 29s.   Ox 1988, Latimer.   95 p. £3.   0-946307-28-8 [-9-6]. – ᴿScotBEv 8 (1990) 135s (D. *McAdam*).

g803 *Burkert* W.,   Die antike Stadt als Festgemeinschaft: → 192*, Zürich, Stadt und Fest 1987, 25-44; ill.

g804 *a) Daiber* K.-F.,   Religion in der Stadt; – *b) Sievernich* M.,   Urbanität und Christentum; – *c) Grünberg* W.,   Die Idee der Stadtkirche: Pastoraltheologie 79 (Gö 1990) 80-94 / 95-115 / 132-151 [< ZIT 90,357].

g805 **Demont** Paul,   La cité grecque archaïque et classique et l'idéal de tranquillité: Coll.ÉtAnc, gr. 118.   P 1990, BLettres.   435 p.   2-251-32633-2. – ᴿRPg 64 (1990) 223-5 (M. *Nouhaud*).

g805* *Finkelstein* Israel,   Early Arad — urbanism of the nomads : ZDPV 106 (1990) 34-50.

g806 ᴱ**Frézouls** Edmond,   Sociétés urbaines, sociétés rurales dans l'Asie mineure et la Syrie hellénistiques et romaines 1985/7 → 4,680.736; 2-990-433715-6: ᴿAntClas 59 (1990) 500s (G. *Raepsaet*); Latomus 49 (1990) 279s (J.-N. *Robert*).

g807 **Fritz** Volkmar,   Die Stadt im alten Israel: ArchBibl. Mü 1990, Beck. 177 p.; 60 fig. DM 38 [ZAW 103, 297, O. *Kaiser*].

g808 *Geus* C. H. J. de,   Steden in het Oude Nabije Oosten: PhoenixEOL 36,2 (1990) 7s; 64-72 Lachis (-83, *al.*).

g809 **Gros** Pierre, *Torelli* Mario,   Storia dell'urbanistica; il mondo romano. R 1988, Laterza.   466 p. – ᴿAnÉCS 45 (1990) 908-911 (Y. *Thébert*).

g810 ᴱ**Harvey** Anthony,   Theology in the city; a theological response to 'Faith in the city'.   L 1989, SPCK.   ix-132 p. £7. – ᴿTLond 93 (1990) 152-4-5 (D. F. *Ford* & P. *Selby*).

g810* **Hemmenway** Scott R.,   Platonic myth and the archeology of the *polis*: diss. Pennsylvania State, ᴰ*Rosen* S. 1989.   283 p. 90-18221. – DissA 51 (1990s) 524-A.

g811 **Herman** Gabriel,   Ritualised friendship and the Greek city 1987 → 3, f917; 4,h535: ᴿAnÉCS 45 (1990) 878s (Pauline *Schmitt Pantel*); AntClas 59 (1990) 476-8 (J.-M. *Hannick*); ClasJ 85 (1989s) 357s (T. W. *Gallant*).

g812 **Hoepfner** W., *Schwandner* E.-L.,   Haus und Stadt im klassischen Griechenland 1985 → 3,f918 ... 5,g491:   ᴿJHS 110 (1990) 263s (J. E. *Jones*).

g813 **Huot** Jean-Louis, *Thalmann* Jean-Paul, *Valbelle* Dominique,   Naissance des cités: Origines.   P 1990, Nathan.   352 p. F 198.

g814 *a) Isaac* Benjamin,   Roman administration and urbanization; – *b) Geiger* Joseph,   Local patriotism in the Hellenistic cities of Palestine: → 540, Greece–Israel 1985/90, 151-9 / 141-150.

g815 **Kolb** Frank,   Die Stadt im Altertum 1984 → 65,d248 ... 5,g493; ᴿJHS 110 (1990) 264s (J. E. *Jones*).

g816 **Lampe** Peter,   Die stadtrömischen Christen ᴰ1987 ²1989 [17-p. addenda] → 3,f759 ... 5,g494: ᴿActuBbg 27 (1990) 43-46 (V. *Fábrega*); JBL 109 (1990) 733-5 (A. E. *Segal*); JEH 41 (1990) 278s (W. H. C. *Frend*); JTS 41 (1990) 228s (H. *Chadwick*); Neotestamentica 24 (1990) 144-6 (W. S. *Vorster*); SvEx 55 (1990) 164-7 (B. *Holmberg*); TüTQ 170 (1990) 227-9 (H. J. *Vogt*); ZkT 112 (1990) 233s (K. H. *Neufeld*).

g817 **Levi** Mario A., La città antica; morfologia e biografia della aggregazione urbana nell'Antichità: Problemi e Ricerche di Storia Antica 12. R 1989, Bretschneider. 514 p.; 88 fig. [Gnomon 63, 143-7, P. *Gros*).

g818 *Lévy* Edmond, La cité grecque; invention moderne ou réalité antique: → 760, Du pouvoir 1983/90, 53-67 (-127, *al.*, la décision politique).

g819 *Lim* David S., The city in the Bible: EvRT 12 (1988) 138-156 [< OTAbs 14,206].

g820 *Ling* R., A stranger in town; finding the way in an ancient city [no street-numbers or signposts; districts named but informally]: GreeceR 37 (1990) 204-214; 3 fig.

g821 *López Paz* P., La relación ciudad-campo; revisión: Veleia 6 (Vitoria 1989) 111-133.

g822 *a*) *Mactoux* Marie-Madeleine, La polis en quête de théologie; – *b*) *Sakellariou* Michel, *Polis* et cité; état-*polis* et état-cité: → 111, ᶠLÉVEQUE P., 4 (1990) 289-313 / 2 (1989) 375-7.

g823 *a*) *Margueron* Jean-Claude, The urbanization of Mari and the Middle Euphrates river; – *b*) *Sürenhagen* Dietrich, Aššur; when and how did it become a city?: → 784, AJA 94 (1990) 305 /305s (summaries).

g823* *Massa-Pairault* Françoise-Hélène, L'art et la définition de la cité: → 811, Crise 1987/90, 199-227.

g824 *Morin* Alfredo, La ciudad en la Biblia [... *Comblin* J.; *Ellul* J.; *Cox* H.]: Medellín 16 (1990) 362-395 [< TContext 8/2, 91].

g825 **Müller** Reimar, Polis und Res publica; Studien zum antiken Gesellschafts- und Geschichtsdenken [20 Art. 1965-85] 1987 → 5,326; DM 58: ᴿHZ 250 (1990) 121s (K.-W. *Welwei*).

ᴱ**Murray** O., *Price* S., The Greek city 1986/90 → 759.

g826 *a*) *Nixon* Lucia, *Price* Simon, The size and resources of Greek cities; – *b*) *Runciman* W. G., Doomed to extinction; the *polis* as an evolutionary dead-end: → 759, Greek city 1986/90, 137-170 / 347-367.

g827 *Osborne* Michael J., Citizens, friends and foreigners in Athens [HERMAN G., Ritualised friendship 1987]: AncHRes 20 (1990) 35-42.

g828 **Osborne** Robin, Classical landscape with figures 1987 → 3,f927 ... 5,g300: ᴿClasJ 85 (1989s) 148-150 (Virginia *Hunter*).

g828* *Ottosson* Magnus, Topography and city planning with special reference to Jerusalem: → 21*, Mem. BJØRNDALEN A., TsTKi 60,4 (1989) 263-9; Eng. 269; map 270.

g829 **Piétri** Charles, présent., L'urbs, espace urbain 1985/7 → 3,832: ᴿAnÉCS 45 (1990) 906-8 (Y. *Thébert*).

g830 **Rykwert** Joseph, The idea of a town; the anthropology of urban form in Rome, Italy and the ancient world 1988 → 5,g504: ᴿRelStR 16 (1990) 70 (A. T. *Kraebel*).

g831 *Simon* Stephen J., The origin of the Greek poleis in Greek thought: AncW 21,1s (1990) 23-26.

g832 **Stambaugh** J., The ancient Roman city 1988 → 4,h557; 5,g509: ᴿAmHR 95 (1990) 468s (K. R. *Bradley*); ClasJ 85 (1989s) 151s (G. M. *Woloch*); Latomus 49 (1990) 896s (J. *Le Gall*).

g833 *Thalmann* Jean-Paul, Les premières civilisations urbaines; deux livres-clef sur la question [HUOT J.-L., Les sumériens 1989; La naissance des cités 1990]: MondeB 67 (1990) 69s.

g834 ᴱ**Uglione** Renato, La città ideale 1985/7 → 3,774 ... 5,g511: ᴿLatomus 49 (1990) 710-2 (H. *Savon*).

g835 **Uphill** Eric P., Egyptian towns and cities. Aylesbury 1988, Shire. 72 p. £2.50. 0-8526-3939-2. – ᴿFolOr 27 (1990) 264s (J. *Śliwa*).

g836 ᴱ**Weiss** Harvey, Origins of cities 1984/6 ⇒ 2,d69 ... 5,g513: ᴿOLZ 85 (1990) 43-45 (E. *Lindemeyer*).

g837 *Weiss* Harvey, Tell Leilan 1989, new data for mid-third millennium urbanization and state formation: MDOG 122 (1990) 193-218; 17 fig.

g838 **Welwei** Karl-W., Die griechische Polis 1983 ⇒ 64,a190 ... 1,f295: ᴿAnz-AltW 43 (1990) 56s (C. *Ulf*).

g839 *Will* Ernest, Les villes de la Syrie à l'époque hellénistique et romaine: ⇒ 481, Syrie II (1989) 223-250; fig. 24-37.

U5.9 *Demographia*, **population-statistics.**

g840 *Bellemore* Jane, *Rawson* Beryl, Alumni [in relation to total population and urbanization]; the Italian evidence: ZPapEp 83 (1990) 1-17.

g841 *Crispell* Diane, How to navigate the Census Bureau: American Demographics 11 (1989) 46-66 [< BS 147 (1990) 231s, A. M. *Malphurs*: this periodical published by Dow Jones furnishes sociological information useful for ministry].

g842 **Hansen** Mogens H., Demography and democracy 1986 ⇒ 3,f947 ... 5,g516: ᴿEos 78 (1990) 404-7 (R. *Turasiewicz* ●); Gnomon 62 (1990) 170-2 (T. P. *Duncan-Jones*).

g843 **McCarthy** Justin, The population of Palestine; population history and statistics of the Late Ottoman period and the Mandate: Institute for Palestine Studies Series. NY 1990, Columbia Univ. xxviii-242 p. 0-231-07110-8.

g844 **Morris** Ian, Burial and ... city-state 1987 ⇒ 4,h577; 5,g517: ᴿAmHR 95 (1990) 793 (E. *Vermeule*); Helios 17 (1990) 263-8 (S. C. *Humphreys*).

g845 *a*) *Safrai* Z., ● The influence of demographic stratification on the agricultural and economic structure during the Mishnaic and Talmudic periods; – *b*) *Broshi* M., ● Demographic changes in ancient Eretz-Israel; methodology and estimates: ⇒ 348, Man and law 1986, 20-46 / 49-56.

g846 **Suder** Wiesław, Census populi; Bibliographie de la démographie de l'antiquité romaine. Bonn 1988, Habelt. vii-127 p. DM 48. – ᴿClasR 40 (1990) 182s (A. *Lintott*).

g847 *Ward* Lorne H., Roman population, territory, tribe, city, and army size from the Republic's founding to the Veientane War, 500 B.C. - 400 B.C.: AmJPg 111 (1990) 5-39.

U6 **Narrationes peregrinorum et exploratorum;** *Loca sancta.*

g848 *Allouche* Adel, A study of IBN BAṬṬŪṬAH's account of his 726/1326 journey through Syria and Arabia: JSS 35 (1990) 283-299.

g849 *Alonso* Carlos, El primer viaje desde Persia a Roma del P. VICENTE de S. Francisco O.C.D. [mandado a Persia 1604] (1609-1611): Teresianum 40 (1989) 517-550.

g850 ᴱ**Babinger** Franz, Hans DERNSCHWAM's Tagebuch einer Reise nach Konstantinopel und Kleinasien (1553-1555) ⇒ 3,953 [Fugger-Archiv]. B 1986 = 1923, Duncker & H. xxxvi-318 p. 3-428-06097-0. – ᴿMitteil. Inst. Österr. G-Forsch. 97 (1989) 245s (K. *Belke*) [ByZ 83,300].

g851 *Bastiaensen* Antoon, Sur quelques passages de l'Itinerarium Egeriae: AnBoll 108 (1990) 271-7; Eng. 277.

g852 **Bermejo Cabrera** Enrique, La proclamación de la Sagrada Escritura en la liturgía de Jerusalén; estudio terminológico del Itinerarium EGERIAE [< Diss. ᴰ*Gibert* J.]. R 1990, Pont. Athenaeum S. Anselmi. 159 p.

g853 ᴱBetrò Maria Carmela, Racconti di viaggio e di avventura dell'antico Egitto: Testi VOAnt 8, eg. 1. Brescia 1990, Paideia. 85 p. 88-394-0443-0.

g854 **Bruce** James, Zu den Quellen des Blauen Nils; die Erforschung Aethiopiens 1768-1773, ᴱ*Gussenbauer* Herbert: Alte abenteuerliche Reiseberichte. Stu 1987, Thienemann. 367 p.; 46 fig.; 3 maps. – ᴿNubica 1s (1990) 379s (P. *Scholz*).

g855 *Brunn* Albert von, Vom Haus des Staubes [Gilgamesch] nach Jerusalem [Franziskanernovizen 1536; *Campos* F., (Roman, novel) 1990]: Orientierung 54 (1990) 250-2.

g856 **Chardin** John, Travels in Persia 1673-7, ᵀᴱ1927, préf. *Penzer* N., *Sykes* P. NY 1988, Dover. 0-486-25636-7 [OIAc JuJ89].

g857 **Chelini** J., *al.*, Histoire des pèlerinages [II.] non chrétiens 1987 ➤ h580*: ᴿRHist 280 (1988) 544-9 (Dominique *Prévot*).

g858 *Conrad* Lawrence I., The Near East study tour diary of Ignaz GOLDZIHER [1873; ᴱ*Patai* Raphael, I. Goldziher and his Oriental diary (Detroit 1987, Wayne State Univ.)]: JRAS (1990) 105-126.

g859 **Coutu** L., Pèlerinage aux Églises d'Orient. Québec 1990, Fides. 517 p.; 6 fig. [NRT 113, 463, J. *Masson*].

g860 **Damiani** Anita, Enlightened observers; British travellers to the Near East 1715-1850, 1979 ➤ 64,d854: ᴿJAOS 110 (1990) 291-303 (R. *Murphey*).

g861 ᵀ*Dams* Thérèse, Le voyage en Orient de DIEGO de Mérida (1507-1512) IIs: MélSR 47 (1990) 21-42.134-155.

g862 ᴱ**Da Schio** Alvise, Filippo PIGAFETTA, Viaggio da Creta in Egitto e al Sinai 1576-1577. Vicenza 1984, Bertoliana. 349 p.; ind. (*Romanato* L.); ill., maps [KirSef 62 (1988s) p. 627].

g863 **Davies** J. G., Pilgrimage yesterday and today; why? where? how? 1989 ➤ 5,g525: ᴿPEQ 121 (1989) 155 (M. *Hannam*).

g863* *Davies* J. G., A fourteenth century 'Processional for pilgrims in the Holy Land': Hispania Sacra 41 (1989) 421-432 [< ZIT 90,763].

g864 *Deluz* Christiane, Pèlerins à Jérusalem à la fin du Moyen-Âge: Social Compass 36 (Lv 1989) 159-174 [139-270, pèlerinage (et modernité) < ZIT 89,617].

g865 **Denon** Vivant, Travels in Upper and Lower Egypt: Middle East series. ... 1989 = 1803, Darf/Ayer. 346 + 332 p. $180/$86 [Books in Print 1990s, 1, p. 1561] 1-85077-098-0; -9-9 / 0-405-05331-2.

g866 *Engelfried* Brigitte, Else LASKER-SCHÜLER, Das zweite Palästinabuch; über den [mangelhaft edierten] Druck eines Manuskripts aus dem Nachlass: Laurentianum 31 (1990) 485-533.

g867 **Firby** Nora R., European travellers and their perceptions of Zoroastrians in the 17th and 18th centuries [ᴰ1984] 1988 ➤ 4,h585; DM 88: ᴿBO 47 (1990) 722-4 (J. W. *Drijvers*).

g868 *Friedmann* Yvonne, Le pèlerinage en Palestine, acte de dévotion aux yeux des Juifs et des Chrétiens: ➤ 521, RÉJ 149 (1990) 485-8.

g869 **Ganz-Blättler** Ursula, Andacht und Abenteuer; Berichte europäischer Jerusalem- und Santiago-Pilger 1320-1520: Jakobus-Studien 4. Tü 1990, Narr. vii-425 p. DM 68 [TR 86,431].

g870* *Gilbert* Maurice, Le pèlerinage d'Iñigo à Jérusalem en 1523: NRT 112 (1990) 660-685.

g871 **Haynes** Jonathan, The humanist as traveler; George SANDYS' relation of a journey begun An.Dom. 1610. Cranbury NJ 1986, Assoc. Univ. 159 p. – ᴿJAOS 110 (1990) 291-303 (R. *Murphey*).

g872 *Hyde* J. K., ᴱ*Waley* Daniel, Italian [Palestine] pilgrim literature in the late Middle Ages: ➤ 84, Mem. HYDE J., BJRyL 72,3 (1990) 13-33.

g872* **Janeras** S., EGÉRIA, pelegrinatge 1986 ➤ 2,d98*: ᴿHelmantica 38 (1987) 437s (J. *Oroz*).

g873 **Jochum** A., Die Beschreibung Palästinas in der englischen Cotton version von MANDEVILLE's Travel (um 1356) [Diss.]: EurHS 14/209. Bern 1990, Lang. ii-61 p.; map; Fs 76 [RHE 85,378*].

g873* **Klatzker** David E., American Christian travellers to the Holy Land 1821-1939: diss. Temple. Ph 1988. – OIAc JJ89.

g874 *Klein* Richard, Die Entwicklung der christlichen Palästinawallfahrt in konstantinischer Zeit: RömQ 85 (1990) 145-181.

g875 *Kowalska* Maria, Bosporus, Schwarzes Meer und Dobrudscha um die Mitte des 17. Jh. im Bericht des arabischen Reisenden PAULS, des Sohnes von Makarios aus Aleppo: FolOr 25 (1989) 181-194.

g876 ᴱ**Laurens** Henry, KLÉBER en Égypte 1798-1800; Kléber et Bonaparte 1798-9: Voyageurs Occ. Ég. 25. Le Caire 1988, IFAO. viii-342 p.; p. 343-579; 2 foldout maps. – ᴿOLZ 85 (1990) 287-9 (W. *Helck*).

g877 *Linage Conde* Antonio, En la Tierra Santa; notas del viaje de Jerusalén al Sinai: RelCu 35 (1990) [no como en bajo] 67-97.

g878 **Magdalena Nom de Déu** José R., Relatos de viajes y epístolas de peregrinos judíos a Jerusalén (1481-1523): 1987 ➤ 4,h590; 5,g550; 84-86329-45-4: ᴿBO 47 (1990) 208 (F. *García Martínez*).

g879 **Maraval** Pierre, Lieux saints et pèlerinages d'Orient 1985 ➤ 1,f342... 4,h592: ᴿRCatalT 13 (1988) 506s (S. *Janeras*).

g880 ᴱ**Mayer** Rolf, Louis de CLERCQ [Voyage en Orient, Ausstellung Köln 1989]. Stu 1989, Cantz. 111 p. 3-89322-163-8 [OIAc Ja91].

g881 *Nakamura* Y., Some aspects of the Russian pilgrimage to the Mediterranean sacred places: ➤ 186, ᶠWATANABE K. 1988, 25-35.

g882 **Ohler** Norbert, Reisen im Mittelalter. Mü 1986, Artemis. 456 p. – ᴿArKulturG 71 (1989) 505s (H.-W. *Goetz*).

g883 *Oroz Reta* José, Del latín cristiano al latín litúrgico; algunas observaciones en torno al Itinerarium Egeriae: ➤ 761, Helmantica 40 (1987/9) 381s.

g884 **Osband** Linda, Famous travellers to the Holy Land; intr. *Morris* Jan. L 1989, Prion. 159 p. 1-85375-031-X [OIAc JJ90].

g884* **Osterhout** Robert, The blessings of pilgrimage. Carbondale 1990, Univ. Illinois [BAR-W 17/3,8].

g885 *Palumbo* Gaetano, Viaggi e esplorazioni nella regione dello Wadi el-Yabis [N. Giordania] dalla tarda antichità al XIX secolo: LA 40 (1990) 375-392; 392-5, bibliog.; Eng. 451s.

g886 ᴱ**Raven** Maarten J., Willem de FAMARS TESTAS Reisschetsen uit Egypte, 1858-1860. Haag 1988, Maarssen/Schwartz-SDU. 232 p. 90-6179-070-0 [OIAc Ja91].

g887 *Rich* Claudius J., Journey to Babylon in the year 1811: BCanadMesop 20 (1990) 15-27.

g888 **Roller** Duane W., Early travellers in Eastern Boiotia [Tanagra]: McGill Univ. MgArch 8. Amst 1988, Gieben. 211 p. – ᴿClasR 40 (1990) 366s (R. *Osborne*); Salesianum 52 (1990) 426 (B. *Amata*).

g889 **Rüger** Hans Peter, Syrien und Palästina nach dem Reiseberichte des Benjamin von TUDELA: AbhDPV 12. Wsb 1990, Harrassowitz. xi-80 p.; 2 maps. 3-447-02881-5 [OIAc S90].

g890 **De Sandoli** Sabino, La liberazione pacifica dei Luoghi Santi nel sec. XIV. J 1990, Franciscan. [TerraS 66,299].

g891 **Schiffer** Reinhold, Turkey; romanticized images of the Turks in early 19th-century English travel literature: Materialia Turcica Beih. 5. Bochum 1982, Brockmeyer. iv-183 p. – ᴿJAOS 110 (1990) 291-303 (R. *Murphey*).

g892 *Schneider* Thomas, Der Ägyptenbesuch des [litauischen Fürstens] Mikolaj Krzysztof Radziwill SIEROTKA von 1583: ZägSpr 117 (1990) 157-171.

g893 *Schmitz* R., Lexikographische Notizen [B. TUDELA...]: ➤ 154, ᶠSACCHI P., 1990, 675-680.

g894 **Simoën** Jean-Claude, Le voyage en Égypte: Les grands voyageurs au XIXᴱ siècle. P 1989, J.-C. Lattès. 315 p. [OIAc JJ90].

g895 ᵀ**Stewart** Aubrey, ²*Musto* Ronald G., THEODORICUS of Würzburg, Guide to the Holy Land. NY 1986, Italica. xxxvi-108 p.; ill., maps [KirSef 62 (1988s), p. 617].

g896 ᴱ**Vatin** Jean-Claude, La fuite en Égypte; supplément aux voyages européens en Orient. Le Caire 1989, CEDEJ. 349 p.; 8 pl. 2-905-838-18-3 [OIAc F91,21 gives titles without pages of the 18 art.].

g897 *Weber* Clifford, EGERIA's Norman homeland: HarvClasPg 92 (1989) 437-456.

g898 **Wilkinson** J., Jerusalem pilgrimage 1099-1185: 1988 ➤ 5,g563: ᴿByZ 83 (1990) 119-121 (Marie-Luise *Favreau-Lilie*); JEH 40 (1989) 452 (J. *Brundage*); LA 40 (1990) 526-8 (E. *Alliata*); RB 97 (1990) 144 (J. *Murphy-O'Connor*); Speculum 64 (1989) 1051s (J. *Folda*).

g899 ᴱ**Wolf-Crome** Editha, Aufbruch nach Armenien; Reise- und Forschungsberichte aus dem Lande Urartu-Armenien. B 1985, Reimer. 280 p.; 3 maps ➤ 1,f352: DM 45. 3-496-00810-5. – ᴿBO 47 (1990) 213s (J. J. S. *Weitenberg*).

U7 *Crucigeri* – **The Crusades.**

g900 **Armstrong** Karen, Holy War [Crusades...]. L c. 1989, Macmillan. £18. – ᴿTablet 243 (1989) 227s (J. *Riley-Smith*).

g901 **Becker** Alfons, Papst Urban II... und der Kreuzzug 1988 ➤ 5,g568: ᴿJTS 41 (1990) 281s (J. *Riley-Smith*).

g902 **Burns** Robert I., Muslims, Christians and Jews in the Crusader kingdom of Valencia; societies in symbiosis [10 art. printed or given at meetings]: Iberian and Latin American Studies, 1984 ➤ 65,d303; 2,d121*: ᴿRHR 207 (1990) 329-331 (S. *Schwarzfuchs*).

g903 [Campo Rey, conde de] **Churruca y de la Plaza** Santiago de, Historia diplomática de España en los Santos Lugares, 1770-1980. M 1982, Min. Ext. 556 p. [KirSef 62 (1988s) p. 185].

g904 **Chazan** Robert, European Jewry and the First Crusade 1987 ➤ 3,g1... 5,g571: ᴿSpeculum 64 (1989) 685 (I. G. *Marcus*).

    Constable Giles, Monks, hermits and crusaders in medieval Europe 1988 ➤ 215.

g905 *Dąbrowska* Malgorzata, L'attitude pro-Byzantine de Saint Louis: BySlav 50 (1989) 11-23.

g906 *Demirkent* Işın, ❶ Recueil des historiens des Croisades I: Belleten 54,210 (1990) 863-898.

g907 **Demurger** Alain, Vie et mort de l'ordre du Temple, 1118-1314²ʳᵉᵛ [= ¹1985 ➤ 2,d124]: Points H 123. P 1989, Seuil. 437 p.; 3 maps. – ᴿSpeculum 65 (1990) 969s (Anne *Gilmour-Bryson*: largely unchanged).

g908 **Demurger** Alain, Vita e morte dell'ordine dei Templari (1118-1314). Mi 1987, Garzanti. 352 p.; ill. Lit. 32.000. – ᴿCC 141 (1990,4) 305s (C. *Capizzi*).

g909 **Edbury** Peter W., *Rowe* John G., WILLIAM of Tyre, historian of the Latin East 1988 → 4,h606; 5,g573; ᴿAmHR 95 (1990) 145s (Leah *Shopkow*); Speculum 65 (1990) 658s (Stephanie E. *Christelow*).

g910 *Engels* Peter, WILHELM von Tripolis [o.p., c. 1270], De statu Sarracenorum; Bemerkungen zu einem neuen Textfund: → 777, Or.-Tag. 1988/90, 77-89.

g911 *Flori* Jean, Guerre sainte et rétributions spirituelles dans la 2ᵉ moitié du XIᵉ siècle (lutte contre l'Islam ou pour la papauté?): RHE 85 (1990) 617-649.

g912 **Holt** F. M., The age of the Crusades 1986 → 2,d127; 3,g7: ᴿSpeculum 65 (1990) 175s (Paula *Sanders*).

g913 ᴱ**Kedar** B. Z., ❺ The Crusaders in their kingdom 1099-1291. J 1987, Yad Ben Zvi. 283 p. 965-217-040-2 [KirSef 62 (1988s) p. 626].

g914 **Kühnel** Gustav, Wall painting in the Latin Kingdom of Jerusalem: Frankfurter Forschungen zur Kunst 14, 1988 → 5,g579: ᴿCahArch 38 (1990) 196 (T. *Velmans*); OLZ 85 (1990) 276-8 (B. *Brentjes*).

g915 **Lawrence** T. E., Crusader castles (diss. 1910, publ. 1936), ᴱ*Pringle* Denys 1988 → 5,g580: ᴿBSO 53 (1990) 512 (J. *Riley-Smith*).

g916 *Leclercq* J., L'ordine del Tempio; monachesimo guerriero e spiritualità medievale: RivAscM 14 (1989) 280-7, 'continuerà' ma non 1989 o 1990.

g917 *Le Goff* Jacques, Saint Louis and the Mediterranean: MeditHistR 5 (1990) 21-43.

g918 **Leistikow** Dankwart, Kreuzritterburgen im lateinischen Königreich Jerusalem; Überblick und Forschungsstand: IstMitt 39 (1989) 341-372; 15 fig.; map.

g919 **Linder** Amnon, The liturgy of the liberation of Jerusalem: MedvSt 52 (1990) 110-131.

g920 **Lloyd** Simon, English society and the crusade, 1216-1307. Ox 1988, Clarendon. xiv-329 p. – ᴿSpeculum 65 (1990) 1010-2 (J. T. *Rosenthal*).

g921 **Maalouf** A., Les Croisades vues par les Arabes. P 1983, Lattès. – ᴿOrMod 69 (1989) 294 (Elizabeth *Vuillemin*).

g922 **Mayer** Hans E., The Crusades [1965 ¹1985], Eng. ²*Gillingham* John, 1988 → 4,h612; 5,g584: ᴿCathHR 85 (1989) 144-6 (J. A. *Brundage*: principal changes on origins and first success).

g923 *Mayer* Hans E., Das syrische Erdbeben von 1170; ein unedierter Brief König Amalrichs von Jerusalem: Deutsches Archiv Erf. Mittelalters 45 (1989) 474-484 [< ZIT 90,479].

g924 **Powell** James M., Anatomy of a Crusade [Fifth] 1213-1221: 1986 → 3,g13: ᴿEngHR 105 (1990) 156s (J. *Riley-Smith*); Speculum 64 (1989) 207-9 (D. E. *Queller*).

g925 **Prawer** Joshua, History of the Jews in the Latin Kingdom 1988 → 5,g585: ᴿJEH 40 (1989) 620 (P. W. *Edbury*).

g926 *Rapp* Francis, Naissance d'une idée-force; la Croisade [< MondeB 61 (1989)]: EsprVie 100 (1990) 184s (J. *Daoust*).

g927 **Regan** Geoffrey, Saladin and the fall of Jerusalem. L 1987, Croom Helm. 186 p.; 5 maps. £22.50. 0-7099-4208-7. – ᴿJEH 40 (1989) 308 (J. *Riley-Smith*).

g928 *Richard* J., La croisade de 1270, premier 'passage général'?: CRAI (1989) 510-523.

g929 **Riley-Smith** Jonathan, The Crusades, a short history. NHv 1990, Yale Univ. 332 p. $15 pa. [0-300-03905-0: 1987, $27.50]. – ᴿCathHR 75 (1989) 146s (J. M. *Powell*); CritRR 2 (1989) 342-4 (M. *Markowski*); Speculum 64 (1989) 703s (R. S. *Avi-Yonah*).

g930 *Riley-Smith* Jonathan,   Kreuzzüge, ᵀ*Schäferdiek* Barbara: ► 857, TRE 20 (1990) 1-10.

g931 **Rotter** Ekkehart, Abendland und Sarazenen; das okzidentale Araberbild und seine Entstehung im Frühmittelalter: Stud. Islam. Or. 11. B 1986, de Gruyter. xii-290 p. DM 158. – ᴿ WZKM 80 (1990) 249-251 (H. *Bobzin*).

g932 *Şeşen* Ramazan, ❶ Armée de Salâhattin à Hittin: Belleten 54,209 (1990) 427-434.

g933 *Severin* Tim,   Retracing the First Crusade: NatGeog 176 (1989) 326-365; color. ill. (P. *Essick*).

g934 *Shinnie* Peter,   Christian Nubia and the Crusades: ► 781, Nubien/ Uppsala 1986/90, 603-610; 2 pl.

g935 *Tanner* Norman P.,   Medieval Crusade decrees and Ignatius's meditation on the Kingdom: HeythJ 31 (1990) 505-515.

g936 **Tibble** Steven,   Monarchy and lordships in the Latin Kingdom of Jerusalem, 1099-1291. Ox 1989, Clarendon. xvii-203 p. £25. – ᴿRHE 85 (1990) 741s (J. *Richard*).

g937 **Tyerman** Christopher,   England and the Crusades 1095-1588;   1988: 5,g593: ᴿJEH 41 (1990) 286-290 (R. B. *Dobson*); JTS 41 (1990) 738-740 (C. *Morris*); ZKG 101 (1900) 113s (G. R. *Elton,* Eng.).

g938 *Vannini* Guido,   Insediamenti di età crociata in Transgiordania: LA 40 (1990) 476-8.

g939 **Zanki** Jamal M. al-,   The emirate of Damascus in the Early Crusading Period - 488-549 / 1095-1154: diss St. Andrews, 281 p. BRDX-91069. – DissA 51 (1990s) 3184-A.

U8   *Communitates Terrae Sanctae* – **The Status Quo.**

Abitbol Michel,   Les deux terres promises; les juifs de France et le Sionisme 1989 ► a343*.

g941 **Ateek** Naim S.,   Justice and only justice 1989 ► 5,g595: ᴿIslamochristiana 16 (1990) 307-315 (M. *Lagarde*); Missiology 18 (1990) 372 (Marcia *Sayre*).

g942 **Bourguet** Pierre du, Les Coptes 1988 ► 5,b390: ᴿBO 47 (1989) 665-670 (G. *Godron*).

g943 **Cannuyer** Christian,   Les Coptes: Fils d'Abraham. Turnhout 1990, Brepols. 230 p.; 28 (color.) fig.; map. 2-503-50003-X.

g944 ᴱ**Carmel** Alex, *al.,* The Jewish settlement in Palestine, 634-1881: TAVO Beih B-88. Wsb 1990, Reichert. 181 p. 3-88226-479-9 [OIAc S90].

g945 **Chacour** Élias,   Fratelli di sangue. ᵀ*Cagiano de Azevedo* M. R 1990, Dehoniane. – ᴿSidic 23,1 (1990) 25-28 (J. A. *Soggin*: réserves).

g946 **Cohen** Amnon [► d940],   Jewish life under Islam; Jerusalem in the sixteenth century 1984 ► 65,d341 ... 3,g36: ᴿRelStT 8,3 (1988) 43-45 (F. *Landy*).

g947 **Colbi** S. P.,   A history of the Christian presence in the Holy Land. Lanham ᴹᴰ 1988, UPA. 377 p. [TerraS 66,89].

g948 **Dieckhoff** Alain,   Les espaces d'Israël; essai sur la stratégie territoriale israélienne²: Références. P 1989, Fond. Nat. Sc. Politiques. 215 p. – ᴿAnÉCS 45 (1990) 475s (H. P. *Jeudy*).

g949 **Facchini** A., † 1949   Le processioni praticate dai Frati Minori nei santuari di Terra Santa [1924]: studio storico-liturgico: StOrChr 19, 1986 ► 4,h633: ᴿRHE 85 (1990) 502 (A. *Haquin*).

g950 *Figliuolo* Bruno, New evidence relating to the condition of Christians in the Holy Land toward the middle of the fifteenth century: MeditHistR 5 (1990) 62-71.

g951 **Findley** Paul, They dared to speak out; people and institutions confront Israel's lobby. Ch 1989, Hill. 390 p. $10. 1-55652-073-5. – ᴿRExp 87 (1990) 508 (H. *Barnette*: 20 publishers refused this book because they didn't want 'the heat').

g952 ᴱ**Friedman** Isaiah, *al.*, The rise of Israel (4+8+7 volumes chiefly of facsimiles). NY 1987, Garland. [KirSef 62 (1988s) p. 632s, titles of items 9-39].

g952* **Friedman** Thomas, From Beirut to Jerusalem [Jewish journalist's defense of Arab Intifada]. L 1990, Collins. £15. – ᴿTablet 244 (1990) 484 (E. C. *Hodgkin*).

g953 **Gerber** Haim, Ottoman rule in Jerusalem 1890-1914: Islamkundliche Untersuchungen 101, 1985 ➤ 2,d166 ... 4,h636: ᴿOLZ 85 (1990) 700s (G. *Barthel*).

g954 **Gerber** Haim, The social origins of the modern Middle East. Boulder CO 1987, Rienner. vii-221 p. [KirSef 62 (1988s) p. 627].

g954* **Giniewski** Paul, L'an prochain à Jérusalem; préhistoire de l'État d'Israël. P 1990, Atlantic. – ᴿFoiVie 89,6 (1990) 106-8 (J. *Ellul*).

g955 *Glassner* Gottfried, Erneuerung im Zeichen der Mönche; das Aufblühen der koptischen Klöster und das Reformwerk des Matta al-Maskin: Erb-Auf 66 (1990) 29-43.

g956 *Hacker* Joseph R., ❸ The Ottoman system of *surgūn* [colonizing banishment] and its influence on the Jewish society in the Ottoman empire: Zion 55 (1990) 27-82; Eng. II-IV.

g957 **Hussar** Bruno, When the cloud lifted [1983 ➤ 65,d354], ᵀ*Megroz* Alison. Dublin 1989, Veritas. £5.25 – ᴿTablet 243 (1989) 1059s (H. *Mowat*: much in few words).

g958 **Irani** George É., Santa Sede e Medio Oriente ᵀ*Marinucci* Elisa. Mi 1989, ViPe. 217 p. Lit. 30.000. – ᴿLetture 45 (1990) 664-6 (P. *Nenci*, anche su Soκoᴌowιcᴢ J.); ViPe 73 (1990) 293-7 (*ipse*).

g959 **Issawi** Charles, The Fertile Crescent 1800-1914, a documentary economic history: MEHistory. NY 1988, Oxford-UP. xv-502 p. £29.50. – ᴿBSO 53 (1990) 140s (A. *Selby*).

g960 **Klein** Herbert A., The peoples of Israel; fifty-seven centuries of presence. Malibu CA 1986, J. Simon. 240 p.; ill., maps [KirSef 62 (1988s) 617].

g961 **Krämer** Gudrun, The Jews in modern Egypt, 1914-1952. Seattle 1989, Univ. Washington. x-319 p. $25. – ᴿRelStR 16 (1990) 363 (A. A. *Ramadan*).

g962 *Lassner* Jacob, The origins of Muslim attitudes towards the Jews and Judaism: Judaism 39 (1990) 494-507.

g963 **Le Strange** Guy, Palestine under the Moslems; a description of Syria and the Holy Land from 650 to 1500, translated from the works of the mediaeval Arab geographers. NY 1975 AMS = Boston 1890. xii-604 p. $47.50 0-04-56288-4 [OIAc F91,15].

g964 **Lewis** Bernard, Die Juden in der islamischen Welt, vom frühen Mittelalter bis ins 20. Jahrhundert [1984 ➤ 65,8735], ᵀ*Julius* Liselotte 1987 ➤ 5,g609: ᴿHZ 250 (1990) 117 (E. *Rotter*).

g965 **Lipman** V. D., Americans and the Holy Land through British eyes 1820-1917: America-Holy Land Project, Hebrew Univ. Institute of Contemporary Jewry. L 1989, auct. 320 p. £15. – ᴿRelStR 16 (1990) 361 (J. D. *Sarna*).

g966 *Longo* C., I domenicani a Cipro, documenti (1451-1587): ArchFrPr 59 (1989) 149-211 [< ZIT 90,262].

g967 **Luz** Ehud, Parallels met; religion and nationalism in the early Zionist movement (1882-1904), ᵀ*Schramm* Lenn J. Ph 1988, Jewish Publ. xix-365 p. $25. – ᴿRelStR 16 (1990) 219s. 222 (C. S. *Liebman*) & 222-5 (M. *Friedman*).

g968 *Martin* Maurice P., Les Coptes catholiques 1880-1920: PrOrChr 40 (1990) 33-55.

g969 *Nakad* Antoine-Pierre, L'Église en Égypte: EsprVie 100 (1990) 58-60 [J. *Daoust* < Œuvre d'Orient 664, févr. 1989].

g969* **Naso** Paolo, Come pietre viventi ... Immagini e testimonianze dei cristiani palestinesi; intr. *Garrone* Daniele: Dossier 25. T 1990, Claudiana, 93 p. Lit. 8500. – ᴿProtestantesimo 45 (1990) 330-3 (J. A. *Soggin*: l'*Intifada* non-violento?).

g970 **Năsturel** Petre S., Le Mont Athos et les Roumains; recherches sur leurs relations du milieu du XIVᵉ siècle à 1654: OrChrAnal 227. R 1986, Pont. Inst. Stud. Orientalium. 375 p. – ᴿRHR 207 (1990) 201-3 (M. *Cazacu*).

g970* **Nicholl** Donald, The testing of hearts [his reflections on five years as rector of Ṭanṭur]. ?L c. 1990, Lamp. £6. – ᴿTablet 244 (1990) 1041 (Rosemary *Hartill*).

g971 **Nimier** Alain, Les Alawites: Minorités 1. P 1989, Asfar. 78 p. – ᴿÉtudes 372 (1990) 710s (J. *Langhade*).

g972 *Orlandi* Tito, Koptische Kirche, ᵀ*Schäferdiek* K.: ➤ 857, TRE 19 (1990) 595-607.

g973 **Parfitt** Tudor, The Jews in Palestine 1800-1882: Royal Hist. Soc. 52. Woodbridge 1987, Boydell. xii-243 p. £25 [KirSef 62 (1988s) p. 627]. – ᴿBSO 52 (1989) 127s (G. *Mandel*).

g973* **Ruether** Rosemary R. & Herman J., The wrath of Jonah ... Israeli-Palestinian conflict 1989 ➤ 5,g612: ᴿSWJT 33,1 (1990s) 71 (F. M. *Graham*: accurately detailed; Arab unity at present unrealizable).

g974 *Sabbah* Michel (pastorale du Patriarche Latin de Jérusalem, Pentecôte 1990), 'Appelez la paix sur Jérusalem' (Ps 122,6): EsprVie 100 (1990) 609-619.

g975 **Sarairah** Hatem A. al-, A British actor on the Bedouin stage; [John B.] GLUBB's career in Jordan, 1930-1956: diss. Indiana Univ, ᴰ*Rodriguez* A. Bloomington 1989. 243 p. 90-20701. – DissA 51 (1990s) 964-A.

g976 **Schneider** Ursula, Land ist unser Leben; galiläische Dörfer ['Ibilin, Mlilyā, Jîš] im Nahostkonflikt Diss. Münster]: Soziologie und Anthropologie 5. Fra 1987, Lang. 512 p. Fs 78 [RB 98, 314, R. J. *Tournay*].

g977 **Schoon** Simon, Christliche Präsenz im jüdischen Staat: Veröff. 17. B 1986, Institut Kirche und Judentum. 210 p. 3-923095-17-1.

g978 *Sélis* Claude, Les Syriens orthodoxes et catholiques 1988 ➤ 5,g616: ᴿNedTTs 44 (1990) 343s (L. van *Rompay*); NRT 112 (1990) 275s (L.-J. *Renard*); OrChrPer 56 (1990) 259s (R. *Lavenant*); StMon 32 (1990) 246s (M. *Nin*).

Stemberger Günter, Juden und Christen im Heiligen Land; Palästina unter Konstantin und Theodosius [II] 1987 ➤ b893.

g980 **Watterson** Barbara, Coptic Egypt. L 1989, Scottish Academic. 187 p. £11. 0-7073-0556-X. – ᴿExpTim 101 (1989s) 87 (J. D. *Ray*).

g981 **Wilson** Mary C., King Abdullah, Britain and the making of Jordan. C 1988, Univ. xxii-289 p. £25. – ᴿBSO 52 (1989) 355s (J. A. *Rudd*).

g982 **Yapp** M. E., The making of the modern Middle East, 1792-1923: 1987
➤ 5,g622: ᴿJSS 35 (1990) 372-4 (R. R. *Pennell*: a college text that sizzles;
he is writing a continuation).

g983 **Zamir** Meir, The formation of modern Lebanon. L 1985, Croom Helm.
– ᴿAcÉCS 45 (1990) 225-7 (A. *Nouschi*).

g984 *Zananiri* G., Le monde arabe et les chrétiens: EsprVie 100 (1990)
696-704.

XX. Historia Scientiae Biblicae

Y1 History of Exegesis .1 General.

g985 ᴱ**Avis** Paul, The history of Christian theology; the science of theology.
Basingstoke 1986, Marshall-Pickering. xi-363 p. £10. – ᴿScotJT 43 (1990)
408s (J. B. *Walker*).

g986 *Basevi* Claudio, Hacia la estructuración de una 'Historia de la exégesis
bíblica'; ensayos y perspectivas: ScripTPamp 22 (1990) 221-241.

g987 **Bosio** Guido, Introduzione ai Padri della Chiesa, secoli I e II: Strumenti
della Corona Patrum. T 1990, SEI. xxxiv-265 p. Lit. 29.000. 88-05-
05172-1.

g988 **Brown** Harold O. J., Heresies; the image of Christ in the mirror of
orthodoxy from the Apostles to the present 1988 = 1944 ➤ 65,d381 ...
5,g626: ᴿCriswT 4 (1989s) 195 (T. *George*).

g989 **Brox** Norbert, Historia de la Iglesia primitiva [1983 ➤ 65,d382 ²1986],
ᵀ*Gancho* Claudio: Biblioteca de Teologia 8. Barc 1986, Herder. 264 p. –
ᴿSalesianum 52 (1990) 719s (F. *Bergamelli*).

g990 *a)* **Camelot** Pierre-T., *Maraval* Pierre, Les conciles œcuméniques I., Le
premier millénaire; – *b)* **Christophe** Paul, *Frost* Francis, II. Le second
millénaire: BtHistChr 15s. P 1988, Desclée. 90 p.; 272 p. ➤ 5,g628: ᴿMél-
SR 47 (1990) 55s (M. *Huftier*).

g990* **Carrara** Paolo, I pagani di fronte al cristianesimo 1984 ➤ 1,b368:
ᴿProtestantesimo 45 (1990) 147 (G. *Scuderi*).

g991 *Cavalcanti* Elena, Quindici anni di studi patristici in Italia (orientamenti
metodologici): ➤ 735, ᴱ*Garzya* A., Metodologie/tarda antichità 1987/9,
189-222.

g992 **Christie-Murray** David, A history of heresy. Ox 1989 = 1976, UP.
viii-243 p. £6 pa. – ᴿTLond 93 (1990) 226 (G. *Irvine*).

g993 **Comby** Jean, Per leggere la storia della Chiesa, I. dalle origini; II. dal
XV al XX secolo; ᵀᴱ*Molinari* Franco: Serie Per leggere ... [AT, NT, Gesù
etc.]. R 1986s, Borla. 162 p.; 200 p. – ᴿBenedictina 37 (1990) 235s (P.
Lunardon).

g994 *Curti* Carmelo, Quintino Cataudella editore di testi patristici [1940 ...
1969]: Orpheus 11 (1990) 211-220.

g995 **Droge** Arthur J., Homer or Moses? HermUnT 26, 1989 ➤ 5,g629: ᴿAr-
TGran 53 (1990) 382s (A. S. *Muñoz*); JTS 41 (1990) 656-9 (E. *Osborn*).

g996 **Faivre** Alexandre, The emergence of the laity in the early Church, ᵀ*Smith*
David. NY 1990, Paulist. iii-242 p. $12. – ᴿTS 51 (1990) 781s (W. P.
Loewe).

g997 **Fédou** M., L'Église des Pères: initiation à la théologie patristique: Média
Sèvres. P 1989, Centre Sèvres. 37 p. [NRT 113, 467, J.-C.M.].

g997* *Flores R.* Mario A., Los Padres de la Iglesia en el estudio de la teología:
EfMex 8 (1990) 341-358.

g998 **Grossi** Vittorino, *Siniscalco* Paolo, La vita cristiana nei primi secoli. R 1988, Studium. 135 p. – RScuolC 117 (1989) 399s (L. *Orsenigo*: secondo volume di una collana sulla spiritualità).

g999 **Hadot** Jean, La formation du dogme chrétien des origines à la fin du 4e siècle: Cahier de la Forel 3. Charleroi 1990, Fac. Religions et Laicité. 167 p. [RTLv 21,402].

k1 *La Potterie* Ignace de, I Padri della Chiesa nello studio 'attuale' della Sacra Scrittura: Seminarium 42 ('Instructio de Patrum Ecclesiae studio in sacerdotali institutione', 1990) 486-494 (389-578, 9 altri commentari; 364-388, summaria polyglotta).

k2 ELöser Werner, *al.,* Dogmengeschichte und katholische Theologie [21 Aufsätze] 1985 ➤ 2,323*... 4,g636: RTPhil 65 (1990) 299-305 (W. *Schneemelcher*: spät, ausführlich).

k3 **Lortz** Joseph, Storia della Chiesa in prospettiva di storia delle idee, I. Antichità e medioevo; II. Evo moderno. CinB 1987, Paoline. 702 p.; 751 p. – RSTEv 1 (1989) 92s (P. *Guccini*).

k4 **McKim** Donald K., Theological turning points; major issues in Christian thought. Atlanta 1988, Knox. 211 p. – RInterpretation 44 (1990) 326.328 (D. H. *Sutton*).

k5 *Maraval* Pierre, Modèles bibliques de l'hospitalité chez les Pères: StMor 28 (1990) 27-42 [< ZIT 90,612].

k6 *Margerie* Bertrand de, Three suggestions about the study and diffusion of the biblical commentaries of the Fathers: DoctComm 42 (1989) 185-8.

k7 **Moda** Aldo, Il cristianesimo nel primo secolo 1986 ➤ 4,h678; 5,g641: RRTPhil 122 (1990) 279s (R. *Petraglio*); Salesianum 52 (1990) 157s (E. *dal Covolo*).

k8 **Pierini** Franco, Mille anni di pensiero cristiano... I. Alla ricerca dei Padri; introduzione e metodologia generale: L'Abside 10, 1988 ➤ 4,h682: RNRT 112 (1990) 129s (A. *Harvengt*); RivStoLR 26 (1990) 367-370 (C. *Gianotto*).

k9 EQuacquarelli Antonio, Complementi interdisciplinari di Patrologia 1989 ➤ 5,503: RRTLv 21 (1990) 486-8 (A. de *Halleux*); Salesianum 52 (1990) 721s (S. *Felici*); Teresianum 41 (1990) 704s (M. *Diego Sánchez*).

k10 **Reventlow** Henning, Epochen der Bibelauslegung I. Vom Alten Testament bis Origenes. Mü 1990, Beck. 238 p. DM 48 [TR 87,73].

k11 *a) Rexine* John E., The Church Fathers and modern man; – *b)* Abp. *Methodios,* The mind (*phronema*) of the Fathers of the Church: Patristic and Byzantine Review 4/1 (1985) 3-13 [39-50, *Azkoul* Michael] / 14-19.

k12 **Robinson** Thomas A., The [1934 Walter] BAUER thesis examined; the geography of heresy in the early Church: StBEC 11, 1988 ➤ 4,h686: REvQ 62 (1990) 280-2 (D. F. *Wright*); CBQ 52 (1990) 568 (R. A. *Wild*: Rechtgläubigkeit not [1]1934 but [2]1964 acclaimed as a seminal classic; Robinson's challenge is more convincing on Ephesus-area than on Edessa); Interpretation 44 (1990) 104s (M. E. *Boring*).

k13 **Sawicki** Marianne, The Gospel in history 1988 ➤ 4,h691; 5,g649: RScripTPamp 22 (1990) 289s (M. *Merino*).

k14 **Schneemelcher** Wilhelm, Il Cristianesimo delle origini [1981], TMorato Gabriella: Univ. pa. 201. Bo 1987, Mulino. 235 p. – RSalesianum 52 (1990) 731s (F. *Bergamelli*).

k15 ESevrin J.-M., The NT in early Christianity: Coll. Bibl. Lov. 36, 1986/9 ➤ 5,606: RRivB 38 (1990) 262s (R. *Mela*).

k16 **Skarsaune** Oskar, Fra Jerusalem til Rom og Bysants: Kristendommen i Europa 1. Oslo 1987, Tano. 167 p. Nk 118. – RNorTTs 91 (1990) 1-6 (Øyvind *Norderval*; *al.* 2-5).

k17 *Starowieyski* Marek, ❷ L'exégèse des Pères de l'Église: AtKap 115 (1990) 25-36.

k18 ᴱ**Tanner** Norman P., Decrees of the ecumenical councils; I. Nicaea I to Lateran IV; II. Trent to Vatican II. L 1990, Sheed & W. xxv-655 p.; p. 657-1342. 0-7220-3010-X / US 0-87340-490-2 (both volumes).

k19 **Trigg** Joseph W., Biblical interpretation: Message of the Fathers 9, 1989 ⮑ 4,b701; 5,g651*: ᴿBibTB 20 (1990) 134s (C.C. *Black*).

k20 **Urban** L., A short history of Christian thought 1987 ⮕ 2,d237; 3,g121: 0-19-503717-0: ᴿBL (1990) 27 (R. *Hammer* would have expected more on Scriptural basis and history of interpretation).

k21 **Vilanova** E., Historia de la Teologia I, 1987 ⮕ 3,g125... 5,g652: ᴿHumT 10 (1989) 125s (A. de *Pinho*); PerspT 21 (1989) 398-401 (D. *Mondoni*); Salesianum 52 (1990) 910s (P.T. *Stella*).

k22 **Viller** Marcel, *Rahner* K. [1939, 1958, 1972]; Ascese und Mystik in der Vaterzeit; ein Abriss der frühchristlichen Spiritualität. FrB 1989, Herder (unveränderte Neuausgabe, Vorw. *Neufeld* Karl H.). 26*-323 p. DM 68. – ᴿGeistL 63 (1990) 151s (A. *Batlogg*).

k23 **Wallace-Hadrill** D.S., Christian Antioch, a study of early Christian thought 1983 ⮕ 63,e481... 65,d414: ᴿCathHR 75 (1989) 125s (S.H. *Griffith*).

Y1.4   *Patres apostolici et saeculi II* – First two centuries.

k24 [Histoire de l'apologétique], *a*) *Fabris* R., judaïsme et NT; – *b*) *Péri* V., grecque avant 300; – *c*) *Paparozzi* M., Orient; – *d*) *Bori* P.C., patristique et moderne; – *e*) *Pizzolato* L.F., Augustin; – *f*) *Kölmel* W., devant l'Islam; – *g*) *Horvath* T., scolastique, réforme; – *h*) *Ruggieri* G., moderne: ⮕ 843, EncTF 1 (1987) 1-14 / 15-60 / 61-112 / 113-131 / 133-219 / 221-246 / 247-274 / 275-340.

k25 **Grant** Robert M., Jesus after the Gospels; the Christ of the second century [Seabury-Western Hale Lectures 1989]. Louisville/L 1990, W-Knox/SCM. 134 p. $15 [CBQ 52,779]. /0-334-02444-7.

k26 **Grant** Robert M., Greek apologists 1988 ⮕ 4,h708; 5,g656: ᴿJRel 90 (1990) 89s (E.V. *Gallagher*); Salmanticensis 37 (1990) 241-3 (R. *Trevijano*).

k27 **Grelot** Pierre, (*Dumais* Marcel), Homélies sur l'Écriture à l'époque apostolique: Intr... 1989 ⮕ 5,g657: ᴿScEsp 42 (1990) 358s (L. *Sabourin*).

k28 **Le Boulluec** Alain, La notion d'hérésie dans la littérature grecque I. JUSTIN-IRÉNÉE; II. CLÉMENT et ORIGÈNE 1985 ⮕ 1,f554... 4,k783: ᴿAnÉCS 45 (1990) 871-3 (D.A. *Bertrand*); RevSR 63 (1989) 154-6 (Mariette *Canévet*).

k29 **Lightfoot** J.B., *Harmer* J.R., The Apostolic Fathers [Gk-Eng 1891 = 1984], ᴱ*Holmes* M.W. GR/Leicester 1989, Baker / Apollos. xvi-347 p.; 2 maps. $18. 0-8010-5655-1 [NTAbs 34,271: *Lightfoot*'s rendition indicated in note where significantly changed].

k30 **Neymeyr** Ulrich, Die christlichen Lehrer im zweiten Jahrhundert; ihre Lehrtätigkeit, ihr Selbstverständnis und ihre Geschichte [kath. Diss. Mainz 1987, ᴰ*Baumeister* T.]: VigChr supp 4. Leiden 1989, Brill. x-279 p. *f* 130. 90-04-08773-7 [NTAbs 34,138]. – ᴿTPhil 65 (1990) 264s (H.J. *Sieben*).

k31 **Orbe** Antonio, Introducción a la teología de los siglos II y III: AnGreg 248, 1987 ⮕ 3,g128... 5,g661: ᴿMaia 42 (1990) 203-6 (C. *Gianotto*); RÉAug 35 (1989) 332-4 (Simone *Deléani*); Teresianum 40 (1989) 237s (M. *Diego Sánchez*); TLZ 115 (1990) 611-3 (G. *Wendelborn*).

k32 **Pilhofer** Peter, *Presbyteron kreitton*; der Altersbeweis der jüdischen und christlichen Apologeten und seine Vorgeschichte [Diss. Münster 1989]: WUNT 2/39. Tü 1990, Mohr. xvii-339 p. 3-16-145584-3. – RArTGran 53 (1990) 331 (A. *Segovia*).

k33 **Schille** Gottfried, Frei zu neuen Aufgaben; Beiträge zum Verständnis der dritten urchristlichen Generation 1986 ➤ 2,d247: RTLZ 115 (1990) 202 (J. *Roloff*).

k34 *Stander* H. F., Die breuk tussen die Christendom en die Jodedom in de eerste twee eeue nC [radical break shown originating in Barnabas, Didache, 1-2 Clement, Ignatius, Justin, Irenaeus, Tertullian]: SkrifKerk 10,1 (1989) 44-60 [< NTAbs 34,211].

k35 **Tugwell** S., The apostolic fathers: Outstanding Christian Thinkers. Harrisburg PA 1990, Morehouse. xii-148 p. $17; pa. $10. 0-8192- 1492-2; -1-4 [NTAbs 34,416].

---

k35* ARISTIDES: *Astås* Reidar, Den aldste bevarte kristne apologi [c. 140; mentioned by EUSEBIUS, JEROME, OROSIUS; c. 1000 Armenian fragment published 1878; *Harnack* TLZ 1879]: TsTKi 61 (1990) 177-192; Eng. 192.

k36 ATHENAGORAS: *Harris* Bruce F., The defence of Christianity in Athenagoras' *Embassy*: JRelHist 15 (1988s) 413-424.

k37 EM*arcovich* Miroslav, Athenagoras, Legatio pro christianis: PatrTStud 31. B/NY 1990, de Gruyter. xii-158 p. DM 118. 3-11-011881-5. – RRSPT 74 (1990) 626s (G.-M. de *Durand*).

k38 **Pouderon** Bernard, Athénagore [diss. Lyon 1986]: THist 82, 1989 ➤ 5, g667: RArTGran 53 (1990) 332 (A. *Segovia*); EsprVie 100 (1990) 473 (Y.-M. *Duval*); ETL 66 (1990) 420-2 (A. de *Halleux*); Gregorianum 71 (1990) 796s (G. *Pelland*); JTS 41 (1990) 651-3 (L. W. *Barnard*); RÉAug 36 (1990) 184s (A. *Wartelle*) RHPR 70 (1990) 345 (P. *Maraval*); RivStoLR 26 (1990) 587-596 (M. *Rizzi*); RSPT 74 (1990) 624-6 (G.-M. de *Durand*, aussi sur EMARCOVICH 1990); TLZ 115 (1990) 838s (K. *Treu*); TPhil 65 (1990) 265s (H. J. *Sieben*).

k39 *Pouderon* Bernard, 'La chair et le sang'; encore sur l'authenticité du traité d'Athénagore [niée par R. GRANT, E. GALLICET, H.-E. LONA]: VigChr 44 (1990) 1-5.

k40 BARNABAS: *Ferguson* Everett, Was Barnabas a chiliast? an example of Hellenistic number symbolism in *Barnabas* and CLEMENT of Alexandria: ➤ 122, FMALHERBE A., Greeks 1990, 157-167.

k41 *Hanson* A. T., The activity of the pre-existent Christ as reflected in the Epistle of Barnabas: ➤ 643, StPatr 18,3 (1983/9) 155-9.

---

k42 CLEMENS A.: *Alexander* Loveday, The living voice; scepticism towards the written word in early Christian and in Graeco-Roman texts: ➤ 166, FSheffield 1990, 221-247.

k43 *Fernández Ardanaz* Santiago, El problema hermenéutico en la interpretación de la obra de Clemente Alejandrino: ScripV 36 (1989) 278-339.

k44 *Grzywaczewski* Józef, ⊕ *Pojęcie...* The concept of contemplation in Clement of Alexandria: STWsz 28,1 (1990) 210-222.

k45 *Hoek* Annewies van den Clement A./PHILO 1988 ➤ 4,a982: RBLitEc 91 (1990) 239s (H. *Crouzel*); JTS 41 (1990) 653-6 (E. *Osborn*); StPhilonAn 2 (1990) 211-4 (Anita *Méasson*).

k46 *Hoek* Annewies van den, How Alexandrian was Clement of Alexandria? Reflections on Clement and his Alexandrian background: HeythJ 31 (1990) 179-194.

k47 *Osborn* E. F., Clement's Hypotyposeis; Macarius revisited: SecC 7 (1989s) 232-5.

k48 *Places* Édouard des, Les citations profanes du VIᵉ / VIIᵉ Stromate de Clément d'Alexandrie: RÉAnc 92 (1990) 109-119 / 297-303.

k49 *Tardif de Lagneau* Henri, Chrétiens devant la philosophie grecque; un point de vue de Clément d'Alexandrie: ➤ 91, ᶠJERPHAGNON L. 1989, 89-98.

k50 CLEMENS ROMANUS: **Bowe** Barbara E., A church in crisis... Clement of Rome, ᴰ1988 ➤ 4,h716: ᴿCritRR 3 (1990) 281-3 (D. A. *Hagner*); RExp 87 (1990) 142s (E. G. *Hinson*); SecC 7 (1989s) 242 (A. F. *Droge*); TS 51 (1990) 175 (Carolyn *Osiek*).

k51 *Fernández-Ardanaz* Santiago, Elementos hebreos en la antropología de la llamada Prima Clementis: ➤ 135, ᶠORBE A., Compostellanum 34 (1989) 51-87.

k52 *Cormode* D. Scott, The influence of Hellenistic Judaism on the concepts of God and the Church in 1 Clement: StudiaBT 17 (Pasadena 1989) 185-197.

k53 *Mees* M. †, ᴱ*Neirynck* Frans, Das Christusbild des ersten Klemensbriefes: ETL 66 (1990) 297-318.

k54 *Serraima Cirici* Enrique, Las 'Cartas a las vírgenes' atribuidas a Clemente Romano: EfMex 8 (1990) 71-81.

k55 *Warns* Rüdiger, Untersuchungen zum 2. Clemensbrief [Inaug. Marburg 1985]. 1989. x-696 p. – ᴿTPhil 65 (1990) 596s (H. J. *Sieben*).

k56 *Snowden* Joe R., The redactors of the 'Pseudo-Clementines' in the Tripolis discourses: diss. Harvard, ᴰ*Strugnell* J. CM 1990. 198 p. 90-28260. – DissA 51 (1990s) 1455-A; RelStR 17,194.

k57 a) *Drijvers* Han J. W., Adam and the True Prophet in the Pseudo-Clementines; – b) *Dihle* Albrecht, Die Gewissensentscheidung des Synesios; – c) *Gladigow* Burkhard, Chresthai theois — Orientierungs- und Loyalitätskonflikte in der griechischen Religion: ➤ 785, ᶠCOLPE C., Loyalitätskonflikte 1990, 314-323 / 324-9 / 237-251.

k58 CONST.AP.: ᵀᴱ**Metzger** Marcel, Constitutions Apostoliques: SChr 320. 329.336; 1985-7 ➤ 1,f494... 5,g677: ᴿMaisD 181 (1990) 143-5 (I. H. *Dalmais*); RBgPg 68 (1990) 181s (J. *Schamp*).

k59 DIDACHE: *Brock* Sebastian, The two ways [Didache; BARNABAS] and the Palestinian Targum: ➤ 183, ᶠVERMES G. 1990, 139-152.

k59* *Grimonprez-Damm* Benoît, Le 'sacrifice' [*thusía* = *koinonía*, 'entraide'] eucharistique dans la *Didachè*: RevSr 64 (1990) 9-25.

k60 *Hills* J. V., Tradition and composition in the Epistula Apostolorum [diss. ᴰ*Koester* H.]: HarvDissRel 24. Mp 1990, Fortress. xvii-172 p. $13 pa. 0-8006-7078-7 [NTAbs 34,409].

k61 **Jefford** C. N., The sayings of Jesus in the Teaching of the Twelve Apostles [diss. Claremont 1988, *Robinson* J.]: VigChr supp 11. Leiden 1989, Brill. xvi-185 p. ƒ100. 90-04-09127-0 [NTAbs 34,269].

k62 ᴱ**Niederwimmer** K., Die Didache: KommApV 1. Gö 1989, Vandenhoeck & R. 329 p. DM 94. 3-525-51670-3 [NTAbs 34,138]. – ᴿNeotestamentica 29 (1990) 369-371 (H. F. *Stander*: first of 8 volumes); NRT 112 (1990) 606s (X. *Jacques*); Salmanticensis 37 (1990) 237-9 (R. *Trevijano*); TLZ (1990) 690s (A. *Lindemann*).

k63 *Schöllgen* Georg, Wandernde oder sesshafte Lehrer in der Didache?: BibNot 52 (1990) 19-26.

k64 *Winslow* Donald F., Poverty and riches, an embarrassment for the early Church [Didache 4. ...]^T: ➤ 643, StPatr 18,2 (1983/9) 317-328.

k65 AD DIOGNETUM: **Rizzi** Mario, La questione dell'unità dell'"Ad Diognetum' 1989 ➤ 5,g681: RETL 66 (1990) 423s (A. de *Halleux*); Gregorianum 71 (1990) 791s (G. *Pelland*); RÁug 36 (1990) 183s (B. *Pouderon*); RivStoLR 26 (1990) 370-2 (L. *Vigna*); ScripTPamp 22 (1990) 648 (A. *Viciano*).

k65* *Blanchetière* François, Au cœur de la cité; le chrétien philosophe selon l'À Diognète 5-6: RevSR 63 (1989) 183-194.

k66 HERMAS: **Haas** C., De Geest bewaren... Hermas [diss. Leiden, ᴰ*Jonge* M. de] 1985 ➤ 1,7017: RNedTTs 44 (1990) 257s (A. *Hilhorst*).

k67 *Henne* Philippe, *a*) Canonicité du 'Pasteur' d'Hermas; – *b*) Le péché d'Hermas: RThom 90 (1990) 81-100 / 640-651.

k68 *Jeffers* J. S., Pluralism in early Roman Christianity [Hermas vs. 1 CLEMENT]: Fides et Historia 22,1 (GR 1990) 4-17 [< NTAbs 35,225].

k69 **Leutzsch** M., Die Warnehmung sozialer Wirklichkeit... Hermas: FRL 150, 1989 ➤ 5,686: RSalmanticensis 37 (1990) 239s (R. *Trevijano*).

k70 *Osiek* Carolyn, The second century through the eyes of Hermas; continuity and change: BibTB 20 (1990) 116-122.

k71 IGNATIUS: *Dehandschutter* B., L'authenticité des épîtres d'Ignace d'Antioche: ➤ 643, StPatr 18,3 (1983/9) 103-110.

k72 *Maier* Harry O., The charismatic authority of Ignatius of Antioch: a sociological analysis [< SR 18 (1989) 185-199, Eng.], E*Bonness* Mary Kay: TDig 37 (1990) 235-240.

k73 E**Paulsen** Henning, Die Briefe... Ignatius/POLYKARP²ʳᵉᵛ 1985 ➤ 1,f500 ... 5,g690: RSecC 7 (1989s) 57s (W. R. *Schoedel*: commentary sparse).

k74 *Pettersen* Alvyn, Sending heretics to Coventry? Ignatius of Antioch on reverencing silent bishops: VigChr 44 (1990) 335-350.

k75 **Schoedel** W. R., Die Briefe des Ignatius voon Antiochien, ein Kommentar [1985 ➤ 1,f502], T*Koester* G. Mü 1990, Kaiser. vi-472 p. DM 139. 3-459-01836-4 [NTAbs 35,133]. – RSNTU A-15 (1990) 220s (A. *Fuchs*).

k76 IRENAEUS: **Torisu** Yoshifumi, Gott und Heilsökonomie; eine Untersuchung der Theologie des Irenäus von Lyon: kath. Diss. ᴰ*Schulte*. Wien 1989s. – TR 86,511.

k77 *Barrett-Lennard* R.J.S., Salvation and healing [Irenaeus]: Prudentia 22,2 (1990) 16-35.

k78 **Birrer** Jakob, Der Mensch als Medium und Adressat der Schöpfungsoffenbarung; eine dogmengeschichtliche Untersuchung zur Frage der Gotteserkenntnis bei Irenäus von Lyon: BaBSt 59. Bern 1989, Lang. 268 p. – RBTAM 14 (1990) p. 774 (E. M.).

k79 *a*) *Norris* Richard A.ᴶ, Irenaeus' use of Paul in his polemic against the Gnostics; – *b*) *Lindemann* Andreas, Paul in the writings of the Apostolic Fathers: ➤ 510, SMU Paul 1987/90, 79-88 / 25-45.

k80 **Orbe** Antonio, Espiritualidad de S. Ireneo: AnGreg 256, 1989 ➤ 5,g698: RArTGran 53 (1990) 330s (C. *Granado*); ETL 66 (1990) 422s (A. de *Halleux*); Teresianum 41 (1990) 705s (M. *Diego Sánchez*).

k81 **Orbe** A., Teologia de S. Ireneo V: 2s, 1987s ➤ 4,h732; 5,g697: RJTS 41 (1990) 239-247 (D. *Minns*).

k82 **Puttanil** Thomas, A comparative study on the theological methodology of Irenaeus of Lyon and SANKARACHARYA [Diss. München]: RelW 4. Fra 1990, Lang. vi-379 p. Fs 79 [TR 87.76].

k83 JUSTINUS: **Cabaniss** A., [Justin: I, 65-67] Pattern in early Christian worship. Macon 1989, Mercer Univ. x-112 p. 0-86554-345-3 [NTAbs 34,261].

k84 *Grant* Robert M., Eternal fire and the occasion of JUSTIN's apology: → 135, ᶠORBE A, Compostellanum 34 (1989) 129-133.

k85 ᴱMarcovich Miroslav, Pseudo-Iustinus, Cohortatio ad Graecos; De monarchia; Oratio ad Graecos: PatrTSt 32. B 1990, de Gruyter. ix-161 p. 3-11-012135-2 / US 0-89925-708-9.

k86 *Panimolle* Salvatore A., L''ora' del Cristo nel 'Dialogo con Trifone': VetChr 27 (1990) 303-332.

k87 *Petersen* William L., Textual evidence of TATIAN's dependence upon Justin's 'apomnēmoneumata': NTS 36 (1990) 512-534.

k88 **Robillard** Edmond, Justin, l'itinéraire philosophique: Recherches NS 23. Montréal/P 1989, Bellarmin/Cerf. 172 p. – ᴿArTGran 53 (1990) 333 (A. S. *Muñoz*); EsprVie 100 (1990) 473 (Y.-M. *Duval*); ETL 66 (1990) 196s (A. de *Halleux*).

k90 **Skarsaune** Oskar, The proof from prophecy... Justin: NT supp 56, 1987 → 3,g166... 5,g701: ᴿCBQ 52 (1990) 365s (J. S. *Siker*); CritRR 2 (1989) 344-6 (W. R. *Schoedel*).

k91 **Visonà** Giuseppe, S. Giustino, Dialogo con Trifone 1988 → 4,b742; 5,g702: ᴿRHE 85 (1990) 246s (P.-A. *Deproost*).

k92 *Young* M. O., Justin, Socrates, and the Middle Platonists; → 643, StPatr 18,2 (1983/9) 161-8.

k93 POLYCARPUS: *Dehandschutter* B., A 'new' text of the Martyrdom of Polycarp [updating his 1979 BiblETL 52 by collation with known-but-unnoticed Athens codex 989]: ETL 66 (1990) 391-4.

k94 *a) Rius-Camps* Josep, La carta de Policarpo a los Filipenses, ¿aval de la recopilación 'policarpiana' o credencial del nuevo obispo Crescente?; – *b) Beatrice* Pier Franco, Der Presbyter des Irenäus, Polycarp von Smyrna und der Brief an Diognet; → 135, ᶠORBE A. Compostellanum 34 (1989) 97-127 / 135-153.

k95 *Tripp* David, The prayer of St. Polycarp and the development of anaphoral prayer: EphLtg 104 (1990) 97-132; lat. 97.

Y1.6 **Origenes.**

k96 *Cavallo* Guglielmo, Scuola, scriptorium, biblioteca a Cesarea [Origene, PANFILO]: → 478, Biblioteche² 1989, 65-77.

k97 **Crouzel** Henri, Origen, the life and thought of the first great theologian 1989 → 5,g707: ᴿAnglTR 72 (1990) 340-2 (J. W. *Trigg*: no feel for Origen's marvelous style of exegesis); NewTR 3,2 (1990) 96s (A. *Chirovsky*); VigChr 44 (1990) 97-99 (J. van *Winden*).

k98 *Crouzel* Henri, Chronique origénienne: BLitEc 91 (1990) 221-6.

k99 *Crouzel* Henri, *a)* Le thème platonicien du 'véhicule de l'âme' chez Origène [< Didaskalia 7 (1977) 225-237; cf. 3 (1973) 3-19]; – *b)* Différences entre les ressuscités selon Origène [< ᶠStuiber A., Jenseitsvorstellung (1982) 107-116]: → 217, Fins dernières 1990, III (225-237; IV. 3-19) / IX (107-116).

k100 *a*) *Crouzel* Henri, Idées platoniciennes et raisons stoïciennes dans la théologie d'Origène; – *b*) *Hennessey* L. R., The scriptural and classical roots of Origen's theology of death; – *c*) *Demura* Miyako, The resurrection of the body and soul in Origen's Contra Celsum: ➤ 643, StPatr 18,3 (1983/9) 365-383 / 403-412 / 385-392.

k101 **Falla** Claire †, L'apologie d'Origène par Pierre HALLOIX (1648): BFac ph/L Liège 238. P 1983, BLettres. xxx-194 p. 2-251-67238-9; pa. 3. – RAnBoll 108 (1990) 457s (J. *Kluyskens*).

k102 **Fédou** Michel, Christianisme et religions païennes dans le Contre Celse d'Origène: THist 81, 1989 ➤ 5,g708: RActuBbg 27 (1990) 231s (J. *Vives*); ArTGran 53 (1990) 323s (E. *Barón*); BBudé (1990) 423-5 (É. des *Places*: tant de perspectives); EsprVie 100 (1990) 474 (Y.-M. *Duval*: bon avec réserves sur Balaam et les Mages); ETL 66 (1990) 424s (A. de *Halleux*: remarquable); Gregorianum 71 (1989) 795s (G. *Pelland*: croise plusieurs questions disputées avec mesure et prudence; moins bien soulève la question 'd'interroger une œuvre du 3ᵉ siècle sur le sujet des religions non chrétiennes'); JTS 41 (1990) 659-661 (M. J. *Edwards*: dubious method); MondeB 65 (1990) 71 (I. H. *Dalmais*); RHPR 70 (1990) 347s (F. *Blanchetière*); RSPT 74 (1990) 629-632 (G.-M. de *Durand*: chenal étroit et malaisé entre écueils); TPhil 65 (1990) 266-9 (H. J. *Sieben*: worthily continues the great French tradition of Origen-interpretation); TS 51 (1990) 739s (G. H. *Ettlinger*: scholarly and extremely interesting).

k103 *Feldman* Louis H., Origen's Contra Celsum and JOSEPHUS' Contra Apionem; the issue of Jewish sources: VigChr 44 (1990) 105-135.

k104 *Foubert* Jean, L'école d'Origène; physique et éthique spirituelles, d'après le Remerciement de GRÉGOIRE le Thaumaturge (VI, §23 - IX, §115): ➤ 91, FJERPHAGNON L. 1989, 99-135.

k105 *Gorday* Peter J., Paulus origenianus; the economic interpretation of Paul in Origen and GREGORY of Nyssa: ➤ 510, SMU Paul 1987/90, 141-163.

k106 *Hauck* R. J., Omnes contra Celsum?: SecC 5 (1985s) 211-225 [< RHE 85,819].

k107 TEHoffmann R. Joseph, Celsus 1987 ➤ 3,gl74; 4,h756: RAnglTR 71 (1989) 214s (Kathleen E. *McVey*); JEH 40 (1989) 255s (S. G. *Hall* 'a constant desire to be outrageous regardless of the facts'; ignores superior SChr).

k107* **Hunstorfer** Karl, F. W. J. SCHELLING und Origenes; ein problemgeschichtlicher Vergleich: Diss. Innsbruck 1989s, ECoreth E. – ZkT 112 (1990) 500s.

k108 EKannengiesser C., Petersen W., Origen 1986/8 ➤ 5,683: RCritRR 3 (1990) 294s (E. J. *Epp*: tit. pp.); RÉAug 36 (1990) 186s (A. *Le Boulluec*);VigChr 44 (1990) 310s (J. van *Winden*).

k109 *König* Hildegard, 'Vestigia antiquorum magistrorum sequi'; Wie liest APPONIUS Origenes?: TüTQ 170 (1990) 129-136.

k110 **Laak** Werner van, Allversöhnung; die Lehre von der Apokatastasis; ihre Grundlegung durch Origenes und ihre Bewertung in der gegenwärtigen Theologie bei Karl BARTH und Hans Urs von BALTHASAR: TTSt 11. Zinzig 1990, St. Meinrad. 175 p.; 12 fig. [TR 87,340].

k111 ELies Lothar, Origeniana quarta 1985/7 ➤ 3,664b... 5,g712: RAsprenas 37 (1990) 236-8 (L. *Fatica*); CrNSt 11 (1990) 384s (P. F. *Beatrice*); DivThom 93 (1990) 163-5 (L. *Elders*); RÉAug 35 (1989) 182-4 (M. *Fédou*); RHE 85 (1990) 80-83 (C. *Kannengiesser*); Salmanticensis 37 (1990) 245-9 (R. *Trevijano*); ScotJT 43 (1990) 122s (R. E. *Heine*).

k112 *Lies* Lothar, Vom Christentum zu Christus nach Origenes Contra Celsum: ZkT 112 (1990) 150-177.

k113 **Meis Wörmer** Annelies, El problema del mal en Origenes... Peri Archon III 1,1-24: AnChile 37/2 1988 ➤ 5,g713; $10: ᴿNRT 112 (1990) 435 (B. *Pottier*); RET 50 (1990) 476-8 (E. *Tourón*); ScripTPamp 22 (1990) 648 (A. *Viciano*); VigChr 44 (1990) 101-3 (P. van der *Eijk*); ZkT 112 (1990) 122 (K. H. *Neufeld*).

k114 [Monaci] **Castagno** Adele, Origene predicatore e il suo pubblico 1987 ➤ 4,h759; 5,g714: ᴿOrpheus 10 (1989) 219-221 (A. V. *Nazzaro*).

k115 **Neuschäfer** Bernhard, Origenes als Philologe 1987 ➤ 3,g177; 5,g715: ᴿRÉAug 35 (1989) 184-6 (A. *Le Boulluec*); RFgIC 118 (1990) 94-98 (M. *Simonetti*).

k116 **Pietras** H., L'amore in Origene 1988 ➤ 4,h761; 5,g716: ᴿNRT 112 (1990) 434s (R. *Godding*).

k117 *a) Sfameni Gasparro* Giulia, AGOSTINO di fronte alla 'eterodossia' di Origene; un aspetto della questione origeniana in Occidente; – *b) Kato* Takeshi, La voix chez Origène et saint Augustin: ➤ 13, ᶠBAVEL T. van, AugLv 40 (1990) 219-243 / 245-258.

k118 ᴱ**Sgherri** Giuseppe, Origene, Sulla Pasqua; il papiro di Tura: LettCr 6. Mi 1989, Paoline. 172 p. – ᴿAsprenas 37 (1990) 112s (L. *Fatica*); Salesianum 52 (1990) 181 (B. *Amata*).

k119 **Torjesen** Karen Jo, Hermeneutical procedure and theological method in Origen's exegesis 1986 ➤ 2,d316... 4,h763: ᴿAntonianum 65 (1990) 666s (M. *Nobile*); NedTTs 44 (1990) 76-78 (J. *Roldanus*); NorTTs 91 (1990) 158s (Øyvind *Norderval*).

k120 *Zandee* Jan, Origène et Les enseignements de Silvain (NHC VII,4): LavalTP 46 (1990) 369-382.

Y1.8 **Tertullianus.**

k121 **Ahlborn** Elke, Naturvorgänge als Auferstehungsgleichnis bei SENECA, Tertullian und Minucius FELIX: WienerSt 103 (1990) 123-137.

k122 ᵀᴱ**Braun** René, Tertullien, Contre Marcion I (livre I), intr. texte critique, tr., notes.: SChr 365. P 1990, Cerf. 315 p. [NRT 113, 588, V. *Roisel*]. 2-204-04281-1.

k123 *Braun* René, *al.,* Chronica Tertullianea et Cypriana [1988] 1989 [... un phénomène nouveau, l'apparition en masse d'articles dupliqués... espérons que (ne soit publiée) qu'une seule version]: RÉAug [35 (1989) 315-345] 36 (1990) 328-354 [74 courts comptes-rendus signés].

k124 *a) Braun* René, Sacralité et sainteté chez Tertullien; – *b) Mandouze* André, *Sacramentum* et *sacramenta* chez saint Augustin; – *c) Ingremeau* Christiane, LACTANCE et le sacré; l'Histoire Sainte racontée aux païens... par les païens; – *d) Fontaine* Jacques, Le 'sacré'... ISIDORE: ➤ 5,786 Écrivains 1988/9, 313s / 318s / 320s / 322s.

k125 **Driver** Charles B.ᴶ, The historical and theological features of [Phrygia-Tertullian and] resurgent Montanism and their effect upon American Christianity: diss. Mid-America Baptist Theol. Sem. 1990. 189 p. 90-27795. – DissA 51 (1990s) 1451s-A.

k126 **Goldhahn-Müller** Ingrid, Die Grenze der Gemeinde... der zweiten Busse... bis Tertullian 1989 ➤ 5,g728: ᴿTLZ 115 (1990) 892s (G. *Schille*); WissWeis 52 (1989) 237s (H. J. *Klauck*).

k127 **González** Justo L., Christian thought revisited; three types of theology [Tertullian: law; ORIGEN: truth; IRENAEUS: history]. Nv 1989, Abingdon. 185 p. $16. 0-687-07629-3 [TDig 37,365].

k128 **Harnack** A. von, Marcion, the gospel of the alien God [Das Ev. vom fremden Gott ²1924], ᵀ*Steely* J. E., *Bierma* L. D.   Durham NC 1990, Labyrinth.   x-182 p. $30.   0-939464-16-0 [NTAbs 34,408].

k129 **Heck** Eberhard,   *mē theomacheîn...* Tertullian 1987 ⇒ 4,b672.h767: ᴿJTS 41 (1990) 247-250 (O. *Nicholson*).

k130 **Heine** Ronald E.,   The Montanist oracles and testimonia: NAm Patristic Soc. Mg 14, 1989 ⇒ 5,g732:   ᴿJTS 41 (1990) 643 (S. G. *Hall*: replaces P. de LABRIOLLE 1913, omitting the 80 post-300 texts).

k131 *Matheson* Peter,   Thomas MÜNTZER's marginal comments on Tertullian: JTS 41 (1990) 76-90.

k132 *Munier* Charles,   *a)* Propagande gnostique et discipline ecclésiale d'après Tertullien: RevSR 63 (1989) 195-205; – *b)* Tertullien: ⇒ 837, DictSpir XV, 96ss (1990) 271-295.

k133 *St.-Arnaud* Guy-Robert, De la 'lettre' à *persona* [et son introduction en théologie par Tertullien, mise en cause par R. CANTALAMESSA]; prolégomènes à une structure: RevSR 64 (1990) 283-305.

k133* *Sider* Robert D.,   Literary artifice and the figure of Paul in the writings of Tertullian: ⇒ 510, SMU Paul 1987/90, 99-120.

k134 **Steiner** Heinrich,   Das Verhältnis Tertullians zur antiken Paideia [kath. Diss. Mü 1987, ᴰ*Schwaiger* G.]: StTGesch 3.   St. Ottilien 1989, EOS. x-285 p. DM 30.   3-88096-903-5. – ᴿScripTPamp 22 (1990) 969-973 (A. *Viciano*).

k135 *Williams* D. H.,   The origins of the Montanist movement; a sociological analysis: Religion 19,4 (Lancaster 1989) 331-351 [< NTAbs 34,222].

Y2   *Patres graeci* – **The Greek Fathers.**

k136 *Armstrong* Arthur R.,   *a)* The self-definition of Christianity in relation to later Platonism [< ᴱ*Sanders* E. P., Jewish and Christian self-definition 1980, 74-90. 224-234]; – *b)* Negative theology; myth and incarnation [< ᶠ*Trouillard* J., Néoplatonisme 1981, 47-62]: ⇒ 197, Hellenic and Christian Studies 1990, VIII. (p. 74 ... 234) / VII. (p. 47-62).

k137 *a)* *Broek* Roelof van den,   Juden und Christen in Alexandrien im 2. und 3. Jahrhundert; – *b)* *Ritter* Adolf M., Juden und Christen im Heiligen Land; Palästina unter Konstantin und Theodosius; – *c)* *Horst* Peter W. van der,   Juden und Christen in Aphrodisias im Licht ihrer Beziehungen in anderen Städten Kleinasiens [⇒ e862*]: ⇒ 506*, Juden/Christen 1989/ 90, 101-115 / 116-124 / 125-143.

k137* *Brun* Jean,   Hellénisme et christianisme: Hokhma 41 (1989) 1-11.

k138 **Cavarnos** Constantine,   The Hellenic-Christian philosophical tradition [Boston Univ. Lectures 1987s]. Belmont MA 1989, Institute for Byzantine. viii-127 p. $10.50; pa. $7.50.   0-914744-83-6; 4-4 [TDig 37,352].

k138* **Davis** Leo D.,   The first seven ecumenical councils 1987 ⇒ 4,h776; 5,g744:   ᴿCathHR 76 (1990) 100s (Frances M. *Young*).

k139 *Elders* Leo J.,   The Greek Christian authors and ARISTOTLE: DoctCom 43 (1990) 26-57.

k140 **Geyer** Carl-Friedrich,   Religion und Diskurs; die Hellenisierung des Christentums aus der Perspektive der Religionsphilosophie [Hab.-Diss. Bochum]. Stu 1990, Steiner.   185 p. DM 36 [TR 87,169].

k141 **Goehring** James E.,   Chalcedonian power politics and the demise of Pachomian monasticism: OccP 15.   Claremont CA 1989, Institute for Antiquity and Christianity.   20 p.

k142 *Jerphagnon* Lucien, Les sous-entendus anti-chrétiens de la Vita PLOTINI ou l'évangile de Plotin selon PORPHYRE: MusHelv 47 (1990) 41-52.

k143 *Kearsely* Roy, Faith and philosophy in the early Church: Themelios 15 (1989s) 81-86.

k144 **Kinneavy** J. L., Greek rhetorical origins of Christian faith 1987 ➤ 3, 3830.g205 ... 5,g745: ᴿBullBiblB 1 (1990) 7-11 (M. *Schoeni*); CritRR 2 (1989) 210-3 (D. F. *Watson*).

Le Boulluec A., La notion d'hérésie dans la littérature grecque 1985 ➤ k28.

k145 **Lochman** J. M., Christ and Prometheus? 1988 ➤ 4,219: ᴿPacifica 3 (1990) 236-8 (G. *Garrett*).

k146 **Meyendorff** John, Imperial unity and Christian divisions; the Church 450-680 A.D.: The Church in history 2. Crestwood NY 1989, St. Vladimir. xv-402 p.; map. – ᴿRHE 85 (1990) 729-732 (V. *Peri*).

k147 ᴱ**Mondésert** Claude, La Bibbia alle origini della Chiesa [< Le monde grec et la Bible, BTT 1, 1984, pp. 19-125], ᵀRigo Caterina, ᴱChiesa Bruno: StBPaid 92. Brescia 1990, Paideia. 170 p. 88-394-0441-4. 6 art; ➤ 4349.

k148 ꟳMONDÉSERT Claude, Alexandrina, 1987 ➤ 3,117: ᴿRTLv 21 (1990) 96-98 (A. de *Halleux*).

k149 *O'Meara* Dominic J., Le problème du discours sur l'indicible chez PLOTIN: RTPhil 122 (1990) 145-156; Eng. 295.

k150 *Quinn* Philip L., A response to HAUERWAS; is Athens revived Jerusalem denied?: AsbTJ 45,1 (1990) [5-48.59-63] 49-57.

k151 *Ryan* P. J., The Greek tradition of allegorization and its influence on the early Christian writers: Prudentia 21,2 (1989) 25-46 [< NTAbs 34,290].

k152 **Simonetti** Manlio, Cristianesimo antico e cultura greca 1983 ➤ 65,d485; 2,d344: ᴿRÉAug 35 (1989) 182 (P. *Jay*; 'on peut ne pas partager le regard très négatif sur la réaction contre l'hellénisme et la décadence' finale).

k153 **Spanneut** M., Les Pères de l'Église, 2. Du IVᵉ au VIIIᵉ siècle: Bibl-HistChr 22. P 1990, Desclée. 357 p. [NRT 113,467]. – ᴿRTLv 21 (1990) 497s (A. de *Halleux*).

k154 *Staats* Reinhart, Die römische Tradition im Symbol von 381 (N[icaeno]C[onst.]) und seine Entstehung auf der Synode von Antiochien 379: VigChr 44 (1990) 209-221.

k155 *Strand* Kenneth A., Sunday Easter and quartodecimanism in the early Christian church: AndrUnS 28 (1990) 127-136.

k156 **Studer** Basil, La riflessione teologica nella Chiesa imperiale (sec. IV e V): Studi patristici 4, 1944 ➤ 5,g752: ᴿAsprenas 37 (1990) 247 (L. *Fatica*); ETL 66 (1990) 419s (D. *Bundy*).

k157 **Thümmel** Hans G., Die Kirche des Ostens im 3. und 4. Jahrhundert: ZKG Einz 1/4. B 1988, Ev.-V. 135 p. M 12. [TLZ 115, 351-3, H.-C. *Brennecke*].

k158 *Young* Frances, The rhetorical schools and their influence on patristic exegesis: ➤ 5,38*, ꟳCHADWICK H., Making of orthodoxy 1989, 182-190.

---

k159 ALEXANDER: *Kannengiesser* Charles, Alexander and ARIUS of Alexandria, the last ante-Nicene theologians: ➤ 135, ꟳORBE A., Compostellanum 35,1s (1990) 93-105.

k160 ARIUS: *Loose* Uta, Zur Chronologie des arianischen Streites: ZKG 101 (1990) 88-92.

Hanson R.P.C., The search for the Christian doctrine of God; the Arian controversy 318-381: 1988 → 7468.

k161 *Ritter* Adolf M., Arius redivivus? Ein Jahrzwölft Arianismusforschung: TRu 55 (1990) 153-187.

k162 *Stead* Christopher, The Arian controversy; a new perspective: → 80, FHÖRNER H., Hermeneumata 1990, 51-59.

k163 ATHANASIUS: **Arnold** Duane Wade-Hampton, The early episcopal career of Athanasius of Alexandria, AD 328-335: diss. Durham 1989. 380 p. BRD-91855. – DissA 51 (1990s) 3786-A.

k164 **Camplani** A., Le lettere festali di Atanasio... studio storico-critico. R 1989, CIM. vi-340 p. – RJTS 41 (1990) 258-264 (R. D. *Barnes*).

k165 *Pettersen* Alvyn, The Arian context of Athanasius of Alexandria's Tomus ad Antiochenos VII: JEH 41 (1990) 183-198.

k166 *Simonetti* Manlio, Sulla recente fortuna del Contra Sabellianos ps. Atanasiano: RivStoLR 26 (1990) 117-132.

k167 *Tetz* Martin, Eine asketische Ermunterung zur Standhaftigkeit aus der Zeit der maximinischen Verfolgung (311/313) ['Athanasius' De patientia]: ZNW 81 (1990) 79-102.

k168 ATHENOGENES: TEMaraval P., La passion inédite de S. Athénogène de Pédachthoé en Cappadoce (BHG 197b): Subsidia Hagiog. 75. Bru 1990, Bollandistes. [vii-] 120 p.; map.

k169 BASILIUS: TEDucatillon Jeanne, Basile de Césarée, Sur le baptême: SChr 357. P 1989, Cerf. 323 p. 2-204-04062-2.

k170 *Rousseau* P., Basil of Caesarea; choosing a past: → 479, Reading 1990, 37-58.

k171 **Sieperski** Paulo D., The liberating *leitourgía* of Basil the Great [... his *koinōnía, kérygma* and *diakonía* from the point of view of the oppressed]: diss. Southern Baptist Theol. Sem., DHinson E. 1989. 262 p. 90-15973. – DissA 51 (1990s) 199-A.

k172 CHRYSOSTOMUS: *Aubineau* Michel, Textes chrysostomiens... 'In Joh. Bapt.': JbÖstByz 40 (1990) 83-90; 2 pl.
Druet François-X., Langage, images et visages de la mort chez Jean Chrysostome [diss. Liège]: 1990 → 9052.

k173 EMalingrey Anne-Marie, (*Leclercq* Philippe), PALLADIOS... vie de Chrysostome: SChr 341s, 1988 → 4,h812; 5,g760: RAntClas 59 (1990) 394-9 (J. *Schamp*); ETL 66 (1990) 202 (A. de *Halleux*); JTS 41 (1990) 690s (J.N.D. *Kelly*: surpasses even R. *Coleman-Norton* 1928); MélSR 47 (1990) 53s (P. M. *Hombert*); RÉAug 36 (1990) 196s (C. *Lepelley*).

k174 EMeyer Robert T., PALLADIUS, Dialogue on the life of St. John Chrysostom: Ancient Christian Writers 45. NY 1985, Paulist. $17. 0-8091-0358-3. – RCathHR 76 (1990) 103s (F. T. *Gignac*).

k175 *Monaci Castagno* Adele, Paideia classica ed esercizio pastorale nel IV secolo; il concetto di 'synesis' nell'opera di G. Crisostomo: RivStoLR 26 (1990) 429-459.

k176 EPiédagnel Auguste, *Doutreleau* A., Jean Chrysostome, Trois catéchèses baptismales: SChr 366. P 1990, Cerf. 288 p. F 200 [NRT 113, 590, A. *Harvengt*]. 2-204-04231-5.

k177 *Ritter* Adolf M., John Chrysostom as an interpreter of Pauline social ethics [*Clark* Elizabeth A., comment]: → 510, SMU Paul 1987/90, 183-192 [-199].

k177* *Roldanus* J., Le chrétien — étranger au monde dans les homélies bibliques de Jean Chrysostome: SacrEr 30 (1987s) 231-251.

k178 ᴱ**Schatkin** Margaret, *al.,* Jean Chrysostome, Discours [+ ᴱ*Grillet* B. *al.,* Homélie] sur Babylas: SChr 562. P 1990, Cerf. 330 p. F 245 [NRT 113, 591, V. *Roisel*]. 2-204-04117-3.

k179 **Schatkin** Margaret A., J. Chrysostom as apologist 1987 ➤ 5,g775: ᴿBLitEc 91 (1990) 67 (H. *Crouzel*); JEH 40 (1989) 450s (H. *Chadwick,* also on her ᵀwith *Harkins* P.); Salesianum 52 (1990) 184-6 (O. *Pasquato*).

k179* *Tidball* Derek J., John Chrysostom's 'On the priesthood': Evangel 8,2 (1990) 8-11.

k180 *Wicker* Kathleen O., 'The politics of Paradise' reconsidered; Chrysostom and PORPHYRY [i. Elaine PAGELS on sexual asceticism]: ➤ 152, ꟳROBINSON J. M., Gnosticism 2 (1990) 116-133.

k181 *Zeegers-Van der Vorst* Nicole, À propos du Dialogue de PALLADE sur la vie de Jean Chrysostome [SChr 341s, 1988]: RHE 85 (1990) 30-41.

k182 CYRILLUS A.: *Adshead* K., De civitate Dei; le vocabulaire politique de saint Cyrille d'Alexandrie: RechSR 78 (1990) 233-240.

k183 ᵀᴱ**McEnerney** John I., St. Cyril of Alexandria, Letters 1-50 / 51-110: Fathers 66s. Wsh 1987, Catholic Univ. xvi-237 p.; xii-204 p. $30 each. – ᴿJEH 40 (1989) 137-9 (G. *Bonner*); RelStR 16 (1990) 347 (R. L. *Wilken*).

k184 CYRILLUS H.: *Cignelli* Lino, Il Cristo liberatore in San Cirillo di Gerusalemme: TerraS 65 (1989) 13-21.

k185 ᴱ**Piédagnel** Auguste, ᵀ*Paris* Pierre, Cyrille de Jerusalem, Catéchèses Mystagogiqucs²: SChr 126 bis. P 1988, Cerf. 222 p. – ᴿEllinika 40 (1989) 165-7 (T. *Detorakis,* franç.); OrChrPer 56 (1990) 235s (J. D. *Baggarly*).

k186 DAMASCENUS: ᴱ**Kotter** Bonifatius †, Die Schriften des Johannes von Damaskus 5. Opera homiletica et hagiographica: PatrTSt 29, 1988 ➤ 5, g780: ᴿBO 47 (1990) 256-8 (G. *Quispel*: an Aquinas of the East); BySlav 50 (1989) 225 (H. G. *Thümmel*); RelStR 16 (1990) 348 (R. L. *Wilken*).

k187 *Odorico* P., La cultura della *syllogē,* 1) Il cosiddetto enciclopedismo bizantino; 2) Le tavole del sapere di Giovanni Damasceno: ByZ 83 (1990) 1-21.

k188 *Orban* A.P., Die lateinische Übersetzung von zwei Predigten des Joannes Damaskenos auf die Koimesis Mariä; Einführung, Ausgabe und Anmerkungen: Byzantion 60 (1990) 232-291.

k189 DIONYSIUS Alex.: *Pietras* Henryk, Lettera *pròs Germanón* di Dionigi Alessandrino; osservazioni e prova di ricostruzione: Gregorianum 71 (1990) 573-583.

k189* DIONYSIUS PSEUD.-A. ᵀ**Luibheid** Colm, ᴱ*Rorem* Paul, Pseudo-Dionysius, the complete works: ClasWSpir 54. 1987 ➤ 3,g437; 4,k18: ᴿCalvinT 25 (1990) 269-272 (J. R. *Payton*: cited 1700 times by AQUINAS, and in general commented more than *Augustine*).

k190 ᵀ**Suchla** Beate R., *a)* Ps.-Dionysius A., Die Namen Gottes 1988 ➤ 5,g782: ᴿJTS 41 (1990) 714s (A. *Louth*); VigChr 44 (1990) 92s (J. van *Winden*). – *b)* De divinis nominibus: Corpus dionysiacum I / PatrTSt 33. B 1990, de Gruyter. xxix-238 p. 3-11-012042-9.

k190* **Louth** Andrew, Denys A. 1989 ➤ 5,k16: ᴿRelStR 16 (1990) 347s (P. *Viscuso*).

k191 EPIPHANIUS: *Adler* William, The origins of the proto-heresies; fragments from a chronicle in the first book of Epiphanius' *Panarion*: JTS 41 (1990) 472-501.

k192 ᵀᴱ**Amidon** Philip R.,   The Panarion of St. Epiphanius, bishop of
Salamis, selected passages.   NY 1990, Oxford-UP.   378 p. $45.   0-19-
506291-4 [TDig 38,57].

k193 *Frickel* Josef,   Der Antinoet-Bericht des Epiphanius als Korrektiv für
den Text von HIPPOLYTS Contra Noetum: → 135, ᶠORBE A., Compostellanum 35 (1990) 39-53.

k194 *Thornton* T. C. G.,   The stories of [= told by] Joseph of Tiberias [Pa-
narion 30]:   VigChr 44 (1990) 54-63.

k195 **Dechow** Jon F.,   Dogma and mysticism in early Christianity; Epiphanius of Cyprus and the legacy of ORIGEN: PatrMg 13, 1988 → 4,h821;
5,g782: ᴿCritRR 3 (1990) 283s (C. L. *Hanson*); JTS 41 (1990) 673-682
(G. *Gould*); RelStR 16 (1990) 263 (Elizabeth A. *Clark*).

k196 EUSEBIUS: ᵀᴱ**Bodogae** T.,   Eusebiu de Cezareea, Scrieri I [Hist. Eccl.;
Mart. Pal.]: Părinţi şi scriitori bisericeşti 13.   Bucureşti 1987.   451 p. –
ᴿSTBuc 40,1 (1988) 121-5 (T. *Baconsky*).

k197 **Christensen** Torben,   RUFINUS of Aquileia and the Historia Ecclesiastica of Eusebius: Hist-F. Med. 58, 1989 → 5,g793: ᴿNorTTs 91
(1990) 163-7 (Hugo *Montgomery*).

k198 ᵀᴱ**Forrat** M.,   (*Places* É. des),   Eusèbe, Contre Hiéroclès: SChr 333,
1986: → 2,d364 ... 5,g785: ᴿEsprVie 100 (1990) 475 (Y.-M. *Duval*);
RBgPg 68 (1990) 174-7 (J. *Schamp*).

k199 **Places** Édouard des, Eusèbe, La préparation évangélique 14s, SChr 338,
1987 → 3,g240 ... 5,g787: ᴿBLitEc 91 (1990) 147-9 (H. *Crouzel*, aussi sur
6 autres SChr); ÉtClas 58 (1990) 399 (F.-X. *Druet*); RBgPg 68 (1990)
177-9 (J. *Schamp*).

k200 *Hollerich* Michael J.,   Myth and History in Eusebius's De vita Con-
stantini; VitConst 1.12 in its contemporary setting: HarvTR 82 (1989)
421-443.

k201 *Louth* Andrew,   The date of Eusebius' Historia ecclesiastica: JTS 41
(1990) 111-123.

k202 *Mortley* R.,   The Hellenistic foundations of ecclesiastical historiography:
→ 479, Reading 1990, 225-250.

k203 **Smith** Mark D.,   Eusebius of Caesarea, scholar and apologist; a study of
his religious terminology and its application to the Emperor Constantine:
diss. California, ᴰDrake H.   Santa Barbara 1989.   171 p. 90-21957. –
DissA 51 (1990s) 962-A.

k204 **Verheyden** Jozef,   De vlucht ... naar Pella ... Eusebius/EPIPHANIUS 1988
→ 4,h833; 5,g796: ᴿCBQ 52 (1990) 764-6 (M. C. de *Boer*: too concerned
to support his teacher NEIRYNCK against R. PESCH); CollatVL 20 (1990)
120s (A. *Denaux*); JTS 41 (1990) 664s (R. M. *Grant*); VigChr 44 (1990) 86s
(A. F. J. *Klijn*: why Pella? source plausible).

k205 *Verheyden* J.,   The flight of the Christians to Pella [Epiphanius depends
on Eusebius, earliest source of the belief, against C. KOESTER CBQ]: ETL
66 (1990) 368-384.

k206 *Walker* P. W. L.,   Gospel sites and 'holy places'; the contrasting attitudes of Eusebius [never linked Transfiguration with Tabor except once
as contender with Hermon; ... 'the true Cross'] and CYRIL: TyndB 41
(1990) 89-108.

k207 ᵀᴱ**Williamson** G. A., ²ʳᵉᵛ *Louth* Andrew, Eusebius; the history of the
Church from Christ to Constantine.   L 1989, Penguin.   xxxix-435 p. £6
[JTS 41,824].

k208 EUNOMIUS: *Keith* Graham A., Our knowledge of God; the relevance of the debate between Eunomius and the Cappadocians: TyndB 41 (1990) 60-88.

k209 ᵀᴱ**Vaggione** Richard P., Eunomius: Early Christian texts. Ox 1987, Clarendon. xvii-209 p. £30. – ᴿHeythJ 31 (1990) 336 (A. *Meredith*); JEH 40 (1989) 258-260 (S.G. *Hall*: splendid, despite some noted errors); RTPhil 122 (1990) 281 (É. *Junod*).

k210 FIRMUS: ᵀᴱ**Calvet-Sebasti** Marie-Ange, *Gatier* Pierre-Louis, Firmus de Césarée, Lettres: SChr 350, 1989 ➤ 5,g797: ᴿRTPhil 122 (1990) 563s (J. *Borel*).

k211 GREGORIUS NAZ.: *Kalamakis* Dionysios C., ⓖ Lexiques des poésies de S. Grégoire de Nazianze, précédés d'un aperçu général de la lexicographie patristique, I. Prolégomènes: Epeteris Etairías Byzantinôn Spoudôn 47 (1987-9) 311-418.

k212 ᵀᴱ**Meier** Beno, Gregor von Nazianz, Über die Bischöfe (Carmen 2,1,12): StGKAlt 2/7. Pd 1989, Schöningh. 174 p. – ᴿTPhil 65 (1990) 597-9 (H.J. *Sieben*).

k213 ᵀᴱ**Moreschini** Claudio, Gregoire de Nazianze, Discours 38-41, ᵀ*Galley* Paul: SChr 358. P 1990, Cerf. 389 p. 2-204-04063-0.

k214 *Tsirpanlis* Constantine N., Saint Gregory [Naz.] the theologian on marriage and family; Patristic and Byzantine Review 4/1 (1985) 33-38.

k215 GREGORIUS NYSS.: **Altenburger** Margarete, *Mann* Friedhelm, Bibliographie zu Gregor von Nyssa 1988 ➤ 4,h838; 5,g802: ᴿJTS 41 (1990) 684s (A. *Meredith*); TLZ 115 (1990) 354 (K. *Treu*).

k216 *Drobner* Hubertus R., Die Himmelfahrtspredigt Gregors von Nyssa: ➤ 80, ᶠHÖRNER Hadwig 1990, 95-115.

k217 **Drobner** Hubertus R., Bibelindex zu den Werken Gregors von Nyssa 1988 ➤ 5,g802: ᴿRHE 85 (1990) 141 (A. de *Halleux*).
ᴱ**Drobner** H., Studien zu Gregor von Nyssa 1990 ➤ 695.

k218 **Fabricius** C., *Ridings* D., A concordance to Gregory of Nyssa: StGrLat 50. Göteborg 1989, Univ. 31 microfiches [NRT 113, 297, B. *Pottier*].

k219 ᴱ**Maraval** Pierre, Grégoire de Nysse, Lettres: SChr 363. P 1990, Cerf. 346 p. F 224 [NRT 113, 589, A. *Harvengt*].

k220 *a*) *Mosshammer* Alden A., Non-being and evil in Gregory of Nyssa: VigChr 44 (1990) 136-167; – *b*) *Winling* Raymond, Mort et résurrection du Christ dans les traités Contre Eunome de Grégoire de Nysse: RevSR 64 (1990) 127-140. 251-269.

k221 KOSMAS H.: *Kazhdan* Alexandre, Kosmas of Jerusalem [or Hagiopolites; part 1 with S. *Gero* > ByZ]; 2. Can we speak of his political views?: Muséon 103 (1990) 329-346.

k222 MAXIMUS: **Gatti** Maria Luisa, Massimo il Confessore; saggio di bibliografia 1987 ➤ 3,g256: ᴿJTS 41 (1990) 719s (A. *Louth*).

k223 MELITO: *Drobner* Hubertus R., Der Aufbau der Paschapredigt Melitos von Sardes: TGL 80 (1990) 205-7.

k224 NESTORIUS: *Kyle* Richard, Nestorius; the partial rehabilitation of a heretic: JEvTS 32 (1989) 73-84 [< ᴢɪᴛ 89,509].

k225 PAULUS SAMOSAT.: *Grillmeier* Alois, Neue Fragmente zu Paul von Samosata? [*Declerck* J.]: TPhil 65 (1990) 392-4.

k226 PETRUS ALEX.: **Vivian** Tim, St. Peter of Alexandria, bishop and martyr [MG 18,467-508 ...]: Studies in Antiquity and Christianity 2. Ph 1988, Fortress. xvii-231 p. $40. – ᴿSecC 7 (1989s) 187s (M. *Slusser*).

k226* ROMANOS: *Barkhuizen* J. H., Romanos' encomium on Joseph; portrait of an athlete: JbÖstByz 40 (1990) 91-106.

k227 SYMEON: **Turner** H. J. M., St. Symeon the new theologian and spiritual fatherhood [< diss. Manchester]: ByzNeerl 11. Leiden 1990, Brill. xvi-257 p. [TR 87,342].

k228 SYNESIUS: **Roques** Denis, Synésios ... et la Cyrénaïque 1987 → 4,h846*; 5,g815: ᴿLatomus 49 (1990) 512-4 (P. *Trousset*); RÉAug 35 (1989) 191-4 (Y. *Modéran*).

k229 THEODORETUS: *Allen* P., The use of heretics and heresies in the Greek Church historians; studies in Socrates and Theodoret: → 479, Reading 1990, 265-289.

k230 *Azéma* Yvan, Théodoret de Cyr: → 837, DictSpir 96ss (1990) 418-435.

k230* **Cope** Glenn M., An analysis of the heresiological method of Theodoret of Cyrus in the 'Haereticarum fabularum compendium': diss. Catholic Univ., ᴰ*Halton* T. Wsh 1990. 425 p. 90-27656. – DissA 51 (1990s) 1651-A: RTLv 22, p. 597.

k231 THEODORUS M.: *Khoury* Nabil el-, Der Mensch als Gleichnis Gottes; eine Untersuchung zur Anthropologie des Theodor von Mopsuestia: OrChr 74 (1990) 62-71.

k231* *Lera* José-M., Théodore de Mopsueste: → 837, DictSpir XV, 96ss (1990) 385-400.

k232 **Zaharopoulos** Dimitri Z., Theodore of Mopsuestia on the Bible 1989 → 5,g818; $12: ᴿScripTPamp 22 (1990) 1011s (A. *Viciano*); TS 51 (1990) 369 (Celia E. *Rabinowitz*: overstresses his anti-allegorizing).

Kabasilas Nikolaos (1320-1363), La vie en Christ, ᵀᴱ*Congourdeau* Marie-Hélène: SChr 355.361, 1989s → 8186.

ᴙ2.4 **Augustinus.**

k233 *a)* Agostino d'Ippona, 'Quaestiones disputatae' 1987/9 ...: ᴿLateranum 56 (1990) 371-4 (O. *Pasquato*); – *b)* Augustinus XVI cent. 1986: De conversione: AugM 32 (1987 → 4,517*a*); – *c)* Congresso: R 1986/7 → 4,517*a*: ᴿBTAM 14 (1990) 778-782 (G. M.).

k233* **Álvarez Turienzo** Saturnino, Regio media salutis. ... hombre, creación, Agustín [→ 5,7173]. S 1988, Univ. Pontificia. 369 p. 84-7299-2144. ᴿEstE 65 (1990) 354s (L. *Vela*); AugM 35 (1990) 172s (J. *Oroz*).

k234 *Anglin* W. S., SIMPLICIAN's reply to Augustine: ChrSchR 19 (1990) 243-251 [< ZIT 90,447].

k235 ᵀᴱ**Babcock** William S., Tyconius, the Book of Rules: SBL TTr 31, 1989 → 5,g819*a:* ᴿTLZ 115 (1990) 691s (H.-U. *Delius*).

k236 — **Bright** Pamela, The book of rules of Tyconius [ᴰ1987, ᴰ*Kannengiesser* C.] 1988 → 5,g819*b:* ᴿCathHR 76 (1990) 350s (K. B. *Steinhauser*).

k237 *Beers* William R., The Confessions of Augustine; 'narcissistic' elements: American Imago, psychoanalytic journal 45 (1988) 107-125 [< RÉAug 35,377].

k238 *Bonner* Gerald, *a)* Augustinus (uita): → 829, AugL 1,4 (1990) 519-550; – *b)* St. Augustine's Confessions: ExpTim 101 (1989s) 163-7.

k239 *a)* *Bonner* Gerald, The significance of Augustine's De gratia Novi Testamenti; – *b)* *Langa* Pedro, La autoridad de la Sagrada Escritura en

Contra Cresconium; – *c*) *Hamman* Adalbert G., Saint Augustin, la Bible et la théologie spirituelle; – *d*) *Kevane* Eugene, Augustine's De doctrina christiana in world-historical perspective: ➤ 13, ᶠBAVEL T. van, AugLv 41 (1990s) 531-559 / 691-721 / 773-782 / 1011-1031.

k240 *a*) *Burns* J. Patout, AMBROSE preaching to Augustine; the shaping of faith; – *b*) *Sweeney* Leo, 'Was St. Augustine a Neoplatonist or a Christian?'; old question new approach: ➤ 688*a*, Collectanea 1986/90, 373-386 / 403-420.

k241 *Canévet* Mariette, Se connaître soi-même en Dieu; un aspect du discernement spirituel dans les Confessions d'Augustin: RevSR 64 (1990) 27-52.

k242 ᴱCaprioli A., *Vaccaro* L., Agostino e la conversione 1986/7 ➤ 4,518*a*; 5,g823: ᴿJTS 41 (1990) 694-6 (A. *Louth*).

k243 **Chadwick** Henry, Augustine 1986 ➤ 2,d387... 5,g824: ᴿAugSt 19 (1988) 195-8 (J. M. *Quinn*).

k244 *Cleary* M., Augustine, affectivity and transforming grace: TLond 93 (1990) 205-212.

k245 *Corcoran* Gervase, Prayer and solidarity in St. Augustine: DowR 108 (1990) 157-174.

k246 **Daraki** Maria, Une religiosité sans Dieu; essai sur les stoïciens d'Athènes et saint Augustin: Armillaire. P 1989, Découverte 223 p. ᴿÉtudes 372 (1990) 279s (M. *Fédou*).

k247 ᴱ**Divjak** Johannes, Augustin Lettres 1*-39⁺: Œuvres 46B, 1987 ➤ 3,g277, 5,g828: ᴿScriptorium 43 (1989) 158-161 (P. *Hamblenne*: plusieurs 'suggestions').

k248 *Doignon* Jean, Augustinus in Cassiciacum und die Kultur seiner Zeit: Verbundenheit und Ablösung! ᵀ*Stolle* Thomas: RömQ 85 (1990) 50-65.

k249 *Dulaey* Martine, La sixième Règle de TYCONIUS et son résumé dans le De doctrina christiana: RÉΛug 35 (1989) 83-103.

k250 *Duval* Yves-Marie, La date du 'De natura' de Pélage; les premières étapes de la controverse sur la nature et la grâce: RÉAug 36 (1990) 257-283.

k251 *Elledge* W. Paul, Embracing Augustine; reach, restraint, and romantic resolution in the Confessions: JScStR 27 (1988) 72-89.

k252 **Ferrier** Francis, Saint Augustin: Que sais-je? 2468. P 1989, PUF. 128 p. – ᴿRÉAug 35 (1989) 368-370 (G. *Madec*); RHPR 70 (1990) 356s (A. *Benoît*: une gageure).

k253 *Finn* Thomas M., It happened one Saturday night; ritual and conversion in Augustine's North Africa: JAAR 50 (1990) 589-616.

k254 *Gunton* Colin, Augustine, the Trinity and the theological crisis of the West: ScotJT 43 (1990) 33-58.

k255 **Hensellek** Werner, *Schilling* Peter, Specimina eines Lexicon Augustinianum CSEL; EDV-Belange, *Divjak* J. W 1987-9, Österr. Akad. 72 p.; 54 p.; 48 p.; DM 36 + 24 + 24. 3-7001-1437-0; -553-9. – ᴿAntClas 59 (1990) 408s (H. *Savon*: the project of a philological dictionary of the 5 million words in all of Augustine had to be reduced to the 2.7 million in already-published CSEL; and cited articles not as planned in alphabetical order).

k257 *Kaufman* Peter I., Augustine, evil, and Donatism; sin and sanctity before the Pelagian controversy [EVANS G. 1982; PAGELS E. 1988]: TS 51 (1990) 115-126.

k258 **Kriegbaum** Bernhard, Kirche der Traditoren oder Kirche der Märtyrer?... Donatismus 1986 ➤ 3,g286... 5,g837: ᴿEstE 65 (1990) 111s (J. B. *Valero*); HZ 250 (1990) 677s (H. *Castritius*).

k259 *Langa* Pedro, Reflexiones agustinianas sobre la riqueza: RelCult 34 (1988) 447-476.

k260 **Lawless** George, Augustine of Hippo and his monastic rule 1987 ➤ 5,g839: ᴿJAAR 58 (1990) 301-3 (B. E. *Daley*).

k261 **Lettieri** Gaetano, Il senso della storia in Agostino d'Ippona; il 'saeculum' e la storia nel 'De Civitate Dei'. R 1988, Borla. 146 p. Lit. 30.000. – ᴿCC 141 (1990,1) 604s (D. *Marafioti*); Studium 86 (R 1990) 307-9 (P. *Miccoli*).

k262 *MacDonald* Scott, Augustine's Christian-Platonist account of goodness: New Scholasticism 63 (Wsh 1989) 485-509 [< ZIT 90,488].

k263 **Madec** Goulven, La patrie et la voie; le Christ dans la vie et la pensée de S. Augustin: JJC 36, 1989 ➤ 5,g841: ᴿBLitEc 91 (1990) 151s (H. *Derycke*: titre 'Goulvem', texte 'Gouvem'); MélSR 47 (1990) 54s (M. *Huftier*); RHR 207 (1990) 212s (J. *Doignon*); ScEsp 42 (1990) 115s (G. *Pelland*); VigChr 44 (1990) 96s (J. van *Winden*).

k264 *Madec* G., Bulletin Augustinien pour 1988/9 / 1989/90 et compléments d'années antérieures: RÉAug 35 (1989) 346-452; 36 (1990) 360-430 [plusieurs centaines de courtes notices, quelques-unes signées].

k265 **Maier** Jean-Louis, Le dossier du donatisme I, 1987 ➤ 4,h864; 5,g842: ᴿRÉAug 35 (1989) 171-9 (N. *Duval*); TS 51 (1990) 559 (R. B. *Eno*).

k265* *a) Mara* Maria G., L'influsso di Paolo in Agostino; – *b) Frend* W. H. C., The Donatist church and St. Paul; – *c) Decret* F., Les Manichéens d'Afrique: ➤ 552, ᴱ*Ries* J., Le epistole paoline nei manichei, i donatisti... 1988/9, 125-162 / 85-123 / 29-83.

k266 **Markus** R. A., Saeculum; history and society in the theology of St. Augustine²ʳᵉᵛ [¹c. 1968] C 1988, Univ. 254 p. £35; pa. £11. 0-521-36306-3; pa. 855-3. – ᴿExpTim 101 (1989s) 87 (T. A. *Hart*).

k267 ᴱ**Mayer** Cornelius, *Chelius* Karl-Heinz, Int. Symposion... Augustinus-Forschung 1987-9 ➤ 5,707: ᴿJTS 41 (1990) 693s (H. *Chadwick*); RSPT 74 (1990) 643-6 (G.-M. de *Durand*: French and German only); TLZ 115 (1990) 601s (G. *Haendler*).

k268 **Mondin** Battista, Il pensiero di Agostino 1988 ➤ 4,h867: ᴿDivinitas 33 (1989) 84s (D. *Composta*); DoctComm 42 (1989) 92-94 (A. *Lobato*).

k269 **O'Connell** Robert J., Imagination and metaphysics in St. Augustine [1986 Aquinas Lecture]. Milwaukee 1986, Marquette Univ. 70 p. – ᴿAugSt 19 (1988) 203-6 (J. M. *Quinn*).

k270 **O'Meara** John J., La jeunesse de. S. Augustin; introduction à la lecture des Confessions, ᵀ*Marrou* Jeanne H.: Vestigia 3. FrS 1988 = 1958, Univ. 279 p. [TZBas 46,93]. – ᴿRHR 207 (1990) 213s (J. *Doignon*).

k271 **Oort** J. van, Augustinus; facetten van leven en werk. Kampen 1989, Kok. 111 p. ƒ22,50. – ᴿKerkT 41 (1990) 256 (G. de *Ru*).

k272 **Oroz Reta** J., San Agustin, cultura clásica y cristianismo [17 ensayos 1954-88]: Bibl. Salm. Estudios 110, 1988 ➤ 5,334: ᴿAnnTh 4 (1990) 227-9 (V. *Reale*); Helmantica 40 (1989) 514-7 (M. A. *Marcos Casquero*).

k273 *Pavel* Constantin C., Le christianisme et la philosophie antique dans la pensée du bienheureux Augustin, en roumain, I: STBuc 42/2 (1990) 20-41; franç. 142.

k274 *Pelikan* Jaroslav, An Augustinian dilemma; Augustine's doctrine of grace versus Augustine's doctrine of the Church [1987 Villanova Augustine lecture]: AugSt 18 (1987) 1-29.

k275 **Pollastri** Alessandra [su Agostino], *Cocchini* Francesca, Bibbia e storia nel cristianesimo latino 1988 ➤ 5, g851: ᴿCC 141 (1990,1) 406s (G. *Pani*); RivB 38 (1990) 122-4 (Clara *Burini*); RivStoLR 26 (1990) 596-9 (P. *Gramaglia*).

k276 *Puryiile-Kpowda* D. Novat, À l'écoute d'Augustin d'Hippone: Écoute, Afrique 1 (Burkina Faso 1989) 52-72 [< TContext 8,26].

k277 ᴱ**Ranson** Patric, Les dossiers H, 1988 → 5,506: ᴿRevSR 64 (1990) 91-93 (Marianne *Canévet*); RHPR 70 (1990) 357 (A. *Benoît*).

k278 **Raveaux** Thomas, Augustinus, Contra adversarium legis et prophetarum [ᴰ1984] 1987 → 5,g854: ᴿJEH 40 (1989) 451s (H. *Chadwick*).

k279 ᴱ**Reale** G., *al.*, L'opera letteraria di Agostino tra Cassiciacum e Milano; Agostino nella terra di Ambrogio (1-4 ott. 1986): AugTestSt 2, 1987 → 4,518b: ᴿGnomon 62 (1990) 11-14 (H. *Chadwick*).

k280 **Rees** B. R., PELAGIUS, a reluctant heretic 1988 → 4,b873; 5,g855: ᴿCathHR 76 (1990) 101s (R. B. *Eno*); RHE 85 (1990) 232 (P. *Brady*).

k281 *Russell* Frederick H., 'Only something good can be evil'; the genesis of Augustine's secular ambivalence: TS 51 (1990) 698-716.

k282 *Sharpe* Richard, GOSCELIN's [c. 1100] St. Augustine and St. Mildreth; hagiography and liturgy in context: JTS 41 (1990) 502-516.

k283 *Siniscalco* Paolo, Dai mediatori al mediatore; la demonologia di APULEIO e la critica di Agostino: → 593, Diavolo 1 (1988/90) 279-294.

k284 **Sordi** M., *al.*, Agostino a Milano. TSt 3. Palermo 1988, Augustinus. 110 p.; 115 fig. – ᴿAthenaeum 78 (1990) 271-8 (Maria Pia *Billanovich*: poco convincente); RHR 207 (1990) 328s (J. *Doignon*).

k285 *Spanneut* M., Saint Augustin et la violence: StMor 28 (1990) 79-116 [< ZIT 90,632].

k286 **Starnes** Colin, Augustine's conversion; a guide to the argument of Confessions I-IX. Waterloo 1990, W. Laurier Univ. xvi-303 p. 0-88920-991-X.

k287 *a) Studer* Basil, Augustine and the Pauline theme of hope [*Markus* R., comment]; – *b) Fredriksen* Paula, Beyond the body-soul dichotomy; Augustine's answer to MANI, PLOTINUS and JULIAN [*Babcock* W., comment]: → 510, SMU Paul 1987/90, 201-221 [-25] / 227-51 [-61].

k288 **Tombeur** Paul, CETEDOC, Thesaurus augustinianus, I. A – Formae. Turnhout 1989, Brepols. lxx-700 p.; 248 microfiches. Fb 35.000. – ᴿCC 141 (1990,4) 351-6 (R. *Busa*: inventario sintetico e analitico di ogni parola di tutti gli scritti di A.); RÉAug 35 (1989) 298-307 (G. *Madec*).

k289 **Trapé** Agostino, Saint Augustine, man, pastor, mystic [1976],ᵀ *O'Connell* M. NY 1985, Catholic Book. 384 p. $7. 0-89942-172-5. – ᴿJEH 40 (1989) 591s (G. *Bonner*).

k290 **Vigini** G., Agostino d'Ippona; l'avventura della grazia e della carità. CinB 1988, Paoline, 158 p. – ᴿStudium 85 (R 1989) 726s (I. *Di Iorio*).

k291 *Vilanova* Evangelista, Teología autobiográfica; Sant Agusti i NEWMAN: QVidCr 150 (1990) 191-5.

k292 **Virgilio** D., Sant'Agostino; I. Itinerario filosofico; II. Cristianesimo e filosofia. Catanzaro 1982, Rubbettino. 411 p.; p. 415-921. – ᴿDivThom 92 (1989) 418-420 (J. J. *Sanguineti*).

k293 *Vitiello* Vincenzo, Dove abita Dio? La divinità in PLOTINO e Agostino: Asprenas 37 (1990) 195-212.

k294 *Weismann* F. J., The problematic of freedom in St. Augustine; towards a new hermeneutics: RÉAug 35 (1989) 104-118; franç. 119.

Y2.5 **Hieronymus.**

k295 **Allegri** Giuseppina, I *damna* della mensa in San Girolamo [litt. 52,6]. Parma 1989, Benedettina. 102 p. Lit 15.000. – ᴿCivClasCr 11 (1990) 96s (Maria F. *Buffa Giolito*).

k296 *Balthasar* H. U. von, Il silenzio della parola; Dürer in cammino con Girolamo [analisi dei 14 ritratti]; [T]*Russo* G., [E]*Graziotto* R. CasM 1989, Piemme. 48 p.; ill. Lit. 8.000. 88-384-1270-7. – [R]RasT 31 (1990) 400-5 (Rosa *Morelli*).

k297 **Berschin** Walter, *a*) Greek letters and the Latin Middle Ages from Jerome to Nicholas of Cusa[2rev] [[1]1980], [T]*Frakes* Jerold C. Wsh 1988, Catholic University of America. xv-415 p. $55. 0-8132-0606-5 [TDig 37,251]; – *b*) Medioevo greco-latino da Gerolamo a Niccoló Cusano [1984], [TE]*Livrea* Enrico. N 1988, Liguori. xv-392 p.; 16 pl. – [R]RÉAug 36 (1990) 203-6 (Anne-Marie *Turcan*).

k298 [TE]**Ceresa-Gastaldo** Aldo, Gerolamo, Gli uomini illustri (De viris illustribus): BiblPatr 12, 1988 → 4,4883: [R]RHPR 70 (1990) 352s (P. *Maraval*: definitive available edition of the Latin text, based on 4 new miss beside the 9 previously used, and with an Italian tr.).

k299 [E]**Ceresa-Gastaldo** Aldo, Gerolamo e la biografia letteraria [corso 1987-8; p. 63-79, *Tibiletti* Carlo, Immagini bibliche nel linguaggio figurato di S. Gerolamo + 5 al.]: D.AR.FI.CL.ET 125. Genova 1989. 123 p.

k300 *Clark* Elizabeth A., Theory and practice in late ancient asceticism; Jerome, CHRYSOSTOM, and AUGUSTINE: JFemRel 5,2 (1989) 25-46 [< ZIT 90,292].

k301 [TE]**Cola** Silvano, Girolamo, Omelie sul Vangelo e su varie ricorrenze liturgiche: Testi Patristici 88. R 1990, Città Nuova. 244 p. 88-311-3088-9.

k302 *Doignon* Jean, Oracles, prophéties, 'on-dit' sur la chute de Rome (395-410); les réactions de Jérôme et d'Augustin: RÉAug 36 (1990) 120-146.

k303 *a*) *Dunphy* Walter, St. Jerome and the Gens Anicia (Ep. 130 to Demetrias); – *b*) *Jay* P., Saint Jérôme et la prophétie: → 643, StPatr 18,4 (1983/90) 139-145 / 152-165.

k304 [E]**Duval** Yves-Marie, Jérôme entre l'Occident et l'Orient 1986/8 → 5,e577* (index!): [R]RHE 85 (1990) 214s (H. *Silvestre*).

k305 *Kaczynski* B. M., Greek glosses on Jerome's Ep. CVI, Ad Sunnian et Fretelam, in E. *Berlin,* Deutsche Staatsbibliothek, ms. Phillips 1674: → 4,h971*, Nectar 1988, 215-227.

k306 **Mastandrea** Paolo, [ARNOBIO, Girolamo ...] Lettori cristiani di SENECA filosofo: AntClasCr 28. Brescia 1988, Paideia. 101 p. – [R]RPg 63 (1989) 326s (J.-C. *Fredouille*).

k307 *a*) *Nautin* Pierre, Notes critiques sur la lettre 27* de Jérôme à Aurélius de Carthage; – *b*) *Lardet* Pierre, Jérôme exégète; une cohérence insoupçonnée: RÉAug 36 (1990) 288-299 / 300-307.

k308 *Opelt* Ilona, Aug. Epist. 27* Divjak; ein Schreiben des Hieronymus an Bischof Aurelius von Karthago: → 13, [F]BAVEL T. van, AugLv 40 (1990) 19-25.

k309 **Russo** Daniel, Saint Jérôme en Italie; étude d'iconographie et de spiritualité (XIIIe-XVe siècle); Images à l'appui 2, 1987 → 4,h888; F 265: [R]AmHR 95 (1990) 147s (R. E. *Lerner*); RHR 207 (1990) 103-5 (G. *Audisio*).

k310 *Salisbury* Joyce E., The Latin doctors of the Church on sexuality [disagreements known to ABELARD: Jerome, AMBROSE; AUGUSTINE ...] Journal of Medieval History 12 (1986) 279-289 [< BTAM 14 (1990) p. 775s].

k311 **White** Carolinne, The correspondence (394-419) between Jerome and

AUGUSTINE of Hippo: Studies in Bible and Early Christianity 23. Lewiston NY 1990, Mellen. [viii-] 252 p.

Y2.6 Patres latini *in ordine alphabetico*.

k312 **Margerie** Bertrand de, Introduction à l'histoire de l'exégèse [I-III, 1980-3 ➤ 61,u595 ... 3,g103], IV. L'Occident latin de Léon le Grand à Bernard de Clairvaux. P 1990, Cerf. 286 p. – RArTGran 53 (1990) 298s (A. *Segovia*); Benedictina 35 (1988) 234-6 (L. *De Lorenzi*, 1,3); EsprVie 100 (1990) 381s (É. *Ricaud*); RTPhil 122 (1990) 434s (J. *Borel*).

k313 *Mathieu* Jean-Marie, De l'univers mythologique à l'univers biblique; une révolution culturelle à la fin du IVème siècle après J.-C.: ➤ 91, FJERPHAGNON L. 1989, 149-166.

k314 AMBROSIUS: **Jacob** Christoph, 'Arkandisziplin', Allegorese, Mystagogie; ein neuer Zugang zur Theologie des Ambrosius von Mailand [Diss. Bonn 1988, DDassmann E.]: Theophaneia 32. Fra 1990, Hain. 299 p. 3-445-09129-3; RRSPT 74 (1990) 639-641 (G.-M. de *Durand*); ScripTPamp 22 (1990) 606-611 (Λ. *Viciano*); TPhil 65 (1990) 599s (A. *Grillmeier*).

k315 *Lizzi* Rita, Ambrose's contemporaries and the Christianization of northern Italy: JRS 80 (1990) 156-173.

k316 **Mazzarino** Santo, Storia sociale del vescovo Ambrogio [1974 conferenze, Ambrogio nella società del suo tempo]. R 1989, Bretschneider. 101 p.; 16 pl. Lit. 50.000 – RClasR 40 (1990) 511s (N. *McLynn*). Gymnasium 97 (1990) 369 (R. *Klein*).

k317 EPasini Cesare, Le fonti greche su sant'Ambrogio: Opere/sussidi 24,1. Mi/R 1990, Biblioteca Ambrosiana / Città Nuova. 466 p. 88-311-9184-5.

k318 *Sordi* Marta, I rapporti fra Ambrogio e il panegirista PACATO: Ist-LombR 122 (1988) 93-100.

k319 **Torvend** Samuel E., The typology of the basilica conflict between Ambrose of Milan and the imperial court; a study in the use of biblical exempla in Ambrosian sermons preached between 385-386: Diss. DGreeley D., St. Louis Univ. 1990. 193 p. 91-02933. DissA 51 (1990s) 2785s-A.

k320 *Wenning* Gregor, Der Einfluss des Manichäismus und des Ambrosius auf die Hermeneutik AUGUSTINS: RÉAug 36 (1990) 80-90.

k321 CASSIODORUS: **Macpherson** Robin, Rome in involution; Cassiodorus' Variae in their literary and historical setting: FgKlas 14. Poznań 1989, Univ. 367 p. – RAtenRom 35 (1990) 120s (A. *Marcone*).

k322 CYPRIANUS: *Robertz* Charles A., The historical context of Cyprian's De unitate: JTS 41 (1990) 107-111.

k323 TEClarke G. W., The letters of St. Cyprian of Carthage [I] II (28-54), III (55-66), IV (67-82): Ancient Christian Writers 44, 46s, 1984-9 ➤ 5,g878: RCathHR 76 (1990) 328-330 (W. H. C. *Frend*, 4); Prudentia 21,2 (1989) 75s (P. *Rousseau*, 4); VigChr 44 (1990) 199s (J. den *Boeft*).

k324 *Djalbonyo* Ajika, La conversion de S. Cyprien: Téléma 15,1 (1989) 7-15.

k325 *Orbán* Árpád P., 'Gerecht' und 'Gerechtigkeit' bei Cyprian von Karthago: ArBegrG 32 (1989) 103-120.

k326 DRACONTIUS: EMoussy Claude, *Camus* Colette, Dracontius, Louanges de Dieu Is/III. P 1985-8, BLettres. 386 p.; 232 p. – RRÉLat 68 (1990)

191-4 (J. *Fontaine*); Scriptorium 43 (1989) 161-6 (P. *Hamblenne*: nombreuses mises au point).

k326* GAUFRIDUS Antissiodorensis: ᴱ**Rochais** Henri, Geoffroy d'Auxerre, Entretien de Simon-Pierre avec Jésus: SChr 364.   P 1990, Cerf.   328 p. 2-204-04287-0.

k327 GREGORIUS M.: **Clark** Francis,   The Pseudo-Gregorian Dialogues 1987 ➤ 3,g342 ... 5,g881:   ᴿRelStR 16 (1990) 76 (T. F. X. *Noble*: totally misguided); Salesianum 52 (1990) 900s (F. *Meyer*); Speculum 64 (1989) 397-9 (Carole *Straw*).

k328 *Clark* Francis, *a*) St. Gregory and the enigma of the Dialogues; a response to Paul MEYVAERT: JEH [39 (1988) 335-381] 40 (1989) 323-343 [344-6, Meyvaert comment]; – *b*) The authorship of the Gregorian Dialogues; a challenge to the traditional view: ➤ 643, StPatr 18,4 (1983/90) 120-132; – *c*) The renewed debate on the authenticity of the Gregorian Dialogues: AugR 30 (1990) 75-105.

k329 —*Cremascoli* Giuseppe,   Se i Dialogi siano opera di Gregorio Magno; due volumi per una vexata quaestio [CLARK F.]: Benedictina 36 (1989) 179-192.

k330 —*Gillet* Robert,   Les Dialogues sont-ils de Grégoire? [CLARK semble avoir raison]: RÉAug 36 (1990) 309-314.

k331 —*Kessler* Stephan C.,   Das Rätsel der Dialoge Gregors des Grossen: Fälschung oder Bearbeitung? zur Diskussion um ein Buch von Francis CLARK: TPhil 65 (1990) 566-578.

k332 ᴱ**Fontaine** Jacques, *al.*,   Gregoire 1982/6 ➤ 2,433: ... 5,g886:   ᴿJEH 40 (1989) 101-3 (R. *Collins*).

k333 **Godding** Robert,   Bibliografia di Gregorio Magno, 1890-1989: Opere, complementi 1.   R 1990, Città Nuova.   x-349 p.   Lit. 42.000 [RHE 85, 354*].   88-311-9417-8. – ᴿAnBoll 108 (1990) 439-442 (J. van der *Straeten*); Benedictina 37 (1990) 523 (L. *Crippa*).

k334 *Grego* Igino,   San Gregorio Magno e la Terra Santa: TerraS 65 (1989) 26-30. 69-72. 115-8.

k335 **Paronetto** Vera,   Gregorio 1985 ➤ 5,g888:   ᴿRTLv 21 (1990) 98 (Marie *Hendrickx*).

k336 **Straw** Carole, Gregory 1988 ➤ 4,h910; 5,g889:   ᴿBLitEc 91 (1990) 153s (R. *Belanger*); CathHR 75 (1989) 128s (J. *Richards*); ETL 66 (1990) 427s (A. de *Halleux* cites high praise of Paul MEYVAERT); Gregorianum 71 (1990) 195-7 (G. *Pelland*); RÉAug 36 (1990) 202s (M. *Doucet*); Speculum 65 (1990) 761-3 (E. Ann *Matter*); StMon 31 (1989) 439s (J. A. *Rocha*).

k337 *Thurn* Hans,   Handschriftenstudien zu Gregors des Grossen Dialogi: Wü DiözGB 52 (1990) 17-24.

k338 HILARIUS: *Doignon* Jean,   La 'lectio' de textes d'Hilaire de Poitiers à la lumière d'études récentes [LÖFSTEDT B.; MILHAU; ROCHER A.; SMULDERS P.]: WienerSt 103 (1990) 179-191.

k339 *Doignon* J.,   *a*) Un cri d'alarme d'Hilaire de Poitiers sur la situation de l'Église à son retour d'exil: RHE 85 (1990) 281-290; – *b*) Peccatrix ecclesia; une formule d'inspiration origénienne chez Hilaire de Poitiers: RSPT 74 (1990) 255-8; – *c*) Une pièce de la tradition parénétique romaine dans le 'discours exégétique' d'Hilaire de Poitiers, l'*adhortatio*: Latomus 49 (1990) 833-8.

k340 *Doignon* Jean,   Innerer Glaube, Bekenntnis und schriftliche Festlegung des Glaubens im westlichen Römerreich des vierten Jahrhunderts; der Fall des Hilarius von Poitiers. ᵀ*Stolle* M., *Sieben* H.: TPhil 65 (1990) 246-255.

k341 *a) Ladaria* Luis F., Adán y Cristo; un motivo soteriológico nel pensiero de Hilario de Poitiers; – *b) Padovese* Luigi, Ministero episcopale e 'memoria' nel pensiero d'Ilario di Poitiers: ➤ 135, ᶠOʀʙᴇ A., Compostellanum 35 (1990) 145-162 / 163-179.

k342 Hɪᴘᴘᴏʟʏᴛᴜs: *Bammel* Caroline P., The state of play with regard to Hippolytus and the Contra Noetum [Fʀɪᴄᴋᴇʟ J. 1988]: HeythJ 31 (1990) 195-9.

k343 **Botte** Bernard, La Tradition Apostolique de Saint Hippolyte; essai de reconstitution, ⁵*Gerhards* Albert [⁴1963]: Liturgiewissenschaftliche Quellen und Forschungen 39. Münster 1989, Aschendorff. xlviii-132 p. 3-402-03360-7.

k344 *Finn* Thomas M., Ritual process and the survival of early Christianity; a study of the Apostolic Tradition of Hippolytus: JRit 3,1 (Pittsburgh 1989) 69-90 [< zɪᴛ 89,497].

k345 **Frickel** Josef, Das Dunkel um Hippolyt von Rom 1988 ➤ 5,g891: ᴿGregorianum 71 (1990) 194s (G. *Pelland*); JTS 41 (1990) 236-9 (R. *Butterworth*); RömQ 85 (1990) 123s (G. *Feige*); TLZ 115 (1990) 36 (Ursula *Treu*).

k346 *Hinson* E. Glenn, Did Hippolytus know Essenes firsthand?: ➤ 643, StPatr 18,3 (1983/9) 283-9.

k347 ᴱ**Marcovich** Miroslav, Hippolytus, Refutatio...: PatrTSt 25, 1986 ➤ 2,d447... 5,g892: ᴿBTAM 14 (1990) p. 774 (G. H.); Latomus 49 (1990) 515-7 (H. *Savon*); NedTTs 44 (1990) 78 (S. de *Boer*); SecC 7 (1989s) 177-180 (D. *Tripp*); ZkT 112 (1990) 304-314 (N. *Kehl*).

k348 ᴱ**Norelli** Enrico, Ippolito, L'Anticristo: BtPatr 10, 1987 ➤ 3,g345; 5,g893: ᴿSalesianum 52 (1990) 750s (S. *Felici*).

k349 *Scholten* Clemens, Hippolytus [I. mythischer Märtyrer; II.] (von Rom): ➤ 853, RAC 15,116 (1990) 492-551.

k350 **Visonà** Giuseppe, Pseudo Ippolito, In sanctum Pascha...: StPatrMediolan 15, 1988 ➤ 4,h918*; 5,g896: ᴿETL 66 (1990) 197s (A. de *Halleux*); JTS 41 (1990) 645-8 (S. G. *Hall*); RasT 31 (1990) 213-5 (E. *Cattaneo*); RÉAug 36 (1990) 189-191 (A. *Le Boulluec*); ScripTPamp 22 (1990) 282s (D. *Ramos-Lissón*).

k351 Jᴜᴠᴇɴᴄᴜs: *Di Terlizzi* Piervincenzo, Interpretazione e prospettive di ricerca negli studi recenti sul poeta Giovenco: StPatav 37 (1990) 359-373; Eng. 374.

k352 *Testard* Maurice, Juvencus et le sacré dans un épisode des Euangeliorum libri IV: BBudé (1990) 3-31.

k353 Lᴀᴄᴛᴀɴᴛɪᴜs: *Buchheit* Vinzenz, Cicero inspiratus — Vergilius propheta? Zur Wertung paganer Autoren bei Laktanz: Hermes 118 (1990) 357-374.

k354 ᵀᴱ**Monat** Pierre, Lactance, Epit. Inst. I-II: SChr 335.337, 1986s ➤ 2,d449 ... 4,h920: ᴿJTS 41 (1990) 665-8 (G. *Nicholson*); MélSR 47 (1990) 201s. 202-4 (M. *Spanneut*); RPg 63 (1989) 140s (R. *Braun*).

k355 *Wlosok* Antonie, Lactantius (250-325): ➤ 857, TRE 20 (1990) 370.

k356 Lᴇᴏ M.: **Piloni** Antonio, La 'Fides christiana' nelle opere di S. Leone Magno; dalla 'celebratio fidei' alla 'vita credentium' (Per una teologia della celebrazione): diss. Pont.Ist. Liturgico 104. R 1985, Pont.Ateneo S. Anselmo. 125 p.

k357 *Studer* Basil, Leo I: → 857, TRE 20 (1990) 737-741.
k358 PRUDENTIUS: *Buchheit* Vinzenz, Göttlicher Heilsplan bei Prudentius (Cath. II, 25-48): VigChr 44 (1990) 222-239.
k359 **Kah** Marianne, 'Die Welt der Römer mit der Seele suchend ...'; die Religiosität des Prudentius im Spannungsfeld zwischen 'pietas christiana' und 'pietas romana': Hereditas 3. Bonn 1990, Börengasser. xx-369 p. – ᴿRSPT 74 (1990) 641-3 (G.-M. de *Durand*).
k360 **Malamud** Martha A., A poetics of transformation; Prudentius and classical mythology: StClasPg 49. Ithaca NY 1989, Cornell Univ. xiii-192 p. $27.50. 0-8014-2249-3. – ᴿAntClas 59 (1990) 405-7 (H. *Savon*).
k361 SEDULIUS: **Springer** Carl P. E., Gospel as epic; Sedulius 1988 → 4,h924; 5,g899: ᴿClasR 40 (1990) 159 (R. P. H. *Green*); Helmantica 41 (1990) 411-3 (J. *Oroz Reta*).
k362 [ᴱ*Simpson* Dean], supp. ᴱ**Dolbeau** François, Sedulius Scottus, Collectaneum Miscellaneum: CCMed 67 supp. Turnhout 1990, Brepols. 63 p. 2-503-90672-9.

Y2.8 Documenta orientalia.

k363 *Brashear* William (griech.), *Quecke* Hans (kopt.), Ein Holzbrett mit zweisprachigen Hymnen auf Christus und Maria: Enchoria 17 (1990) 1-19; pl. 2.
Brock S., The Syriac Fathers on prayer 1987 → 8177.
k364 *Coombs* Stephen, Thematic correspondences in Iberogallic, Egyptian and Ethiopian eucharistic prayers: OstkSt 38 (1989) 281-310.
k365 **Cuming** Geoffrey J. † 24.III.1988, The liturgy of St Mark, edited from the manuscripts with a commentary: OrChrAn 234. R 1990, Pontificium Institutum Studiorum Orientalium. xliii-155 p.
k366 *Dalmais* Irénée-Henri, Les rites orientaux de la célébration eucharistique [< Notre Histoire 50 (mai 1989)]: EsprVie 100 (1990) 247-9 (J. *Daoust*).
k367 **Gamber** Klaus, Liturgische Texte aus der Kirche Äthiopiens: StPatrLtg Beih 13. Rg 1984, Pustet. 73 p. 3-7917-0925-9.
k368 ᶠGUILLAUMONT Antoine: Mélanges... christianismes orientaux 1988 → 4,59: ᴿRSO 63 (1989) 331-9 (R. *Contini*).
k369 **Isaac** Jacques, *Taḳsā d-Ḥūssāyā*, le rite du pardon dans l'Église syriaque orientale: OrChrAn 233, 1989 → 5,g904: ᴿAnBol 108 (1990) 228s (U. *Zanetti*); Muséon 103 (1990) 187s (A. de *Halleux*); RHE 85 (1990) 739s (J.-M. *Fiey*); ZkT 112 (1990) 75s (H. B. *Meyer*).
k371 **Mat'evosyani** A. S., Hayeren dzeragreri hišatakaranner 5.-12. dd [Armenian manuscript colophons]. Erevan 1988, Akad.Wiss. Armen. SSR. [xxvi-] 368 p.
k372 *Pedersen* Kirsten, The Incarnation according to Ethiopian Orthodox catechisms: → 117*, ᶠLØKKEGAARD F., 1990, 259-269.
k373 *a*) *Perrot* C., Littérature et chrétienté syriaques; – *b*) *Colin* G.,... éthiopiennes; – *c*) *Micheau* Françoise, Documents sur la communauté nestorienne de Baghdad à l'époque abbaside: RICathP 35 (1990) 139-164 / 165-175 / 177-191.
k374 **Regnault** Lucien, L'évangile vécu au désert; paroles des Pères du désert traduites et commentées: Paroles de Lumière. P 1990, Fayard-Sarment. 198 p. F 59. – ᴿEsprVie 90 (1990) 352 (G. M. *Oury*).
k375 **Sauget** J.-M., Un gazza chaldéen: ST 326, 1987 → 3,g374; 5,g908. – ᴿOrChrPer 56 (1990) 258s (E. R. *Hambye*); RHE 85 (1990) 91-93 (J. M. *Fiey*).

k376 **Schwaigert** Wolfgang, Das Christentum im Khuzistan im Rahmen der frühen Kirchengeschichte Persiens bis zur Synode von Seleukeia-Ktesiphon im Jahre 410: Inaug.-Diss. Marburg 1989. 371 p. – ᴿRHE 85 (1990) 367s (J. M. *Fiey*).

k377 ᴱ**Vis** Henri de, Homélies coptes de la Vaticane I-II: Bibliothèque Copte Cah 5s. Lv 1990, Peeters. I (= 1922) viii-220 p.; II (= 1929) vii-315 p. 90-6831-213-8; -4-6.

k378 ABERCIUS: *Bundy* David, The Life of Abercius [including the burial inscription (before 215 A.D.) found by W. RAMSAY in 1883]; its significance for early Syriac Christianity: SecC 7 (1989s) 163-176.

k379 ADDAI: *Marston* William, A solution to the enigma of 'Addai and Mari': EphLtg 103 (1989) 79-92; lat. 79.

k380 AMMON: **Goehring** James E., The letter of Ammon and Pachomian monasticism: PatrTSt 27, 1986 → 2,7644; 5,g910: ᴿCathHR 75 (1989) 125 (D. *Johnson*); NedTTs 44 (1990) 75s (R. van den *Broek*).

k381 APHRAATES: **Bruns** Peter, Das Christusbild Aphrahats des persischen Weisen [Diss. Bochum]: Hereditas 4. Bonn 1990, Borengässer. xxiv-234 p. DM 46. 3-923946-15-5.

k382 *McCullough* J.C., Aphrahat the biblical exegete: → 643, StPatr 18,4 (1983/90) 263-8.

k383 ᴱ**Pierre** M.-J., Aphraate, Exposés II (11-23): SChr 359, 1989 → 4,h935; 5,g912: ᴿETL 66 (1990) 428-430 (A. de *Halleux*); NRT 112 (1990) 265 (V. *Roisel*); OrChrPer 56 (1990) 255s (E. R. *Hambye*); RHPR 70 (1990) 351s (P. *Maraval*, 1s).

k384 CHRYSOSTOMUS: *Browne* Gerald M., Ad [-ditions to] Ps.-Chrysostomi In Raphaelem Archangelum sermonem (with PLUMLEY J. 1988): Orientalia 59 (1990) 521-3.

k385 *Esbroeck* Michel van, Une homélie arménienne sur la Dormition attribuée à Chrysostome: OrChr 74 (1990) 199-208; texte 209-220; tr. 220-233.

k386 *Taft* Robert, The authenticity of the Chrysostom [Syriac] Anaphora revisited; determining the authorship of liturgical texts by computer: OrChrPer 56 (1990) 5-51.

k387 CYRILLUS H.: *Coquin* R.-G., *Godron* G., Un encomion copte sur Marie-Madeleine attribué à Cyrille de Jérusalem: BIFAO 90 (1990) 169-212; 2 phot. + texte copte.

k388 DIONYSIUS TM: **Witakowski** Witold, The Syriac Chronicle of Pseudo-Dionysius of Tel-Mahrè 1987 → 3,g867... 5,g917: ᴿAbrNahr 28 (1990) 142-150 (A. N. *Palmer*); BO 47 (1990) 743-6 (J. *Sanders*); BSO 52 (1989) 338s (S. P. *Brock*); JAOS 110 (1990) 529s (L. J. *Conrad*); JEH 40 (1989) 596s (also L. J. *Conrad*); OstkSt 38 (1989) 332s (B. *Plank*); Speculum 65 (1990) 1081-3 (D. G. K. *Taylor*).

k389 EPHRAEM: **Bou-Mansour** Tanios, La pensée symbolique de saint Ephrem 1988 → 5,g919: ᴿJTS 41 (1990) 682-4 (S. *Brock*); RThom 90 (1990) 312-4 (D. *Cerbelaud*).

k390 ᵀᴱ**Brock** Sebastian, Ephraem, Hymns on Paradise. Crestwood NY 1990, St. Vladimir Sem. 240 p. $9. 0-88141-076-4 [TDig 37,359].

k391 *Bruns* Peter, Arius hellenizans? — Ephräm der Syrer und die neoarianischen Kontroversen seiner Zeit; ein Beitrag zur Rezeption des Nizänums im syrischen Sprachraum: ZKG 101 (1990) 21-57.

k392 ᵀᴱMcVey Kathleen E., Ephraem the Syrian; Hymns: Classics of Western Spirituality, NY 1989 ➤ 5,g923; 0-8091-0429-6; pa. -3093-9 [TDig 37,359]. – ᴿETL 66 (1990) 430s (D. *Bundy*).

k393 *McVey* Kathleen E., The anti-Judaic polemic of Ephrem Syrus' hymns on the Nativity: ➤ 173, ᶠStrugnell J., Of scribes 1990, 229-240.

k394 **Ogren** [🅑, given as pronounced 'Agren'] Irina, Parenesis Efrema Sirina, k istorii slaviańskiego perevoda: AcU, Studia slavica 26. Sto 1989, Almqvist & W. 146 p.; Eng. summ. – ᴿETL 66 (1990) 431-3 (D. *Bundy*).

k395 *Schall* Anton, Die syroaramäische Vita Sancti Ephraem Syri; geschichtlicher und sprachlicher Ertrag: ➤ 777, Or.-Tag. 1988/90, 99-104.

k396 Eᴜᴛʏᴄʜɪᴜs: *Horst* Heribert, Eutychios [arabisch 937] und die Kirchengeschichte — das erste Konzil von Nikaia (325): OrChr 74 (1990) 152-167.

k397 G. Sᴀɢʟā: ᵀᴱ**Beyene** Yaqob, Giyorgis di Saglā, Il libro del mistero (*Mashafa Mestir*), parte prima: CSCOr 515s, aethiop. 89s. Lv 1990, Peeters. I/1, xv-277 p., ital. I/2, x-422 p. Ethiop. 0070-0398.

k398 Gʀᴇɢᴏʀɪᴜs Nᴀᴢ.: ᵀᴱ**Camps i Gaset** Montserrat, Gregori de Nazianz, Discursos teològics; cartes i poemes: Clàssics del Cristianisme 12. Barc 1990, Proa. 172 p. 84-7739-114-9.

k399 *Grand'henry* Jacques, Les discours de Grégoire de Nazianze et la tradition manuscrite arabe syrienne: Muséon 103 (1990) 255-265.

k400 Gʀᴇɢᴏʀɪᴜs Nʏss.: *Parmentier* M. F. G., Syriac translations of Gregory of Nyssa [some twenty items, mostly with cited Syriac text]: OrLovPer 20 (1989) 143-193.

k401 Hᴀʙᴛᴀ Māʀʏām: **Raineri** Osvaldo, Atti di Habta Māryām († 1497) e di Iʏāsᴜ († 1508), santi monaci etiopici: OrChrAn 235. R 1990, Pontificium Institutum Studiorum Orientalium. xviii-265 p.

k401* Ḥᴇɴᴀɴɪšᴏ: *Reinink* Gerrit J., Fragmente der Evangelienexegese des Katholikos Ḥenanišo' I: ➤ 779*, Symposium 5, 1988/90, 71-91.

k402 Jᴀᴄᴏʙᴜs S.; **Rilliet** Frédéric, Jacques de Saroug, prédicateur; commentaire aux six homélies festales en prose: diss. ᴰ*Bovon* F. Genève 1990. – RTLv 22, p. 597.

k403 Jᴏʜᴀɴɴᴇs D.: **Beulay** Robert, L'enseignement spirituel de Jean de Dalyatha, mystique syro-oriental du VIIIe siècle [2d part of diss. La lumière sans forme 1987 supra ➤ 8174]. P 1990, Beauchesne. 523 p. F 330 [TS 52, 354, F. G. *McLeod*].

k404 Jᴏʜᴀɴɴᴇs M.: **Marrassini** Paolo, Gadla Yohannes Mesraqawi, vita di Y. l'orientale: QuadSem 10. F 1981, Univ. cix-506 p. Lit. 60.000. – ᴿOrientalia 59 (1990) 91-95 (E. *Hammerschmidt*).

k405 Mᴀᴄᴀʀɪᴜs M.: **Argyriou** Astérios, Macaire Makrès et la polémique contre l'Islam: ST 313, 1986 ➤ 2,9087*: ᴿJbÖsByz 40 (1990) 475-7 (E. *Trapp*); RÉByz 47 (1989) 261s (J. *Darrouzès*).

k406 Mᴇᴛʜᴏᴅɪᴜs: *Reinink* G. J., Der edessenische 'Pseudo-Methodius': ByZ 83 (1990) 31-45.

k407 Nᴀʀsᴀɪ: **Siman** Emmanuel P., Narsaï, cinq homélies sur les paraboles évangéliques 1984 ➤ 2,d473: ᴿZDMG 140 (1990) 158s (Maria *Macuch*).

k408 **Sunquist** Scott W., Narsai and the Persians; a study in cultural contact and conflict: diss. Princeton Theol. Sem. 1990. 313 p. 90-30375. – DissA 51 (1990s) 2055-A.

k409 Pᴀʟʟᴀᴅɪᴜs: **Bunce** Gabriel, Palladiana I [II. ᵀ*Vogüé* Adalbert de] Introduction aux fragments coptes de l'Histoire Lausiaque: StMon 32 (1990) 78-129 [323-339].

k410 SEVERUS A.: *Breydy* Michael, Les témoignages de Sévère d'Antioche dans l'Exposé de la foi de Jean MARON: Muséon 103 (1990) 215-235.

k411 SHENUTE: *Depuydt* Leo, In Sinuthium graecum [Shenute: *Lucchesi* E.]: Orientalia 59 (1990) 67-71.

k412 THEODORETUS: **Parmentier** Martin, A letter from Theodoret of Cyrus to the exiled NESTORIUS (CPG 6270) in a Syriac version: Bijdragen 51 (1990) 234-245; Syriac 242.

k413 THEODORUS: *Spinks* Bryan D., The East Syrian anaphora of Theodore; reflections upon its sources and theology: EphLtg 103 (1989) 441-455.

k414 *Youssif* Pierre, Traduzioni siriache di Teodoro di Mopsuestia: → 733, Autori classici 1984/90, 141-162.

Y3   **Medium aevum,** generalia.

k415 *a) Anton* Hans H., Zur neuen Wertung Pseudo-CYPRIANS ('De duodecim abusivis saeculi') und zu seinem Vorkommen in Bibliothekskatalogen des Mittelalters; – *b) Contreni* John J., The Egyptian origins of the Irish: two ninth-century notes: Würzburger Diözesangeschichtsblätter 51 (1989) 463-474 / 51-54 [< ZIT 89,609s].

k416 L'aveu 1984/6 ➤ 3,750*: ᴿRTAM 57 (1990) 279-282 (G. *Hendrix*).

k417 *Avril* J., L'histoire religieuse des derniers siècles du Moyen Âge; à propos de quelques colloques récents [Mende, 24-26.V; Annecy, 25-28.IV; Avignon, 9-15.IV; Tours 15-16.VI: tous 1990]: RHE 85 (1990) 701-4.

k418 *Bautier* R.-H., Chancellerie et culture au Moyen Âge: ➤ 741, Cancelleria 1985/90, 1-75.

k419 *a) Bischoff* Bernhard, La biblioteca di corte di Carlo Magno [< ᴱ*Braunfels* W., Karl der Grosse (1965) 2, 42-62], ᵀ*D'Alessio* Daniela; – *b) Wilson* Nigel G., Le biblioteche del mondo bizantino [< GrRByz 8 (1967) 53-80], ᵀ*Cataldi Palau* Annaclara: ➤ 478, Biblioteche² 1989, 113-135 / 79-111.

k420 **Brooke** Christopher, The medieval idea of marriage 1989 ➤ 5,g946: ᴿRHE 85 (1990) 861s (P. H. *Daly*); TS 51 (1990) 535-7 (T. *Mackin*).

k421 **Brooke** Christopher N. L., The Church and the Welsh border in the central middle ages. ...1986, Boydell & B. 127 p. $40. – ᴿJAAR 58 (1990) 114s (sr. Alberta *Dieker*).

k422 *Brown* Daniel A., The Alleluia, a thirteenth-century peace movement: ArFrancH 81 (1988) 3-16.

k423 *a) Brown* Stephen P., Theology, schools of; – *b) Wallace* William A., Thomism and its opponents: ➤ 837*, DMA 12 (1989) 20-22 / 38-45.

k424 **Brundage** James A., Law, sex and Christian society in medieval Europe 1988 ➤ 4,h959; 5,g947: ᴿCathHR 76 (1990) 334-6 (M. M. *Sheehan*); JEH 40 (1989) 412s (C. N. L. *Brooke*: rightly titled, though seems to cover sexual attitudes from Hammurabi to John Paul II); Speculum 64 (1989) 674 (R. C. *Figueira*).

k425 *a)* **Burrow** J. A., The ages of man; a study in medieval writing and thought. Ox 1986, Clarendon. vi-211 p.; 12 pl. £19.50. 0-19-811188-6. – *b)* **Sears** Elizabeth, The ages of man; medieval interpretations of the life-cycle. Princeton 1987, Univ. xviii-235 p.; 98 pl. £36.70. 0-691-04037-0. – ᴿJEH 40 (1989) 105-7 (Antonia *Granden*: both excellent).

k426 **Calati** B., *al.,* La spiritualità del Medioevo: StSpG 4, 1988 ➤ 855: ᴿTeresianum 41 (1990) 287s (E. *Pacho*).

k427 *a*) *Chastagnol* André, Le salaire des professeurs à Rome; – *b*) *Mostert* Marco, La magie de l'écrit dans le Haut Moyen Âge; quelques réflexions générales: → 149, ᶠRICHÉ P., Haut Moyen-Âge 1990, 25-31 / 273-281.

k428 ᴱ**Clover** F. M., *Humphreys* R. S., Tradition and innovation in late antiquity [Madison 24-27.IV.1984] 1989, Univ. Wisconsin. xx-343 p. – ᴿRÉAug 36 (1990) 198-202 (K. S. *Frank*).

k429 **Courtenay** William J., Schools and scholars in fourteenth century England 1987 → 5,g951: ᴿSpeculum 65 (1990) 139-141 (Edith D. *Sylla*).

k430 **Dahan** Gilbert, Les intellectuels chrétiens et les Juifs du Moyen Âge: Patrimoines, Judaïsme. P 1990, Cerf. 637 p. 2-204-04165-3.

k431 *Dahan* Gilbert, La connaissance de l'exégèse juive par les chrétiens du XIIᵉ au XIVᵉ siècle: → 521, RÉJ 149 (1990) 483.

k432 *Dionisotti* A. C., Greek grammars and dictionaries in Carolingian Europe: → k447, Nectar 1988, 1-56.

k432* **Eco** Umberto, El péndulo de Foucault 1988 → 5,g954: ᴿLumenVr 39 (1990) 494-528 (F. *García Matarranz*: ¿divertimiento o/y radiografía de la sociedad?).

k433 **Épiney-Burgard** Georgette, *Zum Brunn* Émilie, Femmes troubadours de Dieu: Témoins de notre histoire. Turnhout 1989, Brepols. 235 p.; 9 fig. 2-503-50011-0. – ᴿRÉJ 149 (1990) 220-2 (Colette *Sirat*: excellent de soi-même; important pour les études juives).

k434 **Erdoes** Richard, A.D. 1000; living on the brink of apocalypse 1988 → 5,g955: ᴿRExp 87 (1990) 353s (E. G. *Hinson*); WestTJ 52 (1990) 165-8 (J. L. *Marshall*).

k435 ᴱ**Finke** Laurie A., *Schichtman* Martin B., Medieval texts and contemporary readers. Ithaca NY 1987, Cornell Univ. ix-264 p. $30; pa. $13. – ᴿSpeculum 65 (1990) 661-3 (M. *Quilligan*).

k436 **Fuhrmann** Horst, Einladung ins Mittelalter. Mü 1987 ²1988, Beck. 327 p.; 32 pl. DM 39,50. – ᴿAevum 64 (1990) 307s (M. *Ronzani*); Franz-St 71 (1989) 115-7 (L. *Lehmann*).

k437 *Gabriel* Astrik L., Universities: → 837*, DMA 12 (1989) 282-300.

k438 **Gaybba** R. P., Aspects of the mediaeval history of theology, XIIth to XIVth cent.: Studia Originalia 7. Pretoria 1988, Univ. S. Africa. viii-280 p. [RHE 85,p.269*].

k439 **Goetz** Hans-Werner, Leben im Mittelalter vom 7. bis zum 13. Jahrhundert. Mü 1986, Beck. 302 p.; 34 fig. – ᴿZKG 101 (1990) 96s (W. *Hartmann*).

k440 **Gonnet** Giovanni, Il grano e le zizzanie; tra eresia e riforma (secoli XII-XVI). Soveria Mannelli 1989, Rubbetino. 3 vol. Lit 180.000 [RHR 208, 334-7, G. *Audizio*].

k441 **Gurevich** Aron, Medieval popular culture; problems of belief and perception, ᵀ*Bak* James M., *Hollingsworth* Paul A. C 1988, Univ. 275 p. $44.50. – ᴿJIntdis 20 (1989s) 129-132 (Marcia L. *Colish*).

k442 ᴱ**Graus** František, Mentalitäten im Mittelalter; methodische und inhaltliche Probleme: Konstanzer Vort.For. 35. Sigmaringen 1987, Thorbecke. 344 p.; ill. – ᴿZKG 101 (1990) 93-96 (F. *Göttmann*).

k443 *Gruber* Hans-Günter, Hexenverfolgung und Inquisition; zeit- und kirchengeschichtliche Verstehenszusammenhänge [... 2.3 Das Bild und die Situation der Frau; 2.4 Sexual- und Sinnenfeindlichkeit des Christentums]: MüTZ 41 (1990) 157-172.

k444 **Haines** Roy M., Ecclesia anglicana; studies in the English Church of the later Middle Ages 1989 → 5,g962: ᴿRHE 85 (1990) 809s (D. *Bradley*: ensemble d'essais).

k445 *Hamilton* Bernard, The Cathars and the seven churches of Asia [the reference is to those linked with Paul's epistles rather than with Apc. 2s]: ByzF 13 (1988) 269-295.

k446 **Henry** Avril, The mirour of mans saluacioune; a Middle English translation of the Speculum Humanae Salvationis [surviving in 394 Latin and other manuscripts from around 1400]. Ph 1987, Univ. Pennsylvania. 347 p. $50. – [R]JAAR 58 (1990) 285s (J. *Gutmann*: meticulous research).

k447 [E]**Herren** Michael W., **Brown** Shirley A., The sacred nectar of the Greeks; the study of Greek in the West in the early Middle Ages: Medieval Studies 2, 1988 → 4,h971*, 23 pl.: [R]RÉByz 48 (1990) 316s (A. *Failler*); Speculum 65 (1990) 794 (tit. pp.).

k447* **Kaczynski** Bernice M., Greek in the Carolingian age — the St. Gall manuscripts: Speculum Anniv. Mg 13. Boston 1989, Medieval Acad. x-164 p. $15; pa. $8. 0-910956-96-0; -7-9 [AmHR 96,147, Rosamond *McKitterick*].

k448 **Kaluza** Z., Les querelles doctrinales à Paris; [*Gerson* J.,...] nominalistes et réalistes aux confins du XIVe et du XVIe siècles: Quodlibet 2. Bergamo 1988, Lubrina. 204 p. – [R]RET 50 (1990) 350s (M. *Gesteira*).

k449 **Kerlouégan** François, Le 'De excidio Britanniae' de Gildas; les destinées de la culture latine dans l'île de Bretagne au VIe siècle: diss. P Sorbonne 1977. lxviii-601 + 225 p. – [R]RÉAug 35 (1989) 196-200 (M. *Banniard*).

k450 **Knowles** David, The evolution of medieval thought [[1]1962], [2]*Lipscombe* D. E. *Brooke* C. N. L. L 1988, Longman. xxvi-338 p. – [R]RHist 280 (1988) 579s (J. *Verger*).

k451 **Labarge** Margaret W., *a*) A small sound... women in medieval life 1986 → 4,h975 [N. B. all numbers after this in volume 4 index should be L. **Laberge** book-reviews]: [R]CathHR 75 (1989) 149s (Mary M. *McLaughlin*); – *b*) La mujer en la edad media: Historia. M 1988, Nerea. 318 p. – [R]CommSev 22 (1989) 466 (M. *Sánchez* gives surname as Wade-Labarge).

k452 **Leader** Damian R., A history of the University of Cambridge, I. The university to 1546. C 1988, Univ. xxii-399 p.; 29 fig. £35. – [R]JEH 41 (1990) 98-100 (A. B. *Cobban*); RHE 85 (1990) 560s (D. *Bradley*).

k453 **Leclercq** Jean, La spiritualità del Medioevo (VI-XII secolo), da San Gregorio a San Bernardo: → 854, StSp 4A. Bo 1986, Dehoniane. 352 p. – [R]Teresianum 40 (1989) 269s (D. *Maroto*).

k454 [E]**Leonardi** C., *al.*, Medioevo latino; bollettino bibliografico della cultura europea dal secolo VI al XIII: 10 (1987), 11 (1988). Spoleto 1989s, Centro Medioevo. xlviii-1067 p.; xlvii-1147 p. – [R]RHE 85 (1990) 732-4 (J. *Pycke*).

k455 **Lubac** H. de, Esegesi medievale [II/1 [T]1986] I/2 [1959], [T]*Auletta* G., *Frattini* L. Mi 1988, Jaca. 412 p. – [R]Salesianum 52 (1990) 430s (A. *Isola*).

k456 **Machielsen** Johannes, Clavis patristica pseudepigraphorum medii aevi [i.e. inventory of medieval works (732-1300) wrongly attributed to Latin Fathers], I. A (praef.; Ambrosius-Augustinus); B (Beda-Zeno): Opera homiletica: CCLat. Turnhout 1990, Brepols. xix-1127 p. Fb 14.000 [NRT 113, 930, S. *Hilaire*].

k457 *McNamara* Martin, Monastic schools in Ireland and Northumbria before A.D. 750: MilltSt 25 (1990) 19-36.

k458 *Miethke* Jürgen, Die mittelalterlichen Universitäten und das gesprochene Wort: HZ 251 (1990) 1-44 [< RHE 85,789s].

k459 **Minnis** A. J., Medieval theory of [divine/human biblical] authorship[2] [[1]1984]. Wildwood House, 1988. 323 p. £12. 0-7045-0592-4. – [R]ExpTim 101 (1989s) 250 (A. K. *McHardy*).

k459* *Nelson* Janet L., Women and the Word in the earlier Middle Ages: → 692*, Eccl.Hist.Soc. 1989/90, 53-78.

k460 **Orabona** Luciano, La Chiesa dell'anno mille; spiritualità tra politica ed economia nell'Europa medievale: SpCr 6, 1988 → 4,h987; 5,g978: [R]Benedictina 36 (1989) 265-7 (M. *Dell'Omo*); CC 141 (1990,1) 404 (C. *Capizzi*); ScuolC 117 (1989) 398s (L. *Orsenigo*).

k461 **Pelikan** Jaroslav, The excellent empire 1987 → 4,h989; 5,g981: [R]Cath-HR 75 (1989) 127 (W. E. *Kaegi*); CritRR 2 (1989) 334-6 (W. D. *Lindsey*).

k462 **Peters** Edward, Inquisition 1988 → 5,g982: [R]CathHR 75 (1989) 112-5 (A. C. *Shannon*).

k463 **Poppi** Antonino, Classicità del pensiero medievale; ANSELMO, BONAVENTURA, TOMMASO, Duns SCOTO alla prova dell'élenchos: Univ. S. Cuore. Mi 1988, ViPe. 191 p. – [R]DoctComm 42 (1989) 94s (L. *Elders*).

k464 *Quacquarelli* Antonio, Appunti sulla sticometria cristiana antica: Vet-Chr 27 (1990) 241-256.

k465 **Quaife** G. R., Godly zeal and furions rage; the witch in early modern Europe. NY 1987, St, Martin's. 235 p. $25. – [R]RelStR 16 (1990) 353 (R. M. *Golden*: does not quite replace J. KLAITS or B. LEVACK).

k466 *Raedts* Peter, De christelijke middeleeuwen als mythe; ontstaan en gebruik van een constructie uit de negentiende eeuw: TsTNijm 30 (1990) 146-158; Eng. 158.

k467 *Reedijk* Wim M., Some observations on the influence of Christian scholastic authors on Jewish thinkers in the thirteenth and fourteenth century: Bijdragen 51 (1990) 382-395.

k468 [E]**Riché** P., *Lobrichon* G., Moyen Âge et la Bible: BTT 4, 1984 → 1,308.d605 ... 4,h991: [R]ÉglT 20 (1989) 485-8 (L. *Laberge*).

k469 [**Riché** Pierre] *Chatillon* Jean, *Verger* Jacques, Lo studio della Bibbia nel medioevo latino [< BTT 4,163-282], [T]*Rigo* Caterina: StBPaid 87, 1989 → 5,g984: [R]Antonianum 65 (1990) 667s (M. *Nobile*).

k470 **Riché** Pierre, [→ 149] École et enseignement dans le Haut Moyen Âge. P 1989, Picard. 471 p. – [R]CahHist 34 (1989) 350-3 (Nicole *Gonthier*).

k471 *Roberts* Michael, Biblical epic and rhetorical paraphrase in late antiquity [< [D]1978] 1985 → 1,b719 ... 5,g985: [R]CritRR 3 (1990) 319-321 (W. *Wuellner*).

k472 *Sieben* Hermann J., Griechische Konzilsidee zur Zeit des Florentinums: TPhil 65 (1990) 184-215 (513-548, vom Florentinum zum ersten Vatikanum).

k473 **Smalley** Beryl † 1984, The Gospels in the Schools, c. 1100 - c. 1280: 1985 → 1,131 ... 5,g988: [R]ArFrancH 82 (1989) 197-203 (J. G. *Bougerol*).

k474 **Stroll** Mary, The Jewish pope ... 1130; 1987 → 4,h998; 5,g990: [R]JEH 40 (1989) 110s (H. *Cowdrey*); Speculum 65 (1990) 379-381 (J. C. *Moore*).

k475 *Tristano* Caterina, Economia del libro in Italia tra la fine del XV e l'inizio del XVI secolo; il prezzo del libro 'vecchio': ScrCiv 14 (1990) 199-241.

k476 **Uitz** Erika, Die Frau in der mittelalterlichen Welt. Lp 1988, Ed. Lp. 204 p. – [R]SixtC 21 (1990) 134 (Susan C. *Karant-Nunn*).

k477 **Uytfanghe** Marc Van, Stylisation biblique et condition humaine dans l'hagiographie mérovingienne (600-750) [diss. Gand 1979 → 5,g993: 'Bible et hagiographie dans le royaume mérovingien']: Verhandelingen 49/120.

Bru 1987, Acad. 286 p. – ᴿHelmantica 40 (1989) 507-511 (J. *Oroz Reta*); RÉAug 35 (1989) 200s (F. *Dolbeau*).

k478 ᵀᴱ**Van Engen** John, Devotio moderna; basic writings; pref. *Oberman* Heiko A. NY 1988, Paulist. 331 p. $14 pa. – ᴿSpTod 41 (1989) 270-3 (Susan *Hutchens*).

k479 **Vauchez** André, I laici nel Medioevo; pratiche ed esperienze religiose [1987 ➤ 4,h999]ᵀ. Mi 1989, Saggiatore. 340 p. Lit. 45.000. – ᴿRasT 31 (1990) 100s (A. *Barruffo*).

k480 **Wirth** Jean, L'image médiévale; naissance et développement (viᵉ-xvᵉ s.). P 1989, Méridiens Klincksieck. 395 p. 2-86563-210-5. – ᴿÉTRel 65 (1990) 278 (Dominique *Viaux*).

k481 *Zinn* Grover, History and interpretation; 'Hebrew truth', Judaism, and the Victorine exegetical tradition: ➤ 396, ᴱ*Charlesworth* J., Jews and Christians 1988/90, 100-122. (-126, discussion).

k482 *Zutshi* Patrick, *Ombres* Robert, The Dominicans in Cambridge 1238-1538: ArFrPr 60 (1990) 313-373; pl. II.

Y3.4   **Exegetae mediaevales** (hebraei ➤ K7.2s).

k483 Aɴsᴇʟᴍᴜs: *Clanchy* M. T., Aʙᴇʟᴀʀᴅ's mockery of St. Anselm: JEH 41 (1990) 1-23.

k484 ᵀᴱ**Corbin** M., Anselme de Cantorbéry. La conception virginale et le péché originel...: Œuvres 4. P 1990, Cerf. 461 p. ᴿCarthaginensia 6 (1990) 379 (F. *Martínez Fresneda*).

k485 *Hart* Trevor A., Anselm of Canterbury and John McLeod Cᴀᴍᴘʙᴇʟʟ; where opposites meet?: EvQ 62 (1990) 311-333.

k486 Aǫᴜɪɴᴀs: **Pesch** Otto H., Thomas von Aquin, Grenze 1988 ➤ 4,k6: ᴿLebZeug 44 (1989) 70s (F. *Courth*); RHPR 70 (1990) 486s (A. *Birmelé*: Frenchᵀ needed).

k487 **Schmidl** Wolfgang, Homo discens; Studien zur pädagogischen Anthropologie bei T. von Aquin: Komm. Ph. Pädagogik 22. W 1987, Österr. Akad. 210 p. DM 40. – ᴿSpeculum 65 (1990) 231s (J. A. *Aertsen*: interesting; some queries).

k488 *Schockenhoff* Eberhard, Personsein und Menschenwürde bei Thomas von Aquin und Maᵣtin Lᴜᴛʜᴇʀ: TPhil 65 (1990) 481-512.

k489 ᴱ**Tugwell** Simon, Aʟʙᴇʀᴛ and Thomas, selected writings: Classics of Western Spirituality. NY 1988, Paulist. xv-650 p. $18. – ᴿRHE 85 (1990) 514 (P. H. *Daly*); Thomist 54 (1990) 541-5 (R. *Woods*).

k490 **Valkenberg** Wilhelmus B. M., 'Did not our heart burn?' Place and function of Holy Scripture in the theology of St. Thomas Aquinas: diss. ᴰ*Grijs* F. de. Utrecht 1990. x-440 p. – TsTNijm 30 (1990) 191 & 314; RTLv 22, p. 599; TR 86,430.

k491 **Wohlman** Avital, Thomas / Mᴀɪᴍᴏɴɪᴅᴇ 1988 ➤ 4,k10; 5,k6: ᴿÉTRel 65 (1990) 126s (C. *Izard*); RTPhil 122 (1990) 131s (R. *Imbach*).

k492 Aʀᴀᴛᴏʀ: *Deproost* Paul-Augustin, Notes sur le texte et l'interprétation d'Arator: VigChr 44 (1990) 76-82.

k493 Bᴇᴅᴀ: **Brown** George H., Bede the Venerable: English Authors 443 1987 ➤ 4,k11: ᴿSpeculum 65 (1990) 375-7 (R. W. *Hanning*).

k494 *Holder* Arthur G., Bede and the tradition of patristic exegesis: AnglTR 72 (1990) 390-411.

k495 *Martin* Lawrence T., Aᴜɢᴜsᴛɪɴᴇ's influence on Bede's Homeliae euangelii: ➤ 688*a*, Collectanea 1986/90, 357-369.

k496 **Roera Sans** Javier,   San Beda, exegeta del Nuovo Testamento; criterio[s] de interpretación y exegesis: diss. Pamplona 1990, ᴰ*Basevi* C.   286 p. – RTLv 22, p. 586 'criterior'.

k497 ᵀᴱ**Simonetti Abbolito** Giuseppina,   Venerabile Beda, Omelie sul Vangelo: Testi Patristici 90.   R 1990, Città Nuova.   541 p.   88-311-3090-0.

k498 BERCEO G.: *Ruiz Dominguez* Juan A.,   Un divulgador bíblico del siglo XIII, Gonzalo de Berceo: CommSev 22 (1989) 381-403.

k499 BERNARDUS: **Leclercq** Jean, Bernard ... :   BiblHistChr 19.   P 1989, Desclée.   166 p. – RScEsp 42 (1990) 116s (R. *Potvin*).

k500 *Oury* G.-M.,   Saint Bernard après huit siècles: EsprVie 100 (1990) 529-533.

k501 *Posset* Franz,   St. Bernard's influence on two Reformers; John von STAUPITZ and Martin LUTHER: Cistercian Studies 25 (1990) 175-...

k502 BOETHIUS: **Lluch-Baixauli** M.,   La teología de Boecio, en la transición del mundo clásico al mundo medieval: Teológica 69.   Pamplona 1990, Eunsa.   349 p. pt 3250 [NRT 113, 269, V. *Roisel*].

k503 BONAVENTURA: **Bougerol** Jacques G.,   Introduction à saint Bonaventure; à la recherche de la vérité: LibrPh.   P 1988, Vrin.   xiv-261 p. – ᴿWissWeis 53 (1990) 78s (A. *Speer*).

k504 **Hattrup** Dieter,   Ekstatik der Geschichte; die Entwicklung der christologischen Erkenntnistheorie Bonaventuras: kath. Hab.-Diss. ᴰ*Hünermann*. Tübingen 1989s. – TR 86 (1990) 510.

k505 *Vian* Paolo,   Bonaventura di Bagnoregio di fronte a GIOACCHINO da Fiore e al Gioachimismo; qualche riflessione su recenti valutazioni [REEVES M., LUBAC H. de]: Antonianum 65 (1990) 133-160; Eng. 133.

k506 CUSANUS: *Gerl* Hanna-Barbara,   'Der Friede im Glauben'; zu einem Entwurf religiöser Toleranz des Nikolaus Cusanus: UnSa 45 (1990) 63-69.

k507 *a) Dupré* Louis,   Introduction, and major works of Nicholas of Cusa; – *b) Moran* Dermot,   Pantheism in John Scottus ERIUGENA and Nicholas of Cusa; – *c) Miller* Clyde L.,   Perception, conjecture, and dialectic in Nicholas of Cusa: AmCathPhilosQ 54,1 (Nicholas of Cusa 1990) 1-6 (153s) / 131-152 / 35-54.

k508 ᴱ**Haubst** R.,   Das Sehen Gottes nach Nikolaus von Kues [Trier 25.-27.IX.1986]. Trier 1989, Paulinus. 303 p. – ᴿTR 86 (1990) 383-5 (L. *Hödl*).

k509 *Kandler* Karl-Hermann,   Nikolaus von Kues als Theologe: TLZ 115 (1990) 481-490.

k510 **Schulze** Werner,   Harmonik und Theologie bei Nikolaus Cusanus: Beit. zur harmonikalen Grundlagenforschung 13.   W 1983, Branmüller.   100 p. DM 34. – ᴿZkT 112 (1990) 123s (M. *Illmer*).

k511 DAMIANI: ᴱ**Lucchesi** Giovanni, S. Petrus Damianus, Sermones: CCMed 57; CETEDOC digest *Laviolette* Marie-P., *al.*   Turnhout 1990, Brepols. 44 p.; 8 microfiches.   2-503-73572-X.

k512 ᴱ**Reindel** Kurt,   Petrus Damiani, Briefe II (Nr. 41-90) 1988. – ᴿSpeculum 65 (1990) 740-2 (K. F. *Morrison*).

DIONYSIUS PSEUDO-AREOPAGITA ➤ k189; k190*.

k513 ECKHART: **Libera** Alain de, *al.*, Eckhart, Le commentaire de l'Évangile selon Jean, le Prologue: Œuvre latine 6.   P 1989, Cerf.   463 p. F 380.   2-204-02834-7. – ᴿETL 66 (1990) 214s (A. *Haquin*); Gregorianum 71 (1990) 384 (P. *Gilbert*); NRT 112 (1990) 623s (R. *Escol*); RThom 90 (1990) 336s (S. T. *Bonino*).

k514 ERIUGENA: **Brennan** Mary,   Guides des [Eng. title 'A guide to'] études érigéniennes; bibliographie commentée des publications 1930-1987. FrS/P 1989, Univ./Cerf. 341 p. – ᴿFreibZ 37 (1990) 514-526 (W. *Otten*).

k514* **Jeauneau** Édouard, Études érigéniennes 1988 ➤ 5,k21: RTPhil 122 (1990) 285s (J. *Borel*).

k515 **O'Meara** J.J., Eriugena 1988 ➤ 4,k23; 5,k20: ᴿJEH 41 (1990) 336 (R. *McKitterick*).

k516 *Otten* Willemien, Some perspectives in Eriugenian studies [JEAUNEAU E. 1987; MADEC G. 1988; BRENNAN Mary 1989]: FreibZ 37 (1990) 514-526.

k518 GAUFRIDUS A.: ᴱ**Rochais** H., Geoffroy d'Auxerre, Entretien de Simon-Pierre avec Jésus [De colloquio..., 85 ms]: SChr 364. P 1990, Cerf. 328 p. F 200 [NRT 113, 593, L.-J. *Renard*].

k519 GERSON: **Burger** Christoph, Aedificatio, fructus, utilitas; Johannes Gerson als Professor der Theologie und Kanzler der Universität Paris: BeitHistT 70, 1986 ➤ 4,k24: ᴿJEH 40 (1989) 283-6 (L. B. *Pascoe*, also on BROWN D. Catherine 1987).

k520 GERTRUD H.: *Lewis* Gertrud J., Das Gottes- und Menschenbild im Werk der mittelalterlichen Mystikerin Gertrud von Helfta; ein Beitrag zu der Diskussion 'Frau in der Kirche': GeistL 63 (1990) 53-69.

k521 GOTTSCHALK: *Nineham* D.E., Gottschalk of Orbais [b. c.804]; reactionary or precursor of the Reformation?: JEH 40 (1989) 1-18.

k522 GUERRIC: **Lockey** Paul E., The theology of Guerric of Igny [one of the four fundamental Cistercians]; a study of anthropology, Christology, and eschatology: diss. Dallas Univ. 1989, ᴰ*Sommerfeldt* J. 220 p. 90-17051. – DissA 51 (1990s) 198-A.

k523 GULIELMUS S.T.: *Renna* T., The Jewish Law according to William of Saint Thierry: StMonast 31,1 (Barc 1989) 49-68 [< zɪᴛ 89,736].

k524 HERMANN W.: *Hamburger* Jeffrey F., Hermann of Werden's [1225] Hortus deliciarum Salomonis discovered, lost, and recovered: Scriptorium 43 (Bru 1989) 120-9.

k525 HILTON: *Ross* Ellen M., The use of Scripture and the spiritual journey in Walter Hilton's [14th c. Middle English] Scale of Perfection: AugLv 39 (1989) 119-131.

k525* HRABANUS: *Le Maître* Philippe, Les méthodes exégétiques de Raban Maur: ➤ 149, ᶠRICHÉ P., Haut Moyen-Âge 1990, 343-352.

k526 JOACHIM F.: **Grundmann** Herbert, Studi su Gioacchino di Fiore [c. 1920],ᵀ. Genova 1989, Marietti. 215 p. – ᴿLateranum 56 (1990) 386-8 (G. *Ancona*).

k527 **Lee** Harold, *Reeves* Marjorie, Western Mediterranean prophecy; the school of Joachim of Fiore and the fourteenth-century Breviloquium: StT 88, 1989 ➤ 5,k31: ᴿCathHR 76 (1990) 357s (D.C. *West*); RHE 85 (1990) 753-5 (D. *Verhelst*).

k528 **Reeves** Marjorie, *Gould* Warwick, Joachim of Fiore and the myth of the eternal evangel in the nineteenth century 1987 ➤ 3,g448... 5,k30: ᴿHeythJ 31 (1990) 353s (D. *Jasper*).

k529 JOHANNES G.: **Swanson** Jenny, John of Wales; a study of the works and ideas of a thirteenth-century friar: Studies in Medieval Life. C 1989, Univ. xii-307 p. £32.50. – ᴿRHE 85 (1990) 561 (D. *Bradley*).

k530 JOHANNES L.: *Talvio* Leena, Les citations bibliques dans le Morale Somnium Pharaonis [Juan de Limoges c.1270]: Arctos 24 (1990) 139-146.

k531 JULIANA N.: **Jantzen** Grace, Julian of Norwich, mystic and theologian 1987 ➤ 4,k31; 5,k33: ᴿHeythJ 31 (1990) 239s (Lavinia *Byrne*); JTS 41 (1990) 750s (A.M. *Allchin*); NedTTs 43 (1989) 65s (V. *Brümmer*); RelSt 25 (1989) 403-5 (Ann *Loades*); TorJT 6 (1990) 153-5 (J. *McArdle*).

k532 **Pelphrey** Brant, Christ our mother; Julian of Norwich [➤ 5,k34]: The way of the Christian mystics. Wilmington 1988, Glazier. 271 p. $15 pa. 0-89453-690-3. – ᴿRExp 87 (1990) 500s (E. G. *Hinson*).

k533 KEMPE Margerie, Le livre de ~ [Eng.] ᵀ*Magdinier* L. P 1989, Cerf. x-373 p. – ᴿRSPT 74 (1990) 475s (N. *Bériou*).

k534 KILWARDBY: *Biffi* Inno, Figure della teologia medioevale, tra Scrittura e teologia, II. Roberto Kilwardby: TItSett 15 (1990) 9-66; Eng. 67.

k535 LOMBARDUS P.: *Laarhoven* Jan van, Lombardus zonder bijbel; een 'negatieve' benadering van het schriftgebruik in de Sententiae: TsTNijm 30 (1990) 362-375 [94% of the verses never cited at all, with breakdown by tables].

k536 LULL R.: *Serverat* Vincent, L''irrisio fidei'; encore sur Raymond Lulle et Thomas d'AQUIN [iv. ironie thomiste et ironie lullienne]: RThom 90 (1990) 436-448.

k537 ᴱ**Lohr** Charles, *al.*, Brevicvlvm seu Electorivm Parvvm Thomae Migerii (LE MYÉSIER): Opera Latina supplementi Lulliani 1 / CCMed 77. Turnhout 1990, Brepols. xxvi-414 p. 2-503-03771-2; pa.-2-0.

k538 MASSA M.: *Geith* Karl-E., Die Vita Jesu Christi des Michael von Massa: AugLv 38 (1988) 99-117.

k539 MIRANDOLA P.: *Raspanti* Antonino, Filosofia, teologia, religione; l'unità della visione in Giovanni Pico della Mirandola [1463-94]: Ho Theológos 8 (1990) 225-283.

k540 ᴱ**Roulier** Fernand, Jean Pic de la Mirandole (1463-1494), humaniste, philosophe et théologien; Bibliothèque F. Simone 17. Genève 1989, Slatkine. 667 p. – ᴿJTS 41 (1990) 285-7 (G. R. *Evans* describes this rather as work of a single author).

k541 PHOTIUS: **Schamp** J., Photius historien des lettres; la Bibliothèque et ses notices historiques. P 1987, Belles Lettres. 543 p. F 249. 2-251-66248-0. – ᴿRPg 64 (1988) 156s (E. des *Places*).

k542 RADBERTUS P.: *Silvestre* Hubert, Nouvelles éditions de Paschase Radbert: Scriptorium 42 (Bru 1988) 113-8.

k543 RUFUS R.: **Raedts** P., R. Rufus 1987 ➤ 5,k40: ᴿJTS 41 (1990) 748-750 (J. *McEvoy*).

k544 RUPERTUS T.: **Arduini** Maria Lodovica, Rupert von Deutz (1076-1129) und der 'Status christianitatis' seiner Zeit; symbolisch-prophetische Deutung der Geschichte: ArKulturG Beih 25, 1987 ➤ 5,k41: ᴿTR 86 (1990) 381-4 (H. *Feld*); ZKG 101 (1990) 99-101 (R. *Haacke*).

k545 SCOTUS: *Modrić* Luka, I testi di Duns Scoto sulla dimostrazione di Dio in una strana edizione [piuttosto in una *critica* (V. RICHTER ZkT 1981/8) dell'edizione 'Ordinazio' e 'Lectura']: Antonianum 65 (1990) 312-344; Eng. 312.

k545* **Krop** H. A., De status van de theologie volgens J. D. Scotus; de verhouding tussen theologie en metafysica. Amst 1987, Rodopi. x-279 p. f 48. 90-6203-600-7. – ᴿNedTTs 43 (1989) 343s (H. *Veldhuis*).

k546 *Del Zotto* Cornelio, La 'via Scoti' nell'epistolario di Johann AMERBACH (1443-1513) [ᴱ*Hartmann* A. 1942; contro OCKHAM]: Antonianum 65 (1990) 161-186; eng. 161.

Y4.1 **Luther.**

k547 *a*) *Arnold* Matthieu, Un aspect de l'humanité de Luther; ses lettres aux endeuillés; – *b*) *Hège* Lydie, Le mariage selon Luther: PosLuth 38,1 (1990) 15-44 / 45-68 [< ZIT 90,312].

k548 **Asendorf** Ulrich, Die Theologie Luthers nach seinen Predigten 1988 ⇥ 5,k44: ᴿLuJb 57 (1990) 288-290 (A. *Beutel*).

k549 *Beintker* Horst J. E., Luther und das Alte Testament: TZBas 46 (1990) 219-244.

k550 ᴱ**Cavallotto** Stefano, M. Lutero, Scritti pastorali minori; pref. *Lilianich* B. [⇥ 4,k45; 5,450 'Ulianich'] , 1987: ᴿStEcum 7 (1989) 344 (M. *Cassese*).

k551 **Currà** Gaetano, Il falso profeta Lutero negli scritti di Tommaso CAMPANELLA [diss.]. Cosenza 1989, Progetto 2000. 184 p. Lit. 20.000. – ᴿSapienza 43 (1990) 225s (M. *Miele*).

k552 *a) Dembowski* Hermann, [im Augustinerkloster zu Erfurt] Martin Luther; – *b) Brecht* Martin, Erfahrung-Exegese-Dogmatik; [biblische Quellen von] Luthers Lied 'Nun freut euch, lieben Christen gmein': NSys 31 (1989) 125-140; Eng. 140 / 32 (1990) 94-104; Eng. 104.

k553 **Dithmar** Reinhard, Martin Luthers Fabeln und Sprichwörter: Tb 1094. Fra 1989, Insel. 247 p.; ill. – ᴿLuJb 57 (1990) 287s (M. *Beyer*).

k554 ᴱ**Fabisch** P., *Iserloh* E., Dokumente zur Causa Lutheri I, 1988 ⇥ 4,k50; 5,k56: ᴿCathHR 75 (1989) 697-9 (J. *Wicks*).

k554* **Hammann** Konrad, Ecclesia spiritualis; Luthers Kirchenverständnis in den Kontroversen mit Augustin von ALVELDT und Ambrosius CATHARINUS: ForKDG 44. Gö 1989, Vandenhoeck & R. 330 p. DM 58. 3-525-55151-7. – ᴿLuthTKi 14 (1990) 34s (E. *Volk*).

k555 **Hell** Silvia, Die Dialektik des Wortes bei M. Luther; die Beziehung zwischen Gott und dem Menschen: Diss. ᴰ*Lies* L. Innsbruck 1990. 243 p. – RTLv 22, p. 619.

k556 **Hövelmann** H., Kernstellen der Lutherbibel; eine Anleitung zum Schriftverständnis [Diss.]: Texte und Arbeiten zur Bibel 5. Bielefeld 1989, Luther. 394 p. DM 58 [RHE 85,209*].

k557 **Jüngel** Eberhard, The freedom of a Christian; Luther's significance for contemporary theology 1988 ⇥ 5,k66: ᴿAnglTR 72 (1990) 108-110 (R. C. *Zachman*); TorJT 6 (1990) 316-9 (R. *Topping*).

k558 **Jüngel** Eberhard, Theological essays, ᵀᴱ*Webster* J. B. 1989 ⇥ 5,287: ᴿExpTim 102 (1990s) 57 (C. *Gunton*: very Lutheran, notably in criticism of RAHNER's 'anonymous Christian' and in 'unerringly' exposing pitfalls of Catholic 'Church as sacrament').

k559 **Kittelson** James M., Luther the reformer; the story of the man and his career 1986 ⇥ 3,g484 ... 5,k69: ᴿExpTim 101 (1989s) 96 (C. S. *Rodd*: strong commendation); WestTJ 52 (1990) 168s (W. S. *Barker*).

k560 **Lage** Dietmar, Martin Luther's Christology and ethics: Texts and Studies in Religion 45. Lewiston NY 1990, Mellen, viii-175 p. $50. [RelStR 17, 367, D. R. *Janz*].

k560* **Lehmann** Hartmut, Martin Luther in the American imagination: (German) American Studies 63. Mü 1988, Fink. 349 p. DM 88. 3-7705-2478-0. – ᴿLuthTKi 14 (1990) 181s (J. *Oesch*: 'a book that had to be written but doesn't have to be read').

k561 [*Lell* Joachim, p. 1-14] Deum magnificare — Gott preisen: Luthers Marienverständnis; historische, ökumenische und Frauen-theologische Perspektiven; Tagung vom 14. bis 15. Mai 1983: Ev.Akad.Tagungsprotokoll 13/83. Iserlohn 1983, Haus Ortlohn. 40 p. [p. 20-39, *Wittkemper* Karl; < LuJb p. 321.340].

k562 **Lienhard** Marc, L'Évangile et l'Église chez Luther: CogF, 1989 ⇥ 5,k75; F 145; ᴿTLZ 115 (1990) 280 (A. *Greiner*).

k563 **Lohse** B., M. Luther, ᵀ*Schultz* R. C., 1986 ➤ 3,g488; 5,k58: ᴿCritRR 2 (1989) 319-321 (M. *Hoffman*); EngHR 105 (1990) 727s (B. *Scribner*).

k564 *Lukens* Michael B., Luther's death and the secret Catholic report [COCHLAEUS 1548 ...]: JTS 41 (1990) 545-553 [not suicide].

k565 **McGoldrick** James E., Luther's Scottish connection. Teaneck NJ 1989, F. Dickinson. 128 p. $26.50. – ᴿWestTJ 52 (1990) 387-9 (D. W. *Hall*).

k566 ᴱ**Manns** Peter, M. Luther 'Reformator und Vater im Glauben' 1985/5 ➤ 3,465: ᴿTLZ 115 (1990) 38-41 (S. *Bräuer*).

k567 ᴱ**Manns** Peter, Zur Bilanz des Lutherjahres 1984/6 ➤ 3,671*; 4,k63: ᴿTLZ 115 (1990) 518-520 (S. *Bräuer*).

k568 **Maron** Gottfried, Martin Luther und EPIKUR; ein Beitrag zum Verständnis des alten Luther: Ha Jungius-Ges 1988, 6/1, 1989 ➤ 5,k83: ᴿLuJb 57 (1990) 290-2 (M. *Beyer*: rather on a new way of approaching the aging Luther's attitudes).

k569 *Moe* Steinar, Luthers oppgjør [encounter] i 'De servo arbitrio' (1525) med den humanistiske antropologi: TsTKi 60 (1989) 161-173; Eng. 173.

k570 *a) Mostert* Walter, Die theologische Bedeutung von Luthers antirömischer Polemik; – *b) Scribner* Bob, Luther's anti-Roman polemic and popular belief; – *c) Moeller* Bernd, Die Rezeption Luthers in der frühen Reformation; – *d) Herms* Eilert, Das Evangelium für das Volk; – *e) Schwarz* Reinhard, Luther als Erzieher des Volkes: LuJb 57 (1990) 72-92 / 93-113 / 57-71 / 19-56 / 114-127.

k571 *Müller* Johann B., M. Luther als Anwalt des Liberalismus?: ZRGg 42 (1990) 217-228.

k572 **Oberman** Heiko A., Luther, man between God and the devil [1982 ➤ 64,e263; 65,d667, ital. 5,185], ᵀ*Walliser-Schwarzbart* Eileen. NHv 1989, Yale. xv-380 p. £19. – ᴿExpTim 102 (1990s) 32 [C. S. *Rodd*].

k573 **Peura** Simo, Mehr als ein Mensch? Die Vergöttlichung als Thema der Theologie M. Luthers von 1513 bis 1519: Diss. ᴰ*Mannermaa* T. Helsinki 1990. 315 p. – RTLv 22, p. 600.

k574 *Polenz* Peter von, Martin Luther und die Anfänge der deutschen Schriftlautung: ➤ 737, Kolloq. FRINGS T. 1990, 185-196.

k575 ᵀ ᴱ **Ronchi de Michelis** Laura, Lutero, Replica ad A. Catarino sull'Anticristo (1521); Antitesi ... (1521): Opere scelte 3. T 1989, Claudiana. 208 p.; 46 fig. Lit. 19.000. – ᴿProtestantesimo 45 (1990) 148-150 (U. *Gastaldi*).

k576 **Russell** William R., The Smalcald articles as a confessional document in the context of M. Luther's life and thought: diss. Iowa 1990, ᴰ*Forell* G. - RelStR 17,192.

k577 *Sakrausky* Oskar, Doktor Martin Luther — eine Gestalt der europäischen Geistesgeschichte: Lutherische Kirche in der Welt 37 (Erlangen 1990) 74-94 [< ZIT 90,288].

k578 *Schwarzwäller* Klaus, Luthers Auffassung von Gesetz und Evangelium: EvT 50 (1990) 189-206 [> NSys 33,89].

k579 *Thadden* Rudolf von, Luther in Preussen: ArRefG 79 (1988) 5-25; Eng. 25s.

Y4.3 Exegesis et controversia saeculi XVI.

k580 **Anderson** Marvin W., Evangelical foundations; religion in England, 1378-1683: AmerUnivSt 7/33, 1987 ➤ 5,k99: ᴿJEH 41 (1990) 343s (P. N. *Brooks*).

k581 **Barnes** Robin B., Prophecy and Gnosis; apocalypticism in the wake of the Lutheran Reformation 1988 ➤ 4,k80; 5,k100: ᴿLuthTKi 13 (1989) 77s (R. *Keller*); SixtC 21 (1990) 298s (R. G. *Clouse*).

k582 ᴱ**Bedouelle** Guy, *Roussel* Bernard, Le temps des Réformes et la Bible: BTT 5, 1989 ➤ 5,k101: ᴿÉTRel 65 (1990) 129 (A. *Gounelle*); FreibZ 37 (1990) 278-282 (Simone de *Reyff*); NRT 112 (1990) 417s (V. *Roisel*); RHPR 70 (1990) 379s (M. *Arnold*); RThom 90 (1990) 655s (B. *Montagnes*); SixtC 21 (1990) 751s (M. *Engammare*: some defects); TLZ 115 (1990) 672s (H. *Reventlow*).

k583 *Bedouelle* G., *Roussel* B., La lecture de la Bible en langue vivante au XVIᵉ siècle; chronologie de quelques textes et faits marquants: ➤ 511, Théorie/pratique 1988/90, (39-59) 61-76.

k584 *Bierma* Lyle D., The role of covenant theology in early Reformed orthodoxy: SixtC 21 (1990) 453-462.

k585 **Bietenholz** P. G., *Deutscher* T. R., Contemporaries of Erasmus 3. N-Z. Toronto 1987, Univ. xii-303 p. $80 [3 vol. $195] 0-8020-2575-7. – ᴿJEH 41 (1990) 308s (G. F. *Nuttall*).

k586 *Bilinkoff* Jodi, The social meaning of religious reform; the case of St. Teresa and Avila: ArRefG 89 (1988) 340-356; deutsch 356s.

k587 *Brady* Thomas A.ᴶ, The Reformation's fate in America; a reflection: ➤ 37*, ᶠCHRISMAN M., Process of change 1988, 17-31.

k588 **Brigden** Susan, London and the Reformation. Ox 1989, Clarendon. xx-676 p.; 1 pl., map. – ᴿRHE 85 (1990) 866 (D. *Bradley*).

k589 *Bujanda* J. M. De, Index des livres interdits [1s ➤ 2,d581] 3. Vénise 1549, Vénise ct Milan 1554; 7. Anvers 1569-1571. Genève 1987s, Droz. 528 p.; 976 p. C$50 chaque. 2-7622-0063-9. – ᴿColcFranc 60 (1990) 332-7 (V. *Criscuolo*); JEH 40 (1989) 629 (G. H. *Tucker*, also on 2. Louvain).

k590 **Bundschuh** Benno von, Das Wormser Religionsgespräch von 1557 unter besonderer Berücksichtigung der kaiserlichen Religionspolitik: RefStT 124, 1988 ➤ 5,k105: ᴿRHE 85 (1990) 453s (J.-F. *Gilmont*).

k591 *Cole* Graham, Sola scriptura; some historical and contemporary perspectives: Churchman 104 (1990) 20-34 [< ZIT 90,447].

k592 Contemporary printed literature of the English counter reformation I (*Allison* Antony F., *Rogers* D. M.). L 1989, Scolar. £60. 0-85967-640-4. – ᴿDowR 108 (1990) 77s (D. *Rees*).

k593 **Davidson** N. S., Le Contre-Réforme, ᵀ*Denis* Philippe: Bref. P 1989, Cerf/Fidcs. 123 p. F 40. 2-204-03042-2 / 2-7621-1454-2. – ᴿÉTRel 65 (1990) 130 (H. *Bost*: rappelle clairement l'histoire de ce terme contestable; DELUMEAU plus utile); RHPR 70 (1990) 389 (M. *Chevallier*: as the author notes, not all the reforms were 'Contre').

k594 **Dippel** Stewart A., A study of religious thought at Oxford and Cambridge 1590-1640. Lanham MD 1987, UPA. xiii-122 p. £9.75. 0-8191-6388-0. – ᴿJEH 40 (1989) 463 (H. C. *Porter*: zealous, amateur).

k595 *Donnelly* John P., Padua, Louvain and Paris; three case studies of University-Jesuit confrontation: LvSt 15 (1990) 38-52.

k596 *Edwards* Mark U.ᴶ, Catholic controversial literature, 1518-1555; some statistics: ArRefG 89 (1988) 189-204; Eng. 205.

k597 **Eire** Carlos M. N., War against the idols; the reformation of worship from Erasmus to Calvin 1986 ➤ 2,d586; 5,k107: ᴿHeythJ 31 (1990) 99s (B. D. *Spinks*).

k598 *Ellis* Steven G., Economic problems and the Church; why the Reformation failed in Ireland: JEH 41 (1990) 239-265.

k599 *Engammare* Max,   La Bible en français à la dispute de Lausanne; recherche sur l'autorité et l'utilisation d'une Bible en français dans la première moitié du XVIe siècle: ZtsSchweizKG 83 (1989) 205-232 [< ZIT 90,115].

k600 **Faltenbacher** Karl F.,   Das Colloquium Heptaplomeres [nicht BODEN J. sondern von r. LEONE da Modena inspiriert], ein Religionsgespräch zwischen Scholastik und Aufklärung [Diss.]: EurHS 13/127. Fra 1988, Lang. 126 p. Fs 29. – RKIsr 5 (1990) 79 (Julie *Kirchberg*).

k601 *Ferrario* Fulvio,   L'anabattismo svizzero delle origini nella storiografia recente [GASTALDI U. 1972-81]: Protestantesimo 45 (1990) 179-199.

k602 *Flood* John L.,   Le livre dans le monde germanique à l'époque de la Réforme: ⋟ 411*, EGilmont J.-F., La Réforme et le livre 1990, 29-104; eng. 104.

k603 **Frick** David A.,   Polish sacred philology in the Reformation and the Counter-Reformation; chapters in the history of the controversies 1551-1632: Publ. Modern Philology 123, Berkeley 1989, Univ. California. xi-288 p. [TR 86, 432].

k604 *Friedman* Jerome,   Unitarians and New Christians in sixteenth-century Europe: ArRefG 81 (1990) 216-237; deutsch 238.

k605 **Garrisson** Janine,   Les Protestants au XVIe siècle. P 1988, Fayard. 413 p. 2-213-02220-8. – RÉTRel 65 (1990) 635s (D. *Poton*).

k606 **George** Timothy,   Theology of the Reformers 1988 ⋟ 4,k102; 5,k112: REvQ 62 (1990) 282s (W. P. *Stephens*); ExpTim 102 (1990s) 27 (also W. P. *Stephens*); Interpretation 44 (1990) 190-2 (Jill *Raitt*); TLZ 115 (1990) 901s (E. W. *Gritsch*).

k607 *a) Gestrich* Christof,   Wer darf ihn nennen? Reformation als bussfertige Erneuerung kirchlichen Redens von Gott; – *b) Beintker* Michael, Das reformatorische Zeugnis von der Freiheit heute ... die Bedeutung der Rechtfertigungslehre zu erschliessen?: BTZ 7 (1990) 141-153 / 202-216. EGilmont J.-F.,   La Réforme et le livre 1990 ⋟ 411*.

k608 *a) Goertz* Hans-Jürgen, Träume, Offenbarungen und Visionen in der Reformation; - *b) Talkenberger* Heike, Prophetie und Zeitgeschichte; Texte und Holzschnitte astrologischer Flugschriften zur 'Sintflutdebatte' 1520-4; – *c)* Wohlfeil Schriftenverzeichnis: ⋟ 5,216, FWOHLFEIL R. 1989, 171-192 / 193-223 / 17-22.

k609 Mém. GRIMM H.,   Pietas et societas, new trends in Reformation social history, ESessions K. 1985 ⋟ 2,40: RRHPR 70 (1990) 377-9 (M. *Arnold,* also on FFORELL G. 1984).

k610 *Hagen* K.,   What did the term 'commentarius' mean to 16th century theologians?: ⋟ 511, Théorie/pratique 1988/90, 13-38.

k611 *Halkin* L.-E., *al.*,   Les débuts de la Réforme catholique dans les pays de langue française (1560-1620) [4 évêques, 6 clergé sec./reg.]: Revue d'histoire de l'Église de France 75 (P 1989) c.210 p. [< ZIT 89,796].

k612 *Harline* Craig,   Official religion — popular religion, in recent historiography of the Catholic reformation [HOVIUS M. 1596-1620]: ArRefG 81 (1990) 239-257; deutsch. 257s; bibliog. 258-262.

k613 *Huxtable* John,   Kongregationalismus [(1558-)1662 ...], TWiedermann G.: ⋟ 857, TRE 19 (1990) 452.

k614 EIserloh Erwin,   Katholische Theologen der Reformationszeit 1-5, 1987 ⋟ 1,362 ... 5,k116: RBibHumRen 51 (1989) 510s (Irena *Backus,* 5); FranzSt 71 (1989) 225s (J. *Decorte*); JEH 40 (1989) 625 (A. D. *Wright,* 5); RHPR 70 (1990) 383s (M. *Lienhard,* 4s); ZKG 101 (1990) 122-7 (M. *Beyer,* 1-3; 7 Beiträge von R. *Bäumer*).

k615 **Jacoby** Michael, Bibeltradition und Bibelsprache zwischen Mittelalter und 20. Jahrhundert im nordgermanischen Raum; Der Einfluss der Scholastik aus Paris und der Lutherbibel: Lexemdistribution 2, 1988 ➤ 4,k206*: RTsTKi 60 (1989) 217 (R. *Astås*).

k616 *Jensen* Kristian, Protestant rivalry; metaphysics and rhetoric in Germany c. 1590-1620: JEH 41 (1990) 24-43.

k617 *Kobert-Groch* Marion, Von 'Armen frowen' und 'bösen wibern' — Frauen im Bauernkrieg zwischen Anpassung und Auflehnung: ArRefG 89 (1988) 103-137; Eng. 137 [138-157, *Vice* Roy I.].

k618 **Kolb** Robert, For all the saints; changing perceptions of martyrdom and sainthood in the Lutheran Reformation. Macon GA 1987, Mercer Univ. 186 p. – RZKG 101 (1990) 120-2 (E. *Koch*).

k619 *Lukens* Michael B., LORTZ's view of the Reformation and the crisis of the true Church: ArRefG 81 (1990) 20-31; deutsch 31 [*Gritsch* E. 32-49].

k620 **McGrath** Alister, The intellectual origins of the European Reformation 1987 ➤ 3,g536... 5,k124: RJAAR 58 (1990) 508-511 (J. *Tempest*).

k621 **McGrath** Alister E., Reformation thought; an introduction [1]1988 ➤ 4,k107*; 5,k125: 0-631-15802-2; -3-0: RJEH 40 (1989) 602-5 (E. *Cameron*); RelStR 16 (1990) 158 (D. D. *Martin*).

k622 *McGrath* Alister E., Justification and the Reformation; the significance of the doctrine of justification by faith in sixteenth-century urban communities: ArRefG 81 (1990) 5-18; deutsch 18s.

k623 **Nowicki-Pastuschka** Angelika, Frauen in der Reformation; Untersuchungen zum Verhalten von Frauen in den Reichsstädten Augsburg und Nürnberg zur reformatorischen Bewegung zwischen 1517 und 1537: Forum ev.Gesch. 2. Pfaffenweiler 1990, Centaurus. 167 p. DM 28 [TR 86,343].

k624 **Oberman** Heiko A., The dawn of the Reformation 1986 ➤ 3,g542... 5,k128: REngHR 105 (1990) 170s (H. M. *Höpfl*); HeythJ 31 (1990) 344s (A. *Hamilton*); ScotJT 43 (1990) 124-6 (Susan H. *Moore*: splendid, seminal).

k625 *Prodi* P., Controriforma e/o riforma cattolica, superamento di vecchi dilemmi nei nuovi panorami storiografici: Römische Historische Mitteilungen 31 (Wien 1988) 227-237 [< RHE 85,348*].

k626 ERaitt Jill, Christian spirituality; high Middle Ages and Reformation: EWSp 17, 1987 ➤ 3,862.g545... 5,k133: RCritRR 2 (1989) 338-340 (L. S. *Cunningham*); HeythJ 31 (1990) 240s (P. *Sheldrake*).

k627 **Richardson** Fiona J., A theological study of books printed abroad in English in the first half of the sixteenth century (1535-1548): Diss. St.Andrews. – RTLv 22, p. 601, no date.

k628 ERobinson-Hammerstein Helga [two essays, one on music; *al.*], The transmission of ideas in the Lutheran reformation. Totowa NJ 1989, Rowman & L. 192 p. $45. – RCathHR 76 (1990) 129s (M. U. *Edwards*).

k629 ERodríguez P., Catechismus romanus... Trident. R/Pamplona 1989, Vaticano/Eunsa. lxxx-1378 p.; 26 fig. Lit. 260.000 [NRT 113, 455s A. *Toubeau*].

k630 **Scarisbrick** J. J., The Reformation and the English people. Ox 1984, pa. 1985, Blackwell. viii-203 p. – RJRelHist 15 (1988s) 153-5 (Sybil M. *Jack*).

k631 ESchilling Heinz, Die reformierte Konfessionalisierung in Deutschland 1985/6 ➤ 5,739: RArRefG 89 (1988) 358-362 (R. M. *Kingdon*, Eng.).

k632 **Segert** Stanislav, Unitas Fratrum and the Old Testament: ComViat 33 (1990) 27-35.

k633 **Séguenny** André, Bibliotheca dissidentium [1980 ↠ 61,1331]; 8 [7 polonais] 1987; 224 p. -9, 1988; 207. -10 (M. SERVETUS) 1989, 167 p. -11 [Heidelberg Antitrinitarians] 308 p. -12 [Hungary] 1990, 174 p. Baden-Baden, Koerner. – ᴿRHE 85 (1990) 457s (J.-F. *Gilmont*).

k634 *Shiels* W. J., Protestantism in the English Reformation [HAIGH C. 1988 & ᴱ1987; ᴱLAKE P.]: JEH 41 (1990) 64-68.

k635 **Sieben** Hermann J., Die katholische Konzilsidee [Mittelalter 1984 ↠ 1,f721] von der Reformation bis zur Aufklärung: Konziliengeschichte B. Untersuchungen. Pd 1988, Schöningh. xxiii-560 p. DM 148. – ᴿAnHConc 21 (1989) 451-464 (R. *Bäumer*): TGL 80 (1990) 101s (W. *Beinert*).

k636 **Smahel** František, La révolution hussite, une anomalie historique [conférences 1983 au Collège de France] 1985 ↠ 3,g550: ᴿRHE 85 (1990) 834s (R. *Aubert*).

k637 *Snyder* Arnold, Word and power in Reformation Zurich: ArRefG 81 (1990) 263-284; deutsch 284s.

k638 **Steinhauf** Bernhard, Giovanni L. MADRUZZO (1532-1600); katholische Reformation zwischen Kaiser und Papst; das Konzept zur praktischen Gestaltung der Kirche der Neuzeit im Anschluss an das Konzil von Trient: Diss. ᴰ*Grasmück* E. Bamberg 1990. 171 p. – RTLv 22, p. 601.

k639 *a) Steinmetz* David C., CALVIN and the patristic exegesis of Paul; – *b) Muller* Richard A., The hermeneutic of promise and fulfillment in Calvin's exegesis of the OT prophecies of the Kingdom; – *c) Hendrix* Scott H., The use of Scripture in establishing Protestantism (Urbanus RHEGIUS); – *d) Backus* Irena, Polemic, exegetical tradition, and ontology [M. BUCER on Jn 6,52s.64); – *e) Midelfort* H. C. Erik, Social history and biblical exegesis; – *f) Hagen* Kenneth G., 'De exegetica methodo' (HEMMINGSEN N.): ↠ 556*b*, Bible 16th c. 1982/90, 100-118. 231-5 / 68-82. 214-221 / 37-49. 202-9 / 167-180. 248-252 / 7-20. 197-200 / 181-196. 252-5.

k640 **Unghváry** Alexander S., The Hungarian Protestant Reformation in the sixteenth century under the Ottoman impact: Texts and Studies in Religion 48. Lewiston NY 1989, Mellen. 405 p. – ᴿWestTJ 52 (1990) 389s (M. I. *Klauber*: anti-Luther, pro-Reformed).

k641 **Vilanova** Evangelista, Historia de la teología cristiana II., Prerreforma ... 1989 ↠ 3,g553 ... 5,k142: ᴿCarthaginensia 6 (1990) 237 (V. *Sánchez*); LumenVr 39 (1990) 81s (F. *Ortiz de Urtaran*); PerspTeol 22 (1990) 396-8 (D. *Mondoni*).

k642 *Waite* Gary R., From apocalyptic crusaders to Anabaptist terrorists; Anabaptist radicalism after Müntzer, 1535-1544: ArRefG 80 (1989) 173-192; deutsch 192; map 193.

k643 **Weir** David A., The origins of the federal theology in sixteenth-century Reformation thought. Ox 1990, Clarendon. 244 p. £27.50. 0-19-826690-1. – ᴿÉTRel 65 (1990) 636s (H. *Bost*).

k644 **Wendebourg** Dorothea, Reformation und Orthodoxie ... II. 1573-81: 1986 ↠ 5,k143: ᴿOstkSt 38 (1989) 59-62 (W. *Hryniewicz*, vom ℗ ᵀ*Patock* C.).

k645 **Whiting** Robert, The blind devotion of the people; popular religion and the English Reformation. C 1989, Univ. 320 p. $54.50 [AndrUnS 28,111].

k646 *Wright* Stephen K., The vengeance of our Lord; medieval dramatizations of the destruction of Jerusalem: StT 89. Toronto 1989, Pont.Inst.Med. St. x-233 p.; 3 microfiches. $29. – ᴿSpeculum 65 (1990) 1085-7 (R. *Blasting*).

k647 ᴿ**Zambelli** Paolo, 'Astrologi hallucinati' 1986 ➤ 5,768:   ᴿCathHR 76 (1990) 128s (H. C. E. *Midelfort*: unsatisfactory.

k648 *Ziegler* Walter,   Reformation als Gemeindereformation?: ArKulturG 72 (1990) 441-452 [< TR 87,343].

Y4.4   Periti aetatis reformatoriae.

k649 AMES: **Boerkoel** Benjamin J.,   Uniqueness within the Calvinist tradition; William Ames (1576-1633), primogenitor of the theologia pietatis in English-Dutch Puritanism: diss. Calvin Theol. Sem, ᴰ*Gamble* R. vii-250 p. + bibliog. – CalvinT 25 (GR 1990) 326s.

k650 ANDREAE: *Raeder* Siegfried,   Jakob Andreae; ein Leben für Reformation und Eintracht im Glauben: TBeit 21 (Wu 1990) 244-263 [< ZIT 90,753].

k650* *Mahlmann* Theodor,   Jakob Andreä [† 7.I.1590; Konkordienformel lutherischer Einigung 1580] im Lichte neuerer Forschung: LuthTKi 14 (1990) 138-153; portr.

k651 BELLARMINO: ᴱ**Donnelly** John P., *Teske* Roland J.,   Robert Bellarmine, Spiritual writings 1989 ➤ 5,k148:   ᴿGregorianum 71 (1990) 794 (M. *Ruiz Jurado*).

k652 BOCCHI: **Pinkus** Karen E.,   The 'Symbolicae Quaestiones' of Achille Bocchi; humanist emblems [i.e. 'a literary form combining text and visual image, often collected under a theological rubric'] and Counter-Reformation: diss. City Univ., ᴰ*Schein* Seth.   NY 1990. 324 p. 90-29967. – DissA 51 (1990s) 1605-A.

k653 BUCER: ᴱ**Fraenkel** Pierre,   Martin Bucer & Matthew PARKER,   Florilegium patristicum: Bucer Opera Latina 3/ StMedRefT 41.   Leiden 1988, Brill.   xxvi-237 p. – ᴿRHPR 70 (1990) 375s (R. *Bodenmann*).

k654 **Hammann** Gottfried, M. Bucer 1491-1551, zwischen Volkskirche und Bekenntnisgemeinschaft: Mainz Inst. Eur. RelG 139.   Stu 1989, Steiner. 387 p. DM 68. – ᴿTLZ 115 (1990) 603-5 (M. *Brecht*): TR 86 (1990) 475 (J. V. *Pollet* †).

k655 BUGENHAGEN: *Schorn-Schütte* Luise,   'Papocäsarismus' der Theologen?; vom Amt des evangelischen Pfarrers in der frühneuzeitlichen Stadtgesellschaft bei Bugenhagen: ArRefG 89 (1988) 230-260; Eng. 261.

k656 CALVIN: **Barton** F. Whitfield,   Calvin and the Duchess [Renée of Ferrara, whom his letters influenced].   Louisville 1989, Westminster-Knox. x-242 p. $12 pa. – ᴿCalvinT 25 (1990) 126-9 (J. E. *Kok*).

k657 *Carbonnier* Jean,   Le Calvinisme; entre la fascination et la nostalgie de la Loi: ÉTRel 65 (1990) 507-517.

k658 *Dietrich* Wendell,   CALVIN's Scriptural ethical monotheism; interpretation, moral conscience, and religious system: ➤ 123*a, ᶠMEYER P., Faith 190, 360-377.

k659 **Engel** Mary P.,   John Calvin's perspectival anthropology 1988 ➤ 5,k158: ᴿSixtC 21 (1990) 324s (Jill *Raitt*).

k660 **Ganoczy** Alexandre,   The young Calvin 1987 ➤ 3,g571 ... 5,k159:   ᴿEvQ 62 (1990) 283s (W. P. *Stephens*: splendid translation, but 'deviations from the Catholic tradition' will irritate).

k661 ᴱ**George** Timothy,   John Calvin and the Church; a prism of reform. Louisville 1990, Westminster/Knox.   276 p. $15 [TR 86,431 tit. pp.].

k661* **Gisel** Pierre,   Le Christ de Calvin: JJC 44. P 1990, Desclée. 207 p. [RTLv 21,402].

k662 **Hwang Jung-Uck,** Der junge Calvin und seine Psychopannychia: Diss. ᴰ*Scholl*. Kirchl. Hochschule Wuppertal 1989s. – TR 86 (1990) 520.

k663 **Kerr** Hugh T., Calvin's Institutes, a new compend. Louisville 1989, Westminster-Knox. 180 p. $10 pa. – ᴿCalvinT 25 (1990) 283s (R. C. *Gamble*: not in all ways an improvement on the 1939 and 1964 editions, though based on the better BATTLES instead of ALLEN translation).

k664 **Leith** John H., John Calvin's Doctrine of the Christian Life 1989 ➤ 5,k161: ᴿAndrUnS 28 (1990) 167-9 (D. *Augsburger*); TTod 47 (1990s) 463s (C. *Gunton*).

k665 *a) Leithart* Peter J., That eminent pagan; Calvin's use of CICERO in Institutes 1.1-5; – *b) Butler* Diana, God's visible glory; the beauty of nature in the thought of John Calvin and Jonathan EDWARDS: WestTJ 52 (1990) 1-12 / 13-26.

k666 **McGrath** Alister E., A life of John Calvin; a study in the shaping of western culture. Oxford 1990, Blackwell. xv-332 p.; ill. [TR 87,343].

k667 *Mihály* Márkus, Ⓜ Calvin, the organizer of the European Reformation: TSzem 32 (1989) 274-281; 33 (1990) 34-42.

k668 *Muller* Richard A., Fides and cognitio in relation to the problem of intellect and will in the theology of John Calvin: CalvinT 25 (1990) 207-224.

k669 **Newport** John P., An investigation of factors influencing John Calvin's use of the linguistic and historical principles of biblical exegesis: diss. Edinburgh 1953. 277 p. BRD-89784. – DissA 51 (1990s) 1662-A.

k670 **Olson** Jeannine E., Calvin and social welfare; deacons and the Bourse française. Selingsgrove PA 1989, Susquehanna Univ. 341 p. $55. – ᴿCalvinT 25 (1990) 135-7 (R. A. *Muntzer*); TTod 47 (1990s) 82.84 (Elsie A. *McKee*); WestTJ 52 (1990) 385-7 (M. I. *Klauber*: fine, but more Bourse than Calvin).

k671 **Rainbow** Jonathan H., The will of God and the cross; an historical and theological study of John Calvin's doctrine of limited redemption: Princeton TheolMg 22. Allison Park PA 1990, Pickwick. x-206 p. $24 [TR 87,78].

k672 *Rainbow* Jonathan H., Double grace; John Calvin's view of the relationship of justification and sanctification: ExAud 5 (1989) 99-105.

k672* *Schluchter* Antoine, L'entrée en Cène; la pensée œcuménique et la conception calvinienne en dialogue [Petit traité de la sainte Cène 1541; BEM]: Hokhma 41 (1989) 21-52.

k673 ᴱ**Schnucker** Robert V., Calviniana; ideas and influence of John Calvin: SixtC Essays 10. Kirksville MO 1988, SixtC. 288 p. – ᴿBibHumRen 51 (1989) 506-8 (F. *Higman*).

k674 **Torrance** Thomas F., The hermeneutics of John Calvin 1988 ➤ 4,k151; 5,k168: ᴿÉTRel 65 (1990) 287s (H. *Bost*); EvQ 62 (1990) 191s (A. E. *McGrath*); TLond 93 (1990) 223-6 (C. *Schwöbel*).

k675 **Wallace** Ronald S., Calvin, Geneva and the Reformation 1988 ➤ 4,k153; 5,k169: ᴿSixtC 21 (1990) 320s (W. F. *Graham*).

k676 **Zachman** Randall C., The testimony of conscience in the theology of Martin LUTHER and John Calvin, a comparative study: diss. ᴰ*Gerrish* B. Chicago 1990. – RelStR 17,192; RTLv 22, p. 601.

k677 **Zimmermann** Gunter, Die Argumentation Calvins gegen die Gegner seiner Erwählungslehre: ArRefG 81 (1990) 69-95; Eng. 96.

k678 CANO: **Tapia** Joaquín, Iglesia y teología en Melchior Cano (1509-1560); un protagonista de la restauración eclesial y teológica en la

España del siglo XVI: MgHist 31. Roma 1989, Iglesia Nacional Española. 382 p. [NRT 113,468]. – RAngelicum 67 (1990) 589s (M. F. *Manzanedo*); Burgense 31 (1990) 270-2 (R. *Berzosa Martínez*); CommSev 23 (1990) 111s (M. *Sánchez*).

k679 CASTELLION: **[Gallicet] Calvetti** Carla, Sebastiano Castellion [1515-1563], il riformato umanista contro il riformatore Calvino; per una lettura filosofico-teologica dei Dialogi IV postumi di Castellion, con la prima traduzione italiana: Centro Metafisica. Mi 1989, ViPe. xvi-424 p. Lit. 60.000 [NRT 113,469, L. J. *Renard*]. – RCiVit 45 (1990) 187s (B. *Farnetani*); HumBr 45 (1990) 558 (G. *Penati*).

k680 COCCEIUS: **Asselt** W. J. van, Amicitia Dei; een onderzoek naar de structuur van de theologie van Johannes Coccejus (1603-1691) [diss. Utrecht]. 1988, Ede. xii-257 p. *f*45. 90-9002-142-6. – RNedTTs 44 (1990) 270s (W. *Nijenhuis*).

k681 *Asselt* W. J. van, Missionaire motieven en perspectieven in de theologie van Johannes Coccejus: KerkT 41 (1990) 227-236.

k682 CORTESE: **Cesareo** Francesco, Humanism and Catholic reform; the life and work of Gregorio Cortese (1483-1584): RenBaroque 2. NY 1990, Lang. xviii-203 p. [TR 87,78].

k683 CRANMER: **Brooks** Peter N., Cranmer in context [selections, letters]. ... 1989, Lutterworth. 144 p. £7. 0-7188-2790-2 [ExpTim 101,12].

k684 *Brooks* Peter N., [Thomas] Cranmer from his correspondence: ExpTim 101 (1989s) 8-12.

k685 DIETENBERGER: EIserloh E., *Fabisch* P., J. Dietenberger, Phimostomus Scripturariorum 1532/1985 ➤ 2,1017; 3,g585: RFranzSt 71 (1989) 101s (J. *Decorte*).

k686 DUNGERSHEIM: EFreudenberger T., H. Dungersheim, Schriften gegen LUTHER: CCath 39, 1987 ➤ 3,g587... 5,k147: – RJEH 40 (1989) 460s (R. *Rex*); TLZ 115 (1990) 824-6 (S. *Bräuer*); TüTQ 170 (1990) 67-69 (R. *Reinhardt*, also on ECK etc.).

k687 ECK: EIserloh E., J. Eck im Streit 1986/8 ➤ 5,k177: RBibHumRen 51 (1989) 733-5 (J. v. *Pollet*).

k688 **Ziegelbauer** Max, Johannes Eck, Mann der Kirche im Zeitalter der Glaubensspaltung. St. Ottilien 1987, EOS. DM 138 [RelSt 17,169, W. *Moore*: a bishop's praise for his 500th birthday].

k689 ERASMUS: **De Molen** Richard L., Spirituality of Erasmus 1987 ➤ 4,k156; 5,k179: RCathHR 75 (1989) 162-4 (J. W. *O'Malley*: 'Robert L.').

k690 **Augustijn** C., Erasmus 1986 ➤ 3,g587: RZkT 112 (1990) 245 (M. *Illmer*).

k691 **Inoue** Masami, The philosophia Christi and mens scriptoris; a comparative study of the hermeneutics and humanism of D. Erasmus and J. CALVIN: diss. DGamble R. C., Calvin Theol. Sem. vii-179 p. + bibliog. – CalvinT 25 (GR 1990; no other date assigned) 330s.

k692 *Mehlhausen* Joachim, Forma christianismi; die theologische Bewertung eines kleinen katechetischen Lehrstücks durch LUTHER und Erasmus von Rotterdam: ZTK 87 (1990) 437-455.

k693 **Rummel** Erika, Erasmus and his Catholic critics, I. 1515-1522; II. 1523-1536: BibHumRef 45. Nieukoop 1989, De Graaf. xiv-263; x-220 p. [RelStR 17,169, J. B. *Payne*].

k694 *Rummel* Erika, Erasmus' conflict with LATOMUS, Round Two: ArRefG 80 (1989) 5-23; deutsch 23.

k695 a) *Rummel* Erika, Erasmus and the Louvain theologians — a strategy of defense; – b) *Trapman* J., Ioannes SARTORIUS (ca. 1500-1557), gymnasiarch te Amsterdam en Noordwijk, als erasmiaan en spiritualist: Ned. Archief voor Kerkegeschiedenis 70 (1990) 2-12 / 30-51.

k696 [Seidel] **Menchi** Silvana, Erasmo in Italia 1987 ➤ 4,k163 ... 5,k185: RCathHR 75 (1989) 164s (Erika *Rummel*).

k697 **Vilanova** A., Erasmo y CERVANTES: Palabra Crítica 8. Barc 1989, Lumen. 576 p. – RCommSev 23 (1990) 287s (M. *Sánchez*).

k698 EWeiland Jan S., Erasmus von Rotterdam, die Aktualität seines Denkens, THübner Annemarie, 1986/8 ➤ 5,k188: RDLZ 111 (1990) 6-9 (S. *Wollgast*); SixtC 21 (1990) 297s (R. L. *DeMolen*).

k700 ERSKINE: *Bardgett* F., John Erskine of Dun [1509-1589]; a theological reassessment: ScotJT 43 (1990) 59-85.

k701 FISHER: EBradshaw Brendan, *Duffy* Eamon, Humanism ... John Fisher, 1989 ➤ 5,638: RTablet 243 (1989) 726 (J. *Todd*).

k702 FLACIUS: *Olson* O., The clavis Scripturae sacrae of Matthias Flacius Illyricus: ➤ 511, Théorie/pratique 1988/90, 167-175.

k703 FRANCK: *Hayden-Roy* Priscilla, Hermeneutica gloriae vs. hermeneutica crucis; Sebastian Franck and M. LUTHER on the clarity of Scripture: ArRefG 81 (1990) 50-67; deutsch 67s.

k704 GÜNZBURG: **Peters** Christian, Franziskaner Reformer, Humanist und konservativer Reformator; Wirken und Werke Johann von Günzburg (ca. 1465-1533): Diss. DBrecht. Münster 1990. 455 p. – RTLv 22, p. 600.

k705 HASLER: *Burchill* Christopher J., ARISTOTLE and the Trinity; the case of Johann Hasler in Strasbourg 1574-1575: ArRefG 89 (1988) 282-309; deutsch 310.

k706 HELLBARDT: *Boecker* Hans Jochen, Auslegung des Alten Testaments bei Hans Hellbardt: Monastshefte für ev.KG des Rheinlandes 37s (Dü 1988s) 595-606 [< ZIT 90,185].

k707 HUBMAIER: TEPipkin H. Wayne, *Yoder* John H., Balthasar Hubmaier, theologian of Anabaptism [texts translated]: Classics in the Radical Reformation 5, 1989 ➤ 5,k192: RAndrUnS 28 (1990) 183s (K. A. *Strand*: excellent); ExpTim 101 (1989s) 250s (D. M. *Thompson*).

k708 HUS: **Vidmanová-Schmidtová** Anežka, Johannis Hus opera omnia IX, Leccionarium bipartitum, pars hiemalis. Praha 1988, SAcad. 512 p. – RTPhil 65 (1990) 273-6 (I. *Müller*).

k709 KNOX: EBreslow Marvin A., The political writings of John Knox; The first blast of the trumpet against the monstrous regiment of women; and other selected works. L 1986, Assoc. Univ. (for Folger). 160 p. £17. 0-918016-75-4. – RJEH 40 (1989) 145s (J. P. *Sommerville*).

k710 *Cameron* James C., Knox, John (c. 1514-1572), THall Margarethe D.: ➤ 857, TRE 19 (1990) 281-7.

k711 DE LEÓN: **Guy** A., Fray Luis de León 1528-1591: Ibériques. P 1989, Corti. 163 p. F 85 [NRT 113, 290, P. *Masset*].

k712 LOYOLA I. [➤ 46]: *Álvarez* Dictino, Dos banderas [Loyola I.] i la leyenda del Gran Inquisidor [DOSTOYEVSKI F.]: Manresa 61 (1989) 269-279.

k713 *Cebollada* Pascual, Loyola y ERASMO; aportación al estudio de la relación entre ambos: Manresa 62 (1990) 49-60.

k714 *a) O'Reilly* Terence, Ignatius of Loyola and the Counter-Reformation; the hagiographic tradition; – *b) Koterski* Joseph W., Discerning the more fruitful paths to reform; Pierre FAVRE and the Lutheran Reformation: HeythJ 31 (1990) 439-470 / 488-504.

k715 MELANCHTHON: *Bayer* Oswald, 'Die Kirche braucht liberale Erudition'; das Theologieverständnis Melanchthons; KerDo 36 (1990) 218-243; Eng. 244.

k716 ᵀ**Jundt** Pierre, Philippe Mélanchthon, La Confession d'Augsbourg et l'Apologie de la Confession, préf. *Chaunu* Pierre. P 1989, Cerf. 566 p. – ᴿRHPR 70 (1990) 335-8 (M. *Lienhard*).

k717 *Mager* Inge, 'Es ist nicht gut, dass der Mensch allein sei' (Gen. 2,15); zum Familienleben Philipp Melanchthons: ArRefG 81 (1990) 120-137; Eng. 137.

k718 ᵀᴱ**Keen** Ralph, P. Melanchthon... reader: AmerUnivSt 7/41. NY 1988, Lang. viii-296 p. – ᴿSixtC 21 (1990) 115s (M. E. *Schild*).

k719 *Peterson* Luther D., Justus MENIUS, Philipp Melanchthon, and the 1547 treatise, Von der Notwehr Unterricht: ArRefG 81 (1990) 138-157; deutsch 157.

k720 MORE T.: *Telle* Émile V., Thomas More, LE MOINE et ÉRASME: BibHumRen 51 (1989) 77-105.

k722 MÜNTZER: ᴱ**Bräuer** Siegfried, *Junghans* Helmut, Der Theologe Thomas Müntzer; Untersuchungen zu seiner Entwicklung und Lehre. B/Gö 1989, Ev.-V./VR. 385 p.; ill.; 2 facsimiles [LuJb 57 (1990) p. 322, indicating 15 items cited].

k723 **Bubenheimer** Ulrich, T. Müntzer, Herkunft und Bildung. Leiden 1989, Brill. xx-359 p. – ᴿSixtC 21 (1990) 655-660 (J. M. *Stayer*).

k724 *Dreher* Luis H., Decadência da cristiandade e hermenêutica na teologia de Thomas Müntzer. REB 50 (1990) 858-895.

k725 *Friesen* Abraham, T. Muentzer, a destroyer of the godless; the making of a sixteenth-century religious revolutionary. Berkeley 1990, Univ. California. xiii-332 p. – ᴿSixtC 21 (1990) 660s (J. M. *Stayer*).

k726 *a) Friesen* Abraham, T. Müntzer and M. LUTHER; – *b) Baylor* Michael G., Theology and politics in the thought of T. Müntzer; the case of the elect: ArRefG 79 (1988) 59-79; deutsch 80 / 81-101; deutsch 102.

k727 **Goertz** Hans-Jürgen, T. Müntzer, Mystiker, Apokalyptiker, Revolutionär. Mü 1989, Beck. 215 p. – ᴿSixtC 21 (1990) 665s (J. M. *Stayer*).

k728 **Gritsch** E. W., T. Müntzer, a tragedy of errors 1989 → 5,k197: ᴿCathHR 76 (1990) 844s (A. *Friesen*: a gem); SWJT 33,2 (1990s) 64 (W. R. *Estep*); TLZ 115 (1990) 826-8 (U. *Bubenheimer*).

k729 *Jørgensen* Ninna, Hat Luther Müntzers Liturgiereform abgelehnt?: ArRefG 80 (1989) 47-67; Eng. 67.

k729* **La Rocca** Tommaso, Es ist Zeit; Apocalisse e storia; studio su Thomas Müntzer (1490-1525). Bo 1988, Cappelli. 212 p. Lit. 21.000. – ᴿHumBr 44 (1989) 612 (G. *Sansonetti*).

k730 ᵀᴱ**Matheson** Peter, The collected works of Thomas Müntzer (all except liturgies). E 1988, Clark. 490 p. – ᴿCathHR 76 (1990) 593s (L. II. *Zuck*); LuJb 57 (1990) 292s (E. W. *Gritsch*); ScotJT 43 (1990) 420-3 (W. P. *Stephens*).

k731 *Matheson* Peter, [T. Müntzer] The hammer, the sickle and the rainbow; sixteenth-century radicalism and its interpreters: TLond 93 (1990) 20-26.

k732 *Mau* Rudolf, Rollentausch bei der Müntzerrezeption? Zum Müntzerverständnis im Gedenkjahr 1989: BTZ 7 (1990) 66-77.

k733 **Scott** Tom, Thomas Müntzer; theology and revolution in the German Reformation. NY 1989, St. Martin's. xix-203 p. $30. 0-312-02679-X [TDig 37,384].

k734 *Stayer* James M., Thomas Müntzer in 1989; a review article [GRITSCH E., *al.*]: SixtC 21 (1990) 655-670.

k736 **Steinmetz** Max, Thomas Müntzers Weg nach Allstedt; eine Studie zu seiner Frühentwicklung. B 1988, Deutscher-V. 295 p. DM 45,50. – 3-326-00402-8. – ᴿSixtC 21 (1990) 113 (M. G. *Baylor*).

k737 **Vogler** Günter, Thomas Müntzer. B 1989, Dietz. 326 p. – ᴿSixtC 21 (1990) 667-670 (J. M. *Stayer*).

k738 [Ŝevelev-] *Nasedka* Ivan (1570-1660; in:) Virševaja poezija ❻, Moskva 17° sec. Moskva 1989, Sovetskaja Rossija. 479 p. r 2.50. – ᴿProtestantesimo 45 (1990) 153-5 (C. G. *De Michelis*: due scritti, uno antiluterano; altro antiromano 'sostanzialmente luterano su Mt 16,18').

k738* OETINGER: **Weyer-Menkhoff** Martin, Christus, das Heil der Natur; Entstehung und Systematik der Theologie Friedrich C. Oetingers [Diss. 1984]: Arbeiten zur Geschichte des Pietismus 27. Gö 1990, Vandenhoeck & R. 334 p. DM 98. 3-525-55811-2. – ᴿLuthTKi 14 (1990) 128s (Ingetraut *Ludolphy*).

k739 OLEVIAN: *Holtmann* Wilhelm, *al.*, Caspar Olevian 1546-1587, ein evangelisch-reformierter Theologe aus Trier: Montatshefte für evangelische KG des Rheinlandes 37s (Dü 1988s) 1-12 [-344, < ZIT 90,184].

k740 PALLADIUS: **Ertner** Jørgen, Peder Palladius' lutherske teologi [Hab.-D.]. K 1988, Akademisk. 766 p.; dt. Zsf. – ᴿLuJb 57 (1990) 293s (S. *Kieldegaard-Pedersen*); ST 44 (1990) 149-151.

k740* PETRI: **Gardemeister** Christer, Den suveräne Guden; en studie i Olavus Petris teologi: diss. Lund 1989. Lund 1989, Univ. 304 p. – ST 44 (1990) 151s.

k741 PFLUG: *a) Kremer* Ulrich M., Petrus MOSELLANUS und Julius Pflug; ein Beitrag zur Geschichte des Einflusses von Erasmus in Sachsen; – *b) Stupperich* Robert, MELANCHTHON und J. Pflug: → 670, ᴱ**Neiss** Elmar, *Pollet* J. V., Pflugiana 1990, 3-22 / 43-59.

k741* PROPST: **Rudloff** Ortwin, Bonae litterae et Lutherus; Texte und Untersuchungen zu den Anfängen der Theologie des Bremer Reformators Jakob Propst: Forschungen zur Bremischen Kirchengeschichte 14, 1985 → 2,d662; DM 68: ᴿTLZ 115 (1990) 828-831 (S. *Bräuer*).

k742 SCHATZGEYER: **Schäfer** P., K. Schatzgeyer, Von der waren ... freyheit: CCath 40, 1987 → 4,k180; 5,k201: ᴿJEH 41 (1990) 160s (D. *Bagchi*: he was Franciscan provincial).

k743 SOZZINI L. & F.: ᴱ**Rotondo** Antonio, Lelio Sozzini, opere: ST Cinquecento 1. F 1986, Olschki. 429 p. Lit. 86.000. – ᴿHeythJ 31 (1990) 94s (A. *Hamilton*); Protestantesimo 45 (1990) 152s (U. *Rozzo*); RivStoLR 26 (1990) 622-5 (Lucia *Felici*).

k744 **Gomes** Alan W., Faustus Socinus' 'De Jesu Christo servatore' [1578] Part III; historical introduction, translation and critical notes: diss. Fuller Theol. Sem. Pasadena 1990. 414 p. 91-07407. – DissA 51 (1990s) 3439-A.

k745 STANCARO: *Urban* Wacław, Die grossen Jahre der stancarianischen 'Häresie' (1559-1563), ᵀ*Rommel* Ludwig: ArRefG 81 (1990) 309-318; Eng. 318s, Francesco Stancaro's second stay in Poland.

k746 STAUPITZ: *Foket* Monique, LUTHER et Staupitz I: FoiTemps 20 (1990) 69-83. ...

k747 ᴱ**Wetzel** Richard, Johannes von Staupitz, Tübinger Predigten: Sämtliche Schriften 1. B 1987, de Gruyter. xii-637 p.; 2 facsim. DM 258. – ᴿAugLv 38 (1988) 257s (A. de *Meijer*).

k748 *a) Wetzel* Richard, Staupitz antibarbarus; Beobachtungen zur Rezeption heidnischer Antike in seinen Tübinger Predigten; – *b) Oberman*

Heiko A., Captivitas babylonica; die Kirchenkritik des Johann von Staupitz: ➤ 61, ᶠGRAF ZU DOHNA L., 1989, 107-129 / 97-106.

k749 **Wriedt** Markus, Gnade und Erwählung bei Johann von Staupitz; eine Untersuchung zu den theologiegeschichtlichen Bedingungen der Entwicklung der reformatorischen Theologie M. LUTHERS: ev. Diss. ᴰLohse; Hamburg 1989s. – TR 86,515, RTLv 22, p. 601.

k750 *Zumkeller* Adolar, Johannes von Staupitz [Freund Luthers] und die klosterliche Reformbewegung: AnAug 52 (1989) 31-49.

k751 TURRETTINI: *Klauber* Martin I., *Sunshine* Glenn S., Jean-Alphonse Turrettini on biblical accommodation; Calvinist or Socinian?: CalvinT 25 (1990) 7-27.

k752 TYNDALE: **Smeeton** Donald D., Lollard themes in... Tyndale 1986 ➤ 3,g613 ... 5,k206: ᴿJAAR 58 (1990) 149-152 (M. W. *Anderson*).

k753 VALDÉS: **Otto** Wolfgang, Juan de Valdés und die Reformation in Spanien im 16. Jahrhundert. Fra 1989, P. Lang. 596 p. Fs 82. 3-631-40508-1. – ᴿRivStoLR 26 (1990) 616-621 (L. *D'Ascia*).

k754 WYCLIF: **Hudson** Anne, The premature reformation; Wycliffite... 1988 ➤ 4,k188*; 5,k209: ᴿAnglTR 71 (1989) 317-9 (D. *Siegenthaler*).

k755 *Hudson* Anne, Wyclif, John c. 1335/1384: ➤ 837*, DMA 12 (1989) 706-711.

k756 **Jeffrey** David L., The law of love; English spirituality in the age of Wyclif. GR/Exeter 1988, Eerdmans/Paternoster. x-404 p. £13.25. 0-8028-0299-0. – ᴿExpTim 101 (1989s) 156 (A. *Louth*, also on ALLEN R., ROLLE).

k757 ᴱ**Kenny** Anthony, Wyclif in his time 1986 ➤ 5,k210: ᴿAnglTR 71 (1989) 104s (D. R. *Holeton*); RicStoSocR 83 (1988) 230-3 (A. *Landi*).

k758 *Stacey* John, John Wyclif as theologian: ExpTim 101 (1989s) 134-140.

k759 ZWINGLI: ᵀᴱ**Courvoisier** Jacques † 1988, Huldrych Zwingli, De la Parole de Dieu: TextesDD. P 1989, Beauchesne. 70 p. – ᴿRHPR 70 (1990) 376s (M. *Chevallier* †).

k760 **Hamm** Berndt, Zwinglis Reformation der Freiheit 1988 ➤ 5,k215: ᴿScotJT 43 (1990) 126s (A. *Heron*).

k761 **Hoburg** Ralf, 'In deinem Licht werden wir das Licht sehen'; Hermeneutik und Schriftauslegung bei H Zwingli bis 1522: Diss. Münster 1990, ᴰBrecht. 406 p. – RTLv 22, p. 600.

k762 *Jörg* Ruth, Zwingli und die Reformation in Zürich im Spiegel der Chronik von Johannes SALAT: ArRefG 80 (1989) 88-103; Eng. 104 [105-122, *Wendel* Lee P.].

k763 **Pollet** J. V., Huldrych Zwingli, biographie et théologie: Histoire et société, 1988 ➤ 5,k216b: ᴿBibHumRen 51 (1989) 505s (M. *Campagnolo*: the French original).

k764 **Schindler** Alfred, Zwingli und die Kirchenväter. Z 1984, Waisenhaus/Beer. 112 p. [= ➤ 3,g622]. – ᴿRTPhil 122 (1990) 569s (Iréna *Backus*).

k765 *a) Schindler* Alfred, Zwinglis Randbemerkungern in den Büchern seiner Bibliothek; – *b) Bächtold* Hans U., *Haag* Hans J., Literatur zur zwinglischen Reformation: Zwingliana 18,1s (1989) 1-11 / 166.. [< ZIT 90,116].

Y4.5 *Exegesis post-reformatoria* – **Historical criticism to 1800.**

k766 *Argyriou* Astérios, La Bible dans l'Orthodoxie grecque du XVIIᵉ siècle: RevSR 64 (1990) 141-168.

k767 ᴱ**Armogathe** Jean-R.,   Le grand siècle [XVII, malgré ➤ 5,k291] et la Bible: BTT 6. P 1989, Beauchesne. F 480. 2-7010-1156-6. – ᴿEsprVie 100 (1990) 236s (L. *Monloubou,* surtout sur PASCAL); DivThom 92 (1989) 179-181 (Y. *Poutet*); ÉTRel 65 (1990) 461s (H. *Bost*, très riche, même sans chapîtres sur LE CLERC, LA PEYRÈRE, E. LÉVITA); NRT 112 (1990) 418s (V. *Roisel*).

k768 ᴱ**Besier** G., *Gestrich* C.,   450 Jahre Evangelische Theologie in Berlin [-Brandenburg 1539]. Gö 1989, Vandenhoeck & R. 646p.; ill. DM 98. 3-525-55416-8. – ᴿTsTNijm 30 (1990) 410s (T. *Schoof*).

k769 *Brossier* François,   Les références à la Bible dans les catéchismes du XVIIᵉ siècle: RICathP 29 (1989) 37-43.

k770 **Butler** Jon,   Awash in a sea of faith; Christianizing the American people [1620-1860]. CM 1990, Harvard. xii-360p. $29.50. – ᴿAnglTR 72 (1990) 473-6 (J. F. *Woolverton*); TS 51 (1990) 543-5 (E. G. *Ernst*).

k772 **Dippel** Stewart A.,   A study of religious thought at Oxford and Cambridge, 1590-1640: 1987 ➤ 4,k204*: ᴿJAAR 58 (1990) 491s (J. von *Rohr*).

k773 ᴱ**Dupré** Louis, *Saliers* Don E. (*Meyendorff* John),   Christian spirituality, post-Reformation and modern: EWSp 18. xxvi-566p. $49.50. 0-8245-0766-5 [TDig 37,255].

k774 *Field* Clive D.,   Sources for the study of Protestant nonconformity in the John Rylands University Library of Manchester: BJRyL 71,2 (1989) 141-157.

k775 **Fuchs** Eric, *Grappe* Christian,   Le droit de résister; le protestantisme face au pouvoir: Entrée libre 7. Genève 1900, Labor et fides. 96p. F 55. 2-8309-0599-7. – ᴿÉTRel 65 (1990) 637s (H. *Bost*).

k776 **Funkenstein** Amos,   Theology and the scientific imagination... to 17h cent. 1986 ➤ 4,k205; 5,k227: ᴿSpeculum 64 (1989) 163s (J. D. *North*).

k777 *Hawkes* R. M.,   The logic of assurance in English Puritan theology: WestTJ 52 (1990) 247-261.

k778 *Katz* David S.,   The Abendana brothers and the Christian Hebraists of seventeenth-century England: JEH 40 (1989) 28-52. ➤ k817.

k779 **Olmo Lete** Gregorio del,   Semitistas catalanes del siglo XVIII: OrBarc 5. Sabaudell 1988, AUSA. 276p. 84-86329-29-9. – ᴿBO 47 (1990) 179s (F. *García Martínez*).

k780 **Parker** Kenneth I.,   The English sabbath, 1558-1660; a study of doctrine and discipline from the Reformation to the Civil War. C 1988, Univ. 224p. $42.50. 0-521-30535-7. – ᴿAndrUnS 28 (1990) 181s (W. *Douglas*).

k781 **Podskalsky** Gerhard,   Griechische Theologie... 1453-1821: 1988 ➤ 3, g633 ... 5,k236: ᴿRHE 85 (1990) 758-761 (A. de *Halleux*: théologie sans être 'science systématique rationnelle').

k782 **Primus** John H.,   Holy time; moderate Puritanism and the Sabbath. Macon GA, Mercer Univ. 184p. [JAAR 58,163].

k783 **Reinhardt** Klaus,   Bibelkommentare spanischer Autoren (1500-1700), I: Medi[a]evalia et Humanistica 5. M 1990, Cons.Sup.Inv. xx-283p.

k784 **Rupp** Ernest G.,   Religion in England, 1688-1791: History of the Christian Church 1986 ➤ 3,g635: ᴿHeythJ 31 (1990) 354s (A. *Hamilton*).

k785 **Scholder** K.,   The birth of modern critical theology; origins and problems of biblical criticism in the seventeenth century [Ursprünge und Probleme der Bibelkritik 1966 ➤ 69,9418], ᵀ*Bowden* J. L/Ph 1990, SCM/Trinity. 184p. £10.50. 0-334-02442-0 [BL 91, 120, J. W. *Rogerson*: too little clue to what has happened since 1800 — or 1966].

k786 *Strohm* Stefan, Glaube und Offenbarung im Zeitalter der Aufklärung: Blätter für Württembergische Kirchengeschichte 89 (1989) 99-151 [< ZIT 90,547].

k787 **Todd** Margo, Christian humanism and the Puritan social order. C 1987, Univ. 293 p. – ᴿRTPhil 122 (1990) 287s (Maria-Cristina *Pitassi*).

k788 [*Tudur*] *Jones* R., Union with Christ, the existential nerve of Puritan piety: TyndB 41 (1990) 186-208.

k789 *Walker* Daniele, La confessione di fede Battista del 1689, le sue origini e la sua teologia: STEv 1 NS (1989) 107-131 + 3 facsimile [135-191 (-207), documentazione].

k790 **Washington** Joseph R., Puritan race virtue, vice and values 1620-1820: AmerUnivSt. NY 1988, Lang. 507 p. $58. – ᴿTTod 47 (1990s) 106 (D. A. *Wells*: J. EDWARDS defended Indians but not Blacks).

k791 **Westerkamp** Marilyn J., The triumph of the laity; Scots-Irish piety and the Great Awakening, 1625-1760. Ox 1988, UP. 266 p. $30. – ᴿJAAR 58 (1990) 527-9 (W. G. *McLoughlin*).

---

k792 BAXTER: *Cornick* David, Richard Baxter, Autobiography [1686]: Exp-Tim 101 (1989s) 258-262.

k793 BAYLE: *Bost* Hubert, Histoire et critique de l'histoire chez Pierre Bayle, la Critique générale de l'histoire du Calvinisme de Mr. Maimbourg, 1682-1683: RHPR 70 (1990) 69-108; Eng. 145.

k794 *Whelan* Ruth, Images de la Réforme chez Pierre Bayle, ou l'histoire d'une déception [1682, 'met égalemeut en cause la bonne foi des historiens protestants' p. 87]: RTPhil 122 (1990) 85-107; Eng. 142.

k795 BENGEL: *a) Haug* Richard, Bengels Theologie der Weltgeschichte; – *b) Breymayer* Reinhard, 'Gnomon typusque vitae christianae'; zum emblematischen Hintergrund des 'Gnomon-'Begriffs bei Heinrich ORAEUS (1584-1646) und bei Johann Albrecht Bengel (1687-1752): ➤ 156, ᶠSCHÄFER G., BLWKG 88 (1988) 324-334 / 289-323.

k796 CHAUNCY: *Gibbs* Norman B. & Lee W., Charles Chauncy [1705-1787]; a theology in two portraits: HarvTR 83 (1990) 259-268; 269s, 2 portraits.

k797 CLAUDIUS: *Freund* Winfried, 'Seht ihr den Mond dort stehen?' Matthias Claudius [geb. 1740] und die religiöse Selbsterfahrung im Zeitalter der Vernunft: EvT 50 (1990) 375-390.

k798 COTTON: *Jinkins* Michael, John Cotton and the antinomian controversy, 1636-1638; a profile of experiential individualism in American Puritanism: ScotJT 43 (1990) 321-349.

k799 EDWARDS: **Jenson** Robert W., America's theologian... J. Edwards 1988 ➤ 4,k216; 5,k245: ᴿJAAR 58 (1990) 290-3 (D. L. *Weddle*); ScotJT 43 (1990) 423-5 (M. *Jinkins*).

k800 **Lee Sang Hyun,** The philosophical theology of Jonathan Edwards. Princeton 1988, Univ. 248 p. $35. – ᴿInterpretation 44 (1990) 218.220 (W. S. *Johnson*).

k801 **Vető** Miklos, La pensée de J. Edwards 1987 ➤ 3,g643; 5,k247: ᴿRTLv 21 (1990) 233s (M. *Clairbois*); TR 86 (1990) 475-7 (A. *Ganoczy*).

k802 EICHHORN: *Seidel* B., J. G. Eichhorn; Konstruktionsmechanismen in den Anfängen einer historisch-kritischen Theoriebildung: WZHalle 39 (1990) 73-81 [< ZAW 103,289].

k803 FOX: *Punshon* John, George Fox's journal [d.1691]: ExpTim 102 (1990s) 35-39.

k804 HAMANN: *Marinelli* Giancarlo, Esperienza e rivelazione; le 'Meditazioni bibliche' di J. G. Hamann (1730-1788): Studium 86 (R 1990) 751-775.

k805 HERBERT: **Veith** Gene E., Reformation spirituality; the religion of George Herbert [1593-1633]. Lewisburg 1985, Bucknell Univ. 289 p. – REvQ 62 (1990) 285-8 (A. G. *Newell*).

k806 JANSENIUS: *Ceyssens* Lucien, Autour de la bulle Unigenitus; le cardinal Guillaume DUBOIS (1656-1723): RÉAug 35 (1989) 151-170.

k807 **Ceyssens** L., *Tans* J., Autour de l'Unigenitus 1987 → 3,g648... 5,k256: RColcFranc 60 (1990) 363-5 (C. *Cargnoni*); NedTTs 43 (1989) 341s (J. *Visser*).

k808 E**Eijl** E. J. M. van, Image de Jansénius 1985/7 → 4,557... 5,k261: RJEH 40 (1990) 463s (J. Mc*Manners*).

k809 E**Hamon** Leo, Du Jansénisme à la laïcité; le Jansénisme et les origines de la déchristianisation. P 1987, Sciences de l'Homme. xii-245 p. F 140 [RelStR 17, 265, J. *Gres-Gayer*].

k810 **Orcibal** Jean, Jansénius d'Ypres (1585-1638). P 1989, ÉtAug. 160 p. [RTLv 21,125].

k811 *Lamberigts* M., 'Centrum voor de studie van het Jansenisme': ETL 66 (1990) 236-9 [240s, *Soetens* C., Centre Lumen Gentium].

k812 LESSING: **Freund** G., Theologie im Widerspruch; die Lessing-GOEZE-Kontroverse. Stu 1989, Kohlhammer. viii-289 p. DM 69. 3-17-010577-9. – RLuthTKi 13 (1989) 180s (E. *Volk*); TsTNijm 30 (1990) 95s (T. *Brattinga*).

k813 **Lüpke** Johannes von, Wege der Weisheit; Studien zu Lessings Theologiekritik: GöTArb 41, 1989 → 5,k268; 3-525-87595-6: RGregorianum 71 (1990) 592s (X. *Tilliette*: 'méthodique et sagace', deserving better than the saw-tooth margins of a second-rate thesis); Protestantesimo 45 (1990) 325s (V. *Bernardi*); TPhil 65 (1990) 606s (A. *Schilson*).

k814 **Niewöhner** Friedrich, Veritas sive Varietas, Lessings Toleranzparabel und das Buch Von den drei Betrügern: Bibliothek der Aufklärung 5, Heid 1988 → 5,k270; DM 118 pa.: RTLZ 115 (1990) 288-291 (W. *Gericke*); TPhil 65 (1990) 429-431 (J. *Splett*).

k815 *Seckler* Max, Zu Lessings 'theologiekritischen' Schriften; aus Anlass einer Neuausgabe [SCHILSON A. 1989]: TüTQ 170 (1990) 299-303.

k815* LIGUORI: *Lissa* G., Tra innovazione e tradizione, S. Alfonso M. de Liguori († 1787) nel dibattito sull'utilizzazione dei testi biblici: → 617*, E*Giannantonio* P., Alfonso 1988/90, 161-204.

k816 MENDELSOHN: *a) Schweid* Eliezer, The impact of enlightenment on religion; – *b) Wurzburger* Walter S., The enlightenment, the emancipation and the Jewish religion; – *c) Morgan* Michael L., Mendelsohn's defense of reason in *Jerusalem*: Judaism 38 (1989) 389-398 / 399-407 [-448 *al.*] / 449-459 [-537, *al.*].

k817 SIMON R., *al.*: **McKane** William, Selected Christian Hebraists 1989 → 5,k276: RBL (1990) 19 (S. C. *Reif*); BR 6,6 (1990) 11s (G. *Howard*: they favored knowing, rather than actually knew, Hebrew); CritRR 3 (1990) 158s (M. P. *Graham*); ExpTim 101 (1989s) 118s (J. W. *Rogerson*). → k778.

k817* *a) Iofrida* Manlio, L'originale smarrito; scrittura e storia nell'opera di Richard Simon; – *b) Bonola* Gianfranco, Un filo scoperto; tracce dell'attenzione dell' 'Aufklärung' teologica per il razionalismo radicale (J. S. SEMLER -L. MEIJER); – *c) Cazzaniga* Gian Mario, L'utopia sociale e radicalismo massonico in Nicolas de BONNEVILLE: ➤ 526*, AnStoEseg 7,1 (1990) 139-155 / 157-185 / 293-310.

k818 SPINOZA: *Auwers* Jean-Marie, L'interprétation de la Bible chez Spinoza; ses présupposés philosophiques [BARRET, KRIEGEL, BLANDINE 1988]: RTLv 21 (1990) 199-213; Eng. 279.

k819 *Freedman* R. David, [Spinoza B.] The father of modern biblical scholarship: ➤ 75, Mem. HELD M., JANES 19 (1989) 31-38.

k820 *Klever* W. N. W., Schrift en rede, of: Over een vermeende tegenstelling tussen Spinoza en [Lodewijk] Meyer: NedTTs 44 (1990) 223-241; Eng. 245.

k821 **Krochmalnik** Daniel, Praktische Philosophie als Religionsersatz; Spinozas Auseinandersetzung mit dem Judentum [Diss.München]. Mü 1988, Univ. Fak. Philosophie. 235 p. – ᴿRÉJ 149 (1990) 240s (M.-R. *Hayoun*: étudiant aussi de G. NAHON à l'École Maïmonide).

k821* *Pellecchia* Pasquale, Un caso spinoso di 'Spinozismo' scolastico [risposta alle critiche di MOLINARI A.]: DivThom 93 (1990) [79-117] 118-131.

k822 *Polka* Brayton, Spinoza and the separation between philosophy and theology: JRelSt 16 (Cleveland 1988) 91-119 [< ZIT 90,865].

k823 **Yovel** Yirmiyahu, Spinoza and other heretics, I. The Marrano of reason; II. The adventures of immanence. Princeton 1989, Univ. xiii-244 p.; xv-225 p. $24.50; $29.50; both $45 [RelStR 17,173, J. M. *Harris*].

k824 **Meyer** Louis [ami de Spinoza], La philosophie interprète de l'Écriture sainte [lat.], ᵀ*Lagrée* Jacqueline, *Moreau* Pierre-F.: Horizons. P 1988, Intertextes. 267 p. F 149. – ᴿRHR 207 (1990) 105s (F. *Laplanche*: sur les rapports de l'herméneutique biblique avec la philosophie).

k824* TÖLLNER: **Pfizenmaier** Martin, Mit Vernunft glauben — fides ratione formata; die Umformung der Rechtfertigungslehre in der Theologie der deutschen Aufklärung dargestellt am Werk Johann G. Töllners (1724-1774) ➤ 5,k282 [Diss. ᴰ*Baur* Jörg]: TMg B-10. Stu 1986, Calwer. xxxiii-618 p. DM 68. 3-7668-0784-6. – ᴿLuthTKi 14 (1990) 130-2 (G. *Martens*: mancherlei Pedanterien; ignoriert C. OLEARIUS).

k825 VARLET: *Thériault* Serge A., L'articulation christologique comme forme de la thématique ecclésiologique dans trois textes de Dominique-Marie Varlet [1678-1742] aux origines du vieux-catholicisme: IkiZ 80 (1990) 40-58.

k825* WESLEY: *Baker* Frank, John Wesley, biblical commentator: BJRyL 71,1 (1989) 109-120.

k826 *Brantley* Richard E., The common ground of Wesley and EDWARDS: HarvTR 83 (1990) 271-303.

k827 a) *Maddox* Randy, John Wesley and eastern Orthodoxy; influences, convergences, and differences; – b) *Snyder* Howard, John Wesley and MACARIUS the Egyptian: AsbTJ 45,2 (1990) 29-53 / 55-60.

k828 **Rack** Henry D., Reasonable enthusiast; John Wesley and the rise of Methodism. Ph 1989, Trinity. xvi-656 p. $40. ᴿExpTim 101,5 top choice (1989s) 129s (C. S. *Rodd*); TS 51 (1990) 749-751 (J. D. *Nelson*: heavy).

k829 *Rack* Henry D., John Wesley's 'Journal': ExpTim 101 (1989s) 228-230.

k830 WIEST: **Müller** Bernhard, Vernunft und Theologie... bei Stephan Wiest, ᴰ1988 ➤ 5,k290: ᴿTLZ 115 (1990) 850-2 (U. *Kern*).

Y5   *Saeculum XIX* – **Exegesis** – **19th Century.**

k831 **Bebbington** D. W., Evangelicalism in modern Britain; a history from the 1730s to the 1980s, 1988 ➤ 5,k292; 0-04-941019-9: ᴿExpTim 101 (1989s) 24s (J. *Kent*); ScotBEv 9 (1990) 133s (D. *Smith*).

k832 **Brown** Colin,   Jesus in European Protestant thought 1778-1860[2] [[1]1985],
     1988 ➤ 5,k293:   [R]EvQ 62 (1990) 89s (G. L. *Bray*).

k833 **Brückmann** Hans,   Bibelverbreitung im Rheinland; 175 Jahre Evan-
     gelisches Bibelwerk im Rheinland, gegründet als Bergische Bibelge-
     sellschaft im Jahre 1814.   Köln 1989, Rheinland.   x-404 p. – [R]RHE 85
     (1990) 463 (P.-M. *Bogaert*).

k834 **Cameron** Nigel M.,   Biblical higher criticism and the defense of
     infallibilism in 19th century Britain: TStRel 33, [D]1987 ➤ 3,g684; 5,k264:
     [R]JEH 40 (1989) 315s (B. M. G. *Reardon*); ScotBEv 7 (1989) 133s (F. F.
     Bruce).

k835 **Cashdollar** Charles D.,   The transformation of theology, 1830-1890;
     positivism and Protestant thought in Britain and America 1989 ➤ 5,k295:
     [R]JTS 41 (1990) 768s (D. *Brown*); TS 51 (1990) 158-160 (J. C. *Livingston*).

k836 *Drobner* Hubertus R.,   Die Professoren der theologischen Fakultät
     Paderborn 1773-1989: TGL 80 (1990) 419-441.

k837 **Drury** John,   Critics of the Bible 1724-1873:   1989 ➤ 5,k234; £10 pa. –
     [R]TLond 93 (1990) 242s (R. *Morgan*).

k838 *Fitzmier* John R.,   Becoming proper partners [i.e. history and the social
     sciences]; the Religion in North America series by Indiana University
     Press [6 volumes so far, including *Chidester* D. on Jonestown; *Andrews*
     W., Three black women's autobiographies]: RelStR 16 (1990) 97-103.

k839 **Fogarty** Gerald P.,   American Catholic biblical scholarship 1989 ➤ 4,
     k245; 5,k298:   [R]CalvinT 25 (1990) 279s (A. J. *Griffioen*); [R]Exp 87 (1990)
     351s (E. G. *Hinson*: sorry he stops 1965); Thomist 54 (1990) 355-7 (L.
     Boadt); TS 51 (1990) 157s (J. T. *Ellis*).

k840 **Grane** Leif,   Die Kirche im 19. Jh. — europäische Perspektiven,
     [T]*Wesemann* Monika: UTB 1425.   Gö 1987, Vandenhoeck & R.   291 p.
     DM 27,80 [TR 87,288, K.J. *Rivinius*].

k841 **Gundert** W.,   Geschichte der deutschen Bibelgesellschaften 1987 ➤ 3,
     g686; 4,k246:   [R]TLZ 114 (1989) 289s (M. *Brecht*).

k842 **Hilton** Boyd,   The age of atonement; the influence of evangelicalism on
     social and economic thought, 1785-1865:   [R]JTS 41 (1990) 766-8 (M.
     Hennell).

k843 **Hughes** R.,   *Allen* C.,   Illusions of innocence 1988 ➤ 4,k248; 5,k304:
     [R]CathHR 75 (1989) 729s (E. S. *Gaustad*).

k844 **Hylson-Smith** Kenneth,   Evangelicals in the Church of England 1734-
     1984.   E 1989, Clark.   411 p. £20.   0-567-09454-5. – [R]ExpTim 101 (1989s)
     24s (J. *Kent*: needed replacement of G. R. BALLEINE 1908).

k845 [E]**Kauffmann** Christopher J.,   The bicentennial history of the Catholic
     Church in America 1989 ➤ 5,477:   [R]TorJT 6 (1990) 300-4 (B. *Clarke*);
     TTod 47 (1990s) 86, 88s (A. M. *Greeley*: except for FOGARTY on bishops
     [➤ m64] a disgrace to American Catholic scholarship).

k846 **Kenis** L.,   De theologische faculteit te Leuven in de negentiende
     eeuw 1834-1889: diss. [D]*Boudens* R., Lv 1989.   LI-1053 p. – TsTNijm 30
     (1990) 189.

k847 [E]**Kennelly** Karen,   American Catholic women, a historical exploration.
     NY 1988, Macmillan.   256 p. $25.   0-02-917302-7. – [R]CathHR 76 (1990)
     149s (Margaret S. *Thompson*: a service though in a misnamed series).

k848 **Marty** M.,   Modern American Religion 1, 1986 ➤ 2,d739 ... 5,k305:
     [R]JScStR 27 (1988) 141s (M. *Valeri*).

k849 [E]**Parsons** Gerald,   Religion in Victorian Britain, I. Traditions; II.
     Controversies; III. ([E]**Moore** James R.) Sources; IV. Interpretations.
     Manchester 1988, Univ. [RelStR 17,77, D. L. *Pals*: no pp.].

k850 **Pelikan** Jaroslav, Christian doctrine and modern culture (since 1700): The Christian Tradition 5. Ch 1989, Univ. 416 p. $30. 0-226-65378-1. – RAnglTR 72 (1990) 228-230 (L. *Urban*); TS 51 (1990) 339-341 (D. K. *McKim*).

k851 ESmart Ninian, *al.*, Nineteenth century religious thought in the west 1985/8 ➤ 1,399.f934 ... 5,k309: RRTPhil 122 (1990) 288s (K. *Blaser*, but not 'Swart' as in title; index p. 584 correct).

k852 **Smend** Rudolf, Deutsche Alttestamentler in drei Jahrhunderten 1989 ➤ 5,358: RJTS 41 (1990) 763-5 (Joanna *Davson*); TR 86 (1990) 368s (H. *Reventlow*); ZkT 112 (1990) 90s (R. *Oberforcher*).

k853 **Sykes** Stephen, The identity of Christianity... Schleiermacher to Barth 1984 ➤ 65,d786 ... 4,k259: RTsTKi 60 (1989) 72s (Astri *Hauge*).

k854 **Vilanova** Evangelista, (*Hereu i Bohigas* Josep), Història de la teologia cristiana, III. Segles XVIII, XIX i XX; próleg *Alberigo* Giuseppe. Barc 1989, Fac. Teol. Catalunya / Herder. xviii-785 p. – RAntonianum 65 (1990) 683s (C. *Larrañaga*); QVidCr 152s (1990) 150-7-8 (F. *Manresa*, J. M. *Valverde*: una historia que fa pensar); RCatalT 15 (1990) 226-9 (J. M. *Rovira Bellòso*).

k855 BAUER: **Barnikol** E., Das entdeckte Christentum im Vormärz; Bruno Bauers Kampf gegen Religion und Christentum und Erstausgabe seiner Kampfschrift[2]. Aalen 1989, Scientia. viii-270 p. DM 115. – RWUNT A-15 (1990) 144s (A. *Fuchs*).

k856 **Bauer** Bruno, The trumpet of the last judgement against Hegel the atheist and antichrist [c. 1840], TStepelevich Lawrence: Studies in German thought 5. Lewiston NY 1989, Mellen. 207 p. $50. 0-88946-356-5 [TDig 37,250].

k857 BAUR: **Horton** H., The Tübingen school... Baur[2] [[1]1975]. GR 1990, Baker. xxxvi-288 p. $18. 0-8010-4344-1 [NTAbs 35,94: slightly revised].

k858 BOYCE: EGeorge Timothy, James Petigru Boyce, selected writings. Nv 1989, Broadman. 143 p. $7. – RCriswT 4 (1989s) 204s (B. *Mitchell*: influential Southern Baptist).

k859 BRIGGS: **Massa** M. S., Charles A. Briggs and the crisis of historical criticism [diss. Harvard, DHutchison W.]: HarvDissRel 25. Mp 1990, Fortress. xii-220 p. $17 pa. 0-8006-7079-5 [NTAbs 35,95].

k860 BROWNSON: *Burrows* Mark S., The Catholic revision of an American myth; the eschatology of Orestes Brownson as an apology of American Catholicism: CathHR 76 (1990) 18-43.

k861 BRUMMELKAMP: **Velde** M. te, Anthony Brummelkamp (1811-1888). Barneveld 1988. 572 p. *f* 65. 90-601-5814-8. – RNedTTs 44 (1990) 345s (W. *Nijenhuis*).

k861* CAMPBELL: *Olbricht* Thomas H., Alexander Campbell in the context of American biblical studies, 1810-1874: RestQ 33,1 (Abilene 1991) 13-28 [< ZIT 91,348].

k862 COLENSO: *Nicolson* R. B., The [Bishop William] Colenso sermon: ExpTim 101 (1989s) 369s.

k863 COMBA: **Biagetti** Stefania, Emilio Comba (1839-1904), storico della Riforma italiana e del movimento valdese medievale: Collana Fac. Valdese. T 1989, Claudiana. 127 p. Lit. 22.000. – RProtestantesimo 45 (1990) 226s (E. *Sfredda*).

k864 DREY: **Tiefensee** Eberhard, Die religiöse Anlage... J. S. Dreys 1988 ➤ 5,k316: RRHE 85 (1990) 766s (R. *Reinhardt*).

k865 FINNEY: **Hardman** Keith J., Charles Grandison Finney, 1792-1875, revivalist and reformer 1987 → 5,k318: ᴿAndrUnS 28 (1990) 162-5 (G. R. *Knight*, also on 1989 Finney memoirs).

k866 **Finney** Charles G., Memoirs [1876 ᴱ*Fairchild* James H.], ²ʳᵉᵛ*Rosell* Garth M., *Dupuis* Richard A. G. GR 1989, Zondervan. xlvii-736 p. $25. 0-310-45920-6 [TDig 37,262]. – ᴿAsbTJ 45,2 (1990) 88s (D. *Bundy*).

k867 FRANZELIN: **Walter** Peter, J. B. Franzelin 1987 → 3,g714; 4,k272: ᴿTR 86 (1990) 25s (K.-H. *Menke*); ZkT 112 (1990) 245s (A. *Felderer*).

k868 FYFE: **Gilson** Theo T., Robert Alexander Fyfe [Canadian Baptist † 1878]; his contemporaries and his influence. Burlington ON 1988, Welch. 358 p. – ᴿSR 19 (1990) 116s (Marguerite Van *Die*).

k869 GOLDZIHER: **Simon** Róbert, Ignáz Goldziher, his life and scholarship as reflected in his works and scholarship. Budapest/Leiden 1986, Hungarian Acad./Brill. 457 p.; ill. – ᴿJJS 41 (1990) 115-7 (E. *Ullendorff*: a goldmine, though neither 'pleasure' nor 'biography').

k870 GUNNING: **Lange** A. de, De verhouding tussen dogmatiek en godsdienstwetenschap binnen de theologie; een onderzoek naar de ontwikkeling van het theologiebegrip van J. H. Gunningᴶ (1829-1905) [proefschrift Kampen]. Kampen 1987, Mondiss. 294 p. ƒ 35. 90-6651-084-6. – ᴿTsTNijm 30 (1990) 210 (H. D. van *Hoogstraten*).

k871 HEGEL: **Asendorf** Ulrich, LUTHER und Hegel; Untersuchungen zur Grundlegung einer neuen systematischen Theologie: Mainz Abendl. Rel-G. 107. Wsb 1982, Steiner. 529 p. – ᴿTsTKi 60 (1989) 147s (T. *Austad*).

k872 *Brito* Emilio, Hegel et la religion [CODA P. 1987; D'AQUINO M. 1989; POTTIER B. 1990]: RTLv 21 (1990) 477-483.

k873 **Fessard** Gaston [1897-1978], Hegel, le Christianisme et l'histoire [inedita postuma], ᴱ*Sales* Michel: Théologiques. P 1990, PUF. 320 p. F 195. – ᴿÉtudes 373 (1990) 425 (J.-Y. *Calvez*); ZkT 112 (1990) 465s (W. *Kern*).

k874 O'REGAN Cyril J., The heterodox Hegel; Trinitarian ontotheology and Gnostic narrative: diss. Yale, ᴰ*Dupré* L. NHv 1989. 893 p. 90-15259. – DissA 51 (1990s) 193s-A; RelStR 17,191 without 'The heterodox'.

k875 **Hegel** Georg W. F., Gesammelte Werke, I. ᴱ*Nicolin* F., *Schüler* G. 1989; 15, ᴱ*Hogemann* F., *Jamme* C., 1990; 19 (Enzyklopädie 1827) ᴱ*Bonsiepen* W., *Lucas* H.-C. 1989. Ha 1989s, Meiner. xv-656 p.; v-333 p.; x-552 p. DM 342 + 168 + 186. – ᴿZkT 112 (1990) 437-9 (W. *Kern*).

k876 HODGE Charles (1797-1878), The way of life, ᴱ*Noll* Mark A. NY 1987, Paulist. 291 p. $15. – ᴿCritRR 2 (1989) 328-331 (D. *Jodock*).

k877 **Plaster** David R., The theological method of the Early Princetonians [ALEXANDER A., Hodge C.]: diss. Dallas Theol. Sem., 1989. 257 p. 90-20892. – DissA 51 (1990s) 900-A.

k878 ᴱ**Wells** David F., Reformed theology in America [= The Princeton Theology 1985, but with two parts now published separately as:] Dutch Reformed Theology / Southern Reformed Theology. GR 1989, Baker. xii-127 p. / xii-96 p. / xii-92 p. $8/8/7 pa. – ᴿBS 147 (1990) 252s (J. D. *Hannah*).

k879 **Noll** Mark A., Princeton and the Republic, 1768-1882; the search for a Christian enlightenment in the era of Samuel Stanhope Smith [president 1794-1812]. Princeton 1989, Univ. 340 p. $35. – ᴿTTod 47 (1990s) 188.190 (J. H. *Moorhead*); WestTJ 52 (1990) 390-2 (J. L. *Marshall*: how to un-dour Presbyterianism).

k880 HORT: **Patrick** G. A., F. J. A. Hort 1987 → 4,k276; 5,k321: RAnglTR 71 (1989) 320s (J. *Dunkly*); CritRR 2 (1989) 235-7 (E. J. *Epp*); TLZ 115 (1990) 113s (O. *Merk*).

k881 HUG: **Müller** Gerald, Johann L. Hug (1785-1846); seine Zeit, sein Leben und seine Bedeutung für die neutestamentliche Wissenschaft [Diss. D*Merk* O. – TR 86 (1990) 514; RTLv 22, p. 594]: Erlanger Studien 85. Erlangen 1990, Palm & E. v-292 p.; portr. 3-7896-0185-3.

k882 JOWETT: **Hinchliff** Peter, Benjamin Jowett and the Christian religion 1987 → 4,k278; 5,k322: RCritRR 2 (1989) 310-2 (W. *Baird*); JEH 40 (1989) 442-4 (K. *Robbins*, also on his letters to Florence NIGHTINGALE).

k883 KIERKEGAARD: *Petterson* Elaine, Kierkegaard's exegetical methodology [... in the hundreds of writings about him, there is very little about his use of the Bible]: SR 19 (1990) 351-9.

k884 KUENEN: *Hahn* Joachim, Kuenen, Abraham (1828-1891): → 857, TRE 20 (1990) 129-131.

k885 KUHN: **Wolf** Hubert, Ketzer oder Kirchenvater; Johannes Ev. Kuhn (1806-1887) – eine kirchenpolitische Biographie; zugleich ein Beitrag zur Geschichte des Ultramontanismus und der Römischen Inquisition im 19. Jt.; kath. Diss. D*Reinhardt*. Tübingen 1989s. – TR 96 (1990) 520.

k886 LACHMANN: *Sparks* Irving A., Lachmann, Karl (1791-1851), T*Balz* H. R.: → 857, TRE 20 (1990) 368-370.

k887 LAGARDE: *Heiligenthal* Roman, Lagarde, Paul Anton de (1829-1891): → 857, TRE 20 (1990) 375-8.

k888 LEO XIII: *Aubert* Roger, Leo XIII, T*Schäferdiek* K.: → 857, TRE 20 (1990) 748-753.

k889 LIGHTFOOT: *Bruce* F. F., J. B. Lightfoot (1828-1889), commentator and theologian: Evangel 7,2 (1989) 10-12 [< NTAbs 35,1].

k890 MEYER: *Kaiser* Peter, Heinrich A. W. Meyer, zum 190. Gb. des Begründers des Kritisch-exegetischen Kommentars über das NT: Deutsches Pfarrerblatt 90 (Essen 1990) 9-42 [< ZIT 90,197].

k891 MILLAR: *Davies* Ronald E., Robert Millar, an eighteenth-century Scottish LATOURETTE: EvQ 62 (1990) 143-156.

k892 MÖHLER [→ 6191]: *a) Gritz* Martin, Kirchengeschichte als Geschichte des Christentums; Anmerkungen zur Konzeption eines christlichen Geschichtsbildes bei Johann Adam Möhler; – *b) Rieger* Reinhold, J. A. Möhler Wegbereiter der Ökumene? Ein Topos im Licht neuer Texte; – *c) Kustermann* Abraham P., Pseudepigraphie und literarische Anleihen in der Tübinger Theologie des 19. Jhts.; ein Plädoyer für den kritischen Umgang mit Texten: ZKG 101 (1990) 249-266 / 267-286 / 287-300.

k893 NIETZSCHE: *Bucher* Rainer, Nietzsches Mensch und Nietzsches Gott; das Spätwerk als philosophisch-theologisches Programm: WüStFT 1, 1986 → 5,k329: RSalmanticensis 36 (1989) 233-5 (A. *González Montes*); ZkT 112 (1990) 115s (W. *Kern*).

k894 — *Biser* Eugen, Der Maximal-Gott [BUCHER R. 1986]: MüTZ 41 (1990) 291-3.

k895 *Makarushka* Irena, Nietzsche's critique of modernity; the emergence of hermeneutical consciousness: → 365, Semeia 51 (1990) 193-214.

k896 ORR: **Scorgie** Glen G., A call for continuity; the theological contribution of James Orr [Scots Presbyterian 1844-1913]. Macon GA 1988, Univ. xiv-189 p. – RSR 19 (1990) 264s (J. A. *Vissers*).

k897 OVERBECK: EBrändle R., *Stegemann* E. W., F. Overbecks unerledigte Anfragen 1988 → 5,444: RTZBas 46 (1990) 83-87 (E. *Valyi-Nagy*).

k897* REUSS: **Vincent** J. M., Leben und Werk des frühen Eduard Reuss;

ein Beitrag zu den geistesgeschichtlichen Voraussetzungen der Bibelkritik im zweiten Viertel des 19. Jahrhunderts [< Hab-Diss.Bochum 1984, ᴰ*Reventlow* H.]: BeitEvT 106. Mü 1990, Kaiser. 400 p. DM 135. – ᴿSNTU A-15 (1990) 145s (A. *Fuchs*).

k898 Scheeben: M.-J. Scheeben, teologo cattolico d'ispirazione tomista 1987/8 ⇥ 4,k398*b*; 5,k335: ᴿDivThom 93 (1990) 166-8 (L. *Elders*); ETL 66 (1990) 439s (A. *Vanneste*).

k899 **Murray** J. Courtney, ᴱ*Hughson* D. T., M. Scheeben on faith 1987 ⇥ 3,7277: ᴿCritRR 3 (1990) 441-3 (T. L. *Fallon*).

k899* Scheibel: ᴱ**Hauptmann** Peter, Gerettete Kirche; Studien zum Anliegen des Breslauer Lutheraners Johann G. Scheibel 1783-1843 [Symposion Oberursel 12.XI.1984]: Kirche im Osten 20. Gö 1987, Vandenhoeck & R. 187 p. DM 45. 3-525-56438-4. – ᴿLuthTKi 13 (1989) 177s (W. A. *Beinert*).

k900 Schleiermacher: *Clendenin* Daniel B., A conscious perplexity; Barth's interpretation of Schleiermacher: WestTJ 52 (1990) 281-301.

k900* *Groot* Nicolaas, Schleiermacher en Feuerbach; een confrontatie van Das Wesen des Christentums met de Glaubenslehre: NedTTs 43 (1989) 294-312; Eng. 330.

k901 *a*) *Korsch* D., Wort Gottes oder Frömmigkeit? Über den Sinn einer theologischen Alternative zwischen K. Barth und F. Schleiermacher; – *b*) *Gräb* W., Aktion und Kommunikation; die Lebenswirklichkeit der Gemeinde in der Pneumatologie S's und Barths; – *c*) *Leersum* E. van, Die Rationalität und die Offenbarungstheologie: ZdialektT 5,2 ('Leuenberg 1989' 1989) 195-216 / 237-268 / 279... [*al.*; < ZIT 90,268].

k902 *Meding* Wichmann von, Schleiermachers theologische Promotion: ZTK 87 (1990) 299-322.

k903 *Mildenberger* Friedrich, Die Verhältnisbestimmung von Theologie und Ökonomie als grundlegendes Strukturproblem einer modernen Dogmatik: ZTK 87 (1990) 340-358 ['Ökonomie' im Sinne von 'Konstitution der Wirklichkeit in Gott': on Schleiermacher (and Barth), not finance/poverty].

k904 *Peiter* Hermann, Schleiermachers 'Christliche Sittenlehre' als analytische Handlungstheorie: TZBas 46 (1990) 162-172 [97-124-161 ⇥ 9068; k908].

k905 *Root* Michael, Schleiermacher as innovator and inheritor; God, dependence, and election: ScotJT 43 (1990) 87-110.

k906 **Schleiermacher** F., Theologische Enzyklopädie [1813s], ᴱ*Sachs* W. 1987 ⇥ 5,k344: ᴿTR 86 (1990) 419-421 (H. *Peiter*).

k907 **Schleiermacher** F., Sulla religione; discorsi a quegli intellettuali che la disprezzano, ᵀᴱ*Spera* Salvatore. Brescia 1989, Queriniana. 251 p. Lit. 22.000. – ᴿProtestantesimo 45 (1990) 157s (A. *Sonelli*); RivScR 4 (1990) 277s (V. *Angiuli*).

k908 *Weiss* Peter, Die Hermeneutik F. Schleiermachers und R. Bultmanns in Vergleich: TZBas 46 (1990) 124-161.

k909 Smith Joseph: *Barlow* Philip L., Joseph Smith's revision of the Bible; fraudulent, pathologic, or prophetic?: HarvTR 83 (1990) 43-64.

k910 Smith W. R.: **Riesen** Richard A., Criticism and faith in Late Victorian Scotland... W. R. Smith... 1985 ⇥ 1,f930...4,k296: ᴿCBQ 52 (1990) 724-6 (J. R. *Huddleston*: fine).

k911 Stuart: **Giltner** John H., Moses Stuart 1988 ⇥ 4,k300; 5,k350: ᴿCritRR 3 (1990) 68-71 (M. A. *Noll*).

k912 *Granquist* Mark, The role of 'common sense' in the hermeneutics of Moses Stuart: HarvTR 83 (1990) 305-319.

k913 WHITE: **Mustard** Andrew G., James White and Seventh-Day Adventist organization; historical development, 1844-1881: diss. 12. Berrien Springs MI 1988, Andrews Univ. vii-320 p. $15 pa. – ᴿAndrUnS 28 (1990) 99s (J. *Moon*).

k914 WOLTER: *Petzolt* Stephan, Maurus Wolter [Gustav Rudolph, O.S.B., 4.VI.1825-8.VII.1890], ein Leben im Geist der Liturgie: ErbAuf 66 (1990) 349-359.

Y5.5 *Crisis modernistica* – **The Modernist era.**

k915 *Aubert* Roger, L'intégrisme au début du XXᵉ siècle: Foi Temps 20 (1990) 26-57 [< RHE 85 (1990) 178].

k916 **Azam** Gilbert † (1940-86), ᴱMme *Azam*, El modernismo desde dentro. Barc 1989, Anthropos. 187 p. – ᴿBLitEc 91 (1990) 299s (J. *Darrabat*).

k917 *Cárcel Ortí* Vincente, Católicos liberales e integristas en la España del novecientos: AnSacT 63s (1990) 285-422.

k918 *a) Farley* Edward, The modernist element in Protestantism; – *b) Moorhead* James M., The ambiguous legacy of modernism: TTod 47 (1990s) 131-144 / 145-8.

k919 ᴱ*Fitzer* Joseph, Romance and the rock; nineteenth-century Catholics on faith and reason [part of last section is on modernism]: Fortress texts in modern theology. Minneapolis 1989, Fortress. ix-386 p. $20. 0-8006-3207-9 [TDig 37,383].

k920 *Graf* Friedrich W., *Tanner* Klaus, Kultur, theologiegeschichtlich [... Modernistenkrise]: ➔ 857, TRE 20 (1990) 187-209 [-243 *al.*, Kulturkampf, Kulturprotestantismus].

k921 **Kurtz** Lester R., The politics of heresy; the modernist crisis... 1986 ➔ 2,d806... 5,k354: ᴿHeythJ 31 (1990) 92s (G. *Daly*); JScStR 27 (1988) 137s (J. A. *Varacalli*).

k922 **O'Gara** Margaret, Triumph in defeat 1988 ➔ 4,k310; 5.k356: ᴿArHistConc 20 (1988) 495-7 (M. *Buschkühl*); CathHR 75 (1989) 718s (W. J. *Portier*); Dialog 28 (1989) 240 (J. *Gros*: useful); NewTR 3,1 (1990) 98s (J. E. *Linnan*); SR 19 (1990) 114s (L. F. *Murphy*); TPhil 65 (1990) 607-610 (K. *Schatz*).

k923 *O'Gara* Margaret, Listening to forgotten voices; the French minority bishops of Vatican I and infallibility [Catholic Theological Society, St. Louis 1989, unabridged]: TDig 37 (1990) 3-15.

k924 **Poulat** Émile, L'Église, c'est un monde; l'Ecclésiosphère 1986 ➔ 3,g755: ᴿRHE 85 (1990) 223s (R. *Aubert*); RicStoSocR 81 (1987) 265-7 (G. *de Rosa*).

k925 **Poulat** Émile, Liberté laïcité 1987 ➔ 4,k311; 5,k358: ᴿCahHist 34 (1989) 85s (X. de *Montclos*); ScripTPamp 22 (1990) 620-3 (C. *Izquierdo*); SuppVSp 175 (1990) 193-6 (J. *Morange*).

k926 *a) Schumacher* Joseph, Der Offenbarungsbegriff im Modernismus; – *b) Stöhr* Johannes, Überlegungen zu einigen neueren Theorien nicht-begrifflicher Erfahrung der Offenbarung: ➔ 608, Révélation/Aquin 1989/90, 230-249 / 250-278.

THILS Gustave, Primauté et infaillibilité du pontife romain à Vatican I, 1989 ➔ 309.

---

k927 BLONDEL: *Bertoldi* Francesco, Il dibattito sulla verità tra Blondel e GARRIGOU-LAGRANGE: Sapienza 43 (1990) 293-310.

k928 **Favraux** Paul, Une philosophie du Médiateur, M. Blondel 1987 ➤ 3,g759: ᴿRThom 90 (1990) 464-7 (Y. *Floucat*).

k929 *Greisch* Jean, De l'action à la pragmatique; une nouvelle interprétation de Blondel: RechSR 78 (1990) 175-197; Eng. 161.

k930 *Saint-Jean* Raymond, La philosophie et la mystique d'après Blondel: ScEsp 42 (1990) 77-88.

k931 **Theobald** C., M. Blondel und ... Modernität ᴰ1988 ➤ 5,k368: ᴿActu-Bbg 27 (1990) 82s (J. *Boada*).

k932 CHESTERTON: ᴱ**Nichols** Aidan, [Gilbert K.] Chesterton and the modernist crisis: Chesterton Review (special, May 1989). Saskatoon 1989, St. Thomas More College. £6. – ᴿTablet 244 (1990) 1308 (R. *Butterworth*: V. MORAN unfair to TYRRELL; J. COATES fair but as E. POULAT and G. DALY show, Chesterton can scarcely be blamed for being unable to keep up with a massively changing world).

k933 CORNOLDI: **Malusa** L., Neotomismo e intransigentismo cattolico ... Cornoldi, I-II, 1986-9 ➤ 5,k368: ᴿRasT 31 (1990) 406-8 (G. *Lorizio*, anche su ROSMINI).

k934 DÖLLINGER: **Neuner** Peter, Stationen einer Kirchenspaltung; der Fall Döllinger — ein Lehrstück für die heutige Kirchenkrise. Fra 1990, Knecht. 208 p. DM 28 pa. – ᴿIkiZ 80 (1990) 246-8 (E. *Kessler*); ÖkRu 39 (1990) 381s (W. *Müller*).

k934* a) *Oeyen* Christian, Döllinger [Ignaz von, † 1.I.1890] als Altkatholik; eine Bestandsaufnahme; – b) *Ring* Matthias, 'Ähnlich dem Prophetismus in der hebräischen Zeit...' Anmerkungen zum Charismatischen in der Theologie Ignaz Döllingers und insofern auch zum Verhältnis von Lehramt, Theologie und sensus fidelium; – c) *Kessler* H. Ewald, Ergänzungen und Berichtigungen zur Döllinger-Bibliographie von Stephan *Lösch* [1955]: IkiZ 80 (1990) 67-105 [+ 244s] / 106-136 / 137-153.

k935 **Plummer** Alfred, Conversations with Dr. Döllinger 1870-1890: BtETL 67, 1985 ➤ 1,f995 ... 5,k371: ᴿTLZ 115 (1990) 358-360 (P. F. *Barton*).

k936 a) *Schwaiger* Georg, Ignaz von Döllinger — der Apologet — Jahre der Wandlung; – b) *Weitlauff* Manfred, ... im Schatten des I. Vat.; – c) *Neuner* Peter, ... als Theologe der Ökumene: MüTZ 41 (1990) 197-214 / 215-243 / 245-260.

k937 DUCHESNE: *Bressolette* Claude, a) Louis Duchesne, sa vie, son œuvre et son époque: MaisD 181 (1990) 7-34 [-141]; – b) Louis Duchesne [1843-1922]; sa vie, son œuvre, son époque: RICathP 35 (1990) 55-76.

k938 GÜNTHER: *Schwedt* Herman H., Die Verurteilung der Werke Anton Günthers (1857) und seiner Schüler: ZKG 101 (1990) 301-343.

k939 HEFELE: *Reinhardt* Rudolf, Noch einmal; Carl Joseph von Hefele und das Vatikanum I [RIVINIUS K. in ᶠ*Bäumer* R. 1988]: ZKG 101 (1990) 385-396.

k940 VON HÜGEL: *Barmann* Lawrence, Friedrich von Hügel as modernist and as more than modernist: CathHR 75 (1989) 211-232 (photo as cover).

k941 **Barry** John C., The nature of Christian mysticism in the thought of Baron von Hügel and George TYRRELL: diss. Leeds 1989. 470 p. BRD-88567. - DissA 51 (1990s) 194-A.

k942 *Gentili* A., Spiritualità e rinnovamento culturale nel carteggio von Hügel-SEMERIA [30 lettere recentemente scoperte nel archivio barnabita]: Studi Barnabiti 5 (1988) 195-240 [< RHE 85 (1990) 889].

k943 *Izquierdo* César, History and truth; the exegetical position of Baron von Hügel: DowR 108 (1990) 295-312.

k944 *Rambaldi* Giuseppe, Una memoria inedita del barone Friedrich von Hügel sull'unione tra cattolici e anglicani: ArHistPont 27 (1989) 419-432. LAGRANGE M.-J., École Biblique: *Montagnes* B. 1990 → m40.

k945 LOISY: *Provencher* Normand, Les lettres de Henri BERGSON à Alfred Loisy: ÉglT 20 (1989) 425-438.

k946 **Talar** C.J.T., Metaphor and modernist; the polarization of Alfred Loisy and his neo-Thomist critics. Lanham MD 1988, UPA. x-184 p. $19.50. 0-8191-6654-5. – ᴿJEH 40 (1989) 475s (N. *Sagovsky*: promising but unsteady step in the right direction).

k947 NEWMAN, OXFORD MOVEMENT: *Angelini* Giuseppe, La coscienza nel pensiero di J.H. Newman: TItSett 15 (1990) 243-262; Eng. 263.

k948 *Bedouelle* G., Pusey (Edward Bouverie 1800-1882): → 833, Catholicisme 13,55 (1989) 320-2.

k949 **Biemer** Günter, J.H. Newman 1801-1890, Leben und Werk 1989 → 5, k378: ᴿScripTPamp 22 (1990) 1017 (J. *Morales*; 1018 sobre BIEMER-FRIES 1988); TPQ 138 (1990) 396 (R. *Zinnhobler*); TLZ 115 (1990) 832s (J. *Mann*).

k950 *Biemer* Günter, J.H. Newman als Zeuge und Animateur des Glaubens: TBer 18 (Z 1989) 61-88 [< ZIT 90,174].

k951 **Biemer** Günter, *Holmes* J.D., Gott, das Licht des Lebens, [Newman] Gebete und Meditationen. Mainz 1987, Grünewald. 179 p., DM 19,80. – ᴿGeistL 63 (1990) 393s (R. *Siebenrock*).

k952 **Boudens** R., Vriendelijk Licht; de profetische visie van J.H. Newman. Averbode 1989, Altiora. 258 p. Fb. 585. – ᴿCollatVL 20 (1990) 336 (J. *Bonny*).

k953 *Boudens* Robrecht, De actualiteit van J.H. Newman: CollatVL 20 (1990) 7-20 = TGegw 33 (1990) 336-344, Die Aktualität J.H. Newmans.

k954 *Boudens* Robrecht, Newman and the Roman authorities: → 189, LvSt 15 (1990) 301-317.

k955 *Boyce* Philip, Commenti e impressioni sulla morte di Newman nel 1890: Teresianum 41 (1990) 647-667.

k956 *a) Boyce* Philip, Newman, predicatore di verità e maestro di vita; implicazioni per la teologia e la spiritualità; – *b) Stern* Jean, La Chiesa, il magistero e i teologi secondo J.H. Newman; – *c) González Fernández* Fidel, J.H. Newman, sua incidenza nella vita della Chiesa: EuntDoc 43,3 [colloquio Roma 26-28.IV.1990] 437-455 / 457-476 / 477-522 [431-6, *Ratzinger* J.].

k957 **Chadwick** Owen, John-Henry Newman ᵀ*Dayras* Solange, *d'Haussy* Christiane; préf. *Guitton* J. 1989 → 5,k380: ᴿLavalTP 46 (1990) 414s (T.R. *Potvin*); RHE 85 (1990) 128-130 (J. *Seynaeve*); RHPR 70 (1990) 396s (M. *Arnold*: méritait mieux); RHR 207 (1990) 220-2 (B. *Cottret*).

Chadwick Owen, The spirit of the Oxford Movement; tractarian essays 1990 → 211.

k959 *Cristaldi* Giuseppe, La 'conversione' di J.H. Newman: ViPe 72 (1989) 703-710.

k960 *Crosby* John, What is anthropocentric and what is theocentric in Christian existence; the challenge of J.H. Newman: CommND 16 (1989) 244-256.

k961 *Dulles* Avery, Newman, conversion, and ecumenism [...centenary of his death Aug. 11, 1890]: TS 51 (1990) 717-731.

k962 **Forrester** David, Young Doctor Pusey. L 1989, Mowbray. xviii-271 p.
£27.50. 0-264-67160-0. – ᴿExpTim 101 (1989s) 129 [C. S. *Rodd*].

k963 *Frappell* L. O., J. H. Newman and the two systems of Providence:
JRelHist 15 (1988s) 470-487.

k964 **Gauthier** Pierre, Newman et BLONDEL; tradition et développement du
dogme: CogF 147, 1988 ➤ 4,k335; 5,k382: ᴿGregorianum 71 (1990) 179s
(R. *Fisichella*); HerdKor 43 (1989) 142 (A. R.); JEH 40 (1989) 473s (O.
Chadwick); NRT 112 (1990) 250-4 (P. *Favraux*); RThom 90 (1990)
668-671 (G. *Narcisse*).

k965 *Gauthier* Pierre, Un testigo de la persona; J. H. Newman [< Un témoin
de la personne, RevSR 63 (1989) 227-241], ᵀᴱ*Muñoz* Maxim: SelT 29
(1990) 328-334.

k966 **Gilley** Sheridan, Newman and his age. L 1990, Darton-LT. 485 p.
£25. 0-232-51742-8. – ᴿExpTim 102 (1990s) 128 [C. S. *Rodd*: greatest
modern English theologian]; Tablet 244 (1990) 1376s (J. M. *Cameron*).

k967 *Griffin* Philip, Newman's thought on Church and Scripture: IrTQ 56
(1990) 287-306.

k968 *Holland* James C., 'Toleration' intolerable; [Richard] SIMPSON's suppressed essay [for the Rambler, organ of largely Oxford Movement
converts urging to update 'old' Catholics: withdrawn at Newman's in-
sistence]: CathHR 75 (1989) 21-54.

k969 **Imberg** Rune, Tracts for the times; a complete survey of all the editions.
Lund 1988, Krieger. 175 p. $35.25. 9-179-66019-3. – ᴿJEH 40 (1989)
611s (N. *Sagovsky*).

k970 *a*) *Jaki* Stanley L., Newman and science; – *b*) *Merrigan* Terrence,
'One momentous doctrine which enters into my reasoning'; the unitive
function of Newman's doctrine of Providence: DowR 108 (1990)
282-294 / 254-281.

k971 *Jay* Pierre, J. H. Cardinal Newman (1801-1890); pour le centenaire de
sa mort: EsprVie 100 (1990) 625-634.

k972 **Ker** Ian, Newman, biography 1988 ➤ 5,k385: ᴿAngelicum 67 (1990)
586-9 (A. *Wilder*); AnnTh 4 (1990) 489-493 (R. A. P. *Stork*); CurrTMiss
17 (1990) 312s (A. F. *Weisner*); HeythJ 31 (1990) 327-9 (S. *Thomas*); JEH
41 (1990) 317-9 (O. *Chadwick*); JTS 41 (1990) 305-7 (G. *Rowell*); RHE 85
(1990) 130-3 (J. *Seynaeve*); ScotJT 43 (1990) 427-9 (G. S. *Wakefield*).

k973 **Ker** Ian, The achievement of J. H. Newman. ND 1990, Univ. x-209 p.
0-268-00624-5 [TDig 37,370].

k974 **McRedmond** Louis, Thrown among the strangers; J. H. Newman in
Ireland. Dublin 1990, Veritas. £10. – ᴿTablet 244 (1990) 730 (P. *Hebblethwaite*).

k975 *a*) *Morales* José, La personalidad de John Newman en su teología; en
torno a un centenario; – *b*) *Boyce* Philip, La Iglesia, una y visible, en la
vida y pensamiento de Newman: ScripTPamp 22 (1990) 689-701 [-755,
al.] / 757-767.
Newman centenary essays 1989 ➤ 129.

k976 **Nichols** Aidan, From Newman to CONGAR; the idea of doctrinal
development from the Victorians to the Second Vatican Council. E 1990,
Clark. 256 p. £10. 0-567-29181-2. – ᴿExpTim 102 (1990s) 249 (J. *Kent*).

k977 *Pelikan* Jaroslav, Newman and the Fathers; the vindication of tradition:
➤ 643, StPatr 18,4 (1983/90) 379-390.

k978 ᴱ**Rowell** Geoffrey, Tradition renewed; the Oxford Movement conference
[Keble College 1986; 15 of the 16] papers 1986 ➤ 3,711; 4,k339: ᴿHeythJ
31 (1990) 358s (P. *Butler*).

k979 *Rowell* Geoffrey, J.H. Newman, Apologia: ExpTim 101 (1989s) 196-201.

k980 *Scordato* C., *al.*, Viaggio e malattia di Newman in Sicilia nel 1833, simposio Enna-Leonforte 13.V.1990: Ho Theológos 8 (1990) 17-41 (5-98).

k981 **Trevor** Meriol, J.H. Newman, crónica de un amor a la verdad [Newman's Journey], ᵀ*Boix* Aureli: Rostro de los Santos 8. S 1989, Sígueme. 287 p. 84-301-1093-3. – ᴿActuBbg 27 (1990) 107s (J. *Vives*); EfMex 8 (1990) 405s (E. *Serraima Cirici*); LumenVr 39 (1990) 346-8 (U. *Gil Ortega*); ScripTPamp 22 (1990) 655s (J.L. *Lorda*).

k982 ᴱ**Weaver** Mary Jo, Newman and the Modernists 1986 ➤ 2,d844 ... 5,k392: ᴿJEH 40 (1989) 316 (G. *Rowell*).

k983 ᴱ**Weidner** H.D., The Via Media of the Anglican church by John Henry Newman. Ox 1990, Clarendon. lxxix-479 p. £50. 0-19-826693-6. – ᴿExpTim 102 (1990s) 213 (J. *Kent*: splendid).

k984 **Yakaitis** Michael T., The office of priest, prophet, and king in the thought of John H. Newman: diss. Pont. Univ. Gregoriana, ᴰ*Sharkey* M. Roma 1990. Nº 3648, 320 p. – RTLv 22, p. 605.

k985 Pıus IX: **Martina** Giacomo, Pio IX. R 1-3. 1974, 1986 [➤ 5,k396] 1990, Pont. Univ. Gregoriana. 88-7652-459-2; -543-2; -625-0. – ᴿGregorianum 71 (1990) 811-3 (*ipse*).

k986 Pıus X: *Carcel Ortí* Vicente, San Pio X, los jesuitas y los integristas españoles: ArHistPont 27 (1989) 249-355.

k987 Rosmini: **Lorizio** G., Eschaton e storia nel pensiero di Antonio Rosmini [➤ 4,k345; 5,k399]; Genesi e analisis della Teodicea in prospettiva teologica [diss. Pont. Univ. Gregoriana, Roma 1988]: Aloisiana 21, 1988: ᴿRET 50 (1990) 345-7 (E. *Tourón*).

k988 **Rosmini** Antonio [➤ 9081], Les cinc plagues de la Santa Església, ᵀ*Llopis* Joan: Classics del cristianisme 11. Barc 1990, Fac.Teol./Enc.Catalana. – ᴿQVidCr 154 (1990) 107-111 (M. Adelaide *Raschini*).

k989 **Staglianò** Antonio, La 'teologia' secondo Antonio Rosmini; sistematica — critica — interpretazione del rapporto fede e ragione. Brescia 1988, Morcelliana. 429 p. Lit. 50.000. – ᴿCC 141 (1990,2) 511s (G. *Lorizio*).

k990 Sailer: *Wolf* Hubert, Der Fall [J.M.] Sailer vor der Inquisition; eine posthume Anklageschrift ... 1873: ZKG 101 (1990) 344-370.

k991 Schell: *Hausberger* Karl, Karl Anton von Henle und Herman Schell, ein Briefwechsel im Vorfeld der 'Modernismus-'Kontroverse: ➤ 161, ᶠSchwaiger G., Papsttum 1990, 699-744.

k992 *Sweeney* David F., Herman Schell, 1850-1906; a German dimension to the Americanist controversy: CathHR 76 (1990) 44-70.

k993 Tyrrell: **Afonso Meneo** A., The source of clerical absolutism according to George Tyrrell; an evaluation: diss. Marquette, ᴰ*Misner* P., Milwaukee 1990. 256 p. 91-01408. – DissA 51 (1990s) 3110s-A.

k994 ᴱ**Butterworth** Robert, A Jesuit friendship; letters of George Tyrrell to Herbert Thurston 1988 ➤ 5,k400: ᴿHeythJ 31 (1990) 93s (M.J. *Walsh*: reveal much for which Thurston's biographer J. Crehan lacked warmth).

k995 *Leonard* Ellen, Modernism and The Month; exploring the connections past and present: Month 250 (1989) 461-471 [472-7; 478-481 *Moffatt* Ronald and *Hebblethwaite* Peter on the past 25 years].

k996 **Sagovsky** Nicholas, 'On God's side'; a life of George Tyrrell. Ox 1989, Clarendon. ix-276 p. 0-19-826728-2 [TDig 38,84]. £30. – ᴿExpTim 101 (1989s) 384 [C.S. *Rodd*]; Month 251 (1990) 242s (R. *Butterworth*); TLond 93 (1990) 489 (D. *Nicholls*).

k997 *Sagovsky* Nicholas, [Tyrrell (-Thurston)] A religious genius?: Month 251 (1990) 165-7.

k998 ZIGLIARA: *Raschini* M. Adelaide, Zigliara e ROSMINI [< simposio sul Card. Zigliara O.P., Roma Pont. Univ. S. Tommaso 2.V.1987]: Angelicum 67 (1990) 555-577.

Y6   *Saeculum XX* – **20th Century Exegesis.**

m1 **Doyle** B. Rod, Biblical studies in Australia, a Catholic contribution [➤ 5,k402]: a short survey and bibliography [Australia CBA presidential address for 1988 Australia Bicentennial]. Melbourne 1990, Lovell. 56 p. 1-86355-008-9.

m2 ᴱ**Epp** Eldon J., *MacRae* George W. †, The New Testament and its modern interpreters 1989 ➤ 4180 (5,394): ᴿTorJT 6 (1990) 125-7 (J. S. *Kloppenborg*).

---

m3 BAECK: *Brocke* Edna, Leo Baeck [1873-1956] — ein deutscher Jude: KIsr 5 (1990) 123-134.

m4 *Kurzweil* Zvi, The relevance of Leo Baeck's thought to the mainstreams of Judaism: Judaism 39 (1990) 163-170.

m5 BEA: **Schmidt** S., A. Bea 1987 ➤ 3,g812 ... 5,k407: ᴿHumBr 45 (1990) 88-90 (G. M. *Pizzuti*).

m6 **Schmidt** Stjepan, Augustin Bea, der Kardinal der Einheit 1989 ➤ 5,k408: ᴿAtKap 115 (1990) 331-3 (L. *Górka*).

m7 BUBER: **Biser** Eugen, Buber für Christen 1988 ➤ 5,k411: ᴿMüTZ 41 (1990) 396s (E. *Zwick*).

m8 **Mendes-Flohr** Paul, From mysticism to dialogue; Martin Buber's transformation of German social thought [< diss. Brandeis 1972, deutsch 1978]: Culture of Jewish Modernity. Detroit 1989, Wayne State Univ. 205 p. $30; pa. $16. 0-8143-2028-7; -9-5 [TDig 37,276].

m9 *Morgan* Michael L., Martin Buber, cooperation, and evil: JAAR 58 (1990) 99-109.

m10 *Vendemiati* Aldo, Autenticità e testimonianza in 'Io e Tu' di Martin Buber: ViPe 73 (1990) 857-864.

m11 BULTMANN: **Bockmuehl** Klaus, The unreal God of modern theology [... Bultmann, BARTH] 1988 ➤ 5,k420: ᴿBS 147 (1990) 238 (J. A. *Witmer*).

m12 **Evang** Martin, R. Bultmann in seiner Frühzeit 1988 ➤ 4,k365; 5,k422: ᴿJTS 41 (1990) 308-310 (R. *Morgan*); NorTTs 90 (1989) 245-7 (S. A. *Christoffersen*); SNTU A-15 (1990) 149s (A. *Fuchs*).

m13 *Fergusson* David, Meaning, truth, and realism in Bultmann and LIMBECK: RelSt 26 (1990) 183-198.

m14 *Fuchs* Othmar, Entsicherung statt Entmythologisierung!: R. Bultmann im Horizont aktueller Mythendiskussion: [... zum mythischen Charakter der 'existentialen Interpretation']: UnSa 45 (1990) 28-38.

m15 **Gager** Henri-Jérôme, Bultmann et la question du spécifique chrétien: diss. Inst. Catholique, ᴰ*Doré* J. Paris 1990. 469 p. – BICathP 34 (1990) 189-192; RTLv 22, p. 603.

m15* *Gager* Henri-Jérôme, La foi chez Bultmann et après lui: ➤ 404, ᴱ*Doré* J., Identité 1990, 129-170.

m16 *Jaspert* Bernd, Sachkritik und Widerstand; das Beispiel Rudolf Bultmanns: TLZ 115 (1990) 161-182.

m17 ᴱ**Johnson** Roger, R. Bultmann; interpreting faith for the modern era:
Making of Modern Theology 2, 1987 ➤ 4,k367; 5,k424: ᴿCritRR 3
(1990) 437-9 (S.R. *Gordy*); PerspRelT 17 (1990) 173-5 (D.T. *Priestley*,
also on HARNACK and SCHLEIERMACHER in the series).

m18 *Lührmann* Dieter, Rudolf Bultmann and the History of Religion school:
➤ 24, ᶠBOERS H., Text 1990, 3-14.

m19 *a) Vorster* W.S., Rudolf Bultmann as historikus; – *b) Pelser* G.M.M.,
Die ontmitologiseringsprogram...: HervTSt 45,1s (1987) 138-161 / 162-
191 [< NTAbs 34,9.6].

m20 *Wartenberg* Günther, Verpasste Chance oder vergebliche Mühe? Dokumente um den Versuch, Rudolf Bultmann Anfang des Jahres 1930 nach
Leipzig zu berufen: TLZ 115 (1990) 385-398.

m21 CADBURY J.H.: **Bacon** Margaret H., Let this life speak 1987 ➤ 3,g827;
4,k370: ᴿJRelHist 15 (1988s) 276s (D. *Goodman*).

m22 COHEN Hermann [1842-1918], Jüdische Schriften: Jewish Philosophy.
NY 1980 = 1924, Arno. lxiv-341 p.; viii-482 p.; [vii-] 375 p. 0-405-
12245-4 (all 3; all entirely in German).

m23 DALMAN: **Männchen** Julia, G. Dalmans Leben und Wirken 1987
➤ 3,g828: ᴿBijdragen 51 (1990) 86 (F. De *Meyer*).

m24 DAVIES W.D., My Odyssey in New Testament interpretation: BR 5,3
(1989) 10-18.

m25 DELITZSCH: **Johanning** K., Der Babel-Bibel-Streit [Friedrich Delitzsch
1902-20]: EurHS 23/343, ᴰ1989 ➤ 5,k432: ᴿBL (1990) 18s (R.A. *Mason*:
entertaining as well as informative).

m26 DODD: **Barnes** Oswald, The edifice of exegesis; the structure of C.H.
Dodd's theology: diss. Edinburgh 1989, ᴰ*Templeton* D. 344 p. – RTLv
22,391.

m27 DuBOSE: *Macquarrie* John, William Porcher DuBose: NT scholar and
systematic theologian: ➤ 52, ᶠFULLER R., AnglTR supp 11 (1990)
140-153.

m28 HESCHEL: **Flerman** Morton C., Leap of action; ideas in the theology of
Abraham J. Heschel. Lanham MD 1990, UPA. 312 p. $18.50 [JAAR
58,161].

m29 **Heschel** A., La terra è del Signor; il mondo intero dell'Ebreo in Europa
orientale. ᵀᴱ*Poli* E. Genova 1989, Marietti. xx-136 p. Lit. 19.000. 88-
211-8364-5. – ᴿProtestantesimo 45 (1990) 328s (M. *Abbà*).

m30 **Moore** Donald J., The human and the holy; the spirituality of A.J.
Heschel 1989 ➤ 5,k439: ᴿTTod 47 (1990s) 483 (W. *Harrelson*).

m31 KAUFMANN: **Krapf** Thomas, Yehezkel Kaufmann [100. Gb.]; ein
Lebens- und Erkenntnisweg zur Theologie der Hebräischen Bibel: Stu-
dien zu Kirche und Israel 11. B 1990, Inst. Kirche und Judentum. 154 p.
[ZAW 103,452, H. *Wahl*]. 3-923095-62-7.

m32 KITTEL G.&R.: *Friedrich* Gerard† & Johannes, KITTEL, Gerhard
(1888-1948): ➤ 857, TRE 19 (1990) 221-5.

m33 *Bernhardt* Karl-Heinz, KITTEL, Rudolf (1853-1929): ➤ 857, TRE 19
(1990) 225s.

m34 LAGRANGE: *Bruckberger* Ray, OP., Le père Marie-Joseph Lagrange:
PenséeC 238 (1989) 75-81.

m35 **Gilbert** Maurice, M.-J. Lagrange, L'Écriture en Église; choix de portraits et d'exégèse spirituelle (1980-1937): LDiv 142. P 1990, Cerf. 242 p. F 145. 2-204-04181-5. – REsprVie 100 (1990) 673s (É. *Cothenet*).

m36 *Gilbert* Maurice, Quinze lettres du Père Lagrange au Père LYONNET, 1933-1938: Biblica 71 (1990) 280-298.

Lahutsky Nadia M., Paris and Jerusalem; Alfred Loisy and Père Lagrange on the Gospel of Mark 1990 → 5196.

m37 **Montagnes** Bernard, Exégèse et obéissance... CORMIER-Lagrange 1989 → 5,k444*: REsprVie 100 (1990) 280-4 (É. *Cothenet*); EstFranc 91 (1990) 592-4 (M. *Taradach*); RThom 90 (1990) 671-3 (L. *Devillers*).

m38 *Montagnes* Bernard, Les lettres du P. Lagrange à Mgr de SOLAGES (1925-1937) [all letters addressed to Lagrange, including those of Mgr de Solages, were burned by L.-H. VINCENT in accord with Lagrange's wishes, p. 83]: BLitEc 91 (1990) 83-100.

m39 *Montagnes* B., Premiers combats du père Lagrange; le congrès de Fribourg (1897): ArchFrP 59 (1989) 297-369.

m40 *Montagnes* Bernard [avec lettre à PIE XI de THEISSLING Louis, maître général O.P.], Les séquelles de la crise moderniste; l'École Biblique au lendemain de la grande guerre: RThom 90 (1990) 245-270.

m41 LA POTTERIE: *Valente* Gianni, Incontro con Ignace de la Potterie, un biblista controcorrente: 30 giorni 8,2 (1990) 56-59.

m42 *Valente* G., Ignace de la Potterie, a counter-current biblicist: 30 Days (SF, March 1990) 56-59 [< Trenta Giorni].

m43 LOHMEYER (1890-1946): *a*) *Lührmann* Dieter, Ernst Lohmeyers exegetisches Erbe; – *b*) *Haufe* Günther, E. Lohmeyer — Theologische Exegese aus dem Geist des philosophischen Idealismus [= ZeichZt 44 (1990) 138-140]; – *c*) *Beintker* Horst J.E., E. Lohmeyers Stellung zum Judentum: → 119, FLOHMEYER E., Freiheit 1990, 53-87 / 88-97 / 98-134.

m44 MARGOLIS: *Greenspoon* Leonard, On the Jewishness of modern Jewish biblical scholarship; the case of Max L. Margolis: Judaism 39 (1990) 82-92.

m44* **MARTINI** Carlo M., La presidencia de la caridad [3 homilías]. Bogotá 1987, Paulinas. 51 p. – RTVida 30 (1989) 318s (Anneliese *Meis W.*).

m45 MONTEFIORE: **Kessler** E., An English Jew; the life and writings of Claude Montefiore [1858-1938]. L 1989, Vallentine. xi-205 p.; 3 pl. 0-85303-228-9 [NTAbs 35,233].

m46 MOWINCKEL: **Dagfinn** Kvale & Rian, Sigmund Mowinckel's life and work [1884-1965], a bibliography; intr. *Kapelrud* A.S., OT study: Institutt for Bibelvitenskap Småskrifter 2. Oslo 1984, Universitet. ix-73 p. 0800-4447. – RSvEx 55 (1990) 116s (L. *Eriksson*).

m46* ROBINSON: *a*) **Kee** Alistair, The roots of Christian freedom; the theology of John A.T. Robinson 1988 → 4,k380; 5,k450*: REvQ 62 (1990) 90s (G.L. *Bray*). – *b*) *Knox* John, J.A.T. Robinson and the meaning of New Testament scholarship: TLond 92 (1989) 251-267.

m47 ROSENZWEIG: EMayer Reinhold, Franz Rosenzweig, Der Stern der Erlösung; Gedenkrede, *Scholem* Gershom: Bibliothek 973. Fra 1990= 1921, Suhrkamp. xxxviii-549 p.

m48 **Mendes-Flohr** Paul, The philosophy of Franz Rosenzweig: Tauber Series 8. 1988, Univ. Press New England. 272 p.; ill. $30. 0-87451-298-7. – RCritRR 2 (1989) 398-401 (M.D. *Yaffe*).

m49 **Meyer** F. de, Franz Rosenzweig, leven en werk 1986 → 3,g840: RNedTTs 44 (1990) 73s (S. *Gerssen*).

m50 SCOFIELD: **Canfield** Joseph M., The incredible Scofield and his book [Reference Bible, Oxford-UP]. Vallecito CA 1988 = 1984, Ross. – ᴿBS 147 (1990) 351-364 (J. D. *Hannah*: theonomic-postmillennialist attack).

Y6.4 **Theologi influentes** *in exegesim saeculi XX*.

m51 *Altizer* Thomas J. J., The atheistic ground of America: AnglTR 71 (1989) 261-272.

m52 **Avis** Paul, Anglicanism and the Christian Church; theological resources in historical perspective. Ph 1989, Fortress. 335 p. $25. 0-8006-2416-5 [JAAR 58,157]. – ᴿTDig 37 (1990) 343 (W. C. *Heiser*).

m53 **Bacik** James, Contemporary theologians. Ch 1989, T. More. 292 p. $15. – ᴿHorizons 17 (1990) 339s (Mary Kay *Oosdyke*).

m54 **Balmer** Randall, Mine eyes have seen the glory; a journey into the evangelical subculture in America. NY 1989, Oxford-UP. 246 p. $20. – ᴿTTod 47 (1990s) 92s (J. M. *Mulder*: a wonderful book; gets past television-electronic church to the real heart, not concealing sham healers and commercialized booksellers).

m55 **Boys** Mary C., Educating in faith; maps and visions [cartography images for current movements]. SF 1989, Harper & R. 230 p. $22. 0-06-061037-9. – ᴿRExp 87 (1990) 142s (T. A. *Lines*: high praise).

m56 *Braaten* Carl E., Gott und das Evangelium; Pluralismus und Apostasie in der amerikanischen Theologie, ᵀ*Linss* Wilhelm C. (Gastvorlesung cv. Fak. München): KerDo 36 (1990) 56-70; Eng. 71.

m57 **Bruce** David, A house divided; Protestantism, schism, and secularization. L 1990, Routledge. 122 p. $22.50 [JAAR 58,325].

m58 ᴱ**Carey** Patrick W., American Catholic religious thought; the shaping of a theological and social tradition 1987 → 4,345; 5,k456: ᴿHeythJ 31 (1990) 366 (B. *Aspinwall*).

m59 **Cholvy** Gérard, *Hilaire* Yves-M., Histoire religieuse de la France contemporaine: I, 1985: 1800-1880; II, 1986: -1930; III, 1988: -1985. 351 p. 457 p. 569 p. → 3,g848; 5,k457: ᴿRelStR 16 (1990) 309-313 (J. F. *Byrnes*).

m60 **Clements** Keith W., Lovers of discord 1988 → 4,k390; 5,k458: ᴿAnglTR 71 (1989) 321-7 (D. F. *Winslow*); EvQ 62 (1990) 92s (G. L. *Bray*); ScotBEv 8 (1990) 141s (S. *Williams*); ScotJT 43 (1990) 132s (B. *Russell*); Tablet 243 (1989) 551s (J. *Bowden*); TLZ 115 (1990) 699s (J. *Langer*).

m61 **Edwards** David L., Tradition and truth; the challenge of England's radical theologians 1962-1989 [J. ROBINSON, D. CUPITT, J. HICK ...]. L 1989, Hodder & S. 326 p. £15. – ᴿTLond 93 (1990) 303-5 (K. W. *Clements*).

m62 **Fenn** Richard K., The Church in the world; the Church with the soul of a nation [U. S. Protestantism: *Neville* G. 1987; *Wuthnow* R. 1989]: TTod 47 (1990s) 171-9.

m63 **Fern** Deane W., Contemporary American theologies; a critical survey²ʳᵉᵛ. SF 1990, Harper & R. viii-184 p. $15 [CBQ 53,170].

m64 ᴱ**Fogarty** Gerald, Patterns of episcopal leadership: Centennial. NY 1989, Macmillan. xvi-306 p. – ᴿNewTR 3,1 (1990) 92-94 (J. E. *Linnan*).

m65 ᴱ**Ford** David, The modern theologians; an introduction to Christian theology in the twentieth century 1989 → 5,k461: ᴿAntonianum 65 (1990) 672s (A. *Galeano*); JTS 41 (1990) 315 (M. *Wiles*); Month 251 (1990) 238s (P. *Endean*: a rare theological genre); ScEsp 42 (1990) 370-2 (M. *Spicer*, 1s: Eng.); Tablet 243 (1989) 1278 (J. *Bowden*); TLond 93 (1990) 229s (P. *Avis*).

m65* **Fowler** Robert B., Unconventional partners; religion and liberal culture in the US. GR 1989, Eerdmans. 185 p. $13 pa. 0-8028-0342-3 [JRel 71, 579, J. W. *Carroll*].

m66 **Frank** Douglas W., Less than conquerors; how evangelicals entered the twentieth century. GR 1986, Eerdmans. 310 p. $20 pa. – ᴿCalvinT 25 (1990) 75-82 (S. *Perisho*); GraceTJ 10 (1989) 111-3 (T. *Craigen*); WestTJ 52 (1990) 171-3 (D. G. *Hart*: no broad historical perspectives on Christian use of power).

m66* **Gauly** Thomas M., *a*) Kirche und Politik in der Bundesrepublik Deutschland 1945-1976; – *b*) Katholiken; Machtanspruch und Macht- verlust. Bonn 1990s, Bouvier. 504 p.; DM 178 / 474 p.; DM 68 [TR 87, 403-6, W. *Damberg*].

m67 **Giussani** Luigi (fondatore di Comunione e Liberazione), Grandi linee della teologia protestante americana. Mi 1988 = 1969, Jaca. 200 p. Lit. 22.000. – ᴿProtestantesimo 45 (1990) 159 (M. *Rubboli*: nemmeno gli errori corretti, ma utile).

m68 **Greeley** Andrew M., Religious change in America: Social Trends in the US. CM 1989, Harvard. xi-137 p. $25 [RelStR 17, 48, W. *Silverman*]. – ᴿTTod 47 (1990s) 193s.196 (J. M. *Spencer*: not much change).

m68* **Hastings** Adrian, A history of English Christianity, 1920-1985. L 1987, Collins. 720 p. £8 pa. 0-00-627041-7. – ᴿNedTTs 44 (1990) 269s (P. *Staples*).

m69 **Hatch** Nathan O., The democratization of American Christianity. NHv 1989, Yale Univ. 312 p. $25. – ᴿTTod 47 (1990s) 89s (J. H. *Moorhead*).

m70 **Hummel** Gert, Die Begegnungen von Philosophie und evangelischer Theologie im 20. Jahrhundert. Da 1989, Wiss. 499 p. DM 85. 3-534- 00599-6. – ᴿLuthTKi 13 (1989) 122s (T. *Junker*).

m71 ᴱ**Leimgruber** Stephan, *Schoch* Max, Gegen die Gottvergessenheit; Schweizer Theologen im 19. und 20. Jht. FrB 1990, Herder. 688 p. 85 fig. Fs 84,50. 3-451-21986-7 [Orientierung 54 (1990) 262 adv.].

m71* ᴱ**Marty** Martin E., *Peerman* Dean G., A handbook of [only 38] Christian theologians² [¹c. 1963]. Nv/C 1988, Abingdon/Lutterworth. 735 p. £10. /0-7188-2793-7. – ᴿÉTRel 65 (1990) 469s (A. *Gounelle*: the 38 include TEILHARD, ELLUL, RICŒUR, but not TROELTSCH).

m72 *Nineham* Denis, The last half-century of theology; a personal im- pression: EpworthR 16,3 (1989) 47-57 [< NTAbs 34,6].

m73 **O'Brien** David, Public Catholicism: Bicentennial 1989 ➔ 5,k466: ᴿNewTR 3,1 (1990) 95s (K. R. *Himes*).

m74 **Pinnock** Clark H., Tracking the maze; finding our way through modern theology from an evangelical perspective. SF 1990, Harper & R. 227 p. $25. – ᴿTTod 47 (1990s) 448.450.452 (D. A. *Hubbard*).

m75 **Reher** Margaret M., Catholic intellectual life in America; a historical study of persons and movements: Bicentennial, 1989 ➔ 5,k468: ᴿNewTR 3,1 (1990) 88s (Patricia O. *Killen*).

m76 **Scholder** Klaus †, A requiem for Hitler — and other new perspectives on the German Church struggle [1988], ᵀ*Bowden* John. L 1989, SCM. 203 p. £8.50. 0-334-02295-9. – ᴿExpTim 101 (1989s) 85s (E. *Robertson*: the 1980 Vienna lecture on PACELLI and BARTH roused controversy).

m77 *Smit* D. J., The ethics of interpretation — and South Africa [Reformed exegesis these past 40 years dominated first by apartheid, then by methodology, now by socio-political wave]: Scriptura 33 (1990) 29-43 [16-28, US new voices: < NTAbs 35,11].

m78 ᴱSykes S., *Booty* J.,   The study of Anglicanism 1988 ➤ 4,420; 5,k471: ᴿAnglTR 71 (1989) 447-450 (W. H. *Peterson*); Month 250 (1989) 28s (P. *Vardy*); ScotJT 43 (1990) 406-8 (G. S. *Wakefield*).

---

m79 ADAM: **Kreidler** Hans,   Eine Theologie des Lebens; Grundzüge im theologischen Denken Karl Adams: TüTSt 29.   Mainz 1988, Grünewald. 123 p. – ᴿTGL 80 (1990) 217-9 (R. M. *Bucher*).

m80 BALTHASAR: *Fisichella* Rino,   Rileggendo Hans Urs von Balthasar: Gregorianum 71 (1990) 511-545; Eng. 546.

m81 *Lee* Claudia,   The role of mysticism within the Church as conceived by Hans Urs von Balthasar: CommND 16 (1989) 105-126.

m81* *Meis W.* Anneliese,   El método teológico de H. U. v. Balthasar; un estudio aproximativo desde su obra principal: TVida 30 (1989) 185-206.

m82 *Moda* Aldo,   Struttura e fondamento della logica teologica secondo H. U. von Balthasar, I: RasT 31 (1990) 548-566 ...

m82* *O'Connor* James T.,   Von Balthasar et le salut [< HomP 1989]:   PenséeC 247 (1990) 62-56.

m83 *Ouellet* Marc,   Hans Urs von Balthasar, teologo del 2000:   HumBr 45 (1990) 579-592.

m84 ᴱRiches John,   The analogy of beauty ... Balthasar 1986 ➤ 3,g858; 4,k401: ᴿCritRR 3 (1990) 450-3 (P. C. *Phan*); HeythJ 31 (1990) 87 (J. *O'Donnell*).

m85 **Roberts** Louis,   The theological aesthetics of H. U. v. Balthasar 1987 ➤ 3,g861 ... 5,k483: ᴿHeythJ 31 (1990) 220 (J. *O'Donnell*).

m86 **Schrijver** Georges de,   Le merveilleux accord de l'homme et de Dieu ... Balthasar [< diss. flamande 1976]: BtETL 63, 1983 ➤ 65,d963 ... 2,d913: ᴿRTLv 21 (1990) 99-101 (É. *Gaziaux*).

m87 **Balthasar** Hans Urs von,   La Dramatique divine 2/1, Les personnes dans le Christ, ᵀ*Givord* R. (*Dumont* C.); Horizon 19, 1988 ➤ 4,k409*: ᴿETL 66 (1990) 443s (E. *Brito*). – ᴿRThom 90 (1990) 279-288 (G. *Narcisse*, 1.2,1s).

m88 **Balthasar** H. U. von,   Glory ... [1986 ➤ 3,g864 ... 5,k485]: 7. Theology of the New Covenant, ᵀ*McNeil* Brian; 2. The dramatis personae, man in God, ᵀ*Harrison* Graham.   SF 1989s, St. Ignatius.   571 p.; 437 p. $35 each.   0-89870-249-6; -87-9 [TDig 38,46]. – ᴿDowR 108 (1990) 232-4 (Francesca *Murphy*, 4).

m89 **Balthasar** H. U. v.,   Si vous ne devenez comme cet enfant, ᵀ*Schlegel* Jean-Louis.   P 1989, D-Brouwer.   90 p. F 50. – ᴿEsprVie 100 (1990) 174s (L. *Barbey*: son dernier ouvrage).

m90 **Balthasar** H. U. v.,   The realm of metaphysics in antiquity.   E 1989, Clark.   419 p. £25.   0-567-09326-3. – ᴿExpTim 101 (1989s) 217 (G. *Newlands*).

m90* **Balthasar** H. Urs von,   Truth is symphonic; aspects of Christian pluralism.   SF 1987, Ignatius.   192 p. £7. – ᴿEvangel 7,1 (1989) 20 (S. *Williams*).

m91 BARTH: *Amberg* Ernst-Heinz,   Neuere Barth-Literatur I: TLZ 115 (1990) 561-572 [... BUSCH E., FREY C.; KÖCKERT H., EICHER P.].

m92 ᴱ**Biggar** Nigel,   Reckoning with Barth ... centenary of birth 1988 ➤ 5,18c; 0-264-67173-2: ᴿExpTim 101 (1989s) 52s (D. *Cornick*).

m92* **Blaser** Klauspeter,   K. Barth ...: BaBSt 57, 1987 ➤ 4,k417 ... 5,k490: ᴿTZBas 46 (1990) 187s (E. *Buess*).

m93 *a) Busch* E., Die Entlarvung der Sünde im Licht ihrer Überwindung;
Karl Barths Sündenlehre [LIENEMANN W.]; – *b) Drewermann* E., Sünde
als Hochmut und Angst; – *c) Egmond* A. van, Triumph der Wahrheit
und Triumph der Gnade; René GIRARD und Karl Barth über Offenbarung, Religionen, Kreuz und Gott: ZdialektT 6,2 (1990s) 109-133
[161-172 / 133-148 / 185 ... : < ZIT 91,177].

m93* EDuke J., *Streetman* R., Barth and SCHLEIERMACHER; beyond the
impasse? 1988 ↠ 5,458: RJRel 70 (1990) 467-9 (P. E. *Capetz*).

m94 *a) Dulk* M. den, Die CALVIN-Rezeption in der Soteriologie Karl Barths;
– *b) Eicher* P., Der Geist der Kirche und der Geist des Herrn; – *c) Knijff*
H. W. de, O. NOORDMANS' Radikalisierung der Offenbarungslehre K.
Barths: ZdialektT 4,1 (Kampen 1988) 11-26 / 27-64 / 65-80 [-92, *Becker*
J. T.].

m95 **Dykstra** D. Ivan, The lordship of God in the theology of Karl Barth:
diss. Yale 1945. 256 p. 90-27476. – Diss-A 51 (1990s) 1558s-A.

m96 **Fisher** Simon, Revelatory positivism? [a Bonhoeffer expression]; Barth's
earliest theology and the Marburg school 1988 ↠ 4,k424: RJRel 70
(1990) 102s (M. I. *Wallace*); TS 51 (1990) 160-2 (R. W. *Palmer*); TsTNijm
30 (1990) 211 (H. D. van *Hoogstraten*).

m97 **Frey** Christopher, Die Theologie Barths, eine Einführung 1988
↠ 4,k424*; 5,k491: RTR 86 (1990) 227s (E. *Hübner*); ZRGg 42 (1990)
284s (K. *Ebert*).

m98 EGisel P., TCorset P., K. Barth, genèse et réception 1987 ↠ 3,g888;
4,k425: RLavalTP 46 (1990) 121s (R.-M. *Roberge*).

m99 *Grözinger* Albrecht, Christologie und Ästhetik; die Lichterlehre Karl
Barths in ihrer Bedeutsamkeit für die praktische Theologie: ↠ 26,
FBOHREN R. 1990, 40-46.

m100 *Heron* Alasdair I. C., The theme of salvation in Karl Barth's doctrine
of reconciliation: ExAud 5 (1989) 107-122.

m100* **Hunsinger** George, How to read Karl Barth; the shape of his
theology. NY 1990, Oxford-UP. x-298 p. $32.50. 0-19-505974-3 [TDig
38,271].

m101 **Jüngel** E., K. Barth, a theological legacy 1986 ↠ 2,d934 ... 5,k493:
RCriswT 2 (1988) 451s (C. *Sanders*); HeythJ 31 (1990) 82s (B. R.
Brinkman).

m102 *Körtner* Ulrich H. J., Der handelnde Gott; zum Verständnis der
absoluten Metapher vom Handeln Gottes bei Karl Barth: NSys 31 (1989)
18-40; Eng. 40.

m103 **Leuba** Jean-Louis, Études barthiennes 1986 ↠ 3,g892: RProtestantesimo 45 (1990) 328-330 (A. *Moda*).

m104 **Macken** John, The autonomy theme in the Church Dogmatics; Karl
Barth and his critics. C 1990, Univ. ix-232 p. £27.50. 0-521-34626-6. –
RExpTim 102 (1990s) 187 (C. *Gunton*: human autonomy is theonomous
but real).

m105 *Macken* John, The Catholic reception of Karl Barth's theology:
MilltSt 25 (1990) 95-113.

m106 *a) Marquardt* F.-W., Barths Forderung einer 'biblischen Haltung' und
MISKOTTES biblische Alephbetisierung der Theologie; – *b) Kraus* H.-J.,
Fragen des Judentums an die Kirche in der Theologie K. H. Miskottes; –
c) Rumscheidt M., Im Westen nichts Neues — Tendenzen der Diskussion
um K. Barth in Nordamerika: ZdialektT 5,1 (1989) 31-36 / 65-80 /
95-118 [< ZIT 90,54].

m106* **Miskotte** K. H., Karl Barth; inspiratie en vertolking, essays, briefwisseling: Verzameld Werk 2. Kampen 1987, Kok. 554 p. – ᴿNedTTs 43 (1989) 160-2 (H. J. *Adriaanse*).

m107 *Peck* George †, Karl Barth and beyond; theses for the contemporary Church: ComViat 33 (1990) 7-18.

m108 *Smalbrugge* Matthias, L'indifférence culturelle dans l'héritage Barthien; propos critiques sur la théologie protestante: RTPhil 122 (1990) 203-215; Eng. 296.

m109 *a)* **Torrance** Thomas F., Karl Barth, biblical and evangelical theologian. E 1990, Clark. xii-256 p. £15. 0-567-09572-X. – *b)* *Muller* Richard A., The Barth legacy; new ATHANASIUS or ORIGEN redivivus? A response to T. F. TORRANCE: Thomist 54 (1990) 673-704.

m109* **BERKHOF** Hendrikus, Two hundred years of theology; report of a personal journey, ᵀ*Vriend* John. GR 1989, Eerdmans. 316 p. £25 [JRel 71, 585, C. *Welch*].

m110 BONHOEFFER: **Alonso Alonso** Bernardo, Honestidad intelectual y compromiso del cristiano Dietrich Bonhoeffer: diss. Madrid 1990, ᴰ*Alemany* J. > MiscCom. – RTLv 22,585.

m111 **de Gruchy** John, D. Bonhoeffer [texts], witness 1988 ➤ 4,k444; 5,k511; No. 4 in the series The making of modern theology, of which he is editor; 0-00-599-58-0: ᴿCathHR 75 (1989) 289-291 (G. A. *McCool*, also on 1-3); Themelios 16 (1990s) 31s (S. N. *Williams*).

m112 **Feil** Ernst, The theology of D. Bonhoeffer [1971], ᵀ*Rumscheidt* Martin, 1985 ➤ 1,g170 ... 3,g916: ᴿRExp 87 (1990) 650 (Molly *Marshall-Green*).

m113 *Gallas* Alberto, Non santi ma uomini; l'idea dell'esserci-per-altri in Dietrich Bonhoeffer [... l'indomani dell'attentato contro Hitler di cui si era dichiarato pronto ad essere l'esecutore materiale...]: StPatav 37 (1990) 273-294; Eng. 294.

m114 **Morris** Kenneth E., Bonhoeffer's ethic of discipleship 1986 ➤ 4,k445: ᴿRExp 87 (1990) 152-4 (G. *Stassen*: good).

m115 *Patrick* Graham A., Bonhoeffer, Letters and papers from prison: ExpTim 101 (1989s) 323-7 [and 319, review of *Robertson* E., Bonhoeffer's heritage 1989].

m116 **Robertson** E., The shame and the sacrifice 1987 ➤ 4,k446; 5,k517; pa. 1989: ᴿCathHR 76 (1990) 609s (E. C. *Helmreich*: a fine study); ColcT 59,4 (1989) 172-4 (E. *Morawiec*).

m117 **Robertson** Edwin, Bonhoeffer's heritage. L 1989, Hodder & S. £9. – ᴿPrPeo 4 (1990) 162 (P. M *Pearson*: also on his Shame); Tablet 244 (1990) 146 (J. *Wilcken*).

m118 BOUYER: *Leiva-Merikakis* Erasmo, Louis Bouyer the theologian: CommND 16 (1989) 257-276; 277-282, bibliog. 1938-88; p. 282-291, letter to Father *Duployé* 8.X.1943.

m119 CADOUX: **Kaye** Elaine, C. J. Cadoux, theologian, scholar and pacifist [† 1947; Life of Jesus 1948] 1988 ➤ 5,k523: ᴿJEH 41 (1990) 134s (B. *Kent*: a giant from another age).

m120 CARNELL: *a)* **Nelson** Rudolph, The making and unmaking of an evangelical mind; the case of Edward Carnell [1919-67]. NY 1988, Cambridge-UP. 320 p.; $34.50 [AndrUnS 28,109]. – *b)* **Rosas** L. Joseph ᴵᴵᴵ, The theology of Edward John Carnell [† 1967]: CriswT 4 (1989s) 351-371.

m120* CHADWICK: *Evans* Gillian R.,   Ecumenists of our time; Henry Chadwick: Mid-Stream 28 (1989) 219-237; phot.

m121 CONGAR: **Henn** William,   The hierarchy of truths according to Yves Congar 1987 ➤ 3,7276 ... 5,k526:   ᴿDivThom 93 (1990) 169s (L. *Elders*); HeythJ 31 (1990) 218-220 (R. B. *Brinkman*).

m122 **Leprieur** François, [Congar, CHENU] Quand Rome condamne; Dominicains et prêtres-ouvriers: Terre humaine. P 1989, Plon/Cerf. 785 p. F 190.   2-259-02130-1. – ᴿArTGran 53 (1990) 388s (I. *Camacho*); RHPR 70 (1990) 399s (E. *Goichot*); RThom 90 (1990) 506-9 (M.-J. *Nicolas*, seul survivant des trois provinciaux 'démissionés'); TsTNijm 30 (1990) 413s (J. van *Laarhoven*).

m123 **Nichols** Aidan,   Y. Congar 1989 ➤ 5,k529:   ᴿPrPeo 4 (1990) 201s (P. *McPartland*, also on DENYS, ANSELM); TLond 93 (1990) 490s (G. *Rowell*); TS 51 (1990) 350-2 (W. W. *Dych*).

m124 COSTANTINI: **Butturini** G.,   Alle origini ... Vat. II ... Costantini 1988 ➤ 4,k450!; 5,k530:   ᴿZMissRW 74 (1990) 247-250 (W. *Henkel*).

m124* CUPITT Don,   The sea of faith; Christianity in change.   C 1988, Univ. 268 p. £30 [JRel 71, 277, K. *Surin*].

m125 DÜRCKHEIM: **Ottemann** Christian,   Initiatisches Christentum; Karlfried Graf Dürckheims Lehre vom 'initiatischen' Weg als Herausforderung an die evangelische Theologie [Diss. Hamburg 1989]: EurHS 23/402.   Bern 1990, Lang.   viii-639 p. DM 133 pa. [TR 87, 334, J. *Sudbrack*: fast nur von J. B. LOTZ und A. GOETTEMANN rezipiert].

m126 FALCONER: **Greenlee** James G.,   Sir Robert Falconer [Presbyterian clergyman presiding over Toronto Univ. (1907-) 52]; a biography. Toronto 1988, Univ. xxii-408 p. – ᴿSR 19 (1990) 117s (B. J. *Fraser*).

m127 FEENEY: **Pepper** George B.,   The Boston heresy case in view of the secularization of religion; a case study in the sociology of religion: StRelSoc 18.   Lewiston NY 1988, Mellen.   xx-209 p. £50. – ᴿCathHR 76 (1990) 629-631 (V. A. *Lapomarda*).

m128 FOX: *Peters* Ted,   Matthew Fox and the Vatican wolves [silenced for a year after The coming of the cosmic Christ]: Dialog 28 (1989) 137-141.

m129 GILKEY: *Peters* Ted,   Langdon Gilkey, theologian to the modern mind: Dialog 27 (St. Paul 1988) 55-62.

m130 GUARDINI: *Schilson* Arno,   Romano Guardini und die Theologie der Gegenwart; Aspekte einer vergessenen Wirkungsgeschichte: TGL 80 (1990) 152-164.

m131 **Vloet** J. van der,   Der Christen aan het einde van de moderniteit; de bijdrage van Romano Guardini tot een theologische kritiek van de moderniteit: diss. ᴰ*Willaert* B.   Lv 1989. L-437 p. – TsTNijm 30 (1990) 189.

m132 GUITTON Jean,   Il Cristo della mia vita [1987 ➤ 4,k465],ᵀ.   CinB 1988, Paoline.   345 p. Lit. 20.000. – ᴿViPe 72 (1989) 477s (A. *Pessina*).

m133 HABERMAS: ᴱ**Arens** E.,   Habermas und die Theologie; Beiträge zur theologischen Rezeption, Diskussion und Kritik der Theorie des kommunikativen Handelns.   Dü 1989, Patmos.   270 p. DM 39,80.   3-491-71087-1. – ᴿTsTKi 61 (1990) 308 (J.-O. *Henriksen*); TsTNijm 30 (1990) 101 (A. van *Harskamp*).

m134 HÄRING B.,   Meine Erfahrung mit der Kirche; Einleitung und Fragen von Gianni *Licheri* 1989 ➤ 5,3375.k546:   ᴿTPhil 65 (1990) 316 (K. *Schatz*); TPQ 138 (1990) 189s (H. *Krätzl*); TsTNijm 30 (1990) 419 (W. *Boelens*).

m135 **Häring** B.,   Mi experiencia con la Iglesia: EAS 80.   M 1989, P.S.
170 p. – ᴿCommSev 23 (1990) 132 (M. *Sánchez*, también sobre SCHURR
V.-VIDAL M., 1989).

m136 HAGIN: *Sannes* Kjell O.,   Kenneth E. Hagins lære — et fram-
gangsteologisk helhetssyn: TsTKi 61 (1990) 161-175; Eng. 75 [1917-,
Tulsa, 'Faith Movement'].

m137 HARNACK: *Ritter* Adolf M.,   Hans von CAMPENHAUSEN und Adolf
von Harnack: ZTK 87 (1990) 323-339.

m138 **Smend** F.,   Adolf von Harnack, Verzeichnis seiner Schriften bis 1930.
Lp 1990, Zentralantiquariat.   vi-301 p. DM 135 [NRT 113, 299, P.
Evrard].

m139 HEIDEGGER: **Lotz** J. B.,   Martin Heidegger et Thomas d'Aquin:
homme temps être [1975],ᵀ.   P 1988, PUF.   x-323 p. F 168. – ᴿNRT 112
(1990) 287s (P. *Gilbert*).

m140 *Strolz* Walter,   Martin Heideggers Denkweg und der christliche Glaube:
NSys 31 (1989) 165-194; Eng. 194.

m141 HENRY Carl F. H.,   Confessions of a theologian 1986 ➔ 2,d985; 3,g950:
ᴿPerspRelSt 17 (1990) 167-172 (T. *George*; quest for evangelical/ Southern
Baptist consensus).

m141* **Henry** Carl F. H.,   Toward a recovery of Christian belief; the
Rutherford lectures [Edinburgh 1989].   Wheaton IL 1990, Crossway.
126 p. $8 pa. 0-89107-588-7 [TDig 38,269].

m142 HICK: ᴱ**Badham** Paul, A John Hick reader. Ph 1990, Trinity. viii-
200 p. $15. 0-334-00599-X [TDig 38,65]. – ᴿTS 51 (1990) 788 (C. *Gillis*).

m143 HIRSCH: **Ericksen** R P ,   Theologians under Hitler 1985 ➔ 1,g111 ...
5,k555* (1986 reprint): ᴿJEH 40 (1989) 133s (J. R. C. *Wright*); RelSt 25
(1989) 247-250 (D. M. *MacKinnon*).

m144 **Ericksen** Robert P.,   Theologen onder Hitler; G. KITTEL, P. ALTHAUS,
E. Hirsch. Franckcr 1987, Wever.   243 p. 90-6135-408-0. – ᴿNedTTs 44
(1990) 79s (R. *Süss*).

m145 **Reimer** A. James,   The Emanuel Hirsch and Paul TILLICH debate; a
study in the political ramifications of theology: Toronto Studies in
Theology 42. Lewiston NY 1989, Mellen. xv-384 p. $80 [TR 87, 303, E.
Arens].

m146 HONSELMANN: *Schmalor* Hermann-Josef,   Klemens Honselmann und
die Anfänge der Arbeitsgemeinschaft katholisch-theologischer Bibliotheken: TGL 80 (1990) 391-402 (403-418, Bibliographie, *Honselmann*;
379-390, Pd Bibliothek, *Hengst* Karl).

m146* IWAND: **Martikainen** Eeva,   Evangelium als Mitte; das Verhältnis von
Wort und Lehre in der ökumenischen Methode H. J. Iwands: ArbGTLuth
9. Hannover 1989, Luth.-V.   164 p. [TR 87, 410, G. *Wenz*].

m147 JOHANNES XXIII: ᴱ**Alberigo** Giuseppe,   Giovanni XXIII, transizione
del Papato c della Chiesa [the eight remaining articles of 24 at 1986
Bergamo colloquy ➔ 3,577] 1988 ➔ 4,512*; 88-263-0453-X: ᴿJEH 40
(1989) 302s (P. *Hebblethwaite*); CiVit 45 (1990) 86s (B. *Farnetani*).

m148 **Hebblethwaite** Peter,   Giovanni XXXIII, il Papa del Concilio [1984
➔ 2,d993],ᵀ.   Mi 1989, Rusconi.   730 p. Lit. 38.000. – ᴿCC 141 (1990,4)
303s (M. *Chappin*).

m148* **Kaufmann** Ludwig, *Klein* Nikolaus, Johannes XXIII — Prophetie im
Vermächtnis.   Brig 1990, Exodus.   159 p. Fs 23,80. – ᴿOrientierung 54
(1990) 145s (H. *Vorgrimler*).

m149 *Robertson* E. H.,   Pope John XXIII; journal of a soul [ᴱCAPOVILLA
Loris]: ExpTim 101 (1989s) 100-5.

m150 JOHANNES PAULUS II: *Berzosa Martínez* Raúl, K. Wojtyła, filósofo y moralista: Burgense 31 (1990) 421-431.

m151 **Hogan** Richard M., *LeVoir* John M., Faith for today; the teachings of Pope John Paul II. L 1989, Collins Fount. xvii-293 p. £8 pa. - ᴿTLond 93 (1990) 306-8 (P. *Avis:* a mind massively powerful ...).

m152 **Quiles** Ismael, Filosofía de la persona según K. Wojtyła 1987 ➤ 4,k482: ᴿStromata 45 (1989) 464-7 (F. J. *Weismann*).

m153 *Swieżawski* Stefan, Karol Wojtyła all'Università Cattolica di Lublino, ᵀ*Gobber* Giovanni: ViePe 72 (1989) 242-253.

m154 JOURNET: *Zuberbier* Andrzej, ❷ Charles Journet, szkic teologiczny: STWsz 27,2 (1989) 159-166.

m154* JÜNGEL: *Greiner* Sebastian, Gott ist Liebe; ein Beitrag zur Gespräch mit Eberhard Jüngel: TGL 80 (1990) 131-151.

m155 KARRER: *Conzemius* Victor, Otto Karrer (1888-1976), theological forerunner of aggiornamento: CathHR 75 (1989) 55-72.

m156 KASPER: **Plovanich** Patricia Ann, The theological method of Walter Kaspar: diss. Fordham, ᴰ*McDermott* J. NY 1990. 316 p. 90-20020. - DissA 51 (1990s) 900s-A; RelStR 17,192.

m156* **Madonia** N., Ermeneutica e cristologia in W. Kasper. Palermo 1990, Augustinus. 311 p. Lit. 50.000. - ᴿDivThom 90 (1990) 170s (L. *Elders*).

m157 KIRK: *Hebblethwaite* Brian, Kirk, Kenneth Escott (1886-1954) ['der führende anglikanische Moraltheologe des 20. Jh.'], ᵀ*Schäferdiek* Barbara ➤ 857, TRE 19 (1990) 213-7.

m158 KLAUSER: *Dassmann* Ernst, Klauser, Theodor (1894-1984) ['RAC'; 'JbAC']: ➤ 857, TRE 19 (1990) 241-4.

m159 KÜNG Hans, Under Rome's displeasure [< Welt am Sonntag]: Tablet 244 (1990) 125s.

m161 LEWIS: **Christensen** Michael, C. S. Lewis on Scripture. L 1989 = 1979, Hodder & S. 126 p. £4. 0-340-50271-1. - ᴿExpTim 101 (1989s) 127 [C. S. *Rodd*].

m162 *Howe* Rex, C. S. Lewis, 'surprised by joy': ExpTim 101 (1989s) 356-9.

m163 **Sayer** George, Jack; C. S. Lewis 1988 ➤ 5,k583: ᴿRExp 87 (1990) 156s (H. L. *Poe*).

m164 **Wilson** A. N., C. S. Lewis, a biography. L 1990, Norton. $22.50. 0-393-02813-5. - ᴿTablet 244 (1990) 249 (R. *Billington*).

m165 LINDBECK: *Baasland* Ernst, Intratekstualitet og kontekstualisering; noen (some) tendenser i nordamerikansk teologi [LINDBECK G. 1984]: TsTKi 60 (1989) 41-54.

m166 **LØGSTRUP** K. E. † 1981: *Hansen* Karstein M., [➤ 1044] 'Some en kilde af jorden ...'; ny Løgstrup-litteratur: NorTTs 90 (1989) 219-228.

m167 LONERGAN: *Bernard* Johannes † 1989, Bernard Lonergans Methode der Theologie: TGL 80 (1990) 243-252.

m168 ᴱ**Crowe** Frederick E., *Doran* Robert M., The collected works of Bernard Lonergan, < (first published) Collection. Toronto 1988, Univ. xviii-349 p. £26.50. - ᴿHeythJ 31 (1990) 85s (G. *Walmsley*).

m169 ᴱ**Fallon** Timothy P., *Riley* Phillip B., Religion and culture... Lonergan 1984/6 ➤ 3,668: ᴿHeythJ 31 (1990) 83-85 (G. *Walmsley*).

m170 ᴱ**Gregson** Vernon, The desires of the human heart; an introduction to the theology of Bernard Lonergan 1988 ➤ 5,k584: ᴿNRT 112 (1990) 613s (L. *Renwart*); PerspRelSt 17 (1990) 175-180 (D. W. *Hudson*); TorJT 6 (1990) 310-2 (J. F. *Wallenhorst*); TS 51 (1990) 348-350 (D. L. *Gelpi:* sans critique); TLZ 115 (1990) 532-4 (G. B. *Sala*).

McEvenue S., *Meyer* B., Lonergan's Hermeneutics 1989 ➤ 1294.

m170* LORTZ: **Lautenschläger** Gabriele, Joseph Lortz (1887-1975) — Weg, Umwelt und Werk eines katholischen Kirchenhistorikers [Diss. Würzburg, ᴰWittstadt P.]. Wü 1987, Echter. – ᴿTGL 80 (1990) 345-8 (R. M. *Bucher*).

m171 DE LUBAC: *Bertoldi* Francesco, The religious sense in Henri de Lubac: CommND 16 (1989) 6-31.

m172 *Komonchak* Joseph A., Theology and culture at mid-century; the example of Henri de Lubac: TS 51 (1990) 579-602.

m173 **Lubac** Henri de, Mémoire sur l'occasion de mes écrits 1989 ➤ 5,k594: ᴿTS 51 (1990) 759-761 (D. *Donovan*: highly personal and deeply moving: attacks on DANIÉLOU by confrères were motivated by 'fratricidal hatred'); ZkT 112 (1990) 205-8 (K. H. *Neufeld*).

m174 **Lubac** Henri de, Théologie dans l'histoire; 1. La lumière du Christ, préf. *Sales* Michel; II. Questions disputées et résistance au nazisme. P 1990, D-Brouwer. 222 p.; 420 p. F 130, F 175 [TR 86,428].

m174* **McCool** Gerald A., From unity to pluralism; the internal evolution of Thomism [...de Lubac]. NY 1989, Fordham Univ. 248 p. [JRel 71,583, R. *McInerny*].

m175 **Russo** Antonio, Henri de Lubac, teologia e dogma nella storia; l'influsso di BLONDEL [diss. Tübingen], pref. *Kasper* Walter: La Cultura 11. R 1990, Studium. 433 p. Lit. 42.000 [TR 87,432].

m175* *Russo* Antonio, Henri de Lubac, Il soprannaturale e la vita quotidiana: Studium 85 (R 1989) 359-371.

m176 MACHEN: *Marsden* George, Understanding J. Gresham Machen: PrincSemB 11,1 (1990) 46-60 [< ZIT 90,388].

m177 MACQUARRIE: **Jenkins** David, The scope and limits of John Macquarrie's existential theology [diss. Uppsala]: St.Doct.Chr. 27. U 1987, Univ. 154 p. – ᴿTsTKi 60 (1989) 74 (J.-O. *Henriksen*).

m178 MERSCH: *Malanowski* Gregory E., Émile Mersch, S. J., (1890-1940); un christocentrisme unifié: NRT 112 (1990) 44-66.

m179 **MICHEL** O., Anpassung oder Widerstand; eine Autobiographie. Wu/Z 1989, Brockhaus. 197 p. DM 29,80. 3-417-12577-4 [NTAbs 34,239].

m180 MOLTMANN: **Gómez Sánchez** C., Identidad y relevancia del cristianismo; introducción al pensamiento de J. Moltmann: Aula Abierta 17. M 1987, Univ. a Distancia. 300 p. – ᴿCommSev 22 (1989) 430s (M. *Sánchez*).

Bauckham R., Moltmann, messianic theology 1987 ➤ 7382.

m181 **Moltmann** Jürgen, Theology today 1988 ➤ 4,8161: ᴿExpTim 101 (1989s) 55 (D. *Ferguson*).

m182 MONTEFIORE: **Peart-Binns** John S., Bishop Hugh Montefiore. 1990, Quarter. xviii-364 p. £18.50. – ᴿTLond 93 (1990) 493s (P. *Hinchliff*).

m183 MURRAY: **McElroy** Robert W., The search for an American public theology; the contribution of John Courtney Murray. NY 1989, Paulist. $11. 0-8091-3051-3. – ᴿHorizons 17 (1990) 360-2 (Stephen *Pope*); TS 51 (1990) 164-6 (J. L. *Hooper*).

m184 OTTO: *Minney* Robin, The development of Otto's thought 1898-1917; from LUTHER's view of the Holy Spirit to The holy: RelSt 26 (1990) 505-524.

m185 PANNENBERG [➤ 7257]: **Grenz** Stanley J., Reason for hope; the systematic theology of W. Pannenberg. NY 1990, Oxford-UP. ix-279 p. $32.50. – ᴿTS 51 (1990) 764-6 (Elizabeth A. *Johnson*).

m186 *Martínez Camino* Juan A., La 'Teología sistemática' de W. Pannenberg [I. 1988]: EstE 65 (1990) 215-225.

m187 **Polk** David P.,   On the way to God; an exploration into the theology of
Wolfhart Pannenberg D1989 ➤ 5,k612:   RExpTim 101 (1989s) 250 (G. T.
Eddy: some echoes of K. POPPER's attack on 'historicism'); TS 51 (1990)
352-4 (T. *Peters*); TLZ 115 (1990) 295-7 (G. *Wenz*).

m188 PAULUS VI: *Adornato* Giselda,   Recenti studi su Paolo VI: HumBr 45
(1990) 224-8.

m189 *Chadwick* Henry,   Paul VI and Vatican II [Acta Roma & Brescia 1986]:
JEH 41 (1990) 463-9.

m190 *Paul VI*, Journées d'Études 1984, réforme liturgique; FrS 1985, réformes
institutionnelles. R 1987, Studium. xi-86 p. ix-106 p. Lit. 15.000 each.
88-382-3549-X; -50-3. – RJEH 40 (1989) 613-5 (P. *Hebblethwaite*).

m191 **PELIKAN** Jaroslav,   Melody of theology 1988 ➤ 5,k618:   RCritRR 3
(1990) 471s (C. J. *Peter*); JRel 70 (1990) 112 (E. *TeSelle*).

m192 PETERSON: *Nichtweiss* B.,   Erik Peterson [1890-1960; NT]; Leben,
Werk und Wirkung: StiZt 208 (1990) 529-544 [< NTAbs 35,2].

m193 PRZYWARA: *Neufeld* Karl H.,   Vertiefte und gelebte Katholizität; Erich
Przywara — 100 Jahre [geb. 1889]: TPhil 65 (1990) 161-171.

m194 PUECH: *Ries* J.,   Puech, Henri-Charles, 1902-1986: ➤ 833, Catholicisme 13,55 (1989) 284s.

m195 RAHNER: **Althapilly** Sebastian,   Glaube und Welt; eine Studie über das
Wohl-Heil-Verhältnis bei Karl Rahner: Diss. Graz 70. Graz 1987, DBV.
318 p. Sch 192,50. – RTPQ 138 (1990) 284s (O. *König*).

m196 **Bonsor** Jack A.,   Rahner, HEIDEGGER and truth; Karl Rahner's notion
of Christian truth; the influence of Heidegger; pref. F. *Schüssler Fiorenza*
1987 ➤ 5,k620:   RRTLv 21 (1990) 238s (E. *Brito*).

m197 **Hines** Mary E.,   The transformation of dogma; an introduction to
Karl Rahner on doctrine 1989 ➤ 5,k622:   RNewTR 3,2 (1990) 102 (J. P.
Szura).

m198 **Imhof** P., *Biallowons* H.,   La fe en tiempo de invierno; diálogos con
Karl Rahner en los últimos años de su vida TAlbizu José Luis:
Cristianismo y Sociedad 17, 1989 ➤ 5,k623:   RLumenVr 39 (1990) 190-2
(U. *Gil Ortega*).

m199 EImhof Paul, *Biallowons* Hubert,   Faith in a wintry season [= 1986
➤ 3,g992]; conversations and interviews with Karl Rahner in the last
years of his life, TEgan Harvey D. NY 1990, Crossroad. 207 p. $23.
0-8245-0909-9 [TDig 37,381].

m200 *Miggelbrink* Rolf,   Die Theologie Karl Rahners vor dem Anspruch des
Lehramtes: WissWeis [52 (1989) 21-62, *Vogels* H.-J.] 53 (1990) 185-203.

m201 *Neufeld* Karl H.,   Worte ins Schweigen [Karl Rahner's first book, 1938;
10 editions + 5 translations; theologically rich but overlooked as a
'meditation-book']: ZkT 112 (1990) 427-436.

m201* *Vogels* Heinz-Jürgen,   Erreicht Karl Rahners Theologie den kirchlichen Glauben? Kritik der Christologie und Trinitätslehre: WissWeis 52
(1989) 21-62.

m202 **Rahner** Karl,   Spirito nel mondo [1939, 2Metz J.] TMarassi M., *Zoerle*
A. Mi 1989, ViPe. 384 p. – REuntDoc 43 (1990) 542-4 (P. *Miccoli*).

m202* RAMSEY: **Chadwick** Owen,   Michael Ramsey, a life [1904-1988]. Ox
1990, Clarendon. xi-422 p. $30. 0-19-826189-8 [TDig 38,154: com-
missioned by Ramsey].

m203 RATZINGER: *a*) ENeuhaus R.,   Biblical interpretation in crisis; the
Ratzinger conference 1989 ➤ 5,591a: RCalvinT 25 (1990) 297-9 (T.

Longman). – *b*) Schriftauslegung im Widerstreit: QDisp 117, 1989 ➤ 5,591*b*: ᴿNRT 112 (1990) 895s (X. *Jacques*); TGL 80 (1990) 526s (W. *Knoch*).

m204 **Nichols** Aidan, Theology of J. Ratzinger 1988 ➤ 4,k538; 5,k632: ᴿNorTTs 90 (1989) 252-4 (Ola *Tjørhom*).

m205 **Ratzinger** Joseph, Principles of Catholic theology 1987 ➤ 3,281; 4,8173: ᴿScotBEv 8 (1990) 67s (J. *Atkinson*: good).

m206 RAUSCHENBUSCH: **Minus** Paul M., W. Rauschenbusch, American reformer 1988 ➤ 4,k540*; 5,k635: ᴿJRel 70 (1990) 108-110 (C. E. *Johnson*); JScStR 29 (1990) 137-140 (H. *Cox*); ZRGg 42 (1990) 183s (C. *Bresina*).

m206* **Peden** Creighton, The Chicago school; voices in liberal religious thought. Bristol IN 1987, Wyndham Hall. 171 p. – ᴿJRel 70 (1990) 107 (L. L. *Greenfield*).

m207 **White** Ronald C.ᴶ, Liberty and justice for all; racial reform and the social gospel (1877-1925): Rauschenbusch Lectures 2. SF 1990, Harper & R. xxiv-309 p. $36 [CBQ 53,174].

m208 RITSCHL: **Weyer-Menkhoff** S., Aufklärung und Offenbarung; zur Systematik der Theologie A. Ritschls ➤ 5,k638: [Diss.]; GöTArb 37, 1988; 3-525-87390-5: ᴿÉTRel 65 (1990) 139 (J.-D. *Kraege*).

m209 SCHILLEBEECKX: **Schreiter** R. J., *Hilkert* Mary C., The praxis of Christian experience ... Schillebeeckx 1989 ➤ 5,514: ᴿNewTR 3,1 (1990) 100s (J. *Nilson*); TS 51 (1990) 180 (P. *Chirico*).

Schillebeeckx Edward, Mensen als verhaal van God 1989 ➤ 7190.

m211 **Schillebeeckx** E., Om het behoud van het evangelie: Evangelic verhalen II [I.1982]. Baarn 1988, Nelissen. 213 p. Fb. 650. – ᴿCollatVL 20 (1990) 104s (J. *De Kesel*).

m212 *Schoof* Ted, E. Schillebeeckx; 25 years in Nijmegen [< Mededenken met E. S. (Baarn 1983) 11-39],ᵀ: TDig 37 (1990) 313-332 ...

m213 ᴱSchreiter Robert, The Schillebeeckx reader 1984 ➤ 65,e64; 3,h15: ᴿCritRR 2 (1989) 462-4 (J. B. *Morris*).

m214 SCHNIEWIND: **Kraus** H.-J., Julius Schniewind [1883-1946], Charisma der Theologie² [¹1965]: TVG Mg 241. Giessen 1990, Brunnen. 285 p. DM 39. 3-7655-9241-2 [NTAbs 35,94]. – ᴿSNTU-A 15 (1990) 146s (F. *Kogler*).

m214* STAEHELIN: *Schmidt* Martin A., Ernst STAEHELIN [1889-1980] als ökumenischer Theologe: TZBas 46 (1990) 339-350.

m215 TEILHARD: *Noir* Pierre, Teilhard de Chardin: ➤ 837, DictSpir 96ss (1990) 115-126.

m216 *Schiwy* Günther, Der Gott der Evolution; der kosmische Christus im Werk von Teilhard de Chardin: ➤ 394*, ᴱBresch Carsten, Gott aus Natur? 1990, 102-116.

m217 VAN TIL: *Oliphint* Scott, The consistency of [Cornelius] Van Til's methodology: WestTJ 52 (1990) 27-49.

m218 TILLICH: *Otto* Randall E., The doctrine of God in the theology of Paul Tillich [... 'Is Tillich a theist?']: WestTJ 52 (1990) 303-323: no.

m219 ᴱRatschow Carl H., *al.*, Paul Tillich, Main works / Hauptwerke; 1. ᴱWenz Günther, [13] Philosophical Writings; 2. ᴱPalmer Michel, [28] Writings in the Philosophy of Culture. B/Fra 1989s, de Gruyter / Ev.-V. xiv-420 p.; xiv-382 p. DM 134 + 138 [TR 87, 294, E. *Sturm*].

m220 **Schüssler** Werner, Jenseits von Religion und Nicht-Religion; der Religionsbegriff im Werk Paul Tillichs: Mg Theologie 4. Fra 1989, Athenäum. 264 p. DM 78 [TR 87, 302, G. *Wenz*].

m221 *Thomas* J. Heywood, Tillich's contribution to a world theology: ScotJT 43 (1990) 350-365.

m222 TORRANCE: *Kruger* C. Baxter, The doctrine of the knowledge of God in the theology of T. F. Torrance; sharing in the Son's communion with the Father in the Spirit: ScotJT 43 (1990) 366-389.

m223 TROELTSCH: **Coakley** Sarah, Christ without absolutes... Troeltsch 1988 → 5,7492: ᴿInterpretation 44 (1990) 100s (J. C. *Livingston*); JTS 41 (1990) 769-772 (D. *Ninehan*); Month 251 (1990) 25s (B. R. *Brinkman*: good); RelSt 25 (1989) 399-401 (D. *Pailin*).

m224 **Dietrich** Wendell S., COHEN and Troeltsch; ethical monotheistic religion and theory of culture: BrownJudSt 120, 1986 → 4,k561; 5,k658: ᴿRÉJ 149 (1990) 254-6 (M. R. *Hayoun*: 'brève mais ô combien dense').

m224* **Griener** George E.ᴶ, Ernst Troeltsch and Herman SCHELL; Christianity and the world religions; an ecumenical contribution to the history of apologetics [diss. Tübingen]: EurUnivSt 23/375. NY 1990, P. Lang. 348 p. $64.80 pa. 3-631-40858-7 [TDig 38,162].

m225 WILES: **Rothuizen** Gerard, Apologetics in Oxford; the theology of Maurice F. Wiles. Kampen 1987, Cahiers. 94 p. £6.65. – ᴿModT 7 (1990s) 198s (J. *Draper*).

m225* WILLEBRANDS: **Purdy** William A., Ecumenist of our time, Jan Cardinal Willebrands: Mid-Stream 29 (1990) 120-133.

m226 WITTGENSTEIN: **Kerr** Fergus, Theology after Wittgenstein 1986 → 2,e102 ... 5,k663: ᴿHeythJ 31 (1990) 80s (H. *Meynell*); TLZ 115 (1990) 367-9 (W. *Flach*).

Y6.8 *Tendentiae exeuntis saeculi XX* – **Late 20th Century Movements.**

m227 **Alegre** X., *al.*, Iglesia, ¿de dónde vienes? ¿a dónde vas? Barc 1989, Cristianisme i justicie. 157 p. – ᴿLumenVr 39 (1990) 537s (F. *Ortiz de Urtaran*).

m228 **Allen** Diogenes, Christian belief in a postmodern world 1989 → 5,k667: ᴿHorizons 17 (1990) 349s (Irena *Makarushka*).

m229 *Alves* Angelo, Da pós-modernidade à Era ecuménica; 1989 — inicio de uma nova era?: HumTeol 2 (1990) 89-93.

m230 **Bauberot** Jean, Le Protestantisme doit-il mourir? 1988 → 5,k668: ᴿExpTim 101 (1989s) 59s (W. S. F. *Pickering*).

m231 *Berger* Peter, American Lutheranism at the crossroads: Dialog 27 (St. Paul 1988) 90-96 [-117, responses; 118-120, rejoinder].

m232 *Berzosa Martínez* Raúl, ¿Hacer teología desde la postmodernidad?: Burgense 31 (1990) 201-212.

m232* **Birch** Charles, A purpose for everything; religion in a postmodern worldview. Mystic CT 1990, Twenty-Third. xvii-195 p. $15. 0-89622-453-8 [TDig 38,252].

m233 *Blenkinsopp* Joseph, An agenda for the 21st century: BR 6,1 (1990) 12s.

m234 *Boff* Clodovis M., Para onde irá a Igreja da América Latina? (Análise de proposta central do Documento preparatório a Santo Domingo): REB 50 (1990) [44-75; 191-4] 275-286 (-381, *al.*).

m235 **Breech** James, Jesus and postmodernism. Ph 1989, Augsburg Fortress. 96 p. $8. – ᴿCurrTMiss 17 (1990) 462s (J. C. *Rochelle*).

m235* **Bühlmann** Walbert, With eyes to see; Church and world in the third millennium [1984 → 1,g284], ᵀBarr Robert R. Mkn 1990, Orbis. vi-162 p. $15. 0-85344-683-9 [TDig 38,152].

m236 a) *Burnett* Fred W., Postmodern biblical exegesis; the eve of historical criticism; – b) *Taylor* Mark C., The eventuality of texts [from his Texts 1989]: ➤ 365, Semeia 51 (1990) 51-80 / 215-240.

m237 ᴱCooke Bernard, The Papacy and the Church in the U.S. 1989 ➤ 5,649: ᴿTS 51 (1990) 378s (D.J. *Grimes*).

m238 **Cupitt** Don, Radicals and the future of the Church. L 1989, SCM. 183 p. £7. 0-334-02289-4. – ᴿEcuR 42 (1990) 354s (P. G. *Henry*: 2d-century Gnostic reaction to nightmare 'We are going to become American'); ExpTim 101 (1989s) 86 (J. *Kent*: 'Why should a radical remain in the Church? Hoping to help radicalize it'); Month 250 (1989) 280s (R. *Butterworth*).

m239 Le deuxième concile du Vatican 1986/9 ➤ 5,652: ᴿNRT 112 (1990) 428s (N. *Plumat*).

m239* *Di Noia* J.A., American Catholic theology at century's end; postconciliar, postmodern, post-Thomistic: Thomist 54 (1990) 499-529.

m240 **Drummond** Richard H., Towards a new age in Christian theology 1985 ➤ 1,g291 ... 5,k673: ᴿEstE 65 (1990) 101s (J.J. *Alemany*); Vidyajyoti 53 (1988) 680s (G. V. *Lobo*).

m241 **Edwards** David L., The futures of Christianity 1988 ➤ 3,h53 ... 5,k674: ᴿAnglTR 72 (1990) 110-2 (V. Nelle *Bellamy*).

m242 a) *Feitzer* Heinz, Kirche auf dem Weg ins Jahr 2000 — Krise als Chance zum Aufbruch?; – b) *Bitter* Gottfried, Die verlorene Kirche — die gesuchte Kirche: TrierTZ 98 (1989) 242-261 / 262-279.

m243 *Fick* Ulrich [United Bible Societies secretary, honorary doctorate of Budapest Reformed Theology Academy 7-14.XI.1989], ⓜ Christianity in the next thousand years, ᵀ*Fóris* (Mrs.) Eva K.]: TSzem 33 (1990) 17-32.

m244 **Griffin** David R., God and religion in the postmodern world 1989 ➤ 5,k679: ᴿAnglTR 72 (1990) 209-219 (O.C. *Thomas*, also on three cognate SUNY books edited by Griffin); JRel 70 (1990) 646 (C. Λ. *Wilson*); TLZ 115 (1990) 135s (J. *Langer*).

m245 **Groos** Helmut, Christlicher Glaube und intellektuelles Gewissen; Christentumskritik am Ende des Zweiten Jahrtausends 1987 ➤ 3,h55 ... 5,k682; 3-16-145245-3: ᴿBijdragen 51 (1990) 91s (H.J. *Adriaanse*); TsTKi 61 (1990) 235-7 (S. O. *Thorbjørnsen*).

m246 **Groothuis** Douglas, Confronting the New Age. DG 1988, InterVarsity. 230 p. $8 pa. – ᴿCriswT 4 (1989s) 206 (B. *Vinson*: sequel to his 'Unmasking the New Age').

m247 *Häring* Bernard, The Church I want / Life in the Spirit: Tablet 244 (1990) 944s / 998s.

m248 **Hesselgrave** David J., Today's choices for tomorrow's mission; an evangelical perspective on trends and issues in missions. GR 1988, Zondervan. 304 p. $15 pa. – ᴿCriswT 4 (1989s) 448s (C. R. *Wells*).

m249 ᴱHomerski Józef, *Szulc* Franciszek, ⓟ W dwudziestolecie Soboru Watykańskiego II; recepcja — doświadczenia — perspektywy. Lublin 1987, KUL. 239 p. – ᴿAtKap 114 (1990) 505s (J. *Królikowski*).

m250 *Houdijk* Rinus, De mens onttrond? Het postmoderne denken en de theologie: TsTNijm 30 (1990) 276-296; Eng. 286s, Man dethroned?

m251 **Hunter** James D., Evangelicalism; the coming generation 1987 ➤ 3,h62 ... 5,k685: ᴿRExp 87 (1990) 486 (B.J. *Leonard*).

m252 **Iniesta** Alberto, Memorandum; ayer, hoy y mañana de la Iglesia en España: Cristianismo y Sociedad 19. Bilbao 1989, D-Brouwer. 193 p. – ᴿLumenVr 39 (1990) 76s (U. *Gil Ortega*).

m253 ^E**Jacobs** J., Is Pinksteren voorbij? Het Tweede Vaticaans Oecumenisch Concilie tussen geschiedenis en actualiteit. Hilversum 1989, Gooi & S. 111 p. Fb. 390. – ^RCollatVL 20 (1990) 357s (E. Van *Walderen*).

m254 **Jensen** Anne, Die Zukunft der Orthodoxie; Konzilspläne und Kirchenstrukturen; Vorw. Metrop. *Damaskinos*: ÖkT 14. Z 1986, Benziger. 384 p. – ^ROstkSt 38 (1989) 199-201 (W. *Hryniewicz*, ^T*Patock* C.).

m255 **Jorstad** Erling, The new Christian Right, 1981-1988; prospects for the post-Reagan decade. Lewiston NY 1987, Lampeter. 286 p. $40. 0-88946-669-6. – ^RRExp 87 (1990) 147s (E. G. *Hinson*).

m256 **Küng** Hans, Theology for the third millennium, an ecumenical view 1988 ➤ 4,k607; 5,k693: ^RAsbTJ 45,1 (1990) 87-89 (K. J. *Collins*); EcuR 42 (1990) 175-7 (A. van der *Bent*).

m257 **Küng** Hans, Une théologie pour le troisième millénaire; pour un nouveau départ œcuménique [Theologie im Aufbruch 1987], ^T*Feisthauer* J. P 1989, Seuil. 389 p. F 130. – ^RPastoral Sciences 9 (1990) 213-5 (J. *Gauthier*).

m258 **Küng** Hans, Teología para la postmodernidad. M 1989, Alianza. 204 p. – ^RIter 1 (Caracas 1990) 127-130 (C. *Bazarra*: claro y convincente).

m259 ^E**Küng** H., *Swidler* L., The Church in anguish 1987 ➤ 4,k606; 5,k690: ^RJeevadhara 19 (1989) 309s (R. *Rao*).

m260 ^E**Latourelle** René, Vaticano II, bilancio e prospettive venticinque anni dopo, 1987 ²1988 ➤ 4,k608*; 5,k695: ^RRasT 31 (1990) 515-522 (V. *Caporale*); ViPe 72 (1989) 470s (G. *Cristaldi*).

m260* — **Colombo** G., present., Atto accademico per la presentazione di Vaticano II, bilancio e prospettive: Pubbl. Ist. Paolo VI, 8. Brescia/R 1989, Ist. Paolo VI / Studium. 76 p. 88-382-3604-6.

m261 ^E**Latourelle** R., Vatican II, Assessment 1988s ➤ 5,k697: ^RHorizons 17 (1990) 156-8 (Carmel *McEnroy*).

m262 ^E**Latourelle** R., Vaticano II, balance y perspectivas: Verdad e Imagen 109, 1989 ➤ 5,k698: ^RActuBbg 27 (1990) 209s (J. *Boada*); CommSev 23 (1990) 434s (M. *Sánchez*); LumenVr 39 (1990) 85s (F. *Ortiz de Urtaran*); NatGrac 37 (1990) 130s (A. *Villalmonte*).

m263 **Laurentin** René, Église qui vient; au-delà des crises. P 1990, Desclée. 234 p. – ^REphMar 40 (1990) 175 (T. P. *Iterriaga*); EsprVie 100 (1990) 410-412 (G. *Viard*).

m264 *Leuba* Jean-Louis, Jean-Paul II et la Curie trahissent-ils Vatican II [... les critiques mordantes de GREINACHER-KÜNG ^E1986, s'adressent en fait non plus au gouvernement actuel de l'Église romaine, mais bien à Vatican II lui-même]: RTPhil 122 (1990) 261-8; Eng. 296.

m265 *Löwe* Hartmut, Ein Blick, freundlich und kritisch, auf die evangelische Kirche: ZTK 87 (1990) 271-284.

m266 *Lorizio* G., Prospettive teologiche del post-moderno: RasT 30 (1989) 539-559.

m267 *Lustiger* Jean-Marie card., La nouveauté du Christ et la Post-Modernité [discours pour son doctorat honoris causa]: RICathP 33 (1990) 3-14.

m268 *Martínez Camino* Juan A., Teología y postmodernidad: MiscCom 48 (1990) 21-33.

m269 **Meagher** John C., The truing of Christianity; visions of life and thought for the future. NY 1990, Doubleday. [xi-] 385 p. $22 [CBQ 52,780].

m270 *Melloni* Alberto, Per un approccio storico-critico ai Consilia et vota della fase antepreparatoria del Vaticano II: RivStoLR 26 (1990) 556-576.

m270* a) *Melloni* A., Tensioni e timori nella preparazione del Vaticano II; – b) *Indelicato* A., Lo schema 'De Deposito Fidei pure custodiendo' e la preparazione del Vaticano II: CrNSt 11 (1990) 275-208 / 309-356 [< ZIT 91,37].

m271 *Metz* Johann-B., Das Konzil — 'der Anfang eines Anfangs?': Orientierung 54 (1990) 245-250.

m272 **Moltmann** Jürgen, Creating a just future. L/Ph 1989, SCM/Trinity. 104 p. – ᴿEcuR 42 (1990) 179-181 (J. W. Van *Hoeven*).

m273 *Müller* Hans Martin, Die Postmoderne und die Konfessionen: ZTK 87 (1990) 359-375.

m274 **Muggeridge** Anne R., The desolate city; revolution in the Catholic Church [since Vatican II]. SF 1986, Harper & R. 217 p. $17. – ᴿCathHR 75 (1989) 122s (J. *Hitchcock*: bleakly pessimistic).

m275 *Nestì* Arnaldo, La Religión y el post-modernismo; para una definición histórico-sociológica: CommSev 23 (1990) 379-393.

m276 **Neuhaus** Richard J., The Catholic moment 1987 ⇢ 3,h74 ... 5,k707: ᴿCommND 15 (1988) 474-487 (G. W. *Olsen*) & 488-496 (J. B. *Benestad*); 16 (1989) 552-7 (Neuhaus reaction; 558-560 rejoinders); CurrTMiss 17 (1990) 236s (J. K. *Robbins*).

m277 *O'Collins* Gerald, Teologia católica (1965-1990): Brotéria 130 (1990) 3-9.

m278 **Oden** Thomas C., After modernity... what?; agenda for theology [= Agenda for theology 1979 + 4 chapters]. GR 1990, Zondervan Academie. 224 p. $15. 0-310-75390-2 [TDig 38,77]. – ᴿCalvinT 25 (1990) 318s (R. J. *Feenstra*).

m279 *Olson* Alan M., Postmodernity and faith: JAAR 58 (1990) 37-53.

m280 *Ong* Walter J., Realizing Catholicism; faith, learning, and the future [Dayton Univ. Marianist award lecture, Jan. 26, 1989]: TDig 37 (1990) 333-340.

m281 *Pestka* Jan, 🅿 L'identité chrétienne vis-à-vis des changements dans le monde contemporain: AtKap 112 (1989) 80-90.

m282 **Rigal** J., Préparer l'avenir de l'Église: Théologies. P 1990, Cerf. 194 p. F 99. – ᴿNRT 112 (1990) 742 (A. *Toubeau*).

m283 *Romaniuk* Kazimierz bp. 🄳 Biblistyka ostatniego ćwierćwiecza [last 25 years]: AtKap 115 (1990) 1-16.

m284 **Roof** Wade C., *McKinney* William, American mainline religion; its changing shape and future [BIP: America mainline... shape of the religious establishment]. New Brunswick 1987, Rutgers Univ. 279 p. $32; pa. $12. 0-8135-1215-8; -6-6. – ᴿPerspRelSt 17 (1990) 269-272 (K. H. *Carter*, also on WEIGEL G. 1989 and ᴱMILLER W., al., 1988).

m285 *Russo* Adolfo, La teologia verso il duemila; per una funzione critica del totalitarismo culturale: Asprenas 37 (1990) 131-144.

m286 ᴱ**Seeber** David, Brauchen wir ein neues Konzil? Erfahrungen mit dem II. Vaticanum: Tb 1400, 1987 ⇢ 5,k714: 191 p. DM 11. – ᴿTLZ 115 (1990) 384 (H. *Kirchner*).

m287 *Slater* Peter, Theology in the 1990s: TorJT 6 (1990) 286-297.

m288 **Thils** Gustave, L'après Vatican II un nouvel âge de l'Église? 1985 ⇢ 1,g324: ᴿAtKap 114 (1990) 496-8 (A. *Nowicki*).

m289 **Zulehner** P. M., Pastorale Futurologie; Kirche auf dem Weg ins gesellschaftliche Morgen: Pastoraltheologie 4. Dü 1990, Patmos. 332 p. DM 50. 3-491-77657-0. – ᴿTsTNijm 30 (1990) 426 (G. *Heitink*).

Y7 *(Acta) Congressuum* .2 *biblica:* **nuntii**, rapports, Berichte.

m290 AAR [American Academy of Religion]–SBL annual meeting. New Orleans 1990. 284 p.; program only.

m291 *Abledler* Giovanni, Musica e Bibbia [convegno internazionale BIBLIA (con l'Accademia Chigiana), Siena 24-26 agosto 1990]: CC 141 (1990,4) 590-6.

m292 *a*) *Borgonovo* Gianantonio, Pentateuco come Torah; storiografia e normatività religiosa nell'Israele antico (VI convegno interdisciplinare sull'AT, Prato 11-13 settembre 1989); – *b*) *Ghiberti* Giuseppe, Il Giovannismo alle origini cristiane; III convegno interdisciplinare sul NT, Prato, 14-15 settembre 1989: ScuolC 117 (1989) 670-681 / 682-4.

m293 *Chmiel* Jerzy, ❷ Fifth biblical colloquium in Vienna 1988: RuBi 42 (1989) 396s.

m294 Colloquium œcumenicum paulinum XII (25-30 Sept. 1989) ❻: DeltioVM 18,2 (1989) 99-108.

m295 *Duarte Castillo* Raúl, Encuentro internacional de la Sociedad de Literatura Bíblica [Copenhague 6-9.VIII.1989], algunos puntos de vista: EfMex 8 (1990) 93-102.

m296 *a*) *Fabry* H.-J., Bericht zum XIII. Kongress der IOSOT vom 27.VIII. bis 1.IX.1989 in Leuven/Belgien; – *b*) *Scholtissek* K., *Kertelge* K., 44th general meeting der SNTS vom 24.-28. Juli 1989 in Dublin: BZ 34 (1990) 148-150 / 151-3.

m297 *Fernández Marcos* N., Debate sobre la historia del texto bíblico [Mesa Redonda M 28.III.1990]: Sefarad 50 (1990) 517-9.

m298 *Fernández Marcos* N., *a*) VII Congreso [Septuag.-Cog. 25-26.VIII.1989] (*Ortega Monasterio* María T., Masoretic); – *b*) III Simposio (luso-)español [17-20.IX.1989]: Sefarad 50 (1990) 241-3 (246s) / 243-5.

m299 *Focant* Camille, Jésus et les synoptiques; colloquium biblicum lovaniense XXXIX [7-9.VIII.1990]: RTLv 21 (1990) 517-9.

m300 *Hay* David, Some recent PHILO meetings [with SNTS, Dublin 25-27.VII.1989; with SBL, Anaheim 18-20.XI.1989]: StPhilonAn 2 (1990) 227s.

m301 *a*) *Kapera* Zdzisław J., ❷ Drugie... Second international Qumran colloquium, Kraków-Mogilany (10-15 Aug.) 1989; – *b*) *Mędala* Stanisław, ❷ Sprawozdanie z ... Report of the international Qumran congress in Groningen (20-23 Aug. 1989): RuBi 43 (1990) 160-2 / 158-160.

m302 *Kaplan* Josef, From Christianity to Judaism [❶ 1982]... [EstLul 30 (1990) 221s sobre p. 179-89, ZEPEDA; LULL].

m303 *Karavidopoulos* I.K., ❻ Colloquium biblicum lovaniense 39, 7-9.VIII.1990: DeltioVM 19,2 (1990) 62-71.

m304 *Leonardi* Giovanni, I Vangeli dell'Infanzia di Matteo e di Luca; XXXI Settimana Biblica Nazionale dell'ABI (10-14 settembre 1990): StPatav 37 (1990) 737-749.

m305 *Matras* Tadeusz, ❷ XXVII obrady... 27th conference of the section of Polish biblists, Lublin 1989 (12-13 Sept.): RuBi 43 (1990) 157s.

m306 *Nobile* Marco, Il XIII Congresso dell'IOSOT [Lv 27.VIII.–1.IX. 1989]: Antonianum 65 (1990) 126s.

m307 *Oyen* Geert Van, Bijbelse studiedagen te Leuven ['Johannes en de synoptische evangeliën', 7-9.VIII.1990]: TsTNijm 30 (1990) 401.

m308 *Rothschild* Jean-Pierre, Le colloque 'Manoscritti, frammenti e libri ebraici nell'Italia del '400 et del '500', San Miniato, 7-9 Novembre 1988: RÉJ 149 (1990) 335-8.

m309 *Schäfer* Rolf, 'Sola Scriptura' — Theologenkongress in Dresden: LuthMon 29 (1990) 500s [< ZIT 90,813].

m310 *Schroer* Silvia, Die Bibel in der neuen Evangelisation [4. Kath. Bibelföderation, Bogotá, Juli 1990]: Orientierung 54 (1990) 175-7.

m311 *Segalla* Giuseppe, 45º Congresso della Studiorum Novi Testamenti Societas (SNTS) all'Università Cattolica del Sacro Cuore (Milano 23-27 luglio 1990): StPatav 37 (1990) 425-434.

m312 *Shanks* Hershel, Celebrating at the annual [SBL, ASOR, AAR] meeting [Anaheim Nov. 18-21, 1989]: BAR-W 16,2 (1990) 26-31 [*Tubb* J.: KENYON was a mighty figure but obsessed with sequential minutiae].

m312* *Testa* Giuseppe, XXXI Settimana Biblica Nazionale dell'ABI (10-14 settembre 1990): DivThom 93 (1990) 132-144.

m313 *Tuckett* C.M., Studiorum Novi Testamenti Societas; the forty-fourth general meeting 24-28 July 1989: NTS 36 (1990) 295-7; 298-320, list of members with (residence) addresses.

m314 *Walsh* Jerome T., Report of the Fifty-Third General Meeting of the Catholic Biblical Association of America [Notre Dame, Aug. 13-16, 1990]: CBQ 52 (1990) 698-703; 703-6, participants without addresses.

Y7.4 *(Acta) theologica: nuntii.*

m315 *Ahrens* Theodor, Wie im Himmel, so auf Erden; Notizen zur 'Weltmissionskonferenz' in San Antonio [22.V.–1.VI.1989]: ZMissRW 74 (1990) 19-34.

m316 *Bagrowicz* Jerzy, *Hanc* Wojciech, ❷ L'héritage chrétien byzantino-slave; VI Congrès des théologiens polonais, Lublin KUL 12-14.IX.1989: AtKap 114 (1990) 131-139 (-150, *al.*).

m317 *Barnhouse* Ruth T., Science and religion; a new conversation [1sthmus institute, hints of past meetings and announcement of Dallas 1989]: Angl-TR 71 (1989) 120-3.

m318 *Berentsen* Jan-Martin, Tilbakeblikk på konferanseåret 1989 [San Antonio; Manila]: TsTKi 61 (1990) 145-152.

m318* *Berger* Teresa, Die Inkulturation der Liturgie; XII. internationaler Kongress der Societas Liturgica in York [14.-19.VIII.1989]: LtgJb 39 (1989) 253-264.

m319 *Bof* Giampiero, Il XIII congresso dell'Associazione Teologica Italiana [Brescia 11-15.IX.1989]: ScuolC 117 (1989) 659-669.

m320 *Borgman* Erik, Symposium voor theologen en sociale wetenschappers over secularisatie [Amst Vrije Univ. 1.VI.1990]: TsTNijm 30 (1990) 301s.

m321 *Bouwen* Frans, 'L'unité de l'Esprit par le lien de la paix'; Vᵉ assemblée générale du Conseil d'Églises du Moyen-Orient [Nicosie 22-28 janvier 1990]: PrOrChr 40 (1990) 93-119.

m322 *Cheza* Maurice, Session théologique interdiocésaine, 'Prophétisme et institution' [15-20 Oct. 1989, Blankenberge]: RTLv 21 (1990) 129-131.

m323 *Cheza* Maurice, Le Symposium [plusieurs, 1969-1990] des Conférences épiscopales d'Afrique et de Madagascar; le SCEAM: RTLv 21 (1990) 472-6.

m324 *Chrostowski* Waldemar, ❷ Jewish-Christian seminar in Chicago, June 29 - Aug. 18, 1989: RuBi 42 (1989) 398-401.

m325 *Crippa* Luigi, La concezione [understanding, not biological conception] dell'uomo nella tradizione monastica antica e medievale [Roma, S. Anselmo, 3-4 maggio 1990]: Benedictina 37 (1990) 205-213 (Crippa is the new Editor, successor to Lorenzo DE LORENZI) [*Carr* Ephrem, L'uomo nella cultura monastica della Siria romana, p. 205s].

m326 *Dal Covolo* Enrico, Il XIII convegno di catechesi patristica, La formazione sacerdotale nei Padri della Chiesa [Roma, 15-17 marzo 1990]:

a) Lateranum 56 (1990) 745-759; – *b*) PalCl 69 (1990) 435-448; – *c*) Salesianum 52 (1990) 703-715.

m327 *Dalmais* I. H.,   La conférence syriaque de Kottayam (3-8 sept. 1990): MaisD 183s (1990) 254-6.

m328 *Danese* Attilio,   Persona e sviluppo nel tempo del post-liberalismo: II Convegno Nazionale, Teramo 8-10 gennaio 1990:   MeliT 41,1 (1990) 69-86.

m329 *Deck* Allan F.,   Hispanic theologians and the U.S. Catholic Church [< Berkeley 1990 meeting]:   NewTR 3,4 (1990) 22-27 [3-88, 92-103 *al.*, 10 cognate articles].

m329* *Eisaks* Sheena,   European creationist conference [Leuven 1988]:   Evangel 7,3 (1989) 20s.

m330 *Engel* Lothar,   Spiritualität in der theologischen Ausbildung; Bericht über eine ökumenische Konsultation [Yokyakarta 20.-25. Juni 1989] und deren Vorgeschichte: ÖkRu 39 (1990) 109-116.

m331 *Evers* Georg,   *a*) Aziatische theologen op zoek naar een spiritualiteit van de bevrijding [Suanbo, S. Korea, 3-7.VII. 1989]; – *b*) Aziatische vrouwen over de dialoog tussen de godsdiensten [Kuala Lumpur 1-8.XI.1989]; – *c*) Conferentie over indiase christelijke theologie [Tiruchirapalli 28-31.XII.1989]: TsTNijm 30 (1990) 298 / 298s / 299.

m332 *Evers* Georg,   *a*) The search for a liberation spirituality, the EATWOT-Asia experience: 3d Asian Theological Conference, Suanbo, Korea 3-8.VII.1989; – *b*) Priestly formation, interiorization and integration: Asian Seminary Directors, Tagaytay City: TContext 7,2 (1990) 130s / 131s.

m333 *Farrugia* Edward G.,   Il primo incontro ecumenico di 'monaci' orientali e occidentali [Creta 12-15.V.1989]: CC 141 (1990,2) 471-9.

m333* *Frei* Hans A.,   Bericht über den XXV. Internationalen Altkatholiken-Kongress in Genf, 27.-31. August 1990:   IkiZ 80 (1990) 249-261 (-262) Jugend 24.-26. Aug.; *Seuling* Bernhard).

m334 *Gesteira Garza* Manuel,   Crónica de la 3ª Semana de Teología 1990 [Madrid]: RET 50 (1990) 469-471.

m335 *Giordan* Giuseppe,   Fede e storia in una chiesa di fraternità; Convegno di studi alla Facoltà teologica di Padova (14-15 febbraio 1990): StPatav 37 (1990) 413-424.

m335* *Govaert* Luitgart,   Symposion über J. H. Newman, 'Seine Liebe zu der Wahrheit' [Rom 26.-28.IV.1990]: ForumKT 6 (1990) 237-9.

m336 *Hakenes* Michael,   Ist Christus der einzige Weg zum Heil? Ein Tagungsbericht [St-Augustin 5.-9.VI.1990]:   ZMissRW 74 (1990) 243-5.

m337 *Halleux* André de,   Une commémoration du concile de Florence [1439(-1445): Bru 23-29.IX.1989]: RTLv 21 (1990) 128s.

m338 *Haquin* André,   Colloque de pastorale familiale, 'La sacramentalité du mariage' [Lv 22-23.IV.1989]: RTLv 21 (1990) 132s.

m339 *Heidemanns* Katja,   Zwischen Schwert und Kreuz; 500 Jahre Christentum in Lateinamerika; ein Tagungsbericht [Klagenfurt 7.-13.VII.1990]: ZMissRW 74 (1990) 298-302.

m340 *Hodgson* Peter E.,   The religion-science dialogue [ᴱ*Russell* R., Physics 1988: Vatican observatory conference for Newton's Principia tercentenary]: Month 250 (1989) 138-142.

m341 *Hoogen* T. van den,   Katholieke theologen over scheppingstheologie [19.V.1990]: TsTNijm 30 (1990) 300s.

m341* **Imstepf** Armin,   Die schweizerischen Katholikentage 1903-1954; Geschichte, Organisation, Programmatik und Sozialstruktur: Religion-

Politik-Gesellschaft in der Schweiz 1. FrS 1987, Univ. xxii-472 p. Fs 68 [TR 87, 402, K.-J, *Rivinius*].

m342 *Klimkeit* Hans-J., Zweiter internationaler Kongress zum Manichäismus [Bonn-St. Augustin 6.-10.-VIII.1989]: ZRGg 42 (1990) 70s.

m343 *Koza* Stanisław J., Christós pobedi — Christus siegt [Symposium Lublin 8.-10. März 1988]: OstkSt 38 (1989) 185-191.

m344 *Martínez Fresneda* F., Dios y el problema del mal; III semana de teologia: Carthaginensia 6 (1990) 363-6.

m344* *Meis* Anneliese, Colloquium origenianum quintum [Boston, 14-19.VIII.1989]: TVida 30 (1989) 235-7.

m345 *Miguel González* José M. de, Crónica del XXIV Simposio de teología trinitaria; Eucaristia y trinidad [22-25 oct. 1989]: EstTrin 24 (1990) 282-4 [3-275, 5 art. + ➤ 7567].

m346 *Müller* Karl, 'Thy will be done'; WCC world conference on mission and evangelism in San Antonio, May 22-June 1, 1989: VerbumSVD 30 (1989) 337-343.

m347 *Müller* Karl / *Feder* Angela, Ist Christus der einzige Weg zum Heil? [Bonn 5.-9.VI.1990]: VerbumSVD 31 (1990) 344-7 / 347-351.

m348 *Palsterman* Jean, Églises et santé dans le Tiers-Monde hier et aujourd'hui [LvN 19-21 oct. 1989, centénaire de la mort du P. Damien à Molokai]: RTLv 21 (1990) 268-273.

m349 *Pek* Kazimierz, ❷ Marie au milieu de l'Église pérégrinante [Lublin 18-21.X.1989]: AtKap 114 (1990) 299-303.

m350 *Pelisse* Marcel, 44e congrès eucharistique international, Séoul (5-8 octobre 1989): EsprVie 100 (1990) 92-95.

m351 *Poswick* R.-F., Centenaire de la mort de John-H. NEWMAN[n], colloque Chantilly 2-4 juin 1990: EsprVie 100 (1990) 431s; Newman en texte, 'Newmann' deux fois en titre.

m352 **Prieur** Jean-Marc, Responsables de la création; rassemblement œcuménique paix et justice [Bâle 15-21.V.1989]: Entrée libre 6. Genève 1989, Labor et Fides. 96 p. F 55. 2-8309-0591-1. – RÉTRel 65 (1990) 307 (*ipse*).

m353 *Ries* Julien, Expérience religieuse et expérience esthétique; rituel, art et sacré dans l'histoire des religions [LvN 21-22.III.1990]: RTLv 21 (1990) 408s.

m354 *Rouleau* Jean-Paul, La société québécoise pour l'étude de la religion [rencontres ...]: SR 19 (1990) 360s.

m355 *Ruh* Ulrich, Das Gottesvolk als Subjekt der Überlieferung; Dogmatikertagung [23.-28.IX.] über Tradition und Erneuerung: HerdKorr 44 (1990) 536-9.

m356 *Salzano* Teresa, Il nostro essere — ebrei e cristiani — sulla terra di tutti; colloquio ebraico-cristiano, Camaldoli (Arezzo) 6-10 dicembre 1989: StPatav 37 (1990) 215-220.

m357 *Sievernich* Michael, The historical meaning of the 500 year celebration (1492-1992); Sixteenth Symposium of the Study Commission for Church History in Latin America, Santo Domingo 11-13.X.1989: TContext 7,2 (1990) 137s.

m357* *Stacpoole* Alberic, Symposium Vaticanum Secundum, sources, LvN 22-25 Oct. 1989: PrPeo 4 (1990) 19-28.

m358 *Tiel* Gerhard, Ökumene im Kraftfeld des Reiches Gottes; Bericht über zwei bedeutende ökumenische Ereignisse in Brasilien [CESEP, São Paulo 8.-17. Juli 1989; Rio (Duque de Caxias) 10.-14. Juli 1989]: ÖkRu 39 (1990) 102-9.

m359 *Trentin* Giuseppe, Il convegno di Aquileia (28 aprile - 1 maggio 1990); analisi, progetti, valutazioni: StPatav 37 (1990) 225-255; Eng. 255s.

m360 *Vande Veire* Daniël, Colloquium te Leuven over 'leven over de dood heen' [26-28.III.1990]; Leerstoel A. Dondeyne]: TsTNijm 30 (1990) 299s.

m361 *Vanneste* A., Théologie africaine, bilan et perspectives [Kinshasa 1989; aussi récension des Actes 1989]: ETL 66 (1990) 456-8.

m362 *Vidal* Marciano, [Redemptoristen 26.-30.VI, Aylmer QUE] Die Moraltheologie als Dienst an der Sache des Menschen: TGegw 33 (1990) 3-19.

m363 *Villar* José R., La sucesión de Pedro y el obispo de Roma (en torno al IX Coloquio católico-ortodoxo de Bari) [27-29.V.1990]: ScripTPamp 22 (1990) 917-923.

Y7.6 *Acta congressuum philologica:* **nuntii.**

m364 Compte rendu des séances: RÉLat 68 (1990) 1-9.

m365 *La Rocca* John J., *al.*, The sixty-ninth annual meeting of the American Catholic Historical Association [Cincinnati 28-30.XII.1988]: CathHR 75 (1989) 208-287 [753-5, Apr. 21-22, 1989, at Canisius College, Buffalo, *Hennesey* James].

m366 *Nahon* Gérard, Education in medieval Jewish society; XVIIIth medieval workshop (Univ. British Columbia, Vancouver, 17 et 18 Nov. 1988): RÉJ 149 (1990) 295-8.

m367 *Olshausen* Eckart, 4. Internationales Kolloquium für historische Geographie der Alten Welt ['Grenze und Grenzland' 2.-6. Mai 1990, Stuttgart]: Gnomon 62 (1990) 671.

m367* *Salomone* Serena, La donna nel mondo antico (T 21-23.IV.1986): Maia 42 (1990) 286-291.

Y7.8 *Acta congressuum orientalistica et archaeologica:* **nuntii.**

m368 Berichte DMG 1987-8 / 1988-9: ZDMG 139 (1989) *1-23* / 140 (1990) 1*-23* [21* / 21*s, Dissertationen, teils abgeschlossen vorliegend].

m369 *Decker* Wolfgang, Internationales Symposium über die Olympischen Spiele in der Antike, Athen (und Olympia), 5.-9. September 1988: Nikephoros 2 (1989) 293-301.

m370 *Duval* Noël, Problématique d'une architecture chrétienne au IVe siècle; rapport [Congrès Rome 1975]: RÉAug 35 (1989) 308-313.

m371 *Duval* Noël, Le troisième congrès d'archéologie chrétienne espagnole à Mahon (septembre 1988): RÉAug 36 (1990) 155-180; 9 plans.

m371* *Falsone* Gioacchino, Highlights of the [1991!] Tunis conference on Phoenician and Punic studies: Berytus 38 (1990) 185-190.

m372 *Fowler* P.J., World Archaeological Congress 2 [successor to Southampton, in Venezuela 4-8 Sept. 1990; discreet silence about whether South Africans were again excluded]: Antiquity 64 (1990) 829s.

m373 *Grenet* Frantz, Colloque international du CNRS, 'Histoire et cultes de l'Asie centrale préislamique; sources écrites et documents archéologiques' (Paris, 22-28 Novembre 1988): StIran 18 (1989) 255s.

m374 *Hocker* F., Ships and shipbuilding in antiquity; third Hellenic symposium: IntJNaut 19 (1990) 157s.

m375 *Hood* Sinclair, The third international Congress on Santorini (Thera) [3-9.IX.1989]: Kadmos 29 (1990) 84-86.

m376 *Lavado* Pedro, Coloquio internacional [Hamburgo Mus. Etnología 15-21.II.1990], Investigaciones sobre alfarería y cerámica en los paises mediterráneos: BAsEspOr 26 (1990) 338-340.

m377 [DOlszewski D., Dibble H.], The Zagros paleolithic; new perspectives on ancient humans in the Middle East [symposium Las Vegas, 18-22 April 1990]: Paléorient 16,1 (1990) 131s (A. Minzoni-Deroche).

m378 Poulin Jean, De nouveaux jalons pour la recherche [2e Congrès international d'archéologie biblique, Jérusalem 24 juin-4 juillet 1990]: MondeB 67 (1990) 66s.

m379 Scholz Piotr, a) 5. Congresso internazionale di studi meroitici, Roma 1984; - b) First international conference on the history of Ethiopian art, London 1986; - c) X. Conférence internationale des études éthiopiennes, Paris 1988:   Nubica 1s (1990) 415-421 / 425 / 428s.

m380 Shanks Hershel,   Absorbing archaeology at the Jerusalem congress [June 24-July 4, 1990]: BAR-W 16,6 (1990) 50-54.

m381 a) Wielowiejski Jerzy, ❷ 10th International Congress on ancient bronzes, FrB 18-22.VII.1988; - b) Nowicki Krzysztof, Taracha Piotr, ❷ 2d conference 'Orient and Aegean; language, religion, culture', Wsz 24-25.XI.1988: ArchWroc 40 (1989) 164s / 166.

Y8   Periti, Scholars, Personalia, organizations.

m382 **Arnold** Matthieu,   La faculté de théologie protestante de l'Université de Strasbourg de 1919 à 1945: Travaux 2.   Strasbourg 1990, Fac. prot. 321 p. F 125. – RFoiVie 89,6 (1990) 108s (P. François); RHPR 70 (1990) 403 (ipse).

m383 EBesier G., Gestrich C.,   450 Jahre evangelische Theologie in Berlin. Gö 1989, Vandenhoeck & R.   648 p. DM 98. – RSNTU-A 15 (1990) 141s (A. Fuchs).

m384 a) Bressolette Claude,   La lente formation d'une Faculté de théologie; – b) Doré Joseph,   Les cent ans de la Faculté de Théologie de l'ICP: RICathP 36 (1990) 23-54 / 55-82.

m385 Caquot André,   L'exégèse et l'épigraphic sémitique à l'École Biblique: CRAI (1990) 847-855.

m386 Casado Orcajo Felicísimo,   Memorias de los cursos 1987-88 / 1988-89: Burgense 31 (1990) 235-257.

m387 Citrini Tullio,   I venti anni della facoltà teologica dell'Italia settentrionale: ScuolC 117 (1989) 104-111.

m388 **Danker** Frederick W.,   A century of Greco-Roman philology [AmPg/SBL] 1988 → 4,k736:   RCBQ 52 (1990) 152-3 (J. M. Reese); CritRR 3 (1990) 195-7 (S. Brown); RelStR 16 (1990) 64 (D. B. Martin); TorJT 6 (1990) 342-4 (T. D. Barnes).

m389 Daoust J.,   Le centenaire de l'École Biblique de Jérusalem [< Vesco J.-L., TerreS juillet 1990]: EsprVie 100 (1990) 641-3.

m390 **Doyle** B. R.,   Biblical Studies in Australia, a Catholic contribution; a short survey and bibliography.   Melbourne 1990, Lovell.   iii-56 p. 1-86355-008-9 [NTAbs 35,230].

m391 Ford John T.,   'A centre of light and truth'; a century of theology at the Catholic University of America: CathHR 75 (1989) 566-591.

m392 a) Gross Heinrich,   Tendenzen der gegenwärtigen Erforschung des ATs; – b) Vögtle Anton,   Katholische Exegese des NTs seit dem Zweiten Vatikanischen Konzil: Fünfzig Jahre KBW 1933-83, 71-86 / 87-103 [-168, al.].

m393 **Handy** R.,   History of Union Theol. Sem. NY 1987 → 3,h265 ... 5,k820: RJEH 40 (1989) 478s (W. C. Gilpin).

m394 ⓜ The [Hungarian Catholic] St. Jerome Bible Society is established [13.II.1989]: TSzem 33 (1990) 92.

m395 Institut Catholique de Toulouse, annuaire 1988-89 / 89-90 / 90-91: BInstC-Chr 89,4 (1988) 109 p. / 90, 2-4 (1989) 109 p. / 91, 3s (1990) 111 p.

m396 *Krašovec* Jože, Teološka fakulteta v akademskim letu 1988-1989: BogVest 49 (Ljubljana 1989) 391-9.

m397 *La Potterie* Ignace de, Instituto Biblico; 80 anos de história [< CC (1989,4) 166-172]: REB 50 (1990) 234s.

m397* *Leclant* Jean, Allocution d'accueil [centenaire de l'École biblique de Jérusalem]: CRAI (1990) 841-5 [... attaques 'de plusieurs Jésuites', surtout FONCK p. 843].

m398 *Le Roux* J. H., Die departement Ou Testamen, 'n halwe eeu [J. H. KRITZINGER, A. H. van ZYL, W. S. PRINSLOO, W. VOSLOO]: SkrifK 9 (1988) 160-180 [< OTAbs 14,9].

m399 *Lewek* A., ❷ Kronika: STWsz 27,1s (1989) 293-313. 279-310; 28,1s (1990) 290-315. 162-188 [doktoraty 27/1, 302-6; 28/2, 173-9. 186s].

m400 *a)* ᴱ**Moeller** B., Theologie in Göttingen; eine Vorlesungsreihe: Gö-UnivSchr Al. Gö 1987, Vandenhoeck–R. 412 p. DM 48. – *b)* ᴱ**Lüdemann** G., *Schröder* M., Die Religionsgeschichtliche Schule in Göttingen; eine Dokumentation. Gö 1987, VR. 148 p.; 80 fig. DM 19,80. – ᴿSNTU-A 15 (1990) 142s (A. *Fuchs*) / 143s (C. *Niemand*).

m401 **Murphy-O'Connor** Jerome, (*Taylor* Justin), *a)* The École Biblique and the New Testament; a century of scholarship (1890-1990): NOrb 13. FrS/Gö 1990, Univ./Vandenhoeck & R. 120 p. Fs 29. 3-7278-0682-6/VR 3-525-53914-2 = *b)* Le Nouveau Testament; cent ans d'exégèse à l'École Biblique: CahRB 27. P 1990, Gabalda. 218 p. F 340. 2-85021-045-5. – ᴿExpTim 102,6 2d-top choice (1990s) 163 (C. S. *Rodd*); RB 97 (1990) 466-470 (F. J. *Moloney*).

m401* ᴱ**Natalini** Terzo, Cento anni... Scuola Vaticana di paleografia 1986 ➤ 4,k745: 5,799: ᴿScriptorium 43 (1989) 334-6 (Françoise *Gasparri*).

m402 *Ordon* Hubert, Kronika Instytuta Biblijnego KUL za rok akademicki 1987/8: RoczTK 36,1 (1989) 84-89.

m402* *Pelland* Gilles, Inaugurazione dell'anno accademico 1990s. R 1990, Pont. Univ. Gregoriana, 31 p.

m403 *Puech* Émile, L'École biblique de Jérusalem à cent ans: MondeB 66 (1990) 58s.

m404 Salesianum: Chronica, Università Pontificia Salesiana: Salesianum 52 (1990) 236-253. 513-523. 786-800. 939-947.

m405 *Santi Cucinotto* Filippo, La Facoltà teologica di Atene; la vicenda istituzionale della teologia neoellenica: Ho Theológos 8 (1990) 285-337.

m406 Studium Biblicum Franciscanum, anno accademico 1989-1990 [tesi di licenza ...]: LA 40 (1990) 533-7.

m407 ᴱ*Swetnam* James [secr.; *Valentino* Carlo, assist.], Acta Pontificii Instituti Biblici 9/7 (1990s) 521-626: prolusione del Rettore Klemens *Stock* 13.X.1990, p. 533-545.

m408 ᴱ**Vesco** J.-L., L'Ancien Testament; cent ans d'exégèse à l'École Biblique: CahRB 28. P 1990, Gabalda. 220 p. F 320. 2-85021-046-3 [NRT 113, 902, J.-L. *Ska*].

m409 *Vilanova Bosch* Evangelista, La teología en España en los últimos 50 años: RET 50 (1990) 385-433.

m410 **Vries** S. De, Bible and theology in the Netherlands² [= ¹1968 + list of professors and dissertations since 1850]: AmerUnivSt 7/22. Fra 1989, Lang. xiii-171 p. Fs 49. 3-8204-1052-7 [BL 91,13].

m411 *Wenham* John, Fifty years of evangelical scholarship; retrospect and prospect: Churchman 103 (L 1989) 209-218 [< ZIT 89,640].

Y8.5 *Periti,* in memoriam.

m412 Obituaries / nécrologies: AnFrPraed 97 (1989) 166-9 . 324-327; AnPg 60 (pour 1989) p. 876-881; AntiqJ 69 (1989) 404-413; ETL 66 (1990) 110*-112*; KirSef 62 (1988s) 221s . 652-4; REB 50 (1990) 240-250 . 483-7 . 732-746 . 998-1004; RHE 85 (1990) 132*s . 297*s . 451*s.

m413 Alikhova, Anna Epifanovna, 1.VII.1902-30.VI.1989: SovArch (1990,4) 295; phot. (K. A. *Smirnov*).

m414 Amos, Ashley Crandall (Mrs.), 1951-1989; Old English: MedvSt 52 (1990) ix-xi, phot. (L. K. *Shook*; bibliog.).

m415 Apollonj Ghetti, Bruno Maria [➔ 5,k833], 7.X.1905-27.V.1989; fouilleur de S. Pierre, 'ses dessins ont fait sa réputation': RHE 85 (1990) 267s (L. *Reekmans*).

m417 Atalay, Erol, 13.XI.1935-5.IX.1988: Belleten 53,206ss (1989) 909-914, phot. (Ö. *Özyiğit*; bibliog.).

m418 Atiya, Aziz Suryal, 4.VII.1898-24.IX.1988; ➔ 5,k835; Enc. copte: BSACoptc 29 (1990) 1-7; portr. (Mirrit *Boutros-Ghali*; bibliog.).

m419 Baaren, Theodoor Pietcr van, 1912-4.V.1989; comparative religious art: NedTTs 44 (1990) 51-53 (H. J. W. *Drijvers*).

m420 Baeck Paul de, 1911-1989: RBgNum 135 (1989) 278s (M. *Colaert*).

m421 Bagatti, Bellarmino, 11.XI.1905-7.X.1990; LA 40 (1990) 538-540 (G. C. *Bottini*); scavatore di Nazaret ecc.: Antonianum 65 (1990) 687-9 (A. *Niccacci*); OssR (9.X.1990) p. 3.

m422 Balthasar, Hans Urs von, ➔ 5,k837; 12.VIII.1905-26.VI.1989: KerkT 40 (1989) 51-54 (A. J. *Bronkhorst*: 'Het beste boek over BARTH, 1952', volgens MISKOTTE); ViPe 72 (1989) 82-91 (G. *Marchesi*); CommND 15 (1988) 512-6 (J. *Ratzinger*); 16 (1989) 152-4 (K. M. *Batinovich*); *Henrici* Peter [*al.*], The life and work of Hans Urs von Balthasar: CommND 16 (1989) 306-350 (ᵀ*Saward* John) [-490].

m423 Bándi, Gábor, 1939-1988: AcArchH 42 (1990) 340s (T. *Kovács*; 242s, Bibliog., A. *Kiss*).

m424 Baron, Salo Wittmayer, 1895-1989: Judaism 39 (1990) 36; Midstream 36,4 (NY 1990) 23-25.

m425 Barrau, Paul, 1916-1990; père: RICathP 35 (1990) 269-271 (M.-A. *Santaner*).

m426 Bascour, Hildebrand, O.S.B., 10.XII.1900-19.IV.1990: dernier de l'équipe fondateurs dc BTAM: RHE 85 (1990) 497s (H. *Silvestre*); RTAM 57,1 (1990) i-ii (E. *Manning*).

m427 Bauer, Gleb Mikhailovič, 25.VII.1925-8.X.1989 [South-Arabist]: VDI 193 (1990) 233 (A. M. *Akopyan*).

m428 Bausani, Alessandro, 1921-1988, iranista: RSO 62 (1988) 135-8 (Biancamaria *Scorcia Amoretti*).

m429 Bengtson, Hermann, 2.VII.1909-2.XI.1989, Mitarbeiter: Historia 39 (1990) i, phot.

m429* Béranger, Jean [➔ 4,k771; 5,k844] 25.X.1903-13.IX.1988: Ivra 39 (1988) 257-9 (F. *Sturm*: '12.IX').

m430 Bernardi, Aurelio, 16.III.1912-15.XII.1989: Athenaeum 78 (1990) xiii-xiv (E. *Gabba*, D. *Magnino*).

m431 Bjørndalen, Anders Jørgen, † 14.I.1989: NorTTS 91 (1990) 59 (H.M. *Barstad*); TsTK 60 (1989) fasc. 4 → 21 supra.

m432 Blank, Josef, 8.IX.1926-2.X.1989: Johannes, Paulus: Orientierung 53 (1989) 201s (G. *Dautzenberg*); BiKi 45 (1990) 49s (P. *Hoffmann*); BLtg 63 (1990) 55 (K. *Kertelge*).

m433 Bliss, Kathleen, 1908-IX.1989: WCC leader: EcuR 42 (1990) 68-70 (M. *Conway*).

m434 Blumenkranz, Bernhard, 12.VI.1913-4.XI.1989: Zion 55 (1990) 347s (M. *Catane* ❺).

m435 Boer, Pieter Arie Hendrik de, 14.VI.1910-5.VIII.1989, ed. OTS, VT ...: Henoch 12 (1990) 98s (J.A. *Soggin*); NedTTs 44 (1990) 54s (P.B. *Dirksen*); VT 40 (1990) 1-3 (G.W. *Anderson*).

m436 Bokser, Baruch M., aet. 44, 12.VII.1990: Talmudist at Jewish Theol. Sem. NY: BR 6,5 (1990) 15.

m437 Bonham Carter, Charlotte ...: Iraq 52 (1990) v, phot. (D.O.).

m437* Bonis, Constantine G., 5.VI.1905-6.VI.1990; patrology: TAth 61 (1990) 506-513 (E.D. *Moutsoulas*, ❻); 514-523 bibliog. (I.C. *Constantinidis*).

m438 Boulter, Cedric Gordon, 1912-10.X.1989; Greek vase painting: AJA 94 (1990) 481s (K.T. *Luckner*).

m439 Bréguet, Esther, 1905-13.I.1990: RÉLat 67 (1989) 32 (M. *Chouet*).

m440 Bromley, John Selwyn, 1913-1985: Belleten 54,210 (1990) 903-5; phot. (Sevim *Ünal*).

m441 Brondy, Réjane, 24.XII.1940-10.VI.1989; médiéviste: CahHist 34 (1989) 105s (R. *Fedou*).

m442 Bruce, Frederick Fyvie, 12.X.1910-11.IX.1990; thirty years editor: EvQ 62 (1990) 291; Crux 26,4 (Vancouver 1990) 2.47 (L. & W. *Gasque*) [< NTAbs 35,137].

m442* Bruin, Cebus Cornelis de, 15.V.1905-9.X.1988: kerkhistoricus, De Statenbijbel 1937: NedTTs 43 (1989) 139s (J. *Trapman*).

m443 Brummer, Rudolf, 23.IV.1907-1.X.1989: EstLul 30 (1990) 117s (A. *Llinarès*.

m444 Bussagli, Mario, [→ 4,k777*; 5,k854*] 23.IX.1917-14.VIII.1988, indologo: RSO 62 (1988) 139-141 (L. *Petech*).

m445 Carmignac, Jean, [→ 2,e336 ... 5,k856] 7.VIII.1914-2.X.1986: Mém., ᴱ*García Martínez* F., [→ 4,22] RQum 49-52 (1988); JTS 41 (1990) 581s (H.G.M. *Williamson*).

m446 Cassandro, Giovanni, 21.IV.1913-10.X.1989: StRom 38 (1990) 392-5, phot. (M. *Caravale*).

m447 Cerckel, Auguste, 11.IX.1907-18.VI.?1989: AnBoll 108 (1990) I-II (P. *Devos*).

m448 Chastel, André, 15.XI.1912-18.VII.1990: art de la Renaissance: CRAI (1990) 655-7 (G. *Lazard*).

m449 Châtillon, Jean [→ 5,k861], 1912-29.IX.1988; médiéviste: RÉAug 35 (1989) 3-11 (J. *Longère*, bibliog.).

m450 Chenu, Marie-Dominique [Marcel], O.P., 7.I.1895-11.II.1990; 'Une école de théologie, Le Saulchoir' 1937, mis à l'Index 1942; réédité 1985: ETL 66 (1990) 250; CiTom 117 (1990) 331-340 (G. *Celada*); CrNSt 11 (1990) 1-3 (G. *Alberigo*); EstFranc 91 (1990) 581-4 (M. *Taradach*); HumT 11 (1990) 361-3 (B. *Dominguez*); NewTR 3,4 (1990) 89-91 (E. *Schillebeeckx*); Orientierung 54 (1990) 37-41 (L. *Kaufmann*); Páginas 15,102 (1990) 88-91 (H. *Bellido Moscoso*); RHE 85 (1990) 542 (R. *Aubert*); RICathP 35 (1990) 265-7 (J. *Le Goff*); TsTNijm 30 (1990) 184s (E. *Schillebeecks*); ViPe 73 (1990) 448-455 (A. *Franco*).

m451 Chevallier, Max-Alain: RHPR 70 (1990) 1s (E. *Trocmé*) [† 1991].

m452 Cohen, Daniel J., aet. 68, 20.IX.1989:   Zion 55 (1990) 249s (M. *Hayman*, ❽).

m453 Contini, Gianfranco, 4.I.1912-1.II.1990; origines de la littérature italienne: CRAI (1990) 197s (G. *Lazard*).

m454 Conzelmann, Hans, 22.X.1915-20.VI.1989: Ev. Lukas: TLZ 115 (1990) 865-876 (E. *Lohse*, 'Theologie als Schriftauslegung').

m455 Crépy, Max, 1905-30.VIII.1988: RBgNum 135 277s (J. *Doutriaux*).

m456 Daly, Lloyd William, 6.X.1910-26.II.1989, prof. Greek: Gnomon 62 (1990) 81-83 (R. E. A. *Palmer*).

m457 Darrouzès, Jean, père, 1912-1990: RICathP 35 (1990) 273s (A. *Failler*).

m458 Dart, Raymond Arthur, aet. 95, 22.XI.1988; publicizer of Australopithecus, 'discoverer of the Missing Link': AntiqJ 69 (1989) 404s.

m459 Davis, Norman, 1913 (NZ)-2.XII.1989: Speculum 65 (1990) 822s (G. *Kane, al.*).

m460 Delhaye, Philippe, mgr., 17.II.1912-18.III.1990: Secrétaire de la Commission théologique internationale: RTLv 21 (1990) 264-7 (R. *Gryson*, H. *Wattiaux*); moraliste: ETL 66 (1990) 460 (G. *Thils*); EsprVie 100 (1990) 14 (E. *Vauthier*, R. *Desvoyes*); 194-200 bibliog. (J.-P. *Renard*); RHE 85 (1990) 498 (H. *Wattiaux*).

m461 Dugmore, Clifford, aet. 81, 25.X.1990: Jewish and Christian liturgy; founder of JEH: RHE 85 (1990) 872 (D. *Bradley*).

m462 Duncker, Pieter, aet. 92, 23.VIII.1990: prof. hebr. Angelicum, Biblicum ... AcPIB 9/7, 619.

m463 Dupront, Alphonse, 26.XII.1905-16.VI.1990; 'Le mythe de la croisade; essai de sociologie religieuse' 1956, jamais publié: RHE 85 (1900) 555s (R. *Aubert*).

m464 Egermann, Franz, 13.II.1905-9.VII.1989: Gnomon 62 (1990) 755-7 (J. *Dalfen*).

m465 Eilers, Wilhelm, [➤ 5,k871] 27.IX.1906-3.VII.1989; Iranist: WZKM 80 (1990) 7-12, phot. (Rüdiger *Schmitt*).

m466 Ellacuría, Ignacio, s.J. -16.XI.1989:   MiscCom 48 (1990) 279-286 (Juan *Lorente*).

m467 Ellenberger, Lee C., aet. 75, 2.VI.1990; ASOR archivist: BA 53 (1990) 233; phot. (E. F. *Campbell*).

m468 Erim, Kenan T., aet. 61, 2.XI.1990, Aphrodisias excavator, NYU prof.: BAR-W 17/1, 18.

m469 Fensham, Frank Charles [➤ 5,k871*], 13.X.1925-26.VII.1989: Henoch 12 (1990) 99 (J. A. *Soggin*); JNWS 15 (1989) 1-5; portr. (W. T. *Claassen*).

m470 Firpo, Luigi, 1915-1989: BibHumRen 51 (1989) 621-3 (G. *Busino*).

m471 Flahiff, George Bernard, card. 26.X.1905-22.VIII.1989; former prof.: MedvSt 52 (1990) v-viii, portr. (M. M. *Sheehan*, bibliog.).

m472 Foley, Richard Lonergan, 30.X.1929-21.II.1989: hist. dogm.;   RHE 85 (1990) 519 (R. *Aubert*).

m473 Gambasin, Angelo, 31.III.1926-14?/24?.VI.1990: storia ecclesiastico-sociale: StPatav 37 (1990) (p. 439: '24.VI'; p. 442: '14.VI').

m474 Gamber, Klaus, Mgr., 23.IV.1919-2.VI.1989; Dir. Inst. Ltg.-Wiss., Regensburg: RHE 85 (1990) 158s (K. *Hausberger*).

m475 Gand, Adrien, 23.V.1907-29.X.1990; évéque de Lille; license PIB 1936 [AcPIb 9/7, 619].

m476 Gansiniec, Zofia, 1.I.1919-17.IV.1988: ArchWroc 40 (1989) 197-202, phot. (B. *Rutkowski*, bibliog.).

m477 García Garcés, Narciso, C. M. F., 1904-1989: EphMar 39 (1989) 345-7; 358-66 bibliog. marian.).

m478 Garitte, Gérard, 15.I.1914-27.VIII.1990; grec, copte: RHE 85 (1990) 807s (J. *Mossay*); Muséon 103 (1990) 201, phot. (D. *Donnet*, éloge funèbre).

m479 Gevaryahu, Haim, JBQ = Dor 18,4 (1989s) 203-5 (J. *Adler*).

m480 Gennep, Frederick Onslow van, 1926-9.I.1990; praktische theologie: NedTTs 44 (1990) 148s (M. van der *Velden*); 150-5, *Knijff* H. W. de, on his Terugkeer van de verloren Vader 1989.

m481 Giuliani, Mateus F., s.a.c., 29.V.1924-20.IV.1990; prof. NT: REB 50 (1990) 740s.

m482 Godechot, Jacques, † 26.VIII.1989; doyen de Toulouse momentanément écarté comme israélite: RHE 85 (1990) 231 (R. *Aubert*).

m484 Göransson, Sven, 1910 -23.XI.1989: NorTTs 91 (1990) 115-8 (Ingun *Montgomery*).

m485 Goldberg, Kurt, aet. 88, 19.XII.1989: Zion 55 (1990) 349-351 (N. *Gross*, ❺).

m486 Grabar, André, ?26.VII.1896-5.X.1990; archéologie paléochrétienne et byzantine: RHE 85 (1990) 854 (R. *Aubert*: 26.VII); CRAI (1990) 673s (G. *Lazard*: 16.VII).

m487 Graesser, Carl^J, 1929 -12.V.1989; biblical pillars; Shechem excavation: BASOR 280 (1990) 3s, phot. (R. H. *Smith*).

m488 Gramignoli, Giuseppe, † 8.III.1990 [studente 1960-4: ActaPIB 9,516].

m489 Griffin, William Augustine, 1926-1988; OT: StLuke 32 (1988s) 181-198 [< OTAbs 13,219].

m490 Grossouw, Willem, 6.XI.1906-22.V.1990: helped transform Studia Catholica into: TsTNijm 30 (1990) 229-233 (B. M. F. van *Iersel*).

m491 Gunneweg, Antonius H. J., † 17.VI.1990 [ZAW 102,320].

m492 Gurevich, Frida Davidovna, 1.I.1911-2.IX.1988: SovArch (1990,2) 281s (A. N. *Kirpichnikov*, M. V. *Malevskaya*; 282s bibliog. L. M. *Vseviov*).

m493 Hambye, Édouard-Roger, 3.VII.1916-7.IX.1990: rite syriaque, histoire des missions: RHE 85 (1990) 808 (R. *Aubert*).

m494 Hanoteau, mère Marie-Émilie, aet. 85, 20.VII.1990: RHE 85 (1990) 807.

m495 Hartdegen, Stephen J., o.f.m. [➤ 5,k886*], 16.VI.1907-19.XII.1989: secretary of NAB: CBQ 52 (1990) 1-4 + portr. (A. A. *Di Lella*).

m496 Healy, James, 1929 -11.XII.1989: MilltSt 26 (1990) 5-8; portr. p. 4 (R. *Moloney*).

m497 Henderson, Eugenie J. A., aet. 74, 27.VII.1989: BSO 53 (1990) 503 (H. L. *Shorto*).

m498 Hernando García, Eusebio, 5.III.1932-17.IX.1990; VT; Burgense 31 (1990) 565s (N. *López Martínez*).

m498* Higounet, Charles ... 1911 -8.IV.1988: Citeaux 41,1 (1990) 171-4 (B. *Barrière*).

m499 Hoffman, Michael Allen, 1944 -23.IV.1990; Hierakonpolis field anthropologist: JAmEg 27 (1990) 17s (W. A. *Fairservis*); VarAeg 6 (1990) 107.

m500 Houghton Arthur A.^J, 1906 3.IV.1990, founder of Corning Museum of Glass: JGlass 32 (1990) 11; phot. (T. S. *Buechner*).

m502 Hughes, Philip Edgcumbe, 1915-1.V.1990: NT & church history: WestTJ 52 (1990) before p. 181; phot.; Churchman 104 (1990) 351 (R. *Beckwith*).

m503 Ilan Zvi, 14.V.1936-17.II.1990; synagogues: BAnglsr 9 (1989s) 64s (S. *Dar*); BAR-W 17/2,18.

m504 Joly, Henri, † 1989: RTPhil 122 (1990) 297-302 (J. *Bouveresse*); bibliog. p. 431s.

m505 Jóźwiak, Franciszek, 1931-28.III.1988: RuBi 42 (1989) 69-72 (M. Gołębiewski, bibliog.).
m506 Kadry, Ahmed: VarAeg 6 (1990) 107.
m507 Kambitsis, Ioannis E., 1938 -7.VIII.1990: Ellinika 41,1 (1990) 209-212 (G. M. Sirakis).
m508 Kanatsoulis, Dimitrios, 1907-1989: Makedonika 27 (1989s) xi-xii, phot. (I. Touloumakos).
m509 Kaplan, Jacob [➤ 5,k895], 1910 -14.IV.1989; Tel Aviv antiquities director: IsrEJ 40 (1990) 228.
m510 Kaske, Robert Earl, 1.VI.1921-8.VIII.1980, ed. Traditio: Speculum 65 (1990) 818-820 (F. Robinson, al.).
m511 Kipper, João Balduino, S.J., [➤ 5,k897*], 28.I.1915-20.XI.1988: Persp-Teol 21 (1989) 113s.
m512 Kolitsaras, Ioannes, 1903-1989: GrOrTR 34 (1989) 416s (G. C. Papademetriou).
m513 Kotsones, Ieronymos, abp., 1905-1988: GrOrTR 34 (1989) 333s (G. C. Papademetriou).
m514 Kramer, Samuel N., 1897 -26.X.1990; cunéiformiste; CRAI (1990) 895s; RAss 84 (1990) 99.
m515 Kraus, F. R., RAss 84 (1990) 99 [21.III.1910-19.I.1991].
m516 Kurang, József, 18.IX.1904-26.VIII.1989: VoxPa 17 (1989) 1014-7 (A. Eckmann; bibliog.).
m517 Łączak, József, 2.XII.1926-21.VIII.1989: Finno-Ugrian: FolOr 27 (1990) 281s (T. Porożniak).
m518 Lasserre, François, 1919 -22.XII.1989, philologie grecque: QuadUrb 63 (1990) 165-8 (C. Calame).
m519 Lassus, Jean, 19.VI.1903-9.X.1990; art paléochrétien: CRAI (1990) 745s.
m520 Leach, Edmund, sir, 1910-6.I.1989: ZEthnol 114 (1989) 17-20 (G. Pfeffer).
m522 Lecler, Joseph, S.J., 1895-1988: RcchSR 78 (1990) 5-7 (J. Moingt: 'De la tolérance à la liberté religieuse').
m523 Lefèbvre, Charles, mons., 29.VIII.1904-13.XI.1989; prof. de droit canon à Paris [... de Karol WOJTYŁA]; auditeur de la Rote: RICathP 35 (1990) 255-8 (J. Portemer).
m524 Le Guillou, Marie-Joseph, O.P., 25.XII.1920-25.I.1990: Istina 35 (1990) 196-9 bibliog. ('25.I'); RICathP 35 (1990) 261-3 (M. Carrez, al., '26.I').
m525 Lemerle, Paul, 22.IV.1903-17.VII.1989: Byzantion 60 (1990) 532-7 (C. Delvoye).
m526 Lentz, Wolfgang, 23.II.1990-8.XII.1986; Iranist: ZDMG 139 (1989) 1-20; portr. (H.-P. Schmidt, Bibliog.).
m527 Lernoux, Penny, 1940-1989 Journalistin in Bogotá/Rio: Orientierung 54 (1990) 13 (N. Klein).
m528 Leroy, Maurice, 23.I.1909-3.III.1990; linguistique: CRAI (1990) 171s (G. Lazard).
m529 Lewis, Archibald Ross, 25.VIII.1914-4.II.1990: president of Medieval Academy of America: Speculum 65 (1990) 520-2 (C. T. Wood, al.).
m530 Lindhardt, P. G., 1910-30.IX.1988; sociohistorical theology: NorTTs 90 (1989) 47s (Ingun Montgomery: his 70th-birthday bibliography had 2500 titles].
m531 Loen, Arnoldus Ewoud, 11.V.1896-8.II.1990; NedTTs 44 (1990) 242-4 (V. Brümmer); KerkT 41 (1990) 142-9 (A. J. Bronkhorst: 'Ewout').
m532 Lydka, Władysław, 5.X.1931-16.IV.1987: VoxPa 17 (1989) 1013s (K. Gurda).

m533 McCord, James Iley, 1919-19.II.1990: PrincSemB 11,2 (1990) 121-128-131 (T. W. *Gillespie*; A. F. *Fogartie*); honorary ed. chairman: TTod 47 (1980s) 120s.

m534 Malcovati, Enrica, 21.X.1894-4.I.1990: Athenaeum 78 (1990) iii-xi (G. *Mazzoli*); StRom 38 (1990) 399s, fot. (G. *D'Anna*: decano dei Latinisti italiani).

m536 Maluquer de Motes y Nicolau, Juan, 1916-28.IX.1988; fundador de las revistas Zephyrus y Pyrenae: Veleia 5 (1988) 311s (I. *Barandarán*).

m536* Martins Mario (Gonçalves), 17.II.1908-30.VI.1990; redactor: Brotéria 131 (1990) 243-254 (A. *Leite*).

m537 Men, Alexandre, 1935-9.IX.1990, assassiné: Contacts 32 (1990) 163-167 (Y. *Hamant*).

m538 Meritt Benjamin Dean, 31.III.1899-7.VII.1989; Greek epigraphy: AJA 94 (1990) 483s, phot. (J. S. *Traill*).

m539 Migliorini, Elio, 1902-7.XII.1988; BSocGgIt 11/7 (1990) 289-205; fot. (D. *Ruocco*).

m540 Missir de Lusignan, Remo, 16.XI.1905-21.II.1990: BBudé (1990) 87s (Livie *Missir de L.*); Smyrne: Pensée C. 249 (1990) 40-43 (L. *Missir de L.*).

m541 (Koldo) Mitxelena, Luis, 30.VIII.1915-11.X.1987; filología latina: Veleia 5 (1988) 305-9.

m542 Mócsy, András, 1929-1987; AcArchH 41 (1989) 3-7, phot. (F. *Redö*; Bibliog. 9-15, B. *Lörincz*).

m543 Moghadam, Mohsen, 2-XII.1901-10.XI.1987: archéologue: StIran 18 (1989) 239s (Geneviève *Dollfuss*, B. *Hourcade*).

m544 Molnár, Amedeo, aet. 67, 1990; Church-Dogma history, Praha: ComViat 33 (1990) 119 (L. *Brož*: † 27.I.).; RivStoLR 26 (1990) 577-583 (G. G. *Merlo*, † 31.I).

m545 Mor, Carlo Guido, † 13.X.1990; droit romain: CRAI (1990) 795s (G. *Lazard*).

m546 Morabia, Alfred, 1931-1986: RÉJ 149 (1990) 265-8 (J. *Hassoun*).

m547 Moravia, Alberto, 28.XI.1907-26.IX.1990: CC 141 (1990,4) 257-273 (F. *Castelli*).

m548 Moss, Rosalind, aet. 99: VarAeg 6 (1990) 107.

m549 Mühlmann, Wilhelm Emil, 1.X.1904-11.V.1988; ZEthnol 114 (1989) 1-15; phot. (E. W. *Müller*).

m550 Müller, Gerhard, 3.XI.1907-5.IX.1988; klass. Philologe: Gnomon 62 (1990) 668s (A. *Graeser*).

m551 Muggeridge, Malcolm: Tablet 244 [(1990) 1494 (Lord *Longford*; no dates).

m552 Myśków, Józef, 20.II.1927-23.XI.1988: StWsz 27,2 (1989) 305-8 (A. *Lewek*).

m553 Nardin (Saverio) Giuseppe, abate O.S.B., 7.XII.1931-4.II.1990: Benedictina 37 (1990) 191-3 [S. *Bajocchi*: fra 6 altri recentemente deceduti].

m554 Neher, André, 1914 -23.X.1988: RÉJ 149 (1990) 287-290 (R. *Goetschel*).

m555 Newman, David, aet. 51, 24.I.1990: TorJT 6 (1990) 170.

m556 Nims, Charles Francis [➤ 4,k857], 19.X.1906-19.XI.1988: Ch Oriental Institute Egyptologist; Enchoria 17 (1990) vii-5; portr. (G. R. *Hughes*).

m557 Odendaal, Dirk Hermanus, 1.III.1928-27.VII.1990 (auto): OTEssays 3 (1990) 225; phot.; 227 (J. P. J. *Olivier*).

m557* Orestano, Riccardo, 1909-11.XI.1988: Ivra 39 (1988) 260-2 (A. *Masi*).

m558 Osipova, Kira Aleksandrovna, 1925-1.X.1988: VizVrem 50 (1989) 260.

m558* Osuchowski, Wacław, 26.I.1906-23.XI.1988: Ivra 39 (1988) 262-5 (H. *Kupiszewski*).

m559 Palanque, Jean-Remy [➤ 4,k861], aet. 90, 2.Vi.1988; S. Ambroise; Église en France: RE 85 (1990) 231 (R. *Aubert*).

m560 Pantoni, Angelo Renato O.S.B., 5.VI.1905-4.V.1988: Benedictina 36 (1989) 211-8 (M. *Dell'Omo*).

m561 Paprocki, Tadeusz, 14.X.1927-21.I.1989; prof. S. Scr. Białystok: RuBi 43 (1990) 165s (S. *Strzelecki*, bibliog.).

m562 Pecioru, Dumitru, prof. 18.VII.1905-22.II.1988: STBuc 40,1 (1988) 114-6 (T. *Baconsky*).

m563 Peck, George, aet. 58, 17.I.1990; Pres. Andover Newton: ComViat 33 (1990) 119 (L. *Brož*).

m564 Penar, Tadeusz, 13.XIII.1936-15.IX.1988 [... dyplom z Biblicum nostry- fikowała Rada KUL]: RuBi 42 (1989) 308s (J. *Szlaga*).

m564* Pólay, Elemér, 1915 -30.XI.1988: Ivra 39 (1988) 365-7 (G. *Hamza*).

m565 Pons, Jacques, † 21.VIII.1989: ÉTRel 65 (1990) 3.

m566 Prawer, Joshua, 10.XI.1917- 1990: Crusade Palestine: IsrEJ 40 (1990) 316s (B. Z. *Kedar*, † 30.IV); CRAI (1990) 344 (G. *Lazard*, † 1.V); Med-HistR 5 (1990) 107-116, bibliog. (B. Z. *Kedar*).

m567 Průšek, Jaroslav, 14.IX.1906-7.IV.1980: ArOr 59, 105-119; portr. (A. *Palát*); whole fascicle 2 on sinology.

m568 Raikes, Robert Lawrence, 6.XI.1910-20.XI.1989; E. Mediterranean cli- mate: EWest 40 (1990) 343-5 (R. *Biscione*; bibliog.).

m569 Ramureanu, Ioan, prof., 1910 -27.IX.1988: STBuc 40,5 (1988) 121s, phot. (V. *Ioniţă*).

m570 Rasker, Albert Jan, 10.II.1906-23.VI.1990: KerkT 41 (1990) 325-8 (A. J. *Bronkhorst*).

m571 Ratto, Mario, 6.VIII.1906-8.I.1990: RitNum 92 (1990) 347s (C. *Crippa*).

m572 Reese, James M., O.S.F.S. [➤ 4,k947], 27.V.1926-3.XII.1989: Wisdom books; president of CBA 1989s: CBQ 52 (1990) 499-501 (A. R. *Ceresko*).

m573 Renard, Marcel, 1909-14.V.1990: RÉLat 67 (1989) 34s (J. *Heurgon*).

m574 Reviv, Hanoch, 1929-4.III.1990: Zion 55 (1990) 352s (B. *Oded* ✡).

m575 Richardson, H. Neil, 1916 -19.XII.1988; Palestine excavator: BASOR 279 (1990) 5s, phot. (J. D. *Purvis*); Amos; Ugarit: BR 5,2 (1989) 5 (S. B. *Parker*).

m577 Rozenfeldt, Rostislav Leonidovič, 17.I.1922-29.III.1989: SovArch (1990, 3) 301s, phot. (K. A. *Smirnov*).

m578 Sacon, K. K., † 1990: BL 91,5.

m579 Sami, Ali, 1910 -16.VIII.1989: IrAnt 25 (1990) 189-193, phot. (A. *Mousavi*, bibliog.).

m580 Sapone, Gilbert Jude, F. S. C.: ClasW 83 (1989) 517.

m581 Schachermeyr, Fritz [➤ 4,k886; 5,k954], 10.I.1895-26.XII.1987: Kadmos 29 (1990) 89s (Sigrid *Deger-Jalkotzy*).

m582 Schaeffer, Claude F. A. [➤ 64,e814; 65,e257], 1898-1982: Eblaitica 2 (1990) 141-4 (C. H. *Gordon*).

m583 Schildenberger, Johannes Jakob Anton, O.S.B., aet. 94, 12.II.1990 [S. S. D. 1925-8-: ActaPIB 9,516]; BiKi 45 (1990) 109 (O. *Knoch*).

m583* Schippers, Reinier, 9.II.1907- 1989: GerefTTs 90 (1990) 129-145 (S. *Noorda*: 'een theoloog in rapport met zijn tijd').

m584 Schoterman, Jan Anthony, 1948-29.VI.1989; Indologist: IndIranJ 33 (1990) 277s (T. *Goudriaan*, bibliog.).

m585 Schröder, Heinrich Otto, 8.IV.1906-19.VII.1987: Galenus, Origenes: Gnomon 62 (1990) 474s (C. *Zintzen*).

m586 Schultze, Bernhard, S.J., 19.I.1902-30.I.1990: OrChrPer 56 (1990) 269- 282 (E. G. *Farrugia*).

m587 Scullion, John, S.J., 26.II.1925-24.XI.1990; translator of WESTERMANN's Genesis.

m588 Seidl, Erwin [➤ 4,k888; 5,k963], 6.XI.1905-4.IV.1987: ägyptisches Recht: ZSavR 106 (1989) 766-773 (A. *Kränzlein*).

m589 Siri, Giuseppe, card. aet. 82: Tablet 243 (1989) 559s.

m590 Skinner, Burrhus Frederic, 1904 -18.VIII.1990: Nature 347 (Sept. 27, 1990) 332 (N. J. *Mackintosh*).

m591 Smoleń, Władysław, 1914-20.VI.1988: RuBi 42 (1989) 72s (J. *Kuś*).

m592 Sollberger, Edmond [➤ 5,k969], 12.X.1920-21.VI.1989: RAss 84,2 (1990) 97-99, phot. (P. *Garelli*); 183-187, bibliog. (C. B. F. *Walker*); tous les articles du fascicule sont dédiés à Sollberger; AnRIM 8 (1990) 70 (A. K. *Grayson*).

m593 Spae, Joseph J., 25.XI.1913-8.XII.1989; Missionar in Japan: ZMissRW 74 (1990) 303 (B. H. *Willeke*).

m594 Speier, Hermine [➤ 5,k971], 28.V.1898-11.I.1989: MiDAI-R 96 (1989) 1-6.

m595 Spuler, Bertold, 5.XII.1911-6.III.1990: StAäK 17 (1990) IX (W. *Helck*).

m596 Stephanou, Pelopida, S.J., 25.XII.1911-13.VI.1989; OrChrPer 56 (1990) 265-8 (C. *Capizzi*).

m597 Stern, Menahem [➤ 5,k974], 5.III.1925-22.VI.1989; authority on Greek-Latin Judaism; assassinated en route to Hebrew University library: BR 5,5 (1989) 4; phot.

m598 Streetman, Robert F., † 1.VI.1989: ETL 66,247.

m599 Syme, Ronald, sir [➤ 5,k980], 1903-4.IX.1989: JRS 80 (1990) xi-xiv; phot. (M. T. G.); Prudentia 21,2 (1989) 63-72 (Kath *Beattie, al.*).

m600 Szilágyi, János, 17.X.1907-1988: AcArchH 42 (1990) 335s (K. *Póczy*; bibliog. 336-340, K. *Szirmai*).

m601 Szreder, Feliks, 10.XII.1914-9.V.1989: Rome Biblicum licentiate: RuBi 43 (1990) 166-8 (B. *Micewski*).

m602 Templeton, Richard, 8.XI.1938-23.IV.1989; RICathP 32 (1989) 149-152.

m603 Thomas, Edit B., 10.III.1923-6.III.1988: AcArchH 42 (1990) 331s (E. *Tóth*; bibliog. J. *Jakabffy* 333-5).

m604 Throckmorton, Peter; IntJNaut 19 (1990) 181 (H. *Frost*), no dates.

m605 Titov, Valery Sergeyevič, 16.X.1932-17.I.1990: SovArch (1990,4) 296s; phot. (V. I. *Markovin*).

m606 Trenchs Odena, José, aet. 49, 9.IV.1991: ScrCiv 14 (1990) 333s (F. *Gimeno Blay*).

m607 Tretyakov, Viktor Petrovič, 1940-26.VI.1985; SovArch (1990,4) 293s, phot. (G. P. *Grigoryev, al.*).

m608 Trümpelmann, Leo [➤ 5,k984], 1.IX.1931-15.VIII.1989; Vorderas. Archäol.: MDOG 122 (1990) 7, phot. (B. *Hrouda*); IrAnt 25 (1990) 183-7; phot. (B. *Hrouda*, Bibliog.).

m609 Vanderpool, Eugene, 3.VIII.1906-1.VIII.1989, Athens agora excavator: AJA 94 (1990) 291s, photo (J. M. *Camp*).

m610 Vankina, Lucia Voldemarovna, 3.IV.1908-12.III.1989: SovArch (1990,2) 284 (G. *Kolleg*).

m611 Verete, Meir, 1915-1990: Zion 55 (1990) 455-7 (J. *Heller*).

m612 Vidman, Ladislav, 20.II.1934-26.XII.1989: Aegyptus 70 (1990) 257s (R. *Pintaudi*); ➤ 160, ᶠSCHOW N. (1990) 561-9 (R. *Pintaudi*, bibliog.).

m613 Vischer, Wilhelm, aet. 93, 27.XI.1988: KerkT 40 (1989) 142-153 (A. J. *Bronkhorst*).

m614 Vogel, Heinrich, aet. 87, 26.XII.1989: TSzem 33 (1990) 181s (S. *Szathmáry*).

m615 Vries, Josef de, s.J., 3.I.1898-26.XII.1989: TPhil 65 (1990) 579, Bibliog.
m616 Walsh, Eugene A., s.s., aet. 78, 15.VIII.1989; liturgist, Catholic University of America: ETL 66 (1990) 248s.
m617 Waszink, Jan, 1908 -5.X.1990, latiniste: CRAI (1990) 795 (G. *Lazard*).
m617* Wellesz, Emmy, 8.I.1889-13.VI.1987, art historian and orientalist: WZKM 79 (1989) 339-342 (Dorothea *Duda*, Bibliog.).
m618 Wickert, Lothar, 31.VII.1900-8.II.1989: Gnomon 62 (1990) 475-478; portr. (H. *Kloft*).
m619 Winnett, Frederick Victor, 1903 -22.I.1989; South-Arabic: BASOR 279 (1990) 1s, phot. (A. D. *Tushingham*).
m620 Winquist, Phyllis, 1911-1990: ClasW 83 (1989s) 514 (G. J. *Tiene*).
m621 Wirszyłło, Jerzy, 4.V.1901-23.IV.1990; lingue bibliche: RuBi 43 (1990) 168s (J. *Jazierski*).
m622 Wresinski, Joseph, aet. 71, 14.II.1988: NRT 112 (1990) 356-371 (É. de *Ghellinck*).
m623 Wulf, Friedrich, s.J., 18.VI.1908-2.V.1990: 30 Jahre Chefredakteur: GeistL 63 (1990) 341s (P. *Imhof*) & 243-256 (Corona *Bamberg*).
m624 Yogev Ora, 24.IV.1934-31.X.1989; Nahariya: BAngIsr 10 (1990s) 101s (E. *Braun*).
m625 Zander, Giuseppe, 7.V.1920-19.VII.1990; history of architecture: EWest 40 (1990) 347-350 (E. *Galdieri*; bibliog. oriental subjects).
m626 Ziegler, Adolf Wilhelm [➤ 5,k995], 9.III.1903-30.VIII.1989; Geschichte, Patrologie: RHE 85 (1990) 472 (K. *Hausberger*).
m627 Ziegler, Joseph [➤ 4,k914; 5,k997], 15.III.1902-1.X.1988, BSeptCog 22 (1989) 1 4 (R. *Hanhart*).

Index Alphabeticus: Auctorcs − *Situs (omisso al-., tel, abu etc.)*
Ddiss./dir. Eeditor FFestschrift Mmentio, de co Rrcccnsio Ttranslator † in mem.

ᴰdiss./dir. ᴱeditor ᶠFestschrift ᴹmentio, de eo ᴿrecensio ᵀtranslator † in mem.
Sub **de**, **van** etc.: cognomina *americana* (post 1979) et *italiana* (post 1984); **non** reliqua.

Ddiss./dir. Eeditor FFestschrift Mmentio, de eo Rrecensio Ttranslator † in mem.
Sub **de, van** etc.: cognomina *americana* (post 1979) et *italiana* (post 1984); **non** reliqua.

ᴰdiss./dir. ᴱeditor ᶠFestschrift ᴹmentio, de eo ᴿrecensio ᵀtranslator † in mem. Sub **de, van** etc.: cognomina *americana* (post 1979) et *italiana* (post 1984); **non** reliqua.

Cognomina **italiana** et **americana** *sola* sub praefixo separato *da* etc.

Cognomina **italiana** et **americana** *sola* sub praefixo separato *da* etc.

Cognomina **italiana** et **americana** *sola* sub praefixo separato *da* etc.

Cognomina **italiana** et **americana** *sola* sub praefixo separato *da* etc.

Cognomina **italiana** et **americana** *sola* sub praefixo separato *da* etc.

Cognomina **italiana** et **americana** *sola* sub praefixo separato *da* etc.

Cognomina **italiana** et **americana** *sola* sub praefixo separato *da* etc.

ᴰdiss./dir. ᴱeditor ᶠFestschrift ᴹmentio, de eo ᴿrecensio ᵀtranslator † in mem.
Sub **de**, **van** etc.: cognomina *americana* (post 1979) et *italiana* (post 1984); **non** reliqua.

Ddiss./dir. Eeditor FFestschrift Mmentio, de eo Rrecensio Ttranslator † in mem.
Sub **de, van** etc.: cognomina *americana* (post 1979) et *italiana* (post 1984); **non** reliqua.

Ddiss./dir. Eeditor FFestschrift Mmentio, de eo Rrecensio Ttranslator † in mem.
Sub **de, van** etc.: cognomina *americana* (post 1979) et *italiana* (post 1984); **non** reliqua.

^{D}diss./dir. ^{E}editor ^{F}Festschrift ^{M}mentio, de eo ^{R}recensio ^{T}translator † in mem.
Sub **de**, **van** etc.: cognomina *americana* (post 1979) et *italiana* (post 1984); **non** reliqua.

^{D}diss./dir. ^{E}editor ^{F}Festschrift ^{M}mentio, de eo ^{R}recensio ^{T}translator † in mem.
Sub **de**, **van** etc.: cognomina *americana* (post 1979) et *italiana* (post 1984); **non** reliqua.

Ddiss./dir. Eeditor FFestschrift Mmentio, de eo Rrecensio Ttranslator † in mem.
Sub **de**, **van** etc.: cognomina *americana* (post 1979) et *italiana* (post 1984); **non** reliqua.

Ddiss./dir. Eeditor FFestschrift Mmentio, de eo Rrecensio Ttranslator † in mem. Sub **de**, **van** etc.: cognomina *americana* (post 1979) et *italiana* (post 1984); **non** reliqua.

Ddiss./dir. Eeditor FFestschrift Mmentio, de eo Rrecensio Ttranslator † in mem.
Sub **de, van** etc.: cognomina *americana* (post 1979) et *italiana* (post 1984); **non** reliqua.

ᴰdiss./dir. ᴱeditor ᶠFestschrift ᴹmentio, de eo ᴿrecensio ᵀtranslator † in mem.
Sub **de, van** etc.: cognomina *americana* (post 1979) et *italiana* (post 1984); **non** reliqua.

ᴰdiss./dir. ᴱeditor ꜰFestschrift ᴹmentio, de eo ᴿrecensio ᵀtranslator † in mem.
Sub **de**, **van** etc.: cognomina *americana* (post 1979) et *italiana* (post 1984); **non** reliqua.

ᴰdiss./dir. ᴱeditor ꜰFestschrift ᴹmentio, de eo ᴿrecensio ᵀtranslator † in mem. Sub **de**, **van** etc.: cognomina *americana* (post 1979) et *italiana* (post 1984); **non** reliqua.

Cognomina **americana** *sola* ponuntur sub praefixo separato *van*

Cognomina **americana** *sola* ponuntur sub praefixo separato *van*

VOCES

ordine graeco

helénion g336
eleuthería 6170
empázomai 9732*
exousía 5217
epilígdēn 9747
eqitiwoe eree 9776
ergastērion d128
euangelion, -ízō 9733
eulabeía 6716
eusébeia a930
ephēmería 5385

Záō, zōē 6619f
zētéō 5216

Thámbos a817b
Tharaba 3192
thélō 9734
theodídaktos 6636
Theodótous nom. 9735
theomacheîn a769 k129
theōsis 669*
thlípsis 6136
thriambos 6444
thrikē 9736
thysía = koinōnía k59*

Hierós 9737 9750*
hierosyleîn 6221b
hiketeía 9737
Ioudaîos 9738
hístamai, estôta 5570
hístōr 9738* historêsai
6508
ichthýs 5901

Katheúdō 6639
kaí 9739 9740
kaléō 5233
katéchein 9741 katéchon
6649
katias g522
kalēs d296 d297
kérdos g730
kérygma 5519
kestós a835
kêpos g340
kirita 9778
klêros 7887
klisíē 9778
koimētērion 9742
koinonía 5512b 6357ab
7928ac 9743
kólymbos 9744

kopiázō 4736
kratéō 5460
kreíttōn k32
kryptón 4806
ktêsis d174
Kyría ekklēsía 5906b

Lâos 8108
latreúō 9745
láchanon, -opôloi 9746
leitourgia 8176
líchanos, ligdēn 9747
lógos 9986 b135 logismós
9749

Maria(m) 4725
megalópsychos b744
metánoia 561* 5219 7983
9748
-mos, -mē 9749
mystērion 7849 7852
7853 9750

Naós 9750*
neániskos e603a
neókoros e839
nēpios 6627
nóos 9751 9773
nósos noûsos 9752

Oîda, íste ginōskontes
6548
oîkos 5532 d174 oiko-
domē 6139
ónoma 4829b
opsárion 5901
horáō, idoú 5887
orgē 6624
hóti 9753

Paidagōgós 6520
paîs theoû 5562
palaístra d315
paraskeuē 9758
peirasmós 4752
péplos d400
perì mèn gár 6465
perikátharma 6340
peripatéō 6135
perípsēma 6340
pólis a949 g822b g826b
g831 g838
pónos g938b
porneía 8386
poroekoto 9777*
presbýteron k32

prosábbaton 9758
proseuchē 9754
ptýō 9754*
pygmę 5262

Rhêtorikē 9755
rhís 9756

Sábbaton 9757 9758
saúra g522
sébō 9759 sébas a817
semikinthia 5601
semnótēs 9760
sesarkōménē 7473
spanelaion g421*
stádion d453
stásis 9761
stégē 5237 9241*
stoicheîon 9764
storýnē g552
syllogē k187
symphonía 1895
sýn b547
syniēmi synetós 9762 sý-
nesis k175
syneídēsis 6098
synístēmi 9763
sŷrinx 9765
sôma 6331c
sōtēría 9766 sōteíra a771
a943 sōzō 5836a
sōphrosýne b632a

Te 9767 9768
télos 9090* a915R
tí 4829a
tiphágion g462
tonáchion 9769
tóte 9225 9269

Hypakoē písteōs 6221a
hypokritēs 9770
hypomonē 6762

Phêgos g354
philánthrōpos 9770*
phóros g321
phrēn 9771

Cháris 6174 chárisma
9772
chreia 4190
chréptomai 9754*
chrêsthai theoîs k57c

Psychē 9773

FINIS – Elenchus of Biblica 6, 1990 – END OF INDEX

Finito di stampare il 4 giugno 1993
Tipografia Poliglotta della Pontificia Università Gregoriana
Piazza della Pilotta, 4 – 00187 Roma

F. W. DOBBS-ALLSOPP

WEEP, O DAUGHTER OF ZION:
A STUDY OF THE CITY-LAMENT GENRE
IN THE HEBREW BIBLE

BIBLICA ET ORIENTALIA, 44

ISBN 88-7653-346-X

(1993) pp. XIV-230   L. 30.000

EDITRICE PONTIFICIO ISTITUTO BIBLICO – ROMA

ROBERT A. DI VITO

STUDIES IN THIRD MILLENNIUM
SUMERIAN AND AKKADIAN
PERSONAL NAMES

The Designation and Conception of the Personal God

STUDIA POHL: SERIES MAIOR, 16

ISBN 88-7653-601-9

(1993) pp. XII-328   L. 25.000

EDITRICE PONTIFICIO ISTITUTO BIBLICO – ROMA

PONTIFICAL BIBLICAL INSTITUTE PRESS
1992

ANALECTA BIBLICA

130. FARFAN NAVARRO Enrique: *El desierto transformado. Una imagen deuteroisaiana de regeneración.*
pp. 304. ISBN 88-7653-130-0 Lit. 35.000

131. PITTA Antonio: *Disposizione e messaggio della lettera ai Galati. Analisi retorico-letteraria.*
pp. 272. ISBN 88-7653-131-9 Lit. 30.000

SUBSIDIA BIBLICA

16. SWETNAM James: *An Introduction to the Study of New Testament Greek. (Part One: Morphology).*
Vol. I: Lessons, Vol. II: Key, Lists, Paradigms, Indices. I due Volumi non sono separabili.
pp. LIV-762. ISBN 88-7653-600-0 Lit. 52.500

FUORI COLLANA

ANDERSEN Francis I. – FORBES A. Dean: *The Vocabulary of the Old Testament.* 1ª ristampa.
pp. VIII-724. ISBN 88-7653-575-6 Lit. 85.000

MERK Agostino: *Novum Testamentum graece et latine, apparatu critico instructum.* 11ª edizione.
pp. 48*+1732, 1 tavola. ISBN 88-7653-597-7. Lit. 50.000

NORTH Robert (a cura di): *Elenchus of Biblica.* Vol. 5/1989.
pp. 1096. ISBN 88-7653-598-5 Lit. 160.000

It is possible to subscribe standing orders

Orders and payments to:

AMMINISTRAZIONE PUBBLICAZIONI PIB/PUG
Piazza della Pilotta, 35 – 00187 Roma – Italia
Tel. 06/678.15.67 – Telefax 06/678.05.88

Conto Corrente Postale n. 34903005 – Compte Postal n. 34903005
Monte dei Paschi di Siena – Sede di Roma – c/c n. 54795.37

ISBN 88-7653-599-3

1506 s